SCOTTISH CURRENT LAW
LEGISLATION CITATOR 1988

STATUTES   1972–88
S.I.s AFFECTED . 1947–88

SCOTTISH CURRENT LAW LEGISLATION CITATOR 1988

STATUTES 1972–88
S.I.s AFFECTED . 1947–88

General Editors
PETER A. NICHOLSON, LL.B.
Solicitor

GILLIAN BRONZE, LL.B.

Edinburgh
W. GREEN & SON LTD.
St. Giles Street
1989

ISBN 0 414 00888 X

© CURRENT LAW LEGISLATION CITATOR, Sweet & Maxwell, 1989
© SCOTTISH CURRENT LAW LEGISLATION CITATOR, W. Green & Son Ltd., 1989

Printed in Great Britain by Ipswich Book Ltd.

PREFACE

How to Use this Volume

This Citator Volume together with its companion Case Citator, the *Scottish Case Citator* 1948–76 and the *Scottish Statute Citator* 1948–71 contains all the information necessary to make either a quick last-minute check to see that nothing has been missed or an exhaustive search which will produce all the material which has accumulated in the past forty-one years of legal development.

It contains a formidable mass of data but is so arranged that with very slight application the required answer, positive or negative, can be produced in the minimum of time.

The Case Citator, covering developments in case law 1977–88, has been bound separately to provide a less bulky volume. The preface to the Case Citator indicates its scope.

The Statute Citator

The Statute Citator consolidates the amendments for the period 1972–88; for previous amendments consult the 1971 Statute Citator which consolidates the amendments for the period 1948–71.

An alphabetical table of statutes has been included to assist in locating chapter numbers of Acts noted in the Statute Citator, which is arranged in chronological order. From these Citators it can promptly be ascertained:

(a) in respect of any statute passed between 1948 and 1959, where it is summarised in the *Current Law* volumes and for any statute thereafter the date of Royal Assent;

(b) in respect of any Act of any date, whether it has been repealed, amended or otherwise modified since 1948;

(c) in respect of any Act of any date, what cases have been decided on it since 1948;

(d) in respect of any Act of any date, what rules or orders have been made under it since 1948.

It should be noted that, as regards England and Wales, the year 1947 is also covered by the Statute Citator.

A table of statutory provisions for which no commencement order had been made as at December 31, 1988, is also included at the end of this section.

PREFACE

Statutory Instruments Affected Citator

This table provides an instant reference to S.I.s made and affected from 1947. It is arranged in numerical order for each year. It lists all amendments and revocations to S.I.s made from 1947 to 1988.

April 1989

P.A.N.

CONTENTS

TABLE OF ABBREVIATIONS

A.B.L.R. = Australian Business Law Review.
A.C. = Appeal Cases (Law Reports).
A.J.I.L. = American Journal of International Law.
A.L.J. = Australian Law Journal.
A.L.J.R. = Australian Law Journal Reports.
A.L.M.D. = Australian Legal Monthly Digest.
A.L.Q. = Arab Law Quarterly.
A.L.R. = Australian Law Reports.
A.R. = Alberta Reports 1977–
A.T.R. = Australian Tax Review.
Acct. = Accountant.
Acct.Rec. = Accountants Record.
Accty. = Accountancy.
Admin. = Administrator.
All E.R. = All England Law Reports.
Anglo-Am. = Anglo-American Law Review
Art. = Article.
Aus. = Australia.

BCC = British Company Law Cases.
BCLC = Butterworths Company Law Cases.
B.C.L.R. = British Columbia Law Reports.
B.L.R. = Business Law Review.
B.T.R. = British Tax Review.
Brit.J.Criminol. = British Journal of Criminology.
Build.L.R. = Building Law Reports.
Bull.E.C. = Bulletin of the European Communities.
Bull.J.S.B. = Bulletin of Judicial Studies Board.

c. = Chapter (of Act of Parliament).
C.A. = Court of Appeal.
C.A.T. = Court of Appeal Transcript.
C. & S.L.J. = Company and Securities Law Journal.
C.C.A. = Court of Criminal Appeal.
CCLR = Consumer Credit Law Reports.
C.C.L.T. = Canadian cases on the Law of Torts 1976–
C.I.L.J.S.A. = Comparative and International Law Journal of Southern Africa.
C.I.L.L. = Construction Industry Law Letter.
C.I.P.A. = The Journal of the Chartered Institute of Patent Agents.
C.J.Q. = Civil Justice Quarterly.
C.L. = Current Law.
C.L.B. = Commonwealth Law Bulletin.
C.L.C. = Current Law Consolidation.
C.L.J. = Cambridge Law Journal.
C.L.L.R. = City of London Law Review.
C.L.P. = Current Legal Problems.
C.L.R. = Commonwealth Law Reports.
C.L.Y. = Current Law Year Book.
C.M.L.R. = Common Market Law Reports.
C.M.L.Rev. = Common Market Law Review.
C.Q.S. = Chartered Quantity Surveyor.
C.S.W. = Chartered Surveyor Weekly.
Can. = Canada.
Can. Bar J. = Canadian Bar Journal.
Can.B.R. or Canadian B.R. = Canadian Bar Review.
Can.C.L. = Canadian Current Law.
Ch. = Chancery (Law Reports).
Co.Law. = Company Lawyer.
Co. Law Dig. = Company Law Digest.

Com.Cas. = Commercial Cases.
Commercial Acct. = Commercial Accountant.
Comp.L. & P. = Computer Law & Practice.
ConLR = Construction Law Reports.
Const.L.J. = Construction Law Journal.
Conv.(n.s.) (or Conv. or Conveyancer) = Conveyancer and Property Lawyer (New Series).
Cox C.C. = Cox's Criminal Cases.
Cr.App.R. = Criminal Appeal Reports.
Cr.App.R.(S.) = Criminal Appeal Reports (Sentencing).
Crim.L.R. = Criminal Law Review.
Cts.-Martial App.Ct. = Courts-Martial Appeal Court.

D.C. = Divisional Court.
D.L.R. = Dominion Law Reports.

E. = England.
E.A.T. = Employment Appeal Tribunal.
E.C.C. = European Commercial Cases.
E.C.L.R. = European Competition Law Review.
E.C.R. = European Court Reports.
E.C.S.C. = European Coal and Steel Community.
E.E.C. = European Economic Community.
E.G. = Estates Gazette.
E.G.L.R. = Estates Gazette Law Reports.
E.I.P.R. = European Intellectual Property Review.
E.H.R.R. = European Human Rights Reports.
E.L.Rev. = European Law Review.
E.O.R. = Equal Opportunities Review.
E.P.L. Leaflet = Excess Profits Levy Leaflet.
E.P.T. Leaflet = Excess Profits Tax Leaflet.

F.C.R. = Family Court Reporter.
F.L.R. = Federal Law Reports.
F.L.R. = Family Law Reports.
FLR = Financial Law Reports.
F.S.R. = Fleet Street Reports.
FTLR = Financial Times Law Reports.
Fam. = Family Division (Law Reports).
Fam.Law = Family Law.

G.W.D. = Green's Weekly Digest.

H.L. = House of Lords.
H.L.R. = Housing Law Reports.
Harv.L.R. or Harvard L.R. = Harvard Law Review.

I.B.F.L. = Butterworths Journal of International Banking and Financial Law
I.B.L. = International Business Lawyer.
I.C.L.Q. = International and Comparative Law Quarterly.
I.C.L.R. = International Construction Law Review.
I.C.R. = Industrial Cases Reports.
IFL Rev = International Financial Law Review.
I.L.J. = Industrial Law Journal.
I.L.P. = International Legal Practitioner.
I.L.R.M. = Irish Law Reports Monthly.
I.L.T. or Ir.L.T. = Irish Law Times.
I.L.T.R. = Irish Law Times Reports.

I.M.L. = International Media Law.
Imm.A.R. = Immigration Appeals Reports.
Imm. and Nat.L. & P. = Immigration and Nationality Law and Practice.
Ins.L. & P. = Insolvency Law & Practice.
I.R. or Ir.R. = Irish Reports (Eire).
I.R.L.R. = Industrial Relations Law Reports.
Ir.Jur. = Irish Jurist.
Ir.Jur.(N.S.) = Irish Jurist (New Series).
Ir.Jur.Rep. = Irish Jurist Reports.
I.T.R. = Industrial Tribunal Reports.

J. and JJ. = Justice, Justices.
J.A.L. = Journal of African Law.
J.B.L. = Journal of Business Law.
J.C. = Justiciary Cases.
J.C.L. = Journal of Criminal Law.
J.C.L. & Crim. = Journal of Criminal Law and Criminology.
J.Crim.L., C. & P.S. = Journal of Criminal Law, Criminology and Police Science.
J.E.R.L. = Journal of Energy and Natural Resources Law.
J.I.B. = Journal of the Institute of Bankers.
J.I.B.L. = Journal of International Banking Law.
J.L.A. = Jewish Law Annual.
J.L.H. = Journal of Legal History.
J.L.S. = Journal of the Law Society of Scotland.
J.P. = Justice of the Peace Reports.
J.P.L. = Journal of Planning and Environment Law.
J.P.N. = Justice of the Peace Journal.
J.R. = Juridical Review.
J.S.W.L. = Journal of Social Welfare Law.
Jam. = Jamaica.

K.B. = King's Bench (Law Reports).
K.I.R. = Knight's Industrial Reports.

L.C. = Lord Chancellor.
L.C.J. or C.J. = Lord Chief Justice.
L.Exec. = Legal Executive.
L.G.C. = Local Government Chronicle.
L.G.R. = Local Government Reports.
L.G.Rev. = Local Government Review.
L.J. = Law Journal Newspaper.
L.J. and L.JJ. = Lord Justice, Lords Justices.
L.J.A.C.R. = Law Journal Annual Charities Review.
L.J.N.C.C.R. = Law Journal Newspaper County Court Reports.
L.J.R. = Law Journal Reports.
L.M.C.L.Q. = Lloyd's Maritime and Commercial Law Quarterly.
L.P. = Reference to denote Lands Tribunal decisions (transcripts available from the Lands Tribunal).
L.Q.R. = Law Quarterly Review.
L.R. = Law Reports.
L.R.R.P. = Reports of Restrictive Practices Cases.
L.S. = Legal Studies.
L.S.Gaz. = Law Society's Gazette.
L.T. = Law Times.
L.Teach. = Law Teacher.
L.T.J. = Law Times Journal.
L.V.App.Ct. = Lands Valuation Appeal Court (Scotland).

L.V.C. = Reference to denote Lands Tribunal decisions (transcripts available from the Lands Tribunal).
L. & J. = Law and Justice.
Ll.L.Rep. = Lloyd's List Reports (before 1951).
Ll.P.C. = Lloyd's Prize Cases.
Law M. = The Law Magazine
Lit. = Litigation.
Liverpool L.R. = Liverpool Law Review.
Lloyd's Rep. = Lloyd's List Reports (1951 onwards).

M.L.J. = Malayan Law Journal.
M.L.R. = Modern Law Review.
M.R. = Master of the Rolls.
McGill L.J. = McGill Law Journal.
Mag.Ct. = Magistrates' Court.
Mal. = Malaya.
Mal.L.R. = Malaya Law Review.
Man.Law = Managerial Law.
Med.Sci. & Law = Medicine, Science and the Law.
Melbourne Univ.L.R. = Melbourne University Law Review.
Mel.L.J. = Melanesian Law Journal.

NATO R. = NATO Review.
N.I. = Northern Ireland; Northern Ireland Reports.
N.I.J.B. = Northern Ireland Judgment Bulletin.
N.I.L.Q. = Northern Ireland Legal Quarterly.
N.I.L.R. = Northern Ireland Law Reports.
N.Z.L.R. = New Zealand Law Reports.
N.Z.U.L.R. = New Zealand Universities Law Review.
New L.J. = New Law Journal.
New L.R. = New Law Reports, Ceylon.
Nig.L.J. = Nigerian Law Journal.

O.H. = Outer House of Court of Session.
O.J. = Official Journal of the European Communities.
O.J.L.S. = Oxford Journal of Legal Studies.
Oklahoma L.R. = Oklahoma Law Review.
Ord. = Order.
Osgoode Hall L.J. = Osgoode Hall Law Journal.

P. = Probate, Divorce and Admiralty (Law Reports).
P.A.D. = Planning Appeal Decisions.
P. & C.R. = Property and Compensation Reports.
P.C. = Privy Council.
PCC = Palmer's Company Cases.
P.C.L.J. = Practitioners' Child Law Journal.
P.L. = Public Law.
P.N. = Professional Negligence.
P.S. = Petty Sessions.
P.T. = Profits Tax Leaflet.
Pr.A.S.I.L. = Proceedings of the American Society of International Law.

Q.B. = Queen's Bench (Law Reports).
Q.J.P.R. = Queensland Justice of the Peace Reports.
Q.L.R. = Queensland Law Reporter.
Q.S. = Quarter Sessions.
Q.S.R. = Queensland State Reports.

TABLE OF ABBREVIATIONS

r. = Rule.
R.A. = Rating Appeals.
R. & I.T. = Rating and Income Tax.
R. & V. = Rating and Valuation.
R.C.N. = Rating Case Notes.
R.F.L. = Reports of Family Law (Canadian).
R.I.C.S. = Royal Institution of Chartered Surveyors, Scottish Lands Valuation Appeal Reports.
R.P.C. = Reports of Patent, Design and Trade Mark Cases.
R.P.Ct. = Restrictive Practices Court.
R.P.R. = Real Property Reports (Canada).
R.R.C. = Ryde's Rating Cases.
R.T.R. = Road Traffic Reports.
R.V.R. = Rating and Valuation Reporter.
reg. = Regulation.
Reg.Acct. = Registered Accountant.
Rep. of Ir. = Republic of Ireland.

s. = Section (of Act of Parliament).
S. or Scot. = Scotland.
S.A. = South Africa.
S.A.L.J. = South African Law Journal.
S.A.L.R. = South African Law Reports.
S.A.S.R. = South Australian State Reports.
S.C. = Session Cases.
S.C.C.R. = Scottish Criminal Case Reports.
S.C.(H.L.) = Session Cases (House of Lords).
S.C.(J.) = Session Cases (High Court of Justiciary).
S.C.L.R. = Scottish Civil Law Reports.
SCOLAG = Journal of the Scottish Legal Action Group.
S.I. = Statutory Instrument.
S.J. = Solicitors' Journal.
S.J.Suppl. = Supplement to the Solicitors' Journal.
S.L.C.R. = Scottish Land Court Reports.
S.L.C.R.App. = Scottish Land Court Reports (appendix).
S.L.G. = Scottish Law Gazette.
S.L.R. = Scottish Law Reporter (Reports 1865–1925).
S.L.R. = Scottish Law Review (Articles 1912–63).
S.L.R. = Scottish Law Review (Sheriff Court Reports 1885–1963).
S.L.R. (and date) = Statute Law Reform Act (Statute Citator only).
S.L.R. = Statute Law Revision.
S.L.T. = Scots Law Times.
S.L.T.(Land Ct.) = Scots Law Times Land Court Reports.
S.L.T.(Lands Tr.) = Scots Law Times Lands Tribunal Reports.

S.L.T.(Lyon Ct.) = Scots Law Times Lyon Court Reports.
S.L.T.(News) = Scots Law Times, News section.
S.L.T.(Notes) = Scots Law Times Notes of Recent Decisions (1946–1981).
S.L.T.(Sh.Ct.) = Scots Law Times Sheriff Court Reports.
S.N. = Session Notes.
S.P.L.P. = Scottish Planning Law and Practice.
S.R. & O. = Statutory Rules and Orders.
S.T.C. = Simon's Tax Cases.
Sc.Jur. = Scottish Jurist.
Sh.Ct.Rep. = Sheriff Court Reports (Scottish Law Review) (1885–1963).
Sol. = Solicitor.
Stat.L.R. = Statute Law Review.
Sydney L.R. = Sydney Law Review.

T.C. or Tax Cas. = Tax Cases.
T.C. Leaflet = Tax Case Leaflet.
T.L.R. = Times Law Reports.
T.P.G. = Town Planning and Local Government Guide.
T.U.L.B. = Trade Union Law Bulletin.
Tas.S.R. = Tasmanian State Reports.
Tax. = Taxation.
Tr.L. = Trading Law.
Traff.Cas. = Railway, Canal and Road Traffic Cases.
Trial = Trial.
Trib. = Tribunal.
Trust L. & P. = Trust Law and Practice.
Tulane L.R. = Tulane Law Review.

U.G.L.J. = University of Ghana Law Journal.
U.S. = United States Reports.
U.T.L.J. = University of Toronto Law Journal.

V.A.T.T.R. = Value Added Tax Tribunal Reports.
V.L.R. = Victorian Law Reports.

W.A.L.R. = West Australian Law·Reports.
W.I.A.S. = West Indies Associated States.
W.I.R. = West Indian Reports.
W.L.R. = Weekly Law Reports.
W.N. = Weekly Notes (Law Reports).
W.W.R. = Western Weekly Reports.
Washington L.Q. = Washington Law Quarterly.

Yale L.J. = Yale Law Journal.

ALPHABETICAL TABLE OF
STATUTES

This table lists all the Statutes referred to in this volume

ALPHABETICAL TABLE OF STATUTES

ALPHABETICAL TABLE OF STATUTES

ALPHABETICAL TABLE OF STATUTES

ALPHABETICAL TABLE OF STATUTES

ALPHABETICAL TABLE OF STATUTES

ALPHABETICAL TABLE OF STATUTES

ALPHABETICAL TABLE OF STATUTES

ALPHABETICAL TABLE OF STATUTES

Improvement of Lands (Ecclesiastical Benefices) Act 1854 (c.67)
Improvement of Live Stock (Licensing of Bulls) Act 1931 (c.43)
Incest Act 1567 (c.14)
Incest and Related Offences (Scotland) Act 1986 (c.36)
Incitement to Disaffection Act 1934 (c.56)
Inclosure Act 1801 (c.109)
Inclosure Act 1845 (c.119)
Inclosure Act 1852 (c.79)
Inclosure Act 1854 (c.97)
Inclosure Act 1857 (c.31)
Income and Corporation Taxes Act 1970 (c.10)
Income and Corporation Taxes Act 1988 (c.1)
Income and Corporation Taxes (No. 2) Act 1970 (c.54)
Income Tax Act 1952 (c.10)
Income Tax Management Act 1964 (c.37)
Income Tax (Repayment of Post-War Credits) Act 1959 (c.28)
Increase of Rent and Mortgage Interest (Restrictions) Act 1920 (c.17)
Increased assessments (1861) (c.27)
Incumbents Act 1868 (c.117)
Indecent Advertisements (Amendment) Act 1970 (c.47)
Indecent Advertisements Act 1889 (c.18)
Indecent Displays (Control) Act 1981 (c.42)
Indecency with Children Act 1960 (c.33)
Independent Broadcasting Authority Act 1973 (c.19)
Independent Broadcasting Authority Act 1974 (c.16)
Independent Broadcasting Authority Act 1978 (c.43)
Independent Broadcasting Authority Act 1979 (c.35)
Independent Broadcasting Authority (No. 2) Act 1974 (c.42)
India and Burma (Emergency Provisions) Act 1940 (c.33)
India and Burma (Existing Laws) Act 1937 (c.9)
India and Burma (Miscellaneous Amendments) Act 1940 (c.5)
India and Burma (Postponement of Elections) Act 1941 (c.44)
India and Burma (Temporary and Miscellaneous Provisions) Act 1942 (c.39)
India (Attachment of States) Act 1944 (c.14)
India (Central Government and Legislature) Act 1946 (c.39)
India (Estate Duty) Act 1945 (c.7)
India (Federal Court Judges) Act 1942 (c.7)
India Independence Act 1947 (c.30)
India Military Funds Act 1866 (c.18)
India (Miscellaneous Provisions) Act 1944 (c.38)
India (Proclamations of Emergency) Act 1946 (c.23)
India Stock Certificate Act 1863 (c.73)
India Stock Transfer Act 1862 (c.7)
indian and Colonial Divorce Jurisdiction Act 1926 (c.40)
Indian Church Act 1927 (c.40)
Indian Divorce Act 1945 (c.5)
Indian Divorces (Validity) Act 1921 (c.18)
Indian Franchise Act 1945 (c.2)
Indian Securities Act 1860 (c.5)
Indictable Offences Act 1848 (c.42)
Indictments Act 1915 (c.90)
Indus Basin Development Fund Act 1960 (c.1)
Industrial and Provident Societies Act 1965 (c.12)
Industrial and Provident Societies Act 1967 (c.48)
Industrial and Provident Societies Act 1975 (c.41)
Industrial and Provident Societies Act 1978 (c.34)
Industrial Assurance Act 1923 (c.8)

Industrial Assurance and Friendly Societies Act 1929 (c.28)
Industrial Assurance and Friendly Societies Act 1948 (c.39)
Industrial Assurance and Friendly Societies Act 1948 (Amendment) Act 1958 (c.27)
Industrial Assurance and Friendly Societies (Emergency Protection from Forfeiture) Act 1940 (c.10)
Industrial Common Ownership Act 1976 (c.78)
Industrial Courts Act 1919 (c.69)
Industrial Development Act 1966 (c.34)
Industrial Development Act 1982 (c.52)
Industrial Development Act 1985 (c.25)
Industrial Development (Ships) Act 1970 (c.2)
Industrial Diseases (Notification) Act 1981 (c.25)
Industrial Expansion Act 1968 (c.32)
Industrial Injuries and Diseases (Northern Ireland Old Cases) Act 1975 (c.17)
Industrial Injuries and Diseases (Old Cases) Act 1967 (c.34)
Industrial Injuries and Diseases (Old Cases) Act 1975 (c.16)
Industrial Organisations and Development Act 1947 (c.40)
Industrial Relations Act 1971 (c.72)
Industrial Training Act 1954 (c.16)
Industrial Training Act 1964 (c.16)
Industrial Training Act 1982 (c.10)
Industrial Training Act 1986 (c.15)
Industry Act 1971 (c.17)
Industry Act 1972 (c.63)
Industry Act 1975 (c.68)
Industry Act 1979 (c.32)
Industry Act 1980 (c.33)
Industry Act 1981 (c.6)
Industry Act 1982 (c.18)
Industry (Amendment) Act 1976 (c.73)
Inebriates Act 1888 (c.19)
Inebriates Act 1898 (c.60)
Inebriates Act 1899 (c.35)
Inebriates Amendment (Scotland) Act 1900 (c.28)
Infant Life (Preservation) Act 1929 (c.34)
Infanticide Act 1938 (c.36)
Infants Property Act 1830 (c.65)
Infectious Diseases (Notification) Act 1889 (c.72)
Inferior Courts Act 1844 (c.19)
Inferior Courts Judgments Extension Act 1882 (c.31)
Inheritance (Family Provision) Act 1938 (c.45)
Inheritance (Provision for Family and Dependants) Act 1975 (c.63)
Injuries in War (Compensation) Act 1914 (c.30)
Injuries in War Compensation Act 1914 (Session 2) (c.18)
Inland Revenue Act 1868 (c.124)
Inland Revenue Act 1880 (c.20)
Inland Revenue Regulation Act 1890 (c.21)
Inner Urban Areas Act 1978 (c.50)
Inshore Fishing (Scotland) Act 1984 (c.26)
Insolvency Act 1976 (c.60)
Insolvency Act 1985 (c.65)
Insolvency Act 1986 (c.45)
Insolvency Services (Accounting and Investment) Act 1970 (c.8)
Insurance Brokers (Registration) Act 1977 (c.46)
Insurance Companies Act 1958 (c.72)
Insurance Companies Act 1974 (c.49)
Insurance Companies Act 1980 (c.25)
Insurance Companies Act 1981 (c.31)
Insurance Companies Act 1982 (c.50)

ALPHABETICAL TABLE OF STATUTES

ALPHABETICAL TABLE OF STATUTES

ALPHABETICAL TABLE OF STATUTES

Seamen's and Soldiers' False Characters Act 1906 (c.5)
Secretary for Scotland Act 1885 (c.61)
Secretaries of State Act 1926 (c.18)
Security of Public Officers Act 1812 (c.66)
Seditious Meetings Act 1817 (c.19)
Seeds Act 1920 (c.54)
Selective Employment Payments Act 1966 (c.32)
Sequestration Act 1871 (c.45)
Servants' Characters Act 1792 (c.56)
Settled Estates Act 1877 (c.18)
Settled Land Act 1882 (c.38)
Settled Land Act 1925 (c.18)
Severn Bridge Tolls Act 1965 (c.24)
Sewerage (Scotland) Act 1968 (c.47)
Sex Discrimination Act 1975 (c.65)
Sex Discrimination Act 1986 (c.59)
Sex Disqualification (Removal) Act 1919 (c.71)
Sexual Offences Act 1956 (c.69)
Sexual Offences Act 1967 (c.60)
Sexual Offences Act 1985 (c.44)
Sexual Offences (Amendment) Act 1976 (c.82)
Sexual Offences (Scotland) Act 1976 (c.67)
Seychelles Act 1976 (c.19)
Sheep Stocks Valuation (Scotland) Act 1937 (c.34)
Sheriff Courts and Legal Officers (Scotland) Act 1927 (c.35)
Sheriff Courts (Civil Jurisdiction and Procedure) (Scotland) Act 1963 (c.22)
Sheriff Courts (Scotland) Act 1838 (c.119)
Sheriff Courts (Scotland) Act 1853 (c.80)
Sheriff Courts (Scotland) Act 1876 (c.70)
Sheriff Courts (Scotland) Act 1907 (c.51)
Sheriff Courts (Scotland) Act 1913 (c.28)
Sheriff Courts (Scotland) Act 1971 (c.58)
Sheriff Courts (Scotland) Extracts Act 1892 (c.17)
Sheriffs Act 1887 (c.55)
Sheriffs (Ireland) Act 1835 (c.55)
Sheriffs' Pension (Scotland) Act 1961 (c.42)
Shipbuilding Act 1985 (c.14)
Shipbuilding Industry Act 1967 (c.40)
Shipbuilding Industry Act 1971 (c.46)
Shipbuilding Act 1979 (c.59)
Shipbuilding Act 1982 (c.4)
Shipbuilding Credit Act 1964 (c.7)
Shipbuilding (Redundancy Payments) Act 1978 (c.11)
Shipping Offences Act 1793 (c.67)
Ships and Aircraft (Transfer Restriction) Act 1939 (c.70)
Shops Act 1950 (c.28)
Shops (Airports) Act 1962 (c.35)
Shops (Early Closing Days) Act 1965 (c.35)
Short Titles Act 1896 (c.14)
Sierra Leone Independence Act 1961 (c.16)
Sierra Leone Republic Act 1972 (c.1)
Silver Plate Act 1790 (c.31)
Simony Act 1588 (c.6)
Singapore Act 1966 (c.29)
Sir R. Hitcham's Charity Act 1863 (c.58)
Slaughter of Animals Act 1958 (c.8)
Slaughter of Animals (Amendment) Act 1954 (c.59)
Slaughter of Animals (Pigs) Act 1953 (c.27)
Slaughter of Animals (Scotland) Act 1928 (c.29)
Slaughter of Animals (Scotland) Act 1949 (c.52)
Slaughter of Animals (Scotland) Act 1980 (c.13)
Slaughter of Poultry Act 1967 (c.24)
Slaughterhouses Act 1954 (c.42)
Slaughterhouses Act 1958 (c.70)
Slaughterhouses Act 1974 (c.3)
Slave Trade Act 1843 (c.98)

Slave Trade Act 1873 (c.88)
Small Debt (Scotland) Act 1837 (c.41)
Small Debt (Scotland) Act 1924 (c.16)
Small Debts Act 1845 (c.127)
Small Dwellings Acquisition Act 1899 (c.44)
Small Estates (Representation) Act 1961 (c.37)
Small Holding Colonies Act 1916 (c.38)
Small Holdings Act 1892 (c.31)
Small Holdings and Allotments Act 1908 (c.36)
Small Holdings and Allotment Act 1926 (c.52)
Small Landholders and Agricultural Holdings (Scotland) Act 1931 (c.44)
Small Landholders (Scotland) Act 1911 (c.49)
Small Tenements Recovery Act 1838 (c.74)
Small Testate Estates (Scotland) Act 1876 (c.24)
Social Fund (Maternity and Funeral Expenses) Act 1987 (c.7)
Social Security Act 1971 (c.73)
Social Security Act 1973 (c.38)
Social Security Act 1975 (c.14)
Social Security Act 1979 (c.18)
Social Security Act 1980 (c.30)
Social Security Act 1981 (c.33)
Social Security Act 1985 (c.53)
Social Security Act 1986 (c.50)
Social Security Act 1988 (c.7)
Social Security Amendment Act 1974 (c.58)
Social Security and Housing Benefits Act 1982 (c.24)
Social Security and Housing Benefits Act 1983 (c.36)
Social Security Benefits Act 1975 (c.11)
Social Security (Consequential Provisions) Act 1975 (c.18)
Social Security (Contributions) Act 1981 (c.1)
Social Security (Contributions) Act 1982 (c.2)
Social Security (Miscellaneous Provisions) Act 1977 (c.5)
Social Security (Northern Ireland) Act 1975 (c.15)
Social Security (No. 2) Act 1980 (c.39)
Social Security Pensions Act 1975 (c.60)
Social Work (Scotland) Act 1968 (c.49)
Social Work (Scotland) Act 1972 (c.24)
Societies' Borrowing Powers Act 1898 (c.15)
Societies (Miscellaneous Provisions) Act 1940 (c.19)
Solicitors Act 1934 (c.45)
Solicitors Act 1936 (c.35)
Solicitors Act 1957 (c.27)
Solicitors Act 1965 (c.31)
Solicitors Act 1974 (c.47)
Solicitors (Amendment) Act 1959 (c.42)
Solicitors (Amendment) Act 1974 (c.26)
Solicitors, Public Notaries, etc., Act 1949 (c.21)
Solicitors (Scotland) Act 1933 (c.21)
Solicitors (Scotland) Act 1958 (c.28)
Solicitors (Scotland) Act 1965 (c.29)
Solicitors (Scotland) Act 1976 (c.6)
Solicitors (Scotland) Act 1980 (c.46)
Solicitors (Scotland) Act 1988 (c.42)
Solomon Islands Act 1978 (c.15)
Solvent Abuse (Scotland) Act 1983 (c.33)
Somerset House Act 1984 (c.21)
Sound Broadcasting Act 1972 (c.31)
South Africa Act 1877 (c.47)
South Africa Act 1909 (c.9)
South Africa Act 1962 (c.23)
South African Offences Act 1863 (c.35)
Southern Rhodesia Act 1965 (c.76)
Southern Rhodesia Act 1979 (c.52)
Southern Rhodesia (Constitution) Act 1961 (c.2)
Special Constables Act 1914 (c.61)

ALPHABETICAL TABLE OF STATUTES

Special Roads Act 1949 (c.32)
Spirits (Ireland) Act 1854 (c.89)
Spirits (Ireland) Act 1855 (c.103)
Spiritual Duties Act 1839 (c.30)
Sporting Events (Control of Alcohol etc.) Act 1985 (c.57)
Sporting Lands Rating (Scotland) Act 1886 (c.15)
Spray Irrigation (Scotland) Act 1964 (c.90)
Sri Lanka Republic Act 1972 (c.55)
Stage Carriages Act 1832 (c.120)
Stamp Act 1815 (c.184)
Stamp Act 1853 (c.59)
Stamp Act 1854 (c.83)
Stamp Act 1891 (c.39)
Stamp Duties (Ireland) Act 1842 (c.82)
Stamp Duties Management Act 1891 (c.38)
Stannaries Court (Abolition) Act 1896 (c.45)
State Immunity Act 1978 (c.33)
Statistics of Trade Act 1947 (c.39)
Statute Law (Repeals) Act 1973 (c.39)
Statute Law (Repeals) Act 1974 (c.22)
Statute Law (Repeals) Act 1975 (c.10)
Statute Law (Repeals) Act 1976 (c.16)
Statute Law (Repeals) Act 1977 (c.18)
Statute Law (Repeals) Act 1978 (c.45)
Statute Law (Repeals) Act 1981 (c.19)
Statute Law (Repeals) Act 1986 (c.12)
Statute Law Revision Act 1890 (c.33)
Statute Law Revision Act 1891 (c.67)
Statute Law Revision Act 1892 (c.19)
Statute Law Revision Act 1893 (c.14)
Statute Law Revision Act 1894 (c.56)
Statute Law Revision Act 1898 (c.22)
Statute Law Revision Act 1908 (c.49)
Statute Law Revision Act 1927 (c.42)
Statute Law Revision Act 1948 (c.62)
Statute Law Revision Act 1950 (c.6)
Statute Law Revision Act 1953 (c.5)
Statute Law Revision Act 1958 (c.46)
Statute Law Revision Act 1959 (c.68)
Statute Law Revision Act 1960 (c.56)
Statute Law Revision Act 1963 (c.30)
Statute Law Revision Act 1964 (c.79)
Statute Law Revision Act 1966 (c.5)
Statute Law Revision Act 1969 (c.52)
Statute Law Revision Act 1971 (c.52)
Statute Law Revision (Consequential Repeals) Act 1965 (c.55)
Statute Law Revision (Northern Ireland) Act 1973 (c.55)
Statute Law Revision (Northern Ireland) Act 1976 (c.12)
Statute Law Revision (Northern Ireland) Act 1980 (c.59)
Statute Law Revision (No. 2) Act 1888 (c.57)
Statute Law Revision (No. 2) Act 1890 (c.51)
Statute Law Revision (No. 2) Act 1893 (c.54)
Statute Law Revision (Scotland) Act 1964 (c.80)
Statute of Frauds 1677 (c.3)
Statute of Frauds Amendment Act 1828 (c.14)
Statute of Frauds (Ireland) 1695 (Eire) (c.12)
Statute of Monopolies 1623 (c.3)
(Statute of Westminster II) 1285
Statute of Westminster 1931 (c.4)
Statutes (Definition of Time) Act 1880 (c.9)
Statutory Corporations (Financial Provisions) Act 1974 (c.8)
Statutory Corporations (Financial Provisions) Act 1975 (c.55)

Statutory Declarations Act 1835 (c.62)
Statutory Instruments Act 1946 (c.36)
Statutory Orders (Special Procedure) Act 1965 (c.43)
Steam Trawling (Ireland) Act 1889 (c.74)
Steam Whistles Act 1872 (c.61)
Stipendiary Magistrates Act 1858 (c.73)
Stipendiary Magistrates Jurisdiction (Scotland) Act 1897 (c.48)
Stock Exchange (Completion of Bargains) Act 1976 (c.47)
Stock Transfer Act 1963 (c.18)
Stock Transfer Act 1982 (c.41)
Straits Settlements and Johore Territorial Waters (Agreement) Act 1928 (c.23)
Straits Settlements Offences Act 1874 (c.38)
Street Betting Act 1906 (c.43)
Street Collections Regulations (Scotland) Act 1915 (c.88)
Street Offences Act 1959 (c.57)
Submarine Telegraph Act 1885 (c.49)
Succession Duty Act 1853 (c.51)
Succession (Scotland) Act 1964 (c.41)
Succession (Scotland) Act 1973 (c.25)
Succession to the Crown Act 1707 (c.41)
Sudan (Special Payments) Act 1955 (c.11)
Suffragan Bishops Act 1534 (c.14)
Sugar Act 1956 (c.48)
Suicide Act 1961 (c.60)
Summary Jurisdiction Act 1857 (c.43)
Summary Jurisdiction (Ireland) Act 1851 (c.92)
Summary Jurisdiction (Ireland) Act 1908 (c.24)
Summary Jurisdiction (Scotland) Act 1908 (c.65)
Summary Jurisdiction (Scotland) Act 1954 (c.48)
Summer Time Act 1922 (c.22)
Summer Time Act 1947 (c.16)
Summer Time Act 1972 (c.6)
Sunday Cinema Act 1972 (c.19)
Sunday Entertainments Act 1932 (c.51)
Sunday Theatre Act 1972 (c.26)
Superannuation Act 1935 (c.23)
Superannuation Act 1949 (c.44)
Superannuation Act 1950 (c.2)
Superannuation Act 1965 (c.74)
Superannuation Act 1972 (c.11)
Superannuation (Amendment) Act 1965 (c.10)
Superannuation and other Trust Funds (Validation) Act 1927 (c.41)
Superannuation (Metropolis) Act 1866 (c.31)
Superannuation (Miscellaneous Provisions) Act 1948 (c.33)
Superannuation (Miscellaneous Provisions) Act 1967 (c.28)
Superannuation (President of Industrial Court) Act 1954 (c.37)
Superannuation Schemes (War Service) Act 1940 (c.26)
Superannuation (Various Services) Act 1938 (c.13)
Supplementary Benefits Act 1976 (c.71)
Supplementary Benefit (Amendment) Act 1976 (c.56)
Supplies and Services (Defence Purposes) Act 1951 (c.25)
Supply of Goods and Services Act 1982 (c.29)
Supply of Goods (Implied Terms) Act 1973 (c.13)
Supply Powers Act 1975 (c.9)
Suppression of Terrorism Act 1978 (c.26)
Supreme Court Act 1981 (c.54)
Supreme Court (Northern Ireland) Act 1942 (c.2)
Supreme Court of Judicature Act 1881 (c.68)
Supreme Court of Judicature Act 1891 (c.53)

xliii

ALPHABETICAL TABLE OF STATUTES

Unfair Contract Terms Act 1977 (c.50)
Uniform Laws on International Sales Act 1967 (c.45)
Uniforms Act 1894 (c.45)
Union of Benefices Act 1860 (c.142)
Union of Benefices Act 1898 (c.23)
Union of Benefices Acts Amendment Act 1871 (c.90)
Union with Ireland Act 1800 (c.67)
Union with Scotland Act 1706 (c.11)
United Nations Act 1946 (c.45)
U.S.A. Veterans' Pensions (Administration) Act 1949 (c.45)
Universities and College Estates Act 1925 (c.24)
Universities and College Estates Act 1964 (c.51)
Universities and Colleges (Trust) Act 1943 (c.9)
Universities of Oxford and Cambridge Act 1923 (c.33)
Universities (Scotland) Act 1966 (c.13)
University of London Act 1898 (c.62)
University of London Act 1899 (c.24)
University of London Medical Graduates Act 1854 (c.114)
Unlawful Drilling Act 1819 (c.1)
Unlawful Oaths Act 1797 (c.123)
Unlawful Oaths Act 1812 (c.104)
Unlawful Oaths (Ireland) Act 1810 (c.102)
Unsolicited Goods and Services Act 1971 (c.30)
Unsolicited Goods and Services (Amendment) Act 1975 (c.13)
Urban Development Corporations (Financial Limits) Act 1987 (c.57)
Usury Laws Repeal Act 1854 (c.90)

Vaccine Damage Payments Act 1979 (c.17)
Vagrancy Act 1824 (c.83)
Vagrancy Act 1838 (c.38)
Vagrancy (Ireland) Act 1847 (c.84)
Validation of War-time Leases Act 1944 (c.34)
Valuation and Rating (Exempted Classes) (Scotland) Act 1976 (c.64)
Valuation and Rating (Scotland) Act 1956 (c.60)
Valuation for Rating (Scotland) Act 1970 (c.4)
Valuation of Lands (Scotland) Acts Amendment Act 1894 (c.36)
Valuation of Lands (Scotland) Amendment Act 1867 (c.80)
Valuation of Lands (Scotland) Amendment Act 1879 (c.42)
Valuation of Lands (Scotland) Amendment Act 1887 (c.51)
Value Added Tax Act 1983 (c.55)
Variation of Trusts Act 1958 (c.53)
Vehicle and Driving Licences Act 1969 (c.27)
Vehicles (Excise) Act 1962 (c.13)
Vehicles (Excise) Act 1971 (c.10)
Venereal Disease Act 1917 (c.21)
Veterinary Surgeons Act 1948 (c.52)
Veterinary Surgeons Act 1966 (c.36)
Vexatious Actions (Scotland) Act 1898 (c.35)
Video Recordings Act 1984 (c.39)
Visiting Forces Act 1952 (c.67)
Visiting Forces (British Commonwealth) Act 1933 (c.6)

Wages Act 1986 (c.48)
Wages Attachment Abolition Act 1870 (c.30)
Wages Councils Act 1948 (c.7)
Wages Councils Act 1959 (c.69)
Wages Councils Act 1979 (c.12)
Wages Councils (Northern Ireland) Act 1945 (c.21)

Wales Act 1978 (c.52)
Wales and Berwick Act 1746 (c.42)
War Charities Act 1940 (c.31)
War Damage Act 1941 (c.12)
War Damage Act 1943 (c.21)
War Damage Act 1964 (c.25)
War Damage (Amendment) Act 1942 (c.28)
War Damage (Clearance Payments) Act 1960 (c.25)
War Damage (Public Utility Undertakings, etc.) Act 1949 (c.36)
War Damaged Sites Act 1949 (c.84)
War Emergency Laws (Continuance) Act 1920 (c.5)
War Loan Act 1919 (c.37)
War Loan (Supplemental Provisions) Act 1915 (c.93)
War Memorials (Local Authorities' Powers) Act 1923 (c.18)
War Orphans Act 1942 (c.8)
War Pensions Act 1920 (c.23)
War Pensions Act 1921 (c.49)
War Pensions (Administrative Provisions) Act 1918 (c.57)
War Risks Insurance Act 1939 (c.57)
Washington Treaty (Claims) Act 1875 (c.52)
Water Act 1945 (c.42)
Water Act 1948 (c.22)
Water Act 1958 (c.67)
Water Act 1973 (c.37)
Water Act 1981 (c.12)
Water Act 1983 (c.23)
Water Charges Act 1976 (c.9)
Water Charges Equalisation Act 1977 (c.41)
Water (Fluoridation) Act 1985 (c.63)
Water Officers Compensation Act 1960 (c.15)
Water Resources Act 1963 (c.38)
Water Resources Act 1971 (c.34)
Water (Scotland) Act 1946 (c.42)
Water (Scotland) Act 1949 (c.31)
Water (Scotland) Act 1967 (c.78)
Water (Scotland) Act 1980 (c.45)
Wear Coal Trade Act 1792 (c.29)
Wedding Rings Act 1855 (c.60)
Weeds Act 1959 (c.54)
Weights and Measures Act 1878 (c.49)
Weights and Measures Act 1963 (c.31)
Weights and Measures etc. Act 1976 (c.77)
Weights and Measures Act 1979 (c.45)
Weights and Measures Act 1985 (c.72)
Weights and Measures (Northern Ireland) Act 1967 (c.6)
Wellington Museum Act 1947 (c.46)
Welsh Cathedrals Act 1843 (c.77)
Welsh Courts Act 1942 (c.40)
Welsh Development Agency Act 1975 (c.70)
Welsh Development Agency Act 1988 (c.5)
Welsh Language Act 1967 (c.66)
West Indian Prisons Act 1838 (c.67)
West Indies Act 1962 (c.19)
West Indies Act 1967 (c.74)
Westminster 1861 (c.78)
Westminster Bridge 1864 (c.88)
Whale Fisheries (Scotland) Act Amendment 1922 (c.34)
Whaling Industry (Regulation) Act 1934 (c.49)
White Herring Fishery (Scotland) Act 1821 (c.79)
White Herring Fishery (Scotland) Act 1861 (c.72)
Wild Creatures and Forest Laws Act 1971 (c.47)
Wildlife and Countryside Act 1981 (c.69)
Wildlife and Countryside (Amendment) Act 1985 (c.31)

ALPHABETICAL TABLE OF STATUTES

CURRENT LAW
STATUTE CITATOR 1972–88

This edition of the Current Law Statute Citator covers the period 1972–88.
It comprises in a single table:
  (i) Statutes passed between 1972 and 1988;
  (ii) Statutes judicially considered during this period;
  (iii) Statutes repealed and amended during this period;
  (iv) Statutory Instruments issued under rule-making powers during this period.

(S.) Amendments relating to Scotland only.

Acts of the Parliament of Scotland

CAP.
79. Declinature Act 1681.
repealed in pt.: 1988, c.36, sch.2.
83. Judicial Sale Act 1681.
repealed: S.L.R. 1973.
86. Bills of Exchange Act 1681.
repealed in pt.: 1987, c.18, sch.8.
14. Prescription Act 1685.
repealed: 1973, c.52, sch.5.
21. Winter Herding Act 1686.
repealed: 1987, c.9, sch.
see Brown v. Lord Advocate, 1973 S.L.T. 205,
Outer House; Farquharson v. Walker, 1977
S.L.T.(Sh.Ct.) 22.
49. Judicial Sale Act 1690.
repealed: S.L.R. 1973.
22. Real Rights Act 1693.
repealed in pt.: 1979, c.33, sch.4.
23. Register of Sasines Act 1693.
repealed in pt.: 1979, c.33, sch.4.
7. Cautioners Act 1695.
repealed: 1973, c.52, sch.5.

CAP.
8. Judicial Sale Act 1695.
repealed: 1973, c.39, sch.1.
5. Bankruptcy Act 1696.
repealed: 1985, c.66, sch.8.
see Thomas Montgomery & Sons v.
Gallacher (O.H.), 1982 S.L.T. 138; Grant's Tr.
v. Grant (O.H.), 1986 S.L.T. 220; Gray (Bob)
(Access) v. T. M. Standard Scaffolding
(Sh.Ct.), 1987 S.C.L.R. 720.
9. Prescription Act 1696.
repealed: 1973, c.52, sch.5.
19. Interruptions Act 1696.
repealed: 1973, c.52, sch.5.
35. Salmon Act 1696.
repealed: 1986, c.62, sch.5.
6. Criminal Procedure Act 1701.
see Herron v. A, B, C and D, 1977 S.L.T.(Sh.Ct.)
24; Dunbar Petr. 1986 S.C.C.R. 602.
repealed in pt.(S.): 1975, c.21, sch.10.

Acts of the Parliaments of England, Great Britain, and the United Kingdom

CAP.
21 Hen. 3 (1236)
9. repealed: order 77/1250.

22 Hen. 3 (1237)
9. repealed: order 77/1250.

30 Hen. 3 (1245)
Ireland 1246
repealed: 1973, c.55, sch.

13 Edw. 1 (1285)
(Statute of Westminster II) 1285.
c.15, repealed: 1973, c.55, sch.

4 Edw. 3 (1330)
2. Chap.II, repealed in pt.: 1978, c.23, sch.

25 Edw. 3 St. 5 (1351)
5. repealed: order 79/1575.

35 Edw. 3 (1361)
1. Justices of the Peace Act 1361.
see Goodlad v. Chief Constable of South Yorkshire [1979] Crim.L.R. 51, Sheffield Crown
Ct.; R. v. Randall [1987] Crim.L.R. 254, C.A.
and D.C.; Hughes v. Holley [1987] Crim.L.R.
253; (1988) 86 Cr.App.R. 130, D.C.; Nawrot
and Shaler v. D.P.P. [1988] Crim.L.R. 107,
D.C.

5 Ric. 2, Stat. 1 (1381)
7. Forcible Entry Act 1381.
repealed: 1977, c.45, s.13, sch.13.
see R. v. Brittain [1972] 2 W.L.R. 450; [1972] 1
All E.R. 353.

CAP.
11 Ric. 2 (1387)
10. Delay 1387.
repealed: 1973, c.55, sch.

15 Ric. 2 (1391)
2. repealed: 1977, c.45, s.13, sch.13.
CAP.
9 Hen. 5 St. 2 (1421)
11. repealed: S.L.R. 1978.

8 Hen. 6 (1429)
9. Forcible Entry Act 1429.
repealed: 1977, c.45, s.13, sch.13.

4 Hen. 7 (1488)
14. (Crown Lands).
repealed: S.L.R. 1977.
15. repealed: S.L.R. 1977.

7 Hen. 7 (1491)
16. repealed: S.L.R. 1977.
19. (Priory of Christchurch).
repealed: S.L.R. 1977.

11 Hen. 7 (1495)
9. repealed: S.L.R. 1975.
12. Poor Persons 1495.
repealed: S.L.R. 1973.
34. repealed: S.L.R. 1978.
35. repealed: S.L.R. 1978.
36. repealed: S.L.R. 1978.
37. repealed: S.L.R. 1978.
39. repealed: S.L.R. 1978.
40. repealed: S.L.R. 1978.
44. repealed: S.L.R. 1977.

CAP.

12 Hen. 7 (1496)
8. repealed: S.L.R. 1978.

19 Hen. 7 (1503)
26. repealed: S.L.R. 1978.
28. (Power to reverse attainders).
repealed: S.L.R. 1977.
29. repealed: S.L.R. 1978.
30. repealed: S.L.R. 1978.
33. repealed: S.L.R. 1978.
34. repealed: S.L.R. 1977.
35. repealed: S.L.R. 1977.
37. repealed: S.L.R. 1977.
38. repealed: S.L.R. 1977.
39. repealed: S.L.R. 1977.
40. repealed: S.L.R. 1977.

1 Hen. 8 (1509)
19. repealed: S.L.R. 1977.

3 Hen. 8 (1511)
16. repealed: S.L.R. 1978.
17. repealed: S.L.R. 1977.
18. repealed: S.L.R. 1978.
19. repealed: S.L.R. 1977.
20. repealed: S.L.R. 1977.
21. repealed: S.L.R. 1977.

4 Hen. 8 (1512)
9. repealed: S.L.R. 1977.
10. repealed: S.L.R. 1978.
11. repealed: S.L.R. 1978.
12. repealed: S.L.R. 1978.
13. repealed: S.L.R. 1978.
14. repealed: S.L.R. 1977.
15. repealed: S.L.R. 1977.
16. repealed: S.L.R. 1977.

5 Hen. 8 (1513)
9. repealed: S.L.R. 1978.
10. repealed: S.L.R. 1978.
11. repealed: S.L.R. 1978.
12. repealed: S.L.R. 1978.
13. repealed: S.L.R. 1977.
14. repealed: S.L.R. 1978.
15. repealed: S.L.R. 1977.
18. repealed: S.L.R. 1978.

6 Hen. 8 (1514)
19. repealed: S.L.R. 1978.
20. repealed: S.L.R. 1978.
21. repealed: S.L.R. 1977.
22. repealed: S.L.R. 1977.
23. repealed: S.L.R. 1978.

14 & 15 Hen. 8 (1523)
18. repealed: S.L.R. 1978.
20. repealed: S.L.R. 1977.
21. Thacte of Auctorite.
repealed: S.L.R. 1977.
23. repealed: S.L.R. 1977.

CAP.

14 & 15 Hen. 8 (1523)—cont.
24. repealed: S.L.R. 1978.
25. repealed: S.L.R. 1978.
26. repealed: S.L.R. 1978.
27. repealed: S.L.R. 1978.
30. repealed: S.L.R. 1978.
31. repealed: S.L.R. 1978.
33. repealed: S.L.R. 1978.
34. repealed: S.L.R. 1978.

21 Hen. 8 (1529)
22. repealed: S.L.R. 1978.
26. repealed: S.L.R. 1978.

22 Hen. 8 (1530)
17. repealed: S.L.R. 1978.
19. repealed: S.L.R. 1978.
21. repealed: S.L.R. 1978.
22. repealed: S.L.R. 1978.
23. repealed: S.L.R. 1978.

23 Hen. 8 (1531)
8. repealed: S.L.R. 1978.
21. repealed: S.L.R. 1978.
22. repealed: S.L.R. 1978.
23. repealed: S.L.R. 1978.
24. repealed: S.L.R. 1978.
25. repealed: S.L.R. 1978.
26. repealed: S.L.R. 1978.
27. repealed: S.L.R. 1978.
28. repealed: S.L.R. 1978.
29. repealed: S.L.R. 1978.
30. repealed: S.L.R. 1978.
31. repealed: S.L.R. 1978.
32. repealed: S.L.R. 1978.
33. repealed: S.L.R. 1978.
34. repealed: S.L.R. 1977.

24 Hen. 8 (1532)
14. repealed: S.L.R. 1978.
16. London 1532.
repealed: 1973, c.39, sch.1.

25 Hen. 8 (1533)
23. repealed: S.L.R. 1978.
24. repealed: S.L.R. 1978.
25. repealed: S.L.R. 1977.
26. repealed: S.L.R. 1978.
28. repealed: S.L.R. 1977.
30. repealed: S.L.R. 1978.
31. repealed: S.L.R. 1978.
32. repealed: S.L.R. 1977.
33. repealed: S.L.R. 1978.
34. repealed: S.L.R. 1977.

26 Hen. 8 (1534)
14. Suffragan Bishops Act 1534.
ss. 2, 4, repealed in pt.: 1978, No.1, s.15.
s. 6, amended: *ibid.*
s. 7, repealed: S.L.R. 1977.
20. repealed: S.L.R. 1978.

26 Hen. 8 (1534)—cont.
21. repealed: S.L.R. 1978.
22. repealed: S.L.R. 1977.
23. repealed: S.L.R. 1977.
24. repealed: S.L.R. 1978.
25. repealed: S.L.R. 1977.

27 Hen. 8 (1535)
23. repealed: S.L.R. 1978.
29. repealed: S.L.R. 1978.
30. repealed: S.L.R. 1978.
31. repealed: S.L.R. 1978.
32. repealed: S.L.R. 1978.
33. repealed: S.L.R. 1978.
34. repealed: S.L.R. 1978.
36. repealed: S.L.R. 1978.
37. repealed: S.L.R. 1978.
38. repealed: S.L.R. 1978.
39. repealed: S.L.R. 1978.
40. repealed: S.L.R. 1978.
43. repealed: S.L.R. 1978.
44. repealed: S.L.R. 1978.
45. repealed: S.L.R. 1978.
46. repealed: S.L.R. 1978.
47. repealed: S.L.R. 1978.
48. repealed: S.L.R. 1978.
49. repealed: S.L.R. 1978.
50. repealed: S.L.R. 1978.
51. repealed: S.L.R. 1978.
52. repealed: S.L.R. 1978.
53. repealed: S.L.R. 1978.
54. repealed: S.L.R. 1978.
55. repealed: S.L.R. 1978.
56. repealed: S.L.R. 1978.
57. repealed: S.L.R. 1978.
58. repealed: S.L.R. 1978.
59. repealed: S.L.R. 1977.
61. repealed: S.L.R. 1978.

28 Hen. 8 (1536)
18. repealed: S.L.R. 1977.
19. repealed: S.L.R. 1978.
20. repealed: S.L.R. 1978.
21. repealed: S.L.R. 1978.
22. repealed: S.L.R. 1978.
24. repealed: S.L.R. 1977.
25. repealed: S.L.R. 1978.
26. repealed: S.L.R. 1978.
28. repealed: S.L.R. 1978.
29. repealed: S.L.R. 1978.
30. repealed: S.L.R. 1978.
32. repealed: S.L.R. 1978.
33. repealed: S.L.R. 1978.
34. repealed: S.L.R. 1978.
35. repealed: S.L.R. 1978.
36. repealed: S.L.R. 1978.
37. repealed: S.L.R. 1978.
38. repealed: S.L.R. 1978.
39. repealed: S.L.R. 1978.
40. repealed: S.L.R. 1978.
41. repealed: S.L.R. 1978.
42. repealed: S.L.R. 1978.
43. repealed: S.L.R. 1978.
44. repealed: S.L.R. 1978.

28 Hen. 8 (1536)—cont.
45. repealed: S.L.R. 1977.
46. repealed: S.L.R. 1978.
47. repealed: S.L.R. 1978.
48. repealed: S.L.R. 1978.
49. repealed: S.L.R. 1978.
50. repealed: S.L.R. 1978.
51. repealed: S.L.R. 1978.
52. repealed: S.L.R. 1977.

31 Hen. 8 (1539)
5. repealed: S.L.R. 1978.

32 Hen. 8 (1540)
42. Barbers and Chirurgians Act 1540.
repealed: S.L.R. 1986.

33 Hen. 8 (1541)
13. repealed: S.I.R. 1977.
26. repealed: S.L.R. 1978.
35. repealed: S.L.R. 1978.
37. repealed: S.L.R. 1978.
38. repealed: S.L.R. 1978.
39. Crown Debts Act 1541.
repealed: 1981, c.54, sch.7.

34 & 35 Hen. 8 (1542)
21. repealed: S.L.R. 1978.
26. Laws in Wales Act 1542.
s. 61, repealed: order 74/595.

37 Hen. 8 (1545)
18. repealed: S.L.R. 1978.

2 & 3 Edw. 6 (1548)
12. repealed: S.L.R. 1978.
18. repealed: S.L.R. 1977.

3 & 4 Edw. 6 (1549)
14. repealed: S.L.R. 1977.

1 Mar. Sess. 2 (1553)
16. repealed: S.L.R. 1977.

5 Eliz. 1 (1562)
28. Bible 1562.
repealed: S.L.R. 1973.

10 Eliz. 1 (1567)
14. Incest Act 1567.
see Vaughan v. H.M. Advocate, 1979 S.L.T. 49.

13 Eliz. 1 (1571)
5. see Murdoch v. Murdoch (1977) 26 Rep. Fam.L.
1, Alberta Sup.Ct.
16. repealed: S.L.R. 1977.

CAP.

14 Eliz. 1 (1572)
13. repealed: S.L.R. 1975.

29 Eliz. 1 (1586)
1. repealed: S.L.R. 1977.

31 Eliz. 1 (1588)
6. Simony Act 1588.
ss. 4 (in pt.), 5 (in pt.), 6, 9 (in pt.), repealed: 1986, No. 3, sch.5.
11. Forcible Entry Act 1588.
repealed: 1977, c.45, s.13, sch.13.

35 Eliz. 1 (1592)
5. repealed: S.L.R. 1977.

3 Jac. 1 (1605)
2. repealed: S.L.R. 1977.
5. Presentation of Benefices Act 1605.
s. 13, repealed: 1986, No. 3, s.30, sch.5.

21 Jac. 1 (1623)
3. Statute of Monopolies 1623.
s. 3, see *International Business Machines Corp.'s Application* [1980] F.S.R. 65, Graham J.
s. 6, see *The Welcome Foundation's Application* [1983] F.S.R. 593, New Zealand, C.A.
15. Forcible Entry Act 1623.
repealed: 1977, c.45, s.13, sch.13.
16. Limitation Act 1623.
repealed: S.L.R. 1986.
30. repealed: S.L.R. 1978.

3 Car. 1 (1627)
6. repealed: S.L.R. 1978.

10 Car. 1 Sess. 3 (1634)
18. Oaths Act (Ireland) 1634.
s. 6, amended: order 81/226.

12 Car. 2 (1660)
7. repealed: S.L.R. 1977.
24. Tenures Abolition Act 1660.
s. 9, repealed: 1973, c.29, sch.3.

13 Car. 2, Stat. 1 (1661)
5. Tumultous Petitioning Act 1661.
repealed: 1986, c.64, sch.3.
38. Justices of the Peace Act 1661.
repealed (S.): 1975, c.20, sch.2.

14 Car. 2 (1662)
3. City of London Militia Act 1662.
s. 1, repealed: 1980, c.9, sch.10.
4. Act of Uniformity 1662.
ss. 11, 22, 23, repealed: S.L.R. 1973; ss. 5, 13, amended: *ibid.*

CAP.

22 Car. 2 (1670)
12. Bridges Act 1670.
repealed: S.L.R. 1973.

25 Car. 2 (1672)
40. Courts Act 1672.
ss. 3, 8, 10, repealed (S).: 1975, c.21, sch.10.

29 Car. 2 (1677)
3. Statute of Frauds 1677.
s. 4, see *Compagnie Generale d'Industrie et de Participations* v. *Myson Group* (1984) 134 New L.J. 788, Hirst J.; *Decouvreur* v. *Jordan, The Times*, May 25, 1987, C.A.; *Perrylease* v. *Imecar A.G.* [1987] 2 All E.R. 373, Scott. J.

31 Car. 2 (1679)
2. Habeas Corpus Act 1679.
s. 2, amended: 1976, c.63, sch.2.
s. 5, repealed in pt.: *ibid.*, sch.3.

1 Will. & Mar. (1688)
26. Presentation of Benefices Act 1688.
repealed: 1986, No. 3, Sch. 5.
s. 2, repealed: *ibid.*, s.30, sch.5.

5 & 6 Will. & Mar. (1694)
20. Bank of England Act 1694.
s. 28, repealed: S.L.R. 1976.
43. Criminal Procedure Act 1694.
repealed (S.): 1975, c.21, sch.10.

7 & 8 Will. 3 (1695)
12. Statute of Frauds (Ireland) 1695 (Eire).
see *Kelly* v. *Park Hall Schools* (1978) 111 I.L.T.R. 9, Eire Sup.Ct.; *Casey* v. *Irish Intercontinental Bank* [1979] I.R. 364, Eire Sup.Ct.
s. 2, see *Mulhall* v. *Haren* [1981] I.R. 364, Keane J.
25. Parliamentary Election Act 1695.
s. 7, see *Hobson* v. *Fishburn, The Guardian*, November 1, 1988, D.C.

8 & 9 Will. 3 (1696)
4. repealed: S.L.R. 1977.
5. repealed: S.L.R. 1977.
8. Plate 1696.
repealed: 1973, c.43, sch.7.
20. Bank of England Act 1696.
repealed: S.L.R. 1973.

11 Will. 3 (1698)
2. repealed: S.L.R. 1978.

12 & 13 Will. 3 (1700)
2. Act of Settlement 1700.
s. 3, amended: 1981, c.61, sch.7.

CAP.

13 & 14 Will. 3 (1701)

6. Criminal Procedure Act 1701.
see *Herron* v. *A, B, C and D,* 1977 S.L.T.(Sh.Ct.)
24.
repealed in pt. (S.): 1975, c.21, sch.10.

1 Anne (1702)

3. Counterfeiting 1702.
repealed: 1973, c.43, sch.7.

3 & 4 Anne (1704)

4. repealed: S.L.R. 1978.

6 Anne (1706)

8. Church of England 1706.
s. 1, amended: S.L.R. 1973.
11. Union with Scotland Act 1706.
art. vi, amended: S.L.R. 1973.
art. ix, repealed: *ibid.*
art. xviii, see *Gibson* v. *Lord Advocate* (O.H.),
1975 S.L.T. 134.
art. xix, amended: 1973, c.39, s.3, sch.1.
41. Succession to the Crown Act 1707.
s. 8, repealed: S.L.R. 1973.
s. 26, repealed: S.L.R. 1978.

7 Anne (1708)

14. Parochial Libraries Act 1708.
s. 10, see *Re St. Mary's Warwick* [1981] 3
W.L.R. 781, Const.Ct.
21. Treason Act 1708.
s. 5, repealed in pt.: S.L.R. 1977.
s. 7, repealed: 1980, c.62, sch.8.
s. 8, repealed: S.L.R. 1977.
29. repealed: S.L.R. 1978.

8 Anne (1709)

16. Circuit Courts (Scotland) Act 1709.
repealed: 1987, c.41, sch.2.

9 Anne (1710)

19. Gaming Act 1710.
see *Cumming* v. *Mackie,* 1973 S.L.T. 242, Outer
House.

10 Anne (1711)

10. Scottish Episcopalians Act 1711.
s. 4, repealed: S.L.R. 1977.
s. 7, repealed (S.): 1977, c.15, sch.3.
s. 13, repealed: S.L.R. 1977.
43. Deal 1711.
ss. 1–5, repealed: S.L.R. 1973.

13 Anne (1713)

13. Presentation of Benefices Act 1713.
repealed, except ss. 9, 11: 1986, No. 3, sch.5.
s. 1, repealed: *ibid.,* s.30, sch.5.

1 Geo. 1, Stat. 2 (1714)

5. Riot Act 1714.
repealed: S.L.R. 1973.

CAP.

1 Geo. 1, Stat. 2 (1714)—cont.

10. Queen Anne's Bounty Act 1714.
ss. 6 (in pt.), 7, 8, repealed: 1986, No. 3, sch.5.
16. repealed: S.L.R. 1977.
17. repealed: S.L.R. 1977.
32. repealed: S.L.R. 1977.
42. repealed: S.L.R. 1977.
53. repealed: S.L.R. 1977.
54. Highlands Services Act 1715.
repealed (S.): S.L.R. 1975.

5 Geo. 1 (1718)

20. Revenue of Scotland Act 1718.
repealed: S.L.R. 1986.
29. Church Patronage (Scotland) Act 1718.
repealed: S.L.R. 1974.

6 Geo. 1 (1719)

11. Plate Duty Act 1719.
repealed: 1973, c.43, sch.7.

8 Geo. 1 (1721)

28. repealed: S.L.R. 1977.

9 Geo. 1 (1722)

15. repealed: S.L.R. 1977.
16. repealed: S.L.R. 1977.
17. repealed: S.L.R. 1977.
25. repealed: S.L.R. 1977.

10 Geo. 1 (1723)

19. Court of Session Act 1723.
repealed: S.L.R. 1986.

1 Geo. 2, Stat. 2 (1727)

22. Edinburgh Beer Duties Act 1727.
repealed: 1981, c.19, sch.1.

3 Geo. 2 (1729)

31. repealed: S.L.R. 1977.

6 Geo. 2 (1732)

32. repealed: S.L.R. 1977.

8 Geo. 2 (1734)

22. repealed: S.L.R. 1977.

10 Geo. 2 (1736)

19. repealed: S.L.R. 1978.
37. repealed: S.L.R. 1977.

11 Geo. 2 (1737)

17. Church Patronage Act 1737.
repealed: 1986, No. 3, sch.2.
19. Distress for Rent Act 1737.
s. 15, repealed: S.L.R. 1977.
s. 20, repealed: S.L.R. 1986.

CAP.

12 Geo. 2 (1738)

26. Plate (Offences) Act 1738.
repealed: 1973, c.43, sch.7.
28. Gaming Act 1738.
repealed: 1980, c.59, sch.

13 Geo. 2 (1739)

19. Gaming Act 1739.
repealed: 1980, c.59, sch.

15 Geo. 2 (1741)

13. Bank of England Act 1741.
repealed: S.L.R. 1973.
20. Gold and Silver Thread Act 1741.
repealed: 1973, c.43, sch.7.

16 Geo. 2 (1742)

18. Justices Jurisdiction Act 1742.
repealed: 1979, c.55, sch.3.

18 Geo. 2 (1744)

15. London Barbers and Surgeons Act 1744.
repealed, except ss.12, 15–18; S.L.R. 1986.

19 Geo. 2 (1745)

26. repealed: S.L.R. 1977.

20 Geo. 2 (1746)

30. Treason Act 1746.
repealed: S.L.R. 1973.
42. Wales and Berwick Act 1746.
repealed: 1978, c.30, sch.3.
43. Heritable Jurisdictions (Scotland) Act 1746.
s. 28, repealed: 1987, c.18, sch. 8.
ss. 32–34, 36, 37, 40, repealed: 1987, c.41, sch.2.
50. Tenures Abolition Act 1746.
ss. 12, 13, repealed (S.): 1987, c.18, sch.8.

21 Geo. 2 (1747)

34. Cattle Theft (Scotland) Act 1747.
repealed: S.L.R. 1974.

22 Geo. 2 (1748)

29. Roll of Valuation (1748).
repealed (S.): S.L.R. 1975.
48. Treason Outlawries (Scotland) Act 1748.
repealed: S.L.R. 1977.

24 Geo. 2 (1750)

23. Calendar (New Style) Act 1750.
s. 4, repealed in pt.: S.L.R. 1986.

25 Geo. 2 (1751)

37. Murder Act 1751.
repealed: S.L.R. 1973.

CAP.

27 Geo. 2 (1754)

19. Bedford Level (1754).
s. 49, repealed: S.L.R. 1976.

28 Geo. 2 (1755)

54. repealed: S.L.R. 1978.

29 Geo. 2 (1756)

23. Fisheries (Scotland) Act 1756.
repealed: 1984, c.26, sch.2.

30 Geo. 2 (1757)

21. repealed: S.L.R. 1978.

31 Geo. 2 (1757)

16. repealed: S.L.R. 1978.
25. repealed: S.L.R. 1978.

32 Geo. 2 (1758)

61. repealed: S.L.R. 1978.

2 Geo. 3 (1762)

17. repealed: S.L.R. 1978.

5 Geo. 3 (1765)

26. Isle of Man Purchase Act 1765.
repealed: S.L.R. 1976.
49. Bank Notes (Scotland) Act 1765.
s. 2, repealed: S.L.R. 1973.
s. 4, amended: 1987, c.18, sch.6; repealed in pt.: S.L.R. 1973.
s. 5, repealed in pt.: *ibid.*
s. 6, repealed in pt.: S.L.R. 1973; 1987, c.18, sch.8.

6 Geo. 3 (1766)

23. An Act to prevent frauds (1766).
repealed: S.L.R. 1976.

8 Geo. 3 (1768)

16. Glasgow (Improvement) Act 1768.
repealed: S.L.R. 1981.

10 Geo. 3 (1770)

13. repealed: S.L.R. 1978.
53. An Act to repeal an Act for the relief of coal–heavers (1770).
repealed: S.L.R. 1976.

11 Geo. 3 (1771)

10. repealed: S.L.R. 1978.
56. repealed: S.L.R. 1978.

12 Geo. 3 (1772)

19. repealed: S.L.R. 1978.
35. repealed: S.L.R. 1978.
43. repealed: S.L.R. 1978.
44. repealed: S.L.R. 1978.

12 Geo. 3 (1772)—cont.

59. repealed: S.L.R. 1978.
72. Bills of Exchange (Scotland) Act 1772.
ss. 37, 39, see *Russland (or M'Kinney)* v. *Allen*
[1976] 1 Lloyd's Rep. 48.
ss. 37, 39, 40, repealed: 1973, c.52, sch.5.
ss. 42, 43, repealed in pt.: 1987, c.18, sch. 8.

13 Geo. 3 (1772)

17. repealed: S.L.R. 1977.
52. Plate Assay (Sheffield and Birmingham) Act 1772.
ss. 2 (in pt.), 3, 6, 7, 8 (in pt.), 18, 28–30,
repealed: order 78/639.
59. Plate (Offences) Act 1772.
repealed: 1973, c.43, sch.7.

14 Geo. 3 (1774)

32. Bank of Scotland Act 1774.
repealed: S.L.R. 1981.
48. Life Assurance Act 1774.
s. 2, see *Arif* v. *Excess Insurance Group* (O.H.),
1987 S.L.T. 473.
88. Quebec 1774.
repealed: S.L.R. 1973.

15 Geo. 3 (1775)

52. Porcelain Patent Act 1775.
repealed: S.L.R. 1986.

16 Geo. 3 (1776)

10. repealed: S.L.R. 1977.

17 Geo. 3 (1776)

11. Worsted Act 1776.
repealed: S.L.R. 1986.
13. An Act for continuing 7 Geo. 3, c.23 (1776).
repealed: S.L.R. 1976.
17. repealed: S.L.R. 1978.
24. repealed: S.L.R. 1978.
53. Clergy Residences Repair Act 1776.
ss. 5, 9, repealed: 1972, No. 2, sch.2.
66. repealed: S.L.R. 1977.

18 Geo. 3 (1778)

12. Taxation of Colonies Act 1778.
repealed: S.L.R. 1973.
61. repealed: S.L.R. 1978.

19 Geo. 3 (1779)

11. repealed: S.L.R. 1978.

21 Geo. 3 (1781)

53. repealed: S.L.R. 1977.

22 Geo. 3 (1782)

82. Civil List and Secret Service Money Act 1782.
ss. 24–29, repealed: S.L.R. 1977.

23 Geo. 3 (1783)

34. repealed: S.L.R. 1977.
45. Justiciary and Circuit Courts (Scotland) Act 1783.
repealed: S.L.R. 1981.
61. repealed: S.L.R. 1978.

24 Geo. 3, Sess. 1 (1783)

19. repealed: S.L.R. 1978.

24 Geo. 3, Sess. 2 (1784)

12. Bank of Scotland Act 1784.
repealed: S.L.R. 1981.
26. Recess Elections Act 1784.
repealed: 1975, c.66, sch.2.

25 Geo. 3 (1785)

98. repealed: S.L.R. 1978.

26 Geo. 3 (1786)

24. Forcible Entry (Ireland) Act 1786.
s. 66, repealed in pt.: order 74/2143.
27. repealed: S.L.R. 1978.
83. An Act to explain 7 Geo. 3, c.23 (1786).
repealed: S.L.R. 1976.
109. Clyde Marine Society Act 1786.
repealed: S.L.R. 1981.

28 Geo. 3 (1788)

7. Gold and Silver Thread Act 1788.
repealed: 1973, c.43, sch.7.
63. repealed: S.L.R. 1978.

29 Geo. 3 (1789)

29. Northumberland Fishery Act 1789.
repealed: S.L.R. 1981.

30 Geo. 3 (1790)

31. Silver Plate Act 1790.
repealed: 1973, c.43, sch.7.
51. repealed: S.L.R. 1978.

31 Geo. 3 (1791)

32. Roman Catholic Relief Act 1791.
repealed: S.L.R. 1978.

32 Geo. 3 (1792)

24. repealed: S.L.R. 1978.
25. Bank of Scotland Act 1792.
repealed: S.L.R. 1981.
29. Wear Coal Trade Act 1792.
repealed: S.L.R. 1981.
38. repealed: S.L.R. 1977.
56. Servants' Characters Act 1792.
ss. 1, 4, repealed in pt.: 1981, c.45, sch.
s. 6, repealed in pt.: 1976, c.63, sch.3.
63. Scottish Episcopalians Relief Act 1792.
repealed: S.L.R. 1977.

CAP.

33 Geo. 3 (1793)

13. Acts of Parliament (Commencement) Act 1793.
repealed in pt.: 1978, c.30, sch.3.
46. repealed: S.L.R. 1978.
67. Shipping Offences Act 1793.
repealed: 1986, c.64, sch.3.
86. repealed: S.L.R. 1978.
104. Crinan Canal Act 1793.
s. lxxx, see *Kenneth* v. *British Waterways Board,* Second Division, July 1, 1977.
124. An Act for rebuilding the Iron Church of the City of Glasgow 1793.
repealed: S.L.R. 1976.

34 Geo. 3 (1794)

19. Bank of Scotland Act 1794.
repealed: S.L.R. 1981.

35 Geo. 3 (1795)

40. repealed: S.L.R. 1978.
76. repealed: S.L.R. 1977.

36 Geo. 3 (1796)

52. Legacy Duty Act 1796.
repealed: 1975, c.7, sch.13.
62. repealed: S.L.R. 1978.
63. repealed: S.L.R. 1978.

37 Geo. 3 (1797)

47. repealed: S.L.R. 1978.
123. Unlawful Oaths Act 1797.
repealed: S.L.R. 1981.
127. Meeting of Parliament Act 1797.
ss. 3–5, repealed: 1985, c.50, s.20, sch.5.

38 Geo. 3 (1798)

69. Gold Plate (Standard) Act 1798.
repealed: 1973, c.43, sch.7.

39 Geo. 3 (1799)

34. Partridges Act 1799.
repealed: S.L.R. 1978.

39 & 40 Geo. 3 (1800)

28. Bank of England Act 1800.
repealed: S.L.R. 1973.
36. Transfer of Stock Act 1800.
repealed: 1981, c.54, sch.7.
67. Union with Ireland Act 1800.
s. 1, repealed in pt.: 1978, c.23, sch.7.
s. 1, art. 6, see *Ex p. Molyneux* [1986] 1 W.L.R. 331, Taylor J.
81. Hop Trade Act 1800.
repealed: S.L.R. 1973.
93. Treason Act 1800.
repealed: 1980, c.62, sch.7.
94. Criminal Lunatics Act 1800.
repealed: S.L.R. 1981.

41 Geo. 3 (1801)

32. Irish Charges Act 1801.
repealed: S.L.R. 1986.

CAP.

41 Geo. 3 (1801)—cont.

57. Bank Notes Forgery Act 1801.
repealed: 1981, c.45, sch.
86. Probate Duty Act 1801.
repealed: 1975, c.7, sch.13.
88. Judges' Lodgings (Ireland) Act 1801.
repealed: 1978, c.23, sch.7.
90. Crown Debts Act 1801.
preamble, ss. 1–8, repealed: 1982, c.27, sch.14.
103. Malta Act 1801.
repealed: S.L.R. 1986.
109. Inclosure Act 1801.
s. 35, see *Fisons Horticulture* v. *Bunting* (1976) 240 E.G. 625, Walton J.

42 Geo. 3 (1802)

90. Militia Act 1802.
repealed: 1980, c.9, sch.10.
91. Militia (Scotland) Act 1802.
repealed: 1980, c.9, sch.10.

43 Geo. 3 (1803)

143. Public Officers Protection (Ireland) Act 1803.
s. 6, repealed in pt.: 1980, c.59, sch.

44 Geo. 3 (1804)

25. repealed: S.L.R. 1978.
43. Clergy Ordination Act 1804.
s. 1, repealed in pt.: 1986, No. 3, sch.5.
77. Marriages Confirmation Act 1804.
repealed: S.L.R. 1977.
102. Habeas Corpus Act 1804.
repealed in pt.: order 74/2143.
s. 1, repealed in pt.: 1978, c.23, sch.7.

45 Geo. 3 (1805)

89. Bank Notes (Forgery) Act 1805.
repealed: 1981, c.45, sch.
92. Writ of Subpoena Act 1805.
ss. 3, 4, amended: 1978, c.23, sch.5.
116. repealed: S.L.R. 1978.

46 Geo. 3 (1806)

54. Offences at Sea Act 1806.
repealed: S.L.R. 1981.
143. repealed: S.L.R. 1977.

47 Geo. 3, Sess. 2 (1807)

77. repealed: S.L.R. 1978.

48 Geo. 3 (1808)

73. Duchy of Lancaster Act 1808.
ss. 1, 2, 4, 5, 7, 20, repealed: 1988, c.10, sch.
110. Herring Fishery (Scotland) Act 1808.
repealed: 1984, c.26, sch.2.
127. Marriages Confirmation Act 1808.
repealed: S.L.R. 1977.
145. Judges' Pensions (Scotland) Act 1808.
repealed: 1981, c.20, sch.4.

CAP.

48 Geo. 3 (1808)—cont.

149. Probate and Legacy Duties Act 1808.
ss. 35–37, 39, 41, repealed: 1975, c.7, sch.13.
s. 38, repealed in pt.: *ibid.*
s. 42, amended: *ibid.*, sch.4.
151. Court of Session Act 1808.
repealed: 1988, c.36, sch.2.
s. 17, see *Lord Advocate* v. *Glasgow Corporation,* 1973 S.L.T. 153.

50 Geo. 3 (1810)

6. repealed: S.L.R. 1978.
85. Government Offices Security Act 1810.
repealed: S.L.R. 1974.
102. Unlawful Oaths (Ireland) Act 1810.
repealed: S.L.R. 1981.
108. Sea Fisheries (Scotland) Act 1810.
repealed: 1984, c.26, sch.2.
112. Court of Session Act 1810.
repealed: 1988, c.36,sch.2

51 Geo. 3 (1811)

36. Cinque Ports Act 1811.
repealed: S.L.R. 1977.

52 Geo. 3 (1812)

11. House of Commons (Offices) Act 1812.
repealed: 1978, c.36, sch.3.
66. Security of Public Officers Act 1812.
repealed: S.L.R. 1974.
104. Unlawful Oaths Act 1812.
repealed: S.L.R. 1981.
123. Duchy of Cornwall Act 1812.
repealed, except ss. 6–9: S.L.R. 1978.
124. repealed: S.L.R. 1978.
130. Malicious Damage Act 1812.
repealed: S.L.R. 1973.
146. Parochial Registers Act 1812.
repealed: 1978, No. 2, sch.4.
155. Places of Religious Worship Act 1812.
repealed: S.L.R. 1977.
156. Prisoners of War (Escape) Act 1812.
repealed: S.L.R. 1973.
161. Duchy of Lancaster Act 1812.
ss. 1, 3, repealed: 1988, c.10, sch.

53 Geo. 3 (1813)

64. Court of Session Act 1813.
repealed: 1988, c.36, sch.2.
107. Endowed Schools (Ireland) Act 1813.
s. 16, repealed in pt.: 1980, c.59, sch.
117. Bridges (Scotland) Act 1813.
repealed: S.L.R. 1973.
154. Kilmainham Hospital (Pensions Commutation) Act 1813.
repealed: S.L.R. 1976.

54 Geo. 3 (1814)

67. Justiciary Courts (Scotland) Act 1814.
repealed: S.L.R. 1986.
92. Probate and Legacy Duties (Ireland) Act 1814.
repealed: S.L.R. 1978.

CAP.

54 Geo. 3 (1814)—cont.

123. Hop Trade Act 1814.
repealed: regs. 79/1095.
146. Treason Act 1814.
s. 2, repealed: S.L.R. 1973.
159. Harbours Act 1814.
repealed: S.L.R. 1981.

55 Geo. 3 (1815)

42. Jury Trials (Scotland) Act 1815.
ss. 1–19, repealed: 1988, c.36, sch.2.
s. 20, amended: 1973, c.65, sch.27; 1988, c.36, sch.1; repealed in pt.: *ibid.*, schs.1,2.
ss. 21–41, repealed: *ibid.*, sch.2.
94. Herring Fishery (Scotland) Act 1815.
repealed: 1984, c.26, sch.2.
157. Evidence Ireland Act 1815.
repealed: 1978, c.23, sch.7.
184. Stamp Act 1815.
ss. 2, 37 (in pt.), 38, 42–51, repealed: 1975, c.7, sch.13.
ss. 24, 27, 28, repealed: 1972, c.41, sch.28.
sch. 1, repealed in pt.: *ibid.*; 1975, c.7, sch.13.
188. repealed: S.L.R. 1978.
194. Apothecaries Act 1815.
ss. 5, 18, 20, 21, 25–27, repealed: S.L.R. 1976.
ss. 8, 9, 17, 22, repealed in pt.: *ibid.*
s. 11, repealed in pt.: S.L.R. 1981.

56 Geo. 3 (1816)

46. Civil List Audit Act 1816.
s. 10, repealed in pt.: S.L.R. 1981.
s. 11, repealed: S.L.R. 1977.
56. Probate Duty (Ireland) Act 1816.
s. 115, repealed in pt.: 1975, c.7, sch.13.
ss. 117, 130, 131, repealed in pt.: S.L.R. 1981.
ss. 121–129, sch., repealed: *ibid.*
96. Bank of England (Advance) Act 1816.
repealed: S.L.R. 1973.
98. Consolidated Fund Act 1816.
s. 14, repealed: S.L.R. 1978.
s. 18, repealed: S.L.R. 1978.
100. Habeas Corpus Act 1816.
see *Re Shahid Iqbal* [1978] Crim.L.R. 563, D.C.
ss. 1, 3, repealed in pt.: S.L.R. 1981.
s. 3, see *In re Quigley* [1983] 8 N.I.J.B., Hutton J.
115. repealed: S.L.R. 1977.
125. Malicious Damage (Scotland) Act 1816.
repealed: S.L.R. 1973.
136. repealed: S.L.R. 1978.
138. Pillory Abolition Act 1816.
repealed: S.L.R. 1973.

57 Geo. 3 (1817)

19. Seditious Meetings Act 1817.
repealed: 1986, c.64, sch.3.
53. Murders Abroad Act 1817.
repealed: S.L.R. 1981.
56. Recognizances (Ireland) Act 1817.
repealed: 1978, c.23, sch.7.
93. Distress (Costs) Act 1817.
s. 7, repealed: S.L.R. 1976.

CAP.

57 Geo. 3 (1817)—cont.

108. Tolls (Ireland) Act 1817.
ss. 5, 6, repealed: 1980, c.59, sch.
129. repealed: S.L.R. 1978.

58 Geo. 3 (1818)

29. Fees for Pardons Act 1818.
repealed: S.L.R. 1973.
44. repealed: S.L.R. 1977.
45. Church Building Act 1818.
repealed: S.L.R. 1974.

59 Geo. 3 (1819)

7. Cutlery Trade Act 1819.
repealed: S.L.R. 1976.
27. Felony Act 1819.
repealed (S.): S.L.R. 1975.
35. Jury Trials (Scotland) Act 1819.
repealed: 1988, c.36, sch.2.
38. North American Fisheries Act 1819.
repealed: S.L.R. 1976.
45. Court of Session Act 1819.
repealed: 1988, c.36, sch.2.
62. Savings Bank (Scotland) Act 1819.
ss. 2, 4, amended: 1975, c.20, schs.1,2.
134. Church Building Act 1819.
repealed: S.L.R. 1974.

60 Geo. 3 & 1 Geo. 4 (1819)

1. Unlawful Drilling Act 1819.
s. 2, repealed in pt.: 1980, c.59, sch.
4. Pleading in Misdemeanour Act 1819.
repealed: 1978, c.23, sch.7.

1 Geo. 4 (1820)

5. Transfer of Stock (Ireland) Act 1820.
repealed: 1978, c.23, sch.7.
92. Bank Notes Forgery (Scotland) Act 1820.
repealed: 1981, c.45, sch.
100. Militia (City of London) Act 1820.
s. 48, repealed: S.L.R. 1976.
106. Chaplains in the Navy (1820).
repealed: S.L.R. 1975.
108. Apportionment Act 1820.
repealed: S.L.R. 1975.

1 & 2 Geo. 4 (1821)

36. Public Notaries (Ireland) Act 1821.
repealed: 1978, c.23, sch.7.
38. Court of Session Act 1821.
repealed (exc. s.32): 1988, c.36, sch.2.
53. Common Law Procedure (Ireland) Act 1821.
repealed: 1978, c.23, sch.7.
54. Clerk of Assize (Ireland) Act 1821.
repealed: 1978, c.23, sch.7.
79. White Herring Fishery (Scotland) Act 1821.
repealed: 1984, c.26, sch.2.
121. Commissariat Accounts Act 1821.
repealed: S.L.R. 1973.

CAP.

3 Geo. 4 (1822)

33. Riotous Assemblies (Scotland) Act 1822.
s. 10, amended: 1973, c.65, sch.27; repealed in
pt.: *ibid.*, sch.29.
ss. 11–14, repealed: *ibid.*
63. Crown Lands (Ireland) Act 1822.
s. 12, repealed in pt.: order 81/226.
72. Church Building Act 1822.
The whole Act, except ss. 13 and 28, repealed:
S.L.R. 1974.
s. 13, repealed in pt.: *ibid.*
126. Turnpike Roads Act 1822.
repealed: S.L.R. 1981.

4 Geo. 4 (1823)

5. An Act to render valid certain marriages.
repealed: S.L.R. 1977.
16. Turnpike Roads (Tolls on Lime) Act 1823.
repealed: 1981, c.19, sch.1.
**46. An Act for repealing capital punishments
(1823).**
repealed: S.L.R. 1976.
48. Judgment of Death Act 1823.
repealed: 1980, c.59, sch.
61. Court of Chancery (Ireland) Act 1823.
repealed: 1978, c.23, sch.7.
75. repealed: S.L.R. 1978.
79. Highlands 1823.
repealed: S.L.R. 1973.
89. Law Costs (Ireland) Act 1823.
repealed: 1978, c.23, sch.7.
95. Turnpike Roads Act 1823.
repealed: S.L.R. 1981.
**98. Confirmation of Executors (Scotland) Act
1823.**
s. 2, amended: 1980, c.55, s.5.

5 Geo. 4 (1824)

69. Turnpike Roads Act 1824.
repealed: S.L.R. 1981.
83. Vagrancy Act 1824.
see *R.* v. *Jackson* [1974] 2 W.L.R. 641; [1974]
2 All E.R. 211, C.A.
s. 3, see *R.* v. *Dalton* [1982] Crim.L.R. 375,
Marlborough Street Magistrates' Court; *Gray*
v. *Chief Constable of Greater Manchester*
[1983] Crim.L.R. 45, Manchester Cr.Ct.
s. 3, amended: 1982, c.48, sch.14.
s. 4, see *Evans* v. *Ewels* [1972] 1 W.L.R. 671;
116 S.J. 274; [1972] 2 All E.R. 22; 56
Cr.App.R. 377; *Quatromini* v. *Peck* [1972] 1
W.L.R. 1318; 116 S.J. 728; [1972] 3 All E.R.
521; *Baecker* v. *Gray*, 1973 S.L.T. (Notes) 31,
High Ct. of Justiciary; *Friel* v. *Harrison* [1975]
Crim.L.R. 391, D.C.; *R.* v. *Manchester Crown
Court, ex p. Anderton* [1980] Crim.L.R. 303,
D.C.; *R.* v. *Martin* [1981] Crim.L.R. 109, Leeds
Crown Ct.; *Cole* v. *Cardle*, 1981 S.C.C.R. 132;
R. v. *West London Stipendiary Magistrate, ex
p. Simeon* [1982] 3 W.L.R. 289, H.L.;
Smith v. *Superintendent of Woking Police
Station* [1983] Crim.L.R. 323; (1983) 76
Cr.App.R. 234, D.C.; *Wood* v. *Comr. of Police
of the Metropolis* [1986] 1 W.L.R. 796, C.A.

5 Geo. 4 (1824)—cont.

83. Vagrancy Act 1824—cont.
s. 4, amended: 1982, c.48, sch.14; repealed in
pt.: 1981, c.42, sch.; c.47, s.8, sch.; 1986,
c.64, sch.3; repealed (S.): 1982, c.45, sch.4.
s. 5, amended: 1982, c.48, sch.14.
s. 8, repealed: 1984, c.20, s.7, sch.7.
s. 13, repealed: *ibid.*, sch.7.
103. Church Building Act 1824.
repealed: S.L.R. 1974.
111. Crown Debts Act 1824.
repealed: 1982, c.27, sch.14.

6 Geo. 4 (1825)

22. Jurors (Scotland) Act 1825.
ss. 1, 2, repealed: 1980, c.55, sch.3.
s. 3, substituted: 1973, c.65, sch.27; 1985,
c.73, s.23.
ss. 5, 6, repealed: 1973, c.65, sch.29.
s. 7, substituted: *ibid.*, sch.27; repealed in pt.:
S.L.R. 1974.
ss. 7, 8, Act of Adjournal 75/834.
ss. 8, 9, repealed: 1975, c.21, sch.10.
s. 10, amended: 1973, c.65, sch.27; 1975, c.21,
sch.9; 1985, c.73, sch.2.
s. 11, repealed: *ibid.*, sch.4.
s. 13, amended: 1975, c.21, sch.9.
s. 14, repealed: 1985, c.73, sch.4.
ss. 15, 16, 18, repealed: 1975, c.21, sch.10.
ss. 17, 19, repealed: 1988, c.36, sch.2.
s. 20, repealed: 1975, c.21, sch.10.
23. Sheriff Courts (Scotland) Act 1825.
repealed: S.L.R. 1986.
47. Leasing–making (Scotland) Act 1825.
repealed: S.L.R. 1973.
**48. Justices of the Peace Small Debt (Scotland)
Act 1825.**
repealed: 1975, c.20, sch.2.
50. Juries Act 1825.
ss. 1, 27, 50, repealed: 1972, c.71, sch.6.
s. 29, amended: 1974, c.23, s.12.
51. Assizes (Ireland) Act 1825.
repealed: 1978, c.23, sch.7.
62. Poor Prisoners (Scotland) Act 1825.
repealed: S.L.R. 1978.
75. repealed: S.L.R. 1977.
87. Consular Advances Act 1825.
repealed: S.L.R. 1973.
92. Marriages Confirmation Act 1825.
ss. 1, 4, repealed: S.L.R. 1977.
120. Court of Session Act 1825.
ss. 1–52, 53 (in pt.), 54, repealed: 1988, c.36,
sch.2.
s. 10, see *Johnston* v. *Johnston* (O.H.), July 29,
1983.

7 Geo. 4 (1826)

8. Juries (Scotland) Act 1826.
s. 4, amended: 1980, c.55, sch.2; 1985, c.73,
s.23, sch.2; repealed in pt.: 1975, c.21,
sch.10.
s. 5, repealed in pt.: *ibid.*
16. Chelsea and Kilmainham Hospitals Act 1826.
ss. 4, 6–9, 12, 22, 26, 33, repealed: S.L.R. 1976.
ss. 10, 13, 24, 27, repealed in pt.: *ibid.*

7 Geo. 4 (1826)—cont.

**16. Chelsea and Kilmainhan Hospitals Act
1826**—cont.
s. 28, repealed: order 79/1714.
s. 35, repealed in pt.: 1980, c.59, sch.
ss. 42, 43, sch., repealed: S.L.R. 1977.
s. 46, amended: 1982, c.53, s.46.
38. Admiralty Offences Act 1826.
repealed: S.L.R. 1974.
64. Criminal Law Act 1826.
s. 28, see *R.* v. *Spiteri* [1981] Crim.L.R. 419,
C.A.; *R.* v. *Haigh* [1981] Crim.L.R. 263, C.A.
ss. 28, 29, see *R.* v. *Beard (Graham)* [1974] 1
W.L.R. 1549.
s. 29, amended: order 76/229.
s. 30, repealed: 1988, c.33, schs.15,16.

7 & 8 Geo. 4 (1827)

20. Fraudulent Bankrupts (Scotland) Act 1827.
repealed: S.L.R. 1973.
24. Turnpike Roads Act 1827.
repealed: S.L.R. 1981.
72. Church Building Act 1827.
repealed: S.L.R. 1974.

9 Geo. 4 (1828)

14. Statute of Frauds Amendment Act 1828.
s. 6, see *UBAF* v. *European American Banking
Corp.* [1984] 2 W.L.R. 508, C.A.
24. Bills of Exchange (Ireland) Act 1828.
ss. 15, 16, repealed: S.L.R. 1976.
29. Circuit Courts (Scotland) Act 1828.
ss. 2, 5, 7, 10, 12, 14, 17, 21, 23, repealed (S.):
1975, c.21, sch.10.
s. 13, repealed: 1978, c.19, sch.
ss. 15, 24, repealed: 1987, c.41, sch.2.
32. Civil Rights of Convicts Act 1828.
repealed: S.L.R. 1981.
39. Salmon Fisheries (Scotland) Act 1828.
repealed: S.L.R. 1977.
**51. An Act to alter and amend [the Act 6 Geo. 4,
c.75].**
repealed: S.L.R. 1977.
54. Criminal Law (Ireland) Act 1828.
ss. 22, 26, 27, 34, repealed: 1978, c.23, sch.7.
69. Night Poaching Act 1828.
s. 1, see *Jones* v. *Evans* [1978] Crim.L.R. 230,
D.C.
s. 1, amended: 1977, c.45, ss.15,30, sch.1.
s. 2, see *R.* v. *Crush* [1978] Crim.L.R. 357,
Croydon Crown Ct.
s. 2, amended: 1977, c.45, s.15, sch.12.
s. 4, repealed: *ibid.*, sch.13.
s. 7, repealed: S.L.R. 1976.
s. 9, amended: 1977, c.45, s.15, sch.12.
s. 11, repealed: *ibid.*, sch.13.
77. Turnpike Roads Act 1828.
repealed: S.L.R. 1981.
83. Australian Courts Act 1828.
s. 15, repealed: 1986, c.2, s.11.

10 Geo. 4 (1829)

7. Roman Catholic Relief Act 1829.
preamble, repealed: S.L.R. 1978.
ss. 2, 5, 11, repealed: *ibid.*
s. 15, repealed in pt.: 1986, No. 3, s.30, sch. 5.

CAP.

10 Geo. 4 (1829)—cont.
7. Roman Catholic Relief Act 1829—cont.
s. 16, repealed in pt.: S.L.R. 1978; 1986, No. 3, sch.5.
s. 17, repealed in pt.: *ibid.*, s.30; repealed: *ibid.*, sch.5.
ss. 23, 24, repealed: S.L.R. 1978.
13. Court Funds Act 1829.
repealed: 1981, c.54, sch.7.
25. Greenwich Hospital (1829).
repealed: S.L.R. 1975.
38. Criminal Law (Scotland) Act 1829.
repealed: S.L.R. 1973.
44. Metropolitan Police Act 1829.
s. 1, amended: 1973, c.15, s.1, sch.1; repealed in pt.: *ibid.*, s.1, sch.5.
s. 2, repealed: *ibid.*, sch.5.
ss. 14–16, repealed: S.L.R. 1986.

11 Geo. 4 & 1 Will. 4 (1830)
18. Marriage Confirmation Act 1830.
ss. 1, 4, 5, repealed: S.L.R. 1977.
37. Criminal Law (Scotland) Act 1830.
ss. 8, 12, repealed (S.): 1975, c.21, sch.10.
s. 10, repealed: S.L.R. 1977.
s. 11, repealed: 1985, c.73, sch.4.
41. Army Pensions Act 1830.
repealed: S.L.R. 1976.
43. Demise of the Crown Act 1830.
repealed: S.L.R. 1977.
65. Infants Property Act 1830.
ss. 2, 12, 21, 31, 35, repealed in pt.: 1980, c.59, sch.
s. 14, repealed in pt.: 1978, c.23, sch.7; 1980, c.59, sch.
66. Forgery Act 1830.
s. 21, repealed: 1978, No. 2, sch.4.
68. Carriers Act 1830.
s. 10, repealed: 1980, c.59, sch.; S.L.R. 1986.
69. Court of Session Act 1830.
ss. 1–3, 9, 11, 15, 16, 19, 29 (in pt.), repealed: 1988, c.36, sch.2.
s. 33, amended: 1983, c.12, sch.1; repealed in pt.: 1986, c.9, sch.2.
s. 35, repealed: 1988, c.36, sch.2.
s. 36, repealed: 1988, c.32, sch.
70. Law Terms Act 1830.
repealed: S.L.R. 1986.

1 Will. 4 (1830)
4. Colonial Offices Act 1830.
repealed: S.L.R. 1973.

1 & 2 Will. 4 (1831)
17. Custos Rotulorum (Ireland) Act 1831.
repealed: order 75/816.
22. London Hackney Carriage Act 1831.
ss. 4, 27, 28, 35, 36, 41, 51, 56, 57, repealed in pt.: S.L.R. 1976.
ss. 18, 62, 63, 68, 70, 71, repealed: *ibid.*
ss. 37, 43–5, 59, 60, repealed: S.L.R. 1973.
25. Turnpikes Act 1831.
repealed: S.L.R. 1981.

CAP.

1 & 2 Will. 4 (1831)—cont.
32. Game Act 1831.
s. 18, sch., amended: 1975, c.20, schs.1, 2.
s. 31, repealed in pt.: 1984, c.60, sch.6.
s. 31A, added: *ibid.*, sch.6.
s. 32, amended: 1988, c.33, s.64.
s. 45, repealed: S.L.R. 1976.
37. Truck Act 1831.
repealed: 1986, c.48, schs.1,5.
see *Brooker* v. *Charrington Fuel Oils* [1981] I.R.L.R. 147, Wandsworth County Ct.
ss. 2, 3, see *Williams* v. *Butlers* [1975] I.C.R. 208; [1975] 2 All E.R. 889, D.C.
s. 3, see *Topping* v. *Warne Surgical Products* [1986] 9 N.I.J.B., 14, Hutton J.
s. 25, see *Riley* v. *Joseph Frisby* [1982] I.R.L.R. 479, Industrial Tribunal, Nottingham.
38. Church Building Act 1831.
repealed: S.L.R. 1974.
43. Turnpike Roads (Scotland) Act 1831.
see *Moncrieff* v. *Tayside Regional Council* (O.H.), 1987 S.L.T. 374.
s. 96, amended: 1982, c.48, sch.6.
44. Tumultuous Risings (Ireland) Act 1831.
s. 9, amended: 1978, c.23, sch.5.
50. Illicit Distillation (Ireland) Act 1831.
repealed: S.L.R. 1978.
55. Illicit Distillation (Ireland) Act 1831.
repealed: S.L.R. 1977.

2 & 3 Will. 4 (1832)
5. Court of Session Act 1832.
repealed: 1988, c.36, sch.2.
48. Clerk of the Crown (Ireland) Act 1832.
repealed: 1978, c.23, sch.7.
61. Church Building Act 1832.
repealed: S.L.R. 1974.
65. Representation of the People (Scotland) Act 1832.
repealed: S.L.R. 1981.
68. Game (Scotland) Act 1832.
s. 1, see *Ferguson* v. *MacPhail*, 1987 S.C.C.R. 52.
71. Prescription Act 1832.
see *Newnham* v. *Willison* (1988) 56 P. & C.R. 8, C.A.
s. 3, see *Allen* v. *Greenwood* [1979] 2 W.L.R. 187, C.A.; *Carr-Saunders* v. *McNeil (Dick) Associates* [1986] 1 W.L.R. 922, Millett J.
s. 4, see *Goldsmith* v. *Burrow Construction Co.*, The Times, July 31, 1987, C.A.
75. Anatomy Act 1832.
repealed: 1984, c.14, s.13.
s. 1, repealed in pt. (S).: 1975, c.20, sch.2.
105. House of Commons (Speaker) Act 1832.
repealed: 1972, c.3, sch.4.
111. Lord Chancellor's Pension Act 1832.
s. 3, repealed in pt.: S.L.R. 1981.
120. Stage Carriages Act 1832.
repealed in pt.: S.L.R. 1981.
124. Turnpikes Act 1832.
repealed: S.L.R. 1981.

3 & 4 Will. 4 (1833)
30. Poor Rate Exemption Act 1833.
repealed: S.L.R. 1975.

CAP.

3 & 4 Will. 4 (1833)—cont.

41. Judicial Committee Act 1833.
modified: order 78/1030.
s. 3, see *Thomas* v. *The Queen* [1978] 3 W.L.R. 927, P.C.
s. 9, repealed in pt.: order 79/1714; 1981, c.19, sch.1.
ss. 10–12, repealed: 1980, c.59, sch.
s. 24, rules 76/899; 80/714; orders 79/720; 80/1078; 81/1124; 82/1676; 85/1635.

45. Marriages at Hamburg Act 1833.
repealed: 1988, c.44, sch.

49. Quakers and Moravians Act 1833.
repealed: S.L.R. 1977.

69. Crown Lands (Scotland) Act 1833.
s. 7, repealed: 1974, c.38, s.20, sch.7.

74. Fines and Recoveries Act 1833.
ss. 33, 48, 49, amended: 1983, c.20, sch.4.
s. 67, repealed in pt.: S.L.R. 1976.

80. Turnpike Trusts Returns Act 1833.
repealed: S.L.R. 1981.

83. Bank Notes Act 1833.
repealed: S.L.R. 1973.

85. Government of India Act 1833.
s. 112, orders 75/1211; 83/1113; 87/1268; 88/1842.

98. Bank of England Act 1833.
repealed: S.L.R. 1973.

99. Fines Act 1833.
ss. 23–25, 33, amended: order 76/229.
ss. 26–28, 30–32, 33 (in pt.); repealed: 1981, c.54, sch.7.

4 & 5 Will. 4 (1834)

22. Apportionment Act 1834.
repealed: S.L.R. 1977.

28. Marriage (Scotland) Act 1834.
repealed: 1977, c.15, sch.3.

70. House of Commons Officers Act 1834.
repealed: 1978, c.36, sch.3.

78. Chancery (Ireland) Act 1834.
repealed: 1978, c.23, sch.7.

81. Turnpike Tolls (Allowance of Wagon Weights) Act 1834.
repealed: S.L.R. 1981.

82. Fines and Recoveries (Ireland) Act 1834.
ss. 31, 46, 47, repealed in pt.: 1980, c.59, sch.

5 & 6 Will. 4 (1835)

16. Chancery (Ireland) Act 1835.
repealed: 1978, c.23, sch.7.

18. Turnpike Tolls Act 1835.
repealed: S.L.R. 1981.

26. Assizes (Ireland) Act 1835.
repealed: 1978, c.23, sch.7.

35. Paymaster General Act 1835.
ss. 1, 7, repealed: S.L.R. 1981.
ss. 3, 4, repealed in pt.: *ibid.*
ss. 10, 11, repealed: S.L.R. 1977.

50. Highway Act 1835.
s. 5, repealed in pt.: S.L.R. 1975.
s. 50, repealed: S.L.R. 1973.
s. 72, amended: 1982, c.48, sch.3.
s. 77, repealed: *ibid.*

CAP.

5 & 6 Will. 4 (1835)—cont.

50. Highway Act 1835—*cont.*
s. 78, see *Midlands Electricity Board* v. *Stephenson* [1973]] Crim.L.R. 441.
s. 78, repealed in pt.: S.L.R. 1973.
ss. 103, 110, 114, 115, repealed: 1982, c.48, sch.3.

55. Sheriffs (Ireland) Act 1835.
ss. 6, 11–17, 23, 24, 39–41, repealed: 1978, c.23, sch.7.
sch. 1, repealed: 1980, c.59, sch.

62. Statutory Declarations Act 1835.
s. 12, repealed: 1974, c.39, sch.5.
s. 14, repealed in pt.: S.L.R. 1973.

6 & 7 Will. 4 (1836).

13. Constabulary (Ireland) Act 1836.
s. 16, amended: 1978, c.23, sch.5.
s. 23, repealed: order 74/2143.
s. 24, repealed in pt.: order 79/1714.
s. 50, repealed in pt.: 1980, c.59, sch.

19. Durham (County Palatine) Act 1836.
repealed: S.L.R. 1976.

22. Bastards (Scotland) Act 1836.
repealed: 1986, c.9, sch.2.

24. repealed: S.L.R. 1977.

28. Government Offices Security Act 1836.
repealed: S.L.R. 1974.

43. Judicial Ratifications (Scotland) Act 1836.
repealed: S.L.R. 1978.

69. Plate (Scotland) Act 1836.
repealed: 1973, c.43, sch.7.

74. Court of Chancery (Ireland) Act 1836.
repealed: 1978, c.23, sch.7.

76. Stamp Duties on Newspapers Act 1836.
s. 19, see *Ricci* v. *Chow, The Times,* June 19, 1987, C.A.

77. Ecclesiastical Commissioners Act 1836.
s. 9, repealed in pt.: S.L.R. 1981.

86. Births and Deaths Registration Act 1836.
s. 35, repealed: 1978, No. 2, sch.4.

87. Liberties Act 1836.
repealed: S.L.R. 1976.

92. repealed: S.L.R. 1977.

114. Trials for Felony Act 1836.
repealed: S.L.R. 1986.

116. Grand Jury (Ireland) Act 1836.
ss. 50–52, 54–56, 162, repealed: order 80/1085.
s. 168, amended: order 75/816.
ss. 169, 170, repealed: 1980, c.59, sch.

7 Will. 4 & 1 Vict. (1837)

14. Jury Trials (Scotland) Act 1837.
repealed: 1988, c.36, sch.2.

26. Wills Act 1837.
ss. 7, 11, see *Re Rapley, decd.* [1983] 1 W.L.R. 1069, Finlay J.
s. 9, see *Re Colling* [1972] 1 W.L.R. 1440; 116 S.J. 547; [1972] 3 All E.R. 729.
s. 9, substituted: 1982, c.53, s.7.
s. 11, see *Re Jones (decd.)* [1981] 2 W.L.R. 106; [1981] 1 All E.R. 1, Arnold P.
s. 13, see *Re Whale* [1977] 2 N.Z.L.R. 1, Wild C.J.

CAP.

7 Will. 4 & 1 Vict. (1837)—cont.

26. Wills Act 1837—cont.
ss. 14, 15, see *In the Estate of Crannis (decd.)*, *Mansell* v. *Crannis* (1978) 122 S.J. 489, Browne-Wilkinson J.
s. 15, see *Ross* v. *Caunters* [1979] 3 W.L.R. 605, Megarry V.-C.
s. 18, see *Re Coleman (decd.)* [1975] 2 W.L.R. 213; [1975] 1 All E.R. 675; *Re Whale* [1977] 2 N.Z.L.R. 1, Wild C.J.; *Re Roberts (decd.)* [1978] 1 W.L.R. 653, C.A.
s. 18, substituted: 1982, c.53, s.18.
s. 18A, see *Cherrington (Decd.)*, *Re* [1984] 1 W.L.R. 772, Butler-Sloss J.; *Sinclair (Decd.)*, *Re, Lloyds Bank* v. *Imperial Cancer Research Fund* [1985] 1 All E.R. 1066, C.A.
s. 18A, added: 1982, c.53, s.18; amended: 1986, c.55, s.53.
s. 23, see *Re Fleming's Will Trusts; Ennion* v. *Hampstead Old People's Housing Trust* [1974] 3 All E.R. 323.
s. 32, amended: 1973, c.55, sch.
s. 33, see *Re Freemantle's Will Trusts* (1984) 81 L.S.Gaz. 282, Nourse J.
s. 33, substituted: 1982, c.53, s.19.
31. Demise of the Crown Act 1837.
repealed: S.L.R. 1973.
41. Small Debt (Scotland) Act 1837.
ss. 16, see *Graham & White* v. *Monktonhall Concessionary Coal Delivery Service*, 1976 S.L.T.(Sh. Ct.) 31.
46. Rolls Estate Act 1837.
repealed (except s. 4): S.L.R. 1975.
53. Liberty of Ely Act 1837.
repealed: S.L.R. 1975.
83. Parliamentary Documents Deposit Act 1837.
amended: 1978, c.23, sch.5.
88. Piracy Act 1837.
s. 2, amended: 1973, c.53, sch.5.

1 & 2 Vict. (1837–38)

2. Civil List Act 1837.
s. 5, amended: 1972, c.7, s.4.
23. Parsonages Act 1838.
s. 14, repealed: S.L.R. 1977.
28. Bread (Ireland) Act 1838.
ss. 13, 15, repealed in pt.; 1980, c.59, sch.
s. 23, repealed in pt.: S.L.R. 1976.
38. Vagrancy Act 1838.
repealed: 1981, c.42, sch.
43. Dean Forest (Mines) Act 1838.
s. 56, repealed in pt.: S.L.R. 1978.
56. Poor Relief (Ireland) Act 1838.
ss. 103, 105–107, 109, 112, sch.1, repealed: 1980, c.59, sch.
ss. 114–116, repealed: 1978, c.23, sch.7.
61. Government Offices Security Act 1838.
repealed: S.L.R. 1974.
67. West Indian Prisons Act 1838.
repealed: S.L.R. 1973.
74. Small Tenements Recovery Act 1838.
s. 2, see *Stoker* v. *Stansfield* [1972] 1 W.L.R. 513; [1972] 1 All E.R. 938.
77. Quakers and Moravians Act 1838.
repealed: S.L.R. 1977.
86. Court of Session (No. 1) Act 1838.
repealed: 1988, c.36, sch.2.

CAP.

1 & 2 Vict. (1837–38)—cont.

101. Duchies of Lancaster and Cornwall (Accounts) Act 1838.
title, repealed in pt.: S.L.R. 1978.
preamble, repealed: *ibid.*
s. 1, repealed: *ibid.*
s. 2, amended: 1982, c.47, s.9.
105. Oaths Act 1838.
repealed: 1978, c.19, sch.
106. Pluralities Act 1838.
ss. 2–27, repealed: S.L.R. 1974.
s. 31, repealed in pt.: 1986, No. 3, sch.5.
s. 41, repealed: 1972, No. 2, sch.2.
s. 58, amended: 1986, No. 3, sch.4; repealed in pt.: *ibid.*, sch.5.
ss. 62–69, 72, repealed: 1972, No. 2, sch.2.
s. 95, repealed in pt.: S.L.R. 1974.
ss. 97 (in pt.), 98, repealed, 1988 No. 1, s.7, sch.3.
s. 106, repealed: S.L.R. 1974.
107. Church Building Act 1838.
The whole Act, except s. 14, repealed: S.L.R. 1974.
110. Judgments Act 1838.
s. 17, see *K.* v. *K.* [1977] 2 W.L.R. 55, C.A.; *Parsons* v. *Mather & Platt* [1977] 1 W.L.R. 855, Ackner J; *Ealing London Borough Council* v. *El Isaacs* [1980] 1 W.L.R. 932; [1980] 2 All E.R. 458, C.A.; *Hunt* v. *R.M.Douglas (Roofing), The Times*, November 7, 1988, H.L.
s. 17, amended: orders 77/141; 79/1382; 80/672; 82/696, 1427; 85/437.
ss. 17, 18, see *Erven Warnink BV* v. *J. Townend & Sons (Hull)* [1982] 3 All E.R. 312, C.A.
s. 18, see *K.* v. *K.* [1977] 2 W.L.R. 55, C.A.
114. Debtors (Scotland) Act 1838.
ss. 2–15, repealed: 1987, c.18, sch.8.
s. 21, see *Mowat* v. *Kerr*, 1977 S.L.T. (Sh.Ct.) 62.
s. 22, amended: 1987, c.18, sch.6.
ss. 23–25, repealed: *ibid.*, sch.8.
s. 26, see *New Day Furnishing Stores* v. *Curran*, 1974 S.L.T.(Sh.Ct.) 20; *British Relay* v. *Keay*, 1976 S.L.T. (Sh.Ct.) 23; *City Bakeries* v. *S. & S. Snack Bars & Restaurants*, 1979 S.L.T. (Sh.Ct.) 28; *South of Scotland Electricity Board* v. *Carlyle*, 1980 S.L.T.(Sh.Ct.) 98; *Roboserve* v. *Akerman*, 1978 S.L.T.(Sh.Ct.) 137.
ss. 26–28, repealed: 1987, c.18, sch.8.
ss. 26, 28, see *Cantors* v. *Hardie*, 1974 S.L.T.(Sh.Ct.) 26.
s. 27, see *Wallace Evans & Partners* v. *T. Daly & Co.*, 1984 S.L.T.(Sh.Ct.) 25; *Aalco Glasgow* v. *Harska Engineering*, 1985 S.L.T.(Sh.Ct.) 65.
ss. 29–31, 32 (in pt.), 35, schs. repealed: 1987, c.18, sch.8.
118. Court of Session (No. 2) Act 1838.
repealed (exc. s.27): 1988, c.36, sch.2.
119. Sheriff Courts (Scotland) Act 1838.
repealed: S.L.R. 1986.
120. Tin Duties Act 1838.
repealed: 1983, c.29, sch.3.

2 & 3 Vict. (1839)

30. Spiritual Duties Act 1839.
repealed: S.L.R. 1977.

CAP.

2 & 3 Vict. (1839)—cont.

36. Court of Session Act 1939.
s. 1, repealed: 1988, c.36, sch.2.
45. Highway (Railway Crossings) Act 1839.
s. 1, amended (S.): 1984, c.54, sch.9.
46. Turnpike Tolls Act 1839.
repealed: S.L.R. 1981.
47. Metropolitan Police Act 1839.
s. 4, repealed: 1973, c.15, sch.5.
s. 7, repealed: 1984, c.60, sch.7.
s. 10, repealed: S.L.R. 1978.
s. 32, repealed: S.L.R. 1986.
ss. 34, 38 (in pt.), repealed: 1984, c.60, sch.7.
s. 39, amended: *ibid.*, sch.6; repealed in pt.: *ibid.*, sch.7.
s. 47, amended: 1988, c.29, sch.2; repealed in pt.: 1984, c.60, sch.7.
s. 50, repealed: 1974, c.39, sch.5.
ss. 51, 56, 59, repealed: S.L.R. 1973.
s. 54, see *Myers* v. *Garrett* [1972] Crim.L.R. 232; *Grant* v. *Taylor* [1986] Crim.L.R. 252, D.C.; *Masterson* v. *Holden* [1986] 1 W.L.R. 1017, D.C.
s. 54, amended: 1977, c.43, s.31, sch.6; repealed in pt.: S.L.R. 1973; 1981, c.42, sch.; 1984, c.60, sch.7; 1986, c.64, sch.3.
ss. 62 (in pt.), 63–65, repealed: 1984, c.60, sch.7.
s. 66, see *Daniel* v. *Morrison* (1979) 70 Cr.App.R. 142, D.C.; *King* v. *Gardner* (1980) 71 Cr. App.R. 13, D.C.; *Pedro* v. *Diss* [1981] Crim.L.R. 236, D.C.; *R.* v. *Prince* [1981] Crim.L.R. 638, Wood Green Crown Ct., Judge McMullen; *R.* v. *Hamilton* [1986] Crim.L.R. 187, C.A.
s. 66, repealed: 1984, c.60, s.7, sch.7.
s. 67, repealed: *ibid.*, sch.7.
s. 69, amended: 1976, c.63, sch.2; repealed in pt.: *ibid.*, sch.3.
s. 74, repealed: S.L.R. 1986.
49. Church Building Act 1839.
ss. 1–5, 8–11, repealed: S.L.R. 1974.
ss. 6, 7, repealed: S.L.R. 1977.
51. Pensions Act 1839.
repealed: S.L.R. 1976.
71. Metropolitan Police Courts Act 1839.
s. 24, repealed: 1977, c.45, schs.12,13.
ss. 27, 28, repealed in pt.: 1974, c.39, sch.5.
s. 37, repealed: S.L.R. 1978.
ss. 39, 40, 51, sch.A, repealed: S.L.R. 1986.

3 & 4 Vict. (1840)

2. repealed: S.L.R. 1977.
9. Parliamentary Papers Act 1840.
s. 3, amended: 1984, c.46, sch.5.
20. Queen Anne's Bounty Act 1840.
ss. 2–4, repealed: 1986, No. 3, sch.5.
39. Turnpikes Act 1840.
repealed: S.L.R. 1981.
50. Canals (Offences) Act 1840.
repealed: 1984, c.60, sch.7.
s. 11, repealed: *ibid.*, s.7, sch.7.
51. Turnpike Tolls Act 1840.
repealed: S.L.R. 1981.

CAP.

3 & 4 Vict. (1840)—cont.

59. Evidence (Scotland) Act 1840.
s. 1, see *McGregor* v. *J.*, First Division, Oct. 23, 1974.
ss. 1, 3, 4 (in pt.), repealed (S.): 1975, c.21, sch.10.
60. Church Building Act 1840.
repealed: S.L.R. 1974.
97. Railway Regulation Act 1840.
ss. 13, 16, repealed in pt.: 1980, c.59, sch.
s. 16, amended: 1984, c.60, sch.6.
ss. 17, 21, repealed: S.L.R. 1976.
105. Debtors (Ireland) Act 1840.
repealed: 1978, c.23, sch.7.
108. Municipal Corporations (Ireland) Act 1840.
ss. 22, 51, 130, 139, repealed: 1978, c.23, sch.7.
109. Counties and Boroughs (Ireland) Act 1840.
s. 1, repealed: 1978, c.23, sch.7.
110. Loan Societies Act 1840.
ss. 6 (in pt.), 7 (in pt.), 16 (in pt.), 17 (in pt.), 18, 21 (in pt.), 23 (in pt.), 26, 28 (in pt.), sch. (in pt.), repealed: S.L.R. 1981.
113. Ecclesiastical Commissioners Act 1840.
ss. 32, 71, 72, 74, repealed: S.L.R. 1974.
ss. 37, 70, 77, repealed: S.L.R. 1977.
ss. 42, 48, 73, repealed: 1986, No. 3, sch. 5.

4 & 5 Vict. (1841)

1. Scrabster Harbour Act 1841.
ss. 17, 19, see *Paterson and Matchett* v. *Scrabster Harbour Trs.*, 1983 S.L.T. 174.
33. Turnpike Tolls Act 1841.
repealed: S.L.R. 1981.
38. School Sites Act 1841.
s. 2, see *Re Clayton's Deed Poll* [1979] 2 All E.R. 1133, Whitford J.; *Re Rowhook Mission Hall, Horsham; Chaning-Pearce* v. *Morris; Ladypool Road Old National School, Birmingham, Re; Birmingham Diocesan Board of Finance* v. *Russell* [1984] 3 W.L.R. 710, Nourse J.
s. 14, amended: S.L.R. 1978.
ss. 15, 19, repealed: S.L.R. 1978.
39. Ecclesiastical Commissioners Act 1841.
ss. 3–10, repealed: S.L.R. 1974.
s. 22, repealed: 1986, No. 3, sch.5.
s. 23, repealed: S.L.R. 1977.
59. Application of Highway Rates to Turnpikes Act 1841.
repealed: S.L.R. 1981.

5 & 6 Vict. (1842)

26. Ecclesiastical Houses of Residence Act 1842.
s. 12, amended: 1982, c.53, s.46.
45. Literary Copyright Act 1842.
see *Redwood Music* v. *B. Feldman & Co.* [1979] R.P.C. 385, C.A.
47. Customs Act 1842.
repealed: 1973, c.43, sch.7.
55. Railway Regulation Act 1842.
s. 9, amended (S.): 1984, c.54, sch.9.
s. 17, see *Rodgers* v. *Smith*, 1981 S.L.T. (Notes) 31.

CAP.

5 & 6 Vict. (1842)—cont.

55. Railway Regulation Act 1842—cont.
s. 17, repealed in pt.: 1984, c.60, sch.7.
s. 20, repealed in pt.: S.L.R. 1978.
69. Perpetuation of Testimony Act 1842.
repealed: S.L.R. 1981.
75. Charitable Pawn Offices (Ireland) Act 1842.
repealed: 1974, c.39, sch.5.
78. repealed: S.L.R. 1978.
79. Railway Passenger Duty Act 1842.
repealed: 1975, c.7, sch.13.
82. Stamp Duties (Ireland) Act 1842.
repealed: S.L.R. 1978.
94. Defence Act 1842.
ss. 10, 18, repealed in pt.: S.L.R. 1973.
ss. 14–16, see *Shonleigh Nominees* v. *Att.-Gen.*
[1974] 1 W.L.R. 305; [1974] 1 All E.R. 734,
H.L.
s. 29, repealed in pt.: 1978, c.23, sch.7.
97. Limitation of Actions and Costs Act 1842.
repealed in pt.: 1978, c.23, sch.7.
106. Fisheries (Ireland) Act 1842.
ss. 86, 87, 89–92, 96–103, repealed in pt.: order
81/227.
108. Ecclesiastical Leasing Act 1842.
s. 4, see *Oakley* v. *Boston* [1975] 3 W.L.R. 478;
[1975] 3 All E.R. 405, C.A.
ss. 12, 13, repealed: S.L.R. 1974.
110. Coventry (1842).
repealed: S.L.R. 1975.
113. repealed: S.L.R. 1977.

6 & 7 Vict. (1843)

19. repealed: S.L.R. 1978.
22. The (Colonies) Evidence Act 1843.
repealed: S.L.R. 1976.
37. New Parishes Act 1843.
The whole Act, except s. 6, repealed: S.L.R.
1974.
s. 6, repealed in pt.: *ibid.*
39. repealed: S.L.R. 1977.
77. Welsh Cathedrals Act 1843.
repealed: S.L.R. 1977.
85. Evidence Act 1843.
repealed: S.L.R. 1986.
86. London Hackney Carriages Act 1843.
s. 2, see *Bassam* v. *Green* [1981] R.T.R. 362,
D.C.
s. 2, repealed in pt.: S.L.R. 1976.
s. 4, repealed: S.L.R. 1973.
ss. 7, 8 (in pt.), 10 (in pt.), repealed: S.L.R. 1976.
ss. 15, 17 (in pt.), repealed: S.L.R. 1976.
s. 20, repealed: 1981, c.45, sch.
ss. 21–22, repealed in pt.: S.L.R. 1976.
s. 23, repealed in pt.: *ibid.*; 1985, c.54, sch.27.
s. 24, repealed in pt.: S.L.R. 1976.
s. 25, amended: 1985, c.67, sch.7; repealed in
pt.: S.L.R. 1976.
s. 27, amended: 1984, c.60, sch.6; repealed in
pt.: S.L.R. 1976.
ss. 28 (in pt.), 30, repealed: *ibid.*
s. 32, repealed: S.L.R. 1973.
ss. 33 (in pt.), 35 (in pt.), 36, 37, 38 (in pt.), 39
(in pt.), 40–43, 44 (in pt.), 45, 46, sch.,
repealed: S.L.R. 1976.

CAP.

6 & 7 Vict. (1843)—cont.

98. Slave Trade Act 1843.
s. 4, amended: 1978, c.78, sch.5; repealed in
pt.: S.L.R. 1976; 1978, c.78, sch.7.

7 & 8 Vict. (1844)

19. Inferior Courts Act 1844.
repealed: 1977, c.38, sch.5.
22. Gold and Silver Wares Act 1844.
repealed: 1973, c.43, sch.7.
32. Bank Charter Act 1844.
s. 1, repealed in pt.: S.L.R. 1973.
s. 7, repealed: 1972, c.41, sch.28.
s. 21, repealed: 1979, c.37, s.46, sch.7.
s. 26, repealed: S.L.R. 1973.
**56. Church Building (Banns and Marriages) Act
1844.**
repealed: S.L.R. 1974.
59. Lecturers and Parish Clerks Act 1844.
s. 3, repealed in pt.: S.L.R. 1977.
61. Counties (Detached Parts) Act 1844.
repealed: 1972, c.70, sch.30.
69. Judicial Committee Act 1844.
s. 1, orders 73/1081, 1084; 75/1505, 1507,
1510, 1513; 76/1149; 83/1108, 1109, 1888;
84/1151; 85/445, 450, 1199.
s. 1, repealed in pt.: S.L.R. 1986.
81. Marriages (Ireland) Act 1844.
ss. 9, 22, repealed in pt.: S.L.R. 1981.
s. 80, repealed in pt.: S.L.R. 1976.
92. Coroners Act 1844.
repealed: 1988, c.13, sch.4.
94. New Parishes Act 1844.
repealed: S.L.R. 1974.
96. Execution Act 1844.
repealed: except s. 67; 1981, c.54, sch.7.
101. Poor Law Amendment Act 1844.
repealed: S.L.R. 1974.
105. Duchy of Cornwall (No. 2) Act 1844.
repealed, except ss. 39, 40, 53–70, 92, schs.:
S.L.R. 1978.
s. 92, repealed in pt.: *ibid.*
107. Common Law Offices (Ireland) Act 1844.
repealed: 1978, c.23, sch.7.

8 & 9 Vict. (1845)

16. Companies Clauses Consolidation Act 1845.
s. 3, repealed in pt.: 1980, c. 59, sch.; S.L.R.
1981.
ss. 142 (in pt.), 150, 154 (in pt.), 155, repealed:
1980, c.59, sch.
s. 158, repealed: S.L.R. 1976.
**17. Companies Clauses Consolidation (Scotland)
Act 1845.**
s. 3, repealed in pt.: S.L.R. 1981.
s. 143, repealed: S.L.R. 1986.
18. Lands Clauses Consolidation Act 1845.
s. 3, amended: 1978, c.23, sch.5; repealed in
pt.: 1980, c.5, sch.; S.L.R. 1981.
s. 9, amended: 1978, c.23, sch.5.
s. 10, repealed: 1977, c.30, sch.2.
ss. 59, 60, 61 (in pt.), repealed: S.L.R. 1974.
s. 68, see *Argyle Motors (Birkenhead)* v. *Birkenhead Corporation* [1974] 2 W.L.R. 71; [1974]
1 All E.R. 201, H.L.

CAP.

8 & 9 Vict. (1845)—cont.

18. Lands Clauses Consolidation Act 1845—cont.
ss. 69–71, 73, 76, 78, 84–89, amended: 1978, c.23, sch.5.
ss. 70, 78, 86, amended: 1982, c.53, s.46.
s. 92, see *London Transport Executive v. Congregational Union of England and Wales (Inc.)* (1979) 37 P. & C.R. 155, Goulding J.
ss. 99, 100, 107, 109, 111, 113, 117, amended: 1978, c.23, sch.5.
ss. 135, 140, repealed: S.L.R. 1974.
s. 138, repealed: 1980, c.59, sch.
s. 145, repealed: S.L.R. 1986.
sch.A, amended: 1978, c.23, sch.5.

19. Lands Clauses Consolidation (Scotland) Act 1845.
see *Rogano v. British Railways Board,* 1979 S.C. 297.
s. 3, repealed in pt.: S.L.R. 1981.
ss. 17, 19, 48, see *Park Automobile Co. v. Strathclyde Regional Council,* 1984 S.L.T.(Lands Tr.) 14.
s. 61, amended: 1972, c.60, sch.2.; 1973, c.26, s.67; c.56, s.63.
s. 80, see *Barr v. Glasgow Corporation,* 1972 S.L.T.(Sh.Ct.) 63.
s. 84, see *Birrell v. City of Edinburgh District Council,* 1982 S.L.T. 111.
s. 101, see *McNicol v. Glasgow Corporation,* 1975 S.L.T.(Lands Tr.) 26.
s. 107, see *Barr v. Glasgow Corporation,* 1972 S.L.T.(Sh.Ct.) 63.
s. 108, see *Blythswood Friendly Society v. Glasgow District Council* (H.L.), 1978 S.L.T. 213; 1981 S.L.T.(Lands Trib.) 2.
s. 114, see *Woolfson v. Glasgow Corporation,* 1976 S.L.T. (Lands Tr.) 5; *Smith and Waverley Tailoring Company v. Edinburgh District Council (No. 2),* 1977 S.L.T. (Lands Tr.) 29; *Anderson v. Moray District Council,* 1978 S.L.T. (Lands Tr.) 37.
s. 116, amended: 1975, c.28, sch.3; 1987, c.26, sch. 7.
ss. 129, 132, repealed: S.L.R. 1986.

20. Railways Clauses Consolidation Act 1845.
s. 1, see *Short v. British Railways Board* [1974] 1 W.L.R. 781.
s. 3, repealed in pt.: 1980, c.59, sch.; S.L.R. 1981.
s. 60, repealed: 1980, c.59, sch.
s. 61, see *Thomas v. British Railways Board* [1976] 2 W.L.R. 761, C.A.
s. 68, see *Short v. British Railways Board* [1974] 1 W.L.R. 781; *T. R. H. Sampson Associates v. British Railways Board* [1983] 1 W.L.R. 170, Michael Wheeler, Q.C.; *R. Walker & Sons v. British Railways Board* [1984] 2 All E.R. 249, Goulding J.
s. 104, repealed in pt.: 1980, c.59, sch.; 1984, c.60, sch.7.
s. 139, repealed: S.L.R. 1986.
ss. 142 (in pt.), 148, 153, repealed: 1980, c.59, sch.
s. 156, repealed: S.L.R. 1976.

CAP.

8 & 9 Vict. (1845)—cont.

33. Railways Clauses Consolidation (Scotland) Act 1845.
s. 3, amended: 1984, c.54, sch.9; repealed in pt.: S.L.R. 1981.
s. 6, amended: 1973, c.56, ss.59, 61.
s. 11, amended: 1984, c.54, sch.9; repealed in pt.: *ibid.,* schs.9,11.
s. 12, amended: *ibid.,* sch.9.
s. 16, amended: *ibid.;* repealed in pt.: *ibid.,* sch.11.
s. 18, repealed in pt.: *ibid.*
ss. 39–44, amended: *ibid.,* sch.9.
s. 46, repealed in pt.: *ibid.,* sch.11.
ss. 47, 49, 50–56, amended: *ibid.,* sch.9.
s. 60, see *Sudjic v. British Railways Board,* 1979 S.L.T.(Sh.Ct.) 64.
s. 144, repealed: 1980, c.62, sch.8.

37. Bankers (Ireland) Act 1845.
s. 9, repealed: 1980, c.59, sch.

38. Bank Notes (Scotland) Act 1845.
s. 13, repealed: 1979, c.37, s.46, sch.7.

70. Church Building Act 1845.
repealed: S.L.R. 1974.

72. Rothwell Gaol Act 1845.
repealed: S.L.R. 1986.

76. Revenue Act 1845.
repealed: S.L.R. 1981.

104. repealed: S.L.R. 1978.

109. Gaming Act 1845.
s. 10, order 82/892.
ss. 10–14, repealed: 1987, c.19, sch.
s. 14, see *Foster v. Attard* [1986] Crim.L.R. 627, D.C.
s. 18, see *A. R. Dennis & Co. v. Campbell* [1978] 2 W.L.R. 429, C.A.; *Futures Index, The, Re, The Times,* October 12, 1984, Harman J.; *Lipkin Gorman v. Karpnale, The Financial Times,* October 19, 1988, C.A.
s. 25, repealed: S.L.R. 1976.
sch. 3, repealed: 1987, c.19, sch.

115. Chancery Taxing Master (Ireland) Act 1845.
repealed: 1978, c.23, sch.7.

118. Inclosure Act 1845.
ss. 39, 40, repealed in pt.: S.L.R. 1981.
s. 163, repealed in pt.: 1985, c.54, sch.27.

127. Small Debts Act 1845.
ss. 9–12, 14, 16–21, 23, repealed: 1977, c.38, sch.5;
s. 24, repealed in pt.: *ibid.*
sch. (C.), repealed: *ibid.*

9 & 10 Vict. (1846)

59. Religious Disabilities Act 1846.
s. 4, repealed: S.L.R. 1977.

67. Citations (Scotland) Act 1846.
s. 1, repealed in pt.: 1987, c.18, sch.8.

68. Church Building (Burial Service in Chapels) Act 1846.
repealed: S.L.R. 1974.

72. Marriages (Ireland) Act 1846.
s. 1, amended: 1983, c.32, sch.2.
s. 4, repealed in pt.: S.L.R. 1977.

73. Tithe Act 1846.
s. 9, amended: 1982, c.53, s.46.

CAP.

9 & 10 Vict. (1846)—cont.

77. House of Commons Offices Act 1846.
repealed: 1978, c.36, sch.3.
s. 5, amended: 1978, c.44, sch.16.

88. Church Patronage Act 1846.
repealed: 1986, No. 3, sch.5.

93. Fatal Accidents Act 1846.
repealed: 1976, c.30, sch.2.
see *Davies* v. *Taylor* [1972] 3 W.L.R. 801; 116 S.J. 864; [1972] 3 All E.R. 836; *Cookson* v. *Knowles* [1978] 2 W.L.R. 978, H.L.
s. 2, see *Davies* v. *Whiteways Cyder Co.* [1974] 3 All E.R. 168; *Hay* v. *Hughes* [1975] 2 W.L.R. 34; [1975] 1 All E.R. 257, C.A.; *Payne-Collins* v. *Taylor Woodrow Construction* [1975] 2 W.L.R. 386; *Murray* v. *Shuter; Same* v. *Same* [1975] 3 W.L.R. 597; [1975] 3 All E.R. 375, C.A.; *Dodds* v. *Dodds* [1978] 2 W.L.R. 434, Balcombe J.
s. 3, see *Kaur (Pritam)* v. *Russell* [1973] 2 W.L.R. 147, C.A.

111. Ejectment and Distress (Ireland) Act 1846.
ss. 15, 16, 18, 20, 22, repealed in pt.: order 81/226.

10 & 11 Vict. (1847)

4. Chelsea Pensions (Abolition of Poundage) Act 1847.
repealed: S.L.R. 1976.

14. Markets and Fairs Clauses Act 1847.
see *Halton Borough Council* v. *Cawley* [1985] 1 W.L.R. 15, Blackett-Ord V.C.
s. 3, repealed in pt.: 1980, c.59, sch.; S.L.R. 1981.
s. 13, see *Wakefield City Council* v. *Box* [1982] 3 All E.R. 506, H.H. FitzHugh J.

16. Commissioners Clauses Act 1847.
s. 3, repealed in pt.: 1980, c.59, sch.; S.L.R. 1981.
s. 64, repealed in pt.: 1980, c.59, sch.

27. Harbours, Docks and Piers Clauses Act 1847.
s. 3, amended: 1973, c.65, sch.19; repealed in pt.: 1980, c.59, sch.; S.L.R. 1981.
ss. 7–9, amended: 1973, c.65, sch.19.
ss. 21, 22, 33, 67, see *Coutts* v. *J. M. Piggins* (O.H.), 1982 S.L.T. 213; 1983 S.L.T. 320.
s. 57, see *Peterhead Harbours Trs.* v. *Chalmers* (O.H.), 1984 S.L.T. 130.
s. 57, amended (S.): 1987, c.18, sch.6.
s. 71, order 87/37.
s. 37, see *B. P. Petroleum Development* v. *Esso Petroleum Co.* (O.H.), 1987 S.L.T. 345.
s. 83, byelaws 74/1066; S.R. 1988 No. 362.

32. Landed Property Improvement (Ireland) Act 1847.
s. 3, repealed in pt.: 1980, c.59, sch.
s. 40, amended: order 75/816.

34. Towns Improvements Clauses Act 1847.
s. 3, repealed in pt.: S.L.R. 1981.
ss. 47–63, 66–74, repealed: order 80/1085.
ss. 77, 150, amended: order 81/234.
s. 79, amended: order 81/154.
s. 135, repealed: 1972, c.70, sch.30.
ss. 200–208, repealed: S.L.R. 1975.

58. repealed: S.L.R. 1977.

CAP.

10 & 11 Vict. (1847)—cont.

65. Cemeteries Clauses Act 1847.
s. 3, repealed in pt.: 1980, c.59, sch.; S.L.R. 1981.
s. 10, repealed: 1972, c.70, sch.30.
s. 32, repealed in pt.: 1978, No. 2, sch.4.
s. 33, substituted: 1978, No. 2, sch.3.
s. 48, see *Reed* v. *Madon, The Independent,* July 17, 1988, Morritt J.

69. House of Commons Costs Taxation Act 1847.
s. 10, repealed in pt.: S.L.R. 1981.

84. Vagrancy (Ireland) Act 1847.
s. 6, repealed: S.L.R. 1976.

89. Town Police Clauses Act 1847.
s. 3, repealed in pt.: 1980, c.59, sch.; S.L.R. 1981.
s. 15, repealed in pt.: 1984, c.60, sch.7.
s. 21, amended: 1982, c.48, s.39, sch.3.
s. 22, repealed: S.L.R. 1973.
ss. 24–27, repealed: order 76/1040.
s. 28, see *Wills* v. *Bowley* [1982] 3 W.L.R. 10, H.L.
s. 28, amended: 1982, c.48, sch.6; repealed in pt.: 1974, c.17, sch.; S.L.R. 1975; 1981, c.42, sch.; 1984, c.60, sch.7.
s. 36, repealed: 1988, c.36, sch.2.
s. 37, see *R.* v. *Liverpool Corporation* [1972] 2 Q.B. 299; [1972] 2 W.L.R. 1262; [1972] 2 All E.R. 589; *Hulin* v. *Cook* [1977] R.T.R. 345, D.C.; *Sharpe* v. *Nottingham City Council,* February 27, 1981, Nottingham Crown Ct.; *Tudor* v. *Ellesmere Port and Nelson B.C., The Times,* May 8, 1987, D.C.
s. 37, repealed in pt.: 1985, c.67, sch.8.
ss. 37, 38, see *Britain* v. *ABC Cabs (Camberley)* [1981] R.T.R. 395, D.C.
s. 38, see *R.* v. *Bournemouth Borough Council* (1985) 83 L.G.R. 662, Mann J.; *Young* v. *Scampion, The Times,* August 8, 1988, D.C.
s. 39, repealed: 1981, c.56, sch.12.
s. 40, see *Challoner* v. *Evans, The Times,* November 22, 1986, D.C.
s. 45, see *Hulin* v. *Cook* [1977] R.T.R. 345, D.C.; *Britain* v. *ABC (Cabs) Camberley* [1981] R.T.R. 395, D.C.; *Pettigrew* v. *Barry, The Times,* July 12, 1984, D.C.
s. 45, amended: 1982, c.48, sch.6.
s. 46, amended: 1980, c.65, sch.6; 1985, c.67, sch.7.
ss. 55, 58, see *House* v. *Reynolds* [1977] 1 W.L.R. 88, D.C.
ss. 55, 58, amended: 1982, c.48, sch.6.
s. 68, see *Hulin* v. *Cook* [1977] R.T.R. 345, D.C.
ss. 69, 70, 71, 73, repealed: S.L.R. 1975.

108. Ecclesiastical Commissioners Act 1847.
repealed: S.L.R. 1973.

11 & 12 Vict. (1848)

36. Entail Amendment Act 1848.
s. 26, repealed in pt.: S.L.R. 1974.
s. 41, repealed: *ibid.*
ss. 47, 48, see *Lord Binning, Petr.,* First Division, January 6, 1983.

37. Church Building Act 1848.
repealed: S.L.R. 1974.

CAP.

11 & 12 Vict. (1848)—cont.

42. Indictable Offences Act 1848.
ss. 12, 14, amended: 1978, c.23, sch.5.

44. Justices Protection Act 1848.
repealed: 1979, c.55, sch.3.

55. Paymaster General Act 1848.
s. 2, repealed: S.L.R. 1981.
ss. 3, 6, repealed: S.L.R. 1977.

79. Justiciary (Scotland) Act 1848.
ss. 4, 7, 11, 12, repealed (S.): 1975, c.21, sch.10.
s. 5, repealed: 1987, c.41, sch.2.

83. Assessionable Manors Award Act 1848.
repealed: except ss. 6, 14; S.L.R. 1978.

132. Taxing Masters (Ireland) Act 1848.
repealed: 1978, c.23, sch.7.

12 & 13 Vict. (1849)

16. Justices Protection (Ireland) Act 1849.
repealed: 1985, c.61, sch.8.

18. Petty Sessions Act 1849.
s. 1, repealed: 1972, c.70, sch.30.

34. Justices of the Peace Small Debt (Scotland) Act 1849.
repealed: 1975, c.20, sch.2.

51. Judicial Factors Act 1849.
ss. 5, 19, amended (S.): 1980, c.55, s.7.
s. 25, amended (S.): 1986, c.9, sch.1.

58. Officers of Inland Revenue (1849).
repealed: S.L.R. 1975.

72. House of Commons Offices Act 1849.
repealed: 1978, c.36, sch.3.

78. House of Lords Costs Taxation Act 1849.
s. 5, repealed in pt.: order 79/1714.
s. 14, repealed in pt.: S.L.R. 1981.

87. Turnpikes Acts Continuation Act 1849.
repealed: S.L.R. 1981.

104. Poor Relief (Ireland) Act 1849.
repealed: 1980, c.59, sch.

105. Renewable Leasehold Conversion Act 1849.
s. 21, repealed: 1978, c.23, sch.7.

13 & 14 Vict. (1850)

7. London Hackney Carriages Act 1850.
s. 6, repealed: S.L.R. 1981.

36. Court of Session Act 1850.
repealed (exc. s.16): 1988, c.36, sch.2.
s. 16, repealed in pt.: 1984, c.15, sch.1.

38. repealed: S.L.R. 1977.

59. Australian Constitutions Act 1850.
s. 28, repealed: 1986, c.2, s.11.

60. Trustee Act 1850.
amended: 1978, c.23, sch.5.
ss. 2, 41, 45, 48, amended: ibid.

73. Attachment of Goods (Ireland) Act 1850.
repealed: 1978, c.23, sch.7.

78. repealed: S.L.R. 1977.

85. Assizes (Ireland) Act 1850.
repealed: order 75/816.

94. Ecclesiastical Commissioners Act 1850.
s. 27, repealed: S.L.R. 1974.

98. Pluralities Act 1850.
ss. 4, 7, 8, 11, repealed: S.L.R. 1974.

105. Liberties Act 1850.
repealed: order 74/1351.

CAP.

14 & 15 Vict. (1851)

19. Prevention of Offences Act 1851.
s. 11, repealed: 1984, c.60, sch.7.

20. Fee-Farm Rents (Ireland) Act 1851.
s. 1, repealed in pt.: 1978, c.23, sch.7.

26. Herring Fishery Act 1851.
repealed: 1984, c.26, sch.2; S.L.R. 1986.

67. repealed: S.L.R. 1977.

70. Railways Act (Ireland) 1851.
s. 19, amended: 1978, c.23, sch.5.
s. 25, repealed: ibid., sch.7.

90. Fines Act (Ireland) 1851.
s. 1, amended: 1978, c.23, sch.5.
s. 2, amended: ibid.; repealed in pt.: ibid., sch.7.
s. 3, amended: ibid., sch.5.
s. 4, repealed in pt.: ibid., sch.7.
s. 9, repealed: ibid.
s. 10, amended: ibid., sch.5.
s. 18, repealed in pt.: 1980, c.59, sch.

92. Summary Jurisdiction (Ireland) Act 1851.
s. 9, repealed in pt.: order 80/1085.
s. 10, repealed in pt.: orders 76/1040; 80/1085.
s. 14, repealed in pt.: order 80/1085.
s. 15, repealed: order 78/1050.
ss. 19, 20, repealed: order 76/1040.
s. 21, repealed: 1980, c.59, sch.
s. 24, repealed: S.L.R. 1976.
s. 25, repealed in pt.: 1980, c.59, sch.

93. Petty Sessions (Ireland) Act 1851.
s. 30, amended: 1978, c.23, sch.5.

97. Church Building Act 1851.
repealed: S.L.R. 1974.

99. Evidence Act 1851.
s. 6, repealed: 1981, c.54, sch.7.
s. 7, see R. v. McGlinchey [1985] 9 N.I.J.B. 62, C.A.
s. 13, repealed: 1984, c.60, sch.7.

100. Criminal Procedure Act 1851.
repealed: S.L.R. 1986.

15 & 16 Vict. (1852)

24. Wills Act Amendment Act 1852.
repealed: 1982, c.53, sch.9.

26. Foreign Deserters Act 1852.
s. 1, orders 80/699, 700.

27. Evidence (Scotland) Act 1852.
ss. 1, 3, 4, repealed in pt. (S.): 1975, c.21, sch.10.
s. 3, see Coll, Petitioner, 1977 S.L.T. 58.; Dorona v. Caldwell (O.H.) 1981 S.L.T. (Notes) 91.
s. 3, repealed: 1988, c.32, sch.

28. Commissioners of Works Act 1852.
s. 3, repealed: S.L.R. 1977.
s. 7, repealed: 1974, c.38, s.20, sch.7.

53. Quebec Act 1852.
repealed: S.L.R. 1973.

55. Trustee Act 1852.
ss. 6, 7, amended: 1978, c.23, sch.5.
ss. 10, 11, repealed in pt.: ibid., sch.7.

70. House of Correction (1852).
repealed: S.L.R. 1975.

76. Common Law Procedure Act 1852.
s. 126, repealed: 1981, c.54, sch.7.

79. Inclosure Act 1852.
ss. 18, 19, repealed: S.L.R. 1977.

CAP.

17 & 18 Vict. (1854)—cont.

103. Towns Improvement (Ireland) Act 1854.
ss. 4, 90, repealed in pt.: 1980, c.59, sch.
s. 71, repealed: order 76/1040.
s. 91, sch. (C), repealed: 1980, c.59, sch.
s. 96, repealed: S.L.R. 1976.

112. Literary and Scientific Institutions Act 1854.
ss. 1–3, 5, 6, 13, repealed in pt.: S.L.R. 1976.
ss. 21, 23, 33, see *Clapham* v. *Harwood*, December 10, 1975, Leeds Crown Ct.
ss. 22, 23 (in pt.), repealed: S.L.R. 1986.
s. 33, amended: S.L.R. 1973.

114. University of London Medical Graduates Act 1854.
repealed: S.L.R. 1977.

18 & 19 Vict. (1855)

40. Public Libraries Act (Ireland) 1855.
repealed: order 81/438.

60. Wedding Rings Act 1855.
repealed: 1973, c.43, sch.7.

66. repealed: S.L.R. 1977.

68. Burial Grounds (Scotland) Act 1855.
s. 5, repealed in pt.: S.L.R. 1986.
s. 24, repealed in pt.: 1981, c.23, schs.2,4.

81. Places of Worship Registration Act 1855.
ss. 2, 3, repealed in pt.: S.L.R. 1977.
s. 5, amended: orders 75/1291; 77/1861; 81/241.
s. 11, repealed in pt.: order 77/1861.
s. 13, repealed: S.L.R. 1977.

86. Liberty of Religious Worship Act 1855.
preamble, s.1, repealed: S.L.R. 1977.

102. Provisional Order Confirmation (Turnpikes) Act 1855.
repealed: S.L.R. 1981.

103. Spirits (Ireland) Act 1855.
repealed: S.L.R. 1977.

104. Chinese Passengers Act 1855.
repealed: S.L.R. 1977.

111. Bills of Lading Act 1855.
s. 1, see *The Berkshire* [1974] 1 Lloyd's Rep. 185; *The Blue Wave* [1981] Com.L.R. 131, Sheen J.

113. River Ness Act 1855.
repealed: S.L.R. 1974.

117. Ordnance Board Transfer Act 1855.
ss. 2, 4, repealed in pt.: S.L.R. 1976.

128. Burial Act 1855.
ss. 3–7, 9, 11–17, 18 (in pt.), 19–21, repealed: 1972, c.70, sch.30.

131. School Grants Act 1855.
s. 1, amended: S.L.R. 1978; repealed in pt.: S.L.R. 1981.

19 & 20 Vict. (1856)

2. Metropolitan Police Act 1856.
preamble, ss. 1, 5, repealed: 1973, c.15, sch.5.
s. 2, amended: 1986, c.32, s.35; repealed in pt.: 1973, c.15, s.1, sch.5.

3. Joint Stock Banks (Scotland) Act 1856.
repealed: S.L.R. 1981.

12. Turnpike Trusts Act 1856.
repealed: S.L.R. 1981.

CAP.

19 & 20 Vict. (1856)—cont.

43. Hereditary Revenues Act 1856.
sch., repealed in pt.: S.L.R. 1981.

48. Justices (Scotland) Act 1856.
repealed: 1975, c.20, sch.2.

50. Sale of Advowsons Act 1856.
repealed: 1986, No. 3, sch.5.

56. Exchequer Court (Scotland) Act 1856.
ss. 2–4, 13, 14 (in pt.), 15, 16, 19–23, 25–28, repealed: 1988, c.36, sch.2.
ss. 29–34, 36, 42, repealed: 1987, c.18, s.74, sch.8.
s. 44, sch. G, repealed: 1988, c.36, sch.2.
schs. G–K; repealed: 1987, c.18, s.74, sch.8.

60. Mercantile Law Amendment (Scotland) Act 1856.
s. 6, see *Andrew Oliver & Son* v. *Douglas* (O.H.), March 20, 1981.
s. 8, see *Scottish Metropolitan Property* v. *Christie,* 1987, S.L.T.(Sh.Ct.) 18.
s. 9, see *The Royal Bank of Scotland* v. *Welsh* (O.H.), 1985 S.L.T. 439.
s. 17, see *Graham* v. *The Shore Porters Society* (O.H.), 1979 S.L.T. 119; *Boomsma* v. *Clark & Rose,* 1983 S.L.T.(Sh.Ct.) 67.

63. Grand Jury (Ireland) Act 1856.
repealed: order 78/1051.

70. repealed: S.L.R. 1977.

75. repealed: S.L.R. 1977.

77. Chancery Receivers (Ireland) Act 1856.
repealed: 1978, c.23, sch.7.

91. Debts Securities (Scotland) Act 1856.
s. 6, repealed in pt.: 1987, c.18, sch.8.

92. Chancery Appeal Court (Ireland) Act 1856.
repealed: 1978, c.23, sch.7.

97. Mercantile Law Amendment Act 1856.
s. 5, see *Brown* v. *Cork* [1986] P.C.C. 78, C.A.

100. Joint Stock Banks Act 1856.
repealed: S.L.R. 1973.

102. Common Law Procedure Amendment Act (Ireland) 1856.
repealed: 1978, c.23, sch.7.

103. Nuisances Removal (Scotland) Act 1856.
repealed: S.L.R. 1977.

104. New Parishes Act 1856.
repealed: S.L.R. 1974.

113. Foreign Tribunals Evidence Act 1856.
repealed: S.L.R. 1974.

20 Vict. (1857)

19. Extra-Parochial Places Act 1857.
repealed: S.L.R. 1974.

20 & 21 Vict. (1857)

9. Provisional Order Confirmation (Turnpikes) Act 1857.
repealed: S.L.R. 1981.

18. Bill Chamber Procedure Act 1857.
repealed: 1988, c.36, sch.2.

26. Registration of Leases (Scotland) Act 1857.
s. 1, amended: 1974, c.38, sch.6.
s. 2, repealed in pt.: *ibid.*
s. 3, amended: 1985, c.73, s.3.
s. 15, repealed in pt.: S.L.R. 1976.
ss. 16, 17, amended: 1974, c.38, sch.6.
ss. 18, 19 (in pt.), repealed: *ibid.*, schs.6, 7.

CAP.

20 & 21 Vict. (1857)—cont.

29. repealed: S.L.R. 1977.
31. Inclosure Act 1857.
ss. 6–9, repealed: 1977, c.30, sch.2.
40. Illicit Distillation (Ireland) Act 1857.
repealed: S.L.R. 1977.
43. Summary Jurisdiction Act 1857.
s. 1, repealed: S.L.R. 1977.
s. 6, see *Universal Salvage* v. *Boothby, The Times*, December 14, 1983, D.C.; *Maydew* v. *Flint* (1985) 80 Cr.App.R. 49, D.C.
ss. 6, 10, amended: 1980, c.43, sch.7.
56. Court of Session Act 1857.
repealed: 1988, c.36, sch.2.
58. Lands Valuation (Scotland) Act 1857.
s. 4, repealed in pt. (S.): S.L.R. 1975.
60. Irish Bankrupt and Insolvent Act 1857.
amended: 1978, c.23, sch.5.
s. 4, amended: *ibid.*
s. 9, see *Kwok Keung Lee, Re* [1988] 2 N.I.J.B. 1, Murray J.
ss. 11, 23, 25, 26, 28, 29, 36, 41, 49, 51, 52, repealed: 1978, c.23, sch.7.
s. 59, amended: *ibid.*, sch.5.
ss. 73–75, repealed: 1985, c.65, sch.10.
ss. 78, 86, repealed: 1978, c.23, sch.5.
s. 115, amended: order 81/226.
s. 129, see *Re Crossey* [1975] N.I. 1, Gibson J.
s. 142, amended: order 81/226.
s. 267, see *Re Keaney* [1977] N.I. 67, Murray J.
s. 269, repealed in pt.: S.L.R. 1981; 1985, c.65, sch.10.
s. 298, amended: order 81/226.
s. 305, repealed in pt.: 1978, c.23, sch.5; 1985, c.65, sch.10.
ss. 312, 320, amended: 1978, c.23, sch.5; repealed in pt.: *ibid* ; 1985, c.65, sch.10.
s. 313, amended: 1974, c.39, sch.4.
s. 343, see *JP and AP (Bankrupts), Re* [1985] 11 N.I.J.B. 9, Hutton J.
s. 343. amended: order 81/226.
ss. 366, 367, 369, 372–375, repealed: 1978, c.23, sch.7.
s. 370, repealed in pt.: *ibid.*; 1985, c.65, sch.10.
s. 410, repealed in pt.: *ibid.*
63. Dunbar Harbour Loan Act 1857.
repealed: S.L.R. 1976.
72. Police (Scotland) Act 1857.
s. 33, see *Cormack* v. *The Crown Estate Commissioners*, 1985 S.L.T. 181.
77. Court of Probate Act 1857.
repealed: 1981, c.54, sch.7.
79. Probates and Letters of Administration Act (Ireland) 1857.
s. 2, repealed in pt.: order 79/1575.
ss. 6, 16–18, 23–29, repealed: 1978, c.23, sch.7.
s. 31, repealed: order 79/1575.
s. 32, 34, 36, 41, repealed: 1978, c.23, sch.7.
ss. 50–57, 59, 61, 63, 65 (in pt.), 66 (in pt.), repealed: order 79/1575.
s. 69, repealed: 1978, c.23, sch.7.
ss. 71, 72, 74, 80, 81, 84, 92, 93, 98, repealed: order 79/1575.
s. 99, repealed: 1975, c.7, sch.13.
ss. 99A, 100, repealed: order 79/1575.
ss. 109, 114, 115, sch. A, repealed: 1978, c.23, sch.7.

CAP.

20 & 21 Vict. (1857)—cont.

81. Burial Act 1857.
repealed (except ss. 10, 23–5): 1972, c.70, sch.30.
ss. 10, 23, repealed in pt.: *ibid.*; S.L.R. 1986.
83. Obscene Publications Act 1857.
s. 1, see *Currie (Superintendent, Royal Ulster Constabulary)* v. *McDonald* [1983] 13 N.I.J.B., C.A.
ss. 1, 4, repealed in pt.: 1980, c.59, sch.

21 & 22 Vict. (1858)

27. Chancery Amendment Act 1858.
repealed: 1981, c.54, sch.7.
s. 2, see *Wroth* v. *Tyler* [1973] 2 W.L.R. 405; *Bracewell* v. *Appleby* [1975] 2 W.L.R. 282; *Biggin* v. *Minton* [1977] 1 W.L.R. 701; [1977] 2 All E.R. 647, Foster J.; *Johnson* v. *Agnew* [1979] 2 W.L.R. 487, H.L.; *Malhotra* v. *Choudhury* [1978] 3 W.L.R. 825, C.A.
31. Bristol Charities Act 1858.
repealed: S.L.R. 1981.
36. repealed: S.L.R. 1978.
46. Confirmation of Certain Marriages Act 1858.
repealed: 1988, c.44, sch.
49. Jews Relief Act 1858.
s. 4, repealed in pt.: 1980, c.59, sch.; 1986, No. 3, sch.5.
56. Confirmation of Executors (Scotland) Act 1858.
ss. 9, 17, repealed in pt.: 1975, c.7, sch.13.
ss. 15, 16, repealed: *ibid.*
57. Ecclesiastical Leasing Act 1858.
s. 1, see *Oakley* v. *Boston* [1975] 3 W.L.R. 478; [1975] 3 All E.R. 405, C.A.
s. 10, repealed: S.L.R. 1974.
72. Landed Estates Court (Ireland) Act 1858.
ss. 37, 40, 55, repealed: 1978, c.23, sch.7.
s. 56, amended and repealed in pt.: *ibid.*, sch.5.
s. 57, amended: *ibid.*, sch.5.
s. 65, repealed: *ibid.*, sch.7.
ss. 66, 70, amended: *ibid.*, sch.5.
ss. 74, 75, 77, 78, 86, 89, sch. A, repealed: *ibid.*, sch.7.
73. Stipendiary Magistrates Act 1858.
repealed: S.L.R. 1981.
78. Parliamentary Witnesses Act 1858.
s. 3, repealed: order 79/1714.
80. Provisional Order Confirmation (Turnpikes) Act 1858.
repealed: S.L.R. 1981.
90. Medical Act 1858.
ss. 48–51, repealed: S.L.R. 1986.
s. 53, repealed: S.L.R. 1977.
93. Legitimacy Declaration Act 1858.
repealed: except ss. 9–11; S.L.R. 1977.
ss. 1, 8, see *The Ampthill Peerage* [1976] 2 W.L.R. 777, H.L.
s. 9, amended: 1981, c.61, sch.7.
s. 11, repealed in pt.: S.L.R. 1977.
95. Court of Probate Act 1858.
repealed: 1981, c.54, sch.7.
109. Cornwall Submarine Mines Act 1858.
preamble, repealed: S.L.R. 1978.
ss. 1, 2, 7, 9, repealed: *ibid.*

24 & 25 Vict. (1861)—cont.

69. Tramways (Scotland) Act 1861.
repealed: S.L.R. 1973.

70. Locomotive Act 1861.
s. 6, repealed: 1980, c.65, sch.7.

72. White Herring Fishery (Scotland) Act 1861.
repealed: 1984, c.26, sch.2.

78. Westminster 1861.
repealed: S.L.R. 1973.

79. Metropolis Gas Act 1861.
repealed: S.L.R. 1977.

86. Conjugal Rights (Scotland) Amendment Act 1861.
repealed (exc. ss.6, 20): 1988, c.36, sch.2.
s. 6, repealed in pt.: 1985, c.37, sch.2.
s. 9, see Coyle v. Coyle (O.H.), 1981 S.L.T.(Notes) 129; Neilly v. Neilly (O.H.), 1981 S.L.T.(Notes) 129; Hogg v. Dick (O.H.), 1987, S.L.T. 716.

91. Revenue (No. 2) Act 1861.
repealed: S.L.R. 1977.

92. Probate Duty Act 1861.
repealed: 1975, c.7, sch.13.

94. Accessories and Abettors Act 1861.
s. 8, see Att.-Gen.'s Reference (No. 1 of 1975) [1975] 3 W.L.R. 11; [1975] 2 All E.R. 684, C.A.; R. v. Hollinshead [1985] 1 All E.R. 850, C.A.; R. v. Calhaem [1985] 2 W.L.R. 826, C.A.
s. 8, amended: 1977, c.45, sch.12.

97. Malicious Damage Act 1861.
s. 36, see R. v. Gittins [1982] R.T.R. 363, C.A.
s. 69, repealed: S.L.R. 1976.

98. Forgery Act 1861.
repealed, except ss. 34, 36, 37, 55, 1981, c.45, sch.

100. Offences against the Person Act 1861.
s. 1, amended: 1973, c.53, sch.5.
s. 4, amended: 1977, c.45, s.5; order 77/1249; repealed in pt.: 1977, c.45, s.5, sch.13.
s. 16, see R. v. Cousins [1982] 2 W.L.R. 621, C.A.; R. v. Williams (Clarence) (1987) 84 Cr.App.R. 299, C.A.
s. 16, substituted: 1977, c.45, sch.12.; order 77/1249.
s. 18, see R. v. Abraham [1973] 1 W.L.R. 1270; [1973] 3 All E.R. 694, C.A.; R. v. Austin (1973) 58 Cr.App.R. 163, C.A.; R. v. Belfon [1976] 1 W.L.R. 741, C.A.; R. v. Lambert (1976) 65 Cr.App.R. 12, C.A.; R. v. McCready; R. v. Hurd [1978] 1 W.L.R. 1376, C.A.; R. v. Nicholls [1978] Crim.L.R. 247, C.A.; R. v. Collison (1980) 71 Cr.App.R. 249, C.A.; R. v. Pond [1984] Crim.L.R. 164, C.A.; R. v. Pearman [1985] R.T.R. 39, C.A.; R. v. Gibson; R. v. Gibson (1985) 80 Cr.App.R. 24, C.A.; R. v. Hamand (1985) 82 L.S.Gaz. 1561, C.A.; R. v. Bryson, The Times, June 28, 1985, C.A.; R. v. Morrison, The Times, November 12, 1988, C.A.
ss. 18, 20, see R. v. Monger [1973] Crim.L.R. 301; R. v. Richards [1973] 3 W.L.R. 888; [1973] 3 All E.R. 1088, C.A.; R. v. Stubbs, The Times, March 25, 1988, C.A.; R. v. Jauncey (1988) 8 Cr.App.R.(S.) 401, C.A.

24 & 25 Vict. (1861)—cont.

100. Offences against the Person Act 1861—cont.
s. 20, see R. v. McCready; R. v. Hurd [1978] 1 W.L.R. 1376, C.A.; R. v. Nicholls [1978] Crim.L.R. 247, C.A.; Flack v. Hunt (1979) 70 Cr.App.R. 51, D.C.; R. v. Collison (1980) 71 Cr.App.R. 249, C.A.; R. v. Sullivan [1981] Crim.L.R. 46, C.A.; R. v. Wilson (Clarence), The Times, February 7, 1983, C.A.; C. (A Minor) v. Eisenhower [1983] 3 All E.R. 230; (1984) 78 Cr.App.R. 48, D.C.; R. v. Power, The Times, May 25, 1983, C.A.; R. v. Martyn Leonard Carpenter (1983) 76 Cr.App.R. 320, C.A.; W. (A Minor) v. Dolbey [1983] Crim.L.R. 681, D.C.; Comr. of Police of the Metropolis v. Wilson; R. v. Jenkins [1983] 3 W.L.R. 686, H.L.; R. v. Grimshaw [1984] Crim.L.R. 108, C.A.; R. v. Williams (1983) 5 Cr.App.R.(S.) 134, C.A.; R. v. Bird (Debbie), The Times, March 28, 1985, C.A.; R. v. Gibson (1985) 80 Cr.App.R. 24, C.A.; R. v. Knight (D.) (1985) 7 Cr.App.R.(S.) 5, C.A.; R. v. Dume (Constantine), The Times, October 16, 1986, C.A.
s. 23, see R. v. Cato; R. v. Morris; R. v. Dudley [1976] 1 W.L.R. 110; [1976] 1 All E.R. 260, C.A.; R. v. Sholanke (1977) 66 Cr.App.R. 127, C.A.; R. v. McShane (1977) 66 Cr.App.R. 97, C.A.
s. 24, see R. v. Wood [1975] Crim.L.R. 236; R. v. Marcus, The Times, April 10, 1981. C.A.; R. v. Hill [1986] Crim.L.R. 815; (1986) 83 Cr.App.R. 386, H.L.; R. v. Nalty, June 16, 1987, C.A.; R. v. Dones [1987] Crim.L.R. 682, C.C.C.; R. v. Gillard, The Times, April 7, 1988, C.A.
s. 29, see R. v. James (1979) 70 Cr.App R. 215, C.A.
ss. 32–34, see R. v. Criminal Injuries Compensation Board, ex p. Webb, The Times, March 28, 1985, C.A.
s. 34, see R. v. Criminal Injuries Compensation Board, ex p. Warner [1985] 2 All E.R. 1069, D.C.; R. v. Criminal Injuries Compensation Board, ex p. Webb, The Times, May 9, 1986, C.A.
s. 35, see R. v. Austin [1981] R.T.R. 10, C.A.
s. 42, see R. v. Harrow JJ., ex p. Osaseri [1985] 3 All E.R. 185, D.C.; R v. Blyth Valley Justices, ex p. Dobson, The Times, November 7, 1987, D.C.
ss. 42, 43, repealed: 1988, c.33, sch.16.
s. 44, see Ellis v. Burton [1975] 1 W.L.R. 386; [1975] 1 All E.R. 395, D.C.
s. 44, repealed in pt.: 1988, c.33, schs 15,16.
ss. 44, 45, see Saeed v. Inner London Education Authority [1985] I.C.R. 638; [1986] i.R.L.R. 23, Popplewell J.
s. 45, amended: 1988, c.33, sch.15.
s. 46, see R. v. Blyth Valley Justices, ex p. Dobson, The Times, November 7, 1987, D.C.
s. 46, repealed: 1988, c.33, sch.16.
s. 47, see R. v. McCready; R. v. Hurd [1978] 1 W.L.R. 1376, C.A.; R. v. Nicholls [1978] Crim.L.R. 247, C.A.; R. v. Martyn Leonard Carpenter (1983) 76 Cr.App.R. 320, C.A.;

CAP.

24 & 25 Vict. (1861)—cont.

100. Offences against the Person Act 1861—cont.
Comr. of Police of the Metropolis v. Wilson;
R. v. Jenkins [1983] 3 W.L.R. 686, H.L.; R. v.
Harrow JJ., ex p. Osaseri [1985] 3 All E.R.
185, D.C.; R. v. Blyth Valley Justices, ex p.
Dobson, The Times, November 7, 1987, D.C.
s. 47, repealed in pt.: 1988, c.33, sch.16.
s. 56, see R. v. Jones (1971) 56 Cr.App.R. 212;
R. v. Pryce [1972] Crim.L.R. 307; R. v. Mears
[1975] Crim.L.R. 155; R. v. Austin [1981] 1 All
E.R. 374, C.A.; B. v. B. [1984] Crim.L.R. 352,
C.A.
s. 56, repealed: 1984, c.37, s.11.
s. 57, see R. v. Sagor [1975] 3 W.L.R. 267;
[1975] 2 All E.R. 926, C.A.
s. 58, see R. v. Smith (John) [1973] 1 W.L.R.
1510, C.A.
ss. 61, 62, amended: order 82/1536.
s. 65, repealed in pt.: 1984, c.60, sch.7.
s. 72, repealed: S.L.R. 1976.
124. Metropolitan Police (Receiver) Act 1861.
ss. 5 (in pt.), 8, repealed: S.L.R. 1986.

25 & 26 Vict. (1862)

7. India Stock Transfer Act 1862.
s. 14, repealed: S.L.R. 1981.
19. General Pier and Harbour Act 1861, Amendment Act 1862.
sch. B, amended: 1973, c.65, sch.19; repealed
in pt.: ibid., schs.19,29.
22. Revenue Act 1862.
repealed: 1975, c.7, sch.13.
49. repealed: S.L.R. 1977.
53. Land Registry Act 1862.
s. 135, repealed: S.L.R. 1974.
56. Provisional Orders Confirmation (Turnpikes) Act 1862.
repealed: S.L.R. 1981.
69. Harbours Transfer Act 1862.
s. 10, repealed in pt.: S.L.R. 1977.
s. 16, repealed: S.L.R. 1981.
97. Salmon Fisheries (Scotland) Act 1862.
repealed: 1986, c.62, sch.5.
ss. 6, 16, byelaw 80/1256.
s. 18, see Fraser, Petr., 1980 S.L.T.(Sh. Ct.) 70.
ss 18, 19, 24, see Cormack v. The Crown
Estate Commissioners, 1985 S.L.T. 181.
105. Highland Roads and Bridges Act 1862.
repealed: 1973, c.65, sch.29.
114. Poaching Prevention Act 1862.
s. 1, repealed in pt.. 1980, c.59, sch.
s. 5, repealed: S.L.R. 1976.

26 & 27 Vict. (1863)

10. Salmon Acts Amendment Act 1863.
repealed: 1986, c.62, sch.5.
s. 4, repealed in pt. (S.): S.L.R. 1975.
13. Town Gardens Protection Act 1863.
s. 5, amended: 1984, c.60, sch.6.
20. Elections in the Recess Act 1863.
repealed: 1975, c.66, sch.2.
35. South African Offences Act 1863.
repealed: S.L.R. 1973.

CAP.

26 & 27 Vict. (1863)—cont.

49. Duchy of Cornwall Management Act 1863.
s. 7, repealed in pt.: 1982, c.47, s.2.
ss. 8, 11, 15, 16, amended: ibid., s.10.
ss. 21, 22, repealed in pt.: ibid.,s.5.
ss. 24, 34, amended: ibid., s.10.
50. Salmon Fisheries (Scotland) Act 1863.
repealed: 1986, c.62, s.41, sch.5.
58. Sir R. Hitcham's Charity Act 1863.
repealed: S.L.R. 1981.
60. General Police and Improvement (Scotland) Supplemental Act 1863.
repealed: S.L.R. 1981.
69. Officers of the Royal Naval Reserve Act 1863.
repealed: 1980, c.9, sch.10.
73. India Stock Certificate Act 1863.
ss. 13–15, repealed in pt.: S.L.R. 1981.
76. Colonial Letters Patent Act 1863.
repealed: S.L.R. 1973.
92. Railways Clauses Act 1863.
ss. 5–7, 16, amended (S.): 1984, c.54, sch.9.
98. Provisional Order Confirmation (Turnpikes) Act 1863.
repealed: S.L.R. 1981.
112. Telegraph Act 1863.
repealed, exc. ss. 1, 45: 1984, c.12, sch.7.
s. 45, amended: 1981, c.38, sch.3; 1984. c.12,
sch.4; repealed in pt.: ibid.
114. Salmon Fishery (Ireland) Act 1863.
repealed: S.L.R. 1978.

27 & 28 Vict. (1864)

7. Bills of Exchange (Ireland) Act 1864.
repealed: 1978, c.23, sch.7.
24. Naval Agency and Distribution Act 1864.
ss. 6, 8, amended: 1981, c.55, s.24.
s. 17, repealed in pt.: ibid., sch.5.
s. 25, order 73/232.
s. 26, repealed in pt.: S.L.R. 1986.
25. Naval Prize Act 1864.
s. 2, repealed in pt.: 1981, c 54, sch.7.
ss. 10–12, 14, 15, 45, repealed: ibid.
s. 47, amended: 1979, c.2, sch.4.
s. 48, amended: ibid.
s. 48A, amended: ibid.
s. 49, amended: ibid.
s. 50, repealed: order 79/1714.
s. 54, repealed in pt.: S.L.R. 1986.
56. Revenue (No. 2) Act 1864.
repealed: 1975, c.7, sch.13.
58. Hartlepool Pilotage Order Confirmation Act 1864.
repealed: S.L.R. 1986.
60. repealed: S.L.R. 1977.
62. Isle of Man Harbours Amendment Act 1864.
repealed: S.L.R. 1973.
75. Annual Turnpike Acts Continuance Act 1864.
repealed: S.L.R. 1981.
77. Ionian States Acts of Parliament Act 1864.
repealed: 1988, c.44, sch.
79. Provisional Order Confirmation (Turnpikes) Act 1864.
repealed: S.L.R. 1981.
88. Westminster Bridge 1864.
repealed: S.L.R. 1973.

CAP.

27 & 28 Vict. (1864)—cont.

95. Fatal Accidents Act 1864.
repealed: 1976, c.30, sch.2.
97. Registration of Burials Act 1864.
s. 3, repealed: 1978, No. 2, sch.3.
s. 6, substituted: *ibid.*
114. Improvement of Land Act 1864.
ss. 2, 3, 7, 17, 19, 20, 21, 23, 29, 32, 56, 69, repealed in pt.: S.L.R. 1974.
s. 68, amended: 1983, c.20, sch.4; 1984, c.36, sch.3.
118. Salmon Fisheries (Scotland) Act 1864.
repealed: 1986, c.62, sch.5.

28 & 29 Vict. (1865)

7. General Police and Improvement (Scotland) Supplemental Act 1865.
repealed: S.L.R. 1977.
18. Criminal Procedure Act 1865.
s. 2, see *R.* v. *Ludwick* [1977] Crim.L.R. 158, 210, C.A.; *R.* v. *Morley* [1988] 2 W.L.R. 963, C.A.
s. 3, see *R.* v. *Thompson* (1976) 64 Cr.App.R. 96, C.A.; *R.* v. *Norton and Driver* [1987] Crim.L.R. 687, C.A.
ss. 3, 4, see *R.* v. *Booth* (1982) 74 Cr.App.R. 123, C.A.
s. 4, see *R.* v. *Conway* (1979) 70 Cr.App.R. 4, C.A.
s. 6, amended: 1984, c.60, sch.7.
s. 8, see *R.* v. *Angeli* [1978] 3 All E.R. 950, C.A.; *R.* v. *Ewing, The Times,* March 15, 1983, C.A.
25. Dockyard Act 1865.
s. 7, order 72/443.
28. Isle of Man 1865.
repealed: S.L.R. 1973.
42. District Church Tithes Act 1865.
repealed: S.L.R. 1974.
49. Courts of Justice Concentration (Site) Act 1865.
repealed: S.L.R. 1977.
56. Trespass (Scotland) Act 1865.
s. 2, amended: 1984, c.54, sch.9.
s. 3, repealed in pt.: S.L.R. 1973; 1984, c.54, schs.9,11.
s. 4, amended: 1982, c.48, sch.15.
63. Colonial Laws Validity Act 1865.
see *Gilbertson* v. *State of South Australia* (1977) 121 S.J. 409. P.C.
s. 1, repealed in pt.: S.L.R. 1976.
73. Naval and Marine Pay and Pensions Act 1865.
s. 4, repealed in pt.: S.L.R. 1976.
s. 7, repealed: *ibid.*
s. 12, repealed in pt.: 1981, c.55, sch.5.
74. Tramway Act (1865).
repealed: S.L.R. 1975.
81. repealed: S.L.R. 1977.
89. Greenwich Hospital Act 1865.
s. 5, repealed in pt.: S.L.R. 1976.
s. 8, repealed: *ibid.*
s. 20, orders 76/1774; 83/141; 84/123.
s. 25, repealed: S.L.R. 1975.
s. 43, repealed (N.I.): S.L.R. 1976.
s. 44, repealed: S.L.R. 1973.

CAP.

28 & 29 Vict. (1865)—cont.

89. Greenwich Hospital Act 1865—*cont.*
s. 45, repealed: S.L.R. 1976.
s. 47, amended: 1981, c.55, s.24.
s. 60, repealed in pt.: S.L.R. 1986.
90. Metropolitan Fire Brigade Act 1865.
amended: 1985, c.51, sch.11.
91. Turnpikes (Provisional Orders Confirmation) Act 1865.
repealed: S.L.R. 1981.
100. Harbours Transfer Act 1865.
repealed: S.L.R. 1986.
111. Navy and Marines (Property of Deceased) Act 1865.
s. 18, repealed in pt.: S.L.R. 1986.
124. Admiralty Powers etc. Act 1865.
repealed: S.L.R. 1981.
125. Dockyard Ports Regulation Act 1865.
s. 3, orders 75/1074, 1703; 78/1880, 1881.
s. 5, orders 73/957, 1890; 75/1074, 1703; 76/578; 78/1880, 1881; 80/1075.
s. 6, orders 75/1074, 1703; 76/578; 78/1880; 83/1887; 84/1148.
s. 7, orders 73/957, 1890; 75/1074; 76/578; 78/1881; 80/1075; 83/878(S.), 1887; 84/1148.
ss. 7 (in pt.), 8–10, 26 (in pt.), repealed: S.L.R. 1986.

29 & 30 Vict. (1866)

17. Cattle-sheds in Burghs Act 1866.
repealed: 1973, c.65, sch.29.
18. India Military Funds Act 1866.
repealed: S.L.R. 1981.
31. Superannuation (Metropolis) Act 1866.
repealed: S.L.R. 1976.
37. Hop (Prevention of Frauds) Act 1866.
repealed: regs. 79/1095.
39. Exchequer and Audit Departments Act 1866.
ss. 3, 6, repealed in pt.: S.L.R. 1975.
s. 24, repealed: 1983, c.44, s.10, sch.5.
83. National Gallery Enlargement Act 1866.
repealed, except ss. 1, 3, 16, 17, 20, 29; S.L.R. 1978.
92. Turnpikes (Provisional Orders Confirmation) Act 1866.
repealed: S.L.R. 1981
105. Annual Turnpike Acts Continuance Act 1866.
repealed: S.L.R. 1981.
111. Ecclesiastical Commissioners Act 1866.
s. 23, repealed: S.L.R. 1977.
112. Evidence (Scotland) Act 1866.
repealed: 1988, c.36, sch.2.
s. 1, see *McColl* v. *Strathclyde Regional Council* (O.H.), 1981 S.L.T. (Notes) 70.
122. Metropolitan Commons Act 1866.
s. 25, repealed in pt.: 1985, c.51, sch.17.
sch. 1, amended: *ibid.,* sch.8; repealed in pt.: *ibid.,* sch.17.

30 & 31 Vict. (1867)

2. Odessa Marriage Act 1867.
repealed: 1988, c.44, sch.
3. British North America Act 1867.
Act renamed Constitution Act 1867 (Can.): 1982, c.11, sch.

CAP.

30 & 31 Vict. (1867)—cont.

3. British North America Act 1867—cont.
s. 1, substituted: *ibid*.
ss. 9, 91, 92, see *R.* v. *Secretary of State for Foreign and Commonwealth Affairs, ex p. Indian Association of Alberta* [1982] 2 W.L.R. 641, C.A.
ss. 20, 91 (in pt.), 92 (in pt.), repealed: 1982, c.11, sch.

17. Lyon King of Arms Act 1867.
s. 2, amended (S.): 1987, c.18, sch.6.
s. 10, repealed in pt. (S.): 1985, c.73, schs.2,4.
s. 11, repealed in pt.: S.L.R. 1986.
sch. B, order 79/443; amended: order 75/1299.

35. Criminal Law Amendment Act 1867.
s. 6, amended: 1980, c.43, sch.7.
s. 10, amended: 1976, c.63, sch.2.

39. Metropolitan Police (Receiver) Act 1867.
s. 1, amended: S.L.R. 1974.

41. National Gallery Enlargement Act 1867.
repealed: S.L.R. 1978.

44. Chancery (Ireland) Act 1867.
repealed: 1978, c.23, sch.7.

52. Herring Fisheries (Scotland) Act 1867.
repealed: 1984, c.26, sch.2.

66. Turnpike Trusts Arrangements Act 1867.
repealed: S.L.R. 1981.

75. Office and Oath Act 1867.
repealed: S.L.R. 1978.

79. General Police and Improvement (Scotland) Supplemental Act 1867.
repealed: S.L.R. 1977.

80. Valuation of Lands (Scotland) Amendment Act 1867.
s. 2, repealed: S.L.R. 1975.
s. 5, repealed: 1973, c.65, sch.29.
ss. 6 (in pt.), 8, repealed: S.L.R. 1986.

85. repealed: S.L.R. 1977.

90. Revenue Act 1867.
repealed: S.L.R. 1977.

93. Morro Velho Marriage Act 1867.
repealed: 1988, c.44, sch.

114. Court of Admiralty (Ireland) Act 1867.
repealed: 1978, c.23, sch.7.

121. Annual Turnpike Acts Continuance Act 1867.
repealed: S.L.R. 1981.

129. Chancery and Common Law Offices (Ireland) Act 1867.
repealed: 1978, c.23, sch.7.

134. Metropolitan Streets Act 1867.
ss. 4 (in pt.), 8, 26, repealed: S.L.R. 1973.
s. 17, repealed: S.L.R. 1976.
s. 25, repealed: S.L.R. 1981.

31 & 32 Vict. (1868)

20. Legitimacy Declaration Act (Ireland) 1868.
s. 2, repealed: 1986, c.55, sch.2.
ss. 3, 4, 5, 7, repealed: 1978, c.23, sch.7.

23. Frampton Mansel Marriage Act 1868.
repealed: S.L.R. 1977.

24. Capital Punishment Amendment Act 1868.
s. 2, repealed in pt.: 1973, c.53, sch.5.

CAP.

31 & 32 Vict. (1868)—cont.

37. Documentary Evidence Act 1868.
s. 5, repealed in pt.: S.L.R. 1976.
sch., amended: 1973, c.41, sch.1; functions transferred: order 86/600.

40. Partition Act 1868.
s. 4, see *Northern Bank* v. *Beattie* [1982] 18 N.I.J.B., Murray J.

42. Municipal Rate (Edinburgh) Act 1868.
repealed (S.): S.L.R. 1975.

45. Sea Fisheries Act 1868.
s. 26, substituted: 1988, c.12, sch.6.
s. 69, repealed: S.L.R. 1981.

54. Judgments Extension Act 1868.
see *Wilson Vehicle Distribution* v. *Colt Car Co., The Times,* October 25, 1983, Bingham J.
repealed: 1982, c.27, sch.14.

64. Land Registers (Scotland) Act 1868.
s. 6, amended: 1979, c.33, sch.2; repealed in pt.: *ibid.*, sch.4.
s. 15, repealed: 1973, c.52, sch.5.
s. 24, Act of Sederunt, 75/1009.
s. 25, Acts of Sederunt, 74/1659; 76/468; 77/1623; orders 79/1127; 81/42; substituted: 1979, c.33, s.23.

66. Turnpike Trusts Arrangements Act 1868.
repealed: S.L.R. 1981.

70. Railways Traverse Act 1868.
repealed in pt.: 1978, c.23, sch.7.

72. Promissory Oaths Act 1868.
s. 3, see *Chiene, Petr.,* 1984 S.L.T. 323.
ss. 7, 9, repealed in pt.: S.L.R. 1981.
Pt. II. repealed in pt.: 1981, c.54, sch.7.
ss. 8, 9, 12, 14, repealed in pt.: 1980, c.59, sch.
s. 11, repealed: 1977, c.38, sch.5.
s. 14, sch., repealed in pt.: S.L.R. 1977.
sch., repealed in pt. (S.): 1975, c.20, sch.2.

83. Army Chaplains Act 1868.
s. 4, repealed in pt.: 1986, No. 3, s.34, sch.5.

88. Court of Chancery and Exchequer Funds (Ireland) Act 1868.
repealed: S.L.R. 1978.

95. Court of Justiciary (Scotland) Act 1868.
ss. 1, 10, 16, 18, repealed (S.): 1975, c.21, sch.10.
s. 11, repealed in pt.: S.L.R. 1977.
sch. B. repealed: *ibid*.

96. Ecclesiastical Buildings and Glebes (Scotland) Act 1868.
s. 4, repealed in pt.: 1982, c.27, sch.14.

99. Annual Turnpike Acts Continuance Act 1868.
repealed: S.L.R. 1981.

100. Court of Session Act 1868.
ss. 10, 12, 13, repealed: 1988, c.36, sch.2.
s. 14, amended: 1987, s.18, sch.6; repealed in pt.: 1988, c.36, sch.2.
ss. 15–42, repealed: *ibid*.
s. 24, see *Campbell* v. *Campbell,* 1983 S.L.T. 530.
s. 43, repealed: 1980, c.55, sch.3; 1988, c.36, sch.2.
s. 44, repealed: *ibid*.
s. 45, amended: 1973, c.65, sch.27; repealed in pt.: 1988, c.36, sch.2.
ss. 46, 47 (in pt.), 50–101, repealed: *ibid*.

CAP.

31 & 32 Vict. (1868)—cont.

100. Court of Session Act 1868—cont.
s. 89, see *Maersk Co.* v. *National Union of Seamen* (O.H.), May 4, 1988; *Stirling Shipping Co.* v. *National Union of Seamen* (O.H.), May 5, 1988.
s. 91, see *Edwards* v. *Lothian Regional Council,* 1981 S.L.T.(Sh.Ct.) 41.

101. Titles to Land Consolidation (Scotland) Act 1868.
ss. 3, 157, see *Leeds Permanent Building Society* v. *Aitken Malone & Mackay* (O.H.), 1986 S.L.T. 338.
ss. 52, 54, 55, repealed: S.L.R. 1975.
ss. 122, 123, see *Bank of Scotland* v. *Lord Advocate* (O.H.), August 2, 1976.
s. 138, amended: 1987, c.18, sch.6.
s. 142, amended: 1979, c.33, sch.2; repealed in pt.: *ibid.,* sch.4.
s. 148, repealed: 1985, c.66, sch.8.
ss. 151, 153, repealed: S.L.R. 1975.
s. 158, see *McInally* v. *Kildonan Homes* (O.H.), 1979 S.L.T.(Notes) 89.
s. 159, amended: 1985, c.73, sch.2.
s. 162, repealed in pt.: 1979, c.33, sch.4; S.L.R. 1986.
sch. QQ, see *Murphy's Trs.* v. *Aitken* (O.H.), January 22, 1982.
sch. RR, amended: 1985, c.73, sch.2.

110. Telegraph Act 1868.
repealed, exc. ss.1, 20: 1984, c.12, sch.7.
s. 20, amended: 1981, c.36, sch.3; repealed in pt.: 1984, c.12, sch.4.

113. repealed: S.L.R. 1977.

117. Incumbents Act 1868.
repealed: S.L.R. 1977.

118. Public Schools Act 1868.
ss. 5, 8–11, 26, 32, repealed in pt.: S.L.R. 1973.
ss. 6, 14, 22, 24, repealed: *ibid.*

123. Salmon Fisheries (Scotland) Act 1868.
repealed (exc. ss.1, 11, 15, 18–24, 26, 27, 29, 31–36, 41): 1986, c.62, s.41, sch.5.
s. 3, see *Fraser, Petr.,* 1980 S.L.T. (Sh.Ct.) 70.
ss. 6, 13, see *Cormack* v. *The Crown Estate Commissioners,* 1985 S.L.T. 426 (H.L.).
s. 9, orders 78/1326; 80/1255.
s. 15, amended and repealed in pt.: 1986, c.62, s.5.
ss. 15, 24, sch. D, see *Fishmongers' Company* v. *Bruce,* 1980 S.L.T.(Notes) 35.
s. 18, repealed in pt.: 1986, c.62, sch.4.
s. 19, amended and repealed in pt.: *ibid.*
s. 20, repealed in pt.: *ibid.*
s. 30, repealed: *ibid.,* s.30.
s. 34, repealed in pt.: S.L.R. 1978.
ss. 38–40, repealed: 1986, c.62, s.30.
s. 41, repealed in pt.: *ibid.,* sch.4.
sch. G, amended: 1979, c.11, sch.11.

124. Inland Revenue Act 1868.
s. 6, repealed: S.L.R. 1977.
s. 7, repealed: 1975, c.7, sch.13.

125. Parliamentary Elections Act 1868.
repealed: 1988, c.36, sch.2.
s. 11, repealed: 1981, c.54, sch.7.

CAP.

32 & 33 Vict. (1869)

3. Lord Napier Act 1869.
repealed: S.L.R. 1974.

10. Colonial Prisoners Removal Act 1869.
s. 2, repealed in pt.: S.L.R. 1978.

24. Newspapers, Printers and Reading Rooms Repeal Act 1869.
sch. 2, amended: S.L.R. 1973.

30. preamble, s.1, repealed: S.L.R. 1977.

31. Oyster and Mussel Fisheries Orders Confirmation Act 1869 (No. 2).
repealed: S.L.R. 1973.

36. Juries (Lighthouse Keepers' Exemption) Act 1869.
repealed (S.): 1980, c.55, sch.3.

42. Irish Church Act 1869.
ss. 7, 8, 11, 12, 23, 25–28, 30 in pt., 34 in pt., 35–37, 48, 49, 52 in pt., 54, 56–65, repealed: S.L.R. (N.I.) 1980.

44. Greenwich Hospital Act 1869.
s. 5, order 82/1830.
s. 9, repealed: 1983, c.29, sch.3.

56. Endowed Schools Act 1869.
repealed: 1973, c.16, sch.2.

62. Debtors Act 1869.
s. 6, see *Al Nahkel for Contracting and Trading* v. *Lowe, The Times,* December 21, 1985, Tudor Price J.

68. Evidence Further Amendment Act 1869.
repealed: S.L.R. 1978.

70. Contagious Diseases (Animals) Act 1869.
repealed: S.L.R. 1975.

90. Annual Turnpike Acts Continuance Act 1869.
repealed: S.L.R. 1981.

94. New Parishes Acts and Church Building Acts Amendment Act 1869.
ss. 1, 8, 10–13, repealed: S.L.R. 1974.
s. 9, repealed: S.L.R. 1977.

115. Metropolitan Public Carriage Act 1869.
ss. 2, 4, see *Bassam* v. *Green* [1981] R.T.R. 362, D.C.
s. 5, repealed: S.L.R. 1976.
s. 6, order 82/311.
s. 6, amended: 1981, c.56, s.35; repealed in pt.: *ibid.,* sch.12.
s. 7, amended: 1982, c.48, sch.3; repealed in pt.: 1981, c.56, sch.12.
s. 8, orders 82/311; 87/999.
s. 8, amended: 1981, c.56, s.35; repealed in pt.: *ibid.,* sch.12.
s. 9, orders 73/519; 74/601; 75/1216; 76/1956; 77/2080; 79/706; 80/588, 939; 81/843; 82/610; 83/653; 84/707, 85/933, 1023; 86/857; 88/996.
s. 9, amended: S.L.R. 1973; repealed in pt.: 1981, c.56, sch.12.
s. 15, repealed in pt.: *ibid.*

33 & 34 Vict. (1870)

13. Survey Act 1870.
s. 5, repealed: S.L.R. 1977.

16. Inverness and Elgin County Boundaries Act 1870.
ss. 4–7, 10–16, repealed: S.L.R. 1977.

CAP.

33 & 34 Vict. (1870)—cont.

22. Turnpikes (Provisional Orders Confirmation) Act 1870.
repealed: S.L.R. 1981.

23. Forfeiture Act 1870.
s. 4, see *R.* v. *Ali* [1972] Crim.L.R. 225; (1972) 56 Cr.App.R. 301; *R.* v. *McDevitt* (1972) 56 Cr.App.R. 851, C.A.
s. 4, repealed: 1972, c.71, s.1, sch.6.

28. Attorneys and Solicitors Act 1870.
repealed: 1981, c.54, sch.7.

30. Wages Attachment Abolition Act 1870.
repealed: S.L.R. 1976.

33. Salmon Acts Amendment Act 1870.
repealed: 1986, c.62, sch.5.
s. 4, repealed (S.): S.L.R. 1975.

35. Apportionment Act 1870.
s. 2, see *Parry* v. *Robinson-Wyllie* (1987) 283 E.G. 559; (1987) 54 P. & C.R. 187, Browne-Wilkinson V.-C.

39. Church Patronage Act 1870.
repealed: 1986, No. 3, sch.5.

46. Landlord and Tenant (Ireland) Act 1870.
Pt. III, repealed: 1980, c.59, sch.
s. 70, sch., repealed in pt.: *ibid.*

52. Extradition Act 1870.
see *Wan Ping Nam* v. *Federal German Republic, 1972 S.L.T.* 220; *Beese* v. *Governor of Ashford Remand Centre and the Federal German Republic* [1973] 1 W.L.R. 1426, H.L.
s. 1, order 78/1889.
s. 2, orders 72/960, 1102, 1581; 73/1756; 74/1107, 1108; 75/803, 804, 1034; 76/679, 770, 1037, 2144; 77/1237–1239; 78/455, 782, 1106, 1403, 1623, 1887, 1888; 79/453, 913, 1311; 80/185, 398, 566, 1525; 81/210–213, 731–734, 1544; 82/145–149; 85/751, 1634, 1637, 1989–1993; 86/220, 766, 1300, 2011–2016, 2020; 87/451, 453–456, 2041–2044, 2046, 2206.
s. 3, see *Cheng* v. *Governor of Pentonville Prison* [1973] 2 W.L.R. 746; [1973] 2 All E.R. 204; *R.* v. *Governor of Pentonville Prison, ex p. Herbage (No. 3), The Times,* November 15, 1986, D.C.
s. 3, amended: 1978, c.26, s.2; 1988, c.33, sch.1
ss. 3, 5, see *R.* v. *Chief Metropolitan Stipendiary Magistrate, ex p. Secretary of State for the Home Department, The Independent,* June 3, 1988, D.C.
s. 4, see *R.* v. *Governor of Pentonville Prison, ex p. Dowse, The Times,* April 23, 1983, H.L.
s. 7, see *R.* v. *Secretary of State for the Home Department, ex p. Rees* [1986] 2 W.L.R. 1024, H.L.
s. 8, see *Government of the Federal Republic of Germany* v. *Sotiriadis* [1974] 2 W.L.R. 253; [1974] 1 All E.R. 692, H.L.
s. 9, see *Nielsen, Re* [1984] 2 W.L.R. 737, H.L.; *R.* v. *Governor of Pentonville Prison, ex p. Syal, The Times,* May 18, 1987, D.C.
s. 10, see *Beese* v. *Governor of Ashford Remand Centre and the Federal German Republic* [1973] 1 W.L.R. 1426, H.L.; *R.* v. *Governor of Pentonville Prison, ex p. Zezza*

CAP.

33 & 34 Vict. (1870)—cont.

52. Extradition Act 1870—*cont.*
[1982] 2 W.L.R. 1077, H.L.; *Nielsen, Re* [1984] 2 W.L.R. 737, H.L.; *Government of the United States of America* v. *McCaffery* [1984] 1 W.L.R. 867, H.L.; *R.* v. *Governor of Pentonville Prison, ex p. Voets* [1986] 1 W.L.R. 470, D.C.; *R.* v. *Secretary of State for the Home Department, ex p. Rees* [1986] 2 W.L.R. 1024, H.L.; *R.* v. *Bow Street Magistrates, ex p. Van der Holst* (1986) 83 Cr.App.R. 114, D.C.; *Government of Belgium* v. *Postlethwaite* [1987] 3 W.L.R. 365, H.L.; *Lee* v. *Governor of Pentonville Prison and the Government of the U.S.A.* [1987] Crim.L.R. 635, D.C.; *R.* v. *Chief Metropolitan Stipendiary Magistrate, ex p. Secretary of State for the Home Department, The Independent,* June 3, 1988, D.C.
ss. 10–12, see *Wan Ping Nam* v. *Minister of Justice of German Federal Republic, 1972 S.C.* 43 (J.).
s. 11, see *R.* v. *Secretary of State for the Home Department, ex p. Kirkwood* [1984] 2 All E.R. 390, Mann J.
s. 11A, added: 1988, c.33, sch.1.
ss. 13, 14, see *R.* v. *Governor of Pentonville Prison, ex p. Passingham* (1983) 127 S.J. 308, H.L.
s. 14, see *Dowse* v. *Government of Sweden* [1983] 2 All E.R. 123, H.L.; *R.* v. *Secretary of State for the Home Office, ex p. Rees* [1986] 2 W.L.R. 1024, H.L.
ss. 14, 15, see *R.* v. *Bow Street Magistrates, ex p. Van der Holst* (1986) 83 Cr.App.R. 114, D.C.
s. 15, see *Espinosa, Re* [1986] Crim.L.R. 684, D.C.; *Lee* v. *Governor of Pentonville Prison and the Government of the U.S.A.* [1987] Crim.L.R. 635, D.C.
s. 16, see *Wan Ping Nam* v. *Minister of Justice of German Federal Republic, 1972 S.C.* 43 (J.).
s. 17, orders 72/960, 1102, 1581; 73/1756; 74/1107, 1108; 75/803, 804, 1034; 76/679, 770, 1037, 2144; 77/1237–1239; 78/455, 1887–1889; 79/453, 913, 1311; 80/185, 566; 81/210–213, 731–734; 82/145–149; 85/751, 1634, 1637, 1989–1992; 86/2011–2016, 2020; 87/451, 453–456, 2041, 2042–2044, 2046.
s. 18, order 85/167.
s. 19, see *R.* v. *Kerr; R.* v. *Smith* (1975) 62 Cr.App.R. 210, C.A.; *R.* v. *Davidson* (1976) 64 Cr.App.R. 209, C.A.; *R.* v. *Davies* (1983) 76 Cr.App.R. 120, C.A.
s. 20, see *R.* v. *Governor of Pentonville Prison, ex p. Budlong; R.* v. *Governor of Holloway Prison, ex p. Kember* [1980] 1 All E.R. 701, D.C.
s. 21, orders 72/960, 1102; 74/1107, 1108; 75/803, 804, 1034; 76/679, 770, 1037, 2144; 77/1237–1239; 78/455, 1403, 1523, 1623, 1886–1889; 79/913, 1311; 80/185, 566; 81/209–213, 731–734, 1544; 82/145–149; 85/1634, 1637, 1989–1993; 86/220, 1300, 2011–2016, 2020; 87/451, 453–456, 2041–2044, 2046, 2206.

CAP.

33 & 34 Vict. (1870)—cont.

52. Extradition Act 1870—cont.
s. 23, repealed: S.L.R. 1976.
s. 24, repealed: 1975, c.34, sch.2.
s. 26, see *R.* v. *Governor of Pentonville Prison, ex p. Zezza* [1982] 2 W.L.R. 1077, H.L.; *R.* v. *Governor of Holloway Prison, ex p. Jennings* [1982] 3 W.L.R. 450, H.L.; *Nielsen, Re* [1984] 2 W.L.R. 737, H.L.; *R.* v. *Bow Street Magistrates, ex p. Van der Holst* (1986) 83 Cr.App.R. 114, D.C.
s. 26, amended: 1988, c.33, sch.1.
sch. 1, see *R.* v. *Kerr; R.* v. *Smith* (1975) 62 Cr.App.R. 120, C.A.; *Nielsen, Re* [1984] 2 W.L.R. 737, C.A.
sch. 1, amended: 1973, c.47, s.5; 1978, c.17, s.3; c.26, s.3; c.37, s.1; 1982, c.28, s.3; 1983, c.18, s.5; 1988, c.33, s.136, sch.1; repealed in pt.: 1978, c.26, s.3; 1984, c.37, s.11; 1985, c.38, s.3.
sch. 2, see *R.* v. *Governor of Pentonville Prison, ex p. Budlong; R.* v. *Governor of Holloway Prison, ex p. Kember* [1980] 1 All E.R. 701, D.C.
63. Wages Arrestment Limitation (Scotland) Act 1870.
repealed: 1987, c.18, sch.8.
69. Statute Law Revision Act 1870.
repealed: S.L.R. 1986.
71. National Debt Act 1870.
ss. 2, 4, Pts. IV, V (ss. 22–44) s.73, sch. 2, repealed: S.L.R. 1986.
77. Juries Act 1870.
repealed: 1972, c.71, sch.6; 1974, c.23, sch.3.
78. Tramways Act 1870.
s. 3, amended(S.): 1984, c.54, sch.9.
s. 64, repealed in pt.: S.L.R. 1986.
90. Foreign Enlistment Act 1870.
ss. 21, 26, 30, amended: order 80/399.
s. 30, amended: 1984, c.12, sch.4; repealed in pt.: S.L.R. 1976.
110. Matrimonial Causes and Marriage Law (Ireland) Amendment Act 1870.
s. 7, amended: 1978, c.23, sch.5.
ss. 8, 10, 11, 12, repealed: *ibid.*, sch.7.
s. 13, amended: *ibid.*, sch.5.
ss. 14–17, 23, 28, 29, repealed: *ibid.*, sch.7.
s. 35, repealed in pt.: S.L.R. 1981.

34 & 35 Vict. (1871)

3. Parliamentary Costs Act 1871.
s. 4, repealed in pt.: S.L.R. 1986.
16. Anatomy Act 1871.
repealed: 1984, c.14, s.13.
22. Lunacy Regulation (Ireland) Act 1871.
amended: 1978, c.23, sch.5.
ss. 2 (in pt.), 16, 17, (in pt.), 24, 41 (in pt.), 55 (in pt.), 105 (in pt.), 108, 110 (in pt.), 112, 114 (in pt.), 118 (in pt.) repealed: *ibid.*, sch.7.
ss. 2, 6, 8, 11–13, 17, 22, 28, 30, 35, 38, 41, 47–49, 52, 53, 55, 56, 59, 73, 88, 90, 99, 105, 110, 111, 114, 118, amended: *ibid.*, sch.5.
s. 68, order 81/235; amended: *ibid.*
s. 117, substituted: 1978, c.23, sch.5.
s. 199, added: *ibid.*

CAP.

34 & 35 Vict. (1871)—cont.

24. Irish Presbyterian Church Act 1871.
ss. 4–8, 9 in pt., 10 in pt., 13 in pt., 32, repealed: 1980, c.59, sch.
28. British North America Act 1871.
Act renamed Constitution Act 1871 (Can.): 1982, c.11, sch.
s. 1, substituted: *ibid.*
33. Burial Act 1871.
repealed: 1972, c.70, sch.30.
36. Pensions Commutation Act 1871.
repealed in pt.: 1972, c.11, schs.1,8.
s. 2, amended: 1981, c.55, sch.3.
ss. 4, 7, regs. 74/734, 1441; 77/108; 78/1257; 83/1052.
ss. 4 (in pt.), 5, repealed: 1984, c.7, s.1.
s. 6, repealed in pt.: 1976, c. 4, sch.6; 1984, c.7, s.1.
s. 7, repealed in pt.: 1984, c.7, s.1.
42. Citation Amendment (Scotland) Act 1871.
repealed: S.L.R. 1978.
s. 3, see *Lawrence Jack Collections* v. *Dallas,* 1976 S.L.T.(Sh.Ct.) 21.
43. Ecclesiastical Dilapidations Act 1871.
repealed: 1972,No.2, sch.2.
45. Sequestration Act 1871.
s. 6, repealed: 1986, No. 3, sch.5.
48. Promissory Oaths Act 1871.
s. 2, repealed in pt. (S.): 1975, c.20, sch.2.
49. Matrimonial Causes and Marriage Law (Ireland) Amendment Act 1871.
ss. 3, 9, 11–14, 20, repealed: 1978, c.23, sch.7.
50. Bankruptcy Disqualification Act 1871.
repealed: 1985, c.65, sch.10.
56. Dogs Act 1871.
s. 2, see *Sansom* v. *Chief Constable of Kent* [1981] Crim.L.R. 617, D.C.
s. 3, sch., repealed: 1974, c.17, sch.
s. 5, amended: *ibid.*
65. Juries (Ireland) Act 1871.
s. 3, repealed in pt.: 1978, c.23, sch.7.
ss. 7–9, 12–16, 19, 26, 27, 29, 45, 46, 47, sch. 3, repealed: order 74/2143.
ss. 17, 18, 23, 43, amended: *ibid.*
s. 18, amended: 1978, c.23, sch.5; repealed in pt.: *ibid.*, sch.7.
ss. 18, 23, 30, 32, 42, 43, repealed in pt.: order 74/2143.
s. 32, repealed: 1978, c.23, sch.7.
ss. 41, 42, amended: *ibid.*, sch.5.
ss. 48, 51, repealed: *ibid.*, sch.7.
68. An Act to determine the boundaries of Glasgow 1871.
repealed: S.L.R. 1976.
70. Local Government Board Act 1871.
repealed: S.L.R. 1986.
78. Regulation of Railways Act 1871.
s. 2, amended: 1987, c.53, sch.6.
s. 6, order 80/1941; S.Rs. 1985 No. 10; 1988 No. 145.
83. Parliamentary Witnesses Oaths Act 1871.
s. 1, repealed in pt.: 1977, c.38, sch.5.
86. Regulation of the Forces Act 1871.
repealed: 1980, c.9, sch.10.
90. Union of Benefices Acts Amendment Act 1871.
repealed: S.L.R. 1974.

CAP.

34 & 35 Vict. (1871)—cont.

96. Pedlars Act 1871.
s. 3, see *Watson* v. *Oldrey; Watson* v. *Malloy,
The Times,* May 7. 1988, D.C.
ss. 3, 5, see *Murphy* v. *Duke* [1985] 2 W.L.R.
773, Forbes J.
s. 5, amended: orders 80/580; 81/1604; 82/173;
83/1589; 85/2027.
s. 12, repealed in pt.: 1981, c.45, sch.
s. 18, repealed: 1984, c.60, sch.7.
s. 19, repealed: *ibid.,* s.7, sch.7.

112. Prevention of Crimes Act 1871.
ss. 6, 17, 18, repealed in pt.: S.L.R. 1981.
s. 7, see *Lafferty* v. *Farrell,* 1974 S.L.T. (Notes)
64; *Flynn* v. *Smith,* High Court of Justiciary,
December 15, 1981.
s. 7, repealed (S.): 1982, c.45, sch.4.
s. 9, repealed: S.L.R. 1981.
s. 13, repealed (S.): 1982, c.45, sch.4.
s. 15, see *Baecker* v. *Gray,* 1973 S.L.T. (Notes)
31, High Ct. of Justiciary; *Cole* v. *Cardle,*
1981, S.C.C.R. 132.
s. 15, repealed: 1981, c.47, sch.; (S.) 1982,
c.45, sch.4.
s. 17, repealed in pt.: S.L.R. 1981.
s. 18, repealed in pt.: *ibid.;* 1984, c.60, sch.7.
s. 20, see *Flynn* v. *Smith,* High Court of Justiciary, December 15, 1981.
s. 22, repealed: S.L.R. 1981.
sch., repealed (S.): 1982, c.45, sch.4.

115. Annual Turnpike Acts Continuance Act 1871.
repealed: S.L.R. 1981.

117. Tancred's Charities 1871.
repealed: S.L.R. 1981.

35 & 36 Vict. (1872)

14. Diocesan Boundaries Act 1872.
repealed: S.L.R. 1974.

15. Parks Regulation Act 1872.
ss. 3, 6–8, amended: 1974, c.29, sch.
s. 5, substituted: 1984, c.60, sch.6.

25. Juries (Ireland) Act 1872.
repealed: order 74/2143.

26. Review of Justices' Decisions Act 1872.
see *R.* v. *Daejan Properties, ex p. Merton
London Borough Council, The Times,* April 25,
1978, D.C.

45. Treaty of Washington Act 1872.
repealed: S.L.R. 1976.

**47. An Act to amend [the Act 30 & 31 Vict. c.
85].**
repealed: S.L.R. 1977.

50. Railway Rolling Stock Protection Act 1872.
s. 7, repealed: S.L.R. 1976.

58. Bankruptcy (Ireland) Amendment Act 1872.
s. 2, repealed in pt.: 1985, c.65, sch.10.
s. 4, amended: 1978, c.23, sch.5.
ss. 8, 10, 11, 13–16, repealed: *ibid.,* sch.7.
s. 21, amended: order 81/226.
ss. 40–42, repealed: 1985, c.65, sch.10.
ss. 43, 44, repealed: 1975, c.66, sch.2.
s. 53, see *Industrial Design and Manufacture,
Re* [1984] 10 N.I.J.B., Carswell J.
s. 57, amended: 1978, c.23, sch.5.

CAP.

35 & 36 Vict. (1872)—cont.

**58. Bankruptcy (Ireland) Amendment Act
1872—cont.**
s. 62, amended: orders 79/296; 81/226.
s. 65, repealed in pt.: S.L.R. 1981; 1985, c.65,
sch.10.
ss. 70, 71, repealed: S.L.R 1981.
s. 121, repealed in pt.: 1985, c.65, sch.10.
s. 124, amended: 1978, c.23, sch.5.

61. Steam Whistles Act 1872.
repealed: order 78/1049.

73. Merchant Shipping Act 1872.
repealed: 1980, c.9, sch.10.

75. Commissioners for Oaths (Ireland) Act 1872.
repealed: 1978, c.23, sch.7.

85. Annual Turnpike Acts Continuance Act 1872.
repealed: order 80/1085.
ss. 14, 15, repealed: S.L.R. 1981.

**86. Borough and Local Courts of Record Act
1872.**
repealed: 1977, c.38, sch.5.

93. Pawnbrokers Act 1872.
repealed: 1974, c.39, sch.5.
s. 13, repealed: order 80/50.
s. 36, repealed: 1984, c.60, sch.7.

94. Licensing Act 1872.
s. 12, see *Seamark* v. *Prouse* [1980] 1 W.L.R.
698, D.C.; *Winzar* v. *Chief Constable of Kent,
The Times,* March 28, 1983, D.C.; *Lanham* v.
Rickwood, The Times, May 10, 1984, D.C.;
Neale v. *R. M. J. E. (A Minor)* (1985) 80
Cr.App.R. 20, D.C.
s. 12, amended: 1977, c.45, s.31, sch.6.
s. 39, repealed: S.L.R. 1978.
s. 75, repealed: 1987, c.19, sch.

96. Ecclesiastical Dilapidations Act 1872.
repealed: 1972, No. 2, sch.2.

36 & 37 Vict. (1873)

1. repealed: S.L.R. 1977.

12. Custody of Infants Act 1873.
preamble, s. 2, repealed: 1973, c.29, sch.3.

**16. Marriage Law (Ireland) Amendment Act
1873.**
s. 2, repealed: S.L.R. 1977.

20. repealed: S.L.R. 1977.

22. Australian Colonies Duties Act 1873.
repealed: S.L.R. 1973.

25. repealed: S.L.R. 1977.

28. repealed: S.L.R. 1977.

48. Regulation of Railways Act 1873.
s. 6, amended: 1973, c.55, sch.

55. Medical Act (University of London) 1873.
repealed: S.L.R. 1977.

**57. Consolidated Fund (Permanent Charges
Redemption) Act 1873.**
s. 3, amended: 1978, c.23, sch.5.
s. 7, repealed in pt.: S.L.R. 1976.
s. 8, repealed in pt.: S.L.R. 1986.

59. Slave Trade (East African Courts) Act 1873.
repealed: S.L.R. 1986.

60. Extradition Act 1873.
see *R.* v. *Secretary of State for the Home
Department, ex p. Spermacet Whaling and
Shipping Co. S.A., The Times,* November 14,
1986, D.C.

CAP.

36 & 37 Vict. (1873)—cont.

60. Extradition Act 1873—cont.
s. 3, see *Government of the United States of America* v. *McCaffery* [1984] 1 W.L.R. 867, H.L.
s. 4, see *R.* v. *Governor of Pentonville Prison, ex p. Singh* [1981] 1 W.L.R. 1031, D.C.; *R.* v. *Governor of Pentonville Prison, ex p. Passingham* (1983) 127 S.J. 308, H.L.; *Dowse* v. *Government of Sweden* [1983] 2 All E.R. 123, H.L.
sch., amended: 1978, c.31, s.5; repealed in pt.: S.L.R. 1973; 1978, c.26, sch.2.

62. Public Schools (Eton College Property) Act 1873.
repealed: S.L.R. 1973.

76. Railway Regulation Act (Returns of Signal Arrangements, Workings etc.) 1873.
repealed: 1988, c.13, sch.4.

81. Langbaurgh Coroners Act 1873.
repealed: S.L.R. 1976.

87. Endowed Schools Act 1873.
repealed: 1973, c.16, sch.2.

88. Slave Trade Act 1873.
s. 2, repealed in pt.: S.L.R. 1976; S.L.R. 1986.
s. 3, order 80/399.
s. 18, repealed in pt.: S.L.R. 1976.
s. 29, repealed in pt.: S.L.R. 1986.

37 & 38 Vict. (1874)

14. repealed: S.L.R. 1977.
17. repealed: S.L.R. 1977.
27. Courts (Colonial) Jurisdiction Act 1874.
s. 2, repealed in pt.: S.L.R. 1976.
s. 2A, repealed: *ibid.*

31. Conjugal Rights (Scotland) Amendment Act 1874.
repealed: 1984, c.15, sch.2.

34. Apothecaries Act Amendment Act 1874.
s. 5, repealed: S.L.R. 1976.

38. Straits Settlements Offences Act 1874.
repealed: S.L.R. 1973.

40. Board of Trade Arbitrations etc. Act 1874.
s. 4, repealed: S.L.R. 1976.

42. Building Societies Act 1874.
ss. 1, 4, 32, repealed: 1986, c.53, sch.19.

45. County of Hertford and Liberty of St. Albans Act 1874.
repealed: order 74/1351.

48. Hosiery Manufacture (Wages) Act 1874.
repealed: 1986, c.48, schs.1,5.

62. Infants Relief Act 1874.
repealed: 1987, c.13, ss.1,4.

63. Archdeaconries and Rural Deaneries Act 1874.
repealed: S.L.R. 1974.

72. Fines Act (Ireland) 1851, Amendment Act 1874.
s. 2, amended: 1978, c.23, sch.5.

81. Great Seal (Offices) Act 1874.
s. 8, repealed in pt.: S.L.R. 1973.
s. 9, orders 77/1971; 83/1916; 87/1464.

88. Births and Deaths Registration Act 1874.
s. 28, repealed: 1973, c.32, sch.5.
s. 51, repealed in pt.: S.L.R. 1977.
sch. 4, repealed: *ibid.*

CAP.

37 & 38 Vict. (1874)—cont.

92. Alderney Harbour (Transfer) Act 1874.
repealed: S.L.R. 1977.

94. Conveyancing (Scotland) Act 1874.
ss. 3, 9, see *Mulheron and Others, Petitioners*, 1977 S.L.T.(Sh.Ct.) 65.
s. 10, see *Findlay*, 1975 S.L.T.(Sh.Ct.). 46; *Mulheron and Others, Petrs.*, 1977 S.L.T.(Sh.Ct.) 65; *Grant and Others, Petrs.*, 1977 S.L.T.(Sh.Ct.) 97; *Fraser, Petitioner*, 1978 S.L.T.(Sh.Ct.) 5; *Robertson, Petitioner*, 1978 S.L.T.(Sh.Ct.) 30; *McKenzie, Petitioner*, 1979 S.L.T.(Sh.Ct.) 68.
s. 15, amended: 1981, c.19, sch.2.
s. 32, see *Gorrie and Banks* v. *Burgh of Musselburgh*. 1973 S.C. 33, First Division; *Bachoo* v. *George Wimpey*, 1977 S.L.T.(Lands Tr.) 2.
s. 39, see *McNeill* v. *McNeill*, 1973 S.L.T.(Sh.Ct.) 16.
s. 43, see *McBride*, 1975 S.L.T.(Sh.Ct.) 25; *Robertson, Petr.*, 1980 S.L.T.(Sh.Ct.) 73.

38 & 39 Vict. (1875)

17. Explosives Act 1875.
s. 3, see *R.* v. *Wheatley* [1979] 1 W.L.R. 144, C.A.; *R.* v. *Bouch* [1982] 3 W.L.R. 673, C.A.
s. 4, amended: regs. 74/1885.
s. 5, amended: regs. 74/1885; 84/510.
s. 6, amended: regs. 74/1885.
s. 7, amended: regs. 84/510.
ss. 8–13, amended: regs. 74/1885.
s. 15, amended: orders 78/270; 83/219; regs. 85/1108; 87/52.
s. 16, amended: regs. 84/510.
s. 17, amended: regs. 74/1885; 84/510.
s. 18, amended: orders 78/270; 83/219; regs. 74/1885; 85/1108; 87/52.
s. 19, amended: regs. 74/1885.
s. 21, amended: regs. 77/918; 85/1108; 87/52; order 83/219.
s. 22, amended: regs. 74/1885; 84/510; 1984, c.54, sch.9(S.).
s. 24, amended: regs. 74/1885; 84/510.
s. 25, repealed: regs. 74/1885.
s. 26, amended: regs. 74/1885; 87/52; repealed in pt.: 1972, c.70, sch.30; regs. 74/1885; 83/1450.
ss. 28, 29, amended: regs. 74/1885.
s. 30, amended(S.): 1984, c.54, sch.9.
s. 31, amended: 1976, c.54, s.1; 1987, c.43, sch.4.
s. 32, amended: regs. 84/510.
s. 33, amended: regs. 74/1885.
s. 34, repealed in pt.: order 87/37.
s. 35, amended: 1984, c.32, sch.6.
s. 36, repealed in pt.: order 87/37.
s. 37, repealed: regs. 74/1885.
s. 40, amended: *ibid.*; 1979, c.2, sch.4.
s. 43, order 77/1798; S.R. 1979 No. 290; amended: regs. 74/1885; 1979, c.2, sch.4.
s. 45, amended: regs. 74/1885.
ss. 46, 47, amended: regs. 74/1885; 84/510.
s. 48, amended: regs. 84/510.
s. 49, amended: regs. 74/1885.

CAP.

38 & 39 Vict. (1875)—cont.

17. Explosives Act 1875—cont.
ss. 53–57, repealed: *ibid.*
s. 58, amended: *ibid.*
s. 59, repealed: *ibid.*
s. 60, amended: *ibid.*
s. 62, repealed: *ibid.*
s. 63, amended: regs. 74/1885; 84/510.
s. 64, amended: regs. 74/1885.
ss. 65, 66, repealed: *ibid.*
s. 67, amended: 1972, c.70, sch.29; 1985, c.51, sch.11; repealed in pt.: 1972, c.70, schs.29, 30.
s. 68, repealed: *ibid.*, sch.30.
s. 69, amended, regs. 74/1885.
s. 70, repealed in pt.: 1972, c.70, sch.30.
s. 72, amended: regs. 74/1885.
s. 73, repealed: *ibid.*
s. 74, amended: *ibid.*
ss. 75, 76, repealed: *ibid.*
s. 77, amended: *ibid.*
s. 78, amended: *ibid.*: repealed in pt.: 1984, c.60, sch.7.
s. 79, repealed: regs. 74/1885.
s. 80, amended: 1976, c.26, s.1; 1984, c.54, sch.9(S.); 1987, c.43, sch.4.
s. 81, repealed: regs. 74/1885.
s. 83, S.R. 1979 No. 290.
s. 83, amended: regs. 74/1885; repealed in pt.: S.L.R. 1986.
s. 85, repealed: regs. 74/1885.
s. 86, amended: *ibid.*
ss. 87, 88, 89 (in pt.), 91 (in pt.), 92, 93 (in pt.), 94 (in pt.), 96 (in pt.), repealed: *ibid.*
s. 97, regs. 72/1502–1504; 74/479; order 87/37.
s. 99, repealed: S.L.R. 1977.
s. 103, amended: regs. 74/1885.
s. 104, order 77/1978; S.R. 1979 No. 290.
s. 108, amended (S.): 1984, c.54, sch.9; repealed in pt.: 1972, c.70, sch.30.
s. 109, repealed in pt.: 1973, c.65, sch.29.
ss. 110, 111, amended: *ibid.*, sch.27; repealed in pt.: *ibid.*, sch.29.
s. 112, repealed: *ibid.*
s. 114, amended: regs. 74/1274.
s. 115, repealed: order 87/37.
sch. 1, amended: regs. 84/510.
sch. 2, repealed: regs. 74/1885.
sch. 3, repealed: regs. 83/1450.

18. Seal Fishery Act 1875.
s. 1, repealed in pt.: S.L.R. 1986.

21. Public Entertainments Act 1875.
repealed: S.L.R. 1973.

25. Public Stores Act 1875.
ss. 7, 9, repealed: 1977, c.45, schs.12,13.
s. 10, repealed: *ibid.*, sch.13.
s. 17, repealed: S.L.R. 1976.

34. Bishopric of St. Albans Act 1875.
repealed: S.L.R. 1973.

38. Parliament of Canada Act 1875.
Act renamed Parliament of Canada Act 1875 (Can.): 1982, c.11, sch.

41. Intestates' Widows and Children (Scotland) Act 1875.
s. 3, repealed in pt.: 1975, c.7, sch.13.
ss. 3, 5, amended: 1979, c.22, s.1.

CAP.

38 & 39 Vict. (1875)—cont.

41. Intestates' Widows and Children (Scotland) Act 1875—cont.
s. 7, repealed in pt.: *ibid.*, s.1, sch.
s. 8, repealed: 1975, c.7, sch.13.
schs. A,B, amended: *ibid.*, s.1.
sch. C, repealed: *ibid.*, s.1, sch.

42. Glebe Lands, Representative Church Body, Ireland, Act 1875.
s. 4, see *Re Steele; Northern Bank Executor & Trustee Co.* v. *Linton* [1976] N.I. 66, Murray J.

43. Medical Act (Royal College of Surgeons of England) 1875.
repealed: S.L.R. 1986.

51. Pacific Islanders Protection Act 1875.
repealed: S.L.R. 1986.

52. Washington Treaty (Claims) Act 1875.
repealed: S.L.R. 1977.

53. Canada Copyright Act 1875.
repealed: S.L.R. 1973.

55. Public Health Act 1875.
s. 4, see *Weaver* v. *Family Housing Association (York)* (1975) 74 L.G.R. 255, H.L.
s. 4, repealed in pt.: 1972, c.70, sch.30.
s. 64, see *Gilson* v. *Kerrier District Council* [1976] 1 W.L.R. 904, C.A.
s. 148, repealed: 1974, c.40, sch.4.
s. 149, see *Russell* v. *Barnet London Borough Council* [1985] 83 L.G.R. 152, Tudor Evans J.
s. 172, repealed: 1980, c.65, sch.34.
ss. 253, 262, repealed: *ibid.*, s.27, sch.2.
s. 265, amended: *ibid.*; 1982, c.32, sch.5
s. 276, repealed: 1972, c.70, sch.30.
ss. 293, 294, 299–302, 304, 309, repealed: 1980, c.65, s.27, sch.2.
sch. 5, repealed in pt.: 1972, c.70, sch.30; S.L.R. 1977; S.L.R. 1978.

61. Entail Amendment (Scotland) Act 1875.
s. 3, amended: 1984, c.54, sch.9.

64. Government Officers (Security) Act 1875.
repealed: S.L.R. 1974.

86. Conspiracy and Protection of Property Act 1875.
s. 3, repealed: 1977, c.45, s.5, sch.13.
s. 5, repealed in pt.: *ibid.*, sch.13.
s. 7, see *Elsey* v. *Smith*, [1983] I.R.L.R. 292, High Ct. of Justiciary, Scotland; *Galt* v. *Philp* [1984] I.R.L.R. 156, High Court of Justiciary; *R.* v. *Bonsall* [1985] Crim.L.R. 150, Derby Crown Court; *Thomas* v. *National Union of Mineworkers* [1985] 2 All E.R. 1, C.A.
s. 7, amended: 1986, c.64, sch.2; repealed in pt.: 1977, c.45, sch.13.
s. 9, repealed: *ibid.*, s.15, sch.13.
s. 11, repealed: 1980, c.62, sch.8.
s. 19, repealed in pt.: 1977, c.45, s.15, sch.13.

89. Public Works Loans Act 1875.
s. 41, repealed in pt.: S.L.R. 1986.

90. Employers and Workmen Act 1875.
repealed: S.L.R. 1973.

91. Trade Marks Registration Act 1875.
s. 1, see *Henry Denny & Sons* v. *United Biscuits (U.K.)* [1981] F.S.R. 114, Graham J.

CAP.

39 & 40 Vict. (1876)

18. Treasury Solicitor Act 1876.
s. 5, repealed in pt.: S.L.R. 1986.
ss. 6, 9, repealed: S.L.R. 1981.

24. Small Testate Estates (Scotland) Act 1876.
ss. 3, 5, amended: 1979, c.22, s.1.
s. 7, repealed in pt.: *ibid.*, s.1, sch.
s. 8, repealed: 1975, c.7, sch.13.
sch. A, amended: 1979, c.22, s.1.
sch. C, repealed: *ibid.*, s.1, sch.

28. Court of Admiralty (Ireland) Amendment Act 1876.
repealed: 1978, c.23, sch.7.

33. Trade Marks Registration Amendment Act 1876.
see *Henry Denny & Sons* v. *United Biscuits (U.K.)* [1981] F.S.R. 114, Graham J.

36. Customs Consolidation Act 1876.
s. 42, see *Derrick* v. *Customs and Excise Commissioners* [1972] 2 W.L.R. 359; *Henn and Darby* v. *D.P.P.* [1980] 2 W.L.R. 597, European Ct. and H.L.; *Conegate* v. *H.M. Customs and Excise* [1987] 2 W.L.R. 39, Kennedy J.; *R.* v. *Bow Street Magistrates' Court, ex p. Noncyp, The Times,* May 14, 1988, D.C.
s. 42, repealed: 1981, c.45, sch.
s. 43, repealed: S.L.R. 1986.
s. 283, repealed: 1979, c.58, sch.2.

41. Medical Act 1876.
repealed: S.L.R. 1976.

54. Bishopric of Truro Act 1876.
repealed: S.L.R. 1973.

56. Commons Act 1876.
s. 8, repealed: 1980, c.65, schs.3,34.
s. 24, repealed: S.L.R. 1977.
s. 37, see *Re Britford Common* [1977] 1 W.L.R. 39.

57. Winter Assizes Act 1876.
repealed: order 75/816.

59. Appellate Jurisdiction Act 1876.
s. 3, see *Re Poh* [1983] 1 W.L.R. 2, H.L.
s. 6, amended: S.L.R. 1973.
s. 7, repealed: 1973, c.15, sch.5.
s. 25, amended: 1978, c.23, sch.5.

70. Sheriff Courts (Scotland) Act 1876.
Pt. VII, repealed: S.L.R. 1986.
s. 54, Acts of Sederunt, 75/539; 78/1509; 79/1405; 84/969; 86/267.

77. Cruelty to Animals Act 1876.
repealed: 1986, c.14, s.27.

78. Juries Procedure (Ireland) Act 1876.
s. 4, amended: order 74/2143.
ss. 5, 9, 14, 15, 21, repealed: *ibid.*

40 & 41 Vict. (1877)

2. Treasury Bills Act 1877.
ss. 2, 8, repealed in pt.: S.L.R. 1977.
s. 9, regs. 88/1603.
s. 9, repealed in pt.: S.L.R. 1986.

11. Jurisdiction in Rating Act 1877.
s. 3, repealed in pt.: 1978, c.23, sch.7; 1988, c.36, sch.2.
s. 12, amended: 1980, c.48, s.94; c.55, s.9(S.); repealed in pt.: 1980, c.48, s.94, sch.20; c.55, s.9, sch.3(S.).

CAP.

40 & 41 Vict. (1877)—cont.

14. Evidence Act 1877.
repealed: S.L.R. 1981.

15. Public Libraries (Ireland) Amendment Act 1877.
repealed: order 81/438.

18. Settled Estates Act 1877.
s. 34, amended: 1978, c.23, sch.5.
s. 42, repealed in pt.: *ibid.*, sch.7.

23. Colonial Fortifications Act 1877.
repealed: S.L.R. 1976.

29. Married Women's Property (Scotland) Act 1877.
repealed: 1984, c.15, sch.2.
s. 4, repealed: *ibid.*, s.6.

36. Registration of Leases (Scotland) Amendment Act 1877.
s. 2, repealed: S.L.R. 1975.

40. Writs Execution (Scotland) Act 1877.
s. 3, substituted: 1987, c.18, s.87.

41. Crown Office Act 1877.
s. 3, rules 73/2099; 75/622, 802; order 88/1082.
ss. 3, 5, amended: 1973, c.15, sch.5; repealed in pt.: 1975, c.20, sch.2(S.); S.L.R. 1986.
s. 5, order 88/1162.

43. Justices Clerks Act 1877.
repealed: 1979, c.55, sch.3.

46. Winter Assizes Act 1877.
repealed: order 75/816.

47. South Africa Act 1877.
repealed: S.L.R. 1973.

49. General Prisons (Ireland) Act 1877.
repealed: S.L.R. (N.I.) 1980.

56. County Officers and Courts (Ireland) Act 1877.
repealed: 1978, c.23, sch.7.

57. Supreme Court of Judicature Act (Ireland) Act 1877.
repealed: 1978, c.23, sch.7.

59. Colonial Stock Act 1877.
s. 20, see *Franklin* v. *Att.-Gen.* [1973] 2 W.L.R. 255; *Barclays Bank* v. *The Queen* [1973] 3 W.L.R. 627, Cusack J.
s. 20, amended: 1973, c.27, sch.2; 1978, c.15, sch.; c.20, sch.2; 1979, c.27, sch.; 1981, c.52, sch.2, order 78/1030.
s. 26, repealed in pt.: S.L.R. 1976.

41 & 42 Vict. (1878)

8. Public Parks (Scotland) Act 1878.
repealed: 1982, c.43, sch.4.

14. Baths and Washhouses Act 1878.
repealed: S.L.R. 1976.

15. Customs and Inland Revenue Act 1878.
repealed: S.L.R. 1973.

27. Supreme Court of Judicature Act (Ireland) 1877, Amendment Act 1878.
repealed: order 75/816.

33. Dentists Act 1878.
repealed: S.L.R. 1986.

43. Marriage Notice (Scotland) Act 1878.
repealed: 1977, c.15, sch.3.

49. Weights and Measures Act 1878.
repealed: order 81/231.

41 & 42 Vict. (1878)—cont.

51. Roads and Bridges (Scotland) Act 1878.
repealed: 1984, c.54, sch.11.

52. Public Health (Ireland) Act 1878.
s. 2, amended: order 79/1049.
s. 18, see *Moen* v. *Watson* [1981] 7 N.I.J.B., Hutton J.
ss. 38–40, repealed: order 80/1085.
ss. 50, 51, amended: order 79/1049.
ss. 52, 53, repealed: order 79/1049.
s. 54, amended and repealed in pt.: *ibid.*
ss. 55, 59, 60, repealed: *ibid.*
s. 79, amended: *ibid.*
s. 80, repealed in pt.: order 80/1085.
ss. 82–86, repealed: order 81/156.
ss. 107, 112, 114, amended: order 79/1049.
s. 261, repealed: S.L.R. 1976.
sch. C, amended: order 79/1049.

61. Fiji Marriage Act 1878.
repealed: 1988, c.43, sch.

68. Bishoprics Act 1878.
repealed (except ss. 1, 5): S.L.R. 1973.

69. Petty Sessions Clerks and Fines (Ireland) Act 1878.
s. 9, repealed: 1978, c.23, sch.7.

71. Metropolitan Commons Act 1878.
s. 2, amended: 1985, c.51, sch.8.

73. Territorial Waters Jurisdiction Act 1878.
s. 7, repealed in pt.: S.L.R. 1976; 1987, c.49, sch.2.

76. Telegraph Act 1878.
repealed: 1984, c.12, sch.7.
s. 8, see *Post Office* v. *Hampshire County Council* [1979] 2 W.L.R. 907, C.A.; *Post Office* v. *Mears Construction* [1979] 2 All E.R. 814, Willis J.; *Post Office* v. *Tarmac Construction,* 1983 S.L.T. 586.

77. Highways and Locomotives (Amendment) Act 1878.
s. 26, amended: 1972, c.70, sch.30; 1985, c.51, sch.4.

42 & 43 Vict. (1879)

11. Bankers' Books Evidence Act 1879.
see *Barker* v. *Wilson, The Times,* February 5, 1980, D.C.
s. 6, amended: 1988, c.32, s.7.
s. 7, see *Williams* v. *Summerfield* [1972] 3 W.L.R. 131; [1972] 2 All E.R. 1334; *R.* v. *Andover Justices, ex p. Rhodes* [1980] Crim.L.R. 644, D.C.; *A.* v. *C.* [1980] 2 All E.R. 347, Robert Goff J.; *R.* v. *Marlborough Street Metropolitan Stipendiary Magistrate, ex p. Simpson* (1980) 70 Cr.App.R. 291, D.C.; *Owen* v. *Sambrook* [1981] Crim.L.R. 329, D.C.; *R.* v. *Grossman* [1981] Crim.L.R. 396, C.A.; *R.* v. *Nottingham City JJ., ex p. Lynn* [1984] Crim.L.R. 554; (1984) 79 Cr.App.R. 238, D.C.
ss. 7, 9, see *Williams* v. *Williams; Tucker* v. *Williams* [1987] 3 W.L.R. 790, C.A.
ss. 7, 10, see *Carmichael* v. *Sexton,* 1986 S.L.T. 16.
s. 9, see *Barker* v. *Wilson* [1980] 2 All E.R. 81, D.C.; *R.* v. *Dadson* [1983] Crim.L.R. 540, C.A.

42 & 43 Vict. (1879)—cont.

11. Bankers' Books Evidence Act 1879—*cont.*
s. 9, substituted: 1979, c.37, sch.6; amended: 1981, c.65, sch.6; 1986, c.53, sch.18; 1987, c.22, sch.6; repealed in pt.: 1985, c.58, sch.4.
s. 10, amended: 1974, c.26, sch.2; c.47, s.86.

17. House of Commons Costs Taxation Act 1879.
ss. 1, 2, repealed in pt.: S.L.R. 1986.

19. Habitual Drunkards Act 1879.
repealed: S.L.R. 1976.

21. Customs and Inland Revenue Act 1879.
s. 5, amended: 1979, c.2, sch.4.
s. 8, repealed: S.L.R. 1986.

22. Prosecution of Offences Act 1879.
repealed: 1979, c 31, sch.2.
s. 2, see *Turner* v. *D.P.P.* (1978) 68 Cr.App.R. 70, Mars Jones J.
ss. 2, 5, 8, regs. 78/1357, 1846.
s. 5, repealed in pt.: 1979, c.31, sch.2.
s. 7, repealed: *ibid.*

27. Convention of Royal Burghs (Scotland) Act 1879.
repealed: 1973, c.65, sch.29.

29. Confirmation of Marriages on Her Majesty's Ships Act 1879.
repealed: 1988, c.44, sch.

31. Public Health (Internments) Act 1879.
repealed: 1972, c.70, sch.30.

38. Slave Trade (East African Courts) Act 1879.
repealed: S.L.R. 1986.

42. Valuation of Lands (Scotland) Amendment Act 1879.
s. 7, amended: 1984, c.31, s.13.
ss. 7, 9, see *Lugano* v. *Ayrshire Valuation Appeal Committee,* 1972 S.C. 314.
s. 8, repealed: regs. 78/252.

44. Lord Clerk Register (Scotland) Act 1879.
s. 9, repealed: 1972, c.11, sch.8.

50. Bills of Sale (Ireland) Act 1879.
s. 4, amended: 1978, c.23, sch.5.
ss. 13, 19, substituted: *ibid.*
ss. 17, 21, repealed: *ibid.,* sch.7.

58. Public Offices Fees Act 1879.
s. 2, orders 73/164, 165; 74/1382; 75/1328; 76/184, 1479; 77/346, 1451, 2184; 78/569, 570, 704, 705, 1243, 1256, 1298, 1653, 1654; 79/779, 780, 966–968, 1149, 1589, 1591; 80/509, 773, 819–821, 1060, 1186, 1187, 2007, 2008; 81/54, 861, 898, 1103, 1515; 1642, 1643; 82/541, 542, 859, 860; 84/880, 881, 887; 85/1783, 1784; 86/1399, 2030; S.Rs. 1978 No. 363; 1979 Nos. 160, 161; 1980 No. 264; 1981 Nos. 173, 364; 1984 No. 14; 1986 No. 232.
ss. 2, 3, orders 72/194, 1054, 1055, 1189–91, 1287, 1381, 1383, 1384; 77/346; 85/358, 359, 372, 88/665; rules 74/637, 638, 2095, 2096; 75/1314–1316, 1344; 76/687, 688, 1333, 1363, 1506; S.R. 1984 Nos. 419, 420.
ss. 2, 3, repealed in pt.: S.L.R. 1986.
s. 3, orders 78/569, 570, 704, 705, 1256, 1298, 1653, 1654; 79/779, 780, 966, 968, 1589, 1591; 80/509, 819–821, 1060, 1186, 1187, 2007, 2008; 81/54, 861, 1103, 1515; 86/1399; S.Rs. 1979 Nos. 160, 161; 1980 No. 264; 1981 Nos. 173, 364; 1984 No. 14; 1986 No. 232.

CAP.

42 & 43 Vict, (1879)—cont.

75. Parliamentary Elections and Corrupt Practices Act 1879.
repealed: 1981, c.54, sch.7.
repealed (S.): 1988, c.36, sch.2.

43 Vict. (1880)

7. Roads Amendment Act 1880.
repealed: S.L.R. 1973.

14. Customs and Inland Revenue Act 1880.
repealed: 1975, c.7, sch.13.

43 & 44 Vict. (1880)

4. Judicial Factors (Scotland) Act 1880.
s. 3, amended: 1980, c.55, s.14; 1985, c.66, sch.7.
s. 4, amended: 1980, c.55, s.14; repealed in pt.: *ibid.*, s.14, sch.3.

9. Statutes (Definition of Time) Act 1880.
repealed: 1978, c.30, sch.3.

16. Merchant Seamen (Payment of Wages and Rating) Act 1880.
repealed: S.L.R. 1973.

20. Inland Revenue Act 1880.
s. 47, repealed: 1987, c.19, sch.
s. 57, repealed: 1979, c.37, sch.7.
sch. 3, repealed: *ibid.*

26. Married Women's Policies of Assurance (Scotland) Act 1880.
see *Will* v. *I.R.C.* [1981] S.T.C. 428, H.L.
s. 2, see *Barclay's Tr.* v. *Inland Revenue,* [1975] 1 W.L.R. 106; [1975] 1 All E.R. 168; 1975 S.L.T. 17, H.L.; *Stevenson's Exrs.* v. *Lord Advocate* (H.L.), 1981 S.L.T. 336.
s 2, amended: 1980, c.56, s.1.

34. Debtors (Scotland) Act 1880.
s. 4, amended: 1987, c.18, sch. 6; repealed in pt.: *ibid.*, sch. 8.

41. Burial Laws Amendment Act 1880.
ss. 1, 10, 12, amended: order 74/628.

44 & 45 Vict. (1881)

11. Sea Fisheries (Clam and Bait Beds) Act 1881.
repealed: 1984, c.26, sch.2.

12. Customs and Inland Revenue Act 1881.
Pt. III (except s. 34) repealed: 1975, c.7, sch.13.
s. 34, repealed: 1979, c.22, sch.
s. 38, see *Re Nichols, decd.*; *Nichols* v. *I.R.C.* [1975] 1 W.L.R. 534; [1975] 2 All E.R. 120, C.A.; *Re Stewart's Annuity Trusts; Stewart* v. *I.R.C.* [1981] S.T.C. 91, Megarry V.-C.

21. Married Women's Property (Scotland) Act 1881.
s. 1, repealed in pt.: 1985, c.66, sch.8.
ss. 1–5, 8, sch., repealed: 1985, c.37, sch.2.

24. Summary Jurisdiction (Process) Act 1881.
s. 6, repealed in pt.: S.L.R. 1986.

41. Conveyancing Act 1881.
s. 46, see *Industrial Development Authority* v. *Moran* [1978] I.R. 159, Sup.Ct. of Ireland.
ss. 48, 69, 72, repealed in pt.: 1978, c.23, sch.7.

49. Land Law (Ireland) Act 1881.
s. 57, repealed in pt.: 1980, c.59, sch.

CAP.

44 & 45 Vict. (1881)—cont.

52. Royal University of Ireland Act 1881.
repealed: order 81/610.

60. Newspaper Libel and Registration Act 1881.
s. 5, repealed: 1977, c.45, s.17, sch.13.

68. Supreme Court of Judicature Act 1881.
repealed: 1977, c.38, sch.5.

71. Irish Church Act Amendment Act 1881.
repealed: S.L.R. (N.I.) 1980.

45 & 46 Vict. (1882)

12. Militia Storehouses 1882.
repealed: 1980, c.9, sch.10.

15. Commonable Rights Compensation Act 1882.
sch., amended: 1985, c.51, sch.8.

22. Boiler Explosions Act 1882.
repealed: regs. 80/804.

27. Highway Rate Assessment and Expenditure Act 1882.
repealed: S.L.R. 1973.

29. County Court Amendment (Ireland) Act 1882.
repealed: 1978, c.23, sch.7.

31. Inferior Courts Judgments Extension Act 1882.
repealed: 1982, c.27, sch.14.

37. Corn Returns Act 1882.
ss. 4, 5, 14, regs. 72/1245, 1275; 74/399; 75/675; 76/1081; 79/607, 614; orders 76/1035; 81/293, 927(S.).
ss. 8, 9, amended: orders 76/1034, 1082.

38. Settled Land Act 1882.
s. 2, amended: 1978, c.23, sch.5.
s. 20, amended: 1973, c.55, sch.
s. 25, amended (S.): 1984, c.54, sch.9; repealed in pt. (S.): *ibid.*, schs.9,11.
s. 65, repealed in pt.: 1978, c.23, sch.5.

39. Conveyancing Act 1882.
s. 3, see *Northern Bank* v. *Henry* [1981] I.R. 1, Eire Sup. Ct.; *Ulster Bank* v. *Shanks* [1982] 6 N.I.J.B., Murray J.

42. Civil Imprisonment (Scotland) Act 1882.
s. 4, see *White* v. *White,* 1984 S L.T.(Sh.Ct.) 30.
s. 5, repealed: 1987, c.18, sch.8.
s. 6, see *Morrow* v. *Neil,* 1975 S.L.T. (Sh.Ct.) 65; *Porteous* v. *Rutherford,* 1980 S.L.T.(Sh.Ct.) 129.
s. 8, repealed: S.L.R. 1978.

43. Bills of Sale Act (1878) Amendment Act 1882.
s. 7, amended: 1974, c.39, sch.4.
s. 11, amended: 1985, c.65, sch.8.

44. Pensions Commutation Act 1882.
s. 3, regs. 74/734, 1441; 77/108; 78/1257; 83/1052.

45. Bombay Civil Fund Act 1882.
repealed: S.L.R. 1981.

49. Militia Act 1882.
repealed: 1980, c.9, sch.10.

50. Municipal Corporations Act 1882.
s. 6, repealed: order 74/1351.
s. 7, repealed in pt.: *ibid.*; 1973, c.15, sch.5.
ss. 31, 105, repealed: *ibid.*
s. 146, repealed: order 74/1351.
ss. 154, 156–158, 159 (in pt.), repealed: 1973, c.15, sch.5.

CAP.

45 & 46 Vict. (1882)—cont.

50. Municipal Corporations Act 1882—cont.
ss. 170, 171, 178–184, repealed: 1972, c.70, sch.30.
s. 187, repealed: 1973, c.15, sch.5.
ss. 193. 225, 228, 229, repealed: S.L.R. 1976.
s. 231, repealed: 1973, c.15, sch.5.
s. 232, repealed: S.L.R. 1976.
s. 234, repealed: 1973, c.15, sch.5.
s. 235, repealed: 1981, c.45, sch.
ss. 237, 241, 242 (in pt.), repealed: 1973, c.15, sch.5.
s. 245, repealed: S.L.R. 1976.
s. 248, repealed in pt.: 1988, c.13, sch.14
s. 250, repealed in pt.: 1973, c.15, sch.5.
s. 253, repealed in pt.: S.L.R. 1975.
s. 255, repealed: 1988, c.13, sch.4.
s. 257, repealed in pt.: S.L.R. 1986.
s. 258, repealed: 1973, c.15, sch.5.
sch. 1, repealed: S.L.R. 1974.
sch. 4, repealed: S.L.R. 1975.
sch 5, repealed in pt.: 1973, c.15, sch.5.
sch. 9, repealed in pt.: *ibid.*; S.L.R. 1975.

52. Annual Turnpike Acts Continuance Act 1882.
repealed: S.L.R. 1981.

53. Entail (Scotland) Act 1882.
s. 14, amended: 1977, c.27, sch.1; repealed in pt.: *ibid.*, sch.2.
s. 16, substituted: *ibid.*

56. Electric Lighting Act 1882.
see *R.* v. *Midlands Electricity Board, ex p. Busby; Same* v. *Same, ex p. Williamson, The Times,* October 28, 1987, Schiemann J.
s. 12, amended (S.): 1982, c.48, sch.15.
ss. 12–15, amended (S.): 1984, c.54, sch. 9.
s. 17, see *Christian Salvesen (Properties)* v. *Central Electricity Generating Board* (1984) 48 P. & C.R. 465, Lands Tribunal, V.G. Wellings Esq., Q.C.; *Mayclose* v. *Central Electricity Generating Board* (1987) 283 E.G. 192, C.A.
s. 24, amended: 1983, c.25, s.14.
s. 25, amended: *ibid.*, sch.3.
s. 26, amended: 1981, c.38, sch.3; 1984, c.12, sch.4.
s. 31, amended: orders 74/595; 75/1636.
ss. 31, 36, amended: 1973, c.65, sch.27.
s. 32, amended (S.): 1984, c.54, sch.9.
s. 36, repealed in pt.(S.): *ibid.*, schs.9,11.

61. Bills of Exchange Act 1882.
see *Thompson* v. *J. Barke & Co.* (O.H.), October 30, 1974.
s. 3, see *Dickie* v. *Singh,* 1974 S.L.T.(Notes) 3, Ct. of Session.
ss. 3, 5, see *Aziz* v. *Knightsbridge Gaming and Catering Services and Supplies, The Times,* July 6, 1982, Hobhouse J.
s. 11, see *Korea Exchange Bank* v. *Debenhams (Central Buying)* (1979) 123 S.J. 163, C.A.
s. 21, see *Bank of Cyprus (London)* v. *Jones* (1984) 134 New L.J. 522, Legatt J.
s. 23, see *Ringham* v. *Hackett, The Times,* February 8, 1980, C.A.
s. 26, see *Rolfe, Lubell & Co.* v. *Keith* [1979] 1 All E.R. 860, Kilner Brown J.; *Claydon* v. *Bradley* [1987] 1 All E.R. 522, C.A.

CAP.

45 & 46 Vict. (1882)—cont.

61. Bills of Exchange Act 1882—cont.
s. 27, see *Mackenzie Mills* v. *Buono, The Times,* July 31, 1986, C.A.
ss. 27, 29, see *Bank of Credit and Commerce International S.A.* v. *Dawson and Wright* [1987] FLR 342, Drake J.
s. 29, see *Jade International Steel Stahl und Eisen GmbH & Co., K.G.* v. *Robert Nicholas (Steels)* [1978] 3 W.L.R. 39, C.A.; *Mackenzie Mills* v. *Buono, The Times,* July 31, 1986, C.A.
ss. 29, 30, see *Williams* v. *Williams,* 1980 S.L.T.(Sh.Ct.)25; *Osterreichische Landerbank* v. *S'Elite* [1980] 2 All E.R. 651, C.A.
s. 30, see *Bank of Cyprus (London)* v. *Jones* (1984) 134 New L.J. 522, Legatt J.
s. 32, see *K. H. R. Financings* v. *Jackson,* 1977 S.L.T.(Sh.Ct.) 6.
s. 45, see *Ringham* v. *Hackett, The Times,* February 8, 1980, C.A.
s. 46, see *Aziz* v. *Knightsbridge Gaming and Catering Services and Supplies,The Times,* July 6, 1982, Hobhouse J.
ss. 48, 49, see *Eaglehill* v. *Needham (J.) Builders* [1973] A.C. 992; [1972] 3 W.L.R. 789; [1972] 3 All E.R. 895.
s. 50, see *Barclays Bank* v. *W. J. Simms Son and Cooke (Southern)* [1979] 3 All E.R. 522, Robert Goff J.; *Aziz* v. *Knightsbridge Gaming and Catering Services and Supplies, The Times,* July 6, 1982, Hobhouse J.
s. 53, see *Thompson* v. *Jolly Carters Inn,* 1972 S.C. 215; *Williams* v. *Williams,* 1980 S.L.T.(Sh.Ct.) 25.
s. 53, amended (S.): 1985, c.73, s.11.
s. 55, see *Ladup* v. *Shaikh (Nadeem)* [1982] 3 W.L.R. 172, McCowan J.
s. 57(2), repealed: 1977, c.38, s.4, sch.5.
s. 70, repealed in pt.: 1978, c.23, sch.7.
s. 72, see *Barclays Bank International* v. *Levin Bros. (Bradford)* [1976] 3 W.L.R. 852; [1976] 3 All E.R. 900.
s. 72, repealed in pt.: 1977, c.38, s.4, sch.5.
s. 73, see *Thompson* v. *Jolly Carters Inn,* 1972 S.C. 215; *Aziz* v. *Knightsbridge Gaming and Catering Services and Supplies, The Times,* July 6, 1982, Hobhouse J.
s. 75, see *Thompson* v. *Jolly Carters Inn,* 1972 S.C. 215.
s. 75A, added (S.): 1985, c.73, s.11.
s. 81, see *Ladup* v. *Shaikh (Nadeem)* [1982] 3 W.L.R. 172, McCowan J.
s. 83, see *Creative Press* v. *Harman and Harman* [1973] I.R. 313; *Dickie* v. *Singh,* 1974 S.L.T.(Notes) 3, Ct. of Session; *Claydon* v. *Bradley* [1987] 1 All E.R. 522, C.A.
s. 89, see *Dickie* v. *Singh,* 1974 S.L.T.(Notes) 3, Ct. of Session.
s. 100, see *Thompson* v. *Jolly Carters Inn,* 1972 S.C. 215.
s. 100, amended: 1973, c.52, sch.5.

70. Supreme Court of Judicature (Ireland) Act 1882.
repealed: 1978, c.23, sch.7.

CAP.

45 & 46 Vict. (1882)—cont.

72. Revenue, Friendly Societies and National Debt Act 1882.
s. 6, repealed: S.L.R. 1973.
s. 25, repealed in pt.: 1978, c.23, sch.7.

73. Ancient Monuments Protection Act 1882.
sch., repealed: 1979, c.46, sch.5.

75. Married Women's Property Act 1882.
see *Pearce* v. *Diensthuber* (1978) 81 D.L.R. 286, Ontario C.A.
s. 17, see *Hazell* v. *Hazell* [1972] 1 W.L.R. 301; [1972] 1 All E.R. 923; *Cowcher* v. *Cowcher* [1972] 1 W.L.R. 425; 116 S.J. 142; [1972] 1 All E.R. 943; *Kowalczuk* v. *Kowalczuk* [1973] 1 W.L.R. 930; *Glenn* v. *Glenn* [1973] 1 W.L.R. 1016; [1973] 2 All E.R. 1187; *Steadman* v. *Steadman* [1973] 3 W.L.R. 695; [1973] 3 All E.R. 977, C.A.; *Burke* v. *Burke* [1974] 1 W.L.R. 1063; [1974] 2 All E.R. 944; 118 S.J. 98, C.A.; *Willis* v. *Willis* (1973) 4 Fam.Law 21, C.A.; *Cuzner (formerly Underdown)* v. *Underdown* [1974] 1 W.L.R. 641; [1974] 2 All E.R. 351, C.A.; *Leake (formerly Bruzzi)* v. *Bruzzi* [1974] 2 All E.R. 1196, C.A.; *Baker (formerly Sillence)* v. *Sillence* (1974) 5 Fam.Law 47, C.A.; *Bothe* v. *Amos* [1975] 2 W.L.R. 838; [1975] 2 All E.R. 321, C.A.; *Calderbank* v. *Calderbank* [1975] 3 W.L.R. 586; [1975] 3 All E.R. 333, C.A.; *Coley* v. *Coley* (1975) 5 Fam. Law 195, C.A.; *Chaudhry* v. *Chaudhry* [1976] 1 W.L.R. 221, C.A.; *Shinh* v. *Shinh* [1977] 1 All E.R. 97; *Suthill* v. *Graham* [1977] 1 W.L.R. 819, C.A.; (1977) 121 S.J. 408, C.A.; *Cann* v. *Ayres* [1977] Fam. Law 47, C.A.; *Fielding* v. *Fielding (Note)* [1977] 1 W.L.R. 1146, C.A.; *McKeown* v. *McKeown* [1975] N.I. 139, Lord MacDermott; *Chambers* v. *Chambers* (1979) 123 S.J. 689, Wood J.; *Ward* v. *Ward and Green (Note)* [1980] 1 W.L.R. 4; [1980] 1 All E.R. 176, C.A.; *Thompson* v. *Thompson*, The Times, February 14, 1985, C.A.; *Hamlin* v. *Hamlin*, The Times, May 9, 1985, C.A.
s. 17, amended: 1984, c.42, s.43; order 78/1045.

77. Citation Amendment (Scotland) Act 1882.
s. 3, see *Smith* v. *Conner & Co.*, 1979 S.L.T (Sh.Ct.) 25.
s. 4, see *McCormick* v. *Martin*, 1985 S.L.T.(Sh.Ct.) 57.

78. Fishery Board (Scotland) Act 1882.
repealed: 1986, c.62, sch.5.

46 & 47 Vict. (1883)

1. Consolidated Fund (Permanent Charges Redemption) Act 1883.
s. 2, repealed in pt.: 1985, c.58, sch.4.

3. Explosive Substances Act 1883.
s. 2, see *Bellew* v. *Secretary of State* [1985] 6 N.I.J.B. 86, Hutton J.
s. 2, substituted: 1975, c.59, s.7.
s. 3, see *Black* v. *H.M. Advocate*, 1974 S.L.T. 247.; *R.* v. *Byrne*; *R.* v. *Coughlan*; *R.* v. *Gillespie* (1975) 62 Cr.App.R. 159, C.A.; *R.* v. *Coughlan*; *R.* v. *Young* (1976) 63 Cr.App.R. 33, C.A.; *R.* v. *Bouch* [1982] 3 W.L.R. 637,

CAP.

46 & 47 Vict. (1883)—cont.

3. Explosive Substances Act 1883—cont.
C.A.; *R.* v. *McLaughlin* (1983) 76 Cr.App.R. 42, C.A.
s. 3, substituted: 1975, c.59, s.7; amended: 1977, c.45, s.33, sch.12; order 77/1249; 1978, c.5, s.9.
s. 4, see *Black* v. *H.M. Advocate*, 1974 S.L.T. 247; *R.* v. *Wheatley* [1979] 1 W.L.R. 144, C.A.; *Att.-Gen.'s Reference (No. 2 of 1983)* [1984] 2 W.L.R. 465, C.A.; *R.* v. *Berry* [1984] 3 W.L.R. 1274, H.L.
s. 4, repealed in pt.: 1984, c.60, sch.7.
s. 7, see *R.* v. *Cain*; *R.* v. *Schollick* [1975] 3 W.L.R. 131; [1975] 2 All E.R. 900, C.A.; *R.* v. *Marron* [1981] 1 N.I.J.B., C.A.; *R.* v. *McLaughlin* (1983) 76 Cr.App.R. 42, C.A.
s. 7, repealed in pt.: 1975, c.59, sch.6.
ss. 7, 9, amended: 1982, c.53, s.63.
s. 9, see *R.* v. *Bouch* [1982] 3 W.L.R. 637, C.A.

7. Bills of Sale (Ireland) Act (1879) Amendment Act 1883.
s. 7, amended: 1974, c.39, sch.4.
s. 14, amended: order 77/2157.

18. Municipal Corporations Act 1883.
ss. 2–4, repealed: order 74/1351.
s. 6, repealed: 1977, c.38, sch.5.
s. 12, repealed: S.L.R. 1978.
s. 13, repealed in pt · S.L.R. 1975.
s. 15, repealed: order 74/1351.
ss. 16, 18, repealed: S.L.R. 1975.
ss. 22, 23, repealed: 1977, c.38, sch. 5.
s. 25, repealed in pt.: S.L.R. 1978.
s. 26, repealed in pt.: S.L.R. 1975.
s. 27, repealed: S.L.R. 1978.
sch. 1, repealed: order 74/1351.
sch. 2, repealed: S.L.R. 1975.

22. Sea Fisheries Act 1883.
s. 20, amended (S.): 1987, c.18, sch.6.

31. Payment of Wages in Public-houses Prohibition Act 1883.
repealed: 1986, c.48, schs.1,5.

34. Cheap Trains Act 1883.
repealed: S.L.R. 1978.

38. Trial of Lunatics Act 1883.
see *R.* v. *Sullivan* [1983] 3 W.L.R. 123, H.L.

51. Corrupt and Illegal Practices Prevention Act 1883.
repealed (S.): 1988, c.36, sch.2.
s. 42, repealed: 1981, c.54, sch.7.
s. 49, repealed: 1973, c.55, sch.

52. Bankruptcy Act 1883.
s. 32, amended (S.): 1985, c.66, sch.7.
s. 32, repealed in pt.: S.L.R. 1973; S.L.R. 1975; 1985, c.65, sch.10.
s. 33, repealed in pt.: 1975, sch.2; 1985, c.65, sch.10.
s. 34, repealed in pt.: S.L.R. 1975; 1985, c.65, sch.10.
s. 34A, added (S.): 1985, c.66, sch.7.

55. Revenue Act 1883.
ss. 10, 11, repealed: 1973, c.43, sch.7.

57. Patents, Designs and Trade Marks Act 1883.
see *Polaroid Corp. (Land's) Patent* [1981] R.P.C., 11, C.A.
s. 29, see *Williamson* v. *Moldline* [1986] R.P.C. 556, C.A.

CAP.

46 & 47 Vict. (1883)—cont.

57. Patents, Designs and Trade Marks Act 1883—cont.
s. 76, see *Rolls-Royce Motors* v. *Dodd* [1981] F.S.R. 517, Whitford J.
s. 77, see *Henry Denny & Sons* v. *United Biscuits (U.K.)* [1981] F.S.R. 114, Graham J.

47 & 48 Vict. (1884)

12. Public Health (Confirmation of Byelaws) Act 1884.
repealed: S.L.R. 1975.
17. Metropolitan Police Act 1884.
repealed: S.L.R. 1973.
20. Greek Marriages Act 1884.
repealed: 1986, c.55, s.62, sch.2.
23. National Debt (Conversion of Stock) Act 1884.
ss. 1 (in pt.), 6, 7, 9 (in pt.), repealed: S.L.R. 1986.
31. Colonial Prisoners Removal Act 1884.
s. 2, amended: 1981, c.55, sch.3.
s. 4, repealed in pt.: S.L.R. 1986.
s. 10, amended: 1983, c.20, sch.4; 1984, c.36, sch.3.
s. 13, repealed in pt.: S.L.R. 1986.
ss. 14A, 17, repealed: S.L.R. 1976.
s. 18, repealed in pt. *ibid.*
37. Public Libraries Act 1884.
repealed: order 81/438.
44. Naval Pensions Act 1884.
s. 3, repealed: S.L.R. 1976.
46. Naval Enlistment Act 1884.
repealed: 1980, c.9, sch.10.
52. Annual Turnpike Acts Continuance Act 1884.
repealed: S.L.R. 1981.
55. Pensions and Yeomanry Pay Act 1884.
Title, repealed in pt.: S.L.R. 1976.
s. 2, repealed in pt.: *ibid.*; S.L.R. 1986.
58. Prosecution of Offences Act 1884.
repealed: 1979, c.31, sch.2.
62. Revenue Act 1884.
ss. 4, 5, repealed: 1973, c.43, sch.7.
s. 14, repealed in pt.: 1978, c.30, sch.3.
65. New Parishes Acts and Church Building Acts Amendment Act 1884.
repealed: S.L.R. 1974.
66. Bishopric of Bristol Act 1884.
ss. 2, 3 (in pt.), sch., repealed: S.L.R. 1973.
67. Improvement of Lands (Ecclesiastical Benefices) Act 1884.
repealed: 1972, No.2, Sch.2.
70. Municipal Elections (Corrupt and Illegal Practices) Act 1884.
repealed: S.L.R. 1978.
71. Intestates' Estates Act 1884.
s.5, see *Re Lowe's Will Trusts; More* v. *Att.-Gen.* [1973] 1 W.L.R. 882; [1973] 2 All E.R. 1136.
s. 5, repealed: order 79/1575.
s. 9, repealed in pt.: *ibid.*
72. Disused Burial Grounds Act 1884.
ss. 2, 3, see *Re St. Ann's Church, Kew* [1976] 1 All E.R. 461.

CAP.

47 & 48 Vict. (1884)—cont.

72. Disused Burial Grounds Act 1884—cont.
s. 3, see *Re St. Luke's, Chelsea* [1975] 3 W.L.R. 564; *Re St. Thomas, Lymington* [1980] 2 W.L.R. 267, Phillips Ch., Winchester Consistory.
76. Post Office (Protection) Act 1884.
repealed: 1984, c.12, sch.7.

48 & 49 Vict. (1885)

16. Registration Amendment (Scotland) Act 1885.
repealed: 1975, c.30, sch.7.
s. 3, order 75/805.
21. Burial Boards (Contested Elections) Act 1885.
repealed: 1972, c.70, sch.30.
25. East India Unclaimed Stock Act 1885.
s. 2, repealed in pt.: S.L.R. 1976.
ss. 17–24, repealed: *ibid.*
31. Ecclesiastical Commissioners Act 1885.
repealed: S.L.R. 1975.
40. Polehampton Estates Act 1885.
repealed: S.L.R. 1981.
42. Greenwich Hospital Act 1885.
s. 4, repealed: 1981, c.55, sch.5.
49. Submarine Telegraph Act 1885.
s. 3, amended: 1981, c.61, sch.7.
s. 6, repealed in pt.: S.L.R. 1986.
s. 8, repealed in pt.: 1981, c.45, sch.
61. Secretary for Scotland Act 1885.
sch., repealed in pt.: S.L.R. 1973; 1977, c.15, sch.3.
69. Criminal Law Amendment Act 1885.
repealed: 1976, c.67, sch.2.
s. 11, order 82/1536.
70. Sea Fisheries (Scotland) Amendment Act 1885.
s. 4, byelaws 76/2231; 77/2183
ss. 4, 11, repealed: 1984, c.26, sch.2.
72. Housing of the Working Classes Act 1885.
repealed (S.): S.L.R. 1981.
s. 9, amended: order 78/1049.
73. Purchase of Land (Ireland) Act 1885.
s. 19, repealed: 1978, c.23, sch.7.
74. Evidence by Commission Act 1885.
repealed: 1975, c.34, sch.2.
78. Educational Endowments (Ireland) Act 1885.
ss. 1 (in pt.), 4, 5, 6–9 (in pt.), 11–14 (in pt.), 16 (in pt.), 18 (in pt.), 19–25, 27, 28 (in pt.), 30–36, 38, repealed: S.L.R. (N.I.) 1980.

49 & 50 Vict. (1886)

15. Sporting Lands Rating (Scotland) Act 1886.
s. 6, amended: 1975, c.30, sch.6.
22. Metropolitan Police Act 1886.
s. 4, amended: 1981, c.67, sch.4
s. 5, repealed: 1973, c.26, sch.3.
27. Guardianship of Infants Act 1886.
repealed: 1986, c.9, sch.2.
s. 9, amended: 1986, c.55, sch.1; repealed in pt.: 1978, c.23, sch.7; 1986, c.55, sch.2.
ss. 10, 11, repealed in pt.: 1978, c.23, sch.7.
29. Crofters Holdings (Scotland) Act 1886.
s. 1, see *Arran Properties* v. *Currie*, 1983 S.L.C.R. 92.

CAP.

49 & 50 Vict. (1886)—cont.

29. Crofters Holdings (Scotland) Act 1886—cont.
s. 2, see *Secretary of State for Scotland* v. *Shareholders of Lealt and Culnacnock Common Grazings,* 1982 S.L.T.(Land Ct.) 20; *Barvas Estate* v. *Crofters Sharing in South Bragar Common Grazings,* 1983 S.L.C.R. 47.
s. 6, see *W. C. Johnston* v. *Fitzsimon,* 1983 S.L.C.R. 95.
s. 8, see *Gilmour* v. *Master of Lovat,* 1979 S.L.T.(Land Ct.) 2.
s. 16, see *Kennedy* v. *MacInnes,* 1977 S.L.T. (Land Ct.) 3.
s. 27, repealed: 1976, c.21, sch.3.
s. 29, rules 79/379; 80/1319; 83/1058; 87/643, 88/1933.
s. 29, amended: 1983, c.12, sch.1.
s. 32, amended: 1984, c.26, sch.1; repealed in pt.: *ibid.,* schs.1,2.
s. 34, see *Gilmour* v. *Master of Lovat,* 1979 S.L.T.(Land Ct.) 2, *Fraser* v. *Van Arman,* 1982 S.L.C.R. 79.
sch. amended: 1974, c.45, s.25; 1984, c.54, sch.9; 1987, c.26, sch.23.

35. British North America Act 1886.
Act renamed Constitution Act 1886 (Can.): 1982, c.11, sch.
s. 3, substituted: *ibid.*

38. Riot (Damages) Act 1886.
s. 3, regs. 86/76.
ss. 5, 9, repealed in pt.: 1972, c.70, sch.30.

41. Customs Amendment Act 1886.
repealed: S.L.R. 1986.

48. Medical Act 1886.
repealed: S.L.R. 1986.

53. Sea Fishing Boats (Scotland) Act 1886.
s. 14, order 81/740.

57. Parliamentary Elections (Returning Officers) Act (1875) Amendment Act 1886.
repealed: S.L.R. 1978.

50 & 51 Vict. (1887)

6. Supreme Court of Judicature (Ireland) Act 1887.
repealed: 1978, c.23, sch.7.

20. Criminal Law and Procedure (Ireland) Act 1887.
s. 10, repealed in pt.: order 74/2143.

27. Markets and Fairs (Weighing of Cattle) Act 1887.
s. 9, repealed in pt.: S.L.R. 1975.

32. Open Spaces Act 1887.
s. 4, see *Re St. Ann's Church, Kew* [1976] 1 All E.R. 461.

33. Land Law (Ireland) Act 1887.
s. 7, repealed: 1978, c.23, sch.7.
s. 34, amended: *ibid.,* sch.5.

35. Criminal Procedure (Scotland) Act 1887.
see *H.M. Advocate* v. *Boyle* [1973] Crim.L.R. 769.
ss. 1, 2, repealed: 1975, c.21, sch.10.
s. 3, see *H.M. Advocate* v. *Hanna,* 1975 S.L.T. (Sh.Ct.) 24; repealed in pt.: 1975, c.21, sch.10.

CAP.

50 & 51 Vict. (1887)—cont.

35. Criminal Procedure (Scotland) Act 1887—cont.
ss. 4–35, repealed: 1975, c.21, sch.10.
s. 36, see *Lindie* v. *H.M. Advocate,* 1974 S.L.T. 208.
ss. 37–42, repealed: 1975, c.21, sch.10.
s. 43, see *H.M. Advocate* v. *Boyle,* 1972 S.L.T.(Notes) 16; *H.M. Advocate* v. *McTavish,* 1974 S.L.T. 246.
ss. 43, 44, 47–76, repealed: 1975, c.21, sch.10.
s. 59, see *Christie* v. *Barclay,* 1974 J.C. 68.
s. 67, see *Carberry,* 1976 S.L.T. 38.
s. 76, Act of Adjournal 73/450.
schs. F, G, repealed: 1980, c.62, sch.8.

40. Savings Banks Act 1887.
s. 10, amended: orders 75/1291, 1808; 77/1861, 1961; 81/241; 82/222; repealed in pt.: 1985, c.58, sch.4.

42. Public Libraries Consolidation (Scotland) Act 1887.
s. 2, substituted: 1973, c.65, sch.21; amended: 1982, c.43, sch.3.
ss. 4–6, repealed: 1973, c.65, schs.21,29.
s. 10, amended: *ibid.,* sch.21.
ss. 14, 17–20, repealed: *ibid.,* schs.21, 29.
ss. 21, 22, amended: *ibid.,*sch.21; repealed in pt.: *ibid.,*schs. 21,29.
s. 23, repealed: *ibid.*
s. 24, substituted: *ibid.,*sch.21.
ss. 25–27, 30, schs. A, B, repealed: *ibid.,*schs.21,29.

43. Stannaries Act 1887.
ss. 12, 13, repealed: 1986, c.48, sch.5.

45. Metropolitan Police Act 1887.
s. 4, repealed: S.L.R. 1986.

46. Truck Amendment Act 1887.
repealed: 1986, c.48, schs.1,5.
ss. 12, 13, regs. 74/1887.

51. Valuation of Lands (Scotland) Amendment Act 1887.
repealed: S.L.R. 1976.

53. Escheat (Procedure) Act 1887.
s. 2, repealed in pt.: S.L.R. 1986.

54. British Settlements Act 1887.
orders 72/668; 73/598; 75/1211, 1706; 76/52; 77/423; 82/824; 83/1110, 1113; 85/444, 449; 87/1268; 88/1842.
s. 7, repealed: S.L.R. 1986.

55. Sheriffs Act 1887.
s. 3, repealed in pt.: S.L.R. 1973.
ss. 4, 10, 14, repealed in pt.: 1972, c.70, sch.30.
s. 18, repealed: 1977, c.38, sch.5.
s. 20, orders 73/981; 75/694; 77/416, 2111; 79/1442.
s. 21, 22, amended: order 76/229.
s. 26, repealed: S.L.R. 1981.
s. 29, repealed in pt.: 1972, c.70, sch.30.
s. 30, repealed: S.L.R. 1981.
ss. 34, 36, 38 (in pt.), repealed: 1972, c.70, sch.30.
s. 40, repealed in pt.: 1977, c.38, sch.5.
sch. 2, repealed in pt.: S.L.R. 1978.

57. Deeds of Arrangement Act 1887.
s. 15, amended: 1978, c.23, sch.5.
s. 18, repealed in pt.: *ibid.,* sch.7.

CAP.

50 & 51 Vict. (1887)—cont.

58. Coal Mines Regulation Act 1887.
repealed: 1986, c.48, sch.5.
ss. 12–14, repealed: *ibid.*, sch.1.

65. Military Tramways Act 1887.
s. 6, amended: 1981, c.38, sch.3; 1984, c.12, sch.4.
s. 12, amended: 1984, c.54, sch.9.

68. Pluralities Act 1887.
repealed: S.L.R. 1974.

70. Appellate Jurisdiction Act 1887.
s. 2, repealed: S.L.R. 1977.

71. Coroners Act 1887.
s. 3, see *R.* v. *West Yorkshire Coroner, ex p. Smith* [1982] 3 W.L.R. 920, C.A.; *R.* v. *Inner North London Coroner, ex p. Chambers; R.* v. *Inner North London Coroner, ex p. G.L.C., The Times,* April 30, 1983, Woolf J.; *R.* v. *Greater Manchester Coroner, ex p. Worth, The Times,* August 1, 1987, C.A.
s. 4, see *R.* v. *Surrey Coroner, ex p. Campbell* [1982] 2 W.L.R. 626, D.C.; *R.* v. *West London Coroners' Court, ex p. Gray; Same* v. *Same, ex p. Duncan* [1987] 2 W.L.R. 1020, D.C.
s. 6, see *R.* v. *South London Coroner, ex p. Thompson, The Times,* May 15, 1982, Comyn J.; *R.* v. *Inner North London Coroner, ex p. Chambers; R.* v. *Inner North London Coroner, ex p. G.L.C., The Times,* April 30, 1983, Woolf J.; *R.* v. *Central Cleveland Coroner, ex p. Dent, The Times,* February 17, 1986, D.C.; *Inquest into the Death of Adam Bithell (Decd), Re* (1986) 150 J.P.N. 348, D.C.; *Rapier, Decd, Re* [1986] 3 W.L.R. 830, D.C.; *R.* v. *West London Coroners' Court, ex p. Gray; Same* v. *Same, ex p. Duncan* [1987] 2 W.L.R. 1020, D.C.; *Att.-Gen.* v. *Harte (J. D.)* (1987) 151 J.P.N. 750, Taylor J.; *R.* v. *H.M. Coroner for South Glamorgan, ex p. B.P. Chemicals* (1987) 151 J.P.N. 808, D.C.
s. 7, see *R.* v. *West Yorkshire Coroner, ex p. Smith* [1982] 3 W.L.R. 920, C.A.
s. 25A, regs. 74/1582; 75/1091, 2068; 77/408.

51 & 52 Vict. (1888)

2. National Debt (Conversion) Act 1888.
ss. 2 (in pt.), 19, 25, 27, 28, 32, repealed: S.L.R. 1986.

9. Roads and Bridges (Scotland) Act 1878, Amendment Act 1888.
repealed: 1984, c.54, sch.11.

12. Electric Lighting Act 1888.
repealed: 1983, c.25, sch.4.
s. 4, amended: 1984, c.12, sch.4; c.54, sch.9 (S.); repealed in pt.: 1984, c.12, sch.7 (S.); c.54, schs.9, 11.

15. National Debt (Supplemental) Act 1888.
repealed: S.L.R. 1986.

19. Inebriates Act 1888.
repealed: S.L.R. 1976.

21. Law of Distress Amendment Act 1888.
s. 8, rules 73/474; 79/711; 83/1917.

CAP.

51 & 52 Vict. (1888)—cont.

25. Railway and Canal Traffic Act 1888.
s. 16, amended (S.): 1984, c.54, sch.9; repealed in pt. (S.): *ibid.*, schs.9,11.
s. 40, repealed in pt.: S.L.R. 1986.
s. 54, repealed in pt.: 1972, c.70, sch.30.

27. Supreme Court of Judicature (Ireland) Amendment Act 1888.
repealed: 1978, c.23, sch.7.

28. Marriages Validation Act 1888.
repealed: S.L.R. 1977.

29. Lloyd's Signal Stations Act 1888.
ss. 2, 6, amended: 1981, c.38, sch.3.

36. Bail (Scotland) Act 1888.
repealed (S.): 1975, c.21, sch.10.

41. Local Government Act 1888.
s. 3, repealed: order 74/1351.
ss. 5, 7, 11 (in pt.), 28 (in pt.), 31–39, repealed: 1972, c.70, sch.30.
s. 42, repealed in pt.: 1979, c.55, sch.3.
ss. 46, 48, repealed: 1972, c.70, sch.30.
s. 59, repealed: order 74/1351.
s. 63, repealed in pt.: S.L.R. 1975.
s. 64, repealed: orders 74/595, 1351.
s. 69, amended: order 74/1351.
ss. 79 (in pt.), 82, repealed: S.L.R. 1978.
s. 83, repealed: order 74/1351.
s. 100, repealed in pt.: 1972, c.70, sch.30; S.L.R. 1978.
s. 109, repealed: *ibid.*
sch. 1, repealed in pt.: S.L.R. 1975.
sch. 3, repealed: order 74/1351.

42. Mortmain and Charitable Uses Act 1888.
s. 13, see *Re South Place Ethical Society; Barralet* v. *Att.Gen.* [1980] 1 W.L.R. 1565; [1980] 3 All E.R. 918, Dillon J.

46. Oaths Act 1888.
repealed: 1978, c.19, sch.

57. Statute Law Revision (No. 2) Act 1888.
s. 2, repealed: 1977, c.38, sch.5.

64. Law of Libel Amendment Act 1888.
s. 3, amended: 1984, c.46, sch.5.
s. 8, see *Goldsmith* v. *Pressdram* [1976] 3 W.L.R. 191; *Desmond* v. *Thorn* [1982] 3 All E.R. 268, Taylor J.
s. 9, repealed in pt.: S.L.R. 1986.

52 & 53 Vict. (1889)

6. National Debt Act 1889.
s. 2, repealed in pt.: S.L.R. 1986.
s. 5, regs. 88/1603.

7. Customs and Inland Revenue Act 1889.
repealed: 1975, c.7, sch.13.
s. 11, see *Nichols* v. *I.R.C.* [1973] 3 All E.R. 632, Walton J.

10. Commissioners for Oaths Act 1889.
s. 13, repealed: S.L.R. 1977.

17. London Coal Duties Abolition Act 1889.
repealed: S.L.R. 1976.

18. Indecent Advertisements Act 1889.
repealed: 1981, c.42, sch.
s. 6, repealed: 1984, c.60, sch.7.

CAP.

52 & 53 Vict. (1889)—cont.

23. Herring Fishery (Scotland) Act 1889.
repealed: 1984, c.26, sch.2.
s. 6, see *Aitchison* v. *Taylor,* 1980 S.L.T.(Sh.Ct.)
8.
s. 7, byelaw 73/1122.

24. Master and Servant Act 1889.
repealed: S.L.R. 1977.

25. National Portrait Gallery Act 1889.
repealed: S.L.R. 1978.

27. Advertising Stations (Rating) Act 1889.
repealed: S.L.R. 1975 (S.); S.L.R. 1978.

28. Canada (Ontario Boundary) Act 1889.
Act renamed Canada (Ontario Boundary) Act
1889 (Can.): 1982, c.11, sch.

30. Board of Agriculture Act 1889.
ss. 2 (in pt.), 9, 11, (in pt.), 13, repealed: S.L.R.
1986.
sch. 1, repealed in pt.: S.L.R. 1975; S.L.R. 1978;
S.L.R. 1986.

34. Telegraph (Isle of Man) Act 1889.
repealed: 1984, c.12, sch.7.

**38. Basutoland and British Bechuanaland
Marriage Act 1889.**
repealed: 1988, c.44, sch.

39. Judicial Factors (Scotland) Act 1889.
s. 1, amended: 1972, c.11, sch.6.
s. 2, amended: 1985, c.66, sch.7.
s. 5, repealed in pt.: *ibid.,* sch.8.
ss. 11A, 11B, added: *ibid.,* sch.7.
ss. 14 (in pt.), 15, 16, 22, repealed: *ibid.,* sch.8.

42. Revenue Act 1889.
s. 2, repealed: 1981, c.45, sch.

45. Factors Act 1889.
ss. 1, 2, see *Henderson* v. *Prosser,* May 25,
1982, Peter Pain J.; *Beverley Acceptances* v.
Oakley [1982] R.T.R. 417, C.A.
ss. 2, 9, see *National Employers Mutual General
Insurance Association* v. *Jones* [1987] 3 All
E.R. 385, C.A.
s. 9. see *Martin* v. *Duffy* [1985] 11 N.I.J.B. 80,
Lord Lowry L.C.J.
s. 9, amended: 1974, c.39, sch.4.

48. County Court Appeals (Ireland) Act 1889.
repealed: 1978, c.23, sch.7.

50. Local Government (Scotland) Act 1889.
repealed: S.L.R. 1976.

53. Paymaster General Act 1889.
s. 1, repealed in pt.: S.L.R. 1986.

**54. Clerks of Session (Scotland) Regulation Act
1889.**
s. 8, substituted: 1972, c.11, sch.6.
ss. 6, 7, 9, 12, repealed: 1988, c.36, Sch.2.

57. Regulation of Railways Act 1889.
s. 5, see *Corbyn* v. *Saunders* [1978] 1 W.L.R.
400, D.C.
s. 5, repealed in pt.: 1984, c.60, sch.7.
s. 6, amended: 1984, c.32, sch.6.

63. Interpretation Act 1889.
repealed, except s.13 (in pt.): 1978, c.30, sch.3.
s. 1, see *Williams* v. *Secretary of State* (1971)
23 P. & C.R. 135; *"Cannon" Trade Mark*
[1980] R.P.C. 519, C.A.; *Worthing Rugby
Football Club Trustees* v. *I.R.C.* [1985] 1
W.L.R. 409, Peter Gibson J.

CAP.

52 & 53 Vict. (1889)—cont.

63. Interpretation Act 1889—*cont.*
s. 3, see *Hulton* v. *Esher U.D.C.* [1973] 2 W.L.R.
917; [1973] 2 All E.R. 1123; *I.R.C.* v. *Clydebridge Properties,* Inner House, November 22,
1979.
s. 13, repealed in pt.: 1978, c.23, sch.7.
s. 26, see *Bishop* v. *Helmville* [1972] 2 W.L.R.
149; [1972] 1 All E.R. 365; *Cathrineholm* v.
Norequipment [1972] 2 Q.B. 314; [1972] 2
W.L.R. 1242; [1972] 2 All E.R. 538; *Saga* v.
Avalon [1972] 2 Q.B. 325; [1972] 2 W.L.R.
1250n.; [1972] 2 All E.R. 545n.; *Maltglade* v.
St. Albans R.D.C. [1972] 1 W.L.R. 1230;
[1972] 3 All E.R. 129; *Chiswell* v. *Griffin Land
and Estates* [1975] 2 All E.R. 665, C.A.; *Mig-
wain* v. *Transport and General Workers' Union*
[1979] I.C.R. 597, E.A.T.
s. 32, see *Swansea City Council* v. *Harris* (1983)
L.G.R. 521, C.A.
s. 34, see *Fraser* v. *Van Arman,* 1982 S.L.C.R.
79.
s. 36, see *Bedfordshire C.C.* v. *Clarke* (1974)
230 E.G. 1587.
s. 38, see *Apostolic Church Trustees* v. *Glasgow
District Council (No. 2),* 1978 S.L.T.(Lands Tr.)
17; *R.* v. *Secretary of State for the Foreign
and Commonwealth Office, ex p. Council of
Civil Service Unions, The Times,* July 17,
1984, Glidewell J.

69. Public Bodies Corrupt Practices Act 1889.
s. 1, see *R.* v. *Andrews-Weatherfoil* [1972] 1 All
E.R. 65; [1972] 1 W.L.R. 118, C.A.; *sub nom.
R.* v. *Andrews-Weatherfoil; R.* v. *Sporle; R.* v.
Day (1971) 56 Cr.App.R. 31; *R.* v. *Parker*
[1985] Crim.L.R. 589; (1985) 82 Cr.App.R. 69,
C.A.
s. 2, amended: 1988, c.33, s.47.
s. 4, repealed in pt.: 1975, c.59, sch.6.
s. 7, see *R.* v. *Manners* [1976] 2 W.L.R. 709,
C.A.

72. Infectious Disease (Notification) Act 1889.
s. 2, repealed(S.): 1972, c.58, sch.7.
s. 3, amended(S.): *ibid.,* sch.6; 1978, c.29,
sch.15.
s. 4, regs. 75/308; 76/1240.
ss. 4, (in pt.), 5, repealed(S): 1972, c.58, sch.7.
s. 6, amended(S.): *ibid.,* sch.6; 1978, c.29,
sch.15.
s. 7, substituted(S.): 1972, c.58, s.53.
s. 8, amended(S.): *ibid.;* 1978, c.29, sch.15.
s. 11, repealed(S.): 1972, c.58, sch.7.
s. 13, amended(S.): *ibid.,* sch.6; 1978, c.29,
sch.15.
ss. 14, 16 (in pt.), 17 (in pt.), repealed (S.): 1972,
c.58, sch.7.

74. Steam Trawling (Ireland) Act 1889.
repealed: order 81/227.

53 & 54 Vict. (1890)

8. Customs and Inland Revenue Act 1890.
repealed: S.L.R. 1986.

21. Inland Revenue Regulation Act 1890.
s. 5, repealed: S.L.R. 1974.
s. 8, repealed in pt.: 1972, c.71, sch.6; order
74/2143; 1980, c.55, sch.3(S.); S.L.R. 1986.

53 & 54 Vict. (1890)—cont.

21. Inland Revenue Regulation Act 1890—cont.
ss. 10, 14, 15, 23, repealed: S.L.R. 1978.
s. 24, see B & S Displays v. I.R.C., The Times, February 22, 1978, Goulding J.
s. 33, repealed: S.L.R. 1978.
s. 35, repealed in pt.: ibid.
s. 38, repealed in pt.: 1978, c.30, sch.3; S.L.R. 1978.
s. 39, repealed in pt.: S.L.R. 1974.
s. 40, repealed: S.L.R. 1978.

24. Deeds of Arrangement Amendment Act 1890.
s. 2, amended: 1978, c.23, sch.5.
s. 3, repealed in pt.: ibid., sch.7.

25. Barracks Act 1890.
s. 10, repealed: S.L.R. 1973.

27. Colonial Courts of Admiralty Act 1890.
s. 4, repealed in pt.: S.L.R. 1976.
s. 7, orders 76/1777; 78/276; 84/540.
ss. 7 (in pt.), 9 (in pt.), 13 (in pt.), 14 (in pt.), 16–18, schs. 1, 2, repealed: S.L.R. 1986.
s. 12, orders 75/1511, 1514.

33. Statute Law Revision Act 1890.
s. 4, repealed: 1977, c.38, sch.5

35. Boiler Explosions Act 1890.
repealed: regs. 74/1886.

37. Foreign Jurisdiction Act 1890.
orders 72/449; 73/759, 1758; 74/1262; 75/407–414, 807, 808, 1511, 1514, 1831, 1832; 76/422; 77/49, 590, 1628; 78/783.
s. 5, order 76/579.
ss. 11, 13, 18, repealed in pt.: S.L.R. 1986.
ss. 14, 16, 17, repealed: S.L.R. 1973.
sch. 1, repealed in pt.: ibid.; 1975, c.7, sch.13; c.34, sch.2.

39. Partnership Act 1890.
s. 1, see Walker West Developments v. F. J. Emmett (1978) 252 E.G. 1171, C.A.
s. 4, see Jardine-Paterson v. Fraser, 1974 S.L.T. 93, Ct. of Sess. (O.H.); Highland Engineering v. Anderson (O.H.) 1979 S.L.T. 122.
s. 5, see Hudgell Yeates & Co. v. Watson [1978] 2 W.L.R. 661, C.A.; United Bank of Kuwait v. Hammoud (1987) 137 N.L.J. 921, Stuart-Smith J.
s. 6, see Littlejohn v. Mackay, 1974 S.L.T.(Sh.Ct.) 82.
ss. 6, 9, see Highland Engineering v Anderson (O.H.) 1979 S.L.T. 122.
s. 10, see Kirkintilloch Equitable Co-op. Society v. Livingstone, 1972 S.L.T. 154.
ss. 10, 11, see Re Bell's Indenture; Bell v. Hickley [1980] 1 W.L.R. 1217; [1980] 3 All E.R. 425, Vinelott J.
s. 23, amended: order 81/226.
s. 24, see Walker West Developments v. F. J. Emmett (1978) 252 E.G. 1171, C.A.; Hutcheon and Partners v. Hutcheon, 1979 S.L.T.(Sh.Ct.) 62.
s. 27, see Stekel v. Ellice [1973] 1 W.L.R. 191; [1973] 1 All E.R. 465.
s. 28, see Ferguson v. Mackay (O.H.), 1985 S.L.T. 94.
s. 32, see Millar v. Strathclyde Regional Council, 1988 S.L.T.(Lands Tr.) 9.

53 & 54 Vict. (1890)—cont.

39. Partnership Act 1890—cont.
s. 33, see William S. Gordon & Co. v. Mrs Mary Thomson Partnership, 1985 S.L.T. 122.
ss. 33, 34, see Jardine-Paterson v. Fraser, 1974 S.L.T. 93, Ct. of Sess. (O.H.).
s. 34, see Hudgell, Yeates & Co. v. Watson [1978] 2 W.L.R. 661, C.A.
s. 35, see Roxburgh v. Dinardo (O.H.) January 21, 1981.
s. 38, see Welsh v. Knarston, 1973 S.L.T. 66; D. Forbes Smith & Johnston v. Kaye, 1975 S.L.T.(Sh.Ct.) 33.
s 42, see Barclays Bank Trust Co. v. Bluff [1981] 3 All E.R. 232, H. E. Francis, Q.C.

51. Statute Law Revision (No. 2) Act 1890.
s. 2, repealed: 1977, c.38, sch.5.
s. 3, repealed: S.L.R. 1981.

59. Public Health Acts Amendment Act 1890.
ss. 2 (in pt.), 3, 5, 11 (in pt.), repealed: 1972, c.70, sch.30.
s. 11, amended: order 78/1049.
s. 26, repealed in pt.: ibid.
s. 38, repealed: ibid.
s. 51, see Marsden v. Birmingham Licensing Justices [1975] 3 All E.R. 517; Boyce v. Keighley Licensing Justices, July 21, 1977, Bradford Crown Ct.; R. v. Torbay Licensing JJ., ex p. White [1980] 2 All E.R. 25, D.C.; Lidster v. Owen [1983] 1 All E.R. 1012, C.A.
s. 51, repealed: 1982, c.30, sch.7.

71. Bankruptcy Act 1980.
s. 9, repealed: 1985, c.65, sch 10.

54 & 55 Vict. (1891)

3. Custody of Children Act 1891.
ss. 1, 3, see A. v. N., 1973 S.L.T.(Sh.Ct.) 34.

13. Taxes (Regulation of Remuneration) Act 1891.
repealed: S.L.R. 1973.

22. Museums and Gymnasiums Act 1891.
repealed: order 81/438.

24. Public Accounts and Charges Act 1891.
s. 5, repealed: S.L.R. 1975.

29. Presumption of Life Limitation (Scotland) Act 1891.
repealed: 1977, c.27, sch.2.

32. Roads and Streets in Police Burghs (Scotland) Act 1891.
repealed: 1973, c.65, schs.14,29.

36. Consular Salaries and Fees Act 1891.
repealed: 1980, s.23, s.1.
s. 2, orders 72/1677; 73/597, 1082, 1892; 75/806, 2161; 76/216, 1151; 77/46; 78/177; regs 78/692; 79/875.

38. Stamp Duties Management Act 1891.
s. 9, repealed in pt.: S.L.R. (N.I.) 1973.
s. 23, amended: 1979, c.2, sch.4.
s. 28, repealed: S.L.R. 1981.

39. Stamp Act 1891.
ss. 8, 10, repealed: 1985, c.54, sch.27.
s. 12, see Marx v. Estates and General Investments [1975] 3 All E.R. 1064.
ss. 12, 14, see Dickie v. Singh, 1974 S.L.T.(Notes) 3, Ct. of Session.

54 & 55 Vict. (1891)—cont.

39. Stamp Act 1891—cont.
s. 13, see *Ingram* v. *I.R.C.*, *The Times*, November 18, 1985, Vinelott J.
s. 14, see *Terrapin International* v. *I.R.C.* [1976] 1 W.L.R. 665; [1976] 2 All E.R. 461.
s. 15, amended: 1984, c.43, s.111.
ss. 15, 17, see *Dickie* v. *Singh*, 1974 S.L.T.(Notes) 3, Ct. of Session.
ss. 29–31, repealed: 1972, c.41, sch.28.
s. 54, see *George Wimpey & Co.* v. *I.R.C.* [1975] 2 All E.R. 45, C.A.
s. 56, see *Blenden* v. *I.R.C.*, *Quietlece* v. *I.R.C.* [1984] S.T.C. 95, C.A.
s. 58, amended: 1984, c.43, s.112; 1985, c.54, s.82.
s. 59, repealed in pt.: *ibid.*, sch.27.
s. 75, see *Ingram* v. *I.R.C.*, *The Times*, November 18, 1985, Vinelott J.
s. 75, amended: 1984, c.43, s.111; repealed in pt.: *ibid.*, s.111, sch.23.
ss. 82, 83 (in pt.), 112, 113, repealed: 1973, c.51, sch.22.
s. 115, repealed: 1976, c.40, s.126, sch.15.
sch. 1, see *Marx* v. *Estates and General Investments* [1975] 3 All E.R. 1064; *Coventry City Council* v. *I.R.C.* [1978] 1 All E.R. 1107, Brightman J.; *Cummins Engine Co.* v. *I.R.C.* [1981] S.T.C. 604, Ct. of Session.
sch. 1, amended: 1972, c.41, s.125; 1974, c.30, sch.11; 1980, c.48, s.95; 1982, c.39, s.128; order 81/226; 1986, c.41, s.64; repealed in pt.: 1972, c.41, s.126, sch.28; 1973, c.51, sch.22; S.L.R. 1976; 1985, c.54, s.85, schs.24, 27; 1986, c.41, s.80, sch.23; 1988, c.39, s.140, sch.14.
sch. 2, repealed: 1976, c.40, sch.15.

40. Brine Pumping (Compensation for Subsidence) Act 1891.
s. 28, repealed in pt.: S.L.R. 1986.

43. Forged Transfers Act 1891.
s. 1, amended: 1982, c.41, sch.2.

48. Purchase of Land (Ireland) Act 1891.
s. 25, amended and repealed in pt.: order 81/234.

50. Commissioners for Oaths Act 1891.
s. 1, amended: 1974, c.39, sch.5.

53. Supreme Court of Judicature Act 1891.
s. 5, repealed in pt.: 1981, c.54, sch.7.

66. Local Registration of Title (Ireland) Act 1891.
s. 34, see *Re Skelton* [1976] N.I. 132, Murray J.
s. 45, amended: 1975, c.7, sch.12.

67. Statute Law Revision Act 1891.
s. 2, repealed: 1977, c.38, sch.5.

69. Penal Servitude Act 1891.
s. 7, repealed: 1981, c.47, sch.

70. Markets and Fairs (Weighing of Cattle) Act 1891.
s. 3, repealed: S.L.R. 1975.
s. 4, repealed in pt.: *ibid.*

55 & 56 Vict. (1892)

4. Betting and Loans (Infants) Act 1892.
repealed: 1987, c.13, ss.1, 4.

55 & 56 Vict. (1892)—cont.

6. Colonial Probates Act 1892.
s. 1, order 76/579.
s. 2, rules 82/446; 83/623; 85/1232; 87/2024.
s. 2, amended: 1975, c.7, sch.12; 1981, c.54, sch.5; rules 76/1362; repealed in pt.: 1975, c.7, sch.13.
s. 4, repealed in pt.: S.L.R. 1986.
s. 6, repealed in pt.: 1975, c.7, sch.13.

12. Roads and Bridges (Scotland) Amendment Act 1892.
repealed: 1984, c.54, sch.11.

17. Sheriff Courts (Scotland) Extracts Act 1892.
see *L/F Føroya Fiskasola* v. *Charles Mauritzen*, 1977 S.L.T.(Sh.Ct.) 76.
s. 2, repealed in pt.: S.L.R. 1986.
s. 7, see *Hardie* v. *Hardie*, 1984 S.L.T.(Sh.Ct.) 49.
s. 7, amended: 1987, c.18, s.87; repealed in pt.: *ibid.*, sch.8.
s. 9, substituted: order 75/948.

19. Statute Law Revision Act 1892.
s. 2, repealed: 1977, c.38, sch.5.

23. Foreign Marriage Act 1892.
s. 1, amended: 1988, c.44, s.1.
s. 4, substituted: *ibid.*, s.2.
s. 5, amended: *ibid.*, s.3.
s. 7, amended: *ibid.*, s.2.
s. 8, amended: *ibid.*, s.4.
ss. 9, 10, amended: *ibid.*, s.5.
ss. 14, 15, repealed: *ibid.*, sch.
s. 17, amended: *ibid.*, s.5.
s. 18, amended: *ibid.*, s.1.
s. 20, amended: 1980, c.23, s.1.
s. 21, amended: 1988, c.44, s.1; repealed in pt.: S.L.R. 1986; 1988, c.44, sch.
s. 22, amended: 1977, c.15, sch.2(S.); 1988, c.44, s.6; repealed in pt.: *ibid.*, s.6, sch.
s. 24, amended: *ibid.*, s.1; repealed in pt.: *ibid.*, sch.
s. 26, repealed in pt.: *ibid.*

31. Small Holdings Act 1892.
s. 11, see *Macdonald*, 1973 S.L.T. 26, Lands Tr.

34. Naval Knights of Windsor (Dissolution) Act 1892.
repealed: 1976, c.52, sch.10.

35. Colonial Stock Act 1892.
s. 2, repealed in pt.: S.L.R. 1977.

39. National Debt (Stockholders Relief) Act 1892.
s. 7, repealed: S.L.R. 1986.

43. Military Lands Act 1892.
s. 8, see *Re Edis* [1972] 1 W.L.R. 1135; [1972] 2 All E.R. 769.
s. 9, repealed: S.L.R. 1973.
s. 10, repealed in pt.: 1988, c.10, sch.
s. 13, substituted (S.): 1984, c.54, sch.9.
ss. 13, 16, amended: 1980, c.66, sch.24.
Pt. II (ss. 14–18), see *D.P.P.* v. *Bugg* [1987] Crim.L.R. 625, D.C.
ss. 14, 17, see *Francis* v. *Cardle*, 1987 S.C.C.R. 1.
s. 17, amended: 1982, c.48, schs.3,6(S.).
s. 24, repealed in pt.: S.L.R. 1973.
s. 25, amended (S.): 1984, c.54, sch.9; repealed in pt. (S.): *ibid.*, schs.9,11.
s. 26, repealed in pt.: order 80/1085.

CAP.
55 & 56 Vict. (1892)—cont.

48. Bank Act 1892.
s. 6, repealed: 1983, c.9, s.3, sch.
54. Allotments (Scotland) Act 1892.
ss. 2, 6, 8, 14–6, amended: 1973, c.65, schs.27,29.
55. Burgh Police (Scotland) Act 1892.
repealed (31.12.84): 1973, c.65, s.229; 1978, c.4, s.5; 1982, c.45, ss.134, 135.
s. 132, repealed: 1984, c.12, sch.7.
s. 219, see *Rae v. Burgh of Musselburgh*, 1974 S.L.T. 29.
ss. 270, 271, see *Drummond v. Pendreich*, 1972 J.C. 27.
ss. 270, 277, see *Hamilton District Council v. Johnston & Kerr*, 1981 S.L.T. (Sh.Ct.) 43.
s. 385, see *Loyal Orange Lodge No. 493 Hawick First Purple v. Roxburgh District Council*, Second Division, December 14, 1979.
sch. 5, see *Drummond v. Pendreich*, 1972 J.C. 27.
56. Coroners Act 1892.
repealed: 1988, c.13, sch.4.
59. Telegraph Act 1892.
repealed: 1984, c.12, sch.7.
64. Witnesses (Public Inquiries) Protection Act 1892.
s. 3, amended: 1978, c.23, sch.5.
ss. 3, 6, repealed in pt.: 1977, c.45, s.15, sch.13.

56 & 57 Vict. (1893–94)

5. Regimental Debts Act 1893.
s. 3, repealed in pt.: 1975, c.7, sch.13.
s. 9, repealed in pt.: S.L.R. 1975.
ss. 16, 29, amended: S.L.R. 1973.
14. Statute Law Revision Act 1893.
s. 2, repealed: 1977, c.38, sch.5.
20. Duchy of Cornwall Management Act 1893.
s. 2, amended: 1982, c.47, s.1.
22. Appeal (Forma Pauperis) Act 1893.
repealed: S.L.R. 1973.
32. Barbed Wire Act 1893.
repealed: order 80/1085; 1984, c.54, sch.11(S.).
44. Sheriff Courts Consignations (Scotland) Act 1893.
ss. 2 (in pt.), 6, 7 (in pt.), 8 (in pt.), 9 (in pt.), repealed: S.L.R. 1986.
s. 7, amended: *ibid.*
54. Statute Law Revision (No. 2) Act 1893.
s. 2, repealed: 1977, c.38, sch.5.
71. Sale of Goods Act 1893.
repealed, except s. 26: 1979, c.54, sch.3.
s. 5, see *Sainsbury v. Street* [1972] 1 W.L.R. 834.
s. 8, see *Glynwed Distribution v. S. Koronka & Co.*, 1977 S.L.T. 65.
s. 11, see *Millers of Falkirk v. Turpie*, 1976 S.L.T.(Notes) 66.
s. 12, see *Microleads A.G. v. Vinhurst Road Markings* [1975] 1 W.L.R. 218; [1975] 1 All E.R. 529, C.A.; *Empresa Exportadora de Azucar (Cubazucar) v. Industria Azucarera Nacional SA (IANSA)* [1983] Com.L.R. 58, C.A.
s. 13, see *Hughes v. Hall & Hall* [1981] R.T.R. 430, D.C.; *Berger & Co. v. Gill & Duffus SA, The Times*, December 21, 1983, H.L.

CAP.
56 & 57 Vict. (1893–94)—cont.

71. Sale of Goods Act 1893—*cont.*
ss. 13, 14, see *Britain Steamship Co. v. Lithgows* (O.H.) 1975 S.L.T. (Notes) 20.
s. 14, see *Stuart v. Neil*, 1973 S.L.T. 52; *Crowther v. Shannon Motor Co.* [1975] 1 W.L.R. 30; [1975] 1 All E.R. 139, C.A.; *Cehave N.V. v. Bremer Handelgesellschaft mbH.; The Hansa Nord* [1975] 3 W.L.R. 477; [1975] 3 All E.R. 739, C.A.; *Millers of Falkirk v. Turpie*, 1976 S.L.T.(Notes) 66; *Lee v. York Coach and Marine* [1977] R.T.R. 35, C.A.; *Rasbora v. J. C. L. Marine; Atkinson v. J. C. L. Marine* [1977] 1 Lloyd's Rep. 645, Lawson J.; *D. & M. Trailers (Halifax) v. Stirling* [1978] R.T.R. 468, C.A.; *Leaves v. Wadham Stringer (Cliftons)* [1980] R.T.R. 308, Griffiths J.; *McCrone v. Boots Farm Sales* (O.H.), 1981 S.L.T. 103.
ss. 16, 18, see *Karlshamns Oljefabriker v. Eastport Navigation Corp., The Elafi* [1982] 1 All E.R. 208, Mustill J.
s. 18, see *Edwards v. Ddin* [1976] 1 W.L.R. 942, D.C.; *Lombard North Central v. Lord Advocate* (O.H.), September 8, 1982.
s. 21, see *J. Sargent (Garages) v. Motor Auctions (West Bromwich)* [1977] R.T.R. 121, C.A.
s. 22, see *Reid v. Metropolitan Police* [1973] 2 W.L.R. 576; [1973] 2 All E.R. 97, C.A.
s. 25, see *Blythswood Motors v. Lloyds and Scottish Finance*, 1973 S.L.T. 82, Sheriff Ct.; *Dawber Williamson Roofing v. Humberside County Council*, October 22, Mais J.
s. 26, repealed: 1981, c.54, sch.7.
ss. 30, 31, see *Regent OHG Aisenstadt und Barig v. Francesco of Jermyn St.* [1981] 3 All E.R. 327, Mustill J.
s. 34, see *Berger & Co. v. Gill & Duffus SA, The Times*, December 21, 1983, H.L.
s. 35, see *Central Farmers v. Smith*, 1974 S.L.T.(Sh.Ct.) 87; *Cehave N.V. v. Bremer Handelgesellschaft mbH; The Hansa Nord* [1975] 3 W.L.R. 477; [1975] 3 All E.R. 739, C.A.; *White Cross Equipment v. Farrell* [1983] 2 Tr.L. 21, Garland Q.C.
s. 50, see *Lazenby Garages v. Wright* [1976] 1 W.L.R. 459, C.A.
s. 51, see *Tai Hing Cotton Mill v. Kamsing Knitting Factory (A Firm)* [1978] 2 W.L.R. 62, P.C.
s. 52, see *Societe Des Industries Metallurgiques S.A. v. Bronx Engineering Co.* [1975] 1 Lloyd's Rep. 465, C.A.; *C. N. Marina Inc. v. Stena Line A/B, The Times*, May 11, 1982, Parker J.
s. 55, see *George Mitchell (Chesterhall) v. Finney Lock Seeds, The Times*, July 2, 1983, H.L.
s. 61, see *Sainsbury v. Street* [1972] 1 W.L.R. 834.
s. 62, see *Millers of Falkirk v. Turpie*, 1976 S.L.T.(Notes) 66; *Berger & Co. v. Gill & Duffus SA, The Times*, December 21, 1983, H.L.
73. Local Government Act 1894.
ss. 7, 8 (in pt.), repealed: 1972, c.70, sch.30.
ss. 16, 19 (in pt.), repealed: order 79/1123.
s. 21, repealed in pt.: S.L.R. 1978.

56 & 57 Vict. (1893–94)—cont.

73. Local Government Act 1894—*cont.*
s. 25, repealed in pt.: S.L.R. 1976; S.L.R. 1978.
s. 26, repealed in pt.: *ibid.*
s. 27, repealed in pt.: 1974, c.39, sch.5.
ss. 32, 35, repealed: S.L.R. 1978.
ss. 53, 62, repealed: 1972, c.70, sch.30.
s. 63, repealed: order 79/1123.
ss. 66, 71, 75 (in pt.), 84, repealed: S.L.R. 1978.

57 & 58 Vict. (1894)

2. Behring Sea Award Act 1894.
s. 3, repealed in pt.: S.L.R. 1986.

10. Trustee Act 1893 Amendment Act 1894.
repealed: 1980, c.59, sch.

13. Arbitration (Scotland) Act 1894.
s. 6, amended: 1980, c.55, s.17.

17. Colonial Officers (Leave of Absence) Act 1894.
repealed: S.L.R. 1973.

20. Public Libraries (Scotland) Act 1894.
repealed: 1973, c.65, sch.29.

21. Bishopric of Bristol Amendment Act 1894.
repealed: S.L.R. 1973.

23. Commissioners of Works Act 1894.
s. 1, amended: 1975, c.77, sch.10; 1980, c.65, sch.33.

28. Notice of Accidents Act 1894.
ss. 2, 7, 8, repealed in pt.: S.L.R. 1986.

30. Finance Act 1894.
repealed: 1975, c.7, sch.13.
s. 2, see *Low's Executors* v. *I.R.C.* [1972] T.R. 23; 1972 S.L.T. 197; *Hicks* v. *I.R.C.* [1973] S.T.C. 406, Ct. of Session; *Oppenheim's Trustees* v. *I.R.C.* [1975] T.R. 217; 1975 S.C. 297; *Re Nichols, decd.; Nichols* v. *I.R.C.* [1975] 1 W.L.R. 534; [1975] 2 All E.R. 120, C.A.; *Henry* v. *I.R.C.* [1975] S.T.C. 448; *Royal Bank of Scotland* v. *Inland Revenue,* Second Division, 1977 S.L.T. 45; [1977] S.T.C. 121; *Singer* v. *I.R.C.* [1977] S.T.C. 316, Templeman J.; *Re Buttle's Will Trusts* [1977] 1 W.L.R. 1200, C.A.; *Baird* v. *Lord Advocate* [1978] S.T.C. 282, I.H., 2nd Div.; *Thomson's Trs.* v. *Inland Revenue* (H.L.), 1979 S.L.T. 166; *Stevenson's Exrs.* v. *Lord Advocate* (H.L.), 1981 S.L.T. 336.; *Will* v. *I.R.C.* [1981] S.T.C. 428, H.L.
s. 4, see *Clark's Trustees* v. *I.R.C.* [1972] T.R. 17; 1972 S.L.T. 190; *Hicks* v. *I.R.C.* [1973] S.T.C. 406, Ct. of Session; *Barclay's Tr.* v. *Inland Revenue,* (H.L.) 1975 S.L.T. 17; [1975] 1 W.L.R. 106; [1975] 1 All E.R. 168, H.L.; *Kerr's Trs.* v. *Inland Revenue,* 1974 S.L.T. 193; [1974] S.T.C. 309.
s. 5, see *Bunbury* v. *I.R.C.* [1972] 2 W.L.R. 77; [1972] 1 All E.R. 343; *Singer* v. *I.R.C.* [1977] S.T.C. 316, Templeman J.
s. 7, see *Low's Executors* v. *I.R.C.* [1972] T.R. 23; 1972 S.L.T. 197; *Coles (Mrs.) Executors* v. *I.R.C.,* 1973 S.L.T. 24, Lands Tribunal for Scotland; *Astley's Exors.* v. *I.R.C.* [1975] 3 All E.R. 696; [1975] T.R. 137, C.A.; *Re Whitfield's Estate; I.R.C.* v. *Whitfield* [1976] 2 W.L.R. 657; [1976] 1 All E.R. 807, C.A.

57 & 58 Vict. (1894)—cont.

30. Finance Act 1894—*cont.*
s. 8, orders 79/1689, 1690.
s. 8, amended: orders 82/1584, 1586; 85/561, 562; 86/1942, 1943 (N.I.); 87/892; 88/1276, 1619.
s. 22, see *Oppenheim's Trustees* v. *I.R.C.* [1975] T.R. 217; 1975 S.C. 297; *Re Buttle's Will Trusts* [1977] 1 W.L.R. 1200, C.A.

36. Valuation of Lands (Scotland) Acts Amendment Act 1894.
ss. 2, 3, 5, 6, repealed: 1975, c.30, sch.7.
s. 4, repealed: 1973, c.65, sch.29.
s. 7, amended: 1975, c.30, sch.6.

38. Public Libraries (Ireland) Act 1894.
repealed: order 81/438.

44. Heritable Securities (Scotland) Act 1894.
s. 5, see *Prestwick Investment Trust* v. *Jones,* 1981 S.L.T.(Sh.Ct.) 55.

45. Uniforms Act 1894.
s. 4, substituted: 1981, c.55, sch.3.

47. Building Societies Act 1894.
ss. 8 (in pt.), 29, repealed: 1986, c.53, sch.19.

52. Coal Mines (Check Weigher) Act 1894.
repealed: 1986, c.48, schs.1,5.

56. Statute Law Revision Act 1894.
s. 2, repealed: 1977, c.38, sch. 5.

58. Local Government (Scotland) Act 1894.
ss. 3–25, 42–8, 54 (in pt.), repealed: 1973, c.65, schs.27,29.
s. 29, repealed: 1984, c.54, sch.11.

60. Merchant Shipping Act 1894.
amended: 1982, c.48, s.40.
ss. 1–3, repealed: 1988, c.12, s.1, schs.1, 7.
s. 4, amended: order 80/399; 1988, c.12, sch.1; repealed in pt.: order 88/399; 1988, c.12, schs.1, 7.
s. 5, amended: *ibid.,* sch.1.
s. 6, repealed in pt.: *ibid.,* schs. 1, 7.
s. 7, amended: 1979, c.39, sch.6; 1988, c.12, sch.1; repealed in pt.: *ibid.,* schs.1,7.
s. 9, amended: *ibid.,* sch.1; repealed in pt.: *ibid.,* schs.1, 7.
s. 10, amended: 1979, c.39; sch.6.
ss. 11, 13, repealed in pt.: 1988, c.12, schs.1, 7.
s. 14, amended: *ibid.,* sch.1.
s. 15, amended: 1979, c.39, sch.6.
s. 18, amended: *ibid.;* 1988, c.12, sch.1.
s. 19, repealed: *ibid.;* schs.1, 7.
s. 20, amended: 1979, c.39, sch.6.
s. 21, amended: *ibid.,* 1988, c.12, sch.1.
s. 22, substituted: *ibid.*
s. 23, amended: *ibid.;* repealed in pt.: *ibid.,* schs. 1, 7.
ss. 24, 25, amended: *ibid.,* sch.1.
s. 26, repealed in pt.: *ibid.,* schs.1, 7.
s. 27, amended: *ibid.,* sch.1; repealed in pt.: *ibid.,* schs.1, 7.
ss. 28, 30, 31, amended: *ibid.,* sch.1.
ss. 32, 33, repealed in pt.: *ibid.,* schs.1, 7.
s. 36, repealed: 1985, c.65, sch.10; c.66, sch.8(S.).
s. 37, amended: 1988, c.12, sch.1.
ss. 38 (in pt.), 39–46, repealed: *ibid.,* schs.1, 7.
ss. 47, 48, amended: 1979, c.39, sch.6; repealed in pt.: 1988, c.12, schs.1, 7.

CAP.

57 & 58 Vict. (1894)—cont.

60. Merchant Shipping Act 1894—cont.

s. 49, amended: 1979, c.39, sch.6; 1988, c.12, sch.1.

ss. 50, 53, amended: ibid.

ss. 53A, 53B, added: ibid.

ss. 54, 55, repealed: ibid., schs.1, 7.

s. 56, see Lombard North Central v. Lord Advocate (O.H.), September 8, 1982.

ss 56, 57, repealed in pt.: 1988, c.12, schs.1, 7.

s 59, amended: ibid., sch.1.

ss. 61, 62, repealed in pt.: ibid., schs.1, 7.

ss. 63, 64, amended: ibid., sch.1; repealed in pt.: ibid., schs 1, 7.

s. 65, repealed in pt.: ibid.

s. 66, repealed: 1981, c.45, sch.

ss. 67, 69, amended: 1988, c.12, sch.1.

s 70, substituted: ibid.

s. 71, repealed: ibid., schs.1, 7.

s. 72, substituted: ibid., sch.1.

s. 73, amended: 1979, c.39, sch.6; 1988, c.12, sch.1; repealed in pt.: 1979, c.39, schs.6, 7, 1988, c 12, schs.1, 7.

s. 74, amended: 1979, c.39, sch.1; 1988, c.12, sch.1.

s. 76, amended: ibid., sch.1; repealed in pt.. ibid., schs.1, 7.

s. 84, orders 75/1839; 79/306; 82/1085.

s. 84, amended: 1988, c.12, sch.1.

s. 85, regs 83/439.

s. 85, repealed: 1988, c.12, schs.1, 7.

s. 88, orders 74/1262; 77/424.

ss. 88–91, repealed: 1988, c.12, schs.1, 7.

s. 104, repealed in pt.: 1981, c.45, sch.

ss. 111, 112, amended: 1979, c.39, sch.6.

s. 238, order 79/293.

s. 271, see Secretary of State for Trade v. Booth: The Biche [1984] 1 Lloyd's Rep. 26; [1984] 1 W.L.R. 243, D.C.

ss. 271, 280, 281, 285–287, amended: 1979, c.39, sch.6

s. 272, repealed: regs. 81/568.

s. 282, repealed in pt.: 1981, c.45, sch.

s. 287, amended: 1977, c.45, s.31, sch.6.

s. 356, amended: order 80/399.

s. 360, repealed in pt.: 1979, c.39, schs.6, 7.

s. 368, repealed: S.L.R. 1976.

s. 369, order 76/455.

s. 369, repealed in pt.: 1979, c.39, s.28, sch.7; S.L.R. 1986.

s. 370, repealed: 1988, c.12, sch.7.

s. 373, orders 79/1455; 81/740; 87/1284; 88/252.

ss. 372–374, repealed: 1988, c.12, sch.7.

s. 385, amended: 1979, c.39, sch.6.

s. 386, amended: ibid., s.28.

s. 413, amended: 1979, c.39, sch.6; repealed in pt.: regs. 80/1227.

s. 417, amended: 1979, c.39, sch.6.; repealed in pt.: S.L.R. 1986.

s. 418, orders 72/809, 1267; 74/1890; 77/982, 1301; 78/462, 1059; 79/462; 83/768; 86/1892.

s. 418, repealed in pt.: regs. 83/708.

CAP.

57 & 58 Vict. (1894)—cont.

60. Merchant Shipping Act 1894—cont.

s. 419, see Cashen v. Fitzimmons, February 4, 1980, D.C.; Bradshaw v. Ewart-James [1982] 3 W.L.R. 1000, D.C.; Taylor v. O'Keefe [1984] 1 Lloyd's Rep. 31, Div.Ct.

ss. 419 (in pt.), 420, repealed: regs. 83/708.

ss. 419, 422, see Foreman v. MacNeill, 1979 J.C. 17.

s. 421, orders 73/1230; 78/1062, 1914; 83/770, 771; 86/1893.

s. 422, amended: 1979, c.39, sch.6.

s. 424, orders 77/982, 1301; 78/462; 79/462.

s. 427, rules 72/531, 74/2185; 75/330, 471; 76/432; 77/229, 252, 313, 498, 632; 78/1873, 1874; 80/541, 701; 81/567, 575; 84/955, 1222; 86/1258; regs. 81/1472; 86/1072.

s. 427, amended: 1973, c.27, s.5, sch.2; c.49, sch.; 1976, c.19, sch.; 1978, c.15, sch; c.20, sch.2, 1980, c.2, sch.; c.18, sch.1; rules 78/801; orders 78/1030; 79/1455; 80/701; 81/1105; 83/882, 1985, c.3, sch.

s. 430, amended: 1979, c.39,'sch.6.

s. 431, repealed in pt.: ibid., s.28, sch.7.

s. 446, amended: 1979, c.39, sch.6; repealed in pt.: ibid., schs.6,7.

s. 447, amended: ibid., sch.6.

s. 457, repealed: ibid., s.44, sch.7.

s. 459, amended: ibid., s.28; 1988, c.12, sch.6.

s. 460, amended: regs. 88/1638, 1639, 1641.

s. 462, amended: 1988, c.12, sch.6.

s. 463, repealed: ibid., schs.5, 7.

s. 464, amended: 1979, c.39, s.32.

s. 465, see The State (At the Prosecution of Shannon Atlantic Fisheries) v. The Minister for Transport and Power and D.J. M'Polin [1976] I.R. 93.

s. 465, amended: 1979, c.39, s.28.

s. 466, see R. v. A Wreck Commissioner, ex p. Knight [1976] 3 All E.R. 8, D.C.; European Gateway, The [1986] 3 W.L.R. 756, Steyn J.

s. 468, repealed: 1979, c.39, sch.7.

s. 471, amended: ibid., s.28.

s. 479, repealed in pt.: S.L.R. 1986.

s. 488, amended: 1979, c.39, s.28, sch.6.

s. 489, repealed in pt.: S.L.R. 1986.

s 492, amended: 1979, c.2, sch.4.

Pt. VIII (ss. 502–9), repealed: 1979, c.39, sch.7.

s. 503, see London Dredging Co. v. G.L.C. [1972] 3 W.L.R. 610; [1972] 3 All E.R. 590; Groen (Rederij Erven H.) and Groen v. The England (Owners) [1973] 1 Lloyd's Rep. 373; The "Devotion II," 1979 S.C. 80; The Alastor [1981] 1 Lloyd's Rep. 581, C.A.; The Smjeli [1982] 2 Lloyd's Rep. 75, Sheen. J.; The Garden City [1982] 2 Lloyd's Rep. 382, Staughton J.; Richard Irvin & Sons v. Aberdeen Near Water Trawlers (O.H.), 1983 S.L.T. 26; Grand Champion Tankers v. Norpipe A/S; Marion, The [1984] 2 W.L.R. 942, H.L.

s. 503, amended: 1981, c.10, s.1; 1984, c.5, s.12.

s. 504, see Afromar Inc. v. Greek Atlantic Cod Fishing Co.; The Penelope II [1980] 2 Lloyd's Rep. 17, C.A.

CAP.

57 & 58 Vict. (1894)—cont.

60. Merchant Shipping Act 1894—*cont.*
ss. 510, 518, 523, see *Pierce* v. *Bernis; The Lusitania* [1986] 2 W.L.R. 501; [1986] 1 Lloyd's Rep. 132, Sheen J.
s. 515, amended: 1973, c.65, sch.27.
s. 517, amended: 1979, c.39, s.28.
ss. 518, 519, amended: *ibid.*, sch.6.
s. 531, amended: 1988, c.12, sch.5.
ss. 536, 543, amended: 1979, c.39, sch.6.
ss. 538–542, repealed (S.): 1982, c.45, sch.4.
s. 546, see *Powstaniec Wielkopolski, The, The Times,* July 14, 1988, Sheen J.
s. 546, amended: 1988, c.12, sch.5.
s. 564, repealed in pt.: 1981, c.45, sch.
s. 610. see *Cashen* v. *Fitzimmons,* February 4, 1980, D.C.
s. 634, repealed in pt.: 1988, c.12, schs.5, 7.
s. 634A, added: *ibid.*, s.41.
s. 637, repealed: 1979, c.39, s.33, sch.7.
s. 638, repealed in pt.: *ibid.*, sch.7.
ss. 640, 641, repealed: *ibid.*, s.33, sch.7.
s. 648, amended: 1988, c.12, sch.5; repealed in pt.: *ibid.*, schs.5, 7.
s. 652, repealed in pt.: *ibid.*
s. 658, substituted: *ibid.*, sch.5.
s. 659, amended: *ibid.*
s. 665, repealed: 1972, c.11, s.17, sch.8.
ss. 666, 667, amended: 1979, c.39, sch.6.
s. 668, amended: 1973, c.65, schs.27,29; 1974, c.43, s.18; 1979, c.39, s.33.
s. 669, order 87/171.
ss. 670–672, 675, repealed: 1979, c.39, s.34, sch.7.
s. 677, repealed in pt.: *ibid.*
s. 680, amended: *ibid.*, sch.6.; 1982, c.48, schs.13,15(S.); repealed in pt.: *ibid.*, schs.15(S.),16.
s. 683, amended: 1979, c.39, s.42; repealed in pt.: S.L.R. 1986.
s. 686, see *R.* v. *Liverpool JJ., ex p. Molyneux* [1972] 2 W.L.R. 1033; [1972] 2 All E.R. 471; [1972] 1 Lloyd's Rep. 367; *Cameron* v. *H.M. Advocate,* 1971 S.C. 50; *R.* v. *Kelly* [1981] 3 W.L.R. 387, H.L.
s. 689, amended: 1979, c.39, sch.6.
s. 692, amended: *ibid.*; order 80/399; regs. 88/1638, 1639, 1641.
s. 693, amended (S.): 1987, c.18, sch.6.
s. 695, repealed in pt.: 1981, c.45, sch.
s. 696, amended: 1979, c.39, sch.6.
s. 702, amended (S.): *ibid.*; 1982, c.48, sch.15.
s. 703, substituted (S.): 1979, c.39, sch.6; amended: 1982, c.48, schs.7, 15(S.).
ss. 703–705, see *Ross* v. *Deutsche Dampfschiffahrts Ges Hansa,* 1980 S.L.T. (Sh.Ct.) 141.
s. 722, repealed in pt.: 1981, c.45, sch.
ss. 722, 723, amended: 1979, c.39, sch.6.
s. 724, repealed in pt.: *ibid.*, schs.6,7.
s. 726, amended: *ibid.*, sch.6.
s. 728, amended: *ibid.*, s.26.
ss. 729, 730, repealed: *ibid.*, s.28, sch.7.
s. 731, amended: 1988, c.12, sch.5; repealed in pt.: *ibid.*, schs.5, 7.
s. 734, order 77/982.

CAP.

57 & 58 Vict. (1894)—cont.

60. Merchant Shipping Act 1894—*cont.*
s. 735, orders 72/446; 73/1317; 76/1038; 78/1061; 79/110, 1448; 80/698; 84/357, 1162; 85/1636; 87/932, 933, 1267, 1827; 88/787, 927, 928.
s. 737, order 74/1262.
s. 738, orders 72/809, 1267; 74/1262, 1890; 77/424, 982, 1241, 1242, 1301; 78/462, 1059; 79/293, 462; 81/214–225, 431, 433, 434, 1111, 1539, 1540; 82/1085, 1538; 83/415, 416, 768, 770, 771; 84/543, 1160, 1163; 85/1197; 86/1892, 1893, 2223, 2225; 87/1263, 1284; 88/252, 789, 1850.
ss. 738 (in pt.), 740, repealed: S.L.R. 1986.
s. 742, see *Foreman* v. *MacNeill,* 1979 J.C. 17; *Powstaniec Wielkopolski, The, The Times,* July 14, 1988, Sheen J.
s. 742, amended: order 80/399.
s. 744, repealed: 1988, c.12, schs.5, 7.
s. 746, repealed in pt.: S.L.R. 1977.
sch. 1, amended: 1988, c.12, sch.1; repealed in pt.: *ibid.*, schs.1, 7.

58 & 59 Vict. (1895)

3. Australian Colonies Duties Act 1895.
repealed: S.L.R. 1973.
6. Convention of Royal Burghs (Scotland) Act 1879, Amendment Act 1895.
repealed: 1973, c.65, sch.29.
14. Courts of Law Fees (Scotland) Act 1895.
s. 2, Acts of Sederunt 75/1849, 1850, 1908; 76/282; 77/71, 73, 402; 78/113, 116; 79/347, 348; 80/388, 454; 81/496, 514; 82/652, 654; 84/233, 235; Acts of Adjournal, 75/1848; 77/72; 80/390; 81/498; 82/653, 1824; 84/234; orders 84/251, 252, 256, 257, 466; 85/825–827, 2072; 86/449–451; 87/38, 39, 771, 772; 88/798, 799, 966, 969, 1892, 1893.
s. 2, substituted: 1983, c.12, s.4.
21. Seal Fisheries (North Pacific) Act 1895.
s. 6, repealed in pt.: S.L.R. 1986.
24. Law of Distress Amendment Act 1895.
s 3, rules 83/1917.
s. 5, repealed: 1984, c.60, sch.7.
34. Colonial Boundaries Act 1895.
orders 76/893; 88/1838.
36. Fatal Accidents Inquiry (Scotland) Act 1895.
repealed (S.): 1976, c.14, sch.2.
42. Sea Fisheries Regulation (Scotland) Act 1895.
repealed: 1984, c.26, sch.2.
44. Judicial Committee Amendment Act 1895.
s. 1, orders 78/620; 86/1161.
s. 1, repealed in pt.: S.L.R. 1986.

59 Vict., Session 2 (1895)

3. Canadian Speaker (Appointment of Deputy) Act 1895.
repealed: 1982, c.11, sch.

59 & 60 Vict. (1896)

8. Life Insurance Companies (Payment into Court) Act 1896.
s. 3, amended: 1978, c.23, sch.5.
s. 4, repealed in pt.: *ibid.*, sch.7.

CAP.

59 & 60 Vict. (1896)—cont.

9. Local Government (Determination of Differences) Act 1896.
repealed: S.L.R. 1975.

14. Short Titles Act 1896.
s. 3, repealed: 1978, c.30, sch.3.

25. Friendly Societies Act 1896.
repealed in part: 1974, c.46, sch.11.
s. 22, amended: *ibid.*, schs.9,11.
s. 49, see *Re Bucks Constabulary Widows and Orphans Fund Friendly Society; Thompson* v. *Holdsworth (No. 2)*, [1979] 1 All E.R. 623, Walton J.
s. 79, see *Re Bucks Constabulary Widows' and Orphans' Fund Friendly Society; Thompson* v. *Holdsworth* [1978] 1 W.L.R. 641, Megarry V.-C.
ss. 96, 99, regs. 74/1300.
s. 99, regs. 74/474, 2066.

28. Finance Act 1896.
s. 12, repealed: 1973, c.51, sch.22.
Pt. IV (ss.14–24), repealed: 1975, c.7, sch.13.
s. 39, repealed in pt.: *ibid.*; S.L.R. 1976.

29. Bishopric of Bristol Amendment Act 1896.
repealed: S.L.R. 1973.

30. Conciliation Act 1896.
repealed: 1975, c.71, sch.18.

32. Orkney and Shetland Small Piers and Harbours Act 1896.
repealed: 1973, c.65, sch.29.

33. Royal Naval Reserve Volunteer Act 1896.
repealed: 1980, c.9, sch.10.

35. Judicial Trustees Act 1896.
s. 1, amended: 1985, c.61, s.50; repealed in pt.: 1982, c.53, s.57, sch.9.
s. 4, rules 72/1096; 83/370.
s. 4, amended: 1982, c.53, s.57; repealed in pt.: S.L.R. 1986.

44. Truck Act 1896.
repealed: 1986, c.48, schs.1,5.
s. 1, see *Riley* v. *Joseph Frisby* [1982] I.R.L.R. 479, Industrial Tribu ːl, Nottingham; *Sealand Petroleum* v. *Barratt* [1986] 1 W.L.R. 700, C.A.
ss. 1, 2, 4, see *Bristow* v. *City Petroleum* [1987] 1 W.L.R. 529, H.L.

'45. Stannaries Court (Abolition) Act 1896.
s. 1, see *R.* v. *East Powder JJ., ex p. Lampshire* [1979] 2 W.L.R. 479, D.C.

48. Light Railways Act 1896.
orders 72/545, 1051, 1541; 73/357, 785; 74/642.
s. 3, orders 78/471, 1119; 80/1660; 81/512, 616, 1083; 85/747; 86/174(S.), 277; 87/1443, 1984.
s. 5, repealed: S.L.R. 1986.
s. 7, orders 72/197; 73/998; 74/1024, 1857, 1933; 75/962, 1014, 1480; 77/519, 862; 78/471, 1119, 1937; 79/317, 1091, 1270, 1421; 80/667, 671, 1660, 1969; 81/62, 512, 616, 1083; 82/1456, 1621; 83/1229, 1955; 84/557, 558, 681, 1202; 85/725, 747, 810, 844, 1578; 86/174(S), 277, 343, 690, 1000; 87/75, 950, 1088, 1443, 1984; 88/725(S.).

CAP.

59 & 60 Vict. (1896)—cont.

48. Light Railways Act 1896—cont.
s. 7, amended (S.): 1984, c.54, sch.9.
s. 8, order 87/1443.
s. 9, orders 72/197; 73/998; 74/1024, 1857, 1933; 75/962, 1014, 1480; 77/519, 862; 78/471, 1119, 1937; 79/317, 1091, 1270, 1421; 80/607, 667, 671, 1660, 1969; 81/62, 512, 616, 1083; 82/1456, 1621; 83/1229, 1955; 84/557, 558, 681, 1202; 85/725, 747, 810, 844, 1578; 86/174(S.), 277, 343, 690, 1000, 2150; 87/75, 950, 1088, 1443, 1984; 88/725(S.).
s. 10, orders 72/197; 73/998; 74/1024, 1857, 1933; 75/962, 1014, 1480; 77/519, 862; 78/871; 79/317, 1091, 1270, 1421; 80/607, 667, 671, 1969; 81/62, 512, 616, 1083; 82/1456, 1621; 83/1229, 1955; 84/557, 558, 681, 1202; 85/725, 747, 810, 844, 1578; 86/174(S.), 277, 343, 690, 1000, 2150; 87/950, 1088, 1443; 88/725(S.).
s. 10, repealed in pt.: S.L.R. 1986.
s. 11, orders 77/519, 862; 78/471, 1119; 79/317, 1421; 80/667, 671, 1660, 1969; 81/62, 512, 616, 1083; 82/1456, 1621; 83/1229, 1955; 84/557, 558, 681, 1202; 85/725, 747, 810, 844, 1578; 86/174(S.), 277, 343, 690, 1000, 2150; 87/950, 1088; 88/725(S.).
s. 11, amended: 1982, c.53, s.46.
s. 12, orders 77/862; 78/471, 1119, 1937; 80/1660; 81/1083; 83/1229, 1955; 84/681, 1202; 85/747, 1578; 86/174(S.), 277, 343, 1000, 2150; 87/75, 950, 1088, 1984.
s. 18, orders 74/1857, 1933; 77/862; 78/1937; 79/317, 1270; 81/512, 1083; 84/1202; 85/747, 810, 844, 86/277, 2150; 88/725(S.).
s. 24, orders 72/1695; 73/192, 302, 1874; 74/643, 1024; 75/1014, 1125; 78/952; 79/1091; 80/607; 81/62; 82/1456; 83/1229; 84/681, 1202; 85/810; 86/690; 87/75, 950.
s. 25, repealed: 1984, c.12, sch.7.
s. 26, amended: 1973, c.65, sch.18.

50. Poor Law Officers' Superannuation Act 1896.
repealed: S.L.R. 1981.

54. Public Health (Ireland) Act 1896.
s. 28, repealed: 1980, c.59, sch.
s. 33, repealed in pt.: *ibid.*

60 & 61 Vict. (1897)

17. Supreme Court of Judicature (Ireland) Act 1897.
repealed: 1978, c.23, sch.7.

20. Quarter Sessions Jurors (Ireland) Act 1897.
repealed: 1978, c.23, sch.7.

26. Metropolitan Police Courts Act 1897.
ss. 1, 8, repealed: 1979, c.55, sch.3.

30. Police (Property) Act 1897.
see *R.* v. *Uxbridge JJ., ex p. Commissioner of Police for the Metropolis*, The Times, June 13, 1981, C.A.
s. 1, see *Raymond Lyons & Co.* v. *Metropolitan Police Commissioner* [1975] 2 W.L.R. 197; [1975] 1 All E.R. 335, D.C.; *R.* v. *Chester Justices, ex p. Smith* [1978] Crim. L.R. 226; [1978] R.T.R. 373, D.C.; *R.* v. *Southampton Magistrates' Court, ex p. Newman*, The Guardian, July 28, 1988, D.C.

60 & 61 Vict. (1897)—cont.

30. Police (Property) Act 1897—cont.
s. 1, amended: 1972, c.71, s.58; repealed in pt.: 1974, c.39, sch.5.
s. 2, regs. 75/1474.
s. 2, amended: 1972, c.71, s.66; 1973, c.62, s.43.

38. Public Health (Scotland) Act 1897.
s. 3, see Clydebank District Council v. Monaville Estates, 1982 S.L.T.(Sh.Ct.) 2.
s. 3, amended: 1973, c.65, sch.27; 1984, c.54, sch.9; repealed in pt.: 1972, c.58, sch.7; 1973, c.65, schs.26, 29.
s. 6, amended: ibid., sch.27.
s. 12, substituted: ibid.
s. 15, repealed: ibid., schs.27, 29.
s. 16, see Clydebank District Council v. Monaville Estates, 1982 S.L.T.(Sh.Ct.) 2.
s. 16, amended: 1984, c.54, sch.9; repealed in pt.: ibid., schs.9, 11.
s. 18, amended: 1972, c.58, sch.6; 1973, c.29, sch.15; 1982, c.48, sch.15; repealed in pt.: 1973, c.65, schs.27, 29.
s. 19, repealed in pt.: ibid.
s. 20, see Clydebank District Council v. Monaville Estates, 1982 S.L.T.(Sh.Ct.) 2.
s. 22, amended: 1974, c.40, sch.2; repealed in pt.: 1973, c.65, schs.27, 29.
s. 23, repealed in pt.: ibid.
s. 24, amended: 1974, c.40, sch.2; 1982, c.48, sch.15.
ss. 25–27, repealed in pt.: 1973, c.65, schs.27, 29.
s. 28, repealed: ibid.
s. 29, repealed: 1982, c.43, sch.4.
s. 31, repealed in pt.: 1972, c.58, sch.7: 1973, c.65, schs.27, 29.
s. 32, repealed in pt.: ibid.
s. 33, repealed: 1980, c.13, sch.3.
s. 36, amended: 1972, c.58, sch.6; 1974, c.40, sch.2; 1978, c.29, sch.15; repealed in pt.: 1973, c.65, schs.27, 29; 1981, c.23, schs.2, 4.
s. 37, repealed in pt.: 1973, c.65, schs.27, 29.
s. 39, amended: ibid., sch.27; repealed in pt.: ibid., schs. 27, 29; 1974, c.40, sch.4; 1982, c.48, sch.4; 1984, c.54, schs.9,11.
s. 42, repealed in pt.: 1973, c.65, schs.27, 29.
s. 46, amended: 1972, c.58, sch.6; 1978, c.29, sch.15.
s. 47, amended: 1972, c.58, sch.6; 1978, c.29, sch.15; repealed in pt.: 1973, c.65, schs.27, 29.
ss. 48, 49, 51, amended: 1972, c.58, sch.6; 1978, c.29, sch.15.
s. 52, repealed in pt.: 1973, c.65, schs.27, 29.
s. 53, amended: 1972, c.58, sch.6; 1978, c.29, sch.15.
ss. 54, 55, amended: 1972, c.58, sch.6; 1978, c.29, sch.15; repealed in pt.: 1973, c.65, schs.27, 29.
s. 56, amended: 1972, c.58, sch.6; 1978, c.27, sch.15; 1984, c.54, sch.9.
ss. 57, 59, 62–64, 66, amended: 1972, c.58, sch.6; 1978, c.29, sch.15.

60 & 61 Vict. (1897)—cont.

38. Public Health (Scotland) Act 1897—cont.
s. 69, amended: 1972, c.58, sch.6; 1978, c.29, sch.15; repealed in pt.: 1973, c.65, schs.27, 29.
ss. 70, 73, amended: 1972, c.58, sch.6; 1978, c.29, sch.15.
s. 74, amended: 1984, c.54, sch.9.
s. 94, repealed in pt.: 1973, c.65, schs.27, 29.
ss. 96–98, amended: 1972, c.58, sch.6; 1978, c.29, sch.15.
ss. 102, 103, see Lawrence Building Co. v. Lanark County Council, 1979 S.L.T. 2.
s. 103, see Rae v. Burgh of Musselburgh, 1974 S.L.T. 29.
ss. 118, 121, repealed: 1973, c.65, schs.27, 29.
ss. 146, 154, 155, repealed in pt.: 1973, c.65, schs.27, 29.
s. 157, see Renfrew District Council v. McGourlick (O.H.), 1988 S.L.T. 127.
ss. 157, 158, 162, 177, repealed in pt.: 1973, c.65, schs.27, 29.
ss. 191, 192, repealed: ibid.

39. Yorkshire Coroners Act 1897.
repealed: 1972, c.70, sch.30.

40. Local Government (Joint Committees) Act 1897.
repealed: 1972, c.70, sch.30.

48. Stipendiary Magistrates Jurisdiction (Scotland) Act 1897.
repealed: 1975, c.20, sch.2.

53. Congested Districts (Scotland) Act 1897.
s. 4, amended: 1981, c.38, sch.3; repealed in pt.: 1984, c.12, sch.7.
s. 10, amended: 1973, c.65, sch.19; 1984, c.54, sch.9; repealed in pt.: 1973, c.65, sch.29.

59. Merchant Shipping Act 1897.
s. 1, repealed in pt.: 1988, c.12, sch.7.

63. Foreign Prison-made Goods Act 1897.
s. 1. amended: 1979, c.2, sch.4; regs. 88/1772.
s. 1A, added: ibid.

66. Supreme Court of Judicature (Ireland) (No. 2) Act 1897.
repealed: 1978, c.23, sch.7.

61 & 62 Vict. (1898)

4. Greek Loan Act 1898.
repealed: S.L.R. 1977.

10. Finance Act 1898.
ss. 13, 14, repealed: 1975, c.7, sch.13.

15. Societies' Borrowing Powers Act 1898.
repealed: 1974, c.46, sch.11.

20. Ex-officio Justices of the Peace (Scotland) Act 1898.
repealed: 1975, c.20, sch.2.

22. Statute Law Revision Act 1898.
s. 2, repealed: 1977, c.38, sch.5.

23. Union of Benefices Act 1898.
repealed: S.L.R. 1974.

24. Greenwich Hospital Act 1898.
repealed, S.L.R. 1976.

29. Locomotives Act 1898.
s. 7, repealed: 1980, c.65, sch.7.
s. 17, repealed in pt.: S.L.R. 1975.

CAP

61 & 62 Vict. (1898)—cont.

35. Vexatious Actions (Scotland) Act 1898.
s. 1, see Lord Advocate v. Henderson, 1983 S.L.T. 518; Lord Advocate v. Cooney, 1984 S.L.T. 434.
s. 1A, added: 1980, c.55, s.19.

36. Criminal Evidence Act 1898.
repealed (S.) (except as to courts-martial): 1975, c.21, sch.10.
see R. v. Exton, The Times, July 9, 1981.
s. 1, see R. v. Vickers [1972] Crim.L.R. 101; R. v. Lovett [1973] 1 W.L.R. 241; [1973] 1 All E.R. 744, C.A.; R. v. Conti [1974] Crim.L.R. 247; (1974) 58 Cr.App.R. 387, C.A.; R. v. Bishop [1974] 3 W.L.R. 380; [1974] 2 All E.R. 1206, C.A.; Knowles v. H.M. Advocate, 1975 J.C. 6, R. v. Davis (Alan) [1975] 1 W.L.R. 345; [1975] 1 All E.R. 233, C.A.; R. v. Lee (Paul) [1976] 1 W.L.R. 71, C.A.; H.M. Advocate v. Grundins, 1976 S.L.T. (Notes) 10; R. v. Gunner and Lye [1977] Crim.L.R. 217, C.A.; R. v. Coughlan (1976) 64 Cr.App.R. 11, C.A.; R. v. Hatton (1976) 64 Cr.App.R. 88, C.A.; R. v. Wilson [1977] Crim.L.R. 553, C.A.; R. v. Nightingale [1977] Crim.L.R. 744, C.A.; R. v. Jones (Benjamin) [1978] 1 W.L.R. 195, C.A.; R. v. Lauchlan (Note) [1978] R.T.R. 326, C.A.; R. v. Tanner (1977) 66 Cr.App.R. 56, C.A.; R. v. McLean [1978] Crim.L.R. 430, C.A.; R. v. Hills [1978] 3 W.L.R. 423, H.L.; R. v. Meehan and Meehan [1978] Crim.L.R. 690, C.A.; R. v. Rockman (1978) 67 Cr.App.R. 171, C.A.; R. v. France [1979] Crim.L.R. 48, C.A.; R. v. Nelson (1978) 68 Cr.App.R. 12, C.A.; R. v Coltress (1978) 68 Cr.App.R. 193, C.A.; R. v. McGee and Cassidy (1979) 70 Cr.App.R. 247, C.A.; R. v. Shepherd (1980) 71 Cr.App.R. 120, C.A.; R. v. De Vere [1981] 3 W.L.R. 593, C.A.; R. v. Varley [1982] Crim.L.R. 300, C.A.; [1982] 2 All E.R. 519, C.A.; R. v. Brown and Routh [1983] Crim.L.R. 38, C.A.; R. v. Britzman; R. v. Hall [1983] 1 All E.R. 369, C.A.; R. v. Watts [1983] Crim.L.R. 541, C.A.; R. v. Weekes [1983] Crim.L.R. 801; (1983) 77 Cr.App.R. 207, C.A.; R. v. Naudeer [1984] Crim.L.R. 501; [1984] 3 All E.R. 1036, C.A.; R. v. Rowson [1985] Crim.L.R. 307, C.A.; R. v. Powell [1985] 1 W.L.R. 1364, C.A.; R. v. Burke [1985] Crim.L.R. 660, C.A.; R. v. Owen (A. C.) (1986) 83 Cr.App.R. 100, C.A.; R. v. Phillips (D. M.) (1986) 86 Cr.App.R. 18, C.A.; R. v. Stronach [1988] Crim.L.R. 48, C.A.; R. v. Anderson [1988] 2 All E.R. 549, C.A.
s. 1, amended: 1979, c.16, s.1; repealed in pt.: 1982, c.48, sch.16; 1984, c.60, s.80, sch.7.
s. 4, repealed: ibid., sch.7.
s. 6, amended: 1976, c.52, sch.9; repealed in pt.: S.L.R. 1981; 1984, c.60, sch.7.
sch., repealed: ibid.

37. Local Government (Ireland) Act 1898.
s. 12, repealed: order 80/1085.
s. 69, amended: order 75/816; repealed in pt.: order 74/2143; 1978, c.23, sch.7.
s. 82, repealed in pt.: order 80/1085.
ss. 83, 96, repealed in pt.: order 74/2143.

40. Circuit Clerks (Scotland) Act 1898.
repealed: 1987, c.41, sch.2.

CAP.

61 & 62 Vict. (1898)—cont.

43. Metropolitan Commons Act 1898.
repealed: 1985, c.51, sch.17.

44. Merchant Shipping (Mercantile Marine Fund) Act 1898.
s. 1, substituted: 1988, c.12, sch.5.
s. 1A, added: 1972, c.11, s.17; repealed in pt.: 1972, c.41, sch.28.
s. 2, amended: 1979, c.39, s.36; repealed in pt.: ibid., s.36, sch.7; 1988, c.12, sch.7.
ss. 2A, 2B, added: ibid., s.43.
s. 3, regs. 79/631.
s. 5, orders 72/456; 73/964; 74/868; 75/432, 2194; 77/430; regs. 80/355; 81/354; 83/573, 1080; 86/334; 87/244, 746; 88/330; amended: 1979, c.39, s.36; repealed in pt.: ibid., sch.7.
s. 7, repealed in pt.: ibid.
sch. 2, repealed: ibid.
sch. 3, repealed in pt.: 1973, c.27, s.5; 1979, c.39, s.36, sch.7.

46. Revenue Act 1898.
s. 1, amended: 1979, c.2, sch.4.

48. Benefices Act 1898.
ss. 1, 2 (in pt.), repealed: 1986, No. 3, sch.5.
s. 3, amended: ibid., s.18.
ss. 5, 6, repealed: ibid., sch.5.
s. 11, substituted: ibid., s.18.

60. Inebriates Act 1898.
repealed, except s. 30, sch.1: S.L.R. 1976.
s. 30, amended: S.L.R. 1976; repealed in pt. (S.): 1976, c.66, sch.8.
sch. 1, repealed in pt.: S.L.R. 1976.

62. University of London Act 1898.
repealed: S.L.R. 1977.

62 & 63 Vict. (1899)

5. Public Libraries (Scotland) Act 1899.
repealed: 1973, c.65, sch.29.

7. Metropolis Water Act 1899.
repealed: S.L.R. 1973.

9. Finance Act 1899.
ss. 7, 8, repealed: 1973, c.51, sch.22.
s. 8, see Associated Maltsters v. I.R.C. [1972] 3 All E.R. 192; [1972] T.R. 53; Reed International v. I.R.C. [1975] 2 W.L.R. 622; [1975] 1 All E.R. 484, C.A.; Agricultural Mortgage Corporation v. I.R.C. [1978] 1 All E.R. 248, C.A.
s. 12, repealed: 1985, c.54, s.88, sch.27.
sch., repealed: ibid., sch.27.

19. Electric Lighting (Clauses) Act 1899.
see R. v. Midlands Electricity Board, ex p. Busby, Same v. Same, ex p. Williamson, The Times, October 28, 1987, Schiemann J.
ss. 10, 14, 60, 69, 79, amended: 1981, c.38, sch.3.
s. 27, see Woodcock v. South West Electricity Board [1975] 1 W.L.R. 983; [1975] 2 All E.R. 545.
s. 57, regs. 86/1627; 87/901.
sch., regs. 88/457, 1206.
sch., amended: 1981, c.38, sch.3; 1983, c.25, ss.13,14, schs.1,3; 1984, c.12, sch.4; c.54, sch.9(S.); repealed in pt.: 1982, c.48, sch.16; 1983, c.25, s.20, schs.1,4; 1984, c.12, sch.7; 1986, c.63, sch.12.

CAP.

62 & 63 Vict. (1899)—cont.

24. University of London Act 1899.
repealed: S.L.R. 1977.

27. Marriages Validity Act 1899.
s. 1, repealed in pt.: S.L.R. 1977.

30. Commons Act 1899.
s. 1, repealed in pt.: 1972, c.70, sch.30.
ss. 1, 2, regs. 82/209, 667.
s. 2, amended: 1980, c.65, sch.3; repealed in
pt.: ibid., schs.3,34.
s. 4, repealed: 1972, c.70, sch.30.
s. 11, substituted: 1980, c.65, sch.3.
s. 12, repealed in pt.: ibid., schs.3,34.
s. 13, repealed: 1972, c.70, sch.30.
s. 15, regs. 82/209, 667.
s. 18, amended: 1988, c.4, sch.6.

35. Inebriates Act 1899.
repealed: S.L.R. 1976.

38. Telegraph Act 1899.
s. 2, amended: 1981, c.38, sch.3; 1984, c.12,
sch.4; repealed in pt.: ibid., sch.7.
s. 4, repealed in pt.: ibid.

44. Small Dwellings Acquisition Act 1899.
repealed: 1980, c.52, sch.5(S.); 1985, c.71,
sch.1.
s. 5, amended: 1981, c.54, sch.5.
s. 9, amended: 1972, c.70, sch.22; repealed in
pt.: ibid., sch.30.
s. 12, amended: 1973, c.65, sch.12.

46. Improvement of Land Act 1899.
repealed: 1973, c.55, sch.
s. 6, repealed: S.L.R. 1974.

48. Lincolnshire Coroners Act 1899.
repealed: 1972, c.70, sch 30.

63 & 64 Vict. (1900)

7. Finance Act 1900.
s. 13, repealed: 1975, c.7, sch.13.

**12. Commonwealth of Australia Constitution
Act 1900.**
s. 74, see Shigeo Kitano v. Commonwealth of
Australia [1975] 3 W.L.R. 136, P.C.

14. Colonial Solicitors Act 1900.
s. 2, order 86/1986 (S.).

15. Burial Act 1900.
repealed: S.L.R. 1978.

**27. Railway Employment (Prevention of Acci-
dents) Act 1900.**
s. 11, repealed in pt.: 1980, c.59, sch.

28. Inebriates Amendment (Scotland) Act 1900.
repealed: S.L.R. 1976.

**32. Merchant Shipping (Liability of Shipowners
and Others) Act 1900.**
s. 2, see Mason v. Uxbridge Boat Centre and
Wright [1980] 2 Lloyd's Rep. 592, Lloyd J.
s. 2, amended: 1979, c.39, sch.5; repealed in
pt.: ibid., sch.7; 1984, c.5, sch.2.

**38. Elementary School Teachers Superannua-
tion (Isle of Man) Act 1900.**
repealed: S.L.R. 1977.

44. Exportation of Arms Act 1900.
repealed: S.L.R. 1986.

49. Town Councils (Scotland) Act 1900.
repealed: 1973, c.65, sch.29.

CAP.

63 & 64 Vict. (1900)—cont.

51. Moneylenders Act 1900.
see Re Roe's Legal Charge Park Street Securities v. Roe [1982] 2 Lloyd's Rep. 370, C.A.
repealed: 1974, c.39, sch.5.
s. 4, repealed: order 80/50.
s. 6, see Offen v. Smith, The Times, November
15, 1978. C.A.; Wills v. Wood, The Times,
March 24, 1984, C.A.

52. Naval Reserve Act 1900.
repealed: 1980, c.9, sch.10.

55. Executors (Scotland) Act 1900.
s. 2, see Kennedy, Petr., 1983 S.L.T. (Sh.Ct.)
10.
s. 3, amended: 1980, c.55, sch.2.

62. Colonial Stock Act 1900.
repealed: S.L.R. 1977.

63. Local Government (Ireland) Act 1900.
repealed: 1980, c.59, sch.

1 Edw. 7 (1901)

5. Demise of the Crown Act 1901.
s. 1, repealed in pt.: S.L.R. 1973.

7. Finance Act 1901.
s. 10, amended: 1979, c.2, sch.4.

**16. National Gallery (Purchase of Adjacent Land)
Act 1901.**
repealed: S.L.R. 1978.

17. Lunacy (Ireland) Act 1901.
repealed: 1978, c.23, sch.7.

19. Public Libraries Act 1901.
repealed: order 81/438.

22. Factory and Workshop Act 1901.
s. 149, see Occidental Inc. v. Assessor for
Orkney, 1979 S.L.T. 60; Assessor for Grampian Region v. Claben, 1981 S.L.T.(Notes)
108.

23. Marriages Legalization Act 1901.
repealed: S.L.R. 1977.

38. Fisheries (Ireland) Act 1901.
repealed: order 81/227.

2 Edw. 7 (1902)

5. Royal Naval Reserve Act 1902.
repealed: 1980, c.9, sch.10.

7. Finance Act 1902.
s. 11, repealed: S.L.R. 1986.

8. Cremation Act 1902.
ss. 2, 3, repealed in pt.: S.L.R. 1978.
s. 7, regs. 79/1138; 85/153, 820(S.).
s. 8, amended: 1977, c.45, schs.2,3.
s. 9, repealed in pt.: 1972, c.70, schs.26,30;
1981, c.23, schs.2,4.
s. 10, amended: 1988, c.13, sch.3.
s. 12, repealed in pt.: 1972, c.70, sch.30.

11. Immoral Traffic (Scotland) Act 1902.
repealed: 1976, c.67, sch.2.

13. Labour Bureaux (London) Act 1902.
repealed: S.L.R. 1973.

20. Public Libraries (Ireland) Act 1902.
repealed: order 81/438.

21. Shop Clubs Act 1902.
repealed: 1986, c.48, schs.1,5.

CAP.

2 Edw. 7 (1902)—cont.

28. Licensing Act 1902.
s. 2, amended: 1977, c.45, s.31, sch.6; repealed
in pt.: S.L.R. 1976.
s. 3, repealed: S.L.R. 1976.
s. 6, repealed in pt.: S.L.R. 1976.

41. Metropolis Water Act 1902.
s. 18, repealed in pt.: S.L.R. 1986.
ss. 24, 47, repealed in pt.: S.L.R. 1976.

3 Edw. 7 (1903)

5. Berwickshire County Town Act 1903.
repealed: S.L.R. 1977.

6. Naval Forces Act 1903.
repealed: 1980, c.9, sch.10.

20. Patriotic Fund Reorganisation Act 1903.
sch. 1, amended: orders 74/595; 75/629.

25. Licensing (Scotland) Act 1903.
repealed: 1982, c.45, sch.4.
s. 70, see *Skeen* v. *Speirs*, 1980 S.L.T.(Notes)
86.

26. Marriages Legalization Act 1903.
repealed: S.L.R. 1977.

30. Railways (Electrical Power) Act 1903.
s. 1, repealed in pt.: S.L.R. 1986.

31. Board of Agriculture and Fisheries Act 1903.
s. 1, repealed in pt.: S.L.R. 1978; S.L.R. 1986.
sch., repealed: *ibid.*

33. Burgh Police (Scotland) Act 1903.
repealed (31.12.1984): 1973, c.65, s.229; 1978,
c.4, s.5; 1982, c.45, ss.134,135.
s. 44, repealed: 1982, c.43, sch.4.

37. Irish Land Act 1903.
s. 33, repealed in pt.: 1981, c.35, s.137, sch.19.
ss. 41, 45, 46, rules 73/1850; 74/977.

46. Revenue Act 1903.
s. 5, repealed: 1973, c.51, sch.22.

4 Edw. 7 (1904)

6. Hall-marking of Foreign Plate Act 1904.
repealed: 1973, c.43, sch.7.

13. London Electric Lighting Areas Act 1904.
repealed: S.L.R. 1973.

19. Railways (Private Sidings) Act 1904.
repealed: 1973, c.55, sch.

24. Wireless Telegraphy Act 1904.
repealed: S.L.R. 1973.

30. Bishopric of Southwark and Birmingham Act 1904.
repealed: S.L.R. 1973.

33. Anglo-French Convention Act 1904.
repealed: S.L.R. 1976.

5 Edw. 7 (1905)

1. Leeds Corporation (Consolidation) Act 1905.
s. 178, repealed: order 75/944.

9. Coal Mines (Weighing of Minerals) Act 1905.
repealed: 1986, c.48, schs.1,5.

11. Railway Fires Act 1905.
s. 1, amended: 1981, c.56, s.38.

15. Trade Marks Act 1905.
see *York Trade Mark* [1981] F.S.R. 33, Graham
J.

CAP.

5 Edw. 7 (1905)—cont.

15. Trade Marks Act 1905—*cont.*
s. 3, see *Ind Coope* v. *Paine* [1983] R.P.C. 326,
Whitford J.
ss. 3, 39, see *News Group Newspapers* v. *The
Rocket Record Co.* [1981] F.S.R. 89, Slade J.
s. 22, see *Sterling-Winthrop Group* v. *Farbenfabriken Bayer A.G.* [1976] R.P.C. 469, Kerry J.,
High Ct. of Ireland.
s. 39, see *Gallaher (Dublin), Hergall (1981)* v.
The Health Education Bureau [1982] F.S.R.
464, H.Ct. of Ireland.
s. 42, see *Henry Denny & Sons* v. *United
Biscuits (U.K.)* [1981] F.S.R. 114, Graham J.

6 Edw. 7 (1906)

5. Seamen's and Soldiers' False Characters Act 1906.
ss. 1, 2, repealed in pt.: 1981, c.45, sch.
s. 3, repealed: 1980, c.9, sch.10.

14. Alkali, etc., Works Regulation Act 1906.
ss. 3–5, 8, repealed: 1974, c.40, schs.3,4.
s. 9, repealed in pt.: *ibid.*, sch.4.
ss. 10–13, repealed: regs. 74/2170.
ss. 14, 15, repealed: 1974, c.40, schs.3,4.
s. 16A, repealed: regs. 74/2170.
s. 17, repealed: 1974, c.40, sch.4.
s. 18, repealed: regs. 74/2170.
s. 19, repealed: 1974, c.40, sch.4.
ss. 20, 21, repealed: regs. 74/2170.
s. 22, repealed in pt.: 1974, c.40, sch.4.
s. 27, S.R. 1981 No. 383.
s. 27, amended: 1974, c.40, sch.3; regs.
74/2170; 87/180; repealed in pt.: 1972, c.70,
sch.30; 1974, c.40, sch.3; 87/180.

16. Justices of the Peace Act 1906.
repealed: 1973, c.15, sch.5; 1975, c.20,
sch.2(S.).

25. Open Spaces Act 1906.
see *Third Greytown Properties* v. *Peterborough
Corporation* [1973] 3 All E.R. 731, Templeman
J.
s. 7, see *Re St. George's Church, Oakdale*
[1975] 2 All E.R. 870.
s. 10, see *Laverstoke Property Co.* v. *Peterborough Corporation* [1972] 1 W.L.R. 1400;
[1972] 3 All E.R. 678; *Re St. Luke's, Chelsea*
[1975] 3 W.L.R. 564.
s. 15, repealed in pt.: order 86/1.

31. Local Government (Ireland) Act (1898) (Amendment) Act 1906.
repealed: order 78/1051.

32. Dogs Act 1906.
s. 1, repealed in pt.: order 76/1040; 1987, c.9,
sch.
s. 3, amended: 1982, c.45, ss.75,128(S.); 1984,
c.54, sch.9; 1988, c.9, s.39; repealed in pt.
(S.): 1982, c.45, sch.4.
s. 4, amended: *ibid.*, ss.75,128(S.); 1988, c.9,
s.39.
ss. 8, 9, repealed in pt.: S.L.R. 1976.

33. Local Authorities (Treasury Powers) Act 1906.
repealed: S.L.R. 1981.

CAP.

6 Edw. 7 (1906)—cont.

34. Prevention of Corruption Act 1906.

see *R.* v. *Hirst and McNamee* (1975) 64
Cr.App.R. 151, C.A.

s. 1, see *R.* v. *Barrett* [1976] 1 W.L.R. 946, C.A.;
D.P.P. v. *Holly; D.P.P.* v. *Manners* [1977] 2
W.L.R. 178; [1977] 1 All E.R. 316, H.L.; *R.* v.
Mills (1978) 68 Cr.App.R. 154, C.A.; *R.* v.
Wellburn, Nurdin and Randel (1979) 69
Cr.App.R. 254, C.A.; *R.* v. *Braithwaite; R.* v.
Graham [1983] 1 W.L.R. 385, C.A.; *R.* v.
Tweedie [1984] 2 W.L.R. 608, C.A.; *Temple-
ton* v. *H.M. Advocate*, 1988 S.L.T. 171.

s. 1, amended: order 74/595; 1988, c.33, s.47.

s. 2, repealed in pt.: 1975, c.59, sch.6; 1980,
c.59, sch.

**35. Fatal Accidents and Sudden Deaths Inquiry
(Scotland) Act 1906.**

repealed (S.): 1976, c.14, sch.2.

40. Marriage with Foreigners Act 1906.

s. 1, amended: 1977, c.15, sch.2; 1980, c.23,
s.1; repealed in pt.: order 79/1714.

s. 2, amended: 1977, c.15, sch.2.

s. 5, sch. (in pt.), repealed: *ibid.*, sch.2.

41. Marine Insurance Act 1906.

s. 1, see *Continental Illinois National Bank &
Trading Company of Chicago* v. *Bathhurst, The
Times,* February 12, 1985, Mustill J.

s. 16, see *Berger and Light Diffusers Pty.* v.
Pollock [1973] 2 Lloyd's Rep. 442.

s. 17, see *Black King Shipping Corp.* v. *Massie,
The Times,* December 17, 1984, Hirst J.

s. 18, see *March Cabaret Club & Casino* v.
*London Assurance; March Cabaret Club &
Casino* v. *Thompson & Bryan* [1975] 1 Lloyd's
Rep. 169; *Lambert* v. *Co-operative Insurance
Society* [1975] 2 Lloyd's Rep. 485, C.A.; *Soya
GmbH Mainz Kommanditgesellschaft* v.
White [1983] 1 Lloyd's Rep. 124, H.L.

ss. 18, 20, see *Container Transport International
Inc. and Reliance Group Inc.* v. *Oceanus
Mutual Underwriting Association (Bermuda)*
[1984] 1 Lloyd's Rep. 476, C.A.

s. 28, see *Berger and Light Diffusers Pty.* v.
Pollock [1973] 2 Lloyd's Rep. 442.

s. 33, see *Brady* v. *Irish National Insurance Co.*
[1986] I.R. 698, Supreme Ct., Rep. of Ir.

s. 39, see *Compania Maritima San Basilio S.A.*
v. *Oceanus Mutual Underwriting Association
(Bermuda)* [1976] 3 W.L.R. 265. C.A.

s. 41, see *Euro Diam* v. *Bathurst* [1987] 2 All
E.R. 113, Staughton J.

s. 44, see *Shell International Petroleum Co.* v.
Gibbs [1982] 2 W.L.R. 745, C.A.

s. 50, see *First National City Bank of Chicago* v.
*West of England Shipowners Mutual Protec-
tion and Indemnity Association (Luxembourg);
Elvepidis Era, The* [1981] 1 Lloyd's Rep. 54,
Mocatta J.

s. 55, *Soya GmbH Mainz Kommanditgesellschaft* v. *White* [1983] 1 Lloyd's Rep.
124, H.L.; *Lloyd (J.J.) Instruments* v. *Northern
Star Insurance Co., Financial Times,* October
21, 1986, C.A.

s. 57, see *ICI Fibres* v. *Mat Transport, The
Financial Times,* December 2, 1986, Staughton J.

CAP.

6 Edw. 7 (1906)—cont.

41. Marine Insurance Act 1906—*cont.*

s. 78, see *Integrated Containers Service Inc.* v.
British Traders Insurance Co., The Times,
November 23, 1983, C.A.

s. 83, see *C. T. Bowring Reinsurance* v. *Baxter,
Financial Times,* March 25, 1987, Hirst J.

43. Street Betting Act 1906.

s. 4, repealed: 1980, c.59, sch.

44. Burial Act 1906.

repealed: 1972, c.70, sch.30.

47. Trade Disputes Act 1906.

ss. 1, 3, repealed: order 76/1043.

s. 2, repealed: order 82/528.

ss. 2, 3, see *Becton, Dickinson & Co.* v. *Patrick
Lee* [1973] I.R. 1.

s. 5, amended: order 76/1043.

48. Merchant Shipping Act 1906.

s. 2, repealed in pt.: 1988, c.12, sch.7.

s. 16, amended: 1979, c.39, sch.6.

s. 50, order 78/1533; regs. 79/341; 88/2003.

s. 51, order 80/399.

s. 51, repealed: 1988, c.12, schs.6,7.

s. 52, repealed: *ibid.*, schs.5,7.

s. 69, repealed: 1979, c.39, sch.7; 1984, c.5,
sch.1.

s. 72, see *Pierce* v. *Bernis: The Lusitania* [1986]
2 W.L.R. 501, Sheen J.

ss. 76, 77, amended: 1979, c.39, sch.7.

s. 80, orders 78/1628; 85/1200.

s. 82, repealed in pt.: 1979, c.39, sch.7.

s. 83, repealed: 1988, c.12, sch.7.

50. National Galleries of Scotland Act 1906.

ss. 2, 3, 6, 8, order 78/660.

s. 3, amended: 1985, c.16, s.16.

s. 4, substituted: *ibid.*

ss. 4A–4D, added: *ibid.*

s. 7, amended: *ibid.* sch.2.

s. 8, repealed: S.L.R. 1986.

sch., added: 1985, c.16, s.17.

54. Town Tenants (Ireland) Act 1906.

s. 11, substituted: 1978, c.23, sch.7.

55. Public Trustee Act 1906.

s. 3, rules 83/1050.

s. 8, amended: 1986, c.57, sch.

s. 9, orders 73/408; 74/310; 75/287; 77/508;
78/373; 79/189; 80/370; 81/324; 82/316;
83/443; 84/390; 85/373; 87/403; 88/571.

s. 14, rules 75/1189; 76/836; 81/358; 83/1050;
84/109; 85/132; 87/1891, 2249.

7 Edw. 7 (1907)

**8. Assay of Imported Watch-Cases (Existing
Stocks Exemption) Act 1907.**

repealed: 1973, c.43, sch.7.

11. British North America Act 1907.

Act renamed Constitution Act 1907 (Can.):
1982, c.11 sch.

s. 2, substituted: *ibid.*

13. Finance Act 1907.

Pt. III (ss. 12–16), repealed: 1975, c.7, sch.13.

s. 5, repealed: 1973, c.43, sch.7.

s. 7, amended: 1985, c.54, s.85.

CAP.

7 Edw. 7 (1907)—cont.

13. Finance Act 1907—cont.

s. 10, see *Associated Maltsters* v. *I.R.C.* [1972] 3 All E.R. 192; [1972] T.R. 53.

s. 10, repealed: 1973, c.51, sch.22.

s. 30, repealed in pt.: 1975, c.7, sch.13.

s. 77, repealed in pt.: 1985, c.54, s.86.

23. Criminal Appeal Act 1907.

s. 19. see *R.* v. *Chard, The Times,* November 11, 1983, H.L.

24. Limited Partnerships Act 1907.

s. 4, see *Reed (Inspector of Taxes)* v. *Young* [1986] 1 W.L.R. 649, H.L.

s. 4, repealed in pt.: 1979, c.37, sch.7.

s. 11, repealed: 1973, c.51, sch.22.

s. 17, rules 72/1040; 74/560.

29. Patents and Designs Act 1907.

see *Associated British Combustion's Application* [1978] R.P.C. 582, C.A.; *Polaroid Corp. (Land's) Patent* [1981] R.P.C. 11, C.A.

ss. 23, 24, 35, see *Codex Corp* v. *Racal-Milgo* [1983] R.P.C. 369, C.A.

s. 47, functions transferred: order 81/207.

s. 47, repealed in pt.: 1977, c.37, sch.6; 1983, c.47, sch.6.

ss. 62, 63, amended: 1986, c.39, sch.2.

s. 70, see *Allibert's Exploitation Application* [1978] R.P.C. 261, Whitford J.

s. 82, repealed: S.L.R. 1986.

ss. 88, 91, repealed: 1986, c.39, sch.3.

s. 91A, orders 72/972; 73/773; 74/2146; 75/2195; 76/1785; 77/1633, 1634; 80/571; 82/162; 83/1709; 84/367, 1694; 85/173, 456, 457.

s. 91A, repealed: 1986, c.39, sch.3.

s. 93. see *Lamson v. Industries' Application* [1978] R.P.C. 1, Whitford J., *Dehle's Design Applications* [1982] R.P.C. 526, Registered Designs Appeal Tribunal; *Weir Pumps* v. *C.M.L. Pumps* [1984] F.S.R. 33, Whitford J.

40. Notification of Births Act 1907.

s. 1, amended (S.): 1972, c.58, sch.6; 1978, c.29, sch.15.

s. 4, repealed in pt. (S.): 1972, c.58, sch.7.

41. Whale Fisheries (Scotland) Act 1907.

repealed: 1981, c.29, sch.5.

42. Sea Fisheries (Scotland) Application of Penalties Act 1907.

repealed: 1984, c.26, sch.2.

43. Education (Administrative Provisions) Act 1907.

repealed: S.L.R. 1978.

51. Sheriff Courts (Scotland) Act 1907.

s. 3, see *Cormack* v. *The Crown Estate Comrs.* (O.H.), March 24, 1982; *W. Jack Baillie Associates* v. *Kennedy,* 1985 S.L.T.(Sh.Ct.) 53; *Squire Light & Sound* v. *Vidicom Systems* (Sh.Ct.), 1987 S.C.L.R. 538; *Kerr* v. *Strathclyde Regional Council,* 1988 S.L.T.(Sh.Ct.) 42.

s. 3, repealed in pt.: 1980, c.55, sch.3.

s. 4, see *Banque Indo Suez* v. *Maritime Co. Overseas,* 1985 S.L.T. 117.

s. 4, repealed in pt.: 1975, c.2, sch.10.

CAP.

7 Edw. 7 (1907)—cont.

51. Sheriff Courts (Scotland) Act 1907—cont.

s. 5, see *Scottish Provident Institution* v. *Watson,* 1972 S.L.T.(Sh.Ct.) 66; *Cook* v. *McGinnes,* 1982 S.L.T.(Sh.Ct.) 101; *Brown* v. *Hamilton District Council* (H.L.), 1983 S.L.T. 397; *Milne* v. *Rennet,* 1983 S.L.T.(Sh.Ct.) 81.

s. 5, amended: 1977, c.27, sch.1; 1978, c.22, sch.2; 1983, c.12, s.1; 1985, c.37, sch.1; 1986, c.9, sch.1; repealed in pt.: 1980, c.55, s.15, sch.3; 1982, c.27, sch.14; 1986, c.9, sch.2.

s. 5A, added: 1985, c.73, s.17.

s. 6, see *City of Glasgow District Council* v. *Hamlet Textiles,* 1986 S.L.T. 415; *R.I. Combined Parkinson Services* v. *Barneston,* 1986 S.L.T. (Sh.Ct.) 63.

s. 6, amended: 1973, c.45, sch.4; 1986, c.55, sch.1.

s. 7, repealed in pt.: 1980, c.55, sch.3.

s. 27, see *Iannelli* v. *Stevenson,* 1977 S.L.T.(Sh.Ct.) 5; *C. J. Palombo Building Contractor* v. *James Jack (Hyndford),* 1977 S.L.T.(Sh.Ct.) 95; *Troc Sales* v. *Kirkcaldy District Licensing Board,* 1982 S.L.T.(Sh.Ct.) 77; *Davidson* v. *Duncan,* 1981 S.C. 83; *Duggie* v. *A. Tulloch & Sons,* 1983 S.L.T.(Sh.Ct.) 66; *Spencer* v. *Spencer,* 1983 S.L.T.(Sh.Ct.) 87; *Lamberton* v. *Lamberton,* 1984 S.L.T.(Sh.Ct.) 22; *Trolland* v. *Trolland,* 1987 S.L.T.(Sh.Ct.) 42; *Vag Finance* v. *Smith,* 1988 S.L.T.(Sh.Ct.) 59.

s. 27, repealed in pt.: 1980, c.55, sch.3.

s. 27(B), see *Thomson* v. *Thomson,* 1979 S.L.T.(Sh Ct.) 11; *Cassidy* v. *Cassidy,* 1986 S.L.T.(Sh.Ct.) 17.

s. 29, see *Boss* v. *Lyle Shipping Co.,* 1980 S.L.T.(Sh.Ct.) 65; *Williamson* v. *Harris,* 1981 S.L.T.(Sh.Ct.) 56; *Rediffusion* v. *McIlroy,* 1986 S.L.T.(Sh.Ct.) 33.

s. 30, repealed: 1980, c.55, sch.3.

s. 31, repealed: *ibid.,* s.11, sch.3.

s. 34, see *Gemmell* v. *Andrew,* 1975 S.L.T.(Land Ct.) 5; *Austin* v. *Gibson,* 1979 S.L.T.(Land Ct.) 12; *Milne* v. *Earl of Seafield,* 1981 S.L.T.(Sh.Ct.) 37.

s. 36, see *Gemmell* v. *Andrew,* 1975 S.L.T.(Land Ct.) 5.

s. 38A, added: 1974, c.44, sch.13; 1987, c.26, sch.23.

ss. 38B, 38C, added: 1988, c.36, sch.1.

s. 39, see *Hall* v. *Riverlodge* (O.H.), October 20, 1978; *British Railways Board* v. *Strathclyde Regional Council,* Second Division, November 26, 1980; *Milne* v. *The Earl of Seafield,* 1981 S.L.T.(Sh.Ct.) 37; *Thomson* v. *Wiggins Teape,* 1981 S.L.T.(Sh.Ct.) 85.

s. 40, Acts of Sederunt 72/1673; 73/461, 462; 74/1744; 75/73, 1148, 1300, 1642, 1908; 76/441, 848, 1119, 1287, 1620, 1848, 2198; 77/402, 568, 969; 78/115, 116, 928, 948, 1167, 1423; 79/347, 1034, 1633; 80/454, 908, 1015, 1553, 1678; 81/499, 514, 1136, 1408; 82/182, 466, 652, 803, 1167, 1722; 83/970, 1635; 84/233, 471, 1134, 1135; 85/544, 759; 86/266, 978, 1129; 87/865, 1078; 88/681, 1033, 1502.

CAP.

7 Edw. 7 (1907)—cont.

51. Sheriff Courts (Scotland) Act 1907—cont.
s. 40, amended: 1983, c.12, sch.1; repealed in pt.: ibid., sch.2.
s. 50, see Cigaro (Glasgow) v. City of Glasgow District Licensing Board, First Division, December 8, 1981; TF v. Management Committee and Managers of Ravenscraig Hospital, 1988 S.C.L.R. 327.
s. 51, repealed: S.L.R. 1973.
sch. 1, see Low & Sons v. McKenzie, 1972 S.L.T. 10; Mackie v. Gardner, 1973 S.L.T. (Land Ct.) 11; Craig-na-BrroSales v. Munro Furniture, 1974 S.L.T.(Sh.Ct.) 107; Jarvie v. Laird, 1974 S.L.T.(Sh.Ct.) 75; Gemmell v. Andrew, 1975 S.L.T.(Land Ct) 5; D. Forbes Smith & Johnston v. Kaye, 1975 S.L.T.(Sh.Ct.) 33; G. v. H., 1976 S.L.T.(Sh.Ct) 51; Beverley v. Beverley, 1977 S.L.T.(Sh.Ct.) 3; Mackays v. James Deas & Son, 1977 S.L.T.(Sh.Ct.) 10; Wilson v. Hay, 1977 S.L.T.(Sh.Ct.) 52; C. J. Palombo Building Contractor v. James Jack (Hyndford), 1977 S.L.T.(Sh.Ct.) 95; British Railways Board v. Devol Brushing, 1978 S.L.T.(Sh.Ct.) 34; Orr v. Orr, 1978 S.L.T.(Sh.Ct.) 61; Hall v. Riverlodge (O.H.), October 20, 1978; Austin v. Gibson, 1979 S.L.T.(Land Ct.) 12; Wailes Dove Bitumatic v. Plastic Sealant Services, 1979 S.L.T.(Sh.Ct.), 41; Ellis v. MacDonald, 1980 S.L.T. 11; Dixon Street Motors v. Associated Rentals, 1980 S.L.T.(Sh.Ct.) 46; Tennent Caledonian Breweries v. Gearty, 1980 S.L.T.(Sh.Ct.) 71; Church of Scotland Home Board v. J. C. McGeach & Co., 1980 S.L.T.(Sh.Ct.) 75; Cosgrove v. Cosgrove, 1980 S.L.T.(Sh.Ct.) 105; Milne v. The Earl of Seafield, 1981 S.L.T.(Sh.Ct.) 37; Taylor v. Brick (O.H.), August 11, 1978; British Railways Board v. Strathclyde Regional Council, Second Division, November 26, 1980; Williamson v. Harris, 1981 S.L.T.(Sh.Ct.) 56; Thomson v. Wiggins Teape, 1981 S.L.T.(Sh.Ct.) 85; Petroleum Industry Training Board v. Jenkins, 1982 S.L.T.(Sh.Ct.) 43; The Royal Bank of Scotland v. Briggs, 1982 S.L.T.(Sh.Ct.) 46; Thorniewood United F.C. Social Club v. Hamilton, 1982 S.L.T.(Sh.Ct.) 97; Cormack v. The Crown Estate Comrs. (O.H.), March 24, 1982; Cobb v. Baker Oil Tools (U.K.), 1984 S.L.T. 232; Macinsure Brokers v. Mackenzie & Co., 1984 S.L.T.(Sh.Ct.) 66, Hardy v. Robinson; Johnstone v. W. Y. Walker, 1985 S.L.T.(Sh.Ct.) 40; McCormick v. Martin, 1985 S.L.T. (Sh.Ct.) 57; Cadzow v. White, 1986 S.L.T.(Sh.Ct.), 21; Haliburton Manufacturing and Services v. Picts (Construction) Co., 1986 S.L.T.(Sh.Ct.) 24; Guardian Royal Exchange Group v. Moffat, 1986 S.L.T. 262; Borland v. Lochwinnoch Golf Club, 1986 S.L.T.(Sh.Ct.), 13; Cunningham v. Rowe, 1985 S L.C.R. 154; R.I. Combined Parkinson Services v. Barneston, 1986 S.L.T.(Sh.Ct.) 63; Anderson Brown & Co. v. Morris 1987 S.L.T.(Sh.Ct.) 96; Burmy v. White, 1987 S.L.T.(Sh.Ct.) 120; Strang v. Ross, Harper &

CAP.

7 Edw. 7 (1907)—cont.

51. Sheriff Courts (Scotland) Act 1907—cont.
Murphy (Sh.Ct.) 1987 S.C.L.R. 10; Kristiansen v. Kristiansen (Sh.Ct.), 1987 S.C.L.R. 462; C.J.M. Manufacturing v. Gordon (Sh.Ct.), 1987 S.C.L.R. 534; Kinnerslay v. Husband (Sh.Ct.), 1987 S.C.L.R. 544; Mackenzie v. Mackenzie (Sh.Ct.), 1987 S.C.L.R. 671; Freel v. Freel (Sh.Ct.), 1987 S.C.L.R. 665; Central Farmers v. Watson (Sh.Ct.) 1987 S.C.L.R. 745; Taylor v. Taylor (Sh.Ct.) 1988 S.C.L.R. 60; Colville v. Colville, 1988 S.L.T.(Sh.Ct.) 23; Philp v. Philp (Sh.Ct.), 1988 S.C.L.R. 313; Dryburgh v. Curry's Group (Sh.Ct.), 1988 S.C.L.R. 316; Kerr v. Strathclyde Regional Council, 1988 S.L.T.(Sh.Ct.) 42; Rayment v. Jack, 1988 S.L.T. 647; Girvan v. Girvan, 1988 S.C.L.R. 493.
sch. 1, amended: order 76/744; repealed in pt.: S.L.R. 1973; 1980, c.55, ss. 11,15, sch.3.

53. Public Health Acts Amendment Act 1907.
ss. 2 (in pt.), 3, repealed: 1972, c.70, sch.30.
s. 7, repealed in pt.: 1980, c.59, sch.
ss. 13, 31, 76, repealed in pt.: 1972, c.70, sch.30.
s. 81, repealed in pt.: 1973, c.55, sch.; 1981, c.42, sch.
s. 85, repealed: 1973, c.35, sch.; order 81/839.
s 94, see Weymouth Corporation v. Cook (1973) 71 L.G.R. 458, D.C.
s. 94, amended: 1974, c.7, sch.6; 1976, c.57, s.18; 1980, c.65, s.186.

55. London Cab and Stage Carriage Act 1907.
s. 1, orders 73/519; 74/601; 75/1216; 76/1956; 77/2030; 79/706; 80/588, 939; 81/843; 82/610; 83/653; 84/707; 85/933, 1023; 86/857; 87/999; 88/996.
s. 1, repealed in pt.: S.L.R. 1973; S.L.R. 1976.
ss. 3, 5, repealed: ibid.
s. 6, see Bassam v. Green [1981] R.T.R. 362, D.C.
s. 6, repealed in pt.: S.L.R. 1976.

8 Edw. 7 (1908)

3. Prosecution of Offences Act 1908.
repealed: 1979, c.31, sch.2.
ss. 1, 2. see Turner v. D.P.P. (1978) 68 Cr.App.R. 70, Mars Jones J.
s. 2, repealed in pt.: 1979, c.31, sch.2.
s. 2, regs. 78/1357.

16. Finance Act 1908.
s 6, amended: 1972, c.70, s.213; repealed in pt.: ibid., s.213, sch.30.

17. Cran Measures Act 1908.
repealed: 1979, c.45, sch.7.
s. 4, order 77/55.

24. Summary Jurisdiction (Ireland) Act 1908.
ss. 1, 2. repealed in pt.: 1980, c.59, sch.
ss. 5, 11, repealed: ibid.

26. Naval Marriages Act 1908.
repealed (S.): 1977, c.15, sch.3.

32. Friendly Societies Act 1908.
repealed: 1974, c.46, sch.11.

33. Telegraph (Construction) Act 1908.
repealed: 1984, c.12, sch.7.

CAP.

8 Edw. 7 (1908)—cont.

36. Small Holdings and Allotments Act 1908.
s. 24, repealed: 1972, c 70, sch.30.
s 25, amended: 1981, c.67, sch.4.
s. 27, repealed in pt.: 1972, c.70, sch.30.
s. 28, repealed in pt.: 1980, c.65, schs.5,34.
s. 32, repealed in pt.: 1972, c.70, sch.30; 1980, c.65, schs.5,34.
s. 34, amended: 1972, c.70, sch.29.
ss. 35, 37, repealed: ibid., sch.30.
s. 39, amended: ibid., sch.29; repealed in pt.: S.L.R. 1986
s. 40, repealed in pt.: 1988, c.10, sch.
s. 47, amended: 1986, c.5, sch.14; repealed in pt.: 1980, c.65, schs.5,34.
s. 49, repealed in pt.: ibid.
s. 51, repealed: S.L.R. 1973.
s. 52, amended: 1972, c.70, sch.29.
s. 53, repealed in pt.: ibid., sch.30.
s. 54, repealed: 1980, c.65, schs.5,34.
s. 57, repealed in pt.: 1972, c.70, sch.30.
s. 58, amended: 1986, c.5, sch.14.
s. 59, repealed: 1980, c.65, schs.5,34.
s. 61, repealed in pt.: 1972, c 70, sch.30; 1985, c.51, sch.17.
sch. 1, amended: 1986, c.5, sch.14.

38. Irish Universities Act 1908.
repealed: order 81/610.

44. Commons Act 1908.
s. 1, amended: 1985, c.51, sch.8.

45. Punishment of Incest Act 1908.
s. 6, repealed in pt.: 1975, c.59, sch.6.

49. Statute Law Revision Act 1908.
s. 2, repealed: 1977, c.38, sch.5.

51. Appellate Jurisdiction Act 1908.
s. 2, repealed: S.L.R. 1976.
s. 3, sch., repealed in pt.: S.L.R. 1986.

53. Law of Distress Amendment Act 1908.
s. 1, see Lawrence Chemical Co. v. Rubinstein, [1982] 1 W.L.R. 284; [1982] 1 All E.R. 653, C.A.
ss. 1, 3, 6, see Offshore Ventilation, Re (1987) 3 BCC 486, Harman J.; Rhodes v. Allied Dunbar Pension Services [1987] 1 W.L.R 1703, Harman J.
s. 4, amended: 1986, c.5, sch.14; repealed in pt.: 1974, c.39, sch.5.
s. 4A, added: ibid., sch.4.

57. Coal Mines Regulation Act 1908.
amended: 1975, c.65, s.21; order 76/1042.
s. 2, repealed in pt.: 1986, c.48, schs.4,5.
s. 8, repealed: ibid., sch.4.

59. Prevention of Crime Act 1908.
repealed: order 80/1084

61. Housing of the Working Classes (Ireland) Act 1908.
repealed: order 81/156

62. Local Government (Scotland) Act 1908.
repealed: S.L.R. 1986.

65. Summary Jurisdiction (Scotland) Act 1908.
repealed: S.L.R. 1977.

66. Public Meeting Act 1908.
s. 1, amended: 1977, c.45, sch.1; repealed in pt : 1982, c.2, sch.8; 1984, c.60, sch.7.

CAP.

8 Edw. 7 (1908)—cont.

69. Companies (Consolidation) Act 1908.
s. 93, see Welsh Irish Ferries, Re, Financial Times, June 5, 1985, Nourse J.

9 Edw. 7 (1909)

8. Trawling in Prohibited Areas Prevention Act 1909.
repealed: 1984, c.26, sch.2; S.L.R. 1986.

9. South Africa Act 1909.
repealed: S.L.R. 1976.

12. Marine Insurance (Gambling Policies) Act 1909.
s. 1, repealed in pt.: 1980, c.59, sch.

18. Naval Establishments in British Possessions Act 1909.
repealed: S.L.R. 1976.

20. Telegraph (Arbitration) Act 1909.
repealed: 1984, c.12, sch.7.

30. Cinematograph Act 1909.
repealed: 1985, s.13, sch.3.
s. 1, see British Amusement Catering Trades Association v. Westminster City Council [1988] 2 W.L.R. 485, H.L.
s. 1, regs. 76/1315.
s. 1, substituted: 1982, c.33, s.10; amended: 1984, c.12, sch.4; repealed in pt.: 1984, c.46, schs.5,6.
ss. 1, 2, regs. 82/1856; 83/367(S.).
s. 2, amended: orders 78/1387; 80/1398; 81/1411, 1421: 1982, c.33, sch.1; repealed in pt.: ibid., sch.2.
ss. 3, 4, repealed: ibid.
s. 5, repealed (S.): 1973, c.65, schs.24,29.
ss. 5, 6, repealed: 1972, c.70, s.204, sch.30.
s. 7, regs. 82/1856; 83/367(S.).
s. 7, amended: 1972, c.70, s.204; 1973, c.65, sch.24; 1982, c.33, sch.1; repealed in pt.: ibid., s.10.
s. 8, repealed in pt.: 1973, c.65, schs.24,29.

34. Electric Lighting Act 1909.
see R. v. Midlands Electricity Board, ex p. Busby; Same v. Same, ex p. Williamson, The Times, October 28, 1987, Schiemann J.
s. 23, repealed: 1983, c.25, s.1, sch.4.
s. 25, repealed in pt. (S.): 1984, c.54, sch.11.

39. Oaths Act 1909.
repealed: 1978, c.19, sch.

43. Revenue Act 1909.
s. 9, repealed: 1985, c.54, sch.27.
s. 11, repealed: regs. 74/1885.

47. Development and Road Improvement Funds Act 1909.
Pt. I (ss. 1–6), s. 19, sch., repealed: 1983, c.29, sch.3.
Pt. II (ss. 7–17), repealed (S.): 1984, c.54, sch.11.

10 Edw. 7 & 1 Geo. 5 (1910)

7. Development and Road Improvement Funds Act 1910.
repealed: order 80/1085; 1983, c.29, sch.3.

CAP.

10 Edw. 7 & 1 Geo. 5 (1910)—cont.

8. Finance (1909–10) Act 1910.
Pt. III (ss. 54–64), repealed: 1975, c.7, sch.13.
s. 55, see *Bunbury* v. *I.R.C.* [1972] 2 W.L.R. 77; [1972] 1 All E.R. 343.
s. 59, see *Park, Re (No. 2)*; *I.R.C.* v. *Park* [1972] 2 W.L.R. 276; [1972] 1 All E.R. 394.
s. 74, see *Lap Shun Textiles Industrial Co.* v. *Collector of Stamp Revenue* [1976] 2 W.L.R. 817; [1976] 1 All E.R. 833, P.C.; *Thorn* v. *I.R.C.* [1976] 2 All E.R. 622; *Berkeley* v. *Comrs. of Inland Revenue* [1984] 13 N.I.J.B., Murray J.
s. 74, repealed: 1985, c.54, sch.27.
ss. 77–79, repealed in pt.: *ibid.*, sch.27; repealed (prosp.): 1987, c.16, s.49, sch.16.
s. 96, repealed in pt.: 1975, c.7, sch.13.

28. Civil List Act 1910.
repealed: S.L.R. 1977.

31. Jury Trials Amendment (Scotland) Act 1910.
repealed: 1988, c.36, sch.2.

1 & 2 Geo. 5 (1911)

2. Revenue Act 1911.
repealed: S.L.R. 1973.

6. Perjury Act 1911.
s. 1, see *R.* v. *Millward (Neil)* [1985] 1 W.L.R. 532, C.A; *R.* v. *Rider* (1986) 83 Cr.App.R. 207, C.A.
s. 1A, added: 1975, c.34, sch.1.
ss. 1, 5, see *R.* v. *Power* [1977] 66 Cr.App.R. 159, C.A.
s. 2, see *R.* v. *Stokes* [1988] Crim.L.R. 100, C.A.
s. 3, amended: 1986, c.16, s.4.
ss. 7, 12, repealed in pt.: 1981, c.47, sch.
s. 9, repealed: 1985, c.23, s.28, sch.2.
s. 13, see *R.* v *O'Connor* [1980] Crim. L.R. 43, C.A.; *R.* v. *Hamid* (1979) 69 Cr.App.R. 324, C.A.; *R.* v. *Rider* [1986] Crim.L.R. 626; (1986) 83 Cr.App.R. 207, C.A.
s. 15, repealed in pt.: 1977, c.38, sch.5.

26. Telephone Transfer Act 1911.
repealed: 1981, c.38, sch.6.

27. Protection of Animals Act 1911.
s. 1, amended: 1977, c.45, s.31, sch.6; 1986, c.14, sch.3; 1987, c.35, s.1; 1988, c.31, s.1.
s. 4, repealed: 1972, c.71, s.1, sch.6.
ss. 5A, 5B, added: 1988, c.29, s.2.
s. 8, amended: 1982, c.48, sch.6.
s. 15, see *Wastie* v. *Phillips* [1972] 3 All E.R. 302, D.C.; *Hudnott* v. *Campbell, The Times,* June 27, 1986, D.C.
s. 17, repealed: S.L.R. 1976.

28. Official Secrets Act 1911.
s. 1, see *R.* v. *Shulze and Shulze* (1988) 8 Cr.App.R.(S.) 463, C.A.
s. 2, see *R.* v. *Ponting* [1985] Crim.L.R. 318, C.C.C., McCowan J.; *Loat* v. *James* [1986] Crim.L.R. 744, D.C.; *R.* v. *Galvin* [1987] 3 W.L.R. 93, C.A.
s. 3, order 75/182.
s. 8, repealed in pt.: 1975, c.59, sch.6.

CAP.

1 & 2 Geo. 5 (1911)—cont.

28. Official Secrets Act 1911—cont.
s. 9, see *R.* v. *Prager* [1972] 1 W.L.R. 260; [1972] 1 All E.R. 1114, C.A.; *sub nom. R.* v. *Prager (Nicholas Anthony)* (1971) 56 Cr.App.R. 151.
s. 9, repealed in pt.: 1984, c.60, sch.6.
s. 10, repealed in pt.: 1973, c.55, sch.; 1975, c.62, sch.3.
s. 11, repealed in pt.: S.L.R. 1986.

32. Education (Administrative Provisions) Act 1911.
repealed: S.L.R. 1975.

39. Telegraph (Construction) Act 1911.
repealed: 1984, c.12, sch.7.

42. Merchant Shipping Act 1911.
repealed: S.L.R. 1986.

46. Copyright Act 1911.
see *Geographia* v. *Penguin Books* [1985] F.S.R. 208, Whitford J.; *Butterworth & Co.* v. *Ng Sui Nam; Longman Group* v. *Ng Sui Nam; Royal Academy of Music* v. *Ng Sui Nam* [1987] 2 F.T.L.R. 198, High Court of the Republic of Singapore.
s. 1, see *Computer Edge Pty.* v. *Apple Computer Inc.* [1986] F.S.R. 537, High Ct. of Australia; *Ashmore* v. *Douglas-Home* [1987] F.S.R. 553, Mervyn Davies Q.C.
ss. 1, 2, see *Standen Engineering* v. *Spalding (A.) & Sons* [1984] F.S.R. 554, Falconer J.
ss. 1, 5, see *Bauman* v. *Fussell* [1978] R.P.C. 485, C.A.; *Redwood Music* v. *Chappell & Co.* [1982] R.P.C. 109, Goff J.
s. 2, see *Sillitoe* v. *McGraw-Hill Book Co. (U.K.)* [1983] F.S.R. 545, H.H. Judge Mervyn Davies.
s. 5, see *James Arnold & Co.* v. *Miatern* [1980] R.P.C. 397, Paul Baker, Q.C.; *Chappell & Co.* v. *Redwood Music; Redwood Music* v. *Francis Day and Hunter* [1980] 2 All E.R. 817, H.L.
ss. 5, 16, 24, 35, see *Redwood Music* v. *B. Feldman & Co.* [1979] R.P.C. 385, C.A.
s. 15, order 87/698; regs. 87/918.
s. 15, amended: 1972, c.54, s.4; order 86/600.
s. 21, see *Barson Computers (N.Z.)* v. *Gilbert (John) & Co.* [1985] F.S.R. 489, New Zealand H.C.
s. 34, repealed: S.L.R. 1986.
s. 35, see *Chappell & Co.* v. *Redwood Music; Redwood Music* v. *Francis Day and Hunter* [1980] 2 All E.R. 817, H.L.; *Computer Edge Pty.* v. *Apple Computer Inc.* [1986] F.S.R. 537, High Ct. of Australia.
s. 37, repealed in pt.: S.L.R. 1986.

48. Finance Act 1911.
s. 18, repealed: 1975, c.7, sch.13.
ss. 21, 22 (in pt.), repealed: S.L.R. 1973.

49. Small Landholders (Scotland) Act 1911.
see *McDonald's Exr.* v. *North Uist Estates Trs.,* 1977 S.L.T. (Land Ct.) 10; *Clark* v. *Moffat's Exrs.,* 1982 S.L.C.R. 137.
s. 2, see *Fraser* v. *Van Arman,* 1982 S.L.C.R. 79.
s. 2, amended: regs. 77/2007.
s. 3, rules 76/96; 83/1058; rules of the Scottish Land Court; 77/657.

CAP.

1 & 2 Geo. 5 (1911)—cont.

49. Small Landholders (Scotland) Act 1911— cont.

s. 7, see *Secretary of State for Scotland* v. *Greig,* 1972 S.L.T.(Land Ct) 3; amended: regs. 77/2007.

s. 10, see *Arran Properties* v. *Currie,* 1983 S.L.C.R. 92.

s. 16, amended: regs. 77/2007.

s. 21, see *McGregor* v. *Garrow,* 1973 S.L.T. 3.

s. 25, repealed in pt.: 1976, c 21, sch.3.

s. 26, see *Gilmour* v. *Master of Lovat,* 1979 S.L.T.(Land Ct.) 2.

s. 26, amended: regs. 77/2007.

ss. 26, 32, see *Representatives of the late Hugh Matheson* v. *Master of Lovat,* 1984 S.L.C.R. 82.

s. 28, rules 79/379; 83/1058.

s. 32, amended: 1976, c.21, sch.3.

s. 33, amended: regs. 77/2007.

sch. 1, repealed in pt.: S.L.R. 1973; 1983, c.29, sch.3; S.L.R. 1986.

51. Burgh Police (Scotland) Amendment Act 1911.

repealed (31.12.1984): 1973, c.65, s.229; 1978, c.4, s.5; 1982, c.45, ss.134,135.

52. Rag Flock Act 1911.

s. 1, repealed in pt.: 1980, c.59, sch.

53. House Letting and Rating (Scotland) Act 1911.

repealed: 1973, c.65, sch.29.

57. Maritime Conventions Act 1911.

s. 8, see *The Norwhale; John Franetovich & Co. (Owners)* v. *Ministry of Defence* [1975] 2 W.L.R. 829; *The Albany and The Marie Josanne* [1983] 2 Lloyd's Rep. 195, Sheen J.; *Gaz Fountain, The* [1987] 1 F.T.L.R. 423, Sheen J.

2 & 3 Geo. 5 (1912–13)

8. Finance Act 1912.

repealed: 1975, c.7, sch.13.

10. Seal Fisheries (North Pacific) Act 1912.

s. 4, amended: 1979, c.2, sch.4.

13. London Institution (Transfer) Act 1912.

repealed: S.L.R. 1973.

14. Protection of Animals (Scotland) Act 1912.

s. 1, see *Patchett* v. *Macdougall,* 1984 S.L.T. 152; *Tudhope* v. *Ross,* 1986 S.C.C.R. 467.

s. 1, amended: 1986, c.14, sch.3; repealed in pt.: 1977, c.45, s.31, sch.6.

ss. 1A, 1B, added: 1988, c.29, s.2.

s. 4, repealed: 1980, c.62, sch 8.

s. 7, amended: 1982, c.48, sch.6.

s. 9, repealed in pt.: 1981, c.69, sch.17.

s. 13, repealed in pt.: 1975, c.20, sch.2.

15. Marriages in Japan (Validity) Act 1912.

repealed: 1988, c.44, sch.

17. Protection of Animals Act (1911) Amendment Act 1912.

repealed: 1987, c.35, s.2.

19. Light Railways Act 1912.

order 87/1443.

s. 6, amended (S.): 1984, c.54, sch.9.

20. Criminal Law Amendment Act 1912.

repealed: 1976, c.67, sch.2.

CAP.

2 & 3 Geo. 5 (1912–13)—cont.

28. Sheriff Courts (Scotland) Act 1913.

s. 6, repealed: 1980, c.55, s.11, sch.3.

30. Trade Union Act 1913.

s. 1, repealed in pt.: 1984, c.49, s.17.

s. 2, amended: 1974, c.52, sch.3.

s. 3, see *McCarthy* v. *Association of Professional Executive, Clerical and Computer Staff* [1979] I.R.L.R. 255, Certification Officer; *Parkin* v. *Association of Scientific, Technical and Managerial Staffs* [1980] I.C.R. 662; *Woolf J.; Reeves* v. *Transport and General Workers Union, The Times,* April 24, 1980, E.A.T.; *Coleman* v. *Post Office Engineering Union* [1981] I.R.L.R. 427, Certification Officer; *Richards* v. *National Union of Mineworkers and National Union of Mineworkers (Nottingham Area)* [1981] I.R.L.R. 247, Certification Officer; *Association of Scientific Technical and Managerial Staffs* v. *Parkin* [1984] I.C.R. 127, E.A.T.; *Paul & Fraser* v. *National and Local Government Officers' Association* [1987] I.R.L.R. 413, Browne-Wilkinson V.-C.

s. 3, amended: 1974, c.52, sch.3; 1975, c.71, sch.16; 1984, c.49, s.17; repealed in pt.: 1974, c.52, sch.3; 1975, c.71, sch.18.

s. 4, amended: 1974, c.52, sch.3; 1975, c.71, sch.16; 1984, c.49, s.13; regs. 84/1199; 1988, c.19, s.14, sch.3; repealed in pt.: 1974, c.52, schs.3,5; 1988, c.19, sch.4.

s. 5, amended: 1974, c.52, sch.3; 1975, c.71, sch.16.

s. 5A, added: *ibid.;* amended: 1978, c.44, sch.16.

s. 6, amended: 1974, c.52, sch.3; repealed in pt.: 1984, c.49, s.14.

s. 6A, added: 1974, c.52, sch.3.

s. 7, substituted: 1975, c.71, sch.16.

31. Pilotage Act 1913.

repealed: 1983, c.21, sch.4; S.L.R. 1986 (Isle of Man).

s. 7, orders 72/288; 74/965; 75/897, 1110; 76/748, 938, 1533, 1541, 1770, 1884, 2131; 77/719, 1147, 1366, 1396; 78/1540; 79/712, 1340; 80/95, 903, 1304; 81/193; 82/258, 414.

s. 11, see *McMillan* v. *Crouch* [1972] 1 W.L.R. 1102; [1972] 3 All E.R. 61; *Clayton* v. *Albertsen* [1972] 1 W.L.R. 1443; [1972] 3 All E.R. 364; *Jenkin* v. *Godwin; Godwin* v. *Jenkin; The Ignition* [1983] 1 Lloyd's Rep. 382, D.C.

s. 15, see *Esso Petroleum Co.* v. *Hall Russell & Co.,* 1988 S.L.T. 874.

ss. 23, 27, see *Jensen* v. *The Corporation of Trinity House; Schiller* v. *Same, The Times,* April 23, 1982, C.A.

ss. 30, 32, see *Montague* v. *Babbs* [1972] 1 W.L.R. 176; [1972] 1 All E.R. 240; [1972] 1 Lloyd's Rep. 65; *McMillan* v. *Crouch* [1972] 1 W.L.R. 1102; [1972] 3 All E.R. 61.

sch. 1, orders 81/193; 82/258, 414.

3 & 4 Geo. 5 (1913)

16. Foreign Jurisdiction Act 1913.

order 72/449.

sch., repealed in pt.: 1975, c.7, sch.13.

CAP.

3 & 4 Geo. 5 (1913)—cont.

17. Fabrics (Misdescription) Act 1913.
repealed: 1987, c.43, s.48, sch.5.
s. 1, regs. 80/726.

19. Local Government (Adjustments) Act 1913.
repealed: S.L.R. 1975.

20. Bankruptcy (Scotland) Act 1913.
repealed: 1985, c.6, sch.8.
s. 4, see *Grant's Tr.* v. *Grant* (O.H.), November 15, 1985.
s. 13, see *Burgh of Millport,* 1974 S.L.T. (Notes) 23 (O.H.).; *United Dominions Trust* v. *Dickson,* 1983 S.L.T. 572.
s. 17, see *West of Scotland Refractories,* 1969 S.C. 43.
s. 27, see *Hill* v. *Hill,* 1984 S.L.T.(Sh.Ct.) 21.
s. 29, see *The Royal Bank of Scotland* v. *Aitken,* 1985 S.L.T.(Sh.Ct.) 13; *James Finlay Corporation* v. *McCormack* (O.H.), 1986 S.L.T. 106.
s. 30, see *Murdoch* v. *Newman Industrial Control* (O.H.), 1980 S.L.T. 13.
s. 41, see *Cook's Tr., Petr.* (O.H.), 1985 S.L.T. 33.
s. 44, see *Law Society of Scotland,* 1974 S.L.T.(Notes) 66.
s. 45, regs. 77/1495.
s. 62, see *Clydesdale Bank* v. *Morison's Tr.,* Second Division, November 10, 1981.
s. 63, see *Law Society of Scotland,* 1974 S.L.T.(Notes) 66.
s. 88, see *Paxton* v. *H.M. Advocate,* 1984 S.L.T. 367.
s. 97, see *Robertson's Tr.* v. *Roberts* (O.H.), May 8, 1981; *Dickson* v. *United Dominions Trust* (O.H.), 1988 S.L.T. 19.
ss. 97, 107, see *Cook's Tr., Petr.* (O.H.) 1985 S.L.T. 33.
s. 98, see *Grindall* v. *John Mitchell (Grangemouth)* (O.H.), 1987 S.L.T. 137.
s. 143, see *Spark,* 1974 S.L.T.(Sh.Ct.) 9.
s. 189, repealed in pt.: 1985, c.54, sch.27.

27. Forgery Act 1913.
repealed: 1981, c.45, sch.
see *R.* v. *Donnelly (Ian), The Times,* May 18, 1984, C.A.
s. 1, see *R.* v. *Douce* [1972] Crim.L.R. 105; *R.* v. *Patel* (1973) 48 T.C. 647, C.A.; *R.* v. *Gambling* [1974] 3 All E.R. 479, C.A.; *R.* v. *Hiscox* (1978) 68 Cr.App.R. 411, C.A.; *R.* v. *Abdullah* [1982] Crim.L.R. 122, Croydon Crown Court.
s. 2, see *R.* v. *Vincent* (1972) 56 Cr.App.R. 281.
s. 3, see *Att.-Gen.'s Reference (No. 2 of 1980)* [1981] 1 W.L.R. 148; [1981] 1 All E.R. 493, C.A.; *R.* v. *Turner* (1980) 72 Cr.App.R. 117, C.A.
s. 4, see *R.* v. *Clemo (Note)* [1973] R.T.R. 176, C.A.
s. 6, see *R* v. *Patel* (1973) 48 T.C. 647, C.A.; *R.* v. *Hornett* [1975] R.T.R. 256, C.A.; *R.* v. *Hiscox* (1978) 68 Cr.App.R. 411, C.A.; *R.* v. *Turner* (1980) 72 Cr.App.R. 117, C.A.; *R.* v. *Terry, The Times,* December 23, 1983, H.L.
s. 7, see *R.* v. *Clemo (Note)* [1973] R.T.R. 176, C.A.; *R.* v. *Gambling* [1974] 3 All E.R. 479, C.A.; *R.* v. *Macer* [1979] Crim.L.R. 659, Courts-Martial Appeal Ct.; *R.* v. *Hagan* [1985] Crim.L.R. 598, C.A.

CAP.

3 & 4 Geo. 5 (1913)—cont.

27. Forgery Act 1913—*cont.*
s. 16, see *Frank Truman Export* v. *Metropolitan Police Commissioner* [1977] 3 W.L.R. 257, Swanwick J.; *R.* v. *Peterborough JJ., ex p. Hicks* [1977] 1 W.L.R. 1371, D.C.; *Reynolds* v. *Comr. of Police of the Metropolis* [1984] 3 All E.R. 649; [1984] Crim.L.R. 688, C.A.
s. 17, see *R.* v. *Hornett* [1975] R.T.R. 256, C.A.

32. Ancient Monuments Consolidation and Amendment Act 1913.
repealed: 1979, c.46, sch.5.

34. Bankruptcy and Deeds of Arrangement Act 1913.
s. 15, see *The Observer* v. *Gordon (Cranfield)* [1983] 2 All E.R. 945, Glidewell J.

36. Bishoprics of Sheffield, Chelmsford and for the County of Suffolk Act 1913.
repealed: S.L.R. 1973.

4 & 5 Geo. 5 (1914)

10. Finance Act 1914.
repealed: 1975, c.7, sch.13.
s. 14, see *Bunbury* v. *I.R.C.* [1972] 2 W.L.R. 177; [1972] 1 All E.R. 343.

18. Patents and Designs Act 1914.
repealed: 1986, c.39, sch.3.

30. Injuries in War (Compensation) Act 1914.
scheme 73/1635.
s. 1, schemes 72/1280; 74/1104; 77/1836; 81/1475; 85/299, 1566.

31. Housing Act 1914.
repealed: 1985, c.71, sch.1; 1987, c.26, sch.24(S.).

43. Entail (Scotland) Act 1914.
s. 9, repealed: S.L.R. 1974.

46. Milk and Dairies (Scotland) Act 1914.
s. 2, amended: 1973, c.65, sch.27.
s. 4, amended: 1972, c.58, sch.6; 1978, c.29, sch.5; repealed in pt.: 1972, c.58, sch.7.
s. 5, repealed: *ibid.*
s. 6, amended: *ibid.,* sch.6; 1978, c.29, sch.15; repealed in pt.: 1972, c.58, sch.7.
s. 7, repealed: *ibid.*
s. 12, orders 76/875, 1857, 1888.
s. 15, amended: 1972, c.58, sch.6; 1978, c.29, sch.15.
s. 16, substituted: 1972, c.58, sch.6; amended: 1978, c.29, sch.15.
s. 17, amended: 1972, c.58, sch.6; 1978, c.29, sch.15.
s. 18, amended: 1972, c.58, sch.6; 1978, c.29, sch.15; repealed in pt.: 1972, c.58, sch.7.
ss. 19, 20, amended: *ibid.,* sch.6; 1978, c.29, sch.15.
s. 21, amended: 1972, c.58, sch.6; 1978, c.29, sch.15; repealed in pt.: 1972, c.58, sch.6.
s. 28, repealed in pt.: 1973, c.65, schs.25, 29.
s. 31, amended: *ibid.,* sch.27; repealed in pt.: S.L.R. 1977.

47. Deeds of Arrangement Act 1914.
ss. 3, 11, amended: 1985, c.65, sch.8; 1986, c.45, sch.14.
ss. 13, 14, amended: 1985, c.65, sch.8.
ss. 15, 16, amended: *ibid.;* 1986, c.45, sch.14.

4 & 5 Geo. 5 (1914)—cont.

47. Deeds of Arrangement Act 1914—cont.
s. 19, amended. 1985, c.65, sch.8; repealed in pt.: ibid., sch.10.
s. 23, amended: ibid., sch.8; 1986, c.45, sch.14.
s. 24, repealed in pt.: 1985, c.65, sch.10.
s. 27, repealed: ibid.
s. 30, amended: ibid., sch.8; 1986, c.45, sch.14.
s. 31, repealed: S.L.R. 1977.

48. Feudal Casualties (Scotland) Act 1914.
s. 23, repealed in pt.: S.L.R. 1986.

58. Criminal Justice Administration Act 1914.
s. 19, amended: 1976, c.63. sch.2.
s. 28, repealed in pt.: 1984, c.60, sch.7.
s. 41, repealed: S.L.R. 1977.
s. 43, repealed in pt.: 1973, c.55, sch.

59. Bankruptcy Act 1914.
repealed: 1985, c.65, sch.10.
see Re A Debtor (No. 5982 of 1979); Re A Debtor (No. 5983 of 1979); Re A Debtor (No. 6006 of 1979) (1981) 125 S.J. 203, C.A.; Eyre v. Hall (1986) 18 H.L.R. 509, C.A.
order 77/350.
s. 1, see Re Cartwright, ex p. Cartwright v. Barker [1975] 1 W.L.R. 573, D.C.; Re A Debtor (No. 6864 of 1980); The Debtor v. Slater Walker [1981] 2 All E.R. 987, C.A.; Re Wheeler (A Debtor) [1982] 1 W.L.R. 175, C.A.; Re A Debtor (No. 138 of 1980), The Times, January 29, 1981, C.A.; Re A Debtor (No. 75 of 1982), ex p. The Debtor v. National Westminster Bank [1984] 1 W.L.R. 353, Ch.D.; James v. Amsterdan-Rotterdam Bank N.V. [1986] 3 All E.R. 179, D.C.
s. 2, see Re A Debtor [1973] 1 All E.R. 797, D.C.; Re Durrance, ex p. Durrance v. Hungerford R.D.C. [1973] 1 W.L.R. 738; Re Wheeler (A Debtor) (1981) 125 S.J. 843, C.A.
s. 4, see Re Brauch (A Debtor), ex p. Britannic Securities & Investments [1977] 3 W.L.R. 354, C.A.; Re A Debtor (No. 39 of 1974), ex p. Okill v. Gething [1977] 3 All E.R. 489, D.C.; Re A Debtor (No. 2 of 1977), ex p. The Debtor v. Goacher [1979] 1 All E.R. 870, D.C.; Hastings (A Bankrupt), Re [1985] 1 All E.R. 885, D.C.
ss. 4, 5, see Patel (A Debtor), Re [1986] 1 W.L.R. 221, D.C.
s. 5, see Re Field (A Debtor) [1977] 3 W.L.R. 937, D.C.; Orakpo v. I.R.C. [1977] T.R. 235, C.A.; Re A Debtor (No. 26 of 1982), The Times, October 25, 1983, D.C.
s. 7, see Ezekiel v. Orakpo [1976] 3 W.L.R. 693; [1976] 3 All E.R. 659, C.A.
s. 15, see Re A Debtor (No. 37 of 1976, Liverpool), ex p. Taylor v. The Debtor [1980] 1 All E.R. 129, D.C.
s. 25, see Re A Debtor (No. 26 of 1982), The Times, October 25, 1983, D.C.; Tucker, Re, sub nom. Tucker (A Bankrupt), ex p. Tucker, Re [1988] 1 FTLR 137, C.A.
s. 26, see Re Stern (A Bankrupt), ex p. Keyser Ullman v. The Bankrupt [1982] 2 All E.R. 600, C.A.; Waldron (A Bankrupt), Re, ex p. The Bankrupt v. The Official Receiver [1985] F.L.R. 164, C.A.

4 & 5 Geo. 5 (1914)—cont.

59. Bankruptcy Act 1914—cont.
s. 29, see Re A Debtor (No. 819 of 1970), ex p. Biart v. The Trustee of the Property of the Debtor [1974] 1 W.L.R. 1475; [1974] 3 All E.R. 502; Re Beesley (Audrey), ex p. Beesley (Terence Jack) v. Official Receiver [1975] 1 All E.R. 385, D.C.; Re A Debtor (No. 37 of 1976, Liverpool), ex p. Taylor v. The Debtor [1980] 1 All E.R. 129, D.C.
s. 30, see Re Clark (A Bankrupt), ex p. Trustee of the Property of the Bankrupt v. Texaco [1975] 1 All E.R. 453; Re Hurren (A Bankrupt), ex p. The Trustee v. I.R.C. [1982] 3 All E.R. 982, Walton J.; Re Islington Metal and Plating Works [1983] 3 All E.R. 218, Harman J.
s. 31, see National Westminster Bank v. Halesowen Presswork & Assemblies [1972] 2 W.L.R. 455; [1972] 1 All E.R. 641; Re D. H. Curtis (Builders) [1978] 2 W.L.R. 28, Templeman J.; Re Cushla [1979] 3 All E.R. 415, Vinelott J.; Willment Brothers v. North West Thames Regional Health Authority [1984] 26 Build.L.R. 51, C.A.; Farley v. Housing and Commercial Developments [1984] 26 Build.L.R. 66, Neill J.; Carreras Rothmans v. Freeman Mathews Treasure [1984] 3 W.L.R. 1016, Peter Gibson J.; Unit 2 Windows (in Liquidation), Re [1985] 1 W.L.R. 1383, Walton J.
s. 32, see Re Savundra [1973] 1 W.L.R. 1147; [1973] 3 All E.R. 406, D.C.
s. 33, see Re Rolls-Royce Co. [1974] 1 W.L.R. 1584; [1974] 3 All E.R. 646; Rudd & Son, Re [1984] 3 W.L.R. 831, Nourse J.
s. 33, repealed in pt.: 1985, c.58, sch.4.
s. 36, see Woodstock (A Bankrupt), November 19, 1979, Walton J.
s. 37, see Re Clark (A Bankrupt), ex p. Trustee of the Property of a Bankrupt v. Texaco [1975] 1 All E.R. 543; Re Salaman (A Bankrupt), The Times, October 20, 1983, C.A.
s. 40, see Re Green (A Bankrupt), ex p. Official Receiver v. Cutting [1979] 1 All E.R. 832, Walton J.
s. 41, see Marley Tile Co. v. Burrows [1977] 3 W.L.R. 641, C.A.; Re A Debtor (No. 2 of 1977), ex p. The Debtor v. Goacher [1979] 1 All E.R. 870, D.C.
s. 42, see Re Windle (A Bankrupt), ex p. Trustee of the Property of the Bankrupt v. The Bankrupt [1975] 1 W.L.R. 1628; [1975] 3 All E.R. 987; Re Davies (A Bankrupt); Trustee in Bankruptcy v. Davies, June 24, 1980; Judge Lewis; Gloucester County Ct.; Re Abbott (A Bankrupt), ex p. The Trustee of the Property of the Bankrupt v. Abbott (P.M.) [1982] 3 W.L.R. 86, D.C.
s. 44, see Re F.P. and C.H. Matthews [1982] 1 All E.R. 338, C.A.
s. 45, see Re Green (A Bankrupt), ex p. Official Receiver v. Cutting [1979] 1 All E.R. 832, Walton J.
s. 55, see Ramsey v. Hartley [1977] 1 W.L.R. 686, C.A.

CAP.

4 & 5 Geo. 5 (1914)—cont.

59. Bankruptcy Act 1914—cont.

ss. 55, 56, see Michaelides v. Bank of Cyprus (London), The Times, September 11, 1980, Browne-Wilkinson J.; Weddell v. Pearce (J. A.) and Major [1987] 3 W.L.R. 592, Scott J.

s. 56, see Re A Debtor (No. 26A of 1975) [1984] 3 All E.R. 995, Scott J.

s. 66, see Amalgamated Investment and Property Co., Re [1984] 3 All E.R. 272, Vinelott J.

s. 82, see Colgate,(A Bankrupt), Re, ex p. Trustee of the Property of the Bankrupt [1986] 2 W.L.R. 137, C.A.

s. 83, see Re A Debtor (No. 26A of 1975) [1984] 3 All E.R. 995, Scott. J.

s. 89, see Re Walker [1974] 1 W.L.R. 197; [1974] 1 All E.R. 551, C.A.

s. 93, see Singer v. Trustee of the Property of Munro (Bankrupt) [1981] 3 All E.R. 215, Walton J.

s. 96, orders 76/852; 77/151; 81/1624; 83/713; 84/297, 1075; 86/1361.

s. 100, see Re A Debtor (No. 2A of 1980, Colchester) [1980] 3 All E.R. 641, Goulding J.; Re A Debtor (No. 26A of 1975) [1984] 3 All E.R. 995, Scott J.

s. 105, see Re A Debtor (No. 819 of 1970), ex p. Biart v. The Trustee of the Property of the Debtor [1974] 1 W.L.R. 1475; [1974] 3 All E.R. 502; Colgate (A Bankrupt), Re, ex p. Trustee of the Property of the Bankrupt [1986] 2 W.L.R. 137, C.A.

s. 108, see Re A Debtor (No. 13 of 1964), ex p. Official Receiver and Trustee v. The Debtor [1979] 3 All E.R. 15, D.C.; Podbery v. Peak [1981] 1 All E.R. 699, C.A.; Re Toobman (A Bankrupt), The Times, March 3, 1982, Warner J.; Re Thomas, ex p. Inland Revenue Commissioners v. Falconer [1984] 1 W.L.R. 232, C.A.

s. 109, see Re A Debtor (No. 138 of 1980), The Times, January 29, 1981, C.A.; Re A Debtor (No. 6864 of 1980); The Debtor v. Slater Walker [1981] 2 All E.R. 987, C.A.; Re A Debtor (No. 26 of 1983); Re A Debtor (No. 72 of 1982) [1984] 2 All E.R. 257, D.C.

s. 113, orders 76/687; 80/1186.

s. 115, see Re Jones (E.D.) and Jones (C.V.), ex p. The Debtors v. Hallinan Blackburn Gittings & Co. (1982) 126 S.J. 482, D.C.

ss. 121–123, repealed: 1985, c.65, sch.10.

s. 122, see Re James (An insolvent) (Att.-Gen. invervening) [1977] 2 W.L.R. 1; Re A Debtor, Viscount of the Royal Court of Jersey v. The Debtor, The Times, May 21, 1980, Goulding J.; Tucker, Re [1988] F.L.R. 154, Isle of Man High Ct.

s. 132, rules 72/529; 73/715; 74/205, 1236; 75/213; 76/1932; 77/1394; 78/544, 1224; 79/1590; 80/2044; 82/441, 1148, 1437; 84/1371.

s. 133, orders 72/1054, 1189; 74/637, 2095; 78/1653; 79/780, 1589; 80/683; 81/1642; 82/541, 859, 1785; 83/775; 84/880; 85/1783; 86/2030.

CAP.

4 & 5 Geo. 5 (1914)—cont.

59. Bankruptcy Act 1914—cont.

s. 147, see Re Cartwright, ex p. Cartwright v. Barker [1975] 1 W.L.R. 573, D.C.

s. 148, repealed in pt.: 1985, c.54, sch.27.

s. 155, see R. v. Hartley [1972] 2 W.L.R. 101; [1972] 1 All E.R. 599; R. v. Haynt (1976) 63 Cr.App.R. 181, C.A.; R. v. Miller [1977] Crim.L.R. 562; [1977] 1 W.L.R. 1129, C.A.; Browne v. Phillips [1979] Crim.L.R. 381, D.C.; R. v. Godwin [1980] Crim.L.R. 426, C.A.; (1980) 71 Cr.App.R. 97, C.A.

s. 164, see Browne v. Phillips [1979] Crim.L.R. 381, D.C.

sch. 2, see Re Savundra [1973] 1 W.L.R. 1147; [1973] 3 All E.R. 406, D.C.

61. Special Constables Act 1914.

s. 1, S.Rs. 1977 No. 346; 1979 No. 412; 1980 No. 352; 1981 No. 322; 1982 Nos. 329, 374; 1983 Nos. 22, 306; 1985 No. 255; 1986 No. 279; 1987 No. 380; 1988 No. 391.

s. 4, S.R. 1978 No. 359.

64. Customs (Exportation Prohibition) Act 1914.

repealed: S.L.R. 1986.

76. Death Duties (Killed in War) Act 1914.

repealed: 1975, c.7, sch.13.

78. Courts (Emergency Powers) Act 1914.

repealed: S.L.R. 1976.

83. Army Pensions Act 1914.

repealed in pt.: 1981, c.55, s.26, sch.5.

s. 1, repealed in pt.: S.L.R. 1976.

5 & 6 Geo. 5 (1914–15)

1. Anglo-Portuguese Commercial Treaty Act 1914.

s. 1, repealed in pt.: S.L.R. 1975.

2. Customs (Exportation Restriction) Act 1914.

repealed: S.L.R. 1986.

18. Injuries in War Compensation Act 1914 (Session 2).

s. 1, schemes 75/265, 1696; 76/1461; 78/1629; 79/1506; 80/1731; 83/756, 1713; 86/1095; 87/529; 88/624.

28. Naval Medical Compassionate Fund Act 1915.

s. 1, order 88/1294.

40. Marriage of British Subjects (Facilities) Act 1915.

repealed (S.): 1977, c.15, sch.3.

45. British North America Act 1915.

Act renamed Constitution Act 1915 (Can.): 1982, c.11, sch.

s. 3, substituted: ibid.

48. Fishery Harbours Act 1915.

s. 2, repealed in pt.: S.L.R. 1986.

s. 3, repealed in pt.: 1972, c.70, sch.30.

49. Housing (Rosyth Dockyard) Act 1915.

repealed: S.L.R. 1977.

57. Prize Courts Act 1915.

s. 4, repealed: 1981, c.54, sch.7.

74. Police Magistrates (Superannuation) Act 1915.

repealed: 1973, c.15, sch.5.

CAP.

5 & 6 Geo. 5 (1914–15)—cont.

83. Naval and Military War Pensions, etc. Act 1915.
s. 3, amended: 1981, c.19, sch.2; repealed in pt.: *ibid.*, sch.1.

88. Street Collections Regulations (Scotland) Act 1915.
repealed: 1973, c.65, sch.29.

89. Finance (No. 2) Act 1915.
s. 45, repealed: S.L.R. 1974.
s. 48, repealed in pt.: S.L.R. 1986.

90. Indictments Act 1915.
see *R.* v. *Noe* [1985] Crim.L.R. 97, Snaresbrook Crown Court.
s. 3, see *R.* v. *Clifford*, March 10, 1988; H.H. Judge Croft Q.C. Maidstone Crown Ct.
s. 4, see *R.* v. *Barrell* (1979) 69 Cr.App.R. 250, C.A.; *R.* v. *Blackstock* (1979) 70 Cr.App.R. 34, C.A.; *R.* v. *Bell (Peter)* (1984) 78 Cr.App.R. 305, C.A.
s. 5, see *R.* v. *Johal* [1972] 3 W.L.R. 210; [1972] 2 All E.R. 449; 56 Cr.App.R. 348; *R.* v. *R. G. Radley*; *R.* v. *W. G. Radley*; *R.* v. *B. Radley* (1973) 58 Cr.App.R. 394, C.A.; *R.* v. *Harris* (1975) 62 Cr.App.R. 28, C.A.; *R.* v. *Walters*; *R.* v. *Tovey*; *R.* v. *Padfield* [1979] R.T.R. 220, C.A.; *R.* v. *Collison* (1980) 71 Cr.App.R. 249, C.A.; *R.* v. *Harward* (1981) 73 Cr.App.R. 168, C.A.; *R.* v. *Thomas* [1983] Crim.L.R. 619, C.A.; *R.* v. *McGlinchey* (1984) 78 Cr.App.R. 282, C.A.; *R.* v. *Phillips (D. M.)* (1988) 86 Cr.App.R. 18, C.A.; *R.* v. *Newland* [1988] 2 W.L.R. 382, C.A.
s. 5, amended: 1976, c.63, sch.2; repealed in pt.: 1985, c.23, sch.2.
ss. 5, 6, see *Practice Direction (Costs: Acquittal of Defendants)* [1981] 1 W.L.R. 1383, C.A.
s. 6, repealed in pt.: 1985, c.23, sch.2.
s. 8, repealed in pt.: 1977, c.45, sch.13.

93. War Loan (Supplemental Provisions) Act 1915.
s. 8, repealed in pt.: 1974, c.46, sch.11.

6 & 7 Geo. 5 (1916)

9. Pacific Islands Regulations (Validation) Act 1916.
repealed: S.L.R. 1986.

12. Local Government (Emergency Provisions) Act 1916.
s. 3, repealed: S.L.R. 1977.
s. 5, amended (S.): 1972, c.58, sch.6; 1978, c.29, sch.15.
ss. 6, 13, repealed: S.L.R. 1977.
ss. 21, 22, repealed in pt.: S.L.R. 1977.

13. Courts (Emergency Powers) (Amendment) Act 1916.
repealed: S.L.R. 1976.

18. Courts (Emergency Powers) (No. 2) Act 1916.
repealed: S.L.R. 1976.

21. Marriage of British Subjects (Facilities) Amendment Act 1916.
repealed (S.): 1977, c.15, sch.3.

24. Finance Act 1916.
s. 66, repealed in pt.: S.L.R. 1986.

CAP.

6 & 7 Geo. 5 (1916)—cont.

31. Police, Factories, etc. (Miscellaneous Provisions) Act 1916.
s. 3, repealed: S.L.R. 1973.
s. 5, see *Meaden* v. *Wood* [1985] Crim.L.R. 678, D.C.
s. 5, regs. 79/1230; 86/1696.
s. 5, amended: 1972, c.70, sch.29; 1973, c.65, sch.27(S.); repealed in pt. (S.): 1982, c.45, s.119, sch.4.

38. Small Holding Colonies Act 1916.
ss. 1, 4, 8, 9, 11, 12, repealed in pt.: S.L.R. 1973.
s. 3, repealed in pt : 1983, c.29, sch.3.
s. 7, repealed: S.L.R. 1973.

40. Telegraph (Construction) Act 1916.
repealed: 1984, c.12, sch.7.

46. Law and Procedure (Emergency Provisions) (Ireland) Act 1916.
repealed: 1978, c.23, sch.7.

50. Larceny Act 1916.
repealed (S.): 1975, c.21, sch.10.
ss. 32, 35, see *R.* v. *Fisher* (1975) 60 Cr.App.R. 225, C.A.

52. Trading with the Enemy and Export of Prohibited Goods Act 1916.
repealed: S.L.R. 1986.

58. Registration of Business Names Act 1916.
repealed: 1981, c.62, sch.4.
s. 8, see *Kennedy Contractors* v. *Connell*, 1977 S.L.T.(Sh.Ct.) 32; *Lawrence Vanger & Co.* v. *Company Developments (Property Division)* (1977) 243 E.G. 43, C.A.; *Thomas Montgomery & Sons* v. *W. B. Anderson & Sons* (O.H.), February 7, 1979.
s. 17, rules 77/537.

63. Defence of the Realm (Acquisition of Land) Act 1916.
ss. 10, 12, repealed in pt.: S.L.R. 1973.
s. 15, amended (S): 1984, c.54, sch.9.

64. Prevention of Corruption Act 1916.
see *R.* v. *Hirst and McNamee* (1975) 64 Cr.App.R. 151, C.A.
s. 1, repealed: 1988, c.33, sch.16.
s. 2, see *R.* v. *Joy and Emmony* (1974) 60 Cr.App.R. 132; *R.* v. *Mills* (1978) 68 Cr.App.R. 154, C.A.; *R.* v. *Wellburn, Nurdin and Randel* (1979) 69 Cr.App.R. 254, C.A.; *R.* v. *Braithwaite*; *R.* v. *Graham* [1983] 1 W.L.R. 385, C.A.
ss. 2, 4, see *D.P.P.* v. *Holly*; *D.P.P.* v. *Manners* [1977] 2 W.L.R. 178; [1977] 1 All E.R. 316, H.L.
s. 3, repealed: 1988, c.33, sch.16.

7 & 8 Geo. 5 (1917–18)

21. Venereal Disease Act 1917.
s. 2, repealed in pt.: order 77/2128.

31. Finance Act 1917.
s. 29, repealed: 1975, c.7, sch.13.
s. 30, repealed in pt.: 1985, c.54, sch.27.
s. 34, repealed: S.L.R. 1978.
s. 35, repealed: S.L.R. 1986.
s. 38, repealed in pt.: 1975, c.7, sch.13.

36. Police Constables (Naval and Military Service) Act 1917.
repealed: S.L.R. 1973.

CAP.

7 & 8 Geo. 5 (1917–18)—cont.

37. Naval and Military War Pensions etc. (Transfer of Powers) Act 1917.
repealed: S.L.R. 1981.

51. Air Force (Constitution) Act 1917.
s. 4, amended: 1981, c.55, sch.3.
s. 6, repealed in pt.: S.L.R. 1976.

55. Chequers Estate Act 1917.
sch. amended: 1986, c.5, sch.14.

57. Bishoprics of Bradford and Coventry Act 1918.
repealed: S.L.R. 1973.

58. Wills (Soldiers and Sailors) Act 1918.
s, 1, see *Re Rapley, decd.* [1983] 1 W.L.R. 1069, Finlay J.

64. Representation of the People Act 1918.
repealed: 1985, c.50, sch.5.
s. 21, repealed in pt.: *ibid.*, s.28.

8 & 9 Geo. 5 (1918)

15. Finance Act 1918.
repealed: S.L.R. 1986.

24. Flax Companies (Financial Assistance) Act 1918.
repealed S.L.R. 1986.

39. Education Act 1918.
s. 14, repealed: 1973, c.16, sch.2.
ss. 47, 52, amended: *ibid.*

57. War Pensions (Administrative Provisions) Act 1918.
ss. 8, 9, 18, repealed: 1981, c.19, sch.1.

59. Termination of the Present War (Definition) Act 1918.
repealed: S.L.R. 1978.

9 & 10 Geo. 5 (1919)

20. Scottish Board of Health Act 1919.
s. 4, repealed in pt.(S.): 1977, c.15, sch.3.
sch. 1, repealed in pt.: S.L.R. 1978.

23. Anthrax Prevention Act 1919.
repealed: regs. 74/1775.
ss. 2, 3, repealed: order 78/1039.

32. Finance Act 1919.
s. 8, repealed: 1978, c.42, sch.13
Pt. III, sch. 3, repealed: 1975, c.7, sch.13.
s. 38, repealed in pt.: *ibid.*; 1978, c.42, sch.13.

33. Treaty of Peace Act 1919.
repealed: S.L.R. 1976.

35. Housing, Town Planning, & etc. Act 1919.
repealed: 1985, c.71, sch.1.

37. War Loan Act 1919.
repealed: S.L.R. 1986.

45. Housing (Ireland) Act 1919.
Pt. I, except ss. 26, 33, repealed: order 81/156.
s. 6, S.Rs. 1978 No. 22; 1979 No. 379.

50. Ministry of Transport Act 1919.
repealed: order 80/1085.
sch. 2, repealed (S): 1984, c.54, sch.9.

51. Checkweighing in Various Industries Act 1919.
repealed: 1986, c.48, schs.1,5.

53. War Pensions (Administrative Provisions) Act 1919.
s. 8, sch., repealed in pt.: S.L.R. 1986.

CAP.

9 & 10 Geo. 5 (1919)—cont.

57. Acquisition of Land (Assessment of Compensation) Act 1919.
repealed: order 82/712.
s. 8, see *J. & A. Massie* v. *Aberdeen Corporation,* 1974 S.L.T.(Lands Tr.) 13.

59. Land Settlement (Facilities) Act 1919.
s. 2, amended: 1981, c.67, sch.4; 1986, c.5, sch.14.
s. 7, repealed: 1977, c.30, sch.2.
s. 9, amended: 1972, c.70, sch.29; repealed in pt.: 1977, c.30, sch.2.
s. 11, amended: 1986, c.5, sch.14.
ss. 12, 17, amended: 1972, c.70, sch.29.
s. 22, repealed in pt.: 1980, c.65, schs.5,34.
s. 27, amended: 1986, c.5, sch.14.
sch. 1, repealed in pt.: 1972, c.70, sch.30.

60. Housing, Town Planning, etc. (Scotland) Act 1919.
repealed: S.L.R. 1981.

62. British Mercantile Marine Uniform Act 1919.
s. 2, substituted: 1988, c.48, sch.7.

69. Industrial Courts Act 1919.
ss. 1–3, 4 (in pt.), repealed: 1975, c.71, sch.16.
s. 7, amended: 1974, c.52, sch.3; repealed in pt.: 1975, c.71, schs.16, 18.
s. 8, substituted: 1982, c.46, sch.3.
s. 9, amended: 1974, c.52, sch.3; repealed in pt.: 1975, c.71, schs.16,18.
ss. 10, substituted: 1975, c.71, sch.16.
ss. 11, 12, repealed: *ibid.*, sch.18.

71. Sex Disqualification (Removal) Act 1919.
ss. 1, 4, repealed in pt.: 1972, c.71, sch.6; order 74/2143; 1975, c.21, sch.10; 1980, c.55, sch.3(S.).

75. Ferries (Acquisition by Local Authorities) Act 1919.
s. 1, repealed in pt.: 1972, c.70, s.186, sch.30.

80. Patents and Designs Act 1919.
s. 10, see *Codex Corp.* v. *Racal-Milgo* [1983] R.P.C. 369, C.A.
s. 19, see *Allibert S.A.* v. *O'Connor* [1981] F.S.R. 613, Costello J.

82. Irish Land (Provision for Sailors and Soldiers) Act 1919.
s. 4, repealed: 1987, c.48, sch.

92. Aliens Restriction (Amendment) Act 1919.
s. 4, repealed: 1979, c.39., sch.7.
s. 8, repealed: 1972, c.71, sch.6; 1980, c.55, sch.3(S.).
s. 13, repealed in pt.: S.L.R. 1975.

97. Land Settlement (Scotland) Act 1919.
s. 6, amended: 1976, c.21, sch.2.
s. 18, amended: 1973, c.65, sch.27; repealed in pt.: *ibid.*, sch.29.
s. 24, repealed in pt.: *ibid.*

100. Electricity (Supply) Act 1919.
s. 11, repealed: 1983, c.25, s.1, sch.4.
s. 21, substituted: 1986, c.63, s.44; 1988, c.4, sch.3
s. 22, see *Christian Salvesen (Properties)* v. *Central Electricity Generating Board* (1984) 48 P. & C.R. 465, Lands Tribunal, V. G. Wellings Esq., Q.C.
s. 22, amended: 1981, c.38, sch.3; 1984, c.12, sch.4; c.54, sch.9(S.).

CAP.

9 & 10 Geo. 5 (1919)—cont.

100. Electricity (Supply) Act 1919—cont.
s. 25, repealed. 1984, c.12, sch.7.
s. 36, repealed in pt.: 1983, c.25, sch.4.

101. Government of India Act 1919.
repealed: S.L.R. 1976.

10 & 11 Geo. 5 (1920)

2. Merchant Shipping (Amendment) Act 1920.
s. 1, amended: 1988, c.12, sch.6.

5. War Emergency Laws (Continuance) Act 1920.
repealed: S.L.R. 1978.

8. House Letting and Rating (Scotland) Act 1920.
repealed: 1973, c.65, sch.29.

16. Imperial War Museum Act 1920.
ss. 2, 3, sch., functions transferred: orders 81/207; 86/600.
sch., amended and repealed in pt.: 1973, c.48, s.4; order 88/253.

17. Increase of Rent and Mortgage Interest (Restrictions) Act 1920.
repealed: order 78/1050.
s. 12, see Dyson Holdings v. Fox [1975] 3 W.L.R. 744, C.A.

18. Finance Act 1920.
s. 36, repealed: S.L.R. 1976.
s. 37, repealed: 1974, c.30, sch.14; 1976, c.40, sch.15.
s. 39, repealed: 1973, c.51, sch.22.
s. 42, amended: ibid., sch.21; 1980, c.48, s.100; repealed in pt.: 1986, c.41, s.85, sch.23.

23. War Pensions Act 1920.
s. 9, repealed: S.L.R. 1981.

27. Nauru Island Agreement Act 1920.
repealed: S.L.R. 1986.

33. Maintenance Orders (Facilities for Enforcement) Act 1920.
repealed: 1972, c.18, s.22.
s. 3, see Collister v. Collister [1972] 1 W.L.R. 54; [1972] 1 All E.R. 334.
s. 3, amended: 1978, c.22, sch.2; 1979, c.55, sch.2.
s. 6, amended: 1987, c.42, sch. 2.

41. Census Act 1920.
s. 1, order 80/702.
s. 3, regs. 80/897, 904.
s. 9, regs. 80/904.
s. 9, amended: 1973, c.65, s.168.

45. Public Libraries (Scotland) Act 1920.
repealed: 1973, c.65, schs.21,29.

50. Mining Industry Act 1920.
sch. 2, repealed: S.L.R. 1973.

51. Duchy of Lancaster Act 1920.
s. 2, repealed: 1988, c.10, sch.
s. 3, repealed in pt.: S.L.R. 1981.

53. Jurors (Enrolment of Women) (Scotland) Act 1920.
repealed: 1985, c.73, sch.4.

54. Seeds Act 1920.
licence 73/1032.
s. 1, licence 73/1117.
s. 7, regs. 73/944; 74/897; 78/215
ss. 12 (in pt.), 13 (in pt.), 16, repealed: S.L.R. 1973.

CAP.

10 & 11 Geo. 5 (1920)—cont.

55. Emergency Powers Act 1920.
s. 1, regs. 73/2089; 74/33, 350.
s. 2, regs 72/157, 1164; 73/1881; 74/175.
s. 2, amended: 1982, c.48, s.41; repealed in pt.: S.L.R. 1986.

64. Married Women's Property (Scotland) Act 1920.
repealed: 1985, c.37, sch.2.
s. 5, repealed in pt.: 1985, c.66, sch.8.

65. Employment of Women, Young Persons and Children Act 1920.
ss. 1, 3, 4, sch., repealed in pt.: S.L.R. 1978.

67. Government of Ireland Act 1920.
ss. 1 (in pt.) 4–6, 8 (in pt.), repealed: 1973, c.36, sch.6.
s. 10, see D.P.P. v. McNeill [1975] N.I. 177, C.A.
ss. 11–19, 20 (in pt.), 21 (in pt.), 22–25, 26 (in pt.), repealed: 1973, c.36, sch.6.
s. 28, repealed: 1975, c.7, sch.13.
ss. 31, 32, 34, 37, repealed: 1973, c.36, sch.6.
ss. 38, 40, 41 (in pt.), 44, repealed: 1978, c.23, sch.7.
s. 45, repealed: 1973, c.36, sch.6.
s. 46, repealed: 1978, c.23, sch.7.
s. 47, repealed: 1973, c.36, sch.6.
s. 50, repealed: 1978, c.23, sch.7.
ss. 51–53, repealed: 1973, c.36, sch.6.
s. 56, repealed: 1972, c.11, s.27, sch.8.
ss. 61 (in pt.), 62, 63, repealed: 1973, c.36, sch.6.
s. 64, repealed in pt.: ibid.; order 81/610.
ss. 65 (in pt.), 67, 69, 70, 73, 74 (in pt.), 75 (in pt.), schs.3–6, repealed: 1973, c.36, sch.6.
sch. 7, repealed: 1978, c.23, sch.7.

72. Roads Act 1920.
s. 4, sch. 1, repealed: order 80/1085.
s. 19, repealed in pt.: S.L.R. 1975.

75. Official Secrets Act 1920.
s. 1, repealed in pt.: 1981, c.45, sch.
s. 4, repealed: 1985, c.56, s.11.
s. 5, amended: 1981, c.38, sch.3.; 1984, c.12, sch.4.
s. 7, see R. v. Bingham [1973] 2 W.L.R. 520, C.A.
s. 8, see Att.-Gen. v. Leveller Magazine [1979] 2 W.L.R. 247, H.L.
s. 11, repealed in pt.: S.L.R. 1976.

81. Administration of Justice Act 1920.
s. 10, substituted: 1982, c.27, s.35.
ss. 11, 12, repealed in pt.: 1978, c.23, sch.7.
s. 14, orders 84/129; 85/1994.
s. 14, amended: 1982, c.27, s.37.

11 & 12 Geo. 5 (1921)

16. Importation of Plumage (Prohibition) Act 1921.
repealed: 1976, c.72, s.13

18. Indian Divorces (Validity) Act 1921.
repealed: S.L.R. 1975.

19. Housing Act 1921.
s. 10, repealed in pt.: 1973, c.36, sch.6.

28. Merchant Shipping Act 1921.
s. 1, repealed in pt.: 1979, c.39, sch.7.
s. 2, amended: ibid., sch.6.

CAP.

11 & 12 Geo. 5 (1921)—cont.

30. Coroners Act 1921.
repealed: S.L.R. 1977.

32. Finance Act 1921.
s. 17, repealed: S.L.R. 1986.
Pt. IV, s. 63, repealed: 1975, c.7, sch.13.
s. 65, repealed in pt.: *ibid.*
sch. 3, regs. 82/1829.
sch.3, amended: 1982, c.41, s.4, repealed in pt.: 1985, c.54, sch.27; c.58, sch.4.

35. Corn Sales Act 1921.
s. 1, repealed: 1972, c.62, s.17, sch.6.
s. 5, amended: regs. 79/357.

37. Territorial Army and Militia Act 1921.
repealed: 1980, c.9, sch.10.

49. War Pensions Act 1921.
s. 1, orders 75/1607; 80/1685; 85/1544.
ss. 1 (in pt.), 2 (in pt.), 3 (in pt.), 4, 6 (in pt.), 9 (in pt.), repealed: S.L.R. 1986.

50. Criminal Procedure (Scotland) Act 1921.
repealed: 1975, c.21, sch.10.
s. 2, see *H.M. Advocate* v. *Stern*, 1974 S.L.T. 2.

52. Exchequer and Audit Departments Act 1921.
s. 1, amended: 1983, c.44, s.11; repealed in pt.: *ibid.* s.11, sch.5.
s. 3, order 84/1078.
s. 3, amended: 1983, c.44, s.12; repealed in pt.: *ibid.*, s.12, sch.5.
s. 8, repealed in pt.: S.L.R. 1975; 1983, c.44, sch.5.

55. Railways Act 1921.
ss. 14, 68 (in pt.), 70 (in pt.), 71 (in pt.), 86 (in pt.), schs. 3, 9, repealed: S.L.R. 1978.
Pt. V (ss. 68–74), orders 87/1088, 1443.
s. 70, repealed: S.L.R. 1986.
s. 73, amended (S.): 1984, c.54, sch.9.

58. Trusts (Scotland) Act 1921.
s. 2, see *Fraser, Petr.* (O.H.), 1987, S.C.L.R. 577.
s 2, amended: 1986, c.9, sch.1; repealed in pt.: S.L.R. 1976.
s. 3, see *Kennedy, Petr.*, 1983 S.L.T.(Sh.Ct.) 10.
s. 13, repealed in pt.: S.L.R. 1977.
ss. 22–24, amended: 1980, c.55, s.13.
s. 29A, added: *ibid.*

65. Trade Facilities Act 1921.
repealed: S.L.R. 1974.

67. Local Authorities (Financial Provisions) Act 1921.
repealed: S.L.R. 1975.

12 & 13 Geo. 5 (1922)

10. Kenya Divorces (Validity) Act 1922.
repealed: S.L.R. 1975.

11. Forces Act 1922.
repealed: 1972, c.71, sch.6.

13. Empire Settlement Act 1922.
repealed: S.L.R. 1976.

16. Law of Property Act 1922.
sch. 15, see *Caerphilly Concrete Products* v. *Owen* [1972] 1 W.L.R. 372; *sub nom. Hopkins' Lease, Re; Caerphilly Concrete Products* v. *Owen* [1972] 1 All E.R. 248; *Marjorie Burnett* v. *Barclay, The Times,* December 19. 1980, Nourse J.

CAP.

12 & 13 Geo. 5 (1922)—cont.

17. Finance Act 1922.
s. 45, repealed: 1975, c.7, sch.13.

22. Summer Time Act 1922.
repealed: 1972, c.6, s.6.

34. Whale Fisheries (Scotland) Amendment Act 1922.
repealed: 1981, c.29, sch.5.

35. Celluloid and Cinematograph Film Act 1922.
s. 2, amended: 1985, c.13, sch.2.
s. 9, amended: 1972, c.70, sch.29; 1985, c.51, sch.11.
s. 10, amended (S.): 1973, c.65, sch.27.
s. 11, amended (S.): *ibid.*; repealed in pt.: 1972, c.70, sch.30.

46. Electricity (Supply) Act 1922.
s. 23, repealed: 1983, c.25, s.17, sch.4.
s. 25, amended: 1981, c.38, sch.3; 1984, c.12, sch.4.

50. Expiring Laws Act 1922.
repealed: S.L.R. 1977.

51. Allotments Act 1922.
s. 2, repealed in pt.: S.L.R. 1973.
s. 3, amended: 1986, c.5, sch.14.
s. 8, repealed in pt.: 1972, c.70, sch.30.
s. 9, repealed: 1977, c.30, sch.2.
s. 11, amended: 1986, c.5, sch.14.
s. 14, repealed: 1972, c.70, sch.30.
s. 20, repealed: 1980, c.65, schs.5,34.

52. Allotments (Scotland) Act 1922.
s. 2, repealed in pt.: S.L.R. 1974.
ss. 7, 10, amended: 1973, c.65, sch.27.
s. 16, repealed: *ibid.*, sch.29.
s. 19, amended: *ibid.*. sch.27.

54. Milk and Dairies (Amendment) Act 1922.
s. 2, amended(S.): 1973, c.65, sch.27.
ss. 3, 6, orders 75/1997; 80/1886(S.); 83/939, 1527; 86/788(S.); 1816(S.).
s. 6, orders 76/875, 1857.
s. 14, amended(S.): 1973, c.65, sch.27.

56. Criminal Law Amendment Act 1922.
repealed: 1976, c.67, sch.2.

13 Geo. 5, Sess. 2 (1922)

2. Irish Free State (Consequential Provisions) Act 1922.
s. 2, repealed in pt.: S.L.R. 1975.
s. 3, repealed: 1987, c.48, sch.
sch. 1, repealed: 1978, c.23, sch.7.

4. Trade Facilities and Loans Guarantee Act 1922 (Sess. 2).
repealed: S.L.R. 1977.

13 & 14 Geo. 5 (1923)

4. Fees (Increase) Act 1923.
s. 2, repealed in pt.: 1988, c.12, sch.7.
s. 5, repealed: 1981, c.62, sch.4.
s. 7, order 78/239; amended: orders 76/138, 501; 77/2140; 79/1258; 81/1739; 82/364.
s. 8, orders 72/1677; 73/597, 1082; 75/806, 2161; 76/215, 1151; 77/46; 78/177; regs. 78/692; 79/875.
s. 8, repealed: 1980, c.23, s.1.

CAP.

13 & 14 Geo. 5 (1923)—cont.

8. Industrial Assurance Act 1923.
s. 3, amended: 1974, c.46, sch.9.
s. 4, repealed in pt.: ibid., sch.11.
s. 7, amended: 1982, c.53, s.46.
s. 8, amended: 1974, c.46, sch.9.
s. 16, repealed in pt.: 1980, c.25, sch.5.
s. 18, amended: 1973, c.58, sch.2.
s. 20, amended: 1974, c.46, sch.9.
s. 36, repealed in pt.: ibid., sch.11.
s. 43, regs. 74/1306; 76/341; 79/1549; 80/1740; 81/1754; 83/373; 84/280; 85/338; 86/608; 87/377; 88/453.
s. 43, repealed in pt.: S.L.R. 1986.

11. Special Constables Act 1923.
s. 3, amended and repealed in pt.: 1987, c.4, s.7.

14. Finance Act 1923.
s. 13, repealed: S.L.R. 1977.
s. 39, repealed in pt.: S.L.R. 1976.

15. Alderney (Transfer of Property etc.) Act 1923.
s. 1, order 87/1273.

16. Salmon and Freshwater Fisheries Act 1923.
repealed: 1975, c.51, sch.5.
ss. 37, 38, orders 72/11, 192, 340, 715; 74/591.
s. 38, orders 74/786, 805, 1131.

17. Explosives Act 1923.
s. 3, repealed: regs 74/1885.
s. 4, repealed: order 87/37.

18. War Memorials (Local Authorities' Powers) Act 1923.
s. 2, repealed: 1972, c.70, schs.29,30.
s. 4, repealed in pt.: S.L.R. 1976.

20. Mines (Working Facilities and Support) Act 1923.
s. 3, see BP Development, Re, Financial Times, February 26, 1986, Warner J.

24. Housing, etc., Act 1923.
repealed: 1985, c.71, sch.1.
repealed (S.): S.L.R. 1981.

27. Railway Fires Act (1905) Amendment Act 1923.
s. 1, repealed: 1981, c.56, sch.12.
s. 2, repealed in pt.: ibid., s.38, sch.12.
s. 4, repealed: S.L.R. 1978.

33. Universities of Oxford and Cambridge Act 1923.
ss. 2–4, repealed: S.L.R. 1978.

34. Agricultural Credits Act 1923.
ss. 3 (in pt.), 4, 5 (in pt.), sch., repealed: S.L.R. 1973.

14 & 15 Geo. 5 (1924)

8. Trade Facilities Act 1924.
repealed: S.L.R. 1977.
s. 24, see Mulheron and Others, Petitioners, 1977 S.L.T.(Sh.Ct.) 65.

11. Friendly Societies Act 1924.
repealed: 1974, c.46, sch.11.

15. Auxiliary Air Force and Air Force Reserve Act 1924.
repealed: S.L.R. 1976.

16. Small Debt (Scotland) Act 1924.
repealed: S.L.R. 1981.

CAP.

14 & 15 Geo. 5 (1924)—cont.

17. County Courts Act 1924.
repealed: 1981, c.54, sch.7.

22. Carriage of Goods by Sea Act 1924.
sch., see Ismail v. Polish Ocean Lines [1976] 2 W.L.R. 477; [1976] 1 All E.R. 902, C.A.; Actis Co. v. Sanko Steamship Co. [1982] 1 W.L.R. 119, C.A.

27. Conveyancing (Scotland) Act 1924.
s. 6, repealed: 1985, c.54, sch.27.
ss. 16, 17, repealed: 1973, c.52, sch.5.
s. 23, repealed in pt.: 1982, c.27, sch.14.
s. 44, amended: 1985, c.66, sch.7; c.73, sch.2; repealed in pt.: 1985, c.66, sch.8.
s. 46, amended: 1985, c.73, sch.2.

35. Housing (Financial Provisions) Act 1924.
repealed: S.L.R. 1981.
ss. 2, 3, see Pollock v. Glasgow Corporation, 1973 S.L.T. 77.

15 & 16 Geo. 5 (1924–25)

2. Canals (Continuance of Charging Powers) Act 1924.
repealed: S.L.R. 1973.

3. Irish Free State Land Purchase (Loan Guarantee) Act 1924.
repealed: S.L.R. 1976.

5. Law of Property (Amendment) Act 1924.
sch. 9, repealed in pt.: 1985, c.71, sch.1.

9. Anglo-Italian Treaty (East African Territories) Act 1925.
repealed: S.L.R. 1973.

18. Settled Land Act 1925.
s. 1, see Re Buttle's Will Trusts [1976] 3 All E.R. 289; [1976] S.T.C. 393, D.C.
s. 7, see Leicester v. Wells-next-the-Sea U.D.C. [1972] 3 W.L.R. 486; [1972] 3 All E.R. 77.
s. 42, see Harrison v. Wing [1988] 29 E.G. 101, C.A.
s. 56, amended: 1980, c.66, sch.24.
s. 64, see Raikes v. Lygon [1988] 1 W.L.R. 281, Peter Gibson J.
s. 73, amended: 1986, c.5, sch.14.
s. 103, amended: 1985, c.65, sch.8.
s. 113, amended: orders 77/600; 81/1123; 1982, c.53, sch.3; 1984, c.28, sch.2.

19. Trustee Act 1925.
s. 15, see Re Earl of Strafford (decd.); Royal Bank of Scotland v. Byng [1979] 1 All E.R. 513, C.A.
s. 16, see Moores v. Moores (1974) 232 E.G. 335.
s. 31, see Re Sharp's Settlement Trusts [1972] 3 W.L.R. 765; 116 S.J. 666; [1972] 3 All E.R. 151; Kenny v. Cunningham-Reid, The Times, November 15, 1983; Re Delamere's Settlement Trusts [1984] 1 All E.R. 584, C.A.; Swales v. I.R.C. [1984] 3 All E.R. 16, Nicholls J.
s. 32, see Re Hastings-Bass (Deceased); Hastings v. I.R.C. [1974] 2 W.L.R. 904; [1974] 2 All E.R. 193; [1974] S.T.C. 211, C.A.; Henley v. Wardell, The Times, January 29, 1988, John Mowbray Q.C.

CAP.

15 & 16 Geo. 5 (1924–25)—cont.

19. Trustee Act 1925—cont.

s. 33, see *Re Gordon's Will Trusts; National Westminster Bank* v. *Gordon* [1976] 2 All E.R. 577; *Moore* v. *I.R.C.: Re Trafford's Settlement* [1984] 1 All E.R. 1108, Peter Gibson J.

s. 33, amended: 1987, c.42, sch. 2.

s. 36, see *Re Crowhurst Park; Sims-Hilditch* v. *Simmons* [1974] 1 All E.R. 991.

ss. 36, 41, amended: 1983, c.20, sch.4.

s. 44, see *Jones* v. *Jones* [1971] 3 All E.R. 1201.

s. 54, rules 82/322; 84/2035.

ss. 54, 55, amended: 1983, c.20, sch.4.

s. 57, see *Mason* v. *Farbrother* [1983] 2 All E.R. 1078, H.H. Judge Blackett-Ord; *Thompson* v. *Thompson, The Times*, February 14, 1985, C.A.

s. 61, see *Re Rosenthal* [1972] 1 W.L.R. 1273; 116 S.J. 666; [1972] 3 All E.R. 552; *Bartlett* v. *Barclays Bank Trust Co.* [1980] 1 All E.R. 139, Brightman J.

s. 63A, added: 1984, c.28, sch.2.

s. 69, see *Trustees of the British Museum* v. *Att.-Gen., The Times*, October 25, 1983, Sir Robert Megarry, V.C.; *Re Delamere's Settlement Trusts* [1984] 1 All E.R. 584, C.A.

s. 69, sch. 1, repealed in pt.: S.L.R. 1978.

20. Law of Property Act 1925.

s. 3, amended: 1984, c.28, sch.2; repealed in pt.: 1987, c.15, s.8, sch.

ss. 3, 7, see *Rowhook Mission Hall, Horsham, Chaning Pearce* v. *Morris; Ladypool Road, Old National School, Birmingham, Re; Birmingham Diocesan Board of Finance* v. *Russell* [1984] 3 W.L.R 710, Nourse J.

s. 7, repealed in pt.: 1987, c.15, sch.

s. 14, see *City of London Building Society* v. *Flegg* [1987] 2 W.L.R. 1266, H.L.

ss. 16–18, repealed: 1975, c.7, sch.13.

s. 17, amended: order 75/1455.

s. 22, amended: 1983, c.20, sch.4.

s. 28, see *Harrison* v. *Wing* [1988] 29 E.G. 101, C.A.

s. 30, see *Re McCarthy, a Bankrupt, ex p. Trustee of the Property of the Bankrupt* v. *McCarthy* [1975] 1 W.L.R. 807; *Bizz* v. *Bizz* (1975) 6 Fam.Law 56, C.A.; *Williams* v. *Williams* [1976] 3 W.L.R. 494, C.A.; *Ward* v. *Ward and Green (Note)* [1980] 1 W.L.R. 4; [1980] 1 All E.R. 176, C.A.; *Re Holliday (A Bankrupt), ex p. Trustee of the Bankrupt* v. *The Bankrupt* [1980] 3 All E.R. 385, C.A.; *Evers' Trust, Re.; Papps* v. *Evers* [1980] 1 W.L.R. 1327; [1980] 3 All E.R. 399, C.A.; *Re Lowrie (A Bankrupt), ex p Trustee of the Bankrupt* v. *the Bankrupt* [1981] 3 All E.R. 353, D.C.; *Dennis* v. *McDonald* [1982] 2 W.L.R. 275, C.A.; *Stott* v. *Ratcliffe* [1982] 126 S.J. 310, C.A.; *Bernard* v. *Josephs* [1982] 2 W.L.R. 1052, C.A.; *Norman* v. *Norman* (1983) 13 Fam.Law 17, Wood J.; *Walker* v. *Hall* (1984) 14 Fam.Law 21, C.A.; *First National Securities* v. *Hegerty, The Times*, July 17, 1984, C.A; *Thompson* v. *Thompson,*

CAP.

15 & 16 Geo. 5 (1924–25)—cont.

20. Law of Property Act 1925—cont.

The Times, February 14, 1985, C.A.; *Singh* v. *Singh* (1985) Fam.Law 97, Anthony Lincoln J.. *Mott, Re, ex p. Trustee of the Property of the Bankrupt* v. *Mott and McQuitty*, March 30, 1987, Hoffmann J.; *Midland Bank* v. *Pike* [1988] 2 All E.R. 434, Nugee Q.C.

s. 30, amended: 1984, c.28, sch.2.

ss. 34–36, see *Goodman* v. *Gallant, The Times*, November 7, 1985, C.A.

s. 36, see *Nielson-Jones* v. *Fedden* [1974] 3 All E.R. 38; *Burgess* v. *Rawnsley* [1975] 3 W.L.R. 99, C.A.; *Bernard* v. *Josephs* [1982] 2 W.L.R. 1052, C.A.; *Harris* v. *Goddard* [1983] 3 All E.R. 242, C.A.; *Young* v. *Young* (1984) 14 Fam.Law 271, C.A.

s. 40, see *Law* v. *Jones* [1973] 2 W.L.R. 994; [1973] 2 All E.R. 437; *Hardy* v. *Elphick* [1973] 2 W.L.R. 824; [1973] 2 All E.R. 914; *Richards* v. *Creighton Griffiths (Investments)* (1972) 225 E.G. 2104; *Steadman* v. *Steadman* [1974] 3 W.L.R. 56; [1974] 2 All E.R. 977, H.L.; *Tiverton Estates* v. *Wearwell* [1974] 1 All E.R. 209, C.A.; *Liddell* v. *Hopkinson* (1974) 233 E.G. 513; *New Hart Builders* v. *Brindley* [1975] 2 W.L.R. 595; [1975] 1 All E.R. 1007; *Daulia* v. *Four Millbank Nominees* [1978] 2 W.L.R. 621, C.A.; *Ram Narayan S/O Shanker* v. *Rishad Hussain Shah S/O Tasaduq Hussain Shah* [1979] 1 W.L.R. 1349, P.C.; *Sutton* v. *Sutton* [1984] 1 All E.R. 168, John Mowbray Q.C.

s. 41, see *Rightside Properties* v. *Gray* [1974] 2 All E.R. 1169; *United Scientific Holdings* v. *Burnley B.C.; Cheapside Land Development Co.* v. *Messels Service Co.* [1977] 2 W.L.R. 806, H.L.; *Dean and Chapter of Chichester* v. *Lennards* (1978) 35 P. & C.R. 309, C.A.; *Raineri* v. *Miles; Wiejski (Third Party)* [1980] 2 W.L.R. 847; [1980] 2 All E.R. 145, H.L.

s. 46, see *Stearn* v. *Twitchell* [1985] 1 All E.R. 631, C.A.

s. 49, see *Schindler* v. *Pigault* (1975) 30 P. & C.R. 328; *Universal Corp.* v. *Five Ways Properties* [1979] 1 All E.R. 552, C.A.; *Maktoum* v. *South Lodge Flats, The Times*, April 22, 1980, Mervyn Davies J.; *Dunsdale Development (South East)* v. *De Haan* (1984) 47 P. & C.R. 1, Gerald Godfrey Q.C.

s. 49, amended: 1984, c.28, sch.2.

s. 52, amended: 1985, c.65, sch.8; 1986, c.45, sch.14.

s. 53, see *Re Vandervell's Trusts (No. 2); White* v. *Vandervell Trustees* [1974] 3 W.L.R. 256, C.A.; *Roban Jig & Tool Co. and Elkadart* v. *Taylor* [1979] F.S.R. 130, C.A.; *Brykiert* v. *Jones, The Times*, January 15, 1981, C.A.; *Midland Bank* v. *Dobson and Dobson* (1986) 1 F.L.R. 171, C.A.

s. 56, see *Lyus* v. *Prowsa Developments* [1982] 1 W.L.R. 1044, Dillon J.; *Pinemain* v. *Welbeck International* (1984) 272 E.G. 1166, Mr. E. G. Nugee, Q.C.; *Wiles* v. *Banks* (1985) 50 P. & C.R. 81, C.A.

CAP.

15 & 16 Geo. 5 (1924-25)—cont.

20. Law of Property Act 1925—cont.

s. 62, see *Anderson* v. *Bostock* [1976] 1 All E.R. 560; *Sovmots Investments* v. *Secretary of State for the Environment; Brompton Securities* v. *Same* [1977] 2 W.L.R. 951; [1977] 2 All E.R. 385, H.L. *Re Broxhead Common, Whitehill, Hampshire* (1977) 33 P. & C.R. 451, Brightman J.; *Nickerson* v. *Barraclough* (1980) 125 S.J. 185, C.A.; *Squarey* v. *Harris-Smith* (1981) 42 P. & C.R. 118, C.A.; *Graham* v. *Philcox* [1984] 3 W.L.R. 150, C.A.; *Deen* v. *Andrews* (1986) 52 P. & C.R. 17. Hirst J.; *Kumar* v. *Dunning* (1987) 283 E.G. 59, C.A.; *St. Clement's Leigh-on-Sea, Re* [1988] 1 W.L.R. 720, Chelmsford Consistory Ct.; *M.R.A. Engineering* v. *Trimster Co.* [1988] 56 P. & C.R. 1, C.A.

ss. 62, 78, see *Roake* v. *Chadha* [1983] 3 All E.R. 503; [1984] 1 W.L.R. 40, Judge Paul Baker Q.C.; *Pinemain* v. *Welbeck International* (1984) 272 E.G. 1166, Mr. E. G. Nugee, Q.C.

s. 63, see *Cedar Holdings* v. *Green* [1979] 3 W.L.R. 31, C.A.; *Bridges* v. *Harrow London Borough Council, The Times*, June 18, 1981, Stuart-Smith J., *Boots the Chemist* v. *Street* (1983) 268 E.G. 817, Falconer J.

s. 65, see *St. Edmundsbury and Ipswich Diocesan Board of Finance* v. *Clark (No. 2)* [1975] 1 W.L.R. 468; [1975] 1 All E.R. 772, C.A.

s. 66, amended: 1984, c.28, sch.2.

ss. 76, 77, see *Middlegate* v. *Bilbao* (1972) 24 P. & C.R. 329.

s. 77, see *Johnsey Estates* v. *Lewis and Manley (Engineering) (Chepstow Machine Tool Co., Third Party)* (1987) 284 E.G. 1240, C.A.

s. 78, see *Marchant* v. *Casewell & Redgrave and the N.H.B.R.C.* [1976] J.P.L. 752; *Federated Homes* v. *Mill Lodge Properties* [1980] 1 All E.R. 371, C.A.

s. 84, see *Re Calthorpe Estate, Edgbaston, Birmingham; Anstruther-Gough-Calthorpe* v. *Grey* (1973) 26 P. & C.R. 120, Foster J.; *Griffiths* v. *Band* (1974) 29 P. & C.R. 243; *Gilbert* v. *Spoor* [1982] 2 All E.R. 576, C.A.; *Re Barry's Application* (1980) 41 P. & C.R. 383, Lands Tribunal; *6, 8, 10 and 12 Elm Avenue, New Milton, ex p. New Forest District Council, Re* [1984] 3 All E.R. 632, Scott J.; *Da Costa's Application, Re* (1986) 52 P. & C.R. 99, Lands Tribunal (Ref. No LP/40/1983), V. G. Wellings Esq. Q.C.; *Stockport Metropolitan Borough Council* v. *Alwiyah Developments* (1983) 52 P. & C.R. 278, C.A.; *Martin, Re, The Times*, May 30, 1988, C.A.

s. 84, amended: 1982, c.16, sch.15

ss. 89–92, amended: 1984, c.28, sch.2.

s. 91, see *Twentieth Century Banking Corporation* v. *Wilkinson* [1976] 3 W.L.R. 489.

s. 97, amended: 1972, c.61, sch 3.

s. 101, see *Williams* v. *Wellingborough Borough Council* (1974) 73 L.G.R. 33; [1975] 1 W.L.R. 1327, [1975] 3 All E.R. 462, C.A.; *Twentieth Century Banking Corporation* v. *Wilkinson* [1976] 3 W.L.R. 489.

CAP.

15 & 16 Geo. 5 (1924-25)—cont.

20. Law of Property Act 1925—cont.

s. 109, see *Re John Willment (Ashford)* [1979] 2 All E.R. 615, Brightman J.; *Marshall* v. *Cottingham* (1981) 125 S.J. 411, Megarry V.-C.

s. 110, repealed in pt.: 1985, c.65, sch.10.

s. 136, see *Ramsey* v. *Hartley* [1977] 1 W.L.R. 686, C.A.; *Pfeiffer (E.) Weinkellerei-Weinein-kauf GmbH & Co.* v. *Arbuthnot Factors* [1987] BCLC 522, Phillips J.

s. 136, amended: 1984, c.28, sch 2

s. 140, see *Jelley* v. *Buckman* [1973] 3 W.L.R. 585, C.A.; *William Skelton & Son* v. *Harrison & Pinder* [1975] 2 W.L.R. 238; [1975] 1 All E.R. 182; *Dodson Bull Carpet Co.* v. *City of London Corporation* [1975] 1 W.L.R. 781; [1975] 2 All E.R. 497; *Persey* v. *Bazley* (1983) 267 E.G. 519; (1984) 47 P. & C.R. 59, C.A.; *Neville Long & Co. (Boards)* v. *Firmenich & Co.* (1983) 268 E.G. 572; (1984) 47 P. & C.R. 37, C.A.

ss. 141, 142, see *Pettiward Estates* v. *Shephard*, April 11, 1986; Assistant Recorder Rice; West London County Ct.

s. 142, see *City and Metropolitan Properties* v. *Greycroft* [1987] 1 W.L.R. 1085, Mr. John Mowbray Q.C.

s. 143, see *GMS Syndicate* v. *Gary Elliott, The Times*, October 24, 1980, Nourse J.

s. 146, see *Central Estates* v. *Woolgar (No. 2)* [1972] 1 W.L.R. 1048; 116 S.J. 566; 24 P. & C.R. 103; *Bathurst (Earl)* v. *Fine* [1974] 1 W.L.R. 905; [1974] 2 All E.R. 1160; *Boxrusher Properties* v. *Graham* (1975) 240 E.G. 463, Douglas Frank Q.C.; *Burfort Financial Investments* v. *Chotard* (1976) 239 E.G. 891, Foster J.; *Middlegate Properties* v. *Gidlow-Jackson* (1977) 34 P. & C.R. 4, C.A.; *Halliard Property Co.* v. *Jack Segal* (1977) 245 E.G. 230; [1978] 1 W.L.R. 377, Goulding J.; *Pakwood Transport* v. *15 Beauchamp Place* (1978) 36 P. & C.R. 112, C.A.; *Clifford* v. *Personal Representatives of Johnson decd.* (1979) 251 E.G. 571, C.A.; *Old Grovebury Manor Farm* v. *W. Seymour Plant Sales and Hire* [1979] 1 W.L.R. 263; 3 All E.R. 504, C.A.; *GMS Syndicate* v. *Gary Elliott* [1981] 1 All E.R. 619, Nourse J.; *West Sussex County Council* v. *Wood*, December 2, 1981, Mr. Recorder Willis, Worthing County Court; *Sedac Investments* v. *Tanner* [1982] 3 All E.R. 646, Michael Wheeler, Q.C.; *Starrokate* v. *Burry* (1983) 265 E.G. 871, C.A.; *Cadogan* v. *Dimovic* [1984] 1 W.L.R. 609, C.A.; *Official Custodians of Charities* v. *Parway Estates Developments* [1984] 3 W.L.R. 525, C.A.; *Farimani* v. *Gates* (1984) 271 E.G. 887, C.A.; *Abbey National Building Society* v. *Maybeech* [1984] 3 W.L.R. 793, Nicholls J.; *Official Custodian for Charities* v. *Mackey* [1984] 3 W.L.R. 915, Scott J.; *Export Clothing Service & Sales* v. *Hillgate House* [1985] 3 W.L.R. 359, C.A.; *British Petroleum Pension Trust* v. *Behrendt* (1985) 276 F.G. 199, C.A.; *South Buckinghamshire County*

CAP.

15 & 16 Geo. 5 (1924–25)—cont.

20. Law of Property Act 1925—cont.

Council v. Francis, October 1, 1985, Slough County Ct.; P. S. J. Langan, Q.C.; Smith v. Metropolitan Properties (1985) 277 E.G. 753, Walton J.: Church Comrs. for England v. Nodjoumi (1986) 51 P. & C.R. 155, Hirst J.; Hill v. Griffin (1987) 282 E.G. 85, C.A.; St. Marylebone Property Co. v. Tesco Stores [1988] 27 E.G. 72, Hoffmann J.

ss. 146, 147, amended: 1984, c.28, sch.2.

s. 149, see Bass Holdings v. Lewis (1986) 280 E.G. 771, C.A.

s. 152, see Readymix Concrete v. Farnborough U.D.C. (unreported).

s. 164, see Re Dodwell & Co.'s Trust Deed [1978] 3 All E.R. 738, Walton J.

s. 172, see Lloyds Bank v. Marcan [1973] 1 W.L.R. 1387; [1973] 3 All E.R. 754, C.A.; Cadogan v Cadogan [1977] 1 W.L.R. 1041; [1977] 1 All E.R. 200, C.A.; Re Shilena Hosiery Co. [1979] 2 All E.R. 6, Brightman J.

s. 172, repealed: 1985, c.65, sch.10.

s. 177, see Re Coleman (decd.) [1975] 2 W.L.R. 213; [1975] 1 All E.R. 675.

s. 177, repealed: 1982, c.53, sch.9.

ss. 181, 188, amended: 1984, c.28, sch.2.

s. 189, see Coastplace v. Hartley [1987] 2 W.L.R. 1289, French J.: Kumar v. Dunning (1987) 283 E.G. 59, C.A.

s. 191, repealed: 1977, c.30, sch.2.

s. 193, amended: 1972, c.70, s.189; 1985, c.51, sch.8; repealed in pt.: 1972, c.70, sch.30.

s. 194, amended: 1981, c.38, sch.3.; 1984, c.12, sch.4; 1985, c.51, sch.8; repealed in pt.: 1972, c.70, sch.30.

s. 196, see Holwell Securities v. Hughes [1974] 1 W.L.R. 155; [1974] 1 All E.R. 161, C.A.; New Hart Builders v. Brindley [1975] 2 W.L.R. 595; [1975] 1 All E.R. 1007.

s. 198, see Barber v. Shah (1985) 17 H.L.R. 584, D.C.; Rignall Developments v. Halil [1987] 3 W.L.R. 394, Millett J.

s. 198, amended: 1975, c.76, sch.1.

s. 199, see Midland Bank v. Farmpride Hatcheries (1981) 260 R.G. 493, C.A.; Kingsnorth Finance v. Tizard [1986] 2 All E.R. 54, Judge Findlay, Q.C.

s. 205, amended: 1983, c.20, sch.4; 1984, c.28, sch.2.

sch. 1, amended: ibid.

sch 2, see Middlegate v. Bilbao (1972) 24 P. & C.R. 329; Johnsey Estates v. Lewis and Manley (Engineering) (Chepstow Machine Tool Co., Third Party) (1987) 284 E.G. 1240, C.A.

21. Land Registration Act 1925.

order 72/1139.

s. 1, substituted: 1982, c.53, s.66.

s. 3, see Elias v. Mitchell [1972] 2 W.L.R. 740; [1972] 2 All E.R. 153; Murray v. Two Strokes [1973] 1 W.L.R. 823; Calgary and Edmonton Land Co. v. Dobinson [1974] 2 W.L.R. 143; [1974] 1 All E.R. 484; Williams & Glyn's Bank v. Boland; Same v. Brown [1980] 3 W.L.R. 138, H.L.; City of London Building Society v. Flegg [1986] 2 W.L.R. 616, C.A.

CAP.

15 & 16 Geo. 5 (1924–25)—cont.

21. Land Registration Act 1925—cont.

s. 3, amended: 1975, c.76, sch.1; 1982, c.53, sch.5; repealed in pt.: 1975, c.7, sch.13; 1986, No. 3, s.6.

ss. 5, 9, see Kitney v. M.E.P.C. [1977] 1 W.L.R. 981, C.A.

s. 8, amended: 1986, c.26, ss.2,3.

s. 10, see Murray v. Two Strokes [1973] 1 W.L.R. 823; Re Brickwall Farm; Blacklocks v. J.B. Developments (Godalming), The Times, April 10, 1981, Judge Mervyn Davies, Q.C., sitting as a deputy judge of the High Court.

s. 13, see M.E.P.C. v. Christian-Edwards [1979] 3 W.L.R. 713, H.L.

ss. 18, 19, repealed in pt.: 1986, c.26, s.4.

s. 20, see Abbey National Building Society v. Davis Contractors (1972) 225 E.G. 1917; Peffer v. Rigg [1977] 1 W.L.R. 285; Kitney v. M.E.P.C. [1977] 1 W.L.R. 981, C.A.; Lyus v. Prowsa Developments [1982] 1 W.L.R. 1044, Dillon J.; City of London Building Society v. Flegg [1986] 2 W.L.R. 616, C.A.

s. 20, amended: 1975, c.7, sch.12.

s. 21, see Spectrum Investment Co. v. Holmes [1981] 1 All E.R. 6, Browne-Wilkinson J.

ss. 21, 22, repealed in pt.: 1986, c.26, s.4.

s. 23, see Kitney v. M.E.P.C. [1977] 1 W.L.R. 981, C.A.

s. 23, amended: 1975, c.7, sch.12.

s. 25, see Barclays Bank v. Taylor [1973] 2 W.L.R. 293.

s. 25, amended: 1986, c.53, sch.18.

s. 28, see Coren v. Keighley [1972] 1 W.L.R. 1556; 116 S.J. 904.

s. 34, see Lyus v. Prowsa Developments [1982] 1 W.L.R. 1044, Dillon J.

s. 42, amended: 1985, c.65, sch.8; 1986, c.45, sch.14.

s. 49, see Watts v. Waller [1972] 3 W.L.R. 365.

s. 49, amended: 1979, c.53, s.3; 1986, c.32, s.39; 1987, c.31, sch. 4; 1988, c.33, sch.15.

s. 52, see Kitney v. M.E.P.C. [1977] 1 W.L.R. 981, C.A.; Elias v. Mitchell [1972] 2 W.L.R. 740; [1972] 2 All E.R. 153.

s. 54, see Clayhope Properties v. Evans [1986] 2 All E.R. 795, C.A.

s. 54, repealed in pt.: 1986, c.26, s.5.

s. 55, see Smith v. Morrison; Smith v. Chief Land Registrar [1974] 1 All E.R. 957.

s. 56, see Clearbrook Property Holdings v. Verrier [1973] 3 All E.R. 614, Templeman J.

s. 59, see Peffer v. Rigg [1977] 1 W.L.R. 285; Kling v. Keston Properties (1984) 91 L.S.Gaz. 1683, Vinelott J.; Clayhope Properties v. Evans [1986] 2 All E.R. 795, C.A.

s. 59, amended: 1975, c.7, sch.12; repealed in pt.: ibid., sch.13; 1988, c.3, sch.

s. 61, amended: 1985, c.65, sch.8; repealed in pt.: ibid., sch.10; 1988, c.3, sch.

s. 62, amended: 1985, c.65, sch.8; repealed in pt.: ibid., sch.10.

s. 64, amended: 1975, c.7, sch.12; 1981, c.24, s.4; 1983, c.19, sch.2; 1987, c.31, sch. 4.

s. 69, see Spectrum Investment Co. v. Holmes [1981] 1 All E.R. 6, Browne-Wilkinson J.

CAP.

15 & 16 Geo. 5 (1924-25)—cont.

21. Land Registration Act 1925—cont.

s. 70, see Epps v. Esso Petroleum Co. [1973] 1 W.L.R. 1071; [1973] 2 All E.R. 465; Schwab (G. B.) & Co. v. McCarthy (1975) 31 P. & C.R. 196, D.C.; Bird v. Syme Thompson [1978] 3 All E.R. 1027, Templeman J.; Williams & Glyn's Bank v. Boland; Same v. Brown [1980] 3 W.L.R. 138, H.L.; Blacklocks v. J. B. Developments (Godalming) [1981] 3 W.L.R. 554, Mervyn Davies J.; Kling v. Keston Properties (1984) 81 L.S.Gaz.1683; (1985) 49 P. & C.R. 212, Vinelott J.; Celsteel v. Alton House Holdings [1985] 1 W.L.R. 204, Scott J.; Paddington Building Society v. Mendelsohn (1985) 50 P. & C.R. 244, C.A.; Kingsnorth Finance v. Tizard (1986) 83 L.S.Gaz. 1231, Judge Finlay, Q.C.; Winkworth v. Baron (Edward) Development Co. [1986] 1 W.L.R. 1512, H.L.; City of London Building Society v. Flegg [1987] 2 W.L.R. 1266, H.L.; Regent Indemnity Co. v. Fishley and Fishley, July 21, 1987, Mr. Recorder Walton; Birmingham County Ct.; Ashburn Anstalt v. Arnold (1987) 284 E.G. 1375, C.A.; Ashburn Anstalt v. Arnold (No. 2) [1988] 2 W.L.R. 706, C.A.; Lloyd's Bank v. Rossett, The Times, May 23, 1988, C.A.

s. 70, amended: 1986, c.26, s.4.

s. 73, substituted: 1975, c.7, sch.12; amended: order 75/1455; 1984, c.51, sch.8.

s. 77, substituted: 1986, c.26, s.1.

s. 82, see Watts v. Waller [1972] 3 W.L.R. 365; Epps v. Esso Petroleum Co. [1973] 1 W.L.R. 1071; [1973] 2 All E.R. 465; Lester v. Burgess (1973) 26 P. & C.R. 536; Price Bros. (Somerford) v J. Kelly Homes (Stoke-on-Trent) [1975] 1 W.L.R. 1512; [1975] 3 All E.R. 369, C.A.; Freer v. Unwins [1976] 2 W.L.R. 609; [1976] 1 All E.R. 634; Argyle Building Society v. Hammond (1985) 49 P. & C.R. 148, C.A.; Proctor v. Kidman (1986) 51 P. & C.R. 67, C.A.

s. 82, amended: 1977, c.38, s.24; repealed in pt.: ibid., s.24, sch.5.

s. 83, amended: 1980, c.58, sch.3.

ss. 100, amended: 1972, c.70, sch.29; repealed in pt.: 1985, c.51, sch.17.

s. 101, see Elias v. Mitchell [1972] 2 W.L.R. 740; [1972] 2 All E.R. 153.

s. 102, repealed in pt.: 1986, c.26, s.5.

s. 106, see Barclays Bank v. Taylor [1973] 2 W.L.R. 293.

s. 106, substituted: 1977, c.38, s.26.

s. 110, see Walia v. Naughton (Michael) [1985] 1 W.L.R. 1115, Judge Finlay, Q.C.; Naz v. Raja, The Times, April 11, 1987, C.A.

s. 110, repealed in pt.: 1988, c.3, sch.

s. 111, amended: 1983, c.20, sch.4.

ss. 112–112C, substituted: 1988, c.3, s.1

s. 112A, amended: 1988, c.33, sch.15.

ss. 113, 113A, repealed in pt.: 1988, c.3, sch.

s. 113A, added: 1982, c.53, s.66.

s. 120, orders 73/1764; 74/250, 559; 75/160; 76/1782; 77/828; 84/1579; 85/1999; 87/939; 88/596, 1854.

CAP.

15 & 16 Geo. 5 (1924-25)—cont.

21. Land Registration Act 1925—cont.

s. 120, repealed in pt.: 1972, c.70, schs.29, 30.

s. 123, amended: 1986, c.26, s.2.

s. 126, repealed in pt.: S.L.R. 1986.

s. 132, orders 73/131; 74/445, 1304; 78/1162; 79/1019; 80/1499; 84/1579; 87/360, 2213; 88/1825.

s. 133, orders 73/131; 74/445, 1304; 78/1162; 79/1019; 80/1499; 84/1579; 87/360.

s. 137, repealed in pt.: S.L.R. 1986.

s. 138, substituted: 1982, c.53, sch.5.

s. 144, orders 73/1009; 75/1316; 76/1333; 81/54; 85/359; 88/665; rules 75/367; 76/1332; 77/2089; 78/1600, 1601; 81/1135; 83/40; 86/1534, 1536, 1537, 2116; 87/2214; 88/629.

s. 144, repealed in pt.: 1986, c.26, s.5; 1988, c.3, sch.

s. 145, orders 85/359; 86/1399; 88/665.

22. Land Charges Act 1925.

repealed: 1975, c.76, sch.2.

see Kling v. Keston Properties (1984) 81 L.S.Gaz. 1683, Vinelott J.

s. 6, see Clayhope Properties v. Evans [1986] 2 All E.R. 795, C.A.

s. 10, see Diligent Finance Co. v. Alleyne (1971) 23 P. & C.R. 346; Hooker v. Wyle [1973] 3 All E.R. 707, Templeman J.; Kitney v. M.E.P.C. [1977] 1 W.L.R. 981, C.A.; Property Discount Corp. v. Lyon Group (1981) 1 W.L.R. 300; [1981] 1 All E.R. 379, C.A.

s. 13, see Kitney v. M.E.P.C. [1977] 1 W.L.R. 981, C.A.; Midland Bank Trust Co. v. Green [1981] 2 W.L.R. 28; [1981] 1 All E.R. 153, H.L.

s. 15, rules 72/690.

s. 17, see Diligent Finance Co. v. Alleyne (1971) 23 P. & C.R. 346.

s. 19, rules 72/50; 73/1862; 74/424; 76/48.

s. 23, see Kitney v. M.E.P.C. [1977] 1 W.L.R. 981, C.A.

23. Administration of Estates Act 1925.

s. 2, see Fountain Forestry v. Edwards [1974] 2 W.L.R. 767; [1974] 2 All E.R. 280; Harrison v. Wing [1988] 29 E.G. 101, C.A.

s. 9, see Wirral Borough Council v. Smith (1982) 43 P. & C.R. 312, C.A.

s. 17, amended: 1984, c.28, sch.2.

s. 21A, added: 1980, c.24, s.10; amended: 1980, c.58, sch.3.

s. 30, repealed in pt.: 1981, c.19, sch.1.

s. 34, repealed in pt.: 1985, c.65, sch.10.

s. 38, amended: 1984, c.28, sch.2.

s. 41, see Re Collins (decd.); Robinson v. Collins [1975] 1 W.L.R. 309; [1975] 1 All E.R. 321; Re Phelps (decd.); Wells v. Phelps [1979] 3 All E.R. 373, C.A

s. 41, amended: 1983, c.20, sch.4; 1984, c.28, sch.2

s. 46, see Re Collens, (decd.); Royal Bank of Canada (London) v. Krogh [1986] 1 All E.R. 611, Browne-Wilkinson V.-C.

s. 46, order 83/1374.

s. 46, amended: orders 77/415, 1491, 81/255; 1977, c.38, s.28.

CAP.

15 & 16 Geo. 5 (1924–25)—cont.

23. Administration of Estates Act 1925—cont.
s. 47, see *Hardy* v. *Shaw* [1975] 2 W.L.R. 1002.
s. 47A, amended: 1977, c.38, s.28; 1981, c.54.
sch.5; repealed in pt.: 1977, c.38, sch.5.
s. 49, see *Re Osoba (decd.); Osoba* v. *Osoba*
[1978] 1 W.L.R. 791, Megarry V.-C.
ss. 50, 52, amended: 1987, c.42, sch. 2.
s. 53, repealed in pt.: 1975, c.7, sch.13.
s. 55, see *Re Crispin's Will Trusts, Arkwright* v.
Thurley [1974] 3 W.L.R. 657; [1974] 3 All E.R.
772, C.A.; *Harrison* v. *Wing* [1988] 29 E.G.
101, C.A.
s. 55, amended: 1984, c.28, sch.2; repealed in
pt.: 1981, c.54, sch.7.
sch. 1, repealed in pt.: 1983, c.49, sch.2; 1985,
c.65, sch.10.

24. Universities and College Estates Act 1925.
ss. 10, 15, amended: regs. 78/443.
s. 16, amended: 1980, c.66, sch.24.
s. 26, amended: 1986, c.5, sch.14.
s. 33, repealed in pt.: S.L.R. 1986.

28. Administration of Justice Act 1925.
s. 22, orders 80/509; 84/887.
ss. 28, 29, repealed in pt.: S.L.R. 1973.
s. 53, see *Re Crispin's Will Trusts, Arkwright* v.
Thurley [1973] 2 All E.R. 141.

29. Gold Standard Act 1925.
repealed: S.L.R. 1986.

33. Church of Scotland (Property and Endowments) Act 1925.
ss. 3–6, 10, repealed: S.L.R. 1976.
s. 11, Acts of Sederunt 75/1849; 77/73; 84/235.
s. 11, repealed in pt.: 1983, c.12, sch.2
s. 22, amended: 1973, c.65, sch.27; repealed in
pt.: *ibid.*, schs.27, 29.
ss. 26, 28, amended: *ibid.*, sch.27.
s. 32, amended: *ibid.*; repealed in pt.: *ibid.*,
schs.27, 29.
s. 33, amended: *ibid.*, sch.27.
schs. 3, 4, repealed: S.L.R. 1976.

34. Northern Ireland Land Act 1925.
s. 36, repealed in pt.: 1973, c.36, sch.6.

36. Finance Act 1925.
ss 25, 28, repealed in pt.: S.L.R. 1974.
Pt. III, sch. 4, repealed: 1975, c.7, sch.13.

38. Performing Animals (Regulation) Act 1925.
s. 1, amended: 1973, c.65, sch.25(S.); 1974,
c.7, sch.6; repealed in pt.: 1973, c.65,
schs.25, 29(S.); 1974, c.7, schs.6, 8.
s. 5, amended: 1985, c.51, sch.8; repealed in
pt.: 1973, c.65, schs.25, 29(S.); 1974, c.7,
schs.6, 8.
s. 6, amended(S.): 1973, c.65, sch.24; repealed
in pt.(S.): *ibid.*, schs.24, 29.

42. Merchant Shipping (International Labour Conventions) Act 1925.
s. 4, amended: 1979, c.39, sch.6.
s. 6, order 79/1449.

45. Guardianship of Infants Act 1925.
repealed (S.): 1986, c.9, sch.2.
s. 1, see *Cheetham* v. *Glasgow Corporation*,
1972 S.C. 243, Lord Dunpark, Outer House.
ss. 1 (in pt.) 2, repealed: 1973, c.29, s.10.
s. 3, amended: *ibid.*, sch.4; 1985, c.37,
sch.1(S.); repealed in pt. (S.): *ibid.*, sch.2.

CAP.

15 & 16 Geo. 5 (1924–25)—cont.

45. Guardianship of Infants Act 1925—cont.
s. 4, amended: 1973, c.29, sch.5.
ss. 5 (in pt.), 8, repealed (S.): 1985, c.37, sch.1.

46. Dramatic and Musical Performers Protection Act 1925.
see *Ex p. Island Records* [1978] 3 W.L.R. 23,
C.A.

48. Improvement of Land Act (1899) Amendment Act 1925.
repealed: S.L.R. 1974.

49. Supreme Court of Judicature (Consolidation) Act 1925.
repealed: 1981, c.54, sch.7.
s. 27, see *Podbery* v. *Peak* [1981] 1 All E.R. 699,
C.A.
s. 30, see *Re Edwards' Will Trusts. Edwards* v.
Edwards [1981] 3 W.L.R. 15, C.A.
s. 31, see *Joseph Cartwright* v. *Legal and Merchant Securities* (1975) 1 Build.L.R. 129, C.A.;
Scherer v. *Counting Instruments* [1977] F.S.R.
569, Whitford J.; *R.* v. *Board of Visitors of
Hull Prison, ex p. St. Germain* [1978] 2 W.L.R.
42, C.A.; *R.* v. *D.P.P., ex p. Raymond* (1979)
70 Cr.App.R. 233, C.A.; *Lowe* v. *Lowe* (1980)
10 Fam. Law 186, C.A.; *Merino* v. *Pilcher;
Oakeley Vaughan & Co. (Third Party)* (1980)
124 S.J. 188, C.A.; *Ford* v. *Ford, The Times,*
January 16, 1981, C.A.
s. 36, see *Department of Environment* v. *James*
[1972] 1 W.L.R. 1279; [1972] 3 All E.R. 629.
s. 41, see *Snelling* v. *Snelling (John G.)* [1972]
2 W.L.R. 588; [1972] 1 All E.R. 79; *The
Atlantic Star; Atlantic Star (Owners)* v. *Bona
Spes (Owners)* [1973] 2 W.L.R. 795; [1973] 2
All E.R. 175; *Jefferson* v. *Bhetcha* [1979] 1
W.L.R. 898, C.A.
s. 43, see *G.* v. *G.* (1980) 10 Fam. Law 250,
Eastham J.
s. 44, see *Department of the Environment* v.
James [1972] 1 W.L.R. 1279; [1972] 3 All E.R.
629.
s. 45, see *McGibbon* v. *McGibbon* [1973] 2
W.L.R. 1013; [1973] 2 All E.R. 836; *Nippon
Yasen Kaisha* v. *Karageorgis* [1975] 1 W.L.R.
1093, C.A.; *Gouriet* v. *Union of Post Office
Workers* [1977] 3 W.L.R. 300, H.L.; *Rasu
Maritime S.A.* v. *Perusahaan Pertambangan
Minyak Dan Gas Bumi Negara (Pertamina)
and Government of Republic of Indonesia
(Intervener)* [1977] 3 All E.R. 324, C.A.;
Mareva Compania Naveriri S.A. v. *International Bulkcarriers S.A.; The Mareva (Note)*
(1975) [1980] 1 All E.R. 213, C.A.; *A.* v. *C.*
[1980] 2 All E.R. 347, Robert Goff J.; *A. J.
Bekhor & Co.* v. *Bilton* [1981] 2 W.L.R. 601,
C.A.; *Faith Panton Property Plan* v. *Hodgetts*
[1981] 1 W.L.R. 927; [1981] 2 All E.R. 877,
C.A.; *Chief Constable of Kent* v. *V., The
Times,* May 14, 1982, C.A.; *Astro Exito Navegacion SA* v. *Southland Enterprise Co. (No.
2)* [1982] 3 W.L.R. 296, H.L.; *A* v. *C.* (Note)
[1981] 1 Q.B. 956, Goff J.; *House of Spring
Gardens* v. *Waite* [1985] F.S.R. 173, C.A.

CAP.

15 & 16 Geo. 5 (1924–25)—cont.

49. Supreme Court of Judicature (Consolidation) Act 1925—cont.

s. 47, see *Astro Exito Navegacion SA* v. *Southland Enterprise Co. (No.2)* [1982] 3 W.L.R. 296, H.L.; *Astro Exito Navegacion SA* v. *Southland Enterprise Co. (No. 2) (Chase Manhattan Bank NA Intervening)* [1983] 3 W.L.R. 130, H.L.

s. 50, see *Wright* v. *Westoby* [1973] 3 All E.R. 1078, C.A.; *Stewart* v. *Stewart* [1974] 1 W.L.R. 877; [1974] 2 All E.R. 795, C.A; *Department of Health and Social Security* v. *Envoy Farmers* [1976] 2 All E.R. 173; *Scherer* v. *Counting Instruments* [1977] F.S.R. 569, Whitford J.; *Bacal Contracting* v. *Modern Engineering (Bristol)* [1980] 2 All E.R. 655, Judge Fay Q.C.; *Re Gibson's Settlement Trusts; Mellors* v. *Gibson* [1981] 2 W.L.R. 1; [1981] 1 All E.R. 233, Megarry V.-C.; *E.M.I. Records* v. *Ian Cameron Wallace, The Times,* March 19, 1982, Megarry V.-C.; *Re G. (Minors) (Wardship: Costs)* [1982] 1 W.L.R. 438, C.A.; *Williamson* v. *Moldline* [1986] R.P.C. 556, C.A.

s. 51, see *Re Becker* [1975] 1 W.L.R. 842, D.C.; *Rohrberg* v. *Charkin, The Times,* January 30, 1985, C.A.

s. 53, order 72/968.

s. 58, see *Midland Bank* v. *Stamps* [1978] 1 W.L.R. 635, Donaldson J.

s. 84, orders 75/1781; 76/434, 891; 77/152, 351, 1216; 80/1216; 81/1625.

s. 99, rules 72/813, 1194, 1786, 1898; 73/1114, 1384, 2046; 74/295, 1115, 1360, 75/128, 911; 76/337, 1196, 2097; 77/532, 960, 1955; 78/251, 359, 579, 1066, 1118; 79/35, 402, 522, 1542, 1716; 80/629, 1010, 1908, 2000; 81/562.

s. 99, repealed in pt.: 1977, c.38, s.22, sch.5.

s. 100, rules 74/597; 76/1362.

s. 108, order 81/726.

s. 162, see *Van Hoorn* v. *Van Hoorn, The Times,* November 3ᵒ 1978, Balcombe J.; *Re D. and B.* (1979) 10 Fam. Law 55, Latey J.; *I.R.C.* v. *Stype Investments (Jersey); Re Clore (decd.)* [1982] 3 W.L.R. 228, C.A.

s. 172, regs. 78/1724.

s. 213, orders 72/1190, 1191; 73/164, 165, 1993; 74/1381, 1384; 75/1344; 76/1363, 1506; 78/1244, 1298; 79/968; 80/509, 820, 821, 1060; 81/861, 1103.

s. 216, orders 72/1188; 75/1972; 80/70.

s. 218, regs. 74/1937.

s. 225, see *Moon* v. *Atherton* [1972] 3 W.L.R. 57; [1972] 3 All E.R. 145.

50. Theatrical Employers Registration Act 1925.
repealed: 1982, c.30, s.11, sch.7.

61. Allotments Act 1925.

s. 3, repealed in pt.: 1972, c.70, sch.30; S.L.R. 1978.

s. 12, repealed: 1972, c.70, sch.30.

s. 13, repealed: 1980, c.65, schs.5, 34.

67. Wireless Telegraphy (Explanation) Act 1925.
repealed: S.L.R. 1973.

CAP.

15 & 16 Geo. 5 (1924–25)—cont.

68. Roads Improvement Act 1925.
repealed (S): 1984, c.54, sch.11.

s. 1, amended: 1984, c.12, sch.4.

s. 5, amended: 1981, c.38, sch.3; 1984, c.12, sch.4.

71. Public Health Act 1925.

ss. 1 (in pt.), 2 (in pt.), 3–5, repealed: 1972, c.70, sch.30.

s. 7, repealed in pt.: 1986, c.44, sch.9.

s. 10, amended: 1981, c.38, sch.3; 1984, c.12, sch.4.

s. 16, repealed in pt.: 1972, c.70, schs.14, 30.

ss. 18 (in pt.), 19 (in pt.), 70, repealed: *ibid.,* sch.30.

s. 74, repealed in pt.: 1984, c.60, sch.7.

s 75, repealed in pt.: 1972, c.70, sch.30.

s. 76, see *Hulin* v. *Cook* [1977] R.T.R. 345.

s. 80, repealed: S.L.R. 1975.

schs. 2, 3, repealed: 1972, c.70, sch.30.

73. National Library of Scotland Act 1925.

s. 2, amended: 1985, c.16, sch.19; repealed in pt.: *ibid.,* s.18, sch.2.

s. 2A, added: *ibid.,* s.18.

s. 10, amended: *ibid.,* sch.2.

s. 14, repealed: 1972, c.11, sch.8.

sch, amended: 1985, c.16, sch.18.

76. Expiring Laws Act 1925.
repealed: S.L.R. 1977.

77. Ireland (Confirmation of Agreement) Act 1925.

s. 1, see *D.P.P.* v. *McNeill* [1975] N.I. 177, C.A.

81. Circuit Courts and Criminal Procedure (Scotland) Act 1925.
repealed (S.): 1975, c.21, sch.10.

s. 1, Act of Adjournal 75/834.

82. Roads and Streets in Police Burghs (Scotland) Act 1925.
repealed: 1973, c.65, schs.14,29.

84. Workmen's Compensation Act 1925.

s. 12, see *Park* v. *National Coal Board* [1981] I.C.R. 783, C.A.

86. Criminal Justice Act 1925.

s. 11, repealed in pt.: 1981, c.45, sch.

s. 12, amended: 1980, c.43, sch.7.

s. 13, see *R.* v. *Fisher* [1980] Crim.L.R. 430, Swansea Crown Ct.; *R.* v. *Blithing* [1983] Crim.L.R. 474; [1984] R.T.R. 18, C.A.; *R.* v. *O'Loughlin and McLaughlin* [1987] Crim.L.R. 632; (1987) 85 Cr.App.R. 157, Central Criminal Ct.

s. 28, repealed in pt.: 1977, c.45, sch.13.

s. 33, amended: 1980, c.43, sch.7.

s. 34, repealed: 1979, c.31, sch.2.

s. 35, repealed: 1981, c.45, sch.

s. 36, amended: 1977, c.45, ss.16, 28, sch.3; repealed in pt.: 1981, c.45, sch.

s. 38, see *Hughes* v. *Brook* [1973] Crim.L.R. 526.

s. 38, repealed: 1981, c.45, sch.

s. 39, repealed: 1988, c.33, sch.16.

s. 41, see *Re St. Andrew's, Heddington* [1977] 3 W.L.R. 286, Salisbury Consistory Ct.

CAP.

15 & 16 Geo. 5 (1924–25)—cont.

86. Criminal Justice Act 1925—cont.
s. 47, see R. v. Gary Richman and Ann Richman [1982] Crim.L.R. 507, Bristol Crown Ct.; R. v. Ditta, Hussain and Kara [1988] Crim.L.R. 42, C.A.
sch. 12, repealed in pt.: 1982, c.48, sch.16.

87. Tithe Act 1925.
s. 1, repealed: S.L.R. 1975.

90. Rating and Valuation Act 1925.
s. 2, amended: 1972, c.70, sch.13.
ss. 9 (in pt.), 10, 48, 49, 52, 54, sch.6, repealed: ibid., sch.30.

16 & 17 Geo. 5 (1926)

3. Trade Facilities Act 1926.
repealed: S.L.R. 1974.

7. Bankruptcy (Amendment) Act 1926.
repealed: 1985, c.65, sch.10.
s. 4, see Re Byfield (A Bankrupt), ex p. Hill Samuel & Co. v. The Trustee of the Bankrupt [1982] 1 All E.R. 249, Goulding J.

11. Law of Property (Amendment) Act 1926.
s. 3, amended: 1981, c.54, sch.5.
s. 4, rules 72/50.
s. 4, repealed: 1972, c.61, sch.5.
sch. repealed in pt.: ibid.; 1975, c.76, sch. 2.

15. Criminal Appeal (Scotland) Act 1926.
ss. 1–3, repealed: 1975, c.21, sch.10.
s. 2, see Smith v. H.M. Advocate, 1975 S.L.T.(Notes) 89.
s. 4, repealed in pt.: 1975, c.21, sch.10; S.L.R. 1977.
ss. 5–18, repealed: 1975, c.21, sch.10.
s. 6, see Lindie v. H.M. Advocate, 1974 S.L.T. 208.
s. 11, see Storrie v. Murray, 1974 S.L.T. (Sh.Ct.) 45; McGowan v. Mein, 1976 S.L.T.(Sh.Ct.) 29.
s. 13, see Butterworth v. Herron, 1975 S.L.T.(Notes) 56.
s. 15, Acts of Adjournal 73/450; 75/473.
s. 19, repealed in pt.: S.L.R. 1977.

16. Execution of Diligence (Scotland) Act 1926.
ss. 1, 2, amended: 1987, c.18, sch. 6.
s. 6, Acts of Sederunt 75/73, 74, 1147, 1300; 77/567; 78/114, 115, 1423, 1424; 80/1553, 1554; 82/1166, 1167; 86/255, 266; 88/1502, 1503.

18. Secretaries of State Act 1926.
s. 2, repealed: S.L.R. 1977.

21. Markets and Fairs (Weighing of Cattle) Act 1926.
s. 2, amended and repealed in pt : S.L.R. 1975

26. Chartered Associations (Protection of Names and Uniforms) Act 1926.
s. 1, order 85/611.
s. 1, amended: 1988, c.48, sch.7.

29. Adoption of Children Act 1926.
repealed: 1975, c.72, sch.4.

31. Home Counties (Music and Dancing) Licensing Act 1926.
repealed: 1982, c.30, sch.7.

CAP.

16 & 17 Geo. 5 (1926)—cont.

36. Parks Regulation (Amendment) Act 1926.
s. 2, see Burgess v. McCracken, The Times, June 26, 1986, D.C.
s. 2, regs. 73/214; 77/217, 804, 2088; 78/670; 80/361.
s. 3, regs. 77/2088; 80/361.

38. Local Government (County Boroughs and Adjustments) Act 1926.
repealed: S.L.R. 1975.

40. Indian and Colonial Divorce Jurisdiction Act 1926.
rules 72/774.
repealed: 1986, c.55, sch.2.

41. Naval Reserve (Officers) Act 1926.
repealed: 1980, c.9, sch.10.

43. Public Health (Smoke Abatement) Act 1926.
repealed: regs. 74/2170.

44. Supreme Court of Judicature of Northern Ireland Act 1926.
repealed: 1978, c.23, sch.7.

47. Rating (Scotland) Act 1926.
ss. 2, 12, repealed in pt.: S.L.R. 1975.
s. 14, repealed in pt.: ibid.; 1987, c.47, sch. 6.
s. 26, repealed: S.L.R. 1977.
s. 29, repealed in pt.: S.L.R. 1975; 1975, c.30, sch.7.

48. Births and Deaths Registration Act 1926.
ss. 1, 3, regs. 87/2088.
s. 8, repealed: S.L.R. 1977.
s. 9, amended: order 88/1843.
s. 12, regs. 87/2088.

50. Burgh Registers (Scotland) Act 1926.
ss. 1 (in pt.), 4, sch. 2, repealed: S.L.R. 1974.

51. Electricity (Supply) Act 1926.
s. 24, repealed: 1983, c.25, sch.4.
s. 33, repealed: S.L.R. 1981.
s. 35, amended: 1973, c.65, sch.27(S.); 1985, c.51, sch.4.
s. 44, amended: 1979, c.46, sch.4.
sch. 6, repealed in pt.: 1973, c.65, sch.29(S.); S.L.R. 1978; 1986, c.63, sch.12.

52. Small Holdings and Allotments Act 1926.
ss. 4, 9, amended: 1972, c.70, schs.29, 30.
ss. 17, 22, repealed in pt · S.L.R. 1973.
sch. 1, repealed in pt.: ibid.; 1977, c.30, sch.2.
sch. 2, repealed: S.L.R. 1973.

54. Wireless Telegraphy (Blind Persons Facilities) Act 1926.
repealed: S.L.R. 1974.

56. Housing (Rural Workers) Act 1926.
repealed: 1972, c.46, sch.11; c.47, sch.11.

59. Coroners (Amendment) Act 1926.
repealed: 1988, c.13, sch.4.
s. 13, see R. v. H.M. Coroner at Hammersmith, ex p. Peach [1980] 2 W.L.R. 496, C.A.; R. v. Surrey Coroner, ex p. Campbell [1982] 2 W.L.R. 626, C.A.; R. v. H.M. Coroner of the Eastern District of the Metropolitan County of West Yorkshire, ex p. National Union of Mineworkers, Yorkshire Area (1985) 150 J.P. 58, D.C.
s. 14, see R. v. Bristol Coroner, ex p. Kerr [1974] 2 W.L.R. 816.
s. 18, see R. v. East Sussex Coroner, ex p. Healy, The Guardian, May 13, 1988, D.C.

CAP.

16 & 17 Geo. 5 (1926)—cont.

59. Coroners (Amendment) Act 1926—cont.
s. 19, see *R.* v. *Central Cleveland Coroner, ex p. Dent, The Times,* February 17, 1986, D.C.; *Rapier, Decd., Re* [1986] 3 W.L.R. 830, D.C.; *Att.-Gen.* v. *Harte (J. D.)* (1987) 151 J.P.N. 750, Taylor J.; *R.* v. *H.M.Coroner for South Glamorgan, ex p. B.P. Chemicals* (1987) 151 J.P.N. 808, D.C.

s. 21, see *R.* v. *Greater Manchester North District Coroner, ex p. Worch* [1987] 3 W.L.R. 997, C.A.

s. 25, repealed: 1977, c.45, sch.13.

s. 26, rules 74/2128; 77/1881; 80/557, 668; 83/1539; 84/552; 85/1414.

s. 26, amended: 1983, c.31, s.2.

s. 27, rules 77/1881; 80/557, 668; 83/1539, 84/552; 85/1414.

s. 29, rules 75/1126; 80/969; 81/1191; 82/995.

ss. 32, 33, repealed: 1972, c.70, sch.30.

60. Legitimacy Acts 1926.
repealed: 1976, c.32, schs.1, 2.
s. 1, see *Veasey* v. *Att.-Gen.,* (1981) 11 Fam. Law 249, Ewbank J.

s. 3, see *Re Billson's Settlement Trusts,* [1984] 2 W.L.R. 966, C.A.

s. 10, see *Dunbar of Kilconzie, Petr.,* 1986 S.L.T. 463, H.L.

62. East Africa Loans Act 1926.
repealed: S.L.R. 1976.

17 & 18 Geo. 5 (1927)

4. Royal and Parliamentary Titles Act 1927.
s. 2, repealed in pt.: S.L.R. 1977; 1978, c.30, sch.3.

10. Finance Act 1927.
s. 51, repealed: 1975, c.7, sch.13.
s. 53, repealed: 1976, c.40, sch.15.
s. 55, see *Clarke Chapman-John Thompson* v. *I.R.C.* [1975] 3 All E.R. 701, C.A.; *Crane-Fruehauf* v. *I.R.C.* [1975] 1 All E.R. 429, C.A.; *Chelsea Land & Investment Co.* v. *I.R.C.* [1978] 2 All E.R. 113, C.A.; *I.R.C.* v. *Ufitec Group* [1977] 3 All E.R. 924; [1977] S.T.C. 363, May J.

s. 55, amended: 1986, c.41, s.73; repealed in pt.: 1973, c.51, sch.22; 1986, c.41, s.73; repealed (prosp.): *ibid.,* s.74, sch.23.

s. 56, repealed: 1985, c.54, sch 27.

12. Auctions (Bidding Agreements) Act 1927.
s. 1, see *R.* v. *Jordan,* July 10, 1981, Swansea Crown Ct.

18. Royal Naval Reserve Act 1927.
repealed: 1980, c.9, sch.10.

21. Moneylenders Act 1927.
repealed (except for ss. 1–3, 4 (in pt.), 10, 13 (in pt.), 18 (in pt.)): 1974, c.39, sch.5.
s. 4, repealed in pt.: order 80/50.
ss. 4, 6, see *London and Harrogate Securities* v. *Pitts* [1976] 1 W.L.R. 264; [1976] 1 W.L.R. 1063, C.A.

s. 6, see *Greendon Investments* v. *Mills* (1973) 226 E.G. 1957, Pennycuick V.-C., *Goodman*

CAP.

17 & 18 Geo. 5 (1927)—cont.

21. Moneylenders Act 1927—cont.
& *Sterling (Coventry)* v. *Kent* [1974] 1 C.L. 249a, Coventry Cty.Ct.; *Barclay* v. *Prospect Mortgages* [1974] 1 W.L.R. 837; [1974] 2 All E.R. 672; *Holiday Credit* v. *Erol* [1977] 1 W.L.R. 704; [1977] 2 All E.R. 696, H.L.; *Orakpo* v. *Manson Investments* [1977] 3 W.L.R. 229, H.L.

s. 13, see *Orakpo* v. *Manson Investments* [1977] 3 W.L.R. 229, H.L.

22. Trade Disputes and Trade Unions Act 1927.
s. 5, see *R.* v. *Secretary of State for the Foreign and Commonwealth Office, ex p. Council of Civil Service Unions, The Times,* July 17, 1984, Glidewell J.

26. Criminal Appeal (Scotland) Act 1927.
repealed: S.L.R. 1977.

35. Sheriff Courts and Legal Officers (Scotland) Act 1927.
s. 1, amended: 1972, c.11, sch.6; 1985, c.73, s 47.
s. 6, amended: 1972, c.11, sch.6.
s. 7, amended: *ibid.;* repealed in pt.: *ibid.,* sch.8.
s. 11, order 74/599.
s. 11, repealed: S.L.R. 1975.

36. Landlord and Tenant Act 1927.
s. 1, see *Pelosi* v. *Newcastle Arms Brewery (Nottingham)* (1982) 43 P. & C.R. 18, C.A.

s. 3, see *Deerfield Travel Services* v. *Wardens and Society of the Mistery or Art of the Leathersellers of the City of London* (1983) P. & C.R. 132, C.A.

s. 16, amended: 1977, c.42, sch.23; repealed in pt.: 1980, c.51, sch.26.

s. 17, amended: 1986, c.5, sch.14.

s. 18, see *Hibernian Property Co.* v. *Liverpool Corporation* [1973] 1 W.L.R. 751; [1973] 2 All E.R. 1117; *Family Management* v. *Gray* (1979) 253 E.G. 369, C.A.; *Mather* v. *Barclays Bank* [1987] 2 E.G.L.R. 254, H.H. Judge Paul Baker Q.C.

s. 19, see *Bocardo S.A.* v. *S. & M. Hotels* [1979] 3 All E.R. 737, C.A.; *Guardian Assurance Co.* v. *Gants Hill Holdings* (1983) 267 E.G. 678, Mervyn Davies J.

s. 19, amended: 1980, c.51, s.81; 1986, c.5, sch.14

s. 20, amended: 1977, c.30, sch.1; 1980, c.51, s.143.

s. 23, see *Italica Holdings S.A.* v. *Bayadea* (1985) 273 E.G. 888, French J.

s. 25, see *Pelosi* v. *Newcastle Arms Brewery (Nottingham)* (1982) 43 P. & C.R. 18, C.A.

s. 25, repealed in pt.: 1986, c.44, sch.9.

39. Medical and Dentists Acts Amendment Act 1927.
repealed: order 87/2047

40. Indian Church Act 1927.
repealed: S.L.R. 1976.

41. Superannuation and other Trust Funds (Validation) Act 1927.
s. 3, regs. 74/1301; 76/354; 79/1557.
ss. 7–8, 10, 11 (in pt.), repealed: 1973, c.38, sch.28.

CAP.

17 & 18 Geo. 5 (1927)—cont.

42. Statute Law Revision Act 1927.
s. 2, repealed: 1977, c.38, sch.5.
s. 4, repealed in pt.: 1973, c.36, sch.6.

18 & 19 Geo. 5 (1928)

3. Patents and Designs (Convention) Act 1928.
repealed: 1986, c.39, sch.3.
13. Currency and Bank Notes Act 1928.
s. 3, repealed in pt.: S.L.R. 1973.
ss. 5, 7, repealed: 1983, c.9, sch.
s. 6, amended: 1983, c.9, s.3; repealed in pt.: 1972, c.41, sch.28.
15. Bankers (Northern Ireland) Act 1928.
s. 1, repealed in pt.: 1980, c.59, sch.
17. Finance Act 1928.
s. 6, repealed in pt.: 1975, c.45, sch.14.
s. 26, repealed: S.L.R. 1986.
s. 30, repealed in pt.: 1975, c.7, sch.13.
s. 31, repealed: 1986, c.41, sch.23.
s. 35, repealed in pt.: S.L.R. 1976; S.L.R. 1986.
19. Agricultural Produce (Grading and Marking) Act 1928.
s. 3, repealed in pt.: S.L.R. 1973.
ss. 4, 5, repealed in pt.: 1972, c.70, sch.30; 1973, c.65, sch.29(S.).
s. 6, regs. 76/1833.
s. 8, amended: 1973, c.65, sch.27.
21. Dogs (Amendment) Act 1928.
s. 1, repealed in pt.: 1987, c.9, sch.
23. Straits Settlements and Johore Territorial Waters (Agreement) Act 1928.
repealed: S.L.R. 1973.
24. Northern Ireland (Miscellaneous Provisions) Act 1928.
s. 2, repealed: 1973, c.36, sch.6.
s. 3, repealed: order 79/1575.
26. Administration of Justice Act 1928.
repealed: 1981, c.54, sch.7.
s. 16, repealed (S.): 1986, c.9, sch.2.
29. Slaughter of Animals (Scotland) Act 1928.
repealed: 1980, c.13, sch.3.
32. Petroleum (Consolidation) Act 1928.
s. 1, amended: regs. 74/1942.
s. 2, amended: 1972, c.70, sch.29; regs 74/1942; 1985, c.51, sch.11.
s. 3, substituted. regs. 74/1942.
s. 4, amended: regs. 74/1942; 87/52.
s. 5, amended: regs. 74/1942.
s. 6, regs. 73/1221.
ss. 6, 7 (in pt.), 8 (in pt.), repealed: regs. 74/1942.
ss. 7, 8, order 87/37.
s. 9, amended: regs. 74/1942.
ss. 10, 12, repealed: ibid.
s. 13, repealed: regs. 80/804.
s. 20, amended: 1985, c.72, sch.12.
s. 23, amended and repealed in pt.: regs. 74/1942.
s. 24, amended: 1973, c.65, sch.27.
sch. 1, repealed: regs. 87/52.
34. Reorganisation of Offices (Scotland) Act 1928.
ss. 2, 4, 7, repealed: S.L.R. 1981.
ss. 8, 9, repealed: 1988, c.36, sch.2.
ss. 11, 12, repealed: S.L.R. 1981.
s. 13, repealed in pt.: ibid.

CAP.

18 & 19 Geo. 5 (1928)—cont.

35. Easter Act 1928.
sch., repealed in pt.: 1979, c.60, sch.3.
42. Criminal Law Amendment Act 1928.
repealed: 1976, c.67, sch.2.
43. Agricultural Credits Act 1928.
s. 5, amended: 1979, c.37, sch.6; 1981, c.65, sch.6; 1986, c.5, sch.14; 1987, c.22, sch.6; repealed in pt.: 1985, c.58, sch.4.
ss. 6, 7, see Re Fox (A Bankrupt), ex p. Midland Bank v. The Trustee, April 21, 1975.
s. 7, amended: 1985, c.65, sch.8.
s. 8, repealed in pt.: ibid., sch.10.
s. 9, order 85/372.
s. 9, amended: 1972, c.61, sch.3.
sch., added: ibid.; order 75/1314.
44. Rating and Valuation (Apportionment) Act 1928.
s. 3, see Renfrew Assessor v. McGregor & Sons [1974] S.L.T. 17, Lands Valuation Appeal Ct.; Occidental Inc. v. Assessor for Orkney, 1979 S.L.T. 60; Assessor for West Lothian v. Vibroplant, 1980 S.C. 34; Assessor for Grampian Region v. Claben, 1981 S.L.T. (Notes) 108; Total Oil Marine v. Assessor for Grampian Region, 1982 S.L.T. 253; Assessor for Highland Region v. Highland Omnibuses, 1983 S.L.T. 237; Assessor for Grampion Region v. Bristow Helicopters, 1983 S.C. 206; Assessor for Strathclyde Region v. B.S.R., 1987, S.L.T. 250; Assessor for Lothian Region v. Harper, The Scotsman, July 2, 1988.
ss. 3, 4, see Castrol v. Lanarkshire Assessor, 1974 S.L.T. 302.
s. 5, see B.P. Oil Grangemouth Refinery v. Assessor for Lothian Region, 1985 S.L.T. 228.
s. 5, amended (S.): 1984, c.54, sch.9.
ss. 5, 6, see Clyde Container Services v. Assessor for Renfrewshire, 1971 S.C. 14, Ct. of Sess.; Aberdeen Harbour Board v. Assessor for the City of Aberdeen, 1973 S.L.T. 93; 1973 S.C. 76, L.V.A.C.
s. 9, see Castrol v. Lanarkshire Assessor, 1974 S.L.T. 302.
s. 9, amended: 1975, c.30, sch.6 (S.); 1984, c.31, sch.2.
ss. 9, 10, repealed in pt. (S.): S.L.R. 1975.
46. Theatrical Employers Registration (Amendment) Act 1928.
repealed: 1982, c.30, s.11, sch.7.

19 & 20 Geo. 5 (1929)

8. Appellate Jurisdiction Act 1929.
repealed: S.L.R. 1976.
13. Agricultural Credits (Scotland) Act 1929.
s. 9, amended: 1979, c.37, sch.6; 1981, c.65, sch.6; 1987, c.22, sch.6; repealed in pt.: 1985, c.58, sch.4.
14. Northern Ireland Act 1929.
s. 7, amended: orders 73/2095; 77/2157.
s. 8, repealed in pt.: 1973, c.36, sch.6.
17. Local Government Act 1929.
ss. 30, 31, repealed in pt.: 1972, c.70, sch.30.
ss. 46, 50, repealed: S.L.R. 1975.

CAP.

19 & 20 Geo. 5 (1929)—cont.

17. Local Government Act 1929—cont.
s. 57, repealed in pt.: S.L.R. 1976.
s. 79, repealed: 1972, c.71, sch.6.
s. 85, repealed: S.L.R. 1976.
s. 114, repealed: S.L.R. 1975.
s. 117, repealed in pt.: 1972, c.70, sch.30.
s. 127, repealed: S.L.R. 1976.
s. 134, repealed in pt.: 1972, c.70, sch.30; S.L.R. 1975.
s. 138, repealed in pt.: ibid.
sch. 1, repealed: 1972, c.70, sch.30.
sch. 10, repealed in pt.: S.L.R. 1974.

25. Local Government (Scotland) Act 1929.
ss. 1–3, repealed: 1973, c.65, sch.29.
ss. 5, 6, 10, 11, 18, 24, 26, repealed: ibid., schs.27, 29.
ss. 20, 47, 48, repealed. S.L.R. 1986.
s. 29, amended: 1973, c.65, sch.27.
ss. 34, 41, 49 (in pt.), 50–52, 76, repealed: ibid., schs. 27, 29.
s. 77, amended: ibid., sch.27; repealed in pt.: ibid., schs.27, 29, S.L.R. 1986.
s. 79, schs. 1, 2, 5, repealed: 1973, c.65, schs.27, 29

28. Industrial Assurance and Friendly Societies Act 1929.
ss. 1, 3, 5, repealed in pt.: 1974, c.46, sch.11.

29. Government Annuities Act 1929.
s. 22, repealed in pt.: 1985, c.54, sch.27.
s. 30, repealed: S.L.R. 1974.
s. 43, regs. 79/552.
s. 51, repealed in pt.: 1985, c.58, sch.4.
s. 52, regs. 79/552.
s. 58, repealed in pt.: 1985, c.54, sch.27.
s. 62, repealed in pt.: order 79/1714.
s. 65, repealed: S.L.R. 1974.

33. Bridges Act 1929.
repealed (S.): 1984, c.54, sch.11.
s. 13, amended: 1984, c.12, sch.4.

34. Infant Life (Preservation) Act 1929.
see C. v. S. [1987] 1 All E.R. 1230, C.A.
s. 2, repealed in pt.: 1984, c.60, sch.7.

36. Age of Marriage Act 1929.
repealed (S.): 1977, c.15, sch.3.
s. 1, repealed in pt.: 1976, c.67, sch.2.

37. Police Magistrates Superannuation Amendment Act 1929.
repealed: 1973, c.15, sch.5

39. Salmon and Freshwater Fisheries (Amendment) Act 1929.
repealed: 1975, c.51, sch.5.

20 & 21 Geo. 5 (1929–30)

5. Colonial Development Act 1929.
s. 4, repealed: S.L.R. 1976.

6. Housing (Revision of Contributions) Act 1929.
repealed: S.L.R. 1981.

7. Development (Loan Guarantees and Grants) Act 1929.
repealed: S.L.R. 1973.

20. Land Drainage (Scotland) Act 1930.
s. 4, amended: 1982, c.48, sch.6.

CAP.

20 & 21 Geo. 5 (1929–30)—cont.

24. Railways (Valuation for Rating) Act 1930.
s. 22, amended (S.): 1975, c.30, sch.6.

25. Third Parties (Rights against Insurers) Act 1930.
see Pioneer Concrete (U.K.) v. National Employers Mutual General Insurance Association [1985] 2 All E.R. 395; [1985] 1 Lloyd's Rep. 274, Bingham J.; Aluminium Wire and Cable Co. v. Allstate Insurance Co. [1985] 2 Lloyd's Rep. 280, N. Collier Q.C. (sitting as deputy judge); Firma C-Trade S.A. v. Newcastle Protection and Indemnity Association [1987] 2 Lloyd's Rep. 229, Staughton J.; Socony Mobil Oil Co. Inc. v. West of England Ship Owners Mutual Insurance Association; Padre Island, The (No. 2) [1987] 2 Lloyd's Rep. 529, Saville J.
s. 1, see Socony Mobil Oil Co. Inc., Mobil Oil Co. and Mobil Oil A.-G. v. The West of England Shipowners Mutual Insurance Association (London); Padre Island, The [1984] 2 Lloyd's Rep. 408, Leggatt J.
s. 1, amended: 1985, c.65, sch.8; c.66, sch.7(S.); 1986, c.45, sch.14.
s. 2, amended: 1985, c.65, sch.8; 1986, c.45, sch.14.
s. 3, amended: 1985, c.65, sch.8.
s. 4, amended: ibid.; c.66, sch.7(S.); 1986, c.45, sch.14; repealed in pt. (S.): 1985, c.65, schs.7,8.
s. 4, amended: ibid., c.66, sch.7(S.); repealed in pt.(S.): ibid., schs.7, 8.

26. British North America Act 1930.
Act renamed Constitution Act 1930: 1982, c.11, sch.
s. 1, sch., see R. v. Secretary of State for Foreign and Commonwealth Affairs, ex p. Indian Association of Alberta [1982] 2 W.L.R. 641, C.A.

28. Finance Act 1930.
s. 41, see Chelsea Land & Investment Co. v. I.R.C. [1978] 2 All E.R. 113, C.A.
ss. 41, 45, repealed: 1973, c.51, sch.22.
s. 42, see Canada Safeway v. I.R.C. [1972] 2 W.L.R. 443; [1972] 1 All E.R. 666.
Pt. III (ss.33–40), sch. 2, repealed: 1975, c.7, sch.13.
s. 53, repealed in pt.: ibid.

33. Illegitimate Children (Scotland) Act 1930.
repealed: 1986, c.9, sch.2.
s. 1, see Freer v. Taggart, 1975 S.L.T.(Sh.Ct.) 13; Findlay v. Pallys, 1977 S.L.T.(Sh.Ct.) 13; Bell v. McCurdie, Second Division, October 17, 1980.
s. 2, see A. v. N., 1973 S.L.T.(Sh.Ct.) 34; A. v. G., 1984 S.L.T.(Sh.Ct.) 65.

37. Adoption of Children (Scotland) Act 1930.
repealed: S.L.R. 1977.

39. Housing Act 1930.
repealed: S.L.R. 1981.

40. Housing (Scotland) Act 1930.
repealed: 1972, c.46, sch.11.

43. Road Traffic Act 1930.
Pt. III (ss.45–60), repealed (S.): 1984, c.54, sch.11.

CAP.

20 & 21 Geo. 5 (1929–30)—cont.

43. Road Traffic Act 1930—cont.
s. 54, repealed in pt.: S.L.R. 1975.
s. 101, repealed in pt.: 1985, c.67, schs.7, 8.
s. 107, repealed in pt.: 1972, c.70, sch.30.
s. 108, amended (S.): 1973, c.65, sch.18; repealed in pt.: 1972, c.70, sch.30.
s. 109, amended (S.): 1973, c.65, sch.18.
s. 119, amended (S.): ibid., sch.14; 1984, c.54, sch.9; repealed in pt. (S.): ibid., sch.11.
s. 121, repealed in pt.: 1985, c.51, sch.7; c.67, sch.8.

44. Land Drainage Act 1930.
repealed: 1976, c.60, sch.8.
s. 4, orders 72/1305, 1557, 1738, 1832; 73/114, 126, 250, 438, 989, 995, 996, 1235, 1356, 1507, 1902–1906; 74/199, 334, 347, 534, 589, 590, 1209, 1536, 1537, 1980; 75/543, 1770, 1783; 76/109, 498, 532, 557, 558, 568, 569, 845, 858, 913, 1367, 1392–4, 1502, 1562, 1852; 77/678, 685–687, 1151, 1208, 1398, 1449; 78/79, 506.
s. 8, orders, 74/535; 76/469.
s. 11, order 77/1498.
s. 14, orders 72/1557; 73/114, 126, 438; 74/199, 334, 347, 534, 589, 590, 1536, 1537, 1980.
s. 22, regs. 74/375.
s. 23, amended: regs. 74/595.
s. 34, see Welsh National Water Development Authority (Formerly Gwynedd River Authority) v. Burgess (1974) 28 P. & C.R. 378, C.A.; Rimmer v. River Crossens Drainage Board (1976) 239 E.G. 817.
s. 49, order 75/345.
s. 61, amended: 1972, c.60, sch.6; 1973, c.64, sch.2.
s. 74, regs. 74/375.
ss. 79, 80, amended: 1972, c.11, sch.8.

51. Reservoirs (Safety Provisions) Act 1930.
repealed: 1975, c.23, s.28.
ss. 5, 10, see Braintree D.C. v. Gosfield Hall Settlement Trustees, July 13, 1977, Chelmsford Crown Ct.

21 & 22 Geo. 5 (1930–31)

9. Colonial Naval Defence Act 1931.
s. 2, repealed in pt.: 1981, c.55, sch.5.

16. Ancient Monuments Act 1931.
repealed: 1979, c.46, sch.5.

17. Local Authorities (Publicity) Act 1931.
repealed: 1972, c.70, sch.30; 1973, c.65, sch.29 (S.).

21. East Africa Loans (Amendment) Act 1931.
repealed: S.L.R. 1976.

28. Finance Act 1931.
s. 28, amended: 1972, c.52, sch.21.
s. 35, repealed in pt.: 1985, c.54, s.89, sch.27.
ss. 40, 41, repealed: 1975, c.7, sch.13.
s. 42, repealed: 1973, c.51, sch.22.
sch. 2, amended: 1972, c.52, sch.21.

33. Architects (Registration) Act 1931.
s. 18, repealed in pt.: 1973, c.36, sch.6.

39. Housing (Rural Authorities) Act 1931.
repealed: 1972, c.46, sch.11(S.); S.L.R. 1981.

CAP.

21 & 22 Geo. 5 (1930–31)—cont.

41. Agricultural Land (Utilisation) Act 1931.
ss. 8–10, repealed: S.L.R. 1973.
ss. 11, repealed in pt.: 1972, c.70, sch.30; S.L.R. 1973.
s. 12, amended: 1980, c.65, sch.33.
s. 14, repealed in pt.: 1972, c.70, sch.30; S.L.R. 1973.
ss. 16 (in pt.), 17, 19 (in pt.), 23 (in pt.); repealed: ibid.
s. 24, amended(S.): 1973, c.65, sch.27; repealed in pt.: S.L.R. 1973.

43. Improvement of Live Stock (Licensing of Bulls) Act 1931.
repealed: 1984, c.40, s.12, sch.2.
regs. 72/1261, 1309.

44. Small Landholders and Agricultural Holdings (Scotland) Act 1931.
s. 23, see McGregor v. Garrow, 1973 S.L.T. 3.
s. 41, sch. 1, repealed: S.L.R. 1973.

46. Gold Standard (Amendment) Act 1931.
repealed: S.L.R. 1986.

22 & 23 Geo. 5 (1931–32)

2. Expiring Laws Act 1931.
repealed: S.L.R. 1976.

4. Statute of Westminster 1931.
ss. 4, 7, see R. v. Secretary of State for Foreign and Commonwealth Affairs, ex p. Indian Association of Alberta [1982] 2 W.L.R. 641, C.A.; Manuel v. Att.-Gen. [1982] 3 W.L.R. 321, C.A.
ss. 4, 9, 10, amended: 1986, c.2, s.12.
s. 11, repealed: 1978, c.30, sch.3.

9. Merchant Shipping (Safety and Load Line Conventions) Act 1932.
ss. 12, 24, 27, 29–31, amended: 1979, c.39, sch.6.
s. 36, orders 73/1315, 1316; 75/413; 79/1707; 81/1540.

11. Northern Ireland (Miscellaneous Provisions) Act 1932.
s. 3, repealed: 1973, c.36, sch.6.
s. 5, repealed: 1978, c.23, sch.7.
s. 9, amended: ibid., sch.5; repealed in pt.: 1973, c.36, sch.6.

12. Destructive Imported Animals Act 1932.
s. 2, regs. 75/2222, 2223; 77/2121, 2122; 79/1668, 1669; 82/1882, 1883; 87/2224, 2225.
s. 10, orders 72/1784, 1785; 77/1993, 1994; 82/1744, 1745; 87/2195, 2196.
s. 12, repealed in pt.: 1973, c.36, sch.6.

17. Tanganyika and British Honduras Loans Act 1932.
repealed: S.L.R. 1976.

25. Finance Act 1932.
s. 24, repealed: 1979, c.30, sch.
s. 25, repealed in pt.: ibid.

32. Patents and Designs Act 1932.
repealed: S.L.R. 1986.

34. British Museum Act 1932.
s. 1, amended: 1972, c.54, s.4.
s. 2, repealed in pt.: S.L.R. 1978.

CAP.

22 & 23 Geo. 5 (1931–32)—cont.

39. Extradition Act 1932.
s. 1, repealed in pt.: 1978, c.26, sch.2.

46. Children and Young Persons Act 1932.
repealed: S.L.R. 1977.

47. Children and Young Persons (Scotland) Act 1932.
repealed: 1986, c.9, sch.2.

51. Sunday Entertainments Act 1932.
s. 1, repealed: 1985, c.13, sch.3.
s. 2, repealed: S.L.R. 1978.
s. 4, repealed in pt.: 1985, c.13, sch.3.
s. 5 repealed in pt.: 1972, c.19, sch.; 1985, c.13, sch.3
sch., repealed: 1972, c.19, sch.

53. Ottawa Agreements Act 1932.
repealed: S.L.R. 1986.

55. Administration of Justice Act 1932.
repealed: 1981, c.54, sch.7.

23 & 24 Geo. 5 (1932–33)

12. Children and Young Persons Act 1933.
s. 1, see R. v. Lowe [1973] 2 W.L.R. 281; [1973] 1 All E.R. 805, C.A.; Marsh v. Hodgson [1974] Crim.L.R. 35, D.C.; R. v. Gibbins [1977] Crim.L.R. 741, Woodford Crown Ct.; R. v. Sheppard [1980] 3 W.L.R. 961, H.L; Gibson [1984] Crim.L.R. 615; (1985) 80 Cr.App.R. 24, C.A.; R. v. Lane and Lane [1985] Crim.L.R. 789; (1986) 82 Cr.App.R. 5, C.A.; R. v. Beard (1987) 85 Cr.App.R. 395, C.A.
s. 1, amended: 1988, c.33, s.45; repealed in pt.: ibid., sch.16.
s. 3, amended: 1977, c.45, ss.15,30, sch.1.
s. 5, see Lincoln Corporation v. Parker [1974] 1 W.L.R. 713, D.C.
s. 7, amended and repealed in pt.: 1975, c.72, schs.3,4; 1986, c.34, s.1.
s. 8, repealed: 1974, c.39, sch.5.
ss. 10, 13, 15, repealed: 1984, c.60, sch.7.
s. 12, amended: 1985, c.13, sch.2; c.51, sch 8; repealed in pt.: 1985, c.13, sch.3.
s. 18, amended: 1972, c.44, s.1; (prosp.) 1973, c.24, sch.2.
s. 19, repealed (prosp.): ibid.
s. 21, see Portsea Island Mutual Co-operative Society v. Leyland [1978] Crim.L.R. 554, D.C.
s. 25, order 76/773.
s. 26, repealed in pt.: 1980, c.62, sch.8; 1984, c.60, sch.7.
s. 28, amended: 1973, c.24, sch.2 (prosp.); 1984, c.46, sch.5.
s. 34, amended: 1984, c.60, sch.57.
s. 38, see D.P.P. v. Hester [1972] 3 W.L.R. 910; [1972] 3 All E.R. 1056; R. v. Khan, The Times, February 11, 1981, C.A.; R. v. Campbell, The Times, December 10, 1982, C.A.
s. 38, repealed in pt.: 1988, c.33, s.34, sch.16.
s. 39, amended: 1977, c.45, s.31, sch.6; 1982, c.48, sch.3; 1984, c.46, sch.5.
s. 40, repealed in pt.: 1984, c.60, sch.7.
s. 44, see R. v. Ford; R. v. Johnson; R. v. Wright; R. v. Vernon (1976) 62 Cr.App.R. 303, C.A.
s. 46, amended: 1980, c.43, sch.7.

CAP.

23 & 24 Geo. 5 (1932–33)—cont.

12. Children and Young Persons Act 1933—cont.
s. 47, see R. v. Southwark Juvenile Court, ex p. J. [1973] 1 W.L.R. 1300, D.C.; R. v. Willesden Justices, ex p. Brent London Borough [1988] 2 F.L.R. 95, Sheldon J.
s. 49, amended: 1977, c.45, s.31, sch.6; 1982, c.48, sch.3; 1984, c.46, sch.5.
s. 50, see R. v. F. (A Child), The Times, March 20, 1985, C.A.; R. v. F. (A Child), The Times, April 20, 1985, C.A.
s. 53, see R. v. Storey; R. v. Fuat; R. v. Duignan [1973] 1 W.L.R. 1045, C.A.; R. v. Bosomworth (1973) 57 Cr.App.R. 708, C.A.; R. v. Bryson (1973) 59 Cr.App.R. 464, C.A; R. v. Ford; R. v. Johnson; R. v. Wright; R. v. Vernon (1976) 62 Cr.App.R. 303, C.A.; R. v. Oakes (1983) 5 Cr.App.R.(S.) 389, C.A.; R. v. Massheder (1983) 5 Cr.App.R.(S.) 442, C.A.; R. v. Ward (S.) (1983) 5 Cr.App.R.(S.) 372, C.A.; R. v. South Hackney Juvenile Court, ex p. R. B. (A Minor) and C. B. (A Minor) (1983) 77 Cr.App.R. 294, D.C.; R. v. R., The Times, July 31, 1984, C.A.; R. v. F. (A Child), The Times, March 20, 1985, C.A.; R. v. F. (A Child), The Times, April 20, 1985, C.A.; R. v. Nightingale (1984) 6 Cr.App.R.(S.) 65, C.A.; R. v. Storey (Stephen) (1984) 6 Cr.App.R.(S.) 104, C.A.; R. v. Butler (M. P.) (1984) 6 Cr.App.R.(S.) 263, C.A.; R. v. Horrocks, The Times, February 8, 1986, C.A.; R. v. Burrowes (1985) 7 Cr.App.R.(S.) 106, C.A.; R. v. Gaskin (1985) 7 Cr.App.R.(S.) 28, C.A.; R. v. Mckenna (1985) 7 Cr.App.R.(S) 348, C.A.; R. v. Fairhurst [1986] 1 W.L.R. 1374, C.A.; R. v. Padwick and New (1985) 7 Cr.App.R.(S) 452, C.A.; R. v. Ealand and Standing (1986) 83 Cr.App.R. 241, C.A.; R. v. Brown and Chung (1986) 8 Cr.App.R.(S.) 417, C.A.; R. v. Masters (1986) 8 Cr.App.R.(S.) 421, C.A.; R. v. Learmouth, The Times, June 13, 1988, C.A.; R. v. Godber (1986) 8 Cr.App.R.(S.) 460, C.A.
s. 53, amended: 1988, c.33, s.126.
s. 55, see R. v. Croydon Juvenile Court Justices [1973] 2 W.L.R. 61, D.C.; Somerset C.C. v. Brice [1973] 1 W.L.R. 1169; [1973] 3 All E.R. 438, D.C.; Somerset C.C. v. Kingscott [1975] 1 W.L.R. 283; [1975] 1 All E.R. 326, D.C.; Leicestershire C.C. v. Cross [1976] 2 All E.R. 491, D.C.; Leeds City Council v. West Yorkshire Metropolitan Police [1982] 2 W.L.R. 186, H.L.; R. v. Sheffield Crown Court, ex p. Clarkson (1986) 8 Cr.App.R.(S.) 454, D.C.
s. 55, substituted: 1982, c.48, s.26; 1988, c.33, s.127.
s. 56, see R. v. Billericay JJ., ex p. Johnson [1979] Crim.L.R. 315, D.C.; R. v. South Hackney Juvenile Court, ex p. R. B. (A Minor) and C. B. (A Minor) (1983) 77 Cr.App.R. 294, D.C.
ss. 62, 76, see H. v. H. [1973] 2 W.L.R. 525; [1973] 1 All E.R. 801.
ss. 86–89, 92, 93, repealed: 1980, c.5, sch.6.
s 96, amended: 1980, c.5, sch.5; repealed in pt.: 1981, c.67, sch.6.
s. 102, repealed in pt.: 1980, c.5, sch.6.

CAP.

23 & 24 Geo. 5 (1932–33)—cont.

12. Children and Young Persons Act 1933—cont.

s. 106, amended: 1988, c.33, s.129; repealed in pt.: 1980, c.5, sch.6.

s. 107, see *R.* v. *Croydon Juvenile Court Justices* [1973] 2 W.L.R. 61, D.C.; *Somerset C.C.* v. *Brice* [1973] 1 W.L.R. 1169; [1973] 3 All E.R. 438, D.C.; *Leeds City Council* v. *West Yorkshire Metropolitan Police* [1982] 2 W.L.R. 186, H.L.

s. 107, amended: 1978, c.22, sch.2; 1979, c.55, sch.2; repealed in pt.: 1980, c.5, sch.6; S.L.R. 1986.

sch. 1, see *R.* v. *Geisheimer*, March 26, 1981, Waterhouse J., Cardiff Crown Ct.

sch. 1, amended: 1978, c.37, s.1; 1988, c.33, sch.15.

sch. 2, orders 73/593, 1665; 74/1584; 84/713.

ssh. 2, amended: 1985, c.61, s.61; order 85/1383.

sch. 5, repealed in pt.: S.L.R. 1975.

13. Foreign Judgments (Reciprocal Enforcement) Act 1933.

see *Compagnie Francaise de Télévision* v. *Thorn Consumer Electronics* [1981] F.S.R. 306, Whitford J.; *Interpol* v. *Galani* [1987] 2 All E.R. 981, C.A.

s. 1, orders 73/610–612; 77/2149; 87/2211; 88/1304, 1853.

s. 1, amended: 1982, c.27, sch.10.

ss. 1, 2, 4, 5, see *S.A. Consortium General Textiles* v. *Sun and Sand Agencies* [1978] 2 W.L.R. 1, C.A.

ss. 1, 3, orders 73/1894; 80/1523; 81/735; 86/2027; 87/468.

s. 2, repealed in pt.: 1977, c.38, s.4, sch.5.

ss. 3, 10, amended: 1981, c.54, sch.5.

s. 4, repealed in pt.: 1982, c.27, sch.14.

s. 8, see *Black-Clawson International* v. *Papierwerke Waldhof-Aschaffenburg Aktiengesellschaft* [1975] 2 W.L.R. 513; [1975] 1 All E.R. 810, H.L.; *Maples (Formerly Melamud)* v. *Maples; Maples (Formerly Melamud)* v. *Melamud* [1987] 3 W.L.R. 487, Latey J.

s. 9, repealed in pt.: 1982, c.27, schs.10,14.

s. 10, substituted: *ibid.*, sch.10.

s. 10A, added: *ibid.*

s. 11, amended: *ibid.*: repealed in pt.: *ibid.*, schs.10,14.

s. 12, 13, repealed in pt.: *ibid.*, sch.14.

s. 13, amended: 1978, c.23, sch.5.

14. London Passenger Transport Act 1933.

ss. 19 (in pt.), 24, repealed: 1984, c.32, sch.7.

s. 51, repealed: S.L.R. 1976.

s. 93, repealed in pt.: 1986, c.44, sch.9.

s. 106, regs. 78/1791.

16. Housing (Financial Provisions) (Scotland) Act 1933.

repealed: 1972, c.46, sch.11.

17. Protection of Animals (Cruelty to Dogs) Act 1933.

repealed: 1988, c.29, sch.

19. Finance Act 1933.

s. 41, repealed: 1973, c.51, sch.22.

s. 43, repealed: 1975, c.7, sch.13.

CAP.

23 & 24 Geo. 5 (1932–33)—cont.

20. False Oaths (Scotland) Act 1933.

s. 2, amended: 1975, c.34, sch.1.

s. 7, repealed in pt.: 1977, c.38, sch.5.

21. Solicitors (Scotland) Act 1933.

repealed: 1980, c.46, sch.7.

s. 18, Acts of Sederunt 76/867; 79/1410.

25. Pharmacy and Poisons Act 1933.

Parts I, II, sch. 2, repealed: 1972, s.66, sch.2.

ss. 8–11A, 12 (in pt.), 13, 14, 17 (in pt.), 18 (in pt.), 19, 23 (in pt.), 25 (in pt.), 29 (in pt.), repealed: order 77/2128.

s. 17, orders 74/80, 1556; 75/1072; 76/979.

s. 23, rules 74/81, 1557; 75/1073; 76/978; 77/1519; order 77/1520.

33. Metropolitan Police Act 1933.

repealed: 1986, c.32, s.35.

35. Trout (Scotland) Act 1933.

s. 5, repealed: S.L.R. 1974.

36. Administration of Justice (Miscellaneous Provisions) Act 1933.

s. 2, see *R.* v. *Groom* [1976] 1 W.L.R. 618, C.A.; *R.* v. *Waters; R.* v. *Tovey; R.* v. *Padfield* [1979] R.T.R. 220, C.A.; *R.* v. *Considine* (1979) 70 Cr.App.R. 239, C.A.; *R.* v. *Raymond* (1980) 72 Cr.App.R. 151; [1981] 2 All E.R. 246, C.A.; *R.* v. *Cairns* [1983] Crim.L.R. 478, D.C.; *R.* v. *Peter Anthony Carey* (1983) 76 Cr.App.R. 152, C.A.; *R.* v. *Liverpool Crown Court, ex p. Bray* [1987] Crim.L.R. 51, D.C.; *R.* v. *Morais* (1988) 87 Cr.App.R. 9, C.A.

s. 2, rules 88/1738.

s. 2, amended: 1981, c.54, sch.5; 1987, c.38, sch.2; 1988, c.33, sch.15; repealed in pt.: 1985, c.23, sch.2.

s. 3, repealed: 1975, c.7, sch.13.

s. 6, see *Rothermere* v. *Times Newspapers* [1973] 1 W.L.R. 448; [1973] 1 All E.R. 1013, C.A.; *Williams (John L.) (Solicitor)* v. *Beesley (Terence)* [1973] 1 W.L.R. 1295, C.A.; *Stafford Winfield Cook & Partners* v. *Winfield* [1980] 3 All E.R. 759, Megarry V.-C.

s. 6, repealed: 1981, c.54, sch.7.

s. 16, rules 73/145, 360, 540, 541.

sch. 2, repealed in pt.: S.L.R. 1986.

41. Administration of Justice (Scotland) Act 1933.

s. 1, repealed (S.): S.L.R. 1975.

ss. 2–6, repealed: 1988, c.36, sch.2.

s. 4, Acts of Sederunt 75/1165; 76/1127; 77/186; 78/926; 79/190, 723; 80/84, 1928; 82/122; 83/119; 84/61; 85/317; 86/543; 87/40.

s. 6, see *Gribben* v. *Gribben*, March 30, 1976; *Gilmont Transport Services* v. *Renfrew District Council* (O.H.), 1982 S.L.T. 290; *Maersk Co.* v. *National Union of Seamen* (O.H.), May 4, 1988; *Stirling Shipping Co.* v. *National Union of Seamen* (O.H.), May 5, 1988.

s. 6, amended: 1975, c.34, sch.1.

s. 8, repealed: S.L.R. 1975.

ss. 9–11, repealed: 1988, c.36, sch. 2.

s. 10, see *McGeachy* v. *Standard Life Assurance Co.*, 1972 S.C. 145.

CAP.

23 & 24 Geo. 5 (1932–33)—cont.

41. Administration of Justice (Scotland) Act 1933—cont.

s. 12, repealed in pt.: S.L.R. 1975.

ss. 13–18, repealed: 1988, c.36, sch.2.

s. 16, rules 72/1530, 1672; 73/984, 1991; 74/939, 945, 946, 1603, 1628, 1686; Acts of Sederunt 74/1981, 2090; 75/74, 89, 474, 475, 1106, 1147, 1585, 1850; 76/137, 282, 283, 372, 467, 745, 779, 847, 867, 1061, 1287, 1605, 1606, 1849, 1994, 2020, 2196, 2197; 77/71, 472, 567, 974, 1621; 78/106, 113, 114, 117, 161, 169, 799, 925, 947, 955, 1373, 1424, 1804; 79/226, 348, 516, 613, 670, 1033, 1438, 1631; 80/290, 291, 388, 891, 892, 909, 1016, 1144, 1554, 1727, 1754, 1801, 1803; 81/496, 497, 1137; 82/174, 467, 654, 804, 1166, 1381, 1679, 1723, 1824, 1825; 83/397, 398, 656, 826, 971, 1210, 1438, 1642, 84/235, 472, 499, 919, 920, 997, 1132, 1133; 85/227, 500, 555, 760, 1178, 1426, 1600; 86/255, 341, 514, 515, 694, 799, 967, 1128, 1231, 1937, 1941, 1955, 2298; 87/871, 1079, 1206, 2160; 88/615, 684, 1032, 1503, 1521.

ss. 19, 21, repealed: 1975, c.21, sch.10.

s. 22, repealed: 1980, c.55, sch.3; S.L.R. 1981.

s. 24, repealed in pt.: 1988, c. 36, sch.2.

s. 27, repealed in pt.: S.L.R. 1981.

s. 28, amended: 1972, c.11, sch.6.

s. 29, repealed: ibid., sch.8.

s. 30, repealed: 1988, c.36, sch.2.

ss. 31, 36, repealed: S.L.R. 1981.

s. 34, Acts of Sederunt 75/73, 1300; 78/115, 1423; 80/1553; 82/1167.

s. 38, repealed: 1976, c.14, sch.2.

s. 40, repealed in pt.: 1988, c.36, sch.2.

44. Church of Scotland (Property and Endowments) Amendment Act 1933.

s. 2, amended: 1973, c.65, schs.27, 29.

51. Local Government Act 1933.

repealed: 1972, c.70, sch.30.

s. 61, rules 73/79, 166.

s. 163, see Dowty Boulton Paul v. Wolverhampton Corporation (No. 2) [1973] 2 W.L.R. 618, C.A.

ss. 165, 179, see Laverstoke Property Co. v. Peterborough Corporation [1972] 1 W.L.R. 1400; [1972] 3 All E.R. 678.

s. 228, see Giddens v. Harlow District Auditor [1972] 70 L.G.R. 485; Asher v. Lacey [1973] 1 W.L.R. 1412; [1973] 3 All E.R. 1008, D.C.; Re Armitage [1972] Ch. 438; [1972] 2 W.L.R. 503; [1972] 1 All E.R. 708; Beecham v. Metropolitan District Auditor (1976) 75 L.G.R. 79, D.C.

ss. 228, 229, 236, see Asher v. Secretary of State for the Environment [1974] 2 W.L.R. 466; [1974] 2 All E.R. 156, C.A.

s. 266, see North West Leicestershire District Council v. East Midlands Housing Association [1981] 3 All E.R. 364, C.A.

s. 292, order 73/1396.

53. Road and Rail Traffic Act 1933.

s. 42, order 86/277.

s. 45, amended (S.): 1984, c.54, sch.9.

CAP.

24 & 25 Geo. 5 (1933–34)

5. Air Force Reserve (Pilots and Observers) Act 1934.

repealed: S.L.R. 1976.

7. Rural Water Supplies Act 1934.

repealed: S.L.R. 1975.

13. Marriage (Extension of Hours) Act 1934.

repealed: 1988, c.44, sch.

17. County Courts (Amendment) Act 1934.

s. 6, see Jones v. Barnett [1984] 3 W.L.R. 333, Judge Paul Baker Q.C.

18. Illegal Trawling (Scotland) Act 1934.

s. 1, repealed: 1984, c.26, sch.2.

s. 4, amended: ibid., sch.1.

s. 5, repealed: ibid., sch.2.

s. 6, amended: ibid., sch.1; repealed in pt.: ibid., sch.2.

21. Protection of Animals Act 1934.

s. 2, amended: 1977, c. 45, s.31, sch.6.

22. Assessor of Public Undertakings (Scotland) Act 1934.

ss. 2, 3, repealed: S.L.R. 1986.

25. Protection of Animals (Cruelty to Dogs) (Scotland) Act 1934.

repealed: 1988, c.29, sch.

30. Cotton Manufacturing Industry (Temporary Provisions) Act 1934.

repealed: 1981, c.19, sch.1.

32. Finance Act 1934.

s. 24, repealed: S.L.R. 1986.

s. 29, repealed: 1973, c.51, sch.2.

36. Petroleum (Production) Act 1934.

s. 1, amended: 1982, c.23, s.18; repealed in pt.: 1987, c.12, sch.3.

s. 2, amended: 1982, c.23, s.18.

s. 3, see B.P. Petroleum Development v. Ryder (1987) 27 R.V.R. 211, Peter Gibson J.

ss. 3, 11, 12, see BP Development, Re, Financial Times, February 26, 1986, Warner J.

s. 4, amended: 1982, c.23, s.12, sch.4.

s. 5, repealed: 1975, c.74, s.16.

s. 6, regs. 72/1522; 78/929; 80/721; 82/1000; 84/397, 1832; 86/1021; 88/1213.

s. 10, repealed in pt.: 1982, c.23, sch.4.

s. 11, repealed in pt.: 1987, c. 12, sch.3.

sch., repealed in pt.: S.L.R. 1978.

40. Administration of Justice (Appeals) Act 1934.

sch., amended: 1974, c.40, sch.4.

41. Law Reform (Miscellaneous Provisions) Act 1934.

see Cookson v. Knowles [1978] 2 W.L.R. 978, H.L.; Nutbrown v. Rosier, The Times, March 1, 1982, Aubrey Myerson Q.C.; Clay v. Pooler [1982] 3 All E.R. 570, Hodgson J.; Ashley v. Vickers, The Times, January 18, 1983, Croom-Johnson J.; Adsett v. West, The Times, February 23, 1983, McCullough J.; Wilson v. Stag, The Times, November 27, 1985, C.A.; Holmes v. Bangladesh Biman Corp, Financial Times, March 9, 1988, C.A.

s. 1, see D'Este v. D'Este [1973] 2 W.L.R. 183; Kandalla v. British Airways Board [1980] 1 All E.R. 341, Griffiths J.; Gammell v. Wilson; Furness v. B. & S. Massey [1981] 2 W.L.R. 248; [1981] 1 All E.R. 578, H.L.; Benson v. Biggs Wall & Co. [1982] 3 All E.R. 300, Pain

CAP.

24 & 25 Geo. 5 (1933–34)—cont.

41. Law Reform (Miscellaneous Provisions) Act 1934—cont.
J.; *Harris* v. *Empress Motors* [1982] 3 All E.R. 306, McCowan J.; *Ronex Properties* v. *John Laing Construction* [1982] 3 W.L.R. 875, C.A.; *Warren-Gash* v. *Lane* (1984) 14 Fam.Law 184, Sheldon J.; *R. (Deceased), Re; R.* v. *O.* (1986) 16 Fam.Law 58, Mr. Registrar Garland; *Lane (Deceased), Re, Lane* v. *Lane* (1986) 16 Fam.Law 74, C.A.; *Whytte* v. *Ticehurst* [1986] 2 W.L.R. 700, Booth J.
s. 1, amended: 1982, c.53, s.4; repealed in pt.: *ibid.*, sch.9.
s. 2, repealed: 1976, c.30, sch.2.
s. 3, see *Mason* v. *Harman* [1972] R.T.R. 1; *Bushwall Properties* v. *Vortex Properties* [1975] 2 All E.R. 214; *General Tyre & Rubber Co.* v. *Firestone Tyre & Rubber Co.* [1975] 1 W.L.R. 819; [1975] 2 All E.R. 173, H.L. *The Aldora* [1975] 2 W.L.R. 791; [1975] 2 All E.R. 69; *Tomkins* v. *Tomkins, The Times,* May 24, 1978, Megarry V.-C.; *Gardner Steel* v. *Sheffield Brothers (Profiles)* [1978] 1 W.L.R. 916, C.A.; *Techno-Impex* v. *Gebr. van Weeide Scheepvaartkantoor BV.* [1981] 2 W.L.R. 821, C.A.; *Alex Lawrie Factures* v. *Modern Injection Moulds* [1981] 3 All E.R. 658, Drake J.; *B.P. Exploration Co. (Libya)* v. *Hunt, The Times,* February 5, 1981, H.L.; *Re F.P. & C.H. Matthews* [1982] 1 All E.R. 338, C.A.; *B.P. Exploration* v. *Hunt (No.2)* [1982] 2 W.L.R. 253, H.L.; *Fablaine* v. *Leygill (No. 2)* [1982] Com.L.R. 162, Whitford J.; *Matarazzo* v. *Kent Area Health Authority, The Times,* March 25, 1983, C.A.; *Wright* v. *British Railways Board* [1983] 2 All E.R. 698, H.L.; *President of India* v. *La Pintada Compania Navigacion S.A.* [1984] 3 W.L.R. 10, H.L.; *Knibb and Knibb* v. *National Coal Board* (1986) 26 R.V.R. 123, C.A.

43. National Maritime Museum Act 1934.
ss. 2, 4, 6, functions transferred: orders 81/207; 86/600.

45. Solicitors Act 1934.
repealed: 1980, c.46, sch.7(S.); S.L.R. 1986.

49. Whaling Industry (Regulation) Act 1934.
amended: orders 78/1030; 83/882; 1979, c.27, sch.
s. 1, substituted: 1981, c.29, s.35.
ss. 2–4, 6, 8, amended: *ibid.*
s. 9, amended: *ibid.*, repealed in pt.: 1981, c.45, sch.
s. 10, amended: 1981, c.29, s.35.
s. 17, amended: *ibid.*, repealed in pt.: *ibid.*, sch.5.

50. Road Traffic Act 1934.
repealed (S.): 1984, c.54, sch.11.
s. 10, see *Lambert* v. *Co-operative Insurance Society* [1975] 2 Lloyd's Rep.485, C.A.
s. 23, repealed: 1973, c.65, schs.14, 29.
s. 41, repealed in pt.: S.L.R. 1976.

51. Milk Act 1934.
s. 10, repealed in pt.: S.L.R. 1973.

53. County Courts Act 1934.
repealed: 1981, c.20, sch.4.
s. 180, see *Jones* v. *Barnett* [1984] 3 W.L.R. 333, Judge Baker Q.C.

CAP.

24 & 25 Geo. 5 (1933–34)—cont.

55. Dindings Agreement (Approval) Act 1934.
repealed: S.L.R. 1973.

56. Incitement to Disaffection Act 1934.
ss. 1, 2, see *R.* v. *Arrowsmith* [1975] 2 W.L.R. 484; [1975] 1 All E.R. 463, C.A.
s. 2, amended: 1972, c.71, sch.5.

25 & 26 Geo. 5 (1935)

2. Supreme Court of Judicature (Amendment) Act 1935.
repealed: 1981, c.54, sch.7.

8. Unemployment Insurance Act 1935.
repealed: S.L.R. 1978.

21. Northern Ireland Land Purchase (Winding Up) Act 1935.
s. 1, repealed in pt.: 1973, c.36, sch.6.
s. 2, repealed. 1978, c.23, sch.7.
s. 6, repealed in pt.: 1973, c.36, sch.6; 1978, c.23, sch.7.
ss. 7 (in pt.), 8, repealed: *ibid.*
ss. 11, 15, repealed in pt.: 1973, c.36, sch.6.
sch. 2, repealed: 1973, c.36, sch.6.

23. Superannuation Act 1935.
s. 14, repealed in pt.: 1981, c.20, sch.4.

25. Counterfeit Currency (Convention) Act 1935.
ss. 1 (in pt.), 2, 6 (in pt.), repealed: 1981, c.45, sch.
s. 4, repealed: 1978, c.26, sch.2.

30. Law Reform (Married Women and Tortfeasors) Act 1935.
s. 6, see *Wah Tat Bank* v. *Chan Cheng Kum* [1975] 2 W.L.R. 475, P.C.; *Acrecrest* v. *W. S. Hattrell & Partners* (1982) 264 E.G. 245, C.A.; *Ronex Properties* v. *John Laing Construction* [1982] 3 W.L.R. 875, C.A.; *Southern Water Authority* v. *Lewis and Duvivier (No. 2)* (1984–85), 1 Const.L.J. 74, H.H. Judge Smout, Q.C., O.R.; *Harper* v. *Gray & Walker* [1985] 2 All E.R. 507, Judge John Newey, Q.C.; *Fortes Service Areas* v. *Department of Transport* (1984) 31 Build.L.R. 5, C.A.; *Nottingham Health Authority* v. *Nottingham City Council* [1988] 1 W.L.R. 903, C.A
s. 6, repealed: 1978, c.47, sch.2.

31. Diseases of Animals Act 1935.
repealed: 1981, c.22, sch.6.

40. Housing Act 1935.
repealed: 1985, c.71, sch.1.

41. Housing (Scotland) Act 1935.
repealed: S.L.R. 1981.

42. Government of India Act 1935.
repealed: S.L.R. 1976.

43. Salmon and Freshwater Fisheries Act 1935.
repealed: 1975, c.51, sch.5.

47. Restriction of Ribbon Development Act 1935.
repealed (S.): except ss.17, 23 (in pt.), 24, 26: 1984, c.54, sch.11.
s. 17, amended: 1973, c.65, sch.15(S.); 1984, c.54, sch.8(S.); c.55, sch.6.
s. 21, repealed: S.L.R. 1975.
s. 23, amended: 1981, c.38, sch.3; 1984, c.12, sch.4.
s. 24, amended (S.): *ibid.*, sch.9; repealed in pt.: S.L.R. 1975.
s. 25, amended (S.): 1973, c.65, sch.14.

26 Geo. 5 & 1 Edw. 8 (1935–36)

1. Government of India (Reprinting) Act 1935.
repealed: S.L.R. 1976.

2. Government of India Act 1935.
Whole Act, except ss. 1 and 311 (in pt.), repealed: S.L.R. 1976.
s. 273, rules 73/727.

15. Civil List Act 1936.
s. 8, repealed in pt.: S.L.R. 1977.

16. Coinage Offences Act 1936.
repealed: 1981, c.45, sch.
s. 1, see R. v. Heron, Storey and Thomas [1982] 1 W.L.R. 451, H.L.
ss. 5, 17, see R. v. Walmsley, Dereya and Jackson (1978) 67 Cr.App.R. 30, C.A.

20. Electricity Supply (Meters) Act 1936.
s. 1, amended: 1983, c.25, sch.1; repealed in pt.: ibid. schs.1,4.
s. 3, amended: ibid., sch.1.

22. Hours of Employment (Conventions) Act 1936.
s. 1, sch. 1 (in pt.), repealed: 1986, c.59, s.7, sch.
s. 4, repealed in pt.: ibid., sch.

26. Land Registration Act 1936.
s. 7, amended: 1972, c.11, sch.6.

27. Petroleum (Transfer of Licences) Act 1936.
s. 1, amended: regs. 74/1942; 78/635; 81/1333; 83/1640; 87/52.

34. Finance Act 1936.
Pt. III, s. 34, repealed: 1975, c.7, sch.13.

35. Solicitors Act 1936.
repealed: 1974, c.26, sch.3.

36. Pilotage Authorities (Limitation of Liability) Act 1936.
repealed: 1983, c.21, sch.4; S.L.R. 1986 (Isle of Man).

40. Midwives Act 1936.
repealed: S.L.R. 1986.

43. Tithe Act 1936.
amended: 1977, c.36, s.56.
ss. 3, 4 (in pt.), repealed: 1977, c.36, sch.9.
s. 7, repealed in pt.: S.L.R. 1975.
s. 13, repealed in pt.: 1972, c.61, sch.5; 1977, c.36, sch.9.
s. 14A, repealed: S.L.R. 1975.
ss. 15, 16 (in pt.), 17, 25 (in pt.), 28 (in pt.), 29, repealed: 1977, c.36, sch.9.
s. 30, amended: 1972, c.61, sch.2.
ss. 34, 47 (in pt.), repealed: 1977, c.36, sch.9.

44. Air Navigation Act 1936.
repealed: S.L.R. 1986.

48. Health Resorts and Watering Places Act 1936.
repealed: 1972, c.70, sch.30; 1973, c.65, sch.29.

49. Public Health Act 1936.
regs. 72/317.
see Dutton v. Bognor Regis U.D.C. [1972] 2 W.L.R. 299; sub nom. Dutton v. Bognor Regis United Building Co. [1972] 1 All E.R. 462; [1972] 1 Lloyd's Rep. 227; Loosmore v. Bridport R.D.C. (1971) 22 P. & C.R. 1084; Anns v. Merton London Borough Council [1977] 2 W.L.R. 1024, H.L.; Perry v. Tendring District

26 Geo. 5 & 1 Edw. 8 (1935–36)—cont.

49. Public Health Act 1936—cont.
Council; Thurbon v. Same [1985] C.I.L.L. 145, H.H. Judge John Newey, Q.C., O.R.; Greater London Council v. Tower Hamlets, London Borough of (1983) 15 H.L.R. 57, D.C.
s. 1, substituted: 1972, c.70, sch.14; amended: 1973, c.32, sch.4; 1977, c.49, sch.14.
ss. 2–5, repealed: 1984, c.22, sch.3.
ss. 2, 3, orders 77/1457–1460; 78/383, 685, 819, 1695; 79/134; 80/609, 1024, 1063, 1104, 1320, 1329, 1330, 1469, 1481, 1497; 81/88, 166, 495, 679, 682, 978; 82/1274, 1275, 1327, 1328, 1479.
s. 6, amended: 1984, c.22, sch.2; c.55, sch.6.
s. 7, repealed in pt.: 1972, c.70, schs.14, 30.
s. 8, repealed: ibid., sch.30.
s. 9, orders 73/577; 77/1459, 1460; 78/383, 685, 819; 79/134; 80/609, 1024, 1063, 1104, 1320, 1329, 1330, 1469, 1481, 1497; 81/87, 88, 166, 495, 679, 682, 978; 82/1274, 1275, 1327, 1328, 1479.
ss. 9, 10, repealed in pt.: 1984, c.22, sch.3.
ss. 11–13, repealed: 1972, c.70, sch.30.
s. 14, repealed: 1973, c.37, s.14, sch.9.
s. 15, see Hutton v. Esher U.D.C. [1973] 2 W.L.R. 917; [1973] 2 All E.R. 1123; Royco Homes v. Eatonwill Construction; Three Rivers District Council, Third Party [1978] 2 W.L.R. 957, Hugh Francis, Q.C.
s. 15, amended: 1972, c.70, sch.15; 1973, c.37, s.14, sch.8.
s. 16, repealed: ibid., s.14, sch.9.
s. 17, see R. v. Secretary of State for Wales and A.B. Hutton (Secretary to the Maes Gerddi Residents Association) [1987] J.P.L. 711, MacPherson J.
ss. 17, 18, amended: 1973, c.37, s.14.
s. 19, amended: ibid.; 1974, c.40, sch.2.
s. 20, see Royco Homes v. Eatonwill Construction; Three Rivers District Council, Third Party [1978] 2 W.L.R. 957, Hugh Francis, Q.C.
s. 20, substituted: 1973, c.37, sch.8; amended: ibid., s.14; 1980, c.66, sch.24; repealed in pt.: 1973, c.37, sch.9.
s. 21, amended: ibid., s.14; 1980, c.66, sch.24; 1985, c.51, sch.4.
ss. 22, 23, amended: 1973, c.37, s.14.
s. 24, amended: ibid., s.14, sch.8.
ss. 25, repealed: 1984, c.55, sch.7.
s. 27, amended: 1973, c.37, s.14; 1974, c.40, sch.2.
s. 28, repealed: 1973, c.37, schs.8, 9.
ss. 29–31, amended: ibid., s.14.
s. 32, amended: ibid., sch.8; repealed in pt.: 1985, c.51, sch.17.
s. 33, amended: 1973, c.37, s.14.
s. 34, see Beech Properties v. G. E. Wallis & Sons [1976] J.P.L. 429.
s. 34, amended: 1973, c.37, s.14, sch.8.
s. 35, repealed: ibid., schs.8, 9.
s. 36, amended: ibid., s.14; 1974, c 40, sch.2.
ss. 37–41, repealed: 1984, c.55, sch.7.
s. 39, see R. v. Cannock Justices (1972) 70 L.G.R. 607, D.C.

CAP.

26 Geo. 5 & 1 Edw. 8 (1935–36)—cont.

49. Public Health Act 1936—cont.

s. 42, see *Northern Ireland Trailers* v. *Preston Corporation* [1972] 1 W.L.R. 203; *sub nom. Northern Ireland Trailers* v. *County Borough of Preston* [1972] 1 All E.R. 260.

ss. 43, 44, 46, 47, repealed: 1984, c.55.sch.7.

ss. 48, 50, amended: 1973, c.37, sch.8.

s. 53, regs. 76/1676; 81/1338.

s. 58, see *Farooqi* v. *Bradford City Metropolitan Council*, May 5, 1981, Judge Dean, Leeds Crown Ct.; *R.* v. *Stroud District Council, ex p. Michael Goodenough; Julian Usborne and Stephen Tomlin* [1982] J.P.L. 240, Woolf J.

s. 61, see *Acrecrest* v. *W. S. Hattrell & Partners* (1982) 264 E.G. 245, C.A.; *Dennis* v. *Charnwood Borough Council* [1982] 3 All E.R 486, C.A.

s. 61, regs. 74/1944; 76/1676; 78/723; 79/601; 80/286; 81/1338; 82/547; 83/195, 1611.

s. 62, regs. 74/1944; 76/1676; 78/723; 80/286; 81/1338; 82/547; 83/195, 611.

s. 63, amended: 1974, c.37, ss.74,76.

s. 64, see *Investors in Industry Commercial Properties* v. *South Bedfordshire District Council (Ellison and Partners (A Firm), Third Party)* [1986] 1 All E.R. 787, C.A.

s. 64, regs. 76/1676.

ss. 64–66, repealed: 1984, c.55, sch.7.

s. 66, see *R.* v. *West Devon Borough Council, ex p. North East Essex Building Co.* [1985] J.P.L. 391, Mann J.

ss. 67, 70, 71, repealed: 1984, c.55, sch.7.

s. 72, see *Iron Trades Mutual Employers Insurance Association* v. *Sheffield Corporation* [1974] 1 W.L.R. 107; [1974] 1 All E.R. 182, D.C.; *Exeter City Council* v. *Exeter Shilhay Community* (1981) 79 L.G.R. 605, Forbes J.; *Mattison* v. *Beverley Borough Council, The Times,* February 16, 1987, C.A.; *Dear* v. *Newham London Borough Council, The Times,* February 23, 1988, C.A.

ss. 72, 73, see *Rother District Council* v. *Coghurst Gardens* (1981) 79 L.G.R. 477, D.C.; *Pentewan Sands* v. *Restormel Borough Council* (1980) 78 L.G.R. 642, D.C.; *Craven District Council* v. *Brewer Properties, The Times,* May 7, 1985, Kennedy J.

ss. 72–77, 79, 80, repealed: 1974, c.40, sch 4.

s. 87, repealed in pt.: 1985, c.51, sch.17.

s. 88, repealed: 1984, c.55, sch 7.

s. 89, repealed: 1976, c.57, sch.2.

s. 90, regs. 76/1676.

s. 90, amended: 1974, c.37, sch.6; repealed in pt.: 1973, c.37, sch.9; 1984, c.55, sch.7.

s. 92, see *Nottingham City District Council* v. *Newton; Nottingham Friendship Housing Association* v. *Newton* [1974] 1 W.L.R. 923; [1974] 2 All E.R. 760; *Coventry City Council* v. *Cartwright* [1975] 1 W.L.R. 845; [1975] 2 All E.R. 99, D.C.; *National Coal Board* v. *Thorne* [1976] 1 W.L.R. 543, D.C.; *National Coal Board* v. *Neath B.C.* [1976] 2 All E.R. 478, D.C.; *Lambeth London Borough Council* v. *Stubbs* (1980) 78 L.G.R. 650, D.C.; *Coven-*

CAP.

26 Geo. 5 & 1 Edw. 8 (1935–36)—cont.

49. Public Health Act 1936—cont.

try City Council v. *Doyle* [1981] 2 All E.R. 184, D.C.; *Wivenhoe Port* v. *Colchester Borough Council* [1985] J.P.L. 175, Chelmsford Crown Court; *Birmingham District Council* v. *McMahon* (1987) 17 H.L.R. 452, D.C.

s. 92, amended: 1982, c.30, s.26.

s. 93, see *R.* v. *Kerrier D.C., ex p. Guppys (Bridport)* (1976) 32 P. & C.R 411, C.A.; *Lambeth Borough Council* v. *Stubbs* (1980) 78 L.G.R. 650, D.C.; *Warner* v. *Lambeth, London Borough of* (1984) 15 H.L.R. 42, D.C.

s. 94, see *Northern Ireland Trailers* v. *Preston Corporation* [1972] 1 W.L.R. 203; *sub nom. Northern Ireland Trailers* v. *County Borough of Preston* [1972] 1 All E.R. 260; *Nottingham City District Council* v. *Newton; Nottingham Friendship Housing Association* v. *Newton* [1974] 1 W.L.R. 923; [1974] 2 All E.R. 760; *R.* v. *Newham JJ., ex p. Hunt; R.* v. *Oxted JJ., ex p. Franklin* [1976] 1 W.L.R. 420; [1976] 1 All E.R. 839, D.C.; *R.* v. *Fenny Stratford JJ., ex p. Watney Mann (Midlands)* [1976] 2 All E.R. 888, D.C.; *R.* v. *Secretary of State for the Environment, ex p. Watney Mann (Midlands)* [1976] J.P.L. 368, D.C.; *Coventry City Council* v. *Doyle* [1981] 2 All E.R. 184, D.C.; *Warner* v. *Lambeth, London Borough of* (1984) 15 H.L.R. 42, D.C.

s. 94, amended: 1974, c.40, sch.2.

s. 95, see *Lambeth London Borough Council* v. *Stubbs* (1980) 78 L.G.R. 650, D.C.

s. 95, amended: 1974, c.40, sch.2.

s. 99, see *Nottingham City District Council* v. *Newton; Nottingham Friendship Housing Association* v. *Newton* [1974] 1 W.L.R. 923; [1974] 2 All E.R. 760; *Salford City Council* v. *McNally* [1975] 3 W.L.R. 87; [1975] 2 All E.R. 860, H.L.; *R.* v. *Newham JJ., ex p. Hunt; R.* v. *Oxted JJ., ex p. Franklin* [1976] 1 W.L.R. 420; [1976] 1 All E.R. 839, D.C.; *Lambeth London Borough Council* v. *Stubbs* (1980) 78 L.G.R. 650, D.C.; *Coventry City Council* v. *Doyle* [1981] 2 All E.R. 184, D.C.; *Warner* v. *Lambeth, London Borough of* (1984) 15 H.L.R. 42, D.C.; *Birmingham City Council* v. *Kelly* (1985) 17 H.L.R. 573, D.C.; *Birmingham District Council* v. *McMahon* (1987) 17 H.L.R. 452, D.C.

s. 100, see *Bradford Metropolitan City Council* v. *Brown, The Times,* March 18, 1986, C.A.

s. 107, see *Epping Forest District Council* v. *Essex Rendering* [1983] 1 All E.R. 359, H.L.

s. 107, amended: 1972, c.70, sch.14.

s. 108, repealed in pt.: *ibid.,* schs.14, 18.

ss. 111–122, 124, 125 (in pt.), 126–136, repealed: 1973, c.37, s.11, sch.9.

ss. 137, 138, 142, repealed: 1984, c.55, sch.7.

s. 143, regs. 74/268, 269; 76/1955; 78/286, 287; orders 79/1315, 1316, 1434, 1435; 82/1671, 1672.

s. 143, amended: 1973, c.32, sch.4; 1977, c.49, sch.14; 1980, c.53, sch.1; 1982, c.16, s.36; c.48, sch.3; repealed in pt.: 1973, c.32, sch.5; 1982, c.16, s.36; 1983, c.41, schs.9,10; 1984, c.22, sch.3.

CAP.

26 Geo. 5 & 1 Edw. 8 (1935–36)—cont.

49. Public Health Act 1936—cont.

ss. 147–170, 179, repealed: *ibid.*

ss. 187, 188, repealed: 1975, c.37, sch.3.

ss. 189–91, repealed: 1973, c.32, sch.5.

s. 193, repealed: 1975, c.37, sch.3.

ss. 194, 195, repealed: 1973, c.32, s.41, sch.5.

s. 196, repealed: *ibid.*, sch.5.

s. 199, repealed: 1975, c.37, schs.2, 3.

s. 203, repealed: 1977, c.49, sch.16.

s. 221, amended: 1976, c.57, s.19; repealed in pt.: *ibid.*, sch.2.

s. 222, see *Bradford Metropolitan City Council v. Brown* (1987) 19 H.L.R. 16, C.A.

s. 222, amended: 1976, c.57, s.19.

s. 226, amended: 1982, c.33, sch.1; 1985, c.13, sch.2.

s. 230, repealed: 1972, c.70, sch.30.

s. 231, amended: 1976, c.57, s.17.

Pt. IX (ss. 235–248), repealed: 1985, c.71, sch.1.

ss. 238, 239, see *R. v. London Borough of Hounslow, ex p. Pizzey* [1977] 1 All E.R. 305, D.C.

ss. 249 (in pt.), 251, 253–256, 258, repealed: 1984, c.22, sch.3.

s. 259, repealed in pt.: 1974, c.40, sch.4.

s. 267, amended: 1982, c.30, sch.6; repealed in pt.: 1984, c.22, sch.3.

s. 268, repealed in pt.: *ibid.*

s. 269, amended: 1984, c.55, sch.6.

s. 271, repealed: 1976, c.57, s.27.

ss. 272, 273, repealed: 1972, c.70, sch.30.

s. 274, repealed: 1976, c.57, sch.2.

s. 276, amended: 1972, c.70, sch.14.

s. 277, repealed: 1976, c.57, sch.2.

s. 278, see *George Whitehouse v. Anglian Water Authority* (Ref./157/1977) 247 E.G. 223; *Leonidis v. Thames Water Authority* (1979) 77 L.G.R. 722, Parker J.

s. 278, amended: 1972, c.70, sch.14.

s. 283, see *Epping Forest District Council v. Essex Rendering* [1983] 1 All E.R. 359, H.L.

s. 283, regs. 76/1226, 1955.

s. 283, amended: 1974, c.44, s.126; 1976, c 57, s.78.

s. 286, repealed: *ibid.*, sch.2.

s. 287, amended: *ibid.*, s.35.

s. 288, amended: 1974, c.44, s.126; 1976, c.57, s.35.

s. 289, see *Warner v. Lambeth, London Borough of* (1984) 15 H.L.R. 42, D.C.

s. 290, see *R. v. Cannock JJ.* (1972) 70 L.G.R. 607, D.C.

s. 290, amended: 1977, c.45, s.31, sch.6.

s. 291, repealed in pt.: 1980, c.65, schs.6, 34.

s. 292, repealed: 1974, c.7, sch.8.

ss. 293 (in pt.), 295, repealed: 1976, c.57, s.27, sch.2.

s. 301, see *Farooqi v. Bradford City Metropolitan Council*, May 5, 1981, Judge Dean, Leeds Crown Ct.; *Cook v. Southend Borough Council, The Times*, April 14, 1987, Simon Brown J.

s. 304, amended: 1976, c.57, s.78.

ss. 306, 308, repealed: 1972, c.70, sch.30.

s. 310, repealed: 1973, c.37, sch.9.

CAP.

26 Geo. 5 & 1 Edw. 8 (1935–36)—cont.

49. Public Health Act 1936—cont.

ss. 312–314, repealed: 1976, c.57, s.27, sch.2.

s. 320, repealed: 1972, c.70, sch.30.

s. 321, repealed: *ibid.*, schs.14, 30.

s. 322, see *R. v. Secretary of State for the Environment, ex p. Jaywick Sands Freeholders Association* [1975] J.P.L. 663, D.C.; *R. v. Kensington and Chelsea (Royal) L.B.C., ex p. Birdwood* (1976) 74 L.G.R. 424, D.C.

s. 322, amended: 1976, c.57, s.27; repealed in pt.: *ibid.*, s.27, sch.2; 1984, c.22, sch.3.

s. 323, repealed: 1976, c.57, s.27, sch.2.

s. 324, functions transferred: orders 81/207; 86/600.

ss. 324, 325, repealed in pt.: 1984, c.22, sch.3.

ss. 326, 327, amended: 1984, c.22, sch.2.

s. 343, see *Cook v. Minion* (1978) 37 P. & C.R. 58, Goulding J.; *Rother District Council v. Coghurst Gardens* (1981) 79 L.G.R. 477, D.C.; *Lambeth London Borough Council v. Stubbs* (1980) 78 L.G.R. 650, D.C.; *Exeter City Council v. Exeter Shilhay Community* (1981) 79 L.G.R. 605, Forbes J.; *British Railways Board v. Tunbridge and Malling District Council* (1981) 79 L.G.R. 589, C.A.

s. 343, amended: 1972, c.70, sch.14; 1982, c.30, s.8; 1984, c.22, sch.2; repealed in pt.: 1974, c.37, sch.10; 1984, c.22, sch.3; 1986, c.44, sch.9.

s 344, repealed: 1984, c.55, sch.7.

s. 346, amended: 1982, c.30, sch.6.

sch. 1, substituted: 1980, c.65, sch.2.

50. Public Health (London) Act 1936.

s. 5, see *Cozens v. Brutus* [1972] 1 W.L.R. 484; 116 S.J. 217; [1972] 2 All E.R. 1.

52. Private Legislation Procedure (Scotland) Act 1936.

s. 5, amended: 1985, c.73, s.57.

s. 11, amended: 1973, c.65, sch.27.

s. 15, order 77/132.

1 Edw. 8 & 1 Geo. 6 (1936–37)

5. Trunk Roads Act 1936.

repealed (S.): 1984, c.54, sch.11.

see *Montcrieff v. Tayside Regional Council* (O.H.) 1987 S.L.T. 374.

s. 3, amended: 1972, c.70, sch.21; repealed in pt.: *ibid.*, schs.21, 30.

s. 6, repealed in pt.: S.L.R. 1973; 1974, c.40, sch.4.

s. 12, repealed in pt : S.L.R. 1973; S.L.R. 1978.

s. 13, sch. 3, repealed in pt.: 1972, c.70, sch.30.

6. Public Order Act 1936.

see *Kent v. Metropolitan Police Commissioner, The Times*, May 15, 1981, C.A.

s. 1, see *O'Moran v D.P.P.; Whelan v. D.P.P.* [1975] 2 W.L.R. 413; [1975] 1 All E.R. 473, D.C.

s. 1, amended: 1975, c.59, sch.5; 1976, c.63, sch.2; 1979, c.31, sch.1.

s. 3, see *Loyal Orange Lodge No. 493 Hawick First Purple v. Roxburgh District Council, Second Division*, December 14, 1979.

CAP.

1 Edw. 8 & 1 Geo. 6 (1936–37)—cont.

6. Public Order Act 1936—cont.
ss. 3–5, repealed: 1986, c.64, sch.3.
s. 5, see *Brutus* v. *Cozens* [1972] 3 W.L.R. 521; [1972] 2 All E.R. 1297; *Vernon* v. *Paddon* [1973] 1 W.L.R. 663; *Garfield* v. *Maddocks* [1973] 2 W.L.R. 888; [1973] 2 All E.R. 303; 57 Cr.App.R. 372; *R. v. Ambrose (Peter Thomas)* (1973) 57 Cr.App.R. 538, C.A.; *R. v. Venna* [1975] 3 W.L.R. 737; [1975] 3 All E.R. 788, C.A.; *Hudson* v. *Chief Constable, Avon & Somerset Constabulary* [1976] Crim.L.R. 451, D.C.; *Simcock* v. *Rhodes* [1977] Crim.L.R. 751; (1977) 66 Cr.App.R. 192, D.C.; *R. v. Oakwell* [1978] 1 W.L.R. 32, C.A.; *R. v. Edwards; R. v. Roberts* (1978) 67 Cr.App.R. 228, C.A.; *R. v. Gedge* [1979] Crim.L.R. 167, C.A; *Maile* v. *McDowell* [1980] Crim.L.R. 586, D.C.; *Parkin* v. *Norman; Valentine* v. *Lilley* [1982] 2 All E.R. 583, D.C.; *Lawrenson* v. *Oxford* [1982] Crim.L.R. 185, D.C.; *Marsh* v. *Arscott* (1982) 75 Cr.App.R. 211, D.C.; *Read* v. *Jones* [1983] Crim.L.R. 809; (1983) 77 Cr.App.R. 246, D.C.; *Harrington* v. *Roots* [1984] 2 All E.R. 474, H.L.; *Parrish* v. *Garfitt* [1984] 1 W.L.R. 911, D.C.; *Allen* v. *Ireland* [1984] 1 W.L.R. 903, D.C.; *Nicholson* v. *Gage* (1985) 80 Cr.App.R. 40, D.C., *Joyce* v. *Hertfordshire Constabulary* (1985) 80 Cr.App.R. 298, D.C.; *G.* v. *Chief Superintendent of Police, Stroud* [1987] Crim.L.R. 269; (1988) 86 Cr.App.R. 92, D.C.
s. 5A, see *R.* v. *Pearce* (1980) 72 Cr.App.R. 295, C.A.
s. 5A, repealed: 1986, c.64, sch.3.
s. 7, see *G.* v. *Chief Superintendent of Police, Stroud* (1988) 86 Cr.App.R. 92, D.C.
s. 7, amended. 1976, c.74, s.70; 1977, c.45, schs.6, 11(S.); repealed in pt.: 1986, c.64, sch.3.
s. 8, amended (S.): 1975, c.20, sch.1; repealed in pt.: *ibid.*, sch.2(S.); 1986, c.64, sch.3.
s. 9, see *Cawley* v. *Frost* [1976] 1 W.L.R. 1207; [1976] 3 All E.R. 743, D.C.; *R.* v. *Edwards; R. v. Roberts* (1978) 67 Cr.App.R. 228, C.A.; *Lawrenson* v. *Oxford* [1982] Crim.L.R. 185, D.C.; *Marsh* v. *Arscott* (1982) 75 Cr.App.R. 211, D.C.
s. 9, amended: 1972, c.71, s.33; 1984, c.54. sch.9(S.); repealed in pt.: 1986, c.64, sch.3.

9. India and Burma (Existing Laws) Act 1937.
repealed: S.L.R. 1976.

14. East India Loans Act 1937.
s. 12, repealed in pt.: 1973, c.36, sch.6.

18. Empire Settlement Act 1937.
repealed: S.L.R. 1976.

28. Harbours, Piers and Ferries (Scotland) Act 1937.
functions transferred: order 76/1775.
s. 1, amended: 1973, c.65, sch.19; repealed in pt.: *ibid.*, sch.29.
s. 2, repealed in pt.: *ibid.*
s. 5, amended: *ibid.*, sch.19.
s. 7, amended: 1972, c.29, s.1; 1973, c.65, sch.19.

CAP.

1 Edw. 8 & 1 Geo. 6 (1936–37)—cont.

28. Harbours, Piers and Ferries (Scotland) Act 1937—cont.
s. 10, repealed in pt.: *ibid.*, schs.25, 29.
s. 17, repealed: *ibid.*, sch.29.
s. 18, substituted: *ibid.*, sch.19.
s. 21, amended: *ibid.*, sch.19; repealed in pt.: 1981, c.23, sch.4.
s. 23, repealed: 1973, c.65, sch.29.
s. 31, amended: *ibid.*, sch.19; repealed in pt.: *ibid.*, sch.29.
sch. 3, substituted: *ibid.*, sch.19.

32. Civil List Act 1937.
s. 3, amended: 1972, c.7, s.2; order 84/39.
s. 4, repealed: S.L.R. 1977.
s. 13, repealed in pt.: *ibid.*

33. Diseases of Fish Act 1937.
s. 1, order 86/283.
s. 1, amended: 1979, c.2, sch.4; 1983, c.30, s.1, sch.
s. 2, orders 73/1415; 74/1016, 1595, 1665, 1995; 75/403, 1525, 1527; 77/118, 2080; 78/744, 775; 79/186, 1366, 1367; 80/69; 81/528–532, 1138(S.), 1204, 1245, 1470; 1634(S.), 1835(S.), 1893(S.); 82/49(S.), 167(S.), 531(S.)–534(S.), 617(S.)–621(S.), 682(S.)–685(S.), 792(S.), 1031(S.), 1239(S.), 1240(S.), 1290(S.), 1291(S.), 1312(S.), 1507(S.), 1508(S.), 1870(S.); 83/266(S.), 267(S.), 734, 963(S.), 982(S.)–988(S.), 1282(S.), 1283(S.); 1341(S.)–1343(S.), 1380(S.), 1423(S.), 1496(S.), 1534(S.), 1824(S.); 84/20(S.), 140(S.), 424(S.), 483(S.)–485(S.).
ss. 2, 2A, 2B, substituted: 1983, c.30, s.2.
s. 3, amended and repealed in pt.: 1983, c.30, sch.
ss. 4, 4A, substituted: *ibid.*, s.3.
ss. 5–7, amended: *ibid.*,sch.
s. 8, amended: 1973, c.37, sch.8; 1983, c.30, sch.; 1986, c.62, sch.4.
s. 9, regs. 84/455; 86/538.
s. 9, amended: 1983, c.30, sch.
s. 10, amended: *ibid.*, s 4, sch.; order 78/1022; repealed in pt.: 1983, c.30, s.4.
s. 11, orders 74/1595, 1665; 75/2046; 79/1366, 1367; 81/528–532, 1138(S.), 1204, 1245, 1470, 1634(S.); 82/1239, 1240, 1291, 1312, 1507(S.), 1508(S.); 83/266(S.), 267(S.), 963(S.), 982(S.)–988(S.), 1282(S.), 1283(S.), 1341(S.)–1343(S.), 1380(S.), 1423(S.), 1496(S.), 1534(S.), 1824(S.); 84/140(S.), 483(S.)–485(S.).
s. 11, substituted: 1983, c.30, sch.
s. 13, orders 73/2093; 78/1022; 84/301; 86/213(S.); 88/195.
s. 13, substituted: 1983, c.30, s 4.

34. Sheep Stocks Valuation (Scotland) Act 1937.
s. 1, see *Tufnell and Nether Whitehaugh Co.*, 1977 S.L.T. (Land Ct.) 14.

37. Children and Young Persons (Scotland) Act 1937.
s. 12, see *Kennedy* v. *S.*, 1986 S.L.T. 679.
s. 12, amended 1975, c.72, sch.3; 1988, c.33, s.45; repealed in pt.: 1975, c.72, sch.4.

CAP.

1 Edw. 8 & 1 Geo. 6 (1936–37)—cont.

37. Children and Young Persons (Scotland) Act 1937—cont.

ss. 13, 14, repealed: 1976, c.67, sch.2.

s. 18, amended and repealed in pt.: 1986, c.34, s.2.

s. 19, repealed: 1974, c.39, sch 5.

s. 20, repealed: 1982, c.45, sch.4.

s. 23, repealed in pt.: 1985, c.13, sch.3.

ss. 24, 25; repealed: 1975, c.21, sch.10

s. 28, amended: 1972, c.44, s.1; 1973, c.24, sch.1.

s. 29, repealed: 1973, c.24, sch.2.

s. 31, amended: ibid., sch.1.

s. 36, amended: 1973, c.24, sch.1; 1984, c.46, sch.5.

s. 37, amended: 1973, c.24, sch.1.

ss. 39–45, repealed: 1975, c.21, sch.10.

s. 46, see C. v. S., The Scotsman, September 9, 1988.

s. 46 amended: 1977, c.45, s.31, sch.6; 1984, c.46, sch.5; repealed in pt.: 1975, c.21, sch.10.

ss. 47–55, repealed: ibid.

s. 57, amended: 1975, c.21, sch.9; repealed in pt.: S.L.R. 1975; 1975, c.21, sch.10.

s. 58, amended: ibid., sch.9; repealed in pt.: ibid., sch.10.

s. 58A, repealed: 1987, c.41, s.59, sch.2.

s. 59, repealed: 1975, c.21, sch.10.

s. 62, amended: ibid., sch.9.

s. 67, repealed: ibid., sch.10.

s. 87, amended: ibid., sch.8.

s. 103, repealed: ibid., sch.10.

s. 105, amended: ibid., sch.9.

s. 110, amended: 1973, c.65, schs.27, 29.

sch. 1, repealed: 1975, c.21, sch.10.

40. Public Health (Drainage of Trade Premises) Act 1937.

s. 2, amended: 1974, c.40, sch.2; repealed in pt.: ibid., schs.3, 4.

s. 3, repealed in pt.: ibid.

s. 4, amended: ibid., sch.3; repealed in pt.: 1973, c.37, schs.8, 9; 1974, c.40, sch.4

s. 7, repealed in pt.: ibid., schs.3, 4.

s. 9, amended: ibid., sch.2.

s. 10, amended: ibid., sch.3.

s. 11, repealed: ibid., sch.4.

s. 12, repealed in pt.: 1973, c.37, sch.9.

s. 14, see Thames Water Authority v. Blue and White Launderettes (1979) 78 L.G.R. 237, C.A.

s. 14, repealed in pt.: 1974, c.40, sch.4; S.L.R. 1986.

43. Public Records (Scotland) Act 1937.

s. 1, Acts of Adjournal 72/227, 88/110; Act of Sederunt 76/745.

s. 3, repealed: 1975, c.20, sch.2.

s. 4, repealed: 1981, c.19, sch.1.

s. 5, amended: 1973, c.65, s.200; 1978, c.51, sch.16; repealed in pt.: 1981, c.19, sch. 1.

s. 7, amended and repealed in pt.: 1985, c.16, s.13.

s. 1v, Acts of Sederunt 74/1720; 75/778, 76/375; 77/976; 79/804; 80/1442; 85/1815.

CAP.

1 Edw. 8 & 1 Geo. 6 (1936–37)—cont.

43. Public Records (Scotland) Act 1937—cont.

s. 11A, added: 1985, c.16, s.19.

s. 12, amended: ibid.

s. 13, repealed in pt.: S.L.R. 1981.

s. 14, repealed in pt.: 1975, c.20, sch.2.

sch. 1, repealed: S.L.R. 1981.

45. Hydrogen Cyanide (Fumigation) Act 1937.

s. 1, amended: 74/1840.

s. 2, repealed: regs. 80/804.

ss. 3–5, sch., repealed: 74/1840.

46. Physical Training and Recreation Act 1937.

s. 3, repealed in pt. (S.): 1973, c.65, s.29.

ss. 4, 5, repealed: 1976, c.57, sch.2.

ss. 4 (in pt.), 5, 7, 10 (in pt.), repealed (S.): 1982, c.43, sch.4.

s. 9, repealed in pt.: S.L.R. 1976; 1976, c.57, sch.2.

s. 10, amended (S.): 1973, c.65, s.162; repealed in pt.: ibid., sch.29.

48. Methylated Spirits (Sale by Retail) (Scotland) Act 1937.

s. 1, amended: 1981, c.23, sch.2.

s. 2, amended: 1973, c.65, sch.25; 1981, c.23, sch.2, repealed in pt.: S.L.R. 1986.

s. 3, repealed: ibid.

s. 6, amended: 1973, c.65, sch.24; repealed in pt.: 1981, c.23, schs.2,4.

54. Finance Act 1937.

s. 29, repealed: S.L.R. 1986.

s. 31, repealed: 1972, c.41, sch.28; 1975, c.7, sch.13.

56. Coal (Registration of Ownership) Act 1937.

repealed: S.L.R. 1973.

59. Cinematograph Films (Animals) Act 1937.

s. 1, amended: 1977, c.45, s.31, sch.6.

67. Factories Act 1937.

s. 47, see Bryce v. Swan Hunter Group, The Times, February 19, 1987, Phillips J.

68. Local Government Superannuation Act 1937.

repealed: 1972, c.11, sch.8; regs. 74/520. repealed, except ss. 28, 29, 30 in pt., 35, 36 in pt., 38, 40 in pt., 42, sch. 2 in pt.: regs. 77/1341.

s. 5, see Hertfordshire County Council v. Retirement Lease Housing Association (1988) 86 L.G.R. 222, Hoffmann J.

s. 24, sch. 3, regs. 81/1263.

s. 35, amended: regs. 81/1250.

s. 40, amended: regs. 77/1341.

69. Local Government Superannuation (Scotland) Act 1937.

repealed: 1972, c.11, sch.8; regs. 74/812.

70. Agriculture Act 1937.

repealed: S.L.R. 1986.

1 & 2 Geo. 6 (1937–38)

6. Air–Raid Precautions Act 1937.

repealed: S.L.R. 1976.

8. Unemployment Insurance Act 1938.

repealed: S.L.R. 1978.

13. Superannuation (Various Services) Act 1938.

s. 1, repealed: 1972, c.11, sch.8.

s. 2, regs. 75/1194.

sch., amended: 1972, c.11, schs.6, 8.

CAP.

1 & 2 Geo. 6 (1937–38)—cont.

21. Dogs Amendment Act 1938.
s. 1, amended: 1972, c.71, sch.5.

22. Trade Marks Act 1938.
modified: 1984, c.19, s.1, sch.1.
see *"Predator" Trade Mark* [1982] R.P.C. 387,
Slade J.; *Coca-Cola Co's Applications, Re*
[1986] 2 All E.R. 274, H.L.
s. 1, substituted: 1986, c.39, sch.1.
s. 2, see *Henry Denny & Sons v. United Biscuits
(U.K.)* (1980) 125 S.J. 96, Graham J.; *McGregor–Doniger Inc. v. Sterling McGregor* [1981]
F.S.R. 299, Whitford J.
s. 2, repealed in pt.: 1984, c.19, s.1.
s. 3, see *Tornado Trade Mark* [1979] R.P.C. 155,
Trade Marks Registry.
s. 4, see *British Northrop v. Texteam Blackburn*
[1973] F.S.R. 241, Megarry J.; *Rolls–Royce
Motors v. Zanelli* [1979] R.P.C. 148, Browne–
Wilkinson J.; *Revlon v. Cripps & Lee* (1979)
124 S.J. 184; *News Group Newspapers v.
The Rocket Record Co.* [1981] F.S.R. 89, Slade
J.; *Rolls–Royce Motors v. Dodd* [1981] F.S.R.
517, Whitford J.; *Gallaher (Dublin), Hergall
(1981) v. The Health Education Bureau* [1982]
F.S.R. 464, H.Ct. of Ireland; *Castrol v. Automotive Oil Supplies* [1983] R.P.C. 315, Vivian
Price, Q.C.; *Parker Knoll v. Knoll Overseas*
[1985] F.S.R. 349, Whitford J.; *CPC (United
Kingdom) v. Keenan* [1986] F.S.R. 527, Peter
Gibson J.; *Mars G.B. v. Cadbury* [1987] R.P.C.
387, Whitford J.; *Smith Kline & French Laboratories v. Higson (K.V.) T/A Europharm*
[1988] F.S.R. 115, Whitford J.; *News Group
Newspapers v. Mirror Group Newspapers
(1986), The Guardian,* July 27, 1988, Aldous
J.; *Mothercare U.K. v. Penguin Books* [1988]
R.P.C. 114, C.A.
s. 4, amended: 1984, c.19, sch.2.
s. 5, see *News Group Newspapers v. The
Rocket Record Co.* [1981] F.S.R. 89, Slade J.;
Thermawear v. Vedonis [1982] R.P.C. 44,
Whitford J.; *Castrol v. Automotive Oil Supplies* [1983] R.P.C. 315, Vivian Price Q.C.;
*Williams & Humbert v. International Distillers
and Vintners* [1986] F.S.R. 150, Whitfield J.
s. 7, see *"Keraion" Trade Mark* [1977] R.P.C.
588, Trade Marks Registry; *Caravillas Trade
Mark* [1981] R.P.C. 381, Trade Marks
Registry.
s. 8, see *British Northrop v. Texteam Blackburn*
[1973] F.S.R. 241, Megarry J.; *Imperial Group
v. Philip Morris & Co.* [1982] F.S.R. 72, C.A.;
Parker Knoll v. Knoll Overseas [1985] F.S.R.
349, Whitford J.; *Mars G.B. v. Cadbury* [1987]
R.P.C. 387, Whitford J.
s. 9, see *Blue Paraffin Trade Mark* [1974] F.S.R.
75; *Smith Kline & French Laboratories' Trade
Mark Applications* [1971] F.S.R. 640; *Smith,
Kline & French Laboratories v. Sterling-Winthrop Group* [1975] 1 W.L.R. 914; [1975] 2 All
E.R. 578, H.L.; *Must Trade Mark* [1976] R.P.C.
712; *The International Society of Postmasters
Trade Mark* [1977] R.P.C. 873; *"Cannon"
Trade Mark* [1979] R.P.C. 519, C.A.; *"Kwik*

CAP.

1 & 2 Geo. 6 (1937–38)—cont.

22. Trade Marks Act 1938—*cont.*
Copy" Trade Mark [1982] R.P.C. 102, Nourse
J.; *Gallaher (Dublin), Hergall (1981) v. The
Health Education Bureau* [1982] F.S.R. 464,
H.Ct. of Ireland; *Alfred Dunhill Trade Mark
Application* [1982] R.P.C. 145, Trade Marks
Registry; *L'Amy Trade Mark* [1983] R.P.C.
138, Trade Marks Registry; *Revuetronic Trade
Mark* [1983] R.P.C. 401. Trade Marks Registry; *Coca Cola Trade Marks* [1985] F.S.R. 315,
C.A.; *Milk Marketing Board's Application*
[1988] R.P.C. 124, Aldous Q.C.

ss. 9, 10, see *Waterford Trade Marks* [1972]
F.S.R. 51; [1972] R.P.C. 149; *Tijuana Smalls
Trade Mark* [1973] F.S.R. 235, Graham J.;
Treasury Trade Mark [1973] R.P.C. 551, Whitford J.; *"Discovision" Trade Mark* [1977]
R.P.C. 594, Whitford J.; *Rheumaton Trade
Mark* [1978] R.P.C. 406, Trade Marks Registry; *Safemix Trade Mark* [1978] R.P.C. 397,
Trade Marks Registry; *"Multilight" Trade
Mark* [1978] R.P.C. 601, Board of Trade;
"Barry Artist" Trade Mark [1978] R.P.C. 703,
Trade Marks Registry; *Golden Jet Trade Mark*
[1979] R.P.C. 19, Trade Marks Registry; *The
Chef Trade Mark* [1979] R.P.C. 143; Board of
Trade; *Update Trade Mark* [1979] R.P.C. 165,
Board of Trade; *Imperial Group v. Philip Morris
& Co.* [1982] F.S.R. 72, C.A.; *York Trailer
Holdings v. Registrar of Trade Marks* [1982] 1
All E.R. 257, H.L.; *Telecheck Trade Mark*
[1986] R.P.C. 77, Board of Trade; *A.D.D.-70
Trade Mark* [1986] R.P.C. 89, Trade Marks
Registry; *VEW Trade Mark* [1986] R.P.C. 82,
Board of Trade; *Always Trade Mark* [1986]
R.P.C. 93, Falconer J.; *GI Trade Mark* [1986]
R.P.C. 100, Board of Trade; *Unilever's
(Striped Tooth-paste No. 2) Trade Marks*
[1987] R.P.C. 13, Hoffmann J.; *Exxate Trade
Mark* [1987] R.P.C. 597, Whitford J.; *Photo-Scan Trade Mark* [1987] R.P.C. 213, Board of
Trade; *My Mums COLA Trade Mark* [1988]
R.P.C. 130, Aldous Q.C.

s. 10, see *Esso Trade Mark* [1971] F.S.R. 624;
Re Soflens Trade Mark [1976] R.P.C. 694;
Must Trade Mark [1976] R.P.C. 712; *The
International Society of Postmasters Trade
Mark* [1977] R.P.C. 373; *Ogen Trade Mark*
[1977] R.P.C. 529, Trade Marks Registry;
Philip Morris Inc.'s Trade Mark Application
[1980] R.P.C. 527, Trade Marks Registry;
Thermawear v. Vedonis [1982] R.P.C. 44,
Whitford J.; *"Kwik Copy" Trade Mark* [1982]
R.P.C. 102, Nourse J.; *Alfred Dunhill Trade
Mark Application* [1982] R.P.C. 145, Trade
Marks Registry.

s. 11, see *Frigiking Trade Marks* [1972] F.S.R.
183; *General Electric v. General Electric*
[1972] 1 W.L.R. 729; [1972] 2 All E.R. 507;
Treasury Trade Mark [1973] R.P.C. 551, Whitford J.; *Tonino Trade Mark* [1973] R.P.C. 568,
Trade Marks Registry; *Azoschloramid Trade
Mark* [1974] R.P.C. 655; *Karo Step Trade
Mark* [1977] R.P.C. 255; *The International*

1 & 2 Geo. 6 (1937–38)—cont.
22. Trade Marks Act 1938—cont.

Society of Postmasters Trade Mark [1977] R.P.C. 373; Ogen Trade Mark [1977] R.P.C. 529, Trade Marks Registry; Smith, Kline & French Laboratories v. Sterling–Winthrop Group [1975] 1 W.L.R. 914; [1975] 2 All E.R. 578, H.L.; Re Hallelujah Trade Mark [1976] R.P.C. 605; "Keraion" Trade Mark [1977] R.P.C. 588, Trade Marks Registry; "Pol-rama" Trade Mark [1977] R.P.C. 581, Trade Marks Registry; "Zing" Trade Mark [1978] R.P.C. 47, Trade Marks Registry; "Margaret Rose" Trade Mark [1978] R.P.C. 55, Trade Marks Registry; "Turbogaz" Trade Mark [1978] R.P.C. 206, Trade Marks Registry; "Advo-kaat" Trade Mark [1978] R.P.C. 252, Trade Marks Registry; "Molyslip" Trade Mark [1978] R.P.C. 211, Trade Marks Registry; Safemix Trade Mark [1978] R.P.C. 397, Trade Marks Registry; "Multilight" Trade Mark [1978] R.P.C. 601, Board of Trade; "Barry Artist" Trade Mark [1978] R.P.C. 703, Trade Marks Registry; Golden Jet Trade Mark [1979] R.P.C. 19, Trade Marks Registry; The Chef Trade Mark [1979] R.P.C. 143, Board of Trade; Tornado Trade Mark [1979] R.P.C. 155, Trade Marks Registry: "Oscar" Trade Mark [1979] R.P.C. 197, Trade Marks Registry; "Semigres" Trade Mark [1979] R.P.C. 330, Trade Marks Registry; "Fif" Trade Mark [1979] R.P.C. 355, Whitford J.; "China-Therm" Trade Mark [1980] F.S.R. 21, Whitford J.; "Jägerschoppen" Trade Mark [1980] R.P.C. 11, Trade Marks Registry; "Wee McGlen" Trade Mark [1980] R.P.C. 115, Trade Marks Registry; Re Euroasian Equipment's Trade Mark Application, The Times, May 15, 1980, Graham J.; "Da Vinci" Trade Mark [1980] R.P.C. 237, Trade Marks Registry; "Keebler" Trade Mark [1980] R.P.C. 243, Trade Marks Registry; Philip Morris Inc's Trade Mark Application [1980] R.P.C. 527, Trade Marks Registry; Caravillas Trade Mark [1981] R.P.C. 381, Trade Marks Registry; "Domgarden" Trade Mark [1982] R.P.C. 156, Whitford J.; L'Amy Trade Mark [1983] R.P.C. 138, Trade Marks Registry; Revuetronic Trade Mark [1983] R.P.C. 401, Trade Marks Registry; Photo-Scan Trade Mark [1987] R.P.C. 213, Board of Trade; Lancer Trade Mark [1987] R.P.C. 303, C.A.; Reckitt and Colman Products v. Borden Inc. (No. 3) [1987] F.S.R. 505, Walton J.

s. 12, see Berlei v. Bali [1972] F.S.R. 77; Frigiking Trade Marks [1972] F.S.R. 183; Linpac Trade Marks [1973] R.P.C. 661; Optimal Trade Mark [1977] R.P.C. 163; "Trina" Trade Mark [1977] R.P.C. 131; "Keraion" Trade Mark [1977] R.P.C. 588, Trade Marks Registry; "Pol-rama" Trade Mark [1977] R.P.C. 581, Trade Marks Registry; "Zing" Trade Mark [1978] R.P.C. 47, Trade Marks Registry; "Phantom" Trade Mark [1978] R.P.C. 245, C.A.; "Margaret Rose" Trade Mark [1978]

1 & 2 Geo. 6 (1937–38)—cont.
22. Trade Marks Act 1938—cont.

R.P.C. 55, Trade Marks Registry; "Turbogaz" Trade Mark [1978] R.P.C. 206, Trade Marks Registry; Rheumaton Trade Mark [1978] R.P.C. 406, Trade Marks Registry; Runner Trade Mark [1978] R.P.C. 402, Trade Marks Registry; Bali Trade Mark (No. 2) [1978] F.S.R. 193, Fox J.; Golden Jet Trade Mark [1979] R.P.C. 19, Trade Marks Registry; Revue Trade Mark [1979] R.P.C. 27, Trade Marks Registry; Atlas Trade Mark [1979] R.P.C. 59, Trade Marks Registry; Tornado Trade Mark [1979] R.P.C. 155, Trade Marks Registry; "Oscar" Trade Mark [1979] R.P.C. 197, Trade Marks Registry; Granada Trade Mark [1979] R.P.C. 303, Trade Marks Registry; "Semigres" Trade Mark [1979] R.P.C. 330, Trade Marks Registry; "Fif" Trade Mark [1979] R.P.C. 355, Whitford J.; "Keebler" Trade Mark [1980] R.P.C. 243, Trade Marks Registry; "Sea-horse" Trade Mark [1980] R.P.C. 250, Trade Marks Registry; "Consort" Trade Mark [1980] R.P.C. 160, Trade Marks Registry; Caravillas Trade Mark [1981] R.P.C. 381, Trade Marks Registry; L'Amy Trade Mark [1983] R.P.C. 138, Trade Marks Registry; Revuetronic Trade Mark [1983] R.P.C. 401, Trade Marks Registry; Lancer Trade Mark [1987] R.P.C. 303, C.A.

s. 12, amended: 1984, c.19, sch.2.

s. 13, see Ogen Trade Mark [1977] R.P.C. 529, Trade Marks Registry; "Molyslip" Trade Mark [1978] R.P.C. 211, Trade Marks Registry; "Oscar" Trade Mark [1979] R.P.C. 197, Trade Marks Registry; Mars G.B. v. Cadbury [1987] R.P.C. 387, Whitford J.

s. 14, see Granada Trade Mark [1979] R.P.C. 303, Trade Marks Registry; Philip Morris Inc's Trade Mark Application [1980] R.P.C. 527, Trade Marks Registry; Revuetronic Trade Mark [1983] R.P.C. 401, Trade Marks Registry; Milk Marketing Board's Application [1988] R.P.C. 124, Aldous Q.C.

s. 15, see Ogen Trade Mark [1977] R.P.C. 529, Trade Marks Registry; Thermawear v. Vedonis [1982] R.P.C. 44; Gallaher (Dublin), Hergall (1981) v. The Health Education Bureau [1982] F.S.R. 464, H.Ct. of Ireland.

s. 17, see Re Hallelujah Trade Mark [1976] R.P.C. 605; Karo Step Trade Mark [1977] R.P.C. 255; "Disco-vision" Trade Mark [1977] R.P.C. 594, Whitford J.; Safemix Trade Mark [1978] R.P.C. 397, Trade Marks Registry; Runner Trade Mark [1978] R.P.C. 402, Trade Marks Registry; "Multilight" Trade Mark [1978] R.P.C. 601, Board of Trade; "Barry Artist" Trade Mark [1978] R.P.C. 703, Trade Marks Registry; Update Trade Mark [1979] R.P.C. 165, Board of Trade; "Oscar" Trade Mark [1979] R.P.C. 197, Trade Marks Registry; Philip Morris Inc's Trade Mark Application [1980] R.P.C. 527, Trade Marks Registry; Caravillas Trade Mark [1981] R.P.C. 381, Trade Marks Registry; Alfred Dunhill Trade Mark

CAP.

1 & 2 Geo. 6 (1937–38)—cont.

22. Trade Marks Act 1938—cont.

Application [1982] R.P.C. 145, Trade Marks Registry; Coca Cola Trade Marks [1985] F.S.R. 315, C.A.; Telecheck Trade Mark [1986] R.P.C. 77; VEW Trade Mark [1986] R.P.C. 82, Board of Trade: Always Trade Mark [1986] R.P.C. 93, Falconer J.

s. 18, see Frigiking Trade Marks [1972] F.S.R. 183; "Disco-vision" Trade Mark [1977] R.P.C. 594, Whitford J.; Granada Trade Mark [1979] R.P.C. 303, Trade Marks Registry; Alfred Dunhill Trade Mark Application [1982] R.P.C. 145, Trade Marks Registry; L'Amy Trade Mark [1983] R.P.C. 138, Trade Marks Registry.

s. 18, amended: 1978, c.23, sch.5.

s. 19, see McGregor-Doniger Inc. v. Sterling McGregor [1981] F.S.R. 299, Whitford J.; Alfred Dunhill Trade Mark Application [1982] R.P.C. 145, Trade Marks Registry.

s. 19, amended: 1986, c.39, sch.2, repealed in pt.: ibid., sch.3.

s. 20, see Runner Trade Mark [1978] R.P.C. 402, Trade Marks Registry.

s. 21, see Philip Morris Inc.'s Trade Mark Application [1980] R.P.C. 527, Trade Marks Registry.

s. 22, see "Phantom" Trade Mark [1978] R.P.C. 245, C.A.; "Barry Artist" Trade Mark [1978] R.P.C. 703, Trade Marks Registry; Boot Tree v. Robinson [1984] F.S.R. 545, Nourse J.

s. 22, amended: 1984, c.19, sch.2.

s. 23, see "Phantom" Trade Mark [1978] R.P.C. 245, C.A.; Atlas Trade Mark [1979] R.P.C. 59, Trade Marks Registry; "Fif" Trade Mark [1979] R.P.C. 355, Whitford J.

s. 23, amended: 1984, c.19, sch.2.

s. 26, see Astronaut Trade Mark [1972] F.S.R. 33; "Trina" Trade Mark [1977] R.P.C. 131; Wells Fargo Trade Mark [1977] R.P.C. 503, Trade Marks Registry; Revue Trade Mark [1979] R.P.C. 27, Trade Marks Registry; Atlas Trade Mark [1979] R.P.C. 59, Trade Marks Registry; Update Trade Mark [1979] R.P.C. 165, Board of Trade; "Oscar" Trade Mark [1979] R.P.C. 197, Trade Marks Registry; "Consort" Trade Mark [1980] R.P.C. 160, Trade Marks Registry; Imperial Group v. Phillip Morris & Co. [1982] F.S.R. 72, C.A.; Gallaher (Dublin), Hergall (1981) v. The Health Education Bureau [1982] F.S.R. 464, H.Ct. of Ireland; Williams & Humbert v. International Distillers and Vintners [1986] F.S.R. 150, Whitfield J.; Warrington Inc.'s Application, Re, The Times, February 9, 1987, C.A.; Concord Trade Mark [1987] F.S.R. 209, Falconer J.; Kodiak Trade Mark [1987] R.P.C. 269, C.A.

s. 26, amended: 1984, c.19, sch.2; 1986, c.39, sch.2.

s. 27, see Atlas Trade Mark [1979] R.P.C. 59, Trade Marks Registry.

s. 28, see "Molyslip" Trade Mark [1978] R.P.C. 211, Trade Marks Registry; Update Trade Mark [1979] R.P.C. 165, Board of Trade; Levi Strauss & Co. and Levi Strauss (U.K.) v. French Connection [1982] F.S.R. 443,

CAP.

1 & 2 Geo. 6 (1937–38)—cont.

22. Trade Marks Act 1938—cont.

Falconer J.; Re Holly Hobbie Trade Mark [1983] F.S.R. 581, C.A.; Dristan Trade Mark [1984] F.S.R. 215, High Court of Calcutta; Re American Greetings Corp.'s Application [1984] 1 W.L.R. 189, H.L.

ss. 28, 29, see Dristan Trade Mark [1986] R.P.C. 161, Supreme Court of India.

s. 29, see "Keraion" Trade Mark [1977] R.P.C. 588, Trade Marks Registry; Re Holly Hobbie Trade Mark [1983] F.S.R. 581, C.A.; Dristan Trade Mark [1984] F.S.R. 215, High Court of Calcutta.

s. 30, see Sterling-Winthrop Group v. Farbenfabriken Bayer A.G. [1976] R.P.C. 469, Kerry J., High Ct. of Ireland; Atlas Trade Mark [1979] R.P.C. 59, Trade Marks Registry; "Consort" Trade Mark [1980] R.P.C. 160, Trade Marks Registry.

s. 32, see General Electric v. General Electric [1972] 1 W.L.R. 729; [1972] 2 All E.R. 507; Karo Step Trade Mark [1977] R.P.C. 255; Wells Fargo Trade Mark [1977] R.P.C. 503, Trade Marks Registry; Ogen Trade Mark [1977] R.P.C. 529, Trade Marks Registry; "Molyslip" Trade Mark [1978] R.P.C. 211, Trade Marks Registry; Revue Trade Mark [1979] R.P.C. 27, Trade Marks Registry; Atlas Trade Mark [1979] R.P.C. 59, Trade Marks Registry; "Oscar" Trade Mark [1979] R.P.C. 197, Trade Marks Registry; Imperial Group v. Phillip Morris & Co. [1982] F.S.R. 72, C.A.

s. 32, amended: 1978, c.23, sch.5.

s. 35, see "Pelican" Trade Mark [1978] R.P.C. 424, Board of Trade.

s. 36, rules 86/1319.

s. 39, see Gallaher (Dublin), Hergall (1981) v. The Health Education Bureau [1982] F.S.R. 464, H.Ct. of Ireland.

s. 39, rules 82/713.

s. 39A, orders 86/1303, 1890, 2236; 87/170; 88/1856.

s. 39A, added: 1986, c.39, sch.2.

s. 40, see Sterling-Winthrop Group v. Farbenfabriken Bayer A.G. [1976] R.P.C. 469, Kerry J., High Ct. of Ireland.

s. 40, rules 72/229; 74/1314; 80/1931; 82/298; 85/1099; 86/1319, 1367; 88/894.

s. 40, repealed in pt.: S.L.R. 1986.

ss. 40, rules 75/576, 1532; 78/1120; 80/221; 81/248; 82/713; 83/181; 84/459; 85/921; 86/691, 1447; 87/751, 964; 88/1112.

s. 40A, rules 86/1319.

s. 40A, added: S.L.R. 1986.

s. 43, see Always Trade Mark [1986] R.P.C. 93, Falconer J.

s. 46, see Karo Step Trade Mark [1977] R.P.C. 255.

s. 52, see Bali Trade Mark (No. 2) [1978] F.S.R. 193, Fox J.

s. 53, see "Kwik Copy" Trade Mark [1982] R.P.C. 102, Nourse J.; Telecheck Trade Mark [1986] R.P.C. 77, Board of Trade; VEW Trade Mark [1986] R.P.C. 82, Board of Trade.

1 & 2 Geo. 6 (1937–38)—cont.

22. Trade Marks Act 1938—cont.
ss. 57, 58, repealed: 1986, c.39, sch.3.
ss. 58A–58D, added: 1988, c.48, s.300
s. 61, amended: *ibid.* sch.2.
s. 64A, see *C.B.S. Inc.* v. *Blue Suede Music* [1982] R.P.C. 523, Falconer J.
s. 64A, amended: 1979, c.2, sch.4.
s. 68, see *Smith, Kline & French Laboratories' Trade Mark Applications* [1971] F.S.R. 640; *Smith, Kline & French Laboratories* v. *Sterling-Winthrop Group* [1975] 1 W.L.R. 914; [1975] 2 All E.R. 578, H.L.; *Wells Fargo Trade Mark* [1977] R.P.C. 503, Trade Marks Registry; *"Molyslip" Trade Mark* [1978] R.P.C. 211, Trade Marks Registry; *Revue Trade Mark* [1979] R.P.C. 27, Trade Marks Registry; *Philip Morris Inc.'s Trade Mark Application* [1980] R.P.C. 527, Trade Marks Registry; *News Group Newspapers* v. *The Rocket Record Co.* [1981] F.S.R. 89, Slade J.; *Imperial Group* v. *Phillip Morris & Co.* [1982] F.S.R. 72, C.A.; *Re Coca-Cola Trade Marks* [1985] F.S.R. 315, C.A.; *A.D.D.-70 Trade Mark* [1986] R.P.C. 89, Trade Marks Registry; *Unilever's (Striped Toothpaste No. 2) Trade Marks* [1987] R.P.C. 13, Hoffmann J.; *Mothercare U.K.* v. *Penguin Books* [1988] R.P.C. 114, C.A.
s. 68, amended: 1978, c.23, sch.5; 1984, c.19, s.1.

24. Conveyancing Amendment (Scotland) Act 1938.
s. 4, repealed: 1973, c.52, sch.5.
s. 6, amended: 1979, c.33, sch.2.
s. 9, amended: 1974, c.38, s.13.

25. Eire (Confirmation of Agreements) Act 1938.
repealed: S.L.R. 1981.

28. Evidence Act 1938.
see *R.* v. *Wood Green Crown Court, ex p. P.* (1982) 4 F.L.R 206, McCullough J.
s. 5, repealed: 1981, c.54, sch.7.

29. Patents &c. (International Conventions) Act 1938.
repealed: 1986, c.39, sch.3.

31. Scottish Land Court Act 1938.
s. 1, repealed in pt.: 1972, c.11, sch.6.

34. Leasehold Property (Repairs) Act 1938.
s. 1, see *Middlegate Properties* v. *Messimeris* [1973] 1 W.L.R. 168, C.A.; *Selim* v. *Bickenhall Engineering* [1981] 3 All E.R. 210, Megarry V.-C.: *Swallow Securities* v. *Brand* (1981) 260 E.G. 63; (1983) 45 P. & C.R. 328, McNeill J; *Sedac Investments* v. *Tanner* [1982] 3 All E.R. 646, Michael Wheeler, Q.C.; *Starrokate Ltd.* v. *Bury* (1983) 265 E.G. 871, C.A.; *Land Securities plc* v. *Receiver for the Metropolitan Police District* [1983] 1 W.L.R. 439, Sir Robert Megarry V.-C.; *Hamilton* v. *Martell Securities* [1984] 2 W.L.R. 699, Vinelott J.; *Farimani* v. *Gates* (1984) 271 E.G. 887, C.A.
ss. 1, 2, see *Middlegate Properties* v. *Gidlow-Jackson* (1977) 34 P. & C.R. 4, C.A.
s. 7, amended: 1986, c.5, sch.14.

35. Housing (Rural Workers) Amendment Act 1938.
repealed: 1972, c.46, sch.11; c.47, sch.11.

1 & 2 Geo. 6 (1937–38)—cont.

36. Infanticide Act 1938.
s. 1, see *R.* v. *Smith (K.A.)* [1983] Crim.L.R. 739, St. Albans Crown Ct.

38. Housing (Agricultural Population) (Scotland) Act 1938.
repealed: 1972, c.46, sch.11.

44. Road Haulage Wages Act 1938.
repealed: 1980, c.42, s.19, sch.2.
ss. 4, 5, see *R.* v. *C.A.C., ex p. R.H.M. Foods* [1979] I.C.R. 657, Mocatta J.

45. Inheritance (Family Provision) Act 1938.
repealed: 1975, c.63, sch.
s. 1, see *Millward* v. *Shenton* [1972] 1 W.L.R. 711; [1972] 2 All E.R. 1025.

46. Finance Act 1938.
s. 47, repealed: 1975, c.7, sch.13.
s. 51, repealed: S.L.R. 1976.
s. 55, repealed in pt.: *ibid.*

48. Criminal Procedure (Scotland) Act 1938.
repealed: 1986, c.36, sch.2

50. Divorce (Scotland) Act 1938.
repealed: 1983, c.12, sch.2.
s. 5, see *O'Halloran,* 1974 S.L.T.(Notes) 19 (O.H.)

52. Coal Act 1938.
ss. 1, 3 (in pt.), 4, 6 (in pt.), 7–10, 12, 13, 17 (in pt.), 18, 20, 21, 23–31, repealed: S.L.R. 1973.
s. 34, amended (S.): 1984, c.54, sch.9.
ss. 35–40, repealed: S.L.R. 1973.
s. 42, amended: 1975, c.56, ss.2, 3; repealed in pt.: S.L.R. 1973.
s. 43, repealed in pt.: *ibid.*
s. 44, amended: 1975, c.56, ss.2, 3.
s. 45, amended: *ibid.*; repealed in pt.: S.L.R. 1973; S.L.R. 1986.
ss. 56, 57, repealed: S.L.R. 1973.
sch. 1, repealed: *ibid.*
sch. 2, see *Butterley Building Materials* v. *National Coal Board* (1976) 32 P. & C.R. 34.
sch. 2, repealed in pt.: 1975, c.56, sch.5.
schs. 3–5, repealed: S.L.R. 1973.

54. Architects Registration Act 1938.
s. 3, amended: 1977, c.45, s.31, sch.6.
s. 6, repealed in pt.: 1973, c.36, sch.6.

63. Administration of Justice (Miscellaneous Provisions) Act 1938.
repealed: 1981, c.54, sch.7.

67. Supreme Court of Judicature (Amendment) Act 1938.
repealed: 1981, c.54, sch.7.

69. Young Persons (Employment) Act 1938.
s. 5, amended: orders 75/1291, 1808; 77/1861, 1891; 81/241; 82/222.
s. 6, amended: 1972, c.70, sch.29; repealed in pt.: *ibid.*, sch.30.
s. 7, repealed in pt.: S.L.R. 1986.
s. 10, amended: 1973, c.65, s.160.

70. Holidays with Pay Act 1938.
ss. 1, 2, 3, 5, repealed: S.L.R. 1975.

73. Nursing Homes Registration (Scotland) Act 1938.
s. 1, regs. 74/1182; 81/977.
s. 1, repealed: 1987, c.40, s.6.
s. 1A, added: *ibid.*

CAP.

1 & 2 Geo. 6 (1937–38)—cont.

73. Nursing Homes Registration (Scotland) Act 1938—cont.
s. 2, amended: 1972, c.58, sch.6; 1978, c.29, sch.15; 1980, c.53, sch.4.
s. 2A, added: 1987, c.40, s.5.
s. 3, amended: 1972, c.58, sch.6; 1978, c.29, sch.15.
s. 3A, added; 1980, c.53, sch.4.
s. 4, regs. 74/1182.
s. 4, amended: 1972, c.58, sch.6; 1978, c.29, sch.15; 1980, c.53, sch.4.
s. 5, repealed: *ibid.*, schs.4,7.
s. 6, amended: 1972, c.58, sch.6; 1978, c.29, sch.15.
s. 7, amended: 1980, c.53, sch.4.
s. 8, amended: 1977, c.45, s.31, sch.6.
s. 9, repealed: 1972, c.58, sch.7.
s. 10, amended: 1979, c.36, sch.7; 1980, c.53, sch.4; 1984, c.26, sch.3; repealed in pt.: 1972, c.58, sch.7; 1979, c.36, schs.7,8; 1980, c.53, sch.7.

2 & 3 Geo. 6 (1938–39)

3. Housing (Financial Provisions) (Scotland) Act 1938.
repealed: 1972, c.46, sch.11.

4. Custody of Children (Scotland) Act 1939.
repealed: 1986, c.9, sch.2.

11. Czecho-Slovakia (Restriction on Banking Accounts, etc.) Act 1939.
s. 1, repealed in pt.: S.L.R. 1975.

13. Cancer Act 1939.
s. 4, repealed in pt.: order 77/2128.
ss. 4, 5, 7, repealed in pt.: S.L.R. 1986.

18. Local Government Superannuation Act 1939.
repealed: order 74/520.

21. Limitation Act 1939.
repealed: 1980, c.58, sch.4.
see *Buck* v. *English Electric Co.* [1977] 1 W.L.R. 806, Kilner Brown J.; *Gawthrop* v. *Boulton* (1978) 122 S.J. 297, Walton J.; *Firman* v. *Ellis* [1978] 3 W.L.R. 1, C.A.; *Arnold* v. *Central Electricity Generating Board, The Times,* October 23, 1987, H.L.
s. 2, see *King* v. *Victor Parsons* [1973] 1 W.L.R. 29, C.A.; *Pritam Kaur* v. *Russell* [1973] 2 W.L.R. 147, C.A.; *Higgins* v. *Arfon B.C.* [1975] 1 W.L.R. 524; *Ackbar* v. *C. F. Green & Co.* [1975] 2 W.L.R. 773; [1975] 2 All E.R. 65; *Sparham-Souter* v. *Town and Country Developments (Essex)* [1976] 2 W.L.R. 493, C.A.; *Tito* v. *Waddell (No. 2)*; *Tito* v. *Att.-Gen.* [1977] 2 W.L.R. 496; *Ronex Properties* v. *John Laing Construction* [1982] 3 W.L.R. 875, C.A.; *Pirelli General Cable Works* v. *Oscar Faber & Partners* [1983] 2 W.L.R. 6, H.L.; *Yorkshire Electricity Board* v. *British Telecommunications: Igoe (P.) & Son (A Firm) (Third Party)* (1985) 83 L.G.R. 760, C.A.
ss. 2, 2A, see *Arnold* v. *Central Electricity Generating Board* [1987] 3 W.L.R. 1009, H.L.
s. 2A, see *Cameron* v. *Wordham Bros. (Contractors),* June 30, 1976; *Simpson* v. *Norwest*

CAP.

2 & 3 Geo. 6 (1938–39)—cont.

21. Limitation Act 1939—cont.
Holst Southern [1980] 2 All E.R. 471, C.A.; *Farmer* v. *National Coal Board, The Times,* April 27, 1985, C.A.
ss. 2A, 2D, see *Biss* v. *Lambeth, Southwark and Lewisham Area Health Authority (Teaching)* [1978] 1 W.L.R. 382, C.A.; *Coulson* v. *Ruston-Bucyrus,* July 24, 1980, Russell J.
s. 2D, see *McCafferty* v. *Metropolitan Police Receiver* [1977] 2 All E.R. 756, C.A.; *Firman* v. *Ellis, The Times,* February 6, 1978, C.A.; *Hattam* v. *National Coal Board, The Times,* October 28, 1978, C.A.; *Jones* v. *G. D. Searle & Co.* [1978] 3 All E.R. 654, C.A.; *Deeming* v. *British Steel Corp.* (1978) S.J. 303, C.A.; *Walkley* v. *Precision Forgings* [1979] 1 W.L.R. 606, H.L.; *Browes* v. *Jones & Middleton (A Firm)* (1979) 123 S.J. 489, C.A.; *Mead* v. *Mead,* September 18, 1979, Milmo J., Cardiff Crown Ct.; *Stannard* v. *Stonar School,* August 13, 1979, Judge Hawser; *Soidlaczek* v. *Hymatic Engineering Co.,* July 31, 1979, Lawson J.; *C. Constantinides* v. *C. Birnbaum & Co.; E. Constantinides* v. *C. Birnbaum & Co.,* February 27, 1980, Judge Dow, Clerkenwell County Ct.; *Simpson* v. *Norwest Holst Southern* [1980] 2 All E.R. 471, C.A.; *Liff* v. *Peasley* [1980] 1 All E.R. 623, C.A.; *Chappell* v. *Cooper; Player* v. *Bruguiere* [1980] 2 All E.R. 463, C.A.; *Thompson* v. *Brown (Trading as George Albert Brown (Builders)) & Co.* [1981] 1 W.L.R. 744; [1981] 2 All E.R. 296, H.L.; *Wilson* v. *Banner Scaffolding, The Times,* June 22, 1982, Milmo J.; *Davis* v. *Soltenpur, The Times,* February 16, 1983, Hobhouse J.
s. 4, see *Palfrey* v. *Palfrey* (1973) 229 E.G. 1593, C.A.; *Heslop* v. *Burns* [1974] 1 W.L.R. 1241; [1974] 3 All E.R. 406, C.A.; *Wallis's Cayton Bay Holiday Camp* v. *Shell-Mex and B.P.* [1974] 3 W.L.R. 387; [1974] 3 All E.R. 575, C.A.; *Hyde* v. *Pearce* [1982] 1 All E.R. 1029, C.A.; *B.P. Properties* v. *Buckler, The Times,* August 13, 1987, C.A.
s. 5, see *Basildon District Council* v. *Manning* (1976) 237 E.G. 879.
s. 9, see *Jessamine Investment Co.* v. *Schwartz* [1976] 3 All E.R. 521, C.A.; *Palfrey* v. *Palfrey* (1973) 229 E.G. 1593, C.A.; *Heslop* v. *Burns* [1974] 1 W.L.R. 1241; [1974] 3 All E.R. 406, C.A.
s. 10, see *Wallis's Cayton Bay Holiday Camp* v. *Shell-Mex and B.P.* [1974] 3 W.L.R. 387; [1974] 3 All E.R. 575, C.A.; *Treloar* v. *Nute* [1976] 1 W.L.R. 1295, C.A.; *Hyde* v. *Pearce* [1982] 1 All E.R. 1029, C.A.; *B.P. Properties* v. *Buckler, The Times,* August 13, 1987, C.A.
ss. 13, 16, see *Wallis's Cayton Bay Holiday Camp* v. *Shell-Mex and B.P.* [1974] 3 W.L.R. 387; [1974] 3 All E.R. 575, C.A.
s. 16, see *B.P. Properties* v. *Buckler, The Times,* August 13, 1987, C.A.
s. 17, see *Re Howell* [1972] 2 W.L.R. 1346; (1971) 23 P. & C.R. 266.
s. 21, see *Arnold* v. *Central Electricity Generating Board* [1987] 3 W.L.R. 1009, H.L.

CAP.

2 & 3 Geo. 6 (1938–39)—cont.

21. Limitation Act 1939—cont.

s. 22, see *Tolley* v. *Morris* [1979] 1 W.L.R. 592, H.L.

s. 23, see *Surrendra Overseas* v. *Government of Sri Lanka* [1977] 1 W.L.R. 565; [1977] 2 All E.R. 481, Kerr J.; *Kamouh* v. *Associated Electrical Industries International* [1979] 2 W.L.R. 795, Parker J.; *Re Overmark Smith Warden* [1982] 1 W.L.R. 1195, Slade J.

ss. 23, 24, see *Re Gee & Co. (Woolwich)* [1974] 2 W.L.R. 515; [1974] 1 All E.R. 1149.

s. 26, see *King* v. *Victor Parsons* [1973] 1 W.L.R. 29, C.A.; *Lewisham London Borough* v. *Leslie & Co.* (1979) 250 E.G. 1289, C.A.; *Bartlett* v. *Barclays Bank Trust Co.* [1980] 1 All E.R. 139, Brightman J.; *Morton-Norwich Products* v. *Intercen (No. 2); Same* v. *United Chemicals (London)* [1981] F.S.R. 337, Graham J.; *Frisby* v. *Theodore Goddard & Co., The Times,* March 7, 1984, C.A.; *Waldron (A Bankrupt), Re, ex p. The Bankrupt* v. *The Official Receiver, The Times,* February 12, 1985, C.A.

s. 28, see *Tersons* v. *Colman (E. Alec) Investments* (1973) 225 E.G. 2300; *Henriksens Rederi A/S.* v. *T. H. Z. Rolimpex; The Brede* [1973] 3 W.L.R. 556, C.A.

ss. 31, 32, amended: 1975, c.54, sch.1.

s. 32, see *I.R.C.* v. *Stoke Commissioners and Baddeley's Executrix* [1974] T.R. 207.

22. Camps Act 1939.

repealed: 1973, c.39, sch.1.

31. Civil Defence Act 1939.

Pts. I–IV, (ss. 1–35), repealed: S.L.R. 1976.

Pt. V (ss. 36–42) (exc. ss. 36 (in pt.), 37, 39), repealed: *ibid.*

Pt. VI, VII (ss. 43–55), repealed: *ibid.*

Pt. VIII (ss. 56–73) (exc. s. 62), repealed: *ibid.*

s. 62, amended and repealed in pt.: *ibid.*

s. 83, repealed in pt.: S.L.R. 1976; S.L.R. 1986.

ss. 85–89, repealed: S.L.R. 1976.

s. 90, amended (S.): 1984, c.54, sch.9; repealed in pt.: S.L.R. 1976; 1986, c.44, sch.9.

s. 91, repealed in pt.: 1973, c.65, schs.27,29; S.L.R. 1976.

s. 92, repealed in pt.: 1973, c.36, sch.6.

sch. 2, repealed: S.L.R. 1976.

32. Patents and Designs (Limits of Time) Act 1939.

repealed: S.L.R. 1986.

33. Marriage Act 1939.

ss. 1, 2 in pt., repealed: 1977, c.15, sch.2.

34. Marriage (Scotland) Act 1939.

repealed: 1977, c.15, sch.3.

36. Hall-Marking of Foreign Plate Act 1939.

repealed: 1973, c.43, sch.7.

38. Ministry of Supply Act 1939.

repealed: 1975, c.9, sch.2.

41. Finance Act 1939.

ss. 29–31, repealed: 1975, c.7, sch.13.

s. 35, repealed in pt.: S.L.R. 1976.

s. 37, repealed: 1976, c.40, s.126, sch.15.

s. 38, repealed in pt.: 1975, c.7, sch.13; S.L.R. 1986.

CAP.

2 & 3 Geo. 6 (1938–39)—cont.

44. House to House Collections Act 1939.

repealed (S.): 1982, c.45, s.119, sch.4.

s. 1, see *Hankinson* v. *Dowland* [1974] 1 W.L.R. 1327; [1974] 3 All E.R. 655, D.C.; *Davison* v. *Richards* [1976] C. L.R. 46, D.C.; *Murphy* v. *Duke* [1985] 2 W.L.R. 773, Forbes J.; *Cooper* v. *Coles* [1986] 3 W.L.R. 888, D.C.

s. 2, amended: 1972, c.70, sch.29; repealed in pt.: *ibid.,* schs.29, 30.

s. 5, see *R.* v. *Davison* [1972] 1 W.L.R. 1540; [1972] 3 All E.R. 1121.

s. 7, repealed in pt.: 1972, c.70, sch.30.

s. 9, amended: *ibid.,* sch.29; repealed in pt.: *ibid.,* sch.30.

s. 11, see *Hankinson* v. *Dowland* [1974] 1 W.L.R. 1327; [1974] 3 All E.R. 655, D.C.; *Murphy* v. *Duke* [1985] 2 W.L.R. 773, Forbes J.; *Cooper* v. *Coles* [1986] 3 W.L.R. 888, D.C.

48. Agricultural Development Act 1939.

repealed: S.L.R. 1986.

49. House of Commons Members' Fund Act 1939.

sch. 1, amended: resolutions 74/2061; 75/2038; 77/2073; 79/1667; 80/1899; order 84/2065.

50. Prevention of Violence (Temporary Provisions) Act 1939.

repealed: S.L.R. 1973.

57. War Risks Insurance Act 1939.

repealed: S.L.R. 1981.

66. Government of India Act (Amendment) Act 1939.

repealed: S.L.R. 1976.

69. Import, Export and Customs Powers (Defence) Act 1939.

see *R.* v. *Secretary of State for Trade, ex p. Chris International Foods, The Times,* July 22, 1983, Woolf J.

s. 1, orders 72/89, 266, 1536; 73/106, 532, 1033, 1779, 2126; 74/28, 134, 213, 909, 2189, 2204; 75/149, 1582, 2080, 2117; 76/666; 77/104; 78/271, 796, 806, 945, 1219, 1496, 1812; 79/164, 276, 1437, 1671; 80/735, 1370; 81/60, 668, 925, 1206, 1641; 82/1446, 1556; 83/1006, 1266; 84/90, 553, 694, 819, 85/34, 148, 849, 1085, 1293, 1294; 86/82, 1446, 1934; 87/215, 271, 1350, 2070; 88/1487.

ss. 1, 3, amended: 1979, c.2, sch.4.

s. 2, repealed in pt.: S.L.R. 1986.

ss. 3, 9, see *Att.-Gen. of New Zealand* v. *Ortiz, The Times,* May 22, 1982, C.A.

s. 9, amended: 1979, c.2, sch.4

70. Ships and Aircraft (Transfer Restriction) Act 1939.

repealed: S.L.R. 1977.

72. Landlord and Tenant (War Damage) Act 1939.

ss. 25, 26 (in pt.), repealed: 1973, c.36, sch.6.

73. Housing (Emergency Powers) Act 1939.

repealed: S.L.R. 1981.

75. Compensation (Defence) Act 1939.

s. 2. repealed in pt.: S.L.R. 1973.

s. 7, see *McDermott* v. *Department of Agriculture for Northern Ireland* [1984] 2 N.I.J.B., Hutton J.; *McDermott* v. *Department of*

CAP.

2 & 3 Geo. 6 (1938–39)—cont.

75. Compensation (Defence) Act 1939—cont.
Agriculture for Northern Ireland and H.M.
Treasury (R/11/1986).
s. 13, amended: 1974, c.39, sch.4.
s. 17, amended: ibid.; repealed in pt.: S.L.R.
1973; S.L.R. 1976.
s. 18, repealed in pt.: 1974, c.39, sch.4.

82. Personal Injuries (Emergency Provisions) Act 1939.
s. 1, schemes 76/585; 83/686; 84/1675;
85/1313; 86/628; 87/191; 88/367.
s. 2, schemes 72/1177; 73/1369; 74/1044;
75/392, 1518; 76/585, 1167; 77/404, 1640;
78/384, 1426; 79/270, 1232; 80/1102, 1103,
1950; 81/1143, 1678; 82/810, 1047; 83/686,
1164, 1540; 84/1289, 1675; 85/1313; 86/628;
87/191; 88/367.

83. Pensions (Navy, Army, Air Force and Mercantile Marine) Act 1939.
ss. 3, 4, 7, schemes 72/1434; 88/639.
s. 4, amended: 1983, c.21, sch.3; 1987, c.21,
sch.2.
s. 5, amended: 1981, c.55, sch.3.
ss. 5, 7, scheme 72/1436.
ss. 6, 7, scheme 82/1023.
s. 7, scheme 87/585; order 88/568.

86. Isle of Man (War Legislation) Act 1939.
repealed: S.L.R. 1973.

89. Trading with the Enemy Act 1939.
s. 1, repealed in pt.: 1975, c.59, sch.6.

94. Local Government Staffs (War Service) Act 1939.
repealed: S.L.R. 1975.
ss. 3, 9, repealed in pt.: regs. 77/1341.

95. Teachers Superannuation (War Service) Act 1939.
ss. 12, 13 (in pt.), repealed: 1973, c.36, sch.6.

102. Liability for War Damage (Miscellaneous Provisions) Act 1939.
s. 1, amended: 1974, c.39, sch.4.
ss. 4, 5 (in pt.), repealed: ibid., sch.5.
ss. 7, 8 (in pt.), repealed: 1973, c.36, sch.6.

103. Police and Firemen (War Service) Act 1939.
ss. 1 (in pt.), 3, 6, 8, 9, 10 (in pt.), 12, 13 (in pt.),
repealed: S.L.R. 1975.
ss. 15, 16 (in pt.), repealed: 1973, c.36, sch.6.

107. Patents, Designs, Copyright and Trade Marks (Emergency) Act 1939.
ss. 1, 2, amended: 1988, c.48, sch.7.
s. 4, amended: 1986, c.39, sch.2.
s. 5, amended: 1988, c.48, sch.7.
s. 6, amended: S.L.R. 1986; c.39, sch.2.
s. 7, amended: ibid.
s. 10, amended: ibid.; 1988, c.48, sch.7;
repealed in pt.: ibid., sch.8.

109. Finance (No. 2) Act 1939.
s. 23, repealed: 1975, c.7, sch.13.
s. 24, repealed in pt.: ibid.

114. Execution of Trusts (Emergency Provisions) Act 1939.
repealed: S.L.R. 1973.

120. Restriction of Advertisement (War Risks Insurance) Act 1939.
s. 1, repealed in pt.: S.L.R. 1981.
s. 5, repealed: S.L.R. 1974.

CAP.

3 & 4 Geo. 6 (1939–40)

4. Czecho-Slovakia (Financial Claims and Refugees) Act 1940.
repealed: S.L.R. 1981.

5. India and Burma (Miscellaneous Amendments) Act 1940.
repealed: S.L.R. 1976.

10. Industrial Assurance and Friendly Societies (Emergency Protection from Forfeiture) Act 1940.
repealed: S.L.R. 1974.

13. Old Age and Widows Pensions Act 1940.
repealed: 1972, c.11, sch.8.

14. Agriculture (Miscellaneous Provisions) Act 1940.
ss. 14, 16–21, 23–6, sch. 5, repealed: S.L.R.
1973.
ss. 22, 30–32, repealed in pt.: ibid.
s. 27, repealed: S.L.R. 1986.

19. Societies (Miscellaneous Provisions) Act 1940.
ss. 8–10, 12, repealed: 1974, c.46, sch.11.
s. 11, repealed: 1973, c.36, sch.6.

21. Treachery Act 1940.
repealed: S.L.R. 1973.

23. National Loans (No. 2) Act 1940.
repealed: S.L.R. 1986.

26. Superannuation Schemes (War Service) Act 1940.
ss. 2, 3 (in pt.), repealed: 1973, c.36, sch.6.

28. Evidence and Powers of Attorney Act 1940.
s. 4, repealed in pt.: 1981, c.54, sch.7.

29. Finance Act 1940.
Pt. IV (ss. 43–59), repealed: 1975, c.7, sch.13.
ss. 46, 47, 58, see I.R.C. v. Standard Industrial
Trust [1979] S.T.C. 372, C.A.
s. 64, repealed: 1975, c.7, sch.13.
s. 65, repealed in pt.: ibid.
sch. 7, see I.R.C. v. Standard Industrial Trust
[1979] S.T.C. 372, C.A.
sch. 7, repealed: 1975, c. 7, sch. 13.

31. War Charities Act 1940.
s. 7, amended (S.): 1982, c.45, s.119; repealed
in pt.: ibid., s.119, sch.4.
s. 10, amended: 1972, c.70, s.210.
s. 12, amended: 1973, c.65, sch.24; repealed in
pt.: ibid., sch.29.
s. 13, repealed: 1973, c.36, sch.6.
s. 14, amended: ibid.

33. India and Burma (Emergency Provisions) Act 1940.
repealed: S.L.R. 1976.

35. Indian and Colonial Divorce Jurisdiction Act 1940.
repealed: 1986, c.55, sch.2.

36. British North America Act 1940.
Act renamed Constitution Act 1940 (Can.):
1982, c.11, sch.
s. 2, substituted: ibid.

38. Truck Act 1940.
repealed: 1986, c.48, schs.1,5.

41. Confirmation of Executors (War Service) (Scotland) Act 1940.
repealed: S.L.R. 1973.

CAP.

3 & 4 Geo. 6 (1939–40)—cont.

42. Law Reform (Miscellaneous Provisions) (Scotland) Act 1940.
see *Anderson* v. *Wilson*, 1972 S.L.T. (Notes) 27.
s. 1, see *Ford* v. *Bell Chandler*, 1977 S.L.T.(Sh.Ct.) 90.
s. 2, repealed (S.): 1976, c.13, sch.2.
s. 2, repealed in pt.: 1975, c.72, sch.4.
s. 3, see *Bacon* v. *Blair*, 1972 S.L.T. 11, Sh.Ct.; *National Coal Board* v. *Knight Bros.*, 1972 S.L.T.(Notes) 24; *Watson* v. *Traill*, 1972 S.L.T.(Notes) 38; *Harley* v. *Forth Ports Authority* (O.H.), 1973 S.L.T.(Notes) 7; *Central S.M.T. Co.* v. *Cloudsley*, 1974 S.L.T.(Sh.Ct.) 70; *Buchan* v. *Thomson*, 1976 S.L.T. 42; *Magee & Co. (Belfast)* v. *Bracewell Harrison & Cotton* (O.H.), 1981 S.L.T. 107; *Hardy* v. *British Airways Board*, Second Division, January 28, 1982; *Singer* v. *Gray Tool Co. (Europe)*, 1984 S.L.T. 149; *Comex Houlder Diving* v. *Colne Fishing Co.*, House of Lords, 1987 S.L.T. 433.
s. 4, amended: 1982, c.27, sch.12; repealed in pt.: 1974, c.39, sch.5.
s. 7, repealed: 1978, c.33, s.23.
s. 8, repealed: 1975, c.21, sch.10.

48. Finance (No. 2) Act 1940.
Pt. IV (ss.16, 17), sch. 6, repealed: 1975, c.7, sch.13.
s. 42, repealed in pt.: *ibid.*

50. Agriculture (Miscellaneous War Provisions) (No. 2) Act 1940.
ss. 2 (in pt.), 5–9, 10 (in pt.), repealed: S.L.R. 1973.
s. 11, repealed: 1980, c.12, s.5.
s. 12, repealed in pt.: *ibid.*

4 & 5 Geo. 6 (1940–41)

3. Local Elections and Register of Electors (Temporary Provisions) Act 1940.
repealed: S.L.R. 1978.
s. 2, repealed (S.): order 74/812.

7. Diplomatic Privileges (Extension) Act 1941.
repealed: S.L.R. 1973.

12. War Damage Act 1941.
repealed: S.L.R. 1981.

13. Land Drainage (Scotland) Act 1941.
s. 2, amended: 1982, c.48, sch.6.

25. Rating (War Damage) (Scotland) Act 1941.
repealed (S.): S.L.R. 1975.

28. Trustee (War Damage Insurance) Act 1941.
repealed: S.L.R. 1981.

30. Finance Act 1941.
ss. 45, 46, repealed: 1975, c.7, sch.13.

34. Repair of War Damage Act 1941.
repealed: S.L.R. 1981.

35. Colonial War Risks Insurance (Guarantees) Act 1941.
repealed: S.L.R. 1973.

36. Financial Powers (U.S.A. Securities) Act 1941.
repealed: S.L.R. 1973.

41. Landlord and Tenant (War Damage) (Amendment) Act 1941.
s. 1, repealed in pt.: S.L.R. 1976.
s. 18, repealed: 1973, c.36, sch.6.

CAP.

4 & 5 Geo. 6 (1940–41)—cont.

42. Pharmacy and Medicines Act 1941.
repealed: order 77/2128.

44. India and Burma (Postponement of Elections) Act 1941.
repealed: S.L.R. 1976.

50. Agriculture (Miscellaneous Provisions) Act 1941.
s. 1, repealed: S.L.R. 1986.
s. 3, repealed: 1976, c.70, sch.8.
ss. 4–6, repealed: S.L.R. 1973.
s. 8, repealed in pt.: 1975, c.76, sch.2.
ss. 9, 10, repealed: S.L.R. 1973.
s. 11, repealed in pt.: 1972, c.62, s.21, sch.5.
ss. 12–14, repealed: S.L.R. 1986.
s. 15. repealed in pt.: S.L.R. 1973.
schs. 1, 2, 4, repealed: *ibid.*

5 & 6 Geo. 6 (1941–42)

7. India (Federal Court Judges) Act 1942.
repealed: S.L.R. 1976.

8. War Orphans Act 1942.
s. 1, repealed in pt.: 1981, c.55, sch.5.

9. Restoration of Pre-War Trade Practices Act 1942.
repealed: S.L.R. 1986.

10. Securities (Validation) Act 1942.
repealed: S.L.R. 1986.

19. Coal (Concurrent Leases) Act 1942.
repealed: S.L.R. 1973.

20. Marriage (Scotland) Act 1942.
repealed: 1977, c.15, sch.3.

21. Finance Act 1942.
s. 44, repealed: 1985, c.54, sch.27.
s. 47, regs. 81/1004; 85/1146.
s. 47, amended: 1982, c.41, sch.2.
sch. 11, repealed in pt.: S.L.R. 1974; S.L.R. 1986.

28. War Damage (Amendment) Act 1942.
repealed: S.L.R. 1981.

32. Housing (Rural Workers) Act 1942.
repealed: 1972, c.46, sch.11; c.47, sch.11.

39. India and Burma (Temporary and Miscellaneous Provisions) Act 1942.
repealed: S.L.R. 1976.

40. Welsh Courts Act 1942.
s. 3, rules 72/97; amended: 1977, c.38, sch.2.

6 & 7 Geo. 6 (1942–43)

2. Supreme Court (Northern Ireland) Act 1942.
repealed: 1978, c.23, sch.7.

5. Town and Country Planning Act 1943.
s. 8, orders 77/1296; 80/560.

9. Universities and Colleges (Trust) Act 1943.
s. 2, see *Sylvester* v. *Master and Fellows of University College, Oxford; Re Freeston's Charity* [1978] 1 W.L.R. 741, C.A.

16. Agriculture (Miscellaneous Provisions) Act 1943.
repealed, except ss.18, 24, sch. 3: S.L.R. 1986.

18. Evidence and Powers of Attorney Act 1943.
repealed, except ss. 4, 5: S.L.R. 1977.
s. 5, repealed in pt.: *ibid.*

CAP.

6 & 7 Geo. 6 (1942–43)—cont.

21. War Damage Act 1943.
repealed: S.L.R. 1981.

28. Finance Act 1943.
s. 26, repealed: 1975, c.7, sch.13.

30. British North America Act 1943.
repealed: 1982, c.11, sch.

32. Hydro-Electric Development (Scotland) Act 1943.
repealed, except ss. 2 (in pt.), 16 (in pt.), 17, 27 (in pt.), 28, sch. 4: 1979, c.11, sch.12.
s. 10A, see *South of Scotland Electricity Board* v. *Elder*, 1980 S.L.T.(Notes) 83.
ss. 12, 13, regs. 75/1799.

38. Coal Act 1943.
ss. 4–6, 8–10, 12, 13, 15, 16, schs. 1, 3, repealed: S.L.R. 1973.
s. 11, sch. 2, repealed: 1975, c.56, sch.5.

39. Pensions Appeal Tribunals Act 1943.
order 81/1541.
s. 5, amended: 1980, c.30, s.16.
s. 6, rules 80/1120; 81/500; S.Rs. 1981 No. 231; 1982 No. 201; 1983 No. 23.
s. 6, amended: 1978, c.23, sch.5; 1980, c.30, s.16.
s. 8, repealed in pt.: *ibid.*, s.16, sch.5.
s. 10, rules 86/366.
s. 12, amended: orders 81/1541; 88/1843; repealed in pt.: 1981, c.55, sch.5.
s. 13, rules 74/1968; 75/1764, 2198; 86/373(S.).
s. 14, amended: 1978, c.23, sch.5; 1980, c.30, s.16.
sch., rules 72/1466, 1783; 73/1346, 1714; 74/1764, 1968; 75/519, 1188, 1764, 1782, 2198; 78/607, 977, 1780; 79/94 (S.), 1744; 80/839, 1120; 81/500; 86/373(S.); S.Rs. 1978 Nos. 117, 169; 1979 No. 397; 1980 No. 4; 1981 No. 231; 1983 No. 23.
sch., amended: 1977, c.38, sch.2; 1978, c.23, sch.5; 1980, c.30, s.16; repealed in pt.: 1977, c.38, sch.5; 1980, c.30, sch.5; 1985, c.61, s.59.

40. Law Reform (Frustrated Contracts) Act 1943.
ss. 1, 2, see *B.P. Exploration Co. (Libya)* v. *Hunt, The Times*, February 5, 1981, H.L.: *B.P. Exploration* v. *Hunt (No. 2)* [1982] 2 W.L.R. 253, H.L.
s. 2, amended: 1979, c.54, sch.2.

7 & 8 Geo. 6 (1943–44)

2. Local Elections and Register of Electors (Temporary Provisions) Act 1943.
repealed: S.L.R. 1978.
s. 2, repealed (S.): order 74/812.

5. Landlord and Tenant (Requisitioned Land) Act 1944.
s. 5, repealed in pt.: S.L.R. 1976.

7. Prize Salvage Act 1944.
s. 1, repealed in pt.: S.L.R. 1976.

8. Guardianship (Refugee Children) Act 1944.
repealed: S.L.R. 1973.

9. Supreme Court of Judicature (Amendment) Act 1944.
repealed: 1981, c.54, sch.7.

CAP.

7 & 8 Geo. 6 (1943–44)—cont.

10. Disabled Persons (Employment) Act 1944.
ss. 2–5, repealed: 1973, c.50, schs.3,4.
s. 7, repealed in pt.: 1981, c.55, sch.5.
s. 9, see *Seymour* v. *British Railways Board* [1983] I.C.R. 148, E.A.T.; *Hobson* v. *G.E.C. Telecommunications* [1985] I.C.R. 777, E.A.T.
s. 16, repealed in pt.: 1973, c.50, schs.3, 4; 1981, c.55, sch.5.
s. 22, repealed in pt.: 1973, c.36, sch.6.
sch. 1, repealed: 1981, c.55, sch.5.

14. India (Attachment of States) Act 1944.
repealed: S.L.R. 1976.

15. Reinstatement in Civil Employment Act 1944.
repealed: S.L.R. 1981.

22. Police and Firemen (War Service) Act 1944.
ss. 3, 4, repealed in pt.: S.L.R. 1975.
s. 6, repealed in pt.: 1973, c.36, sch.6; S.L.R. 1975.
s. 7, repealed in pt.: 1973, c.36, sch.6.

23. Finance Act 1944.
Pt. VI, (ss.35–41) sch. 3, repealed: 1975, c.7, sch.13.
ss. 42, 49, sch. 4, repealed in pt.: *ibid.*

25. Law Officers Act 1944.
s. 2, see *H.M. Advocate* v. *Hanna*, 1975 S.L.T.(Sh.Ct.) 24.
s. 3, repealed: 1973, c.36, sch.6.

26. Rural Water Supplies and Sewerage Act 1944.
s. 1, amended: 1973, c.37, sch.8; (S.) 1975, c.30, s.3; repealed in pt.: 1973, c.37, sch.9; S.L.R. 1975.
s. 2, repealed: 1973, c.37, schs.8, 9.
s. 4, repealed: *ibid.*, sch.9.
s. 6, amended: 1972, c.70, sch.13; repealed in pt.: *ibid.*, sch.30.
s. 7, amended: 1973, c.65, sch.17.

28. Agriculture (Miscellaneous Provisions) Act 1944.
s. 1, order 72/1137.
s. 1, repealed: 1986, c.49, sch.4.
ss. 2, 3, repealed in pt.: S.L.R. 1977.
s. 6, repealed in pt.: 1972, c.62, s.8, sch.6; 1984, c.40, sch.2.
ss. 7, 9 (in pt.), repealed: S.L.R. 1973.
sch. 1, repealed: 1986, c.49, sch.4.

29. Food and Drugs (Milk and Dairies) Act 1944.
repealed: S.L.R. 1975.

31. Education Act 1944.
see *Birmingham City Council* v. *Equal Opportunities Commission, The Times*, May 17, 1968, C.A.
s. 1, see *Secretary of State for Education and Science* v. *Tameside Metropolitan B.C.* [1976] 3 W.L.R. 641, H.L.; *Smith* v. *Inner London Education Authority* [1978] 1 All E.R. 411, C.A.
s. 4, repealed: 1986, c.61, s.59, sch.6.
s. 5, repealed: *ibid.*, s.60, sch.6.
s. 6, see *R.* v. *Brent London Borough Council, ex p. Gunning* (1985) 84 L.G.R. 168, Hodgson J.
s. 6, repealed in pt.: 1972, c.70, sch.30.
Pt. II (ss.6–69), see *R.* v. *Secretary of State of Education and Science, ex p. Birmingham District Council, The Times*, July 18, 1984, McCullough J.

CAP.

7 & 8 Geo. 6 (1943–44)—cont.

31. Education Act 1944—cont.

s. 8, see *Secretary of State for Education and Science* v. *Tameside Metropolitan B.C.* [1976] 3 W.L.R. 641, H.L.; *Smith* v. *Inner London Education Authority* [1978] 1 All E.R. 411, C.A.; *Winward* v. *Cheshire County Council* (1978) 77 L.G.R. 172, Judge Mervyn Davies, Q.C.; *Meade* v. *Haringey London Borough Council* [1979] 1 W.L.R. 637, C.A.; *R.* v. *Hereford and Worcester Local Education Authority, ex p. Jones* [1981] 1 W.L.R. 768, D.C.; *Honeyford* v. *City of Bradford Metropolitan Council* [1986] I.R.L.R. 32, C.A.; *R.* v. *Mid-Glamorgan County Council, ex p. Greig, The Independent,* June 1, 1988, Simon Brown J.

s. 8, amended: 1981, c.60, s.2; 1988, c.40, s.120; repealed in pt.: 1980, c.20, sch.7; 1988, c.40, s.120, sch.13.

s. 9, repealed in pt.: 1980, c.20, s.28, sch.7.

s. 10, regs. 72/1255; 81/909.

s. 10, amended: 1988, c.40, sch.12.

s. 11, repealed: 1980, c.20, sch.7.

s. 12, repealed: *ibid.,* s.30, sch.7.

s. 13, see *Legg* v. *Inner London Education Authority* [1972] 1 W.L.R. 1245; [1972] 3 All E.R. 177; *Coney* v. *Choyce; Ludden* v. *Choyce* [1975] 1 W.L.R. 422; [1975] 1 All E.R. 979; *North Yorkshire County Council* v. *Department of Education and Science* (1978) 77 L.G.R. 457, Browne-Wilkinson J.

s. 13, repealed: 1980, c.20, s.16, sch.7.

s. 14, repealed in pt.: 1980, c.20, sch.1.

s. 15, amended: 1986, c.61, sch.4; repealed in pt.: 1930, c.20, sch.1.

s. 16, amended: *ibid.,* sch.3; repealed in pt.: *ibid.,* sch.1.

s. 17, see *Jones* v. *Lee, The Times,* November 21, 1979, C.A.; *Att -Gen.* v. *Schonfield* [1980] 3 All E.R. 1, Megarry V.-C.; *R.* v. *Manchester City Council, ex p. Fulford* (1983) 81 L.G.R. 292, D.C.; *R.* v. *Powys County Council, ex p. Smith* (1983) 81 L.G.R. 342, Woolf J.; *Noble* v. *Inner London Education Authority* (1984) 82 L.G.R. 291, C.A.; *Honeyford* v. *City of Bradford Metropolitan Council* [1986] I.R.L.R. 32, C.A.; *McGoldrick* v. *Brent London Borough Council, The Times,* November 20, 1986, C.A.

ss. 17, 18, repealed: 1986, c.61, sch.4.

s. 19, see *Happe* v. *Lay* (1977) 76 L.G.R. 313, D.C.

ss. 19–21, repealed: 1986, c.61, sch.6.

s. 22, amended: *ibid.,* sch.4; repealed in pt.: 1980, c.20, sch.1.

s. 23, repealed: 1986, c.61, sch.6.

ss. 23, 24, see *Honeyford* v. *City of Bradford Metropolitan Council* [1986] I.R.L.R. 32, C.A.

s. 24, see *Jones* v. *Lee, The Times,* November 21, 1979, C.A.; *R.* v. *Governors of Litherland High School, ex p. Corkish, The Times,* December 4, 1982, C.A.; *R.* v. *Powys County Council, ex p. Smith* (1983) 81 L.G.R. 342, Woolf J.; *Noble* v. *Inner London Education*

CAP.

7 & 8 Geo. 6 (1943–44)—cont.

31. Education Act 1944—cont.

Authority (1984) 82 L.G.R. 291, C.A.; *McGoldrick* v. *Brent London Borough Council* [1987] I.R.L.R. 67, C.A.

s. 24, repealed in pt.: 1975, c.65, sch.6; 1980, c.20, sch.1; 1986, c.61, sch.6.

s. 25, repealed: 1988, c.40, sch.13.

s. 26, substituted: *ibid.,* sch.1.

s. 27, see *Honeyford* v. *City of Bradford Metropolitan Council* [1986] I.R.L.R. 32, C.A.

s. 27, amended: 1988, c.40, sch.1; repealed in pt.: 1980, c.20, sch.1; 1986, c.61, sch.6.

s. 28, amended: 1988, c.40, sch.1.

s. 29, amended: *ibid.;* repealed in pt.: 1980, c.20, sch. 1; 1988, c.40, sch. 13.

s. 30, see *Ahmad* v. *Inner London Education Authority* [1977] I.C.R. 490, C.A.

s. 30, amended: 1988, c.40, sch. 1.

s. 31, repealed in pt.: 1980, c.20, schs.1,7.

s. 32, repealed: *ibid.,* sch.7.

s. 33, regs. 73/340, 2021; 75/1962; 77/278; 78/1146; 80/888; 81/1087; 82/129.

ss. 33, 34, repealed: 1981, c.60, sch.4.

s. 34, regs. 75/328.

s. 35, order 72/444.

s. 36, see *Winward* v. *Cheshire County Council* (1978) 77 L.G.R. 172, Judge Mervyn Davies, Q.C.

ss. 36, 37, see *Enfield London Borough Council* v. *F.* (1987) 85 L.G.R. 526, D.C.

s. 37, amended: 1981, c.60, sch.3, repealed in pt.: *ibid.,* sch.4.

s. 38, repealed: *ibid.*

s. 39, see *Myton* v. *Wood, The Times,* July 12, 1980, C.A.; *Jarman* v. *Mid-Glamorgan Education Authority, The Times,* February 11, 1985, D.C.; *Rogers* v. *Essex County Council* [1986] 3 W.L.R. 689, H.L.; *R.* v. *Devon County Council, ex p. G.* [1988] 3 W.L.R. 49, C.A.

s. 39, repealed in pt.: 1980, c.20, sch.1.

ss. 39, 40, see *Happe* v. *Lay* (1977) 76 L.G.R. 313, D.C.

s. 40, amended: 1977, c.45, s.31, sch.6.

s.41, substituted: 1988, c.40, s.120.

ss. 42–46, repealed: *ibid.,* s.120, sch.13.

s. 48, amended: 1973, c.32, sch.4; 1977, c.49, sch.15; 1988, c.40, sch.12; repealed in pt.: 1973, c.32, sch.5.

s. 49, regs. 72/1098; 73/271, 1299; 74/1125; 75/311, 1619; 76/402, 1705; 77/385, 1193, 1684; 78/959, 1301; 79/695, 1686.

s. 49, repealed: 1980, c.20, sch.7.

s. 50, amended: 1981, c.60, sch.3; 1988, c.40, s.100; repealed in pt.: *ibid.,* sch.13.

s. 52, amended: 1981, c.60, sch.3; repealed in pt.: 1988, c.40, sch. 13.

s. 53, amended: *ibid.,* sch. 12; repealed in pt.: 1981, c.60, s.30, sch.7.

s. 54, repealed in pt.: 1988, c.40, sch.13.

s. 55, see *Myton* v. *Wood, The Times,* July 12, 1980, C.A.; *R.* v. *Devon County Council, ex p. G.* [1988] 3 W.L.R. 49, C.A.

s. 55, amended: 1986, c.61, s.53; 1988, c.40, s.100, sch.12.

7 & 8 Geo. 6 (1943–44)—cont.

31. Education Act 1944—*cont.*

s. 59, repealed: 1973, c.24, sch.2.

s. 60, repealed: 1988, c.40, sch.13.

s. 61, see *R.* v. *Hereford and Worcester Local Education Authority, ex p. Jones* [1981] 1 W.L.R. 768, D.C.

s. 61, repealed: 1988, c.40, sch.13.

s. 62, amended: *ibid.*, sch. 12; repealed in pt.: *ibid.*, schs.12, 13.

s. 63, repealed in pt.: 1974, c.37, sch.10; 1984, c.55, sch.7.

s. 65, repealed in pt.: 1980, c.20, sch.1.

s. 66, repealed: *ibid.*, sch.7.

s. 67, amended: 1988, c.40, s.120, schs.1, 12; repealed in pt.: 1980, c.20, sch.1; 1986, c.61, sch.4.

s. 68, see *Secretary of State for Education and Science* v. *Tameside Metropolitan B.C.* [1976] 3 W.L.R. 641, H.L.

s. 68, repealed in pt.: 1972, c.70, sch.30; 1980, c.20, sch.1.

s. 69, repealed in pt.: 1973, c.32, sch.5; 1988, c.40, sch.13.

s. 70, orders 78/467; 82/1730.

s. 70, amended and repealed in pt.: 1980, c.20, s.34.

ss. 70, 73, amended: 1982, c.48, sch.3.

ss. 71, 76, see *R.* v. *Secretary of State for Education and Science, ex p. Talmud Torah Machzikei Hadass School Trust, The Times,* April 12, 1985, D.C.

s. 75, rules 72/42; 74/563, 1574, 1972; 75/854, 1298.

s. 75, repealed in pt.: 1976, c.81, s.6.

s. 76, see *Winward* v. *Cheshire County Council, The Times,* July 21, 1978; (1978) 77 L.G.R. 172, Judge Mervyn Davies, Q.C.

s. 77, amended: 1982, c.48, sch.3; 1988, c.40, schs.1, 12; repealed in pt.: 1980, c.20, sch.1.

s. 78, repealed in pt.: 1973, c.32, sch.5.

s. 79, repealed: *ibid.*

s. 80, regs. 87/1285; 88/1185.

s. 80, amended: 1988, c.40, sch.12; repealed in pt.: 1980, c.20, sch.1.

s. 81, see *R.* v. *Hampshire County Council, The Times,* December 5, 1985, Taylor J.; *R.* v. *Oxfordshire Education Authority, ex p. W., The Times,* November 22, 1986, D.C.; *R.* v. *Inner London Education Authority, ex p. F., The Times,* June 16, 1988, McCowan J.

s. 81, regs. 75/1198; 77/1443; 79/542.

s. 81, amended: 1988, c.40, sch.12.

ss. 82, 83, repealed in pt.: 1980, c.20, s.30, sch.7.

s. 84, repealed: 1988, c.40, sch.13.

s. 85, amended: 1980, c.20, sch.3.

s. 86, repealed: 1973, c.16, sch.2.

s. 88, repealed in pt.: 1972, c.70, sch.30.

s. 90, amended: 1988, c.40, sch.12; repealed in pt.: 1980, c.20, schs.1,7.

s. 91, repealed: 1972, c.70, sch.30.

s. 94, amended: orders 74/1291; 77/1861; 81/241; 82/222.

7 & 8 Geo. 6 (1943–44)—cont.

31. Education Act 1944—*cont.*

s. 95, repealed in pt.: 1980, c.20, sch.1.

s. 97, repealed: *ibid.*, sch.7.

s. 99, see *Coney* v. *Choyce; Ludden* v. *Choyce* [1975] 1 W.L.R. 422; [1975] 1 All E.R. 979; *Meade* v. *Haringey London Borough Council* [1979] 1 W.L.R. 637, C.A.; *R.* v. *Northampton County Council, ex p. Gray, The Times,* June 10, 1986, D.C.

s. 99, repealed in pt.: 1980, c.20, sch.1.

s. 100, regs. 72/1678; 73/370, 1535; 75/1054, 1198, 1929, 1964; 76/1191; 77/278; 78/1145; 79/1552; 80/1861; 81/786, 1086, 1788, 1839; 82/106; 83/74, 169, 1017; 84/113; 85/684; 86/989; 87/1126, 1138, 1182, 1314; 88/240, 1212.

s. 100, repealed in pt.: 1973, c.16, sch.2; 1980, c.20, sch.7.

s. 102, amended: 1975, c.2, s.3; 1980, c.20, sch.3; repealed in pt.: *ibid.*, sch.1.

s. 103, amended: 1975, c.2, s.3; 1980, c.20, sch.1.

s. 105, repealed in pt.: *ibid.*

s. 106, repealed: S.L.R. 1975.

s. 107, repealed: S.L.R. 1978.

ss. 108–110, repealed: S.L.R. 1975.

s. 111, order 78/467; regs. 81/1839.

s. 111A, added: 1988, c.40, s.229.

s. 114, regs. 82/1730.

s. 114, amended: 1972, c.70, s.192; 1973, c.32, sch.4; regs. 77/293, 1977, c.49, sch.14; 1980, c.20, ss.24, 34, sch.1; 1988, c.40, ss.120, 234, schs.1, 12; repealed in pt.: 1973, c.32, sch.5; regs. 74/595; S.L.R. 1975; 1976, c.5, sch.; 1980, c.20, schs.1, 7; 1981, c.60, sch.3; 1988, c.40, s.234, sch.13.

s. 120, repealed in pt.: S.L.R. 1978; 1980, c.20, sch.1.

s. 121, repealed in pt.: 1973, c.16, sch.2.

sch. 1, see *R.* v. *Liverpool City Council, ex p. Professional Association of Teachers, The Times,* March 22, 1984, Forbes J.; *R.* v. *Brent London Borough Council, ex p. Gunning* (1985) 84 L.G.R. 168, Hodgson J.; *R.* v. *Croydon London Borough Council, ex p. Leney* (1987) 85 L.G.R. 466, D.C.; *R.* v. *Kirklees Metropolitan Borough Council, ex p. Molloy* (1987) 86 L.G.R. 115, C.A.; *R.* v. *Gateshead Metropolitan Borough Council, ex p. Nichol, The Times,* June 2, 1988, D.C.; *R.* v. *Secretary of State for Education and Science, ex p. Threapleton, The Times,* June 2, 1988, D.C.

sch. 1, repealed in pt.: 1972, c.70, s.192, sch.30; 1980, c.20, sch.7.

sch. 2, repealed in pt.: *ibid.*, sch.1.

sch. 3, amended: *ibid.*, sch.3; repealed in pt.: *ibid.*, schs.1,7.

sch. 4, repealed: *ibid.*, s.4, sch.7; repealed in pt.: *ibid.*, sch.1.

sch. 5, amended: 1988, c.40, sch.1.

sch. 7, repealed: S.L.R. 1975.

sch. 8, repealed in pt.: 1972, c.44, sch.; S.L.R. 1978.

sch. 9, repealed: 1973, c.16, sch.2.

7 & 8 Geo. 6 (1943–44)—cont.

34. Validation of War-time Leases Act 1944.
repealed: S.L.R. 1976.

36. Housing (Temporary Accommodation) Act 1944.
repealed: 1972, c.46, sch.11; c.47, schs.8,11.

38. India (Miscellaneous Provisions) Act 1944.
repealed: S.L.R. 1976.

43. Matrimonial Causes (War Marriages) Act 1944.
repealed: 1986, c.55, sch.2.

8 & 9 Geo. 6 (1944–45)

5. Representation of the People Act 1945.
repealed: S.L.R. 1978.
s. 34, repealed (S.): order 74/812.

7. India (Estate Duty) Act 1945.
repealed: S.L.R. 1976.

10. Compensation of Displaced Officers (War Service) Act 1945.
ss. 1, 6, 8, 9, repealed in pt.: S.L.R. 1975.
ss. 2–5, sch., repealed: ibid.
s. 10, repealed in pt.: 1973, c.36, sch.6.

12. Northern Ireland (Miscellaneous Provisions) Act 1945.
ss. 1, 2, repealed: 1973, c.36, sch.6.
s. 8, repealed: 1978, c.23, sch.7.

16. Limitation (Enemies and War Prisoners) Act 1945.
s. 1, amended: 1973, c.52, sch.4; 1984, c.45, sch.1(S.).
s. 2, amended: 1973, c.18, sch.2; 1978, c.47, sch.1; 1980, c.58, sch.3; 1984, c.16, s.2; repealed in pt.: 1974, c.39, sch.5; 1988, c.48, sch.8.
s. 4, repealed in pt.: ibid.

18. Local Authorities Loans Act 1945.
order 74/989.
s. 2, regs. 74/989; 82/1089.
s. 8, repealed: 1972, c.70, sch.30.

19. Ministry of Fuel and Power Act 1945.
s. 1, repealed in pt.: regs. 74/2012.

26. Camps Act 1945.
repealed: S.L.R. 1973.

28. Law Reform (Contributory Negligence) Act 1945.
see De Meza and Stuart v. Apple, Van Staten Shena and Stone [1974] 1 Lloyd's Rep. 508; Jeyes v. IMI (Kynoch) Ltd., The Times, October 20, 1984, C.A.; Tennant Radiant Heat v. Warrington Development Corp., The Times, December 19, 1987, C.A.
s. 1, see Boothman v. British Northrop [1972] 13 K.I.R. 112, C.A.; Parnell v. Shields [1973] R.T.R. 414; Toperoff v. Mor [1973] R.T.R. 419; McGee v. Francis Shaw & Co. [1973] R.T.R. 409; James v. I.M.I. (Kynoch) [1985] I.C.R. 155, C.A.; Lancashire Textiles (Jersey) v. Thomson Shepherd & Co. (O.H.), November 29, 1984; A.B. Marintrans v. Comet Shipping Co.: Shinjitsu Maru No. 5, The [1985] 3 All E.R. 442, McNeill, L.J.; Banque Keyser Ullrnan S.A. v. Skandia (U.K.) Insurance Co. [1987] 2 W.L.R. 1300, Steyn J.; Fitzgerald v. Lane [1988] 3 W.L.R. 356, H.L.

8 & 9 Geo. 6 (1944–45)—cont.

28. Law Reform (Contributory Negligence) Act 1945—cont.
s. 1, repealed in pt.: 1976, c.30, sch.2; 1978, c.47, sch.2.
ss. 1, 4, see Basildon District Council v. J.E. Lesser (Properties) [1984] 3 W.L.R. 812, Judge Newley Q.C.
s. 4, repealed in pt.: 1976, c.30, sch.2.
s. 5, amended (S.): 1978, c.47, sch.1.

33. Town and Country Planning (Scotland) Act 1945.
repealed: 1972, c.52, sch.23.
s. 62, sch. 6, see City of Glasgow District Council v. Morrison McChlery & Co., Second Division, June 19, 1984.
sch. 6, see Renfrew's Trs. v. Glasgow Corporation, 1972 S.L.T. 2; Smith & Waverley Tailoring Co. v. Edinburgh District Council, 1976 S.L.T.(Lands Tr.) 19; Apostolic Church Trs. v. Glasgow District Council, 1977 S.L.T. (Lands Tr.) 24; Apostolic Church Trustees v. Glasgow District Council (No. 2), 1978 S.L.T. (Lands Tr.) 17, Birrell v. City of Edinburgh District Council, 1982 S.L.T. 111.

37. Education (Scotland) Act 1945.
sch. 4, repealed in pt.: 1972, c.44, sch.; S.L.R. 1978

39. Housing (Temporary Accommodation) Act 1945.
repealed: 1972, c.47, sch.11; (S.) 1973, c.46, sch.11.

42. Water Act 1945.
see Royco Homes v. Southern Water Authority (1978) 122 S.J. 627, Forbes J.
ss. 1–5, repealed: 1973, c.37, sch.9.
s. 7, amended: 1977, c.45, ss.15,30, sch.1.
s. 8, repealed: 1973, c.37, sch.9.
s. 9, orders 72/251, 267, 498, 525, 1270, 1311, 1360, 1443, 1463, 1688, 1744; 73/257–63, 333, 353, 378, 453, 589, 1048, 1447, 1604, 1669, 1837, 2235, 2236; 74/644, 915, 1422; 75/1840.
s. 9, repealed in pt.: 1973, c.36, sch.9.
s. 10, orders 72/525; 73/938.
s. 10, amended: 1973, c.37, sch.8.
s. 11, orders 74/439, 440.
s. 11, repealed: 1973, c.37, sch.9.
s. 12, substituted: ibid., sch.4.
s. 13, see R. v. Secretary of State for the Environment, ex p. Jaywick Sands Freeholders Association [1975] J.P.L. 663, D.C.
s. 13, substituted: 1973, c.37, sch.4.
s. 13A, added: ibid.
s. 14, amended: ibid., sch.8; 1977, c.45, sch.6.
s. 15, amended: 1973, c.37, sch.8; repealed in pt.: ibid., sch.9.
s. 16, amended: 1977, c.45, sch.6.
s. 18, repealed: 1974, c.40, sch.4.
s. 19, orders 73/1612, 1723–6, 1777, 1778, 1809, 1914–6, 1937, 1970, 2017, 2018, 2127, 2141, 2142; 74/48, 76, 77, 79, 114, 152–4, 228, 308, 393, 462, 751, 893, 962, 987, 1034, 1207, 1227, 1308, 1341, 1394, 1396, 1466, 1550, 1568, 1589, 1590, 1641–3, 1645, 1647,

CAP.

8 & 9 Geo. 6 (1944–45)—cont.

42. Water Act 1945—cont.

1649, 1650, 1677, 1716, 1723, 1724, 1745, 1751, 1753, 1814, 1858, 1882, 1947, 1956–8, 1961; 75/23, 34, 35, 47, 48, 77–83, 96, 105–8, 134, 317, 318, 451, 600, 680, 722–5, 784–6, 912, 1018–20, 1069, 1070, 1103, 1104, 1167, 1168, 1501, 1540–2, 1550, 1601–3, 1605, 1655, 1734, 1735, 1754, 1755, 1772, 1774, 1786–8, 1934, 2034, 2151; 76/6–13, 33, 34, 83–85, 108, 148, 176, 240, 313, 415, 562–564, 643, 644, 682, 683, 774, 799, 862, 864, 947–949, 1047–1050, 1078, 1140, 1141, 1183, 1327–1329, 1359, 1420, 1500, 1501, 1551–1554, 1596, 1752, 1787–1790, 1834–1838, 1949–1951, 1993, 2036, 2037; 77/33, 173, 241, 332–334, 515, 565, 664, 694, 725, 796–798, 909, 1029, 1431, 1542, 1543, 1594, 1690, 1799, 1800, 1920, 1976–1980, 2043–2045, 2116–2119, 2166; 78/19, 27, 39, 51, 52, 60, 61, 86, 166, 213, 261–265, 403, 404, 406, 509, 511, 572, 636, 666–668, 853, 902–906, 1084, 1184, 1193, 1229–1232, 1369, 1380, 1381, 1414–1416, 1447, 1448, 1506, 1561, 1620, 1666, 1667, 1672–1674, 1740, 1849, 1940, 1955; 79/7, 8, 28, 39, 48, 57, 101, 128, 147, 161, 199, 248, 335, 343, 344, 479, 502, 505, 536, 537, 557, 561, 593, 596, 684, 1329, 1330; 80/72, 1422; 81/133, 724; 86/1618, 1733, 1776; 88/1380.

s. 19, amended: 1973, c.37, sch.8; 1974, c.40, sch.2; repealed in pt.: 1973, c.37, sch.9.

s. 21, amended: 1974, c.40, sch.2.

s. 22, amended: 1973, c.37, sch.8.

s. 23, orders 72/75, 147, 180, 398, 412, 476, 477, 594, 681, 750, 783, 789, 837, 921, 948, 1197, 1228, 1286, 1386, 1387, 1412, 1418, 1432, 1441, 1442, 1483, 1525, 1546, 1601, 1605, 1646, 1685, 1743, 1795, 1863, 1935; 73/25, 53, 151, 255, 348, 487, 497, 498, 623, 626, 627, 700, 738, 786, 787, 834, 891, 911, 918, 919, 938, 1151, 1183, 1184, 1247, 1294, 1296, 1389, 1434, 1467, 1589, 1597–9, 1604, 1663, 1691, 1692, 1703, 1770, 1837, 1917, 1918, 2127, 2141, 2142; 74/26, 113, 123, 195, 236, 237, 304, 621, 622, 640, 641, 699, 700, 895, 915, 996, 997, 1035, 1141, 1203–5, 1395, 1443, 1465, 1693, 1750, 1873, 1948, 2182; 75/92, 114, 115, 139, 397–9, 587, 852, 967, 993, 1017, 1604, 1733, 1756, 1771, 1773; 76/35, 109, 241, 266, 267, 312, 335, 861, 863, 1142, 1499, 1753, 1792, 2035, 2106, 2170; 77/34, 35, 62, 207, 295, 296, 514, 564, 566, 584, 744, 745, 761, 762, 799, 800, 805, 810, 839, 868, 896, 1004, 1116, 1407, 1422, 1435, 1531, 1646, 1800, 1837, 1852, 2179; 78/142, 143, 268, 510, 628, 653, 827, 829, 899, 1194, 1198, 1200, 1240, 1276, 1482, 1586, 1645, 1782, 1932; 79/175, 176, 509, 512, 513, 562, 679, 801, 831, 901, 1065, 1078, 1168, 1361, 1369, 1457, 1498, 1527, 1560; 80/125, 128, 176, 217, 435–438, 441, 526, 722, 731, 863, 911, 1106, 1114, 1116, 1205, 1431, 1432, 1588, 1633, 1739, 2020; 81/75, 89, 90, 294, 391, 729, 1010, 1036,

CAP.

8 & 9 Geo. 6 (1944–45)—cont.

42. Water Act 1945—cont.

1100, 1187, 1213, 1310, 1311, 1382, 1458, 1477, 1494, 1514, 1607, 1610, 1644; 82/30, 223–225, 389, 403, 576, 725, 744, 816, 822, 823, 912, 1150, 1371, 1579, 1600, 1625, 1694, 1695, 1714, 1716, 1718, 1818, 1863; 83/2, 78, 156, 560, 629, 918, 965, 966, 1055, 1161–1163, 1189, 1809; 84/36, 108, 1353, 1354, 2050, 2051; 85/72, 73, 88, 93, 96, 121, 231, 240, 513, 709, 716, 815, 819, 990, 1668, 1706, 1725; 86/2, 13, 136, 245–247, 401, 740, 1277, 1532, 1986; 87/234, 1434.

ss. 23, 24, repealed in pt.: 1973, c.37, sch.9.

s. 25, order 80/87.

s. 27, amended: 1973, c.37, s.11.

s. 28, see *Hey and Croft* v. *Lexden and Winstree R.D.C.* (1972) 70 L.G.R. 531, D.C.

s. 28, order 78/986.

s. 28, repealed: 1973, c.37, sch.9.

ss. 29, 30, repealed: 1984, c.55, sch.7.

s. 30, order 76/439.

s. 32, orders 72/720, 752, 791, 867, 878, 1744; 73/1629; 75/967, 978, 1733; 76/911, 974, 1142, 1791, 2123, 2243; 77/799, 963, 1079, 1406, 1598, 1608, 1647, 1915; 78/405, 881, 1240; 79/801, 1079, 1528; 80/722, 1106, 1205; 82/102, 1579, 1718; 83/2, 156, 560, 1809; 84/108, 806, 905, 1319; 85/60, 81, 121, 266, 513, 709, 716, 990, 1677; 86/2, 13, 136, 249, 1733; 87/234.

s. 32, repealed in pt.: 1973, c.37, sch.9.

s. 33, orders 72/30, 370, 525, 601, 720, 752, 791, 867, 878, 1418; 73/486, 498, 642, 938, 1604; 74/894, 1948; 75/1237, 1251; 77/647, 2195; 78/1240, 1249, 1823; 79/1079, 1527; 80/1106, 1633; 81/1310; 82/390, 1579, 1718, 1818; 83/78, 156, 1188, 1189, 1216, 1809, 1923; 84/108; 85/74, 240, 513, 716, 1677; 86/136, 249, 401, 1532, 1733; 87/234, 1434.

s. 33, repealed in pt.: 1973, c.37, sch.9.

s. 34, amended: *ibid.*, sch.8; 1977, c.45, ss.15, 30, sch.1; repealed in pt.: 1973.c.37, sch.9.

s. 35, repealed in pt.: *ibid.*

s. 36, amended: *ibid.*, sch.8.

s. 37, see *Banbury Corporation* v. *Oxfordshire and District Water Board* [1974] 1 W.L.R. 848; [1974] 2 All E.R. 929, C.A.; *Cherwell District Council* v. *Thames Water Authority* [1975] 1 W.L.R. 448; [1975] 1 All E.R. 763, H.L.; *Royco Homes* v. *Southern Water Authority* [1979] 1 W.L.R. 1366, H.L.

s. 37, amended: 1973, c.37, sch.8.

s. 38, see *West Pennine Water Board* v. *Jon Migael (North West)* (1975) 73 L.G.R. 420, C.A.

s. 38, amended: 1973, c.37, sch.8; repealed in pt.: *ibid.*, sch.9.

s. 40, orders 72/257–61, 298, 324, 343–6, 397, 427, 439, 461, 499, 501–4, 523, 524, 720, 937, 1034, 1196, 1464, 1506; 73/89, 256, 552, 575, 576, 587, 588, 624, 625, 628–30, 641, 701, 1045, 1133–6, 1246, 1248, 1250, 2127, 2141, 2142.

CAP.

8 & 9 Geo. 6 (1944–45)—cont.

42. Water Act 1945—cont.
s. 40, repealed: 1973, c.37, sch.9.
s. 41, see *Sutton District Water Co.* v. *I.R.C.* [1982] S.T.C. 459, Nourse J.
s. 41, repealed in pt.: S.L.R. 1986; 1988, c.19, sch.14.
s. 42, amended: 1973, c.37, sch.8.
s. 46, repealed in pt.: *ibid.*, sch.9.
s. 50, orders 72/75, 251, 267, 468, 523, 594, 681, 720, 752, 791, 867, 878, 921, 937, 1196, 1270, 1311, 1360, 1387, 1443, 1688, 1744; 73/256–63, 353, 378, 453, 497, 498, 552, 576, 588, 623, 911, 938, 1045, 1134, 1136, 1447, 1629; 74/622, 1203, 1422, 1750; 75/92, 967, 978, 993, 1733, 1756, 1771, 1773, 1840; 76/35, 335, 911, 1753, 1791, 1792, 2123; 77/295, 564, 744, 799, 963, 1079, 1406, 1526, 1598, 1608, 1647, 1915; 78/405, 881, 1240, 1482, 1923; 79/48, 801, 1079, 1168, 1369, 1528; 80/722, 863, 1106, 1205, 1633; 81/1311, 1658; 82/1579, 1716, 1718, 1818; 83/2, 156, 560, 629, 965, 1188, 1216, 1809; 84/108, 1319; 85/60, 81, 96, 240, 266, 716, 990, 1677; 86/2, 13, 136, 249, 401, 1277, 1532, 1733; 87/234, 1434.
s. 55, amended: 1973, c 37, sch.8; repealed in pt.: *ibid.*, sch.9.
s. 59, see *Cakebread (V.O.)* v. *Severn Trent Water Authority* [1988] R.A. 290, C.A.
s. 59, orders 87/1434; 88/1380.
s. 59, amended: 1973, c.37, sch.8; repealed in pt.: *ibid.*, sch.9; S.L.R. 1986.
s. 60, amended: 1984, c.12, sch.4.
sch. 1, amended: 1973, c.37, sch.8; order 74/2044; 1985, c.51, sch.8; repealed in pt.: 1973, c.37, sch.9; order 74/2044.
sch. 2, repealed in pt.: 1973, c.37, sch.9.
sch. 3, see *George Whitehouse* v. *Anglian Water Authority* (Ref./157/1977) 247 E.G. 223; *Morgan Grenfell Group* v. *Mid Kent Water Co.*, *The Times*, July 1, 1988, C.A.
sch. 3, orders 74/122, 123, 607, 699; 75/40, 978, 993, 1017; 76/1142.
sch. 3, amended: 1973, c.37, sch.8; 1977, c.45, ss.15,30,31, schs.1,6; 1981, c.12, s.4; c.38, sch.3; 1984, c.12, sch.4; orders 73/1393; 77/293; 86/1; repealed in pt.: 1972, c.70, schs.15, 30; 1973, c.37, sch.9; 1977, c.45, sch.13; 1981, c.38, sch.3; 1984, c.12, schs.4,7; 1986, c.44, sch.9; 1988, c.15, sch.3.
sch. 4, repealed in pt.: 1973, c.37, sch.9; 1984, c.55, sch.7.

43. Requisitioned Land and War Works Act 1945.
s. 15, amended (S.): 1984, c.54, sch.9.
s. 21, repealed: S.L.R. 1973.
Pt. IV (ss.23–25), repealed: 1984, c.12, sch.7.
ss. 33 (in pt.), 34 (in pt.), 40–43, 45, 46, repealed: S.L.R. 1973.
s. 52, repealed: 1982, c.43, sch.4(S.); 1986, c.63, s.48, sch.12.
s. 53, repealed in pt.; S.L.R. 1986.
s. 54, repealed: S.L.R. 1973.
s. 59, repealed in pt.: S.L.R. 1976.
s. 60, amended (S.): 1984, c.54, sch.9; repealed in pt.: S.L.R. 1973.

CAP.

8 & 9 Geo. 6 (1944–45)—cont.

44. Treason Act 1945.
repealed: 1980, c.62, sch.8.

9 & 10 Geo. 6 (1945–46)

2. Indian Franchise Act 1945.
repealed: S.L.R. 1976.
5. Indian Divorce Act 1945.
repealed: S.L.R. 1976.
7. British Settlements Act 1945.
orders 72/668; 73/598; 75/1211, 1706; 76/52; 77/423; 82/824; 85/444, 449; 87/1268; 88/1842.
12. Civil Defence (Suspension of Powers) Act 1945.
repealed: S.L.R. 1976.
13. Finance (No. 2) Act 1945.
s. 54, repealed: 1975, c.7, schs.7,13.
ss. 55–57, 62 (in pt.), repealed: *ibid.*, sch.13.
15. Public Health (Scotland) Act 1945.
s. 1, regs. 74/1003, 1017; 77/206; 78/369, 370; 83/1008; 88/1550.
s. 1, amended: 1972, c.58, sch.6; 1973, c.65, sch.27; 1978, c.29, sch.15; 1982, c.48, sch.6; 1983, c.41, sch.9; repealed in pt.: 1972, c.58, sch.7; 1973, c 65, sch.29; 1983, c.41, sch.9.
s. 2, repealed: S.L.R. 1981.
17. Police (Overseas Service) Act 1945.
ss. 1–3, repealed in pt.: S.L.R. 1986.
18. Statutory Orders (Special Procedure) Act 1945.
s. 1, see *R.* v. *Minister of Agriculture, Fisheries and Food, ex p. Wear Valley District Council*, *The Times*, March 6, 1988, D.C.
19. Bretton Woods Agreements Act 1945.
repealed: 1980, c.63, sch.2.
s. 3, order 77/825.
20. Building Materials and Housing Act 1945.
repealed: S.L.R. 1981.
22. Dock Workers (Regulation of Employment) Act 1946.
s. 1, see *Gibbons* v. *Associated British Ports* [1985] I.R.L.R. 376, Tudor Price J.
s. 2, orders 80/1940; 88/1492.
23. India (Proclamations of Emergency) Act 1946.
repealed: S.L.R. 1976.
26. Emergency Laws (Transitional Provisions) Act 1946.
s. 16, amended: 1973, c.39, sch.1.
sch. 2, amended: 1972, c.62, sch.6; repealed in pt.: 1976, c.70, sch.8; 1984, c.40, sch.2.
27. Bank of England Act 1946.
s. 5, sch. 2, repealed in pt.: S.L.R. 1976.
28. Assurance Companies Act 1946.
repealed: 1973, c.36, sch.6.
29. Agriculture (Artificial Insemination) Act 1946.
ss. 2–4, 6 (in pt.), repealed: S.L.R. 1973.
30. Trunk Roads Act 1946.
repealed (S.): 1984, c.54, sch.11.
see *Moncrieff* v. *Tayside Regional Council* (O.H.), 1987 S.L.T. 374.
s. 5, amended: 1973, c.56, s.20.
s. 9, repealed: S.L.R. 1978.
s. 14, amended: 1973, c.65, sch.14.

CAP.

9 & 10 Geo. 6 (1945–46)—cont.

31. Ministers of the Crown (Transfer of Functions) Act 1946.
repealed: 1975, c.26, sch.3.
s. 1, orders 74/691, 692, 1274, 1896.
ss. 1, 1A, order 74/1264.

35. Building Restrictions (War Time Contraventions) Act 1946.
ss. 3, 4, see *R.* v. *Secretary of State for the Environment, ex p. Bulk Storage* [1985] J.P.L. 35, McCullough J.
s. 8, amended and repealed in pt. (S.): 1972, c.52, sch.21.

36. Statutory Instruments Act 1946.
s. 1, see *R.* v. *Secretary of State for Social Services, ex p. Camden London Borough Council, The Times,* March 6, 1987, C.A.
s. 1, amended: 1978, c.51, sch.16; c.52, sch.11.
s. 4, amended: 1978, c.51, sch.16.
s. 5, orders 75/1517, 1830; 77/603; 79/459, 1375.
s. 5A, added: 1978, c.51, sch.16.
s. 6, orders 78/1022; 86/2239; regs. 81/1004; 82/670.
s. 6A, added: 1978, c.51, sch.16.
s. 7, orders 83/605, 606, 1841.
ss. 7, 8, amended: 1978, c.51, sch.16.
s. 8, regs. 72/1205; 77/641; 82/1728.
s. 9, repealed in pt.: S.L.R. 1986.
s. 10, repealed in pt.: S.L.R. 1977.

39. India (Central Government and Legislature) Act 1946.
repealed: S.L.R. 1976.

40. Miscellaneous Financial Provisions Act 1946.
s. 2, repealed: S.L.R. 1981.
s. 3, amended: 1974, c.18, s.1; repealed in pt.: *ibid,* sch.

42. Water (Scotland) Act 1946.
repealed: 1980, c.45, sch.11.
order 78/208.
s. 21, orders 75/198; 77/1385.
ss. 21, 44, orders 72/32, 571, 639, 697; 73/159, 1399, 1655, 1656, 1695, 2153, 2154, 2156, 2227; 75/69, 268, 270–2, 309, 486, 860, 863; 76/1306; 77/79, 1961, 2040; 78/1166, 1513, 1607; 79/455, 973, 1471, 1513, 1531.
ss. 21, 44, 75, orders 72/1238; 74/415, 787, 1310, 1765, 2155; 75/25, 862; 76/1286; 77/80.
s. 26, see *Central Regional Council* v. *Ferns,* 1980 S.L.T. 126.
s. 75, orders 77/80, 1385, 2040.
s. 76, regs. 75/930.

44. Patents and Designs Act 1946.
repealed: S.L.R. 1986.

45. United Nations Act 1946.
s. 1, orders 72/1584, 1585; 78/277, 1034, 1052–1054, 1624, 1894–1898; 79/1655; 81/1671; 82/153, 154, 1531; repealed in pt.: 1979, c.60, sch.3.

48. Housing (Financial and Miscellaneous Provisions) Act 1946.
repealed: 1972, c.47, sch.11.

CAP.

9 & 10 Geo. 6 (1945–46)—cont.

49. Acquisition of Land (Authorisation Procedure) Act 1946.
repealed except ss. 6 (in pt.), 10, sch. 4 (in pt.): 1981, c.67, sch.6.
s. 1, sch. 1, see *Wilson* v. *Secretary of State for the Environment* [1973] 1 W.L.R. 1083, Browne J.
sch. 1, see *McMeehan* v. *Secretary of State for the Environment* [1974] J.P.L. 411; *R.* v. *Secretary of State for the Environment, ex p. Ostler* [1976] 3 W.L.R. 288, C.A.; *George* v. *Secretary of State for the Environment* (1979) 38 P. & C.R. 609, C.A.; *Varsani* v. *Secretary of State for the Environment* (1980) 40 P. & C.R. 354, Sir Douglas Frank, Q.C.; *E.O.N. Motors* v. *Secretary of State for the Environment and Newbury District Council* [1981] J.P.L. 576, Sir Douglas Frank, Q.C.; *Islington London Borough Council* v. *Secretary of State for the Environment; Stockport Metropolitan Borough Council* v. *Secretary of State for the Environment* [1982] 43 P. & C.R. 300, C.A.
sch. 4, order 76/1775; modified: order 77/84.
sch. 4, repealed in pt.: 1972, c.70, sch.30; S.L.R. 1973; S.L.R. 1976; 1976, c.17, sch.3; c.57, sch.2; 1980, c.45, sch.11; 1983, c.25, sch.4; c.29, sch.3.

50. Education Act 1946.
s. 1, amended: 1980, c.20, sch.13; repealed in pt.: 1988, c.40, sch.13.
s. 2, amended: 1980, c.20, sch.3; repealed in pt.: *ibid.,* sch.1.
s. 3, repealed in pt.: *ibid.*
s. 4, amended: 1973, c.32, sch.4; 1977, c.49, schs.14, 15; repealed in pt.: 1980, c.20, sch.1.
s. 5, repealed: S.L.R. 1975.
s. 6, repealed in pt.: 1980, c.20, sch.1.
s. 7, repealed: 1988, c.40, sch.13.
s. 8, repealed in pt.: S.L.R. 1978; 1988, c.40, sch.13.
ss. 10, 12, 13 (in pt.), 14 (in pt.), repealed: 1972, c.70, sch.30.
s. 15, repealed: S.L.R. 1978.
s. 16, amended: 1988, c.40, sch.12; repealed in pt.: 1972, c.70, sch.30.
sch. 1, amended: 1980, c.20, sch.3.
sch. 2, repealed in pt.: 1972, c.70, sch.30; S.L.R. 1975; S.L.R. 1978; 1980, c.20, sch.7.

52. Trade Disputes and Trade Unions Act 1946.
see *R.* v. *Secretary of State for the Foreign and Commonwealth Office, ex p. Council of Civil Service Unions, The Times,* July 17, 1984, Glidewell J.
s. 1 (in pt.), sch., repealed: S.L.R. 1973.

58. Borrowing (Control and Guarantees) Act 1946.
ss. 1, 3, orders 72/1218; 75/12; 79/794; 85/1150; 86/1770; 88/295.
s. 3, order 77/1602.
s. 3, repealed in pt.: S.L.R. 1986.
s. 6, repealed in pt.: 1973, c.36, sch.6.

59. Coal Industry Nationalisation Act 1946.
see *R.* v. *British Coal Corp, ex p. Union of Democratic Mineworkers* [1988] I.C.R. 36, E.A.T.

9 & 10 Geo. 6 (1945–46)—cont.

59. Coal Industry Nationalisation Act 1946—cont.
s. 1, amended: 1977, c.39, sch.4; 1987, c.3, sch.1.
s. 2, amended: 1973, c.8, sch.1; 1987, c.3, sch.1.
s. 3, amended: 1977, c.39, sch.4; 1987, c.3, sch.1.
s. 4, amended: 1987, c.3, sch.1; repealed in pt.: 1972, c.68, sch.3.
ss. 5 (in pt.), 10–25, repealed: S.L.R. 1973.
s. 27, amended: 1973, c.8, sch.1; 1983, c.29, s.4, sch.2; 1987, c.3, sch.1.
s. 28, amended: ibid.; repealed in pt.: S.L.R. 1973.
ss. 29, 30, amended: 1987, c.3, sch.1.
ss. 31, 36, amended: 1977, c.39, sch.4; 1987, c.3, sch.1.
s. 37, amended: 1977, c.39, s.12; 1987, c.3, sch.1.
s. 38, amended: ibid.; repealed in pt.: S.L.R. 1973.
s. 42, repealed in pt.: regs. 74/2011.
s. 46, see R. v. National Coal Board, ex p. National Union of Mineworkers, The Times, March 8, 1986, D.C.; National Coal Board v. National Union of Mineworkers [1986] I.C.R. 736, Scott J.
ss. 46–49, amended: 1987, c.3, sch.1.
s. 50, amended: ibid.; repealed: S.L.R. 1986.
s. 51–53, amended: 1987, c.3, sch.1.
s. 54, amended: 1977, c.39, sch.4; 1987, c.3, sch.1.
s. 55, repealed in pt.: S.L.R. 1973.
s. 62, repealed in pt.: S.L.R. 1986.
s. 63, regs. 77/1452; amended: 1977, c.39, sch.4.
s. 64, amended: 1987, c.3, sch.1; repealed in pt.: S.L.R. 1973; S.L.R. 1986.
sch. 2A, added: 1977, c.39, sch.3; amended 1987, c.3, sch.1.
sch. 3, repealed in pt.: S.L.R. 1973.

62. National Insurance (Industrial Injuries) Act 1946.
repealed: 1975, c.18, sch.1.
see Park v. National Coal Board [1981] I.C.R. 783, C.A.

63. British North America Act 1946.
repealed: 1982, c.11, sch.

64. Finance Act 1946.
Pt. V (ss.46, 47), s. 49, repealed: 1975, c.7, sch.13.
ss. 48, 50, 51, repealed: 1980, c.17, s.15, sch.2.
s. 52, repealed in pt.: 1973, c.51, sch.22.
s. 53, repealed: 1988, c.39, s.140, sch.14.
s. 54, repealed in pt.: 1976, c.40, sch.15; 1987, c.16, sch.16.
s. 57, see Arbuthnot Financial Services v. I.R.C. [1985] S.T.C. 211, Walton J.
s. 57, regs. 88/268.
s. 57, amended: 1987, c.16, s.48; repealed in pt.: 1985, c.54, sch.27.
s. 63, repealed: 1979, c.30, sch.
s. 66, repealed in pt.: 1985, c.64, sch.4.

9 & 10 Geo. 6 (1945–46)—cont.

64. Finance Act 1946—cont.
s. 67, repealed in pt.: 1975, c.7, sch.13.
sch. 10, repealed in pt.: 1975, c.7, sch.13.

67. National Insurance Act 1946.
repealed: 1973, c.38, sch.28.

68. New Towns Act 1946.
ss. 2, 3, see Basildon District Council, ex p. Brown (1981) 79 L.G.R. 655, C.A.
s. 11, see Midlothian County Council v. Secretary of State for Scotland, 1975 S.L.T. 122.

72. Education (Scotland) Act 1946.
s. 81, see Trapp v. Mackie (O. H.), 1977 S.L.T. (Notes) 68.

73. Hill Farming Act 1946.
s. 3, repealed in pt.: 1972, c.62, sch.6.
s. 9, repealed: 1986, c.5, sch.15.
s. 10, regs. 73/974, 990; 75/1547, 1577.
s. 12, repealed in pt.: S.L.R. 1986.
ss. 13–15, schemes 72/725, 1616, 1659; 73/828, 866; 74/1863, 1906, 1997; 75/1951, 1952, 1957, 1958, 2130, 2131.
ss. 13–17, repealed: S.L.R. 1986.
s. 14, orders 72/628, 629, 726, 1617, 1660; 73/828, 866; 74/794, 1864; 75/1140.
s. 17, orders 72/628, 629, 726; 74/794, 1864; 75/1140; schemes 72/725, 1616, 1659; 73/828, 866; 74/1863, 1906, 1997; 75/1951, 1952, 1957, 1958, 2130, 2131.
s. 18, regs. 81/892.
s. 19, repealed in pt.: 1981, c.45, sch.
s. 20, regs. 74/2078; 75/112; 83/425, 1439; 86/428; 87/1208.
s. 20, amended: 1981, c.69, s.72; 1985, c.32, s.1.
s. 23, amended: regs. 77/2007.
s. 27, amended: 1981, c.69, s.72.
s. 28, order 86/1823(S.).
s. 28, amended (S.): 1985, c.73, s.32.
s. 32, repealed in pt.: S.L.R. 1986.
s. 33, repealed: 1972, c.62, sch.6.
s. 34, repealed in pt.: ibid.
ss. 37, 39, repealed in pt.: S.L.R. 1986.
s. 38, amended: order 78/272.

77. Association of County Councils (Scotland) Act 1946.
repealed: 1973, c.65, sch.29.

80. Atomic Energy Act 1946.
s. 2, amended: 1975, c.9, s.8.
s. 12, repealed in pt.: 1977, c.37, sch.6.
s. 20, repealed in pt.: 1973, c.36, sch.6.
sch. 1, repealed in pt.: S.L.R. 1974.

81. National Health Service Act 1946.
repealed: 1977, c.49, sch.16.
see Department of Health and Social Security v. Kinnear, The Times, July 7, 1984, Stuart-Smith J.
regs. 73/1468.
s. 2, orders 74/186, 196.
s. 3, regs. 74/284, 609, 1377; 75/1687, 1946.
s. 11, orders 72/47, 60, 408, 409, 474, 475, 618, 748, 1022, 1543, 1779; 73/452, 515, 1022, 2193; 74/341; regs. 82/202; 83/305.
s. 14, regs. 82/276.
s. 21, regs. 74/287.

CAP.

9 & 10 Geo. 6 (1945–46)—cont.

81. National Health Service Act 1946—cont.
s. 32, regs. 74/160, 455.
s. 33, regs. 74/160, 285, 455; 75/719; 76/1407.
s. 34, regs. 74/160.
s. 35, see Hensman v. Traill, The Times, October 22, 1980, Bristow J.
s. 36, regs. 73/1200.
s. 38, regs. 74/160, 285, 455, 627; 75/718, 719; 76/690, 1821.
s. 39, regs. 74/160; 75/719.
s. 40, regs. 72/82, 1336, 1842, 1899; 74/285, 451, 455; 75/1945.
s. 41, regs. 74/287, 455; 75/1945.
s. 42, regs. 74/455.
s. 44, regs. 74/287, 527; 75/1687, 1946; 77/434.
s. 45, regs. 74/160, 287.
s. 54, regs. 74/282, 541.
s. 55, regs. 74/282.
s. 66, regs. 72/1822.
s. 74, regs. 74/160, 287, 455; 75/719.
s. 75, orders 72/60, 474, 475, 1779; 73/1022, 2193; 74/196, 341.
s. 79, regs. 74/287.
sch. 1, regs. 74/187.
sch. 3, regs. 82/202; 83/305.
sch. 6, regs. 74/160.
sch. 7, regs. 74/455.

82. Cable and Wireless Act 1946.
ss. 1 (in pt.), 2, 4 (in pt.), 5, 6, 7 (in pt.), repealed: S.L.R. 1978.
s. 3, repealed in pt.: S.L.R. 1981.

10 & 11 Geo. 6 (1946–47)

4. Burma Independence Act 1947.
see R. v. Secretary of State for the Home Department, ex p. Bibi (Mahaboob) [1985] Imm.A.R. 134, Mann J.

9. Malta (Reconstruction) Act 1947.
repealed: S.L.R. 1973.

14. Exchange Control Act 1947.
repealed: 1987, c.16, s.68, sch.16.
s. 1, orders 72/146, 386, 930.
s. 2, order 79/1331.
s. 5, see SA Ancien Maison Marcel Bauche v. Woodhouse Drake and Carey (Sugar) [1982] 2 Lloyd's Rep. 516, Parker J.
s. 7, see Shelley v. Paddock (1979) 123 S.J. 706, C.A.
s. 8, see Re Transatlantic Life Assurance Co. [1979] 3 All E.R. 352, Slade J.
s. 15, order 79/1333.
s. 17, see Swiss Bank Corp. v. Lloyds Bank [1980] 2 All E.R. 419, C.A.
s. 22, see Credit Lyonnais v. P. T. Barnard & Associates [1976] 1 Lloyd's Rep. 557.
s. 23, order 79/1335.
s. 31, orders 72/137; 73/1997; 75/313, 369, 609; 76/212, 1564; 77/1734, 1938, 2021; 78/756, 1683; 79/647, 648, 1331–1334, 1336, 1337, 1660.
s. 33, see SA Ancien Maison Marcel Bauche v. Woodhouse Drake and Carey (Sugar) [1982] 2 Lloyd's Rep. 516, Parker J.

CAP.

10 & 11 Geo. 6 (1946–47)—cont.

14. Exchange Control Act 1947—cont.
s. 35, order 84/1459.
s. 36, orders 72/132, 137, 146, 386, 556, 1011, 1398, 1821; 73/42, 451, 615, 775, 1154, 1623, 1949, 1997; 74/588, 838, 1199, 1572, 1813, 2206; 75/313, 369, 571, 609, 1495; 76/16, 212, 1275, 1564, 2208; 77/501, 1734, 1938, 1957, 2021; 78/581, 756, 1599, 1638, 1942; 79/321, 647, 648, 740, 1331–1334, 1338, 1660; directions 79/1194.
s. 37, order 79/1660; directions 79/1339, 1662.
s. 42, orders 72/132, 556, 1011, 1398, 1821; 73/42, 451, 615, 775, 1154, 1623, 1949; 74/588, 838, 1199, 1572, 1813, 2206; 75/571, 1495; 76/16, 1275; 76/2208; 77/501, 1957; 78/581, 1599, 1942; 79/321, 740, 1194; directions 79/1335.
sch. 5, see D.P.P. v. Ellis [1973] 1 W.L.R. 722; [1973] 2 All E.R. 504; A. v. H.M. Treasury; B. v. H.M. Treasury [1979] 2 All E.R. 586, T. P. Russell Q.C.

16. Summer Time Act 1947.
repealed: 1972, c.6, s.6.

19. Polish Resettlement Act 1947.
s. 1, orders 72/95, 1435; 74/1045; 81/1876.
s. 3, amended: 1976, c.71, sch.7; 1980, c.30, schs.4,5; repealed in pt.: ibid.
s. 4, amended: 1972, c.58, sch.6(S.); 1973, c.32, sch.4; 1976, c.71, sch.6; 1977, c.49, schs.14,15; 1978, c.29, sch.15(S.); 1980, c.30, sch.4; c.53, sch.1; 1983, c.20, sch.4; repealed in pt.; 1972, c.58, sch.7(S.); 1973, c.32, sch.5.
ss. 6, 7, amended: 1980, c.30, sch.4.
s. 11, amended: 1978, c.29, sch.16(S); 1983, c.20, sch.4; 1984, c.36, sch.3.
s. 12, amended: 1980, c.30, sch.4.
sch. amended: 1976, c.71, sch.7; 1980, c.30, schs.4,5; repealed in pt.: ibid.

22. Civic Restaurants Act 1947.
repealed (S.): 1982, c.43, sch.4..
ss. 1 (in pt.), 2, repealed: 1972, c.70, sch.30.
s. 3, repealed in pt.: ibid.; 1974, c.7, schs.6,8.
s. 4, repealed in pt.: 1972, c.70, sch.30.

26. Cotton (Centralised Buying) Act 1947.
repealed: S.L.R. 1973.

27. National Health Service (Scotland) Act 1947.
repealed: 1978, c.29, sch.17.
s. 3, regs. 74/486, 1440, 1910; 75/1715, 1988; 76/1874.
s. 8, order 72/222.
s. 14, regs. 72/467.
s. 27, see Glasgow Assessor v. Nuffield Nursing Homes Trust, 1976 S.L.T. 101.
s. 34, regs. 73/1063; 74/504, 506, 508, 647; 75/696; 76/1574; 78/1762.
ss. 35, 36, regs. 74/506.
s. 37, regs. 73/1219.
s. 39, regs. 72/96, 1348, 1862; 73/1063; 74/504, 505, 507, 508, 522, 647, 2048; 75/1987; 77/471.
s. 40, regs. 73/1063; 74/504–508, 647; 75/695, 696, 1716; 76/733, 1873.
s. 41, regs. 74/505–507; 75/696.

10 & 11 Geo. 6 (1946–47)—cont.

27. National Health Service (Scotland) Act 1947—cont.
s. 42, regs. 72/828; 74/504, 505, 507, 522; 75/789, 1987; 77/471.
s. 43, regs. 72/827; 74/504.
s. 45, regs. 74/505, 507, 1440, 1522; 75/1715, 1988; 76/1825, 1874; 77/471.
s. 46, regs. 74/505–507.
s. 65, regs. 73/63.
s. 72, regs. 72/827; 74/504–507; 75/696.
schs. 6, 8, regs. 72/827.
sch. 7, regs. 74/506.

30. India Independence Act 1947.
ss. 2–5, 8–12, 16, 19, schs. 1, 2, repealed: S.L.R. 1976.
ss. 6, 14, 15, 18, repealed in pt.: ibid.
s. 17, repealed: 1986, c.55, sch.2.

32. Agriculture (Emergency Payments) Act 1947.
repealed: S.L.R. 1973.

33. Foreign Marriage Act 1947.
ss. 1, 5, repealed: 1988, c.44, sch.

35. Finance Act 1947.
Pt. V (ss.49–51), repealed: 1975, c.7, sch.13.
s. 53, repealed: 1974, c.30, sch.14.
ss. 54–57, repealed: 1975, c.7, sch.13.
s. 58, repealed: S.L.R. 1986.
s. 59, repealed: 1973, c.51, sch.22.
ss. 62, 74, repealed in pt.: 1975, c.7, sch.13.

37. Northern Ireland Act 1947.
ss. 1, 3–7, repealed: 1973, c.36, sch.6.
ss. 8, 9, amended: 1972, c.11, s.27; repealed in pt.: 1973, c.36, sch.6.
ss. 10, 11, 14 (in pt.), repealed: ibid.

39. Statistics of Trade Act 1947.
ss. 1, 9, amended: 1978, c.51, sch.16; c.52, sch.11.
ss. 2, 11, orders 72/1598; 73/1841; 74/1803; 75/1760; 76/1801; 77/1752; 78/1573; 79/1484; 80/1835; 81/1487; 84/1762.
s. 5, order 87/669.
s. 19, repealed in pt.: S.L.R. 1978.
sch., amended: order 87/669.

40. Industrial Organisation and Development Act 1947.
ss. 1–6, order 86/1110.
ss. 1, 2, 4, order 81/1767.
s. 8, orders 75/142; 80/623, 2001; 81/1142; 86/1372.
s. 9, orders 76/1016; 79/748, 1740; 82/485, 486; 83/1149; 86/995.
s. 10, repealed: S.L.R. 1978.
s. 14, orders 81/1767; 86/1110.

41. Fire Services Act 1947.
regs. 77/1118.
title, repealed in pt.: 1972, c.70, sch.30.
s. 1, see Hallett v. Nicholson, 1979 S.C. 1.
s. 3, amended: 1981, c.67, sch.4; 1984, c.54, sch.9(S.); repealed in pt.: 1981, c.67, sch.6.
s. 4, amended: 1985, c.51, sch.11; repealed in pt.: 1972, c.70, sch.30.
s. 5, order 72/1764.
s. 5, repealed in pt.: 1972, c.70, sch.30.
s. 6, repealed in pt.: ibid., s.197, sch.30.
s. 8, amended: ibid., s.197; 1985, c.43, sch.2; repealed in pt.: 1972, c.11, sch.8; c.70, sch.30; 1981, c.67, sch.6; 1982, c.32, sch.6.

10 & 11 Geo. 6 (1946–47)—cont.

41. Fire Services Act 1947—cont.
s. 9, order 72/1764.
s. 9, repealed in pt.: 1972, c.70, sch.30.
s. 10, amended: ibid., s.197; repealed in pt.: ibid., sch.30.
s. 14, amended (S.): 1982, c.48, schs.3,6; 1984, c.54, sch.9.
s. 17, regs. 85/930, 1758(S.).
s. 17, see R. v. Leicestershire Fire Authority, ex p. Thompson (1978) 77 L.G.R. 373, D.C.
s. 18, regs. 72/932; 76/2017, 2159; 78/436, 1727; 81/787; 85/1176; 88/31, 1362.
s. 21, regs. 75/2132.
s. 23, repealed in pt.: 1982, c.13, s.1.
s. 26, orders 72/522, 1643; 73/318, 966, 1814; 74/1797; 75/1717; 76/1273, 1708; 77/1680, 1704; 78/1228, 1349, 1577; 79/407, 855, 1286, 1360; 80/273, 1587, 1615; 82/114; 83/614, 1409; 85/318; 86/1663; 87/1302.
s. 26, amended: 1972, c.11, s.16; 1973, c.38, sch.27; orders 74/264; 76/551; repealed in pt.: 1972, c.11, s.16, sch.8; 1975, c.18, sch.1.
s. 27, repealed in pt.: 1973, c.38, sch.28.
s. 30, amended (S.): 1982, c.48, schs.3,6; 1984, c.54, sch.9.
ss. 30, 31, see R. v. Eastbourne Justices, ex p. Kisten, The Times, December 22, 1984, D.C.
s. 31, amended: 1977, c.45, s.31, sch.6.
s. 36, orders 75/487, 829; 82/232(S.); 83/282(S.).
s. 36, amended: 1973, c.65, s.147; 1980, c.45, sch.10(S.); order 74/812; repealed in pt.: 1972, c.11, sch.8; 1973, c.65, s.147, sch.29; S.L.R. 1986.
s. 38, amended: 1973, c.65, s.147; 1984, c.54, sch.9(S.).
sch. 4, repealed: 1973, c.65, s.147, sch.29.
sch. 5, repealed in pt.: 1972, c.70, sch.30.

42. Acquisition of Land (Authorisation Procedure) (Scotland) Act 1947.
amended: 1974, c.45, s.26.
s. 1, amended: 1978, c.29, sch.16; 1982, c.16, s.3; repealed in pt.: 1979, c.46, sch.5.
s. 3, amended: 1984, c.12, sch.4; repealed in pt.: S.L.R. 1973.
s. 5, repealed in pt.: 1988, c.41, sch.13.
s. 5, sch. 1, see McCowan v. Secretary of State, 1972 S.L.T. 163.
s. 7, repealed in pt.: 1979, c.46, sch.5; 1986, c.44, sch.9.
sch. 1, see Hamilton v. Secretary of State for Scotland, 1972 S.L.T. 233 (O.H.) Martin v. Bearsden and Milngavie District Council (O.H.), 1987 S.L.T. 300.
sch. 1, regs. 76/820.
sch. 1, amended: 1973, c.56, s.60; 1975, c.30, sch.6; 1976, c.21, sch.2; 1981, c.23, sch.2; 1984, c.54, sch.9; repealed in pt.: 1979, c.46, sch.5.
sch. 2, amended: 1973, c.56, s.54.

43. Local Government (Scotland) Act 1947.
ss. 1–178, 179 (in pt.), 180–186, repealed: 1973, c.65, sch.29.

10 & 11 Geo. 6 (1946–47)—cont.

43. Local Government (Scotland) Act 1947— *cont.*

s. 52, see *Zetland County Council* v. *Thomson,* 1974 S.L.T.(Sh.Ct.) 67.

s. 106, see *Lord Advocate* v. *Glasgow Corporation,* 1973 S.L.T. 33 (H.L.).

s. 132, see *Aitken* v. *Buckhaven Burgh,* Second Division, January 7, 1972.

ss. 175, 177, 210–212, see *Midlothian C.C.* v. *Secretary of State for Scotland,* 1975 S.L.T. 122.

s. 187, repealed: 1975, c.20, sch.2.

ss. 188–192, 194, repealed: 1973, c.65, sch.29.

s. 195, amended: *ibid.,* sch.9.

ss. 196–215, repealed: *ibid.,* sch.29.

s. 216, regs. 86/411; 87/2167.

s. 216, amended: 1973, s.65, sch.9.

ss. 217–220, repealed: *ibid.,* sch.29.

ss. 221, 223, repealed: 1975, c.30, sch.7.

ss. 224–227, repealed: 1973, c.65, sch.29.

ss. 228, 229, repealed: 1975, c.30, sch.7.

s. 230, repealed: 1973, c.65, sch.29.

ss. 231, 232, repealed: 1975, c.30, sch.7.

s. 233, substituted: *ibid.,* s.11.

s. 234, repealed: *ibid.,* sch.7.

s. 235, amended: *ibid.,* sch.6; repealed in pt.: 1973, c.65, sch.29; 1975, c.30, schs.6,7.

s. 237, amended: 1973, c.65, sch.9; 1987, c.47, sch.1; repealed in pt.: 1973, c.65, schs.9, 29.

s. 238, see *British Railways Board* v. *Glasgow Corporation,* 1976 S.C. 224.

s. 238, amended: 1981, c.23, sch.3; 1984, c.31, sch.2; repealed in pt.: 1973, c.65, schs.9, 29; 1984, c.31, sch.3.

ss. 239, 240 (in pt.), 241 (in pt.), repealed: 1973, c.65, sch.29.

s. 243, amended: 1975, c.30, sch.6; 1981, c.23, s.6; 1984, c.31, sch.2; repealed in pt.: 1973, c.65, schs.9, 29.

s. 243A, added: 1984, c.31, s.6.

s. 243B, added: *ibid.,* s.7; amended: 1987, c.47, sch.1.

ss. 245, 246, repealed: 1973, c.65, sch.29.

s. 247, see *Ross* v. *Glasgow Corporation,* 1972 S.L.T. 174.

ss. 247, 247A, substituted: 1987, c.18, sch.4.

s. 248, repealed: *ibid.,* s.74, sch.8.

s. 249, repealed: *ibid.,* sch.8.

s. 250, amended: *ibid.,* sch.4; repealed in pt.: *ibid.,* sch.8.

ss. 251, 252, repealed: *ibid.*

ss. 255–257, repealed: *ibid.,* sch.29.

Pt. XII (ss. 258–296), repealed: 1975, c.30, sch.7.

ss. 297–316, repealed: 1973, c.65, sch.29.

s. 317, see *Dunbarton C.C.* v. *Cumbernauld Burgh* (O.H.), 1973 S.L.T. 155.

ss. 317, 319, 320–376, repealed: 1973, c.65, sch.29.

s. 377, amended: 1984, c.26, sch.2; repealed in pt.: S.L.R. 1973; S.L.R. 1976.

s. 379, see *Lord Advocate* v. *Glasgow Corporation,* 1973 S.L.T. 33 (H.L.); *Zetland County Council* v. *Thomson,* 1974 S.L.T.(Sh Ct.) 67.

s. 379, repealed: 1987, c.47, sch.6.

10 & 11 Geo. 6 (1946–47)—cont.

43. Local Government (Scotland) Act 1947— *cont.*

schs. 1–5, repealed: 1973, c.65, sch.29.

schs. 6–8, repealed: 1975, c.30, sch.7.

schs. 9, 10, repealed: 1973, c.65, sch.29.

44. Crown Proceedings Act 1947.

s. 2, see *Trawnik* v. *Ministry of Defence* [1984] 2 All E.R. 791, Sir Robert Megarry V.-C.; *O'Neill* v. *Department of Health and Social Services* [1986] 5 N.I.J.B. 60, Carswell J.; *Jones* v. *Department of Employment* [1988] 2 W.L.R 493, C.A.

s. 2, repealed in pt.: S.L.R. 1981.

s. 3, substituted: 1988, c.48, sch.7.

s. 4, repealed in pt.: 1978, c.47, sch.2.

s. 5, substituted: 1979, c.39, sch.5.

s. 10, see *Brown* v. *Lord Advocate* (O.H.), 1984 S.L.T. 146; *Smith* v. *Ministry of Defence,* January 25, 1985, Woolf J.; *Bell* v. *Secretary of State for Defence* [1985] 3 All E.R. 661, C.A.; *Pearce* v. *Secretary of State for Defence* [1988] 2 W.L.R. 1027, H.L.

s. 10, repealed: 1987, c.25, s.1.

s. 14, amended: 1972, c.41, s.55; 1975, c.7, sch.12; 1984, c.51, sch.8.

s. 17, see *Trawnik* v. *Ministry of Defence* [1984] 2 All E.R. 791, Sir Robert Megarry V -C.

s. 20, repealed in pt.: 1981, c.54, sch.7.

s. 21, see *Goldstein* v. *Secretary of State for the Home Department, The Times,* January 3, 1974; *R.* v. *Secretary of State for the Home Department, ex p. Kirkwood* [1984] 2 All E.R. 390, Mann J.; *R.* v. *Secretary of State for the Home Department, ex p. Herbage* [1986] 3 W.L.R. 504, Hodgson J.; *British Medical Association* v. *Greater Glasgow Health Board,* 1988 S.L.T. 538.

s. 23, repealed in pt.: 1973, c.16, sch.2.

s. 24, amended: 1982, c.53, s.15, sch.1; 1984, c.28, sch.2.

s. 26, repealed in pt.: 1972, c.41, s.54, sch.28.

s. 27, see *Brooks Associates Inc.* v. *Basu* [1983] 2 W.L.R. 141, Woolf J.

s. 27, amended: 1981, c.54, s.139; repealed in pt.: *ibid.,* s.139, sch.7.

s. 34, repealed: 1977, c.38, sch.5.

s. 38, see *R.* v. *Secretary of State for the Home Department, ex p. Herbage* [1986] 3 W.L.R. 504, Hodgson J.

s. 38, repealed in pt.: 1981, c.55, sch.5.

ss. 39, 40, see *Franklin* v. *Att.-Gen.* [1973] 2 W.L.R. 255.

s. 40, see *Tito* v. *Waddell (No. 2); Tito* v. *Att.-Gen.* [1977] 2 W.L.R. 496; *Mutasa* v. *Att.-Gen.* [1979] 3 All E.R. 257, Boreham J.; *R.* v. *Secretary of State for Foreign and Commonwealth Affairs, ex p. Indian Association of Alberta* [1982] 2 W.L.R. 641, C.A; *Trawnik* v. *Ministry of Defence* [1984] 2 All E.R. 791, Sir Robert Megarry V.-C.; *Trawnick* v. *Lennox (Gordon)* [1985] 2 All E.R. 368, C.A.; *R.* v. *Secretary of State for Foreign and Commonwealth Affairs, ex p Trawnick, The Times,* February 21, 1986, C.A.

s. 46, amended (S.): 1985, c.73, s.49; repealed in pt. (S.): *ibid.,* sch.4; 1987, c.18, sch.8.

10 & 11 Geo. 6 (1946–47)—cont.

44. Crown Proceedings Act 1947—cont.
s. 49, repealed in pt.: 1972, c.41, s.54, sch.28.
s. 50, see *Laing (Liquidator of Inverdale Construction Co.)* v. *Lord Advocate,* 1973 S.L.T.(Notes) 81, Outer House; *Smith* v. *Lord Advocate (No. 2)* (O.H.), First Division, February 29, 1980.
s. 53, order 81/233.
s. 53, repealed in pt.: 1973, c.36, sch.6.
sch. 2, see *Franklin* v. *Att.-Gen.* [1973] 2 W.L.R. 255.

46. Wellington Museum Act 1947.
functions transferred: order 86/600.
s. 4, repealed in pt.: 1982, c.39, sch.22.

47. Companies Act 1947.
s. 58, repealed: 1981, c.62, sch.4.
s. 91, repealed: 1985, c.65, sch.10; c.66, sch.8(S.).
ss. 92, 99, repealed: 1985, c.65, sch.10.
s. 115, repealed: *ibid.*; c.66, sch.8(S.).
s. 116, repealed: 1981, c.62, sch.4.
ss. 121, 123, repealed: 1985, c.65, sch.10.

48. Agriculture Act 1947.
s. 2, repealed in pt.: 1972, c.68, sch.3.
ss. 71, 72, repealed: 1972, c.62, s.21, sch.6.
s. 73, orders 72/1207; 74/66, 67; 76/208, 2183; 78/259; 82/97; 84/1301.
s. 73, amended: 1986, c.5, sch.14.
ss. 75, repealed in pt.: 1972, c.62, sch.6.
s. 77, repealed: *ibid.*, s.18, sch.6.
s. 78, repealed in pt. (S.): S.L.R. 1986.
ss. 78–81, repealed: 1979, c.13, sch.2.
s. 85, repealed: S.L.R. 1973.
s. 86, amended: 1981, c.67, sch.4.
s. 92, amended: *ibid.*; repealed in pt.: S.L.R. 1973; 1981, c.67, sch.6.
s. 93, amended: *ibid.*, sch.4.
s. 97, repealed: S.L.R. 1986.
s. 103, order 72/704.
s. 103, repealed: 1986, c.49, sch.4.
s. 104, repealed in pt.: 1972, c.62, sch.6
s. 108, order 84/1301.
s. 109, see *Jones* v. *Metropolitan Borough of Stockport* (1985) 50 P. & C.R. 299, C.A.; *South Oxfordshire District Council* v. *East (Geoffrey) and Secretary of State for the Environment* [1987] J.P.L. 866, Simon Brown J.
s. 109, amended: regs. 78/446.
sch. 2, amended: regs. 78/446; 1986, c.5, sch.14.
schs. 9 (in pt.), 10, repealed: 1972, c.62, sch.6.

49. Transport Act 1947.
ss. 12–14, 28, 69, 125, 126, 128, sch. 3, repealed: S.L.R. 1974.

51. Town and Country Planning Act 1947.
ss. 49, 119, repealed in pt.: 1981, c.67, sch.6.
ss. 113, 120, repealed in pt.: S.L.R. 1975.
sch. 8, repealed in pt.: 1974, c.37, sch.10; S.L.R. 1975; 1981, c.67, sch.6; 1986, c.36, sch.12.

53. Town and Country Planning (Scotland) Act 1947.
ss. 1–43, repealed: 1972, c.52, sch.23.

10 & 11 Geo. 6 (1946–47)—cont.

53. Town and Country Planning (Scotland) act 1947—cont.
s. 10, see *Alexandra Transport Co.* v. *Secretary of State for Scotland,* 1974 S.L.T. 81; 27 P. & C.R. 352, Ct. of Session.
ss. 10, 11, see *Alexander Russell* v. *Secretary of State for Scotland,* 1984 S.L.T. 81.
s. 12, regs. 72/904.
s. 44, amended: 1972, c.52, sch.21; repealed in pt.: *ibid.*, sch.23; 1984, c.54, sch.11.
s. 45, repealed: *ibid.*
ss. 46 (in pt.), 47–108, 109 (in pt.), 110–112, repealed: 1972, c.52, sch.23.
s. 113, amended: 1973, c.65, sch.23; repealed in pt.: 1972, c.52, sch.23; 1973, c.65, sch.29; S.L.R. 1975; 1984, c.54, sch.11.
schs. 1–7, repealed: 1972, c.52, sch.23.
sch. 8, repealed in pt.: *ibid.*; 1973, c.65, sch.29; S.L.R. 1975; 1984, c.54, sch.11; c.55, sch.7.
sch. 11, see *Renfrew's Trs.* v. *Glasgow Corporation,* 1972 S.L.T. 2; *Apostolic Church Trustees* v. *Glasgow District Council (No. 2),* 1978 S.L.T. (Lands Tr.) 17; *City of Glasgow District Council* v. *Morrison McChlery & Co.,* Second Division, June 19, 1984.

54. Electricity Act 1947.
repealed: except ss. 1 (in pt.), 2 (in pt.), 4 (in pt.), 11 (in pt.), 13, 19 (in pt.), 22, 54 (in pt.), 57 (in pt.), 60, 67, 68 (in pt.), 69, schs. 2, 4 (in pt.): 1979, c.11, sch.12.
see *R.* v. *Midlands Electricity Board, ex p. Busby; Same* v. *Same, ex p. Williamson, The Times,* October 28, 1987, Schiemann J.
s. 1, amended: 1983, c.25, sch.3.
s. 2, amended: *ibid.*, sch.3; repealed in pt.: *ibid.*,schs.3,4.
s. 3, amended: *ibid.*, sch.3.
s. 4, order 73/2050.
s. 7, regs. 77/710.
s. 7, amended: 1983, c.25, s.22.
s. 7A, regs. 78/962, 963.
s. 9, amended: 1981, c.38, sch.3; c.67, sch.4; 1984, c.12, sch.4; repealed in pt.: 1981, c.67, sch.6.
s. 19, orders 73/1348; 74/1092, 1445, 1951; 75/831, 1150, 1896, 1897, 2245; 76/131, 1138; 77/504.
s. 19, repealed in pt.: 1972, c.17, s.3, sch.
s. 37, amended: 1983, c.25, s.17, sch.3; repealed in pt.: *ibid.*, sch.4.
s. 50, order 72/152.
s. 50, amended: 1983, c.25, s.19.
s. 54, regs. 83/353; 88/1271.
s. 60, repealed: 1983, c.25, sch.4; repealed in pt.: S.L.R. 1986.
s. 63, amended: 1983, c.25, sch.3.
s. 64, regs. 88/1057, 1206.
ss. 64, 66, amended: 1983, c.25, sch.3.
s. 67, amended: order 74/595.
s. 68, amended: 1973, c.65, sch.27; repealed in pt.: S.L.R. 1977; order 78/1175 (S.).
sch. 4, amended: order 75/1636; repealed in pt.: S.L.R. 1978; 1983, c.25, sch.4, 1986, c.63, sch.12.

CAP.

11 & 12 Geo. 6 (1947–48)

3. Burma Independence Act 1947.
s. 2, sch. 1, repealed: 1981, c.61, sch.9.
s. 3, repealed: S.L.R. 1977.
s. 4, repealed in pt.: 1986, c.55, sch.2.

7. Ceylon Independence Act 1947.
s. 3, repealed: 1986, c.55, sch.2.
s. 4, repealed in pt.: 1978, c.30, sch.3.
sch. 2, repealed in pt.: S.L.R. 1977; 1986, c.55, sch.2.

10. Emergency Laws (Miscellaneous Provisions) Act 1947.
sch. 2, amended and repealed in pt.: 1987, c.4, s.7.

11. Medical Practitioners and Pharmacists Act 1947.
repealed: 1978, c.12, sch.7.

17. Requisitioned Land and War Works Act 1948.
ss. 1, 2, 5, 9, repealed: S.L.R. 1973.
ss. 3, 4, 10, 11, repealed in pt.: *ibid.*
s. 14, amended: 1975, c.76, sch.1; repealed in pt.: *ibid.*, sch.2.
s. 18, amended (S.): 1980, c.45, sch.10; repealed in pt.: S.L.R. 1973.
s. 20, repealed in pt.: *ibid.*
sch. amended: 1981, c.38, sch.3; repealed in pt.: 1982, c.43, sch.4(S.); 1984, c.12, sch.7; 1986, c.63, s.48, sch.12.

20. Supreme Court of Judicature (Amendment) Act 1948.
repealed: S.L.R. 1973.

21. Army and Air Force (Women's Service) Act 1948.
s. 3, repealed in pt.: 1981, c.55, sch.5.
s. 4, repealed: S.L.R. 1977.

22. Water Act 1948.
s. 1, see *Cakebread (V.O.)* v. *Severn Trent Water Authority* [1988] R.A. 290, C.A.
s. 1, repealed: 1973, c.37, sch.9.
ss. 2, 4, repealed in pt.: *ibid.*, s.12, sch.9.
s. 8, repealed in pt.: *ibid.*, sch.9.
s. 9, substituted: *ibid.*, sch.8.
ss. 12, 13, repealed: *ibid.*, sch.9.
s. 14, amended: *ibid.*, sch.8.
s. 15, amended: order 76/1775; repealed in pt.: 1986, c.44, sch.9.
sch. amended: 1981, c.67, sch.4; repealed in pt.: *ibid.*, sch.6.

24. Police Pensions Act 1948.
repealed: 1976, c.35, sch.3.
regs. 73/1773; order 76/444.
s. 1, regs. 72/1642, 1844; 73/1815; 74/1533, 1673, 1796, 1899; 75/1718; 76/306.
ss. 1, 5, regs. 73/428, 429.

25. Royal Marines Act 1948.
repealed: 1980, c.9, sch.10.

26. Local Government Act 1948.
Pt. I (ss. 1–16) repealed: S.L.R. 1975.
ss. 17, 21, 22, 24, 26–32, repealed: 1973, c.65, sch.29.
s. 68, repealed: S.L.R. 1976.
s. 85, see *British Railways Board* v. *Glasgow Corporation* (O.H.), July 30, 1974.
s. 85, repealed (S.): orders 78/1174, 1175.
s. 86, repealed (S.): order 78/1174.
s. 87, amended and repealed in pt. (S.): *ibid.*

CAP.

11 & 12 Geo. 6 (1947–48)—cont.

26. Local Government Act 1948—*cont.*
s. 90, repealed: S.L.R. 1975.
ss. 91, 92, repealed (S.): order 78/1175.
s. 94, repealed (S.): order 78/1174; repealed in pt.: S.L.R. 1978.
ss. 96–99, repealed (S.): order 78/1175.
s. 100, repealed (S.): orders 78/1174, 1175; repealed in pt.: S.L.R. 1978.
s. 101, repealed (S.): 1973, c.65, sch.29.
ss. 102, 105, repealed (S.): orders 78/1174, 1175.
s. 107, repealed (S.): order 78/1175.
s. 108, order 82/330.
s. 108, amended: 1973, c.11, sch.6.
s. 109, order 72/1237.
ss. 109, 110, repealed (S.): order 78/1174; repealed in pt.: S.L.R. 1978.
Pt. VI (ss. 111–119), repealed: 1972, c.70, sch.30; 1973, c.65, sch.29(S.).
s. 112, regs. 73/1031, 1047; 74/1464.
s. 113, regs. 72/1566, 1572; 73/1300, 1453; 74/125, 652; 75/628.
s. 117, regs. 72/1565, 1566, 1572; 73/1031, 1047, 1300, 1453, 1464; 74/125, 652, 1464; 75/628.
s. 118, regs. 73/1031; 74/125, 652.
s. 124, amended (S.): 1973, c.65, sch.9; order 78/1174; repealed in pt. (S.): 1975, c.30, sch.7; order 78/1174.
ss. 129–132, repealed: 1972, c.70, sch.30; 1973, c.65, sch.29(S.).
s. 133, amended (S.): 1973, c.65, s.170, sch.27; 1982, c.43, sch.3; repealed in pt.: 1972, c.70, sch.30.
ss. 134, 135, repealed: 1972, c.70, sch.30; 1973, c.65, sch.29(S.).
s. 136, repealed: 1972, c.70, sch.30.
s. 138, repealed in pt.: 1973, c.65, schs.25, 29(S.); 1974, c.7, schs.6, 8.
ss. 139, 141, repealed: S.L.R. 1975.
s. 142, order 82/330.
s. 143, repealed: S.L.R. 1978.
s. 144, amended (S.): 1984, c.54, sch.9; repealed in pt. (S.): 1973, c.65, sch.9.
s. 145, amended (S.), *ibid.*; 1987, c.47, sch.1: repealed in pt.: 1973, c.65, schs.9, 29.

27. Palestine Act 1948.
repealed: S.L.R. 1981.

29. National Assistance Act 1948.
s. 21, amended: 1972, c.70, sch.23; 1973, c.32, sch.4; 1977, c.49, schs.14, 15; repealed in pt.: 1972, c.70, schs.23, 30; 1973, c.32, schs.4, 5; 1977, c.48, sch.
ss. 21, 24, see *R.* v. *Waltham Forest Borough Council, ex p. Vale, The Times,* February 25, 1985, Taylor J.
s. 22, regs. 72/1240, 1347; 73/1497, 1500; 74/118, 1126; 75/347, 472, 1325, 1628; 76/1659, 1670; 77/1069, 1359 (S.); 78/1073, 1190; 79/823, 1084; 80/954, 1301 (S.); 81/968, 1227; 82/1399, 1552(S.); 83/1465(S.), 1492; 84/1356, 1558(S.); 85/1317, 1350(S.); 86/861, 1050(S.); 87/364(S.), 370; 88/234, 331(S.).

CAP.

11 & 12 Geo. 6 (1947–48)—cont.

29. National Assistance Act 1948—cont.
s. 22, amended: 1976, c.71, schs. 6, 7; 1980, c.3, sch.4; 1983, c.41, s.20; 1986, c.50, sch.10; repealed in pt.: 1977, c.48, sch.; 1980, c.3, schs.4,5.
s. 24, amended: 1972, c.58, sch.6; c.70, sch.3; 1973, c.32, sch. 4; 1977, c.49, sch.14; 1978, c.29, sch.15; repealed in pt.: 1977, c.48, sch.
s. 25, repealed: 1977, c.48, s.20, sch.
s. 26, regs. 84/1558(S.); 85/1530(S.); 86/1050(S.).
s. 26, amended: 1972, c.70, sch.23; repealed in pt.: 1977, c.48, sch.; 1983, c.41, s.20; c.48, sch.
s. 27, repealed: 1980, c.3, schs.4,5.
s. 29, see *Royal Cross School for the Deaf* v. *Morton* [1975] 1 W.L.R. 1002; [1975] 2 All E.R. 519, C.A.; *Wyatt* v. *Hillingdon London Borough Council* (1978) 76 L.G.R. 727, C.A.
s. 29, amended: 1972, c.70, sch.23; 1973, c.50, sch.3; 1977, c.49, sch.15; repealed in pt.: 1972, c.70, schs.23,30; 1983.c.41, sch.10.
s. 30, amended: 1972, c.20, sch.23.
s. 30A, added: 1983, c.41, sch.9.
s. 31, repealed: 1980, c.7, sch.2.
s. 33, amended: 1972, c.70, sch.23; (S.) 1973, c.65, sch.27; repealed in pt.: 1972, c.70, sch.30.
s. 34, repealed: *ibid.*
s. 35, regs. 88/234, 331(S.).
s. 35, repealed: 1972, c.70, sch.30.
s. 36, see *R.* v. *Kent County Council, ex p. Bruce, The Times,* February 8, 1986, D.C.
ss. 37–40, repealed: 1980, c.7, sch.2.
s. 41, amended: 1972, c.70, sch.23; (S.) 1973, c.65, sch.27; 1980, c.7, sch.1; 1983, c.41, sch.9; 1984, c.23, sch.1
s. 42, amended: 1986, c.9, sch.1(S.); 1987, c.42, sch.2; repealed in pt.: *ibid.*, sch.4.
s. 43, amended: 1976, c.71, sch.7; 1978, c.22, sch 2; 1979, c.55, sch.2; 1987, c.42, sch.2; repealed in pt.: 1978, c.22, sch.3; 1986, c.50, schs.10,11.
s. 44, repealed: 1987, c.42, schs.2, 4.
s. 44, repealed (S.): 1986, c.9, sch.2.
s. 47, amended: 1972, c.58, sch.6; c.70, sch.29; (S.) 1973, c.65, sch.27; 1977, c.49, sch.15; 1978, c.29, schs.15,16; repealed in pt.: 1973, c.32, sch.5.
s. 50, repealed: 1984, c.22, sch.3; repealed in pt.: 1986, c.50, sch.11.
s. 53, repealed: 1986, c.50, sch.11.
s. 55, amended: 1977, c.45, s.31, schs.6,11.
s. 56, amended: 1972, c.70, sch.23; 1987, c.42, sch.2.
s. 58, repealed: S.L.R. 1978; 1981, c.67, sch.9.
s. 59, repealed: 1972, c.70, sch.30.
ss. 60, 61, repealed in pt.: S.L.R. 1977.
s. 64, regs. 88/234, 220(S.).
s. 64, amended: 1975, c.18, sch.2; 1978, c.23, sch 16(S.); repealed in pt. (S.): 1973, c.65, sch.29.
s. 65, amended: 1973, c.65, sch.27; repealed in pt.: *ibid.*, sch.29.

CAP.

11 & 12 Geo. 6 (1947–48)—cont.

29. National Assistance Act 1948—cont.
s. 66, order 80/326.
s. 67, repealed in pt.: 1973, c.36, sch.6.
sch. 6, amended: 1976, c.71, schs.6,7; (S.) 1978, c.29, sch.16; 1980, c.30, sch.4; repealed in pt.: 1973, c.32, sch.5; S.L.R. 1977.

30. Lord High Commissioner (Church of Scotland) Act 1948.
repealed: 1974, c.19, s.3.

31. Cotton Spinning (Re–equipment Subsidy) Act 1948.
repealed: S.L.R. 1977.

33. Superannuation (Miscellaneous Provisions) Act 1948.
s. 1, amended: 1972, c.11, sch.6.
s. 2, rules 72/63, 328, 521, 527, 532, 933, 1693, 1742, 1761, 1778; 74/162, 777, 778, 1738, 1992; 81/1681; regs. 78/425.
s. 2, amended: 1972, c.11, sch.6.
ss. 6, 7, repealed: *ibid.*, sch.8; repealed: regs. 77/1341.
s. 15, rules 72/63, 328, 521, 527, 532, 933, 1742, 1778; 74/162, 1992; 81/1681; regs. 78/425.
s. 17, orders 74/520, 812.
s. 17, amended: 1972, c.11, sch.6. repealed in pt.: *ibid.*, schs.7,8; regs. 77/1341. sch., repealed in pt.: 1972, c.11, sch.8.

36. House of Commons Members' Fund Act 1948.
s. 3, orders 75/2038; 76/1878; 84/2065; resolutions 77/2073; 79/1667; 80/1899; 85/2082; 87/511; 88/742.
s. 4, amended: 1984, c.52, sch.12.
s. 6, repealed: S.L.R. 1986.

37. Radioactive Substances Act 1948.
s. 2, amended: 1979, c.2, sch.4.
ss. 3, 4, repealed: order 77/2128.
s. 5, S.Rs. 1983 No. 344; 1986 No. 61; regs. 85/1729.
s. 5, amended: order 74/1821; regs. 74/1735; 75/1522.
s. 8, amended: 1982, c.48, schs.3,6(S.).
s. 12, repealed in pt.: order 77/2128.

38. Companies Act 1948.
repealed: 1985, c.9, sch.1.
see *British Airways Board* v. *Parish* (1979) 123 S.J. 139, C.A.
orders 73/482; 79/1545, 1547.
s. 10, see *Cane* v. *Jones* [1980] 1 W.L.R. 1451, Michael Wheeler, Q.C.
s. 12, see *Baby Moon (U.K.), Re, The Times,* November 12, 1984, Harman J.; *South India Shipping Corp.* v. *Bank of Korea* [1985] 1 W.L.R. 585, C.A.
s. 15, order 77/530.
s. 18, see *Richards & Wallington (Earthmoving* v. *Whatlings* (O.H.) 1982 S.L.T. 66; *Lin Pac Containers (Scotland)* v. *Kelly* (O.H.), 1983 S.L.T. 422.
s. 20, see *Scottish Fishermen's Organisation* v. *McLean,* 1980 S I T (Sh.Ct.) 76.
s. 27, see *Stenhouse London* v. *Allwright,* 1972 S.L.T. 87.

11 & 12 Geo. 6 (1947–48)—cont.

38. Companies Act 1948—cont.

s. 52, regs. 83/1021; order 77/530.

s. 54, see *Wallersteiner* v. *Moir; Moir* v. *Wallersteiner* [1974] 1 W.L.R. 991, C.A.; *Belmont Finance Corp.* v. *Williams Furniture* [1978] 3 W.L.R. 712, C.A.; *Belmont Finance Corp.* v. *Williams Furniture (No. 2)* [1980] 1 All E.R. 393, C.A.; *Armour Hick Northern* v. *Whitehouse* [1980] 1 W.L.R. 1520, Mervyn-Davies J.; *Charterhouse Investment Trust* v. *Tempest Diesels, Financial Times*, June 28, 1985, Hoffman J.

s. 56, see *Shearer* v. *Bercain* [1980] 3 All E.R. 295, Walton J.

s. 62, regs. 82/674.

s. 65, see *Re St. Piran, The Times*, July 11, 1981, Dillon J.

s. 66, see *Barry Artist, Re* [1985] 1 W.L.R. 1305, Nourse J.

ss. 66, 68, see *Jupiter House Investments (Cambridge), Re* [1985] 1 W.L.R. 975, Harman J.; *Grosvenor Press, Re* [1985] 1 W.L.R. 980, Nourse J.

s. 74, see *Westminster Property Group, Re, The Times*, July 10, 1984, Nourse J.

s. 94, see *I.R.C.* v. *Goldblatt* [1972] 2 W.L.R. 953; [1972] 2 All E.R. 202; *Re Christonette International* [1982] 3 All E.R. 227, Vinelott J.; *G. L. Saunders, Re* [1986] 1 W.L.R. 215, Nourse J.

s. 95, see *Re Wallis & Simmonds (Builders)* [1974] 1 All E.R. 561; *Burston Finance* v. *Speirway* [1974] 1 W.L.R. 1648; [1974] 3 All E.R. 735; *Lloyds and Scottish Finance* v. *Prentice, The Times*, November 3, 1977, C.A.; *Re Bond Worth* [1979] 3 W.L.R. 629, Slade J.; *Borden (U.K.)* v. *Scottish Timber Products* [1979] 3 W.L.R. 672, C.A.; *NV Slavenburg's Bank* v. *International Natural Resources* [1980] 1 All E.R. 955, Lloyd J.; *Property Discount Corp.* v. *Lyon Group* (1981) 1 W.L.R. 300; [1981] 1 All E.R. 379, C.A.; *Re R. M. Arnold & Co., The Times*, May 10, 1984, Harman J.; *Carreras Rothmans* v. *Freeman Matthews Treasure* [1984] 3 W.L.R. 1016, Peter Gibson J.; *Clough Mill* v. *Martin* [1984] 3 All E.R. 982, C.A.; *Welsh Irish Ferries, Re* [1985] 3 W.L.R. 610, Nourse J.; *Oriel, Re* [1985] 3 All E.R. 216, C.A.; *Pfeiffer (E.) Weinkellerei-Weineinkauf GmbH & Co.* v. *Arbuthnot Factors* [1987] BCLC 522, Phillips J.

ss. 95, 96, see *Foster, Re, Foster* v. *Crusts* (1985) 129 S.J. 333, Judge Finlay Q.C. sitting as a High Court Judge.

ss. 95, 97, regs. 83/1021.

ss. 95, 98, see *R.* v. *Registrar of Companies, ex p. Central Bank of India* [1986] 1 All E.R. 105, C.A.

s. 98, see *R.* v. *Registrar of Companies, ex p. Esal (Commodities) (in liquidation), The Times*, November 26, 1984, Mervyn Davies J.

s. 100, regs. 83/1021.

s. 101, see *Re Resinoid and Mica Products* [1982] 3 All E.R. 677, C.A.; *Victoria Housing*

11 & 12 Geo. 6 (1947–48)—cont.

38. Companies Act 1948—cont.

Estates v. *Ashpurton Estates* [1982] 3 All E.R. 665, C.A.; *Re R. M. Arnold & Co., The Times*, May 10, 1984, Harman J.

s. 106, see *NV Slavenburg's Bank* v. *International Natural Resources* [1980] 1 All E.R. 955, Lloyd J.; *Oriel, Re* [1985] 3 All E.R. 216, C.A.

s. 106, regs. 83/1021.

ss. 106A, 106C, 106D, 106F, 106K, order 72/1636.

s. 108, see *British Airways Board* v. *Parish* [1979] 2 Lloyd's Rep. 361, C.A.; *East Midlands Electricity Board* v. *Grantham*, June 3, 1980, Judge McGregor; *Kettering County Ct.*; *Banque de l'Indochine et de Suez* v. *Euroseas Group Finance Co.* [1981] 3 All E.R. 198, Robert Goff J.; *Maxform S.p.A.* v. *Mariani and Goodville* [1981] 2 Lloyd's Rep. 54, C.A.; *Wilkes (John) (Footwear)* v. *Lee International (Footwear), The Times*, July 20, 1985, C.A.; *Blum* v. *O.C.P. Repartition S.A.* [1988] BCLC 170, C.A.

ss. 110, 113, see *Re Performing Right Society* [1978] 1 W.L.R. 1197, C.A.

s. 116, see *Re Transatlantic Life Assurance Co.* [1979] 3 All E.R. 352, Slade J.

s. 125, order 77/1369; regs. 83/1021.

s. 127, see *Stockdale* v. *Coulson* [1974] 3 All E.R. 154.

s. 132, see *Re Windward Islands Enterprises (U.K.)*, July 29, 1982, Nourse J.

s. 139, see *Hillman* v. *Crystal Bowl Amusements* [1973] 1 W.L.R. 162, C.A.; *Re Herbert Berry Associates (In Liquidation)* [1977] 1 W.L.R. 617, C.A.

s. 141, see *Re Moorgate Mercantile Holdings* [1980] 1 W.L.R. 227, Slade J.; *Cane* v. *Jones* [1980] 1 W.L.R. 1451, Michael Wheeler, Q.C.

s. 142, see *Pedley* v. *Inland Waterways Association* [1977] 1 All E.R. 209.

s. 143, see *Re M. J. Shanley Contracting (in Voluntary Liquidation)* (1979) 124 S.J. 239, Oliver J.

s. 147, see *Conway* v. *Petronius Clothing Co.* [1978] 1 W.L.R. 72, Slade J.

s. 164, see *Bryanston Finance* v. *de Vries (No. 2)* [1976] 2 W.L.R. 41; [1976] 1 All E.R. 25, C.A.

s. 165, see *Maxwell* v. *Department of Trade and Industry* [1974] 2 W.L.R. 338, C.A.; *R.* v. *Cheltenham JJ., ex p. Secretary of State for Trade* [1977] 1 W.L.R. 95, D.C.; *Norwest Holst* v. *Secretary for Trade* [1978] 3 W.L.R. 73, C.A.; *Re St. Piran* [1981] 1 W.L.R. 1300, Dillon J.

s. 167, see *London and County Securities* v. *Nicholson (formerly trading as Harmood Banner & Co.)* [1980] 1 W.L.R. 948, Browne-Wilkinson J.

s. 168, regs. 81/1686.

ss. 172, 174, see *Westminster Property Group, Re, The Times*, July 10, 1984, Nourse J.

11 & 12 Geo. 6 (1947–48)—cont.

38. Companies Act 1948—*cont.*

s. 174, see *Re Ashbourne Investments* [1978] 2 All E.R. 418, Templeman J.; *Westminster Property Group, Re* [1985] 1 W.L.R. 676, C.A.

s. 188, see *Re Civica Investments, The Times,* June 9, 1982, Nourse J.; *R. v. Campbell* (1984) 78 Cr.App.R. 95, C.A.; *R. v. Corbin* (1984) 6 Cr.App.R.(S.) 17, C.A.; *R. v. Austin* (1985) 82 L.S.Gaz. 2499, C.A.; *Arctic Engineering, Re* [1986] 1 W.L.R. 686, Hoffmann J.

s. 189, see *Owens v. Multilux,* 1974 S.L.T. 189; [1974] I.R.L.R. 113.

s. 190, see *Thompson v. J. Barke & Co.* (O.H.), October 30, 1974; *Wallersteiner v. Moir; Moir v. Wallersteiner* [1974] 1 W.L.R. 991, C.A.

ss. 191, 194, see *Gibson's Exr. v. Gibson* (O.H.), 1980 S.L.T. 2.

s. 196, see *Parsons v. Albert J. Parsons and Sons* [1979] I.C.R. 271, C.A.

s. 200, order 77/531; regs. 83/1021.

s. 205, see *Movitex v. Butfield* [1988] BCLC 104, Vinelott J.

s. 206, see *Re N.F.U. Development Trust* [1972] 1 W.L.R. 1548; 116 S.J. 679; *Singer Manufacturing Co. v. Robinow,* 1971 S.C. 11; *Re Calgary and Edmonton Land Co. (In Liquidation)* [1975] 1 W.L.R. 355; *Re Savoy Hotel* [1981] 3 W.L.R. 441, Nourse J.

ss. 206, 209, see *Re Hellenic & General Trust* [1975] 3 All E.R. 382.

s. 207, see *Minster Assets, Re* [1985] P.C.C. 105, Harman J.

s. 209, see *Re Ashbourne Investments,* [1978] 2 All E.R. 418, Templeman J.

s. 209, regs. 80/2016.

s. 210, see *Re Burton & Deakin* [1977] 1 W.L.R. 390; *Re A Company (No. 003324 of 1979)* [1981] 1 W.L.R. 1059, Vinelott J.; *Re A Company (No. 003420 of 1981), The Times,* November 4, 1983, Nourse J.; *London School of Electronics, Re* [1985] 3 W.L.R. 474, Nourse J.

s. 212, see *Holliday (L. B.) & Co., Re* [1986] 2 All E.R. 367, Mervyn Davies J.

s. 216, see *Re Wolverhampton Steel and Iron Co.* [1977] 1 W.L.R. 153, 860, C.A.; [1977] 1 All E.R. 417.

s. 218, see *Fabric Sales v. Eratex* [1984] 1 W.L.R. 863, C.A.; *Baby Moon (U.K.), Re, The Times,* November 12, 1984, Harman J.

s. 218, orders 76/852; 77/151, 350; 81/1624; 83/713; 84/297, 1075.

s. 218, repealed in pt.: 1984, c.9, s.28.

Pt. V (ii) (iii), (ss.218–310) see *Ross v. Smith,* 1986 S.L.T.(Sh.Ct) 59.

s. 222, see *Ebrahimi v. Westbourne Galleries* [1972] 2 W.L.R. 1289; [1972] 2 All E.R. 492; *Re A. & B.C. Chewing Gum; Topps Chewing Gum Inc. v. Coakley* [1975] 1 W.L.R. 579; [1975] 1 All E.R. 1017; *Bryanston Finance v. de Vries (No. 2)* [1976] 2 W.L.R. 41; [1976] 1 All E.R. 25, C.A.; *Re Southard & Co.* [1979] 1 W.L.R. 1198, C.A.; *Gammack, Petr.* (O.H.), July 7, 1982; *Teague, Petr.* (O.H.), May 15, 1984.

11 & 12 Geo. 6 (1947–48)—cont.

38. Companies Act 1948—*cont.*

ss. 222, 223, see *Re Bryant Investment Co.* [1974] 1 W.L.R. 826; [1974] 2 All E.R. 683.

s. 223, see *Holt Southey v. Catnic Components* [1978] 1 W.L.R. 630, Goulding J.; *Re Capital Annuities* [1978] 3 All E.R. 704, Slade J.; *Stonegate Securities v. Gregory* [1980] 1 All E.R. 241, C.A.; *Company (No. 003729 of 1982), A, Re* [1984] 1 W.L.R. 1090, Mervyn Davies J; *Byblos Bank v. Al Khudhairy, Financial Times,* November 7, 1986, C.A.

s. 223, regs. 84/1199.

ss. 223, 224, see *Re Lympne Investments* [1972] 1 W.L.R. 523; [1972] 2 All E.R. 385; *Furmston, Petr.,* 1987 S.L.T.(Sh.Ct.) 10.

s. 224, see *Re A Company* [1973] 1 W.L.R. 1566; *Re Lubin, Rosen and Associates* [1975] 1 W.L.R. 122; *Re JN 2* [1977] 3 All E.R. 1104, Brightman J.; *Holt Southey v. Catnic Components* [1978] 1 W.L.R. 630, Goulding J.

s. 225, see *Foxhall & Gyle (Nurseries) Petitioners* (O.H.), 1978 S.L.T.(Notes) 29; *Re Camburn Petroleum Products* [1979] 3 All E.R. 297, Slade J.; *Re A Company (No. 002567 of 1982)* [1983] 2 All E.R. 854, Vinelott J.

s. 225, repealed in pt.: 1980, c.22, sch.4.

s. 226, see *Re Dynamics Corporation of America* [1972] 3 All E.R. 1046; *Re A Company* [1973] 1 W.L.R. 1566; *Re Bellaglade* [1977] 1 All E.R. 319; *Herbert Berry Associates v. I.R.C.* [1977] 1 W.L.R. 1437, H.L.

s. 227, see *Sullivan v. Henderson* [1973] 1 All E.R. 48; *Re Argentum Reductions (U.K.)* [1975] 1 W.L.R. 186; [1975] 1 All E.R. 608; *Re J. Leslie Engineers Co. (In Liquidation)* [1976] 1 W.L.R. 292; *Re Burton & Deakin* [1977] 1 W.L.R. 390; [1977] 1 All E.R. 631; *United Dominions Trust,* (O.H.), 1977 S.L.T. (Notes) 56; *Peak v. Midland Commercial Services,* November 22, 1977, Judge F.L. Clark, Q.C.; *Banbury County Ct.; Re Gray's Inn Construction Co.* [1980] 1 All E.R. 814, C.A.; *Tramway Building and Construction Co., Re* (1987) BCC 443, Scott J.; *Webb Electrical, Re* (1988) 4 BCC 230, Harman J.

s. 229, see *Haig v. Lord Advocate* (O.H.), 1976 S.L.T.(Notes) 16.

s. 231, see *Re Aro Co.* [1980] 2 W.L.R. 453; [1980] 1 All E.R. 1067, C.A.; *Re Berkeley Securities (Property)* [1980] 1 W.L.R. 1589; [1980] 3 All E.R. 513, Vinelott J.; *Wilson v. Banner Scaffolding, The Times,* June 22, 1982, Milmo J.; *Aziz v. Knightsbridge Gaming and Catering Services and Supplies, The Times,* July 6, 1982, Hobhouse J.; *G. & A. (Hotels) v. T.H.B. Marketing Services* (O.H.), 1983 S.L.T. 497; *Memco Engineering, Re* [1985] 3 All E.R. 267, Mervyn Davies J.

s. 235, see *Re Overmark Smith Warden* [1982] 1 W.L.R. 1195, Slade J.

s. 238, see *Union Accident Insurance Co.* [1972] 1 W.L.R. 640; [1972] 1 All E.R. 1105, [1972] 1 Lloyd's Rep. 297, 340; *Re A Company* [1973] 1 W.L.R. 1566.

11 & 12 Geo. 6 (1947–48)—cont.

38. Companies Act 1948—cont.

s. 245, see *Liquidator of Upper Clyde Shipbuilders* (O.H.), 1974 S.L.T. (Notes) 52; *Re Associated Travel Leisure and Services (In Liquidation)* [1978] 1 W.L.R. 547, Templeman. J.; *Ross* v. *Smith*, 1986 S.L.T.(Sh.Ct) 59.

s. 246, see *Re Wyvern Developments* [1974] 1 W.L.R. 1097; [1974] 2 All E.R. 535.

ss. 252, 253, see *Souter, Petr.*, 1981 S.L.T.(Sh.Ct.) 89.

s. 256, see *Re Wolverhampton Steel and Iron Co.* [1977] 1 W.L.R. 153, 860, C.A.; [1977] 1 All E.R. 417.

s. 256, see *Re Calgary and Edmonton Land Co. (In Liquidation)* [1975] 1 W.L.R. 355; *Re Orthomere; Re Gilgate Securities; Re South Bucks Properties* (1981) 125 S.J. 495, Vinelott J.

s. 263, see *Re U.S., The Times,* October 10, 1983, Nourse J.

s. 264, see *Butler* v. *Broadhead* [1974] 2 All E.R. 401.

s. 265, see *Liverpool and District Hospital for Diseases of the Heart* v. *Att.-Gen.* [1981] 2 W.L.R. 379; [1981] 1 All E.R. 994, Slade J.

s. 267, see *Re Mesco Properties* [1980] 1 All E.R. 117, C.A.

s. 268, see *Re Bletchley Boat Co.* [1974] 1 W.L.R. 630; [1974] 1 All E.R. 1225; *Re Castle New Homes* [1979] 2 All E.R. 775, Slade J.; *Re Spiraflite (1974)* [1979] 2 All E.R. 766, Megarry J.; *Re Highgrade Traders, The Times,* December 9, 1982, Mervyn Davies J.; *Rhodes (John T.), Re* [1986] P.C.C. 366, Hoffmann J.

s. 276, see *Re Dynamics Corporation of America* [1972] 3 All E.R. 1046.

s. 293, see *E. V. Saxton and Sons* v. *R. Miles (Confectioners)* [1983] 1 W.L.R. 952, H.H. Judge Finlay.

s. 301, see *Orthomere; Re Gilgate Securities; Re South Bucks Properties* (1981) 125 S.J. 495, Vinelott J.

s. 302, see *British Eagle International Air Lines* v. *Campagnie Nationale Air France* [1973] 1 Lloyd's Rep. 414; [1975] 1 W.L.R. 758; [1975] 2 All E.R. 390, H.L.; *Re Compania de Electricidad de la Provincia de Buenos Aires* [1978] 3 All E.R. 668, Slade J.; *Liverpool and District Hospital for Diseases of the Heart* v. *Att.-Gen.* [1981] 2 W.L.R. 379; [1981] 1 All E.R. 994, Slade J.; *Carreras Rothmans* v. *Freeman Matthews Treasure* [1984] 3 W.L.R. 1016, Peter Gibson J.

s. 307, see *Booth* v. *Thomson*, 1972 S.L.T.(Notes) 18; *Knoll Spinning Co.* v. *Brown* (O.H.), 1977 S.L.T.(Notes) 62; *Re Compania de Electricidad de la Provincia de Buenos Aires* [1978] 3 All E.R. 668, Slade J.; *Re R.-R. Realisations* [1980] 1 All E.R. 1019, Megarry V.-C.; *Re J. Burrows (Leeds) (In Liquidation)* (1982) 126 S.J. 227, Slade J.; *Ross* v. *Smith*, 1986 S.L.T.(Sh.Ct.) 59.

ss. 316, 317, see *Re Islington Metal and Plating Works* [1983] 3 All E.R. 218, Harman J.

11 & 12 Geo. 6 (1947–48)—cont.

38. Companies Act 1948—cont.

s. 317, see *Re Rolls-Royce Co.* [1974] 1 W.L.R. 1584; [1974] 3 All E.R. 646; *Re Berkeley Securities (Property)* [1980] 1 W.L.R. 1589; [1980] 3 All E.R. 513, Vinelott J.; *Amalgamated Investment and Property Co., Re* [1984] 3 All E.R. 272, Vinelott J.

s. 319, see *Herbert Berry Associates* v. *I.R.C.* [1977] 1 W.L.R. 1437, H.L.; *Re Piccadilly Estate Hotels* (1978) 77 L.G.R. 79, Slade J.; *Re Nadler Enterprises* [1980] 124 S.J. 219, Dillon J.; *Re Christonette International* [1982] 3 All E.R. 227, Vinelott J.; *Memco Engineering, Re* [1985] 3 All E.R. 267, Mervyn Davies J.

s. 320, see *Re F. P. & C. A. Matthews* [1982] 1 All E.R. 338, C.A.; *Johnstone* v. *Peter H. Irvine* (O.H.), 1984 S.L.T. 209; *Bob Gray (Access)* v. *T.M. Standard Scaffolding* (Sh.Ct.), 1987 S.C.L.R. 720.

s. 322, see *Libertas-Kommerz GmbH, Appellants* (O.H.), March 22, 1978; *Mace Builders (Glasgow)* v. *Lunn* [1986] 3 W.L.R. 921, C.A.

s. 323, see *Re H. H. Realisations* (1975) 31 P. & C.R. 249; *Warnford Investments* v. *Duckworth* [1978] 2 W.L.R. 741, Megarry V.-C.; *Potters Oils, Re,* [1985] P.C.C. 148, Harman J.

s. 325, see *D. Wilson (Birmingham)* v. *Metropolitan Property Developments* [1975] 2 All E.R. 814, C.A.; *Re Bellaglade* [1977] 1 All E.R. 319.

s. 326, see *Hellyer* v. *Sheriff of Yorkshire* [1974] 2 W.L.R. 844; [1974] 2 All E.R. 712, C.A.

s. 327, see *Lord Advocate* v. *Royal Bank of Scotland* (O.H.), 1976 S.L.T. (Notes) 23; First Division, February 24, 1977; *Manley, Petr.* (O.H.), 1985 S.L.T. 42; *Commercial Aluminium Windows* v. *Cumbernauld Development Corporation*, 1987 S.L.T.(Sh.Ct.) 91.

s. 332, see *Liquidator of Upper Clyde Shipbuilders* (O.H.), 1974 S.L.T.(Notes) 52; *Re Gerald Cooper Chemicals* [1978] 2 All E.R. 49, Templeman J.; *Re Sarflax* [1979] 2 W.L.R. 202, Oliver J.; *R.* v. *Cox and Hodges* (1982) 75 Cr.App.R. 291, C.A.; *R.* v. *Davies* (1983) 76 Cr.App.R. 120, C.A.; *R.* v. *Sutcliffe-Williams and Gaskell* [1983] Crim.L.R. 255, Oxford Crown Ct.; *R.* v. *Redmond and Redmond* [1984] Crim.L.R. 292, C.A.; *R.* v. *Grantham* [1984] 2 W.L.R. 815, C.A.; *Augustus Barnett & Son, Re* [1986] P.C.C. 167, Hoffman J.; *Rossleigh* v. *Carlaw*, 1986 S.L.T. 204; *R.* v. *Lockwood* [1986] Crim.L.R. 244, C.A.; *R.* v. *Kemp* (1988) 4 BCC 203, C.A.

s. 333, see *Gibson's Exr.* v. *Gibson* (O.H.), 1980 S.L.T. 2; *Re Halt Garage* [1982] 3 All E.R. 1016, Oliver J.; *Blin* v. *Johnstone*, 1988 S.L.T. 335.

s. 346, see *Re Camburn Petroleum Products* [1979] 3 All E.R. 297, Slade J.; *Re Southard & Co.* [1979] 1 W.L.R. 1198, C.A.

ss. 352, 353, see *Re Thompson & Riches (in Liquidation)* [1981] 1 W.L.R. 682; [1981] 2 All E.R. 477, Slade J.

CAP.

11 & 12 Geo. 6 (1947–48)—cont.

38. Companies Act 1948—cont.

s. 353, see Re Court Lodge Development Co. [1973] 1 W.L.R. 1097; [1973] 3 All E.R. 425, Megarry J.; A.G.A. Estate Agencies, Re [1986] P.C.C. 358, Harman J.

ss. 357–359, repealed: 1984, c.9, s.28.

s. 365, orders 72/1055, 1190, 1404; 74/638, 1382, 1384, 2096; 75/214, 1328; 76/688, 1479, 1506; 77/1451, 2184; 78/569, 705, 1243, 1654; 79/968, 1149; 80/2008; 81/1643; 84/881; 85/574; rules 74/1237; 77/365, 1395; 78/543; 79/209, 1591, 1592; 80/773, 821, 1060, 1187; 81/788, 1309; 82/542, 860, 1706, 1707; 83/1645; 85/95.

s. 369, see Nicholl v. Cutts, 1985 P.C.C. 311, C.A.

s. 371, see Potters Oils, Re [1986] 1 W.L.R. 201, Hoffman J.

s. 372, see Smiths v. Middleton [1979] 3 All E.R. 842, Blackett Ord, V.-C.

ss. 372, 373, see Re Overmark Smith Warden [1982] 1 W.L.R. 1195, Slade J.

ss. 382, 384, 386, regs. 83/1021.

ss. 382, 384, 385, 394, repealed in pt.: 1984, c.9, s.28.

ss. 398, 399, see Nourse Self Build Association, Re (1985) 82 L.S. Gaz. 1709, Harman J.

s. 399, see Re Eloc Electro-Optieck and Communicatie B.V. [1981] 3 W.L.R. 176, Nourse J.

ss. 399, 400, see Re Compania Merabello [1972] 3 W.L.R. 471; [1972] 3 All E.R. 448; Inland Revenue v. Highland Engineering (O.H.), 1975 S.L.T. 203.

s. 407, regs. 82/674; 83/1021.

ss. 407, 416, see Curragh Investment v. Cork [1974] 1 W.L.R. 1559; [1974] 3 All E.R. 658.

s. 409, order 77/531.

s. 415, order 77/1367; regs. 83/1021.

ss. 424, 434, repealed: 1985, c.9, s.28.

s. 435, regs. 75/597; 80/926, 1784; 84/682.

s. 437, see Bishop (Thomas) v. Helmville [1972] 2 W.L.R. 149; [1972] 1 All E.R. 365; Cathrineholm v. Norequipment [1972] 2 Q.B. 314; [1972] 2 W.L.R. 1242; [1972] 2 All E.R. 538; Saga v. Avalon [1972] 2 Q.B. 325; [1972] 2 W.L.R. 1250n.; [1972] 2 All E.R. 545n; Blake v. Charles Sullivan Cars, The Times, June 26, 1986, D.C.

s. 441, see Re A Company [1980] 2 W.L.R. 241; [1980] 1 All E.R. 284, C.A.; Re Racal Communications [1980] 3 W.L.R. 181; [1980] 2 All E.R. 634, H.L.

s. 445, order 80/1786.

s. 447, see Parkinson v. Triplan [1973] 2 W.L.R. 632; [1973] 2 All E.R. 273, C.A.; Bishop v. National Union Bank [1973] 1 All E.R. 707; Pearson v. Naydler [1977] 1 W.L.R. 899, Megarry V.-C.; Dean Warwick v. Borthwick (O.H.), 1981 S.L.T.(Notes) 18; Wilson Vehicle Distribution v. Colt Car Co., The Times, October 25, 1983, Bingham J.; Speed Up Holdings v. Gouch [1986] F.S.R. 330, Evans-Lombe Q.C.

CAP.

11 & 12 Geo. 6 (1947–48)—cont.

38. Companies Act 1948—cont.

s. 448, see Customs and Excise Comrs. v. Hedon Alpha [1981] 2 W.L.R. 791; [1981] 2 All E.R. 697, C.A.

s. 450, repealed: 1985, c.9, s.28.

s. 454, regs. 73/1150; 77/1368; 79/54, 1618; 80/1055, 1160; 82/1092, 1698; 83/1023; 84/1717, 1859, 1860; 85/805.

s. 455, see Fabric Sales v. Eratex (1984) 128 S.J. 330, C.A.

s. 455, orders 77/166, 530, 531, 775, 1367, 1369, 1370; 82/673; regs. 80/2016; 81/1622, 1686; 82/674; 83/1021.

s. 455, repealed in pt.: 1985, c.9, s.28.

sch. 1, see Re Emmadart [1979] 1 All E.R. 599, Brightman J.; Re M. J. Shanley Contracting (In Voluntary Liquidation) (1979) 124 S.J. 239, Oliver J.; Re Halt Garage [1982] 3 All E.R. 1016, Oliver J.; Re Zinotty Properties [1984] 1 W.L.R. 1249, Mervyn Davies J.

sch. 14, regs. 75/597; 80/926, 1784; 84/682.

39. Industrial Assurance and Friendly Societies Act 1948.

s. 1, amended: 1974, c.46, sch.9; repealed in pt.: ibid., sch.11.

s. 2, amended: ibid., sch.9; regs. 77/1144; repealed in pt.: ibid., sch.11; 1985, c.65, sch. 10; c.66, sch.8(S.).

ss. 3, 4 (in pt.), repealed: 1974, c.46, sch. 11.

s. 6, amended: 1974, c.52, sch.3; repealed in pt.: 1974, c.46, sch.11.

s. 7, amended: 1973, c.38, sch.27; 1974, c.46, schs.6,9; repealed in pt.: 1975, c.18, sch.1.

s. 8, regs. 77/1353.

ss. 10, 11, amended: 1974, c.46, sch.9.

s. 12, amended and repealed in pt.: ibid.

s. 13, repealed in pt.: 1980, c.25, sch.5.

s. 15, repealed: 1974, c.46, schs.10,11.

s. 16, amended: ibid., sch.9; c.52, sch.3; repealed in pt.: 1974, c.46, sch.11.

s. 17, repealed: ibid.

s. 17A, added; S.L.R. 1974.

ss. 18, 19, repealed: 1974, c.46, sch.11.

s. 23, amended: ibid., sch.9; c.52, sch.3.

s. 24, repealed in pt.: 1973, c.36, sch.6.

s. 25, repealed in pt.: 1974, c.46, sch.11.

sch. 1, regs. 87/2088.

sch. 1, amended: 1974, c.46, schs.5,9; repealed in pt.: ibid., sch.11.

sch. 2, repealed in pt.: ibid.

sch. 3, amended: ibid., sch.9.

sch. 4, repealed: ibid., sch.11.

40. Education (Miscellaneous Provisions) Act 1948.

s. 2, repealed: 1973, c.16, sch.2.

s. 4, repealed in pt.: 1980, c.20, sch.1.

s. 5, regs. 80/545, amended: 1980, c.20, s.29; 1981, c.60, sch.3; 1988, c.40, s.100, sch.12.

s. 6, regs. 73/1676; repealed: 1980, c.20, sch.7.

s. 7, repealed in pt.: ibid.

s. 10, amended: 1988, c.40, sch.12; repealed in pt.: 1980, c.20, sch.1.

s. 11, repealed in pt.: 1973, c.16, sch.2.

s. 13, repealed: S.L.R. 1978.

CAP.

11 & 12 Geo. 6 (1947–48)—cont.

40. Education (Miscellaneous Provisions) Act 1948—*cont.*

s. 14, repealed in pt.: 1973, c.16, sch.2.

sch. 1, repealed in pt.: 1972, c.44, sch; 1973, c.16, sch.2; S.L.R. 1978; 1980, c.20, sch.7.

41. Law Reform (Personal Injuries) Act 1948.

s. 1, see *Brodin* v. *A/R Seljan,* 1973 S.L.T. 198, Outer House.

s. 2, see *Rudy* v. *Tay Textiles* (O.H.), 1978 S.L.T.(Notes) 62; *Lim Poh Choo* v. *Camden and Islington Area Health Authority* [1979] 3 W.L.R. 44, H.L.; *Bowers* v. *Strathclyde Regional Council,* 1981 S.L.T. 122; *Barnes* v. *Bromley London Borough Council, The Times,* November 16, 1983, H.H. Judge David Smout; *Denman* v. *Essex Area Health Authority; Haste* v. *Sandell Perkins* [1984] 3 W.L.R. 73, Q.B.D., Peter Pain J. and Hirst J.; *Foster* v. *Tyne and Wear County Council* [1986] 1 All E.R. 567, C.A.; *Jackman* v. *Corbett* [1987] 2 All E.R. 699, C.A.; *Rodriquez* v. *Rodriquez, The Times,* April 6, 1988, C.A.

s. 2, amended: 1975, c.18, sch.2; c.60, sch.4; 1977, c.49, sch.15; 1978, c.29, sch.16(S.); 1984, c.48, sch.4; repealed in pt. (S.): 1976, c.13, sch.2.

s. 5, repealed in pt.: 1973, c.36, sch.6.

43. Children Act 1948.

repealed: 1980, c.5, sch.6.

see *W.* v. *Nottinghamshire County Council, The Times,* October 26, 1981, C.A.

s. 1, see *Bawden* v. *Bawden* (1975) 74 L.G.R. 347, C.A.; *Tilley* v. *Wandsworth London Borough Council, The Times,* February 5, 1981, C.A.; *Re W. (A Minor)* (1981) 12 Fam.Law 27, C.A.

ss. 1, 2, see *Halvorsen* v. *Hertfordshire C.C.* (1974) 5 Fam. Law 79, D.C.; *Re D. (A Minor), The Times,* February 14, 1978, Balcombe J.; *Johns* v. *Jones* [1978] 3 W.L.R. 792, C.A.; *Lewisham London Borough Council* v. *Lewisham Juvenile Court JJ.* [1979] 2 W.L.R. 513, H.L.; *Wheatley* v. *Waltham Forest London Borough Council (Note)* [1979] 2 W.L.R. 543, D.C.; *W.* v. *Nottinghamshire County Council* [1981] 3 W.L.R. 959, C.A.

s. 2, see *Re K.* (1972) 116 S.J. 664; *R.* v. *Oxford City Justices, ex p. H.* [1974] 3 W.L.R. 1; [1974] 2 All E.R. 356; *S.* v. *Huddersfield Borough Council* [1974] 3 All E.R. 296, C.A.; *Re H. (A Minor), The Times,* October 29, 1977, C.A.; *Re D. F. (A Minor)* (1977) 76 L.G.R. 133, Dunn J.; *Re D. (A Minor)* (1978) 76 L.G.R. 653, Balcombe J.; *Re M. (Minors)* (1979) 123 S.J. 284, D.C.; *M.* v. *Wigan Metropolitan Borough Council* [1979] 2 All E.R. 958, D.C.; *Re M. (Review of Care Order)* (1979) 9 Fam.Law 186, D.C.; *W.* v. *Sunderland Borough Council* [1980] 2 All E.R. 514, D.C.; *O'D* v. *South Glamorgan County Council* (1980) 78 L.G.R. 522, D.C.; *Re Begum* (1982) 12 Fam. Law 61, D.C.; *Re W. (A Minor)* (1981) 12 Fam. Law 27, C.A.; *R.* v. *Corby Juvenile Court, ex p. M* [1987] 1 W.L.R. 55, Waite J.

s. 4, see *Re H. (A Minor), The Times,* October 29, 1977, C.A.

CAP.

11 & 12 Geo. 6 (1947–48)—cont.

43. Children Act 1948—*cont.*

s. 12, see *Re D. (A Minor), The Times,* February 14, 1978, Balcombe J.; *Att.-Gen.* v. *Hammersmith and Fulham London Borough Council, The Times,* December 18, 1979, Dillon J.

s. 13, see *Lincoln Corporation* v. *Parker* [1974] 1 W.L.R. 713, D.C.; *Re. Y (A Minor) (Child in Care: Access)* [1975] 3 W.L.R. 342, C.A.; *Leicestershire C.C.* v. *Cross* [1976] 2 All E.R. 491, D.C.; *Leeds City Council* v. *West Yorkshire Metropolitan Police* [1982] 2 W.L.R. 186, H.L.

44. Merchant Shipping Act 1948.

ss. 1, 3, regs. 75/341; 76/346, 1098; 77/2049; 78/600; 79/798; 80/270; 81/363.

s. 4, order 78/1522.

s. 5, regs. 75/341; 76/346, 1098; 77/627, 2049; 78/600; 79/798; 80/270; 81/363; 83/1167; orders 72/1105; 75/1045; 78/1532; 80/1143; 82/355; 85/1607; 86/2220; 87/63; 88/1485.

s. 23, rules 72/666.

45. Agriculture (Scotland) Act 1948.

ss. 8, 25, repealed: S.L.R. 1973.

s. 39, amended: 1981, c.69, s.72.

ss. 39–42, repealed in pt.: 1982, c.19, sch.3.

s. 43, repealed in pt.: *ibid.,* s.13, sch.3.

s. 50, orders 75/1722; 82/91.

ss. 50, 50A, amended: 1977, c.45, s.31, sch.6.

ss. 58, 62, repealed: S.L.R. 1973.

s. 64, amended: regs. 77/2007.

ss. 68, 69, repealed: 1972, c.62, s.21, sch.6.

s. 74, repealed: S.L.R. 1973.

s. 75, repealed in pt.: S.L.R. 1973.

s. 79, repealed: 1973, c.65, sch.29.

s. 80, amended: 1972, c.62, sch.6.

s. 85, order 75/1722.

s. 86, amended: regs. 77/2007.

sch. 3, amended: regs. 77/2007.

sch. 5, see *Ross* v. *Donaldson,* 1983 S.L.T.(Land Ct.) 26; *Sinclair* v. *Mackintosh,* 1983 S.L.T (Land Ct.) 29.

schs. 5, 6, see *Jedlitschka* v. *Fuller,* 1985 S.L.C.R. 90.

sch. 6, see *Austin* v. *Gibson,* 1979 S.L.T.(Land Ct.) 12; *Ross* v. *Donaldson,* 1983 S.L.T.(Land Ct.) 26; *Sinclair* v. *Mackintosh,* 1983 S.L.T.(Land Ct.) 29; *Buchanan* v. *Buchanan,* 1983 S.L.T.(Land Ct.) 31; *McGill* v. *Bichan,* 1982 S.L.C.R. 33; *Luss Estates Co.* v. *Firkin Farm Co.,* 1984, S.L.C.R. 1.

sch. 7, repealed: 1973, c.65, sch.29.

sch. 8, repealed in pt.: 1972, c.72, sch.6.

46. Employment and Training Act 1948.

repealed: 1973, c.50, sch.4.

ss. 10, 18, amended: 1972, c.70, s.209, sch.30.

47. Agricultural Wages Act 1948.

s. 1, regs. 82/1181.

s. 2, regs. 80/1005; 82/1181, 1182; orders 74/515; 81/9, 179.

ss. 3–5, 11, amended: 1975, c.71, sch.9.

s. 12, amended: *ibid.;* repealed in pt.: *ibid.,* sch.18.

s. 17, regs. 80/1005; 82/1181, 1182.

s. 18, order 74/515.

sch. 4, repealed in pt.: 1975, c.71, sch.18.

CAP.

11 & 12 Geo. 6 (1947–48)—cont.

49. Finance Act 1948.

s. 73, repealed: 1973, c.51, sch.22.

s. 75, repealed: S.L.R. 1976.

s. 81, repealed: S.L.R. 1975.

s. 82, repealed in pt.: 1975, c.7, sch.13.

52. Veterinary Surgeons Act 1948.

repealed: S.L.R. 1986.

53. Nurseries and Child-Minders Regulation Act 1948.

ss. 1, 2, amended: 1972, c.70, sch.23.

s. 3, amended: ibid.; 1983, c.41, sch.9.

s. 8, amended: 1980, c.6, sch.2; (S.) 1984, c.56, sch.2.

s. 11, amended: 1972, c.70, sch.23.

s. 13, amended: ibid.; 1977, c.49, sch.15; 1978, c.29, sch.16(S.); 1980, c.6, sch.2; 1984, c.56, sch.2(S.); repealed in pt.: 1975, c.72, sch.4.

56. British Nationality Act 1948.

repealed except ss. 3, 32 (in pt.), 33 (in pt.), 34 (in pt.), 1981, c.61, sch.9.

s. 5A, see R. v. Secretary of State for the Home Department, ex p. Sultan Mahmood (Note) [1980] 3 W.L.R. 312, C.A.; R. v. Secretary of State for the Home Department, ex p. Margueritte [1982] 3 W.L.R. 754, C.A.

s. 6, see R. v. Secretary of State for the Home Department, ex p. Puttick, The Times, November 15, 1980, D.C.

s. 7, see R. v. Secretary of State for the Home Department, ex p. Akhtar [1980] 3 W.L.R. 302; [1980] 2 All E.R. 735, C.A; Gowa v. Att.-Gen. [1985] 1 W.L.R. 1003, H.L.

s. 20, see R. v. Secretary of State for the Home Department, ex p. Akhtar [1980] 3 W.L.R. 302; [1980] 2 All E.R. 735, C.A.; R. v. Secretary of State for the Home Department, ex p. Sultan Mahmood (Note) [1980] 3 W.L.R. 312, C.A.

s. 29, regs. 73/1491; 74/1895, 2136; 75/225, 1937; 76/1520; 78/91; 79/240, 1072; orders 78/1026; 80/197, 358; 82/283.

ss. 30, 32, orders 74/1895; 78/1026.

s. 32, amended: 1978, c.15, s.4; repealed in pt.: 1980, c.2, s.3.

57. Public Registers and Records (Scotland) Act 1948.

s. 2, repealed in pt. (S.): S.L.R. 1975.

s. 4, Act of Sederunt, 77/70.

58. Criminal Justice Act 1948.

s. 2, repealed: S.L.R. 1977.

s. 3, see R. v. Jackson (Alan) [1974] 2 W.L.R. 641; [1974] 2 All E.R. 211, C.A.; R. v. Tucker [1974] 1 W.L.R. 615; [1974] 2 All E.R. 639; R. v. Marquis [1974] 1 W.L.R. 1087; [1974] 2 All E.R. 1216, C.A.

ss. 3–7, repealed: 1973, c.62, sch.6.

s. 8, see R. v. Isherwood (1974) 59 Cr.App.R. 162, C.A.

ss. 8–11, repealed: 1973, c.62, sch.6.

s. 12, see R. v. Akan [1972] 3 W.L.R. 866; [1972] 3 All E.R. 285; R. v. Maizone [1974] Crim.L.R. 112, C.A.; R. v. Tucker [1974] 1 W.L.R. 615; [1974] 2 All E.R. 639; R. v. Isherwood (1974) 59 Cr.App.R. 162, C.A.

CAP.

11 & 12 Geo. 6 (1947–48)—cont.

58. Criminal Justice Act 1948—cont.

ss. 12, 14, 17 (in pt.), repealed: 1973, c.62, sch.6.

ss. 19, 20, repealed: 1982, c.48, sch.16.

s. 27, amended: 1980, c.43, sch.7.

s. 29, repealed: 1973, c.62, sch.6.

s. 30, repealed: S.L.R. 1977.

s. 35, repealed: 1974, c.23, sch.3.

s. 37, amended: 1976, c.63, sch.2; 1981, c.54, sch.5; repealed in pt.: 1976, c.63, sch.3; 1981, c.54, sch.7.

ss. 43, 45, repealed: 1973, c.62, sch.6.

s. 46, rules 74/1065.

ss. 46, 47, repealed: 1973, c.62, sch.6.

s. 48, repealed in pt.: 1982, c.48, sch.16.

s. 52, rules 78/1919.

s. 52, repealed: 1982, c.48, sch.16.

s. 66, repealed: S.L.R. 1977.

s. 68, repealed: 1984, c.60, sch.7.

s. 70, repealed in pt.: S.L.R. 1977.

s. 73, repealed: ibid.

s. 76, repealed in pt.: 1982, c.48, sch.16.

s. 77, repealed in pt.: 1972, c.71, s.56, sch.6; 1973, c.62, sch.6.

s. 80, repealed in pt.: 1972, c.71, sch.6; 1973, c.62, sch.6.

ss. 81–83, repealed in pt.: S.L.R. 1977.

sch. 1, repealed: 1973, c.62, sch.6.

sch. 5, rules 72/803, 1208, 1400, 1657; 73/1175, 1746; 74/746, 1064.

schs. 5, 8 (in pt.), repealed: 1973, c.62, sch.6.

sch. 9, repealed in pt.: 1976, c.35, sch.3; S.L.R. 1977.

sch. 10, repealed: ibid.

59. Laying of Documents before Parliament (Interpretation) Act 1948.

s. 1, see R. v. Secretary of State for the Environment, ex p. Leicester City Council (1985) 25 R.V.R. 31, Woolf J.

62. Statute Law Revision Act 1948.

s. 2, repealed: 1977, c.38, s.2.

s. 6, amended: 1973, c.36, sch.6.

63. Agricultural Holdings Act 1948.

repealed: 1986, c.5, sch.15.

see Wetherall v. Smith [1980] 2 All E.R. 530, C.A.

s. 1, see Hickson and Welch v. Cann (Note) (1977) 40 P. & C.R. 218, C.A.; Russell v. Booker (1982) 263 E.G. 513, C.A.; Short v. Greeves [1988] 08 E.G. 109, C.A.

s. 2, see Epps v. Ledger (1972) 225 E.G. 1373; Bahamas International Trust Co. v. Threadgold [1974] 1 W.L.R. 1514; [1974] 3 All E.R. 881, H.L.; Bedfordshire C.C. v. Clarke (1974) 230 E.G. 1587; Avon County Council v. Clothier (1977) 242 E.G. 1048, C.A.; 75 L.G.R. 344, C.A.; Cox v. Husk (1976) 239 E.G. 123, Griffiths J.; Somerset County Council v. Pearse, September 13, 1977, Judge Willcock, Q.C., Taunton C.C.; Midgley v. Stott (1977) 244 E.G. 883, C.A.; James v. Lock (1977) 246 E.G. 395, C.A.; Luton v. Tinsey (1978) 249 E.G. 239, C.A.; Short Bros. (Plant) v. Edwards (1978) 249 E.G. 539, C.A.; Milton v. Farrow (1980) 255 E.G. 449, C.A.; Stone v. Whit-

CAP.

11 & 12 Geo. 6 (1947–48)—cont.

63. Agricultural Holdings Act 1948—*cont.*
combe (1980) 40 P. & C.R. 296, C.A.; *Epsom and Ewell Borough Council* v. *C. Bell (Tadworth)* [1983] 1 W.L.R. 379, Rubin J.; *South West Water Authority* v. *Palmer, The Times,* May 9, 1983, C.A.; *Keen* v. *Holland* (1983) 127 S.J. 764; [1984] 1 All E.R. 75, C.A.; *Chaloner* v. *Bower* (1984) 269 E.G. 275, C.A.; *Lampard* v. *Barker* (1984) 81 L.S.Gaz. 2381; (1984) 272 E.G. 783, C.A.; *Collier* v. *Hollinshead* (1984) 272 E.G. 941, Scott J.; *Watts* v. *Yeend* [1987] 1 W.L.R. 323, C.A.; *Harrison* v. *Wing* [1988] 29 E.G. 101, C.A.
s. 6, regs. 73/1473.
s. 7, regs. 73/1482.
s. 8, see *Llanover* v. *Bevan* (unreported); *Stiles* v. *Farrow* (1976) 241 E.G. 623, Judge Stock Q.C.; *Personal Representatives of the Estate of the Late Dr. Cotton* v. *Gardener,* November 28, 1979, Judge Whitehead, Spalding County Ct.; *Tummon* v. *Barclays Bank Trust Co.* (1979) 250 E.G. 980; (1979) 39 P. & C.R. 300, Judge Goodall, Bodmin County Ct.; *Pennington-Ramsden* v. *McWilliam,* July 10, 1980, H.H. Judge Leech, Whitehaven County Court; *University College, Oxford* v. *Durdy* [1982] 1 All E.R. 1108, C.A.; *Buckinghamshire County Council* v. *Gordon* (1986) 279 E.G. 853, H.H. Judge Barr.
s. 23, see *Paddock Investments* v. *Lory* (1975) 236 E.G. 803, C.A.; *Elsden* v. *Pick* [1900] 1 W.L.R. 899, C.A.
ss. 23, 24, see *Rugby Water Board* v. *Foottit* [1972] 2 W.L.R. 757; [1972] 1 All E.R. 1057.
s. 24, see *Stoneman* v. *Brown* [1973] 1 W.L.R. 459, C.A.; *Jones* v. *Lewis* (1973) 117 S.J. 373, C.A.; *Magdalen College, Oxford* v. *Heritage* [1974] 1 W.L.R. 441; [1974] 1 All E.R. 1065, C.A.; *Wykes* v. *Davis* [1975] 2 W.L.R. 131; [1975] 1 All E.R. 399, C.A.; *Pickard* v. *Bishop* (1975) 31 P. & C.R. 108, C.A.; *Beevers* v. *Mason* (1978) 37 P. & C.R. 452, C.A.; *Johnson* v. *Moreton* [1978] 3 All E.R. 37, H.L.; *Newman* v. *Keedwell* (1978) 35 P. & C.R. 393, Fox J.; *Persey* v. *Bazley* (1983) 267 E.G. 519, C.A.
ss. 24, 25, see *Gisbourne* v. *Burton* [1988] 38 E.G. 129, C.A.
s. 25, see *N.C.B.* v. *Nayler* [1972] 1 W.L.R. 908; [1972] 1 All E.R. 1153; *Greaves* v. *Mitchell* (1971) 222 E.G. 1395; *R.* v. *Agricultural Land Tribunal for the South Eastern Area, ex p. Parslow* (1979) 251 E.G. 667, D.C.
s. 34, see *Davis* v. *Powell* [1977] 1 W.L.R. 258; [1977] 1 All E.R. 471; *Parry* v. *Million Pigs* (1981) 260 E.G. 281, Ewbank J.
s. 50, order 78/259.
s. 51, regs. 72/864; 75/11; 76/818; 78/809; 80/751; 81/822; 83/1475.
s. 56, see *Parry* v. *Million Pigs* (1981) 260 E.G. 281, Ewbank J.
s. 58, see *Lady Hallinan* v. *Jones & Jones,* November 13, 1984, Mr. Assistant Recorder Langdon Davies, Aberystwyth County Ct.

CAP.

11 & 12 Geo. 6 (1947–48)—cont.

63. Agricultural Holdings Act 1948—*cont.*
s. 65, see *Parry* v. *Million Pigs* (1981) 260 E.G. 281, Ewbank J.
s. 66, see *Lloyds Bank* v. *Marcan* [1973] 1 W.L.R. 1387; [1973] 3 All E.R. 754, C.A.
s. 70, see *Lady Hallinan* v. *Jones & Jones,* November 13, 1984, Mr. Assistant Recorder Langdon Davies, Aberystwyth County Ct.
s. 77, order 85/1829.
s. 78, order 78/742.
s. 79, regs. 78/809; 80/751; 81/822; 83/1475.
s. 92, see *Newborough (Lord)* v. *Jones* [1974] 3 W.L.R. 52, C.A.; *Lady Hallinan* v. *Jones & Jones,* November 13, 1984, Mr. Assistant Recorder Langdon Davies, Aberystwyth County Ct.
s. 94, see *Hickson and Welch* v. *Cann* (Note) (1977) 40 P. & C.R. 218, C.A.; *Russell* v. *Booker* (1982) 263 E.G. 513, C.A.
sch. 6, see *University College, Oxford* v. *Durdy* [1982] 1 All E.R. 1108, C.A.; *E.D. & A.D. Cooke Bourne (Farms)* v. *Mellows* [1982] 2 All E.R. 208, C.A.; *Burton* v. *Timmis* [1987] 281 E.G. 795, C.A.
sch. 6, rules 78/444.
64. National Service Act 1948.
repealed: 1985, c.17, sch.5.
65. Representation of the People Act 1948.
repealed: 1986, c.56, sch.4.
66. Monopolies and Restrictive Practices (Inquiry and Control) Act 1948.
order 73/1643.
repealed: 1973, c.41, sch.13.
s. 10, orders 73/55, 720, 925, 1093, 1155, 1487.
s. 11, see *Hoffmann-La Roche (F.) & Co.* v. *Secretary of State for Trade and Industry* [1974] 2 All E.R. 1128, H.L.
67. Gas Act 1948.
repealed: 1972, c.60, schs.6,8.
s. 1, see *R.* v. *Manners* [1976] 2 W.L.R. 709, C.A.; *R.* v. *Hirst and McNamee* [1975] 64 Cr.App.R. 151, C.A.
s. 54, regs. 72/695.
s. 58, regs. 72/630.
s. 67, regs. 72/1178.

12, 13 & 14 Geo. 6 (1948–49)

1. Colonial Stock Act 1948.
s. 1, amended: 1982, c.41, sch.2.
2. Debts Clearing Offices Act 1948.
repealed: S.L.R. 1986.
4. Judges Pensions (India and Burma) Act 1948.
amended: 1974, c.21, sch.1.
5. Civil Defence Act 1948.
s. 2, regs. 74/68–70; 75/848, 849; 83/1634, 1650(S.).
s. 2, repealed in pt.: 1972, c.70, sch.30; 1973, c.65, sch.29(S.).
s. 3, regs. 83/1633, 1651(S.); 87/622, 677(S.).
ss. 3, 6, repealed in pt.: S.L.R. 1986.
s. 4, amended (S.): 1984, c.54, sch.9.
s. 8, regs. 74/68–70; 75/848, 849; 83/1633, 1634, 1650(S.), 1651(S.); 87/622, 677(S.).
s. 9, orders 73/1759; 83/609(S.).
s. 10, repealed in pt.: 1973, c.36, sch.6.

CAP.

12, 13 & 14 Geo. 6 (1948–49)—cont.

6. National Service (Amendment) Act 1948.
repealed: S.L.R. 1981.

7. Wages Councils Act 1948.
s. 1, repealed in pt.: 1980, c.42, sch.2.

8. Recall of Army and Air Force Pensioners Act 1948.
repealed: 1980, c.9, sch.10.
sch., amended: 1980, c.23, sch.1.

9. Prize Act 1948.
repealed: S.L.R. 1977.

10. Administration of Justice (Scotland) Act 1948.
repealed: 1988, c.36, sch.2.
s. 2, Acts of Sederunt 73/361; 74/336; 75/88; 76/14; 77/21; 78/148; 79/190; 80/84, 1928; 82/122; 83/119; 84/61; 85/317; 86/543; 87/40.
s. 3, Act of Sederunt 88/682.

11. Railway and Canal Commission (Abolition) Act 1949.
s. 2, repealed: 1984, c.12, sch.7.
ss. 6, 7, repealed: S.L.R. 1978.

16. National Theatre Act 1949.
functions transferred: orders 81/207; 86/600.
s. 1, amended: 1973, c.2, s.1; 1974, c.55, s.1; repealed in pt.: *ibid.*

18. Colonial Naval Defence Act 1949.
s. 1, repealed in pt.: 1981, c.55, sch.5.

20. Cinematograph Film Production (Special Loans) Act 1949.
repealed: 1981, c.15, sch.3.

21. Solicitors, Public Notaries, etc., Act 1949.
repealed: 1974, c.27, sch.4.

22. British North America Act 1949.
Act renamed Newfoundland Act 1949 (Can.): 1982, c.11, sch.
s. 3, substituted: *ibid.*

25. Tenancy of Shops (Scotland) Act 1949.
s. 1, see *McMahon v. Associated Rentals*, 1987, S.L.T.(Sh.Ct.) 94.

26. Public Works (Festival of Britain) Act 1949.
repealed: S.L.R. 1986.

27. Juries Act 1949.
repealed (except (S.)): S.L.R. 1978.
s. 1, regs. 72/1001; 73/935, 991, 1171, 1601, 1898; 74/733, 935.
s. 24, regs. 73/1129, 1686; 74/666, 1484; 75/747, 1936; 77/445.
s. 24, amended (S.): 1980, c.55, sch.2.
s. 25, regs. 73/643.
s. 25, amended (S.): 1980, c.55, sch.2; 1987, c.41, sch.1; repealed in pt. (S.): 1980, c.55, sch. 3.
s. 26, amended (S.): 1983, c.12, sch.1; repealed in pt. (S.): *ibid.*, schs.1, 2.
s. 30, repealed: S.L.R. 1978.
s. 32, regs. 73/643, 1129, 1686; 74/666, 1484; 75/747, 1936; 77/445.
s. 34, repealed: 1973, c.36, sch.6.
s. 35, repealed in pt.: S.L.R. 1978.
sch. 1, repealed in pt.(S.): 1988, c.36, sch.2.

29. Consular Conventions Act 1949.
s. 1, amended: 1981, c.54, sch.5.
s. 6, orders 76/1150, 1216; 86/216.
s. 8, order 78/779.

CAP.

12, 13 & 14 Geo. 6 (1948–49)—cont.

30. Agricultural Wages (Scotland) Act 1949.
ss. 1 (in pt.), 2, repealed: 1972, c.62, schs.5, 6.
s. 3, substituted: 1975, c.71, sch.10.
s. 4, amended: *ibid.*
ss. 5, 6, amended: 1972, c.62, sch.5; 1975, c.71, sch.10; repealed in pt.: 1972, c.62, schs.5, 6.
s. 7, amended: *ibid.*, sch.5; repealed in pt.: *ibid.*, schs.5, 6.
s. 8, repealed: *ibid.*
s. 9, amended: *ibid.*, sch.5; repealed in pt.: *ibid.*, schs.5, 6.
s. 11, amended: 1975, c.71, sch.10.
s. 12, amended: *ibid.*; repealed in pt.: 1972, c.62, schs.5, 6; 1975, c.71, schs.10, 18.
ss. 13–15, repealed in pt.: 1972, c.62, schs.5, 6.
sch. 2, repealed: *ibid.*
sch. 3, amended: *ibid.*, sch.5; repealed in pt.: *ibid.*, schs.5, 6; 1975, c.71, schs.10, 18.

31. Water (Scotland) Act 1949.
repealed: 1980, c.45, sch.11.
s. 20, regs. 75/930.

32. Special Roads Act 1949.
repealed (S.): 1984, c.54, sch.11.
s. 3, amended: 1973, c.65, sch.15.
s. 9, repealed in pt.: 1972, c.52, sch.23.
s. 20, substituted: 1984, c.12, sch.4.
s. 21, amended: 1973, c.65, sch.14; repealed in pt.: *ibid.*, schs.14, 29.
sch. 1, see *Lithgow v. Secretary of State for Scotland*, 1973 S.L.T. 81, Court of Session (O.H.).
sch. 1, amended: 1973, c.65, sch.14.

34. Milk (Special Designations) Act 1949.
ss. 10, 11, orders 83/939, 1527; 86/788(S.).

35. British Film Institute Act 1949.
s. 1, functions transferred: orders 81/207; 86/600.
s. 1, amended: 1972, c.19, sch.

36. War Damage (Public Utility Undertakings, etc.) Act 1949.
repealed: S.L.R. 1981.

37. Agriculture (Miscellaneous Provisions) Act 1949.
s. 1–5, repealed: S.L.R. 1973.
s. 8, repealed in pt.: 1973, c.50, sch.4.
ss. 9, 14, 15 (in pt.), 16 (in pt.), repealed: S.L.R. 1973.
s. 10, repealed: 1986, c.5, sch.15.
s. 12, repealed: S.L.R. 1986.
sch. 1, repealed in pt.: 1986, c.5, sch.15.

39. Commonwealth Telegraphs Act 1949.
s. 6, amended: 1978, c.44, sch.10; 1984, c.12, sch.5; repealed in pt.: 1972, c.11, sch.8.

41. Ireland Act 1949.
s. 1, repealed in pt.: 1973, c.36, sch.6.
s. 2, see *ex p. Molyneaux* [1986] 1 W.L.R. 331, Taylor J.
s. 3, see *R. v. McGlinchey* [1985] 9 N.I.J.B. 62, C.A.
ss. 3, 7, amended: 1981, c.61, sch.7.
s. 5, repealed: *ibid.*, sch.9.

CAP.

12, 13 & 14 Geo. 6 (1948–49)—cont.

42. Lands Tribunal Act 1949.
s. 1, see *J. & A. Massie* v. *Aberdeen Corporation*, 1974 S.L.T.(Lands Tr.)13; *Park Automobile Co.* v. *Glasgow Corporation*, 1975 S.L.T.(Lands Tr.) 23; *Cupar Trading Estate* v. *Fife Regional Council*, 1979 S.L.T. (Lands Tr.) 2.

s. 1, amended: 1984, c.31, s.12.
s. 2, repealed in pt.: 1981, c.20, sch.4.
s. 3, see *Pepys* v. *London Transport Executive* [1975] 1 W.L.R. 234, C.A.; *R.* v. *Lands Tribunal, ex p. City of London Corporation* [1982] 1 W.L.R. 258, C.A.; *Watneys of London* v. *City of London Corp.* (1982) 261 E.G. 1089, C.A.; *Imperial College of Science and Technology* v. *Ebdon (V.O.) and Westminster City Council* [1986] R.A. 233, C.A.

s. 3, rules 75/299; 77/432, 1820; 81/105, 600, 632; 83/1428(S.); 84/793; 85/581(S.); 86/1322; 87/1139(S.).

s. 3, amended: 1974, c.38, s.19; 1975, c.77, sch.10; 1980, c.65, sch.33.

43. Merchant Shipping (Safety Convention) Act 1949.
modified: 1977, c.24, s.1; regs. 80/539.
s. 1, rules 75/927; 76/302.
s. 1, amended: 1977, c.24, s.1.
s. 2, amended: 1973, c.27, sch.2; c.49, sch.; 1976, c.19, sch.; 1978, c.15, sch.; c.20, sch.2; order 78/1899.
s. 3, rules 74/1919; 82/1292.
ss. 3, 5, amended: 1979, c.39, sch.6.
s. 6, rules 76/302.
s. 6, amended: 1979, c.39, sch.6.
s. 7, amended: regs. 81/568.
s. 12, amended: 1979, c.39, sch.6; repealed in pt.: regs. 81/568.
s. 13, repealed in pt.: *ibid.*
s. 14, repealed in pt.: 1979, c.39, s.28; regs. 81/568.
s. 16, repealed: *ibid.*
s. 19, amended: 1979, c.39, sch.6.
s. 21, rules 77/1010.
s. 21, amended: 1979, c.39, sch.6; regs. 83/703; repealed in pt.: *ibid.*
s. 23, rules 78/1543; 79/976; 80/789, 1502; regs. 81/1747; 86/1069.
s. 23, amended: 1979, c.39, sch.6.
s. 24, amended: 1977, c.24, s.1; 1979, c.2, sch.4; c.39, sch.6; repealed in pt.: 1977, c.24, s.1; 1979, c.39, sch.7; regs. 80/536.
s. 26, see *Secretary of State for Trade* v. *Booth; The Biche* [1984] 1 W.L.R. 243; [1984] 1 Lloyd's Rep. 26, D.C.
s. 31, orders 77/1876; 81/237.
s. 33, regs. 75/341; 76/346, 1098; 77/627, 2049; 78/600; 79/798; 80/270, 572, 1143; 81/363, 624; 82/355, 864; 83/1167; 85/936, 1607; 86/837; 87/63, 548, 854; 88/478, 1485.
s. 36, amended: regs. 81/568; 85/212.

44. Superannuation Act 1949.
repealed: 1972, c.11, sch.8.

CAP.

12, 13 & 14 Geo. 6 (1948–49)—cont.

45. U.S.A. Veterans' Pensions (Administration) Act 1949.
s. 1, amended: 1983, c.20, sch.4.

47. Finance Act 1949.
s. 8, repealed: 1973, c.51, sch.22.
s. 15, repealed: S.L.R. 1978.
ss. 27–29, repealed: 1975, c.7, sch.13.
s. 28, see *Trustees Executors & Agency Co.* v. *I.R.C.* [1973] 2 W.L.R. 248; *Standard Chartered Bank* v. *I.R.C.* [1978] 1 W.L.R. 1160, Goulding J.
ss. 31–33, repealed: 1975, c.7, sch.13.
s. 34, repealed: S.L.R. 1976.
s. 40, repealed in pt.(S.): S.L.R. 1986.
s. 48, repealed in pt.: *ibid.*
s. 49, repealed in pt.: 1973, c.36, sch.6.
s. 52 (in pt.), sch. 7, repealed: 1975, c.7, sch.13.
sch. 8, repealed in pt.: S.L.R. 1976; 1985, c.54, sch.27.
sch. 11, repealed in pt.: 1975, c.7, sch.13.

50. Colonial Loans Act 1949.
repealed: 1980, c.63, sch.2.

51. Legal Aid and Advice Act 1949.
repealed: 1974, c.4, sch.5.
see *Din (Taj)* v. *Wandsworth London Borough Council (No. 3), The Times*, April 28, 1983, Lloyd J.
regs. 72/1749.
s. 1, see *Fakes* v. *Taylor Woodrow* [1973] 2 W.L.R. 161, C.A.
s. 1, regs. 73/349.
s. 2, regs. 73/1782, 2036.
s. 3, see *Till* v. *Till* [1974] 2 W.L.R. 447; [1974] 1 All E.R. 1096, C.A.; *Cooke* v. *Head (No. 2)* [1974] 1 W.L.R. 972; [1974] 2 All E.R. 1124, C.A.; *Currie & Co.* v. *The Law Society* [1976] 2 W.L.R. 785.
s. 3, regs. 73/1782.
s. 4, regs. 73/349, 1474, 1475.
s. 7, regs. 72/1747.
s. 12, regs. 72/1747, 1748; 73/349, 535, 1474, 1475, 1716, 1782, 1783, 2036.
s. 15, see *Roberts* v. *Duce* [1974] Crim. L.R. 107, D.C.
s. 17, order 73/2035.
sch. 3, regs. 73/2036.

52. Slaughter of Animals (Scotland) Act 1949.
repealed: 1972, c.62, sch.6.

53. Coal Industry Act 1949.
s. 1, amended: 1987, c.3, sch.1.
s. 2, order 75/1219; repealed: 1977, c.39, s.11, sch.5.

54. Wireless Telegraphy Act 1949.
order 80/184.
s. 1, see *Monks* v. *Pilgrim* [1979] Crim.L.R. 595, D.C.; *D. (A Minor)* v. *Yates* [1984] Crim.L.R. 430, D.C.; *Walkinshaw* v. *McIntyre*, 1985 S.C.C.R. 389; *Rudd* v. *Secretary of State for Trade and Industry* [1987] 1 W.L.R. 786, H.L.; *Irving* v. *Jessop*, 1988 S.L.T. 53.
s. 1, regs. 80/1848; 82/1697; 84/1053; 87/775, 776; 88/1648.
ss. 1, 2, see *Congreve* v. *Home Office* [1976] 2 W.L.R. 291; [1976] 1 All E.R. 697, C.A.

CAP.

12, 13 & 14 Geo. 6 (1948–49)—cont.

54. Wireless Telegraphy Act 1949—cont.
s. 2, regs. 75/212, 1693; 76/2031; 77/1286; 78/12, 1680; 79/841, 1490; 80/798, 1848, 1850; 81/882, 1432, 1706; 83/670; 84/1053; 85/490; 86/1039; 88/135, 376, 899.

s. 3, regs. 88/47.

s. 3A, added: 1984. c.12, s.74.

s. 5, see *Paul* v. *Ministry of Posts and Telecommunications* [1973] R.T.R. 245; *Francome* v. *Mirror Group Newspapers* [1984] 2 All E.R. 408, C.A.

s. 6, amended: 1982, c.48, s.50.

s. 9, regs. 78/1267, 1268.

ss. 9, 10, repealed in pt.: 1984, c.12, sch.7.

s. 10, regs. 73/1217; 78/1267, 1268; 82/635; 85/807, 808; 88/1216.

s. 12A, added: 1984, c.12, s.78.

s. 14, see *Rudd* v. *Secretary of State for Trade and Industry* [1987] 1 W.L.R. 786, H.L.

s. 14, amended: 1977, c.45, s.31, sch.6; 1984, c.12, s.82, sch.3.

s. 15, see *Oldfield, Complainer*, 1988 S.L.T. 734.

s. 15, amended: 1984, c.12, s.92.

s. 19, amended: *ibid.*, c.46, sch.6.

sch. 2, amended: 1984, c.12, s.92.

55. Prevention of Damage by Pests Act 1949.
s. 1, repealed in pt.: 1972, c.70, sch.30.

s. 2, repealed in pt.: 1980, c.65, schs.1,34.

s. 4, repealed in pt.: 1972, c.62, sch.5.

s. 7, amended: 1980, c.45, sch.10(S.); repealed in pt.: 1974, c.7, sch.8.

s. 8, regs. 76/42, 1236; 78/1614.

s. 9, repealed: 1976, c.57, sch.2.

s. 12, repealed in pt.: 1980, c 65, schs.1,34.

s. 21, repealed in pt.: *ibid.*, sch.34.

s. 29, repealed in pt.: 1973, c 36, sch.6.

60. Housing Act 1949.
ss. 5, 43, repealed: S.L.R. 1981.

s. 44, repealed: 1985, c.71, sch.6.

s. 45, repealed: 1972, c.47, sch.11.

s. 50, repealed: S.L.R. 1981; 1985, c.71, sch.6.

s. 51, repealed: S.L.R. 1981.

61. Housing (Scotland) Act 1949.
repealed: S.L.R. 1981.

62. Patents and Designs Act 1949.
repealed: 1986, c.39, sch.3.

s. 33, see *Fairfax (Dental) Equipment* v. *Filhol (S.J.)* [1986] R.P.C. 499, C.A.

s. 85, see *Allmanna Svenska Elektriska Aktiebolaget's Application* [1976] R.P.C. 464.

s. 100, see *International Business Machines Corp.'s Application* [1980] F.S.R. 565, Graham J.

63. Legal Aid and Solicitors (Scotland) Act 1949.
Pt. II (ss. 18–28), repealed in pt.: 1980, c.46, sch.7.

s. 20, see *Sharp* v. *Council of the Law Society of Scotland*, 1984 S.L.T. 313.

s. 20, amended: 1972, c.50, sch.2; 1976, c.6, s.5.

s. 25, repealed: 1985, c.73, schs.1,4.

schs. 4–7, repealed: 1980, c.46, sch.7.

CAP.

12, 13 & 14 Geo. 6 (1948–49)—cont.

66. House of Commons (Redistribution of Seats) Act 1949.
repealed: 1986, c.56, sch.4.

s. 2, order 82/1838; 83/417, 418, 422(S.).

s. 2, sch. 2, see *R.* v. *Boundary Commission for England, ex p. Foot; R.* v. *Boundary Commission for England, ex p. Gateshead Borough Council* [1983] 2 W.L.R. 458, C.A.

s. 3, orders 73/604–8, 764–70; 78/1911; 83/417, 418, 422(S.); 84/548; 85/1776; 86/597, 2231.

67. Civil Aviation Act 1949.
orders 72/129, 445, 452–4; 76/421, 1776; 77/422, 820; 78/1520.

ss. 1, 6, repealed: 1982, c.16, sch.16.

s. 8, orders 72/455, 672, 1266, 1723; 73/71, 1750; 74/111, 1114, 1275; 75/429, 1515, 1836; 76/583, 1783; 77/1255, 2160; 78/284, 1627; 79/929, 930, 1318; 80/965; 82/161.

ss. 8–11, repealed: 1982, c.16, sch.16.

s. 10, regs. 72/962; 74/1519; 75/1516.

s. 15, repealed, 1980, c.60, sch.3.

s. 16, repealed in pt.: *ibid.*; 1982, c.16, sch.16.

ss. 17–20, 23–35, repealed: *ibid.*

s. 36, repealed: 1982, c.1, schs.1,2.

ss. 37–41, repealed: 1982, c.16, sch.16.

s. 40, see *Bernstein* v. *Skyviews and General* [1977] 3 W.L.R. 136, Griffiths J.

ss. 40, 41, see *Steel-Maitland* v. *British Airways Board* (O.H.), 1981 S.L.T. 110.

s. 41, orders 74/1114; 76/1783; 79/929; 80/1965.

ss. 51–53, repealed: 1982, c.16, sch.16.

s. 53, orders 72/696; 77/829.

s. 55, regs. 72/323, 1513.

ss. 55, 56, repealed: 1982, c.16, sch.16.

s. 56, regs. 72/1027.

s. 57, orders 72/455, 672, 1266, 1723; 73/71, 1750; 74/111, 1114, 1275; 75/429, 1515, 1836; 76/583, 1783; 77/1255, 2160; 78/284, 1627; 79/929, 930, 1318; 80/1965; 82/161.

ss. 57, 58, repealed: 1982, c.16, sch.16.

s. 58, orders 74/1114; 76/1783; 79/929, 930; 80/1965.

ss. 59, orders 72/672, 1266, 1723; 73/71, 1750; 74/1114; 76/1783; 78/1627; 79/930; 80/1965.

s. 59, amended: 1978, c.8, sch.1.; 1982, c.1, sch.1; c.16, sch.16.

ss. 60–65, repealed: 1982, c.16, sch.16.

s. 61, orders 74/1114; 76/1783; 79/930; 80/1965.

s. 63, order 75/1516.

s. 66, repealed in pt.: 1979, c.60, sch.3.

s. 67, regs. 74/1519.

s. 68, repealed: 1973, c.39, sch.1.

ss. 69–71, schs.1–4, 8, 9, 11, repealed: 1982, c.16, sch.16.

68. Representation of the People Act 1949.
repealed: 1983, c.2, sch.9.

see *James* v. *Davies* (1977) 76 L.G.R. 189, D.C.; *Webster* v. *Southwark London Borough, The Times*, November 13, 1982, Forbes J.

rules 73/166.

s. 1, see *Dumble* v. *Electoral Registration Officer for Borders*, 1980 S.L.T.(Sh.Ct.) 60.

CAP.

12, 13 & 14 Geo. 6 (1948–49)—cont.

68. Representation of the People Act 1949—cont.

ss. 1, 4, see *Scott* v. *Phillips*, 1973 S.L.T.(Notes) 75; *Scott* v. *Electoral Registration Officer for Kinross and West Perthshire*, 1980 S.L.T.(Sh.Ct.) 126.

s. 9, see *Marshall* v. *B.B.C.* (1979) 123 S.J. 336, C.A.

s. 12, see *Electoral Registration Officer for Strathclyde* v. *Boylan*, 1980 S.C. 266.

ss. 12, 13, see *Moore* v. *Electoral Registration Officer for Borders*, 1980 S.L.T.(Sh.Ct.) 39.

s. 18, order 74/243.

s. 20, regs. 74/179, 180, 1497; 79/429–431, 538, 589.

s. 29, rules 73/79, 229.

s. 37, see *Morgan* v. *Simpson* [1973] 3 W.L.R. 893; [1974] 3 W.L.R. 517; [1974] 3 All E.R. 722, C.A.; *Gunn* v. *Sharpe* [1974] 3 W.L.R. 7, D.C.; *Ruffle* v. *Rogers, The Times,* February 13, 1982, C.A.

s. 39, see *Metropolitan Properties & Co.* v. *Griffiths* (1982) 43 P. & C.R. 138, C.A.

s. 42, regs. 73/427, 1177, 1272; 74/648, 651; 75/850, 1329; 77/105, 106, 111; 78/197, 198; 79/434, 1657, 1659, 1770; 80/1031–1033, 1133; 81/63.

s. 63, see *Meek* v. *Lothian Regional Council* (O.H.), 1983 S.L.T. 494.

ss. 63, 95, see *D.P.P.* v. *Luft; Duffield* v. *D.P.P.* [1976] 3 W.L.R. 32; [1976] 2 All E.R. 569, H.L.

s. 78, rules 73/1910.

s. 91, see *Fairbairn* v. *Scottish Nationalist Party* (O.H.), April 26, 1976.

s. 95, see *Re Berry* [1978] Crim.L.R. 357, D.C.

ss. 115, 125, 137, see *R.* v. *Cripps, ex p. Muldoon* [1984] 3 W.L.R. 53, C.A.

s. 145, see *Re Berry* [1978] Crim.L.R. 357, D.C.

s. 160, Acts of Sederunt 79/516, 521, 543; S.R. 1979 No. 179.

s. 165, rules 73/79, 1910; 74/84.

s. 171, regs. 73/427, 1177, 1272; 74/648, 651; 75/850, 1329; 77/105, 106, 111; 78/197, 198; 79/434, 1657, 1679, 1770; 80/1031–1033, 1133; 81/63.

sch. 4, regs. 73/427, 1177; 74/648, 651; 75/850; 79/1770; 80/1133.

69. New Forest Act 1949.

s. 1, amended: order 76/315.

s. 9, see *Newman* v. *Bennett, The Times,* May 22, 1980, D.C.

s. 9, orders 74/1462; 81/550.

sch. 1, amended: order 78/440.

70. Docking and Nicking of Horses Act 1949.

ss. 1, 2, amended: 1977, c.45, s.31, sch.6.

72. Iron and Steel Act 1949.

repealed: 1975, c.64, sch.7.

s. 40, regs. 72/27, 696, 1132, 1826; 73/478.

ss. 40, 41, amended: 1978, c.44, sch.16.

74. Coast Protection Act 1949.

s. 1, amended (S.): 1973, c.65, s.138; repealed in pt.: 1972, c.70, sch.30; 1973, c.65, sch.29(S.).

CAP.

12, 13 & 14 Geo. 6 (1948–49)—cont.

74. Coast Protection Act 1949 —cont.

s. 2, repealed in pt.: 1972, c.70, sch.30; order 85/442.

s. 3, repealed: *ibid.*; 1973, c.65, sch.29(S.).

s. 5, regs. 88/957.

s. 5, repealed in pt.: order 85/442.

s. 8, regs. 88/957.

s. 8, amended: 1975, c.76, sch.1; repealed in pt.: 1972, c.70, sch.30; order 85/442.

s. 10, amended: 1972, c.70, s.171; 1973, c.65, s.121(S.); 1980, c.65, sch.6.

s. 14, amended: 1981, c.67, sch.4; repealed in pt.: *ibid.*, sch.6.

s. 17, amended: 1984, c.54, sch.9.

s. 18, see *British Dredging (Services)* v. *Secretary of State for Wales and Monmouthshire; Hayes Metals* v. *Same* [1975] 1 W.L.R. 687.

s. 18, amended: 1987, c.49, sch.1.

s. 20, amended: 1972, c.70, sch.29; 1973, c.65, s.138(S.); 1984, c.54, sch.9; repealed in pt.(S.): 1973, c.65, sch.29.

s. 21, amended: 1972, c.70, sch.29; 1984, c.54, sch.9; repealed in pt.: 1972, c.70, sch.30; 1973, c.65, sch.29(S.).

s. 22, amended: *ibid.*, s.138; repealed in pt.: 1972, c.70, sch.30.

s. 27, amended: 1981, c.67, sch.4.

s. 29, repealed in pt.: 1972, c.70, sch.30; 1973, c.65, sch.29(S.).

s. 30, amended (S.): *ibid.*, s.138; repealed in pt.: 1972, c.70, sch.30.

ss. 34, 36, amended: 1988, c.12, s.36.

s. 36A, added: *ibid.*

s. 42, repealed: 1972, c.70, sch.30; 1973, c.65, sch.29(S.).

s. 42, repealed: *ibid.*; 1973, c.65, sch.29(S.).

s. 45, amended (S.): *ibid.*, s.138; repealed in pt.: 1972, c.70, sch.30.

s. 46, amended (S.): 1973, c.65, s.138.

s. 47, amended: 1979, c.46, sch.4; 1981, c.38, sch.3.; 1984, c.12, sch.4.

s. 49, regs.99/957.

s. 49, amended: 1987, c.49, sch.1; 1988, c.12, s.36; repealed in pt.: 1972, c.70, sch.30; 1973, c.65, sch.29(S.).

sch. 1, amended (S.): *ibid.*, s.138; repealed in pt.: 1972, c.70, sch.30.

sch. 2, repealed in pt.: order 85/442.

sch. 4, regs. 83/1203, 1503.

75. Agricultural Holdings (Scotland) Act 1949.

s. 2, see *Gairneybridge Farm and King,* 1974 S.L.T.(Land Ct.) 8; *Maclean* v. *Galloway,* 1979 S.L.T.(Sh.Ct.) 32; *Love* v. *Montgomerie,* 1982 S.L.T.(Sh.Ct.) 60.

s. 5, see *Haggart and Brown, Joint Applicants,* 1983 S.L.C.R. 13.

s. 5, see *Cormack* v. *McIldowie,* 1972 S.L.T.(Notes) 40.

s. 7, see *Stroyan* v. *McEwan,* 1971 S.L.C.R.App. 104; *Witham* v. *Stockdale,* 1981 S.L.T.(Land Ct.) 27; *Dunbar and Anderson, Joint Applicants,* 1985 S.L.C.R. 1; *Kinnaird Trust and Boyne, Joint Applicants,* 1985 S.L.C.R. 19; *MacKenzie* v. *Bocardo S.A.,* 1986 S.L.C.R. 53;

12, 13 & 14 Geo. 6 (1948–49)—cont.

75. Agricultural Holdings (Scotland) Act 1949— *cont.*

McGill v. *Bury Management*, 1986 S.L.C.R. 32; *Buccleuch Estates and Kennedy*, 1986 S.L.C.R. 1; *Strathclyde Regional Council v. Arneil*, 1988 S.L.T.(Land Ct.) 2; *British Aluminium Co. and Shaw*, 1987 S.L.C.R. 1; *National Coal Board v. Wilson*, 1987 S.L.C.R. 15; *Shand v. Trustees of the Late Major S. F. Christie*, 1987 S.L.C.R. 29.

s. 7, amended: 1983, c.46, s.2; repealed in pt.: *ibid.*, sch.2; S.L.R. 1986.

s. 9, see *Cormack v. McIldowie*, 1972 S.L.T.(Notes) 40.

s. 15, amended: regs. 77/2007.

s. 17, regs. 79/799.

s. 20, see *Coats v. Logan* (O.H.), 1985 S.L.T. 221; *Macrae v. MacDonald*, 1986 S.L.C.R. 69.

ss. 20, 21, see *Reid's Trs. v. Macpherson* (O.H.), 1975 S.L.T.(Notes) 18; *Rotherwick's Trs. v. Hope* (O.H.), 1975 S.L.T. 187.

s. 21, see *Garvie's Trs. v. Still*, 1972 S.L.T. 29; *Garvie's Trs. v. Garvie's Tutors* (O.H.), 1975 S.L.T. 94; *Morrison-Low v. Paterson* (H.L.), 1985 S.L.T. 255; *Coats v. Logan* (O.H.), 1985 S.L.T. 221.

s. 24, see *Mackie v. Gardner*, 1973 S.L.T.(Land Ct.) 11; *Gemmell v. Andrew*, 1975 S.L.T.(Land Ct.) 5; *Gilmour v. Cook*, 1975 S.L.T. (Land Ct.) 10; *Austin v. Gibson*, 1979 S.L.T.(Land Ct.) 12; *Milne v. The Earl of Seafield*, 1981 S.L.T.(Sh.Ct.) 37; *Crawford v. Dun*, 1981 S.L.T.(Sh.Ct.) 66; *Morrison's Exrs. v. Rendall*, 1986 S.L.T. 227.

s. 25, see *Barns Graham v. Lamont*, 1971 S.L.T. 341; *Nicholl's Trustees v. Maclarty*, 1971 S.L.C.R.App. 85; *Gordon v. Rankin*, 1972 S.L.T.(Land Ct.) 7; *Allan-Fraser's Trs. v. Macpherson*, 1981 S.L.T.(Land Ct.) 17; *Smoor v. Macpherson*, 1981 S.L.T. (Land Ct.) 25; *Luss Estates Co. v. Colquhoun*, 1982 S.L.C.R. 3; *Ritson v. McIntyre*, 1982 S.L.C.R. 13.

s. 25, amended: 1983, c.46, s.3.

ss. 25, 26, see *Skinner v. Cooper*, 1971 S.L.C.R.App. 83; *Geddes v. Mackay*, 1971 S.L.C.R.App. 94; *Gemmell v. Robert Hodge & Sons*, 1974 S.L.T.(Land Ct.) 2; *Altyre Estate Trs. v. McLay*, 1975 S.L.T.(Land Ct.) 12; *Austin v. Gibson*, 1979 S.L.T.(Land Ct.) 12; *Somerville v. Watson*, 1980 S.L.T.(Land Ct.) 14; *Hutchison v. Buchanan*, 1980 S.L.T.(Land Ct.) 17; *Eagle Star Insurance Co. v. Simpson*, 1984 S.L.T.(Land Ct.) 37; *McRobbie v. Halley*, 1984 S.L.C.R. 10; *Edmondton v. Smith*, 1986 S.L.C.R. 97.

s. 26, see *Arbroath Town Council v. Carrie*, 1972 S.L.C.R.App. 114; *Gemmell v. Andrew*, 1975 S.L.T.(Land Ct.) 5; *Allan-Fraser's Trs. v. Macpherson*, 1981 S.L.T.(Land Ct.) 17; *Leask v. Grains*, 1981 S.L.T.(Land Ct.) 11; *Smoor v. Macpherson*, 1981 S.L.T.(Land Ct) 25; *Ritson v. McIntyre*, 1982 S.L.C.R. 13; *Macdonald's Exrs. v. Taylor*, 1984 S.L.T.(Land Ct.) 49; *Prior v. J. & A. Henderson*, 1984 S.L.T.(Land Ct.)

12, 13 & 14 Geo. 6 (1948–49)—cont.

75. Agricultural Holidings (Scotland) Act 1949— *cont.*

51; *Peace v. Peace*, 1984 S.L.T.(Land Ct.) 6; *Clamp v. Sharp*, 1985 S.L.R.C. 95; *Lindsay MacDougall v. Peterson*, 1987 S.L.C.R. 59.

s. 26, amended: 1983, c.46, s.4.

s. 26A, see *Trustees of the Main Calthorpe Settlement v. Calder*, 1988 S.L.T.(Land Ct.) 30; *Macdonald v. Macrae*, 1987 S.L.C.R. 72.

s. 26A, added: 1983, c.46, s.4.

s. 27, see *Gemmell v. Robert Hodge & Sons*, 1974 S.L.T.(Land Ct.) 2.

s. 28, see *McCrindle v. Andrew*, 1972 S.L.C.R.App. 117; *Austin v. Gibson*, 1979 S.L.T.(Land Ct.) 12; *Ross v. Donaldson*, 1983 S.L.T.(Land Ct.) 26; *Sinclair v. Mackintosh*, 1983 S.L.T.(Land Ct.) 29; *Buchanan v. Buchanan*, 1983 S.L.T.(Land Ct.) 31; *McGill v. Bichan*, 1982 S.L.C.R. 33; *Luss Estates Co. v. Firkin Farm Co.*, 1984 S.L.C.R. 1; *Jedlitschka v. Fuller*, 1985 S.L.C.R. 90.

s. 31, see *Gordon v. Rankin*, 1972 S.L.T.(Land Ct.) 7.

s. 49, see *MacEwen and Law*, 1986 S.L.C.R. 109.

s. 52, see *Renwick v. Rodger*, 1988 S.L.T.(Land Ct.) 23.

s. 63, amended: regs. 77/2007.

s. 68, see *Cormack v. McIldowie's Exors.*, 1974 S.L.T. 178.

s. 70, amended: 1980, c.45, sch.10.

s. 74, see *Taylor v. Brick* (O.H.), August 11, 1978; *Craig, Applicant*, 1981 S.L.T.(Land Ct.) 12; *Love v. Montgomerie*, 1982 S.L.T.(Sh.Ct.) 60; *Exven v. Lumsden*, 1982 S.L.T.(Sh.Ct.) 105.

s. 75, see *Aberdeen Endowments Trust v. Will*, 1985 S.L.T.(Land Ct.) 23; *Earl of Seafield v. Stewart*, 1985 S.L.T.(Land Ct.) 35; *Macgregor v. Glencruitten Trust*, 1985 S.L.C.R. 77.

s. 75, amended: 1983, c.46, s.5.

s. 78, see *Craig, Applicant*, 1981 S.L.T. (Land Ct.) 12; *Witham and Stockdale*, 1981 S.L.T.(Land Ct.) 27.

s. 79, order 78/798.

s. 82, amended: 1980, c.45, sch.10.

s. 93, see *Gordon v. Rankin*, 1972 S.L.T.(Land Ct.) 7; *Mackie v. Gardner*, 1973 S.L.T.(Land Ct.) 11; *Cromack v. McIldowie's Exors*, 1974 S.L.T. 178; *Austin v. Gibson*, 1979 S.L.T.(Land Ct.) 12; *Crawford v. Dun*, 1981 S.L.T. (Sh.Ct.) 66.

sch. 1, repealed in pt.: order 78/798.

sch. 6, see *Johnson v. Gill*, 1978 S.C. 74; *Earl of Seafield v. Stewart*, 1985 S.L.T.(Land Ct.) 35; *Suggett v. Shaw*, 1985 S.L.C.R. 80.

sch. 6, instrument 79/800; order 83/1073.

sch. 6, amended: 1983, c.46, s.5.

sch. 8, repealed in pt.: S.L.R. 1973.

sch. 9, see *Trustees of the Main Calthorpe Settlement v. Calder*, 1988 S.L.T.(Lands Ct.) 30; *MacDonald v. Macrae*, 1987 S.L.C.R. 72.

sch. 9, added: 1983, c.46, s.4, sch.1.

CAP.

12, 13 & 14 Geo. 6 (1948–49)—cont.

76. Marriage Act 1949.
s. 1, amended: 1986, c.16, sch.1.
s. 3, rules 74/706.
s. 3, amended: 1975, c.72, sch.3; 1978, c.22, sch.2; 1979, c.55, sch.2; 1987, c.42, sch.2.
s. 5, amended: 1986, c.16, sch.1.
s. 5A, added: *ibid.*, s.3.
s. 15, amended: order 88/165.
s. 16, amended: 1986, c.16, sch.1; 1987, c.42, sch.2; repealed in pt.: S.L.R. 1975.
s. 17, amended: 1983, c.32, sch.1.
s. 20, repealed in pt.: 1986, No. 3, sch.5.
s. 23, repealed in pt.: 1986, c.7, s.1.
ss. 25, 26, amended: 1983, c.32, sch.1.
s. 27, regs. 74/572; 84/460, 461; 86/1442, 1445; order 87/50.
s. 27, amended: 1983, c.32, sch.1; orders 75/1291; 77/1861; 81/241; 82/222.
s. 27A, regs. 84/460, 461; 86/1442, 1445.
s. 27A, added: 1983, c.32, sch.1.
s. 27B, regs. 86/1442, 1445.
ss. 27B, 27C, added: 1986, c.16, sch.1.
s. 28, amended: 1987, c.42, sch.2.
s. 31, regs. 74/572; 84/460, 461; 86/1442, 1445.
s. 32, regs. 74/572; 86/1442, 1445; order 87/50.
s. 32, amended: orders 75/1291; 77/1861; 81/1241; 82/222; repealed in pt.: S.L.R. 1975.
s. 34, amended: 1983, c.32, sch.1.
s. 35, regs. 74/572; 86/1442, 1445.
s. 37, amended: 1977, c.15, sch.2; 1983, c.32, sch.1; repealed in pt.: 1977, c.15, sch.3.
s. 38, amended: 1983, c.32, sch.1.
s. 39, amended: *ibid.*; 1986, c.16, sch.1.
s. 41, order 87/50.
s. 41, amended: orders 75/1291; 77/1861; 81/241.
s. 45A, added: 1983, c.32, sch.1.
ss. 46, 49, 50, amended: *ibid.*
s. 51, order 87/50.
s. 51, amended: 1983, c.32, sch.1; orders 75/1291; 77/1861; 81/241; 82/222.
s. 53, amended: 1983, c.32, sch.1.
s. 55, regs. 74/572; 84/460, 461; 86/1442, 1445.
s. 55, amended: 1983, c.32, sch.1.
s. 57, regs. 86/1442.
s. 57, amended: 1972, c.70, sch.29; orders 75/1291; 77/1861; 81/241.
s. 59, amended: 1983, c.32, sch.1.
ss. 63–65, amended: orders 75/1291; 77/1861; 81/241; 82/222.
s. 67, amended: 1983, c.32, sch.1.
s. 68, amended: 1981, c.55, sch.3; repealed in pt.: 1975, c.72, sch.4; 1981, c.55, sch.5.
s. 74, regs. 74/572, 573; 84/460, 461; 86/1442, 1444, 1445.
s. 74, amended: 1978, c.52, sch.11.
s. 75, amended: 1983, c.32, sch.1.
s. 76, regs. 86/1442.
s. 78, amended: 1983, c.32, sch.1; 1986, c.16, sch.1; 1987, c.42, sch.2.
sch. 1, amended: 1975, c.72, sch.3; 1986, c.16, sch.1; repealed in pt.: *ibid.*
sch. 2, amended: 1975, c.72, sch.3; 1987, c.42, s.9, sch.2.

CAP.

12, 13 & 14 Geo. 6 (1948–49)—cont.

76. Marriage Act 1949—cont.
sch. 3, repealed: 1981, c.55, sch.5.
sch. 6, repealed in pt.: 1986, c.7, s.1.
78. Married Women (Restraint upon Anticipation) Act 1949.
s. 1, repealed in pt.: S.L.R. 1975.
81. British North America (No.2) Act 1949.
repealed: 1982, c.11, sch.
84. War Damaged Sites Act 1949.
repealed: S.L.R. 1986.
86. Electoral Registers Act 1949.
repealed: 1983, c.2, sch.9.
87. Patents Act 1949.
see *Beechams Group* v. *Bristol Laboratories* [1973] F.S.R. 546; *I.C.O.S.'s Application* [1977] F.S.R. 551; *Associated British Combustion's Application* [1978] R.P.C. 582, C.A.; *Wavin Pipes* v. *The Hepworth Iron Co.* [1982] F.S.R. 32, Costello J.; *Agfa-Gevaert (Engelsmann) AG Application* [1982] R.P.C. 441, Falconer J.
s. 1, see *Engel and Anderson's Application* [1978] R.P.C. 608, Whitford J.; *Canon K. K.'s Application* [1980] R.P.C. 133, Graham J.; *Polaroid Corp. (Land's) Patent* [1981] R.P.C. 11, C.A.; *Dehle's Design Applications* [1982] R.P.C. 526, Registered Designs Appeal Tribunal; *Ishihara Sangyo Kaisha* v. *Dow Chemical Co.* [1987] F.S.R. 137, C.A.
s. 3, see *Mediline A.G.'s Patent* [1973] R.P.C. 91; *Re R, B & F's Application* [1976] R.P.C. 680, C.A.; *A.B.C.'s Application* [1978] F.S.R. 289, C.A.
s. 4, see *Illinois Tool Works* v. *Autobars* [1972] F.S.R. 67; *U.C.B. Société Anonyme's Application* [1973] F.S.R. 433, Graham J.; *Beloit Corporation's Application (No. 2)* [1974] R.P.C. 478; *Pfizer Incorporated (Dezeeuw's) Application* [1974] R.P.C. 689; *Microcell's Application* [1977] F.S.R. 163; *Raychem Corp.'s Application* [1977] F.S.R. 155; *Beecham Group* v. *Bristol Laboratories* [1978] R.P.C. 153, H.L.; *Fuji Photo Film Co. (Kiritani's) Application* [1978] R.P.C. 413, Whitford J.; *Holtite* v. *Jost (Great Britain)* [1979] R.P.C. 81, H.L.; *American Cyanamid Co.* v. *Ethicon* [1979] R.P.C. 215, Graham J.; *Dunlop Holding's Application* [1979] R.P.C. 523, C.A.; *Garcock Inc.'s Application* [1979] F.S.R. 604, Whitford J.; *Canon K.K.'s Application* [1980] R.P.C. 133, Graham J.; *Monsanto Co.* v. *Maxwell Hart (London)* [1981] R.C.C. 201, Graham J.; *Standard Brands Incorporated's Patent (No. 2)* [1981] R.P.C. 499, C.A.; *Poseidon Industri AB* v. *Cerosa* [1982] F.S.R. 209, C.A.; *Proctor & Gamble's Application* [1982] R.P.C. 473, C.A.
s. 5, see *C.I.B.A.'s Patent* [1971] F.S.R. 616; *Daikin Kogyo Kabushiki Kaisha's Patent* [1973] R.P.C. 101; *Farbenfabriken Bayer A.G. (Zirngibl's) Application* [1973] R.P.C. 698; *Stauffer Chemical Co.'s Application* [1977] R.P.C. 33, C.A.; *Hughes Tool Co.* v. *Ingersoll-Rand Co.* [1977] F.S.R. 406, Graham J.; *Canon K.K.'s*

CAP.
12, 13 & 14 Geo. 6 (1948–49)—cont.
87. Patents Act 1949—cont.

Application [1980] R.P.C. 133, Graham J.; *International Paint Co's Application* [1982] R.P.C. 247, C.A.; *Dehle's Design Applications* [1982] R.P.C. 526, Registered Designs Appeal Tribunal; *Ishihara Sangyo Kaisha* v. *Dow Chemical Co.* [1987] F.S.R. 137, C.A.

s. 6, see *Armstrong-Krupp Development Corporation's Applications* [1974] R.P.C. 268; *D's Application* [1974] F.S.R. 291; [1975] R.P.C. 447; *Standard Magnet A.G.'s Application* [1974] F.S.R. 393, D.C.; *Re R, B & F's Application* [1976] R.P.C. 680, C.A.; *Re S.'s Application* [1977] R.P.C. 367, C.A.; *A.B.C.'s Application* [1978] F.S.R. 289, C.A.; *American Cyanamid Co.* v. *Ethicon* [1979] R.P.C. 215, Graham J.; *V.'s Application* [1981] R.P.C. 245, C.A.; *T's Application* [1982] F.S.R. 173, C.A.

s. 6, amended: 1977, c.37, sch.1.

s. 7, see *Koch-Light Laboratories Application* [1978] R.P.C. 291, Whitford J.; *Dehle's Design Applications* [1982] R.P.C. 526, Registered Designs Appeal Tribunal.

s. 9, see *Institut Francais du Petrole des Carburants et Lubrifiants (Cosyns') Application* [1973] R.P.C. 891; *Xerox Corp. (Chatterji's) Application* [1979] R.P.C. 375, Whitford J.

s. 10, see *Ashe Chemical's Application* [1972] R.P.C. 613.

s. 11, repealed in pt.: 1977, c.37, sch.1.

s. 12, see *D's Application* [1974] F.S.R. 291; [1975] R.P.C. 447; *Re S.'s Application* [1977] R.P.C. 367, C.A.; *A.B.C.'s Application* [1978] F.S.R. 289, C.A.; *V's Application* [1981] R.P.C. 245, C.A.; *T's Application* [1982] F.S.R. 173, C.A.

s. 13, see *General Tire & Rubber Co.* v. *Firestone Tyre & Rubber Co.* [1975] 1 W.L.R. 819; [1975] 2 All E.R. 173, H.L.; *Re S.'s Application* [1977] R.P.C. 367, C.A.; *Sevcon* v. *Lucas CAV* [1986] 1 W.L.R. 462, H.L.

s. 13, amended: 1988, c.48, sch.5.

s. 14, see *Kessler's (J.) Application* [1971] F.S.R. 393; [1971] R.P.C. 360; *Union Carbide's Application* [1972] R.P.C. 854; *R.* v. *Patents Appeal Tribunal* [1973] 2 W.L.R. 66, C.A.; *Daikin Kogyo Kabushiki Kaisha's Patent* [1973] R.P.C. 101; *Westinghouse Electric Corporation (Frost's) Application* [1973] R.P.C. 173; *Jacques Kessler's Application* [1973] F.S.R. 189, Whitford J.; *Daikin Kogyo Co. (Shingu's) Application* [1973] F.S.R. 272, C.A.; *Technic Incorporated's Application* [1973] R.P.C. 383, C.A.; *Minnesota Mining and Manufacturing Co. (Vogel's) Application* [1973] R.P.C. 578, Whitford J.; *E. I. Du Pont de Nemours & Co. (Chantrys') Application* [1974] R.P.C. 484; *Bristol-Myers Co.* v. *Beecham Group* [1974] 2 W.L.R. 79; [1974] 1 All E.R. 333, H.L.; *Imperial Chemical Industries (Haggis') Application* [1975] R.P.C. 403, C.A.; *Templeborough Rolling Mills' Application* [1975] R.P.C. 511, C.A.; *Colgate-Palmolive Co. (Hendrickson's Application)* [1977] R.P.C. 233; *Badische Anilin and*

CAP.
12, 13 & 14 Geo. 6 (1948–49)—cont.
87. Patents Act 1949—cont.

Soda Fabrik A.G. (Distiller's) Application [1977] F.S.R. 137; *Tetra Molectric's Application* [1976] F.S.R. 424, C.A.; *General Electric Co. (Cox's) Patent* [1977] R.P.C. 421, C.A.; *L. B. Holliday & Co.'s Application* [1977] F.S.R. 391, Whitford J.; *Globe Industries Corp.'s Patent* [1977] R.P.C. 563, C.A.; *Muto Industrial Co.'s Application* [1978] R.P.C. 70, Graham J.; *Asea Aktiebolag's Application* [1978] F.S.R. 115, Whitford J.; *Amchem Products Inc.'s Patent* [1978] R.P.C. 271, Whitford J.; *Fuji Photo Film Co. (Kiritani's) Application* [1978] R.P.C. 413, Whitford J.; *Bristol-Myers Co.* v. *Beecham Group* [1978] F.S.R. 553, Sup.Ct. of Israel; *General Tyre and Rubber Co. (Hofelt & Corl's) Application* [1977] F.S.R. 402, Whitford J.; *Dunlop Holding's Application* [1979] R.P.C. 523, C.A.; *BOC International's Application* [1980] R.P.C. 122, Graham J.; *Canon K.K.'s Application* [1980] R.P.C. 133, Graham J.; *Standard Oil Co. (Fahrig's) Application* [1980] R.P.C. 359, Whitford J.; *Blendax-Werke's Application* [1980] R.P.C. 491, Graham J.; *Polaroid Corp. (Land's) Patent* [1980] R.P.C. 441, Whitford J.; *Standard Brands Incorporated Patent (No. 2)* [1981] R.P.C. 499, C.A.; *E.I. Du Pont De Nemours & Co. (Witsiete's) Application* [1982] F.S.R. 303, H.L.; *Hauni-Werke Korber & Co. K.G.'s Application* [1982] R.P.C. 327, C.A.; *International Paint Co's Application* [1982] R.P.C. 247, C.A.; *Proctor & Gamble's Application* [1982] R.P.C. 473, C.A.; *Canon K. K.'s Application* [1982] R.P.C. 549, Whitford J.; *Jamesigns (Leeds) Application* [1983] R.P.C. 68, C.A.; *Re Wheatley's Application* (1984) 81 L.S.Gaz. 741, C.A.

s. 14, repealed: 1977, c.37, schs.3,6.

s. 15, see *Ford Motor Co. (Lee's) Application* [1974] F.S.R. 30.

ss. 16(6), 18, repealed: 1977, c.37, sch.6.

s. 21, see *Illinois Tool Works* v. *Autobars* [1972] F.S.R. 67.

s. 22, see *Dutton's Patent* [1972] R.P.C. 216; *Convex's Patent* [1980] R.P.C. 423, C.A.

s. 22, amended: 1977, c.37, sch.1; repealed in pt.: *ibid.*, sch.6.

s. 23, see *National Research Patent* [1972] F.S.R. 157; *N.R.D.C.'s Patent (No. 2)* [1977] F.S.R. 76; *Hoechst A.G.'s Patent Extension* [1977] R.P.C. 521, Graham J.; *Hovercraft Development's Patent Extension* [1979] F.S.R. 481, Whitford J.; *Golden Promise Spring Barley* [1981] F.S.R. 562, Plant Varieties and Seeds Tribunal; *J.R. Geigy A.G.'s Irish Patent Extension* [1982] F.S.R. 278, Costello J.

s. 23, repealed in pt.: 1977, c.37, sch.6.

s. 24, see *E. I. Du Pont's War Loss Extension Application* [1975] R.P.C. 1; *Brupal* v. *Sandford Marine Products* [1983] R.P.C. 61, C.A.

s. 24, repealed in pt.: 1977, c.37, s.6.

s. 25, see *Sterling-Winthrop Group's War Loss Extension Application* [1976] R.P.C. 400.

CAP.

12, 13 & 14 Geo. 6 (1948–49)—cont.

87. Patents Act 1949—*cont.*

s. 26, see *Hughes Tool Co.* v. *Ingersoll-Rand Co.* [1977] F.S.R. 406, Graham J.; *Aktiebolaget Celloplast's Application* [1978] R.P.C. 239, Whitford J.; *Hauni-Werke Korber & Co. K.G.'s Application* [1982] R.P.C. 327, C.A.

s. 26, amended: 1977, c.37, sch.1.

s. 27, see *Dutton's Patent* [1972] R.P.C. 216; *Minnesota Mining* v. *Bondina* [1972] F.S.R. 331; *KSM Products Incorporated's Patents* [1974] R.P.C. 229; *Re Cousins' Application* [1976] R.P.C. 587; *Dynamics Research and Manufacturing Inc.'s Patent* [1980] R.P.C. 179, Whitford J.; *Convex's Patent* [1980] R.P.C. 423, C.A.

s. 27, repealed: 1977, c.37, sch.6.

s. 29, see *Westinghouse Application* [1972] F.S.R. 47; *Owens-Corning Fiberglas Corpn.'s Application* [1973] F.S.R. 451, Whitford J.; *Fossco International Patent* [1976] F.S.R. 244; *Re S.'s Application* [1977] R.P.C. 367, C.A.; *Imperial Chemical Industries (Whyte's) Patent* [1978] R.P.C. 11, Patents Appeal Tribunal; *Aktiebolaget Celloplast's Application* [1978] R.P.C. 239, Whitford J.; *S.C.M. Corp's Application* [1979] R.P.C. 341, C.A.; *Bentley Engineering Co.'s Patent* [1981] R.P.C. 361, Graham J.; *Jamesigns (Leeds) Application* [1983] R.P.C. 68, C.A.; *Donaldson Co. Inc's Patent* [1986] R.P.C. 1, Falconer J.; *Waddington's Patent* [1986] R.P.C. 158, Patent Office.

s. 30, see *Bristol-Myers Co.* v. *Beecham Group* [1974] 2 W.L.R. 79; [1974] 1 All E.R. 333, H.L.; *American Cyanamid Co. (Wilkinson and Shepherd's Patent)* [1975] F.S.R. 518; *Holtite* v. *Jost (Great Britain)* [1979] R.P.C. 81, H.L.; *American Cyanamid Co.* v. *Ethicon* [1979] R.P.C. 215, Graham J.

s. 31, see *Polymer Corporation's Patent, The* [1972] R.P.C. 39; *General Tire Patent* [1972] F.S.R. 317; *Screen Printing Machinery's Application* [1974] R.P.C. 628; *Imperial Chemical Industries (Whyte's) Patent* [1978] R.P.C. 11, Patents Appeal Tribunal; *Amchem Products Inc.'s Patent* [1978] R.P.C. 271, Whitford J.; *Holtite* v. *Jost (Great Britain)* [1979] R.P.C. 81, H.L.; *American Cyanamid Co.* v. *Ethicon* [1979] R.P.C. 215, Graham J.; *S.C.M. Corp's Application* [1979] R.P.C. 341, C.A.; *Blendax-Werke's Application* [1980] R.P.C. 491, Graham J.; *Egyt Gyogyszervegyeszeti Gyar's Patent* [1981] R.P.C. 99, Graham J.; *Dow Chemical AG* v. *Spence Bryson & Co. (No. 2)* [1982] F.S.R. 598, Falconer J.; *Donaldson Co. Inc's Patent* [1986] R.P.C. 1, Falconer J.; *P.P.G. Industries Inc.'s Patent* [1987] R.P.C. 470, C.A.

s. 32, see *General Tire & Rubber Co.* v. *Firestone Tyre & Rubber Co.* [1971] F.S.R. 417; *Minnesota Mining* v. *Bondina* [1972] F.S.R. 331; *Universal Oil Products Co.* v. *Monsanto Co.* [1973] R.P.C. 212, High Ct. of Australia; *Tetra Molectric's Application* [1976] F.S.R. 424, C.A.; *Globe Industries Corp.'s Patent*

CAP.

12, 13 & 14 Geo. 6 (1948–49)—cont.

89. Patents Act 1949—*cont.*

[1977] R.P.C. 563, C.A.; *American Cyanamid Co.* v. *Ethicon* [1977] F.S.R. 593, C.A.; *Harrison* v. *Project and Design Co. (Redcar)* [1978] F.S.R. 81, Graham J.; *Bristol-Myers Co.* v. *Beecham Group* [1978] F.S.R. 553, Sup.Ct. of Israel; *American Cyanamid Co.* v. *Ethicon* [1979] R.P.C. 215, Graham J.; *Monsanto Co.* v. *Maxwell Hart (London)* [1981] R.P.C. 201, Graham J.; *Poseidon Industri AB* v. *Cerosa* [1982] F.S.R. 209, C.A.; *E.I. Du Pont De Nemours & Co (Witsiete's) Application* [1982] F.S.R. 303, H.L.; *Dow Chemical AG* v. *Spence Bryson & Co. (No. 2)* [1982] F.S.R. 598, Falconer J.; *Canon K.K.'s Application* [1982] R.P.C. 549, Whitford J.; *Hickman* v. *Andrews* [1983] R.P.C. 147, C.A.; *Therm-A-Stor* v. *Weatherseal Windows* [1984] F.S.R. 323, C.A.; *Reckitt & Colman Products* v. *Biorex Laboratories* [1985] F.S.R. 94, Falconer J.; *Du Pont de Nemours (E.I.) & Co.* v. *Enka B.V.* [1988] F.S.R. 69, Falconer J.; *Greenwich Inc.'s Patent* [1988] R.P.C. 553, Whitford J.; *Rhone Poulenc A.G.* v. *Dikloride Herbicides* [1988] F.S.R. 282, Malaysia H.C.; *W. L. Gore & Associates Inc.* v. *Kimal Scientific Products* [1988] R.P.C. 137, Whitford J.

s. 32, amended: 1977, c.37, schs.1,3; repealed in pt.: *ibid.*, sch.6.

s. 33, see *Telesco Brophey's Patent* [1972] F.S.R. 257; *Owens-Corning Fiberglas Corporation's Patent* [1972] R.P.C. 684; *Airoil Burner Company (G.B.)'s Patent* [1973] F.S.R. 155; *Addressograph-Multigraph Corporation's Patent* [1974] R.P.C. 264; *E. I. Du Pont de Nemours Co. (Dahlstrom and Bunting's) Patent* [1975] F.S.R. 559, C.A.; *Dual Manufacturing and Engineering Inc.'s Patent* [1977] R.P.C. 189; *Fossco International Patent* [1976] F.S.R. 244; *Globe Industries Corp.'s Patent* [1977] R.P.C. 563, C.A.; *Morrish's Patent* [1977] F.S.R. 429, Whitford J.; *Hayashibara Co.* v. *Patent* [1977] F.S.R. 582, C.A.; *Standard Brands' Patent* [1980] R.P.C. 187, C.A.; *Polaroid Corp. (Land's) Patent* [1980] R.P.C. 441, Whitford J.; *Standard Brands Incorporated's Patent (No. 2)* [1981] R.P.C. 499, C.A.; *Canon K.K.'s Application* [1982] R.P.C. 549, Whitford J.

s. 33, amended: 1977, s.37, sch.1; repealed in pt.: *ibid.*, sch.6.

s. 34, see *Canon K.K.'s Application* [1982] R.P.C. 549, Whitford J.

s. 34, repealed: 1977, c.37, sch.6.

s. 35, see *R.* v. *Comptroller-General of Patents, Designs and Trade Marks, ex p. Gist-Brocades N.V., The Times,* August 5, 1985, H.L.; *Allen & Hanbury (Salbutamol) Patent* [1987] R.P.C. 327, C.A.

ss. 35, 26, see *Glaverbel's Patent* [1987] F.S.R. 153, C.A.

ss. 35–39, repealed: 1977, c.37, schs.4, 6.

ss. 37–39, see *Penn Engineering and Manufacturing Corp.'s Patent* [1972] F.S.R. 533.

CAP.

12, 13 & 14 Geo. 6 (1948–49)—cont.

87. Patents Act 1949—cont.

s. 40, repealed: 1977, c.37, schs.,6.

s. 41, see *Hoffmann-La Roche (F.) & Co. A.G.'s Patents* [1971] F.S.R. 522; [1971] R.P.C. 311; *Farbwerke Hoechst A.G. (Sturm's) Patent* [1973] R.P.C. 253, Patents Appeal Tribunal; *Hoffmann-La Roche (F.) & Co. A.G.'s Patent* [1973] R.P.C. 601, Whitford J.; *The Wellcome Foundation v. Plantex and Pharmaplantex* [1974] R.P.C. 514; *Microcell's Application* [1977] F.S.R. 163, *Hoffman-La Roche & Co. v. Harris Pharmaceuticals* [1977] F.S.R. 200, Whitford J.; *Nolan's Application* [1977] F.S.R. 425, Graham J.; *Lee Pharmaceutical's Applications* [1978] R.P.C. 51, Patents Office; *Syntex Corporation's Patent* [1986] R.P.C. 585, Whitford J.; *Allen & Hanbury (Salbutamol) Patent* [1987] R.P.C. 327, C.A.; *Shirley Inc.'s Patent* [1988] R.P.C. 97, Whitford J.

ss. 41, 42, repealed: 1977, c.37, schs.3,4,6.

s. 43, repealed: *ibid.*, schs.4,6.

s. 44, see *Tetra Molectric's Application* [1976] F.S.R. 424, C.A.

ss. 44, 45, repealed: 1977, c.37, schs.4,6.

ss. 46, 47, see *Microcell's Application* [1977] F.S.R. 163.

s. 47, amended: 1988, c.48, sch.7.

ss. 50, 51, see *Ralph M. Parsons Co. (Beavon's) Application* [1978] F.S.R. 226, Patents Office.

s. 51, see *Re Perard Engineering (Hubbard's) Application* [1976] R.P.C. 36, C.A.; *Monsanto v. Stauffer Chemical Co.* [1985] F.S.R. 55, Falconer J.

ss. 51, 52, see *International Paint Co's Application* [1982] R.P.C. 247, C.A.

s. 52, see *Letraset v. Rexel* [1975] F.S.R. 62, C.A.

s. 53, see *X's Application* [1982] F.S.R. 143, C.A.

s. 54, repealed: 1977, c.37, sch.6.

s. 57, see *Solar Thomson Engineering Co. v. Barton* [1977] R.P.C. 537, C.A.

s. 57, repealed: 1977, c.37, sch.6.

s. 58, see *Hansen v. Magnavox Electronics Co.* [1977] R.P.C. 301, C.A.

s. 58, repealed: 1977, c.37, sch.6.

s. 59, see *Illinois Tool Works v. Autobars* [1972] F.S.R. 67; *Lancer Boss v. Henley Forklift Co. and H. & M. Sideloaders* [1974] F.S.R. 14.

ss. 59, 60, see *Codex Corp. v. Racal-Milgo* [1983] R.P.C. 369, C.A.

s. 62, see *David Kahn Inc. v. Conway Stewart & Co.* [1974] R.P.C. 279.

s. 63, see *Morton-Norwich Products v. Intercen (No.2); Same v. United Chemicals (London)* [1981] F.S.R. 337, Graham J.

s. 65, see *Alpi Pietro e figlio v. Wright (John) & Sons (Veneers)* [1971] F.S.R. 510; *Speedcranes v. Thomson* (O.H.) 1972 S.L.T. 226; 1972 S.C. 324, Lord Emslie, Outer House; *Cerosa v. Poseidon Industries A.B.* [1973] F.S.R. 223, Whitford J.; *Bristol-Myers Co. v. Beecham Group* [1974] 2 W.L.R. 79; [1974] 1 All E.R. 333, H.L.; *Scherer v. Counting Instruments* [1977] F.S.R. 569, Whitford J.

CAP.

12, 13 & 14 Geo. 6 (1948–49)—cont.

87. Patents Act 1949—cont.

s. 66, see *Hoe-Crabtree v. Miehle-Goss-Dexter* [1971] F.S.R. 502; *Mallory Metallurgical Products v. Black Siwall and Bryson Inc.* [1977] R.P.C. 321, C.A.; *Plasticisers v. Pixdane* [1978] F.S.R. 595, D. W. Falconer, Q.C.; *Martinez's Patent* [1983] R.P.C. 307, Patent Office; *Reckitt & Colman Products v. Biorex Laboratories* [1985] F.S.R. 94, Falconer J.

s. 68, orders 72/972; 73/773; 74/2146; 75/2195; 76/1785; 77/1633, 1634, 2161; 78/187.

s. 68, repealed: 1977, c.37, sch.6.

ss. 68, 69, see *Dehle's Design Applications* [1982] R.P.C. 526, Registered Designs Appeal Tribunal.

s. 69, see *American Cyanamid Co. v. Ethicon* [1979] R.P.C. 215, Graham J.; *Ishihara Sangyo Kaisha v. Dow Chemical Co.* [1987] F.S.R. 137, C.A.

s. 70, repealed: 1977, c.37, sch.6.

ss. 71, 72, repealed: 1977, c.37, schs.3,6.

ss. 73–75, 77–79, repealed: 1977, c.37, sch.6.

s. 76, see *Mobil Oil Corporation (Ciric's) Application* [1974] R.P.C. 507.

s. 81, see *Re S.'s Application* [1977] R.P.C. 367, C.A.

ss. 81–86, repealed: 1977, c.37, sch.6.

s. 85, see *Bristol-Myers Co. v. Beecham Group* [1978] F.S.R. 553, Sup.Ct. of Israel.

s. 85, order 73/164.

s. 87, see *Imperial Chemical Industries (Haggis') Application* [1975] R.P.C. 403, C.A.; *Templeborough Rolling Mills' Application* [1975] R.P.C. 511, C.A.; *Hauni-Werke Korber & Co. K.G.'s Application* [1982] R.P.C. 327, C.A.; *International Paint Co's Application* [1982] R.P.C. 247, C.A.

s. 87, repealed in pt.: 1977, c.37, sch.6.

ss. 88–91, 93, repealed: *ibid.*

s. 94, see *Morrish's Patent* [1977] F.S.R. 429, Whitford J.

s. 94, rules 73/66; 74/87; 75/371, 891, 1021, 1262, 1467.

ss. 94, 95, 97–99, repealed: 1977, c.37, sch.6.

s. 99, rules 74/87; 75/371, 891, 1262.

s. 100, see *Tetra Molectric's Application* [1976] F.S.R. 424, C.A.; *Raychem Corp.'s Application* [1977] F.S.R. 155.

s. 100, repealed: 1977, c.37, sch.6.

s. 101, see *Rhodes' Application* [1973] R.P.C. 243, Patents Appeal Tribunal; *Jacques Kessler's Application* [1973] F.S.R. 189, Whitford J.; *Burroughs Corporation's Application* [1973] F.S.R. 439, D.C.; *Bio-Digital Sciences Incorporated's Application* [1973] R.P.C. 668; *Calmic Engineering Co.'s Application* [1973] R.P.C. 684; *Ciba Geigy A.G. (Dürr's) Application* [1977] R.P.C. 83, C.A.; *The Upjohn Co. (Robert's) Application* [1977] R.P.C. 94, C.A.; *Nolan's Application* [1977] F.S.R. 425, Graham J.; *Lee Pharmaceutical's Applications* [1978] R.P.C. 51, Patents Office; *I.T.S. Rubber's Application* [1979] R.P.C. 318, Whitford J.; *Blendax-Werke's Application* [1980] R.P.C. 491, Graham J.; *Morton-Norwich Products v. Intercen (No. 2); Same v. United Chemicals*

12, 13 & 14 Geo. 6 (1948–49)—cont.

87. Patents Act 1949—cont.

(London) [1981] F.S.R. 337, Graham J.; Ishihara Sangyo Kaisha v. Dow Chemical Co. [1987] F.S.R. 137, C.A.

s. 101, amended: 1977, c.37, sch.1.

s. 102, repealed in pt.: ibid., sch.6.

sch. 1, repealed: ibid., sch.6.

sch. 3, repealed in pt.: ibid.

88. Registered Designs Act 1949.

text as amended: 1988, c.48, s.273, sch.4.

see Agfa-Gevaert (Engelsman) AG Application [1982] R.P.C. 441, Falconer J.; Dehle's Design Applications [1982] R.P.C. 526, Registered Designs Appeal Tribunal.; Sommer Allibert (U.K.) v. Flair Plastics, The Times, June 6, 1987, C.A.

s. 1, see Amp Inc. v. Utilux [1971] F.S.R. 572; [1972] R.P.C. 103; Aspro-Nicholas' Design Application [1974] R.P.C. 645; Lamson v. Industries' Application [1978] R.P.C. 1, Whitford J.; P. Ferrero and C.S.p.A.'s Application [1978] R.P.C. 473, Whitford J.; Cook & Hurst's Design Application [1979] R.P.C. 197, Whitford J.; Vernon & Co. Pulp Products v. Universal Pulp Containers [1980] F.S.R. 179, Megarry V.-C.; Vlisco B.V.'s Application [1980] R.P.C. 509, Design Registry; Caron International Design Application [1981] R.P.C. 179, Whitford J.; Silent Gliss International A.G. v. Module Four Curtain Rail Co. [1981] F.S.R. 423, Nourse J.; Coffey's Registered Design [1982] F.S.R. 227, C.A.; K. K. Suwa Seikosha's Design Application [1982] R.P.C. 166, Falconer J.; Kevi A/S v. Suspa-Verein U.K. [1982] R.P.C. 173, Falconer J.; Dyrno Industries Inc.'s Application [1982] R.P.C. 437, Stephen Gratwick Q.C.; Gardex v. Sorata [1986] R.P.C. 623, Falconer J.; Interlego A.G. v. Tyco Industries Inc. [1988] 3 W.L.R. 678, P.C.

s. 1, rules 84/1989.

s. 1, substituted: 1988, c.48, s.265.

ss. 1, 4, see Interlego A.C. v. Folley (Alex) (Vic.) Pty. [1987] F.S.R. 238, Whitford J.

s. 2, amended: 1988, c.48, s.267.

s. 3, see Tomy Kogyo Design Applications [1983] R.P.C. 207, Whitford J.

s. 3, rules 84/1989.

s. 3, amended: 1988, c.48, sch.3; repealed in pt.: ibid., sch.8.

s. 4, see On Tat Bakellite Electric and Metal Works Design Application [1983] R.P.C. 297, Falconer J.

s. 4, amended: 1988, c.48, sch.3.

s. 5, rules 84/1989.

s. 5, amended: 1988, c.48, sch.3; repealed in pt.: ibid., schs.3,8.

s. 6, see Bampal Materials Handling Design [1981] R.P.C. 44, Design Registry.

s. 6, amended: 1988, c.48, sch.3.

s. 7, see Caron International Design Application [1981] R.P.C. 179, Whitford J.; Weir Pumps v. C.M.L. Pumps [1984] F.S.R. 33, Whitford J.

s. 7, substituted: 1988, c.48, s.268.

12, 13 & 14 Geo. 6 (1948–49)—cont.

88. Registered Designs Act 1949—cont.

s. 8, see On Tat Bakellite Electric and Metal Works Design Application [1983] R.P.C. 297, Falconer J.

s. 8, rules, 84/1989.

s. 8, substituted: 1988, c.48, s.269.

ss. 8A, 8B, added: ibid.

s. 9, amended: ibid., sch.3.

s. 11, see Vlisco B.V.'s Application [1980] R.P.C. 509, Design Registry.

s. 11, rules 84/1989.

s. 11, amended: 1988, c.48, sch.3; repealed in pt.: ibid., schs.3, 8.

ss. 11A, 11B, added: ibid., s.270.

s. 13, orders 72/972; 73/773; 74/2146; 75/2195; 76/1785; 77/1633, 1634, 2161; 78/187; 82/162; 83/1709; 84/367, 1694; 85/173, 456, 457; 88/1856.

s. 13, repealed in pt.: S.L.R. 1986.

s. 14, see Allibert's Exploitation Application [1978] R.P.C. 261, Whitford J.

s. 14, amended: 1988, c.48, sch.3; repealed in pt.: ibid., sch.8.

ss. 15, 16, amended: ibid., sch.3.

s. 17, substituted: 1986, c.39, sch.1.

ss. 17–23, rules 84/1989.

ss. 19, 20, amended: 1988, c.48, sch.3.

s. 21, see Allibert's Exploitation Application [1978] R.P.C. 261, Whitford J.

s. 22, amended: 1988, c.48, sch.3.

s. 23, substituted: ibld.

s. 24, repealed: 1986, c.39, sch.3.

ss. 25, 25, amended: 1988, c.48, sch.3.

s. 27, substituted: ibid.

s. 28, order 73/165.

s. 28, amended: 1988, c.48, sch.3.

s. 29, see Tomy Kogyo Design Applications [1983] R.P.C. 207, Whitford J.

s. 29, amended: 1988, c.48, sch.3.

s. 30, substituted: ibid.

s. 31, rules 84/1989.

s. 31, substituted: 1988, c.48, sch.3.

s. 32, rules 84/1989.

s. 32, repealed: 1988, c.48, schs.3,8.

s. 33, amended: ibid., sch.3; repealed in pt.: ibid., schs.3,8.

ss. 34, 35, amended: ibid., sch.3.

s. 35A, added: ibid.

s. 36, rules 74/86, 2043; 75/372, 890; 78/907; 80/1794; 82/299, 86/584; 87/287; 88/856.

s. 36, amended: 1988, c.48, sch.3.

s. 37, amended: ibid.; repealed in pt.: ibid., schs.3,8.

s. 38, repealed: ibid., schs.3,8

s. 39, rules 84/1989; 87/287

s. 39, amended: 1988, c.48, sch.3.

s. 40, rules 74/86; 75/372, 890; 78/907, 1151; 80/96; 81/71; 84/1989; 85/784; 86/584; 88/856.

s. 40, amended: 1988, c.48, sch.3.

s. 42, amended: 1977, c.37, sch.5.

s. 44, amended: ibid.; 1988, c.48, sch.3; repealed in pt.: ibid., schs. 3,8.

s. 45, repealed in pt.: ibid.

CAP.

12, 13 & 14 Geo. 6 (1948–49)—cont.

88. Registered Designs Act 1949—cont.

s. 46, amended: *ibid.*, sch.3; repealed in pt.: *ibid.*, schs.3,8.

s. 47, substituted: *ibid.*, sch.3.

s. 47A, added: *ibid.*

s. 48, repealed in pt.: *ibid.*, schs.3,8.

sch. 1, amended: 1973, c.4, s.5; 1988, c.48, s.271, schs.3,8.

sch. 2, repealed: *ibid.*, schs.3,8.

92. Commonwealth (India (Consequential Provisions)) Act 1949.

s. 1, repealed in pt.: S.L.R. 1974; S.L.R. 1976.

93. National Health Service (Amendment) Act 1949.

s. 3, repealed in pt.: 1972, c.58, sch.7(S.); 1973, c.32, sch.5.

ss. 8, 10, 11, repealed: 1977, c.49, sch.16(S.); 1978, c.29, sch.17.

s. 12, repealed: 1972, c.58, sch.7(S.); 1973, c.32, sch.5.

s. 13, repealed: 1975, c.71, sch.18.

ss. 14–18, repealed: 1977, c.49, sch.16; 1978, c.29, sch.17(S.).

s. 20, repealed: 1973, c.32, sch.5; 1977, c.49, sch.16; 1978, c.29, sch.17(S.).

s. 21, repealed: 1977, c.49, sch.16; 1978, c.29, sch.17(S.).

s. 23, repealed: 1977, c.49, schs.14,16; (S.) 1978, c.29, schs.15,17.

s. 24, repealed: 1973, c.32, sch.5.

s. 25, repealed: 1977, c.49, sch.16.

s. 28, repealed: *ibid.*; 1978, c.29, sch.17(S.).

s. 29, repealed: 1972, c.58, sch.7(S.); 1973, c.32, sch.5; 1977, c.49, sch.16.

s. 32, repealed in pt.: 1977, c.49, sch.16; 1978, c.29, sch.17(S.).

sch., repealed: 1977, c.49, sch.16; 1978, c.29, sch.17(S.).

94. Criminal Justice (Scotland) Act 1949.

ss. 1–20, repealed: 1975, c.21, sch.10.

s. 2, see *McPherson* v. *Henderson*, 1984 S.C.C.R. 294.

s. 21, repealed: 1980, c.62, sch.8.

ss. 22–41, repealed: 1975, c.21, sch.10.

s. 42, amended: *ibid.*, sch.9.

ss. 43–49, 67, repealed: *ibid.*, sch.10.

s. 75, repealed in pt.: 1980, c.62, sch.8.

s. 78, repealed in pt.: 1973, c.65, schs.27,29; S.L.R. 1977.

s. 79, repealed in pt.: 1975, c.21, sch.10; S.L.R. 1977.

sch. 2, repealed: 1975, c.21, sch.10.

sch. 11, repealed in pt.: 1973, c.62, sch.6; 1975, c.21, sch.10(S.); 1976, c.35, sch.3; S.L.R. 1977.

sch. 12, repealed: S.L.R. 1977.

96. Auxiliary and Reserve Forces Act 1949.

repealed: 1980, c.9, sch.10.

97. National Parks and Access to the Countryside Act 1949.

see *R.* v. *Secretary of State for the Environment, ex p. Pearson* [1979] J.P.L. 765, D.C.

ss. 2, 4, repealed: 1981, c.69, sch.17.

ss. 8, 10, repealed: 1972, c.70, sch.30.

CAP.

12, 13 & 14 Geo. 6 (1948–49)—cont.

97. National Parks and Access to the Countryside Act 1949—cont.

s. 11, amended: 1981, c.69, s.72.

s. 13, amended: 1973, c.54, sch.1.

s. 20, see *Evans* v. *Godber* [1974] 1 W.L.R. 1317; [1974] 3 All E.R. 341, D.C.

s. 20, amended: 1984, c.12, sch.4.

s. 21, amended: 1972, c.70, sch.17; 1973, c.65, sch.27(S.); 1982, c.43, s.10(S.).

s. 22, amended: 1972, c.70, sch.17.

s. 23, amended (S.): 1973, c.65, sch.27; repealed in pt.: 1981, c.69, sch.17.

s. 25, repealed: 1973, c.54, sch.4.

s. 27, see *R.* v. *Secretary of State for the Environment, ex p. Hood* [1975] 3 W.L.R. 172, C.A.; *Suffolk County Council* v. *Mason* [1979] 2 W.L.R. 571, H.L.

ss. 27–32, repealed: 1981, c.69, sch.17.

s. 31, regs. 72/93.

ss. 31, 32, see *Armstrong* v. *Whitfield* [1973] 2 W.L.R. 720, D.C.

s. 32, see *Att.-Gen.* v. *Honeywill* [1972] 1 W.L.R. 1506; 116 S.J. 801; [1972] 3 All E.R. 641; *R.* v. *Secretary of State for the Environment, ex p. Hood* [1975] 3 W.L.R. 172, C.A.; *L. G. Walwin & Partners* v. *West Sussex C.C.* [1975] 3 All E.R. 604; *Suffolk County Council* v. *Mason* [1979] 2 W.L.R. 571, H.L.

ss. 32, 33, see *R.* v. *Secretary of State for the Environment, ex p. Stewart* (1979) 37 P. & C.R. 279, D.C.

s. 33, see *Pearson* v. *Secretary of State for the Environment* (1981) 42 P. & C.R. 40, C.A.

ss. 33–35, repealed: 1981, c.69, sch.17.

s. 37, repealed: 1980, c.65, schs.3,34.

s. 38, repealed: 1981, c.69, sch.17.

ss. 51, 52, repealed in pt.: 1972, c.70, sch.30.

s. 53, repealed in pt.: 1980, c.65, schs.7,34.

s. 57, amended: 1972, c.70, s.188, sch.21.

s. 60, amended: 1984, c.12, sch.4.

s. 61, amended: 1972, c.70, sch.17; repealed in pt.: 1980, c.65, schs.3,34.

s. 62, repealed in pt.: *ibid.*

ss. 64, 65, repealed in pt.: 1974, c.7, schs.6,8.

ss. 67, 68, amended: 1972, c.70, sch.17.

s. 69 substituted: 1980, c.65, sch.3.

s. 70, amended: 1972, c.70, sch.17.

s. 77, repealed in pt.: 1980, c.65, schs.23,34.

s. 79, repealed: *ibid.*, schs.3,34.

s. 80, repealed in pt.: *ibid.*

ss. 81, 82, amended: 1972, c.70, sch.17.

s. 89, amended: 1982, c.42, s.3; repealed in pt.: 1972, c.70, schs.17,30.

s. 90, amended: *ibid.*, sch.17; repealed in pt.: *ibid.*, schs.17,30.

s. 95, repealed: 1981, c.69, sch.17.

s. 97, repealed: 1982, c.42, ss.1,2, sch.

s. 98, repealed: 1974, c.7, schs.1,8.

s. 99, amended: 1972, c.70, sch.17; (S.) 1973, c.65, sch.27; repealed in pt.: 1972, c.70, sch.30.

s. 102, repealed: *ibid.*

s. 103, amended: 1973, c.54, sch.1; c.65, sch.27(S.); 1981, c.67, sch.4; repealed in pt.: *ibid.*, sch.6.

12, 13 & 14 Geo. 6 (1948–49)—cont.

**97. National Parks and Access to the Country-
side Act 1949**—*cont.*

s. 104, see *R.* v. *Plymouth City Council and
Cornwall County Council, ex p. Freeman*
(1988) 28 R.V.R. 89, C.A.

s. 104, amended(S.): 1973, c.65, sch.27;
repealed in pt.: *ibid.*, sch.29; 1974, c.7,
schs.6,8.

s. 105, repealed: *ibid.*

s. 106, regs. 73/1687; 75/1543, 1970;
84/918(S.).

s. 111, order 73/1395.

s. 111, amended: 1972, c.70, sch.17.

s. 111A, added: 1985, c.4, sch.3.

sch. 1, see *R.* v. *Secretary of State for the
Environment, ex p. Stewart* (1979) 37 P. &
C.R. 279, D.C.

sch. 1, amended: 1972, c.70, sch.17.

98. Adoption of Children Act 1949.

s. 13, repealed in pt.: 1975, c.72, sch.4; 1980,
c.5, sch.6.

**100. Law Reform (Miscellaneous Provisions) Act
1949.**

ss. 1, 2, repealed: S.L.R. 1975.

s. 2, see *Cabel* v. *Cabel* (O.H.), 1974 S.L.T. 295.

s. 3, see *Alex Lawrie Factors* v. *Modern Injection
Moulds, The Times*, May 19, 1981, Drake J.

s. 4, repealed in pt.: S.L.R. 1975.

s. 9, see *A.* v. *Liverpool City Council, The Times*,
May 21, 1981, H.L.

s. 9, repealed: 1981, c.54, sch.7.

ss. 10, 11 (in pt.) repealed: 1973, c.36, sch.6.

101. Justices of the Peace Act 1949.

repealed (S.): 1975, c.20, sch.2.

ss. 1, 3, 5, repealed: 1979, c.55, sch.3.

ss. 4, 6, repealed: 1973, c.15, sch.5.

s. 8, regs. 72/1401, 1425; 73/1116, 1174, 1489,
1560; 74/530, 673, 1474.

ss. 8, 10, repealed: 1973, c.15, sch.5.

s. 13, rules 78/1163.

s. 13, repealed: 1979, c.55, sch.3.

s. 15, rules 73/790, 1118, 1119; 74/444, 668,
706; 75/126, 127, 286, 300, 301, 488, 519,
2236; 76/1505, 1767–1769; 77/1174, 1175,
1890; 78/146, 147, 754, 757, 758, 869;
79/170, 570, 757, 758, 952, 953, 1220–1222,
1561; 80/108, 510, 511, 1582–1585,
1895–1897.

s. 15, amended: 1972, c.18, ss.18,21,27,39;
1973, c.29, ss.2,3, sch.4; 1976, c.36, s.66;
repealed in pt.: 1973, c.15, s.19, sch.5; 1979,
c.55, sch.3.

ss. 16, 17, repealed: 1979, c.55, sch.3.

s. 18, orders 72/1123, 1481, 1482; 73/426, 982;
74/2046; 75/90, 352, 1000, 1872; 2064;
76/139, 162, 399, 1928, 1972; 77/556, 1521,
1604, 1664; 78/644, 671, 777, 1124, 1365,
1952; 79/1284; 80/213.

s. 20, amended: 1974, c.47, sch.3; repealed in
pt.: 1972, c.70, schs.27,30; 1974, c.26, sch.3;
1979, c.55, sch.3.

ss. 21, 23, 25–27, repealed: *ibid.*

s. 27, regs. 73/579.

s. 28, repealed: 1972, c.71, s.62, sch.6.

ss. 29, 32–34, repealed: 1973, c.15, sch.5.

12, 13 & 14 Geo. 6 (1948–49)—cont.

101. Justices of the Peace Act 1949—*cont.*

ss. 36, 37, repealed: 1973, c.6, sch.6.

s. 41, repealed in pt.: 1982, c.30, sch.7; 1987,
c.19, sch.

s. 42, regs. 78/1682.

s. 42, repealed: 1979, c.55, sch.3.

s. 43, repealed in pt.: 1977, c.45, sch.13.

s. 44, repealed: 1979, c.55, sch.3.

ss. 45, 46, repealed in pt.: S.L.R. 1978.

sch. 2, repealed: 1973, c.15, sch.5.

sch. 3, repealed: 1972, c.70, sch.30.

sch. 4, regs. 73/1522.

sch. 4, repealed: 1979, c.55, sch.3.

**102. Festival of Britain (Supplementary Pro-
visions) Act 1949.**

repealed: S.L.R. 1986.

103. Parliament Act 1949.

s. 1, repealed in pt.: S.L.R. 1986.

14 Geo. 6 (1950)

**5. Newfoundland (Consequential Provisions)
Act 1950.**

repealed: 1981, c.61, sch.9.

6. Statute Law Revision Act 1950.

s. 2, repealed: 1977, c.38, sch.5.

s. 5, repealed in pt.: 1973, c.36, sch.6.

9. Merchant Shipping Act 1950.

s. 4, repealed: 1988, c.12, sch.7.

s. 7, repealed in pt.: 1983, c.21, schs.3,4.

12. Foreign Compensation Act 1950.

order 81/240.

s. 1, repealed in pt.: S.L.R. 1974.

s. 3, orders 75/410; 76/1154; 80/1720; 82/1073;
86/2222; 87/663, 2201.

s. 4, rules 72/219; order 82/1073; instruments
85/697; 88/153.

ss. 4, 8, instruments 76/1646; 82/1110; 87/143.

s. 7, orders 72/303; 73/234, 760; 74/249;
75/409; 76/220; 77/239, 2148; 78/180;
79/109; 80/186; 82/150, 1073; 83/145;
84/128; 85/168; 86/219; 87/164, 1028;
88/244.

15. Finance Act 1950.

Pt. IV (ss.43–48), repealed: 1975, c.7, schs.4,13.

s. 50, repealed in pt.: *ibid.*, sch.13.

**17. Agriculture (Miscellaneous Provisions) Act
1950.**

repealed: S.L.R. 1986.

**20. Colonial and Other Territories (Divorce Jur-
isdiction) Act 1950.**

repealed: 1986, c.55, sch.2.

21. Miscellaneous Financial Provisions Act 1950.

repealed: S.L.R. 1986.

23. Coal Mining (Subsidence) Act 1950.

repealed: S.L.R. 1973.

**24. Highways (Provision of Cattle Grids) Act
1950.**

repealed (S.): 1984, c.54, sch.11.

s. 11, repealed: 1981, c.23, schs.2,4.

27. Arbitration Act 1950.

see *Japan Line* v. *Aggeliki Charis Compania
Maritima S.A.* (1979) 123 S.J. 487, C.A.

s. 1, see *Property Investments (Development)*
v. *Byfield Building Services* (1985) 31
Build.L.R. 47, Steyn J.

14 Geo. 6 (1950)—cont.

27. Arbitration Act 1950—*cont.*

s. 3, amended: 1985, c.65, sch.8; 1986, c.45, sch.14.

s. 4, see *Phoenix* v. *Pope* [1974] 1 All E.R. 512; *The Golden Trader* [1974] 3 W.L.R. 16; [1974] 2 All E.R. 686; *Camilla Cotton Oil Co.* v. *Granadex SA and Tracomin SA; Shawnee Processors Inc.* v. *Same* [1975] 1 Lloyd's Rep. 470, C.A.; *Modern Buildings Wales* v. *Limmer and Trinidad Co.* [1975] 2 All E.R. 549, C.A.; *Paczy* v. *Haendler & Natermann GmbH* [1979] F.S.R. 420, Whitford J.; *G. Dew & Co.* v. *Tarmac Construction* (1978) 15 Build.L.R. 22, C.A.; *Turner* v. *Fenton* [1982] 1 All E.R. 8, Warner J.; *Goodman* v. *Winchester and Alton Railway* [1984] 3 All E.R. 594, C.A.; *Turner & Goudy (A Firm)* v. *McConnell* [1985] 2 All E.R. 34, C.A.; *Chatbrown* v. *Alfred McAlpine Construction (Southern)* (1987) 35 Build.L.R. 44, C.A.; *Skopos Design Group (T/A Anker Contract Carpets)* v. *Homelife Nursing, The Times,* March 24, 1988, C.A.; *Cunningham-Reid* v. *Buchanan-Jardine* [1988] 1 W.L.R. 678; [1988] 2 All E.R. 438, C.A.

s. 4, repealed in pt.: 1975, c.3, s.8.

s. 7, see *Laertis Shipping Corp.* v. *Ex Portadora Espanola de Cementos Portland S.A., The Times,* December 8, 1981, Bingham J.; *Ministry of Food, Government of Bangladesh* v. *Bengal Liner: The Bengal Pride* [1986] 1 Lloyd's Rep. 167, Leggatt J.

s. 7, order 84/1168.

s. 8, amended: 1979, c.42, s.6.

ss. 8, 9, see *Termarea S.R.L.* v. *Rederiaktiebolaget Sally* [1979] 2 All E.R. 989, Mocatta J.

s. 9, substituted: 1979, c.42, s.6.

s. 10, see *National Enterprises* v. *Racal Communications* [1974] 1 All E.R. 1118; [1974] 3 All E.R. 1010, C.A.; *Abu Dhabi Gas Liquifaction Co.* v. *Eastern Bechtel Corp.; Eastern Bechtel Corp.* v. *Ishikawajima Harima Heavy Industries, The Times,* June 24, 1982, C.A.

s. 10, amended: 1979, c.42, s.6; repealed in pt.: *ibid.,* ss.6,8; 1985, c.61, s.58.

s. 11, see *Northern Regional Health Authority* v. *Derek Crouch Construction Co.* [1984] 2 W.L.R. 676, C.A.

s. 12, see *Crawford* v. *Prowting* [1972] 2 W.L.R. 749; 116 S.J. 195; [1972] 1 All E.R. 1199; *Mavani* v. *Ralli Bros.* [1973] 1 All E.R. 555; *Bank Mellat* v. *Helleniki Techniki SA* [1983] 3 All E.R. 428, C.A.; *Vasso (Owners)* v. *Vasso (Owners of Cargo Lately Laden on Board)* [1983] 1 W.L.R. 838, Lloyd J.; *The Tuyuti* [1984] 3 W.L.R. 231, C.A.; *Dorval Tankships Pty.* v. *Two Arrows Maritime and Port Services; Pakistan Edible Oils Corp. intervening, The Times,* August 9, 1984, C.A.; *Richo International* v. *International Food Co. Sal, Financial Times,* July 13, 1988, Hirst J.

s. 14, amended: 1979, c.42, s.7.

s. 17, see *Mutual Shipping Corp. of New York* v. *Bayshore Shipping Co. of Monrovia; Montan, The* [1985] 1 All E.R. 520, C.A.

14 Geo. 6 (1950)—cont.

27. Arbitration Act 1950—*cont.*

s. 18, see *Perkins (H. G.)* v. *Brent-Shaw* [1973] 1 W.L.R. 975; [1973] 2 All E.R. 924; *Windvale* v. *Darlington Insulation Co., The Times,* December 22, 1983, Walton J.

ss. 18, 19, see *Kurkjian (SN) (Commodity Brokers)* v. *Marketing Exchange for Africa, Financial Times,* June 11, 1986, Staughton J.

s. 19A, see *Food Corp. of India* v. *Marastro Cia. Naviera S.A.; Trade Fortitude, The* [1986] 3 All E.R. 500, C.A.

s. 19A, added: 1982, c.53, s.15, sch.1.

s. 20, see *Rocco Giuseppe & Figli* v. *Tradax Export SA* [1983] 2 Lloyd's Rep. 434; [1984] 1 W.L.R. 742, Parker J.; *Continental Grain Co.* v. *Bremer Handelsgesellschaft mbH (No. 2); Deutsche Conti-Handelsgesellschaft mbH* v. *Bremer Handelsgesellschaft mbH* [1984] 2 Lloyd's Rep. 121, Bingham J.; *Coastal States Trading (U.K.)* v. *Niebro Minaeroloel GmbH* [1986] 1 Lloyd's Rep. 465, Hobhouse J.: *Knibb and Knibb* v. *National Coal Board* (1986) 26 R.V.R. 123, C.A.

s. 21, see *Halfdan Greig & Co. A/S* v. *Sterling Coal & Navigation Corp.* [1973] 2 W.L.R. 904; *Imperial Metal Industries (Kynoch)* v. *Amalgamated Union of Engineering Workers (Technical, Administrative and Supervisory Section)* [1979] I.C.R. 23, C.A.; *Antco Shipping* v. *Seabridge Shipping* [1979] 1 W.L.R. 1103, C.A.; *Glafki Shipping Co. S.A.* v. *Pinios Shipping Co. No. 1; The Maira, The Times,* October 8, 1981, C.A.; *Compagne General Maritime* v. *Diakaw Spirit SA* [1982] Com.L.R. 228, Goff J.; *Aire* v. *Phonographic Performance and the Musicians' Union* [1983] F.S.R. 637, Falconer J.

s. 21, repealed: 1979, c.42, ss.1,8.

s. 22, see *Mutual Shipping Corp. of New York* v. *Bayshore Shipping Co. of Monrovia; Montan, The* [1985] 1 All E.R. 520, C.A.; *Shield Properties & Investments* v. *Anglo-Overseas Transport Co.* (1985) 273 E.G. 69, Bingham J.; *Learmonth Property Investment Co.* v. *Hinton (Amos) & Sons* (1985) 274 E.G. 725, Walton J.; *Compagnie Nationale Algerienne de Navigation* v. *Hecate Shipping Co.* [1985] 2 Lloyd's Rep. 588, Leggatt J.

ss. 22, 23, see *Moran* v. *Lloyd's* [1983] W.L.R. 672, C.A.

s. 23, see *Prodexport* v. *Man* [1972] 3 W.L.R. 845; 116 S.J. 663; *Micklewright* v. *Mullock* (1974) 232 E.G. 337, *Modern Engineering (Bristol)* v. *C. Miskin & Son, The Times,* July 12, 1980, C.A.; *Zermat Holdings S.A.* v. *Nu-Life Upholstery Repairs* (1985) 275 E.G. 1134, Bingham J.; *Top Shop Estates* v. *C. Danino; Same* v. *Tandy Corp.* (1985) 273 E.G. 197, Leggatt J.; *Shield Properties Investments* v. *Anglo-Overseas Transport Co.* (1985) 273 E.G. 69, Bingham J.; *Cook International Inc.* v. *B.V. Handelmaat Schappij Jean Devaux, The Times,* April 10, 1985, Leggatt J.; *Agromet Motoimport* v. *Maulden Engineering Co.(Beds.)* [1985] 2 All E.R 436, Otton J.;

CAP.

14 Geo. 6 (1950)—cont.

27. Arbitration Act 1950—cont.

Tracomin S.A. v. Gibbs Nathaniel (Canada) and Bridge (George Jacob) [1985] 1 Lloyd's Rep. 586, Staughton J.

s. 24, see Camilla Cotton Oil Co. v. Granadex SA and Tracomin SA; Shawnee Processors Inc. v. Same [1975] 1 Lloyd's Rep. 470, C.A.; Paczy v. Haendler & Natermann GmbH [1979] F.S.R. 420, Whitford J.; Cunningham-Reid v. Buchanan-Jardine [1988] 1 W.L.R. 678; [1988] 2 All E.R. 438, C.A.; Ashville Investments v. Elmer Contractors (1987) 37 Build.L.R. 55, C.A.

s. 25, see Socony Mobil Oil Company Inc. v. West of England Ship Owners Mutual Insurance Association (London), The Times, June 6, 1984, Leggatt J.

s. 26, see Middlemiss Gould v. Hartlepool Corporation [1972] 1 W.L.R. 1643, C.A.; Jugoslavenska Oceanska Plovidba v. Castle Investment Co. Inc. [1973] 3 W.L.R. 847; [1973] 3 All E.R. 498, C.A.; Hall & Wodehouse v. Panorama Hotel Properties [1974] 2 Lloyd's Rep. 413, C.A.; Dalmia Cement v. National Bank of Pakistan [1974] 3 W.L.R. 138; Leonidis v. Thames Water Authority (1979) 251 E.G. 669, Parker J.; Continental Grain Co. v. Bremer Handelgesellschaft mbH (No. 2); Deutsche Conti-Handelsgesellschaft mbH v. Bremer Handelsgellschaft mbH [1984] 2 Lloyd's Rep. 121, Bingham J.; Agromet Motoimport v. Maulden Engineering Company (Beds.), The Times, April 17, 1984, Otton J.; Coastal States Trading (U.K.) v. Niebro Minaeroloel GmbH [1986] 1 Lloyd's Rep. 465, Hobhouse J.

s. 26, amended: 1977, c.38, s.17; 1984, c.28, sch.2.

s. 27, see Richmond Shipping Co. v. Agro Co. of Canada, The Simonburn (No. 2) [1973] 2 Lloyd's Rep. 145, Kerr J.; The Angeliki [1973] 2 Lloyd's Rep. 226; International Tank and Pipe S.A.K. v. Kuwait Aviation Fuelling Co. K.S.C. [1974] 3 W.L.R. 721, C.A.; Nea Agrex S.A. v. Baltic Shipping Co [1976] 2 W.L.R. 925, C.A.; Intermare Transport GmbH v. Naves Transoceanica's Amadore SA; The Aristokratis [1976] 1 Lloyd's Rep. 552; Consolidated Investment and Contracting v. Saponaria Shipping [1978] 1 W.L.R. 986, C.A.; S.I. Pension Trustees v. William Hudson (1977) 35 P. & C.R. 54, Forbes. J.; Mogul Line v. Commerce International Inc., The Times, April 19, 1980, C.A.; The American Sioux (No. 2) [1980] 1 Lloyd's Rep. 623, Sheen J.; Sioux Inc. v. China Salvage, Kwangchow Branch [1980] 1 W.L.R. 996, C.A.; H. Kruidenier (London) v. The Egyptian Navigation Co.; The El Amria (No. 2) [1980] 2 Lloyd's Rep. 166, Sheen J.; Tradax International S.A. v. Cerrahogullari T.A.S. [1981] 3 All E.R. 344, Kerr J.; Babanaft International Co. SA v. Avant Petroleum, The Times, April 23, 1982, C.A.; [1982] 1 W.L.R. 871; Federal Commerce & Navigation v. Xcan Grain (Europe); The Ratna

CAP.

14 Geo. 6 (1950)—cont.

27. Arbitration Act 1950—cont.

Vandana [1982] 1 Lloyd's Rep.499, Webster J.; C. M. Van Stillevoldt BV v. El Carriers Inc, The Times, July 8, 1982, Staughton J.; Tradax Export SA v. Italcarbo Societa Di Navigazione SpA; The Sandalion [1983] 1 Lloyd's Rep. 514, Lloyd J.; Plovidba v. Oleagine SA; The Luka Botic [1983] 3 All E.R. 602, C.A.; Chartered Trust v. Maylands Green Estate Co. (1984) 270 E.G. 845, Vinelott J.; Casillo Grani v. Napier Shipping Co. [1984] 2 Lloyd's Rep. 481, Neill J.; Tote Bookmakers v. Development and Property Holding Co. [1985] 2 W.L.R. 603, Peter Gibson J.; Davies (Graham) (U.K.) v. Rich (Marc) & Co., The Times, August 5, 1985, C.A.; European Grain & Shipping v. Dansk Landbrugs Grovvareslskab [1985] 1 Lloyd's Rep. 163, Leggatt J.; Pittallis v. Sherefettin (1986) 278 E.G. 153, C.A.; Mariana Islands Steamship Corp. v. Marimpex Mineraloel-Handelsgesellschaft mbH & Co. K.G.; Medusa, The [1986] 2 Lloyd's Rep. 328, C.A.; Irish Agricultural Wholesale Society v. Partenreederei: M.S. Eurotrader; Eurotrader, The [1987] 1 Lloyd's Rep. 418, C.A.; First Steamship Co. v. C.T.S. Commodity Transport Shipping Schiffartsgesellschaft m.b.H; Ever Splendor, The [1988] 1 Lloyd's Rep. 245, Phillips J.

s. 28, see Anico Shipping v. Seabridge Shipping [1979] 1 W.L.R. 1103, C.A.; Glafki Shipping Co. S.A. v. Pinios Shipping Co. No. 1; The Maira, The Times, October 8, 1981, C.A.; Warde v. Feedex International Inc., The Times, November 2, 1983, Staughton J.

ss. 28, 30, 31, amended: 1979, c.42, s.7; repealed in pt.: 1975, c.3, s.8.

s. 32, see Imperial Metal Industries (Kynoch) v. Amalgamated Union of Engineering Workers (Technical, Administrative and Supervisory Section) [1979] I.C.R. 23, C.A.; Excomm v. Ahmed Abdul-Qawi Barnaodah; The St. Raphael [1985] 1 Lloyd's Rep. 403, C.A.

s. 32, amended: 1979, c.42, s.7.

s. 34, repealed in pt.: 1975, c.3, s.8.

s. 35, orders 78/186; 79/304; 84/1168.

ss. 35, 36, see Dalmia Cement v. National Bank of Pakistan [1974] 3 W.L.R. 138.

Pt. II (ss.35–43), see Masinimport v. Scottish Mechanical Light Industries (O.H.) January 30, 1976; 1976 S.L.T. 245, Ct. of Session.

s. 38, amended: 1978, c.23, sch.5; 1981, c.54, sch.5.

s. 42, repealed in pt.: ibid., sch.7.

s. 43, repealed: S.L.R. 1978.

28. Shops Act 1950.

see R. v. London Committee of Deputies of British Jews, ex p. Helmcourt, The Times, July 16, 1981, A.C.; Wickes Building Supplies v. Kirklees Metropolitan Borough Council, The Times, July 30, 1983, D.C.; Wychavon District Council v. Midland Enterprises (Special Events) (1988) L.G.R. 83, Millett J.

s. 2, see Havering London Borough Council v. L. F. Stone & Son (1973) 72 L.G.R. 223, D.C.

14 Geo. 6 (1950)—cont.

28. Shops Act 1950—*cont.*

ss. 2 (in pt.), 4 (in pt.), 5, 6 (in pt.), 7, repealed: S.L.R. 1974.

s. 8, repealed in pt.: *ibid.*; 1980, c.65, schs.4,34.

ss. 9 (in pt.), 10, repealed: *ibid.*

s. 11, substituted: *ibid.*, sch.4.

s. 14, see *Havering London Borough Council v. L. F. Stone & Son* (1973) 72 L.G.R. 223, D.C.

s. 22, amended: 1973, c.32, sch.4; 1977, c.49, sch.14; 1980, c.53, sch.1; 1985, c.13, sch.2; order 85/39.

s. 35, amended: orders 75/1291, 1808; 77/1861, 1891; 81/241; 82/222.

ss. 41, 42, repealed in pt.: S.L.R. 1974.

s. 47, see *Waller v. Hardy* (1972) 116 S.J. 237; *Maby v. Warwick Corporation* [1972] 2 Q.B. 242; [1972] 3 W.L.R. 25; [1972] 2 All E.R. 1198; *Randall v. D. Turner (Garages)* [1973] 1 W.L.R. 1052; [1973] 3 All E.R. 369, D.C.; *Hudson v. Marshall* (1977) 75 L.G.R. 13, D.C.; *Stafford Borough Council v. Elkenford* [1977] 1 W.L.R. 324, C.A.; *Solihull Metropolitan Borough Council v. Maxfern* (1977) 57 L.G.R. 392, Oliver J.; *Jarmain v. Wetherell* (1977) 75 L.G.R. 537, D.C.; *Baker v. Arthurs*, February 28, 1980; Judge J. G. Baker, Q.C.; *Bradford Crown Ct.*; *Bury Metropolitan Council v. Law; Bury Metropolitan Borough Council v. Cowburn* [1983] Crim.L.R. 748, D.C.; *Stoke-on-Trent City Council v. B. & Q. (Retail)* [1983] 3 W.L.R. 78, C.A.; *Barking and Dagenham London Borough Council v. Essexplan* (1983) 81 L.G.R. 408, Whitford J.; *Stoke on Trent City Council v. B & Q (Retail)* [1984] 2 W.L.R. 929, C.A.; *Lewis v. Rogers; Gardner v. Duffield* [1984] Crim.L.R. 426, D.C.; *B. & Q. (Retail) v. Dudley Metropolitan Borough Council* (1987) 86 L.G.R. 137, D.C.; *Hadley v. Texas Homecare, The Times*, December 31, 1987, D.C.; *North West Leicester District Council v. Gramlo, The Daily Telegraph*, May 20, 1988, C.A.; *Parker v. Ilkeston Consumer Co-operative Society, The Independent*, July 5, 1988, D.C.; *Palmer v. Bugler, The Independent*, November 10, 1988, D.C.

s. 49, see *York City Council v. The Little Gallery, The Times*, December 2, 1985, D.C.

s. 51, see *Hudson v. Marshall* (1977) 75 L.G.R. 13, D.C.

s. 53, see *Thanet District Council v. Ninedrive* [1978] 1 All E.R. 703, Walton J.; *Chichester District Council v. Flockglen* (1977) 122 S.J. 61, Fox J.; *Barking and Dagenham London Borough Council v. Essexplan* (1983) 81 L.G.R. 408, Whitford J.; *North West Leicester District Council v. Gramlo, The Daily Telegraph*, May 20, 1988, C.A.; *Waltham Forest London Borough Council v. Scott Markets, The Independent*, June 24, 1988, Wright Q.C.

s. 56, see *Solihull Metropolitan Borough Council v. Maxfern* (1977) 57 L.G.R. 392, Oliver J.; *R. v. Braintree District Council, ex p. Willingham* (1983) 81 L.G.R. 70, D.C.

s. 57, see *York City Council v. The Little Gallery, The Times*, December 2, 1985, D.C.

14 Geo. 6 (1950)—cont.

28. Shops Act 1950—*cont.*

s. 58, see *Maby v. Warwick Corporation* [1972] 2 Q.B. 242; [1972] 3 W.L.R. 25; [1972] 2 All E.R. 1198; *Randall v. D. Turner (Garages)* [1973] 1 W.L.R. 1052; [1973] 3 All E.R. 369, D.C.; *Jarmain v. Wetherell* (1977) 75 L.G.R. 537, D.C.; *Thanet District Council v. Ninedrive* [1978] 1 All E.R. 703, Walton J.; *Chichester District Council v. Flockglen* (1977) 122 S.J. 61, Fox J.; *Newark District Council v. E. & A. Market Promotions* (1978) 77 L.G.R. 6, C.A.; *Palmer v. Bugler, The Independent*, November 10, 1988, D.C.

s. 59, see *Jarmain v. Wetherell* (1977) 75 L.G.R. 537, D.C.; *Lewis v. Rogers; Gardner v. Duffield* [1984] Crim.L.R. 426, D.C.; *Hadley v. Texas Homecare, The Times*, December 31, 1987, D.C.; *Palmer v. Bugler, The Independent*, November10, 1988, D.C.

ss. 59, 64, 67, amended: 1972, c.71, s.31.

s. 69, regs. 79/1294.

s. 71, see *Stafford Borough Council v. Elkenford* [1977] 1 W.L.R. 324, C.A.; *R. v. Braintree District Council, ex p. Willingham* (1983) 81 L.G.R. 70, D.C.; *Stoke-on-Trent City Council v. B. & Q. (Retail)* [1983] 3 W.L.R. 78, C.A.; *Stoke on Trent City Council v. B & Q (Retail)* [1984] 2 W.L.R. 929, C.A.; *Kirklees Metropolitan Council v. Wickes Building Supplies* [1984] L.G.R. 467, D.C.; *R. v. North West Leicestershire District Council, ex p. Dakin* [1985] Crim.L.R. 390, D.C.

s. 73, amended: 1972, c.70, sch.29; 1973, c.65, s.157; repealed in pt.: 1972, c.70, sch.30.

s. 74, see *Maby v. Warwick Corporation* [1972] 2 Q.B. 242; [1972] 3 W.L.R. 25; [1972] 2 All E.R. 1198; *Chichester District Council v. Flockglen* (1977) 122 S.J. 61, Fox J.; *Lewis v. Rogers; Gardner v. Duffield* [1984] Crim.L.R. 426, D.C.

s. 74, amended: 1982, c.33, sch.1; 1985, c.13, sch.2; repealed in pt.: S.L.R. 1974.

sch. 5, see *Hadley v. Texas Homecare, The Times*, December 31, 1987, D.C.

sch. 5, amended: 1973, c.32, sch.4; 1980, c.53, sch.1; order 85/39.

sch. 7, see *Hudson v. Marshall* (1977) 75 L.G.R. 13, D.C.; *Stafford Borough Council v. Elkenford* [1977] 1 W.L.R. 324, C.A.; *Solihull Metropolitan Borough Council v. Maxfern* (1977) 57 L.G.R. 392, Oliver J.; *Jarmain v. Wetherell* (1977) 75 L.G.R. 537, D.C.

sch. 8, repealed: S.L.R. 1974.

29. Medical Act 1950.

repealed: 1978, c.12, sch.7.

30. National Service Act 1950.

repealed: S.L.R. 1977.

31. Allotments Act 1950.

ss. 1–3, 12, 15, repealed in pt.: S.L.R. 1973.

s. 10, see *Harwood v. Borough of Reigate and Banstead* (1982) 43 P. & C.R. 336, Vivian Price, Q.C.

sch., repealed: S.L.R. 1973.

32. Army Reserve Act 1950.

repealed: 1980, c.9, sch.10.

CAP.

14 Geo. 6 (1950)—cont.

33. Air Force Reserve Act 1950.
repealed: 1980, c.9, sch.10.

34. Housing (Scotland) Act 1950.
repealed: 1987, c.26, sch.24.

36. Diseases of Animals Act 1950.
repealed: 1981, c.22, sch.6.
see R. v. Sands (1976) 63 Cr.App.R. 297, C.A.
orders 72/242, 287, 761, 1375, 1413, 1521, 1539, 1644; 73/101, 470, 1377, 1698, 1964.
s. 1, orders 72/738, 759, 760, 1173, 1219, 1509; 73/100, 690, 1936, 2173; 74/799, 839, 1183, 1185, 2211, 2212; 75/95, 154, 203, 346, 979, 1024, 1051, 1702; 76/32, 189, 244, 597, 695, 708, 776, 919, 1093, 1117, 1604; 77/36, 361, 944, 945, 948, 949, 958, 1132, 1139, 1173, 1284, 1721, 1751, 1838; 78/32, 206, 541, 663, 689, 934, 943, 944, 975, 1197, 1279, 1480, 1875 (S.); 79/37, 702, 703, 773, 815, 1013, 1596 (S.), 1701; 80/12, 14, 25, 79, 145, 890, 955, 1212, 1673 (S.), 1689, 1934; 81/7, 555, 676, 677, 747.
s. 2, order 76/919.
s. 5, orders 72/161, 738, 759, 1173–1175, 1219; 73/100, 590, 987, 988; 74/839, 1151; 75/143, 154, 1702; 76/244, 245, 614, 1117, 1403, 1604, 1640, 1853; 77/692, 949, 958, 1132, 1284, 1751; 78/206, 541, 663, 689, 943, 944, 1480, 1875 (S.); 79/789 (S.), 1288, 1596 (S.); 80/890, 1673 (S.), 1689.
s. 8, orders 74/1185, 2212; 75/888, 889; 77/1173, 1838; 80/79.
s. 9, order 72/1509.
s. 10, orders 74/1185, 2212; 75/888, 889; 77/1173, 1838; 80/145.
s. 11, orders 74/799, 1185, 2212; 75/95, 888, 889; 76/32, 1093; 77/1139, 1173, 1838; 78/934, 1875 (S.); 79/773, 815; 80/25, 145, 955; 81/7.
s. 17, orders 72/814, 825, 1500, 1538; 74/2212; 76/256–259, 2195; 77/946, 947, 989, 990, 1284, 1751, 1905, 1906, 1908, 1909; 78/975, 976, 1480, 1483, 1485, 1875(S.); 80/79, 80, 145, 148.
s. 19, orders 72/814, 1500, 1538; 77/946, 947, 989, 990, 1284, 1751, 1905, 1906, 1908, 1909; 78/976, 1480, 1483, 1485, 1875(S.); 80/80.
s. 20, orders 73/690, 1936, 2173; 74/799, 2212; 75/95, 203, 346, 979, 1024, 1051; 76/32, 695, 919, 1093; 77/944, 1139, 1173, 1838; 78/32, 934, 1197, 1279; 79/773, 1013; 80/12, 25, 79, 145; 81/7.
s. 22, order 75/1024.
s. 23, see Air India v. Wiggins [1980] 1 W.L.R. 815; [1980] 2 All E.R. 593, H.L.
s. 23, order 77/944.
s. 24, orders 74/2211; 76/189, 597; 77/994, 1838; 79/1701–1703; 80/12, 14, 79, 1934; 81/677.
s. 33, orders 74/1183, 2211; 76/708.
s. 37, orders 73/1178; 78/1748.
s. 42, orders 76/695; 77/1173; 81/747.
s. 45, orders 73/2173; 74/1183; 79/1702; 80/12, 14, 1934; 81/676, 677.
s. 49, order 74/1183.

CAP.

14 Geo. 6 (1950)—cont.

36. Diseases of Animals Act 1950—cont.
s. 50, orders 74/799; 75/95, 979, 1051; 76/32, 1093; 77/1139; 78/934; 79/37, 773; 80/25; 81/7.
s. 53, order 81/555.
s. 59, orders 76/2101; 78/163.
s. 61, see City of London Corporation v. British Caledonian Airways, The Times, May 21, 1981, C.A.
s. 77, orders 72/1509; 74/2211, 2212; 75/1024; 78/975; 80/79.
s. 78, repealed in pt.: 1981, c.45, sch.
s. 84, orders 73/2173; 74/1183, 1185, 2211, 2212; 75/888, 889; 76/189, 708; 77/1838; 78/1197, 1279; 79/815, 1701, 1702; 80/12, 14, 79, 145, 1212, 1934; 81/676.
s. 85, orders 72/738, 814, 825, 1173, 1219; 73/590, 1936, 2173; 74/799, 820, 1183, 1185, 2211, 2212; 75/95, 203, 346, 888, 889, 979, 1024, 1051; 76/32, 244, 245, 256–259, 597, 695, 708, 776, 919, 1093, 1117, 1118, 1640, 1853; 77/361, 692, 944–949, 957, 989, 990, 1133, 1139, 1173, 1284, 1751, 1905, 1906, 1908, 1909; 78/32, 207, 541, 689, 934, 943, 944, 1480, 1483, 1485, 1748; 1875 (S.); 79/37, 773, 789 (S.), 1013, 1288, 1365, 1701–1703; 80/12, 14, 25, 79, 80, 890, 1673 (S.), 1689, 1934; 81/7, 555, 747.

37. Maintenance Orders Act 1950.
s. 2, repealed in pt.: 1978, c.22, sch.3.
s. 3, repealed: 1987, c.42, sch.4.
s. 4, amended: 1976, c.71, sch.7; 1986, c.50, sch.10; repealed in pt.: 1976, c.71, sch.7; 1980, c.5, sch.6.
s. 6, repealed: 1982, c.27, sch.14; repealed in pt. (S.): 1984, c.15, sch.1; 1985, c.37, sch.2.
s. 7, repealed: 1986, c.55, sch.2; repealed in pt.(S.): 1985, c.37, sch.2.
s. 8, repealed: 1982, c.27, sch.14.
s. 9, amended: 1976, c.71, sch.7; 1986, c.50, sch.10.
s. 10, amended and repealed in pt.: order 80/564.
ss. 11, 12, amended: 1976, c.71, sch.7; order 77/2158; 1986, c.50, sch.10.
s. 13, amended: 1978, c.23, sch.5; repealed in pt.: ibid., sch.7.
s. 14, repealed: 1980, c.5, sch.6.
s. 15, amended: 1972, c.18, s.41; 1975, c.72, sch.3; 1977, c.38, sch.3; 1978, c.22, sch.2; 1980, c.5, sch.5; 1982, c.27, s.16, sch.12; order 80/564.
s. 16, see Tayside Regional Council v. Thaw, 1987 S.L.T. 69.
s. 16, amended: 1973, c.18, sch.2; c.29, s.9, sch.5; 1975, c.72, sch.3; (S.) 1976, c.39, sch.1; c.71, sch.7; 1977, c.38, sch.3; 1978, c.22, sch.2; 1980, c.5, sch.5; 1982, c.24, sch.4; 1984, c.42, sch.1; orders 77/2158; 80/564; 1985, c.37, sch.1(S.); 1986, c.50, sch.10; 1987, c.42, sch.2; repealed in pt.: 1982, c.27, sch.14; 1987, c.42, sch.2,4.
Pt. II (ss. 16–25), Acts of Sederunt 80/1727, 1732.

CAP.

14 Geo. 6 (1950)—cont.

37. Maintenance Orders Act 1950—*cont.*
s. 18, amended: 1977, c.38, sch.3; 1982, c.27, schs.11,12; 1984, c.42, sch.1; 1987, c.42, sch.2.
ss. 21, amended: 1977, c.38, sch.3; 1982, c.27, sch.12.
s. 22, amended: 1978, c.22, sch.2.
s. 23, substituted: 1977, c.38, sch.3.
s. 24, amended: *ibid.*; 1982, c.27, sch.12.
s. 25, amended: 1978, c.23, sch.5; 1980, c.43, sch.7; order 77/2158.
s. 28, amended: 1978, c.23, sch.5.
s. 31, repealed in pt.: 1973, c.36, sch.6.
sch. 1, repealed: 1980, c.5, sch.6.

38. Allotments (Scotland) Act 1950.
ss. 1–4, repealed in pt.: S.L.R. 1974.
ss. 9, 13, amended: 1973, c.65, sch.27.
s. 14, sch., repealed: S.L.R. 1974.

39. Public Utilities Street Works Act 1950.
s. 1, see *Strathclyde Regional Council* v. *British Railways Board,* 1978 S.L.T. (Sh.Ct.) 8.
ss. 1, 2, amended: 1972, c.70, sch.21.
ss. 1–22, amended (S.): 1984, c.54, sch.9.
ss. 3, 4, 6, 10, amended: 1984, c.12, sch.4.
s. 12, repealed in pt. (S.): 1984, c.54, schs.9,11.
s. 18, see *Department of Transport* v. *North-West Water Authority* [1983] 3 W.L.R. 707, H.L.
s. 19, amended: 1978, c.47, sch.1.
s. 20, repealed in pt.: 1984, c.12, sch.7.
s. 21, amended: 1972, c.70, sch.21.
s. 23, repealed in pt. (S.): 1984, c.54, sch.11.
s. 26, see *Yorkshire Electricity Board* v. *British Telecom* [1986] 2 All E.R. 961, H.L.
ss. 26, 28, amended: 1984, c.12, sch.4.
ss. 26–29, 31, 33, 34, amended (S.): 1984, c.54, sch.9.
s. 30, repealed in pt. (S.): *ibid.,* sch.11; 1982, c.30, s.21.
s. 33, repealed in pt.: S.L.R. 1978.
s. 36, amended: 1973, c.65, sch.14.
ss. 36, 39, amended (S.): 1984, c.54, sch.9; repealed in pt. (S.): *ibid.,* sch.11.
s. 39, amended: 1972, c.70, sch.21; 1976, c.44, s.2; 1980, c.66, sch.24; repealed in pt.: 1972, c.70, sch.30; 1984, c.12, sch.7.
sch. 1, amended (S.): 1984, c.54, sch.9.
schs. 1, 3, amended: 1984, c.12, sch.4.
sch. 2, substituted (S.): 1984, c.54, sch.9.
schs. 3–6, amended (S.): *ibid.*
sch. 5, amended: 1972, c.52, sch.23; s.60, sch.8; order 74/595; S.L.R. 1978; repealed in pt.: 1980, c.45, sch.11; 1984, c.12, sch.7 (S.).
sch. 6, amended: 1972, c.70, sch.21.
sch. 7, amended: 1984, c.12, sch.4; repealed in pt.: 1972, c.70, sch.30; 1975, c.76, sch.2.

14 & 15 Geo. 6 (1950–51)

2. Superannuation Act 1950.
repealed: 1981, c.20, sch.4.

3. Exchequer and Audit Departments Act 1950.
ss. 2–4, repealed: 1972, c.11, sch.8.

9. Restoration of Pre-War Trade Practices Act 1950.
repealed: S.L.R. 1986.

CAP.

14 & 15 Geo. 6 (1950–51)—cont.

10. Reinstatement in Civil Employment Act 1950.
repealed: 1985, c.17, sch.5.

11. Administration of Justice (Pensions) Act 1950.
repealed: 1981, c.20, sch.4.
s. 6, order 79/1275.

15. Local Government (Scotland) Act 1951.
repealed: 1973, c.65, sch.29.

18. Livestock Rearing Act 1951.
s. 1, repealed in pt.: 1984, c.41, sch.4.
s. 8, repealed in pt.: S.L.R. 1986.
ss. 9, 10, repealed: 1972, c.62, sch.6.

19. Town and Country Planning (Amendment) Act 1951.
repealed: 1972, c.52, sch.23.

21. Alkali, etc., Works Regulation (Scotland) Act 1951.
repealed: regs. 74/2170.
s. 1, order 72/1330.

22. Workmen's Compensation (Supplementation) Act 1951.
see *Park* v. *National Coal Board* [1981] I.C.R. 783, C.A.

23. Reserve and Auxiliary Forces (Training) Act 1951.
repealed: S.L.R. 1976.

25. Supplies and Services (Defence Purposes) Act 1951.
repealed: S.L.R. 1978.

26. Salmon and Freshwater Fisheries (Protection) (Scotland) Act 1951.
s. 1, amended: 1986, c.62, sch.4.
ss. 1–3, 13, see *MacDougall* v. *Livingstone,* 1986 S.C.C.R. 527.
s. 2, see *Lockhart* v. *Cowan,* 1980 S.L.T.(Sh.Ct.) 91.
s. 2, amended: 1986, c.62, s.21.
s. 7, see *Corbett* v. *MacNaughton,* 1985 S.L.T. 312; *Walls* v. *McDougall,* 1987 S.C.C.R. 552.
s. 7A, added: 1986, c.62, s.22.
s. 7B, added: *ibid.,* s.25.
s. 9, amended: 1974, c.40, sch.3; 1986, c.62, sch.4; repealed in pt.: *ibid.*
s. 11, amended: *ibid.,* s.22.
s. 14, repealed: *ibid.,* sch.5.
s. 15, repealed in pt.: *ibid.,* sch.4.
s. 19, see *Bain* v. *Wilson,* 1987 S.C.C.R. 270.
s. 19, repealed in pt.: 1986, c.62, schs.4,5.
s. 21, amended: *ibid.,* s.26.
s. 22, amended: *ibid.,* sch.4.
s. 24, see *Lockhart* v. *Cowan,* 1980 S.L.T.(Sh.Ct.) 91.
s. 24, amended: 1986, c.62, s.8, sch.4.
s. 25 (in pt.), sch. 2, repealed: S.L.R. 1974.

27. Fire Services Act 1951.
s. 2, amended: 1973, c.38, sch.27.
s. 2, repealed in pt.: 1975, c.18, sch.1.

28. Long Leases (Temporary Provisions) Act 1951.
repealed: S.L.R. 1975.

30. Sea Fish Industry Act 1951.
s. 26, repealed: 1981, c.19, sch.1.
s. 29 (in pt.), sch. 5, repealed: S.L.R. 1974.

CAP.

14 & 15 Geo. 6 (1950–51)—cont.

31. National Health Service Act 1951.
repealed: 1977, c.49, sch.16; 1978, c.29, sch.17
(S.).
s. 1, regs. 74/1910.
s. 1, sch., regs. 73/1468; 74/284, 287, 505, 507,
522; 75/1945, 1987; 77/471.

32. British North America Act 1951.
repealed: 1982, c.11, sch.

33. Fraudulent Mediums Act 1951.
s. 2, see *R.* v. *Martin* [1981] Crim.L.R. 109,
Leeds Crown Ct.

35. Pet Animals Act 1951.
s. 1, repealed in pt.: 1973, c.65, schs.25,29;
1974, c.7, schs.6,8.
s. 2, amended: 1983, c.26, s.1.
ss. 2, 7, amended (S.): 1984, c.54, sch.9.
s. 7, see *Chalmers* v. *Diwell* (1975) L.G.R. 173,
D.C.
s. 7, amended: 1973, c.65, sch.24; 1983, c.26,
s.1; repealed in pt.: 1972, c.70, sch.30.

36. Criminal Law Amendment Act 1951.
repealed: S.L.R. 1974.

**38. Leasehold Property (Temporary Provisions)
Act 1951.**
repealed: S.L.R. 1975.

39. Common Informers Act 1951.
s. 2, repealed: 1973, c.36, sch.6.
sch., amended: 1973, c.15, sch.5; c.43, sch. 7;
repealed in pt.: S.L.R. 1976; S.L.R. 1977;
S.L.R. 1978; 1984, c.26, sch.2; 1986, c.48,
sch.5.

41. Coal Industry Act 1951.
repealed: S.L.R. 1973.

43. Finance Act 1951.
s. 4, repealed: 1973, c.51, sch.22.
ss. 33–35, repealed: 1975, c.7, sch.13.
s. 44, repealed in pt.: S.L.R. 1974; 1975, c.7,
sch.13.
sch. 7, repealed: S.L.R. 1974.

46. Courts-Martial (Appeals) Act 1951.
s. 34, repealed: 1981, c.20, sch.4.
s. 35, amended: 1972, c.11, sch.6.

**47. Festival of Britain (Additional Loans) Act
1951.**
repealed: S.L.R. 1981.

53. Midwives Act 1951.
repealed: 1979, c.36, sch.8.
s. 1, orders 74/731; 75/1986; 83/134.
s. 17, regs. 77/1580.
ss. 23, 29, amended: 1980, c.53, sch.1.
s. 30, rules 74/496; instrument 80/1468.
s. 31, substituted: 1980, c.53, sch.1.
s. 34, instrument 82/1787.
sch. 1, instrument 80/1468.

54. Midwives (Scotland) Act 1951.
repealed: 1979, c.36, sch.8.
ss. 4, 5, sch. 1, instrument 80/1968.
s. 27, repealed: 1980, c.55, sch.3.

55. Nurses (Scotland) Act 1951.
Pts. I, II, repealed: 1979, c.36, sch.8.
ss. 6A, 6B, added: order 79/1604.
s. 6A, amended: orders 81/432; 82/1076.
s. 6B, amended: order 81/432.
s. 7, amended: *ibid.*

CAP.

14 & 15 Geo. 6 (1950–51)—cont.

55. Nurses (Scotland) Act 1951—cont.
s. 19, sch. 4, order 74/703.
ss. 19, 20, 22, 32, amended: 1972, c.58,
schs.6,7.
s. 22, amended (S.): 1978, c.29, sch.16.
ss. 27, 29, amended: 1979, c.36, sch.7.
s. 32, repealed in pt.: *ibid.*, schs.7,8.
Pt. IV (except s. 36 in pt.), repealed: 1979, c.36,
sch.8.
schs. 1, 4, repealed: *ibid.*
sch. 3A, added: order 79/1604; amended: order
80/1721.
sch. 5, repealed: S.L.R. 1974.

58. Fireworks Act 1951.
ss. 1, 2, 4, amended: regs. 74/1885.

60. Mineral Workings Act 1951.
repealed (exc. ss. 28, 32, 40 (in pt.)–42 (in pt.),
43): 1985, c.12, s.1, sch.2.
s. 31, repealed: 1972, c.52, sch.23.
s. 32, substituted (S.): 1984, c.54, sch.9.
s. 41, amended: 1985, c.12, s.6.
s. 43, amended: 1972, c.52, sch.23; S.L.R.
1974.

62. Tithe Act 1951.
amended: 1977, c.36, s.56.
s. 1, repealed in pt.: *ibid.*, sch.9.
ss. 2–5, repealed: *ibid.*
s. 10, repealed in pt.: *ibid.*
s. 11, order 81/232.
sch. 1, repealed: 1977, c.36, sch.9

**63. Rag, Flock and Other Filling Materials Act
1951.**
s. 2, amended: 1980, c.65, sch.6.
ss. 6, 7, amended: *ibid.*, schs.6,34; repealed in
pt.: *ibid.*, sch.1.
ss. 9, 15, 30, 33, 34, regs. 81/1218.
s. 10, amended: 1974, c.39, sch.4.
s. 15, repealed in pt.: 1980, c.65, schs.1,34.
s. 20, amended: 1980, c.43, sch.7.
s. 27, repealed: 1980, c.65, sch.33.
s. 35, amended: 1972, c.58, sch.6; c.70, sch.30.
s. 36, amended: 1973, c.65, sch.27.
s. 37, repealed: S.L.R. 1974.

64. Rivers (Prevention of Pollution) Act 1951.
repealed: 1974, c.40, sch.4.
s. 2, see *Price* v. *Cromack* [1975] 2 All E.R. 113,
D.C.; *F. J. H. Wrothwell* v. *Yorkshire Water
Authority, The Times,* October 31, 1983, C.A.
s. 6, order 75/787.
s. 7, see *Att.-Gen.* v. *Wellingborough U.D.C.*
(1974) 72 L.G.R. 507, C.A.

**65. Reserve and Auxiliary Forces (Protection of
Civil Interests) Act 1951.**
s. 2, amended: 1973, c.29, s.9; 1987, c.42,
sch.2.
s. 4, amended: 1974, c.39, sch.4; 1977, c.42,
sch.23; 1988, c.50, sch.17.
s. 5, amended: order 79/1573.
s. 8, amended: 1973, c.29, sch.5.
s. 10, substituted: 1974, c.39, sch.4.
s. 14, amended: 1976, c.80, sch.8; 1977, c.42,
sch.24.
s. 15, amended: *ibid.*, schs.23,24; 1980, c.51,
sch.25; c.52, s.39(S.); 1984, c.58, sch.8(S.).

14 & 15 Geo. 6 (1950–51)—cont.

65. Reserve and Auxiliary Forces (Protection of Civil Interests) Act 1951—cont.

s. 16, repealed in pt.: 1973, c.9, schs.5,6; 1980, c.51, sch.26; c.52, s.39, sch.5(S.); 1988, c.43, sch.10; substituted: 1988, c.50, sch.17.

s. 17, amended: 1977, c.42, schs.23,24; 1980, c.51, sch.25; c.52, s.39(S.); 1984, c.58, sch.8(S.); 1988, c.50, sch.17; repealed in pt.: 1980, c.52, sch.5(S.).

s. 18, amended: 1976, c.80, sch.8; 1977, c.42, schs.23,24; 1980, c.51, sch.25; c.52, s.39(S.); 1988, c.50, sch.17; repealed in pt.: 1980, c.52, sch.5(S.); 1988, c.50, schs. 17,18.

s. 19, repealed in pt.: 1980, c.52, sch.5(S.); 1988, c.50, sch.17.

s. 20, amended: 1977, c.42, schs.23,24; 1984, c.58, sch.8(S.); 1988, c.50, sch.17.

s. 21, repealed: 1977, c.12, sch.2.

s. 22, amended: 1977, c.42, sch.23; c.43, sch.1; 1984, c.58, sch.8(S.); 1988, c.50, sch.17; repealed in pt.: 1977, c.12, sch.2.

s. 23, amended: 1977, c.42, sch.23; 1984, c.58, sch.8(S.); 1988, c.50, sch.17.

s. 27, amended: 1986, c.5, sch.14.

s. 29, amended: order 79/1573.

s. 41, repealed: 1972, c.11, sch.8.

s. 43, repealed: 1976, c.35, sch.3.

s. 44, repealed in pt.: 1972, c.11, sch.8; 1976, c.35, sch.3.

s. 46, amended: 1972, c.11, sch.6.

s. 50, repealed in pt. (S.): 1972, c.58, sch.7.

s. 52, repealed in pt.: S.L.R. 1977.

s. 57, amended: order 79/1573.

s. 60, repealed in pt.: S.L.R. 1977.

s. 63, amended: 1976, c.35, sch.2.

s. 64, amended: 1972, c.11, sch.6; 1974, c.39, sch.4; S.L.R. 1977; 1981, c.55, sch.5; repealed in pt.: S.L.R. 1977.

s. 65, order 79/291.

s. 65, repealed in pt.: 1973, c.36, sch.6.

sch. 1, amended: 1985, c.17, sch.4; repealed in pt.: S.L.R. 1977; 1981, c.55, sch.5.

sch. 2, amended: 1972, c.11, sch.6; 1972, c.58, sch.6(S.); 1977, c.49, sch.15; 1978, c.29, schs.15,16(S.); order 79/1573; repealed in pt.: 1980, c.20, sch.1.

66. Rivers (Prevention of Pollution) (Scotland) Act 1951.

repealed, except ss. 1, 6 (in pt.), 7, 9, 10 (in pt.), 12 (in pt.), 13, 16, 17, 18 (in pt.), 19, 32 (in pt.), 35 (in pt.), sch.4: 1974, c.40, sch.4.

s. 1, repealed in pt.: 1981, c.23, s.31, sch.4.

s. 2, see Alphacell v. Woodward [1972] 2 W.L.R. 1320; [1972] 2 All E.R. 475.

ss. 2–5, repealed: 1973, c.65, sch.29.

s. 6, amended: ibid., sch.16; repealed in pt.: ibid., sch.29.

ss. 6, 7, orders 75/232, 237, 310.

s. 7, repealed: 1975, c.30, sch.7.

s. 8, repealed: 1973, c.65, sch.29.

s. 10, amended: ibid., sch.16; repealed in pt.: ibid., sch.29.

s. 11, repealed: ibid.

14 & 15 Geo. 6 (1950–51)—cont.

66. Rivers (Prevention of Pollution) (Scotland) Act 1951—cont.

s. 12, amended: ibid., sch.16; 1974, c.40, sch.3.

s. 13, substituted: 1973, c.65, sch.16.

s. 14, repealed: 1972, c.11, schs.7,8.

s. 15, repealed: 1973, c.65, sch.29.

s. 17, amended: ibid., sch.16; 1974, c.40, sch.3.

s. 18, amended: 1973, c.65, sch.16; 1974, c.40, sch.3; repealed in pt.: 1973, c.65, sch. 29.

s. 19, amended: 1974, c.40, sch.3.

s. 21, amended: 1982, c.48, sch.6.

s. 22, see Lockhart v. National Coal Board, 1981 S.L.T. 161.

s. 26, amended: 1973, c.65, sch.16; repealed in pt.: ibid., sch.29.

s. 28, repealed in pt.: ibid.

s. 29, orders 72/103, 1161; 73/1244.

s. 29, repealed in pt.: 1973, c.65, schs.16,29.

s. 30, amended: ibid., sch.16; repealed in pt.: ibid., sch.29.

s. 35, amended: ibid., sch.16; 1980, c.45, sch.10; repealed in pt.: 1973, c.65, sch.29.

s. 36, repealed in pt.: S.L.R. 1974.

sch. 1, repealed in pt.: 1973, c.65, sch.29.

sch. 3, repealed: ibid.

sch. 4, repealed: S.L.R. 1974.

15 & 16 Geo. 6 & 1 Eliz. 2 (1951–52)

8. Home Guard Act 1951.

s. 1, repealed in pt.: 1980, c.9, sch.10.

s. 2, amended: ibid., sch.9.

10. Income Tax Act 1952.

see McMann v. Shaw [1972] 1 W.L.R. 1578; [1972] 3 All E.R. 732.

ss. 2, 12, see Murphy v. Ingram [1974] 2 W.L.R. 782; [1974] 2 All E.R. 187, C.A.

s. 47, see R. v. Special Commissioners of Income Tax, ex p. Martin (1971) 48 T.C. 1; R. v. Special Commissioners of Income Tax, ex p. Morey (1972) 49 T.C. 71, C.A.

s. 52, see Jonas v. Bamford [1973] T.R. 225.

s. 56, see Redditch Electro-Plating Co. v. Ferrebe; Harris Hardeners v. Ferrebe [1973] T.R. 57.

s. 64, see Rose v. Humbles [1972] 1 W.L.R. 33; R. v. H.M. Inspector of Taxes, ex p. Clarke [1972] 1 All E.R. 545; R. v. Freshwell Commissioners, ex p. Clark [1971] T.R. 353; Bath and West Counties Property Trust v. Thomas [1977] 1 W.L.R. 1423, Walton J.

s. 122, see Simpson v. John Reynolds & Co. (Insurances) [1975] 1 W.L.R. 617; [1975] 2 All E.R. 88, C.A.; I.R.C. v. Falkirk Ice Rink [1975] S.T.C. 434; 1975 S.L.T. 245.

ss. 122, 123, see Simpson v. John Reynolds & Co. (Insurance) [1974] 2 All E.R. 545; Ransom v. Higgs [1974] 1 W.L.R. 1594, H.L.

s. 123, see Nothman v. Cooper [1971] T.R. 513; Duff v. Williamson [1973] T.R. 171, Plowman J.; Aplin v. White [1973] 2 All E.R. 637; Taylor v. Good [1973] 2 All E.R. 785; [1974] 1 All E.R. 1137, C.A.

s. 124, see Sargent v. Eayrs [1973] 1 W.L.R. 236; [1973] 1 All E.R. 277.

CAP.

15 & 16 Geo. 6 & 1 Eliz. 2
(1951–52)—cont.

10. Income Tax Act 1952—*cont.*

s. 127, see *I.R.C.* v. *Helical Bar* [1972] 2 W.L.R. 880; [1972] 1 All E.R. 1205; [1972] T.R. 1.

s. 131, see *Sinsbury* v. *O'Brien* [1971] T.R. 397.

s. 132, see *Buswell* v. *I.R.C.* [1973] T.R. 27; [1974] 2 All E.R. 520, C.A.

s. 135, see *Sinsbury* v. *O'Brien* [1971] T.R. 397.

s. 137, see *Odeon Associated Theatres* v. *Jones* [1972] 2 W.L.R. 331; [1972] 1 All E.R. 681; *Bamford* v. *A.T.A. Advertising* [1972] 1 W.L.R. 1261; [1972] 3 All E.R. 535; *Heather* v. *P.E. Consulting Group* [1972] 3 W.L.R. 833; [1973] 1 All E.R. 8; *Sargent* v. *Eayrs* [1973] 1 W.L.R. 236; [1973] 1 All E.R. 277; *Ransom* v. *Higgs* [1974] 1 W.L.R. 1594, H.L.; *Hammond Engineering Co.* v. *I.R.C.* [1975] S.T.C. 334.

s. 143, see *Moore* v. *Mackenzie* [1972] 1 W.L.R. 359; [1972] 2 All E.R. 549; [1971] T.R. 457.

s. 148, see *Aplin* v. *White* [1973] 2 All E.R. 637; *Aplin* v. *White (No. 2)* [1973] T.R. 231; *Way* v. *Underdown (No. 2)* [1974] 2 All E.R. 595; *Dunmore* v. *McGowan* [1978] 1 W.L.R. 617, C.A.

s. 150, see *R.* v. *Special Commissioners of Income Tax, ex p. Rogers* (1972) 48 T.C. 46; *R.* v. *General Commissioners of Income Tax for Tavistock, ex p. Adams (No. 2)* (1971) 48 T.C. 56.

s. 152, see *Sargent* v. *Fayrs* [1973] 1 W.L.R. 236; [1973] 1 All E.R. 277.

s. 156, see *Harmel* v. *Wright* [1974] 1 W.L.R. 325; [1974] 1 All E.R. 945.

ss. 156, 160, see *Taylor* v. *Provan* [1974] 2 W.L.R. 394; [1974] 1 All E.R. 1201, H.L.

s. 169, see *Ceylon I.R.C.* v. *Rajaratnam* [1971] T.R. 451; *Fitzleet Estates* v. *Cherry* [1977] 1 W.L.R. 1345, H.L.

s. 170, see *Fitzleet Estates* v. *Cherry* [1977] 1 W.L.R. 1345, H.L.

s. 175, see *T. & E. Homes* v. *Robinson* [1979] 1 W.L.R. 452, C.A.

s. 177, see *I.R.C.* v. *Church Commissioners for England* [1976] 3 W.L.R. 214; [1976] 2 All E.R. 1037, H.L.

s. 211, see *Northend* v. *White & Leonard and Corbin Greener* [1975] 1 W.L.R. 1037; [1975] 2 All E.R. 481.

s. 212, see *Murphy* v. *Ingram* [1973] 2 W.L.R. 983.

s. 229, see *R.* v. *Special Comrs. of Income Tax, ex p. Morey* (1972) 49 T.C. 71, C.A.; *Knight* v. *I.R.C.* [1974] T.R. 19; [1974] S.T.C. 156, C.A.

ss. 245, 246, see *Hanstead Investments* v. *I.R.C.* [1974] 2 All E.R. 299.

s. 354, see *Murphy* v. *Ingram* [1973] 2 W.L.R. 983.

s. 361, see *Gubay* v. *Kington* [1984] 1 W.L.R. 163, H.L.

s. 404, see *I.R.C.* v. *Cookson* [1977] 2 All E.R. 331, C.A.

ss. 405, 409, 411, see *I.R.C.* v. *Mills* [1974] 1 All E.R. 722, H.L.

CAP.

15 & 16 Geo. 6 & 1 Eliz. 2
(1951–52)—cont.

10. Income Tax Act 1952—*cont.*

s. 412, see *Lord Chetwode* v. *I.R.C.* [1977] 1 W.L.R. 248; [1977] 1 All E.R. 638, H.L.; *Vestey* v. *I.R.C.* [1979] 3 W.L.R. 915, H.L.; *I.R.C.* v. *Pratt* [1982] S.T.C. 756, Walton J.

s. 414, see *Royal Bank of Canada* v. *I.R.C.* [1972] 2 W.L.R. 106.

ss. 425, 426, see *United Friendly Insurance Company* v. *Eady* [1973] T.R. 37.

s. 430, see *"B": Sun Life Assurance Co. of Canada* v. *Pearson* [1986] S.T.C. 335, C.A.

s. 447, see *I.R.C.* v. *Church Comrs. for England* [1976] 3 W.L.R. 214; [1976] 2 All E.R. 1037, H.L.

s. 501, see *I.R.C.* v. *Adams* (1971) 48 T.C. 67.

s. 510, see *Scorer (Inspector of Taxes)* v. *Olin Energy Systems, The Times*, March 29, 1985, H.L.

s. 514, see *Murphy* v. *Elders* [1974] S.T.C. 34; *Bath and West Counties Property Trust* v. *Thomas* [1977] 1 W.L.R. 1423, Walton J.

s. 524, see *Aplin* v. *White* [1973] 2 All E.R. 637; *Nicholson* v. *I.R.C.* [1974] S.T.C. 230; [1975] S.T.C. 245, C.A.

s. 525, see *Pegler* v. *Abell* [1973] 1 All E.R. 53; *Northend* v. *White & Leonard and Corbin Greener* [1975] 1 W.L.R. 1037; [1975] 2 All E.R. 481.

s. 526, see *Taylor* v. *Good* [1973] 2 All E.R. 785; [1974] 1 All E.R. 1173, C.A.; *Ransom* v. *Higgs* [1974] 1 W.L.R. 1594, H.L.

sch. 9, see *Owen* v. *Burden* [1972] 1 All E.R. 356; *Lucas* v. *Cattell* [1972] T.R. 83; *Taylor* v. *Provan* [1974] 2 W.L.R. 394; [1974] 1 All E.R. 1201, H.L.

11. Northern Ireland (Foyle Fisheries) Act 1952.
repealed: 1973, c.36, sch.6.

12. Judicial Officers (Salaries, etc.) Act 1952.
s. 1, repealed: 1973, c.15, sch.5.
s. 2, amended (S.): 1987, c.41, sch.1.
s. 4, repealed in pt.: 1978, c.23, sch.7.
s. 5, repealed: 1981, c.20, sch.4.
s. 6, repealed: in pt.: S.L.R. 1974.
sch., repealed: *ibid.*

13. Festival Pleasure Gardens Act 1952.
repealed: S.L.R. 1986.

15. Agriculture (Fertilisers) Act 1952.
repealed: S.L.R. 1986.

20. Cinematograph Film Production (Special Loans) Act 1952.
repealed: 1980, c.41, sch.

23. Miners' Welfare Act 1952.
ss. 1, 18, repealed: in pt.: S.L.R.1974.
ss. 13, 14, 16, amended: 1987, c.3, sch.1.
sch. 2, repealed: S.L.R. 1974.

25. National Health Service Act 1952.
repealed: 1977, c.49, sch.16; 1978, c.29, sch.17 (S.).
s. 1, regs. 74/627, 1377, 1440; 75/695, 718, 1687, 1688, 1715, 1716, 1988; 76/1821, 1873, 1874.
ss. 1, 2, 7, regs. 74/284, 285, 505, 508, 522, 647; 75/1987; 77/471.

CAP.

15 & 16 Geo. 6 & 1 Eliz. 2
(1951–52)—cont.

25. National Health Service Act 1952—cont.
s. 2, regs. 75/1945.
ss. 2, 7, regs. 73/1468.
ss. 3, 44, regs. 76/1823.

31. Cremation Act 1952.
s. 1, repealed in pt.: 1980, c.65, sch.34.
s. 3, amended: 1972, c.70, sch.30.
s. 4, repealed: S.L.R. 1978.

33. Finance Act 1952.
s. 30, repealed in pt.: 1985, c.9, sch.1; c.65, sch.10; c.66, sch.8 (S.).
s. 71, see *Barty King* v. *Ministry of Defence* [1979] 2 All E.R. 80, May J.
ss. 71, 72, repealed: 1975, c.7, sch.13.
s. 74, amended: 1974, c.30, sch.12; 1988, c.1, sch.29.
s. 76, repealed in pt.: S.L.R. 1974.
sch. 5, amended: order 75/1185.
sch. 13, repealed: 1975, c.7, sch.13.
sch. 14, repealed in pt.: S.L.R. 1974.

35. Agriculture (Ploughing Grants) Act 1952.
repealed: S.L.R. 1986.

37. Civil List Act 1952.
s. 9, schs. 1, 2, repealed: 1972, c.7, sch.
ss. 2–7, 13, amended: *ibid.*, ss.2,4, sch.
ss. 3–5, amended: order 39/84.

39. Motor Vehicles (International Circulation) Act 1952.
s. 1, orders 75/1208; 80/1095; 85/459.
s. 2, S.R. 1980 No. 262.
s. 3, repealed: S.L.R. 1976.
s. 4, repealed in part: S.L.R. 1974.
s. 5, repealed: 1973, c.36, sch.6.
sch., repealed: S.L.R. 1974.

41. Affiliation Orders Act 1952.
repealed (S.): 1985, c.37, sch.2.
s. 3, amended: 1980, c.5, sch.5.

43. Disposal of Uncollected Goods Act 1952.
repealed: 1977, c.32, s.15.

44. Customs and Excise Act 1952.
see *R.* v. *Smith (Donald)* [1973] 3 W.L.R. 88; [1973] 2 All E.R. 1161.
Pts. I–III (ss. 1–92), repealed, except ss. 35–37, 41–43; 1979, c.2, sch.6.
s. 2, order 74/2143.
s. 10, see *Logdon* v. *D.P.P.* [1976] Crim.L.R. 121, D.C.
s. 13, orders 73/1001, 2082.
s. 16, order 77/763.
s. 34, regs. 72/1739.
ss. 35–37, repealed: 1979, c.3, sch.3.
s. 40, regs. 73/997; 76/1099.
ss. 41–43, repealed: 1979, c.3, sch.3.
s. 44, see *Mizel* v. *Warren* [1973] 1 W.L.R. 899; [1973] 2 All E.R. 1149; *Allgemeine Gold-und-Silber–scheideanstalg* v. *Customs and Excise Comrs., The Times,* December 11, 1979, C.A.
s. 56, see *R.* v. *Hurford-Jones* (1977) 65 Cr.App.R. 263, C.A.
Pt. IV (ss. 93–172), repealed: 1979, c.4, sch.4.
s. 127, regs. 78/893, 1186.
ss. 128, 131, regs. 78/893.
s. 140, regs. 75/1790; 78/1786.

CAP.

15 & 16 Geo. 6 & 1 Eliz. 2
(1951–52)—cont.

44. Customs and Excise Act 1952—cont.
s. 171, regs. 78/893, 1186.
Pt. V (ss.173–194), repealed: 1977, c.36, s.3, sch.9.
ss. 219–222, repealed: 1979, c.6, sch.
s. 221, regs. 75/1891.
s. 225, see *Commissioners of Customs and Excise* v. *Tan* [1977] 2 W.L.R. 181, H.L.
ss. 226–228, repealed: 1979, c.4, sch.4.
Pt. IX (ss. 233–254), repealed: except ss.237, 241–243: 1979, c.2, sch.6.
ss. 237, 241–243, repealed: 1979, c.4, sch.4.
s. 250, regs. 78/893, 1186.
Pt. X (ss. 255–273), repealed, except ss.263 (in pt.), 271 (in pt.), 272: 1979, c.2, sch.6.
s. 255A, order 77/2042.
ss. 258, 260, see *Commissioners of Customs and Excise* v. *Tan* [1977] 2 W.L.R. 181, H.L.
s. 263, regs. 75/1790.
s. 263, amended: 1975, c.45, sch.3; 1976, c.40, sch.3; 1978, c.42, sch.12; repealed in pt.: 1979, c.4, sch.4.
s. 271, repealed in pt.: 1979, c.3, sch.3.
s. 272, repealed: *ibid.*
Pt. XI (ss.274–291), repealed: 1979, c.2, sch.6.
s. 281, see *R.* v. *Whitehead* [1982] 3 W.L.R. 543, C.A.
s. 283, see *Att.-Gen.'s Reference (No. 3 of 1975)* [1976] 1 W.L.R. 737; [1976] 2 All E.R. 798, C.A.
s. 283, amended: 1982, c.48, sch.14.
s. 288, see *Patel* v. *Spencer* [1976] 1 W.L.R. 1268.
s. 290, see *Mizel* v. *Warren* [1973] 1 W.L.R. 899; [1973] 2 All E.R. 1149; *R.* v. *Watts and Stack* (1979) 70 Cr.App.R. 187, C.A.
Pt. XII (ss. 292–321), repealed, except ss.307 (in pt.), 309 (in pt.), 310, 315 (in pt.): 1979, c.2, sch.6.
s. 301, see *Att.-Gen.'s Reference (No. 3 of 1975)* [1976] 1 W.L.R. 737; [1976] 2 All E.R. 798, C.A.
s. 304, see *R.* v. *Ardalan* [1972] 1 W.L.R. 463; [1972] 2 All E.R. 257; 56 Cr.App.R. 320; *R.* v. *Borro and Abdullah* [1973] Crim.L.R. 513, C.A.; *R.* v. *Wall* [1974] 2 All E.R. 245; *R.* v. *Green (Harry)* [1976] 2 W.L.R. 57; [1975] 3 All E.R. 1011, C.A.; *Commissioners of Customs and Excise* v. *Tan* [1977] 2 W.L.R. 181, H.L.; *Geismar* v. *Sun Alliance and London Insurance* [1977] Crim.L.R. 475, D.C.; *R.* v. *Watts and Stack* (1979) 70 Cr.App.R. 187, C.A.; *Henn and Darby* v. *D.P.P.* [1980] 2 W.L.R. 597, European Ct. and H.L.; *R.* v. *Whitehead* [1982] 3 W.L.R. 543, C.A.
ss. 304, 305, see *Byrne* v. *Law* [1972] 1 W.L.R. 1282; [1972] 3 All E.R. 526.
s. 307, see *Dean* v. *Scottish and Newcastle Breweries,* 1978 S.L.T.(Notes) 24.
ss. 309, 310, amended: 1978, c.42, sch.12.
ss. 309 (in pt.), 311, repealed: *ibid.*, s.13.
sch. 2, amended: 1978, c.42, sch.12; repealed in pt.: *ibid.*, sch.13.

CAP.

15 & 16 Geo. 6 & 1 Eliz. 2
(1951–52)—cont.

44. Customs and Excise Act 1952—cont.

sch. 4, repealed: 1972, c.68, sch.3.

sch. 7, see *McAfee* v. *Gilliland* [1979] N.I. 97, N.I.C.A.

sch. 7, repealed in pt.: 1979, c.2, sch.6.

sch. 8, repealed: 1978, c.42, sch.13.

sch. 10, repealed in pt.: 1973, c.43, sch.7; S.L.R. 1977; 1979, c.2, sch.6; c.4, sch.4.

schs. 11, 12, repealed: S.L.R. 1974.

46. Hypnotism Act 1952.

s. 2, amended: 1973, c.65, sch.24; 1982, c.30, sch.2; repealed in pt.: 1972, c.70, sch.30.

47. Rating and Valuation (Scotland) Act 1952.

s. 1, amended: 1973, c.65, sch.9.

s. 3, orders 75/2232; 85/62.

s. 3, amended: 1973, c.65, sch.9; 1975, c.30, sch.6; 1984, c.31, sch.2; repealed in pt.: 1975, c.30, schs.6,7.

s. 4, amended: order 75/2232; 1975, c.30, sch.6; repealed in pt.: *ibid.*, schs.6,7.

s. 5, orders 75/2232; 78/1464; 85/62.

s. 6, Acts of Sederunt, 76/778, 850; 78/924; 79/1408, 1409; 82/1506; 85/499; 86/641.

s. 8, amended: 1973, c.65, sch.9; repealed in pt.: S.L.R. 1974.

sch. 2, repealed: *ibid.*

48. Costs in Criminal Cases Act 1952.

repealed: 1973, c.14, sch.2.

ss. 5, 9, see *R.* v. *Chertsey JJ., ex p. Edwards & Co.* [1973] 1 W.L.R. 1545; [1974] 1 All E.R. 156, D.C.

s. 6, see *R.* v. *Lewes Crown Court, ex p. Rogers* [1974] 1 W.L.R. 196; [1974] 1 All E.R. 589, D.C.

s. 12, regs. 72/49; 73/922.

51. Isle of Man (Customs) Act 1952.

s. 5, amended: S.L.R. 1974.

52. Prison Act 1952.

see *R.* v. *Board of Visitors of Hull Prison, ex p. St. Germain, The Times,* October 4, 1978, C.A.

s. 4, see *R.* v. *Deputy Governor of Camp Hill Prison, ex p. King, The Times,* August 15, 1984, C.A.; *R.* v. *Secretary of State for the Home Department, ex p. Dew, The Independent,* February 19, 1987, McNeill J; *Leech* v. *Deputy Governor of Parkhurst Prison, sub nom. R.* v. *Deputy Governor of Parkhurst Prison, ex p. Leech; R.* v. *Deputy Governor of Long Lartin Prison, ex p. Prevot* [1988] 2 W.L.R. 290, H.L.

s. 5A, added: 1982, c.48, s.57.

s. 7, see *Freeman* v. *The Home Office* [1983] 3 All E.R. 589, McGowan J.

s. 7, repealed in pt.: 1975, c.65, s.18.

s. 8, see *Home Office* v. *Robinson* [1982] I.C.R. 31, E.A.T.

s. 12, see *Williams* v. *Home Office (No. 2)* [1981] 1 All E.R. 1211, Tudor Evans J.; *R.* v. *Secretary of State for the Home Department, ex p. McAvoy* [1984] 3 All E.R. 417, Webster J.

CAP.

15 & 16 Geo. 6 & 1 Eliz. 2
(1951–52)—cont.

52. Prison Act 1952—cont.

s. 13, see *Nicoll* v. *Catron* (1985) 81 Cr.App.R. 339, D.C.: *R.* v. *Moss and Hartle* [1986] Crim.L.R. 659; (1985) 82 Cr.App.R. 116, C.A.

s. 13, amended: 1982, c.48, sch.14.

s. 19, repealed in pt.: 1972, c.70, sch.30.

s. 22, amended: 1982, c.48, sch.14.

s. 25, rules 72/1860; 81/70; 82/260; 83/568–570; 87/1256; 88/1421, 1422.

s. 36, amended: 1981, c.67, sch.4; repealed in pt.: *ibid.*, sch.6.

s. 37, amended: 1982, c.48, sch.14.

s. 38, repealed in pt.: 1972, c.71, sch.6.

s. 39, see *Nicoll* v. *Catron* (1985) 81 Cr.App.R. 339; [1985] Crim.L.R. 223, D.C.; *R.* v. *Moss and Harte* [1986] Crim.L.R. 659; (1985) 82 Cr.App.R. 116, C.A.

s. 43, see *Nicoll* v. *Catron* (1985) 81 Cr.App.R. 339, D.C.

s. 43, rules 83/569, 570; 88/1422.

s. 43, substituted: 1982, c.48, s.11; amended: 1988, c.33, sch.15; repealed in pt.: *ibid.*, sch.16.

ss. 44–46, repealed: 1982, c.48, sch.16.

s. 47, see *Fraser* v. *Mudge* [1975] 1 W.L.R. 1132; [1975] 3 All E.R. 78, C.A; *R.* v. *Hull Prison Board of Visitors, ex p. St. Germain (No. 2)* [1979] 3 All E.R. 545, D.C.; *R.* v. *Secretary of State for the Home Department, ex p. Tarrant* [1984] 2 W.L.R. 613, D.C.; *R.* v. *Secretary of State for the Home Department, ex p. Anderson* [1984] 2 W.L.R. 725, D.C.; *R.* v. *Secretary of State for the Home Department, ex p. Benwell* [1984] 3 W.L.R. 843, Hodgson J.; *R.* v. *Deputy Governor of Camp Hill Prison, ex p. King, The Times,* August 15, 1984, C.A.; *R.* v. *Secretary of State for the Home Department, ex p. Broom* [1985] 3 W.L.R. 778, Kennedy J.; *R.* v. *Secretary of State for the Home Department, ex p. Hickling* (1986) 16 Fam. Law 140, C.A.; *R.* v. *Secretary of State for the Home Department, ex p. Simmons, The Times,* October 5, 1988, D.C.

s. 47, rules 72/1012, 1860; 74/713, 1923; 75/1263; 76/502, 503; 81/70; 82/260; 83/568–570; 87/1256, 2176; 88/89, 747, 1421, 1422.

s. 49, amended: 1982, c.48, sch.14; repealed in pt.: *ibid.*, sch.16.

ss. 51–53, see *Becker* v. *Home Office* [1972] 2 W.L.R. 1193; [1972] 2 All E.R. 676.

s. 53, amended: 1982, c.48, sch.14.

s. 54, repealed in pt: S.L.R. 1974.

s. 55, repealed in pt.: 1982, c.48, sch.16.

sch. 4, repealed: S.L.R. 1974.

54. Town Development Act 1952.

s. 1, amended and repealed in pt.: 1972, c.70, s.185.

s. 2, amended: 1973, c.37, sch.8; repealed in pt.: 1972, c.47, sch.11; c.70, schs.18,30; 1973, c.37, sch.9.

s. 3, repealed in pt.: 1972, c.47, sch.11.

s. 4, amended: 1972, c.70, sch.18; 1985, c.51, sch.8; repealed in pt.: 1980, c.65, sch.34.

CAP.

15 & 16 Geo. 6 & 1 Eliz. 2
(1951–52)—cont.

54. Town Development Act 1952—cont.
s. 5, repealed in pt.: ibid., s.185, sch.30.
s. 6, amended: 1981, c.67, sch.4; repealed in pt.: ibid., sch.6.
s. 7, amended: 1972, c.70, sch.18; 1973, c.37, sch.8; 1985, c.51, sch.8; repealed in pt.: 1980, c.65, sch.34.
s. 8, amended: 1972, c.70, sch.18; 1973, c.37, sch.8; repealed in pt.: 1972, c.47, sch.11; c.70, schs.18,30; 1973, c.37, schs.8,9; 1980, c.65, sch.34.
s. 9, repealed in pt.: 1973, c.37, sch.9.
s. 10, amended: 1972, c.70, sch.18; 1985, c.51, sch.8; repealed in pt.: 1972, c.70, s.185, sch.30; 1980, c.65, sch.34.
s. 11, repealed: 1980, c.65, s.124, sch.34.
s. 12, repealed: 1972, c.70, sch.30.
s. 13, repealed in pt.: ibid.
s. 14, amended: 1972, c.47, sch.9; repealed in pt.: ibid., sch.11.
s. 15, repealed: 1973, c.37, sch.9.

55. Magistrates' Courts Act 1952.
repealed: 1980, c.43, sch.9.
see R. v. Colchester Stipendiary Magistrate, ex p. Beck [1979] Crim.L.R. 250, D.C.; R. v. Gateshead JJ., ex p. Tesco Stores; R. v. Birmingham JJ. ex p. D. W. Parkin Construction [1981] 2 W.L.R. 419; [1981] 1 All E.R. 1027, D.C.; Maher v. Gower, The Times, November 7, 1981, Purchas J.
s. 1, see R. v. West London Justices, ex p. Klahn [1979] 2 All E.R. 221, D.C.
s. 2, see R. v. East Powder JJ., ex p. Lampshire [1979] 2 W.L.R. 479, D.C.
s. 4, see R. v. Colchester Stipendiary Magistrate, ex p. Beck [1979] 2 W.L.R. 637, P.C.
s. 7, see R. v. Horsham JJ., ex p. Reeves [1981] Crim.L.R. 566, D.C.; R. v. Peter Anthony Carey (1983) 76 Cr.App.R. 152, C.A.
s. 13, see R. v. Gowerton JJ., ex p. Davies [1974] Crim.L.R. 253, D.C.
s. 14, see R. v. Talgarth Justices, ex p. Bithell [1973] 2 All E.R. 717.
s. 15, see R. v. Maidstone JJ., ex p. Booth, The Times, May 17, 1980, D.C.
s. 18, see Collins v. Spring [1975] Crim.L.R. 100, D.C.; R. v. Manchester Crown Court, ex p. McKenzie [1975] Crim.L.R. 347, D.C.; R. v. Greater Manchester JJ., ex p. Martyn [1976] Crim.L.R. 574, D.C.
s. 19, see R. v. Lymm Justices [1973] 1 All E.R. 716, D.C.; R. v. McLean, ex p. Metropolitan Commissioner of Police [1975] Crim.L.R. 289, D.C.
s. 25, see R. v. Khan [1974] Crim.L.R. 45, C.A.
s. 28, see R. v. O'Connor [1976] 1 W.L.R. 368, C.A.; R. v. T. (A Juvenile) [1979] Crim.L.R. 588, Snaresbrook Crown Ct.; R. v. Folkestone and Hythe Juvenile Court Justices, ex p. R. (A Juvenile) (1982) 74 Cr.App.R. 58, D.C.
s. 29, see R. v. Blackpool JJ. (ex p. Charlson) [1972] 1 W.L.R. 1456; [1972] 3 All E.R. 854; R. v. Lymm Justices [1973] 1 All E.R. 716,

CAP.

15 & 16 Geo. 6 & 1 Eliz. 2
(1951–52)—cont.

55. Magistrates' Courts Act 1952—cont.
D.C.; R. v. Hartlepool JJ., ex p. King [1973] Crim.L.R. 637, D.C.; R. v. Rugby JJ., ex p. Prince [1974] 2 All E.R. 116, D.C.; R. v. Harlow JJ., ex p. Galway [1975] Crim.L.R. 288, D.C.; R. v. Manchester Crown Court, ex p. McKenzie [1975] Crim.L.R. 347, D.C.; R. v. Colchester JJ., ex p. North Essex Building Co. [1977] 1 W.L.R. 1109, D.C.; R. v. Brentwood JJ., ex p. Jones [1979] Crim.L.R. 115, D.C.; R. v. Derby and South Derbyshire Magistrates, ex p. McCarthy and McGovern (1980) 2 Cr.App.R.(S.) 140, D.C.; R. v. Warrington JJ., ex p. Mooney (1980) 2 Cr.App.R.(S.) 40, D.C.
s. 35, see Stanton v. Webber [1973] R.T.R. 86, D.C.; Cassady v. Reg Morris (Transport) [1975] R.T.R. 470, D.C.; Ullah v. Luckhurst [1977] R.T.R. 401, D.C.; Makeham v. Donaldson [1981] R.T.R. 511, D.C.
s. 38, see R. v. McGregor [1975] Crim.L.R. 514; R. v. Houghton; R. v. Franciosy (1978) 68 Cr.App.R. 197, C.A.; R. v. Hudson (1980) 72 Cr.App.R. 163, D.C.; Re Sherman and Apps [1981] 2 All E.R. 612; (1981) 72 Cr.App.R. 266, D.C.; R. v. Nycander, The Times, December 9, 1982, C.A.; R. v. Boyd Mackintosh (1983) 76 Cr.App.R. 177, C.A.
s. 40, see R. v. Jones (Yvonne) [1978] R.T.R. 137, C.A.; George v. Coombe [1978] Crim.L.R. 47, D.C.
s. 54, see Re K. (A Minor) (Access Order: Breach) [1977] 1 W.L.R. 533, D.C. (Note).
s. 55, see R. v. Uxbridge JJ., ex p. Met. Police Comr., The Times, June 13, 1981, C.A.
s. 57, see Tomlinson v. Tomlinson [1980] 1 W.L.R. 322; [1980] 1 All E.R. 593, D.C.
s. 63, see R. v. Bunce (1977) 66 Cr.App.R. 109, C.A.
s. 64, see R. v. Southampton JJ., ex p. Davies [1981] 1 W.L.R. 374; [1981] 1 All E.R. 722, D.C.
ss. 65, 71, see R. v. Clerkenwell Stipendiary Magistrate, ex p. Mays [1975] 1 W.L.R. 52; [1975] 1 All E.R. 65, D.C.
s. 76, see Ross v. Pearson (formerly Ross) [1976] 1 W.L.R. 224, D.C.; R. v. Halifax JJ., ex p. Woolverton (1978) 123 S.J. 123, D.C.
s. 77, see R. v. Greenwich Justices, ex p. Carter [1973] Crim.L.R. 444; R. v. Greenwich Juvenile Court, ex p. Greenwich London Borough Council (1977) 76 L.G.R. 99, D.C.
s. 81, see Ross v. Hodges [1975] R.T.R. 55, D.C.
ss. 83, 87, see Sivalingham v. D.P.P., October 13, 1975.
s. 87, see Michael v. Gorland [1977] 1 W.L.R. 296, D.C.; Kirk v. Civil Aviation Authority, May 16, 1978, Judge Clarke, Exeter Crown Ct.; Robinson v. Whittle (1980) 124 S.J. 807, D.C.; R. v. Bromley Magistrates' Court, ex p. Waitrose [1980] 3 All E.R. 464, D.C.; R. v. Petersfield JJ., ex p. Levy [1981] R.T.R. 204, D.C.; R. v. Winchester Crown Court, ex p. Lewington [1982] 1 W.L.R. 1277, D.C.

CAP.

15 & 16 Geo. 6 & 1 Eliz. 2
(1951–52)—cont.

55. Magistrates' Courts Act 1952—cont.

s. 90, see *R.* v. *Preston JJ., ex p. Pamplin, The Times,* April 1, 1981, D.C.

s. 96, see *R.* v. *Southampton JJ., ex p. Green* [1975] 3 W.L.R. 277; [1975] 2 All E.R. 1073, C.A.; *R.* v. *Tottenham Magistrates' Court, ex p. Riccardi* (1977) 66 Cr.App.R. 150, D.C.; *R.* v. *Wells St. Magistrates' Court, ex p. Albanese* [1981] 3 W.L.R. 694; (1982) 74 Cr.App.R. 180, Gibson J.

s. 98, see *R.* v. *Denbigh Justices, ex p. Williams; R.* v. *Denbigh Justices, ex p. Evans* [1974] 3 W.L.R. 45; [1974] 2 All E.R. 1052, D.C.

s. 100, see *Taylor* v. *Grey* [1973] R.T.R. 281; *Darnell* v. *Holliday* [1973] R.T.R. 276; *R.* v. *Godstone JJ., ex p. Secretary of State for the Environment* [1974] Crim.L.R. 110, D.C.; *Allan* v. *Wiseman* [1975] Crim.L.R. 37; [1975] R.T.R. 217, D.C.; *R.* v. *Newcastle-upon-Tyne JJ., ex p. John Bryce (Contractors)* [1976] 1 W.L.R. 517, D.C.; *Tuberville* v. *Wyer; Bryn Motor Co.* v. *Wyer* [1977] R.T.R. 29, D.C.; *Morriss* v. *Lawrence* [1977] R.T.R. 205, D.C.; *Roberts* v. *Griffiths* [1978] R.T.R. 362, D.C.; *R.* v. *Sandwell JJ., ex p. West Midlands Passenger Transport Board* [1979] R.T.R. 17, D.C.; *Lee* v. *Wiltshire Chief Constable* [1979] R.T.R. 349, D.C.

s. 102, see *De Costa Small* v. *Kirkpatrick* (1978) 68 Cr.App.R. 186, D.C.

s. 104, see *R.* v. *Bicester JJ., ex p. Unigate* [1975] 1 W.L.R. 207; [1975] 1 All E.R. 449, D.C.; *R.* v. *Newcastle-upon-Tyne JJ., ex p. John Bryce (Contractors)* [1976] 1 W.L.R. 517, D.C.; *Mitchell* v. *Lepine-Smith* (1977) 75 L.G.R. 474, D.C.; *St. Albans District Council* v. *Norman Harper Autosales* (1977) 245 E.G. 1029, D.C.; *R.* v. *Eastbourne JJ., ex p. Barsoum,* January 26, 1979; *R.* v. *Sandwell JJ., ex p. West Midlands Passenger Transport Board* [1979] R.T.R. 17, D.C.; *R.* v. *Coventry JJ., ex p. Sayers* [1979] R.T.R. 22, D.C.; *R.* v. *Brentford Justices, ex p. Wong* [1981] 2 W.L.R. 203, D.C.; *R.* v. *Leeds JJ., ex p. Hanson; R.* v. *Manchester Stipendiary Magistrate, ex p. Hill; R.* v. *Edmonton JJ., ex p. Hughes; R.* v. *Gateshead JJ., ex p. Ives; R.* v. *Dartford JJ., ex p. Rhesi; Moody* v. *Anderton, The Times,* June 25, 1981, D.C.; *R.* v. *Oxford City Justices, ex p. Smith* [1982] R.T.R. 201, D.C.; *R.* v. *Watford JJ., ex p. Outrim* [1983] R.T.R. 26, D.C.

s. 107, see *R.* v. *Bunce* (1977) 66 Cr.App.R. 109, C.A.; *R.* v. *Greenwich JJ., ex p. Carter* [1973] Crim.L.R. 444.

s. 108, see *R.* v. *Metropolitan Stipendiary Magistrate for South Westminster, ex p. Green* [1977] 1 All E.R. 353, D.C.

ss. 108, 126, see *R.* v. *Uxbridge JJ., ex p. Fisc* [1980] 2 Cr.App.R.(S.) 112, D.C.

sch. 2, see *R.* v. *Colchester JJ., ex p. North Essex Building Co.* [1977] 1 W.L.R. 1109, D.C.

sch. 3, see *R.* v. *Southampton JJ., ex p. Davies* [1981] 1 W.L.R. 374; [1981] 1 All E.R. 722, D.C.

CAP.

15 & 16 Geo. 6 & 1 Eliz. 2
(1951–52)—cont.

56. Insurance Contracts (War Settlement) Act 1952.

repealed: S.L.R. 1981.

57. Marine and Aviation Insurance (War Risks) Act 1952.

s. 11, repealed in pt.: S.L.R. 1974.

sch., repealed: *ibid.*

58. Irish Sailors and Soldiers Land Trust Act 1952.

repealed: 1987, c.48, sch.

59. Cockfighting Act 1952.

s. 1, amended: 1977, c.45, s.31, sch.6.

60. Agriculture (Poisonous Substances) Act 1952.

ss. 1–3 repealed: order 75/45.

s. 4, amended: 1972, c.62, s.14; repealed in pt.: order 75/45.

s. 5, repealed: *ibid.*

s. 6, amended: orders 75/45; 76/1247.

s. 8, repealed: *ibid.*

s. 9, repealed: order 75/45.

s. 10, repealed in pt.: order 76/1247.

s. 11, repealed in pt.: order 75/45.

61. Prisons (Scotland) Act 1952.

s. 6A, added: 1982, c.48, s.57.

s. 7, rules 84/2058; 87/2231; 88/537.

s. 7, amended: 1973, c.65, sch.27; repealed in pt.: 1980, c.62, sch.8; 1985, c.73, s.42, sch.4.

s. 12, see *McAllister* v. *H.M. Advocate,* 1986 S.C.C.R. 688.

s. 14, rules 74/982.

s. 14, amended: 1973, c.65, sch.27; 1980, c.62, sch.7.

s. 16, amended: 1973, c.65, sch.7; 1985, c.73, s.42.

s. 17, amended: *ibid.*

s. 18, repealed in pt.: *ibid.,* sch.4.

s. 19, repealed: 1980, c.62, sch.8.

s. 20, rules 83/1739.

s. 25, repealed in pt. (S.): 1976, c.14, sch.2.

s. 28, amended: 1980, c.62, sch.7.

s. 31, rules 83/1739.

s. 31, amended: 1980, c.62, sch.7; 1988, c.33, sch.9; repealed in pt.: 1973, c.65, sch.29; 1980, c.62, schs.7,8; 1988, c.33, sch.16.

ss. 32, 33, repealed: *ibid.,* sch.8.

s. 34, amended: *ibid.,* sch.7; 1985, c.73, s.42; repealed in pt.: 1988, c.33, sch.16.

s. 35, rules 76/1889; 79/1630; 81/1222, 1223; 83/1739; 84/2058; 87/2231; 88/537.

s. 35, amended: 1980, c.62, sch.7; repealed in pt.: *ibid.,* sch.8; 1985, c.73, s.42, sch.4; 1988, c.33, sch.16.

s. 37, repealed in pt.: 1973, c.65, sch.29; 1980, c.62, schs.7,8; 1988, c.33, sch.16.

ss. 38, 41, repealed: 1973, c.65, sch.29.

s. 42, repealed in pt.: *ibid.*

s. 43, repealed in pt.: S.L.R. 1974.

sch. 4, repealed in pt.: *ibid.*

62. Agriculture (Calf Subsidies) Act 1952.

repealed: S.L.R. 1986.

s. 1, scheme 73/533.

ss. 1, 4, schemes 73/717; 74/630, 1123, 1282; 75/535; 77/453.

15 & 16 Geo. 6 & 1 Eliz. 2 (1951–52)—cont.

63. Housing (Scotland) Act 1952.
repealed: 1972, c.46, sch.11.

64. Intestates' Estates Act 1952.
s. 7, sch. 3, repealed: 1975, c.63, sch.
sch. 2, see *Re Collins (decd.); Robinson* v. *Collins* [1975] 1 W.L.R. 309; [1975] 1 All E.R. 321; *Re Phelps (decd.), Wells* v. *Phelps* [1979] 3 All E.R. 373, C.A.

66. Defamation Act 1952.
ss. 3, 7, amended: 1984, c.46, s.28.
s. 5, see *Pamplin* v. *Express Newspapers, The Times*, March 18, 1985, C.A.; *Polly Peck (Holdings)* v. *Trelford* [1986] 2 W.L.R. 845, C.A.
s. 7, see *Blackshaw* v. *Lord* [1983] 2 All E.R. 311, C.A.
s. 10, see *Fairbairn* v. *Scottish National Party* (O.H.), April 26, 1976.
s. 15, repealed: 1973, c.36, sch.6.
s. 16, amended: 1984, c.12, sch.4; repealed in pt.: 1984, c.46, sch.6.
s. 18, repealed in pt.: 1973, c.36, sch.6; S.L.R. 1974.
sch., see *Blackshaw* v. *Lord* [1983] 2 All E.R. 311, C.A.
sch., amended: 1981, c.61, sch.7; 1985, c.43, sch.2.

67. Visiting Forces Act 1952.
s. 1, see *R.* v. *Thames Metropolitan Stipendiary Magistrate, ex p. Brindle* [1975] 1 W.L.R. 1400, C.A.
s. 1, amended: 1973, c.27, sch.2; c.49, sch.; 1976, c.19, sch.; 1978, c.15, sch.; c.20, sch.2; 1979, c.27, sch.; 1980, c.2, sch.; c.16, sch.1; 1981, c.52, sch.2; orders 78/1030; 80/701; 81/1105; 83/882; 1985, c.3, sch.; repealed in pt.: 1973, c.48, sch.4.
s. 3, amended: 1973, c.47, s.6; 1982, c.45, s.52.
s. 5, amended: 1988, c.33, sch.15.
s. 8, order 87/928.
s. 10, amended: 1978, c.15, sch.; 1979, c.27, sch.; 1981, c.52, sch.2.
s. 12, amended: 1988, c.33, sch.15.
ss. 12, 13, see *R.* v. *Thames Met. Stipendiary Magistrate, ex p. Brindle* [1975] 1 W.L.R. 1400, C.A.
s. 13, see *Re Narinder Singh Virdee, The Times*, March 13, 1980, D.C.
ss. 13, 14, see *R.* v. *Tottenham Magistrates' Court, ex p. Williams* [1982] 2 All E.R. 705, D.C.
s. 15, repealed in pt.: 1981, c.61, sch.9.
s. 18, repealed: S.L.R. 1974.
sch., amended: 1978, c.17, s.2: c.31, s.5; c.37, s.1; 1982, c.45, s.52 (S); 1983, c.18, s.4; 1984, c.37, s.11; 1985, c.38, s.3; orders 78/1047, 1407; 1988, c.33, sch.15.

68. Cinematograph Act 1952.
repealed: 1985, c.13, sch.3.
s. 2, regs. 82/1856.
s. 5, regs. 83/367 (S.).
s. 8, sch., regs. 76/1315.

1 & 2 Eliz. 2 (1952–53)

1. Colonial Loans Act 1952.
repealed: 1980, c.63, sch.2.

7. Law Reform (Personal Injuries) (Amendment) Act 1953.
repealed (S.): 1976, c.13, sch.2.

12. Leasehold Property Act and Long Leases (Scotland) Act Extension Act 1953.
repealed: S.L.R. 1975.

13. Transport Act 1953.
s. 24, repealed: S.L.R. 1978.

14. Prevention of Crime Act 1953.
see *R.* v. *Spanner, Poulter and Ward* [1973] Crim.L.R. 704, C.A.
s. 1, see *R.* v. *Brown (D. W.)* (1971) 55 Cr.App.R. 478; *Evans* v. *Hughes* [1972] 1 W.L.R. 1452; [1972] 3 All E.R. 412; *R.* v. *Dayle* [1973] 3 All E.R. 1151, C.A.; *Bradley* v. *Moss* [1974] Crim.L.R. 430, D.C.; *R.* v. *Allamby; R.* v. *Medford* [1974] 3 All E.R. 126, C.A.; *Ohlson* v. *Hylton* [1975] 1 W.L.R. 724, D.C.; *R.* v. *Giles* [1976] Crim.L.R. 253; *Bryan* v. *Mott* (1976) 62 Cr.App.R. 71, D.C.; *Pittard* v. *Mahoney* [1977] Crim.L.R. 169, D.C.; *R.* v. *Williamson* (1978) 67 Cr.App.R. 35, C.A.; *Bates* v. *Bulman* (1978) 68 Cr.App.R. 21, D.C.; *R.* v. *Ambrose*, January 31, 1979, London Crown Court, Judge Layton; *R.* v. *Rapier* (1979) 70 Cr.App.R. 17, C.A.; *Lopez* v. *MacNab*, 1978 J.C. 41; *R.* v. *Morris*, February 5, 1981, Kingston-upon-Thames Crown Ct., Judge Bax, Q.C.; *R.* v. *Heffey* [1981] Crim.L.R. 111, Liverpool Crown Ct.; *Tudhope* v. *O'Neill*, 1982 S.L.T. 360; *R.* v. *McCogg* [1982] Crim.L.R. 685, Inner London Crown Ct.; *Gibson* v. *Wales* [1983] 1 All E.R. 869, D.C.; *Hemming* v. *Annan*, 1982 S.C.C.R. 432; *Knox* v. *Anderton* (1983) 76 Cr.App.R. 156, C.A.; *Addison* v. *Mackinnon*, 1983 S.C.C.R. 52; *R.* v. *Simpson (Calvin)* [1983] 3 All E.R. 789, C.A.; *Kincaid* v. *Tudhope*, 1983 S.C.C.R. 389; *R.* v. *Forbes* [1984] Crim.L.R. 482, C.A.; *O'Rourke* v. *Lockhart*, 1984 S.C.C.R. 322; *R.* v. *Russell (Raymond)* [1985] Crim.L.R. 231, C.A.; *R.* v. *Flynn* [1986] Crim.L.R. 239; (1986) 82 Cr.App.R. 319, C.A.; *Coull* v. *Guild*, 1986 S.L.T. 184; *Houghton* v. *Chief Constable of Greater Manchester, The Times*, July 24, 1986, C.A.; *Southwell* v. *Chadwick, The Times*, January 8, 1987, D.C.; *Campbell* v. *H.M. Advocate*, 1986 S.C.C.R. 516; *Ralston* v. *Lockhart*, 1986 S.C.C.R. 400; *Smith* v. *Wilson*, 1987 S.C.C.R. 191, *Houghton* v. *Chief Constable of Greater Manchester* (1987) 84 Cr.App.R. 320, C.A.; *Glendinning* v. *Guild*, 1987 S.C.C.R. 304; *Southwell* v. *Chadwick* (1987) 85 Cr.App.R. 235, C.A.; *McLaughlin* v. *Tudhope*, 1987 S.C.C.R. 456; *R.* v. *McCalla, The Times*, April 12, 1988, C.A.; *Woods* v. *Heywood*, 1988 S.L.T. 849.
s. 1, amended (S.): 1984, c.54, sch.9; 1986, c.64, sch.2; 1988, c.33, s.46; repealed in pt.: 1984, c.60, sch.7.
ss. 1, 4, see *Harrison* v. *Thornton (Note)* (1979) 68 Cr.App.R. 28, D.C.
s. 4, see *R.* v. *Flynn (James)* (1986) 82 Cr.App.R. 319, C.A.

CAP.

1 & 2 Eliz. 2 (1952–53)—cont.

15. Iron and Steel Act 1953.
repealed: 1975, c.64, sch.7.

16. Town and Country Planning Act 1953.
repealed: 1972, c.52, sch.23.

18. Coastal Flooding (Emergency Provisions) Act 1953.
repealed: S.L.R. 1977.

20. Births and Deaths Registration Act 1953.
s. 1, regs, 74/572; 85/1133, 1134; 87/2088.
s. 1, amended: 1975, c.72, sch.3.
s. 3, amended: *ibid.*; repealed in pt.: *ibid.*, sch.4.
3A, regs. 76/2081, 2092; 87/2088.
s. 3A, added: 1975, c.72, s.92.
ss. 4, 5, amended: *ibid.*, sch.3.
s. 5, regs. 74/572; 87/2088.
ss. 6–8, repealed in pt.: 1975, c.72, sch.4.
s. 7, regs. 74/572; 87/2088.
s. 9, regs. 74/572; 76/2081, 2092; 87/2088.
s. 9, amended: 1975, c.72, s.93; 1987, c.42, sch.2.
s. 10, substituted: *ibid.*, s.24.
ss. 10, 10A, regs. 76/2081, 2092; 87/2088.
s. 10A, substituted: 1987, c.42, s.25.
s. 11, regs. 74/572; 85/1133, 1134; 87/2088.
s. 11, amended: 1979, c.36, sch.7.
s. 12, regs. 87/2088.
s. 13, regs. 74/572; 87/2088; order 75/1291.
s. 13, amended: orders 77/1861; 81/241.
s. 14, regs. 74/572; 87/2088.
s. 14, amended: 1975, c.72, sch.3; 1976, c.31, sch.1; 1987, c.42 sch.2; repealed in pt.: *ibid*
s. 14A, regs. 87/2088; 88/638, 687.
s. 14A, added: 1987, c.42, s.26.
ss. 15, 20, regs. 74/572; 82/265, 266; 87/2088.
s. 21, regs. 74/572; 87/2088.
s. 22, regs. 74/572; 85/568, 569, 1133, 1134; 87/2088.
s. 23, regs. 74/572, 2088.
s. 23, amended: 1988, c.13, sch.3; repealed in pt.: *ibid.*, schs.3,4.
ss. 23, 29, see *Att.-Gen.* v. *Harte (J.D.)* (1987) 151 J.P.N. 750, Taylor J.
s. 24, regs. 74, 572; 87/2088.
s. 25, regs. 74/572.
s. 26, regs. 87/2088.
s. 29, regs. 74/572; 87/2088; 88/638.
s. 29, amended: 1977, c.45, sch.12; 1988, c.13, sch.3.
s. 30, amended: 1975, c.72, sch.3; orders 75/1291; 77/1861; 81/241; 82/222.
ss. 31–33, amended: orders 75/1291, 77/1861; 81/241; 82/222.
s. 33, regs. 74/572; 76/2081, 2092; 87/2088.
s. 34, amended: 1975, c.72, sch.3; 1987, c.42, sch.2.
s. 36, repealed in pt.: 1975, c.72, sch.4
s. 37, repealed in pt.: 1981, c.45, sch.
s. 38, repealed in pt.: 1972, c.71, sch.6.
s. 39, regs. 74/572; 76/2080, 2081, 2092; 77/1912; 82/265, 266; 85/568, 569, 1133, 1134; 87/2088; 88/638, 687.
s. 39, amended: 1978, c.52, sch.11.
s. 41, regs. 74/572; 87/2088; 88/638, 687.
s. 41, amended: 1975, c.72, sch.3; repealed in pt.: *ibid.*, sch.4.

CAP.

1 & 2 Eliz. 2 (1952–53)—cont.

20. Births and Deaths Registration Act 1953— cont.
s. 43, repealed in pt.: S.L.R. 1974.
sch. 1, repealed in pt.: S.L.R. 1977.
sch. 2, repealed: S.L.R. 1974.

23. Accommodation Agencies Act 1953.
s. 1, see *Saunders* v. *Soper* [1974] 3 W.L.R. 777; [1974] 3 All E.R. 1025, H.L.

25. Local Government Superannuation Act 1953.
repealed: 1972, c.11, sch.8; c.70, sch.30.
repealed, except ss. 1 (in pt.), 18, 21, 27, 29, sch. 4, regs. 77/1341.
ss. 1, 18, amended: *ibid.*
s. 15, see *Hertfordshire County Council* v. *Retirement Lease Housing Association, The Independent*, February 19, 1987, Hoffmann J.; *Hertfordshire County Council* v. *Retirement Lease Housing Association*, (1988) 86 L.G.R. 222, Hoffmann J.

26. Local Government (Miscellaneous Provisions) Act 1953.
ss. 1–3, repealed: 1972, c.70, sch.30.
s. 4, amended: 1980, c.34, sch.5; 1981, c.14, sch.7.
s. 5, amended: 1980, c.65, sch.7.
s. 6, amended: 1981, c.38, sch.3; 1984, c.12, sch.4.
s. 8, repealed: 1974, c.40, sch.4
s. 12, substituted: 1973, c.37, sch.8.
s. 13, amended: *ibid.*, s. 14.
s. 14, repealed: 1972, c.70, sch.30.
ss. 15–17, repealed: S.L.R. 1976.
s. 18, repealed in pt.: 1972, c.70, sch.30; S.L.R. 1976.
s. 19, repealed in pt.: *ibid.*

27. Slaughter of Animals (Pigs) Act 1953.
repealed: 1980, c.13, sch.3.

28. Dogs (Protection of Livestock) Act 1953.
s. 1, amended: 1977, c.45, s.31, sch.6; 1981, c.69, sch.7.
s. 2A, added: 1984, c.60, sch.6.

30. Rhodesia and Nyasaland Federation Act 1953.
repealed: S.L.R. 1976.

33. Education (Miscellaneous Provisions) Act 1953.
s. 2, amended: 1980, c.20, sch.3; 1988, c.40, s.114, sch.12.
s. 4, repealed: 1973, c.32, sch.5.
ss. 5–7, see *R.* v. *Hampshire County Council, The Times*, December 5, 1985, Taylor J.
s. 6, amended: 1981, c.60, sch.3; repealed in pt.: 1980, c.20, s.28, sch.7.
s. 7, repealed: *ibid.*, sch.7.
s. 8, repealed in pt.: *ibid.*, sch.1.
s. 9, repealed: *ibid.*, sch.7.
s. 12, repealed: 1980, c.34, sch.9.
s. 13, repealed: S.L.R. 1978.
s. 14, repealed: 1973, c.16, sch.2.
s. 16, repealed: 1980, c.20, sch.7.
s. 17, repealed in pt.: 1973, c.16, sch.2.
s. 19, repealed: S.L.R. 1978.
sch. 1, repealed in pt.: 1973, c.32, sch.5; 1976, c.81, s.10; 1980, c.20, sch.7.
sch. 2, repealed: 1973, c.16, sch.2.

CAP.

1 & 2 Eliz. 2 (1952–53)—cont.

34. Finance Act 1953.
s. 2, repealed: 1979, c.4, sch.4.
s. 3, amended: 1975, c.45, sch.3; repealed in pt.: *ibid.*, sch.14; 1978, c.42, sch.13; 1979, c.6, sch.
s. 20, see *Wilmot Breeden* v. *Haddock* [1975] S.T.C. 255, H.L.
s. 30, repealed: 1975, c.7, sch.13; 1980, c.17, sch.2.
s. 30, functions transferred: orders 81/207; 86/200.
s. 33, repealed in pt.: 1979, c.2, sch.6.
s. 35, repealed in pt.: S.L.R. 1974; 1979, c.2, sch.6.
sch. 3, repealed: S.L.R. 1974.

36. Post Office Act 1953.
ss. 3, 4, repealed: 1981, c.38, sch.6.
s. 11, see *R.* v. *Anderson; Neville; Dennis; R.* v. *Oz Publications Ink* [1971] 3 W.L.R. 939; [1971] 3 All E.R. 1152; 56 Cr.App.R. 115; *R.* v. *Stamford* [1972] 2 W.L.R. 1055; [1972] 2 All E.R. 430; 56 Cr.App.R. 398; *Kosmos Publications* v. *D.P.P.* [1975] Crim.L.R. 345, D.C.
s. 16, regs. 73/411; 75/1992; 86/260; order 86/1019.
s. 16, amended: 1979, c.9, sch.4; repealed in pt.: 1987, c.16, sch.16.
s. 17, amended: 1979, c.9, sch.4.
s. 23, repealed in pt.: 1981, c.45, sch.
s. 51, amended: 1972, c.70, sch.29; 1973, c.65, sch.27; repealed in pt.: 1972, c.70, schs.29,30; 1973, c.65, sch.29.
s. 56, amended: 1977, c.45, ss.15,30, sch.1.
s. 58, see *Gouriet* v. *Union of Post Office Workers* [1977] 3 W.L.R. 300, H.L.; *Harold Stephen & Co.* v. *Post Office* [1977] 1 W.L.R. 1172, C.A.
s. 58, amended: 1985, c.56, s.11.
ss. 60, 61, repealed in pt.: 1981, c.38, sch.6.
s. 63, amended: 1981, c.45, s.29.
s. 64, repealed in pt.: 1981, c.38, sch.6.
s. 65A, repealed: *ibid.*
s. 68, see *Gouriet* v. *Union of Post Office Workers* [1977] 3 W.L.R. 300, H.L.
s. 87, repealed in pt.: 1981, c.38, sch.6.
s. 91, repealed: S.L.R. 1974.
sch. 3, repealed: *ibid.*

37. Registration Service Act 1953.
see *R.* v. *Barrett* [1976] 1 W.L.R. 946, C.A.
ss. 5–7, 9, 10, 13, 14, 18, amended: 1972, c.70, sch.29.
s. 6, see *Miles* v. *Wakefield Metropolitan District Council* [1985] 1 All E.R. 905, C.A.
ss. 6, 16, regs. 74/571.
s. 17, repealed: S.L.R. 1986.
s. 19, amended: 1978, c.52, sch.11.
s. 20, regs. 74/571, 572; 77/1912; 82/955; 84/460, 461; 86/1442, 1445; 87/2088.
s. 20, amended: 1972, c.70, sch.29; 1975, c.14, s.160; 1978, c.52, sch.11.
s. 21, regs. 87/2088.
s. 21, amended: 1972, c.70, sch.29; repealed in pt.: S.L.R. 1976.
s. 23, repealed in pt.: S.L.R. 1974.
sch. 1, repealed in pt.: S.L.R. 1977.
sch. 2, repealed: *ibid.*

CAP.

1 & 2 Eliz. 2 (1952–53)—cont.

41. Hospital Endowments (Scotland) Act 1953.
repealed (S.): 1978, c.29, sch.17.

47. Emergency Laws (Miscellaneous Provisions) Act 1953.
s. 2, repealed in pt.: S.L.R. 1976.
s. 3, amended: order 74/1885; repealed in pt.: S.L.R. 1976.
s. 5, amended: 1973, c.65, sch.27; repealed in pt.:1972, c.70, sch.30; S.L.R. 1976.
s. 6, repealed: 1979, c.36, sch.8.
s. 9, repealed: S.L.R. 1974; S.L.R. 1976.
s. 10, amended: 1981, c.55, s.19.
s. 11, repealed: S.L.R. 1976.
s. 12, repealed in pt.: *ibid.*
ss. 13, 14, repealed in pt.: S.L.R. 1974; S.L.R. 1976.
sch. 1, repealed in pt.: S.L.R. 1973; S.L.R. 1974.

49. Historic Buildings and Ancient Monuments Act 1953.
s. 1, repealed: 1983, c.47, sch.6.
ss. 2, 3, amended: *ibid.*, sch.4; repealed in pt.: *ibid.*, sch.6.
s. 3A, added: *ibid.*, sch.4.
s. 4, amended: 1974, c.32, s.12; 1983, c.47, sch.4.
s. 4A, added: 1979, c.46, s.48; amended: 1983, c.47, sch.4.
s. 5, amended: 1979, c.46, sch.4; 1983, c.47, sch.4; 1985, c.16, s.21 (S.).
ss. 5A, 5B, added: 1983, c.47, sch.4.
s. 6, amended: *ibid.*; 1985, c.16, s.21 (S.).
s. 7, repealed: 1980, c.17, s.15, sch.2.
s. 8, amended: 1979, c.46, sch.4; 1983, c.47, sch.4; 1985, c.16, s.21 (S.).
ss. 8A–8C, added: 1983, c.47, sch.4.
s. 9, amended: *ibid.*
ss. 10–19, repealed: 1979, c.46, sch.5.
s. 12, see *Hoveringham Gravels* v. *Secretary of State for the Environment* [1975] 2 W.L.R. 897, C.A.
s. 19, repealed in pt.: 1975, c.76, sch.2.
s. 20, repealed: 1979, c.46, sch.5; 1981, c.67, sch.6.
s. 22, repealed in pt.: *ibid.*
sch., repealed: *ibid.*

50. Auxiliary Forces Act 1953.
repealed: 1980, c.9, sch.10.
s. 39, repealed in pt. (S.): 1980, c.55, sch.3.

52. Enemy Property Act 1953.
repealed, except ss. 4 (in pt.), 16, 18: S.L.R. 1976.
s. 4, amended: *ibid.*

2 & 3 Eliz. 2 (1953–54)

5. Statute Law Revision Act 1953.
s. 2, repealed: 1977, c.38, sch.5.
s. 4, repealed in pt.: 1973, c.36, sch.6.
schs. 1–3, repealed: S.L.R.1974.
sch. 4, repealed in pt.: *ibid.*

8. Electoral Registers Act 1953.
repealed: 1983, c.2, sch.9.

10. Navy, Army and Air Force Reserves Act 1954.
repealed: S.L.R. 1976.

2 & 3 Eliz. 2 (1953–54)—cont.

12. Currency and Bank Notes Act 1954.
s. 2, orders 72/154; 74/405; 76/232; 78/224; 80/192; 82/198.
s. 2, repealed: 1983, c.9, s.2, sch.
s. 3, repealed in pt.: *ibid.*, sch.
s. 4, amended: 1973, c.39, sch.1.

13. Local Government (Financial Provisions) (Scotland) Act 1954.
repealed: S.L.R. 1976.
s. 2, see *Midlothian C.C.* v. *Secretary of State for Scotland,* 1975 S.L.T. 122.

14. National Museum of Antiquities of Scotland Act 1954.
repealed: 1985, c.16, sch.2.

15. Cinematograph Film Production (Special Loans) Act 1954.
repealed: 1981, c.15, sch.3.

16. Industrial Training Act 1954.
s. 9, order 79/1595.

17. Royal Irish Constabulary (Widows' Pensions) Act 1954.
s. 1, regs. 72/1310; 75/484; 77/1949; 78/1692; 79/1401; 80/1486; 81/1321; 82/1316; 83/1379; 84/1350; 85/1319; 86/1381; 87/1461.

21. Rights of Entry (Gas and Electricity Boards) Act 1954.
s. 1, 2, amended: 1972, c.60, schs.6,8; 1986, c.44, sch.7.
s. 3, amended: 1972, c.60, schs.6,8; 1986, c.44, sch.7; repealed in pt.: *ibid.*, schs.7,9.

23. Hill Farming Act 1954.
s. 2, amended: 1972, c.70, sch.30; 1973, c.36, sch.6; 1975, c.76, sch.1; repealed in pt.: *ibid.*, sch.2.

24. Cotton Act 1954.
repealed: S.L.R. 1973.

30. Protection of Birds Act 1954.
repealed: 1981, c.69, sch.17.
s. 3, orders 74/1596; 78/1074, 1075; 80/401–404, 1839.
ss. 4, 5, see *Robinson* v. *Whittle* [1980] 1 W.L.R. 1476; [1980] 3 All E.R. 459, D.C.
s. 5, see *Jipps* v. *Lord, The Times,* May 24, 1982, D.C.
ss. 5, 9, 13, order 76/1416.
s. 7, order 79/1007.
s. 9, orders 77/408, 496, 2079; 78/96, 1071 (S.), 1872; 79/423, 437, 438; 81/650, 854 (S.).
s. 13, orders 77/496; 78/96; 79/70, 99 (S.), 141 (S.), 423, 437, 438; 80/944; 81/1890 (S.); 82/23, 59, 74 (S.), 234, 1218, 1234 (S.).

31. Coroners Act 1954.
repealed: 1988, c.13, sch.4.
s. 1, rules 72/980; 73/921, 1173, 1899; 74/936, 1581, 2178; 75/1090, 2066; 77/406.

32. Atomic Energy Authority Act 1954.
s. 1, amended and repealed in pt.: 1986, c.3, s.7.
s. 2, repealed in pt.: 1973, c.4, s.6.
s. 4, amended: 1981, c.48, s.4.
s. 5, amended: 1981, c.67, sch.4; 1984, c.54, sch.9(S.); c.55, sch.6; repealed in pt.: 1974, c.37, sch.10; 1981, c.67, sch.6; 1983, c.25, s.34, sch.4; 1984, c.55, sch.6.

2 & 3 Eliz. 2 (1953–54)—cont.

32. Atomic Energy Authority Act 1954—*cont.*
s. 6, see *Pearce* v. *Secretary of State for Defence, The Times,* April 29, 1988, H.L.
s. 6, amended: 1978, c.25, s.2.
s. 9, amended: 1981, c.67, sch.4.
sch. 3, amended: 1976, c.23, s.2; 1987, c.4, s.7.

34. Law Reform (Enforcement of Contracts) Act 1954.
repealed: S.L.R. 1974.

36. Law Reform (Limitation of Actions etc.) Act 1954.
repealed: S.L.R. 1978.
ss. 1, 7, see *Arnold* v. *Central Electricity Generating Board* [1987] 3 W.L.R. 1009, H.L.
s. 6, see *Comrie* v. *National Coal Board,* 1974 S.L.T.(Notes) 12; *Kerr* v. *J. A. Stewart (Plant),* First Division, February 27, 1976; *Boyle* v. *Glasgow Corporation,* 1978 S.L.T.(Notes) 77.

37. Superannuation (President of Industrial Court) Act 1954.
repealed: S.L.R. 1978.

38. Supreme Court Officers (Pensions) Act 1954.
repealed: 1981, c.54, sch.7.

39. Agriculture (Miscellaneous Provisions) Act 1954.
s. 2, order 74/1325.
s. 2, repealed: S.L.R. 1986.
ss. 5, 6, see *Wickington* v. *Bonney* (1983) 266 E.G. 434, Stephen Brown J.
s. 6, see *Clegg* v. *Fraser* (1982) 264 E.G. 144, McCullough J.
s. 6, order 78/259.
s. 7, repealed: 1976, c.55, sch.4.
s. 9, repealed in pt.: 1972, c.70, sch.30.
s. 10, orders 78/683; 79/587, 1588.
s. 10, repealed: 1980, c.12, s.5.
s. 11, repealed: 1981, c.22, sch.6.
s. 12, repealed in pt.: 1973, c.36, sch.6.
s. 13, repealed: S.L.R. 1973.
s. 16, repealed in pt.: 1973, c.36, sch.6; S.L.R. 1973.
s. 17, repealed in pt.: *ibid.*
sch. 2, repealed: 1981, c.22, sch.6.
sch. 3, repealed: S.L.R. 1973.

40. Protection of Animals (Amendment) Act 1954.
s. 1, amended: order 78/272; 1988, c.29, s.1.
ss. 1, 4, see *Wastie* v. *Phillips* [1972] 3 All E.R. 302, D.C.
s. 3, repealed: 1977, c.45, sch.13; 1988, c.29, sch.

41. Juries Act 1954.
repealed: S.L.R. 1974.

42. Slaughterhouses Act 1954.
repealed: 1980, c.13, sch.3; 1981, c.19, sch.1.
s. 7, see *Kelly* v. *Castle-Douglas Mags.,* Second Division, Nov. 1, 1974.

44. Finance Act 1954.
Pt. IV (ss. 28–33), repealed: 1975, c.7, sch.13.
s. 17, see *Crisp Malting* v. *Bourne* [1972] 1 W.L.R. 286; [1972] 1 All E.R. 700; [1971] T.R. 417; *J. H. & S. (Timber)* v. *Quirke* [1972] T.R. 311; *Ayerst* v. *C. & K. (Construction)* [1975] 3 W.L.R. 16; [1975] 2 All E.R. 537, H.L.

CAP.

2 & 3 Eliz. 2 (1953–54)—cont.

44. Finance Act 1954—cont.
s. 33, see Clark's Trustees v. I.R.C. [1972] T.R.
17; 1972 S.L.T. 190; Elliott v. I.R.C. [1974]
S.T.C. 80.
s. 35, repealed in pt.: S.L.R. 1974; 1975, c.7,
sch.13.
sch. 6, repealed: S.L.R. 1974.

**46. Protection of Animals (Anaesthetics) Act
1954.**
s. 1, order 82/1626.
s. 1, amended: order 78/272.
s. 2, repealed in pt.: S.L.R. 1974.
sch. 1, amended: order 82/1626; 1986, c.14,
sch.3.

48. Summary Jurisdiction (Scotland) Act 1954.
ss. 1–73, schs. 1, 4, repealed: 1975, c.21,
sch.10.
s. 7, see McGunnigal v. Copeland, 1972
S.L.T.(Notes) 70.
s. 8, see Adair v. Morton, 1972 S.L.T. (Notes)
70.
s. 15, see McCoull v. Skeen, 1974 S.L.T. (Notes)
48; Campbell v. McLeod, 1975 S.L.T.(Notes)
6.
s. 31, see Herron v. Nelson, 1976 S.L.T. (Sh.Ct.)
42.
ss. 52, 53, sch. 3, see Lord Advocate v. Aberdeen Corporation, 1977 S.L.T. 234.
s. 68, see Anderson v. H.M. Advocate, 1974
S.L.T. 239.
s. 71, see Wilson v. Milne, 1974 S.L.T. (Notes)
60.
ss. 71, 73, see Christie v. Barclay, 1974 J.C. 68.
s. 74, repealed in pt.: 1975, c.21, sch.10.
s. 75, repealed: ibid.
s. 76, Acts of Adjournal 72/308; 73/450, 672;
75/473, 837; 84/232.
s. 76, amended: 1983, c.12, sch.1; repealed in
pt.: 1975, c.21, sch.10.
s. 77, repealed in pt.: ibid.
s. 78, repealed: ibid.
sch. 1, repealed: ibid.
sch. 2, see Anderson v. Allan, 1985 S.C.C.R.
399.
ˉsch. 2, repealed in pt.: Act of Adjournal 78/834.
sch. 4, repealed: 1975, c.21, sch.10.

49. Long Leases (Scotland) Act 1954.
s. 4, amended: 1973, c.65, sch.27.
s. 27, amended: 1974, c.38, sch.6; repealed in
pt.: ibid., sch.7.

**50. Housing (Repairs and Rents) (Scotland) Act
1954.**
repealed: 1987, c.26, sch.24.

53. Housing Repairs and Rents Act 1954.
Part I, repealed: 1972, c.47, sch.11.
s. 25, see West Lothian C.C. v. Ferguson, Lin-
lithgow Sheriff Court, July 22, 1968.
s. 41, see Maunsell v. Olins [1974] 3 W.L.R.
835; [1975] 1 All E.R 16, H.L.

56. Landlord and Tenant Act 1954.
see Bond v. Graham (1975) 236 E.G. 563; Secretary of State for the Environment v. Pivot
Properties (1980) 256 E.G. 1176, C.A.; Turone
v. Howard de Walden Estates [1982] 262 E.G.

CAP.

2 & 3 Eliz. 2 (1953–54)—cont.

56. Landlord and Tenant Act 1954—cont.
1189, C.A.; Nevill Long & Co. (Boards) v.
Firmenich & Co. (1982) 44 P. & C.R. 12,
Whitford J.
s. 1, see Pelosi v. Newcastle Arms Brewery
[1981] 259 E.G. 247, C.A.
s. 1, amended: 1977, c.42, sch.24.
ss. 1, 2, see Regalian Securities v. Ramsden
[1981] 1 W.L.R. 611; [1981] 2 All E.R. 65, H.L.
s. 2, see Re Hennessey's Agreement; Hillman
v. Davison [1975] 2 W.L.R. 159; [1975] 1 All
E.R. 60.
s. 2, amended: 1977, c.42, sch.23.
s. 3, see Baron v. Phillips (1979) 38 P. & C.R.
91, C.A.
s. 4, see Galinski v. McHugh, The Times, October 13, 1988, C.A.
s. 7, see Etablissement Commercial Kamira v.
Schiazzano [1984] 3 W.L.R. 95, C.A.
ss. 10, 12, amended: 1977, c.42, sch.23.
s. 11, see Dinefwr Borough Council v. Jones,
The Times, June 27, 1987, C.A.
s. 17, see Re Hennessey's Agreement; Hillman
v. Davison [1975] 2 W.L.R. 159; [1975] 1 All
E.R. 60.
s. 21, amended: 1980, c.51, s.73.
s. 22, see Regalian Securities v. Ramsden [1981]
1 W.L.R. 611; [1981] 2 All E.R. 65, H.L.
s. 22, amended: 1977, c.42, sch.23; repealed in
pt.: ibid., sch.25.
Pt. II (ss. 23–46), see Garner v. Heath Park
Engineering Co., July 31, 1975; Chapman v.
Freeman [1978] 1 W.L.R. 1298, C.A.; Pivot
Properties v. Secretary of State for the
Environment (1979) 39 P. & C.R. 386, Phillips.
J.; A. Plesser & Co. v. Davis, The Times,
January 21, 1983, French J.
s. 23, see Lee-Verhulst v. Harwood Trust [1972]
3 W.L.R. 772; [1972] 3 All E.R. 619; Hodson
v. Cashmore (1972) 226 E.G. 1203, Brightman
J.; William Skelton & Son v. Harrison & Pinder
[1975] 2 W.L.R. 238; [1975] 1 All E.R. 182;
Morrison Holdings v. Manders Property (Wol-
verhampton) [1976] 2 All E.R. 205, C.A.; Wm.
Boyer & Sons v. Adams (1975) 32 P. & C.R.
89; Lewis v. Weldcrest, The Times, April 15,
1978, C.A.; Buchmann v. May [1978] 2 All
E.R. 993, C.A.; Parkes v. Westminster Roman
Catholic Diocese Trustee (1978) 39 P. & C.R.
22, C.A.; Cheryl Investments v. Saldanha;
Royal Life Saving Society v. Page [1978] 1
W.L.R. 1329, C.A.; Hillil Property & Invest-
ment Co. v. Naraine Pharmacy (1979) 39 P.
& C.R. 67, C.A.; Land Reclamation Co. v.
Basildon District Council [1979] 1 W.L.R. 767,
C.A.; Ross Auto Wash v. Herbert (1979) 250
E.G. 971, Fox J.; Bell v. Frank (Alfred) &
Bartlett Co. [1980] 1 All E.R. 356, C.A.; Cam
Gears v. Cunningham (1981) 258 E.G. 749,
C.A.; Manchester City Council v. National Car
Parks (1982) 262 E.G. 1297, C.A.; Groveside
Properties v. Westminster Medical School
(1983) 267 E.G. 593; (1984) 47 P. & C.R. 507,
C.A.; Harley Queen v. Forsyte Kerman (A
Firm), May 9, 1983, H.H. Judge Head; Bloom-

2 & 3 Eliz. 2 (1953–54)—cont.

56. Landlord and Tenant Act 1954—*cont.*
sbury and Marylebone County Ct.; *Neville Long & Co. (Boards)* v. *Firmenich & Co.* (1983) 268 E.G. 572; (1984) 47 P. & C.R. 59, C.A.; *Edwards (J. H.) & Sons* v. *Central London Commercial Estates; Eastern Bazaar* v. *Same* (1984) 271 E.G. 697, C.A.; *Simmonds* v. *Egyed,* February 12, 1985, Bloomsbury County Ct.; *Christina* v. *Seear* (1985) 275 E.G. 898, C.A.; *Linden* v. *Department of Health and Social Security* [1986] 1 W.L.R. 164, Scott J.; *Trans-Britannia Properties* v. *Darby Properties* (1986) 278 E.G. 1254, C.A.; *Nozari-Zadeh* v. *Pearl Assurance* (1987) 283 E.G. 457, C.A.

s. 24, see *Hodson* v. *Cashmore* (1972) 226 E.G. 1203, Brightman J.; *Junction Estates* v. *Cope* (1974) 2 P. & C.R. 482; *Meah* v. *Sector Properties* [1974] 1 All E.R. 1074, C.A.; *Watney* v. *Boardley* [1975] 1 W.L.R. 857; *William Skelton & Son* v. *Harrison & Pinder* [1975] 2 W.L.R. 238; [1975] 1 All E.R. 182; *Tegerdine* v. *Brooks* (1978) 36 P. & C.R. 261, C.A.; *Meadows* v. *Clerical, Medical and General Life Assurance Society* [1980] 1 All E.R. 454, Sir Robert Megarry V.-C.; *Dodds* v. *Walker* [1980] 2 All E.R. 507, C.A.; *Joan Barrie* v. *G.U.S. Property Management* (1981) 259 E.G. 628, C.A.; *Robert Baxendale* v. *Davstone (Holdings), The Times,* July 9, 1982, C.A.; *Hancock and Willis (A Firm)* v. *G.M.S. Syndicate* (1983) 265 E.G. 473, C.A.; *Neville Long & Co. (Boards)* v. *Firmenich & Co.* (1983) 268 E.G. 572; (1984) 47 P. & C.R. 59, C.A.; *Curtis* v. *Calgary Instruments* (1984) 47 P. & C.R. 13, C.A.; *Cadogan* v. *Dimovic* [1984] 1 W.L.R. 690, C.A.; *Riley (E. J.) Investments* v. *Eurostile Holdings* [1985] 3 All E.R. 181, C.A.; *Hill* v. *Griffin* (1987) 282 E.G. 85, C.A.

s. 24A, see *Stream Properties* v. *Davis* [1972] 1 W.L.R. 645; [1972] 2 All E.R. 746; *English Exporters* v. *Eldonwall* [1973] 2 W.L.R. 435; [1973] 1 All E.R. 726; *Bailey Organisation* v. *United Kingdom Temperance and General Provident Institution* [1975] J.P.L. 94, C.A.; *Michael Kramer & Co.* v. *Airways Pension Fund Trustees* (1976) 246 E.G. 911, C.A.; *Lovely & Orchard Services* v. *Daejan Investments* (1977) 246 E.G. 651, Judge Finlay Q.C.; *Fawke* v. *Viscount Chelsea* [1979] 3 W.L.R. 508, C.A.; *Victor Blake (Menswear)* v. *Westminster City Council* (1979) 38 P. & C.R. 448, Deputy Judge Michael Wheeler, Q.C.; *Janes (Gowns)* v. *Harlow Development Corporation* (1979) 253 E.G. 799, Judge Finlay, Q.C.; *Ratners (Jewellers)* v. *Lemnoll* (1980) 255 E.G. 987, Dillon J.; *U.D.S. Tailoring* v. *B.L. Holdings* (1982) 261 E.G. 49, Vivian Price Q.C.; *Bloomfield* v. *Ashwright* (1983) 266 E.G. 1095; (1984) 47 P. & C.R. 78, C.A.; *Texaco* v. *Benton & Bowles Holdings* (1983) 267 E.G. 355, Falconer J.; *Artoc Bank & Trust* v. *Prudential Assurance Co.* [1984] 1 W.L.R. 1181, Ch.D., Falconer J.; *Halberstam* v. *Tandalco Corp. N.V.* (1985) 274 E.G. 393, C.A.; *Thomas*

2 & 3 Eliz. 2 (1953–54)—cont.

56. Landlord and Tenant Act 1954—*cont.*
v. *Hammond-Lawrence* [1986] 1 W.L.R. 456, C.A.; *Follett (Charles)* v. *Cabtell Investments* (1987) 283 E.G. 195, C.A.; *Short* v. *Greeves* [1988] 08 E.G. 109, C.A.

s. 25, see *Re Crowhurst Park; Sims-Hilditch* v. *Simmons* [1974] 1 All E.R. 991; *Sun Alliance and London Assurance Co.* v. *Hayman* [1975] 1 W.L.R. 177; [1975] 1 All E.R. 248, C.A.; *Dodson Bull Carpet Co.* v. *City of London Corporation* [1975] 1 W.L.R. 781; [1975] 2 All E.R. 497; *Winter* v. *Mobil Oil Co.,* March 24, 1975; *Lewis* v. *M.T.C. (Cars)* [1975] 1 W.L.R. 457; [1975] 1 All E.R. 874, C.A.; *Snook* v. *Schofield* (1975) 234 E.G. 197, C.A.; *Chiswell* v. *Griffin Land and Estates* [1975] 2 All E.R. 665, C.A.; *Germax Securities* v. *Speigal* (1978) 123 S.J. 164, C.A.; *R.* v. *Secretary of State for the Environment and Buckinghamshire County Council, ex p. A. G. Powis* [1980] J.P.L. 673, D.C.; *Safeway Food Stores* v. *Morris* (1980) 254 E.G. 1091, Walton J.; *Philipson-Stow* v. *Trevor Square* (1981) 257 E.G. 1262, Goulding J.; *Jones* v. *Daniels & Davidson (Holdings),* April 27, 1981, Judge Woolley, Brecon County Ct.; *Pelosi* v. *Newcastle Arms Brewery* [1981] 259 E.G. 247, C.A.; *British Railways Board* v. *A. J. A. Smith Transport* (1981) 259 E.G. 766, Fitzhugh Q.C.; *Robert Baxendale* v. *Davstone (Holdings); Carobene* v. *John Collier Menswear* [1982] 3 All E.R. 496, C.A.; *Watkins* v. *Elmslie* (1982) 261 E.G. 1192, C.A.; *Evans Construction Co.* v. *Charrington & Co.* (1982) 264 E.G. 347, C.A.; *Lewington* v. *Trustees of the Society for the Protection of Ancient Buildings, The Times,* February 12, 1983, C.A.; *Neville Long & Co. (Boards)* v. *Firmenich & Co.* (1983) 268 E.G. 572; (1984) 47 P. & C.R. 59, C.A.; *Hutchinson* v. *Lambeth* (1984) 270 E.G. 545, C.A.; *Cadogan* v. *Dimovic* [1984] 1 W.L.R. 609, C.A.; *Artoc Bank & Trust* v. *Prudential Assurance Co.* [1984] 1 W.L.R. 1181, Ch.D., Falconer J.; *Italica Holdings S.A.* v. *Bayadea* (1985) 273 E.G. 888, French J.; *Southport Old Links* v. *Naylor* (1985) 273 E.G. 767, C.A.; *Earthcare Cooperative* v. *Troveworth,* May 13, 1985; Durham County Ct.; *Hogg* v. *Bullimore & Co.* v. *Co-operative Insurance Society* (1985) 50 P. & C.R. 105, Whitford J.; *Trustees of National Deposit Friendly Society* v. *Beatties of London* (1985) 275 E.G. 55, Goulding J.; *Aireps* v. *Bradford City Metropolitan Council* (1985) 267 E.G. 1067; *Morrow* v. *Nadeem* [1986] 1 W.L.R. 1381, C.A.; *Short* v. *Greeves* [1988] 08 E.G. 109, C.A.; *Moss* v. *Mobil Oil Co.* [1988] 06 E.G. 109, C.A.; *Herongrove* v. *Wates City of London Properties* [1988] 24 E.G. 108, Harman J.

s. 26, see *Meah* v. *Sector Properties* [1974] 1 All E.R. 1074, C.A.; *Bristol Cars* v. *R. K. H. Hotels (In Liquidation)* (1979) 38 P. & C.R. 411, C.A.; *Polyviou* v. *Seeley* [1979] 3 All E.R. 853, C.A.; *Stile Hall Properties* v. *Gooch*

CAP.

2 & 3 Eliz. 2 (1953-54)—cont.

56. Landlord and Tenant Act 1954—cont.

[1979] 3 All E.R. 848, C.A.; Watkins v. Elmslie (1982) 261 E.G. 1192, C.A.; Cadogan v. Dimovic [1984] 1 W.L.R. 609, C.A.

s. 28, see Stratton (R. J.) v. Wallis Tomlin & Co. (1985) 277 E.G. 409, C.A.

s. 29, see Harris v. Monro (1972) 225 E.G. 1551; Meah v. Sector Properties [1974] 1 All E.R. 1074, C.A.; Chiswell v. Griffin Land and Estates [1975] 2 All E.R. 665, C.A.; Amika Motors v. Colebrook Holdings [1981] 259 E.G. 243, C.A.; Dodds v. Walker, The Times, June 29, 1981, H.L.; Lewington v. Trustees for the Protection of Ancient Buildings (1983) 266 E.G. 997, C.A.; Mehmet v. Dawson (1984) 270 E.G. 139, C.A.; Riley (E. J.) Investments v. Eurostile Holdings [1985] 3 All E.R. 181, C.A.; Sharma v. Knight, The Times, January 30, 1986, C.A.; Bar v. Pathwood Investments (1987) 54 P. & C.R. 178; (1987) 282 E.G. 1538, C.A.

s. 30, see Heath v. Drown [1972] 2 W.L.R. 1306; [1972] 2 All E.R. 561; Hunt v. Decca Navigator Co. (1972) 222 E.G. 625; Re Crowhurst Park; Sims-Hilditch v. Simmons [1974] 1 All E.R. 991; Decca Navigator Co. v. Greater London Council [1974] 1 All E.R. 1178, C.A.; Turner & Bell (Trading as Avro Luxury Coaches v. Searles (Stanford-Le-Hope) (1977) P. & C.R. 208, C.A.; Lightcliffe and District Cricket and Lawn Tennis Club v. Walton (1977) 245 E.G. 393, C.A.; Parkes v. Westminster Roman Catholic Diocese Trustee (1978) 36 P. & C.R. 22, C.A.; Redfern v. Reeves (1978) 37 P. & C.R. 364, C.A.; Harvey Textiles v. Hillel (1979) 249 E.G. 1063, Whitford J.; Safeway Food Stores v. Morris (1980) 254 E.G. 1091, Walton J.; Price v. Esso Petroleum Co. (1980) 255 E.G. 243, C.A.; A. J. A. Smith Transport v. British Railways Board (1981) 257 E.G. 1257, C.A.; Philipson-Stow v. Trevor Square (1981) 257 E.G. 1262, Goulding J.; Geo. Akin v. Ward, April 29, 1981, Judge Heald, Mansfield County Co.; Cam Gears v. Cunningham (1982) 43 P. & C.R. 114, C.A.; Lloyds Bank v. City of London Corporation [1982] 3 W.L.R. 1138, C.A.; DAF Motoring Centre (Gosport) v. Hutfield and Wheeler (1982) 263 E.G. 976, C.A.; Chez Gerard v. Greene (1983) 268 E.G. 575, C.A.; Botterill and Cheshire v. Bedfordshire County Council, The Times, May 24, 1984, C.A.; Hutchinson v. Lambeth (1984) 270 E.G. 545, C.A.; Leathwoods v. Total Oil (Great Britain) (1984) 270 E.G. 1083, Vivian Price Q.C.; Westminster City Council v. British Waterways Board [1984] 3 W.L.R. 1047, H.L.; Botterill v. Bedfordshire County Council (1985) 273 E.G. 1217, C.A.; Europark (Midlands) v. Town Centre Securities (1985) 274 E.G. 289, Warner J.; Trustees of National Deposit Friendly Society v. Beatties of London (1985) 275 E.G. 55, Goulding J.; Morar v. Chauhan [1985] 3 All E.R. 493, C.A.; Mularczyk v. Azralnove Investments (1985) 276 E.G. 1064,

CAP.

2 & 3 Eliz. 2 (1953-54)—cont.

56. Landlord and Tenant Act 1954—cont.

C.A.; Aireps v. Bradford City Metropolitan Council (1985) 267 E.G. 1067; Leathwoods v. Total Oil Great Britain (1986) 51 P. & C.R. 20, C.A.; Jones v. Jenkins (1985) 277 E.G. 644, C.A.; Cerex Jewels v. Peachey Property Corp., The Times, May 12, 1986, C.A.; Beard (Formerly Coleman) v. Williams (1986) 278 E.G. 1087, C.A.; Thornton (J.W.) v. Blacks Leisure Group (1986) 279 E.G. 588; (1987) 53 P. & C.R. 223, C.A.; Capocci v. Goble (1987) 284 E.G. 230, C.A.; Ahern (P. F.) & Sons v. Hunt [1988] 21 E.G. 69, C.A.; Spook Erection v. British Railways Board [1988] 21 E.G. 73, C.A.; Blackburn v. Hussain [1988] 22 E.G. 78, C.A.

s. 31A, see Decca Navigator Co. v. Greater London Council [1974] 1 All E.R. 1178, C.A.; Redfern v. Reeves (1978) 37 P. & C.R. 364, C.A.; Price v. Esso Petroleum Co. (1980) 255 E.G. 243, C.A.; Mularczyk v. Azralnove Investments (1985) 276 E.G. 1064, C.A.; Cerex Jewels v. Peachey Property Corp. (1986) 52 P. & C.R. 127, C.A.; Blackburn v. Hussain [1988] 22 E.G. 78, C.A.

s. 32, see G. Orlik (Meat Products) v. Hastings and Thanet Building Society (1974) 29 P. & C.R. 126, C.A.; Kirkwood v. Johnson (1979) 38 P. & C.R. 392, C.A.; Neville Long & Co. (Boards) v. Firmenich & Co. (1983) 268 E.G. 572; (1984) 47 P. & C.R. 59, C.A.

s. 33, see Derby & Co. v. I.T.C. Pension Trust [1977] 2 All E.R. 890, Oliver J.; Chipperfield v. Shell (U.K.); Warwick & Warwick (Philately) v. Shell (U.K.) (1980) 257 E.G. 1042; (1981) 42 P. & C.R. 136, C.A.; CBS (U.K.) v. London Scottish Properties (1985) 275 E.G. 718, H.H. Judge Micklem.

s. 34, see Hyams v. Titan Properties (1972) 24 P. & C.R. 359, C.A.; English Exporters v. Eldonwall [1973] 2 W.L.R. 435; [1973] 1 All E.R. 726; Derby & Co. v. T.T.C. Pension Trust [1977] 2 All E.R. 890, Oliver J.; Lovely & Orchard Services v. Daejan Investments (1977) 246 E.G. 651, Judge Finlay Q.C.; Fawke v. Viscount Chelsea [1979] 3 W.L.R. 508, C.A.; Family Management v. Gray (1979) 253 E.G. 369, C.A.; Janes (Gowns) v. Harlow Development Corporation (1979) 253 E.G. 799, Judge Finlay, Q.C.; Chipperfield v. Shell (U.K.); Warwick & Warwick (Philately) v. Shell (U.K.) (1980) 257 E.G. 1042; (1981) 42 P. & C.R. 136, C.A.; W. J. Barton v. Long Acre Securities [1982] 1 All E.R. 465, C.A.; U.D.S. Tailoring v. B.L. Holdings (1982) 261 E.G. 49, Vivian Price Q.C.; Euston Centre Properties v. H. & J. Wilson (1982) 262 E.G. 1079, Cantley J.; O'May v. City of London Real Property Co. [1982] 2 W.L.R. 407, H.L.; National Car Parks v. Colebrook Estates (1983) 266 E.G. 810, Foster J.; Newey & Eyre v. Curtis (J.) & Son (1984) 271 E.G. 891, E.C. Evans-Lombe Q.C.; Halberstam v. Tandalco Corp. N.V. (1985) 274 E.G. 393, C.A.; Brett v. Brett Essex Golf Club, The Times, May 12, 1986, H.L.; Oriani v. Dorita Properties (1987) 282 E.G. 1001, C.A.

CAP.

2 & 3 Eliz. 2 (1953–54)—cont.

56. Landlord and Tenant Act 1954—cont.
s. 35, see G. Orlik (Meat Products) v. Hastings and Thanet Building Society (1974) 29 P. & C.R. 126, C.A.; Derby & Co. v. I.T.C. Pension Trust [1977] 2 All E.R. 890, Oliver J.; Charles Clements (London) v. Rank City Wall (1978) 246 E.G. 739, Goulding J.; Kirkwood v. Johnson (1979) 38 P. & C.R. 392, C.A.; O'May v. City of London Real Property Co. [1982] 2 W.L.R. 407, H.L.; Cairnplace v. CBL (Property Investment) Co. [1984] 1 All E.R. 315, C.A.; Etablissement Commercial Kamira v. Schiazzano (1984) 81 L.S.Gaz. 1684, C.A.
s. 37, see Re Crowhurst Park; Sims-Hilditch v. Simmons [1974] 1 All E.R. 991; Young Austen & Young v. British Medical Association [1977] 1 W.L.R. 881, Whitford J.; Ove Arup Inc. v. Howland Property Investment Co. (1982) 261 E.G. 149, Michael Wheeler Q.C.; International Military Services v. Capital and Counties P.L.C. [1982] 2 All E.R. 20, Slade J.; Cardshops v. John Lewis Properties [1982] 3 W.L.R. 803, C.A.; Lloyds Bank v. City of London Corporation [1982] 3 W.L.R. 1138, C.A.; Sperry v. Hambro Life Assurance (1983) 265 E.G. 233, Goulding J.; Edicron v. William Whiteley [1984] 1 W.L.R. 59, C.A.; Drummond (Inspector of Taxes) v. Austin Brown [1984] 3 W.L.R. 381, C.A.; Breeze v. Elden & Hyde, December 3, 1986, Mr. Deputy Registrar Sheriff; Norwich County Ct.; Department of the Environment v. Royal Insurance (1987) 54 P. & C.R. 26; (1987) 282 E.G. 208, Falconer J.
s. 37, regs. 81/69; order 84/1932.
s. 37, amended: 1980, c.65, sch.33; 1986, c.63, s.13.
s. 38, see Tottenham Hotspur Football & Athletic Co. v. Princegrove Publishers [1974] 1 W.L.R. 113; [1974] 1 All E.R. 17; Stevenson and Rush (Holdings) v. Langdon (1979) 38 P. & C.R. 208, C.A.; Allnatt London Properties v. Newton (1983) 45 P. & C.R. 94, C.A.; Tarjomani v. Panther Securities (1983) 46 P. & C.R. 32, Gibson J.; Cardiothoracic Institute v. Shrewdcrest [1986] 1 W.L.R. 368, Ch.D., Knox J.; Essexcrest v. Evenlex [1988] 01 E.G. 56, C.A.
s. 39, amended: 1973, c.26, s.47; repealed in pt.; ibid., s.47, sch.3.
s. 40, amended: 1977, c.42, sch.23.
s. 41, see Hodson v. Cashmore (1972) 226 E.G. 1203, Brightman J.; Carshalton Beeches Bowling Club v. Cameron (1979) 249 E.G. 1279, C.A.; Morar v. Chauhan [1985] 3 All E.R. 493, C.A.
s. 41A, see Cairnplace v. CBL (Property Investment) Co. [1984] 1 All E.R. 315, C.A.
s. 42, amended: 1985, c.9, sch.2.
s. 43, see Grant v. Gresham (1979) 252 E.G. 55, C.A.; Lansley v. Adda Properties, June 7, 1982, Judge Curtis-Raleigh, Bloomsbury and Marylebone County Court; Ye Old Cheshire Cheese v. Daily Telegraph, The Independent, May 19, 1988, Browne-Wilkinson V.-C.

CAP.

2 & 3 Eliz. 2 (1953–54)—cont.

56. Landlord and Tenant Act 1954—cont.
s. 43, amended: 1986, c.5, sch.14; repealed in pt.: 1980, c.51, sch.26.
s. 44, see Lewis v. M.T.C. (Cars) [1974] 1 W.L.R. 1499; [1974] 3 All E.R. 423; Geo. Akin v. Ward, April 29, 1981, Judge Heald, Mansfield County Ct.; Neville Long & Co. (Boards) v. Firmenich & Co. (1983) 268 E.G. 572; (1984) 47 P. & C.R. 59, C.A.
s. 45, repealed: S.L.R. 1974.
s. 53, see Tollbench v. Plymouth City Council [1988] 23 E.G. 132, C.A.
s. 53, amended: 1984, c.28, sch.2.
s. 56, see Linden v. Department of Health and Social Security [1986] 1 W.L.R. 164, Scott J.
s. 56, amended: 1980, c.51, s.73.
s. 57, see R. v. Secretary of State for the Environment, ex p. Powis [1981] 1 All E.R. 788, C.A.
s. 57, amended: 1973, c.32, sch.5; 1977, c.49, sch.15; 1980, c.51, sch.1; order 85/39.
s. 59, amended: 1975, c.70, s.11; 1976, c.75, sch.7.
s. 60, amended: 1972, c.5, sch.3; 1981, c.13, s.9; 1982, c.52, sch.2; repealed in pt.: 1972, c.63, sch.4.
s. 60A, added: 1975, c.70, s.11.
s. 60B, added: 1976, c.75, sch.7.
s. 63, amended: 1973, c.15, sch.2.
s. 64, see Rumsey v. Owen White and Catlin (1976) 241 E.G. 611, Sir Douglas Frank, Q.C.; Covell Matthews & Partners v. French Wools (1977) 35 P. & C.R. 107; [1978] 2 All E.R. 800, C.A.; Lovely & Orchard Services v. Daejan Investments (1977) 246 E.G. 651, Judge Finlay Q.C.; Bristol Cars v. R. K. H. Hotels (In Liquidation) (1979) 251 E.G. 1279, C.A.; Warwick & Warwick (Philately) v. Shell (U.K.); Chipperfield v. Shell (U.K.) (1980) 257 E.G. 1042, C.A.; Turone v. Howard de Walden Estates (1983) 267 E.G. 440, C.A.
s. 66, see Sun Alliance and London Assurance Co. v. Hayman [1975] 1 W.L.R 177; [1975] 1 All E.R. 248, C.A.
s. 66, regs. 73/792; 83/133; 86/2181.
s. 68, repealed in pt.: S.L.R. 1974.
s. 69, see Stratton (R. J.) v. Wallis Tomlin & Co. (1985) E.G. 409, C.A.
s. 69, amended: 1985, c.51, sch.14; order 85/1884; 1986, c.5, sch.14; 1987, c.3, sch.1; amended: 1988, c4, sch.6; repealed in pt. (prosp.): 1988, c.40, sch.13.
schs. 1, 3, amended: 1977, c.42, sch.23.
sch. 6, see Lewis v. M.T.C. (Cars) [1974] 1 W.L.R. 1499; [1974] 3 All E.R. 423.
sch. 9, repealed in pt.: S.L.R. 1976.

57. Baking Industry (Hours of Work) Act 1954.
repealed: 1986, c.59, s.8, sch.
s. 9, order 74/878.

58. Charitable Trusts (Validation) Act 1954.
s. 3, amended: 1980, c.58, sch.3.
s. 5, repealed: 1973, c.36, sch.6.

59. Slaughter of Animals (Amendment) Act 1954.
repealed: 1980, c.13, sch.3; 1981, c.19, sch.1.

CAP.

2 & 3 Eliz. 2 (1953–54)—cont.

60. Electricity Reorganisation (Scotland) Act 1954.
repealed, except ss. 1 (in pt.), 15 (in pt.), 16, 17, sch. 1 (in pt.): 1979, c.11, sch.12.
s. 1, repealed in pt.: 1983, c.25, sch.4.
s. 15, sch. 1, see *South of Scotland Electricity Board* v. *Elder*, 1980 S.L.T.(Notes) 83.
s. 15, repealed in pt.: S.L.R. 1974.
sch. 1, amended: 1972, c.17, sch.; repealed in pt.: S.L.R. 1978; 1983, c.25, sch.4.

61. Pharmacy Act 1954.
ss. 2, 4, 5, amended: order 87/2202.
s. 4A, added: *ibid.*
s. 8, see *R.* v. *Pharmaceutical Society of Great Britain, ex p. Sokoh, The Times,* December 4, 1986, Webster J.
s. 8, amended: order 87/2202.
s. 19, repealed: order 77/2128.
s. 20, repealed in pt.: 1981, c.45, sch.
s. 21, amended: 1980, c.43, sch.7.
s. 24, amended: 1972, c.66, s.12.
s. 25, repealed in pt.: S.L.R. 1974.
sch. 1, order 78/20.
sch. 1A, added: order 87/2202.
sch. 3, repealed in pt.: 1972, c.66, s.12, sch.2.
sch. 4, repealed: S.L.R. 1974.

64. Transport Charges, etc. (Miscellaneous Provisions) Act 1954.
s. 1, repealed: 1985, c.67, schs.7,8.
s. 2, repealed: 1980, c.34, s.65, sch.9.
s. 6, orders 73/1486; 76/470.
s. 6, amended: 1972, c.70, s.186, sch.30; 1973, c.65, sch.18.
s. 7, repealed in pt.: 1982, c.16, sch.16.
ss. 12, 13, repealed in pt.: 1985, c.67, sch.8.
s. 14, repealed in pt.: S.L.R. 1974.
sch. 1, repealed: 1980, c.34, s.65, sch.9.
sch. 2, repealed: S.L.R. 1974.

65. National Gallery and Tate Gallery Act 1954.
ss. 2–4, functions transferred: order 81/207.
ss. 3, 8, amended: S.L.R. 1974.
s. 4, orders 73/1313, 2109.
s. 4, repealed in pt.: 1983, c.47, schs.5,6.
s. 6, repealed: S.L.R. 1974.
sch. 1, amended: 1983, c.47, sch.5; 1985, c.16, sch.2(S.); repealed in pt. (S.): *ibid.*
sch. 2, repealed: S.L.R. 1974.

68. Pests Act 1954.
s. 6, amended: 1974, c.7, schs.6,8; 1975, c.30, sch.6 (S.).
s. 8, orders 75/1647; 82/53.
s. 8, amended: 1977, c.45, s.31, sch.6; repealed in pt.: S.L.R. 1973.
s. 9, amended: 1977, c.45, s.31, sch.6.
s. 12, amended: *ibid*; 1986, c.14, sch.3.
s. 15 (in pt.), sch., repealed: S.L.R. 1973.

70. Mines and Quarries Act 1954.
regs. 73/194.
see *Hills* v. *N.C.B.* (1972) 13 K.I.R. 486.
s. 1, amended: order 74/2013.
s. 4, repealed in pt.: *ibid.*
s. 5, amended: regs. 76/2063.
s. 10, amended: order 74/2013.
s. 12, repealed in pt.: *ibid.*
s. 14, see *Malone* v. *N.C.B.*, 1972 S.L.T.(Notes) 56.

CAP.

2 & 3 Eliz. 2 (1953–54)—cont.

70. Mines and Quarries Act 1954—*cont.*
ss. 15, 19, 20, amended: order 74/2013.
s. 21, repealed: *ibid.*
ss. 22–25, repealed: regs. 88/1729.
s. 26, amended: order 74/2013.
s. 27, repealed: order 75/1102.
s. 28, amended: regs. 76/2063.
ss. 29, 31 (in pt.), 32, repealed: order 74/2013.
ss. 33–35, repealed: regs. 88/1729.
s. 34, see *Connolly* v. *National Coal Board* (O.H.), 1979 S.L.T. 51; *Jennings* v. *National Coal Board* [1983] I.C.R. 636, C.A.
s. 37, see *Storey* v. *National Coal Board* [1983] 1 All E.R. 375, Mustill J.
s. 40, amended: regs. 76/2063.
s. 42, repealed in pt.: order 74/2013.
s. 45, amended: regs. 76/2063; repealed in pt.: order 74/2013.
s. 47, repealed: *ibid.*
s. 48, see *O'Hara* v. *N.C.B.*, 1973 S.L.T.(Notes) 25; *Aitken* v. *N.C.B.*, 1973 S.L.T.(Notes) 48; *McFarlane* v. *National Coal Board*, 1974 S.L.T.(Notes) 16 (O.H.); *Anderson* v. *National Coal Board*, 1970, S.C. 42, Ct. of Session; *Hill* v. *National Coal Board*, 1976 S.L.T. 261; *Richardson* v. *National Coal Board*, March 14, 1980, C.A.; *Weir* v. *National Coal Board* (O.H.), January 14, 1982; *Aitken* v. *National Coal Board*, 1982 S.L.T. 545; *Shevchuk* v. *National Coal Board*, 1982 S.L.T. 557; *Hammond* v. *National Coal Board* [1984] 3 All E.R. 321, C.A.; *Mettam* v. *N.C.B., The Guardian,* July 14, 1988, C.A.
s. 48, amended: regs. 88/1729.
s. 49, see *McDerment* v. *N.C.B.*, 1973 S.L.T.(Notes) 60.
s. 49, regs. 74/1075.
s. 49, repealed in pt.: orders 74/2013; 75/1102.
s. 50, repealed: order 74/2013.
s. 51, repealed in pt.: *ibid.*; 1986, c.48, schs.1,5.
s. 54, regs. 74/1075.
s. 55, repealed in pt.: order 74/2013.
s. 57, repealed: order 75/1102.
s. 59, amended: regs. 76/2063.
s. 60, repealed in pt.: order 74/2013.
s. 62, repealed in pt.: order 75/1102.
s. 63, repealed: order 74/2013.
s. 64, amended: *ibid.*
s. 68, regs. 74/1853.
s. 68, repealed in pt.: orders 74/2013; 75/1102.
s. 69, repealed in pt.: order 74/2013.
s. 70, repealed: regs. 88/1729.
ss. 71, 72 (in pt.), repealed: order 74/2013.
s. 74, amended and repealed in pt.: *ibid.*
ss. 75–77, repealed: regs. 79/318.
s. 78, repealed: order 75/1102.
s. 81, see *Hughes* v. *N.C.B.* (1971) 12 K.I.R. 419; *Samson* v. *National Coal Board* (O.H.), 1980 S.L.T. (Notes) 57; *Harkin* v. *National Coal Board* (O.H.) 1981 S.L.T.(Notes) 37; *Brebner* v. *British Coal Corporation,* Second Division, 1988 S.L.T. 736.
s. 81, repealed in pt.: order 74/2013.
s. 82, see *Ewing* v. *National Coal Board* (O.H.), 1987 S.L.T. 414.

CAP.

2 & 3 Eliz. 2 (1953–54)—cont.

70. Mines and Quarries Act 1954—cont.
s. 83, amended: order 74/2013.
s. 84, amended and repealed in pt.: ibid.
s. 88, see Thompson v. National Coal Board [1982] I.C.R. 15, C.A.; England v. Cleveland Potash, The Times, July 1, 1986, C.A.
s. 89, see McMullen v. National Coal Board [1982] I.C.R. 148, Caulfield J.
ss. 91 (in pt.), 92, 95 (in pt.), 96, 104, repealed: order 74/2013.
s. 105, amended: ibid.
s. 106, repealed: ibid.
s. 107, amended: ibid.
s. 108, repealed in pt.: ibid.
ss. 108, 109, see English v. Cory Sand & Ballast Company, The Times, April 2, 1985, Stocker J.
s. 112, amended and repealed in pt.: order 74/2013.
s. 114, repealed: ibid.
s. 115, repealed in pt.: ibid.; regs. 81/917.
Pt. VI (ss. 116–122), repealed: regs. 80/804.
s. 123, amended: ibid.; 85/2023.
s. 124, amended: 1975, c.65, s.21; repealed in pt.: order 74/2013.
ss. 125, 126, repealed in pt.: 1986, c.59, s.7, sch.
s. 128, amended: order 74/2013; repealed in pt.: 1986, c.59, s.7, sch.
s. 129, repealed; order 74/2013.
s. 131, amended: ibid, repealed in pt.: 1986, c.59, s.7, sch.
ss. 133, 136, 137, amended: ibid.
s. 138, repealed: ibid.
s. 141, regs. 72/631; 74/1075, 1853.
s. 141, amended and repealed in pt.: order 74/2013.
s. 142, repealed: ibid.
s. 143, regs. 74/1075, 1853.
ss. 144, 145, repealed: order 74/2013.
s. 146, repealed: order 75/1102.
s. 147, amended: order 74/2013.
s. 148, amended: orders 74/2013; 78/1951.
ss. 149, 150, 152, amended: order 74/2013.
s. 151, amended (S.): 1984, c.54, sch.9.
s. 153, amended: 1980, c.43, sch.7.
s. 155, repealed in pt.: order 74/2013.
s. 156, amended: ibid.
s. 157, see Shevchuck v. National Coal Board, 1982 S.L.T. 557; Storey v. National Coal Board [1983] 1 All E.R. 375, Mustill J.; Hammond v. National Coal Board [1984] 3 All E.R. 321, C.A.; Mettam v. N.C.B., The Guardian, July 14, 1988, C.A.
s. 157, amended: order 74/2013.
ss. 161, 163 (in pt.), 164 (in pt.), repealed: ibid.
s. 166, repealed in pt.: 1973, c.16, sch.2.
s. 167, repealed: 1972, c.71, sch.6.
s. 172, repealed: order 74/2013.
s. 173, amended: ibid.
s. 174, substituted: ibid.
s. 175, repealed: ibid.
s. 176, amended: ibid.
s. 177, repealed: ibid.

CAP.

2 & 3 Eliz. 2 (1953–54)—cont.

70. Mines and Quarries Act 1954—cont.
s. 180, see Brook v. National Coal Board (1975) 234 E.G. 479, C.A.
s. 182, amended: order 74/2013; regs. 83/710; repealed in pt.: regs. 80/804.
s. 184, repealed in pt.: order 74/2013.
s. 185, repealed: 1986, c.48, sch.5.
s. 187, amended: ibid., sch.4; repealed in pt.: ibid., sch.5.
s. 189, repealed: S.L.R. 1974.
s. 190, schs. 1, 2, repealed: order 74/2013.
sch. 4, repealed in pt.: 1973, c.16, sch.2; 1986, c.59, sch.
sch. 5, repealed: S.L.R. 1974.

72. Town and Country Planning Act 1954.
s. 53, repealed in pt.: S.L.R. 1973.
s. 69, repealed in pt.: S.L.R. 1975.

73. Town and Country Planning (Scotland) Act 1954.
ss. 1–54, repealed: 1972, c.52, sch.23.
s. 55, repealed in pt.: S.L.R. 1973.
ss. 56–68, 70, repealed: 1972, c.52, sch.23.
ss. 69, 71, repealed in pt.: S.L.R. 1975.
schs. 1–9, repealed: 1972, c.52, sch.23.

3 & 4 Eliz. 2 (1954–55)

2. Wireless Telegraphy (Validation of Charges) Act 1954.
repealed: S.L.R. 1973.

5. Cocos Islands Act 1955.
repealed: S.L.R. 1976.

7. Fisheries Act 1955.
s. 3, repealed: S.L.R. 1986.
ss. 4, 6 (in pt.), repealed: S.L.R. 1978.
s. 7, repealed in pt.: S.L.R. 1974.
sch. repealed: ibid.

8. Northern Ireland Act 1955.
repealed: order 79/1573.

11. National Service Act 1955.
repealed: S.L.R. 1977.

13. Rural Water Supplies and Sewerage Act 1955.
s. 1, amended: 1973, c.37, sch.8; repealed in pt. (S.): 1975, c.30, sch.7.

14. Imperial War Museum Act 1955.
s. 1, order 88/253.
s. 2, repealed: in pt.: S.L.R. 1974.
s. 2, functions transferred: orders 81/207; 86/600.

18. Army Act 1955.
rules 72/316.
continued in force: orders 74/2147; 77/1231; 82/1069; 1981, c.54, s.1; orders 83/1104; 84/1147; 85/1196; 1986, c.21, s.1; orders 87/1262; 88/1293.
see Riley v. Riley (1988) 18 Fam.Law 167, Swinton Thomas J.
s. 14, repealed: order 72/1955.
s. 17, repealed in pt.: 1976, c.52, sch.10.
s. 20, repealed: S.L.R. 1977.
s. 26, repealed in pt.: 1981, c.55, s.23.
ss. 28, 29, 33, repealed in pt.: 1986, c.21, s.4, sch.2.
s. 44B, added: ibid., s.2.

3 & 4 Eliz. 2 (1954–55)—cont.
18. Army Act 1955—cont.

s. 55, repealed in pt.: *ibid.*, s.4, sch.2.

s. 57, amended: 1982, c.48, sch.8.

s. 62, amended: 1986, c.21, s.3.

s. 65, repealed in pt.: *ibid.*, s.4, sch.2.

s. 69, see *R.* v. *Davies; R.* v. *Hamilton* [1980] Crim.L.R. 582, Courts Martial Appeal Ct.; *R.* v. *Miller* [1983] Crim.L.R. 622, Courts Martial Appeal Court.

s. 69, amended: 1986, c.21, s.4.

s. 70, amended: 1974, c.6, s.5; 1976, c.52, s.10; 1981, c.47, s.7.

s. 71, amended: 1976, c.52, s.10; 1981, c.55, s.2; 1986, c.21, sch.1.

s. 71A, added: 1976, c.52, s.10; amended: 1982, c.48, sch.8; repealed in pt.: *ibid.*, schs.8,16.

s. 71AA, added: 1981, c.55, s.2; amended: 1982, c.48, sch.8; 1985, c.73, s.46(S.); 1986, c.21, sch.1; 1988, c.33, schs. 8, 9(S.).

s. 71B, added: 1976, c.52, sch.6; amended: 1982, c.48, s.69, sch.8; 1986, c.21, s.5; repealed in pt.: *ibid,* sch.2.

s. 77, amended: 1981, c.55, s.2.

s. 78, amended: 1976, c.52, s.5; 1981; c.55, s.3, sch.2; repealed in pt.: 1976, c.52, sch.10.

s. 79, amended: *ibid.*, s.5; 1981, c.55, s.3, sch.2.

s. 80, amended: 1976, c.52, sch.3.

s. 82, repealed in pt.: 1981, c.55, schs.2,5.

s. 85, amended: 1982, c.48, sch.8.

s. 86, repealed in pt.: 1976, c.52, schs.9,10.

s. 91, amended: 1981, c.55, sch.2.

s. 93, see *Kamarul Azman bin Jamaluddin* v. *Wan Abdul Majid bin Abdullah* [1983] 1 W.L.R. 579, P.C.

s. 93, amended: 1976, c.52, s.12; 1981, c.55, sch.2; repealed in pt.: 1976, c.52, s.12, sch.10.

s. 99, amended: 1976, c.52, sch.5; 1984, c.60, sch.6; repealed in pt.: 1981, c.55, schs.2,5.

s. 99A, regs. 77/86.

s. 99A, added: 1976, c.52, sch.5; 1984, c.60, sch.6.

s. 102, repealed in pt.: 1977, c.38, sch.5.

s. 103, rules 74/761; 77/92; 81/1220; 82/369; 83/719; 84/1670; 86/2126.

ss. 103, 104, amended: 1981, c.55, sch.2.

s. 104, rules 74/761; 77/92; 83/719; 84/1670.

ss. 105, 106, rules 74/761; 77/92; 82/369; 83/719; 84/1670; 86/2126.

ss. 107, 108, amended: 1986, c.21, sch.1.

s. 110, continued: 1981, c.54, sch.5; amended: 1981, c.55, s.5.

s. 113, amended: *ibid.*; 1986, c.21, sch.1.

s. 114, repealed: *ibid.*, s.6, sch.2.

s. 116, amended: 1982, c.51, sch.3; 1983, c.20, sch.4; 1984, c.36, sch.3.

s. 119, rules 74/702; 75/1086; 77/90, 91; 79/1456.

s. 120, repealed in pt.: 1986, c.21, sch.2.

ss. 122, 123, rules 74/702; 75/1086; 77/90, 91; 79/1456; 80/723; 83/1853.

ss. 124, 126, 127, rules 74/702; 75/1086; 77/90, 91; 79/1456.

3 & 4 Eliz. 2 (1954–55)—cont.
18. Army Act 1955—cont.

s. 128, amended: 1988, c.13, sch.3.

s. 129, rules 74/702; 75/1086; 77/90, 91; 79/1456.

s. 131, amended: 1981, c.55, s.6; repealed in pt.: *ibid.*, s.6, sch.5.

s. 132, amended: *ibid.*, s.6.

ss. 133, 134, amended: *ibid.*, s.5.

ss. 133, 134, 138, extended: 1976, c.52, sch.8.

s. 133A, added: *ibid.*, sch.8; amended: 1986, c.21, sch.1; repealed in pt.: *ibid.*, sch.2.

s. 134, see *R.* v. *Bissett* [1980] 1 W.L.R. 335, Courts-Martial Appeal Ct.; *R.* v. *Amos, The Times,* March 18, 1986, Courts-Martial Appeal Court.

s. 135, rules 72/847; 82/366, 370.

s. 135, amended: 1981, c.44, s.23.

s. 138, amended: 1976, c.52, sch.7.

s. 141, amended: 1981, c.55, ss.7,8.

s. 141A, added: *ibid.*, s.8.

s. 145, amended: 1982, c.48, sch.8.

s. 150, amended: 1972, c.18, sch.; 1982, c.27, sch.12; repealed in pt.: 1975, c.72, sch.4; 1987, c.42, sch.4.

ss. 150, 153, see *Smith* v. *Chuter* (1988) 18 Fam. Law 339, Booth J.

s. 151, amended: 1976, c.52, s.18; 1981, c.55, sch.2.

s. 153, amended: *ibid.*, s. 18; repealed in pt.: *ibid.*, s.18, sch.5.

s. 163, repealed in pt.: S.L.R. 1976.

s. 183, repealed: 1972, c.71, sch.6; 1980, c.55, sch.3 (S).

ss. 187, see *R.* v. *Thames Metropolitan Stipendiary Magistrate, ex p. Brindle* [1975] 1 W.L.R. 1400, C.A.; *R.* v. *Tottenham Magistrates' Court, ex p. Williams* [1982] 2 All E.R. 705, D.C.

s. 187, amended: 1980, c.43, sch.7.

ss. 189, 190A, regs. 72/318.

s. 195, amended: 1984, c.60, sch.7.

s. 198, amended: 1981, c.55, s.9; repealed in pt.: 1984, c.60, sch.7.

s. 198A, renumbered s. 198C: 1981, c.55, s.9.

ss. 198A, 198B, repealed: 1984, c.60, sch.7.

s. 200A, added: *ibid,* sch.6.

s. 203, see *Walker* v. *Walker* [1983] 2 All E.R. 909, C.A.; *Roberts* v. *Roberts* [1986] 1 W.L.R. 437, Wood J.

s. 204, amended: 1981, c.55, s.19.

s. 205, repealed in pt.: 1986, c.21, sch.2.

s. 209, rules 81/1220; 83/719; 84/1670; 86/2126.

s. 209, amended: 1976, c.52, s.9, sch.9; 1981, c.55, sch.1; 1986, c.21, s.8; repealed in pt.: 1981, c.55, schs.2,5; rules 77/92.

s. 210, amended: 1981, c.55, sch.4.

s. 211, amended: 1980, c.9, sch.9.

s. 213, repealed in pt.: 1986, c.21, s.14, sch.2.

s. 214, amended: 1973, c.65, sch.27; 1988, c.13, sch.3.

s. 215, amended: 1976, c.52, schs.8,9; 1980, c.43, sch.7; 1988, c.13, sch.3; repealed in pt.: 1973, c.53, sch.5; S.L.R. 1977.

3 & 4 Eliz. 2 (1954–55)—cont.

18. Army Act 1955—*cont.*
s. 221, repealed.: 1972, c.71, sch.6.
s. 225, amended: 1973, c.27, s.4; c.49, sch.;
1976, c.19, sch.; c.52, sch.9; 1978, c.15, s.7;
c.20, s.4; orders 78/1030, 1899; 1979, c.27,
sch.; 1980, c.2, sch.; c.9, sch.9; c.16, sch.1;
1981, c.52, sch.2; rules 77/92; 1978, c.15,
s.7; c.20, s.4; orders 78/1030; 80/701;
81/1105; 83/882; 1985, c.3, sch.; 1986, c.21,
sch.1; repealed in pt.: 1973, c.48, sch.4;
1976, c.52, sch.10; 1981, c.55, sch.5.
sch. 2, repealed: S.L.R. 1977.
sch. 3, repealed in pt.: 1986, c.21, sch.2.
sch. 5A, regs. 82/365; 83/717; 86/1241;
87/1999.
sch. 5A, added: 1976, c.52, sch.4; regs. 77/87;
amended: 1981, c.55, sch.1; 1982, c.48,
sch.8; order 80/1088; 1985, c.73, s.46(S.);
1986, c.21, ss.9–11, sch.1; 1988, c.33,
schs.8,9(S.); repealed in pt.: 1986, c.33, s.10,
sch.2.
sch. 6, amended: *ibid.*, sch.1.
sch. 7, amended: 1976, c.52, sch.1; 1980, c.9,
sch.9; 1981, c.55, sch.4; repealed in pt.:
1976, c.52, schs.1,10; S.L.R. 1977; 1981,
c.55, s.4, sch.5; regs. 88/1395.

19. Air Force Act 1955.
rules 72/419.
continued in force: orders 74/2147; 77/1231;
82/1069; 83/1104; 1981, c.55, s.1; orders
84/1147; 85/1196; 1986, c.21, s.1; orders
87/1262; 88/1293.
ss. 12, 13, see *R.* v. *Garth* [1986] 2 W.L.R. 80,
H.L.
s. 17, amended: regs. 77/1097; repealed in pt.:
1976, c.52, sch.10.
s. 20, amended: regs. 77/1097; repealed: S.L.R.
1977.
s. 26, repealed in pt.: 1981, c.55, s.23.
ss. 28, 29, 33, repealed in pt.: 1986, c.21, s.4,
sch.2.
s. 44B, added: *ibid.*, s.2.
s. 55, repealed in pt.: *ibid.*, s.4, sch.2.
s. 57, amended: 1982, c.48, sch.8
s. 62, amended: 1986, c.21, s.3.
s. 65, repealed in pt.: *ibid.*, s.4, sch.2.
s. 69, amended: *ibid.*, s.4.
s. 70, amended: 1974, c.6, s.5; 1976, c.52,
s.10; 1981, c.47, s.7.
s. 71, amended: 1976, c.52, s.10; 1981, c.55,
s.2; 1986, c.21, sch.1.
s. 71A, added: 1976, c.52, s.10; amended:
1982, c.48, sch.8; repealed in pt.: *ibid.*,
schs.8,16.
s. 71AA, added: 1981, c.55, s.2; amended:
1982, c.48, sch.8; 1985, c.73, s.46 (S.); 1986,
c.21, sch.1; 1988, c.33, schs.8, 9(S.).
s. 71B, added: 1976, c.52, sch.6; amended:
1982, c.48, s.69, sch.8; 1986, c.21, s.5;
repealed in pt.: *ibid.*, sch.2.
s. 77, amended: 1981, c.55, s.3.
s. 77A, added: *ibid.*
s. 78, amended: 1976, c.52, s.5; 1981, c.55,
s.3, sch.2.; repealed in pt.: 1976, c.52, sch.10.

3 & 4 Eliz. 2 (1954–55)—cont.

19. Air Force Act 1955—*cont.*
s. 79, amended: *ibid.*, s.5; 1981, c.55, s.3,
sch.2.
s. 80, amended: 1976, c.52, sch.3.
s. 82, repealed in pt.: *ibid.*, schs.2,5.
s. 85, amended: 1982, c.48, sch.8.
s. 86, repealed in pt.: 1976, c.52, sch.9.
s. 91, amended: 1981, c.55, sch.2.
s. 93, amended: 1976, c.52, s.12; 1981, c.55,
sch.2; repealed in pt.: 1976, c.52, s.12,
sch.10.
s. 99, amended: 1976, c.52, sch.5; 1984, c.60,
sch.6; repealed in pt.: 1981, c.55, schs.2,5.
s. 99A, added: 1976, c.52, sch.5; amended:
1984, c.60, sch.6.
s. 102, repealed in pt.: 1977, c.38, sch.5.
s. 103, rules 74/752; 77/94; 81/1219; 82/368;
83/1104; 84/1670; 86/2125; 87/2000, 2172.
ss. 103, 104, amended: 1981, c.55, sch.2.
s. 104, rules 74/752; 77/94; 83/1104; 84/1670.
ss. 105, 106, rules 74/752; 77/94; 82/368;
83/1104; 84/1670; 86/2125.
ss. 107, 108, amended: 1986, c.21, sch.1.
s. 110, continued: 1981, c.54, sch.5; amended:
1981, c.55, s.5.
s. 113, amended: *ibid.*; 1986, c.21, sch.1.
s. 114, repealed: *ibid.*, s.6, sch.2.
s. 116, amended: 1982, c.51, sch.3; 1983, c.20,
sch.4; 1984, c.36, sch.3.
s. 119, rules 76/2165; 77/93; 80/2005.
s. 120, repealed in pt.: 1986, c.21, sch.2.
ss. 122, 123, rules 76/2165; 77/93; 80/2005;
83/1854.
ss. 124, 126, 127, rules 76/2165; 77/93;
80/2005.
s. 128, amended: 1988, c.13, sch.3.
s. 129, rules 76/2165; 77/93, 80/2005.
s. 131, amended: 1981, c.55, s.6; repealed in
pt.: *ibid.*, s.6, sch.5.
s. 132, amended: *ibid.*, s.6; 1986, c.21, s.7.
ss. 133, 134, amended: 1981, c.55, s.5.
s. 133A, added: 1976, c.52, sch.8; amended:
1981, c.55, sch.1; repealed in pt.: *ibid.*, sch.2.
s. 135, amended: 1981, c.55, s.23.
s. 138, amended: 1976, c.52, schs.3,7.
s. 141, amended: 1981, c.55, ss.7,8.
s. 141A, added: *ibid.*, s.8.
s. 144, amended: 1976, c.52, s.19.
s. 145, amended: 1982, c.48, sch.8.
s. 150, amended: 1972, c.18, sch; 1982, c.27,
sch.12; repealed in pt.: 1975, c.72, sch.4;
1986, c.42, sch.4.
s. 151, amended: 1976, c.52, s.18; 1981, c.55,
sch.2.
s. 153, amended: *ibid.*, s.18; repealed in pt.:
ibid., s.18, sch.5.
s. 163, repealed in pt.: S.L.R. 1976.
s. 183, repealed: 1972, c.71, sch.6; 1980, c.55,
sch.3 (S.).
s. 187, amended: 1980, c.43, sch.7.
ss. 189, 190A, regs. 72/286.
s. 195, amended: 1984, c.60, sch.6.
s. 198, amended: 1981, c.55, s.9; repealed in
pt.: 1984, c.60, sch.7.

CAP.

3 & 4 Eliz. 2 (1954–55)—cont.

19. Air Force Act 1955—cont.

s. 198A, renumbered s. 198C: 1981, c.55, s.9.

ss. 198A, 198B, repealed: 1984, c.60, sch.7.

s. 200A, added: *ibid.*, sch.6.

s. 203, see *Ranson* v. *Ranson* [1988] 1 W.L.R. 183, C.A.

s. 205, repealed in pt.: 1986, c.21, sch.2.

s. 209, rules 81/1219; 83/718; 84/1669; 86/2125; 87/2000, 2172.

s. 209, amended: 1976, c.52, s.9, sch.9; 1981, c.55, sch.1; 1986, c.21, s.8; repealed in pt.: 1981, c.55, schs.2,5; rules 77/94.

s. 210, amended: 1980, c.9, sch.9.

s. 212, amended: 1973, c.65, sch.27; 1988, c.13, sch.3.

s. 213, amended: 1976, c.52, schs.8,9; 1980, c.43, sch.7; 1988, c.13, sch.3; repealed in pt.: 1973, c.52, sch.5; S.L.R. 1977.

s. 219, repealed in pt.: 1972, c.71, sch.6.

s. 223, amended: 1973, c.27, s.4; c.49, sch.; 1976, c.19, sch.; c.52, sch.9; 1978, c.15, s.7; c.20, s.4; 1979, c.27, sch.; 1980, c.2, sch.; c.9, sch.9; c.16, sch.1; 1981, c.52, sch.2; rules 77/94; orders 78/1030, 1899; 80/701; 81/1105; 83/882; 1985, c.3, sch.; 1986, c.21, sch.1; repealed in pt.: 1973, c.48, sch.4; 1976, c.52, sch.10; 1981, c.55, sch.5.

sch. 2, repealed: S.L.R. 1977.

sch. 3, repealed in pt.: 1986, c.21, sch.2.

sch. 5A, regs. 77/87; 82/365; 83/717; 86/1241; 87/1999.

sch. 5A, added: 1976, c.52, sch.4; amended: 1981, c.55, sch.1; 1982, c.48, sch.8; order 80/1088; 1985, c.73, s.46(S.); 1986, c.21, ss.9–11, sch.1; 1988, c.33, schs.8,9(S.); repealed in pt.: 1986, c.21, s.10, sch.2.

sch. 6, amended: 1976, c.52, sch.1; 1986, c.21, sch.1.

20. Revision of the Army and Air Force Acts (Transitional Provisions) Act 1955.

s. 5, repealed: S.L.R. 1974.

sch. 2, repealed in pt.: S.L.R. 1977; 1980, c.9, sch.10.

sch. 3, repealed in pt.: S.L.R. 1977.

sch. 4, repealed: S.L.R. 1974.

21. Crofters (Scotland) Act 1955.

see *Byrne* v. *Guthrie*, 1974 S.L.T. (Land Ct.) 6.

s. 1, amended: 1976, c.21, sch.2.

s. 2, amended: *ibid.*; repealed in pt.: *ibid.*, schs.2,3.

s. 3, see *Laird*, 1973 S.L.T. 4; *Bray* v. *Morrison*, 1973 S.L.T. 6; *Libberton Properties* v. *Mackay*, 1973 S.L.T.(Land Ct.) 13; *MacDonald's Exr.* v. *North Uist Estates Trs.*, 1977 S.L.T. (Land Ct.) 10; *Fraser* v. *Van Arman*, 1982 S.L.C.R. 79; *Representatives of the Late Hugh Matheson* v. *Master of Lovat*, 1984 S.L.C.R. 82; *MacLaren* v. *MacLaren*, 1984 S.L.C.R. 43.

s. 3, amended: 1976, c.21, s.14.

s. 5, see *Secretary of State for Scotland* v. *Love*, 1972 S.L.C.R.App. 46; *Hitchcock's Trs.* v. *McCuish*, 1982 S.L.C.R. 101.

s. 8, amended: 1976, c.21, sch.2.

CAP.

3 & 4 Eliz. 2 (1954–55)—cont.

21. Crofters (Scotland) Act 1955—cont.

s. 11, see *Maclennan's Excrx.* v. *Maclennan*, 1974 S.L.T.(Land Ct.) 3.

s. 12, see *Watson* v. *Maclennon*, 1972 S.L.T.(Land Ct.) 2; *Libberton Properties* v. *Mackay*, 1973 S.L.T.(Land Ct.) 10; *Martin* v. *Luib Common Grazing Shareholders*, 1973 S.L.T. (Land Ct.) 9; *Sumburgh Co.* v. *Mail*, 1975 S.L.T. (Land Ct.) 9; *Beardsell* v. *Bell*, 1975 S.L.T. (Land Ct.) 2; *Galston Estate* v. *Crofters of Fivepenny Borve*, 1975 S.L.T. (Land Ct.) 4; *Foljambe* v. *Crofters of Melness*, 1979 S.L.T.(Land Ct.) 9; *Macrae* v. *Secretary of State, Cameron* v. *Secretary of State, Macleod* v. *Secretary of State*, 1981 S.L.T.(Land Ct.) 18; *Secretary of State for Scotland* v. *Shareholders of Lealt and Culnacnock Common Grazings*, 1982 S.L.T.(Land Ct.) 20; *Cameron* v. *Corpach Common Graziers*, 1984 S.L.T. (Land Ct.) 41; *Barvas Estate* v. *Crofters in South Bragar Common Grazings*, 1983 S.L.C.R. 47; *South Uist Estates* v. *MacDonald*, 1983 S.L.C.R. 86; *Secretary of State for Scotland* v. *Sutherland*, 1984 S.L.C.R. 53; *Fountain Forestry* v. *W. H. Ross*, 1985 S.L.C.R. 115; *Shaw* v. *Cummings*, 1987 S.L.C.R. 157.

s. 12, amended: 1985, c.73, s.30; repealed in pt.: 1976, c.21, sch.3.

s. 13, see *Secretary of State for Scotland* v. *Campbell*, 1971 S.L.C.R. App. 35.

s. 14, see *Maclennan's Excrx.* v. *Maclennan*, 1974 S.L.T. (Land Ct.) 3; *Gilmour* v. *Master of Lovat*, 1979 S.L.T.(Land Ct.) 2.

s. 15, amended: 1976, c.21, sch.2.

s. 16, see *Watson* v. *Maclennon*, 1972 S.L.T.(Land Ct.) 2; *Laird*, 1973 S.L.T. 4; *Gray* v. *Crofters Commission*, 1980 S.L.T.(Land Ct.) 2; *Steven* v. *Crofters Commission*, 1984 S.L.C.R. 30.

s. 16, amended: 1976, c.13, sch.2; repealed in pt.: *ibid.*, sch.3.

s. 16A, see *Gray* v. *Crofters Commission*, 1980 S.L.T.(Land Ct.) 2; *Steven* v. *Crofters Commission*, 1984 S.L.C.R. 30; *MacColl* v. *Crofters Commission*, 1985 S.L.C.R. 142; *Moray Estates Development Co.* v. *Crofters Commission*, 1988 S.L.T.(Land Ct.) 14.

s. 16A, added: 1976, c.21, s.13.

s. 17, see *Anderson* v. *MacLeod's Trs.*, 1973 S.L.T. 2.

s. 17, amended: 1974, c.38, s.14; 1976, c.21, sch.2; repealed in pt.: *ibid.*, sch.3.

s. 18, repealed: 1976, c.21, sch.3.

s. 22, schemes 72/407, 1338; 73/1550; 74/118, 1604, 1870, 2152; 88/559; regs. 82/1419.

s. 22, amended: 1976, c.21, s.12, sch.2; 1985, c.73, s.31; repealed in pt.: 1976, c.21, sch.3.

s. 23, see *Secretary of State for Scotland* v. *Campbell*, 1971 S.L.C.R.App. 35.

s. 24, amended: 1976, c.21, s.16.

s. 25, amended: *ibid.*, s.16; repealed in pt.: *ibid.*, sch.3.

ss. 25, 26, see *Sikorski* v. *Noble*, 1985 S.L.C.R. 139.

3 & 4 Eliz. 2 (1954–55)—cont.

21. Crofters (Scotland) Act 1955—cont.
s. 26, amended: 1976, c.21, s.16.
s. 27, amended: ibid., s.16, sch.2.
s. 28, see MacDonald's Exr. v. North Uist Estates Trs., 1977 S.L.T.(Land Ct.) 10; Duke of Argyll's Trs. v. Macneill, 1983 S.L.T.(Land Ct.) 35.
ss. 30, 31, 34, amended: 1976, c.21, sch.2.
s. 37, amended: 1973, c.65, sch.27; 1984, c.54, sch.9.
sch. 1, amended: 1976, c.21, s.18.
sch. 2, see Bray v. Morrison, 1973 S.L.T. 6; Libberton Properties v. Mackay, 1973 S.L.T.(Land Ct.) 13; Gilmour v. Master of Lovat, 1979 S.L.T.(Land Ct.) 2; Hitchcock's Trs v. McCuish, 1982 S.L.C.R. 101; MacLaren v. MacLaren, 1984 S.L.C.R. 43; Crofters Sharing in Keil Common Grazings v. MacColl, 1986 S.L.C.R. 142; MacAskill v. Basil Baird & Sons, 1987 S.L.T.(Land Ct.) 34.
sch. 3, amended: 1976, c.21, sch.2; repealed in pt.: ibid., sch.3.
sch. 5, see Gilmour v. Master of Lovat, 1979 S.L.T.(Land Ct.) 2.
sch. 5, amended: 1974, c.45, s.25; 1987, c.26, sch.23.

22. Pensions (India, Pakistan and Burma) Act 1955.
repealed: 1973, c.21, sch.2.

24. Requisitioned Houses and Housing (Amendment) Act 1955.
repealed: S.L.R. 1978.

25. Oil in Navigable Waters Act 1955.
s. 1, regs. 72/1928.
s. 1, see Federal Steam Navigation Co. v. Department of Trade and Industry [1974] 1 W.L.R. 505; [1974] 2 All E.R. 97, H.L.
s. 2, orders 72/676, 1592.
s. 7, regs. 72/1929.
s. 18, orders 72/675, 1591.

26. Public Service Vehicles (Travel Concessions) Act 1955.
repealed: 1985, c.67, sch.8.

27. Public Libraries (Scotland) Act 1955.
s. 1, repealed: S.L.R. 1986.
s.-3, repealed: 1973, c.65, schs.21,29.
s. 4, amended: 1988, c.48, sch.7.
s. 5, amended: 1973, c.65, sch.21.

28. Children and Young Persons (Harmful Publications) Act 1955.
s. 3, repealed in pt.: 1984, c.60, sch.7.

4 & 5 Eliz. 2 (1955–56)

2. German Conventions Act 1955.
s. 1, repealed in pt.: 1975, c.34, sch.2.

5. International Finance Corporation Act 1955.
repealed: 1980, c.63, sch.2.
s. 3, order 76/221.

6. Miscellaneous Financial Provisions Act 1955.
s. 1, repealed: S.L.R. 1977.
s. 4, repealed in pt.: S.L.R. 1974.
s. 5, amended: 1972, c.65, s.15; repealed in pt.: S.L.R. 1974; S.L.R. 1986.
sch. 2, repealed: S.L.R. 1974.

4 & 5 Eliz. 2 (1955–56)—cont.

9. Rating and Valuation (Miscellaneous Provisions) Act 1955.
s. 6, see British Gas Corporation (formerly North Thames Gas Board) v. Anglian Water Authority (formerly Essex River Authority) (1975) 73 L.G.R. 376.
ss. 6, 14, sch. 4, repealed (S.): S.L.R. 1975.
s. 17, repealed in pt. (S.): ibid.

11. Sudan (Special Payments) Act 1955.
repealed: 1972, c.11, sch.8.

16. Food and Drugs Act 1955.
repealed: 1984, c.30, sch.11.
regs. 72/1117; 81/1063; 83/1810.
see Widnes Corporation v. Ranger (1972) 12 K.I.R. 324; Ricketts v. Havering London Borough Council, The Times, July 17, 1980, Whitford J.
s. 2, see French's Dairies (Sevenoaks) v. Davis [1973] Crim.L.R. 630, D.C.; Tesco Stores v. Roberts [1974] 3 All E.R. 74, D.C.; Grimsby Borough Council v. Louis C. Edwards & Sons (Manufacturing) [1976] Crim.L.R. 512, D.C.; Meah v. Roberts; Lansley v. Roberts [1977] 1 W.L.R. 1187, D.C.; Greater Manchester Council v. Lockwood Foods [1979] Crim.L.R. 593, D.C.; Goldup v. John Manson [1981] 3 All E.R. 257; [1981] 3 W.L.R. 833, D.C.; T. W. Lawrence & Sons v. Burleigh (1982) 80 L.G.R. 631, D.C.; Barber v. Co-operative Wholesale Society [1983] Crim.L.R. 476, D.C.; R. v. Uxbridge JJ., ex p. Gow; R. v. Uxbridge JJ., ex p. Cooperative Retail Services [1986] Crim.L.R. 177, D.C.; Shearer v. Rowe (1986) 84 L.G.R. 296, D.C.; Arun District Council v. Argyle Stores [1986] Crim.L.R. 685, D.C.
s. 2, regs. 77/1854.
ss. 2, 3, see Smedleys v. Breed [1974] 2 W.L.R. 575; [1974] 2 All E.R. 21, H.L.
s. 4, regs. 72/205, 1391, 1843; 73/1052, 1053, 1340; 74/1119–1122; 75/1484–1488; 76/295, 509, 541, 1832, 1886, 1887, 2086; 77/645, 691, 927, 928; 78/105, 1420, 1787; 79/752, 1254; 80/36, 931, 1831–1834, 1849; 82/14–17, 254, 255, 264, 1066, 1700, 1727; 83/1211, 1508, 1509; 84/649, 1304, 1305.
s. 7, regs. 72/1391, 1510; 73/161, 1340; 74/1119–1122; 75/1485–1488; 76/103, 295, 509, 541, 859, 1832, 1886, 1887, 2086; 77/645, 927, 928; 78/105, 646, 1420, 1787; 79/752, 1570; 80/931, 1831–1834, 1849; 82/14–17, 254, 255, 1066, 1700, 1727; 83/1211, 1508; 84/649, 1304, 1305; order 81/1174.
s. 8, see Hooper v. Petrou [1973] Crim.L.R. 298, D.C.; Macpherson, Train & Co. v. Christchurch B.C. [1976] Crim. L.R. 568, D.C.; Meah v. Roberts; Lansley v. Roberts [1977] 1 W.L.R. 1187, D.C.; Walker v. Baxter's Butchers (1977) 76 L.G.R. 183, D.C.
s. 9, see R. v. Archer, ex p. Barrow Lane & Ballard, The Times, August 13, 1983; (1984) 82 L.G.R. 361, C.A.
s. 12, regs. 81/1084.

CAP.

4 & 5 Eliz. 2 (1955–56)—cont.

16. Food and Drugs Act 1955—cont.
  s. 13, regs. 73/1351; 75/654; 76/882; 77/1805;
    79/693, 1426, 1427; 81/454, 1085; 82/1018,
    1727; 83/173, 174, 1508; orders 81/1168;
    84/604.
  s. 28, regs. 73/1064.
  s. 29, regs. 73/1070; 76/1883; 77/171; 79/1567;
    82/1358; 83/1509, 1511.
  s. 30, regs. 77/171; 79/1567; 82/1703.
  s. 35, regs. 80/488, 1863; 82/1359.
  ss. 35, 43, regs. 74/62; 77/1033; 83/15.
  s. 49, see *R.* v. *Basildon District Council, ex p.
    Brown* (1981) 79 L.G.R. 655, C.A.; *East Lind-
    sey District Council* v. *Hamilton, The Times,*
    April 2, 1984, C.A.
  Pt. III (ss. 49–61), see *Halton Borough Council*
    v. *Cawley* [1985] 1 W.L.R. 15, Blackett-Ord
    V.C.
  s. 55, see *Leicester Corporation* v. *Maby* (1971)
    70 L.G.R. 209.
  s. 82, regs. 76/509, 1209, 1832, 1886, 1887,
    2086; 77/927, 928, 1805; 78/105, 646, 1420;
    79/1427; 80/931, 1831–1834; 81/454, 1085;
    82/14–17, 254, 255, 1018, 1066; orders
    81/1168, 1174; 82/1700.
  s. 86, regs. 74/391, 1211, 1806; 78/884.
  s. 87, regs. 73/1064; 74/62; 76/1883; 77/1033;
    80/1863; 83/1508–1511.
  s. 88, repealed in pt.: 1984, c.22, sch.3.
  ss. 91, 92, see *Arun District Council* v. *Argyle
    Stores* [1986] Crim.L.R. 685; (1987) 85 L.G.R.
    59, D.C.
  s. 93, see *Skeate* v. *Moore* [1972] 1 W.L.R. 110.
  s. 108, see *Widnes Corporation* v. *Ranger* (1972)
    12 K.I.R. 324; *Manson* v. *Louis C. Edwards
    & Sons (Manufacturing)* (1976) 74 L.G.R. 545,
    D.C.; *Benfell Farm Produce* v. *Surrey County
    Council* [1983] 1 W.L.R. 1213, D.C.; *R.* v.
    *Harvey (J.P. for Shropshire), ex p, Select Live-
    stock Producers* [1985] Crim.L.R. 510, D.C.;
    R. v. *Uxbridge JJ., ex p. Gow; R.* v.
    *Uxbridge JJ., ex p. Cooperative Retail Ser-
    vices* [1986] Crim.L.R. 177, D.C.; *Arun District
    Council* v. *Argyle Stores* [1986] Crim.L.R. 685;
    (1987) 85 L.G.R. 59, D.C.
  s. 111, see *Hooper* v. *Petrou* [1973] Crim.L.R.
    298, D.C.
  s. 113, see *Macpherson, Train & Co.* v. *Christ-
    church B.C.* [1976] Crim.L.R. 568, D.C.; *R.* v.
    Bacister II, ex p. Unigate [1975] 1 W.L.R. 207;
    [1975] 1 All E.R. 449, D.C.; *Meah* v. *Roberts;
    Lansley* v. *Roberts* [1977] 1 W.L.R. 1187,
    D.C.; *Benfell Farm Produce* v. *Surrey County
    Council* [1983] 1 W.L.R. 1213, D.C.; *R.* v.
    Uxbridge JJ., ex p. Gow; R. v. *Uxbridge JJ.,
    ex p. Cooperative Retail Services* [1986]
    Crim.L.R. 177, D.C.
  s. 115, see *Tesco Stores* v. *Roberts* [1974] 3 All
    E.R. 74, D.C.; *Walker* v. *Baxter's Butchers*
    (1977) 76 L.G.R. 183, D.C.; *Rochdale Metro-
    politan Borough Council* v. *F.M.C. (Meat)*
    [1980] 1 W.L.R. 461, D.C.; *Dover District
    Council* v. *C. R. Barron* (1980) 78 L.G.R. 126,
    D.C.

CAP.

4 & 5 Eliz. 2 (1955–56)—cont.

16. Food and Drugs Act 1955—cont.
  s. 123, regs. 72/205, 1391, 1510, 1843; 73/161,
    1052, 1053, 1064, 1070, 1340, 1351; 74/62,
    1119–1122; 75/654, 1484–1488; 76/103, 295,
    509, 541, 859, 882, 1832, 1883, 1886, 1887,
    2086; 77/171, 645, 691, 1033, 1805; 78/646,
    1420, 1787; 79/693, 752, 1254, 1426, 1427,
    1567, 1570; 80/36, 488, 931, 1831–1834,
    1849, 1863; 81/454, 1084, 1085, 1168, 1174;
    82/14–17, 254, 255, 264, 1018, 1066, 1311,
    1358, 1359, 1700, 1703, 1727; 83/173, 174,
    1211, 1508–1511; 84/604, 649, 1304, 1305.
  s. 123A, regs. 73/369; 74/1119–1122; 75/1487;
    76/295, 541, 1883, 1887; 77/645, 1854;
    79/752; 80/931; 82/15, 17, 254, 255, 264,
    1066, 1602; 84/1145.
  s. 134, regs. 79/1427; 81/1084.
  s. 135, see *Meah* v. *Roberts; Lansley* v. *Roberts*
    [1977] 1 W.L.R. 1187, D.C.; *Fleming* v.
    Edwards, The Times, March 15, 1986, D.C.
  sch. 7, see *Skeate* v. *Moore* [1972] 1 W.L.R.
    110.
  sch. 10, regs. 79/1427; 81/1084.
18. Aliens' Employment Act 1955.
  s. 2, repealed in pt.: 1973, c.36, sch.6.
19. Friendly Societies Act 1955.
  ss. 1, 2, 3 (in pt.), 4, repealed: 1974, c.46,
    sch.11.
  s. 5, repealed: S.L.R. 1978.
  s. 8, repealed: 1974, c.46, sch.11.
  s. 9, amended: 1973, c.38, sch.27; 1974, c.46,
    sch.9; repealed in pt.: 1973, c.38, sch.28;
    1974, c.46, schs.9,11; 1975, c.18, sch.1.
**20. Agriculture (Improvement of Roads) Act
    1955.**
  repealed: 1984, c.54, sch.11 (S.); S.L.R. 1986.
23. Leeward Islands Act 1956.
  repealed: S.L.R. 1986.
25. Therapeutic Substances Act 1956.
  Part II, repealed: order 77/2128.
  s. 4, amended: 1975, c.4, s.6; order 88/1843.
  s. 8, regs. 73/855.
  s. 9, regs. 72/190, 1315, 1687; 73/201, 640,
    1733; 74/242; 75/1906.
  s. 17, repealed: 1973, c.36, sch.6.
29. Dentists Act 1956.
  repealed: 1983, c.38, sch.3.
30. Food and Drugs (Scotland) Act 1956.
  ss. 1–3, repealed in pt.: order 77/2128.
  s. 2, see *Burrell* v. *Walls,* 1972 S.L.T.(Sh.Ct.) 27;
    [1973] Crim.L.R. 766; *Skinner* v. *MacLean,*
    1979 S.L.T.(Notes) 35; *McLeod* v. *Morton,*
    1981 S.L.T.(Sh.Ct.) 107; 1982 S.L.T.(Sh.Ct.)
    102.
  s. 3, amended: 1979, c.4, sch.3; repealed in
    pt.: 1981, c.35, s.19.
  s. 4, regs. 72/307, 1489, 1906; 73/1310;
    74/1337–1340, 1356; 75/594, 1594–1598;
    76/442, 914, 916, 1818, 1910, 1911, 2232;
    77/860, 1026–1028, 1883; 78/492; 79/107,
    383, 1073, 1641; 80/289, 1232, 1886–1889;
    81/137, 1320; 82/18, 108, 410, 514–516,
    1209, 1619, 1779; 83/270, 940, 1497, 1514,
    1515, 1526, 1815; 84/847, 1518, 1519, 1714;
    85/1068, 1222, 1438; 86/789–791, 836, 1288;
    87/26, 1985, 2014; 88/1815.

CAP.

4 & 5 Eliz. 2 (1955–56)—cont.

30. Food and Drugs (Scotland) Act 1956—*cont.*
s. 4, amended: 1972, c.68, sch.4.
s. 5, regs. 87/1985, 2014.
s. 6, repealed in pt.: order 77/2128.
s. 7, regs. 72/1489, 1790: 73/249;
74/1337–1340, 1356; 75/1595–1598; 76/294,
442, 914, 916, 1176, 1818, 1910, 1911, 2232;
77/860, 1026, 1027, 1883; 78/492, 927;
79/107, 383, 1073, 1693; 80/1232,
1886–1889; 81/1319, 1320; 82/108, 409, 410,
514–516, 1209, 1619, 1779; 83/270, 940,
1497, 1514, 1526, 1815; 84/847, 1518, 1519,
1714; 85/1068, 1222; 86/789, 790, 836, 1288;
87/26.
s. 12, amended: 1980, c.13, sch.1.
s. 13, regs. 73/1471; 75/685; 76/874, 1221;
78/173, 1273; 79/768, 1537, 1563; 81/996,
1035, 1169; 83/702–704, 1515; 84/842, 1885;
85/913, 1068, 1222, 1856; 86/789, 790, 1808;
87/800, 1957; 88/1484.
s. 16, regs. 85/1068.
s. 17, repealed in pt.: 1972, c.68, sch.4.
s. 20, amended: 1973, c.65, sch.27.
s. 21, amended: *ibid.*; repealed in pt.: *ibid.*,
schs.25,29.
s. 22, amended: 1972, c.58, sch.6; 1978, c.29,
sch.15; repealed in pt.: 1973, c.65,
schs.25,29.
s. 24, amended: 1972, c.58, sch.6; 1978, c.29,
sch.15.
s. 25, repealed: 1981, c.23, s.30, sch.4.
s. 26, regs. 74/1356; 76/914, 916, 1818,
77/1026–1028, 1883; 78/492; 79/383, 1073;
80/289, 1232, 1888, 1889; 81/1320; 83/940,
1497, 1514, 1515, 1526; 84/1518, 1519,
1714; 85/913; 86/836; 87/26, 800; 88/1484.
s. 26, amended: 1973, c.65, sch.27; 1982, c.43,
s.22; repealed in pt.: *ibid.*, s.22, sch.4.
ss. 26–29, see *McLeod* v. *Morton*, 1981
S.L.T.(Sh.Ct.) 102.
s. 27, amended: 1973, c.65, sch.27; repealed in
pt.: *ibid.*, sch.29.
s. 27A, added: 1982, c.43, s.22.
s. 28, repealed in pt.: order 77/2128.
s. 29, amended: 1973, c.65, sch.27; 1982, c.43,
s.22.
s. 35, amended: 1973, c.65, sch.27; repealed in
pt.: 1981, c.23, schs.2,4.
s. 36, amended: 1981, c.22, sch.5.
s. 40, repealed in pt.: 1985, c.73, s.41.
s. 41, see *McLeod* v. *Morton*, 1981
S.L.T.(Sh.Ct.) 107.
s. 56, regs. 72/307, 1489, 1790, 1906; 73/249,
914, 1310, 1471; 74/1337–1340, 1356;
75/594, 685, 1594–1598; 76/122, 294, 442,
874, 914, 916, 1176, 1818, 1888, 1910, 1911,
2232; 77/860, 1026–1028, 1883; 78/173, 492,
927, 1273; 79/107, 383, 768, 1073, 1537,
1563, 1641, 1693; 80/289, 1232, 1886, 1887;
81/996, 1035, 1169, 1319, 1320; 82/18, 108,
409, 410, 514–516, 1209, 1619, 1779; 83/270,
702–704, 940, 1497, 1514, 1515, 1526, 1815;
84/842, 847, 1518, 1519, 1714, 1885; 85/913,
1068, 1222, 1438, 1856; 86/789–791, 836,
1288, 1808; 87/26, 800, 1957, 1985, 2014;
88/1484, 1815.

CAP.

4 & 5 Eliz. 2 (1955–56)—cont.

30. Food and Drugs (Scotland) Act 1956—*cont.*
s. 56, amended: 1982, c.48, sch.15.
s. 56A, added: 1972, c.68, sch.4.
s. 56A, regs. 73/914; 76/1888; 77/1804;
79/1073; 80/232; 82/18, 108, 409, 410, 516,
938, 1372; 84/1576; 87/2014.
s. 58, amended: 1972, c.58, sch.6; 1978, c.29,
sch.15; 1979, c.2, sch.4; repealed in pt.:
1972, c.58, sch.7.
s. 60, regs. 79/1641; 85/1068.
s. 60, repealed in pt.: S.L.R. 1974.
sch. 3, repealed: *ibid.*
**31. Pakistan (Consequential Provisions) Act
1956.**
repealed: 1973, c.48, sch.4.
33. Housing Subsidies Act 1956.
repealed: 1972, c.47, sch.11.
34. Criminal Justice Administration Act 1956.
repealed: 1973, c.15, sch.5.
36. Local Authorities (Expenses) Act 1956.
repealed: 1972, c.70, sch.30.
38. Agricultural Mortgage Corporation Act 1956.
s. 2, amended: 1972, c.62, s.13.
43. Local Government Elections Act 1956.
repealed: 1972, c.70, sch.30.
**44. Magistrates' Courts (Appeals from Binding
Over Orders) Act 1956.**
s. 1, see *Shaw* v. *Hamilton* [1982] 2 All E.R.
718, D.C.
s. 1, amended: 1980, c.43, sch.7.
s. 2, see *R.* v. *Preston Crown Court, ex p.
Pamplin* [1981] Crim.L.R. 338, D.C.
46. Administration of Justice Act 1956.
Pts. I, II (ss. 1–20), repealed: 1981, c.54, sch.7.
s. 1, see *The Eschersheim* [1976] 1 W.L.R. 430;
[1976] 1 All E.R. 920, H.L.; *Techno-Impex* v.
Gebr. van Weelde Scheepvaartkantoor B.V.
[1981] 2 W.L.R. 821, C.A.; *The Stella Nova,
The Times,* July 24, 1981, Sheen J.; *Gatoil
International* v. *Arkwright-Boston Manufacturers Mutual Insurance Co.* [1985] 2 W.L.R.
74, H.L.
ss. 1, 3, see *The Conoco Britannia* [1972] 2
W.L.R. 1352; [1972] 2 All E.R. 238; [1972] 1
Lloyd's Rep. 342; *The Halcyon Skies* [1976] 2
W.L.R. 514; [1976] 1 All E.R. 856.
s. 3, see *The Berny* [1978] 2 W.L.R. 387, Brandon J.; *Re I Congreso del Partido* [1977] 3
W.L.R. 778, Goff J.; *The Ledesco Uno* [1978]
2 Lloyd's Rep. 99, Li J. (Hong Kong); *Unitramp*
v. *Maritime Trader; The Maritime Trader*
[1981] Com.L.R. 27, Sheen J.
s. 15, see *Giles & Co.* v. *Morris* [1972] 1 W.L.R.
307; *Whiteoaks Clifton Property Services* v.
Jackson [1975] 1 W.L.R. 658; [1975] 2 All
E.R. 85.
s. 25, repealed: 1981, c.20, sch.4.
ss. 34, 36, 38, 42–44, repealed: 1981, c.54,
sch.7.
s. 35, see *A. & M. Records Inc.* v. *Darakdjian;
Capital Records Inc.* v. *Same* [1975] 1 W.L.R.
1610; [1975] 3 All E.R. 983; *National Westminster Bank* v. *Stockton, The Times,* August
19, 1980, Russell J.; *Roberts Petroleum* v.
Bernard Kenny [1983] 2 W.L.R. 305, H.L.
s. 35, repealed: 1979, c.53, s.7.

4 & 5 Eliz. 2 (1955–56)—cont.

46. Administration of Justice Act 1956—cont.

s. 36, amended: *ibid.*; repealed in pt.: 1985, c.65, sch.10.

s. 37, order 80/26.

s. 37, repealed in pt.: S.L.R. 1975.

s. 38, see *Choice Investments* v. *Jeromnimon (Midland Bank, Garnishee)* [1981] 1 All E.R. 225, C.A.

s. 40, amended: 1965, c.65, sch.8; repealed in pt.: *ibid.*, schs.8,10.

s. 47, see *West of Scotland Ship Owners' Mutual Protection & Indemnity Association (Luxembourg)* v. *Aifanourios Shipping S.A.* (O.H.), June 26, 1980; *Gatoil International Inc.* v. *Arkwright-Boston Manufacturers Mutual Insurance Co.* [1985] 2 W.L.R. 74, H.L.; *William Batey (Exports)* v. *Kent,* 1987 S.L.T. 557; *Clipper Shipping Co.* v. *San Vincente Partners, The Scotsman,* June 24, 1988.

s. 49, repealed in pt.: 1981, c.22, sch.6.

s. 51, repealed in pt.: 1982, c.27, sch.14.

s. 54, repealed: 1981, c.54, sch.7.

s. 55, repealed in pt.: 1973, c.36, sch.6; S.L.R. 1974.

s. 56, orders 74/2148; 75/1506, 1509, 1511, 1514.

s. 56, repealed: 1981, c.54, s.149, sch.7.

s. 57, repealed in pt.: S.L.R. 1974.

sch. 1, amended: 1978, c.23, sch.5; regs. 83/708; repealed in pt.: S.L.R. 1974; 1978, c.23, s.30, sch.7.

sch. 2, repealed: S.L.R. 1974.

48. Sugar Act 1956.

repealed: 1984, c.30, sch.11.

s. 18, orders 72/105, 224; 73/410; 74/370; 76/324; 77/338; 78/320; 79/222; 81/292; 82/274; 83/294; 84/250.

s. 19, order 75/1939.

49. Agriculture (Safety, Health and Welfare Provisions) Act 1956.

s. 1, regs. 73/1977; 74/2034.

ss. 1, 2, repealed in pt.: order 75/46.

s. 3, amended: order 76/1247; regs. 77/746; repealed in pt.: *ibid.*

s. 4, repealed: order 75/46.

s. 5, amended and repealed in pt.: regs. 77/746.

s. 6, repealed in pt.: order 75/46; regs. 81/917.

ss. 7 (in pt.), 8, 10, repealed: order 75/46.

s. 11, repealed: regs. 77/746.

ss. 12–15, 17–21, repealed: order 75/46.

ss. 14, 24, see *O'Sullivan* v. *Thompson-Coon* (1972) 14 K.I.R. 108.

s. 23, repealed: order 76/1247.

s. 24, amended: *ibid.*; repealed in pt.: 1972, c.70, sch.30; order 76/1247; regs. 77/746; 1986, c.5, sch.14.

s. 25, amended and repealed in pt.: order 75/46; regs. 77/746.

52. Clean Air Act 1956.

s. 4, repealed: 1980, c.65, schs.2,34.

s. 6, repealed in pt.: *ibid.*

s. 10, amended: 1973, c.65, sch.15 (S.); 1983, c.25, sch.3; 1984, c.55, sch.6.

4 & 5 Eliz. 2 (1955–56)—cont.

52. Clean Air Act 1956—cont.

s. 11, orders 72/438, 611, 935, 1008; 73/2166; 74/83, 762, 855, 1325; 75/989, 1001, 1111, 1643; 78/1609; 81/249 (S.), 1568; 82/448, 1615; 83/277, 426, 1018, 1472, 1573; 84/1649, 1805 (S.); 85/315 (S.), 864; 86/638; 87/383 (S.), 1394; 88/2282.

s. 11, repealed in pt.: 1980, c.65, schs.2,34.

s. 12, amended: 1980, c.65, sch.2; 1987, c.26, sch.23 (S.); repealed in pt.: 1980, c.65, sch.34.

s. 13, amended: *ibid.*, sch.2.

s. 14, amended: 1974, c.39, sch.4.

s. 16, amended: 1982, c.30, s.26; repealed in pt.: 1974, c.40, sch.4.

s. 17, repealed in pt.: regs. 74/2170.

s. 23, repealed: 1980, c.65, s.189, sch.34.

s. 24, regs. 72/317; 76/1676.

s. 24, repealed: 1974, c.37, sch.10.

s. 25, amended: 1974, c.40, s.79; repealed in pt.: *ibid.*, s.79, sch.4.

s. 26, repealed in pt.: *ibid.*

s. 27, amended: *ibid.*, sch.2.

s. 30, amended: *ibid.*, sch.3.

s. 31, amended (S.): 1987, c.26, sch.23; repealed in pt.: 1972, c.70, sch.30; 1980, c.65, schs.2,34.

s. 33, regs. 81/192; 82/639; 85/1812; 86/162, 892(S.), 1480; orders 87/1394; 88/2282; repealed in pt.: S.L.R. 1981.

s. 34, regs. 72/986; 73/1767; 78/99; 80/1773(S.); 81/192, 664(S.); 82/449, 639; 85/1812; 86/162, 892(S.), 1480; 87/625, 2159; 88/1270(S.), 1607.

s. 34, amended: 1973, c.65, sch.27; 1974, c.39, sch.4.

s. 35, repealed in pt.: S.L.R. 1974; 1980, c.65, schs.2,34.

s. 36, repealed in pt.: 1973, c.36, sch.6.

sch. 2, repealed in pt.: 1974, c.40, sch.4; S.L.R. 1981.

sch. 3, amended (S.): 1987, c.26, sch.23; repealed in pt.: S.L.R. 1981.

sch. 4, repealed: S.L.R. 1974.

54. Finance Act 1956.

s. 2, repealed: 1975, c.45, sch.14.

s. 10, see *Moore* v. *Griffiths* [1972] 1 W.L.R. 1024; [1972] T.R. 61.

s. 26, amended: 1988, c 1, sch.29; repealed in pt : 1974, c.46, sch.11.

ss. 33, 34, 36, repealed: 1975, c.7, sch.13.

s. 34, functions transferred: orders 81/207; 86/600.

ss. 40, 41, repealed: 1975, c.7, sch.13.

s. 44, repealed in pt.: S.L.R. 1974; 1975, c.7, sch.13.

sch. 2, see *Graham* v. *White* [1972] 1 W.L.R. 874; [1972] 1 All E.R. 1159; [1971] T.R. 477; *Harmer* v. *Wright* [1974] 1 W.L.R. 325; [1974] 1 All E.R. 945; *Tyrer* v. *Smart* [1979] 1 W.L.R. 113, H.L.

sch. 5, repealed: S.L.R. 1974.

59. Underground Works (London) Act 1956.

s. 6, amended: 1975, c.76, sch.1; 1981, c.67, sch.4; repealed in pt.: *ibid.*, sch.6.

4 & 5 Eliz. 2 (1955–56)—cont.

60. Valuation and Rating (Scotland) Act 1956.
s. 1, repealed in pt.: 1973, c.65, schs.9,29.
s. 3, amended: 1981, c.23, s.11.
s. 4, repealed: 1973, c.65, sch.29.
s. 5, repealed: 1975, c.30, sch.7.
s. 6, see *Scottish Malt Distillers* v. *Banffshire Assessor*, 1973 S.L.T. 127; 1973 S.C. 63, L.V.A.C.; *Paisley Burgh* v. *Renfrewshire Assessor*, 1973 S.L.T. 222; *Glasgow Assessor* v. *Glasgow Corporation*, 1974 S.L.T. 69; *Edinburgh Assessor* v. *Forces Help Society*, 1974 S.L.T. 287; *Fife Assessor* v. *Game Fisheries*, 1975 S.L.T. 224; *Assessor for Central Region* v. *United Glass*; (2) *United Glass Containers* v. *Assessor for Fife Region*, 1981 S.L.T.(Notes) 114; *Milligan* v. *Assessor for Strathclyde Region*, Lands Valuation Appeal Court, August 6, 1981; *Distillers Co. (Bottling Services)* v. *Assessors for the Fife Region*, 1988 S.L.T.(Lands Tr.) 49.
s. 6, order 84/1112.
s. 6, amended: 1981, c.23, s.4; 1988, c.41, sch.12; repealed in pt.: 1981, c.23, s.3, sch.4; 1987, c.47, sch.6.
s. 7, see *McCowan* v. *Secretary of State*, 1972 S.L.T. 163; *Glasgow Assessor* v. *Berridale Allotments Association*, 1973 S.L.T. 178; *Roxburgh Assessor* v. *West Cumberland Farmers Trading Society*, Lands Val.Appeal Ct., Dec. 14, 1973; *Lowlands Cereals* v. *Assessor for Lothian Region*, Lands Valuation Appeal Court, June 2, 1979; *Rennie* v. *Assessor for Lothian Region* v. *Isle of Jura Fish Farm*, 1981 S.L.T.(Notes) 121; *Assessor for Tayside Region* v. *D.B. Marshall (Newbridge)*, 1983 S.C. 54.
s. 7, amended: 1976, c.21, sch.2; regs. 77/2007; 1984, c.31, s.16; 1987, c.47, sch.1; repealed in pt.: *ibid.*, sch.6.
s. 7A, added: 1980, c.65, s.32; repealed in pt.: 1987, c.47, sch.6.
s. 8, see *Angus Assessor* v. *Dundee Society for the Blind*, 1969 S.C. 342; *Edinburgh Assessor* v. *Forces Help Society*, 1974 S.L.T. 287; *Glasgow Assessor* v. *Nuffield Nursing Homes Trust*, 1976 S.L.T. 101; *Edinburgh Assessor* v. *Brodie*, 1976 S.L.T. 234; *Assessor for Lothian Region* v. *Thistle Foundation*, 1978 S.L.T. 162.
s. 8, repealed in pt.: 1978, c.40, sch.2.
s. 8A, added: 1984, c.31, s.17.
s. 8AA, added: *ibid.*, s.18.
s. 9, see *Renfrewshire Assessor* v. *Hendry*, 1969 S.C. 211; *Aberdeen Harbour Board* v. *Aberdeen Assessor*, 1973 S.L.T. 93; *Glasgow Assessor* v. *Glasgow Corporation*, 1974 S.L.T. 69; *Ferguson* v. *Assessor for Glasgow*, 1977 S.L.T. 142; *Assessor for Fife* v. *W. & J. B. Eastwood*, 1978 S.L.T. 48.
ss. 9–11, repealed: 1975, c.30, sch.7.
s. 12, repealed: order 78/252.
s. 13, orders 72/1544; 75/2232; 77/1694; 78/1464; 80/267, 1875; 81/928; 84/1504; 85/62; 87/432, 794; 88/337.

4 & 5 Eliz. 2 (1955–56)—cont.

60. Valuation and Rating (Scotland) Act 1956— *cont.*
s. 13, amended: 1975, c.30, sch.6; repealed in pt.: *ibid.*, sch.7.
s. 15, see *Faulkner* v. *Talbot* [1981] 3 All E.R. 468, D.C.
s. 15, repealed: 1975, c.30, sch.7.
s. 16, repealed in pt.: 1973, c.65, sch.29.
s. 18, repealed: 1980, c.45, sch.11.
s. 19, repealed: 1975, c.30, sch.7.
s. 21, repealed in pt.: 1973, c.65, schs.9,29.
s. 22, order 75/2232.
s. 22, amended: 1987, c.47, sch.1; 1988, c.41, sch.12.
s. 22A, added: *ibid.*
s. 24, repealed: order 78/1176.
ss. 26, 31, 37, 40, repealed: 1973, c.65, sch.29.
s. 42, orders 72/1544; 77/1694; 80/267; 81/928; 84/1504; 85/62; 87/794; 88/337.
s. 43, amended: 1972, c.60, sch.6; 1975, c.30, sch.6; 1987, c.47, sch.1; repealed in pt.: 1972, c.60, schs.6,8; 1975, c.30, schs.9,29; 1987, c.47, sch.6.
s. 44, repealed: S.L.R. 1974.
sch. 1, repealed: 1987, c.47, sch.6.
sch. 2, repealed: 1975, c.30, sch.7.
sch. 4, repealed: order 78/1176.
sch. 6, repealed: 1973, c.65, sch.29.
sch. 7, repealed: S.L.R. 1974.

63. British Caribbean Federation Act 1956.
repealed: S.L.R. 1986.

66. Sanitary Inspectors (Change of Designation) Act 1956.
repealed: S.L.R. 1977.

67. Road Traffic Act 1956.
repealed (S.): 1984, c.54, sch.11.
s. 8, see *Re Gail Anne Jennings, The Times*, August 2, 1982, H.L.
s. 45, amended: 1973, c.65, sch.14.

68. Restrictive Trade Practices Act 1956.
ss. 1, 6–17, 19–22, 30, repealed: 1976, c.34, sch.6.
ss. 2–5, repealed: 1976, c.33, sch.
ss. 6, 20, see *Re National Federation of Retail Newsagents' Agreement* [1973] I.C.R. 649; [1973] 3 All E.R. 283, R.P.Ct.
ss. 7, 8, see *Re Cadbury Schweppes' Agreement* [1975] 2 All E.R. 307.
ss. 11, 19, regs. 72/196; 73/950; 76/183.
s. 20, see *Re British Concrete Pipe Association's Agreement* [1982] I.C.R. 182, R.P.Ct.
s. 22, see *Re Cement Makers' Federation's Agreement (No. 2)* [1974] 2 All E.R. 219.
s. 23, rules 73/1653, 2010.
ss. 29, 31, 33, repealed: 1973, c.41, sch.13.
Pt. II, ss. 35–38, repealed: 1976, c.53, sch.3.

69. Sexual Offences Act 1956.
s. 1, see *D.P.P.* v. *Morgan; Same* v. *McDonald* [1975] 2 W.L.R. 913; [1975] 2 All E.R. 347, H.L.; *R.* v. *Gaston* (1981) 73 Cr.App.R. 164, C.A.; *R.* v. *Olugboja* [1981] 3 W.L.R. 585, C.A.
s. 1, amended: 1976, c.82, s.1.

CAP.

4 & 5 Eliz. 2 (1955–56)—cont.

69. Sexual Offences Act 1956—cont.

s. 2, see *R.* v. *Wilson* (1973) 58 Cr.App.R. 304, C.A.

s. 6, see *R.* v. *Dodd* (1977) 66 Cr.App.R. 87, C.A.; *Gillick* v. *West Norfolk and Wisbech Area Health Authority* [1983] 3 W.L.R. 859, Woolf J.

s. 6, amended: 1977, c.45, schs.2,3.

ss. 10, 11. see *R.* v. *Whitehouse* [1977] 2 W.L.R. 925, C.A.

s. 12, see *R.* v. *Gaston* (1981) 73 Cr.App.R. 164, C.A.; *R.* v. *Courtie* [1984] 2 W.L.R. 331, H.L.

s. 12, repealed in pt.: 1984, c.60, sch.6.

s. 13, see *R.* v. *Preece*; *R.* v. *Howells* [1976] 2 W.L.R. 749, C.A.; *R.* v. *Mucklow*, January 4, 1984, H.H. Judge Galpin, Newport, Isle of Wight Crown Court; *R.* v. *Spight* [1986] Crim.L.R. 817; *Chief Constable of Hampshire* v. *Mace* (1987) 84 Cr.App.R. 40, D.C.

s. 13, amended: 1977, c.45, sch.3.

s. 14, see *R.* v. *Hodgson* [1973] 2 W.L.R. 570, C.A.; *R.* v. *Kimber* [1983] Crim.L.R. 630; [1983] 1 W.L.R. 1118, C.A.; *R.* v. *Court* [1988] 2 W.L.R. 1071, H.L.; *R.* v. *Hall* (J.H.) [1986] 86 Cr.App.R. 159, C.A.

ss. 14, 15, see *R.* v. *Thomas* (E.) (1985) 81 Cr.App.R. 331, C.A.

s. 15, see *R.* v. *Sutton* [1977] 1 W.L.R. 1086, C.A.

ss. 15, 16, repealed in pt.: 1984, c.60, sch.7.

s. 20, see *R.* v. *Jones* (*James William*) [1973] Crim.L.R. 621, Swanwick J.; *R.* v. *Tegerdine* (1982) 75 Cr.App.R. 298, C.A.

s. 22, see *R.* v. *Broadfoot* [1976] 3 All E.R. 753, C.A; *R.* v. *Brown* (*Raymond Andrew*) [1984] 1 W.L.R. 1211, C.A.; *R.* v. *Morris-Lowe* [1985] 1 W.L.R. 29, C.A.

s. 26, see *R.* v. *McPherson, Farrell and Kajal* [1980] Crim.L.R. 654, Leicester Crown Ct.

s. 26, amended: 1977, c.45, schs.2,3.

s. 28, see *R.* v. *Drury* (1975) 60 Cr.App.R. 195, C.A.; *Gillick* v. *West Norfolk and Wisbech Area Health Authority* [1983] 3 W.L.R. 859, Woolf J.

s. 28, repealed in pt.: 1975, c.72, sch.4.

s. 30, see *R.* v. *Ansell* [1974] 3 W.L.R. 430; [1974] 3 All E.R. 568, C.A.; *R.* v. *N. A. Clarke* [1976] 2 All E.R. 696, C.A.; *R.* v. *Bell* [1978] Crim.L.R. 233, C.A.; *R.* v. *Farrugia, Borg, Agius and Gauchi* (1979) 69 Cr.App.R. 108, C.A.; *R.* v. *Tan* [1983] 2 All E.R. 12, C.A.; *R.* v. *Wilson* [1984] Crim.L.R. 173; (1984) 78 Cr.App.R. 247, C.A.; *R.* v. *Grant* [1985] Crim.L.R. 387, C.A.; *R.* v. *Stewart* [1986] Crim.L.R. 805; (1986) 83 Cr.App.R. 327, C.A.

s. 31, see *R.* v. *O.* [1983] Crim.L.R. 401, Knightsbridge Crown Ct.; *R.* v. *Hanton, The Times,* February 14, 1985, C.A.

s. 32, see *R.* v. *Ford* [1977] 1 W.L.R. 1083, *The Times,* C.A.; *R.* v. *Dodd* (1977) 66 Cr.App.R. 87, C.A.; *R.* v. *Redgrave* (1982) 74 Cr.App.R. 10, C.A.; *R.* v. *Gray* (1982) 74 Cr.App.R. 324, C.A.

s. 33, see *Woodhouse* v. *Hall* (1980) 72 Cr.App.R. 39, D.C.; *Anderton* v. *Cooper* (1980)

CAP.

4 & 5 Eliz. 2 (1955–56)—cont.

69. Sexual Offences Act 1956—cont.

72 Cr.App.R. 232, D.C.; *Kelly* v. *Purvis* [1983] 2 W.L.R. 299, D.C.; *Stevens and Stevens* v. *Christy* [1987] Crim.L.R. 503; (1987) 85 Cr.App.R. 249, D.C.

s. 37, see *R.* v. *Rogina* (1975) 64 Cr.App.R. 79, C.A.

s. 37, amended: 1980, c.43, sch.7.

s. 38, substituted: 1973, c.29, sch.1; amended: 1983, c.20, sch.4.

ss. 39, 40, repealed: 1984, c.60, sch.7.

s. 41, amended: *ibid.*, sch.6.

s. 43, repealed in pt.: *ibid.*, sch.7.

s. 44, see *R.* v. *Gaston* (1981) 73 Cr.App.R. 164, C.A.

s. 45, see *R.* v. *Hall* (J. H.) (1988) 86 Cr.App.R. 159, C.A.

s. 45, amended: 1982, c.51, sch.3.

s. 46, see *R.* v. *Thomas* (E.) (1985) 81 Cr.App.R. 331, C.A.

s. 49, repealed: 1976, c.67, sch.2.

s. 50, repealed in pt.: 1973, c.36, sch.6.

s. 51, repealed: S.L.R. 1974.

s. 60, see *R.* v. *O'Grady* (1978) 66 Cr.App.R. 279, C.A.

sch. 2, see *R.* v. *Rogina* (1975) 64 Cr.App.R. 79, C.A.

sch. 2, amended: 1977, c.45, sch.12; 1980, c.43, sch.7; 1984, c.44, s.3; repealed in pt.: 1975, c.59, sch.6; 1977, c.45, sch.13.

sch. 3, repealed in pt.: *ibid.*; 1978, c.26, sch.2; 1984, c.60, sch.7.

sch. 4, repealed: S.L.R. 1974.

70. Marriage (Scotland) Act 1956.

s. 1, amended: 1977, c.15, sch.2; repealed in pt.: 1975, c.72, sch.4; 1977, c.15, sch.3.

ss. 2, 3, repealed: *ibid.*

s. 4, repealed in pt.: *ibid.*

74. Copyright Act 1956.

repealed: 1988, c.48, sch.8.

see *Lady Anne Tennant* v. *Associated Newspapers Group* [1979] F.S.R. 298, Megarry V.-C.

s. 1, see *British Northrop* v. *Texteam Blackburn* [1973] F.S.R. 241, Megarry J.; *Redwood Music* v. *Francis, Day & Hunter* [1978] R.P.C. 429, Goff J.; *Nichols Advanced Vehicle System Inc.* v. *Rees, Oliver* [1979] R.P.C. 128, Templeman J.; *Spelling Goldberg Productions Inc.* v. *B.P.C. Publishing* [1979] F.S.R. 494, Judge Mervyn Davies, Q.C.; *Performing Right Society* v. *Harlequin Record Shops* [1979] 1 W.L.R. 851, Browne-Wilkinson J.; *Ravenscroft* v. *Herbert and New English Library* [1980] R.P.C. 193, Brightman J.; *James Arnold & Co.* v. *Miafern* [1980] R.P.C. 397; Paul Baker Q.C.; *Reditune* v. *The Performing Right Society* [1981] F.S.R. 165, Whitford J.; *J. Bernstein* v. *S. Murphy* [1981] R.P.C. 303, Fox J.; *C.B.S. Inc.* v. *Ames Records and Tapes* [1981] 2 W.L.R. 973, Whitford J.; *Standen Engineering* v. *Spalding (A.) & Sons* [1984] F.S.R. 554, Falconer J.; *Jaytex* [1985] F.S.R. 75, Jeffs Q.C.; *Evans (C.) & Sons* v. *Spritebrand* [1985] 1 W.L.R. 317,

CAP.

4 & 5 Eliz. 2 (1955–56)—cont.

74. Copyright Act 1956—cont.

C.A.; *Barson Computers (N.Z.)* v. *Gilbert (John) & Co.* [1985] F.S.R. 489, New Zealand H.C.; *Amstrad Consumer Electronics* v. *British Phonographic Industry* [1986] F.S.R. 159, C.A.; *Def-Lepp Music* v. *Stuart-Brown* [1986] R.P.C. 273, Browne-Wilkinson V.-C.

s. 2, see *Performing Right Society* v. *Harlequin Record Shops* [1979] 1 W.L.R. 851, Browne-Wilkinson J.; *Ravenscroft* v. *Herbert and New English Library* [1980] R.P.C. 193, Brightman J.; *Reditune* v. *The Performing Right Society* [1981] F.S.R. 165, Whitford J.; *Exxon Corp.* v. *Exxon Insurance Consultants International* [1981] 3 All E.R. 241, C.A.; *Redwood Music* v. *Chappell & Co.* [1982] R.P.C. 109, Goff J.; *Independent Television Companies Association* v. *Performing Right Society, The Times,* November 23, 1982, Whitford J.; *Sillitoe* v. *McGraw-Hill Book Co. (U.K.)* [1983] F.S.R. 545, H.H. Judge Mervyn Davies.; *Independent Television Publications and British Broadcasting Corp.* v. *Time Out* [1984] F.S.R. 64, Whitford J.; *Express Newspapers* v. *Liverpool Daily Post and Echo* [1985] 1 W.L.R. 1089, Whitford J.; *Williamson Music* v. *Pearson Partnership* [1987] F.S.R. 97, Judge Paul Baker Q.C.

s. 2, amended: 1984, c.46, sch.5.

s. 3, see *British Northrop* v. *Texteam Blackburn* [1973] F.S.R. 241, Megarry J.; *Hensher (George)* v. *Restawile Upholstery (Lancs.)* [1974] 2 W.L.R. 700; [1974] 2 All E.R. 420, H.L.; *E. Gomme* v. *Relaxateze Upholstery* [1976] R.P.C. 377; *Solar Thompson Engineering Co.* v. *Barton* [1977] R.P.C. 537, C.A.; *L.B. (Plastics)* v. *Swish Products* [1979] F.S.R. 145, H.L.; *Nichols Advanced Vehicle System Inc.* v. *Rees, Oliver* [1979] R.P.C. 128, Templeman J.; *Oscar Trade Mark* [1979] R.P.C. 197, Trade Marks Registry; *James Arnold & Co.* v. *Miafern* [1980] R.P.C. 397, Paul Baker, Q.C.; *Reditune* v. *The Performing Right Society* [1981] F.S.R. 165, Whitford J.; *J. Bernstein* v. *S. Murphy* [1981] R.P.C. 303, Fox J.; *Infabrics* v. *Jaytex* [1981] 2 W.L.R. 646; [1981] 1 All E.R. 1057, H.L.; *Brigid Foley* v. *Ellot* [1982] R.P.C. 433, Megarry V.-C.; *The Durion Co. Inc.* v. *Hugh Jennings & Co.* [1984] F.S.R. 1, C.A.; *Merlet* v. *Mothercare* [1984] F.S.R. 358, Walton J.; *British Leyland Motor Corp.* v. *Armstrong Patents Co., The Times,* July 2, 1984, C.A.; *Smith* v. *Greenfield* [1984] 6 N.I.J.B., Murray J.; *Geographia* v. *Penguin Books* [1985] F.S.R. 208, Whitford J.; *Howard Clark* v. *David Allan & Co.* (O.H.), February 6, 1986; *Spectravest Inc.* v. *Aperknit* [1988] F.S.R. 161, Millett J.; *Interlego A.G.* v. *Tyco Industries Inc.* [1988] 3 W.L.R. 678, P.C.

s. 3, order 73/1089.

s. 3, amended: 1984, c.46, sch.5.

s. 4, see *Beloff* v. *Pressdram* [1973] 1 All E.R. 241; *Roban Jig & Tool Co. and Elkadart* v. *Taylor* [1979] F.S.R. 130, C.A.; *James Arnold*

CAP.

4 & 5 Eliz. 2 (1955–56)—cont.

74. Copyright Act 1956—cont.

& Co. v. *Miafern* [1980] R.P.C. 397, Paul Baker, Q.C.; *J. Bernstein* v. *S. Murphy* [1981] R.P.C. 303, Fox J.; *Plix Products* v. *Winstone (Frank M.) (Merchants)* [1986] F.S.R. 608, N.Z.C.A.; *Gardex* v. *Sorata* [1986] R.P.C. 623, Falconer J.

s. 5, see *Carlin Music Corp.* v. *Collins* [1979] F.S.R. 548, C.A.; *James Arnold & Co.* v. *Miafern* [1980] R.P.C. 397, Paul Baker, Q.C.; *CBS United Kingdom* v. *Charmdale Record Distributors* [1980] 2 All E.R. 807, Browne-Wilkinson J.; *Roberts* v. *Jump Knitwear* [1981] F.S.R. 527, Falconer J.; *Politechnika Ipan Szovetkezet* v. *Dallas Print Transfers* [1982] F.S.R. 529, Dillon J.; *Rexnold* v. *Ancon* [1983] F.S.R. 662, Whitford J.; *Standen Engineering* v. *Spalding (A.) & Sons* [1984] F.S.R. 554, Falconer J.; *Infabrics* v. *Jaytex* [1985] F.S.R. 75, Jeffs Q.C.; *Def-Lepp Music* v. *Stuart-Brown* [1986] R.P.C. 273, Browne-Wilkinson V.-C.

s. 6, see *Hubbard* v. *Vosper* [1972] 2 W.L.R. 389; [1972] 1 All E.R. 1023; *Beloff* v. *Pressdram* [1973] 1 All E.R. 241; *Sillitoe* v. *McGraw-Hill Book Co. (U.K.)* [1983] F.S.R. 545, H.H. Judge Mervyn Davies.; *Independent Television Publications and British Broadcasting Corp.* v. *Time Out* [1984] F.S.R. 64, Whitford J.; *Associated Newspapers Group* v. *News Group Newspapers* [1986] R.P.C. 515, Walton J.

ss. 6, 7, amended: 1984, c.46, sch.5.

s. 8, see *Carlin Music Corp.* v. *Collins* [1979] F.S.R. 548, C.A.; *Discount Inter-Shopping Co.* v. *Micrometro* [1984] 2 W.L.R. 919, Vinelott J.

s. 8, regs. 73/409; 74/2190.

s. 9, see *Antocks Lairn* v. *Bloohn* [1971] F.S.R. 490; *Temple Instruments* v. *Hollis Heels* [1971] F.S.R. 634; *British Northrop* v. *Texteam Blackburn* [1973] F.S.R. 241, Megarry J.; *E. Gomme* v. *Relaxateze Upholstery* [1976] R.P.C. 377; *L. B. (Plastics)* v. *Swish Products* [1979] F.S.R. 145, H.L.; *Solar Thompson Engineering Co.* v. *Barton* [1977] R.P.C. 537, C.A.; *Nichols Advanced Vehicle System Inc.* v. *Rees, Oliver* [1979] R.P.C. 128, Templeman J.; *J. Bernstein* v. *S. Murphy* [1981] R.P.C. 303, Fox J.; *Dymo Industries Inc.'s Application* [1982] R.P.C. 437, Stephen Gratwick Q.C.; *John Michael (Design Consultants)* v. *Morgan Grampian,* November 9, 1982, Goulding J.; *Politechnika Ipan Szovetkezet* v. *Dallas Print Transfers* [1982] F.S.R. 529, Dillon J.; *Merlet* v. *Mothercare, The Times,* November 6, 1985, C.A.; *Howard Clark* v. *David Allan & Co.* (O.H.), February 6, 1986; *Rubycliff* v. *Plastic Engineers* [1986] R.P.C. 573, Browne-Wilkinson V.-C.; *Interlego A.G.* v. *Tyco Industries Inc.* [1988] 3 W.L.R. 678, P.C.

s. 9, amended: 1984, c.46, sch.5.

s. 10, see *Bampal Materials Handling Design* [1981] R.P.C. 44, Designs Registry; *Silent Gliss International A.G.* v. *Module Four Curtain*

CAP.

4 & 5 Eliz. 2 (1955–56)—cont.

74. Copyright Act 1956—cont.

Rail Co. [1981] F.S.R. 423, Nourse J.; Weir Pumps v. C.M.L. Pumps [1984] F.S.R. 33, Whitford J.; British Leyland Motor Corp. v. Armstrong Patents Co., The Times, July 2, 1984, C.A.; Smith v. Greenfield [1984] 6 N.I.J.B., Murray J.; Interlego A.G. v. Folley (Alex) (Vic.) Pty. [1987] F.S.R. 283, Whitford J.

s. 12, see Reditune v. The Performing Right Society [1981] F.S.R. 165, Whitford J.; A.I.R.C. v. Phonographic Performance and the Musician's Union [1983] F.S.R. 637, Falconer J.; Silly Wizard v. Shaughnessy, El Fakir [1983] F.S.R. 163, Ct. of Session; Def-Lepp Music v. Stuart-Brown [1986] R.P.C. 273, Browne-Wilkinson V.-C.; CBS/Sony Hong Kong v. Television Broadcasts [1987] F.S.R. 262, Supreme Ct. Hong Kong.

s. 12, amended: 1984, c.46, sch.24

s. 13, see Spelling Goldberg Productions Inc. v. B.P.C. Publishing [1979] F.S.R. 494, Judge Mervyn Davies, Q.C.; Reditune v. The Performing Right Society [1981] F.S.R. 165, Whitford J.; Adventure Film Productions v. Tully, The Times, October 14, 1982, Whitford J.; Musa v. Le Maitre [1987] F.S.R. 212, D.C.; CBS/Sony Hong Kong v. Television Broadcasts [1987] F.S.R. 262, Supreme Ct. Hong Kong.

s. 13, amended: 1984, c.46, sch.24; 1985, c.21, s.7; repealed in pt.: ibid., s.7, sch.2.

s. 14, amended: 1984, c.46, s.23, sch.5.

ss. 14, 15, Reditune v. The Performing Right Society [1981] F.S.R. 165, Whitford J.

s. 14A, added: 1984, c.46, s.22.

s. 16, see CBS United Kingdom v. Charmdale Record Distributors [1980] 2 All E.R. 807, Browne-Wilkinson J.; The British Phonographic Industry v. Cohen [1984] F.S.R. 159, Ct. of Session (Inner House); Barson Computers (N.Z.) v. Gilbert (John) & Co. [1985] F.S.R. 489, New Zealand H.C.; Columbia Picture Industries v. Robinson [1986] F.S.R. 367, Scott J.; Def-Lepp Music v. Stuart-Brown [1986] R.P.C. 273, V.-C.

s. 16, amended: 1984, c.46, sch.5.

s. 17, see Beloff v. Pressdram [1973] 1 All E.R. 241; Hunter v. Fitzroy Robinson and Partners [1978] F.S.R. 167, Oliver J.; Rank Film Distributors v. Video Information Centre (A Firm) (1979) 124 S.J. 48, Whitford J.; Nichols Advanced Vehicle System Inc. v. Rees. Oliver [1979] R.P.C. 128, Templeman J.; Ravenscroft v. Herbert and New English Library [1980] R.P.C. 193, Brightman J.; James Arnold & Co. v. Miafern [1980] R.P.C. 397, Paul Baker, Q.C.; Monadress v. Bourne and Hollingsworth [1981] F.S.R. 118, C.A.; Richmark Camera Services Inc. v. Neilson-Hordell [1981] F.S.R. 413, Dillon J.; Sillitoe v. McGraw-Hill Book Co. (U.K.) [1983] F.S.R. 545, H.H. Judge Mervyn Davies; Overseas Programming Co. v. Cinematographische Commerz-Anstalt and Induna Film GmbH, The

CAP.

4 & 5 Eliz. 2 (1955–56)—cont.

74. Copyright Act 1956—cont.

Times, May 14, 1984, French J.; Lewis Trusts v. Bambers Stores [1984] F.S.R. 453, C.A.; Infabrics v. Jaytex [1985] F.S.R. 75, Jeffs, Q.C.; Goswami v. Hammons (1985) 129 S.J. 653, C.A.; Besson (A.P.) v. Fulleon and Amlani [1986] F.S.R. 319, Harman J.; Paterson Zochonis & Co. v. Merfarken Packaging [1986] 3 All E.R. 522, C.A.; Nichols Advanced Vehicle Systems Inc. v. Rees (No. 3) [1988] R.P.C. 71, C.A.

s. 18, see WEA Records v. Benson King (Sales) [1974] 3 All E.R. 81; Redwood Music v. Francis, Day & Hunter [1978] R.P.C. 429, Goff J.; Nichols Advanced Vehicle System Inc. v. Rees, Oliver [1979] R.P.C. 128, Templeman J.; Ravenscroft v. Herbert and New English Library [1980] R.P.C. 193, Brightman J.; James Arnold & Co. v. Miafern [1980] R.P.C. 397, Paul Baker, Q.C.; J. Bernstein v. S. Murphy [1981] R.P.C. 303, Fox J.; Infabrics v. Jaytex [1981] 2 W.L.R. 646; [1981] 1 All E.R. 1057, H.L.; Richmark Camera Services Inc. v. Neilson-Hordell [1981] F.S.R. 413, Dillon J.; Redwood Music v. Chappell & Co. [1982] R.P.C. 109, Goff J.; R. v. Storrow and Poole [1983] Crim.L.R. 332, Central Criminal Ct.; Sillitoe v. McGraw-Hill Book Co. (U.K.) [1983] F.S.R. 545, H.H. Judge Mervyn Davies; Lewis Trusts v. Bambers Stores [1983] F.S.R. 453, C.A.; Staver & Co. v. Digitext Display [1984] F.S.R. 512, Scott J.; Infabrics v. Jaytex [1985] F.S.R. 75, Jeffs Q.C.; Amstrad Consumer Electronics v. British Phonographic Industry [1986] F.S.R. 159, C.A.; Besson (A. P.) v. Fulleon and Amlani [1986] F.S.R. 319, Harman J.; Colombia Picture Industries v. Robinson [1986] F.S.R.. 367, Scott J.; Rubycliffe v. Plastic Engineers [1986] R.P.C. 573, Browne-Wilkinson V.-C.; Musa v. Le Maitre [1987] F.S.R. 212, D.C.; C.B.S. Songs v. Amstrad Consumer Electronics (No. 2), 1987 R.P.C. 429, C.A.; Nichols Advanced Vehicle Systems Inc. v. Rees (No. 3) [1988] R.P.C. 71, C.A.

s. 18, amended: 1984, c.46, sch.5.

s. 19, see Columbia Picture Industries v. Robinson [1986] F.S.R. 367, Scott J.; Western Front v. Vestron Inc. [1987] F.S.R. 66, Gibson J.

s. 20, see Roban Jig & Tool Co. and Elkadart v. Taylor [1979] F.S.R. 130, C.A.

s. 21, see Thorn EMI Video Programmes v. Kitching and Busby [1984] F.S.R. 342, New Zealand H.C.; C.B.S. Songs v. Amstrad Consumer Electronics, The Times, May 9, 1986, Whitford J.; Amstrad Consumer Electronics v. British Phonographic Industry [1986] F.S.R. 159, C.A.; Reid v. Kennet [1986] Crim.L.R. 456, D.C.; Musa v. Le Maitre [1987] F.S.R. 212, D.C.; C.B.S. Songs v. Amstrad Consumer Electronics (No. 2), 1987 R.P.C. 429, C.A.; R. v. Ward [1988] Crim.L.R. 57, Teesside Crown Ct; C.B.S. Songs v. Amstrad Consumer Electronics [1988] 2 W.L.R. 1191; [1988] 2 All E.R. 484, H.L.; Phillips v. Holmes (1988) 152 J.P.N. 738, D.C.

CAP.

4 & 5 Eliz. 2 (1955–56)—cont.

74. Copyright Act 1956—cont.

s. 21, amended: 1982, c.35, s.1; 1983, c.42, s.1.

ss. 21A, 21B, added: *ibid.*, s.2.

s. 22, regs. 82/766.

s. 22, amended: 1979, c.2, sch.4.

ss. 23–30, see *Phonographic Performance* v. *Grosvenor Leisure* [1984] F.S.R. 24, Whitford J.

s. 24, amended: 1984, c.46, sch.5.

ss. 24, 25, 27, 30, see *A.I.R.C.* v. *Phonographic Performance and the Musician's Union* [1983] F.S.R. 637, Falconer J.

ss. 24, 27, see *Reditune* v. *The Performing Right Society* [1981] F.S.R. 165, Whitford J.

s. 27B, added: 1984, c.46, s.23.

s. 28, amended: *ibid.*, sch.5.

s. 31, orders 72/673, 1729; 73/72, 772, 963, 1751; 74/1276; 75/2193; 76/227, 1784, 2153; 77/56, 830, 1256, 1632; 78/1060; 79/577, 910, 1715, 80/1723; 83/1708; 84/541, 549, 1985–1988; 86/1299, 2235; 87/940, 1030, 1826, 1833, 2060, 2200; 88/250, 1297, 1307, 1855.

ss. 31, 32, amended: 1984, c.46, sch.5.

s. 32, see *Spelling Goldberg Productions Inc.* v. *B.P.C. Publishing* [1979] F.S.R. 494, Judge Mervyn Davies, Q.C.

s. 32, orders 73/72, 772, 963, 1089, 1751; 74/1276; 75/2193; 76/227, 1784, 2153; 77/56, 830, 1256, 1632; 78/1060; 79/910, 1715; 80/1723; 83/1708; 84/549, 1987; 85/1777; 86/2235; 87/940, 1030, 2060; 88/250, 797, 1297, 1307, 1855.

s. 36, see *Karo Step Trade Mark* [1977] R.P.C. 225; *Roban Jig & Tool Co. and Elkadart* v. *Taylor* [1979] F.S.R. 130, C.A.; *Reditune* v. *The Performing Right Society* [1981] F.S.R. 165, Whitford J.; *Western Front* v. *Vestron Inc.* [1987] F.S.R. 66, Gibson J.

s. 40, amended: 1984, c.46, s.23, sch.5

s. 40A, added: *ibid.*, s.24.

s. 41, see *L.B. (Plastics)* v. *Swish Products* [1979] F.S.R. 145, H.L.; *Sillitoe* v. *McGraw-Hill Book Co. (U.K.)* [1983] F.S.R. 545, H.H. Judge Mervyn Davies.

s. 41, amended: 1984, c.46, sch.5.

s. 42, order 73/963.

s. 43, see *Moore* v. *News of the World* [1972] 2 W.L.R. 419; [1972] 1 All E.R. 915; *John Michael (Design Consultants)* v. *Morgan Grampian plc*, November 9, 1982, Goulding J.

s. 43, amended: 1984, c.46, sch.5.

s. 45, see *Apple Corps.* v. *Lingasong* [1977] F.S.R. 345, Megarry V.-C.

ss. 45, 46, see *Rickless* v. *United Artists Corp.* [1986] F.S.R. 502, Hobhouse J.

s. 47, orders 73/72, 409, 772, 1089, 1751; 74/1276; 75/2193; 76/227, 673, 1784, 2153; 77/56, 830, 1256, 1632; 78/1060; 79/910, 1715; 80/1723; 83/1708; 84/549, 1987; 85/1775, 1985–1988, 86/1299, 2235; 87/940, 1030, 1826, 2060; 88/250, 797, 1297, 1307, 1855.

CAP.

4 & 5 Eliz. 2 (1955–56)—cont.

74. Copyright Act 1956—cont.

s. 48, see *E. Gomme* v. *Relaxateze Upholstery* [1976] R.P.C. 377; *Solar Thompson Engineering Co.* v. *Barton* [1977] R.P.C. 537, C.A.; *L.B. (Plastics)* v. *Swish Products* [1979] F.S.R. 145, H.L.; *Nichols Advanced Vehicle System Inc.* v. *Rees, Oliver* [1979] R.P.C. 128, Templeman J.; *Spelling Goldberg Productions Inc.* v. *B.P.C. Publishing* [1979] F.S.R. 494, Judge Mervyn Davies, Q.C.; *James Arnold & Co.* v. *Miafern* [1980] R.P.C. 397, Paul Baker, Q.C.; *Independent Television Publications and British Broadcasting Corp.* v. *Time Out* [1984] F.S.R. 64, Whitford J.; *British Leyland Motor Corp.* v. *Armstrong Patents Co.*, *The Times*, July 2, 1984, C.A.; *Express Newspapers* v. *Liverpool Daily Post and Echo* [1985] 1 W.L.R. 1089, Whitford J.

s. 48, amended: 1984, c.46, sch.5.

s. 49, see *Temple Instruments* v. *Hollis Heels* [1971] F.S.R. 634; *Bodley Head* v. *Flegon* [1972] 1 W.L.R. 680; *L.B. (Plastics)* v. *Swish Products* [1979] F.S.R. 145, H.L.; *Spelling Goldberg Productions Inc.* v. *B.P.C. Publishing* [1979] F.S.R. 494, Judge Mervyn Davies, Q.C.; *Ravenscroft* v. *Herbert and New English Library* [1980] R.P.C. 193, Brightman J.; *CBS United Kingdom* v. *Charmdale Record Distributors* [1980] 1 All E.R. 807, Browne-Wilkinson J.; *Infabrics* v. *Jaytex* [1981] 2 W.L.R. 646; [1981] 1 All E.R. 1057, H.L.; *Sillitoe* v. *McGraw-Hill Book Co. (U.K.)* [1983] F.S.R. 545, H.H. Judge Mervyn Davies; *Smith* v. *Greenfield* [1984] 6 N.I.J.B., Murray J.; *Barson Computers (N.Z.)* v. *Gilbert (John) & Co.* [1985] F.S.R. 489, New Zealand H.C.; *Williamson Music* v. *Pearson Partnership* [1987] F.S.R. 97, Judge Paul Baker Q.C.

s. 50, see *Redwood Music* v. *Francis, Day & Hunter* [1978] R.P.C. 429, Goff J.

s. 50, repealed in pt.: 1974, c.22, sch.

sch. 6, see *Apple Corps.* v. *Lingasong* [1977] F.S.R. 345, Megarry V.-C.

sch. 7, see *Redwood Music* v. *B. Feldman & Co.* [1979] R.P.C. 1, Goff J.; *Weir Pumps* v. *C.M.L. Pumps* [1984] F.S.R. 33, Whitford J.; *Interlego A.G.* v. *Tyco Industries Inc.* [1988] 3 W.L.R. 678, P.C.

sch. 7, amended: 1984, c.46, sch.5; repealed in pt.: S.L.R. 1986.

sch. 9, repealed: S.L.R. 1974.

76. Medical Act 1956.

repealed: 1983, c.54, sch.7.

s. 7, order 73/68.

s. 7B, order 81/432.

s. 10, orders 75/809; 76/898.

s. 19, orders 77/1720; 78/283.

ss. 28, 33, see *Tarnesby* v. *Kensington, Chelsea and Westminster Area Health Authority (Teaching)* [1981] I.C.R. 615, H.L.

s. 36, see *Libman* v. *General Medical Council* [1972] 2 W.L.R. 272; [1972] 1 All E.R. 798.

s. 37, order 78/1796.

5 Eliz. 2 (1956)

1. Police, Fire and Probation Officers' Remuneration Act 1956.
repealed: 1977, c.45, sch.13.
rules 74/1352, 1955.
s. 1, rules 72/803,1657; 75/910; 76/1314.

5 & 6 Eliz. 2 (1957)

6. Ghana Independence Act 1957.
s. 2, repealed: 1981, c.61, sch.9.
s. 3, repealed: S.L.R. 1976.
s. 4, repealed in pt.: 1978, c.30, sch.3.
sch. 2, repealed in pt.: S.L.R. 1977; 1988, c.48, sch.8.

11. Homicide Act 1957.
s. 1, see *R.* v. *Williamson and Ellerton* (1978) 67 Cr.App.R. 63, C.A.
s. 2, see *R.* v. *Fenton* (1975) 61 Cr.App.R. 261, C.A.; *R.* v. *Turnbull* (1977) 65 Cr.App.R. 242, C.A.; *R.* v. *Kiszko* (1978) 68 Cr.App.R. 62, C.A.; *R.* v. *Vinagre* (1979) 69 Cr.App.R. 104, C.A.; *R.* v. *Kooken* (1982) 74 Cr.App.R. 30, C.A.; *R.* v. *Dix* (1982) 74 Cr.App.R. 306, C.A.; *R.* v. *Gittens* [1984] 3 W.L.R. 327, C.A.; *R.* v. *Seers* (1984) 79 Cr.App.R. 261, C.A.; *R.* v. *Campbell, The Times,* November 4, 1986, C.A.; *R.* v. *Tandy, The Times,* December 23, 1987, C.A.
s. 3, see *R.* v. *Brown* [1972] 2 Q.B. 229; [1972] 3 W.L.R. 11; [1972] 2 All E.R. 1328; (1972) 56 Cr.App.R. 564; *R.* v. *Davies (Peter)* [1975] 2 W.L.R. 586; [1975] 1 All E.R. 890, C.A.; *D.P.P.* v. *Camplin* [1978] 2 W.L.R. 679, H.L.; *R.* v. *Gilbert* (1977) 66 Cr.App.R. 237, C.A.; *R.* v. *Newell* (1980) 71 Cr.App.R. 331, C.A.; *R.* v. *Ibrams; R.* v. *Gregory* (1982) 74 Cr.App.R. 154, C.A.; *R.* v. *Doughty* [1986] Crim.L.R. 625; (1986) 83 Cr.App.R. 319, C.A.
s. 14, repealed: S.L.R. 1973.
s. 16, repealed: S.L.R. 1977.
s. 17, repealed in pt.: S.L.R. 1974.
sch. 2, repealed: *ibid.*

15. Nurses Act 1957.
repealed: 1979, c.36, sch.8.
see *Kingston and Richmond Area Health Authority* v. *Kaur, The Times,* June 4, 1981, E.A.T.
s. 2, regs. 84/1400.
s. 3A, amended: order 82/1076.
ss. 3A, 3B, added: order 79/1604; amended: order 81/432.
s. 4, amended: *ibid.*
s. 7, regs. 84/1400.
ss. 11, 13, 14, 16, amended: 1980, c.53, sch.1.
ss. 11, 32, sch. 2, orders 74/235, 320.
s. 32, rules 73/1077; instruments, 75/167; 76/1188; 79/49; 80/1837, 1974.
s. 42, instrument 81/1432.
sch. 1A, added: order 79/1604; amended: order 80/1721.
sch. 2, amended: 1980, c.53, sch.1.

16. Nurses Agencies Act 1957.
ss. 1, 2, 7, regs. 78/1443; 81/1574.
ss. 1, 3, amended: 1979, c.36, sch.7.
s. 2, amended: 1972, c.70, sch.29.
ss. 2, 7, regs. 86/1414.

5 & 6 Eliz. 2 (1957)—cont.

16. Nurses Agencies Act 1957—*cont.*
s. 5, repealed: 1972, c.70, sch.29.
s. 6, repealed in pt.: S.L.R. 1981.
s. 8, repealed in pt.: 1979, c.36, schs.7,8.
s. 9, repealed in pt.: S.L.R. 1974.
sch., repealed: *ibid.*

19. Public Health Officers (Deputies) Act 1957.
repealed: 1972, c.70, sch.30.

20. House of Commons Disqualification Act 1957.
repealed: 1975, c.24, sch.3; c.25, sch.3; c.26, sch.3.

21. Cinematograph Films Act 1957.
repealed: 1981, c.16, sch.2.
s. 2, regs. 73/728; 75/1885; 77/1330; 78/1092; 79/1751; 80/1178.
s. 3, regs. 79/1750; 80/1179.

24. House of Commons Members' Fund Act 1957.
s. 1, order 81/748.

25. Rent Act 1957.
s. 16, regs. 75/2196.
s. 16, repealed: 1977, c.43, sch.3.

26. National Insurance Act 1957.
repealed: 1973, c.38, sch.28.

27. Solicitors Act 1957.
repealed: 1974, c.47, sch.4.
s. 18, see *Hudgell, Yeates & Co.* v. *Watson* [1978] 2 W.L.R. 661, C.A.
ss. 18, 20, 22, see (*Homes*) *Parkling Court* v. *London Borough of Lewisham,* Feb. 6, 1974.
s. 20, see *Reynolds* v. *Hoyle* [1975] 3 All E.R. 934, D.C.; *Green* v. *Hoyle* [1976] 1 W.L.R. 575; [1976] 2 All E.R. 633, D.C.; *R.* v. *Wells Street Stipendiary Magistrate, ex p. Watson* (1977) 243 E.G. 50, D.C.
s. 23, see *Hudgell, Yeates & Co.* v. *Watson* [1978] 2 W.L.R. 661, C.A.
s. 56, see *Bates* v. *Hailsham* [1972] 1 W.L.R. 1373; [1972] 3 All E.R. 1019.
s. 56, rules 72/1096, 1139.
s. 60, see *Re Eastwood; Lloyds Bank* v. *Eastwood* [1973] 3 W.L.R. 795; [1973] 3 All E.R. 1079, Brightman J.
s. 64, see *Carlton* v. *Theodore Goddard & Co.* [1973] 1 W.L.R. 623.

28. Dentists Act 1957.
repealed: 1984, c.24, sch.6.
s. 2B, order 81/432.
s. 25, see *Peter Ziderman* v. *General Dental Council* [1976] 1 W.L.R. 330, P.C.; *McEniff* v. *General Dental Council* [1980] 1 All E.R. 461, P.C.
s. 41, regs. 74/544; 78/1128.

29. Magistrates' Courts Act 1957.
repealed: 1980, c.43, sch.9.
s. 1, see *R.* v. *Liskerrett JJ., ex p. Child* [1972] R.T.R. 141.

31. Occupiers' Liability Act 1957.
see *Vollans* v. *Simco Supermarkets,* January 13, 1982, H.H. Judge Pickles; *Holden* v. *White, The Times,* March 23, 1982, C.A.; *Collier* v. *Anglian Water Authority, The Times,* March 26, 1983, C.A.; *Page* v. *Read* (1984) 134 New L.J. 723, Stocker J.

CAP.

5 & 6 Eliz. 2 (1957)—cont.

31. Occupiers' Liability Act 1957—*cont.*
s. 1, see *Wheeler* v. *Copas* [1981] 3 All E.R. 405, Chapman J.; *Holden* v. *White* [1982] 2 All E.R. 328, C.A.

s. 2, see *Clare* v. *L. Whittaker & Son (London)* [1976] I.C.R. 1; *Simkiss* v. *Rhondda Borough Council* (1983) 81 L.G.R. 460, C.A.; *McDonagh* v. *Kent Area Health Authority* (1984) New L.J. 567, Beldam J.; *Ferguson* v. *Welsh* [1987] 3 All E.R. 777, H.L.

ss. 2, 5, see *Sole* v. *Hallt* [1973] 2 W.L.R. 171; [1974] 1 W.L.R. 1575, C.A.

s. 4, repealed: 1972, c.35, s.6.

32. Naval and Marine Reserves Pay Act 1957.
repealed: 1980, c.9, sch.10.

36. Cheques Act 1957.
s. 4, see *Prescott Meat Co.* v. *Northern Bank* [1981] 4 N.I.J.B., Hutton J.; *Thackwell* v. *Barclays Bank* [1986] 1 All E.R. 676, Hutchison J.

s. 6, repealed in pt.: S.L.R. 1974.

s. 7, repealed in pt.: 1973, c.36, sch.6.

sch., repealed: S.L.R. 1974.

38. Housing and Town Development (Scotland) Act 1957.
ss. 1–7, repealed: 1972, c.46, sch.11.

s. 9, amended: 1972, c.46, s.69, repealed in pt.: *ibid*, s.69, sch.11; S.L.R. 1974.

s. 13, repealed in pt.: *ibid.*

s. 14, regs. 77/273.

s. 16, amended: 1973, c.65, sch.12.

s. 23, repealed: 1972, c.46, sch.11.

s. 28, repealed in pt.: S.L.R. 1974.

sch. 1, repealed in pt.: 1972, c.46, sch.11; S.L.R. 1981.

sch. 3, repealed: S.L.R. 1974.

39. Legitimation (Registration of Births) Act 1957.
repealed: S.L.R. 1974; 1976, c.31, sch.2.

40. Thermal Insulation (Industrial Buildings) Act 1957.
repealed (S.): order 79/594.

ss. 1, 3, 7, regs. 72/87.

s. 2, repealed: regs. 79/601.

s. 3, amended: 1973, c.66, sch.15.

s. 10, amended: regs. 79/601.

s. 12, amended: 1973, c.65, sch.15; repealed in pt.: *ibid.*, schs.15,29.

42. Parish Councils Act 1957.
s. 3, amended: 1972, c.70, schs.13,14; 1980, c.66, sch.24; repealed in pt.: 1972, c.70, sch.30.

s. 5, amended: 1985, c.51, sch.4.

ss. 6, 8, repealed in pt.: 1972, c.70, sch.30.

ss. 9, 10, 12, 15, sch. 1, repealed: 1972, c.70, sch.30.

sch. 2, repealed: S.L.R. 1974.

44. National Health Service (Amendment) Act 1957.
repealed: 1973, c.32, sch.5.

45. Exchequer and Audit Departments Act 1957.
s. 1, amended: 1976, c.48, s.6.

s. 3, repealed in pt.: S.L.R. 1974.

CAP.

5 & 6 Eliz. 2 (1957)—cont.

46. Judicial Offices (Salaries and Pensions) Act 1957.
repealed: 1973, c.15, sch.5.

s. 1, order 72/1078.

48. Electricity Act 1957.
see *R.* v. *Midlands Electricity Board, ex p. Busby; Same* v. *Same, ex p. Williamson, The Times,* October 28, 1987, Schiemann J.

s. 1, repealed: S.L.R. 1977.

s. 2, repealed in pt.: 1983, c.25, schs.3,4.

s. 5, regs. 78/963.

s. 15, order 74/1295.

s. 15, amended: 1972, c.17, s.1; 1974, c.8, sch.2.

s. 16, regs. 81/1763.

ss. 16, 20, repealed in pt.: S.L.R. 1977.

s. 17, amended: 1974, c.8, sch.2; 1983, c.29, sch.2.

s. 19, amended: 1975, c.55, s.5.

s. 25, repealed in pt.: S.L.R. 1977.

s. 26, repealed: *ibid.*

s. 28, repealed: 1979, c.11, sch.12; amended: 1981, c.38, sch.3; 1984, c.12, sch.4; repealed in pt.: *ibid.*, sch.17.

s. 29, repealed in pt.: *ibid.*

s. 30, orders 75/56; 77/1970; 82/1442; 87/730

s. 30, amended: 1983, c.25, sch.1; repealed in pt.: *ibid.*, schs.1,4.

ss. 33, repealed in pt.: 1973, c.65, sch.29 (S.); 1986, c.63, sch.12.

s. 34, amended: 1973, c.65, sch.27 (S); 1986, c.63, s.44.

s. 35, see *R.* v. *Chief Constable of Devon and Cornwall, ex p. Central Electricity Generating Board* [1982] 3 W.L.R. 967, C.A.

s. 35, repealed: 1979, c.11, sch.12.

s. 39, repealed: S.L.R. 1978.

ss. 42, 43, repealed in pt.: S.L.R. 1974.

sch. 2, amended(S): 1973, c.65, sch.27.

sch. 3, repealed in pt.: S.L.R. 1977.

sch. 4, repealed: 1979, c.11, sch.12 (S.); 1983, c.25, sch.4.

sch. 5, repealed: S.L.R. 1974.

49. Finance Act 1957.
s. 5, repealed: 1979, c.2, sch.6.

s. 38, see *Battle* v. *I.R.C.* [1980] S.T.C. 86.

Pt. V (ss. 38, 39), repealed: 1975, c.7, sch.13.

s. 42, repealed in pt.: S.L.R. 1974; 1975, c.7, sch.13; 1979, c.2, sch.6.

sch. 2, order 73/2038; repealed: 1979, c.2, sch.6.

sch. 9, repealed: S.L.R. 1974.

51. Road Transport Lighting Act 1957.
repealed: 1972, c.20, sch.9.

s. 10, regs. 72/176, 557.

52. Geneva Conventions Act 1957.
s. 4, amended: 1978, c.32, sch.5; 1980, c.47, sch.4.

s. 8, order 74/1262.

53. Naval Discipline Act 1957.
continued in force: orders 74/2147; 77/1231; 1981, c.55, s.1; orders 82/1069; 83/1104; 84/1147; 85/1196; 1986, c.21, s.1, orders 87/1262; 88/1293.

5 & 6 Eliz. 2 (1957)—cont.

53. Naval Discipline Act 1957—cont.

ss. 6, 11, repealed in pt.: 1986, c.21, s.4, sch.2.

s. 24, amended: 1981, c.55, s.1; repealed in pt.: 1986, c.21, s.4, sch.2.

s. 29B, added: ibid., s.2.

s. 33B, repealed in pt.: ibid., s.4, sch.2.

s. 35, amended: ibid., s.3.

s. 36A, repealed in pt.: ibid., s.4, sch.2.

s. 38, amended: 1982, c.48, sch.8; 1986, c.21, sch.1.

s. 39, amended: ibid., s.4.

s. 42, amended: 1976, c.52, s.10; repealed in pt.: 1981, c.47, s.7; 1986, c.21, schs.1,2.

s. 43, amended: 1976, c.52, s.10; 1981, c.55, s.2; 1982, c.48, sch.6; 1986, c.12, sch.1.

s. 43A, added: 1976, c.52, s.10; amended: 1982, c.48, sch.8; repealed in pt.: ibid., schs.8,16.

s. 43AA, added: 1981, c.55, s.2; amended: 1982, c.48, sch.8; 1985, c.73, s.46 (S.); 1986, c.21, sch.1; 1988, c.33, schs.8,9(S.).

s. 43B, added: 1976, c.52, sch.6; amended: 1986, c.21, s.5; repealed in pt.: ibid., sch.2.

s. 48, amended: 1974, c.6, s.5.

s. 49, amended: 1981, c.55, s.15.

s. 51, repealed in pt.: ibid., s.6, sch.5.

s. 52, amended: ibid., s.6; 1986, c.21, s.7.

s. 52A, added: 1981, c.55, s.3.

s. 54, amended: 1976, c.52, sch.2.

s. 58, order 72/966; amended: 1976, c.52, sch.7.

s. 60, amended: 1978, c.19, s.7; repealed in pt.: 1976, c.52, s.12; 1977, c.38, sch.5.

s. 66, amended: 1981, c.55.s.7.

s. 66A, added: ibid., s.8.

s. 70, amended: 1986, c.21, sch.1.

s. 71, amended: 1982, c.51, sch.3; 1983, c.20, sch.4; 1984, c.36, sch.3.

s. 72, amended: ibid., s.5.

s. 76, amended: 1976, c.52, sch.7; 1983, c.20, sch.7; repealed in pt.: 1976, c.52, schs.7, 10.

s. 77, amended: ibid., sch.7; 1983, c.20, sch.7.

s. 82, rules 73/270; 75/227; 76/892; 80/724.

s. 82, amended: 1988, c.13, sch.3.

s. 93, repealed in pt.: 1981, c.55, sch.5.

ss. 93, 94, 96–98, amended: 1976, c.52, s.15.

s. 100, repealed in pt.: 1972, c.71, sch.6.

s. 101, amended: 1972, c.18, sch.; 1981, c.55, s.18; 1982, c.27, sch.12; repealed in pt.: 1981, c.55, s.18, sch.5; 1987, c.42, sch.4.

ss. 103, 110, regs. 72/430.

s. 106, repealed in pt.: 1984, c.60, sch.7.

s. 111, amended: 1976, c.52, sch.2; 1980, c.9, sch.9, repealed in pt.: ibid., sch.10.

s. 113, repealed in pt.: 1976, c.52, sch.2.

s. 117, amended: 1986, c.21, sch.1

s. 118, amended: 1976, c.52, sch.9.

s. 123, amended: 1988, c.13, sch.3.

s. 124, amended: 1976, c.52, sch.8, repealed in pt.: 1973, c.53, sch.5.

ss. 128A, 128D, amended: 1986, c.21, sch.1.

s. 128F, added: 1976, c.52, sch.8; repealed in pt.: 1986, c.21, sch.2.

s. 129E, added: 1976, c.52, sch.9.

s. 132, amended: 1976, c.52, schs.2,9; 1981, c.55, s.21.

5 & 6 Eliz. 2 (1957)—cont.

53. Naval Discipline Act 1957—cont.

s. 135, amended: 1973, c.27, s.4; c.49, sch.; 1976, c.19, sch.; 1978, c.15, s.7; c.20, s.4; 1981, c.52, sch.2; orders 78/1030, 1899; 1979, c.27, sch.; 1980, c.2, sch.; c.16, sch.1; orders 80/701; 81/1105; 83/882; 1985, c.3, sch.

s. 137, repealed in pt.: S.L.R. 1974; S.L.R. 1977.

sch. 4, amended: 1981, c.55, sch.1; 1986, c.21, s.8.

sch. 4A, added: 1976, c.52, sch.4; 1985, c.73, s.46 (S.); amended: 1986, c.21, ss.10, 11, sch.1; repealed in pt.: ibid., s.10, sch.2.

sch. 4A, regs. 77/87; 82/365; 83/717; 86/1241; 87/1999; amended: order 80/1088; 1981, c.55, .sch.1; 1982, c.48, sch.8; 1988, c.33, schs. 8, 9(S.).

sch. 6, repealed: 1981, c.55, sch.1.

sch. 7, repealed: S.L.R. 1977.

54. Tanganyika Agricultural Corporation Act 1957.

repealed: S.L.R. 1976.

55. Affiliation Proceedings Act 1957.

repealed: 1987, c.42, s.17, sch.4.

see Haroutunian v. Jennings [1977] Fam. Law 210, Sir George Baker P.; Haldane v. Bourne, July 30, 1982, Assistant Recorder Scott, Birmingham Crown Court.

s. 2, see Willett v. Wells [1985] 1 W.L.R. 237, Hollings J.; T. v. B., The Times, November 30, 1985, D.C.

s. 4, see Foy v. Brooks [1977] 1 W.L.R. 160, D.C.; Osborn v. Sparks (1982) 12 Fam.Law 146, Waterhouse J.; Turner v. Blunden [1986] 2 W.L.R. 491, D.C.; McVeigh v. Beattie [1988] 2 W.L.R. 992, Wood J.

s. 4, order 88/1069.

ss. 4, 5, see R. v. Harrow Magistrates Court, ex p. Weiser (1985) 15 Fam.Law 153, Webster J.

s. 5, see Boniface v. Harris (1983) 13 Fam.Law 117, D.C.

s. 8, see R. v. Hereford City JJ., ex p. [1982] 1 W.L.R. 1252, Reeve J.

56. Housing Act 1957.

repealed: 1985, c.71, sch.1.

see R. S. Wahiwala v. Secretary of State for the Environment [1977] J.P.L. 511, C.A.; R. v. Cardiff County Council, ex p. Cross, The Times, April 11, 1981, Woolf J.; R. v. Hillingdon London Borough Council, ex p. Pulhofer, The Times, February 7, 1986, H.L.

s. 4, see Victoria Square Property Co. v. London Borough of Southwark [1978] 1 W.L.R. 463, C.A.

Pt. II (ss. 4–41), see R. v. Cardiff City Council, ex p. Cross, The Times, October 6, 1982, C.A.

s. 5, see Chorley Borough Council v. Barratt Developments (North West) [1979] 3 All E.R. 634, Blackett-Ord V.-C.

s. 5, repealed: 1980, c.51, schs.25,26.

s. 9, see R. v. Kerrier D. C., ex p. Guppys (Bridport) (1976) 32 P. & C.R. 411, C.A.; Inworth Property Co. v. Southwark London

5 & 6 Eliz. 2 (1957)—cont.

56. Housing Act 1957—cont.

Borough Council (1977) 34 P. & C.R. 186, C.A.; *Ellis Copp & Co.* v. *Richmond-upon-Thames London Borough Council* (1976) 245 E.G. 931, C.A.; *Hillbank Properties* v. *Hackney London Borough Council; Talisman Properties* v. *Same* [1978] 3 W.L.R. 260, C.A.; *Elliott* v. *Brighton Borough Council* (1980) 258 E.G. 441; (1981) 79 L.G.R. 506, C.A.; *Church of Our Lady of Hal* v. *Camden London Borough Council* (1980) 3 P. & C.R. 472, C.A.; *McGreal* v. *Wake* (1984) 269 E.G. 1254, C.A.; *Kenny* v. *Kingston-upon-Thames Royal London Borough Council* (1985) 274 E.G. 395, C.A.; *Pollway Nominees* v. *Croydon London Borough Council* [1986] 2 All E.R. 849, H.L.; *R.* v. *Lambeth London Borough, ex p. Clayhope Properties* (1987) 19 H.L.R. 426, C.A.

s. 9, amended: 1980, c.51, s.149.

s. 10, see *Elliott* v. *Brighton Borough Council* (1980) 258 E.G. 441; (1981) 79 L.G.R. 506, C.A.

s. 10, amended: 1980, c.65, sch.6; repealed in pt.: *ibid.*, schs.6,34.

s. 11, see *Inworth Property Co.* v. *Southwark London Borough Council* (1977) 34 P. & C.R. 186, C.A.; *Ellis Copp & Co.* v. *Richmond-upon-Thames London Borough Council* (1976) 245 E.G. 931, C.A.; *Hillbank Properties* v. *Hackney London Borough Council* [1978] 3 W.L.R. 260, C.A.; *Church of Our Lady of Hal* v. *Carnden London Borough Council* (1980) 3 P. & C.R. 472, C.A.; *Elliott* v. *Brighton Borough Council* (1980) 258 E.G. 441; (1981) 79 L.G.R. 506, C.A.; *Phillips* v. *Newham London Borough Council* (1982) 43 P. & C.R. 54, C.A.; *Pollway Nominees* v. *Croydon London Borough Council* [1986] 2 All E.R. 849, H.L.

s. 15, amended: 1984, c.55, sch.6.

s. 16, see *R.* v. *Kerrier D.C., ex p. Guppys (Bridport)* (1976) 32 P. & C.R. 411, C.A.; *Victoria Square Property Co.* v. *London Borough of Southwark* [1978] 1 W.L.R. 436, C.A.; *Dudlow Estates* v. *Sefton Metropolitan Borough Council* (1979) 249 E.G. 1271, C.A.; *R.* v. *Ealing London Borough, ex p. Richardson* (1983) 265 E.G. 691, C.A.

s. 16, amended: 1976, c.80, sch.8; 1977, c.42, sch.23.

s. 17, see *Victoria Square Property Co.* v. *London Borough of Southwark* [1978] 1 W.L.R. 463, C.A.; *R.* v. *Ealing London Borough, ex p. Richardson* (1983) 265 E.G. 691, C.A.

s. 20, see *Victoria Square Property Co.* v. *London Borough of Southwark* [1978] 1 W.L.R. 463, C.A.; *Dudlow Estates* v. *Sefton Metropolitan Borough Council* (1979) 249 E.G. 1271, C.A.

s. 22, amended: 1976, c.80, sch.8; 1977, c.42, sch.23; c.43, sch.2.

s. 27, see *Wrekin District Council* v. *Shah* (1985) 149 J.P. 703, D.C.; *Barber* v. *Shah* (1985) 17 H.L.R. 584, D.C.

5 & 6 Eliz. 2 (1957)—cont.

56. Housing Act 1957—cont.

s. 27, amended: 1972, c.71, s.32; 1976, c.57, c.10; c.80, sch. 8; 1977, c.42, sch. 23.

s. 32, repealed: 1973, c.26, sch.3.

ss. 37, 39, see *Pollway Nominees* v. *Croydon Borough Council* [1985] 2 All E.R. 849, H.L.

s. 39, see *Inworth Property Co.* v. *Southwark London Borough Council* (1977) 34 P. & C.R. 186, C.A.; *Ellis Copp & Co.* v. *Richmond-upon-Thames London Borough Council* (1976) 245 E.G. 931, C.A.; *Hillbank Properties* v. *Hackney London Borough Council; Talisman Properties* v. *Same* [1978] 3 W.L.R. 260, C.A.; *Dudlow Estates* v. *Sefton Metropolitan Borough Council* (1979) 249 E.G. 1271, C.A.; *Phillips* v. *Newham London Borough Council* (1982) P. & C.R. 54, C.A.; *R.* v. *Ealing London Borough, ex p. Richardson* (1983) 265 E.G. 691, C.A.

s. 42, see *Williams* v. *Secretary of State* (1971) 23 P. & C.R. 135; *Gordondale Investments* v. *Secretary of State* (1971) 70 L.G.R. 158; (1971) 23 P. & C.R. 334; *Savoury* v. *Secretary of State for Wales* (1974) 31 P. & C.R. 344; *Wahiwala* v. *Secretary of State for the Environment* (1977) 75 L.G.R. 651, C.A.; *Att.-Gen., ex rel. Rivers-Moore* v. *Portsmouth City Council* (1978) 76 L.G.R. 643, Walton J.; *R.* v. *Secretary of State for the Environment, ex p. Wellingborough Borough Council and Runnymede Borough Council* (1982) 80 L.G.R. 603, Skinner J.; *R.* v. *Birmingham City Council, ex p. Sale* (1984) 82 L.Q.R. 69, D.C.

s. 42, repealed in pt.: 1973, c.26, sch.3.

Pt. III (ss. 42–75), see *Eckersley* v. *Secretary of State for the Environment* (1977) 34 P. & C.R. 124, C.A.; *Islington London Borough Council* v. *Secretary of State for the Environment; Stockport Metropolitan Borough Council* v. *Secretary of State for the Environment* (1982) 43 P. & C.R. 300, C.A.

s. 43, see *Williams* v. *Secretary of State* (1971) 23 P. & C.R. 135; *Gosling* v. *Secretary of State for the Environment* [1975] J.P.L. 406; *R.* v *Secretary of State for the Environment, ex p. Wellingborough Borough Council and Runnymede Borough Council* (1982) 80 L.G.R. 603, Skinner J.

s. 43, repealed in pt.: 1974, c.44, sch.15; 1980, c.51, sch.26.

ss. 44–46, repealed: 1974, c.44, sch.15.

s. 48, see *Salford City Council* v. *McNally* [1975] 1 W.L.R. 365; [1975] 1 All E.R. 597, D.C.; *R.* v. *Birmingham City Council, ex p. Sale* (1984) 82 L.Q.R. 69, D.C.

s. 50, repealed in pt.: 1974, c.44, sch.15.

ss. 51, 53, 54, repealed: *ibid.*

s. 59, see *Barnett* v. *Wirral Borough Council* (1976) 239 E.G. 662.

s. 60, regs. 74/1511.

s. 60, amended: 1974, c.44, sch.9.

s. 63, repealed in pt.: 1973, c.26, sch.3.

s. 64, see *E. A. Wyse* v. *Secretary of State for the Environment* [1984] J.P.L. 256, Forbes J.

s. 64, amended: 1981, c.38, sch.3.

CAP.

5 & 6 Eliz. 2 (1957)—cont.

56. Housing Act 1957—cont.

s. 67, repealed in pt.: 1974, c.44, sch.15.

s. 68, amended: 1977, c 42, schs.23, 24.

s. 70, amended: 1974, c.44, sch.13.

s. 71, see Williams v. Khan (1982) 43 P. & C.R. 1, C.A.

s. 73, amended: 1976, c.80, sch.8; 1977, c.42, sch.23; c.43, sch.2.

s. 74A, added: 1984, c.12, sch.4.

s. 79, repealed: 1975, c.6, sch.6.

s. 85, amended: 1977, c.43, sch.2.

s. 86, repealed: 1972, c.70, schs.22, 30.

s. 89, see Williams v. Khan (1982) 43 P. & C.R. 1, C.A.

s. 90, see Ali v. Wolkind [1975] 1 W.L.R. 170; [1975] 1 All E.R. 193, D.C.

s. 90, substituted: 1980, c.51, s.146.

s. 91, repealed in pt.: ibid., s.90, sch.26.

Pt. V (ss. 91–134), see C. D. Brinklow and Croft Bros. (London) v. Secretary of State for the Environment [1976] J.P.L. 299; Vassily v. Secretary of State for the Environment [1976] J.P.L. 364; Lester and Butler v. Secretary of State for the Environment and Hillingdon London Borough [1978] J.P.L. 308, Sir Douglas Frank, Q.C.; Islington London Borough Council v. Secretary of State for the Environment; Stockport Metropolitan Borough Council v. Secretary of State for the Environment (1982) 43 P. & C.R. 300, C.A.; Hemsted v. Lees and Norwich City Council (1986) 18 H.L.R. 424, McCowan J.

s. 92, see Vassily v. Secretary of State for the Environment [1976] J.P.L. 364.

s. 93, repealed in pt.: 1985, c.51, sch.17.

s. 94, substituted: 1974, c.39, sch.4.

s. 96, see Meravale Builders v. Secretary of State for the Environment (1978) 36 P. & C.R. 87, Willis J.; Att.-Gen., ex rel. Rivers-Moore v. Portsmouth City Council (1978) 76 L.G.R. 643, Walton J.

s. 96, repealed in pt.: 1980, c.51, schs.25,26.

s. 100, repealed: 1973, c.26, sch.3.

s. 104, see Williams v. Willingborough Borough Council (1974) 73 L.G.R. 33; First National Securities v. Chiltern District Council [1975] 2 All E.R. 766.

s. 104, substituted: 1980, c.51, s.91.

ss. 104A, 104B, 104C, added: ibid., s.92.

s. 104B, amended: 1984, c.29, s.23, sch.6.

s. 104C, amended: ibid.; repealed in pt.: ibid., s.23, schs.6,12.

s. 105, see Att.-Gen., ex rel. Rivers-Moore v. Portsmouth City Council (1978) 76 L.G.R. 643, Walton J.

s. 105, repealed in pt.: 1977, c.30, sch.2; 1980, c.51, s.91, sch.26.

s 106, repealed: ibid., sch.26.

ss. 108, 109, amended: 1972, c.70, sch.22; repealed in pt.: ibid., schs.22, 30.

s. 110A, added: 1980, c.51, s.95.

s. 111, see Bristol District Council v. Clark [1975] 1 W.L.R. 1443, C.A.; Sevenoaks District Council v. Emmott (1979) 39 P. & C.R. 404, C.A.; Parker v. Camden London Borough

CAP.

5 & 6 Eliz. 2 (1957)—cont.

56. Housing Act 1957—cont.

Council [1985] 2 All E.R. 141, C.A.; R. v. Secretary of State for Health and Social Security, ex p. Sheffield (1985) 18 H.L.R. 6, Forbes J.; Wandsworth London Borough Council v. Winder (No. 2) (1987) 137 New L.J. 124, Mervyn Davies J.

s. 111, repealed in pt.: 1975, c.6, s.1, sch.6.

s. 113, amended: ibid, s.1; 1977, c.48, s.6; repealed in pt.: 1972, c.47, sch.11; 1980, c.51, s.35, sch.26.

s. 114, repealed: 1972, c.47, sch.11.

ss. 115–118, repealed: 1972, c.70, schs.22, 30.

s. 119, amended: 1972, c.47, s.78, repealed in pt.: 1980, c.51, schs.25,26.

s. 120, repealed: 1972, c.47, s.78, sch.11.

s. 121, repealed: 1974, c.44, schs. 13, 15.

s. 123, repealed: 1972, c.47, s.78, sch.11.

s. 125, repealed in pt.: ibid., sch.11.

s. 126, amended: 1980, c.51, sch.25.

s. 130, repealed in pt.: 1972, c.60, schs.6,8.

s. 134, repealed: 1972, c.47, s.103, sch.11.

s. 135, repealed: 1972, c.70, schs.22,30.

s. 141, repealed in pt: ibid.

s. 143, repealed: 1975, c.6, s.13, sch.6.

s. 144, repealed: 1973, c.26, sch.3.

s. 145, repealed: 1972, c.70, schs.22,30.

s. 146, amended: 1985, c.51, sch.8.

ss. 147, 148, repealed: 1972, c.70, schs.22,30.

s. 149, repealed in pt.: S.L.R. 1977.

s. 152, amended: 1972, c.47, sch.9.

s. 156, repealed: 1972, c.70, schs.22,30.

s. 157, amended: ibid., sch.22; repealed in pt.: ibid., schs.22,30.

s. 158, see Bristol District Council v. Clark [1975] 1 W.L.R. 1443, C.A.; Lambeth London Borough Council v. Udechuka, The Times, April 30, 1980, C.A.

s. 158, amended: 1976, c.80, sch.8; 1977, c.42, sch.23.

s. 159, repealed in pt.: 1974, c.44, sch.15.

s. 160, repealed in pt.: 1972, c.70, schs.22,30.

s. 161, see Canterbury City Council v. Bern (1982) 44 P. & C.R. 178, D.C.

s. 161, repealed in pt.: 1972, c.70, schs.22,30.

ss. 162, 163, repealed in pt.: 1974, c.44, sch.15.

s. 166, see Graddage v. Haringey London Borough Council [1975] 1 W.L.R. 241; [1975] 1 All E.R. 224.

s. 166, amended: 1972, c.70, sch.22; repealed in pt.: 1974, c.44, sch.15; 1985, c.51, sch.17.

s. 170, repealed: 1976, c.57, sch.2.

ss. 171–176, repealed: 1972, c.70, schs. 22, 30.

s. 178, regs. 72/228; 74/1511; 75/500; 81/1347.

s. 178, amended: 1975, c.6, sch.5.

s. 181, repealed in pt.: 1972, c.70, schs.22,30.

s. 189, see Sovmots Investments v. Secretary of State for the Environment; Brompton Securities v. Same [1977] 2 W.L.R. 951; [1977] 2 All E.R. 385, H.L.

s. 189, amended: 1972, c.70, sch.22; 1974, c.44, sch.13; 1985, c.51, sch.8.

s. 191, amended: 1980, c.43, sch.7; repealed in pt.: S.L.R. 1977.

sch. 1, amended: 1981, c.67, sch.4; repealed in pt.: ibid., sch.6.

CAP.

5 & 6 Eliz. 2 (1957)—cont.

56. Housing Act 1957—cont.
sch. 2, orders 72/1792; 73/753; 82/1112.
sch. 2, amended: 1973, c.26, s.73; 1974, c.44, sch.13; 1975, c.72, sch.3; 1976, c.80, sch.8; 1977, c.42, sch.23; repealed in pt.: 1974, c.44, sch.15.
sch. 3, see *Williams* v. *Secretary of State* (1971) 23 P. & C.R. 135; *Hibernian Property Co.* v. *Secretary of State for the Environment* (1973) 27 P. & C.R. 197; *Harris* v. *Birkenhead Corporation* [1975] 1 W.L.R. 379; [1975] 1 All E.R. 1001; *R.* v. *Secretary of State for the Environment, ex p. Wellingborough Borough Council and Runnymede Borough Council* (1982) 80 L.G.R. 603, Skinner J.; *E. A. Wyse* v. *Secretary of State for the Environment* [1984] J.P.L. 256, Forbes J.
sch. 3, amended: 1980, c.51, sch.25.
sch. 4, see *Williams* v. *Secretary of State* (1971) 23 P. & C.R. 135; *Gordondale Investments* v. *Secretary of State* (1971) 70 L.G.R. 158; (1971) 23 P. & C.R. 334; *Islington London Borough Council* v. *Secretary of State for the Environment; Stockport Metropolitan Borough Council* v. *Secretary of State for the Environment* (1982) 43 P. & C.R. 300, C.A.
sch. 4, amended: 1974, c.44, sch.10; repealed in pt.: *ibid.*, sch.15.
sch. 5, repealed: *ibid.*
sch. 7, amended: 1981, c.67, sch.4; repealed in pt.: *ibid.*, sch.6.
sch. 9, repealed: 1973, c.26, sch.3.
sch. 10, see *Williams* v. *Khan* (1982) 43 P. & C.R. 1, C.A.
sch. 10, repealed: S.L.R. 1978.
sch. 11, repealed: S.L.R. 1977.
sch. 14, see *Eckersley* v. *Secretary of State for the Environment, The Times,* June 29, 1977; [1977] J.P.L. 580, C.A.
57. Agriculture Act 1957.
s. 1, orders 73/352, 501; 76/95, 249, 602, 918; 80/1564; 85/63.
s. 2, repealed in pt.: 1972, c.68, sch.3.
s. 3, repealed: *ibid.*
s. 4, repealed: *ibid.*; order 75/1164.
s. 5, orders 72/492; 73/204, 502, 591; 75/357; 76/250; 78/17, 1660; 79/1541; 80/1562, 1563, 1811; 81/751; 82/726; 83/1009; 85/64.
s. 5, amended: 1972, c.68, s.6.
s. 6, orders 78/17; 80/1563.
s. 8, repealed in pt.: 1972, c.68, sch.3; S.L.R. 1973.
s. 9, orders 72/492; 73/352, 502, 591; 76/249, 250; 85/64.
s. 10, repealed: S.L.R. 1973.
s. 11, repealed in pt.: 1972, c.68, sch.3.
s. 25, amended: 1980, c.13, sch.1.
s. 35, orders 72/492; 73/352, 501, 502, 591; 76/95, 249, 250; 602; 78/17, 1660; 79/1541; 80/1562, 1563, 1811; 81/751; 82/726; 83/1009; 85/63, 64.
s. 36, repealed in pt.: 1972, c.68, s.4; S.L.R. 1973; order 75/1164.
sch. 1, order 76/918.
sch. 1, amended: order 76/918; repealed in pt.: orders 77/2053; 80/1564; 1986, c.49, sch.4.
sch. 4, repealed: S.L.R. 1973.

CAP.

5 & 6 Eliz. 2 (1957)—cont.

58. Registration of Births, Deaths and Marriages (Special Provisions) Act 1957.
ss. 1–3, 5, 6, order 88/1295.
59. Coal Mining (Subsidence) Act 1957.
s. 1, amended: 1973, c.65, sch.27; 1984, c.54, sch.9 (S.); 1985, c.71, sch.2.; 1987, c.3, sch.1; c.26, sch.23 (S.)
s. 1, see *Knibb* v. *National Coal Board* [1986] 3 W.L.R. 895, C.A.
ss. 2–7, amended: 1987, c.3, sch.1.
s. 8, repealed: S.L.R. 1973; amended: 1987, c.3, sch.1.
s. 9, amended: 1979, c.46, sch.6; 1987, c.3, sch.1.
s. 10, amended: 1986, c.5, sch.14; 1987, c.3, sch.1.
s. 13, see *Knibb* v. *National Coal Board* [1986] 3 W.L.R. 895, C.A.
ss. 13, 15, 17, amended: 1987, c.3, sch.1.
s. 18, repealed in pt.: S.L.R. 1973.
schs. 1, 2, amended: 1985, c.71, sch.2; 1987, c.3, sch.1; c.23, sch.23 (S.).
60. Federation of Malaya Independence Act 1957.
s. 2, repealed in pt.: S.L.R. 1976.
s. 3, order 78/182.
s. 4, repealed in pt.: S.L.R. 1974.
sch. 1, repealed in pt.: S.L.R. 1977; 1981, c.61, sch.9; 1988, c.48, sch.8.
sch. 2, repealed: S.L.R. 1974.
61. Winfrith Heath Act 1957.
repealed: S.L.R. 1976.
62. Governors' Pensions Act 1957.
repealed: 1973, c.21, sch.2.
ss. 3, 9, order 72/229.
s. 11, amended: 1972, c.11, sch.6.
63. Appropriation Act 1957.
ss. 6, 7, repealed: 1972, c.11, s.28, sch.8.

6 & 7 Eliz. 2 (1957–58)

6. Import Duties Act 1958.
repealed (except ss. 4–10, 12 (in pt.) 13, 15, 16 (in pt.), schs. 3, 5: 1972, c.68, sch.3.
order 73/144.
s. 1, orders 72/677; 73/393, 648, 874, 973, 1166, 1344, 1569, 1616, 2152, 2169; 74/166, 887, 1020, 1318, 1350, 1371, 2020, 2120, 2121, 2135, 2163, 2164; 75/263, 975, 1003, 1005, 1064, 1159, 1266, 1320, 1492, 1744, 1795, 1944, 1977, 1978, 1998, 2022, 2027, 2049, 2056–2058, 2073–2077, 2093, 2114, 2128, 2129, 2203, 2238; 76/125, 370, 719, 912, 976, 977, 1012, 1017, 1138, 1383, 1399, 1677, 1687, 2053, 2072, 2077, 2078; 77/435, 616, 713, 838, 1046, 1087, 1093, 1499.
ss.1–3, repealed: order 77/2028.
s. 2, orders 72/677; 73/393, 648, 1166, 2152, 2169; 74/166, 887, 1020, 1318, 1350, 1371, 2020, 2120, 2135, 2163; 75/263, 1064, 1266, 1744, 1977, 2073, 2076, 2128, 2203; 76/370, 912.
s. 3, orders 73/51, 874, 1569, 2152, 2169; 74/166, 887, 1020, 1318, 1350, 1371, 2120, 2121, 2135, 2163, 2164; 75/263, 975, 1003,

CAP.

6 & 7 Eliz. 2 (1957–58)—cont.

6. Import Duties Act 1958—cont.
1005, 1064, 1266, 1320, 1795, 1944, 1977, 1978, 1998, 2027, 2056–2058, 2073–2077, 2093, 2128, 2129, 2203, 2238; 76/125, 370, 719, 912, 976, 977, 1012, 1017, 1383, 1399, 1677, 2053, 2072, 2077, 2078; 77/435, 616, 713, 838, 1046, 1087, 1093, 1499.
s. 4, repealed: 1979, c.3, sch.3.
s. 5, orders 73/293, 1109, 1699, 2065, 2174, 2224–2226; 74/25, 96, 676, 677, 1014, 1093, 1133, 1145, 1375, 1376, 1610, 1658, 2023, 2084, 2085, 2165, 2181, 2188; 75/39, 960, 963, 1063, 1290, 1296, 1791, 2003, 2059, 2060, 2072, 2081, 2228–2230; 76/118, 534, 868, 1013, 1786, 1860, 2076, 2105, 2108, 2116, 2179, 2193, 2206; 77/76, 971, 1082, 1722, 2048; 78/194, 820, 878, 1866, 1933; 79/121, 153.
ss. 5, 6, repealed: 1979, c.3, sch.3.
s. 7, repealed in pt.: regs. 77/910.
s. 8, order 73/863.
s. 9, repealed: 1977, c.36, s.12, sch.9.
s. 10, amended: regs. 77/910; repealed in pt.: 1977, c.37, s.9, sch.9; 1979, c.3, sch.3.
s. 11, repealed: order 77/2028.
s. 12, regs. 72/338; 73/2067, 2069, 2071, 2227, 2229; 74/1019, 1971, 2076; 75/1109, 2082, 2100; 76/995; 77/972, 1081, 2047; repealed in pt.: order 77/2028; 1979, c.3, sch.3.
s. 13, orders 72/677; 73/393, 648, 651, 874, 973, 1166, 1344, 1569, 1616, 2065, 2152, 2169, 2174, 2224–2226; 74/25, 96, 166, 676, 677, 887, 1014, 1020, 1093, 1133, 1145, 1318, 1350, 1371, 1375, 1376, 1610, 1658, 2020, 2023, 2120, 2121, 2135, 2163, 2164; 75/263, 975, 1003, 1005, 1064, 1159, 1266, 1320, 1492, 1744, 1795, 1944, 1977, 1978, 1998, 2022, 2027, 2049, 2056–2058, 2073–2077, 2093, 2114, 2128, 2129, 2203, 2238; 76/125, 370, 719, 868, 912, 976, 977, 1012, 1017, 1382, 1383, 1399, 1677, 1687, 1786, 1860, 2053, 2072, 2077, 2078; 77/435, 616, 713, 838, 1046, 1082, 1087, 1093, 1499, 1722; 78/820, 878; 79/153.
s. 13, repealed: 1979, c.3, sch.3.
ss. 15, 16, repealed: ibid.
sch. 1, repealed: order 77/2028.
sch. 3, orders 73/2065, 2174, 2224–2226; 74/25, 96, 676, 677, 1014, 1093, 1133, 1145, 1375, 1376, 1610, 1658, 2023, 2084, 2085, 2165, 2181, 2188; 75/960, 963, 1063, 1290, 1296, 1791, 2003, 2059, 2060, 2072, 2081, 2228–2230; 76/118, 1013, 1786, 1860, 2076, 2108, 2116, 2179, 2193, 2206; 77/1722; 78/820, 1806, 1933; 79/121, 153; repealed in pt.: 1977, c.36, s.12, sch.9; 1979, c.3, sch.3.
sch. 4, order 77/971.
sch. 4, repealed in pt.: 1972, c.68, sch.3; order 77/2028; regs. 78/1704; 1979, c.3, sch.3.
sch. 5, repealed: 1977, c.36, s.12, sch.9.
10. British Nationality Act 1958.
repealed: 1981, c.61, sch.9.
11. Isle of Man Act 1958.
repealed: 1979, c.58, sch.2.
s. 2, order 78/273.

CAP.

6 & 7 Eliz. 2 (1957–58)—cont.

14. Overseas Service Act 1958.
amended: 1974, c.21, sch.1.
s. 2, repealed: 1973, c.21, schs.1,2.
s. 3, amended: 1972, c.11, sch.6, repealed in pt.: ibid., sch.8; 1973, c.21, sch.2.
s. 4, repealed: ibid., schs.1,2.
s. 5 (in pt.), sch.2, repealed: 1976, c.35, sch.3.
16. Commonwealth Institute Act 1958.
s. 7, repealed in pt.: 1975, c.24, sch.3.
s. 8, repealed in pt.: S.L.R. 1974.
sch. 3, repealed: ibid.
17. Recreational Charities Act 1958.
s. 1, see I.R.C. v. McMullen [1980] 2 W.L.R. 416; [1980] 1 All E.R. 884, H.L.
s. 4, repealed: 1973, c.36, sch.6.
22. Road Transport Lighting (Amendment) Act 1958.
repealed: 1972, c.20, sch.9.
23. Milford Haven Conservancy Act 1958.
ss. 1, 4, 7, 9, 11–13, 23, sch. 1, amended: order 80/1987.
s. 5, amended: 1981, c.38, sch.3.
ss. 13, 23, repealed in pt.: ibid.
sch. 1, amended: orders 74/1351; 75/1828.
24. Land Drainage (Scotland) Act 1958.
s. 5, regs. 74/1213.
s. 11, amended: 1982, c.48, sch.6.
s. 17, substituted: 1984, c.12, sch.4.
s. 19, repealed in pt.: S.L.R. 1974.
sch. 1, order 78/1154.
sch. 1, amended: 1973, c.65, sch.27; regs. 77/2007; order 78/1154.
sch. 2, amended: 1981, c.38, sch.3; 1984, c.12, sch.4.
25. Christmas Island Act 1958.
repealed: S.L.R. 1976.
26. House of Commons (Redistribution of Seats) Act 1958.
repealed: 1986, c.56, sch.4.
orders 83/417, 418, 422.
27. Industrial Assurance and Friendly Societies Act 1948 (Amendment) Act 1958.
ss. 1, 3, repealed in pt.: 1974, c.46, sch.11.
28. Solicitors (Scotland) Act 1958.
repealed: 1980, c.46, sch.7.
s. 5A, see A & B, Petitioners, 1978 S.L.T.(Notes) 71.
s. 15, see Ross v. Gordon's J. F. (O.H.), 1973 S.L.T.(Notes) 91.
s. 16, see Pontifical Society v. McGregor's J. F., 1974 S.C. 106.
30. Land Powers (Defence) Act 1958.
s. 1, repealed in pt.: S.L.R. 1978.
s. 6, amended: 1979, c.46, sch.4; repealed in pt.: ibid., schs.4,5.
s. 9, amended (S.): 1984, c.54, sch.9.
s. 17, amended: 1975, c.76, sch.1; repealed in pt.: 1972, c.70, sch.30; 1975, c.76, schs.1,2.
s. 20, repealed: 1984, c.12, sch.7.
s. 25, see McDermott v. Department of Agriculture for Northern Ireland [1984] 2 N.I.J.B., Hutton J.; McDermott v. Department of Agriculture for Northern Ireland and H.M. Treasury (R/11/1986).
sch. 3, order 80/1085.

CAP.

6 & 7 Eliz. 2 (1957–58)—cont.

31. First Offenders Act 1958.
repealed: 1972, c.71, s.14, sch.6.

32. Opticians Act 1958.
order 81/1821.
s. 7, orders 73/1450, 2215; 76/157; 77/176; 79/1638; 80/1936; 83/1; 85/2024; rules 75/51; 87/1887.
s. 9, amended: 1984, c.48, sch.2.
s. 9, order 83/545.
ss. 10A, 10B, 10C, added: 1984, c.48, sch.2.
s. 11, see *Lowe* v. *General Optical Council* (1980) 124 S.J. 829, P.C.; *Le Scroog* v. *General Optical Council* [1982] 3 All E.R. 257, P.C.
s. 12, amended: 1984, c.48, sch.2.
s. 13, repealed in pt.: *ibid.*, sch.8.
s. 13A, added: *ibid.*, sch.2.
s. 14, amended: *ibid.*
s. 15, order 85/1580.
ss. 15, amended: 1984, c.48, sch.2.
s. 17, rules 74/149.
s. 20, rules 74/1329.
s. 20, amended: 1977, c.45, sch.1.
s. 20A, orders 85/856; 88/1305.
s. 20A, added: 1984, c.48, sch.2.
s. 20B, added: 1988, c.49, s.14.
s. 21, see *Elsner* v. *Mirams* [1975] Crim.L.R. 519, D.C.; *Smith* v. *Mackeith*, 1985 S.C.C.R. 164; *S.A. Magnivision NV* v. *Generai Optical Council, The Tims*, February 19, 1987, D.C.
s. 21, order of council 84/1778.
s. 21, amended: 1973, c.32, sch.4; 1977, c.45, sch.1; c.49, schs.14,15; 1978, c.29, sch.16 (S.); 1988, c.49, s.13; repealed in pt.: 1972, c.58, sch.7; 1973, c.23, schs.4,5; 1984, c.48, sch.1.
s. 22, amended: 1977, c.45, sch.1; 1984, c.48, s.3.
ss. 23, 24, amended: *ibid.*, sch.2.
s. 25, orders 81/522; 85/203; 88/1305.
s. 25, amended: 1984, c.48, ss.1,2.
s. 27, amended: *ibid.*, sch.2; 1985, c.9, sch.2.
s. 29, amended: 1984, c.48, sch.2.
s. 30, see *Smith* v. *Mackeith*, 1985 S.C.C.R. 164.
s. 30, amended: 1977, c.49, sch.15; 1978, c.29, sch.16 (S.); 1984, c.48, sch.2.
s. 31, repealed in pt.: 1973, c.36, sch.6.
sch., orders 73/268; 78/1410; 83/1842; 85/664; 86/309; amended: order 78/1410.

33. Disabled Persons (Employment) Act 1958.
s. 3, amended: 1972, c.70, sch.23; 1973, c.65, sch.27; 1977, c.49, sch.15; repealed in pt.: 1972, c.70, schs. 23, 30; 1973, c.65, schs.27,29; 1985, c.51, sch.17.
sch., amended: 1972, c.70, sch.23; repealed in pt.: *ibid.*, schs.23,30; S.L.R. 1978; repealed (S.): 1973, c.65, schs.27, 29.

34. Litter Act 1958.
repealed: 1983, c.34, sch.2.
s. 1, see *Witney* v. *Cattanach* [1979] Crim.L.R. 461, D.C.

35. Matrimonial Causes (Property and Maintenance) Act 1958.
s. 7, amended: 1984, c.42, sch.1.

CAP.

6 & 7 Eliz. 2 (1957–58)—cont.

36. Physical Training and Recreation Act 1958.
repealed: 1976, c.57, sch.2; 1982, c.43, sch.4 (S.).

37. Drainage Rates Act 1958.
repealed: 1976, c.70, sch.8.

38. Defence Contracts Act 1958.
s. 4, amended: 1977, c.37, sch.5.
s. 7, repealed in pt.: S.L.R. 1974.

39. Maintenance Orders Act 1958.
s. 1, amended: 1972, c.18, sch.; 1977, c.38, sch.3; 1982, c.27, sch.12.
Pt. I (ss. 1–5), Acts of Sederunt 80/1727, 1732.
s. 2, amended: 1977, c.38, sch.3; 1982, c.27. sch.11.
s. 2A, added: *ibid.*
s. 3, amended: 1984, c.42, sch.1; 1987, c.42, sch.2.
ss. 3, 4, see *Allen* v. *Allen* [1984] 2 W.L.R. 65, Booth J.
s. 4, see *Smethurst* v. *Smethurst* [1977] 3 W.L.R. 472, D.C.; *Goodall* v. *Jolley* (1984) 14 Fam.Law 23, Wood J.; *Berry* v. *Berry* [1986] 3 W.L.R. 257, C.A.
s. 4, amended: 1977, c.38, sch.3; 1984, c.42, sch.1; repealed in pt.: 1977, c.38, sch.5.
s. 5, amended: *ibid.*, sch.3.
s. 16, repealed: 1980, c.43, sch.9.
s. 18, see *Slater* v. *Slater* (1984) S.J. 32, D.C.; *R.* v. *Cardiff JJ., ex p. Salter* (1986) 1 F.L.R. 162, Wood J.; *R.* v. *Horseferry Road Magistrates' Court, ex p. Bernstein, The Times*, November 4, 1986, Arnold J.
s. 18, amended: 1980, s.43, sch.7.
s. 19, orders 74/557; 75/2188; 79/116; 83/1124; repealed: 1972, c.18, s.22.
s. 20, repealed in pt.: 1980, c.43, sch.9.
s. 21, amended: *ibid.*, sch.7; repealed in pt.: 1987, c.42, sch.4.
s. 22, repealed: 1973, c.36, sch.6.
s. 23, amended: 1977, c.38, sch.3; 1982, c.27, sch.12; repealed in pt.: 1972, c.18, s.22; 1973, c.36, sch.6; S.L.R. 1975.

40. Matrimonial Proceedings (Children) Act 1958.
s. 7, repealed: 1986, c.9, sch.2.
s. 7, repealed in pt. (S.): 1976, c.37, sch.2.
s. 8, see *Hunter* v. *Hunter* (O.H.), 1976 S.L.T.(Notes) 2.
s. 8, amended: 1986, c.55, sch.1; repealed in pt.: 1986, c.9, sch.2.
s. 9, amended (S.): *ibid.*, sch.1.
s. 9, amended: 1986, c.55, sch.1; repealed in pt.: 1984, c.15, sch.2; 1985, c.37, sch.2(S.).
s. 10, amended: 1973, c.65, sch.27; 1986, c.55, sch.1.
s. 11, amended: *ibid.*; repealed in pt.: 1986, c.9, sch.2.
s. 12, see *Hunt* v. *Hunt* (O.H.) 1987 S.L.T. 672.
s. 12, amended: 1973, c.65, sch.27.
s. 13, repealed: 1986, c.55, sch.2.
s. 13, amended (S.): 1985, c.73, s.16.
s. 14, repealed: 1986, c.9, sch.2.
s. 15, repealed in pt.: 1973, c.65, sch.29.

CAP.

6 & 7 Eliz. 2 (1957–58)—cont.

42. Housing (Financial Provisions) Act 1958.
repealed: 1985, c.71, sch.1.
s. 43, see *Harris* v. *Wyre Forest District Council*
(1987) 1 E.G.L.R. 231, Schiemann J.

43. Horse Breeding Act 1958.
repealed: 1984, c.40, s.12, sch.2.
ss. 1, 13, rules 82/813.
ss. 2, 3, 5, 13, rules 80/592.
ss. 2, 3, 5, 13, 16, rules 74/1962; 75/1777.
ss. 2, 3, 13, 16, rules 76/1992.

44. Dramatic and Musical Performers' Protection Act 1958.
repealed: 1988, c.48, sch.8.
see *Ex p. Islands Records, The Times*, March
22, 1978, C.A.; *Shelley* v. *Cunane* (1983) 133
New L.J. 377, Harriman J.; *Rickless* v. *United
Artists Corporation, The Times*, December 12,
1986, C.A.
s. 1, see *Warner Bros. Records Inc.* v. *Parr*
[1982] 2 All E.R. 455, Julian Jeffs Q.C.; *R.C.A.
Corp.* v. *Pollard* [1982] 3 All E.R. 771, C.A.;
Silly Wizard v. *Shaughnessy, El Fakir* [1983]
F.S.R. 163, Ct. of Session.
ss. 1, 4, see *Helliwell* v. *Piggott Sims* [1980]
F.S.R. 582, Whitford J.
s. 2, see *Ekland* v. *Scripglow* [1982] F.S.R. 432,
Peter Gibson J.; *Rickless* v. *United Artists
Corp.* [1987] 1 All E.R. 679, C.A.

45. Prevention of Fraud (Investments) Act 1958.
repealed: 1986, c.60, sch.17.
s. 3, regs. 76/1600; 77/1607; 80/350; 82/342;
83/586, 587; 84/738; 85/974.
s. 4, regs. 78/917; 83/1943.
s. 5, regs. 83/587.
s. 7, rules 83/585.
s. 13, see *Secretary of State for Trade* v. *Markus*
[1975] 2 W.L.R. 708; [1975] 1 All E.R. 958,
H.L.; *R.* v. *Brown (Kevin), The Times*, December 9, 1983, C.A.
s. 14, see *Hudson* v. *Bishop Cavanagh Commodities* [1982] Crim.L.R. 114, D.C.
s. 15, regs. 84/562.
s. 21, regs. 74/2042; 76/1600; 77/1607; 80/350;
82/342; 83/586, 587, 1943; 84/562, 738;
85/974.
s. 26, order 80/701.

46. Statute Law Revision Act 1958.
ss. 1–3, 4 (in pt.), repealed: S.L.R. 1974.
s. 5, repealed: 1973, c.36, sch.6.
schs. 1–3, repealed: S.L.R. 1974.

47. Agricultural Marketing Act 1958.
s. 1, order 84/464 (S.).
s. 2, orders 72/1427; 74/2030; 80/1238; 82/616,
970; 84/464 (S.), 1330; 85/312; 86/83;
87/282, 740 (S.).
s. 2, amended: 1986, c.49, sch.3.
s. 5, amended: 1979, c.13, sch.1.
s. 19A, added: 1973, c.41, s.127; amended:
1980, c.21, s.15.
s. 22, amended: 1972, c.62, s.12; repealed in
pt.: *ibid.*, sch.6.
s. 23, repealed: 1972, c.62, s.12, sch.6.
s. 24, amended: *ibid.*, s.12; repealed in pt.:
ibid., sch.6.
s. 25, repealed in pt.: *ibid.*, s.12, sch.6.

CAP.

6 & 7 Eliz. 2 (1957–58)—cont.

47. Agricultural Marketing Act 1958—*cont.*
s. 34, amended: order 77/899.
s. 41, order 84/463.
s. 41A, added: regs. 81/864.
s. 47, amended: 1973, c.41, sch.12; 1980, c.21,
s.19.
s. 53, repealed in pt.: 1972, c.62, s.12, sch.6;
1973, c.36, sch.6.
s. 54, repealed in pt.: S.L.R. 1974.
sch. 1, orders 84/1330; 85/312; 86/83; 87/282,
740 (S.).
sch. 1, amended: 1986, c.49, s.11.
sch. 2, orders 82/616, 970.
sch. 2, amended: 1985, c.9, sch.2; 1986, c.45,
sch.14.
sch. 3, repealed in pt.: 1972, c.62, s.12, sch.6.
sch. 4, repealed: S.L.R. 1974.
sch. 7, order 80/1238.

49. Trading Representations (Disabled Persons) Act 1958.
s. 1, see *Murphy* v. *Duke* [1985] 2 W.L.R. 773,
Forbes J.
s. 1, amended: 1972, c.45, s.1; c.70, sch.29;
1973, c.65, sch.27(S.); repealed in pt.: 1972,
c.45, s.1; c.70, sch.30; 1985, c.51, sch.17.
ss. 2, 3, repealed: 1972, c.45, s.2.

50. Local Government (Omnibus Shelters and Queue Barriers) (Scotland) Act 1958.
amended: 1984, c.54, s.49.
ss. 1, 2, amended: *ibid.*, sch.9.
s. 3, amended: 1981, c.38, sch.3; 1984, c.12,
sch.4.
s. 7, amended: 1973, c.65, sch.18; 1980, c.34,
sch.5; 1981, c.14, s.7; 1984, c.54, sch.9;
repealed in pt.: 1980, c.34, sch.9.

51. Public Records Act 1958.
s. 2, regs. 73/1401; 77/288; 86/697; 87/444;
88/1385.
s. 8, repealed in pt.: 1981, c.54, sch.7.
s. 11, repealed: 1988, c.48, sch.8.
s. 12, repealed in pt.: 1973, c.36, sch.6.
s. 13, repealed in pt.: S.L.R. 1974.
sch. 1, orders 84/546, 547.
sch. 1, amended: 1973, c.32, sch.4; c.38,
sch.27; c.41, sch.12; 1975, c.71, sch.16;
1977, c.49, schs.14, 15; 1978, c.29, sch.15;
1979, c.43, sch.6; 1980, c.53, sch.1; 1982,
c.16, sch.15; 1983, c.44, sch.2; c.47, sch.5;
1984, c.35, sch.3; 1987, c.3, sch.1; 1988,
c.34, sch.5; repealed in pt.: 1975, c.60, sch.5;
c.71, sch.18; 1983, c.47, sch.6; order 85/39;
1987, c.3, sch.3.
sch. 2, amended: 1979, c.13, sch.1; 1981, c.16,
s.10; repealed in pt.: S.L.R. 1973; c.41,
sch.13; 1974, c.4, sch.5; 1975, c.9, sch.2;
S.L.R. 1977; 1979, c.13, sch.2; 1981, c.16,
s.10, sch.2; c.19, sch.1; 1988, c.3, sch.
sch. 3, repealed: 1988, c.48, sch.8.

52. Costs of Leases Act 1958.
s. 1, see *Cairnplace* v. *CBL (Property Investment) Co.* [1984] 1 All E.R. 315, C.A.

53. Variation of Trusts Act 1958.
see *Practice Direction (Ch.D.) (Procedure: Applications under the Variation of Trusts Act 1958)
(No. 3 of 1987)*, December 8, 1987.

CAP.

6 & 7 Eliz. 2 (1957–58)—cont.

53. Variation of Trusts Act 1958—cont.
s. 1, see Re Whittall; Whittall v. Faulkner [1973] 1 W.L.R. 1027; [1973] 3 All E.R. 35, Brightman J.; Allen v. Distillers Co. (Biochemicals); Albrice v. Same [1974] 2 W.L.R. 481; Knocker v. Youle [1986] 1 W.L.R. 934, Warner J.
s. 1, amended: 1983, c.20, sch.4.
s. 2, repealed in pt.: 1973, c.36, sch.6.

54. Divorce (Insanity and Desertion) Act 1958.
repealed (S.): 1976, c.39, sch.2.

55. Local Government Act 1958.
Part I (ss. 1–16), repealed: S.L.R. 1975.
Pts. II, III (ss. 17–53), s.55, repealed: 1972, c.70, sch.30.
s. 56, repealed in pt.: 1972, c.47, sch.11; c.70, sch.30; S.L.R. 1974; S.L.R. 1978.
ss. 57–59, 60 (in pt.), repealed: 1972, c.70, sch.30.
s. 58, see ILEA v. Secretary of State for the Environment, The Times, May 26, 1984, C.A.
ss. 61, 63 (in pt.), 64, repealed: S.L.R. 1978.
s. 65, repealed in pt.: 1972, c.70, sch.30.
s. 66, repealed in pt.: 1972, c.60, sch.8; S.L.R. 1978.
s. 67, repealed in pt.: ibid.
sch. 1, repealed: S.L.R. 1975.
sch. 7, repealed: 1972, c.70, sch.30.
sch. 8, rules 73/79, 166.
sch. 8, repealed in pt.: 1972, c.70, sch.30; S.L.R. 1974; S.L.R. 1975; S.L.R. 1978; 1980, c.5, sch.6; c.20, sch.7, 1983, c.2, sch.9.
sch. 9, repealed: S.L.R. 1974.

56. Finance Act 1958.
s. 6, repealed: 1979, c.4, sch.4.
s. 22, see Blausten v. I.R.C. [1972] 2 W.L.R. 376; [1972] 1 All E.R. 41; [1971] T.R. 363.
Pt. V (ss. 28–33), repealed: 1975, c.7, sch.13.
s. 35, repealed in pt.: 1974, c.57, sch.14.
s. 37, repealed: 1975, c.7, sch.13.
s. 38, repealed: 1977, c.36, sch.9.
s. 40, repealed in pt.: S.L.R. 1974; 1975, c.7, sch.13; 1979, c.2, sch.6.
sch. 8, repealed: 1975, c.7, sch.13.
· sch. 9, repealed: S.L.R. 1974.

58. Medical Act 1956 (Amendment) Act 1958.
repealed. 1983, c.54, sch.7.

60. Chequers Estate Act 1958.
s. 2, amended: order 87/2039.
s. 3, amended: S.L.R. 1974.

61. Interest on Damages (Scotland) Act 1958.
see McCuaig v. Redpath, 1972 S.L.T.(Notes) 42; MacDonald v. Glasgow Corporation, 1973 S.L.T. 107.
s. 1, see Smith v. Middleton, 1972 S.L.T.(Notes) 3; Ross v. British Ry., 1972 S.L.T. 174; Orr v. Metcalfe, 1973 S.L.T. 133; Buchanan (James) & Co. v. Stewart Cameron (Drymen), 1973 S.L.T.(Notes) 78; Mouland v. Ferguson (O.H.), 1979 S.L.T.(Notes) 85; Plaxton v. Aaron Construction (Dundee) (O.H.), 1980 S.L.T.(Notes) 6.
s. 2, repealed: 1980, c.55, sch.3.

CAP.

6 & 7 Eliz. 2 (1957–58)—cont.

62. Merchant Shipping (Liability of Shipowners and Others) Act 1958.
repealed (except s. 11 in pt.): 1979, c.39, sch.7.
see The Penelope II, The Times, November 21, 1979, C.A.; The Marion, The Times, May 24, 1983, C.A.
s. 1, orders 72/734; 73/1190; 74/536; 75/1615; 76/1031, 2189; 78/54, 1468; 79/790; 80/280, 1872; 81/1240; 83/36, 582; 84/1548.
s. 1, amended: 1981, c.10, s.1; repealed in pt.: ibid., s.1, sch.
ss. 1, 2, see London Dredging Co. v. G.L.C. [1972] 3 W.L.R. 610; [1972] 3 All E.R. 590.
ss. 1, 3, see Mason v. Uxbridge Boat Centre and Wright [1980] 2 Lloyd's Rep. 592, Lloyd J.
s. 2, see Grand Champion Tankers v. Norpipe A/S; The Marion, The Times, May 21, 1984, H.L.
s. 3, see The Alastor [1981] 1 Lloyd's Rep. 581, C.A.; McDermid v. Wash Dredging and Reclamation Co. [1987] 3 W.L.R. 212, H.L.
s. 4, repealed in pt.: 1984, c.5, sch.2.
s. 5, see The Wladyslaw Lokotiek, The Times, June 16, 1978, Brandon J.
s. 5, amended: 1981, c.10, s.1.
s. 10, repealed in pt.: order 81/233.
s. 11, orders 74/1262; 77/50, 1629; 82/335, 336, 527.

63. Park Lane Improvement Act 1958.
s. 4, order 73/578.

64. Local Government and Miscellaneous Financial Provisions (Scotland) Act 1958.
ss. 1–6, repealed: 1973, c.65, sch.29.
s. 7, repealed in pt.: 1987, c.47, sch.6.
s. 8, repealed: 1973, c.65, schs.9,29.
ss. 10, 11, repealed: S.L.R. 1974.
s. 15, repealed in pt.: 1972, c.58, sch.7.
s. 17, regs. 74/1502; 75/1810.
s. 17, repealed: 1977, c.15, sch.3.
s. 18, repealed: 1973, c.65, sch.29.
s. 21, repealed in pt.: S.L.R. 1976.
s. 22, repealed: S.L.R. 1974.
schs. 1–3, repealed: 1973, c.65, sch.29.
sch. 4, repealed in pt.: 1973, c.65, sch.29; S.L.R. 1974; S.L.R. 1975; S.L.R. 1976; 1983, c.2, sch.9; S.L.R. 1986.
sch. 5, repealed: S.L.R. 1976.
sch. 6, repealed: S.L.R. 1974.

65. Children Act 1958.
repealed, except sch. 2 (in pt.): 1980, c.6, sch.3.
repealed (S.): 1984, c.56, sch.3.
s. 6, amended (S.): 1980, c.6, sch.2.
s. 7, amended: 1980, c.5, sch.5; 1983, c.41, sch.2.
s. 13, see Western Heritable Investment Co. v. Husband, The Times, August 10, 1983, H.L.
s. 17, amended: 1973, c.65, sch.27 (S.); 1978, c.28, sch.3 (S.); 1980, c.44, sch.4 (S.).
sch. 2, repealed in pt.: 1980, c.5, sch.6.

66. Tribunals and Inquiries Act 1958.
repealed: 1975, c.24, sch.3; c.25, sch.3.
s. 11, see Hamilton v. Secretary of State, 1972 S.L.T. 233 (O.H.); Watt v. Lord Advocate (O.H.), 1977 S.L.T. 130; 1979 S.L.T. 137.

6 & 7 Eliz. 2 (1957–58)—cont.

s. 12, see *Glasgow Heritable Trust*, 1977 S.L.T. 44; *Guppy's Properties* v. *Knott* (1979) 124 S.J. 81, Sir Douglas Frank, Q.C.

67. Water Act 1958.
repealed: 1976, c.44, s.5; 1980, c.45, sch.11 (S.); S.L.R. 1986.

69. Opencast Coal Act 1958.
order 81/599.
s. 1, see *Nicholson* v. *Secretary of State for Energy and National Coal Board* [1978] J.P.L. 38, Sir Douglas Frank, Q.C.
ss. 1, 2, repealed: 1986, c.63, s.39, sch.12.
s. 3, substituted: *ibid.*, sch.8; amended: 1987, c.3, sch.1.
s. 4, regs. 87/1915.
s. 4, amended: 1975, c.56, s.4; 1981, c.67, sch.4; 1986, c.63, sch.8; repealed in pt.: 1975, c.56, schs.3, 5; 1981, c.67, sch.6.
s. 5, amended: 1975, c.56, sch.3; 1986, c.63, sch.8.
s. 6, repealed: 1975, c.56, schs.3,5.
s. 7, see *Wigan Borough Council* v. *Secretary of State for Energy and the National Coal Board* [1979] J.P.L. 610, Deputy Judge Michael Kempster, Q.C.
ss. 7, 8, repealed in pt.: 1975, c.56, schs.3,5.
s. 9, amended: *ibid.*, sch.3; repealed in pt.: 1986, c.63, s.39, sch.12.
s. 11, amended: 1975, c.56, sch.1; repealed in pt.: 1972, c.70, sch.30; 1975, c.27, schs.1,2.
s. 13, amended: 1984, c.54, sch.9(S.); 1986, c.63, sch.8; repealed in pt. (S.): 1984, c.54, schs.9, 11.
s. 14, substituted: 1986, c.63, sch.8.
s. 14A, substituted: *ibid.*; amended: 1987, c.3, sch.1.
ss. 15, 15A, substituted: 1986, c.63, sch.8.
s. 15A, regs. 87/1915.
s. 16, repealed; 1981, c.67, sch.6; amended: 1986, c.63, sch.8.
s. 18, amended: *ibid.*; repealed in pt.: *ibid.*, sch.12.
s. 23A, added: 1975, c.12, s.6.
s. 24, amended: 1984, c.41, sch.3; 1986, c.5, sch.14.
ss. 25–28, amended: *ibid.*
s. 35, amended: 1975, c.12, s.6.
ss. 35, 49, orders 72/373, 1216; 73/75, 850, 1544, 2074; 74/888; 75/208, 603, 1858; 76/235, 960, 1586, 1799; 77/302, 722, 878, 1466; 78/255, 735, 1419, 1802; 79/942; 80/44, 1365, 1978; 81/1457; 82/402, 1008, 1298, 1543, 1642, 1821; 83/1269; 84/607, 1049, 1903; 85/187, 1130; 87/700; 88/890.
s. 36, amended: 1975, c.56, sch.3; repealed in pt.: *ibid.*, schs.3,5.
s. 38, amended: 1986, c.63, sch.8.
s. 39, amended: *ibid.*; repealed in pt.: *ibid.*, sch.12.
s. 45, amended: 1981, c.38, sch.3; 1984, c.12, sch.4; 1986, c.63, sch.8; repealed in pt.: 1975, c.56, sch.5.
s. 46, repealed in pt.: 1986, c.63, sch.12.
s. 47, repealed in pt.: 1981, c.67, sch.6.

6 & 7 Eliz. 2 (1957–58)—cont.

69. Opencast Coal Act 1958—*cont.*
s. 48, repealed: 1986, c.63, sch.12.
s. 49, regs. 87/1915.
s. 49, amended: 1975, c.56, sch.3.
s. 51, amended: *ibid.*; order 76/1775; 1981, c.38, sch.3; 1986, c.5, sch.14; c.63, sch.8; 1987, c.3, sch.1; repealed in pt.: 1975, c.56, schs.3,5; 1981, c.38, sch.6; 1986, c.44, sch.9; c.63, sch.12; 1987, c.3, sch.3.
s. 52, amended: 1973, c.65, sch.27; order 76/1775; 1986, c.63, sch.8; repealed in pt.: 1973, c.65, sch.29; S.L.R. 1981.
s. 53, repealed in pt.: 1986, c.63, sch.12.
sch. 1, see *Wigan Borough Council* v. *Secretary of State for Energy and the National Coal Board* [1979] J.P.L. 610, Deputy Judge Michael Kempster, Q.C.
sch. 1, repealed: 1986, c.63, sch.12.
sch. 2, amended: 1975, c.56, sch.3; 1986, c.63, sch.8; repealed in pt.: 1981, c.38, sch.6.
sch. 6, amended: 1975, c.56, s.6; 1986, c.5, sch.14; c.63, sch.12.
s. 7, amended: 1986, c.5, sch.14; c.63, sch.12.
sch. 9, amended: 1981, c.38, sch.4; repealed in pt.: 1986, c.63, sch.12.
sch. 10, repealed: *ibid.*

70. Slaughterhouses Act 1958.
repealed: 1974, c.3, sch.6; S.L.R. 1978.

71. Agriculture Act 1958.
s. 2, repealed: 1983, c.46, sch.2; 1984, c.41, sch.4.
s. 3, see *Geddes* v. *MacKay*, 1971 S.L.C.R.App. 94; *McCryndle* v. *Andrew*, 1972 S.L.C.R.App. 117; *Gemmell* v. *Robert Hodge & Sons*, 1974 S.L.T.(Land Ct.) 2.
s. 3, repealed: 1977, c.12, sch.2.
s. 4, repealed: 1986, c.5, sch.15.
s. 6, repealed in pt.: S.L.R. 1973; 1983, c.46, sch.2.
s. 8, order 74/67.
s. 8, repealed in pt.: 1975, c.24, sch.3.
s. 9, repealed in pt.: 1986, c.5, sch.15.
s. 10, repealed in pt.: S.L.R. 1973; 1985, c.12, sch.2.
s. 11, repealed in pt.: 1975, c.24, sch.3.
sch. 1, orders 74/66, 67; repealed in pt.: 1976, c.55, sch.4; 1977, c.12, sch.2; S.L.R. 1977; 1985, c.12, sch.2; 1986, c.5, sch.15.
schs. 2, 3, repealed: S.L.R. 1973.
sch. 4, repealed in pt.: S.L.R. 1977; 1986, c.5, sch.15.

72. Insurance Companies Act 1958.
repealed (except ss. 19 (1), 20, 34, 36 (4) (5) (7), 37 (1) (3)): 1974, c.49, sch.2.
s. 20, regs. 74/493; amended: 1974, c.49, sch.1; 1981, c.31, sch.4; 1982, c.53, s.46.

7 & 8 Eliz. 2 (1958–59)

1. Armed Forces (Housing Loans) Act 1958.
s. 3, repealed in pt.: S.L.R. 1974.

2. Agricultural Mortgage Corporation Act 1958.
repealed: S.L.R. 1977.

5. Adoption Act 1958.
repealed: 1976, c.36, sch.4; 1978, c.28, sch.4 (S.).

CAP.

7 & 8 Eliz. 2 (1958–59)—cont.

5. Adoption Act 1958—cont.

s. 1, see *Re F. (Infants) (Adoption Order: Validity)* [1977] 2 W.L.R. 488, C.A.

s. 4, see *Re P. (A Minor)*; *H.* v. *H.* (1973) 4 Fam.Law. 73, C.A.

ss. 4, 5, see *A.B.* v. *C.D.*, 1970 S.C. 268; *H. and H.*, First Division, October 24, 1975; *A. and B.* v. *C.*, 1977 S.C. 27.

s. 5, see *Re B. (A Minor)*; *S.* v. *B.* (1973) 4 Fam.Law. 75, C.A.; *Re B. (A Minor) (Adoption by Parent)* [1975] 2 W.L.R. 569, D.C.; *Re B. (An Infant) (Adoption: Parental Consent)* [1976] 2 W.L.R. 755; *Re P. (An Infant) (Adoption: Parental Consent)* [1976] 3 W.L.R. 924, C.A.; *Re D. (An Infant) (Adoption: Parents' Consent)* [1977] 2 W.L.R. 79, H.L.; *A. and B.* v. *C.*, 1977 S.L.T.(Sh.Ct.) 55; *A.* v. *B.*, 1987, S.L.T.(Sh.Ct.) 121.

ss. 5, 7, see *Re D. (Minors) (Adoption by Parent)* [1973] 3 W.L.R. 595.

s. 7, see *Re J. (Adoption Order: Conditions)* [1973] 2 W.L.R. 782; *Re S. (A Minor) (Adoption Order: Access)* [1975] 2 W.L.R. 250; [1975] 1 All E.R. 109, C.A.

s. 8, see *S.* v. *Huddersfield Borough Council* [1974] 3 All E.R. 296, C.A.

s. 9, rules 73/1541; 76/1644, 1645; 78/417, 1518, 1519; 79/978; 82/3, 4; 84/265.

s. 9, amended: 1980, c.43, sch.7.

s. 11, Acts of Sederunt 77/977; 78/1373.

s. 13, see *Re J. (Adoption Order: Conditions)* [1973] 2 W.L.R. 782; *H. (A Minor) (Adoption)*, *Re*, (1985) 15 Fam.Law 133, C.A.

s. 19, repealed: 1981, c.61, sch.9.

s. 20A, regs. 76/1743.

s. 21, regs. 75/1959.

s. 22, amended: regs. 75/1809; 77/1892; (S): 1976, c.36, sch.3.

s. 23, regs. 75/2091.

s. 28, see *M. & M.* v. *Glasgow Corporation*, 1976 S.L.T.(Sh.Ct.) 45; *R.* v. *Birmingham City District Council, ex p. O.* (1980) 78 L.G.R. 497, D.C.

s. 29, see *Re K. (A Minor)*, December 20, 1982, Eastham J.; *R.* v. *Children's Hearing for the Border Region*, Second Division, May 13, 1983; *S. (A Minor) (Adoption)*, *Re* (1985) 15 Fam.Law 132, C.A.; *Gatehouse* v. *R.* [1986] 1 W.L.R. 18, D.C.; *A. (Adoption: Placement)*, *Re, sub nom Adoption Application AA113/67*, *Re* [1988] 1 W.L.R. 229, Lincoln J.

s. 29, amended (S): 1976, c.36, sch.3.

s. 32, regs. 73/1203; 81/1818; 82/34 (S.), 1289 (S.); 83/1964.

s. 32, amended: 1978, c.22, sch.2.; 1983, c.41, sch.2.

s. 34, see *T. (A Minor) (Adoption: Parental Consent)*, *Re* [1986] 1 All E.R. 817, C.A.

s. 34, amended: 1976, c.36, sch.3 (S.); 1978, c.22, sch.2.

s. 34A, amended: 1976, c.36, sch.3 (S.); 1983, c.41, sch.2.

s. 37, amended (S.): 1976, c.36, sch.3.

s. 48, amended: 1980, c.43, sch.7.

CAP.

7 & 8 Eliz. 2 (1958–59)—cont.

5. Adoption Act 1958—cont.

s. 50, see *Adoption Application (Payment for Adoption)*, *Re* [1987] 3 W.L.R. 31, Latey J.

s. 50, amended: 1977, c.45, sch.12.

s. 52, amended (S.): 1976, c.36, sch.3.

ss. 52, 53, see *Re M. (an infant)* [1973] 2 W.L.R. 515; [1973] 1 All E.R. 852.

s. 53, amended: orders 78/1433, 1440.

s. 56, regs. 75/1959, 2091; 76/1743.

s. 57, see *S. (A Minor) (Adoption)*, *Re*, (1985) 15 Fam.Law 132, C.A.

s. 57, amended: 1976, c.36, sch.3 (S.); 1983, c.41, sch.2.

s. 57A, added: *ibid.*

s. 60, repealed in pt.: 1981, c.61, sch.9.

sch. 3, see *R.* v. *Birmingham City Council, ex p. O.* [1983] 2 W.L.R. 189, H.L.

6. National Debt Act 1958.

repealed: 1972, c.65, sch.

s. 12, regs. 72/641, 765.

7. Manoeuvres Act 1958.

s. 3, amended (S.): 1984, c.54, sch.9; repealed in pt. (S.): *ibid.*, schs.9, 11.

s. 9, amended: 1980, c.43, sch.7; 1984, c.54, sch.9 (S.).

s. 10, repealed in pt.: S.L.R. 1974.

8. Slaughter of Animals Act 1958.

repealed: 1974, c.3, sch.6.

11. European Monetary Agreement Act 1959.

repealed: 1979, c. 29, sch.

12. Agriculture (Small Farmers) Act 1959.

repealed: S.L.R. 1986.

17. International Bank and Monetary Fund Act 1959.

repealed: 1980, c.63, sch.2.

19. Emergency Laws (Repeal) Act 1959.

ss. 3, 4, repealed: S.L.R. 1977.

s. 6, repealed in pt.: S.L.R. 1974.

s. 8, repealed in pt.: 1973, c.36, sch.6.

s. 9, repealed: S.L.R. 1981.

s. 10, repealed in pt.: S.L.R. 1974.

sch. 4, repealed: *ibid.*

22. County Courts Act 1959.

repealed (except ss. 99 (in pt.), 168–174, 174A, 176): 1984, c.28, sch.4.

s. 2, orders 72/1746; 73/1278, 2045; 74/1004; 75/33; 76/29, 201, 281, 604, 605, 797, 850, 890; 77/149, 348, 1189, 1911; 78/817; 80/694, 1215, 1918.

s. 43, see *Stiffel* v. *Industrial Dwelling Society* [1973] 1 W.L.R. 855.

s. 47, see *Perkins (H. G)* v. *Brent-Shaw* [1973] 1 W.L.R. 975; [1973] 2 All E.R. 924; *Vehicle and General Insurance Co. (In Liquidation)* v. *H. & W. Christie* [1976] 1 All E.R. 747; *Chic-Grit* v. *Weatherhead* (1982) 126 S.J. 658, Balcombe J.; *Matarazzo* v. *Kent Area Health Authority, The Times*, March 25, 1983, C.A.

s. 48, see *P. B. Frost* v. *Green* [1978] 2 All E.R. 206, Slade J.

s. 55, orders 84/297, 1075.

s. 74, see *Jennison* v. *Baker* [1972] 2 W.L.R. 429; [1972] 1 All E.R. 997; *Hatt & Co. (Bath)* v. *Pearce* [1978] 2 All E.R. 474, C.A.; *Re W. (A Minor)* [1981] 3 All E.R. 401, C.A.; *Peart* v. *Stewart* [1983] 2 W.L.R. 451, H.L.

CAP.

7 & 8 Eliz. 2 (1958–59)—cont.

22. County Courts Act 1959—cont.

s. 92, see *Leung* v. *Garbett* [1980] 2 All E.R. 436, C.A.

s. 94, see *Harmsworth* v. *London Transport Executive* (1979) 123 S.J. 825, C.A.

s. 98, see *R.* v. *Bloomsbury and Marylebone County Court, ex p. Villerwest* [1975] 2 All E.R. 562, D.C.

s. 99, see *Re A Debtor* [1973] 1 All E.R. 797, D.C.; *Re Durrance, ex p. Durrance* v. *Hungerford R.D.C.* [1973] 1 W.L.R. 733.

s. 102, see *Faulkner* v. *Love (Trading as W. Love & Son)* [1977] 2 W.L.R. 477; [1977] 1 All E.R. 791, C.A.

s. 102, rules 72/1593; 73/345, 1412; 74/178, 636, 1138; 75/285; 76/2137; 77/600; 78/911; 79/1045; 80/329, 628; 81/1181, 1687, 1775; 82/436, 786.

s. 107, see *Pearlman* v. *Keepers and Governors of Harrow School* [1978] 3 W.L.R. 736, C.A.

s. 109, see *Connor* v. *Maunder* [1972] 1 W.L.R. 914; [1972] 2 All E.R. 1195.

s. 113, see *Gatrell* v. *Industrial Services (High Wycombe)* [1984] 134 New L.J. 408, C.A.

s. 139A, order 84/1141.

s. 143, see *Choice Investments* v. *Jeromnimon (Midland Bank, Garnishee)* [1981] 1 All E.R. 225, C.A.

s. 168, rules 72/334; 73/230; 74/206; 76/2234; 78/750; 79/705, 1619; 80/1857; 81/1588; 82/124, 586, 1140, 1141; 83/291.

s. 177, orders 74/1382; 75/1328; 76/1479; 77/1451, 2184; 78/1243; 79/967, 1149; 80/773; 81/898; 82/1706.

s. 191, see *R.* v. *A Circuit Judge (sitting as Norwich Crown Court), ex p. Wathen* (1977) 33 P. & C.R. 423, D.C.; *West Sussex County Council* v. *Wood*, December 2, 1981, Mr. Recorder Willis, Worthing County Court; *Jones* v. *Barnett* [1984] 3 W.L.R. 333, Judge Paul Baker Q.C.; *Clays Lane Housing Co-operative* v. *Patrick, The Times*, December 1, 1984, C.A.; *Di Palma* v. *Victoria Square Property Co.* [1985] 2 All E.R. 676, C.A.

s. 200, see *P. B. Frost* v. *Green* [1978] 2 All E.R. 206, Slade J.

23. Overseas Resources Development Act 1959.

repealed: 1978, c.2, sch.2.

order 76/611.

sch. 1, regs. 77/2186.

24. Building (Scotland) Act 1959.

s. 1, repealed: 1973, c.65, schs.15,29.

s. 2, regs. 75/550; 77/2189; 80/1756; 81/1499; 87/1232.

s. 2, amended: 1973, c.65, sch.15; repealed in pt.: *ibid.*, schs.15, 19.

s. 3, regs. 73/794; 75/404; 79/310; 80/1772; 81/1596; 82/1878; orders 79/594; 84/1660; 86/1278; 87/1231.

s. 3, amended: 1974, c.37, sch.7; 1986, c.65, s.19.

s. 4, regs. 75/547, 550; 81/1499; 85/1272.

s. 4, amended: 1973, c.65, sch.15; 1974, c.37, sch.7.

s. 4A, see *Glasgow District Council* v. *Secretary of State* (O.H.), 1981 S.L.T.(Notes) 63.

CAP.

7 & 8 Eliz. 2 (1958–59)—cont.

24. Building (Scotland) Act 1959—cont.

s. 4A, regs. 75/550; 81/1499.

s. 4B, substituted: 1986, c.65, s.19.

s. 5, regs. 75/549.

s. 6, regs. 75/550; 81/1596.

s. 6, amended: 1974, c.37, sch.7; repealed in pt.: 1973, c.65, schs.15,29.

ss. 6A, 6B, regs. 75/550.

s. 6AA, added: 1986, c.65, s.19.

s. 7, repealed: 1973, c.65, schs.15,29.

s. 8, repealed: 1984, c.54, sch.11.

s. 9, regs. 75/550.

s. 9, amended: 1974, c.37, sch.7; 1986, c.65, s.19; repealed in pt.: 1973, c.65, schs.15,29.

s. 10, amended: *ibid.*, sch.15; repealed in pt.: *ibid.*, schs.15,29.

s. 11, amended: 1974, c.37, sch.7.

s. 13, see *Howard* v. *Hamilton District Council*, 1985 S.L.T.(Sh.Ct.) 42; *City of Edinburgh District Council* v. *Co-operative Wholesale Society*, 1986 S.L.T.(Sh.Ct.) 57; *Pegg* v. *City of Glasgow District Council*, 1988 S.L.T.(Sh.Ct.) 49.

ss. 13, 14, amended: 1973, c.65, sch.15.

s. 16, see *Waddell* v. *Dumfries and Galloway Regional Council*, 1979 S.L.T.(Sh.Ct.) 45.

s. 17, amended: 1972, c.52, sch.21; 1979, c.46, sch.4; 1986, c.65, sch.2; repealed in pt.: 1979, c.46, schs.4,5.

s. 18, amended: 1973, c.65, sch.15; repealed in pt.: *ibid.*, schs.15,19.

s. 19, amended: 1974, c.37, sch.7.

s. 19A, added: *ibid.*

s. 20, regs. 75/550; 87/1232.

s. 20, substituted: 1986, c.65, s.19.

s. 21, repealed: 1973, c.65, schs.15,29.

s. 23, amended: *ibid.*, sch.15.

s. 24, regs. 73/794; 75/440, 548–550; 81/1499, 1522.

s. 25, amended: 1973, c.65, sch.15; repealed in pt.: *ibid.*, schs.15,19.

s. 26, amended: 1974, c.37, sch.7.

s. 27, repealed: 1973, c.65, schs.15,29.

s. 29, regs. 87/1232.

s. 29, amended: 1973, c.65, sch.15; 1984, c.54, sch.9; repealed in pt.: 1973, c.65, schs.15,29.

s. 30, repealed in pt.: *ibid.*

s. 31, repealed in pt.: S.L.R. 1974.

schs. 1, 2, repealed: 1973, c.65, schs.15,29.

sch. 2, see *Sawers* v. *Clackmannan County Buildings Authority*, 1973 S.L.T. (Sh.Ct.) 4.

sch. 3, regs. 75/550; 81/1499.

sch. 3, repealed in pt.: 1973, c.65, sch.29.

sch. 4, regs. 73/794; 75/404; 82/1878; 84/1660; 86/1278; 87/1231.

sch. 6, see *Howard* v. *Hamilton District Council*, 1985 S.L.T.(Sh.Ct.) 42.

sch. 6, amended: 1987, c.26, sch.23; repealed in pt.: 1973, c.65, schs.15,29.

sch. 7, amended: *ibid.*, sch.15.

sch. 8, repealed: *ibid.*, schs.15,29.

sch. 9, amended: *ibid.*, sch.15; repealed in pt.: *ibid.*, schs.15,29.

sch. 10, repealed: S.L.R. 1974.

CAP.

7 & 8 Eliz. 2 (1958–59)—cont.

25. Highways Act 1959.
repealed: 1980, c.66, sch.25.
see *Hall* v. *H. B. Howlett & Partners* (1976) 237
E.G. 875, D.C.
s. 6, order 73/2147.
s. 7, see *Waters* v. *Secretary of State for the
Environment* (1977) 3 P. & C.R. 410, Slynn J.
ss. 7, 9, 13, see *Lovelock* v. *Secretary for
Transport* [1979] R.T.R. 250, C.A.
s. 11, instruments 75/216; 80/359.
s. 34, see *Att.-Gen.* v. *Honeywill* [1972] 1 W.L.R.
1506; [1972] 3 All E.R. 641; *R.* v. *Secretary of
State for the Environment, ex p. Stewart*
(1979) 37 P. & C.R. 279, D.C.
s. 40, see *National Employers Mutual General
Insurance Association* v. *Herne Bay U.D.C.*
(1972) 70 L.G.R. 542.
s. 44, see *Pridham* v. *Hemel Hempstead Corporation* (1970) 69 L.G.R. 523; *Rider* v. *Rider*
[1973] 2 W.L.R. 190, C.A.; *Hereford and
Worcester County Council* v. *Newman* [1975]
1 W.L.R. 901; [1975] 2 All E.R. 673, C.A.;
Waters v. *Secretary of State for the Environment* (1977) 3 P. & C.R. 410, Slynn J.; *Haydon*
v. *Kent County Council* [1978] 2 W.L.R. 485,
C.A.; *Allison* v. *Corby District Council* [1980]
R.T.R. 111, Peter Pain J.; *Bartlett* v. *Department of Transport* (1984) 83 L.G.R. 579, Boreham J.; *McKenna* v. *Scottish Omnibuses and
Northumberland County Council,* March 13,
1985, C.A.
s. 55, order 83/713.
s. 59, see *Riggall* v. *Hereford C.C.* [1972] 1
W.L.R. 171; [1972] 1 All E.R. 301; *Hereford
and Worcester County Council* v. *Newman*
[1975] 1 W.L.R. 901; [1975] 2 All E.R. 673,
C.A.
s. 70, see *R.* v. *Surrey County Council, ex p.
Send Parish Council* (1980) 40 P. & C.R. 390,
D.C.
s. 82, see *Russell* v. *Barnet London Borough
Council* [1985] 83 L.G.R. 152, Tudor Evans J.
s. 103, see *Johnston* v. *Essex C.C.* (1971) 69
L.G.R. 498.
s. 110, see *Wood* v. *Secretary of State for the
Environment* [1977] J.P.L.307; *R.* v. *Secretary
of State for the Environment, ex p. Stewart*
(1979) 39 P. & C.R. 354, Phillips J.
s. 111, see *Roberton* v. *Secretary of State for
the Environment* [1976] 1 W.L.R. 371; [1976]
1 All E.R. 689.
s. 116, see *R.* v. *Lancashire County Council*
(1977) 76 L.G.R. 290, D.C.; *R.* v. *Surrey
County Council, ex p. Send Parish Council*
[1979] J.P.L. 613, D.C.; *Allison* v. *Corby District Council* [1980] R.T.R. 111, Peter Pain J.;
Re Guyer's Application [1980] 2 All E.R. 520,
C.A.
s. 121, see *Broome* v. *D.P.P.* [1974] 2 W.L.R.
58; [1974] 1 All E.R. 314, H.L.; *Brook* v.
Ashton [1974] Crim.L.R. 105, D.C.; *Absalom*
v. *Martin* [1974] R.T.R. 145, D.C.; *Dixon* v.
Atfield [1975] 1 W.L.R. 1171, D.C.; *Lewis* v.
Dickson [1976] Crim.L.R. 442; [1976] R.T.R.
431, D.C.; *Atfield* v. *Ipswich Borough Council*

CAP.

7 & 8 Eliz. 2 (1958–59)—cont.

25. Highways Act 1959—*cont.*
(1975) 238 E.G. 415, D.C.; *R.* v. *Bierton* [1983]
Crim.L.R. 392, Southwark Crown Ct.
ss. 121, 127, see *Waltham Forest London Borough Council* v. *Mills* [1980] Crim.L.R. 243,
D.C.
s. 127, see *Cambridgeshire C.C.* v. *Rust* [1972]
3 W.L.R. 226; [1972] 3 All E.R. 232; *Waltham
Forest London Borough Council* v. *Mills* [1980]
Crim.L.R. 243, D.C.; *Remet Co.* v. *Newham
London Borough Council* [1981] R.T.R. 502,
D.C.
s. 129, see *Haydon* v. *Kent County Council*
[1978] 2 W.L.R. 485, C.A.
ss. 146, 150, see *Drury* v. *Camden B.C.* [1972]
R.T.R. 391.
s. 192, see *Ramsden* v. *Bowercastle* (1982) 80
L.G.R. 182, D.C.
s. 193, see *National Employers Mutual General
Insurance Association* v. *Herne Bay U.D.C.*
(1972) 70 L.G.R. 542.
s. 214, see *Lovelock* v. *Minister of Transport*
(1980) 40 P. & C.R. 336, C.A.
s. 286, instruments 75/216; 80/359, 1006.
s. 295, see *Rider* v. *Rider* [1973] 2 W.L.R. 190,
C.A.; *Haydon* v. *Kent County Council* [1978]
2 W.L.R. 485, C.A.; *Allison* v. *Corby District
Council* [1980] R.T.R. 111, Peter Pain J.
s. 312, orders 72/595; 74/645; 77/502; 80/457.
sch. 1, see *Shorman* v. *Secretary of State for
the Environment* [1977] J.P.L. 98; *Lovelock* v.
Secretary of State for Transport [1979] R.T.R.
250, C.A.
sch. 2, see *R.* v. *Secretary of State for the
Environment, ex p. Ostler* [1976] 3 W.L.R.
288, C.A.; *Bushell* v. *Secretary of State for
the Environment, The Times,* February 12,
1980, H.L.
sch. 14, orders 72/601; 73/230.
**26. Terms and Conditions of Employment Act
1959.**
repealed: 1975, c.71, sch.18.
**27. Sea Fisheries (Compensation) (Scotland) Act
1959.**
repealed: 1984, c.26, sch.2.
**28. Income Tax (Repayment of Post-War Credits)
Act 1959.**
ss. 1, 3, 5, regs. 72/374.
ss. 1, 5, regs. 72/1840.
30. National Assistance (Amendment) Act 1959.
s. 1, amended (S.): 1972, c.58, sch.6; 1978,
c.29, sch.15.
32. Eisteddfod Act 1959.
s. 2, repealed: S.L.R. 1975.
33. House Purchase and Housing Act 1959.
repealed: 1985, c.71, sch.1; 1987, c.26, sch.24
(S.).
s. 1, see *R.* v. *Chief Registrar of Friendly Societies, ex p. New Cross Building Society* [1984]
2 All E.R. 370, C.A.
s. 1, regs. 72/1577; 82/36; 83/1766; 84/8.
s. 1, repealed (S.): 1985, c.71, sch.1.
ss. 3, 31, repealed in pt. (S.): 1980, c.52, sch.5.
34. Housing (Underground Rooms) Act 1959.
repealed: 1985, c.71, sch.1.

7 & 8 Eliz. 2 (1958–59)—cont.

37. Restriction of Offensive Weapons Act 1959.
see *Tudhope* v. *O'Neill*, 1982 S.L.T. 360.
s. 1, see *Gibson* v. *Wales* [1983] Crim.L.R. 113, D.C.; *R.* v. *Simpson (Calvin)* [1983] 3 All E.R. 789, C.A.
s. 1, amended: 1988, c.33, s.46.
39. Supreme Court of Judicature (Amendment) Act 1959.
repealed: 1981, c.54, sch.7.
40. Deer (Scotland) Act 1959.
s. 1, amended: 1973, c.54, sch.1; 1982, c.19, s.1.
s. 2, amended: *ibid.*, s.2.
s. 3, amended: *ibid.*, s.1.
s. 4, amended: *ibid.*, ss.1, 2; repealed in pt.: *ibid.*, s.1, sch.3.
s. 5, amended: *ibid.*, s.1, sch.1.
s. 6, amended: *ibid.*, s.3.
s. 6A, added: *ibid.*, s.4.
ss. 7, 8, amended: *ibid.*, s.1.
s. 9, amended: *ibid.*, sch.1.
s. 11, amended: *ibid.*, s.1.
s. 12, amended: *ibid.*; repealed in pt.: *ibid.*, sch.3.
ss. 14, 15, amended: *ibid.*, s.1.
s. 17, amended: *ibid.*, sch.1.
ss. 19, 20, amended: *ibid.*, s.1.
s. 21, amended: *ibid.*, ss.6, 7, sch.1.
s. 22, amended: *ibid.*, s.6, sch.1.
ss. 22–25, see *Miln* v. *Maher*, 1979 S.L.T.(Notes) 10.
s. 23, amended: 1982, c.19, ss.6, 8, 9, sch.1; repealed in pt.: *ibid.*, s.14, sch.3.
s. 23A, order 85/1168.
s. 23A, added: 1982, c.19, s.10.
s. 24, amended: *ibid.*, s.10, sch.1; repealed in pt.: *ibid.*, schs.1,3.
s. 25A, order 84/922.
ss. 25A–25F added: 1982, c.19, s.11.
s. 25B, order 84/899.
s. 26, amended: 1982, c.19, sch.1.
s. 27, amended: *ibid.*, s.14, sch.2.
s. 28A, added: *ibid.*, sch.2.
s. 29, repealed: *ibid.*, sch.3.
s. 33, amended: *ibid.*, ss.12,13.
s. 35, amended: *ibid.*, sch.2.
s. 36, repealed: S.L.R. 1974.
s. 37, repealed in pt.: 1975, c.24, sch.3.
sch. 1, amended: 1982, c.19, s.5.; repealed in pt.: 1975, c.24, sch.3.
sch. 2, amended: 1973, c.65, sch.27.
sch. 3, repealed: S.L.R. 1974.
42. Solicitors (Amendment) Act 1959.
repealed: 1974, c.26, sch.3.
44. Fire Services Act 1959.
ss. 1, 5 (in part), 6 (in part), repealed: S.L.R. 1974.
s. 7, amended: 1973, c.65, s.147, sch.29.
s. 14, (in part), sch., repealed: S.L.R. 1974.
45. Metropolitan Magistrates' Courts Act 1959.
s. 2, repealed: 1979, c.55, sch.3.
s. 3, amended: 1973, c.62, sch.5.
sch., repealed: S.L.R. 1974.
48. Cotton Industry Act 1959.
repealed: S.L.R. 1977.

7 & 8 Eliz. 2 (1958–59)—cont.

49. Chevening Estate Act 1959.
s. 2, amended: 1987, c.20, s.4.
sch. amended: 1986, c.5, sch.14.
51. Licensing (Scotland) Act 1959.
repealed: 1976, c.66, sch.8.
s. 31, order 75/495.
ss. 78, 80, amended: 1977, c.16, s.6.
s. 121, see *Colthard* v. *Reeves*, 1973 S.L.T.(Notes) 34.
s. 130, order 76/637.
s. 171, see *United Biscuits (Tollcross) Sports and Social Club, Applicants*, 1973 S.L.T.(Sh.Ct.) 25; *Three Steps Social Club* v. *Chief Constable of Strathclyde*, 1977 S.L.T.(Sh.Ct.) 18; *Chief Constable of Strathclyde* v. *Hamilton and District Bookmakers Club*, 1977 S.L.T.(Sh.Ct.) 78.
s. 172, see *Chief Constable of Strathclyde* v. *Hamilton and District Bookmakers Club*, 1977 S.L.T.(Sh.Ct.) 78.
s. 173, see *Hibernian Club*, 1972 S.L.T.(Sh.Ct.) 38.
s. 174, see *Lodge Regal*, 1972 S.L.T.(Sh.Ct.) 61; *Ashton Dance Club* v. *Chief Constable of Strathclyde*, 1977 S.L.T.(Sh.Ct.) 43.
s. 182, see *Chief Constable of Strathclyde* v. *Hamilton and District Bookmakers Club*, 1977 S.L.T.(Sh.Ct.) 78.
53. Town and Country Planning Act 1959.
s. 22, repealed in pt.: 1985, c.12, sch.2.
s. 23, see *Dowty* v. *Wolverhampton Corporation* [1973] 2 W.L.R. 618, C.A.
s. 23, amended: 1980, c.65, sch.23; repealed in pt.: *ibid.*, schs.23, 34.
ss. 26, 29, see *R.* v. *Plymouth City Council and Cornwall County Council, ex p. Freeman* (1988) 28 R.V.R. 89, C.A.
s. 26, amended: 1980, c.65, sch.23; 1985, c.71, schs.1, 2; repealed in pt.: 1980, c.65, schs. 23, 24; 1985, c.71, schs. 1, 2.
s. 27, repealed in pt.: S.L.R. 1976.
s. 28, repealed: 1972, c.70, sch.30.
s. 29, amended: 1972, c.70, s.128.
s. 30, repealed in pt.: 1980, c.65, schs.23,34.
s. 34, repealed: S.L.R. 1975.
ss. 48, 49, repealed: 1980, c.66, sch.25.
s. 57, amended: 1972, c.47, sch.11; repealed in pt.: S.L.R. 1975.
s. 58, repealed in pt.: *ibid.*; 1985, c.71, sch.1.
sch. 7, repealed in pt.: *ibid.*
54. Weeds Act 1959.
s. 3, repealed in pt.: 1975, c.76, sch.2.
s. 5, amended: 1985, c.51, sch.8; repealed in pt.: 1972, c.70, sch.30.
s. 10 (in pt.), sch., repealed: S.L.R. 1974.
s. 11, amended: 1984, c.54, sch.9.
55. Dog Licences Act 1959.
repealed: 1988, c.9, s.38, sch.7.
56. Rights of Light Act 1959.
s. 1, repealed: S.L.R. 1974.
s. 2, amended: 1975, c.76, sch.1.
s. 5, amended: *ibid.*, repealed in pt.: *ibid.*, sch.2.
s. 6, repealed: 1973, c.36, sch.6.
s. 7, amended: 1975, c.76, sch.1.
s. 8, repealed in pt.: 1973, c.36, sch.6.

CAP.

7 & 8 Eliz. 2 (1958–59)—cont.

57. Street Offences Act 1959.

s. 1, see *Knight* v. *Fryer* [1976] Crim.L.R. 322, D.C.; *Behrendt* v. *Burridge* [1976] 3 All E.R. 285, D.C.

s. 1, amended; 1977, c.45, s.31, sch.6; 1982, c.48, s.71.

s. 1, 2, see *Collins* v. *Wilcock* [1984] 1 W.L.R. 1172, D.C.

s. 2, amended: 1980, c.43, sch.7.

s. 5 (in pt.), sch., repealed: S.L.R. 1974.

58. Finance Act 1959.

ss. 2, 3, repealed in pt.: 1979, c.4, sch.4.

s. 9, repealed: 1977, c.36, sch.9.

s. 30, repealed in pt.: S.L.R. 1976.

s. 32, repealed: *ibid.*

ss. 34, 35, repealed: 1975, c.7, sch.13.

s. 37, repealed in pt.: 1979, c.2, sch.6.

sch. 2, see *Ye Old Cheshire Cheese* v. *Daily Telegraph, The Independent,* May 19, 1988, Browne-Wilkinson V.-C.

60. Education Act 1959.

s. 1, repealed in pt.: 1980, c.20, sch.1.

62. New Towns Act 1959.

repealed: 1981, c.64, sch.13.

65. Fatal Accidents Act 1959.

see *Dodds* v. *Dodds, The Times,* July 29, 1977, Balcombe J.; *Cookson* v. *Knowles* [1978] 2 W.L.R. 978, H.L.

s. 1, repealed in pt.: 1975, c.72, sch.4; 1976, c.30, sch.2; 1977, c.45, s.53, sch.13; 1978, c.47, sch.2.

s. 2, repealed: 1976, c.30, sch.2.

s. 3, repealed in pt.: S.L.R. 1974; S.L.R. 1976, sch., repealed: S.L.R. 1974.

66. Obscene Publications Act 1959.

s. 1, see *D.P.P.* v *Whyte* [1972] A.C. 849; [1972] 3 W.L.R. 410; [1972] 3 All E.R. 12; *R.* v. *Wells Street Stipendiary Magistrates, ex p. Golding* [1979] Crim.L.R. 254, D.C.; *Re Att.-Gen.'s Ref. (No. 5 of 1980), The Times,* September 2, 1980, C.A.

s. 1, repealed in pt.: 1977, c.45, s.53, sch.13.

ss. 1, 2, see *Att.-Gen.'s Reference (No. 2 of 1975)* [1976] 1 W.L.R. 710; [1976] 2 All E.R. 753, C.A.

ss. 1–3, see *R.* v. *Commissioner of Metropolitan Police* [1973] 2 W.L.R. 43; [1973] 1 All E.R. 324, C.A.

ss. 1, 2, 4, see *R.* v. *Anderson; Neville; Dennis; R.* v. *Oz Publications Ink* [1971] 3 W.L.R. 939; [1971] 3 All E.R. 1152; 56 Cr.App.R. 115.

ss. 1, 3, see *Gold Star Publications* v. *Metropolitan Police Comr.* (1980) 71 Cr.App.R. 185, D.C.

ss. 1, 4, see *R.* v. *Bow Street Magistrates' Court, ex p. Noncyp, The Times,* May 14, 1988, D.C.

s. 2, see *D.P.P.* v. *Jordan* [1976] 3 W.L.R. 887; [1976] 3 All E.R. 775, H.L.; *R.* v. *Sumner* [1977] Crim.L.R. 362, Liverpool Crown Ct.; *R.* v. *Bristol Crown Court, ex p. Willets, The Times,* January 25, 1985, D.C.; *R.* v. *Skirving; R.* v. *Grossman (Beth)* [1985] 2 W.L.R. 1001, C.A.

CAP.

7 & 8 Eliz. 2 (1958–59)—cont.

66. Obscene Publications Act 1959—*cont.*

s. 2, amended: 1977, c.45, s.53; 1982, c.33, sch.1; 1985, c.13, sch.2; repealed in pt.: 1982, c.33, sch.13.

ss. 2, 3, see *R.* v. *Metropolitan Police Commissioner, ex p. Blackburn, The Times,* December 1, 1979, D.C.; *R.* v. *Adams* [1980] 1 All E.R. 473, C.A.; *Dunraven Securities* v. *Holloway* (1982) 264 E.G. 709, C.A.

s. 3, see *Roandale* v. *Metropolitan Police Commissioner,* December 15, 1978, Park J.; *Gold Star Publications* v. *D.P.P.* [1981] 1 W.L.R. 732; [1981] 2 All E.R. 257, H.L.; *R.* v. *Croydon Metropolitan Stipendiary Magistrate, ex p. Richman, The Times,* March 8, 1985, D.C.; *R.* v. *Snaresbrook Crown Court, ex p. Comr. of Police for the Metropolis* (1984) 79 Cr.App.R. 184, D.C.

s. 3, amended: 1977, c.45, s.53, sch.12; repealed in pt.: 1984, c.60, sch.7.

ss. 3, 4, see *Olympia Press* v. *Hollis* [1973] 1 W.L.R. 1520; [1974] 1 All E.R. 108, D.C.

s. 4, see *D.P.P.* v. *Jordan* [1976] 3 W.L.R. 887; [1976] 3 All E.R. 775, H.L.; *R.* v. *Sumner* [1977] Crim.L.R. 362, Liverpool Crown Ct.; *Att.-Gen.'s Reference (No. 3 of 1977), The Times,* July 14, 1978, C.A.

s. 4, amended: 1977, c.45, s.53.

68. Statute Law Revision Act 1959.

repealed: S.L.R. 1974.

69. Wages Councils Act 1959.

repealed: 1979, c.12, sch.7.

orders 73/39, 122, 146, 155–7, 175, 183, 184, 190, 191.

s. 4, orders 73/1780, 1781, 2062; 74/654, 843, 844, 1739; 75/41, 199, 646, 758, 1156; 76/756; 77/1688, 1689; 79/862, 863.

s. 11, orders 72/9, 16, 168, 264, 581, 680, 718, 782, 818, 819, 854, 869, 928, 943, 944, 1087, 1088, 1116, 1223, 1224, 1430, 1431, 1484, 1485, 1532, 1819, 1820, 1858, 1859; 73/218–21, 264, 311, 312, 342, 343, 953, 954, 1016, 1017, 1115, 1140, 1141, 1159, 1160, 1198, 1218, 1237, 1243, 1255, 1256, 1261, 1514, 1563, 1594, 1866, 1867, 1883, 1955, 2075, 2076, 2134, 2148, 2149, 2171; 74/11, 12, 41, 42, 45, 46, 139, 234, 261, 278, 305, 331, 332, 437, 438, 478, 537, 538, 574, 575, 631, 632, 655, 674, 675, 685, 686, 732, 743, 744, 754, 755, 770, 771, 810, 811, 834, 835, 853, 879, 880, 934, 999, 1009, 1010, 1042, 1068, 1096, 1162, 1216, 1278, 1297, 1355, 1411, 1479, 1480, 1493, 1494, 1558, 1559, 1567, 1586, 1612, 1613, 1618–1620, 1695–1698, 1718, 1769, 1825, 1874, 1875, 1904, 1916, 1927, 2021, 2022, 2134, 2175; 75/8, 9, 18, 19, 20, 42, 66, 67, 93, 94, 99, 100, 118, 165, 255, 256, 304–306, 323, 362, 363, 365, 490, 508, 509, 580, 581, 625, 626, 690, 691, 914, 934, 936, 946, 947, 964, 965, 992, 1047, 1048, 1116–1119, 1136, 1171, 1482, 1530, 1531, 1571, 1608, 1641, 1648, 1685, 1779, 1824, 1825, 1826, 1865, 1880, 1910, 2051, 2096, 2097, 2247, 2248.

CAP.

7 & 8 Eliz. 2 (1958–59)—cont.

69. Wages Councils Act 1959—cont.
s. 22, orders 75/2136–2138.
sch. 1, orders 74/654, 843, 844, 1739; 75/199,
646; 76/756; 77/1688, 1689; 79/862, 863.

70. Town and Country Planning (Scotland) Act 1959.
ss. 1–13, 17–22, repealed: 1972, c.52, sch.23.
s. 24, amended: 1981, c.23, schs.2,3.
s. 27, amended: 1972, c.52, sch.21; 1981, c.23,
schs.2,3; repealed in pt.: 1973, c.65, sch.23;
1981, c.23, schs.3,4.
s. 28, repealed: 1973, c.65, sch.29.
s. 29, repealed in pt.: *ibid.*
s. 30, repealed in pt.: 1981, c.23, sch.4.
ss. 31–37, repealed: 1972, c.52, sch.23.
s. 34, see *Church of Scotland General Trs.* v.
Helensburgh Town Council, 1973 S.L.T.
(Lands.Tr.) 21.
s. 38, see *Trustees of St. John's Church, Galashiels* v. *Borders Regional Council,* 1976
S.L.T.(Lands Tr.) 39.
s. 38, repealed: 1972, c.52, schs.22,23.
ss. 38, 39, see *Campbell (Malcolm)* v. *Glasgow
Corporation,* 1972 S.L.T. 8.
ss. 39–42, repealed: 1972, c.52, sch.23.
s. 41, see *Church of Scotland General Trs.* v.
Helensburgh Town Council, 1973
S.L.T.(Lands Tr.) 21.
s. 43, repealed: 1972, c.52, sch.23.
s. 47, repealed: 1984, c.54, sch.11.
ss. 49, 50 (in pt.), 51–53, repealed: 1972, c.52,
sch.23.
s. 54, repealed in pt.: 1972, c.46, sch.11; S.L.R.
1975.
s. 55, repealed in pt.: 1972, c.52, sch.23; S.L.R.
1975.
schs. 1–3, repealed: *ibid.*, sch.23.
sch. 4, amended: 1972, c.52, sch.21; 1973,
c.65, sch.23; 1980, c.45, sch.10; 1981, c.23,
sch.3.
schs. 5, 6, repealed: 1972, c.52, sch.23.
sch. 7, repealed in pt.: *ibid.*; S.L.R. 1975.
schs. 8, 9, repealed: 1972, c.52, sch.23.

71. Colonial Development and Welfare Act 1959.
repealed: S.L.R. 1976.

72. Mental Health Act 1959.
ss. 1–5, repealed: 1983, c.20, sch.6.
s. 4, see *W.* v. *L.* [1973] 3 W.L.R. 859; [1973] 3
All E.R. 884, C.A.
s. 8, amended: 1972, c.70, sch.23; 1977, c.49,
sch.15; 1980, c.7, sch.1; repealed in pt.:
1977, c.49, sch.16.
s. 9, amended: 1972, c.70, sch.23; 1977, c.49,
sch.15; 1980, c.5, sch.5; 1983, c.41, sch.2.
s. 10, repealed: 1983, c.20, sch.6.
ss. 14–18, repealed: 1975, c.37, sch.3.
ss. 19–21, repealed: 1980, c.7, sch.2.
s. 22, repealed: 1983, c.20, sch.6.
s. 23, repealed in pt.: 1975, c.37, sch.3; 1980,
c.7, sch.2.
ss. 25–35, repealed: 1983, c.20, sch.6.
s. 26, see *Re Mental Health Act* [1972] 3 W.L.R.
669.
ss. 26, 27, see *W.* v. *L.* [1973] 3 W.L.R. 859;
[1973] 3 All E.R. 884, C.A.

CAP.

7 & 8 Eliz. 2 (1958–59)—cont.

72. Mental Health Act 1959—cont.
s. 36, repealed: 1982, c.51, sch.4.
ss. 37–43, repealed: 1983, c.20, sch.6.
s. 44, repealed: 1982, c.51, sch.4.
ss. 45–59, repealed: 1983, c.20, sch.6.
s. 52, see *W.* v. *L.* [1973] 3 W.L.R. 859; [1973]
3 All E.R. 884, C.A.; *B.* v. *B. (Mental Health
Patient)* [1979] 3 All E.R. 494, C.A.
s. 60, see *R.* v. *Lincoln (Kesteven) JJ., ex p.
O'Connor* [1983] 1 W.L.R. 335, D.C.; *R.* v.
Harding (Bernard), The Times, June 15, 1983,
C.A.; *R.* v. *Ramsgate JJ., ex p. Kazmarek,
The Times,* May 15, 1984, D.C.; *R.* v. *Nordon,
The Times,* November 29, 1984, C.A.
s. 60, repealed: 1983, c.20, sch.6.
ss. 60, 65, see *R.* v. *Toland* (1973) 58 Cr.App.R.
453, C.A.; *R.* v. *Blackwood* (1974) 59
Cr.App.R. 170, C.A.; *R.* v. *McFarlane* (1975)
60 Cr.App.R. 320, C.A.; *Kynaston* v. *Secretary
of State for Home Affairs, The Times,* February 19, 1981, C.A.
ss. 62–68, repealed: 1983, c.20, sch.6.
s. 66, see *X.* v. *United Kingdom,* November 5,
1981, European Court of Human Rights.
ss. 70–76, repealed: 1983, c.20, sch.6.
s. 72, see *R.* v. *Nordon, The Times,* November
29, 1984, C.A.
ss. 77, 78, repealed: 1982, c.51, sch.4.
s. 80, see *R.* v. *Astill,* Jan. 20, 1977.
ss. 80, 81, 85, 87, 89, 90, 92–96, repealed:
1983, c.20, sch.6.
s. 90, see *R.* v. *Secretary of State for the Home
Department, ex p. Alghali, The Times,* July
22, 1986, D.C.
ss. 97, 98, repealed: 1973, c.32, sch.5.
ss. 99–119, repealed: 1983, c.20, sch.6.
ss. 100, 102, 103, see *Re D, (J.)* [1982] 2 W.L.R.
373, Sir Robert Megarry V.-C.
ss. 101, 103, see *Re S.* [1973] 1 W.L.R. 178.
s. 103, see *Re C. W. H. T.* [1977] 3 W.L.R. 880,
Fox J.
ss. 103, 103A, see *Re Davey (decd.)* [1980] 3
All E.R. 342, Fox J.
s. 105, see *Re N., decd.* [1977] 1 W.L.R. 676,
C.A.
ss. 105, 109, see *Re W.* (1972) 116 S.J. 218.
ss. 112, 114, rules 73/791; 75/1253; 80/1164;
82/322.
s. 113, rules 82/322.
ss. 121–126, repealed: 1983, c.20, sch.6.
s. 123, see *Re Mental Health Act* [1972] 3
W.L.R. 669.
s. 124, rules 76/447.
s. 126, see *R.* v. *Holmes* [1979] Crim.L.R. 52,
Bodmin Crown Ct.; *R.* v. *Spencer, The Times,*
November 8, 1984, C.A.
s. 127, repealed in pt.: 1973, c.29, sch.3.
s. 128, amended: 1977, c.49, sch.15; 1980, c.7,
sch.1; 1983, c.20, sch.4; c.41, sch.9; 1984,
c.23, sch.1; repealed in pt.: 1977, c.49,
sch.16.
ss. 129, 130, repealed: 1983, c.20, sch.6.
s. 131, amended: 1972, c.70, sch.23; repealed
in pt.: 1982, c.51, sch.4.
ss. 132, 133, repealed: 1983, c.20, sch.6.

CAP.

7 & 8 Eliz. 2 (1958–59)—cont.

72. Mental Health Act 1959—cont.
s. 134, repealed: 1982, c.51, sch.4.
ss. 135–141, repealed: 1983, c.20, sch.6.
ss. 136, 141, see Carter v. Commissioner of Police of the Metropolis [1975] 1 W.L.R. 507, C.A.
s. 141, see Pountney v. Griffiths [1975] 3 W.L.R. 410; [1975] 2 All E.R. 881, H.L.; R. v. Runighian [1977] Crim.L.R. 361, Warwick County Ct.; Kynaston v. Secretary of State for Home Affairs, The Times, February 19, 1981, C.A.
s. 142, amended: 1970, c.20, sch.23; 1977, c.49, sch.15.
s. 144, repealed in pt.: 1982, c.51, s.60; 1983, c.20, sch.6.
s. 145, repealed in pt.: ibid.
s. 146, repealed: 1982, c.51, s.64, sch.4.
s. 147, amended: 1972, c.70, sch.23; 1973, c.32, sch.4; 1975, c.37, sch.1; 1977, c.49, schs.14,15; 1980, c.53, sch.1; 1982, c.51, s.63, sch.3; 1983, c.54, sch.5; repealed in pt.: 1982, c.51, sch.4; 1983, c.20, sch.6.
s. 148, repealed: 1983, c.20, sch.6.
s. 149, amended: S.L.R. 1974; repealed in pt.: 1983, c.20, sch.6.
s. 150, repealed in pt.: 1975, c.24, sch.3; 1983, c.20, sch.6.
s. 151, repealed: 1973, c.36, sch.6.
s. 152, repealed in pt.: ibid.; 1975, c.24, sch.3; 1982, c.51, sch.4; 1983, c.20, sch.6.
s. 153, repealed: ibid.
s. 154, amended: 1977, c.49, sch.15.
schs. 1, 3, 5, repealed: 1983, c.20, sch.6.
sch. 6, amended: 1982, c.51, sch.3; repealed in pt.: 1983, c.20, sch.6.
sch. 7, repealed in pt.: 1972, c.11, sch.8; c.66, sch.2; 1973, c.14, sch.2; c.62, sch.6; 1974, c.26, sch.3, 1975, c.37, sch.3; c.72, sch.4; S.L.R. 1975; S.L.R. 1976; S.L.R. 1977; 1977, c.49, sch.16; 1979, c.36, sch.8; 1980, c.6, sch.3; c.7, sch.2; c.43, sch.9; c.58, sch.4; 1981, c.20, sch.4; c.45, sch.; c.54, sch.7; 1982, c.51, sch.4; 1983, c.20, sch.6.
sch. 8, repealed: S.L.R. 1974.
73. Legitimacy Act 1959.
repealed: 1987, c.42, sch.4.
s. 2, see Dunbar of Kilconzie, Petr., 1986 S.L.T. 463, H.L.

8 & 9 Eliz. 2 (1959–60)

1. Mr. Speaker Morrison's Retirement Act 1959.
repealed: S.L.R. 1986.
3. Marshall Scholarships Act 1959.
s. 1, order 72/961.
6. Commonwealth Scholarships Act 1959.
amended: 1974, c.21, sch.1.
8. Lord High Commission (Church of Scotland) Act 1959.
repealed: 1974, c.19, s.3.
9. Judicial Pensions Act 1959.
s. 1, repealed: 1981, c.20, sch.4.
s. 2, repealed in pt.: 1973, c.15, sch.5; 1981, c.20, sch.4.
ss. 3 (in pt.), 4, 6, 8–11, repealed: ibid.

CAP.

8 & 9 Eliz. 2 (1959–60)—cont.

9. Judicial Pensions Act 1959—cont.
sch. 1, repealed in pt.: 1973, c.15, schs.4, 5; 1981, c.20, sch.4; c.54, sch.7.
sch. 2, repealed: 1981, c.20, sch.4.
sch. 3, repealed: S.L.R. 1974.
15. Water Officers Compensation Act 1960.
s. 1, regs. 75/734; 83/264 (S.).
s. 1, amended (S.): 1980, c.45, sch.10.
16. Road Traffic Act 1960.
Pts. I, II (ss. 1–116), repealed: 1972, c.20, sch.9.
s. 1, see R. v. Thorpe [1972] 1 W.L.R. 342; [1972] 1 All E.R. 929; [1972] R.T.R. 118; (1972) 56 Cr.App.R. 293; R. v. Dutton [1972] Crim.L.R. 321; [1972] R.T.R. 186; Bensley v. Smith [1972] R.T.R. 221; R. v. Guilfoyle [1973] R.T.R. 272; [1973] 2 All E.R. 844.
ss. 1, 6, see R. v. Kashyap [1972] R.T.R. 78; [1972] Crim.L.R. 257.
s. 2, see Trentham v. Rowlands [1974] R.T.R. 164, D.C.
s. 3, see Butty v. Davey [1972] R.T.R. 75; Squires v. Botwright [1972] R.T.R. 462, D.C.; Cheyne v. Macneill, High Court of Justiciary, July 5, 1972; Bensley v. Smith [1972] R.T.R. 221.
ss. 3, 6, see Seaton v. Allan, 1974 S.L.T. 234.
s. 4, amended: 1980, c.34, s.42.
s. 5, see R. v. Sibthorpe (John Raymond) (1973) 57 Cr.App.R. 447, C.A.
s. 6, see Norman v. Magill [1972] R.T.R. 81; Reynolds v. Roche [1972] R.T.R. 282; R. v. Lawrence (Paul Antony) [1973] 1 W.L.R. 329; [1973] 1 All E.R. 364, C.A.; Wimperis v. Griffin [1973] Crim.L.R. 533, D.C.; R. v. Mayne [1973] R.T.R. 448, C.A.
s. 7, amended: 1980, c.34, s.42.
s. 12, regs. 72/336.
s. 14, see Walton v. Hawkins [1973] R.T.R. 366; [1973] Crim.L.R. 187, D.C.; Rumbles v. Poole [1980] R.T.R. 449, D.C.
ss. 14, 17–19, amended: 1980, c.34, s.42.
s. 20, see Roberts v. Warne; Davies v. Warne [1973] R.T.R. 217; Williams v. Jones [1975] R.T.R. 433, D.C.
ss. 22, 24–26, amended: 1980, c.34, s.42.
s. 64, see Goosey v. Adams [1971] R.T.R. 465; Renouf v. Franklin [1971] R.T.R. 469; Hill v. Hampshire Chief Constable [1972] R.T.R. 29; Crawford v. Haughton [1972] 1 W.L.R. 572; [1972] 1 All E.R. 534; [1972] R.T.R. 125; Baker v. Esau [1973] R.T.R. 49, D.C.; Garrett v. Hooper [1973] R.T.R. 1, D.C.; Drysdale v. Harrison [1973] R.T.R. 45, D.C.; Kenyon v. Thorley [1973] R.T.R. 60, D.C.; Reeve v. Webb [1973] R.T.R. 130, D.C.; Ashmore, Benson Pease & Co. v. A. V. Dawson [1973] 1 W.L.R. 828, [1973] 2 All E.R. 856; Borthwick v. Vickers [1973] R.T.R. 390; [1973] Crim.L.R. 317, D.C.; Stowers v. Darnell [1973] R.T.R. 459, D.C.; Wurzel v. Reade Bros. [1974] R.T.R. 283, D.C.
s. 64, regs. 72/751, 805, 842, 843, 987.
s. 65, see Artingstoll v. Hewen's Garages [1973] R.T.R. 197.
s. 65, regs. 72/898.

8 & 9 Eliz. 2 (1959–60)—cont.

16. Road Traffic Act 1960—*cont.*

s. 66, see *Gosling* v. *Howard* [1975] R.T.R. 429, D.C.

s. 68, see *British Car Auctions* v. *Wright* [1972] 1 W.L.R. 1519; [1972] 3 All E.R. 462.

s. 74, see *Andrews* v. *Watts* [1971] R.T.R. 484; *Powell* v. *Phillips* [1972] 3 All E.R. 864.

s. 77, see *Campbell* v. *Copeland*, 1972 S.C.(J.) 24.

s. 97, see *Kinsey* v. *Herts C.C.* [1972] R.T.R. 498, D.C.

ss. 100, 103, see *Guest* v. *Kingsnorth* [1972] Crim.L.R. 243; [1972] R.T.R. 265.

s. 104, see *McPherson* v. *Henderson*, 1984 S.C.C.R. 294.

s. 110, see *R.* v. *Bowsher* [1973] R.T.R. 202, C.A.

ss. 114, 117, see *Traffic Commissioners for the South Wales Traffic Area* v. *Snape* [1977] R.T.R. 367, D.C.

s. 117, regs. 77/1496.

ss. 117, 118, see *Middlemass* v. *McAleer* [1979] R.T.R. 245, D.C.

Pt. III (ss. 117–163), repealed: 1981, c.14, sch.8.

ss. 117, 127, see *Westacott* v. *Centaur Overland Travel* [1981] R.T.R. 182, D.C.

s. 121, regs. 80/916.

s. 127, see *Robinson* v. *Secretary of State for the Environment* [1973] 1 W.L.R. 1139; [1973] 3 All E.R. 1045, D.C.; *Vickers* v. *Bowman* [1976] Crim.L.R. 77; [1976] R.T.R. 165, D.C.

ss. 127, 129, see *Middlemass* v. *McAleer* [1979] R.T.R. 245, D.C.

s. 129, regs. 72/751; 76/726; 80/141, 1097.

s. 130, regs. 80/635; 81/257.

ss. 134, 135, 143, see *R.* v. *Traffic Commissioners for the N.W. Traffic Area, ex p. B.R. Board* [1977] R.T.R. 179, D.C.

s. 139A, regs. 78/1315.

s. 144, see *Westacott* v. *Centaur Overland Travel* [1981] R.T.R. 182, D.C.

s. 146, see *Edwards* v. *Rigby* [1980] R.T.R. 353, D.C.; *Steff* v. *Beck* [1987] R.T.R. 61, D.C.

ss. 146, 147, regs. 75/461.

s. 148, regs. 80/76; 81/260.

s.ˉ158, regs. 72/1061; 78/1315; 80/635, 1354; 81/258.

s. 159, regs. 76/1113, 1114; 78/1315; 80/634, 635, 1354; 81/257, 258, 264, 265, 462.

s. 160, regs. 72/341, 461, 751, 1061; 73/806; 76/726, 1113, 1114; 77/1496; 78/1313, 1315, 1684; 79/654; 80/76, 141, 144, 634, 635, 914–916, 1097, 1313, 1354, 1459, 1460; 81/257–260, 262–265, 269, 461, 462, 886.

ss. 183–185, 187, 189–191, Pts. V, VI (ss.192–216), repealed: 1972, c.20, sch.9.

s. 195, see *Crawford* v. *Scottish Traffic Area Licensing Authority*, 1974 S.L.T.(Sh.Ct.) 11.

s. 198, see *Metropolitan Traffic Area Licensing Authority* v. *Blackman* [1973] R.T.R. 525, D.C.

s. 201, see *Sheldon* v. *Willis* [1972] R.T.R. 217; *Leathley* v. *Drummond* [1972] Crim.L.R. 227; [1972] R.T.R. 293; *Nichol* v. *Leach* [1972] R.T.R. 416, D.C.; *Cobb* v. *Williams* [1973] R.T.R. 113, D.C.; *Gosling* v. *Howard* [1975] R.T.R. 429, D.C.

8 & 9 Eliz. 2 (1959–60)—cont.

16. Road Traffic Act 1960—*cont.*

ss. 201, 203, see *Bridgeford* v. *Weston* [1975] R.T.R. 189.

s. 205, see *Moore* v. *Crowe* [1972] 2 Lloyd's Rep. 563.

s. 214, amended: 1972, c.58, sch.6.

ss. 217–221, 223–231, repealed: 1972, c.20, sch.9.

s. 220, see *Allison* v. *Corby District Council* [1980] R.T.R. 111, Peter Pain J.

s. 224, see *Wurzal* v. *Reader Bros.* [1973] Crim.L.R. 640; [1974] R.T.R. 283, D.C.

s. 228, see *Squires* v. *Botwright* [1972] R.T.R. 462, D.C.

s. 232, amended: regs. 77/1462; 1980, c.34, s.42; repealed in pt.: 1972, c.20, sch. 9; 1980, c.34, sch.9; 1981, c.14, sch.8.

s. 233, amended: 1974, c.50, sch.5; regs. 77/1461, 1462; 1980, c.34, sch.5; 1981, c.45, s.12; regs. 84/176; 1988, c.54, sch.3; repealed in pt.: 1972, c.20, sch.9.

s. 234, repealed: 1980, c.34, sch.9.

s. 235, amended: 1974, c.50, sch.5; regs. 77/1461, 1462; 1980, c.34, schs.4,5; regs. 84/176; repealed in pt.: 1972, c.20, sch.9.

ss. 236–238, repealed: 1972, c.20, sch.9.

s. 239, repealed: 1981, c.14, sch.8.

s. 240, repealed: 1980, c.34, sch.9.

s. 241, see *Phipps* v. *McCormick* [1972] R.T.R. 21; *Nicholson* v. *Tapp* [1972] 1 W.L.R. 1044; [1972] 3 All E.R. 245; [1972] R.T.R. 313.

s. 241, repealed: 1972, c.20, sch.9.

s. 244, amended: regs. 77/1461; 1988, c.54, sch.3; repealed in pt.: 1972, c.20, sch.9.

s. 246, repealed: 1980, c.62, sch.8.

s. 247, amended: 1972, c.20, sch.7; 1988, c.54, sch.3; repealed in pt.: 1972, c.20, sch.9; c.71, sch.6; 1980, c.34, sch.9; 1981, c.45, s.2.

s. 248, repealed: *ibid.*, sch.5; repealed in pt.: 1984, c.32, sch.7.

s. 249, amended: 1981, c.45, sch.4.

s. 250, repealed: 1972, c.20, sch.9.

s. 252, repealed: 1981, c.14, sch.8.

s. 253, see *Nichol* v. *Leach* [1972] R.T.R. 416, D.C.

s. 253, regs. 81/1373; amended: regs. 81/1374; 1984, c.27, sch.13.

ss. 254, 255 (in pt.), repealed: 1972, c.20, sch.9.

s. 257, see *Cheyne* v. *MacNeill*, High Court of Justiciary, July 5, 1972; *Borthwick* v. *Vickers* [1973] R.T.R. 390; [1973] Crim.L.R. 317, D.C.

s. 257, amended: 1973, c.65, sch.14; 1980, c.34, sch.5; c.43, sch.7; 1984, c.54, sch.9 (S.); repealed in pt.: 1972, c.20, sch.9; 1980, c.34, sch.9; 1981, c.14, sch.8.

s. 258, repealed: *ibid.*

s. 259, repealed: 1972, c.20, sch.9.

s. 260, regs. 76/1113; 77/1496; 78/1313, 1684; 80/76, 141, 914–916; 81/259, 260, 262–265, 269, 461, 462, 886, 1373.

s. 260, repealed: 1981, c.14, sch.8.

ss. 261, 262, repealed: 1972, c.20, sch.9.

s. 263, repealed in pt.: *ibid.*; 1981, c.14, sch.8.

s. 265, repealed in pt.: *ibid.*

s. 267, repealed in pt.: S.L.R. 1974.

CAP.

8 & 9 Eliz. 2 (1959–60)—cont.

16. Road Traffic Act 1960—cont.
schs. 8, 9, repealed: 1972, c.20, sch.9.
sch. 12, repealed: 1980, c.34, s.1, sch.9.
sch. 15, see Metropolitan Traffic Area Licensing Authority v. Blackman [1973] R.T.R. 525, D.C.; Crawford v. Scottish Traffic Area Licensing Authority, 1974 S.L.T.(Sh. Ct.) 11.
schs. 15, 16, repealed: 1972, c.20, sch.9.
sch. 17, repealed in pt.: 1972, c.20, sch.9; S.L.R. 1975; 1980, c.34, sch.9.
sch. 18, repealed; S.L.R. 1974.
sch. 19, repealed in pt.: 1972, c.20, sch.9.
sch. 20, repealed in pt.: S.L.R. 1975.

18. Local Employment Act 1960.
repealed: S.L.R. 1978.

19. European Free Trade Association Act 1960.
repealed: 1972, c.68, sch.3.

20. Requisitioned Houses Act 1960.
repealed: S.L.R. 1978.

21. Wages Arrestment Limitation (Amendment) (Scotland) Act 1960.
repealed: 1987, c.18, sch.8.

22. Horticulture Act 1960.
s. 1, amended: 1986, c.5, sch.14.
ss. 1, 2, 6, order 73/2206.
ss. 3 (in pt.), 8 (in pt.), 9–12, repealed: S.L.R. 1973.
s. 13, amended and repealed in pt.: ibid.
s. 14, amended: ibid.; 1985, c.9, sch.2; repealed in pt.: S.L.R. 1973.
s. 15, amended and repealed in pt.: ibid.
ss. 16, 17 (in pt.), 18 (in pt.), 19, schs. 1 (in pt.), 2, repealed: ibid.

23. First Offenders (Scotland) Act 1960.
repealed: 1975, c.21, sch.10.
s.1, see Binnie v. Farrell, 1972 S.L.T. 212.

24. Pawnbrokers Act 1960.
repealed: 1974, c.39, sch.5.

25. War Damage (Clearance Payments) Act 1960.
repealed: S.L.R. 1981.

27. Gas Act 1960.
repealed: 1972, c.60, sch.8.

28. Legal Aid Act 1960.
repealed: S.L.R. 1974.

29. Marriage (Enabling) Act 1960.
repealed (S.): 1977, c.15, sch.3.
s. 1 (in pt.), sch., repealed: S.L.R. 1974.

30. Occupier's Liability (Scotland) Act 1960.
s. 2, see Telfer v. Glasgow Corporation, 1974 S.L.T.(Notes) 51; McQueen v. Ballater Golf Club (O.H.), 1975 S.L.T.(Notes) 39; Davie v. Edinburgh Corporation (O.H.), 1977 S.L.T. (Notes) 5; Sibbald or Bermingham v. Sher Brothers (A Firm), The Times, February 1, 1980, H.L.; Pollock v. Stead & Simpson (O.H.), 1980 S.L.T.(Notes) 76; Poliskie v. Lane (O.H.) August 29, 1980; McGinlay or Titchener v. British Railways Board [1983] 1 W.L.R. 1427; 1984 S.L.T. 192, H.L.; Wallace v. City of Glasgow District Council, Second Division, May 11, 1984; Johnstone v. Sweeney, 1985 S.L.T.(Sh.Ct.) 2; Johnstone v. City of Glasgow District Council, First Division, March 29, 1985.

CAP.

8 & 9 Eliz. 2 (1959–60)—cont.

30. Occupiers Liability (Scotland) Act 1960—cont.
ss. 2, 3, see Murray v. Edinburgh District Council (O.H.), January 8, 1981; Hughes' Tutrix v. Glasgow District Council, 1982 S.L.T.(Sh.Ct.) 70.
s. 3, see Lamb v. Glasgow District Council (O.H.), 1978 S.L.T.(Notes) 64.

31. Highlands and Islands Shipping Services Act 1960.
s. 5, sch., amended: 1973, c.65, schs.19,29.

33. Indecency with Children Act 1960.
s. 1, see R. v. Speck [1977] 2 All E.R. 859, C.A.; R. v. Francis, The Times, April 26, 1988, C.A.
s. 1, repealed in pt.: 1984, c.60, sch.7.
s. 2, amended: 1985, c.44, s.5; repealed in pt.: ibid., sch.

34. Radioactive Substances Act 1960.
order 80/184.
s. 2, orders 74/487, 488, 500, 501; 80/1599(S.); 86/1002; regs. 80/953; S.Rs. 1980 No. 304; 1986 Nos. 10–12; orders 85/1047–1049.
s. 4, orders 80/1599(S.); 85/1049; S.R. 1986 No. 12.
s. 6, orders 74/487, 488, 500, 501; 80/1599(S.); 86/1002; regs. 80/953; S.R. 1980 No. 304; orders 85/1047–1049; S.Rs. 1986 Nos. 10–12.
s. 7, orders 74/487. 488, 500, 501; 80/1599(S.); 86/1002; S.R. 1980 No. 304; orders 85/1047–1049; S.Rs. 1986 Nos. 10–12.
s. 13, amended: 1974, c.40, schs.2,4; order 78/1049.
s. 14, amended: 1972, c.58, sch.6; 1973, c.32, sch.4; 1977, c.49, sch.14; 1978, c.29, sch.15 (S.); 1980, c.53, sch.1; repealed in pt.: 1973, c.32, sch.4,5.
s. 15, orders 74/487, 488; regs. 80/953.
s. 19, amended: order 85/1884; repealed in pt.: 1972, c.70, sch.30; 1985, c.51, sch.17.
s. 20, orders 74/487, 488; 85/1047–1049.
s. 20, amended: 1973, c.65, sch.27.
s. 21, S.Rs. 1980 No. 304; 1986 Nos. 10–12.
s. 21, repealed in pt.: 1973, c.36, sch.6.
sch. 1, amended: 1974, c.40, schs.2,4; orders 76/959; 84/863; 1980, c.45, sch.10(S.); 1984, c.55, sch.6; regs. 80/1709; 85/708; 1986, c.36, schs.7, 7(S.); repealed in pt.: regs. 79/654; 1984, c.26, sch.2.

35. International Development Association Act 1960.
repealed: 1980, c.63, sch.2.
s. 3, order 76/221.

36. Game Laws (Amendment) Act 1960.
s. 1, repealed: 1984, c.60, sch.7.
ss. 2, 4, amended: ibid., sch.6.

37. Payment of Wages Act 1960.
repealed: 1986, c.48, schs.1,5.
see Brooker v. Charrington Fuel Oils [1981] I.R.L.R. 147, Wandsworth County Ct.
ss. 1, 2, 7, amended: 1986, c.53, sch.18.

38. Civil Aviation (Licensing) Act 1960.
s. 5, repealed in pt.: 1982, c.1, sch.2; c.16, sch.16.
s. 6, amended: 1982, c.1, sch.1; repealed in pt.: 1982, c.16, sch.16.
ss. 7, 10, 12, repealed: ibid.

8 & 9 Eliz. 2 (1959–60)—cont.

39. Dock Workers (Pensions) Act 1960.
repealed: 1973, c.38, sch.28.

40. Commonwealth Teachers Act 1960.
repealed: 1980, c.63, sch.2.

41. Ghana (Consequential Provisions) Act 1960.
s. 2, repealed: S.L.R. 1977.

42. Merchant Shipping (Minicoy Lighthouse) Act 1960.
repealed: S.L.R. 1986.

44. Finance Act 1960.
s. 3, repealed: 1979, c.4, sch.4.
s. 7, repealed in pt.: 1975, c.45, sch.14; 1979, c.6, sch.
s. 10, repealed in pt.: 1979, c.3, sch.3.
s. 28, see *Marks* v. *I.R.C.* [1973] T.R. 185, C.A.; *Howard* v. *Borneman (No. 2)* [1975] 2 W.L.R. 971, H.L.; *Addy* v. *I.R.C.* [1975] S.T.C. 601; *Green* v. *I.R.C.* [1975] S.T.C. 633, C.A.; *I.R.C.* v. *Goodwin* [1976] 1 W.L.R. 191; [1976] 1 All E.R. 481, H.L.
s. 38, see *Basnett* v. *J. & A Jackson* [1976] I.C.R. 63.
ss. 47, 48, 56, see *I.R.C.* v. *Adams* (1971) 48 T.C. 67.
s. 51, see *Pearlberg* v. *Varty* [1972] 1 W.L.R. 534; [1972] 2 All E.R. 6; [1972] T.R. 5.
s. 58, see *R.* v. *Special Commissioners of Income Tax, ex p. Morey* (1972) 49 T.C. 71, C.A.
Pt. IV (ss. 64–66), repealed: 1975, c.7, sch.13.
s. 73, repealed: 1975, c.7, sch.13.
s. 74, amended: 1973, c.36, sch.6.
s. 79, repealed in pt.: 1975, c.7, sch.13; 1979, c.2, sch.6
sch. 1, repealed: 1979, c.4, sch.4.
sch 8, repealed: S.L.R. 1974.

46. Corporate Bodies' Contracts Act 1960.
s. 2, amended: 1985, c.9, sch.2.
s. 3, repealed: 1973, c.36, sch.6.
s. 4, repealed in pt.: *ibid.*; S.L.R. 1974.
sch. repealed: *ibid.*

48. Matrimonial Proceedings (Magistrates' Courts) Act 1960.
repealed: 1978, c.22, sch.3.
see *Gengler* v *Gengler* [1976] 1 W.L.R. 275, D.C.; *M.* v. *M.* [1977] Fam.Law 17, D.C.
s. 1, see *Brannan* v. *Brannan* [1973] 2 W.L.R. 7; [1973] 1 All E.R. 38, D.C.
s. 2, see *McEwan* v. *McEwan* [1972] 2 All E.R. 708; *Cann* v. *Cann* [1977] 1 W.L.R. 938, D.C.; *Khan* v. *Khan* [1980] 1 W.L.R. 355; [1980] 1 All E.R. 497, D.C.
ss. 2, 16, see *Snow* v. *Snow* [1971] 3 W.L.R 951.

49. Public Health (Laboratory Service) Act 1960.
repealed: 1977, c.49, sch.16.

51. Road Traffic (Amendment) Act 1960.
repealed: 1972, c.20, sch.9.

52. Cyprus Act 1960.
s. 3, sch., see *Franklin* v. *Att.-Gen.* [1973] 2 W.L.R. 255.
s. 4, regs. 80/358.
s. 4, repealed in pt.: 1981, c.61, sch.9.
s. 5, repealed: S.L.R. 1977.
s. 6, amended: 1981, c.61, sch.7.

8 & 9 Eliz. 2 (1959–60)—cont.

52. Cyprus Act 1960—cont.
sch. repealed in pt.: *ibid.*, sch.9; 1986, c.55, sch.2; 1987, c.16, sch.16; 1988, c.48, sch.8.

54. Clean Rivers (Estuaries and Tidal Waters) Act 1960.
repealed: 1974, c.40, sch.4.

55. Nigeria Independence Act 1960.
s. 2, repealed: 1981, c.61, sch.9.
s. 3, repealed in pt.: 1978, c.30, sch.3.
sch. 2, repealed in pt.: S.L.R. 1977; 1986, c.55, sch.2; 1988, c.48, sch.8.

56. Statute Law Revision Act 1960.
s. 1, repealed in pt.: S.L.R. 1974.
s. 2, repealed: 1973, c.36, sch.6.
sch. 1, repealed: S.L.R. 1974.

57. Films Act 1960.
repealed: 1985, c.21, s.1, sch.2.
s. 4, order 77/1306.
s. 7, order 81/1155.
ss. 13, 32, regs. 72/1925.
s. 19, orders 75/623, 1838; 83/610.
s. 44, regs. 72/1925, 1926; 74/2129–2132; 75/1656–1659; 76/1252–1255; 77/1666–1669; 78/1632; 80/1180, 1181, 1188, 1819; 82/372–374, 1021.

58. Charities Act 1960.
ss. 2, 3 (in pt.), 4 (in pt.), repealed: 1973, c.16, s.1, sch.2.
s. 4, see *I.R.C.* v. *Trustees of the Football Association Youth Trust* [1977] T.R. 189, Walton J.; *I.R.C.* v. *Sir Andrew Stephen, The Times,* October 19, 1978, C.A.; *I.R.C.* v. *McMullen* [1980] 2 W.L.R. 416; [1980] 1 All E.R. 884, H.L.; *I.R.C.* v. *White, Re Clerkenwell Green Association for Craftsmen* [1980] T.R. 155, Fox J.
ss. 4, 5, see *McGovern* v. *Att.-Gen.* [1981] 3 All E.R. 493, Slade J.
s. 5, see *Murawski's Will Trust, Re; Lloyds Bank* v. *R.S.P.C.A.* [1971] 1 W.L.R. 707; [1971] 2 All E.R. 328.
s. 6, repealed in pt.: 1972, c.70, sch.30.
ss. 6, 8, see *Jones* v. *Att.-Gen.* [1973] 3 W.L.R. 608; [1973] 3 All E.R. 518, C.A.
s. 8, regs. 76/929.
s. 8, amended: 1985, c.9, sch.2.
s. 9, amended: 1986, c.41, s.33.
s. 10, amended: 1972, c.70, s.210; repealed in pt.: *ibid.*, sch.30; 1973, c.16, s.1, sch.2.
ss. 11, 12, amended: 1972, c.70, s.210; repealed in pt.: *ibid.*, sch. 30.
s. 13, see *Re J. W. Laing Trust; Stewards' Co.* v. *Att.-Gen.* [1983] 3 W.L.R. 886, Peter Gibson J.
s. 18, see *Bateman,* 1972 S.L.T.(Notes) 78; *Childs* v. *Att.-Gen.* [1973] 1 W.L.R. 497; [1973] 2 All E.R. 108.
s. 18, repealed in pt.: 1972, c.70, s.210, sch.30; 1973, c.16, sch.2.
s. 19, orders 72/163; 73/169, 196; 74/690, 1839; 75/1155, 1304; 76/147, 1809; 77/223, 456, 2104, 2105; 78/1155; 79/284; 80/1790; 82/1326; 83/175, 588, 910; 85/1935; 86/2003; 88/1068.
ss. 19, 20, repealed in pt.: 1973, c.16, sch.2.

CAP.

8 & 9 Eliz. 2 (1959–60)—cont.

58. Charities Act 1960—cont.

s. 20, see Jones v. Att.-Gen. [1973] 3 W.L.R. 608; [1973] 3 All E.R. 518, C.A.

s. 22, amended: 1986, c.60, sch.16; repealed in pt.: 1973, c.16, sch.2; 1986, c.60, schs.16,17.

ss. 23, 28, see Bateman, 1972 S.L.T.(Notes) 78.

s. 28, see Hauxwell v. Barton-upon-Humber U.D.C. [1973] 3 W.L.R. 41; Brooks v. Richardson [1986] 1 W.L.R. 385, Warner J.; Bradshaw v. University College of Wales, Aberystwyth [1987] 3 All E.R. 200, Hoffmann J.; Hampton Fuel Allotment Charity, Re; Richmond-upon-Thames London Borough Council v. Rogers [1988] 2 All E.R. 761, C.A.

ss. 28, 29, see Haslemere Estates v. Baker [1982] 1 W.L.R. 1109, Megarry V.-C.

s. 29, see Michael Richards Properties v. Corporation of Warders of St. Saviour's Parish, Southwark [1975] 3 All E.R. 416.

s. 29, regs. 78/1386.

s. 29, amended: 1974, c.44, s.2.

s. 30, amended: 1985, c.9, sch.2; 1986, c.45, sch.14.

s. 32, repealed in pt.: 1972, c.70, sch.30.

s. 37, amended: ibid., s.210; 1988, c.40, sch.12; repealed in pt.: 1972, c.70, s.210, sch.30.

s. 38, repealed in pt.: 1973, c.16, sch.1; c.36, sch.6.

s. 39, repealed in pt.: ibid.

s. 42, repealed in pt.: 1977, c.38, sch.5.

s. 43, amended: 1973, c.16, s.1, sch.1.

ss. 43, 45, regs. 76/929; 78/1386.

s. 44, repealed in pt.: 1972, c.11, sch.8; c.70, sch.30; 1973, c.16, s.1, sch.2.

s. 45, see Construction Training Board v. Att.-Gen. [1972] 3 W.L.R. 187; [1972] 2 All E.R. 1339; I.R.C. v. White, Re Clerkenwell Green Association for Craftsmen [1980] T.R. 155, Fox J.

s. 47, repealed: 1973, c.36, sch.6.

s. 48, repealed in pt.: 1973, c.16, s.1, sch.2.

s. 49, repealed in pt.: ibid.; c.36, sch.6; 1975, c.24, sch.3; S.L.R. 1978.

sch. 1, repealed in pt.: 1973, c.16, s.1, sch.2.

sch. 2, orders 78/453; 83/1516; 84/1976; 87/1823.

sch. 2, amended: 1972, c.54, s.4; 1983, c.47, sch.5; 86/453.

sch. 3, amended: 1972, c.70, s.210.

sch. 4, amended: 1973, c.16, s.2.

sch. 5, repealed: ibid., s.1, sch.2.

sch. 6, repealed in pt.: 1973, c.16, s.1, sch.2; 1977, c.38, sch.5; S.L.R. 1986.

sch. 7, repealed: 1973, c.16, s.1, sch.2.

59. Adoption Act 1960.

repealed: 1976, c.36, sch.4; 1978, c.28, sch.4(S.).

61. Mental Health (Scotland) Act 1960.

repealed: 1984, c.36, sch.5.

s. 63, see H.M. Advocate v. Aitken, 1975 S.L.T.(Notes) 86.

s. 90, regs. 84/294; order 84/389.

s. 107, see Skinner v. Robertson, 1980 S.L.T.(Sh.Ct.) 43.

sch. 2A, regs. 84/294.

sch. 4, repealed in pt.: 1984, c.56, sch.3.

CAP.

8 & 9 Eliz. 2 (1959–60)—cont.

62. Caravan Sites and Control of Development Act 1960.

see Beaconsfield JJ., ex p. Stubbings, The Times, May 7, 1986, D.C.

Pt. I (ss. 1–32), see Hooper v. Eagleston (1977) 245 E.G. 572, D.C.

s. 1, see James v. Brecknock R.D.C. (1973) 226 E.G. 2353, C.A.; North v. Brown (1974) 231 E.G. 737, D.C.; Bromsgrove District Council v. Carthy (1975) 30 P. & C.R. 34, D.C.; National By-Products v. Brice (1983) 81 L.G.R. 652, C.A.; R. v. Secretary of State for the Environment, London Borough of Hammersmith and Fulham, Royal Borough of Kensington and Chelsea and G.L.C., ex p. Ward [1984] J.P.L. 90, Woolf J.; Holmes v. Cooper [1985] 1 W.L.R. 1060, C.A.

s. 1, 3, see Balthasar v. Mullane (1986) 84 L.G.R. 55, C.A.

s. 3, see Willis v. Edmunds, The Times, November 20, 1984, D.C.

s. 3, amended: 1980, c.65, sch.3.

s. 5, see Att.-Gen. v. Maidstone R.D.C., ex rel. Lamb (1973) 226 E.G. 805, Plowman J.; Babbage v. North Norfolk District Council, The Times, July 20, 1988, D.C.

ss. 5, 8, amended: 1982, c.30, s.8.

ss. 5, 9, see Penton Park Homes v. Chertsey U.D.C. (1973) 26 P. & C.R. 531, D.C.

s. 9, see Cameron v. Charles Simpson Motors, June 30, 1980, D.C.

s. 13, see James v. Brecknock R.D.C. (1973) 226 E.G. 2353, C.A.

ss. 14, 17, see Hereford City Council v. Edmunds (1985) 274 E.G. 1030, D.C.

s. 17, see Loosmore v. Bridport R.D.C. (1971) 22 P. & C.R. 1084.

ss. 21, 22, repealed: 1972, c.52, sch.23.

s. 23, amended: 1972, c.70, sch.29; order 75/1636.

s. 24, see R. v. Secretary of State for the Environment and Cheshire County Council, ex p. Halton B.C. [1984] J.P.L. 97, Taylor J.; R. v. Secretary of State for Wales, ex p. Price [1984] J.P.L. 87, McCullough J.; R. v. Secretary of State for the Environment, London Borough of Hammersmith and Fulham, Royal Borough of Kensington and Chelsea and G.L.C., ex p. Ward [1984] J.P.L. 90, Woolf J.; West Glamorgan County Council v. Rafferty; R. v. Secretary of State for Wales, ex p. Gilhaney, The Times, June 4, 1986, C.A.

s. 24, amended: 1981, c.67, sch.4; 1982, c.30, s.8; c.43, s.13 (S.); repealed in pt.: ibid., sch.6.

s. 26, see Cameron v. Charles Simpson Motors, June 30, 1980, D.C.

s. 27, repealed: 1973, c.65, sch.29.

s. 29, see Backer v. Secretary of State for the Environment [1983] 2 All E.R. 1021, David Widdicombe Q.C.

s. 29, amended: 1982, c.30, s.8; repealed in pt.: 1972, c.70, sch.30.

s. 32, amended: 1973, c.65, sch.23; repealed in pt.: ibid., sch.29; 1982, c.43, sch.4 (S.).

CAP.

8 & 9 Eliz. 2 (1959–60)—cont.

62. Caravan Sites and Control of Development Act 1960—*cont.*

s. 48, repealed: S.L.R. 1974.

sch. 1, see *North* v. *Brown* (1974) 231 E.G. 737, D.C.; *Holmes* v. *Cooper* [1985] 1 W.L.R. 1060, C.A.

sch. 1, amended: 1980, c.65, s.176.

sch. 2, amended: 1974, c.7, sch.8; 1982, c.43, sch.3 (S.); repealed in pt.: 1972, c.70, sch.30; 1974, c.7, schs.6,8.

sch. 4, repealed: S.L.R. 1974.

63. Road Traffic and Roads Improvement Act 1960.

repealed (S.): 1984, c.54, sch.11.

s. 1, see *Lord Advocate* v. *Aberdeen Corporation*, 1977 S.L.T. 234.

ss. 18–20, repealed: 1980, c.66, sch.25.

s. 21, repealed: 1972, c.20, sch.9.

s. 22, repealed in pt.: S.L.R. 1978.

s. 23, repealed in pt.: 1980, c.66, sch.25.

s. 24, sch., repealed: 1981, c.14, sch.8.

64. Building Societies Act 1960.

ss. 72, 73 (in pt.), repealed: 1986, c.53, sch.19.

s. 75, repealed: 1973, c.36, sch.6.

s. 77, sch. 5 (in pt.), repealed: 1986, c.53, sch.19.

65. Administration of Justice Act 1960.

ss. 1–3, repealed in pt.: 1978, c 23, sch.7.

ss. 1, 5, 15, see *Government of the United States of America* v. *McCaffery* [1984] 1 W.L.R. 867, H.L.

s. 4, amended: 1976, c.63, sch.2; repealed in pt.: *ibid.*, sch.3; 1978, c.23, sch.7.

s. 5, amended: 1982, c.51, sch.3.; 1983, c.20, sch.4; repealed in pt.: 1978, c.23, sch.7.

s. 6, amended: 1976, c.63, sch.2; repealed in pt.: 1978, c.23, sch.7.

s. 9, repealed in pt.: *ibid.*

s. 11, repealed: 1981, c.49, s.3.

ss. 11, 12, see *Re F. (A Minor) (Publication of Information)* [1976] 3 W.L.R. 813, C.A.

s. 12, see *Re R. (M. J.) (A Minor) (Publication of Transcript)* [1975] 2 W.L.R. 978; *S. (Minors) (Wardship: Police Investigation), Re* [1987] 3 W.L.R. 847, Booth J.; *W. (Minors), Re, The Times,* April 30, 1988, Stephen Brown P.: *L. (A Minor) (Wardship: Freedom of Publication), Re* [1981] 1 All E.R. 418, Booth J.; *Wolverhampton Metropolitan Borough Council* v. *M.* (1988) 152 J.P.N. 508, Bush J.

s. 13, see *R.* v. *Goult, The Times,* November 15, 1982, C.A.; *Linnett* v. *Coles* [1986] 3 W.L.R. 843, D.C.

s. 13, amended: 1980, c.43, sch.7; 1984, c.28, sch.2; repealed in pt.: 1978, c.23, sch.7; 1981, c.54, sch.7.

s. 14, see *Re Tarling* [1979] 1 All E.R. 981, Gibson J.

s. 15, repealed in pt.: 1978, c.23, sch.7.

s. 16, repealed: 1981, c.54, sch.7.

s. 17, repealed in pt.: 1978, c.23, sch.7.

s. 18, repealed in pt.: 1973, c.36, sch.6; 1978, c.23, sch.7; S.L.R. 1978.

s. 19, repealed in part: S.L.R. 1974.

s. 19, sch.3, see *R.* v. *Chard, The Times,* November 11, 1983, H.L.

CAP.

8 & 9 Eliz. 2 (1959–60)—cont.

65. Administration of Justice Act 1960—*cont.*

sch. 2, amended: 1978, c.23, sch.5; repealed in pt.: *ibid.*, sch.7.

sch. 3, repealed in pt.: S.L.R. 1978.

sch. 4, repealed: S.L.R. 1974.

66. Professions Supplementary to Medicine Act 1960.

s. 2, orders 75/1691; 79/365; 80/968; 81/178; 83/1799; 86/660.

s. 10, order 86/630.

s. 14, repealed in pt.: 1973, c.36, sch.6.

sch. 1, amended: 1985, c.9, sch.2; order 88/1843; repealed in pt.: 1972, c.11, sch.8.

sch. 2, amended: 1978, c.23, sch.5; 1981, c.54, sch.5.

67. Public Bodies (Admission to Meetings) Act 1960.

s. 1, see *R.* v. *Liverpool City Council, ex p. Liverpool Taxi Fleet Operators' Association* [1975] 1 All E.R. 379, D.C.; *R.* v. *Brent Health Authority, ex p. Francis* [1984] 3 W.L.R. 1317, Forbes J.

s. 1, amended: 1984, c.46, sch.5; 1985, c.43, sch.2; repealed in pt.: *ibid.*, sch.3.

s. 2, repealed in pt.: *ibid.*, schs.2,3.

sch., amended: 1972, c.58, sch.6; 1973, c.32, sch.4; c.37, sch.3; c.65, sch.27; 1975, c.77, sch.3; 1978, c.29, sch.16 (S.); 1980, c.53, sch.1; 1983, c.41, sch.9; 1985, c.43, sch.2; c.51, sch.14; 1988, c.24, s.1; repealed in pt.:1972, c.70, sch.30; 1973, c.32, schs. 4,5; order 74/1351; 1983, c.23, sch.5; 1985, c.43, schs.2,3; order 85/1884.

68. Noise Abatement Act 1960.

repealed: 1974, c.40, sch.4.

69. Road Traffic (Driving of Motor Cycles) Act 1960.

repealed: 1972, c.20, sch.9.

9 & 10 Eliz. 2 (1960–61)

1. Indus Basin Development Fund Act 1960.

repealed: S.L.R. 1977.

2. British North America Act 1960.

Act renamed Constitution Act 1960 (Can.): 1982, c.11, sch.

s. 2, substituted: *ibid.*

3. Administration of Justice (Judges and Pensions) Act 1960.

repealed: 1981, c.54, sch.7.

6. Ministers of the Crown (Parliamentary Secretaries) Act 1960.

s. 4, repealed in pt.: S.L.R. 1974; S.L.R. 1978.

s. 5, repealed: *ibid.*

sch. 1, repealed in pt.: *ibid.*

sch. 2, repealed: S.L.R. 1974.

11. Diplomatic Immunities (Conferences with Commonwealth Countries and Republic of Ireland) Act 1961.

repealed: 1981, c.9, sch.

s. 1, amended: order 81/1105.

s. 2, order 77/821.

14. Nurses (Amendment) Act 1961.

repealed: 1979, c.36, sch.8.

s. 9, amended: 1981, c.54, sch.5.

CAP.

9 & 10 Eliz. 2 (1960–61)—cont.

15. Post Office Act 1961.
ss. 2, 27, repealed in pt.: 1973, c.36, sch.6.
s. 24, repealed in pt.: 1972, c.71, sch.6.

16. Sierra Leone Independence Act 1961.
s. 2, repealed: 1981, c.61, sch.9.
s. 3, repealed in pt.: 1978, c.30, sch.3.
sch. 3, repealed in pt.: S.L.R. 1977; 1981, c.9, sch.; 1986, c.55, sch.2; 1988, c.48, sch.8.

17. Betting Levy Act 1961.
repealed: 1975, c.24, sch.3.

19. National Health Service Act 1961.
repealed: 1977, c.49, sch.16; 1978, c.29, sch.17 (S.)
ss. 1, 2, regs. 74/284, 287, 505, 507.
s. 2, regs. 73/1468; 75/1987; 77/471.

20. Home Safety Act 1961.
ss. 1, 2, repealed in pt.: S.L.R. 1975.

21. Oaths Act 1961.
repealed: 1978, c.19, sch.

23. Republic of South Africa (Temporary Provisions) Act 1961.
repealed: S.L.R. 1973.

24. Private Street Works Act 1961.
repealed: 1980, c.66, sch.25.

25. Patents and Designs (Renewals, Extensions and Fees) Act 1961.
repealed: 1988, c.48, sch.8.
s. 2, order 74/2145.

27. Carriage by Air Act 1961.
see Holmes v. Bangladesh Biman Corp., Financial Times, March 9, 1988, C.A.
s. 1, see Goldman v. Thai International [1983] 1 W.L.R. 1186, C.A.
ss. 1–3, amended: 1979, c.28, sch.2.
s. 2, orders 72/970; 75/430; 76/56, 1159; 77/240, 1631; 78/1058; 88/243.
s. 3, amended: order 77/1251.
s. 4, orders 73/1189; 74/528; 75/1613; 76/1032; 77/1; 78/31; 79/765; 80/281, 1873; 81/1252; 83/43, 593; 84/1582; 85/229, 1428; 86/1778.
s. 4, amended: 1978, c.47, sch.1; 1979, c.28, sch.2; repealed in pt.: 1978, c.47, sch.2; 1979, c.28, s.6, sch.2.
s. 4A, added: ibid., s.2.
s. 5, amended: 1978, c.47, sch.1; 1980, c.58, sch.3.
s. 8A, added: 1979, c.28, s.3; amended: 1983, c.14, sch.2..
s. 10, orders 79/931; 81/440; 84/701.
s. 11, amended: 1973, c.52, sch.4.
sch: 1, see Fothergill v. Monarch Airlines [1980] 3 W.L.R. 809; [1980] 2 All E.R. 696, H.L.; Rothmans of Pall Mall (Overseas) v. Saudi Arabian Airlines Corp. [1980] 3 W.L.R. 642; [1980] 3 All E.R. 359, Mustill J.; Collins v. British Airways Board [1982] 2 W.L.R. 165, C.A.; American Express v. British Airways Board [1983] 1 All E.R. 557, Lloyd J.; Goldman v. Thai International [1983] 1 W.L.R. 1186, C.A.; Swiss Bank Corp. v. Brinks MAT [1986] 2 All E.R. 188, Bingham J.
sch. 1, amended: order 76/1032; 1979, c.28, s.4; substituted: ibid., s.1, sch.1.
sch. 2, repealed: S.L.R. 1974.

CAP.

9 & 10 Eliz. 2 (1960–61)—cont.

29. Rural Water Supplies and Sewerage Act 1961.
repealed: 1973, c.37, sch.9.
s. 1, amended: 1972, c.70, sch.30.

31. Printer's Imprint Act 1961.
s. 1, amended: 1986, c.39, sch.2.

32. Local Authorities (Expenditure on Special Purposes) (Scotland) Act 1961.
repealed: 1973, c.65, sch.29.

33. Land Compensation Act 1961.
see Johnson v. Sheffield City Council (1982) 43 P. & C.R. 272, Lands Tribunal.
s. 1, see Duttons Brewery v. Leeds City Council (1981) 42 P. & C.R. 152, Nourse J.
s. 2, amended: 1975, c.77, sch.10; 1980, s.65, sch.33.
s. 4, see Pepys v. London Transport Executive [1975] 1 W.L.R. 234, C.A.
s. 4, see Trustees for Methodist Church Purposes v. North Tyneside Metropolitan Borough Council (1979) 38 P. & C.R. 665, Browne-Wilkinson J.
s. 5, see Salop C.C. v. Craddock (1969) 213 E.G. 633; Zoar Independent Church Trustees v. Rochester Corporation [1974] 3 All E.R. 5, C.A.; Trocette Property Co. v. G.L.C. (1974) 28 P. & C.R. 408, C.A.; W. & S. (Long Eaton) v. Derbyshire C.C. (1975) 31 P. & C.R. 99, C.A.; D.H.N. Food Distributors v. Tower Hamlets L.B.C.; Bronze Investments v. Same [1976] 1 W.L.R. 852, C.A.; Hoveringham Gravels v. Chiltern District Council (1978) 35 P. & C.R. 295, C.A.; Stoke on Trent City Council v. Wood Mitchell & Co. [1979] 2 All E.R. 65, C.A.; Service Welding v. Tyne and Wear County Council (1979) 250 E.G. 1291, C.A.; Khan v. Birmingham City Council (1980) 40 P. & C.R. 412, C.A.; Wilkinson v. Middlesbrough Borough Council (1983) 45 P. & C.R. 142, C.A.; Harrison and Hetherington v. Cumbria County Council (1985) 275 E.G. 457; (1985) 50 P. & C.R. 396, H.L.; Palatine Graphic Art Co. v. Liverpool City Council [1986] 2 W.L.R. 285, C.A.; Hughes v. Doncaster Metropolitan Borough Council (1987) 55 P. & C.R. 383, Lands Tribunal.
s. 5, amended: order 76/1218.
s. 6, amended: 1980, c.65, s.145; 1988, c.50, s.78.
s. 8, amended: 1980, c.66, sch.24; repealed in pt.: 1983, c.29, sch.3; 1985, c.71, sch.1.
s. 9, see Jelson v. Blaby District Council [1977] 1 W.L.R. 1020, C.A.
ss. 14, 15, see Williamson and Stevens v. Cambridgeshire County Council, REF/143/1976 (1977) 242 E.G. 369.
s. 15, see Myers v. Milton Keynes Development Corporation [1974] 1 W.L.R. 696.
s. 15, amended: 1975, c.77, sch.10; 1980, c.65, sch.33.
s. 16, see Provincial Properties (London) v. Caterham & Warlingham U.D.C. [1972] 2 W.L.R. 44; [1972] 1 All E.R. 60.

CAP.

9 & 10 Eliz. 2 (1960–61)—cont.

33. Land Compensation Act 1961—cont.

s. 17, see *Car Rim Properties* v. *Secretary of State for Wales* [1974] J.P.L. 719; *Williamson and Stevens* v. *Cambridgeshire County Council, REF/143/1976* (1977) 242 E.G. 369; *Scunthorpe Borough Council* v. *Secretary of State for the Environment and Humberside County Council and Hawley (Builders)* [1977] J.P.L. 653, Sir Douglas Frank Q.C.; *Hoveringham Gravels* v. *Chiltern District Council* (1978) 35 P. & C.R. 295, C.A.; *Skelmersdale Development Corp.* v. *Secretary of State for the Environment* [1980] J.P.L. 322, Griffith J.; *T. D. White* v. *Secretary of State for the Environment and Stockton-on-Tees Borough Council* [1982] J.P.L. 506, David Widdicombe Q.C; *Sutton* v. *Secretary of State for the Environment* (1985) 50 P. & C.R. 147, McCullough J.

s. 17, amended: 1975, c.77, s.47, sch.9; 1980, c.65, s.121, sch.24; 1988, c.4, sch.3.

ss. 17, 18, 22, see *Robert Hitchins Builders* v. *Secretary of State for the Environment; Wakeley Brothers (Rainham, Kent)* v. *Secretary of State for the Environment* (1979) 37 P. & C.R. 140, Sir Douglas Frank Q C.

ss. 17, 21, see *Sutton* v. *Secretary of State for the Environment* (1984) 270 E.G. 144, McCullough J.

s. 19, amended: 1975, c.77, sch.10; 1980, c.65, sch.33.

s. 20, orders 74/539; 86/435.

s. 22, see *Hoveringham Gravels* v. *Chiltern District Council* (1978) 35 P. & C.R. 295, C.A.

s. 30, repealed: 1973, c.26, sch.3.

s. 31, see *Trustees for Methodist Church Purposes* v. *North Tyneside Metropolitan Borough Council* (1979) 38 P. & C.R. 665, Browne-Wilkinson J.

s. 32, regs. 72/949, 1126; 73/76, 573, 848, 1542, 2072; 74/721; 75/209, 602, 1856; 76/233, 1124, 1660, 1798; 77/300, 720, 876, 1656, 1657; 78/886, 1418, 1741; 79/616, 1166, 1743; 80/1026, 1944; 81/564, 1153, 1981; 82/442, 945, 1351, 1541; 83/33, 863, 1735; 84/1456, 1647, 1967; 85/157, 1131; 87/405, 889; 88/874.

s 39, see *Hoveringham Gravels* v. *Chiltern District Council* (1978) 35 P. & C.R 295, C.A.

s. 39, amended: order 76/315.

s. 40, repealed in pt.: S.L.R. 1974.

sch. 1, amended: 1980, c.65, s.145, sch.25; 1988, c.50, s.78

sch. 2, amended: 1974, c.44, sch.13; 1975, c.77, sch.10; 1980, c.65, sch.33; repealed in pt.: *ibid.*, sch.34; 1985, c.51, sch.17; substituted: 1985, c.71, sch 2.

sch. 4, repealed in pt.: 1981, c.67, sch.6; 1985, c.71, sch.1.

sch. 5, repealed: S.L.R. 1974.

34. Factories Act 1961.

see *Bowie* v. *Great International Plate Glass Insurance Cleaning Co., The Times,* May 14, 1981, C.A.

ss. 1–5, repealed: regs. 74/1941.

ss. 1, 4, see *Brooks* v. *J. & P. Coates (U.K.)* [1984] I.C.R. 158, Boreham J.

CAP.

9 & 10 Eliz. 2 (1960–61)—cont.

34. Factories Act 1961—cont.

ss. 1, 7, regs. 74/426, 427.

ss. 2, 3, amended: regs. 83/978.

s. 4, see *Wallhead* v. *Ruston & Hornsby* (1973) 14 K.I.R. 285; *Hornett* v. *Associated Octel,* November 6, 1986, Russell J., Manchester Crown Ct.

s. 5, see *Davies* v. *Massey Ferguson Perkins* [1986] I.C.R. 580, Evans J.

s. 6, see *Gay* v. *St. Cuthberts Cooperative Association,* 1977 S.C. 212.

s. 7, repealed in pt.: regs. 74/1941.

s. 8, repealed: regs. 77/746.

ss. 9, 10, repealed: regs. 74/1941.

ss. 11, 13, amended and repealed in pt.: regs. 74/1941.

s. 13, see *Boyes* v. *Carnation Foods* (O.H.), January 15, 1985.

s. 14, see *Sarwar* v. *Simmons & Hawker* (1971) 11 K.I.R. 300; *McGuiness* v. *Key Markets* (1973) 13 K.I.R. 249; *Weaving* v. *Pirelli* [1977] 1 W.L.R. 48, H.L.; *Ballard* v. *Ministry of Defence* [1977] I.C.R. 513, C.A.; *Stevenson* v. *J. Drummond & Sons* (O.H.), 1978 S.L.T.(Notes) 13; *Cope* v. *Nickel Electro,* May 8, 1980, Sheldon J.; *Humphreys* v. *Silent Channel Products,* February 20, 1981, French J., Cardiff Crown Ct.; *Mirza* v. *Ford Motor Co.* [1981] I.C.R. 757, C.A.; *Jayes* v. *IMI (Kynoch) Ltd.* [1985] I.C.R. 155, C.A.; *Walker* v. *Dick Engineering Co. (Coatbridge)* (O.H.), 1985 S.L.T. 465; *TBA Industrial Products* v. *Lainé* [1987] I.C.R. 75, D.C.; *Price* v. *Steinberg,* January 27, 1987, H.H. Judge Hywel Robert, Pontypridd, County Ct.; *Clews* v. *B.A. Chemicals* (O.H.), July 21, 1987.

s. 14, repealed in pt.: regs. 74/1941.

s. 15, repealed in pt.: 1975, c.65, sch.5.

s. 16, see *Joy* v. *News of the World* (1972) 13 K.I.R. 57; *Stevenson* v. *J. Drummond & Sons* (O.H.), 1978 S.L.T.(Notes) 13.

s. 17, regs. 74/903.

s. 17, repealed: regs. 74/1941.

s. 18, amended: regs. 83/978; repealed in pt.. regs. 74/1941.

s. 19, amended: regs. 83/978.

s. 20, see *Stevenson* v. *J. Drummond & Sons* (O.H.), 1978 S.L.T.(Notes) 13.

s. 22, see *Oldfield* v. *Reid & Smith* [1972] 2 All E.R. 104.

s. 25, see *Ross* v. *British Steel Corporation,* 1973 S L.T.(Notes) 34 (O.H.).

s. 25, repealed in pt.: regs. 74/1941.

ss. 26, 27, amended: regs. 83/978.

s. 27, see *McKendrick* v. *Mitchell Swire* (O.H.), 1976 S.L.T.(Notes) 65; *McDowell* v. *British Leyland Motor Corporation* (O.H.), 1982 S.L.T. 71; *Walker* v. *Andrew Mitchell & Co.,* 1982 S.L.T. 266.

s. 28, see *Henderson* v. *Redpath Dorman Long,* 1975 S.L.T.(Sh.Ct.) 27; *Moffat* v. *Marconi Space and Defence Systems,* 1975 S.L.T.(Notes) 60; *Gillies* v. *Glynwed Foundries,* 1977 S.L.T. 97, Ct. of Session 1st Div.; *Gray* v. *St. Cuthberts Co-operative Associ-*

9 & 10 Eliz. 2 (1960–61)—cont.

34. Factories Act 1961—*cont.*
ation, 1977 S.C. 212; *Bennett* v. *Rylands Whitecross* [1978] I.C.R. 1031, Kilner Brown J.; *Devine* v. *Costain Concrete Co.* (O.H.), 1979 S.L.T.(Notes) 97; *Sanders* v. *F. H. Lloyd & Co.* [1982] I.C.R. 360, Drake J.; *Brown* v. *Rowntree Mackintosh,* 1983 S.L.T. (Sh.Ct.) 47; *Johnston* v. *Caddies Wainwright* [1983] I.C.R. 407, C.A.; *Allen* v. *Avon Rubber Co.* [1986] I.C.R. 695, C.A.; *McCart* v. *Queen of Scots Knitwear,* 1987 S.L.T.(Sh.Ct.) 57; *Lynch* v. *Babcock Power* (O.H.), 1988 S.L.T. 307.
ss. 28, 29, see *Ashdown* v. *Jonas Woodhead & Sons* [1975] K.I.L.R. 27, C.A.; *Hemmings* v. *British Aerospace,* May 22, 1986, Swinton-Thomas J., Bristol.
ss. 28–30, amended: regs. 83/978.
s. 29, see *Geddes* v. *United Wires,* 1973 S.L.T.(Notes) 50; 1974 S.L.T. 170 (O.H.); *Bowen* v. *Mills & Wright* [1973] 1 Lloyd's Rep. 580, Ashworth J.; *Thompson* v. *Bowaters United Kingdom Paper Co.* [1975] K.I.L.R. 47, C.A.; *Ball* v. *Vaughan Bros.* (*Drop Forgings*), June 26, 1979, Hodgson J., Birmingham Crown Ct.; *Hunter* v. *British Steel Corporation,* 1980 S.L.T. 31; *Woodward* v. *Renold* [1980] I.C.R. 387, Lawson J.; *Cox* v. *Angus* (*H.C.B.*) [1981] I.C.R. 683, Lloyd J.; *Smith* v. *British Aerospace* [1982] I.C.R. 98, C.A.; *Wilson* v. *Wallpaper Manufacturers,* March 10, 1981, C.A.; *Fildes* v. *International Computers,* January 24, 1984, C.A.; *Rice* v *Central Electricity Generating Board, The Times,* February 23, 1985, Pain J.; *Darby* v. *G.K.N. Screws and Fasteners* [1986] I.C.R. 1, Pain J.; *Davies* v. *Massey Ferguson Perkins* [1986] I.C.R. 580, Evans J.; *Allen* v. *Avon Rubber Co.* [1986] I.C.R. 695, C.A.; *Harkins* v. *McCluskey* (O.H.), 1987 S.L.T. 289; *Kirkpatrick* v. *Scott Lithgow* (O.H.), 1987 S.L.T. 654; *Yates* v. *Rockwell Graphic Systems* [1988] I.C.R. 8, Steyn J.
ss. 29, 36, see *Nixon* v. *G. D. Searle and Co.,* December 21, 1981.
s. 31, see *Haigh* v. *Charles W. Ireland,* 1973 S.L.T. 142; [1974] 1 W.L.R. 43; [1973] 3 All E.R. 1137, H.L.
ss. 32, 33, amended and repealed in pt.: regs. 74/1941.
s. 35, repealed in pt.: *ibid.*
s. 39, amended: regs. 83/978.
ss. 40–52, repealed: regs. 76/2004.
s. 48, see *L. Bresler* v. *H.M. Inspector of Factories,* 1975 S.L.T.(Notes) 74.
s. 50, regs. 72/917.
ss. 53–55, 56 (in pt.), 58 (in pt.), 59 (in pt.), repealed: regs. 74/1941.
s. 61, repealed: regs. 81/917.
s. 62, regs. 74/209.
s. 62, repealed: regs. 74/1941.
s. 63, see *Wallhead* v. *Ruston & Hornsby* (1973) 14 K.I.R. 285; *Cartwright* v. *G.K.N. Sankey* (1973) 14 K.I.R. 349, C.A.; *Brooks* v. *J. & P. Coates (U.K.)* [1984] I.C.R. 158, Boreham J.; *Hornett* v. *Associated Octel,* November 6, 1986, Russell J., Manchester Crown Ct.

9 & 10 Eliz. 2 (1960–61)—cont.

34. Factories Act 1961—*cont.*
s. 64, repealed in pt.: regs. 74/1941; 80/1248.
s. 65, see *Hay* v. *Dowty Mining Equipment* [1971] 3 All E.R. 1136; *Rogers* v. *Blair,* (1971) 11 K.I.R. 391.
s. 65, regs. 74/1681.
s. 66, repealed: regs. 74/1941.
s. 68, amended: regs. 83/978.
s. 69, amended: regs. 74/1941.
ss. 70, 71, repealed: *ibid.*
ss. 71, 72, see *Brown* v. *Allied Ironfounders,* 1973 S.L.T. 230. Ct. of Session, First Division; [1974] 1 W.L.R. 527; [1974] 2 All E.R. 135; 1974 S.L.T. 146, H.L.
s. 72, see *Bailey* v. *Rolls Royce* (1971) [1984] I.C.R. 688, C.A.; *Power* v. *Greater Glasgow Health Board* (O.H.), 1987 S.L.T. 567.
ss. 72, 73, repealed in pt.: regs. 74/1941.
s. 75, repealed: regs. 80/1248.
s. 76, see *Smith* v. *Wimpey* [1972] 2 Q.B. 329; [1972] 2 W.L.R. 1166; [1972] 2 All E.R. 723.
s. 76, regs. 72/917, 1512; 73/9; 74/903, 1681.
ss. 76, 77 (in pt.), 78 (in pt.), repealed: regs. 74/1941.
s. 80, repealed: regs. 80/804.
s. 81, repealed: regs. 74/1941.
s. 82, order 73/6.
s. 82, repealed: regs. 85/2023.
ss. 83, 84, repealed: regs. 74/1941.
s. 85, repealed: 1972, c.28, sch.3.
s. 86, repealed in pt : 1986, c.59, s.7, sch.
Pt. VI (ss. 86–119), order 86/2312.
s. 87, repealed in pt.: regs. 74/1941.
s. 88, repealed in pt.: 1986, c.59, s.7, sch.
s. 89, amended: regs. 74/1941; repealed in pt.: *ibid.*; 1986, c.59, s.7, sch.
s. 90, repealed in pt.: *ibid.,* sch.
ss. 91–93, repealed in pt.: *ibid.,* s.7, sch.
s. 94, amended: 1973, c.65, s.155; repealed in pt.: *ibid.,* s.155, sch.29; 1986, c.59, s.7, sch.
s. 95, repealed: *ibid.,* sch.
s. 96, amended: regs. 74/1941; repealed in pt.: 1986, c.59, sch.
s. 97, amended: regs. 74/1941; 1988, c.40, sch.12; repealed in pt.: 1986, c.59, sch.
s. 98, amended: regs. 74/1941; repealed in pt.: 1986, c.59, sch.
s. 99, repealed in pt.: 1972, c.28, sch.3; 1986, c.59, sch.
s. 100, repealed in pt.: *ibid.*
s. 101, amended: regs. 74/1941; repealed in pt.: 1986, c.59, sch.
ss. 102 (in pt.), 106 (in pt.)–109 (in pt.), 110, 111, 112 (in pt.)–115 (in pt.), repealed: *ibid.*
s. 117, orders 72/1669; 73/1852; 74/1627.
s. 118, repealed: 1972, c.28, sch.3.
s. 119, amended: *ibid.,* sch.2; repealed: *ibid.,* sch 3.
s. 119A, added: *ibid.,* s.5; amended: 1973, c.50, sch.3.
s. 120, repealed: regs. 76/2004.
ss. 121, 122, repealed in pt.: regs. 74/1941.
s. 123, amended and repealed in pt.: *ibid.*
s. 124, see *MacDonald* v. *Secretary of State for Scotland,* 1979 S.L.T.(Sh.Ct.) 8.

CAP.

9 & 10 Eliz. 2 (1960–61)—cont.
34. Factories Act 1961—cont.
s. 124, repealed in pt.: regs. 74/1941.
s. 125, amended: *ibid.*; regs. 88/1655, repealed in pt.: 1972, c.28, sch.3; regs. 74/1941; order 75/1012.
s. 126, repealed in pt.: 1972, c.28, sch.3; regs. 74/1941; order 75/1012.
s. 127, see *Davies* v. *Camerons Industrial Services* [1980] 2 All E.R. 680, D.C.
s. 127, amended: regs. 74/1941; repealed in pt.: 1972, c.28, sch.3; regs. 74/1941; order 75/1012.
s. 128, repealed in pt.: regs. 74/1941, 80/1248.
ss. 129, 130, repealed: *ibid.*
ss. 135, 135A, repealed: 1986, c.48, schs.1,5.
s. 136, repealed: regs. 75/1012.
s. 137, repealed in pt.: regs. 74/1941.
s. 138, order 73/7.
s. 138, amended: 1972, c.28, sch.2; regs. 74/1941.
s. 139, orders 73/37; 74/1587.
s. 139, amended: regs. 74/1941.
s. 140, order 73/8.
s. 140, repealed in pt.: regs. 76/2004; 80/804; 85/2023.
s. 141, amended: 1972, c.28, sch.2.
s. 142, repealed: regs. 74/1941.
s. 143, repealed: regs. 75/1012.
s. 145, repealed: 1972, c.71, sch.6; regs. 74/1941.
ss. 146–148, repealed: 76/2004.
ss. 149, 150, repealed: regs. 74/1941.
ss. 151, 152, repealed: 1972, c.28, sch.3.
s. 153, amended (S.): 1972, c.58, sch.6; 1978, c.29, sch.15; repealed in pt. (S.): 1973, c.65, sch.29; regs. 74/1941; 77/746.
s. 154, repealed in pt.: regs. 74/1941.
s. 155, see *Maurice Graham* v. *Brunswick* (1974) 16 K.I.R. 158, D.C.; *Davies* v. *Camerons Industrial Services* [1980] 2 All E.R. 680, D.C.; *R.* v. *A.I. Industrial Products* [1987] I.C.R. 418, C.A.; *Morganite Crucible* v. *Nurse, The Times,* May 16, 1988, D.C.; *Gorrie* v. *CIBA Geigy* (O.H.), 1988 S.L.T. 518.
s. 155, repealed in pt.: regs. 74/1941; 75/1012.
s. 156, repealed: regs. 76/2004.
s. 157, repealed in pt.: regs. 74/1941.
s. 158, amended: *ibid.*
s. 159, repealed: *ibid.*
ss. 160, 161, repealed: regs. 76/2004.
s. 164, repealed in pt.: 1972, c.71, sch.6; regs. 74/1941; 76/2004.
s. 165, repealed: regs. 76/2004.
s. 166, repealed in pt.: regs. 74/1941.
s. 167, repealed in pt.: 1973, c.16, sch.2.
s. 168, repealed in pt.: regs. 74/1941.
s. 173, amended: *ibid.*
s. 174, repealed in pt.: *ibid.*
s. 175, see *Findlay* v. *Miller Construction (Northern),* 1977 S.L.T.(Sh.Ct.) 8; *MacDonald* v. *Secretary of State for Scotland,* 1979 S.L.T.(Sh.Ct.) 8; *Bromwich* v. *National Ear, Nose and Throat Hospital* [1980] I.C.R. 450; [1980] 2 All E.R. 663, Cantley J.; *Dunsby* v. *B.B.C., The Times,* July 25, 1983, Pain J.

CAP.

9 & 10 Eliz. 2 (1960–61)—cont.
34. Factories Act 1961—cont.
s. 175, amended: regs. 83/978.
s. 176, see *Drysdale* v. *Kelsey Roofing Industries* (O.H.), 1981 S.L.T.(Notes) 118; *Shepherd* v. *Pearson Engineering Services (Dundee),* 1980 S.C. 268, Outer House.
s. 176, amended: 1973, c.65, s.155; regs. 74/1941; 1976, c.20, sch.1 (S.); 1980, c.43, sch.7; c.44, sch.4 (S.); repealed in pt.: 1972, c.70, sch.30; regs. 74/1941; 83/978.
s. 177, repealed: regs. 74/1941.
s. 178, amended: orders 75/1291, 1808; 77/1861, 1891; 81/241.
s. 179, repealed: regs. 74/1941.
s. 180, regs. 72/917; 73/7–9, 37; 74/903, 1681.
s. 180, amended: 1972, c.28, s.2; regs. 74/1941; repealed in pt.: *ibid.*
s. 181, repealed in pt.: 1973, c.65, s.155, sch.29 (S.); regs. 74/1941; 77/746.
s. 182, amended: 1973, c.65, s.155 (S.); regs. 74/1941; repealed in pt.: 1973, c.65, s.155, sch.29 (S.); regs. 74/1941.
s. 183, repealed in pt.: regs. 74/1941; S.L.R. 1974.
s. 184, repealed in pt.: 1972, c.28, sch.3.
s. 185, repealed in pt.: S.L.R. 1974.
sch. 1, substituted: regs. 83/978.
sch. 2, repealed: regs. 76/2004.
schs. 3, 4, repealed: regs. 74/1941.
sch. 5, amended (S.): 1972, c.58, sch.6; 1978, c.29, sch.15; repealed in pt.: regs. 77/746.
sch. 6, repealed in pt.: S.L.R. 1986.
sch. 7, repealed: S.L.R. 1974.
35. Police Pensions Act 1961.
s. 1, regs. 79/76; 87/1698 (S.).
ss. 1, 2, amended: 1976, c.35, sch.2; repealed in pt.: *ibid.,* sch.8.
36. Finance Act 1961.
s. 5, repealed in pt.: 1979, c.58, sch.2.
s. 9, repealed: 1979, c.8, sch.2.
s. 11, repealed: 1979, c.2, sch.6.
s. 34, repealed: 1986, c.41, sch.23.
s. 35, repealed: 1972, c.65, sch.
s. 37, amended: S.L.R. 1974; 1979, c.2, sch.4; repealed in pt.: *ibid.,* sch.6.
schs. 3, 4, repealed: 1979, c.8, sch.2.
sch. 7, repealed: S.L.R. 1974.
37. Small Estates (Representation) Act 1961.
repealed: 1979, c.22, sch.
39. Criminal Justice Act 1961.
s. 1, amended: 1980, c.43, sch.7; 1982, c.48, sch.16; repealed in pt.: 1980, c.43, sch.9.
s. 2, see *R.* v. *Storey; R.* v. *Fuat; R.* v. *Duignan* [1973] 1 W.L.R. 1045, C.A.; *Darch* v. *Weight* [1984] 1 W.L.R. 659; [1984] Crim.L.R. 168, D.C.
s. 2, repealed in pt.: 1973, c.62, sch.6; 1988, c.33, sch.16.
ss. 2, 3, see *R.* v. *Bosomworth* (1973) 57 Cr.App.R. 708, C.A.
s. 3, see *R.* v. *Lyons* (1971) 55 Cr.App.R. 565, C.A.; *R.* v. *Halse* [1971] 3 All E.R. 1149; *R.* v. *Gillespie* [1973] 1 W.L.R. 1483, C.A.; *R.* v. *Farndale* (1973) 58 Cr.App.R. 336, C.A.; *R.* v. *Taylor (Victor)* (1974) 60 Cr.App.R. 143, C.A.;

CAP.
9 & 10 Eliz. 2 (1960–61)—cont.
39. Criminal Justice Act 1961—cont.
R. v. *Quinn* (1975) 60 Cr.App.R. 314, C.A.; R. v. *Harnden* (1978) 66 Cr.App.R. 281, C.A; R. v. *Mellor* [1981] 1 W.L.R. 1044; [1981] 2 All E.R. 1049, C.A.; R. v. *Orpwood* [1981] 1 W.L.R. 1048; [1981] 2 All E.R. 1053, C.A.; R. v. *Lowery, The Times,* December 13, 1982, C.A.
ss. 3–7, repealed: 1982, c.48, sch.16.
s. 8, amended: 1977, c.45, s.58; repealed in pt.: 1972, c.71, sch.6; 1977, c.45, sch.13; 1980, c.43, sch.9.
s. 9, repealed: 1973, c.62, sch.6.
s. 11, repealed in pt.: 1977, c.45, sch.13.
s. 12, amended: 1972, c.71, s.42, sch.5; 1977, c.45, sch.12; 1980, c.43, sch.7.
s. 21, repealed: S.L.R. 1974.
s. 22, see *Darch* v. *Weight* [1984] 1 W.L.R. 659; [1984] Crim.L.R. 168, D.C.; *Nicoll* v. *Catron* [1985] Crim.L.R. 223; (1985) 81 Cr.App.R. 339, D.C.
s. 23, amended: 1982, c.48, sch.14.
s. 26, amended: 1977, c.45, sch.12; 1980, c.62, sch.7(S.); order 80/1088; 1982, c.48, sch.14; repealed in pt.: 1977, c.45, sch.13; 1980, c.62, schs.7,8 (S.); order 80/1088.
s. 28, amended: 1977, c.45, sch.12; repealed in pt.: *ibid.,* schs.12,13.
s. 29, see *Becker* v. *Home Office* [1972] 2 W.L.R. 1193; [1972] 2 All E.R. 676; R. v. *Governor of Brixton Prison, ex p. Walsh* [1984] 3 W.L.R. 205, H.L., R. v. *Secretary of State for the Home Department, ex p. Greenwood, The Times,* August 2, 1986, Macpherson J.
s. 29, amended: 1977, c.45, sch.12.
ss. 29, 30, amended: 1980, c.62, sch.7 (S.); order 80/1088; 1982, c.48, sch.14.
s. 32, amended: 1975, c.21, sch.9 (S.); 1980, c.62, sch.7 (S.); order 80/1088; 1982, c.48, sch.14; repealed in pt.: order 76/226; 1980, c.62, schs.7,8 (S.); 1982, c.48, sch.16.
s. 33, amended: *ibid.,* sch.14.
s. 34, repealed in pt.: *ibid.,* sch.16.
s. 36, order 88/1654.
s. 38, see R. v. *Taylor (Victor)* (1974) 60 Cr.App.R. 143, C A
s. 38, orders 83/1314, 1695; 88/1654.
s. 38, amended: 1980, c.62, sch.7 (S.); order 80/1088; 1982, c.48, sch.14; repealed in pt.: 1980, c.62, schs.7,8 (S.); 1982, c.48, sch.16.
s. 39, see R. v. *Farndale* (1973) 58 Cr.App.R. 336, C.A.
s. 39, amended: 1977, c.45, sch.12; 1980, c.62, sch.7 (S.); order 80/1088; 1982, c.48, sch.14; repealed in pt.: 1980, c.62, schs.7,8 (S.); 1982, c.48, sch.16.
s. 40, amended: 1973, c.36, sch.6.
s. 41, repealed in pt.: S.L.R. 1974; 1980, c.43, sch.9.
s. 42, amended: 1982, c.48, sch.14.
sch.1, repealed: *ibid.,* sch.16.
sch. 4, repealed in pt.: 1978, c.22, sch.3; 1980, c.43, sch.9; 1981, c.54, sch.7; 1982, c.48, sch.16.
sch. 5, repealed: S.L.R. 1974.
sch. 6, repealed: 1982, c.48, sch.16.

CAP.
9 & 10 Eliz. 2 (1960–61)—cont.
40. Consumer Protection Act 1961.
repealed: 1978, c.38, sch.3.
s. 1, regs. 76/2, 1208; 78/1354; 83/1477.
ss. 1, 2, regs. 76/454; 77/167, 931; 78/836, 1372; 79/1125; 84/1260; 85/1279, 2043, 2047.
ss. 1, 2, 6, sch., regs. 73/2106; 74/226, 1367.
s. 2, regs. 75/1241.
s. 2, see *London Borough of Southwark* v. *Charlesworth* (1983) 2 Tr.L 95, D.C.
s. 3, see *Riley* v. *Webb* [1987] Crim.L.R. 477, D.C.
sch., regs. 77/167; 78/836, 1372; 79/1125; 85/2047.
41. Flood Prevention (Scotland) Act 1961.
s. 3, amended: 1979, c.46, sch.4; 1984, c.12, sch.4.
s. 5, repealed: 1973, c.65, sch.29.
s. 11, repealed in pt.: *ibid.,* sch.29.
s. 15, amended: *ibid.,* sch.27; 1984, c.54, sch.9; repealed in pt.: 1973, c.65, sch.29.
schs. 1, 2, amended: 1981, c.38, sch.3; 1984, c.12, sch.4.
42. Sheriffs' Pension (Scotland) Act 1961.
ss. 1 (in pt.), 8 (in pt.), sch. 2, repealed: S.L.R. 1974.
43. Public Authorities (Allowances) Act 1961.
repealed: S.L.R. 1976.
44. Barristers (Qualification for Office) Act 1961.
s. 1, amended: 1974, c.47, sch.3.
45. Rating and Valuation Act 1961.
s. 29, repealed in pt.: 1975, c.7, sch 13
46. Companies (Floating Charges) (Scotland) Act 1961.
repealed (except s. 7): 1972, c.67, s.30.
see *Royal Bank of Scotland* v. *Williamson,* 1972 S.L.T.(Sh.Ct.) 45.
s. 7, repealed: 1985, c.9, sch.1.
47. Mock Auctions Act 1961.
see R. v. *Ingram* (1976) 64 Cr.App.R. 119, C.A.
s. 1, see *Aitchison* v. *Cooper,* 1982 S.L.T.(Sh.Ct.) 41.
ss. 1, 3, see *Allen* v. *Simmons* [1978] 1 W.L.R. 79; [1978] Crim.L.R. 362, D.C.; *Clements* v. *Rydeheard* [1978] 1 All E.R. 658, D.C.; R. v. *Pollard* (1984) 148 J.P.N. 683, C.A.
48. Land Drainage Act 1961.
repealed: 1976, c.70, sch.8.
s. 22, see *British Gas Corporation (formerly North Thames Gas Board)* v. *Anglian Water Authority (formerly Essex River Authority)* (1975) 73 L.G.R. 376.
s. 29, see *Rimmer* v. *River Crossens Drainage Board* (1976) 239 E.G. 817.
49. Covent Garden Market Act 1961.
s. 29, repealed in pt.: 1977, c.2, s.4.
ss. 37, 42, 44, substituted: *ibid.,* s.3.
s. 38, amended and repealed in pt.: 1974, c.8, sch.2.
s. 43, repealed in pt.: 1977, c.2, s.3.
ss. 45, 46, amended: *ibid.*
s. 47, repealed: 1975, c.24, sch.3.
s. 48, amended: 1975, c.76, sch.1; repealed in pt.: *ibid.,* sch.2.
sch. 1, amended: 1972, c.11, sch.6; repealed in pt.: *ibid.,* schs.4,8.

CAP.

9 & 10 Eliz. 2 (1960–61)—cont.

50. Rivers (Prevention of Pollution) Act 1961.
repealed (except ss. 10, 12, 13 (1), 15 (1) (3)):
1974, c.40, sch.4.
s. 6, amended: 1981, c.54, sch.9.
s. 13, amended: 1973, c.37, sch.9.
s. 14, repealed in pt.: 1985, c.51, sch.17.
s. 15, repealed in pt.: S.L.R. 1974.

51. Post Office Act 1961.
repealed: 1981, c.38, sch.6.

52. Army and Air Force Act 1961.
s. 13, amended: regs. 77/1097.
s. 24, repealed: 1981, c.55, sch.5.
s. 26, repealed in pt.: *ibid.*
s. 29, repealed in pt.: S.L.R. 1974.
sch. 2, amended: regs. 77/1097; repealed in
pt.: S.L.R. 1974; 1980, c.9, sch.10.

54. Human Tissue Act 1961.
s. 1, see *R.* v. *Lennox-Wright* [1973] Crim.L.R.
529, Lawson J.
s. 1, amended: 1986, c.18, s.1.
ss. 2 (in pt.), 3, repealed: 1984, c.14, s.13.
s. 4, repealed in pt.: S.L.R. 1974.

55. Crown Estate Act 1961.
s. 1, see *Walford* v. *Crown Estate Commissioners* (O.H.), 1988 S.L.T. 377.
s. 3, amended: 1976, c.4, sch.5; 1983, c.29,
s.5.
s. 6, regs. 73/1113.
ss. 9, 10, repealed in pt.: S.L.R. 1974.
sch. 2, amended: 1974, c.38, s.20.
sch. 3, repealed: *ibid.*

57. Trusts (Scotland) Act 1961.
s. 1, see *Nimmo*, 1972 S.L.T.(Notes) 68; *Henderson, Petr.*, 1981 S.L.T.(Notes) 40; *Lord
Binning, Petr.*, First Division, January 6, 1983;
Morris, Petr., 1985 S.L.T. 252.
s. 2, Act of Sederunt 80/1803.
s. 2, amended: 1980, c.55, s.8.
s. 5, see *McIver* v. *I.R.C.* [1973] T.R. 133; 1974
S.L.T. 202; *Baird* v. *Lord Advocate* [1979] 2
W.L.R. 369, H.L.; *Thompson's Trs.* v. *Inland
Revenue* (H.L.), 1979 S.L.T. 166.

58. Crofters (Scotland) Act 1961.
see *Byrne* v. *Guthrie*, 1974 S.L.T.(Land Ct.) 6.
s. 2, amended: 1976, c.21, sch.2; repealed in
pt.: S.L.R. 1974; 1976, c.21, schs.2,3.
s. 3, amended: *ibid.*, sch.2.
s. 4, see *Laird*, 1973 S.L.T. 4; *MacLennan's
Excrx.* v. *MacLennan*, 1974 S.L.T.(Land Ct.) 3;
Duke of Argyll's Trs. v. *Macneill*, 1983 S.L.T.
(Land Ct.) 35; *Fraser* v. *Van Arman*, 1982
S.L.C.R. 79.
s. 4, amended: 1976, c.21, sch.2; repealed in
pt.: S.L.R. 1974.
s. 6, see *Thomson* v. *Stewart*, 1972
S.L.C.R.App. 105; *MacDonald's Exr.* v. *Wills*,
1972 S.L.C.R.App. 108.
s. 6, repealed in pt.: S.L.R. 1974; 1976, c.21,
sch.3.
s. 7, repealed: 1976, c.21, sch.3.
s. 8, repealed in pt.: *ibid.*
ss. 9 (in pt.), 10, 11 (in pt.), repealed: S.L.R.
1974.
ss. 11, 13, see *Carnach Crofts* v. *Robertson*,
1973 S.L.T. 8.

CAP.

9 & 10 Eliz. 2 (1960–61)—cont.

58. Crofters (Scotland) Act 1961—*cont.*
ss. 12–15, amended: 1976, c.21, sch.2.
s. 14, schemes 72/407, 1338; 74/118, 1604,
1870, 2152; 88/559; regs. 82/1419.
ss. 14, 15, amended: 1976, c.21, sch.2.
s. 18, repealed in pt.: S.L.R. 1974.
sch. 1, see *Watson* v. *Maclennan*, 1972
S.L.T.(Land.Ct.) 2.
schs. 1 (in pt.), 3, repealed: S.L.R. 1974.

60. Suicide Act 1961.
see *R.* v. *Inner West London Coroner, ex p. De
Luca* [1988] 3 W.L.R. 286, D.C.
ss. 1, 2, see *R.* v. *McShane* [1977] Crim. L.R.
737, C.A.; (1977) 66 Cr.App.R. 97, C.A.
s. 2, see *Att.-Gen.* v. *Able* [1984] 1 All E.R. 277,
Woolf J.
s. 2, repealed in pt.: 1975, c.59, sch.6.
s. 3, repealed in pt.: S.L.R. 1974.
sch. 1, repealed in pt.: 1977, c.45, sch.13.
sch. 2, repealed: S.L.R. 1974.

62. Trustee Investments Act 1961.
see *Mason* v. *Farbrother* [1983] 2 All E.R. 1078,
H.H. Judge Blackett-Ord; *R.* v. *Chief Registrar
of Friendly Societies, ex p. New Cross Building Society, The Times*, January 14, 1984,
C.A.; *Trustees of the British Museum* v.
Att.-Gen. [1984] 1 All E.R. 337, Megarry V.-C.;
Fraser, Petr. (O.H.), 1987 S.C.L.R. 577.
s. 1, see *Trustees of the British Museum* v.
Att.-Gen., The Times, October 25, 1983, Sir
Robert Megarry V.-C.
s. 6, see *Cowan* v. *Scargill* [1984] 3 W.L.R. 501,
Sir Robert Megarry V.-C.
s. 7, amended (S.): 1982, c.43, sch.3.
s. 8, order 75/2039.
s. 11, amended: 1972, c.11, sch.6; 1985, c.51,
sch.14; order 85/1884; 1986, c.60, sch.16;
1988, c.4, sch.6; repealed in pt.: 1972, c.70,
sch.30; 1985, c.51, sch.17; 1988, c.40, sch.13
(prosp.).
s. 12, orders 73/1332; 75/1710; 77/831, 1878;
81/1547; 82/1086; 83/772, 1525; 85/1780;
86/601; 88/2254.
s. 15, see *Henderson, Petr.*, 1981 S.L.T.(Notes)
40.
s. 16, repealed in pt.: S.L.R. 1974.
s. 17, repealed in pt.: 1985, c.58, sch.4.
sch. 1, amended: orders 77/831, 1878;
81/1547; 82/1086; 83/772, 1525; 1982, c.39,
s.150; 1985, c.71, sch.2; order 85/1780;
1986, c.53, schs.18,19; c.60, sch.16;
repealed in pt.: 1972, c.70, sch.30; 1976, c.4,
sch.6; S.L.R. 1981.
sch. 4, repealed in pt.: 1985, c.71, sch.1.
sch. 5, repealed: S.L.R. 1974.

**63. Highways (Miscellaneous Provisions) Act
1961.**
repealed: 1980, c.66, sch.25.
s. 1, scheme 73/1008.
s. 1, see *Pridham* v. *Hemel Hempstead Corporation* (1970) 69 L.G.R. 523; *Rider* v. *Rider*
[1973] 2 W.L.R. 190, C.A.; *Tarrant* v. *Rowlands* [1979] R.T.R. 144, Cantley J.; *Hughlock*
v. *Department of Transport*, June 18, 1981,
Mars-Jones J.

CAP.

9 & 10 Eliz. 2 (1960–61)—cont.

63. Highways (Miscellaneous Provisions) Act 1961—cont.
s. 3, schemes 72/1296, 1332, 1476, 1884; 73/1511; 74/1646, 1660, 1661; 76/279; 77/2190; 79/1664, 1674, 1675; 80/106, 1006, 1113, 1223, 1242, 1444, 1728, 1729; instruments 74/725, 955; 75/1076; 76/1036, 2240; 77/31, 751; 78/830, 1296; 79/606, 1260; 80/2002.
s. 4, amended: 1972, c.70, sch.21.
s. 7, repealed: 1976, c.57, sch.2.
s. 12, repealed: S.L.R. 1974.
s. 14, repealed in pt.: 1972, c.70, sch.30.

64. Public Health Act 1961.
see *Fuller* v. *Nicholas, The Times,* April 18, 1984, D.C.; *Investors in Industry Commercial Properties* v. *South Bedfordshire District Council, The Times,* December 31, 1985, C.A.
s. 1, amended: 1974, c.37, s.76; repealed in pt.: 1984, c.22, sch.3.
s. 2, repealed in pt.: 1972, c.70, sch.30.
s. 4, see *Bassetlaw District Council* v. *Dyson* (1976) 241 E.G. 837, D.C.; *Estate Products (Frozen Foods)* v. *Doncaster Borough Council* [1980] Crim.L.R. 108, Doncaster Crown Ct.
s. 4, regs. 72/317; 73/1276; 78/723; 79/601; 80/286; 81/1338; 82/577; 83/195, 1611.
ss. 4–11, repealed: 1984, c.55, sch.7.
s. 9, regs. 78/723; 83/195.
ss. 12–14, amended: 1973, c.37, s.14.
s. 14, see *Hertsmere Borough Council* v. *Dunn (Alan) Building Contractors* [1985] Crim.L.R. 726, D.C.
s. 15, repealed: 1973, c.37, sch.9.
s. 16, repealed: 1972, c.70, schs.14,30.
s. 17, see *Rotherham Metropolitan Borough Council* v. *Dodds* [1986] 2 All E.R. 867, C.A.
s. 17, substituted: 1982, c.30, s.27; amended: 1984, c.55, sch.6.
s. 18, substituted: 1982, c.30, s.27.
ss. 19–21, 23–33, repealed: 1984, c.55, sch.7.
ss. 25, 27, see *Re All Saints', Plymouth* [1980] 3 W.L.R. 876, Exeter Consistory Ct.
s. 34, amended: 1972, c.70, sch.14; 1974, c.40, sch.3.
ss. 38–42, repealed: 1984, c.22, sch.8.
s. 41, amended: 1984, c.30, sch.10.
ss. 43, 44, 46–50, repealed: 1980, c.66, sch.25.
s. 51, repealed: 1983, c.35, sch.2.
ss. 52, 53, amended: 1972, c.70, sch.14.
s. 54, amended: *ibid.*; repealed in pt.: *ibid.,* sch.30.
ss. 55–57, repealed: 1974, c.40, sch.4.
s. 58, repealed: S.L.R. 1974.
s. 63, repealed in pt.: 1974, c.40, sch.4.
s. 65, repealed: 1973, c.37, sch.9.
s. 66, amended: 1981, c.54, sch.5.
s. 73, amended: 1985, c.51, sch.11.
s. 74, amended: 1981, c.69, s.72.
s. 75, see *Walker* v. *Leeds City Council; Greenwich L.B.C.* v. *Hunt* [1976] 3 W.L.R. 736; [1976] 3 All E.R. 709, H.L.
s. 75, amended: 1976, c.57, s.22; repealed in pt.: *ibid.,* sch.2.
s. 76, repealed in pt.: *ibid.,* s.17, sch.2.

CAP.

9 & 10 Eliz. 2 (1960–61)—cont.

64. Public Health Act 1961—cont.
s. 78, repealed: 1981, c.12, s.5.
s. 79, repealed: S.L.R. 1974.
s. 80, repealed: 1976, c.57, sch.2.
s. 81, repealed in pt.: 1985, c.51, sch.17.
s. 82, order 72/582.
s. 86, repealed in pt.: S.L.R. 1974.
sch. 1, repealed: 1984, c.55, sch.7.
sch. 2, amended: 1973, c.37, sch.8.
sch. 3, amended: 1980, c.65, sch.7.
sch. 4, amended: 1981, c.38, sch.3.
sch. 5, repealed: S.L.R. 1974.

65. Housing Act 1961.
repealed: 1985, c.71, sch.1.
ss. 12, 15, 19, see *R.* v. *Camden London Borough Council, ex p. Rowton (Camden Town)* [1984] L.G.R. 614, McCullough J.
s. 13, see *Neville* v. *Mavroghenis* [1984] Crim.L.R. 42, D.C.
ss. 15, 16, see *Honig* v. *Islington L.B.C.* [1972] Crim.L.R. 126.
ss. 15, 19, see *Simmons* v. *Pizzey* [1977] 2 All E.R. 432, H.L.; *R.* v. *Hackney London Borough Council, ex p. Thrasyvoulou* (1986) 84 L.G.R. 823, C.A.; *R.* v. *Hackney London Borough Council, ex p. Evenbray, The Times,* September 15, 1987, Kennedy J.
s. 17, see *Berg* v. *Trafford Borough Council, The Times,* July 14, 1987, C.A.
s. 19, see *Black* v. *Oliver* [1978] 2 W.L.R. 923, C.A.; *Topfell* v. *Galley Properties, The Times,* October 27, 1978, Templeman J.; *Hackney London Borough* v. *Ezedinma* [1981] 3 All E.R. 438, D.C.
s. 32, see *O'Brien* v. *Robinson* [1973] 2 W.L.R. 393; [1973] 1 All E.R. 583, H.L.; *Sheldon* v. *West Bromwich Corporation* (1973) 25 P. & C.R. 360, C.A.; *Hopwood* v. *Cannock Chase District Council (formerly Rugeley U.D.C.)* [1975] 1 W.L.R. 373; [1975] 1 All E.R. 796, C.A.; *Liverpool City Council* v. *Irwin* [1976] 2 W.L.R. 562; [1976] 2 All E.R. 39, H.L.; *Campden Hill Towers* v. *Gardner* [1977] 2 W.L.R. 159, C.A.; *Newham London Borough* v. *Patel* [1979] J.P.L. 303, C.A.; *Wycombe Area Health Authority* v. *Barnett* (1982) 264 E.G. 619, C.A.; *Douglas-Scott* v. *Scorgie* [1984] 1 All E.R. 1086, C.A.; *McGreal* v. *Wake* (1984) 269 E.G. 1254, C.A.; *Wainwright* v. *Leeds City Council* (1984) 270 E.G. 1289; (1984) 82 L.G.R. 657, C.A.; *McCoys & Co.* v. *Clark* (1982) 13 H.L.R. 89, C.A.; *Taylor* v. *Knowsley Borough Council* (1985) 17 H.L.R. 376, C.A.; *Quick* v. *Taff-Ely Borough Council* [1985] 3 All E.R. 321, C.A.; *Bradley* v. *Chorley Borough Council* (1985) 83 L.G.R. 623; (1985) 17 H.L.R. 305, C.A.; *Fraser* v. *Hopewood Properties,* October 29, 1985, H.H. Judge Parker, West London County Ct.; *Murray* v. *Birmingham City Council* (1987) 283 E.G. 962, C.A.; *Palmer* v. *Sandwell Metropolitan Borough* (1987) 284 E.G. 1487, C.A.; *Morris* v. *Liverpool City Council* [1988] 14 E.G. 59, C.A.

CAP.

9 & 10 Eliz. 2 (1960–61)—cont.

65. Housing Act 1961—*cont.*
ss. 32, 33, see *Parker* v. *O'Connor* [1973] 1
W.L.R. 1160; [1974] 3 All E.R. 257, C.A.;
Brikom Investments v. *Seaford* [1981] 1
W.L.R. 863, C.A.; *Department of Transport* v.
Egoroff (1986) 278 E.G. 1361, C.A.

10 & 11 Eliz. 2 (1961–62)

1. Tanganyika Independence Act 1961.
s. 2, repealed: 1981, c.61, sch.9.
s. 3, repealed in pt.: 1978, c.30, sch.3.
s. 4, repealed: S.L.R. 1976.
sch. 2, repealed: 1981, c.9, sch.; repealed in
pt.: 1986, c.55, sch.2; 1988, c.48, sch.8.

2. Southern Rhodesia (Constitution) Act 1961.
repealed: 1979, c.60, sch.3.

8. Civil Aviation (Eurocontrol) Act 1962.
ss. 1–4, repealed: 1982, c.16, sch.16.
ss. 4, 7, regs. 72/108, 188, 905; 73/1196, 1678,
2070; 74/564, 1132, 1144, 2064; 75/122,
1631, 1968, 2071; 76/369, 883, 2084, 2085;
77/287, 314, 340, 1437, 2033; 78/241, 245,
317, 554, 693, 837, 1799; 79/154, 237, 267,
1274, 1599; 80/317, 356, 1349, 1892; 81/355,
362, 803, 1237, 1746; 82/175, 261, 356, 1093.
s. 5, repealed in pt.: 1982, c.16, sch.16.
ss. 6–8, repealed: *ibid.*
s. 9, repealed: 1981, c.1, schs.1,2; c.16, sch.16.
s. 10, repealed: *ibid.*

**9. Local Government (Financial Provisions, etc.)
(Scotland) Act 1962.**
s. 1, repealed: 1973, c.65, sch.29.
s. 2, repealed: orders 78/1174, 1175.
s. 3, regs. 78/1096; repealed: order 78/1176;
amended: 1980, c.45, sch.10.
s. 4, regs. 78/1096; orders 83/534; 84/193.
s. 4, amended: 1976, c.45, s.1; 1981, c.23, s.5;
1982, c.43, s.5; 1987, c.47, sch.1; 1988, c.41,
sch.12; repealed in pt.: 1975, c.30, sch.7;
1981, c.23, s.5, sch.4.
s. 5, repealed: S.L.R. 1986.
ss. 6, 7, 9, repealed: 1975, c.30, sch.7.
s. 11, repealed: 1973, c.65, sch.29.
s. 12, repealed in pt.: S.L.R. 1974.
sch. 2, repealed in pt.: 1973, c.65, sch.29; order
78/1175.
sch. 3, repealed: S.L.R. 1974.

10. Army Reserve Act 1962.
repealed: 1980, c.9, sch.10.

12. Education Act 1962.
see *R.* v. *Haringey London Borough, ex p. Lee,
The Times,* July 31, 1984, Glidewell J.; *R.* v.
*Hertfordshire County Council, ex p. Cheung:
R.* v. *Sefton Metropolitan Borough Council, ex
p. Pau, The Times,* April 4, 1986, C.A.
s. 1, see *Cicutti* v. *Suffolk County Council* [1980]
3 All E.R. 689, Megarry V.-C.; *R.* v. *Barnet
London Borough Council, ex p. Nilish Shah*
[1983] 2 W.L.R. 16, H.L.; *R.* v. *West Glamorgan County Council, ex p. Gheissary; R. v.
East Sussex County Council, ex p. Khatib-
shahidi, The Times,* December 18, 1985,
Hodgson J.; *R.* v. *Lancashire County Council,
ex p. Huddleston* [1986] 2 All E.R. 941, C.A.

CAP.

10 & 11 Eliz. 2 (1961–62)—cont.

12. Education Act 1962—*cont.*
s. 1, regs. 72/1124; 73/1233, 1234, 1298, 1644;
74/1231, 1540; 75/1207, 1697; 76/1087;
77/536, 1409; 78/1097; 79/889; 80/974,
1149, 1247; 81/943, 1193; 82/954, 1295;
83/114, 477, 1135; 84/1116, 1240; 85/1126;
86/1306, 1397; 87/1261, 2199; 88/477, 1360.
s. 1, amended: 1984, c.11, s.4.
ss. 1–4, substituted: 1980, c.20, s.19, sch.5.
s. 3, regs. 73/1234; 74/1231; 75/940, 1225;
76/613; 77/1308; 79/333; 81/1328; 82/559,
1041; 83/188, 431, 481, 920, 1274, 1747;
84/446, 893; 85/741, 1220, 1883; 86/1324,
1346; 87/96, 499, 1365, 1393; 88/1360.
s. 3, repealed in pt.: 1986, c.61, sch.6.
s. 4, regs. 77/1409, 1443; 78/1097; 79/333,
889; 80/974, 1352; 81/943, 1193, 1328;
82/954, 1295; 83/114, 188, 431, 477, 481,
920, 1135, 1274, 1747; 84/446, 893, 1116,
1240; 85/741, 1126, 1220, 1883; 86/1306,
1324, 1346, 1397; 87/96, 499, 1261, 1365,
1393, 2199; 88/477, 1360, 1392.
s. 4, amended: 1986, c.61, sch.4; repealed in
pt.: *ibid.,* sch.6.
s. 7, repealed: S.L.R. 1975.
s. 8, repealed: S.L.R. 1977.
s. 9, order 87/275.
s. 9, amended: 1976, c.5, s.1, repealed in pt.:
1975, c.18, sch.1; 1976, c.5, sch.
s. 11, repealed: S.L.R. 1978.
ss. 12, 14, repealed in pt.: *ibid.*
s. 13, repealed in pt.: S.L.R. 1974.
s. 14, regs. 77/1307.
sch. 1, regs. 77/1307; 78/1097; 80/974, 1352;
81/943, 1193; 82/954; 83/1135; 84/1116,
1240; 85/1126; 86/1306; 87/1261;88/1360.
sch. 1, amended: 1976, c.81, s.8; substituted:
1980, c.20, s.19, sch.5.
sch. 2, repealed: *ibid.*

13. Vehicles (Excise) Act 1962.
repealed: S.L.R. 1975.
ss. 7, 12, see *Seeney* v. *Dean* [1972] R.T.R. 25.

15. Criminal Justice Administration Act 1962.
repealed: S.L.R. 1981.
sch. 3, repealed in pt.: 1981, c.45, sch.

**16. Forth and Clyde Canal (Extinguishment of
Rights of Navigation) Act 1962.**
repealed: S.L.R. 1977.

19. West Indies Act 1962.
s. 4, order 83/1112.
s. 5, orders 72/1101; 73/599, 759; 76/55, 1156,
2145; 79/919; 82/151, 1075; 84/126;
86/1157; 87/934, 1271, 1829.
ss. 5, 7, orders 72/808; 79/1603; 83/1112, 2199;
88/247.
sch., repealed: S.L.R. 1974.

20. International Monetary Fund Act 1962.
repealed: 1979, c.29, sch.

21. Commonwealth Immigrants Act 1962.
s. 2, see *R.* v. *Immigration Appeals Adjudicator,
ex p. Khan* [1972] 1 W.L.R. 1058.
s. 4, see *Nawaz* v. *Lord Advocate,* 1983 S.L.T.
653.

10 & 11 Eliz. 2 (1961–62)—cont.

21. Commonwealth Immigrants Act 1962—*cont.*
ss. 4, 4A, see *Azam* v. *Secretary of State for the Home Department; Khera* v. *Same; Sidhu* v. *Same* [1973] 2 W.L.R. 1058; [1973] 2 All E.R. 765.
s. 7, see *R.* v. *Hussain* (1971) 56 Cr.App.R. 165.
s. 12, repealed in pt.: 1981, c.61, sch.9.
s. 20, repealed: 1973, c.45, sch.6.
sch. 1, see *R.* v. *Chief Immigration Officer Manchester Airport* [1973] 1 W.L.R. 141, C.A.

22. Coal Consumers' Councils (Northern Irish Interests) Act 1962.
s. 1, amended: 1972, c.68, sch.3.

23. South Africa Act 1962.
s. 1, repealed in pt.: 1981, c.61, sch.9.
ss. 1, 2, repealed in pt.: S.L.R. 1974.
s. 3, amended: 1973, c.36, sch.6.
sch. 1, repealed: 1973, c.61, sch.3.
sch. 2, amended: 1972, c.18, s.22; c.68, sch.3.
sch. 3, repealed in pt.: S.L.R. 1976; 1983, c.38, sch.3; c.54, sch.7; 1986, c.55, sch.2.
sch. 4, repealed in pt.: 1986, c.60, sch.17.
sch. 5, repealed: S.L.R. 1974.

24. National Assistance Act 1948 (Amendment) Act 1962.
s. 1, repealed in pt.: 1980, c.7, sch.2.

26. Animals (Cruel Poisons) Act 1962.
s. 1, amended: 1977, c.45, s.31, sch.6.

27. Recorded Delivery Service Act 1962.
s. 3, repealed in pt.: 1973, c.36, sch.6.
sch., repealed in pt.: 1981, c.54, sch.7.

28. Housing (Scotland) Act 1962.
repealed: 1987, c.26, sch.24.

29. Agricultural and Forestry Associations Act 1962.
repealed: 1976, c.34, sch.6.
s. 1, order 74/1836.

30. Northern Ireland Act 1962.
ss. 1–5, repealed: 1978, c.23, sch.7.
s. 7, S.R.s 1977 No. 348; 1978 Nos. 128, 180, 181, 287.
ss. 7–11, repealed: 1978, c.23, sch.7.
ss. 12–21, 22 (in pt.), repealed: 1973, c.36, sch.6.
s. 25, repealed in pt.: S.L.R. 1974; S.L.R. 1978.
s. 27, repealed: 1978, c.30, sch.3.
s. 28, repealed: S.L.R. 1974.
s. 29, repealed in pt.: 1973, c.36, sch.6; S.L.R. 1978.
s. 30, repealed in pt.: S.L.R. 1974.
sch. 1, repealed: 1978, c.23, sch.7.
sch. 2, repealed in pt.: 1984, c.12, sch.7.
schs. 3, 4, repealed: S.L.R. 1974.

31. Sea Fish Industry Act 1962.
s. 37, sch. 4, repealed: S.L.R. 1974.

33. Health Visiting and Social Work (Training) Act 1962.
repealed: 1983, c.41, sch.10.
s. 3, orders 74/1265; 77/1240.

35. Shops (Airports) Act 1962.
s. 1, orders 74/1124; 77/1397, 1919; 80/774; 85/654, 1739; 86/981; 87/837 (S.), 1983.
s. 1, amended: 1986, c.31, s.70.

10 & 11 Eliz. 2 (1961–62)—cont.

36. Local Authorities (Historic Buildings) Act 1962.
s. 1, amended: 1988, c.4, sch.3; repealed in pt.: S.L.R. 1976.
s. 2, see *Canterbury City Council* v. *Quine* (1987) 284 E.G. 507, C.A.
s. 3, repealed: S.L.R. 1976

37. Building Societies Act 1962.
repealed: 1986, c.53, sch.19.
s. 1, see *Nationwide Building Society* v. *Registry of Friendly Societies* [1983] 3 All E.R. 296, Peter Gibson J.
s. 21, orders 75/1205; 79/1639; 80/2003; 82/1056.
ss. 21, 22, see *R.* v. *Chief Registrar of Friendly Societies, ex p. New Cross Building Society* [1984] 2 All E.R. 370, C.A.
s. 25, see *Martin* v. *Bell-Ingram*, 1986 S.L.T. 575.
s. 32, see *Re Abbots Park* [1972] 1 W.L.R. 598; [1972] 2 All E.R. 177; *Nash* v. *Halifax Building Society* [1979] 2 W.L.R. 184, Browne-Wilkinson J.
s. 34, amended (S.): 1985, c.73, sch.1.
s. 43, see *Halifax Building Society* v. *Registrar of Friendly Societies* [1978] 3 All E.R. 403, Templeman J.
s. 48, see *R.* v. *Chief Registrar of Friendly Societies, ex p. New Cross Building Society* [1984] 2 All E.R. 370, C.A.
s. 58, orders 75/1995; 77/851, 2052, 79/1301; 82/1761; 83/1769; 86/406.
ss. 78, 88, regs. 72/70.
ss. 78, 88, 91, regs. 76/1935; 80/1472; 81/1497; 83/1768.
s. 123, regs. 74/1305; 76/342; 77/2000; 78/1752; 79/1550; 81/1753; 83/372; 84/279; 85/339; 86/406.
sch. 3, amended (S.): 1980, c.52, s.31; repealed in pt. (S.): 1986, c.65, sch.3.
sch. 5, amended: 1973, c.65, sch.27.
sch. 10, repealed: S.L.R. 1974.

38. Town and Country Planning Act 1962.
see *R.* v. *Yeovil B.C.* (1971) 116 S.J. 78; 70 L.G.R. 142; 23 P. & C.R. 39.
s. 12, see *Lewis* v. *Secretary of State* (1971) 23 P. & C.R. 125; 70 L.G.R. 291; *David* v. *Penybont R.D.C.* [1972] 1 W.L.R. 1526; [1972] 3 All E.R. 1092.
s. 17, see *R.M.C.* v. *Secretary of State* (1972) 222 E.G. 1593.
ss. 17, 18, 23, see *London Corporation* v. *Secretary of State* (1971) 23 P. & C.R. 169.
s. 29, see *Barnet B.C.* v. *Eastern Electricity Board* [1973] 1 W.L.R. 430, D.C.
s. 34, regs. 72/489.
s. 45, see *Stevens* v. *Bromley B.C.* [1972] Ch. 400; [1972] 2 W.L.R. 605; [1972] 1 All E.R. 712.
s. 73, see *Wilson* v. *Secretary of State for the Environment* [1973] 1 W.L.R. 1083, Browne J.
s. 129, see *Essex Incorporated Congregational Union* v. *Colchester Borough Council* (Ref./49/1980) (1982) 263 E.G. 167.

CAP.

10 & 11 Eliz. 2 (1961–62)—cont.

38. Town and Country Planning Act 1962—*cont.*
ss. 129, 130, see *Zoar Independent Church Trustees* v. *Rochester Corporation* [1974] 3 All E.R. 5, C.A.
ss. 129, 132, see *Plymouth Corporation* v. *Secretary of State* [1972] 1 W.L.R. 1347; [1972] 3 All E.R. 225.
s. 133, see *Provincial Properties (London)* v. *Caterham & Warlingham U.D.C.* [1972] 2 W.L.R. 44; [1972] 1 All E.R. 60.
s. 179, see *Vale Estates, Acton* v. *Secretary of State for the Environment* (1970) 69 L.G.R. 543.
s. 199, see *Molton Builders* v. *City of Westminster L.B.C.* (1975) P. & C.R. 182, C.A.
s. 214, see *Maltglade* v. *St. Albans R.D.C.* [1972] 1 W.L.R. 1230; [1972] 3 All E.R. 129.
s. 217, regs. 72/489.
s. 221, see *R.* v. *Plymouth City Council and Cornwall County Council, ex p. Freeman* (1988) 28 R.V.R. 89, C.A.
s. 224, repealed in pt.: S.L.R. 1975.
sch. 12, repealed in pt.: 1982, c.16, sch.16.
sch. 13, see *Bedfordshire C.C.* v. *Secretary of State* (1972) 71 L.G.R. 420.

39. Drainage Rates Act 1962.
repealed: 1976, c.70, sch.8.

40. Jamaica Independence Act 1962.
s. 2, repealed: 1981, c.61, sch.9.
s. 3, repealed in pt.: 1978, c.30, sch.3.
sch. 2, repealed in pt.: S.L.R. 1977; 1981, c.9, sch.; 1986, c.55, sch.2; 1988, c.48, sch.8.

41. Colonial Loans Act 1962.
repealed: 1980, c.63, sch.2.

42. Law Reform (Damages and Solatium) (Scotland) Act 1962.
repealed (S.): 1976, c.13, sch.2.

43. Carriage by Air (Supplementary Provisions) Act 1962.
s. 3, repealed in pt.: 1978, c.47, sch.2.
s. 4, amended: 1979, c.28, sch.2.
s. 4A, added: *ibid.*, s.3.
sch. amended: *ibid.*, sch.2.

44. Finance Act 1962.
s. 1, repealed in pt.: S.L.R. 1975; 1975, c.45, sch.14.
s. 2, repealed: 1973, c.51, sch.22.
s. 3, repealed: 1972, c.68, sch.3.
s. 10, see *McBrearty* v. *I.R.C.* [1975] T.R. 45.
ss. 12, 13, see *Thompson* v. *Salan* [1972] 1 All E.R. 530.
s. 13, see *Lord Chetwode* v. *I.R.C.* [1976] 1 W.L.R. 310; [1976] 1 All E.R. 641, C.A.
s. 16, see *Macpherson* v. *Hall* [1972] T.R. 41.
ss. 28, 29, repealed: 1975, c.7, sch.13.
s. 30, repealed: 1988, c.39, s.140, sch.14.
s. 32, repealed: 1977, c.36, sch.9.
s. 33, orders 73/1407; 74/1935; 75/692; 77/1536.
s. 33, repealed in pt.: S.L.R. 1974.
s. 34, repealed in pt.: 1975, c.7, sch.13; 1979, c.2, sch.6.
sch. 5, repealed: 1972, c.68, sch.3.
sch. 9, see *Macpherson* v. *Hall* [1972] T.R. 41.
sch. 10, see *Lord Chetwode* v. *I.R.C.* [1976] 1 W.L.R. 310; [1976] 1 All E.R. 641, C.A.
sch. 11, repealed in pt.: S.L.R. 1974.

CAP.

10 & 11 Eliz. 2 (1961–62)—cont.

46. Transport Act 1962.
s. 1, repealed in pt.: 1981, c.56, sch.12.
s. 1, see *Botwood* v. *Phillips* [1976] R.T.R. 260, D.C.
s. 3, amended: 1985, c.67, sch.7; 1987, c.53, s.39.
s. 4, amended: 1980, c.34, sch.5 repealed in pt.: 1985, c.67, sch.8.
s. 4A, added: *ibid.*, s.118.
s. 5, repealed in pt.: order 84/1747.
s. 9, repealed: 1981, c.56, sch.12.
s. 15, amended: 1981, c.67, sch.4, repealed in pt.: *ibid.*, sch.6.
s. 19, order 83/1957.
s. 19, amended: 1974, c.8, sch.2; 1977, c.20, s.3; 1981, c.12, s.1; repealed in pt.: 1977, c.20, s.3; 1981, c.56, sch.12.
s. 21, amended: 1983, c.29, s.4, sch.2; repealed in pt.: 1974, c.8, sch.4.
ss. 22, 23, repealed: S.L.R. 1974.
s. 24, amended: 1985, c.9, sch.2.
s. 27, amended: 1974, c.48, s.4; 1982, c.49, s.3.
s. 31, see *Botwood* v. *Phillips* [1976] R.T.R. 260, D.C.
ss. 33, 34 (in pt.), 36 (in pt.), 38, repealed: S.L.R. 1974.
s. 41, repealed in pt.: 1973, c.51, sch.22.
s. 43, repealed in pt.: S.L.R. 1974; 1977, c.50, sch.4.
s. 52, amended: 1984, c.32, sch.4.
s. 54, amended: *ibid.*, s.42.
s. 56, see *R.* v. *British Railways Board, ex p. Bradford City Metropolitan Council, The Times*, December 8, 1987, C.A.
s. 56, amended: 1981, c.32, s.1; 1984, c.32, s.42; repealed in pt.: S.L.R. 1974.
s. 56A, added: 1981, c.32, s.1.
s. 57, repealed in pt.: S.L.R. 1978; 1985, c.67, sch.8.
s. 60, repealed: S.L.R. 1974.
s. 66, repealed (S.): order 78/1174.
s. 67, see *Hulin* v. *Cook* [1977] R.T.R. 345, D.C.; *Khan* v. *Evans* [1985] R.T.R. 33, D.C.; *Grieve* v. *Hillary*, 1987, S.C.C.R. 317.
s. 67, amended: 1981, c.56, s.37; 1984, c.32, sch.4; repealed in pt.: *ibid.*, sch.7.
s. 68, repealed: *ibid.*, sch.7.
s. 70, amended: *ibid.*, sch.4.
s. 73, amended: *ibid.*, s.25.
s. 74, orders 72/51; 73/1390, 2019; 74/526, 2001, 2045; 75/361; 77/699; 78/1290, 1358; 80/657, 1351; 88/962.
s. 74, amended: 1978, c.44, sch.10; 1984, c.32, s.25.
s. 85, repealed: 1975, c.24, sch.3; c.25, sch.3.
s. 86, functions transferred: order 76/1775; amended: *ibid.*; 1984, c.32, sch.4; repealed in pt.: S.L.R. 1974.
s. 87, amended: 1984, c.32, sch.4.
s. 92, amended: 1985, c.9, sch.2, repealed in pt.: 1985, c.67, sch.8.
s. 93, repealed in pt.: 1973, c.36, sch.6.
sch. 1, amended: 1982, c.49, s.67.

CAP.

10 & 11 Eliz. 2 (1961–62)—cont.

46. Transport Act 1962—cont.

sch. 2, amended: 1984, c.32, sch.4; repealed in pt.: 1980, c.34, sch.9; c.66, sch.25; 1981, c.14, sch.8; c.22, sch.6; 1984, c.30, sch.11; c.32, sch.7.

schs. 2, 3, see *Botwood* v. *Phillips* [1976] R.T.R. 260, D.C.

schs. 3–5, 6 (in pt.), 7 (in pt.), repealed: S.L.R. 1974.

sch. 6, amended: 1984, c.32, sch.4.

sch. 9, repealed in pt.: 1981, c.56, sch.12.

sch. 10, rules 73/934.

sch. 10, repealed: 1985, c.67, sch.8.

sch. 11, repealed in pt.: 1975, c.24, sch.3; c.25, sch.3.

sch. 12, repealed in pt.: S.L.R. 1974.

47. Education (Scotland) Act 1962.

trust scheme 81/739.

repealed (except ss. 136, 137, 145 (in pt.), 148 (in pt.), 149 (in pt.), sch. 8 (in pt)).: 1980, c.44, sch.5.

schemes 73/1813; 74/598, 1188, 1666, 1667; 75/254, 677–99; 76/93, 158, 1366, 1480, 1503; 77/140, 655; 78/776, 1085, 1463; 79/81, 82, 173, 451, 496, 760, 1227; 80/135, 589, 715, 854, 1174; orders 78/372, 561.

s. 1, see *Malloch* v. *Aberdeen Corporation* [1973] 1 W.L.R. 71; [1973] 1 All E.R. 304, H.L.; *Edwards* v. *Lothian Regional Council*, 1981 S.L.T.(Sh.Ct.) 41.

s. 2, regs. 72/776; 73/321, 322.

ss. 2, 5, 10, regs. 75/1135.

s. 19, regs. 79/1185, 1186.

s. 29, see *Kidd* v. *New Kilpatrick School Council*, 1978 S.L.T.(Sh.Ct.) 56; *Brown* v. *Lothian Regional Council*, 1980 S.L.T.(Sh.Ct.) 14; *Sinclair* v. *Lothian Regional Council*, [1981] S.L.T.(Sh.Ct.) 13; *Edwards* v. *Lothian Regional Council*, 1981 S.L.T.(Sh.Ct.) 41.

s. 30, see *Grieve* v. *Lothian Regional Council*, 1978 S.L.T.(Sh.Ct.) 24.

s. 32, regs. 72/59.

s. 33A, order 76/1027.

ss. 35, 36, see *Lanarkshire County Council* v. *Vincent*, 1976 J.C. 5, High Ct. of Justiciary

s. 38, see *Grieve* v. *Lothian Regional Council*, 1978 S.L.T.(Sh.Ct.) 24; *Kidd* v. *New Kilpatrick School Council*, 1978 S.L.T.(Sh.Ct.) 56; *Brown* v. *Lothian Regional Council*, 1980 S.L.T.(Sh.Ct.) 14; *Sinclair* v. *Lothian Regional Council*, 1981 S.L.T.(Sh.Ct.) 13.

s. 39, see *Kent* v. *Glasgow Corporation*, 1974 S.L.T.(Sh.Ct.) 44.

s. 49, regs. 72/844; 73/1176; 74/1173; 75/1228; 76/1104; 77/1150, 1356; 78/998; 79/840; 80/988.

s. 53, regs. 72/1220; 73/423, 1258; 74/708, 1134; 75/296, 1629; 76/1702; 77/362, 1203, 1654; 78/504, 969, 1278; 79/824, 1682.

ss. 70, 71, see *Lord Advocate* v. *Glasgow Corporation*, 1973 S.L.T. 33 (H.L.).

s. 71, see *Edwards* v. *Lothian Regional Council*, 1981 S.L.T.(Sh.Ct.) 41.

s. 75, regs. 74/1187; 75/1135; 76/475, 1431; 79/766; 80/799, 800.

CAP.

10 & 11 Eliz. 2 (1961–62)—cont.

47. Education (Scotland) Act 1962—cont.

s. 76, regs. 72/1753; 74/102, 1187, 1410; 75/520, 1135; 76/66. 475; 77/953.

s. 81, regs. 72/1753, 1891; 74/102, 1410; 75/520, 640, 1135; 76/66, 77/634.

s. 85, see *Scott* v. *Aberdeen Corporation*, First Division, January 22, 1976.

s. 101, see *Lanarkshire County Council* v. *Vincent*, 1976 J.C. 5, High Ct. of Justiciary.

s. 116, rules 74/1701; 77/1261.

ss. 118, 125, schemes 72/1184, 1185, 1508.

ss. 118, 129, scheme 73/1811.

s. 126, orders 72/967; 80/715; 81/739.

s. 137, repealed: 1973, c.24, sch.2.

s. 144, regs. 72/844, 1753; 73/423, 864, 1176, 1258, 1812; 74/102, 708, 1134, 1173, 1187, 1410; 75/296, 640, 1098, 1135, 1228, 1629; 76/475, 1104, 1431, 1702; 77/362, 634, 953, 1150, 1208, 1356, 1654; 78/504, 969, 998, 1278; 79/824, 840, 1682; 80/988.

s. 145, regs. 73/1812; 75/1098, 1135.

s. 145, amended: 1972, c.11, sch.6; c.58, sch. 6; 1973, c.65, sch.11; 1976, c.20, sch.1; 1978, c.29, sch.16; repealed in pt.: 1972, c.58, sch.7; 1973, c.65, sch.29.

s. 147, repealed in pt.: S.L.R. 1974.

sch. 8, repealed: *ibid.*

48. Law Reform (Husband and Wife) Act 1962.

s. 1, repealed in pt.: 1984, c.28, sch.4.

s. 3 (in pt.), sch., repealed: S.L.R. 1974.

49. London County Council (Improvements) Act 1962.

ss. 17, 50, see *Tate and Lyle Industries* v. *G.L.C.* [1983] 2 W.L.R. 649, H.L.

50. Landlord and Tenant Act 1962.

repealed; 1985, c.71, sch.1.

s. 2, regs. 72/1827; 73/1055; 76/378; 82/1474.

s. 6, regs. 82/1474.

51. Licensing (Scotland) Act 1962.

repealed: 1976, c.66, sch.8.

52. Penalties for Drunkenness Act 1962.

s. 1, repealed in pt.: 1976, c.66, sch.8; 1977, c.45, sch.13; 1980, c.62, sch.8.

53. House of Commons Members' Fund Act 1962.

s. 2 (in pt.), sch., repealed: S.L.R. 1974.

54. Trinidad and Tobago Independence Act 1962.

s. 2, repealed: 1981, c.61, sch.9.

s. 3, repealed in pt.: 1978, c.30, sch.3.

sch. 2, repealed in pt.: S.L.R. 1977; 1981, c.9, sch.; 1986, c.55, sch.2; 1988, c.48, sch.8.

56. Local Government (Records) Act 1962.

s. 2, order 86/803.

s. 2, amended: 1985, c.51, schs.8,14; repealed in pt.: 1972, c.70, sch.30; 1988, c.40, sch.13 (prosp.).

s. 3, repealed: *ibid.*

s. 4, repealed in pt.: S.L.R. 1975.

s. 7, repealed in pt.: S.L.R. 1978.

s. 8, amended: 1985, c.51, sch.14; 1988, c.4, sch.3; repealed in pt.: 1972, c.70, sch.30; 1985, c.51, sch.17; 1988, c.40, sch.13 (prosp.).

CAP.

10 & 11 Eliz. 2 (1961–62)—cont.

57. Uganda Independence Act 1962.
s. 2, repealed: 1981, c.61, sch.9.
s. 3, repealed in pt.: 1978, c.30, sch.3.
sch. 3, repealed in pt.: S.L.R. 1977; 1981, c.9, sch.; 1986, c.55, sch.2.

58. Pipelines Act 1962.
s. 5, amended: 1978, c.51, sch.16; c.52, sch.11.
s. 13, amended: regs. 74/1986.
s. 15, functions transferred: order 76/1775.
s. 15, amended: 1980, c.66, sch.24.
ss. 15, 16, amended (S.): 1984, c.54, sch.9.
s. 18, repealed: 1985, c.51, sch.17.
s. 19, repealed: 1980, c.66, sch.25.
s. 20, amended and repealed in pt.: regs.74/1986.
s. 21, amended: ibid.
s. 22, amended and repealed in pt.: ibid.
s. 23, amended: regs. 74/1986; 81/695; repealed in pt.: regs. 74/1986.
s. 24, repealed: order 76/1775.
s. 26, amended and repealed in pt.: regs. 74/1986.
s. 26A, added: 1987, c.12, s.26.
s. 27, amended: 1972, c.60, s.39.
s. 28, amended: 1985, c.71, sch.2.
s. 30, amended: ibid.; 1987, c.26, sch.23 (S.).
s. 31, amended: 1972, c.60, sch.39.
s. 33, repealed: regs. 80/804.
s. 35, repealed in pt.: orders 74/595; 75/1636.
s. 40, amended: 1981, c.38, sch.3; 1984, c.12, sch.4.
s. 42, amended: regs. 74/1986.
s. 46, repealed in pt.: regs. 74/1986.
s. 47, repealed in pt.: ibid.; 1987, c.12, sch.3.
s. 49, amended: 1975, c.74, s.48.
s. 56, repealed: 1979, c.2, sch.6.
s. 57, see BP Development, Re, Financial Times, February 26, 1986, Warner J.
s. 58, amended: 1972, c.60, s.38; 1986, c.44, sch.7; 1987, c.12, s.26; repealed in pt.: regs. 74/1986.
s. 59, amended: 1987, c.12, s.26; repealed in pt.: regs. 74/1986.
ss. 60, 61, repealed in pt.: ibid.
s. 66, amended: 1980, c.66, sch.24; repealed in pt.: regs. 74/1986; 1984, c.54, sch. 11 (S.); 1986, c.44, sch.9.
s. 67, repealed in pt.: S.L.R. 1986.
sch. 1, amended: 1987, c.12, s.25; repealed in pt.: ibid., s.25, sch.3.
sch. 5, repealed: order 76/1775.

59. Road Traffic Act 1962.
repealed (except ss. 49, 51, 52, schs.1,4): 1972, c.20, sch.9.
s. 2, see Langridge v. Taylor [1972] R.T.R. 157; R. v. Banks [1972] 1 W.L.R. 346; 116 S.J. 80; [1972] 1 All E.R. 1041; [1972] R.T.R. 179; 56 Cr.App.R. 310; Kierman v. Willcock [1972] Crim.L.R. 248; [1972] R.T.R. 270; Dickson v. Atkins [1972] Crim.L.R. 185; [1972] R.T.R. 209; Clark v. Stenlake [1972] R.T.R. 276; Piggott v. Sims [1973] R.T.R. 15, D.C.; Hudson v. Hornsby [1973] R.T.R. 4, D.C.; Nicholson v. Watts [1973] R.T.R. 208, D.C.

CAP.

10 & 11 Eliz. 2 (1961–62)—cont.

59. Road Traffic Act 1962—cont.
s. 5, see R. v. Kashyap [1972] R.T.R. 78; Flewitt v. Horvath [1972] Crim.L.R. 103; [1972] R.T.R. 121; R. v. Andersen [1972] Crim.L.R. 245; [1972] R.T.R. 113, C.A.; Coombs v. Kehoe [1972] 1 W.L.R. 797; 116 S.J. 486; [1972] 2 All E.R. 55; [1972] R.T.R. 224; R. v. Middlesex Area Q.S., ex p. Bull [1972] Crim.L.R. 189; [1972] R.T.R. 205; Lambie v. Woodage [1972] 1 W.L.R. 754; 116 S.J. 376; [1972] 2 All E.R. 462; James v. Hall [1972] R.T.R. 228; Reynolds v. Roche [1972] R.T.R. 282; Milliner v. Thorne [1972] Crim.L.R. 245; [1972] R.T.R. 279; Owen v. Imes [1972] R.T.R. 489, D.C.; Alexander v. Latter [1972] R.T.R. 441, D.C.; Pugsley v. Hunter [1973] 1 W.L.R. 578; [1973] 2 All E.R. 10, D.C.; R. v. Bain [1973] R.T.R. 213, C.A.; Holroyd v. Berry [1973] R.T.R. 145, D.C.; R. v. Messom [1973] R.T.R. 140, C.A.; R. v. Messe [1973] 1 W.L.R. 675; R. v. Guilfoyle [1973] R.T.R. 272; [1973] 2 All E.R. 844; Maynard v. Andrews [1973] R.T.R. 398, D.C.; R. v. Hollier [1973] R.T.R. 395, C.A.; R. v. Slade [1974] R.T.R. 20, C.A.
ss. 5, 7, sch. 1, see Kenyon v. Thorley [1973] R.T.R. 60, D.C.
s. 5, sch. 1, see R. v. Bowsher [1973] R.T.R. 202, C.A.
ss. 47, 52, regs. 72/577.
s. 49, repealed in pt.: S.L.R. 1975.
s. 51, sch. 4, see Phipps v. McCormick [1972] R.T.R. 21; Nicholson v. Tapp [1972] 1 W.L.R. 1044; [1972] 3 All E.R. 245; [1972] R.T.R. 313.
schs. 1, 4, repealed in pt.: 1974, c.50, sch.7.
sch. 4, see British Car Auctions v. Wright [1972] 1 W.L.R. 1519; [1972] 3 All E.R. 462.

11 Eliz. 2 (1962)

1. Tanganyika Republic Act 1962.
s. 2, repealed: S.L.R. 1977.

4. Foreign Compensation Act 1962.
s. 3, orders 72/302; 73/234; 74/249; 75/409; 76/220; 77/239, 2148; 78/180; 79/109; 80/186; 81/240; 82/150; 83/145; 84/128; 85/168; 86/219; 87/164.

6. Coal Industry Act 1962.
s. 2, amended: 1987, c.3, sch.1.

1963

2. Betting, Gaming and Lotteries Act 1963.
see Jack v. Edinburgh Corporation, 1973 S.L.T. 64; Low v. Kincardineshire Licensing Court, 1974 S.L.T.(Sh.Ct.) 54; Smillie v. Hamilton Burgh Licensing Court, 1975 S.L.T.(Sh.Ct.) 45.
ss. 5 (in pt.), 6 (in pt.), 7, repealed: 1985, c.18, sch.
s. 8, amended: 1984, c.60, sch.6.
s. 9, see Ladbrokes the Bookmakers v. Hamilton District Council, 1977 S.L.T.(Sh.Ct.) 86; Ladbroke Racing (Strathclyde) v. Cunninghame District Licensing Court and Others, 1978 S.L.T.(Sh.Ct.) 50.

CAP.

2. Betting, Gaming and Lotteries Act 1963— cont.

ss. 9, 10, see *R.* v. *Wenlock Betting Licensing Committee, ex p. Pooler (E.R.)* [1973] 1 W.L.R. 1330; [1973] 3 All E.R. 654, C.A.

s. 10, see *Simpson* v. *Coral (Joe) & Tavern Press* [1972] Crim.L.R. 36; *Windsors (Sporting Investments)* v. *Oldfield; Boulton* v. *Coral Racing* [1981] 1 W.L.R. 1176; [1981] 2 All E.R. 718, D.C.

s. 10, regs. 86/102, 120 (S.).

s. 10, amended: 1984, c.25, ss.1,2.

s. 12, amended: 1972, c.69, s.2; 1985, c.53, s.25.

s. 13, amended: 1972, c.69, s.5

s. 14, amended: *ibid.*, ss.1,4.

s. 16, see *Poole Stadium* v. *Squires* [1982] 1 All E.R. 404, D.C.

s. 16, amended: 1985, c.18, s.2; repealed in pt.: *ibid.*, sch.

s. 18, see *Midland Greyhound Racing Co.* v. *Foley* [1973] 1 W.L.R. 324, D.C.

s. 24, amended: 1985, c.53, s.25.

s. 25, amended: 1972, c.69, s.4.

s. 26, regs. 76/1237; 82/1464.

s. 28, amended: 1982, c.48, schs.3,6 (S.).

ss. 28, 29, amended: 1981, c.30, sch.

s. 29, rules 82/270, 829(S.); 83/72 (S.).

s. 41, see *Atkinson* v. *Murrell* [1972] 3 W.L.R. 465; [1972] 2 All E.R. 1131.

Pts. III, IV (ss. 41–50), repealed: 1976, c.32, sch.6.

s. 42, see *Atkinson* v. *Murrell* [1972] 3 W.L.R. 465; [1972] 2 All E.R. 1131; *Reader's Digest Association* v. *Williams* [1976] 1 W.L.R. 1109; [1976] 3 All E.R. 737, D.C.

s. 47, see *News of the World* v. *Friend* [1973] 1 W.L.R. 249; [1973] 1 All E.R. 422, H.L.

s. 49, see *Bell* v. *Dooks* [1974] Crim.L.R. 549; *Walker* v. *Leeds City Council; Greenwich L.B.C.* v. *Hunt* [1976] 3 W.L.R. 736; [1976] 3 All E.R. 709, H.L.

s. 49, orders 75/607, 672.

s. 51, repealed in pt.: 1984, c.60, sch.7.

s. 52, amended: 1977, c.45, sch.1; repealed in pt.: 1975, c.58, sch.5; 1976, c.32, sch.5.

s. 54, repealed: *ibid.*

s. 55, regs. 85/1513 (S.); 86/120 (S.).

s. 55, amended: 1972, c.25, sch.5; c.69, s.5; 1981, c.63, sch.5; 1985, c.9, sch.2; repealed in pt.: 1976, c.32, sch.5.

s. 56, repealed in pt.: 1987, c.19, sch.

s. 57, amended: 1974, c.22, sch.

sch. 1, see *R.* v. *Inner London Licensing Committee, ex p. Pearcy* [1972] 1 W.L.R. 421; [1972] 1 All E.R. 932; *Murphy* v. *Alloa Licensing Authority,* 1973 S.L.T.(Sh.Ct.) 2; *Murphy* v. *Renfrew Burgh Licensing Court,* 1973 S.L.T.(Sh.Ct.) 18; *R.* v. *Betting Licensing Committee for Ross-on-Wye, ex p. Smith,* July 7, 1975; *Williamson* v. *Edinburgh Licensing Authority,* 1976 S.L.T.(Sh.Ct.) 35; *Ladbrokes the Bookmakers* v. *Hamilton District Council,* 1977 S.L.T.(Sh.Ct.) 86; *Ladbroke Racing (Strathclyde)* v. *Cunninghame District Licen-*

CAP.

2. Betting, Gaming and Lotteries Act 1963— cont.

sing Court and Others, 1978 S.L.T.(Sh.Ct.) 50; *Joe Coral (Racing)* v. *Hamilton District Council,* 1981 S.L.T.(Notes) 106; *Mecca Bookmakers (Scotland)* v. *East Lothian District Licensing Board* (O.H.), 1988 S.L.T. 520; *R.* v. *Forest Betting Licensing Committee, ex p. Noquet, The Times,* June 21, 1988, Schiemann J.; *Art Wells (T/A Corals)* v. *Glasgow District Licensing Board,* 1988, S.C.L.R. 531.

sch. 1, Act of Sederunt 78/229; orders 87/93 (S.), 95.

sch. 1, amended: 1972, c.69, s.3; 1973, c.65, sch.24 (S.); 1976, c.66, s.133 (S.); 1980, c.55, sch.2; 1981, c.30, sch.; 1984, c.25, s.3; order 87/95; repealed in pt.: 1972, c.70, sch.30; 1973, c.65, schs.24, 29; 1975, c.20, sch.2; 1976, c.66, sch.8.

sch. 2, amended: 1972, c.70, sch.29; 1973, c.65, sch.24 (S.); 1976, c.69, sch.2; order 82/572; 1985, c.9, sch.2; repealed in pt.: 1972, c.70, sch.3; 1973, c.65, schs.24,29(S.).

sch. 3, amended: 1972, c.70, sch.29; 1973, c.65, sch.24 (S.); order 82/572; 1985, c.9, sch.2; repealed in pt.: 1972, c.70, sch.30; 1973, c.65, schs.24, 29 (S.); 1985, c.51, schs. 8,17.

sch. 4, amended: 1984, c.46, sch.5.

sch. 5, orders 75/1331; 80/1771; regs. 85/1476, 1513 (S.)

sch. 6, see *R.* v. *Herrod, ex p. Leeds City District Council* [1976] 2 W.L.R. 18; [1976] 1 All E.R. 273, C.A.; *Walker* v. *Leeds City Council; Greenwich L.B.C.* v. *Hunt* [1976] 3 W.L.R. 736; [1976] 3 All E.R. 709, H.L.

sch. 6, repealed: 1976, c.32, sch.5.

sch. 7, repealed: 1975, c.58, sch.5.

sch. 8, repealed: S.L.R. 1974.

3. Betting Duties Act 1963.

repealed: 1972, c.25, sch.7.

5. County Courts (Jurisdiction) Act 1963.

repealed: 1973, c.15, sch.5.

6. Commonwealth Scholarships (Amendment) Act 1963.

repealed: 1980, c.63, sch.2.

9. Purchase Tax Act 1963.

repealed: 1972, c.41, sch.28.

s. 1, amended: 1979, c.2, sch.5.

s. 2, order 72/1745.

s. 2, sch. 1, see *Customs and Excise Commissioners* v. *Beecham Foods* [1972] 1 W.L.R. 241; [1972] 1 All E.R. 498.

s. 25, amended and repealed in pt.: 1979, c.2, sch.5.

s. 31, regs. 72/1146.

s. 34, sch. 2, amended: 1979, c.2, sch.5.

s. 37, repealed: 1973, c.36, sch.6.

s. 41, repealed in pt.: S.L.R. 1974.

sch. 1, see *Esso Petroleum Co.* v. *Customs and Excise Commissioners* [1976] 1 W.L.R. 1; [1976] 1 All E.R. 117, H.L.

sch. 1, repealed in pt.: order 77/2128.

sch. 4, repealed: S.L.R. 1974.

CAP.

1963—cont.

10. Drainage Rates Act 1963.
repealed: 1976, c.70, sch.8.

11. Agriculture (Miscellaneous Provisions) Act 1963.
ss. 4, 5, schemes 72/815; 73/976.
ss. 4, 5, 9, 10, 12, repealed: S.L.R. 1986.
s. 10, scheme 72/861.
ss. 10, 12, schemes 75/882, 2231.
s. 11, repealed: S.L.R. 1973.
ss. 13, 14, repealed: 1981, c.22, sch.6.
s. 15, repealed: S.L.R. 1976.
s. 16, orders 72/863; 76/453, 988; 77/377, 962; 78/708, 1188; 79/751, 1281; 80/1383.
s. 16, amended: 1981, c.22, sch.5; order 78/272; repealed in pt.: 1972, c.62, sch.6; S.L.R. 1973; 1981, c.62, schs.5,6; 1984, c.40, sch.2.
s. 17, repealed: 1972, c.62, s.8, sch.6.
s. 19, see *Mercantile and General Reinsurance Co.* v. *Groves* [1973] 3 W.L.R. 248, C.A.; *Jones* v. *Lewis* (1973) 25 P. & C.R. 375, C.A.; *Wykes* v. *Davis* [1975] 2 W.L.R. 131; [1975] 1 All E.R. 399, C.A.
s. 19, repealed: 1977, c.12, sch.2.
s. 20, repealed in pt.: 1984, c.41, sch.4, 1986, c.5, sch.15.
s. 22, amended: *ibid.*, sch.14.
s. 25, repealed: 1972, c.68, sch.3.
s. 26, amended: order 78/272.
ss. 28, 29 (in pt.) sch., repealed; S.L.R. 1973.

12. Local Government (Financial Provisions) (Scotland) Act 1963.
ss. 1, 2, repealed: 1973, c.65, sch.29.
s. 2, see *Midlothian C.C.* v. *Secretary of State for Scotland,* 1975 S.L.T. 122.
s. 3, repealed: 1975, c.30, sch.7.
ss. 4, 5, repealed: 1973, c.65, sch.29.
s. 7, amended: *ibid.,* sch.9; 1975, c.30, sch.6; repealed in pt.: 1973, c.65, sch.29; 1987, c.47, sch.6.
s. 8, repealed: *ibid.*
s. 9, orders 73/666; 74/612; 75/251, 2215; 76/2212, 77/2137; 79/64; 82/194, 1897; rules 73/631; 80/128; 84/102; 85/94; 86/140; regs. 79/227, 235; 82/1843; 85/246; 86/407; 87/2279; 88/19.
s. 9, amended: 1973, c.65, sch.9; 1975, c.30, sch.6; repealed in pt.: 1973, c.65, schs.9,29; 1975, c.38, schs.6,7.
s. 10, orders 73/859; 75/95; 78/371; 81/537; 82/1900; 85/101.
s. 10, amended: 1980, c.65, s.46; repealed in pt.: 1987, c.47, sch.6.
s. 11, order 72/1237.
s. 11, repealed: order 78/1174.
s. 12, repealed: order 78/1176.
s. 13, see *Occidental Inc.* v. *Assessor for Orkney,* 1979 S.L.T. 60.
s. 13, order 72/1115.
s. 13, repealed: 1975, c.30, sch.7.
s. 15, see *Heart of Midlothian Football Club* v. *Assessor for Lothian Region; Hibernian Football Club* v. *Assessor for Lothian Region,* 1988 S.L.T.(Lands Tr.) 61.
s. 15, regs. 75/1261; 78/252; 84/1506.

CAP.

1963—cont.

12. Local Government (Financial Provisions) (Scotland) Act 1963—*cont.*
s. 15, amended: 1975, c.30, sch.6; 1984, c.31, ss.12,19, sch.2; repealed in pt.: 1987, c.47, sch.6.
s. 16, repealed: 1973, c.65, sch.29.
s. 18, repealed in part: S.L.R. 1974.
s. 19, see *Assessor for Dumfries and Galloway* v. *Wigtown District Council,* 1977 S.C. 299; *Oban Tennis Club* v. *Assessor for Strathclyde,* 1982 S.L.T. 209; *Trustees of Paisley Golf Club* v. *Assessor for Strathclyde Region,* 1986 S.L.T. 493; *Hamilton District Council* v. *Assessor for Strathclyde Region,* 1986 S.L.T. 370; *East Kilbride Sports Club* v. *Assessor for Strathclyde Region,* 1986 S.L.T. 379.
s. 19, repealed in pt.: 1973, c.65, schs.9,29.
s. 20, amended: 1981, c.23, sch.3; repealed in pt.: 1973, c.65, schs.9,29.
s. 21, repealed: 1975, c.30, sch.7.
s. 22, orders 72/1544; 77/1694; 80/267; 81/928.
s. 22, amended: 1975, c.30, sch.6; repealed in pt.: *ibid.,* sch.7
s. 23, repealed: S.L.R. 1975.
s. 26, amended: 1973, c.65, sch.9; 1975, c.30, sch.6; 1981, c.23, sch.3; repealed in pt.: 1987, c.47, sch.6.
s. 27, repealed: S.L.R. 1974.
sch. 1, repealed: 1973, c.65, sch.29.
sch. 3, repealed: S.L.R. 1974.

13. Nursing Homes Act 1963.
repealed: 1975, c.37, sch.3.

16. Protection of Depositors Act 1963.
repealed: 1979, c.37, sch.7.
s. 1, amended: *ibid.,* s.39.
s. 13, regs. 76/1954; 78/1065.
s. 26, amended: 1984, c.46, sch.5.

17. Town and Country Planning Act 1963.
repealed: 1972, c.52, sch.23.

18. Stock Transfer Act 1963.
s. 1, amended: 1985, c.9, sch.2; 1986, c.53, sch.18; c.60, sch.16.
s. 2, amended: 1985, c.9, sch.2.
s. 3, orders 74/1214; 79/277; amended: 1976, c.47, s.6.
s. 4, order 73/536.
s 5, repealed in pt.: 1973, c.36, sch.6.
sch. 1, amended: order 79/277.

19. Local Employment Act 1963.
repealed: S.L.R. 1978.

21. Education (Scotland) Act 1963.
repealed: 1980, c.44, sch.5.

22. Sheriff Courts (Civil Jurisdiction and Procedure) (Scotland) Act 1963.
s. 3, orders 83/1445; 85/626.
s. 3, substituted: 1985, c.37, s.23.

24. British Museum Act 1963.
ss. 1, 10, functions transferred: order 81/207; 86/600.
s. 8, amended: order 88/1836.
s. 9, amended: 1983, c.47, sch.5.
s. 10, orders 72/653; 73/1126; 79/1086; 82/1238; 84/1181; 85/462; 88/1836.
s. 13, repealed in part, S.L.R. 1974; S.L.R. 1978.

1963—cont.

24. British Museum Act 1963—*cont.*
sch. 3, amended: orders 79/1086; 84/1181; 85/462.
sch. 4, repealed: S.L.R. 1974.

25. Finance Act 1963.
s. 2, repealed: S.L.R. 1976.
s. 3, repealed: 1973, c.51, sch.22.
s. 4, repealed in pt.: *ibid.*; 1975, c.45, sch.14; 1979, c.6, sch.
s. 6, repealed: 1979, c.4, sch.4.
s. 7, repealed: 1979, c.2, sch.6.
s. 22, see *Banning* v. *Wright* [1972] 1 W.L.R. 972; [1972] T.R. 105.
s. 47, see *Langley* v. *Appleby* [1976] 3 All E.R. 391; (1976) 53 T.C. 1, D.C.
Pt. III (ss. 52–54), repealed: 1975, c.7, sch.13.
s. 55, amended: 1972, c.41, s.125; 1974, c.30, sch.11; 1980, c.48, c.95; 1982, c.39, s.128; 1984, c.43, s.109; 1986, c.41, s.64.
s. 56, repealed in pt.: 1972, c.41, sch.28; 1974, c.30, s.49, sch.14.
s. 57, repealed in pt.: 1973, c.51, sch.22; 1974, c.30, s.49, sch.14.
s. 58, repealed: *ibid.*, sch.14.
s. 59, amended: 1986, c.41, s.65; repealed in pt.: 1973, c.51, sch.22.
s. 62, amended: 1974, c.30, sch.11; repealed in pt.: 1973, c.51, sch.22; 1976, c.40, sch.15; 1986, c.41, s.79, sch.23.
s. 64, repealed: 1985, c.54, sch.27.
s. 65, repealed in pt.: 1988, c.39, sch.14.
s. 67, repealed in pt.: 1985, c.54, sch.27.
s. 71, amended: 1972, c.65, s.15; repealed in pt.: S.L.R. 1986; 1987, c.16, sch.16.
s. 73, repealed in pt.: 1975, c.7, sch.13; 1979, c.2, sch.6.
sch. 1, repealed: 1973, c.51, sch.22.
sch. 2, repealed: 1979, c.4, sch.4.
sch. 11, amended: 1974, c.30, sch.11; 1980, c.48, s.95; repealed in pt.: 1984, c.43, sch.23.
sch. 12, repealed: S.L.R. 1986.
sch. 14, repealed in pt.: *ibid.*

27. Oaths and Evidence (Overseas Authorities and Countries) Act 1963.
s. 4, repealed: 1975, c.34, sch.2; order 72/1722.
s. 5, orders 72/116; 84/857.

29. Local Authorities (Land) Act 1963.
s. 1, repealed: 1972, c.70, sch.30.
s. 2, amended: 1974, c.7, schs.6,8.
s. 3, amended: 1982, c.30, s.43.
s. 6, repealed in pt.: 1982, c.42, s.3, sch.
s. 8, repealed: S.L.R. 1974.
s. 13, repealed: 1972, c.70, sch.30.
sch. repealed: S.L.R. 1974.

30. Statute Law Revision Act 1963.
repealed: S.L.R. 1974.

31. Weights and Measures Act 1963.
repealed: 1985, c.72, sch.13.
s. 4, regs. 76/2168; 79/1436; 83/1653.
s. 5, regs. 79/1719; 83/1653.
s. 9A, order 83/1077.
s. 10, regs. 76/1664.
s. 11, see *F. E. Charman* v. *Clow* [1974] 1 W.L.R. 1384; [1974] 3 All E.R. 371, D.C.; *Evans* v. *Clifton Inns* (1987) 85 L.G.R. 119, D.C.

1963—cont.

31. Weights and Measures Act 1963—*cont.*
s. 11, regs. 72/767, 1551; 76/1330, 1807, 1981; 77/1932, 1933; 78/1362; 79/41, 729, 1359, 1605, 1612, 1720; 80/1878, 1993; 81/1306; 83/592, 914, 1390, 1655, 1656; orders 77/2162; 84/273, 1446; 85/209, 1532.
s. 12, regs. 76/1330; 79/1605, 1720; 80/1878, 1993; 81/1306; 83/592, 914, 1390, 1656; 85/209.
s. 14, see *North Yorkshire County Council* v. *Holmesterne Farm Co.* (1985) 150 J.P.N. 111, D.C.
s. 14, regs. 72/767, 1551; 74/1326; 75/1319; 76/1330, 1981; 77/1683, 1932, 1933; 78/1362; 79/41, 729, 1605, 1720; 80/1878, 1993; 81/1306; 83/592, 914, 1390, 1655, 1656; 84/273, 1446; 85/209, 1532.
s. 16, see *Bellerby* v. *Carle* [1983] 1 All E.R. 1031, H.L.
s. 21, orders 73/1967, 1968; 74/874, 875, 1166; 75/1177–9, 1319; 77/1333, 2058, 2059; 78/741, 1080, 1081; 79/1752; 81/1780–1782; 83/1078; regs. 76/795; 77/1683; 78/238; 79/1752, 1753; 80/8, 246; 84/1314–1316; 85/778, 988, 1980.
s. 22, see *Dean* v. *Scottish and Newcastle Breweries*, 1978 S.L.T.(Notes) 24; *Church* v. *Lee & Co-operative Retail Services*, (1985) 150 J.P.N. 335, D.C.; modified: order 78/1081.
s. 24, see *Bibby-Cheshire* v. *Golden Wonder* [1972] 1 W.L.R. 1487; [1972] 3 All E.R. 738; *Wigdor* v. *Hogg*, 1974 S.L.T.(Notes) 59; *Mac-Donald* v. *Smith*, 1979 J.C. 55; *Heron Service Stations* v. *Hunter* [1981] Crim.L.R. 418, D.C.; *Bennett* v. *Markham* [1982] 1 W.L.R. 1230, D.C.
ss. 24, 26, see *Paterson* v. *Ross Poultry*, 1974 S.L.T.(Sh.Ct.) 38; *North Yorkshire County Council* v. *Holmesterne Farm Co.* (1985) 150 J.P.N. 111, D.C.
s. 26, see *Bibby-Cheshire* v. *Golden Wonder* [1972] 1 W.L.R. 1487; [1972] 3 All E.R. 738; *Pickover* v. *Smith* [1975] Crim.L.R. 529, D.C.; *Urwin* v. *Toole* [1976] Crim.L.R 583; (1976) 75 L.G.R. 98, D.C.; *Westminster City Council* v. *Turner, Gow* (1984) 4 Tr.L. 130, D.C.
s. 33, regs. 76/2061.
s. 43, regs. 76/1807; 79/1359.
s. 48, regs. 79/1359.
ss. 48, 49, see *Brunner* v. *Williams* [1975] Crim.L.R. 250, D.C.
s. 51, see *Bakerboy (Hot Bread)* v. *Barnes* (1985) 4 Tr.L. 52, D.C.
s. 54, orders 76/111, 430, 431, 794, 1120, 1294–1297; 77/558, 1332, 1333, 1335, 2058, 2059; 78/741, 1080, 1081; 81/1780–1782; 83/1077, 1078; 84/1314–1316; 85/435, 778, 998; regs. 75/1319; 77/1638, 1933; 79/955, 1605, 1612, 1752; 80/8, 1878, 1993; 81/1306; 83/592, 914, 1390, 1653, 1656; 84/273, 1446; 85/209, 1532, 1980.
s. 58, regs. 72/767, 1551; 76/1330, 1807, 1981; 76/2061, 2168; 80/1878, 1993; 81/1306; 83/592, 1390, 1653, 1655, 1656; 84/1446; 85/209, 1532; orders 77/2162; 78/1362; 79/41, 729, 1436, 1605, 1720.

1963—cont.

31. Weights and Measures Act 1963—*cont.*

s. 58, amended: 1979, c.4, sch.3; c.45, sch.5; 1984, c.30, sch.10; c.54, sch.9 (S.).

s. 59, repealed: 1979, c.4, sch.4.

s. 60, repealed: 1979, c.45, schs.5,7.

s. 61, repealed: S.L.R. 1974.

s. 62, repealed in pt.: S.L.R. 1977.

s. 63, repealed in pt.: S.L.R. 1974.

sch. 1, substituted: regs. 80/1070.

sch. 1A, added: 1976, c.77, s.2; substituted: regs. 80/1070.

sch. 3, regs. 80/1070.

sch. 3, substituted: 1976, c.77, s.2; amended: order 83/1077.

sch. 4, repealed: orders 84/1314–1316.

sch. 5, see *F. E. Charman* v. *Clow* [1974] 1 W.L.R. 1384; [1974] 3 All E.R. 371, D.C.

schs. 5–7, amended: regs. 80/1070.

sch. 6, see *Church* v. *Lee & Co-operative Retail Services,* (1986) 150 J.P.N. 335, D.C.; *Gaunt* v. *Nelson* [1987] R.T.R. 1, D.C.

sch. 6, regs. 78/238.

sch. 6, amended: 1973, c.65, s.149; 1976, c.77, sch.4; 1977, c.45, sch.11; order 79/1753; 1984, c.54, sch.9 (S.).

sch. 8, amended: order 84/1316.

sch. 9, repealed: S.L.R. 1974; order 77/1335.

sch. 10, amended: 1973, c.36, sch.6; 1984, c.30, sch.10; repealed in pt.: S.L.R. 1974; S.L.R. 1977; 1979, c.4, sch.4.

32. Public Lavatories (Turnstiles) Act 1963.

s. 1, repealed in pt.: S.L.R. 1981.

33. London Government Act 1963.

s. 1, repealed in pt.: 1972, c.70, schs.2,30; 1978, c.30, sch.3; S.L.R. 1978.

s. 2, repealed in pt.: 1972, c.70, sch.30; 1985, c.51, sch.17.

s. 3, repealed: 1972, c.70, sch.30.

s. 4, repealed in pt.: 1985, c.51, sch.17; 1986, c.56, sch.4.

s. 5, amended: 1985, c.51, sch.14; order 85/1884; repealed in pt.: 1985, c.51, sch.17; 1988, c.40, sch.13 (prosp.).

s. 6, repealed: 1972, c.70, sch.30.

s. 7, repealed: 1985, c.51, sch.17.

s. 8, repealed in pt.: S.L.R. 1978; 1986, c.56, sch.4.

s. 9, repealed in pt.: 1972, c.20, sch.9; 1980, c.34, sch.9; 1985, c.51, sch.17.

s. 14, repealed in pt.: 1972, c.20, sch.9; 1980, c.34, sch.9; c.66, sch.25.

ss. 16–18, repealed: *ibid.*

s. 18, amended: 1984, c.27, sch.13.

s. 19, repealed in pt.: 1972, c.70, sch.30; 1985, c.51, sch.17.

s. 21, repealed: 1985, c.71, sch.1.

s. 22, repealed: 1985, c.51, sch.17.

s. 23, see *Brent London Borough Council* v. *Greater London Council* (1980) 79 L.G.R. 179, C.A.; *Fleming* v. *Wandsworth London Borough Council, The Times,* December 23, 1985, C.A.; *R.* v. *Secretary of State for the Environment, ex p. Newham London Borough Council* (1987) 19 H.L.R. 298, C.A.

1963—cont.

33. London Government Act 1963—*cont.*

s. 23, orders 72/171–173; 73/417; 78/240, 763; 80/320; 81/289, 536, 644, 1313; 82/301; 83/250; 84/1390; 85/828, 993.

s. 23, amended: 1985, c.51, sch.8; repealed in pt.: 1972, c.47, sch. 11; 1985, c.51, sch. 17.

s. 30, see *ILEA* v. *Secretary of State for the Environment, The Times,* May 26, 1984, C.A.

s. 30, repealed in pt.: 1985, c.51, sch.17.

s. 31, amended: 1980, c.20, s.31, sch.3; repealed in pt.: S.L.R. 1975; 1980, c.20, sch.7; 1985, c.51, sch.17; 1986, c.61, sch.6; 1988, c.40, sch.13.

ss. 31, 32, repealed in pt. (prosp.): *ibid.*

s. 32, repealed: 1973, c.32, schs.4,5.

s. 33, repealed: 1980, c.20, sch.7.

s. 34, repealed: 1973, c.50, sch.4.

ss. 35, 36, 37 (in pt.), 38, repealed: 1973, c.37, sch.9.

s. 39, order 72/478.

s. 40, amended: 1975, c.37, sch.1; 1984, c.23, sch.1; repealed in pt.: 1974, c.40, sch.4; 1975, c.37, schs.2,3; 1985, c.51, sch.17.

s. 41, order 80/215.

s. 41, repealed: 1984, c.22, sch.3.

s. 43, repealed in pt.: 1985, c.51, sch.17.

s. 44, repealed in pt.: 1972, c.70, sch.30.

s. 45, repealed in pt.: *ibid.*; 1973, c.32, sch.5.

s. 46, amended: 1972, c.70, sch.29; repealed in pt.: *ibid.*, sch.30; 1984, c.22, sch.3.

s. 47, amended: 1980, c.5, sch.5; repealed in pt.: 1972, c.70, sch. 30; 1985, c.51, sch. 17.

s. 48, repealed in pt.: *ibid.*

s. 49, regs. 83/1634.

ss. 49, 50 (in pt.), 51 (in pt.), repealed: 1985, c.51, sch.17.

s. 52, amended: 1972, c.19, sch; repealed in pt.: *ibid.*; 1985, c.13, sch.3.

s. 53, repealed in pt.:1985, c.51, sch.17.

s. 54, amended: 1974, c.3, sch.3; 1981, c.22, sch.5; 1984, c.30, sch.10; repealed in pt.: 1972, c.62, sch.6; c.70, sch.30; 1974, c.3, schs.5,6; 1981, c.22, sch.6; 1984, c.30, sch.11.

s. 55, repealed in pt.: 1972, c.62, sch.6; 1985, c.51, sch.17.

s. 57, repealed in pt.: 1972, c.70, sch.30; 1985, c.51, sch.17.

s. 58, amended: 1980, c.65, sch.3; repealed in pt.: 1972, c.70, sch. 30; 1985, c.51, sch. 17.

s. 59, repealed in pt.: *ibid.*

s. 60, repealed in pt.: 1981, c.69, sch.17; 1985, c.51, sch.17.

s. 61, repealed in pt.: 1972, c.70, sch.30.

s. 62, repealed in pt.: 1972, c.66, sch.3; c.70, sch. 30; S.L.R. 1978; 1985, c.51, sch. 17.

ss. 64, 65, repealed: S.L.R. 1975; S.L.R. 1976.

s. 66, amended: 1985, c.51, s.83; repealed in pt.: S.L.R. 1975; 1985, c.51, sch.17; repealed (prosp.): 1988, c.41, sch.13.

s. 68, repealed in pt. (prosp.): *ibid.*

ss. 69, 70, repealed: 1972, c.70, sch.30.

ss. 71, 72, repealed: 1985, c.51, sch.17.

s. 73, amended: 1972, c.70, s.144; 1985, c.51, sch.16; repealed in pt.: 1980, c.65, s.190, sch.34.

CAP.

33. London Government Act 1963—*cont.*

s. 74, repealed: 1972, c.70, sch.30.

s. 75, amended: 1985, c.51, sch.14; order 85/1884; repealed in pt.: 1985, c.51, sch.17; 1988, c.40, sch.13 (prosp.).

s. 77, repealed: 1972, c.11, schs.7,8.

s. 78, see *R. v. Inner North London Coroner, ex p. Chambers; R. v. Inner North London Coroner, ex p. G.L.C., The Times,* April 30, 1983, Woolf J.

s. 78, repealed:1985, c.51, sch.17.

s. 79, repealed: 1975, c.76, sch.2.

s. 80, orders 74/250; 75/160; 76/1782; 77/828; 84/1693; 85/1999; 87/939; 88/596.

s. 81, amended: order 76/315; repealed in pt.: 1973, c.16, sch.2; 1985, c.51, sch.17; 1988, c.40, sch.13 (prosp.).

s. 82, repealed: 1985, c.51, sch.17.

s. 83, repealed in pt.: *ibid.*; 1988, c.40, sch.13 (prosp.).

s. 84, orders 72/171–173; 74/449, 595; 77/293, 1596; 78/440; 79/1737; 80/320; 81/289, 536, 644, 1313, 1856; 85/828, 993; 86/918.

s. 84, amended: 1980, c.9, sch.9.

ss. 84, 85, see *Fleming v. Wandsworth London Borough Council* (1984) 83 L.G.R. 277.

s. 85, orders 72/171–173; 79/1737; 80/646; 81/1856; 86/918.

s. 85, repealed in pt.: 1972, c.70, sch.30; 1985, c.51, sch.17.

s. 86, repealed: 1972, c.70, sch.30.

s. 87, repealed in pt.: 1985, c.51, sch.17.

s. 89, repealed in pt.: S.L.R. 1976; 1985, c.51, sch.17; 1988, c.40, sch.13 (prosp.).

s. 90, orders 74/250, 75/160; 76/1782; 77/828, 1596; 84/1693; 85/828, 993, 1999; 87/939; 88/596.

s. 92, repealed: 1975, c.24, sch.3; c.25, sch.3.

s. 93, repealed in pt.: 1972, c.60, sch.8; S.L.R. 1974.

s. 94, repealed in pt.: 1975, c.24, sch.3; c.25, sch.3.

sch. 1, repealed in pt.: 1972, c.70, sch.30.

sch. 2, order 72/924.

sch. 2, amended: 1980, c.65, sch.13; repealed in pt.: 1972, c.60, sch.8; c.70, sch.30; S.L.R. 1975; S.L.R. 1978; 1980, c.65, schs. 13,34; 1983, c.35, sch.2.

sch. 3, rules 73/79.

sch. 3, amended: 1983, c.2, sch.3; repealed in pt.: 1972, c.70, sch.30; 1983, c.2, sch.9; 1986, c.56, sch.4.

sch. 4, repealed: 1972, c.70, sch.30.

sch. 5, repealed in pt.: 1972, c.20, sch.9; 1980, c.34, sch.9; c.66, sch.25.

sch. 6, repealed: *ibid.*

sch. 8, repealed: 1985, c.71, sch.1.

sch. 9, see *Governors of the Peabody Donation Fund v. Sir Lindsay Parkinson & Co.* [1984] 3 W.L.R. 953, H.L.

sch. 9, amended: 1976, c.70, sch.7; 1980, c.66, sch.24; repealed in pt.: 1973, c.37, sch.9; 1980, c.66, sch.25; 1984, c.55, sch.7.

sch. 10, repealed: 1973, c.40, sch.9.

CAP.

33. London Government Act 1963—*cont.*

sch. 11, amended: 1974, c.37, s.70; 1984, c.55, sch.6; 1985, c.51, sch.5; repealed in pt.: 1972, c.70, sch.30; 1974, c.40, sch.4; S.L.R. 1977; 1980, c.66, sch.25; 1984, c.22, sch.3; c.55, sch.7; 1985, c.51, sch.17.

sch. 12, amended: 1982, c.30, s.1; c.33, sch.1; 1985, c.51, sch.8; 1987, c.27, s.42, sch.3; repealed in pt.: 1974, c.7, schs.6,8; 1985, c.13, sch.3; 1987, c.27, schs.3,4.

sch. 13, repealed in pt.: 1972, c.70, sch.30; 1974, c.3, schs.5,6; 1981, c.22, sch.6; 1984, c.30, sch.11.

sch. 14, repealed in pt.: 1973, c.37, sch.9; 1976, c.70, sch.8; 1981, c.67, sch.6; 1985, c.51, sch.17.

sch. 16, repealed: 1972, c.70, sch.30.

sch. 17, repealed in pt.: *ibid.*; S.L.R. 1974; 1984, c.12, sch.7; 1985, c.51, sch.17.

sch. 18, repealed: 1984, c.12, sch.7.

35. Malaysia Act 1963.

s. 2, repealed: 1981, c.61, sch.9.

s. 6, repealed in pt.: S.L.R. 1974.

sch. 1, repealed: 1981, c.61, sch.9.

sch. 2, repealed in pt.: S.L.R. 1977; 1981, c.9, sch.

sch. 3, repealed: S.L.R. 1974.

36. Deer Act 1963.

ss. 1, 3, 10, 12, amended: 1981, c.69, sch.7.

s. 5, amended: 1984, c.60, sch.6; repealed in pt.: *ibid.*, sch.7.

ss. 5–8, substituted: 1980, c.49, s.7, sch.2.

s. 10, see *Traill v. Buckingham* [1972] 1 W.L.R. 459; [1972] 2 All E.R. 389.

s. 10, amended: 1987, c.28, s.1.

s. 10A, added: 1981, c.69, sch.7.

s. 11, amended: 1973, c.54, sch.1.

sch. 1, amended: 1977, c.4, s.1.

sch. 2, repealed in pt.: 1981, c.69, schs.7,17.

37. Children and Young Persons Act 1963.

s. 1, see *R. v. Local Commissioner for Administration for the North and East Area of England, ex p. Bradford Metropolitan City Council* [1979] 2 W.L.R. 1, C.A.; *Tilley v. Wandsworth London Borough Council, The Times,* February 5, 1981, C.A.

s. 1, repealed: 1980, c.5, sch.6.

s. 21, repealed: S.L.R. 1974.

s. 23, amended: 1976, c.36, sch.3; 1980, c.6, sch.2.

s. 27, repealed: 1980, c.43, sch.9.

s. 28, amended: 1978, c.19, s.2.

s. 29, see *R. v. Amersham Juvenile Court, ex p. Wilson* [1981] 2 W.L.R. 887; [1981] 2 All E.R. 315, D.C.; *R. v. Tottenham Juvenile Court, ex p. A. R. C. (A Minor); R. v. Islington North Juvenile Court, ex p. C. D. (A Minor); R. v. Eltham JJ., ex p. N. C. (A Minor)* [1982] 2 W.L.R. 945, D.C.

ss. 30, 45–47, repealed: 1980, c.5, sch.6.

s. 37, amended: 1984, c.46, sch.5.

ss. 48, 54, repealed: 1975, c.72, sch.4.

ss. 49, 55, 58, repealed: 1980, c.5, sch.6.

s. 57, repealed in pt. (S.): 1975, c.21, sch.10.

ss. 62, 64 (in pt.), repealed: S.L.R. 1977.

CAP.

1963—cont.

37. Children and Young Persons Act 1963—cont.
s. 63, amended: 1980, c.5, sch.5.
sch. 2, amended:1985, c.61, s.61; repealed in pt.: 1972, c.70, sch.30.
sch. 3, repealed in pt.: 1972, c.44, sch.; S.L.R. 1974; 1980, c.5, sch.6; S.L.R. 1986.
sch. 4, repealed: S.L.R. 1977.
sch. 5, repealed: S.L.R. 1974.

38. Water Resources Act 1963.
functions transferred: order 76/1775.
s. 1, orders 88/46, 1758.
ss. 1 (in pt.), 3 (in pt.), 4–9, repealed: 1973, c.37, sch.9.
s. 10, orders 74/561, 562.
ss. 10–15, repealed: 1973, c.37, sch.9.
s. 12, order 87/1360.
s. 16, amended: 1973, c.37, sch.8; repealed in pt.: ibid., sch.9.
ss. 18, 19 (in pt.), 21, 22, repealed: ibid.
ss. 23, 24, see Cargill v. Gotts [1981] 1 W.L.R. 441; [1981] 1 All E.R. 682, C.A.
s. 24, amended: 1973, c.37, sch.8.
s. 25, order 73/1953.
ss. 25 (in pt.), 32, 33 (in pt.), repealed: 1973. c.37, sch.9.
s. 38, amended: ibid., sch.8.
s. 48, repealed in pt.: ibid., sch.9.
s. 54, amended: 1988, c.4, sch.3.
ss. 57–59, repealed: 1973, c.37, sch.9.
s. 60, amended: ibid., sch.8; 1981, c.17, s.16.
ss. 61, 62, repealed: 1973, c.37, sch.9.
s. 63, amended: ibid., sch.8; 1988, c.15, sch.2; repealed in pt.: 1973, c.37, sch.9.
s. 64, repealed in pt.: ibid.
s. 67, orders 72/1091, 1417, 1424; 73/265; 74/122, 883, 1163; 75/40, 853, 1285; 77/1527; 78/898, 1945; 79/1499; 81/1437, 86/1575.
s. 67, amended: 1976, c.70, sch.7; 1984, c.12, sch.4.
s. 68, amended: 1981, c.67, sch.4.
s. 69, amended: 1976, c.70, sch.7; repealed in pt.: 1973, c.37, sch.9.
s. 71, amended: 1976, c.70, sch.7; repealed in pt.: 1975, c.51, sch.5; 1981, c.67, sch.6.
ss. 72–76, repealed: 1974, c.40, sch.4.
s. 77, amended: 1974, c.40, sch.3.
s. 79, amended: 1973, c.37, sch.8; repealed in pt.: 1974, c.40, sch.4.
s. 80, repealed: 1973, c.37, sch.9.
s. 81, repealed in pt.: ibid.
s. 82, orders 79/1196; 83/52; 87/1360.
s. 82, amended: 1973, c.37, sch.8; order 76/1775; repealed in pt.: 1973, c.37, sch.9.
ss. 83–87, 88 (in pt.), 89, 90, repealed: ibid.
s. 91, amended: order 76/1775.
ss. 92–104, 107 (in pt.), repealed: 1973, c.37, sch.9.
s. 93, repealed in pt.: S.L.R. 1986.
s. 108, amended: order 76/1775; repealed in pt.: 1973, c.37, sch.9.
s. 109, amended: order 76/1775.
s. 110, repealed: 1973, c.37, sch.9.
s. 111, amended: order 76/1775.
s. 113, amended: 1974, c.40, sch.3.

CAP.

1963—cont.

38. Water Resources Act 1963—cont.
ss. 114, 115, repealed in pt.: ibid., sch.4.
s. 119, repealed: 1973, c.37, sch.9.
s. 120, amended: ibid., sch.8.
ss. 121, 123 (in pt.), 124, 125, repealed: ibid., sch.9.
s. 126, repealed in pt.: ibid.; 1975, c.51, sch.5.
ss. 127, 129, repealed: 1973, c.37, sch.9.
s. 130, substituted: 1984, c.12, sch.4.
s. 131, repealed: 1973, c.37, sch.9.
s. 133, orders 73/1664; 75/2134; 76/608, 830; 77/637, 938; 81/317, 515, 1346; 82/959; 83/589, 625; 84/818, 908; 85/1469; 86/58, 1670; 88/46, 1758.
s. 134, order 74/1163.
s. 134, repealed in pt.: S.L.R. 1986.
s. 135, orders 88/46, 1758.
s. 135, amended: 1973, c.37, sch.8; order 76/1775; repealed in pt.: 1973, c.37, sch.9; 1974, c.40, sch.4.
s. 136, repealed in pt.: 1973, c.37, sch.9.
s. 137, repealed in pt.: 1975, c.24, sch.3; S.L.R. 1986.
schs. 1–6, repealed: 1975, c.24, sch.3.
sch. 7, amended: order 78/272; repealed in pt.: 1973, c.37, sch.9.
sch. 8, amended: 1981, c.67, sch.4; repealed in pt.: ibid., sch.6.
sch. 10, amended: order 76/1775.
schs. 11–14, repealed: 1973, c.37, sch.9.

39. Criminal Justice (Scotland) Act 1963.
see Binnie v. Farrell, 1972 S.L.T. 212.
ss. 1, 3, 6–8, repealed (S.): 1975, c.21, sch.10.
ss. 2, 4, 5, repealed: 1980, c.62, sch.8.
s. 9, amended: 1975, c.21, sch.9; 1980, c.62, sch.5; repealed in pt.: ibid., sch.8; 1981, c.55, sch.5.
s. 10, amended: 1975, c.21, sch.9; 1980, c.62, sch.5.
s. 11, repealed: ibid., sch.8.
s. 12, substituted: 1980, c.62, sch.5; amended: 1985, c.73, s.45.
ss. 13, 16, 17, 23–25, repealed: 1975, c.21, sch.10.
s. 26, repealed: 1977, c.45, sch.13.
ss. 27–47, repealed: 1975, c.21, sch.10.
s. 37, see Ward v. H.M. Advocate, 1972 S.L.T.(Notes) 22.
s. 50, repealed in pt.: 1980, c.62, sch.8.
s. 51, amended: ibid., sch.5.
s. 53, repealed in pt. (E.) & (S.): 1975, c.21, sch.10; S.L.R. 1977; 1977, c.45, sch.13.
sch. 1, amended: 1975, c.21, sch.9; repealed in pt.: ibid., sch.10.
sch. 3, repealed in pt.: 1975, c.21, sch.10; 1977, c.45, sch.13.
sch. 5, repealed in pt.: 1972, c.71, sch.6; 1975, c.21, sch.10; 1984, c.36, sch.5.

40. Commonwealth Development Act 1963.
repealed: 1978, c.2, sch.2.

41. Offices, Shops and Railway Premises Act 1963.
s. 1, see Westwood v. Post Office [1973] 3 W.L.R. 287; [1973] 3 All E.R. 184, H.L.; Oxfordshire County Council v. Chancellor,

1963—cont.

41. Offices, Shops and Railway Premises Act 1963—*cont.*

Master and Scholars of Oxford University, The Times, December 10, 1980, D.C.

s. 3, repealed in pt.: regs. 74/1943.

s. 4, amended and repealed in pt.: *ibid.*

s. 5, amended: regs. 82/827.

s. 6, amended: *ibid.*; repealed in pt.: regs. 74/1943.

ss. 7–10, 12, repealed in pt.: *ibid.*

s. 9, amended: 1984, c.55, sch.6.

s. 14, see *Wray* v. *Greater London Council,* January 16, 1986, Mr. M. Ogden Q.C. (sitting as a deputy High Court judge).

s. 16, see *Westwood* v. *Post Office* [1973] 3 W.L.R. 287; [1973] 3 All E.R. 184, H.L.; *Mackay* v. *Dryborough & Co.,* 1986 S.L.T. 624.

ss. 20–22, repealed: regs. 74/1943.

s. 23, see *Hamilton* v. *Western S.M.T. Co.* (O.H.), 1977 S.L.T.(Notes) 66, Lord Maxwell, Outer House; *Black* v. *Carricks (Caterers)* [1980] I.R.L.R. 448, C.A.; *Watson* v. *Foster Menswear* (O.H.), January 22, 1982; *Osarak* v. *Hawker Siddeley Water Engineering, The Times,* October 29, 1982, Comyn J.

s. 23, repealed in pt.: regs. 74/1943.

s. 24, repealed: regs. 81/917.

ss. 25, 26, 27 (in pt.), repealed: regs. 74/1943.

ss. 28–41, repealed: regs. 76/2005.

ss. 42, 43, repealed in pt.: regs. 74/1943; 76/2005.

s. 45, order 72/1086.

s. 45, repealed: regs. 74/1943.

s. 46, amended and repealed in pt.: *ibid.*

s. 48, repealed: regs. 80/804.

s. 49, amended and repealed in pt.: regs. 74/1943.

s. 50, repealed: *ibid.*

s. 52, amended: 1985, c.51, sch.8; repealed in pt.: 1973, c.65, s.156, sch.29; regs. 74/1943, 76/2005; 77/746.

s. 53, repealed: regs. 76/2005.

s. 54, repealed: regs. 74/1943.

s. 55, repealed: regs. 76/2005.

ss. 56–58, 59 (in pt.), repealed: regs. 74/1943.

s. 60, repealed: regs. 76/2005.

ss. 61, 62, repealed: regs. 74/1943.

s. 63, amended: regs. 74/1943; repealed in pt.: regs. 76/2005.

s. 64, repealed: *ibid.*

ss. 65, 66, 68, repealed: regs. 74/1943.

s. 69, amended: *ibid.*

ss. 70, 71, repealed: regs. 74/1943; 76/2005.

s. 73, repealed in pt.: regs. 76/2005.

ss. 74, 75, repealed in pt.: regs. 74/1943.

s. 76, repealed in pt.: regs. 76/2005.

s. 80, amended and repealed in pt.: regs. 74/1943.

s. 81, repealed: *ibid.*

s. 83, amended: *ibid.*; repealed in pt.: regs. 74/1943; 76/2005.

s. 84, amended: 1973, c.49, sch.; 1980, c.2, sch.; c.16, sch.1; 1985, c.3, sch.; repealed in pt.: 1973, c.48, sch.4.

1963—cont.

41. Offices, Shops and Railway Premises Act 1963—*cont.*

s. 85, repealed in pt.: regs.74/1943.

s. 87, repealed: 1973, c.36, sch.6.

s. 88, amended: 1972, c.70, sch.29.

s. 89, repealed: regs. 77/746.

s. 90, amended: 1985, c.13, sch.2; repealed in pt.: regs. 77/746.

s. 91, repealed in pt.: 1973, c.36, sch.6.

sch. 1, repealed: regs. 74/1943.

43. Animal Boarding Establishments Act 1963.

s. 1, repealed in pt.: 1973, c.65, schs.25,29; 1974, c.7, schs.6,8; 1988, c.29, sch.

s. 5, amended: 1973, c.65, sch.24; 1981, c.43, sch.5; repealed in pt.: 1972, c.70, sch.30.

s. 6, repealed: S.L.R. 1976.

s. 7, repealed in pt.: S.L.R. 1974; S.L.R. 1976.

44. Wills Act 1963.

s. 1, see *Re Kanani (decd.)* (1978) 122 S.J. 611, Judge Mervyn Davies.

s. 7, repealed in pt.: 1973, c.36, sch.6.

46. Local Government (Financial Provisions) Act 1963.

ss. 1–4, repealed: 1972, c.70, sch.30.

s. 5, repealed in pt.: S.L.R. 1976.

ss. 6–11, repealed: 1972, c.70, sch.30

s. 13, repealed: S.L.R. 1976.

s. 14, repealed in pt.: 1972, c.70, sch.30; S.L.R. 1976.

s. 15, repealed in pt.: *ibid.*

s. 16, repealed: S.L.R. 1974.

sch. 1, repealed: 1972, c.70, sch.30.

sch. 2, repealed: S.L.R. 1974.

47. Limitation Act 1963.

see *Walford* v. *Richards* [1976] 1 Lloyd's Rep. 526, C.A.

s. 1, see *Knipe* v. *British Railways Board* [1972] 2 W.L.R. 127; [1972] 1 All E.R. 673; *Central Asbestos* v. *Dodd* [1972] 3 W.L.R. 333; [1972] 2 All E.R. 1135; *Harper* v. *National Coal Board (Intended Action)* [1974] 2 W.L.R. 775; [1974] 2 All E.R. 441, C.A.; *Arnold* v. *Central Electricity Generating Board* [1987] 3 W.L.R. 1009, H.L.

ss. 1–3B, 6, repealed: 1975, c.54, sch.2.

ss. 4, 5, repealed: 1980, c.58, sch.3.

s. 7, see *Knipe* v. *British Railways Board* [1972] 2 W.L.R. 127; [1972] 1 All E.R. 673; *Central Asbestos* v. *Dodd* [1972] 3 W.L.R. 333; [1972] 2 All E.R. 1135; *Comrie* v. *National Coal Board,* 1974 S.L.T.(Notes) 12.

s. 7, repealed in pt.: 1975, c.54, sch.2; 1980, c.58, sch.3.

ss. 7, 8, 13, see *Hunter* v. *Glasgow Corporation,* 1971 S.C. 220.

Pt. II (ss. 8–13), see *Kerr* v. *J. A. Stewart (Plant),* 1976 S.L.T. 255.

ss. 8–13, repealed: 1973, c.52, sch.5.

s. 14, repealed in pt.: 1973, c.36, sch.6; 1980, c.58, sch.3.

ss. 15, 16, repealed: 1980, c.58, sch.3.

48. Peerage Act 1963.

s. 7 (in pt.), sch. 2, repealed: S.L.R. 1974.

CAP.

1963—cont.

49. Contracts of Employment Act 1963.
repealed: 1972, c.53, sch.3.
s. 4, see *Gascol Conversions* v. *Mercer* [1974]
I.C.R. 420, C.A.
sch. 1, see *Bloomfeld* v. *Springfield* [1972] 1
W.L.R. 386; [1972] 1 All E.R. 609; *Clarke
Chapman* v. *Walters* [1972] 1 W.L.R. 378;
[1972] 1 All E.R. 614; *Woodhouse* v. *Brotherhood* [1972] 3 W.L.R. 215; [1972] 3 All E.R.
91; *McGorry* v. *Earls Court Stand Fitting Co.*
[1973] I.C.R. 100, N.I.R.C.; *De Rosa* v. *John
Barrie (Contractor)* [1973] I.C.R. 553, Ct. of
Session; *Deaway Trading* v. *Calverley* [1973]
I.C.R. 546; [1973] 3 All E.R. 776, Ct. of Ses-
sion; *Lord Advocate* v. *De Rosa* [1974] 1
W.L.R. 946; [1974] 2 All E.R. 849, H.L.;
Newlin Oil Co. v. *Trafford* [1974] I.R.L.R. 205;
Kolatsis v. *Rockware Glass* [1974] I.R.L.R.
240; [1974] I.C.R. 580; [1974] 3 All E.R. 555;
Smith v. *Lord Advocate*, 1979 S.L.T. 233.
sch. 2, see *Allison's Freightlines* v. *Smylie* [1971]
I.T.R. 175; *Mole Mining* v. *Jenkins* [1972]
I.C.R. 282; *Redpath Dorman Long* v. *Sutton*
[1972] I.C.R. 477, N.I.R.C.; *Adams* v. *Wright*
[1972] I.C.R. 463, N.I.R.C.; *Tarmac Roadstone
Holdings* v. *Peacock* [1973] 1 W.L.R. 594,
C.A. *McBride* v. *British Railways*, 1974 S.L.T.
22, Ct. of Session; *S. & U. Stores* v. *Wilkes*
[1974] 3 All E.R. 401, N.I.R.C.

51. Land Compensation (Scotland) Act 1963.
s. 1, see *Robertson* v. *Mackenzie*, 1975 S.L.T.
221.
ss. 2, 3, see *Miller & Partners* v. *Edinburgh
Corporation*, 1978 S.C. 1.
s. 8, see *Ibbotson* v. *Tayside Regional Council*,
1978 S.L.T.(Lands Tr.) 25; *Park Automobile
Co.* v. *Strathclyde Regional Council*, 1984
S.L.T.(Lands Tr.) 14.
s. 9, amended: 1975, c.77, sch.10; 1980, c.65,
sch.33.
s. 12, see *Hoey* v. *Glasgow Corporation*, 1972
S.L.T.(Notes) 36; *Glasgow Corporation* v.
McArdle, 1972 S.L.T. 223; *Scottish & Newcastle Breweries* v. *Glasgow Corporation*,
1973 S.L.T.(Lands Tr.) 13; *Odeon Associated
Theatres* v. *Glasgow Corporation* (O.H.), Sept.
24, 1973; *Sisters of Charity of the Order of
St. Vincent de Paul* v. *Lanark Town Council*,
1974 S.L.T.(Lands Tr.) 3; *David Lowe & Sons*
v. *Burgh of Musselburgh*, 1974 S.L.T. 5, Ct of
Sess.; *Park Automobile Co.* v. *Glasgow Corporation*, 1975 S.L.T.(Lands Tr.) 23; *Kahn* v.
Glasgow District Council, 1977 S.L.T.(Lands
Tr.) 35; *Smith and Waverley Tailoring Company* v. *Edinburgh District Council (No. 2)*
1977 S.L.T.(Lands Tr.) 29; *Mitchell* v. *Hamilton District Council*, 1978 S.L.T.(Lands Tr.) 2;
Cupar Trading Estate v. *Fife Regional Council*,
1979 S.L.T. (Lands Tr.) 2; *Murray Bookmakers*
v. *Glasgow District Council*, 1979 S.L.T.(Lands
Tr.) 8; *Woolfson* v. *Strathclyde Regional Council* (1979) 38 P. & C.R. 521, H.L.; *Miller &
Partners* v. *Edinburgh Corporation*, 1978, S.C.
1; *Sim* v. *City of Aberdeen District Council*,
1980 S.L.T.(Lands Tr.) 10; *Smith* v. *Strath-*

CAP.

1963—cont.

51. Land Compensation (Scotland) Act 1963—
cont.
clyde Regional Council, 1982 S.L.T.(Lands Tr.)
2; *Campbell Douglas & Co.* v. *Hamilton District Council*, 1984 S.L.T.(Lands Tr.) 44;
Edmonstone v. *Central Regional Council*,
1985 S.L.T.(Lands Tr.) 57; *McLean* v. *City of
Glasgow District Council*, 1987 S.L.T.(Lands
Tr.) 2; *Mclaren's Discretionary Tr.* v. *Secretary
of State for Scotland*, 1987 S.L.T.(Lands Tr.)
25; *Sloan* v. *City of Edinburgh District Council*,
1988 S.L.T.(Lands Tr.) 25.
s. 13, amended: 1980, c.55, s.145, sch.25.
s. 14, see *James Miller & Partners* v. *Lothian
Regional Council (No. 2)*, 1984 S.L.T.(Lands
Tr.) 2.
ss. 14, amended: 1980, c.55, sch.25.
s. 15, amended: *ibid.*; 1987, c.26, sch.23;
repealed in pt.: 1983, c.29, sch.3.
s. 16, see *Grampian Regional Council* v. *Secretary of State for Scotland, The Times*, November 16, 1983, H.L.
s. 20, see *Blythswood Friendly Society* v. *Glasgow District Council*, (H.L.) 1978 S.L.T. 213;
1981 S.L.T. (Lands Tr.) 2.
ss. 22, 23, see *David Lowe & Sons* v. *Burgh of
Musselburgh*, 1974 S.L.T. 5, Ct. of Sess.
ss. 22, 24, see *Glasgow Corporation* v. *McArdle*,
1972 S.L.T. 223; *Menzies Motors* v. *Stirling
District Council*, Second Division, Nov. 19,
1976; *James Miller & Partners* v. *Lothian
Regional Council (No. 2)*, 1984 S.L.T.(Lands
Tr.) 2.
s. 23, amended: 1975, c.77, sch.10; 1980, c.55,
sch.33.
s. 24, see *James Miller & Partners* v. *Lothian
Regional Council*, 1981 S.L.T.(Lands Tr.) 3.
s. 25, see *David Lowe & Sons* v. *Burgh of
Musselburgh*, 1974 S.L.T. 5, Ct. of Sess.;
Trustees of St. John's Church, Galashiels v.
Borders Regional Council, 1976 S.L.T.(Lands
Tr.) 39; *Edmonstone* v. *Central Regional
Council*, 1985 S.L.T.(Lands Tr.) 57.
s. 25, amended: 1975, c.77, s.47, sch.9; 1980,
c.65, s.121, sch.24.
ss. 25, 26, see *London & Clydeside Estates* v.
Aberdeen District Council [1979] 3 All E.R.
876; 1980 S.L.T. 81, H.L.
ss. 25, 30, see *Grampian Regional Council* v.
Secretary of State for Scotland [1983] 1
W.L.R. 1340; 1984 S.L.T. 212, H.L.
s. 27, amended: 1975, c.77, sch.10; 1980, c.65,
sch.33.
s. 28, order 75/1287.
s. 30, see *Low* v. *Kincardineshire Licensing
Court*, 1974 S.L.T.(Sh.Ct.) 54.
s. 38, repealed in pt.: 1973, c.26, sch.3.
s. 40, regs. 72/950, 1127; 73/77, 574, 849,
1543; 74/22; 75/210, 601; 1857; 76/234,
1125, 1661, 1800; 77/301, 721, 876, 877,
1657; 78/887, 1417, 1742; 79/615, 1165,
1742; 80/1027, 1945; 81/563, 1154, 1492;
82/443, 946, 1352, 1542; 83/34, 864, 1736;
84/1097, 1457, 1648, 1968; 85/158, 1132;
87/397, 890, 1842; 88/875.

CAP.

1963—cont.

51. Land Compensation (Scotland) Act 1963—
cont.
s. 47, repealed in pt.: S.L.R. 1974.
s. 1, see *James Miller & Partners v. Lothian Regional Council (No. 2)*, 1984 S.L.T.(Lands Tr.) 2.
sch. 1, amended: 1980, c.65, s.145, sch.25.
sch. 2, substituted: 1987, c.26, sch.23.

52. Public Order Act 1963.
s. 1, see *Cozens* v. *Brutus* [1972] 1 W.L.R. 484; [1972] 2 All E.R. 1.
s. 1, repealed in pt.: 1977, c.45, sch.13.

53. Performers' Protection Act 1963.
repealed: 1988, c.48, sch.8.
see *Ex p. Island Records, The Times*, March 22, 1978, C.A.; *Ekland* v. *Scripglow* [1982] F.S.R. 432, Peter Gibson J.
s. 1, see *Apple Corps.* v. *Lingasong* [1977] T.S.R. 345, Megarry V.-C.; *R.C.A. Corp.* v. *Pollard* [1982] 2 All E.R. 468, Vinelott J.; *Warner Bros. Records Inc.* v. *Parr* [1982] 2 All E.R. 455, Julian Jeffs Q.C.; *Shelley* v. *Cunane* (1983) 133 New L.J. 377, Harriman J.

54. Kenya Independence Act 1963.
ss. 2, 3, repealed: 1981, c.61, sch.9.
s. 4, repealed in pt.: 1978, c.30, sch.3.
s. 5, repealed: S.L.R. 1976.
s. 6, repealed: S.L.R. 1977.
s. 7, repealed: 1986, c.55, sch.2.
sch. 2, repealed in pt.: 1981, c.9, sch.

55. Zanzibar Act 1963.
s. 2, sch. 2, repealed: 1981, c.61, sch.9.
ss. 3, 5, repealed: S.L.R. 1977.
s. 6, repealed in pt.: S.L.R. 1974.
sch. 1, repealed in pt.: S.L.R. 1976; S.L.R. 1977; 1981, c.9, sch.
sch. 3, repealed: S.L.R. 1974.

56. Bahama Islands (Constitution) Act 1963.
s. 1, order 73/1080.

57. Nigeria Republic Act 1963.
s. 1, repealed in pt.: S.L.R. 1977.

59. Electricity and Gas Act 1963.
s. 1, repealed: 1972, c.17, sch.
s. 2, amended: *ibid.*, s.1; repealed in pt.: *ibid.*, sch.; c.60, sch.8; 1979, c.11, sch.12.
s. 3, repealed in pt.: 1972, c.60, sch.8; 1979, c.11, sch.12.
s. 4, sch. 1, repealed in pt.: *ibid.*
sch. 2, repealed: S.L.R. 1974.
sch. 3, repealed: 1979, c.11, sch.12.

60. Malaysia Act 1963.
s. 5, order 78/182.

1964

5. International Headquarters and Defence Organisations Act 1964.
s. 1, order 87/927.
s. 2, repealed in pt.: 1981, c.61, sch.9.

7. Shipbuilding Credit Act 1964.
repealed: S.L.R. 1986.

9. Public Works Loans Act 1964.
s. 6, amended: 1975, c.30, sch.6.
s. 8, repealed: S.L.R. 1976.

11. Navy, Army and Air Force Reserves Act 1964.
repealed: 1980, c.9, sch.10.

CAP.

1964—cont.

12. Episcopal Church (Scotland) Act 1964.
s. 1, repealed in pt.: S.L.R. 1974.

13. International Development Association Act 1964.
repealed: 1980, c.63, sch.2.

14. Plant Varieties and Seeds Act 1964.
regs. 73/1049; 74/1343.
s. 1, schemes 72/85, 86; 77/142–146; 80/318, 319, 321, 331; 82/1095–1100, 1114; 85/1090, 1091, 1093–1097; orders 78/297–308.
ss. 1, 2, 4, 6, see *Moulin Winter Wheat* [1985] F.S.R. 283, Plant Varieties and Seeds Tribunal.
s. 3, schemes 72/85, 86; 77/142–146; 80/318, 319, 321, 331; 82/1095–1100, 1114; 85/1090, 1091, 1093–1095; regs. 78/294; orders 78/297–308.
s. 3, amended: 1983, c.17, s.1; repealed in pt.: *ibid.*, s.1, sch.2.
ss. 3, 4, see *Golden Promise Spring Barley* [1981] F.S.R. 562, Plant Varieties and Seeds Tribunal.
s. 4, amended: 1983, c.17, sch.1.
s. 5, regs. 78/294; orders 78/297–308; schemes 80/318, 319, 321, 331; 82/1095–1100, 1114; 85/1090–1095.
s. 5, repealed in pt.: 1972, c.68, sch.3.
s. 5A, amended: 1983, c.17, sch.1; repealed in pt.: *ibid.*, schs.1,2.
s. 7, schemes 80/319, 331; 82/1097, 1114; 85/1090, 1091, 1096, 1097.
s. 7, amended: 1983, c.17, s.3.
s. 8, amended: 1976, c.34, sch.5.
s. 9, regs. 72/84, 506; 76/123; 77/146, 359; 78/294, 295; 80/316, 351; 81/357; 82/1101, 1102; 83/292, 1501; 84/242; 85/357, 1092; 86/339; 88/356.
s. 10, regs. 72/84; 78/294.
s. 10, amended: 1972, c.68, sch.4.
s. 11, regs. 82/1101; 85/1092.
s. 13, repealed in pt.: 1983, c.17, schs.1, 2.
s. 15, amended: *ibid.*, sch.1.
s. 16, regs. 73/944, 994, 1050, 1108; 74/736, 760, 877, 897–900; 75/1348, 1665, 1694; 76/124, 1068, 1133, 1283, 1284, 1389, 1831; 77/358, 891, 1049, 1264; 78/215, 296, 428, 559, 1010; 79/133, 366, 774, 888, 1003–1005; 80/330, 480, 501 (S.), 898–901; 81/342, 490, 548 (S.), 938, 939, 1699; 82/698, 721 (S.), 844, 897, 1756, 1757; 83/293, 544 (S.), 707, 928, 1500; 84/199, 243, 412, 445, 661 (S.), 910, 1872, 1873; 85/356, 385 (S.), 438, 975–981, 1529; 86/338, 1114; 87/188, 498 (S.), 547, 649, 1091–1093, 1097, 1098, 1148; 88/357, 671(S.), 1759.
s. 16, amended: 1972, c.68, sch.4; regs. 77/1112; 1986, c.49, s.2.
s. 17, regs. 74/897–900; 75/1694; 76/1068, 1133, 1283, 1284; 79/774, 1004, 1005; 80/899, 900; 81/938; 85/975–979; 87/1091–1093, 1097.
s. 18, regs. 74/897–900.
s. 18, amended: 1972, c.68, sch.4.
ss. 20–23A, repealed: 1972, c.68, sch.3.
s. 22, regs. 72/647.
s. 23, amended: 1980, c.43, sch.7.

1964—cont.

14. Plant Varieties and Seeds Act 1964—*cont.*
s. 23A, regs. 72/507.
s. 24, regs. 74/897–900; 76/1068, 1133, 1283, 1284; 79/774, 1004, 1005; 80/899, 900; 81/938; 85/980; 87/1098.
s. 25, amended: 1972, c.68, sch.4; 1982, c.48, schs.3,6 (S.); regs. 78/215; repealed in pt.: 1972, c.68, sch.4; regs. 78/215.
s. 26, regs. 74/897–900; 76/1068, 1133, 1283, 1284; 79/774, 1003–1005; 80/899, 900; 81/938; 85/980; 87/1098.
s. 26, repealed in pt.: regs. 78/215.
s. 27, amended: 1982, c.48, schs.3,6 (S.).
s. 28, amended: 1980, c.43, sch.7.
s. 29, amended: 1972, c.68, sch.4.
s. 30, repealed in pt.: *ibid.*
s. 32, repealed: *ibid.*, sch.3
s. 33, order 79/882.
s. 34, repealed in pt.: 1972, c.68, sch.4.
s. 36, regs. 72/84, 506; 74/736, 760, 877, 897–900; 75/720; 76/123, 1068, 1133, 1283, 1284; 77/146, 359; 78/294, 295; 79/774, 1003–1005; 80/316, 351, 899, 900, 81/357, 938, 1699; 82/1102, 1756, 1757; 83/292, 1501; 84/199, 242, 412, 1872, 1873; 85/357, 975–980, 1092; 86/339; 87/547, 1091–1093, 1097, 1098; 88/356, 1759.
s. 38, regs. 84/412; 88/356, 357.
s. 38, amended: 1972, c.68, sch.4; order 78/272; 1983, c.17, sch.1.
s. 39, amended: *ibid.*; repealed in pt.: 1973, c.36, sch.6; 1983, c.17, schs.1, 2.
s. 40, order 87/2210.
s. 41, orders 73/928, 78/1002.
sch. 1, amended: 1983, c.17, sch.1; repealed in pt.: *ibid.*, schs.1, 2.
sch. 2, see *Moulin Winter Wheat* [1985] F.S.R. 283, Plant Varieties and Seeds Tribunal.
sch. 2, orders 72/403; 78/1649; 82/1094; 85/1098; regs. 78/294.
sch. 2, amended: 1983, c.17, sch.1.
sch. 3, schemes 77/144, 145; 80/331; 85/1090, 1091, 1093–1097.
sch. 3, amended: 1983, c.17, s.2.
sch. 4, rules 74/1136
sch. 4, repealed in pt.: 1975, c.24, sch.3; c.25, sch.3; rules 74/1136.
sch. 5, regs. 72/507.
sch. 5, repealed: 1972, c.68, sch.3.

15. Defence (Transfer of Functions) Act 1964.
s. 1, order 82/1830.
s. 1, schemes 75/1696; 76/1461; 77/1836
s. 1, repealed in pt.: S.L.R. 1974.
s. 2, repealed in pt.: 1974, c.21, sch.3.

16. Industrial Training Act 1964.
repealed, except s.16: 1982, c.9, sch.2; c.10, sch.4.
s. 1, orders 82/657–663, 665, 771–778.
s. 2, orders 72/268; 73/295.
s. 2, see *Construction Training Board v. Att.-Gen.* [1972] 3 W.L.R. 187; [1972] 2 All E.R. 1339.
s. 4, see *Road Transport Industry Training Board v. John Duncan Removals*, 1975 S.L.T. (Sh.Ct.) 2.

1964—cont.

16. Industrial Training Act 1964—*cont.*
ss. 4, 12, see *Road Transport v. Wyatt* [1973] 2 W.L.R. 79; [1972] 3 All E.R. 913.
s. 7, orders 75/1971; 76/926; 81/1849.
s. 9, orders 73/2005, 2006; 80/1273.
s. 9A, orders 76/396, 1635, 2110; 77/1951; 78/448, 1225, 1643; 79/793; 80/586, 1753; 81/1041.
s. 10, amended: 1982, c.24, sch.4.
s. 12, see *J. Wyatt Jnr. (Haulage) v. Road Haulage Industry Training Board* (1973) 15 K.I.R. 147, D.C.
s. 12, regs. 72/638; 77/1473, 1474.
s. 16, repealed (S.): 1980, c.44, sch.5; repealed in pt.: 1988, c.40, sch.13.

19. Married Women's Property Act 1964.
repealed (S.): 1985, c.37, sch.2.

20. Uganda Act 1964.
s. 3, repealed: S.L.R. 1977.

21. Television Act 1964.
repealed: 1973, c.19, sch.3.
ss. 3, 18, 24, see *Att.-Gen. ex rel. McWhirter v. Independent Broadcasting Authority* [1973] 2 W.L.R. 344, C.A.

22. British Nationality Act 1964.
repealed: 1981, c.61, sch.9.
s. 3, regs. 80/358; 81/1571.

24. Trade Union (Amalgamations, etc.) Act 1964.
s. 1, see *R. v. Certification Officer, ex p. Amalgamated Union of Engineering Workers* [1983] I.C.R. 125, C.A.
ss. 1, 4, see *Rothwell v. Association of Professional Executive, Clerical and Computer Staff* [1976] I.C.R. 211.
s. 1, amended: 1974, c.52, sch.3; 1975, c.71, sch.16.
ss. 2, 3, amended: 1974, c.52, sch.3.
s. 4, amended: *ibid.*; 1975, c.71, sch.16; 1978, c.44, sch.16; repealed in pt.: 1988, c.19, sch.4.
s. 5, amended: 1974, c.52, sch.3.
s. 6, amended: *ibid.*; 1975, c.71, sch.16.
s. 7, regs. 75/536; 78/1344; 79/1385; 80/1708; 81/1631; 85/300; 86/302; 87/258; 88/310.
ss. 7, 9, amended: 1974, c.52, sch.3; 1975, c.71, sch.16; repealed in pt.: *ibid.*, sch.18.
s. 10, amended: 1974, c.52, sch.3; repealed in pt.: 1973, c.36, sch.6.
schs.1, 2, amended: 1974, c.52, sch.3.

25. War Damage Act 1964.
repealed: S.L.R. 1981.

26. Licensing Act 1964.
see *R. v. Leicester Justices, ex p. Watchorn, The Times,* June 9, 1978, D.C.; *Gate v. Bath J.J., The Times,* March 8, 1983, D.C.
s. 1, see *R. v. Dudley JJ., ex p. Curlett* [1974] 1 W.L.R. 457; [1974] 2 All E.R. 38, D.C.
s. 2, order 85/1383.
s. 2, amended: 1972, c.70, sch.25; repealed in pt.: *ibid*, sch.30; 1988, c.17, s.14, sch.4.
s. 3, see *R. v. Torbay Licensing JJ., ex p. White* [1980] 2 All E.R. 25, D.C.; *R. v. Edmonton Licensing JJ., ex p. Baker, The Times,* November 23, 1982, Woolf J.; *Ray v. Fareham JJ.,* August 5, 1983, H.H. Judge Inskip Q.C.,

CAP.

1964—cont.

26. Licensing Act 1964—cont.

Portsmouth Crown Court; *R. v. Haringey London Borough Council, ex p. Sandhu* (1988) 86 L.G.R. 56, D.C.

ss. 3–6, see *R. v. Licensing JJ. for the City of London, ex p. Davys of London Wine Merchants* (1985) 149 J.P. 507, MacPherson J.

s. 4, see *R. v. Leeds Crown Court, ex p. Bradford Chief Constable* [1974] 3 W.L.R. 715, D.C.

s. 5, see *Patel v. Wright, The Times*, November 19, 1987, D.C.

s. 6, see *R. v. Dudley Crown Court, ex p. Pask, The Times*, June 18, 1983, Taylor J.

s. 6, amended: 1988, c.17, s.9; repealed in pt.: *ibid.*, sch.4.

s. 7, see *R. v. Windsor JJ., ex p. Hodes* [1983] 1 W.L.R. 685, C.A.

s. 7, amended: 1988, c.17, sch.3; repealed in pt.: *ibid.*, schs.3,4.

s. 8, see *R. v. Melksham Justices, ex p. Collins, The Times*, April 10, 1978, D.C.; *R. v. Buckingham JJ., ex p. Walker, The Times*, February 20, 1981, D.C.

s. 8, amended: 1985, c.65, sch.8; 1986, c.45, sch.14.

s. 9, amended: 1980, c.66, sch.24; 1988, c.17, s.10; repealed in pt.: *ibid.*, schs.3,4.

s. 10, see *R. v. Birminghm City Magistrates, ex p. Bass Mitchells & Butlers, The Times*, June 15, 1988, Schiemann J.

s. 10, amended: 1985, c.65, sch.8; 1986, c.45, sch.14.

s. 12, amended: 1983, c.2, sch.8.

s. 14, amended: 1975, c.7, sch.12.

s. 16, amended: 1972, c.70, sch.25; repealed in pt.: *ibid.*, sch.30.

s. 20, see *R. v. Sheffield Crown Court, ex p. Mecca Leisure* (1984) 148 J.P. 225, D.C.; *R. v. Croydon Crown Court, ex p. Bromley Licensing Justices, The Times*, February 29, 1988, D.C.

s. 20A, added: 1988, c.17, s.12

s. 21, amended: 1988, c.17, sch.3.

s. 22, amended: 1980, c.43, sch.7, 1988, c.17, sch.3.

s. 23, see *R. v. Exeter Crown Court, ex p. Beattie* [1974] 1 W.L.R. 428; [1974] 1 All E.R. 1183, D.C.

s. 23, amended: 1988, c.17, sch.3.

s. 26, amended: *ibid.*, s.11.

s. 28, amended: 1980, c.43, sch.7.

s. 29, orders 76/1858; 78/1644; 80/1543; 88/1186.

s. 30, repealed in pt.: 1977, c.45, schs.12,13, 1983, c.28, s.9, sch.10.

s. 36, repealed in pt.: 1981, c.45, sch.

s. 37, amended: 1980, c.40, s.1.

s. 38, rules 72/44.

s. 38, repealed: 1981, c.28, sch.2.

s. 39, see *Lansley v. Adda Properties*, June 7, 1982, Judge Curtis-Raleigh, Bloomsbury and Marylebone County Court.

s. 43, amended: 1988, c.17, sch.3.

s. 48, amended: 1980, c.43, sch.7.

CAP.

1964—cont.

26. Licensing Act 1964—cont.

s. 49, see *R. v. Torbay JJ., ex p. The Royal British Legion (Paignton) Social Club*, February 10, 1981, Forbes J.

s. 51, amended: 1988, c.17, sch.1.

s. 55, repealed in pt.: 1975, c.45, sch.14.

s. 56, amended: 1987, c.3, sch.1.

s. 58, repealed in pt.: 1972, c.70, sch.30.

s. 59, see *Taylor v. Speed* [1979] Crim.L.R. 114, D.C.

s. 60, amended: 1988, c.17, s.1, sch.1; repealed in pt.: *ibid.*, s.1, sch.4.

s. 61, amended: *ibid.*, sch.1.

s. 62, amended: *ibid.*, s.1, sch.1; repealed in pt.: *ibid.*, sch.4.

s. 63, see *Jackson v. Sinclair* [1973] 1 W.L.R. 840.

s. 63, amended: 1988, c.17, s.2.

s. 65, amended: *ibid.*, sch.3.

s. 66, amended: 1972, c.70, sch.25.

s. 67, amended: *ibid.*; 1983, c.2, sch.8.

ss. 67A–67D, added: 1988, c.17, s.3.

s. 68, amended: 1987, c.2, s.1; 1988, c.17, sch.1.

s. 70, repealed in pt.: 1985, c.40, s.1.

s. 71, amended: 1988, c.17, s.4; repealed in pt.: *ibid.*, sch.4.

s. 72, amended: *ibid.*, s.4; repealed in pt.: *ibid.*, s.4, sch.4.

s. 73, repealed in pt.: *ibid.*, sch.4.

s. 74, see *R. v. Metropolitan Police Commissioner, ex p. Ruxton* [1972] 1 W.L.R. 232; [1972] 1 All E.R. 310; *R. v. Wenlock Justices, ex p. Furber, The Times*, July 26, 1978, *Martin v. Spalding* [1979] 2 All E.R. 1193, D.C.; *Knole Park Golf Club v. Chief Superintendent, Kent County Constabulary* [1979] 3 All E.R. 829, D.C.; *R. v. Corwen Justices, ex p. Edwards* [1980] 1 All E.R. 1035, D.C.; *R. v. Metropolitan Police Comr., ex p. Maynard, The Times*, June 9, 1982, D.C.; *Chief Constable of Kent v. Deayer, The Times*, May 6, 1983, Forbes J.; *R. v. Doncaster Justices, ex p. Langfield* (1985) 149 J.P. 26, Nolan J.; *Workman George Grosvenor v. Blaenau Ffestiniog Magistrates' Court, The Times*, January 28, 1987, Taylor J.

s. 74, amended: 1988, c.17, s.6.

s. 76, amended: 1980, c.40, s.2; 1988, c.17, s.1, sch.3; repealed in pt.: 1976, c.18, s.1; 1985, c.40, s.1.

ss. 76, 77, see *R. v. South Westminster Licensing Justices, ex p. Raymond* [1973] 1 W.L.R. 1303, D.C.; *Carter v. Bradbeer* [1975] 1 W.L.R. 665, D.C.

s. 77, see *Young v. O'Connell, The Times*, May 25, 1985, Glidewell J.

ss. 77, 78, amended: 1988, c.17, s.4; repealed in pt.: 1982, c.30, sch.7.

s. 78A, added: 1988, c.17, s.4.

s. 79, amended: 1982, c.30, sch.2; 1988, c.17, s.6; repealed in pt.: 1982, c.30, schs.2,7.

s. 80, amended: 1988, c.17, s.5; repealed in pt.: *ibid.*, s.5, sch.4.

CAP.
1964—cont.

26. Licensing Act 1964—*cont.*
s. 81, see *Mason* v. *Pearce, The Times,* October 7, 1981, Comyn J.
s. 81, amended: 1981, c.40, s.1.
s. 81A, substituted: 1988, c.17, s.5.
ss. 81A, 81B, added: 1980, c.40, s.3.
s. 81B, amended: 1988, c.17, s.5, sch.3.
s. 87, orders 72/1335; 73/1871; 77/1113; 78/225; 82/204; 83/1217; 85/653, 1730; 86/525, 971; 87/1982.
s. 87, amended: 1979, c.2, sch.4.
s. 87A, added: 1988, c.17, s.8.
s. 89, amended: *ibid.,* sch.3.
s. 91, rules 82/1384; 88/1188, 1338.
s. 91, amended: 1980, c.40, s.2; 1988, c.17, sch.3.
s. 92, repealed in pt.: *ibid.,* sch.4.
s. 94, amended: 1987, c.2, s.1.
s. 95, repealed in pt.: 1988, c.17, schs. 3,4.
s. 100, see *R.* v. *Ioannou* [1975] 1 W.L.R. 1297; [1975] 3 All E.R. 400, C.A.
ss. 102, 104–107, repealed: order 79/1977.
s. 112, repealed in pt.: 1980, c.65, s.131, sch.34.
s. 115, amended: 1976, c.75, sch.7.
ss. 116, 117, amended: 1981, c.64, sch.12.
s. 118, amended: 1972, c.70, s.204; repealed in pt.: S.L.R. 1981.
s. 119, see *R.* v. *Birmingham Licensing Committee, ex p. Kennedy* [1972] 2 Q.B. 140; [1972] 2 W.L.R. 939; [1972] 2 All E.R. 305; *Fletcher* v. *London (Metropolis) Licensing Planning Committee* [1975] 3 W.L.R. 148; [1975] 2 All E.R. 916, H.L.
ss. 119–131, amended: 1972, c.70, s.204.
s. 125, repealed in pt.: 1981, c.19, sch.1.
s. 133, amended; 1988, c.17, s.11.
s. 134, order 82/1837.
s. 136, repealed: 1981, c.19, sch.1.
s. 142, amended: 1988, c.17, s.11.
s. 143, order 82/1837.
s. 144, repealed in pt.: 1981, c.19, sch.1.
s. 150A, added: 1988, c.17, sch.3.
s. 151, amended: *ibid.,* s.11, sch.3; repealed in pt.: *ibid.,* sch.4.
s. 153A, added: *ibid.,* s.12.
s. 154, amended: *ibid.,* sch.3.
s. 156A, added: *ibid.,* s.3.
s. 159, repealed: 1981, c.45, sch.
s. 160, see *R.* v. *Edwards* [1974] 3 W.L.R. 285; [1974] 2 All E.R. 1085, C.A.; *Southall* v. *Haime* [1979] Crim.L.R. 249, D.C.; *Anderton* v. *Rogers* [1981] Crim.L.R. 404, D.C.
s. 160, amended: 1983, c.24, s.4.
s. 167, amended: regs. 79/1476.
s. 168, amended: 1988, c.17, sch.3.
s. 169, see *Howker* v. *Robinson* [1972] 3 W.L.R. 234; [1972] 2 All E.R. 786; *Rowlands* v. *Gee* [1977] Crim.L.R. 481, D.C.; *Buxton* v. *Chief Constable of Northumbria, The Times,* July 19, 1983, D.C.; *Woby* v. *B. and O.* [1986] Crim.L.R. 183, D.C.
s. 169, amended: 1977, c.45, s.31, schs.6,12; 1988, c.17, s.16, sch.3; repealed in pt: *ibid.,* s.16, sch.4.
s. 171A, added: *ibid.,* s.18.

CAP.
1964—cont.

26. Licensing Act 1964—*cont.*
s. 174, amended: *ibid.,* s.31, sch.6.
s. 180, see *Southall* v. *Haime* [1979] Crim.L.R. 249, D.C.; *R.* v. *Bow Street Metropolitan Stipendiary Magistrate, ex p. Comr. of Police of the Metropolis* [1983] Crim.L.R. 39; [1983] 2 All E.R. 915, Glidewell J.
s. 180, amended: 1972, c.70, sch.25.
s. 181, repealed: 1988, c.25, s.1.
s. 181A, added: 1988, c.17, s.17.
s. 182, amended: 1984, c.46, sch.5; repealed in pt.: 1987, c.19, sch.
s. 185, amended: 1988, c.17, sch.3.
s. 186, see *Valentine* v. *Jackson* [1972] 1 W.L.R. 528.
s. 186, amended: 1977, c.26, s.1.
s. 187, repealed in pt.: 1984, c.60, sch.7.
s. 192, amended: 1980, c.43, sch.7.
s. 192A, added: 1988, c.17, s.14.
s. 193, repealed in pt.: 1972, c.70, sch.30.
s. 193A, added: 1988, c.17, s.13.
s. 193B, added: *ibid.,* s.15.
s. 196A, added: *ibid.,* sch.3.
s. 198, orders 77/1113; 78/1644; 80/1543; 83/1136, 1217; 85/1730; 88/1186; rules 88/1188.
s. 200, see *R.* v. *South Westminster Licensing JJ., ex p. Raymond* [1973] 1 W.L.R. 1303, D.C.
s. 201, see *Carter* v. *Bradbeer* [1975] 1 W.L.R. 665, D.C.; *Grieve* v. *Hillary,* 1987 S.C.C.R. 317.
s. 201, amended: 1975, c.45, sch.3; 1979, c.4, sch.3; c.55, sch.2; 1981, c.35, sch.8; 1982, c.30, sch.2; 1988, c.17, ss.3,11; c.25, s.1; repealed in pt.: 1981, c.28, sch.2.
s. 202, orders 73/1958; 83/1136.
s. 202, amended: 1983, c.24, s.4.
s. 203, order 77/1113.
s. 203, repealed in pt.: S.L.R. 1974.
sch. 1, amended: 1988, c.17, s.14.
sch. 2, see *R.* v. *Bristol Licensing Planning Committee, ex p. Bristol City and Council Retail Licensed Trade Association, The Times,* October 13, 1977, D.C.
sch. 2, amended: 1972, c.70, sch.25; 1980, c.43, sch.7; repealed in pt.: 1988, c.17, sch.4.
schs. 3, 4, repealed: 1981, c.28, sch.2.
sch. 6, amended: 1980, c.43, sch.7.
sch. 8, amended: 1972, c.70, sch.25; repealed in pt.: *ibid.,* schs.25,30.
sch. 8A, added: 1988, c.17, s.3, sch.2.
sch. 9, repealed: order 79/1977.
sch. 10, amended: 1976, c.75, sch.7.
sch. 14, repealed in pt.: S.L.R. 1978.
sch. 15, repealed: S.L.R. 1974.

27. Salmon and Freshwater Fisheries Act 1923 (Amendment) Act 1964.
repealed: S.L.R. 1974.

28. Agriculture and Horticulture Act 1964.
s. 1, orders 72/15, 21, 25, 57, 58, 83, 94, 170, 193, 215, 230, 254, 277, 299, 347, 372, 399, 400, 488, 530, 609, 790, 824, 851, 991, 998, 1030, 1350, 1388, 1406, 1465, 1603, 1628, 1767, 1883; 73/85, 117, 140–2, 292, 294.

1964—cont.

28. Agriculture and Horticulture Act 1964—*cont.*
s. 1, amended: 1979, c.2, sch.4; repealed in
pt.: 1973, c.36, sch.6; 1979, c.58, sch.2.
s. 7, order 73/827; repealed in pt.: S.L.R. 1974.
s. 10, order 72/999.
s. 11, regs. 73/22; 83/1053.
s. 11, amended: 1972, c.68, sch.4.
s. 13, regs. 82/387.
ss. 13, 21, amended (S.): 1984, c.54, sch.9.
s. 19, repealed in pt.: 1986, c.20, s.7.
s. 20, amended: 1982, c.48, s.42, sch.3; regs.
83/1053; repealed in pt.: 1986, c.20, s.7.
ss. 22, 24, amended: 1972, c.68, sch.4.
s. 23, regs. 73/22; 82/387; 83/1053.
s. 26, amended: order 78/272; repealed in pt.:
1973, c.36, sch.6.
sch., regs. 73/294.
sch., amended: 1979, c.2, sch.4; c.3, sch.2;
repealed in pt.: 1977, c.36, s.9, sch.9.

29. Continental Shelf Act 1964.
s. 1, orders 74/1489; 76/1153; 77/1871;
78/1029; 79/1447; 80/184; 82/1072; 87/1265.
s. 1, amended: 1982, c.23, sch.3; 1987, c.3,
sch.1; repealed in pt.: 1987, c.12, sch.3.
s. 2, orders 72/883; 73/284; 75/511, 981, 1080;
76/332, 954, 1308, 1497; 77/712, 966, 1035,
1344; 78/260, 673, 733, 890, 935, 1411;
79/641, 1058, 1083, 1136, 1273; 80/251, 666,
758, 943, 946, 960–962, 1366, 1374, 1393,
1417, 1418, 1426, 1606, 1607, 1796–1799;
81/29, 267, 402, 403, 468, 469, 613, 640,
641, 699, 869–873, 902, 903, 930, 1144,
1270–1273, 1429, 1430, 1587, 1637; 82/81,
82, 190, 239, 240, 587–589, 703–705, 1040,
1183, 1184, 1214, 1215, 1248–1251, 1392,
1393.
s. 2, repealed: 1982, c.23, s.21, sch.4.
s. 3, see *Johnston* v. *Heerema Offshore Contractors* (O.H.), 1987 S.L.T. 407; *Fraser* v.
John N. Ward & Son (O.H.), 1987 S.L.T. 513.
s. 3, order 75/1708.
s. 3, repealed: 1982, c.23, s.22, sch.4.
ss. 3, 6, 7, orders 74/1490; 75/1517; 78/454,
1024; 80/184, 559; 82/1523.
s. 6, amended: 1982, c.23, sch.3; 1984, c.12,
s.107.
ss. 6, 7, order 87/2179.
s. 8, amended: 1975, c.74, s.45; repealed in
pt.: S.L.R. 1974.
s. 9, repealed: 1976, c.76, sch.4.
s. 11, amended: 1982, c.23, sch.3.
s. 11A, added: *ibid.*
s. 12, repealed: 1973, c.36, sch.6.

30. Legal Aid Act 1964.
repealed: 1974, c.4, sch.5.
s. 1, see *Clifford* v. *Walker* [1972] 1 W.L.R. 724;
[1972] 2 All E.R. 806; *General Accident* v.
Foster [1972] 3 W.L.R. 657; [1972] 3 All E.R.
877; *Lewis* v. *Averay, The Times*, Feb. 15,
1973, C.A.; *Davies* v. *Taylor* [1973] 2 W.L.R.
610; [1973] 1 All E.R. 959, H.L.; *Shiloh Spin-
ners* v. *Harding* [1973] 1 W.L.R. 518; [1973]
1 All E.R. 966, H.L.; *O'Brien* v. *Robinson*
[1973] 1 W.L.R. 515; [1973] 1 All E.R. 969n.,
H.L.; *Stewart* v. *Stewart* [1974] 1 W.L.R. 877;
[1974] 2 All E.R. 795, C.A.

1964—cont.

31. Election (Welsh Forms) Act 1964.
repealed: 1983, c.2, sch.9.
s. 1, regs. 75/1330.

32. National Health (Hospital Boards) Act 1964.
repealed: 1973, c.32, sch.5.

**33. Burgh Police (Amendment) (Scotland) Act
1964.**
repealed: 1984, c.54, sch.11.

34. Criminal Procedure (Right of Reply) Act 1964.
s. 1, amended: S.L.R. 1974.

**35. Pharmacy and Poisons (Amendment) Act
1964.**
repealed: S.L.R. 1975.

37. Income Tax Management Act 1964.
ss. 3, 5, 17, sch. 6, see *R.* v. *General Commissioners of Tax for Tavistock, ex p. Adams* (*No.
2*) (1971) 48 T.C. 56.
ss. 5, 6, see *R.* v. *Special Commissioners of
Income Tax, ex p. Morey* (1972) 49 T.C. 71,
C.A.
ss. 5, 6, 11, sch. 3, see *I.R.C.* v. *Adams* (1971)
48 T.C. 67.
s. 6, see *Pearlberg* v. *Varty* [1972] 1 W.L.R. 534;
[1972] 2 All E.R. 6; *Knight* v. *I.R.C.* [1972] T.R.
323, C.A.; *R.* v. *Special Commissioners of
Income Tax, ex p. Martin* (1971) 48 T.C. 1.;
Fen Farming Co. v. *Dunsford* (*No. 2*) [1973]
T.R. 209.
s. 11, see *Murphy* v. *Elders* [1974] S.T.C. 34.
s. 12, see *Way* v. *Underdown* [1973] T.R. 199,
Plowman J.
s. 17, sch. 6, see *Knight* v. *I.R.C.* [1974] S.T.C.
156, C.A.
sch. 4, see *I.R.C.* v. *Helical Bar* [1972] 2 W.L.R.
880; [1972] 1 All E.R. 1205.

**39. Protection of Animals (Anaesthetics) Act
1964.**
s. 1, amended: S.L.R. 1974.

40. Harbours Act 1964.
ss. 1–8, repealed: 1981, c.56, sch.12.
s. 4, orders 73/1620; 75/1612; 77/1725.
s. 9, orders 81/19; 84/522.
ss. 9, 10, repealed: 1985, c.30, sch.
s. 11, amended: 1972, c.16, s.4; repealed in
pt.: 1981, c.56, sch.12.
s. 12, substituted: order 82/1488.
s. 14, orders 72/275, 300, 733, 1155, 1703,
1704; 73/926, 1284, 1394, 1984, 2135, 2136;
74/697, 924, 925, 991, 1142, 1652; 75/121,
348, 568, 627, 693, 1224, 1252, 1272, 1273,
1828, 1890, 2135, 2205–2207; 76/817, 1067;
77/494, 607, 933, 1354, 2082, 2125; 78/427,
647, 919, 1069; 79/1656; 80/364, 365, 1068,
1870, 1987; 81/124, 125 (S), 318, 352, 1015,
1095–1097, 1632, 1819; 82/723, 1281, 1294,
1370, 1488; 83/125 (S.), 179, 1345, 1490,
1605; 84/50, 59, 206, 207, 803 (S.), 998,
1027, 1067, 1878, 1974; 85/992, 1026, 1251,
1449, 1473, 1554, 1667, 1678, 1803; 86/124,
137, 301, 1038 (S.), 1626, 2130, 2356;
87/420, 1016, 1514, 1790, 2985; 88/72, 1480,
1493–1497, 1499, 1500, 1519, 1626–1629,
1702–1704, 1706, 1707, 1711, 1928, 1940,
1946, 1947.
s. 14, amended: order 80/364; 1981, c.56,
sch.6; repealed in pt.: *ibid.*, schs.6,12.

1964—cont.

40. Harbours Act 1964—*cont.*
s. 15, orders 74/923; 76/1907; 78/941.
s. 15, repealed in pt.: 1981, c.56, sch.12.
s. 15A, added: *ibid.*, sch.6.
s. 15A, orders 85/1504; 87/222.
s. 16, orders 73/252; 88/904(S.), 1040, 1677.
s. 16, amended: 1981, c.56, sch.6; repealed in *ibid.*, schs.6,12.
s. 17, amended: *ibid.*, sch.5; repealed in pt.: *ibid.*, sch.12.
s. 18, amended: *ibid.*, sch.6; repealed in pt.: *ibid.*, sch.12.
ss. 20–25, repealed: *ibid.*, schs.6,12.
s. 27A, added: *ibid.*, sch.6.
s. 29, repealed in pt.: S.L.R. 1974.
s. 30, amended: order 78/272; amended: 1981, c.56, sch.5; repealed in pt.: *ibid.*, schs.6,12.
s. 31, amended: 1981, c.29, sch.3; c.56, schs.5,6; repealed in pt.: *ibid.*, schs. 5, 6, 12.
ss 32–34, 35 (in pt.), repealed: *ibid.*, schs.6,12.
ss. 36, 37, repealed in pt.: *ibid.*, sch.12.
ss. 38, 39, repealed in pt.: S.L.R. 1974.
s. 41, amended: 1981, c.56, schs.5,6; repealed in pt.: *ibid.*, sch.12.
s. 42, regs. 83/931.
s. 42, substituted: 1981, c.56, sch.6; amended: 1985, c.9, sch.2.
s. 43, repealed in pt.: 1981, c.56, sch.12.
s. 44, amended: *ibid.*, sch.6; repealed in pt.: *ibid.*, sch.12.
ss. 45, 46, amended: *ibid.*, sch.6; repealed in pt.: *ibid.*, sch.12; 1985, c.30, sch.
s. 47, amended: 1981, c.56, sch.6; repealed in pt.: *ibid.*, schs.6,12.
s. 49, repealed in pt.: *ibid.*, sch.12.
s. 53, substituted: 1984, c.12, sch.4.
s. 54, amended: 1981, c.56, sch.12; repealed in pt.: *ibid.*, sch.12.
s. 57, amended: 1973, c.65, sch.19; 1978, c.51, sch.16; regs. 88/1336; repealed in pt.: 1973, c.65, sch.29; 1980, c.34, sch.9; 1981, c.56, schs.4,12.
s. 58, amended: 1973, c.37, sch.8.
s. 59, repealed: 1973, c.36, sch.6.
s. 62, repealed in pt.: 1981, c.56, sch.12.
s. 63, repealed in pt.: *ibid*; S.L.R. 1974; 1975, c.24, sch.3.
sch. 1, amended: 1972, c.11, sch.6, repealed in pt.: *ibid.*, schs.4,8; 1975, c.24, sch.3; 1981, c.56, sch.12.
sch. 3, orders 75/2135, 2205–2207; 76/855, 77/553; 78/427; 84/998; regs. 88/1336.
sch. 3, amended: 1981, c.56, schs.5,6; repealed in pt.: *ibid.*, schs.6,12; 1986, c.44, sch.9.
sch. 4, amended: 1981, c.56, schs.5,6; repealed in pt.: *ibid.*, sch.12.
sch. 5, repealed: *ibid.*, schs.6,12.
sch. 6, repealed: S.L.R. 1974.

41. Succession (Scotland) Act 1964.
ss. 4, 6 (in pt.), repealed: 1986, c.9, sch.2.
s. 8, orders 81/806; 88/633.
s. 8, amended: 1973, c.25, s.1.
s. 9, orders 81/805, 806; 88/633.

1964—cont.

41. Succession (Scotland) Act—*cont.*
s. 9, amended: 1973, c.25, s.1; order 77/2110; 1980, c.55, s.4; repealed in pt.: 1986, c.9, sch.2.
s. 9A, added: 1980, c.55, s.4.
s. 9A, orders 81/805, 806; 88/633.
ss. 10A, 11 (in pt.), 13 (in pt.), repealed: 1986, c.9, sch.2.
s. 14, see *Robertson, Petitioner,* 1978 S.L.T.(Sh.Ct.) 30; *Re Dougal* [1981] S.T.C. 514, Ct. of Session.
ss. 14, 16, see *Garvie's Trs. v. Still,* 1972 S.L.T. 29; *Cormack v. McIldowie's Exors.,* 1974 S.L.T. 178; *Garvie's Trs. v. Garvie's Tutors* (O.H.), 1975 S.L.T. 94; *Rotherwick's Trs. v. Hope* (O.H.), 1975 S.L.T. 187; *Morrison-Low v. Paterson* (H.L), 1985 S.L.T. 255.
ss. 14, 19, see *Cowie Trs., Petrs.,* First Division, June 5, 1981.
s. 16, see *Reid's Trs. v. Macpherson* (O.H.), 1975 S.L.T.(Notes) 18; *Gifford v. Buchanan,* Second Division, March 23, 1983; *Coats v. Logan* (O.H.), 1985 S.L.T. 221.
ss. 16, 20, see *Inglis v. Inglis,* 1983 S.L.T. 437.
s. 19, repealed. 1975, c.7, sch.13.
s. 22, repealed in pt.: *ibid.*
s. 23, amended: 1975, c.72, sch.2, 1978, c.28, sch.3.
s. 24, amended: 1975, c.72, sch.2; repealed in pt.: 1978, c.28, sch.4.
ss. 25, 26, see *Fraser v. Fraser* (O.H.) 1976 S.L.T.(Notes) 69; *Dunbar v. Dunbar* (O.H.), 1977 S.L.T.(Notes) 55.
ss. 25–27, repealed: 1976, c.39, sch.2.
s. 27, see *MacLean v. MacLean,* First Division, November 7, 1975.
s. 30, see *Stirling's Trs.,* 1977 S.L.T. 229; *Marshall v. Marshall's Exr.* (O.H.), 1987 S.L.T. 49.
s. 31, see *Lamb v. Lord Advocate,* 1975 S.L.T.(Notes) 78; Second Division, February 27, 1976.
s. 33, see *Thomson v. Thomson,* 1982 S.L.T. 521.
s. 33, amended: 1976, c.39, sch.1; 1984, c.42, sch.1; 1985, c.37, sch.1; 1986, c.9, sch.1; repealed in pt.: *ibid.*, sch.2.
s. 34, repealed in pt.: S.L.R. 1974.
s. 36, see *Cormack v. McIldowie's Exors.,* 1974 S.L.T. 178.
s. 36, amended: 1986, c.9, sch.1; repealed: *ibid.*, sch.2.
ss 36, 37, see *McBride,* 1975 S.L.T.(Sh.Ct.) 25.
s. 37, see *Findlay,* 1975 S.L.T.(Sh.Ct.) 46; *MacMillan, Petr.* 1987 S.L.T.(Sh.Ct.) 50.
s. 37, amended: 1975, c.72, sch.2; 1978, c.28, sch.3.
sch. 2, see *Reid's Trs. v. Macpherson* (O.H.), 1975 S.L.T.(Notes) 18.
schs. 2 (in pt.), 3, repealed in pt.: S.L.R. 1974.

42. Administration of Justice Act 1964.
s. 2, order 77/1521.
ss. 2, 3, 9, 10, repealed: 1979, c.55, sch.3.
s. 11, repealed: 1980, c.43, sch.9.
ss. 13–17, repealed: 1979, c.55, sch.3.
s. 18, repealed in pt.: 1972, c.70, sch.30; S.L.R. 1975; 1980, c.9, sch.10.

CAP.

1964—cont.

42. Administration of Justice Act 1964—cont.
s. 19, repealed in pt.: 1972, c.70, sch.30.
s. 21, repealed: 1972, c.71, sch.6.
s. 22, repealed: 1973, c.62, sch.6.
s. 25, repealed: 1973, c.15, sch.5.
ss. 27, 28, repealed: 1979, c.55, sch.3.
s. 28, amended: 1981, c.54, sch.5.
s. 30, repealed: 1979, c.55, sch.3.
s. 31, repealed: 1975, c.20, sch.2 (S.); S.L.R. 1978.
ss. 32, 36, repealed: 1979, c.55, sch.3.
s. 37, amended: 1973, c.62, sch.5; repealed in pt.: S.L.R. 1978; 1979, c.55, sch.3; 1985, c.51, sch.17.
s. 38, amended: 1979, c.55, sch.2; 1980, c.43, sch.7.
s. 40, repealed in pt.: S.L.R. 1974.
s. 41, repealed in pt.: ibid.; 1975, c.24, sch.3; S.L.R. 1978.
sch. 3, amended: 1972, c.70, sch.27; repealed in pt.: 1972, c.11, sch.8; c.70, sch.30; c.71, sch.6; 1973, c.15, s.20, sch.5; 1973, c.62, sch.6; S.L.R. 1974; 1975, c.24, sch.3; 1978, c.22, sch.3; S.L.R. 1978; 1979, c.55, sch.3; 1980, c.43, sch.7.

43. Criminal Appeal Act 1964.
repealed: 1981, c.54, sch.7.

44. Nurses Act 1964.
repealed: 1979, c.36, sch.8.

46. Malawi Independence Act 1964.
ss. 2, 3, repealed: 1981, c.61, sch.9.
s. 4, repealed in pt.: 1978, c.30, sch.3.
s. 5, repealed: S.L.R. 1977.
s. 6, repealed: 1986, c.55, sch.2.
sch. 2, repealed in pt.: S.L.R. 1977; 1981, c.9, sch.; 1988, c.48, sch.8.

47. Merchant Shipping Act 1964.
modified: 1977, c.24, s.1; regs. 80/539.
s. 1, order 81/1540.
s. 1, repealed in pt.: 1977, c.24, s.1.
s. 2, rules 75/750, 927; 76/302; regs. 83/1167.
s. 2, amended: 1977, c.24, s.1.
s. 3, amended: regs. 81/568; 85/212; repealed in pt.: regs. 81/568.
s. 5, amended: 1979, c.39, sch.6; regs. 81/568; 85/212.
s. 6, amended: regs. 81/568.
s. 7, amended: 1979, c.39, sch.6; repealed in pt.: ibid., s.28, sch.7.
s. 9, amended: S.L.R. 1974.
s. 10, rules 82/1292.
s. 18, amended: S.L.R. 1974; repealed in pt.: 1977, c.24, s.1.
s. 20, amended: regs. 81/568; 85/212.

48. Police Act 1964.
see Wiltshire Police Authority v. Wynn, The Times, June 18, 1980, C.A.
s. 1, amended: 1985, c.51, sch.11; repealed in pt.: 1972, c.70, sch.30.
s. 2, rules 73/733.
s. 2, amended: 1972, c.70, s.196, sch.27; 1985, c.51, sch.11; repealed in pt.: 1972, c.70, sch.30; 1985, c.51, schs.11,17.
s. 2A, added: 1985, c.51, sch.11.
s. 3, amended: 1985, c.43, sch.2.

CAP.

1964—cont.

48. Police Act 1964—cont.
s. 4, see R. v. Lancashire County Police Authority, ex p. Hook (1980) 78 L.G.R. 397, C.A.; R. v. Secretary of State for the Home Department, ex p. Northumbria Police Authority [1987] 2 W.L.R. 998, Q.B.D.
s. 5, see R. v. Knightsbridge Crown Court, ex p. Umeh [1979] Crim.L.R. 727, D.C.; Ostler v. Elliott [1980] Crim.L.R. 584, D.C.
s. 6, amended: 1984, c.60, s.108.
s. 6A, added: ibid.
s. 7, amended: ibid., sch.6.
s. 8, amended: 1972, c.70, s.196; 1982, c.32, sch.5; 1985, c.51, sch.11; repealed in pt.: 1972, c.70, sch.30; 1982, c.32, sch.6.
s. 9, amended: 1972, c.70, s.196; 1981, c.67, sch.4; repealed in pt.: 1972, c.70, sch.30; 1981, c.67, sch.6.
s. 10, repealed in pt.: 1972, c.11, sch.8; c.70, sch.30.
s. 11, amended: 1985, c.51, sch.11; repealed in pt.: 1972, c.70, sch.30.
s. 14, see R. v. Secretary of State for the Home Department, ex p. Devon and Cornwall Police Authority, The Times, March 16, 1987, D.C.
s. 15, see Harris v. Sheffield United Football Club [1987] 3 W.L.R. 305, C.A.
s. 17, see Wiltshire Police Authority v. Wynn [1980] 3 W.L.R. 445, C.A.
s. 19, amended: 1972, c.70, s.196; repealed in pt.: ibid., sch.30.
s. 21, orders 72/693; 73/1046, 1238, 1715, 1739, 1927, 2049, 2112; 74/165, 417, 800; 76/928; 88/564.
s. 21, repealed in pt.: 1972, c.70, sch.30.
s. 22, orders 72/693; 73/1046, 1238, 2112; 74/165, 417, 800; 76/928; 88/564.
s. 22, repealed in pt.: 1972, c.70, sch.30.
s. 23, orders 73/1046, 1238, 1715, 1739, 1927, 2049, 2112; 74/165, 417.
s. 23, amended: 1972, c.70, s.196; repealed in pt.: ibid., sch.30.
s. 25, rules 73/735.
s. 25, repealed in pt.: 1972, c.70, sch.30.
s. 26, order 74/165.
s. 26, repealed in pt.: S.L.R. 1977.
s. 27, repealed in pt.: 1972, c.70, sch.30.
s. 29, amended: 1984, c.60, sch.6.
s. 31, orders 72/1574; 74/1277, 2184; 86/455.
s. 31, amended: 1985, c.51, sch.11.
s. 33, see Crosby v. Sandford [1979] Crim.L.R. 668, C.A.; R. v. Lancashire County Police Authority, ex p. Hook (1980) 78 L.G.R. 397, C.A.; R. v. Chief Constable of South Wales, ex p. Thornhill [1987] I.R.L.R. 313, C.A.
s. 33, regs. 72/74, 339, 1195; 73/33, 356, 1368; 74/649, 1217, 1365, 1973, 1974; 75/183, 378, 915, 1324, 1844; 76/538, 1274; 77/580–582, 1006, 1989; 78/1169; 79/694, 991, 1216, 1470; 80/405, 803, 1455; 81/41, 919, 1371; 82/271, 1486, 1607; 83/160; 84/1214, 1590, 1808; 85/130, 131, 518, 519, 885, 1045, 1577, 1808; 86/784, 2032, 2241; 87/851, 1753; 88/727, 1821.
s. 33, repealed in pt.: 1976, c.46, s.10.

1964—cont.

48. Police Act 1964—cont.

s. 34, regs. 72/1845; 73/431, 1816; 74/1535, 1900; 77/1948; 79/76; 80/1259; 87/159, 343.

s. 35, regs. 72/706; 73/430, 1156; 74/1153, 1534; 75/933; 76/1595; 77/1005, 1989; 78/1239; 79/75, 1543, 1727; 80/1260; 81/477; 82/350, 1487; 83/161, 990, 1348, 1349; 84/1633; 85/686, 1909; 86/2033; 87/157, 158, 342, 1754; 88/728, 1820.

s. 37, see *Calveley* v. *Merseyside Police* [1986] I.R.L.R. 177, C.A.

s. 37, substituted: 1984, c.60, s.103.

s. 40, repealed: 1976, c.35, sch.3.

s. 41, see *R.* v. *Secretary of State for the Home Department, ex p. Northumbria Police Authority, The Times,* November 19, 1987, C.A.

s. 43, amended: 1976, c.35, sch.2; 1984, c.60, sch.6; repealed in pt.: 1976, c.35, sch.3.

s. 44, regs. 73/706, 1252; 75/630, 1739; 77/583; 85/809, 1531 (S.); 86/1846; 87/1062.

s. 44, amended: 1972, c.39, s.1; 1984, c.60, s.109.

s. 46, regs. 75/1844; 77/577–581, 758; 79/1470; 81/919; 82/350, 1607; 84/1214, 1590; 85/130, 131, 518, 519, 1045, 1808.

s. 46, amended: 1980, c.10, s.2.

s. 48, see *Hill* v. *Chief Constable of West Yorkshire, The Times,* April 29, 1988, H.L.

ss. 48, 49, see *Hehir* v. *Comr. of Police of the Metropolis* [1982] 2 All E.R. 335, C.A.; *Peach* v. *Comr. of Police for the Metropolis* [1986] 2 All E.R. 129, C.A.

s. 49, see *Neilson* v. *Laugharne* [1981] 2 W.L.R. 537; [1981] 1 All E.R. 829, C.A.; *Conerney* v. *Jacklin* [1985] Crim.L.R. 234, C.A.; *R.* v. *Comr. of Police for the Metropolis, ex p. Ware, The Times,* July 31, 1985, Forbes J.

ss. 49, 50, repealed: 1984, c.60, sch.7.

s. 51, see *Squires* v. *Botwright* [1972] R.T.R. 462, D.C.; *Stunt* v. *Bolton* [1972] R.T.R. 435, D.C.; *Cunliffe* v. *Bleasdale* [1973] R.T.R. 90, D.C.; *R.* v. *Inwood* [1973] 1 W.L.R. 647; *R.* v. *Gormley* [1973] R.T.R. 483, C.A.; *King* v. *Hodges* [1974] Crim.L.R. 424, D.C.; *Johnson* v. *Phillips* [1975] 3 All E.R. 682, D.C.; *R.* v. *Roff; R.* v. *Dowie* [1976] R.T.R. 7, C.A.; *Evans* v. *Macklen* [1976] Crim.L.R. 120, D.C.; *Kay* v. *Hibbert* [1977] Crim.L.R. 226, D.C.; *Hickman* v. *O'Dwyer* [1979] Crim.L.R. 309, D.C.; *Wershof* v. *Metropolitan Police Commissioner* (1978) 68 Cr.App.R. 82; *Daniel* v. *Morrison* (1979) 70 Cr.App.R. 142, D.C.; *Grant* v. *Gorman* [1980] R.T.R. 119, D.C.; *Re Prescott* (*Note*) (1979) 70 Cr.App.R. 244, C.A.; *Syce* v. *Harrison* [1980] Crim.L.R. 649, D.C.; *Albert* v. *Lavin, The Times,* December 5, 1980, D.C.; *Lindley* v. *Rutter* [1980] 3 W.L.R. 660, D.C.; *Coffin* v. *Smith* (1980) 71 Cr.App.R. 221, D.C.; *Pedro* v. *Diss* [1981] Crim.L.R. 236, D.C.; *Ashton* v. *Merseyside Police,* May 13, 1981, Judge Arthur, Birkenhead Crown Ct.; *Pamplin* v. *Fraser* [1981] R.T.R. 494, D.C.; *Moore* v. *Green, The Times,* November 12, 1981, D.C.; *Ricketts* v. *Cox* (1982) 74 Cr.App.R. 298, D.C.; *McLorie* v. *Oxford* [1982] 3 W.L.R. 423, D.C.;

1964—cont.

48. Police Act 1964—cont.

Bentley v. *Brudzinski* (1982) 75 Cr.App.R. 217, D.C.; *Ludlow* v. *Burgess* (1982) 75 Cr.App.R. 227, C.A.; *McBean* v. *Parker,* [1983] Crim.L.R. 399, D.C.; *Hills* v. *Ellis* [1983] 2 W.L.R. 235, D.C.; *Moore* v. *Green* [1983] 1 All E.R. 663, D.C.; *Brazil* v. *Chief Constable of Surrey* [1983] 1 W.L.R. 1155, D.C.; *Read* v. *Jones* (1983) 77 Cr.App.R. 246, D.C.; *Collins* v. *Wilcock* [1984] 1 W.L.R. 1172, D.C.; *Lewis* v. *Cox* [1984] 3 W.L.R. 875, D.C.; *Liepins* v. *Spearman* [1986] R.T.R. 24, D.C.; *Bennett* v. *Bale* [1986] Crim.L.R. 404, D.C.; *Smith* v. *Reynolds* [1986] Crim.L.R. 559, D.C.; *Smith* v. *Hancock* [1986] Crim.L.R. 560; *Smith* v. *Lowe* [1986] Crim.L.R. 561, D.C.; *Weight* v. *Long* [1986] Crim.L.R. 746, D.C.; *G.* v. *Chief Superintendent of Police,* Stroud, *Gloucestershire* [1987] Crim.L.R. 269, D.C.; *Nicholas* v. *Parsonage* [1987] R.T.R. 199, D.C.

s. 51, amended: 1977, c.45, ss.15, 30, 31, schs.1,6.

ss. 51, 53, see *Neal* v. *Evans* [1976] R.T.R. 333, D.C.; *Willmott* v. *Atack* [1976] 3 W.L.R. 753, D.C.

s. 52, see *Turner* v. *Shearer* [1972] 1 W.L.R. 1387.

s. 52, amended: 1982, c.48, sch.3.

s. 58, amended: 1984, c.60, s.108.

s. 60, order 74/1277.

s. 62, repealed in pt.: 1978, c.30, sch.3.

s. 64, repealed in pt.: S.L.R. 1974.

schs. 1, 3, repealed in pt.: 1972, c.70, sch.30.

sch. 4, repealed in pt.: 1972, c.11, schs.7,8; order 74/520; regs. 77/1341.

sch. 5, see *R.* v. *Secretary of State for the Home Department, ex p. Chief Constable of Nottingham, The Times,* March 10, 1984, Hodgson J.

sch. 5, rules 77/759; 85/576.

sch. 5, substituted: 1984, c.60, s.103; amended: 1985, c.51, sch.11.

sch. 6, repealed: 1976, c.35, sch.3.

sch. 8, repealed in pt.: 1972, c.70, sch.30.

sch. 9, repealed in pt.: *ibid.*; c.71, sch.6; S.L.R. 1974; order 74/595; 1976, c.35, sch.3.

sch. 10, repealed: S.L.R. 1974.

sch. 11, repealed in pt.: 1972, c.70, sch.30; order 74/520; regs. 77/1341.

49. Finance Act 1964.

s. 1, amended: 1978, c.42, sch.12; repealed in pt.: 1972, c.41, sch.28; 1973, c.51, sch.22; 1975, c.45, sch.14.

s. 2, repealed in pt.: 1973, c.51, sch.22; 1975, c.45, sch.14.

s. 3, repealed: 1975, c.45, sch.14.

s. 4, repealed: 1977, c.36, s.3, sch.9.

s. 7, repealed: 1972, c.25, sch.7.

s. 8, repealed: 1979, c.8, sch.2.

s. 10, amended: 1979, c.2, sch.5; repealed in pt.: 1972, c.41, sch.28; 1979, c.2, sch.6.

s. 22, repealed: 1972, c.68, sch.3.

s. 26, repealed: 1979, c.2, sch.5.

schs. 1–4, repealed: 1975, c.45, sch.14.

sch. 5, repealed: 1977, c.36, sch.9.

schs. 8, 9, repealed in part: S.L.R. 1974.

1964—cont.

50. Tenancy of Shops (Scotland) Act 1964.
repealed: S.L.R. 1974.

51. Universities and College Estates Act 1964.
s. 4, repealed in pt.: S.L.R. 1974.
sch. 3, repealed in pt.: *ibid.*; S.L.R. 1981; 1986, c.5, sch.15.
sch. 4, repealed: S.L.R. 1974.

52. Films Act 1964.
repealed: 1985, c.21, s.1, sch.2.

53. Hire-Purchase Act 1964.
whole Act, except Pt. III (ss.27–29) and s. 37, repealed: 1974, c.39, sch.5.
s. 27, see *North West Securities* v. *Barrhead Coachbuilders*, 1975 S.L.T.(Sh.Ct.) 34; *Stevenson* v. *Beverley Bentinck* [1976] 1 W.L.R. 483, C.A.
s. 27, amended: 1979, c.54, sch.2.
ss. 27, 28, 29, see *Soneco* v. *Barcross Finance* [1978] R.T.R. 444, C.A.
ss. 27, 29, see *North-West Securities* v. *Barrhead Coachworks* (O.H.), 1976 S.L.T. 99.

54. British Nationality (No. 2) Act 1964.
repealed: 1981, c.61, sch.9.
s. 5, orders 74/1895; 78/1026.
s. 6, regs. 80/358; 81/1571.

55. Perpetuities and Accumulations Act 1964.
s. 1, see *Green's Will Trusts, Re* [1985] 3 All E.R. 455, Nourse J.
s. 4, amended: 1975, c.72, sch.3.

56. Housing Act 1964.
see *Silbers* v. *Southwark London Borough Council* (1978) 76 L.G.R. 421, C.A.; *Milford Properties* v. *Hammersmith London Borough* [1978] J.P.L. 766, D.C.
Pt. I (ss.1–12), repealed: 1985, c.71, sch.1.
Pt. I (ss.1–12), repealed (S): *ibid.*
s. 9, order 74/698.
ss. 13–44, repealed: 1974, c.44, sch.15.
s. 34, amended: 1977, c.42, sch.23.
ss. 57, 59, repealed: 1974, c.44, sch.15; regs. 74/1791.
s. 63, repealed: S.L.R. 1981.
Pt. IV (ss.64–91), repealed: 1985, c.71, sch.1.
s. 67, see *Hackney London Borough* v. *Ezedinma* [1981] 3 All E.R. 438, D.C.
s. 73, see *R.* v. *London Borough of Southwark, ex p. Lewis Levy* (1983) 267 E.G. 1040, Stephen Brown J.
s. 78, regs. 81/781; 84/1629.
s. 92, repealed: 1972, c.46, sch.11 (S.); c.47, sch.11.
s. 93, repealed: 1972, c.46, schs.8,11 (S.); c.47, schs.8,11.
s. 94, repealed: *ibid.*, sch.11.
s. 95, amended: 1974, c.40, sch.3; repealed in pt.: 1980, c.65, sch.34.
s. 96, repealed: 1985, c.71, sch.1.
s. 97, repealed: 1972, c.47, sch.11.
s. 98, repealed (S.): 1972, c.46, sch.11.
s. 101, amended: 1973, c.65, sch.12; repealed (S.): 1987, c.26, sch.24.
ss. 102, 103, repealed: 1985, c.71, sch.1.
s. 104, repealed: 1972, c.47, sch.11.
s. 105, repealed: S.L.R. 1981.
s. 106, repealed in pt.: 1985, c.71, sch.17; repealed: 1985, c.71, sch.1.

1964—cont.

56. Housing Act 1964—*cont.*
s. 108, repealed in pt.: 1975, c.24, sch.3; regs. 81/781; 1985, c.71, sch.1.
schs. 1–4, repealed: *ibid.*
sch. 5, repealed: S.L.R. 1981.

57. Adoption Act 1964.
repealed: 1976, c.36, sch.4; 1978, c.28, sch.4 (S.).
ss. 1, 4, repealed in pt.: 1981, c.61, sch.9.

58. Resale Prices Act 1964.
ss. 1–5, 7, 10–14, sch., repealed: 1976, c.53, sch.3.
s. 3, see *J.J.B.* (*Sports*) v. *Milbro Sports*; *Same* v. *Richard Forshaw & Co.* [1975] I.C.R. 73, C.A.
ss. 6, 8, repealed: 1976, c.53, sch.3.

59. Protection of Birds Act 1954 (Amendment) Act 1964.
repealed: 1981, c.69, sch.17.

60. Emergency Laws (Re-enactments and Repeals) Act 1964.
s. 1, orders 73/2129, 2130; 74/1868; 75/711, 712, 2139, 2140; 76/1135; 77/770, 771; 78/553; 79/1223; 81/746; 82/1034.
s. 1, amended: 1974, c.39, sch.4; repealed in pt.: *ibid.*, sch.5.
s. 2, directions 72/982; 79/1661; 82/512, 1296, 1297, 1307, 1583.
s. 3, repealed: S.L.R. 1977.
s. 4, orders 73/289; 75/686; 76/517, 1682, 1856; 77/25, 1492, 1620; 78/269, 1876; 79/1568; 80/1648, 1836; 81/1292; 83/379; regs. 85/1932.
s. 4, repealed: 1988, c.7, sch.5.
s. 5, order 74/377.
s. 5, repealed: 1977, c.49, sch.16; 1978, c.29, sch.17 (S.).
s. 6, orders 72/366, 367; 74/565, 1549, 1707; 75/179, 1230, 2139; 76/639, 1271, 2059; 77/858, 859, 1441, 2055; 78/469, 1382, 1491, 1498; 79/604, 700, 1289, 1290, 1602; 80/48, 49, 1175, 1176, 1294 (S.), 1295, 1296, 2022, 2023; 81/628, 629, 1027, 1261, 1852, 1854; 82/456 (S.), 464; 83/491; 84/142, 166; continued in force: order 79/1602.
s. 7, orders 72/366, 367, 982; 73/289, 2068, 2080, 2087, 2091, 2092, 2119, 2120, 2129, 2130, 2137, 2146, 2172; 74/78, 117, 137, 197, 198, 245, 511, 565, 620, 948, 986, 1225, 1549, 1707, 1868, 1898; 75/179, 711, 712, 1230, 1686, 2139, 2140; 76/517, 639, 1135, 1271, 1682, 1856, 2059; 77/25, 770, 771, 1441, 1492, 1620, 2054, 2055; 78/269, 469, 470, 553, 1382, 1491, 1498, 1876; 79/604, 700, 1289, 1290, 1568; 80/48, 49, 1175, 1176, 1294(S.), 1295, 1296, 1648, 1836, 2022, 2023; 81/628, 629, 746, 1027, 1292, 1852, 1854; 82/456 (S.), 464, 1034; 83/379, 491; 84/142, 166; directions 79/1661; 82/1296, 1307; regs. 85/1932.
s. 9, amended: 1981, c.61, sch.7.
s. 14, repealed in pt.: S.L.R. 1977.
s. 15, repealed in pt.: 1977, c.49, sch.16; 1978, c.29, sch.17 (S.).
s. 16, repealed: S.L.R. 1977.

1964—cont.

60. Emergency Laws (Re-enactments and Repeals) Act 1964—*cont.*
s. 20, repealed in pt.: 1973, c.36, sch.6.
s. 21, repealed: S.L.R. 1981.
s. 22, orders 77/2055; 78/470, 1491; 79/604, 1289; 80/49, 1176, 1296; direction 72/982.
sch. 2, repealed: S.L.R. 1974.

61. Animals (Restriction of Importation) Act 1964.
repealed: 1976, c.72, s.13.
s. 2, order 75/1008.

63. Law of Property (Joint Tenants) Act 1964.
s. 1, amended: 1985, c.65, sch.8.

64. Drugs (Prevention of Misuse) Act 1964.
repealed: 1971, c.38, sch.6.
s. 1, see *R.* v. *Buswell* [1972] 1 W.L.R. 64, C.A.; *R.* v. *Peevey* (1973) 57 Cr.App.R. 554, C.A.

65. Zambia Independence Act 1964.
ss. 3, 4, repealed: 1981, c.61, sch.9.
ss. 5, 6, 10, repealed: S.L.R. 1977.
s. 7, repealed: 1985, c.55, sch.2.
s. 11, repealed in pt.: S.L.R. 1974.
sch. 1, repealed in pt.: S.L.R. 1976; 1981, c.9, sch.; 1988, c.48, sch.8.
sch. 3, repealed: S.L.R. 1974.

67. Local Government (Development and Finance) (Scotland) Act 1964.
s. 1, repealed in pt.: 1973, c.65, sch.29.
ss. 2, 3, amended: 1982, c.43, sch.1.
s. 4, repealed; 1983, c.35, sch.2.
s. 5, repealed: 1973, c.65, sch.29.
s. 6, amended: *ibid.*, sch.27; repealed in pt.: *ibid.*, sch.29.
s. 7, amended: 1982, c.43, s.49.
ss. 8–12, repealed: 1975, c.30, sch.7.

69. Scrap Metal Dealers Act 1964.
ss. 1, 9, see *Such* v. *Gibbons* [1981] R.T.R. 126, D.C.
s. 9, repealed in pt.: 1972, c.70, sch.30.

70. Riding Establishments Act 1964.
s. 1, amended: 1973, c.65, sch.25(S.); 1974, c.7, sch.6; repealed in pt.: 1988, c.29, sch.
s. 6, amended: 1972, c.70, sch.29; 1973, c.65, sch.24(S.); repealed in pt.: 1972, c.70, schs.29, 30.
ss. 7, 8, repealed: S.L.R. 1976.

71. Trading Stamps Act 1964.
s. 1, amended: 1985, c.9, sch.2.
ss. 2, 3, amended: 1974, c.39, sch.4.
s. 4, substituted: 1973, c.13, s.16.
s. 10, amended: 1974, c.39, sch.4; repealed in pt.: *ibid.*, sch.5; order 80/50.

72. Fishery Limits Act 1964.
s. 1, repealed: 1976, c.86, ss.9,10, sch.4.
s. 3, repealed in pt.: S.L.R. 1974; 1976, s.86, ss.9,10, sch.4; S.L.R. 1978.
s. 4, repealed in pt.: 1973, c.36, sch.6.
sch. 1, repealed in pt.: S.L.R. 1974; order 81/227; 1984, c.26, sch.2.
sch. 2, repealed: S.L.R. 1974.

73. British North America Act 1964.
Act renamed Constitution Act 1964 (Can.): 1982, c.11, sch.

1964—cont.

74. Obscene Publications Act 1964.
s. 1, see *R.* v. *Anderson; Neville; Dennis; R.* v. *Oz Publications Ink* [1971] 3 W.L.R. 939; [1971] 3 All E.R. 1152; (1971) 56 Cr.App.R. 115; *R.* v. *Bristol Crown Court, ex p. Willets, The Times,* January 25, 1985, D.C.; *R.* v. *Skirving; R.* v. *Grossman (Beth), The Times,* March 9, 1985, C.A.
ss. 1, 4, see *Att.-Gen.'s Reference (No. 3 of 1977)* [1978] 1 W.L.R. 1123, C.A.

75. Public Libraries and Museums Act 1964.
functions transferred: orders 81/207; 86/600.
s. 2, amended: orders 81/207; 86/600.
s. 4, amended: 1972, c.70, s.208; repealed in pt.: *ibid.*, sch.30.
s. 5, amended: *ibid.*, s.208.
s. 6, amended: *ibid.*; repealed in pt.: *ibid.*, sch.30.
s. 7, see *Att.-Gen.* v. *Observer; Application by Derbyshire County Council, Re* [1988] 1 All E.R. 385, Knox J.
s. 7, repealed in pt.: 1972, c.70, sch.30.
ss. 7, 10, see *R.* v. *Ealing London Borough Council, ex p. Times Newspapers; R.* v. *Hammersmith and Fulham London Borough Council, ex p. Same; R.* v. *Camden London Borough Council, ex p. Same* (1987) 85 L.G.R. 316, D.C.
s. 8, amended: 1988, c.48, sch.7; repealed in pt.: 1980, c.65, schs.6, 34.
s. 10, amended: 1972, c.70, s.208; repealed in pt.: *ibid.*, sch.30.
s. 11, amended: *ibid.*, s.208.
s. 12, repealed in pt.: *ibid.*, sch.30.
ss. 14, 15, amended: *ibid.*, s.208; repealed in pt.: *ibid.*, sch.30.
s. 16, amended: *ibid.*, s.208.
s. 18, repealed: *ibid.*, sch.30.
s. 21, amended: *ibid.*, s.208; repealed in pt.: *ibid.*, s.208, sch.30.
s. 22, repealed: S.L.R. 1975.
s. 24, amended: 1972, c.70, s.208.
s. 25, amended in pt.: *ibid.*, sch.30.
s. 26, repealed in pt.: *ibid.*; S.L.R. 1974.
sch. 1, repealed in pt.: 1972, c.11, schs.7,8; regs. 74/520; 77/1341.
sch. 2, repealed in pt.: 1972, c.70, s.208, sch.30.
sch. 3, repealed: S.L.R. 1974.

77. Local Government (Pecuniary Interests) Act 1964.
repealed: 1972, c.70, sch.30.

79. Statute Law Revision Act 1964.
repealed: S.L.R. 1974.

80. Statute Law Revision (Scotland) Act 1964.
s. 1, sch. 1, repealed: S.L.R. 1974.

81. Diplomatic Privileges Act 1964.
see *R.* v. *Guildhall Magistrates' Court, ex p. Jarrett-Thorpe, The Times,* October 5, 1977.
s. 2, amended: 1973, c.38, sch.27; 1979, c.2, sch.4; repealed in pt.: 1975, c.18, sch.1.
s. 3, amended: 1981, c.61, sch.7.
s. 5, repealed in pt.: *ibid.*, sch.9.
s. 7, amended: 1979, c.2, sch.4.
s. 8, repealed in pt.: S.L.R. 1974; 1979, c.60, sch.3.

CAP.

1964—cont.

81. Diplomatic Privileges Act 1964—cont.
sch. 1, see Shaw v. Shaw [1979] 3 W.L.R. 24.
Balcombe J.; Intpro Properties (U.K.) v. Sauvel
[1983] 2 W.L.R. 1, Bristow J.; R. v. Lambeth
JJ., ex p. Yusufu [1985] Crim.L.R. 510, D.C.;
Fayed v. Tajir [1987] 2 All E.R. 396, C.A.;
Shearson Lehman Brothers Inc. v. Maclaine
Watson & Co. (No. 2) (International Tin Council Intervener) [1988] 1 W.L.R. 16, H.L.
sch. 1, amended: 1987, c 46, sch.2.
sch. 2, repealed: S.L.R. 1974.

82. Education Act 1964.
s. 1, regs. 80/918; amended: 1980, c.20, sch.3.
s. 2, repealed: 1976, c.5, sch.
ss. 3, 4, repealed: S.L.R. 1978.
s. 5, repealed in pt.: 1976, c.5, sch.; S.L.R.
1978; repealed (S.): 1980, c.44, sch.5.

83. New Forest Act 1964.
s. 3, amended: 1976, c.70, sch.7; 1980, c.66,
sch.24.

84. Criminal Procedure (Insanity) Act 1964.
s. 2, see R. v. Sullivan [1983] 3 W.L.R. 123, H.L.
s. 4, see R. v. Berry (1977) 66 Cr.App.R. 156,
C.A.; R. v. Metropolitan Stipendiary Magistrate, ex p. Anufowsi, The Times, August 5,
1985, D.C.
s. 4, repealed in pt.: 1983, c.20, sch.6.
s. 8, amended: ibid.; repealed in pt.: S.L.R.
1974.
sch. 1, see R. v. Astill, Jan. 20, 1977
sch. 1, amended: 1982, c.51, sch.3.
sch. 2, repealed in pt.: S.L.R. 1974.

86. Malta Independence Act 1964.
ss. 2, 3, repealed: 1981, c.61, sch.9.
s. 4, repealed in pt.: S.L.R. 1974; 1978, c.30,
sch.3.
sch. 1, repealed in pt.: 1988, c.48, sch.8.
sch. 2, repealed in pt.: S.L.R. 1977; 1981, c.9,
sch.
sch. 4, repealed: S.L.R. 1974.

89. Hairdressers (Registration) Act 1964.
s. 13, amended: 1985, c.9, sch.2.

90. Spray Irrigation (Scotland) Act 1964.
s. 1, amended: 1980, c.45, sch.10.
s. 9, amended: 1974, c.40, sch.3.

91. Divorce (Scotland) Act 1964.
repealed: 1976, c.39, sch.2.
s. 3, see Hamilton v. Hamilton (O.H.), 1975
S.L.T.(Notes) 49.
s. 5, see Grant v. Grant (O.H.), 1974
S.L.T.(Notes) 59.

92. Finance (No. 2) Act 1964.
repealed: S.L.R. 1986.
s. 9, amended: 1979, c.2, sch.4.
s. 10, amended: ibid; repealed in pt.: 1972,
c.41, sch.28; S.L.R. 1974.
sch. 4, repealed: ibid.

93. The Gambia Independence Act 1964.
ss. 2, 3, repealed: 1981, c.61, sch.9.
s. 4, repealed in pt.: 1978, c.30, sch.3.
sch. 2, repealed in pt.: S.L.R. 1977, 1981, c.9,
sch.; 1988, c.48, sch.8.

95. Travel Concessions Act 1964.
repealed: 1985, c.67, sch.8.

CAP.

1964—cont.

98. Ministers of the Crown Act 1964.
repealed, so far as unrepealed: 1975, c.26,
sch.3.
s. 4, orders 74/692. 1264.

1965

2. Administration of Justice Act 1965.
s. 1, scheme 72/528.
ss. 1–16, repealed: 1982, c.53, sch.9.
s. 2, orders 72/683. 771, 1082.
s. 4, rules 75/1803.
s. 6, see The Halcyon the Great [1975] 1 W.L.R.
515; [1975] 1 All E.R. 882.
s. 7, rules 73/231, 239; 74/207; 75/1803;
77/2235; 78/751; 79/1620; 80/1858;
81/1589; 82/123, 787; 83/290; 84/285;
86/1142, 2115.
s. 12, regs. 78/468.
s. 14, regs. 83/1943.
s. 14, repealed in pt.: 1986, c.60, sch.17.
s. 18, repealed: 1982, c.53, sch.9; amended:
1983, c.20, sch.4.
s. 20, orders 72/1103; 77/601; 81/1122.
s. 20, amended: 1976, c.60, ss.1, 12, sch.1;
regs. 84/1199; repealed in pt.: 1982, c.53,
sch.9; 1984, c.28, sch.4.
s. 21, repealed: 1976, c.60, s.13, sch.3.
s. 22, repealed in pt.: S.L.R. 1974.
s. 23, repealed: 1984, c.28, sch.4.
s. 27, regs. 78/1357.
s. 27, repealed: 1979, c.31, sch.2.
s. 28, repealed: S.L.R. 1977.
ss. 30, 32, 33, repealed: 1978, c.23, sch.7.
s. 31, repealed: 1973, c.36, sch.6.
ss. 34, 36, repealed in pt.: S.L.R. 1974.
sch. 1, amended: 1982, c.53, s.46; repealed in
pt.: 1972, c.20, sch.9; S.L.R. 1974; S.L.R.
1981; c.54, sch.7; 1982, c.27, sch.14; c.53,
sch.9; 1983, c.20, sch.6; 1986, c.60, sch.17;
1987, c.16, sch.16.
schs. 2, 3, repealed: S.L.R. 1974.

3. Remuneration of Teachers Act 1965.
repealed in pt.: 1987, c.1, s.1, sch.2.
see Vaughan v. Solihull Metropolitan Borough,
The Times, November 26, 1980, D.C.
s. 1, see R. v. Burnham Primary and Secondary
Committee, ex p. Professional Association of
Teachers, The Times, March 30, 1985, Mac-
Pherson J.
s. 1, orders 74/959; 76/169, 824; 77/61, 1501;
78/1019, 1226, 1409, 1773; 79/339, 1193;
80/247, 1611; 81/1188; 82/1231, 1232;
83/1463, 1464; 85/1663.
ss. 1, 2, see Lewis v. Dyfed County Council
(1978) 77 L.G.R. 339, C.A.
s. 2, orders 72/255, 276; 73/956, 1222, 1223;
74/747, 958, 960, 1048–1050, 1644, 1990,
1991, 2098, 2099; 75/152, 277, 278, 280,
1226, 1227, 1416, 1417, 1558; 76/656, 1192,
2228; 77/292; 78/982, 1019, 1773; 79/428,
1193; 80/247, 965, 966, 1197, 1331, 1611;
81/65, 66, 1188, 1236; 82/1231, 1232, 1416,
1417; 83/385, 572, 1463, 1464; 84/1650,
2043; 85/38, 495, 944, 1248; 86/176, 559;
87/137, 236, 398.

1965—cont.

3. Remuneration of Teachers Act 1965—*cont.*
s. 3, orders 80/1611; 82/1416.
s. 3, amended: 1975, c.71, sch.16; repealed in pt.: *ibid.*, schs.16,18.
s. 4, orders 72/255; 80/1611; 82/1416.
s. 6, repealed: S.L.R. 1978.
s. 7, orders 78/982, 1019, 1773; 79/428; 80/247, 965, 966, 1331, 1611; 81/65, 66; 83/385, 572, 1463, 1464; 84/1650, 2043; 85/38, 495, 944, 1248; 86/559; 87/137, 236, 398.
s. 8, amended: 1986, c.1, s.2.
s. 9, repealed in pt.: S.L.R. 1978.

4. Science and Technology Act 1965.
s. 1, repealed in pt.: 1973, c.54, schs.2,4.
s. 3, amended: *ibid.*, sch.2; repealed in pt.: *ibid.*, schs.2,4.
s. 5, amended: order 74/692.
sch. 2, repealed in pt.: 1973, c.37, sch.9; c.54, sch.4; S.L.R. 1974; 1980, c.45, sch.11(S.).
sch. 4, repealed in pt.: S.L.R. 1974.

6. National Insurance Act 1965.
s. 49, see *R.* v. *National Insurance Commissioner, ex p. Warry* [1981] I.C.R. 90; [1981] 1 All E.R. 229, D.C.

9. Armed Forces (Housing Loans) Act 1965.
s. 1, sch., repealed in pt.: S.L.R. 1974.

10. Superannuation (Amendment) Act 1965.
s. 5, repealed: 1981, c.20, sch.4.
s. 24, order 80/1610.
sch. 1, repealed: 1973, c.36, sch.6; 1975, c.24, sch.3; c.25, sch.3.
sch. 2, orders 79/680, 1275; 80/1610.
sch. 2, repealed: 1981, c.20, sch.4.

11. Ministerial Salaries and Members' Pensions Act 1965.
repealed: 1972, c.48, sch.4.
s. 7, repealed in pt.: 1978, c.56, sch.2.
s. 14, amended: orders 75/1137; 84/539.

12. Industrial and Provident Societies Act 1965.
s. 1, amended: 1985, c.9, sch.2.
s. 2, amended: 1979, c.34, ss.2,6.
s. 6, amended: 1975, c.41, s.1; 1985, c.71, sch.2.
s. 7, amended: 1978, c.34, s.1.
s. 10, amended: 1979, c.34, s.4.
s. 11, amended: 1974, c.46, sch.9.
s. 16, amended: 1979, c.34, s.6.
s. 31, amended: 1986, c.53, sch.18.
s. 42, amended: 1984, c.28, sch.2.
s. 52, amended: 1985, c.9, sch.2.
s. 53, amended: 1975, c.41, s.3; 1979, c.34, ss.6,23; 1985, c.9, sch.2.
s. 55, see *Nourse Self Build Association, Re* (1985) 82 L.S.Gaz. 1709, Harman J.
s. 55, amended: 1985, c.9, sch.2; 1986, c.45, sch.14.
s. 61, amended: 1982, c.48, schs.3,6 (S.).
ss. 61–66, 68, amended: 1979, c.34, s.28.
s. 70, regs. 74/1299; 76/355; 77/2022; 78/1729; 79/937, 1556, 1558; 80/1751, 1752; 81/1832, 1833; 83/350, 352; 84/307, 308; 85/344, 345; 86/621, 622; 87/393, 394; 88/450, 451.
s. 71, regs. 74/1299; 76/355; 79/1556; 80/1752; 81/1832; 85/344, 345; 86/621, 622; 87/393, 394; 88/450, 451.

1965—cont.

12. Industrial and Provident Societies Act 1965—*cont.*
s. 74, amended: 1985, c.9, sch.2.
s. 77, repealed in pt.: S.L.R. 1974.
sch. 5, repealed: *ibid.*

13. Rivers (Prevention of Pollution) (Scotland) Act 1965.
repealed, except ss. 10, 13 (in pt.), 15 (in pt.), 17 (in pt.): 1974, c.40, sch.4.
s. 2, amended: 1984, c.26, sch.1; repealed in pt.: *ibid.*, schs.1,2.
s. 8, orders 72/1661; 73/1244.
s. 10, amended: 1974, c.40, sch.3.
s. 11, amended: 1982, c.48, sch.6.

14. Cereals Marketing Act 1965.
s. 1, orders 79/782; 82/896; 84/892.
s. 1, amended: 1986, c.49, s.4, sch.3.
ss. 2–5, repealed: *ibid.*, s.4, sch.4.
s. 6, amended: *ibid.*, s.4.
s. 7, amended: *ibid.*, sch.3.
Pt. II, repealed: *ibid.*, s.4, sch.4.
s. 12, repealed in pt.: *ibid.*, sch.4.
s. 13, orders 72/870, 871; 74/2094; 75/1050; 76/1189; 77/1034; 78/883; 80/862; 81/207; 82/896; 83/946; 84/892; 85/1013; 86/138; 87/1194; 88/1132.
s. 13, amended: regs. 79/26; repealed in pt.: 1986, c.49, sch.4.
s. 14, order 84/892.
ss. 14, 15, repealed: 1986, c.49, sch.4.
s. 16, orders 74/2083; 84/892; 87/671.
s. 16, amended: 1972, c.62, s.16; regs. 79/26; 1986, c.49, s.5, sch.3.
ss. 18, 19, repealed in pt.: *ibid.*, sch.4.
s. 20, amended: *ibid.*, s.5.
s. 21, amended: 1985, c.19, sch.2.
s. 23, orders 87/671, 1194; 88/1132.
s. 23, repealed in pt.: 1986, c.49, sch.4.
s. 24, amended: 1972, c.62, s.16; regs. 77/181; 1986, c.49, ss.5,6; repealed in pt.: *ibid.*, s.5, sch.4.
sch. 1, amended: 1976, c.34, sch.5; 1986, c.49, s.4, sch.3; repealed in pt.: 1975, c.24, sch.3; c.25, sch.3.
sch. 2, repealed: 1986, c.49, sch.4.
sch. 3, order 72/870.
sch. 3, amended: 1986, c.49, s.5, sch.3; repealed in pt.: *ibid.*, sch.4.

15. Dangerous Drugs Act 1965.
s. 2, see *R.* v. *Borro and Abdullah* [1973] Crim.L.R. 513, C.A.
s. 5, see *Christison* v. *Hogg*, 1974 J.C. 55, Court of Justiciary; *R.* v. *Ashdown*; *R.* v. *Howard* (1974) 59 Cr.App.R. 193, C.A.; *R.* v. *Thomas*; *R.* v. *Thomson* (1976) 63 Cr.App.R. 65, C.A.; *R.* v. *Mogford* (1970) 63 Cr.App.R. 168.
s. 13, see *Searle* v. *Randolph* [1972] Crim.L.R. 779; *Bocking* v. *Roberts* [1973] 3 W.L.R. 465; [1973] 3 All E.R. 962, D.C.

16. Airports Authority Act 1965.
repealed: 1975, c.78, sch.6.
s. 9, see *Robertson* v. *Bannister* [1973] R.T.R. 109, D.C.
s. 12, order 76/363.
s. 15, order 72/1291.

CAP.

1965—cont.

16. Airports Authority Act 1965—*cont.*
s. 15, schemes 73/617; 74/2051.
s. 16, regs. 72/1027.
s. 19, amended (S.): 1980, c.45, sch.10.

17. Museum of London Act 1965.
functions transferred: orders 81/207, 86/600.
s. 1, repealed in pt.: 1985, c.51, sch.17; 1986, c.8, sch.
s. 2, order 75/614.
ss. 3, 8, substituted: 1986, c.8, s.2.
s. 9, amended: 1985, c.51, s.43; 1986, c.8, s.2; repealed in pt.: 1985, c.51, sch.17.
s. 10, repealed: regs. 77/1341.
s. 13, repealed: 1986, c.8, sch.
s. 14, amended: 1985, c.51, s.43; 1986, c.8, s.4; repealed in pt.: *ibid.*, sch.
s. 15, amended: 1985, c.51, s.43; 1986, c.8, s.3.
sch., amended: 1985, c.51, s.43; repealed in pt.: *ibid.*, sch.17.

19. Teaching Council (Scotland) Act 1965.
see *Malloch* v. *Aberdeen Corpn.*, First Div., June 1, 1973.
s. 2, amended: 1981, c.58, sch.7.
s. 5, regs. 86/1353.
s. 5, amended: 1981, c.58, s.17.
s. 7, regs. 73/864.
s. 7, amended: 1981, c.58, s.17, sch.7; repealed in pt.: S.L.R. 1981.
s. 10, sch. 2, rules 81/721.
s 11, see *Johnstone* v. *General Teaching Council for Scotland*, 1981 S.C. 51.
sch. 1, order 77/1980; amended: 1975, c.30, sch.6; 1985, c.9, sch.2.

20. Criminal Evidence Act 1965.
repealed: 1984, c.60, sch.7.
see *R.* v. *Schreiber and Schreiber* [1988] Crim.L.R. 112, C.A.
s. 1, see *R.* v. *Tirado* (1974) 59 Cr.App.R. 80, C.A.; *R.* v. *Nicholls* (1976) 63 Cr.App.R. 187, C.A.; *R.* v. *Jones*; *R.* v. *Sullivan* (1977) 122 S.J. 94, C.A.; *R.* v. *Crayden* [1978] 1 W.L.R. 604, C.A.; *R.* v. *Pettigrew*; *R.* v. *Newark* (1980) 71 Cr.App.R. 39, C.A.; *R.* v. *Cook* (1980) 71 Cr.App.R. 205, C.A.; *R.* v. *Patel* (1981) 73 Cr.App.R. 117, C.A.; *R.* v. *Abdullah* [1982] Crim.L.R. 122, Croydon Crown Court; *R.* v. *Cook* [1982] Crim.L.R. 169, Kingston Crown Ct.; *R.* v. *Ewing*, The Times, March 15, 1983, C.A.; *R.* v. *Shone* (1983) 76 Cr.App.R. 33, C.A.; *R.* v. *Wood* (1983) 76 Cr.App.R. 23, C.A.
s. 1, amended: 1981, c.38, sch.3.

22. Law Commissions Act 1965.
s. 1, amended: 1982, c.53, s.64.
s. 2, repealed in pt. (S.): 1985, c.73, sch.2.
s. 6, repealed in pt.: 1975, c.24, sch.3; c.25, sch.3.

24. Severn Bridge Tolls Act 1965.
ss. 1, 2, 15, 16, amended: 1980, c.66, sch.24.
ss. 1, 3, 4, sch. 2, see *R.* v. *Secretary of State for Transport, ex p. Gwent County Council* [1987] 1 All E.R. 161, C.A.
s. 2, orders 73/120; 74/745; 79/883; 85/726.
s. 3, amended: regs. 74/595.

CAP.

1965—cont.

24. Severn Bridge Tolls Act 1965—*cont.*
s. 5, regs. 73/121.
s. 7, regs. 75/1269; 82/326.
s. 20, repealed in pt.: 1972, c.71, sch.6.
s. 22, amended: 1980, c.66, sch.24; repealed in pt.: *ibid.*, sch.25.

25. Finance Act 1965.
s. 2, repealed: 1972, c.68, sch.3; 1977, c.36, sch.9.
s. 3, repealed: 1972, c.41, sch.28.
ss. 6, 15, see *Floor* v. *Davis* [1976] 3 All E.R. 314, D.C.
s. 15, see *Associated Newspapers* v. *Fleming* [1972] 2 W.L.R. 1273; [1972] 2 All E.R 574.
s. 19, see *Caren* v. *Keighley* [1972] 1 W.L.R. 1556; *Turner* v. *Follett* [1973] T.R. 13; *I.R.C.* v. *Montgomery* [1975] 2 W.L.R. 326; *Aberdeen Construction Group* v. *I.R.C.* [1978] A.C. 885, H.L.; *Lang (H.M. Inspector of Taxes)* v. *Rice* [1983] 5 N.I.J.B., C.A.; *Worthing Rugby Football Club Trustees* v. *I.R.C.* [1985] 1 W.L.R. 409, Peter Gibson J.; *Craven (Inspector of Taxes)* v. *White*; *I.R.C.* v. *Bowater Property Developments*; *Baylis (Inspector of Taxes)* v. *Gregory*, The Times, July 22, 1988, H.L.
Pt. III (ss.19–45), except s. 45 (in pt.), repealed: 1979, c.14, sch.8.
s. 20, see *Chinn* v. *Hochstrasser*, *Chinn* v. *Collins* [1979] 2 W.L.R. 411, C.A.; *Ritchie* v. *McKay* [1984] S.T.C. 422, D.C.; *Young* v. *Phillips* [1984] S.T.C. 520, D.C.
s. 21, repealed: 1978, c.42, s.44, sch.13.
s. 22, see *Cleveleys Investment Trust* v. *I.R.C.*, 1972 S.L.T. 54; *Caren* v. *Keighley* [1972] 1 W.L.R. 1556; *Cochrane* v. *I.R.C.* [1974] S.T.C. 335; *Kidson* v. *MacDonald* [1974] 1 All E.R. 849; *Stephenson* v. *Barclays Bank Trust Co.* [1975] 1 All E.R. 625; *Crowe* v. *Appleby* [1975] 1 W.L.R. 1539; [1975] 3 All E.R. 625; *Davis* v. *Powell* [1977] 1 W.L.R. 258; [1977] 1 All E.R. 471; *Harrison* v. *Nairn Williamson* [1978] 1 W.L.R. 145, C.A.; *O'Brien* v. *Benson's Hosiery (Holdings)* [1979] 3 W.L.R. 572, H.L.; *Harthan* v. *Mason* [1980] S.T.C. 94, (1982) 53 T.C. 272, Fox J.; *Marson* v. *Marriage* [1980] S.T.C. 177, Fox J.; *Booth* v. *Ellard* [1980] 3 All E.R. 569, C.A.; *Marren* v. *Ingles* [1980] 1 W.L.R. 983; [1980] 3 All E.R. 95, H.L.; *Prest* v. *Bettinson* [1980] S.T.C. 607, Dillon J.; *I.R.C.* v. *Burmah Oil Co.* [1982] S.T.C. 30, H.L.; *Aspden (Inspector of Taxes)* v. *Hildesley* [1982] S.T.C. 206, Nourse J.; *Berry* v. *Warnett* [1982] 1 W.L.R. 698; [1982] S.T.C. 396, H.L.; *O'Brien* v. *Benson's Hosiery (Holdings)* (1982) 53 T.C. 241, H.L.; *Davenport* v. *Chilver* [1983] S.T.C. 426; [1983] 3 W.L.R. 481, Nourse J.; *Strange* v. *Oppenshaw* [1983] S.T.C. 416, Peter Gibson J.; *Lang* v. *Rice* [1984] S.T.C. 172, C.A.; *Drummond* v. *Austin Brown* [1984] 3 W.L.R. 381, C.A.; *Golding* v. *Kaufman* [1985] S.T.C. 152, Ch.D.; *Worthing Rugby Football Club Trustees* v. *I.R.C.* [1985] 1 W.L.R. 409, Peter Gibson J.; *Zim Properties* v. *Procter* [1985] S.T.C. 90, D.C.; *Mashiter* v. *Pearmain*

1965—cont.

25. Finance Act 1965—*cont.*

[1985] S.T.C. 165, C.A.; *Anders Utkilens Rederi A/S* v. *O/Y Lovisa Stevedoring Co. A/B; The Golfstraum* [1985] 2 All E.R. 669, Goulding J.; *Bell* v. *I.R.C.*, 1985 S.L.T.(Lands Tr.) 52; *Kirby (Inspector of Taxes)* v. *Thorn E.M.I.* [1987] S.T.C 621, C.A.; *Welbeck Securities* v. *Poulson (Inspector of Taxes)* [1987] S.T.C. 468; [1987] 2 FTLR 298, C.A.

s. 23, see *Caren* v. *Keighley* [1972] 1 W.L.R. 1556; *Cleveleys Investment Trust Co.* v. *Inland Revenue*, 1975 S.L.T. 237; [1975] S.T.C. 457; *Williams* v. *Bullivant* [1983] S.T.C. 107, Vinelott J.; *Ritchie* v. *McKay* [1984] S.T.C. 422, D.C.; *Larner* v. *Warrington* [1985] S.T.C. 442, Nicholls J.

s. 24, see *Larter* v. *Skone James* [1976] 1 W.L.R. 607; [1976] 2 All E.R. 615; *Bentley* v. *Pike* [1981] S.T.C. 360, Vinelott J.

s. 25, see *Stephenson* v. *Barclays Bank Trust Co.* [1975] 1 All E.R. 625; *Pexton* v. *Bell; Crowe* v. *Appleby* [1976] 2 All E.R. 914, C.A.; *Chinn* v. *Hochstrasser, Chinn* v. *Collins* [1979] 2 W.L.R. 411, C.A.; *Hoare Trustees* v. *Gardner; Hart* v. *Briscoe* [1978] 1 All E.R. 791, Brightman J.; *Roome* v. *Edwards, The Times,* February 10, 1981, H.L.; *Berry* v. *Warnett* [1982] 1 W.L.R. 698, H.L.; [1982] S.T.C. 396, H.L.; *Bond* v. *Pickford* [1983] S.T.C. 517, C.A.

s. 29, see *Sassoon* v. *Peay* [1976] 1 W.L.R. 1073; [1976] 3 All E.R. 375; *Varty* v. *Lynes* [1976] 1 W.L.R. 1091; [1976] 3 All E.R. 447; *Makins* v. *Elson* [1977] 1 W.L.R. 221; [1977] 1 All E.R. 572; *Batey (Inspector of Taxes)* v. *Wakefield* [1982] 1 All E.R. 61, C.A.; *Green* v. *I.R.C.*, 1983 S.L.T. 282.

s. 33, see *Anderton* v. *Lamb* [1981] S.T.C. 43, Goulding J.; *Williams* v. *Evans* (1982) 126 S.J. 346, Nourse J.

s. 34, see *Smethurst* v. *Cowtan* [1977] S.T.C. 60; *McGregor* v. *Adcock* [1977] 1 W.L.R. 864, Fox J.; *Davenport* v. *Hasslacher* [1977] 1 W.L.R. 869, Slade J.; *Harthan* v. *Mason* [1980] S.T.C. 94; (1982) 53 T.C. 272, Fox J.; *Hepworth* v. *Williams Smith Group* [1981] S.T.C. 354, Vinelott J.

s. 35, see *Hart* v. *Briscoe, The Times,* November 25, 1977, Brightman J.; *Prest* v. *Bettinson* [1980] S.T.C. 607, Dillon J.; *I.R.C.* v. *Helen Slater Charitable Trust* [1981] 3 W.L.R. 377, C.A.

s. 39, orders 74/1269; 75/2191; 77/57; 78/282, 785–787, 1056; 79/117, 300–302.

ss. 40, 41, see *Van Arkadie* v. *Plunket* [1983] S.T.C. 54, Warner J.

s. 42, see *Chinn* v. *Collins* [1981] 2 W.L.R. 14; [1981] 1 All E.R. 189, H.L.; *Leedale* v. *Lewis* [1982] 1 W.L.R. 1319, H.L.; *Bayley* v. *Garrod, The Times,* March 1, 1982; [1983] S.T.C. 287, Mervyn Davies J.; *Ewart* v. *Taylor* [1983] S.T.C. 721, Vinelott J.; *Ritchie* v. *McKay* [1984] S.T.C. 422, D.C.

s. 45, see *Kidson* v. *MacDonald* [1974] 1 All E.R. 849; *Booth* v. *Ellard* [1980] 3 All E.R. 569, C.A.; *Gubay* v. *Kington* [1984] 1 W.L.R. 163, H.L.

1965—cont.

25. Finance Act 1965—*cont.*

ss. 46–48, see *Waller & Hartley* v. *I.R.C.* [1972] T.R. 149.

s. 47, see *Addy* v. *I.R.C.* [1975] S.T.C. 601; *John Paterson (Motors)* v. *I.R.C.*, 1978 S.L.T. 202.

s. 52, see *Willingdale* v. *Islington Green Investment Co.* [1972] 1 W.L.R. 1533; [1972] 3 All E.R. 849.

s. 56, see *Ellis (Inspector of Taxes)* v. *B.P. Northern Ireland Refinery; Ellis (Inspector of Taxes)* v. *B.P. Tyne Tanker Co.* [1987] 1 F.T.L.R. 253; [1987] S.T.C. 52, C.A.

s. 58, see *Bank Line* v. *I.R.C.* [1974] S.T.C. 342.

s. 61, see *Crisp Malting* v. *Bourne* [1972] 1 W.L.R. 286; [1972] 1 All E.R. 700; [1971] T.R. 417.

s. 74, see *Redditch Electro-Plating Co.* v. *Ferrebe; Harris Hardeners* v. *Ferrebe* [1973] T.R. 57.

s. 75, see *Stephens* v. *T. Pittas* [1983] S.T.C. 576, Goulding J.

s. 77, see *MacTaggart Scott & Co.* v. *I.R.C.* [1973] S.T.C. 180, Ct. of Session.

s. 78, see *Clark (C. & J.)* v. *I.R.C.* [1975] 1 W.L.R. 413; [1975] 3 All E.R. 801, C.A.

s. 82, see *Lord Chetwode* v. *I.R.C.* [1976] 1 W.L.R. 310; [1976] 1 All E.R. 641, C.A.

s. 83, see *Waller & Hartley* v. *I.R.C.* [1972] T.R. 149; *I.R.C.* v. *Ocean Wilsons Holdings* [1973] 1 W.L.R. 935; *R.* v. *Patel* (1973) 48 T.C. 647, C.A.; *Halsack Developments* v. *I.R.C.* [1976] S.T.C. 440.

s. 84, regs. 73/1590.

s. 84, repealed: 1988, c.1, sch.31.

s. 88, repealed: 1975, c.7, ss.50,52,59, sch.13.

s. 90, amended: 1985, c.54, s.82; repealed in pt.: *ibid.*, sch.27.

s. 92, regs. 85/1886.

s. 92, amended: 1974, c.30, s.54; 1977, c.36, s.4; 1979, c.5, sch.6; c.8, sch.1; 1980, c.34, c.62, sch.5; c.43, sch.7; c.48, s.3; 1981, c.14, s.92; c.35, s.4; 1984, c.32, sch.6; 1985, c.67, s.110; repealed in pt.: 1973, c.36, sch.6; 1980, c.34, sch.9; 1985, c.67, s.110, sch.8.

s. 93, repealed: 1985, c.71, sch.1.

s. 93, repealed (S.): *ibid.*

s. 94, repealed: 1979, c.14, sch.8.

sch. 1, see *Frost* v. *Feltham* [1981] S.T.C. 115, Nourse J.

schs. 1–4, repealed: S.L.R. 1986.

sch. 2, see *Tyrer* v. *Smart* [1979] S.T.C. 34, H.L.

sch. 5, see *Esslemont* v. *Estill* [1979] S.T.C. 624, Oliver J.

sch. 6, see *I.R.C.* v. *Chubb's Tr.*, 1972 S.L.T. 81; *Caren* v. *Keighley* [1972] 1 W.L.R. 1556; *Randall* v. *Plumb* [1975] 1 W.L.R. 633; [1975] 1 All E.R. 734; *Cleveleys Investment Trust Co.* v. *Inland Revenue*, 1975 S.L.T. 237; [1975] S.T.C. 457; *Allison* v. *Murray* [1975] 1 W.L.R. 1578; [1975] 1 All E.R. 561; *Emmerson* v. *Computer Time International (In Liquidation)* [1976] 2 All E.R. 131, D.C.; *Aberdeen Construction Group* v. *I.R.C.* [1978] A.C. 885, H.L.; *Eilbeck* v. *Rawling* [1979] S.T.C. 16, Slade J.; *Watkins* v. *Kidson* [1979] 1 W.L.R. 876, H.L.;

1965—cont.

25. Finance Act 1965—cont.

I.R.C. v. *Beveridge*, First Division, July 19, 1979; *Oram* v. *Johnson* [1980] 1 W.L.R. 558; [1980] 2 All E.R. 1, Walton J.; *Marson* v. *Marriage* [1980] S.T.C. 177, Fox J.; *Gibbon* v. *Inland Revenue*, 1980 S.L.T.(Lands Tr.) 3; *Bayley* v. *Rogers* [1980] S.T.C. 544; [1980] T.R. 245, Browne-Wilkinson J.; *Butler* v. *Evans* [1980] S.T.C. 613, Dillon J.; *Whitaker* v. *Cameron* [1982] S.T.C. 665, Walton J.; *Stanton* v. *Drayton Commercial Investment Co.* [1982] 3 W.L.R. 214, H.L.; *Henderson* v. *Executors of David Karmel (decd.)* [1984] S.T.C. 572, D.C.; *Mashiter* v. *Pearmain* [1985] S.T.C. 165, C.A.; *Passant* v. *Jackson* [1986] S.T.C. 164, C.A.; *Tod (Inspector of Taxes)* v. *South Essex Motors (Basildon)* [1988] S.T.C. 392, Knox J.

schs. 6–9 repealed: 1979, c.14, sch.8.

sch. 7, see *Kidson* v. *MacDonald* [1974] 1 All E.R. 849; *I.R.C.* v. *Montgomery* [1975] 2 W.L.R. 326; *Aberdeen Construction Group* v. *I.R.C.* [1978] A.C. 885, H.L.; *Floor* v. *Davis* [1979] 2 W.L.R. 830, H.L.; *Rank Zerox* v. *Lane* [1979] 3 W.L.R. 594, H.L.; *Harthan* v. *Mason* [1980] S.T.C. 94; (1982) 53 T.C. 272, Fox J.; *Marson* v. *Marriage* [1980] S.T.C. 177, Fox J; *Marren* v. *Ingles* [1980] 1 W.L.R. 983; [1980] 3 All E.R. 95, H.L.; *I.R.C.* v. *Burmah Oil Co.* [1982] S.T.C. 30, H.L.; *Innocent (Inspector of Taxes)* v. *Whaddon Estates* [1982] S.T.C. 115, Walton J.; *Berry* v. *Warnett* [1982] 1 W.L.R. 698, H.L.; *Strange* v. *Oppenshaw* [1983] S.T.C. 416, Peter Gibson J.; *Gubay* v. *Kington* [1984] 1 W.L.R. 163, H.L.; *Furniss* v. *Dawson* [1984] S.T.C. 153, H.L.; *Coates* v. *Arndale Properties, The Times*, November 27, 1984, H.L.; *Young* v. *Phillips, The Times*, July 12, 1984, Nicholls J.; *Golding* v. *Kaufman* [1985] S.T.C. 152, Ch.D.; *Reed* v. *Nova Securities* [1985] 1 W.L.R. 193, H.L.; *Welbeck Securities* v. *Poulson (Inspector of Taxes)* [1987] S.T.C. 468; [1987] 2 FTLR 298, C.A.; *Westcott (Inspector of Taxes)* v. *Woolcombers* [1987] S.T.C. 600, C.A.; *Dunstan (Inspector of Taxes)* v. *Young, Austen & Young* [1987] S.T.C. 709, Warner J.

sch. 10, see *Roome* v. *Edwards* [1981] 2 W.L.R. 268, H.L.

sch. 10, amended: 1972, c.41, s.117; 1975, c.45, s.57; 1976, c.40, s.52; repealed in pt.: 1978, c.42, sch.13; 1979, c.14, sch.8; 1985, c.65, sch.10; c.66, sch.8 (S.).

sch. 11, see *Willingdale* v. *Islington Green Investment Co.* [1972] 1 W.L.R. 1533; [1972] 3 All E.R. 849; *Addy* v. *I.R.C.* [1975] S.T.C. 601; *John Paterson (Motors)* v. *I.R.C.*, 1978 S.L.T. 202.

sch. 12, see *R.* v. *Patel* (1973) 48 T.C. 647, C.A.

sch. 13, see *Innocent (Inspector of Taxes)* v. *Whaddon Estates* [1982] S.T.C. 115, Walton J.; *Westcott (Inspector of Taxes)* v. *Woolcombers* [1987] S.T.C. 600, C.A.

1965—cont.

25. Finance Act 1965—cont.

sch. 17, see *W. T. Ramsay* v. *I.R.C.*; *Eilbeck* v. *Rawling* [1981] 2 W.L.R 449; [1981] 1 All E.R. 865, H.L.; *Craven* v. *White* [1985] S.T.C. 531; [1985] 1 W.L.R. 1024, D.C.; *Bell* v. *I.R.C.*, 1985 S.L.T.(Lands Tr.) 52.

sch. 18, see *Willingdale* v. *Islington Green Investment Co.* [1972] 1 W.L.R. 1533; [1972] 3 All E.R. 849; *Craigengillan Estates Co.* v. *I.R.C.* [1975] S.T.C. 233.

sch. 20, repealed: 1988, c.1, sch.31.

26. Criminal Justice Act 1965.

repealed: 1974, c.23, sch.3.

27. Lost Property (Scotland) Act 1965.

repealed as from Jan. 1, 1980: S.L.R. 1976.

28. Justices of the Peace Act 1965.

repealed: 1979, c.55, sch.3.

29. Solicitors (Scotland) Act 1965.

repealed: 1980, c.46, sch.7.

30. Highways (Amendment) Act 1965.

repealed: 1980, c.66, sch.25.

31. Solicitors Act 1965.

repealed: 1974, c.47, sch.4.

s. 30, order 72/642.

32. Administration of Estates (Small Payments) Act 1965.

s. 1, amended: orders 75/1137, 1253; 84/539; repealed in pt.: 1972, c.65, sch.

s. 2, amended: orders 75/1137; 84/539.

s. 4, repealed in pt.: 1975, c.7, sch.13.

s. 5, amended: 1972, c.65, s.6; 1974, c.46, sch.9; 1981, c.65, sch.6; repealed in pt.: 1985, c.58, sch.4.

s. 6, order 84/539.

s. 6, amended: 1972, c.48, s.24; c.65, s.6; c.70, s.119; 1974, c.46, sch.9; 1981, c.65, sch.6; repealed in pt.: 1972, c.48, s.24; 1974, c.46, sch.9; 1981, c.20, sch.4; 1985, c.58, sch.4; S.L.R. 1986; 1987, c.45, sch.4.

sch. 1, repealed in pt.: 1974, c.46, sch.11; S.L.R. 1977; 1986, c.53, sch.19.

sch. 2, repealed in pt.: 1974, c.46, sch.11.

sch. 3, repealed in pt.: S.L.R. 1974; 1986, c.53, sch.19.

sch. 4, repealed: S.L.R. 1974.

33. Control of Office and Industrial Development Act 1965.

repealed: 1972, c.52, sch.23; S.L.R. 1986.

ss. 6, 8, see *R.K.T. Investments* v. *Hackney London Borough Council* (1978) 36 P. & C.R. 442, Sir Douglas Frank, Q.C.

ss. 19, 23, orders 72/903, 996.

34. British Nationality Act 1965.

repealed: 1981, c.61, sch.9.

s. 5, regs. 80/358; 81/1571.

35. Shops (Early Closing Days) Act 1965.

s. 1, see *Boyd* v. *Bell*, 1970 S.C. 1, Ct. of Justiciary.

36. Gas Act 1965.

Pt. I (ss. 1–3), repealed: 1972, c.60, sch.8.

Pt. II (ss. 4–28), amended: *ibid.*, sch.6; 1986, c.44, sch.7.

s. 4, amended: 1972, c.52, sch.21 (S.); repealed in pt.: 1972, c.60, sch.6; 1974, c.40, sch.4; 1986, c.44, schs.7,9.

CAP.

1965—cont.

36. Gas Act 1965—*cont.*
s. 5, amended: 1975, c.76, sch.1; 1986, c.44, sch.7.
s. 6, amended: *ibid.*
s. 11, amended: 1975, c.76, sch.1.
s. 12, repealed in pt.: 1972, c.60, schs.6,8; 1981, c.67, sch.6.
s. 13, amended: 1986, c.44, sch.7; repealed in pt.: 1981, c.67, sch.6.
s. 15, amended: 1980, c.45, sch.10 (S.); 1986, c.44, sch.7.
s. 16, amended: 1972, c.60, sch.6; 1986, c.44, sch.7.
s. 17, amended: 1972, c.60, sch.6; 1976, c.14, sch.1 (S.); 1986, c.44, sch.7. ·
s. 19, amended: 1972, c.60, sch.6; 1986, c.44, sch.7.
s. 21, amended: 1972, c.60, sch.6; 1980, c.43, sch.7; 1986, c.44, sch.7; repealed in pt.: *ibid.*
s. 22, amended: 1972, c.60, sch.6; 1986, c.44, sch.7.
s. 23, amended (S.): 1980, c.45, sch.10.
s. 27, amended: 1975, c.76, sch.1; repealed in pt.: 1972, c.70, sch.30; 1975, c.76, schs.1,2.
s. 28, amended: 1972, c.52, sch.21 (S.); c.60, sch.6; 1973, c.65, sch.27 (S.); order 74/595; 1980, c.45, sch.10 (S.); 1986, c.44, sch.7; repealed in pt.: 1972, c.60, sch.6, S.L.R. 1978; 1985, c.51, sch.17; 1986, c.44, schs.7,9.
ss. 29, 30, repealed: 1972, c.60, sch.8.
s. 31, repealed in pt.: S.L.R. 1978.
s. 32, amended: 1986, c.44, sch.7.
sch. 1, repealed: 1972, c.60, sch.8, repealed in pt.: (S.): 1984, c.54, sch.11.
sch. 2, amended: 1972, c.60, sch.6; c.70, sch.29; 1986, c.44, sch.7; repealed in pt.: 1972, c.60, schs.6,8.
sch. 3, amended (S.): 1972, c.52, sch.21; 1980, c.45, sch.10.
sch. 4, repealed in pt.: 1981, c.67, sch.6.
sch. 6, amended: 1972, c.60, sch.6; 1973, c.65, sch.27; 1986, c.44, sch.7; repealed in pt.: 1972, c.60, schs.6,8.

37. Carriage of Goods by Road Act 1965.
see *Chloride Industrial Batteries* v. *F. & W. Freight, The Times,* October 25, 1988, Sheen J.
s. 1, see *Muller Batavier* v. *Laurent Transport Co.* [1977] R.T.R. 499, May J.; *SGS-Ates Componenti Eletronici S.P.A.* v. *Grappo* [1977] R.T.R. 442, Goff J.; *Arctic Electronics Co. (U.K.)* v. *McGregor Sea and Air Services* [1986] R.T.R. 207, Hobhouse J.
s. 2, orders 73/596; 80/697.
s. 5, amended: 1978, c.47, sch.1.
s. 7, amended: 1980, c.58, sch.3.
s. 8A, added: 1979, c.28, s.3; amended: 1983, c.14, sch.2.
ss. 9, 12, regs. 81/604, 1543; 86/1882.
s. 10, see *General Trading Corporation* v. *James Mills (Montrose)*, 1982 S.L.T.(Sh.Ct.) 30.
s. 11, repealed in pt.: 1973, c.36, sch.6.
s. 12, order 80/697.

CAP.

1965—cont.

37. Carriage of Goods by Road Act 1965—*cont.*
sch., see *William Tatton & Co.* v. *Ferrymasters* [1974] 1 Lloyd's Rep. 203; *James Buchanan & Co.* v. *Babco Forwarding & Shipping (U.K.)* [1977] 3 W.L.R. 907, H.L.; *SGS-Ates Componenti Electronici S.P.A.* v. *Grappo* [1977] R.T.R. 442, Goff J.; *Muller Batavier* v. *Laurent Transport Co.* [1977] R.T.R. 499, May J.; *Thermo Engineers and Anhydro A.S.* v. *Ferrymasters* [1981] 1 All E.R. 1142, Neill J.; *Cummins, Engine Co.* v. *Davis Freight Forwarding (Hull)* [1981] 1 W.L.R. 1363, C.A.; *Impex Transport Aktieselskabet* v. *A. G. Thames Holdings* [1981] 1 W.L.R. 1547, Goff J.; *General Trading Corporation* v. *James Mills (Montrose)*, 1982 S.L.T.(Sh.Ct.) 30; *Michael Galley Footwear (In Liquidation)* v. *Laboni* [1982] 2 All E.R. 200, Hodgson J.; *Worldlife Carriers* v. *Ardtran International* [1983] 1 All E.R. 692, Parker J.; *W. Donald & Son (Wholesale Meat Contractors)* v. *Continental Freeze (O.H.)*, 1984 S.L.T. 182; *R. H. & D. International* v. *I.A.S. Animal Air Service* [1984] 1 W.L.R. 573, Neill J.; *Arctic Electronics Co. (U.K.)* v. *McGregor Sea and Air Services* [1986] R.T.R. 207, Hobhouse J.
sch., amended: 1979, c.28, s.4.

38. Overseas Development and Service Act 1965.
repealed: 1980, c.63, sch.2.

39. Criminal Procedure (Scotland) Act 1965.
repealed (S.): 1975, c.21, sch.10.

41. Local Government (Scotland) Act 1947 (Amendment) Act 1965.
repealed: 1973, c.65, sch.29.

42. Public Health (Notification of Births) Act 1965.
repealed: 1977, c.49, sch.16.

43. Statutory Orders (Special Procedure) Act 1965.
ss. 1 (in pt.), 2 (in pt.), sch., repealed: S.L.R. 1974.

45. Backing of Warrants (Republic of Ireland) Act 1965.
see *R.* v. *Durham Prison Governor, ex p. Carlisle* [1979] Crim.L.R. 175, D.C.
s. 1, see *Re Lawlor* (1977) 66 Cr.App.R. 75, D.C.; *R.* v. *Governor of Risley Remand Centre, ex p. Marks* [1984] Crim.L.R. 238, D.C.; *Malinowski, Re* [1987] Crim.L.R. 324, D.C.
s. 2, see *R.* v. *Governor of Winson Green Prison, Birmingham, ex p. Littlejohn* [1975] 1 W.L.R. 893, D.C.; *R.* v. *Farringdon Police Station, Officer in Charge, ex p. Nobbs* [1977] Crim.L.R. 422, D.C.; *Re Lawlor* (1977) 66 Cr.App.R. 75, D.C.; *Re Nobbs* [1978] 3 All E.R. 390, D.C.; *R.* v. *Governor of Pentonville Prison, ex p. Healy, The Times,* May 11, 1984, D.C.; *Simpson* v. *McLeod,* 1986 S.C.C.R. 237.
s. 2, amended: 1975, c.59, sch.3; 1978, c.26, s.2.
s. 2A, added: 1988, c.33, sch.1.
s. 5, amended: 1976, c.63, sch.2; repealed in pt.: *ibid.*, sch.3.
s. 7, see *Hawkins (Francis), Re, The Times,* February 11, 1987, D.C.

1965—cont.

45. Backing of Warrants (Republic of Ireland) Act 1965—cont.
s. 8, repealed in pt.: S.L.R. 1986.
s. 9, repealed in pt.: S.L.R. 1978.
s. 11, repealed: 1973, c.36, sch.6.
sch., amended: 1973, c.14, sch.1; 1979, c.55, sch.2; 1980, c.43, sch.7; order 81/228.

46. Highlands and Islands Development (Scotland) Act 1965.
s. 1, orders 75/843; 79/1461; 86/1956.
s. 1, amended: 1973, c.65, sch.27.
s. 3, amended: 1978, c.51, sch.16.
s. 5, repealed in pt.: 1972, c.5, sch.4; 1975, c.69, sch.5.
s. 10, repealed in pt.: 1982, c.43, sch.4.
s. 13, amended: 1972, c.5, sch.3; repealed in pt.: 1975, c.69, sch.5.
s. 18, amended: 1973, c.65, sch.27.
s. 19, sch. 1, repealed in pt.: 1975, c.24, sch.3.

47. Merchant Shipping Act 1965.
order 74/1345.
s. 1, regs. 72/656; 75/594; 79/1519; 80/282, 642, 744; 82/841; order 79/306.
s. 1, amended: 1979, c.39, s.31, sch.6; repealed in pt.: ibid., sch.7.
s. 5, repealed in pt.: order 81/233.
s. 6, orders 72/447; 84/1160; 88/1850.
s. 7, repealed in pt.: S.L.R. 1974.
sch. 1, repealed in pt.: ibid.; 1988, c.12, sch.7.
sch. 2, repealed: S.L.R. 1974.

49. Registration of Births, Deaths and Marriages (Scotland) Act 1965.
ss. 5, 6, amended: 1973, c.65, s.166.
s. 7, regs. 75/734; 83/264.
s. 7, amended: 1972, c.11, sch.6; repealed in pt.: regs. 74/812.
s. 8, repealed in pt.: 1973, c.65, s.166, sch.29.
s. 9, amended: ibid., s.166.
ss. 11, 12, amended: 1977, c.15, sch.2.
s. 14, amended: 1986, c.9, sch.1.
s. 15, amended: 1973, c.65, s.166.
s. 18, amended: 1986, c.9, sch.1; repealed in pt.: ibid., sch.2.
ss. 18, 18A, regs. 86/1984.
s. 18A, added: 1986, c.9, sch.1.
s. 20, amended: ibid.
s. 21, amended: 1975, c.65, sch.5; 1979, c.36, sch.7; repealed in pt.: ibid., schs.7,8.
s. 21, regs. 86/1984.
s. 28A, regs. 85/2005; 86/21, 2256; 88/80.
s. 28A, added: 1985, c.73, s.50.
s. 28B, added: 1988, c.41, sch.12.
ss. 29–31, repealed in pt.: 1977, c.15, sch.3.
s. 32, regs. 86/21.
s. 32, amended; 1977, c.15, sch.2.
s. 37, regs. 85/1890; 86/2256; 88/80.
s. 37, amended: regs. 75/1809; 77/1892; 81/203.
s. 38, regs. 85/268, 1890; 86/2256; 88/80.
s. 38, amended: regs. 75/1809; 77/1892; 81/203.
s. 40, regs. 85/1890; 86/2256; 88/80.
s. 40, amended: regs. 75/1809; 77/1892; 81/203.
s. 43, regs. 85/268, 1890; 86/2256; 88/80.

1965—cont.

49. Registration of Births, Deaths and Managers (Scotland) Act 1965—cont.
s. 43, amended: regs. 75/1809; 77/1892; 81/203; 1986, c.9, sch.1; repealed in pt.: ibid., sch.2.
s. 47, regs. 85/268, 1890; 86/2256; 88/80.
s. 47, amended: regs. 75/1809; 77/1892; 81/203.
s. 48, amended: 1985, c.73, s.50.
s. 48, regs. 86/1984.
s. 51, amended: 1972, c.58, sch.6; 1978, c.29, sch.15.
s. 52, amended: 1977, c.15, sch.2.
s. 54, regs. 74/1501; 75/1809; 77/1892; 78/160; 79/143; 80/244; 81/203; 82/192; 83/221, 1795; 84/43, 266, 267; 85/268, 1890, 2005; 86/21, 1984, 2256; 88/80.
s. 54, amended: 1975, c.14, s.160; repealed in pt.: 1975, c.72, sch.4; 1977, c.15, sch.3; S.L.R. 1981.
s. 56, amended: 1986, c.9, sch.1; repealed in pt.: 1973, c.65, s.166, sch.9; 1975, c.72, sch.4.
s. 58, repealed in pt.: S.L.R. 1974.
sch. 1, repealed in pt.: 1978, c.28, sch.4.
sch. 2, repealed: S.L.R. 1974.

50. Monopolies and Mergers Act 1965.
repealed: 1973, c.41, sch.13.
s. 3, see F. Hoffman-La Roche & Co. v. Secretary of State for Trade and Industry [1974] 3 W.L.R. 104; [1974] 2 All E.R. 1128, H.L.
s. 3, orders 72/130; 73/925, 1093, 1137.
s. 6, orders 72/130, 131, 1880; 73/924, 1137, 1273.

51. National Insurance Act 1965.
repealed: 1975, c.18, sch.1.
regs. 72/166, 606, 1301, 1302; 73/548, 1124, 1480.
s. 1, regs. 72/555, 1287; 73/1441; 74/10, 416, 1036.
s. 4, regs. 72/235, 1259, 1363; 73/776, 1013, 1417, 1444, 1547; 74/906, 1129, 1157.
s. 8, see Morgan v. Quality Tools & Engineering (Stourbridge) [1972] 1 W.L.R. 196; [1972] 1 All E.R. 744; Chesterfield F.C. v. Secretary of State for Social Services [1973] 2 W.L.R. 120.
s. 8, regs. 72/1287; 73/1441; 74/1036.
s. 10, regs. 74/1243; 77/1341.
s. 12, regs. 73/398, 1106.
s. 14, regs. 73/1444; 74/1129.
s. 16, regs. 72/555; 74/10.
s. 20, regs. 74/593, 1243.
s. 22, see Watt v. Lord Advocate, 1979 S.L.T. 137.
s. 22, regs. 73/693; 74/1243.
s. 25, see Freer v. Taggart, 1975 S.L.T.(Sh.Ct.) 13.
s. 29, regs. 73/1078.
s. 36, regs. 75/1748; 78/391; continued in force: ibid.; amended: orders 78/912; 80/1245; 82/1130; 83/1244; 84/1104; 85/1245; 87/45, 1978.
s. 37, regs. 78/391; continued in force: ibid.
s. 45, regs. 74/1128.
s. 48, regs. 74/1243.

CAP.

1965—cont.

51. National Insurance Act 1965—cont.
s. 49, regs. 74/1128.
s. 50, regs. 72/394, 603, 604; 74/416, 593.
s. 51, regs. 72/604.
s. 55, regs. 72/394; 73/1478.
s. 57, regs. 72/428, 1031.
s. 62, regs. 74/1135.
s. 64, see *Secretary of State* v. *McLean*, 1972 S.L.T. 34; *Department of Health and Social Security* v. *Envoy Farmers* [1976] 2 All E.R. 173.
s. 66, see *Gara, Appellant*, 1979 S.L.T.(Notes) 29.
s. 75, see *Watt* v. *Lord Advocate*, 1979 S.L.T. 137.
s. 75, regs. 74/416.
s. 81, regs. 72/167, 1232; 74/2008, 2079.
s. 90, see *Smith* v. *Hawkins* [1972] 1 W.L.R. 141; [1972] 1 All E.R. 910; *Stott* v. *Hefferon* [1974] 1 W.L.R. 1270; [1974] 3 All E.R. 673, D.C.
s. 95, see *Department of Health & Social Security* v. *Wayte* [1972] 1 W.L.R. 19; [1972] 1 All E.R. 255; *Morgan* v. *Quality Tools & Engineering (Stourbridge)* [1972] 1 W.L.R. 196; [1972] 1 All E.R. 744.
s. 97, see *Secretary of State* v. *McLean*, 1972 S.L.T. 34; *Department of Health and Social Security* v. *Envoy Farmers* [1976] 2 All E.R. 173.
s. 99, regs. 72/1363; 73/776; 74/1157.
s. 100, regs. 73/1444; 74/1129.
s. 102, regs. 73/693.
s. 104, regs. 73/776.
s. 105, orders 72/1586–8; 73/763; 74/555; 75/415.
s. 106, regs. 72/235; 73/1013.
s. 110, regs. 72/1537, 1604; 73/731, 746, 1649, 1713; 74/520, 812, 1047, 1135, 1357; 76/1450, 1742; 78/266, 1378; 79/1534; 80/216, 342 (S.); 86/24; 87/1850 (S.).
s. 113, regs. 73/693, 1073.
s. 114, regs. 72/909.
s. 118, continued in force: regs. 78/391.
sch. 11, regs. 74/1128.

52. National Insurance (Industrial Injuries) Act 1965.
repealed: 1975, c.18, sch.1.
regs. 72/1231; 73/1429.
s. 3, see *Chesterfield F.C.* v. *Secretary of State for Social Services* [1973] 2 W.L.R. 120.
s. 3, regs. 72/1287; 73/1441; 74/1036.
s. 5, see *R.* v. *National Insurance Commissioner, ex p. Michael* [1977] 1 W.L.R. 109, C.A.
s. 5, see *Jones* v. *Secretary of State for Social Services, Hudson* v. *Same* [1972] 2 W.L.R. 210; [1972] 1 All E.R. 145.
s. 12, regs. 74/1041; 75/125.
s. 14, see *R.* v. *Industrial Injuries Comr., ex p. Langley* [1976] I.C.R. 36, D.C.
ss. 14, 15, regs. 74/1041; 75/125.
s. 16, regs. 73/1479; 74/1041; 75/125.
s. 18, regs. 74/1041.
s. 25, regs. 72/375; 73/905.
s. 27, regs. 73/905.

CAP.

1965—cont.

52. National Insurance (Industrial Injuries) Act 1965—cont.
s. 29, regs. 73/1479.
s. 30, regs. 72/605; 73/1479.
s. 31, regs. 73/905.
s. 33, regs. 72/605.
s. 34, regs. 72/393.
ss. 37, 50, see *Jones* v. *Secretary of State for Social Services, Hudson* v. *Same* [1972] 2 W.L.R. 210; [1972] 1 All E.R. 145.
s. 50, see *R.* v. *National Insurance Commissioner, ex p. Viscusi* [1974] 1 W.L.R. 646, C.A.
s. 50, regs. 74/464.
s. 54, regs. 72/375.
ss. 56, 57, regs. 72/910, 1258; 73/1950; 74/1414, 1415.
ss. 67, 75, regs. 72/1276; 73/1445; 74/1130.
s. 78, regs. 74/1041; 75/125.
s. 79, regs. 72/1433; 74/8.
s. 84, orders 72/1586–1588; 74/555.
s. 85, regs. 72/1258; 73/1950; 74/1414, 1415.
sch. 1, regs. 72/1433; 74/464.
sch. 4, regs. 75/125.

53. Family Allowances Act 1965.
repealed: 1975, c.61, sch.5.
s. 2, amended: 1976, c.5, s.2; repealed in pt.: *ibid.*, sch.
s. 8, regs. 72/167; 75/1250.
s. 12, regs. 75/561.
s. 13, regs. 75/1661; 76/651.

54. National Health Service Contributions Act 1965.
repealed: 1973, c.38, sch.28.

55. Statute Law Revision (Consequential Repeals) Act 1965.
repealed: 1986, c.50, sch.11.

56. Compulsory Purchase Act 1965.
Pt. I, modified: 75/40; adapted: 1976, c.57, sch.1; c.75, sch.4.
s. 1, amended: 1981, c.67, sch.4; repealed in pt.: *ibid.*, sch.7.
s. 4, amended: 1974, c.44, s.116; repealed in pt.: 1985, c.71, sch.1.
s. 5, see *Cohen* v. *Haringey London Borough Council* (1981) 42 P. & C.R. 6, C.A.
s. 6, see *Cohen* v. *Haringey London Borough Council* (1981) 42 P. & C.R. 6, C.A.; *Duttons Brewery* v. *Leeds City Council* (1981) 42 P. & C.R. 152, Nourse J.
s. 7, see *Hoveringham Gravels* v. *Chiltern District Council* (1978) 35 P. & C.R. 295, C.A.; modified: order 77/84.
s. 9, repealed in pt.: 1973, c.39, sch.4.
s. 10, see *6, 8, 10 and 12 Elm Avenue, New Milton, ex p. New Forest District Council, Re* [1984] 3 All E.R. 632, Scott J.
s. 11, see *Cohen* v. *Haringey London Borough Council* (1981) 42 P. & C.R. 6, C.A.; *Chilton* v. *Telford Development Corp.* (1987) 281 E.G. 1443, C.A.
s. 11, amended: 1981, c.67, sch.4; repealed in pt.: 1985, c.71, sch.1.
s. 20, see *Runcorn Association Football Club* v. *Warrington and Runcorn Development Corp.* (1983) 45 P. & C.R. 183, Lands Tribunal.

CAP.

1965—cont.

56. Compulsory Purchase Act 1965—*cont.*
s. 24, repealed: 1977, c.30, s.17, sch.2.
s. 25, repealed: S.L.R. 1973.
s. 27, amended: 1985, c.71, sch.2.
s. 29, repealed in pt.: S.L.T. 1974.
s. 30, see *Fagan* v. *Knowsley Metropolitan Borough* (1985) 275 E.G. 717; (1985) P. & C.R. 363, C.A.
s. 30, substituted: 1981, c.67, sch.4.
ss. 31, 32, amended: *ibid.*
s. 33, order 73/1296.
s. 33, amended: order 74/700; 1981, c.67, sch.4; repealed in pt.: 1973, c.37, sch.9; S.L.R. 1974.
ss. 34, 35, repealed: 1985, c.71, sch.1.
s. 36, orders 72/1424; 73/265; 74/122, 883, 1163; 75/40, 853, 1285; 78/1945; 79/1499; 81/1437; 86/1575.
ss. 36–39, amended: 1981, c.67, sch.4.
s. 39, see *Argyle Motors (Birkenhead)* v. *Birkenhead Corporation* [1974] 2 W.L.R. 71; [1974] 1 All E.R. 201, H.L.
sch. 1, amended: 1983, c.20, sch.4; repealed in pt.: S.L.R. 1974.
sch. 2, repealed in pt.: S.L.R. 1973; S.L.R. 1974.
sch. 3, amended: 1973, c.26, s.57, repealed in pt.: S.L.R. 1973.
sch. 6, repealed in part.: S.L.R. 1974; 1975, c.51, sch.5; c.78, sch.6; S.L.R. 1978; 1980, c.66, sch.25; 1985, c.12, sch.2.
sch. 7, repealed in pt.: 1973, c.26, sch.3; 1981, c.67, sch.7; 1985, c.71, sch.1.
sch. 8, see *Argyle Motors (Birkenhead)* v. *Birkenhead Corporation* [1974] 2 W.L.R. 71; [1974] 1 All E.R. 201, H.L.

57. Nuclear Installations Act 1965.
s. 1, amended and repealed in pt.: regs. 74/2056.
s. 3, amended: *ibid.*; repealed in pt.: 1973, c.65, sch.29(S.).
ss. 4, 5, amended and repealed in pt.: regs. 74/2056.
s. 6, repealed: regs. 74/2056.
ss. 13, 16, amended: 1983, c.25, s.27.
s. 14, repealed in pt.: 1979, c.39, sch.7.
s 16, regs. 83/910.
s. 17, amended: 1983, c.25, ss.28,31; repealed in pt.: *ibid.*, s.28, sch.4.
s. 18, amended: *ibid.*, s.28.
ss. 19, 20, amended: *ibid.*, s.27.
s. 21, amended: *ibid.*, s.28; regs. 27/2171.
ss. 22, 25, amended and repealed in pt.: regs. 74/2056.
ss. 25A, 25B, added: 1983, c.25, c.30.
s. 26, regs. 78/1779.
s. 26, amended: regs. 74/2056; 1983, c.25, ss.27,32.
s. 27, repealed in pt.: 1973, c.36, sch.6.
s. 28, orders 72/121–8; 73/235; 77/429; 78/1528; 80/1527; 83/1889–1893; 85/752, 1985; 86/2018; 87/668, 2207.
s. 29, repealed in pt.: S.L.R. 1974.
sch. 1, amended: regs. 74/2056; 1976, c.23, s.2; 1978, c.25, s.2; 1987, c.4, s.7; repealed in pt.: *ibid.*
sch. 2, repealed: regs. 74/2056.

CAP.

1965—cont.

58. Ministerial Salaries Consolidation Act 1965.
repealed: 1972, c.48, sch.4.

59. New Towns Act 1965.
repealed: 1981, c.64, sch.13.
s. 10, regs. 77/549.
s. 41, orders 80/112, 596, 1284.
s. 43, orders 76/828; 79/204; 81/741.
s. 51, regs. 77/549.
s. 53, orders 76/828; 79/204; 80/112, 596, 1284; 81/741; regs. 77/549.
schs. 3, 4, regs. 77/549.
sch. 6, see *Chilton* v. *Telford Development Corp.* [1987] 1 W.L.R. 872, C.A.
sch. 10, orders 80/112, 596.

61. Judges' Remuneration Act 1965.
repealed: 1973, c.15, sch.5.
s. 1, order 72/1104.

62. Redundancy Payments Act 1965.
see *Simms Motor Units* v. *Hindes* [1971] I.T.R. 113; *Allied Ironfounders* v. *Macken* [1971] I.T.R. 109; *Malton* v. *Crystal of Scarborough* [1971] I.T.R. 106; *Blakely* v. *Chemetron* [1972] I.T.R. 224; *Farmer* v. *Willow Dye Works* [1972] I.T.R. 226; *Trevillion* v. *Hospital of St. John and St. Elizabeth* [1973] I.R.L.R. 176; *Robert Normansell (Birmingham)* v. *Barfield* [1973] I.T.R. 171.
s. 1, see *Bagga* v. *Heavy Electricals (India)* [1971] 12 K.I.R. 154; [1972] I.T.R. 70; *Bromby & Hoare* v. *Evans* [1972] I.T.R. 76; *Woodhouse* v. *Brotherhood* [1972] 3 W.L.R. 215; [1972] 3 All E.R. 91; *Chapman* v. *Goonvean and Rostowrack China Clay Co.* [1973] 1 W.L.R. 678, C.A.; *Stocks* v. *Magna Merchants* [1973] 1 W.L.R. 1505; *Amos* v. *Max-Arc* [1973] I.C.R. 46, N.I.R.C; *O'Neill* v. *Merseyside Plumbing Co.* [1973] I.C.R. 96, N.I.R.C.; *Runnalls* v. *Richards & Osborne* [1973] I.C.R. 225; *Sutton* v. *Revlon Overseas Corporation* [1973] I.R.L.R. 73; *Sutcliffe* v. *Hawker Siddeley Aviation* [1973] I.C.R. 560, N.I.R.C.; *Delanair* v. *Mead* [1976] I.C.R. 522; *Higgs & Hill* v. *Singh* [1977] I.C.R. 193; *Lesney Products & Co.* v. *Nolan* [1977] I.C.R. 235, C.A.; *Dean* v. *Eastbourne Fishermen's and Boatmen's Protection Society and Club* [1977] I.C.R. 556, E.A.T.; *Thomas* v. *Jones* [1978] I.C.R. 274, E.A.T.; *Robinson* v. *British Island Airways* [1978] I.C.R. 304, E.A.T.; *Ranson* v. *G. & W. Collins* [1978] I.C.R. 765, E.A.T.; *Nottinghamshire County Council* v. *Lee* [1980] I.C.R. 635, C.A.; *Secretary of State for Employment* v. *Globe Elastic Thread Co.* [1979] 3 W.L.R. 143, H.L.; *Smith* v. *Lord Advocate*, 1979 S.L.T 233; *Pillinger* v. *Manchester Area Health Authority* [1979] I.R.L.R. 430, E.A.T.; *Wilson* v. *National Coal Board*, 1981 S.L.T. 67.
ss. 1–26, repealed: 1978, c.44, sch.17.
s. 2, see *Morganite* v. *Street* [1972] 1 W.L.R. 918; [1972] 2 All E.R. 411; [1972] I.T.R. 182; *Lonmet* v. *Green* [1972] I.T.R. 86; *Johnston* v. *St. Cuthberts*, 1969 S.C. 98; *Lane Fox & Co.* v. *Binns* [1972] I.T.R. 125; *Devonald* v. *J. D. Insulating Co.* [1972] I.C.R. 209; *Davis* v. *Chatterway* [1972] I.C.R. 267; *Simpson* v.

CAP.

1965—cont.
62. Redundancy Payments Act 1965—cont.
Dickinson [1972] I.C.R. 474, N.I.R.C.; *Harris* v.
Turner [1973] I.C.R. 31, N.I.R.C.; *Jones* v.
Aston Cabinet Co. [1973] I.C.R. 292; *Kaye* v.
Cook's (Finsbury) [1973] 3 All E.R. 434,
N.I.R.C.; *Litster* v. *Fram Gerrard and Leonard
Fairclough* [1973] I.R.L.R. 302, N.I.R.C.; *Chapman* v. *Goonvean and Rostowrack China Clay
Co.* [1973] 1 W.L.R. 678, C.A.; *United Kingdom Atomic Energy Authority* v. *Claydon*
[1974] I.C.R. 128, N.I.R.C.; *Johnson* v. *Nottinghamshire Combined Police Authority*
[1974] 1 W.L.R. 358; [1974] 1 All E.R. 1082,
C.A.; *Thomson & MacIntyre (Patternmakers)*
v. *McCreadie*, 1970 S.C. 235, Ct. of Sess.;
1971 S.C. 124, H.L.; *Kane* v. *Paine & Co.*
[1974] I.C.R. 300; *Rowbotham* v. *Arthur Lee
& Sons* [1974] I.R.L.R. 377; [1975] I.C.R. 109;
John Fowler (Don Foundry) v. *Parkin* [1975]
I.R.L.R. 89; *Thomas Wragg & Sons* v. *Wood*
[1976] I.C.R. 313; *British Steel Corporation* v.
Dingwall, 1976 S.L.T. 230; *Kennedy* v. *Werneth Ring Mills* [1977] I.C.R. 206; *M. S. Rose
(Heating)* v. *Edgington* [1977] I.C.R. 844,
E.A.T.; *Forrester* v. *Strathclyde Regional
Council* (1977) 12 I.T.R. 424, E.A.T.; *Paton
Calvert & Co.* v. *Westerside* [1979] I.R.L.R.
108, E.A.T.; *Hindes* v. *Supersine* [1979] I.C.R.
517, E.A.T.

s. 3, see *Ramseyer Motors* v. *Broadway and
Magee* (1971) 11 K.I.R. 169; *G.K.N.* v. *Lloyd*
[1972] I.C.R. 214; *Eaton* v. *R.K.B.* [1972] I.C.R.
273; *Ubsdell* v. *Paterson* [1973] I.C.R. 86,
N.I.R.C.; *Cartin* v. *Botley Garages* [1973] I.C.R.
144, N.I.R.C.; *Oldham & Son* v. *Heyd-Smith*
(1973) 16 K.I.R. 177; *Secretary of State for
Employment* v. *Wellworthy* [1973] I.C.R. 477;
[1973] 2 All E.R. 488, N.I.R.C.; *Maher* v. *Fram
Gerrard* [1974] I.C.R. 31; [1974] 1 All E.R. 449,
N.I.R.C.; *Harold Fielding* v. *Mansi* [1974] 1 All
E.R. 1035, N.I.R.C.; *Lord Advocate* v. *De Rosa*
[1974] 1 W.L.R. 946; [1974] 2 All E.R. 849,
H.L.; *Burton, Allton & Johnson* v. *Pick* [1975]
I.C.R. 193; *Secretary of State for Employment*
v. *Wellworthy (No. 2)* [1976] I.C.R. 13; *Bailey's
Exors.* v. *Co-op Wholesale Society* (O.H.),
1976 S.L.T. 92; *D. & J. Mackenzie* v. *Smith*
(O.H.) 1976 S.L.T. 216; *Breach* v. *Epsylon
Industries* [1976] I.C.R. 316; *British Steel
Corporation* v. *Bennett*, 1976 S.L.T (Notes)
55; *McKenzie* v. *Smith* [1976] I.R.L.R. 345;
Tunnell Holdings v. *Woolf* [1976] I.C.R. 387;
Allman v. *Rowland* [1977] I.C.R. 201; *Camelo*
v. *Sheerlyn Productions* [1976] I.C.R. 531;
Secretary of State for Employment v. *Rooney*
[1977] I.C.R. 440, E.A.T.; *Burroughs Machines*
v. *Timmoney*, 1978 S.L.T.(Notes) 10; *Turvey*
v. *C. W. Cheyney & Son* [1979] I.C.R. 341,
E.A.T.; *Air Canada* v. *Lee* [1978] I.C.R. 1202;
Glencross v. *Dymoke* [1979] I.C.R. 536,
E.A.T.; *Smith* v. *Lord Advocate*, 1979 S.L.T.
233; *Melon* v. *Powe (Hector)* [1981] I.C.R. 43;
[1981] 1 All E.R. 313, H.L.; *Wilson* v. *National
Coal Board*, 1981 S.L.T. 67.

CAP.

1965—cont.
62. Redundancy Payments Act 1965—cont.
s. 4, see *McAlwane* v. *Boughton Estates* [1973]
2 All E.R. 299; *Pritchard-Rhodes* v. *Boon and
Milton* [1979] I.R.L.R. 19, E.A.T.

ss. 5, 6, see *Powell Duffryn Wagon Co.* v.
House [1974] I.C.R. 123, N.I.R.C.

s. 6, see *Neepsend Steel* v. *Vaughan* [1972]
I.C.R. 278; *Wilson-Undy* v. *Instrument and
Control* [1976] I.C.R. 508; *Farbar Construction*
v. *Race* [1979] I.C.R. 529, E.A.T.

s. 8, see *Deaway Trading* v. *Calverley* [1973]
I.C.R. 546; [1973] 3 All E.R. 776, N.I.R.C.;
Harold Fielding v. *Mansi* [1974] 1 All E.R.
1035, N.I.R.C.; *Dean* v. *Eastbourne Fishermen's and Boatmen's Protection Society and
Club* [1977] I.C.R. 556, E.A.T.; *Rastill* v. *Automatic Refreshment Services* [1978] I.C.R.
289, E.A.T.; *Wood* v. *York City Council* [1978]
I.C.R. 840, C.A.; *Smith* v. *Lord Advocate*,
1979 S.L.T. 233.

s. 9, see *Simpson* v. *Dickinson* [1972] I.C.R.
474, N.I.R.C.; *Rigley* v. *British Steel Corporation* [1973] I.C.R. 160, N.I.R.C.; *Midland Foot
Comfort Centre* v. *Richmond* [1973] 2 All E.R.
294; *Secretary of State for Employment* v.
Wellworthy [1973] I.C.R. 477; [1973] 3 All
E.R. 488, N.I.R.C.; *Burton, Allton & Johnson*
v. *Pick* [1975] I.C.R. 193; *Evenden* v. *Guildford
City Association Football Club* [1975] 3 W.L.R.
251, C.A.; *Secretary of State for Employment*
v. *Wellworthy (No. 2)* [1976] I.C.R. 13; *Lesney
Products & Co.* v. *Nolan* [1977] I.C.R. 235,
C.A.; *Wood* v. *York City Council* [1978] I.C.R.
840, C.A.; *Secretary of State for Employment*
v. *Globe Elastic Thread Co.* [1979] 3 W.L.R.
143, H.L.

s. 10, see *Lignacite Products* v. *Krollman* [1979]
I.R.L.R. 22, E.A.T.

s. 13, see *Ramseyer Motors* v. *Broadway and
Magee* (1971) 11 K.I.R. 169; *Ubsdell* v. *Paterson* [1973] I.C.R. 86, N.I.R.C.; *Cartin* v. *Botley
Garages* [1973] I.C.R. 144, N.I.R.C.; *Newlin
Oil Co.* v. *Trafford* [1974] I.R.L.R. 205; *Lord
Advocate* v. *De Rosa* [1974] 1 W.L.R. 946;
[1974] 2 All E.R. 849, H.L.; *Crompton* v. *Truly
Fair (International)* [1975] I.C.R. 359; *Bailey's
Exors* v. *Co-op Wholesale Society* (O.H.), 1976
S.L.T. 92; *Camelo* v. *Sheerlyn Productions*
[1976] I.C.R. 531; *Secretary of State for
Employment* v. *Rooney* [1977] I.C.R. 440,
E.A.T.; *M. S. Rose (Heating)* v. *Edgington*
[1977] I.C.R. 844, E.A.T.; *Rastill* v. *Automatic
Refreshment
Services* [1978] I.C.R. 289, E.A.T.; *Smith* v.
Lord Advocate, 1979 S.L.T. 233; *Melon* v.
Powe (Hector) [1981] I.C.R. 43; [1981] 1 All
E.R. 313, H.L.

s. 15, see *Ioannou* v. *B.B.C.* [1974] I.C.R. 414;
[1975] 3 W.L.R. 63; [1975] 2 All E.R. 999,
C.A.; *The Open University* v. *Triesman* [1978]
I.C.R. 524, E.A.T.

s. 16, see *Bagga* v. *Heavy Electricals (India)*
[1971] 12 K.I.R. 154; [1972] I.T.R. 70.

s. 16, order 73/1281.

CAP.

1965—cont.

62. Redundancy Payments Act 1965—*cont.*

s. 17, see *Roux International* v. *Licudi* [1975] I.C.R. 424; *Costain Civil Engineering* v. *Draycott* [1977] I.C.R. 335, E.A.T.

s. 21, see *Secretary for Employment* v. *Atkins* [1972] 1 W.L.R. 507; [1972] 1 All E.R. 987; *Bentley Engineering* v. *Crown* [1976] I.C.R. 225; *Watts* v. *Rubery Owen Conveyancer* [1977] 2 All E.R. 1; *Nash* v. *Ryan Plant International* [1977] I.C.R. 560, E.A.T.; *Price* v. *Smithfield & Zwanenberg Group* [1978] I.C.R. 93, E.A.T.; *Pritchard-Rhodes* v. *Boon and Milton* [1979] I.R.L.R. 19, E.A.T.

s. 22, see *British Airports Authority* v. *Fenerty* [1976] I.C.R. 361.

ss. 27–9, repealed: 1973, c.38, sch.28.

s. 30, see *Secretary of State for Employment* v. *Atkins* [1972] 1 W.L.R. 507; [1972] 1 All E.R. 987; *Secretary of State for Employment* v. *Globe Elastic Thread Co.* [1979] 3 W.L.R. 143, H.L.; *North East Coast Shiprepairers* v. *Secretary of State for Employment* [1978] I.C.R. 755, E.A.T.

ss. 30–44, repealed: 1978, c.44, sch.17.

s. 32, see *Smith* v. *Lord Advocate*, 1979 S.L.T. 233.

s. 34, see *Secretary of State for Employment* v. *Wellworthy (No. 2)* [1976] I.C.R. 13.

s. 35, order 72/174.

s. 45, repealed: 1981, c.57, sch.3.

ss. 46–54, repealed: 1978, c.44, sch.17.

s. 48, see *Spanlight Structures* v. *Jarrett* [1973] I.C.R. 465, N.I.R.C.

s. 53, see *Fabar Construction* v. *Race* [1979] I.C.R. 529, E.A.T.

ss. 55 (in pt.), 56–58, repealed: 1978, c.44, sch.17.

s. 59, repealed in pt.: 1972, c.53, sch.3; 1978, c.44, sch.17.

sch. 1, see *Allison's Freightlines* v. *Smylie* [1971] I.T.R. 175; *Mole Mining* v. *Jenkins* [1972] I.C.R. 282; *Adams* v. *Wright* [1972] I.C.R. 463, N.I.R.C.; *Woodhouse* v. *Brotherhood* [1972] 3 W.L.R. 215; [1972] 3 All E.R. 91; *McBride* v. *British Railways* [1974] S.L.T. 22, Ct. of Sess.; *Murphy Telecommunications (Systems)* v. *Henderson* [1973] I.C.R. 581, N.I.R.C.; *Ogden* v. *Ardphalt Asphalt* [1977] 1 All E.R. 267; *Weevsmay* v. *Kings* [1977] I.C.R. 244, E.A.T.

sch. 1, orders 74/1327; 77/2031; repealed: 1978, c.44, sch.17.

sch. 2, repealed: 1978, c.44, sch.17.

sch. 3, amended: 1978, c.29, sch.16(S.); repealed: 1978, c.44, sch.17.

sch. 4, see *Ranger* v. *Brown* [1978] I.C.R. 603, E.A.T.

sch. 4, regs. 76/663.

schs. 4–9, repealed: 1978, c.44, sch.17.

63. Public Works Loans Act 1965.

s. 2, amended (S.): 1975, c.30, sch.6; 1987, c.47, sch.1; repealed in pt.: 1972, c.70, sch.30; 1975, c.30, sch.7(S.).

sch., amended: 1976, c.70, sch.7; repealed in pt.: 1972, c.70, sch.30; 1975, c.30, sch.7(S.).

CAP.

1965—cont.

64. Commons Registration Act 1965.

see *Wilkes* v. *Gee* [1973] 1 W.L.R. 111; *Crowle Waste, Boothferry District, Humberside, Re* (Ref. No. 24/D/17–47); *Mynydd Preseli, Re* (Ref. No. 272/D/967–1042).

s. 1, see *New Windsor Corporation* v. *Mellor* [1974] 2 All E.R. 510; [1975] 3 W.L.R. 25, C.A.; *Central Electricity Generating Board* v. *Clwyd County Council* [1976] 1 W.L.R. 151; [1976] 1 All E.R. 251; *Re Turnworth Down* [1977] 2 All E.R. 105; *Re The Rye, High Wycombe, Bucks* (1977) 242 E.G. 811; *Re Box Hill Common* [1979] 2 W.L.R. 177, C.A.

s. 2, amended: 1985, c.51, sch.8; repealed in pt.: 1972, c.70, sch.30.

s. 3, regs. 72/437.

s. 4, see *Re Bachelors' Acre, New Windsor, Berkshire* (1974) 28 P. & C.R. 85.

ss. 4–7, see *Re Tillmire Common, Heslington* [1982] 2 All E.R. 615, Dillon J.

s. 5, see *Re Sutton Common, Wimborne* [1982] 1 W.L.R. 647, Walton J.; *R.* v. *Commons Comr., ex p. Bostock, G. S.,* May 27, 1982, Comyn J.

s. 5, regs. 73/815.

ss. 5, 6, see *Wilkes* v. *Gee* [1973] 1 W.L.R. 742; *Re West Anstey Common* [1985] 1 All E.R. 618, C.A.

s. 6, regs. 72/437.

s. 7, see *Smith* v. *East Sussex County Council* (1977) 76 L.G.R. 332, Templeman J.

s. 8, amended: 1972, c.70, s.189.

s. 10, see *Cooke* v. *Amey Gravel Co.* [1972] 1 W.L.R. 1310; [1972] 3 All E.R. 579.

ss. 10, 13, see *President and Scholars of Corpus Christi College, Oxford* v. *Gloucestershire County Council* [1982] 3 W.L.R. 849, C.A.

s. 13, see *Re Tillmire Common, Heslington* [1982] 2 All E.R. 615, Dillon J.

ss. 14, 18, see *Wilkes* v. *Gee* [1973] 1 W.L.R. 742.

s. 18, see *R.* v. *Chief Commons Commissioner, ex p. Constable* (1977) 76 L.G.R. 127, D.C.; *R.* v. *Chief Commons Comr., ex p. Winnington, The Times,* November 26, 1982, Woolf J.; *Re West Anstey Common, The Times,* October 17, 1983, Whitford J.

s. 19, regs. 72/437; 80/1195.

s. 22, see *New Windsor Corporation* v. *Mellor* [1974] 2 All E.R. 510; [1975] 3 W.L.R. 25, C.A.; *Central Electricity Generating Board* v. *Clwyd County Council* [1976] 1 W.L.R. 151; [1976] 1 All E.R. 251; *Re Britford Common* [1977] 1 W.L.R. 39; *Re Yateley Common, Hampshire; Arnold* v. *Dodd* [1977] 1 All E.R. 505; *Re Turnworth Down* [1977] 2 All E.R. 105; *Re The Rye, High Wycombe, Bucks* [1977] 3 All E.R. 521; 242 E.G. 811, Brightman J.; *Re Chewton Common, Christchurch; Borough of Christchurch* v. *Milligan* [1977] 3 All E.R. 509, Slade J.; *Re Box Hill Common* [1979] 2 W.L.R. 177, C.A.; *Baxendale* v. *Instow Parish Council* [1981] 2 W.L.R. 1055; [1981] 2 All E.R. 620, Megarry V.-C.; *Re Tillmire Common, Heslington* [1982] 2 All E.R. 615, Dillon J.

CAP.

1965—cont.

66. Hire-Purchase Act 1965.
repealed: 1974, c.39, sch.5.
s. 2, amended: orders 78/461; 83/611.
s. 3, orders 78/461; 83/611.
ss. 9, 10, see *V. L. Skuce & Co.* v. *Cooper*
[1975] 1 W.L.R. 593; [1975] 1 All E.R. 612,
C.A.
ss. 20, 54, 58, amended: 1979, c.54, sch.2.
s. 27, see *Wadham Stringer Finance* v. *Meancy,
TheTimes*, July 26, 1980, Woolf J.
s. 34, see *Lombank* v. *Dowdall* (1973) 118 S.J.
96, C.A.; *Chartered Trust* v. *Pitcher* [1988]
R.T.R. 72, C.A.
s. 42, amended: 1984, c.28, sch.2.

67. Hire-Purchase (Scotland) Act 1965.
repealed: 1974, c.39, sch.5.
s. 2, amended: orders 78/461; 83/611.
s. 3, orders 78/461; 83/611.
ss. 8, 16, 25, see *Broadwood Finance Co.* v.
Calder, 1976 S.L.T.(Sh.Ct.) 34.
ss. 20, 50, 54, amended: 1979, c.54, sch.2.

69. Criminal Procedure (Attendance of Witnesses) Act 1965.
ss. 1, 7, repealed in pt.: S.L.R. 1974.
s. 2, see *R.* v. *Skegness Magistrates' Court, ex
p. Cardy; R.* v. *Manchester Crown Court, ex
p. Williams* [1985] R.T.R. 49, D.C.; *Day v.
Grant; R.* v. *Manchester Crown Court, ex p.
Williams* [1985] R.T.R. 299, C.A.; *R.* v. *Morley*
[1988] 2 W.L.R. 963, C.A.
s. 8, amended: 1980, c.43, sch.7.
s. 9, repealed: 1973, c.36, sch.6.
s. 10, repealed in pt.: *ibid.*; S.L.R. 1974.
s. 10, sch. 2, see *R.* v. *Blithing* [1984] R.T.R. 18,
C.A.
sch. 2, repealed in pt.: S.L.R. 1974; 1980, c.43,
sch.9.

71. Murder (Abolition of Death Penalty) Act 1965.
s. 1, see *R.* v. *Flemming* [1973] 2 All E.R. 401;
repealed in part (S.): 1975, c.21, sch.10.
s. 3, repealed in part: S.L.R. 1974.
s. 4, repealed: S.L.R. 1973.
sch., repealed: S.L.R. 1974.

72. Matrimonial Causes Act 1965.
repealed (except ss. 8, 25–8A, 38, 42, 43, 46):
1973, c 18, sch.3.
s. 2, see *McGibbon* v. *McGibbon* [1973] 2
W.L.R. 1013.
s. 6, see *Kaur* v. *Singh* [1972] 1 W.L.R. 105;
[1972] 1 All E.R. 292.
s. 8, see *Dryden* v. *Dryden* [1973] 3 W.L.R. 524;
[1973] 3 All E.R. 526, Baker P.
s. 9, see *Potter* v. *Potter* (1975) 5 Fam. Law
161, C.A.
s. 10, see *Kaur* v. *Singh* [1972] 1 W.L.R. 105;
[1972] 1 All E.R. 292.
s. 17, see *D'Este* v. *D'Este* [1973] 2 W.L.R. 183.
s. 25, repealed in pt.: 1975, c.63, sch.
s. 26, see *Lusternik* v. *Lusternik* [1972] 2 W.L.R.
203; [1972] 1 All E.R. 592.
ss. 26–28A, repealed: 1975, c.63, sch.
s. 38, repealed: S.L.R. 1976.
s. 40, see *Kern* v. *Kern* [1972] 1 W.L.R. 1224;
[1972] 3 All E.R. 207.

CAP.

1965—cont.

72. Matrimonial Causes Act 1965—*cont.*
s. 42, repealed: 1978, c.22, sch.3.
s. 43, repealed in pt.: 1984, c.60, s.80, sch.7.
s. 46, repealed in pt.: S.L.R. 1977.

73. Race Relations Act 1965.
repealed: 1976, c.74, sch.5.
s. 7, see *Brutus* v. *Cozens* [1972] 3 W.L.R. 521;
[1972] 2 All E.R. 1297; *Garfield* v. *Maddocks*
[1973] 2 W.L.R. 888; [1973] 2 All E.R. 303;
Hudson v. *Chief Constable, Avon and Somerset Constabulary* [1976] Crim.L.R. 451, D.C.;
Allen v. *Ireland* [1984] 1 W.L.R. 903, D.C.

74. Superannuation Act 1965.
repealed (except ss. 38, 39, 39A, 42, 95, 97, 98,
104, 106, schs. 8, 10): 1972, c.11, sch.8.
s. 38, rules 72/1762; 75/1183; 82/1207; 87/376.
s. 38, amended: 1972, c.11, sch.6.
s. 39, amended: 1973, c.54, sch.3; repealed in
pt.: 1973, c.36, sch.6; 1979, c.43, sch.7.
s. 39A, rules 72/1277; 79/668.
s. 39A, amended: 1981, c.20, sch.3.
s. 42, rules 72/1762.
s. 42, amended: 1972, c.11, sch.6.
s. 93, repealed in pt.: 1975, c.7, sch.13.
s. 95, amended: 1972, c.11, sch.6.

75. Rent Act 1965.
repealed: 1977, c.43, sch.3; 1984, c.58,
sch.10(S.).
s. 27, see *Learmonth Property Investment Co.*
v. *Aitken*, 1971 S.L.T. 349.
s. 30, see *Thurrock U.D.C.* v. *Shira*, (1972) 23 P.
& C.R. 205; 70 L.G.R. 301; *Olidawura* v.
Fulmyk, January 17, 1975, Shoreditch Cty.
Ct.; *R.* v. *Bokhari* (1974) 59 Cr.App.R. 303,
C.A.; *McCall* v. *Abelesz* [1976] 2 W.L.R. 151,
C.A.; *R.* v. *Blankley* [1979] Crim.L.R. 166,
Knightsbridge Crown Ct.
s. 32, amended (S.): 1980, c.52, s.42.

76. Southern Rhodesia Act 1965.
repealed: order 80/394.
s. 1, see *Mutasa* v. *Att.Gen.* [1979] 3 All E.R.
257, Boreham J.
ss. 1, 2, see *Lonrho* v. *Shell Petroleum Co.* (*No.
2*) [1981] 3 W.L.R. 33; [1981] 2 All E.R. 456,
H.L.
s. 2, orders 72/1583; 73/1226; 77/591; 79/820,
1374.
s. 3, orders 72/1717; 73/1895; 74/1894;
75/1833; 76/1913; 77/1872; 78/1625.

81. Housing (Slum Clearance Compensation) Act 1965.
repealed: 1985, c.71, sch.1.

82. Coal Industry Act 1965
s. 1, orders 72/468; 74/1296; 79/1012; 80/1101;
81/1132; 83/1047.
s. 1, amended: 1973, c.8, s.2, sch.1; 1975,
c.55, sch.4; 1976, c.1, s.1; 1977, c.39, s.1,
sch.; 1980, c.50, s.1; 1982, c.15, s.1; 1983,
c.60, s.1; order 83/1047; 1985, c.9, sch.2;
1987, c.3, sch.1; repealed in pt.: 1977, c.39,
sch.5.
s. 2, amended: 1987, c.3, sch.1; repealed in
pt.: 1973, c.8, sch.2.
s. 3, repealed: 1977, c.39, sch.5.
s. 4, amended: 1987, c.3, sch.1.
s. 5, repealed in part: S.L.R. 1974.
sch. 2, repealed: *ibid.*

CAP.

1966

4. Mines (Working Facilities and Support) Act 1966.
s. 1, see *Re W.J. King & Sons' Application* [1976] 1 W.L.R. 521; [1976] 1 All E.R. 770, C.A.
s. 1, amended: 1974, c.36, s.1; 1987, c.3, sch.1.
ss. 1–5, 8, see *B.P. Petroleum Development* v. *Ryder* (1987) 27 R.V.R. 211, Peter Gibson J.
s. 2, amended: 1981, c.36, s.33; 1987, c.12, s.27; repealed in pt.: *ibid.*, s.27, sch.3.
s. 4, amended: 1987, c.3, sch.1.
s. 7, amended: 1979, c.46, sch.4; repealed in pt.: *ibid.*, schs.4,5.
s. 9, amended: 1987, c.3, sch.1.
sch. 1, repealed: S.L.R. 1974.
sch. 2, repealed in pt.: 1972, c.52, sch.23.

5. Statute Law Revision Act 1966.
repealed: S.L.R. 1974.

6. National Insurance Act 1966.
repealed: 1975, c.18, sch.1; c.24, sch.3.; c.25, sch.3.
s. 2, amended: 1980, c.53, s.17.
ss. 2, 4, regs. 72/909.
s. 6, amended: 1980, c.53, s.18.
s. 11, regs. 72/166; 74/1128.
sch., amended: 1980, c.53, s.19.

7. Local Government (Pecuniary Interests) (Scotland) Act 1966.
repealed (S.): S.L.R. 1975.
s. 18, see *British Railways Board* v. *Glasgow Corporation*, 1976 S.C. 224.

8. National Health Service Act 1966.
ss. 1–9, repealed: 1988, c.49, s.3.
s. 2, amended: 1978, c.29, sch.16(S.).
s. 2A, added: 1988, c.49, s.3.
s. 6, orders 78/921; 81/777; 84/580.
s. 6, amended: *ibid.*; 1984, c.48, s.8; 1988, c.49, s.3.
s. 10, amended: 1977, c.49, sch.15.
ss. 10, 11, amended (S.): 1978, c.29, sch.16.
s. 11, amended: order 88/1843; repealed: 1988, c.49, sch.3.
s. 12, repealed in pt.: 1977, c.49, sch.16; 1978, c.29, sch.17(S.); 1988, c.49, sch.3.
sch., repealed: 1988, c.49, sch.3.

9. Rating Act 1966.
repealed: S.L.R. 1986.
ss. 2–4, repealed (S.): 1975, c.30, sch.7.
s. 7, orders 72/112; 73/197.

10. Commonwealth Secretariat Act 1966.
sch., amended: 1973, c.38, sch.27; 1981, c.61, sch.7; 1988, c.41, sch.12 (prosp.); repealed in pt.: 1975, c.18, sch.1.

13. Universities (Scotland) Act 1966.
s. 12, amended: 1985, c.9, sch.2.
s. 14, sch. 7, repealed: S.L.R. 1974.
sch. 2, amended: 1981, c.58, s.18.
sch. 6, repealed in pt.: 1978, c.12, sch.7; 1983, c.54, sch.7.

14. Guyana Independence Act 1966.
ss. 2, 3, repealed: 1981, c.61, sch.9.
s. 5, repealed in pt.: 1978, c.30, sch.3.
s. 7, repealed: S.L.R. 1977.
sch. 2, repealed in pt.: *ibid.*; 1981, c.9, sch.

CAP.

1966—cont.

17. Transport Finances Act 1966.
repealed: S.L.R. 1974.

18. Finance Act 1966.
s. 1, repealed in pt.: regs. 77/910.
s. 2, amended: 1979, c.2, sch.4; c.8, sch.1; repealed in pt.: 1972, c.41, sch.28.
s. 3, repealed: 1977, c.36, sch.9.
s. 7, repealed: 1978, c.42, sch.13.
s. 9, repealed: 1972, c.68, sch.3.
ss. 10, 11, repealed: 1979, c.2, sch.6.
s. 12, amended: 1972, c.25, sch.5; repealed in pt.: *ibid.*, sch.7.
s. 15, repealed in pt.: *ibid.*
s. 29, repealed: S.L.R. 1978.
s. 31, see *Hewitt* v. *I.R.C.* [1972] 1 W.L.R. 411; [1972] 2 All E.R. 453.
s. 31, order 72/465.
ss. 31, 32, repealed: 1972, c.41, sch.28.
s. 32, order 72/464.
ss. 41, 42, repealed: 1975, c.7, sch.13.
s. 43, repealed: 1979, c.14, sch.8.
s. 44, repealed in pt.: 1972, c.41, sch.28; 1973, c.36, sch.6.
s. 46, repealed: 1985, c.54, sch.27.
s. 52, repealed: 1972, c.68, sch.3.
s. 53, amended: 1979, c.2, sch.4; repealed in pt.: 1975, c.7, sch.13; S.L.R. 1978.
sch. 1, amended: 1979, c.2, sch.4.
sch. 2, repealed in pt.: 1977, c.36, sch.9; 1979, c.2, sch.6; c.4, sch.4.
sch. 3, repealed in pt.: 1972, c.25, sch.7.
sch. 6, repealed in pt.: 1985, c.9, sch.1.
sch. 8, order 73/1868.
sch. 8, repealed in pt.: 1974, c.46, sch.11; 1975, c.45, sch.14.
sch. 9, see *Hewitt* v. *I.R.C.* [1972] 1 W.L.R. 411; [1972] 2 All E.R. 453.
sch. 9, repealed: 1972, c.41, sch.28.
sch. 10, see *Re McMeekin, A Bankrupt* (1973) 48 T.C. 725, N.I.D.C.
sch. 10, repealed: 1979, c.14, sch.8.
sch. 11, repealed: 1972, c.41, sch.28.

19. Law Reform (Miscellaneous Provisions) (Scotland) Act 1966.
see *Trustees of the Late Sir James Douglas Wishart Thomson* v. *I.R.C.* [1978] T.R. 171, Ct. of Session.
ss. 2, 3, repealed: 1987, c.18, sch.8.
s. 4, repealed: 1975, c.72, sch.4.
s. 7, see *McGowan* v. *Mein*, 1976 S.L.T.(Sh.Ct.) 29; *Docherty* v. *McGlynn* (O.H.), 1985 S.L.T. 237.
s. 7, repealed: 1988, c.32, sch.
s. 8, see *McGuire* v. *McGuire* (Sh.Ct.), 1987 S.C.L.R. 378.
s. 8, Act of Sederunt 84/667.
s. 8, amended: 1973, c.29, sch.5; 1976, c.39, sch.1; 1984, c.42, sch.1; 1985, c.37, sch.1; 1986, c.55, sch.1; repealed in pt.: 1976, c.39, sch.2; 1986, c.55, sch.2.
s. 9, repealed (S.): 1975, c.21, sch.10.
s. 11, repealed in pt.: S.L.R. 1974.
sch., repealed: *ibid.*

1966—cont.

20. Supplementary Benefit Act 1966.
repealed: 1976, c.71, sch.8.
see *R. v. Preston Supplementary Benefits Appeal Tribunal, ex p. Moore; R. v. Sheffield Supplementary Benefits Appeal Tribunal, ex p. Shine* [1975] 1 W.L.R. 624, C.A.; *R. v. West London Supplementary Benefits Appeal Tribunal, ex p. Taylor* [1975] 1 W.L.R. 1048; [1975] 2 All E.R. 790, D.C.
s. 4, see *R. v. Bristol Supplementary Benefits Appeal Tribunal, ex p. Southwell, The Times,* July 21, 1977, D.C.
ss. 4, 5, see *R. v. West London Supplementary Benefits Appeal Tribunal, ex p. Clarke* [1975] 1 W.L.R. 1396; [1975] 3 All E.R. 513, D.C.
s. 5, regs. 72/1145; 74/854; 75/464, 1097; 76/1030.
ss. 11, 17, regs. 74/1416.
s. 17, regs. 72/329, 1493; 75/1335.
s. 26, see *Secretary of State for Social Services v. Solly* [1974] 3 All E.R. 922, C.A.
s. 26, repealed: 1986, c.50, sch.11.
s. 29, see *Clear v. Smith* [1980] Crim.L.R. 246, D.C.
sch. 2, regs. 74/2100; see *R. v. Barnsley Supplementary Benefits Appeal Tribunal, ex p. Atkinson* [1977] 1 W.L.R. 917, C.A.

21. Overseas Aid Act 1966.
repealed: 1980, c.63, sch.2.

23. Botswana Independence Act 1966.
ss. 3, 4, repealed: 1981, c.61, sch.9.
ss. 5, 6, 7, repealed: S.L.R. 1977.
sch., repealed in pt.: 1973, c.36, sch.6; S.L.R. 1976; 1981, c.9, sch.

24. Lesotho Independence Act 1966.
ss. 3, 4, repealed: 1981, c.61, sch.9.
ss. 5, 6, 7, repealed: S.L.R. 1977.
sch., repealed in pt.: 1973, c.36, sch.6; S.L.R. 1976; 1981, c.9, sch.; 1988, c.48, sch.8.

27. Building Control Act 1966.
repealed: 1984, c.29, s.61, sch.12.
sch., amended: 1987, c.3, sch.1.

28. Docks and Harbours Act 1966.
s. 2, orders 73/94; 75/257; 81/918.
s. 2, amended: 1976, c.79, s.12.
ss. 6–12, 15, 40, repealed in pt.: 1981, c.56, sch.12.
ss. 25, 32, amended: order 74/1820.
s. 30, functions transferred: order 76/1775.
s. 42, amended: 1981, c.56, sch.6; repealed in pt.: *ibid.,* sch.12.
s. 44, repealed: *ibid.*
s. 47, amended: *ibid.,* sch.4.
ss. 48, 49, repealed: *ibid.,* sch.12.
s. 51, see *National Dock Labour Board v. Hull Fish Landing Co., The Times,* May 17, 1988, Simon Brown J.
s. 51, amended: 1982, c.10, sch.3.
s. 52, repealed in pt.: 1981, c.56, sch.12.
s. 58, amended: order 74/1820; repealed in pt.: 1981, c.56, sch.12.
s. 60, orders 73/889; 81/918.
sch. 1, amended: orders 74/595; 81/918.

1966—cont.

29. Singapore Act 1966.
s. 2, repealed: 1986, c.55, sch.2.
sch. repealed in pt.: 1980, c.9, sch.; 1981, c.61, sch.9; 1985, c.9, sch.1; c.21, sch.2.

30. Reserve Forces Act 1966.
repealed: 1980, c.9, sch.10.

31. Criminal Appeal Act 1966.
repealed: 1981, c.54, sch.7.
s. 1, see *R. v. Rose* [1982] 3 W.L.R. 192, H.L.

32. Selective Employment Payments Act 1966.
repealed: 1972, c.41, sch.28.
see *Laing v. Lord Advocate,* 1973 S.L.T.(Notes) 81, Outer House; *Norwest Holst Group Administration v. Secretary of State for Employment* [1974] 2 Lloyd's Rep. 89, D.C.
s. 1, see *Lord Advocate v. Babcock & Wilcox* [1972] 1 W.L.R. 488; [1972] 1 All E.R. 1130.
ss. 1, 3, 7, 10, amended: 1974, c.30, schs.13,14.

33. Prices and Incomes Act 1966.
repealed: 1973, c.9, sch.6.

34. Industrial Development Act 1966.
s. 8, repealed in pt.: 1977, c.45, sch.13; 1985, c.23, sch.2.
s. 14, repealed: 1973, c.36, sch.6.
s. 15, repealed: 1972, c.5, sch.4.
s. 16, repealed in pt.: S.L.R. 1978.
ss. 18, 19, repealed: 1972, c.5, sch.4.
ss. 20, 21, repealed: S.L.R. 1978.
Pt. III (ss. 22–27): repealed: 1972, c.52, sch.23.
s. 31, repealed in pt.: 1972, c.5, sch.4; c.52, sch.23; 1973, c.36, sch.6; S.L.R. 1974; 1975, c.24, sch.3; c.25, sch.3.
sch. 1, amended: 1972, c.5, sch.3; repealed in pt.: 1972, c.63, sch.4.
sch. 2, amended: 1981, c.38, sch.3; 1987, c.3, sch.1; repealed in pt.: 1980, c.34, sch.9; 1986, c.31, sch.6.
sch. 3, repealed in pt.: 1972, c.5, sch.4; c.52, sch.23; S.L.R. 1974; 1975, c.24, sch.3; c.25, sch.3; 1984, c.29, sch.12.

35. Family Provision Act 1966.
repealed except ss. 1, 10 (in pt.): 1975, c.63, sch.
s. 1, orders 72/916; 77/415; 81/255; 87/799.
s. 11, order 78/1809.
sch. 3, see *Millward v. Shenton* [1972] 1 W.L.R. 711; [1972] 2 All E.R. 1025.

36. Veterinary Surgeons Act 1966.
ss. 2, 6, amended: order 80/1951.
s. 5A, added: *ibid.*
s. 6, regs 76/1168; order 84/1072.
s. 11, regs 75/2212; orders 80/2004; 84/2009.
s. 19, orders 73/308; 80/1003; 81/988; 82/1627, 1885; 83/6; 88/526, 1090.
s. 19, amended: 1986, c.14, sch.3; repealed in pt.: 1977, c.45, sch.13.
s. 20, repealed in pt.: *ibid.*
s. 21, order 88/784.
s. 24, repealed in pt.: 1972, c.71, sch.6; order 74/2143; 1980, c.55, sch.3 (S.).
s. 25, regs. 75/70; orders 78/1809; 80/999, 2004.
s. 27, amended: orders 78/272; 80/1951.
s. 29, order 73/45.
s. 29, repealed in pt.: 1973, c.36, sch.6.

CAP.

1966—cont.

36. Veterinary Surgeons Act 1966—cont.
s. 61, order 80/999.
sch. 1A, added: order 80/1951; amended: orders 81/205; 87/447.
sch. 2, amended: 1978, c.23, sch.5; order 80/1003; 1981, c.54, sch.5.
sch. 3, substituted: order 88/526; amended: 1988, c.40, sch.12.

37. Barbados Independence Act 1966.
ss. 2, 3, repealed: 1981, c.61, sch.9.
s. 4, repealed in pt.: 1978, c.30, sch.3.
sch. 2, repealed in pt.: S.L.R. 1977; 1981, c.9, sch.; 1988, c.48, sch.8.

38. Sea Fisheries Regulation Act 1966.
s. 1, orders 73/2194–2204; 78/438, 1715; 80/805–813, 822, 823; 86/647, 648, 1201.
ss. 1–3, amended: 1985, c.51, sch.8; repealed in pt.: 1972, c.70, sch.30.
s. 2, order 86/1201.
s. 5, regs. 85/1785(S.).
s. 5, repealed in pt.: 1974, c.40, sch.4.
s. 11, see *Alexander* v. *Tonkin* [1979] 1 W.L.R. 629, D.C.
s. 11, amended: 1976, c.86, sch.1.
s. 17, amended: 1985, c.51, sch.8.
s. 18, orders 78/74, 1715; 80/805–813, 822, 823; 86/647, 1201.
s. 18, amended: 1973, c.37, sch.8.
s. 19, amended: 1985, c.51, sch.8; repealed in pt.: 1972, c.70, sch.30.
s. 20, repealed in pt.: *ibid.*
s. 21, repealed in part: S.L.R. 1974.
sch., repealed: *ibid.*

39. Land Registration Act 1966.
ss. 1, 2, repealed in part: S.L.R. 1974.
sch., repealed: *ibid.*

41. Arbitration (International Investment Disputes) Act 1966.
s. 1, repealed in pt.: 1977, c.38, s.4, sch.5.
ss. 1, 2, amended: 1981, c.54, sch.5.
ss. 3, 7, repealed in pt.: 1975, c.34, sch.2.
s. 6, order 79/572.
s. 8, amended: 1978, c.23, sch.5.

42. Local Government Act 1966.
order 73/2187.
ss. 1–5, repealed: 1974, c.7, sch.8.
s. 3, order 73/2180.
s. 4, regs. 74/259.
s. 5, regs. 73/895.
ss. 8, 10, repealed: 1974, c.7, sch.8.
s. 9, repealed: 1982, c.42, ss.1,2, sch.
s. 11, amended: 1985, c.51, sch.14; repealed in pt.: 1988, c.40, sch.13 (prosp.).
ss. 12, 13, repealed: S.L.R. 1975.
s. 14, repealed: 1980, c.20, sch.7.
Pt. III (ss. 27–34), repealed: 1980, c.66, sch.25.
s. 35, orders 75/336, 605; 76/593; 78/473, 1387; 80/580, 1398; 81/1411, 1604; 82/572; 83/1589; 85/2027.
s. 35, repealed in pt.: S.L.R. 1974.
s. 37, repealed: S.L.R. 1978.
s. 39, repealed in pt.: *ibid.*
s. 40, orders 75/605; 76/593; 78/473, 1387; 80/580, 1398; 81/1411, 1604; 82/572; 83/1589; 85/2027.

CAP.

1966—cont.

42. Local Government Act 1966—cont.
s. 40, repealed in pt.: 1988, c.9, sch.7.
s. 41, repealed in pt.: S.L.R. 1978; 1985, c.51, sch.17.
s. 43, repealed in pt.: S.L.R. 1974.
ss. 47, 48, 51, orders 81/1597, 1628, 1629, 1649, 1667, 1682.
s. 48, regs. 74/428.
s. 67, orders 81/1628, 1629, 1649, 1667, 1682.
sch. 1, repealed: 1974, c.7, sch.8.
sch. 3, orders 75/605; 76/593; 78/1387; 80/580, 1398; 81/1411, 1604; 82/572; 83/1589; 85/2027.
sch. 3, repealed in part: 1974, c.7, sch.8; S.L.R. 1974; c.39, sch.5; 1975, c.37, schs.2,3; c.58, sch.5; 1976, c.32, sch.5; 1980, c.7, sch.1; c.65, sch.34; 1982, c.30, sch.7; 1983, c.41, sch.10; 1985, c.13, sch.3; 1988, c.9, sch.7.
sch. 5, repealed in pt.: S.L.R. 1976; 1980, c.65, sch.31; 1984, c.22, sch.3; 1986, c.61, sch.6.
sch. 6, repealed: S.L.R. 1974.

44. New Towns Act 1966.
repealed: 1981, c.64, sch.13.

45. Armed Forces Act 1966.
s. 2, regs. 72/8, 355, 517, 558, 1864; 73/916; 74/818; 75/224, 281, 1900; 76/729; 77/701, 1097; 79/192, 215; 80/61, 746–748, 1494; 81/404; 83/343, 897–899; 85/1819, 1820, 2003; 86/2027–2074; 88/1395.
s. 2, amended: 1976, c.52, s.2.
s. 4, amended: 1980, c.9, sch.9.
s. 11, repealed: S.L.R. 1974.
s. 13, repealed in pt.: 1976, c.52, sch.10.
ss. 19 (in pt.), 20 (in pt.), 34, 37 (in pt.), sch. 2, repealed: S.L.R. 1974.
s. 29, repealed: 1986, c.21, sch.2.
sch. 3, repealed in pt.: S.L.R. 1974; 1976, c.52, sch.10.
sch. 4, repealed in pt.: S.L.R. 1974; 1980, c.9, sch.10.

46. Bus Fuel Grants Act 1966.
s. 1, repealed: 1973, c.36, sch.6.

47. National Coal Board (Additional Powers) Act 1966.
s. 1, amended: 1987, c.3, sch.1; repealed in pt.: 1977, c.39, sch.5.

48. Films Act 1966.
s. 2, repealed: 1981, c.15, sch.3.
s. 7, repealed in pt.: *ibid.*; c.16, sch.2.

49. Housing (Scotland) Act 1966.
repealed: 1987, c.26, sch.24.
s. 8, see *Hastie* v. *City of Edinburgh District Council*, 1981 S.L.T.(Sh.Ct.) 61, 92.
s. 17, repealed in pt.: 1980, c.52, s.76, sch.5.
s. 18, amended: 1972, c.52, sch.21.
ss. 19, 21, 23, 25, amended: 1974, c.45, sch.3.
s. 47, see *Mitchell* v. *Hamilton District Council*, 1978 S.L.T.(Lands Tr.) 2.
s. 57A, added: 1984, c.12, sch.4.
s. 66, regs. 78/965.
ss. 80, 87, revived and amended: 1974, c.45, s.25.
s. 91, repealed: 1980, c.52, s.75, sch.5.
s. 98, repealed: 1973, c.65, schs.12,29.
ss. 100, 102, 103, amended: 1980, c.52, s.65.

CAP.

CAP.

49. Housing (Scotland) Act 1966—*cont.*

s. 107, amended: 1982, c.43, s.52; repealed in pt.: 1973, c.65, schs.12,29.

s. 110, amended: 1977, c.45, s.31, schs.6,12; 1980, c.52, s.65.

ss. 111, 112, amended: *ibid.*

s. 123, amended: 1984, c.58, sch.8.

s. 125, amended: 1981, c.23, sch.3.

s. 127, amended: *ibid.*, schs.2,3.

s. 130, amended: *ibid.*, sch.2.

s. 135, amended: 1974, c.44, sch.13.

s. 137, amended: 1974, c.45, sch.3.

s. 138, amended: 1978, c.14, sch.2.

s. 140, amended: 1974, c.39, sch.4.

s. 143, amended: 1974, c.45, sch.3; repealed in pt.: *ibid.*, schs.3,5.

s. 145, amended: 1972, c.46, sch.9; 1978, c.14, sch.2; 1980, c.52, ss.8,76; repealed in pt.: *ibid.*, s.8, sch.5.

s. 146, amended: 1972, c.45, sch.9.

s. 147, repealed in pt.: 1973, c.65, schs.12,29.

s. 149, amended: 1972, c.46, s.71; repealed in pt.: *ibid.*, sch.11.

s. 151, amended: *ibid.*, sch.9; 1977, c.48, s.6; repealed in pt.: 1972, c.46, schs.9,11; 1980, c.52, sch.5.

s. 152, repealed: 1985, c.71, sch.1.

ss. 153–155, repealed: 1974, c.44, schs. 13,15.

s. 156, repealed: 1985, c.71, sch.1.

s. 157, repealed: 1972, c.46, sch.11.

s. 158, repealed: 1985, c.71, sch.1.

s. 159, repealed: 1974, c.44, schs.13,15.

s. 160, amended: 1974, c.45, sch.3; repealed in pt.: 1973, c.26, sch.3.

s. 167, amended: 1980, c.52, s.75, sch.5.

s. 168, repealed: 1973, c.26, sch.3.

ss. 173, 174, repealed: 1973, c.65, schs.12,29.

s. 175, amended: 1972, c.46, sch.9; 1974, c.44, sch.13; 1985, c.71, sch.2.

s. 177, amended: 1981, c.23, sch.3; repealed in pt.: 1980, c.52, s.77, sch.5.

s. 181, amended: 1974, c.45, sch.3.

s. 184, amended: 1982, c.48, sch.6; repealed in pt.: 1973, c.65, schs.12,29.

s. 185, amended: 1980, c.52, s.65; 1982, c.48, sch.6; repealed in pt.: 1973, c.65, schs.12,29; 1982, c.48, sch.16.

s. 193, repealed in pt.: 1972, c.46, sch.11; 1973, c.65, schs.12,29.

s. 195, repealed: 1975, c.28, schs.3,4.

s. 197, regs. 74/1982; 75/1644; 78/965; 80/1647; 81/638.

s. 201, repealed: 1973, c.65, schs.12,29.

s. 208, amended: 1974, c.44, sch.13; c.45, sch.3; 1985, c.71, sch.2; repealed in pt.: 1973, c.65, schs.12,29; S.L.R. 1974.

s. 209, repealed: S.L.R. 1981.

s. 212, repealed: S.L.R. 1974.

sch. 2, regs. 78/965.

sch. 7, amended: 1975, c.30, sch.6.

sch. 8, repealed: 1973, c.26, sch.3.

sch. 10, repealed in pt.: S.L.R. 1974.

51. Local Government (Scotland) Act 1966.

s. 1, repealed: S.L.R. 1976.

s. 2, orders 75/251, 2215; 79/64; 81/128; 82/194, 1897; 83/1648; 84/102, 1686; 85/94; 86/140; 87/2279.

ss. 2–7, repealed: 1987, c.47, sch.6.

s. 3, orders 75/251, 2215; 76/2212; 77/2137; 79/64; 81/128; 82/194, 1897; 83/1648; 84/102, 1686; 85/94, 556, 1705; 86/140, 1965; 87/1329, 2279; 88/1286.

s. 4, orders 72/262, 263; 73/667, 2021; 74/613, 614; 75/252, 253, 1149, 2215; 81/128; 82/173, 194, 1897; 83/1648; 84/102, 1686; 85/94, 556, 1705; 86/140, 1965; 87/132, 2279; 88/1286.

s. 5, see *Commission for Local Authority Accounts in Scotland* v. *Stirling District Council,* 1984 S.L.T. 442; *Lord Advocate* v. *Stirling District Council,* 1986 S.L.T. 179.

s. 5, order 83/1074.

s. 5A, order 82/50.

s. 6, regs. 72/1090, 75/653; 76/456; 77/1862.

s. 8, repealed: 1972, c.52, sch.23.

s. 9, repealed: order 81/127.

s. 10, repealed: 1975, c.69, s.8, sch.5.

s. 11, repealed in pt.: 1973, c.65, sch.29.

s. 13, repealed in pt.: 1975, c.30, sch.7.

s. 14, repealed: 1987, c.47, sch.6.

s. 15, see *Bustin* v. *Assessor for Strathclyde Region,* 1985 S.L.T. 204; *Assessor for Borders Region* v. *A. M. S. Leisure,* 1986 S.L.T. 689; *Assessor for Central Region* v. *Fleming's Trs.,* 1987 S.L.T. 793.

s. 15, amended: 1975, c.30, sch.6.

s. 17, order 72/1138.

s. 17, amended: orders 78/1173–1176; repealed in pt.: order 78/1175.

s. 18, see *British Railways Board* v. *Glasgow Assessor,* 1969 S.C. 347; *Assessor for Edinburgh* v. *South of Scotland Electricity Board,* 1970 S.C. 125, Ct. of Session.

s. 18, amended: 1972, c.60, sch.6; 1984, c.31, sch.2; 1986, c.44, sch.7; repealed in pt.: 1972, c.60, schs.6,8; orders 78/1174–1176.

s. 19, repealed: orders 78/1174, 1176.

s. 22, amended: 1976, c.15, s.3.

s. 24, amended: 1975, c.30, sch.6; repealed in pt.: *ibid.*, schs.6,7; 1987, c.47, sch.6.

s. 25, regs. 86/34.

s. 25, amended: 1972, c.52, sch.21; 1975, c.30, sch.6; repealed in pt.: *ibid.*, schs.6,7; 1981, c.23, sch.4; revived in pt.: 1984, c.31, sch.2.

ss. 26, 27, repealed: 1987, c.47, sch.6.

Pt. III (ss.28–34), repealed: 1984, c.54, sch.11.

ss. 36, 37, 39, repealed: *ibid.*, sch.29.

s. 41, amended: 1972, c.52, sch.21.

s. 42, orders 75/666; 76/616; 78/1545; 80/1780; 81/1421; 82/173, 680; 83/1626; 85/2054.

s. 42, repealed in pt.: S.L.R. 1974.

s. 43, repealed: 1988, c.9, sch.7.

s. 45, orders 75/666; 76/616; 78/1178, 1545; 79/64; 80/1780; 81/1421; 82/680; 83/1626; 85/94, 556, 1705, 2054; 86/140, 1965; 87/1329, 2279; 88/1286.

CAP.

1966—cont.

51. Local Government (Scotland) Act 1966— cont.

s. 46, amended: 1972, c.46, sch.9; 1973, c.65, sch.9; 1975, c.30, sch.6; 1984, c.54, sch.9; 1987, c.26, sch.23; c.47, s.27; repealed in pt.: 1975, c.30, sch.7; 1984, c.54, sch.11.

s. 48, repealed in pt.: S.L.R. 1974.

sch. 1, see *Midlothian C.C.* v. *Secretary of State for Scotland,* 1975 S.L.T. 122.

sch. 1, regs. 72/1090; 75/653, 2215; 77/1862; orders 73/667; 79/64; 81/128; 82/1897; 84/102; 85/94, 1705; 86/140, 1965; 87/1329, 2279; 88/1286.

sch. 1, amended: 1973, c.65, sch.9; 1975, c.30, sch.2; 1981, c.23, s.16; 1984, c.31, s.1, sch.1; 1987, c.47, s.27; repealed in pt.: 1973, c.65, schs.9,29; 1982, c.43, sch.4; 1987, c.47, sch.6.

sch. 2, orders 78/1178; 83/1626.

sch. 3, amended: 1975, c.30, sch.6; 1987, c.26, sch.23; c.47, sch.1.

sch. 4, orders 76/616; 78/1545; 80/1780; 81/1421; 82/173, 680; 85/2054.

sch. 4, amended: 1981, c.23, sch.3; 1984, c.36, sch.3; repealed in pt.: 1972, c.58, sch.7; S.L.R. 1974: c.39, sch.5; 1975, c.58, sch.5; order 75/666; 1976, c.32, sch.5; 1980, c.65, sch.34; 1985, c.13, sch.3; 1988, c.9, sch.7.

sch. 5, repealed in pt.: 1973, c.65, sch.29.

sch. 6, repealed: S.L.R. 1974.

1967

1. Land Commission Act 1967.

s. 11, repealed in pt.: 1975, c.76, sch.2.

ss. 15, 58, 89, 99, schs. 15, 16, amended: 1972, c.52, sch.21.

s. 25, repealed in pt.: 1985, c.54, sch.27.

ss. 27, 32, 36, 38, 44, 46, 47, 100, see *Secretary of State for Scotland* v. *Ravenstoke Securities,* 1976 S.C. 171.

s. 46, see *Secretary of State for Scotland* v. *Tronsite,* First Division, November 25, 1977.

s. 51, order 74/974.

s. 56, amended: 1988, c.50, sch.17.

s. 82, repealed in pt.: 1977, c.45, sch.13.

s. 99, see *Alexandra Transport Co.* v. *Secretary of State for Scotland,* 1974 S.L.T. 81.

3. Education Act 1967.

s. 1, amended: 1975, c.2, s.3; 1980, c.20, sch.3; repealed in pt.: 1975, c.2, sch.; 1980, c.20, sch.1.

s. 3, repealed: 1988, c.40, sch.13.

s. 4, regs. 83/74.

s. 4, amended: 1988, c.40, s.229.

4. West Indies Act 1967.

repealed, except ss. 6, 8, 17 (in pt.), 19, 21: S.L.R. 1986.

s. 5, orders 72/301; 73/412, 2155; 75/2160; 78/1027, 1521, 1901; 79/916; 81/1106; 83/881.

s. 6, orders 82/334; 83/1108; amended: order 83/1107.

s. 10, orders 73/2157; 79/918.

s. 13, orders 73/2156; 78/1030, 1622, 1899; 79/917; 81/603, 1105; 83/882, 1107.

CAP.

1967—cont.

4. West Indies Act 1967—cont.

s. 13, amended: order 86/984.

s. 14, orders 78/1030, 1899; 79/917; 81/1105; 83/882.

s. 15, orders 78/1030; 81/603; 83/1107.

s. 17, orders 78/1622, 1900; 79/918; 81/1104; 82/334; 83/880, 1108.

5. London Government Act 1967.

repealed: 1972, c.70, sch.30.

6. Weights and Measures (Northern Ireland) Act 1967.

ss. 38, 45, repealed: order 81/231.

7. Misrepresentation Act 1967.

s. 2, see *Davis & Co.* (*Wines*) v. *Afa-Minerva* (*E.M.I*) [1974] 2 Lloyd's Rep. 27; *Watts* v. *Spence* [1975] 2 W.L.R. 1039; [1975] 2 All E.R. 528; *Howard Marine and Dredging Co.* v. *A. Ogden & Sons* (*Excavations*) [1978] 2 W.L.R. 515, C.A.; *Resolute Maritime Inc.* v. *Nippon Kaiji Kyokai, The Skopas* [1983] 2 All E.R. 1, Mustill J.; *Chesneau* v. *Interhome, The Times,* June 9, 1983, C.A.; *Sharneyford Supplies* [1985] 1 All E.R. 976, Mervyn Davies J.; *Highland Insurance Company* v. *Continental Insurance Company* [1987] 1 Lloyd's Rep. 109, Steyn J.; *Corner* v. *Mundy,* January 7, 1987, Judge Hewitt, Middlesborough County Ct.; *Production Technology Consultants* v. *Bartlett* [1988] 25 E.G. 121, C.A.; *Cooper* v. *Tamms* [1988] 1 E.G.L.R. 2357, Mr. P. J. Crawford Q.C.

s. 3, see *Overbrooke Estates* v. *Glencombe Properties* [1974] 1 W.L.R. 1335; [1974] 3 All E.R. 511; *Cremdean Properties* v. *Nash* (1977) 241 E.G. 837, Fox J.; *Howard Marine and Dredging Co.* v. *A. Ogden and Sons* (*Excavations*) [1978] 2 W.L.R. 515, C.A.; *Walker* v. *Boyle* [1982] 1 All E.R. 634, Dillon J.; *South Western General Property Co.* v. *Marton* (1983) 2 Tr.L. 14, Croom-Johnson J.; *White Cross Equipment* v. *Farrell* (1983) 2 Tr.L. 21, Garland Q.C.

s. 3, substituted: 1977, c.50, s.8.

s. 4, repealed: 1979, c.54, sch.3.

s. 6, repealed in pt.: *ibid.*

8. Plant Health Act 1967.

s. 1, orders 87/428, 880(S.); 88/736, 1427, 1882(S.).

s. 1, repealed in pt.: 1972, c.68, sch.4.

s. 2, orders 73/1107; 74/1, 2; 77/901; 80/420, 449, 1942; 82/599; 83/807, 1953; 84/306, 416, 839, 1871, 1892; 85/873, 1230; 86/195, 196, 1135; 87/19, 340, 428, 880(S.), 1679; 1758; 88/736, 1427, 1882(S.).

s. 2, amended: 1972, c.68, sch.4; 1979, c.2, sch.4.

s. 3, orders: 72/1742, 1937; 73/1059, 1060, 1107; 74/1, 2, 767, 768, 830, 1152, 1159, 1816; 75/55, 1163, 1618, 1842, 1904, 1905, 2225; 76/734, 975; 77/901, 988, 1074, 1075; 78/505; 79/638, 639; 80/420, 449, 450, 499, 1942; 81/1170; 82/599, 1457; 83/807, 1485, 1953; 84/306, 416, 686-688, 839, 1871, 1892; 85/242, 637(S.), 873, 1230;

CAP.

1967—cont.

8. Plant Health Act 1967—cont.

86/194–197, 476, 1135, 1342; 87/19, 340, 428, 880(S.), 1679, 1758; 88/45, 604, 605, 736, 971, 1427, 1882(S.).

s. 3, amended: 1972, c.68, sch.4; 1982, c.48, s.42; repealed in pt.: 1972, c.48, sch.4.

s. 4, orders 75/2225; 87/1758.

s. 4A, orders 87/340; 88/1427, 1882(S.).

s. 4A, added: 1986, c.49, s.3.

s. 5, orders 74/768, 830, 1816; 75/55, 1163; 76/975; 77/1074; 79/638; 84/687; 86/1342; 88/604.

s. 5, amended: 1972, c.70, sch.29; repealed in pt.: 1973, c.65, sch.29(S.); 1974, c.7, schs.6,8.

s. 6, amended: 1972, c.68, sch.4; repealed in pt.: 1973, c.65, sch.29(S.); 1974, c.7, schs.6, 8.

9. General Rate Act 1967.

repealed (prosp.): 1988, c.41, sch.13.

see *R.* v. *Liverpool City JJ., ex p. Lanchrist* [1977] Crim.L.R. 299; *R.* v. *Ealing Justices, ex p. Coatsworth, The Times,* March 1, 1980, D.C.; *Rendall* v. *Duke of Westminster* (1987) 19 H.L.R. 345, C.A.; *Westminster City Council* v. *Tomlin, The Times,* August 25, 1988, Henry J.

s. 1, see *Banister* v. *Islington London Borough Council* (1973) 71 L.G.R. 239, D.C.

ss. 1–5, see *Smith* v. *Skinner; Gladden* v. *McMahon* (1986) 26 R.V.R. 45, D.C.

s. 2, see *B. Kettle* v. *Newcastle-under-Lyme Borough Council* [1979] 77 L.G.R. 700, C.A.; *Debenhams* v. *Ealing London Borough Council* (1981) 79 L.G.R. 589, Glidewell J.; *R.* v. *Hackney London Borough Council, ex p. Fleming* (1986) 26 R.V.R. 182, Woolf J.; *Lloyd* v. *McMahon* (1986) 26 R.V.R. 188, C.A.; *R.* v. *Hackney London Borough Council, ex p. S. G. Warburg Group Management* (1988) 28 R.V.R. 75, D.C.

s. 2, amended: 1972, c.70, sch.13; repealed in pt.: *ibid.,* sch.30; 1982, c.32, sch.6.

s. 3, see *R.* v. *Hackney London Borough Council, ex p. Fleming* (1986) 26 R.V.R. 182, Woolf J.

s. 3, repealed in pt.: 1982, c.32, sch.6.

s. 4, amended: 1980, c.65, s.44; repealed in pt.: *ibid.,* sch.34.

s. 5, amended: 1972, c.70, sch.13; repealed in pt.: 1980, c.65, schs.33, 34.

s. 6, see *B. Kettle* v. *Newcastle-under-Lyme Borough Council* [1979] 77 L.G.R. 700, C.A.; *Debenhams* v. *Ealing London Borough Council* (1981) 79 L.G.R. 589, Glidewell J.; *Trendworthy Two* v. *Islington London Borough Council* [1988] 2 W.L.R. 681, H.L.

s. 7, see *Newport Borough Council* v. *Williams, The Times,* May 8, 1982, Stephen Brown J.; *Verrall* v. *Hackney London Borough Council* [1983] 1 All E.R. 277, C.A.; *Investors in Industry Commercial Properties* v. *Norwich City Council* [1986] 3 W.L.R. 925, H.L.; *Polo Pictures* v. *Trafford Metropolitan Borough Council* (1987) 27 R.V.R. 74, Manchester Crown Court.

CAP.

1967—cont.

9. General Rate Act 1967—cont.

s. 7, repealed in pt.: 1982, c.32, sch.6.

ss. 7, 9, see *R.* v. *Rochdale Metropolitan Borough Council, ex p. Cromer Ring Mill* [1982] 3 All E.R. 761, Forbes J.; *Rialto Builders* v. *Barnet London Borough Council* (1986) 26 R.V.R. 120, Wood Green Crown Court.

s. 8, amended: 1980, c.65, s.35.

s. 9, see *White* v. *Bromidge* (1979) 251 E.G. 469, C.A.; *R.* v. *Tower Hamlets London Borough Council, ex p. Chetnik Developments* [1988] 2 W.L.R. 654, H.L.; *Stubbs* v. *Richmond upon Thames London Borough Council* (1988) 28 R.V.R. 35, Kennedy J.

s. 9, repealed in pt.: 1988, c.41, s.120.

s. 11, see *Manchester City Council* v. *Greater Manchester County Council* (1980) 78 L.G.R. 560, H.L.; *Lloyd* v. *McMahon* (1986) 26 R.V.R. 188, C.A.

ss. 11, 12, see *Smith* v. *Skinner; Gladden* v. *McMahon* (1986) 26 R.V.R. 45, D.C.

s. 12, rules 82/1224.

s. 12, amended: 1974, c.7, sch.7; rules 74/1322; 1985, c.51, sch.68; repealed in pt.: 1982, c.32, sch.6.

ss. 12, 14, rules 81/327; 86/1236.

s. 16, see *Re Briant Colour Printing Co.* [1977] 1 W.L.R. 942, C.A.; *R.* v. *Ealing JJ., ex p. Coatsworth* (1980) 78 L.G.R. 439, D.C.; *Routhan* v. *Arun District Council* [1982] 2 W.L.R. 144, C.A.; *Verrall* v. *Hackney London Borough Council, The Times,* November 22, 1982, C.A.; *R.* v. *Harrow JJ., ex p. Harrow London Borough Council* (1983) 81 L.G.R. 514, D.C.; *Locker* v. *Stockport Metropolitan Borough Council* (1985) 83 L.G.R. 652, Glidewell J.; *Hastings Borough Council* v. *Tarmac Properties* (1985) 274 E.G. 925, C.A.; *Channel Shipping (Newport)* v. *Newport Borough Council* [1988] 16 E.G. 87, Kennedy J.

s. 17, see *Bexley Congregational Church* v. *Bexley L.B.C.* [1972] 2 Q.B. 222; [1972] 2 W.L.R. 1161; [1972] 2 All E.R. 662; *Post Office* v. *Nottingham City Council* [1976] 1 W.L.R. 624, C.A.; *Dixon* v. *Harding* [1977] 1 W.L.R. 122, D.C.; *Sheffield City Council* v. *Graingers Wines* [1977] 1 W.L.R. 1119; 242 E.G. 687, C.A.; *Camden London Borough Council* v. *Post Office* [1977] 1 W.L.R. 812, C.A.; *J.L.G. Investments* v. *Sandwell District Council* (1977) 75 L.G.R. 643, C.A.; *Tower Hamlets London Borough Council* v. *London Electricity Board* (1977) 75 L.G.R. 810, D.C.; *Windsor Securities* v. *Liverpool City Council* (1978) 77 L.G.R. 502, C.A.; *Bar Hill Development* v. *South Cambridgeshire District Council* (1979) 252 E.G. 915, D.C.; *Provident Mutual Life Insurance* v. *Derby City Council; Fenclose Securities* v. *Derby City Council* [1981] 1 W.L.R. 173, H.L.; *Brent London Borough Council* v. *Ladbroke Rentals* (1980) 258 E.G. 857, C.A.; *Drake Investments* v. *Lewisham London Borough Council* (1983) 23 R. & V.R. 150, Sir Douglas Frank Q.C.; *Camden London*

1967—cont.

9. General Rate Act 1967—cont.

Borough Council v. Bromley Park Gardens Estates, The Times, October 7, 1985, McPherson J.; Hastings Borough Council v. Tarmac Properties (1985) 83 L.G.R. 629, C.A.; Trendworthy Two v. Islington London Borough Council (1987) 282 E.G. 1125, C.A.

s. 17, amended: 1974, c.7, s.15; repealed in pt.: ibid., sch.8.

s. 17A, see Dixon v. Harding [1977] 1 W.L.R. 122, D.C.; Royal Borough of Kensington and Chelsea v. Victoria Wine (1977) 75 L.G.R. 835, D.C.; Nuneaton Borough Council v. Groatlan Property Holdings (1977) 243 E.G. 455, D.C.; Brent London Borough Council v. Alfa-Romeo (G.B.) (1977) 242 E.G. 1053; 75 L.G.R. 685, D.C.; Windsor Securities v. Liverpool City Council (1978) 77 L.G.R. 502, C.A.; Post Office v. Oxford City Council (1979) 77 L.G.R. 534, D.C.; Westminster City Council v. Haymarket Publishing [1981] 1 W.L.R. 677, C.A.

ss. 17A, 17B, repealed: order 80/2015.

s. 17B, see Royal Borough of Kensington and Chelsea v. Victoria Wine (1977) 75 L.G.R. 835, D.C.; Westminster City Council v. Haymarket Publishing [1981] 1 W.L.R. 677, C.A.

s. 17B, regs. 75/1022.

s. 19, see Gilbard v. Amey Roadstone Corporation (1974) 73 L.G.R. 43, C.A.; Baker, Britt and Co. v. Hampsher (1976) 239 E.G. 971, H.L.; Eldred v. Playle (1976) 240 E.G. 219, C.A.; Black v. Oliver [1978] 2 W.L.R. 923, C.A.; Edmondson v. Teesside Textiles [1984] R.A. 247; (1985) 83 L.G.R. 317, C.A.; Imperial College of Science and Technology v. Ebdon (V.O.) and Westminster City Council [1986] R.A. 233, C.A.; R. v. Hackney London Borough Council, ex p. S. G. Warburg Group Management (1988) 28 R.V.R. 75, D.C.

s. 19, amended: 1980, c.65, s.29; 1984, c.33, sch.1; 1986, c.44, sch.7; repealed in pt.: 1980, c.65, s.29, sch.34; 1986, c.44, sch.7.

s. 19A, order 87/604.

s. 19A, added: 1980, c.65, s.30.

ss. 19, 20, see Addis v. Clement (Valuation Officer) (1987) 85 L.G.R. 489; (1987) 281 E.G. 683, C.A.

s. 20, see K Shoe Shops v. Hardy [1983] 1 W.L.R. 1273, H.L.; Clement (V.O.) v. Addis [1988] 1 W.L.R. 301, H.L.

s. 20, amended: 1980, c.65, s.30; repealed in pt.: ibid.sch.34; 1984, c.33, sch.1.

s. 21, see Manchester Marine v. Duckworth [1973] 1 W.L.R. 1431; [1973] 3 All E.R. 838, C.A.; Edmondson v. Teesside Textiles [1984] R.A. 247; (1985) 83 L.G.R. 317, C.A.

s. 21, order 74/413.

s. 21, amended: 1974, c.7, s.18; repealed in pt.: ibid., sch.8.

s. 22, repealed: ibid.

s. 23, amended: 1984, c.33, sch.1.

s. 24, see Arsenal Football Club v. Ende [1976] 3 W.L.R. 508, C.A.; Arsenal Football Club v. Smith [1977] 2 W.L.R. 974; [1977] 2 All E.R. 267, H.L.

1967—cont.

9. General Rate Act 1967—cont.

s. 25, amended: 1984, c.33, sch.1.

s. 26, see Cresswell v. B.O.C. [1980] 3 All E.R. 443, C.A.; Corser v. Gloucester- shire Marketing Society (1980) 257 E.G. 825, C.A.; Prior (Valuation Officer) v. Sovereign Chicken [1984] 2 All E.R. 289, C.A.; Hayes v. Lloyd [1985] 1 W.L.R. 714, H.L.; Hemens (V.O.) v. Whitsbury Farm and Stud [1988] 2 W.L.R. 72; [1988] 1 All E.R. 72, H.L.

s. 26, amended: regs. 78/318.

s. 26A, added: 1980, c.65, s.31.

s. 28, amended: 1984, c.33, sch.1.

s. 30, amended: 1980, c.65, sch.33; repealed in pt.: ibid., sch.34.

s. 31, see Cakebread (V.O.) v. Severn Trent Water Authority [1988] R.A. 290, C.A.

s. 31, substituted: 1988, c.41, s.122.

ss. 32, 32A, 32B, substituted: 1984, c.33, sch.1.

s. 32A, amended: 1985, c.9, sch.2.

s. 33, orders 72/1625; 73/1459; 76/391; 79/1373; 86/1365.

s. 33, substituted: 1986, c.44, sch.7.

s. 33A, added: 1982, c.23, sch.3; 1986, c.44, sch.7.

s. 34, see Tower Hamlets London Borough Council v. London Electricity Board (1977) 75 L.G.R. 810, D.C.

s. 34, amended: 1984, c.33, sch.1.

s. 34A, added: ibid.

s. 35, see Milford Haven Conservancy Board v. I.R.C. (1975) 73 L.G.R. 390; [1976] 1 W.L.R. 817, C.A.; Harwich Dock Co. v. I.R.C. (1978) 76 L.G.R. 238, H.L.

s. 35, orders 72/1910; 73/654.

s. 35, repealed: 1974, c.7, sch.8.

s. 36, repealed: 1977, c.11, sch.

s. 37, see Rendall v. Duke of Westminster (1987) 281 E.G. 1197, C.A.

s. 38, amended: 1972, c.70, sch.13; repealed in pt.: ibid., sch.30; 1985, c.51, sch.17.

s. 39, see Swansea City Council v. Edwards and Trustees of Our Lady of Lourdes Roman Catholic Church (1976) 239 E.G. 731; Att-Gen. v. British Broadcasting Corp., The Times, June 13, 1980, H.L.; Broxtowe Borough Council v. Birch [1983] 1 All E.R. 641, C.A.; Liverpool Roman Catholic Arch-diocesan Trustees Inc. v. Mackay (V.O.) [1988] R.A. 90, Lands Tribunal.

s. 40, see Bexley Congregational Church v. Bexley L.B.C. [1972] 2 Q.B. 222; [1972] 2 W.L.R. 1161; [1972] 2 All E.R. 662; Ealing London B.C. v. Ladysholme Co. [1975] J.P.L. 32, D.C.; Oxfam v. Birmingham City Council [1975] 2 W.L.R. 874; [1975] 2 All E.R. 289, H.L.; Forces Help Society v. Canterbury City Council (1978) 77 L.G.R. 541, Slade J.

s. 40, order 78/218.

s. 40, amended: 1976, c.45, s.1.

s. 44, amended: 1988, c.4, sch.6; repealed in pt.: 1972, c.70, sch.30; 1985, c.51, sch.17.

s. 45, see Vandyk v. Oliver [1976] 2 W.L.R. 235; [1976] 1 All E.R. 466, H.L.; Royal Cross School for the Deaf v. Morton [1975] 1 W.L.R. 1002; [1975] 2 All E.R. 519, C.A.

1967—cont.

9. General Rate Act 1967—*cont.*

s. 45, repealed: 1978, c.40, sch.2.

s. 46A, see *Sheafbank Property Trust* v. *Sheffield Metropolitan District Council* [1988] R.A. 33, Schiemann J.

s. 46A, added: 1984, c.33, sch.1.

s. 48, see *Skittrall* v. *South Hams District Council* [1976] 3 All E.R. 1; *Stubbs* v. *Richmond upon Thames London Borough Council* (1988) 28 R.V.R. 35, Kennedy J.

s. 48, regs. 74/428, 1987; 75/1950; 77/1941; 78/1701; 79/1514; 81/326.

s. 48, amended: 1974, c.7, sch.7; 1980, c.65, s.33; 1984, c.33, sch.1; repealed in pt.: 1980, c.65, s.34; 1982, c.32, sch.6.

s. 49, repealed: 1974, c.7, sch.8.

s. 50, see *Smith* v. *Skinner; Gladden* v. *McMahon* (1986) 26 R.V.R. 45, D.C.

s. 50, orders 80/2011; 83/1298.

s. 50, amended: 1980, c.65, s.34; 1984, c.33, sch.1; repealed in pt.: 1980, c.65, s.34, sch.34; 1984, c.33, sch.1.

s. 51, repealed in pt.: 1974, c.7, schs.7,8.

s. 52, repealed: *ibid.*

s. 53, see *Windsor Securities* v. *Liverpool City Council* (1978) 77 L.G.R. 502, C.A.; *Investors in Industry Commercial Properties* v. *Norwich City Council* [1986] 2 W.L.R. 925, H.L.; *Polo Pictures* v. *Trafford Metropolitan Borough Council* [1987] 27 R.V.R. 74, Manchester Cown Court.

s. 54, amended: 1974, c.7, sch.7.

s. 55, see *R.* v. *Nottingham City Council, ex p. Nottinghamshire County Council; R.* v. *Mansfield District Council, ex p. Nottingham County Council, The Times*, June 17, 1988, C.A.

ss. 55, 56, amended: 1980, c.65, s.36.

s. 60, substituted: *ibid.*, s.37.

s. 67, see *County and Nimbus Estates* v. *Ealing London Borough Council* (1978) 76 L.G.R. 624, D.C.; *R.* v. *Hackney London Borough Council, ex p. S. G. Warburg Group Management* (1988) 28 R.V.R. 75, D.C.

s. 67, rules 72/1612.

s. 67, amended: 1972, c.70, sch.13.

ss. 67, 70, see *R.* v. *Valuation Officer, ex p. High Park Investments* (1987) 27 R.V.R. 84, Nolan J.

s. 68, see *K Shoe Shops* v. *Hardy* [1983] 1 W.L.R. 1273, H.L.

s. 68, order 87/921.

s. 68, amended: 1975, c.5, s.1; order 78/993; 1980, c.65, s.28, sch.33; 1984, c.33, sch.1.

s 69, see *Arsenal Football Club* v. *Ende* [1976] 3 W.L.R. 508, C.A.; *Arsenal Football Club* v. *Smith* [1977] 2 W.L.R. 974; [1977] 2 All E.R. 267, H.L.

s. 69, regs. 74/2213.

s. 69, amended: 1974, c.7, s.21; 1977, c.11, s.1; 1984, c.33, sch.1; repealed in pt.: *ibid.*

s. 70, amended: *ibid.*

s. 71, repealed in pt.: *ibid.*

s. 72, amended: *ibid.*

s. 73, repealed in pt.: *ibid.*

ss. 73, 74, see *Knight* v. *Morton (V.O.)* (1988) 28 R.V.R. 55, Lands Tribunal.

1967—cont.

9. General Rate Act 1967—*cont.*

s. 74, substituted: 1984, c.33, sch.1.

s. 75, amended: *ibid.*

s. 76, see *Att.-Gen.* v. *B.B.C.; Dible* v. *B.B.C.* [1978] 1 W.L.R. 477, D.C.; *Ellesmere Port and Neston Borough Council* v. *Shell U.K.* [1980] 1 W.L.R. 205; [1980] 1 All E.R. 283, C.A.; *R.* v. *Oxfordshire Local Valuation Panel, ex p. Oxford City Council* (1981) 259 E.G. 46, Woolf J.

s. 76, amended: 1984, c.33, sch.1.

ss. 76, 77, see *Electricity Supply Nominees* v. *Sharma (V.O.)* (1985) 276 E.G. 299, C.A.

s. 79, see *Ravenseft Properties* v. *Newham London Borough Council* [1976] 2 W.L.R. 131, C.A.; *Re Piccadilly Estate Hotels* (1978) 77 L.G.R. 79, Slade J.; *Hastings Borough Council* v. *Tarmac Properties* (1985) 83 L.G.R. 629, C.A.; *MacFarquhar* v. *Phillimore; Marks* v. *Phillimore* (1986) 279 E.G. 584, C.A.; *Rendall* v. *Duke of Westminster* (1987) 281 E.G. 1197, C.A.

s. 80, amended: 1984, c.33, sch.1.

s. 85, amended: 1985, c.51, sch.14; order 85/1884; 1988, c.4, sch. 6; repealed in pt.: 1972, c.70, sch.30; 1985, c.51, sch.17.

s. 87, see *County and Nimbus Estates* v. *Ealing London Borough Council* (1978) 76 L.G.R. 624, D.C.

s. 90, amended: 1985, c.65, sch.8.

s. 91, amended: 1985, c.51, s.14; repealed in pt.: 1972, c.70, sch.30

s. 92, amended: 1976, c.70, s.79; 1980, c.65, s.43; repealed in pt.: 1972, c.11, sch.8.

s. 94, repealed in pt.: 1985, c.51, sch.17.

s. 96, see *Evans* v. *Caterham and Warlingham U.D.C.* (1974) 72 L.G.R. 448, D.C.; *Pearce* v. *Croydon JJ.* (1977) 242 E.G. 207, D.C.

s. 96, amended: 1980, c.65, s.34.

ss. 96, 97, see *Newport Borough Council* v. *Williams, The Times,* May 8, 1982, Stephen Brown J.

s. 97, see *Banister* v. *London Borough of Islington* (1972) 225 E.G. 2301; *Hounslow London Borough Council* v. *Peake* [1974] 1 W.L.R. 26; *Ratford* v. *North- avon District Council* [1986] 3 All E.R. 193, C.A.

ss. 97, 98, amended: 1980, c.43, sch.7.

s. 99, see *R.* v. *Liverpool City JJ, ex p. Greaves; Greaves* v. *Liverpool City Council* (1979) 77 L.G.R. 440, D.C.

s. 101, see *Brintons* v. *Wyre Forest District Council* [1976] 3 W.L.R. 749.

s. 101, orders 72/820; 79/1038; 80/2013.

s. 101, amended: 1980, c.65, s.38.

s. 102, see *R.* v. *Richmond JJ., ex p. Atkins* (1983) 23 R. & V.R. 148, D.C.; *Smith (S. J.) (A Bankrupt), ex p. Braintree District Council; Braintree District Council* v. *The Bankrupt* [1988] 3 W.L.R. 327, Warner J.; *R.* v. *Birmingham Magistrates' Court, ex p. Mansell* [1988] 28 R.V.R. 112, D.C.

ss. 102, 103, see *R.* v. *Lambeth Borough Council, ex p. Sterling (Ahijah)* (1986) 26 R.V.R. 27, C.A.

1967—cont.

9. General Rate Act 1967—*cont.*

ss. 102, 103, amended: 1980, c.65, s.39.

s. 103, see *R.* v. *Liverpool City Justices, ex p. Lanckriet* (1977) 75 L.G.R. 605, D.C.; *Pearce* v. *Croydon JJ.* (1977) 242 E.G. 207, D.C.; *R.* v. *Liverpool City JJ., ex p. Greaves; Greaves* v. *Liverpool City Council* (1979) 77 L.G.R. 440, D.C.; *R.* v. *Poole JJ., ex p. Fleet* [1983] 2 All E.R. 897, Forbes J.; *R.* v. *Richmond JJ., ex p. Atkins* (1983) 23 R. & V.R. 148, D.C.; *R.* v. *Manchester City Justices, ex p. Davies (No. 1)* (1988) 152 J.P.N. 302, Webster J.; *R.* v. *Manchester City Justices, ex p. Davies (No. 2), The Independent,* August 5, 1988, C.A.; *Smith (S. J.) (A Bankrupt), ex p. Braintree District Council; Braintree District Council* v. *The Bankrupt* [1988] 3 W.L.R. 327, Warner J.; *R.* v. *Birmingham Magistrates Court, ex p. Mansell* [1988] 28 R.V.R. 112, D.C.

s. 104, amended: 1980, c.43, sch.7.

s. 105, see *Brintons* v. *Wyre Forest District Council* [1976] 3 W.L.R. 749.

s. 107, amended: 1980, c.43, sch.7.

s. 107A, added: 1980, c.65, s.40.

s. 108, substituted: 1984, c.33, sch.1

s. 112, repealed: *ibid.*

s. 113, rules 72/1612; 74/362–364; 77/454; 81/327–329; 82/1224; 83/268; 85/6, 1486; 86/1236.

s. 114, regs. 74/2213; orders 72/1625; 73/654, 1459; 76/206, 207, 490, 535; 77/454; 79/1516; 83/547, 1298; 86/1365; 88/974; rules 83/268; 86/1236.

s. 115, see *Skittrall* v. *South Hams District Council* [1976] 3 All E.R. 1; *Camden London Borough Council* v. *Post Office* [1977] 1 W.L.R. 812, C.A.; *Royal Borough of Kensington and Chelsea* v. *Victoria Wine* (1977) 242 E.G. 207, D.C.; *Westminster City Council* v. *Hailbury Investments, The Times,* December 24, 1984, D.C.; *Cakebread (V.O.)* v. *Severn Trent Water Authority* [1988] R.A. 290, C.A.; *Stubbs* v. *Richmond upon Thames London Borough Council* (1988) 28 R.V.R. 35, Kennedy J.

s. 115, amended: 1972, c.70, sch.13; 1974, c.7, sch.7; 1980, c.65, s.37; repealed in pt.: 1974, c.7, schs.7,8; 1982, c.32, sch.6.

s. 116, repealed in pt.: 1972, c.70, sch.30.

s. 117, order 73/494.

sch. 1, see *Bexley Congregational Church* v. *Bexley L.B.C.* [1972] 2 Q.B. 222; [1972] 2 W.L.R. 1161; [1972] 2 All E.R. 662; *Banister* v. *Islington London Borough Council* (1973) 71 L.G.R. 239, D.C.; *Camden London Borough Council* v. *Post Office* [1977] 1 W.L.R. 812, C.A.; *J.L.G. Investments* v. *Sandwell District Council* (1977) 75 L.G.R. 643, C.A.; *Tower Hamlets London Borough Council* v. *London Electricity Board* (1977) 75 L.G.R. 810, D.C.; *Graylaw Investments* v. *Ipswich Borough Council* (1978) 77 L.G.R. 297, C.A.; *Windsor Securities* v. *Liverpool City Council* (1978) 77 L.G.R. 502, C.A.; *Bar Hill Development* v. *South Cambridgeshire District Council*

1967—cont.

9. General Rate Act 1967—*cont.*

(1979) 252 E.G. 915, D.C.; *Provident Mutual Life Insurance* v. *Derby City Council; Fenclose Securities* v. *Derby City Council* [1981] 1 W.L.R. 173, H.L.; *Brent London Borough Council* v. *Ladbroke Rentals* (1980) 258 E.G. 857, C.A.; *Tower Hamlets London Borough Council* v. *St. Katherine by the Tower* (1982) 264 E.G. 529, McCullough J; *Drake Investments* v. *Lewisham London Borough Council* (1983) 23 R. & V.R. 150, Sir Douglas Frank, Q.C.; *R.* v. *Liverpool City Council, ex p. Caplin* (1983) 24 R. & V.R. 132, Nolan J.; *Camden London Borough Council* v. *Bromley Park Gardens Estates* (1985) 276 E.G. 928, McPherson J.; *Hastings Borough Council* v. *Tarmac Properties* (1985) 83 L.G.R. 629; (1985) 274 E.G. 925, C.A.; *Trendworthy Two* v. *Islington London Borough* (1985) 277 E.G. 539, Mervyn Davies J.; *Investors in Industry Commercial Properties* v. *Norwich City Council* [1986] 2 W.L.R. 925, H.L.; *Rialto Builders* v. *Barnet London Borough Council* (1986) 26 R.V.R. 120, Wood Green Crown Court; *Hailbury Investments* v. *Westminster City Council, The Times,* October 17, 1986, H.L.; *Debenhams* v. *Westminster City Council* [1986] 3 W.L.R. 1063, H.L.; *London Merchant Securities* v. *Islington London Borough Council* [1987] 3 W.L.R. 173, H.L.; *Trendworthy Two* v. *Islington London Borough Council* [1988] 2 W.L.R. 681, H.L.; *Stubbs* v. *Richmond upon Thames London Borough Council* (1988) 28 R.V.R. 35, Kennedy J.

sch. 1, regs. 74/1563, 75/226; 76/982; 77/1515; 84/221; 85/258; order 80/2012.

sch. 1, amended: 1974, c.7, s.15; 1979, c.46, sch.4; 1980, c.65, s.42; 1985, c.51, sch.14; repealed in pt.: 1972, c.70, sch.30; 1979, c.46, schs.4,5; 1980, c.65, sch.34; 1985, c.51, sch.17.

sch. 2, repealed: 1980, c.65, sch.34.

sch. 3, amended: 1972, c.60, s.6; 1986, c.44, sch.7.

sch. 4, see *Cakebread (V.O.)* v. *Severn Trent Water Authority* [1988] R.A. 290, C.A.

sch. 4, orders 72/907; 73/1962; regs. 75/540.

sch. 4, amended: regs. 75/540; repealed in pt.: 1972, c.70, sch.30; regs. 75/540.

sch. 5, orders 73/2140; 77/481, 585; 80/494; 81/506; amended: orders 77/585; 80/494; 81/506; 1984, c.33, sch.1; repealed in pt.: order 78/1174(S.); 1984, c.33, sch.1.

sch. 6, orders 72/1692; 79/1373.

sch. 6, substituted: 1986, c.44, sch.7.

sch. 7, order 72/1691; amended: order 76/489; repealed in pt.: *ibid.*: 1982, c.32, sch.6.

sch. 8, amended: order 78/218.

sch. 9, order 72/81.

schs. 9, 11, repealed: 1974, c.7, sch.8.

sch. 10, see *Evans* v. *Caterham and Warlingham U.D.C.* (1974) 72 L.G.R. 448, D.C.; *Smith* v. *Skinner; Gladden* v. *McMahon* (1986) 26 R.V.R. 45, D.C.

CAP.

1967—cont.

9. General Rate Act 1967—cont.
sch. 10, amended: 1980, c.65, s.34; repealed in pt.: ibid., s.34, sch.34; 1982, c.32, sch.6.
sch. 13, see Skittrall v. South Hams District Council [1976] 3 All E.R. 1; Royal Borough of Kensington and Chelsea v. Victoria Wine (1977) 242 E.G. 207, D.C.
sch. 13, amended: 1985, c.71, sch.2.

10. Forestry Act 1967.
s. 1, amended: 1985, c.31, s.4.
s. 2, amended: 1981, c.39, s.5.
s. 4, repealed: 1979, c.21, sch.2.
s. 8A, added: 1981, c.39, s.4.
s. 9, regs. 72/91; 74/1817; 77/1954; 81/1476; 85/1572, 1958; 88/970.
s. 9, amended: 1972, c.52, sch.21; 1979, c.21, sch.1; regs. 85/1958; repealed in pt.: 1979, c.21, sch.2.
ss. 10, 11, 14–16, 19–21, 23–26, regs. 79/791.
ss. 10, 17B, 24, 25, regs. 87/632.
s. 17, see Cullen v. Jardine [1985] Crim.L.R. 688, D.C.
ss. 17A–17C, added: 1986, c.30, sch.1.
s. 24, amended: 1982, c.48, schs.3,6(S.).
s. 25, regs. 88/970.
s. 27, amended; 1986, c.30, sch.1.
s. 32, regs. 72/91; 74/1817; 77/1954; 79/791, 792; 81/1476; 85/1572, 1958; 85/1958; 87/632.
s. 35, amended: 1972, c.52, sch.21; 1986, c.30, s.1.
s. 39, amended: 1981, c.39, s.1; repealed in pt.: ibid., sch.
s. 40, amended: 1973, c.65, sch.27; 1981, c.39, s.5; order 74/595; repealed in pt.: 1986, c.44, sch.9.
s. 41, amended: 1981, c.39, s.3; repealed in pt.: ibid., s.3, sch.
s. 43, amended: 1979, c.21, sch.1.
s. 46, amended: 1972, c.71, sch.6; bye-laws 72/303; 75/918, 919.
ss. 46, 47, bye-laws 82/648.
ss. 46, 48, amended: 1982, c.48, schs.3, 6(S.).
sch. 1, amended: 1972, c.11, s.28, schs.6,8; c.41, sch.28; orders 75/1137; 84/539.
sch. 3, amended: 1972, c.52, sch.21.
sch. 5, repealed in part: S.L.R. 1974.

12. Teachers' Superannuation Act 1967.
repealed: 1972, c.11, sch.8.
s. 7, regs. 72/360.

13. Parliamentary Commissioner Act 1967.
order 87/661.
s. 1, amended: 1987, c.39, s.2; repealed in pt.: 1975, c.24, sch.3; c.25, sch.3.
s. 2, amended: 1976, c.48, s.6; repealed in pt.: ibid., sch.
s. 3, amended: 1987, c.39, s.3.
s. 3A, added: ibid., s.6.
s. 4, orders 72/1716; 75/1033; 77/816; 78/616; 79/1705; 81/1537; 86/1889; 88/585.
s. 4, substituted: 1987, c.39, s.1.
s. 5, orders 79/915; 81/736; 83/1707; 86/1168; 87/661.
s. 6, amended: 1978, c.51, sch.16; c.52, sch.11; 1981, c.11, s.1.

CAP.

1967—cont.

13. Parliamentary Commissioner Act 1967—cont.
s. 7, repealed in pt. (S.): 1978, c.29, s.95.
s. 8, amended: 1978, c.51, sch.16; repealed in pt. (S.): 1978, c.29, s.95.
s. 11, amended: 1978, c.51, sch.16; c.52, sch.11; 1987, c.39, s.4.
s. 11A, added: ibid.
s. 12, amended: 1978, c.51, sch.16.
ss. 13, 14, amended: 1987, c.39, s.1.
sch. 1, amended: 1972, c.11, sch.6; 1981, c.20, sch.3; regs. 72/494.
sch. 2, substituted: 1987, c.39, s.1, sch.1; order 87/2039; 1988, c.19, sch. 3; c.34, sch.5; c.40, sch.12; c.43, sch.2; c.50, sch.17; order 88/1843; repealed in pt.: orders 87/2039; 88/1843; 1988, c.19, sch.4.
sch. 3, amended: 1972, c.58, sch.6; 1973, c.32, sch.4; 1977, c.49, sch.14; 1978, c.29, sch.15; 1980, c.53, sch.1; orders 79/915; 81/736; 83/1707; 86/1168; 87/661; 1987, c.39, s.1; . repealed in pt.: order 87/661.

14. Licensing (Certificates in Suspense) (Scotland) Act 1967.
repealed: 1976, c.66, sch.8.

16. Teachers of Nursing Act 1967.
repealed: 1979, c.36, sch.8.

17. Iron and Steel Act 1967.
repealed: 1975, c.64, sch.7.
s. 4, see British Steel Corporation v. Chant; British Steel Corporation v. Portman [1974] 1 I.T.R. 110, D.C.; [1974] I.C.R. 540, C.A.
s. 31, repealed in pt.: 1978, c.44, sch.17.

18. Local Government (Termination of Reviews) Act 1967.
repealed: S.L.R. 1976.

19. Private Places of Entertainment (Licensing) Act 1967.
s. 1, amended: 1972, c.70, sch.29; 1982, c.30, sch.2.
s. 2, amended: 1982, c.30, sch.2; 1984, c.46, sch.5; repealed in pt.: 1985, c.13, sch.3.
s. 6, repealed: 1982, c.30, sch.7.
sch., amended: 1972, c.70, sch.29; 1982, c.30, sch.2; 1985, c.51, sch.8; repealed in pt.: 1972, c.70, sch.30; 1985, c.51, sch.17.

20. Housing (Financial Provisions, Etc.) (Scotland) Act 1967.
repealed: 1987, c.26, sch.24.

22. Agriculture Act 1967.
s. 1, amended: 1986, c.49, s.7.
s. 1A, added: 1976, c.55, s.3.
ss. 2, substituted: ibid., sch.1.
ss. 4, 7, amended: 1984, c.30, sch.10.
s. 8, amended: 1985, c.72, sch.12.
s. 9, amended: 1976, c.34, sch.5; order 79/578.
ss. 10–12, repealed; S.L.R. 1986.
s. 12, orders 72/700, 701, 727, 728, 779, 780; 73/865; 76/2058; schemes 74/1905, 1998; 76/2057.
s. 13, orders 75/721; 79/393; 81/1066; 88/838.
s. 13, amended: 1981, c.22, sch.5; 1986, c.49, s.7; repealed in pt.: ibid, s.7, sch.4.
s. 13A, order 87/1303.
s. 16, order 72/460.

1967—cont.

22. Agriculture Act 1967—cont.

s. 19, amended: 1985, c.9, sch.2.

s. 21, repealed in pt.: 1977, c.38, sch.5.

s. 23, amended (S.): 1984, c.54, sch.9.

s. 25, amended: 1976, c.55, sch.1; 1984, c.30.sch.10; repealed in pt.: 1976, c.55, sch.4.

ss. 26, orders 76/2125, 2126; scheme 73/1404.

s. 26, amended: 1972, c.62, s.9, sch.4; scheme 73/1404; 1985, c.5, sch.14; repealed in pt.: 1972, c.62, sch.6; S.L.R. 1986.

s. 27, orders: 73/1403; 76/2125, 2126; schemes 81/1709; 83/1882.

s. 27, amended: 1972, c.62, s.9; orders 73/1403; 76/1771; 1986, c.5, sch.14.

s. 28, amended: *ibid.*

s. 29, amended: *ibid.*; repealed in pt.: 1977, c.12, sch.2.

s. 34, order 72/435.

s. 35, orders 73/1403; 76/2125, 2126; schemes 73/1404; 83/1949.

s. 40, see *R.* v. *Agricultural Land Tribunal (Wales), ex p. Hughes* (1980) 225 E.G. 703, D.C.

s. 40, scheme 73/1404; orders 76/2125, 2126.

ss. 43, 44, repealed; S.L.R. 1986.

s. 45, amended: 1975, c.76, sch.1; repealed in pt.: *ibid.*, sch.2.

s. 48, amended: 1977, c.12, sch.1; 1986, c.5, sch.14.

s. 50, amended: 1981, c.67, sch.4.

ss. 50, 52, amended: 1972, c.52, sch.21.

s. 51, amended: 1981, c.67, sch.4; repealed in pt.: *ibid.*, sch.6.

ss. 51, 52, amended: regs. 78/244.

s. 58, amended: 1983, c.3, sch.2; repealed in pt.: *ibid.*, sch.3.

s. 59, repealed in pt.: *ibid.*

s. 60, amended: *ibid.*, sch.2.

s. 61, amended; order 86/817; repealed in pt.: S.L.R. 1986.

ss. 61, 62, schemes 77/846; 80/1382; 83/1157, 1949; 85/334; orders 77/847; 80/636; 83/744; 86/817.

s. 62, amended. order 86/817.

s. 64, orders 73/2102; 79/323; 84/275.

s. 64, amended: 1984, c.20, s.1; repealed in pt.: 1972, c.68, sch.3.

s. 65, repealed in pt.: 1972, c.68, sch.3.

s. 66, repealed: 1981, c.22, sch.6.

s. 67, amended: 1975, c.18, sch.2; c.60, sch.4.

s. 69, repealed in pt.: S.L.R. 1986.

s. 70, orders 72/492; 73/204, 502.

s. 72, amended: 1973, c.36, sch.6.

s. 73, repealed: 1975, c.24, sch.3; c.25, sch.3.

s. 75, amended: 1972, c.70, sch.30.

sch. 1, amended: 1976, c.55, sch.1; repealed in pt.: 1972, c.11. schs. 4, 8; 1976, c.55, sch. 4.

sch. 3, amended: 1972, c.62, s.10; 1975, c.76, sch.1; 1980, c.58, sch.3; 1986, c.5, sch.14; repealed in pt.: 1975, c.76, schs.1,2.

sch. 5, amended: 1981, c.67, sch.4; repealed in pt.: *ibid.*, sch.6.

sch. 6, repealed in pt.: 1983, c.3, sch.3.

1967—cont.

24. Slaughter of Poultry Act 1967.

s. 1, amended: 1974, c.3, sch.3; 1984, c.40, s.5, sch.1; 1986, c.14, sch.3; repealed in pt.: 1984, c.40, ss.5, 17, sch.2.

s. 2, see *Malins* v. *Cole & Attard,* Knightsbridge Crown Court.

s. 2, amended and repealed in pt.: 1984, c.40, sch.1.

s. 3, regs. 83/687; 84/2056.

s. 3, substituted: 1984, c.40, s.6.

s. 3A, added: *ibid.*, s.7.

s. 4, substituted: *ibid.*, s.8.

s. 6, substituted: *ibid.*, s.9.

s. 7, order 78/201.

s. 7, repealed in pt.: 1984, c.40, schs.1,2.

s. 8, amended: 1972, c.70, sch.30; 1973, c.65, sch.27: order 78/272; 1984, c.40, schs.1,2.

25. National Insurance (Industrial Injuries) (Amendment) Act 1967.

repealed: 1975, c.18, sch.1.

27. Merchant Shipping (Load Lines) Act 1967.

s. 2, rules 75/595; 79/1267; 80/641.

s. 3, order 81/236.

s. 3, amended: 1979, c.39, sch.6.

s. 4, amended: *ibid.*, sch.6; repealed in pt.: *ibid.*, schs.6,7.

ss. 5, 9, amended: *ibid.*, sch.6.

s. 10, regs. 72/1841.

s. 11, repealed in pt.: 1979, c.39, s.28, sch.7.

s. 13, amended: *ibid.*, sch.6.

s. 17, repealed in pt.: *ibid.*, s.28, sch.7.

s. 24, amended: *ibid.*, sch.6; repealed in pt.: *ibid.*, sch.7.

s. 26, regs. 81/363; 82/120; 83/1167; 85/1607; 87/63; 88/1485.

s. 27, repealed in pt.: 1979, c.39, sch.7.

s. 28, orders 75/412; 81/1540.

s. 31, order 77/1875.

sch. 1, repealed in pt.: 1979, c.39, sch.7.

28. Superannuation (Miscellaneous Provisions) Act 1967.

s. 1, repealed: 1972, c.11, sch.8.

s. 2, repealed in pt.: *ibid.*; 1981, c.20, sch.4.

s. 3, amended: 1976, c.33, s.11; 1981, c.20, sch.3; repealed in pt.: 1973, c.15, sch.5; c.41, sch.13; 1981, c.54, sch.7.

s. 4, order 72/229.

ss. 4, 5, repealed: 1973, c.21, sch.2.

s. 6, amended: 1977, c.49, sch.15.

s. 7, amended: 1972, c.11, sch.9; 1977, c.49, sch.15; 1978, s.29, sch.16(S.); repealed in pt.: 1972, c.11, sch.8; 1973, c.32, sch.5.

s. 8, repealed: 1972, c.11, sch.8.

s. 9, repealed: 1978, c.44, sch.17.

s. 10, repealed: 1972, c.48, sch.4.

s. 11, repealed in pt.: 1972, c.11, sch.8; 1976, c.35, sch.3.

s. 13, regs. 83/990; 87/157, 158, 1699(S.), 1700(S.).

s. 13, amended: 1973, c.38, sch.27; repealed in part: 1975, c.18, sch.1.

s. 14, repealed: 1984, c.36, sch.5.

s. 15, amended: 1972, c.11, s.14; order 74/520.

1967—cont.

28. Superannuation (Miscellaneous Provisions) Act 1967—cont.
s. 16, repealed: 1972, c.11, sch.8.
s. 18, amended: ibid., sch.6.

29. Housing Subsidies Act 1967.
repealed: 1985, c.71, sch.1.
s. 26, regs. 75/1302, 1303.
s. 27, orders 72/1507; 74/473; 75/1451; 78/10; 80/1636, 2040; 81/253, 520, 979.
s. 28, orders 73/1928; 74/1005; 75/1240; 77/1336; 78/1699; 79/894.
s. 32, regs. 75/1303; orders 72/1507; 74/473; 75/1451; 78/10; 80/1636, 2040; 81/253, 520, 979.

30. Road Safety Act 1967.
repealed: 1972, c.20, sch.9.
see Smith v. Fyfe [1972] Crim.L.R. 252; 1971 S.L.T. 89; Farrell v. Brown [1972] Crim.L.R. 250; 1971 S.L.T. 40; McIlhargey v. Herron [1973] Crim.L.R. 768
s. 1, see Gill v. Forster [1970] R.T.R. 45; Ritchie v. Pine, 1972 S.L.T. 2; [1972] Crim.L.R. 251; Kiernan v. Willcock [1972] Crim.L.R. 248; [1972] R.T.R. 270; Coombs v. Kehoe [1972] 1 W.L.R. 797; [1972] 2 All E.R. 55; [1972] R.T.R. 224; James v. Hall [1972] R.T.R. 228; Pugh v. Knipe [1972] Crim.L.R. 247; [1972] R.T.R. 286; Milliner v. Thorne [1972] Crim.L.R. 245; [1972] R.T.R. 279; Darnell v. Portal [1972] R.T.R. 483; Everitt v. Trevorrow [1972] Crim.L.R. 566; Rowlands v. Harper [1972] R.T.R. 469, D.C.; Alexander v. Latter [1972] R.T.R. 441, D.C.; Hudson v. Hornsby [1973] R.T.R. 4, D.C.; R. v. Stratford-upon-Avon Justices [1973] Crim.L.R. 241, D.C.; R. v. Lawrence (Paul Antony) [1973] 1 W.L.R. 329, [1973] 1 All E.R. 364, C.A.; Endean v. Evans [1973] Crim.L.R. 448; R. v. Thomas [1973] R.T.R. 325; Wimperis v. Griffin [1973] Crim.L.R. 533, D.C.; R. v. Britton [1973] R.T.R. 502, C.A.; R. v. Bedford and Sharnbrook JJ., ex p. Ward [1974] Crim.L.R. 109, D.C.; Seaton v. Allan, 1974 S.L.T. 234.
ss. 1, 2, see Harris v. Croson [1973] R.T.R. 57, D.C.; R. v. Herd [1973] R.T.R. 165, C.A.; R. v. Tulsiani [1973] Crim.L.R. 186; Hogg v. Veitch, 1973 S.L.T. 61.
ss. 1–3, see Goodley v. Kelly [1973] R.T.R. 125, D.C.; R. v. Porter [1973] R.T.R. 116, C.A.
ss. 1, 3, see R. v. Orrell [1972] R.T.R. 14; R. v. Welsby [1972] Crim.L.R. 512; [1972] R.T.R. 301.
ss. 1, 3, 7, see McIlhargey v. Herron, 1972 S.L.T. 185; Clark v. Stenlake [1972] R.T.R. 276; Kiernan v. Willcock [1972] Crim.L.R. 248; [1972] R.T.R. 270.
ss. 1, 3, 32, sch. 1, see Norman v. Magill [1972] R.T.R. 81.
ss. 1, 5, see Milliner v. Thorne [1972] Crim.L.R. 245; [1972] R.T.R. 279; Owen v. Innes [1972] R.T.R. 489, D.C.
ss. 1, 5, 7, see R. v. Slade [1974] R.T.R. 20, C.A.
ss. 1, 7, see R. v. Parsons [1972] R.T.R. 425, C.A.

1967—cont.

30. Road Safety Act 1967—cont.
s. 2, see R. v. Morris [1972] 1 W.L.R. 228; [1972] 1 All E.R. 384; 56 Cr.App.R. 175; Williams v. Jones [1972] R.T.R. 5; Mendham v. Lawrence [1972] Crim.L.R. 113; 116 S.J. 80; [1972] R.T.R. 153; Taylor v. Houston, 1971 S.L.T. 39; Bryant v. Morris [1972] Crim.L.R. 115; [1972] R.T.R. 214; Sakhuja v. Allan [1972] 2 W.L.R. 1116; 116 S.J. 375; [1972] 2 All E.R. 311; [1972] R.T.R. 315; 56 Cr.App.R. 464; R. v. Masters [1972] R.T.R. 492, D.C.; Swankie v. Milne, 1973 S.L.T.(Notes) 28, High Court of Justiciary; Edkins v. Knowles [1973] 2 W.L.R. 977; [1973] 2 All E.R. 503; R. v. Bates [1973] 1 W.L.R. 718; [1973] 2 All E.R. 509; R. v. Fardy [1973] R.T.R. 268; R. v. Mayne [1973] R.T.R. 448, C.A.; R. v. Gready [1974] R.T.R. 16, C.A.; R. v. Needham [1974] R.T.R. 201, C.A.
ss. 2, 3, see R. v. Haslam [1972] R.T.R. 297; Brooks v. Ellis [1972] 2 All E.R. 1204; R. v. Kelly [1972] R.T.R. 447, C.A.; Glendinning v. Bell [1973] R.T.R. 52, D.C.; R. v. Guttridge [1973] R.T.R. 135, C.A.; Bourlet v. Porter [1973] 1 W.L.R. 866; [1973] 2 All E.R. 800.
ss. 2, 7, see Halbert v. Stewart, 1971 S.L.T. 43; Darnell v. Portal [1972] R.T.R. 483, D.C.; R. v. Holah [1973] 1 W.L.R. 127; [1973] 1 All E.R. 106, C.A.
s. 3, see R. v. Wallace [1972] R.T.R. 9; [1972] Crim.L.R. 186, C.A.; Burke v. Jobson [1972] R.T.R. 59; [1972] Crim.L.R. 187; Macneil v. England [1972] Crim.L.R. 255; 1971 S.L.T. 103; R. v. Nicholls [1972] 1 W.L.R. 502; 116 S.J. 298; [1972] 2 All E.R. 186; [1972] R.T.R. 308; 56 Cr.App.R. 382; Dickson v. Atkins [1972] Crim.L.R. 185; [1972] R.T.R. 209; R. v. Walter [1972] Crim.L.R. 381; R. v. Hyams [1973] 1 W.L.R. 13; 116 S.J. 886; [1972] 3 All E.R. 651; R. v. Weir [1972] 3 All E.R. 906; Rushton v. Higgins [1972] R.T.R. 456, D.C.; Jones v. Roberts [1973] R.T.R. 26, D.C.; Cunliffe v. Bleasdale [1973] R.T.R. 90, D.C.; Hogg v. Lockhart, 1973 S.L.T.(Sh.Ct.) 40; R. v. Lennard [1973] 1 W.L.R. 483, C.A.; R. v. Chippendale [1973] R.T.R. 236; R. v. Paduch (1972) 57 Cr.App.R. 676, C.A.; R. v. Reid (Phillip) [1973] 1 W.L.R. 1283, C.A.; R. v. Najran [1973] R.T.R. 451, C.A.; R. v. Mayne [1973] R.T.R. 448, C.A.
ss. 3, 5, see Hockin v. Weston [1972] R.T.R. 136.
s. 9, regs. 72/195, 806.
s. 19, sch. 1, see Crawford v. Scottish Traffic Area Licensing Authority, 1974 S.L.T.(Sh.Ct.) 11.

31. Commonwealth Settlement Act 1967.
repealed: S.L.R. 1976.

32. Development of Inventions Act 1967.
s. 1, regs. 86/431.
s. 4, order 78/382.
s. 4, amended: 1975, c.68, s.26; order 78/382.
s. 12, amended: 1985, c.9, sch.2.
s. 14, repealed: 1973, c.36, sch.6.
sch., regs. 86/431.
sch., amended: 1972, c.11, sch.8.

1967—cont.

33. Air Corporations Act 1967.
repealed: 1978, c.8, sch.2.

34. Industrial Injuries and Diseases (Old Cases) Act 1967.
repealed: 1975, c.18, sch.1.
s. 2, schemes 72/1288; 73/1440; 74/943; 75/513.
ss. 5, 7, schemes, 72/1289; 73/1439; 74/944; 75/514.

36. Remuneration of Teachers (Scotland) Act 1967.
repealed: 1980, c.44, sch.5.
s. 2, orders 77/1530, 1756.
ss. 2, 4, 8, order 72/1281.
ss. 2, 8, orders 73/86, 544; 74/1721; 75/1928; 76/692, 1959; 77/44; 78/68, 1747.

39. National Health Service (Family Planning) Act 1967.
repealed: 1973, c.32, sch.5.

40. Shipbuilding Industry Act 1967.
repealed: 1972, c.63, sch.4.

41. Marine, etc., Broadcasting (Offences) Act 1967.
s. 3, amended: 1981, c.61, sch.7; order 86/948.
s. 5, amended: 1988, c.48, sch.7.
s. 6, repealed in pt.: 1975, c.59, sch.6.
s. 9, repealed in pt.: 1987, c.49, sch.2.

42. Advertisements (Hire-Purchase) Act 1967.
repealed: 1974, c.39, sch.5; *order 80/50.

43. Legal Aid (Scotland) Act 1967.
repealed: 1986, c.47, sch.5.
s. 1, see *Rae, Petr.* High Court of Justiciary, December 16, 1981; *Harper, Petr.,* 1982 S.L.T. 232; *McColl* v. *Strathclyde Regional Council* (O.H.), 1983 S.L.T. 616; *McLachlan, Petr.,* 1987 S.C.C.R. 195.
s. 1, regs. 76/512; 79/1522; 82/1877.
s. 2, see *Hanley* v. *James Bowen & Sons* (O.H.), 1976 S.L.T.(Notes) 32; *Hill* v. *McMillan,* 1980 S.L.T.(Sh.Ct.) 3; *Cameron* v. *Parker* (O.H.), 1980 S.L.T.(Notes) 21; *Boughen* v. *Scott,* 1983 S.L.T.(Sh.Ct.) 94; *Roy, Nicholson, Becker & Day* v. *Clarke,* 1984 S.L.T.(Sh.Ct.) 16; *Johnston* v. *Johnston* (O.H.), July 29, 1983; *Jeffrey* v. *Jeffrey,* 1987 S.L.T. 488; *Clelland* v. *Clelland* (O.H.), 1988 S.L.T. 674; *Austin* v. *Austin* (O.H.), 1988 S.L.T. 676; *Gilbert's Tr.* v. *Gilbert* (O.H.), 1988 S.L.T. 680; *Stewart* v. *Stewart,* 1988 S.C.L.R. 477.
s. 2, regs. 73/1802; 74/1311; 75/901, 1862; 76/1847; 77/1981; 78/1817; 79/409, 1521, 1522; 83/532, 1835, 1865; 85/1859.
s. 3, regs. 73/1802; 74/1311; 75/901, 1862; 76/1847; 77/1981; 78/622, 1817; 79/409, 1521; 83/532, 1835, 1865; 85/1859; 86/1358.
s. 4, regs. 72/1756, 1757; 73/1561, 1562; 77/1761, 1762; 78/1565, 1566; 79/324, 325, 1390; 80/1792, 1793; 86/253, 254.
s. 5, regs. 72/1757; 74/1311.
s. 6, see *Drummond* v. *Law Society of Scotland,* 1980 S.C. 175.
s. 8, scheme: Legal Aid (Scot.) (Crim. Proceed.) Scheme 1975.
s. 11, regs. 77/1663; 79/1390, 1522.

1967—cont.

43. Legal Aid (Scotland) Act 1967—*cont.*
s. 13, see *Bell* v. *Fife County Council,* 1975 S.L.T.(Notes) 4; *McKee* v. *McKee,* 1980 S.L.T.(Sh.Ct.) 6; *Wilson* v. *Wilson* (O.H.), 1980 S.L.T.(Notes) 68.
ss. 13, 14, see *Walker* v. *Walker* (O.H.), 1987 S.L.T. 129.
s. 14A, regs. 84/210, 519, 520; 85/337, 554, 557; 86/673, 674, 681; 87/894, 1355, 1357; 88/422, 922, 1108, 1110, 1111.
s. 15, regs. 72/1755–1757; 73/545, 1561, 1562, 1738, 1802, 1803; 74/1197, 1312; 75/678, 717, 901, 902, 1746, 1862, 1863; 76/333, 512, 1706, 1846, 1847; 77/213, 507, 1663, 1761, 1762, 1981, 1982; 78/622, 1564, 1817, 1818; 79/156, 409, 410, 1390, 1521, 1522; 80/1151, 1791; 82/216, 507, 622, 1533, 1877; 83/384, 532, 533, 1665, 1777, 1835, 1836; 84/210, 519, 520, 1677, 1865, 1866; 85/337, 554, 557, 1628, 1859, 1860; 86/673, 674, 681, 1154, 1358, 1359; 87/894, 1355, 1357; 88/422, 922, 1108, 1110, 1111.
s. 16, rules 73/673, 1145, 1774; Acts of Adjournal 75/835, 836; 76/339, 371; 78/1686; 79/95, 1632; 81/387, 388, 1443; 82/121, 468; 83/972; Acts of Sederunt 76/373, 1062; 78/1889; 81/213, 734.
s. 18, see *Skeen* v. *Simpson,* 1973 S.L.T.(Sh.Ct.) 8.
s. 20, see *Walker* v. *Walker* (O.H.), 1987 S.L.T. 129.
s. 22, order 75/716.

45. Uniform Laws on International Sales Act 1967.
s. 1, order 87/2061.
s. 1, amended: 1973, c.13, s.5; 1979, c.54, sch.2; repealed in pt.: 1977, c.50, sch.4.
ss. 1, 2, order 72/973.
sch. 2, see *Butler Machine Tool Co.* v. *Ex-Cell-O Corp.* [1979] 1 W.L.R. 401, C.A.

46. Protection of Birds Act 1967.
repealed: 1981, c.69, sch.17.
s. 4, orders 80/401, 402, 404, 1839.
s. 7, orders 79/70, 99 (S.), 141 (S.); 82/23, 59.
s. 12, order 82/59.

47. Decimal Currency Act 1967.
repealed: S.L.R. 1986.

48. Industrial and Provident Societies Act 1967.
s. 3, substituted: 1985, c.9, s.26.
s. 4, amended: 1972, c.67, s.10; 1985, c.9, s.26.
s. 5, amended: *ibid.*
s. 7, regs. 84/307, 308; 86/621, 622; 88/450, 451.
sch., amended: 1972, c.67, s.10.

50. Farm and Garden Chemicals Act 1967.
s. 4, amended: 1984, c.30, sch.10.
s. 5, amended: order 78/272.

52. Tokyo Convention Act 1967.
ss. 1, 2, repealed: 1982, c.16, sch.16.
s. 2, orders 72/960; 73/762; 77/1239; 78/1889; 82/149; 85/1993.
ss. 3, 5, 6, repealed: 1982, c.16, sch.16.
s. 4, repealed in pt.: 1982, c.36, sch.3.

CAP.

1967—cont.

52. Tokyo Convention Act 1967—*cont.*
s. 4, sch., see *Cameron* v. *H. M. Advocate,*
1971 S.C. 50.
s. 6, regs. 72/187.
s. 7, orders 77/1258; 78/1534.
s. 7, repealed in pt.: 1982, c.16, sch.16; c.36,
sch.3.
s. 8, order 87/456.
s. 8, repealed in pt.: 1982, c.1, sch.2; c.16,
sch.16.
s. 9, repealed in pt.: *ibid.*

53. Prices and Incomes Act 1967.
repealed (except ss. 4 (2), (5)): 1973, c.9, sch.6.

54. Finance Act 1967.
s. 1, repealed in pt.: 1979, c.4, sch.4.
s. 2, repealed: 1979, c.3, sch.3.
s. 3, repealed: 1979, c.2, sch.6.
s. 4, repealed in pt.: 1973, c.36, sch.6; 1977,
c.36, sch.9; 1979, c.2, sch.6; c.4, sch.4.
s. 5, amended (S.): 1976, c.66, sch.7; repealed
in pt.: *ibid.,* sch.8(S.); 1979, c.2, sch.6.
s. 6, repealed: 1979, c.4, sch.4.
s. 7, amended: 1979, c.2, sch.4; repealed in
pt.: 1972, c.25, sch.7.
s. 8, repealed: 1972, c.41, sch.28.
s. 9, repealed: *ibid.;* amended: 1979, c.2, sch.5.
s. 20, see *A. W. Chapman* v. *Hennessey* [1982]
S.T.C. 214, Nourse J.
s. 25, repealed: 1972, c.41, sch.28.
s. 26, see *Lord Advocate* v. *Babcock & Wilcox*
[1972] 1 W.L.R. 488; [1972] 1 All E.R. 1130;
12 K.I.R. 329; [1972] T.R. 31; [1972] I.T.R.
168.
s. 26, repealed: 1972, c.41, sch.28.
s. 26, orders 75/1284; 76/1227.
s. 27, see *Canada Safeway* v. *I.R.C.* [1972] 2
W.L.R. 443; [1972] 1 All E.R. 666.
s. 28, see *Clarke Chapman-John Thompson* v.
I.R.C. [1974] 1 All E.R. 465.
s. 28, repealed: 1973, c.51, sch.22.
s. 29, repealed: 1986, c.41, s.79, sch.23.
s. 30, amended: 1987, c.16, s.51; repealed in
pt.: *ibid.,* s.51, sch.16.
ss. 32, 35, 37, repealed: 1979, c.14, sch.8.
s. 38, repealed: 1975, c.7, sch.13.
s. 40, orders 74/966, 1148; 79/1687; 82/1587;
85/563; 86/1181, 1832; 87/513, 898, 1492,
1988; 88/756, 1278, 1621, 2185.
s. 45, amended: 1979, c.2, sch.4; repealed in
pt.: 1979, c.14, sch.8.
sch. 5, repealed in pt.: 1979, c.4, sch.4.
sch. 6, repealed in pt.: 1973, c.36, sch.6; 1976,
c.40, sch.15; 1979, c.2, sch.6; c.4, sch.4.
sch. 7, repealed in pt.: 1977, c.45, sch.13; 1981,
c.28, sch.2; 1983, c.12, sch.2; 1988, c.17,
sch. 4; c.25, s.3.
sch. 8, repealed (S.): 1976, c.66, sch.8.
sch. 9, repealed in pt.: 1979, c.2, sch.6; c.4,
sch.4.
sch. 10, see *A. W. Chapman* v. *Hennessey*
[1982] S.T.C. 214, Nourse J.
sch. 12, repealed: 1972, c.41, sch.28.
sch. 13, repealed: 1979, c.14, sch.8.

55. Road Transport Lighting Act 1967.
repealed: 1972, c.20, sch.9.

CAP.

1967—cont.

56. Matrimonial Causes Act 1967.
repealed: 1984, c.42, sch.3.
s. 1, orders 72/1746; 73/1278; 74/1004;
75/1002, 1869; 76/17, 676, 1222, 2233;
77/939, 1624; 78/818, 1759; 80/790, 1217;
82/1769; 83/659, 713; 84/297, 1075.
s. 2, see *Re F. (A Minor)* (*Access out of Jurisdiction*) [1973] 3 W.L.R. 461; [1973] 3 All E.R.
493, Baker P.
s. 7, rules 72/1095; 73/350, 770, 1413, 1414.
s. 8, order 72/194.

57. Control of Liquid Fuel Act 1967.
repealed: 1973, c.39, sch.1.

58. Criminal Law Act 1967.
s. 1, see *Webley* v. *Buxton* [1977] 2 W.L.R. 766,
D.C.
s. 2, see *Swales* v. *Cox* (1980) 72 Cr.App.R.
171, D.C.; *Wills* v. *Bowley, The Times,* May
27, 1982, H.L.; *George* v. *Comr. of Police of
the Metropolis, The Times,* March 31, 1984,
Park J.; *Mohammed-Holgate* v. *Duke* [1984]
2 W.L.R. 600, H.L.; *Reynolds* v. *Comr. of
Police of the Metropolis, The Times,* August
4, 1984, C.A.; *R.* v. *Jackson (Kenneth)* [1985]
R.T.R. 257, C.A.; *R.* v. *Richards; R.* v. *Leeming*
(1985) 81 Cr.App.R. 125, C.A.; *Ward* v. *Chief
Constable of Avon and Somerset Constabulary, The Times,* June 26, 1986, C.A.; *Houghton* v. *Chief Constable of Greater Manchester,
The Times,* July 24, 1986, C.A.; *Castorina* v.
Chief Constable of Surrey, The Times, June
15, 1988, C.A.
s. 2, repealed: 1984, c.60, sch.7.
s. 3, see *R.* v. *Coroner for Durham County, ex
p. Att.-Gen., The Times,* June 29, 1978, D.C.;
Allen v. *Commissioner of Metropolitan Police,
The Times,* March 25, 1980, May J.; *R.* v.
Cousins [1982] 2 W.L.R. 621, C.A.; *R.* v.
Jackson (Kenneth) [1985] R.T.R. 257, C.A.; *R.*
v. *Renouf* [1986] 1 W.L.R. 522, C.A.
s. 4, see *R.* v. *Morgan* (1971) 56 Cr.App.R. 181;
R. v. *Vincent* (1972) 56 Cr.App.R. 281; *R.* v.
Kerrigan (1973) 57 Cr.App.R. 269, C.A.; *R.* v.
Spinks [1982] 1 All E.R. 587, C.A.; *R.* v.
Donald and Donald [1986] Crim.L.R. 535,
C.A.; *Holtham* v. *Commissioner of Police for
the Metropolis, The Independent,* November
26, 1987, C.A.
s. 4, amended: 1977, c.45, schs.2, 3; 1984,
c.60, sch.6; repealed in pt.: 1975, c.59, sch.6;
1977, c.45, sch.13.
ss. 4, 5, see *R.* v. *Panyiotou; R.* v. *Antoniades*
[1973] 1 W.L.R. 1032; [1973] 3 All E.R. 112,
C.A.
s. 5, amended: 1977, c.45, schs.2, 3; repealed
in pt.: *ibid.,* sch.13.
s. 6, see *R.* v. *Snewing* [1972] Crim.L.R. 267; *R.*
v. *Hodgson* [1973] 2 W.L.R. 570, C.A.; *R.* v.
Tennant [1976] Crim.L.R. 133; *R.* v. *Lambert*
[1977] Crim.L.R. 164, C.A.; (1976) 65
Cr.App.R. 12, C.A.; *R.* v. *McCready; R.* v.
Hurd [1978] 1 W.L.R. 1376, C.A.; *R.* v.
Nicholls [1978] Crim.L.R. 247, C.A.; *R.* v.
Barnard (1979) 70 Cr.App.R. 28, C.A.; *R.* v.
Collison (1980) 71 Cr.App.R. 249, C.A.; *R.* v.
Martyn Leonard Carpenter (1983) 76

1967—cont.

58. Criminal Law Act 1967—*cont.*
Cr.App.R. 320, C.A.; *Comr. of Police of the Metropolis* v. *Wilson*; *R.* v. *Jenkins* [1983] 3 W.L.R. 686, H.L.; *George* v. *Comr. of Police of the Metropolis, The Times*, March 31, 1984, Park J.; *R.* v. *Saunders* [1987] 3 W.L.R. 355, H.L.: *R.* v. *Whiting* (1987) 85 Cr.App.R. 78; [1987] Crim.L.R. 473, C.A.

s. 7, repealed: 1973, c.62, sch.6.

s. 11, amended: 1973, c.36, sch.6; repealed in pt.: 1986, c.64, sch.3.

sch. 2, amended: 1972, c.20, sch.9; c.71, sch.6; repealed in pt.: 1981, c.45, sch.; c.47, sch.; 1986, c.64, sch.3.

sch. 3, see *R.* v. *Blackpool JJ.* [1972] 1 W.L.R. 1456; [1972] 3 All E.R. 854.

60. Sexual Offences Act 1967.
s. 1, see *Knuller* v. *D.P.P.* [1972] 3 W.L.R. 143; *R.* v. *Ford* [1977] 1 W.L.R. 1083, C.A.

s. 1, amended: 1982, c.51, sch.3; repealed in pt.: *ibid.*, schs.3,4.

s. 1, 3, see *R.* v. *Courtie* [1984] 2 W.L.R. 331, H.L.

ss. 1, 4, see *R.* v. *Mucklow*, January 4, 1984, H.H. Judge Galpin, Newport, Isle of Wight Crown Court; *R.* v. *Spight* [1986] Crim.L.R. 817, C.A.

ss. 4, 5, 7, repealed in pt.: 1977, c.45, sch.13.

s. 5, see *R.* v. *Tan* [1983] 2 All E.R. 12, C.A.

s. 7, see *R.* v. *Lewis* [1979] 2 All E.R. 665, C.A.

s. 8, repealed in pt.: 1975, c.59, sch.6; 1981, c.47, sch.

s. 9, repealed: 1977, c.45, sch.13.

62. Post Office (Data Processing Service) Act 1967.
repealed: 1981, c.38, sch.6.

63. Bermuda Constitution Act 1967.
s. 1, orders 73/233; 79/459, 1310.

64. Anchors and Chain Cables Act 1967.
s. 1, regs. 87/854; 88/1485.

65. Antarctic Treaty Act 1967.
s. 1, amended: 1981, c.61, sch.7; order 86/948.

s. 6, order 88/1296.

s. 7, orders 73/1755; 77/1234, 1235; 84/1150; 86/2221; 88/587, 786.

s. 9, order 74/1109.

s. 10, orders 84/1150; 86/2221; 88/586, 587, 786.

sch.2, amended: order 87/586.

66. Welsh Language Act 1967.
rules 74/2184.

ss. 1, 2, see *Collector of Taxes* v. *Morgan*, Jan. 12, 1977.

s. 2, rules 73/358, 1272; 86/1079; regs. 74/2213; 75/1329; 76/513; 77/106; 81/63; 85/36, 713; 86/1445, 1460; orders 75/841, 1538; 78/1953; 79/368, 434; 80/1032; 87/561, 562; regs. 87/2088, 2089; 88/1265.

s. 2, amended: 1978, c.52, sch.11.

ss. 2, 3, order 76/1766; regs. 82/667; 85/1133, 1134.

s. 3, regs. 86/1445; 87/2089.

s. 4, repealed: 1978, c.30, sch.3.

1967—cont.

67. Irish Sailors and Soldiers Land Trust Act 1967.
repealed: 1987, c.48, sch.

68. Fugitive Offenders Act 1967.
s. 1, see *R.* v. *Governor of Pentonville Prison, ex p. Khubchandani* (1980) 71 Cr.App.R. 241, D.C.

s. 2, orders 74/110; 75/1213; 76/771, 1918, 2142; 78/1905; 79/460, 1712; 81/1808; 83/1901; 86/2022.

s. 2, amended: 1981, c.61, sch.7.

s. 3, substituted: 1988, c.33, sch.1.

ss. 3, 7, see *R.* v. *Governor of Pentonville Prison, ex p. Elliott* [1975] Crim.L.R. 516, D.C.; *R.* v. *Governor of Pentonville Prison, ex p. Khubchandani* [1980] Crim.L.R. 436; (1980) 71 Cr.App.R. 241, D.C.

ss. 4–7, amended: 1988, c.33, sch.1.

s. 4A, added: 1982, c.28, s.3.

s. 5, see *R.* v. *Governor of Pentonville Prison, ex p. Elliott* [1975] Crim.L.R. 516, D.C.

ss. 6–10, see *Jones* v. *H.M. Advocate*, 1975 J.C. 23.

s. 7, see *Jones* v. *Milne*, 1975 S.L.T. 2; *Government of Australia* v. *Harrod* [1975] 1 W.L.R. 745; [1975] 2 All E.R. 1, H.L.

ss. 7, 11, see *R.* v. *Governor of Pentonville Prison, ex p. Kirby (Note)* [1979] 1 W.L.R. 541, D.C.; *R.* v. *Governor of Gloucester Prison, ex p. Miller* [1979] 1 W.L.R. 587, D.C.

s. 7A, added: 1988, c.33, sch.1.

s. 8, see *Higgison* v. *Secretary of State for Scotland*, 1973 S.L.T.(Notes) 35; *R.* v. *Governor of Pentonville Prison, ex p. Narang* [1977] 2 W.L.R. 862, H.L.; *Kakis* v. *Governor of the Republic of Cyprus* [1978] 1 W.L.R. 779, H.L.; *Re Tarling* [1979] 1 All E.R. 981, Gibson J.; *Oskar* v. *Government of Australia* [1988] 2 W.L.R. 82; [1988] 1 All E.R. 183, H.L.

s. 8, amended: 1988, c.33, sch.1; repealed in pt.: *ibid.*, schs. 1, 16.

s. 9, amended: *ibid.*, sch. 1.

ss. 9, 11, see *R.* v. *Governor of Pentonville Prison, ex p. Oscar, The Times*, May 29, 1987, D.C..

s. 10, see *Oskar, Re, The Guardian*, March 2, 1988, C.A.

s. 10, amended: 1988, c.33, sch.1.

s. 11, repealed in pt.: *ibid.*, sch. 16.

s. 14, amended: *ibid.*, sch. 1.

s. 15, amended: 1973, c.62, sch.5.

s. 16, amended: 1988, c.33, sch.1; repealed in pt.: *ibid.*, sch.16.

s. 17, orders 75/2163; 79/456; 81/1803; 82/1540; 87/451–455.

s. 19, amended: 1988, c.33, sch.1.

s. 20, orders 75/2163; 76/2142; 81/1803; 87/452.

s. 22, order 81/1745.

sch.1, see *R.* v. *Governor of Pentonville Prison, ex p. Khubchandani* (1980) 71 Cr.App.R. 241, D.C.

sch. 1, repealed: 1988, c.33, sch.16.

1967—cont.

69. Civic Amenities Act 1967.
ss. 1, 3, 6, 8, 11–14, 15 (in pt.), 16, 17, repealed (S): 1972, c.52, sch.23.
s. 5, amended: 1973, c.65, sch.23.
ss. 18–24, 27, 28, repealed: 1978, c.3, sch.2.
ss. 21, 22, regs. 74/1809; 75/1894.
s. 25, repealed: S.L.R. 1976.
ss. 25, 27, order 75/1949.
s. 30, repealed in pt.: 1978, c.3, sch.2.

70. Road Traffic (Amendment) Act 1967.
repealed (except ss. 8, 10): 1972, c.20, sch.9.
s. 1, see *Wright* v. *Howard* [1973] R.T.R. 12, D.C.
ss. 1, 3, see *Piggott* v. *Sirns* [1973] R.T.R. 15, D.C.
s. 6, see *Goosey* v. *Adams* [1971] R.T.R. 465; [1972] Crim.L.R. 49; *Renouf* v. *Franklin* [1971] R.T.R. 469; [1972] Crim.L.R. 115; *Hill* v. *Hampshire Chief Constable* [1972] R.T.R. 29; *Crawford* v. *Haughton* [1972] 1 W.L.R. 572; [1972] 1 All E.R. 534; [1972] R.T.R. 125; *Baker* v. *Esau* [1973] R.T.R. 49, D.C.; *Garrett* v. *Hooper* [1973] R.T.R. 1, D.C.; *Kenyon* v. *Thorley* [1973] R.T.R. 60, D.C.

71. Aden, Perim and Kuria Muria Islands Act 1967.
s. 2, sch. repealed: 1981, c.59, sch.9.
s. 4, repealed: 1973, c.21, sch.2.
s. 5, repealed: S.L.R. 1977.
s. 6, repealed in pt.: *ibid.*
s. 8, amended: 1973, c.36, sch.6.

72. Wireless Telegraphy Act 1967.
ss. 1, 2, 13, regs. 79/563.
s. 6, amended: 1984, c.46, sch.5; repealed in pt.: *ibid.*schs.5,6.
s. 7, see *R.* v. *Goldstein* [1983] 1 W.L.R. 157, H.L.
s. 7, orders 82/636; 87/774; 88/1215.
s. 7, substituted: 1984, c.12, s.77.
s. 9, repealed in pt.: *ibid.*, sch.7; 1987, c.49, sch.2.
s. 11, repealed: 1984, c.12, sch.7.
s. 13, regs. 79/563; orders 81/1113; 82/636.
s. 15, orders 78/1055; 81/1113.
sch., amended and repealed in pt.: regs. 79/563.

73. National Insurance Act 1967.
repealed: 1975, c.18, sch.1.

75. Matrimonial Homes Act 1967.
repealed, except s.2 (in pt.), sch.(in pt.): 1983, c.19, sch.1.
see *Re V. (A Minor) (Wardship)* (1979) 123 S.J. 201, Sir George Baker P.
s. 1, see *Tarr* v. *Tarr* [1972] 2 W.L.R. 1068; 116 S.J. 353; [1972] 2 All E.R. 299; *Wroth* v. *Tyler* [1973] 2 W.L.R. 405; *Collins* v. *Collins* (1973) 4 Fam.Law 133, C.A.; *Grange Lane South Flats* v. *Cook, The Times,* November 28, 1979, C.A.; *Hoggett* v. *Hoggett* (1979) 39 P. & C.R. 121, C.A.; *S.* v. *S.* (1980) 10 Fam.Law 153, French J.; *Barnett* v. *Hassett* [1981] 1 W.L.R. 1385, Wood J; *Richards* v. *Richards* [1983] 3 W.L.R. 173, H.L.; *Lee* v. *Lee* (1983) 127 S.J. 696, C.A.

1967—cont.

75. Matrimonial Homes Act 1967—*cont.*
ss. 1, 2, see *Watts* v. *Waller* [1972] 3 W.L.R. 365.
s. 2, see *Baggott* v. *Baggott* (1986) 16 Fam.Law 129, C.A.
s. 2, amended: 1972, c.61, sch.3; 1981, c.24, ss.1,4,5, sch.1; repealed in pt.: 1972, c.61, sch.5; 1981, c.24, s.4, sch.3; 1984, c.28, sch.4.
s. 7, see *Buckingham* v. *Buckingham,* May 12, 1978, Judge Kingham, Luton Cty.Ct.; *Terry-Smith* v. *Terry-Smith* (1981) 125 S.J. 375, Sir John Arnold P.
sch. 1, amended: 1983, c.19, sch.2; repealed in pt.: 1972, c.61, sch.5; 1984, c.28, sch.4.
sch. 2, see *Lewis* v. *Lewis* [1985] 2 W.L.R. 962, H.L.
sch. 2, added: 1981, c.24, s.6.

76. Road Traffic Regulation Act 1967.
repealed (except ss.109, 113, sch.6); 1984, c.27, sch.14.
s. 1, see *Houghton* v. *Scholfield* [1973] R.T.R. 239; *Phillips* v. *Prosser* [1976] R.T.R. 300, D.C.; *Gribben* v. *Skeen,* 1980 S.L.T.(Notes) 32; *Hawkins* v. *Phillips* [1980] R.T.R. 197, D.C.; *Bulman* v. *Godbold* [1981] R.T.R. 242, D.C.; *Gouldie* v. *Pringle* [1981] R.T.R. 525, D.C.; *Freight Transport Association* v. *Royal Berkshire C.C.* [1981] R.T.R. 95, C.A.; *Corfe Transport* v. *Gwynedd County Council* (1983) 81 L.G.R. 745, D.C.
s. 6, orders 72/3, 4, 274, 364, 920, 1014, 1052, 1368, 1524, 1607, 1608, 1834; 73/3, 84, 162, 213, 400, 403, 404, 483, 554, 698, 755, 807, 871, 872, 875, 906, 1007, 1075, 1152, 1153, 1241, 1526, 1856; 74/14, 49, 144, 251, 912, 954, 1506, 1623, 1953, 2125; 75/241, 588, 589, 742–744, 990, 1010, 1068, 1152, 1247, 1566, 1712; 84/622.
s. 9, see *Freight Transport Association* v. *Royal Berkshire County Council* [1981] R.T.R. 95, C.A.
s. 9, regs. 81/1042.
s. 12, see *Platten* v. *Growing* [1983] Crim.L.R. 184, D.C.
s. 13, regs. 72/109, 247, 553, 554, 679; 73/1021, 2059; 74/436, 502, 1855; 75/1233; 80/1414; 81/1575; 82/1163; 83/374; 84/1479.
s. 15, amended (S.): 1973, c.65, sch.14.
s. 20, regs. 78/1345; 81/990.
s. 20, amended (S.): 1973, c.65, sch.14.
s. 21, order 72/1099.
s. 21, substituted: 1980, c.65, sch.7.
s. 23, see *Moulder* v. *Neville* [1974] R.T.R. 53, D.C.; *Connor* v. *Paterson* [1977] R.T.R. 379, D.C.; *Tudhope* v. *Birbeck,* 1979 S.L.T.(Notes) 47; *Crank* v. *Brooks* [1980] R.T.R. 441, D.C.; *Oakley-Moore* v. *Robinson* [1982] R.T.R. 74, D.C.
s. 23, regs. 79/401.
s. 24, amended (S.): 1973, c.65, sch.14.
s. 25, see *Wall* v. *Walwyn* [1973] Crim.L.R. 376; [1974] R.T.R. 24, D.C.
s. 25, directions 75/1536; 81/859.

CAP.

CAP.

1967—cont.

76. Road Traffic Regulation Act 1967—*cont.*
s. 26, amended (S.): 1973, c.65, sch.14.
s. 28, see *Freight Transport Association* v. *Lothian Regional Council*, 1978 S.L.T. 14; *Startin* v. *Solihull Metropolitan Borough Council* [1979] R.T.R. 228, O'Connor J.
s. 28, amended (S.): 1973, c.65, sch.14.
s. 29, repealed in pt. (S.): 1973, c.65, schs.25,29.
s. 29A, repealed in pt. (S.): 1984, c.54, sch.9.
s. 30, see *Spence* v. *Lanarkshire County Council*, 1976 S.L.T.(Lands Tr.) 2.
s. 31, see *Boxer* v. *Snelling* [1972] R.T.R. 472, D.C.; *Freight Transport Association* v. *Lothian Regional Council*, 1978 S.L.T. 14; *Startin* v. *Solihull Metropolitan Borough Council* [1979] R.T.R. 228, O'Connor J.; *Crossland* v. *Chichester District Council* (1983) 81 L.G.R. 787, C.A.
s. 31, repealed in pt. (S.): 1973, c.65, schs.25,29.
s. 35, amended (S.): 1973, c.65, sch.14.
s. 37, amended (S.): 1973, c.65, sch.24; repealed in pt.: *ibid.*, schs.25,29.
s. 41, see *Freight Transport Association* v. *Lothian Regional Council*, 1978 S.L.T. 14.
s. 42, see *Wilson* v. *Arnott* [1977] 1 W.L.R. 331, D.C.
s. 42, amended: 1982, c.48, schs.3,6(S.).
s. 43, amended (S.): 1982, c.48, sch.6.
s. 44, repealed in pt. (S.): 1973, c.65, schs.25,29.
ss. 52, 53, regs. 74/1809; 75/1894; 78/1345, 1346; 80/69; 81/989, 990; 82/1682, 1696.
s. 54, see *Sharples* v. *Blackmore* [1973] R.T.R. 249; *Walton* v. *Hawkins* [1973] R.T.R. 366, D.C.; *Tudhope* v. *Birbeck*, 1979 S.L.T.(Notes) 47; *Cotterill* v. *Chapman* [1984] R.T.R. 73, D.C.
s. 54, regs.75/49; 77/952; 79/401; 80/1854; 82/1879; 83/1088; 84/966; directions 75/1536; 81/859.
s. 55, see *West* v. *Buckinghamshire County Council* (1985) 83 L.G.R. 449, Caulfield J.
s. 55, regs. 79/401; directions 75/1536; 81/859; 82/1880; 83/1086.
s. 59, regs.75/49; 80/1854.
s. 65, amended (S.): 1973, c.65, sch.14.
s. 69, amended (S.): 1973, c.65, sch.14; repealed in pt. (S.): *ibid.*, schs.14,29.
s. 71, see *Hood* v. *Lewis* [1976] Crim.L.R. 74; [1976] R.T.R. 99, D.C.; *Westwater* v. *Milton*, 1980 S.L.T.(Sh.Ct.) 63; *Gibson* v. *Dalton* [1980] R.T.R. 410, D.C.; *Burton* v. *Gilbert* [1984] R.T.R. 162, D.C.
ss. 71, 72, see *Spittle* v. *Kent County Constabulary* [1985] Crim.L.R. 744; [1986] R.T.R. 142, D.C.
s. 72, see *Walker* v. *Rawlinson* [1976] R.T.R. 94, D.C.
ss. 72, 73, orders 72/940; 84/615, 621.
s. 74, orders 72/1833; 81/812, 813; regs. 82/41; 83/561, 1918; 84/615, 621, 728.
s. 75, see *Sharples* v. *Blackmore* [1973] R.T.R. 249; *Smith* v *Rankin*, 1977 S.L.T.(Notes) 12; regs. 77/952.

1967—cont.

76. Road Traffic Regulation Act 1967—*cont.*
s. 76, amended (S.): 1973, c.65, sch.14; repealed in pt. (S.): *ibid.*, schs.14, 19.
s. 77, orders 75/1895; 76/1872; 78/1548.
s. 78, see *Swain* v. *Gillett* [1974] R.T.R. 446, D.C.; *Hood* v. *Lewis* [1976] Crim.L.R. 74; [1976] R.T.R. 99, D.C.; *Jones* v. *Nicks* [1977] R.T.R. 72, D.C.; *Plume* v. *Suckling* 1977 R.T.R. 271, D.C.; *Lyon* v. *Oxford* [1983] R.T.R. 257, D.C.
s. 78, regs. 73/747, 748, 2058; 74/619; 81/202, 1372; 84/325.
s. 78A, see *Swain* v. *Gillett* [1974] Crim.L.R. 433, D.C.; *R.* v. *Petersfield JJ., ex p. Levy* [1981] R.T.R. 204, D.C.; *Westwater* v. *Milton*, 1980 S.L.T. (Sh.Ct.) 63; *Gibson* v. *Dalton* [1980] R.T.R. 410, D.C.; *Platten* v. *Growing* [1983] Crim.L.R. 184, D.C.; *Lyon* v. *Oxford* [1983] R.T.R. 257, D.C.; *Burton* v. *Gilbert* [1984] R.T.R. 162, D.C; *Collinson* v. *Mabbott*, *The Times*, October 10, 1984; *Spittle* v. *Kent County Constabulary* [1986] R.T.R. 142, D.C.
s. 80, see *Lord Advocate* v. *Aberdeen Corporation*, 1977 S.L.T. 234.
s. 80, regs. 72/333, 1399; 73/319; 74/476, 1235, 1475; 75/312; 77/311, 1711; orders 75/1153; 76/261, 1401; 82/137.
s. 80, amended (S.): 1980, c.62, s.31; 1982, c.48, schs.3,6.
s. 81, see *Rumbles* v. *Poole* [1980] R.T.R. 449, D.C.
s. 83C, regs. 75/267, 881, 1498.
s. 84, see *Freight Transport Association* v. *Lothian Regional Council*, 1978 S.L.T. 14.
s. 84, regs. 72/729; 78/707, 932; orders 74/912; 954.
s. 84C, regs. 73/1028, 1103, 1121; 75/1562, 1586, 2029–2031; 78/1347; 79/213, 214; 82/291–293, 614(S.), 615(S.).
s. 84D, see *Startin* v. *Solihull Metropolitan Borough Council* [1979] R.T.R. 228, O'Connor J.
s. 84D, regs. 75/1233, 1712; orders 72/920, 1608, 1833; 73/400, 404, 483, 807, 872, 906, 1007, 1241, 1526, 1856; 81/812, 813; 83/561, 1918; 84/615, 621, 728.
s. 85, see *Pamplin* v. *Gorman* [1980] R.T.R. 54, D.C.; *Lowe* v. *Lester* [1986] Crim.L.R. 339, D.C.
s. 93, repealed (S.): 1980, c.62, sch.8.
s. 94, see *Lord Advocate* v. *Aberdeen Corporation*, 1977 S.L.T. 234.
s. 96, amended (S.): 1982, c.48, sch.6.
s. 99, regs. 81/1373.
s. 103, regs. 83/1168.
s. 104, amended (S.): 1973, c.65, s.14.
s. 107, regs. 77/952; 78/707, 932, 1347; 79/401; 80/169, 1414, 1854; 81/202, 989, 990, 1372, 1373; 82/291–293, 1163, 1682, 1696, 1879; 83/1168; 84/966, 1479; directions 81/859.
s. 113, repealed in pt.: 1980, c.65, sch.34.
sch. 5, see *Plume* v. *Suckling* [1977] R.T.R. 271, D.C.
sch. 6, repealed in pt.: 1972, c.20, sch.9; S.L.R. 1976; 1978, c.55, sch.4; 1980, c.34, sch.9; c.66, sch.25.

1967—cont.

77. Police (Scotland) Act 1967.
s. 1, amended: 1973, c.65, s.146.
s. 2, amended: *ibid.*; repealed in pt.: 1981, c.23, sch.2,4.
s. 4, repealed in pt.: 1973, c.65, s.146, sch.29.
s. 5, amended: 1984, c.60, s.108; repealed in pt.: *ibid.*, s.108, sch.7.
s. 5A, added: *ibid.*, s.108.
s. 6, amended: *ibid.*, sch.6.
s. 7, regs. 72/777, 1206; 76/1073.
s. 7, amended: 1984, c.60, sch.6.
s. 16, regs. 72/777; 76/1073.
s. 16, amended: 1975, c.20, sch.1.
s. 17, see *Caldwell* v.*Caldwell*, 1983 S.L.T. 610.
s. 17, amended: 1975, c.20, sch.1; repealed in pt.: 1973, c.65, sch.29; 1984, c.60, s.110, sch.7.
ss. 17, 18, see *Binnie* v. *Donnelly*, High Court of Justiciary, June 25, 1981.
s. 18, amended: 1972, c.70, sch.29; 1973, c.65, s.146; 1975, c.20, sch.1.
s. 19, amended: regs. 74/812; repealed in pt.: 1973, c.65, sch.29.
ss. 19, 21, order 82/231.
s. 20, amended: 1973, c.65, s.146.
s. 21A, orders 75/632, 633.
s. 21A, added: 1973, c.65, s.146.
s. 23, substituted: *ibid.*, amended: 1976, c.35, sch.2; 1984, c.60, s.108.
s. 26, regs. 72/136, 777, 1206, 1847; 73/119, 391, 433, 1458, 1609; 74/489, 1348, 1515, 1630, 1902; 75/269, 983, 1286, 2070; 76/260, 1018, 1073, 1433; 77/1016, 2008; 78/528, 1170, 1510; 79/767, 784, 1263; 80/1050, 1411; 81/67, 86, 1679; 82/681, 902, 1113, 1628; 83/317, 1354, 1850; 84/648, 1651; 85/111, 1325, 1733; 86/576; 87/423, 1698, 1914, 2226; 88/260, 1501.
s. 26, amended: 1980, c.10, s.2.
s. 27, regs. 72/778; 73/434, 1138; 74/1248, 1629; 77/1131, 2009; 78/999, 1171; 79/783, 1968; 80/1410; 81/361; 82/273, 1660, 1768; 83/318, 1368; 84/2029; 86/121; 87/424, 1699, 1700, 1878.
s. 27, amended: 1984, c.60, s.111.
s. 29, amended: 1973, c.65, s.146.
s. 31, amended: 1984, c.60, sch.6.
s. 32, orders 72/24; 73/362; 75/1056; 86/390.
s. 35, repealed: 1976, c.35, sch.3.
s. 36, orders 73/278; 75/1254; 87/1537.
s. 38, amended: 1976, c.35, sch.2; repealed in pt.: *ibid.*, sch.3.
s. 41, see *Skeen* v. *Shaw*, 1979 S.L.T.(Notes) 58; *Wither* v. *Reid*, 1979 S.L.T. 192; *Annan* v. *Tait*, 1981 S.C.C.R. 326; *Stirton* v. *McPhail*, High Court of Justiciary, June 9, 1982; *Kinney* v. *Tudhope*, 1985 S.C.C.R. 393.
s. 41, amended: 1977, c.45, s.31, sch.6; 1980, c.62, s.57.
ss. 43, 44, amended: 1982, c.48, sch.6.
s. 45, amended: 1975, c.20, sch.1.
s. 46, repealed in pt.: 1981, c.23, schs.2,4.
s. 48, regs. 81/1679; 82/273; order 87/1537.
s. 50, repealed in pt.: 1978, c.30, sch.3.

1967—cont.

77. Police (Scotland) Act 1967—*cont.*
s. 51, see *Binnie* v. *Donnelly*, High Court of Justiciary, June 25, 1981.
s. 51, amended: 1973, c.65, s.146; repealed in pt.: *ibid.*, sch.29; 1978, c.30, sch.3.
s. 52, repealed in pt.: S.L.R. 1973.
sch. 1, repealed: 1973, c.65, sch.29.
sch. 4, repealed in pt.: S.L.R. 1973; 1976, c.35, sch.3; 1980, c.63, sch.2; 1984, c.27, sch.14.
sch. 5, repealed in pt.: 1982, c.45, sch.4.

78. Water (Scotland) Act 1967.
repealed: (except s. 4 (in pt.), sch. 2 (in pt.)): 1980, c.45, sch.11.
see *Zetland County Council* v. *Thomson*, 1974 S.L.T.(Sh.Ct.) 67.
s. 4, amended: 1973, c.65, sch.17; repealed in pt.: *ibid.*, sch.29.
s. 5, orders 77/547; 78/1185.
sch. 2, amended: 1973, c.37, sch.9.
sch. 3, order 75/231.

79. Road Traffic (Driving Instruction) Act 1967.
repealed: 1972, c.20, sch.9.

80. Criminal Justice Act 1967.
see *Payne* v. *Lord Harris of Greenwich, The Times*, March 26, 1981, C.A.
s. 1, see *R.* v. *William* [1972] Crim.L.R. 436; *R.* v. *Scott, The Times*, June 29, 1978, C.A.; *R.* v. *Hall* [1982] 1 All E.R. 75, C.A.
ss. 1, 2, see *R.* v. *Brooker* (1977) 65 Cr.App.R. 181, C.A.; *R.* v. *Blithing* [1984] R.T.R. 18, C.A.
ss. 1–6, repealed: 1980, c.43, sch.9.
s. 2, see *R.* v. *Cairns* [1983] Crim.L.R. 478, D.C.
s. 3, see *R.* v. *Blackpool Licensing Justices, ex p. Beaverbrook Newspapers* [1972] 1 W.L.R. 95; *R.* v. *Horsham JJ., ex p. Farquarson and the N.U.J.*; *R.* v. *Horsham JJ., ex p. West Sussex County Times, The Times*, November 4, 1981, D.C.
s. 3, amended: 1977, c.45, sch.12; 1981, c.27, s.1.
s. 7, amended: 1980, c.43, sch.7.
s. 8, see *R.* v. *Lowe* [1973] 2 W.L.R. 481; [1973] 1 All E.R. 805, C.A.; *Hyam* v. *D.P.P.* [1974] 2 W.L.R. 607; [1974] 2 All E.R. 41, H.L.; *R.* v. *Mohan* [1975] 2 W.L.R. 859; [1975] 2 All E.R. 193, C.A.; *R.* v. *Majewski* [1976] 2 W.L.R. 625; [1976] 2 All E.R. 142, H.L.
s. 9, see *Ellis* v. *Jones* [1973] 2 All E.R. 893; *Chapman* v. *Ingleton* (1973) 57 Cr.App.R. 476, D.C.; *French's Dairies (Sevenoaks)* v. *Davis* [1973] Crim.L.R. 630, D.C.; *Lister* v. *Quaife* [1983] 1 W.L.R. 48, D.C.; *Collins* v. *Lucking* [1983] R.T.R. 312, D.C.
ss. 9, 11, modified: order 77/86.
s. 10, see *R.* v. *Horseferry Road Metropolitan Stipendiary Magistrate, ex p. O'Regan, The Times*, May 17, 1986, D.C.
s. 11, see *R.* v. *Jackson and Robertson* [1973] Crim.L.R. 356; *R.* v. *Lewis* (1973) 57 Cr.App.R. 860, C.A.; *R.* v. *Gibbs* [1974] Crim.L.R. 474; *R.* v. *Cooper* (1979) 69 Cr.App.R. 229, C.A.; *R.* v. *Watts* (1980) 71 Cr.App.R. 136, C.A.; *R.* v. *Rossborough* [1985] Crim.L.R. 372; (1985) 81 Cr.App.R. 139, C.A.

1967—cont.

80. Criminal Justice Act 1967—*cont.*

s. 11, amended: 1980, c.43, sch.7; 1987, c.38, sch.2.

s. 12, regs. 77/86; amended: 1976, c.52, sch.5.

s. 13, see *R. v. Wright* (1974) 58 Cr.App.R. 444, C.A.; *R. v. Barry (Christopher)* [1975] 1 W.L.R. 1190; [1975] 2 All E.R. 760, C.A.

s. 13, repealed: 1974, c.23, sch.3.

ss. 14–6, repealed: 1972, c.71, sch.6.

s. 18, repealed: 1976, c.63, sch.3.

s. 19, repealed: 1980, c.43, sch.9.

s. 20, repealed in pt.: *ibid.*

s. 21, repealed: 1976, c.63, sch.3.

s. 22, see *R. v. Kwame* [1975] R.T.R. 106, C.A.

s. 22, amended: 1976, c.63, sch.2; 1977, c.45, sch.12; repealed in pt.: 1976, c.63, sch.3; 1977, c.45, schs.12, 13.

s. 23, repealed: 1976, c.63, sch.3; amended: 1977, c.45, sch.12.

s. 24, see *R. v. Brighton Justices* [1973] 1 W.L.R. 69, D.C.; *R. v. Power* (1977) 66 Cr.App.R. 159, C.A.

s. 24, repealed: 1980, c.43, sch.9.

s. 26, see *R. v. Talgarth Justices, ex p. Bithell* [1973] 2 All E.R. 717.

ss. 26, 28–30, repealed: 1980, c.43, sch.9.

s. 27, repealed: 1977, c.45, sch.13.

s. 31, repealed: 1973, c.14, sch.2.

s. 32, amended: 1973, c.14, schs.1,2; c.62, sch.5; 1985, c.23, sch.1; repealed in pt.: 1973, c.14, sch.2; 1985, c.23, schs.1,2.

s. 33, repealed in pt.: 1973, c.14, sch.9.

s. 35, see *R. v. Blackpool Licensing Justices, ex p. Beaverbrook Newspapers* [1972] 1 W.L.R. 95.

s. 35, repealed: 1977, c.45, sch.13.

s. 36, amended: 1980, c.43, sch.7; repealed in pt.: *ibid.,* sch.9.

s. 37, see *R. v. Hulme* [1972] Crim.L.R. 123; (1971) 56 Cr.App.R. 203; *R. v. Spearpoint* [1973] Crim.L.R. 36, C.A.; *R. v. Newton* [1973] 1 W.L.R. 233; [1973] 1 All E.R. 758, C.A.; *R. v. McKenna* [1974] 1 W.L.R. 267; [1974] 1 All E.R. 637, C.A.; *R. v. Johnson* [1976] 1 W.L.R. 426; [1976] 1 All E.R. 869, C.A.

ss. 37, 38, see *R. v. Isherwood* (1974) 59 Cr.App.R. 162, C.A.

ss. 37–42, repealed: 1973, c.62, sch.6.

s. 38, see *R. v. Bangs* (1983) 5 Cr.App.R.(S.) 453, C.A.

s. 39, see *R. v. Butters; R. v. Fitzgerald* (1971) 55 Cr.App.R. 515; *R. v. Arkle* (1972) 56 Cr.App.R. 722, C.A.

s. 40, see *R. v. McDonald* (1971) 55 Cr.App.R. 573; *R. v. Arkle* (1972) 56 Cr.App.R. 722, C.A.; *R. v. Goodlad* [1973] 2 All E.R. 1200.

s. 43, repealed: 1977, c.45, sch.13.

s. 44, see *R. v. Dudley JJ, ex p. Payne* [1979] 1 W.I..R. 891, D.C.; *R. v. Brighton Magistrates' Court, ex p. Hamilton; R. v. Marylebone Magistrates' Court, ex p. Forrest, The Times,* June 19, 1981, H.L.

ss. 44, 44A, 45, repealed: 1980, c.43, sch.9.

s. 47, repealed: 1973, c.62, sch.6.

1967—cont.

80. Criminal Justice Act 1967—*cont.*

s. 48, repealed: *ibid.;* 1975, c.21, sch.10(S.).

s. 49, repealed: 1988, c.33, sch.16.

s. 50, repealed in pt.: 1973, c.62, sch.6; 1980, c.43, sch.9.

s. 51, see *Owen* v. *Imes* [1972] R.T.R. 489, D.C.

s. 51, repealed: 1972, c.20, sch.9.

ss. 52, 53, repealed: 1973, c.62, sch.6.

s. 54, repealed in pt.: 1972, c.71, sch.6; 1973, c.62, sch.6; 1975, c.21, sch.10.

s. 55, repealed: 1973, c.62, sch.6.

s. 56, see *R. v. Blackpool JJ.* [1972] 1 W.L.R. 1456; [1972] 3 All E.R 854; *R. v. O'Connor* [1976] 1 W.L.R. 368, C.A.; *R. v. Guildhall JJ., ex p. Cooper, The Times,* May 6, 1983, Glidewell J.

s. 56, amended: 1988, c.33, s.42; c.54, sch.3.

s. 57, repealed: 1973, c.62, sch.6.

s. 59, see *Payne v. Lord Harris of Greenwich* [1981] 1 W.L.R. 754, C.A.

s. 59, rules 73/4; 75/1528; 76/237; 78/1325; 83/622, 1694.

s. 59, amended (S.): 1985, c.73, s.44.

s. 60, see *R. v. Hulme* [1972] Crim.L.R. 123; (1971) 56 Cr.App.R. 203; *R. v. Mellor* [1981] 1 W.L.R. 1044; [1981] 2 All E.R. 1049, C.A.; *R. v. McKinnon (William Harold)* [1987] 1 W.L.R. 234, C.A.

s. 60, order 83/1958.

s. 60, amended: 1972, c.71, ss.35,66; 1977, c.45, sch.12; 1980, c.62, sch./(S.); 1982, c.48, s.33, sch.14; repealed in pt.: 1972, c.71, schs.5,6; 1977, c.45, schs.12,13; 1980, c.62, sch.8(S.); 1982, c.48, s.33, sch.14.

ss. 60, 61, see *Findlay, Re* [1984] 3 W.L.R. 1159, H.L.

s. 61, see *R. v. Secretary of State for the Home Department, ex p. Handscomb* (1988) 86 Cr.App.R. 59, D.C.

s. 61, amended: 1975, c.21, sch.9(S.); 1980, c.62, sch.7(S.); 1982, c.48, sch.14; repealed in pt. (S.): 1980, c.62, sch.7.

s. 62, see *Payne v. Lord Harris of Greenwich* [1981] 1 W.L.R. 574, C.A.; *R. v. Secretary of State for the Home Department, ex p. Gunnell* [1985] Crim.L.R. 105, C.A.; *R. v. McKinnon (William Harold)* [1987] 1 W.L.R. 234, C.A.

s. 62, amended: 1973, c.62, sch.5; 1975, c.21, sch.9(S.); 1980, c.43, sch.7; c.62, sch.7(S.); 1982, c.48, sch.14; 1988, c.33, sch.15; repealed in pt. (S.): 1975, c.21, sch.10.

s. 63, repealed: 1982, c.48, sch.16.

s. 64, amended: 1980, c.62, sch.7(S.); 1982, c.48, sch.14; repealed in pt.: 1975, c.21, sch.10.

s. 66, repealed in pt.: 1982, c.48, sch.16.

s. 67, see *R. v. Governor of Blundeston Prison, ex p. Gaffney* (1982) 75 Cr.App.R. 42, C.A.; *R. v. McIntyre* (1985) 7 Cr.App.R.(S.) 196, C.A.; *R. v. Towers* (1988) 86 Cr.App.R. 355, C.A.

s. 67, amended: 1972, c.71, sch.5; 1973, c.62, sch.5; 1977, c.45, sch.9; 1982, c.48, ss.10,34, sch.14; 1984, c.60, s.49; 1988, c.33, s.130, sch.15; repealed in pt.: 1982, c.48, sch.16.

CAP.

1967—cont.

80. Criminal Justice Act 1967—cont.
s. 68, repealed (S.): 1975, c.2, sch.10.
s. 72, amended: 1982, c.51, sch.3; 1983, c.20, sch.4; 1984, c.36, sch.3; repealed in pt. (S.): 1975, c.21, sch.10.
Pt. IV (ss. 73–84), repealed: 1974, c.4, sch.5.
s. 76, see R. v. Cardiff Crown Court, ex p. Jones [1973] 3 W.L.R. 497, D.C.
s. 89, amended: 1976, c.52, sch.9; repealed in pt.: 1980, c.62, sch.9.
s. 90, repealed: 1988, c.34, sch.6.
s. 91, see Lanham v. Rickwood, The Times, May 10, 1984, D.C.; Neale v. E. (A Minor) [1984] Crim.L.R. 485, D.C.
s. 91, amended: 1972, c.71, s.34; repealed in pt.: 1977, c.45, schs.12,13.
s. 92, repealed in pt.: 1977, c.45, sch.13.
s. 93, repealed: 1975, c.21, sch.10(S.); 1977, c.45, sch.13; repealed in pt.: 1979, c.2, sch.6.
s 94, see R. v. Preston JJ., ex p. Pamplin, The Times, April 1, 1981, D.C.
s. 94, repealed: 1980, c.62, sch.9.
s. 95, repealed in pt.: 1973, c.62, sch.6; 1982, c.48, sch.16.
ss. 96, 99, repealed: 1973, c.62, sch.6.
s. 100, rules 83/622.
s. 100, amended: 1982, c.48, s.33; repealed in pt.: 1974, c.4, sch.5.
s. 101, repealed in pt.: ibid.
s. 104, see R. v. Arkle (1972) 56 Cr.App.R. 722, C.A.
s. 104, amended: 1973, c.62, sch.5.
s. 105, repealed in pt.: 1973, c.36, sch.6.
s. 106, order 77/2139.
s. 106, amended: 1973, c.62, sch.5; 1982, c.48, s.33; repealed in pt.: 1973, c.62, sch.6; 1977, c.45, sch.13; 1978, c.23, sch.7; 1979, c.2, sch.6; 1980, c.62, sch.9.
sch. 2, repealed in pt.: 1975, c.24, sch.3.
sch. 3, repealed in pt.: 1973, c.18, sch.3; c.32, sch.5; c.50, sch.4; 1974, c.3, sch.6; c.27, sch.(S.); c.40, sch.4; c.46, sch.11; c.50, sch.7; 1975, c.37, sch.3; 1976, c.77, sch.7; S.L.R. 1977; 1977, c.37, sch.6; c.45, sch.13; 1978, c.22, sch.3; 1979, c.36, sch.8; c.46, sch.5; 1980, c.5, sch.6; c.9, sch.10; c.44, sch.5; c.66, sch.25; 1981, c.22, sch.6; c.42, sch.; c.56, sch.12; 1982, c.30, sch.3; c.33, sch.2; 1984, c.22, sch.3; c.28, sch.4; c.30, sch.11; 1987, c.43, sch.5; 1988, c.33, sch. 16; c.48, sch.8.
sch. 4, repealed in pt.: 1978, c.23, sch.7.
sch. 6, see R. v. Blackpool JJ. [1972] 1 W.L.R. 1456; [1972] 3 All E.R. 854.
sch. 6, repealed in pt.: 1972, c.20, sch.9; 1973, c.62, sch.6; 1974, c.4, sch.5; 1975, c.21, sch.10(S.); 1977, c.45, sch.13; 1979, c.31, sch.2; 1980, c.43, sch.9; 1988, c.13, sch.4.

81. Companies Act 1967.
orders 79/1545, 1547.
repealed (exc. Pt. II (ss.58–108) (in pt.)): 1985, c.9, sch.1.
s. 22, see Fletcher Challenge v. Fletcher Challenge Pty. [1982] F.S.R. 1, Powell J.

CAP.

1967—cont.

81. Companies Act 1967—cont.
s. 26, see Parsons v. Albert J. Parsons and Sons [1979] I.C.R. 271, C.A.
s. 26, order 77/1367.
s. 35, see Re Lubin, Rosen and Associates [1975] 1 W.L.R. 122; Re Golden Chemical Products [1976] 3 W.L.R. 1; [1976] 2 All E.R. 543; Re St. Piran [1981] 1 W.L.R. 1300, Dillon J.; Highfield Commodities, Re [1984] 3 All E.R. 884, Megarry V.C.
s. 43, regs. 79/1546.
s. 44, regs. 79/1546.
s. 48, regs. 73/2060; 75/596.
s. 50, see London and County Securities v. Nicholson (formerly trading as Harmood Banner & Co.) [1980] 1 W.L.R. 948, Browne-Wilkinson J.
s. 56, regs. 79/1546, 1618.
ss. 58, 59, repealed: 1974, c.49, sch.2.
s. 60, repealed in pt.: ibid.
ss. 61–85, 88, repealed: ibid.
s. 89, amended: ibid., sch.1; 1982, c.50, sch.5.
s. 90, substituted: 1985, c.9, sch.3.
ss. 92–95, repealed in pt.: 1974, c.49, sch.1.
ss. 98, 100, 101, 103–106, repealed: ibid., sch.2.
s. 109, see Norwest Holst v. Secretary of State for Trade [1978] 3 W.L.R. 73, C.A.; R. v. Secretary of State for Trade, ex p. Perestrello [1980] 3 W.L.R. 1, Woolf J.
s. 120, regs. 82/530.

83. Sea Fisheries (Shellfish) Act 1967.
s. 1, orders 72/45, 315, 1128; 73/77; 74/27, 981; 75/705, 710; 78/243, 1596, 1854; 79/1066, 1087; 80/1373; 82/135; 84/907; 85/847; 86/497, 1896, 1901; 87/217, 218; 88/1024.
s. 7, amended: 1977, c.45, s.31, sch.6.
s. 12, orders 74/1555; 78/560; 81/994; 83/159.
ss. 12, 14, amended: 1983, c.30, s.6.
s. 13, order 81/995.
s. 16, amended: 1973, c.30, s.1.
s. 17, amended: order 78/272.
sch. 1, orders 72/756; 76/153; 78/243; 79/38, 1137; 80/1373; 84/907.
sch. 2, repealed in pt.: 1984, c.26, sch.2.

84. Sea Fish (Conservation) Act 1967.
see Dunkley v. Evans [1981] 3 All E.R. 285, D.C.
s. 1, orders 76/305, 1826; 79/741, 742, 1995; 81/535, 551, 1870; 82/454, 1373, 1846; 83/552, 1384; 84/907, 1522; 85/100; 86/497.
s. 1, substituted: 1981, c.29, s.19; amended: 1988, c.12, sch.6.
s. 2, amended: 1981, c.29, s.19.
s. 3, orders 72/23; 73/2167; 74/192; 76/1324; 77/440; 78/946; 79/744; 80/1994; 81/98, 281, 465, 592, 906, 1163, 1869; 82/453, 573, 874, 1372, 1844.
s. 3, amended: 1976, c.86, sch.2; 1984, c.26, sch.1.
s. 4, orders 72/470, 1477, 1857; 73/1983, 2000, 2084, 2185; 74/75, 738, 1766, 2208; 75/340, 998, 1465, 1466, 1646; 76/1102, 1322, 1323; 77/194, 624, 942, 1083, 1388, 1389, 1497, 1638, 2086; 78/1285, 1537, 1538, 1652;

1967—cont.

84. Sea Fish (Conservation) Act 1967—*cont.*
79/268, 509, 711; 80/332–334; 81/1183, 1184, 1293, 1295, 1662; 82/281, 1850; 83/1204, 1206, 1879, 1881; 86/1438, 1439; 87/1564, 1565.

s. 4, substituted: 1976, c.86, s.3; amended: 1981, c.29, s.20.

s. 4A, orders 82/281; 83/1139.

s. 4A, added: 1981, c.29, s.21.

s. 5, see *Skinner* v. *Patience*, 1982 S.L.T.(Sh.Ct.) 81; *Mehlich* v. *Mackenzie, Gewiese* v. *Mackenzie*, 1984 S.L.T. 449.

s. 5, orders 72/1093, 1662, 1964, 1965; 73/188, 189, 207, 346, 1259, 1496, 1983, 1999, 2020, 2185; 74/107, 1100, 1215, 1361, 1966, 2208; 75/170, 844, 1201; 76/440, 1101, 1311, 1325, 1563, 2023; 77/200, 290, 291, 961, 1101, 1291, 1377, 1508, 1756, 2182; 78/930, 1374, 1379; 79/1176, 1422(S.); 80/374, 478, 1480, 1809, 1868(S.), 1906; 81/97, 282, 463, 585, 594, 907, 1163, 1184, 1185, 1294, 1296, 1297, 1298, 1873; 82/169, 455, 875, 1374, 1845, 1847–1849; 83/14, 15, 59, 60; 84/1935; 86/988, 1115, 1620, 1936, 1982, 2060, 2075, 2122; 87/718, 1227, 1900, 2100, 2192; 88/683, 1264, 1761.

s. 5, amended: 1976, c.86, sch.2; 1981, c.29, c.22.

s. 6, orders 72/471, 1649, 1793, 1966; 73/347, 1038, 2004; 74/74, 106, 397, 881, 2207; 75/639; 76/38, 2023, 2094, 2095; 77/781; 78/1286, 1287, 1413; 79/398, 743; 80/335, 1657; 83/58, 1205, 1880; 84/92; 86/496, 1437; 87/1566.

ss. 6, 7, amended: 1981, c.29, s.23.

s. 9, amended: *ibid.*, ss.19,21.

s. 11, amended: 1976, c.86, schs.1,2; 1981, c.29, s.24.

s. 12, amended: *ibid.*, ss.19,28.

s. 14, amended: *ibid.*, s.29.

s. 15, see *Mehlich* v. *Mackenzie, Gewiese* v. *Mackenzie*, 1984 S.L.T. 449.

s. 15, orders 72/23, 470, 471, 1093, 1477, 1649, 1662, 1793, 1857; 73/112, 210, 346, 347, 1038, 1259, 1496, 1999, 2000, 2004, 2020, 2034, 2185; 74/74, 75, 106, 107, 397, 738, 881, 1100, 1215, 1361, 1766, 1966, 2207, 2208; 75/170, 340, 998, 1201, 1465, 1466, 1646; 76/38, 440, 1101, 1102, 1311, 1322–1325, 1563, 2023, 2094, 2095; 77/194, 200, 290, 291, 440, 624, 781, 942, 961, 1101, 1291, 1377, 1388, 1389, 1497, 1508, 1756, 2182; 78/930, 946, 1285–1287, 1374, 1379, 1413; 79/268, 398, 503, 711, 741–743, 1176, 1422(S.); 80/332–335, 374, 478, 1480, 1657, 1808–1810, 1868(S.), 1994; 81/97, 98, 281, 282, 463, 465, 535, 551, 585, 592, 594, 906, 907, 1183, 1184, 1293, 1295, 1297, 1298, 1662, 1869, 1873; 82/80, 454, 873–875, 1372–1374, 1844–1850; 83/14, 15, 1204, 1206, 1384, 1879, 1881; 84/1447(S), 1522, 1523, 1627, 1935; 85/100; 86/497, 988, 1115, 1437–1439, 1620, 1936, 1982, 2060, 2075, 2122; 87/718, 1227, 1564–1566, 1900, 2100, 2192; 88/683, 1264, 1761.

1967—cont.

84. Sea Fish (Conservation) Act 1967—*cont.*
s. 15, amended: 1976, c.86, sch.2; 1981, c.29, s.25.

s. 16, amended: 1981, c.29, s.25.

s. 18, amended: 1975, c.51, s.42; 1976, c.86, sch.2.

s. 19, repealed in pt.: *ibid.*, schs.2,4.

s. 20, orders 73/2167; 74/192; 75/639, 844; 77/1083, 1291, 1638, 1756, 2086; 78/1286, 1379, 1538, 1652; 79/398, 503; 80/1657, 1808–1810, 1994, 1995; 81/97, 98, 281, 282, 463, 465, 585, 592, 594, 906, 907, 1163, 1184, 1294–1296, 1298, 1662; 82/169, 281, 453–455, 573, 873–875, 1372–1374; 83/1139, 1204–1206, 1879–1881; 84/92, 1522, 1935; 85/100; 86/497, 988, 1437–1439, 2075; 87/1564–1566, 1900; 88/1761.

s. 20, amended: 1981, c.29, s.21.

s. 22, orders 73/2000; 81/1183, 1184, 1293–1298, 1662.

s. 22, amended: 1981, c.29, ss.19,21,45; repealed in pt.: *ibid.*, s.45, sch.5.

s. 23, amended: 1976, c.86, sch.2; 1981, c.29, s.19; repealed in pt.: 1973, c.36, sch.6; 1981, c.29, s.22, sch.5.

s. 24, orders 73/237, 238, 1887, 1888; 77/1244; 78/280, 281; 81/737, 1662.

86. Countryside (Scotland) Act 1967.
s. 1, repealed in pt.: 1975, c.24, sch.3.

s. 2, repealed in pt.: 1973, c.65, sch.29.

s. 5, amended: 1981, c.44, sch.1; repealed in pt.: *ibid.*, sch.2.

s. 7, substituted: *ibid.*, s.1.

s. 9, repealed: *ibid.*, sch.2.

s. 10, amended: *ibid.*, s.2.

s. 11, amended: 1984, c.12, sch.4.

s. 12, amended: 1982, c.43, sch.1.

s. 13, amended: 1976, c.21, sch.2; 1981, c.44, s.3; repealed in pt.: *ibid.*, sch.2; 1982, c.43, sch.1.

s. 14, regs. 75/1032; 82/1467.

s. 14, repealed in pt.: 1981, c.44, sch.2; 1982, c.43, sch.1; repealed: *ibid.*, sch.4.

ss. 16–18, 20, amended: 1982, c 43, sch.1.

s. 22, regs. 75/1032; 82/1467.

s. 24, amended: 1981, c.44, s.4; 1982, c.43, sch.1; repealed in pt.: 1981, c.44, sch.2.

s. 26, regs. 75/1032; 82/1467.

s. 27, amended: 1982, c.43, sch.1; repealed in pt.: 1981, c.44, sch.2.

ss. 28–30, amended: 1982, c.43, sch.1.

s. 31, regs. 75/1032; 82/1467.

s. 31, amended: 1982, c.43, schs.1,3.

ss. 32, 33, amended: *ibid.*, sch.1; repealed in pt.: 1981, c.44, sch.2.

s. 34, amended: 1982, c.43, schs.1,3; repealed in pt.: *ibid.*, schs.3,4.

ss. 34, 35, regs. 75/1032; 82/1467.

s. 35, amended: 1982, c.43, schs.1,3.

s. 35A, repealed: 1982, c.43, sch.4.

s. 36, amended: *ibid.*, sch.1; repealed in pt.: 1981, c.44, sch.2.

s. 37, regs. 75/1032; 82/1467.

s. 37, repealed in pt.: 1984, c.54, sch.11.

CAP.

1967—cont.

86. Countryside (Scotland) Act 1967—*cont.*
s. 38, amended: 1981, c.38, sch.3; 1982, c.43, sch.1; 1984, c.12, sch.4.
s. 41, repealed in pt.: 1973, c.65, schs.25,29.
s. 43, amended: 1981, c.44, s.6, sch.1; repealed in pt.: *ibid.*, sch.2.
s. 44, amended: *ibid.*, s.6.
s. 45, repealed in pt.: *ibid.*, sch.2.
s. 46, amended: *ibid.*, s.7; 1984, c.54, sch.9.
s. 47, amended: *ibid.*
s. 48, repealed in pt.: 1981, c.44, sch.2.
s. 48A, added: *ibid.*, s.8.
s. 49, amended: 1982, c.43, sch.1; repealed in pt.: 1973, c.65, sch.29.
s. 49A, added: 1981, c.44, s.9.
s. 50, amended: 1982, c.43, sch.1.
s. 51, amended: *ibid.*; 1984, c.27, sch.13; c.54, sch.9.
s. 52, amended: 1982, c.43, sch.1.
s. 54, amended: 1981, c.44, s.10; 1984, c.12, sch.4; c.54, sch.9; repealed in pt.: 1981, c.44, sch.2; 1982, c.43, sch.1; 1984, c.54, schs.9,11.
s. 55, repealed in pt.: 1981, c.44, sch.2; 1982, c.43, sch.1.
s. 56, repealed: 1982, c.45, sch.4.
s. 56A, added: 1981, c.44, s.11.
s. 57, amended: 1973, c.65, sch.27; 1978, c.4, sch.; repealed in pt.: 1982, c.45, sch.4.
s. 59, repealed in pt.: 1981, c.39, sch.
s. 60, amended: 1981, c.44, s.6; repealed in pt.: S.L.R. 1986.
s. 62, regs. 75/1032; 82/1467.
ss. 63, 65, amended: 1980, c.45, sch.10.
s. 65, amended: 1981, c.44, s.12, sch.1; 1982, c.43, sch.1.
ss. 67, 68, repealed: 1981, c.44, sch.2.
s. 69, amended: 1982, c.43, sch.1.
s. 75, amended: 1981, c.44, s.6.
s. 78, regs. 75/1032; 82/1467.
s. 78, amended: 1973, c.65, sch.27; 1976, c.66, sch.7; 1981, c.44, sch.2; 1984, c.12, sch.9; repealed in pt.: 1975, c.65, sch.29.
s. 79, repealed in pt.: 1975, c.24, sch.3.
sch. 1, amended: 1981, c.44, s. 13; repealed in pt.: *ibid.*, sch.2.
sch. 3, regs. 75/1032; 82/1467.
sch. 3, amended: 1982, c.43, sch.3; repealed in pt.: *ibid.*, schs.3,4.
sch. 4, added: 1981, c.44, s.3.

87. Abortion Act 1967.
s. 1, see *R.* v. *Smith (John)* [1973] 1 W.L.R. 1510, C.A.; *Paton* v. *Trustees of B.P.A.S.* [1978] 2 All E.R. 987, Sir George Baker P.; *Royal College of Nursing* v. *Department of Health and Social Security* [1981] 2 W.L.R. 279; [1981] 1 All E.R. 545, H.L.; *Re P. (A Minor)* (1982) 80 L.G.R. 301, Butler-Sloss J.; *C.* v. *S.* [1987] 1 All E.R. 1230, C.A.
s. 1, amended: 1980, c.53, sch.1.
s. 2, regs. 74/1309; 76/15, 127; 80/1724, 1864; amended: 1977, c.45, s.31, sch.6.
s. 2, amended: order 88/1843.
s. 3, amended: 1980, c.53, sch.1.

CAP.

1967—cont.

87. Abortion Act 1967—*cont.*
s. 4, see *R.* v. *Salford Health Authority, ex p. Janaway*, [1988] 2 W.L.R. 442, C.A.
s. 6, amended: 1977, c.49, sch.15; 1978, c.29, sch.16(S.); repealed in pt.: 1980, c.53, sch.7.

88. Leasehold Reform Act 1967.
see *Lang* v. *Cornock* (1976) 241 E.G. 605; *Witham* v. *Collins* (1976) 239 E.G. 737; *Pearlman* v. *Keepers and Governors of Harrow School, The Times,* July 18, 1978, C.A.; *Methuen-Campbell* v. *Waters* (1978) 122 S.J. 610, C.A.; *James* v. *U.K.* (1986) 26 R.V.R. 139, European Court of Human Rights; *Rendall* v. *Duke of Westminster* (1987) 19 H.L.R. 345, C.A.
s. 1, see *Re Fairview, Church Street, Bromyard* [1974] 1 W.L.R. 579; [1974] 1 All E.R. 1233; *Parsons* v. *Viscount Gage (Trustees of Henry Smith's Charity)* [1974] 1 W.L.R. 435; [1974] 1 All E.R. 1162, H.L.; *Bates* v. *Pierrepoint* (1978) 37 P. & C.R. 420, C.A.; *Baron* v. *Phillips* (1979) 38 P. & C.R. 91, C.A.; *Poland* v. *Earl Cadogan* (1980) 40 P. & C.R. 331; [1980] 3 All E.R. 544, C.A.; *Harris* v. *Plentex* (1980) 40 P. & C.R. 483, Vinelott J.; *Duke of Westminster* v. *Oddy* (1984) 270 E.G. 945, C.A.; *McFarquhar* v. *Phillimore; Marks* v. *Phillimore* (1986) 18 H.L.R. 397, C.A.; *Gratton-Storey* v. *Lewis* (1987) 137 N.L.J. 789; (1987) 283 E.G. 1562, C.A.; *Dixon* v. *Allgood* [1987] 1 W.L.R. 1689, H.L.
s. 1, amended: 1974, c.44, s.118; 1977, c.42, sch.23; 1980, c.51, sch.20; 1986, c.5, sch.14; c.63, sch.4.
Pt. I (ss.1–37), see *Sharpe* v. *Duke Street Securities N.V., The Times,* June 13, 1987, C.A.
s. 1A, amended: 1986, c.63, sch.4.
s. 2, see *Parsons* v. *Viscount Gage (Trustees of Henry Smith's Charity)* [1974] 1 W.L.R. 435; [1974] 1 All E.R. 1162, H.L.; *Gaidowski* v. *Gonville and Caius College, Cambridge* [1975] 1 W.L.R. 1066; [1975] 2 All E.R. 952, C.A.; *Methuen-Campbell* v. *Walters* [1979] 2 W.L.R. 113, C.A.; *Tandon* v. *Trustees of Spurgeons Homes* [1982] 2 W.L.R. 735, H.L.; *Cresswell* v *Duke of Westminster* (1985) 275 E.G. 461, C.A.; *Sharpe* v. *Duke Street Securities N.V.* (1987) 283 E.G. 1558, C.A.
s. 3, see *Austin* v. *Dick Richards Properties* [1975] 2 All E.R. 75, C.A.; *Bates* v. *Pierrepoint* (1978) 37 P . & C.R. 420, C.A.; *Eton College* v. *Bard* [1983] 3 W.L.R. 231, C.A.
s. 3, amended: 1984, c.29, sch.11; 1985, c.71.sch.2; 1986, c.63, sch.4.
s. 4, see *Gidlow-Jackson* v. *Middlegate Properties* [1974] 2 W.L.R. 116, C.A.; *Manson* v. *Duke of Westminster* [1981] 2 W.L.R. 428, C.A.; *Johnston* v. *Duke of Westminster* [1986] 3 W.L.R. 18, H.L.; *Griffiths* v. *Birmingham City District Council,* January 26, 1987, H.H. Judge Clive Taylor, Q.C., Stafford County Ct.; *McDonald* v. *Trustees of Henry Smith's Charity, The Times,* July 30, 1987, C.A.; *Hembry*

1967—cont.

88. Leasehold Reform Act 1967—cont.
v. *Henry Smith's Charity Trustees* (1987) 284 E.G. 369, C.A.; *Dixon* v. *Allgood* [1987] 1 W.L.R. 1689, H.L.
ss. 4, 6, see *McFarquhar* v. *Phillimore*; *Marks* v. *Phllimore* (1986) 18 H.L.R. 397, C.A.
s. 5, see *Pollock* v. *Brook Shepherd* (1983) 45 P. & C.R. 357, C.A.
ss. 5, 8, see *Johnson* v. *Sheffield City Council* (1982) 43 P. & C.R. 272, Lands Tribunal.
s. 7, repealed in pt.: 1975, c.72, sch.4.
s. 8, see *Collins* v. *Duke of Westminster* [1985] 1 All E.R. 463, C.A.; *Gratton-Storey* v. *Lewis* (1987) 137 N.L.J. 789; (1987) 283 E.G. 1562, C.A.
s. 8, amended: 1977, c.30, sch.1.
s. 9, see *Re Howell* [1972] 2 W.L.R. 1346; *Gallagher Estates* v. *Walker* (1973) 28 P. & C.R. 113, C.A.; *Official Custodian for Charities* v. *Goldridge* (1973) 26 P. & C.R. 191, C.A.; *Miller* v. *St. John Baptist's College, Oxford* (1977) 243 E.G. 535; *Jones* v. *Wrotham Park Settled Estates* [1979] 2 W.L.R. 132, H.L.; *Re London and Winchester Properties' Appeal* (1983) 45 P. & C.R. 429, Lands Tribunal; *Mosley* v. *Hickman*; *Same* v. *Hagan*; *Same* v. *Francis* (1986) 278 E.G. 728, C.A.
s. 9, amended: 1980, c.51, sch.20; repealed in pt.: 1977, c.30, sch.2; 1986, c.63, s.23.
s. 11, amended: 1977, c.30, sch.1; repealed in pt.: *ibid.*, sch.2.
ss. 14,15, see *Official Custodian for Charities* v. *Goldridge* (1973) 26 P. & C.R. 191, C.A.
s. 16, amended: 1976, c.80, sch.8; 1977, c.42, sch.13; 1980, c.51, sch.20.
s. 18, repealed in pt.: 1975, c.72, sch.4.
s. 19, see *Re Abbots Park* [1972] 1 W.L.R. 598; [1972] 2 All E.R. 177; *Cadbury* v. *Woodward* (1972) 24 P. & C.R. 335; *Re Calthorpe Estate, Edgbaston, Birmingham*; *Anstruther-Gough-Calthorpe* v. *Grey* (1973) 26 P. & C.R. 120, Foster J.; *Re Dulwich College Estates' Application* (1973) 231 E.G. 845.
s. 19, amended: 1975, c.76, sch.1.
s. 20, see *Collins* v. *Duke of Westminster* [1985] 1 All E.R. 463, C.A.
s. 21, see *Re London and Winchester Properties' Appeal* (1983) 45 P. & C.R. 429, Lands Tribunal.
s. 21, regs. 81/271.
s. 21, amended: 1980, c.51, s.142, sch.22; 1984, c.28, sch.2; repealed in pt.: 1980, c.51, schs.22,26.
s. 23, see *Jones* v. *Wrotham Park Settled Estates* [1979] 2 W.L.R. 132, H.L.
s. 23, amended: 1980, c.51, sch.20.
s. 26, amended: 1983, c.20, sch.4.
s. 27, see *Re Howell* [1972] 2 W.L.R. 1346.
s. 28, amended: 1973, c.32, sch.4; 1976, c.75, sch.7; 1977, c.49, sch.15; 1980, c.53, sch.1; 1985, c.51, sch.14; orders 85/39, 1884; 1988, c.4, sch.6; c.50, sch.17; repealed in pt.: 1985, c.51, sch.14; 1988, c.40, sch.12 (prosp.).
s. 29, see *Gaidowski* v. *Gonville and Caius College* [1975] 1 W.L.R. 1066; [1975] 2 All E.R. 952, C.A.

1967—cont.

88. Leasehold Reform Act 1967—cont.
s. 29, amended: 1976, c.75, sch.7; 1980, c.51, sch.20; 1988, c.50, sch.17.
s. 30, amended: 1976, c.75, sch.7; repealed in pt.: 1985, c.71, sch.1.
s. 31, amended: 1980, c.51, sch.22; 1988, No. 1, s.10; repealed in pt.: *ibid.*.
s. 33A, added: 1986, c.63, sch.4.
s. 37, see *McFarquhar* v. *Phillimore*; *Marks* v. *Phillimore* (1986) 18 H.L.R. 397, C.A.
s. 37, amended: 1977, c.42, sch.23.
s. 39, see *Investment & Freehold English Estates* v. *Casement* (1987) 283 E.G. 748, H.H. Judge Paul Baker, Q.C.
s. 39, amended: 1973, c.9, sch.6; repealed in pt.: S.L.R. 1976.
sch. 1, amended: 1980, c.51, schs.20,22; repealed in pt.: 1977, c.42, s.17, sch.2; 1980, c.51, sch.26.
sch. 2, amended: 1976, c.80, sch.8; 1977, c.42, sch.23; 1980, c.51, sch.22; repealed in pt.: *ibid.*, schs.22,26.
sch. 3, see *Duke of Westminister* v. *Oddy* (1984) 270 E.G. 945, C.A.; *Cresswell* v. *Duke of Westminster* (1985) 275 E.G. 461, C.A.
sch. 3, amended: 1980, c.51, sch.21.
sch. 4, amended: 1976, c.75, sch.7; 1981, c.67, sch.4.
sch. 4A, regs. 87/1940.
sch. 4A, added: 1986, c.63, sch.4; amended: 1988, c.50, sch.17.
sch. 5, amended: 1972, c.47, schs.9,11; 1977, c.42, sch.23; repealed in pt.: 1972, c.47, sch.11; 1985, c.71, sch.1.

90. Family Allowances and National Insurance Act 1967.
ss. 1–3, sch. 1, amended: 1973, c.38, schs.27,28.
ss. 1, 2, 4, sch. 3, repealed in pt.: 1975, c.18, sch.1.
s. 2, repealed in pt.: 1976, c.5, sch.
sch. 2, repealed: 1975, c.18, sch.1.

91. Coal Industry Act 1967.
s. 1, repealed: 1973, c.8, sch.2.
s. 2, repealed: 1977, c.39, sch.5.
s. 3, orders 72/335; 73/1268; 75/545; 76/491, 495; 77/524.
s. 3, repealed 1977, c.39, sch.5.
s. 4, amended: 1987, c.3, sch.1; repealed in pt.: 1977, c.39, sch.5.
ss. 5, 6, repealed: *ibid.*
s. 7, repealed in pt.: *ibid.*; 1987, c.3, sch.3.
sch., repealed in pt.: 1977, c.39, sch.5.

1968

2. Provisional Collection of Taxes Act 1968.
s. 1, amended: 1972, c.41, s.1, sch.7; 1975, c.22, s.11; 1981, c.35, s.128; 1983, c.53, s.10, sch.9; 1985, c.54, s.97; 1986, c.41, s.86; 1988, c.1, sch.29; repealed in pt.: 1972, c.41, sch.28.
s. 3, regs. 76/546; amended: 1979, c.2, sch.4.
s. 4, amended: *ibid.*

1968—cont.

2. Provisional Collection of Taxes Act 1968—
cont.
s. 5, amended: 1972, c.41, sch.24; 1988, c.1, sch.29.
s. 6, repealed in pt.: 1973, c.36, sch.6.

3. Capital Allowances Act 1968.
s. 1, amended: 1975, c.7, s.13; 1978, c.42, sch.6; 1981, c.35, s.73; 1984, c.43, sch.12; modified: 1980, c.48, s.75, sch.13; 1982, c.39, s.74; repealed in pt.: 1980, c.48, s.76, sch.20.
s. 2, modified: 1980, c.48, sch.13; amended: 1981, c.35, s.74.
s. 3, amended: *ibid.*, ss.74,75.
s. 4, amended: *ibid.*, s.75; 1988, c.39, s.90.
s. 6, amended: 1981, c.35. s.74.
s. 7, see *Buckingham* v. *Securitas Properties* [1980] 1 W.L.R. 380, Slade J.; *Vibroplant* v. *Holland* [1982] S.T.C. 164, C.A.; [1982] 1 All E.R. 792, C.A.; *Copol Clothing* v. *Hindmarsh* [1984] 1 W.L.R. 411, C.A.; *Crusabridge Investments* v. *Casings International* [1979] 54 T.C. 246, D.C.
s. 7, amended: 1982, c.39, ss.74,75; 1983, c.28, s.30.
s 12, amended: 1988, c.1, sch.29.
s. 14, amended: 1986, c 41, s.86.
s. 15, amended: 1988, c.1, sch.29.
s. 18. see *Benson* v. *Yard Arm Club* [1979] 1 W.L.R. 347, C.A.
ss. 18, 19, see *Corke* v. *Beach Station Caravans* [1974] 3 All E.R. 159; *St. John's School (Mountford and Knibbs)* v. *Ward* [1975] S.T.C. 7, C.A.; *Bolton* v. *International Drilling Co.* [1983] S.T.C. 70, Vinelott J.
s. 20, amended: 1976, c.40, s.39; repealed in pt.: *ibid.*, sch.15.
s. 24, repealed in pt.: *ibid.*
s. 26, amended: 1982, c.39, sch.21; 1988, c.1, sch.29; repealed in pt.: 1976, c.40, sch.15.
s. 31, repealed in pt.: *ibid.*
s. 33, see *Costain-Blankwoort (U.K.) Dredging Co.* v. *Davenport, The Times,* November 17, 1978, Walton J.
s. 33, amended: 1976, c.40, sch.9; 1988, c.1, sch.29.
s. 34, amended: 1976, c.40, sch.9; 1987, c 16, sch.15; 1988, c.1, sch.29.
s. 47, amended: *ibid.*, repealed in pt. (prosp.): 1988, c.39, sch.14.
ss. 48, 60, amended: 1988, c.1, sch. 29.
ss. 51–66, repealed: 1986, c.41, sch.23.
s. 67, amended: 1988, c.1, sch.29.
s. 68, repealed: 1986, c.41, s.56, sch. 23; substituted: *ibid,* s.56,.
s. 69, amended: *ibid;* 1988, c.1, sch.29; c.39, s.91; repealed in pt. (prosp.): *ibid.,* sch.14.
s. 70, amended: 1981, c.35, s.77; 1988, c.1, sch. 29; repealed in pt.: 1986, c.41, sch.23; 1988, c.39, sch.14 (prosp.).
s. 72, amended: 1988, c.1, sch. 29.
s. 74, amended: 1978, c.42, s.39; repealed in pt.: 1986, c.41, sch.23.
s. 75, repealed in pt.: *ibid.*
s. 78, amended: 1981, c.35, s.77; 1988, c.1, sch.29; repealed in pt.: 1986, c.41, sch.23.

1968—cont.

3. Capital Allowances Act 1968—*cont.*
s. 79, amended: 1988, c.1, sch.29; repealed in pt.: 1986, c.41, sch.23; 1988, c.39, sch.14 (prosp.).
s. 80, amended: 1988, c.1, sch.29.
s. 82, repealed in pt.: 1985, c.54, s.56, sch.27.
s. 83, see *Schofield* v. *R. & H. Hall* [1975] S.T.C. 353, C.A.
s. 83, order 82/1237.
s. 83, amended: 1973, c.65, sch.27: 1984, c.32, sch.6; repealed in pt.: 1986, c.41, sch.23.
s. 84, orders 78/53; 80/1071; 82/1228; 83/498; 84/407; 86/539; 87/362.
s. 84, amended: 1972, c.41, s.67; 1982, c.52, sch.2.
s. 85, amended: 1976, c.40, s.42; 1986, c.51, s.56; 1988, c.1, sch. 29; c.39, s.91; repealed in pt.: 1986, c.51, sch.23; 1988, c.39, sch.14 (prosp.).
s. 87, amended: 1986, c.51, sch.13; repealed in pt. (prosp.): 1988, c.39, sch.14.
s. 90, amended: 1988, c.1, sch.29.
s. 91, see *Gaspet (formerly Saga Petroleum (U.K.))* v. *Elliss (Inspector of Taxes)* [1987] 1 W.L.R. 769, C.A.
ss. 91, amended: 1985, c.54, s.63; 1988, c.1, sch.29.
s. 92, amended: 1985, c.54, s.63.
s. 93, amended: 1986, c.41, sch.13.
s. 94, repealed in pt.: 1985, c.54, sch.27.
s. 95, orders 78/53; 80/1071; 82/1228; 83/498; 84/407; 86/539; 87/362
s. 95, amended: 1972, c.41, s.67; 1982, c.52, sch.2.
s. 100, sch. 2, amended: 1988, c.1, sch.29.
sch. 4, repealed in pt.: 1976, c.40, sch.15.
schs. 5, 6, repealed: 1986, c.41, sch.23.
sch. 7, amended: 1981, c.35, s.76; 1986, c.41, sch.13; 1987, c.51, s.64; 1988, c.1, sch.29; c.9, s.91; repealed in pt.: 1986, c.41, sch.23.
sch 9, repealed in pt. (prosp.): 1988, c.9, sch.14.

4. Erskine Bridge Tolls Act 1968.
s. 2, orders 74/1877; 81/1375(S.).
ss. 5, 7, 9, regs. 73/668.

5. Administration of Justice Act 1968.
repealed (S.): 1988, c.36, sch.2.
s. 1, orders 78/1057; 81/439; 85/1213(S.); 86/2233(S.).
s. 1, amended: orders 75/1215; 77/602; 78/1057; 81/439; 85/1213(S.); repealed in pt.: 1978, c.23, sch.7; 1981, c.54, sch.7.

7. London Cab Act 1968.
s. 1, orders 79/906; 85/933, 1023; 87/999; 88/996.
s. 2, order 72/1047.
s. 3, amended: 1984, c.27, sch.13.
s. 4, see *Green* v. *Turkington; Green* v. *Cater, Craig* v. *Cater* [1975] Crim.L.R. 242, D.C.; *Armitage* v. *Walton* [1976] R.T.R. 160, D.C.
s. 4, amended: 1973, c.20, s.1; 1984, c.46, sch.5.
s. 4A, added: 1973, c.20, s.1.
s. 4A, order 73/1671.

1968—cont.

8. Mauritius Independence Act 1968.
see *R. v. Secretary of State for the Home Department, ex p. Bibi (Mahaboob)* [1985] Imm.A.R. 134, Mann J.
ss. 2, 3, repealed: 1981, c.61, sch.9.
s. 4, repealed in pt.: 1978, c.30, sch.3.
sch. 2, repealed in pt.: S.L.R. 1977; 1981, c.9, sch.

9. Commonwealth Immigration Act 1968.
s. 2, see *R. v. Immigration Appeals Adjudicator, ex p. Khan* [1972] 1 W.L.R. 1058.
s. 3, see *Azam v. Secretary of State for the Home Department; Khera v. Same; Sidhu v. Same* [1973] 2 W.L.R. 1058; [1973] 2 All E.R. 765.

11. Revenue Act 1968.
repealed: S.L.R. 1986.
s. 1, see *Lord Advocate v. Babcock & Wilcox* [1972] 1 W.L.R. 488; [1972] 1 All E.R. 1130.
sch. order 72/202.

12. Teachers' Superannuation (Scotland) Act 1968.
repealed (except s. 13): 1972, c.11, sch.8.
s. 7, regs. 72/442.

13. National Loans Act 1968.
s. 1, repealed in pt.: 1975, c.7, sch.13; 1978, c.30, sch.3.
s. 2, repealed in pt.: 1980, c.63, sch.2.
s. 3, amended: 1984, c.43, s.125; repealed in pt.: *ibid.*, s.125, sch.23.
s. 4, orders 86/129; 88/635.
s. 4, substituted: 1984, c.43, s.125.; amended: orders 86/129; 88/635; 1986, c.41, s.112.
s. 5, substituted: 1982, c.39, s.153; amended: 1983, c.28, s.44.
s. 6, amended: 1972, c.46, sch.11; c.47, sch.11; repealed in pt.: 1975, c.30, sch.7; 1980, c.66, sch.25; 1985, c.71, sch.1.
s. 7, repealed: 1979, c.30, sch.
s. 10, repealed in pt.: S.L.R. 1976; 1978, c.2, sch.2; 1980, c.41, sch.; c.63, sch.2; 1981, c.15, sch.3.
s. 11, repealed: 1972, c.52, sch.23.
s. 12, amended: 1982, c.39, s.152; repealed in pt.: S.L.R. 1973.
s. 14, rules 79/1678; 85/1147.
s. 16, repealed in pt.: 1972, c.65, sch.; 1981, c.35, sch.19.
s. 21, repealed in pt.: S.L.R. 1973.
s. 23, repealed in pt.: 1973, c.36, sch.6.
sch. 1, amended: 1982, c.39, s.153; repealed in pt.: 1972, c.60, sch.8; c.63, sch.4; c.68, sch.3; 1974, c.44, sch.15; 1975, c.64, sch.7; c.78, sch.6; 1976, c.55, sch.4; 1977, c.36, sch.9; 1978, c.44, sch.17; 1981, c.56, sch.12; c.64, sch.13; 1985, c.71, sch.1; S.L.R. 1986.
sch. 2, repealed: 1980, c.63, sch.2.
sch. 4, amended: 1975, c.30, sch.6(S.); 1980, c.63, sch.6; 1985, c.71, sch.2; 1987, c.26, sch.23(S.); c.47, sch.1(S.); repealed in pt.: 1988, c.12, sch.7.
sch. 5, repealed in pt.: 1972, c.65, sch.; 1973, c.36, sch.6; 1975, c.64, sch.7; 1981, c.38, sch.6; S.L.R. 1986.

1968—cont.

14. Public Expenditure and Receipts Act 1968.
ss. 1, 2, repealed: 1973, c.38, sch.28.
s. 5, orders 72/890, 911; 75/1291, 1299, 1808; 76/138; 77/1861, 1891, 2140; 79/569, 1443; 80/111, 242(S.), 265, 295(S.), 1612; 81/241, 929, 976(S.), 1739; 83/1072, 1778; 85/202, 281(S.), 1960; 86/368, 408(S.), 977(S.); 87/50, 353; 88/165, 1653.
s. 6, repealed: 1972, c.5, sch.4.
s. 7, repealed in pt.: 1973, c.38, sch. 28.
sch. 2, repealed: *ibid.*
sch. 3, orders 72/890; 75/1291, 1299, 1808; 76/138; 77/1861, 1891. 2140; 79/569, 1448; 80/111, 242(S.), 265, 295(S.), 1612; 81/241, 929, 976(S.), 1739; 83/1072, 1778; 85/202, 281(S.), 1960; 86/368, 408(S.), 977(S.); 87/50, 353; 88/165, 1653.
sch. 3, amended: 1972, c.52, sch.21; 1974, c.46, sch.9; 1975, c.18, sch.2; repealed in pt.: 1973, c.32, sch.5; 1974, c.46, sch.11; 1986, c.63, sch.12.
sch. 3, repealed in pt.: (S.): *ibid.*

15. Representation of the People Act 1968.
s. 27, order 76/2064.

16. New Towns (Scotland) Act 1968.
s. 1, orders 73/491, 1245.
s. 1A, added: 1985, c.5, s.10.
ss. 1, 2, amended: 1977, c.16, s.1.
s. 4, amended: 1974, c.8, sch.3.
s. 5, amended: 1977, c.16, s.1.
s. 6, orders 73/1010, 1682; 75/908.
s. 6, amended: 1973, c.65, sch. 23; 1984, c.54, sch. 9; repealed in pt.: 1987, c.26, schs.23, 24.
ss. 8, 10, amended: *ibid.*
s. 11, repealed: 1973, c.26, sch.3.
s. 14, amended: 1984, c.12, sch.4.
s. 18, amended: 1976, c.66, sch.7; 1980, c.65, sch.25.
ss. 18A–18C, added: 1985, c.5, sch.3.
s. 18AA, added: 1988, c.43, s.71.
s. 19, amended: 1984, c.12, sch.4; c.54, sch.9.
ss. 20, 21, amended: *ibid.*
s. 22, amended: *ibid.*; c.58, sch.8, repealed in pt.: 1973, c.26, sch.3.
s. 23, amended: 1973, c.65, sch.23; 1984, c.54, sch.9.
s. 24, substituted: 1984, c.12, sch.4; amended: 1984, c.54, sch.9.
s. 25, repealed: *ibid.*, sch.11.
s. 26, amended: 1984, c.12, sch.4; c.54, sch.9.
s. 32, amended: *ibid.*
ss. 33, repealed: 1973, c.65, sch.29.
s. 34, repealed in pt.: *ibid.*
ss. 35, 36, amended: *ibid.*, sch.23.
s. 36A, added: 1984, c.12, sch.4.
ss. 37A, 38A, added: 1974, c.8, sch.3.
s. 38A, amended: 1983, c.29, s.4, sch.2.
s. 38B, added: 1975, c.28, s.6; 1987, c.26, sch.23.
s. 41, amended: 1973, c.65, sch.23; repealed in pt.: 1972, c.11, sch.8; 1984, c.54, sch.11.
s. 42, amended: *ibid.*, sch.9.
s. 46, orders 73/491, 1245; regs. 75/1567.

CAP.

1968—cont.

16. New Towns (Scotland) Act 1968—*cont.*
s. 47, amended: 1973, c.65, sch.23; 1976, c.66, sch.7; order 76/1775; 1981, c.38, sch.3; 1984, c.54, sch.9; repealed in pt.: 1973, c.65, sch.29; 1976, c.66, sch.8; 1986, c.44, sch.9.
sch. 1, amended: 1973, c.65, sch.23.
sch. 1A, added: 1985, c.5, s.10, sch.1.
sch. 2, amended: 1975, c.42, s.2.
schs. 3, 4, regs. 75/1567.
schs. 3, 4, amended: 1984, c.54, sch.9.
sch. 6, repealed in pt.: 1973, c.26, sch.3.
sch. 10, repealed in pt.: 1975, c.42, s.3.

17. Education Act 1968.
s. 1, amended: 1980, c.20, sch.3; repealed in pt.: *ibid.*, sch.7.
s. 3, amended: *ibid.*, sch.3; repealed in pt.: *ibid.*, schs.1,7.
s. 5, schs. 1, 3, repealed in pt.: *ibid.*, sch.7.
sch. 1, amended: 1973, c.16, sch.2.

18. Consular Relations Act 1968.
s. 1, order 84/1978.
s. 1, amended: 1973, c.38, sch.27; 1979, c.2, sch.4; 1981, c.61, sch.7; order 86/948; repealed in pt.: 1975, c.18, sch.1.
s. 3, orders 78/1028; 84/1978.
s. 4, orders 76/768, 1152; 78/275; 86/217.
s. 5, amended: 1979, c.2, sch.4.
ss. 5, 6, orders 76/768, 1152; 78/275.
s. 7, repealed: 1981, c.61, sch.9.
s. 8, amended: 1979, c.2, sch.4.
s. 10, amended: 1982, c.53, s.28.
s. 12, order 85/1983.
ss. 12, 14, orders 74/109, 1709; 76/51; 77/1627; 78/780; 84/1977.
s. 13, repealed in pt.: 1980, c.23, s.1.
s. 14, orders 78/1028; 84/1977, 1978.
s. 16, orders 76/768, 1152; 78/275; 86/217.
sch. 1, amended: 1987, c.46, sch.2.

19. Criminal Appeal Act 1968.
s. 1, see *R.* v. *Smith* [1974] 2 W.L.R. 20, C.A.; *R.* v. *Pinfold* [1988] 2 W.L.R. 635, C.A.
s. 1, amended: 1980, c.43, sch.7.
s. 2, see *R.* v. *Brown* (*D. W.*) (1971) 55 Cr.App.R. 478; *R.* v. *Lewis* (1973) 57 Cr.App.R. 860, C.A.; *R.* v. *Gray* (1973) 58 Cr.App.R. 177, C.A.; *R.* v. *Deacon* [1973] 1 W.L.R. 696; *Stafford* v. *D.P.P.*; *Luvaglio* v. *D.P.P.* [1973] 3 W.L.R. 719; [1973] 3 All E.R. 762, H.L.; *R.* v. *Rivers* [1974] R.T.R. 31, C.A.; *R.* v. *Mitcham* [1974] R.T.R. 205, C.A.; *D.P.P.* v. *Shannon* [1974] 3 W.L.R. 155; [1974] 2 All E.R. 1009, H.L.; *R.* v. *Brown* (*John*) [1974] R.T.R. 377, C.A.; *R.* v. *Shaw* (*Derek*) [1974] R.T.R. 458, C.A.; *R.* v. *Thorpe* (*Thomas*) [1974] R.T.R. 465, C.A.; *R.* v. *Lamb* (1974) 59 Cr.App.R. 196, C.A.; *R.* v. *Shaw* (*Kenneth*) [1975] R.T.R. 160, C.A.; *R.* v. *Vickers* [1975] 1 W.L.R. 811, C.A.; *D.P.P.* v. *Morgan*; *Same* v. *McDonald* [1975] 2 W.L.R. 913; [1975] 2 All E.R. 347, H.L.; *R.* v. *Callum* [1975] R.T.R. 415, C.A.; *R.* v. *Shepherd* [1975] R.T.R. 497, C.A.; *R.* v. *Foster* [1975] R.T.R. 553, C.A.; *R.* v. *Graham* (1975) 61 Cr.App.R. 292, C.A.; *R.* v. *Segal* [1976] R.T.R. 319, C.A.; *R.* v. *Paley* (1976) 63 Cr.App.R. 172, C.A.; *R.* v. *Gilbert* (1977) 66

CAP.

1968—cont.

19. Criminal Appeal Act 1968—*cont.*
Cr.App.R. 237, C.A.; *R.* v. *Lidiard* (1978) 122 S.J. 743, C.A.; *R.* v. *Wallace*; *R.* v. *Short* (1978) 67 Cr.App.R. 291, C.A.; *R.* v. *Hamid* (1979) 69 Cr.App.R. 334, C.A.; *R.* v. *Dempster* (1980) 71 Cr.App.R. 302, C.A.; *R.* v. *Molyneux*; *R.* v. *Farmborough* (1980) 72 Cr.App.R. 111, C.A.; *R.* v. *Jenkins* (1981) 72 Cr.App.R. 354, C.A.; *R.* v. *Bogdal* [1982] R.T.R. 395, C.A.; *R.* v. *Edwards* (*Webb*), *The Times*, March 1, 1983, C.A.; *R.* v. *John Paraskeva* (1983) 76 Cr.App.R. 162, C.A.; *R.* v. *Home Office, ex p. Graham* [1983] 1 W.L.R. 1281, D.C.; *R.* v. *Ayres*, *The Times*, February 18, 1984, H.L.; *R.* v. *Foster*, *The Times*, March 31, 1984, C.A.; *R.* v. *Lee* [1984] 1 All E.R. 1080, C.A.; *R.* v. *Bell* (*Peter*) (1984) 78 Cr.App.R. 305, C.A.; *R.* v. *St. Louis and Case* (1984) 79 Cr.App.R. 53, C.A.; *R.* v. *Tonner*; *R.* v. *Evans* (*Ronald*) [1985] 1 W.L.R. 344, C.A.; *R.* v. *Drew* [1985] 1 W.L.R. 914, C.A.; *R.* v. *Khan* [1985] R.T.R. 365, C.A.; *R.* v. *Grant* [1986] Crim.L.R. 235, C.A.; *R.* v. *Stewart* [1986] 83 Cr.App.R. 327, C.A.; *R.* v. *Garwood* [1987] 1 W.L.R. 319, C.A.; *R.* v. *Gorman* [1987] 1 W.L.R. 545, C.A.; *McVey, The Times*, October 24, 1987, C.A.; *R.* v. *Pope* (1987) 85 Cr.App.R. 201, C.A.; *R.* v. *Pinfold* [1988] 2 W.L.R. 635, C.A.; *R.* v. *Silverman* (1988) 86 Cr.App.R. 213, C.A.; *R.* v. *Donoghue* (1988) 86 Cr.App.R. 267, C.A.
s. 2, amended: 1977, c.45, s.44.
s. 3, see *R.* v. *Deacon* [1973] 1 W.L.R. 696; *R.* v. *Spratt* [1980] 1 W.L.R. 554; [1980] 2 All E.R. 269, C.A.; *R.* v. *Lee* [1984] 1 All E.R. 1080, C.A.; *R.* v. *Tonner*; *R.* v. *Evans* (*Ronald*) [1985] 1 W.L.R. 334, C.A.
s. 4, see *R.* v. *Thompson* (1978) 66 Cr.App.R. 130, C.A.; *R.* v. *Fairhurst*, *The Times*, August 2, 1986, C.A.
s. 5, amended: 1973, c.39, sch.1.
s. 6, amended: 1983, c.20, sch.4.
s. 7, see *R.* v. *Wallace*; *R.* v. *Short* (1978) 67 Cr.App.R. 291, C.A.
s. 7, repealed in pt.: 1988, c.33, s.43, sch.16.
s. 8, amended: 1976, c.63, sch.2; 1982, c.51, sch.3; 1983, c.20, sch.4; 1988, c.33, s.43.
s. 9, see *R.* v. *Tucker* [1974] 1 W.L.R. 615; [1974] 2 All E.R. 639; *R.* v. *Hayden* [1975] 1 W.L.R. 852, C.A.; *R.* v. *Ioannou* [1975] 1 W.L.R. 1297; [1975] 3 All E.R. 400, C.A.; *R.* v. *McQuaide* (1975) 60 Cr.App.R. 239, C.A.; *R.* v. *Robinson* [1979] Crim.L.R. 785, C.A.; *R.* v. *Welch* [1982] 1 W.L.R. 976, C.A.; *R.* v. *Raeburn* [1982] 74 Cr.App.R. 21, C.A.; *R.* v. *Bentham* [1982] R.T.R. 357, C.A.; *R.* v. *Wintour* (*Note*) [1982] R.T.R. 361, C.A.; *R.* v. *Williams* (*Carl*) [1982] 1 W.L.R. 1398, C.A.
s. 9, amended: 1988, c.33, sch.15.
s. 10, see *R.* v. *Wilson*; *R.* v. *Keelan* (1975) 61 Cr.App.R. 212; [1980] 1 W.L.R. 376; [1980] 1 All E.R. 1093, C.A.; *R.* v. *Harding* (1983) 5 Cr.App.R.(S.) 197, C.A.
s. 10, amended: 1972, c.71, sch.5; 1973, c.62, sch.4; 1982, c.48, sch.14; 1988, c.33, sch.15; repealed in pt.: *ibid.*, sch.16.

CAP.

1968—cont.

19. Criminal Appeal Act 1968—cont.

s. 11, see *R.* v. *Lambert* [1974] R.T.R. 244, C.A.; *R.* v. *Quinn* (1975) 60 Cr.App.R. 314, C.A.; *R.* v. *Keelan* (1975) 61 Cr.App.R. 212, C.A.; *R.* v. *Berry* (1976) 63 Cr.App.R. 44, C.A.; *R.* v. *Thompson* (1978) 66 Cr.App.R. 130, C.A.; *R.* v. *Midgley* [1979] R.T.R. 1, C.A.; *R.* v. *Mah-Wing, The Times,* October 18, 1983, C.A.; *R.* v. *Ardani* (1983) 77 Cr.App.R. 302, C.A.; *R.* v. *Sandwell* [1985] R.T.R. 45, C.A.

s. 11, amended: 1973, c.62, sch. 5; 1982, c.48, s.29; c.51, sch. 3; 1983, c.20, sch. 4; 1988 c.33, sch.15; repealed in pt.: 1981, c.54, sch. 7.

s. 14, amended: 1982, c.51, sch.3; 1983, c.20, sch.4.

s. 16, amended: 1976, c.65, sch.2; 1983, c.20, sch.4.

s. 17, see *R.* v. *Saunders* (1973) 58 Cr.App.R. 248, C.A.; *Stafford* v. *D.P.P.*; *Luvaglio* v. *D.P.P.* [1973] 3 W.L.R. 719; [1973] 3 All E.R. 762, H.L.; *R.* v. *Graves* [1978] Crim.L.R. 216, C.A.; *R.* v. *McMahon* (1978) 68 Cr.App.R. 18, C.A.; *R.* v. *Chard* [1983] 3 W.L.R. 835, H.L.

s. 18, see *R.* v. *Howitt* (1975) 61 Cr.App.R. 327, C.A.; *R.* v. *Suggett* (1985) 81 Cr.App.R. 243, C.A.

s. 18A, added: 1988, c.33, sch.15.

s. 19, substituted: 1982, c.48, s.29; amended: 1988, c.33, sch.15.

s. 20, see *R.* v. *Taylor* [1979] Crim.L.R. 649, C.A.

s. 20, substituted: 1988, c.33, s.157.

s. 23, see *R.* v. *Beresford* (1971) 56 Cr.App.R. 143; *R.* v. *Melville* [1976] 1 W.L.R. 181; [1976] 1 All E.R. 395, C.A.; *R.* v. *Lattimore*; *R.* v. *Salih*; *R.* v. *Leighton* (1975) 62 Cr.App.R. 53, C.A.; *R.* v. *Shields and Patrick* [1977] Crim.L.R. 281, C.A.; *R.* v. *McMahon* (1978) 68 Cr.App.R. 18, C.A.; *R.* v. *Wallace*; *R.* v. *Short* (1978) 67 Cr.App.R. 291, C.A.; *R.* v. *Conway* (1979) 70 Cr.App.R. 4, C.A.; *R.* v. *Malcherek*; *R.* v. *Steel* [1981] 1 W.L.R. 690; [1981] 2 All E.R. 422, C.A.; *R.* v. *Kooken* (1982) 74 Cr.App.R. 30, C.A; *R.* v. *Foster, The Times,* March 31, 1984, C.A.; *R.* v. *Lee* (1984) 81 L.S.Gaz. 970, C.A.; *R.* v. *Callaghan*; *R.* v. *Hill (Patrick)*; *R.* v. *Hunter (Robert)*; *R.* v. *McIlkenny*; *R.* v. *Power*; R. v. *Walker* [1988] 1 W.L.R. 1, C.A.; *R.* v. *Pinfold* [1988] 2 W.L.R. 635, C.A.

s. 24, see *R.* v. *Benyon* (1972) 57 Cr.App.R. 259, C.A.; *R.* v. *Arron (Note)* [1973] 2 All E.R. 1221, C.A.

ss. 24–8, repealed: 1973, c.14, sch.2.

ss. 24, 25, 28, see *R.* v. *Rimmer* [1972] 1 W.L.R. 268; [1972] 1 All E.R. 604.

s. 29, amended: 1988, c.33, sch.15.

ss. 29, 31, see *R.* v. *Howitt* (1975) 61 Cr.App.R. 327, C.A.

s. 30, substituted: 1988, c.33, sch.15.

s. 31, see *R.* v. *Suggett* (1985) 81 Cr.App.R. 243, C.A.

s. 31, amended: 1973, c.14, sch.1; 1974, c.50, sch.6; 1976, c.63, sch.2; c.82, s.5; 1988, c.33, sch.15; c.54, sch. 3; repealed in pt.: 1973, c.14, sch.2.

CAP.

1968—cont.

19. Criminal Appeal Act 1968—cont.

s. 33, see *R.* v. *Ashdown* [1974] 1 W.L.R. 270; [1974] 1 All E.R. 800, C.A.; *R.* v. *Delgado, The Times,* January 18, 1984, C.A.

s. 33, amended: 1981, c.54, sch.5; 1987, c.38, sch.2.

s. 35, see *Stafford* v. *D.P.P.*; *Luvaglio* v. *D.P.P.* [1973] 3 W.L.R. 719; [1973] 3 All E.R. 762, H.L.

s. 36, amended: 1976, c.63, sch.2; 1987, c.38, sch.2.

s. 37, amended: 1982, c.51, sch.3; 1983, c.20, sch.4.

s. 38, amended; 1987, c.38, sch.2.

ss. 39–41, repealed: 1973, c.14, sch.2.

s. 42, see *Gooch* v. *Ewing (Allied Irish Bank, Garnishee)* [1985] 3 All E.R. 654, C.A.

s. 42, repealed: 1988, c.33, sch 16.

s. 43, amended: 1976, c.63, sch.2.

s. 44, amended: 1973, c.14, sch.1; 1974, c.50, sch.6; 1988, c.33, sch.15; c.54, sch.3; repealed in pt.: 1973, c.14, sch.2.

s. 46, rules 72/1786; 73/1114; 78/1118.

s. 46, repealed: 1981, c.54, sch.7.

s. 50, see *R.* v. *Tucker* [1974] 1 W.L.R. 615; [1974] 2 All E.R. 639; *R.* v. *Hayden* [1975] 1 W.L.R. 852, C.A.; *R.* v. *Ioannou* [1975] 1 W.L.R. 1297; [1975] 3 All E.R. 400, C.A.; *R.* v. *Robinson* [1979] Crim.L.R. 785, C.A.

s. 50, amended: 1982, c.48, s.66; 1983, c.20, sch.4.

s. 51, see *R.* v. *Mealey and Sheridan* [1975] Crim.L.R. 154, C.A.

s. 51, amended: 1983, c.20, sch.4; repealed in pt.: 1981, c.54, sch.5.

s. 52, repealed in pt.: S.L.R. 1973.

sch. 1, amended: 1982, c.51, sch.3; 1983, c.20, sch.4.

sch. 2, amended: 1973, c.14, sch.1; 1976, c.63, sch.2; 1988, c.33, sch.15; repealed in pt.: 1985, c.23, sch.2.

sch. 3, amended: 1983, c.20, sch.4; repealed in pt.: 1976, c.63, sch.4.

sch. 5, amended: 1978, c.23, sch.5; 1979, c.31, sch.2; repealed in pt.: 1973, c.14, sch.2; S.L.R. 1973; 1981, c.54, sch.7.

20. Courts-Martial (Appeals) Act 1968.

ss. 2, 3, repealed in pt.: 1981, c.54, s.145, sch.7.

s. 5, substituted: *ibid.,* s.145.

s. 7, amended: 1972, c.11, sch.6.

s. 8, see *R* v. *Herbert* [1983] Crim. L.R. 332, Court-Martial Appeal Ct.

ss. 8, 17, amended: 1976, c.52, sch.9.

s. 13, see *R.* v. *Swabey (No. 2)* (1972) 117 S.J. 90.

s. 17A, added: 1976, c.52, sch.9.

s. 20, amended: 1983, c.20, sch.4; 1984, c.36, sch.3.

s. 23, amended: 1982, c.51, sch.2; 1983, c.20, sch.4; 1984, c.36, sch.3.

s. 25, amended: 1983, c.20, sch.4; 1984, c.36, sch.3.

s. 33A, added: 1977, c.38, s.5.

CAP.

1968—cont.

20. Courts-Martial (Appeals) Act 1968—*cont.*

s. 34, see *R. v. Swabey* [1972] 1 W.L.R. 925; [1972] 2 All E.R. 1094; amended: 1977, c.38, s.5.

s. 35, see *R. v. Swabey (No. 2)* (1972) 117 S.J. 90.

s. 35, repealed: 1977, c.38, s.5, sch.5.

s. 36, amended: 1976, c.82, s.5; 1981, c.54, s.145.

s. 37A, added: 1984, c.60, sch.6.

s. 43, amended: 1983, c.20, sch.4; 1984, c.36, sch.3.

s. 44, see *Druid Development Co. (Bingley) v. Kay* (1982) 44 P. & C.R. 76, C.A.

s. 45, amended: 1976, c.63, sch.2.

s. 47, amended: 1977, c.38, s.5.

s. 49, rules 72/798.

s. 52, rules, 73/270; 75/227, 1086; 76/892, 2165; 77/90, 91, 93; 79/1456; 80/2005.

sch. 4, repealed in pt.: 1983, c.20, sch.6; 1984, c.36, sch.5.

21. Criminal Appeal (Northern Ireland) Act 1968.

Pt. I (ss. 1–7), repealed: 1978, c.23, sch.7.

s. 9, amended: 1977, c.45, s.44.

s. 14, amended: 1978, c.23, sch.5; repealed in pt.: *ibid.*, sch.7.

ss. 20, 23–25, 27, amended: 1978, c.23, sch.5.

s. 30, repealed in pt.: *ibid.*, sch.7.

s. 32, amended: *ibid.*, sch.5.

s. 33, amended: *ibid.*, s.37.

ss. 34, 36, amended: *ibid.*, sch.5.

s. 46, amended: *ibid.*, sch.5; repealed in pt.: *ibid.*, sch.7.

s. 48, amended: *ibid.*, sch.5.

s. 48A, added: 1972, c.71, sch.4; amended: 1978, c.23, sch.5.

ss. 49, 50, amended: *ibid.*; repealed in pt.: *ibid.*

s. 52, repealed: 1973, c.36, sch.6.

ss. 53 (in pt.), 54, schs. 3 (in pt.), 4, 5, repealed: 1978, c.23, sch.7.

22. Legitimation (Scotland) Act 1968.

s. 1, amended: 1975, c.72, sch.2.

ss. 2, 4, 7, 8, see *Dunbar of Kilconzie, Petr.,* 1986 S.L.T. 463, H.L.

s. 6, amended: 1975, c.72, sch.2; 1978, c.28, sch.3; repealed in pt.: 1975, c.72, sch.4.

23. Rent Act 1968.

repealed: 1977, c.42, sch.25.

regs. 73/176.

see *Guppys (Bridport) v. Sandoe; Same v. Moyle; Same v. Radcliffe; Same v. Spencer* (1975) 30 P. & C.R. 69, D.C.

s. 1, see *Jelley v. Buckman* [1973] 3 W.L.R. 585, C.A.; *Horford Investments v. Lambert* [1973] 3 W.L.R. 872, C.A.; *R. v. Westminster (City) London Borough Council Rent Officer, ex p. Rendall* [1973] 3 W.L.R. 109; *Newman v. Dorrington Developments* [1975] 1 W.L.R. 1642; [1975] 3 All E.R. 928.

s. 2, see *Woodward v. Docherty* [1974] 1 W.L.R. 996; [1972] 2 All E.R. 844, C.A.; *Marchant v. Charters* [1977] 1 W.L.R. 1181, C.A.; regs. 74/1366; 75/1054; 76/905.

CAP.

1968—cont.

23. Rent Act 1968—*cont.*

s. 3, see *Walker v. Ogilvy* (1974) 28 P. & C.R. 288, C.A.; *Colin Smith Music v. Ridge* [1975] 1 W.L.R. 463; [1975] 1 All E.R. 290, C.A.; *Smalley v. Quarrier* [1975] 1 W.L.R. 938, C.A.; *Lloyd v. Sadler* [1978] 2 W.L.R. 721, C.A.; *Featherstone v. Staples, The Times,* November 7, 1984, Nourse J.; *Hampstead Way Investments v. Lewis-Weare* [1985] 1 W.L.R. 164, H.L.

s. 5A, see *Bardrick v. Haycock; Same v. Vernon; Same v. Robinson* (1976) 31 P. & C.R. 420, C.A.; *Stubbs v. Assopardi* [1978] 1 W.L.R. 646, C.A.

s. 6, see *R. v. Westminster (City) London Borough Council Rent Officer, ex p. Rendall* [1973] 3 W.L.R. 109.

s. 7, see *Newman v. Dorrington Developments* [1975] 1 W.L.R. 1642; [1975] 3 All E.R. 928.

s. 9, see *Lewis v. Weldcrest, The Times,* April 15, 1978, C.A.

s. 10, see *Redspring v. Francis* [1973] 1 W.L.R. 134, C.A.; *Kennealy v. Dunne* [1977] 2 W.L.R. 421, C.A.; *Tilling v. Whiteman* [1979] 2 W.L.R. 401, H.L.

s. 18, see *Maunsell v. Olins* [1974] 3 W.L.R. 835; [1975] 1 All E.R. 16, H.L.

ss. 22, 38, see *Avenue Properties (St. John's Wood) v. Aisinzon* [1976] 2 W.L.R. 740, C.A.

s. 37, regs. 72/1306, 1615; 75/541.

s. 44, see *R. v. Lambeth Rent Officer, ex p. Fox* (1978) 35 P. & C.R. 65, D.C.

ss. 44, 46, see *London Housing and Commercial Properties v. Cowan* [1976] 3 W.L.R. 115; [1976] 2 All E.R. 385, D.C.

s. 44A, regs. 72/1307.

s. 46, see *Nicoll v. First National Developments* (1972) 226 E.G. 301, D.C.; *Palmer v. Peabody Trust* [1974] 3 W.L.R. 575; [1974] 3 All E.R. 355, D.C.; *Metropolitan Property Holdings v. Finegold* [1975] 1 W.L.R. 349; [1975] 1 All E.R. 389, D.C.; *Campbell v. Gardner* (1976) 238 E.G. 115, D.C.; *Guppys Properties v. Knott; Guppys Properties v. Strutt* (1977) 245 E.G. 1023, D.C.

s. 47, see *Dominal Securities v. McLeod* (1978) 37 P. & C.R. 411, C.A.

s. 50, regs. 72/1306, 1307, 1615; 75/541.

s. 66, regs. 75/315.

Pt. VI (ss. 68–84), see *R. v. Kensington and Chelsea Rent Tribunal, ex p. Barrett* (1977) 245 E.G. 397, D.C.

s. 70, see *R. v. South Middlesex Rent Tribunal, ex p. Beswick* (1976) 32 P. & C.R. 67, D.C.

s. 72, see *R. v. Barnet and Camden Rent Tribunal, ex p. Frey Investments* [1972] 2 Q.B. 342; [1972] 2 W.L.R. 619; [1972] 1 All E.R. 1185.

s. 73, see *R. v. Kensington and Chelsea Rent Tribunal, ex p. MacFarlane* [1974] 1 W.L.R. 1486; [1974] 3 All E.R. 390, D.C.

ss. 85, 86, 90, see *Farell v. Alexander* [1976] 3 W.L.R. 145, H.L.

ss. 85, 91, 92, see *R. v. Ewing* (1977) 65 Cr.App.R. 4, C.A.

CAP.

1968—cont.

23. Rent Act 1968—cont.

ss. 86, 88, 89, 90, see *Ailion* v. *Spiekermann* [1976] 1 All E.R. 497.

s. 105, see *R.* v. *Brent London Borough Rent Officer, ex p. Ganatra* [1976] 2 W.L.R. 330, D.C.; *R.* v. *Croydon and South West London Rent Tribunal, ex p. Ryzewska* [1977] 2 W.L.R. 389; [1977] 1 All E.R. 312, D.C.; *R.* v. *Rent Officer for Kensington and Chelsea, ex p. Noel* [1977] 1 All E.R. 356, D.C.; *Somma* v. *Hazlehurst; Somma* v. *Savelli* [1978] 1 W.L.R. 1014, C.A.

ss. 108, 109, repealed in pt.: 1977, c.43, sch.3.

s. 114, regs. 72/1306, 1307, 1615; 75/315, 541.

sch. 1, see *Joram Developments* v. *Sharratt* [1979] 1 W.L.R. 928, H.L.

sch. 3, see *Redspring* v. *Francis* [1973] 1 W.L.R. 134, C.A.; *Arain* v. *Steel*, October 13, 1975; *Rowe* v. *Truelove* (1976) 241 E.G. 533, C.A.; *Kennealy* v. *Dunne* [1977] 2 W.L.R. 421, C.A.; *Tilling* v. *Whiteman* [1978] 3 W.L.R. 137, C.A.

sch. 6, see *R.* v. *Westminster (City) London Borough Council Rent Officer, ex p. Rendall* [1973] 3 W.L.R. 109; *Metropolitan Property Holdings* v. *Laufer* (1974) 29 P. & C.R. 172, D.C.; *Hanson* v. *Church Commissioners for England* [1977] 2 W.L.R. 848, C.A.

sch. 15, repealed in pt.: 1977, c.12, sch.2; c.43, sch.3; 1981, c.24, sch.3.

24. Commonwealth Telecommunications Act 1968.

s. 2, repealed in pt.: 1975, c.24, sch.3; c.25, sch.3.

25. Local Authorities' Mutual Investment Trust 1968.

ss. 1, 2, amended: 1986, c.60, sch.16.

26. Export Guarantees Act 1968.

repealed: 1975, c.38, s.12.

s. 4, repealed: *ibid.*

27. Firearms Act 1968.

s. 1, see *Sullivan* v. *Earl of Caithness* [1976] 2 W.L.R. 361, D.C.; *R.* v. *Howells* [1977] 2 W.L.R. 716, C.A.; *Richards* v. *Curwen* [1977] 1 W.L.R. 747, D.C.; *Creaser* v. *Tunnicliffe* [1977] 1 W.L.R. 1493, D.C.; *R.* v. *Hucklebridge; Att.-Gen.'s Reference (No. 3 of 1980)* (1980) 71 Cr.App.R. 171, C.A.; *Bennett* v. *Brown* (1980) 71 Cr.App.R. 109, D.C.; *R.* v. *Hussain* [1981] 1 W.L.R. 416, C.A.; *R.* v. *Thorpe* [1987] 1 W.L.R. 383, C.A.

s. 1, amended: 1988, c.45, s.2.

ss. 1, 2, see *R.* v. *Burke* (1978) 67 Cr.App.R. 220, C.A.

ss. 1, 4, see *Kelly* v. *Mackinnon*, High Court of Justiciary, May 11, 1982.

s. 2, amended: 1988, c.33, sch. 8.

ss. 2, 3, see *Hall* v. *Cotton* [1986] 3 W.L.R. 681, D.C.

s. 4, amended: 1988, c.45, s.23.

s. 5, see *R.* v. *Titus* [1971] Crim.L.R. 279; *R.* v. *Jobling* [1981] Crim.L.R. 625, Taylor J.; *R.* v. *Pannell* [1982] Crim.L.R. 752; (1983) 76 Cr.App.R. 53, C.A.; *R.* v. *Clarke (Frederick)* [1986] 1 W.L.R. 209, C.A.; *Jessop* v. *Steven-*

CAP.

1968—cont.

27. Firearms Act 1968—cont.

son, 1988 S.L.T. 223; *Flack* v. *Baldry* [1988] 1 W.L.R. 393, H.L.

s. 5, amended: 1988, c.45, s.1.

s. 6, amended: *ibid.*, s.20; repealed in pt.: *ibid.*

s. 7, see *R.* v. *Wakefield Crown Court, ex p. Oldfield* [1978] Crim.L.R. 164, D.C.

s. 8, see *Woodage* v. *Moss* [1974] 1 All E.R. 584, D.C.

s. 10, amended: 1974, c.3, sch.3; 1980, c.13, sch.1.

s. 11, repealed in pt.: 1988, c.45, s.15.

ss. 12, 13, amended: *ibid.*, s.23.

s. 14, repealed: *ibid.*

s. 16, see *R.* v. *Bentham* [1972] 3 W.L.R. 398; 116 S.J. 598; *R.* v. *El Hakkaoui* [1975] 1 W.L.R. 396, C.A.; *R.* v. *Rex Norton* [1977] Crim.L.R. 478, Norwich Crown Ct.; *Urquhart* v. *H.M. Advocate*, 1987 S.C.C.R. 31.

s. 17, see *R.* v. *McGrath* [1987] Crim.L.R. 143; (1986) 8 Cr.App.R.(S.) 372, C.A.

s. 18, see *R.* v. *Titus* [1971] Crim.L.R. 279; *R.* v. *Faulkner* (1972) 56 Cr.App.R. 594; *R.* v. *Kelt* [1977] Crim.L.R. 556; [1977] 1 W.L.R. 1365, C.A.; *R.* v. *Houghton* [1982] Crim.L.R. 112, C.A.; *R.* v. *French* (1982) 75 Cr.App.R. 1, C.A.

s. 19, see *Anderson* v. *Miller* (1977) 64 Cr.App.R. 178, D.C.; *Ross* v. *Collins* [1982] Crim.L.R. 368, D.C.; *McLeod* v. *McLeod*, 1982 S.C.C.R. 130.

s. 20, see *Ferguson* v. *Mcphail*, 1987 S.C.C.R. 52.

s. 21, see *Davies* v. *Tomlinson* (1980) 71 Cr.App.R. 279, D.C.

s. 21, amended: 1972, c.71, ss.29,66; 1977, c.45, sch.9; 1982, c.48, sch.14; repealed in pt.: 1988, c.33, sch. 16.

ss. 22–24, amended: 1988, c.45, s.23.

s. 26, see *R.* v. *Kitt* [1977] Crim.L.R. 220; *Ogston* v. *Miller, The Times*, October 31, 1980, D.C.; *Burditt* v. *Joslin* [1981] 3 All E.R. 203, D.C.

s. 26, amended: 1988, c.45, ss. 9, 10.

s. 27, see *Milligan* v. *Glasgow Chief Constable*, 1976 S.L.T.(Sh.Ct.) 55; *Hutchinson* v. *Chief Constable of Grampian*, 1977 S.L.T. 98, Sheriff Ct.

s. 27, amended: 1988, c.45, s.23.

ss. 27, 28, see *Kavanagh* v. *Chief Constable of Devon and Cornwall* [1974] 2 W.L.R. 762, C.A.

s. 28, amended: 1988, c.45, s.3.

s. 30, see *Ackers* v. *Taylor* [1974] 1 W.L.R. 405; [1974] 1 All E.R. 771, D.C.; *Cunning* v. *Fife Chief Constable*, 1975 S.L.T.(Sh.Ct.) 18; *Jarvis* v. *Chief Constable of Strathclyde*, 1976 S.L.T.(Sh.Ct.) 66; *Hamilton* v. *Chief Constable of Strathclyde*, 1978 S.L.T.(Sh.Ct.) 69; *Luke* v. *Little*, 1980 S.L.T.(Sh.Ct.) 138; *McBride* v. *Frizzell*, 1982 S.L.T.(Sh.Ct.) 8; *R.* v. *Acton Crown Court, ex p. Varney* [1984] Crim.L.R. 683, D.C.

s. 32, amended: orders 75/956, 991; 76/1446, 2157; 78/267, 360 (S.); 79/86, 91 (S.); 80/574, 604 (S.); 86/986; 1988, c.45, s.15.

CAP.

1968—cont.

27. Firearms Act 1968—cont.

s. 33, amended: *ibid.*, s.13.
s. 34, see *Kavanagh* v. *Chief Constable of Devon and Cornwall* [1974] 2 W.L.R. 762, C.A.
s. 34, amended: 1988, c.45, s.13.
s. 35, amended: orders 75/956, 991, 76/1446, 2157; 78/267, 360(S.); 79/86, 91(S.); 80/574, 604(S.); 86/986.
s. 38, amended: 1988, c.45, s.13.
s. 39, see *Staravia* v. *Gordon* [1973] Crim.L.R. 298.
s. 40, rules 83/1441, 1495(S.).
s. 40, amended: 1988, c.45, ss.13, 23.
s. 42, amended: *ibid.*, s.23.
s. 43, orders 75/956, 991; 76/1446, 2157, 2158; 78/267, 360 (S.); 79/86, 91 (S.), 411, 459; 80/574, 604 (S.); 86/986, 996(S.).
s. 44, see *Cunning* v. *Fife Chief Constable* 1975 S.L.T.(Sh.Ct.) 18; *Milligan* v. *Glasgow Chief Constable,* 1976 S.L.T.(Sh.Ct.) 55; *Hamilton* v. *Chief Constable of Strathclyde,* 1978 S.L.T.(Sh.Ct.) 69; *R.* v. *Acton Crown Court, ex p. Varney* [1984] Crim.L.R. 683, D.C.
s. 45, amended: 1979, c.2, sch.4.
s. 46, amended: 1973, c.65, sch.29; repealed in pt.: 1984, c.60, sch.7.
s. 49, amended: 1988, c.45, s.23.
s. 50, repealed: 1984, c.60, sch.7.
s. 51, amended: 1980, c.43, sch.7.
s. 52, see *Goodlad* v. *Chief Constable of South Yorkshire* [1979] Crim.L.R. 51, Sheffield Crown Ct.
s. 52, repealed in pt.: 1988, c.33, sch.16.
s. 53, rules 83/1495(S.).
s. 55, rules 83/1441, 1495(S.).
s. 57, see *R.* v. *Titus* [1971] Crim.L.R. 279; *Anderson* v. *Miller* (1977) 64 Cr.App.R. 178, D.C.; *Creaser* v. *Tunnicliffe* [1977] 1 W.L.R. 1493, D.C.; *Kelly* v. *Mackinnon,* High Court of Justiciary, May 11, 1982; *R.* v. *Pannell* (1983) 76 Cr.App.R. 53, C.A.; *R.* v. *Morris; R.* v. *King* [1984] Crim.L.R. 422, C.A.; *R.* v. *Clarke (Frederick)* [1986] 1 W.L.R. 209, C.A.; *Hall* v. *Cotton* [1986] 3 W.L.R. 681, D.C.; *R.* v. *Thorpe* [1987] 1 W.L.R. 383, C.A.
s. 57, amended (S.): 1984, c.54, sch.9; repealed in pt.: 1977, c.45, sch.13.
s. 58, see *R.* v. *Howells* [1977] 2 W.L.R. 716, C.A.; *Richards* v. *Curwen* [1977] 1 W.L.R. 747, D.C.; *R.* v. *Burke* (1978) 67 Cr.App.R. 220, C.A.; *Bennett* v. *Brown* (1980) 71 Cr.App.R. 109, D.C.
sch. 1, amended: 1984, c.37, s.11; repealed in pt.: 1981, c.47, sch.; 1984, c.37, s.11.
sch. 2, substituted: 1972, c.20, sch.7; amended: 1982, c.45, sch.3(S.).
sch. 6, see *R.* v. *McGrath* [1987] Crim.L.R. 143, C.A.
sch. 6, amended: 1972, c.71, ss.28, 66; 1977, c.45, sch.12; 1980, c.43, sch.7; 1981, c.47, s.7; 1988, c.33, s.44; c.45, s.13; repealed in pt.: 1972, c.71, ss.28,66, sch.6; 1980, c.62, sch.8; 1988, c.45, s.23.

CAP.

1968—cont.

29. Trade Descriptions Act 1968.

see *R.* v. *Gupta (Kuldip)* (1985) 7 Cr.App.R.(S.) 172, C.A.
s. 1, see *Wycombe* v. *Fowler* [1972] 1 W.L.R. 1156; [1972] 3 All E.R. 248; *Robertson* v. *Dicicco* (1972) 70 L.G.R. 589, D.C.; *Cottee* v. *Seaton* [1972] 1 W.L.R. 1408; [1972] 3 All E.R. 750; *Hall* v. *Wickens* [1972] 1 W.L.R. 1418; 116 S.J. 744; [1972] R.T.R. 519; *Kensington & Chelsea B.C.* v. *Riley* [1973] R.T.R. 122, D.C.; *Fletcher* v. *Stedmore* [1973] Crim.L.R. 195; 71 L.G.R. 179; *Furniss* v. *Scott* [1973] R.T.R. 314; *Tarleton Engineering* v. *Nattrass* [1973] 1 W.L.R. 1261; [1973] 3 All E.R. 699, D.C.; *R.* v. *Haesler* [1973] R.T.R. 486, C.A.; *Clode* v. *Barnes* [1974] 1 W.L.R. 544; [1974] 1 All E.R. 1166, D.C.; *Chidwick* v. *Beer* [1974] Crim.L.R. 267; [1975] R.T.R. 415, D.C.; *Furniss* v. *Scholes* [1974] R.T.R. 133, D.C.; *Taylor* v. *Smith* [1974] R.T.R. 190, D.C.; *Fletcher* v. *Budgen* [1974] 1 W.L.R. 1056; [1974] 2 All E.R. 1243, D.C.; *Aitchison* v. *Reith and Anderson (Dingwall and Tain),* 1974 S.L.T. 282; *Norman* v. *Bennett* [1974] 1 W.L.R. 1229; [1974] 3 All E.R. 351, D.C.; *R.* v. *Ford Motor Co.* [1974] 1 W.L.R. 1220; [1974] 3 All E.R. 489, C.A.; *Butler* v. *Keenway Supermarkets* [1974] Crim.L.R. 560, D.C.; *Rees* v. *Munday* [1974] 1 W.L.R. 1284; [1974] 3 All E.R. 506, D.C.; *Zawadski* v. *Sleigh* [1975] R.T.R. 113, D.C.; *Simmons* v. *Potter* [1975] Crim.L.R. 354; [1975] R.T.R. 347, D.C.; *R.* v. *Anthony Lloyd,* February 13, 1976; *Harringey L.B.C.* v. *Piro Shoes* [1976] Crim.L.R. 462, D.C.; *R.* v. *Hammerstons Cars* [1976] 1 W.L.R. 1243, C.A.; *Waltham Forest London Borough Council* v. *T. G. Wheatley (Central Garage)* [1977] Crim.L.R. 761, D.C.; *Waltham Forest London Borough Council* v. *T. G. Wheatley (Central Garage) (No. 2)* [1978] R.T.R. 333, D.C.; *Hawkins* v. *Smith* [1978] Crim.L.R. 578, Portsmouth Crown Ct.; *Kinchin* v. *Haines* [1979] Crim.L.R. 329, D.C.; *K. Jill Holdings (Trading as Stratford Motor Co.)* v. *White* [1979] R.T.R. 120, D.C.; *Stainthorpe* v. *Bailey* [1979] Crim.L.R. 677, D.C.; *Routledge* v. *Ansa Motors (Chester Le Street)* [1980] Crim.L.R. 65, D.C.; *Wandsworth London Borough Council* v. *Bentley* [1980] R.T.R. 429, D.C.; *Crook* v. *Howells Garages (Newport)* [1980] R.T.R. 434, D.C.; *Holloway* v. *Cross,* The Times, November 20, 1980, D.C.; "*Wee McGlen*" *Trade Mark* [1980] R.P.C. 115, Trade Marks Registry; *Blair* v. *Keane,* 1981 S.L.T.(Notes) 4; *Hackney London Borough* v. *Measureworth and Newman* [1981] Crim.L.R. 503, Snaresbrook Crown Ct.; *Barker* v. *Hargreaves* [1981] R.T.R. 197, D.C.; *Roberts* v. *Severn Petroleum & Trading Co.* [1981] R.T.R. 312, D.C.; *Miller* v. *F.A. Sadd & Son* [1981] 3 All E.R. 265, D.C.; *Corfield* v. *Starr* [1981] R.T.R. 380, D.C.; *Newman* v. *Hackney London Borough Council* (1982) 80 L.G.R. 611, D.C.; *R.* v. *R. McMillan Aviation and McMillan* [1981] Crim.L.R. 785, Rubin J.; *Blakemore* v. *Bellamy*

CAP.

1968—cont.

29. Trade Descriptions Act 1968—cont.
[1983] R.T.R. 303, D.C.; *Davies v. Summer, The Times,* August 11, 1983, D.C.; *Simmons v. Ravenhill* [1983] Crim.L.R. 749, D.C.; *Benfell Farm Produce v. Surrey County Council* [1983] 1 W.L.R. 1213, D.C.; *R. v. Inner London JJ., ex p. Wandsworth London Borough Council* [1983] R.T.R. 425, D.C.; *Robertson v. Tudhope,* 1984 S.L.T. 277; *Norman (Alec) Garages v. Phillips, The Times,* August 3, 1984, D.C.; *Davies v. Summer* [1984] 1 W.L.R. 1301, H.L.; *Simmons v. Ravenhill* [1984] R.T.R. 412, D.C.; *Davis v. Allan, The Times,* February 11, 1985, D.C.; *Cavendish Woodhouse v. Wright, The Times,* March 8, 1985, D.C.; *R. v. Beaconsfield Justices, ex p. Johnston and Sons, The Times,* March 23, 1985, D.C.; *Norman (Alec) Garages v. Phillips* [1985] R.T.R. 164, D.C.; *Lewis v. Bland* [1985] R.T.R. 171, D.C.; *Newham London Borough v. Co-operative Retail Services* (1984) 149 J.P. 421, D.C.; *Queensway Discount Warehouses v. Burke, The Times,* October 14, 1985, D.C.; *Olgeirsson v. Kitching, The Times,* November 16, 1985, D.C.; *Wolkind and Northcott v. Pura Foods, The Times,* January 30, 1987, D.C.; *Hirschler v. Birch* [1987] R.T.R. 13, D.C.; *Denard v. Abbas* (1987) 151 J.P.N. 348, D.C.; *Blunden v. Gravelle* (1987) 151 J.P.N. 348, D.C.; *Newham London Borough Council v. Singh, The Times,* December 10, 1987, D.C.; *Rotherham Metropolitan Borough Council v. Raysun (U.K.), The Times,* April 27, 1988, D.C.; *R. v. Southwood* [1987] R.T.R. 273, C.A.; *Dixons v. Barnett, The Guardian,* June 14, 1988, D.C.
ss. 1, 2, see *R. v. Coventry City Justices, ex p. Farrand* [1988] R.T.R. 273, D.C.
ss. 1–3, see *Corfield v. Sevenways Garage* [1985] R.T.R. 109, D.C.; *R. v. Anderson, The Times,* December 31, 1987, C.A.
s. 2, see *Wycombe v. Fowler* [1972] 1 W.L.R. 1156; [1972] 3 All E.R. 248; *Robertson v. Dicicco* (1972) 70 L.G.R. 589, D.C.; *British Gas Corporation v. Lubbock* [1974] 1 W.L.R. 37; [1974] 1 All E.R. 188, D.C.; *Cadbury v. Halliday* [1975] 1 W.L.R. 649; [1975] 2 All E.R. 226, D.C.; *Stainthorpe v. Bailey* [1979] Crim.L.R. 677, D.C.; *Routledge v. Ansa Motors (Chester Le Street)* [1980] Crim.L.R. 65, D.C.; *Roberts v. Severn Petroleum & Trading Co.* [1981] R.T.R. 312, D.C.; *R. v. Inner London J.', ex p. Wandsworth London Borough Council* [1983] R.T.R. 425, D.C.; *Davies v. Sumner* [1984] 1 W.L.R. 1301, H.L.
s. 2, amended: 1972, c.20, s.63; c.68, s.4, sch.4; 1978, c.38, s.7; 1984, c.30, sch.10; 1987, c.43, sch.4; repealed in pt.: 1972, c.68, s.4, sch.3.
s. 3, see *Robertson v. Dicicco* (1972) 70 L.G.R. 589, D.C.; *Cadbury v. Halliday* [1975] 1 W.L.R. 649; [1975] 2 All E.R. 226, D.C.; *Routledge v. Ansa Motors (Chester Le Street)* [1980] Crim.L.R. 65, D.C.; *Holloway v. Cross, The Times,* November 20, 1980, D.C.; *R. v. Inner*

CAP.

1968—cont.

29. Trade Descriptions Act 1968—cont.
London JJ., ex p. Wandsworth London Borough Council [1983] R.T.R. 425, D.C.; *Simmons v. Ravenhill* [1984] R.T.R. 412, D.C.
s. 4, see *Rees v. Munday* [1974] 1 W.L.R. 1284; [1974] 3 All E.R. 506, D.C.; *Roberts v. Severn Petroleum & Trading Co.* [1981] R.T.R. 312, D.C.; *Norman (Alec) Garages v. Phillips* [1985] R.T.R. 164, D.C.
s. 6, see *Stainthorpe v. Bailey* [1980] R.T.R. 7, D.C.; *Miller v. F.A. Sadd & Son* [1981] 3 All E.R. 265, D.C.
s. 8, orders 72/1041; 80/1150; 81/121; 86/193.
s. 9, orders 80/1150; 81/121; 86/193.
s. 11, see *Doble v. Greig (David)* [1972] 1 W.L.R. 703; [1972] 2 All E.R. 195; 71 L.G.R. 411; *Feiner v. Barnes* (1973) 71 L.G.R. 477, D.C.; *Whitehead v. Collett* [1975] Crim.L.R. 53, D.C.; *Richards v. Westminster Motors* (1975) 61 Cr.App.R. 228, D.C.; *Read Bros. Cycles (Leyton) v. Waltham Forest London Borough Council* [1978] R.T.R. 397, D.C.; *Barnes v. Watts Tyre and Rubber Co.* [1978] R.T.R. 405 (Note), D.C.; *Stainthorpe v. Bailey* [1980] R.T.R. 7, D.C.; *Miller v. F. A. Sadd & Son* [1981] 3 All E.R. 265, D.C.; *Heron Service Stations v. Hunter* [1981] Crim.L.R. 418, D.C.; *Westminster City v. Ray Alan (Manshops)* [1982] 1 All E.R. 771, D.C.
s. 11, repealed: 1987, c.43, sch. 5.
s. 12, see *Rotherham Metropolitan Borough Council v. Raysun (U.K.), The Times,* April 27, 1988, D.C.
s. 14, see *Herron v. Lunn Poly (Scotland),* 1972 S.L.T. 2; *Becket v. Cohen* [1972] 1 W.L.R. 1593; 116 S.J. 882; [1973] 1 All E.R. 120; *R. v. Clarksons* (1972) 57 Cr.App.R. 38, C.A.; *M.F.I. Warehouses v. Nattrass* [1973] 1 W.L.R. 307; [1973] 1 All E.R. 762, D.C.; *R. v. Breeze* [1973] 1 W.L.R. 994; [1973] 2 All E.R. 1141; *Parsons v. Barnes* [1973] Crim.L.R. 537, D.C.; *Coupe v. Guyett* [1973] 1 W.L.R. 669; *R. v. Sunair Holidays* [1973] 2 All E.R. 1233, C.A.; *R. v. Thomson Holidays* [1974] 2 W.L.R. 371; [1974] 1 All E.R. 823, C.A.; *British Airways Board v. Taylor* [1976] 1 W.L.R. 13; [1976] 1 All E.R. 65, H.L.; *Westminster City v. Ray Alan (Manshops)* [1982] 1 All E.R. 771, D.C.; *Cowburn v. Focus Television Rentals* [1983] Crim.L.R. 563, D.C.; *Newell v. Taylor* (1984) 148 J.P. 308, D.C.; *Dixons v. Roberts, The Times,* May 3, 1984, D.C.; *Kinchin v. Ashton Park Scooters* (1984) J.P.N. 459, D.C.; *Thomson Travel v. Roberts* (1984) 148 J.P.N. 637, D.C.; *Wings v. Ellis* [1984] 3 W.L.R. 965, H.L.; *Dixons v. Roberts* (1984) 82 L.G.R. 689, D.C.; *Cahalne v. Croydon London Borough* (1985) 4 Tr.L. 199, D.C.; *R. v. Bow Street Magistrates' Court, ex p. Joseph* (1986) 130 S.J. 593, D.C.; *Smith v. Dixons,* 1986 S.C.C.R. 1; *Best Travel Co. v. Patterson* (1987) 151 J.P.N. 348, D.C.; *Yugotours v. Wadsley, The Guardian,* June 3, 1988, D.C.

1968—cont.
29. Trade Descriptions Act 1968—*cont.*
s. 19, see *Rees* v. *Munday* [1974] 1 W.L.R.
1284; [1974] 3 All E.R. 506, D.C.; *Tudhope* v.
Lawson, 1983 S.C.C.R. 435; *Robertson* v.
Tudhope, 1984 S.L.T. 277; *Newham London
Borough* v. *Co-operative Retail Services*
(1984) 149 J.P. 421, D.C.; *R.* v. *Beaconsfield
JJ., ex p. Johnston & Sons* (1985) 4 Tr.L. 212,
D.C.; *R.* v. *Pain, Jory and Hawkins* (1986) 82
Cr.App.R. 141, C.A.
s. 19, amended: 1980, c.43, sch.7.
s. 20, see *R.* v. *R. McMillan Aviation and McMillan* [1981] Crim.L.R. 785, Rubin J.; *Lewin* v.
Bland [1985] R.T.R. 171, D.C.; *R.* v. *Burridge*
(1985) 7 Cr.App.R.(S.) 125, C.A.; *Hirschler* v.
Birch [1987] R.T.R. 13, D.C.
s. 22, see *Heron Service Stations* v. *Hunter*
[1981] Crim.L.R. 418, D.C.
s. 22, amended: 1972, c.68, s.4, sch.4; order
81/231; 1984, c.30, sch. 10; 1985, c.72, sch.
12.
s. 23, see *Cottee* v. *Seaton* [1972] 1 W.L.R.
1408; [1972] 3 All E.R. 750; *Coupe* v. *Guyett*
[1973] 1 W.L.R. 669; *Tarleton Engineering* v.
Nattrass [1973] 1 W.L.R. 1261; [1973] 3 All
E.R. 699, D.C.; *Nattrass* v. *Timpson Shoes*
[1973] Crim.L.R. 197, D.C.; *K. Jill Holdings*
(*Trading as Stratford Motor Co.*) v. *White*
[1979] R.T.R. 120, D.C.; *Hicks* v. *Grewal*
(1985) 4 Tr.L. 92, D.C.; *Olgeirsson* v. *Kitching*
[1986] 1 W.L.R. 304, D.C.; *Hirschler* v. *Birch*
[1987] R.T.R. 13, D.C.; *Rotherham Metropolitan Borough Council* v. *Raysun (U.K.), The
Times,* April 27, 1988, D.C.
s. 24, see *Nattrass* v. *Timpson Shoes* [1973]
Crim.L.R. 197, D.C.; *Coupe* v. *Guyett* [1973]
1 W.L.R. 669; *Furniss* v. *Scott* [1973] R.T.R.
314; *R.* v. *Haesler* [1973] R.T.R. 486, C.A.; *R.*
v. *Southampton JJ., ex p. Atherton* [1974]
Crim.L.R. 108, D.C.; *Butler* v. *Keenway Supermarkets* [1974] Crim.L.R. 560, D.C.; *Whitehead* v. *Collett* [1975] Crim.L.R. 53, D.C.;
Zawadski v. *Sleigh* [1975] R.T.R. 113, D.C.;
Simmons v. *Potter* [1975] Crim.L.R. 354;
[1975] R.T.R. 347, D.C.; *Lewis* v. *Mahoney*
[1977] Crim.L.R. 436, D.C.; *Waltham Forest
London Borough Council* v. *T. G. Wheatley*
(*Central Garage*) [1977] Crim.L.R. 761, D.C.;
Department of Commerce v. *Elliott* [1980] 12
N.I.J.B., C.A.; *Stainthorpe* v. *Bailey* [1980]
R.T.R. 7, D.C.; *Crook* v. *Howells Garages
(Newport)* [1980] R.T.R. 434, D.C.; *Wandsworth London Borough Council* v. *Bentley*
[1980] R.T.R. 429, D.C.; *Barker* v. *Hargreaves*
[1981] R.T.R. 197, D.C.; *Simmons* v. *Ravenhill*
[1983] Crim.L.R. 749; [1984] R.T.R. 412, D.C.;
Wandsworth Borough Council v. *Fontana*
(1983) 146 J.P. 196, D.C.; *Lewin* v. *Rothersthorpe Road Garage* (1984) 148 J.P. 87, D.C.;
Davis v. *Allen, The Times,* February 11, 1985,
D.C.; *Norman (Alec) Garages* v. *Phillips* [1985]
R.T.R. 164, D.C.; *Hicks* v. *Grewal* (1985) 4
Tr.L. 92, D.C.; *Amos* v. *Melcon (Frozen Foods)*
(1985) 4 T.L.R. 247, D.C.; *Hirschler* v. *Birch*

1968—cont.
29. Trade Descriptions Act 1968—*cont.*
[1987] R.T.R. 13, D.C.; *Denard* v. *Abbas*
[1987] Crim.L.R. 424, D.C.; *R.* v. *Southwood,
The Times,* July 1, 1987, C.A.; *Texas Homecare* v. *Stockport Metropolitan Borough Council* [1987] Crim.L.R. 709, D.C.; *Rotherham
Metropolitan Borough Council* v. *Raysun
(U.K.), The Times,* April 27, 1988, D.C.
s. 26, amended (S.): 1973, c.65, sch.27;
repealed in pt.: *ibid.;* 1980, c.65, schs.4,34;
1985, c.72, sch.13.
s. 28, amended: 1974, c.39, sch.4; 1987, c.43,
sch.4.
ss. 28, 29, see *Barge* v. *British Gas Corp.* (1983)
81 L.G.R. 53, D.C.
s. 30, see *v. R.* v. *Thomson Holidays* [1974] 2
W.L.R. 371; [1974] 1 All E.R. 823, C.A.
s. 30, amended: 1973, c.41, sch.13.
s. 32, amended: 1979, c.2, sch.4; 1985, c.72,
sch.12.
s. 34, see *Waltham Forest London Borough
Council* v. *T. G. Wheatley (Central Garage)*
(*No. 2*) [1978] R.T.R. 333, D.C.
s. 36, order 81/122.
s. 38, orders 72/1041; 80/1150; 84/91; 86/193;
88/1771.
s. 39, amended: 1984, c.46, sch.5.
s. 40, amended: 1973, c.36, sch.6; 1980, c.43,
sch.7.
s. 41, repealed in pt.: S.L.R. 1975.
s. 42, sch. 2, repealed: *ibid.*
sch. 1, repealed in pt.: 1972, c.20, sch.9.
**31. Housing (Financial Provisions) (Scotland) Act
1968.**
repealed, except ss.20, 67, 71: 1987, c.26, sch.
24.
s. 3, regs. 73/757.
s. 25, orders 74/1284; 78/401; 80/740; 85/926.
ss. 29, 31, regs. 72/1740.
s. 49, see *Vaughan* v. *City of Edinburgh District
Council* (O.H.), 1988 S.L.T. 191.
s. 54, regs. 72/1740.
s. 67, amended: 1974, c.45, sch.3; repealed in
pt.: *ibid.,* schs.3, 5.
32. Industrial Expansion Act 1968.
s. 8, order 72/1243.
s. 8, amended: 1973, c.7, s.1.
s. 9, repealed: S.L.R. 1986.
s 10, repealed: 1972, c.63, sch.4.
s. 13, sch. 3, repealed: 1975, c.9, sch.2.
s. 16, see *Howard* v. *Secretary of State for the
Environment* [1974] 1 All E.R. 644, C.A.
s. 17, repealed: 1973, c.36, sch.6.
**34. Agriculture (Miscellaneous Provisions) Act
1968.**
s. 1, amended: 1986, c.14, sch.3.
s. 2, regs. 74/1061, 1062; 78/1800; 80/1004;
82/1884; 87/114, 2020, 2021.
s. 5, order 74/798.
s. 7, amended: 1977, c.45, s.31, sch.6; 1982,
c.48, sch.6(S.).
s. 8, orders 80/593, 685.
s. 8, amended and repealed in pt.: 1981, c.22,
sch.5.
ss. 9, 10, repealed: 1986, c.5, sch.15.

CAP.

1968—cont.

34. Agriculture (Miscellaneous Provisions) Act 1968—cont.
ss. 9, 11, see *Barns Graham* v. *Lamont*, 1971 S.L.T. 341; *Copeland* v. *McQuaker*, 1973 S.L.T. 186.
s. 11, amended (S.): 1976, c.21, sch.2; repealed in pt.: S.L.R. 1977.
s. 12, see *Anderson* v. *Moray District Council*, 1978 S.L.T.(Lands Tr.) 37.
s. 12, amended: 1986, c.5, sch.14.
s. 13, amended: 1976, c.75, sch.7; 1986, c.5, sch.14.
s. 14, amended: 1972, c.52, sch.21.
s. 15, repealed in pt.: 1973, c.26, s.48, sch.3; 1986, c.5, sch.15.
s. 17, amended: 1984, c.41, sch.3; 1986, c.5, sch.14; repealed in pt.: *ibid.*, sch.15.
s. 18, see *Altyre Estate Trs.* v. *McLay*, 1975 S.L.T.(Land Ct.) 12; *Earl of Seafield* v. *Currie*, 1980 S.L.T.(Land Ct.) 10; *Haddo House Estate Trs.* v. *Davidson*, 1982 S.L.T.(Land Ct.) 14; *Mackenzie* v. *Lyon*, 1984 S.L.T.(Land Ct.) 30.
Pt. III, repealed (S.): 1983, c.46, sch.2.
Pt. IV (ss. 21–37), repealed: 1976, c.70, sch.8.
s. 22, order 73/1309.
ss. 38, 39, scheme 73/330.
ss. 38–40, repealed: S.L.R. 1986.
s. 42, amended: 1986, c.5, sch.14; repealed in pt.: 1973, c.26, sch.3.
s. 44, repealed: 1976, c.34, sch.6.
s. 45, amended: *ibid.*, sch.5; repealed in pt.: order 82/1080.
s. 46, repealed in pt.: 1972, c.62, schs.5, 6.
s. 49, repealed: 1973, c.36, sch.6.
s. 50, order 73/1309: scheme 73/330.
s. 50, repealed in pt.: 1973, c.37, sch.9.
s. 54, repealed in pt.: 1973, c.36, sch.6.
schs. 1, 2, repealed: S.L.R. 1977.
sch. 3, amended: 1986, c.5, sch.14.
sch. 6, repealed: 1976, c.70, sch.8.
sch. 7, repealed in pt.: 1972, c.68, sch.3.

36. Maintenance Orders Act 1968.
s. 1, sch., see *McEwan* v. *McEwan* [1972] 2 All E.R. 708.
sch., repealed in pt.: S.L.R. 1977; 1978, c.22, sch.3.

37. Education (No. 2) Act 1968.
repealed: 1988, c.40, sch.13.
s. 1, see *Winder* v. *Cambridgeshire County Council* (1977) 76 L.G.R. 176, Sir Douglas Frank, Q.C.
s. 4, order 72/212.

38. Sale of Venison (Scotland) Act 1968.
repealed: 1982, c.19, sch.3.
ss. 1, 2, amended; 1982, c.48, sch.6.

39. Gas and Electricity Act 1968.
repealed: 1979, c.11, sch.12.
s. 2, repealed in pt.: 1987, c.16, sch. 16.
s. 5, repealed: 1980, c.63, sch.2.

40. Family Allowances and National Insurance Act 1968.
repealed: 1975, c.18, sch.1.

41. Countryside Act 1968.
see *Pearson* v. *Secretary of State for the Environment* [1981] J.P.L. 108, C.A.

CAP.

1968—cont.

41. Countryside Act 1968—cont.
s. 1, repealed in pt.: 1975, c.24, sch.3; 1981, c.69, sch.17.
s. 2, amended: 1981, c.69, s.72; repealed in pt.: 1974, c.7, sch.8.
ss. 3, 5, repealed: 1981, c.69, s.72.
s. 6, repealed in pt.: 1972, c.70, sch.30; 1985, c.51, sch.17.
ss. 6, 7, see *R.* v. *Plymouth City Council and Cornwall County Council, ex p. Freeman* (1988) 28 R.V.R. 89, C.A.
s. 14, orders 72/458, 1049.
s. 15, amended: 1973, c.54, sch.1; repealed in pt.: 1981, c.72, sch.17.
s. 17, repealed: 1980, c.65, schs.3,34.
s. 22, amended: 1973, c.37, sch.8; repealed in pt.: *ibid.*, sch.9; 1974, c.40, sch.4.
ss. 23, 24, repealed in pt.: 1981, c.39, sch.
ss. 25, 26, repealed (S.): 1972, c.52, sch.23.
s. 27, amended: 1980, c.66, sch.24; 1981, c.69, s.65; repealed in pt.: 1984, c.27, sch.14.
ss. 28, 29, repealed: 1980, c.66, sch.25.
s. 30, amended: 1972, c.20, schs.7,9; 1988, c.54, sch.3; repealed in pt.: 1972, c.20, sch.9.
s. 32, repealed: 1984, c.27, sch.14; amended(S.): 1984, c.54, sch.9.
ss. 33–35, repealed: 1974, c.7, schs.1, 8.
s. 36, repealed: 1982, c.42, sch.
s. 37, amended: 1973, c.54, sch.1; 1981, c.69, s.72.
s. 39, repealed: 1972, c.70, sch.30.
s. 41, amended: 1980, c.66, s.342; 1984, c.12, sch.4.
s. 42, amended: 1983, c.35, s.12.
s. 46, see *R.* v. *Plymouth City Council and Cornwall County Council, ex p. Freeman* (1988) 28 R.V.R. 89, C.A.
s. 47, repealed in pt.: 1980, c.66,sch.25.
s. 47A, added: 1988, c.4, sch.3.
s. 49, repealed in pt.: 1972, c.70, sch.30; 1973, c.37, sch.9; 1980, c.66, sch.24.
s. 50, repealed in pt.: 1975, c.24, sch.3.
sch. 2, amended: 1981, c.67, sch.4; 1984, c.12, sch.4.
sch. 3, see *R.* v. *Secretary of State for the Environment, ex p. Hood* [1975] 3 W.L.R. 172, C.A.; *Pearson* v. *Secretary of State for the Environment* (1981) 42 P. & C.R. 40, C.A.
sch. 3; amended: 1980, c.66, schs.24,25; 1984, c.27, sch.13; repealed in pt.: 1975, c.56, sch.5; 1981, c.67, sch.6; c.69, sch.17.

42. Prices and Incomes Act 1968.
repealed: 1985, c.71, sch.1.
s. 12, amended: 1972, c.47, schs.9,11; 1980, c.51, sch.25.
s. 54, order 73/745.

43. Appropriation Act 1968.
repealed: 1974, c.31, s.4, sch.

44. Finance Act 1968.
s. 1, repealed in pt.: 1979, c.4, sch.4.
s. 3, repealed: 1973, c.51, sch.22.
s. 4, repealed: 1972, c.25, sch.7.
s. 5, repealed: 1972, c.41, sch.28.
s. 6, repealed: 1979, c.2, sch.6.
s. 7, orders 72/838, 872, 1770; 73/955; 74/1514; 75/1132; 76/684; 78/1882, 1883.

CAP.

1968—cont.

44. Finance Act 1968—cont.
s. 7, repealed: 1979, c.3, sch.3.
s. 10, repealed in pt.: 1979, c.8, sch.2.
s. 23, amended: 1974, c.30, sch.14.
ss. 32, 34, repealed: 1979, c.14, sch.8.
ss. 35–37, repealed: 1975, c.7, sch.13.
s. 41, see *Neubergh* v. *I.R.C.* [1978] S.T.C. 181, Brightman J.
s. 41, repealed in pt.: 1973, c.36, sch.6.
s. 43, amended: 1973, c.51, s.44.
s. 46, see *Stein* v. *I.R.C.* [1973] T.R. 167, Plowman J.
ss. 51, 52, repealed: 1972, c.41, sch.28.
s. 55, repealed in pt.: 1977, c.36, sch.9.
s. 56, repealed: 1973, c.51, sch.22.
s. 58, repealed: 1972, c.68, sch.3.
s. 61, repealed in pt.: 1975, c.7, sch.13; 1979, c.2, sch.; c.14, sch.8.
sch. 5, repealed: 1972, c.25, sch.7.
sch. 6, repealed: 1972, c.41, sch.28.
schs. 11, 12, repealed: 1979, c.14, sch.8.
sch. 12, see *Burman (Inspector of Taxes)* v. *Westminster Press* [1987] S.T.C. 669, Knox J.
sch. 14, repealed: 1975, c.70, sch.13.
sch. 17, repealed: 1972, c.41, sch.28.

45. British Standard Time Act 1968.
repealed: 1972, c.6, s.6.

46. Health Services and Public Health Act 1968.
Pt. I (ss. 1–43), repealed: 1977, c.49, sch.16; 1978, c.29, sch.17 (S.).
s. 5, order 74/6.
s. 11, order 74/32.
s. 19, regs. 74/1522.
s. 28, regs. 74/541.
s. 29, see *Glanvill* v. *Secretary of State for Health and Social Services, The Times*, November 20, 1979, C.A.
s. 29, regs. 73/1468; 74/160, 282, 468, 505, 507.
s. 30, regs. 74/285, 508.
s. 38, regs. 74/287, 507.
s. 39, regs. 74/1522.
s. 45, amended: 1972, c.70, sch.23; 1977, c.49, sch.15; repealed in pt.: S.L.R. 1978; 1983, c.41, sch.10.
s. 46, repealed (S.): *ibid.*, s.3.
ss. 47–50, repealed: 1984, c.22, sch.3.
s. 51, repealed: 1972, c.70, schs.14,30.
ss. 52–58, repealed: 1984, c.22, sch.3.
s. 59, amended: 1977, c.49, sch.15; 1978, c.29, sch.16 (S.).
s. 60, amended: 1980, c.6, sch.2; 1984, c.56, sch.2(S.); repealed in pt.: *ibid* (S.); S.L.R. 1986.
s. 61, repealed: 1988, c.7, sch. 5.
s. 62, amended: 1973, c.32, sch.4; 1977, c.49, sch.14; 1978, c.29, sch.15 (S.); 1984, c.30, sch.11; repealed in pt.: *ibid.*, schs.11,12.
s. 63, amended: 1972, c.58, sch.6 (S.); 1973, c.32, sch.4; 1977, c.49, schs.14,15; 1978, c.29, sch. 16 (S.); order 85/39; 1988, c.49, s.20; repealed in pt.: 1972, c.58, sch.7 (S.); 1973, c.32, sch.5; 1977, c.49, sch.16 (S.); 1978, c.29, sch.17 (S.); 1980, c.53, sch.1, 1985, c.51, sch.17; 1988, c.49, sch.3.

CAP.

1968—cont.

46. Health Services and Public Health Act 1968—cont.
s. 64, amended: 1973, c.32, sch.4; 1975, c.72, sch.3; 1976, c.36, sch.3; 1977, c.49, schs.14,15; 1978, c.22, sch.2; c.29, sch.15; 1980, c.5, sch.5; c.6, sch.2; c.53, sch.1; order 85/39; repealed in pt.: 1973, c.32, sch.5; 1976, c.36, sch.4; 1977, c.49, schs.15,16; 1978, c.29, sch.17; 1980, c.5, sch.6; repealed (S.): 1983, c.41, sch.10.
s. 65, amended: 1972, c.70, sch.23; 1973, c.32, sch.4; c.65, sch.27 (S.); 1975, c.72, sch.3; 1976, c.36, sch.3; 1977, c.49, schs.14,15; 1978, c.22, sch.2; c.29, sch.16 (S.); 1980, c.5, sch.5; c.6, sch.2; repealed in pt.: 1973, c.23, sch.5; c.65, schs.27,29 (S.); 1976, c.36, sch.4; 1977, c.49, schs.15,16; 1980, c.5, sch.6; 1985, c.51, sch.17.
s. 67, amended: 1973, c.65, sch.27 (S.); repealed: 1972, c.58, sch.7 (S.); 1973, c.32, sch.5.
s. 69, repealed: *ibid.*
s. 70, repealed: 1984, c.22, sch.3.
s. 71, amended: 1972, c.58, sch.6; 1973, c.65, sch.27; 1978, c.29, sch.15.
s. 71A, added: 1983, c.41, s.26.
s. 72, amended (S.): 1972, c.58, sch.6; 1978, c.29, sch.15.
s. 73, amended (S.): 1972, c.58, sch.6; 1978, c.29, sch.15; repealed in pt.: 1972, c.58, sch.7.
s. 74, repealed in pt.: S.L.R. 1981.
s. 75, repealed: 1984, c.36, sch.5.
s. 76, repealed (S.): order 81/127.
s. 79, orders 72/826; 74/286, 317; repealed in pt.: 1977, c.49, sch.16; 1978, c.29, sch.17 (S.).
sch. 1, repealed: 1973, c.32, sch.5.
sch. 2, repealed in pt.: 1977, c.49, sch.16; 1978, c.29, sch.17 (S.).
sch. 3, repealed in pt.: 1972, c.58, sch.7 (S.); 1973, c.32, sch.5 (S.); 1978, c.29, sch.17 (S.); 1979, c.36, sch.8.
sch. 5, repealed in pt.: S.L.R. 1986.

47. Sewerage (Scotland) Act 1968.
s. 1, see *James Miller & Partners v. Lothian Regional Council (No. 2)*, 1984 S.L.T.(Lands Tr.) 2.
s. 2, see *RHM Bakeries (Scotland)* v. *Strathclyde Regional Council*, Second Division, December 20, 1983.
s. 3, see *Central Regional Council* v. *Barbour European*, 1982 S.L.T.(Sh.Ct.) 49.
s. 3, amended: 1973, c.65, sch.27; 1984, c.54, sch.9; repealed in pt.: 1973, c.65, sch.29.
ss. 5, 6 (in pt.): repealed: *ibid.*
s. 7, amended and repealed in pt.: *ibid.*, sch.27.
s. 10, repealed in pt.: *ibid.*, sch.30.
s. 12, amended: 1974, c.40, sch.2; 1984, c.54, sch.9.
s. 14, amended: 1974, c.40, sch.2.
s. 16, see *Lawrence Building Co.* v. *Lanark County Council*, 1979 S.L.T. 2.
s. 16, repealed in pt.: 1973, c.65, sch.29.

1968—cont.

47. Sewerage (Scotland) Act 1968—*cont.*

s. 18, amended: *ibid.*, sch.27; repealed in pt.: *ibid.*, sch.29; 1987, c.47, sch.6.

s. 19, repealed: *ibid.*

s. 20, see *Strathclyde Regional Council* v. *James Waddell & Son* (O.H.), January 22, 1982.

s. 22, amended: 1975, c.78, sch.5; 1984, c.12, sch.4.

s. 24, amended: 1974, c.40, sch.2.

s. 41, amended: 1984, c.54, sch.9.

s. 44, amended: 1982, c.48, sch.6.

ss. 45, 46, amended: 1974, c.40, sch.2.

s. 47, amended: 1980, c.45, sch.10.

ss. 48, 50, amended: 1982, c.48, sch.6.

s. 54, order 73/745.

s. 59, amended: 1973, c.65, sch.27; 1984, c.54, sch.9; repealed in pt.: 1973, c.65, sch.29; 1984, c.54, schs.9,11; 1987, c.47, sch.6.

s. 61, order 72/363.

sch. 1, repealed in pt.: 1973, c.65, sch.29.

48. International Organisations Act 1968.

s. 1, orders 72/113, 115, 117, 119, 120; 73/958, 1083; 74/1251–1261; 75/411, 1209, 1210; 77/825; 78/1105; 83/1111; 84/1152, 1980–1982; 85/750, 753; 86/2017; 88/245.

s. 1, amended: 1981, c.9, sch.1.

s. 2, order 72/118.

s. 2, amended: 1988, c.41, sch.12.

s. 3, repealed: 1972, c.68, sch.3.

s. 4, amended: *ibid.*; repealed in pt.: 1981, c.9, s.1, sch.

s. 4A, added: *ibid.*, s.2.

s. 5, orders 74/1251–1261.

s. 5A, added: 1981, c.9, s.3.

s. 6, orders 72/448, 1262.

s. 6, amended: 1981, c.9, s.1.

s. 9, amended: 1972, c.41, s.55; 1979, c.2, sch.4.

s. 10, orders 72/669, 670; 74/2158; 75/158, 159, 411, 1209; 76/216, 219–222, 224; 77/824, 825; 78/179, 181, 1105, 1884, 1893; 79/911, 912, 914; 80/1076, 1096; 81/1108, 1109, 1802, 1804; 82/709, 1071, 1074; 83/142–144, 1111; 84/127, 1152; 85/446, 451, 750, 753; 88/926, 1298, 1299.

s. 12, orders 72/120; 74/1251–1261.

s. 12, repealed in pt.: 1982, c.16, sch.16.

ss. 32, 42, see *L.* v. *McGregor*, Second Division, January 26, 1979.

sch. 1, amended: 1973, c.38, sch.27; 1979, c.2, sch.4; 1981, c.9, s.5; repealed in pt.: 1975, c.18, sch.1.

49. Social Work (Scotland) Act 1968.

s. 1, amended: 1973, c.65, sch.27; 1984, c.36, sch.3; repealed in pt.: 1972, c.58, sch.7; 1973, c.65, sch.27.

s. 2, see *Central Regional Council* v. *Mailley*, 1977 S.L.T.(Sh.Ct.) 36; *Lothian Regional Council* v. *B.*, 1984 S.L.T.(Sh.Ct.) 83.

s. 2, amended: 1973, c.29, sch.5; c.65, sch.27; 1975, c.72, sch.3; 1977, c.48, s.20; 1978, c.28, sch.3; 1984, c.56, sch.2; 1986, c.33, s.12; repealed in pt.: 1973, c.65, sch.29.

s. 3, regs. 78/1284.

s. 3, repealed in pt.: 1981, c.23, schs.2,4.

1968—cont.

49. Social Work (Scotland) Act 1968—*cont.*

s. 5, regs. 75/790; 85/1798, 1799; 87/2233; 88/841.

s. 5, amended: 1975, c.72, sch.3; 1978, c.28, sch.3.

s. 6, amended: 1975, c.72, sch.3; 1977, c.45, sch.11; 1978, c.28, sch.3; 1984, c.56, sch.2.

s. 7, repealed: 1981, c.23, s.29, sch.4.

s. 10, amended: 1975, c.72, sch.3; 1978, c.28, sch.3; 1983, c.41, sch.9.

s. 12, see *Edinburgh Assessor* v. *Brodie*, 1976 S.L.T. 234; *Assessor for Lothian Region* v. *Thistle Foundation*, 1978 S.L.T. 162.

Pt. II (ss. 12–29), III (ss. 30–58), see *Central Regional Council* v. *B.*, 1985 S.L.T. 413.

s. 14, repealed in pt.: 1972, c.58, sch.7; 1983, c.41, sch.9.

s. 15, amended: 1975, c.72, s.73; 1983, c.41, sch.2.

ss. 15, 16, see *Central Regional Council* v. *B.*, 1985 S.L.T. 413; *Lothian Regional Council* v. *S.*, 1986 S.L.T.(Sh.Ct.) 37.

s. 16, see *Central Regional Council* v. *Mailley*, 1977 S.L.T.(Sh.Ct.) 36; *Strathclyde Regional Council* v. *McNair*, 1980 S.L.T.(Sh.Ct.) 16; *Strathclyde Regional Council* v. *D.*, 1981 S.L.T.(Sh.Ct.) 34; *MacInnes* v. *Highland Regional Council* (O.H.), 1982 S.L.T. 288; *Lothian Regional Council* v. *H.*, 1982 S.L.T.(Sh.Ct.) 65; *Strathclyde Regional Council* v. *M.*, 1982 S.L.T.(Sh.Ct.) 106; *Strathclyde Regional Council* v. *T.*, 1984 S.L.T.(Sh.Ct.) 18; *Beagley* v. *Beagley*, 1984 S.L.T. 202, H.L.; *Lothian Regional Council* v. *T.*, 1984 S.L.T.(Sh.Ct.) 74; *Lothian Regional Council* v. *B.*, S.L.T.(Sh.Ct.) 83.

s. 16, substituted: 1975, c.72, s.74; amended: 1976, c.36, sch.3; 1978, c.28, sch.3; 1983, c.41, s.7; 1984, c.36, sch.3; 1985, c.60, 25; 1986, c.9, sch.1; repealed in pt.: 1983, c.41, s.7.

s. 16A, added: 1975, c.72, s.75.

s. 17, amended: *ibid.*, sch.3; repealed in pt.: *ibid.*, sch.4.

s. 17A, order 83/1913.

ss. 17A–17E, added: 1983, c.41, s.7.

s. 18, amended: *ibid.*, sch.3; 1978, c.28, sch.3; 1986, c.9, sch.1; repealed in pt.: 1975, c.72, sch.4.

s. 18A, Act of Sederunt 85/780.

s. 18A, added: 1975, c.72, s.78; amended: 1983, c.41, s.7.

s. 19, repealed: 1984, c.56, sch.3.

s. 20, amended: 1975, c.72, s.79; 1983, c.41, sch.2.

s. 20A, added: 1975, c.72, s.81.

s. 21, amended: 1980, c.5, sch.5; 1985, c.73, sch.2.

s. 22, repealed in pt.: 1973, c.65, schs.25, 29.

s. 23, amended: 1983, c.41, sch.2.

s. 25A, added: 1975, c.72, s.81.

s. 27, amended: 1978, c.49, sch.2.

s. 27A, added: *ibid.*, s.9.

s. 27B, added: 1980, c.62, s.79.

1968—cont.

49. Social Work (Scotland) Act 1968—cont.

s. 28, amended: 1975, c.18, sch.2; repealed in pt.: 1986, c.50, sch.11.

s. 30, amended: 1972, c.24, s.1.

s. 31, see *M.* v. *Dean*, 1974 S.L.T. 229.

s. 31, amended: 1983, c.41, sch.2, repealed in pt.: *ibid.*, sch.10.

s. 32, see *Kennedy* v. *B.* 1973 S.L.T. 38; *K.* v. *Finlayson*,1974 S.L.T. (Sh.Ct.) 51; *McGregor* v. *T.*, First Division, October 23, 1974; *McGregor* v. *D.*, 1977 S.L.T. 182; *McGregor* v. *L.*, 1981, S.L.T. 194; *McGregor* v. *D.*, 1981 S.L.T.(Notes) 97; *M.* v. *McGregor*, Second Division, March 10, 1981; *McGregor* v. *C.A.*, Second Division, March 25, 1981; *McGregor* v. *K.*, Second Division, June 11, 1981; *McGregor* v. *H.*, First Division, February 16, 1983; *Kennedy* v. *S.*, 1986 S.L.T. 679; *Merrin* v. *S.*, 1987 S.L.T. 193; *S.* v. *Kennedy*, 1987 S.L.T. 667; *B.* v. *Kennedy*, 1987 S.L.T. 765; *D.* v. *Kennedy*, 1988 S.L.T. 55; *F.* v. *Kennedy*, 1988 S.L.T. 404.

s. 32, amended: 1975, c.72, sch.3; 1983, c.33, s.1; c.41, s.8.

s. 34, rules 86/2291.

s. 34A, rules 85/843; Act of Sederunt 85/781.

s. 34A, added: 1975, c.72, s.66.

s. 35, rules 83/1424; 84/100, 1867; 85/843, 1724; 86/518, 2291.

s. 35, amended: 1975, c.72, sch.3.

s. 36, rules 84/100.

s. 36, amended: 1973, c.65, sch.27; repealed in pt.: *ibid.*, schs.27, 29.

s. 36A, added: 1975, c.72, s.82.

s. 36A, regs. 75/2251.

s. 37, see *Humphries, Petr.*, First Division, December 11, 1981; *Humphries* v. *S.*, 1986 S.L.T. 683.

s. 37, amended: 1975, c.21, sch.9; c.72, s.83.

s. 39, see *Kennedy* v. *B.*, 1973 S.L.T. 38.

s. 40, amended: 1975, c.72, s.84.

s. 42, see *Holmes* v. *McGregor*, 1973 S.L.T. (Notes) 5; *K.* v. *Finlayson*, 1974 S.L.T. (Sh.Ct.) 51; *D.* v. *Kennedy*, 1974 S.L.T. 168; *McGregor* v. *T.*, First Division, October 23, 1974; *H.* v. *Mearns*, 1974 S.L.T.(Notes) 21; 1974 S.L.T. 184; *Kennedy* v. *O.*, 1975 S.L.T. 235; *C.* v. *McGregor*, 1976 S.L.T.(Notes) 13; *McGregor* v. *D.*, 1977 S.L.T. 182; *H. and H.* v. *M*'*Gregor*, 1973, S.C. 95, Second Division; *Strathclyde Regional Council* v. *X and Another*, 1978 S.L.T.(Sh.Ct.) 46; *McGregor* v. *D.*, 1981 S.L.T.(Notes) 97; *J.F. and Others* v. *McGregor*, Second Division, March 25, 1981; *M.* v. *McGregor*, Second Division, March 10, 1981; *McGregor* v. *C.A.*, Second Division, March 25, 1981; *McGregor* v. *H.*, First Division, February 16, 1983; *McGregor* v. *L.*, 1983 S.L.T. (Sh.Ct.) 7; *Merrin* v. *S.*, 1987 S.L.T. 193; *B.* v. *Kennedy*, 1987 S.L.T. 765; *F.* v. *Kennedy*, 1988 S.L.T. 404.

s. 42, amended: 1980, c.62, sch.7; 1983, c.41, sch.2; 1985, c.73, s.25.

s. 43, see *K.* v. *Finlayson*, 1974 S.L.T.(Sh.Ct.) 51.

1968—cont.

49. Social Work (Scotland) Act 1968—cont.

s. 44, see *Aitken* v. *Aitken*, 1978 S.L.T. 183; *R.* v. *Children's Hearing for the Borders Region*, Second Division, May 13, 1983; *D.* v. *Strathclyde Regional Council*, 1985 S.L.T. 114; *Central Regional Council* v. *B.*, 1985 S.L.T. 413.

s. 44, rules 84/100; 86/518.

s. 44, amended: 1975, c.72, sch.3; 1985, c.73, s.28.

s. 46, amended: 1984, c.36, sch.3.

s. 48, rules 85/1724.

s. 48, amended: 1985, c.73, s.29.

s. 49, see *Holmes* v. *McGregor*, 1973 S.L.T.(Notes) 5; *D.* v. *Sinclair*, 1973 S.L.T.(Sh.Ct.) 47; *K.* v. *Finlayson*, 1974 S.L.T.(Sh.Ct.) 51; *H. and H.* v. *M*'*Gregor*, 1978 S.C. 95, Second Division; *S. Appellants*, 1979 S.L.T.(Sh.Ct.) 37; *Kennedy* v. *H.*, 1988 S.L.T. 586.

s. 49, amended: 1975, c.72, sch.3.

s. 50, see *D.* v. *Kennedy*, 1974 S.L.T. 168.

s. 53, repealed: 1986, c.47, sch.5.

s. 56, amended: 1975, c.21, sch.9; repealed in pt.: *ibid.*, sch.10.

s. 57, amended: *ibid.*, sch.9; repealed in pt.: *ibid.*, sch.10.

s. 58, amended: 1984, c.46, sch.5.

s. 58A, regs. 83/1912; 88/841.

ss. 58A–58G, added: 1983, c.41, s.8.

s. 58B, regs. 83/1912.

s. 58B, amended: 1985, c.73, s.26, sch.2.

s. 58C, regs. 83/1912; 88/841.

s. 58E, amended: 1985, c.73, s.26.

s. 58F, regs. 83/1912; 88/841.

s. 58G, regs. 83/1912.

s. 59A, added: 1975, c.21, s.72; amended: 1983, c.41, s.8; repealed in pt.: *ibid.*, sch.10.

s. 60, regs. 83/1912.

s. 60, amended: 1977, c.45, sch.11; 1978, c.29, sch.16; 1983, c.41, s.8.

s. 61, amended: 1977, c.45, sch.11; 1987, c.40, s.1.

s. 61A, added: *ibid.*, s.2.

s. 62, order, 88/1673.

s. 62, amended: 1977, c.45, sch.11; 1987, c.40, s.3.

s. 63A, added: *ibid.*, s.4.

s. 63B, added: *ibid.*, s.5.

s. 64, rules 83/71.

s. 64A, order 88/1671.

s. 64A, amended: 1987, c.40, s.6.

s. 65, amended: 1977, c.45, sch.11; 1987, c.40, s.7.

ss. 69–71, amended: 1975, c.72, sch.3.

s. 78, Act of Sederunt 85/780.

s. 78, amended: 1983, c.41, s.19; 1986, c.50, sch.10; repealed in pt.: 1983, c.41, s.19, sch.10.

ss. 78, 80, 82, see *Tayside Regional Council* v. *Thaw*, 1987 S.L.T. 69.

s. 78A, added: 1983, c.41, s.19.

s. 80, repealed in pt.: 1987, c.18, sch. 8.

s. 81, amended: 1986, c.9, sch.1; repealed in pt.: *ibid*, schs.1,2.

1968—cont.

49. Social Work (Scotland) Act 1968—cont.

s. 85, regs. 75/734; 83/264.

s. 85, repealed: 1982, c.43, sch.4.

s. 86, amended: 1977, c.49, sch.15; 1978, c.29, sch.16; 1980, c.5, sch.5; repealed in pt.: 1972, c.58, sch.7.

s. 87, regs. 77/1359; 78/1190; 79/1084.

s. 87, amended: 1980, c.30, sch.4; 1983, c.41, ss.18, 20; 1986, c.50, sch.10; repealed in pt.: 1980, c.30, schs.4,5.

s. 88, amended: 1986, c.9, sch.1.

s. 90, orders 72/466; 74/169; 75/359; 76/270; 77/656; 79/320; 81/285; 82/331; 83/430; 85/1514; 88/1673.

s. 92, orders 72/262, 263.

s. 93, orders 79/320; 81/285; 82/331; 83/430; 85/1514.

s. 94, see *Kennedy* v. *H.,* 1988 S.L.T. 586.

s. 94, rules 84/100; order 88/1673.

s. 94, amended: 1973, c.62, sch.5; c.65, sch.27; 1976, c.20, sch.1; 1978, c.29, sch.16; 1980, c.44, sch.4; 1984, c.36, sch.3; 1986, c.9, sch.1; 1987, c.40, s.6; repealed in pt.: 1975, c.72, sch.4; 1977, c.48, sch.

s.94A, order 88/1671.

s. 95, regs. 83/1912.

s. 96, repealed: 1973, c.36, sch.6.

s. 97, repealed in pt.: *ibid.*

sch. 1, repealed: 1984, c.56, sch.3.

sch. 2, repealed in pt.: 1975, c.21, sch.10; 1987, c.41, sch.2.

sch. 3, amended: 1973, c.65, sch.27; 1975, c.30, s.33; 1985, c.73, s.24; repealed in pt.: 1973, c.65, schs.27,29.

sch. 4, repealed: 1986, c.47, sch.5.

sch. 5, rules 83/71; 88/1672.

sch. 7, orders 72/466; 74/169; 75/359; 76/270; 77/656; 79/320; 81/285; 83/430; 85/1514.

sch. 8, repealed in pt.: 1975, c.21, sch.10; c.61, sch.5; 1978, c.28, sch.4; c.40, sch.2; 1979, c.36, sch.8; 1980, c.5, sch.6; c.6, sch.3; c.44, sch.5; 1983, c.20, sch.4; c.39, sch.3; 1984, c. 36, sch.5; c.56, sch.3.

50. Hearing Aid Council Act 1968.

ss. 9, 10, 15, amended: 1975, c.39, ss.1,2.

s. 10, amended: 1981, c.54, sch.5.

s. 12, amended: 1985, c.9, sch.2.

52. Caravan Sites Act 1968.

see *Brown* v. *Secretary of State for the Environment* (1980) 40 P. & C.R. 285, Forbes J.; *Beaconsfield JJ., ex p. Stubbings, The Times,* May 7, 1986, D.C.; *Avon County Council* v. *Buscott* [1988] 1 All E.R. 841, C.A.

s. 1, see *Balthasar* v. *Mullane* (1985) 17 H.L.R. 561; (1986) 84 L.G.R. 55, C.A.

ss. 1, 3, see *Hooper* v. *Eaglestone* (1977) 76 L.G.R. 308, D.C.

s. 5, substituted (S.): 1975, c.49, sch.; amended: 1977, c.43, sch.1.

s. 6, see *Greater London Council* v. *Jones* [1974] J.P.L. 281; 72 L.G.R. 320; *R.* v. *Secretary of State for the Environment, ex p. Ward* [1984] 1 W.L.R. 834, Woolf J.; *R.* v. *Secretary of State for Wales, ex p. Price* [1984] J.P.L. 87, McCullough J.

1968—cont.

52. Caravan Sites Act 1968—cont.

s. 6, amended: 1972, c.70, s.190; 1985, c.51, sch.8; repealed in pt.: 1972, c.7, sch.30; 1980, c.65, s.173, sch.34.

Pt.II (ss.6–12), see *West Glamorgan County Council* v. *Rafferty; R.* v. *Secretary of State for Wales, ex p. Gilhaney* (1986) 18 H.L.R. 375, C.A.

ss. 6, 8, see *R.* v. *Sheffield City Council, ex p. Mansfield* (1978) 37 P. & C.R. 1, D.C.

ss. 6, 9, see *Kensington and Chelsea L.B.C.* v. *Wells* (1973) 72 L.G.R. 289, C.A.; *R.* v. *Secretary of State for the Environment, ex p. Lee; R.* v. *Secretary of State for the Environment, ex p. Bond* [1985] J.P.L. 724; (1987) 54 P. & C.R. 311, Mann J.

s. 7, repealed in pt.: 1972, c.70, sch.30.

ss. 7, 8, see *R.* v. *Secretary of State for Wales, ex p. Price* [1984] J.P.L. 87, McCullough J.; *R.* v. *Secretary of State for the Environment and Cheshire County Council, ex p. Halton B.C.* [1984] J.P.L. 97; (1984) 48 P. & C.R. 28, Taylor J.

s. 9, see *R.* v. *Secretary of State for the Environment, ex p. Ward* [1984] 1 W.L.R. 834, Woolf J.

s. 9, substituted: 1980, c.65, sch.3.

ss. 9, 10, 12, see *R.* v. *Secretary of State for Wales, ex p. Price* [1984] J.P.L. 87, McCullough J.

s. 10, see *Stubbings* v. *Beaconsfield JJ.* (1987) 284 E.G. 233, C.A.

ss. 10, 11, see *R.* v. *Havering JJ., ex p. Smith* [1974] 3 All E.R. 484, D.C.; *R.* v. *Beaconsfield Justices, ex p. Stubbings* (1987) 85 L.G.R. 821, C.A.

s. 11, substituted: 1980, c.65, s.174; repealed in pt.: 1984, c.60, sch.7.

s. 12, orders 72/1449–51; 73/445–9, 879–81; 74/4, 5, 919–22, 1788; 75/316, 647, 648, 1083; 78/1221; 79/419, 420; 81/665, 666, 1337, 1592; 82/67–69, 1255, 1501, 1570, 1799; 83/387, 388, 410, 1218, 1358, 1391, 1392, 1945; 84/16, 200, 267, 1017, 1296, 1469, 1780, 1797, 1958, 1959, 1964; 85/324, 382, 407, 1652, 1764, 1795, 1885; 86/688, 1145, 1170, 1572, 2048, 2286; 88/26, 454, 669, 1242, 1458.

s. 12, substituted: 1980, c.65, s.175; amended: 1985, c.51, sch.8.

s. 13, amended (S.): 1984, c.54, sch.9.

s. 16, see *Greenwich London Borough Council* v. *Powell, The Times,* February 24, 1988, C.A.; *Hammond* v. *Secretary of State for the Environment; Smith* v. *Same, The Times,* July 1, 1988, C.A.

s. 16, substituted (S): 1975, s.49, sch.

s. 17, amended (S): *ibid.*

sch. 1, amended: 1980, c.65, schs.6,34.

53. Adoption Act 1968.

repealed: 1976, c.36, sch.4; 1978, c.28, sch.4 (S.).

s. 4, orders 73/19; 78/1432, 1441.

ss. 7, 11, orders 78/1431, 1432, 1441, 1442.

ss. 9, 14, repealed in pt.: 1981, c.61, sch.9.

CAP.

1968—cont.

53. Adoption Act 1968—cont.
s. 12, rules 78/417, 1519; Acts of Sederunt 78/1373; 84/265; 87/73, 556, 1639–1641, 1709.
s. 14, orders 73/18; 78/1430.

54. Theatres Act 1968.
s. 2, repealed in pt.: 1981, c.42, sch.; 1982, c.45, sch.4 (S.).
s. 5, repealed: 1986, c.64, sch.3.
s. 6, amended: 1977, c.45, ss.15,30, sch.1.
s. 7, amended: 1984, c.46, sch.5; repealed in pt.: ibid., schs.5, 6; 1986, c.64, sch.3.
ss. 8–10, repealed in pt.: ibid.
s. 12, see R. v. South Westminster Licensing Justices, ex p. Raymond [1973] 1 W.L.R. 1303, R.C.
s. 13, sch. 1, see Fischer's Restaurant v. Greater London Council (1980) 78 L.G.R. 672, D.C.
s. 15, repealed in pt.: 1973, c.65, schs.24,29; 1986, c.64, sch.3.
s. 18, amended: 1972, c.70, s.204; 1973, c.65, s.24(S.); 1985, c.51, sch.8; repealed in pt.: 1986, c.64, sch.3.
s. 19, repealed in pt.: S.L.R. 1977.
ss. 19, 20, sch. 2, see R. v. South Westminster Licensing Justices, ex p. Raymond [1973] 1 W.L.R. 1303, D.C.
sch. 1, orders 78/1388, 1544.
sch. 1, amended: 1980, c.65, schs.6,34.
sch. 2, repealed in pt.: S.L.R. 1977; 1979, c.4, sch.4; 1982, c.36, sch.7.
sch. 3, repealed: S.L.R. 1977.

55. Friendly and Industrial and Provident Societies Act 1968.
s. 7, amended: 1985, c.9, sch.2; repealed in pt.: 1974, c.46, sch.11.
s. 8, amended: 1985, c.9, sch.2.
ss. 9, 11, 12, repealed in pt.: 1974, c.46, sch.11.
s. 16, repealed: ibid.
s. 17, amended: ibid., sch.9; repealed in pt.: ibid., sch.11.
ss. 20, 21, 23, schs.1 (in pt.), 2,3 (in pt.): repealed: ibid.

56. Swaziland Independence Act 1968.
ss. 3, 4, repealed: 1981, c.61, sch.9.
ss. 5, 6, repealed: S.L.R. 1977.
sch., amended: 1973, c.36, sch.6; repealed in pt.: S.L.R. 1976; 1981, c.9, sch.; 1988, c.48, sch.8.

57. Overseas Aid Act 1968.
repealed: 1980, c.63, sch.2.
order 75/480.
s. 1, orders 74/1881; 75/1088; 77/1839; 78/472.
s. 2, orders 73/1446; 76/1121; 77/1381, 1590; 78/154, 1152; 79/1160, 1225.
s. 3, orders 72/1048; 76/231.

58. International Monetary Fund Act 1968.
repealed: 1977, c.6, sch.2.

59. Hovercraft Act 1968.
s. 1, orders 72/674, 971, 1576; 77/1257; 78/1913; 79/305, 1309; 82/715; 83/769; 86/1305; 87/1835.
s. 1, amended: 1974, c.40, sch.3; 1978, c.8, sch.1; 1981, c.54, sch.5; 1983, c.21, sch.3.
s. 2, amended: ibid.: 1984, c.28, sch.2; repealed in pt.: 1983, c.21, sch.7.

CAP.

1968—cont.

59. Hovercraft Act 1968—cont.
s. 3, order 87/1835.
s. 5, amended: 1973, c.36, sch.6.
s. 7, order 72/979.
sch., amended: 1972, c.20, sch.9; repealed in pt.: 1979, c.2, sch.6; 1981, c.61, sch.9; order 82/1083; 1984, c.27, sch.14.

60. Theft Act 1968.
see Oteri v. The Queen [1976] 1 W.L.R. 1272, P.C.; R. v. Clow, The Times, August 9, 1978, C.A.
s. 1, see R. v. Gilks [1972] 1 W.L.R. 1341; [1972] 3 All E.R. 280; R. v. Falconer-Attlee (1973) 58 Cr.App.R. 348, C.A.; Stapylton v. O'Callaghan [1973] 2 All E.R. 782; R. v. Feely [1973] 2 W.L.R. 201; [1973] 1 All E.R. 341, C.A.; Low v. Blease [1975] Crim.L.R. 513, D.C.; Edwards v. Ddin [1976] 1 W.L.R. 942, D.C.; R. v. McHugh [1977] R.T.R. 1, C.A.; Pilgram v. Rice-Smith [1977] 1 W.L.R. 671, D.C.; R. v. Bhachu (1977) 65 Cr.App.R. 261, C.A.; R. v. Hircock (1978) 67 Cr.App.R. 278, C.A.; Davies v. Leighton (1978) 68 Cr.App.R. 4, D.C.; R. v. Hale (1978) 68 Cr.App.R. 415, C.A.; Oxford v. Moss (1978) 68 Cr.App.R. 183, D.C.; R. v. Monaghan [1979] Crim.L.R. 673, C.A.; R. v. Kohn (1979) 69 Cr.App.R. 395, C.A.; R. v. Brewster (1979) 69 Cr.App.R. 375, C.A.; Corcoran v. Anderton [1980] Crim.L.R. 385, D.C.; Kaur v. Chief Constable for Hampshire, The Times, January 30, 1981, D.C.; Oxford v. Peers (1980) 72 Cr.App.R. 19, D.C.; Anderton v. Wish (Note) (1980) 72 Cr.App.R. 23, D.C.; Eddy v. Niman [1981] Crim.L.R. 502, D.C.; R. v. McIvor [1982] 1 All E.R. 491, C.A.; R. v. Davies [1982] 1 All E.R. 513, C.A.; R. v. Ghosh [1982] 3 W.L.R. 110, C.A.; R. v. Woolven [1983] Crim.L.R. 623, C.A.; (1983) 77 Cr.App.R. 231, C.A.; R. v. Gregory (1983) 77 Cr.App.R. 41, C.A.; R. v. Morris (David); Anderton v. Burnside [1983] 3 W.L.R. 697, H.L.; Heaton v. Costello, The Times, May 10, 1984, D.C.; Att.-Gen.'s Reference (No. 1 of 1983) [1984] 3 W.L.R. 686, C.A.; R. v. Lloyd (Sidney); R. v. Bhuee; R v. Ali (Chaukal) [1985] 3 W.L.R. 30, C.A.; R. v. Shelton (1986) 83 Cr.App.R. 379, C.A.; R. v. Shadrokh-Cigari (Hamid), The Times, February 23, 1988, C.A.
s. 2, see R. v. Falconer-Attlee (1973) 58 Cr.App.R. 348, C.A.; R. v. Robinson [1977] Crim.L.R. 173, C.A.; R. v. Andrews & Hedges [1981] Crim.L.R. 106, Cent.Crim.Ct.; R. v. Hammond [1982] Crim.L.R. 611, Lincoln Crown Ct.; R. v. Woolven [1983] Crim.L.R. 623; (1983) 77 Cr.App.R. 231, C.A.; Att.-Gen.'s Reference (No. 2 of 1982) [1984] 2 W.L.R. 447, C.A.
s. 3, see R. v. Falconer-Attlee (1973) 58 Cr.App.R. 348, C.A.; Stapylton v. O'Callaghan [1973] 2 All E.R. 782; R. v. Hale (1978) 68 Cr.App.R. 415, C.A.; R. v. Monaghan [1979] Crim.L.R. 673, C.A.; R. v. Kohn (1979) 69 Cr.App.R. 395, C.A.; Corcoran v. Anderton

1968—cont.

60. Theft Act 1968—*cont.*

(1980) 71 Cr.App.R. 104, D.C.; *Oxford* v. *Peers* (1980) 72 Cr.App.R. 19, D.C.; *Anderton* v. *Wish (Note)* (1980) 72 Cr.App.R. 23, D.C.; *R.* v. *Hammond* [1982] Crim.L.R. 611, Lincoln Crown Ct.; *R.* v. *Stuart, The Times,* December 14, 1982, C.A.; *R.* v. *Brooks and Brooks* (1983) 76 Cr.App.R. 66, C.A.; *R.* v. *Drameh* [1983] Crim.L.R. 322, Manchester Crown Ct.; *R.* v. *Gregory* (1983) 77 Cr.App.R. 41, C.A.; *R.* v. *Morris (David); Anderton* v. *Burnside* [1983] 3 W.L.R. 697, H.L.; *R.* v. *Navvabi* [1986] 3 All E.R. 102, C.A.

s. 4, see *Low* v. *Blease* [1975] Crim.L.R. 513, D.C.; *Oxford* v. *Moss* (1978) 68 Cr.App.R. 183, D.C.; *R.* v. *Kohn* (1979) 69 Cr.App.R. 395, C.A.; *Att.-Gen.'s Reference (No. 1 of 1983)* [1984] 3 W.L.R. 686, C.A.

s. 5, see *R.* v. *Gilks* [1972] 1 W.L.R. 1341; [1972] 3 All E.R. 280; *R.* v. *Hall* [1972] 3 W.L.R. 381; 116 S.J. 598; [1972] 2 All E.R. 1009; 56 Cr.App.R. 547; *R.* v. *Meech; R.* v. *Parslow; R.* v. *Joliffe* [1973] 3 W.L.R. 507; *Wakeman* v. *Farrar* [1974] Crim.L.R. 136, D.C.; *R.* v. *Woodman* [1974] 2 W.L.R. 821, C.A.; *R.* v. *Hayes* (1976) 64 Cr.App.R. 82, C.A.; *R.* v. *Williams* [1979] Crim.L.R. 736, Knightsbridge Crown Ct.; *R.* v. *Brewster* [1979] Crim.L.R. 798, C.A.; *R.* v. *Mainwaring; R.* v. *Madders* (1982) 74 Cr.App.R. 99, C.A.; *R.* v. *Cording* [1983] Crim.L.R. 175, Snaresbrook Crown Court; *R.* v. *Storrow and Poole* [1983] Crim.L.R. 332, Central Criminal Ct.; *Davidge* v. *Bunnett* [1984] Crim.L.R. 207, D.C.; *Att.-Gen.'s Reference (No. 1 of 1983)* [1984] 3 W.L.R. 686, C.A.; *Att.-Gen's Ref. (No. 1 of 1985)* [1986] 2 W.L.R. 733, C.A.; *Lewis* v. *Lethbridge* [1987] Crim.L.R. 59, D.C.; *D.P.P.* v. *Huskinson, The Times,* May 24, 1988, D.C.

s. 6, see *R.* v. *Asghar* [1973] Crim.L.R. 701, C.A.; *R.* v. *Kohn* (1979) 69 Cr.App.R. 395, C.A.; *R.* v. *Johnstone, Comerford and Jalil* [1982] Crim.L.R. 454, Newcastle-upon-Tyne Crown Ct; *R.* v. *Downes* [1983] Crim.L.R. 819; (1983) 77 Cr.App.R. 260, C.A.; *R.* v. *Lloyd (Sidney); R.* v. *Bhuee; R.* v. *Ali (Chaukal)* [1985] 3 W.L.R. 30, C.A.; *R.* v. *Sobel* [1986] Crim.L.R. 261, C.A.; *R.* v. *Coffey* [1987] Crim.L.R. 498, C.A.

s. 8, see *R.* v. *Tennant* [1976] Crim.L.R. 133; *R.* v. *Dawson; R.* v. *James* (1978) 68 Cr.App.R. 170, C.A.; *R.* v. *Hale* (1979) 68 Cr.App.R. 415, C.A.; *Corcoran* v. *Anderton* (1980) 71 Cr.App.R. 104, D.C.; *R.* v. *French* (1982) 75 Cr.App.R. 1, C.A.

s. 9, see *R.* v. *Collins* [1972] 3 W.L.R. 243; 116 S.J. 432; [1972] 2 All E.R. 1105; 56 Cr.App.R. 554; *Low* v. *Blease* [1975] Crim.L.R. 513, D.C.; *R.* v. *Jones; R.* v. *Smith* [1976] 1 W.L.R. 672; 63 Cr.App.R. 47, C.A.; *R.* v. *Greenhoff* [1979] Crim.L.R. 108, Huddersfield Crown Ct.; *B. and S.* v. *Leathley* [1979] Crim.L.R. 314, Carlisle Crown Ct.; *R.* v. *Walkington* [1979] 2 All E.R. 716, C.A.; *Att.-Gen.'s References (Nos.* 1 *and*

1968—cont.

60. Theft Act 1968—*cont.*

2 *of* 1979) [1979] 3 All E.R. 143, C.A.; *R.* v. *Francis* [1982] Crim.L.R. 363, C.A.; *R.* v. *Gregory* (1983) 77 Cr.App.R. 41, C.A.; *Comr. of Police of the Metropolis* v. *Wilson; R.* v. *Jenkins* [1983] 3 W.L.R. 686, H.L; *R.* v. *Brown (Vincent)* [1985] Crim.L.R. 212, C.A.; *Norfolk Constabulary* v. *Seekings and Gould* [1986] Crim.L.R. 167, Norwich Crown Court; *R.* v. *O'Neill, McMullen and Kelly, The Times,* October 17, 1986, C.A.; *R.* v. *Whiting* (1987) 85 Cr.App.R. 78; [1987] Crim.L.R. 473, C.A.

s. 10, see *R.* v. *Jones,* November 30, 1979, Solomon J., Middlesex Crown Ct.

s. 11, see *R.* v. *Barr* [1978] Crim.L.R. 244, Bristol Crown Ct.

s. 12, see *R.* v. *MacPherson* [1973] R.T.R. 157, C.A.; *R.* v. *Bogacki* [1973] 2 W.L.R. 937; *R.* v. *Pearce* [1973] Crim.L.R. 321; *McKnight* v. *Davies* [1974] R.T.R. 4, D.C.; *Blayney* v. *Knight* [1975] Crim.L.R. 237; [1975] R.T.R. 279, D.C.; *R.* v. *Earle* [1976] R.T.R. 33, C.A.; *R.* v. *Miller* [1976] Crim.L.R. 147, C.A.; *R.* v. *Bow* [1977] R.T.R. 6, C.A.; *Neal* v. *Gribble* [1978] R.T.R. 409, D.C.; *R.* v. *Mulroy* [1979] R.T.R. 214, C.A.; *R.* v. *Ambler* [1979] R.T.R. 217, C.A.; *A. C. (A Minor)* v. *Hume* [1979] R.T.R. 424, D.C.; *R.* v. *Bonner* [1980] R.T.R. 187, C.A.; *R.* v. *Digin* [1981] R.T.R. 83, C.A.; *R.* v. *Clotworthy* [1981] R.T.R. 477, C.A.; *R.* v. *Donovan* [1982] R.T.R. 126, C.A.; *R.* v. *Stokes* [1983] R.T.R. 59, C.A.; *R.* v. *Kent, The Times,* May 13, 1983, C.A.; *Whittaker* v. *Campbell* [1983] 3 W.L.R. 676, D.C.; *R.* v. *Cooper (Frederick)* [1983] R.T.R. 183, C.A.; *R.* v. *Marchant* (1985) 80 Cr.App.R. 361, C.A.; *Chief Constable of Avon and Somerset Constabulary* v. *Jest* [1986] R.T.R. 372, D.C.; *R.* v. *Briggs* [1987] Crim.L.R. 708, C.A.

s. 12, amended: 1972, c.20, sch.4; 1988, c.33, s.37; repealed in pt.: 1984, c.60, sch.7.

s. 13, see *Low* v. *Blease* [1975] Crim.L.R. 513, D.C.; *Boggeln* v. *Williams* [1978] 1 W.L.R. 873, D.C.; *Collins and Fox* v. *Chief Constable of Merseyside* [1988] Crim.L.R. 247, D.C.

s. 15, see *Halstead* v. *Patel* [1972] 1 W.L.R. 661; [1972] 2 All E.R. 147; 56 Cr.App.R. 334; *R.* v. *Dabek* [1973] Crim.L.R. 527, C.A.; *R.* v. *Asghar* [1973] Crim.L.R. 701, C.A.; *D.P.P.* v. *Ray* [1973] 3 W.L.R. 359; [1973] 3 All E.R. 131, H.L.; *R.* v. *Duru* [1973] 3 All E.R. 715, C.A.; *R.* v. *Tirado* (1974) 59 Cr.App.R. 80, C.A.; *Etim* v. *Hatfield* [1975] Crim.L.R. 234, D.C.; *R.* v. *Staines* (1975) 60 Cr.App.R. 160, C.A.; *R.* v. *Greenstein; R.* v. *Green* [1975] 1 W.L.R. 1353, C.A.; *R.* v. *Lewis (Joseph)* (1975) 62 Cr.App.R. 206, C.A; *Levene* v. *Pearcey* [1976] Crim.L.R. 63, D.C.; *R.* v. *Clegg,* March 15, 1977; *R.* v. *Rashid* [1977] 1 W.L.R. 298, C.A.; *R.* v. *Doukas* [1978] 1 W.L.R. 372, C.A.; *R.* v. *Hircock* (1978) 67 Cr.App.R. 278, C.A.; *R.* v. *Banaster* [1979] R.T.R. 113, C.A.; *Chan Wai Lam* v. *The Queen; Woo Yin Lung* v. *The Queen; Chau Lei Sheung* v. *The Queen* [1981] Crim.L.R. 497, Hong Kong C.A.; *R.* v. *Hartley & Hartley* [1981] R.T.R. 373, C.A.;

CAP.

1968—cont.

60. Theft Act 1968—*cont.*
R. v. *Lambie* [1981] 3 W.L.R. 88; [1981] 2 All
E.R. 776, H.L.; *R. v. Abdullah* [1982] Crim.L.R.
122, Croydon Crown Court; *R. v. Davies* [1982]
1 All E.R. 513, C.A.; *R. v. Ghosh* [1982] 3
W.L.R. 110, C.A.; *R. v. Gilmartin* [1983] 1 All
E.R. 829, C.A.; *R. v. Morris (David)* [1983] 2
W.L.R. 768, C.A.; *R. v. Woolven* [1983]
Crim.L.R. 623, C.A.; (1983) 77 Cr.App.R. 231,
C.A.; *R. v. Thompson* (1984) 79 Cr.App.R. 191;
[1984] 1 W.L.R. 962, C.A.; *R. v. Zemmel; R. v.
Mecik* [1985] Crim.L.R. 213, C.A.; *R. v. Cooke*
[1986] 3 W.L.R. 327, H.L.; *R. v. Silverman*
(1988) 86 Cr.App.R. 213, C.A.; *R. v. Young; R.
v. Kassim, The Times,* March 8, 1988, C.A.
s. 16, see *R. v. Royle* [1971] 1 W.L.R. 1764;
[1971] 3 All E.R. 1359; 56 Cr.App.R. 131;
Davies v. Flackett [1973] R.T.R. 8, D.C.; *R. v.
Fazackerley* [1973] 1 W.L.R. 632; *R. v. Plunkett*
[1973] Crim.L.R. 367; *R. v. Dabek* [1973]
Crim.L.R. 527, C.A.; *D.P.P. v. Ray* [1973] 3
W.L.R. 359; [1973] 3 All E.R. 131, H.L.; *D.P.P.
v. Turner* [1973] 3 W.L.R. 352; [1973] 3 All E.R.
124, H.L.; *R. v. Kovacs* [1974] 1 W.L.R. 370,
C.A.; *R. v. Charles* [1976] 3 W.L.R. 431; [1976]
3 All E.R. 112, H.L.; *R. v. Watkins* [1976] 1 All
E.R. 578; *R. v. Nordeng* (1975) 62 Cr.App.R.
123, C.A.; *R. v. Harris* (1975) 62 Cr.App.R. 28,
C.A.; *R. v. Lewis (Joseph)* (1975) 62 Cr.App.R.
206, C.A.; *Richardson v. Skells* [1976] Crim.L.R.
448; *Bale v. Rosier* [1977] 1 W.L.R. 263, C.A.;
R. v. McHugh [1977] R.T.R. 1, C.A.; *R. v.
Bhachu* (1977) 65 Cr.App.R. 261, C.A.; *R. v.
Ewing* (1977) 65 Cr.App.R. 4, C.A.; *Smith v.
Koumourou* [1979] R.T.R. 355, D.C.; *R. v. Alex-
ander* [1981] Crim.L.R. 183, C.A.; *R. v. Lambie*
[1981] 3 W.L.R. 88; [1981] 2 All E.R. 776, H.L.;
R. v. Waites [1982] Crim.L.R. 369, C.A.; *R. v.
Gilmartin* [1983] 1 All E.R. 829, C.A.; *R. v.
McNiff* [1986] Crim.L.R. 57, C.A.; *R. v. Bevan*
[1987] Crim.L.R. 129; (1987) 84 Cr.App.R. 143,
C.A.; *R. v. King (David); R. v. Stockwell* [1987]
2 W.L.R. 746, C.A.
s. 16, repealed in pt.: 1978, c.31, s.5.
s. 17, see *R. v. Mallett* [1978] 1 W.L.R. 820, C.A.;
R. v. Keatley [1980] Crim.L.R. 505, Knightsbridge Crown Ct.; *Att.-Gen.'s Reference (No. 1
of 1980)* [1981] Crim.L.R. 41, C.A.; *Edwards v.
Toombs* [1983] Crim.L.R. 43, D.C.
s. 20, see *R. v. Clegg,* March 15, 1977; *R. v.
Governor of Pentonville Prison, ex p. Khubchandani* (1980) 71 Cr.App.R. 241, D.C.; *R. v. Ben-
stead and Taylor* (1982) 75 Cr.App.R. 276, C.A.;
R. v. Ghosh [1982] 3 W.L.R. 110, C.A.; *R. v.
Beck* [1985] 1 W.L.R. 22, C.A.; *R. v. Nannay-
akkara; R. v. Khor; R. v. Tan* [1987] 1 W.L.R.
265, C.A.; *R. v. Young; R. v. Kassim, The
Times,* March 8, 1988, C.A.
s. 21, see *R. v. Lawrence* (1971) 57 Cr.App.R. 64,
C.A.; *R. v. Parkes* [1973] Crim.L.R. 358; *R. v.
Harry* [1974] Crim.L.R. 32; *R. v. Harvey, Ulyett
and Plummer* (1980) 72 Cr.App.R. 139, C.A.; *R.
v. Garwood* [1987] 1 W.L.R. 319, C.A.; *R. v.
Bevans (Ronald), The Times,* December 1,
1987, C.A.

CAP.

1968—cont.

60. Theft Act 1968—*cont.*
s. 22, see *R. v. Marshall* (1972) 56 Cr.App.R. 263;
R. v. Alt (1972) 56 Cr.App.R. 457; *R. v. Willis*
[1972] 1 W.L.R. 1605; 116 S.J. 944; [1972] 3
All E.R. 797; *R. v. Deakin* [1972] 1 W.L.R. 1618;
116 S.J. 944; [1972] 3 All E.R. 803; *R. v.
Pitchley* (1973) 57 Cr.App.R. 30, C.A.; *R. v.
McCullum* (1973) 57 Cr.App.R. 645, C.A.; *R. v.
Dabek* [1973] Crim.L.R. 527, C.A.; *Stapylton v.
O'Callaghan* [1973] 2 All E.R. 782; *R. v. Grange*
[1974] 1 All E.R. 928, C.A.; *R. v. Griffiths* (1974)
60 Cr.App.R. 14, C.A.; *R. v. Dolan* (1975) 62
Cr.App.R. 36, C.A.; *R. v. Nicklin* [1977] 1 W.L.R.
403, C.A.; *R. v. Pitham and Hehl* (1976) 65
Cr.App.R. 45, C.A.; *R. v. Smith (Albert)* (1976)
64 Cr.App.R. 217, C.A.; *R. v. Reader* (1977) 66
Cr.App.R. 33, C.A.; *R. v. Reeves* (1978) 69
Cr.App.R. 331, C.A.; *R. v. Hulbert* (1979) 69
Cr.App.R. 243, C.A.; *R. v. Pethick* [1980]
Crim.L.R. 242, C.A.; *R. v. McDonald* (1980) 70
Cr.App.R. 288, C.A.; *Greater London Met.
Police Comr. v. Streeter* (1980) 71 Cr.App.R.
113, D.C.; *R. v. Bloxham, The Times,* February
24, 1981, H.L.; *R. v. Smythe* (1980) 72
Cr.App.R. 8, C.A.; *R. v. Gregory, The Times,*
December 1, 1981, C.A.; *R. v. De Acetis, The
Times,* January 22, C.A.; *R. v. Bloxham* [1982]
2 W.L.R. 392, H.L.; *R. v. Kanwar* [1982] 2 All
E.R. 528, C.A.; *R. v. Saunders* (1982) 75
Cr.App.R. 84, C.A.; *R. v. Korniak* (1983) 76
Cr.App.R. 145, C.A.; *R. v. Ball* [1983] 1 W.L.R.
C.A.; *R. v. Cash (Noel)* C.A.; *R. v. Hall (Edward),
The Times,* March 14, 1985, C.A.; *Anderton v.
Ryan, The Times,* May 13, 1985, H.L.; *R. v. Hall*
[1985] Crim.L.R. 376; (1985) 81 Cr.App.R. 260,
C.A.: *R. v. Roberts (William)* (1987) 84 Cr.App.R.
117, C.A.: *R. v. Shelton* (1986) 83 Cr.App.R.
379, C.A.; *R. v. Park, The Times,* December 4,
1987, C.A.
s. 23, see *Denham v. Scott* [1983] Crim.L.R. 558;
(1983) 77 Cr.App.R. 210, D.C.
s. 24, see *R. v. Smith (Roger)* [1973] 2 W.L.R.
942; *Haughton v. Smith* [1974] 2 W.L.R. 1;
[1973] 2 All E.R. 1109, H.L.; *Att.-Gen.'s Reference (No. 1 of 1974)* [1974] 2 W.L.R. 891;
[1974] 2 All E.R. 899, C.A.; *Greater London
Met. Police Comr. v. Streeter* (1980) 71
Cr.App.R. 113, D.C.; *Att.-Gen.'s Reference (No.
4 of 1979)* (1980) 71 Cr.App.R. 341, C.A.;
Solomon v. Metropolitan Police Comr. [1982]
Crim.L.R. 606, Milmo J.
s. 25, see *R. v. Mandry; R. v. Wooster* [1973] 1
W.L.R. 1232, C.A.; *R. v. Ellames* [1974] 3 All
E.R. 130, C.A.; *R. v. Rashid* [1977] 1 W.L.R.
298, C.A.; *R. v. Bundy* [1977] 2 All E.R. 382,
C.A.; *R. v. Doukas* [1978] 1 W.L.R. 372, C.A.;
R. v. Coboz [1984] Crim.L.R. 629, C.A.; *R. v.
Cooke* [1986] 3 W.L.R. 327, H.L.; *Minor v.
D.P.P.* (1988) 86 Cr.App.R. 378, D.C.
s. 25, amended: 1972, c.20, sch.4.
s. 26, repealed in pt.: 1972, c.71, sch. 6; 1984,
c.60, sch.7.
s. 27, see *R. v. Davis* [1972] Crim.L.R. 431; *R. v.
Knott* [1973] Crim.L.R. 36; *R. v. Airlie* [1973]
Crim.L.R. 310; *R. v. French* [1973] Crim.L.R.

1968—cont.

60. Theft Act 1968—*cont.*

621, Swanwick J.; *R.* v. *Wilkins* [1975] 2 All E.R. 734, C.A.; *R.* v. *Anderson* [1978] Crim.L.R. 223, Newcastle-upon-Tyne Crown Ct.; *R.* v. *Bradley* (1979) 70 Cr.App.R. 200, C.A.; *R.* v. *Perry* [1984] Crim.L.R. 680, C.A.; *R.* v. *Rasini, The Times,* March 20, 1986, C.A.: *R.* v. *Simmons* [1986] Crim.L.R. 397, C.A.; *R.* v. *Wood (William Douglas)* [1987] 1 W.L.R. 779, C.A.; *R.* v. *Fowler* [1987] Crim.L.R. 769; (1988) 86 Cr.App.R. 219, C.A.

s. 28, see *R.* v. *Blackpool JJ.* [1972] 1 W.L.R. 1458; 116 S.J. 729; [1972] 3 All E.R. 854; *Malone* v. *Met. Police Commissioner* [1979] 1 All E.R. 256, C.A.; *Chief Constable of Kent* v. *V., The Times,* May 14, 1982, C.A.; *R.* v. *Thibeault* [1983] Crim.L.R. 102, C.A.

s. 28, amended: 1972, c.71, sch.5; 1977, c.45, sch.12; 1988, c.33, s.163, sch.15.

s. 29, repealed in pt.: 1977, c.45, sch.13.

s. 30, see *R.* v. *Noble* [1974] 1 W.L.R. 894; [1974] 2 All E.R. 811, C.A.; *R.* v. *Withers* [1975] Crim.L.R. 657; *Woodley* v. *Woodley* [1978] Crim.L.R. 629, D.C.

s. 30, amended: 1975, c.59, sch.5; 1979, c.31, sch.1; repealed in pt.: 1975, c.59, sch.6; 1984, c.60, sch.7.

s. 31, see *Khan* v. *Khan* [1982] 2 All E.R. 60, C.A.; *Overseas Programming Co.* v. *Cinematographische Commerz-Anstalt and Iduna Film GmbH, The Times,* May 16, 1984, French J.

s. 34, see *R.* v. *Parkes* [1973] Crim.L.R. 358.

s. 36, repealed in pt.: 1973, c.36, sch.6.

sch. 1, repealed in pt.: 1980, c.49, s.9.

sch. 2, repealed in pt.: 1972, c.20, sch.9; 1974, c.39, sch.5; 1977, c.45, sch.13; 1981, c.38, sch.6; 1985, c.65, sch.10.

61. Civil Aviation Act 1968.

ss. 1–6, 8, 13 (in pt.), 14–23, 26–28, repealed: 1982, c.16, sch.16.

ss. 2, 4, see *Re Koscot* [1972] 3 All E.R. 829.

s. 3, amended: 1973, c.65, sch.27.

s. 8, orders 72/107; 74/101; 75/30; 76/1709; 77/1164.

s. 9, order 72/540.

ss. 9–12, repealed: 1975, c.78, sch.6.

s. 13, repealed in pt.: 1973, c.36, sch.6.

s. 14, see *Air Canada* v. *Secretary of State for Trade* [1981] 3 All E.R. 336, Parker J.

s. 14, order 72/189, 385, 1736.

s. 15, orders 72/108, 905; 73/1196, 1678; 74/1132; regs. 75/1184, 1631, 1968; 76/2084; 77/340; 78/241, 693, 837; 79/154, 267, 1274; 80/317, 356, 1349; 81/355, 362, 1237.

s. 16, see *Nast* v. *Nast* [1972] Fam. 142; [1972] 2 W.L.R. 901; [1972] 1 All E.R. 1171.

s. 16, order 72/1288.

s. 18, order 81/611.

s. 19, order 79/930.

s. 21, amended: 1975, c.76, sch.1; repealed in pt.: 1972, c.70, sch.30; 1975, c.76, schs.1,2.

s. 24, repealed: 1977, c.13, sch.2.

s. 25, repealed: 1975, c.78, sch.6.

s. 28, amended: 1973, c.65, sch.27; repealed in pt.: 1972, c.70, sch.30.

1968—cont.

62. Clean Air Act 1968.

s. 1, see *Sheffield City Council* v. *A.D.H. Demolition* (1984) 82 L.G.R. 177, D.C.

ss. 1, 2, 3, 4, 6, 9, amended: 1974, c.40, sch.2.

s. 3, amended: 1980, c.65, sch.2.

ss. 4, 6, repealed in pt.: *ibid.,* schs.2,34.

s. 6, amended: 1983, c.25, sch.3.

s. 8, amended (S.): 1987, c.26, sch.23.

ss. 10, 12, repealed in pt.: 1980, c.65, sch.34.

s. 11, repealed in pt.: regs. 74/2170.

s. 14, repealed in pt.: 1980, c.65, schs.2,34.

63. Domestic and Appellate Proceedings (Restriction of Publicity) Act 1968.

s. 2, amended: 1973, c.18, schs.2,3; 1986, c.55, sch.1; 1987, c.42, sch.2; repealed in pt.: 1986, c.55, schs.1,2; 1987, c.42, sch.4.

s. 3, amended: 1973, c.18, schs.2,3.

s. 4, amended: *ibid.,* c.36, sch.6; repealed in pt.: 1978, c.23, sch.7.

64. Civil Evidence Act 1968.

see *R.* v. *Wood Green Crown Court, ex p. P.* (1982) 4 F.L.R. 206, McCullough J.; *Lego System Aktieselskab* v. *Lego m. Lemelstrich* [1983] F.S.R. 155, Falconer J.

s. 1, see *Forth Investments* v. *I.R.C.* [1976] S.T.C. 399; *Minnesota Mining and Manufacturing Co.* v. *Johnson & Johnson* [1976] F.S.R. 6, C.A.

s. 2, see *Morris* v. *Stratford-on-Avon R.D.C.* [1973] 1 W.L.R. 1059, C.A.; *Forth Investments* v. *I.R.C.* [1976] S.T.C. 399; *Khan* v. *Edwards* [1977] T.R. 143, Walton J.; *Lawrence* v. *Newham London Borough Council* [1978] I.C.R. 10, E.A.T.; *Piermay Shipping Co. S.A.* v. *Chester* [1978] 1 W.L.R. 411, C.A.; *Savings and Investment Bank* v. *Gasco Investments (Netherlands) B.V. (No. 2)* [1988] 1 All E.R 975, C.A.

ss. 2, 4, see *D. (A Minor) (Wardship: Evidence), Re,* (1986) 16 Fam.Law 263; (1986) 2 F.L.R. 189, Wood J.

s. 4, see *H.* v. *Schering Chemicals* [1983] 1 W.L.R. 143, Bingham J.; *Savings & Investment Bank* v. *Gasco Investments (Netherlands) BV* [1984] 1 W.L.R. 271, Peter Gibson J.

s. 5, see *Khan* v. *Edwards* [1977] T.R. 143, Walton J.

s. 8, see *Rasool* v. *West Midlands Passenger Transport Executive* [1974] 3 All E.R. 638; *Piermay Shipping Co. S.A.* v. *Chester* [1978] 1 W.L.R. 411, C.A.; *Minnesota Mining and Manufacturing Co.* v. *Johnson & Johnson* [1976] F.S.R. 6, C.A.

s. 8, amended: 1980, c.43, sch.7; 1984, c.28, sch.2; repealed in pt.: 1981, c.54, sch.7.

s. 9, see *Humberside C.C.* v. *D.P.R. (An Infant), The Times,* June 24, 1977.

s. 10, amended: 1984, c.28, sch.2.

s. 11, see *Re Raphael (Decd.); Raphael* v. *D'Antin* [1973] 1 W.L.R. 998; [1973] 3 All E.R. 19; *McIlkenny* v. *Chief Constable of the West Midlands; Walker* v. *Same; Power* v. *Chief Constable of the Lancashire Police Force; Hunter* v. *Same* [1980] 2 W.L.R. 689, C.A.; *Union Carbide Corp.* v. *Naturin* [1987] F.S.R. 538, C.A.

s. 12, amended: 1987, c.42, s.29.

CAP.

1968—cont.

64. Civil Evidence Act 1968—*cont.*

s. 14, see *Re Westinghouse Electric Corp. Uranium Contract Litigation M.D.L. Docket No. 235 (No. 1) (No. 2); Rio Tinto Zinc Corp. v. Westinghouse Electric Corp.* [1978] 2 W.L.R. 81, H.L.; *Overseas Programming Co. v. Cinematographische Commerz-Anstalt and Iduna Film GmbH, The Times,* May 16, 1984, French J.; *Garvin v. Domus Publishing* [1988] 3 W.L.R. 344, Walton J.

s. 15, see *"Dormeuil" Trade Mark* [1983] R.P.C. 132, Nourse J.

s. 15, repealed: 1977, c.37, sch.6.

s. 17, repealed in pt.: 1975, c.34, sch.2.

s. 18, see *Khan v. Edwards* [1977] T.R. 143, Walton J.; *Chocoladefabriken Lindt & Sprungli A.G. v. Nestlé* [1978] R.P.C. 287, Megarry V.-C.

s. 19, repealed: 1973, c.36, sch.6.

s. 20, amended: *ibid.*

sch., amended: 1973, c.38, sch.28; repealed in pt.: 1979, c.12, sch. 7; S.L.R. 1981; 1983, c.2, sch. 9; 1986, c.59, sch.

65. Gaming Act 1968.

s. 1, amended: 1976, c.32, sch.4.

ss. 1, 5, 8, see *Brown v. Plant,* 1985 S.L.T. 371.

s. 5, repealed in pt.: 1984, c.60, sch.7.

s. 6, amended (S.): 1976, c.66, sch.7; repealed in pt.: *ibid.,* schs. 7, 8; S.L.R. 1986.

s. 7, repealed in pt.: S.L.R. 1986.

s. 8, amended: 1976, c.66, sch.7 (S.); 1977, c.45, s.31, schs.6,12.; *ibid.,* schs.11,12(S.); repealed in pt.: S.L.R. 1986.

Pt. II (ss.9–25), see *Lock v. Rank Leisure, The Times,* February 24, 1984, D.C.

s. 10, repealed in pt.: 1975, c.24, sch.3.

s. 13, see *Re De Keller's Application, The Times,* April 28, 1983, Forbes J.

s. 14, regs. 73/355, 359; 78/38, 76; orders 75/604, 606, 665, 671; 76/1902, 1904, 1921, 1924; 80/27, 143; 82/84, 130 (S.); 83/5, 80 (S.); 84/248, 470 (S.); 87/609, 613 (S.).

s. 16, see *Aziz v. Knightsbridge Gaming and Catering Services and Supplies, The Times,* July 6, 1982, Hobhouse J.; *Ladup v. Shaikh (Nadeem)* [1982] 3 W.L.R. 172, McCowan J.; *R. v. Knightsbridge Crown Court, ex p. Marcrest Properties* [1983] 1 W.L.R. 300, C.A.; *Ladup v. Siu, The Times,* November 24, 1983, C.A.

s. 16, amended: 1986, c.11, s.7.

s. 18, amended and repealed in pt.: 1987, c.11, s.1.

s. 20, orders 75/608, 664; 76/1901, 1923; orders 80/1429, 1679 (S.); 81/2, 58 (S.); 82/85, 131 (S.); 84/247, 468 (S.); 85/575, 641 (S.); 87/608, 630 (S.).

s. 20, amended: orders 75/608; 76/1901, 1923; 1980, c.8, s.1; orders 80/1429, 1679 (S.); 81/2, 58 (S.); 82/131 (S.); 84/247; 87/608.

s. 21, orders 75/608, 664; 80/28, 148; 82/85, 131 (S.); 84/247, 468 (S.); 88/1026, 1050(S.).

s. 21, amended: orders 75/608; 80/28, 148; 82/131 (S.); 84/247; 85/575; 88/1050(S.).

s. 22, regs. 84/248, 470 (S.); 88/1027, 1052, 1251, 1416.

s. 22, amended: 1986, c.11, s.2.

CAP.

1968—cont.

65. Gaming Act 1968—*cont.*

s. 23, see *Bentley v. Palace Cinema (Gorleston)* [1973] Crim.L.R. 300.

Pt. III (ss.26–39), s.30, see *Chief Constable, Tayside v. Dundee Snooker Centre,* 1987 S.L.T.(Sh.Ct.) 65.

s. 31, orders 76/1901, 1923; 81/2, 58 (S.); 85/575, 641(S.).

s. 31, amended: orders 76/1901, 1923; 81/2, 58 (S.); 85/575.

s. 32, see *Mecca Leisure v. City of Glasgow District Licensing Board* (O.H.), 1987 S.L.T. 483.

s. 33, amended: 1975, c.58, sch.4; repealed in pt.: 1976, c.32, sch.5.

s. 34, see *Brown v. Plant,* 1985 S.L.T. 371; *J. E. Sheeran (Amusement Arcades) v. Hamilton District Council,* 1986 S.L.T. 289.

s. 34, orders 75/608, 664, 1901, 1923; 78/37, 75; 81/2, 58 (S.); 83/1740, 1954 (S.); 86/1981, 2035 (S.).

s. 34, amended: orders 75/608; 76/1901, 1923; 78/37; 81/2, 58 (S.); 83/1740; 86/1981; 1976, c.32, sch.4.

s. 40, orders 75/670; 76/1903, 1922; 80/1127, 1161 (S.); 81/1, 59 (S.); 84/246, 469 (S.); 88/1028, 1051(S.).

s. 40, amended: 1973, c.12, s.1; orders 75/670, 788; repealed in pt.: 1973, c.12, s.1.

s. 41, orders 75/608, 664; 76/1901, 1923; 81/2, 58 (S.); 84/247, 468 (S.); 88/1026, 1050(S).

s. 41, amended: orders 75/608; 76/1901, 1923; 81/2, 58 (S.); 1976, c.32, sch.4; orders 84/247; 1050(S.); repealed in pt.: 1976, c.32, sch.5.

s. 42, see *R. v. Brighton Gaming Licensing Committee, ex p. Cotedale* [1978] 1 W.L.R. 1140, C.A.

s. 42, amended: 1984, c.46, sch.5.

s. 43, repealed in pt.: 1984, c.60, sch.7.

s. 44, amended: 1973, c.65, sch.24; repealed in pt.: 1972, c.70, sch.30; 1985, c.51, sch.17.

s. 48, orders 76/592, 608, 623, 664; 77/570, 633; 78/1847; 79/380; 80/299, 502; 81/456, 546 (S.); 82/1171, 1253; 83/127, 333 (S.); 84/338 (S.); regs. 84/166; orders 88/15, 109(S.), 373(S.).

s. 48, amended: orders 75/608; 76/592, 623; 77/570, 633; 78/1847; 79/380; 81/456; 82/1171, 1253; 83/127; 88/15.

s. 51, orders 75/604, 606, 665, 670, 671, 788; 76/592, 623, 1901–1904, 1921–1924; 77/570, 633; 78/37, 75, 1847; 79/380; 80/27, 28, 143, 148, 299, 502, 1127; 81/1, 2, 58 (S.), 456, 546 (S.); 82/84, 85, 130 (S.), 131 (S.), 1171, 1253; 83/127, 333 (S.), 1740, 1954 (S.); 84/166, 246, 247, 338 (S.), 469 (S.); 85/575, 641 (S.); 86/1981, 2035 (S.); 87/242, 255 (S.), 608, 631 (S.); 88/15, 109(S), 373(S.), 1027, 1028, 1051(S.); regs. 73/355, 359; 78/38; 83/5, 80 (S.); 84/248, 470 (S.); 87/609; 88/1052, 1251, 1416.

s. 51A, added: 1976, c.32, sch.4.

s. 52, amended: *ibid.*; 1987, c.3, sch.1.

s. 54, repealed in pt.: 1975, c.24, sch.3.

sch. 1, amended: 1985, c.53, s.25.

1968—cont.

65. Gaming Act 1968—*cont.*

sch. 2, see *W. M. T. Entertainments* v. *Glasgow Burgh Licensing Court,* 1974 S.L.T.(Sh.Ct.) 76; *Fehilly and Hope* v. *Stirling Licensing Court,* 1975 S.L.T.(Sh.Ct.) 16; *W. M. T. Entertainments* v. *Glasgow Burgh Licensing Court,* 1975 S.L.T.(Sh.Ct.) 39; *Mecca* v. *Kirkcaldy Burgh Licensing Court,* 1975 S.L.T.(Sh.Ct.) 50; *R.* v. *Newcastle upon Tyne Gaming Licensing Committee, ex p. White Hart Enterprises* [1977] 1 W.L.R. 1135; *The Times,* June 28, 1977, C.A.; *R.* v. *Brighton Gaming Licensing Committee, ex p. Cotedale* [1978] 1 W.L.R. 1140, C.A.; *Mecca* v. *Glasgow District Licensing Court,* 1979 S.L.T.(Sh.Ct.) 42; *R.* v. *Knightsbridge Crown Court, ex p. International Sporting Club (London)* [1981] 3 W.L.R. 640, D.C.; *Cigaro (Glasgow)* v. *City of Glasgow District Licensing Board,* First Division, December 8, 1981; *R.* v. *Knightsbridge Crown Court, ex p. Marcrest Properties* [1983] 1 W.L.R. 300, C.A.; *Patmor* v. *City of Edinburgh District Licensing Board* (O.H.), 1987 S.L.T. 492.

sch. 2, Act of Sederunt 78/229.

sch. 2, amended: 1972, c.25, sch.5; 1973, c.65, sch.24 (S.); 1976, c.66, s.133 (S.); 1981, c.63, sch.5; repealed in pt.: 1972, c.25, sch.7; c.70, sch.30; 1975, c.20, sch.2 (S.); 1976, c.66, sch.8 (S.); 1982, c.22, sch.1.

sch. 3, amended: 1972, c.25, sch.5; 1981, c.63, sch.5; repealed in pt.: 1972, c.25, sch.7; 1982, c.22, sch.1.

sch. 4, amended: 1972, c.25, sch.5; repealed in pt.: *ibid.,* sch.7; 1982, c.22, sch.1.

sch. 7, see *Chief Constable, Strathclyde* v. *Pollokshaws Road Snooker Centre,* 1977 S.L.T.(Sh.Ct.) 72.

schs. 7, 8, see *Chief Constable, Tayside* v. *Dundee Snooker Centre,* 1987 S.L.T. (Sh.Ct.) 65.

sch. 9, see *Dawson* v. *Lanark Licensing Court,* 1972 S.L.T.(Sh.Ct.) 68; *Prise* v. *Aberdeen Licensing Court,* 1974 S.L.T.(Sh.Ct.) 48.

sch. 9, amended (S.): 1973, c.65, sch.24; 1976, c.66, sch.7; repealed in pt.: 1972, c.70, sch.30; (S.) 1973, c.65, schs.24,29; (S.) 1976, c.66, sch.8; S.L.R. 1986.

sch. 11, amended: orders 75/606, 666; repealed in pt.: 1972, c.25, sch.7; (S.) 1973, c.65, sch.29; 1975, c.58, sch.5; 1976, c.32, sch.5.

66. Restrictive Trade Practices Act 1968.

repealed, except ss. 12, 14, 15, 16 in pt., 17 in pt., sch. 1: 1976, c.34, sch.6.

ss. 6, 7, see *Re Flushing Cistern Makers' Agreement* [1973] 3 All E.R. 817, R.P.Ct.

ss. 12, 14, 15, sch. 1, repealed: 1976, c.53, sch.3.

ss. 16, 17, repealed in pt.: 1976, c.53, sch.3.

67. Medicines Act 1968.

Commencement order 85/1539.

orders 72/1200; 78/20.

s. 1, regs. 78/1121; order 87/1980.

s. 2, repealed in pt.: 1975, c.24, sch.3; c.25, sch.3.

1968—cont.

67. Medicines Act 1968—*cont.*

s. 3, order 84/1261.

s. 4, orders 75/1006, 1473; 78/1005; 79/1535; 82/1335; 84/1261.

s. 6, see *R.* v. *Licensing Authority, ex p. Smith Kline and French Laboratories, The Times,* January 2, 1988, Henry J.

s. 7, see *McColl* v. *Strathclyde Regional Council* (O.H.), 1983 S.L.T. 616.

ss. 7, 8, amended: regs. 77/1050; 83/1724.

s. 11, amended: 1979, c.36, sch.7; repealed in pt.: *ibid.,* schs.7,8.

s. 13, orders 74/316, 498, 1150; 77/161, 640; 78/1139, 1461; 79/1585; 84/673; 86/228.

s. 15, orders 72/640, 1199; 73/2079; 74/316, 498, 1150; 75/762; 77/161, 1054; 78/1139, 1461; 79/1114, 1585, 1745; 81/164; 83/1728; 84/673; 86/228, 1180, 2217; 87/2217.

s. 16, orders 78/1138; 79/1539; 85/1539.

s. 17, orders 72/1198; 74/1149; 75/761; 80/1467; 81/1690.

s. 18, regs. 72/1201; 74/832; 75/681; 77/1051, 1052; 78/1138; 79/1760; 82/1789; 83/1725, 1726.

s. 18, amended: regs. 77/1050; 83/1724.

s. 19, see *Wellcome Foundation* v. *Secretary of State for Social Services, sub nom. R.* v. *Secretary of State for Social Services, ex p. Wellcome Foundation* [1988] 1 W.L.R. 635, H.L.

s. 19, regs. 77/1038.

s. 20, see *R.* v. *Licensing Authority, ex p. Smith Kline and French Laboratories, The Times,* January 2, 1988, Henry J.

s. 20, amended: regs. 77/1050.

s. 23, orders 78/1139; 79/1585.

s. 24, regs. 74/832; 82/1789; amended: regs. 77/1050.

s. 28, amended: order 75/1169; regs. 77/1050; repealed in pt.: 1984, c.40, s.13.

s. 35, orders 74/316, 498, 1150; regs. 78/1139; 79/1585; 81/164; 86/1180.

s. 36, regs. 72/1201; 74/832; 75/681; 77/1051; 82/1789; order 79/1760.

s. 37, order 72/1198.

s. 38, regs. 82/1789.

s. 40, regs. 85/1533; 88/976.

s. 40, substituted: 1984, c.40, s.13.

ss. 41, 42, 46 (in pt.), repealed: *ibid.,* schs.1,2.

s. 47, regs. 72/1226; 74/1523; 77/675, 1039, 1053; 83/1730.

s. 51, orders 77/2129; 79/315; 80/1922; 82/26; 84/768, 769; 85/1540; 87/910.

s. 52, see *Pharmaceutical Society of Great Britain* v. *Logan* [1982] Crim.L.R. 443, Croydon Crown Ct.

s. 52, order 77/2126.

s. 53, regs. 80/1923; 82/28.

s. 55, order 77/2133.

ss. 55, amended: 1973, c.32, sch.4; 1977, c.49, sch.14; 1978, c.29, sch.15.

s. 56, order 77/2130.

CAP.

1968—cont.

67. Medicines Act 1968—cont.

s. 57, orders 77/2130, 2133, 2167; 78/988, 1001, 1421; 79/45, 1008; 80/283, 1560, 1924; 81/793, 1872; 82/27, 1019, 1805; 83/274, 1156; 84/349, 1861; 85/310, 857, 1823; 86/982, 1997; 87/1123, 1980; 88/1015.

s. 57, amended: 1984, c.40, s.14

s. 58, see *Pharmaceutical Society of Great Britain v. Storkwain* [1986] 2 All E.R. 635, H.L.

s. 58, orders 77/2127; 78/189, 987; 79/36, 1040; 80/24, 1921; 81/80; 82/29, 1596, 1801; 83/341, 957, 1212, 1213, 1506, 1792; 84/756, 1862; 85/309, 1288; 86/586; 87/674, 1250.

s. 59, orders 77/2127; 80/1921; 82/29; 83/1212, 1213; 85/1288.

s. 60, regs. 78/1006.

s. 61, regs. 77/2132; 78/989; 80/1923.

s. 62, orders 73/1120; 74/711, 1082, 2167; 76/1861; 77/172, 670, 2127, 2131; 79/382, 1181; 80/263; 82/518; 86/1368; 87/2216; S.R.s 1977 No. 359; 1981 No. 182.

s. 66, regs. 77/2132; 78/989; 80/1923.

s. 67, regs. 77/2132; 80/1923.

s. 67, amended: 1977, c.45, s.31.

s. 69, order 73/1849.

s. 70, amended: order 87/2202.

s. 71, amended and repealed in pt.: *ibid.*

s. 72, regs. 81/1713.

s. 72, amended: 1985, c.65, sch.8; 1986, c.45, sch.14.

ss. 75, 76, regs. 73/1822; 76/667, 1961; 77/2077; 80/1806; 82/1719; 83/1787; 84/1886; 85/1878; 87/2099.

s. 76, regs. 77/511; 81/1713.

s. 85, regs. 73/1530; 76/1726; 77/996, 2168; 78/41, 190, 1140; 85/1558, 2008; orders 79/1759; 81/1689, 1791; 83/1729; 88/1009.

s. 86, regs. 73/1530; 76/1726; 77/1055; 78/41, 1140; 85/2008; orders 79/1759; 81/1689; 83/1727; 88/1009.

s. 87, regs. 78/40; 87/877.

ss. 87, 88, regs. 75/2000; 76/1643.

s. 91, regs, 73/1530; 75/2000; 76/1643, 1726; 77/996, 1055, 2168; 78/40, 41, 1140; 81/1689; 83/1729; 85/1558, 2008; 88/1009; order 79/1759.

s. 92, amended: 1984, c.46, sch.5; 1988, c.48, sch.7.; repealed in pt.: 1984, c.46, schs.5,6; 1988, c.48, schs.7,8.

s. 93, see *R. v. Roussel Laboratories; R. v. Good, The Times*, June 13, 1988, C.A.

s. 95, regs. 75/298, 1326; 78/41, 1020.

ss. 95, 96, order 79/1760.

s. 96, regs. 81/1633.

s. 98, repealed: 1988, c.48, sch.8.

s. 103, regs. 85/803, 804; 86/26, 144; 88/1547; S.R. 1985 No. 131.

s. 103, amended: 1988, c.49, s.22.

s. 104, orders 73/1164; 75/533; 76/968; 78/1004; 84/187.

s. 105, regs. 73/367; orders 82/425; 85/1403.

s. 108, amended: 1984, c.40, sch.1; order 88/1955; repealed in pt.: 1972, c.70, sch.30.

ss. 108, 109, regs. 77/2132.

CAP.

1968—cont.

67. Medicines Act 1968—cont.

s. 109, amended: 1973, c.65, sch.27.

s. 112, see *Mistry v. Norris, The Times*, October 16, 1985, D.C.

ss. 112, 113, 115, modified: regs. 76/30; 85/273.

ss. 112, 115, regs. 76/1970; 77/1399.

s. 116, amended: 1979, c.2, sch.4.

s. 117, regs. 76/30; 77/1584; 83/62; 85/273; order 76/31.

s. 117, amended: 1984, c.40, s.15, sch.1.

s. 126, amended: *ibid.*, sch.1.

s. 129, orders 72/1199, 1201; 77/640, 2127; 78/189, 190, 987, 988, 1001, 1140; 79/36, 45, 315, 1008, 1040, 1535, 1585, 1745, 1759, 1760; 80/7, 24, 263, 283, 1560, 1921, 1922, 1924; 81/80, 793, 1872; 82/26–29, 425, 518, 1019, 1335, 1501, 1596, 1805; 83/274, 341, 957, 1156, 1212, 1506, 1729; 84/187, 349, 673, 756, 769, 1261, 1861, 1862; 85/309, 310, 857, 1288, 1403, 1539, 1540, 1823, 1878; 86/982, 1997; 87/674, 910, 1123, 1250, 1980, 2216; 88/1015; regs. 78/40, 41, 1020; 80/1923; 81/1633, 1689, 1791; 82/1121, 1789; 83/62, 1787; 84/1886; 85/1558; 87/877, 2099; 88/976, 1009.

s. 130, orders 77/1488; 86/2177.

s. 130, amended: 1984, c.40, s.13, sch.1; repealed in pt.: *ibid.*, schs.1,2.

s. 131, amended: 1973, c.32, sch.4; 1977, c.49, schs.14, 15; (S.) 1978, c.29, schs.15,16.

s. 132, regs. 87/2099.

s. 132, amended: 1972, c.70, s.198; 1973, c.32, sch.4; 1977, c.49, schs.14,15; (S.) 1978, c.29, schs.15, 16; 1983, c.54, sch.5; order 80/703; 1984, c.24, sch.5; c.30, sch.10; c.40, s.13.

s. 134, S.Rs. 1977 No. 359; 1981 No. 182.

s. 134, amended: 1973, c.36, sch.6.

s. 136, orders 72/788, 1225; 73/1529, 1851; 76/74; 77/1068.

sch. 3, see *Mistry v. Norris, The Times*, October 16, 1985, D.C.

sch. 3, regs. 76/1970; 77/1399.

sch. 3, amended: 1984, c.30, sch.10.

sch. 4, S.R.s 1977 No. 359; 1981 No. 182.

sch. 4, amended: order 79/1753; repealed in pt.: 1984, c.40, schs.1,2.

sch. 5, repealed in pt.: 1972, c.66, sch.2; 1978, c.29, sch.17.

sch. 6, repealed in pt.: 1981, c.22, sch.6.

schs. 19, 20, regs. 76/1970.

68. Design Copyright Act 1968.

repealed: 1988, c.48, sch.8.

see *Smith v. Greenfield* [1984] 6 N.I.J.B., Murray J.

69. Justices of the Peace Act 1968.

repealed (S.): 1975, c.20, sch.2.

s. 1, see *R. v. Swindon Crown Court, ex p. Pawittar Singh* [1984] 1 W.L.R. 449, D.C.; *R. v. Kingston-upon-Thames Crown Court, ex p. Guarino* [1986] Crim.L.R. 325, C.A.; *R. v. Inner London Crown Court, ex p. Benjamin* (1987) 85 Cr.App.R. 267, D.C.

s. 1, repealed in pt.: 1972, c.70, sch.3; 1973, c.15, sch.5; 1979, c.55, sch.3.

CAP.

1968—cont.

69. Justices of the Peace Act 1968—*cont.*
s. 2, repealed: 1973, c.15, sch.5.
ss, 3, 5, repealed: 1979, c.55, sch.3.
s. 4, repealed: 1973, c.15, sch.5; c.62, sch.6.
ss. 7, 8, repealed in pt.: 1973, c.15, sch.5.
sch. 1, repealed: 1973, c.15, sch.5.
sch. 2, repealed: 1979, c.55, sch.3.
sch. 3, amended: 1972, c.70, sch.27; order 74/520; repealed in pt.: 1972, c.11, sch.8; 1973, c.15, sch.5; 1979, c.55, sch.3; 1980, c.43, sch.2.
sch. 4, amended: 1973, c.38, sch.27; repealed: 1973, c.15, sch.
sch. 5, repealed: *ibid.*

70. Law Reform (Miscellaneous Provisions) (Scotland) Act 1968.
ss. 1–6, repealed: 1986, c.9, sch.2.
s. 7, amended: *ibid*, sch.1; repealed in pt.: *ibid.*, sch.2.
s. 9, see *McGowan* v. *Lord Advocate*, 1972 S.L.T. 188; *McLaren* v. *Caldwell's Paper Mill Co.*, 1973 S.L.T. 158; *Thomson* v. *Tough Ropes* (O.H.), 1978 S.L.T.(Notes) 5; *Mason* v. *S. L. D. Olding* (O.H.), 1982 S.L.T. 385; *McArthur* v. *Organon Laboratories* (O.H.), 1982 S.L.T. 425; *Comerford* v. *Strathclyde Regional Council* (Sh.Ct.), 1987 S.C.L.R. 758; *MacIntosh* v. *National Coal Board*, 1988 S.L.T. 348.
s. 9, repealed: 1988, c.32, sch.
s. 10, see *Wanless* v. *Glasgow Corporation*, 1976 S.L.T.(Sh.Ct.) 84; *Hayhoe* v. *Hydro Plant*, 1976 S.L.T.(Sh.Ct.) 78; *Guardian Royal Exchange Group* v. *Moffat*, 1986 S.L.T. 262.
s. 10, amended: 1973, c.62, sch.5.
s. 11, amended: 1976, c.39, sch.1; repealed in pt.: 1986, c.9, sch.2.
ss. 13–16, 17 (in pt.), repealed: 1988, c.32, sch.
sch. 1, repealed: 1986, c.9, sch.2.

71. Race Relations Act 1968.
repealed: 1976, c.74, sch.5.
ss. 1, 2, 12, see *Applin* v. *Race Relations Board* [1974] 2 W.L.R. 541; [1974] 2 All E.R. 73, H.L.
ss. 1, 3, see *Race Relations Board* v. *Mecca* [1976] I.R.L.R. 15.
ss. 1, 5, 19, see *London Borough of Ealing* v. *Race Relations Board* [1972] 2 W.L.R. 71; [1972] 1 All E.R. 105.
s. 2, see *Charter* v. *Race Relations Board* [1973] 2 W.L.R. 299; [1973] 1 All E.R. 512, H.L.; *Dockers' Labour Club and Institute* v. *Race Relations Board* [1974] 3 W.L.R. 533; [1974] 3 All E.R. 592, H.L.
ss. 2, 19, see *Commission for Racial Equality* v. *Ealing London Borough Council* [1978] 1 W.L.R. 112; [1978] 1 All E.R. 497, C.A.
s. 6, see *Commission for Racial Equality* v. *Associated Newspapers Group* [1978] 1 W.L.R. 905, C.A.
s. 15, see *R.* v. *Race Relations Board, ex p. Selvarajan* [1975] 1 W.L.R. 1686; [1976] 1 All E.R. 12, C.A.

72. Town and Country Planning Act 1968.
s. 15, see *Iddenden* v. *Secretary of State* [1972] 1 W.L.R. 1433; [1972] 3 All E.R. 883; *Eldon Garages* v. *Kingston-upon-Hull County Borough Council* [1974] 1 All E.R. 358.

CAP.

1968—cont.

72. Town and Country Planning Act 1968—*cont.*
ss. 15, 16, see *Howard* v. *Secretary of State for the Environment* [1972] 3 W.L.R. 51; 116 S.J. 315; (1972) 23 P. & C.R. 324; 71 L.G.R. 430.
s. 16, see *Trevor's Warehouses* v. *Secretary of State for the Environment* (1972) 23 P. & C.R. 215.
s. 17, see *Bolivian Tin Trust* v. *Secretary of State* [1972] 1 W.L.R. 1481; [1972] 3 All E.R. 918.
s. 30, regs. 72/1313; 76/300.
s. 30, repealed: 1981, c.66, sch.5.
s. 31, repealed: 1981, c.67, sch.6.
s. 32, see *Plymouth Corporation* v. *Secretary of State* [1972] 1 W.L.R. 1347; [1972] 3 All E.R. 225.
s. 39, repealed: 1980, c.51, s.91, sch.26.
s. 59, repealed: 1979, c.46, sch.5; 1981, c.67, sch.6.
s. 104, sch. 3, regs. 72/1313; 76/300.
sch. 9, repealed in pt.: 1980, c.66.sch.25.

73. Transport Act 1968.
see *Tuck* v. *National Freight Corp.*, The Times, July 13, 1977, Donaldson J.
order 72/1094.
ss. 1–6, repealed: 1980, c.34, sch.9.
s. 7, amended: 1978, c.55, s.15; 1980, c.34, sch.7; repealed in pt.: *ibid.*, sch.9.
s. 8, amended: 1980, c.34, sch.7; repealed in pt.: *ibid.*, sch.9.
s. 9, orders 73/153, 457.
s. 9, amended: 1973, c.65, sch.18(S.); 1985, c.67, ss.57, 58 (prosp.), sch. 3; repealed in pt.: 1972, c.70, schs.24,30; 1973, c.65, schs.18,29 (S.); 1985, c.67, s.51, schs.3;8.
ss. 9, 11, 13, 15, see *R.* v. *Merseyside County Council, ex p. Great Universal Stores* (1982) 80 L.G.R. 639. Woolf J.
s. 9A, see *R.* v. *Merseyside Passenger Transport Authority, ex p. Crosville Motor Services*, The Times, April 4, 1987, D.C.
ss. 9A, 9B, added: 1985, c.67, sch.57.
s. 9B, amended (prosp.): *ibid.*, s.58.
s. 10, amended: 1973, c.65, sch.18(S.); 1981, c.67, sch.4; 1985, c.67, schs.3, 7; repealed in pt.: 1973, c.65, schs.18, 29(S.); 1974, c.7, schs.6,8; 1985, c.67, schs.3,8.
s. 11, amended: 1972, c.70, sch.24; 1973, c.65, sch.18 (S.); repealed in pt.: 1973, c.65, schs.18,29 (S.); 1974, c.7, schs.6,8; 1985, c.67, schs.3,8.
s. 12, amended: 1975, c.30, sch.6 (S.); 1985, c.67, sch.3; repealed in pt.: 1973, c.65, schs.25,29 (S.); 1974, c.7, schs.6,8; 1985, c.67, schs.3,8.
s. 13, regs. 72/1596.
s. 13, substituted: 1973, c.65, sch.18 (S.); 1985, c.67, sch.3.
s. 14, amended: 1972, c.70, sch.24; 1973, c.65, sch.18 (S.); 1982, c.32, sch.5; 1985, c.9, sch.2; repealed in pt.: 1973, c.65, schs.18,29 (S.); 1982, c.32, sch.6; 1985, c.67, schs.3,8 (S.).
s. 15, amended: 1972, c.70, sch.24; 1973, c.65, sch.18 (S.); 1983, c.10, s.9; 1985, c.67,

1968—cont.

73. Transport Act 1968—cont.

schs.3,7; repealed in pt.: 1974, c.7, sch.8; 1975, c.30, sch.7 (S.); 1985, c.67, schs.3,8.

s. 15, repealed in pt. (S.): *ibid.*

s. 15A, added: 1972, c.70, sch.24; 1973, c.65, sch.18(S.); repealed in pt.: 1985, c.67, schs.3,8.

s. 16, amended: 1972, c.70, sch.24; 1973, c.65, sch.18 (S.); 1985, c.67, schs.3,7; repealed in pt.: 1973, c.65, schs. 18,29 (S.); 1974, c.7, schs.6, 8; 1985, c.67, schs.3,8.

s. 17, orders 73/154, 780.

ss. 17–19, repealed: 1985, c.67, schs.3,8.

s. 18, repealed in pt. (S.): 1973, c.65, schs.18,29.

s. 19, amended (S.): 1975, c.30, sch.6.

s. 20, orders 74/1247; 75/870, 871.

s. 20, amended: 1974, c.7, sch.1 (S.); 1975, c.30, s.14 (S.); 1985, c.67, sch.3; repealed in pt.: 1985, c.67, schs.3,8,

s. 21, repealed: *ibid.*

s. 21, repealed in pt. (S.): 1973, c.65, schs.18,29.

s. 22, orders 72/1596; 76/457.

s. 22, repealed in pt.: 1985, c.67, schs.3,8.

s. 23, amended: 1972, c.70, sch.24; 1973, c.65, sch.18 (S.); 1985, c.67, sch.3.

s. 24, amended: *ibid.*, s.113, sch.3; repealed in pt.: *ibid.*, s.113, sch.8.

s. 26, amended (S.): 1973, c.65, sch.18.

s. 27, amended: 1975, c.55, s.4; 1982, c.6, s.4.

s. 29, amended: 1980, c.34, sch.7; repealed in pt.: 1985, c.67, sch.8.

s. 30, order 73/153.

s. 30, repealed: 1980, c.34, s.1, sch.9.

s. 32, order 80/1105; amended: 1980, c.34, s.62.

s. 34, amended: 1985, c.67, sch.7; repealed in pt.: 1972, c.70, sch.30; 1974, c.7, schs.1,8; 1985, c.67, schs.3,8.

s. 34, substituted (S.): 1973, c.65, sch.18; amended (S.): 1975, c.30, s.14; 1982, c.43, s.12; repealed in pt. (S.): 1985, c.67, schs.3,8.

s. 35, see *Robinson* v. *Secretary of State for the Environment* [1973] 1 W.L.R. 1139, D.C.

s. 35, amended: (S.) 1973, c.65, sch.18; 1976, c.3, s.2; regs.77/777, repealed in pt.: 1972, c.70, sch.30; 1975, c.71, sch.18; 1980, c.34, sch.9; 1981, c.14, sch.8.

s. 36, repealed. 1985, c.67, sch.8.

s. 36, repealed in pt. (S.): 1973, c.65, schs.25,29.

s. 37, repealed in pt.: *ibid.* (S.); 1974, c.7, schs.6,8.

s. 38, repealed in pt.: S.L.R. 1974.

s. 39, repealed: 1974, c.48, s.3.

ss. 41, repealed in pt.: 1981, c.56, sch.12.

s. 42, order 79/944.

s. 42, amended: 1974, c.48, s.2; 1978, c.55, s.15; 1982, c.6, s.1.

s. 43, repealed in pt.: S.L.R. 1974; 1977, c.20, s.3.

s. 44, repealed: 1980, c.45, sch.9.

s. 45, amended: *ibid.*, sch.7; repealed in pt.: *ibid.*, sch.9.

1968—cont.

73. Transport Act 1968—cont.

s. 49, repealed in pt.: S.L.R. 1974.

s. 50, repealed in pt.: 1981, c.56, sch.12.

s. 52, repealed in pt.: 1980, c.45, sch.9.

s. 53, orders 72/1024; 73/290, 338, 366.

s. 54, amended: 1985, c.67, s.123, sch.3; repealed in pt.: S.L.R. 1974; 1984, c.32, s.42; 1985, c.67, s.123, sch.8.

s. 55, repealed in pt.: S.L.R. 1974; 1980, c.45, sch.9.

s. 56, amended: 1973, c.65, sch.18 (S.); 1974, c.7, sch.1; 1975, c.30, s.14 (S.); 1985, c.51, sch.12; repealed in pt.: 1984, c.32, sch.7; 1985, c.51, sch.12; c.67, sch.7.

s. 58, repealed (S.): 1973, c.65, schs.18,29.

s. 59, amended: 1981, c.56, sch.7; 1985, c.67, s.3; repealed in pt.: 1982, c.49, sch.6; 1985, c.67, sch.8.

Pt. V. (ss.59–94) modified: order 75/1046; regs. 77/1462.

s. 60, see *Alderton* v. *Richard Burgon Associates (Manpower)* [1974] Crim.L.R. 318; [1974] R.T.R. 422, D.C.; *Bowra* v. *Dann Catering Co.* [1982] R.T.R. 120, D.C.; *Annar* v. *Duncan*, 1982, S.C.C.R. 584; *Stirk* v. *McKenna* [1984] R.T.R. 330, D.C.; *Creek* v. *Fossett, Eccles and Supertents* [1986] Crim.L.R. 256; *Smith* v. *Holt Brothers*, 1986 S.L.T.(Sh.Ct.) 49; *Kennet* v. *Holding & Barnes; Harvey (T. L.)* v. *Hall* [1986] R.T.R. 334, D.C.

s. 60, regs. 77/1737; 82/226; 84/176; 87/841, 2170.

s. 60, amended: 1972, c.27, s.1, sch.2.

s. 62, amended: 1974, c.50, s.16, sch.4; 1976, c.3, s.2; regs. 77/777; 1988, c.54, sch.3; repealed in pt.: 1982, c.49, sch.6.

s. 63, regs. 76/292; 77/1737; 84/176.

s. 63, amended: 1973, c.65, sch.18(S.); 1982, c.49, sch.4; repealed in pt.: 1972, c.70, sch.30; 1982, c.49, schs.4,6; 1985, c.51, sch.17.

s. 64, amended: 1974, c.50, sch.4; 1976, c.3, s.2, regs. 77/777; 84/176; 1982, c.49, sch.4; repealed in pt.: *ibid.*, sch.6.

ss. 65, 66, repealed: *ibid.*

s. 67, regs. 77/1737; 84/176.

s. 67, amended: 1974, c.50, sch.4.

s. 68, amended: regs. 77/1462; 84/176; 1982, c.49, sch.4.

s. 69, see *R.* v. *Eastern Traffic Area Licensing Authority, ex p. J. Wyatt jnr. (Haulage)* [1974] R.T.R. 480, D.C.

s. 69, regs. 77/1737; 84/176; 86/1391.

s. 69, amended: 1972, c.12, sch.6; c.20, sch.7; 1974, c.50, sch.4; 1975, c.46, s.3; regs. 77/777, 1462; 1979, c.5, sch.6; 1984, c.27, sch.13; regs. 84/176; 1985, c.9, sch.2; regs. 87/841; 1988, c.54, sch.3; repealed in pt.: 1980, c.42, sch.2; 1982, c.49, sch.6.

ss. 69A–69G, added: *ibid.*, sch.4.

ss. 69C–69E, 69G, regs. 84/176.

s. 70, amended: 1974, c.50, sch.4; 1982, c.49, sch.4.

s. 71, regs. 77/1737; 84/176.

1968—cont.

73. Transport Act 1968—*cont.*
s. 71, repealed in pt.: 1980, c.34, sch.9.
ss. 72–80, repealed: *ibid.*
s. 81, repealed in pt.: *ibid.*
s. 82, amended: 1972, c.20, sch.7; 1980, c.34, s.66; 1988, c.54, sch.3; repealed in pt.: 1980, c.34, sch.9; 1982, c.49, sch.6.
ss. 83–87, repealed in pt.: *ibid.*
s. 84, amended: regs. 77/1462; 84/176; repealed in pt.: 1982, c.49, sch.6.
s. 85, regs. 87/841.
s. 85, repealed in pt.: 1982, c.49, sch.5.
ss. 85, 86, regs. 77/1737; 84/176.
s. 86, see *Green* v. *Harrison* [1979] R.T.R. 483, D.C.
s. 86, amended: 1985, c.65, sch.8.
s. 87, regs. 84/176.
s. 87, amended: regs. 77/1462; 84/176; 1982, c.49, sch.4.; repealed in pt.: *ibid.*, sch.6.
s. 88, repealed: 1985, c.67, sch.8.
s. 89, regs. 72/716; 74/2060; 75/1046; 76/460; 79/1732; 80/637; 84/176, 179; 86/666; 87/841.
s. 89, repealed in pt.: 1980, c.34, sch.9; 1982, c.49, sch.6.
s. 90, repealed: 1985, c.67, sch.8.
s. 91, regs. 72/716, 1535; 73/793; 74/313, 2060; 75/1046, 1713; 76/292, 460, 1257; 77/1737, 2172; 78/1110; 79/1732; 80/637; 81/37, 527; 82/1713; 83/1832; 84/176, 177, 179, 1835; 85/30; 86/666, 1391; 87/841; 88/1811.
s. 91, amended: 1972, c.27, sch.2; 1980, c.34, s.66; 1982, c.49, sch.4; regs. 77/1462; 84/176; repealed in pt.: 1980, c.34, sch.9; 1982, c.49, sch.6.
s. 92, amended: 1972, c.20, sch.7; regs. 77/1462; 84/176; 1982, c.49, sch.4; 1985, c.9, sch.2; 1988, c.54, sch.3; repealed in pt.: 1980, c.34, sch.2; 1982, c.49, sch.6.
s. 94, regs. 81/37.
s. 94, repealed in pt.: S.L.R. 1974; 1980, c.34, sch.2; 1982, c.49, sch.6.
s. 95, see *Carter* v. *Walton* [1985] R.T.R. 378, D.C.
s. 95, regs. 73/379; 78/1157; 79/1746; 86/1458.
s. 95, amended: 1976, c.3, s.2.
s. 96, see *Knowles Transport* v. *Russell* [1974] Crim.L.R. 717; [1975] R.T.R. 87, D.C.; *Lawson* v. *Fox* [1974] 2 W.L.R. 247; [1974] 1 All E.R. 783, H.L.; *Whitby* v. *Stead* [1975] R.T.R. 169, D.C.; *Green* v. *Harrison* [1979] Crim.L.R. 395, D.C.; *Paterson* v. *Richardson* [1982] R.T.R. 49, D.C.; *Carter* v. *Walton, The Times*, May 28, 1984, D.C.; *Licensing Authority for Goods Vehicles in Metropolitan Traffic Area* v. *Coggins, The Times*, February 28, 1985, D.C.; *Carter* v. *Walton* [1985] R.T.R. 378, D.C.; *Brown* v. *W. Burns Tractors*, 1986 S.C.C.R. 146; *Williams* v. *Boyd* [1986] R.T.R. 185; [1986] Crim.L.R. 564, D.C.
s. 96, regs. 72/574; 73/379; 78/1157; 82/1554; 86/1492; 87/28, 98; order 86/1459.
s. 96, amended: 1985, c.67, sch.2.

1968—cont.

73. Transport Act 1968—*cont.*
s. 97, see *Amman* v. *Duncan*, 1982, S.C.C.R. 584; *Oxford* v. *Thomas Scott and Sons Bakery* [1983] R.T.R. 369, D.C.; *Universal Salvage* v. *Boothby* [1984] R.T.R. 289, D.C.; *R.* v. *Scott (Thomas)* & *Sons Bakers* [1984] R.T.R. 337, European Ct. of Justice; *D.P.P.* v. *Hackett (Sidney)* (*Nos. 91/84 and 92/84*) [1985] R.T.R. 209, European Ct.; *Creek* v. *Fossett, Eccles and Supertents* [1986] Crim.L.R. 256; *Brown* v. *W. Burns Tractors*, 1986 S.C.C.R. 146; *Ross-Taylor* v. *Houston*, 1986 S.C.C.R. 210; *Gaunt* v. *Nelson* [1987] R.T.R. 1, D.C.; *Redhead Freight* v. *Shulman, The Times*, May 12, 1988, D.C.
s. 97, amended: 1972, c.27, s.1; 1982, c.48, schs.3,6 (S.); regs. 84/144.
ss. 97, 98, see *Weir* v. *Tudhope*, 1987 S.C.C.R. 307.
s. 97A, amended: 1982, c.48, schs.3,6 (S.).
s. 98, see *Alderton* v. *Richard Burgon Associates (Manpower)* [1974] Crim.L.R. 318; [1974] R.T.R. 422, D.C. *Lawson* v. *Fox* [1974] 2 W.L.R. 247; [1974] 1 All E.R. 783, H.L.; *Cassady* v. *Ward* & *Smith* [1975] R.T.R. 353, D.C.; *Cassady* v. *Reg. Morris* (*Transport*) [1975] R.T.R. 470, D.C.; *Lackenby* v. *Browns of WEM* [1980] R.T.R. 363, D.C.; *Alcock* v. *G. C. Griston* [1980] Crim.L.R. 653, D.C.; *Pearson* v. *Rutherford* [1982] R.T.R. 54, D.C.; *Bowra* v. *Dann Catering Co.* [1982] R.T.R. 120, D.C.; *Oxford* v. *Spencer* [1983] R.T.R. 63, C.A.
s. 98, regs. 72/1019; 73/380; 76/1447; 77/777; 86/1493; 87/1421.
s. 98, amended: 1972, c.27, sch.2; c.68, sch.4; 1976, c.3, s.2; 1985, c.67, sch.2.
s. 99, see *Keane* v. *Jackson*, 1981 S.L.T.(Sh.Ct.) 32; *Pearson* v. *Rutherford* [1982] R.T.R. 54, D.C.; *R.* v. *Parkinson* (1984) 6 Cr.App.R.(S.) 423, C.A.
s. 99, amended: 1972, c.20, sch.7; c.27, sch.1; c.68, sch.4; 1976, c.3, s.2; 1985, c.67, sch.2; 1988, c.54, sch.3; repealed in pt.: 1976, c.3, s.2.
s. 100, amended: 1972, c.27, s.1.
s. 101, regs. 72/1019; 73/380; 76/1447; 77/777; 78/1364, 1938; 79/1746; 81/1373; 86/1493; 87/1421; order 86/1459.
s. 101, amended: 1976, c.3, s.2.
s. 102, amended: 1982, c.49, s.64; 1988, c.54, sch.3.
s. 102A, added: 1972, c.20, sch.7; 1988, c.54, sch.3.
s. 103, see *Lawson* v. *Fox* [1974] 2 W.L.R. 247; [1974] 1 All E.R. 783, H.L.; *Whitby* v. *Stead* [1975] R.T.R. 169, D.C.; *Green* v. *Harrison* [1979] R.T.R. 483, D.C.; *Alcock* v. *G. C. Griston* [1980] Crim.L.R. 653, D.C.; *Paterson* v. *Richardson* [1982] R.T.R. 49, D.C.; *Oxford* v. *Spencer* [1983] R.T.R. 63, C.A.; *Carter* v. *Walton* [1985] R.T.R. 378, D.C.
s. 103, regs. 81/1373.
s. 103, amended: 1972, c.68, sch.; 1976, c.3, ss.2,3; 1985, c.67, sch.3; repealed in pt.: *ibid.*, sch.8.

CAP.
1968—cont.

73. Transport Act 1968—*cont.*

s. 104, repealed in pt.: 1981, c.66, sch.5.

s. 107, see *R.* v. *Hitchin JJ., ex p. Hilton* [1974] Crim.L.R. 319; [1974] R.T.R. 380, D.C.

s. 107, repealed in pt.: S.L.R. 1974.

s. 108, amended: 1972, c.52, sch.21.

s. 109, amended: 1986, c.44, sch.7.

s. 112, orders 73/96, 1488.

s. 112, amended: 1972, c.52, sch.21; repealed in pt.: S.L.R. 1974.

s. 113, orders 73/1465; 86/870.

s. 115, amended: (S.) 1973, c.65, sch.18; repealed in pt.: 1972, c.70, sch.30; 1973, c.37, sch.9; 1985, c.51, sch.17.

s. 116, amended: 1984, c.32, sch.4; repealed in pt.: 1972, c.70, sch.30.

ss. 116–118, amended (S.): 1984, c.54, sch.9.

s. 117, order 72/1705.

s. 117, amended: 1984, c.27, sch.13; c.32, sch.4.

s. 118, amended: *ibid.*

s. 119, amended: 1980, c.66, sch.24; 1984, c.32, sch.4; c.54, sch.9(S.); repealed in pt.(S.): *ibid.*, sch.11.

s. 120, repealed: 1980, c.65, sch.34.

s. 121, orders 80/1660; 81/512, 1083; 84/557, 558, 1202; 85/1578; 86/277, 343; 87/1443; 88/725(S.).

s. 121, amended: 1980, c.34, sch.2; c.66, sch.24; 1984, c.32, sch.4; c.54, sch.9(S.); repealed in pt.(S.): *ibid.*, sch.11.

s. 122, amended (S.): 1984, c.54, sch.9; repealed in pt. (S): *ibid.*, schs.9, 11.

s. 123, amended (S): 1984, c.54, sch.9; repealed in pt.: 1972, c.70, sch.30; 1973, c.65, schs.14, 29(S.); 1985, c.51, sch.17.

s. 124, amended (S.): 1973, c.65, sch.14; 1984, c.54, sch.9; repealed in pt.: 1972, c.70, sch.30; 1985, c.51, sch.17.

s. 125, amended: 1984, c.32, sch.4; repealed in pt.: 1980, c.34, sch.2.

ss. 126–132, repealed: 1984, c.27, sch.14.

ss. 127, 130, see *Lowe* v. *Lester* [1987] R.T.R. 30, D.C.

s. 130, see *Hawkins* v. *Phillips* [1980] R.T.R. 197, D.C.

s. 130, repealed in pt.: 1972, c.20, sch.9; 1980, c.66, sch.25; 1981, c.14, sch.8.

s. 131, repealed in pt.: 1977, c.45, sch.13; 1982, c.49, sch.6.

s. 133, repealed: S.L.R. 1974.

s. 134, amended: 1985, c.67, sch.3; repealed in pt.: 1980, c.34, sch.9.

s. 135, see *Tuck* v. *National Freight Corp.* [1978] 1 W.L.R. 37, H.L.

s. 135, amended: 1978, c.44, sch.16; repealed in pt.: 1978, c.51, sch.16.

s. 137, amended: order 76/1775; 1985, c.67, sch.3.

s. 138, amended (S.): 1973, c.65, sch.18; repealed: 1985, c.67, sch.8.

s. 139, repealed in pt.: 1980, c.66, sch.25; repealed (S.): 1984, c.54, sch.11.

s. 140, repealed: 1980, c.66, sch.25.

CAP.
1968—cont.

73. Transport Act 1968—*cont.*

s. 141, amended: 1972, c.52, sch.21(S.); 1984, c.32, sch.4; 1985, c.67, sch.3.

s. 144, functions transferred: order 76/1775; amended: 1984, c.32, sch.4..

s. 145, repealed in pt.: 1972, c.20, sch.9; 1981, c.14, sch.8.

ss. 146, 148, repealed: 1972, c.20, sch.9.

s. 149, see *Kellett* v. *Daisy, The Times,* June 28, 1977, D.C.; order 77/548.

s. 149, orders 74/797, 1202; 78/749, 802; 83/217.

s. 149, repealed: 1984, c.27, sch.14.

s. 150, repealed: 1980, c.34, sch.9.

s. 151, repealed (S.): 1973, c.65, sch.29.

s. 152, repealed (S.): 1972, c.29, s.1.

s. 154, repealed: 1981, c.19, sch.1.

s. 155, repealed: 1975, c.24, sch.3; c.25, sch.3.

s. 156, repealed in pt.: 1980, c.34, sch.9.

s. 157, regs. 72/1596; 79/1746; orders 73/153, 154; 74/797, 1202; 76/457; 77/548; 78/749, 802; 83/217; 86/1459.

s. 159, amended: 1972, c.20, sch.7; 1973, c.65, sch.14(S.); 1980, c.34, sch.5; c.66, sch.24; 1981, c.14, sch.7; 1984, c.54, sch.9; 1985, c.67, sch.1; 1988, c.54, sch.3; repealed in pt.: 1980, c.34, sch.9; 1984, c.54, sch.11(S.); 1985, c.67, sch.8.

s. 160, amended: 1973, c.51, schs.19,22; 1985, c.67, sch.3; repealed in pt.: 1980.c.34, sch.9; 1988, c.39, sch.14.

s. 162, amended: order 78/1174(S.); 1984, c.32, s.42; repealed in pt.: 1980, c.34, sch.9; 1984, c.33, sch.1.

s. 164, repealed in pt.: 1973, c.36, sch.6.

sch. 1, repealed in pt.: 1980, c.34, sch.9.

sch. 2, orders 72/1020, 1023; 76/329.

sch. 2, amended: 1978, c.55, s.15; repealed in pt.: *ibid.*, sch.4; 1980, c.34, sch.9.

sch. 3, repealed: *ibid.*; 1981, c.66, sch.5.

sch. 3A, repealed: 1981, c.66, sch.5.

sch. 4, repealed in pt.: 1980, c.34, sch.9.

sch. 5, order 76/457.

sch. 5, amended: 1973, c.65, sch.18; 1985, c.67, sch.3; repealed in pt.: 1972, c.11, sch.8; c.70, schs.24,30; 1973, c.65, schs. 18,19 (S.); 1974, c.7, schs.6,8; 1985, c.67, schs.3,8.

sch. 6, repealed: *ibid.*, sch.8.

sch. 8, repealed in pt.: 1977, c.45, sch.13; 1985, c.23, sch.2.

sch. 9, repealed: 1982, c.49, sch.6.

sch. 10, repealed in pt.: 1972, c.20, sch.9; 1980, c.34, sch.9; c.42, sch.2; 1981, c.14, sch.8; 1985, c.67, sch.8.

sch. 11, amended: 1972, c.20, sch.9; repealed in pt.: 1979, c.12, sch.7; 1980, c.42, sch.2.

sch. 13, order 76/1084.

sch. 14, see *Hawkins* v. *Phillips* [1980] R.T.R. 197, D.C.; *Lowe* v. *Lester* [1987] R.T.R. 30, D.C.

sch. 14, repealed: 1984, c.27, sch.14.

sch. 16, amended: 1980, c.34, sch.7; 1981, c.22, sch.5; 1984, c.30, sch.10; c.32, sch.4; repealed in pt.: 1980, c.34, sch.9; c.66, sch.25; 1981, c.56, sch.12; 1984, c.29, sch.12.

CAP.

1968—cont.

73. Transport Act 1968—*cont.*
sch. 17, repealed in pt.: 1975, c.24, sch.3; c.25, sch.3.
sch. 18, repealed: S.L.R. 1974.

74. Customs (Import Deposits) Act 1968.
repealed: S.L.R. 1975.

75. Miscellaneous Financial Provisions Act 1968.
s. 1, repealed: 1974, c.18, sch.

77. Sea Fisheries Act 1968.
s. 5, amended: 1981, c.29, s.24.
s. 7, orders 73/1998; 75/171; 76/1103.
s. 7, repealed in pt.: 1981, c.29, s.26, sch.5.
ss. 7, 18, orders 72/758, 868; 73/127, 789, 1701; 74/701, 1807.
s. 8, amended: 1981, c.29, s.26.
s. 10, amended: *ibid.*, ss.24,26.
s. 12, amended: 1980, c.43, sch.7; 1987, c.18, sch.6 (S.).
s. 13, amended: 1982, c.48, sch.7.
s. 16, repealed: 1981, c.29, sch.5.
s. 19, amended: 1988, c.12, sch.6.
s. 20, repealed: 1973, c.36, sch.6.
s. 21, orders 73/236, 1319, 1320.
sch. 1, repealed in pt.: 1984, c.26, sch.2; 1988, c.12, sch.7.

1969

1. Electricity (Scotland) Act 1969.
repealed: 1979, c.11, sch.12.

2. Local Government Grants (Social Need) Act 1969.
s. 1, amended: 1985, c.51, sch.14; repealed in pt. (prosp.): 1988, c.40, sch.13.

3. Administration of Justice Act 1969.
ss. 12, 13, see *York Trade Mark* [1981] F.S.R. 33, Graham J.

4. National Insurance, etc., Act 1969.
repealed: 1973, c.38, sch.28.

8. Redundancy Rebates Act 1969.
repealed: 1978, c.44, sch.17.

10. Mines and Quarries (Tips) Act 1969.
s. 1, repealed in pt.: regs. 74/2013.
s. 2, amended: orders 74/2013; 75/1102.
s. 3, amended: order 74/2013.
ss. 7, 10, amended: *ibid.*
ss. 8, 9, repealed: *ibid.*
s. 11, amended: 1973, c.65, sch.27 (S.); 1985, c.51, s.11; repealed in pt.: 1972, c.70, sch.30.
ss. 19, 36, see *Lanark County Council* v. *Frank Doonin*, 1974 S.L.T.(Sh.Ct.) 13.
s. 23, amended: 1972, c.70, s.171; 1973, c.65, s.121(S.); 1980, c.65, sch.6; repealed in pt.: 1974, c.7.sch.8.
s. 25, amended: 1972, c.70, sch.29.
s. 28, amended: 1984, c.28, sch.2.
s. 33, repealed in pt.: 1976, c.57, sch.2.
sch. 1, repealed in pt.: regs. 80/804.
sch. 3, amended: 1980, c.58, sch.3.

12. Genocide Act 1969.
s. 1, repealed in pt.: 1978, c.23, sch.7.
s. 2, amended: 1988, c.33, sch.15; repealed in pt.: 1978, c.26, sch.2; 1988, c.33, sch.16.
s. 3, order 74/1113.

13. Licensing (Scotland) Act 1969.
repealed: 1973, c.65, sch.29.

CAP.

1969—cont.

14. Horserace Betting Levy Act 1969.
s. 1, orders 78/496; 81/753; amended: orders 78/496; 81/753.
ss. 2, 3, amended: 1981, c.30, sch.

15. Representation of the People Act 1969.
repealed: 1983, c.2, sch.9.
s. 9, see *Marshall* v. *British Broadcasting Corp.* [1979] 1 W.L.R. 1071, C.A.; *McAlishey* v. *British Broadcasting Corp.* [1980] N.I. 44, Murray J.

16. Customs Duties (Dumping and Subsidies) Act 1969.
orders 72/1361; 73/419, 2037.
repealed: 1972, c.68, sch.3.
s. 1, orders 72/569, 1371; 74/277, 724, 1103, 1541; 75/54, 113, 140, 368, 373, 701, 987, 1025, 1714, 1741; 76/112, 638, 697, 736, 737, 763, 986, 1100, 1179, 1193, 1471, 1712, 1940, 1969, 2098, 2115, 2177; 77/112, 184, 569, 666, 695, 716, 861, 954, 1072, 1073, 1134, 1767; 79/104, 842, 1182; 80/35, 279; 81/699.
ss. 1–4, amended: 1978, c.42, sch.1.
s. 2, orders 72/569; 74/1541; 75/140, 368, 373, 987; 76/763, 986, 1100; 77/695, 1072, 1073; 1134.
s. 5, amended: 1978, c.42, sch.1, repealed in pt.: 1978, c.42, schs.1,13.
s. 6, amended: *ibid.*, sch.1.
s. 7, orders 75/987; 76/638, 1179; 77/1072, 1973.
s. 8, orders 72/1907; 74/1541, 2069; 75/140, 368, 373; 76/638, 1179, 1471, 1712, 1969, 2098, 2115, 2177; 77/60, 112, 184, 506, 569, 666, 716, 793, 861, 954, 1080, 1134.
s. 9, orders 74/1541; 75/140, 368, 373; 76/763, 1471, 1712.
s. 9, amended: 1979, c.2, sch.4.
s. 10, orders 74/277, 724, 1103; 75/54, 113, 701, 1025, 1714, 1741; 76/112, 697, 986, 1940; 77/695, 1072, 1967; 79/104.
s. 10, repealed in pt.: 1978, c.42, schs.1,13; amended: 1979, c.2, sch.4.
ss. 11, 12, repealed: *ibid.*, sch.13.
ss. 13, 14, repealed in pt.: *ibid.*, schs.1,13.
s. 15, orders 74/277, 724, 1103; 75/54, 113, 368, 373, 701, 987, 1025, 1714, 1741; 76/112, 697, 737, 986, 1193, 1471, 1712, 1940, 1969, 2098, 2115, 2177; 77/112, 184, 569, 666, 695, 861, 954, 1072, 1073, 1767; 78/1497.
s. 15, amended: 1978, c.42, sch.12.
s. 16, repealed: 1981, c.35, s.11, sch.19.
s. 17, amended: 1979, c.2, sch.4.

18. Nuclear Installations Act 1969.
s. 2, repealed: 1983, c.25, sch.4.

19. Decimal Currency Act 1969.
s. 6, amended: order 79/1574.
s. 7, repealed in pt.: 1974, c.46, sch.11; order 79/1573.
s. 18, repealed in pt.: 1973, c.36, sch.6.
sch. 2, repealed in pt.: 1972, c.70, sch.30; 1973, c.37, sch.9; c.65, sch.29; 1974, c.39, sch.5; 1977, c.45, sch.13; 1980, c.65, sch.34; 1988, c.41, sch.13 (prosp.).

CAP.

1969—cont.

20. Foreign Compensation Act 1969.
s. 1, repealed in pt.: S.L.R. 1976.

22. Redundant Churches and other Religious Buildings Act 1969.
s. 1, orders 74/1206; 79/478; 84/203.
s. 4, repealed in pt.: 1973, c.16, sch.2.
ss. 4, 5, amended: 1983, c.47, sch.4.
s. 6, repealed: 1980, c.17, sch.2.

23. Army Reserve Act 1969.
repealed: S.L.R. 1976.

26. Agriculture (Spring Traps) (Scotland) Act 1969.
repealed (S.): S.L.R. 1975.

27. Vehicle and Driving Licences Act 1969.
s. 2, regs. 77/1316.
s. 2, repealed in pt.: regs. 74/520, 812.
ss. 13, 15, see *Guest* v. *Kingsnorth* [1972] Crim.L.R. 243; [1972] R.T.R. 265.
ss. 13–15, repealed: 1972, c.20, sch.9.
s. 16, see *Lowe* v. *Lester* [1987] R.T.R. 30, D.C.
s. 16, repealed in pt.: 1972, c.20, sch.9; 1984, c.27, sch.14.
ss. 18, 20 (in pt.), 22, 23, 25 (in pt.)–27 (in pt.), repealed: 1972, s.20, sch.9.
s. 29, repealed in pt.: S.L.R. 1975; 1978, c.3, sch.2.
ss. 31, 32, repealed: 1972, c.20, sch.9.
s. 33, amended: 1973, c.65, sch.24; repealed in pt.: 1972, c.70, sch.30.
s. 35, schs.1 (in pt.), 2 (in pt.), repealed: 1972, c.20, sch.9.

28. Ponies Act 1969.
repealed: 1981, c.22, sch.6.

29. Tanzania Act 1969.
s. 1, repealed: 1981, c.61, sch.9.
s. 2, repealed: 1986, c.55, sch.2.
s. 3, repealed in pt.: S.L.R. 1977.
s. 4, amended: 1981, c.61, sch.7; repealed in pt.: 1986, c.55, sch.2.
s. 7, repealed in pt.: 1981, c.61, sch.9; 1986, c.55, sch.2.

30. Town and Country Planning (Scotland) Act 1969.
ss. 1–27, 29–31, 33–8, 40–57, repealed: 1972, c.52, sch.23.
s. 28, repealed: S.L.R. 1975.
s. 39, repealed: 1972, c.46, sch.11.
s. 59, repealed: 1979, c.64, sch.5.
ss. 60–97, repealed: 1972, c.52, sch.23.
ss. 66, 67, see *Alexander Russell* v. *Secretary of State for Scotland*, 1984 S.L.T. 81.
ss. 99–101, repealed: 1972, c.52, sch.23.
s. 102, repealed in pt.: *ibid.*
s. 103, repealed in pt.: S.L.R. 1975.
s. 104, order 72/667.
ss. 105, 107, repealed: 1972, c.52, sch.23.
s. 108, repealed in pt.: *ibid.* S.L.R. 1975; 1975, c.24, sch.3.
sch. 1–9, repealed: 1972, c.52, sch.23.
sch. 10, see *Church of Scotland General Trs.* v. *Helensburgh Town Council*, 1973 S.L.T. 21, Lands Tr.
sch. 10, repealed: S.L.R. 1975.
sch. 11, repealed: 1972, c.52, sch.23.

CAP.

1969—cont.

31. Appropriation Act 1969.
repealed: 1974, c.31, s.4, sch.

32. Finance Act 1969.
see *Astley* v. *I.R.C.* [1974] S.T.C. 367.
s. 1, amended: 1975, c.45, s.16; repealed in pt.: 1972, c.41, sch.8; 1973, c.51, sch.22; 1979, c.4, sch.4; 1983, c.28, sch.10.
s. 3, repealed in pt.: 1972, c.25, sch.7; S.L.R. 1974.
s. 5, repealed: S.L.R. 1974.
s. 6, see *Seeney* v. *Dean* [1972] R.T.R. 25.
s. 16, repealed: S.L.R. 1975.
s. 33, see *Vestey* v. *I.R.C.* [1979] 3 W.L.R. 915, H.L.
Pt. III (ss.35–40), repealed: 1975, c.7, sch.13.
s. 36, see *Royal Bank of Scotland* v. *Inland Revenue*, Second Division, 1977 S.L.T. 45; *Re Buttle's Will Trusts* [1977] 1 W.L.R. 1200, C.A.; *Thomson's Trs.* v. *Inland Revenue* (H.L.) 1979 S.L.T. 166.
ss. 36, 37, see *Stevenson's Exrs.* v. *Lord Advocate* (H.L.), 1981 S.L.T. 336.
s. 37, see *Royal Bank of Scotland* v. *Inland Revenue*, Second Division, 1977 S.L.T. 45.
s. 40, see *Oppenheim's Trustees* v. *I.R.C.* [1975] T.R. 217.
s. 41, orders 72/244, 1015; 73/241, 716, 1769; 74/693, 1071, 1907; 75/354, 1129, 1757; 76/698, 1859; 77/347, 919, 1136, 1614; 78/141, 1312, 1838.
ss. 41, 42, repealed: 1979, c.14, sch.8.
s. 51, repealed: 1972, c.41, sch.28.
s. 52, amended: 1972, c.65, sch; repealed in pt.: 1985, c.58, sch.4; 1988, c.1, sch.31.
s. 54, repealed: 1979, c.3, sch.3.
s. 55, repealed: 1972, c.41, sch.28.
s. 56, repealed: 1973, c.51, sch.22.
s. 58, amended: 1973, c.50, s.4; 1987, c.51, s.69; 1988, c.1, sch.29.
s. 61, amended: 1979, c.2, sch.4; repealed in pt.: 1972, c.41, sch.28; 1975, c.7, sch.13; 1979, c.14, sch.8.
sch. 1, repealed: 1972, c.41, sch.28.
schs. 2–5, repealed: 1973, c.51, sch.22.
sch. 6, repealed: 1972, c.41, sch.28.
sch. 7, amended: 1988, c.22, s.3; repealed in pt.: 1983, c.28, s.9; repealed: *ibid.*, sch.10.
sch. 9, repealed in pt.: 1972, c.25, sch.7.
sch. 11, repealed: *ibid.*
sch. 12, see *Seeney* v. *Dean* [1972] R.T.R. 25.
sch. 17, repealed: 1975, c.7, schs.11,13.
schs. 18, 19, repealed: 1979, c.14, sch.8.
sch. 19, see *Cochrane* v. *I.R.C.* [1974] S.T.C. 335; *Stephenson* v. *Barclays Bank Trust Co.* [1975] 1 All E.R. 625; *Crowe* v. *Appleby* [1975] 1 W.L.R. 1539; [1975] 3 All E.R. 529; *Stoke-on-Trent City Council* v. *Wood Mitchell & Co.* [1979] 2 All E.R. 65, C.A.; *Worthing Rugby Football Club Trustees* v. *I.R.C.* [1985] 1 W.L.R. 409, Peter Gibson J.
sch. 20, see *United Friendly Insurance Co.* v. *Eady* [1973] T.R. 37.
sch. 20, repealed in pt.: 1972, c.60, sch.8.

CAP.

1969—cont.

33. Housing Act 1969.
ss. 1–21, repealed: 1974, c.44, schs.14, 15.
s. 4, amended: 1977, c.42, s.116.
s. 6, see *Ealing London Borough Council* v. *El Isaacs* [1980] 1 W.L.R. 932; [1980] 2 All E.R. 548, C.A.
ss. 6, 7, regs. 72/37.
s. 21, order 73/1102.
s. 22, order 72/953.
ss. 22–27, repealed: 1974, c.44, schs.14, 15.
Pt. II (ss. 28–42), repealed: 1985, c.71, sch.1.
s. 37, orders 72/440; 80/857.
ss. 39 (in pt.), 40, repealed: 1985, c.51, sch.17.
Pt. III (ss.43–57), repealed: 1972, c.47, sch.11.
s. 58, see *Simmons* v. *Pizzey* [1977] 2 All E.R. 432, H.L.
Pt. IV (ss. 58–64), repealed: 1985, c.71, sch.1.
s. 59, order 72/457.
s. 59, amended: 1985, c.71, sch.2.
Pt. V (ss. 65–69), repealed: 1985, c.71, sch.1.
s. 68, see *Hunter* v. *Manchester City Council* [1975] 3 W.L.R. 245; [1975] 2 All E.R. 966, C.A.; *Laundon* v. *Hartlepool Borough Council* (1977) 244 E.G. 885; [1978] 2 W.L.R. 732, C.A.; *Khan* v. *Birmingham City Council* (1980) 40 P. & C.R. 412, C.A.; *Patel* v. *Leicester City Council* (86/1979) (1982) 43 P. & C.R. 278, Lands Tribunal; *Manzur Hussain* v. *Tameside Metropolitan Borough Council* (1982) 43 P. & C.R. 441, Lands Tribunal; *Mit Singh* v. *Derby City Council* (1982) 44 P. & C.R. 258, C.A.; *Westerman* v. *St. Helen's Metropolitan Borough Council* (1983) 46 P. & C.R. 236, Lands Tribunal, V. G. Wellings, Q.C.
ss. 70–72, repealed: 1985, c.71, sch.1.
s. 73, repealed: 1976, c.57, sch.2.
s. 74, repealed: 1974, c.7, sch.8.
s. 75, repealed: 1985, c.71, sch.1.
ss. 76, 77, repealed: 1974, c.44., sch.15.
ss. 78, 79, repealed: 1982, c.39, sch.22.
s. 80, see *Investment & Freehold English Estates* v. *Casement* (1987) 283 E.G. 748, H.H. Judge Paul Baker, Q.C.
ss. 80, 81, 83, repealed: 1977, c.42, sch.25.
s. 82, see *Official Custodian for Charities* v. *Goldridge* (1973) 26 P. & C.R. 191, C.A.
ss. 84–90, 91 (in pt.), repealed: 1985, c.71, sch.1.
s. 85, order 73/1102.
s. 86, order 72/440.
schs. 2, 3, repealed: 1972, c.47, sch.11.
schs. 4–9, repealed: 1985, c.71, sch.1.
sch. 5, see *Hunter* v. *Manchester City Council* [1975] 3 W.L.R. 245; [1975] 2 All E.R. 966, C.A.; *Laundon* v. *Hartlepool Borough Council* (1977) 244 E.G. 885; [1978] 2 W.L.R. 732, C.A.; *Khan* v. *Birmingham City Council* (1980) 40 P. & C.R. 412, C.A.; *Mohammed Niaz* v. *Metropolitan Borough of Rochdale* (1980) 41 P. & C.R. 113, Lands Tribunal; *Patel* v. *Leicester City Council* (86/1979) (1982) 43 P. & C.R. 278, Lands Tribunal; *Manzur Hussain* v. *Tameside Metropolitan Borough Council* (1982) 43 P. & C.R. 441, Lands Tribunal; *Mit Singh* v. *Derby City Council* (1982) 44 P. & C.R. 258,

CAP.

1969—cont.

33. Housing Act 1969—*cont.*
C.A.; *Westerman* v. *St. Helen's Metropolitan Borough Council* (1983) 46 P. & C.R. 236, Lands Tribunal, V. G. Wellings, Q.C.
34. Housing (Scotland) Act 1969.
repealed: 1987, c.26, sch.24.
ss. 4, 10, see *Gray* v. *Glasgow District Council*, 1980 S.L.T. (Lands Tr.) 7.
ss 4, 10, 18, see *Hugh MacDonald's Reps.* v. *Sutherland District Council*, 1977 S.L.T.(Lands Tr.) 7.
ss. 7, 10, see *McNicol* v. *Glasgow Corporation*, 1975 S.L.T.(Lands Tr.) 26.
s. 18, see *Jackson* v. *Glasgow District Council*, 1981 S.L.T.(Lands Tr.) 6; *Vaughan* v. *City of Edinburgh District Council* (O.H.), 1988 S.L.T. 191.
s. 21, order 83/1804.
s. 24, regs. 78/965.
s. 25, regs. 78/965.
s. 59, orders 79/253; 80/1496; 83/271.
35. Transport (London) Act 1969.
s. 1, see *R.* v. *Merseyside County Council, ex p. Great Universal Stores, The Times,* February 18, 1982, Woolf J.
ss. 1–3, see *R.* v. *London Transport Executive, ex p. G.L.C.* [1983] 2 W.L.R. 702, D.C.
Pts. I, II (ss.1–15), repealed: 1984, c.32, s.1, sch.7.
ss. 5, 7, see *R.* v. *Greater London Council, ex p. Bromley London Borough Council, The Times,* December 18, 1981, H.L.; *R.* v. *London Transport Executive, ex p. G.L.C.* [1983] 2 W.L.R. 702, D.C.
s. 8, order 75/1131.
Pts. III, IV (ss.16–28), repealed: 1984, c.32, sch.7.
s. 18, orders 73/1390; 74/526; 75/361.
ss. 29, 31, repealed: 1980, c.66, sch.25.
s. 30, repealed: 1985, c.51, sch.17.
ss. 32–36, repealed: 1984, c.27, sch.14.
ss. 37–41, repealed: 1984, c.32, sch.7.
s. 42, amended: 1984, c.27, sch.13.
s. 43, regs. 80/1355.
ss. 44, 45 (in pt.), repealed: 1984, c.32, sch.7.
s. 47, orders 72/1097; 74/407.
s. 47, repealed in pt.: 1975, c.24, sch.3; c.25, sch.3, 1984, c.32, sch.7.
s. 59, amended: 1980, c.52, s.32.
s. 62, amended: *ibid.*, s.17.
schs. 1–4; repealed: 1984, c.32, sch.7.
sch. 4, regs. 72/1269.
sch. 5, regs. 77/1317.
sch. 5, repealed: 1984, c.27, sch.14.
36. Overseas Resources Development Act 1969.
repealed: 1978, c.2, sch.2.
ss. 12, 13, order 76/611.
37. Employers' Liability (Defective Equipment) Act 1969.
see *Clarkson* v. *Jackson (William) & Sons, The Times,* November 21, 1984, C.A.
s. 1, see *Yuille* v. *Daks Simpson* (O.H.), 1984 S.L.T. 115; *Coltman* v. *Bibby Tankers, Derbyshire, The* [1987] 3 All E.R. 1068, H.L.; *Ralston* v. *Greater Glasgow Health Board* (O.H.), 1987 S.L.T. 386.

CAP.

1969—cont.

37. Employer's Liability (Defective Equipment) Act 1969—cont.

s. 2, amended: 1973, c.36, sch.6.

39. Age of Majority (Scotland) Act 1969.

sch. 1, amended: 1973, c.52, sch.5; 1974, c.46, sch.11; repealed in pt.: 1979, c.2, sch.6; 1984, c.36, sch.5.

sch. 2, repealed in pt.: 1983, c.2, sch.9.

40. Medical Act 1969.

repealed: 1983, c.54, sch.7.

s. 4, orders 77/1266; 79/844.

s. 5, orders 72/429; 78/1772; 80/1779; order in council, 76/403; regs. 77/1950.

s. 18, orders 75/1044; 76/898; 80/872.

41. National Mod. (Scotland) Act 1969.

repealed: 1973, c.65, sch.29.

42. Architects Registration (Amendment) Act 1969.

s. 4, amended: 1973, c.36, sch.6.

43. Air Corporations Act 1969.

s. 1, sch. 1, repealed in pt.: S.L.R. 1976.

44. National Insurance Act 1969.

repealed: S.L.R. 1978.

s. 8, regs. 73/1013.

sch. 6, regs. 72/1302; 74/1041, 1128; 75/125, 458.

45. Iron and Steel Act 1969.

repealed: 1975, c.64, sch.7.

s. 6, order 73/2044.

s. 8, see *Re British Concrete Pipe Association* (1983) 1 All E.R. 203, C.A.

46. Family Law Reform Act 1969.

s. 2, repealed in pt.: 1988, c.44, sch.

s. 5, repealed in pt.: 1975, c.63, sch.; 1978, c.22, sch.3.

s. 6, amended: 1978, c.23, sch.5.; 1982, c.53, s.50; 1987, c.42, sch. 2; repealed in pt.: *ibid.*, sch. 2.

s. 7, see *Re Y (A Minor) (Child in Care: Access)* [1975] 3 W.L.R. 342, C.A.; *Re B. (A Minor), The Times,* June 4, 1980, C.A.; *Re C.B. (Minor)* [1981] 1 All E.R. 16, C.A.; *Re Clare* v. *Tower Hamlets London Borough* (1980) 10 Fam.Law 243, C.A.; *Lewisham London Borough Council* v. *M.* [1981] 1 W.L.R. 1248, Hollings J.; *Re C. (A Minor) Wardship: Care Order)* [1982] 1 W.L.R. 1462, Balcombe J.; *M.* v. *Lambeth London Borough Council and Liverpool City Council* (1984) 14 Fam.Law 211, Balcombe J.; *G.-U. (A Minor) (Wardship), Re* (1984) 14 Fam.Law 248, Balcombe J.; *L (A Minor), Re, The Times,* July 25, 1984, Hollings J.; *L. (A Minor) Re, The Times,* November 2, 1984, Hollings J.; *M.* v. *Lambeth London Borough Council (No. 2), The Times,* December 20, 1984, Sheldon J.; *W. (A Minor), Re* (1985) 129 S.J. 523, Sheldon J.; *S. W. (A Minor) (Wardship: Jurisdiction), Re,* (1985) Fam.Law 322, Sheldon J.; *M. (A Minor), Re, The Times,* January 24, 1986, C.A.; *D. (A Minor), Re,* [1987] 1 W.L.R. 1400, C.A.

s. 7, amended: 1973, c.18, sch.2; 1980, c.5, sch.5; 1983, c.41, sch.2.

s. 13, repealed: 1973, c.36, sch.6.

CAP.

1969—cont.

46. Family Law Reform Act 1969—cont.

s. 14, see *Re Trott (decd.); Whitton* v. *Trott,* May 14, 1980, Judge Mervyn Davies.

ss. 14, 15, repealed: 1987, c.42, sch.4.

s. 16, repealed: 1982, c.53, sch.9.

s. 17, repealed: 1987, c.42, s.20, sch.4.

s. 19, repealed in pt. (S.): 1980, c.56, s.5.

s. 20, see *R.* v. *R. (Blood Test: Jurisdiction)* [1973] 1 W.L.R. 1115, Baker P.; *Re J. S. (A Minor)* [1980] 1 All E.R. 1061, C.A.

s. 20, amended: 1987, c.42, s.23, sch.2.

s. 21, see *Hodgkiss* v. *Hodgkiss and Walker* (1985) 15 Fam. Law 87, C.A.

s. 21, amended: 1983, c.20, sch.4; 1987, c.42, sch.2.

s. 22, regs. 75/896; 78/1266; 79/1226; 80/887; 82/1244; 83/1346; 85/1416; 86/1357; 87/1199; 88/1198.

ss. 22–24, amended: 1987, c.42, sch.2.

s. 25, amended: *ibid.,* s.23.

s. 26, see *Serio* v. *Serio* (1983) 13 Fam.Law 255, C.A.

s. 27, repealed: 1987, c.42, sch.4.

s. 28, repealed in pt.: 1973, c.36, sch.6; 1981, c.61, sch.9; 1988, c.44, sch.

sch. 1, amended: 1973, c.29, sch.3; 1974, c.46, sch.11; repealed in pt.: 1979, c.2, sch.6; 1981, c.54, sch.7; c.61, sch.9; 1983, c.20, sch.6; 1986, c.53, sch.19.

sch. 2, repealed in pt.: 1983, c.2, sch.9.

47. Nurses Act 1969.

repealed: 1979, c.36, sch.8.

48. Post Office Act 1969.

see *R.* v. *Hunstanton JJ., ex p. Clayton (T.E.); R.* v. *Hunstanton JJ., ex p. Clayton (E.A.), The Times,* July 6, 1982, D.C.

ss. 1, 2 (in pt.), 6 (in pt.), repealed: 1981, c.38, sch.6.

s. 2, amended: order 74/691.

s. 3, amended: 1973, c.19, sch.3.

s. 6, amended: 1977, c.44, s.1.

s. 7, amended: 1976, c.10, s.1; 1981, c.38, sch.3; 1984, c.12, s.99, sch.4; c.32, sch.6; 1985, c.67, schs.3,7; 1986, c.44, sch.7; repealed in pt.: 1984, c.32, schs.6,7; 1985, c.67, schs.7,8.

s. 8, repealed in pt.: 1980, c.63, sch.2.

s. 9, see *Gouriet* v. *Union of Post Office Workers* [1977] 3 W.L.R. 300, H.L.; *Harold Stephen & Co.* v. *Post Office* [1977] 1 W.L.R. 1172, C.A.

s. 11, see *A.S.T.M.S. (Telephone Contracts Officers' Section)* v. *The Post Office* [1980] I.R.L.R. 475, C.A.

s. 11, repealed in pt.: 1981, c.38, sch.6.

s. 12, repealed in pt.: *ibid.*; 1988, c.9, sch.7.

s. 13, repealed: 1981, c.38, sch.6.

s. 14, amended: order 74/595; repealed in pt.: 1975, c.24, sch.3; 1981, c.38, sch.6.

ss. 17, 19, 23, 27, repealed: *ibid.*

s. 21, repealed in pt.: 1984, c.12, sch.7.

s. 29, see *Gouriet* v. *Union of Post Office Workers* [1977] 3 W.L.R. 300, H.L.; *Harold Stephen & Co.* v. *Post Office* [1977] 1 W.L.R. 1172, C.A.; *American Express* v. *British Airways Board* [1983] 1 All E.R. 557, Lloyd J.

CAP.

1969—cont.

48. Post Office Act 1969—*cont.*

s. 29, amended: 1981, c.38, sch.3; repealed in pt.: *ibid.*, sch.6; 1984, c.12, s.99, sch.7.

ss. 31, 32, 34–36, repealed: *ibid.*

s. 37, amended and repealed in pt.: *ibid.*, sch.3.

s. 38, amended: 1983, c.29, s.4, sch.2.

s. 39, amended: 1976, c.10, s.5.

s. 40, repealed in pt.: 1979, c.37, sch.7.

s. 42, repealed: 1981, c.38, sch.6.

s. 43, repealed in pt.: 1972, c.11, schs.4, 8.

s. 44, amended: *ibid.*, sch.6.

s. 45, repealed: *ibid.*, sch.8.

s. 46, amended: *ibid.*, sch.6.

s. 50, repealed: 1981, c.38, sch.6.

s. 51, repealed: 1973, c.42, sch.7.

s. 52, order 72/1794; amended: order 76/206; 1981, c.38, sch.3; repealed in pt.: order 76/206.

s. 53, amended: 1973, c.65, sch.9; 1975, c.30, sch.6; order 76/177; repealed (S.): order 78/1173.

s. 54, order 76/309.

s. 54, repealed: 1981, c.38, sch.6.

s. 55, amended: 1981, c.67, sch.4; repealed in pt.: *ibid.*, sch.6.

s. 58, amended: 1972, c.52, sch.21.

ss. 65, 68, repealed: 1981, c.38, sch.6.

s. 69, amended: *ibid.*, sch.3; repealed in pt.: *ibid.*, sch.6.

s. 72, amended: 1983, c.2, sch.8; repealed in pt.: 1981, c.38, sch.6.

s. 74, amended: 1979, c.14, sch.7; repealed in pt.: 1981, c.38, sch.6.

s. 76, see *R.* v. *Stamford* [1972] 2 W.L.R. 1055; [1972] 2 All E.R. 430; 56 Cr.App.R. 398.

s. 77, repealed in pt.: 1984, c.12, sch.7.

s. 78, repealed: 1981, c.38, sch.6.

s. 80, amended: 1981, c.38, sch.3.

s. 81, amended: 1979, c.12, sch.6; repealed in pt.: 1980, c.42, schs.1,2; 1981, c.38, sch.6.

ss. 82, 85, repealed: *ibid.*

s. 83, repealed: *ibid.*; 1984, c.12, sch.7.

s. 86, amended: 1972, c.58, sch.6; 1973, c.32, sch.4; c.65, sch.27; 1978, c.29, sch.16(S.); 1980, c.53, sch.1; 1981, c.38, sch.3; 1984, c.12, s.99; 1985, c.9, sch.2; c.51, sch.14; order 85/1884; repealed in pt.: 1981, c.38, sch.6; 1985, c.51, sch.17; 1988, c.40, sch.13(S.).

s. 87, orders 73/959, 960.

s. 87, amended: 1981, c.38, sch.3; repealed in pt.: *ibid.*, sch.6.

s. 88, repealed in pt.: *ibid.*; 1982, c.1, sch.2; 1984, c.12, sch.7.

Pt. IV (ss.89–92), repealed: *ibid.*, sch.7.

s. 93, repealed in pt.: 1972, c.65, sch.; 1984, c.60, sch.7; 1987, c.39, sch.2.

s. 94, repealed in pt.: order 81/233.

ss. 106, 107, repealed: 1981, c.38, sch.6.

s. 108, repealed in pt.: 1972, c.65, sch.

ss. 110–112, repealed: *ibid.*

ss. 115,116, repealed: S.L.R. 1976.

s. 121, repealed: 1973, c.38, sch.28.

s. 122, repealed: 1972, c.65, sch.

CAP.

1969—cont.

48. Post Office Act 1969—*cont.*

ss. 127, 129 (in pt.), 130, 131, repealed: 1981, c.38, sch.6.

ss. 134, 135, repealed in pt.: 1988, c.9, sch.7.

s. 139, repealed in pt.: 1973, c.36, sch.6.

sch. 1, see *T.S.A.* v. *Post Office* [1973] I.C.R. 173, N.I.R.C.; *R.* v. *Post Office, ex p. A.S.T.M.S. (Telephone Contracts Officers' Section)*, *The Times*, July 24, 1980, C.A.

sch. 1, repealed in pt.: 1975, c.24, sch.3.

sch. 4, order 76/1775.

sch. 4, amended: 1972, c.52, sch.21; 1974, c.26, sch.3; c.39, sch.5; 1979, c.2, sch.4; 1980, c.65, sch.33; 1981, c.23, sch.3; c.38, sch.3; order 81/156; 1987, c.26, sch.23(S.); repealed in pt.: 1972, c.52, schs. 21, 23; 1973, c.36, sch.6; 1974, c.26, sch.3; c.39, sch.5; 1975, c.78, sch.6; S.L.R. 1976; 1976, c.70, sch.8; S.L.R. 1977; 1980, c.34, sch.9; c.45, sch.11(S.); c.66, sch.25; 1981, c.56, sch.12; c.64, sch.13; c.67, sch.6; 1982, c.16, sch.16; c.51, sch.4; 1983, c.2, sch.9; c.25, sch.4; orders 80/1085; 82/1083; 1984, c.12, sch.7; c.29, sch.12; c.60, sch.7; 1985, c.65, sch.10; c.66, sch.8 (S.); S.L.R. 1986; 1986, c.48, sch.5.

sch. 5, amended: 1985, c.56, s.11; repealed in pt.: 1984, c.12, sch.7.

sch. 6, amended: 1973, c.39, sch.1; c.58, schs.2,5; repealed in pt.: 1973, c.36, sch.6; 1979, c.37, sch.7; 1981, c.54, sch.7.

sch. 7, repealed in pt.: 1981, c.38, sch.6.

sch. 9, amended: (S.) 1972, c.52, sch.21; 1978, c.44, sch.16; repealed in pt.: (S.) 1972, c.52, sch.23; 1973, c.38, sch.28; 1978, c.44, sch.17; 1981, c.38, sch.6.

sch. 10, amended: 1988, c.48, sch.7.

49. Education (Scotland) Act 1969.

repealed: 1980, c.44, sch.5.

schemes 73/1813; 74/598, 1188, 1666, 1667; 75/254, 697–699; 76/93, 158, 1366, 1480, 1503; 77/140, 655; 78/776, 1085, 1463; 78/81, 82, 173, 451, 496, 760, 1227; 80/135, 589, 715, 854, 1174; orders 78/372, 561; 81/739.

s. 19, schemes 72/1184, 1185, 1508.

50. Trustee Savings Banks Act 1969.

repealed: 1981, c.65, sch.7.

s. 17, order 74/932.

s. 28, regs. 79/259; 80/1061.

s. 29, order 75/1137.

s. 34, orders 72/1751; 73/835; 74/1912; 75/1256; 76/1202; 77/216; 78/605; 80/584.

s. 82, orders 72/495, 1029, 1278; 73/1405.

s. 86, regs. 79/259; 80/1061.

s. 88, warrants 74/2003; 76/738; 77/482; 78/615; 79/258, 1761; 82/285.

s. 99, orders 76/2149, 2150.

51. Development of Tourism Act 1969.

order 77/1877.

s. 1, amended: 1978, c.51, sch.16; repealed in pt.: 1975, c.24, sch.3; 1978, c.51, sch.16.

s. 5, amended: order 74/1264; 1980, c.63, sch.2.

s. 11, amended: 1972, c.5, sch.3; 1982, c.52, sch.2; repealed in pt.: 1972, c.63, sch.4.

CAP.

CAP.

1969—cont.

51. Development of Tourism Act 1969—cont.
s. 14, amended: 1973, c.65, sch.27; 1985, c.9, sch.2.
s. 21, repealed in pt.: 1975, c.24, sch.3.
sch. 2, repealed in pt.: 1977, c.45, sch.13.

52. Statute Law Revision Act 1969.
s. 5, amended: 1973, c.36, sch.6.

53. Late Night Refreshment Houses Act 1969.
s. 1, see *Portsmouth Corporation v. Nishar Ali* [1973] 1 All E.R. 236, D.C.; *Bucknell v. Croydon B.C.* [1973] 1 W.L.R. 534; [1973] 2 All E.R. 165.
s. 1, amended: 1982, c.30, s.7.
s. 2, amended: 1972, c.70, s.204.
s. 3, amended: 1974, c.7, sch.6; repealed in pt.: *ibid.*, sch.8.
ss. 3, 4, 5, amended: 1974, c.7, sch.6.
s. 11, amended: 1977, c.45, s.31, sch.6.
s. 12, repealed: 1974, c.7, sch.8.

54. Children and Young Persons Act 1969.
see *E. v. E. and Cheshire County Council (Intervener)* (1978) 9 Fam.Law 185, C.A.; *R. v. Wood Green Crown Court, ex p. P.* (1982) 4 F.L.R. 206, McCullough J.; *M. v. Westminster City Council, The Times,* July 13, 1984, D.C.
s. 1, see *Surrey County Council v. S.* [1973] 3 W.L.R. 579, C.A.; *Re B (A Minor) (Wardship: Child in Care)* [1974] 3 All E.R. 915; *R. v. Worthing JJ., ex p. Stevenson* [1976] 2 All E.R. 194, D.C.; *R. v. Lincoln (Kesteven) County Justice, ex p. M. (A Minor); R. v. Lincoln (Kesteven) Juvenile Court, ex p. Lincolnshire C.C.* [1976] 2 W.L.R. 143, D.C.; *Re D. (A Minor) Justices' Decision; Review)* [1977] 2 W.L.R. 1006, Dunn J.; *Humberside County Council v. R.* [1977] 1 W.L.R. 1251, D.C.; *Re H. (A Minor), The Times,* October 29, 1977, C.A.; *Re S. (A Minor) (Care Order: Education)* [1977] 3 W.L.R. 575; [1977] 3 All E.R. 582, C.A.; *Re H. (A Minor) (Wardship: Jurisdiction)* [1978] 2 W.L.R. 608; *D. v. National Society for the Prevention of Cruelty to Children* (1978) 76 L.G.R. 5, H.L.; *Essex County Council v. T.L.R. and K.B.R. (Minors)* (1979) 9 Fam.Law 15, D.C.; *R. v. Milton Keynes JJ., ex p. R.* (1979) 123 S.J. 321, D.C.; *Re W. (Minors) (Wardship: Jurisdiction)* [1979] 3 W.L.R. 252, C.A.; *F. v. Suffolk County Council* (1981) 99 L.G.R. 554, McNeill J.; *Leeds City Council v. West Yorkshire Metropolitan Police* [1982] 2 W.L.R. 186, H.L.; *Clarke (A Minor) v. Southwark London Borough Council* (1982) 12 Fam. Law 94, D.C.; *Re E (Minors), (Wardship: Jurisdiction)* [1983] 1 W.L.R. 541, C.A.; *Re. J. (A Minor) (Wardship) Jurisdiction)* (1984) 1 All E.R. 29, C.A.; *N. (A Minor) v. Birmingham Distict Council, The Times,* March 20, 1984, Sir John Arnold P.; *R. v. Birmingham Juvenile Court, ex p. S (A Minor)* [1984] 3 W.L.R. 387, Sir John Arnold; *R. v. F. (A Child), The Times,* April 20, 1985, C.A.; *M. v. Westminster City Council* (1985) 15 Fam. Law 93, D.C.; *A.-R. v. Avon County Council, The Times,* April 25, 1985,

1969—cont.

54. Children and Young Persons Act 1969—cont.
D.C.; *W. (A Minor) (Wardship Jurisdiction), Re* [1985] 2 W.L.R. 892, H.L.; *sub nom. W. v. Hertfordshire C.C.* [1985] 2 All E.R. 301, H.L.; *A. v. Wigan Metropolitan Borough Council* (1986) 16 Fam.Law 162, Ewbank J.; *D. (A Minor), Re* [1986] 3 W.L.R. 85, C.A.; *Berkshire County Council v. D.-P.* (1986) 16 Fam.Law 264; (1986) 2 F.L.R. 276, C.A.; *D. (A Minor) Re* [1986] 3 W.L.R. 1080, H.L.; *B. (A Minor) (Wardship: Sterilisation), Re* [1987] 2 W.L.R. 1213, H.L.; *R. v. Bedfordshire County Council, ex p. C.; R. v. Hertfordshire County Council, ex p. B.* (1987) 85 L.G.R. 218, Ewbank J.; *R. v. Birmingham Juvenile Court, ex p. G.; Same v. Same, ex p. R.* [1988] 1 W.L.R. 950, Sir Stephen Brown P.
s. 1, amended: 1975, c.72, sch.3; 1981, c.60, sch.3; 1983, c.20, sch.4; c.41.sch.2.
ss. 1, 2, see *R. v. Croydon Juvenile Court, ex p. N.* (1987) J.P.N. 151, Garland J.
s. 2, see *R. v. Gloucestershire County Council* [1980] 2 All E.R. 746, D.C.; *Clarke (A Minor) v. Southwark London Borough Council* (1982) 12 Fam.Law 94, D.C.; *R. v. Manchester JJ., ex p. Salford City Council* (1983) 81 L.G.R. 755, D.C.; *R. v. Birmingham Juvenile Court, ex p. S.* [1984] 1 All E.R. 393, Ewbank J.; *R. v. Birmingham City Juvenile Court, ex p. Birmingham City Council* [1988] 1 W.L.R. 337, C.A.; *Northamptonshire County Council v. H.* [1988] 2 W.L.R. 389, Sheldon J.; *T. (Minors), Re, The Times,* June 17, 1988, Booth J.
s. 2, amended: 1977, c.45, s.58; 1980, c.43, sch.7; 1982, c.48, s.28; c.51, sch.3; 1983, c.20, sch.4; 1986, c.28, s.2.
s. 3, amended: 1972, c.71, sch.5; 1973, c.62, sch.5; 1977, c.45, s.58; 1985, c.23, s.27; repealed in pt.: 1977, c.45, sch.13; 1982, c.48, s.27.
s. 6, see *R. v. Newham JJ., ex p. Knight* [1976] Crim.L.R. 323, D.C.; *R. v. St. Albans Juvenile Court, ex p. Goodman* [1981] 2 W.L.R. 882; [1981] 2 All E.R. 311, D.C.; *R. v. Tottenham Juvenile Court, ex p. A.R.C. (A Minor); R. v. Islington North Juvenile Court, ex p. C.D. (A Minor); R. v. Feltham Justices, ex p. N.C. (A Minor)* [1982] 2 W.L.R. 945, D.C.
s. 6, repealed: 1980, c.43, sch.9.
s. 7, see *R. v. K.* (1977) 121 S.J. 728, Judge Collinson; *R. v. Billericay JJ., ex p. Johnson* [1979] Crim.L.R. 315, D.C.; *Re C. (A Minor), (Wardship: Care Order)* [1982] 1 W.L.R. 1462, Balcombe J.; *R. v. Barnet Juvenile Court, ex p. London Borough of Barnet* (1982) 4 Cr.App.R. (S.) 221, D.C.; *W. v. Heywood, The Times,* March 15, 1985, D.C.; *R. v. F. (A Child), The Times,* April 20, 1985, C.A.
s. 7, amended: 1972, c.71, sch.5; 1980, c.43, sch.7; 1982, c.48, s.23; repealed in pt.: 1973, c.62, sch.6; 1982, c.48, sch.16.
s. 7A, added: *ibid.*, s.24.
s. 8, amended: 1980, c.43, sch.7.
s. 10, repealed in pt.: *ibid.*, sch.9.

CAP.

54. Children and Young Persons Act 1969—*cont.*
s. 11A, added: 1975, c.72, sch.3.
s. 12, substituted: 1988, c.33, sch.10.
ss. 12A–12D, added: *ibid.*
s. 13, amended: 1973, c.62, sch.5; 1977, c.45, sch.12; repealed in pt.: *ibid.*, sch.13.
s. 14A, added: 1983, c.41, sch.2.
s. 15, see *W.* v. *Nottinghamshire County Council* (1986) Fam.Law 185, C.A.
s. 15, amended: 1977, c.45, ss.37,58; 1988, c.33, sch.10; repealed in pt.: 1977, c.45, schs.12,13; 1982, c.48, s.20.
s. 16, amended: 1977, c.45, sch.12; 1980, c.43, sch.7; 1982, c.48, s.20; 1986, c.28, s.2.; 1988, c.33, sch.10; repealed in pt.: *ibid.*, sch.16.
s. 16A, added: 1988, c.33, sch.10.
s. 17, amended: 1985, c.60, s.25.
s. 18, amended: 1980, c.43, sch.7; 1982, c.48, s.20; 1988, c.33, sch.10.
s. 19, substituted: 1982, c.48, s.20; amended: 1988, c.33, sch.10.
s. 20, see *R.* v. *Lincoln (Kesteven) County Justice, ex p. M. (A Minor)*; *R.* v. *Lincoln (Kesteven) Juvenile Court, ex p. Lincolnshire C.C.* [1976] 2 W.L.R. 143, D.C.; *Re H. (A Minor)*, *The Times*, October 29, 1977, C.A.
s. 20, amended: 1983, c.41, sch.2.
s. 20A, see *R.* v. *F. (A Child)*, *The Times*, March 20, 1985, C.A.; *R.* v. *F. (A Child)*, *The Times*, April 20, 1985, C.A.
s. 20A, added: 1982, c.48, s.22.
s. 21, see *R.* v. *Lincoln (Kesteven) County Justice, ex p. M. (A Minor)*; *R.* v. *Lincoln (Kesteven) Juvenile Court, ex p. Lincolnshire C.C.* [1976] 2 W.L.R. 143, D.C.; *Re D. (A Minor) (Justices' Decision; Review)* [1977] 2 W.L.R. 1006, Dunn J.; *Re H. (A Minor)*, *The Times*, October 29, 1977, C.A.; *R.* v. *Wandsworth West Juvenile Court, ex p. Stanley* (1982) 12 Fam. Law 145, D.C.; *R.* v. *Snaresbrook Crown Court, ex p. S.* [1982] Crim.L.R. 682, D.C.; *Re. J. (A Minor) (Wardship: Jurisdiction)* [1984] 1 All E.R. 29, C.A.; *R.* v. *Tower Hamlets Juvenile Justices, ex p. London Borough of Tower Hamlets* (1984) 14 Fam. Law 307, Bush J.; *R.* v. *Salisbury and Tilsbury and Mere Combined Juvenile Court, ex p. Ball* (1985) 15 Fam. Law 313, Kennedy J.; *R.* v. *Chertsey Justices, ex p. E.* [1987] 2 F.L.R. 415, Hollings, J.; *R.* v. *Poole Juvenile Court, ex p. P.*; *R.* v. *Southwark Juvenile Court, ex p. C.* [1988] F.C.R. 1; [1988] 1 F.L.R. 8, Eastham J.
s. 21, amended: 1986, c.28, s.2.
ss. 21, 22, see *Re J. (Minors)*, September 28, 1979, Waterhouse J.
s. 21A, added: 1975, c.72, sch.3; amended: 1976, c.36, sch.3; substituted: 1983, c.41, sch.2.
s. 22, see *Northamptonshire County Council* v. *H.*, *The Times*, November 7, 1987, Sheldon J.
s. 22, amended: 1980, c.5, sch.5; 1983, c.41, sch.2; 1986, c.28, s.2; repealed in pt.: 1988, c.33, s.125, sch.16.

CAP.

54. Children and Young Persons Act 1969—*cont.*
s. 23, see *R.* v. *K.* (1977) 121 S.J. 728, Judge Collinson; *R.* v. *Slough Juvenile Court, ex p. Royal Berkshire County Council* (1983) 127 S.J. 840, D.C.; *R.* v. *Leicester Juvenile Court, ex p. K.D.C.* (1985) 80 Cr.App.R. 320, D.C.; *R.* v. *Dudley Magistrates' Court, ex p. G.*, *The Times*, February 13, 1988, D.C.
s. 23, amended: 1980, c.43, sch.7; 1982, c.48, sch.14.
s. 24, repealed: 1980, c.5, sch.6.
s. 25, amended: 1983, c.41, sch.2.
s. 26, order 72/1074.
s. 26, amended and repealed in pt.: 1980, c.5, sch.5.
s. 27, repealed: *ibid.*, sch.6.
s. 28, see *R.* v. *Lincoln (Kesteven) County Justice, ex p. M. (A Minor)*; *R.* v. *Lincoln (Kesteven) Juvenile Court, ex p. Lincolnshire C.C.* [1976] 2 W.L.R. 143, D.C.; *Re B. (A Minor)*, *The Times*, January 19, 1980, Dunn J.; *Nottinghamshire County Council* v. *Q.* [1982] 2 W.L.R. 954, D.C.; *H.* v. *Southwark London Borough Council* (1982) 12 Fam. Law 211, Comyn J.; *R.* v. *Bristol J.J., ex p. Broome* [1987] 1 W.L.R. 352, Booth J.
s. 28, amended: 1984, c.60, sch.6.
s. 29, substituted: *ibid*; repealed in pt.: 1988, c.33, sch.16.
s. 31, see *R.* v. *Coleman* (1976) 64 Cr.App.R. 124, C.A.
s. 31, repealed: 1982, c.48, sch.16.
s. 32, amended: 1975, c.72, s.68; 1980, c.5, sch.6; 1983, c.41, sch.2; repealed in pt.: 1975, c.72, s.68.
s. 32A, see *R.* v. *Wandsworth West Juvenile Court, ex p. S.* (1984) 14 Fam. Law 303, C.A.; *A.-R.* v. *Avon County Council* [1985] 3 W.L.R. 311, D.C.; *R.* v. *Plymouth Juvenile Court, ex p. F.*, *The Times*, August 8, 1986, Waterhouse J.; *R.* v. *Croydon Juvenile Court, ex p. N.* (1987) J.P.N. 151, Garland J.; *R.* v. *Poole Juvenile Court, ex p. P.*; *R.* v. *Southwark Juvenile Court, ex p. C.* [1988] F.C.R. 1; [1988] 1 F.L.R. 8, Eastham J.; *R.* v. *Croydon Juvenile Court, ex p. M.* [1988] F.C.R. 11, Waterhouse J.; *R.* v. *Newcastle upon Tyne Council, ex p. S. and T.* [1988] 1 F.L.R. 535, Latey J.; *R.* v. *North Yorkshire County Council, ex p. M.*, *The Times*, September 10, 1988, Ewbank J.
s. 32A, amended: 1986, c.28, s.3.
ss. 32A, 32B, added: 1975, c.72, s.64.
s. 32B, see *R.* v. *Newcastle upon Tyne Council, ex p. S. and T.* [1988] 1 F.L.R. 535, Latey J.; *R.* v. *Birmingham Juvenile Court, ex p. G.*; *Same* v. *Same, ex p. R.* [1988] 1 W.L.R. 950, Sir Stephen Brown P.
s. 32C, rules, 88/952.
s. 32C, added: 1986, c.28, s.3.
s. 33, repealed: 1974, c.4, sch.5.
s. 34, orders 73/485; 74/1083; 77/420; 79/125; 81/81.
s. 34, repealed in pt.: 1977, c.45, sch.13; 1982, c.48, sch.16; 1988, c.33, sch.16.

CAP.

1969—cont.

54. Children and Young Persons Act 1969—*cont.*
s. 35, order 74/163.
ss. 35–42, repealed: 1980, c.5, sch.6.
s. 43, regs. 72/319.
s. 44, 45, repealed: 1980, c.5, sch.6.
s. 46, orders 73/506–13, 516–8, 526, 527, 558–59, 580–6, 635–9, 657, 898, 1495, 1501, 1537, 1538, 1551–3, 1564–8, 1575–8, 1580, 1688, 1694, 2081; 74/349, 414, 670, 671, 806, 937, 1520; 75/968, 969, 982, 2035; 78/629.
s. 46, amended: 1983, c.41, sch.2.
s. 47, orders 79/285; 81/123.
ss. 47–50, repealed: 1980, c.5, sch.6.
ss. 51, 52 (in pt.), 53–57, repealed: 1980, c.6, sch.3.
ss. 56, 57 (in pt.), repealed (S.): 1984, c.56, sch.3.
ss. 58, 59, repealed: 1980, c.5, sch.6.
s. 60, repealed in pt.: 1988, c.33, sch.16.
s. 61, repealed: 1980, c.43, sch.9.
ss. 62–64A, repealed: 1980, c.5, sch.6.
s. 65, amended: 1983, c.41, sch.2; repealed in pt.: 1975, c.72, sch.4; 1980, c.5, sch.6.
s. 68, repealed: 1972, c.70, sch.30.
s. 69, orders 73/1613, 1631; 74/163, 414, 497; 77/420; 79/125; 81/81; regs. 75/465; 76/474.
s. 69, amended: 1982, c.48, sch.14; repealed in pt.: 1980, c.5, sch.6.
s. 70, see *Re H. (A Minor)*, *The Times*, October 29, 1977, C.A.; *R. v. Gloucestershire County Council* [1980] 2 All E.R. 746, D.C.; *D. (A Minor), Re* [1986] 3 W.L.R. 85, C.A.; *Berkshire County Council v. D.-P.* (1986) 16 Fam.Law 264; (1986) 2 F.L.R. 276, C.A.; *R. v. Poole Juvenile Court, ex p. P.*; *R. v. Southwark Juvenile Court, ex p. C.* [1988] F.C.R. 1; [1988] 1 F.L.R. 8, Eastham J.
s. 70, amended: 1972, c.70, sch.23; 1980, c.43, sch.9; 1987, c.42, s.8, sch.2; repealed in pt.: 1980, c.5, sch.6.
s. 71, order 80/327.
s. 72, repealed in pt.: 1980, c.6, sch.3.
s. 73, amended: 1983, c.41, sch.2; repealed in pt.: 1973, c.36, sch.6.
sch. 1, repealed: 1974, c.4, sch.5.
sch. 2, repealed: 1980, c.5, sch.6.
sch. 2, regs. 73/241; 75/465; 76/474; 77/473; order 74/497.
sch. 3, amended: 1973, c.63, sch.5; 1977, c.45, sch.12.
sch. 4, amended: 1973, c.62, sch.5; 1977, c.45, sch.12; 1980, c.43, sch.7; 1983, c.20, sch.4; repealed in pt.: 1973, c.62, sch.6; 1980, c.6, sch.3; c.43, sch.8; 1982, c.48, sch.16; 1983, c.41, sch.10.
sch. 5, see *Somerset County Council v. Brice* [1973] 1 W.L.R. 1169; [1973] 3 All E.R. 438, D.C.
sch. 5, amended: (S.) 1975, c.21, sch.9; 1980, c.5, sch.5; c.43, sch.7; repealed in pt.: 1972, c.71, sch.6; 1973, c.62, sch.6; 1975, c.21, sch.10; c.61, sch.5; 1976, c.36, sch.4; 1977,

CAP.

1969—cont.

54. Children and Young Persons Act 1969—*cont.*
c.45, sch.13; 1978, c.28, sch.4; 1980, c.5, sch.6; c.6, sch.3; 1982, c.48, sch.16; c.51, sch.4; 1983, c.20, sch.6; 1984, c.36, sch.5.
sch. 7, repealed: 1980, c.6, sch.3.
55. Divorce Reform Act 1969.
repealed: 1973, c.18, sch.3.
s. 2, see *Price v. Price*, unreported, December 3, 1971; *McGill v. Robson* [1972] 1 W.L.R. 237; *sub nom. McG. (formerly R.) v. R.* [1972] 1 All E.R. 362; *Pheasant v. Pheasant* [1972] 2 W.L.R. 353; [1972] 1 All E.R. 587; *Ash v. Ash* [1972] 2 W.L.R. 347; [1972] 1 All E.R. 582; *Santos v. Santos* [1972] 2 W.L.R. 889; 116 S.J. 196; [1972] 2 All E.R. 246; *Collins v. Collins* [1972] 1 W.L.R. 689; 116 S.J. 296; [1972] 2 All E.R. 658; *Spill v. Spill* [1972] 1 W.L.R. 793; 116 S.J. 434; [1972] 3 All E.R. 9; *Katz v. Katz* [1972] 1 W.L.R. 955; 116 S.J. 546; [1972] 3 All E.R. 219; *Richards v. Richards* [1972] 1 W.L.R. 1073; 116 S.J. 599; *Mason v. Mason* [1972] Fam. 302; [1972] 3 W.L.R. 405; 116 S.J. 485; [1972] 3 All E.R. 315; *Roper v. Roper* [1972] 1 W.L.R. 1314; 116 S.J. 712; [1972] 3 All E.R. 668; *Chapman v. Chapman* [1972] 1 W.L.R. 1544; 116 S.J. 843; [1972] 3 All E.R. 1089; *Fuller v. Fuller* [1973] 1 W.L.R. 730; [1973] 2 All E.R. 650; *Bradley v. Bradley* [1973] 1 W.L.R. 1291; [1973] 3 All E.R. 750, C.A.; *Griffiths v. Griffiths* [1973] 1 W.L.R. 1454, Arnold J.; *Cleary v. Cleary and Hutton* [1974] 1 W.L.R. 73, C.A.; *Harris v. Harris* (1973) 4 Fam.Law 10, C.A.; *Strelley-Upton v. Strelley-Upton* (1973) 4 Fam.Law 9, C.A.; *Mamane v. Mamane* (1974) 4 Fam.Law 87, C.A.; *Poon v. Tan* (1973) 4 Fam.Law 161, C.A.
ss. 2, 3, see *Mouncer v. Mouncer* [1972] 1 W.L.R. 321; [1972] 1 All E.R. 289; *Carr v. Carr* [1974] 1 All E.R. 1193, C.A.
ss. 2, 4, 5, 6, see *Rule v. Rule*; *Tunstall v. Tunstall*; *Martin v. Martin and Hart* [1971] 3 All E.R. 1368.
ss. 2, 7, see *Beales v. Beales* [1972] 2 W.L.R. 972; 116 S.J. 196; [1972] 2 All E.R. 667.
s. 4, see *Parker v. Parker* [1972] 2 W.L.R. 21; [1972] 1 All E.R. 410; *Mathias v. Mathias* [1972] 3 W.L.R. 201; 116 S.J. 394; [1972] 3 All E.R. 1; *Dorrell v. Dorrell* [1972] 1 W.L.R. 1087; 116 S.J. 617; [1972] 3 All E.R. 343; *Banik v. Banik* [1973] 1 W.L.R. 860; *Brickell v. Brickell* [1973] 3 W.L.R. 602; [1973] 3 All E.R. 508, C.A.; *Olds v. Olds* (1973) 4 Fam.Law 82, C.A.; *Allan v. Allan* (1973) 4 Fam.Law 83; *Rukat v. Rukat* [1975] 2 W.L.R. 201; [1975] 1 All E.R. 343, C.A.
s. 6, see *Trippas v. Trippas* [1973] 2 W.L.R. 585; [1973] 2 All E.R. 1, C.A.; *Wilson v. Wilson* [1973] 1 W.L.R. 555; [1973] 2 All E.R. 17, C.A.; *Krystman v. Krystman* [1973] 1 W.L.R. 927; *Lombardi v. Lombardi* [1973] 1 W.L.R. 1276; [1973] 3 All E.R. 625, C.A.; *Dryden v. Dryden* [1973] 3 W.L.R. 524; [1973] 3 All E.R. 526, Baker P.; *Grigson v. Grigson* [1974] 1

CAP.

1969—cont.

55. Divorce Reform Act 1969—*cont.*
W.L.R. 228; [1974] 1 All E.R. 478, C.A.; *Cumbers* v. *Cumbers* [1974] 1 W.L.R. 1331, C.A.; *Wright* v. *Wright* [1976] 2 W.L.R. 269.

56. Auctions (Bidding Agreements) Act 1969.
s. 1, repealed in pt.: 1977, c.45, sch.13.

57. Employers' Liability (Compulsory Insurance) Act 1969.
s. 1, amended: 1974, c.49, sch.1; 1981, c.31, sch.4; 1982, c.50, sch.5.
ss. 1, 4, 5, modified: order 75/1289.
s. 3, regs. 81/1489.
s. 3, amended: 1972, c.70, sch.30; 1973, c.65, s.159; 1985, c.51, sch.14; order 85/1884; 1988, c.4, sch.6; repealed in pt.: 1985, c.51, sch.17; 1988, c.40, sch.13 (prosp.).
ss. 3, 4, 6, regs. 74/208; 75/1443.
s. 4, regs. 75/194.
ss. 4, 5, amended: 1977, c.45, s.31, sch.6.

58. Administration of Justice Act 1969.
ss. 1–9, repealed: 1984, c.28, sch.4.
s. 10, repealed in pt.: 1973, c.15, sch.5.
s. 11, repealed: 1984, c.28, sch.4.
s. 12, repealed in pt.: 1978, c.23, sch.7; 1981, c.54, sch.7.
s. 13, see *Fitzleet Estates* v. *Cherry* [1977] 1 W.L.R. 1345, H.L.
s. 15, repealed in pt.: 1977, c.38, sch.5.
s. 16, order 78/1045.
s. 16, amended: 1978, c.23, sch.5; repealed in pt.: 1978, c.23, sch.7.
ss. 17–19, repealed: 1983, c.20, sch.6.
s. 20, amended: 1978, c.23, sch.5; repealed in pt.: 1981, c.54, sch.7; 1984, c.28, sch.4.
s. 21, amended: 1978, c.23, sch.5; repealed in pt.: 1981, c.54, sch.7.
s. 22, see *Mason* v. *Harman* [1972] R.T.R. 1.
s. 23, repealed: 1981, c.54, sch.7.
s. 24, repealed in pt.: 1977, c.37, sch.6.
ss. 25, 26, repealed: 1981, c.54, sch.7.
s. 27, repealed in pt.: S.L.R. 1978; order 79/1575; 1981, c.54, sch.7.
s. 28, repealed: S.L.R. 1978.
s. 31, repealed: 1981, c.20, sch.4.
s. 33, repealed: 1973, c.36, sch.6.
s. 34, repealed in pt.: 1981, c.54, sch.7.
s. 35, repealed in pt.: S.L.R. 1978.
s. 36, amended: 1973, c.36, sch.6; 1981, c.20, sch.4.
sch. 1, repealed in pt.: 1974, c.47, sch.4; 1978, c.23, sch.7.
sch. 2, repealed: S.L.R. 1978.

59. Law of Property Act 1969.
s. 16, order 74/221.
s. 19, regs. 73/1992.
s. 25, amended: 1980, c.58, sch.3; repealed in pt.: 1972, c.61, sch.5.
ss. 26, 27, repealed: *ibid.*
s. 28, rules 75/299; 81/600; 84/793; 86/1322.
s. 28, repealed in pt.: 1982, c.16, sch.16.

60. Transport (London) Amendment Act 1969.
repealed: S.L.R. 1976.
ss. 1, 3–7, 11, see *Bromley London Borough Council* v. *Greater London Council* [1982] 2 W.L.R. 62, H.L.

CAP.

1969—cont.

61. Expiring Laws Act 1969.
repealed: S.L.R. 1975.

62. Rent (Control of Increases) Act 1969.
repealed: S.L.R. 1976.
ss. 5, 6, repealed: 1977, c.42, sch.25.

63. Police Act 1969.
s. 1, amended: 1973, c.36, sch.6.
s. 4, regs. 74/1365; 75/1844; 76/538, 1274; 77/580, 581, 582, 1005, 1006, 1988, 1989; 78/1239; 79/75, 694, 1216, 1470, 1543; 80/405.
s. 4, repealed: 1980, c.10, s.3.

64. Customs (Import Deposits) Act 1969.
repealed: S.L.R. 1975.

65. Ulster Defence Regiment Act 1969.
repealed: 1980, c.9, sch.10.

1970

1. Consolidated Fund Act 1970.
repealed: 1974, c.31, s.4, sch.

2. Industrial Development (Ships) Act 1970.
s. 2, repealed: 1973, c.36, sch.6.

3. Food and Drugs (Milk) Act 1970.
repealed: 1984, c.30, sch.11.

4. Valuation for Rating (Scotland) Act 1970.
s. 1, repealed in pt.: 1987, c.47, sch. 6.
s. 2, repealed in pt.: 1975, c.30, sch.7.

5. Housing (Amendment) (Scotland) Act 1970.
repealed: 1976, c.11, s.1.

7. Local Employment Act 1970.
ss. 1–4, 6, repealed: 1972, c.5, sch.4.
s. 7, repealed: 1972, c.41, sch.28.
ss. 8, 9, sch., amended: 1972, c.5, sch.4.

8. Insolvency Services (Accounting and Investment) Act 1970.
repealed: 1986, c.45, sch.12.

9. Taxes Management Act 1970.
see *I.R.C.* v. *Adams* (1971) 48 T.C. 67; *Baker* v. *Superite Tools, The Times*, July 19, 1985, E.A.T.
s. 1, see *R.* v. *General Commissioners of Tax for Tavistock, ex p. Adams (No. 2)* (1971) 48 T.C. 56.
s. 1, amended: 1976, c.24, sch.8.
s. 2, orders 78/3, 18.
s. 2, amended: 1975, c.7, s.57; 1988, c.39, s.134; repealed in pt.: 1975, c.7, s.57, sch.13; 1988, c.39, sch.14.
s. 3, amended: 1972, c.11, sch.6.
ss. 4, 4A, substituted: 1984, c.43, sch.22.
s. 5, repealed in pt.: 1972, c.71, sch.6; 1973, c.65, sch.29; order 74/2143; 1980, c.55, sch.3(S.).
s. 6, amended: 1988, c.1, sch.9; repealed in pt.: 1982, c.39, sch.22.
s. 7, substituted: 1988, c.39, s.120.
s. 8, see *Dunk* v. *General Commissioners for Havant* [1976] S.T.C. 460; *Garnham* v. *I.R.C.* [1977] T.R. 307, D.C.; *Napier* v. *I.R.C.* [1978] T.R. 403, C.A.; *Moschi* v. *The Commissioners for the General Purposes of the Income Tax for the Division of Kensington in Greater London and I.R.C.* [1979] T.R. 279, Goulding J.; *Cox* v. *Poole General Commissioners and I.R.C.* [1988] S.T.C. 66, Knox J.

1970—cont.

9. Taxes Management Act 1970—cont.

s. 8, amended: 1972, c.41, sch.24; 1973, c.51, s.16; 1988, c.1, sch.29; repealed in pt. (prosp.): 1988, c.39, sch.14.

. s. 9, amended: 1988, c.1, sch.29.

s. 10, substituted: 1988, c.39, s.121.

s. 11, amended: 1972, c.41, sch.24; 1979, c.14, sch.7; 1987, c.51, s.82; 1988, c.1, sch.29.

s. 11A, added: 1988, c.39, s.122; repealed in pt. (prosp.): ibid., sch.14.

s. 12, amended: 1978, c.42, s.45; 1979, c.14, sch.7; 1982, c.39, s.81; 1988, c.1, sch.29; c.39, s.122.

s. 13, amended: ibid., s.123; repealed in pt. (prosp.): ibid., sch.14.

s. 15, amended: 1976, c.40, sch.9; 1977, c.36, sch.8; 1981, c.35, ss.71,72; 1988, c.1, sch.29.

s. 16, amended: ibid., c.39, s.124; c.48, sch.7.

s. 16A, added 1988, c.1, sch.29.

s. 17, see Eke v. Knight [1977] T.R. 7, C.A.

s. 17, amended: 1988, c.39, s.123.

s. 18, amended: 1988, c.1, sch.29; c.39, s.123; repealed in pt.: ibid., sch.14.

s. 18A, added: ibid., s.125.

s. 19, amended: 1988, c.1, sch.29; c 39, s.123.

s. 20, see B. & S. Displays v. I.R.C. [1978] S.T.C. 331, Goulding J.; Monarch Assurance Co. v. Special Commissioners [1986] S.T.C. 311, Ch.D.; R. v. Board of Inland Revenue, ex p. Goldberg, The Times, May 3, 1988, D.C.

s. 20, substituted: 1976, c.40, s.57, sch.6; amended: 1988, c.39, s.126.

s. 20B, amended: ibid.

s. 20C, see R. v. I.R.C., ex p. Rossminster [1980] 2 W.L.R. 1, H.L.

s. 21, amended: 1973, c.51, sch.21; 1986, c.41, sch.18; repealed in pt.: 1973, c.51, schs.21,22.

s. 25, amended: 1978, c.42, s.45; 1979, c.14, sch.7; 1982, c.39, s.81; 1986, c.41, sch.18.

s. 27, amended: 1979, c.14, sch.7; 1988, c.1, sch.29.

s. 28, amended: 1979, c.14, sch.7.

s. 29, see R. v. General Comrs. of Tax for Tavistock, ex p. Adams (No. 2) (1971) 48 T.C. 56; Vickerman (Inspector of Taxes) v. Mason's Personal Representatives [1984] 2 All E.R. 1, Scott J.; Honig v. Sarsfield [1985] S.T.C. 31, Gibson J.; Duchy Maternity v. Hodgson [1985] S.T.C. 764, Walton J.; Jones (Inspector of Taxes) v. O'Brien, The Times, June 15, 1988; Financial Times, June 17, 1988, Hoffmann J.; Lord Advocate v. Mckenna (O.H.), 1988 S.L.T. 523.

s. 29, amended: 1972, c.41, sch.24; 1975, c.45, s.44; 1976, c.24, sch.8; 1988, c.1, sch.29; c.39, s.119; repealed in pt.: (prosp.): ibid., sch.14.

s. 30, substituted: 1982, c.39, s.149; amended: 1987, c.51, s.89; 1988, c.1, sch.29.

s. 31, see Hallamshire Industrial Finance Trust v. I.R.C. [1979] 1 W.L.R. 620, Browne-Wilkinson J.; Lord Advocate v. Mckenna (O.H.), 1988 S.L.T. 523.

1970—cont.

9. Taxes Management Act 1970—cont.

s. 31, amended: 1972, c.41, sch.24; 1973, c.51, sch.15; 1976, c.24, sch.8; 1981, c.35, s.45; 1984, c.43, s.89, sch.22; 1988, c.1, sch.29; repealed in pt.: 1972, c.41, schs.24,28; 1985, c.54, sch.27.

s. 32, see Martin v. O'Sullivan [1984] S.T.C. 258, C.A.; Bye v. Coren [1985] S.T.C. 113, D.C.; Lord Advocate v. Mckenna (O.H.), 1988 S.L.T. 523.

s. 32, amended: 1976, c.24, sch.8.

s. 33, see Arranmore Investment Co. v. I.R.C. [1973] S.T.C. 195, N.I.C.A.

s. 33, modified: regs. 74/896; 1975, c.22, sch.2; amended: 1976, c.24, sch.8.

s. 34, see Larter v. Skone James [1976] 1 W.L.R. 607; [1976] 2 All E.R. 615; Johnson v. I.R.C. [1977] T.R. 243; [1978] 2 All E.R. 65, C.A.; Honig v. Sarsfield [1986] S.T.C. 246, C.A.

s. 34, modified: regs. 74/896; amended: 1976, c.24, sch.8.

s. 35, see Bray v. Best, The Times, January 21, 1986, Walton J.

s. 35, amended: 1988, c.1, sch.29; repealed in pt.: 1976, c.40, schs.9,15.

s. 36, see Knight v. I.R.C. [1972] T.R. 323, C.A.; Nicholson v. Morris [1976] S.T.C. 269; Johnson v. Scott [1978] T.R. 121, C.A.; Ottley v. Morris, The Times, June 24, 1978, Fox J.; Theodore P. Kovak v. Morris [1981] T.R. 345, Vinelott J.; Read v. Rollinson [1982] S.T.C. 370, Goulding J.; Hawkins v. Fuller [1982] S.T.C. 468, Goulding J.; Kovak v. Morris [1985] S.T.C. 183, C.A.; Pleasants v. Atkinson (Inspector of Taxes) [1987] S.T.C. 728, Hoffmann J.

s. 36, modified: 1975, c.22, sch.2.

s. 37, see Pearlberg v. Varty [1972] 1 W.L.R. 534; [1972] 2 All E.R. 6; [1972] T.R. 5; R. v. Havering Commissioners, ex p. Knight [1973] T.R. 235, C.A.; Johnson v. Scott [1977] T.R. 121, C.A.; Read v. Rollinson [1982] S.T.C. 370, Goulding J.; Hawkins v. Fuller [1982] S.T.C. 468, Goulding J.

s. 37A, added (prosp.): 1988, c.39, sch.3.

s. 38, amended: 1976, c.24, sch.8; 1985, c.54, sch.25.

s. 39, see Johnson v. Scott [1977] T.R. 121, C.A.

s. 40, see Ex p. Martin [1971] T.R. 391; Larter v. Skone James [1976] 1 W.L.R. 607; [1976] 2 All E.R. 615; Honig v. Scarsfield [1986] S.T.C. 246, C.A.

s. 40, modified: regs. 74/896; amended: 1976, c.24, sch.8; 1985, c.54, sch.25.

s. 41, see Ex p. Martin [1971] T.R. 391; Pearlberg v. Varty [1972] 1 W.L.R. 534; [1972] 2 All E.R. 6; Nicholson v. Morris [1977] T.R. 1, C.A.; Hawkins v. Fuller [1982] S.T.C. 468, Goulding J.; R. v. Comr. for the Special Purposes of the Income Tax Acts, ex p. Stipple Choice [1985] 2 All E.R. 465, C.A.

s. 41, amended: 1976, c.24, sch.8.

CAP.

1970—cont.

9. Taxes Management Act 1970—cont.
s. 42, see Decision No. R(SB) 25/86.
s. 42, amended: 1976, c.24, sch.8; 1988, c.1, sch.29.
s. 43, see R. v. Havering Commissioners, ex p. Knight [1973] T.R. 235, C.A.
s. 43, modified: regs. 74/896; amended: 1976, c.24, sch.8.
s. 44, see R. v. General Commissioners of Income Tax for Kingston and Elmbridge, ex p. Adams (1972) 48 T.C. 75; R. v. Havering Comrs., ex p. Knight [1973] T.R. 235, C.A.; Toogood v. Bristol General Comrs. [1977] S.T.C. 116.
s. 44, amended: 1984, c.43, sch.22; 1988, c.39, s.133.
s. 45, amended: ibid.; repealed in pt.: ibid., schs.22, 23.
s. 46, see R. v. Epping and Harlow General Comrs., ex p. Goldstraw [1983] S.T.C. 693; [1983] 3 All E.R. 257, C.A.
s. 47, amended: 1975, c.7, s.54; 1979, c.14, sch.7; repealed in pt.: 1974, c.30, sch.10; 1979, c.14, sch.8.
s. 47A, added: 1976, c.24, sch.8.
s. 47B, added: 1986, c.41, sch.9; amended: 1988, c.1, sch.29.
s. 48, amended: 1975, c.45, s.45.
s. 49, see R. v. Special Comrs. of Income Tax, ex p. Magill [1981] S.T.C. 479; (1982) 53 T.C. 135, Gibson J.; Reed (Inspector of Taxes) v. Clark [1985] 3 W.L.R. 142, Nicholls J.; Bye v. Coren [1986] S.T.C. 393, C.A.
s. 50, see Jonas v. Bamford [1973] T.R. 225; Johnson v. Scott [1977] T.R. 121, C.A.; Slater v. Richardson and Bottoms [1979] S.T.C. 630; [1979] 3 All E.R. 439, Oliver J.; R. & D. McKerron v. I.R.C. [1978] T.R. 489, Ct. of Session; Eke v. Knight [1977] T.R. 7, C.A.; Hallamshire Industrial Finance Trust v. I.R.C. [1979] 1 W.L.R. 620, Browne-Wilkinson J.; D.I.K. Transmissions (Dundee) v. Commissioners of Inland Revenue, 1981 S.L.T. 87; Cutmore v. Leach [1982] S.T.C. 61, Walton J.; Wicker v. Fraser [1982] S.T.C. 505, Goulding J.; Banin v. Mackinlay [1984] 1 All E.R. 1116, Harman J.; Owton Fens Properties v. Redden [1984] S.T.C. 618, D.C.; Banin v. MacKinlay (Inspector of Taxes) [1985] 1 All E.R. 482, C.A.; Duchy Maternity v. Hodgson [1985] S.T.C. 764, Walton J.
s. 50, modified: 1975, c.22, sch.2; amended: 1975, c.45, s.67; repealed in pt.: 1988, c.39, sch.14.
s. 51, see Script & Play Productions v. I.R.C. [1972] 1 W.L.R. 392; [1972] 1 All E.R. 577; Shah v. General Comrs. for Hampstead [1974] S.T.C. 438; Chapman v. General Comrs. of Income Tax for the District of Sheaf [1975] S.T.C. 170; Campbell v. Rochdale General Comrs. [1975] 2 All E.R. 385; Toogood v. Bristol General Commissioners [1977] S.T.C. 116; Eke v. Knight [1977] T.R. 7, C.A.; Galleri v. Wirral General Comrs. [1979] S.T.C. 216,

CAP.

1970—cont.

9. Taxes Management Act 1970—cont.
Walton J.; D.I.K. Transmissions (Dundee) v. Comrs. of Inland Revenue, 1981 S.L.T. 87; Beach v. Willesden General Comrs. [1982] S.T.C. 157, Walton J.
s. 53, see Script & Play Productions v. I.R.C. [1972] 1 W.L.R. 392; [1972] 1 All E.R. 577; Campbell v. Rochdale General Comrs. [1975] 2 All E.R. 385; Q.T. Discount Foodstores v. General Comrs. of Income Tax for Warley, The Times, July 4, 1981, Vinelott J.; Rujaib v. Kensington General Commissioners and I.R.C. [1982] S.T.C. 40, Vinelott J.; Beach v. Willesden General Comrs. [1982] S.T.C. 157, Walton J.
s. 53, amended: 1972, c.41, s.129; repealed in pt.: 1979, c.14, sch.8.
s. 54, see Delbourgo v. Field [1978] 2 All E.R. 193, C.A.; Beach v. Willesden General Comrs. [1982] S.T.C. 157, Walton J.; Scorer (Inspector of Taxes) v. Olin Energy Systems, The Times, March 29, 1985, H.L.; Tod (Inspector of Taxes) v. South Essex Motors (Basildon) [1988] S.T.C. 392, Knox J.
s. 55, see Parikh v. Currie [1978] S.T.C. 473, C.A.; Hallamshire Industrial Finance Trust v. I.R.C. [1979] 1 W.L.R. 620, Browne-Wilkinson J.
s. 55, substituted: 1975, c.45, s.45; modified: ibid.; amended: 1976, c.24, sch.8; 1982, c.39, s.68; 1984, c.43, s.89; 1988, c.1, sch. 29; repealed in pt.: 1984, c.43, sch.23.
s. 56, see Rose v. Humbles; Aldersgate Textile v. I.R.C. [1972] 1 W.L.R. 33; R. v. Freshwell Commissioners, ex p. Clark [1971] T.R. 353; Barry v. Hughes [1971] T.R. 475; Fen Farming Co. v. Dunsford [1973] T.R. 191, Walton J.; Way v. Underdown [1973] T.R. 199, Plowman J.; Inland Revenue v. Titaghur Jute Factory Co., First Division, December 30, 1977; Yoannou v. Hall [1978] S.T.C. 600, Fox J.; Thomas v. Ingram [1979] S.T.C. 1, Fox J.; R. v. I.R.C. ex p. Emery, The Times, July 8, 1980, D.C.; R. & D. McKerron v. I.R.C. [1982] 53 T.C. 28, Ct. of Session; R. v. Special Commissioners of Income Tax, ex p. Magill (1982) 53 T.C. 135, Gibson J.; Furniss v. Ford [1981] T.R. 255, Vinelott J.; Dutta v. Doig (No. 1) [1979] T.R. 231, Goulding J.; Dutta v. Doig (No. 2) [1979] T.R. 407, Fox J.; Jeffries v. Stevens [1982] S.T.C. 639, Walton J.; Valleybright (In Liquidation) v. Richardson [1985] S.T.C. 70, Ch.D.; Furniss v. Ford (1981) 55 T.C. 561, D.C.; Hughes (Inspector of Taxes) v. Viner [1985] 3 All E.R. 40, Walton J.; Verdon v. Honour (Inspector of Taxes), The Times, November 1, 1988, Morritt J.
s. 56, amended: 1975, c.45, s.45; 1976, c.24, sch.8; 1984, c.43, sch.22.
s. 56A, order 87/1422.
ss. 56A, 56B, added: 1984, c.43, sch.22.
s. 57, amended: 1974, c.30, sch.10; 1979, c.14, sch.7.
s. 57A, added: 1976, c.24, sch.8.

1970—cont.

9. Taxes Management Act 1970—cont.

s. 57A, regs. 81/1038.

s. 58, amended: 1978, c.23, sch.5; 1988, c.1, sch.29; c.39, s.135; repealed in pt.: 1980, c.48, sch.20; 1988, c.39, s.134.

s. 59, repealed: *ibid.*

s. 61, see *Herbert Berry Associates* v. *I.R.C.* [1977] 1 W.L.R. 1437, H.L.

s. 62, amended: 1976, c.24, sch.8.

s. 63, amended: 1988, c.1, sch.29.

ss. 63, 63A, substituted (S.): 1987, c.18, sch. 4.

s. 64, amended: 1976, c.24, sch.8.

s. 65, amended: 1984, c.43, s.57.

s. 66, see *Oxley (Collector of Taxes* v. *Raynham* [1984] T.C. 779, Weston-Super-Mare County Court.

s. 66, amended: 1984, c.28, sch.2; c.43, s.57.

s. 67, amended and repealed in pt.: 1976, c.40, s.58, sch.15.

s. 69, amended: 1987, c.51, s.86.

s. 70, see *Lord Advocate* v. *McKenna* (O.H.), 1988 S.L.T. 523.

s. 70, amended: 1980, c.48, s.115; 1985, c.54, sch.25; 1987, c.51, sch.6.

s. 71, amended: 1988, c.1, sch.29.

s. 77A, added: 1976, c.24, sch.8.

s. 78, amended: 1985, c.54, s.50; 1988, c.1, sch.29.

s. 85, amended: 1987, c.51, sch. 6.

s. 85A, added: 1976, c.24, sch.8.

s. 86, substituted: 1975, c.45, s.46; modified: *ibid.*; amended: 1980, c.48, ss.61,62; 1982, c.39, s.69; 1988, c.1, sch.29; repealed in pt.: 1987, c.16, sch.16; c.51, s.86.

s. 86A, added: 1976, c.24, sch.8; amended: 1980, c.48, s.115, sch.20; 1984, c.43, s.123; repealed in pt.: 1980, c.48, s.115, sch.20.

s. 87, substituted: 1972, c.41, sch.24; amended: 1975, c.45, s.46; 1980, c.48, s.62; 1988, c.1, sch.29.

s. 87A, added: 1987, c.51, s.85; amended: 1988, c.1, sch.29.

s. 88, see *Nicholson* v. *Morris* [1977] T.R. 1, C.A.

s. 88, amended: 1972, c.41, sch.24; 1975, c.45, s.46; 1976, c.24, sch.8; 1980, c.48, s.61; 1987, c.51, s.86; 1988, c.1, sch.29; repealed in pt.: 1987, c.51, s.86; 1988, c.1, sch.31.

s. 89, orders 74/966; 79/1687; 82/1587; 85/563; 86/1181, 1832; 87/513, 898, 1492, 1988; 88/756, 1278, 1621, 2185.

s. 89, amended: 1976, c.24, sch.8; 1987, c.51, s.89; 1988, c.1, sch.29.

s. 91, amended: 1976, c.24, sch.8; 1987, c.51, s.86; 1988, c.1, sch.29.

s. 91A, added: 1976, c.24, sch.8.

s. 93, see *Kenny* v. *General Commissioners for Wirral* [1975] S.T.C. 61; *Napier* v. *I.R.C.* [1977] T.R. 289, D.C.; *Moschi* v. *The Commissioners for the General Purposes of the Income Tax for the Division of Kensington in Greater London and I.R.C.* [1979] T.R. 279, Goulding J.; *Re Hurren (A Bankrupt), ex p. The Trustee* v. *I.R.C.* [1982] 3 All E.R. 982, Walton J.; *Stableford* v. *Liverpool General Comrs.* [1983]

1970—cont.

9. Taxes Management Act 1970—cont.

S.T.C. 162, Vinelott J.; *Jolley* v. *Bolton General Comrs. and I.R.C.* [1986] S.T.C. 414, Scott J.; *Cox* v. *Poole General Commissioners and I.R.C.* [1988] S.T.C. 66, Knox J.

s. 93, amended: 1988, c.1, sch.29, repealed in pt. (prosp.): 1988, c.39, sch.14.

s. 94, substituted: 1987, c.51, s.83; amended: 1988, c.1, sch.29.

s. 95, see *R.* v. *Havering Comrs., ex p. Knight* [1973] T.R. 235, C.A.; *Williams* v. *Commissioners for the Special Purposes of the Income Tax Acts* [1975] S.T.C. 167; *Taylor* v. *Bethnal Green Commissioners* [1977] S.T.C. 44; *Sparks* v. *West Brixton General Commissioners* [1976] S.T.C. 212, Ch.D.; *B. & S. Displays* v. *I.R.C.* [1978] S.T.C. 331, Goulding J.; *Re Hurren (A Bankrupt), ex p. The Trustee* v. *I.R.C.* [1982] 3 All E.R. 982, Walton J.; *Jolley* v. *Bolton General Comrs. and I.R.C.* [1986] S.T.C. 414, Scott J.; *Lear* v. *Leek General Comrs. and I.R.C.* [1986] S.T.C. 542, Vinelott J.; *Brodt* v. *Wells General Comrs. and I.R.C.* [1987] S.T.C. 207, Scott J.

s. 95, amended: 1988, c.1, sch.29; repealed in pt.: (prosp.); 1988, c.39, sch.14.

s. 97A, added: *ibid.*, s.129.

s. 98, see *Script & Play Productions* v. *I.R.C.* [1972] 1 W.L.R. 392; [1972] 1 All E.R. 577; *Shah* v. *General Comrs. for Hampstead* [1974] S.T.C. 438; *Chapman* v. *General Comrs. of Income Tax for the District of Sheaf* [1975] S.T.C. 170; *Toogood* v. *British General Comrs.* [1976] S.T.C. 250; *R.* v. *Board of Inland Revenue ex p. Goldberg, The Times,* May 3, 1988, D.C.; *Boulton* v. *Poole General Commissioners, The Times,* June 18, 1988, Vinelott J.

s. 98, amended: 1972, c.41, ss.78,79, 81,82, schs.12,24; 1973, c.51, ss.21,32,38, sch.15; 1974, c.30, sch.10; 1975, c.7, ss.9,17, sch.1; c.45, ss.34,69,70, sch.8; 1976, c.40, sch.4; 1978, c.42, s.53; 1981, c.35, s.138; 1982, c.39, schs.7,9; 1983, c.28, s.26; 1984, c.43, ss.26, 35, 38, 40, 90, schs.8. 14; 1985, c.54, ss.38, 40, schs. 13, 22, 23; 1986, c.41, s.28, schs.9, 11, 12; 1987, c.16, s.35; c.51, ss.14, 51, sch.5; 1988, c.1, sch.29; c.39, s.85; repealed in pt.: 1978, c.42, sch.14; 1985, c.54, sch.27; 1988, c.39, sch.14; modified: 1975, c.22, sch.2.

s. 99, see *Lord Advocate* v. *Ruffle* (O.H.), March 16, 1979.

s. 100, see *Script & Play Productions* v. *I.R.C.* [1972] 1 W.L.R. 392; [1972] 1 All E.R. 577; *Stableford* v. *Liverpool General Comrs.* [1983] S.T.C. 162, Vinelott J.; *Brodt* v. *Wells General Comrs. and I.R.C.* [1987] S.T.C. 207, Scott J.; *Cox* v. *Poole General Commissioners and I.R.C.* [1988] S.T.C. 66, Knox J.

s. 100, amended: 1976, c.24, sch.8.

ss. 100, 103, see *Willey* v. *I.R.C.* [1985] S.T.C. 56, Scott J.

s. 101, see *Sparks* v. *West Brixton General Commissioners* [1976] S.T.C. 212, Ch.D.

s. 101, amended: 1976, c.24, sch.8.

CAP.

1970—cont.

9. Taxes Management Act 1970—*cont.*

s. 103, see *R.* v. *I.R.C., ex p. Knight* [1973] 3 All E.R. 721, C.A., *sub nom. R.* v. *Havering Comrs., ex p. Knight* [1973] T.R. 235, C.A.; *Carco Accessories* v. *I.R.C.* [1985] S.T.C. 518, C.A.

s. 103, amended: 1976, c.24, sch.8.

s. 108, amended: *ibid.*; 1985, c.9, sch.2.

s. 109, substituted: 1972, c.41, sch.24; amended: 1975, c.45, s.46; 1987, c.51, s.91; 1988, c.1, sch.29; repealed in pt.: 1987, c.51, s.91.

s. 111, amended: 1976, c.24, sch.8; 1979, c.14, sch.7.

s. 112, amended: 1976, c.24, sch.8.

s. 114, see *Baylis (Inspector of Taxes)* v. *Gregory, The Times,* April 2, 1987, C.A.

s. 118, see *Johnson* v. *Scott* [1977] T.R. 151, Walton J.; *R.* v. *General Comrs. of Tax for Tavistock, ex p. Adams (No. 2)* (1971) 48 T.C. 56; *Napier* v. *I.R.C.* [1977], T.R. 289, D.C.; *Johnson* v. *Scott* [1978] T.R. 121, C.A.

s. 118, amended: 1976, c.24, sch.8; c.40, s.57; 1979, c.14, sch.7; 1987, c.51, s.94; 1988, c.1, sch.29; repealed in pt.: *ibid.*, sch.31.

sch. 1, substituted: 1972, c.41, sch.24; amended: 1975, c.7, s.57; 1980, c.48, s.121.

sch. 2, amended: 1988, c.1, sch.29; repealed in pt.: *ibid.*, sch.31.

sch. 3, see *I.R.C., ex p. Knight* [1973] 3 All E.R. 721, C.A.; *sub nom. R.* v. *Havering Comrs., ex p. Knight* [1973] T.R. 235, C.A.

sch. 3, amended: 1972, c.41, sch.24; 1975, c.45, s.66; 1976, c.24, sch.8; c.40, sch.9; 1984, c.43, sch.22; 1988, c.1, sch.29; repealed in pt.: 1972, c.41, schs.24,28; 1975, c.45, sch.14; 1988, c.39, sch.14.

sch. 4, see *R.* v. *General Comrs. of Tax for Tavistock, ex p. Adams (No. 2)* (1971) 48 T.C. 56.

sch. 4, repealed in pt.: 1975, c.45, sch.14; 1978, c.23, sch.7; 1982, c.39, sch.22.

sch. 8, see *Worthing Rugby Football Club Trustees* v. *I.R.C.* [1985] 1 W.L.R. 409, Gibson J.

10. Income and Corporation Taxes Act 1970.

s. 1, see *Wilson* v. *Alexander* [1986] S.T.C. 365, Harman J.

s. 1, repealed in pt.: 1988, c.39, sch.14.

ss. 1–8, repealed: 1988, c.1, sch.31.

s. 4, see *Bird* v. *I.R.C.; Breams Nominees* v. *I.R.C.* [1988] 2 W.L.R. 1237, H.L.

s. 8, see *Binks* v. *Department of the Environment* [1975] Crim.L.R. 244, D.C.; *Nabi (Ghulam)* v. *Heaton* [1983] 1 W.L.R. 626, C.A.

s. 8, amended: order 88/503.

ss. 9–107, repealed: 1988, c.1, sch.31.

s. 10, see *Barry* v. *Hughes* [1973] 1 All E.R. 537; *Murphy* v. *Ingram* [1973] 2 W.L.R. 983; *Robertson* v. *Walton* [1977] 1 W.L.R. 177; [1977] 1 All E.R. 465; *Eke* v. *Knight* [1977] T.R. 7, C.A.; *Buxton* v. *Buxton* [1978] S.T.C. 122, Brightman J.; *Nwagbo* v. *Rising* [1978] S.T.C. 558, Fox J.; *Aspden* v. *Baxi* [1979] S.T.C. 566;

CAP.

1970—cont.

10. Income and Corporation Taxes Act 1970—*cont.*

(1979) 52 T.C. 586, Brightman J.; *Gibbs* v. *Randall* [1981] S.T.C. 106, Goulding J.; *Aspen* v. *Prinja* [1981] S.T.C. 526, Vinelott J.

s. 11, see *Buxton* v. *Buxton* [1978] S.T.C. 122, Brightman J.

s. 11, amended: 1988, c.39, s.134.

s. 16, see *Eke* v. *Knight* [1977] T.R. 7, C.A.; *Eglen (Inspector of Taxes)* v. *Butcher, The Times,* July 3, 1988, Morritt J.

s. 18, see *Edwards* v. *Clinch, The Times,* May 10, 1980, C.A.

s. 27, see *I.R.C* v. *Addison* [1984] 1 W.L.R. 1264, Mervyn Davies J.

s. 30, see *McCartney* v. *Freilich* [1981] S.T.C. 79; [1981] 1 W.L.R. 431, Goulding J.

s. 34, see *Vaughan-Neil* v. *I.R.C.* [1979] 1 W.L.R. 1283, Oliver J.

s. 37, see *Murphy* v. *Ingram* [1973] 2 W.L.R. 983; *Hotter* v. *Spackman* [1982] S.T.C. 483, C.A.; *I.R.C.* v. *Addison* [1984] 1 W.L.R. 1264, Mervyn Davies J.

s. 38, see *Hotter* v. *Spackman* [1982] S.T.C. 483, C.A.

s. 40, see *Johnson* v. *I.R.C.* [1977] T.R. 243; [1978] 2 All E.R. 65, C.A.

s. 42, see *Gubay* v. *Kington* [1984] 1 W.L.R. 163, H.L.

s. 49, see *Reed* v. *Clark* [1985] S.T.C. 323, D.C.

s. 50, see *Robson* v. *Dixon* [1972] 1 W.L.R. 1493; [1972] 3 All E.R. 671; *Donnelly* v. *Platten (H.M. Inspector of Taxes)* [1980] 10 N.I.J.B., C.A.

ss. 51A, 51B, added: 198, c.39, s.36.

s. 52, see *I.R.C.* v. *Plummer* [1979] 3 W.L.R. 689, H.L.; *McBurnie (Inspector of Taxes)* v. *Tacey* [1984] 1 W.L.R. 1019, Gibson J.; *Essex County Council* v. *Ellam (Inspector of Taxes* [1988] T.C.T. 370, Hoffmann J.

ss. 52, 53, see *I.R.C.* v. *Crawley* [1987] S.T.C. 147, Vinelott J.

s. 53, see *I.R.C.* v. *Plummer* [1979] 3 W.L.R. 689, H.L.

s. 54, see *Re Euro Hotel (Belgravia)* [1975] 3 All E.R. 1075; *Chevron Petroleum (U.K.)* v. *B.P. Petroleum Development* [1981] S.T.C. 689, Megarry V.-C.; *Hafton Properties* v. *McHugh (Inspector of Taxes)* [1987] S.T.C. 16, Gibson J.

s. 62, see *Law* v. *Coburn* [1972] 1 W.L.R. 1238; [1972] 3 All E.R. 1115.

s. 65, see *McBurnie (Inspector of Taxes)* v. *Tacey* [1984] 1 W.L.R. 1019, Gibson J.; *Finnie* v. *Finnie* [1984] S.T.C. 598, Ct. of Session.

s. 65, orders 72/436; 80/951; 86/328.

s. 67, see *Gittos* v. *Barclay* [1982] S.T.C. 390, Goulding J.; *Jeffries* v. *Stevens* [1982] S.T.C. 639, Walton J.; *Griffiths* v. *Jackson; Griffiths* v. *Pearman* [1983] S.T.C. 184, Vinelott J.; *McClure (Inspector of Taxes)* v. *Petre, The Times,* July 14, 1988, Browne-Wilkinson V.-C.

s. 67, amended: 1988, c.39, sch.6; repealed in pt.: *ibid.*, sch.14.

s. 68, see *Aplin* v. *White* [1973] 2 All E.R. 637.

CAP.

1970—cont.

10. Income and Corporation Taxes Act 1970— *cont.*

s. 80, see *Banning* v. *Wright* [1972] 1 W.L.R. 972; [1972] T.R. 105.

ss. 91, 92, see *Russell* v. *Hird* [1983] S.T.C. 541, Warner J.

Pt. IV (ss.91, 92), repealed: 1988, c.39, sch.14.

s. 98, see *B. & S. Displays* v. *I.R.C.* [1978] S.T.C. 331, Goulding J.

s. 100, see *Nothman* v. *Cooper* [1971] T.R. 513.

s. 108, see *McMann* v. *Shaw* [1972] 1 W.L.R. 1578; [1972] 3 All E.R. 732; *Willingale* v. *International Commercial Bank* [1978] 2 W.L.R. 452, H.L.; *Inland Revenue* v. *Titaghur Jute Factory Co.*, First Division, December 30, 1977; *Alloway* v. *Phillips* [1980] 1 W.L.R. 888, C.A.; *Griffiths* v. *Jackson; Griffiths* v. *Pearman* [1983] S.T.C. 184, Vinelott J.; *Ditchfield* v. *Sharp* [1983] S.T.C. 590; [1983] 3 All E.R. 681, C.A.; *Reed (Inspector of Taxes)* v. *Clark* [1985] 3 W.L.R. 142, Nicholls J.; *Aspin* v. *Estill* [1986] S.T.C. 323, Ch.D.; *Dawson* v. *I.R.C.* [1987] 1 W.L.R. 716, Vinelott J.; *Marson* v. *Morton* [1986] 1 W.L.R. 1343, Browne-Wilkinson V.-C.; *Dawson* v. *I.R.C.*, *The Daily Telegraph*, May 27, 1988, C.A.; *Jones (Inspector of Taxes)* v. *O'Brien*, *The Times*, June 15, 1988, Hoffmann J.

ss. 108, 109, see *I.R.C.* v. *Aken*, *The Times*, December 15, 1987, Piers Ashworth Q.C.

ss. 108, 109, repealed in pt.: 1988, c.39, sch.14.

ss. 108–129, repealed: 1988, c.1, sch.31.

s. 109, see *Peck* v. *Morton* [1972] T.R. 137; *McMann* v. *Shaw* [1972] 1 W.L.R. 1578; [1972] 3 All E.R. 732; *Duff* v. *Williamson* [1973] T.R. 171, Plowman J.; *Aplin* v. *White* [1973] 2 All E.R. 637; *Ransom* v. *Higgs* [1973] 2 All E.R. 657; *Taylor* v. *Good* [1973] 2 All E.R. 785; *Inland Revenue* v. *Titaghur Jute Factory Co.*, First Division, December 30, 1977; *I.R.C.* v. *Plummer* [1979] 3 W.L.R. 689, H.L.; *Ockenden* v. *Mackley* [1982] 1 W.L.R. 787, Nourse J.; *Griffiths* v. *Jackson; Griffiths* v. *Pearman* [1983] S.T.C. 184, Vinelott J.; *Ditchfield* v. *Sharp* [1983] S.T.C. 590, C.A.; *Parkside Leasing* v. *Smith (Inspector of Taxes)* [1985] 1 W.L.R. 310, Scott J.; *Aspin* v. *Estill* [1986] S.T.C. 323, Ch.D.

s. 110, see *Sargent* v. *Eayrs* [1973] 1 W.L.R. 236; [1973] 1 All E.R. 277; *Webb (Inspector of Taxes)* v. *Conlee Properties* [1982] S.T.C. 913, Warner J.

s. 110, amended: 1988, c.39, sch.6.

s. 111, repealed: *ibid.*, schs. 6, 14.

s. 114, see *Aplin* v. *White* [1973] 2 All E.R. 637; *Ransom* v. *Higgs* [1973] 2 All E.R. 657; *Macpherson* v. *Bond (Inspector of Taxes)* [1985] 1 W.L.R. 1157; [1985] S.T.C. 675, Vinelott J.; *Dawson* v. *I.R.C.* [1987] 1 W.L.R. 716, Vinelott J.

s. 116, see *R.* v. *Havering Commissioners, ex p. Knight* [1973] T.R. 235, C.A.

s. 117, amended: 1987, c.16, sch. 15.

CAP.

1970—cont.

10. Income and Corporation Taxes Act 1970— *cont.*

s. 118, see *I.R.C.* v. *Helical Bar* [1972] 2 W.L.R. 880; [1972] 1 All E.R. 1205; *Watts (Trading as A.A. Watts)* v. *Hart* [1984] S.T.C. 548, Mervyn Davies J.

ss. 119, 120, see *Beese* v. *Mackinlay* [1980] S.T.C. 228, Vinelott J.; *Moore* v. *Austin* [1985] S.T.C. 673, Browne-Wilkinson V.-C.

s. 120, see *Sinsbury* v. *O'Brien* [1971] T.R. 397.

s. 122, see *Buswell* v. *I.R.C.* [1973] T.R. 27; *Newstead* v. *Frost* [1980] 1 W.L.R. 135, H.L.; *I.R.C.* v. *Duchess of Portland* [1982] 2 W.L.R. 367, Nourse J.; *Ockenden* v. *Mackley* [1982] 1 W.L.R. 787, Nourse J.

s. 122, amended: 1974, c.30, sch.1; 1979, c.47, s.10; 1987, c.16, sch.16; repealed in pt.: 1972, c.41, s.75, sch.28; 1974, c.30, s.23, sch.14.

s. 125, see *Sinsbury* v. *O'Brien* [1971] T.R. 397.

s. 129, see *Marshall Hus & Partners* v. *Bolton* [1981] S.T.C. 18, Goulding J.

s. 130, see *Odeon Associated Theatres* v. *Jones* [1972] 2 W.L.R. 331; [1972] 1 All E.R. 681; *Bamford* v. *A.T.A. Advertising* [1972] 1 W.L.R. 1261; [1972] 3 All E.R. 535; *Heather* v. *P.-E. Consulting Group* [1972] 3 W.L.R. 833; [1973] 1 All E.R. 8; *Sargent* v. *Eayrs* [1973] 1 W.L.R. 236; [1973] 1 All E.R. 277; *Caillebotte* v. *Quinn* [1975] 1 W.L.R. 731; *Milnes* v. *J. Beam Group* [1975] T.R. 127; *Wynne-Jones* v. *Bedale Auction* [1977] S.T.C. 50; *Sargent* v. *Barnes* [1978] 1 W.L.R. 823, Oliver J.; *Tucker* v. *Granada Motorway Services* [1979] 1 W.L.R. 683, H.L.; *Bolton* v. *Halpern & Woolf (A Firm)* [1979] S.T.C. 761, Oliver J.; *Mason* v. *Tyson*, *The Times*, February 20, 1980, Walton J.; *Brown* v. *Burnley Football and Athletic Co.* [1980] 3 All E.R. 244, Vinelott J.; *Garforth* v. *Tankard Carpets* [1980] S.T.C. 251, Walton J.; *Dollar (Trading as I. J. Dollar)* v. *Lyon* [1981] S.T.C. 333, Vinelott J.; *Robinson* v. *Scott Bader Co.* [1981] 1 W.L.R. 1135, C.A.; *Pattison* v. *Marine Midland* [1981] 3 W.L.R. 673, Vinelott J.; *Walker* v. *Joint Credit Card Co.* [1982] S.T.C. 427, Walton J.; *Watney Combe Reid & Co.* v. *Pike; Watneys London* v. *Pike* [1982] S.T.C. 733, Walton J.; *Webb* v. *Conlee Properties*, *The Times*, November 3, 1982, Warner J.; *Mallalieu* v. *Drummond* [1983] 3 W.L.R. 409, H.L.: *Whitehead* v. *Tubbs (Elastics)* [1984] S.T.C. 1, C.A.; *O'Keefe* v. *Southport Printers* [1984] S.T.C. 433, Nourse J.; *Watkis (Inspector of Taxes)* v. *Ashford Sparkes & Harward* [1985] S.T.C. 693; [1985] 1 W.L.R. 994, Nourse J.; *Bott (E.)* v. *Price*, *The Times*, December 8, 1986, Hoffmann J.; *Mackinlay (Inspector of Taxes)* v. *Arthur Young McClelland Moores & Co.* [1986] 1 W.L.R. 1468, Vinelott J.; *Bott (E.)* v. *Price (Inspector of Taxes)* [1987] S.T.C. 100; Hoffmann J.; *R.T.Z. Oil and Gas* v. *Elliss (Inspector of Taxes* [1987] 1 W.L.R. 1442, Vinelott J.; *Mackinlay* v. *Arthur Young McClelland Moores & Co.* [1988] S.T.C. 116, C.A.;

1970—cont.

10. Income and Corporation Taxes Act 1970—cont.

Beauchamp (Inspector of Taxes) v. Woolworth (F. W.), The Times, August 1, 1988, C.A.

ss. 130–180, repealed: 1988, c.1, sch.31.

s. 137, see Moore v. Mackenzie & Sons [1972] 1 W.L.R. 359; [1972] 2 All E.R. 549; [1971] T.R. 457; Walker v. Cater Securities [1974] 3 All E.R. 63.

s. 154, see Watts (Trading as A.A. Watts) v. Hart [1984] S.T.C. 548, Mervyn Davies J.

s. 156, see Holland v. Geoghegan [1972] 1 W.L.R. 1473; [1972] 3 All E.R. 333.

s. 167, see Macpherson v. Hall [1972] T.R. 41.

s. 168, see R. v. Havering Comrs., ex p. Knight [1973] T.R. 235, C.A.; Salt v. Chamberlain (1979) S.T.C. 750, Oliver J.; Butt v. Haxby [1983] S.T.C. 239, Vinelott. J.; Reed v. Young [1986] 1 W.L.R. 649, H.L.

ss. 168, 169, 171, amended: 1988, c.39, sch.6; repealed in pt.: (prosp.): ibid., sch.14.

s. 174, repealed in pt. (prosp.): ibid.

s. 177, see Robroyston Brickworks v. I.R.C. [1976] S.T.C. 329; Willis (H.M. Inspector of Taxes) v. Peeters Picture Frames [1982] 12 N.I.J.B., C.A.; Whitehead v. Tubbs (Elastic) [1984] S.T.C. 1, C.A.

s. 181, see Graham v. White [1972] 1 W.L.R. 874; [1972] 1 All E.R. 1159; [1971] T.R. 477; Moore v. Griffiths [1972] 1 W.L.R. 1024; [1972] T.R. 61; Fall v. Hitchen [1973] 1 All E.R. 368, McMann v. Shaw [1972] 1 W.L.R. 1578; [1972] 3 All E.R. 732; Gare v. Parry [1975] S.T.C. 79; Bramby v. Milner; Day v. Quick [1976] 1 W.L.R. 1096; [1976] 3 All E.R. 636, H.L.; Esslemont v. Estill [1980] S.T.C. 620, C.A.; Edwards v. Clinch [1981] 3 W.L.R. 707, H.L.; Donnelly v. Williamson [1982] S.T.C. 88, Walton J., Bird v. Martland; Bird v. Allen [1982] S.T.C. 603, Walton J.; Williams v. Simmonds [1981] S.T.C. 715, Vinelott J.; Glantre Engineering v. Goodhand [1983] 1 All E.R. 542, Warner J.; McGregor (Inspector of Taxes) v. Randall [1984] 1 All E.R. 1092, Scott J.; Richardson v. Worrall; Westall v. McDonald [1985] S.T.C. 693, Scott J.; Wilson v. Alexander [1986] S.T.C. 365, Harman J.; Hamblett v. Godfrey (Inspector of Taxes) [1987] 1 W.L.R. 357, C.A.; Bray (Inspector of Taxes) v. Best [1988] S.T.C. 103, C.A.

ss. 181–188, repealed: 1988, c.1, sch.31.

s. 182, see Gare v. Parry [1975] S.T.C. 79.

s. 183, see Brumby v. Milner, Day v. Quick [1976] 1 W.L.R. 1096; [1976] 3 All E.R. 636, H.L.; Jenkins v. Horn [1979] 2 All E.R. 1141, Browne-Wilkinson J.; Perrons v. Spackman, The Times, July 7, 1981, Vinelott J.; Bird v. Martland; Bird v. Allen [1982] S.T.C. 603, Walton J.; Donnelly v. Williamson [1982] S.T.C. 88; (1981) 80 L.G.R. 289, Walton J.; Glantre Engineering v. Goodhand [1983] 1 All E.R. 542, Warner J.; Beecham Group v. Fair [1984] S.T.C. 15, Walton J.; McGregor v. Randall [1984] 1 All E.R. 1092, Scott J.

1970—cont.

10. Income and Corporation Taxes Act 1970—cont.

Wilson v. Alexander [1986] S.T.C. 365, Harman J.; Hamblett v. Godfrey (Inspector of Taxes) [1987] 1 W.L.R. 357, C.A.

s. 184, see Caldicott v. Varty [1976] 3 All E.R. 329; [1976] S.T.C. 418.

s. 186, see Williamson v. Dalton [1981] S.T.C. 753, Vinelott J.; McGregor (Inspector of Taxes) v. Randall [1984] 1 All E.R. 1092, Scott J.

s. 187, see March v. Pearson [1976] S.T.C. 22; Williams v. Simmonds [1981] S.T.C. 715, Vinelott J.; McGregor (Inspector of Taxes) v. Randall [1984] 1 All E.R. 1092, Scott J.

ss. 187, 188, see Wienand v. Anderton [1977] S.T.C. 12; [1977] 1 All E.R. 384; Warnett v. Jones [1980] I.C.R. 539; [1980] 1 W.L.R. 413; (1982) 53 T.C. 283, Slade J.

s. 189, see Owen v. Burden [1972] 1 All E.R. 356; Lucas v. Cattell [1972] T.R. 83; Taylor v. Provan [1973] 2 W.L.R. 675; [1973] 2 All E.R. 65, C.A.; Woodcock v. I.R.C. [1977] T.R. 147, Walton J.; Ward v. Dunn [1979] S.T.C. 178, Walton J.; Perrons v. Spackman, The Times, July 7, 1981, Vinelott J.; Donnelly v. Williamson [1982] S.T.C. 88; (1981) 80 L.G.R. 289, Walton J.; Shaw v. Tonkin (Inspector of Taxes) [1988] S.T.C. 186, Walton J.; Parikh v. Sleeman (Inspector of Taxes), The Times, May 25, 1988, Vinelott J.; Bhadra v. Ellam (Inspector of Taxes) [1988] S.T.C. 239, Knox J.; Elderkin (Inspector of Taxes) v. Hindmarsh [1988] S.T.C. 267, Vinelott J.

ss. 189–237, repealed: 1988, c.1, sch.31.

ss. 191, 192, see Shaw v. Tonkin (Inspector of Taxes [1988] S.T.C. 186, Walton J.

s. 195, see Wilson v. Alexander. [1986] S.T.C. 365, Harman J.

ss. 195–203, repealed: 1976, c.40, schs.9,15.

s. 196, see Taylor v. Provan [1973] 2 W.L.R. 675; [1973] 2 All E.R. 65, C.A.

s. 204, see Garforth v. Newsmith Stainless [1979] 1 W.L.R. 409; [1979] S.T.C. 129, Walton J.; R. v. General Comrs. for Income Tax, ex p. Wilson, The Times, April 14, 1981, Slade J.; Clark v. Oceanic Contractors Inc. (1982) 56 T.C. 183; [1983] 2 W.L.R. 94, H.L.; I.R.C. v. Findlay McClure & Co. (O.H.), 1986 S.L.T. 417.

s. 204, regs. 72/552, 1186; 73/334; 74/340, 2102; 75/91, 728; 76/381, 950; 77/700; 78/326, 1196; 79/747; 80/505; 81/44; 82/1, 66; 84/1858; 85/350; 86/2212; 88/637, 640.

s. 204, amended: 1987, c.51, s.92.

s. 205, see Woodcock v. I.R.C. [1977] T.R. 147, Walton J.

s. 206, regs. 81/1648.

s. 219, see Peter Willows v. Lewis [1981] T.R. 439, Sir Douglas Frank Q.C.; McBurnie v. Tacey [1984] 1 W.L.R. 1019, Gibson J.

s. 226, repealed in pt.: 1988, c.39, sch.14.

s. 238, amended: 1972, c.41, s.111; repealed in pt.: 1988, c.1, sch.31; (prosp.) c.39, sch.14.

CAP.

1970—cont.

10. Income and Corporation Taxes Act 1970— cont.

ss. 238, 243, see *Inland Revenue* v. *Titaghur Jute Factory Co.*, First Division, December 30, 1977.

ss. 239–266, repealed: 1988, c.1, sch.31.

s. 247, see *Inland Revenue* v. *Titaghur Jute Factory Co.*, First Division, December 30, 1977; *R. v. Comr. for the Special Purposes of the Income Tax Acts, ex p. Stipple Choice* [1985] 2 All E.R. 465, C.A.

s. 248, see *Willingdale* v. *Islington Green Investment Co.* [1972] 1 W.L.R. 1533; [1972] 3 All E.R. 849; *Wilcock* v. *Frigate Investments* [1982] S.T.C. 198, Nourse J.

s. 250, see *Owton Fens Properties* v. *Redden* [1984] S.T.C. 618, D.C.

s. 252, see *J. H. & S. (Timber)* v. *Quirke* [1972] T.R. 311.

s. 258, see *Pilkington Bros.* v. *I.R.C.*, *The Times*, December 23, 1980, Nourse J.; *Irving* v. *Tesco Stores (Holdings)* [1982] S.T.C. 881, Walton J.

s. 267, amended: 1977, c.36, s.41; 1979, c.14, sch.7; 1980, c.48, s.81; 1987, c.51, sch.6; 1988, c.1, sch.29; repealed in pt.: 1987, c.51, s.81, sch.20.

s. 268A, substituted for s. 268; 1977, c.36, s.42; amended: 1979, c.14, sch.7.

s. 269, see *Clark (C. & J.)* v. *I.R.C.* [1973] 1 W.L.R. 905; [1973] 2 All E.R. 513.

s. 269, amended: 1979, c.14, sch.7; 1981, c.61, s.38; repealed in pt.: *ibid.*, s.38, sch.19.

s. 270, amended: 1984, c.43, sch.13; 1985, c.54, s.67; repealed in pt.: 1977, c.36, sch.9; 1985, c.54, sch.27.

s. 271, repealed in pt.: 1977, c.36, sch.9.

s. 272, amended: 1984, c.32, sch.6; c.43, s.44; 1985, c.9, sch.2; 1987, c.51, s.79; 1988, c.1, sch.29; repealed in pt.: 1984, c.32, schs.6, 7.

ss. 272, 273, see *Burman* v. *Hedges & Butler* [1979] 1 W.L.R. 160, Walton J.

s. 273, see *Innocent (Inspector of Taxes)* v. *Whaddon Estates* [1982] S.T.C. 115, Walton J.

s. 273, amended: 1979, c.14, sch.7; 1980, c.48, s.81; 1987, c.51, s.64; 1988, c.1, sch.29.

s. 274, see *Coates (Inspector of Taxes)* v. *Arndale Properties* [1984] 1 W.L.R. 1328, H.L.; *Reed* v. *Nova Securities* [1985] 1 W.L.R. 193, H.L.

s. 274, amended: 1979, c.14, sch.7.

s. 275, amended: *ibid.*; 1980, c.48, s.81.

s. 276, amended: 1979, c.14, sch.7; 1987, c.51, s.64; 1988, c.1, sch.29.

s. 277, repealed: *ibid.*, sch.31.

s. 278, amended: 1979, c.14, sch.7; 1987, c.51, sch.6; 1988, c.1, sch.29; repealed in pt.: 1977, c.51, sch.6.

s. 279, amended: 1979, c.14, sch.7.

s. 280, repealed: 1988, c.39, sch.14.

ss. 282–305, repealed: 1988, c.1, sch.31.

s. 285, see *Willingdale* v. *Islington Green Investment Co.* [1972] 1 W.L.R. 1533; [1972] 3 All E.R. 849.

CAP.

1970—cont.

10. Income and Corporation Taxes Act 1970— cont.

s. 290, see *Noble* v. *Laygate Investments* [1978] 2 All E.R. 1067, Oliver J.; *Shearer* v. *Bercain* [1980] 3 All E.R. 295, Walton J.

ss. 296, 298, see *Lothbury Investment Corp.* v. *I.R.C.* [1979] 3 All E.R. 860; (1982) 53 T.C.223, Goulding J.

ss. 297, 298, see *Clark (C. & J.)* v. *I.R.C.* [1973] 1 W.L.R. 905; [1973] 2 All E.R. 513.

s. 303, see *Willingdale* v. *Islington Green Investment Co.* [1972] 1 W.L.R. 1533; [1972] 3 All E.R. 849; *Sherwood Philip Piratin* v. *I.R.C.* [1981] T.R. 93, D.C.

s. 304, see *Hoechst Finance* v. *Gumbrell* [1983] S.T.C. 150, C.A.

s. 306, amended: 1988, c.1, sch.29.

ss. 307–341A, repealed: *ibid.*, sch.31.

s. 312, see *United Friendly Insurance Co.* v. *Eady* [1973] T.R. 37.

s. 316, see *"B": Sun Life Assurance Co. of Canada* v. *Pearson* [1986] S.T.C. 335, C.A.

s. 342, amended: 1985, c.71, sch.1; 1988, c.50, sch.17.

s. 342A, added: 1974, c.44, s.11; amended: 1985, c.71, sch.1.

s. 342B, added: 1984, c.43, s.56.

s. 343, see *R.* v. *I.R.C.*, *ex p. Woolwich Equitable Building Society* [1987] S.T.C. 654, Nolan J.

s. 343, regs. 86/482; 87/844.

ss. 343–535, repealed: 1988, c.1, sch.31.

s. 351, repealed in pt.: 1988, c.39, sch.14.

s. 353, see *Essex County Council* v. *Ellam (Inspector of Taxes)*, *The Times*, November 6, 1987, Hoffmann J.

s. 354A, regs. 88/267.

s. 360, see *I.R.C.* v. *Helen Slater Charitable Trust* [1981] 3 W.L.R. 377, C.A.

s. 360, repealed in pt.: 1988, c.39, sch.14.

s. 365, amended: order 88/1843.

s. 375, see *Mason* v. *Harman* [1972] R.T.R. 1; *Wicks* v. *Firth (Inspector of Taxes)*; *Johnson* v. *Firth* [1983] 2 W.L.R. 34, H.L.

s. 411, see *Fleming* v. *Associated Newspapers* [1971] 3 W.L.R. 551; [1971] 2 All E.R. 1526.

s. 434, see *I.R.C.* v. *Plummer* (1979) 3 W.L.R. 689, H.L.

s. 437, see *Harvey (Inspector of Taxes)* v. *Sivyer* [1985] 3 W.L.R. 261; [1985] S.T.C. 434, Nourse J.; *I.R.C.* v. *Craw* [1985] S.T.C. 512, Ct. of Sessions; First Division, June 5, 1985; *Butler (Inspector of Taxes)* v. *Wildin (Garry)*; *Same* v. *Gildin (Graham)*, *The Times*, November 16, 1988, Vinelott J.

ss. 437, 444, see *d'Abreu* v. *I.R.C.* [1978] S.T.C. 538, Oliver J.

s. 444, see *Harvey (Inspector of Taxes)* v. *Sivyer* [1985] 3 W.L.R. 261; [1985] S.T.C. 434, Nourse J.

s. 447, see *Mills* v. *I.R.C.* [1972] 3 W.L.R. 980; [1972] 3 All E.R. 977.

s. 448, see *Blausten* v. *I.R.C.* [1972] 2 W.L.R. 376; [1972] 1 All E.R. 41; [1971] T.R. 363.

ss. 451, 454, 455, see *Piratin* v. *I.R.C.* [1981] S.T.C. 441; [1981] T.R. 93, Slade J.

1970—cont.

10. Income and Corporation Taxes Act 1970— cont.

ss. 452, 454, see *Mills* v. *I.R.C.* [1972] 3 W.L.R. 980; [1972] 3 All E.R. 977.

s. 453, see *Wilover Nominees* v. *I.R.C.* [1973] 2 All E.R. 977; [1973] S.T.C. 420; [1974] 1 W.L.R. 1342; [1974] 3 All E.R. 496, C.A.

s. 454, see *I.R.C.* v. *Levy, The Times*, April 21, 1982; [1982] S.T.C. 442, Nourse J.

s. 457, see *I.R.C.* v. *Plummer* [1979] 3 W.L.R. 689, H.L.; *Ang* v. *Parrish* [1980] 1 W.L.R. 940; [1980] 2 All E.R. 790; (1982) 53 T.C. 304, Walton J.; *Watson* v. *Holland* [1984] S.T.C. 372; [1985] 1 All E.R. 290, Gibson J.

s. 460, see *Marks* v. *I.R.C.* [1973] T.R. 185, C.A.; *I.R.C.* v. *Goodwin*; *I.R.C.* v. *Baggley* [1973] 3 All E.R. 545, Walton J.; *Thomas Wade & Sons* v. *I.R.C.* [1975] T.R. 165; *Balen* v. *I.R.C.* [1978] S.T.C. 420, C.A.; *I.R.C.* v. *Wiggins, The Times*, November 21, 1978, Walton J.; *Clark* v. *I.R.C.* [1978] S.T.C. 614; [1979] 1 All E.R. 385, Fox J.; *R.* v. *I.R.C., ex p. Preston* [1984] 3 W.L.R. 945, C.A.; *R.* v. *I.R.C., ex p. Preston* [1985] 2 W.L.R. 836, H.L.

ss. 460–468, see *Anysz* v. *I.R.C.*; *Manolescue* v. *I.R.C.* [1978] S.T.C. 296, Browne-Wilkinson J.; *I.R.C.* v. *Wiggins* [1979] 1 W.L.R. 325, Walton J.; *Williams* v. *I.R.C.* [1980] 3 All E.R. 321, H.L.

ss. 460, 461, see *I.R.C.* v. *Garvin and Rose* [1981] T.R. 215, H.L.; *Bird* v. *I.R.C.*; *Breams Nominees* v. *Same* [1987] 1 F.T.L.R. 361, C.A.

ss. 460, 461, 466, see *Emery* v. *I.R.C.* [1981] S.T.C. 150, Nourse J.

ss. 460, 461, 467, see *I.R.C.* v. *Joiner* [1975] 1 W.L.R. 1701; [1975] 3 All E.R. 1050, H.L.

ss. 460, 463, see *Howard* v. *Borneman (No. 2)*; *Ryan* v. *Borneman (No. 2)* [1973] 3 All E.R. 641, Pennycuick V.-C.

ss. 460, 465, see *R.* v. *I.R.C., ex p. Preston* [1983] 2 All E.R. 300, Woolf J.

ss. 460, 466, see *Bird* v. *I.R.C.*; *Breams Nominees* v. *I.R.C.* [1988] 2 W.L.R. 1237, H.L.

s. 462, see *Balen* v. *I.R.C.* [1978] S.T.C. 420, C.A.

s. 478, see *Vestey* v. *I.R.C., The Times*, August 2, 1977, Walton J.; *Vestey* v. *I.R.C., The Times*, June 5, 1978, Walton J.; *I.R.C.* v. *Schroder* [1983] S.T.C. 480, Vinelott J.; *I.R.C.* v. *Brackett* [1987] 1 F.T.L.R. 8, Hoffmann J.

ss. 478–81, see *Clinch* v. *I.R.C.* [1973] 1 All E.R. 977.

s. 481, see *Royal Bank of Canada* v. *I.R.C.* [1972] 2 W.L.R. 106.

s. 482, see *R.* v. *H.M. Treasury, ex p. Daily Mail and General Trust* [1987] 1 F.T.L.R., Macpherson J.

s. 482, amended: 1988, c.39, s.105; repealed in pt.: *ibid.*, s.105, sch.14.

s. 483, see *Willis (H.M. Inspector of Taxes)* v. *Peeters Picture Frames* [1983] S.T.C. 453, C.A.(N.I.).

s. 488, see *Winterton* v. *Edwards*; *Byfield* v. *Edwards* [1980] 2 All E.R. 56, Slade J.; *R. (Magill)* v. *Special Comrs. of Income Tax*

1970—cont.

10. Income and Corporation Taxes Act 1970— cont.

[1979] N.I. 111, Gibson L.J.; *Chilcott* v. *I.R.C.* [1982] S.T.C. 1, Vinelott J.; *Page* v. *Lowther* [1983] S.T.C. 799, C.A.; *Yuill* v. *Fletcher* [1984] S.T.C. 401, C.A.; *Sugarwhite* v. *Budd (Inspector of Taxes) The Times*, May 23, 1988, C.A.

ss. 488, 489, see *Yuill* v. *Wilson* [1980] 1 W.L.R. 910; [1980] 3 All E.R. 7, H.L.

s. 490, see *Essex* v. *I.R.C.* [1980] S.T.C. 378, C.A.

s. 497, see *Padmore* v. *I.R.C.* [1987] S.T.C. 36, Gibson J.; *Collard (Inspector of Taxes)* v. *Mining and Industrial Holdings* [1988] S.T.C. 15, C.A.; *Union Texas International Corp.* v. *Critchley (Inspector of Taxes), The Times*, September 10, 1988, Harman J.

s. 497, orders 72/1721; 73/1325–30, 1331, 1763, 2096–8; 74/558, 1269–72, 2149; 75/425, 426, 1043, 2189–2191; 76/1342, 1919, 2151, 2152; 77/57, 1297–1300, 1719; 78/183, 184, 282, 785, 787, 1056, 1408; 79/117, 300–303; 80/567, 568, 707–713, 1091, 1528–1532, 1960, 1963; 81/1119, 1120, 1121, 1546, 1815, 1816; 82/714, 1841, 1842; 83/1902, 1903; 84/133, 362–366, 1825, 1826; 85/1996–1998; 86/224; 87/169, 466, 467, 2053–2058.

ss. 501, 505, see *Collard (Inspector of Taxes)* v. *Mining and Industrial Holdings* [1988] S.T.C. 15, C.A.

s. 515, repealed in pt. (prosp.): 1988, c.39, sch.14.

s. 517, regs. 73/317; 80/779, 780; 87/2071.

s. 526, see *R.* v. *General Commissioners of Income Tax for Tavistock, ex p. Adams (No. 2)* (1972) 48 T.C. 46; *Taylor* v. *Good* [1973] 2 All E.R. 785; *Burman* v. *Hedges & Butler* [1979] 1 W.L.R. 160, Walton J.; *Conservative and Unionist Central Office* v. *Burrell* [1982] S.T.C. 317, C.A.; *Tilcon* v. *Holland* [1981] S.T.C. 365, Vinelott J.; *Marson* v. *Morton* [1986] 1 W.L.R. 1343, Browne-Wilkinson V.-C.; *Union Texas International Corp.* v. *Critchley (Inspector of Taxes), The Times*, September 10, 1988, Harman J.

s. 528, see *Aplin* v. *White* [1973] 2 All E.R. 637; *I.R.C.* v. *Addison* [1984] 1 W.L.R. 1264, Mervyn Davies J.; *I.R.C.* v. *Crawley* [1987] S.T.C. 147, Vinelott J.

s. 530, see *Pegler* v. *Abell* [1973] 1 All E.R. 53; *Evans* v. *Pearce* [1974] S.T.C. 46.

s. 530, repealed in pt.: 1988, c.39, sch.14.

s. 534, see *Irving* v. *Tesco Stores (Holdings)* [1982] S.T.C. 881, Walton J.

s. 540, amended: 1979, c.14, sch.7; 1988, c.1, sch.29.

schs. 1–13, repealed: *ibid.*, sch.31.

sch. 7, see *Macpherson* v. *Hall* [1972] T.R. 41.

sch. 10, amended: 1988, c.39, s.61; repealed in pt.: *ibid.*, s.61, sch.14.

sch. 14, amended: 1972, c.41, sch.24; repealed in pt.: *ibid.*, s.75, sch.28; 1988, c.1, sch.31.

sch. 15, order 73/1763.

CAP.

1970—cont.

10. Income and Corporation Taxes Act 1970— *cont.*
sch. 15, repealed in pt.: 1972, c.11, sch.8; 1973, c.36, sch.6; c.38, sch.28; c.51, sch.22; 1974, c.30, sch.14; c.46, sch.11; 1975, c.7, sch.13; c.45, sch.14; 1978, c.42, sch.13; 1982, c.39, sch.22; 1985, c.65, sch.10; c.66, sch.8 (S.); 1987, c.16, sch.16; 1988, c.1, sch.31.
sch. 16, repealed: *ibid.*

11. Sea Fish Industry Act 1970.
repealed except ss. 14, 42, 62: 1981, c.29, sch.5,pt.I.
s. 1, order 78/1822.
s. 6, orders 74/1032; 80/506, 527, 1199.
s. 17, order 80/379.
s. 23, orders 72/1162; 75/111; 76/2230; 78/1821; 80/1972.
s. 35, order 76/2209.
ss. 44, 45, scheme 76/304.
ss. 44, 45, 57, schemes 73/116, 194; 75/360; 76/2136; 77/2136; 78/1820; 79/1692; 80/1973.
s. 49, schemes 72/1171; 74/88; 75/970, 1720, 2224; 79/421.
ss. 57, 58, 61, order 80/506.

12. Consolidated Fund (No. 2) Act 1970.
repealed: 1974, c.31, s.4, sch.

15. Export Guarantees and Payments Act 1970.
repealed: 1975, c.38, s.12.

16. National Health Service Contributions Act 1970.
repealed: 1973, c.38, sch.28.

17. Proceedings Against Estates Act 1970.
repealed: S.L.R. 1986.
s. 2, see *Harris* v. *Monro* (1972) 225 E.G. 1551; *Re Amirteymour (decd.)* [1978] 3 All E.R. 637, C.A.

19. General Rate Act 1970.
repealed (prosp.): 1988, c.41, sch.13.

20. Roads (Scotland) Act 1970.
repealed: 1984, c.54, sch.11.
s. 1, regs. 76/856.
s. 12, see *Grampian Regional Council* v. *City of Aberdeen District Council, The Times,* December 3, 1983, H.L.
ss. 12, 13, regs. 76/63.

21. New Forest Act 1970.
s. 4, repealed: 1974, c.7, sch.8.

22. Tonga Act 1970.
s. 2, repealed: 1981, c.61, sch.9.
sch. amended: 1973, c.36, sch.6; repealed in pt.: S.L.R. 1976; 1981, c.9, sch.9.

23. Road Traffic (Disqualification) Act 1970.
repealed: 1972, c.20, sch.9.
s. 1, see *R.* v. *Bain* [1973] R.T.R. 213, C.A.; *R.* v. *Bowsher* [1973] R.T.R. 202, C.A.; *R.* v. *Sibthorpe* (1973) 57 Cr.App.R. 447, C.A.

24. Finance Act 1970.
s. 1, repealed: 1974, c.22, sch.; 1979, c.2, sch.6.
s. 2, repealed in pt.: 1972, c.25, sch.7; S.L.R. 1976.
s. 3, repealed: 1972, c.25, sch.7.
s. 4, repealed: 1977, c.36, sch.9.
s. 5, repealed in pt.: *ibid.*

CAP.

1970—cont.

24. Finance Act 1970— *cont.*
s. 6, amended: 1975, c.45, sch.3; repealed in pt.: 1979, c.4, sch.4.
s. 7, repealed in pt.: 1973, c.51, sch.22; 1979, c.2, sch.6; c.4, sch.4.
s. 10, repealed: 1973, c.51, sch.22.
ss. 11–14, repealed: 1988, c.1, sch.31.
s. 15, amended: 1972, c.5, sch.3.
s. 16, repealed: 1988, c.1, sch.31.
s. 17, repealed: 1972, c.41, sch.28.
ss. 19–26, repealed: 1988, c.1, sch.31.
s. 28, repealed in pt.: 1979, c.14, sch.8.
s. 29, amended: 1979, c.14, sch.7; 1988, c.1, sch.29; repealed in pt.: *ibid.*, sch.31.
s. 30, orders 79/1690; 82/1584; 85/561; 86/1942; 87/892; 88/1276, 1619.
ss. 30, 31, repealed: 1975, c.7, sch.13.
s. 33, amended: 1976, c.40, s.127; 1986, c.41, s.83; repealed in pt.: 1976, c.40, sch.15.
s. 34, order 72/1750.
s. 34, repealed: 1980, c.48, sch.20.
s. 35, repealed: 1975, c.83, sch.
s. 36, repealed in pt.: 1979, c.2, sch.6.
sch. 1, repealed in pt.: 1972, c.25, sch.7; S.L.R. 1974.
sch. 2, repealed in pt.: 1972, c.68, sch.3; 1977, c.36, sch.9; 1979, c.2, sch.6.
sch. 3, amended: 1979, c.14, sch.7; 1984, c.32, sch.6; repealed in pt.: *ibid.*, schs.6, 7; 1988, c.1, sch.31.
sch. 4, repealed in pt.: 1972, c.41, s.75, sch.28; 1988, c.1, sch.31.
sch. 5, regs. 87/1749; order 88/504.
sch. 5, repealed: 1988, c.1, sch.31; amended: order 88/504.
sch. 6, amended: 1979, c.14, sch.7; 1988, c.1, sch.29.
sch. 7, repealed in pt.: 1972, c.41, sch.28; 1973, c.51, sch.22; 1974, c.30, sch.14; 1985, c.54, sch.27; 1987, c.51, sch.3.
sch. 8, repealed in pt.: 1972, c.41, sch.28.
sch. 15, repealed in pt.: 1979, c.14, sch.8.

25. Appropriation Act 1970.
repealed: 1974, c.31, s.4, sch.

26. Films Act 1970.
repealed: 1985, c.21, s.1, sch.2.

27. Fishing Vessels (Safety Provisions) Act 1970.
s. 1, rules 75/330; 76/432; 81/567.
s. 1, amended: 1979, c.39, sch.6; repealed in pt.: *ibid.*, s.28, sch.7.
s. 2, rules 75/330; 76/432; 77/313; 78/1598; 84/955.
s. 2, amended: 1986, c.23, s.5.
s. 3, amended and repealed in pt.: *ibid.*
s. 4, amended: 1979, c.39, sch.6.
s. 6, regs. 75/954; 76/2205; 79/631; 81/363; 83/1167; 85/1607; 87/63, 548, 854; 88/1485.
s. 7, rules 76/432; 77/498; 78/1873.
s. 9, amended: 1988, c.12, sch.6.
s. 11, order 75/337.

28. Local Government (Footpath and Open Spaces) (Scotland) Act 1970.
ss. 1, 2, 5 (in pt.), repealed: 1984, c.54, sch.11.
s. 5, amended: 1975, c.30, sch.6; repealed in pt.: 1984, c.54, sch.11.
s. 8, amended: 1973, c.65, sch.14.

1970—cont.

29. Parish Councils and Burial Authorities (Miscellaneous Provisions) Act 1970.
s. 1, amended: order 74/628.
s. 3, repealed: 1984, c.27, sch.14.
s. 5, amended: 1972, c.70, sch.30.

30. Conservation of Seals Act 1970.
ss. 3, 14, order 73/1079.
s. 4, repealed in pt.: 1984, c.60, sch.7.
s. 5, amended: 1977, c.45, s.31, sch.6.
s. 10, amended: 1973, c.54, sch.1; 1981, c.69, sch.7; repealed in pt.: *ibid.*, schs.7,17.

31. Administration of Justice Act 1970.
s. 1, repealed in pt.: 1981, c.54, sch.7.
s. 2, repealed in pt.: S.L.R. 1977; 1981, c.54, sch.7.
ss. 3, 5, 6, 9, repealed: *ibid.*
s. 10, amended: 1977, c.37, sch.5; repealed in pt.: *ibid.*, sch.6.
s. 11, amended: 1973, c.38, sch.27.
s. 12, repealed: 1980, c.43, sch.9.
s. 17, see *Re Davies (decd.)*; *Panton* v. *Jones, The Times,* May 23, 1978, Judge Mervyn Davies.
ss. 28, 30, repealed in pt.: 1980, c.43, sch.9.
s. 29, repealed in pt.: 1976, c.60, sch.3; 1984, c.28, sch.4.
s. 31, see *Dunning* v. *United Liverpool Hospitals* [1973] 1 W.L.R. 586, C.A.; *Shaw* v. *Vauxhall Motors* [1974] 1 W.L.R. 1035; [1974] 2 All E.R. 1185, C.A.; *Deistung (A minor)* v. *South West Metropolitan Regional Hospital Board* [1975] 1 W.L.R. 213; [1975] 1 All E.R. 573, C.A.; *Gaskin* v. *Liverpool City Council* [1980] 1 W.L.R. 1549, C.A.; *Campbell* v. *Tameside Metropolitan Borough Council* [1982] 3 W.L.R. 74, C.A.
s. 32, see *Paterson* v. *Chadwick* [1974] 1 W.L.R. 890; [1974] 2 All E.R. 772; *Davidson* v. *Lloyd Aircraft Services* [1974] 1 W.L.R. 1042; [1974] 3 All E.R. 1, C.A.; *McIvor* v. *Southern Health and Social Services Board, Northern Ireland* [1978] 1 W.L.R. 757, H.L.; *O'Sullivan* v. *Herdmans* [1987] 1 W.L.R. 1047, H.L.
s. 34, amended: 1978, c.23, sch.5.
s. 36, see *Halifax Building Society* v. *Clark* [1973] 2 W.L.R. 1; *First Middlesbrough Trading and Mortgage Co.* v. *Cunningham* (1974) 28 P. & C.R. 69, C.A.; *Royal Trust Co. of Canada* v. *Markham* [1975] 1 W.L.R. 1416; [1975] 3 All E.R. 433, C.A.; *Western Bank* v. *Schindler* [1976] 2 All E.R. 393, C.A.; *Centrax Trustees* v. *Ross* [1979] 2 All E.R. 952, Goulding J.; *Peckham Mutual Building Society* v. *Registe* (1981) 42 P. & C.R. 186, Vinelott J.; *Habib Bank* v. *Tailor* [1982] 1 W.L.R. 1218, C.A.; *Bank of Scotland* v. *Grimes* [1985] 2 All E.R. 254, C.A.; *Citibank Trust* v. *Ayivor* [1987] 1 W.L.R. 1157, Mervyn Davies J.
ss. 36, 37, see *Lord Marples of Wallasey* v. *Holmes* (1975) 31 P. & C.R. 94.
s. 37, see *P. B. Frost* v. *Green* [1978] 2 All E.R. 206, Slade J.; *National Westminster Bank* v. *Oceancrest, The Times,* April 24, 1985, C.A.
s. 37, repealed: 1984, c.28, sch.4.

1970—cont.

31. Administration of Justice Act 1970—*cont.*
ss. 37, 38, see *Trustees of Manchester Unity Life Insurance Collecting Society* v. *Sadler* [1974] 1 W.L.R. 770; [1974] 2 All E.R. 410.
s. 38, see *Universal Showcards & Display Manufacturing* v. *Brunt, The Times,* March 26, 1984, C.A.
s. 38, repealed: 1984, c.28, sch.4.
s. 38A, added: 1974, c.39, sch.4.
s. 41, see *R.* v. *Bradburn* (1973) 57 Cr.App.R. 948, C.A.; *R.* v. *Bunce* (1978) 66 Cr.App.R. 109, C.A.; *R.* v. *O'Donoghue and Dallas-Cope* (1978) 66 Cr.App.R. 116, C.A.; *R.* v. *Cain* (1983) 147 J.P.N. 833, C.A.
s. 41, amended: 1980, c.43, sch.7; 1984, c.28, sch.2; 1988, c.33, s.106; repealed in pt.: 1977, c.45, sch.13; 1980, c.43, sch.9; 1988, c.33, sch.16.
s. 42, repealed: 1980, c.43, sch.9.
s. 43, repealed: 1974, c.4, sch.5.
s. 44, see *Rocco Giuseppe & Figli* v. *Tradax Export SA* [1983] 2 Lloyd's Rep. 434; [1984] 1 W.L.R. 742, Parker J.
s. 44, orders 77/41; 79/1382; 80/672; 82/696, 1427; 85/437.
s. 45, repealed in pt.: 1981, c.54, sch.7; 1984, c.28, sch.4.
s. 46, repealed: 1973, c.15, sch.5.
s. 47, repealed: 1977, c.42, sch.25.
s. 50, repealed: 1980, c.43, sch.9.
s. 51, repealed in pt.: 1977, c.45, sch.13; 1980, c.43, sch.9.
s. 53, repealed: 1973, c.36, sch.6.
s. 54, amended: 1974, c.39, sch.4; repealed in pt.: 1973, c.36, sch.6.
sch. 1, repealed: 1981, c.54, sch.7.
sch. 2, repealed in pt.: 1973, c.15, sch.5; c.18, sch.3; 1975, c.63, sch.; 1981, c.20, sch.4; c.54, sch.7; 1984, c.28, sch.4.
sch. 3, repealed in pt.: 1979, c.42, s.8.
sch. 4, amended: 1975, c.18, sch.2; c.60, sch.4.
sch. 8, amended: 1972, c.18, sch.; 1973, c.18, s.54, sch.2; c.29, s.9; 1975, c.72, sch.3; 1976, c.71, sch.7; 1978, c.22, sch.2; 1980, c.5, sch.5; 1982, c.27, sch.12; 1984, c.42, sch.1; 1986, c.50, sch.10; 1987, c.42, sch.2; repealed in pt.: 1976, c.71, sch.7; 1986, c.50, sch.10; 1987, c.42, schs.2, 4.
sch. 9, see *R.* v. *Bradburn* (1973) 57 Cr.App.R. 948, C.A.; *R.* v. *Bunce* (1977) Cr.App.R. 109, C.A.; *R.* v. *Cain* (1983) 147 J.P.N. 833, C.A.
sch. 9, amended: 1973, c.14, sch.1; c.62, sch.5; 1985, c.23, sch.1; repealed in pt.: 1972, c.71, sch.6; 1973, c.14, schs.1,2; 1977, c.45, sch.13; 1985, c.23, schs.1,2.

32. Riding Establishments Act 1970.
s. 4, repealed in pt.: S.L.R. 1986.

33. Law Reform (Miscellaneous Provisions) Act 1970.
s. 2, see *Mossop* v. *Mossop* [1988] 2 All E.R. 202, C.A.
s. 3, see *Simmons* v. *Polak,* March 26, 1986; H.H. Judge Lowe; Willesden County Ct.
s. 4, repealed: 1973, c.18, sch.3.
s. 6, repealed: 1975, c.63, sch.

1970—cont.

34. Marriage (Registrar General's Licence) Act 1970.
s. 1, amended: 1983, c.32, s.2.
ss. 2, 7, 18, regs. 86/1442.
s. 18, amended: 1978, c.52, sch.11.

35. Conveyancing and Feudal Reform (Scotland) Act 1970.
s. 1, see *Devlin* v. *Conn*, 1972 S.L.T. 11; *Main* v. *Doune*, 1972 S.L.T.(Lands Tr.) 14; *Bolton* v. *Aberdeen Corporation*, 1972 S.L.T.(Lands Tr.) 26; *West Lothian Co-operative* v. *Ashdale Land and Property Co.*, 1972 S.L.T.(Lands Tr.) 30; *Smith* v. *Taylor*, 1972 S.L.T.(Lands Tr.) 34; 1972 S.C. 258; *McQuiban* v. *Eagle Star*, 1972 S.L.T.(Lands Tr.) 39; *Solway Cedar* v. *Hendry*, 1972 S.L.T.(Lands Tr.) 42; *Crombie* v. *Heriot* 1972 S.L.T.(Lands Tr.) 40; *Mans* v. *Butter's Trustees*, 1973 S.L.T.(Lands Tribunal) 2; *Morris* v. *Waverley Park Feuars*, 1973 S.L.T.(Lands Tribunal) 6; *McVey* v. *Glasgow Corporation*, 1973 S.L.T.(Lands Tr.) 15; *Macdonald*, 1973 S.L.T.(Lands Tr.) 26; *James Miller & Partners* v. *Hunt*, 1974 S.L.T.(Lands Tr.) 9; *Robinson* v. *Hamilton*, 1974 S.L.T.(Lands Tr.) 2; *Gorrie & Banks* v. *Musselburgh Town Council*, 1974 S.L.T.(Lands Tr.) 5; *Owen* v. *MacKenzie*, 1974 S.L.T.(Lands Tr.) 11; *Sinclair* v. *Gillon*, 1974 S.L.T. (Lands Tr.) 18; *Co-operative Wholesale Society* v. *Ushers Brewery*, 1975 S.L.T.(Lands Tr.) 9; *Clarebrooke Holdings* v. *Glentanar's Trs.* 1975 S.L.T.(Lands Tr.) 8; *McArthur* v. *Mahoney*, 1975 S.L.T.(Lands Tr.) 2; *Pickford* v. *Young*, 1975 S.L.T.(Lands Tr.) 17; *Robertson* v. *Church of Scotland General Trs.*, 1976 S.L.T.(Lands Tr.) 11; *Bachoo* v. *George Wimpey*, 1977 S.L.T.(Lands Tr.) 2; *Mercer* v. *MacLeod*, 1977 S.L.T.(Lands Tr.) 14; *Keith* v. *Texaco*, 1977 S.L.T.(Lands Tr.) 16; *Highland Regional Council* v. *Macdonald-Buchanan*, 1977 S.L.T.(Lands Tr.) 37; *Murrayfield Ice Rink* v. *Scottish Rugby Union Trustees*, 1973 S.C. 21, Second Division; *Ness* v. *Shannon and Others*, 1978 S.L.T.(Lands Tr.) 13; *Mrs Young and Others, Applicants*, 1978 S.L.T. (Lands Tr.) 28; *Bruce* v. *Modern Homes Investment Company*, 1978 S.L.T.(Lands Tr.) 34; *Reid* v. *Stafford*, 1979 S.L.T.(Lands Tr.) 16; *Winston* v. *Patrick*, Second Division, March 12, 1980; *Nicholson* v. *Campbell's Trs.*, 1981 S.L.T.(Lands Tr.) 10; *Leney* v. *Craig*, 1982 S.L.T.(Lands Tr.) 9; *Scott* v. *Fulton*, 1982 S.L.T.(Lands Tr.) 18; *Ross and Cromarty District Council* v. *Ullapool Property Co.*, 1983 S.L.T.(Lands Tr.) 9; *Strathclyde Regional Council* v. *Mactaggart & Mickel*, 1984 S.L.T. (Lands Tr.) 13; *Lothian Regional Council* v. *George Wimpey & Co.*, 1985, S.L.T.(Lands Tr.) 2; *Grampian Regional Council* v. *Viscount Cowdray*, 1985 S.L.T.(Lands Tr.) 6; *Hughes* v. *Frame*, 1985 S.L.T.(Lands Tr.) 12; *George T. Fraser* v. *Aberdeen Harbour Board*, 1985 S.L.T. 314; *MacDonald* v. *Stornoway Trust*, 1987 S.L.T. 240; *Cameron* v. *Stirling*, 1988

1970—cont.

35. Conveyancing and Feudal Reform (Scotland) Act 1970—*cont.*
S.L.T.(Lands Tr.) 18; *Banff and Buchan District Council* v. *Earl of Seafield's Estate*, 1988, S.L.T.(Lands Tr.) 21.
s. 2, see *Gorrie & Banks* v. *Musselburgh Town Council*, 1974 S.L.T.(Lands Tr.) 5.
s. 2, amended: 1974, c.38, s.19.
s. 4, see *Barr* v. *Bass*, 1972 S.L.T. 5.
s. 8, see *Lock* v. *Taylor* (O.H.), December 19, 1975.
s. 8, repealed: 1973, c.52, sch.5.
s. 9, repealed in pt.: 1980, c.52, sch.5.
ss. 9, 11, see *McLeod* v. *Cedar Holdings* (O.H.), 1988 S.L.T. 199.
ss. 9, 11, 16, 19, 20, see *Trade Development Bank* v. *Warriner & Mason* (*Scotland*), First Division, December 26, 1979.
s. 18, amended: 1974, c.38, s.19.
s. 19, amended: 1981, c.59, s.20.
ss. 20, 24, 27, see *Skipton Building Society* v. *Wain* (O.H.), 1986 S.L.T. 96.
s. 24, see *United Dominions Trust* v. *Site Preparations (No. 1)*, 1978 S.L.T.(Sh.Ct.) 14; *Bradford & Bingley Building Society* v. *Walker*, 1988 S.C.T.(Sh.Ct.) 33.
ss. 24, 29, see *National & Provincial Building Society* v. *Riddell*, 1986 S.L.T.(Sh.Ct.) 6; *Mountstar Metal Corporation* v. *Cameron*, 1987 S.L.T.(Sh.Ct.) 106; *Bradford and Bingley Building Society* v. *Roddy*, 1987 S.L.T.(Sh.Ct.) 109.
s. 25, see *Associated Displays* v. *Turnbeam* (Sh.Ct.), 1988 S.C.L.R. 220.
ss. 26, 27, see *Halifax Building Society* v. *Smith*, 1985 S.L.T.(Sh.Ct.) 25.
s. 27, see *Sowman* v. *City of Glasgow District Council*, 1984 S.L.T. 65.
s. 28, amended: 1979, c.33, sch.2.
s. 29, see *Provincial Building Society* v. *Menzies*, 1984 S.L.T.(Sh.Ct.) 81; *Bradford & Bingley Building Society* v. *Walker*, 1988 S.L.T.(Sh.Ct.) 33.
s. 41, repealed: 1985, c.73, sch.2.
schs. 2–4, see *Trade Development Bank* v. *Warriner & Mason* (*Scotland*), First Division, December 26, 1979.
sch. 3, see *United Dominions Trust* v. *Site Preparations (No. 1)*, 1978 S.L.T.(Sh.Ct.) 14; *United Dominions Trust Site Preparations (No. 2)*, 1978 S.L.T.(Sh.Ct.) 21; *Trade Development Bank* v. *Crittall Windows*, 1983 S.L.T. 510; *Trade Development Bank* v. *David W. Haig (Bellshill)* 1983 S.L.T. 510; *Skipton Building Society* v. *Wain* (O.H.), 1986 S.L.T. 96; *National & Provincial Building Society* v. *Riddell*, 1986 S.L.T.(Sh.Ct.) 6; *Bradford and Bingley Building Society* v. *Roddy*, 1987 S.L.T.(Sh.Ct.) 109; *Armstrong, Petr.* (O.H.), 1988 S.L.T. 255.
sch. 3, amended: 1985, c.65, sch.8; c.66, sch.7; repealed in pt.: 1986, c.45, sch.14.

36. Merchant Shipping Act 1970.
Commencement orders: 72/1977; 74/1194, 1908; 75/2156; 78/797; 79/809; 81/1186; 82/840, 1617; 86/2066.

CAP.

1970—cont.

36. Merchant Shipping Act 1970—cont.
amended: 1982, c.48, s.49.
regs. 72/918, 919, 1294.
ss. 1–3, amended: 1979, c.39, sch.6.
s. 2, regs. 79/1519.
s. 3, regs. 78/1756; 79/1519.
s. 6, amended: 1979, c.39, sch.6; repealed in pt.: *ibid.*, schs.6,7.
s. 7, amended: 1988, c.12, s.46.
s. 8, regs. 72/1701.
s. 8, amended: 1979, c.39, sch.6; 1988, c.12, s.46.
s. 9, regs. 72/1700, 1701; 78/1757; 79/97; 85/340.
s. 11, regs. 72/1699.
s. 11, amended: 1979, c.39, s.39; repealed in pt. (S.): 1987, c.18, sch. 8.
s. 13, regs. 72/1698.
s. 15, amended: 1979, c.39, s.37; repealed in pt.: *ibid.*, sch.7.
s. 17, regs. 72/1875; 88/479.
s. 17, repealed in pt.: 1980, c.30, sch.5.
ss. 19–22, amended: 1979, c.39, sch.6.
s. 20, regs. 75/2220; 78/795; 79/491; 84/41.
s. 21, regs. 72/1871, 1872; 75/733; 78/36.
s. 23, repealed: 1988, c.12, schs.5,7.
s. 24, regs. 74/1192, 1193; 75/1581; 80/407.
s. 24, repealed: regs. 88/1547.
s. 27, see *Hodge* v. *Higgins*; *The Harcourt* [1980] 2 Lloyd's Rep. 589, D.C.; *Foreman* v. *MacNeill*, 1979 J.C. 17; *Jenkin* v. *Godwin*; *Godwin* v. *Jenkin* [1983] 1 Lloyd's Rep. 382, D.C.
s. 27, substituted: 1988, c.12, s.32.
s. 28, amended: 1979, c.39, s.45, sch.6; 1986, c.23, s.10.
s. 29, repealed: 1974, c.43, s.19.
s. 30, amended: *ibid.*; 1979, c.39, sch.6; repealed in pt.: 1988, c.12, schs.5,7.
s. 31, repealed: 1974, c.43, s.19.
s. 32, repealed in pt.: *ibid.*; 1988, c.12, sch.7.
s. 33, amended: *ibid.*, sch.6.
s. 34, regs. 74/2047; 78/1754.
ss. 34–38, repealed: 1979, c.39, sch.7.
s. 42, amended: 1974, c.52, sch.3; repealed in pt.: *ibid.*, schs.3,5; 1988, c.12, schs.5,7.
s. 43, regs. 77/1152, 2072; 78/430; 79/599; 80/2025, 2026; 81/1065, 1076; 82/1699; 84/94–96, 1115; 85/1306; 86/1935; 87/884.
s. 43, amended: 1979, c.39, s.37, sch.6.
ss. 45–48, 50, 51, amended: *ibid.*, sch.6.
s. 50, regs. 82/1699.
s. 52 (in pt.), 54 (in pt.), 55, repealed: 1988, c.12, sch.7.
ss. 52, 56, see *Herald of Free Enterprise, Re: Appeal by Captain Lewry, The Independent*, December 18, 1987, D.C.
s. 56, amended: 1979, c.39, s.32; 1980, c.43, sch.7; 1988, c.12, schs.5,6.
s. 58, rules 82/1752; 85/1001.
s. 58, amended: 1988, c.12, sch.6.
s. 59, amended: 1979, c.39, sch.6.
s. 61, amended: 1976, c.14, sch.1 (S.); 1979, c.39, ss.28,29.
s. 62, regs. 79/97, 1519; amended: 1979, c.39, sch.6.

CAP.

1970—cont.

36. Merchant Shipping Act 1970—cont.
s. 65, regs. 72/1697; 79/1519; 83/1801.
s. 65, repealed: 1988, c.12, schs.5,7.
s. 66, order 84/539.
s. 66, repealed: 1988, c.12, schs.15,17.
s. 67, amended: *ibid.*, sch.6.
s. 68, regs. 72/1697, 1873, 1874; 77/628; 1152, 2027; 78/795, 1978; 79/97, 1519; 80/2025, 2026; 81/569, 570; 83/1801; 85/1306, 1828; 86/1935.
s. 68, amended: 1979, c.39, sch.6.
s. 69, regs. 77/45; 79/1519; 83/478.
ss. 69–71, amended: 1979, c.39, sch.6.
s. 70, amended: 1981, c.61, sch.7.
ss. 70, 71, regs. 71/1295; 79/1519; 87/408.
s. 71, regs. 71/1295; 74/1734; 77/1181; 78/107, 979, 1758; 79/1519; 81/313.
s. 72, regs. 72/1523; 79/1755; amended: 1979, c.39, s.30, sch.6.
s. 73, repealed: 1988, c.12, sch.7.
s. 74, amended: 1979, c.39, sch.6.
s. 75, repealed in pt.: 1988, c.12, sch.7.
s. 75A, added: *ibid.*, sch.5.
s. 76, amended: 1979, c.39, s.37, sch.6.
ss. 77, 78, amended: *ibid.*, sch.6.
s. 84, regs. 72/1930; 74/1777; 75/1692; 76/2015, 2205; 77/627, 1152; 79/631; 80/1143; 81/363, 589; 83/1167; 85/1607, 1727; 86/680; 87/63, 548, 854; 2113; 88/1485.
s. 85, rules 76/302; 82/1292, 1525.
s. 86, rules 75/330, 700.
s. 86, amended: 1979, c.39, sch.6.
s. 89, orders 79/120; 80/716; 81/1538; 85/174.
s. 89, repealed: 1988, c.12, schs.5,7.
s. 90, regs. 73/1979.
s. 92, regs. 72/1293, 1876, 1877; 74/1192, 1193; 75/1581, 2220; 78/795; 79/1755; 80/407; 87/884.
s. 92, amended: 1979, c.39, s.37; 1988, c.12, sch.5; repealed in pt.: *ibid.*, schs.5,7.
s. 93, amended: 1981, c.61, sch.7.
s. 94, orders 79/1706; 81/1809, 1812; 82/710, 1667; 84/1164; 88/246, 1085, 1086, 1991.
s. 95, amended: 1974, c.43, s.19; 1979, c.39, s.45; orders 79/296, 81/226; 1988, c.12, sch.6; repealed in pt.: 1979, c.39, sch.7; order 79/296; 1988, c.12, sch.7.
s. 96, amended: *ibid.*, sch.5.
s. 97, amended: 1979, c.39, s.29.
s. 99, regs. 72/1635; 77/45, 628, 1152, 1181; 78/107, 430, 795, 979, 1757, 1758; 79/97, 491, 599, 1519; 80/407; 81/313, 1065, 1076, 1789; 82/1699; 83/478; 84/41, 94–96, 1115; 85/340, 1306; 87/408.
s. 99, repealed: 1979, c.39, sch.7.
s. 101, orders 74/1194, 1908; 75/2156; 78/797; 79/809; 81/1186; 82/840, 1617; 86/2066.
s. 101, amended: 1979, c.39, s.37.
sch. 1, rules 76/302.
sch. 2, amended: 1979, c.39, s.28, sch.6; repealed in pt.: 1974, c.43, s.19; 1979, c.39, sch.7.
sch. 3, repealed in pt.: 1984, c.26, sch.2.

CAP.

1970—cont.

36. Merchant Shipping Act 1970—cont.
sch. 4, regs. 72/1304.
sch. 5, repealed in pt.: 1979, c.39, sch.7.

37. Republic of Gambia Act 1970.
ss. 2, repealed in pt.: S.L.R. 1986.

38. Building (Scotland) Act 1970.
sch. 1, repealed in pt.: S.L.R. 1976; S.L.R. 1977;
1980, c.45, sch.11.

39. Local Authorities (Goods and Services) Act 1970.
s. 1, orders 78/1761; 81/1049.
s. 1, amended: 1972, c.70, sch.30; 1973, c.65,
sch,27; 1985, c.51, sch.14; orders 72/853;
75/193; 85/1884; 1988, c.4, sch.6; repealed
in pt.: 1985, c.51, sch.17; 1988, c.40, sch.13
(prosp.).
s. 2, amended: 1973, c.65, sch.27; repealed in
pt.: *ibid.*, sch.29.
s. 29, schemes 79/876, 877.

40. Agriculture Act 1970.
Commencement order: 86/707.
regs. 73/1521.
ss. 1–24, repealed: 1986, c.49, sch.4.
s. 2, orders 76/366; 77/439; 78/389; 80/325;
81/343.
s. 5, scheme 76/547.
s. 10, orders 76/366; 78/389; 81/343.
s. 13, orders 73/592; 74/605, 606; 75/273;
76/366; 78/389; 80/103; 81/343; 82/278,
1777; 84/249; 85/311; 86/441.
s. 16, orders 74/605, 606.
ss. 25, 26, repealed: 1986, c.49, s.10, sch.4.
s. 27, repealed: *ibid.*; sch.4.
s. 28, orders 80/104, 929; schemes 72/368;
73/492, 1965; 76/547, 1870; 78/380, 768;
80/103, 930, 1072; 81/1533; 82/273, 923;
83/1764; 84/619, 1923; 85/1029; 86/57;
88/1056, 1398; orders 87/1948, 1949.
s. 28, amended: 1986, c.49, s.22.
s. 29, see *Ryrie (Blingery) Wick* v. *Secretary of
State for Scotland* (O.H.), 1988 S.L.T. 806.
s. 29, schemes 72/368, 1404; 73/492, 1945,
1965; 74/1072; 76/547, 761, 1870, 2125,
2126; 78/380, 768; 80/103, 930, 1072;
81/1533; 82/273, 923; 83/1764; 84/619,
1923; 85/1029; 86/57; 88/1056, 1398; order
87/1949.
s. 29, amended: 1976, c.55, s.15; repealed in
pt.: S.L.R. 1986.
s. 32, schemes 73/1404; 76/2125, 2126.
ss. 32, 33, repealed in pt.: 1972, c.62, s.26,
sch.6.
s. 34, repealed in pt.: S.L.R. 1986.
s. 35, orders 75/1546, 1578.
ss. 35, 36, repealed: S.L.R. 1986.
s. 38, repealed in pt.: 1972, c.70, sch.30; 1985,
c.51, sch.17.
s. 44, regs. 76/2001.
s. 48, repealed in pt.:1972, c.70, sch.30.
s. 50, schemes 73/1404; 76/2125, 2126.
s. 50, amended: 1972, c.62, s.9; repealed in
pt.: *ibid.*, s.26, sch.6.
s. 51, schemes 72/368; 73/492, 1965; 76/1870.
s. 52, amended: order 74/396.
s. 57, repealed: 1972, c.70, sch.30.

CAP.

1970—cont.

40. Agriculture Act 1970—cont.
s. 60, amended: order 74/396; repealed in pt.:
1972, c.70, sch.30.
s. 61, repealed in pt.: 1988, c.10, sch.
s. 62, repealed in pt.: 1972, c.70, sch.30.
s. 63, regs. 76/2001.
s. 64, see *Saul* v. *Norfolk County Council* [1984]
3 W.L.R. 84, C.A.
s. 66, regs. 76/840; 77/115, 1489; 78/1108;
79/1617; 80/1130; 81/10; 82/386, 985, 1143,
1144; 84/51, 52, 1592; 85/1119; 86/177,
1735; 88/396; S.Rs. 1980 No. 404; 1981 No.
17; 1982 Nos. 80, 245, 337, 338; 1984 Nos.
26, 27, 363; 1985 No. 194; 1986 Nos. 67,
334; 1988 No. 188.
s. 66, amended: order 78/272; regs. 82/980,
1143, 1144.
s. 67, regs. 78/1108; 82/1144.
s. 67, amended: 1973, c.65, s.171, sch.27;
1985, c.51, sch.8; repealed in pt.: 1972, c.70,
sch.30; 1980, c.65, schs.1,34.
s. 68, regs. 76/840; 77/115, 1489; 79/1617;
82/985, 1143; 84/51, 1592; 86/177, 1735;
88/396; S.Rs. 1980 No. 404; 1982 Nos. 245,
337; 1984 Nos. 27, 363; 1986 Nos. 67, 334;
88/396.
s. 68, amended: regs 82/980, 1144; 88/396.
s. 69, regs. 76/840; 77/115, 1489; 82/1143;
84/51, 1592; 86/177, 1735; 88/396; S.Rs.
1980 No. 404; 1982 No. 337; 1984 Nos. 27,
363; 1986 Nos. 67, 334; 1988 No. 188.
s. 69, modified: regs. 82/1143.
s. 70, regs. 76/840; 77/1489; 84/51, 1592;
86/177, 1735; 88/396; S.Rs. 1982 No. 337;
1984 Nos. 27, 363; 1986 Nos. 67, 334; 1988
No. 188.
s. 73, regs. 82/1143; 84/51; 86/177, 1735;
88/396; S.Rs. 1982 No. 337; 1984 No. 27;
1986 Nos. 67, 334; 1988 No. 188.
s. 73, amended: regs. 82/1980.
s.73A, added: *ibid.*
s. 74, regs. 76/840; 77/1489; 82/1143, 1144;
84/51, 1592; 86/177, 1735; 88/396; S.Rs.
1982 No. 337; 1984 No. 27; 1986 Nos. 67,
334; 1988 No. 188.
s. 74A, added: 1972, c.68, sch.4.
s. 74A, regs. 77/115; 78/1108; 79/1617;
80/1130; 81/10; 82/386, 985, 1143, 1144;
84/51, 52, 1592; 86/177, 1735; 88/396; S.Rs.
1980 No. 404; 1981 No. 17; 1982 Nos. 80,
245, 337, 338; 1984 Nos. 26, 27, 363; 1986
Nos. 67, 334; 1988 No. 188.
ss. 75–77, regs. 78/1108; 80/1130; 82/1144;
84/52; 85/1119; S.Rs. 1982 No. 338; 1984
No. 26; 1985 No. 194.
s. 76, amended: regs. 82/1144.
ss. 78, 79, regs. 78/1108; 80/1130; 82/1144;
S.R. 1982 No. 338.
s. 80, repealed in pt.: 1980, c.65, schs.1,34.
s. 82, amended: regs. 82/1143; 86/1735.
s. 84, regs. 77/115, 1489; 78/1108; 79/1617;
80/1150; 81/10; 82/386, 985, 1143, 1144;
84/51, 52, 1592; 85/1119; 86/177, 1735;
88/396; S.Rs. 1980 No. 404; 1981 No. 17;

1970—cont.

40. Agriculture Act 1970—*cont.*
1982 Nos. 80, 245, 337, 338; 1984 Nos. 26,
27, 363; 1985 No. 194; 1986 Nos. 67, 334;
1988 No. 188.

s. 86, S.Rs. 1980 No. 404; 1981 No. 17; 1982
Nos. 80, 245, 338; 1985 No. 194; 1986 Nos.
67, 334; 1988 No. 188.

s. 86, repealed in pt.: 1980, c.65, sch.34.

s. 87, order 73/1520.

ss. 88–91, repealed: 1976, c.70, sch.8.

s. 92, amended: 1973, c.65, sch.27; 1982, c.43,
s.21(S.); repealed in pt.: 1984, c.12, sch.7.

s. 93, repealed: 1973, c.65, sch.29.

s. 94, amended (S.): 1982, c.43, s.21.

ss. 95, 96, repealed (S.): *ibid.*,s.21, sch.4.

s. 97, repealed (S.): order 81/127; repealed in
pt.: 1973, c.65, sch.29.

s. 98, amended: 1973, c.37, sch.8; 1982, c.43,
s.21(S.).

s. 99, repealed: 1977, c.43, sch.3.

s. 100, repealed: 1977, c.42, sch.25.

s. 103, repealed: 1986, c.49, sch.4.

s. 104, orders 72/268, 289.

s. 104, repealed: 1973, c.50, sch.4.

s. 105, order 73/100; repealed in pt.: 1975,
c.40, sch.2; 1981, c.22, sch.6.

s. 106, orders 72/1219, 1329; 75/154; schemes
73/644; 75/2211; 76/387; 77/1303; 78/594.

s. 106, amended: 1981, c.22, sch.5; repealed in
pt.: 1972, c.68, sch.3; 1981, c.22, sch.6.

s. 107, repealed: 1986, c.49, sch.4.

s. 108, orders 81/142, 926 (S.).

ss. 109, 112, repealed: 1973, c.36, sch.6.

s. 113, order 86/707.

sch. 1, repealed: 1986, c.49, sch.4.

sch. 3, see *Saul* v. *Norfolk County Council* [1984]
3 W.L.R. 84, C.A.

sch. 4, regs. 78/1108.

sch. 4, repealed in pt.: 1972, c.62, sch.6; 1977,
c.12, sch.2; 1985, c.5, sch.15.

sch. 5, order 86/707.

sch. 5, repealed in pt.: S.L.R. 1986.

41. Equal Pay Act 1970.
amended: 1975, c.65, sch.1.

see *Pointon* v. *The University of Sussex* [1979]
I.R.L.R. 119, C.A.

s. 1, see *Sorbie* v. *Trust Houses Forte Hotels*
[1976] 3 W.L.R. 918; *Dugdale* v. *Kraft Foods*
[1976] 1 W.L.R. 1288; *Capper Pass* v. *Lawton*
[1977] 2 W.L.R. 26; *Navy, Army and Air Force
Institutes* v. *Varley* [1977] I.C.R. 11; [1977] 1
W.L.R. 149; *Green* v. *Broxtowe District Council* [1977] 1 All E.R. 694; *Snoxell and Davies*
v. *Vauxhall Motors; Charles Early & Marriott
(Witney)* v. *Smith and Ball* [1977] I.R.L.R. 121;
Murray v. *Lothian Regional Council,* December 8, 1976, E.A.T.; *Electrolux* v. *Hutchison*
[1977] I.C.R. 252, E.A.T.; *Waddington* v.
Leicester Council for Voluntary Service [1977]
I.C.R. 266; [1977] 1 W.L.R. 544, E.A.T.; *Eaton*
v. *Nuttall* [1977] I.C.R. 272, E.A.T.; *Ainsworth*
v. *Glass Tubes and Components* [1977] I.C.R.
347, E.A.T.; *Redland Roof Tiles* v. *Harper*
[1977] I.C.R. 349, E.A.T.; *Kerr* v. *Lister* [1977]
I.R.L.R. 259, E.A.T.; *Edmonds* v. *Computer*

1970—cont.

41. Equal Pay Act 1970—*cont.*
Services (South-West) [1977] I.R.L.R. 359,
E.A.T.; *A. R. W. Transformers* v. *Cupples*
(1977) 12 I.T.R. 355, E.A.T.; *United Biscuits*
v. *Young* [1978] I.R.L.R. 15, E.A.T.; *MacCar-
thys* v. *Smith* [1978] I.R.L.R. 10, E.A.T.; *England* v. *Bromley London Borough Council*
[1978] I.C.R. 1, E.A.T.; *British Leyland* v.
Powell [1978] I.R.L.R. 57, E.A.T.; *National
Vulcan Engineering Insurance Group* v. *Wade*
[1978] 3 W.L.R. 214, C.A.; *Outlook Supplies*
v. *Parry* [1978] I.C.R. 388, E.A.T.; *Hebbes* v.
*Rank Precision Industries (Trading as Rank
Hilger)* [1978] I.C.R. 489, E.A.T.; *Sun Alliance
and London Insurance* v. *Dudman* [1978]
I.C.R. 551, E.A.T.; *De Brito* v. *Standard Char-
tered Bank* [1978] I.C.R. 650, E.A.T.; *National
Coal Board* v. *Sherwin* [1978] I.C.R. 700,
E.A.T.; *Shields* v. *E. Coomes (Holdings)* [1978]
1 W.L.R. 1408, C.A.; *Clay Cross (Quarry Ser-
vices)* v. *Fletcher* [1979] 1 All E.R. 474, C.A.;
Handley v. *H. Mono* [1979] I.C.R. 147, E.A.T.;
Maidment v. *Cooper & Co. (Birmingham)*
[1978] I.C.R. 1094, E.A.T.; *Durrant* v. *North
Yorkshire Area Authority and Secretary of
State for Social Services* [1979] I.R.L.R. 401,
E.A.T.; *Capper Pass* v. *Alcan* [1980] I.C.R.
194, E.A.T.; *O'Brien* v. *Sim-Chem* [1980] 1
W.L.R. 1011, H.L.; *Methuen* v. *Cow Industrial
Polymers* [1980] I.C.R. 463, C.A.; *Noble* v.
David Gold & Son (Holdings) [1980] I.C.R. 543,
C.A.; *Ministry of Defence* v. *Farthing* [1980]
I.C.R. 705, C.A.; *Avon and Somerset Police
Authority* v. *Emery* [1981] I.C.R. 229, E.A.T.;
Jenkins v. *Kingsgate (Clothing Productions)*
[1981] I.C.R. 715, E.A.T.; *Albion Shipping
Agency* v. *Arnold* [1982] I.C.R. 22, E.A.T.;
Worringham v. *Lloyds Bank* [1982] 1 W.L.R.
841, C.A.; *Arnold* v. *Beecham Group* [1982]
I.C.R. 744, E.A.T.; *Re Equal Pay for Equal
Work; E.C. Commission* v. *United Kingdom
(No. 61/81)* [1982] I.C.R. 578, European Ct.;
1985 S.L.T. 518; *Quinnen* v. *Hovells* [1984]
I.C.R. 525, E.A.T.; *Rainey* v. *Greater Glasgow
Health Board* [1986] 3 W.L.R. 1017; 1987
S.L.T. 146, H.L.; *Hayward* v. *Cammell Laird
Shipbuilders (No. 2)* [1986] I.C.R. 862, E.A.T.;
Leverton v. *Clwyd County Council* [1987] 1
W.L.R. 65, E.A.T.; *Forex Neptune (Overseas)*
v. *Miller* [1987] I.C.R. 170, E.A.T.; *McGregor*
v. *General Municipal Boilermakers and Allied
Trades Union* [1987] I.C.R. 505, E.A.T.;
Lawson v. *Britfish* [1987] I.C.R. 726, E.A.T.;
Thomas v. *National Coal Board; Barker* v.
Same [1987] I.R.L.R. 451, E.A.T.; *R.* v. *Sec-
retary of State for Social Services, ex p. Clarke*
[1988] I.R.L.R. 22, D.C.; *Reed Packaging* v.
Boozer [1988] I.C.R. 391, E.A.T.; *Hayward* v.
Cammell Laird Shipbuilders [1988] 2 All E.R.
257, H.L.; *Leverton* v. *Clwyd County Council*
[1988] I.R.L.R. 239, C.A.; *Bromley* v. *Quick
(H. & J.)* [1988] I.R.L.R. 249, C.A.; *Pickstone*
v. *Freemans* [1988] 2 All E.R. 803, H.L.

s. 1, amended: 1975, c.65, s.8, sch.1; repealed
in pt.: *ibid.*; 1981, c.55, sch.5.

1970—cont.

41. Equal Pay Act 1970—*cont.*

s. 2, see *Worringham* v. *Lloyds Bank* [1982] 1 W.L.R. 841, C.A.; *Dennehy* v. *Sealink U.K.* [1987] I.R.L.R. 120, E.A.T.; *British Railways Board* v. *Paul* [1988] I.R.L.R. 20, E.A.T.; *R.* v. *Secretary of State for Social Services, ex p. Clarke* [1988] I.R.L.R. 22, D.C.

s. 2, repealed: 1978, c.44, sch.17.

s. 2A, see *Neil* v. *Ford Motor Co.* [1984] I.R.L.R. 339, London North Industrial Tribunal; *Forex Neptune (Overseas)* v. *Miller, The Times,* November 18, 1986, E.A.T.; *R.* v. *Secretary of State for Social Services, ex p. Clarke* [1988] I.R.L.R. 22, D.C.; *Leverton* v. *Clwyd County Council* [1988] I.R.L.R. 239, C.A.; *Bromley* v. *Quick (H. & J.)* [1988] I.R.L.R. 249, C.A.

s. 3, see *R.* v. *Central Arbitration Committee, ex p. Hy-Mac* [1979] I.R.L.R. 461, D.C.

s. 3, repealed: 1986, c.59, sch.

s. 4, repealed: 1986, c.48, sch.5.

s. 5, amended: 1975, c.65, sch.1; c.71, sch.16.

s. 6, see *Worringham* v. *Lloyds Bank* [1982] 1 W.L.R. 841, C.A.; *Newstead* v. *Department of Transport and H.M. Treasury* [1985] I.R.L.R. 299, E.A.T.; *Duke* v. *G.E.C. Reliance (formerly Reliance Systems), The Times,* February 12, 1988, H.L.

s. 6, amended: 1975, c.65, sch.1; 1986, c.59, ss.2,9; repealed in pt.: *ibid.,* sch.

s. 7, amended: 1975, c.71, sch.16; repealed in pt.: 1981, c.55, sch.5.

s. 8, repealed: 1975, c.65, sch.1.

s. 8, sch. 1, see *Lawson* v. *Britfish* [1987] I.C.R. 726, E.A.T.

s. 9, repealed in pt.: 1975, c.65, sch.1

s. 10, repealed: 1986, c.59, sch.

42. Local Authority Social Services Act 1970.

s. 1, amended: 1972, c.70, s.195.

s. 2, amended: 1973, c.29, s.2; repealed in pt.: 1973, c.32, sch.5.

ss. 2, 3, see *R.* v. *Birmingham City Council, ex p. O.* [1982] 1 W.L.R. 679, C.A.

s. 3, substituted: 1980, c.65, s.183.

s. 3A, added: *ibid.*

s. 5, amended: 1972, c.70, sch.29; 1985, c.67, sch.7.

s. 6, repealed in pt.: 1972, c.70, sch.30; 1980, c.65, sch.34.

s. 7, repealed in pt.: 1972, c.70, sch.30.

ss. 8, 10, repealed: *ibid.*

s. 11, repealed: 1983, c.41, sch.10.

s. 12, order 80/328.

s. 13, repealed in pt.: 1980, c.65, sch.34.

s. 15, amended: 1973, c.36, sch.6; repealed in pt.: 1980, c.65, sch.34; 1983, c.41, sch.10.

sch. 1, amended: 1973, c.18, sch.2; c.32, sch.4; 1975, c.37, sch.1; c.72, sch.3; 1976, c.36, sch.3; c.71, sch.7; 1977, c.48, s.20; c.49, schs.14,15; 1978, c.22, sch.2; 1980, c.5, sch.5; c.6, sch.2; c.7, sch.1; c.30, sch.4; 1982, c.20, s.15; c.51, sch.3; 1983, c.20, sch.4; c.41, sch.9; 1984, c.22, sch.2; c.23, sch.1; c.36, sch.3; 1985, c.71, sch.2; 1987, c.26, sch.23(S.); repealed in pt.: 1973, c.18, schs.2,3; c.32, sch.5; 1975, c.72, sch.4;

1970—cont.

42. Local Authority Social Services Act 1970—*cont.*

1976, c.36, sch.4; c.71, schs.7,8; 1977, c.49, sch.16; 1978, c.22, schs.2,3; S.L.R. 1978; 1980, c.5, sch.6; c.6, schs.2,3; 1983, c.20, schs.4, 6; 1984, c.22, sch.3; 1985, c.71, sch.1.

sch. 2, repealed in pt.: 1980, c.5, sch.6.

43. Trees Act 1970.

s. 1, repealed: 1972, c.52, sch.23.

44. Chronically Sick and Disabled Persons Act 1970.

s. 1, order 72/1420.

s. 1, amended: 1986, c.33, s.9.

s. 2, see *R.* v. *Ealing London Borough Council, ex p. Leaman, The Times,* February 10, 1984, Mann J.; *R.* v. *Kent County Council, ex p. Bruce, The Times,* February 8, 1986, D.C.

s. 2, repealed in pt.: 1972, c.70, sch.30.

s. 3, substituted: 1985, c.71, sch.2; amended (S.): 1987, c.26, sch. 23; repealed in pt. (S.): *ibid.,* sch. 24.

s. 4, amended: 1976, c.49, s.1; 1981, c.28, s.37; c.43, s.6.

s. 5, amended: 1973, c.65, s.141; 1981, c.28, s.37; c.43, s.6.

s. 6, amended: 1976, c.57, s.20; 1981, c.28, s.37; c.43, s.6; repealed in pt.: 1976, c.57, sch.2.

s. 7, substituted: 1981, c.43, s.5.

s. 8, amended: 1988,c.40, sch.12.

s. 8A, added: 1976, c.49, s.2; amended: 1981, c.23, s.37; c.43, s.6.

s. 8B, added: *ibid.,* s.7.

s. 10, repealed in pt.: 1975, c.6, sch.6; repealed (S.): 1980, c.52, sch.5.

s. 11, repealed: 1973, c.38, sch.28.

s. 13, amended: 1972, c.50, sch.3; repealed in pt.: *ibid.,* schs.3,4.

s. 14, amended: 1972, c.60, sch.6; 1983, c.25, sch 2; 1986, c.44, sch.7.

s. 17, amended: 1973, c.32, sch.4; 1977, c.49, sch.14; (S.) 1978, c.29, sch.16.

s. 18, amended: 1984, c.36, sch.3.

s. 20, amended: 1972, c.20, sch.7; 1980, c.66, sch.24; 1984, c.27, sch.13; 1988. c.54, sch.3.

s. 21, regs. 72/906; 75/266; 82/1740; 86/178.

s. 21, amended: 1973, c.65, sch.14; 1982, c.49, s.68; 1984, c.27, sch.13; 1985, c.51, sch.4; repealed in pt.: 1972, c.70, sch.30.

ss. 25–27, repealed: 1980, c.44, sch.5(S.); 1981, c.60, sch.4.

s. 28, amended: 1981, c.23, s.37; c.43, s.6.

s. 29, amended: 1972, c.51, s.1; 1986, c.44, s.12(S.).

45. Matrimonial Proceedings and Property Act 1970.

see *Chamberlain* v. *Chamberlain* [1973] 1 W.L.R. 1557; [1974] 1 All E.R. 33, C.A.

Pt. I (ss. 1–29), repealed: 1973, c.18, sch.3; S.L.R. 1977.

s. 2, see *Coleman* v. *Coleman* [1972] 3 W.L.R. 681; [1972] 3 All E.R. 886; *Glenn* v. *Glenn* [1973] 1 W.L.R. 1016; *Wachtel* v. *Wachtel*

CAP.

1970—cont.

45. Matrimonial Proceedings and Property Act 1970—cont.

[1973] 2 W.L.R. 366, C.A.; *Trippas* v. *Trippas* [1973] 2 W.L.R. 585; [1973] 2 All E.R. 1, C.A.; *Harnett* v. *Harnett* [1974] 1 W.L.R. 219; [1974] 1 All E.R. 764, C.A.; *Griffiths* v. *Griffiths* [1974] 1 All E.R. 932, C.A.; *Chaterjee* v. *Chaterjee* [1976] 2 W.L.R. 397; [1976] 1 All E.R. 719, C.A.

s. 4, see *Jones* v. *Jones* [1971] 3 All E.R. 1201; *Kowalczuk* v. *Kowalczuk* [1973] 1 W.L.R. 930; *Hunter* v. *Hunter* [1973] 1 W.L.R. 958; *Glenn* v. *Glenn* [1973] 1 W.L.R. 1016; *Hector* v. *Hector* [1973] 1 W.L.R. 1122, C.A.; *D'Este* v. *D'Este* [1973] 2 W.L.R. 183; *Wachtel* v. *Wachtel* [1973] 2 W.L.R. 366, C.A.; *Jackson* v. *Jackson* [1973] 2 W.L.R. 735; [1973] 2 All E.R. 395; *Willis* v. *Willis* (1973) 4 Fam.Law 21, C.A.; *Harnett* v. *Harnett* [1974] 1 W.L.R. 219; [1974] 1 All E.R. 764, C.A.; *Cuzner (formerly Underdown)* v. *Underdown* [1974] 1 W.L.R. 641; [1974] 2 All E.R. 351, C.A.; *Moisi* v. *Moisi* (1974) 5 Fam.Law 26, C.A.; *S.* v. *S.* [1975] 2 W.L.R. 615; [1975] 2 All E.R. 19; *Chaterjee* v. *Chaterjee* [1976] 2 W.L.R. 397; [1976] 1 All E.R. 719, C.A.

s. 5, see *Barnes* v. *Barnes* [1972] 1 W.L.R. 1381; [1972] 3 All E.R. 872; *Kowalczuk* v. *Kowalczuk* [1973] 1 W.L.R. 930; *Hunter* v. *Hunter* [1973] 1 W.L.R. 958; *Hector* v. *Hector* [1973] 1 W.L.R. 1122, C.A.; *Lombardi* v. *Lombardi* [1973] 1 W.L.R. 1276; [1973] 3 All E.R. 625, C.A.; *Wachtel* v. *Wachtel* [1973] 2 W.L.R. 366, C.A.; *Trippas* v. *Trippas* [1973] 2 W.L.R. 585; [1973] 2 All E.R. 1, C.A.; *Harris* v. *Harris* (1973) 4 Fam.Law 10, C.A.; *Harnett* v. *Harnett* [1974] 1 W.L.R. 219; [1974] 1 All E.R. 764, C.A.; *Griffiths* v. *Griffiths* [1974] 1 All E.R. 932, C.A.; *Moisi* v. *Moisi* (1974) 5 Fam.Law 26, C.A.; *Dopson* v. *Cherry* (1974) 5 Fam.Law 57, C.A.; *S.* v. *S.* [1975] 2 W.L.R. 615; [1975] 2 All E.R. 19.

s. 7, see *Jackson* v. *Jackson* [1973] 2 W.L.R. 735; [1973] 2 All E.R. 395; *Madden* v. *Madden* [1974] 1 W.L.R. 247; [1974] 1 All E.R. 673; *Bonning* v. *Dodsley (formerly Bonning)* [1982] 1 W.L.R. 279, C.A.

s. 9, see *Jones* v. *Jones* [1971] 3 All E.R. 1201.

s. 12, repealed: S.L.R. 1977.

s. 18, see *H.* v. *H.* [1973] 2 W.L.R. 525; [1973] 1 All E.R. 801.

s. 27, see *A.* v. *A. (Family: Unborn Child)* [1974] 2 W.L.R. 106.

s. 30, repealed in pt.: 1972, c.18, s.42; 1978, c.22, sch.3.

ss. 31–33, repealed: *ibid.*, sch.3.

ss. 34, 35, repealed: 1973, c.18, sch.3.

s. 36, repealed: 1975, c.63, sch.

s. 37, see *Kowalczuk* v. *Kowalczuk* [1973] 1 W.L.R. 930; *Griffiths* v. *Griffiths* [1973] 1 W.L.R. 1454, Arnold J.; *Harnett* v. *Harnett* [1973] 3 W.L.R. 1; [1973] 2 All E.R. 593; *Re Nicholson, decd., Nicholson* v. *Perks* [1974] 1 W.L.R. 376; *Samuels (W. A.)'s Trustee* v. *Samuels* (1973) 233 E.G. 149; *Cann* v. *Ayres* [1977] Fam.Law 47, C.A.

CAP.

1970—cont.

45. Matrimonial Proceedings and Property Act 1970—cont.

s. 38, repealed: 1983, c.19, sch.3.

ss. 40–42, repealed: 1973, c.18, sch.3.

s. 43, repealed in pt.: *ibid.*; S.L.R. 1977.

schs. 1–3, repealed: 1973, c.18, sch.3.

46. Radiological Protection Act 1970.

s. 1, order 74/1230.

ss. 1, 2, amended: 1974, c.37, s.77.

ss. 1, 5, amended: order 78/1039.

s. 2, order 80/970; amended: *ibid.*

s. 4, repealed: 1983, c.41, s.27, sch.10.

s. 5, amended: 1973, c.36, sch.6.

s. 6, repealed in pt.: 1983, c.41, sch.10.

sch. 1, repealed in pt.: 1975, c.24, sch.3.

47. Indecent Advertisements (Amendment) Act 1970.

repealed: 1981, c.42, sch.

48. Appropriation (No. 2) Act 1970.

repealed: 1974, c.31, s.4, sch.

49. International Monetary Fund Act 1970.

repealed: 1979, c.29, sch.

50. Fiji Independence Act 1970.

ss. 2, 3, repealed: 1981, c.61, sch.9.

s. 4, repealed in pt.: 1978, c.30, sch.3.

sch. 2, repealed in pt.: S.L.R. 1977; 1981, c.9, sch.

51. National Insurance (old persons' and widows' pensions and attendance allowance) Act 1970.

repealed: 1973, c.38, sch.28.

s. 1, regs. 72/1302; 73/1480; 74/1128.

s. 4, see *R.* v. *National Insurance Commissioner, ex p. Secretary of State for Social Services* [1974] 1 W.L.R. 1290; [1974] 3 All E.R. 522, D.C.

ss. 4, 6, 7, 13, amended: 1972, c.57, s.6, sch.6.

s. 6, regs. 72/1232.

s. 10, sch. 2, repealed in pt.: 1975, c.24, sch.3.

53. Harbours (Amendment) Act 1970.

repealed: 1972, c.16, s.4.

54. Income and Corporation Taxes (No. 2) Act 1970.

repealed: 1988, c.1, sch.31.

55. Family Income Supplements Act 1970.

repealed: 1986, c.50, sch.11.

see *Freer* v. *Taggart*, 1975 S.L.T.(Sh.Ct.) 13; *Decision No. R(FIS)* 2/85.

s. 1, see *R.* v. *Supplementary Benefits Commission, ex p. Lewes* [1982] 1 All E.R. 680, C.A.; *Decision No. R(FIS)* 3/83; *Decision No. R(FIS)* 4/83; *Taylor* v. *Supplementary Benefits Officer* (1986) 1 F.L.R. 16, C.A.; *Webb* v. *Macaulay* (O.H.), 1988 S.L.T. 138.

s. 1, regs. 83/1003.

s. 1, amended: 1980, c.30, s.7; repealed in pt.: 1983, c.41, sch.10.

ss. 1, 4, see *Chief Adjudication Officer* v. *Hogg, The Times*, June 11, 1985, C.A.; *Lowe* v. *The Adjudication Officer, The Times*, June 11, 1985, C.A.

s. 2, see *Chief Adjudication Officer, The Times*, June 11, 1985, C.A.

CAP.

CAP.

1970—cont.

55. Family Income Supplements Act 1970—*cont.*
s. 2, regs. 72/135; 73/177, 1362; 74/905; 75/879; 76/801; 77/586, 1324; 78/1137; 79/939, 1430; 80/1167; 81/1159; 83/1201; 84/1081; 85/1188; 86/1120; 87/32.
s. 2, substituted: 1975, c.61, sch.4; amended: regs. 74/905; 75/879; 76/801; 77/1324.
s. 3, regs. 72/135; 73/1362; 74/905; 75/879; 76/801; 77/586, 1324; 78/1137; 79/939, 1430; 81/1159; 83/1201; 84/1081; 85/1188; 86/1120; 87/32.
s. 3, amended: 1975, c.61, sch.4; regs. 74/905; 75/879; 76/801; 77/1324.
s. 4, regs. 72/1282; 74/59; 76/289; 77/324; 79/1504; 80/1437; 85/1946.
s. 5, regs. 84/458.
s. 6, see *Decision No. R(FIS) 3/85.*
s. 6, regs. 74/59; 76/289; 77/324; 79/1504; 80/1437; 84/451, 979, 1991; 87/281.
s. 6, amended: 1983, c.41, sch.8.
s. 7, repealed: 1983, c.41, sch.10.
s. 8, amended: 1973, c.38, sch.27; 1975, c.18, sch.2; c.60, sch.4; c.61, sch.4; 1977, c.5, s.22; 1982, c.24, s.41; 1983, c.41, sch.8.
s. 10, regs. 72/1282; 73/177, 1362; 74/59, 905; 75/879; 76/289, 801; 77/324, 586, 1324; 78/1137; 79/160, 939, 1430, 1504, 1505; 80/1437, 1438; 81/1159; 82/1107, 1635; 83/1003; 84/451, 458, 979, 1081, 1991; 85/1188; 86/1120; 87/32.
s. 10, amended: 1979, c.18, sch.3; 1980, c.30, s.7; 1982, c.24, sch.4; repealed in pt.: 1980, c.30, s.7; 1983, c.41, sch.10.
s. 11, amended: 1977, c.5, s.22; 1981, c.33, sch.1.
s. 12, repealed in pt.: 1984, c.60, sch.7.
s. 13, repealed in pt.: 1975, c.11, sch.6; c.61, sch.5; 1976, c.71, sch.8.
s. 14, see *Lowe v. Rigby* [1985] 2 All E.R. 903, C.A.
s. 17, amended: 1980, c.30, s.7; repealed in pt.: *ibid.*, s.7, sch.5; 1983, c.41, sch.10.

56. Contingencies Fund Act 1970.
s. 2, repealed: 1974, c.18, sch.

57. Town and Country Planning Regulations (London) (Indemnity) Act 1970.
repealed: S.L.R. 1976.

1971

1. Consolidated Fund Act 1971.
repealed: 1974, c.31, s.4, sch.

3. Guardianship of Minors Act 1971.
text as amended: 1987, c.42, sch.1.
amended: *ibid.*, sch.2.
see *Faulkner v. Faulkner* (1979) 123 S.J. 751, D.C.; *Ainsbury v. Millington* [1986] 1 All E.R. 73, C.A.; *Essex County Council v. T., The Times,* March 15, 1986, C.A.
s. 1, see *Re K. (Minors) (Children: Care and Control)* [1977] 2 W.L.R. 33, C.A.; *Richards v. Richards* [1983] 3 W.L.R. 173, H.L.; *W. v. P., The Times,* October 26, 1987, Ewbank J.
s. 1, amended: 1973, c.29, sch.3; 1978, c.22, s.36.

1971—cont.

3. Guardianship of Minors Act 1971—*cont.*
s. 2, repealed: 1973, c.29, sch.3.
s. 4, amended: 1978, c.22, s.36.
s. 5, see *Re N. (Minors) (Parental Rights)* [1973] 3 W.L.R. 866, D.C.
s. 5, amended: 1980, c.5, sch.5; 1987, c.42, sch.2; repealed in pt.: 1975, c.72, sch.4.
s. 8, see *Smith v. Koumourou* [1979] R.T.R. 355, D.C.
s. 8, repealed: 1973, c.29, sch.3.
s. 9, see *Jussa v. Jussa* [1972] 1 W.L.R. 881; [1972] 2 All E.R. 600; *Re K.* [1972] 116 S.J. 664; *Re D.; Re F. (A Minor) (Access out of Jurisdiction)* [1973] 3 W.L.R. 461; [1973] 3 All E.R. 493, Baker P.; *Re R. (An Infant) (Custody to Non-Parent)* [1974] 1 All E.R. 1033, D.C.; *R. v. Oxford City Justices, ex p. H.* [1974] 3 W.L.R. 1; [1974] 2 All E.R. 356, D.C.; *Re Thompson (Minors),* 1976, D.C.; *C. v. H.* (1979) 123 S.J. 537, D.C.; *Re W. (A Minor)* [1981] 3 All E.R. 401, C.A.; *C. v. C., The Times,* December 2, 1981, C.A. *Davies v. Davies (sub nom. F. v. D.)* (1983) 13 Fam. Law 111, D.C.; *Fernandez v. Fernandez* (1984) 14 Fam.Law 177, D.C.; *O. (A Minor), Re,* (1985) Fam.Law 135, C.A.; *T. D. (A Minor) (Wardship: Jurisdiction), Re* (1986) 16 Fam.Law 18, Sheldon J.: *R. v. Oxford JJ., ex p. D.* [1986] 3 W.L.R. 447, Waite J.; *M. and H. (Minors) (Local Authority: Parental Rights) Re, sub nom. M. v. H.* [1988] 3 All E.R. 5, H.L.; *P. (Minors: Access, Re; P. v. P. (Gateshead Metropolitan Borough Council Intervening), The Times,* February 19, 1988, C.A.; *M. and H. (Minors) (No. 2), Re* (1988) 152 J.P.N. 127, Booth J; *Staffordshire County Council v. C. and M.* (1988) 152 J.P.N. 238, Latey J.
s. 9, substituted: 1987, c.42, s.9.
ss. 10, 11, substituted: *ibid.*, s.11.
s. 11A, added 1978, c.22, s.37; amended: 1987, c.42, sch.2.
s. 11B, added: *ibid.*, s.12.
s. 11C, added: *ibid.*, s.13.
s. 11D, added: *ibid.*, s.14.
s. 12, substituted: 1978, c.22, s.42; amended: 1987, c.42, sch.2.
s. 12A, added: 1978, c.22, s.43; amended: 1987, c.42, sch.2.
s. 12B, order 88/1069.
s. 12B, added: 1978, c.22, s.43; amended: 1987, c.42, sch.2; repealed in pt.: *ibid.*, schs.2, 4.
s. 12C, added: 1978, c.22, s.43; amended: 1987, c.42, sch.2.
s. 12D, added: *ibid.*
s. 13, see *R. v. Dover Magistrates' Court, ex p. Kidner* [1983] 1 All E.R. 475, D.C.
s. 13, amended: 1973, c.29, s.2, sch.2; 1975, c.72, sch.3; 1978, c.22, s.36, sch.2; 1980, c.43, sch.7; 1987, c.42, sch.2.
s. 13A, added: 1978, c.22, s.39; amended: 1987, c.42, sch.2.
s. 13B, added: *ibid.*
s. 14, see *Re K.* [1972] 116 S.J. 664; *R. v. Oxford City Justices, ex p. H.* [1974] 3 W.L.R.

CAP.

1971—cont.

3. Guardianship of Minors Act 1971—cont.

1; [1974] 2 All E.R. 356, D.C.; *F. v. D., The Times,* December 2, 1982, D.C.; *Davies v. Davies (sub nom. F. v. D.)* (1983) 13 Fam.Law 111, D.C.; *O. (A Minor), Re,* (1985) Fam.Law 135, C.A.

s. 14, repealed: 1987, c.42, schs.2, 4.

s. 14A, added: 1978, c.22, s.40; amended: 1980, c.5, sch.5; 1987, c.42, sch.2.

s. 15, see *Re D.; Re F. (A Minor) (Access out of Jurisdiction)* [1973] 3 W.L.R. 461; [1973] 3 All E.R. 493, Baker J.; *Re Irving (Minors), The Times.* April 25, 1978, D.C.

s. 15, rules 88/329.

s. 15, amended: 1973, c.29, s.2, sch.2; 1978, c.22, ss.36,47; 1979, c.55, sch.2; 1986, c.55, sch.1; repealed in pt.: 1979, c.55, s.38; 1986, c.55, schs.1,2.

s. 15A, added: 1986, c.55, sch.1; amended: 1987, c.42, sch.2; repealed in pt.: *ibid.,* schs.2, 4.

s. 16, amended: 1973, c.29, s.2, sch.2; 1975, c.72, sch.3; 1979, c.55, s.48, sch.2; 1980, c.43, sch.7; 1987, c.42, sch.2; repealed in pt.: 1975, c.72, sch.4; 1984, c.42, sch.3.

s. 17, repealed in pt.: 1986, c.55, schs.1,2.

s. 18, repealed in pt.: S.L.R. 1977.

s. 19, repealed: *ibid.*

s. 20, amended: 1978, c.22, s.36; 1987, c.42, sch.2; repealed in pt.: S.L.R. 1977.

sch. 1, amended: 1973, c.18, sch.3; 1974, c.4, sch.5; repealed in pt.: 1973, c.29, sch.3; 1976, c.36, sch.4; S.L.R. 1977; 1981, c.54, sch.7.

sch. 2, repealed: S.L.R. 1977.

4. Copyright (Amendment) Act 1971.

repealed: 1988, c.48, sch.8.

7. Local Authorities (Qualification of Members) Act 1971.

repealed: 1972, c.70, sch.30; 1973, c.65, sch.29.

8. Hospital Endowments (Scotland) Act 1971.

repealed: 1978, c.29, sch.17.

s. 2, regs. 72/390.

ss. 2, 5, 6, regs. 74/859.

s. 7, schemes 72/391; 74/860.

s. 12, order 72/389.

10. Vehicles (Excise) Act 1971.

Commencement order. 84/1619.

see *Lockhart v. Ayrshire Commercial Spares,* 1983 S.L.T.(Sh.Ct.) 74.

regs. 72/850, 1865.

s. 1, see *Smith v. Koumourou* [1979] R.T.R. 355, D.C.; *R. v. Department of Transport, ex p. Lakeland Plastics (Windermere)* [1983] R.T.R. 82, D.C.

s. 1, amended: 1988, c.39, sch.2.

s. 2, order 80/1183.

s. 2, amended: 1972, c.20, sch.7; 1977, c.36, s.5; 1982, c.39, s.5; 1983, c.28, s.4; 1985, c.54, s.4; 1988, c.54, sch.3; repealed in pt.: 1988, c.39, s.4, sch.14.

s. 2A, orders 80/1183; 86/1428.

s. 2A, amended: 1980, c.48, s.4; 1986, c.41, sch.2.

CAP.

1971—cont.

10. Vehicles (Excise) Act 1971—cont.

s. 3, amended: 1979, c.2, sch.4.

s. 4, see *Coote v. Winfield* [1980] R.T.R. 42, D.C.

s. 4, amended: order 74/168; 1980, c.48, s.4; 1986, c.41, sch.2; repealed in pt.: 1975, c.45, sch.14.

s. 5, amended: 1972, c.20, sch.7; 1988, c.54, sch.3.

s. 6, amended: 1972, c.41, s.55; 1983, c.55, sch.9.

s. 7, order 85/722, regs. 86/1467.

s. 7, amended: 1978, c.29, sch.16(S.); c.42, s.8; 1980, c.48, s.4; 1984, c.43, s.5; 1986, c.41, sch.2.

s. 8, see *Pilgrim v. Dean* [1974] 1 All E.R. 601, D.C.; *Holliday v. Henry* [1974] Crim.L.R. 126; [1974] R.T.R. 101, D.C.; *Binks v. Department of the Environment* [1975] R.T.R. 318, D.C.; *Richardson v. Baker* [1976] R.T.R. 56, D.C.; *McEachran v. Hurst* [1978] R.T.R. 462, D.C.; *Smith v. Koumourou* [1979] R.T.R. 355, D.C.; *Coote v. Winfield* [1980] R.T.R. 42, D.C.; *Cummings v. Tudhope* 1985, S.C.C.R. 125; *Chief Constable of Kent v. Mather, The Times,* August 1, 1985, D.C.; *Algar v. Shaw* [1986] Crim.L.R. 750, D.C.; *Kennet v. Holding & Barnes; Harvey (T.L.) v. Hall* [1986] R.T.R. 334, D.C.; *Guyll v. Bright* [1987] R.T.R. 104, D.C.; *Algar v. Shaw* [1987] R.T.R. 229, D.C.

s. 9, see *Chief Constable of Kent v. Mather, The Times,* August 1, 1985, D.C.

s. 9, repealed in pt.: 1985, c.73, sch.4(S.); 1987, c.16, schs.1, 16.

s. 10, repealed in pt.: 1988, c.39, sch.14.

s. 12, see *Pilgrim v. Dean* [1974] 1 W.L.R. 601, D.C.; *Strowger v. John* [1974] R.T.R. 124, D.C.; *Kennet v. Holding & Barnes; Harvey (T.L.) v. Hall* [1986] R.T.R. 334, D.C.

s. 12, regs. 75/1341; 76/1680; 81/931; 86/607; 87/2122; 88/847.

s. 13, amended: 1985, c.54, sch.9; repealed in pt.: 1988, c.39, sch.14.

s. 14, repealed in pt.: *ibid.*

s. 16, see *Pearson v. Richardson* [1972] 1 W.L.R. 1152; [1972] 3 All E.R. 277; *Hunters the Bakers v. Hills* [1973] R.T.R. 361, D.C.; *McNeill v. Calligan,* 1973 S.L.T.(Sh.Ct.) 54; *Scott v. Gutteridge Plant Hire* [1974] Crim.L.R. 125; [1974] R.T.R. 292, D.C.; *Robertson v. Crew* [1977] R.T.R. 141, D.C.; *Bowers v. Worthington* [1982] R.T.R. 400, D.C.; *Squires v. Mitchell* [1983] R.T.R. 400, D.C.; *Gibson v. Nutter* [1984] R.T.R. 8, D.C.; *Smith v. Holt Brothers,* 1986 S.L.T.(Sh.Ct.) 49; *Kennet v. Holding & Barnes; Harvey (T.L.) v. Hall* [1986] R.T.R. 334, D.C.

s. 16, regs. 76/1680; 81/931; 86/1177, 2100, 2101; 87/2122, 2123.

s. 16, amended: 1977, c.36, s.5; 1980, c.48, s.4; 1981, c.35, s.7.; 1982, c.39, s.5; 1983, c.28, s.4; 1984, c.43, s.4; 1985, c.54, s.4; 1986, c.41, s.3, sch.2; 1987, c.16, sch.1; repealed in pt.: *ibid.,* schs. 1, 16.

s. 17, see *McNeill v. Calligan,* 1973 S.L.T.(Sh.Ct.) 54.

CAP.

1971—cont.

10. Vehicles (Excise) Act 1971—cont.

s. 17, repealed in pt.: 1986, c.41, sch.2.

s. 18, see *Blue Band Motors* v. *Kyle*, 1972 S.L.T. 250; *Bullen* v. *Picking* [1974] R.T.R. 46, D.C.; *McKenzie* v. *Griffiths Contractors (Agricultural)* [1976] Crim.L.R. 69; [1976] R.T.R. 40, D.C.; *Cambrian Land* v. *Allan* [1981] R.T.R. 109, D.C.

s. 18A, added: 1982, c.39, s.7; 1987, c.16, sch.1; repealed in pt.: *ibid.*, schs.1, 16.

s. 19, see *Clifford* v. *Bloom* [1977] Crim.L.R. 485; [1977] R.T.R. 351, D.C.

s. 22, see *Balfour Beatty & Co.* v. *Grindley (Note)* [1975] R.T.R. 156, D.C.

s. 22, amended: 1972, c.20, sch.7; 1988, c.54, sch.3.

s. 23, regs. 73/870; 75/1089; 76/1680, 2089; 78/1536; 81/366, 931; 84/814; 85/610; 86/607, 1177.

s. 23, amended: 1987, c.16, sch.1; repealed in pt.: 1986, c.41, schs 2, 23.

s. 26, see *Cook* v. *Lanyon* [1972] R.T.R. 496, D.C.; *Heumann* v. *Evans* [1977] Crim.L.R. 229, D.C.; [1977] R.T.R. 250, D.C.; *Clifford* v. *Bloom* [1977] Crim. L.R. 485; [1977] R.T.R. 351, D.C.; *R.* v. *Clayton* (1980) 71 Cr.App.R. 135, C.A.; *R.* v. *Terry* [1984] 2 W.L.R. 23, H.L.

s. 26, amended: regs. 78/1536.

s. 28, see *Algar* v. *Shaw* [1986] Crim.L.R. 750; [1987] R.T.R. 229, D.C.

s. 28, amended: 1979, c.2, sch.4.

s. 29, see *Walkingshaw* v. *McLaren*, 1985 S.C.C.R. 293.

s. 31, see *Cardle* v. *Wilkinson*, 1982 S.L.T. 315.

s. 34, amended: 1980, c.43, sch.7.

s. 35, amended: 1972, c.71, sch.6; 1979, c.2, sch.4.

s. 37, see *Scott* v. *Gutteridge Plant Hire* [1974] Crim.L.R. 125; [1974] R.T.R. 292, D.C.

s. 37, regs. 72/1217; 75/1089, 1341, 1342; 76/1680, 2089; 77/230; 78/1536; 81/366, 931; 82/1802; 83/1248; 84/814; 85/610; 86/607, 1177, 2100; 87/2085, 2122, 2123; 88/847.

s. 37, amended: 1985, c.54, s.9; 1987, c.16, sch.1.

s. 38, amended: 1974, c.39, sch.4; 1982, c.39, s.5; 1984, c.54, sch.9(S.); repealed in pt.: 1988, c.39, sch.14.

s. 39, regs. 73/870; 75/1089; 76/1680, 2089; 78/1536; 84/1619, 85/610; 86/607.

sch. 1, regs. 85/610.

sch. 1, substituted: 1977, c.36, s.5, sch.4; amended: 1980, c.48, s.4, sch.3; 1981, c.35, s.7, sch.3; 1982, c.39, s.5, sch.3; 1983, c.28, s.4, sch.3; 1984, c.43, s.4, sch.2; 1985, c.54, s.4, sch.2; 1988, c.39, sch.2.

sch. 2, substituted: 1977, c.36, s.5, sch.4; amended: 1980, c.48, s.4, sch.3; 1981, c.35, s.7, sch.3; 1982, c.39, s.5, sch.3; 1983, c.28, s.4, sch.3; 1984, c.43, s.4, sch.2; 1985, c.54, s.4, sch.2; 1986, c.41, sch.2.

sch. 3, regs. 87/2120.

CAP.

1971—cont.

10. Vehicles (Excise) Act 1971—cont.

sch. 3, substituted: 1977, c.36, s.5, sch.4; amended: 1980, s.49, s.4, sch.3; 1981, c.35, s.7, sch.3; 1982, c.39, s.5, sch.3; 1983, c.28, s.4, sch.3; 1984, c.43, s.4, sch.2; 1985, c,54, s.4, sch.2; 1987, c.16, sch.1; 1988, c.39, s.4, sch.2.

sch. 4, see *Howard* v. *Grass Products* [1972] 1 W.L.R. 1323; [1972] 3 All E.R. 530; *Anderson & Heeley* v. *Paterson* [1975] 1 W.L.R. 228; [1975] 1 All E.R. 523, D.C.; *Cambrian Land* v. *Allan* [1981] R.T.R. 109, D.C.; *R.* v. *Department of Transport, ex p. Lakeland Plastics (Windermere)*, The Times, May 10, 1982, Stephen Brown J.

sch. 4, substituted: 1977, c.36, s.5, sch.4; amended: 1980, c.48, s.4, sch.3; 1981, c.35, s.7, sch.3; 1982, c.39, sch.5; 1983, c.28, s.4, sch.3; 1984, c.43, s.4, sch.2; 1985, c.54, s.4, sch.2; 1986, c.41, sch.2; 1988, c.39, s.4, sch.2; c.54, sch.3.

sch.4A, added: 1988, c.39, sch.2.

sch. 5, substituted: 1977, c.36, s.5, sch.4; amended: 1980, c.48, s.4, sch.3; 1981, c.35, s.7, sch.3; 1982, c.39, s.5, sch.3; 1983, c.28, s.4, sch.3; 1984, c.43, s.4, sch.2; 1985, c.54, s.4, sch.2; 1988, c.39, s.4, sch.2.

sch. 6, repealed in pt.: 1982, c.39, sch.22.

sch. 7, regs. 73/870; 75/1089; 76/1680, 2089; 78/1536; 86/607; 87/2085.

sch. 7, amended: 1987, c.16, sch.1; repealed in pt.: 1986, c.41, sch.23; 1987, c.16, schs.1, 16.

11. Atomic Energy Authority Act 1971.

s. 10, amended: 1978, c.44, sch.16.

ss. 11, 12, amended: 1977, c.7, s.2.

s. 13, order 76/1298; repealed: 1977, c.7, s.2.

s. 14, amended: 1985, c.9, sch.2.

ss. 17, 18, amended: 1973, c.36, sch.6.

s. 19, order 73/17.

s. 19, amended: 1976, c.23, s.2.

s. 22, amended: 1973, c.51, sch.19; repealed in pt.: 1988, c.39, sch.14.

12. Hydrocarbon Oil (Customs and Excise) Act 1971.

regs. 73/1311.

repealed, except s. 22, sch. 6 in pt.: 1979, c.5, sch.7.

ss. 10, 11, see *Customs and Excise Comrs.* v. *George Wimpey & Co.* (1980) 124 S.J. 346, C.A.

s. 11, orders 81/850, 868.

s. 11, amended: 1981, c.48, s.1.

s. 19, regs. 76/443; 77/1868.

s. 20, regs. 77/1868.

s. 21, regs. 74/379; 77/1868.

s. 22, repealed: 1979, c.2, sch.6.

sch. 6, repealed in pt.: 1979, c.2, sch.6; c.8, sch.2.

13. Mr. Speaker King's Retirement Act 1971.

s. 1, amended: 1972, c.48, sch.3; 1987, c.45, s.4.

14. Consolidated Fund (No. 2) Act 1971.

repealed: 1974, c.31, s.4, sch.

1971—cont.

15. Consumer Protection Act 1971.
repealed: 1978, c.38, sch.3.

16. Coal Industry Act 1971.
s. 1, repealed: 1977, c.39, sch.5.
s. 2, repealed: *ibid.*, s.7, sch.5.
s. 3, order 72/469.
s. 3, repealed: 1973, c.8, sch.2.
s. 4, amended: 1987, c.3, sch.1; repealed in
  pt.: 1973, c.8, sch.2.
s. 5, repealed: 1980, c.63, sch.2.
ss. 6–8, amended: 1987, c.3, sch.1.
s. 9, amended: *ibid.*; repealed in pt.: 1977, c.39,
  sch.5.
s. 10, amended: 1985, c.9, sch.2; 1987, c.3,
  sch.1.

17. Industry Act 1971.
repealed: S.L.R. 1986.

18. Land Commission (Dissolution) Act 1971.
s. 7, repealed in pt.: 1975, c.24, sch.3.
sch. 2, amended: 1972, c.52, sch.23; repealed
  in pt.: 1981, c.66, sch.5.

19. Carriage of Goods by Sea Act 1971.
see *Mayhew Foods* v. *Overseas Containers*
  (1983) New L.J. 1103; [1984] 1 Lloyd's Rep.
  317, Bingham J.
order 85/443
s. 1, see *The Morviken, The Times,* January 14,
  1982, C.A.; *The Hollandia* [1982] 3 W.L.R.
  1111, H.L.
s. 1, orders 77/1044; 78/1468; 79/790; 80/280,
  1872; 81/1240; 83/36, 582.
s. 1, amended: 1981, c.10, s.2; repealed in pt.:
  *ibid.,*sch.
s. 2, orders 77/1236; 78/1885; 82/1665.
s. 4, orders 80/1507, 1508, 1954;
  82/1662–1664.
s. 6, order 77/981; amended: 1979, c.39, sch.5.
sch., see *The Hollandia* [1982] 3 W.L.R. 1111,
  H.L.; *The Benarty* [1984] 3 W.L.R. 1082, C.A.;
  *China Ocean Shipping Co. (Owners of Xingch-
  eng)* v. *Andros (Owners of the Andros* [1987]
  1 W.L.R. 1213, P.C.
sch., amended: 1981, c.10, sch.

20. Mines Management Act 1971.
s. 1, amended: regs. 74/2013; 80/804; 85/2023;
  modified: order 75/1102.
ss. 1, 3, repealed in pt.: *ibid.*
ss. 1–3, regs. 72/631.

21. Oil in Navigable Waters Act 1971.
s. 12, order 72/1927.

22. Animals Act 1971.
s. 2, see *Kite* v. *Napp, The Times,* June 1, 1982,
  Stephen Brown J.; *Wallace* v. *Newton*
  [1982] 1 W.L.R. 375, Park J.
ss. 2, 5, see *Cummings* v. *Grainger* [1976] 3
  W.L.R. 842, C.A.
s. 4, see *Morris* v. *Blaenau Gwent District Council* (1982) 80 L.G.R. 793, C.A.
ss. 4, 5, see *Matthews* v. *Wicks, The Times,*
  May 25, 1987, C.A.
s. 8, see *Davies* v. *Davies* [1974] 3 W.L.R. 607;
  [1974] 3 All E.R. 817, C.A.
s. 10, amended: 1980, c.58, sch.3.

1971—cont.

23. Courts Act 1971.
Pts. I, II (ss. 1–13), repealed: 1981, c.54, sch.7.
s. 7, see *R.* v. *Urbanowski* [1976] 1 All E.R. 679,
  C.A.; *R.* v. *H. B. Edwards* (1975) 62 Cr.App.R.
  166, C.A.
ss. 8, 9, see *Maker* v. *Gower (formerly Kubilius)*
  (1981) 12 Fam.Law 32, Purchas J.
s. 9, see *R.* v. *Birmingham JJ., ex p. Wyatt*
  [1975] 3 All E.R. 897, D.C.; *R.* v. *Burn* (1976)
  63 Cr.App.R. 289, C.A.; *Killington* v. *Butcher*
  [1979] Crim.L.R. 458, D.C.; *R.* v. *Inner London
  Crown Court, ex p. Obajuwana* (1979) 69
  Cr.App.R. 125, D.C. *R.* v. *Battle JJ., ex p.
  Shepherd, The Times,* April 26, 1983, D.C.;
  Investors in Industry Commercial Properties
  v. *Norwich City Council* (1985) 83 L.G.R. 64,
  Hodgson J.; *R.* v. *Croydon Crown Court, ex
  p. Claire, The Times,* April 3, 1986, D.C.
s. 10, see *Ex p. Meredith* [1973] 1 W.L.R. 435,
  D.C.; *R.* v. *Cardiff Crown Court, ex p. Jones*
  [1973] 3 W.L.R. 497, D.C.; *R.* v. *Smith* (*Martin*)
  [1974] 1 All E.R. 651, C.A.; *R.* v. *Exeter Crown
  Court, ex p. Beattie* [1974] 1 W.L.R. 428;
  [1974] 1 All E.R. 1183, D.C.; *R.* v. *Leeds
  Crown Court, ex p. Bradford Chief Constable*
  [1974] 3 W.L.R. 715, D.C.; *Harris Simon &
  Co.* v. *Manchester City Council* [1975] 1
  W.L.R. 100; [1975] 1 All E.R. 412, D.C.; *R.* v.
  Sheffield Crown Court, ex p. Brownlow [1980]
  2 W.L.R. 892, C.A.; *R.* v. *Ipswich Crown
  Court, ex p. Baldwin* (*Note*) [1981] 1 All E.R.
  596, D.C.; *R.* v. *St. Albans Crown Court, ex p.
  Cinnamond* [1981] 1 All E.R. 802, D.C.; *Samp-
  son, Re* [1987] 1 W.L.R. 194, H.L.
s. 11, see *R.* v. *Gilbert* [1975] 1 All E.R. 742,
  C.A.; *R.* v. *Michael* [1975] 3 W.L.R. 731;
  R. v. *Annesley* [1976] 1 W.L.R. 106, C.A.; *R.*
  v. *Menocal* [1979] 2 W.L.R. 876, H.L.; *R.* v.
  Grice (1977) 66 Cr.App.R. 167, C.A.; *R.* v.
  Sodhi (1978) 66 Cr.App.R. 260, C.A.; *R.* v.
  McGlen [1980] Crim.L.R. 66, Croydon Crown
  Ct.; *R.* v. *Saville* [1980] 1 All E.R. 561, C.A.;
  R. v. *Reilly* [1982] 3 W.L.R. 149, C.A.; *R.* v.
  Iqbal (1985) 81 Cr.App.R. 145, C.A.
s. 13, see *R.* v. *K.* (1977) 121 S.J. 728; *R.* v. *P.*
  [1980] Crim.L.R. 796, Winchester Crown Ct.
s. 13, rules 78/439.
ss. 14, 15, rules 72/1787; 76/1532, 2164;
  78/439.
s. 16, amended: 1977, c.38, s.12.
s. 17, repealed in pt.: 1975, c.24, sch.3; c.25,
  sch.3.
s. 19, amended: 1981, c.20.sch.3; repealed in
  pt.: *ibid.,*sch.4.
s. 20, repealed in pt.: 1984, c.28, sch.4.
s. 23, repealed: 1981, c.54, sch.7.
s. 24, substituted: *ibid.,*s.146; amended: 1982,
  c.53, s.59.
ss. 25, 26, repealed: 1981, c.54, sch.7.
s. 27, amended: 1972, c.11, sch.6.
Pt. V (ss. 31–40), repealed: 1974, c.23, sch.3.
s. 43, see *R.* v. *Khan*; *R* v. *Crawley, The Times,*
  August 7, 1982, C.A.
s. 44, regs. 73/2009.

1971—cont.

23. Courts Act 1971—cont.

s. 45, amended: 1973, c.18, sch.2; 1984, c.28, sch.2; repealed in pt.: 1973, c.18, sch.2; 1975, c.63, sch.; 1984, c.42, sch.3.

s. 46, repealed: 1977, c.37, sch.6.

ss. 47–9, repealed: 1973, c.14, sch.2.

s. 48, see *R.* v. *Yoxall* (1972) 57 Cr.App.R. 263, C.A.

s. 50, repealed: 1981, c.54, sch.7.

s. 51, repealed in pt.: 1973, c.14, sch.2.

s. 52, see *R.* v. *Lewes Crown Court, ex p. Rogers* [1974] 1 W.L.R. 196; [1974] 1 All E.R. 589, D.C.

s. 52, amended: 1980, c.43, sch.7; repealed in pt.: 1973, c.14, sch.2.

s. 53, orders 72/518, 519, 1728.

s. 53, amended: 1973, c.62, sch.5; repealed in pt.: 1972, c.71, sch.6; 1973, c.62, sch.6, 1979, c.55, sch.3; 1981, c.28, sch.2.

s. 54, repealed in pt.: 1972, c.70, sch.30.

s. 56, see *R.* v. *Midgley* [1979] R.T.R. 1, C.A.; *Day* v. *Grant; R.* v. *Manchester Crown Court, ex p. Williams* [1985] R.T.R. 299, C.A.

s. 57, see *R.* v. *Sodhi* (1978) 66 Cr.App.R. 260, C.A.; *R.* v. *Menocal* [1979] 2 W.L.R. 876, H.L.; *R.* v. *Maidstone Crown Court, ex p. Grill, The Times,* July 15, 1986, C.A.

s. 57, amended: 1983, c.20, sch.4; repealed in pt.: 1977, c.45, sch.13; 1984, c.54, sch.7.

s. 58, repealed: 1973, c.36, sch.6.

s. 59, repealed in pt.: 1973, c.36, sch.6; 1975, c.24, sch.3; c.25, sch.3; 1977, c.45, sch.13.

sch. 1, repealed: 1981, c.54, sch.7.

sch. 2, rules 79/668.

sch. 2, amended: 1981, c.54, sch.7; repealed in pt.: S.L.R. 1973.

sch. 3, amended: order 74/595; 1981, c.67, sch.4.

sch. 4, see *R.* v. *Midgley* [1979] R.T.R. 1, C.A.

sch. 4, repealed: 1974, c.23, sch.3.

sch. 6, repealed in pt.: 1973, c.14, sch.2; 1974, c.4, sch.5.

sch. 7, repealed in pt.: 1972, c.70, sch.30; 1979, c.55, sch.3; 1981, c.28, sch.2.

sch. 8, see *Day* v. *Grant; R.* v. *Manchester Crown Court, ex p. Williams* [1985] R.T.R. 299, C.A.

sch. 8, amended: 1981, c.54, sch.5; repealed in pt.: 1972, c.70, sch.30; c.71, sch.6; 1973, c.18, sch.3; c.62, sch.6; 1974, c.4, sch.5; 1977, c.35, sch.5; c.38, sch.5; c.45, sch.13; 1979, c.31, sch.2; c.55, sch.3; 1980, c.43, sch.9; c.66, sch.25; 1981, c.20, sch.4; c.54, sch.7; c.69, sch.17; 1982, c.48, sch.16; c.51, sch.4; 1983, c.2, sch.9; c.20, sch.6; S.L.R. 1986.

sch. 9, repealed in pt.: 1972, c.11, sch.8; 1973, c.14, sch.2; 1974, c.39, sch.5; c.46, sch.16; 1975, c.23, s.28; 1976, c.32, sch.5; .c.70, sch.8; 1979, c.2, sch.6; c.45, sch.7; 1980, c.6, sch.3; c.43, sch.9; c.66, sch.25; 1981, c.22, sch.6; c.69, sch.17; 1982, c.30, sch.7; c.33, sch.2; 1983, c.20, sch. 6.; 1984, c.30, sch. 11; 1985, c.71, sch. 1; 1986, c.5, sch.15; 1988, c.41, sch.13 (prosp.); c.48, sch.8.

1971—cont.

23. Courts Act 1971—cont.

sch. 10, amended: 1972, c.11, sch.6; order 74/520; repealed in pt.: 1972, c.11, schs.6–8; 1981, c.20, sch.4.

24. Coinage Act 1971.

s. 1, substituted: 1983, c.9, s.1.

s. 2, see *Jenkins* v. *Horn* [1979] 2 All E.R. 1141, Browne-Wilkinson J.

s. 2, amended: 1983, c.9, s.1.

s. 3, amended: *ibid.*; repealed in pt.: *ibid.,* s.1, sch.

s. 4, amended and repealed in pt.: 1973, c.63, s.7.

s. 5, repealed: *ibid.*

s. 6, amended: 1983, c.9, s.1.

s. 8, orders 75/2192; 78/185; 80/1967; 83/612.

s. 12, amended: 1983, c.9, s.1.

sch. 1, repealed in pt.: *ibid.,* s.1, sch.

25. Administration of Estates Act 1971.

s. 8, repealed: 1981, c.54, sch.7.

s. 11, amended: *ibid.,* sch.5; repealed in pt.: *ibid.,*schs.5,7.

s. 12, repealed in pt.: *ibid.,*sch.7.

s. 13, repealed: 1973, c.36, sch.6.

s. 14, amended: 1981, c.54, sch.5.

26. Betting, Gaming and Lotteries (Amendment) Act 1971.

repealed: 1985, c.18, sch.

27. Powers of Attorney Act 1971.

s. 1, see *T.C.B.* v. *Gray, Financial Times,* November 27, 1985, Browne-Wilkinson V.-C.

ss. 2, 11 (in pt.), repealed: 1981, c.54, sch.7.

s. 7, see *Clauss* v. *Pir* [1987] 2 All E.R. 752, Francis Ferrie Q.C.

s. 10, see *Walia* v. *Naughton (Michael)* [1985] 1 W.L.R. 1115, Judge John Finlay Q.C.

28. Rent (Scotland) Act 1971.

repealed, except sch. 18 (in pt.): 1984, c.58, sch.10.

regs. 72/1221, 1333.

s. 1, see *Campbell* v. *McQuillan* (O.H.), June 17, 1982.

s. 1, order 80/1669.

ss. 1, 3, see *Ronson Nominees* v. *Mitchell,* 1982 S.L.T.(Sh.Ct.) 18.

s. 2, see *Holiday Flat Co.* v. *Luczera and Another,* 1978 S.L.T.(Sh.Ct.) 47; *Gavin* v. *Lindsay,* 1987 S.L.T.(Sh.Ct.) 12.

s. 2, regs. 74/1374; 82/702.

s. 35, regs. 73/1410; 75/791; 76/1469; 80/1671, 1672.

s. 37, see *Ronson Nominees* v. *Mitchell,* 1982 S.L.T.(Sh.Ct.) 18.

s. 40, see *Pollock* v. *Glasgow Corporation,* 1973 S.L.T. 77.

s. 42, see *Paisley Burgh* v. *Renfrewshire Assessor,* 1973 S.L.T. 222; *Mason* v. *Skilling* [1974] 1 W.L.R. 1437, H.L.; *sub. nom. Skilling* v. *Arcari's Executrix,* 1974 S.L.T. 46, H.L.; *Albyn Properties* v. *Knox,* 1977 S.L.T. 41; *Western Heritable Investment Co* v. *Husband,* 1983 S.L.T. 578; [1983] 3 W.L.R. 429, H.L.

s. 46, regs. 72/1211; 75/791; 80/1665, 1670, 1672; 82/259.

CAP.

1971—cont.

28. Rent (Scotland) Act 1971—*cont.*
s. 58, regs. 75/792.
s. 68, regs 75/792; 76/1469.
s. 86, order 80/1669.
s. 99, regs. 76/1469; 80/1665; 82/259.
s. 131, see *Hamilton District Council* v. *Maguire,* 1983 S.L.T.(Sh.Ct.) 76.
s. 131, regs. 76/46; 80/1667.
sch. 3, see *Kerr* v. *Gordon,* 1977 S.L.T. (Sh.Ct.) 53.

29. National Savings Bank Act 1971.
regs. 72/764.
s. 2, regs. 74/553; 75/1190, 2153; 77/1807; 78/888; 1594; 80/619; 81/484; 82/294, 487, 1282, 1762; 83/1367; 84/9, 602; 85/342; 88/1166.
s. 2, repealed in pt.: 1985, c.58, sch.4.
s. 3, regs. 74/553.
ss. 3–8, amended: 1982, c.39, sch.20.
s. 4, orders 74/931; 77/1210; 81/108; 84/640; 86/1217; 87/329, 330.
s. 5, orders 72/1750; 76/2112; 82/1806; 85/1875; 86/2161; 87/2096.
s. 6, regs. 83/1750.
s. 8, regs. 82/294; 84/9; 88/1166.
s. 9, regs 75/1190.
s. 9, amended: order 75/1137; regs. 84/539.
s. 11, warrants 74/2003; 76/738; 77/372, 482; 78/615.
s. 12, amended: 1988, c.39, s.126.
ss. 13, 14, repealed: 1985, c.58, sch.4.
s. 21, amended: 1981, c.65, sch.6.
ss. 21–23, repealed: 1980, c.48, sch.20.
s. 22, order 78/1839.
s. 24, amended: 1972, c.11, sch.6.
ss. 24–26, repealed in pt.: 1980, c.48, sch.20.
s. 27, amended: 1981, c.65, sch.6; 1982, c.39, sch.20; repealed in pt.: 1985, c.58, sch.4.
sch. 1, repealed: 1980, c.48, sch.20.

30. Unsolicited Goods and Services Act 1971.
s. 2, see *Readers Digest Assoc.* v. *Pirie,* 1973 S.L.T. 170, High Ct. of Judiciary.
ss. 3, 6, amended: 1975, c.13, s.2.
s. 3A, added: *ibid.*, s.1; regs. 75/732.
s. 4, see *D.P.P.* v. *Beate Uhse (U.K.)* [1974] 2 W.L.R. 50, D.C.

31. Interest on Damages (Scotland) Act 1971.
see *McCuaig* v. *Redpath Dorman Long,* 1972 S.L.T.(Notes) 42.
s. 1, see *Smith* v. *Middleton,* 1972 S.L.T.(Notes) 3; *Picken* v. *J. Smart & Co. (Contractors),* 1972 S.L.T.(Notes) 12; *Ross* v. *British Ry.,* 1972 S.L.T. 174; *Andrew* v. *Scottish Omnibuses* (O.H.) 1972 S.L.T.(Notes) 72; *Orr* v. *Metcalfe,* 1973 S.C. 57, First Division; *Mac-Donald* v. *Glasgow Corporation,* 1973 S.L.T. 107; *Buchanan, James & Co.* v. *Stewart Cameron (Drymen),* 1973 S.L.T.(Notes) 78; *Mouland* v. *Ferguson* (O.H.), 1979 S.L.T.(Notes) 85; *Plaxton* v. *Aaron Construction (Dundee)* (O.H.) 1980 S.L.T.(Notes) 6.
s. 1, repealed in pt.: 1980, c.55, sch.3.

32. Attachment of Earnings Act 1971.
ss. 1, 3, see *Whibley* v. *Cross,* October 13, 1976, Wandsworth County Ct.

CAP.

1971—cont.

32. Attachment of Earnings Act 1971—*cont.*
s. 3, amended: 1973, c.38, sch.27; 1980, c.43, sch.7.
s. 4, amended: 1976, c.60, s.13, sch.3; 1984, c.28, sch.2; repealed in pt.: 1976, c.60, s.13, sch.3.
s. 6, see *Billington* v. *Billington* [1974] 2 W.L.R. 53, D.C.; amended: 1977, c.38, s.19.
s. 7, orders 75/1868; 80/558.
s. 8, amended: 1980, c.43, sch.7.
s. 13, see *Green (A Bankrupt), ex p. Official Receiver* v. *Cutting* [1979] 1 All E.R. 832, Walton J.
s. 14, amended: 1982, c.53, s.53.
s. 17, see *Whibley* v. *Cross,* October 13, 1976, Wandsworth County Ct.
ss. 17, 19, amended: 1980, c.43, sch.7.
s. 22, amended: order 87/2039.
s. 23, amended: 1981, c.49, sch.2; 1982, c.48, sch.4; c.53, s.53; 1984, c.28, sch.2.
s. 24, see *Miles* v. *Miles, The Times,* November 29, 1978, C.A.
s. 24, amended: 1975, c.60, sch.4; 1979, c.39, s.39; 1985, c.53, sch.4; 1986, c.50, sch.10.
s. 25, amended: 1974, c.4, sch.4; 1980, c.43, sch.7; 1984, c.28, sch.2; 1988, c.34, sch.5.
s. 27, repealed in pt.: 1976, c.60, sch.3.
s. 28, repealed: 1973, c.36, sch.6.
s. 29, repealed in pt. *ibid.*
sch. 1, amended: 1972, c.18, sch.; 1973, c.18, sch.2; c.29, s.9; 1975, c.72, sch.3; 1976, c.71, sch.7; 1978, c.22, sch.2; 1980, c.5, sch.5; 1982, c.27, sch.12; 1986, c.50, sch.10; 1987, c.42, sch.2; repealed in pt.: *ibid.*, schs.2, 4.
sch. 2, amended: 1975, c.18, sch.2; c.60, sch.4; repealed in pt.: 1973, c.38, sch.28.
sch. 3, amended: 1975, c.18, sch.2; 1979, c.12, sch.6; 1982, c.53, s.54; 1986, c.48, sch.4; repealed in pt.: 1975, c.60, sch.5.
sch. 4, repealed: 1986, c.50, sch.10.

33. Armed Forces Act 1971.
s. 1, orders 73/2153; 74/2147; 75/2159; repealed: 1976, c.52, s.1, sch.10.
ss. 26, 33, 54, sch. 1, repealed in pt.: 1986, c.21, sch.2.
ss. 64, 69, 76, sch.3, repealed in pt.: 1980, c.9, sch.10.
s. 67, schs. 1, 3, repealed in pt.: 1976, c.52, sch.10.

34. Water Resources Act 1971.
order 77/1851.
s. 1, orders 72/549, 1424; 73/185, 377, 1061, 1808; 74/124, 883, 1002; 75/28, 40, 853, 1285, 1841, 1870; 76/909, 1597; 77/1527; 78/325, 898, 1199; 79/994, 995, 1020, 1767; 80/17, 129, 1115, 1283, 1286, 1470, 1738; 81/1437, 1593, 1594, 1784; 82/250; 83/1085; 85/320, 633, 816, 1472; 86/774, 775, 1531, 1575, 1690, 1739; 87/107, 1354; 88/828.
s. 2, orders 81/1593; 88/828.
s. 2, amended: 1973, c.37, sch.9.

36. Motor Vehicles (Passenger Insurance) Act 1971.
repealed: 1972, c.20, sch.9.

1971—cont.

36. Motor Vehicles (Passenger Insurance) Act 1971—cont.

see *R.* v. *Goodchild; Att-Gen.'s Reference (No. 1 of 1977), The Times,* July 2, 1977, C.A.; *R.* v. *Carver, The Times,* July 14, 1978, H.L.; *R.* v. *Webb* [1979] Crim.L.R. 462, Canterbury Crown Ct.; *R.* v. *Taaffe* [1984] 2 W.L.R. 326, H.L.; *R.* v. *Hunt (Richard), The Times,* December 13, 1986, H.L.

regs. 73/797.

s. 2, see *R.* v. *Best; R.* v. *Rawlinson; R.* v. *Healey; R.* v. *Tighe; R.* v. *McCowan* (1979) 70 Cr.App.R. 21, C.A.; *R.* v. *S. Jakeman* (1983) 76 Cr.App.R. 223, C.A.; *R.* v. *Greensmith* [1983] 1 W.L.R. 1124, C.A.; *R.* v. *Watts (Nigel Blair)* [1984] 1 W.L.R. 757, C.A.

s. 2, orders 73/771; 75/421; 77/1243; 79/299; 83/765; 84/859; 85/1995; 86/2230.

s. 3, see *R.* v. *Watts and Stack* (1979) 70 Cr.App.R. 187, C.A.; *R.* v. *Whitehead* [1982] 3 W.L.R. 543, C.A.; *R.* v. *S. Jakeman* (1983) 76 Cr.App.R. 223, C.A.; *R.* v. *Ellis and Street; R.* v. *Smith (Gloria Marie), The Times,* August 12, 1986, C.A.

s. 4, see *Mieras* v. *Rees* [1979] Crim.L.R. 224, D.C.; *Haggard* v. *Mason* [1976] 1 W.L.R. 187; [1976] 1 All E.R. 337, D.C.; *R.* v. *Blake; R.* v. *O'Connor* (1978) 68 Cr.App.R. 1, C.A.; *R.* v. *Buckley* [1979] Crim.L.R. 665, C.A.; *R.* v. *Harris* (1979) 69 Cr.App.R. 122, C.A.; *R.* v. *Moore* [1979] Crim.L.R. 789, Surbiton Crown Ct.; *R.* v. *Kemp* (1979) 69 Cr.App.R. 330, C.A.; *R.* v. *Buckley* (1979) 69 Cr.App.R. 371, C.A.; *R.* v. *Cuthbertson* [1980] 3 W.L.R. 89, H.L.; *R.* v. *Farr* [1982] Crim.L.R. 745, C.A.; *R.* v. *Greenfield* [1983] Crim.L.R. 397, C.A.; *R.* v. *Hughes* (1985) 81 Cr.App.R. 344, C.A.; *R.* v. *Dempsey and Dempsey* (1986) 82 Cr.App.R. 291, C.A.; *Kerr* v. *H.M. Advocate,* 1986 S.C.C.R. 81; *R.* v. *Taylor* [1986] Crim.L.R. 680, St. Alban's Crown Court; *R.* v. *Maginnis* [1987] 2 W.L.R. 765, H.L.; *Trotter* v. *H.M. Advocate,* 1987 S.C.C.R. 131; *Tudhope* v. *McKee,* 1988 S.L.T. 153.

s. 5, see *R.* v. *Colyer* [1974] Crim.L.R. 243; *Allan* v. *Milne,* 1974 S.L.T.(Notes) 76; *Balloch* v. *Pagan,* 1976 S.L.T.(Notes) 5; *Arnott* v. *Mac-Farlane,* 1976 S.L.T.(Notes) 39; *R.* v. *Garland,* April 13, 1976; *R.* v. *Wright (Brian)* (1975) 62 Cr.App.R. 169, C.A.; *R.* v. *Pragliola* [1977] Crim.L.R. 612, Middlesex Crown Court; *R.* v. *Ashton-Rickhardt* (1977) 65 Cr.App.R. 67, C.A.; *Muir* v. *Smith* [1978] Crim.L.R. 293, D.C.; *R.* v. *King* [1978] Crim.L.R. 228, Maidstone Crown Ct.; *Nocher* v. *Smith,* 1978 S.L.T.(Notes) 32; *Walsh* v. *MacPhail,* 1978 S.L.T.(Notes) 29; *R.* v. *Carver* [1978] *The Times,* July 14, 1978, H.L.; *R.* v. *Peaston* (1978) 69 Cr.App.R. 203, C.A.; *R.* v. *Best* [1979] Crim.L.R. 787, C.A.; *R.* v. *Moore* [1979] Crim.L.R. 789, Surbiton Crown Ct.; *R.* v. *Chatwood* [1980] 1 All E.R. 467, C.A.; *Keane* v. *Gallacher,* High Court of Justiciary, January 11, 1980; *R.* v. *Best; R.* v. *Rawlinson; R.* v. *Healey; R.* v. *Tighe; R.* v. *McCowan* (1979)

1971—cont.

36. Motor Vehicles (Passenger Insurance) Act 1971—cont.

70 Cr.App.R. 21, C.A.; *Tarpy* v. *Rickard* [1980] Crim.L.R. 375, D.C.; *Meider* v. *Rattee,* June 12, 1980, D.C.; *Mingay* v. *Mackinnon,* 1980 J.C. 33; *R.* v. *Dunbar* [1981] 1 W.L.R. 1536, C.A.; *R.* v. *Boyesen* [1982] 2 All E.R. 161, H.L. *R.* v. *Greenfield* [1983] Crim.L.R. 397, C.A.; *McKenzie* v. *Skeen,* 1983 S.L.T. 121; *Morrison* v. *Smith,* 1983 S.C.C.R. 171; *R.* v. *Greensmith* [1983] 1 W.L.R. 1124, C.A.; *Chief Constable of Cheshire Constabulary* v. *Hunt* (1983) 147 J.P. 567, D.C.; *R.* v. *Delgado* [1984] 1 W.L.R. 89, C.A.; *R.* v. *Downes* [1984] Crim.L.R. 552, C.A.; *R.* v. *Watts (Nigel Blair)* [1984] 1 W.L.R. 757, C.A.; *Murray* v. *MacNaughton,* 1984 S.C.C.R. 361; *Donnelly* v. *H.M. Advocate,* 1984 S.C.C.R. 419; *Varley* v. *H.M. Advocate,* 1985 S.C.C.R. 55; *Miller* v. *H.M. Advocate,* 1985 S.C.C.R. 314; *Kerr* v. *H.M. Advocate,* 1986 S.C.C.R. 81; *R.* v. *Dempsey and Dempsey* (1986) 82 Cr.App.R. 291, C.A.; *Guild* v. *Ogilvie,* 1986 S.L.T. 343; *R.* v. *Martindale* [1986] 1 W.L.R. 1042, C.A.; *Allan* v. *Taylor,* 1986 S.C.C.R. 202; *R.* v. *Hunt (Richard)* [1986] 3 W.L.R. 1115, H.L.; *Campbell* v. *H.M. Advocate,* 1986 S.C.C.R. 403, *R.* v. *Maginnis* [1987] 2 W.L.R. 765, H.L.; *Young* v. *H.M. Advocate,* 1986 S.C.C.R. 583, *R.* v. *Walker* [1987] Crim.L.R. 565, C.A.; *Grundison* v. *Brown,* 1987 S.C.C.R. 186; *Heywood* v. *Macrae,* 1988 S.L.T. 218; *Gill* v. *Lockhart,* 1988 S.L.T. 189; *Wood* v. *Allen,* 1988 S.L.T. 341; *Simpson* v. *Hamilton,* 1988 S.C.C.R. 163.

s. 5, repealed in pt.: 1981, c.47, sch.

s. 6, see *Tudhope* v. *Robertson,* 1980 S.L.T. 60; *R.* v. *Champ* [1982] Crim.L.R. 108, C.A.

s. 7, see *R.* v. *Dunbar* [1981] 1 W.L.R. 1536, C.A.

s. 7, regs. 74/402, 1449; 75/499, 1623; 77/291; 84/1143; 88/916; orders 73/796; 75/498; 77/1379; 79/326; 83/788; 84/1144; 85/2066; 86/52, 2330, 2331; S.Rs. 1983 No. 151; 1984 Nos. 364, 365; 1987 Nos. 66, 68; 1988 No. 206.

s. 8, see *R.* v. *Tao* [1976] 3 W.L.R. 25, C.A.; *R.* v. *Thomas; R.* v. *Thomson* (1976) 63 Cr.App.R. 65, C.A.; *R.* v. *Josephs* (1977) 65 Cr.App.R. 253, C.A.; *Taylor* v. *Chief Constable of Kent* [1981] 1 W.L.R. 606, D.C.; *R.* v. *Campbell and Campbell* [1982] Crim.L.R. 595, Kingston Crown Ct.; *R.* v. *Farr* [1982] Crim.L.R. 745, C.A.

s. 9A, added: 1986, c.32.s.34.

s. 10, regs. 73/798, 799; 74/402, 1449; 75/294, 499, 1623; 77/290, 1380; 83/788; 84/17, 1143, 1146; 85/2066, 2067; 86/52, 53, 2330, 2332; 87/67; 88/916; S.Rs. 1979 No. 258; 1983 No. 151; 1984 Nos. 353, 365; 1987 No. 68; 1988 No. 206.

s. 12, amended: 1979, c.2, sch.4; repealed in pt.: 1981, c.47, s.7.

s. 19, see *Mieras* v. *Rees* [1975] Crim. L.R. 224, D.C.

1971—cont.

36. Motor Vehicles (Passenger Insurance) Act 1971—cont.

s. 19, repealed: 1981, c.47, sch.

s. 20, see *R.* v. *Vickers* [1975] 1 W.L.R. 811, C.A.; *R.* v. *Faulkner; R.* v. *Thomas* (1976) 63 Cr.App.R. 295, C.A.; *R.* v. *Evans (Ian)* [1977] Crim.L.R. 223; (1976) 64 Cr.App.R. 237, C.A.; *R.* v. *Panayi and Karte* [1987] Crim.L.R. 764; (1988) 86 Cr.App.R. 261, C.A.

s. 22, regs. 77/1380; 84/17; 85/2066; 86/52.

s. 22, amended: 1979, c.2, sch.4.

s. 23, see *R.* v. *Littleford* [1978] Crim.L.R. 48, Doncaster Crown Ct.; *Nocher* v. *Smith*, 1978 S.L.T.(Notes) 32; *R.* v. *Green* [1982] Crim.L.R. 604, C.A.; *H.M. Advocate* v. *Cumming*, 1983 S.C.C.R. 15; *R.* v. *Forde (James)* [1985] Crim.L.R. 323; (1985) 81 Cr.App.R. 19, C.A.; *Carmichael* v. *Brannen*, 1985 S.C.C.R. 234; *Foster* v. *Attard, The Times*, January 4, 1986, D.C.; *Allan* v. *Tant*, 1986 S.C.C.R. 175; *H.M. Advocate* v. *Welsh*, 1988 S.L.T. 402; *McCarron* v. *Allan*, 1988 S.C.C.R. 9; *Guthrie* v. *Hamilton, The Scotsman*, September 9, 1988; *Johns* v. *Hamilton*, 1988 S.C.C.R. 282; *Bell* v. *H.M. Advocate*, 1988 S.L.T. 820.

ss. 23, 24, see *Farrow* v. *Tunnicliffe* [1976] Crim.L.R. 126, D.C.; *Wither* v. *Reed*, 1979 S.L.T. 192.

s. 24, repealed: 1984, c.60, sch.7.

s. 25, amended: 1980, c.43, sch.7; 1981, c.47, sch.

s. 26, repealed: 1979, c.2, sch.6.

s. 27, see *R.* v. *Glover*, Sept. 9, 1974; *R.* v. *Beard (Graham)* [1974] 1 W.L.R. 1549; *Haggard* v. *Mason* [1976] 1 W.L.R. 187; [1976] 1 All E.R. 337, D.C.; *R.* v. *Menocal* [1979] 2 W.L.R. 876, H.L.; *R.* v. *Kemp* (1979) 69 Cr.App.R. 330, C.A.; *R.* v. *Cuthbertson* [1980] 3 W.L.R. 89, H.L.; *R.* v. *Khan; R.* v. *Crawley, The Times*, August 7, 1982, C.A.; *R.* v. *Ribeyre* (1982) Cr.App.R.(S.), 165, C.A.; *R.* v. *Marland and Jones* (1986) 82 Cr.App.R. 134, C.A.; *R.* v. *Maidstone Crown Court, ex p. Gill* [1986] Crim.L.R. 737, [1986] 1 W.L.R. 1405, D.C.; *R.* v. *Llewellyn (Kevin Anthony)* (1985) 7 Cr.App.R.(S.); 225, C.A.; *R.* v. *Cox* [1987] Crim.L.R. 141, C.A.; *R.* v. *Boothe* [1987] Crim.L.R. 347, C.A.; *R.* v. *Churcher* (1986) 8 Cr.App.R.(S.) 94, C.A.; *R.* v. *Askew* [1987] Crim.L.R. 584, C.A.; *R.* v. *Cox* (1986) 8 Cr.App.R. 384, C.A.; *R.* v. *Simms* [1988] Crim.L.R. 186, C.A.

s. 27, amended: 1988, c.33, s.70.

s. 28, see *R.* v. *Ashton-Rickhardt* (1977) 65 Cr.App.R. 67, C.A.; *R.* v. *Champ* [1982] Crim.L.R. 108, C.A.; *McKenzie* v. *Skeen*, 1983 S.L.T. 121; *R.* v. *Young (Robert Gordon)* [1984] 1 W.L.R. 654, C.A.; *H.M. Advocate* v. *Bell*, 1985 S.L.T. 349; *R.* v. *Ellis and Street; R.* v. *Smith (Gloria Marie), The Times*, August 12, 1986, C.A.; *R.* v. *McNamara, The Times*, February 16, 1988, C.A.; *Tudhope* v. *McKee*, 1988 S.L.T. 153.

1971—cont.

36. Motor Vehicles (Passenger Insurance) Act 1971—cont.

s. 30, regs. 74/962; 77/587; 79/218; 80/160; 81/152; 82/219; 83/196; 84/165; 85/138; 86/416; 87/298; 88/311; S.Rs. 1978 No. 6; 1979 No. 57; 1980 No. 64; 1981 No. 55; 1982 No. 52; 1984 No. 52; 1985 No. 32.

s. 31, regs. 73/798, 799; 74/402, 962, 1449; 75/294, 499, 1623; 77/290, 587, 1380; 79/218, 326; 80/160; 81/152; 82/219; 83/196, 788; 84/17, 165, 1143, 1146; 85/138, 2066, 2067; 86/52, 53, 416, 2330, 2332; 87/67, 298; 88/311, 916; S.R. 1978 No. 6; 1979 Nos. 57, 258; 1980 No. 64; 1981 No. 55; 1982 No. 52; 1983 No. 25; 1984 Nos. 353, 365; 1985 No. 32; 1987, No. 68; 1988 No. 206.

s. 34, repealed: 1978, c.22, sch.3.

s. 37, see *R.* v. *Berridale Johnston* [1976] Crim.L.R. 306; *R.* v. *Mitchell* [1977] 1 W.L.R. 753; [1977] 2 All E.R. 168, C.A.; *R.* v. *McMillan* (1977) 64 Cr.App.R. 104, C.A.; *R.* v. *Goodchild (No.2); Att.-Gen's Reference (No. 1 of 1977)* [1977] 1 W.L.R. 1213, C.A.; *D.P.P.* v. *Goodchild* [1978] 1 W.L.R. 578, H.L.; *R.* v. *Malcolm, The Times*, May 3, 1978, C.A.; *R.* v. *Buckley* (1979) 69 Cr.App.R. 371, C.A.; *R.* v. *Thomas* [1981] Crim.L.R. 496, C.A.; *Taylor* v. *Chief Constable of Kent* [1981] 1 W.L.R. 606, D.C.; *R.* v. *Delgado* [1984] 1 W.L.R. 89, C.A.

s. 37, regs. 87/298; 88/311.

s. 37, amended: 1977, c.45, s.52; 1983, c.54, sch.5; order 80/703; 1984, s.24, sch.4.

s. 38, regs. 77/290; 84/17; 86/52, 53; 87/67; S.Rs. 1978 No. 6; 1979 Nos. 57, 258; 1981 No. 55; 1982 No. 52; 1983 No. 151; 1984 Nos. 52, 353, 365; 1985 No. 32; 1987 No. 68; 1988 No. 206.

s. 38, repealed in pt.: 1973, c.36, sch.6.

s. 39, see *R.* v. *Goodchild* [1977] 1 W.L.R. 473; [1977] 1 All E.R. 163, C.A.

s. 40, order 73/795.

sch. 2, see *R.* v. *Goodchild (No. 2); Att.-Gen.'s Reference (No. 1 of 1977)* [1977] 1 W.L.R. 1213, C.A.; *D.P.P.* v. *Goodchild* [1978] 1 W.L.R. 578, H.L.; *R.* v. *Kemp* (1979) 69 Cr.App.R. 330, C.A.; *Keane* v. *Gallacher*, High Court of Justiciary, January 11, 1980; *R.* v. *Best; R.* v. *Rawlinson; R.* v. *Healey; R.* v. *Tighe; R.* v. *McCowan* (1979) 70 Cr.App.R. 21, C.A.; *R.* v. *Watts and Stack* (1979) 70 Cr.App.R. 187, C.A.; *R.* v. *Stevens* [1981] Crim.L.R. 568, C.A.; *R.* v. *Greensmith* [1983] 1 W.L.R. 1124, C.A.; *R.* v. *S. Jakeman* (1983) 76 Cr.App.R. 223, C.A.; *R.* v. *Watts (Nigel Blair)* [1984] 1 W.L.R. 757, C.A.; *Murray* v. *MacNaughton*, 1984 S.C.C.R. 361; *R.* v. *Cunliffe* [1986] Crim.L.R. 547, C.A.; *R.* v. *Walker* [1987] Crim.L.R. 565, C.A.; *Heywood* v. *Macrae*, 1988 S.L.T. 218.

sch. 2, amended: orders 75/421; 77/1243; 79/299; 83/765; 84/859; 85/1995; repealed in pt.: orders 84/859; 85/1995.

sch. 3, rules 74/85, 459; amended: 1978, c.23, sch.5; 1981, c.54, sch.5.

1971—cont.

36. Motor Vehicles (Passenger Insurance) Act 1971—cont.

sch. 4, see *Kerr* v. *H.M. Advocate*, 1986 S.C.C.R. 81.

sch. 4, amended: 1977, c.45, s.31, sch.6; 1985, c.39, s.1; 1986, c.32, s.34.

39. Rating Act 1971.

ss. 1, 2, see *Cresswell* v. *B.O.C.* [1980] 3 All E.R. 443, C.A.; *Hemens (V.O.)* v. *Whitsbury Farm and Stud* [1988] 2 W.L.R. 72, H.L.

Pt. I (ss.1–4), repealed (prosp.): 1988, c.41, sch.13.

s. 2, amended: regs. 78/318.

s. 4, see *Corser* v. *Gloucestershire Marketing Society, The Times*, November 21, 1980, C.A.; *Prior (Valuation Officer)* v. *Sovereign Chicken* [1984] 2 All E.R. 289, C.A.

s. 5, see *Wallace* v. *Perth & Kinross Assessor*, 1975 S.L.T.(Notes) 12; *Ayrshire Assessor* v. *Macster Poultry*, 1977 S.L.T. 158; amended: regs. 77/2007; *Lothian Regional Assessor* v. *Hood* (1987) 27 R.V.R. 132, Lands Valuation Appeal Ct.

ss. 5, 6, see *Assessor for Lothian Region* v. *Hood*, 1988 S.L.T. 161.

ss. 5, 7, see *Assessor for Tayside Region* v. *D. B. Marshall (Newbridge)*, 1983 S.C. 54.

s. 7, see *Lowlands Cereals* v. *Assessor for Lothian Region*, Lands Valuation Appeal Court, June 2, 1979.

ss. 7, 8, see *Roxburgh Assessor* v. *West Cumberland Farmers Trading Society*, Lands Val.Appeal Ct., December 14, 1973.

s. 9, see *Glasgow Assessor* v. *Berridale Allotments*, 1973 S.L.T. 178.

40. Fire Precautions Act 1971.

s. 1, orders 72/238, 382; 76/2009.

s. 1, amended: 1987, c.27, s.1.

s. 2, repealed in pt.: *ibid.*, s.13, sch.4.

s. 5, regs. 72/237, 392; 76/2008.

s. 5, amended: 1987, c.27, ss.1, 4, 8; repealed in pt.: *ibid.*, s.15, sch.4.

ss. 5, 9, see *McGovern* v. *Central Regional Council*, 1982 S.L.T.(Sh.Ct.) 110.

ss. 5, 10, see *Hallett* v. *Nicholson*, 1979 S.C. 1, Ct. of Session.

ss. 5A, 5B, added: 1987, c.27, s.1.

s. 6, repealed in pt.: *ibid.*, sch.4.

s. 7, see *Berry* v. *Smith*, 1984 S.L.T. 79; *R.* v. *Mabbott* [1987] Crim.L.R. 826; (1988) R.V.R. 131, C.A.

s. 7, amended: 1987, c.27, ss.8, 14.

s. 8A, added: *ibid.*, s.2.

s. 8B, added: *ibid.*, s.3.

s. 9A, see *Oxfordshire County Council* v. *Chancellor, Master and Scholars of Oxford University, The Times*, December 10, 1980, D.C.

s. 9A, substituted: 1987, c.27, s.5.

ss. 9B, 9C, added: *ibid.*, s.6.

ss. 9D, 9E, 9F, added: *ibid.*, s.7.

s. 10, substituted: *ibid.*, s.9.

ss. 10A, 10B, amended: *ibid.*

s. 11, repealed: 1974, c.37, sch.10.

s. 12, regs. 76/2010.

1971—cont.

40. Fire Precautions Act 1971—cont.

s. 12, amended: 1974, c.37, s.78; 1985, c.13, sch.3; 1987, c.27, s.13; repealed in pt.: 1985, c.13, sch.3; 1987, c.27, s.13, sch.4.

s. 13, repealed in pt.: 1984, c.55, sch.7.

s. 14, amended: 1987, c.27, s.7.

s. 15, repealed: 1984, c.55, sch.7.

s. 17, amended: 1973, c.65, sch.15; 1974, c.37, s.78; 1987, c.27, s.7; repealed in pt.: 1973, c.65, schs.15, 29; 1974, c.37, s.78, sch.10; order 88/1955.

s. 18, amended: 1974, c.37, s.78; 1987, c.27, s.10.

s. 19, amended: *ibid.*, s.2.

s. 21, amended: *ibid.*, s.11.

s. 22, repealed in pt.: 1981, c.45, sch.

s. 26, amended: 1980, c.43, sch.7.

s. 27, repealed in pt.: S.L.R. 1986.

s. 27A, added: 1987, c.27, s.12.

s. 28, amended: 1977, c.42, sch.23; 1984, c.58, sch.8(S.); repealed in pt.: S.L.R. 1978.

s. 28A, added: 1987, c.27, s.16.

s. 30, amended: 1984, c.55, sch.6; repealed in pt.: *ibid.*, sch.7.

s. 34, amended: 1972, c.46, sch.9; 1977, c.42, sch.23; 1984, c.58, sch.8(S.); 1987, c.27, s.16; repealed in pt.: 1972, c.46, schs.9, 11; 1984, c.58, sch.10(S.).

s. 35, amended: 1987, c.27, s.17.

s. 36, amended: 1985, c.71, sch.2.

s. 37, regs. 76/2010.

s. 40, amended: 1974, c.37, s.78; 1982, c.48, sch.14; 1987, c.27, s.18; repealed in pt.: 1984, c.55, sch.7; 1988, c.33, sch.16.

s. 42, repealed: 1973, c.36, sch.6.

s. 43, regs. 72/237.

s. 43, amended: 1973, c.65, sch.27; 1974, c.37, s.78; 1987, c.27, ss.4, 9; repealed in pt.: 1974, c.37, sch.10; order 74/595; 1987, c.27, ss.12, 16, sch.4.

s. 44, orders 72/236; 76/2006.

s. 44, repealed in pt.: 1973, c.36, sch.6.

sch. renumbered sch. 1: 1987, c.27, s.16, sch.1; amended: 1972, c.46, sch.9; 1975, c.28, sch.2; 1984, c.58, sch.8(S.); repealed in pt.: 1972, c.46, sch.11; c.47, sch.11; 1977, c.42, sch.25; 1980, c.52, sch.5(S); 1984, c.58, sch.10(S.); 1988, c.43, sch.10.

sch. 2, added: 1987, c.27, s.16, sch.1.

41. Highways Act 1971.

repealed: 1980, c.66, sch.25.

s. 4, see *Lovelock* v. *Secretary of State for Transport* [1979] R.T.R. 250, C.A.

s. 8, see *Walters* v. *Secretary of State for the Environment* [1977] J.P.L. 172.

s. 11, schemes 73/1008; 79/1664; 80/1006.

s. 18, regs. 73/686; 74/735.

s. 31, see *Lambeth London Borough Council* v. *Saunders Transport* [1974] Crim.L.R. 311; [1974] R.T.R. 319, D.C.; *Barnet L.B.C.* v. *S. & W. Transport* [1975] R.T.R. 211, D.C.; *York District Council (formerly York City Council)* v. *Pollen* (1975) 73 L.G.R. 522, D.C.; *P.G.M.*

1971—cont.

41. Highways Act 1971—cont.
Building Co. v. Kensington and Chelsea (Royal) London Borough Council [1982] R.T.R. 107, D.C.
s. 87, order 77/2003.

42. Education (Scotland) Act 1971.
repealed: 1980, c.44, sch.5.

43. Law Reform (Miscellaneous Provisions) Act 1971.
ss. 1–3, repealed: 1973, c.52, sch.5(S.); 1975, c.54, sch.2.
s. 4, see Howitt v. Heads [1972] 2 W.L.R. 183; sub nom. Howitt (Widow of R. A. Howitt) v. Heads [1972] 1 All E.R. 491; Thompson v. Price [1973] 2 W.L.R. 1037; [1973] 2 All E.R. 846; McKinnon v. Reid, 1975 S.C. 233.
ss. 4, 5, repealed: 1976, c.30, sch.2.
ss. 4, 6, see Wilson v. Dagnall [1972] 1 Q.B. 509; [1972] 2 W.L.R. 823; [1972] 2 All E.R. 44.
s. 6, repealed in pt.: 1973, c.36, sch.6.
schs. 1, 2, repealed: 1973, c.52, sch.5(S.); 1975, c.54, sch.2.

44. Nullity of Marriage Act 1971.
repealed: 1973, c.18, sch.3.
s. 1, see Dryden v. Dryden [1973] 3 W.L.R. 524; [1973] 3 All E.R. 526, Baker P.

45. Redemption of Standard Securities (Scotland) Act 1971.
s. 2, amended: 1985, c.9, sch.2.

46. Shipbuilding Industry Act 1971.
repealed: 1972, c.63, sch.4.

47. Wild Creatures and Forest Laws Act 1971.
s. 2, amended: 1973, c.36, sch.6.

48. Criminal Damage Act 1971.
see R. v. Briggs (1976) 63 Cr.App.R. 215, C.A.
s. 1, see R. v. Parker (1976) 63 Cr.App.R. 211, C.A.; R. v. O'Driscoll [1977] Crim.L.R. 560, C.A.; R. v. Criminal Injuries Compensation Board, ex p. Clowes [1977] 3 All E.R. 854, D.C.; R. v. Stephenson [1979] 2 W.L.R. 193, C.A.; A.C. (A Minor) v. Hume [1979] R.T.R. 424, D.C.; R. v. Mullins [1980] Crim.L.R. 37, C.A.; R. v. Orpin [1980] 2 All E.R. 321, C.A.; R. v. Considine (1979) 70 Cr.App.R. 239, C.A.; R. v. Hoof [1980] Crim.L.R. 719; (1980) 72 Cr.App.R. 126, C.A.; R. v. Caldwell [1981] 1 All E.R. 961, H.L.; M. (A Minor) v. Oxford [1981] R.T.R. 246, D.C.; Pike v. Morrison [1981] Crim.L.R. 492, D.C; R. v. Miller [1983] 2 W.L.R. 539; [1983] 77 Cr.App.R. 17, H.L.; Elliott v. C. (A Minor) [1983] 2 All E.R. 1005, D.C.; R. v. R., The Times, July 31, 1984, C.A.; R. v. Hardie [1984] 3 All E.R. 848, C.A.; R. v. R. (S.M.) (1984) 79 Cr.App.R. 334, C.A.; R. v. Appleyard (1985) 81 Cr.App.R. 319, C.A.; Hardman v. Chief Constable of Avon & Somerset Constabulary [1986] Crim.L.R. 330, Bristol Crown Court; Cox v. Riley [1986] Crim.L.R. 460; (1986) 83 Cr.App.R. 54, D.C.; Chief Constable of Avon and Somerset Constabulary v. Shimmen (1987) 84 Cr.App.R. 7, D.C.; R. v. Steer [1987] 3 W.L.R. 205, H.L.; R. v. Sangha [1988] 1 W.L.R. 519, C.A.; R. v. Morrison, The Times, November 12, 1988, C.A.

1971—cont.

48. Criminal Damage Act 1971—cont.
ss. 1, 5, see R. v. Smith [1974] 2 W.L.R. 20, C.A.; R. v. Denton [1981] 1 W.L.R. 1446, C.A.
ss. 1, 7, see R. v. Aylesbury Crown Court [1972] 3 All E.R. 574.
s. 2, see R. v. Harrison (1973) 57 Cr.App.R. 206, C.A.
s. 3, see R. v. Buckingham (1976) 63 Cr.App.R. 159, C.A.; R. v. Fancy [1980] Crim.L.R. 171, Inner London Crown Ct.
s. 5, see R. v. Hunt [1977] Crim.L.R. 740, C.A.; Jaggard v. Dickinson [1980] 3 All E.R. 716, D.C.
s. 7, amended: 1972, c.71, sch.6.
s. 8, repealed: ibid.,s.1, sch.6.
s. 10, see Cox v. Riley [1986] Crim.L.R. 460; (1986) 83 Cr.App.R. 54, D.C.
s. 11, sch., see R. v. Bentham [1972] 3 W.L.R. 398.

50. National Insurance Act 1971.
repealed: 1975, c.18, sch.1.
s. 12, regs. 72/1150.
s. 16, sch. 6, order 72/1149.

51. Investment and Building Grants Act 1971.
s. 1, orders 72/34; 73/384; 74/646; 75/32; 76/41; 77/12; 78/75.
s. 1, amended: 1972, c.9, s.2; 1985, c.9, sch.2.
ss. 2, 3 (in pt.), repealed: 1972, c.5, sch.4.

52. Statute Law Revision Act 1971.
s. 2, repealed in pt.: 1973, c.36, sch.6.

53. Recognition of Divorces and Legal Separations Act 1971.
repealed: 1986, c.55, sch 2.
see Viswalingham v. Viswalingham (1979) 123 S.J. 604, C.A.; R. v. Immigration Appeal Tribunal, ex p. Secretary of State for the Home Department, The Times, July 15, 1983, Taylor J.; Lawrence v. Lawrence, The Times, July 18, 1984, Lincoln J.
s. 2, see Radwan v. Radwan [1972] 3 W.L.R. 735; [1972] 3 All E.R. 967; Quazi v. Quazi [1979] 3 W.L.R. 833, H.L.; Chaudhary v. Chaudhary [1984] 3 All E.R. 1017, C.A.
ss. 2, 3, see R. v. Registrar General of Births, Deaths and Marriages, ex p. Minhas [1976] 2 W.L.R. 473, D.C., R. v. Secretary of State for the Home Department, ex p. Fatima [1986] 2 W.L.R. 693, H.L.
ss. 2–5, see Sharif v. Sharif (1980) 10 Fam. Law 216, Wood J.
s. 3, see Cruse v. Chittum (formerly Cruse) [1974] 2 All E.R. 940; Lawrence v. Lawrence [1985] 3 W.L.R. 125, C.A.
ss. 3, 5, see Torok v. Torok [1973] 1 W.L.R. 1066; [1973] 3 All E.R. 101, Ormrod J.
s. 6, see Chaudhary v. Chaudhary [1984] 3 All E.R. 1017, C.A.
s. 7, see Lawrence v. Lawrence [1985] 3 W.L.R. 125, C.A.
s. 8, see Kendall v. Kendall [1977] 3 W.L.R. 251, Hollings J.; Newmarch v. Newmarch [1977] Fam.Law 143; [1977] 3 W.L.R. 832, Rees J.; Joyce v. Joyce and O'Hare [1979] 2 All E.R. 156, Lane J.; Sharif v. Sharif (1980) 10

CAP.

1971—cont.

53. Recognition of Divorces and Legal Separations Act 1971—cont.

Fam.Law 216, Wood J.; *Zaal* v. *Zaal* (1982) 12 Fam.Law 173, Bush J.; *Chaudhary* v. *Chaudhary* [1984] 3 All E.R. 1017, C.A.; *Mamdani* v. *Mamdani* (1985) 15 Fam.Law 122, C.A.; *Sabbagh* v. *Sabbagh* (1985) 15 Fam.Law 187, Balcombe J.

54. Land Registration and Land Charges Act 1971.

s. 4, rules 72/985.

ss. 5–11, sch.1, repealed: 1972, c.61, sch.5.

ss. 12, 15, repealed in pt. *ibid.*

s. 14, repealed in pt.: 1975, c.76, sch.2.

55. Law Reform (Jurisdiction in Delict) (Scotland) Act 1971.

repealed: 1982, c.27, sch.14.

see *Kirkcaldy District Council* v. *Household Manufacturing* (O.H.), 1987 S.L.T. 617.

s. 1, see *Pollock* v. *Pollock*, 1973 S.L.T. (Notes) 66; *Buchan* v. *Thomson*, 1974 S.L.T. 124 (O.H.); *Russell* v. *F. W. Woolworth & Co.* (O.H.), November 6, 1981; *Comex Houlder Diving* v. *Colne Fishing Co.*, 1987 S.L.T. 13.

s. 2, see *Rogers* v. *Rogers* [1974] 1 W.L.R. 709; [1974] 2 All E.R. 361.

56. Pensions (Increase) Act 1971.

s. 1, amended: 1974, c.9, s.3.

s. 2, orders 72/1298; 73/1370; 74/1373; 76/1356; 77/1387.

s. 2, repealed in pt.: 1975, c.60, sch.5.

s. 3, amended: 1974, c.9, s.3; order 72/1299; repealed in pt.: 1974, c.9, s.3; 1975, c.72, sch.4.

s. 4, amended: 1972, c.11, sch.6.

s. 5, see *Hertfordshire County Council* v. *Retirement Lease Housing Association* (1988) 86 L.G.R. 222, Hoffmann J.; *R.* v. *Hill; R.* v. *Hall, The Times*, October 6, 1988, C.A.

s. 5, regs. 72/71, 550, 990, 1653–1656, 1905; 73/382, 432, 495, 965, 1794, 1838; 74/983, 984, 1094, 1333, 1740, 2029; 75/931, 1478; 76/348, 889; 77/136, 320, 1652; 78/210, 211, 1808; 79/762, 771; 83/1315; 86/391.

s. 5, amended: 1972, c.11, sch.6;c.48, s.31; order 74/1264; 1975, c.60, sch.4; repealed in pt.: order 79/1451.

s. 9, orders 72/1298; 73/1370; 77/1387.

s. 9, amended: 1972, c.11, sch.6; repealed in pt.: 1975, c.60, sch.5.

s. 10, regs. 72/990; 73/1794; 79/1276.

s. 11, regs. 72/550, 1675; 74/1867; 75/1260; 76/1519, 1830, 2013, 2024; 77/320, 1675; 79/1277; 82/686.

s. 11, amended: 1973, c.21, s.4; repealed in pt.: *ibid.*,sch.2.

s. 11A, regs. 73/1792–1794; 75/1260; 76/1519, 1830; 76/2013, 2024; 77/320, 1675; 79/1276, 1277; 82/686.

s. 11A, added: 1973, c.21, s.4.

s. 12, regs. 73/1793; 77/320.

s. 13, regs. 72/387, 395, 877, 931, 1222, 1241, 1354, 1355; 73/942, 1068; 74/737; 75/503, 2045; 76/1451, 1690; 77/286; 80/1869; 84/1751.

CAP.

1971—cont.

56. Pensions (Increase) Act 1971—cont.

s. 13, amended: 1972, c.11, sch.6; 1974, c.9, s.3; order 74/1264; repealed in pt.: order 79/1451.

s. 14, repealed: 1972, c.11, sch.8.

s. 15, amended: 1975, c.60, sch.4; repealed in pt.: 1972, c.11, sch.8.

s. 17, amended: 1974, c.9, ss.1,3.

s. 18, regs. 72/550, 990, 1241.

s. 19, amended: 1976, c.4, sch.5; repealed in pt.: *ibid.*

sch. 2, amended: 1972, c.11, sch.6; c.48, s.31; 1973, c.15, ss.5, 11, 20, schs. 1, 4; 1973, c.21, s.4; c.32, sch. 4; c.41, sch. 12; 1975, c.18, s.1, sch. 2; 1975, c.69, sch. 4; 1976, c.35, sch. 2(S.); 1977, c.16, s.3; c.42, sch. 23; 1977, c.49, sch. 14; 1978, c.29, sch. 15(S.); 1979, c.50, s.4; 1980, c.9, sch. 9; 1981, c.20, sch. 3; 1984, c.27, sch. 13; 1985, c.51, s.61; regs. 74/1264; 78/210, 211; order 76/146; 1987, c.45, sch.3; 1988, c.13, sch.3; c.40, s.179; repealed in pt.: 1972, c.11, schs. 6, 8; 1976, c.4, schs. 5, 6; 1981, c.20, sch. 3; 1985, c.51, sch. 17; S.L.R. 1986.

sch. 3, amended: 1972, c.11, sch.6; 1974, c.9, ss.2,3; orders 74/595; 75/944; 1985, c.51, sch.61; c.67, sch.3; 1988, c.40, s.179.

sch. 4, regs. 72/1222.

sch. 4, repealed in pt.: 1973, c.21, sch.2.

sch. 6, regs. 72/1354; 76/1451, 1690.

sch. 6, amended: order 74/520.

57. Pool Competitions Act 1971.

continued in force: orders 83/1033; 85/1069; 86/1234.

s. 2, amended: 1976, c.32, sch.4; repealed in pt.: *ibid.*,sch.5.

s. 5, order 73/1076.

s. 6, repealed in pt.: 1975, c.59, sch.6.

s. 8, orders 77/907; 79/763; 80/876; 81/1028; 82/1010; 83/1033; 84/977; 85/1069; 86/1234.

s. 8, amended: orders 76/939; 78/778; 80/876; 82/1010; continued in force: order 84/977.

58. Sheriff Courts (Scotland) Act 1971.

s. 2, order 74/2087.

s. 3, orders 75/637, 1539; 77/672; 78/152; 83/1028.

s. 4, repealed in pt.: 1978, c.30, sch.3.

s. 6, repealed in pt.: 1985, c.73, s.20, sch.4.

ss. 10, 11, amended: 1980, c.55, s.10.

s. 21, repealed: 1975, c.24, sch.3; c.25, sch.3.

s. 23, regs. 73/402.

s. 27, regs. 75/734; 83/264.

s. 30, order 73/277.

s. 32, rules 72/1671; 74/939, 1981.

s. 32, Acts of Sederunt 73/542, 543, 1860; 75/474, 475; 76/374, 467, 476, 744, 1581, 1606, 2160; 77/973, 1180, 1622, 1723; 78/112, 162, 229, 1805, 1979; 79/226, 613, 1520; 80/291, 423, 455, 1443, 1732, 1802, 1803; 81/1591; 82/1432; 83/747, 1438, 1546; 84/255, 667, 921, 1013; 85/821, 1427, 1976; 86/513, 517, 545, 692, 1230, 1946, 1947, 1966, 2296, 2297; 88/613, 614, 1976, 1978, 2013, 2059.

s. 32, amended: 1977, c.28, s.29; 1985, c.73, sch.2; 1988, c.32, s.2.

1971—cont.

58. Sheriff Courts (Scotland) Act 1971—cont.

s. 33, repealed in pt.: 1985, c.73, schs.2, 4.

s. 35, see *Tennent Caledonian Breweries* v. *Gearty*, 1980 S.L.T. (Sh.Ct.) 71; *Prestwick Investment Trust* v. *Jones*, 1981 S.L.T.(Sh.Ct.) 55; *Monklands District Council* v. *Johnstone* (Sh.Ct.), 1987 S.C.L.R. 480.

s. 35, amended: 1985, c.73, s.18, sch.2.

s. 36, repealed in pt.: 1987, c.18, sch.8.

ss. 36A, 36B, added: 1985, c.73, s.18, sch.2.

s. 37, see *Hamilton District Council* v. *Sneddon*, 1980 S.L.T.(Sh.Ct.) 36; *Butler* v. *Thom*, 1982 S.L.T.(Sh.Ct.) 57; *Forsyth* v. *John Dickinson Group*, 1984 S.L.T.(Sh.Ct.) 51; *Monklands District Council* v. *Baird* (Sh.Ct.), 1987 S.C.L.R. 88; *Shaw* v. *Lanarkshire Health Board* (Sh.Ct.), 1988 S.C.L.R. 13.

s. 37, amended: 1980, c.55, s.16; 1983, c.12, sch.1; 1985, c.73, s.18, sch.2; 1986, c.9, sch.1.

s. 38, see *Rediffusion* v. *McIlroy*, 1986 S.L.T.(Sh.Ct.) 33; *Webster Engineering Services* v. *Gibson*, 1987 S.L.T.(Sh.Ct.) 101.

s. 38, amended: 1985, c.73, s.18, sch.2.

ss. 38, 45, see *W. Jack Baillie Associates* v. *Kennedy* 1985 S.L.T.(Sh.Ct.) 53.

ss. 39, 40, repealed: 1983, c.12, sch.3.

s. 41, orders, 76/900; 81/842.

s. 41, repealed in pt.: 1980, c.55, sch.3.

s. 43, orders 74/2087; 75/637.

s. 47, repealed in pt.: 1975, c.24, sch.3; c.25, sch.3; order 76/236.

sch. 1, amended: 1972, c.46, s.11; Act of Sederunt 77/1723; repealed in pt.: 1984, c.58, sch.10.

59. Merchant Shipping (Oil Pollution) Act 1971.

extended: orders 75/2184–2186; 76/53.

ss. 1, 6, see *Esso Petroleum* v. *Hall Russell & Co.*, 1988 S.L.T. 33.

ss. 1–4, substituted: 1988, c.12, sch.4.

s. 4, orders 75/868, 1614; 76/1031, 2189; 78/54, 1468; 79/790; 80/280, 1872.

s. 5, amended: 1979, c.39, s.38, sch.5; 1988, c.12, sch.4.

s. 7, amended: 1979, c.39, sch.5; 1988, c.12, sch.4.

s. 8, amended: 1974, c.43, s.9.

s. 8A, orders 75/1036; 76/1039; 77/48, 826; 79/1450; 83/416.

s. 8A, repealed: 1979, c.39, sch.7.

s. 9, amended: 1988, c.12, sch.4.

s. 10, regs. 75/1234, 1759; 76/154, 857, 1177, 1440; 77/85; 81/912.

s. 10, amended: 1979, c.39, sch.6; 1988, c.12, sch.4; repealed in pt.: *ibid.*, schs.4,7.

s. 11, regs. 75/869, 2002; 77/85; 79/1593; 81/912; 82/257.

s. 11, amended: 1979, c.39, s.37.

s. 12, amended: 1988, c.12, sch.4.

s. 13, amended: 1981, c.54, sch.5; 1888, c.12, sch.4.

s. 14, amended: 1979, c.30, s.38; 1988, c.12, sch.4.

s. 15, amended: 1979, c.39, sch.5; 1988, c.12, sch.4; repealed in pt.: *ibid.*, sch.7.

1971—cont.

59. Merchant Shipping (Oil Pollution) Act 1971—cont.

s. 17, amended: *ibid.*, sch.4.

s. 18, orders 75/2164–2175, 2184, 2185, 2186; 76/53, 223, 2143; 81/214–224, 431, 433, 434; 83/1519; 84/543; 85/1197; 87/1263.

s. 19, orders 75/1036; 76/1039; 77/48, 826; 79/1450; 83/416; 86/2225.

s. 20, substituted: 1988, c.12, sch.4.

s. 21, order 75/867.

60. Prevention of Oil Pollution Act 1971.

amended: 1982, c.48, s.49.

s. 1, regs. 84/1684.

s. 1, repealed in pt.: order 83/1106.

s. 2, see *Rankin* v. *De Coster* [1975] 1 W.L.R. 606, D.C.; *Davies* v. *Smith*, 1983 S.L.T. 644.

s. 2, amended: 1986, c.6, s.1; repealed in pt.: order 83/1106.

ss. 4, 8 (in pt.), repealed: order 83/1106.

ss. 9–11, amended: 1979, c.39, sch.6.

s. 15, repealed in pt.: 1985, c.9, sch.2.

s. 16, orders 79/1453; 80/1093, 1522; 82/1669.

s. 17, amended: 1979, c.39, sch.6.

s. 18, amended: *ibid.*, s.28, sch.6; repealed in pt.: *ibid.*, s.28, sch.7.

s. 20, amended (S.): 1987, c.18, sch.6.

s. 21, orders 73/1752; 76/1160; 78/188; 79/721; 80/717, 1521; 81/612.

s. 23, amended: 1975, c.74, s.45.

s. 25, orders 79/1452; 80/1520; 82/1668.

s. 30, amended: 1973, c.36, sch.6.

s. 34, order 73/203.

61. Mineral Workings (Offshore Installations) Act 1971.

regs. 72/703; 73/1842; amended: 1975, c.74, s.44.

s. 1, order 82/1524.

s. 1, substituted: 1982, c.23, s.24; 1987, c.49, sch.1.

s. 2, regs. 72/702.

s. 3, regs. 74/289, 388, 1299; 76/1019; 84/419.

ss. 3–5, amended: 1982, c.23, sch.3.

s. 6, regs. 72/1542; 74/289, 388, 1299; 75/1280; 76/931, 1019, 1542; 79/1203; 80/322; 81/364; 82/360; 83/1258; 84/419; 85/1612; 87/129.

s. 6, amended (S.): 1976, c.14, sch.1; 1982, c.23, sch.3; repealed in pt. *ibid.*, schs.3,4.

s. 7, regs. 72/702, 1542; 74/289, 388, 1299; 75/1289; 76/1019, 1542; 77/486; 78/611; 80/1759; 84/419.

s. 8, repealed: 1982, c.23, sch.4.

s. 9, repealed in pt.: *ibid.*

s. 10, repealed: *ibid.*, s.27, sch.4.

s. 11, amended: order 77/1251.

s. 12, regs. 72/702.

s. 12, amended: 1975, c.74, s.44; 1982, c.23, sch.3; repealed in pt.: *ibid.*, schs.3,4.

s. 14, amended: 1973, c.36, sch.6.

s. 14, order 72/644.

sch., regs. 72/1542; 74/289, 388, 1299; 75/1289; 76/1019, 1542; 77/486; 78/611; 80/1759; 84/419.

1971—cont.

62. Tribunals and Inquiries Act 1971.
see *Re Leeds Federated Housing Association* (1981) 260 E.G. 813, Sir Douglas Frank Q.C.
s. 6, repealed: 1972, c.70, sch.30.
s. 7, amended: 1976, c.71, sch.7; 1977, c.5, s.22, sch.2; 1983, c.41, sch.9; repealed in pt.: 1980, c.51, sch.26.
s. 8, regs. 80/1640.
s. 8, amended: 1974, c.39, s.3; 1976, c.83, sch.1; 1979, c.38, s.24; 1984, c.35, sch.2; 1985, c.65, sch.1; 1987, c.22, sch.6; 1988, c.33, sch.15; repealed in pt.: 1980, c.53, sch.7.
s. 9, repealed: 1985, c.17, sch.5.
s. 10, regs. 77/644, 1033; orders 76/191, 308; 78/259, 540; 79/5, 514; 80/377, 637, 1622, 1640; 82/38–40, 844; 83/550; 84/176; 85/967, 980, 1092; rules 76/447; 78/607, 1780; 80/1605; 82/270, 718, 1400, 1489; 83/180, 942; 84/793, 1346, 1989; 85/784, 785, 921; 86/366, 952; orders 84/1300, 1301.
s. 11, rules 74/419, 420; 75/2040, 2068; 76/721, 746; 80/1676, 1677; 81/1743, 1841; 84/999; 86/420, 1700(S.), 1761, 1957; 87/1522(S.), 2182; 88/944, 945.
s. 12, see *Metropolitan Property Holdings* v. *Laufer* (1974) 29 P. & C.R. 172, D.C.; *Albyn Properties* v. *Knox*, 1977 S.L.T. 41; *Crake* v. *Supplementary Benefits Commission; Butterworth* v. *Supplementary Benefits Commission* [1982] 1 All E.R. 498, Woolf J.; *R.* v. *London Rent Assessment Committee, ex p. St. George's Court* (1983) 265 E.G. 984, McCullough J.; *Westminster City Council* v. *Secretary of State for the Environment and City Commercial Real Estates Investments* [1984] J.P.L. 27, David Widdicombe Q.C.; *R.* v. *Secretary of State for Social Services, ex p. Connolly* [1986] 1 W.L.R. 421, C.A.
s. 12, order 80/1637.
ss. 12, 14, see *Islington London Borough Council* v. *Secretary of State for the Environment; Stockport Metropolitan Borough Council* v. *Secretary of State for the Environment* (1982) 43 P. & C.R. 300, C.A.
s. 13, see *Midanbury Properties (Southampton)* v. *Houghton; T. Clark & Son* v. *Heathfield (No. 2)* (1982) 263 E.G. 797, Sir Douglas Frank Q.C.; *Ellis and Son Fourth Amalgamated Properties* v. *Southern Rent Assessment Panel* (1984) 270 E.G. 39, Mann J.
s. 13, rules 73/540; Act of Sederunt 76/847.
s. 13, amended: 1978, c.23, sch.5; c.44, sch.16; 1980, c.20, s.7; 1981, c.54, sch.5; 1983, c.41, sch.9; 1984, c.31, sch.2; 1985, c.65, sch.1; repealed in pt.: 1977, c.38, sch.5; 1980, c.34, sch.9; c.51, sch.26; 1983, c.41, sch.10.
s. 14, see *R.* v. *Registrar of Companies, ex p. Central Bank of India* [1986] 1 All E.R. 105, C.A.; *R.* v. *Secretary of State for Foreign and Commonwealth Affairs, ex p. Trawnick, The Times,* February 21, 1986, C.A.
s. 14, amended: order 75/816; repealed in pt.: 1981, c.58, sch.9.

1971—cont.

62. Tribunals and Inquiries Act 1971—*cont.*
s. 15, orders 72/1210; 73/1600; 74/1478, 1964; 75/1937; 77/1735; 79/659; 80/1601; 84/1094.
s. 16, orders 80/1601; 83/1287.
s. 19, order 83/1287.
s. 19, amended: 1974, c.39, s.3; 1979, c.38, s.24.
sch. 1, amended: 1972, c.11, sch.6; c.58, sch.6; c.68, sch.4; 1973, c.32, sch.4; c.38, schs.27,28; 1974, c.39, ss.3,42; 1975, c.18, sch.2; c.68, sch.3; 1976, c.35, sch.2; c.71, sch.7; c.83, sch.1; 1977, s.42, sch.2; 1978, c.29, sch.16(S.); 1980, c.5, sch.5; c.20, s.7; c.53, sch.1; 1981, c.58, s.1; rules 78/1780; 79/659; 1982, c.10, sch.3; c.20, s.15; c.25, sch.6; 1983, c.20, sch.4; c.41, sch.9; 1984, c.23, sch.1; c.30, sch.10; c.35, sch.2; 1985, c.17, sch.4; c.65, sch.1; c.67, schs.2, 7; 1986, c.5, sch.14; 1988, c.33, sch.15; c.40, sch.12; c.41, sch.12; c.48, sch.7; repealed in pt.: 1980, c.34, sch.9; c.51, sch.26; c.53, sch.7; 1982, c.39, sch.22; c.45, s.18; order 75/1404; 1983, c.41, sch.10; 1984, c.48, sch.8; c.45, sch.14; 1986, c.60, sch.17; 1987, c.22, sch.6; 1988, c.34, sch.2; c.48, sch.8.
schs. 1, 3, continued in force in pt.: order 74/2058.
sch. 3, amended: 1972, c.52, sch.23; 1973, c.38, schs.27,28; repealed in pt.: 1977, c.42, sch.25; 1984, c.27, sch.14.
sch. 9, see *Westminster City Council* v. *Secretary of State for the Environment and City Commercial Real Estates Investments* [1984] J.P.L. 27, David Widdicombe Q.C.

63. Anguilla Act 1971.
repealed: 1980, c.67, s.1.
s. 1, order 76/50.

64. Diplomatic and Other Privileges Act 1971.
s. 1, amended: 1979, c.2, sch.4.
s. 2, repealed: 1981, c.9, sch.
s. 4, order 74/109.

65. Licensing (Abolition of State Management) Act 1971.
repealed: 1976, c.66, sch.8(S.); S.L.R. 1986.
s. 5, orders 76/678; 79/977.

66. Friendly Societies Act 1971.
repealed (except ss. 11 (5) (6), 15 (4) (5)): 1974, c.48, sch.11.
s. 11, repealed in pt.: S.L.R. 1978.

67. Appropriation Act 1971.
repealed: 1974, c.31, s.4, sch.

68. Finance Act 1971.
s. 1, orders 72/1620, 1791; 73/16, 892, 2218; 74/886, 2071; 75/26, 207, 1067, 1978, 2094; 77/2028.
s. 1, repealed in pt.: 1972, c.68, sch.3; 1977, c.36, sch.9.
s. 2, repealed: 1977, s.36, sch.9.
s. 3, regs. 72/567, 846; 77/1869; order 77/1867.
s. 3, amended: 1977, c.36, s.4; order 77/1866; repealed in pt.: 1979, c.5, sch.7; c.8, sch.2.
ss. 4, 5, repealed: 1972, c.41, sch.28.
s. 6, amended: 1976, c.40, sch.14; repealed in pt.: 1979, c.5, sch.7.

CAP.

1971—cont.

68. Finance Act 1971—cont.

s. 7, amended: 1974, c.30, s.50; 1977, c.49, sch.15; 1978, c.42, s.8.

ss. 8–10, repealed: 1972, c.25, sch.7.

s. 11, repealed: 1979, c.2, sch.6.

s. 12, repealed: 1973, c.51, sch.22.

ss. 13–20, repealed: 1988, c.1, sch.31.

s.19, see Mason v. Harman [1972] R.T.R. 1.

s. 21, amended: 1988, c.1, sch.29; repealed in pt.: ibid., sch.31.

ss. 22–28, repealed: ibid.

s. 29, see Ladkarn v. McIntosh [1983] S.T.C. 113, Vinelott J.

s. 29, regs. 72/1799.

ss. 29, 30, see Slater v. Richardson and Bottoms [1979] S.T.C. 630; [1979] 3 All E.R. 439, Oliver J.

ss. 29–31, repealed: 1975, c.45, sch.14.

s. 30, regs. 72/1798.

s. 31, amended: 1985, c.9, sch.2.

s. 32, see Ang v. Parrish [1980] 1 W.L.R. 940; [1980] 2 All E.R. 790; (1982) 53 T.C. 304, Walton J.

s. 32, order 86/529.

s. 32, amended: order 88/503.

ss. 32–36, repealed: 1988, c.1, sch.31.

s. 36, see I.R.C. v. Crawley [1987] S.T.C. 147, Vinelott J.

s. 39, repealed: 1988, c.1, sch.31.

s. 40, amended: ibid., sch.29.

s. 41, see Dixon v. Fitch's Garage [1975] 3 All E.R. 455; Ben-Odeco v. Powlson [1978] 1 W.L.R. 1093, H.L.; Benson v. Yard Arm Club [1979] 1 W.L.R. 347, C.A.; Hampton v. Fortes Autogrill [1979] T.R. 377, Fox J.; Brown v. Burnley Football and Athletic Co. [1980] 3 All E.R. 244, Vinelott J.; I.R.C. v. Scottish and Newcastle Breweries [1981] S.T.C. 50, Ct. of Session; Cole Bros. v. Phillips [1982] 2 All E.R. 247, H.L.; I.R.C. v. Scottish & Newcastle Breweries [1982] 1 W.L.R. 322, H.L.; Leeds Permanent Building Society v. Proctor [1982] 3 All E.R. 925, Goulding J.; Van Arkadie v. Sterling Coated Materials [1983] S.T.C. 95, Vinelott J.; Stokes v. Costain Property Investments [1984] 1 All E.R. 849, C.A.; Wimpey International v. Warland (Inspector of Taxes): Associated Restaurants v. Warland (Inspector of Taxes) [1988] S.T.C. 49, Hoffmann J.

s. 41, amended: 1985, c.54, s.55; repealed in pt.: ibid., s.55, sch.27.

ss. 41, 44, see Thomas (Inspector of Taxes) v. Reynolds [1987] S.T.C. 135, Walton J.

s. 42, see Hampton v. Fortes Autogrill [1979] T.R. 377, Fox J.

s. 42, amended: 1972, c.41, s.67; 1984, c.43, sch.12; repealed in pt.: 1972, c.41, s.67, sch.28.

s. 43, order 84/2060.

s. 43, amended: 1979, c.47, s.14; 1984, c.43, s.61.

s. 44, amended: 1972, c.41, s.68; 1976, c.40, ss.39,40; 1980, c.48, s.51; 1984, c.43, s.59; 1985, c.54, s.55, sch.14; 1986, c.41, s.55; 1987, c.51, s.64; 1988, c.1, sch.29; repealed in pt.: 1985, c.54, s.55, sch.27.

CAP.

1971—cont.

68. Finance Act 1971—cont.

s. 46, amended: ibid., s.54, sch.14.

s. 47, see Munby v. Furlong [1977] 3 W.L.R 271, C.A.; White v. Higginbottom [1983] S.T.C. 143, Vinelott J.

s. 47, amended: 1988, c.1, sch.29; repealed in pt.(prosp.): 1988, c.39, sch.14.

s. 48, amended: 1980, c.48, s.70.

s. 50, see Van Arkadie v. Sterling Coated Materials [1983] S.T.C. 95, Vinelott J.

s. 50, amended: 1986, c.41, s.55; repealed in pt.: 1985, c.54, s.56, sch.27; 1988, c.1, sch.31.

s. 52, repealed: 1986, c.41, sch.23.

s. 54, repealed: 1988, c.1, sch.31.

s. 55, repealed in pt.: 1979, c.14, sch.8.

s. 56, see Ennis Cropper Johnson v. Edwards [1981] T.R. 269, Vinelott J.

ss. 56, 58–60, repealed: 1979, c.14, sch.8.

s. 57, amended: ibid.,ss.51,52; repealed in pt.: 1978, c.42, s.44, sch.13.

ss. 61, 62, repealed: 1975, c.7, sch.13.

s. 63, repealed: 1972, c.41, sch.28.

s. 64, repealed in pt.: 1985, c.54, sch.27.

s. 65, repealed: 1976, c.40, s.126, sch.15.

s. 66, repealed: 1982, c.39, sch.22.

s. 67, repealed in pt.: 1973, c.36, sch.6.

s. 69, amended: 1988, c.1, sch.29; repealed in pt.: 1972, c.25, sch.7; 1979, c.2, sch.2; c.14, sch.8.

sch. 1, repealed: 1979, c.2, sch.6.

sch. 2, repealed: 1988, c.1, sch.31.

sch. 3, amended: 1972, c.41, s.74; 1988, c.1, sch.29; repealed in pt.: 1974, c.30, sch.14; 1979, c.14, sch.8; 1988, c.1, sch.31.

sch. 4, repealed: ibid.

sch. 5, repealed: 1975, c.45, sch.14.

sch. 6, amended: 1972, c.41, s.65; repealed in pt.: ibid.,schs.11, 28; 1973, c.51, sch.22; 1974, c.30, sch.14; 1975, c.7, ss.50, 52, sch.13; c.45, sch.14; 1979, c.14, sch.8; 1980, c.48, sch.20; 1981, c.35, sch.19; 1982, c.39, sch.22; 1985, c.54, sch.27; 1988, c.1, sch.31.

sch. 7, repealed: ibid.

sch. 8, amended: 1972, c.41, ss.67,68; 1976, c.40, s.43; 1979, c.47, s.14; 1984, c.43, ss.58, 59; 1985, c.54, s.59, schs.14, 16; 1987, c.51, s.64; 1988,c.1, sch.29; repealed in pt.: 1972, c.41, ss.68,75, sch.28; 1979, c.14, sch.8; 1982, c.16, sch. 16; 1985, c.54, s.58, schs. 14, 17; 1986, c.41, ss.55,57; 1988, c.1, sch.31.

sch. 9, repealed in pt.: 1979, c.14, sch.8; 1988, c.1, sch.31.

sch. 10, see Johnson v. Edwards [1981] T.R. 269, Vinelott J.; Magnavox Electronics Co. (In Liquidation) v. Hall [1986] S.T.C. 561, C.A.

schs. 10, 12, repealed: 1979, c.14, sch.8.

sch. 11, repealed: 1978, c.42, sch.13.

sch. 13, amended: 1977, c.49, sch.15; 1978, c.29, sch.16(S.).

sch. 14, repealed in pt.: 1975, c.45, sch.14; 1983, c.21, schs.3, 4.

CAP.

1971—cont.

69. Medicines Act 1971.
regs. 76/1145.
s. 1, regs. 75/366; 76/347; 77/1056, 1374; 79/899; 80/16, 1126; 82/1121; 83/1731; 85/1231; 87/1439.
s. 1, amended: 1988, c.49, s.21.
s. 129, regs. 85/1231.

70. Hijacking Act 1971.
repealed: 1982, c.36, sch.3.
s. 1, see *R.* v. *Moussa Membar* [1983] Crim.L.R. 618, C.A.
ss. 3, 6, orders 72/1102; 74/1107; 75/803; 76/769; 77/1237; 78/1887; 81/210, 731; 82/146.
s. 6, order 73/1893.

71. Mineral Workings Act 1971.
repealed: 1985, c.12, s.1, sch.2.
ss. 1, 2, orders 72/210; 76/107; 77/134; 78/195, 196; 80/249.
s. 3, orders 72/211; 74/1053; 75/181; 76/106; 77/133; 78/196; 79/211; 80/250; 81/277; 82/248.
s. 5, orders 78/195, 196; 79/211; 80/249, 250; 81/277; 82/248.

72. Industrial Relations Act 1971.
repealed: 1974, c.52, s.1, sch.5.
s. 24, see *Bessenden Properties* v. *Corness* [1977] I.C.R. 821 (Note), C.A.; *Carr* v. *Alexander Russell (Note)* [1979] I.C.R. 469, Ct. of Session.
ss. 25, 26, 167, see *Express & Star* v. *Bunday* [1987] I.R.L.R. 422, C.A.
ss. 96, 101, 116, 167, see *General Aviation Services (U.K.)* v. *Transport and General Workers Union* [1985] I.C.R. 615, H.L.

73. Social Security Act 1971.
repealed: 1976, c.71, sch.8.

74. Education (Milk) Act 1971.
repealed: 1980, c.20, sch.7.
s. 1, regs. 77/1193, 1684; 78/959, 1301.
s. 1, repealed in pt.: 1980, c.20, s.22.
s. 2, regs. 78/969(S.).
s. 2, repealed in pt. (S.): 1980, c.20, s.23.
ss. 2, 3, repealed in pt. (S.): 1971, c.20, s.3, sch.2.

75. Civil Aviation Act 1971.
regs. 72/178, 223.
s. 1, regs. 72/862.
ss. 1–36, repealed: 1982, c.16, sch.16.
s. 3, see *Laker Airways* v. *Department of Trade* [1977] 2 W.L.R. 234, C.A.
s. 5, regs. 72/862; 73/1929; 74/1389; 75/532, 1196; 76/1026; 79/514.
s. 9, regs. 72/150, 1272; 73/92, 1978; 75/10, 1673; 76/1396; 77/647.
s. 14, order 72/410.
s. 16, rules 72/690.
s. 19, regs. 72/187.
s. 23, regs. 76/1026.
s. 24, regs. 76/1026; 79/514; 81/61.
s. 25, order 72/139.
s. 26, regs. 74/1802; 75/1196, 1409; 79/5; 81/314.

CAP.

1971—cont.

75. Civil Aviation Act 1971—*cont.*
s. 29, regs. 72/431; 76/26; schemes 75/916, 917; 77/813, 814, 1319; 78/1797, 1798; 79/414; 80/153, 154.
s. 29A, schemes 78/1797, 1798; 81/652, 653.
s. 29A, repealed: 1980, c.60, sch.3.
s. 29B, order 81/651.
Pt. III (ss. 37–60), repealed: 1977, c.13, sch.2.
s. 46, order 76/1893.
s. 51, order 76/1892.
s. 57, order 73/2175.
s. 60, order 72/139.
ss. 61–70, repealed: 1982, c.16, sch.16.
s. 63, orders 76/1892, 1893; regs. 81/61.
s. 66, orders 72/450, 451; 73/1891; 76/1912; 80/188.
s. 70, orders 72/138; 76/1593.
schs. 1–7, repealed: 1982, c.16, sch.16.
sch. 2, order 72/140.
sch. 8, repealed: 1977, c.13, sch.2.
schs. 9–11, repealed: 1982, c.16, sch.16.
sch. 10, regs. 75/1184; 78/241, 693, 837; 79/154; 80/356; 81/355, 1237; orders 72/108. 905.

76. Housing Act 1971.
repealed: 1985, c.71, sch.1; 1986, c.26, sch.24(S.).
s. 1, order 72/422.

77. Immigration Act 1971.
see *R.* v. *Secretary of State for Home Affairs, ex p. Ram, The Times,* August 3, 1978, D.C.; *R.* v. *Secretary of State for the Home Department, ex p. Mahmood, The Times,* August 2, 1978, C.A.; *R.* v. *Immigration Appeal Tribunal, ex p. Shaikh, The Times,* March 3, 1981, D.C.; *R.* v. *Immigration Appeal Tribunal, ex p. Yau, The Times,* February 25, 1982, C.A.; *R.* v. *Secretary of State for the Home Department, ex p. Bugdaycay, The Times,* November 12, 1985, C.A.; *R.* v. *Secretary of State for the Home Department, ex p. H., The Times,* August 5, 1987, D.C.; *R.* v. *Immigration Appeal Tribunal, ex p. Jones (Ross), The Times,* December 9, 1987, C.A.
regs. 81/534.
s. 1, see *Azam* v. *Secretary of State for the Home Department* [1973] 2 W.L.R. 1058; [1973] 2 All E.R. 765; *R.* v. *Secretary of State for the Home Department, ex p. Mughal* [1973] 3 W.L.R. 647; [1973] 3 All E.R. 796, C.A.; *R.* v. *Chief Immigration Officer, Heathrow Airport, ex p. Salamat Bibi* [1976] 1 W.L.R. 979, C.A.; *W. (A Minor) (Adoption: Non-Patrial), Re, The Times,* July 27, 1985, C.A.: *R.* v. *Secretary of State for the Home Department, ex p. Huseyin (Zalihe), The Times,* October 31, 1987, C.A.; *R.* v. *Immigration Appeal Tribunal, ex p. Ruhul Amin; Same* v. *Same, ex p. Rahman; Same* v. *Same, ex p. Haque* [1987] 1 W.L.R. 1538, C.A.; *R.* v. *Secretary of State for the Home Department, ex p. Dhahan, The Times,* January 15, 1988, Kennedy J.; *R.* v. *Immigration Appeal Tribunal, ex p. Singh (Bahadur), The Times,* July 2, 1988, C.A.; *R.* v. *Secretary of State for the*

1971—cont.

77. Immigration Act 1971—*cont.*

Home Department, ex p. Ullah [1988] 3 All
E.R. 1, C.A.

s. 1, repealed in pt.: 1988, c.14, s.1.

s. 1, 2, see Nawaz v. Lord Advocate, 1983 S.L.T.
653.

ss. 1–3, see Kaur v. Lord Advocate (O.H.), 1981
S.L.T. 322.

s. 2, see Azam v. Secretary of State for the
Home Department [1973] 2 W.L.R. 1058;
[1973] 2 All E.R. 765; R. v. Secretary of State
for the Home Office, ex p. Phansopkar; R. v.
Secretary of State for the Home Office, ex p.
Begum [1977] 3 W.L.R. 322, C.A.; R. v.
Immigration Appeal Tribunal, ex p. Manek,
The Times, January 24, 1978, D.C.; Taneja v.
Entry Clearance Officer, Chicago [1977]
Imm.A.R. 9; Decision No. R(U) 1/82; R. v.
Secretary of State for the Home Department,
ex p. Margueritte [1982] 3 W.L.R. 754, C.A.;
R. v. Immigration Appeals Adjudicator, ex p.
Crew, The Times, November 26, 1982, C.A.;
Re H. (A Minor) [1982] 3 W.L.R. 501, Hollings
J.; R. v. Immigration Appeal Tribunal, ex p.
Coomasaru [1983] 1 W.L.R. 14, C.A.; Brahmb-
hatt v. Chief Immigration Officer at Heathrow
Airport [1984] Imm.A.R. 202, C.A.

s. 2, substituted: 1981, c.61, s.39; amended:
1988, c.14, s.3.

s. 3, see R. v. Secretary of State for the Home
Department, ex p. Mughal [1973] 3 W.L.R.
647; [1973] 3 All E.R. 796, C.A.; R. v. Secretary of State for the Home Department, ex p.
Thakrar [1974] 2 W.L.R. 593; [1974] 2 All E.R.
261, C.A.; R. v. Secretary of State for the
Home Department, ex p. Akhtar [1975] 1
W.L.R. 1717; [1975] 3 All E.R. 1987, D.C.;
Suthendran v. Immigration Appeal Tribunal
[1976] 3 W.L.R. 725; [1976] 3 All E.R. 611,
H.L.; R. v. Secretary of State for Home Affairs,
ex p. Hosenball [1977] 1 W.L.R. 766, C.A.; R.
v. Secretary of State for the Home Office, ex
p. Phansopkar; R. v. Secretary of State for
the Home Office, ex p. Begum [1977] 3
W.L.R. 322, C.A.; Khan v. Secretary of State
for the Home Department [1977] 3 All E.R.
538, C.A.; Zamir v. Secretary of State for the
Home Department [1980] 3 W.L.R. 249, H.L.;
R. v. Nazari; R. v. Dissanayake; R. v.
Anyanwu; R. v. Fernandez; R. v. Adamson
(1980) 71 Cr.App.R. 87, C.A.; Re H. (A Minor)
[1982] 3 W.L.R. 501, Hollings J.; R. v. Immigration Appeal Tribunal, ex p. Ullah, Cheema,
Hawol, The Times, January 14, 1983, C.A.;
Salehi v. Smith, 1982 S.C.C.R. 552; R. v.
Secretary of State for the Home Department,
ex p. Mustafa, The Times, February 22, 1984,
McCullough J.; R. v. Immigration Appeal Tribunal, ex p. Nashouki, The Times, October
17, 1985, C.A.; Genec v. Secretary of State
for the Home Department [1984] Imm.A.R.
180, Immigration Appeal Tribunal; R. v. Immigration Appeal Tribunal, ex p. Singh
(Bakhtaur), The Times, June 27, 1986, H.L.;

1971—cont.

77. Immigration Act 1971—*cont.*

R. v. Secretary of State for the Home Office,
ex p. Erdogan, The Times, June 30, 1986,
Nolan J.; Owusu-Sekeyere's Application, Re,
The Times, April 22, 1987, C.A.; R. v. Immigration Appeal Tribunal, ex p. Patel, The Independent, August 21, 1987, C.A.; R. v.
Secretary of State for the Home Department,
ex p. Sivakumaran; Same v. Same, ex p.
Vaithialingam; Same v. Same, ex p. Vilvarajah;
Same v. Same ex p. Vathahan; Same v. Same,
ex p. Navaratnam (United Nations High Commissioner for Refugees Intervening), The
Times, December 17, 1987, H.L.; R. v. Immigration Appeal Tribunal, ex p. Ibrahim, The
Guardian, March 17, 1988, D.C.; R. v. Immigration Appeal Tribunal, ex p. Chundawadra
[1987] Imm.A.R. 227, Taylor J; R. v. Immigration Appeal Tribunal, ex p. Sheikh, The Times,
March 17, 1988, C.A.; R. v. Secretary of State
for the Home Department, ex p. Kusi-Boahen,
The Times, June 18, 1988, Schiemann J.; R.
v. Immigration Appeal Tribunal, ex p. Patel
(Anilkumar Rabindrabhal) [1988] 2 W.L.R.
1165, H.L.; R. v. Secretary of State for the
Home Department, ex p. Mokuolu, The
Times, October 5, 1988, C.A.

s. 3, orders 72/1647; 76/1572.

s. 3, amended: 1981, c.61, s.39, sch.4; 1988,
c.14, s.3, sch.

s. 4, see R. v. Secretary of State for the Home
Department, ex p. Ram [1979] 1 W.L.R. 148,
D.C.; Nawaz v. Lord Advocate, 1983 S.L.T.
653; R. v. Secretary of State for the Home
Department, ex p. Patel, The Times, October
27, 1986, C.A.; Baljinder Singh v. Hammond
[1987] 1 W.L.R. 283, D.C.; Bugdaycay v. Sec-
retary of State for the Home Department;
Nelidow Santis v. Same; Norman v. The
Same; Musisi, Re [1987] 2 W.L.R. 606, H.L.;
R. v. Secretary of State for the Home Office,
ex p. Betancourt, The Times, October 5, 1987,
Kennedy J.; R. v. Secretary of State for the
Home Department, ex p. Ounejma and
Hussan, The Times, October 26, 1988, D.C.

s. 4, regs. 72/1689, 1758; 75/999; 76/2018;
78/24; 80/451; 83/442; orders 72/1047;
76/1572; 82/502, 1024.

ss. 4, 5, see R. v. Secretary of State for the
Home Department, ex p. Mustafa, The Times,
February 22, 1984, McCullough J.

s. 4, amended: 1981, c.61, sch.4.

s. 5, see R. v. Zaman (1975) 61 Cr.App.R. 227,
C.A.; R. v. Secretary of State for the Home
Department, ex p. Alghali, The Times, July
22, 1986, D.C.

s. 5, amended: 1981, c.61, sch.4; 1988, c.14,
sch.

s. 6, see R. v. Nazari; R. v. Dissanayake; R. v.
Anyanwu; R. v. Fernandez; R. v. Adamson
(1980) 71 Cr.App.R. 87, C.A.; R. v. Bayam
and Bayam, The Times, June 9, 1981, C.A; R.
v. Secretary of State for the Home Department, ex p. Dannenberg, The Times, March

CAP.

1971—cont.

77. Immigration Act 1971—cont.
14, 1984, C.A.; *R.* v. *Secretary of State for the Home Department, ex p. Kusi-Boahen, The Times,* June 18, 1988, Schiemann J.

s. 6, amended: 1972, c.71, sch.5; 1975, c.21, sch.9; 1980, c.43, sch.7; 1982, c.48, sch.15; repealed in pt.: (S.): 1980, c.62, sch.8; 1982, c.48, s.16.

s. 7, see *Mehmet* v. *Secretary of State for the Home Department* [1977] Imm.A.R. 68, C.A.; *O'Connor* v. *Secretary of State for the Home Department* [1977] Imm.A.R. 29; *R.* v. *Secretary of State for the Home Office, ex p. Uwabor* [1978] Crim.L.R. 360, D.C.

s. 8, see *R.* v. *Immigration Appeal Tribunal, ex p. Coomasuru* [1983] 1 W.L.R. 14, C.A.; *Tusin* v. *Secretary of State for the Home Department* [1984] Imm.A.R. 42, Imm.A.T.; *R.* v. *Immigration Appeal Tribunal, ex p. Ali, The Guardian,* October 20, 1988, Farquharson J.

s. 8, orders 72/1613; 75/617; 77/693; 82/1649; 85/1809.

s. 8, amended: 1981, c.61, s.39, sch.4; 1988, c.14, s.4.

s. 9, orders 72/1610; 79/730; 80/1859; 82/1028; 85/1854; 87/2092.

s. 9, amended: 1981, c.61, sch.4; repealed in pt.: *ibid.,*sch.9.

s. 11, see *R.* v. *Singh* [1972] 1 W.L.R. 1600; [1973] 1 All E.R. 122; *R.* v. *Secretary of State for the Home Department, ex p. Coonhye, The Independent,* May 14, 1987, D.C.

Pt. II (ss. 12–23), see *R.* v. *Immigration Adjudicator, ex p. Bowen, The Times,* April 8, 1982, McNeill J.

s. 13, see *R.* v. *Entry Clearance Officer, Bombay, ex p. Amin* [1983] 3 W.L.R. 258, H.L., *R.* v. *Immigration Appeal Tribunal, ex p. Coomasuru* [1983] 1 W.L.R. 14, C.A.; *R.* v. *Secretary of State for the Home Department, ex p. Swat* [1986] 1 All E.R. 717, C.A.; *Bugdaycay* v. *Secretary of State for the Home Department; Nedilow Santis* v. *Same; Norman* v. *The Same; Musisi, Re* [1987] 2 W.L.R. 606, H.L.

s. 13, amended: 1981, c.61, s.39, sch.4; 1988, c.14, s.3.

s. 14, see *Suthendran* v. *Immigration Appeal Tribunal* [1976] 3 W.L.R. 725; [1976] 3 All E.R. 611, H.L.; *R.* v. *Hamid, The Times,* October 19, 1978, C.A.; *Horne* v. *Gaygusuz* [1979] Crim.L.R. 594, C.A.; *R.* v. *Secretary of State for the Home Department, ex p. Khawaja* [1982] 1 W.L.R. 625, C.A.; *R.* v. *Immigration Officer (Heathrow Airport), ex p. Ali, The Times,* October 25, 1982, C.A.; *Zoltak* v. *Sussex Constabulary,* November 12, 1982, Lewes Crown Court.; *R.* v. *Immigration Appeal Tribunal, ex p. Bastiampillai* [1983] 2 All E.R. 844, Glidewell J.; *R.* v. *Immigration Appeal Tribunal, ex p. Enwia; R.* v. *Immigration Appeal Tribunal, ex p. A.S.* [1983] 2 All E.R. 1045, C.A.; *R.* v. *Immigration Appeal Tribunal, ex p. Coomasuru* [1983] 1 W.L.R. 14, C.A.; *R.* v. *Secretary of State for the*

CAP.

1971—cont.

77. Immigration Act 1971—cont.
Home Department, ex p. Musisi, The Times, June 8, 1985, C.A.; *Tusin* v. *Secretary of State for the Home Department* [1984] Imm.A.R. 42, Imm.A.T.

s. 14, amended: 1981, c.61, sch.4; 1988, c.14, s.3.

ss. 14, 15, see *R.* v. *Immigration Appeal Tribunal, ex p. Subramanian* [1976] 3 W.L.R. 630, C.A.

s. 15, see *R.* v. *Secretary of State for Home Affairs, ex p. Hosenball* [1977] 1 W.L.R. 766, C.A.; *R.* v. *Bayam and Bayam, The Times,* June 9, 1981, C.A.; *R.* v. *Immigration Appeal Tribunal, ex p. Bakhtaur Singh, The Times,* March 12, 1984, Hodgson J.; *R.* v. *Immigration Appeal Tribunal, ex p. Chumsun and Bano-Ovais, The Times,* December 3, 1986, Hodgson J.; *R.* v. *Secretary of State for the Home Department, ex p. Kusi-Boahen, The Times,* June 18, 1988, Schiemann J.

s. 16, see *R.* v. *Immigration Adjudicator, ex p. Hussain, The Times,* June 23, 1982, Woolf J.

s. 17, see *R.* v. *Immigration Appeal Tribunal, ex p. Muraganandarajah, The Times,* July 23, 1984, C.A.

s. 18, see *R.* v. *Immigration Appeals Tribunal, ex p. Mehmet* [1977] 2 All E.R. 602, D.C.; *R.* v. *Immigration Appeal Tribunal, ex p. Tong, The Times,* December 8, 1981, Glidewell J.; *R.* v. *Immigration Appeal Tribunal, ex p. Hubbard, The Times,* July 16, 1985, D.C.; *R.* v. *Secretary of State for the Home Department, ex p. Daydalen, The Times,* May 7, 1988, C.A.

s. 18, regs. 72/1683; 82/1027; 84/2040.

s. 19, see *R.* v. *Secretary of State for the Home Department, ex p. Malik, The Times,* November 18, 1981, Forbes J.; *R.* v. *Immigration Appeal Tribunal, ex p. Tong, The Times,* December 8, 1981, Glidewell J.; *R.* v. *Immigration Appeal Tribunal, ex p. Weerasuriya* [1983] 1 All E.R. 195, Webster J.; *R.* v. *Immigration Appeal Tribunal, ex p. Coomasuru* [1983] 1 W.L.R. 14, C.A.; *R.* v. *Immigration Appeal Tribunal, ex p. Kotecha* [1983] 1 W.L.R. 487, C.A.; *R.* v. *Entry Clearance Officer, Bombay, ex p. Amin* [1983] 3 W.L.R. 258, H.L.; *Deva* v. *Secretary of State for the Home Department* [1981] Imm.A.R. 48, Immigration Appeal Tribunal; *R.* v. *Immigration Appeal Tribunal, ex p. Wirdestedt, The Times,* December 12, 1984, C.A.; *R.* v. *Immigration Appeal Tribunal, ex p. Hassanin, Kandemir and Farooq* [1986] 1 W.L.R. 1448, C.A.

s. 20, see *R.* v. *Immigration Appeal Tribunal, ex p. Lila, The Times,* October 29, 1977, D.C.; *R.* v. *Immigration Appeal Tribunal, ex p. Tong, The Times,* December 8, 1981, Glidewell, J.; *Tusin* v. *Secretary of State for the Home Department* [1984] Imm.A.R. 42, Imm.A.T.

s. 22, see *R.* v. *Immigration Appeal Tribunal, ex p. Jones (Ross)* [1988] 1 W.L.R. 477, C.A.

s. 22, rules 72/1684; 82/1026; 84/2041.

s. 22, amended: 1981, c.61, sch.4.

CAP.

1971—cont.

77. Immigration Act 1971—*cont.*

s. 24, see *Singh (Gurder)* v. *The Queen* [1973] 1 W.L.R. 1444, D.C.; *Waddington* v. *Miah* [1974] 1 W.L.R. 683; [1974] 2 All E.R. 377, H.L.; *R.* v. *Bello* [1978] Crim.L.R. 551, C.A.; (1978) 67 Cr.App.R. 288, C.A.; *R.* v. *Tzanatos*, March 17, 1978, C.A.; *R.* v. *Hamid, The Times,* October 19, 1978, C.A.; *Horne* v. *Gaygusuz* [1979] Crim.L.R. 594, D.C.; *R.* v. *Eastbourne JJ., ex p. Barsoum,* January 26, 1979, D.C.; *R.* v. *Inner London Crown Court, ex p. Obajuwana* (1979) 69 Cr.App.R. 125; *Skeen* v. *Shaikh,* 1981 S.L.T.(Sh.Ct.) 2; *Lamptey* v. *Owen* (1981) 125 S.J. 725, D.C.; *Grant* v. *Borg* [1982] 1 W.L.R. 638, H.L.; *Zoltak* v. *Sussex Constabulary,* November 12, 1982, Lewes Crown Court; *R.* v. *Immigration Appeal Tribunal, ex p. Muruganandarah, The Times,* July 23, 1984, C.A.; *Enaas* v. *Dovey, The Times,* November 25, 1986, D.C.; *Manickavasagar* v. *Comr. of Metropolitan Police* [1987] Crim.L.R. 50, D.C.; *Gursan,* April 3, 1987, H.H. Judge Phillips, Knutsford Crown Ct.

s. 24, amended: 1972, c.58, sch.6(S.); 1978, c.29, sch.15(S.); 1988, c.14, s.6.

s. 24, amended: 1981, c.61, sch.4.

s. 25, see *R.* v. *Singh* [1972] 1 W.L.R. 1600; [1973] 1 All E.R. 122; *R.* v. *Mistry; R.* v. *Asare* [1980] Crim.L.R. 177, C.A.

s. 25, amended: 1981, c.61, sch.4; 1984, c.60, sch.6.

s. 26, see *Waddington* v. *Miah* [1974] 1 W.L.R. 683; [1974] 2 All E.R. 377, H.L.; *R.* v. *Gill* [1976] 2 All E.R. 893, C.A.; *R.* v. *Gunay* [1984] Crim.L.R. 102, C.A.; *R.* v. *Secretary of State for the Home Department, ex p. Addo, The Times,* April 18, 1985, D.C.; *R.* v. *Clarke (Ediakpo)* [1985] 3 W.L.R. 113, H.L.; *R.* v. *Secretary of State for the Home Department, ex p. Patel, The Times,* October 27, 1986, C.A.; *Baljinder Singh* v. *Hammond* [1987] 1 W.L.R. 283, D.C.

s. 26, amended: 1981, c.61, sch.4.

s. 28, see *R.* v. *Eastbourne JJ., ex p. Barsoum,* January 26, 1979, D.C.; *Horne* v. *Gaygusuz* [1979] Crim.L.R. 594, D.C.; *Skeen* v. *Shaikh,* 1981 S.L.T.(Sh.Ct.) 2; *Grant* v. *Borg* [1982] 1 W.L.R. 638, H.L.; *Enaas* v. *Dovey, The Times,* November 25, 1986, D.C.

s. 29, see *Kassan* v. *Immigration Appeal Tribunal* [1980] 2 All E.R. 330, C.A.

s. 30, see *R.* v. *Secretary of State for the Home Department, ex p. Alghalia, The Times,* July 22, 1986, D.C.

s. 30, repealed: 1984, c.36, sch.5.

s. 31, repealed in pt.: 1981, c.61, sch.9.

s. 32, orders 79/730; 82/1028; 85/1854; 87/2092.

s. 33, see *Azam* v. *Secretary of State for the Home Department* [1973] 2 W.L.R. 1058; [1973] 2 All E.R. 765; *Khan* v. *Secretary of State for the Home Department* [1977] 3 All E.R. 538, C.A.; *O'Connor* v. *Secretary of State for the Home Department* [1977] Imm.A.R.

CAP.

1971—cont.

77. Immigration Act 1971—*cont.*

29; *R.* v. *Secretary of State for the Home Department, ex p. Choudhary* [1978] 1 W.L.R. 1177, C.A.; *R.* v. *Secretary of State for the Home Department, ex p. Mangoo Khan* [1980] 1 W.L.R. 569; [1980] 2 All E.R. 337, C.A.; *Zamir* v. *Secretary of State for the Home Department* [1980] 3 W.L.R. 249, H.L.; *R.* v. *Secretary of State for the Home Department, ex p. Margueritte* [1982] 3 W.L.R. 754, C.A.; *Khawaja* v. *Secretary of State for the Home Department* [1983] 1 All E.R. 765, H.L.; *R.* v. *Governor of Ashford Remand Centre, ex p. Bouzagon, The Times,* July 4, 1983, C.A., sub nom. *Re Ahmed Bouzagou* (1984) 134 New L.J. 407, C.A.; *R.* v. *Entry Clearance Officer, Bombay, ex p. Amin* [1983] 3 W.L.R. 258, H.L.; *Nawaz* v. *Lord Advocate,* 1983, S.L.T. 653; *R.* v. *Secretary of State for the Home Department, ex p. Rouse, The Times,* November 25, 1985, Woolf J.; *R.* v. *Secretary of State for the Home Department, ex p. Bugdaycay* [1986] 1 W.L.R. 155, C.A.; *R.* v. *Secretary of State for the Home Department, ex p. Khaled, The Times,* November 13, 1986, Otton J.; *R.* v. *Secretary of State for the Home Department, ex p. Mokuolu, The Times,* October 5, 1988, C.A.

s. 33, orders 72/1668; 75/2221; 79/1635; 87/177.

s. 33, amended: 1976, c.36, sch.3; 1981, c.61, sch.4; 1988, c.14, sch.

s. 34, see *Waddington* v. *Miah* [1974] 1 W.L.R. 683; [1974] 2 All E.R. 377, H.L.; *Suleman* v. *Secretary of State for the Home Office, The Times,* July 21, 1981, Thompson J.

s. 34, order 72/1647.

s. 35, order 72/1514.

s. 35, repealed in pt.: S.L.R. 1986.

s. 36, orders 72/1719, 1720; 73/1318; 82/1834–1836; 83/1897, 1898; 84/1690.

sch. 1, see *R.* v. *Secretary of State for the Home Department, ex p. Margueritte* [1982] 3 W.L.R. 754, C.A.

sch. 1, repealed in pt.: 1981, c.61, sch.9.

sch. 2, see *Azam* v. *Secretary of State for the Home Department* [1973] 2 W.L.R. 1058; [1973] 2 All E.R. 765; *R.* v. *Secretary of State for the Home Department, ex p. Hussain* [1978] 1 W.L.R. 700, C.A.; *R.* v. *Secretary of State for the Home Department, ex p. Choudhary* [1978] 1 W.L.R. 1177, C.A.; *R.* v. *Secretary of State for the Home Department, ex p. Ram* [1979] 1 W.L.R. 148, D.C.; *Re Shahid Iqbal (Note)* [1979] 1 W.L.R. 425, C.A.; *R.* v. *Secretary of State for the Home Department, ex p. Khan, The Times,* February 14, 1980, C.A.; *R.* v. *Secretary of State for the Home Department, ex p. Sultan Mahmood (Note)* [1980] 3 W.L.R. 312, C.A.; *Zamir* v. *Secretary of State for the Home Department* [1980] 3 W.L.R. 249, H.L.; *R.* v. *Secretary of State for the Home Department, ex p. Khawaja* [1982] 1 W.L.R. 625, C.A.; *R.* v. *Immigration Officer, ex p. Shah* [1982] 1 W.L.R. 544, Woolf J.; *R.* v. *Secretary of State for the Home Depart-*

1971—cont.

77. Immigration Act 1971—cont.

ment, ex p. Awa, The Times, March 12, 1983, Woolf J.; Nawaz v. Lord Advocate, 1983 S.L.T. 653; R. v. Secretary of State for the Home Department, ex p. Mustafa, The Times, February 22, 1984, McCullough J.; R. v. Secretary of State for the Home Department, ex p. Lapinid [1982] 3 All E.R. 257, C.A.; R. v. Secretary of State for the Home Department, ex p. Swat [1986] 1 All E.R. 717, C.A.; Baljinder Singh v. Hammond [1987] 1 W.L.R. 283, D.C.; Kaur v. Secretary of State for the Home Department (O.H.), 1987 S.C.L.R. 550; R. v. Secretary of State for the Home Department, ex p. Malik, The Independent, October 6, 1987, Kennedy J.; R. v. Secretary of State for the Home Department, ex p. Ali, The Independent, January 19, 1888, C.A.; R. v. Secretary of State for the Home Department, ex p. V., The Guardian, June 25, 1988, D.C.; R. v. Secretary of State for the Home Department, ex p. Mokuolu, The Times, October, 5, 1988, C.A.

sch. 2, orders 72/1666, 1667; 75/65, 980; rules 72/1684; 84/2041.

sch. 2, amended: 1972, c.58, sch.6(S.); 1978, c.29, sch.15(S.); 1979, c.55, sch.2; 1981, c.61, sch.4; 1988, c.14, sch.; repealed in pt.: 1972, c.58, schs.6,7(S.); c.71, sch.6; 1984, c.60, sch.7.

sch. 3, see R. v. Zaman (1975) 61 Cr.App.R. 227, C.A.; R. v. Inner London Crown Court, ex p. Obajuwana (1979) 69 Cr.App.R. 125; R. v. Governor of Holloway Prison, ex p. Giambi [1982] 1 W.L.R. 535; [1982] 1 All E.R. 434, D.C.; Lamptey v. Owen [1982] Crim.L.R. 42, D.C.; R. v. Governor of Durham Prison, ex p. Hardial Singh [1984] 1 W.L.R. 704; [1984] 1 All E.R. 983, Woolf J.

sch. 3, amended: 1982, c.48, s.59, sch.9; 1988, c.14, sch.

sch. 5, repealed in pt.: 1975, c.24, sch.3; c.25, sch.3.

sch. 9, order 72/139.

78. Town and Country Planning Act 1971.

see Aston v. Secretary of State for the Environment (1982) 43 P. & C.R. 331, D.C.; Bernard Wheatcroft v. Secretary of State for the Environment (1982) 43 P. & C.R. 233, C.A.; Surrey Heath Borough Council v. Secretary of State for the Environment (1987) 53 P. & C.R. 428, Kennedy J.; Windsor & Maidenhead Borough Council v. Secretary of State for the Environment, The Times, January 6, 1988, Mann J.; London Residuary Body v. Secretary of State for the Environment; Lambeth London Borough Council v. Same, The Independent, March 29, 1988, Simon Brown J.

regs. 72/1154, 1362; 73/31; 81/1826.

s. 1, see Co-operative Retail Services v. Taff-Ely Borough Council (1979) 39 P. & C.R. 223, C.A.; R. v. Basildon District Council, ex p. Martin Grant Homes (1987) 53 P. & C.R. 397, McCowan J.

1971—cont.

78. Town and Country Planning Act 1971—cont.

s. 1, amended: 1972, c.70, sch.16; 1981, c.36, s.2; 1985, c.51, s.3; 1986, c.63, sch.11; 1988, c.4, sch.3.

s. 1A, added: 1986, c.63, s.30; amended: 1988, c.4, sch.3.

s. 1B, added: 1986, c.63, s.30.

s. 2, see North Warwickshire Borough Council v. Secretary of State for the Environment, The Times, December 23, 1983, Woolf J.

s. 2, repealed: 1972, c.70, sch.30.

s. 3, repealed: ibid.,schs.16,30.

s. 4, repealed: ibid.,sch.30.

s. 5, see R. v. Secretary of State for the Environment, ex p. Hampshire County Council (1982) 44 P. & C.R. 343, D.C.

s. 5, regs. 74/450.

s. 5, repealed: 1985, c.51, sch.17.

s. 6, amended: 1972, c.70, s.183; repealed in pt.: 1980, c.65, schs.14,34.

s. 7, regs. 74/1486; 79/1738; 82/555; 84/6.

s. 7, amended: 1972, c.70, s.183; 1980, c.65, sch.14; 1982, c.30, sch.6; repealed in pt.: 1980, c.65, schs.14,34.

ss. 7–9, see Greater London Council v. Secretary of State for the Environment [1984] J.P.L. 424, Hodgson J.

s. 8, regs. 74/1486; 82/555; 84/6.

s. 8, amended: 1972, c.70, s.183, sch.16; repealed in pt.: 1980, c.65, sch.14.

s. 9, see Edwin H. Bradley & Sons v. Secretary of State for the Environment (1982) 264 E.G. 926, Glidewell J.; Barnham v. Secretary of State for the Environment (1986) 52 P. & C.R. 10, Farquharson J.

s. 9, regs. 74/1486; 79/1738; 82/555.

s. 9, amended: 1972, c.42, s.3; c.70, s.183; repealed in pt.: 1980, c.65, sch.14.

s. 10, see R. v. Camden London Borough Council, ex p. Comyn Ching & Co. (London) (1984) 47 P. & C.R. 417, Woolf J.; Groveside Homes v. Elmbridge Borough Council (1987) 284 E.G. 940, D.C.

s. 10, substituted: 1980, c.65, sch.14; amended: 1982, c.30, sch.6.

s. 10A, added: 1972, c.42, s.1.

s. 10B, added: ibid.,s.2.

s. 10C, added: 1972, c.70, s.183; amended: 1980, c.65, sch.14; repealed in pt.: ibid.,schs.14,34.

ss. 11–15B, substituted: (exc. G.L.): 1986, c.63, s.41, sch.10.

ss. 11, 12, regs. 74/1486; 82/555.

s. 12, see Vaughan v. Secretary of State for the Environment and Mid-Sussex District Council [1986] J.P.L. 840, McNeill J.

s. 12A, regs. 87/1760.

s. 13, see Greater London Council v. Secretary of State for the Environment [1984] J.P.L. 424, Hodgson J.

s. 13, regs. 82/555; 83/1190.

s. 14, see Kenwood (Travel, Employment, and Estates) and Z. I. Gourgey v. Secretary of State for the Environment and Westminster City Council [1984] J.P.L. 36, Stephen Brown J.; R. v. Secretary of State for the Environ-

CAP.

78. Town and Country Planning Act 1971—*cont.*
ment, ex p. Southwark London Borough
Council (1987) 54 P. & C.R. 226, D.C.

s. 14, amended: 1972, c.42, s.3; c.70, s.182,
sch.16; 1980, c.65, sch.14.

s. 15, amended: 1972, c.70, sch.16; 1980, c.65,
sch.14; 1982, c.30, sch.6; repealed in pt.:
1972, c.42, s.3.

s. 15A, amended: 1982, c.30, sch.6.

ss. 15A, 15B, added: 1980, c.65, s.88.

s. 16, amended: 1980, c.66, sch.24; repealed in
pt.: *ibid.*,schs.24,25.

s. 17, amended: 1972, c.70, sch.16.

s. 18, regs. 74/1481, 1486; 79/1738; 82/555;
83/1190; 84/6.

s. 18, amended: 1972, c.70, s.182, sch.16;
1986, c.63, sch.11.

s. 19, regs. 74/1481; 83/1190.

s. 19, substituted: 1972, c.42, s.4.

ss. 19, 20, see *City of Glasgow District Council
v. Secretary of State for Scotland*, Second
Division, December 14, 1979.

s. 20, amended: 1972, c.42, s.4; 1980, c.65,
sch.24.

s. 21, orders 72/1060, 1151–3, 1314, 1408,
1519, 1520, 1559; 73/87, 88, 523, 524, 750,
751, 1069, 1279, 1280, 1426, 1584, 1585,
1657, 1834, 2222, 2223; 74/1069, 1070;
75/780–783, 1276–1279; 76/104, 105, 814,
815, 1162, 1163; 77/469, 470, 1363, 1364,
1768, 1769; 78/556, 557, 724–727;
79/200–203, 328, 329, 890, 891, 1042, 1043,
1187, 1189, 1485, 1486, 1622–1629; 80/2, 3,
40, 41, 65, 66, 101, 102, 174, 175, 300, 301,
458–461, 492, 493, 575–578, 828, 829, 932,
933, 963, 964, 1098, 1099, 1155, 1156, 1209,
1210, 1403, 1404, 1451, 1452, 1547, 1548,
1560, 1599, 1634, 1635.

s. 21, amended: 1980, c.65, sch.14.

s. 22, see *David* v. *Penybont R.D.C.* [1972] 1
W.L.R. 1526; [1972] 3 All E.R. 1092; *Lipson
v. Secretary of State for the Environment*
(1976) 33 P. & C.R. 95, D.C.; *Brooks and
Burton* v. *Secretary of State for the Environment* [1977] 1 W.L.R. 1924, C.A.; *Wakelin* v.
Secretary of State for the Environment (1978)
77 L.G.R. 101, C.A.; *Parks* v. *Secretary of
State for the Environment* [1978] 1 W.L.R.
1308, C.A.; *Bilboe* v. *Secretary of State for
the Environment* (1980) 39 P. & C.R. 495,
C.A.; *Northavon District Council* v. *Secretary
of State for the Environment* [1980] 40 P. &
C.R. 332, D.C.; *Hewlett* v. *Secretary of State
for the Environment and Brentwood District
Council* [1981] J.P.L. 187, D.C.; *Sykes* v. *Secretary of State for the Environment; South
Oxfordshire District Council* v. *Secretary of
State for the Environment* [1980] 257 E.G.
821; (1981) 42 P. & C.R. 19, D.C.; *Crowborough Parish Council* v. *Secretary of State for
the Environment and Wealden District Council*
[1981] J.P.L. 281, D.C.; *William R. Winton* v.
*Secretary of State for the Environment and
Guildford Borough Council*, January 27, 1982,
Woolf J.; *Kensington and Chelsea Royal*

CAP.

78. Town and Country Planning Act 1971—*cont.*
London Borough Council v. C.G. Hotels (1980)
41 P. & C.R. 40, D.C.; *Forkhurst* v. *Secretary
of State for the Environment* (1983) 46 P. &
C.R. 89, Hodgson J.; *Camden London Borough* v. *Peaktop Properties (Hampstead)*
(1983) 267 E.G. 841, C.A.; *Winton* v. *Secretary of State for the Environment* (1983) 46 P.
& C.R. 205, Woolf J.; *Wakelin* v. *Secretary of
State for the Environment* (1983) 46 P. & C.R.
214, C.A.; *North Warwickshire Borough Coun-
cil* v. *Secretary of State for the Environment
and Amri Singh Gill* [1984] J.P.L. 434, Woolf
J.; *Lydcare* v. *Secretary of State for the
Environment* (1984) 272 E.G. 175; (1985)
L.G.R. 33, C.A.; *North Warwickshire Borough
Council* v. *Secretary of State for the Environ-
ment* (1985) P. & C.R. 47, Woolf J.; *R.* v.
*Runnymede Borough Council, ex p. Sarvan
Singh Seehra* (1987) 151 J.P. 80, Schiemann
J.; *Somak Travel* v. *Secretary of State for the
Environment, The Times*, June 2, 1987,
Stuart-Smith J.; *R.* v. *Basildon District Council,
ex p. Martin Grant Homes* (1987) 53 P. & C.R.
397, McCowan J.; *Wealden District Council*
v. *Secretary of State for the Environment*
[1988] 08 E.G. 112, C.A.; *Somak Travel* v.
Secretary of State for the Environment (1988)
55 P. & C.R. 250, Stuart-Smith J.

s. 22, orders 72/1385; 83/1614; 87/764.

s. 22, amended: 1981, c.36, s.1; 1986, c.63,
sch.11.

s. 23, see *LTSS Print and Supply Services* v.
Hackney London Borough Council [1976] 2
W.L.R. 253; [1976] 1 All E.R. 311, C.A.; *W. T.
Lamb & Sons* v. *Secretary of State for the
Environment*, March 7, 1975, D.C.; *Day* v.
Secretary of State for the Environment (1979)
78 L.G.R. 27, D.C.; *Young* v. *Secretary of
State for the Environment* [1983] 2 All E.R.
1105, H.L.; *Balco Transport Services* v. *Sec-
retary of State for the Environment* (1983) 45
P. & C.R. 216, Glidewell J.; *Smith* v. *Secretary
of State for the Environment* (1984) 47 P. &
C.R. 194, Woolf J.; *Carmichael* v. *Brannan*,
1985 S.C.C.R. 234; *Cynon Valley Borough
Council* v. *Secretary of State for Wales* (1986)
280 E.G. 195, C.A.; *Fairchild* v. *Secretary of
State for the Environment and Eastleigh Borough Council* [1988] J.P.L. 472, Judge Marder
Q.C.

s. 23, amended: 1982, c.30, sch.6.

s. 24, orders 74/418, 539; 76/301; 77/289, 665,
815, 1781, 2085; 78/523; 80/1946; 81/245,
246, 560, 1082, 1569; 82/796, 817; 85/1011,
1012, 1579; 86/8, 435, 812, 1176; 87/265,
702, 738, 1343–1345; 88/1272, 1400, 1813.

s. 24, amended: 1972, c.70, sch.16; 1980, c.65,
sch.15; c.66, sch.24; 1984, c.12, sch.4; 1986,
c.63, sch.11.

ss. 24A–24E, added: *ibid.*, s.25.

s. 24E, order 87/1849.

s. 24E, amended: 198, c.4, sch.3.

s. 25, orders 74/418; 77/289; 81/1082; 86/435;
regs. 88/1812.

1971—cont.

78. Town and Country Planning Act 1971—*cont.*
s. 26, see *Chalgray* v. *Secretary of State for the Environment* [1977] J.P.L. 176; *Steeples* v. *Derbyshire County Council* [1984] 3 All E.R. 468, Webster J.; *R.* v. *Torfaen Borough Council, ex p. Jones,* September 2, 1985, Woolf J.
s. 26, orders 74/418; 77/289, 1781; 88/1813.
s. 27, see *Main* v. *Swansea City Council* (1985) 49 P. & C.R. 26, C.A.
s. 27, orders 74/418; 76/301; 77/289; 88/1813.
s. 27, amended: 1975, c.77, sch.10; 1980, c.65, sch.15; 1981, c.36, s.4; repealed in pt.: 1986, c.5, sch.14.
s. 28, see *Wain and L.D.R.S.* v. *Secretary of State for the Environment and Waltham Forest London Borough* [1979] J.P.L. 231, Stocker J.
s. 28, amended: 1972, c.70, sch.16; 1974, c.32, s.4; 1983, c.47, sch.4; 1985, c.51, sch.2; repealed in pt.: 1974, c.7, ss.35, 42, schs. 6, 8.
s. 29, see *Murphy* v. *Secretary of State for the Environment* [1973] 1 W.L.R. 550; [1973] 2 All E.R. 26; *Enfield London Borough* v. *Secretary of State for the Environment* [1975] J.P.L. 155; *Clyde & Co.* v. *The Secretary of State for the Environment* [1977] 1 All E.R. 333; [1977] 1 W.L.R. 926, C.A.; *K.C.C.* v. *Secretary of State for the Environment and Burmah-Total Refineries Trust* (1976) 33 P. & C.R. 70, D.C.; *A. I. & P. (Stratford)* v. *London Borough of Tower Hamlets* [1976] J.P.L. 234; *R.* v. *Sheffield City Council, ex p. Mansfield* (1978) 37 P. & C.R. 1, D.C.; *Price Brothers (Rode Heath)* v. *Department of the Environment* (1979) 38 P. & C.R. 579, Forbes J.; *Newbury District Council* v. *Secretary of State for the Environment; Newbury District Council* v. *International Synthetic Rubber Co.* [1980] 2 W.L.R. 379; [1980] 1 All E.R. 731, H.L.; *Co-operative Retail Services* v. *Taff-Ely Borough Council* (1979) 39 P. & C.R. 223, C.A.; *South Oxfordshire District Council* v. *Secretary of State for the Environment and Faherty Bros.,* December 5, 1980, Woolf J.; *R.* v. *East Yorkshire Borough of Beverley Council, ex p. Wilson,* September 8, 1982, D.C.; *Hollis* v. *Secretary of State for the Environment* (1983) 265 E.G. 476; *Richmond-upon-Thames London Borough Council* v. *Secretary of State for the Environment, The Times,* May 16, 1983, Glidewell J.; *Westminster City Council* v. *British Waterways Board* (1983) 268 E.G. 145, C.A.; *Grampian Regional Council* v. *City of Aberdeen District Council, The Times,* December 3, 1983, H.L; *R.* v. *Amber Valley District Council, ex p. Jackson* [1984] 3 All E.R. 501, Woolf J.; *R.* v. *Royal County of Berkshire, ex p. Magnall* [1985] J.P.L. 258, Nolan J.; *Gransden (E. C.) & Co. and Falkbridge* v. *Secretary of State for the Environment and Gillingham Borough Council* [1986] J.P.L. 519 Woolf J.; *R.* v. *Basildon District Council, ex p. Martin Grant Homes* (1987) 53 P. & C.R. 397, McCowan J.; *R.* v. *Great*

1971—cont.

78. Town and Country Planning Act 1971—*cont.*
Yarmouth Borough Council, ex p. Botton Brothers Arcades [1988] 56 P. & C.R. 99, Otton J.
s. 29, amended: 1986, c.63, sch.11.
s. 29A, added: 1981, c.43, s.3; amended: 1986, c.63, sch.11; repealed in pt.: *ibid.,* sch.12.
s. 29B, added: 1981, c.43, s.3; amended: 1986, c.63, sch.11; 1988, c.40, sch.12; repealed in pt.: 1986, c.63, sch.11.
s. 30, see *Kingston-upon-Thames Royal London Borough Council* v. *Secretary of State for the Environment* [1973] 1 W.L.R. 1549, D.C.; *A. I. & P. (Stratford)* v. *London Borough of Tower Hamlets* [1976] J.P.L. 234; *Penwith District Council* v. *Secretary of State for the Environment* (1977) 34 P. & C.R. 269, Sir Douglas Frank, Q.C.; *George Wimpey & Co.* v. *New Forest District Council* (1979) 250 E.G. 249, Sir Douglas Frank Q.C.
s. 30, amended: 1981, c.36, sch.1.
s. 30A, added: *ibid.,*s.5.
s. 31, see *Newbury District Council* v. *Secretary of State for the Environment; Newbury District Council* v. *International Synthetic Rubber Co.* [1980] 2 W.L.R. 379; [1980] 1 All E.R. 731, H.L.; *Co-operative Retail Services* v. *Taff-Ely Borough Council* (1979) 39 P. & C.R. 223, C.A.
s. 31, orders 73/273; 74/418; 76/301; 77/289, 1781, 1946; 81/560, 1082; 86/435; 88/1272, 1813.
s. 31, amended: 1972, c.70, sch.16; 1980, c.65, sch.15; repealed in pt.: 1972, c.70, sch.30; 1974, c.7, ss.35, 42, schs.6,8.
s. 31A, added: 1986, c.63, sch.11.
s. 32, see *Kerrier District Council* v. *Secretary of State for the Environment and Brewer* (1981) 41 P. & C.R. 284, D.C.
s. 32, repealed in pt.: 1986, c.63, sch.12.
s. 33, see *City of Glasgow District Council* v. *Secretary of State for Scotland,* Second Division, December 14, 1979; *Pioneer Aggregates (U.K.) Ltd.* v. *Secretary of State for the Environment* [1984] 3 W.L.R. 32, H.L.; *R.* v. *Hammersmith and Fulham London Borough Council, ex p. Greater London Council, The Times,* October 16, 1985, C.A.
s. 34, orders 74/418; 77/289, 1781; 81/560, 1082; 86/435; 88/1813.
s. 34, amended: 1972, c.70, sch.16; 1975, c.77, sch.10; 1980, c.65, sch.15; 1986, c.63, sch.6.
s. 35, see *Richmond-upon-Thames London Borough Council* v. *Secretary of State for the Environment, The Times,* May 16, 1983, Glidewell J.; *R.* v. *Secretary of State for the Environment and Cheshire County Council, ex p. Halton District Council, The Times,* July 14, 1983, Taylor J.; *Sir Brandon Meredith Rhys Williams* v. *Secretary of State for Wales and the Welsh Water Authority and Taff Ely Borough Council* [1985] J.P.L. 29, C.A.
s. 35, amended: 1981, c.63, sch. 11; 1986, c.63, sch.11.

1971—cont.

78. Town and Country Planning Act 1971—cont.
s. 36, see *Chalgray* v. *Secretary of State for the Environment* (1976) 33 P. & C.R. 19, Slynn J.; *Robert Hitchens Builders* v. *Secretary of State for the Environment; Britannia (Cheltenham)* v. *Same* (1979) 251 E.G. 467, C.A.; *Price Brothers (Rode Heath)* v. *Department of the Environment* (1979) 38 P. & C.R. 579, Forbes J.; *Co-operative Retail Services* v. *Secretary of State for the Environment* [1980] 1 W.L.R. 271; [1980] 1 All E.R. 449, C.A.; *South Oxfordshire District Council* v. *Secretary of State for the Environment and Faherty Bros.*, December 5, 1980, Woolf J.; *Ryan* v. *Secretary of State for the Environment*, June 14, 1982, Forbes J.; *Griffiths* v. *Secretary of State for the Environment* [1983] 2 W.L.R. 172, H.L.; *Hollis* v. *Secretary of State for the Environment* (1983) 265 E.G. 476; *J. A. Pye (Oxford) Estates* v. *West Oxfordshire District Council* (1984) 47 P. & C.R. 125, David Widdicombe Q.C.; *Thrasyvoulou* v. *Secretary of State for the Environment* [1988] 10 E.G. 131, C.A.
s. 36, orders 74/418; 86/435; 87/702.
s. 36, amended: 1980, c.65, sch.15; 1981, c.36, sch.1; 1986, c.63, sch. 11.
s. 37, orders 74/418; 76/301; 86/435; 88/1813.
s. 40, amended: 1978, c.52, sch.11; 1988, c.4, sch.3.
s. 41, see *L. A. H. Ames* v. *North Bedfordshire Borough Council* (1979) 253 E.G. 55, C.A.
s. 41, amended: 1980, c.65, sch.32; 1981, c.36, s.6; 1986, c.63, sch.6.
ss. 41, 42, see *Grampian Regional Council* v. *City of Aberdeen District Council, The Times,* December 3, 1983, H.L.
s. 42, see *R.* v. *Bromley London Borough, ex p. Sievers* (1980) 255 E.G. 355; (1981) 41 P. & C.R. 294, D.C.
s. 42, orders 74/418; 77/289; 86/435; 88/1813.
s. 43, see *Spackman* v. *Secretary of State for the Environment* [1977] 1 All E.R. 257; *South Oxfordshire District Council* v. *Secretary of State for the Environment and Faherty Bros.*, December 5, 1980, Woolf J.; *Malvern Hills District Council* v. *Secretary of State for the Environment* (1982) 262 E.G. 1190; (1983) 81 L.G.R. 13, C.A.
s. 44A, added: 1981, c.36, s.7.
s. 45, amended: 1972, c.70, sch.16; 1981, c.36, s.8.
s. 46, regs. 74/596.
s. 46, repealed in pt.: 1974, c.7, schs.6,8.
s. 47, repealed in pt.: 1975, c.24, sch.3.
ss. 48, 49, amended: 1972, c.70, sch.16.
s. 50, repealed: 1980, c.65, sch.34.
s. 51, see *Parkes* v. *Secretary of State for the Environment* [1978] 1 W.L.R. 1308, C.A.; *Western Fish Products* v. *Penwith District Council and the Secretary of State for the Environment* [1978] J.P.L. 627, C.A.
s. 51, amended: 1972, c.70, sch.16; 1981, c.36, s.9.
ss. 51A–51F, added: *ibid.*,s.10.

1971—cont.

78. Town and Country Planning Act 1971—cont.
s. 52, see *Lewis Jones* v. *Secretary of State for Wales* [1974] J.P.L. 415; 28 P. & C.R. 280, C.A.; *Tarmac Properties* v. *Secretary of State for Wales* [1976] J.P.L. 576; *L. A. H. Ames* v. *North Bedfordshire Borough Council* (1979) 253 E.G. 55, C.A.; *Windsor and Maidenhead Royal Borough Council* v. *Brandrose Investments, The Times,* February 3, 1983, C.A.; *Avon County Council* v. *Millard* (1985) 274 E.G. 1025; (1985) 50 P. & C.R. 275, C.A.; *City of Bradford Metropolitan Council* v. *Secretary of State for the Environment and McLean Homes Northern* [1986] J.P.L. 292, Farquarson J.; *Abbey Homesteads (Developments)* v. *Northamptonshire County Council* (1986) 278 E.G. 1249, C.A.; *City of Bradford Metropolitan Council* v. *Secretary of State for the Environment and McLean Homes Northern* [1986] J.P.L. 598, C.A.; *Martin's Appplication, Re* (No. LP/40/1985) (1987) 53 P. & C.R. 146, Lands Tribunal; *R.* v. *Gillingham Borough Council, ex p. Parham (F.)* [1988] J.P.L. 366, Roch J.
s. 53, see *East Suffolk C.C.* v. *Secretary of State* (1972) 70 L.G.R. 595, D.C.; *English Speaking Union of the Commonwealth* v. *Westminster City Council* (1973) 226 E.G. 1963; (1973) 26 P. & C.R. 575, Pennycuick V.-C; *Western Fish Products* v. *Penwith District Council* (1978) 77 L.G.R. 185, C.A.; *Property Investment Holdings* v. *Secretary of State for the Environment and Reigate and Banstead Borough Council* [1984] J.P.L. 587, McCullough J.; *Trustees of the Earl of Lichfield's Estate* v. *Secretary of State for the Environment and Stafford Borough Council* [1985] J.P.L. 251, McNeill J.; *South Oxfordshire District Council* v. *Secretary of State for the Environment* (1986) 52 P. & C.R. 1, McCullough J.; *Moran* v. *Secretary of State for the Environment and Mid-Sussex District Council* [1988] J.P.L. 24, McCullough J.; *Camden London Borough Council* v. *Secretary of State for the Environment, The Times,* June 3, 1988, Farquharson J.
s. 53, orders 74/418; 77/289; 86/435; 88/1813.
s. 53, amended: 1980, c.65, sch.32; 1986, c.63, sch. 6.
s. 54, see *Amalgamated Investment and Property Co.* v. *John Walker & Sons* [1977] 1 W.L.R. 164, C.A.; *General Accident, Fire & Life Assurance Corp.* v. *Secretary of State for the Environment* (1977) 241 E.G. 842, Slynn J.; *Att.-Gen., ex rel. Sutcliffe* v. *Calderdale Borough Council* (1983) 46 P. & C.R. 399, C.A.; *Cotswold District Council* v. *Secretary of State for the Environment* (1986) 61 P. & C.R. 139, D.C.; *Debenhams* v. *Westminster City Council* [1986] 3 W.L.R. 1063, H.L.; *Leominster District Council* v. *British Historic Buildings and S.P.S. Shipping* [1987] J.P.L. 350, Hoffmann J.
s. 54, regs. 77/228; 87/349.
s. 54, amended: 1972, c.70, sch.16; 1975, c.76, sch.1; 1983, c.47, sch.4; 1985, c.51, sch.2;

CAP.

1971—cont.

78. Town and Country Planning Act 1971—cont.
1986, c.63, sch.9; 1988, c.4, sch.3; repealed in pt.: 1972, c.70, sch.30.
ss. 54, 55, see *Att.-Gen. at the Relation of Robin Sutcliffe, John Rouse and Tony Hughes* v. *Calderdale Borough Council* [1983] J.P.L. 310, C.A.
s. 54A, added: 1980, c.65, sch.15; amended: 1985, c.51, sch.2; 1988, c.4, sch.3.
s. 55, see *R.* v. *Endersby Properties* [1976] J.P.L. 507, C.A.; (1975) 32 P. & C.R. 399, C.A.; *Att.-Gen., ex rel. Bedfordshire C.C.* v. *Howard United Reformed Church Trustees, Bedford* [1975] 2 All E.R. 337, H.L.; *General Accident, Fire & Life Assurance Corp.* v. *Secretary of State for the Environment* (1977) 241 E.G. 842, Slynn J.; *R.* v. *North Hertfordshire District Council, ex p. Sullivan* [1981] J.P.L. 752, Comyn J.; *R.* v. *Stroud District Council, ex p. Michael Goodenough; Julian Usborne and Stephen Tomlin* [1982] J.P.L. 240, Woolf J.; *Bath City Council* v. *Secretary of State for the Environment* (1984) 47 P. & C.R. 663, Woolf J.; *Cotswold District Council* v. *Secretary of State for the Environment* (1986) 61 P. & C.R. 139, D.C.; *R.* v. *Wells Street Stipendiary Magistrate, ex p. Westminster City Council* [1986] 1 W.L.R. 1046, D.C.; *Windsor and Maidenhead Royal Borough Council* v. *Secretary of State for the Environment* (1988) 86 L.G.R. 402, Mann J.
s. 55, amended: 1972, c.70, sch.16; 1980, c.65, sch.15; 1986, c.63, sch.9; repealed in pt.: 1980, c.65, schs.15,34; 1986, c.63, schs.11,12.
s. 56, see *Att.-Gen., ex rel. Bedfordshire C.C.* v. *Howard United Reformed Church Trustees, Bedford* [1975] 2 All E.R. 337, H.L.
s. 56, amended: 1972, c.70, sch.16; 1979, c.46, sch.4; 1980, c.65, sch.15; 1986, c.63, sch.9; repealed in pt.: 1980, c.65, schs.15,34.
s. 56A, added: 1980, c.65, sch.15.
s. 56B, regs. 87/349.
ss. 56B, 56C, added: 1986, c.63, sch.9.
s. 57, amended: *ibid.*, sch.11.
s. 58, amended: 1972, c.42, s.7; 1979, c.46, sch.4; 1980, c.65, sch.15; 1985, c.51, sch.2.
s. 58A, added: *ibid.*
s. 58AA, added: 1986, c.63, sch.9.
ss. 58B–58N, added: *ibid.*, s.31.
s. 60, see *Bullock* v. *Secretary of State for the Environment* (1980) 40 P. & C.R. 246, Phillips J.; *Bell* v. *Canterbury City Council, The Times,* March 11, 1988, C.A.; *Bush* v. *Secretary of State for the Environment and Reddich Borough Council* [1988] J.P.L. 108, Graham Eyre Q.C.
s. 60, regs. 75/148; 81/14; 88/963.
s. 60, amended: 1974, c.32, s.10; 1980, c.65, sch.15; repealed in pt.: *ibid.*, schs.15,34; 1986, c.63, sch.12.
s. 61, repealed in pt.: 1980, c.65, schs.15,34.
s. 61A, see *Bath City Council* v. *Pratt (T/A Crescent Investments),* October 10, 1987, Mr. Assistant Recorder Viscount Colville of Calross; Bristol Crown Ct.

CAP.

1971—cont.

78. Town and Country Planning Act 1971—cont.
s. 61A, regs. 75/148.
s. 61A, added: 1974, c.32, s.8.
s. 62, see *Bush* v. *Secretary of State for the Environment* [1988] 56 P. & C.R. 58; [1988] J.P.L. 108, Graham Eyre Q.C.
s. 62, amended: 1974, c.32, s.10; 1985, c.52, s.1.
s. 63, regs. 74/185; 75/898; 84/421; 87/804, 2227.
s. 63, amended: 1972, c.70, sch.16; 1974, c.32, s.3; 1986, c.63, s.45.
s. 65, see *Red House Farms (Thorndon)* v. *Mid-Suffolk District Council* (1980) 40 P. & C.R. 119, D.C.
s. 65, substituted: 1986, c.63, s.46.
ss. 66–72, repealed: *ibid.*, s.48, sch. 12.
ss. 67, 68, regs. 72/904; 73/149; 74/1418; 77/682, 705; 79/838, 1643; 81/867.
s. 69, orders 72/903, 996; 74/1054, 1283, 1419, 2028; 76/565; 79/839.
ss. 73–80, repealed: 1986, c.63, sch.12.
s. 74, see *B. L. Holdings* v. *Robert J. Wood and Partners* (1979) 123 S.J. 570, C.A.
s. 74, orders 74/1054, 1283, 1419.
s. 75, orders 76/652; 77/848.
s. 78, see *Richmond-upon-Thames London Borough Council* v. *Secretary of State for the Environment* (1979) 37 P. & C.R. 151, Sir Douglas Frank, Q.C.
s. 81, see *R.* v. *Secretary of State for the Environment, ex p. Hillingdon London Borough Council* [1986] (Note) 2 All E.R. 273, C.A.
ss. 81–83, repealed: 1986, c.63, sch.12.
s. 84, see *Harper's Application, Re* (1986) 52 P. & C.R. 104, Lands Tribunal (Ref. No. LP/43/1984), V. G. Wellings Esq. Q.C.
ss. 84–86, repealed: 1986, c.63, sch.12.
s. 86, order 79/908.
s. 87, see *Whitfield* v. *Gowling* (1974) 28 P. & C.R. 386, D.C.; *Tidswell* v. *Secretary of State for the Environment and Thurrock B.C.* [1977] J.P.L. 104, D.C.; *Lipson* v. *Secretary of State for the Environment* (1976) 33 P. & C.R. 95, D.C.; *Copeland B.C.* v. *Secretary of State for the Environment* (1976) 31 P. & C.R. 403, D.C.; *London Borough of Redbridge* v. *Perry* (1976) 75 L.G.R. 90, D.C.; *Bristol Stadium* v. *Brown* (1979) 252 E.G. 803, D.C.; *Rochdale Metropolitan Borough Council* v. *Simmonds* (1980) 256 E.G. 607; (1980) 40 P. & C.R. 432, D.C.; *Sykes* v. *Secretary of State for the Environment; South Oxfordshire District Council* v. *Secretary of State for the Environment* (1980) 257 E.G. 821, D.C.; *Perkins* v. *Secretary of State for the Environment, and the Rother District Council* [1981] J.P.L. 755, Glidewell J.; *W. F. Nicholls* v. *Secretary of State for the Environment and Bristol City Council,* April 10, 1981, McNeill J.; *London Borough of Camden* v. *Backer and Aird* [1982] J.P.L. 516, C.A.; *Lee* v. *Bromley London Borough Council* (1983) 45 P. & C.R. 342, D.C.; *Scarborough Borough Council* v. *Adams*

1971—cont.

78. Town and Country Planning Act 1971—cont.
(1984) 47 P. & C.R. 133, D.C.; *Backer v. Secretary of State for the Environment* (1984) 47 P. & C.R. 149, David Widdicombe Q.C.; *Peacock Homes v. Secretary of State for the Environment* (1984) 42 P. & C.R. 20, C.A.; *Ragsdale v. Creswick* (1984) 271 E.G. 1268, D.C.; *Lydcare v. Secretary of State for the Environment* (1985) 83 L.G.R. 33, C.A.; *R. v. Greenwich London Borough Council, The Times,* July 5, 1985, C.A.; *Balco Transport Services v. Secretary of State for the Environment, The Times,* August 8, 1985, C.A.; *R. v. Secretary of State for the Environment, ex p. Hillingdon London Borough Council* [1986] 1 W.L.R. 192, Woolf J.; *R. v. Greenwich London Borough Council, ex p. Patel* (1986) 84 L.G.R. 241, C.A.; *R. v. Runnymede Borough Council, ex p. Sarvan Singh Seehra* (1987) 151 J.P. 80, Schiemann J.
ss. 87, 88, regs. 81/1742.
s. 88, see *Ipswich County Borough Council v. Secretary of State for the Environment* (1972) E.G. 797; *Hammersmith L.B.C. v. Secretary of State for the Environment* (1975) 73 L.G.R. 288, D.C.; *Button v. Jenkins* [1975] 3 All E.R. 585, D.C.; *Morris v. Secretary of State for the Environment* (1975) 31 P. & C.R. 216, D.C.; *R. v. Melton and Belvoir JJ., ex p. Tynan* [1977] J.P.L. 368, D.C.; *Lipson v. Secretary of State for the Environment* (1976) 33 P. & C.R. 95; [1977] 75 L.G.R. 544, D.C.; *Copeland B.C. v. Secretary of State for the Environment* (1976) 28 P. & C.R. 386, D.C.; *Tynan v. Melton Mowbray District Council* (1977) 242 E.G. 205, D.C.; *Re Land at Banstead Railway Station Goods Yard, Banstead, Surrey, Ref. No. 309/77; Skinner v. Secretary of State for the Environment* (1978) 247 E.G. 1179, D.C.; *Stanton v. Secretary of State for the Environment* (1978) 248 E.G. 227, D.C.; *Dudley Borough Council v. Secretary of State for the Environment and Electronic and Mechanical and Engineering Co.* [1980] J.P.L. 181, D.C.; *Wain v. Secretary of State for the Environment* (1978) 39 P. & C.R. 82, Stocker J.; *Newport v. Secretary of State for the Environment and Bromley London Borough Council* (1980) 40 P. & C.R. 261, D.C.; *Murfitt v. Secretary of State for the Environment and East Cambridgeshire District Council* (1980) 40 P. & C.R. 254, D.C.; *Rochdale Metropolitan Borough Council v. Simmonds* (1980) 256 E.G. 607, D.C.; 40 P. & C.R. 432, D.C.; *W. F. Nicholls v. Secretary of State for the Environment and Bristol City Council,* April 10, 1981, McNeill J.; *South Cambridgeshire District Council v. Stokes* [1981] Crim.L.R. 261, D.C.; *TLG Building Materials v. Secretary of State for the Environment* (1980) 41 P. & C.R. 243, D.C.; *King and King v. Secretary of State for the Environment and Nuneaton Borough Council* [1981] J.P.L. 813, D.C.; *P.A.D. Entertainment v. Secretary of State for the Environment and the City of Westminster; Moorchat*

1971—cont.

78. Town and Country Planning Act 1971—cont.
v. *The Same* [1982] J.P.L. 706, Stephen Brown J.; *Davy v. Spelthorne District Council* [1983] 3 All E.R. 278, H.L.; *Kenwood (Travel, Employment, and Estates) and Z. I. Gourgey v. Secretary of State for the Environment and Westminster City Council* [1984] J.P.L. 36, Stephen Brown J.; *R. v. Smith (Thomas George)* (1984) 48 P. & C.R. 392, C.A.; *Dover District Council v. McKeen* (1985) 50 P. & C.R. 250, D.C.; *R. v. Greenwich London Borough Council. The Times,* July 5, 1985, C.A.; *Lenlyn v. Secretary of State for the Environment; R. v. Secretary of State for the Environment, ex p. Lenlyn* (1985) 50 P.& C.R. 129, Hodgson J.; *R. v. Secretary of State for the Environment, ex p. Crossley (Theresa)* [1985] J.P.L. 632, Webster J.; *Pearcy (John) Transport v. Secretary of State for the Environment, The Times,* January 31, 1986, Mr. David Widdicombe Q.C., sitting as a deputy High Court Judge; *R. v. Greenwich London Borough Council, ex p. Patel* (1986) 84 L.G.R. 241, C.A.; *Vaughan v. Secretary of State for the Environment and Mid-Sussex District Council* [1986] J.P.L. 840, McNeill J.; *Masefield v. Taylor, The Times,* December 16, 1986, D.C.; *R. v. Runnymede Borough Council, ex p. Sarvan Singh Seehra* (1987) 151 J.P. 80; (1987) 53 P. & C.R. 281, Schiemann J.; *R. v. Secretary of State and Bromley London Borough Council, ex p. Jackson* [1987] J.P.L. 790, MacPherson J.; *Thrasyvoulou v. Secretary of State for the Environment* [1988] 10 E.G. 131, C.A.; *R. v. Kuxhaus* [1988] 2 W.L.R. 1005, C.A.; *E.L.S. Wholesale Wolverhampton v. Secretary of State for the Environment* [1988] 56 P. & C.R. 69, D.C.
ss. 88–246, see *Choudry v. Secretary of State for the Environment* (1983) 265 E.G. 384, Stephen Brown J.
s. 88A, see *Burner, Burner and Burner v. Secretary of State for the Environment and the South Hams District Council* [1983] J.P.L. 459, Glidewell J.; *Lydcare v. Secretary of State for the Environment and Westminster City Council* [1984] J.P.L. 39, McCullough J.; *Hughes (H.T.) & Sons v. Secretary of State for the Environment* (1986) 51 P. & C.R. 134, D.C.
ss. 88A, 88B, added: 1981, c.41, sch.
s. 88B, repealed in pt.: 1986, c.63, sch.12.
s. 89, see *Whitfield v. Gowling* (1974) 28 P. & C.R. 386, D.C.; *Johnston v. Secretary of State for the Environment* (1974) 28 P. & C.R. 424, D.C.; *Duffy v. Pillory* (1977) 75 L.G.R. 159, D.C.; *London Borough of Redbridge v. Perry* (1976) 75 L.G.R. 90, D.C.; *St. Albans District Council v. Norman Harper Autosales Ltd.* (1977) 76 L.G.R. 300, D.C.; *Parry v. Forest of Dean District Council* (1976) 34 P. & C.R. 209, D.C.; *South Cambridgeshire District Council v. Stokes* [1981] Crim.L.R. 261, D.C.; *Tandridge District Council v. Powers* (1980) 80 L.G.R. 453, D.C.; *Hodgetts v. Chiltern District Council* [1983] 2 W.L.R. 577; [1983] 1 All E.R.

CAP.

1971—cont.

78. Town and Country Planning Act 1971—*cont.*
1057, H.L.; *Scarborough Borough Council v. Adams* (1984) 47 P. & C.R. 133, D.C.; *Ragsdale* v. *Creswick* (1984) 271 E.G. 1268, D.C.; *R.* v. *Smith (Thomas George)* (1984) 48 P. & C.R. 392, C.A.; *R.* v. *Greenwich London Borough Council, The Times,* July 5, 1985, C.A.; *Prosser* v. *Sharp* (1985) 274 E.G. 1249, D.C.; *R.* v. *Jefford* [1986] J.P.L. 912, Judge Rubin; *Coventry Scaffolding Co. (London)* v. *Parker (John Brian)* [1987] J.P.L. 127, D.C.; *R.* v. *Keeys, The Times,* July 17, 1987, C.A.; *R.* v. *Fyfield Equipment* [1987] Crim.L.R. 507, Snaresbrook Crown Ct.

s. 89, amended: 1981, c.41, sch.; 1986, c.63, sch.11.

ss. 89, 91, see *R.* v. *Greenwich London Borough Council, ex p. Patel* (1986) 84 L.G.R. 241, C.A.

s. 90, see *Scott Markets* v. *Waltham Forest London Borough* (1979) 77 L.G.R. 565, C.A.; *Bristol Stadium* v. *Brown* (1979) 252 E.G. 803, D.C.; *R.* v. *Jenner* [1983] 2 All E.R. 46, C.A; *R.* v. *Runnymede Borough Council, ex p. Sarvan Singh Seehra* (1987) 151 J.P. 80, Schiemann J.; *Runnymede Borough Council* v. *Smith* [1987] 53 P. & C.R. 132, Millett J.

s. 90, substituted: 1977, c.29, s.1; amended: 1981, c.41, sch.; 1986, c.63, sch.11; repealed in pt.: 1981, c.41, sch.

s. 91, regs. 74/596; 77/228; 87/349.

s. 91, amended: 1972, c.70, sch.16; 1981, c.41, sch.; repealed in pt.: 1974, c.7, sch.8.

s. 92, see *Havering London Borough Council* v. *Secretary of State for the Environment* (1983) 45 P. & C.R. 258, Hodgson J.

s. 92, amended: 1981, c.41, sch.

ss. 92, 93, see *Prosser* v. *Sharp* (1985) 274 E.G. 1249, D.C.

s. 92A, orders 86/435; 88/1813.

s. 92A, amended: 1985, c.51, s.3; repealed in pt.: *ibid.*sch.17.

s. 93, see *Broxbourne Borough Council* v. *Small,* April 21, 1980, Judge Goldstone, Edmonton County Ct.; *R.* v. *Fyfield Equipment* [1987] Crim.L.R. 507, Snaresbrook Crown Ct.

s. 93, amended: 1972, c.70, sch.16; 1981, c.41, sch.

s. 94, see *Western Fish Products* v. *Penwith District Council* (1978) 77 L.G.R. 185, C.A.; *Broxbourne Borough Council* v. *Secretary of State for the Environment* [1979] 2 All E.R. 13, D.C.; *Vaughan* v. *Secretary of State for the Environment and Mid-Sussex District Council* [1986] J.P.L. 840, McNeill J.

s. 94, amended: 1981, c.41, sch.

ss. 94, 95, see *Bristol City Council* v. *Secretary of State for the Environment* [1988] 56 P. & C.R. 49, Stuart-Smith J.

ss. 96, 97, see *Leominster District Council* v. *British Historic Buildings and S.P.S. Shipping* [1987] J.P.L. 350, Hoffmann J.

ss. 96, 97, substituted: 1981, c.41, sch.

ss. 96, 97, 97A, see *Bath City Council* v. *Secretary of State for the Environment* (1984) 47 P. & C.R. 663, Woolf J.

CAP.

1971—cont.

78. Town and Country Planning Act 1971—*cont.*
s. 97, see *Royal Borough of Windsor and Maidenhead* v. *Secretary of State for the Environment* [1988] J.P.L. 410, Mann J.

s. 97, amended: 1986, c.63, sch.9.

s. 98, amended: *ibid.,* sch.11.

s. 99, regs. 77/228; 87/349.

s. 99, amended: 1972, c.70, sch.16.

s. 99A, added: 1980, c.65, sch.15.

s. 99B, added: 1985, c.51, sch.2.

s. 100, substituted: 1981, c.41, sch.; amended: 1983, c.47, sch.4; repealed in pt.: 1985, c.51, sch.17.

s. 101, see *R.* v. *Secretary of State for the Environment, ex p. Hampshire County Council* [1981] J.P.L. 47, D.C.; *R.* v. *Stroud District Council, ex p. Michael Goodenough; Julian Usborne and Stephen Tomlin* [1982] J.P.L. 240, Woolf J.; *R.* v. *Secretary of State for the Environment, ex p. Hampshire County Council* (1982) 44 P. & C.R. 343, D.C.

s. 101, substituted: 1986, c.63, sch.9; amended: 1988, c.4, sch.3.

s. 101A, substituted: 1986, c.63, sch.9.

s. 101B, added: *ibid.,* s.32.

s. 102, see *Maidstone Borough Council* v. *Mortimer* (1982) 43 P. & C.R. 67, C.A.; *Vale of Glamorgan Borough Council* v. *Palmer* [1983] Crim.L.R. 334, D.C.; *Groveside Homes* v. *Elmbridge Borough Council, The Times,* September 5, 1987, D.C.

s. 102, amended: 1974, c.32, s.10.

s. 103, see *Bush* v. *Secretary of State for the Environment and Redditch Borough Council* [1988] J.P.L. 108, Graham Eyre Q.C.

s. 103, amended and repealed in pt.: 1981, c.41, sch.

s. 104, see *Red House Farms (Thorndon)* v. *Mid-Suffolk District Council* (1980) 40 P. & C.R. 119, D.C.

s. 104, substituted: 1981, c.41, sch.; amended: 1986, c.63, sch.11.

s. 105, amended: *ibid.;* repealed in pt.: *ibid.,* schs.11,12.

s. 106, amended: 1972, c.70, sch.16.

ss. 106, 107, amended: 1981, c.41, sch.

s. 108, substituted: 1981, c.36, s.11.

s. 109, see *Royal Borough of Kensington and Chelsea* v. *Elmton* (1978) 246 E.G. 1011, D.C.; *Preston* v. *British Union for the Abolition of Vivisection, The Times,* July 24, 1985, Mann J.; *Porter* v. *Honey* [1988] 2 All E.R. 449, D.C.

s. 109, regs. 84/421; 87/804.

s. 109, amended: 1972, c.70, sch.16; 1981, c.41, sch.; 1986, c.36, sch.11.

s. 109A, added: 1982, c.30, s.36.

s. 110, see *Marshal* v. *Ruttle, The Times,* July 20, 1988, D.C.

s. 110, repealed in pt.: 1986, c.36, sch.12.

s. 112, see *Company Developments (Property)* v. *Secretary of State for the Environment and Salisbury District Council* [1978] J.P.L. 107, Sir Douglas Frank, Q.C.; *R.* v. *Secretary of State for the Environment, ex p. Leicester City Council* [1987] J.P.L. 787; (1987) 55 P. & C.R. 364, McCullough J.

1971—cont.

78. Town and Country Planning Act 1971—cont.

s. 112, amended: 1980, c.65, s.91; 1981, c.67, sch.4; repealed in pt.: 1972, c.70, sch.30; 1981, c.67, sch.6.

s. 113, amended: 1975, c.77, sch.30; 1981, c.67, sch.4; repealed in pt.: *ibid.*,sch.6.

s. 114, see *Rolf* v. *North Shropshire District Council* (1988) 55 P. & C.R. 242, C.A.; *Robbins* v. *Secretary of State for the Environment and Ashford Borough Council* [1988] J.P.L. 349, Pill Q.C.

s. 114, amended: 1972, c.70, sch.16; 1981, c.67, sch.4; 1983, c.47, sch.4; 1985, s.51, sch.2; 1988, c.4, sch.3; repealed in pt.: 1972, c.70, sch.30; 1981, c.67, sch.6.

s. 115, see *R.* v. *Stroud District Council, ex p. Michael Goodenough; Julian Usborne and Stephen Tomlin* [1982] J.P.L. 240, Woolf J.; *Rolf* v. *North Shropshire District Council* (1988) 55 P. & C.R. 242, C.A.; *Robbins* v. *Secretary of State for the Environment, The Times,* May 21, 1988, C.A.

s. 115, amended: 1972, c.70, sch.16; 1981, c.67, sch.4; 1983, c.47, sch.4; 1985, c.51, sch.2; 1988, c.4, sch.3.

s. 116, repealed in pt.: 1974, c.32, s.6.

s. 117, amended: 1974, c.7, sch.6; 1981, c.67, sch.4; 1985, c.51, sch.2; 1988, c.4, sch.3; repealed in pt.: 1981, c.67, schs.6,8.

s. 118, amended: 1984, c.12, sch.4.

s. 119, amended: 1972, c.70, sch.16; repealed in pt.: *ibid.*,sch.30; 1980, c.65, schs.23,24; order 86/452.

s. 121, see *Third Greytown Properties* v. *Peterborough Corporation* [1973] 3 All E.R. 731, Templeman J.

s. 121, amended: 1981, c.67, sch.4; repealed in pt.: 1972, c.70, sch.30; 1980, c.65, schs.23,24.

ss. 122, 123, amended: 1980, c.65, sch.23; repealed in pt.: *ibid.*,schs.23,34.

s. 124, amended: 1972, c.5, sch.3; repealed in pt.: *ibid.*; 1974, c.7, schs.6,8.

s. 125, repealed in pt: *ibid.*

s. 126, see *Rolf* v *North Shropshire District Council* (1988) 55 P. & C.R. 242, C.A.

s. 126, amended: 1972, c.70, sch.16; 1985, c.51, sch.2; 1988, c.4, sch.3.

s. 127, see *Dowty Boulton Paul* v. *Wolverhampton Corporation, The Times,* March 1, 1973, C.A.

s. 127, amended: 1984, c.12, sch.4.

s. 130, repealed in pt.: 1973, c.26, sch.3.

s. 132, amended: 1981, c.67, sch.4.

s. 134, amended: 1972, c.70, sch.16.

s. 145, regs. 74/1242.

s. 147, amended: 1973, c.37, sch.8; repealed in pt.: 1986, c.63, sch.12.

s. 151, repealed: *ibid.*

ss. 154, 156, regs. 74/1242.

s. 158, amended: 1975, c.76, sch.1; repealed in pt.: 1972, c.70, sch.30.

s. 162, regs. 74/1242.

s. 164, see *Pennine Raceway* v. *Kirklees Metropolitan Council* [1982] 3 All E.R. 628, C.A.

1971—cont.

78. Town and Country Planning Act 1971—cont.

s. 164, regs. 74/596; 76/1419.

s. 164, amended: 1972, c.70, sch.16; 1981, c.36, s.12, sch.1; repealed in pt.: 1974, c.7, schs.6,8.

ss. 164, 165, see *Jones* v. *Stockport Metropolitan Borough* (1984) 269 E.G. 408; (1985) 50 P. & C.R. 299, C.A.

s. 164A, added: 1981, c.36, s.13.

s. 165, amended: 1985, c.19, s.1; repealed in pt.: 1986, c.63, sch.12.

s. 167, regs. 74/1242.

s. 169, see *Camden London Borough Council* v. *Peaktop Properties (Hampstead)* (1983) 267 E.G. 841, C.A.

s. 169, amended: 1972, c.70, sch.16; 1985, c.19, s.1; repealed in pt.: 1986, c.63, sch.12.

ss. 169, 170, regs. 74/596; 76/1419.

s. 170, amended: 1972, c.70, sch.16; 1981, c.36, s.4, sch.1.

ss. 170A, 170B, added: *ibid.*,s.15.

ss. 171, 172, regs. 77/228; 87/349.

ss. 171, 172, amended: 1972, c.70, sch.16.

s. 173, regs. 77/228; 87/349.

ss. 173, 176, amended: 1972, c.70, sch.16.

s. 174, see *Bell* v. *Canterbury City Council* [1988] 22 E.G. 86, C.A.

s. 176, regs. 84/421.

s. 177, see *Sample (Warkworth)* v. *Alnwick District Council* (1984) 48 P. & C.R. 474, Lands Tribunal; *Texas Homecare* v. *Lewes District Council* (1986) 51 P. & C.R. 205, Lands Tribunal.

s. 177, regs. 74/596.

s. 177, amended: 1974, c.70, sch.16; 1977, c.29, s.2; 1982, c.30, sch.6; repealed in pt.: 1977, c.29, s.2.

s. 178, amended: 1981, c.36, sch.12.

s. 178A, regs. 85/698; 88/726.

ss. 178A–178C, added: 1981, c.36, s.16.

s. 179, amended: *ibid.*,s.17.

s. 180, see *Purbeck District Council* v. *Secretary of State for the Environment* [1982] 80 L.G.R. 545, Woolf J.; *Wain* v. *Secretary of State for the Environment* (1982) 80 L.G.R. 438, C.A.; *Bremer* v. *Haringey London Borough Council, The Times,* May 12, 1983, Vivian Price Q.C.; *Balco Transport Services* v. *Secretary of State for the Environment* [1985] 3 All E.R. 689, C.A.

s. 180, regs. 74/596; 76/1419.

s. 180, repealed in pt.: 1972, c.70, sch.30.

ss. 180, 184, 186, see *Sheppard* v. *Secretary of State for the Environment* [1975] J.P.L. 352.

s. 181, amended: 1986, c.63, sch.11; 1988, c.4, sch.3.

s. 182, amended: 1972, c.70, sch.16; 1988, c.4, sch.3.

s. 184, amended: 1986, c.63, sch.11.

s. 185, repealed: *ibid.*, sch.12.

s. 186, amended: *ibid.*, sch.11.

ss. 187–189, regs. 74/596; 76/1419.

ss. 188, 189, repealed in pt.: 1972, c.70, sch.16.

s. 190, regs. 77/228; 87/349.

s. 190, repealed in pt.: S.L.R. 1975.

CAP.

1971—cont.

78. Town and Country Planning Act 1971—*cont.*
s. 191, repealed in pt.: 1986, c.63, sch.12.
s. 191A, added: 1984, c.12, sch.4.
s. 192, see *R. v. Secretary of State for the Environment, ex p. Bournemouth Borough Council* (1987) 281 E.G. 539, Mann J.
s. 192, order 73/425.
s. 192, amended: 1972, c.70, sch.16; 1973, c.26, ss.68–76,82; 1975, c.77, s.23; 1980, c.66, sch.24; 1985, c.51, sch.1; c.71, sch.2; 1987, c.3, sch.1.
s. 193, regs. 74/596; 76/1419.
s. 193, amended: 1973, c.26, ss.77,82; repealed in pt.: *ibid.*,ss.77,86.
s. 194, see *Mancini v. Coventry City Council* (1985) 49 P. & C.R. 127, C.A.
s. 194, regs. 74/596; 76/1419.
s. 194, amended: 1973, c.26, ss.75,82; 1975, c.77, sch.10; 1980, c.65, sch.15; 1985, c.51, sch.1; repealed in pt.: 1973, c.26, ss.75,86, sch.3; 1975, c.77, schs.10,11.
s. 195, see *Binns v. Secretary of State for Transport* (1985) 50 P. & C.R. 468. Lands Tribunal.
ss. 195–199, amended: 1973, c.26, s.82.
s. 197, amended: 1981, c.67, sch.4; 1985, c.71, sch.2.
s. 200, amended: 1973, c.26, ss.81,82.
s. 201, regs. 74/596.
s. 201, amended: 1973, c.26, ss.77,82; repealed in pt.: *ibid.*,ss.77,86, sch.3.
ss. 202–205, amended: 1973, c.26, s.82.
s. 205, see *R. v. Secretary of State for the Environment, ex p. Bournemouth Borough Council* (1987) 281 E.G. 539, Mann J.
s. 206, amended: 1973, c.26, s.82; 1980, c.66, sch.24.
s. 207, amended: 1973, c.26, s.82; repealed in pt.: *ibid.*,s.86, sch.3.
s. 209, see *Ashby v. Secretary of State for the Environment* [1980] 1 All E.R. 508, C.A.; *Grampian Regional Council v. City of Aberdeen District Council, The Times*, December 3, 1983, H.L.
s. 209, amended: 1972, c.70, sch.16; 1980, c.65, sch.32; c.66, sch.24; 1981, c.67, sch.4; 1985, c.51, sch.4; repealed in pt.: *ibid.*, sch.17.
s. 210, amended: 1972, c.70, sch.16.
s. 212, regs. 74/596.
s. 212, amended: 1972, c.70, sch.16; 1982, c.30, sch.5; 1988, c.4, sch.3; repealed in pt.: 1974, c.7, sch.8.
s. 213, repealed: 1982, c.30, schs.5,7.
s. 214, amended: 1988, c.4, sch.3.
s. 215, amended: 1981, c.38, sch.3; 1985, c.51, sch.14; 1988, c.50, sch.17; repealed in pt.: 1972, c.70, sch.30; 1985, c.51, sch.17; 1988, c.40, sch.13 (prosp.).
s. 216, amended: 1985, c.51, sch.4; 1987, c.3, sch.1; 1988, c.40, sch.12 (prosp.); repealed in pt.: 1972, c.70, sch.30; 1986, c.63, sch.12.
s. 217, regs. 83/22.
s. 218, amended: 1981, c.67, sch.4; repealed in pt.: *ibid.*,sch.6.
s. 219, regs. 74/596.

CAP.

1971—cont.

78. Town and Country Planning Act 1971—*cont.*
s. 220, substituted: 1984, c.12, sch.4.
s. 222, see *North Surrey Water Co. v. Secretary of State for the Environment* (1976) 34 P. & C.R. 140, Slynn J.
s. 223, amended: 1972, c.60, s.4; 1981, c.38, sch.3; 1984, c.32, sch.6; 1986, c.31, sch. 4; c.44, sch.7.
s. 224, amended: orders 74/692; 76/1775; 1981, c.38, sch.3; repealed in pt.: 1986, c.31, sch.6; c.44, sch.9.
s. 225, amended: 1981, c.41, sch.
s. 229, repealed: 1981, c.67, sch.6.
ss. 230, 232, amended: 1984, c.12, sch.4.
s. 238, amended: 1981, c.36, sch.1; c.67, sch.4.
s. 235, see *Richmond-upon-Thames London Borough Council v. Secretary of State for the Environment, The Times*, May 16, 1983, Glidewell J.
s. 237, repealed in pt.: 1986, c.63, sch.12.
s. 242, see *Co-operative Retail Services v. Secretary of State for the Environment* [1980] 1 W.L.R. 271; [1980] 1 All E.R. 449, C.A.; *Griffiths v. Secretary of State for the Environment* [1983] 2 W.L.R. 172, H.L.; *Westminster City Council v. Secretary of State for the Environment and City Commercial Real Estate Investments* [1984] J.P.L. 27, David Widdicombe Q.C.; *G.L.C. v. Secretary of State for the Environment, The Times*, July 18, 1985, Woolf J.
s. 242, amended: 1981, c.36, sch.1.; 1982, c.30, sch.6; 1985, c.51, sch.1; 1986, c.63, schs.6,7.
ss. 242, 243, see *Chalgray v. Secretary of State for the Environment* (1976) 33 P. & C.R. 10; [1977] J.P.L. 176, Slynn J.
s. 243, see *Square Meals Frozen Foods v. Dunstable Corporation* [1974] 1 W.L.R. 59; [1974] 1 All E.R. 441, C.A.; *Rochdale Metropolitan Borough Council v. Simmonds* (1982) 256 E.G. 607; 40 P. & C.R. 432, D.C.; *Scarborough Borough Council v. Adams, The Times*, July 4, 1983, D.C.; *Davy v. Spelthorne Borough Council* [1983] 3 All E.R. 278, H.L.; *Scarborough Council v. Adams* (1984) 47 P. & C.R. 133; *R. v. Smith (Thomas George)* [1984] Crim.L.R. 630; (1984) 48 P. & C.R. 392, C.A.; *Prosser v. Sharp* (1985) 274 E.G. 1249, D.C.; *R. v. Greenwich London Borough Council, ex p. Patel* (1986) 84 L.G.R. 241, C.A.; *Vaughan v. Secretary of State for The Environment and Mid-Sussex District Council* [1986] J.P.L. 840, McNeill J.; *R. v. Keeys* [1987] Crim.L.R. 829, C.A.
s. 243, amended: 1981, c.41, sch.
s. 244, see *Edwin H. Bradley & Sons v. Secretary of State for the Environment* (1982) 264 E.G. 926, Glidewell J.; *Fourth Investments v. Bury Metropolitan Borough Council, The Times*, July 27, 1984, McCullough J.; *Barham v. Secretary of State for the Environment; Pye v. Secretary of State for the Environment, The Times*, May 25, 1985, Farquharson J.
s. 244, amended: 1980, c.65, sch.15; 1985, c.51, sch.1; 1986, c.63, sch.6.

1971—cont.

78. Town and Country Planning Act 1971—cont.
s. 245, see *Miller* v. *Weymouth and Melcombe Regis Corporation* (1974) 27 P. & C.R. 468; *Turner* v. *Secretary of State for the Environment* (1973) 72 L.G.R. 380; *Ellinas* v. *Department of the Environment and Torbay B.C.* [1977] J.P.L. 249; *Chalgray* v. *Secretary of State for the Environment* [1977] J.P.L. 176; *Davies* v. *Secretary of State for Wales* (1977) 33 P. & C.R. 330, Sir Douglas Frank, Q.C.; *Performance Cars* v. *Secretary of State for the Environment* (1977) 34 P. & C.R. 92, C.A.; *North Surrey Water Co.* v. *Secretary of State for the Environment* (1976) 34 P. & C.R. 140, Slynn J.; *Preston Borough Council* v. *Secretary of State for the Environment and E.L.S. Wholesale (Wolverhampton)* [1978] J.P.L. 548, Slynn J.; *Winchester City Council* v. *Secretary of State for the Environment* (1978) 36 P. & C.R. 455, Forbes J.; *Sheffield City Council* v. *Secretary of State for the Environment* (1979) 251 E.G. 165, Drake J.; *Charles Church* v. *Secretary of State for the Environment* (1979) 251 E.G. 674, Sir Douglas Frank, Q.C.; *Elmbridge Borough Council* v. *Secretary of State for the Environment, The Times,* January 19, 1980, Bristow J.; *Price Brothers (Rode Heath)* v. *Department of the Environment* (1979) 38 P. & C.R. 579, Forbes J.; *Bullock* v. *Secretary of State for the Environment* (1980) 254 E.G. 1097, Phillips J.; *Purbeck District Council* v. *Secretary of State for the Environment* (1982) 263 E.G. 261,Woolf J,; *Ryan* v. *Secretary of State for the Environment,* June 14, 1982, Forbes J.; *Granada Theatres* v. *Secretary of State for the Environment* (1982) 43 P. & C.R. 253, Forbes J.; *Griffiths* v. *Secretary of State for the Environment* [1983] 2 W.L.R. 172, H.L.; *Hollis* v. *Secretary of State for the Environment* (1983) 265 E.G. 476, *Robert Hitchens* v. *Secretary of State for the Environment* (1983) 265 E.G. 696, Sir Douglas Frank Q.C.; *Westminster Renslade* v. *Secretary of State for the Environment, The Times,* May 13, 1983, Forbes J.; *Hatfield Construction* v. *Secretary of State for the Environment, The Times,* June 1, 1983, David Widdicombe Q.C.; *London Borough of Richmond upon Thames* v. *Secretary of State for the Environment and Hutchinson Locke and Monk* [1984] J.P.L. 24, Glidewell J.; *Graysmark* v. *Secretary of State for the Environment and the South Hams District Council* [1984] J.P.L. 115, David Widdicombe Q.C.; *Beverley Borough Council* v. *Secretary of State for the Environment, The Times,* June 26, 1984, Judge Dobry Q.C.; *Etheridge* v. *Secretary of State for the Environment* (1984) 42 P. & C.R. 35, Woolf J.; *Property Investment Holdings* v. *Secretary of State for the Environment and Reigate and Banstead Borough Council* [1984] J.P.L. 587, McCullough J.; *Nash* v. *Secretary of State for the Environment and Epping Forest District Council* [1985] J.P.L. 474, Widdicombe Q.C.; *G.L.C.* v. *Secretary of State for the Environment and*

1971—cont.

78. Town and Country Planning Act 1971—cont.
Harrow London Borough Council [1985] J.P.L. 868, Woolf J.; *Penwith District Council* v. *Secretary of State for the Environment* (1985) 277 E.G. 194, Woolf J.; *Chelmsford Borough Council* v. *Secretary of State for the Environment and Alexander (E.R.)* [1985] J.P.L. 112, Glidewell J.; *Gransden (E.C.) & Co. and Falkbridge* v. *Secretary of State for the Environment and Gillingham Borough Council* [1986] J.P.L. 519, Woolf J.; *Surrey Heath Borough Council* v. *Secretary of State for the Environment, The Times,* November 3, 1986, Kennedy J.; *Centre 21* v. *Secretary of State for the Environment* (1986) 280 E.G. 889, C.A.; *Martin Grant Homes* v. *Secretary of State for the Environment, The Times,* April 19, 1988, Hodgson J.; *R.* v. *Secretary of State for the Environment, ex p. Kent, The Times,* May 5, 1988, Pill J.; *West Midlands Cooperative Society* v. *Secretary of State for the Environment and Dudley Metropolitan Borough Council* (1988) J.P.L. 121, Graham Eyre, Q.C.; *Kingswood District Council* v. *Secretary of State for the Environment* [1988] J.P.L. 248, Graham Eyre Q.C.
s. 245, amended: 1972, c.70, sch.16.
s. 246, see *Horsham District Council* v. *Fisher* [1977] J.P.L. 17; *Day* v. *Secretary of State for the Environment* (1979) 251 E.G. 163, D.C.; *Wain* v. *Secretary of State for the Environment* (1978) 39 P. & C.R. 82, Stocker J.; *W. F. Nicholls* v. *Secretary of State for the Environment and Bristol City Council,* April 10, 1981, McNeill J.; *Backer* v. *Secretary of State for the Environment* (1982) 246 E.G. 535, David Widdicombe Q.C.; *Welsh Aggregates* v. *Secretary of State for Wales* [1983] 265 E.G. 43, C.A.; *Weitz* v. *Secretary of State for the Environment* (1983) 43 P. & C.R. 150, Q.B.D., Woolf J.; *Kenwood (Travel, Employment, and Estates) and Z. I. Gourgey* v. *Secretary of State for the Environment and Westminster City Council* [1984] J.P.L. 36, Stephen Brown J.; *Alderson* v. *Secretary of State for the Environment* (1984) 270 E.G. 225, C.A.; *Rhymney Valley District Council* v. *Secretary of State for Wales and G. Isaac* [1985] J.P.L. 27, Nolan J.; *Lenlyn* v. *Secretary of State for the Environment; R.* v. *Secretary of State for the Environment, ex p. Lenlyn* (1985) 50 P. & C.R. 129, Hodgson J.; *Gabbitas* v. *Secretary of State for the Environment and Newham Borough Council* [1985] J.P.L. 630, Judge Dobry Q.C.; *Pearcy (John) Transport* v. *Secretary of State for the Environment, The Times,* January 31, 1986, Mr. David Widdicombe Q.C., sitting as a deputy High Court Judge; *Miah* v. *Secretary of State for the Environment and Hillingdon Borough Council* [1986] J.P.L. 756, Woolf J.; *London Parachuting and Rectory Farm (Pampisford)* v. *Secretary of State for the Environment and South Cambridgeshire District Council* (1986) 52 P. & C.R. 376, C.A.; *Newbury District Council* v.

1971—cont.
78. Town and Country Planning Act 1971—cont.
Secretary of State for the Environment (1988) 55 P. & C.R. 100, Kennedy J.; *Bush* v. *Secretary of State for the Environment and Reddich Borough Council* [1988] J.P.L. 108, Graham Eyre Q.C.; *Gwillim (Leslie)* v. *Secretary of State for the Environment and Ashford Borough Council* [1988] J.P.L. 263, Graham Eyre Q.C.; *R.* v. *Kuxhaus* [1988] 2 W.L.R. 1005, C.A.

s. 246, amended: 1981, c.36, s.1; c.41, sch.; c.54, sch.5; 1985, c.51, sch.2; 1987, c.3, sch.1; repealed in pt.: 1977, c.38, sch.5.

s. 247, see *Camden London Borough Council* v. *Secretary of State for the Environment, The Times,* June 3, 1988, Farquharson J.

s. 247, repealed in pt.: 1977, c.38, sch.5.

s. 250, regs. 85/1152.

ss. 250–252, repealed: 1986, c.63, s.48, sch.12.

s. 254A, added: 1978, c.52, sch.11.

s. 255, amended: 1980, c.66, sch.24; 1985, c.51, sch.1.

s. 256, amended: 1980, c.65, sch.15; repealed in pt.: 1972, c.70, sch.30.

s. 260, repealed in pt.: 1986, c.63, s.48, sch.12.

s. 264, regs. 82/975.

s. 264A, added: 1981, c.36, s.3.

s. 265, repealed: 1974, c.36, s.2.

s. 266, amended: 1981, c.36, sch.1; c.41, sch.; 1985, c.51, sch.1; 1986, c.63, sch.7.

s. 269, orders 73/1285; 84/986.

s. 269, amended: 1981, c.36, s.18; 1982, c.30, s.36.

s. 270, see *Steeples* v. *Derbyshire County Council* [1984] 3 All E.R. 468, Webster J.; *R.* v. *Lambeth London Borough Council, ex p. Sharp* [1987] J.P.L. 440; (1988) 55 P. & C.R. 232, C.A.

s. 270, regs. 74/596; 81/558.

s. 270, amended: 1981, c.41, sch.

s. 271, regs. 87/349.

s. 271, substituted: 1974, c.32, s.7.

s. 271A, added: 1986, c.63, sch.7.

s. 273, regs. 74/1006.; 87/1936.

s. 273, amended: 1987, c.3, sch.1.

s. 273A, added: 1988, c.4, sch.3.

s. 274, amended: 1981, c.41, sch.; c.67, sch.4.

s. 276, amended: 1972, c.70, sch.16; repealed in pt.: 1974, c.7, schs.6,8; 1981, c.36, sch.1; c.41, sch.

s. 277, amended: 1975, c.76, sch.1; 1983, c.47, sch.4; 1985, c.51, sch.2; repealed in pt.: 1980, c.65, schs.15,34.

s. 277A, see *Windsor and Maidenhead Royal Borough* v. *Brandrose Investments* [1981] 3 All E.R. 38, Fox J.

s. 277A, regs. 87/349.

s. 277A, added: 1974, c.32, s.1; 1985, c.51, sch.2; amended: 1986, c.63, sch.9; repealed in pt.: 1980, c.65, schs.15,34; 1986, c.63, sch.9.

s. 277B, added: 1974, c.32, s.1; 1980, c.65, sch.15; repealed in pt.: *ibid.,* schs.15,34.

s. 280, amended: 1981, c.41, sch.; 1982, c.30, s.36; 1985, c.51, schs.1,2; 1986, c.63, sch.7; 1988, c.4, sch.3.

1971—cont.
78. Town and Country Planning Act 1971—cont.
s. 281, see *R.* v. *Chief Constable of Devon and Cornwall, ex p. Central Electricity Generating Board* [1981] 3 W.L.R. 967, C.A.

s. 282, amended: 1986, c.63, sch.11.

ss. 282A, 282B, added: *ibid.*

s. 282B, regs. 87/701.

s. 283, see *Lenlyn* v. *Secretary of State for the Environment; R.* v. *Secretary of State for the Environment, ex p. Lenlyn* (1985) 50 P. & C.R. 129, Hodgson J.; *R.* v. *Secretary of State and Bromley London Borough Council, ex p. Jackson* [1987] J.P.L. 790, MacPherson J.

s. 283, regs. 74/596; 76/1419.

s. 284, see *R.* v. *Greenwich London Borough Council, The Times,* July 5, 1985, C.A.

s. 284, amended: 1977, c.29, s.3; 1981, c.41, sch; 1988, c.4, sch.3.

s. 287, regs. 72/1652; 74/185, 596, 1242, 1481, 1486; 75/898, 1680; 77/477; 80/443, 1403, 1404, 1451, 1452, 1547, 1548, 1560, 1599, 1634, 1635; 85/1152; orders 72/903, 996; 73/425, 1285; 74/418, 1054, 1283, 1419, 2028; 75/148, 780–783, 1276–1279; 76/104, 105, 301, 565, 652, 814, 815, 1162, 1163; 77/289, 469, 470, 665, 815, 848, 1363, 1364, 1768, 1769, 1781, 1939, 2085; 78/523, 556, 557, 602, 724–727; 79/200–203, 328, 329, 839, 890, 891, 1042, 1043, 1187, 1189, 1485, 1486, 1622–1629; 80/2, 3, 40, 41, 65, 66, 101, 102, 174, 175, 300, 301, 458–461, 492, 493, 575–578, 828, 829, 932, 933, 963, 964, 1098, 1099, 1155, 1156, 1209, 1210, 1946; 81/14, 558, 560, 804, 1082, 1569, 1742; 82/555, 796, 817, 975; 86/623; 87/2227; 88/139, 963; orders 80/1946; 81/560, 1082, 1569; 82/796, 817; 83/22, 1190, 1614; 84/6, 421, 1015, 1016; 85/1011, 1012, 1579; 86/8, 435, 632, 812, 1176; 87/349, 804, 1750, 1760; 87/702, 764; 88/1272, 1400, 1812, 1813.

s. 287, amended: 1977, c.40, s.3; 1986, c.63, schs.6,9; repealed in pt: *ibid.,* sch.12.

s. 290, see *Wilcock* v. *Secretary of State for the Environment* [1975] J.P.L. 150; *Parkes* v. *Secretary of State for the Environment* [1978] 1 W.L.R. 1308, C.A.; *Sykes* v. *Secretary of State for the Environment; South Oxfordshire District Council* v. *Secretary of State for the Environment* (1980) 257 E.G. 821; (1981) 42 P. & C.R. 19, D.C.; *Lake District Special Planning Board* v. *Secretary of State for the Environment and Impey* [1981] J.P.L. 363, D.C.; *Crowborough Parish Council* v. *Secretary of State for the Environment* (1982) 43 P. & C.R. 229; *North Warwickshire Borough Council* v. *Secretary of State for the Environment, The Times,* December 23, 1983, Woolf J.; *Impey* v. *Secretary of State for the Environment; Lake District Special Planning Board* v. *Secretary of State for the Environment* (1984) 47 P. & C.R. 157, D.C.; *Bacher* v. *Secretary of State for the Environment* (1984) 47 P. & C.R. 149, David Widdicombe Q.C.; *North Warwickshire Borough Council* v. *Secretary of*

1971—cont.

78. Town and Country Planning Act 1971—*cont.*
State for the Environment (1985) 50 P. & C.R.
47, Woolf J.; *R. v. Plymouth City Council and Cornwall County Council, ex p. Freeman* (1988)
28 R.V.R. 89, C.A.

s. 290, regs. 74/596, 1481; 77/228; 87/349, 1750, 1760; 88/139.

s. 290, amended: 1980, c.65, sch.32; c.66, sch.24; 1981, c.36, sch.1; 1985, c.51, sch.1; 1986, c.63, schs.6,7; 1988, c.4, sch.3; repealed in pt.: 1972, c.70, sch.30; 1985, c.51, sch.17; 1986, c.44, sch.9; c.63, sch.12.

s. 295, repealed in pt.: 1975, c.24, s.10, sch.3.

sch. 1, amended: 1972, c.70, sch.16.

sch. 2, repealed: *ibid.,* sch.30.

sch. 3, order 78/602; regs. 74/450; 80/443.

sch. 3, repealed: 1985, c.51, sch.17.

sch. 4, see *Greater London Council v. Secretary of State for the Environment* [1984] J.P.L. 424, Hodgson J.; *Westminster City Council v. Great Portland Estates* [1984] 3 W.L.R. 1035, H.L.

sch. 4, regs. 74/1481; 83/1190.

sch. 4, substituted: 1972, c.42, s.4, sch.1; amended: 1972, c.70, sch.16; 1980, c.65, sch.14; 1982, c.30, sch.6; repealed in pt.: *ibid.,* schs.14, 34; 1985, c.51, sch.17.

sch. 5, regs. 75/1680.

sch. 5, amended: 1972, c.70, sch.16; order 77/469; 1980, c.66, sch.24; repealed in pt.: orders 76/1162; 77/1364, 1781; 78/724; 79/1623; 80/3, 40, 102.

sch. 6, amended: order 77/469; repealed in pt.: orders 76/1162; 77/1364, 1781; 78/724; 79/1623; 81/3, 40, 102; 1985, c.51, sch.17.

sch. 7, see *R. v. Secretary of State for the Environment, ex p. Great Grimsby Borough Council* [1986] J.P.L. 910, Russell J.

sch. 7, amended: 1980, c.65, sch.14; c.66, sch.24; repealed in pt.: 1985, c.51, sch.17.

sch. 8, see *Camden London Borough Council v. Peaktop Properties (Hampstead)* (1983) 267 E.G. 841, C.A.

sch. 8A, regs. 87/1750.

sch. 8A, added. 1986, c.63, s.25, sch.6.

sch. 9, see *W. F. Nicholls v. Secretary of State for the Environment and Bristol City Council,* April 10, 1981, McNeill J.; *Ryan v. Secretary of State for the Environment,* June 14, 1982, Forbes J.; *Graysmark v. Secretary of State for the Environment and the South Hams District Council* [1984] J.P.L. 115, David Widdicombe Q.C.

sch. 9, regs. 72/1652; 77/477, 1939; 81/804; 86/623.

sch. 9, amended: 1981, c.41, sch.; 1986, c.63, sch.11.

sch. 11, regs. 77/228; 87/349; order 73/273.

sch. 11, amended: 1983, c.47, sch.5; 1985, c.51, sch.2; 1986, c.63, schs.7, 9; repealed in pt.: 1974, c.7, schs.6, 8; 1980, c.65, schs.15, 34; 1985, c.51, sch.17; 1986, c.63, sch.9.

schs. 12, 13, repealed: *ibid.,* sch.12.

sch. 14, orders 73/273; 74/418; 76/301; 86/435; 88/1813.

1971—cont.

78. Town and Country Planning Act 1971—*cont.*
sch. 16, repealed in pt.: 1980, c.65, sch.15.

sch. 19, amended: 1986, c.63, sch.11; 1988, c.4, sch.3.

sch. 20, regs. 83/22.

sch. 20, amended: 1981, c.69, sch.16; 1985, c.51, sch.14; repealed in pt.: 1981, c.69, schs.16,17; 1985, c.51, sch.17; 1988, c.40, sch.13 (prosp.).

sch. 21, regs. 81/558.

sch. 21, amended: 1977, c.40, s.4; 1982, c.36, sch.5; 1986, c.63, schs.9,11; repealed in pt.: *ibid.,* sch.12.

sch. 22, amended: 1980, c.66, sch.24; 1985, c.51, sch.4; repealed in pt.: *ibid.,* sch.17.

sch. 23, repealed in pt.: 1972, c.5, sch.4; 1975, c.78, sch.6; 1978, c.3, sch.2; 1979, c.46, sch.5; 1980, c.66, sch.25; 1981, c.64, sch.13; 1982, c.16, sch.16; c.42, sch.23; 1984, c.27, sch.14; c.29, sch.12; 1985, c.71, sch.1; 1988, c.41, sch.13 (prosp.).

sch. 24, see *R. v. Secretary of State for the Environment, ex p. Percy Bilton Industrial Properties* (1975) 31 P. & C.R. 154, D.C.; *Young v. Secretary of State for the Environment, The Times,* February 8, 1983, C.A.; *Etheridge v. Secretary of State for the Environment* (1984) 42 P. & C.R. 35, Woolf J.

sch. 24, regs. 82/975.

sch. 24, amended: 1972, c.42, s.5; 1981, c.38, sch.3; c.67, sch.4; 1984, c.12, sch.4; repealed in pt.: 1972, c.70, sch.30; S.L.R. 1975; 1986, c.63, sch.12.

79. Consolidated Fund (No. 3) Act 1971.
repealed: 1974, c.31, s.4, sch.

80. Banking and Financial Dealings Act 1971.
s. 1, amended: 1978, c.51, sch.16; c.52, sch.11; 1987, c.16, s.69.

s. 2, amended: 1981, c.35, s.136; 1986, c.53, sch.11; repealed in pt.: 1981, c.35, sch.19.

s. 5, amended: 1973, c.36, sch.6.

81. New Towns Act 1971.
repealed: 1975, c.42, s.3.

1972

1. Sierra Leone Republic Act 1972.
Royal Assent, February 10, 1972.
s. 1, repealed in pt.: S.L.R. 1977.

2. Island of Rockall Act 1972.
Royal Assent, February 10, 1972.
s. 1, amended: 1973, c.65, sch.27.

3. Ministerial and other Salaries Act 1972.
Royal Assent, February 10, 1972.
repealed: 1975, c.24, sch.3; c.25, sch.3.

4. National Insurance Regulations (Validation) Act 1972.
Royal Assent, February 10, 1972.
repealed: 1973, c.38, sch.28.

5. Local Employment Act 1972.
Royal Assent, February 10, 1972.
s. 1, orders 72/421, 585; 74/1372; 77/683, 706; 79/837, 1642; 80/1013; 82/934.

s. 1, repealed: 1982, c.52, sch.3.

s. 2, amended: 1972, c.63, s.13, sch.4.

1972—cont.

5. Local Employment Act 1972—*cont.*
ss. 3, 4, repealed: *ibid.*
s. 5, repealed: 1975, c.69, sch.5 (S.); 1982, c.52, sch.3.
s. 6, repealed: 1973, c.50, sch.4.
s. 7, repealed: 1982, c.52, sch.3.
s. 8, orders 72/421, 585; 74/692, 1372; 78/691; 79/334; 80/1890; 82/935.
s. 8, repealed: 1975, c.69, sch.5 (S); 1982, c.42, ss.1,2, sch.
s. 9, order 74/692.
s. 9, repealed: 1982, c.52, sch.3.
s. 10, repealed: 1981, c.13, sch.2.
ss. 10–12, repealed (S.): 1975, s.69, sch.5.
s. 11, amended: 1972, c.63, s.13, sch.4; repealed in pt.: 1980, c.33, ss.10,13,15, sch.2; 1981, c.13, sch.2.
s. 12, repealed: *ibid.*
ss. 13, 14, repealed: 1982, c.52, sch.3
s. 15, repealed: 1972, c.63, s.13, sch.4.
ss. 16–18, repealed: 1982, c.52, sch.3.
s. 18, orders 72/585; 77/683, 706; 78/691; 79/334, 837, 1642; 80/1890; 82/934.
s. 19, amended: 1972, c.63, s.13, sch.4.
s. 20, repealed: 1982, c.52, sch.3.
s. 21, amended: 1972, c.52, schs.21,23; c.63, sch.4; repealed in pt.: 1981, c.13, sch.2; 1982, c.52, sch.3.
s. 22, repealed in pt.: S.L.R. 1978; 1982, c.52, sch.3.
sch. 1, repealed: 1981, c.13, sch.2.
sch. 2, amended: 1972, c.63, s.13, sch.4; 1980, c.33, sch.2; repealed in pt.: 1982, c.52, sch.3.
sch. 3, amended: 1972, c.52, schs.21,23; repealed in pt.: S.L.R. 1978; 1980, c.51, sch.26; 1982, c.52, sch.3; 1984, c.29, sch.12.
sch. 4, repealed: S.L.R. 1978.

6. Summer Time Act 1972.
Royal Assent, February 10, 1972.
s. 2, orders 80/1089; 82/1673; 86/223; 88/931.
s. 2, amended: 1978, c.51, sch.16.
s. 2A, added: *ibid.*
s. 4, amended: 1973, c.36, sch.6; 1978, c.51, sch.16.
s. 5, amended: 1978, c.51, sch.16.

7. Civil List Act 1972.
Royal Assent, February 24, 1972.
ss. 1, 3, amended: order 75/133.
ss. 1–3, amended: order 84/39.
ss. 2, 6, repealed: S.L.R. 1977.
s. 5, repealed in pt.: 1975, c.82, s.1.
s. 6, orders 75/133; 84/39.

8. Airports Authority Act 1972.
Royal Assent, February 24, 1972.
repealed: 1975, c.78, sch.6.

9. Mineral Exploration and Investment Grants Act 1972.
Royal Assent, February 24, 1972.

10. Northern Ireland Act 1972.
Royal Assent, February 24, 1972.
repealed: 1973, c.36, sch.6.

11. Superannuation Act 1972.
Royal Assent, March 1, 1972.
s. 1, orders 75/338, 599; 79/1540; 83/1942; 85/1855; 86/223.

1972—cont.

11. Superannuation Act 1972—*cont.*
s. 1, amended: 1984, c.60, sch.4.
s. 4, amended: order 75/1137.
s. 5, amended: 1985, c.65, sch.8; c.66, sch.7 (S.); repealed in pt.: 1986, c.45, sch.14.
s. 7, see *Secretary of State for the Environment v. Cumbria County Council* [1983] I.C.R. 52, H.L.
s. 7, regs. 73/313, 503, 1996; 74/520, 812; 75/638; 77/1121, 1341, 1845, 1956; 78/266, 822, 1378, 1738, 1739, 1794 (S.), 1926 (S.); 79/2, 592, 1534; 80/198 (S.), 216, 233, 234, 342 (S.), 1885; 81/1250, 1509, 1892 (S.); 82/385 (S.), 908, 1303, 1514; 83/178, 1268–1271, 1421 (S.); 84/201, 254, 1232 (S.); 85/489, 1515, 1920, 1922; 86/24, 214 (S.), 380, 1449; 87/1850 (S.); 88/466, 625(S.).
s. 8, regs. 73/503; 74/520, 812; 77/1341; 85/1922; 87/1850 (S.).
s. 9, regs. 72/551, 568, 1092, 1239; 73/215, 399, 547, 936, 1383; 74/260, 376, 390, 769, 1135, 1388, 1993, 1994; 75/98, 276, 872, 931; 76/84, 910; 77/1360, 1808; 78/422, 1422, 1507, 1512; 79/47, 1206; 80/344 (S.), 919, 1043; 81/934; 82/46, 496, 967, 1302; 83/639 (S.), 1431 (S.); 84/2028 (S.); 85/1844; 88/387, 816, 1374, 1618, 1652.
s. 10, regs. 72/1339, 1537, 1604; 73/242, 304, 731, 746, 1649; 74/223, 441, 1047, 1357, 1547, 1838; 77/1922, 2138; 78/1353, 1508; 80/343 (S.), 362, 1177 (S.), 1949; 81/1018 (S.), 1205, 1680 (S.).; 82/1765; 83/272; 84/1970 (S.); 85/1492, 1626; 86/199, 587 (S.), 701 (S.); 87/2218; 88/1956 (S).
s. 10, amended: 1972, c.58, sch.7; 1973, c.32, sch.5.
s. 11, regs. 78/1353; 80/919.
s. 12, regs. 73/213, 242, 304, 503, 731, 746, 1649; 74/223, 441, 520, 812, 1047, 1357, 1547, 1838; 75/638, 931; 76/910; 77/1341, 1360, 1808, 1922, 2138; 78/266, 422, 822, 1378, 1422, 1507, 1508, 1512, 1738, 1739, 1794 (S.), 1926 (S.); 79/47, 592, 1206, 1534; 80/198 (S.), 233, 234, 344 (S.), 362, 1043, 1177 (S.), 1885, 1949; 81/934, 1018 (S.), 1205, 1250, 1509, 1680 (S.), 1892 (S.); 82/46, 385 (S.), 496, 908, 967, 1302, 1303, 1514, 1765; 83/178, 272, 639 (S.), 990, 1268, 1269, 1421 (S.), 1431 (S.); 84/1232 (S.); 1970 (S.), 2028 (S.); 85/489, 1492, 1515, 1626, 1844, 1920, 1922; 86/24, 199, 214 (S.), 380, 587 (S.), 701 (S.), 1449; 87/157, 158, 1698 (S.)–1700 (S.), 1850 (S.), 2218; 88/625 (S.), 816, 1374, 1618, 1652, 1956 (S.).
s. 13, regs. 72/493; amended: 1981, c.20, sch.3; repealed in pt.: 1976, c.48, sch.
s. 15, regs. 83/990; 87/157, 158, 1689 (S.)–1700 (S.).
s. 15, repealed in pt.: 1976, c.35, sch.3.
s. 17, amended: 1972, c.41, sch.28.
s. 18, repealed in pt.: 1974, c.4, sch.5; 1986, c.47, sch.5 (S.).
s. 21, repealed: 1977, c.13, sch.2.
s. 22, repealed in pt.: 1981, c.15, sch.3.
s. 23, amended: 1973, c.21, sch.2; repealed in pt.: 1981, c.20, sch.4.

1972—cont.

11. Superannuation Act 1972—*cont.*
s. 24, regs. 74/463, 540, 1748, 1869; 75/734, 1092, 1864; 77/1410, 1777; 79/785 (S.); 80/646, 1254 (S.); 81/1054 (S.), 1088, 1263, 1785; 82/917, 918, 1009; 83/264 (S.), 856; 84/740, 845 (S.), 846 (S.); 85/1181, 1659, 2036 (S.); 86/151, 409 (S.), 412 (S.).
s. 24, amended: 1976, c.35, sch.2.
s. 25, repealed: 1975, c.60, sch.5.
s. 30, orders 72/325, 384.
s. 30, amended: 1972, c.48, s.34; repealed in pt.: 1977, c.13, sch.2.
sch. 1, amended: 1973, c.50, sch.3; 1976, c.46, sch.; 1983, c.47, sch.1; (S.): 1985, c.16, sch.1 (S.); order 85/1855; 1986, c.51, s.1; 1988, c.33, sch.6; c.40, s.224, sch.2; repealed in pt.: 1975, c.71, sch.18; 1976, c.74, sch.5; 1980, c.53, sch.7; 1984, c.27, sch.14.
sch. 3, regs. 78/422, 1422, 1512; 79/1206; 80/362, 919, 1949; 81/934, 1205, 1263; 82/46, 496, 967, 1765; 85/1492, 1626, 1659, 1844; 86/199; 87/2218; 88/387, 816, 1374, 1618, 1652.
sch. 4, amended: 1973, c.19, sch.3; repealed in pt.: 1975, c.78, sch.6; 1976, c.55, sch.4; 1981, c.15, sch.3; c.16, sch.2; c.29, sch.5.
sch. 5, repealed in pt.: 1981, c.20, sch.4.
sch. 6, amended: 1972, c.41, sch.28; 1973, c.19, sch.3; c.21, sch.2; c.38, sch.28; repealed in pt.: 1976, c.4, sch.6; c.33, sch.; c.35, sch.3; 1977, c.13, sch.2; c.42, sch.25; regs. 77/1341; 1978, c.44, sch.17; 1981, c.14, sch.8; c.20, sch.4; c.54, sch.7; c.56, sch.12, c.64, sch.13; 1982, c.16, sch.16; 1983, c.29, sch.3; 1984, c.27, sch.14; 1985, c.71, sch.1; S.L.R. 1986; 1988, c.49, sch.3.
sch. 6; repealed in pt. (S.): 1980, c.44, sch.5; 1985, c.71, sch.1.
sch. 7, regs. 73/313; 77/1341; 81/1250; 82/1514; 83/178, 1421 (S.); 86/24.

12. Iron and Steel Act 1972.
Royal Assent, March 1, 1972.
repealed: 1975, c.64, sch.7.

13. Consolidated Fund Act 1972.
Royal Assent, March 23, 1972.
repealed: 1974, c.31, s.4, sch.

14. Transport Holding Company Act 1972.
Royal Assent, March 23, 1972.
s. 2, amended: 1978, c.44, sch.16.
s. 2, regs. 72/632.
s. 3, amended: 1973, c.36, sch.6.

15. Transport (Grants) Act 1972.
Royal Assent, March 23, 1972.

16. Harbours (Loans) Act 1972.
Royal Assent, March 23, 1972.
s. 1, repealed in pt.: 1981, c.56, sch.12.
s. 2, amended: *ibid.,* sch. 5.

17. Electricity Act 1972.
Royal Assent, March 23, 1972.
repealed, except ss. 2, 4.
s. 2, amended: 1976, c.76, s.16.
s. 4, repealed in pt.: S.L.R. 1978.

18. Maintenance Orders (Reciprocal Enforcement) Act 1972.
Royal Assent, March 23, 1972.
see *Armitage* v. *Nanchen* (1982) 13 Fam.Law 14, D.C.

1972—cont.

18. Maintenance Orders (Reciprocal Enforcement) Act 1972—*cont.*
Pt. 1, order 75/2187.
s. 1, orders 75/2187; 79/115; 83/1125.
s. 2, S.R. 1986 No. 359.
s. 2, amended: 1982, c.27, sch.11.
s. 3, repealed in pt.: 1987, c.42, sch.4.
s. 4, amended: 1982, c.27, sch.12; repealed in pt.: 1984, c.15, sch.1.
s. 5, see *Horn* v. *Horn* (1985) Fam.Law 260, Wood J.
s. 5, amended: 1978, c.22, s.54.
s. 6, amended: 1982, c.27, sch.11.
ss. 7, 14, see *Killen* v. *Killen,* 1981 S.L.T.(Sh.Ct.) 77.
s. 8, S.R. 1986 No. 359.
s. 8, amended: 1982, c.27, sch.11; 1987, c.42, sch.2.
s. 9, amended: 1978, c.22, s.54; 1982, c.27, sch.11.
ss. 10, 11, amended: *ibid.*
s. 14, amended: 1980, c.43, sch.7.
s. 17, amended: 1972, c.49, ss.1–3; repealed in pt.: 1978, c.22, sch.3.
s. 18, amended: 1980, c.43, sch.7.
s. 21, amended: 1978, c.22, s.55; 1980, c.43, sch.7; 1982, c.27, sch.11; repealed in pt.: 1978, c.22, s.55.
s. 22, repealed in pt.: 1980, c.43, sch.9.
s. 24, orders 74/556; 79/115; 83/1125.
s. 24, amended: 1982, c.27, sch.11.
s. 25, orders 75/423; 78/279; 82/1530.
s. 26, amended: order 79/1314.
s. 27, amended: 1978, c.22, s.56, sch.2; 1979, c.55, sch.2; 1980, c.43, sch.7; 1982, c.27, s.37; order 80/564; 1987, c.42, sch.2; repealed in pt.: 1978, c.22, s.56, sch.3; order 80/564; 1987, c.42, schs.2,4.
s. 28, substituted: 1978, c.22, s.57; 1987, c.42, sch.2.
s. 28A, added: 1978, c.22, s.58; amended: 1984, c.42, s.26, sch.1; 1987, c.47, sch.2; repealed in pt.: 1984, c.42, s.26, sch.1.
ss. 29, 29A, substituted: order 80/564.
s. 29A, added: 1978, c.22, s.59; amended and repealed in pt.: 1984, c.42, s.45.
s. 30, amended: 1972, c.49, ss.1–3; 1987, c.42, sch.2; repealed in pt.: *ibid.,* schs.2, 4.
s. 31, amended: 1978, c.22, s.60; 1984, c.42, s.31; 1985, c.37, sch.1; 1986, c.47, sch.3 (S.); repealed in pt.: 1985, c.37, schs.1,2.
s. 32, amended (S.): 1986, c.47, sch.3; repealed in pt. (S.): *ibid.,* schs.3,5.
s. 33, S.R. 1986 No. 359.
s. 33, amended: 1987, c.42, sch.2.
s. 34, amended: 1978, c.22, s.60; 1986, c.47, sch.3 (S.).
s. 35, amended: *ibid.,*sch.2; order 80/564.
s. 36, amended: 1978, c.22, s.60.
s. 38, amended: 1980, c.43, sch.7.
s. 39, amended: 1978, c.22, c.60; 1985, c.37, sch.1.
s. 40, orders 74/2140; 79/1314, 1317; 81/606, 837, 1545, 1674; 83/885, 1523; 84/1824; 87/1282.

1972—cont.

18. Maintenance Orders (Reciprocal Enforcement) Act 1972—*cont.*
s. 40, repealed in pt.: 1982, c.27, sch.14.
s. 41, amended: 1978, c.22, sch.2; 1980, c.43, sch.7; 1987, c.42, sch.2; repealed in pt.: *ibid.*, schs,2,4.
s. 42, amended: 1978, c.33, sch.2; order 80/564.
s. 43, repealed in pt.: 1974, c.4, sch.5; order 81/228.
s. 43A, added: 1978, c.22, s.61; amended: 1986, c.47, sch.3 (S.).
s. 44, amended: 1975, c.34, sch.1.
s. 45, orders 78/279; 79/115; 81/837, 1545, 1674; 82/1530; 83/885, 1125, 1523; 84/1824; 87/1282.
s. 47, amended: 1982, c.27, sch.11; repealed in pt.: *ibid.*, schs.11,14.
s. 48, amended: 1973, c.36, sch.6.
s. 49, orders 74/517; 75/377.

19. Sunday Cinema Act 1972.
Royal Assent, March 30, 1972.
repealed: 1985, c.13, sch.3.

20. Road Traffic Act 1972.
Royal Assent, March 30, 1972.
repealed: 1988, c.54, sch.1.
see *Penman* v. *Parker, The Times,* April 14, 1986, D.C.
regs. 72/1217; 73/24, 1006, 2015.
s. 1, see *R.* v. *Milburn* [1974] R.T.R. 431, C.A.; *R.* v. *Robinson* [1975] R.T.R. 99, C.A.; *R.* v. *Rowe (Frederick)* [1975] R.T.R. 309, C.A.; *R.* v. *Burt* [1977] R.T.R. 340, C.A.; *R.* v. *Yarnold* [1978] R.T.R. 526, C.A.; *R.* v. *Wheeler,* January 25, 1979, Judge ap Robert, Newport Crown Ct.; *R.* v. *Midgley* [1979] R.T.R. 1, C.A.; *R.* v. *Wright (Ernest)* [1979] R.T.R. 15, C.A.; *R.* v. *Clancy* [1979] R.T.R. 312, C.A.; *R.* v. *Davis* [1979] R.T.R. 316, C.A.; *R.* v. *O'Connor* [1979] R.T.R. 467, C.A.; *R.* v. *Murphy* [1980] 2 W.L.R. 743, C.A.; *R.* v. *Lawrence* (1981) 73 Cr.App.R. 1, H.L.; *R.* v. *Ford* [1982] R.T.R. 5, C.A.; *Cooper* v. *H.M. Advocate,* 1982 S.C.C.R. 87; *R.* v. *Governor of Holloway Prison, ex p. Jennings* [1982] 3 W.L.R. 450, H.L.; *R.* v. *Coventry Magistrates' Court, ex p. Wilson* [1982] R.T.R. 177, D.C.; *R.* v. *Seymour (Edward)* [1983] 3 W.L.R. 349; [1983] R.T.R. 455, H.L.; *R.* v. *McLaren* [1984] R.T.R. 126, C.A.; *R.* v. *Boswell* [1984] 1 W.L.R. 1047; (1984) 6 Cr.App.R.(S.) 257; *R.* v. *Krawec* [1985] R.T.R. 1, C.A; *R.* v. *Khan* [1985] R.T.R 365, C.A.: *R.* v. *Crossman* [1986] R.T.R. 49, C.A.; *Anderson* v. *H.M. Advocate,* 1987 S.C.C.R. 529.
s. 2, see *R.* v. *Pashley* [1974] R.T.R. 149, C.A.; *R.* v. *Ball* [1974] R.T.R. 296, C.A.; *R.* v. *Segal* [1976] R.T.R. 319, C.A.; *Richards* v. *Gardner* [1976] R.T.R. 476, D.C.; *Walker* v. *Dowsell* [1977] R.T.R. 215, D.C.; *R.* v. *Banks* [1978] R.T.R. 535, C.A.; *Killington* v. *Butcher* [1979] Crim.L.R. 458, D.C.; *Allan* v. *Patterson* [1980] R.T.R. 97, High Ct. of Justiciary, December 4, 1979; *R.* v. *Murphy* [1980] 2 W.L.R. 743, C.A.; *Jarvis* v. *Norris* [1980] R.T.R. 424, D.C.;

1972—cont.

20. Road Traffic Act 1972—*cont.*
R. v. *Austin* [1981] R.T.R. 10, C.A.; *R.* v. *Lawrence* (1981) 73 Cr.App.R. 1, H.L.; *Deans* v. *Skinner,* 1981 S.C.C.R. 49; *R.* v. *Ford* [1982] R.T.R. 5, C.A.; *Campbell* v. *Johnston,* 1981 S.C.C.R. 179; *Connorton* v. *Annan,* 1981 S.C.C.R. 307; *R.* v. *Madigan* (1982) 75 Cr.App.R. 145, C.A.; *R.* v. *Boswell* [1984] 1 W.L.R. 1047; (1984) 6 Cr.App.R.(S.) 257, C.A.; *Hughes* v. *Challes* [1984] R.T.R. 283, D.C.; *R.* v. *Bell (David)* [1984] 3 All E.R. 842, C.A.; *Frame* v. *Lockhart,* 1985 S.L.T. 193; *R.* v. *Hazell* [1985] R.T.R. 369, C.A.; *O'Toole* v. *MacDougall,* 1986, S.C.C.R. 56; *R.* v. *Denton* [1987] R.T.R. 129; (1987) 85 Cr.App.R. 246, C.A.; *R.* v. *Conway, The Times,* July 19, 1988, C.A.
s. 3, see *Scott* v. *Warren* [1974] R.T.R. 104, D.C.; *Jarvis* v. *Fuller* [1974] R.T.R. 160, D.C.; *Griffiths* v. *Skeen,* 1975 S.L.T. (Notes) 26; *Hume* v. *Ingleby* [1975] R.T.R. 502; *Pagan* v. *Fergusson,* 1976 S.L.T. (Notes) 44; *Hawkins* v. *Roots; Hawkins* v. *Smith* [1976] R.T.R. 49, D.C.; *Botwood* v. *Phillips* [1976] R.T.R. 260, D.C.; *Gubby* v. *Littman* [1976] R.T.R. 470, D.C.; *Walker* v. *Tolhurst* [1976] R.T.R. 513, D.C.; *Wood* v. *Richards* [1977] R.T.R. 201, D.C.; *Kellett* v. *Daisy* [1977] R.T.R. 396, D.C.; *Farrell* v. *Stirling* [1978] Crim.L.R. 696, Sheriff Ct.; *Killington* v. *Butcher* [1979] Crim.L.R. 458, D.C.; *Lockhart* v. *Smith,* 1979 S.L.T.(Sh.Ct.) 52; *Jarvis* v. *Williams* [1979] R.T.R. 497, D.C.; *MacNab* v. *Feeney,* 1980 S.L.T. (Notes) 52; *Webster* v. *Wall* [1980] R.T.R. 284, D.C.; *Stickings* v. *George* [1980] R.T.R. 237, D.C.; *Scruby* v. *Beskeen* [1980] R.T.R. 420, D.C.; *Dicks* v. *Bowman-Shaw* [1981] R.T.R. 4, D.C.; *Moses* v. *Winder* [1980] Crim.L.R. 232; [1981] R.T.R. 37, D.C.; *Barnes* v. *Gevaux* [1981] R.T.R. 236, D.C.; *Lord St. Oswald* v. *Ball* [1981] R.T.R. 211, D.C.; *King* v. *Cardle,* 1981 S.C.C.R. 22; *Sigournay* v. *Douglas,* 1981 S.C.C.R. 302; *R.* v. *Preston JJ., ex p. Lyons* [1982] R.T.R. 173, D.C.; *Keane* v. *Perrie,* 1983 S.L.T. 63; *Jones* v. *Pratt* [1983] R.T.R. 54, D.C.; *Horrix* v. *Malam, The Times,* March 28, 1983, D.C.; *Tariq* v. *Carmichael,* 1982 S.C.C.R. 488; *Lodwick* v. *Jones* [1983] R.T.R. 273, D.C.; *Coles* v. *Underwood, The Times,* November 2, 1983, D.C.; *Horrix* v. *Mallam* [1984] R.T.R. 112, D.C.; *Dunlop* v. *Allen,* 1984 S.C.C.R. 329; *R.* v. *Krawec* [1985] R.T.R. 1, C.A.; *Donaldson* v. *Aitchison,* 1985 S.C.C.R. 43; *Melville* v. *Lockhart,* 1985 S.C.C.R. 242; *R.* v. *Hazell* [1985] R.T.R. 369, C.A.; *McCallum* v. *Hamilton,* 1986 S.L.T. 156; *McLean* v. *Annan,* 1986 S.C.C.R. 52; *R.* v. *Bristol Crown Court, ex p. Jones; Jones* v. *Chief Constable of Avon and Somerset Constabulary* [1986] R.T.R. 259, D.C.; *Farquhar* v. *MacKinnon,* 1986 S.C.C.R. 524; *Broome* v. *Perkins* [1987] R.T.R. 321, D.C.
s. 4, see *Deacon* v. *A.T. (A Juvenile)* [1976] Crim.L.R. 135, D.C.
s. 4, regs. 75/1730.
s. 5, see *R.* v. *Richards (Stanley)* [1974] 3 All E.R. 696, C.A.; *Campbell* v. *McLeod,* 1975 S.L.T.(Notes) 6; *MacPhail* v. *Forbes,* 1975

1972—cont.

20. Road Traffic Act 1972—*cont.*

S.L.T.(Sh.Ct.) 48; *Woodage* v. *Jones (No.* 2) [1975] R.T.R. 119, D.C.; *Williams* v. *Osborne* [1975] R.T.R. 181, D.C.; *R.* v. *Moore (Richard)* [1975] R.T.R. 285, C.A.; *R.* v. *Mayer* [1975] R.T.R. 411, C.A.; *R.* v. *Callum* [1975] R.T.R. 415, C.A.; *R.* v. *Roff; R.* v. *Dowie* [1976] R.T.R. 7, C.A.; *MacNeill* v. *Fitzgerald,* 1976 S.L.T.(Notes) 46; *Breen* v. *Pirie,* 1976 S.L.T. 136; *Comr. of Police of the Metropolis* v. *Curran* [1976] 1 W.L.R. 87; [1976] 1 All E.R. 162, H.L.; *R.* v. *Vaughan* [1976] R.T.R. 184, C.A.; *R.* v. *Estop* [1976] R.T.R. 493, C.A.; *Dunne* v. *Keane,* 1976 J.C. 39; *R.* v. *Hillman* [1977] R.T.R. 124, C.A.; *R.* v. *Hegarty* [1977] R.T.R. 337, C.A.; *R.* v. *Moore* [1978] R.T.R. 384, C.A.; *R.* v. *Wright (Ernest)* [1979] R.T.R. 15, C.A.; *Sharpe* v. *Perry* [1979] R.T.R. 235, D.C.; *R.* v. *Hunt* [1980] R.T.R. 29, C.A.; *R.* v. *Dixon* [1980] R.T.R. 17, C.A.; *R.* v. *Trump* (1979) 70 Cr.App.R. 300, C.A.; *R.* v. *Littell* [1981] 1 W.L.R. 1146, C.A.; *Tee* v. *Gough* [1981] R.T.R. 73, D.C.; *Waters* v. *Bigmore* [1981] R.T.R. 356, D.C.; *R.* v. *Coventry Magistrates' Court, ex p. Wilson* [1982] R.T.R. 177, D.C.; *Kelly* v. *Hogan* [1982] R.T.R. 352, D.C.; *R.* v. *Page* [1981] R.T.R. 132, C.A.; *Bradford* v. *Wilson* [1983] Crim.L.R. 482, D.C.; *Smith* v. *Ross,* 1983 S.L.T. 491; *Awadia* v. *Keane,* 1983 S.C.C.R. 20; *Haime* v. *Walklett* [1983] Crim.L.R. 556, D.C.; *Duffy* v. *Tudhope,* 1984 S.L.T. 107; *Bradford* v. *Wilson* [1984] R.T.R. 116, D.C.; *Muat* v. *Thynne, The Times,* May 28, 1984, D.C.; *Kenny* v. *Tudhope,* 1984 S.C.C.R. 290; *Oxford* v. *Baxendale, The Times,* April 28, 1986, D.C.; *Archbold* v. *Jones* [1986] R.T.R. 178, D.C.; *Redmond* v. *Parry* [1986] R.T.R. 146, D.C.; *Thompson* v. *Thynne* [1986] R.T.R. 293, D.C.; *Pearson* v. *Comr. of Police of the Metropolis, The Times,* June 29, 1987, D.C.; *D.P.P.* v. *Webb, The Times,* October 19, 1987, D.C.; *Chief Constable of Avon and Somerset* v. *Kelliher* [1987] R.T.R. 305, D.C.; *D.P.P.* v. *Frost, The Times,* June 27, 1988, D.C.; *D.P.P.* v. *Singh* [1988] R.T.R. 209, D.C.; *Pearson* v. *Comr. of Police of the Metropolis* [1988] R.T.R. 276, D.C.

s. 6, see *Harding* v. *Oliver* [1973] R.T.R. 497, D.C.; *R.* v. *England,* March 12, 1974, Bristol Crown Ct.; *Hay* v. *Shepherd* [1974] R.T.R. 64, D.C.; *Witts* v. *Williams* [1974] Crim.L.R. 259, D.C.; *R.* v. *Pashley* [1974] R.T.R. 149, C.A.; *R.* v. *Mitcham* [1974] R.T.R. 205, C.A.; *R.* v. *Sharman* [1974] R.T.R. 213, C.A.; *R.* v. *Mills* [1974] R.T.R. 215, C.A.; *Sandy* v. *Martin* [1974] R.T.R. 263, D.C.; *R.* v. *Bowell* [1974] R.T.R. 273, C.A.; *Carter* v. *Richardson* [1974] R.T.R. 314, D.C.; *Wheater* v. *Campbell,* 1974 S.L.T.(Notes) 63; *McGuiness* v. *Thaw,* 1974 S.L.T. 237; *Taylor* v. *Rajan; Frazer* v. *Barton* [1974] 2 W.L.R. 385; [1974] 1 All E.R. 1007, D.C.; *Ratledge* v. *Oliver* [1974] R.T.R. 396, D.C.; *R.* v. *Richards (Stanley)* [1974] 3 All E.R. 696; *Gibson* v. *Skeen,* 1975 S.L.T.(Notes) 52; *McCallum* v. *Herron,* 1975 S.L.T. 75; *Walker* v. *Lovell* [1975] R.T.R. 61,

1972—cont.

20. Road Traffic Act 1972—*cont.*

D.C.; *Woodgate* v. *James (No.* 2) [1975] R.T.R. 119, D.C.; *R.* v. *Shaw (Kenneth)* [1975] R.T.R. 160, C.A.; *R.* v. *Wright (John)* [1975] R.T.R. 193, C.A.; *Roney* v. *Matthews* [1975] R.T.R. 273, D.C.; *Blayney* v. *Knight* [1975] Crim.L.R. 237, D.C.; *Adams* v. *Valentine* [1975] Crim.L.R. 238, D.C.; *Redman* v. *Taylor* [1975] Crim.L.R. 348, D.C.; *R.* v. *Moore (Richard)* [1975] R.T.R. 285, C.A.; *Standen* v. *Robertson* [1975] R.T.R. 329, D.C.; *R.* v. *Sodo* [1975] R.T.R. 357, C.A.; *Hawkins* v. *Ebbutt* [1975] R.T.R. 363, D.C.; *Frogatt* v. *Allcock* [1975] R.T.R. 372, D.C.; *R.* v. *Aspden* [1975] R.T.R. 456, C.A.; *R.* v. *Foster* [1975] R.T.R. 553, C.A.; *R.* v. *Alyson* [1976] R.T.R. 15, C.A.; *MacNeill* v. *Fitzgerald,* 1976 S.L.T.(Notes) 46; *R.* v. *Burdekin* [1976] R.T.R. 27, C.A.; *R.* v. *Beckett* [1976] Crim.L.R. 140; *Williams* v. *Mohamed* [1976] Crim.L.R. 577, D.C.; *R.* v. *Elliott* [1976] R.T.R. 308, C.A.; *R.* v. *Kershberg* [1976] R.T.R. 526, C.A.; *R.* v. *Dawson* [1976] R.T.R. 533; *Spicer* v. *Holt* [1976] 3 W.L.R. 398; [1976] 3 All E.R. 71, H.L.; *Powell* v. *MacNeill,* 1976 J.C. 30, High Ct. of Justiciary; *Tudhope* v. *Williamson,* 1977 S.L.T. 18; *R.* v. *Tate* [1977] R.T.R. 17, C.A.; *R.* v. *Powles* [1977] R.T.R. 69, C.A.; *R.* v. *Rutter* [1977] R.T.R. 105, C.A.; *R.* v. *Krebbs* [1977] R.T.R. 406, C.A.; *R.* v. *Ingram* [1977] R.T.R. 420, C.A.; *R.* v. *Sittingbourne JJ., ex p. Parsley* [1978] R.T.R. 153, D.C.; *R.* v. *Nokes* [1978] R.T.R. 101, C.A.; *R.* v. *Farrance* [1978] R.T.R. 225, C.A.; *R.* v. *Neilson* [1978] R.T.R. 232, C.A.; *McLeary* v. *Douglas,* 1978 S.L.T. 140; *R.* v. *Hatton (Francis)* [1978] R.T.R. 357, C.A.; *R.* v. *Moore* [1978] R.T.R. 384, C.A.; *Topping* v. *Scott,* 1979 S.L.T.(Notes) 21; *R.* v. *Midgley* [1979] R.T.R. 1, C.A.; *Shersby* v. *Klippel* [1979] R.T.R. 116, D.C.; *Ferns* v. *Tudhope,* 1979 S.L.T.(Notes), 23; *R.* v. *Wedlake* [1978] R.T.R. 529, C.A.; *Park* v. *Hicks* [1979] Crim.L.R. 57, D.C.; *Griffiths* v. *Willett* [1979] Crim.L.R. 320, D.C.; *Beck* v. *Watson* [1979] Crim.L.R. 533, D.C.; *Sutherland* v. *Aitchison,* 1975 J.C. 1; 1979 S.L.T.(Notes) 37; *Grant* v. *Gorman* [1979] Crim.L.R. 669, D.C.; *Mulcaster* v. *Wheatstone* [1979] Crim.L.R. 728, D.C.; *R.* v. *Beardsley* [1979] R.T.R. 472, C.A.; *R.* v. *Salters* [1979] R.T.R. 470, C.A.; *Sharpe* v. *Perry* [1979] R.T.R. 235, D.C.; *Winter* v. *Barlow* [1980] R.T.R. 209, D.C.; *MacKinnon* v. *Virhia,* High Court of Justiciary, November 28, 1979; *Allan* v. *Douglas,* 1978 J.C. 7; *Tudhope* v. *Miller,* 1978 J.C. 26; *R.* v. *Dixon* [1980] R.T.R. 17, C.A.; *R.* v. *Gibson* [1980] R.T.R. 39, C.A.; *R.* v. *South Western Magistrates' Court, ex p. Beaton* [1980] R.T.R. 35, D.C.; *Watt* v. *MacNeill,* High Court of Justiciary, March 18, 1980; *Tee* v. *Gough* [1980] Crim.L.R. 380, D.C.; *R.* v. *Birtwhistle* [1980] R.T.R. 342, C.A.; *Poole* v. *Lockwood* [1980] Crim.L.R. 730, D.C.; *R.* v. *Green* [1980] R.T.R. 415, C.A.; *Tudhope* v. *Stevenson,* 1980 S.L.T.(Notes) 94; *Sanaghan* v. *Galt,* High Court of Justiciary, June 24, 1980; *Valentine* v. *Mackie,* 1980 S.L.T. (Sh.Ct.) 122; *McNaughtan* v. *Buchan,* 1980 S.L.T.(Notes)

CAP.

1972—cont.

20. Road Traffic Act 1972—*cont.*

160; *MacNeill* v. *Perrie,* 1981 S.L.T.(Notes) 29; *Tudhope* v. *Heenan,* 1981 S.L.T.(Notes) 30; *Dryburg* v. *Galt,* 1981 S.L.T. 151; *Poole* v. *Lockwood* [1981] R.T.R. 285, D.C.; *Waters* v. *Bigmore* [1981] R.T.R. 356, D.C.; *McNaughton* v. *Deenan,* 1981 S.L.T.(Notes) 105; *Sinclair* v. *Heywood,* 1981 S.L.T.(Notes) 98; *Makeham* v. *Donaldson* [1981] R.T.R. 511, D.C.; *English* v. *Smith,* 1981 S.L.T.(Notes) 113; *Donlon* v. *Mackinnon,* 1982 S.L.T. 93; *Galt* v. *Goodsir,* 1982 S.L.T. 94; *Lee* v. *Smith,* 1982 S.L.T. 200; *Campbell* v. *Mackenzie,* 1982 S.L.T. 250; *Prosser* v. *Dickeson* [1982] R.T.R. 96, D.C.; *Gwyn-Jones* v. *Sutherland* [1982] R.T.R. 102, D.C.; *Williamson* v. *Aitchison,* 1982 S.L.T. 399; *R.* v. *Oxford JJ., ex p. Smith* [1982] R.T.R. 201, D.C.; *Snook* v. *Mannion* [1982] R.T.R. 321, D.C.; *R.* v. *Newman* [1978] R.T.R. 107, C.A.; *Collins* v. *Lucking, The Times,* November 13, 1982, C.A.; *Steel* v. *Goacher* [1983] R.T.R. 98, C.A.; *Burgoyne* v. *Phillips* [1983] R.T.R. 49, D.C.; *Jones* v. *Pratt* [1983] R.T.R. 54, D.C.; *Walker* v. *Hodgins, The Times,* March 1, 1983, C.A.; *R.* v. *Watford JJ., ex p. Outrim* [1983] R.T.R. 26, D.C.; *McGarry* v. *Chief Constable of Bedfordshire* [1983] R.T.R. 172, D.C.; *Clark* v. *Price, The Times,* June 15, 1983, D.C.; *Monaghan* v. *Corbett, The Times,* June 23, 1983, D.C.; *Riddell* v. *MacNeill,* 1983 S.C.C.R. 26; *Collins* v. *Lucking* [1983] R.T.R. 312, D.C.; *Thomas* v. *Henderson* [1983] R.T.R. 293, D.C.; *Tudhope* v. *Grubb,* 1983 S.C.C.R. 350; *Walker* v. *Hodgins* [1984] R.T.R. 34, D.C.; *Fawcett* v. *Tebb* [1982] Crim.L.R. 175, D.C.; *Lomas* v. *Bowler* [1984] Crim.L.R. 178, D.C.; *R.* v. *Newcastle JJ.* [1984] 1 All E.R. 770, D.C.; *Hall* v. *Allan,* 1984, S.L.T. 199; *Bentley* v. *Northumbria Police* [1984] R.T.R. 276, D.C.; *Smith* v. *Macdonald; Smith* v. *Davie,* 1984 S.L.T. 398; *Tudhope* v. *McAllister,* 1984 S.L.T. 395; *Jones* v. *Macphail,* 1984 S.L.T. 396; *Orttewell* v. *Allan,* 1984 S.C.C.R. 208; *Duddy* v. *Gallagher, The Times,* December 5, 1984, D.C.; *Blackmore* v. *Chief Constable of Devon and Cornwall, The Times,* December 6, 1984, D.C.; *Howard* v. *Hallett* [1984] R.T.R. 353, D.C.; *Lodwick* v. *Brow* [1984] R.T.R. 394, D.C.; *Brown* v. *Braid,* 1985 S.L.T. 37; *R.* v. *Skegness Magistrates' Court, ex p. Cardy; R.* v. *Manchester Crown Court, ex p. Williams* [1985] R.T.R. 49, D.C.; *Anderton* v. *Lythgoe* [1985] 1 W.L.R. 222, D.C.; *R.* v. *Burley Magistrates, ex p. Dixon (Allan Timothy)* [1984] Crim.L.R. 759, D.C.; *Wright* v. *Taplin, The Times,* February 13, 1985, D.C.; *Owen* v. *Chesters* [1985] Crim.L.R. 156; [1985] R.T.R. 191, D.C.; *Morgan* v. *Lee, The Times,* April 17, 1985, D.C.; *Anderton* v. *Royle* [1985] R.T.R. 91, D.C.; *Sparrow* v. *Bradley* [1985] R.T.R. 122, D.C.; *Over* v. *Musker* [1985] R.T.R. 84, D.C.; *Gatens* v. *Wilson,* 1985 S.C.C.R. 47; *Snelson* v. *Thompson* [1985] R.T.R. 220, D.C.; *Hughes* v. *McConnell* [1985] R.T.R. 224, D.C.; *Chief Constable of Surrey* v. *Wickens* [1985] R.T.R. 277, D.C.; *Tudhope* v. *Craig,* 1985 S.C.C.R. 214; *Step-*

CAP.

1972—cont.

20. Road Traffic Act 1972—*cont.*

niewski v. *Comr. of Police of the Metropolis* [1985] R.T.R. 330, D.C.; *McDonald* v. *Skelt* [1985] R.T.R. 321, D.C.; *R.* v. *Fox* [1985] 1 W.L.R. 1126, H.L.; *Lockhart* v. *Deighan,* 1985 S.L.T. 549; *Rowan* v. *Chief Constable of Merseyside, The Times,* December 10, 1985, D.C.; *Graham* v. *Albert* [1985] R.T.R. 352, D.C.; *Duddy* v. *Gallagher* [1985] R.T.R. 401, D.C.; *Broadbent* v. *High* [1985] R.T.R. 359, D.C.; *Reid* v. *Tudhope,* 1986 S.L.T. 136; *Anderton* v. *Kinnard* [1986] R.T.R. 11, D.C.; *Chief Constable of the Avon and Somerset Constabulary* v. *Creech* [1986] Crim.L.R. 62, D.C.; [1986] R.T.R. 18, D.C.; *Walton* v. *Rimmer* [1986] R.T.R. 31, D.C.; *Chief Constable of Gwent* v. *Dash* [1986] R.T.R. 41, D.C.; *Gilligan* v. *Tudhope,* 1986 S.L.T. 299; *Denneny* v. *Harding* [1986] Crim.L.R. 254, D.C.; *Oxford* v. *Baxendale, The Times,* April 28, 1986, D.C.; *Woodburn* v. *McLeod,* 1986 S.L.T. 325; *Ross* v. *Allan,* 1986 S.L.T. 349; *Sivyer* v. *Parker* [1986] Crim.L.R. 410, D.C.; *Johnson* v. *West Yorkshire Metropolitan Police* [1986] R.T.R. 167, D.C.; *Owen* v. *Morgan* [1986] R.T.R. 151, D.C.; *Waite* v. *Smith* [1986] Crim.L.R. 405, D.C.; *Price* v. *Nicholls* [1986] R.T.R. 155, D.C.; *Burditt* v. *Roberts* (1986) 150 J.P. 344, D.C.; *Davidson* v. *Aitchison,* 1986 S.L.T. 402; *Harvie* v. *Cardle,* 1986 S.C.C.R. 41; *Smith* v. *Geraghty* [1986] R.T.R. 222, D.C.; *Perry* v. *McGovern* [1986] R.T.R. 240, D.C.; *Dawson* v. *Lunn* [1986] R.T.R. 234, D.C.; *Valentine* v. *McPhail,* 1986 S.L.T. 598; *Lang* v. *Hindhaugh* [1986] R.T.R. 271, D.C.; *Lloyd* v. *Morris* [1986] R.T.R. 299, D.C.; *Blake* v. *Pope* [1986] 1 W.L.R. 1152, D.C.; *Rynsard* v. *Spalding* [1986] R.T.R. 303, D.C.; *McGrath* v. *Field, The Times,* November 20, 1986, D.C.; *Chief Constable of Kent* v. *Berry* [1986] R.T.R. 321, D.C.; *Burridge* v. *East* [1986] R.T.R. 328, D.C.; *Gordon* v. *Thorpe* [1986] R.T.R. 338, D.C.; *Denneny* v. *Harding* [1986] R.T.R. 350, D.C.; *R.* v. *Kingston upon Thames JJ., ex p. Khanna* [1986] R.T.R. 364, D.C.; *Fawcett* v. *Gasparics* [1986] R.T.R. 375, D.C.; *Burditt* v. *Roberts* (Note) [1986] R.T.R. 391, D.C.; *Gunn* v. *Brown,* 1987 S.L.T. 94; *O'Brien* v. *Ferguson,* 1987 S.L.T. 96; *MacLeod* v. *Fraser,* 1987 S.L.T. 142; *Wright* v. *Tudhope,* 1986 S.C.C.R. 431; *Jones* v. *Thomas (John Barrie)* [1987] Crim.L.R. 133; [1987] R.T.R. 111, D.C.; *Newton* v. *Woods* [1987] R.T.R. 41, D.C.; *McKoen* v. *Ellis* [1987] R.T.R. 26, D.C.; *Sivyer* v. *Parker* [1987] R.T.R. 169, D.C.; *Wakeley* v. *Hyams* [1987] R.T.R. 49, D.C.; *Haghigat-Khou* v. *Chambers* [1987] Crim.L.R. 340, D.C.; *Pearson* v. *Comr. of Police of the Metropolis, The Times,* June 29, 1987, D.C.; *Rawlins* v. *Brown* [1987] R.T.R. 238, D.C.; *R.* v. *Brentford Magistrates' Court, ex p. Clarke* [1987] R.T.R. 205, D.C.; *R.* v. *Tower Bridge Metropolitan Stipendiary Magistrate, ex p. D.P.P., The Times,* May 15, 1987, D.C.; *Smith* v. *Mellors and Soar* (1987) 84 Cr.App.R. 279, D.C.; *Stephenson* v. *Clift, The Times,* July 28, 1987, D.C.; *Donnelly*

1972—cont.

20. Road Traffic Act 1972—cont.

v. *Hamilton,* 1987 S.C.C.R. 313; *Gumbley* v. *Cunningham; Gould* v. *Castle* [1987] 3 All E.R. 733, D.C.; *Cracknell* v. *Willis* [1987] 3 W.L.R. 1082, H.L.; *Matto* v. *Wolverhampton Crown Court, sub nom. Matto* v. *D.P.P.* [1987] R.T.R. 337, D.C.; *McGrath* v. *Field* [1987] R.T.R. 349, D.C.; *Nugent* v. *Ridley* [1987] R.T.R. 412, D.C.; *Liddell* v. *McNaughton,* 1987 S.C.C.R. 437; *Anderson* v. *H.M. Advocate,* 1987 S.C.C.R. 529; *Maharaj* v. *Soloman* [1987] R.T.R. 295, D.C.; *Young* v. *Flint* [1987] R.T.R. 300, D.C.; *Hobbs* v. *Clark* [1988] R.T.R. 36, D.C.; *Benton* v. *Cardle,* 1988 S.L.T. 310; *McConnachie* v. *Scott,* 1988 S.L.T. 480; *Watson* v. *Hamilton,* 1988 S.L.T. 316; *R.* v. *Tower Bridge Magistrates' Court, ex p. D.P.P.* (1988) 86 Cr.App.R. 257, D.C.; *Lunney* v. *Cardle,* 1988 S.L.T. 440; *D.P.P.* v. *Frost, The Times,* June 27, 1988, D.C.; *Badkin* v. *Chief Constable of South Yorkshire* [1987] Crim.L.R. 830, D.C.; *D.P.P.* v. *Singh* [1988] R.T.R. 209, D.C.; *D.P.P.* v. *White* [1988] R.T.R. 267, D.C.; *Pearson* v. *Comr. of Police of the Metropolis* [1988] R.T.R. 276, D.C.; *Mayon* v. *D.P.P.* [1988] R.T.R. 281, D.C.

s. 7, see *R.* v. *Richards (Stanley)* [1974] 3 All E.R. 696, C.A.; *R.* v. *Hillman* [1977] R.T.R. 124, C.A.; *R.* v. *Moore* [1978] R.T.R. 384, C.A.; *R.* v. *Hunt* [1980] R.T.R. 29, C.A.; *R.* v. *Trump* (1979) 70 Cr.App.R. 300; *Tee* v. *Gough* [1981] R.T.R. 73, D.C.; *Howard* v. *Hallett* [1984] Crim.L.R. 565, D.C.; *Cotter* v. *Kamil* [1984] Crim.L.R. 569, D.C.; *Anderton* v. *Royle* [1985] R.T.R. 91, D.C.; *Woon* v. *Maskell* [1985] R.T.R. 289, D.C.; *Graham* v. *Albert* [1985] R.T.R. 352, D.C., *Bunyard* v. *Hayes* (Note) [1985] R.T.R. 348, D.C.; *Chief Constable of the Avon and Somerset Constabulary* v. *Creech* [1986] Crim.L.R. 62, D.C.; *Redmond* v. *Parry* [1986] R.T.R. 146, D.C.; *Teape* v. *Godfrey* [1986] R.T.R. 213, D.C.; *Blake* v. *Pope* [1986] 1 W.L.R. 1152, D.C.; *Gallagher* v. *MacKinnon,* 1986 S.C.C.R. 704; *Gull* v. *Scarborough* (Note) [1987] R.T.R. 261, D.C.; *Matto* v. *Wolverhampton Crown Court, sub nom. Matto* v. *D.P.P.* [1987] R.T.R. 337, D.C.; *MacMillan* v. *Scott,* 1988 S.C.C.R. 219; *D.P.P.* v. *White* [1988] R.T.R. 267, D.C.

s. 8, see *Newsome* v. *Hayton* [1974] R.T.R. 9, D.C.; *Hollingsworth* v. *Howard* [1974] R.T.R. 58, D.C.; *R.* v. *Pearson* [1974] R.T.R. 92, C.A.; *R.* v. *Auker-Howlett* [1974] R.T.R. 109, C.A.; *R.* v. *Gaughan* [1974] R.T.R. 195, C.A.; *R.* v. *Mitcham* [1974] R.T.R. 205, C.A.; *R.* v. *McGall* [1974] R.T.R. 216, C.A.; *R.* v. *Evans (Terence)* [1974] R.T.R. 232, C.A.; *Cruickshank* v. *Devlin,* 1974 S.L.T.(Sh.Ct.) 81; *McGuinness* v. *Thaw,* 1974 S.L.T. 237; *Witts* v. *Williams* [1974] Crim.L.R. 259, D.C.; *R.* v. *Coleman* [1974] R.T.R. 359, C.A.; *Ratledge* v. *Oliver* [1974] R.T.R. 394, D.C.; *R.* v. *Thorpe (Thomas)* [1974] R.T.R. 465, C.A.; *R.* v. *Cooper* [1974] R.T.R. 489, C.A.; *Parker* v. *Smith* [1974] R.T.R. 500, D.C.; *Moss* v. *Jenkins* [1975] R.T.R. 25, D.C.; *Taylor* v. *Armand* [1975] R.T.R. 225, D.C.; *Att.-Gen.'s Reference (No. 2 of 1974)* [1975] 1

1972—cont.

20. Road Traffic Act 1972—cont.

W.L.R. 328; [1975] 1 All E.R. 658, C.A.; *R.* v. *Dilley* [1975] Crim.L.R. 393; *Morrison* v. *Pirie,* 1975 S.L.T. 230; *R.* v. *Mayer* [1975] R.T.R. 411, C.A.; *R.* v. *Callum* [1975] R.T.R. 415, C.A.; *Butcher* v. *Catterall* [1975] R.T.R. 436, D.C.; *R.* v. *Aspden* [1975] R.T.R. 456, C.A.; *R.* v. *Foster* [1975] R.T.R. 553, C.A.; *R.* v. *Broomhead* [1975] R.T.R. 558, C.A.; *Adams* v. *Valentine* [1975] R.T.R. 563, D.C.; *Walker* v. *Lovell* [1975] 1 W.L.R. 1141, H.L.; *R.* v. *Burdekin* [1976] R.T.R. 27, C.A.; *McKenna* v. *Smith* [1976] Crim.L.R. 256, D.C.; *Atkinson* v. *Walker* [1976] R.T.R. 117, D.C.; *Taylor* v. *Baldwin* [1976] R.T.R. 265, C.A.; *R.* v. *Maidment* [1976] R.T.R. 294, C.A.; *Jeffrey* v. *MacNeill,* 1976 S.L.T. 134; *Spicer* v. *Holt* [1976] 3 W.L.R. 398; [1976] 3 All E.R. 71, H.L.; *Cannings* v. *Houghton* [1977] R.T.R. 55, D.C.; *Merry* v. *Doherty,* Jan. 26, 1977; *Stoddart* v. *Balls* [1977] R.T.R. 113, D.C.; *R.* v. *Brown* [1977] Crim.L.R. 291, C.A.; *R.* v. *Mackey* [1977] R.T.R. 146, C.A.; *Ely* v. *Marle* [1977] Crim.L.R. 294; [1977] R.T.R. 412, D.C.; *R.* v. *Chapman* [1977] R.T.R. 190, C.A.; *Morriss* v. *Lawrence* [1977] R.T.R. 205, D.C.; *R.* v. *Crowley* [1977] R.T.R. 153, C.A.; *R.* v. *Rees* [1977] R.T.R. 181, C.A.; *R.* v. *Brown* [1977] R.T.R. 160, C.A.; *Att.-Gen.'s Reference (No. 1 of 1976)* [1977] 1 W.L.R. 646, C.A.; *R.* v. *Sittingbourne Justices, ex p. Parsley* [1978] R.T.R. 153, D.C.; *R.* v. *Kaplan* [1978] R.T.R. 119, C.A.; *Seneviratne* v. *Bishop* [1978] R.T.R. 92, D.C.; *Clements* v. *Dams* [1978] R.T.R. 206, D.C.; *R.* v. *Vardy* [1978] R.T.R. 202, C.A.; *Rickwood* v. *Cochrane* [1978] R.T.R. 218, D.C.; *Sloan* v. *Smith,* 1978 S.L.T. (Notes) 27; *Parsley* v. *Beard* [1978] R.T.R. 263, D.C.; *Att.-Gen.'s Reference No. 1 of 1978, The Times,* July 4, 1978, C.A.; *R.* v. *Hatton (Francis)* [1978] R.T.R. 357, C.A.; *R.* v. *Moore* [1978] R.T.R. 384, C.A.; *Att.-Gen.'s Reference (No. 1 of 1978)* [1978] R.T.R. 377, C.A.; *R.* v. *Rey* [1978] R.T.R. 413, C.A.; *Morrison* v. *Pirie* [1978] Crim.L.R. 695, High Ct. of Justiciary; *Manz* v. *Miln,* 1977 J.C. 78; *Blyth* v. *Macphail,* 1977 J.C. 74; *Topping* v. *Scott,* 1979 S.L.T.(Notes) 21; *Stewart* v. *Fekkes,* 1977 J.C. 85; *R.* v. *Wedlake* [1978] R.T.R. 529, C.A.; *Williams* v. *Critchley* [1979] R.T.R. 47, D.C.; *Shersby* v. *Klippel* [1979] R.T.R. 116, D.C.; *R.* v. *Moore (George)* [1979] R.T.R. 98, C.A.; *Mallows* v. *Harris* [1979] Crim.L.R. 320; *Knight* v. *Taylor* [1979] Crim.L.R. 319, D.C.; *Siddiqui* v. *Swain* [1979] R.T.R. 454, D.C.; *Chief Constable of West Midlands Police* v. *Billingham* [1979] 2 All E.R. 182, D.C.; *Price* v. *Davies* [1979] R.T.R. 204, D.C.; *Knight* v. *Taylor* [1979] R.T.R. 304, D.C.; *Sharp* v. *Perry* [1979] R.T.R. 235, D.C.; *Lee* v. *Wiltshire Chief Constable* [1979] R.T.R. 349, D.C.; *R.* v. *Miles* [1979] R.T.R. 509, C.A.; *Winter* v. *Barlow* [1980] R.T.R. 209, D.C.; *Allan* v. *Douglas,* 1978 J.C. 7; *Baker* v. *Oxford* [1980] R.T.R. 315, D.C.; *R.* v. *Carpenter* [1980] R.T.R. 65, C.A.; *Regan* v. *Anderton* [1980] R.T.R. 126, D.C.; *R.* v. *Birtwhistle* [1980] R.T.R. 342, C.A.; *Grant* v. *Gorman* [1980] R.T.R. 119, D.C.; *Mul-*

1972—cont.

20. Road Traffic Act 1972—*cont.*

caster v. *Wheatstone* [1980] R.T.R. 190, D.C.; *Richards* v. *West* [1980] R.T.R. 215, D.C.; *Morris* v. *Beardmore* [1980] 3 W.L.R. 283; [1980] 2 All E.R. 753, H.L.; *R.* v. *Trump* (1979) 70 Cr.App.R. 300, C.A.; *R.* v. *Grant* [1980] R.T.R. 280, C.A.; *Sheridan* v. *Webster* [1980] R.T.R. 349, D.C.; *R.* v. *Green* [1980] R.T.R. 415, C.A.; *McNaughtan* v. *Buchan,* 1980 S.L.T.(Notes) 100; *R.* v. *Littell* [1981] 1 W.L.R. 1146, C.A.; *Tudhope* v. *Heenan,* 1981 S.L.T.(Notes) 30; *R.* v. *Allen* [1981] Crim.L.R. 324, C.A.; *Finnigan* v. *Sandiford, The Times,* May 15, 1981, H.L.; *Waters* v. *Bigmore* [1981] Crim.L.R. 408, D.C.; *Clowser* v. *Chaplin* [1981] Crim.L.R. 412, H.L.; *Such* v. *Ball* [1981] Crim.L.R. 411, D.C.; *Dryburgh* v. *Galt,* 1981 S.L.T. 151; *Lambert* v. *Roberts* [1981] Crim.L.R. 257, D.C.; *Binnie* v. *Donnelly,* High Court of Justiciary, June 25, 1981; *McNaughton* v. *Deenan,* 1981 S.L.T.(Notes) 105; *Sinclair* v. *Heywood,* 1981 S.L.T.(Notes) 98; *Nelson* v. *MacGillivray,* 1981 S.C.C.R. 70; *Chief Constable of Staffordshire* v. *Lees* [1981] R.T.R. 506, D.C.; *Pamplin* v. *Fraser* [1981] R.T.R. 494, D.C.; *Topping* v. *Scott* [1981] Crim.L.R. 780, High Ct. of Justiciary, Scotland; *O'Sharkey* v. *Smith,* 1982 S.L.T. 91; *Pryde* v. *Brown,* 1982 S.L.T. 314; *Smith* v. *McLean,* 1982 S.C.C.R. 39; *Gwyn-Jones* v. *Sutherland* [1982] R.T.R. 102, D.C.; *Ronex Properties* v. *John Laing Construction, The Times,* July 28, 1982, C.A.; *Edwards* v. *Davies* [1982] R.T.R. 279, D.C.; *Faulkner* v. *Willetts* [1982] R.T.R. 159, D.C.; *Such* v. *Ball* [1982] R.T.R. 140, D.C.; *Gilham* v. *Breidenbach* (Note) [1982] R.T.R. 328, D.C.; *Snook* v. *Mannion* [1982] R.T.R. 321, D.C.; *Revel* v. *Jordan; Hillis* v. *Nicholson, The Times,* October 28, 1982, D.C.; *Steel* v. *Goacher* [1983] R.T.R. 98, C.A.; *Johnson* v. *Whitehouse, The Times,* March 26, 1983, C.A.; *Lewis* v. *Ursell, The Times,* April 23, 1983, D.C.; *Corp* v. *Dalton* [1983] R.T.R. 160, D.C.; *Smith* v. *Ross,* 1983 S.L.T. 491; *Wilson* v. *Cummings* (1983) R.T.R. 347, D.C.; *Hart* v. *Chief Constable of Kent* [1983] R.T.R. 484, D.C.; *Gage* v. *Jones* [1983] R.T.R. 508, D.C.; *Revel* v. *Jordan; Hillis* v. *Nicholson* [1983] R.T.R. 497, D.C.; *Cairns* v. *Keane,* 1983 S.C.C.R. 277; *Johnson* v. *Whitehouse* [1984] R.T.R. 38, D.C.; *McGrath* v. *Vipas* [1984] R.T.R. 58, D.C.; *Kelly* v. *Dolbey* [1984] R.T.R. 67, D.C.; *Walker* v. *Hodgkins* [1984] R.T.R. 34, D.C.; *Fawcett* v. *Tebb* [1984] Crim.L.R. 175, D.C.; *Howard* v. *Hallett* [1984] Crim.L.R. 565, D.C.; *Hayward* v. *Eames, The Times,* October 10, 1984, C.A.; *Tudhope* v. *McAllister,* 1984 S.L.T. 395; *Bunyard* v. *Hayes, The Times,* November 3, 1984, D.C.; *Duddy* v. *Gallagher, The Times,* December 5, 1984, D.C.; *Slender* v. *Boothby, The Times,* December 4, 1984, D.C.; *Cotter* v. *Kamil* [1984] R.T.R. 371, D.C.; *Castle* v. *Cross* [1984] 1 W.L.R. 1372, D.C.; *Howard* v. *Hallett* [1984] R.T.R. 353, D.C.; *Tudhope* v. *Quinn,* 1984 S.C.C.R. 255; *Stewart* v. *Aitchison,* 1984

1972—cont.

20. Road Traffic Act 1972—*cont.*

S.C.C.R. 357; *Reeves* v. *Enstone, The Times,* January 15, 1985, D.C.; *R.* v. *Skegness Magistrates' Court ex p. Cardy; R.* v. *Manchester Crown Court, ex p. Williams* [1985] R.T.R. 49, D.C.; *Hayward* v. *Eames* [1985] R.T.R. 12, D.C.; *Anderton* v. *Lythgoe* [1985] 1 W.L.R. 222, D.C.; *Pritchard* v. *Jones* [1985] Crim.L.R. 52, D.C.; *Smith* v. *Nixon,* 1985, S.L.T. 192; *Morgan* v. *Lee, The Times,* April 17, 1985, D.C.; *Anderton* v. *Royle* [1985] R.T.R. 91, D.C.; *Sparrow* v. *Bradley* [1985] R.T.R. 122, D.C.; *Spalding* v. *Paine, The Times,* May 21, 1985, D.C.; *Knox* v. *Lockhart,* 1985 S.L.T. 248; *Owen* v. *Chesters* [1985] R.T.R. 191, D.C.; *Kelly* v. *MacKinnon,* 1985 S.C.C.R. 97; *Chief Constable of Avon and Somerset Constabulary* v. *Creech, The Times,* August 5, 1985, C.A.; *Nichols* v. *Bulman* [1985] R.T.R. 236, D.C.; *Hughes* v. *McConnell* [1985] R.T.R. 244, D.C.; *Pine* v. *Collacott* [1985] R.T.R. 282, C.A.; *Woolman* v. *Lenton* [1985] Crim.L.R. 516, D.C.; *Chief Constable of West Yorkshire Metropolitan Police* v. *Johnson, The Times,* August 27, 1985, D.C.; *Oldfield* v. *Anderton, The Times,* October 9, 1985, D.C.; *Green* v. *Lockhart,* 1985 S.C.C.R. 257; *Stepniewski* v. *Comr. of the Police of the Metropolis* [1985] R.T.R. 330, D.C.; *Chief Constable of Gwent* v. *Dash* [1985] Crim.L.R. 674, D.C.; *Gull* v. *Scarborough, The Times,* November 15, 1985, D.C.; *R.* v. *Fox* [1985] 1 W.L.R. 1126, H.L.; *Archbold* v. *Jones* [1985] Crim.L.R. 740, D.C.; *Lockhart* v. *Deighan,* 1985 S.L.T. 549; *McCormick* v. *Hitchens, The Times,* December 10, 1985, D.C.; *Bunyard* v. *Hayes* (Note) [1985] R.T.R. 348, D.C.; *Graham* v. *Albert* [1985] R.T.R. 352, D.C.; *Duddy* v. *Gallagher* [1985] R.T.R. 401, D.C.; *Broadbent* v. *High* [1985] R.T.R. 359, D.C.; *Reid* v. *Tudhope,* 1985 S.C.C.R. 268; 1986 S.L.T. 136; *Harris* v. *Tudhope,* 1985 S.C.C.R. 305; *Anderton* v. *Kinnard* [1986] R.T.R. 11, D.C.; *Patterson* v. *Charlton* [1986] R.T.R. 18, D.C.; *Walton* v. *Rimmer* [1986] R.T.R. 31, D.C.; *Chief Constable of Kent* v. *Mather* [1986] R.T.R. 36, D.C.; *Chief Constable of Gwent* v. *Dash* [1986] R.T.R. 41, D.C.; *Oldfield* v. *Anderton* [1986] Crim.L.R. 189, D.C.; *Bain* v. *Tudhope,* 1985 S.C.C.R. 412; *Gilligan* v. *Tudhope,* 1986 S.L.T. 299; *Chief Constable of the Avon and Somerset Constabulary* v. *Creech* [1986] Crim.L.R. 62; [1986] R.T.R. 87, D.C.; *Denneny* v. *Harding* [1986] Crim.L.R. 254, D.C.; *Burridge* v. *East, The Times,* May 6, 1986, D.C.; *Clarke* v. *Hegarty, The Times,* May 19, 1986, D.C.; *Dye* v. *Manns* [1986] Crim.L.R. 337, D.C.; *Rawlins* v. *Brown, The Times,* June 6, 1986, D.C.; *Woodburn* v. *McLeod,* 1986 S.L.T. 325; *Ross* v. *Allan,* 1986 S.L.T. 349; *Sivyer* v. *Parker* [1986] Crim.L.R. 410, D.C.; *Archbold* v. *Jones* [1986] R.T.R. 178, D.C.; *Johnson* v. *West Yorkshire Metropolitan Police* [1986] R.T.R. 167, D.C.; *Owen* v. *Morgan* [1986] R.T.R. 151, D.C.; *Waite* v. *Smith* [1986] Crim.L.R. 405, D.C.; *Price* v. *Nicholls* [1986] R.T.R. 155, D.C.; *Burditt* v. *Roberts* (1986) 150 J.P. 344,

1972—cont.

20. Road Traffic Act 1972—*cont.*
D.C.; *Davidson* v. *Aitchison*, 1986 S.L.T. 402;
Smith v. *Geraghty* [1986] R.T.R. 222, D.C.;
Perry v. *McGovern* [1986] R.T.R. 240, D.C.;
Horrocks v. *Binns* [1986] R.T.R. 202, D.C.;
Dempsey v. *Catton* [1986] R.T.R. 194, D.C.;
Teape v. *Godfrey* [1986] R.T.R. 213, D.C.;
McCormick v. *Hitchins* (1986) 83 Cr.App.R.
11, D.C.; *R.* v. *Brentford Magistrates' Court,
ex p. Clarke* [1986] Crim.L.R. 633, D.C.;
Oxford v. *Baxendale* [1986] Crim.L.R. 631,
D.C.; *Thompson* v. *Thynne* [1986] R.T.R. 293;
[1986] Crim.L.R. 629, D.C.; *Chief Constable
of Avon and Somerset Constabulary* v. *Kelliher*
[1986] Crim.L.R. 635, D.C.; *Valentine* v.
McPhail, 1986 S.L.T. 598; *Houston* v.
McLeod, 1986 S.C.C.R. 219; *Manuel* v. *Stew-
art*, 1986 S.L.T. 593; *Smith* v. *Hand* [1986]
R.T.R. 265, D.C.; *Oldfield* v. *Anderton* [1986]
R.T.R. 314, D.C.; *Chief Constable of Kent* v.
Berry [1986] R.T.R. 321; *Burridge* v. *East*
[1986] R.T.R. 328, D.C.; *Gordon* v. *Thorpe*
[1986] R.T.R. 338, D.C.; *Denneny* v. *Harding*
[1986] R.T.R. 350, D.C.; *R.* v. *Kingston upon
Thames JJ., ex p. Khanna* [1986] R.T.R. 364,
D.C.; *Fawcett* v. *Gasparics* [1986] R.T.R. 375,
D.C.; *Slender* v. *Boothby* [1986] R.T.R. 385,
D.C.; *Wright* v. *Taplin* (Note) [1986] R.T.R.
388, D.C.; *Burditt* v. *Roberts* (Note) [1986]
R.T.R. 391, D.C.; *Beveridge* v. *Allan*, 1986
S.C.C.R. 542; *Sutch* v. *Crown Prosecution
Service*, January 30, 1987, H.H. Judge Comp-
ton, Wood Green Crown Ct.; *McLeod* v.
Murray, 1986 S.C.C.R. 369; *Hynd* v. *Guild*,
1986 S.C.C.R. 406; *Goldie* v. *Tudhope*, 1986
S.C.C.R. 414; *Douglas* v. *Stevenson*, 1986
S.C.C.R. 519; *Tudhope* v. *O'Kane*, 1986
S.C.C.R. 538; *Newton* v. *Woods* [1987] R.T.R.
41, D.C.; *Grix* v. *Chief Constable of Kent, The
Times*, March 19, 1987, D.C.; *Chief Constable
of Avon and Somerset Constabulary* v. *Singh,
The Times*, April 11, 1987, D.C.; *R.* v. *Ashford
and Tenterden Magistrates' Court, ex p.
Wood, The Times*, May 8, 1987, D.C.;
McGrath v. *Field* [1985] Crim.L.R. 275, D.C.;
Gallagher v. *MacKinnon*, 1986 S.C.C.R. 704;
Dye v. *Manns* [1987] R.T.R. 90, D.C.; *Kemp*
v. *Chief Constable of Kent* [1987] R.T.R. 66,
D.C.; *Sivyer* v. *Parker* [1987] R.T.R. 169, D.C.;
Wakeley v. *Hyams* [1987] R.T.R. 49, D.C.;
Chief Constable of Avon and Somerset v.
O'Brien [1987] R.T.R. 182, D.C.; *Cotgrove* v.
Cooney [1987] R.T.R. 124, D.C.; *Haghigat-
Khou* v. *Chambers* [1987] Crim.L.R. 340, D.C.;
Cole v. *Boon, The Times*, June 19, 1987,
D.C.; *Sharp* v. *Spencer* [1987] Crim.L.R. 420,
D.C.; *D.P.P.* v. *Billington, Chappell, Rumble
and East, The Independent*, July 22, 1987,
D.C.; *Pearson* v. *Comr. of Police of the
Metropolis, The Times*, June 29, 1987, D.C.;
Grix v. *Chief Constable of Kent* [1987] R.T.R.
193, D.C.; *Gull* v. *Scarborough* (Note) [1987]
R.T.R. 261, D.C.; *Oxford* v. *Baxendale* [1987]
R.T.R. 247, D.C.; *Rawlins* v. *Brown* [1987]
R.T.R. 238, D.C.; *R.* v. *Brentford Magistrates'
Court, ex p. Clarke* [1987] R.T.R. 205, D.C.;
Hartland v. *Alden* [1987] R.T.R. 253, D.C.;

1972—cont.

20. Road Traffic Act 1972—*cont.*
Bodkin v. *Chief Constable of South Yorkshire,
The Times*, August 29, 1987, D.C.; *D.P.P.* v.
Webb, The Times, October 19, 1987, D.C.;
Davis v. *D.P.P., The Times*, October 23, 1987,
D.C.; *Aitchison* v. *Johnstone*, 1987 S.C.C.R.
225; *Fraser* v. *McLeod*, 1987 S.C.C.R. 294;
Reynolds v. *Tudhope*, 1987 S.C.C.R. 340;
Nugent v. *Ridley* [1987] Crim.L.R. 640, D.C.;
Hobbs v. *Clark* [1988] R.T.R. 36, D.C.; *Crack-
nell* v. *Willis* [1987] 3 W.L.R. 1082, H.L.;
Matto v. *Wolverhampton Crown Court, sub
nom. Matto* v. *D.P.P.* [1987] R.T.R. 337, D.C.;
McGrath v. *Field* [1987] R.T.R. 349, D.C.;
Askew v. *Richardson, The Times*, January 18,
1988, D.C.; *Nugent* v. *Ridley* [1987] R.T.R.
412, D.C.; *Chief Constable of Avon and
Somerset* v. *Kelliher* [1987] R.T.R. 305, D.C.;
Maharaj v. *Solomon* [1987] R.T.R. 295, D.C.;
Young v. *Flint* [1987] R.T.R. 300, D.C.; *Emms*
v. *Lockhart*, 1988 S.L.T. 222; *Benton* v.
Cardle, 1988 S.L.T. 310; *McConnachie* v.
Scott, 1988 S.L.T. 480; *D.P.P.* v. *Billington;
Chappell* v. *D.P.P.; D.P.P.* v. *Rumble; Cory-
wright* v. *East* [1988] 1 All E.R. 435; [1988] 1
W.L.R. 535, D.C.; *Lunney* v. *Cardle*, 1988
S.L.T. 440; *Stokes* v. *Sayers* [1988] R.T.R. 89,
D.C.; *Haghigat-Khou* v. *Chambers* (Note)
[1988] R.T.R. 95, D.C.; *Lamb* v. *Heywood*,
1988 S.C.C.R. 42; *Fountain* v. *D.P.P.* [1988]
Crim.L.R. 123, D.C.; *Davies* v. *D.P.P.* [1988]
R.T.R. 156, D.C.; *White* v. *Proudlock* (Note)
[1988] R.T.R. 163, D.C.; *McGregor* v. *Jessop*,
1988 S.L.T. 719; *Scott* v. *Hamilton*, 1988
S.C.C.R. 262; *D.P.P.* v. *Singh* [1988] R.T.R.
209, D.C.; *Francis* v. *Chief Constable of Avon
and Somerset Constabulary*]1988] R.T.R. 250,
D.C.; *Grennan* v. *Wescott* [1988] R.T.R. 253,
D.C.; *D.P.P.* v. *White* [1988] R.T.R. 267, D.C.;
Pearson v. *Comr. of Police of the Metropolis*
[1988] R.T.R. 276, D.C.; *Mayon* v. *D.P.P.*
[1988] R.T.R. 281, D.C.; *D.P.P.* v. *Magill, The
Times*, August 10, 1988, D.C.; *Pringle* v.
Annan, 1988 S.L.T. 899; *D.P.P.* v. *Gordon;
D.P.P.* v. *Griggs, The Independent*, October
28, 1988, D.C.

s. 9, see *R.* v. *Gormley* [1973] R.T.R. 483, C.A.;
R. v. *John* [1974] 1 W.L.R. 624, C.A.; *R.* v.
Auker-Howlett [1974] R.T.R. 109, C.A.; *R.* v.
Harding [1974] R.T.R. 325, C.A.; *O'Hara* v.
Farrell, 1974 S.L.T.(Notes) 48; *Milne* v. *Elliott*,
1974 S.L.T.(Notes) 71; *McGuinness* v. *Thaw*,
1974 S.L.T. 237; *Ratledge* v. *Oliver* [1974]
R.T.R. 394, D.C.; *R.* v. *Horton* [1974] R.T.R.
399, C.A.; *R.* v. *McAllister* [1974] R.T.R. 408,
C.A.; *Parker* v. *Smith* [1974] R.T.R. 500, D.C.;
R. v. *Taylor* (*Thomas*) [1974] R.T.R. 554, C.A.;
Ross v. *Hodges* [1975] R.T.R. 55, D.C.; *Mac-
Phail* v. *Forbes*, 1975 S.L.T.(Sh.Ct.) 48; *Gibson*
v. *Skeen*, 1975 S.L.T.(Notes) 52; *MacDonald*
v. *MacKenzie*, 1975 S.L.T. 190; *R.* v. *Richardson* (*John*) [1975] 1 W.L.R. 321, C.A.; *Baker*
v. *Foulkes* [1975] 1 W.L.R. 1551; [1975] 3 All
E.R. 651, H.L.; *Woodage* v. *Jones* (*No. 2*)

1972—cont.

20. Road Traffic Act 1972—cont.

[1975] R.T.R. 119, D.C.; Williams v. Osborne [1975] R.T.R. 181, D.C.; Roney v. Matthews [1975] R.T.R. 273, D.C.; R. v. Moore (Richard) [1975] R.T.R. 285, C.A.; Standen v. Robertson [1975] R.T.R. 329, D.C.; R. v. Callum [1975] R.T.R. 415, C.A.; R. v. Aspden [1975] R.T.R. 456, C.A.; R. v. Burdekin [1976] R.T.R. 27, C.A.; Pettigrew v. Northumbria Police Authority [1976] R.T.R. 177, D.C.; Gabrielson v. Richards [1976] R.T.R. 223, D.C.; R. v. Reynolds [1976] R.T.R. 229, C.A.; R. v. Trott [1976] R.T.R. 233, C.A.; Taylor v. Baldwin [1976] R.T.R. 265, C.A.; R. v. Maidment [1976] R.T.R. 294, C.A.; R. v. Coward [1976] R.T.R. 425, C.A.; R. v. Estop [1976] R.T.R. 493, C.A.; R. v. Beckett [1976] Crim.L.R. 140; McKenna v. Smith [1976] Crim.L.R. 256, D.C.; Comr. of Police of the Metropolis v. Curran [1976] 1 W.L.R. 87; [1976] 1 All E.R. 162, H.L.; Spicer v. Holt [1976] 3 W.L.R. 398; [1976] 3 All E.R. 71, H.L.; R. v. Powles [1977] R.T.R. 69, C.A.; Ely v. Marle [1977] Crim.L.R. 294; [1977] R.T.R. 412, D.C.; R. v. Rothery [1976] R.T.R. 550, C.A.; R. v. Radcliffe [1977] R.T.R. 99, C.A.; R. v. Hillman [1977] Crim.L.R. 752; R.T.R. 124, C.A.; Shepherd v. Kavulok [1978] R.T.R. 85, D.C.; Seneviratne v. Bishop [1978] R.T.R. 92, D.C.; Hier v. Read [1978] R.T.R. 114, D.C.; Powell v. MacNeill, 1976 J.C. 30, High Ct. of Justiciary; Oxford v. Lowton [1978] R.T.R. 237, D.C.; Roberts v. Griffiths [1978] R.T.R. 362, D.C.; Bayliss v. Thames Valley Police Chief Constable [1978] R.T.R. 328, D.C.; Wilkinson v. Button [1978] Crim.L.R. 436, D.C.; MacDonald v. Mackenzie [1978] Crim.L.R. 694, High Ct. of Justiciary; R. v. Moore [1978] R.T.R. 384, C.A.; R. v. Rey [1978] R.T.R. 413, C.A.; R. v. Wedlake [1978] R.T.R. 529, C.A.; Williams v. Critchley [1979] R.T.R. 47, D.C.; Blyth v. Macphail, 1977 J.C. 74; Brown v. Ridge [1979] R.T.R. 138, D.C.; Beck v. Sager [1979] R.T.R. 475, D.C.; Mallows v. Harris [1979] Crim.L.R. 320, D.C.; Griffiths v. Willett [1979] R.T.R. 195, D.C.; Price v. Davies [1979] R.T.R. 204, D.C.; Sharpe v. Perry [1979] R.T.R. 235, D.C.; Lee v. Wiltshire Chief Constable [1979] R.T.R. 349, D.C.; Glickman v. MacKinnon, 1978 J.C. 81; Allan v. Douglas, 1978 J.C. 7; R. v. Dixon [1980] R.T.R. 17, C.A.; Alcock v. Read [1980] R.T.R. 71, D.C.; Beck v. Watson [1980] R.T.R. 90, D.C.; Payne v. Diccox [1980] R.T.R. 82, D.C.; Baker v. Oxford [1980] R.T.R. 315, D.C.; R. v. Carpenter [1980] R.T.R. 65, C.A.; Watt v. MacNeill, High Court of Justiciary, March 18, 1980; Tee v. Gough [1980] Crim.L.R. 380, D.C.; Anderton v. Goodfellow [1980] R.T.R. 302, D.C.; R. v. Birtwhistle [1980] R.T.R. 342, C.A.; R. v. Green [1980] R.T.R. 415, C.A.; Tudhope v. Stevenson, 1980 S.L.T.(Notes) 94; R. v. Littell [1981] 1 W.L.R. 1146, C.A.; Edwards v. Wood [1981] Crim.L.R. 414, D.C.; Clowser v. Chaplin [1981] Crim.L.R. 412, H.L.; Poole v. Lockwood [1980] Crim.L.R. 730;

1972—cont.

20. Road Traffic Act 1972—cont.

[1981] R.T.R. 285, D.C.; Pascoe v. Nicholson [1981] 1 W.L.R. 1061; [1981] 2 All E.R. 769, H.L.; Stewart v. Aitchison, 1981 S.C.C.R. 107; Chief Constable of Staffordshire v. Lees [1981] R.T.R. 506, D.C.; R. v. Murray, The Times, February 23, 1982, C.A.; Earnshaw v. H.M. Advocate, 1982 S.L.T. 179; Prosser v. Dickeson [1982] R.T.R. 96, D.C.; Gwyn-Jones v. Sutherland [1982] R.T.R. 102, D.C.; Carmichael v. Gilhooly, 1982 S.C.C.R. 119; Edwards v. Davies [1982] R.T.R. 279, D.C.; Gilham v. Breidenbach [1982] R.T.R. 328, D.C.; Snook v. Mannion [1982] R.T.R. 321, D.C.; R. v. Page [1981] R.T.R. 132, C.A.; Corp v. Dalton [1983] R.T.R. 160, D.C.; Palmer v. Killion [1983] R.T.R. 138, D.C. Smith v. Ross, 1983 S.L.T. 491; Collins v. Lucking [1983] R.T.R. 312, D.C.; Sykes v. White [1983] R.T.R. 419, D.C.; Hart v. Chief Constable of Kent [1983] R.T.R. 484, D.C.; Johnson v. Whitehouse [1984] R.T.R. 38, D.C.; Hall v. Allan, 1984 S.L.T. 199; Muat v. Thynne, The Times, May 28, 1984, D.C.; Bentley v. Northumbria Police [1984] R.T.R. 276, D.C.; Franklin v. Jeffries, The Times, March 11, 1985, D.C.; Over v. Musker [1985] R.T.R. 84, D.C.; Nichols v. Bulman [1985] R.T.R. 236, D.C.; Chief Constable of Kent v. Mather [1986] R.T.R. 36, D.C.; D.P.P. v. Fountain, The Times, October 20, 1987, D.C.

s. 10, see R. v. Jones (Colin) [1974] R.T.R. 117, C.A.; R. v. Shaw (Derek) [1974] R.T.R. 458, C.A.; Gibson v. Skeen, 1975 S.L.T.(Notes) 52; R. v. Wright (John) [1975] R.T.R. 193, C.A.; R. v. Moore (Richard) [1975] R.T.R. 285, C.A.; R. v. Sodo [1975] R.T.R. 357, C.A.; Hawkins v. Ebbutt [1975] R.T.R. 363, D.C.; Frogatt v. Allcock [1975] R.T.R. 372, D.C.; R. v. Vaughan [1976] R.T.R. 184, C.A.; R. v. Elliott [1976] R.T.R. 308, C.A.; R. v. Coward [1976] R.T.R. 425, C.A.; Handley v. Pirie, 1977 S.L.T. 30; Williams v. Mohamed [1977] R.T.R. 12, D.C.; R. v. Tate [1977] R.T.R. 17, C.A.; R. v. Rutter [1977] R.T.R. 105, C.A.; McLeary v. Douglas, 1978 S.L.T. 140; Ferns v. Tudhope, 1979 S.L.T.(Notes) 23; Sutherland v. Aitchison, 1979 S.L.T.(Notes) 37; Mackinnon v. Virhia, High Court of Justiciary, November 28, 1979; Donlon v. Mackinnon, 1982 S.L.T. 93; R. v. Murray, The Times, February 23, 1982, C.A.; Williamson v. Aitchison, 1982 S.L.T. 399; Buonaccorsi v. Tudhope, 1982 S.L.T. 528; McMillan v. H.M. Advocate, 1983 S.L.T. 24; Tudhope v. Corrigall, 1982 S.C.C.R. 558; Gaimster v. Marlow [1984] 2 W.L.R. 16, D.C.; Howard v. Hallett [1984] Crim.L.R. 565; [1984] R.T.R. 353, D.C.; Annan v. Mitchell, 1984 S.C.C.R. 32; Aitchison v. Matheson, 1984 S.C.C.R. 83; Bentley v. Northumbria Police [1984] R.T.R. 276, D.C.; Smith v. Macdonald; Smith v. Davie, 1984 S.L.T. 398; Jones v. Macphail, 1984 S.L.T. 396; Reeves v. Enstone, The Times, January 15, 1985, D.C.; Hayward v. Eames [1985] R.T.R. 12, D.C.;

CAP.

1972—cont.

20. Road Traffic Act 1972—cont.
Patterson v. Charlton [1985] Crim.L.R. 449,
D.C.; Annan v. Crawford, 1984 S.C.C.R. 382;
McNamee v. Tudhope, 1985 S.C.C.R. 423;
Owen v. Chesters [1985] Crim.L.R. 156;
[1985] R.T.R. 191, D.C.; Donoghue v. Allan,
1985 S.C.C.R. 93; McDerment v. O'Brien,
1985 S.C.C.R. 50; Snelson v. Thompson
[1985] R.T.R. 220, D.C.; Hughes v. McConnell
[1985] R.T.R. 244, D.C.; Chief Constable of
Surrey v. Wickens [1985] R.T.R. 277, D.C.;
Temple v. Botha [1985] Crim.L.R. 517, D.C.;
Allan v. Miller, 1985 S.C.C.R. 227; Duddy v.
Gallagher [1985] R.T.R. 401, D.C.; Reid v.
Tudhope, 1986 S.L.T. 136; Anderton v. Kin-
nard [1986] R.T.R. 11, D.C.; Patterson v.
Charlton [1986] R.T.R. 18, D.C.; Walton v.
Rimmer [1986] R.T.R. 31, D.C.; Rynsard v.
Spalding [1985] Crim.L.R. 795, D.C.; Beck v.
Scammell [1985] Crim.L.R. 794, D.C.; Chief
Constable of the Avon and Somerset Consta-
bulary v. Creech [1986] Crim.L.R. 62; [1986]
R.T.R. 87, D.C.; Archbold v. Jones [1986]
R.T.R. 178, D.C.; Johnson v. West Yorkshire
Metropolitan Police [1986] R.T.R. 167, D.C.;
Beck v. Scammell [1986] R.T.R. 162, D.C.;
Price v. Nicholls [1986] R.T.R. 155, D.C.;
Penman v. Parker [1986] 1 W.L.R. 882, D.C.;
O'Brien v. Ferguson, 1986 S.C.C.R. 155;
Toovey v. Chief Constable of Northumbria
[1986] Crim.L.R. 475, D.C.; Smith v. Geraghty
[1986] R.T.R. 222, D.C.; Perry v. McGovern
[1986] R.T.R. 240, D.C.; R. v. Brentford Mag-
istrates' Court, ex p. Clarke [1986] Crim.L.R.
633, D.C.; Dawson v. Lunn [1986] R.T.R. 234,
D.C.; Lloyd v. Morris [1986] R.T.R. 299, D.C.;
Rynsard v. Spalding [1986] R.T.R. 303, D.C.;
Burridge v. East [1986] R.T.R. 328, D.C.; Denneny v. Harding [1986] R.T.R. 350, D.C.; Fawcett v. Gasparics [1986] R.T.R. 375, D.C.;
Wright v. Taplin (Note) [1986] R.T.R. 388,
D.C.; Burditt v. Roberts (Note) [1986] R.T.R.
391, D.C.; Gunn v. Brown, 1987 S.L.T. 94;
O'Brien v. Ferguson, 1987 S.L.T. 96;
MacLeod v. Fraser, 1987 S.L.T. 142; Newton
v. Woods [1987] R.T.R. 41, D.C.; Wakeley v.
Hyams [1987] R.T.R. 49, D.C.; Tobi v. Nicholas, The Independent, July 3, 1987, D.C.; R.
v. Brentford Magistrates' Court, ex p. Clarke
[1987] R.T.R. 205, D.C.; Bodkin v. Chief Constable of South Yorkshire, The Times, August
29, 1987, D.C.; Gumbley v. Cunningham;
Gould v. Castle [1987] 3 All E.R. 733, D.C.;
Cracknell v. Willis [1987] 3 W.L.R. 1082, H.L.;
Tobi v. Nicholas [1987] Crim.L.R. 774; (1988)
86 Cr.App.R. 323, D.C.; Mackinnon v. Westwater, 1987 S.C.C.R. 730; Dear v. D.P.P.
[1988] R.T.R. 148, D.C.; D.P.P. v. Singh [1988]
R.T.R. 209, D.C.
s. 12, see Gibson v. Skeen, 1975 S.L.T.(Notes)
52; Walker v. Lovell [1975] R.T.R. 61, D.C.;
Roney v. Matthews [1975] R.T.R. 273, D.C.;
R. v. Aspden [1975] R.T.R. 456, C.A.; R. v.
Burdekin [1976] R.T.R. 27, C.A.; Jeffrey v.
MacNeill, 1976 S.L.T. 134; R. v. Mackey

CAP.

1972—cont.

20. Road Traffic Act 1972—cont.
[1977] R.T.R. 146, C.A.; R. v. Radcliffe [1977]
R.T.R. 99, C.A.; Ely v. Marle [1977] R.T.R.
412, D.C.; R. v. Kaplan [1978] R.T.R. 119,
C.A.; Sloan v. Smith, 1978 S.L.T.(Notes) 27;
Parsley v. Beard [1978] R.T.R. 263, D.C.;
Bayliss v. Thames Valley Police Chief Con-
stable [1978] R.T.R. 328, D.C.; R. v. Rey
[1978] R.T.R. 413, C.A.; Brown v. Ridge
[1979] R.T.R. 138, D.C.; Price v. Davies [1979]
R.T.R. 204, D.C.; Sheridan v. Webster [1980]
R.T.R. 349, D.C.; R. v. Littell [1981] 1 W.L.R.
1146, C.A.; McGarry v. Chief Constable of
Bedfordshire, [1983] R.T.R. 172, D.C.; Corp v.
Dalton [1983] R.T.R. 160, D.C.; Walker v.
Hodgins [1984] R.T.R. 34, D.C.; Bentley v.
Northumbria Police [1984] R.T.R. 276, D.C.;
Castle v. Cross [1984] 1 W.L.R. 1372, D.C.;
Anderton v. Royle [1985] R.T.R. 91, D.C.;
Snelson v. Thompson [1985] R.T.R. 220, D.C.;
Hughes v. McConnell [1985] R.T.R. 244, D.C.;
Stepniewski v. Comr. of Police of the Metrop-
olis [1985] R.T.R. 330, D.C.; Duddy v. Gal-
lagher [1985] R.T.R. 401, D.C.; Patterson v.
Charlton [1986] R.T.R. 18, D.C.; Anderton v.
Waring [1986] R.T.R. 74, D.C.; Johnson v.
West Yorkshire Metropolitan Police [1986]
R.T.R. 167, D.C.; Price v. Nicholls [1986]
R.T.R. 155, D.C.; Smith v. Geraghty [1986]
R.T.R. 222, D.C.; Thompson v. Thynne [1986]
R.T.R. 293, D.C.; Lloyd v. Morris [1986] R.T.R.
299, D.C.; Rynsard v. Spalding [1986] R.T.R.
303, D.C.; Denneny v. Harding [1986] R.T.R.
350, D.C.; R. v. Kingston upon Thames JJ.,
ex p. Khanna [1986] R.T.R. 364, D.C.; Newton
v. Woods [1987] R.T.R. 41, D.C.; Oxford v.
Baxendale [1987] R.T.R. 247, D.C.; R. v.
Brentford Magistrates' Court, ex p. Clarke
[1987] R.T.R. 205, D.C.; Maharaj v. Solomon
[1987] R.T.R. 295, D.C.; D.P.P. v. Singh [1988]
R.T.R. 209, D.C.; D.P.P. v. White [1988] R.T.R.
267, D.C.; Mayon v. D.P.P. [1988] R.T.R. 281,
D.C.
s. 14, see Hay v. Police, January 2, 1979, Judge
Bennett, Q.C., Wakefield Crown Ct.; Ferrari
v. McNaughton, 1979 S.L.T.(Notes) 62.
s. 15, regs. 74/1674; 76/1657, 2019; 78/481;
79/1101 (S.); 80/495; 82/1103; 83/354 (S.);
87/346 (S.).
s. 18, see Nicholas v. Parsonage [1987] R.T.R.
199, D.C.
s. 20, see Sutherland v. Aitchison, 1975 J.C. 1.
s. 20, regs. 73/274; 74/401; 75/202; 76/247;
77/270; 78/245; 79/233; 80/225, 1185;
82/1639; 88/215.
s. 22, see Hoffman v. Thomas [1974] 1 W.L.R.
374, D.C.; Griffiths v. Skeen, 1975
S.L.T.(Notes) 26; R. v. Saunders [1978]
Crim.L.R. 98, Nottingham Crown Ct.; Skeen
v. Smith, 1979 S.L.T. 295; Kentesber v.
Waumsley [1980] R.T.R. 462, D.C.; Cotterill v.
Chapman [1984] R.T.R. 73, D.C.
s. 22, directions 81/859.

CAP.

1972—cont.

20. Road Traffic Act 1972—cont.

s. 25, see *Bulman* v. *Bennett* [1974] R.T.R. 1, D.C.; *Roper* v. *Sullivan* [1978] Crim.L.R. 233; [1978] R.T.R. 181, D.C.; *Ward* v. *Rawson* [1978] R.T.R. 498, D.C.; *Britton* v. *Loveday* [1981] Crim.L.R. 49, D.C.; *Lawson* v. *Ingram*, 1981 S.C.C.R. 240; *Brown* v. *McLeod*, 1981 S.C.C.R. 254; *Jackson* v. *Smith*, 1982 S.C.C.R. 138; *Paterson* v. *MacNeill*, 1982 S.C.C.R. 141; *Croll* v. *Smith*, 1982 S.C.C.R. 292; *Wisdom* v. *MacDonald* [1983] R.T.R. 186, D.C.; *Johnson* v. *Finbow* [1983] 1 W.L.R. 879, D.C.; *Mutton* v. *Bates (Nos. 1 & 2)* [1984] R.T.R. 256, D.C.; *Britton* v. *Mackenzie*, 1985 S.C.C.R. 115; *R.* v. *Jackson (Kenneth)* [1985] R.T.R. 257, C.A.; *McNamee* v. *Carmichael*, 1985 S.C.C.R. 289; *Bentley* v. *Mullen* [1986] R.T.R. 7, D.C.; *Selby* v. *Chief Constable of Avon and Somerset, The Times*, February 18, 1987, D.C.; *Singh* v. *McLeod*, 1986 S.C.C.R. 656; *Cruickshanks* v. *MacPhail*, 1988 S.C.C.R. 165.

s. 28, repealed: 1988, c.13, sch.4.

s. 32, see *R.* v. *Aylesbury Crown Court, ex p. Chanul* [1976] R.T.R. 489, D.C.; regs. 77/129.

s. 32, regs. 73/180; 77/129; 80/1279; 81/374; 86/472.

s. 33, see *Losexis* v. *Clarke* [1984] R.T.R. 174, D.C.

s. 33, regs. 74/2000; 76/2241; 77/128; 80/1279; 81/374; 86/472.

s. 33A, see *Webb* v. *Crane* [1988] R.T.R. 204, D.C.

s. 33A, regs. 82/1203; 87/675; 88/1031.

s. 33AA, regs. 85/1593.

s. 33B, regs. 82/1342.

s. 33C, added: 1988, c.23.

s. 34, regs. 78/1017; 84/1809; 86/1078.

s. 37, see *Jarvis* v. *Fuller* [1974] R.T.R. 160, D.C.; *Hoadley* v. *Dartford District Council* [1979] R.T.R. 359, C.A.

s. 40, see *Stonely* v. *Richardson* [1973] R.T.R. 229; *Stowers* v. *Darnell* [1973] R.T.R. 459, D.C.; *Phillips* v. *Thomas* [1974] R.T.R. 28, D.C.; *Smith* v. *North-Western Traffic Area Licensing Authority* [1974] R.T.R. 236, D.C.; *Thurrock District Council* v. *L. A. & A. Pinch* [1974] R.T.R. 269, D.C.; *Hawkins* v. *Holmes* [1974] R.T.R. 436, D.C.; *Ross Hillman* v. *Bond* [1974] 2 W.L.R. 436, D.C.; *Howard* v. *G. T. Jones & Co.* [1974] Crim.L.R. 606, D.C.; *P. Lowery & Sons* v. *Wark* [1975] R.T.R. 45, D.C.; *Smith of Maddiston* v. *Macnab*, 1975 S.L.T. 86; *Howard* v. *G. T. Jones & Co.* [1975] R.T.R. 150, D.C.; *Balfour Beatty & Co.* v. *Grindey (Note)* [1975] R.T.R. 156, D.C.; *Kennet* v. *British Airports Authority* [1975] R.T.R. 164, D.C.; *Cornish* v. *Ferry Masters* [1975] R.T.R. 292, D.C.; *Kingdom* v. *Williams* [1975] R.T.R. 333, D.C.; *Eden* v. *Mitchell* [1975] R.T.R. 425, D.C.; *Friend* v. *Western British Road Services* [1975] Crim.L.R. 521, D.C.; *Coombes* v. *Cardiff City Council* [1975] R.T.R. 491, D.C.; *Cook* v. *Briddon* [1975] R.T.R. 505, D.C.; *Farrell* v. *Moggach*, 1976

CAP.

1972—cont.

20. Road Traffic Act 1972—cont.

S.L.T.(Sh.Ct.) 8; *Leathley* v. *Robsons Border Transport; Leathley* v. *Wisely* [1976] R.T.R. 503, D.C.; *Coote* v. *Parkin* [1977] R.T.R. 61, D.C.; *Wakeman* v. *Catlow* [1977] R.T.R. 174, D.C.; *Nelmes* v. *Rhys Howells Transport* [1977] R.T.R. 266, D.C.; *Thurrock Borough Council* v. *William Blythe & Co.* [1977] R.T.R. 301, D.C.; *Mickleborough* v. *B.R.S. (Contracts)* [1977] R.T.R. 389, D.C.; *Wade* v. *Grange* [1977] R.T.R. 417, D.C.; *Sever* v. *Duffy* [1977] R.T.R. 429, D.C.; *William Swan & Co.* v. *MacNab*, High Court of Justiciary, June 3, 1977; *Dent* v. *Coleman* [1978] R.T.R. 1, D.C.; *Sandford* v. *Butcher* [1978] R.T.R. 132, D.C.; *R.* v. *Sandwell JJ., ex p. West Midlands Passenger Transport Board* [1979] R.T.R. 17, D.C.; *Patterson* v. *Redpath Brothers* [1979] Crim.L.R. 187, D.C.; *Passmore* v. *Gibbons* [1979] R.T.R. 53, D.C.; *Lovett* v. *Payne* [1980] R.T.R. 103, D.C.; *Keene* v. *Muncaster* [1980] R.T.R. 377, D.C.; *Bennett* v. *Richardson* [1980] R.T.R. 358, D.C.; *Bindley* v. *Willett* [1981] R.T.R. 19, D.C.; *Barnett* v. *French* [1981] 1 W.L.R. 848; [1981] R.T.R. 173, D.C.; *Secretary of State for the Environment* v. *Hooper* [1981] R.T.R. 169, D.C.; *St. Albans Sand & Gravel* v. *Minnis* [1981] R.T.R. 231, D.C.; *Bulman* v. *Godbold* [1981] R.T.R. 242, D.C.; *R.* v. *Tiverton JJ., ex p. Smith* [1981] R.T.R. 280, D.C.; *Connor* v. *Graham* [1981] R.T.R. 291, D.C.; *MacNeill* v. *Wilson*, 1981 S.L.T.(Notes) 109; *Corp.* v. *Toleman International; Toleman Delivery Services* v. *Pattison* [1981] R.T.R. 385, D.C.; *Hudson* v. *Bushrod* [1982] R.T.R. 87, D.C.; *Swift* v. *Spencer* [1982] R.T.R. 116, D.C.; *McDermott Movements* v. *Horsfield* [1983] R.T.R. 42, D.C.; *Halliday* v. *Burl* [1983] R.T.R. 21, D.C.; *Mounsey* v. *Campbell* [1983] R.T.R. 36, D.C.; *Brown* v. *Cardie*, 1983 S.L.T. 218; *Hawkins* v. *Harold A. Russett* [1983] R.T.R. 406, D.C.; *Streames* v. *Copping, The Times*, February 25, 1984, D.C.; *Target Travel (Coaches)* v. *Roberts, The Times*, June 20, 1985, D.C.; *Simpson* v. *Vant* [1986] Crim.L.R. 473; [1986] R.T.R. 247, D.C.; *Percy* v. *Smith* [1986] R.T.R. 252, D.C.; *Valentine* v. *MacBrayne Haulage*, 1986 S.C.C.R. 692; *Carmichael* v. *Hannaway*, 1987 S.C.C.R. 236.

s. 40, regs. 72/1473, 1690; 73/736, 1347, 1706, 1864; 74/64, 765, 973; 75/186, 238, 239, 245, 528, 641, 1736; 76/317, 1256, 1507; 77/154, 790–792, 809, 1401, 1560, 1639, 2103; 78/1017, 1233–1235, 1260–1263, 1313, 1317; 79/803, 843, 1062, 1145; 80/116, 139, 140, 142, 144, 287, 610, 880, 1166, 1789, 1855; 81/257, 261, 697, 915, 1042; 82/20, 430, 1057, 1058, 1132, 1223, 1272, 1422, 1480, 1482–1484, 1576; 83/112, 471, 932, 1859; 84/195, 331, 386, 679, 748, 812–814, 817, 1543, 1711, 1809; 85/91, 730, 1363, 2039, 2051; 86/1078, 1597, 1812, 1813; 87/675, 1133, 1315; 88/271, 1102, 1177, 1178, 1287, 1524, 1871.

1972—cont.

20. Road Traffic Act 1972—cont.

s. 41, regs. 78/1260; 81/261, 915; 84/195, 679, 812; 86/1597; 87/1315; 88/1524, 1871.

s. 42, orders 72/1609; 73/1101; 74/117; 76/323; 79/1198; 81/1664; 84/1810; 85/745; 86/313; 87/1327, 2161.

s. 43, regs. 75/1130; 76/1977, 2155; 78/1574; 79/439, 1215; 80/616; 81/951, 1692, 1694; 82/783; 83/1147, 1434; 84/401, 727, 815, 1126; 85/834, 1923; 86/372, 904; 87/1144; 88/339, 989, 1894.

s. 44, see *Hewer* v. *Cutler* [1974] R.T.R. 155, D.C.; *Tudhope* v. *Every*, 1976 J.C. 42, High Ct. of Justiciary; *McEachran* v. *Hurst* [1978] R.T.R. 462, D.C.; *McColl* v. *Skeen*, 1980 S.L.T.(Notes) 53; *Thomas* v. *Hooper* [1986] R.T.R. 1, D.C.

s. 44, regs. 74/1203; 76/1977, 2155; 81/1694; 82/814, 1477, 1715; 85/45; order 82/1550.

s. 45, regs. 73/1105; 74/99; 75/36; 76/242; 78/867, 1018; 80/656; 81/1428, 1693; 82/1478; 83/1800; 84/178, 402, 816, 1024; 85/1525; 86/371, 1090; 88/338, 1478.

ss. 45, 46, see *Gibson* v. *Nutter* [1984] R.T.R. 8, D.C.; *Kennet* v. *Holding & Barnes*; *Harvey (T.L.)* v. *Hall* [1986] R.T.R. 334, D.C.; *Weir* v. *Tudhope*, 1987 S.C.C.R. 307.

s. 46, see *Balfour Beatty & Co.* v. *Grindey (Note)* [1975] R.T.R. 156, D.C.; *Creek* v. *Fossett, Eccles and Supertents* [1986] Crim.L.R. 256.

s. 46, regs. 82/1478; 88/1478.

s. 47, see *British Leyland* v. *E.C. Commission (Merson Intervening) (No. 226/84)* [1987] R.T.R. 136, European Ct.

s. 47, regs. 76/937; 77/1438, 1917; 78/293, 1237, 1318, 1319, 1811; 79/1092; 80/879, 1165; 81/1340, 1619; 82/8, 1271; 83/328; 84/697, 981, 1401, 1402, 1404, 1761; 85/46, 1651; 86/427, 739, 1089; 87/1508, 1509; 88/1522, 1523.

s. 48, regs. 81/1340; 82/1271; 84/697.

s. 49, regs. 76/937; 79/1092; 80/879; 81/696, 1340; 82/1271; 84/697, 981.

s. 50, regs. 76/937, 1466; 77/1438, 1439, 1917; 78/293, 1237, 1318–1320, 1810, 1811; 79/1092; 80/879, 1165; 81/696; 82/8, 638, 1271; 83/328, 536; 84/697, 981, 1401, 1402, 1404, 1761; 85/46, 1651, 1656; 86/427, 739, 1089; 87/315, 1508, 1509, 1556.

s. 51, see *R.* v. *Hartley & Hartley* [1981] R.T.R. 373, C.A.

s. 51, regs. 76/937; 78/293; 79/1092; 84/981; 88/14787.

s. 52, regs. 76/937; 79/1092; 80/879; 81/696, 1340; 82/8, 1271; 84/697, 981; amended: 1974, c.50, s.10, sch.2.

s. 53, see *Stoneley* v. *Richardson* [1973] R.T.R. 229; *Phillips* v. *Thomas* [1974] R.T.R. 28, D.C.

s. 57, see *Smith* v. *North-Western Traffic Area Licensing Authority* [1974] R.T.R. 236, D.C.

ss. 57, 58, regs. 87/1149.

s. 60, see *Thornley* v. *Clegg* [1982] R.T.R. 405, D.C.; *Streames* v. *Copping, The Times,* February 25, 1984, D.C.

1972—cont.

20. Road Traffic Act 1972—cont.

s. 62, see *R.* v. *Hartley & Hartley* [1981] R.T.R. 373, C.A.

s. 63, regs. 72/1303; 73/550, 1194; 74/764; 75/635, 77/1400; 78/1111, 1870; 79/1088; 80/582, 2027; 81/126, 1732; 82/1479; 83/1602; 85/113; 86/748.

s. 65, regs. 78/1017.

s. 66, regs. 83/1176; 84/812.

s. 68, see *Bunting* v. *Holt* [1977] R.T.R. 373, D.C.; *Payne* v. *Harland* [1980] R.T.R. 478, D.C.; *Such* v. *Ball* [1982] R.T.R. 140, D.C.; *Gilham* v. *Breidenbach* (Note) [1982] R.T.R. 328, D.C.; *Gatens* v. *Wilson*, 1985 S.C.C.R. 47; *R.* v. *Derby Crown Court, ex p. Sewell* [1985] R.T.R. 251, D.C.

s. 68, regs. 75/1736; 77/1560; 78/1261.

s. 69, regs. 77/1560.

s. 71, regs. 80/116.

s. 72, regs. 77/1560.

s. 73, regs. 75/29, 239, 1736, 2111; 77/1560; 78/1261; 80/116, 1855; 81/1042.

s. 75, regs. 79/803.

s. 78, see *Bunting* v. *Holt* [1977] R.T.R. 373, D.C.; *R.* v. *Derby Crown Court, ex p. Sewell* [1985] R.T.R. 251, D.C.

s. 78, regs. 75/29, 239, 1494, 2111; 77/1560; 78/1261; 79/803; 80/116; 81/1042; 82/430.

s. 79, regs. 77/1560.

s. 80, see *Balfour Beatty & Co.* v. *Grindey (Note)* [1975] R.T.R. 156, D.C.

s. 81, see *Bunting* v. *Holt* [1977] R.T.R. 373, D.C.; *Such* v. *Ball* [1982] R.T.R. 140, D.C.; *Gilham* v. *Briedenbach* (Note) [1982] R.T.R. 328, D.C.; *R.* v. *Derby Crown Court, ex p. Sewell* [1985] R.T.R. 251, D.C.

s. 84, see *Tynan* v. *Jones* [1975] R.T.R. 465, D.C.; *McKissock* v. *Rees-Davies* [1976] R.T.R. 419, D.C.; *Milne* v. *Whaley* [1978] Crim.L.R. 695, High Ct. of Justiciary; *Ferrymasters* v. *Adams* [1980] R.T.R. 139, D.C.; *Heidak* v. *Winnett* (1981) R.T.R. 445, D.C.; *R.* v. *Reading JJ., ex p. Bendall* [1982] R.T.R. 30, D.C.; *R.* v. *Coventry Magistrates' Court, ex p. Wilson* [1982] R.T.R. 177, D.C.; *Ogilvie* v. *O'Donnell*, 1983 S.C.C.R. 257; *Farrall* v. *Department of Transport* [1983] R.T.R. 279, Stephen Brown J.

s. 84, regs. 76/1076; 79/1412; 81/952, 1128; 87/1378.

s. 85, see *R.* v. *Bonner* [1980] R.T.R. 187, C.A.; *Farrall* v. *Secretary of State for Transport*, [1983] R.T.R. 279, Stephen Brown J.

s. 85, regs. 75/521; 76/1076; 77/81; 78/697; 80/180; 81/952; 82/99, 230; 83/1662; 85/1161; order 84/737; regs. 87/560, 1378; 88/965.

s. 86, regs. 76/1076; 81/952; 87/1378; 88/965.

s. 87, see *Secretary of State for Transport* v. *Adams* [1982] R.T.R. 369, Hodgson J.

s. 87, regs. 75/757, 2037; 76/1076; 81/952; 82/423; 87/1378.

s. 87A, regs. 75/2037.

s. 88, see *Scott* v. *Jelf* [1974] R.T.R. 256, D.C.; *Cosgrove* v. *Milne*, 1975 S.L.T.(Notes) 25; *Ullah* v. *Luckhurst* [1977] R.T.R. 401, D.C.; *Heidak* v. *Winnett* (1981) R.T.R. 445, D.C.

1972—cont.
20. Road Traffic Act 1972—cont.

s. 88, regs. 75/1471; 76/1076, 1764; 78/697, 1109; 81/952; 82/937; 84/274; 87/1378; 88/1062.

s. 89, regs. 75/2037; 76/1076; 81/952; 82/937; 84/274; 87/1378.

s. 90, see *Secretary of State for Transport* v. *Adams* [1982] R.T.R. 369, Hodgson J.

s. 93, see *Glendinning* v. *Batty* [1973] R.T.R. 405, D.C.; *Jacobs* v. *Reed* [1974] R.T.R. 81, D.C.; *R.* v *Northamptonshire JJ., ex p. Nicholson* [1974] R.T.R. 97, D.C.; *Kerr* v. *Armstrong* [1974] R.T.R. 139, D.C.; *Taylor* v. *Rajan; Fraser* v. *Barton* [1974] 1 All E.R. 1007, D.C.; *R.* v. *Sharman* [1974] R.T.R. 213, C.A.; *R.* v. *Mills* [1974] R.T.R. 215, C.A.; *R.* v. *Shaw* [1974] R.T.R. 225, C.A.; *Scott* v. *Jelf* [1974] R.T.R. 256, D.C.; *R.* v. *Ball* [1974] R.T.R. 296, C.A.; *R.* v. *Brown (John)* [1974] R.T.R. 377, C.A.; *Farrell* v. *Moir*, 1974 S.L.T. (Sh.Ct.) 89; *McLeod* v. *Scoular*, 1974 S.L.T.(Notes) 44; *R.* v. *Newton* [1974] R.T.R. 451, D.C.; *Bullen* v. *Keay* [1974] R.T.R. 559; *R.* v. *Robinson* [1975] R.T.R. 99, C.A.; *R.* v. *Dawtrey* [1975] R.T.R. 101, C.A.; *R.* v. *Kwame* [1975] R.T.R. 106, C.A.; *Adams* v. *Bradley* [1975] R.T.R. 233, D.C.; *Dyson* v. *Ellison* [1975] 1 All E.R. 276, D.C.; *R.* v. *Donnelly* [1975] 1 All E.R. 785, C.A.; *R.* v. *Mallender* [1975] R.T.R. 246, C.A.; *Weatherson* v. *Connop* [1975] Crim.L.R. 239, D.C.; *R.* v. *Reed (Paul)* [1975] R.T.R. 313, C.A.; *R.* v. *Aspden* [1975] R.T.R. 456, C.A.; *Cornwall* v. *Coke*, May 30, 1976, Judge Lee, Worcester County Ct.; *R.* v. *Earle* [1976] R.T.R. 33, C.A.; *Damer* v. *Davison* [1976] R.T.R. 45, D.C.; *Hill* v. *Howell* [1976] R.T.R. 270, D.C.; *R.* v. *McIntyre* [1976] R.T.R. 330, C.A.; *R.* v. *Marshall* [1976] R.T.R. 483; *Skinner* v. *Ayton*, 1977 S.L.T. (Sh.Ct.) 48; *Copeland* v. *Sweeney*, 1977 S.L.T.(Sh.Ct.) 28; *Evans* v. *Bray* [1977] R.T.R. 24, D.C.; *Ullah* v. *Luckhurst* [1977] Crim.L.R. 295; [1977] R.T.R. 401, D.C.; *R.* v. *Mills* [1977] R.T.R. 188, C.A.; *R.* v. *Jones* [1977] R.T.R. 385, C.A.; *Anderton* v. *Anderton* [1977] R.T.R. 424, D.C.; *R.* v. *Krebbs* [1977] R.T.R. 406, C.A.; *R.* v. *Miller* [1978] R.T.R. 98, C.A.; *R.* v. *Kennedy* [1978] R.T.R. 418, C.A.; *Courtman* v. *Masterson* [1978] R.T.R. 457, D.C.; *R.* v. *Banks* [1978] R.T.R. 535, C.A.; *R.* v. *Yarnold* [1978] R.T.R. 526, C.A.; *Smith* v. *Peaston*, 1977 J.C. 81; *Urry* v. *Gibb*, 1979 S.L.T.(Notes) 19; *Smith* v. *Baker*, 1979 S.L.T.(Notes) 19; *Powell* v. *Gliha* [1979] R.T.R. 126, D.C.; *R.* v. *Mulroy* [1979] R.T.R. 214, C.A.; *Smith* v. *Craddock*, 1979 S.L.T.(Notes) 46; *Park* v. *Hicks* [1979] R.T.R. 259, D.C.; *R.* v. *O'Connor* [1979] R.T.R. 467, C.A.; *R.* v. *Fenwick* [1979] R.T.R. 506; C.A.; *R.* v. *Beardsley* [1979] R.T.R. 472, C.A.; *R.* v. *Salters* [1979] R.T.R. 470, C.A.; *R.* v. *Cunningham* [1979] R.T.R. 465, C.A.; *MacNab* v. *McPherson*, 1978 J.C. 21; *R.* v. *Gibson* [1980] R.T.R. 39, C.A.; *R.* v. *Bonner* [1980] R.T.R. 187, C.A.; *Jones* v. *Ridley* [1981] R.T.R. 341, D.C.; *Soanes* v. *Ahlers* [1981] R.T.R. 337, D.C.;

1972—cont.
20. Road Traffic Act 1972—cont.

Rozanski v. *Ingram*, 1981 S.C.C.R. 100; *Doyle* v. *Leroux* [1981] R.T.R. 438, C.A.; *Makeham* v. *Donaldson* [1981] R.T.R. 511, D.C.; *De Munthe* v. *Stewart* (1982) R.T.R. 27, D.C.; *R.* v. *Reading JJ., ex p. Bendall* [1982] R.T.R. 30, D.C.; *Holland* v. *Phipp* [1982] 1 W.L.R. 1150, D.C.; *R.* v. *Coventry Magistrates' Court, ex p. Wilson* [1982] R.T.R. 177, D.C.; *R.* v. *Kent, The Times*, May 13, 1983, C.A.; *Tariq* v. *Carmichael*, 1982 S.C.C.R. 488.; *R.* v. *Afan JJ., ex p. Chaplin* [1983] R.T.R. 168, D.C.; *R.* v. *Macclesfield JJ., ex p. Jones* [1983] R.T.R. 143, D.C.; *R.* v. *Cooper (Frederick)* [1983] R.T.R. 183, C.A.; *McGarry* v. *Chief Constable of Bedfordshire* [1983] R.T.R. 172, D.C.; *Riddell* v. *MacNeill*, 1983 S.C.C.R. 26; *Haime* v. *Walklett* [1983] Crim.L.R. 556; [1983] R.T.R. 512, D.C.; *Donnelly* v. *Shotton*, 1983 S.L.T. 657; *R.* v. *Farnes* [1983] R.T.R. 441, D.C.; *R.* v. *McLaren* [1984] R.T.R. 126, C.A.; *Porter* v. *Manning, The Times*, March 23, 1984, D.C.; *Bolliston* v. *Gibbons, The Times*, March 31, 1984, D.C.; *Hughes* v. *Challes* [1984] R.T.R. 283, D.C.; *Orttewell* v. *Allan*, 1984 S.C.C.R. 208; *White* v. *Metropolitan Police Comr.* [1984] Crim.L.R. 687, Snaresbrook Crown Court; *Vaughan* v. *Dunn* [1984] R.T.R. 376, D.C.; *Lodwick* v. *Brow* [1984] R.T.R. 394, D.C.; *R.* v. *Lazzari* (1984) 6 Cr.App.R.(S.) 83, C.A.; *R.* v. *Sandwell* [1985] R.T.R. 45, C.A.; *Smith* v. *Nixon*, 1985 S.L.T. 192; *Pridige* v. *Gant* [1985] R.T.R. 196, D.C.; *Thompson* v. *Diamond* [1985] R.T.R. 316, D.C.; *Redmond* v. *Parry* [1986] R.T.R. 146, D.C.; *Chatters* v. *Burke* [1986] 3 All E.R. 168, D.C.; *McLean* v. *Annan*, 1986 S.C.C.R. 52; *Harvie* v. *Cardle*, 1986 S.C.C.R. 41; *Denneny* v. *Harding* [1986] R.T.R. 350, D.C.; *Sutch* v. *Crown Prosecution Service*, January 30, 1987; H.H. Judge Compton; Wood Green Crown Ct.; *Tudhope* v. *O'Kane*, 1986 S.C.C.R. 538; *Grix* v. *Chief Constable of Kent* [1987] R.T.R. 193, D.C.; *Watson* v. *Hamilton*, 1988 S.L.T. 316; *Lamb* v. *Heywood*, 1988 S.C.C.R. 42; *Scott* v. *Hamilton*, 1988 S.C.C.R. 262.

s. 93, amended: 1988, c.33, s.68.

ss. 93, 95, see *R.* v. *Bentham* [1982] R.T.R. 357, C.A.; *R.* v. *Wintour* (Note) [1982] R.T.R. 361, C.A.

s. 94, see *Taylor* v. *Comr. of Police of the Metropolis* [1987] R.T.R. 118, D.C.

s. 95, see *R.* v. *Lobley* (1974) 59 Cr.App.R. 63, C.A.; *Damer* v. *Davison* [1976] R.T.R. 45, D.C.; *Ullah* v. *Luckhurst* [1977] R.T.R. 401, D.C.

s. 96, see *R.* v. *Southend-on-Sea Justices, ex p. Sharp* [1980] R.T.R. 25, D.C.; *G. (A Minor)* v. *Jarrett* [1981] R.T.R. 186, D.C.; *Smith* v. *Allan*, 1985 S.L.T. 565.

s. 96, regs. 76/472, 1076, 1764; 80/1734; 81/952; 84/274; 87/1378.

s. 98, see *Scott* v. *Jelf* [1974] R.T.R. 256, D.C.

s. 99, see *Scott* v. *Jelf* [1974] R.T.R. 256, D.C.; *R.* v. *MacDonagh* [1974] 2 W.L.R. 529; [1974] 2 All E.R. 257, C.A.; *R.* v. *Lambert* [1974]

1972—cont.

20. Road Traffic Act 1972—cont.

R.T.R. 244, C.A.; *R.* v. *Miller* [1975] 1 W.L.R. 1222; [1975] 2 All E.R. 974, C.A.; *R.* v. *Shepperd* [1975] R.T.R. 497, C.A.; *Herron* v. *Nelson,* 1976 S.L.T.(Sh.Ct.) 59; *Mitchell* v. *Dean,* 1979 S.L.T.(Notes) 12; *Boustead* v. *MacLeod,* 1979 S.L.T.(Notes) 48; *R.* v. *Bonner* [1980] R.T.R. 187, C.A.; *McQuaid* v. *Anderton* [1980] R.T.R. 371, D.C.; *R.* v. *Redbridge JJ., ex p. Sainty* [1981] R.T.R. 13, D.C.; *Caise* v. *Wright; Fox* v. *Wright* [1981] R.T.R. 49, D.C.; *Robertson* v. *Aitchison* 1981 S.L.T.(Notes) 127; *G. (A Minor)* v. *Jarrett* [1981] R.T.R. 186, D.C.; *Andrews* v. *McLeod,* 1982 S.L.T. 456; *Moffat* v. *Smith,* 1983 S.C.C.R. 392; *R.* v. *Murray (Gerrard)* [1984] R.T.R. 203, C.A.; *Smith* v. *Allan,* 1985 S.L.T. 565; *R.* v. *Sandwell* [1985] R.T.R. 45, C.A.; *Lang* v. *Hindhaugh* [1986] R.T.R. 271, D.C.; *McKenzie* v. *Lockhart,* 1986 S.C.C.R. 663.

s. 100, repealed in pt.: 1988, c.33, sch.16.

s. 101, see *Nicholson* v. *Brown* [1974] R.T.R. 177, D.C.; *Dyson* v. *Ellison* [1975] 1 All E.R. 276, D.C.; *Pirie* v. *Ricard,* 1976 S.L.T.(Sh.Ct.) 59; *Hawkins* v. *Roots; Hawkins* v. *Smith* [1976] R.T.R. 49, D.C.; *Bradburn* v. *Richards* [1976] R.T.R. 275, D.C.; *Jones* v. *Nicks* [1977] R.T.R. 72, D.C.; *Ullah* v. *Luckhurst* [1977] R.T.R. 401, D.C.; *Smith* v. *Peaston,* 1977 J.C. 81; *Urry* v. *Gibb,* 1979 S.L.T.(Notes) 19; *Tudhope* v. *Birbeck,* 1979 S.L.T.(Notes) 47; *Graham* v. *Annan,* High Court of Justiciary, October 9 1979; *MacNab* v. *Feeney,* 1980 S.L.T. (Notes) 52; *Barnett* v. *French* [1981] 1 W.L.R. 848; [1981] R.T.R. 173, D.C.; *Barnes* v. *Gevaux* [1981] R.T.R. 236, D.C.; *Jones* v. *Ridley* [1981] R.T.R. 341, D.C.; *Soanes* v. *Ahlers* [1981] R.T.R. 337, D.C.; *Marks* v. *West Midlands Police* [1981] R.T.R. 471, D.C.; *Burgess* v. *West* [1982] R.T.R. 269, D.C.; *Keane* v. *Perrie,* 1983 S.L.T. 63; *R.* v. *Kent, The Times,* May 13, 1983, C.A.; *Donnelly* v. *Shotton,* 1983 S.L.T. 657; *Miller* v. *Allan,* 1984 S.L.T. 280; *Anderton* v. *Allan,* 1985 S.C.C.R. 262; *Johnston* v. *Over* [1985] R.T.R. 240, D.C.; *R.* v. *Preston* [1986] R.T.R. 136, C.A.; *Simpson* v. *Vant* [1986] R.T.R. 247, D.C.; *Sutch* v. *Crown Prosecution Service,* January 30, 1987; H.H. Judge Compton; Wood Green Crown Ct.; *Chief Constable of West Mercia Police* v. *Williams* [1987] R.T.R. 188, D.C.; *Barnett* v. *Fieldhouse* [1987] R.T.R. 266, D.C.; *Mawson* v. *Oxford. sub nom. Mawson* v. *Chief Constable of Merseyside* [1987] R.T.R. 398, D.C.

s. 101, regs. 75/1471.

s. 105, see *Barnes* v. *Gevaux* [1981] R.T.R. 236, D.C.; *R.* v. *Kent, The Times,* May 13, 1983, C.A.

s. 107, regs. 75/521, 1471, 2037; 76/472, 555, 1076, 1764; 77/871; 78/697, 1109; 79/1412; 80/180, 1734; 81/952, 1128; 82/99, 230, 423, 937; 84/274, 737; 85/1161; 86/748; 87/560, 1378, 88/965, 1062.

s. 108, regs. 76/1076; 81/952; 82/230; 87/1378.

1972—cont.

20. Road Traffic Act 1972—cont.

s. 110, regs. 76/555; orders 84/672; 85/65, 1461.

s. 112, see *McPhail* v. *Allan and Dey,* 1980 S.L.T.(Sh.Ct.) 136; *Anderton* v. *Frost* [1934] R.T.R. 106, D.C.

s. 114, see *North West Traffic Area Licensing Authority* v. *Brady* [1981] R.T.R. 265, C.A.

s. 114, regs. 75/1731; 76/473; 77/309; 83/1232; 84/1925.

s. 115, see *McGowan* v. *Scottish Traffic Area Licensing Authority,* 1976 S.L.T. (Sh.Ct.) 26; *Warrender* v. *Scottish Traffic Area Licensing Authority,* 1976 S.L.T.(Sh.Ct.) 76.

s. 115, regs. 75/1731; 77/309; 83/1232.

ss. 115, 116, see *Bennington* v. *Peter* [1984] R.T.R. 383, Woolf J.

s. 117, see *R.* v. *Gormley* [1973] R.T.R. 483, C.A.

s. 118, see *Crawford* v. *Scottish Traffic Area Licensing Authority,* 1974 S.L.T. (Sh.Ct.) 11; *McGowan* v. *Scottish Traffic Area Licensing Authority,* 1976 S.L.T.(Sh.Ct.) 26; *Bennington* v. *Peter* [1984] R.T.R. 383, Woolf J.

s. 119, regs. 73/1212, 1685; 74/1492, 75/1731; 76/473, 1075; 77/309, 2714; 78/669; 80/1733, 1821; 81/631, 1127; 82/429, 1174; 83/1232; 84/98, 1925; 85/832; 86/752, 868; 88/959, 1101.

s. 120, regs. 75/1731; 77/309; 78/669; 80/1821; 82/1174; 84/98; 85/832; 86/868; 88/1101.

s. 121. regs. 75/1731; 76/473; 77/309.

s. 123, see *Anderton* v. *Frost* [1983] Crim.L.R. 553; [1984] R.T.R. 106, D.C.

s. 124, regs. 75/1731; 76/473; 77/309; 78/669; 80/1821; 81/1127; 82/429, 1174; 84/98, 1925; 85/832, 86/868; 88/959, 1101.

s. 125, regs. 77/1309.

s. 126, regs. 86/1338.

s. 128, regs. 73/2013; 76/1077; 77/1043; 78/1316; 82/1206; 84/1834; 85/577.

s. 129, regs. 76/1077; 77/1043; 78/1316; 82/1206.

s. 131, regs. 76/1077; 77/1043; 82/1206; 84/1834; 85/577; 86/882, 1338.

s. 133, regs. 77/1043; 78/1316; 82/1206; 84/1834; 85/577.

ss. 134, 135, regs. 77/1043.

s. 135, regs. 86/882, 1338.

s. 142, regs. 73/2013; 77/1043; 78/1316; 82/1206; 84/1834, 85/577.

s. 143, see *Davey* v. *Towle* [1973] R.T.R. 328; *Newbury* v. *Davis* [1974] R.T.R. 367, D.C.; *Balfour Beatty & Co.* v. *Grindey (Note)* [1975] R.T.R. 156, D.C.; *Baugh* v. *Crago* [1975] R.T.R. 453, D.C.; *Milne* v. *Whaley,* 1975 S.L.T.(Notes) 75; *Tudhope* v. *Every,* 1976 J.C. 42, High Ct. of Justiciary; *Police* v. *Hepper,* May 23, 1978, Deputy Judge Raw, Knightsbridge Crown Ct.; *Adams* v. *Dunne* [1978] R.T.R. 281. D.C.; *Milne* v. *Whaley* [1978] Crim.L.R. 695, High Ct. of Justiciary; *Mitchell* v. *Dean,* 1979 S.L.T.(Notes) 12; *Boustead* v. *MacLeod,* 1979 S.L.T.(Notes) 48; *Lockhart* v. *Smith,* 1979 S.L.T.(Sh.Ct.) 52; *Graham* v. *Annan,* High Court of Justiciary, October 9,

1972—cont.

20. Road Traffic Act 1972—cont.

1979; *Leathley* v. *Tatton* [1980] R.T.R. 21, D.C.; *Ferrymasters* v. *Adams* [1980] R.T.R. 139, D.C.; *Boldizsar* v. *Knight* [1980] Crim.L.R. 653, D.C.; *Bennett* v. *Richardson* [1980] R.T.R. 358, D.C.; *Sands* v. *O'Connell* [1980] R.T.R. 42, D.C.; *R.* v. *Coventry Magistrates' Court, ex p. Wilson* [1982] R.T.R. 177. D.C.; *B (A Minor)* v. *Knight* [1981] R.T.R. 136, D.C.; *Thomson* v. *Lodwick* [1983] R.T.R. 76, D.C.; *Gardner* v. *Moore* [1984] 2 W.L.R. 714, H.L.; *Reid* v. *McLeod,*1984 S.C.C.R. 333; *Cooper* v. *Motor Insurers' Bureau* [1985] 2 W.L.R. 248, C.A.; *Johnston* v. *Over* [1985] R.T.R. 240, D.C.; *Thomas* v. *Hooper* [1986] R.T.R. 1, D.C.; *MacDonald* v. *MacGillivray,* 1986 S.C.C.R. 28; *Chief Constable of Avon and Somerset Constabulary* v. *Jest* [1986] R.T.R. 372, D.C.; *Dickson* v. *Valentine,* 1988 S.C.C.R. 325.

ss. 143, 144, see *Jones* v. *Chief Constable of Bedfordshire* [1987] Crim.L.R. 502; [1987] R.T.R 332, D.C.

s. 144, amended: 1988, c.4, sch.6.

s. 145, see *Ladd* v. *Jones* [1975] R.T.R. 67; *Gardner* v. *Moore* [1984] 2 W.L.R. 714, H.L.; *Cooper* v. *Motor Insurers' Bureau* [1985] 2 W.L.R. 248, C.A.

s. 147, regs. 81/1567.

s. 148, see *Gregory* v. *Kelly* [1978] R.T.R. 426, Kenneth Jones J.; *Winnick* v. *Dick,* 1984 S.L.T. 185.

s. 149, see *Doherty* v. *Norwich Union Fire Insurance Society,* 1974 S.L.T.(Notes) 37.

s. 157, regs. 74/791, 2186; 77/895; 81/1567.

s. 159, see *Smith* v. *Peaston,* 1977 J.C. 81; *Beard* v. *Wood* [1980] R.T.R. 454, D.C.; *Winter* v. *Barlow* [1980] R.T.R. 209, D.C.; *Steel* v. *Goacher* [1983] R.T.R. 98, C.A.; *Keane* v. *McSkimming,* 1983 S.C.C.R. 220; *Lodwick* v. *Sanders* [1985] 1 W.L.R. 382, D.C; *Gatens* v. *Wilson,* 1985 S.C.C.R. 47; *Chief Constable of Gwent* v. *Dash* [1986] R.T.R. 41, D.C.; *Sanders* v. *Lodwick, The Times,* May 19, 1988, D.C.

s. 160, regs. 78/1180.

s. 161, see *Boyce* v. *Absalom* [1974] R.T.R. 248, D.C.; *Sparks* v. *Worthington* [1986] R.T.R. 64, C.A.

s. 162, see *Davey* v. *Towle* [1973] R.T.R. 328; *Boyce* v. *Absalom* [1974] R.T.R. 248, D.C.; *Smith* v. *Peaston,* 1977 J.C. 81.

s. 162, regs. 73/1821; 74/792, 2187.

s. 166, see *Wisdom* v. *MacDonald* [1983] R.T.R. 186, D.C.

s. 168, see *Jacob* v. *Garland* [1974] R.T.R. 40, D.C.; *Hunter* v. *Mann* [1974] 2 W.L.R. 742; [1974] 2 All E.R. 414, D.C.; *Pamplin* v. *Gorman* [1980] R.T.R. 54, D.C.; *McNaughton* v. *Buchan,* 1980 S.L.T.(Notes) 100; *Galt* v. *Goodsir,* S.L.T. 94; *Blake* v. *Charles Sullivan Cars, The Times,* June 26, 1986, D.C.; *Clarke* v. *Allan,* 1987 S.C.C.R. 333; *Duncan* v. *MacGillivray,* 1989 S.L.T. 48.

s. 169, see *Holloway* v. *Brown* [1978] R.T.R. 537, D.C.; *McColl* v. *Skeen,* 1980 S.L.T.(Notes) 53; *R.* v. *Pilditch* [1981] R.T.R. 303, C.A.; *R.* v. *Howe* [1982] R.T.R. 45, C.A.

1972—cont.

20. Road Traffic Act 1972—cont.

s. 171, see *Essendon Engineering Co.* v. *Maile* [1982] R.T.R. 260, D.C.

s. 172, regs. 83/910; 86/1078; 87/1326.

s. 173, see *Offen* v. *Ranson* [1980] R.T.R. 484, D.C.

s. 175, see *Barclay* v. *Douglas,* 1983 S.C.C.R. 224; *Ashcroft's Curator Bonis* v. *Stewart* (O.H.) 1988 S.L.T. 163.

s. 176, see *McColl* v. *Skeen,* 1980 S.L.T. (Notes) 53; *Valentine* v. *Mackie,* 1980 S.L.T.(Sh.Ct.) 122; *Robertson* v. *Aitchison,* 1981 S.L.T.(Notes) 127; *Manion* v. *Smith,* 1989 S.L.T. 69.

s. 177, see *R.* v. *Ball* [1974] R.T.R. 296, C.A.; *Hawkins* v. *Holmes* [1974] R.T.R. 436, D.C.; *Sands* v. *O'Connell* [1980] R.T.R. 42, D.C.; *R.* v. *Reading JJ., ex p. Bendall* [1982] R.T.R 30, D.C.; *R.* v. *Page* [1981] R.T.R. 132, C.A.; *R.* v. *McLaren* [1984] R.T.R. 126, C.A.; *Bentley* v. *Mullen* [1986] R.T.R. 7, D.C.

s. 179, see *McGlynn* v. *Stewart,* 1974 S.L.T. 230; *Haughton* v. *Harrison* [1976] Crim.L.R. 141; [1976] R.T.R. 208, D.C.; *Metropolitan Police* v. *Scarlett* [1978] Crim.L.R. 234, Inner London Crown Court; *R.* v. *Okike* [1978] R.T.R. 489, C.A.; *Shield* v. *Crighton* (Note) [1978] R.T.R. 494, C.A.; *Gibson* v. *Dalton* [1980] R.T.R. 410, D.C.; *R.* v. *Stacey,* [1982] R.T.R. 20, C.A.; *Bentley* v. *Dickinson* [1983] Crim.L.R. 403; [1983] R.T.R. 356, D.C.; *Sage* v. *Townsend, The Times,* May 27, 1986, D.C.

s. 182, see *Taylor* v. *Comr. of Police of the Metropolis, The Times,* November 3, 1986, D.C.

s. 188, see *Barnett* v. *French* [1981] 1 W.L.R. 848; [1981] R.T.R. 173, D.C.

s. 188, regs. 77/1309.

s. 190, see *Tudhope* v. *Every,* 1976 J.C. 42, High Ct. of Justiciary; *McEachran* v. *Hurst* [1978] R.T.R. 462, D.C.; *Percy* v. *Smith* [1986] R.T.R. 252, D.C.; *Chief Constable of Avon and Somerset* v. *Fleming* [1987] 1 All E.R. 318, D.C.; *Reader* v. *Bunyard* (1987) 85 Cr.App.R. 185, D.C.

s. 190, regs. 81/1373.

s. 190, repealed in pt.: regs. 88/1036.

s. 191, regs. 81/1373.

s. 193, regs. 83/1168.

s. 196, see *Dunne* v. *Keane,* 1976 J.C. 39, High Ct. of Justiciary; *Deacon* v. *A. T. (A Minor)* [1976] R.T.R. 244, D.C.; *Cox* v. *White* [1976] R.T.R. 248, D.C.; *Kellett* v. *Daisy* [1977] R.T.R. 396, D.C.; *Lock* v. *Leatherdale* [1979] R.T.R. 201, D.C.; *Adams* v. *Met. Police Comr.; Aberdeen Park Maintenance Co. (Third Party)* [1980] R.T.R. 289, D.C.; *Oxford* v. *Austin* [1981] R.T.R. 416, D.C.; *R.* v. *Inner London JJ., ex p. Wandsworth London Borough Council,* [1983] R.T.R. 425, D.C.; *R.* v. *Murray (Gerrard)* [1984] R.T.R. 203, C.A.; *Lang* v. *Hindhaugh* [1986] R.T.R. 271, D.C.

s. 199, see *R.* v. *Aylesbury Crown Court, ex p. Cholat* [1976] Crim.L.R. 635, D.C.

CAP.

1972—cont.

20. Road Traffic Act 1972—*cont.*
s. 199, regs. 75/528, 2037, 2111; 76/242, 247, 472, 473, 555, 1075, 1507, 1657, 2155; 77/129, 154, 790–792, 809, 871, 895, 1400, 1560, 1639; 78/481, 669, 697, 867, 1017, 1018, 1109, 1111, 1180, 1237, 1261, 1262, 1313, 1317, 1318, 1574, 1810, 1870; 79/439, 803, 843, 1215, 1412; 80/139, 140, 180, 222, 225, 287, 616, 880, 1855; 81/261, 374, 696, 952, 1127, 1330, 1340, 1534, 1567, 1619, 1663, 1688, 1732; 82/20, 423, 429, 638, 783, 937, 1057, 1058, 1132, 1174, 1223, 1271, 1272, 1342, 1422, 1477, 1478, 1482–1484; 83/471, 910, 1168, 1434, 1859; 84/178, 195, 679, 697, 727, 737, 748, 812–817, 981, 1024, 1126, 1401, 1402, 1404, 1543, 1711, 1761, 1809; 85/45, 46, 91, 113, 713, 730, 832, 834, 1161, 1363, 1525, 1651, 1656; 86/371; 87/1149; directions 81/859.
s. 199, amended: 1988, c.23, s.1.
s. 203, see *Hill* v. *Howell* [1976] R.T.R. 270, D.C.; *Westwater* v. *Milton*, 1980 S.L.T.(Sh.Ct.) 63; *R.* v. *Petersfield JJ., ex p. Levy* [1981] R.T.R. 204, D.C.; *Kent* v. *Stamps* [1982] R.T.R. 273, D.C.; *Burton* v. *Gilbert* [1984] R.T.R. 162, D.C.; *Spittle* v. *Kent County Constabulary* [1986] R.T.R. 142, C.A.
s. 204, order 73/193.
sch. 4, see *R* v. *Sharman* [1974] R.T.R. 213, C.A.; *R.* v. *Mills* [1974] R.T.R. 215, C.A.; *R.* v. *Shaw* [1974] R.T.R. 225, C.A.; *R.* v. *Brown (John)* [1974] R.T.R. 377, C.A.; *Farrell* v. *Moir*, 1974 S.L.T.(Sh.Ct.) 89; *McLeod* v. *Scoular*, 1974 S.L.T.(Notes) 44; *R.* v. *Newton* [1974] R.T.R. 451, D.C.; *Bullen* v. *Keay* [1974] R.T.R. 559; *R.* v. *Dawtrey* [1975] R.T.R. 101, C.A.; *R.* v. *Kwame* [1975] R.T.R. 106, C.A.; *Adams* v. *Bradley* [1975] R.T.R. 233, D.C.; *R.* v. *Reed (Paul)* [1975] R.T.R. 313, C.A.; *R.* v. *Earle* [1976] R.T.R. 33, C.A.; *Damer* v. *Davison* [1976] R.T.R. 45, D.C.; *Hill* v. *Howell* [1976] R.T.R. 270, D.C.; *Comr. of Police of the Metropolis* v. *Curran* [1976] 1 All E.R. 162, H.L.; *Bradburn* v. *Richards* [1976] R.T.R. 275, D.C.; *R.* v. *McIntyre* [1976] R.T.R. 330, C.A.; *R.* v. *Marshall* [1976] R.T.R 483, C.A.; *Evans* v. *Bray* [1977] R.T.R. 24, D.C.; *Jones* v. *Nicks* [1977] R.T.R. 72, D.C.; *R.* v. *Mills* [1977] R.T.R. 188, C.A.; *R.* v. *Jones* [1977] R.T.R. 385, C.A.; *Ullah* v. *Luckhurst* [1977] Crim.L.R. 295; [1977] R.T.R. 401, D.C.; *Anderton* v. *Anderton* [1977] R.T.R. 424, C.A.; *R.* v. *Krebbs* [1977] R.T.R. 406, C.A.; *R.* v. *Miller* [1978] R.T.R. 98, C.A.; *R.* v. *Kennedy* [1978] R.T.R. 418, C.A.; *Courtman* v. *Masterson* [1978] R.T.R. 457, D.C.; *R.* v. *Yarnold* [1978] R.T.R. 526, C.A.; *R.* v. *Wedlake* [1978] R.T.R. 529, C.A.; *R.* v. *Okike* [1978] R.T.R. 489, C.A.; *R.* v. *Coventry JJ., ex p. Sayers* [1979] R.T.R. 22, D.C.; *Powell* v. *Gliha* [1979] R.T.R. 126, D.C.; *R.* v. *Mulroy* [1979] R.T.R. 214, C.A.; *Killington* v. *Butcher* [1979] Crim.L.R. 458, D.C.; *Park* v. *Hicks* [1979] R.T.R. 259, D.C.; *R.* v. *O'Connor* [1979] R.T.R. 467, C.A.; *R.* v. *Fenwick* [1979] R.T.R. 506, C.A.; *R.* v. *Cunningham* [1979] R.T.R. 465, C.A.; *Webster* v. *Wall* [1980]

CAP.

1972—cont.

20. Road Traffic Act 1972—*cont.*
Crim.L.R. 186, D.C.; *R.* v. *Bonner* [1980] R.T.R. 187, C.A.; *Barnett* v. *French* [1981] 1 W.L.R. 848; [1981] R.T.R. 173, D.C.; *Barnes* v. *Gevaux* [1981] R.T.R. 236, D.C.; *Jones* v. *Ridley* [1981] R.T.R. 341, D.C.; *Soanes* v. *Ahlers* [1981] R.T.R. 337, D.C.; *Stewart* v. *Aitchison*, 1981 S.C.C.R. 107; *De Munthe* v. *Stewart* (1982) R.T.R. 27, D.C.; *R.* v. *Reading JJ., ex p. Randall* [1982] R.T.R. 30, D.C.; *R.* v. *Page* [1981] R.T.R. 132, C.A.; *R.* v. *Kent, The Times*, May 13, 1983, C.A.; *R.* v. *Macclesfield JJ., ex p. Jones* [1983] R.T.R. 143, D.C.; *R.* v. *Cooper (Frederick)* [1983] R.T.R. 183, C.A.; *McGarry* v. *Chief Constable of Bedfordshire* [1983] R.T.R. 172, D.C.; *Bentley* v. *Rickinson* [1983] R.T.R. 356, D.C.; *Haime* v. *Walklett* [1983] R.T.R. 512, D.C.; *R.* v. *McLaren* [1984] R.T.R. 126, C.A.; *Hughes* v. *Challes* [1984] R.T.R. 283, C.A.; *Vaughan* v. *Dunn* [1984] R.T.R. 376, D.C.; *Lodwick* v. *Brow* [1984] R.T.R. 394, D.C.; *R.* v. *Krawec* [1985] R.T.R. 1, C.A.; *R.* v. *Sandwell* [1985] R.T.R 45. C.A.; *McLellan* v. *Tudhope*, 1984 S.C.C.R. 397; *Pridige* v. *Gant* [1985] R.T.R. 196, D.C.; *Johnston* v. *Over* [1985] R.T.R. 240, D.C.; *Thompson* v. *Diamond* [1985] R.T.R. 316, D.C.; *Cardle* v. *Campbell*, 1985 S.C.C.R. 309; *Bentley* v. *Mullen* [1986] R.T.R. 7, D.C.; *R.* v. *Preston* [1986] R.T.R. 136, C.A.; *Redmond* v. *Parry* [1986] R.T.R. 146, D.C.; *Simpson* v. *Vant* [1986] Crim.L.R. 473; [1986] R.T.R. 247, D.C.; *Aird* v. *Valentine*, 1986 S.C.C.R. 353; *Denneny* v. *Harding* [1986] R.T.R. 350, D.C.; *Sutch* v. *Crown Prosecution Service*, January 30, 1987; H.H. Judge Compton; Wood Green Crown Ct.; *Tudhope* v. *O'Kane*, 1986 S.C.C.R. 538; *Emms* v. *Lockhart*, 1988 S.L.T. 222; *Lamb* v. *Heywood*, 1988 S.C.C.R. 42; *Scott* v. *Hamilton*, 1988 S.C.C.R. 262; *D.P.P.* v. *White* [1988] R.T.R. 267, D.C.
sch. 4, directions 75/1536; 81/859.
sch. 4, amended: 1988, c.23, s.1; c.33, s.37; c.39, sch.2.
sch. 5, regs. 73/1212.
sch. 10, see *R.* v. *Bentham* [1982] R.T.R. 357, C.A.; *R.* v. *Wintour* (Note) [1982] R.T.R. 361, C.A.

21. Deposit of Poisonous Waste Act 1972.
Royal Assent, March 30, 1972.
repealed: 1974, c.40, sch.4.
s. 2, amended: 1980, c.58, sch.3.
s. 3, regs. 72/1017.
s. 8, order 72/1016.

22. Northern Ireland (Temporary Provisions) Act 1972.
Royal Assent, March 30, 1972.
sch., repealed in pt.: S.L.R. 1977.

23. Consolidated Fund (No. 2) Act 1972.
Royal Assent, May 11, 1972.
repealed: 1974, c.31, s.4, sch.

24. Social Work (Scotland) Act 1972.
Royal Assent, May 11, 1972.

25. Betting and Gaming Duties Act 1972.
Royal Assent, May 11, 1972.
repealed: 1981, c.63, sch.7.

CAP.

1972—cont.

25. Betting and Gaming Duties Act 1972—cont.
s. 2, see *Customs and Excise Comrs.* v. *Hedon Alpha* [1981] 2 W.L.R. 791; [1981] 2 All E.R. 697, C.A.
s. 14, repealed: 1980, c.48, sch.20.
s. 16, regs. 80/1147.
s. 24, repealed: 1980, c.48, schs.6,20.
sch. 1, see *Customs and Excise Commissioners* v. *Guile, The Times*, November 17, 1978, Sheen J.; *Lord Advocate* v. *Mackay*, 1984 S.L.T.(Sh.Ct.) 36.
sch. 1, regs. 73/118
sch. 2, regs. 80/1147.
sch. 3, order 80/19
sch. 4, orders 78/44; 81/21.

26. Sunday Theatre Act 1972.
Royal Assent, May 11, 1972.

27. Road Traffic (Foreign Vehicles) Act 1972.
Royal Assent, May 11, 1972.
s. 1, amended: 1978, c.55, s.9, sch.3; 1982, c.49, s.10; 1988, c.54, sch.3; repealed in pt.: *ibid.*, sch.1.
s. 2, amended: 1978, c.55, s.9, sch.3; 1982, c.49, s.10, sch.5; 1988, c.54, sch.2 (prosp.), 3.
s. 3, amended: 1982, c.48, schs.3,6 (S.); repealed in pt.: 1984, c.60, sch.7.
s. 4, amended: 1980, c.34, sch.5; 1981, c.14, sch.7.
s. 5, repealed: 1974, c.50, sch.7.
s. 6, repealed: 1973, c.36, sch.6.
s. 7, amended: 1978, c.55, s.9, sch.3; 1980, c.34, sch.5; 1981, c.14, sch.7; 1982, c.49, sch.5; 1984, c.54, sch.9 (S.); 1988, c.54, sch.3; repealed in pt.: 1974, c.50, sch.5.
s. 8, order 72/1018
s. 8, repealed in pt.: 1973, c.36, sch.6.
sch. 1, amended: regs. 77/777; 1980, c.34, sch.5; 1981, c.14, sch.7; 1988, c.54, sch.3.
sch. 2, amended: 1972, c.68, sch.4; regs. 77/777; 1988, c.54, sch.3; repealed in pt.: *ibid.*, sch.1.

28. Employment Medical Advisory Service Act 1972.
Royal Assent, May 11, 1972.
s. 1, amended: 1972, c.58, sch.6; 1973, c.32, sch.4.
ss. 1, 5, amended: 1973, c.50, schs.3, 4.
ss. 1, 6, sch. 1, repealed: 1974, c.37, s.60, sch.10.
s. 7, repealed: regs. 74/1941.
s. 8, order 73/36.
s. 8, sch. 2, amended: regs.74/1941.

29. Harbours, Piers and Ferries (Scotland) Act 1972.
Royal Assent, June 12, 1972.

30. Civil Evidence Act 1972.
Royal Assent, June 12, 1972.
see *Khan* v. *Edwards* [1977] T.R. 143, Walton J.; *R.* v. *Wood Green Crown Court, ex p. P.* (1982) 4 F.L.R. 206, McCullough J.; *Lego System Aktieselskab* v. *Lego m. Lemelstrich* [1983] F.S.R. 155, Falconer J.
s. 2, amended: 1980, c.43, sch.7; 1984, c.28, sch.2; repealed in pt.: 1981, c.54, sch.7.
s. 6, orders 74/280, 1137.

CAP.

1972—cont.

31. Sound Broadcasting Act 1972.
Royal Assent, June 12, 1972.
repealed: 1973, c.19, sch.3.
s. 13, orders 73/1087, 1088.

32. Dramatic and Musical Performers Protection Act 1972.
Royal Assent, June 29, 1972.
repealed: 1988, c.48, sch.8.
see *ex p. Island Records* [1978] 3 W.L.R. 23, C.A.; *Shelley* v. *Cunane* (1983) 133 New L.J. 377, Harriman J.

33. Carriage by Railway Act 1972.
Royal Assent, June 29, 1972.
repealed: 1983, c.14, sch.3.
ss. 1, 13, order 72/1579.
s. 2, order 72/1580.
ss. 2, 11, orders 73/2088; 75/1035.
s. 3, repealed in pt. (S.): 1976, c.13, sch.2.
s. 9, order 74/1250.

34. Trade Descriptions Act 1972.
Royal Assent, June 29, 1972.
repealed: 1987, c.43, s.48, sch.5.
s. 1, see *R.* v. *Thomson Holidays* [1974] 2 W.L.R. 371; [1974] 1 All E.R. 823, C.A.
s. 1, directions 72/1886, 1887; 73/50, 51, 1027, 2031, 2177; 74/1046, 2032; 75/949, 2047; 76/160, 260; 78/1153.

35. Defective Premises Act 1972.
Royal Assent, June 29, 1972.
s. 1, see *Alexander* v. *Mercouris* [1979] 1 W.L.R. 1270, C.A.
s. 2, orders 73/1843; 75/1462; 77/642; 79/381.
s. 4, see *Smith* v. *Bradford Metropolitan Council* (1982) 44 P. & C.R. 171, C.A.; *McDonagh* v. *Kent Area Health Authority* (1984) 134 New L.J. 567, Beldam J.

36. National Insurance (Amendment) Act 1972.
Royal Assent, June 29, 1972.
repealed: 1973, c.38, sch.28.
s. 3, order 72/1176.

37. Salmon and Freshwater Fisheries Act 1972.
Royal Assent, June 29, 1972.
repealed: 1975, c.51, sch.5.

38. Matrimonial Proceedings (Polygamous Marriages) Act 1972.
Royal Assent, June 29, 1972.
ss. 1, 4, repealed: 1973, c.18, sch.3.
s. 2, see *Poon* v. *Tan* (1973) 4 Fam.Law 161, C.A.
s. 2, amended: 1983, c.12, sch.1; 1985, c.37, sch 1 (S.); repealed in pt.: 1984, c.15, sch.1; S.L.R. 1986.
ss. 3, 5, repealed in pt.: order 78/1045.
s. 5, repealed in pt.: 1973, c.36, sch.6.

39. Police Act 1972.
Royal Assent, June 29, 1972.

40. Overseas Investment and Export Guarantees Act 1972.
Royal Assent, June 29, 1972.
repealed: 1980, c.63, sch.2.

41. Finance Act 1972.
Royal Assent, July 27, 1972.
Commencement order: 82/87.
see *Commissioners of Customs and Excise* v. *Holvey, The Times*, November 11, 1977, Peter Pain J.

1972—cont.

41. Finance Act 1972—*cont.*
regs. 72/1147; 73/244.
Pt. I (ss. 1–51), repealed: 1983, c.55, sch.11.
s. 1, see *Carlton Lodge Club* v. *Customs and Excise Commissioners* [1974] 3 All E.R. 798, D.C.; *Customs and Excise Comrs.* v. *Oliver* [1980] 1 All E.R. 353, Griffiths J.
s. 2, see *Comrs. of Customs and Excise* v. *Automobile Association* [1974] 1 All E.R. 1257, D.C.; *Commissioners of Customs and Excise* v. *Morrison's Academy Boarding Houses Association,* 1977 S.L.T. 197, First Division; *R.H.M. Bakeries (Northern)* v. *Customs and Excise Commissioners* [1979] S.T.C. 72, Neill J.; *Church of Scientology of California* v. *Customs and Excise Commissioners* [1979] S.T.C. 297, Neill J., *Customs and Excise Comrs.* v. *Royal Exchange Theatre Trust* [1979] S.T.C. 728, Neill J.; *Customs and Excise Comrs.* v. *Oliver* [1980] 1 All E.R. 353, Griffiths J.; *Customs and Excise Comrs.* v. *Lord Fisher* [1981] 2 All E.R. 147, Gibson J.; *Three H. Aircraft Hire (A Firm)* v. *Customs and Excise Comrs.* [1982] S.T.C. 653, Webster J.; *Lord Advocate* v. *Largs Golf Club* [1985] S.T.C. 226, Ct. of Session.
s. 3, see *C. & E. Comrs.* v. *British Railways Bd.* [1976] 3 All E.R. 100, C.A.; *Ashtree Holdings* v. *Customs and Excise Comrs.* [1979] S.T.C. 818, Neill J.; *Customs and Excise Comrs.* v. *Westbury Developments (Worthing)* [1981] S.T.C. 72, C.A.; *Manchester Ship Canal Co.* v. *Customs and Excise Comrs.* [1982] S.T.C. 351, Hodgson J.; *Celtic Football and Athletic Club* v. *Comrs. of Customs and Excise,* First Division, May 19, 1983.
s. 3, regs. 74/328, 329, 1379, 1882; 75/616, 745, 2004, 2006, 2204; 76/1234; 77/1759; orders 72/1165–1167; 75/624; 77/1795, 1796; 78/532, 972, 819; 79/1648; 80/442, 1536; 81/1080, 1530, 1740; 82/1471; 83/1099.
s. 4, see *Customs and Excise Comrs.* v. *C. & A. Modes* [1979] S.T.C. 433, Drake J.; *Celtic Football and Athletic Club* v. *Comrs. of Customs and Excise,* First Division, May 19, 1983.
s. 4, regs. 77/1759; 78/532; 80/1536; 83/295, 475.
s. 5, see *Comrs. of Customs and Excise* v. *Automobile Association* [1974] 1 All E.R. 1257, D.C.; *National Transit Insurance Co.* v. *Customs and Excise Comrs.* [1975] 1 All E.R. 303, D.C.; *Customs and Excise Comrs.* v. *Thorn Electrical Industries* [1975] 3 All E.R. 881, H.L.; *Customs and Excise Comrs.* v. *Tilling Management Services* [1979] S.T.C. 365, Neill J.; *Tynewydd Labour Working Men's Club and Institute* v. *Customs and Excise Comrs.* [1979] S.T.C. 570, Forbes J.; *Customs and Excise Comrs.* v. *Oliver* [1980] 1 All E.R. 353, Griffiths J.
s. 5, orders 72/1170; 73/325, 326, 335, 336; 75/2005, 2007; regs. 80/1537.
s. 6, see *National Coal Board* v. *Customs and Excise Comrs.* [1982] S.T.C. 863, Woolf J.

1972—cont.

41. Finance Act 1972—*cont.*
s. 6, orders 72/1168, 1169; 73/388; 77/1259, 1795, 1796; 79/1648; 80/442, 1603; 81/1740.
s. 7, see *Rowe & Maw (A Firm)* v. *C. & E. Comrs.* [1975] 2 All E.R. 444, D.C.; *Customs & Excise Comrs.* v. *Thorn Electrical Industries* [1975] 3 All E.R. 881, H.L.; *Customs and Excise Comrs.* v. *Woolfold Motor Co.* [1983] S.T.C. 715, McNeil J.; *Pattni (Purshotam M.) & Sons* v. *Customs and Excise Comrs.* [1987] S.T.C. 1, Russell J.
s. 7, regs. 74/1379; 75/1275, 2204; 77/1759; 80/1536; 82/1088.
s. 8B, regs. 77/1759; 80/1536.
s. 9, see *Davies* v. *Customs and Excise Comrs.* [1975] 1 W.L.R. 204; [1975] 1 All E.R. 309, D.C.
s. 9, order 74/1224.
s. 10, see *Davies* v. *Customs and Excise Comrs.* [1975] 1 W.L.R. 204; [1975] 1 All E.R. 309, D.C.; *Customs and Excise Comrs.* v. *Scott* [1978] S.T.C. 191, D.C.; *Tynewydd Labour Working Men's Club and Institute* v. *Customs and Excise Commissioners* [1979] S.T.C. 570, Forbes J.; *Customs and Excise Commissioners* v. *Tilling Management Services* [1979] S.T.C. 365, Neill J.; *Customs and Excise Comrs.* v. *Pippa-Dee Parties* [1981] S.T.C. 495, D.C.; *Exeter Golf and Country Club* v. *Customs and Excise Comrs.* [1981] S.T.C. 211, C.A.
s. 12, see *Comrs. of Customs and Excise* v. *Blackpool Pleasure Beach Co.* [1974] 1 All E.R. 1011, D.C.; *British Railways Board* v. *Customs and Excise Comrs.* [1977] 1 W.L.R. 588, C.A.; *Customs and Excise Comrs.* v. *Scott* [1978] S.T.C. 191, D.C.; *Customs and Excise Comrs.* v. *Bushby* [1979] S.T.C. 8, Neill J.; *Henry Moss of London* v. *Customs and Excise Comrs.* [1981] S.T.C. 139; [1981] 2 All E.R. 86, C.A.; *St. Luke's Parochial Church Council, Great Crosby* v. *Customs and Excise Comrs.* (1982) 126 S.J. 710, Woolf J.; *Sharman* v. *Customs and Excise Comrs., The Times,* October 29, 1983, Webster J.
s. 12, regs. 73/1885, 2123; 74/1379; 75/2204; 77/1759; 78/972; orders 73/324, 385–387, 2151; 74/542, 821, 822, 1146, 1331, 2080; 75/128, 517, 746, 2011–2013; 76/2025, 2026, 2029; 77/1789, 1791–1793, 1849; 79/242, 244–246, 657, 1554; 80/1536; 81/1530; orders 79/1554, 1646; 80/303, 305, 440; 81/365, 1740; 82/321, 1007.
s. 13, see *Customs and Excise Comrs.* v. *Guy Butler (International)* [1975] 2 All E.R. 245, D.C.; *Trewby* v. *Customs and Excise Comrs.* [1976] 2 All E.R. 199, D.C.; *Customs and Excise Comrs.* v. *The Little Spain Club* [1979] S.T.C. 170, Neill J.; *Tynewydd Labour Working Men's Club and Institute* v. *Customs and Excise Comrs.* [1979] S.T.C. 570, Forbes J.
s. 13, orders 73/324, 2151; 74/542, 1146; 75/128, 1185, 2008, 2009; 76/2024; 77/1787, 1788, 1793, 1794, 1797, 2092; 78/1064; 80/1602, 1604, 1909; 81/1740; 82/476; 83/499, 809.

CAP.

1972—cont.

41. Finance Act 1972—cont.

s. 14, see *Customs and Excise Commissioners v. J. H. Corbitt (Numismatists)* [1980] 2 W.L.R. 653, H.L.

s. 14, orders 73/328, 329, 1308; 75/745, 2004, 2006; 77/1795, 1796; 79/1648; 80/442; 81/1741; 83/1099.

s. 15, orders 73/522, 2121; 76/2028.

s. 15A, see *Customs and Excise Comrs. v. Perry* [1983] S.T.C. 383, Woolf J.

s. 15A, regs. 75/649.

s. 16, regs. 74/1379; 75/1275, 2204; 77/1759; 79/1614; 80/1536; orders 73/327; 74/1708; 75/1491; 77/1790; 78/273; 83/499.

s. 17, regs. 74/1379; 75/2204; 80/1536.

s. 18, regs. 74/1379; 75/2204; 78/532; 80/1536.

s. 19, orders 72/1168, 1169.

s. 21, see *Customs and Excise Commissioners v. Save and Prosper Group* [1979] S.T.C. 205, Neill J.; *Re Nadler Enterprises* [1980] S.T.C. 457, Dillon J.

s. 21, orders 77/1259, 1795, 1796; 79/1648; 80/183, 442; 81/1741.

s. 22, see *Commissioners of Customs and Excise v. Glassborow* [1974] 1 All E.R. 1041, D.C.; *Customs and Excise Comrs. v. Evans (T./A The Grape Escape Wine Bar)* [1982] S.T.C. 342, D.C.

s. 23, regs. 74/1379; 75/2204; 80/1536.

s. 25, regs. 80/1536.

s. 26, orders 73/173; 75/385; 80/304; 81/338, 955.

s. 27, regs. 74/1379; 75/2204; 80/1536.

s. 29, regs. 73/293.

s. 30, see *Customs and Excise Comrs. v. J. H. Corbitt (Numismatists)* [1980] 2 W.L.R. 653, H.L.

s. 30, regs. 72/1148; 74/1379, 1876; 75/274, 616, 2204; 76/1234; 77/205; 78/972; 79/224; 80/1536; 81/663, 1080; 82/1088.

s. 31, see *Customs and Excise Commissioners v. Holvey,* (1977) 121 S.J. 776, Peter Pain J.; *S. J. Grange v. Customs and Excise Comrs.* [1979] 1 W.L.R. 239, C.A.; *Customs and Excise Comrs. v. J. H. Corbitt (Numismatists)* [1980] 2 W.L.R. 653, H.L.; *Tynewydd Labour Working Men's Club and Institute v. Customs and Excise Comrs.* [1979] S.T.C. 570, Forbes J.; *Abedin v. Customs and Excise Comrs.* [1979] S.T.C. 426, Neill J.; *Van Boeckel v. Customs and Excise Comrs.* [1981] S.T.C. 290; [1981] 2 All E.R. 505, Woolf J.; *Stephen You Seto v. Customs and Excise Comrs.* [1981] S.T.C. 698, Ct. of Session; *Customs and Excise Comrs. v. Evans (T./A The Grape Escape Wine Bar)* [1982] S.T.C. 342, D.C.; *International Language Centres v. Customs and Excise Comrs. (No. 2)* [1983] S.T.C. 394, Woolf J.; *Parekh v. Customs and Excise Comrs.* [1984] S.T.C. 284, Q.B.D.; *Comrs. of Customs and Excise v. Johnson,* Second Division, January 18, 1985; *Lord Advocate v. Johnson* [1985] S.T.C. 527, Ct. of Session.

s. 32, see *Ang v. Parrish* [1980] 1 W.L.R. 940; [1980] 2 All E.R. 790, Walton J.

CAP.

1972—cont.

41. Finance Act 1972—cont.

s. 33, see *Customs and Excise Commissioners v. Holvey* (1977) 121 S.J. 776, Peter Pain J.; *Customs and Excise Comrs. v. Wells* [1982] 1 All E.R. 920, Piers Ashworth, Q.C.; *Comrs. of Customs and Excise v. Johnson,* Second Division, January 18, 1985.

s. 33, regs. 73/1882; 74/1379; 75/2204; 78/532; 80/1536.

ss. 34, 35, see *Christodoulou v. H.M. Customs and Excise,* April 8, 1976, Inner London Crown Ct.

s. 35, see *Customs and Excise Comrs. v. A. E. Hamlin & Co.* [1984] 1 W.L.R. 509, Falconer J.

s. 35, regs. 74/1379; 75/2204; 77/1759; 78/532; 80/1536.

s. 37, see *Bulloch v. H.M. Advocate,* 1980 S.L.T.(Notes) 5; *Comrs. of Customs and Excise v. A. E. Hamlin & Co. (A Firm), The Times,* July 15, 1983, Falconer J.

s. 38, see *Christodoulou v. H.M. Customs and Excise,* April 8, 1976, Inner London Crown Ct.; *Keogh v. Gordon* [1978] 1 W.L.R. 1383, D.C.; *Grice v. Needs* [1979] 3 All E.R. 501, D.C.; *R. v. McCarthy* [1981] S.T.C. 298, C.A.; *R. v. Tonner; R. v. Evans* [1984] Crim.L.R. 618, C.A.; *R. v. Gamer; R. v. Bullen; R. v. Howard, The Times,* August 10, 1985, C.A.; *R. v. Asif* [1985] Crim.L.R. 679; (1985) 82 Cr.App.R. 123, C.A.

s. 40, see *R. v. Value Added Tax Tribunal Centre (Belfast), ex p. Customs and Excise Commissioners* [1977] S.T.C. 323, C.A.(N.I.); *Customs and Excise Commissioners v. Holvey* (1977) 121 S.J. 776, Peter Pain J.; *Tynewydd Labour Working Men's Club and Institute v. Customs and Excise Comrs.* [1979] S.T.C. 570, Forbes J.; *Abedin v. Customs and Excise Comrs.* [1979] S.T.C. 426, Neill J.; *Shahbag Restaurant v. Customs and Excise Comrs.* [1978] T.R. 467, Neill J.; *Customs and Excise Comrs. v. J. H. Corbitt (Numismatists)* [1980] 2 W.L.R. 653, H.L.; *R. v. V.A.T. Tribunal, ex p. Happer* (1982) 126 S.J. 593, Stephen Brown J.; *Customs and Excise Comrs. v. Hubbard Foundation Scotland* [1982] S.T.C. 593, Ct. of Session.

s. 41, see *Re Nadler Enterprises* [1980] S.T.C. 457, Dillon J.

s. 43, orders 73/385, 388, 1308; 74/542, 1146; 75/128, 517, 746, 1185, 2008, 2009, 2011–2013; 76/2024–2027, 2029; 77/1786–1789, 1791–1797, 1849, 2092; 78/1064; 79/242–246, 657, 819, 1554, 1646, 1648; 80/303–305, 440, 1009, 1603; 81/338, 365, 955, 1741.

s. 44, substituted: 1983, c.28, sch.9.

s. 45, see *Comrs. of Customs and Excise v. Automobile Association* [1974] 1 All E.R. 1257, D.C.; *Trewby v. Customs and Excise Comrs.* [1976] 2 All E.R. 199, D.C.; *Commissioners of Customs and Excise v. Morrison's Academy Boarding Houses Association,* 1977

CAP.

1972—cont.

41. Finance Act 1972—cont.

S.L.T. 197, First Division; *Lord Advocate* v. *Largs Golf Club* [1985] S.T.C. 226, Ct. of Session.

s. 50, orders 73/595, 1749; 74/554, 1708; 75/2158; 76/1773; 77/818; 78/273, 1621.

s. 52, repealed: 1983, c.53, sch.3.

ss. 53, 54, repealed: S.L.R. 1986.

s. 54, see *Collard (Inspector of Taxes)* v. *Mining and Industrial Holdings* [1988] S.T.C. 15, C.A.

s. 54, regs. 72/1146; 82/87.

s. 55, order 81/233.

s. 55, repealed in pt.: 1979, c.2, sch.6; c.3, sch.3.

s. 56, repealed: 1973, c.51, sch.22.

s. 57, repealed in pt.: 1979, c.4, sch.4.

s. 58, repealed: 1981, c.63, sch.7.

ss. 60, 61, repealed: 1973, c.51, sch.22.

ss. 62–66, repealed: 1988, c.1, sch.31.

s. 67, repealed in pt.: 1985, c.54, sch.27; 1988, c.1, sch.31.

s. 68, amended: *ibid.*, sch.29; repealed in pt.: 1976, c.40, s.40, sch.15.

s. 69, amended: 1988, c.1, sch.29.

s. 70, amended (S.): 1978, c.29, sch.16.

ss. 70–77, repealed: 1988, c.1, sch.31.

s. 75, see *Hendy* v. *Hadley* [1980] 2 All E.R. 554, Vinelott J.; *Walcot-Bather* v. *Golding* [1979] S.T.C. 707, Oliver J.; *Cairns* v. *MacDiarmid* [1983] S.T.C. 178, C.A.

s. 75, amended: 1974, c.30, s.19; 1976, c.40, s.49; repealed in pt.: 1974, c.30, s.19, sch.14.

s. 76, repealed: 1987, c.16, sch.16.

s. 77, see *Williamson* v. *Dalton* [1981] S.T.C. 753, Vinelott J.

s. 78, repealed: 1974, c.30, sch.14.

s. 79, see *Cheatle* v. *I.R.C.* [1982] S.T.C. 376; [1982] 1 W.L.R. 834, Nourse J.

s. 79, repealed: 1988, c.1, sch.31; c.39, s.88, sch.14.

ss. 80–95, repealed: 1988, c.1, sch.31.

s. 85, see *Ellis* v. *I.C.I. Petroleum* [1983] S.T.C. 675, Gibson J.; *Collard (Inspector of Taxes)* v. *Mining and Industrial Holdings* (1988) S.T.C. 15, C.A.

s. 86, see *Union Texas International Corp.* v. *Critchley (Inspector of Taxes), The Times,* September 10, 1988, Harman J.

s. 87, amended: 1988, c.39, s.61.

s. 93, restored in pt.: *ibid.*

s. 96, repealed: 1984, c.43, sch.23.

ss. 97–110, repealed: 1988, c.1, sch.31.

s. 98, orders 75/2191; 76/1919; 77/57, 1719; 78/282, 785–787, 1056; 79/117, 302.

s. 100, see *Collard (Inspector of Taxes)* v. *Mining & Industrial Holdings* [1988] S.T.C. 15, C.A.

s. 111, repealed in pt: 1988, c.1, sch.31.

ss. 112–119, repealed: 1979, c.14, sch.8.

ss. 120, 121, repealed: 1978, c.42, sch.13.

s. 122, order 76/2192.

s. 122, repealed: S.L.R. 1986.

s. 123, repealed: 1974, c.30, s.28, sch.14.

s. 124, repealed: 1988, c.1, sch.31.

s. 125, repealed in pt.: 1974, c.30, s.49, sch.14; 1980, c.48, sch.20.

CAP.

1972—cont.

41. Finance Act 1972—cont.

s. 128, repealed in pt.: 1978, c.42, sch.13.

s. 130, regs. 73/900.

s. 131, order 78/662.

s. 131, amended: 1976, c.40, s.59.

s. 132, repealed: 1984, c.43, sch.23; orders 73/1312; 74/91, 1842.

s. 133, repealed: 1981, c.65, sch.8.

s. 134, amended: 1988, c.1, sch.29; repealed in pt.: 1979, c.2, sch.6; c.14, sch.8.

sch. 1, see *Three H. Aircraft Hire (A Firm)* v. *Customs and Excise Comrs.* [1982] S.T.C. 653, Webster J.

sch. 1, regs. 74/1379; 75/2204; 77/1759; 80/1536; order 83/401.

schs. 1–6, repealed: 1953, c.55, sch.11.

sch. 2, see *Customs and Excise Comrs.* v. *Sooner Foods* [1983] S.T.C. 376, Forbes J.

sch. 3, see *GUS Merchandise Corp.* v. *Customs and Excise Comrs.* [1981] S.T.C. 569; [1981] 1 W.L.R. 1309, C.A.; *Elga and Aska Co.* v. *Customs and Excise Comrs.* [1983] S.T.C. 628, H.H. Judge Doby; *Customs and Excise Commissioners* v. *Technequip* [1987] S.T.C. 664, Otton J.

sch. 4, see *Comrs. of Customs and Excise* v. *Blackpool Pleasure Beach Co.* [1974] 1 All E.R. 1011, D.C.; *Barton* v. *Customs and Excise Commissioners* [1974] 1 W.L.R. 1447; [1974] 3 All E.R. 337, D.C.; *British Railways Board* v. *Customs and Excise Commissioners* [1977] 1 W.L.R. 588, C.A.; *Customs and Excise Comrs.* v. *Bushby* [1979] S.T.C. 8, Neill J.; *Customs and Excise Comrs.* v. *G. & B. Practical Management Development* [1979] S.T.C. 280, Q.B.D.; *Customs and Excise Comrs.* v. *Morrison Dunbar and Mecca* [1978] T.R. 267, Neill J.; *Customs and Excise Comrs.* v. *Johnson* [1980] S.T.C. 624, Woolf J.; *ACT Construction* v. *Customs and Excise Comrs.* [1982] 1 All E.R. 84; [1981] 1 W.L.R. 1542, H.L.; *Customs and Excise Comrs.* v. *Cope* [1981] S.T.C. 532, Sir Douglas Frank Q.C.; *Customs and Excise Comrs.* v. *Smitmit Design Centre; Customs and Excise Comrs.* v. *Sharp's Bedroom Design* [1982] S.T.C. 525, Glidewell J.; *Geoffrey E. Snushall (A Firm)* v. *Customs and Excise Comrs.* [1982] S.T.C. 537, Webster J.; *Pilley* v. *Customs and Excise Comrs.* [1982] S.T.C. 662; Stephen Brown J.; *Parochial Church Council of St. Luke's* v. *Customs and Excise Comrs.* [1982] S.T.C. 826, Woolf J.; *Customs and Excise Comrs.* v. *Campbell* [1982] S.T.C. 719, Comyn J.; *Cottage Holiday Associates* v. *Customs and Excise Comrs.* [1983] 2 W.L.R. 861, Woolf J.; *Customs and Excise Comrs.* v. *Sutton Housing Trust* [1983] S.T.C. 399, Woolf J.; *Sharman* v. *Customs and Excise Comrs.* [1983] S.T.C. 809, Q.B.D.; *Customs and Excise Comrs.* v. *Viva Gas Appliances* [1983] 1 W.L.R. 1445, H.L.; *Home Protection Co.* v. *Customs and Excise Comrs.* [1984] S.T.C. 278, D.C.; *Sutton Housing Trust* v. *Customs and Excise Comrs.* [1984] S.T.C. 352, C.A.

CAP.

1972—cont.

41. Finance Act 1972—cont.

sch. 4, orders 73/392, 2150; amended: 1977, c.36, s.14, sch.6; 1979, c.2, sch.4; c.5, sch.6; orders 74/1331, 2080; 75/517, 2012, 2013; 76/128, 2024–6, 2029; 77/1789, 1791–3, 1849, 2092; 78/1064; 79/242–6, 657, 1554, 1646; 80/183, 303, 305, 866; 81/365, 1740; 82/321, 1007; repealed in pt: 1977, c.36, sch.9; 1979, c.5, sch.7; orders 80/1602, 1604, 1909; 81/1740.

sch. 5, see *National Transit Insurance Co. v. Customs and Excise Comrs.* [1975] 1 All E.R. 203, D.C.; *Trewby v. Customs and Excise Comrs.* [1976] 3 All E.R. 199, D.C.; *C. & E. Comrs. v. Guy Butler (International)* [1976] 2 All E.R. 700, C.A.; *British Airports Authority v. Customs and Excise Commissioners* [1977] 1 W.L.R. 302; [1977] 1 All E.R. 497, C.A.; *Customs and Excise Comrs. v. The Little Spain Club* [1979] S.T.C. 170, Neill J.; *Tynewydd Labour Working Men's Club and Institute v. Customs and Excise Comrs.* [1979] S.T.C. 570, Forbes J.

sch. 5, amended: orders 75/2008, 2009; 76/128; 77/1787, 1788, 1793, 1794, 1797, 2092; 78/1064; 79/243, 246; 80/1602, 1604, 1909; 81/1740; 83/809; repealed in pt.: order 82/476.

sch. 6, rules 74/1934; 77/1017, 1760.

sch. 6, amended: 1973, c.51, s.8; 1974, c.30, s.6; 1977, c.41, sch.12; orders 73/1595; 74/1708; 78/273; 80/132; repealed in pt.: 1974, c.30, s.6; 1975, c.24, sch.3; c.25, sch.3; 1980, c.55, sch.3 (S.).

sch. 7, regs. 72/1345; 73/418, 594, 1748; 76/91; orders 75/2175; 77/817; 80/182; 81/365, 1079; 82/1438.

sch. 7, repealed: 1983, c.53, sch.3.

sch. 8, repealed: 1973, c.51, sch.2.

sch. 9, see *Hughes (Inspector of Taxes) v. Viner* [1985] 3 All E.R. 40; [1985] S.T.C. 235, Walton J.

schs. 9–23, repealed: 1988, c.1, sch.31.

sch. 12, regs. 72/1131.

sch. 12, repealed in pt.: 1988, c.39, sch.14.

sch. 16, see *Wilson & Garden v. I.R.C.* [1982] 1 W.L.R. 1069, H.L.; *R. v. H.M. Inspector of Taxes, ex p. Lansing Bagnall* [1986] S.T.C. 453, C.A.

sch. 16, repealed in pt.: 1988, c.39, sch.14.

sch. 23, see *Sime Darby London v. Sime Darby Holdings* [1975] 3 All E.R. 691; *Tilcon v. Holland* [1981] S.T.C. 365, Vinelott J.

sch. 24, repealed in pt.: 1979, c.14, sch.8; 1988, c.1, sch.31.

sch. 25, amended: 1974, c.30, s.51, sch.12; repealed in pt.: 1975, c.7, sch.13.

sch. 26, repealed: 1978, c.42, sch.13.

sch. 27, repealed S.L.R. 1986.

sch. 28, amended: 1979, c 2, s.177; repealed in pt.: S.L.R. 1986.

42. Town and Country Planning (Amendment) Act 1972.

Royal Assent, July 27, 1972.

s. 1, repealed: 1972, c.70, sch.30; sch.1, amended: *ibid.*

CAP.

1972—cont.

42. Town and Country Planning (Amendment) Act 1972—cont.

s. 3, see *Barham v. Secretary of State for the Environment; Pye v. Secretary of State for the Environment, The Times,* May 25, 1985, Farquharson J.

ss. 5, 6, repealed: 1986, c.63, sch.12.

s. 7, amended: 1972, c.52, sch.23.

s. 8, regs. 72/1362; repealed: 1974, c.32, s.13, sch.

s. 9, repealed: *ibid.*

s. 10, amended: 1972, c.52, schs.21,23; 1980, c.65, sch.15; 1983, c.47, sch.4; repealed in pt.: *ibid.*, sch.6.

s. 10A, amended: *ibid.*, sch. 4.

s. 10B, added: 1980, c.65, sch.15; amended: 1983, c.47, sch.4; 1988, c.4, sch.3; repealed in pt.: 1983, c.47, schs.4,6.

s. 10C, added: 1986, c.63, s.51.

s. 12, amended: 1972, c.52, schs.21,23; 1974, c.32, s.13, sch.

sch. 2, regs. 72/1362; repealed: 1974, c.32, s.13, sch.

sch. 3, repealed: *ibid.*

43. Field Monuments Act 1972.

Royal Assent, July 27, 1972.

repealed: 1979, c.46, sch.5.

44. Children Act 1972.

Royal Assent, July 27, 1972.

45. Trading Representations (Disabled Persons) Amendment Act 1972.

Royal Assent, July 27, 1972.

s. 1, sch., repealed in pt.: 1985, c.51, sch.17.

46. Housing (Financial Provisions) (Scotland) Act 1972.

Royal Assent, July 27, 1972.

repealed, except ss.69, 78, 81, sch.9 (in pt.): 1987, c.26, sch.24.

s. 16, regs. 73/788.

s. 17, regs. 73/546, 1517; 74/723, 1097, 1316, 1505, 2019; 75/381, 1725; 76/1755; 77/1581; 78/1392; 79/1308; 80/720, 1552; 81/368; 82/1147, 1505.

s. 20, regs. 72/1377; 73/1411; 82/1317.

s. 23A, see *City of Edinburgh District Council v. Secretary of State for Scotland,* 1985 S.L.T. 551; *Lord Advocate v. Stirling District Council,* 1986 S.L.T. 179.

s. 23A, orders 85/3; 86/7; 87/11.

s. 34, orders 73/782; 74/2006.

s. 63, orders 80/1668; 81/278; 84/501.

s. 71, see *Glasgow Corporation v. Anderson,* First Division, December 18, 1975.

s. 78, amended: 1973, c.65, sch.12; 1975, c.28, sch.3; 1978, c.14, sch.2; 1980, c.52, s.80.

s. 81, repealed in pt.: 1984, c.58, sch.10.

sch. 2, regs. 77/1310; 78/1011; 79/1308; 80/1109; 81/1162.

sch. 9, repealed in pt.: 1974, c.45, schs.3,5; 1975, c.28, sch.4; c.30, sch.7; 1976, c.71, sch.8; 1984, c.58, sch.10.

47. Housing Finance Act 1972.

Royal Assent, July 27, 1972.

repealed: 1985, c.71, sch.1.

order 75/290.

1972—cont.

47. Housing Finance Act 1972—cont.
s. 1, repealed in pt.: 1975, c.6, sch.6; 1982, c.24, sch.5.
ss. 2–6, repealed: 1975, c.6, sch.6.
s. 6, order 78/1412.
s. 7, repealed: 1975, c.6, sch.6.
s. 8, orders 75/2110; 78/34; 79/234; 80/31; repealed: 1980, c.51, sch.26.
ss. 9, 10, repealed: 1975, c.6, sch.6.
s. 11, regs. 74/618; 84/244; repealed in pt.: 1974, c.44, sch.15.
s. 12, see *Hemsted* v. *Lees and Norwich City Council* (1986) 18 H.L.R. 424, McCowan J.
s. 12, amended: 1974, c.44, sch.13; repealed in pt.: 1975, c.6, sch.6.
s. 13, repealed: *ibid.*
s. 14, repealed: 1981, c.64, sch.13.
s. 15, repealed in pt.: 1975, c.6, sch.6.
s. 16, order 74/1099.
s. 17, regs. 81/1513.
s. 17, repealed in pt.: 1975, c.6, sch.6; 1982, c.24, sch.5.
ss. 18–26, repealed: 1982, c.24, sch.5.
s. 19, regs. 73/676.
s. 19A, orders 75/1564, 1565.
s. 20, regs. 73/614, 1387; 74/421, 516, 1076; 75/246, 342; 76/1470; 77/1467; 78/217, 1302; 80/730, 1555; 81/331, 332.
s. 25, regs. 72/1203; 74/1477, 1499, 1936; 75/343; 76/1242; 77/1290; 78/1078; 79/1014, 1319; 80/1141; 81/1150; 82/1061.
ss. 27 34, repealed: 1977, c.42, sch.25.
s. 35, orders 73/752; 74/615, 1884, 1909; repealed: 1975, c.6, sch.6.
s. 36, repealed: *ibid.*
ss. 37–39, repealed: 1977, c.42, sch.25.
s. 40, repealed: 1975, s.6, sch.6.
ss. 41–48, repealed: 1977, c.42, sch.25.
Pts. V, VI (ss.49–70) repealed: 1975, c.6, s.1, sch.6.
s. 77, repealed: 1974, c.44, schs.13,15.
s. 77, repealed in pt. (S.): 1985, c.71, sch.1.
s. 80, orders 72/1193; 74/1891; repealed: 1975, c.6, sch.6.
ss. 81–88, repealed: 1977, c.42, sch.25.
s. 89, order 73/869.
s. 89, repealed: 1974, c.51, s.11, sch.4.
s. 90, see *Legal and General Assurance Society* v. *Keane* (1978) P. & C.R. 399, C.A.
ss. 90–91A, substituted: 1980, c.51, s.136, sch.19; repealed: *ibid.*, sch.26.
s. 91A, see *Cleve House Properties* v. *Schidlof*, December 21, 1979, Deputy Judge R. M. K. Gray, Bloomsbury and Marylebone County Ct.; *Frobisher (Second Investments)* v. *Kiloran Trust Co.* [1980] 1 All E.R. 488, Walton J.; *Yorkbrook Investments* v. *Batten* (1986) 52 P. & C.R. 51, C.A.
s. 92, amended: 1974, c.44, s.35.
s. 94, repealed: 1973, c.26, sch.3.
ss. 95–99, repealed: 1975, c.6, schs.5,6.
s. 102, order 74/1892; regs. 80/341; 81/290; 82/1061.
s. 103, orders 72/1204; 73/538, 886; 75/512.
s. 103, substituted: 1975, c.6, sch.5; repealed in pt.: 1977, c.42, sch.25.

1972—cont.

47. Housing Finance Act 1972—cont.
s. 104, amended: 1973, c.6, sch.1; repealed in pt.: 1975, c.6, sch.6; 1982, c.24, sch.5; 1985, c.51, sch.17.
s. 105, amended: 1975, c.6, sch.1.
sch. 1, see *Hemsted* v. *Lees and Norwich City Council* (1986) 18 H.L.R. 424, McCowan J.
sch. 1, order 74/1099; amended: 1974, c.44, schs.7, 13; 1975, c.6, sch.5; 1976, c.68, s.9; 1980, c.51, s.135; amended: 1982, c.24, sch.4; repealed in pt.: 1972, c.70, sch.30; 1974, c.44, schs.13, 15; 1975, c.6, sch.6; 1982, c.24, sch.5.
schs. 3, 4, repealed: *ibid.*
schs. 5, 6, repealed: 1977, c.42, sch.25.
sch. 8, amended: 1974, c.44, sch.15.
sch. 9, amended: 1974, c.7, sch.8; regs. 74/421, 516, 595; repealed in pt.: 1975, c.6, sch.6; 1976, c.71, sch.8; 1977, c.42, sch.25; c.43, sch.3.
sch. 10, amended: 1973, c.6, sch.1; repealed in pt.: 1975, c.6, sch.6; 1977, c.42, sch.25.

48. Parliamentary and other Pensions Act 1972.
Royal Assent, July 27, 1972.
Pt. I (ss.1–25), repealed: 1987, c.45, sch.4.
s. 4, orders 79/905; 80/1073.
s. 7, order 84/1909.
s. 10, order 84/1909.
s. 27, amended: 1987, c.45, sch.3.
s. 29, orders 79/905; 80/1073.
s. 29, amended: 1976, c.48, s.5.
s. 30, repealed: 1987, c.45, sch.4.
s. 31, amended: 1978, c.56, sch.1; repealed in pt.: 1987, c.45, sch.4.
ss. 33, 34, repealed: *ibid.*
s. 35, amended: 1978, c.56, ss.15,20, sch.1; repealed in pt.: 1987, c.45, sch.4.
s. 36 (in pt.), schs. 1–4, repealed: *ibid.*

49. Affiliation Proceedings (Amendment) Act 1972.
Royal Assent, July 27, 1972.
s. 1, see *Maher* v. *Gower (formerly Kubilins)* (1981) 12 Fam. Law 32, Purchas J.
repealed: 1987, c.42, sch.4.

50. Legal Advice and Assistance Act 1972.
Royal Assent, July 27, 1972.
repealed: 1974, c.4, sch. 5; 1986, c.47, sch. 5 (S.).
s. 1, regs. 73/1803; 74/1312; 75/1863; 76/1846; 77/1982; 78/1818; 82/507 (S.); 83/533 (S.), 1836 (S.); 85/1860 (S.).
s. 1, amended (S.): 1979, c.26, sch.1; regs. 75/1863.
s. 2, amended: 1975, c.20, s.21; amended and repealed in pt. (S.): 1979, c.26, s.6; repealed in pt.: *ibid.*, sch.2.
s. 3, regs. 80/1151 (S.); 83/1777 (S.).
s. 3, amended: 1979, c.26, s.7 (S.), sch.1; regs. 80/1151 (S.); 1983, c.12, sch.1; repealed in pt.: *ibid.*, schs.1,2.
s. 4, regs. 74/1197; 75/1746; 76/1706; 77/213, 1663; 78/1564; 79/156 (S.), 82/216 (S.); 83/384 (S.), 1665 (S); 85/1628 (S.).
s. 4, amended: 1979, c.26, s.8 (S.); regs. 75/1746; 77/1663; 79/156 (S.); 82/216 (S.); 1983, c.12, sch.1; repealed in pt.: 1979, c.26, sch.2; *ibid.*, s.8 (S.).

CAP.

50. Legal Advice and Assistance Act 1972—*cont.*
s. 5, regs. 82/622; 86/1359 (S.).

s. 5, amended: 1983, c.12, sch.1; 1985, c.73, sch.1 (S.); repealed in pt.: 1983, c.12, schs.1,2.

s. 6, amended: *ibid.*, sch.1; repealed in pt.: 1977, c.38, sch.5.

s. 11, regs. 73/1803; 74/1197, 1312; 75/1746, 1863; 76/1706, 1846; 77/213, 1663, 1982; 78/1564; 79/156; 80/1151 (S.); 82/216 (S.), 507 (S.), 622; 83/384 (S.), 533 (S.), 1665(S); 1777 (S.), 1836 (S.); 85/1628 (S.), 1860 (S.).

s. 11, amended: 1979, c.26, sch.1.

s. 14, orders 73/299, 320; amended: 1979, c.26, sch.1.

sch. 1, regs. 77/1663; amended: regs. 75/1746; orders 75/678 (S.); 79/156 (S.); repealed (S.): 1979, c.26, sch.2.

sch. 2, repealed in pt.: *ibid.*, sch.1.

sch. 4, amended (S.): order 75/678.

51. Chronically Sick and Disabled Persons (Scotland) Act 1972.
Royal Assent, July 27, 1972.

52. Town and Country Planning (Scotland) Act 1972.
Royal Assent, July 27, 1972.

regs. 73/1742.

ss. 1–3, repealed: 1973, c.65, sch.29.

s. 3, see *Inverclyde District Council* v. *The Lord Advocate* (1982) 43 P. & C.R. 375, H.L.

s. 4, repealed in pt.: 1981, c.23, schs.2,4.

s. 5, amended: *ibid.*, sch.2; repealed in pt.: *ibid.*, schs.2,4.

ss. 5, 6, regs. 76/1995; 83/1590.

s. 7, regs. 76/1995; 83/1590; amended: 1973, c.65, s.175; 1982, c.43, s.36.

s. 9, regs. 76/1995; 83/1590; amended: 1977, c.10, s.2 repealed in pt.: 1973, c.65, sch.29.

s. 10, regs. 76/1995; 83/1590; amended: 1977, c.10, s.2; 1981, c.23, schs.2,3; repealed in pt.: 1973, c.65, sch.29; 1981, c.23, schs.2,4.

s. 11, regs. 76/1995; 83/1590.

s. 11, amended: 1982, c.43, s.38.

s. 12, amended: 1973, c.65, s.175; 1977, c.10, s.2; 1982, c.43, s.39; 1986, c.63, sch.11; repealed in pt.: 1982, c.43, sch.4.

s. 13, amended: 1973, c.65, sch.23; 1981, c.23, sch.2; 1982, c.43, s.40; repealed in pt.: 1981, c.23, sch.29.

s. 14, amended: 1984, c.54, sch.9.

s. 15, amended: 1973, c.65, sch.23.

s. 16, regs. 76/1995; 83/1590.

s. 16, amended: 1982, c.43, sch.2.

s. 18, orders 75/379, 380; 77/794; 78/1172.

s. 18, amended: 1977, c.10, ss.2–5.

s. 19, orders 73/1165; 83/1619.

s. 19, amended: 1981, c.36, s.19; 1984, c.54, sch.9; 1986, c.63, sch.11.

ss. 19, 20, see *Argyll and Bute District Council* v. *Secretary of State for Scotland*, Second Division, August 4, 1976; *City of Aberdeen District Council* v. *Secretary of State for Scotland*, 1986 S.L.T. 458; *Lord Advocate* v. *Strathclyde Regional Council*, 1988 S.L.T. 546.

CAP.

52. Town and Country Planning (Scotland) Act 1972—*cont.*

s. 21, see *Inverclyde District Council* v. *Secretary of State for Scotland*, Second Division, July 11, 1980.

s. 21, orders 73/1030, 1682; 75/679, 908, 1287; 76/1307; 77/1346; 79/198; 81/830; 83/1620; 84/327; 85/1014, 2007; 88/977, 1249.

s. 21, amended: 1984, c.12, sch.4; 1986, c.63, sch.11.

ss. 21A–21E, added: *ibid.*, s.26.

s. 22, amended: 1982, c.43, sch.2.

ss. 22, 23, orders 75/679; 81/830; 84/237.

s. 23, substituted: 1982, c.43, s.41.

s. 24, orders 75/679; 76/1307; 81/830.

s. 24, amended: 1975, c.77, sch.10; 1980, c.65, s.92; 1981, c.36, s.21; 1982, c.43, sch.2.

s. 25, amended: 1974, c.32, s.4; 1982, c.43, sch.2; repealed in pt.: 1973, c.65, sch.29; 1974, c.32, s.4.

s. 26, see *Bovis Homes (Scotland)* v. *Inverclyde District Council* [1983] J.P.L. 171, Outer House, Lord Wylie; *Inverclyde District Council* v. *Inverkip Building Co.*, 1983 S.L.T. 563; *Grampian Regional Council* v. *City of Aberdeen District Council*, 1984 S.L.T. 197; (1984) 47 P. & C.R. 633, H.L.; *Grampian Regional Council* v. *Secretary of State for Scotland*, 1983 S.L.T. 526.

s. 26, amended: 1981, c.23, s.36; 1982, c.43, sch.2; 1986, c.63, sch.11; repealed in pt.: 1982, c.43, sch.4.

ss. 26, 27, see *British Airports Authority* v. *Secretary of State for Scotland*, First Division, November 22, 1978.

s. 27, see *Inverclyde District Council* v. *Inverkip Building Co.*, 1983 S.L.T. 563.

s. 27, amended: 1981, c.23, sch.2.

s. 27A, added: *ibid.*, s.22.

s. 28, orders 75/679; 76/693, 1307; 81/830; 88/1249.

s. 28, amended: 1982, c.43, sch.2; repealed in pt.: 1973, c.65, sch.29.

s. 28A, added: 1986, c.63, sch.11.

s. 29, amended: 1982, c.43, sch.2; repealed in pt.: 1986, c.63, sch.12.

s. 30A, added: 1982, c.43, sch.2.

s. 31, orders 75/679; 81/830; 84/2337.

s. 31, amended: 1975, c.77, sch.10; 1982, c.43, sch.2; 1986, c.63, sch.6; repealed in pt.: 1980, c.65, sch.34; 1982, c.43, sch.4.

ss. 31, 33, 34, see *Inverclyde District Council* v. *Secretary of State for Scotland*, House of Lords, November 12, 1981.

s. 31A, added: 1982, c.43, s.46.

s. 32, amended: 1981, c.36, sch.2; 1982, c.43, sch.2; 1986, c.63, sch.11; repealed in pt.: 1982, c.43, schs.2,4.

ss. 32, 33, see *Bellway* v. *Strathclyde Regional Council* (O.H.), August 17, 1978; *Lakin* v. *Secretary of State for Scotland*, 1988 S.L.T. 780.

s. 33, see *British Airports Authority* v. *Secretary of State for Scotland*, First Division, November 22, 1978.

1972—cont.

52. Town and Country Planning (Scotland) Act 1972—*cont.*
s. 33, orders 75/679; 76/693; 81/830.
s. 33, amended: 1982, c.43, sch.2; 1986, c.63, sch.11.
ss. 33, 34, see *Inverclyde District Council* v. *Secretary of State for Scotland,* House of Lords, November 12, 1981; *Alexander Russell* v. *Secretary of State for Scotland,* 1984 S.L.T. 81.
s. 34, see *Bovis Homes (Scotland)* v. *Inverclyde District Council* (O.H.), November 17, 1981.
s. 34, orders 75/679; 76/1307; 81/830.
s. 34, amended: 1982, c.43, sch.2.
s. 35, amended: 1981, c.36, sch.2.
s. 37, amended: 1978, c.51, sch.16; repealed in pt.: 1982, c.43, sch.4.
s. 38, see *Alexander Russell* v. *Secretary of State for Scotland,* 1984 S.L.T. 81.
s. 38, amended: 1980, c.65, sch.32; 1981, c.36, s.23; 1986, c.63, sch.6.
s. 39, see *Inverclyde District Council* v. *Secretary of State for Scotland,* House of Lords, November 12, 1981; *Inverclyde District Council* v. *Inverkip Building Co.,* 1983 S.L.T. 563, *Alexander Russell* v. *Secretary of State for Scotland,* 1984 S.L.T. 81.
s. 39, orders 75/679; 81/830.
s. 40, see *Inverclyde District Council* v. *Secretary of State for Scotland,* House of Lords, November 12, 1981.
s. 41A, added: 1981, c.36, s.24.
s. 42, amended: *ibid.,* s.25.
s. 43, repealed in pt.: 1973, c.65, schs.23,29.
ss. 44, 47, repealed in pt.: 1975, c.24, sch.3.
s. 48, repealed: 1981, c.23, schs.2,4.
s. 49, amended: 1981, c.36, s.26.
ss. 49A–49G, added: *ibid.,* s.27.
s. 51, orders 75/679; 76/693; 81/830.
s. 51, amended: 1980, c.65, sch.32; 1986, c.63, sch.6.
s. 52, regs. 75/2069; 87/1529; amended: 1973, c.65, sch.23; 1986, c.63, sch.9.
s. 53, amended: *ibid.;* repealed in pt.: *ibid.,* schs.11, 12.
s. 54, regs. 75/2069
s. 54, amended: 1979, c.46, sch.4; 1982, c.43, sch.2; 1986, c.63, sch.9; repealed in pt.: 1982, c.43, sch.4.
s. 54A, added: 1982, c.43, sch.2; amended: 1986, c.63, sch.9.
s. 54B, added: 1982, c.43, s.2.
s. 54C, added: *ibid.,* s.42.
s. 54D, regs. 87/1529.
ss. 54D, 56AA, added: 1986, c.63, sch.9.
s. 55, amended: 1986, c.63, sch.11.
s. 56, amended: 1979, c.46, sch.4.
s. 56A–56O, added: 1986, c.63, s.35.
s. 58, regs. 75/1204; 84/329.
s. 58, amended: 1974, c.32, s.11; 1981, c.23, sch.2; 1984, c.10, s.2; repealed in pt.: regs. 75/1203; 1981, c.23, schs.2,4; 1986, c.63, sch.12.
s. 59, regs. 75/1204; repealed in pt.: regs. 75/1203; 1981, c.23, schs.2,4.

1972—cont.

52. Town and Country Planning (Scotland) Act 1972—*cont.*
s. 59A, regs. 75/1204.
s. 60, amended: 1974, c.32, s.11; 1985, c.52, s.2.
s. 61, regs. 84/467.
s. 61, amended: 1974, c.32, s.3; repealed in pt.: 1982, c.43, sch.4
s. 62, see *City of Glasgow District Council* v. *Secretary of State for Scotland, The Scotsman,* December 9, 1988.
s. 63, see *Stevenson* v. *Midlothian District Council* (H.L.), 1983 S.L.T. 433.
s. 63, amended: 1973, c.65, sch.23; 1982, c.43, sch.2; 1986, c.63, sch.11; repealed in pt.: 1973, c.65, schs.25,29; 1986, c.63, sch.12.
s. 63A, added: 1982, c.43, sch.2; amended: 1986, c.63, sch.11.
ss. 64–83, repealed: *ibid.,* sch.12.
ss. 65, 66, order 74/1418; regs. 77/682, 705; 79/838.
s. 67, orders 74/1283, 1419, 2028; 76/565; 78/327.
s. 84, see *Midlothian District Council* v. *Stevenson,* 1985 S.L.T. 424; *Lord Advocate* v. *Strathclyde Regional Council,* 1988 S.L.T. 546.
s. 84, amended: 1982, c.43, sch.2; 1986, c.63, sch.11; repealed in pt.: 1973, c.65, schs.25,29; 1982, c.43, sch.4.
ss. 84, 85, see *James Barrie (Sand and Gravel)* v. *Lanark District Council* (O.H.), September 9, 1978; *McDaid* v. *Clydebank District Council,* 1984 S.L.T. 162.
ss. 84, 85, regs. 84/236.
ss. 84–87, see *Pirie* v. *Brauld,* 1975 S.L.T. (Sh.Ct.) 6.
ss. 84, 85, 87, see *Central Regional Council* v. *Clackmannan District Council,* 1983 S.L.T. 666; *Earl Car Sales (Edinburgh)* v. *City of Edinburgh District Council,* First Division, June 3, 1982.
s. 84A, added: 1982, c.43, s.43.
s. 85, see *Adam* v. *Secretary of State for Scotland* (O.H.), 1987 S.C.L.R. 697; 1988 S.L.T. 300; *Hands* v. *Kyle and Carrick District Council,* 1988 S.C.L.R. 470.
s. 85, amended: 1982, c.43, sch.2; repealed in pt.: *ibid.,* sch.4; 1986, c.63, sch.12.
s. 86, amended: 1982, c.43, sch.2; 1986, c.63, sch.11.
s. 87, see *Marine Associates* v. *City of Aberdeen Corporation* (O.H.), 1978 S.L.T. (Notes) 41.
s. 87, substituted: 1977, c.10, s.4; amended: 1982, c.43, sch.2; 1986, c.63, sch.11.
ss. 87, 88, see *Lord Advocate* v. *Strathclyde Regional Council,* 1988 S.L.T. 546.
s. 87A, added: 1982, c.43, s.44.
s. 87A, regs. 84/326.
s. 88, see *Midlothian District Council* v. *Stevenson* [1986] J.P.L. 913, Court of Session.
s. 88, regs. 75/2069.
s. 88, amended: 1980, c.45, sch.10; 1982, c.43, sch.2.
s. 89, amended: *ibid.,* sch.2.
s. 89A, added: *ibid.*

CAP.

1972—cont.

52. Town and Country Planning (Scotland) Act 1972—cont.

s. 90, orders 75/679; 81/830.

s. 91, repealed in pt.: 1981, c.23, schs.2,4.

s. 92, amended: 1982, c.43, sch.2; repealed in pt.: ibid., sch.4.

s. 93, amended: ibid., sch.2; 1986, c.63, sch.9; repealed in pt.: 1982, c.43, sch.4.

s. 94, amended: ibid., sch.2; 1986, c.63, sch.11.

s. 95, regs. 75/2069.

s. 95A, amended: 1986, c.63, sch.9.

s. 96, amended: 1973, c.65, sch.29.

ss. 97, 97A, substituted: 1986, c.63, sch.9.

s. 97B, added: ibid., s.36.

s. 98, see White v. Hamilton, 1987 S.C.C.R. 12.

s. 98, amended: 1982, c.43, sch.2; 1986, c.63, sch.11.

s. 99, amended: ibid.

s. 100, substituted: 1981, c.36, s.28; amended: 1982, c.43, sch.2; 1986, c.63, sch.11.

s. 101, regs. 84/467.

s. 101, amended: 1982, c.43, sch.2; 1986, c.63, sch.11.

s. 102, amended: 1973, c.65, sch.23; 1980, c.65, s.92.

s. 107, amended: ibid.; repealed in pt.: ibid., schs. 23, 29.

s. 108, amended: 1984, c.12, sch.4.

s. 109, amended: 1980, c.65, sch.23; repealed in pt.: ibid., sch.29.

ss. 111, 112, repealed: 1981, c.23, sch.4.

s. 113, repealed in pt.: 1980, c.65, s.92, sch.29; 1981, c.23, sch.4.

s. 114, repealed in pt.: 1980, c.65, sch.29; 1982, c.52, sch.2.

s. 115, amended: 1980, c.65, sch.23; repealed in pt.: ibid., sch.29.

s. 117, amended: 1984, c.12, sch.4.

s. 118, repealed in pt.: 1980, c.65, sch. 29.

s. 120, repealed in pt.: 1973, c.26, sch.3; S.L.R. 1986.

s. 136, amended: 1982, c.43, sch.2; 1984, c.54, sch.9; repealed in pt.: 1986, c.63, sch.12.

s. 140, repealed: ibid.

s. 153, amended: 1981, c.36, sch.2; repealed in pt.: 1973, c.65, schs.23,29

s. 153A, added: 1981, c.36, s.29.

s. 154, amended: 1985, c.19, s.2; repealed in pt.: 1982, c.43, sch.4; 1986, c.63, sch.12.

s. 158, amended: 1985, c.19, s.2; 1986, c.63, sch.11; repealed in pt.: ibid., sch.12.

s. 159, amended: 1982, c.43, sch.2.

ss. 159A, 159B, added: ibid., s.30.

ss. 160–162, regs. 75/2069; 87/1529.

s. 164, repealed in pt.: 1982, c.43, sch.4.

s. 165, regs. 84/467.

s. 166, see Central Regional Council v. Clackmannan District Council, 1983 S.L.T. 666; Earl Car Sales (Edinburgh) v. City of Edinburgh District Council, First Division, June 3, 1982.

s. 166, amended: 1977, c.10, s.5.

s. 167, amended: 1981, c.36, sch.2.

ss. 167A–167C, added: ibid., s.31.

s. 167C, repealed in pt.: 1982, c.43, sch.4.

s. 168, amended: ibid., s.132.

CAP.

1972—cont.

52. Town and Country Planning (Scotland) Act 1972—cont.

s. 169, amended: 1982, c.43, sch.2; repealed in pt.: 1986, c.63, sch.12.

ss. 170, 173, amended: ibid., sch.11.

s. 173, see Strathclyde Regional Council v. Secretary of State for Scotland, 1987 S.L.T. 724.

s. 174, repealed: 1986, c.63, sch.12.

s. 175, amended: ibid., sch.11.

s. 179, regs. 75/2069; 87/1529.

s. 180, repealed in pt.: 1986, c.63, sch.12.

s. 180A, added: 1984, c.12, sch.4.

s. 181, orders 78/324; 85/291.

s. 181, amended: 1973, c.56, ss. 64–71, 77; 1984, c.12, sch.4; c.54, sch.9; 1987, c.3, sch.1; 1988, c.41, sch.12.

ss. 181–184, see Trustees of St. John's Church, Galashiels v. Borders Regional Council, 1976 S.L.T.(Lands Tr.) 39.

s. 182, amended: 1972, c.56, ss.72,77; repealed in pt.: 1973, c.26, sch.3.

ss. 182, 185, see Campbell Douglas & Co. v. Hamilton District Council, 1984 S.L.T.(Lands Tr.) 44.

s. 183, amended: 1973, c.56, ss.71,77; 1975, c.77, sch.10; 1980, c.65, s.92.

s. 184, see Ibbotson v. Tayside Regional Council, 1978 S.L.T.(Lands Tr.) 25.

ss. 184, 185, amended: 1973, c.56, s.77.

s. 186, amended: ibid.; 1974, c.45, sch.3; 1987, c.26, sch.23.

ss. 187, 188, amended: 1973, c.56, s.77.

s. 189, amended: ibid., ss.76,77.

s. 190, amended: ibid., ss.72,77; repealed in pt.: 1973, c.26, s.86.

s. 191, amended: 1973, c.56, ss.54,77.

ss. 192–194, amended: ibid., s.77.

s. 194, see Ibbotson v. Tayside Regional Council, 1978 S.L.T.(Lands Tr.) 25.

ss. 194, 195, amended: 1984, c.54, sch.9.

s. 195, amended: 1973, c.56, ss.71,77.

s. 196, amended: ibid., s.77.

s. 198, see Grampian Regional Council v. City of Aberdeen District Council, 1984 S.L.T. 197; (1984) 47 P. & C.R. 663, H.L.

s. 198, amended: 1980, c.65, sch.32; 1984, c.54, sch.9; repealed in pt.: ibid., sch.11.

s. 198A, added: 1981, c.23, sch.2; amended: 1984, c.54, sch.9; repealed in pt.: ibid., schs.9, 11.

s. 200, repealed: ibid., sch.11.

s. 201, amended: 1973, c.65, sch.23; 1981, c.23, sch.2; 1984, c.54, sch.9; repealed in pt.: ibid., schs.9, 11.

s. 202, amended: 1984, c.12, sch.4; c.54, sch.9.

s. 203, repealed in pt.: 1981, c.23, schs.2,4.

s. 204, amended: 1984, c.54, sch.9; repealed in pt.: 1973, c.65, sch.29; 1981, c.23, sch.4; 1984, c.54, sch.11.

s. 205, amended: ibid., sch.9; 1986, c.63, sch.11; 1987, c.3, sch.1; repealed in pt.: 1984, c.54, sch.11; 1986, c.63, sch.12.

s. 205A, added: 1981, c.23, sch.3; amended: 1986, c.63, sch.11; repealed in pt.: 1984, c.54, sch.11; 1986, c.63, sch.12.

1972—cont.

52. Town and Country Planning (Scotland) Act 1972—*cont.*

s. 206, amended: 1981, c.23, sch.3; 1984, c.54, sch.9; repealed in pt.: *ibid.*, sch.11.

s. 207, amended: *ibid.*

s. 208, amended: 1981, c.23, sch.3; 1984, c.54, sch.9; repealed in pt.: *ibid.*, sch.11.

s. 209, substituted: 1984, c.12, sch.4; amended: 1984, c.54, sch.9; repealed in pt.: *ibid.*, sch.11.

s. 210, repealed: *ibid.*

s. 210A, added: 1982, c.43, s.45; amended: 1984, c.54, sch.9; repealed in pt.: *ibid.*, sch.11.

ss. 211, 214, 233, see *British Airports Authority v. Secretary of State for Scotland,* First Division, November 22, 1978.

s. 212, amended: 1972, c.60, s.40; 1981, c.38, sch.3; 1986, c.31, sch.4; c.44, sch.7.

s. 213, amended: orders 74/692; 76/1775; 1981, c.38, sch.3; repealed in pt.: 1986, c.31.sch.6; c.44, sch.9.

s. 215, repealed in pt.: 1982, c.43, sch.4.

ss. 219, 221, amended: 1984, c.12, sch.4.

s. 226, repealed in pt.: 1986, c.63, sch.12.

s. 227, amended: 1981, c.36, sch.2.

s. 229A, added: 1982, c.43, sch.2.

s. 231, amended: 1981, c.36, sch.2; 1982, c.43, s.47, sch.2; 1986, c.63, schs.6,7,11; repealed in pt.: 1982, c.43, s.47, sch.4.

s. 232, amended: *ibid.*, sch.2; 1986, c.63, sch.6; repealed in pt.: 1984, c.54, sch.11.

s. 233, see *Midlothian District Council v. Secretary of State for Scotland,* 1980 S.C. 210; *Grampian Regional Council v. Secretary of State for Scotland,* 1983 S.L.T. 526.

s. 233, repealed in pt.: 1986, c.63, sch.12.

s. 236, repealed in pt.: 1984, c.54, sch.11.

ss. 237–239, regs. 83/108.

ss. 237–239, repealed: 1986, c.63, sch.12.

s. 241A, added: 1978, c.51, sch.16.

s. 242, amended: 1973, c.65, s.133, sch.14; 1984, c.54, sch.9; repealed in pt.: 1973, c.65, sch.29.

s. 243, amended: *ibid.*,sch.23.

s. 247, regs. 83/108.

s. 247, repealed in pt.: 1986, c.63, sch.12.

s. 250, amended: 1973, c.65, sch.23; 1984, c.54, sch.9.

s. 251, amended: 1987, c.3, sch.1.

s. 251, regs. 82/973.

s. 251A, added: 1981, c.36, s.20.

s. 252, repealed: 1974, c.36, s.2.

s. 253, amended: 1981, c.36, sch.2; 1986, c.63, sch.7.

s. 254, amended: 1982, c.43, sch.2.

s. 256, regs. 75/677; 81/829; 84/238.

s. 257, regs. 75/2069; 87/1529; substituted: 1974, c.32, s.7.

s. 257A, added: 1986, c.63, sch.7.

s. 259, regs. 75/1280; 87/1937.

s. 259, amended: 1987, c.3, sch.1.

s. 260, amended: 1973, c.65, sch.23; 1981, c.36, sch.2; 1986, c.63, sch.11; repealed in pt.: 1973, c.65, s.209, schs.25,29; 1981, c.23, sch.4.

1972—cont.

52. Town and Country Planning (Scotland) Act 1972—*cont.*

s. 261, repealed: 1973, c.65, sch.29.

s. 262, repealed in pt.: 1982, c.43, sch.4.

s. 262A, regs. 75/2069; 87/1529; added: 1974, c.32, s.2, amended: 1982, c.43, sch.2; 1986, c.63, sch.9; repealed in pt.: 1982, c.43, sch.4.

s. 262B, added: 1974, c.32, s.2; amended: 1982, c.43, sch.2; repealed in pt.: *ibid.*, sch.4.

s. 262C, added: 1986, c.63, sch.11.

s. 265, amended: 1977, c.10, s.5; 1982, c.43, sch.2; 1986, c.63, sch.7.

s. 266, amended: 1982, c.43, sch.2

s. 267, amended: 1986, c.63, sch.11; 1987, c.18, sch.6.

ss. 267A, 267B, added: 1986, c.63, sch.11.

s. 269, see *Adam v. Secretary of State for Scotland* (O.H), 1987 S.C.L.R. 697; 1988 S.L.T. 300.

s. 270, amended: 1977, c.10, sch.5; 1986, c.63, sch.11.

s. 272, amended 1982, c.43, sch.2.

s. 273, regs. 73/1165; 75/677, 2069; 76/210, 820, 1307, 1995, 2022; 77/255; 78/892; 80/1675; 81/829, 830; 83/108; 84/238, 329, 995, 996; orders 73/1165; 74/1283, 1419, 2028; 75/679, 1204, 1287; 76/565, 693; 78/324, 327; 82/973; 83/1590, 1619, 1620; 84/237; 85/291, 1014, 2007; regs. 87/1529, 1531, 1532; 88/977, 1249.

s. 273, amended: 1981, c.23, sch.3; 1986, c.63, schs.6,9; repealed in pt.: *ibid.*, sch.12.

s. 275, see *Argyll and Bute District Council v. Secretary of State for Scotland,* Second Division, August 4, 1976.

s. 275, regs. 75/2069; 87/1529, 1531, 1532.

s. 275, amended: 1973, c.65, sch.23; 1980, c.65, sch.32; 1981, c.36, sch.2; 1984, c.54, sch.9; 1986, c.63, schs.6,7,11; repealed in pt.: 1981, c.36, sch.29; S.L.R. 1986; 1986, c.44, sch.9; c.63, sch.12.

s. 277, see *Apostolic Church Trustees v. Glasgow District Council (No. 2),* 1978 S.L.T.(Lands Tr.) 17.

s. 278, see *Ware v. Edinburgh District Council,* 1976 S.L.T.(Lands Tr.) 21; *Murray Bookmakers v. Glasgow District Council,* 1979 S.L.T.(Lands Tr.) 8; *Smith v. Strathclyde Regional Council,* 1982 S.L.T. (Lands Tr.) 2.

s. 279, orders 75/1203; 76/464.

s. 281, repealed in pt.: 1975, c.24, sch.3.

schs. 1, 2, repealed: 1973, c.65, sch.29.

sch. 3, repealed: order 77/794.

sch. 4, regs. 76/820; repealed: order 77/794.

sch. 5, order 78/1172; amended: 1977, c.10, s.5.

sch. 6A, regs. 87/1532.

sch. 6A, added: 1986, c.63, s.26, sch.6.

sch. 7, regs. 76/210; 78/892; 80/1675; 87/1532.

sch. 7, amended: 1986, c.63, sch.11.

sch. 10, regs. 75/2069; 87/1529; amended: 1973, c.65, sch.23; 1982, c.43, sch.2; 1986, c.63, sch.9; repealed in pt.: 1973, c.65, sch.29; 1982, c.43, sch.4.

sch. 12, orders 75/679, 76/1307; 81/830.

1972

1972—cont.

52. Town and Country Planning (Scotland) Act 1972—cont.

sch. 17, amended: 1986, c.63, sch.11.

sch. 18, amended: 1973, c.65, sch.23; 1981, c.23, sch.3; 1984, c.54, sch.9; repealed in pt.: ibid., sch.11.

sch. 19, see Argyll and Bute District Council v. Secretary of State for Scotland, Second Division, August 4, 1976.

sch. 19 amended: 1986, c.63, schs.9,11; repealed in pt.: ibid., sch.12.

sch. 20, repealed in pt.: 1984, c.54, sch.11.

sch. 21, amended: 1974, c.32, s.13, sch.; repealed in pt: 1975, c.78, sch.6; 1978, c.3, sch.2; 1979, c.46, sch.5; 1982, c.16, sch.16; c.52, sch 2; 1984, c.29, sch.12.

sch. 22, see Argyll and Bute District Council v. Secretary of State for Scotland, Second Division, August 4, 1976. Alexander Russell v. Secretary of State for Scotland, 1984 S.L.T. 81.

sch. 22, amended: 1981, c.38, sch.3; 1984, c.12, sch.4; repealed in pt.: 1973, c.65, sch.29; 1986, c.63, sch.12.

schs. 22, 23, see Apostolic Church Trustees v. Glasgow District Council (No. 2), 1978 S.L.T.(Lands Tr.) 17.

sch. 24, see Smith v. Strathclyde Regional Council, 1982 S.L.T.(Lands Tr.) 2; McMillan v. Strathclyde Regional Council, 1984 S.L.T.(Lands Tr.) 25.

sch. 24, modified: 1975, c.8, sch.2.

53. Contracts of Employment Act 1972.

Royal Assent, July 27, 1972.

see Adams v. Wright [1972] I.C.R. 463, N.I.R.C.; Construction Industry Training Board v. Leighton, The Times, October 26, 1977, E.A.T.; Active Elderly Housing Association v. Sparrow (1978) 13 I.T.R. 395, E.A.T.

s. 1, see Leigh v. Arnold (James) & Co. [1973] I.T.R. 364, N.I.R.C.; Johnson v. Cross [1977] I.C.R. 872, E.A.T.

ss. 1, 2, 4, amended: 1975, c.71, s.120, sch.16.

s. 4, see Owens v. Multilux [1974] I.R.L.R. 113; Wiltshire County Council v. National Association of Teachers in Further and Higher Education [1980] I.C.R. 455, C.A.; amended: 1974, c.52, schs.3,5; 1975, c.60, s.30.

s. 5, see British Steel Corporation v. Dingwall, 1976 S.L.T. 230.

s. 5, repealed: 1978, c.44, sch.17.

s. 6, amended: 1973, c.38, s.91; repealed in pt.: 1975, c.60, sch.5.

s. 8, see Grimes v. Sutton London Borough Council [1973] I.C.R. 240; Wood v. Leeds Area Health Authority (Training) [1974] I.C.R. 539; Hodges v. Probeit [1976] I.R.L.R. 28; [1976] I.C.R. 95; W.P.M. Retail v. Lang [1978] I.R.L.R. 243, E.A.T.; Leighton v. Construction Industry Training Board [1978] I.C.R. 577; [1978] 2 All E.R. 723, E.A.T.

s. 9, amended: 1975, c.71, s.120, sch.16; repealed in pt.: 1976, c.79, sch.6.

s. 10, amended: 1975, c.71, s.120, sch.16.

1972—cont.

53. Contracts of Employment Act 1972—cont.

s. 11, see Tyne and Clyde Warehouses v. Hamerton [1978] I.C.R. 661, E.A.T.; Bullock v. Merseyside County Council [1979] I.C.R. 79, C.A.

s. 11, amended: 1974, c.52, sch.5.

s. 13, see Wood v. York City Council [1978] I.C.R. 840, C.A.

s. 35, see Lloyds Bank v. Secretary of State for Employment (1978) 123 S.J. 47, E.A.T.

sch. 1, see Spanlite Structures v. Jarrett [1973] I.C.R. 465, N.I.R.C.; Haque v. Stitchen & Co. (1937) [1973] I.C.R. 474, N.I.R.C.; Harold Fielding v. Mansi [1974] 1 All E.R. 1035, N.I.R.C.; Bentley Engineering v. Crown [1976] I.C.R. 225; Coulson v. City of London Polytechnic [1976] 1 W.L.R. 834; Rashid v. I.L.E.A. [1976] I.T.R. 215; [1977] I.C.R. 157; Dean v. Eastbourne Fishermen's and Boatmen's Protection Society & Club [1977] I.R.L.R. 143; [1977] I.C.R. 556, E.A.T.; Rowley, Holmes & Co. v. Barber [1977] 1 W.L.R. 371; Dhami v. Top Spot Night Club [1977] I.R.L.R. 231, E.A.T.; Secretary of State for Employment v. Rooney [1977] I.C.R. 440, E.A.T.; Young v. Daniel Thwaites & Co. [1977] I.C.R. 877, E.A.T.; I.T.T. Components Group (Europe) v. Kolah [1977] I.C.R. 740, E.A.T.; Zarb and Samuels v. British & Brazilian Produce Co. (Sales) [1978] I.R.L.R. 78, E.A.T.; Mailway (Southern) v. Willsher [1978] I.C.R. 511, E.A.T.; Murphy v. Birrell & Sons [1978] I.R.L.R. 458, E.A.T.; Green v. Wavertree Heating and Plumbing Co. [1978] I.C.R. 928, E.A.T.; Wood v. York City Council [1978] I.C.R. 840, C.A.; Wynne v. Hair Control [1978] I.C.R. 870, E.A.T.; Opie v. John Gubbins (Insurance Brokers) [1978] I.R.L.R. 541, E.A.T.; Lloyds Bank v. Secretary of State for Employment (1978) 123 S.J. 47, E.A.T.; Larkin v. Cambos Enterprises (Stretford) [1978] I.C.R. 1247, E.A.T.; Wessex National v. Long (1978) 13 I.T.R. 413, E.A.T.; Scarlett v. Godfrey Abbot Group [1978] I.C.R. 1106, E.A.T.; Bullock v. Merseyside County Council [1979] I.C.R. 79, C.A.; Cookson & Zinn v. Morgan [1979] I.C.R. 425, E.A.T.; Hillingdon Area Health Authority v. Kauders [1979] I.C.R. 472, E.A.T.; Southwood Hostel Management Committee v. Taylor [1979] I.C.R. 813, E.A.T.; Fisher v. York Trailer Co. [1979] I.C.R. 834, E.A.T.; Teesside Times v. Drury [1980] I.C.R. 338, C.A.; Secretary of State for Employment v. Newcastle-upon-Tyne City Council [1980] I.C.R. 407, E.A.T.

sch. 1, amended: 1975, c.71, s.120, sch.16.

sch. 2, see Friend v. P.M.A. Holdings [1976] I.C.R. 330; Ogden v. Ardphalt Asphalt [1977] 1 All E.R. 267; Weevsmay v. Kings [1977] I.C.R. 244, E.A.T.; J. & S. Bickley v. Washer [1977] I.C.R. 425, E.A.T.; Fox v. C. Wright (Farmers) [1978] I.C.R. 98, E.A.T.

sch. 2, substituted: 1975, c.71, s.85, sch.5.

sch. 16, see Lloyds Bank v. Secretary of State for the Environment [1979] I.C.R. 258, E.A.T.

CAP.

1972—cont.

54. British Library Act 1972.
Royal Assent, July 27, 1972.
functions transferred: order 86/600.
s. 3, order 73/1125.
s. 3, amended: 1983, c.47, sch.5.
sch. amended: 1978, c.44, sch.16; repealed in pt.: 1975, c.24, sch.3; 1978, c.44, sch.17.

55. Sri Lanka Republic Act 1972.
Royal Assent, July 27, 1972.
s. 1, repealed in pt.: 1981, c.61, sch.9.

56. Appropriation Act 1972.
Royal Assent, August 9, 1972.
repealed: 1974, c.31, s.4, sch.

57. National Insurance Act 1972.
Royal Assent, August 9, 1972.
repealed: 1975, c.18, sch.1.
s. 2, regs. 72/1232.
s. 6, order 73/833.
s. 6, sch. 4, orders 72/1229, 1230, 1665; 73/1355.
s. 13, order 73/691.
s. 65, order 73/372.

58. National Health Service (Scotland) Act 1972.
Royal Assent, August 9, 1972.
repealed, except ss. 24 (in pt.), 26–28, 32–36, 52, 53, 61 (in pt.), sch.4; 1978, c.29, sch.17.
ss. 5, 8, regs. 74/548; 76/540.
s. 13, regs. 75/197; 76/1679; orders 74/266, 267, 466, 503, 504, 1031.
s. 14, regs. 74/468, 2177.
s. 16, regs. 74/505–507.
s. 19, regs. 75/196; 76/1679; order 74/467.
s. 21, regs. 74/470.
ss. 22, 23, regs. 74/733; order 74/1491.
s. 25, order 74/509.
s. 26, orders 74/467, 521.
s. 27, order 74/471.
s. 31, order 74/265.
ss. 32, 33, order 74/265.
s. 34, orders 74/265, 469; amended: 1973, c.32, sch.4.
s. 34A, regs. 74/182, 824; 75/7; order 74/265.
s. 35, orders 74/265, 469.
s. 37, order 74/510.
s. 38, order 74/510; scheme 74/860.
s. 39, order 75/457.
ss. 42, 43, 46, 55, amended: 1978, c.51, sch.16.
s. 52, repealed in pt.: 1983, c.39, sch.3; 1984, c.36, sch.5.
ss. 57, 60, regs. 74/468.
s. 61, orders 74/265, 469, 509, 510, 521, 861, 1158; 75/457.
s. 62, orders 74/266, 267, 470, 503, 504, 2177.
s. 65, orders, 72/1256; 73/1421; 74/145.
sch. 1, regs. 74/276, 485, 504–507, 549, 667, 858; 75/197; 76/1679; orders 74/466, 1031.
sch. 3, regs. 74/276, 485, 858; 75/196; 76/1679.
sch. 6, repealed in pt.: 1978, c.44, sch.17; 1984, c.36, sch.5.

59. Administration of Justice (Scotland) Act 1972.
Royal Assent, August 9, 1972.
s. 1, see *Connolly* v. *Edinburgh Northern Hospitals* (O.H.), 1974 S.L.T.(Notes) 53; *Lunan* v. *Forresterhill Hospital* (O.H.), 1975

CAP.

1972—cont.

59. Administration of Justice (Scotland) Act 1972—*cont.*
S.L.T.(Notes) 61; *Baxter* v. *Lothian Health Board* (O.H.), 1976 S.L.T.(Notes) 37; *McGown* v. *Erskine and Ors.* (O.H.), 1978 S.L.T.(Notes) 4; *Moore* v. *Greater Glasgow Health Board,* First Division, February 9, 1978; *Falkingham* v. *Lothian Regional Council,* 1983 S.L.T. (Sh.Ct.) 2; *P. Cannon (Garages)* v. *Lord Advocate,* 1983 S.L.T. (Sh.Ct.) 50: *Micosta S.A.* v. *Shetland Islands Council,* 1983 S.L.T. 483; *Thorne* v. *Strathclyde Regional Council* (O.H.), 1984 S.L.T. 161; *The British Phonographic Industry* v. *Cohen* [1984] F.S.R. 159, Ct. of Session (Inner House); *Yau* v. *Ogilvie & Co.* (O.H.), 1985 S.L.T. 91; *Smith, Petr.* (O.H.), July 14, 1983; *Bank of Scotland, Petrs.* (O.H.), 1988 S.L.T. 282; *Civil Service Building Society* v. *MacDougall,* 1988 S.L.T. 687.
s. 1, Act of Sederunt 87/1206.
s. 1, amended: 1985, c.73, s.19, sch.2.
s. 2, repealed: 1988, c.36, sch.3.
s. 3, see *Fairlie Yacht Slip* v. *Lumsden* [1977] S.L.T.(Notes) 41; *Clydebank District Council* v. *Clink,* First Division, January 25, 1977; *Gunac* v. *Inverclyde District Council,* Second Division, February 14, 1980; *O'Neill* v. *Scottish Joint Negotiating Committee for Teaching Staff* (O.H.), 1987, S.L.T. 648.
s. 3, amended: 1974, c.52, schs.3,5; 1982, c.46, sch.3.
s. 4, Acts of Sederunt 75/948; 83/409; 85/1179.
s. 5, order 73/339.

60. Gas Act 1972.
Royal Assent, August 9, 1972.
s. 1, regs. 72/1440, 1879.
ss. 1 (in pt.), 2 (in pt.), 3–5, repealed: 1986, c.44, sch.9.
s. 6, repealed in pt.: 1980, c.63, sch.2; 1986, c.44, sch.9.
s. 7, directions 81/1459.
ss. 7–13, Pts. II, III (ss. 14–31), 32–50, schs. 1–8, repealed: 1986, c.44, sch.9.
s. 21, regs. 81/1764; 85/1149.
s. 25, regs. 72/1878; 74/847; 80/1851.
s. 26, regs. 78/230; 80/1851.
s. 29B, regs. 83/363.
s. 30, regs. 74/848; 75/1071, 1873, 80/1851; 81/504; 82/565; 83/684, 1246, 1247; 84/1785.
s. 31, see *R.* v. *Clerkenwell Metropolitan Stipendiary Magistrates, ex p. D.P.P., The Times,* August 4, 1983, D.C.; *Mackenzie* v. *Brougham,* 1985 S.L.T. 276.
s. 31, regs. 76/1882; 80/1851; 83/1757; 84/1358.
s. 34, repealed in pt. (S.): order 78/1176.
s. 36, regs. 80/1782; 81/1611.
s. 41, regs. 80/1581.
s. 42, regs. 76/1882; 83/363, 1575; 84/1358.
s. 43, see *R.* v. *Clerkenwell Metropolitan Stipendiary Magistrate, ex p. D.P.P.* [1984] 2 W.L.R. 244, D.C.
s. 45, regs. 84/1358.

CAP.

1972—cont.

60. Gas Act 1972—cont.
s. 48, regs. 72/1737.
sch. 3, regs. 72/1765; 83/1749.
sch. 4, see Keane v. Bathgate, 1983 S.L.T. 651.
sch. 4, orders 78/1848; 82/655.
sch. 4, repealed in pt. (S.): 1984, c.54, sch.11.
sch. 6, repealed in pt. (S.): order 78/1176.

61. Land Charges Act 1972.
Royal Assent, August 9, 1972.
s. 1, see Norman v. Hardy [1974] 1 All E.R. 1170; Northern Development (Holdings) v. U.D.T. Securities [1976] 1 W.L.R. 1230; Allen v. Greehi Builders [1978] 3 All E.R. 1163, Browne-Wilkinson J.
s. 1, amended: 1975, c.76, s.17; 1984, c.28, sch.2.
s. 2, see Greene v. Church Commissioners for England [1974] 3 W.L.R. 349; [1974] 3 All E.R. 609, C.A.; First National Securities v. Chiltern District Council [1975] 2 All E.R. 766; Haslemere Estates v. Baker [1982] 1 W.L.R. 1109, Megarry V.-C.
s. 2, amended: 1975, c.7, sch.12; c.76, s.17; 1983, c.19, sch.1, 1984, c.51, sch.8; repealed in pt.: 1977, c.36, sch.9.
s. 3, see Barrett v. Hilton Developments [1974] 3 W.L.R. 545, C.A.; Property Discount Corp. v. Lyon Group [1981] 1 W.L.R. 300; [1981] 1 All E.R. 379, C.A.
s. 3, amended: 1975, c.7, sch.12; 1985, c.9, sch.2; repealed in pt.: ibid.
s. 4, amended: ibid.; 1984, c.51, sch.8.
s. 5, see Price Bros. (Somerford) v. J. Kelly Homes (Stoke-on-Trent) [1975] 1 W.L.R. 1512; [1975] 3 All E.R. 369, C.A.; Whittingham v. Whittingham; National Westminster Bank (Intervener) [1978] 2 W.L.R. 936. C.A.; Selim v. Bickenhall Engineering [1981] 3 All E.R. 210, Megarry V.-C.; Regan & Blackburn v. Rogers [1985] 2 All A.R. 180, Scott J.; Perez-Adamson v. Perez-Rivas [1987] 2 W.L.R. 500, C.A.
s. 5, amended: 1984, c.28, sch.2; repealed in pt.: 1985, c.65, schs.8,10.
s. 6, see Stockler v. Fourways Estates [1983] 3 All E.R. 501, Kilner Brown J.
s. 6, amended: 1981, c.54, sch.5; 1984, c.28, sch.2; 1985, c.65, sch.8; repealed in pt.: ibid., schs.8,10.
s. 16, rules 74/1286, 1287; orders 75/1315; 85/358.
s. 16, amended: 1985, c.65, sch.8; 1986, c.45, sch.14.
s. 17, see Calgary and Edmonton Land Co. v. Dobinson [1974] 2 W.L.R. 143; [1974] 1 All E.R. 484; Whittingham v. Whittingham; National Westminster Bank (Intervener) [1978] 2 W.L.R. 936, C.A.; Selim v. Bickenhall Engineering [1981] 3 All E.R. 210, Megarry V.-C.; Haslemere Estates v. Baker [1982] 1 W.L.R. 1109, Megarry V.-C.; Sowerby v. Sowerby (1982) 44 P. & C.R. 192, Megarry V.-C.; Regan & Blackburn v. Rogers [1985] 2 All E.R. 180, Scott J.

CAP.

1972—cont.

61. Land Charges Act 1972—cont.
s. 17, amended: 1975, c.7, sch.12.
sch. 2, amended: 1976, c.70, sch.7; 1986, c.5, sch.14; repealed in pt.: ibid., sch.15.
sch. 3, repealed in pt.: 1983, c.19, sch.2.
sch. 4, repealed: 1975, c.76, sch.2; rules 73/1862; 74/424.

62. Agriculture (Miscellaneous Provisions) Act 1972.
Royal Assent, August 9, 1972.
s 1, order 81/677.
ss. 1–3, repealed: 1981, c.22, sch.6.
ss. 4, 7, amended: 1973, c.65, sch.27.
s. 5, repealed: 1974, c.3, sch.6.
ss. 6, 7, repealed: 1980, c.13, sch.3.
s. 8, orders 76/1459, 1491.
s. 8, repealed in pt.: 1975, c.40, sch.2; 1984, c.40, sch.2.
ss. 9, 10, orders 76/2125, 2126.
s. 13, repealed: 1976, c.55, sch.4.
s. 15, repealed: 1986, c.5, sch.15.
s. 16, repealed in pt.: 1986, c.49, sch.4.
s. 17, orders 72/1246, 1274; 76/1034, 1082.
s. 18, repealed: 1979, c.13, sch.1.
s. 19, order 73/744.
s. 20, orders 77/901; 78/505; 79/638; 81/1170; 82/1457; 83/807, 1953; 84/686, 687, 1871, 1892; 85/637 (S.); 86/1342; 88/736.
s. 24, amended: 1977, c.42, sch.23; repealed in pt.: ibid., sch.25.
s. 27, order 72/1260; amended: 1974, c.3, sch.6; repealed in pt.: 1975, c.24, sch.3.
schs. 1, 2, repealed: 1980, c.13, sch.13.
sch. 3, orders 76/1459, 1491.

63. Industry Act 1972.
Royal Assent, August 9, 1972.
Pts. I (ss. 1–6), II (ss. 7–9), repealed: 1982, c.52, sch.3.
s. 1, see Jaka Foods Group v. Secretary of State for Industry, The Times, January 17, 1980, Bristow J.
s. 1, orders: 72/1234; 78/1141; 79/269, 837, 1642; 80/1110; 82/934.
s. 3, orders 73/243; 76/1573; 79/975.
s. 5, orders 76/1573; 79/837, 975, 1642; 80/1110; 82/934.
s. 7, see Burman v. Thorn Domestic Appliances (Electrical) [1982] S.T.C. 179, Walton J.; Ryan (Inspector of Taxes) v. Crabtree Denims [1987] S.T.C. 402, Hoffmann J.
s. 8, orders 75/383; 76/155; 77/1135; 78/812; 79/109; 81/980.
s. 10, amended: order 75/138; 1979, c.59, s.10; 1985, c.9, sch.2; regs. 87/1807.
ss. 13–16, 17 (in pt.), repealed: 1982, c.52, sch.3.
s. 18, amended: 1973, c.36, sch.6; repealed in pt.: 1982, c.52, sch.3.
s. 19, repealed in pt.: ibid.
sch.1, repealed in pt.: 1977, c.45, sch.13; 1982, c.52, sch.3.
sch. 2, orders 74/1372; 77/706; 79/837, 975, 1642; 80/1110; 82/934.
schs. 2, 4 (in pt.), repealed: 1982, c.52, sch.3.

1972—cont.

64. Harbours Development (Scotland) Act 1972.
Royal Assent, August 9, 1972.

65. National Debt Act 1972.
Royal Assent, August 9, 1972.
s. 2, repealed in pt.: 1976, c.4, sch.6.
s. 3, regs. 76/2012, 2100; 79/553, 1677; 81/485; 82/489; 83/998; 84/600; 87/1635; 88/1167, 1355.
s. 3, amended: 1976, c.4, sch.5; repealed in pt.: *ibid.*,sch.6.
s. 5, repealed in pt.: *ibid.*
s. 6, regs. 76/2012.
s. 6, amended: orders 75/1137; 84/539.
s. 7, amended: 1976, c.4, sch.5; repealed in pt.: *ibid.*, sch.6.
s. 9, amended: 1975, c.69, sch.4.
s. 10, amended: 1975, c.68, ss.23–25.
s. 11, regs. 73/389; 74/552; 75/714, 1191–1193; 76/1543, 1962, 2111; 77/545, 1447, 1448, 1456, 1916; 78/788; 1297, 1334, 1855; 79/1388, 1533; 80/45, 452, 767, 1614, 1986; 81/310, 372, 486, 670, 1172, 1460, 1482; 82/488, 1013, 1227, 1574; 83/495, 1063; 84/388, 599, 601, 603, 779, 1052, 1564; 85/146, 861, 891, 1035, 1479; 88/1356–1358.
s. 11, repealed in pt.: 1976, c.4, sch.6.
s. 13, repealed in pt. (S.): 1975, c.69, sch.5.
s. 14, repealed: 1976, c.4, sch.6.
s. 15, repealed in pt.: 1976, c.4, sch.6.
s. 16, amended: 1975, c.69, sch.4; repealed in pt.: 1976, c.4, sch.6.
s. 18, repealed: 1973, c.36, sch.6.

66. Poisons Act 1972.
Royal Assent, August 9, 1972.
s. 2, orders 78/2, 80/126; 82/217; 86/9.
ss. 5, 6, amended: 1980, c.65, sch.6.
s. 6, amended: 1977, c.45, s.31, sch.6.
s. 7, rules 78/1, 672; 80/127; 82/218; 85/1077; 86/10, 1704.
s. 8, amended: 1977, c.45, s.31, sch.6; 1984, c.30, sch.10.
s. 9, amended: 1977, c.45, s.31, sch.6.
s. 11, amended: 1973, c.65, sch.24; order 80/703; 1983, c.54, sch.5; 1984, c.24, sch.5; 1985, c.51, sch.8; repealed in pt.: S.L.R. 1978.

67. Companies (Floating Charges and Receivers) (Scotland) Act 1972.
Royal Assent, October 17, 1972.
repealed: 1985, c.9, sch.1.
rules 73/145.
s. 1, see *Site Preparations* v. *Buchan Development Co.* (O.H.), July 22, 1982.
ss. 1, 13, see *Ross* v. *Taylor*, 1985 S.L.T. 387.
s. 5, see *Cumbernauld Development Corporation* v. *Mustone*, 1983 S.L.T. (Sh.Ct.) 55.
s. 13, see *Forth & Clyde Construction Co.* v. *Trinity Timber & Plywood Co.* 1984 S.L.T. 94; *Cumbernauld Development Corporation* v. *Mustone*, 1983 S.L.T. (Sh.Ct.) 55.
s. 15, see *Lord Advocate* v. *Royal Bank of Scotland*, First Division, February 24, 1977; *Gordon Anderson (Plant)* v. *Campsie Construction*, July 25, 1975; *Imperial Hotel (Aber-*

1972—cont.

67. Companies (Floating Charges and Receivers) (Scotland) Act 1972—*cont.*
deen) v. *Vaux Breweries* (O.H.), 1978 S.L.T. 113; *McPhail* v. *Lothian Regional Council* (O.H.), January 13, 1981; *Cumbernauld Development Corporation* v. *Mustone*, 1983 S.L.T.(Sh.Ct.) 55; *Manley, Petr.* (O.H.), 1985 S.L.T. 42; *Shanks* v. *Central Regional Council* (O.H.), 1987 S.L.T. 410.
ss. 15, 17, see *Taylor, Petr.* (O.H.), August 13, 1981.
s. 17, see *Macleod* v. *Alexander Sutherland* (O.H.) 1977 S.L.T.(Notes) 44; *Mace Builders (Glasgow)* v. *Lunn, The Times*, October 11, 1986, C.A.; *Hill Samuel & Co.* v. *Laing* (O.H.), 1988 S.L.T. 452.
ss. 20, 21, see *Armour and Mycroft, Petrs.* (O.H.), 1983 S.L.T. 543.
s. 31, see *Cumbernauld Development Corporation* v. *Mustone*, 1983 S.L.T. (Sh.Ct) 55.
s. 37, see *Forth & Clyde Construction Co.* v. *Trinity Timber & Plywood Co.*, 1984 S.L.T. 94.

68. European Communities Act 1972.
Royal Assent, October 17, 1972.
Commencement order: 82/1048.
orders 77/654, 1092.
s. 1, orders 73/2154; 74/1263; 75/408, 2162; 76/217, 218; 77/822, 2145–2147; 78/617–619, 781, 1032, 1103, 1104; 79/1446; 81/1125; 82/341, 707; 84/1820; 85/1198, 1772; 87/2040.
s. 1, amended: 1979, c.57, s.1; 1985, c.64, s.1; c.75, s.1; 1986, c.58, s.1; 1988, c.46, s.1.
ss. 1, 2, see *R.* v. *H.M. Treasury, ex p. Smedley* [1985] 2 W.L.R. 576, C.A.; *British Leyland* v. *E.C. Commission (Merson Intervening) (No. 226/84)* [1987] R.T.R. 136, European Ct.
s. 2, see *Schorsch Meier G.m.b.H.* v. *Hennin* [1974] 3 W.L.R. 823; [1975] 1 All E.R. 152, C.A.; *Gibson* v. *Lord Advocate* (O.H.), 1975 S.L.T. 134; *Amies* v. *Inner London Education Authority* [1977] 2 All E.R. 100; [1977] I.C.R. 308, E.A.T., *Macarthys* v. *Smith, The Times*, April 18, 1980, C.A.; *Imperial Chemical Industries* v. *Berk Pharmaceuticals* [1981] F.S.R. 1, Megarry V.-C.; *Albion Shipping Agency* v. *Arnold* [1982] I.C.R. 22, E.A.T.; *R.* v. *H.M. Treasury, ex p. Daily Mail and General Trust* [1987] 1 F.T.L.R. 394, Macpherson J.; *Duke* v. *G.E.C. Reliance (formerly Reliance Systems), The Times*, February 12, 1988, H.L.
s. 2, regs. 73/15, 806, 1012, 1193, 1199, 1351, 1402, 1642, 1820, 1889, 1952, 2124; 74/54, 65, 678, 763, 791, 908, 980, 1175, 1930, 2186; 75/292, 485, 655, 928, 1169, 1173, 1265, 1475, 1873, 2036, 2125, 2210, 2226; 76/195, 202, 316, 406, 743, 798, 1265, 1674, 1771, 1870, 1890, 2163, 2187; 77/27, 181, 276, 312, 777, 910, 932, 1021, 1050, 1091, 1140, 1287, 1304, 1327, 1402, 1461, 1462, 1552, 1553, 1559, 1577, 1718, 1753, 1785, 1804, 1854, 1960, 2112; 78/7, 25, 77, 209, 214, 463, 484, 564, 598, 720, 861, 960, 1086, 1112, 1122, 1158, 1236, 1248, 1330, 1537 (S.), 1546, 1559, 1592, 1602–4, 1748, 1755;

CAP.

1972—cont.

68. European Communities Act 1972—*cont.*

80/97, 124, 419, 754, 762, 765, 865, 886, 927, 928, 956, 1012, 1070, 1182, 1198, 1239, 1298, 1394, 1459, 1565, 1577, 1578, 1721, 1742, 1749, 1770, 1787, 1788, 1795, 1825, 1838, 1851, 1912, 1951, 1979, 1990, 1997, 2018, 2028; 81/2, 100, 199, 205, 266, 283, 322, 323, 407, 432, 445 (S.), 447 (S.), 454, 461, 464, 493, 593, 669, 678, 792, 864, 908, 935, 1034 (S.), 1077, 1102, 1164, 1168, 1169 (S.), 1339, 1374, 1488, 1536, 1549, 1692, 1700, 1707, 1708, 1727, 1776, 1794, 1843; 82/7, 529, 578, 767, 793, 969, 980, 996 (S.), 1043, 1045, 1324, 1496, 1555, 1590, 1602, 1623, 1637, 1683, 1700–1702, 1725, 1726, 1886, 83/61, 70, 507, 508, 530, 624, 641, 703, 709, 877, 884, 924, 925, 938, 1010, 1042, 1098, 1158, 1184, 1246, 1372 (S.), 1600, 1706, 1724, 1732, 1762, 1763, 1794; 84/144, 176, 618, 620, 716, 748, 1048, 1145, 1244, 1260, 1270, 1313 (S.), 1318, 1360 (S.), 1369, 1500, 1519 (S.), 1538, 1576 (S.), 1592, 1618, 1640, 1739, 1765, 1787, 1885 (S.), 1902, 1917, 1918, 1922, 1927, 2005; 85/67, 71, 216, 306, 475, 498 (S.), 509, 615, 777, 913 (S.), 1025, 1068 (S.), 1072, 1154, 1155, 1266, 1271, 1279, 1310, 1377, 1851, 1857, 1968, 2075; 86/23, 68, 560, 666, 890, 938, 947, 1082, 1233, 1272, 1295, 1352, 1373, 1391, 1447, 1456, 1457, 1500, 1501, 1542, 1611, 1613(S.), 1669, 1735, 1795, 1876, 1894, 1980, 2076, 2148; orders 72/1590; 73/2143, 2205; 75/427, 1707; 76/901, 987, 998, 1203, 1221, 2141; 77/827, 980; 78/1033, 1832, 1910, 1927, 1938; 79/80, 132, 221, 249, 319, 555, 586, 654, 693, 749, 768, (S.), 847, 941, 956, 1089, 1094, 1095, 1175, 1205, 1224, 1379, 1426, 1427, 1459, 1476, 1748, 1755; 80/703, 1164; 81/905, 1026; 82/847, 1076; 84/1075; 85/749, 1027, 1773, 1801; 86/23; regs. 87/27, 97, 116, 149, 410, 425 (S.), 442, 524, 735, 736, 800 (S.), 805, 881 (S.), 909, 949, 1497, 1521, 1523, 1755, 1771, 1783, 1807, 1824, 1843, 1902, 1950, 1991, 2093, 2097, 2105, 2117, 2118, 2129, 2130, 2132, 2171, 2202; orders 87/447, 448, 926, 973; regs. 88/132, 186, 296, 361–363, 481(S.), 534, 538, 705, 760, 778, 785, 802, 848, 849, 896, 915, 958, 1000, 1001, 1103, 1128, 1180, 1199, 1201, 1207, 1217, 1218, 1241, 1267, 1336, 1349, 1350, 1476, 1522, 1523, 1532, 1562, 1567, 1640, 1669, 1736, 1772, 1790; order 88/249; scheme 76/547; S.Rs. 1977 No. 310; 1978 Nos. 18, 300, 366, 393; 1979 Nos. 121, 261, 401, 443, 465; 1980 Nos. 14, 139, 410, 458; 1981 Nos. 119, 199, 399, 414; 1982 Nos. 144, 155, 279, 383, 386, 397, 398, 401, 422; 1983 Nos. 3, 28, 282, 286, 368; 1984 Nos. 16, 45, 199, 407; 1985 Nos. 4, 63, 81, 120, 123, 175, 352; 1986, Nos. 188, 299, 334; 1987 Nos. 78, 85, 92, 114, 154–156, 217, 218, 225, 285, 306, 317, 328, 351, 383, 407, 425, 431, 442, 445, 452, 457; 88/40, 188, 211, 253, 263, 265, 279, 288, 297, 310, 344, 358, 388, 403.

CAP.

1972—cont.

68. European Communities Act 1972—*cont.*

s. 2, amended: 1978, c.51, sch.16; c.52, sch.11.

ss. 2, 3, see *R.* v. *Goldstein* [1983] 1 W.L.R. 157, H.L.

s. 2, amended: 1973, c.36, sch.6.

s. 3, amended: 1986, c.58, s.2.

s. 4, see *Paterson* v. *Richardson* [1982] R.T.R. 49, D.C.; *Oxford* v. *Spencer* [1983] R.T.R. 63, C.A.

s. 4, regs. 73/806; 77/1489, 1854; orders 73/135, 806, 1019, 2176; 75/1164; 76/548, 1304, 2016; 77/2028; 78/1003, 1938; 81/1192; 82/1048; 87/2106.

s. 4, amended: 1973, c.36, sch.6.

s. 5, regs. 76/838, 2130; 77/910; 78/1148, 1704; orders 74/166, 1350, 1371, 1376; 75/2238; 76/1399; 77/983, 1117, 2041, 2056, 2143; 78/78, 81–85, 109–111, 155, 192, 193, 237, 246, 601, 640, 641, 674, 698, 765, 909, 1142, 1143, 1205, 1342, 1593, 1941; 79/155, 1649; 80/67, 1911, 1999; 81/1768, 1769; 82/1773, 1780; 83/342, 1782, 1802; 84/1306, 1452, 1754, 1969; 85/12, 118, 1299, 1630, 2019, 2020; 86/346–348, 813, 2179; 87/1053, 1125, 1218, 1804, 2183, 2184; 88/1065, 1259–1261, 1314.

s. 5, amended: 1978, c.42, s.6; 1979, c.3, sch.2; repealed in pt.: 1979, c.2, sch.6; c.3, sch.3.

s. 6, orders 72/1578, 1679; 76/918; 77/2053; 78/17; 79/1541; 80/1564; regs. 79/433; 82/1502; 85/135.

s. 6, amended: 1979, c.2, sch.4; c.3, sch.2; repealed in pt.: 1975, c.45, sch.14; regs. 77/910; modified: 1978, c.42, sch.12.

s. 7, repealed in pt.: 1976, c.55, sch.4; amended: order 78/272.

s. 8, repealed: 1985, c.21, sch.2.

s. 9, see *Phonogram* v. *Lane* [1981] 3 All E.R. 182, C.A.; *International Sales and Agencies* v. *Marcus* [1982] 3 All E.R. 551, Lawson J; *Official Custodians of Charities* v. *Parway Estates Development* [1984] 3 W.L.R 525, C.A.; *TCB* v. *Gray* [1986] 1 All E.R. 587, Browne-Wilkinson V.-C.; *Oskosh B'Gosh Inc.* v. *Dan Marble Inc. and Craze,* November 11, 1987, Sir Neil Lawson.

s. 9, repealed: 1985, c.9, sch.1.

s. 10, regs. 73/950.

s. 10, repealed: 1976, c.34, sch.6.

s. 11, amended: order 79/1714; 1986, c.58, s.2; repealed in pt.: 1985, c.23, sch.2.

s. 12, amended: 1979, c.13, sch.1.

s. 24, regs. 86/470.

sch. 1, see *British Leyland* v. *E.C. Commission (Merson Intervening) (No. 226/84* [1987] R.T.R. 136, European Ct.

sch. 2, regs. 84/716; orders 85/2020; 86/813, 2179; 87/1053, 1125, 1804, 2183; 88/1065, 1259, 1314.

sch. 2, amended: 1977, c.45, s.32; 1978, c.51, sch.16; c.52, sch.11; 1979, c.3, sch.2.

sch. 3, orders 73/135, 1019, 2176; 75/1164; 76/548, 1304; 77/2028, 2143; 78/1003; 81/1192; 87/2106; repealed in pt.: 1978, c.42, s.6, sch.13.

CAP.

1972—cont.

68. European Communities Act 1972—*cont.*
sch. 4, see *Paterson* v. *Richardson* [1982] R.T.R.
49, D.C.; *Oxford* v. *Spencer* [1983] R.T.R. 63,
C.A.

sch. 4, regs. 73/806; 76/1399; 77/1489, 1854;
78/1938; orders 74/96, 166, 1350, 1371,
1376; 75/2230, 2238; 76/1399; 82/1048;
repealed in pt.: 1975, c.24, sch.3; c.25, sch.3;
c.40, sch.2; c.45, sch.14; 1976, c.3, sch.3;
c.40, sch.15; 1978, c.42, sch.13; 1979, c.2,
sch.6; c.3, sch.3; c.12, sch.7; 1980, c.34,
sch.9; c.42, sch.2; regs. 78/1603; 1981, c.22,
sch.6.

**69. Horserace Totalisator and Betting Levy
Boards Act 1972.**
Royal Assent, October 17, 1972.
s. 1, repealed in pt.: 1981, c.63, sch.7.

70. Local Government Act 1972.
Royal Assent, October 26, 1972.
see *Bradford Metropolitan City Council* v. *Brown*
(1987) 19 H.L.R. 16, C.A.
rules 73/1910, 2061; order 86/1190.
s. 2, amended: 1973, c.15, sch.5; 1985, c.51,
sch.16.
s. 5, order 79/710.
s. 6, amended: 1983, c.2, sch.8; 1985, c.51,
sch.16.
s. 7, orders 84/924; 85/59.
s. 7, amended: 1985, c.51, sch.16.
s. 8, order 76/213.
s. 8, repealed in pt.: 1984, c.53, s.2; 1985, c.51,
sch.17.
ss. 9, 11, 16, amended: 1983, c.2, sch.8.
s. 13, see *Taylor* v. *Masefield* (1987) 85 L.G.R.
108, C.A.
s. 13, amended: 1980, c.51, sch.25.
s. 20, order 73/34.
ss. 25, 28, 29, amended: 1983, c.2, sch.8.
s. 32, see *Re A Complainant against Liverpool
City Council* [1975] 2 All E.R. 650, D.C.
s. 35, amended: 1983, c.2, sch.8.
Pt. III (ss. 39–45), repealed: *ibid.,* sch.9.
s. 40, order 74/243.
s. 42, rules 73/79, 166, 358, 2184; 74/84;
76/2065, 2066.
s. 47, see *Enfield London Borough Council* v.
*Local Government Boundary Commission for
England* [1979] 3 All E.R. 747, H.L.
s. 47, orders 76/187, 188; 77/218, 219, 299;
78/129; 79/90; 80/32, 302, 363, 415, 1558,
1876, 1920, 1939; 81/134, 148, 186, 268,
286–288, 1074, 1075, 1326, 1343, 1348,
1349, 1352, 1353, 1696, 1715; 82/128, 141,
185, 195–197, 1235, 1256, 1369, 1599, 1618,
1636, 1658, 1747, 1748, 1759, 1813, 1814,
1864, 1865; 83/84, 288, 329, 412, 433, 434,
460, 1330, 1339, 1376, 1531–1533, 1844,
1868, 1869, 1874, 1936; 84/60, 66, 67, 89,
115–118, 151, 152, 258, 348, 387, 411, 1793,
1906; 85/1891.
s. 47, amended: 1985, c.51, schs.9,16; repealed
in pt.: *ibid.,* sch.17; 1988, c.40, sch.13
(prosp.).
s. 48, orders 79/90; 80/32, 271, 302, 363, 387,
415, 1285, 1876; 81/134, 148, 186, 268,

CAP.

1972—cont.

70. Local Government Act 1972—*cont.*
286–288, 1074, 1075, 1326, 1343, 1348,
1349, 1452, 1453, 1715, 1773, 1774, 1827,
1844; 82/128, 185, 196, 197, 392, 1235, 1256,
1369, 1599, 1618, 1747, 1748, 1864, 1865;
83/96, 138, 167, 192, 288, 329, 412, 433,
434, 460, 1330, 1531–1533, 1839, 1840,
1843, 1844, 1847, 1867–1870, 1873, 1874,
1937, 1941; 84/60, 66, 67, 89, 115–118, 151,
152, 258, 348, 387, 411.
s. 48, amended: 1985, c.51, sch.16.
s. 50, amended: *ibid.,* sch.9; repealed in pt.
(prosp.): 1988, c.40, sch.13.
s. 51, orders 73/2230; 74/694; 75/1667–1672,
1681, 1698–1700, 1811–1818, 1912–1922;
76/65, 67, 114, 115, 161, 174, 180–182, 196,
197, 204, 248, 284–288, 296–298, 318, 319,
343, 379, 380, 401, 750–755, 764, 765,
808–812, 822, 823, 831–833, 876, 992, 1001,
1053, 1063, 1064, 1130–1132, 1238, 1383,
1545–1550, 1691–1695, 1704, 1757, 1763,
1819, 1820, 1867, 1927, 1965–1968, 1974,
2069, 2169; 77/218, 219, 237, 299, 379, 381,
412–4, 437, 438, 510, 538, 546, 681, 723,
731, 732, 864–866, 1064–1066, 1273–1279,
1390–1393, 1414, 1415, 1427, 1433, 1442,
1545, 1546, 1564–1567, 1588, 1613, 1673,
1674, 1763–1766, 1810, 1811, 1817–1819,
1864, 1865, 1885, 1894, 1895, 1962, 2037,
2067, 2068, 2141; 78/43, 45–49, 63, 87–90,
129, 231, 437, 482, 753, 1246, 1247, 1299,
1300, 1356, 1370, 1434–1439, 1465, 1473,
1494, 1495, 1505, 1552, 1553, 1591,
1604–1606, 1611–1613, 1639, 1640, 1664,
1665, 1690, 1694, 1722, 1749–1751, 1768,
1783, 1792, 1793, 1806, 1813, 1814,
1841–1843, 1859–1864; 79/90, 1015, 1016,
1027, 1028, 1071, 1107–1113, 1131,
1264–1266, 1295, 1320–1324, 1327, 1328,
1341, 1346–1349, 1368, 1411, 1472–1474,
1494–1496, 1523–1525, 1615, 1616, 1663,
1670, 1695; 80/32, 43, 63, 85, 138, 181, 196,
231, 297, 302, 363, 380, 415, 516, 581, 594,
643, 652, 653, 732, 733, 738, 739, 756, 757,
777, 778, 795, 842, 1054, 1069, 1128, 1297,
1340, 1341, 1343, 1344, 1402, 1463, 1487,
1558, 1572, 1702, 1725, 1769, 1805, 1829,
1830, 1876, 1920, 1939; 81/43, 49, 51, 79,
85, 118, 131, 134, 141, 148, 165, 167, 186,
190, 268, 284, 286–288, 478, 1074, 1075,
1696, 1715, 1748; 82/128, 141, 185, 195–197,
392, 440, 535, 556, 590, 606, 1235, 1256,
1369, 1599, 1618, 1636, 1658, 1747, 1748,
1759, 1813, 1814, 1864, 1865; 83/84, 96,
138, 166, 167, 192, 288, 329, 411, 412, 433,
434, 460, 829, 830, 842, 1330, 1339, 1376,
1529, 1531–1533, 1664, 1844, 1867–1869,
1874, 1936; 84/60, 66, 67, 89, 115–120, 151,
152, 258, 348, 387, 411, 1752, 1793; 84/1906,
1944; 85/139, 140, 219, 264, 335, 336, 402,
634, 1753, 1891, 1892, 2048–2050, 2061;
86/281, 321, 1619, 1909, 2278, 2279; 87/221,
305, 338, 339, 1576, 1598, 1737, 2228, 2247;
88/61, 65, 70, 71, 241, 259, 314, 315.

1972—cont.

70. Local Government Act 1972—cont.

s. 54, orders 81/113, 145, 146.

s. 58, orders 81/113, 145, 146, 667; 82/1395; 83/381, 447, 448; 84/1799; 85/265; 86/526, 533, 535, 556.

s. 60, amended: 1985, c.51, sch.9; repealed in pt. (prosp.): 1988, c.40, sch.13.

s. 62, amended: 1985, c.51, sch.16.

s. 67, regs. 76/246; 85/110; orders 73/2230; 74/694; 75/1667–1671, 1681, 1698–1700; 78/129, 247; 80/32, 302, 363, 380, 415, 1558, 1876, 1919, 1920, 1939; 81/113, 145, 146, 148, 182, 268, 286, 287, 453, 1074, 1075, 1348, 1349, 1696, 1715; 82/98, 127, 141, 185, 195–197, 376, 1256, 1369, 1395, 1599, 1636, 1658, 1747, 1751, 1759, 1813, 1814, 1864, 1865; 83/84, 96, 124, 138, 154, 166, 167, 192, 206, 269, 288, 329, 411, 412, 433, 434, 460, 1330, 1339, 1376, 1530–1533, 1664, 1788, 1867, 1868, 1874; 84/60, 66, 67, 89, 115–118, 151, 152, 258, 348, 387, 411, 473, 739, 1441, 1562, 1752, 1782, 1793, 1799, 1875, 1906, 1930, 1944, 2023, 2049; 85/59, 89, 129, 219, 264, 265, 335, 336, 1753, 1763, 1816, 1892, 2048–2050, 2061–2064, 86/4, 281, 321, 526, 533, 535, 556, 1364, 1619, 1909, 2008, 2077, 2278, 2279; 87/124, 221, 305, 338, 339, 1576, 1598, 1737, 2228, 2247; 88/61, 65, 70, 71, 241, 259, 314, 315.

s. 67, amended: order 77/1710; 1985, c.51, sch.9; repealed in pt. (prosp.): 1988, c.40, sch.13.

s. 68, repealed in pt.: 1985, c.51, sch.17.

s. 70, amended: *ibid.*, sch.14; order 85/1884; 1988, c.40, sch.12 (prosp.); repealed in pt. (prosp.): *ibid.*, sch.13.

s. 73, orders 77/335, 382; 80/1919; 82/1746.

s. 77, repealed: order 85/1884; 1985, c.51, sch.17.

s. 78, amended: *ibid.*, sch.9; 1988, c.40, sch.12 (prosp.); repealed in pt. (prosp.): *ibid.*, sch.13.

s. 79, amended: 1985, c.51, sch.14; repealed in pt. (prosp.): 1988, c.40, sch.13.

s. 80, amended: 1982, c.32, sch.5; 1983, c.2, sch.8; 1984, c.53, s.10; 1985, c.51, sch.14; order 85/1884; repealed in pt.: 1982, c.32, sch.6; 1985, c.67, sch.8; 1988, c.40, sch.13 (prosp.).

s. 81, amended: 1974, c.7, sch.7; 1985, c.65, sch.8; order 77/1710; repealed in pt.: 1984, c.32, sch.7; 1985, c.51, sch.17; 1988, c.40, sch.13.

s. 82, amended: 1985, c.51, sch. 14; order 85/1884; 1988, c.4, sch.6; repealed in pt. (prosp.): 1988, c.40, sch.13.

s. 83, rules 73/79, 166, 358, 2184.

s. 83, amended: 1985, c.51, sch.14; repealed in pt.: order 77/1710; 1985, c.51, sch.17; 1988, c.40, sch.13 (prosp.).

ss. 84, 85, amended: 1985, c.51, sch.14; order 85/1884; repealed in pt. (prosp.): 1988, c.40, sch.13.

s. 86, amended: 1982, c.32, sch.5; 1983, c.2, sch.8; 1984, c.53, s.10; 1985, c.51, sch.14; order 85/1884; repealed in pt. (prosp.): 1988, c.40, sch.13.

1972—cont.

70. Local Government Act 1972—cont.

s. 87, amended: 1982, c.32, sch.5; 1984, c.53, s.10; 1985, c.51, sch.14; repealed in pt.: order 77/1710; 1988, c.40, sch.13 (prosp.).

s. 88, amended: 1985, c.51, sch.14; repealed in pt.: order 77/1710; S.L.R. 1978, 1988, c.40, sch.13 (prosp.).

s. 89, amended: 1983, c.2, sch.8; 1985, c.50, s.19; c.51, sch.14; repealed in pt.: *ibid.*, schs.14,17; 1988, c.40, sch.13 (prosp.).

s. 90, amended: 1985, c.50, sch.14; order 85/1884; repealed in pt. (prosp.): 1988, c.40, sch.13.

s. 92, amended: 1985, c.50, sch.14; order 85/1884; 1988, c.4, sch.6; repealed in pt. (prosp.): 1988, c.40, sch.13.

s. 93, repealed: 1985, c.51, sch.17.

s. 94, see *R. v. Newham London Borough Council, ex p. Haggerty, The Times,* April 11, 1986, Mann J.

s. 94, order 80/1871.

s. 98, order 85/1781.

s. 98, amended: 1985, c.51, sch.14; order 85/1884; 1986, c.60, sch.16; repealed in pt. (prosp.): 1988, c.40, sch.13.

s. 99, amended: 1985, c.51, sch.14; order 85/1884; repealed in pt. (prosp.): 1988, c.40, sch.13.

s. 100, amended: 1985, c.43, sch.2; repealed in pt.: *ibid.*, schs.2,3.

ss. 100A–100K, added: *ibid.*, s.1.

s. 100E, amended: 1988, c.4, sch.6.

s. 100G, order 86/854.

s. 100J, amended: order 85/1884; 1988, c.4, sch.6; repealed in pt. (prosp.): 1988, c.40, sch.15.

s. 101, see *R. v. Birmingham City Council, ex p. National Union of Public Employees, The Times,* April 24, 1984, Mann J.; *R. v. Secretary of State for Education and Science, ex p. Birmingham District Council, The Times,* July 18, 1984, McCullough J.; *R. v. Secretary of State for the Environment, ex p. Hillingdon London Borough Council* [1986] (Note) 2 All E.R. 273, C.A.

s. 101, order 85/1781.

s. 101, amended: 1985, c.51, sch.14; order 85/1884; repealed in pt.: 1985, c.51, sch.17; S.L.R. 1986; 1988, c.40, sch.13 (prosp.).

s. 102, amended: 1983, c.41, sch.9.

s. 104, repealed in pt.: 1988, c.40, sch.13.

s. 109, order 86/854.

s. 111, see *R. v. Greater London Council, ex p. Burgess* [1978] I.C.R. 991, D.C.; *Provident Mutual Life Assurance Association* v. *Derby City Council; Fenclose Securities* v. *Same* [1981] 1 W.L.R. 173, H.L.; *R. v. Greater London Council, ex p. Westminster City Council, The Times,* December 27, 1984, Glidewell J.; *Smith* v. *Skinner; Gladden* v. *McMahon* (1986) 26 R.V.R. 45, D.C.; *Westminster City Council, Re* [1986] 2 W.L.R. 807, H.L.; *R. v. Oxfordshire Education Authority, ex p. W, The Times,* November 22, 1986, D.C.

1972—cont.

70. Local Government Act 1972—*cont.*
s. 112, see *R.* v. *Hertfordshire County Council, ex p. National Union of Public Employees; R.* v. *Sussex County Council, ex p. National Union of Public Employees* [1985] I.R.L.R. 258, C.A.; *R.* v. *District Auditor for Leicester, ex p. Leicester City Council* (1985) 25 R.V.R. 191, Woolf J.
s. 112, amended: 1984, c.30, sch.10; repealed in pt.: 1985, c.51, sch.17; c.72, sch.13.
s. 113, amended: 1973, c.32, schs.4,5; 1980, c.53, sch.1.
s. 118, regs. 83/1402.
s. 118, amended: 1983, c.20, sch.4.
s. 119, amended: orders 75/1137; 84/539; repealed in pt.: 1986, c.50, sch.11.
s. 120, see *Costello* v. *Dacorum District Council* (1983) 147 L.G.R.1, C.A.
ss. 121, 125, amended: 1981, c.67, sch.4; repealed in pt.: *ibid.,* sch.6.
ss. 122, 123, amended: 1980, c.65, sch.23; repealed in pt.: *ibid.,* schs.23,34.
s. 123, see *R.* v. *Doncaster Metropolitan Borough Council, ex p. Braim* (1987) 85 L.G.R. 233, McCullough J.; *Manchester City Council* v. *Secretary of State for the Environment* (1987) 27 R.V.R. 75; (1987) 54 P. & C.R. 212, C.A.
s. 123A, repealed: 1980, c.65, schs.23,34.
s. 125, regs. 74/423; 76/300; 82/6.
s. 125, substituted: 1986, c.63, s.43.
s. 126, amended: 1980, c.65, sch.23; repealed in pt.: *ibid.,* schs.23,34.
s. 128, see *R.* v. *Plymouth City Council and Cornwall County Council, ex p. Freeman* (1988) 28 R.V.R. 89, C.A.
s. 131, amended: 1974, c.44, s.43; 1979, c.46, sch.4; 1985, c.71, sch.2; repealed in pt.: 1982, c.1, sch.2; 1985, c.71, sch.1.
s. 134, amended: 1988, c.40, sch.12.
s. 137, see *Manchester City Council* v. *Greater Manchester Metropolitan County Council* (1980) 78 L.G.R. 560, H.L.; *R.* v. *District Auditor for Leicester, ex p. Leicester City Council* (1985) 25 R.V.R. 191, Woolf J.; *R.* v. *District Auditor No. 3 Audit District of West Yorkshire Metropolitan County Council, ex p. West Yorkshire Metropolitan County Council* [1986] 26 R.V.R. 24, D.C.
s. 137, order 84/197.
s. 137, amended: 1982, c.30, s.44; c.32, sch.5; 1986, c.10, s.3.
s. 138, repealed in pt.: 1980, c.65, schs.1,34.
s. 140, amended: 1982, c.30, s.39; c.50, sch.5; repealed in pt.: 1982, c.30, s.39, sch.7; 1984, c.32, sch.7.
ss. 140A, 140B, added: 1982, c.30, s.39.
s. 140B, repealed in pt.: 1985, c.51, sch.17.
s. 140C, added: 1982, c.30, s.39; amended: 1982, c.50, sch.5.
s. 141, amended: 1985, c.51, sch.16.
s. 142, see *R.* v. *Greater London Council, ex p. Westminster City Council, The Times,* December 27, 1984, Glidewell J.; *R.* v. *Greater London Council, ex p. Westminster*

1972—cont.

70. Local Government Act 1972—*cont.*
City Council, The Times, January 22, 1985, Nolan J.; *R.* v. *Inner London Education Authority, ex p. Westminster City Council* [1986] 1 All E.R. 19, Glidewell J.
s. 142, amended: 1986, c.10, s.3; repealed in pt. (prosp.): 1988, c.40, sch.13.
s. 143, see *R.* v. *G.L.C., ex p. Bromley London Borough Council, The Times,* March 27, 1984, Forbes J.
s. 143, regs. 74/274.
s. 144, repealed in pt.: 1976, c.57, sch.2; 1980, c.65, s.190, sch.34; 1985, c.51, sch.17.
s. 146, amended: 1986, c.60, sch.16.
s. 146A, added: 1985, c.51, sch.14; amended: order 85/1884; 1988, c.40, sch.12 (prosp.); repealed in pt. (prosp.): *ibid.,* sch.13.
s. 147, see *Randall* v. *Tendring District Auditor* (1980) 79 L.G.R. 207, D.C.; *R.* v. *District Auditor for Leicester, ex p. Leicester City Council* (1985) 25 R.V.R. 191, Woolf J.
s. 148, repealed in pt.: 1985, c.51, sch.17.
s. 149, repealed in pt.: 1982, c.32, sch.6; 1985, c.51, sch.19.
s. 151, see *Provident Mutual Life Assurance Association* v. *Derby City Council; Fenclose Securities* v. *Same* [1981] 1 W.L.R. 173, H.L.; *ILEA* v. *Secretary of State for the Environment, The Times,* May 26, 1984, C.A.; *Smith* v. *Skinner; Gladden* v. *McMahon* (1986) 26 R.V.R. 45, D.C.; *R.* v. *Hackney London Borough Council, ex p. Fleming* (1986) 26 R.V.R. 182, Woolf J.
s. 153, amended: 1985, c.51, sch.14; order 85/1884; 1988, c.50, s.132; repealed in pt. (prosp.): 1988, c.40, sch.13.
ss. 154–158, repealed: 1982, c.32, sch.6.
s. 156, see *Derby City Council* v. *Secretary of State for the Environment* (1983) 81 L.G.R. 134, Forbes J.
s. 159, see *London Borough of Hillingdon* v. *Paullson* [1977] J.P.L. 518, Middlesex Crown Court; *R.* v. *Farmer, ex p. Hargrave* (1981) 79 L.G.R. 676, D.C.
ss. 159–162, repealed: 1982, c.32, sch.6.
s. 161, see *Pickwell* v. *Camden London Borough Council* (1982) 80 L.G.R. 798; *Graham* v. *Teesdale* (1983) 81 L.G.R. 117, Webster J.; *Wilkinson* v. *Doncaster Metropolitan Borough Council* (1986) 84 L.G.R. 257, C.A.
s. 163, regs. 74/1380; 82/349.
ss. 163–167, repealed: 1982, c.32, sch.6.
ss. 166, 167, regs. 74/1169; 83/249.
s. 169, regs. 73/514.
s. 170, repealed: 1984, c.33, s.16.
s. 171, repealed: 1980, c.65, sch.34.
s. 173, see *Hopson* v. *Devon County Council* [1978] 1 All E.R. 1205, Megarry V.-C.; regs. 77/107, 1745; repealed in pt.: order 77/1710.
s. 173, regs. 74/447, 1808; 75/1984; 77/107, 1745; 78/1795, 1917; 79/1565; 80/193; 81/180; 82/125, 275; 83/574; 84/698; 85/426; 86/724; 87/1483; 88/358.
s. 173, amended: 1980, c.65, s.24.

CAP.

1972—cont.

70. Local Government Act 1972—*cont.*

s. 173A, added: *ibid.*; amended: 1983, c.28, sch.5; order 85/1884.

s. 174, amended: 1980, c.65, s.25; repealed in pt.: *ibid.*, s.25, sch.34.

s. 175, amended: *ibid.*, s.25; repealed in pt.: 1983, c.23, sch.5.

s. 176, amended: 1985, c.51, sch.14; order 85/1884; repealed in pt. (prosp.): 1988, c.40, sch.14.

s. 177, regs. 74/447, 1808; 77/833; 79/1122; 83/111; 86/724; 87/1483.

s. 177, amended: 1973, c.37, schs.8,9; 1980, c.65, s.25; 1985, c.51, sch.14; 1986, c.10, s.11; 1988, c.4, sch.6; c.40, sch.12 (prosp.); repealed in pt.: 1983, c.23, sch.5; 1985, c.51, sch.17; 1988, c.40, sch.13.

s. 177A, regs. 81/316; 82/125; 83/574; 84/698; 85/426; 86/299, 724; 87/1483; 88/358.

s. 177A, amended: 1985, c.51, sch.14; 1988, c.4, sch.6; repealed in pt.: 1985, c.51, sch.17; 1988, c.40, sch.13 (prosp.).

s. 178, regs. 74/447, 1808; 75/1984; 77/107, 1745; 78/1795, 1917; 79/1565; 80/193; 82/125, 275; 83/574; 84/698; 86/299, 724; amended: 1980, c.65, s.26.

s. 179, regs. 74/274.

s. 180, amended: 1974, c.40, sch.4; repealed in pt.: 1984, c.22, sch.3.

s. 181, amended: 1973, c.37, schs.8,9; 1984, c.55, sch.6; repealed in pt.: 1985, c.51, sch.17.

s. 182, see *Co-operative Retail Services v. Taff-Ely Borough Council* (1979) 39 P. & C.R. 223, C.A.

s. 182, orders 74/418; 77/289.

s. 182, amended: 1985, c.51, s.3, sch.3; 1986, c.63, sch.11; repealed in pt.: *ibid.*, sch.12.

s. 183, repealed in pt.: 1980, c.65, sch.14; 1986, c.63, sch.12.

s. 184, amended: 1985, c.51, sch.3.

s. 185, repealed in pt.: 1980, c.65, sch.34.

s. 186, repealed in pt.: 1978, c.3, sch.2; 1980, c.34, sch.9; 1985, c.67, sch.8; 1988, c.54, sch.1.

s. 187, repealed in pt.: 1980, c.66, sch.25.

s. 188, see *Allison v. Corby District Council* [1980] R.T.R. 111, Peter Pain J.; *R. v. Surrey County Council, ex p. Send Parish Council* (1980) 40 P. & C.R. 390, D.C.

s. 188, repealed: 1980, c.66, sch.25.

s. 190, repealed in pt.: 1980, c.65, s.173, sch.34.

s. 192, order 73/1010.

ss. 193, 194, repealed: 1985, c.71, sch.1.

s. 195, amended: 1980, c.53, s.23.

s. 197, repealed in pt.: 1982, c.32, sch.6.

ss. 198, 199, repealed: 1984, c.30, sch.11.

s. 201, amended: 1973, c.41, sch.12; 1985, c.51, sch.8; repealed: 1985, c.72, sch.13.

s. 202, order 73/1727–32.

s. 202, amended: 1985, c.51, sch.12; repealed in pt.: 1985, c.67, schs.3,8.

s. 203, repealed: 1978, c.55, sch.4.

s. 204, repealed in pt.: 1982, c.30, sch.7; c.33, sch.2; 1985, c.13, sch.3; c.51, sch.17.

CAP.

1972—cont.

70. Local Government Act 1972—*cont.*

s. 205, repealed: 1977, c.42, sch.25.

s. 206, repealed in pt.: 1985, c.51, sch.17.

s. 207, orders 74/616; 75/119, 120; 88/1789.

s. 209, repealed: 1973, c.50, sch.4.

s. 212, repealed: 1975, c.76, sch.2.

s. 213, amended: 1974, c.39, sch.5; repealed in pt.: 1988, c.9, sch.7.

s. 214, orders 74/628; 77/204; 86/1782.

s. 216, amended: 1973, c.32, schs.4,5; repealed in pt.: 1979, c.55, sch.3.

s. 217, amended: 1973, c.62, sch.6; order 74/72; 1979, c.55, sch.2; repealed in pt.: *ibid.*, sch.3.

s. 218, orders 73/1754; 74/430, 1570.

s. 218, repealed: 1980, c.9, sch.10.

s. 219, order 74/222.

s. 220, repealed: 1988, c.13, sch.4.

s. 222, see *Solihull Metropolitan B.C. v. Maxfern* [1977] 1 W.L.R. 127; *Kent County Council v. Batchelor (No. 2)*, [1978] 76 L.G.R. 714, Talbot J.; *Westminster City Council v. Jones* [1980] J.P.L. 750, Whitford J.; *Stoke-on-Trent City Council v. B. & Q. (Retail)* [1983] 3 W.L.R. 78, C.A.; *Barking and Dagenham London Borough Council v. Essexplan* (1983) 81 L.R.G. 408, Whitford J.; *Stoke-on-Trent City Council v. B. & Q. (Retail)* [1984] 2 W.L.R. 929, C.A.; *R. v. North West Leicestershire District Council, ex p. Dakin* [1985] Crim.L.R. 390, D.C.; *Runnymede Borough Council v. Ball* [1986] 1 All E.R. 629, C.A.; *London Docklands Corp. v. Rank Hovis* (1985) 84 L.G.R. 101, C.A.; *Waverley Borough Council v. Hilden* [1988] 1 W.L.R. 246, Scott J.

s. 223, amended: 1973, c.37, schs.8,9; 1974, c.47, sch.3; 1985, c.51, sch.14; order 85/1884; repealed in pt. (prosp.): 1988, c.40, sch.13.

ss. 224, 225, amended: 1985, c.51, sch.14; order 85/1884; repealed in pt. (prosp.): 1988, c.40, sch.13.

ss. 225, 228, see *Brookham v. Green* [1984] L.G.R. 228, C.A.

s. 226, order 73/2001.

s. 226, amended: 1985, c.51, sch.8.

s. 228, see *Russell-Walker v. Gimblett, The Times,* March 14, 1985, D.C.

s. 228, amended: 1985, c.51, schs.2,14; order 85/1884; 1988, c.4, sch.6; repealed in pt.: 1982, c.32, sch.6; 1988, c.40, sch.13 (prosp.).

ss. 229, 230, amended: 1985, c.51, sch.14; order 85/1884; repealed in pt. (prosp.): 1988, c.40, sch.13.

s. 231, see *R. v. Bromley London Borough, ex p. Sievers* (1980) 255 E.G. 355; (1981) 41 P. & C.R. 294, D.C.

ss. 231, 232, amended: 1985, c.51, sch.14; order 85/1884; repealed in pt. (prosp.): 1988, c.40, sch.13.

s. 233, amended: 1985, c.51, sch.14; order 85/1884; repealed in pt.: 1976, c.57, sch.2; 1988, c.40, sch.13 (prosp.).

s. 234, amended: 1985, c.51, sch.14; order 85/1884; repealed in pt. (prosp.): 1988, c.40, sch.13.

1972—cont.

70. Local Government Act 1972—*cont.*

s. 236, amended: 1974, c.40, sch.4; 1985, c.51, sch.14; 1988, c.40, sch.12; adapted: regs. 75/1970; modified: order 75/2267.

s. 238, adapted: regs. 75/1970; amended: 1985, c.51, sch.14; 1988, c.40, sch.12.

s. 239, amended: 1985, c.15, sch.14; order 85/1884; repealed in pt. (prosp.): 1988, c.40, sch.13.

s. 241, see *R.* v. *Park Joint Planning Board* (1976) 74 L.G.R. 376, D.C.

s. 241, orders 80/393; 81/91, 92; 86/561.

s. 243, amended: 1985, c.50, s.19; c.51, sch.14; repealed in pt.: 1983, c.2, sch.9; 1985, c.50, s.19, sch.5; 1988, c.40, sch.13 (prosp.).

s. 246, amended: 1982, c.32, sch.5.

s. 247, orders 74/869; 75/621; 76/767; 77/1233; 78/1025; 79/909; 80/1506; 82/708; 83/1105; 87/162; 88/1837.

s. 249, amended: 1980, c.65, s.180.

s. 250, repealed in pt.: 1986, c.63, sch.12.

s. 254, see *Walters* v. *Babergh District Council* [1984] L.G.R. 235, Woolf J.

s. 254, orders 73/167, 444, 477, 688, 734, 840, 943, 1010, 1466, 1593, 1616, 1625, 1654, 1847, 1861, 1863, 2025; 74/39, 140, 142, 147, 177, 273, 309, 339, 351, 389, 396, 403, 404, 406, 425, 432, 433, 435, 459, 472, 482–484, 499, 514, 529, 533, 551, 594, 595, 607, 750, 968, 1081, 1351, 1892, 2044; 75/244, 289, 290, 339, 396, 481, 514, 615, 944, 1636; 76/315, 1421; 77/293, 315, 1596; 78/440, 1210; 79/228, 1123; 80/229, 1401, 1421; 81/130; 88/1789.

s. 255, regs. 76/246; orders 73/1654, 1847; 74/147, 339, 403, 404, 406, 435, 461, 483, 499, 533, 551, 595, 968, 1351; 75/1636; 76/315; 88/1789.

s. 259, see *Mallett* v. *Restormel Borough Council* [1978] I.C.R. 725, C.A.; *Walsh* v. *Rother District Council* [1978] 3 All E.R. 881, C.A.

s. 259, regs. 74/463, 540, 759; 75/353.

s. 259, amended: 1984, c.30, sch.10.

s. 260, regs. 73/1260, 1944, 1951, 2023, 2024; 74/73.

s. 262, orders 74/215, 219, 595, 1165; 78/1595; 79/969; 80/883; 83/619, 915; 84/906; 86/114, 1133, 1190, 1461, 2068, 2160; 87/1533.

s. 262, amended: 1973, c.37, schs.8,9.

s. 264, repealed: 1985, c.51, sch.17.

s. 265, orders 74/547; 78/1844; 79/72; 82/701, 1659.

s. 265A, added: 1988, c.4, sch.6.

s. 266, see *R.* v. *Park Joint Planning Board* (1976) 74 L.G.R. 376, D.C.

s. 266, regs. 75/905; 80/2010; 86/299; orders 73/1466; 74/147, 399, 403, 404, 406, 499, 533, 551, 595, 968, 1351, 2044; 75/244, 289, 944, 1636; 77/204, 293, 1596; 78/1844; 79/72; 81/91, 92; 82/991, 992; 83/1402; 85/402, 634; 86/561, 854.

s. 268, repealed: 1975, c.24, sch.3; c.25, sch.3.

s. 269, repealed in pt.: 1978, c.30, sch.3.

s. 270, see *London Docklands Corp.* v. *Rank Hovis* (1985) 84 L.G.R. 101, C.A.

1972—cont.

70. Local Government Act 1972—*cont.*

s. 270, regs. 80/2010; 83/1402.

s. 270, amended: 1980, c.65, sch.23; 1985, c.51, schs.14,16; 1988, c.4, sch.6; repealed in pt.: 1985, c.51, sch.17.

s. 272, see *R.* v. *Surrey County Council, ex p. Send Parish Council* (1980) 40 P. & C.R. 390, D.C.

s. 273, see *R.* v. *Park Joint Planning Board* (1976) 74 L.G.R. 376, D.C.

s. 273, orders 73/373, 375.

s. 274, repealed in pt.: 1975, c.24, sch.3; c.25, sch.3.

sch. 1, orders 73/297, 1110, 1939; 74/569.

sch. 2, orders 76/213; 77/1710; amended: 1983, c.2, sch.8; repealed in pt.: S.L.R. 1978; 1984, c.53, s.2; 1985, c.51, sch.17.

sch. 3, orders 72/1861; 73/383, 551, 1528.

sch. 5, order 72/1861.

sch. 10, regs. 76/246; 78/247; orders 81/1738; 82/98, 127, 376, 1751; 83/124, 154, 206, 269, 1530, 1788; 84/473, 739, 1441, 1562, 1782, 1875, 1930, 2049; 85/89, 129, 1763, 1816, 2063, 2064; 86/4, 1364, 2008, 2077; 87/124.

sch. 11, see *Enfield London Borough Council* v. *Local Government Boundary Commission for England* [1979] 3 All E.R. 747, H.L.

sch. 11, amended: 1985, c.51, sch.9; repealed in pt.: *ibid.*, sch.17; 1988, c.40, sch.13 (prosp.).

sch. 12, rules 73/1911; 76/2067; 83/1151; 87/1, 262.

sch. 12, amended: 1983, c.2, sch.8; 1985, c.51, sch.14; order 85/1844; 1986, c.10, s.10; repealed in pt.: order 77/1710; 1985, c.51, sch.17; 1988, c.40, sch.13 (prosp.).

sch. 12A, added: 1985, c.43, s.1, sch.1; amended: 1986, c.24, s.2; c.53, sch.18; 1988, c.24, s.1.

sch. 13, regs. 74/518, 519, 905; 83/529; 1148; 86/282, 345.

sch. 13, amended: 1974, c.7, schs.7,8; 1976, c.57, s.28; 1982, c.32, s.5; c.41, s.5; 1985, c.51, s.70; 1988, c.40, sch.12 (prosp.); repealed in pt.: 1985, c.51, s.70; c.71, sch.1.

sch. 14, amended: 1973, c.32, schs.4,5; 1974, c.37, sch.10; c.40, sch.4; 1985, c.51, sch.6; order 85/1844; repealed in pt.: 1978, c.3, sch.2; 1982, c.30, sch.7; 1983, c.35, sch.2; 1984, c.22, sch.3; c.55, sch.7; 1985, c.51, sch.17.

sch. 16, see *Co-operative Retail Services* v. *Taff-Ely Borough Council* (1979) 39 P. & C.R. 223, C.A.

sch. 16, orders 74/418; 80/1946, 2010; 86/435; 88/1813.

sch. 16, amended: 1974, c.32, s.13, sch.; 1975, c.77, sch.10; 1980, c.65, s.86, schs.14,33; c.66, sch.24; 1981, c.36, s.2, sch.1; c.41, sch.; 1985, c.51, sch.3; order 86/452; 1988, c.4, sch.3; repealed in pt.: 1980, c.65, sch.34; 1981, c.41, sch.; c.64, sch.13; 1982, c.30, sch.7; 1985, c.51, sch.17; 1986, c.63, sch.12.

sch. 17, orders 73/2001; 81/91, 92; 82/991, 992; 86/561.

CAP.

1972—cont.

70. Local Government Act 1972—cont.

sch. 17, amended: 1978, c.52, sch.11; 1985, c.51, sch.3; repealed in pt.: 1980, c.65, sch.34.

sch. 18, repealed in pt.: *ibid.*

sch. 19, repealed: 1988, c.54, sch.1.

sch. 20, repealed: 1980, c.66, sch.25.

sch. 21, see *Allison* v. *Corby District Council* [1980] R.T.R. 111, Peter Pain J.; *R.* v. *Surrey County Council, ex p. Send Parish Council* (1980) 40 P. & C.R. 390, D.C.

sch. 21, repealed in pt.: S.L.R. 1977; 1980, c.66, sch.25.

sch. 22, repealed: 1985, c.71, sch.1.

sch. 23, repealed: 1978, c.22, sch.3; repealed in pt.: 1980, c.5, sch.6; c.6, sch.3; c.7, sch.2; 1983, c.20, sch.6; c.41, sch.10; 1984, c.22, sch.23.

sch. 24, amended: 1974, c.7, schs.7,8; repealed in pt.: 1982, c.32, sch.6; 1985, c.67, schs.3,8.

sch. 25, repealed in pt.: 1981, c.28, sch.2; 1982, c.30, sch.7.

sch. 26, amended: orders 74/595, 628.

sch. 27, amended: 1973, c.15, sch.5; repealed in pt.: 1979, c.55, sch.3; 1980, c.43, sch.9; 1985, c.51, sch.17.

sch. 29, regs. 74/274; amended: 1973, c.37, schs.8,9; 1976, c.17, sch.2; repealed in pt.: 1975, c.76, sch.2; 1976, c.17, sch.6; c.70, sch.8; 1978, c.38, sch.3; 1981, c.64, sch.13; 1982, c.30, sch.7; c.32, sch.6; 1983, No. 1, sch.9; 1984, c.2, sch.23; 1985, c.51, sch.17; 1987 c.43, sch.5.

71. Criminal Justice Act 1972.

Royal Assent, October 26, 1972.

Pt. I (ss. 1–24), except ss. 6, 23, 24, repealed: 1973, c.62, sch.6.

s. 1, see *R.* v. *Bradburn* (1973) 57 Cr.App.R. 948, C.A.; *R.* v. *Grundy* [1974] 1 W.L.R. 139; [1974] 1 All E.R. 292, C.A.; *R.* v. *Daly* [1974] 1 W.L.R. 133; [1974] 1 All E.R. 290, C.A.; *R.* v. *Kneeshaw* [1974] 2 W.L.R. 432; [1974] 1 All E.R. 896, C.A.; *Hammertons Cars* v. *Redbridge London Borough Council* [1974] 1 W.L.R. 484; [1974] 2 All E.R. 216, D.C.; *R.* v. *Oddy* [1974] 2 All E.R. 666, C.A.; *R.* v. *Wylie* [1975] R.T.R. 94, C.A.; *Berkeley* v. *Orchard* [1975] Crim.L.R. 225, D.C.; *R.* v. *Miller* (Note) [1976] 68 Cr.App.R. 56, C.A.

s. 22, see *R.* v. *Ingle* [1974] 3 All E.R. 811, C.A.; *R.* v. *Dwyer* (1974) 60 Cr.App.R. 39, C.A.; *R.* v. *McQuaide* (1975) 60 Cr.App.R. 239, C.A.

s. 23, see *Lloyds & Scottish Finance* v. *H.M. Advocate,* 1974 S.L.T. 3; *R.* v. *Brown* [1975] R.T.R. 36, C.A.

s. 23, amended: 1973, c.62, sch.5; repealed (S.): 1975, c.21, sch.10.

s. 24, see *R.* v. *Mathews* [1975] R.T.R. 32, C.A.; *R.* v. *Brown* [1975] R.T.R. 36, C.A.; *R.* v. *Thomas* [1975] R.T.R. 38, C.A.

s. 24, amended: 1988, c.54, sch.3.

Pt. II (ss. 25–27), repealed: 1974, c.23, sch.3.

s. 28, repealed in pt.: 1988, c.33, sch.16.

s. 30, repealed: 1977, c.43, sch.3; 1984, c.58, sch.10 (S.).

CAP.

1972—cont.

71. Criminal Justice Act 1972—cont.

s. 31, see *York City Council* v. *The Little Gallery, The Times,* December 2, 1985, D.C.

s. 32, repealed: 1985, c.71, sch.1.

s. 34, amended: 1984, c.60, sch.6; repealed in pt.: 1977, c.45, schs.12,13; 1984, c.60, sch.7.

s. 35, see *R.* v. *Secretary of State for the Home Department, ex p. Findlay, The Times,* May 23, 1983, D.C.

s. 36, see *Att.-Gen.'s Reference (No. 4 of 1979)* (1980) 71 Cr.App.R. 341, C.A.; *Att.-Gen.'s Reference (No. 1 of 1982)* [1983] 3 W.L.R. 72; *Att.-Gen.'s Reference (No. 2 of 1982), The Times,* November 25, 1983, C.A.

s. 37, repealed: 1973, c.62, sch.6.

s. 38, repealed: 1974, c.4, sch.5.

s. 39, see *R.* v. *Arron* (Note) [1973] 2 All E.R. 1221, C.A.

s. 39, repealed: 1973, c.14, sch.2.

s. 40, see *R.* v. *Bradburn* (1973) 57 Cr.App.R. 948, C.A.

s. 40, repealed: 1973, c.62, sch.6.

s. 41, see *Bradburn* v. *Richards* [1976] R.T.R. 275, D.C.; *R.* v. *Gravesend JJ., ex p. Dexter* [1977] Crim.L.R. 298, D.C.; *R.* v. *Maidstone Justices, ex p. Booth, The Times,* May 17, 1980, D.C.; *R.* v. *Wells Street JJ., ex p. Collett* [1981] R.T.R. 272, D.C.

ss. 41, 44, 45, repealed: 1980, c.43, sch.9.

s. 42, repealed: 1982, c.48, sch.16.

s. 43, repealed: 1976, c.63, sch.3.

s. 46, amended: 1980, c.43, sch.7.

s. 47, repealed: 1977, c.43, sch.3.

s. 49, amended: 1973, c.62, sch.5; 1980, c.43, sch.7.

s. 50, repealed: *ibid.,* sch.9.

s. 51, amended: 1975, c.21, sch.9 (S.); 1979, c.55, sch.2; repealed in pt.: 1973, c.62, sch.6.

ss. 52–57, repealed: *ibid.*

ss. 61, 62, repealed: 1979, c.55, sch.3.

s. 63, amended: 1973, c.36, sch.6.

ss. 63, 66, repealed in pt.: 1980, c.47, sch.5.

s. 66, orders 72/1763; 73/272, 1472; 76/299.

sch. 2, repealed: 1974, c.23, sch.3.

sch. 3, see *R.* v. *Arron* (Note) [1973] 2 All E.R. 1221, C.A.

sch. 4, repealed: 1980, c.47, sch.5.

sch. 5, repealed in pt.: 1973, c.14, sch.2; c.62, sch.6; 1974, c.4, sch.5; c.23, sch.3; S.L.R. 1977; 1980, c.43, sch.9; 1982, c.30, sch.7; c.48, sch.16; 1986, c.60, sch.17; 1988, c.33, sch.16.

72. National Health Service (Family Planning) Amendment Act 1972.

Royal Assent, October 26, 1972.

repealed: 1973, c.32, sch.5.

73. Museums and Galleries Admission Charges Act 1972.

Royal Assent, October 26, 1972.

s. 1, orders 73/1274, 1718.

s. 1, amended(S): 1985, c.16, sch.2.

74. Counter Inflation (Temporary Provisions) Act 1972.

Royal Assent, November 30, 1972.

s. 1, order 73/73.

CAP.

74. Counter Inflation (Temporary Provisions) Act 1972—*cont.*
s. 2, repealed: 1973, c.9, s.3(2).
s. 2, see *Summerfield* v. *London Co-operative Society* [1973] I.C.R. 568, Bow County Ct.
s. 2, orders 72/1850–1853; 73/98, 148, 269, 774.
ss. 2, 5, see *Co-operative Employers Association* v. *Pay Board* [1974] I.C.R. 159.
ss. 3, 5, see *Mackay* v. *Peter Pan Playthings* [1973] I.R.L.R. 232, N.I.R.C.
s. 10, orders 72/1848–1851; 73/269, 647, 774.
s. 13, order 73/570.
sch., regs. 72/1854–1856; orders 72/1848–1853; 73/98, 148, 209, 269, 285, 556, 557, 647, 774.

75. Pensioners and Family Income Supplement Payments Act 1972.
Royal Assent, November 30, 1972.
repealed: 1986, c.50, sch.11.
s. 3, regs. 76/289.

76. Northern Ireland (Financial Provisions) Act 1972.
Royal Assent, December 7, 1972.
s. 1, repealed: 1975, c.83, sch.
s. 2, repealed: 1973, c.36, sch.6.

77. Northern Ireland (Border Poll) Act 1972.
Royal Assent, December 7, 1972.
repealed: 1973, c.36, sch.6.

78. Consolidated Fund (No. 3) Act 1972.
Royal Assent, December 12, 1972.
repealed: 1975, c.44, sch.C.

79. Post Office (Borrowing Powers) 1972.
Royal Assent, December 21, 1972.
repealed: 1981, c.38, sch.6.

80. Pensioners' Payments and National Insurance Contributions Act 1972.
Royal Assent, December 21, 1972.
repealed: 1986, c.50, sch.11.

1973

1. Consolidated Fund Act 1973.
Royal Assent, February 13, 1973.
repealed: 1975, c.44, sch.C.

2. National Theatre and Museum of London Act 1973.
Royal Assent, February 13, 1973.
repealed: 1986, c.8, sch.

3. Sea Fish Industry Act 1973.
Royal Assent, February 13, 1973.
repealed: 1981, c.29, sch.5.
s. 1, orders 74/88; 75/110; 76/2135; 77/2135; 79/1691; 80/1971.

4. Atomic Energy Authority (Weapons Group) Act 1973.
Royal Assent, March 6, 1973.
ss. 1, 4, see *Pearce* v. *Secretary of State for Defence* [1988] 2 W.L.R. 1027, H.L.
s. 1, order 73/463.
s. 5, amended: 1977, c.37, sch.5.

5. Housing (Amendment) Act 1973.
Royal Assent, March 6, 1973.
repealed: 1985, c.71, sch.1; 1987, c.26, sch.24 (S.).

CAP.

6. Furnished Lettings (Rent Allowances) Act 1973.
Royal Assent, March 22, 1973.
repealed: 1982, c.24, sch.5.

7. Concorde Aircraft Act 1973.
Royal Assent, March 22, 1973.

8. Coal Industry Act 1973.
Royal Assent, March 22, 1973.
s. 2, order 74/1296; amended: 1977, c.39, s.1, sch.1; 1980, c.50, s.4; 1987, c.3, sch.1; repealed in pt.: 1977, c.39, schs.2,5.
s. 3, order 76/493; repealed: 1977, c.39, sch.5; amended: 1980, c.50, s.4.
s. 4, repealed: 1977, c.39, s.7, sch.5.
s. 6, repealed: *ibid.*; amended: 1980, c.50, s.4.
s. 7, order 76/494; repealed: 1977, c.39, sch.5.
s. 8, order 76/492.
s. 8, repealed: 1983, c.60, s.2, sch.
s. 9, repealed: 1977, c.39, s.8, sch.5.
s. 10, amended: 1987, c.3, sch.1.
s. 12, orders 76/492–494.
s. 12, amended: 1985, c.9, sch.2; repealed in pt.: 1977, c.39, sch.5.
sch. 1, repealed in pt.: *ibid.*

9. Counter Inflation Act 1973.
Royal Assent, March 22, 1973.
see *London Transport Executive* v. *Gray Brothers (East Finchley)* (1981) 259 E.G. 629, Forbes J.
order 73/967
Pts. I (ss. 1, 2), II (ss. 3, 4), V (ss. 15–23), repealed: 1980, c.21, sch.2.
s. 1, orders 77/1078; 79/795.
s. 2, see *British Leyland U.K.* v. *Pay Board* [1974] I.C.R. 134.
s. 2, orders 73/658, 1785; 74/661, 785; 2113, 2158; 75/864, 1293; 76/71, 630, 1170, 2207; 77/1272; 78/1082.
s. 5, orders 73/662, 664, 1786, 1788, 2118; 74/184, 543, 775, 840, 933, 1500, 1793, 2114, 2195; 75/1294, 1583, 1947, 2208; 76/73, 496, 1378; 77/1281; 78/1083; 79/60, 178, 568; continued: orders 76/228, 1161; amended: 1977, c.33, ss.14,21, sch.2.
s. 6, continued: orders 76/228, 1161; amended: 1977, c.33, ss.7,14,21; repealed in pt.: *ibid.*, sch.3.
s. 7, continued: order 76/1161.
s. 8, orders 73/616, 620, 646, 675, 810; 74/2116; 77/1302; continued: orders 76/228, 1161; 77/1302; amended: 1977, c.33, s.14.
s. 9, continued: orders 76/228, 1161; amended: 1977, c.33, s.14.
s. 10, orders 73/659, 1801; 74/1223; 75/615, 1081, 1674; 77/1302; 78/1454; continued: orders 76/228, 1161; 77/1302; 1978, c.54, s.1; amended: 1977, c.33, s.14.
s. 11, orders 73/682, 741, 1717, 1741, 2118; 74/184, 380–383, 434, 1030, 1294, 1482, 1924, 1928, 1988; 75/21, 590; 76/73.
ss. 11, 12, repealed: 1977, c.33, schs.2,3.
s. 13, order 73/619.
s. 14, repealed: 1977, c.42, sch.25.

CAP.

1973—cont.

9. Counter Inflation Act 1973—cont.

s. 15, orders 73/662–664, 778, 784, 968, 1786–1789, 1840; 74/543, 775, 776, 840, 933, 1500, 2114, 2115; 75/865, 1294, 1295, 1948, 2209; 76/72, 1172, 1377; 77/1281; 78/1083; 79/60, 178, 568.

s. 23, regs. 77/1222; orders 73/645, 682, 741, 1065, 1717, 1741; 74/380–383, 434, 1030, 1294, 1482, 1924, 1928, 1988; 75/21, 590; 77/1223, 1225.

sch. 1, amended: 1977, c.33, s.1, sch.2; repealed in pt.: 1975, c.24, sch.3; c.25, sch.3; 1977, c.33, s.1, schs.2,3.

sch. 2, orders 73/616, 620, 646, 661, 662, 664, 784, 1786, 1788, 2118; 74/184, 543, 775, 840, 933, 1500, 2114; 75/1294; 76/73; 77/1281.

sch. 3, orders 73/659, 682, 741, 1717, 1741, 1801; 74/380–383, 434, 543, 775, 840, 933, 1030, 1223, 1294, 1482, 1500, 1793, 1924, 1928, 1988, 2114, 2116, 2199; 75/21, 590, 615, 1081, 1294, 1583, 1674, 1947, 2208; 76/496; 77/1225, 1281; 78/1083, 1454; 79/60, 178, 568; regs. 73/621, 660; 77/1222; amended: 1977, c.33, s.14; regs. 77/1220; repealed in pt.: 1977, c.33, sch.3.

sch. 4, orders 73/645, 1065; 77/1223; amended: regs. 77/1220; repealed in pt.: 1977, c.33, schs.2,3; c.42, sch.25.

sch. 5, repealed: 1977, c.42, sch.25.

10. Consolidated Fund (No. 2) Act 1973.

Royal Assent, March 29, 1973.

repealed: 1975, c.44, sch.C.

11. Fire Precautions (Loans) Act 1973.

Royal Assent, March 29, 1973.

s. 1, order 73/1271.

12. Gaming (Amendment) Act 1973.

Royal Assent, April 18, 1973.

13. Supply of Goods (Implied Terms) Act 1973.

Royal Assent, April 18, 1973.

ss. 1–7, repealed: 1979, c.54, sch.3.

s. 3, see Smith v. Park, 1980 S.L.T. (Sh.Ct.) 62.

s. 4, see White Cross Equipment v. Farrell (1983) 2 Tr.L. 21, Garland Q.C.

ss. 8, 9, amended: 1974, c.39, sch.4.

s. 10, see Laurelgates v. Lombard North Central [1983] 133 New L.J. 720, Webster J.

s. 10, amended: 1974, c.39, sch.4; 1982, c.39, s.17.

ss. 10, 12, see McCann v. Patterson [1984] 16 N.I.J.B., Lord Lowry L.C.J.

s. 11, amended: 1974, c.39, sch.4.

s. 12, see Robotics v. First Co-Operative Finance, November 1, 1982, Assistant Recorder G. G. Brown, Poole County Ct.

s. 12, amended: 1974, c.39, sch.4; repealed in pt.: 1977, c.50, sch.4.

s. 13, repealed: 1977, c.50, sch.4.

s. 14, repealed in pt.: 1981, c.19, sch.1.

s. 15, amended: 1977, c.50, sch.3; 1979, c.54, sch.3; repealed in pt.: 1977, c.50, sch.4.

s. 17, amended: 1973, c.36, sch.6.

s. 18, repealed in pt.: 1979, c.54, sch.3.

CAP.

1973—cont.

14. Costs in Criminal Cases Act 1973.

Royal Assent, April 18, 1973.

repealed: 1985, c.23, sch.2.

s. 1, see R. v. Stockport Magistrates' Court, ex p. Cooper [1984] Crim.L.R. 233, D.C.; R. v. Stafford Stone and Eccleshall Magistrates' Court, ex p. Robinson [1988] 1 All E.R. 430, Simon Brown J.

s. 2, see R. v. Tottenham JJ., ex p. Dwarkados Joshi [1982] 1 W.L.R. 631, D.C.; Bunston v. Rawlings [1982] 2 All E.R. 697, D.C.; Sierzant v. Anderton [1982] Crim.L.R. 823, D.C.; Neville v. Gardner Merchant (1984) 5 Cr.App.R.(S.) 349, D.C.; R. v. Scunthorpe Justices, ex p. Holbrey, The Times, May 24, 1985 D.C.; R. v. Nottingham JJ., ex p. Fohmann (1987) 84 Cr.App.R. 316, D.C.

s. 3, see R. v. Michael [1975] 3 W.L.R. 731; Practice Direction (Costs: Acquittal of Defendants) [1981] 1 W.L.R. 1383, C.A.; R. v. Miller (Raymond) [1983] 3 All E.R. 186; (1984) 78 Cr.App.R. 71, Lloyd J.; R. v. Maher (1983) 5 Cr.App.R.(S.) 39, C.A.

ss. 3, 4, see Sampson, Re, The Independent, February 12, 1987, H.L.

s. 4, see R. v. Hayden [1975] 1 W.L.R. 852, C.A.; R. v. Rowe (Frederick) [1975] R.T.R. 309, C.A.; R. v. Hier (1976) 62 Cr.App.R. 233, C.A.; R. v. Newlove [1978] R.T.R. 150, C.A.; R. v. Smith (1978) 67 Cr.App.R. 332, C.A.; R. v. Mountain; R. v. Kilminster (1978) 68 Cr.App.R. 41, C.A.; R. v. Lewes Crown Court, ex p. Castle (1979) 70 Cr.App.R. 278, D.C.; R. v. Maher, Barclay, Russell and Sinclair [1983] 2 W.L.R. 764, C.A; (1983) 5 Cr.App.R.(S.) 39, C.A.

s. 5, see Cannings v. Houghton (No. 2) [1977] R.T.R. 507, D.C.

s. 7, see R. v. Whitby (1977) 65 Cr.App.R. 257, C.A.; R. v. Agritraders [1983] 2 W.L.R. 412, C.A.

s. 9, see R. v. Howitt (1975) 61 Cr.App.R. 327, C.A.

s. 12, see R. v. Bolton JJ., ex p. Wildish (1983) 147 J.P. 309, D.C.; Patel v. Blakey [1977] Crim.L.R. 683, D.C.; [1988] R.T.R. 65, D.C.

s. 17, regs. 73/1172, 1745; 74/831, 1580; 75/2067; 77/248, 407, 709, 2069; 84/330.

sch. 1, repealed in pt.: 1988, c.33, sch.16.

15. Administration of Justice Act 1973.

Royal Assent, April 18, 1973.

s. 1, repealed in pt.: 1979, c.55, sch.3.

s. 2, amended: ibid., sch.2; repealed in pt.: ibid., sch.3; 1981, c.20, sch.4.

s. 3, repealed: ibid.

s. 4, repealed: 1974, c.47, sch.4.

s. 5, substituted: 1979, c.55, sch.2.

s. 7, repealed; 1984, c.28, sch.4.

s. 8, see Centrax Trustees v. Ross [1979] 2 All E.R. 952, Goulding J.; Habib Bank v. Taylor [1982] 1 W.L.R. 1218, C.A.; Bank of Scotland v. Grimes [1985] 2 All E.R. 254, C.A.; Citibank Trust v. Ayivor [1987] 1 W.L.R. 1157, Mervyn Davies J.

1973—cont.

15. Administration of Justice Act 1973—*cont.*
s. 9, amended: 1977, c.45, sch.12; 1979, c.55,
sch.2; 1981, c.20, sch.3; repealed in pt.:
1981, c.54, sch.7.
ss. 10 (in pt.) 11, repealed: 1981, c.20, sch.4.
s. 10, regs. 79/210; 87/101, 160; S.R. 1978, No.
15.
ss. 10, 14, 18, amended: 1973, c.36, sch.6;
regs. 74/44, 229.
s. 12, repealed in pt.: 1981, c.54, sch.7.
s. 13, repealed: 1981, c.20, sch.4.
s. 15, repealed: 1981, c.54, sch.7.
s. 16, repealed in pt.: *ibid.*; 1984, c.28, sch.4.
s. 17, repealed in pt.: 1985, c.23, sch.2.
s. 18, amended: 1978, c.23, sch.5; repealed in
pt.: *ibid.*, sch.7; 1980, c.47, sch.5.
s. 19, repealed in pt.: 1981, c.54, sch.7.
s. 20, order 74/43.
s. 20, repealed in pt.: 1979, c.55, sch.3; 1981,
c.20, sch.4.
sch. 1, amended: 1973, c.38, sch.27; 1974,
c.47, sch.4; 1977, c.38, sch.2; 1979, c.55,
sch.2; repealed in pt.: 1975, c.18, sch.1;
1977, c.38, sch.5; 1979, c.55, sch.3; regs.
74/1507; 75/593; 76/117, 2118; 1981, c.54,
sch.7; 1985, c.51, sch.17.
sch. 2, repealed in pt.: 1984, c.28, sch.4.
sch. 3, regs. 87/101, 160; S.Rs. 1978, No. 15;
1979 No. 67.
sch. 4, repealed: 1981, c.20, sch.4.

16. Education Act 1973.
Royal Assent, April 18, 1973.
s. 1, order 73/1661.
s. 1, amended: 1980, c.20, sch.3; 1981, c.60,
sch.3; repealed in pt.: 1980, c.20, sch.1.
s. 2, amended: 1988, c.40, s.112; repealed in
pt.: 1987, c.15, sch.
s. 3, regs. 78/1098; 79/900; 80/1111; 81/981;
83/1185; 84/1179; 85/1160; 86/1325;
87/1261; 88/1360.
s. 3, repealed in pt.: 1975, c.72, sch.4; regs.
73/1234; 74/1231; 75/1225; 76/1087;
77/1308.
s. 4, regs. 73/1232.
s. 4, repealed: 1980, c.20, sch./.

17. Northern Ireland Assembly Act 1973.
Royal Assent, May 3, 1973.
ss. 1, 2, 4, repealed in pt.: 1982, c.38, sch.3.
ss. 2, 3, order 82/1135.
ss. 2, 5, orders 85/1268; 86/1811.
s. 3, amended: 1973, c.36, s.30; 1975, c.25,
sch.2.
sch., amended: 1982, c.38, sch.2.

18. Matrimonial Causes Act 1973.
Royal Assent, May 23, 1973.
see *Fielding* v. *Fielding* [1977] 1 W.L.R. 1146
(Note), C.A.; *De Lasala* v. *De Lasala* [1979] 2
All E.R. 1146, P.C.; [1980] A.C. 546, P.C.;
Matz v. *Matz, The Times,* December 14, 1983,
C.A.
s. 1, see *Livingstone-Stallard* v. *Livingstone-Stal-
lard* [1974] 2 All E.R. 766; *Andrews* v.
Andrews [1974] 3 All E.R. 643; *Warr* v. *Warr*
[1975] 2 W.L.R. 62; [1975] 1 All E.R. 85;
O'Neill v. *O'Neill* [1975] 1 W.L.R. 1118, C.A.;

1973—cont.

18. Matrimonial Causes Act 1973—*cont.*
Thurlow v. *Thurlow* [1975] 3 W.L.R. 161;
[1975] 2 All E.R. 979; *Parsons* v. *Parsons*
[1975] 1 W.L.R. 1272; [1975] 3 All E.R. 344;
Stringfellow v. *Stringfellow* [1976] 1 W.L.R.
645; [1976] 2 All E.R. 539, C.A.; *Welfare* v.
Welfare [1978] Fam.Law 55, Bush J., *Grenfell*
v. *Grenfell* [1977] 3 W.L.R. 738, C.A.; *Patel* v.
Patel (1977) 121 S.J. 408; [1977] Fam.Law
215, Payne J.; *Dowden* v. *Dowden* [1977] 8
Fam.Law 106, C.A.; *Reiterbund* v. *Reiterbund*
[1975] 2 W.L.R. 375; [1975] 1 All E.R. 280,
C.A.; *Biggs* v. *Biggs* [1976] 2 W.L.R. 942; *Day*
v. *Day* [1979] 2 All E.R. 187, C.A.; *Stevens* v.
Stevens [1979] 1 W.L.R. 885, Sheldon J.;
Bannister v. *Bannister* (1980) 10 Fam.Law
240, C.A.; *Bergin* v. *Bergin* (1982) 12
Fam.Law 212, D.C.; *Sutton* v. *Sutton* (1984)
1 All E.R. 168, John Mowbray Q.C.; *Quoraishi*
v. *Quoraishi* (1985) 15 Fam.Law 308, C.A.;
Cahill v. *Cahill* (1986) 16 Fam.Law 102, C.A.
s. 1, amended: 1984, c.42, sch.1.
ss. 1, 2, see *Newman* v. *Newman*; *McLean* v.
McLean; *Jones* v. *Jones (Queen's Proctor
Intervening)* (1985) Fam.Law 52, Sir John
Arnold P.
s. 2, see *Brice* v. *Brice* (1974) 4 Fam.Law, 88;
Biggs v. *Biggs* [1976] 2 W.L.R. 942; *C.* v. *C.,
The Times,* November 24, 1978, C.A.; *Piper*
v. *Piper* (1978) 8 Fam. Law 243, C.A.; *Savage*
v. *Savage* [1982] 3 W.L.R. 418, Wood J.
s. 3, see *Montague* v. *Montague* (1974) 4
Fam.Law 88, C.A.; *Lamb* v. *Lamb* (1976) 6
Fam.Law 83, C.A.; *C.* v. *C. (Divorce—Excep-
tional Hardship)* [1979] 2 W.L.R. 95, C.A.;
Woolf v. *Woolf* (1978) 9 Fam.Law 216, C.A.;
Fletcher v. *Titt* (1979) 10 Fam.Law 151, C.A.;
Cooper v. *Cooper,* March 30, 1981, C.A.; *Fay*
v. *Fay* [1983] 3 W.L.R. 206, H.L.; *Iles* v. *Iles*
(1983) 13 Fam.Law 14, Purchas J.; *Quoraishi*
v. *Quoraishi* (1983) 13 Fam.Law 86, Butler-
Sloss J.; *Nota* v. *Nota* (1984) 14 Fam.Law
310, C.A.
s. 3, substituted: 1984, c.42, s.1.
s. 4, amended: 1978, c.22, s.62, sch.2; 1983,
c.19, sch.2; c.41, sch.9.
s. 5, see *Reiterbund* v. *Reiterbund* [1975] 2
W.L.R. 375; [1975] 1 All E.R. 280, C.A.; *Le
Marchant* v. *Le Marchant* [1977] 1 W.L.R.
559, C.A.; *Patel* v. *Patel* (1977) 121 S.J. 408;
[1977] Fam. Law 215, Payne J.; *Grenfell* v.
Grenfell [1977] 3 W.L.R. 738, C.A.; *Balraj* v.
Balraj (1980) 11 Fam.Law 110, C.A.; *Johnson*
v. *Johnson* (1982) 12 Fam.Law 116, Reeve J.
s. 6, see *Birch* v. *Birch* [1977] Fam.Law 172,
C.A.
s. 8, see *Ali Ebrahim* v. *Ali Ebrahim (Queen's
Proctor Intervening)* [1983] 1 W.L.R. 1336, Sir
John Arnold P.
s. 9, see *Biggs* v. *Biggs* [1976] 2 W.L.R. 942;
Newman v. *Newman*; *McLean* v. *McLean*;
Jones v. *Jones (Queen's Proctor Intervening)*
(1985) 15 Fam.Law 52, Sir John Arnold P.
s. 10, see *Le Marchant* v. *Le Marchant* [1977] 1
W.L.R. 559, C.A.; *Patel* v. *Patel* (1977) 121

CAP.

1973—cont.

18. Matrimonial Causes Act 1973—cont.

S.J. 408; [1977] Fam. Law 215, Payne J.; Grenfell v. Grenfell [1977] 3 W.L.R. 738, C.A.; Bridge v. Bridge (1977) 122 S.J. 95, Balcombe J.; Bateman v. Bateman [1979] 2 W.L.R. 377, Purchas J.; Hardy v. Hardy, The Times, June 11, 1981, C.A.; Robertson v. Robertson (1982) 12 Fam.Law 181, Balcombe J.; Balraj v. Balraj (1980) 11 Fam.Law 110, C.A.

s. 11, see Hussain v. Hussain [1982] 3 All E.R. 369, C.A.

s. 11, amended: 1983, c.32, s.2; 1986, c.16, s.6.

s. 12, see Re Roberts (decd.) [1978] 1 W.L.R. 653, C.A.; Harper v. Harper, November 25, 1980, Judge Baker, Kingston County Ct.

s. 13, see D. v. D. [1979] 3 W.L.R. 185, Dunn J.

s. 13, amended: 1984, c.42, s.2.

s. 16, see Rowe v. Rowe (1974) 5 Fam. Law 62.

s. 17, see Kennedy v. Kennedy, July 3, 1978, Judge Monier-Williams.

s. 19, amended: 1973, c.45, s.6, sch.6.

s. 22, see Offord v. Offord (1981) 11 Fam.Law 208, French J.; F. v. F. (Maintenance Pending Suit) (1983) 13 Fam.Law 16, Balcombe J.; Peacock v. Peacock [1984] 1 W.L.R. 532, Booth J.

s. 23, see Baker (formerly Sillence) v. Sillence (1974) 5 Fam.Law 47, C.A.; Doherty v. Doherty [1975] 3 W.L.R. 1; [1975] 2 All E.R. 635, C.A.; H. v. H. (Family Provision; Remarriage) [1975] 2 W.L.R. 124; [1975] 1 All E.R. 367; O'D. v. O'D. [1975] 3 W.L.R. 308; [1975] 2 All E.R. 993, C.A.; Wilson v. Wilson [1975] 3 W.L.R. 587; [1975] 3 All E.R. 464, C.A.; Chaterjee v. Chaterjee [1976] 2 W.L.R. 397; [1976] 1 All E.R. 719, C.A.; Downing v. Downing (Downing Intervening) [1976] 3 W.L.R. 335; Martin v. Martin [1976] 3 W.L.R. 580, C.A.; Ladbrook v. Ladbrook [1977] Fam.Law 213, Dunn J.; Saunders v. Saunders [1978] 8 Fam.Law 206, C.A.; Minton v. Minton [1979] 2 W.L.R. 31, H.L.; Pearce v. Pearce (1979) 10 Fam.Law 209, C.A.; Carter v. Carter [1980] 1 W.L.R. 390; [1980] 1 All E.R. 827, C.A.; Dipper v. Dipper [1980] 2 All E.R. 722, C.A.; Ward v. Ward and Green (Note) [1980] 1 W.L.R. 4; [1980] 1 All E.R. 176, C.A.; Milne v. Milne, The Times, February 6, 1981; Hardy v. Hardy, The Times, June 11, 1981, C.A.; B. v. B. (1982) 12 Fam.Law 92, C.A.; Nicholas v. Nicholas (1984) 14 Fam.Law 118, C.A.; Banyard v. Banyard (1985) 15 Fam.Law 120, C.A.; Sandford v. Sandford (1985) 15 Fam.Law 230, Ewbank J.; Davies v. Davies, The Times, November 2, 1985, C.A.; Sherdley v. Sherdley [1986] 2 All E.R. 202, C.A.; Collins v. Collins, The Times, August 12, 1986, C.A.; Roberts v. Roberts [1986] 1 W.L.R. 437, Wood J.; Board (Orse Checkland) v. Checkland (Board Intervening), The Times, January 10, 1987, C.A.) R. v. Rushmoor Borough Council, ex p. Barrett [1986] 3 W.L.R. 998, Reeve J.; Dinch v. Dinch [1987] 1 W.L.R. 252, H.L.; Sherdley v. Sher-

CAP.

1973—cont.

18. Matrimonial Causes Act 1973—cont.

dley [1987] 2 W.L.R. 1071, H.L.; Kiely v. Kiely (1988) 18 Fam.Law 51, C.A.; Thompson v. Thompson [1988] 1 W.L.R. 562, Ewbank J.

s. 23, amended: 1982, c.53, s.16.

s. 24, see Baker (formerly Sillence) v. Sillence (1974) 5 Fam.Law 47, C.A.; Allen v. Allen [1974] 1 W.L.R. 1171; [1974] 3 All E.R. 385, C.A.; Brent v. Brent [1974] 3 W.L.R. 296; [1974] 2 All E.R. 1211; Hale v. Hale [1975] 1 W.L.R. 931, C.A.; Jones (M. A.) v. Jones (W.) [1975] 2 W.L.R. 606; [1975] 2 All E.R. 12, C.A.; Thompson v. Thompson [1975] 2 W.L.R. 868; [1975] 2 All E.R. 208, C.A.; Doherty v. Doherty [1975] 3 W.L.R. 1; [1975] 2 All E.R. 635, C.A.; Wilson v. Wilson [1975] 3 W.L.R. 537; [1975] 3 All E.R. 464, C.A.; Coley v. Coley (1975) 5 Fam.Law 195, C.A.; Chaterjee v. Chaterjee [1976] 2 W.L.R. 397; [1976] 1 All E.R. 719, C.A.; Daubney v. Daubney [1976] 2 W.L.R. 959; [1976] 2 All E.R. 453, C.A.; Martin v. Martin [1976] 3 W.L.R. 580, C.A.; Martin (B. H.) v. Martin (D.) [1977] 3 W.L.R. 101, C.A.; Ladbrook v. Ladbrook [1977] Fam.Law 213, Dunn J.; Whittingham v. Whittingham; National Westminster Bank (Intervener) [1978] 2 W.L.R. 936, C.A.; Lilford (Lord) v. Glynn [1979] 1 W.L.R. 78, C.A.; Ward v. Ward and Green (Note) [1980] 1 W.L.R. 4; [1980] 1 All E.R. 176, C.A.; Re Holliday (A Bankrupt), ex p. Trustee of the Bankrupt v. The Bankrupt [1980] 3 All E.R. 385, C.A.; Evers' Trust, Re; Papps v. Evers [1980] 1 W.L.R. 1327; [1980] 3 All E.R. 399, C.A.; Hardy v. Hardy, The Times, June 11, 1981, C.A.; L. v. L. (1980) 11 Fam.Law 57, Balcombe J.; Tebbutt v. Haynes [1981] 2 All E.R. 238, C.A.; Re Abbott (A Bankrupt), ex p. Trustee of the Property of the Bankrupt v. Abbott [1982] 3 W.L.R. 86, D.C.; B. v. B. (1982) 12 Fam.Law 92, C.A.; Cartwright v. Cartwright (1982) Fam.Law 252, Sheldon J.; Norman v. Norman [1983] 1 W.L.R. 296; [1983] 1 All E.R. 486, Wood J.; Carson v. Carson [1983] 1 All E.R. 478, C.A.; Harris v. Goddard, The Times, August 18, 1983, C.A.; Nicholas v. Nicholas (1984) 14 Fam.Law 118, C.A.; First National Securities v. Hegerty [1984] 3 W.L.R. 769, C.A.; Banyard v. Banyard (1985) 15 Fam.Law 120, C.A.; Thompson v. Thompson [1985] 2 All E.R. 243, C.A.; Teschner v. Teschner (1985) 15 Fam.Law. 250, C.A.; Dinch v. Dinch [1987] 1 W.L.R. 252, H.L.; Mossop v. Mossop [1988] 2 All E.R. 202, C.A.; R. v. Rushmoor Borough Council, ex p. Barrett, The Times, March 15, 1988, C.A.

s. 24A, see Norman v. Norman [1983] 1 W.L.R. 296; [1983] 1 All E.R. 486; Wood J.; Thompson v. Thompson [1985] 2 All E.R. 243, C.A.; R. v. Rushmoor Borough Council, ex p. Barrett [1986] 3 W.L.R. 998, Reeve J.; Burton v. Burton (1986) 2 F.L.R. 419, Butler-Sloss J.

s. 24A, added: 1981, c.24, s.7; amended: 1984, c.42, sch.1.

1973—cont.

18. Matrimonial Causes Act 1973—cont.

s. 25, see *H.* v. *H. (Family Provision: Remarriage)* [1975] 2 W.L.R. 124; [1975] 1 All E.R. 367; *Jones (M. A.)* v. *Jones (W.)* [1975] 2 W.L.R. 606; [1975] 2 All E.R. 12, C.A.; *O'D.* v. *O'D.* [1975] 3 W.L.R. 308; [1975] 2 All E.R. 993, C.A.; *Calderbank* v. *Calderbank* [1975] 3 W.L.R. 586; *W.* v. *W. (Financial Provision: Lump Sum)* [1975] 3 W.L.R. 752; [1975] 3 All E.R. 970; *Gray* v. *Gray* [1976] 3 W.L.R. 181; *Campbell* v. *Campbell* [1976] 3 W.L.R. 572; *Martin* v. *Martin* [1976] 3 W.L.R. 580, C.A.; *S.* v. *S.* [1976] 3 W.L.R. 775; [1977] Fam.Law 127, C.A.; *Morgan* v. *Morgan* [1977] 2 W.L.R. 712; *West* v. *West* [1977] 2 W.L.R. 933, C.A.; *Martin (B. H.)* v. *Martin (D.)* [1977] 3 W.L.R. 101, C.A.; *Dean* v. *Dean* [1978] 3 W.L.R. 288, Bush J.; *P.* v. *P. (Financial Provision: Lump Sum)* [1978] 1 W.L.R. 483, C.A.; *Backhouse* v. *Backhouse* [1978] 1 W.L.R. 243, Balcombe J.; *Hanlon* v. *Hanlon* [1978] 1 W.L.R. 592, C.A.; *Lilford (Lord)* v. *Glynn* [1979] 1 W.L.R. 78, C.A.; *Bateman* v. *Bateman* [1979] 2 W.L.R. 377, Purchas J.; *Kokosinski* v. *Kokosinski* [1980] 1 All E.R. 1106, Wood J.; *Priest* v. *Priest* (1978) 9 Fam.Law 252, C.A.; *Wilkinson* v. *Wilkinson* (1979) 10 Fam.Law 48, Booth J.; *Pearce* v. *Pearce* (1979) 10 Fam.Law 209, C.A.; *Page* v. *Page, The Times,* January 30, 1981, C.A.; *Foley* v. *Foley, The Times,* May 19, 1981, C.A.; *S.* v. *S.* (1980) 10 Fam.Law. 240, Balcombe J.; *Sharpe* v. *Sharpe* (1981) 11 Fam.Law 121, C.A.; *Preston* v. *Preston* [1981] 3 W.L.R. 619, C.A.; *C.* v. *C.* (1981) 125 S.J. 844, D.C.; *Walker* v. *Walker, The Times,* February 19, 1982, C.A.; *Harvey* v. *Harvey* [1982] 2 W.L.R. 283, C.A.; *Walsh* v. *Corcoran, The Times,* March 1, 1982, C.A.; *Stockford* v. *Stockford* (1982) 12 Fam.Law 30, C.A.; *B.* v. *B.* (1982) 12 Fam.Law 92, C.A.; *Potter* v. *Potter* [1982] 3 All E.R. 321, C.A.; *Robinson* v. *Robinson, The Times,* October 30, 1982, C.A.; *Prow (formerly Brown)* v. *Brown* (1982) 12 Fam.Law 24, C.A.; *Walker-Arnott* v. *Walker-Arnott* (1983) 4 F.L.R. 1, Heilbron J.; *Re Snoek (decd.)* (1983) 13 Fam.Law 19, Wood J.; *Resai* v. *Resai* (1983) 13 Fam.Law 46, Lincoln J.; *H. (formerly W.)* v. *H. (Short Second Marriage)* (1983) 13 Fam.Law 180, Ewbank J.; *Hall* v. *Hall* (1984) 14 Fam.Law 54, C.A.; *Freeman* v. *Swatridge* (1984) 14 Fam.Law 215, C.A.; *Besterman (decd.), Re* [1984] 3 W.L.R. 280, C.A.; *Jenkins* v. *Livesey (formerly Jenkins)* [1985] 2 W.L.R. 47, H.L.; *Leadbeater* v. *Leadbeater* (1985) 15 Fam.Law 280, Balcombe J.; *Michael* v. *Michael, The Times,* May 28, 1986, C.A.; *Sherdley* v. *Sherdley* [1986] 2 All E.R. 202, C.A.; *Roberts* v. *Roberts* [1986] 1 W.L.R. 437, Wood J.; *Collins* v. *Collins, The Times,* August 12, 1986, C.A.; *Kyte* v. *Kyte* [1987] 3 W.L.R. 1114, C.A.; *Kiely* v. *Kiely* (1988) 18 Fam.Law 51, C.A.; *Tandy* v. *Tandy* (1988) 152 J.P.N. 526, C.A.

1973—cont.

18. Matrimonial Causes Act 1973—cont.

ss. 25, 25A, see *Suter* v. *Suter and Jones* [1987] 3 W.L.R. 9, C.A.

ss. 25, 25A, substituted: 1984, c.42, s.3.

s. 25A, see *Morris* v. *Morris* (1986) 16 Fam.Law 24, C.A.; *Seaton* v. *Seaton, The Times,* February 24, 1986, C.A.; *Thompson* v. *Thompson* [1988] 1 W.L.R. 562, Ewbank J.; *Barrett* v. *Barrett, The Times,* June 22, 1988, C.A.

s. 27, see *Lewis* v. *Lewis* (1976) 6 Fam. Law 111, C.A.; *Newmarch* v. *Newmarch* [1977] 3 W.L.R. 832; [1977] Fam.Law 143, Rees J.

s. 27, amended: 1973, c.45, sch.6; 1978, c.22, s.63; 1984, c.42, s.4, sch.1; 1987, c.42, sch.2; repealed in pt.: 1978, c.22, s.63, sch.3.

s. 28, see *Rowe* v. *Rowe* (1974) 5 Fam. Law 62; *Hargood (formerly Jenkins)* v. *Jenkins* [1978] 2 W.L.R. 969, Wood J.; *Nixon* v. *Fox* [1978] 3 W.L.R. 565, Dunn J.

s. 28, amended: 1984, c.42, sch.5.

s. 29, see *Downing* v. *Downing (Downing Intervening)* [1976] 3 W.L.R. 335; *R.* v. *Luton County Court, ex p. Fosdike* [1977] Fam.Law 177, D.C.; *Kiely* v. *Kiely* [1988] 18 Fam.Law 51, C.A.

s. 29, amended: 1984, c.42, s.5.

s. 31, see *Beighton* v. *Beighton* (1974) Fam.Law 119, C.A.; *Stephenson* v. *Stephenson* (1974) 4 Fam.Law 124, C.A.; *Lewis* v. *Lewis* [1977] 1 W.L.R. 409, C.A.; *Ladbrook* v. *Ladbrook* (1977) 121 S.J. 710; [1977] Fam.Law 213, Dunn J.; *Jessel* v. *Jessel* [1979] 1 W.L.R. 1148, C.A.; *J. (H. D.)* v. *J. (A. M.)* [1980] 1 All E.R. 156, Sheldon J.; *Tilley* v. *Tilley* (1979) 10 Fam.Law 89, C.A.; *Pearce* v. *Pearce* (1979) 10 Fam.Law 209, C.A.; *Thwaite* v. *Thwaite, The Times,* February 5, 1981; *L.* v. *L.* (1980) 11 Fam.Law 57, Balcombe J.; *Norman* v. *Norman* [1983] 1 W.L.R. 296; [1983] 1 All E.R. 486; *Carson* v. *Carson* [1983] 1 All E.R. 478, C.A.; *Morris* v. *Morris, The Times,* June 17, 1985, C.A.; *Thompson* v. *Thompson* [1985] 2 All E.R. 243, C.A.; *Sandford* v. *Sandford* (1985) 15 Fam.Law 230, Ewbank J.; *Whitfield* v. *Whitfield* (1985) 15 Fam.Law 226, Wood J.; *Morley-Clarke* v. *Jones* [1985] 3 All E.R. 193, C.A.; *Morris* v. *Morris* (1986) 16 Fam.Law 24, C.A.; *Sandford* v. *Sandford* (1986) 16 Fam.Law 104, C.A.; *S.* v. *S., The Times,* July 9, 1986, Walker J.; *S.* v. *S.* [1986] 3 W.L.R. 518, Waite J.; *Whiting* v. *Whiting* [1988] 1 W.L.R. 565, C.A.; *Atkinson* v. *Atkinson* [1988] 2 W.L.R. 204, C.A.

s. 31, amended: 1981, c.24, s.8; 1982, c.53, s.51; 1984, c.42, s.6.

ss. 31, 35, see *M.* v. *M., The Times,* January 9, 1982, Wood J.

s. 33A, added: 1984, c.42, s.7.

s. 34, see *Saunders* v. *Saunders* [1978] 8 Fam.Law 206, C.A.; *Jessel* v. *Jessel* [1979] 1 W.L.R. 1148, C.A.

s. 35, see *Carr (D. V.)* v. *Carr (G. A.)* [1974] 3 W.L.R. 449; [1974] 3 All E.R. 366; *Pace* v. *Doe* [1976] 3 W.L.R. 865; *Ladbrook* v. *Lad-*

1973

CAP.

1973—cont.

18. Matrimonial Causes Act 1973—cont.
brook (1977) 121 S.J. 710; [1977] Fam.Law
213, Dunn J.; *Warden* v. *Warden* [1981] 3
W.L.R. 435, C.A.
s. 35, amended: 1984, c.42, sch.1.
s. 36, amended: 1975, c.63, s.26.
s. 37, see *Whittingham* v. *Whittingham, National
Westminster Bank (Intervener)* [1978] 2
W.L.R. 936, C.A.; *H.* v. *H. and W. and Barclays
Bank* (1979) 10 Fam.Law 152, Purchas J.; *G.*
v. *G.* (1980) 10 Fam.Law 250, Eastham J.;
Roche v. *Roche* (1981) 11 Fam.Law 243, C.A.;
Green v. *Green* [1981] 1 W.L.R. 391, Eastham
J.; *Walker* v. *Walker* (1982) 12 Fam.Law 249,
Sheldon J.; *K.* v. *K. (Avoidance of Reviewable
Distribution)* (1982) 12 Fam.Law 143; (1983)
4 F.L.R. 31, C.A.; *Hamlin* v. *Hamlin* [1985] 2
All E.R. 1037, C.A.; *Kemmis* v. *Kemmis (Wel-
land Intervening); Lazard Brothers & Co.
(Jersey)* v. *Norah Holdings, The Times,* February 22, 1988, C.A.
s. 39, see *Re Abbott (A Bankrupt), ex p. Trustee
of the Property of the Bankrupt* v. *Abbott*
[1982] 3 W.L.R. 86, D.C.
s. 39, amended: 1985, c.65, sch.8; 1986, c.45,
sch.14.
s. 41, see *Scott* v. *Scott* (1977) 121 S.J. 391;
[1977] Fam.Law 142, Baker P.; *Cook* v. *Cook*
[1978] 1 W.L.R. 994, C.A.; *Ashley* v. *Ashley*
(1979) 9 Fam.Law 219, C.A.; *A.* v. *A. (Children: Arrangements)* [1979] 1 W.L.R. 533,
C.A.; *England* v. *England* (1979) 10 Fam.Law
86, C.A.; *McDermott* v. *McDermott* (1979) 10
Fam.Law 145, C.A.; *Hughes* v. *Hughes* (1984)
14 Fam.Law 23, C.A.; *H.* v. *H. (Queen's
Proctor Intervening), The Times,* June 30,
Anthony Lincoln J.; *Yeend* v. *Yeend* (1984) 14
Fam.Law 314, C.A.; *Healey* v. *Healey* [1984]
3 W.L.R. 806, Anthony Lincoln J.
s. 41, amended: 1986, c.55, sch.1.
s. 42, see *Bowden* v. *Bowden* (1975) 74 L.G.R.
347, C.A.; *Buckley* v. *Buckley* [1977] 3 All E.R.
544 (Note), Baker P.; *Rowe* v. *Rowe* (1979)
123 S.J. 352, C.A.; *Re D. (Minors)* (1980) 10
Fam.Law 246, C.A.; *Re H. (Adoption by
Step-Parent: Preliminary Examination)* (1983)
4 F.L.R. 261, Hollings J.
s. 43, see *R. & Y. (A Minor) (Child in Care:
Access)* [1975] 3 W.L.R. 342, C.A.; *M.* v. *M.*
(1978) 10 Fam.Law 18, C.A.; *Turney* v. *Turney
and Devon County Council* (1983) 4 F.L.R.
199, C.A.; *Re P. (A Minor) (Custody)* (1983) 4
F.L.R. 401, C.A.; *Re R. (A Minor) (Child in
Care: Access)* [1983] 2 All E.R. 929, C.A.; *R.*
v. *G.* [1984] 3 W.L.R. 667, C.A.; *J.* v. *Devon
County Council (Wardship: Jurisdiction)*
(1986) 16 Fam.Law 162, Swinton Thomas J.;
W. (Minors), Re, The Times, July 23, 1988,
C.A.
s. 43, amended: 1980, c.5, sch.5; 1983, c.41,
sch.2; 1985, c.28, s.1; repealed in pt.: 1980,
c.5, sch.6.; 1984, c.42, sch.3; 1985, c.51,
sch.17.
ss. 43, 44, see *Baczowski* v. *Baczowski* (1980)
10 Fam.Law 218, C.A.

CAP.

1973—cont.

18. Matrimonial Causes Act 1973—cont.
s. 44, amended: 1975, c.72, sch.3; repealed in
pt.: 1984, c.42, sch.3; 1985, c.51, sch.17.
s. 45, see *Puttick* v. *Att.-Gen. and Puttick* [1979]
3 W.L.R. 542, Sir George Baker P.; *Vervaeke*
v. *Smith (Messina and Att.-Gen. Intervening)*
[1982] 2 All E.R. 144, H.L.; *Williams* v. *Att.-
Gen., The Times,* October 29, 1986, Latey J.
s. 45, repealed: 1986, c.55, sch.2.
s. 46, repealed: 1973, c.45, sch.6.
s. 47, see *Chaudhry* v. *Chaudhry* [1975] 3 W.L.R.
559; [1975] 3 All E.R. 687; *Onobrauche* v.
Onobrauche (1978) 122 S.J. 210, Comyn J.;
Hussain v. *Hussain* [1982] 3 All E.R. 369, C.A.
s. 47, amended: 1978, c.22, sch.2; 1984, c.42,
sch.1; 1986, c.55, sch.1.
s. 49, see *Bradley* v. *Bradley (Queen's Proctor
Intervening)* (1986) 16 Fam.Law 25, Eastham
J.
s. 50, rules 73/1973, 2016; 74/2168; 76/606,
607, 2166, 2167; 77/344, 345; 78/922;
79/400; 80/977, 1484; 81/5, 1099; 82/1853;
84/1511; 85/144, 1315; 86/634, 1096;
88/226, 1328.
s. 50, repealed: 1984, c.42, sch.3; amended:
1986, c.55, sch.1; repealed in pt.: *ibid.,*
schs.1,2.
s. 51, orders 74/1383; 75/1346; 77/346;
78/1256; 79/966; 80/819; 81/1515; 82/1708;
83/1686; 86/696; 88/870.
s. 51, repealed: 1984, c.42, sch.3.
s. 52, see *C.* v. *G.,* February 19, 1975; *Re M. (A
Minor)* (1980) 10 Fam.Law 184, C.A.; repealed
in pt.: 1975, c.72, sch.4.
s. 52, amended: 1984, c.42, sch.1.
s. 54, repealed in pt.: S.L.R. 1977.
s. 55, order 73/1972; repealed in pt.: S.L.R.
1977.
sch. 2, amended: 1975, c.63, s.26; repealed in
pt.: *ibid.,*sch.; S.L.R. 1977; 1980, c.5, sch.5;
1981, c.54, sch.7; 1984, c.42, sch.3.
sch. 3, repealed: S.L.R. 1977.

**19. Independent Broadcasting Authority Act
1973.**
Royal Assent, May 23, 1973.
repealed: 1981, c.68, sch.9.
ss. 2, 22, see *Wilson* v. *Independent Broadcasting Authority* (O.H.), February 11, 1979.
ss. 39, 40, orders 76/1778; 79/114.

20. London Cab Act 1973.
Royal Assent, May 23, 1973.

21. Overseas Pensions Act 1973.
Royal Assent, May 23, 1973.

22. Law Reform (Diligence) (Scotland) Act 1973.
Royal Assent, May 23, 1973.
repealed: 1987, c.18, sch.8.

23. Education (Work Experience) Act 1973.
Royal Assent, May 23, 1973.
repealed (S.): 1980, c.44, sch.5.
s. 1, amended: 1988, c.40, sch.1-2.

24. Employment of Children Act 1973.
Royal Assent, May 23, 1973.

25. Succession (Scotland) Act 1973.
Royal Assent, May 23, 1973.
s. 1, repealed in pt.: 1980, c.55, sch.3.

CAP.

1973—cont.

26. Land Compensation Act 1973.

Royal Assent, May 23, 1973.

see *R.* v. *Cardiff City Council, ex p. Cross, The Times,* October 6, 1982, C.A.

s. 1, see *Shepherd* v. *Lancashire County Council* [1977] 33 P. & C.R. 296, Lands Tribunal; *Hickmott* v. *Dorset County Council* [1977] 35 P. & C.R. 195, C.A.

ss. 1, 3, amended: 1980, c.65, s.112.

ss. 2, 3, repealed in pt.: 1973, c.56, sch.2.

s. 4, amended: 1975, c.78, sch.5; 1980, c.60, s.20; c.65, s.112; repealed in pt.: 1973, c.56, sch.2.

ss. 5, 6, repealed in pt.: *ibid.*

s. 8, rules 73/1862.

s. 8, amended: 1975, c.76, sch.1; repealed in pt.: 1973, c.56, sch.2; 1975, c.76, sch.1.

ss. 10, 11, repealed in pt.: 1973, c.56, sch.2.

s. 12, amended: 1980, c.65, s.112.

s. 14, repealed in pt.: *ibid.,* sch.34.

s. 16, see *Hickmott* v. *Dorset County Council* (1977) 35 P. & C.R. 195, C.A.

s. 16, amended: 1973, c.56, sch.2; 1980, c.65, s.112, repealed in pt.: 1973, c.56, sch.2.

s. 18, amended: 1980, c.65, s.112; repealed in pt.: 1973, c.56, sch.2.

s. 19, amended: 1980, c.65, s.112; c.66, sch.24; 1985, c.51, sch.4; repealed in pt.: 1973, c.65, sch.2; 1980, c.65, s.112, sch. 34.

s. 20, regs. 73/1363; 75/1763.

s. 20, amended: 1984, c.27, sch 13; repealed in pt.: 1973, c.56, sch.2; 1977, c.42, sch.25; 1980, c,66, sch.25.

s. 21, repealed: 1975, c.78, sch.6.

ss. 22–25, repealed: 1980, c.66, sch.25.

ss. 26–28, repealed in pt.: 1973, c.56, sch.2.

s. 29, see *G.L.C.* v. *Holmes, The Times,* December 10, 1985, C.A.; *Newery* v. *Liverpool City Council* (1982) 14 H.L.R. 75; *Greater London Council* v. *Holmes* [1986] 1 All E.R. 739, C.A.: *Casale* v. *Islington, London Borough of* (1985) 18 H.L.R. 146, Taylor J.

s. 29, amended: 1973, c.56, sch.2; 1974, c.44, sch.13; 1975, c.6, sch.5; 1977, c.42, sch.23; 1980, c.51, sch 24; 1985, c.71, sch.2; 1986, c.63, s.9; repealed in pt.: 1973, c.56, sch.2; 1974, c.44, schs.13,15.

s. 30, repealed in pt.: 1973, c.56, sch.2.

s. 31, repealed: *ibid.*

s. 32, amended: 1980, c.65, s.114; 1986, c.63, s.9; 1988, c.50, sch.17; repealed in pt.: 1973, c.56, sch.2; 1980, c.65, sch.34.

s. 33, amended: 1973, c.56, sch.2.

s. 34, amended: 1986, c.5, sch.14; repealed in pt.: 1973, c.56, sch.2.

ss. 35, 36, repealed in pt.: *ibid.*

s. 37, see *Prasad* v. *Wolverhampton B.C.* [1983] 2 All E.R. 140, C.A.; *R.* v. *Islington London Borough Council, ex p. Knight* [1984] 1 All E.R. 154, McCullough J.; *Newery* v. *Liverpool City Council* (1982) 14 H.L.R. 75.

s. 37, amended: 1973, c.56, sch.2; 1974, c.44, schs.13,15; 1975, c.6, sch.5; 1977, c.42, sch.23; 1985, c.71, sch.2; repealed in pt.: 1973, c.56, sch.2; 1985, c.71, sch.1.

CAP.

1973—cont.

26. Land Compensation Act 1973—*cont.*

s. 38, repealed in pt.: 1973, c.56, sch.2.

s. 39, see *R.* v. *Bristol Corporation, ex p. Hendy* [1974] 1 All E.R. 1047, C.A.

s. 39, amended: 1974, c.44, sch.13; 1976, c.75, sch.7; 1985, c.71, sch.2; repealed in pt.: 1973, c.56, sch.2; 1985, c.51, sch.17; c.71, sch.1.

s. 41, amended: 1974, c.7, s.37; repealed in pt.: 1973, c.56, sch.2.

s 42, amended: 1980, c.51, s.138; 1985, c.71, sch.2; repealed in pt.: 1973, c.56, sch.2.

s. 43, amended: 1974, c.44, sch.13.

s. 44, amended: 1980, c.66, sch.24; 1973, c.56, sch.2; 1986, c.44, sch.7.

s. 46, amended: 1973, c.56, sch.2.

s. 48, see *Wakerley* v. *St. Edmundsbury Borough Council* (1979) 38 P. & C.R. 551, C.A.; amended: 1974, c.56, sch.2; 1977, c.12, sch.1.

s. 48, amended: 1986, c.5, sch.14.

s. 49, repealed: 1973, c.56, sch.2.

s. 50, amended: 1981, c.66, sch.3; repealed in pt.: 1973, c.56, sch.2.

s. 51, repealed in pt.: *ibid.*

s. 52, rules 73/1862.

s. 52, amended: 1975, c.76, sch.1; 1985, c.71, sch.2; repealed in pt.: 1973, c.56, sch.2; 1975, c.76, sch.1.

s. 53, amended: 1981, c.66, sch.3; repealed in pt.: 1973, c.56, sch.2.

ss. 54, 55, repealed in pt.: *ibid.*

s. 56, amended: 1986, c.5, sch.14; repealed in pt.: 1973, c.56, sch.2.

s. 57, amended: 1981, c.66, sch.3; 1985, c.71, sch.2; repealed in pt.: 1973, c.56, sch.2.

s. 58, amended: 1980, c.66, sch.24; 1986, c.44, sch.7; repealed in pt.: 1973, c.56, sch.2; 1981, c.66, sch.5.

s. 59, see *Dawson* v. *Norwich City Council* (1979) 37 P. & C.R. 516, Lands Tribunal.

s. 59, amended: 1973, c.56, sch.2; 1977, c.12, sch.1; 1986, c.5, sch.14.

ss. 60, 61 (in pt.) 62, 63 (in pt.): repealed: *ibid.*

s. 64, repealed: 1981, c.67, sch.6.

ss. 65–67, repealed: 1973, c.56, sch.2.

s. 69, amended: 1980, c.66, sch.24.

s. 72, repealed in pt.: 1981, c.64, sch.13.

s. 73, amended: 1985, c.71, sch.2; 1986, c.63, sch.5; repealed in pt.: 1974, c.44, sch.15; 1985, c.71, sch.1.

s. 74, amended: 1980, c.66, sch.24; repealed in pt.: *ibid.,* sch.25.

s. 76, amended: *ibid.,* sch.24.

s. 78, regs. 74/596; 76/1419.

s. 78, repealed in pt.: 1980, c.66, sch.25.

s. 83, repealed: 1973, c.56, sch.2.

s. 87, amended: *ibid.*; 1975, c.6, sch.5; 1985, c.71, sch.2; 1986, c.5, sch.14; repealed in pt.: 1973, c.56, sch.2; 1980, c.66, schs.24,25; 1985, c.71, sch.1.

s. 89, amended: 1973, c.56, sch.2.

schs. 1, 2, repealed: *ibid.*

CAP.

1973—cont.

27. Bahamas Independence Act 1973.
Royal Assent, June 14, 1973.
s. 2, repealed in pt.: 1981, c.61, sch.9.
s. 4, repealed in pt.: 1978, c.30, sch.3.
s. 5, repealed: S.L.R. 1986.
sch. 2, repealed in pt.: S.L.R. 1977; 1981, c.9,
　　sch., 1982, c.1, sch.2.

28. Rate Rebate Act 1973.
Royal Assent, June 14, 1973.
repealed: 1973, c.65, sch.29.

29. Guardianship Act 1973.
Royal Assent, July 5, 1973.
amended: 1987, c.42, sch.2.
see *Re R (An infant) (Custody to Non-Parent)*
　　[1974] 1 All E.R. 1033, D.C.; *L (A Minor), Re*
　　(1984) 14 Fam.Law 281, C.A.; *Essex County
　　Council v. T, The Times*, March 15, 1986, C.A.
s. 1, amended: 1978, c.22, s.36; 1983, c.20,
　　sch.4; 1986, c.55, sch.1; 1987, c.42, ss.2, 5;
　　repealed in pt.: 1983, c.20, schs.4,6; 1986,
　　c.55, schs.1,2.
s. 2, see *C. v. C., The Times*, December 2,
　　1981, C.A.; *Cooke* v. *Cooke* (1982) 12
　　Fam.Law, D.C.; *P. (Minors: Access), Re; P.
　　v. P. (Gateshead Metropolitan Borough Coun-
　　cil Intervening), The Times*, February 19, 1988,
　　C.A.
s. 2, amended: 1978, c.22, ss.36,38,44,45;
　　1987, c.42, s.3, sch.2; repealed in pt.: 1975,
　　c.72, sch.4; 1978, c.22, s.45, sch.3; 1986,
　　c.55, schs.1,2; 1987, c.42, schs.2,4.
s. 3, amended: 1978, c.22, ss.36,38; 1980,
　　c.43, sch.7; 1987, c.42, s.6; repealed in pt.:
　　1975, c.72, sch.4; 1978, c.22, sch.3.
s. 4, amended: 1975, c.72, sch.3; 1978, c.22,
　　ss.36,38,44, sch.2; 1980, c.5, sch.5; 1987,
　　c.42, s.6, sch.2; repealed in pt.: *ibid.*,
　　schs.2,4.
s. 5, amended: 1978, c.22, s.36, sch.2; 1987,
　　c.42, s.6, sch.2; repealed in pt.: 1986, c.55,
　　schs.1,2.
s. 5A, added: 1978, c.22, s.46; amended: 1987,
　　c.42, s.6, sch.2.
s. 6, amended: 1975, c.72, s.90, sch.3; 1980,
　　c.43, sch.7.
s. 8, repealed: 1978, c.22, sch.3.
s. 8A, added: 1987, c.42, sch.2.
s. 9, amended: 1974, c.4, sch.5; repealed in
　　pt.: 1980, c.43, sch.9; 1981, c.54, sch.7.
s. 10, amended: 1986, c.55, sch.1; repealed in
　　pt.: 1984, c.36, sch.3.
ss. 10, 11 (in pt.), 12 (in pt.), repealed (S.): 1986,
　　c.9, sch.2.
ss. 11, 12, amended: 1975, c.72, s.48.
s. 13, amended (S.): 1986, c.55, sch.1.
s. 15, orders 74/695, 836.
s. 15 (in pt.), schs. 4, 5 (in pt.), repealed (S.):
　　1986, c.9, sch.2.
sch. 2, repealed in pt.: 1978, c.72, s.48; 1986,
　　c.55, schs.1,2.

30. Sea Fisheries (Shellfish) Act 1973.
Royal Assent, July 5, 1973.

31. Dentists (Amendment) Act 1973.
Royal Assent, July 5, 1973.
repealed: 1984, c.24, sch.6.

CAP.

1973—cont.

**32. National Health Service Reorganisation Act
1973.**
Royal Assent, July 5, 1973.
repealed (S.): 1978, c.29, sch.17.
regs. 73/1286, 2217.
s. 2, regs. 74/465; 76/516.
ss. 2–4, repealed: 1977, c.49, sch.16.
s. 5, regs. 75/1101; orders 78/1191, 1192, 1275,
　　1305, 1624, 2077, 2192; 74/9; 75/1099, 1100;
　　repealed: 1977, c.49, sch.16.
s. 6, regs. 73/2012; 74/361, 455, 477, 907;
　　75/1101; 76/334; orders 73/1624, 2192; 74/9;
　　75/1099, 1101; 77/1102; repealed: 1977,
　　c.49, sch.16.
s. 7, regs. 73/2012; 74/24, 29, 36, 160, 191,
　　282, 455; repealed 1977, c.49, sch.16.
s. 8, repealed: *ibid.*
s. 9, regs. 74/282; 76/791; 77/874; repealed:
　　1977, c.49, sch.16.
s. 10, order 74/190; repealed: 1977, c.49,
　　sch.16.
s. 11, regs. 74/191; order 74/168; repealed:
　　1977, c.49, sch.16.
s. 12, repealed: *ibid.*
s. 13, order 74/168.
s. 14, orders 74/248; 82/75, 203; 84/168;
　　amended: 1977, c.49, sch.15; 1980, c.53,
　　sch.1.
s. 15, orders 74/281; 79/51; 80/1193; 81/1548;
　　82/75, 143, 201, 244, 276; 83/304; 84/168;
　　amended: 1977, c.49, sch.15; repealed in pt.:
　　ibid., sch.16; 1980, c.53, sch.7.
s. 16, see *Sheffield Area Health Authority* v.
　　Sheffield City Council [1983] 2 All E.R. 384,
　　Lloyd J.
s. 16, orders 74/330; 75/325; 76/273.
s. 17, order 74/216.
s. 18, amended: 1980, c.53, sch.1; 1984, c.30,
　　sch.10.
ss. 18, 19, orders 74/35, 318, 378; 75/984,
　　1765; 82/296.
s. 19, order 87/1428.
ss. 21, 22, repealed: 1977, c.49, sch.16.
s. 23, order 74/1915.
s. 24, orders 74/103; 82/296; 84/167.
s. 24, amended: 1980, c.53, sch.1; order 82/75;
　　repealed in pt: *ibid.*
s. 25, order 74/246.
s. 26, order 76/1464.
s. 28, repealed: 1977, c.49, sch.16.
s. 29, amended and repealed in pt.: order 82/75.
Part III (ss. 31–39) repealed: 1977, c.49, sch.16.
s. 32, amended: 1976, c.48, s.7; repealed in
　　pt.: *ibid.*, sch.
s. 34, amended: 1976, c.83, sch.1; repealed in
　　pt.: *ibid.*, sch.5.
s. 37, amended: 1976, c.83, sch.1.
s. 38, regs. 74/247.
s. 40, see *R.* v. *McFarlane* (1975) 60 Cr.App.R.
　　320, C.A.; repealed: 1977, c.49, sch.16.
s. 41, repealed: 1975, c.37, sch.3.
ss. 42, 43, repealed: 1977, c.49, sch.16.
s. 44, regs. 74/189, 801; 75/302.
s. 45, repealed: 1977, c.49, sch.16.

CAP.

1973—cont.

32. National Health Service Reorganisation Act 1973—cont.

s. 46, regs. 74/319.

s. 46, repealed: 1977, c.49, sch.16.

s. 47, regs. 74/282; repealed: 1977, c.49, sch.16.

s. 48, repealed: ibid.

s. 50, regs. 74/1377, 1440; 75/1687, 1715, 1988; 76/1874; 77/471; repealed: 1977, c.49, sch.16.

ss. 51–53, repealed: 1977, c.49, sch.16.

s. 54, regs. 74/282, 287, 378; orders 74/63, 248; 75/364, 984; 77/1204; 82/75, 203; 84/168; 87/1428.

s. 54, repealed in pt.: 1977, c.49, sch.16.

s. 55, repealed in pt.: ibid., sch.15.

s. 56, regs. 74/801, 1377; 75/1687; 77/434; orders 75/325, 364, 984, 1765; 76/273; 87/1428.

s. 56, repealed in pt.: 1975, c.37, sch.3; 1977, c.49, sch.16.

s. 57, orders 74/53, 188, 241, 307, 1191.

s. 58, orders 73/1185, 1523, 1935; 74/188, 1191.

sch. 1, see R. v. Central Arbitration Committee, ex p. North Western Regional Health Authority [1978] I.C.R. 1228, D.C.; R. v. Secretary of State for Social Services, ex p. Clarke (1988) I.R.L.R. 22, D.C.

sch. 1, regs. 73/2012, 74/183, 296, 361, 455, 477, 494, 495; 75/1101; 76/334; order 73/1771.

sch. 3, repealed: 1977, c.49, sch.16.

sch. 4, regs. 76/1226; repealed: 1977, c.49, sch.16; repealed in pt.: 1978, c.40, sch 2; c.44, sch.17; 1984, c.24, sch.6; c.30, sch.11.

33. Protection of Wrecks Act 1973.

Royal Assent, July 18, 1973.

order 88/287.

s. 1, orders 73/1531; 74/55–8, 457, 458, 910; 75/174, 262, 726; 77/764, 1357; 78/199, 321, 664, 764; 79/31, 56; 80/645, 1306, 1456; 81/827; 82/47, 83/128, 1400; 84/2, 521, 802, 1658, 1963; 85/699; 86/1020, 1441.

s. 2, order 73/1690.

s. 3, orders 75/262; 79/6, 56; 80/1307; 83/128; 84/2 802; 86/1020.

34. Ulster Defence Regiment Act 1973.

Royal Assent, July 18, 1973.

repealed: 1980, c.9, sch.10.

35. Employment Agencies Act 1973.

Royal Assent, July 18, 1973.

s. 1, amended: 1975, c.17, sch.13.

ss. 1, 9, 13, see McCabe v. Edwards [1981] I.C.R. 468.

s. 2, regs. 76/712, 713; 78/390; 79/770; 82/142.

s. 2, amended: 1975, c.71, sch.13; repealed in pt.: ibid., sch. 18.

ss. 3, 4, amended: 1975, c.71, sch.13.

s. 5, regs. 76/715; 78/805; 81/1481.

s. 6, regs. 76/714; 78/805; 81/1481.

s. 9, amended: 1978, c.71, sch.13; repealed in pt.: ibid., sch.18.

s. 12, regs. 76/710, 712–715; 78/390, 805; 79/770, 1741; 81/1481; 82/142, 809; 84/490, 978.

CAP.

1973—cont.

35. Employment Agencies Act 1973—cont.

s. 13, regs. 76/710; 79/342, 1741; 82/809; 84/490, 978.

s. 13, amended: 1973, c.65, sch.27; 1975, c.71, sch.13; 1984, c.46, sch.5; 1985, c.51, sch.14; order 85/1884; 1988, c.4, sch.6; c.33, sch.8; repealed in pt.: 1975, c.71, sch.8; 1984, c.46, schs.5, 6; 1985, c.51, sch.17; 1988, c.40, sch.13 (prosp.).

s. 14, orders 76/709, 711.

36. Northern Ireland Constitution Act 1973.

Royal Assent, July 18, 1973.

regs. 88/1667.

s. 1, order 82/1078.

s. 7, amended: 1973, c.69, s.1; repealed in pt.: 1982, c.38, schs.2,3.

s. 8, amended: 1973, c.69, s.1; 1982, c.38, sch.2.

s. 9, order 84/358.

s. 10, repealed in pt.: 1981, c.19, sch.1.

s. 11, amended: 1981, c.38, sch.3.

s. 13, repealed in pt.: 1982, c.38, sch.3.

s. 15, regs. 77/1879; 83/1599.

s. 19, see McCartney's Application, Re [1987] 11 N.I.J.B. 94, C.A.

s. 19, amended: 1981, c.38, sch.3.

ss. 19, 20, amended: 1976, c.25, sch.6.

ss. 19, 23, see Purvis v. Magherafelt District Council [1978] N.I. 26, Murray J.

s. 20, repealed in pt.: 1976, c.25, s.58.

s. 21, see French's Application, Re [1985] 7 N.I.J.B. 48, Carswell J.

s. 25, repealed in pt.: 1981, c.38, schs.2,3.

s. 26, orders 82/1079; 84/358, 1823; 86/222.

ss. 26, 27, amended: 1982, c.38, sch.2; repealed in pt.: ibid., sch.3.

s. 27, order 82/1078.

s. 28, order 82/1838.

s. 28, amended: 1979, c.15, s.1; 1986, c.56, sch.3; repealed in pt.: ibid., sch.4.

s. 30, repealed in pt.: 1975, c.25, sch.3.

s. 38, orders 77/2158; 79/927, 1576; 80/562, 564, 1088; 81/157, 160, 229, 234; 83/1122; 84/360; 85/169, 454; 87/168, 1628.

s. 38, amended: 1982, c.38, sch.2; repealed in pt.: ibid., sch.3.

s. 39, sch. 2, amended: ibid., sch.2.

sch. 3, repealed: 1978, c.23, sch.7; 1981, c.38, sch.3; amended: 1984, c.46, sch.5; repealed in pt.: 1981, c.38, schs.3,6; 1985, c.58, sch.4.

37. Water Act 1973.

Royal Assent, July 18, 1973.

Commencement order: 84/71.

s. 1, amended: 1978, c.52, sch.11.

s. 2, orders 73/1287–1289, 1306, 1307, 1345, 1359–1361, 1437; 74/1208, 2077; 76/307; 77/724; 78/520; 79/466–474; 80/170, 677, 841; 81/1883; 82/944.

s. 2, repealed in pt.: 1978, c.30, sch.3.

s. 3, orders 73/1287–1289, 1306, 1307, 1345, 1359–1361, 1437; 74/208, 2077; 77/724; 79/466–474; 81/1883; substituted: 1983, c.23, s.1.

s. 4, orders 73/1373; 80/170; 82/944.

ss. 4, 5 (in pt.), 6, repealed: 1983, c.23, sch.5.

s. 7, amended: ibid., sch.4.

s. 8, orders 76/307; 80/841.

CAP.

1973—cont.

37. Water Act 1973—cont.

s. 11, see *Cakebread (V.O.)* v. *Severn Trent Water Authority* [1988] R.A. 290, C.A.

s. 11, repealed in pt.: 1985, c.51, sch.17.

s. 14, amended: 1976, c.40, sch.3; repealed in pt.: 1984, c.55, sch.7; 1985, c.51, sch.17.

s. 15, substituted: 1983, c.23, s.6.

s. 16, see *George Wimpey & Co.* v. *Secretary of State for the Environment and Maidstone District Council* [1978] J.P.L. 773, Forbes, J.; *William Leech (Midlands)* v. *Severn-Trent Water Authority, The Times*, June 5, 1981; [1982] J.P.L. 110, C.A.

s. 16, amended: 1980, c.65, ss.105,158; repealed in pt.: 1985, c.51, sch.17.

s. 17, regs. 75/450; amended: 1974, c.40, sch.4; repealed in pt.: 1983, c.23, sch.5.

s. 18, repealed: 1975, c.51, sch.5.

ss. 18, 20, see *Cakebread (V.O.)* v. *Severn Trent Water Authority* [1988] R.A. 290, C.A.

s. 19, repealed: 1976, c.70, sch.8.

s. 22, repealed in pt.: 1981, c.69, sch.17.

s. 23, repealed: 1983, c.23, sch.5.

s. 24, amended: 1974, c.40, sch.3; repealed in pt.: 1983, c.23, sch.5.

s. 24A, added: *ibid.*, s.7.

s. 24A, order 84/71.

s. 25, repealed: 1985, c.51, sch.17.

s. 26, amended: 1983, c.33, sch.4; repealed in pt.: *ibid.*, sch.5.

s. 27, order 74/525; regs. 88/1377.

s. 29, orders 81/826; 82/1060, 1087; 83/782, 1592; 84/1470, 1995; 85/1805; 86/1952; 87/2022.

s. 29, repealed in pt.: 1983, c.23, sch.5.

ss. 29-31, see *Severn Trent Water Authority* v. *Cardshops* (1987) 27 R.V.R. 133, C.A.

s. 30, see *Daymond* v. *Plymouth City Council* [1976] A.C. 609; [1976] 1 All E.R. 39, H.L.; *South West Water Authority* v. *Rumble's* [1985] 2 W.L.R. 405, H.L.; *South West Water Authority* v. *Rumble's, The Times*, May 7, 1986, C.A.; *South West Water Authority* v. *Rumble's (No. 2)* (1986) 26 R.V.R. 144, C.A.

s. 30, amended: 1976, c.9, s.2; repealed in pt.: 1983, c.23, sch.5; 1988, c.15, sch.3.

ss. 30, 31, see *Anglian Water Authority* v. *Castle, The Times*, February 23, 1983, C.A.

s. 32A, added: 1974, c.7, s.38.

s. 33, see *Cakebread (V.O.)* v. *Severn Trent Water Authority* [1988] R.A. 290, C.A.

s. 34, see *London Electricity Board* v. *Redbridge London Borough Council* (1985) 84 L.G.R. 146, Stocker J.

s. 34, orders 74/595, 968, 1351, 2044; 75/944, 1636; 76/315; 77/293, 1434; 78/1210; 80/1421; 82/199; 85/914.

s. 34, repealed in pt.: 1985, c.51, sch.17.

s. 36, orders 74/1208, 2077; 76/307; 77/724; 79/466–474; 80/841; 81/130, 1883.

s. 36, amended: 1974, c.40, sch.3; 1976, c.70, sch.7.

CAP.

1973—cont.

37. Water Act 1973—cont.

s. 38, amended: *ibid.;* 1978, c.30, sch.3; 1980, c.45, sch.10 (S.); order 86/208; repealed in pt.: 1985, c.51, sch.17.

ss. 38, 40, see *Cakebread (V.O.)* v. *Severn Trent Water Authority* [1988] R.A. 290, C.A.

s. 40, repealed in pt.: 1975, c.24, sch.3; c.51, sch.5; S.L.R. 1977.

sch. 2, orders 76/307; 80/841; amended: 1974, c.40, sch.4; 1976, c.70, sch.7; repealed in pt.: *ibid.*, sch.8.

sch. 3, orders 80/170; 82/944; regs. 83/1318; 84/1056.

sch. 3, amended: 1976, c.70, sch.7; 1982, c.32, s.32, schs.4, 5; 1983, c.23, ss.1, 2, sch.1; c.29, s.4, sch.2; 1985, c.9, sch.2; repealed in pt.: 1976, c.70, sch.8; 1980, c.65, sch.34; 1982, c.32, sch.6; 1983, c.29, s.4, sch.2.

sch. 4A, added: *ibid.*, sch.5.

sch. 4A, regs. 84/1788.

sch. 5, orders 73/1919–1926, 2014; 74/47; repealed: 1976, c.70, sch.8.

sch. 6, see *Daymond* v. *Plymouth City Council* [1976] A.C. 609; [1976] 1 All E.R. 39, H.L.

sch. 6, orders 74/47; 77/1434; 80/1107, 1421; 82/199, 1646; 85/914.

sch. 6, repealed in pt.: 1974, c.7, sch.7; 1976, c.9, ss.1,2.

sch. 7, amended: 1974, c.40, sch.3; 1976, c.70, sch.7; repealed in pt.: *ibid.*, sch.8.

sch. 8, repealed: 1983, c.23, sch.5; repealed in pt.: 1984, c.55, sch.7; 1985, c.51, sch.17.

sch. 9, see *Cakebread (V.O.)* v. *Severn Trent Water Authority* [1988] R.A. 290, C.A.

38. Social Security Act 1973.

Royal Assent, July 18, 1973.

regs. 73/1264, 1470, 1498, 1854.

s. 1, regs. 72/1244; 74/988, 2035, 2171; 75/219, 516; amended: 1974, c.58, s.1, schs.1,2; repealed in pt.: 1975, c.18, sch.1; c.60, sch.5; order 75/1503.

s. 2, regs. 72/1244; 74/2035; 75/1244; repealed: 1975, c.18, sch.1.

s. 3, regs. 74/988; order 74/2123; repealed: 1975, c.18, sch.1.

s. 4, regs. 74/988; repealed: 1975, c.18, sch.1.

s. 5, regs. 74/988, 2035, 2171; repealed: 1975, c.18, sch.1.

s. 6, regs. 72/1244; 74/988, 2035; repealed: 1975, c.18, sch.1.

ss. 7, 8, repealed: *ibid.*

s. 9, regs. 74/2010; repealed: 1975, c.18, sch.1.

ss. 10, 11, repealed: *ibid.*

s. 12, regs. 74/2192; 75/529; repealed: 1975, c.18, sch.1.

s. 13, repealed : *ibid.*

s. 14, regs. 75/529; repealed: 1975, c.18, sch.1.

ss. 15–22, repealed: *ibid.*

s. 23, order 75/1503; repealed in pt.: 1975, c.18, sch.1; c.60, sch.5.

s. 24, regs. 74/2059; repealed: 1975, c.18, sch.1.

s. 25, repealed: *ibid.*

ss. 26–28, regs. 74/2059; repealed: 1975, c.18, sch.1.

1973—cont.

38. Social Security Act 1973—cont.

ss. 29–31, repealed: *ibid.*

s. 32, regs. 74/2059, 2079; repealed: 1975, c.18, sch.1.

s. 33, repealed: *ibid.*

s. 34, regs. 74/2079; repealed: 1975, c.18, sch.1.

s. 35, regs. 74/2079; 75/458; repealed: 1975, c.18, sch.1.

s. 36, repealed: *ibid.*

s. 37, regs. 74/2010, 2059; repealed: 1975, c.18, sch.1.

s. 38, regs. 74/1911; repealed: 1975, c.18, sch.1.

s. 39, repealed: *ibid.*

s. 40, regs. 74/2035, 2171; 75/529; repealed: 1975, c.18, sch.1.

s. 41, regs. 74/2035, 2171; repealed: 1975, c.18, sch.1.

s. 42, regs. 73/1376; 74/2009, 2010; repealed: 1975, c.18, sch.1.

s. 43, regs. 74/2035, 2171; repealed: 1975, c.18, sch.1.

s. 45, regs. 75/75; repealed: 1975, c.18, sch.1.

ss. 46–50, repealed: *ibid.*

s. 51, regs. 73/1469; 74/1324; 78/289, 1355; 79/1645; 80/288; 84/614.

s. 51, amended: 1975, c.60, s.56, sch.4; 1980, c.30, s.4; repealed in pt.: 1975, c.60, sch.5; order 75/1503.

s. 52, repealed: 1975, c.60, sch.5; order 75/1503.

ss. 53–57, repealed: 1975, c.60, sch.5; order 75/1503.

s. 58, repealed: 1975, c.60, sch.5; amended: 1986, c.50, sch.10.

s. 59, repealed in pt.: 1975, c.60, sch.5.

ss. 60–62, repealed: 1975, c.60, sch.5; order 75/1503.

s. 64, orders 78/407, 1368; amended: 1975, c.60, s.65, sch.4; 1986, c.50, s.12, sch.10; regs. 87/1116.

s. 65, orders 75/740; 76/444, 551; 77/717, 1653, 1858, 2102, 2185; 78/374, 407, 408, 552, 891, 1368; 85/1975; 86/111, 465, 940, 946, 87/373, 374; 88/1418–1420; repealed: order 75/1503.

s. 66, regs. 73/1776; 76/185, 1827; 86/1716; 87/1114; 88/137; amended: 1975, c.60, s.56, sch.4; 1981, c.33, sch.2; 1985, c.53, sch.5; 1986, c.50, sch.10; repealed in pt.: 1975, c.24, sch.3; c.25, sch.3.

s. 67, regs. 73/1776; 76/185; 87/1114; amended: 1975, c.60, s.56, sch.4; 1986, c.50, schs.5,10; repealed in pt.: order 75/1503.

s. 68, amended: 1979, c.18, sch.3; 1986, c.50, sch.10.

s. 69, regs. 73/1431; 75/957.

s. 69, amended: 1975, c.60, s.65, sch.4; 1986, c.50, sch.10; repealed in pt.: order 75/1503.

s. 70, repealed: order 75/1503; 1986, c.48, sch.5.

s. 71, regs. 73/1432; 76/598; repealed: order 75/1503.

s. 72, repealed: *ibid.*

1973—cont.

38. Social Security Act 1973—cont.

ss. 73–76, repealed: 1975, c.60, sch.5.

s. 77, regs. 74/988; repealed: 1975, c.60, sch.5.

ss. 78–83, repealed: *ibid.*

s. 84, repealed: 1975, c.18, sch.1.

s. 85, repealed: order 75/1503; 1975, c.60, sch.5.

s. 86, Act of Sederunt 76/779; repealed: order 75/1503; repealed in pt.: 1977, c.38, sch.5.

s. 87, repealed: 1975, c.18, sch.1.

s. 88, repealed: 1975, c.60, sch.5; order 75/1503.

s. 89, amended: 1974, c.58, s.1, schs.1,2; 1975, c.18, sch.2; c.60, s.56, sch.4; 1985, c.53, sch.5; repealed in pt.: 1975, c.18, sch.1, c.60, sch.5.

s. 90, repealed: 1975, c.18, sch.1.

s. 91, repealed: 1975, c.60, sch.5; order 75/1503.

s. 92, regs. 73/1776; amended: 1974, c.58, s.1, schs.1,2; 1975, c.18, sch.2; repealed in pt.: *ibid.*, sch.1; c.60, sch.5; 1986, c.50, sch.11.

s. 93, repealed: 1975, c.60, sch.5; order 75/1503.

s. 94, repealed: 1975, c.18, sch.1.

s. 95, amended: 1974, c.58, s.1, schs.1,2; 1975, c.18, sch.2; repealed in pt.: *ibid.*, sch.1; order 75/1503.

s. 96, orders 74/823; 78/374; amended: 1974, c.58, ss.1,5, schs.1,2; repealed in pt.: 1975, c.18, sch.1; order 75/1503.

s. 97, amended: 1974, c.58, ss.1,5, schs.1,2; 1975, c.18, sch.2; repealed in pt.: *ibid.*, sch.1.

s. 98, amended: 1974, c.58, s.1, schs.1,2; repealed in pt.: 1975, c.18, sch.1; c.60, sch.5.

s. 99, regs. 74/988, 2008, 2035, 2079, 2171; 84/614; 85/1323, 1926; 86/1716, 2171.

s. 99, amended: 1974, c.14, schs.4,6; c.58, s.1, schs.1,2; 1975, c.18, sch.2; c.60, s.56, sch.4; 1986, c.50, sch.10; repealed in pt.: 1975, c.18, sch.1; c.60, sch.5; c.71, sch.8; order 75/1503; 1986, c.50, sch.11.

s. 100, regs. 74/1757, 1810, 1911, 2008, 2079, 2192; 75/557; repealed in pt.: 1975, c.18, sch.1.

s. 101, orders 73/1249, 1433; 74/164, 823; 75/124.

sch. 1, regs. 74/988, 2035, 2171; 75/75, 219; repealed: 1975, c.18, sch.1.

sch. 2, repealed: 1975, c.18, sch.1; repealed in pt.: 1975, c.60, sch.5.

sch. 3, repealed: 1975, c.18, sch.1; repealed in pt.: 1975, c.60, sch.5.

schs. 4–6, repealed: 1975, c.18, sch.1.

sch. 6, regs. 84/614.

sch. 7, repealed: 1975, c.18, sch.1; repealed in pt.: 1975, c.24, sch.3; c.25, sch.3.

schs. 8, 9, repealed: 1975, c.18, sch.1.

sch. 10, regs. 74/973, 1911, 2008, 2059, 2079; 75/458; repealed: 1975, c.18, sch.1.

sch. 11, repealed: 1975, c.11, sch.6; c.18, sch.1.

schs. 12–14, repealed: *ibid.*

sch. 15, repealed: 1975, c.60, sch.5; order 75/1503.

CAP.

1973—cont.

38. Social Security Act 1973—cont.

sch. 16, regs. 73/1469, 1784; 74/1324; 76/140; 77/1187; 78/1089; 81/129; 85/1323, 1926; 86/1716, 2171; 88/476.

sch. 16, repealed: order 75/1503; amended: 1985, c.53, sch.5; 1986, c.50, s.10, sch.10; regs. 87/1116; repealed in pt.: 1985, c.53, s.1, sch.6.

sch. 17, amended: 1975, c.60, s.56, sch.4.

sch. 18, repealed: 1975, c.60, sch.5.

sch. 19, regs. 74/988; repealed: 1975, c.60, sch.5.

sch. 20, regs. 86/2171.

sch. 20, repealed: 1975, c.60, sch.5.

sch. 21, regs. 86/2171.

sch. 21, repealed: 1975, c.18, sch.1.

sch. 22, regs. 74/2010, 2059; repealed: 1975, c.60, sch.5; order 75/1503.

sch. 23, amended: 1973, c.62, sch.5; 1974, c.14, schs.4,6; c.58, s.1, schs.1,2; 1975, c.18, sch.2; 1986, c.50, sch.11; repealed in pt.: 1975, c.60, sch.5; order 75/1503; 1984, c.60, sch.7.

sch. 24, repealed: 1975, c.60, sch.5; order 75/1503.

sch. 25, repealed: ibid.

sch. 26, regs. 74/141, 988, 1757, 1810, 1911, 2008–2010, 2035, 2059, 2079, 2171, 2192; 75/458, 557; repealed: 1975, c.18, sch.1.

sch. 27, amended: 1974, c.14, schs.4,6; c.46, sch.9; repealed in pt.: 1975, c.18, sch.1; c.24, sch.3; c.25, sch.3; c.71, sch.18; 1976, c.5, sch.; c.30, sch.2; c.71, sch.8; 1978, c.44, sch.17; 1979, c.12, sch.7; 1980, c.43, sch.9; orders 75/1503, 1504; 76/427, 1043; 77/1251; 1984, c.22, sch.3; 1985, c.9, sch.1.

sch. 28, amended, 1974, c.14, sch.4,6; repealed in pt.: 1975, c.11, sch.6.

39. Statute Law (Repeals) Act 1973.

Royal Assent, July 18, 1973.

s. 2, orders 76/54; 84/1692; repealed in pt.: S.L.R. 1977.

sch. 2, repealed in pt.: 1975, c.24, sch.3; S.L.R. 1977.

40. Appropriation Act 1973.

Royal Assent, July 25, 1973.

repealed: 1975, c.44, sch.C.

41. Fair Trading Act 1973.

Royal Assent, July 25, 1973.

see *Director General of Fair Trading* v. *Smith's Bakeries (Westfield)*, *The Times*, May 12, 1978, Restrictive Practices Court; *R.* v. *Monopolies and Mergers Commission, ex p. Brown (Matthew)* [1987] 1 All E.R. 463, Macpherson J.

s. 3, amended: 1985, c.72, sch.12.

s. 4, orders 77/2081, 82/815.

s. 10, amended: 1976, c.34, sch.5.

s. 16, repealed in pt.: 1984, c.12, sch.7.

s. 17, orders 76/1812, 1813.

s. 22, see *Cavendish-Woodhouse* v. *Mancey* (1984) 82 L.G.R. 376, D.C.

s. 22, orders 77/1918; 78/127.

ss. 22, 23, see *Hughes* v. *Hall & Hall* [1981] R.T.R. 430, D.C.

CAP.

1973—cont.

41. Fair Trading Act 1973—cont.

s. 23, see *Blakemore* v. *Bellamy* [1983] R.T.R. 303, D.C.

s. 27, repealed in pt.: 1985, c.72, sch.13.

s. 34, see *R.* v. *Director General of Fair Trading, ex p. F. H. Taylor & Co.* [1981] I.C.R. 292, D.C.

s. 34, order 73/2104.

ss. 41, 42, see *Director-General of Fair Trading* v. *Boswell*, 1979 S.L.T.(Sh.Ct.) 9.

s. 43, amended: 1974, c.4, sch.5; repealed in pt.: order 81/228; 1986, c.47, sch.5 (S.).

s. 50, order 84/1887.

s. 50, repealed in pt.: 1984, c.12, sch.7.

s. 51, amended: order 74/691; 1984, c.12, sch.7.

s. 54, amended: 1976, c.34, sch.5; repealed in pt.: *ibid.*, sch.6.

s. 56, orders 82/1146; 88/1017.

Pt. 5 (ss.57–77), see *R.* v. *Monopolies and Mergers Commission, ex p. Matthew Brown, The Times*, July 18, 1986, Macpherson J.

s. 64, orders 80/373; 81/1762; 82/460; 84/932.

s. 64, amended: *ibid.*

s. 69, orders 81/1762; 82/460.

ss. 72, 75, see *R.* v. *Monopolies and Mergers Commission, ex p. Air Europe, The Times*, January 2, 1988, D.C.

s. 73, see *R.* v. *Secretary of State for Trade, ex p. Anderson Strathclyde* [1983] 2 All E.R. 233, D.C.

s. 74, orders 73/1879, 2104; 74/688, 1249; 82/460, 782.

s. 75, see *R.* v. *Monopolies and Mergers Commission, ex p. Argyll Group* [1986] 2 All E.R. 257, C.A.

s. 78, amended: 1976, c.34, sch.5.

s. 83, amended: 1980, c.21, s.22.

s. 90, orders 82/1146; 88/1017.

s. 90, repealed in pt.: order 82/1080.

s. 91, orders 75/2127; 82/1146.

s. 92, amended: 1985, c.9, sch.2.

s. 94, repealed in pt.: 1976, c.34, sch.6; c.53, sch.3.

ss. 95–106, repealed: 1976, c.34, sch.6.

s. 107, see *Ravenseft Properties* v. *Director-General of Fair Trading* [1977] 1 All E.R. 47.

ss. 107–110, repealed: 1976, c.34, sch.6.

s. 111, order 76/98; repealed: 1976, c.34, sch.6.

ss. 112–117, repealed: *ibid.*

s. 119, regs. 73/1740.

ss. 124, 133, see *R.* v. *Director General of Fair Trading, ex p. F. H. Taylor & Co.* [1981] I.C.R. 292, D.C.

s. 125, amended: 1974, c.39, s.5, sch.4.

s. 126, repealed: 1977, c.37, sch.6.

s. 128, repealed: 1976, c.34, sch.6.

s. 129, amended: 1980, c.43, sch.7.

s. 130, amended: 1987, c.43, sch.4.

s. 131, amended: 1979, c.38, s.9.

s. 133, see *R.* v. *Monopolies and Mergers Commission, ex p. Elders IXL* [1987] 1 All E.R. 451, Mann J.

1973—cont.

41. Fair Trading Act 1973—cont.
s. 133, amended: 1976, c.34, sch.5; 1979, c.38, s.9; 1980, c.21, s.19; 1984, c.12, sch.4; 1986, c.31, sch.4; c.44, sch.7; c.60, sch.13; repealed in pt.: 1976, c.34, sch.6.
s. 134, orders 74/1249; 78/127.
s. 136, repealed: S.L.R. 1977.
s. 137, amended: 1976, c.34, sch.5; 1980, c.21, s.23; 1985, c.9, c.67, s.116; repealed in pt.: 1976, c.34, sch.6; c.58, sch.3.
s. 138, amended: 1974, c.39, s.5, sch.4.
s. 140, orders 73/1545, 1652; repealed in pt.: 1976, c.34, sch.6.
sch. 1, repealed in pt.: 1975, c.24, sch.3; c.25, sch.3.
sch. 3, repealed in pt.: 1977, c.37, sch.6.
sch. 4, amended: ibid., sch.5; 1984, c.24, sch.5; 1985, c.61, s.60; 1988, c.48, sch.7.
sch. 5, amended: 1981, c.38, sch.3; 1984, c.12, sch.4; 1985, c.67, s.114; 1986, c.44, sch.7; repealed in pt.: 1984, c.12, sch.4.
sch. 7, amended: 1984, c.46, sch.5; order 84/1887; repealed in pt.: 1986, c.31, sch.6.
sch. 8, orders 73/1879, 2104; 74/688, 1249; 82/1146; 88/1017; amended: 1976, c.34, sch.5.
sch. 10, repealed: 1976, c.34, sch.6.
sch. 11, repealed in pt.: ibid.
sch. 12, repealed in pt.: 1975, c.64, sch.7; 1976, c.33, sch.; c.34, sch.6; 1977, c.37, sch.6; 1981, c.20, sch.4; order 82/1080.

42. National Insurance and Supplementary Benefit Act 1973.
Royal Assent, July 25, 1973.
repealed: 1981, c.19, sch.1.
s. 9, sch. 6, order 73/1349.

43. Hallmarking Act 1973.
Royal Assent, July 25, 1973.
s. 1, see Chilvers v. Rayner [1984] 1 W.L.R. 328, D.C.
s. 1, schs. 1, 2, see Barge v. Brown (Oasis Trading) [1981] 3 All E.R. 360, D.C.
s. 2, orders 76/730; 81/559; 83/1389, 1608; 84/1131; 87/1892.
s. 4, regs. 86/1757.
s. 4, amended: ibid.
s. 16, orders 78/639; 79/1587.
s. 20, amended: 1973, c.65, sch.27.
s. 21, orders 81/559; 83/1839, 1608; 84/1131; 86/1757; 87/1892.
s. 22, orders 76/730; 83/1839, 1608; 87/1892.
s. 24, repealed in pt.: S.L.R. 1977.
sch. 1, orders 75/1; 82/256; 86/1758.
sch. 1, amended: orders 75/1883; 82/256; 86/1758; repealed in pt.: order 82/256.
sch. 2, amended: order 86/1757.
sch. 3, repealed in pt.: 1977, c.45, sch.13.
sch. 4, amended: 1985, c.9, sch.2.
sch. 6, orders 78/639; 79/1587.

44. Heavy Commercial Vehicles (Controls and Regulations) Act 1973.
Royal Assent, July 25, 1973.
repealed: 1988, c.54, sch.1.

1973—cont.

45. Domicile and Matrimonial Proceedings Act 1973.
Royal Assent, July 25, 1973.
see Lyndon v. Lyndon (O.H.), 1978 S.L.T.(Notes) 7; R. v. Immigration Appeal Tribunal, ex p. Secretary of State for the Home Department, The Times, July 15, 1983, Taylor J.
Pt. IV, repealed: order 78/1045.
s. 1, see Puttick v. Att.-Gen. [1979] 3 W.L.R. 542, Sir George Baker P.; I.R.C. v. Duchess of Portland [1982] 2 W.L.R. 367, Nourse J.
s. 2, repealed: 1986, c.55, sch.2.
s. 4, see Williams (O.H.), 1977 S.L.T.(Notes) 2.
s. 4, repealed in pt.: 1975, c.72, sch.4.
s. 5, see Oundjian v. Oundjian (1979) 10 Fam.Law 90, French J.; Kapur v. Kapur (1985) 15 Fam.Law 22, Bush J.
s. 5, amended: 1984, c.42, sch.1.
ss. 5, 9, see Shemshadfard v. Shemshadfard [1981] 1 All E.R. 726, Purchas J.
s. 6, repealed in pt.: 1984, c.42, sch.3.
s. 7, repealed in pt.: 1977, c.27, sch.2.
s. 8, amended: 1983, c.12, sch.1.
s. 9, repealed (S.); 1980, c.55, sch.3.
s. 15, repealed: 1986, c.55, sch.2.
s. 16, see Chaudhary v. Chaudhary [1984] 3 All E.R. 1017, C.A.; Maples (Formerly Melamud) v. Maples (Formerly Melamud) v. Melamud [1987] 3 W.L.R. 487, Latey J.
s. 16, repealed: 1986, c.55, sch.2.
s. 17, repealed in pt.: order 78/1045; 1979, c.50, sch.3.
s. 89, order 80/1478.
sch. 1, see Mytton v. Mytton [1977] Fam. Law 244, C.A.; Shemshadfard v. Shemshadfard [1981] 1 All E.R. 726, Purchas J.; Gadd v. Gadd [1984] 1 W.L.R. 1435, C.A.; Thyssen-Bornemisza v. Thyssen-Bornemisza [1985] 1 All E.R. 328, C.A.; K. v. K. (1986) 2 F.L.R. 411, Hollis J.; De Dampierre v. De Dampierre [1987] 2 W.L.R. 1006, H.L.
sch. 1, amended: 1981, c.24, s.8.
sch. 2, amended: 1976, c.39, sch.1; 1985, c.37, sch.1 (S.); 1986, c.9, sch.1 (S.); repealed in pt. (S): 1985, c.37, sch.1, 1986, c.9, sch.2.
sch. 3, amended: 1983, c.12, sch.1; repealed in pt.: ibid., schs.1,2; 1985, c.9, sch.1.
sch. 4, repealed in pt.: 1977, c.27, sch.2.
sch. 5, repealed: order 78/1045.

46. International Cocoa Agreement Act 1973.
Royal Assent, July 25, 1973.
s. 2, order 73/1617.

47. Protection of Aircraft Act 1973.
Royal Assent, July 25, 1973.
repealed: 1982, c.36, sch.3.
s. 5, orders 73/1756; 74/1108; 75/804; 76/770; 77/1238; 78/1888; 81/212, 733; 82/148.
s. 27, orders 73/1756, 1757, 1760–1762; 74/1108; 75/804; 76/770; 77/1238; 78/1888; 81/212, 733; 82/148.
s. 28, order 73/1753.

48. Pakistan Act 1973.
Royal Assent, July 25, 1973.
s. 1, repealed in pt.: 1974, c.34, s.2; 1981, c.61, sch.9.

1973—cont.

48. Pakistan Act 1973—cont.
s. 3, amended and repealed in pt.: 1974, c.34, s.2.
s. 4, repealed in pt.: *ibid.*; 1986, c.55, sch.2.
s. 5, repealed: S.L.R. 1977.
schs. 1, 2, repealed in pt.: 1981, c.61, sch.9.
sch. 3, repealed in pt.: 1983, c.35, sch.3; c.54, sch.7.
sch. 4, repealed: 1974, c.34, s.2.

49. Bangladesh Act 1973.
Royal Assent, July 25, 1973.
s. 2, repealed: 1981, c.61, sch.9.
sch., repealed in pt.: S.L.R. 1977; 1981, c.9, sch.; 1983, c.35, sch.3; c.54, sch.7; 1985, c.21, sch.2.

50. Employment and Training Act 1973.
Royal Assent, July 25, 1973.
s. 1, amended: 1975, c.71, sch.14; 1981, c.57, sch.2; 1988, c.19, s.24; repealed in pt.: 1981, c.57, schs.2,3.
s. 2, see *Ojutiku* v. *Manpower Services Commission* [1982] I.C.R. 661, C.A.; *Decision No. R(FIS)* 1/83.
ss. 2, 3, substituted: 1988, c.19, s.25.
s. 4, amended: 1975, c.69, s.11; c.70, s.24; 1976, c.75, s.17; 1981, c.57, sch.2; 1982, c.10, sch.3; 1988, c.19, s.28; repealed in pt.: 1981, c.57, schs.2,3; 1988, c.19, sch.4.
s. 5, amended: 1975, c.71, sch.14; repealed in pt.: 1978, c.6, s.3; 1981, c.57, schs.2,3; 1988, c.19, sch.4.
s. 6, repealed in pt.: 1982, c.9, sch.2; c.10, sch.4.
s. 7, order 74/1571; repealed: 1975, c.71, schs.14,18.
s. 8, order 81/494; repealed in pt.: *ibid.*
ss. 8–10, repealed (S.): 1980, c.44, sch.5.
s. 9, repealed in pt.: order 81/494.
s. 11, amended: 1975, c.18, sch.2; 1982, c.10, sch.3; 1988, c.19, sch.2; repealed in pt.: 1981, c.57, schs.2,3; 1988, c.19, sch.4.
s. 12, order 81/494.
s. 12, amended: 1975, c.18, sch.2; c.60, sch.4; 1976, c.71, sch.7; 1980, c.30, sch.4; 1986, c.50, sch.10; 1988, c.7, sch.4; c.19, sch.2; repealed in pt.: S.L.R. 1977; order 81/494; 1988, c.19, sch.4.
s. 13, orders 74/398, 1463; amended: 1975, c.71, sch.14; repealed in pt.: *ibid.*, schs. 14,18; 1981, c.57, schs.2,3.
s. 14, repealed in pt.: 1982, c.9, sch.2; c.52, sch.3.
s. 15, orders 73/2063; 74/398, 1463; 75/689; repealed in pt.: 1975, c.24, sch.3; c.71, schs.14,18.
sch. 1, amended: 1975, c.71, sch.14; repealed in pt.: *ibid.*, schs.14,18; 1981, c.57, schs.2,3.
sch. 2, repealed in pt.: 1978, c.44, sch.17; 1981, c.57, sch.3.
sch. 3, amended: 1973, c.38, sch.28; 1974, c.37, sch.10; repealed in pt.: 1975, c.24, sch.3; c.71, schs.14,18; 1976, c.74, sch.5; 1982, c.52, sch.3; 1987, c.39, sch.2.

1973—cont.

51. Finance Act 1973.
Royal Assent, July 25, 1973.
s. 1, orders 73/1570, 1948; 74/1105, 1349, 2036; 75/1943, 2095, 2239; 77/921, 1058, 1315.
s. 1, amended: 1976, c.40, s.8; 1977, c.36, s.1; repealed in pt.: 1975, c.45, sch.4; 1976, c.40, sch.15.
s. 2, orders 73/1492, 2069, 2229; 74/1019, 1971, 2076; 75/1109; regs. 75/2082, 2100; 76/995.
s. 2, repealed: 1979, c.2, sch.6.
s. 3, repealed: 1974, c.30, sch.14.
s. 4, see *Revell Fuels* v. *Customs and Excise Commissioners* [1975] 1 All E.R. 312, D.C.; *R.* v. *Value Added Tax Tribunal Centre (Belfast), ex p. Customs and Excise Commissioners* [1977] S.T.C. 323, C.A.(N.I.).
ss. 4–8, repealed: 1983, c.55, sch.11.
s. 9, repealed: 1975, c.45, sch.14.
s. 10, see *James* v. *I.R.C.* [1977] 1 W.L.R. 835, Slade J.
ss. 10–22, repealed: 1988, c.1, sch.31.
s. 14, amended: 1988, c.39, s.57.
s. 16, see *I.R.C.* v. *Regent Trust Co.* (1979) 53 T.C. 54; [1980] 1 W.L.R. 688, Slade J.; *I.R.C.* v. *Berrill* [1981] 1 W.L.R. 1449, Vinelott J.; *Bosanquet* v. *Allen*; *Carver* v. *Duncan* [1985] W.L.R. 1010, H.L.
s. 17, see *Stevenson (Inspector of Taxes)* v. *Wishart* [1987] 2 All E.R. 428, C.A.
s. 19, repealed: 1988, c.39, sch.14.
s. 23, see *Ward-Stemp* v. *Griffin (Inspector of Taxes)* [1988] S.T.C. 47, Walton J.
ss. 23–31, repealed: 1988, c.1, sch.31.
s. 28, see *Tilcon* v. *Holland* [1981] S.T.C. 365, Vinelott J.
s. 29, see *Pilkington Bros.* v. *I.R.C.* [1982] 1 All E.R. 715; [1982] S.T.C. 103, H.L.; *Irving* v. *Tesco Stores (Holdings)* [1982] S.T.C. 881, Walton J.
s. 32, amended: 1988, c.1, sch.29; repealed in pt.: *ibid.*, sch.31.
ss. 33–36, repealed: *ibid.*
s. 37, repealed: 1979, c.14, sch.8.
s. 38, see *Clark* v. *Oceanic Contractors Inc.* (1982) 56 T.C. 183; [1983] 2 W.L.R. 94, H.L.
s. 38, amended: 1979, c.14, sch.7; 1984, c.43, s.81; 1988, c.1, sch.29; repealed in pt.: *ibid.*, sch.31.
s. 39, repealed: *ibid.*; amended: 1988, c.39, s.58.
s. 40, repealed: 1988, c.1, sch.31.
s. 42, repealed: 1976, c.40, s.49, sch.15.
s. 43, repealed: 1988, c.1, sch.31.
s. 44, repealed: 1987, c.16, sch.16.
ss. 45, 46, repealed: 1975, c.7, sch.13.
s. 46, functions transferred: orders 81/207; 86/600.
s. 47, see *Cambridge Petroleum Royalties* v. *I.R.C.* [1982] S.T.C. 325, Nourse J.
ss. 47, 48, repealed: 1988, c.39, s.141, sch.14.
s. 49, repealed in pt.: 1985, c.54, sch.27.
s. 50, repealed in pt.: order 81/107.
s. 51, repealed: 1979, c.14, sch.8.

CAP.

1973—cont.

51. Finance Act 1973—*cont.*
ss. 52, 53, repealed: 1988, c.1, sch.31.
s. 54, repealed in pt.: 1975, c.7, sch.13; 1979, c.14, sch.8; 1988, c.1, sch.31.
s. 55, repealed: 1983, c.55, sch.11.
s. 56, regs. 73/2100; 75/1732, 1874; 76/625, 1465, 1701, 2062, 2199; 77/1413, 1440, 1754, 2196; 78/26, 62, 1321, 1831; 79/42, 1257, 1342, 1376; 80/168, 223, 615, 766; 81/36, 176, 279, 505, 969, 1329, 1535, 1825; 82/805, 811, 1775; 83/280, 537, 1247, 1663, 1831, 1855; 84/748, 1404; 85/307, 386, 852, 1656; 86/589, 831, 1043, 2128; 87/315, 802, 803, 869, 1556, 2012; 88/370, 1184, 1808; order 87/1131; S.Rs. 1978 No. 310; 1979 No. 443; 1980 No. 174; 1981 No. 386; S.R. 1984 No. 32; S.R. 1985 No. 14; 1987 Nos. 217, 383, 390.
s. 56, repealed in pt.: S.L.R. 1977.
s. 57, repealed: 1976, c.55, sch.4.
s. 58, order 73/1393.
s. 59, amended: 1974, c.30, ss.7,8,20,22, schs.7,14; 1979, c.14, sch.7; 1988, c.1, sch.29; repealed in pt.: 1979, c.2, sch.6; 1983, c.55, sch.11; 1984, c.43, schs.7, 23.
s. 90, order 87/1131.
schs. 1–4, repealed: 1975, c.45, sch.14.
sch. 5, amended: order 77/921; repealed: 1977, c.36, sch.9.
schs. 6, 7, repealed: 1975, c.45, sch.14.
sch. 8, orders 73/1797; 87/1131.
sch. 8, repealed: 1988, c.1, sch.31; c.39, sch.14.
schs. 9–14, repealed: 1988, c.1, sch.31.
sch. 15, amended: 1978, c.42, sch.15; 1984, c.43, s.124; 1988, c.1, sch.29; repealed in pt.: *ibid.*, sch.31.
sch. 16, regs. 74/896, 1330.
sch. 16, amended: 1988, c.39, ss.58, 61; repealed in pt.: *ibid.*, s.58, sch.14; repealed: 1988, c.1, sch.1.
sch. 16A, added: 1988, c.39, s.58, sch.5.
sch. 17, repealed: 1976, c.40, s.49, sch.15.
sch. 18, repealed: 1975, c.7, sch.13.
sch. 19, see *Cambridge Petroleum Royalties* v. *I.R.C.* [1982] S.T.C. 325, Nourse J.; *National Smokeless Fuels* v. *I.R.C.* [1986] S.T.C. 300, Ch.D.; *Rothschild (J.) Holdings* v. *I.R.C.*, *The Times*, December 22, 1987, Vinelott J.
sch. 19, repealed: 1988, c.39, s.141, sch.14.
sch. 20, repealed: 1979, c.14, sch.8.
sch. 21, repealed in pt.: *ibid.*; 1986, c.41, sch.23; 1988, c.1, sch.31.

52. Prescription and Limitation (Scotland) Act 1973.
Royal Assent, July 25, 1973.
s. 1, see *Scammell* v. *Scottish Sports Council* (O.H.), October 14, 1982.
s. 1, amended: 1979, c.33, s.10.
s. 3, see *Richardson* v. *Cromarty Petroleum Co.* (O.H.), 1982 S.L.T. 237; *Strathclyde (Hyndland) Housing Society* v. *Cowie*, 1983 S.L.T.(Sh.Ct.) 16.
s. 4, see *British Railways Board* v. *Strathclyde Regional Council* 1982 S.L.T. 55.

CAP.

1973—cont.

52. Prescription and Limitation (Scotland) Act 1973—*cont.*
s. 6, see *Macleod* v. *Sinclair* (O.H.), 1981 S.L.T.(Notes) 38; *Lawrence* v. *J. D. McIntosh & Hamilton*, 1981 S.L.T. (Sh.Ct.) 73; *Muir and Black* v. *Nee*, 1981 S.L.T.(Sh.Ct.) 68; *British Railways Board* v. *Strathclyde Regional Council* 1982 S.L.T. 55; *Riddick* v. *Shaughnessy, Quigley and McColl* (O.H.) 1981 S.L.T. 128; *The Royal Bank of Scotland* v. *Brown*, Second Division, February 5, 1982; *McPhail* v. *Cunninghame District Council, William Loudon & Son* v. *Cunninghame District Council* (O.H.), 1985 S.L.T. 149; *Hobday* v. *Kirkpatrick's Trs.* (O.H.), 1985 S.L.T. 197; *East Hook Purchasing Corporation* v. *Ben Nevis Distillery (Fort William)* (O.H.), 1985, S.L.T. 442; *Fyfe* v. *Croudace* (O.H.), 1986 S.L.T. 528; *Grindall* v. *John Mitchell (Grangemouth)* (O.H.), 1987 S.L.T. 137; *Kirkcaldy District Council* v. *Household Manufacturing* (O.H.), 1987 S.L.T. 617; *Liebermann* v. *G. W. Tait and Sons* (O.H.), 1987 S.L.T. 585; *Scott Lithgow* v. *Secretary of State for Defence*, 1988 S.L.T. 697; *Fisher & Donaldson* v. *Steven* (Sh.Ct.), 1988 S.C.L.R. 337; *Miller* v. *City of Glasgow District Council*, 1989 S.L.T. 44.
ss. 6, 9, see *George A. Hood & Co.* v. *Dumbarton District Council* (O.H.), June 24, 1982; *Barclay* v. *Chief Constable, Northern Constabulary* (O.H.), 1986 S.L.T. 562; *Shanks* v. *Central Regional Council* (O.H.), 1987 S.L.T. 410.
ss. 6, 11, see *Highland Engineering* v. *Anderson* (O.H.), 1979 S.L.T. 122. *Renfrew Golf Club* v. *Ravenstone Securities* (O.H.), 1984 S.L.T. 170.
ss. 6, 11, 14, see *Dunlop* v. *McGowans* (H.L.) 1980 S.L.T. 129.
s. 7, see *Macdonald* v. *Scott* (O.H.), 1981 S.L.T. 128.
s. 7, amended: 1984, c.45, s.5, sch.1; 1987, c.43, sch.1.
ss. 7, 10, see *Gibson* v. *Carson*, 1980 S.C. 356.
s. 8A, added: 1984, c.54, s.1.
s. 9, see *British Railways Board* v. *Strathclyde Regional Council* [1982] S.L.T. 55.
ss. 9, amended: 1984, c.45, sch.1; 1985, c.9, sch.2; c.66, sch.7; 1987, c.36, s.1; repealed in pt.: *ibid.*
s. 10, see *Fortunato's J.F.* v. *Fortunato* (O.H.), June 26, 1981; *Liebermann* v. *G. W. Tait and Sons* (O.H.), 1987 S.L.T. 585.
s. 10, amended: 1984, c.45, sch.1.
s. 11, see *Dunfermline District Council* v. *Blyth & Blyth Associates* (O.H.), 1985 S.L.T. 345.
s. 11, repealed in pt.: 1984, c.45, sch.2.
ss. 11, 12, see *Riddick* v. *Shaughnessy, Quigley and McColl* (O.H.), 1981 S.L.T.(Notes) 89.
ss. 11, 13, see *McPhail* v. *Cunninghame District Concil, William Loudon & Son* v. *Cunninghame District Council* (O.H.), 1985 S.L.T. 149.
ss. 13–15, amended: 1984, c.45, sch.1.
s. 16A, added: 1987, c.43, sch.1.

1973—cont.

52. Prescription and Limitation (Scotland) Act 1973—cont.

s. 17, see *Cross* v. *Noble* (O.H.), 1975 S.L.T.(Notes) 33; *Shaw* v. *Renton & Fisher* (O.H.), 1977 S.L.T.(Notes) 60; *Wilson* v. *Morrington Quarries* (O.H.), 1979 S.L.T. 82; *Morrison* v. *Scotstoun Marine* (O.H.), 1979 S.L.T.(Notes) 76; *Hynd* v. *West Fife Co-operative*, 1980 S.L.T. 41; *Greenhorn* v. *J. Smart & Co. (Contractors)*, First Division, June 28, 1979; *Davies* v. *B.I.C.C.*, 1980 S.L.T.(Sh.Ct.) 17; *McArthur* v. *Raynesway Plant* (O.H.), 1980 S.L.T. 74; *Rollo* v. *British Railways Board*, 1980 S.L.T.(Notes) 103; *Marshall* v. *Black* (O.H.), June 20, 1980; *Cunningham* v. *National Coal Board* (O.H.), 1981 S.L.T.(Notes) 74; *Black* v. *British Railways Board* (O.H.), March 26, 1982; *Robertson* v. *Crane Hire (Paisley)* (O.H.), 1982 S.L.T. 505; *Williams* v. *Forth Valley Health Board* (O.H.), December 3, 1982; *McGrattan* v. *Renfrew District Council* (O.H.), 1983 S.L.T. 678; *Meek* v. *Milne* (O.H.), 1985 S.L.T. 318; *Sellars* v. *I.M.I. Yorkshire Imperial*, 1986 S.L.T. 629; *Barclay* v. *Chief Constable, Northern Constabulary* (O.H.), 1986 S.L.T 562; *Grindall* v. *John Mitchell (Grangemouth)* (O.H.), 1987 S.L.T. 137; *Grimason* v. *National Coal Board*, 1987, S.L.T. 714; *Dormer* v. *Melville Dundas & Whitson* (O.H.), 1987 S.C.L.R. 655; *Webb* v. *BP Petroleum Development* (O.H.), May 3, 1988.

ss. 17–19, substituted: 1984, c.45, s.2.

ss. 17, 18, 19, 22, see *Provan* v. *Glynwed* (O.H.), 1975 S.L.T. 192.

ss. 17, 18, 22, see *Comer* v. *James Scott & Co. (Electrical Engineers)* (O.H.), 1978 S.L.T. 235.

ss. 17, 19A, see *McCullough* v. *Norwest Socea* (O.H.), January 27, 1981; *Carson* v. *Howard Doris* (O.H.), May 22, 1981.

ss. 17, 20, see *Singer* v. *Gray Tool Co. (Europe)*, 1984 S.L.T. 149.

s. 18, see *Hamill* v. *Newalls Insulation Co.* (O.H.), 1987 S.L.T. 478; *Forbes* v. *House of Clydesdale* (O.H.), 1988 S.L.T. 594.

ss. 18, 22, see *Shaw* v. *Renton & Fisher* (O.H.), 1977 S.L.T.(Notes) 60; *Love* v. *Haran Sealant Services* (O.H.), 1979 S.L.T. 89; *McIntyre* v. *Armitage Shanks*, 1979 S.L.T. 110; *Black* v. *British Railways Board* (O.H.), March 26, 1982.

s. 18A, added: 1985, c.73, s.12.

s. 19A, see *Boslem* v. *Paterson* (O.H.), October 14, 1981; *Henderson* v. *Singer (U.K.)* (O.H.), May 21, 1982; *Black* v. *British Railways Board* (O.H.), March 26, 1982; *Donald* v. *Rutherford* (O.H.), July 9, 1982; *Hobbs* v. *Fawcett*, 1983 S.L.T.(Sh.Ct) 15; *Williams* v. *Forth Valley Health Board* (O.H.), December 3, 1982; *Munro* v. *Anderson-Grice Engineering Co.* (O.H.), June 8, 1982; *Whyte* v. *Walker* (O.H.), 1983 S.L.T. 441; *Harris* v. *Roberts* (O.H.), 1983 S.L.T. 452; *Donald* v. *Rutherford*, 1984 S.L.T. 70; *Forsyth* v. *A. F. Stoddart & Co.*, Second Division, July 11, 1984; *Anderson* v. *City of Glasgow District Council*, 1987 S.L.T.

1973—cont.

52. Prescription and Limitation (Scotland) Act 1973—cont.

279; *Forbes* v. *House of Clydesdale* (O.H.), 1987 S.C.L.R. 136; *Dormer* v. *Melville Dundas & Whitson* (O.H.), 1987 S.C.L.R. 655; *Craw* v. *Gallagher* (O.H.), 1988 S.L.T. 204; *Bell* v. *Greenland* (O.H.), 1988 S.L.T. 215; *Henshaw* v. *Carnie* (O.H.), 1988 S.C.L.R. 305; *Webb* v. *BP Petroleum Development* (O.H.), May 3, 1988; *Millar* v. *Newalls Insulation Co.* (Sh.Ct.), 1988 S.C.L.R. 359.

s. 19A, added: 1980, c.55, s.23; amended: 1984, c.45, sch.1; 1985, c.73, s.12.

ss. 20, 21, repealed: 1984, c.45, sch.2.

s. 22, see *Barclay* v. *Chief Constable, Northern Constabulary* (O.H.), 1986 S.L.T. 562.

s. 22, amended: 1985, c.73, s.12; repealed in pt.: 1984, c.45, sch.3.

ss. 22A–22D, added: 1987, c.43, sch.1.

s. 23, repealed: *ibid.*, schs.1,5.

s. 23A, added: 1984, c.45, sch.4.

s. 25, amended: 1980, c.55, s.23; repealed in pt.: 1984, c.45, sch.2.

sch. 1, see *Muir and Black* v. *Nee*, 1981 S.L.T.(Sh.Ct.) 68; *British Railways Board* v. *Strathclyde Regional Council* [1982] S.L.T. 55; *Miller* v. *City of Glasgow District Council*, 1989 S.L.T. 44.

sch. 1, amended: 1985, c.73, s.12; 1987, c.43, sch.1.

schs. 1, 2, see *Riddick* v. *Shaughnessy, Quigley and McColl* (O.H.), 1981, S.L.T.(Notes) 89.

sch. 2, see *The Royal Bank of Scotland* v. *Brown*, Second Division, February 5, 1982; *Robertson (H. G.)* v. *Murray International Metals* (O.H.), 1988 S.L.T. 747.

sch. 4, repealed in pt.: 1984, c.45, sch.2.

53. Northern Ireland (Emergency Provisions) Act 1973.

Royal Assent, July 25, 1973.

ss. 2–4, repealed: 1978, c.5, sch.6.

ss. 3, 6, amended: 1975, c.62, s.3.

s. 5, repealed: *ibid.*, s.7, sch.3.

s. 6, see *R.* v. *Hetherington* [1975] N.I. 164, Lowry L.C.J.; *R.* v. *Thomson* [1977] N.I. 74, C.C.A; *R.* v. *McCormick* [1977] N.I. 105, McGonigal L.J.; *R.* v. *Milne* [1978] N.I. 110, McGonigal L.J.; *R.* v. *O'Halloran* [1979] N.I. 45, N.I.C.A.

s. 6, repealed: 1978, c.5, sch.6.

s. 7, see *R.* v. *Lavery* [1976] N.I. 148, Murray J.

ss. 7, 8, 10–15, repealed: 1978, c.5, sch.6.

s. 16, amended: *ibid.*, ss.10,12,13; repealed in pt.: *ibid.*, sch.6.

ss. 17, 18, repealed: 1978, c.5, sch.6.

s. 19, amended: 1977, c.34, s.1; 1978, c.5, ss.10,12,13; repealed in pt.: 1978, c.5, sch.6.

ss. 20, 21, repealed: *ibid.*

s. 22, repealed: 1975, c.62, s.14, sch.3.

ss. 23–26, repealed: 1978, c.5, sch.6.

s. 25, see *R. (McCreesh)* v. *County Court Judge for Armagh* [1978] N.I. 164, C.A.; *R. (Secretary of State)* v. *County Court Judge for Armagh* [1980] 12 N.I.J.B., C.A.

CAP.

1973—cont.

53. Northern Ireland (Emergency Provisions) Act 1973—cont.
s. 27, order 77/1265; repealed: 1978, c.5, sch.6.
s. 28, repealed in pt.: 1975, c.62, sch.3; 1978, c.5, sch.6.
s. 29, repealed: *ibid.*
s. 30, order 77/2142; amended: 1975, c.62, ss.6,22; repealed in pt.: *ibid.*, sch.3; 1978, c.5, sch.6.
s. 31, repealed in pt.: *ibid.*
sch. 1, repealed: 1975, c.62, s.9, sch.3.
schs. 2–5, repealed: 1978, c.5, sch.6.

54. Nature Conservation Council Act 1973.
Royal Assent, July 25, 1973.
s. 1, order 73/1721.
s. 1, amended: 1978, c.51, sch.16; c.52, sch.11.
s. 3, repealed: 1981, c.69, sch.17.
s. 5, sch. 1, repealed in pt.: *ibid.*
s. 5, sch. 3, repealed in pt.: 1975, c.24, sch.3.
sch. 1, regs. 73/1687.
sch. 3, orders 73/1722, 1829; 74/1241; 77/2169.

55. Statute Law Revision (Northern Ireland) Act 1973.
Royal Assent, July 25, 1973.
s. 3, repealed in pt.: S.L.R. 1977.

56. Land Compensation (Scotland) Act 1973.
Royal Assent, July 25, 1973.
s. 1, see *Stuart* v. *British Airports Authority*, 1983 S.L.T.(Lands Tr.) 42.
s. 1, amended: 1984, c.54, sch.9.
ss. 1–3, 14, see *Inglis* v. *British Airports Authority*, 1978 S.L.T.(Lands Tr.) 30.
ss. 1–4, see *Inglis* v. *British Airports Authority (No. 2)*, 1979 S.L.T.(Lands Tr.) 11.
ss. 1, 3, amended: 1980, c.65, s.112.
s. 4, amended: 1975, c.78, sch.5; 1980, c.60, s.20; c.65, s.112.
s. 9, amended: 1984, c.54, sch.9.
s. 12, repealed: 1980, c.65, sch.34.
s. 13, amended: 1984, c.54, sch.9.
ss. 14, 16, amended: 1980, c.65, s.112.
s. 17, amended: *ibid.*; 1984, c.54., sch.9; repealed in pt.: 1980, c.65, s.112, sch.34; 1984, c.54, sch.11.
s. 18, regs. 75/460.
s. 19, repealed: 1975, c.78, sch.6.
ss. 20–23, repealed: 1984, c.54, sch.11.
s. 26, amended: *ibid.*, sch.9; repealed in pt.: *ibid.*, sch.11.
s. 27, amended: 1974, c.44, schs.13,15; c.45, schs.3,5; 1975, c.28, sch.3; 1978, c.14, sch.2; 1986, c.65, s.20; 1987, c.26, sch.23; 1988, c.43, sch.9; repealed in pt.: 1987, c.26, sch.23.
s. 28, order 85/292.
s. 28, amended: order 78/323.
s. 29, amended: 1980, c.65, s.114; 1986, c.65, s.20; 1987, c.26, sch.23; repealed in pt.: 1980, c.65, sch.34.
s. 34, see *Smith and Waverley Tailoring Company* v. *Edinburgh District Council (No. 2)*, 1977 S.L.T.(Lands Tr.) 29.
s. 34, amended: 1974, c.44, schs.13,15; c.45, schs.3,5; 1975, c.28, sch.3; 1978, c.14, sch.2; 1987, c.26, sch.23.

CAP.

1973—cont.

56. Land Compensation (Scotland) Act 1973—cont.
ss. 34, 35, see *Evans* v. *Glasgow District Council*, 1978 S.L.T.(Lands Tr.) 5; *Millar* v. *Strathclyde Regional Council*, 1988 S.L.T.(Lands Tr.) 9.
s. 35, see *Glasgow Corporation* v. *Anderson*, First Division, 1976 S.L.T. 225.
s. 36, amended: 1974, c.44, schs.13,15; c.45, schs.3,5; 1978, c.14, sch.2; 1987, c.26, sch.23.
s. 38, amended: 1974, c.44, schs.13,15; c.45, schs.3,5; 1987, c.26, sch.23.
s. 39, amended: *ibid.*
s. 40, amended: 1974, c.44, schs.13,15; c.45, schs.3,5.
s. 41, amended: 1986, c.44, sch.7.
s. 44, see *Anderson* v. *Moray District Council*, 1978 S.L.T.(Lands Tr.) 37.
s. 48, see *Khan* v. *Glasgow District Council*, 1977 S.L.T.(Lands Tr.) 35.
s. 52, see *Simpson* v. *Stoke-on-Trent City Council* (1982) 262 E.G. 673, W. H. Rees, F.R.I.C.S.
s. 53, amended: 1987, c.26, sch.23.
s. 54, amended: 1986, c.44, sch.7.
s. 65, amended: 1984, c.54, sch.9; repealed in pt.: *ibid.*, sch.11.
s. 68, amended: 1976, c.21, sch.1.
s. 69, amended: 1974, c.44, schs.13,15; c.45, schs.3,5; 1987, c.26, sch.23.
ss. 70, 73, repealed in pt.: 1984, c.54, sch.9.
s. 73, regs. 76/2022.
ss. 74, 76, amended: 1976, c.21, sch.1.
s. 77, amended: 1984, c.54, sch.9.
s. 80, amended: 1975, c.28, sch.3; 1984, c.54, sch.9; 1987, c.26, sch.23; repealed in pt.: 1984, c.54, sch.11.
s. 81, repealed in pt.: S.L.R. 1976.

57. Badgers Act 1973.
Royal Assent, July 25, 1973.
ss. 1, 2, amended: 1981, c.69, sch.7; 1985, c.31, s.1.
s. 6, order 79/1249.
ss. 6, 7, repealed: 1981, c.69, schs.7,17.
s. 8, amended: *ibid.*, sch.7; 1986, c.14, sch.3; repealed in pt.: 1981, c.69, schs.7,17.
s. 9, amended: 1973, c.54, sch.1; 1975, c.48, s.16; 1981, c.69, sch.7.
s. 10, amended: *ibid.*; repealed in pt.: 1984, c.60, sch.7.
s. 11, amended: 1973, c.54, sch.1; c.65, sch.27; 1981, c.69, sch.7; repealed in pt.: S.L.R. 1976; 1981, c.69, schs.7,17.

58. Insurance Companies Amendment Act 1973.
Royal Assent, July 25, 1973.
repealed, except ss. 50, 57 (in part): order 76/59.
s. 41, regs. 74/901, 1052.
s. 42, see *R.* v. *Clegg*, March 15, 1977.
s. 43, regs. 74/902, 1051.
s. 53, regs. 74/901, 902, 1051, 1052.
s. 56, repealed in pt.: S.L.R. 1977.
s. 56, schs. 3–5, repealed: 1980, c.25, sch.5.
sch. 1, repealed in pt.: 1981, c.31, sch.5.

CAP.

1973—cont.

59. Education (Scotland) Act 1973.
Royal Assent, October 25, 1973.
repealed: 1980, c.44, sch.5.
s. 1, see *Scott* v. *Aberdeen Corporation* (O.H.),
March 12, 1975; First Division, Jan. 22, 1976.

60. Breeding of Dogs Act 1973.
Royal Assent, October 25, 1973.
amended (S.): 1982, c.45, sch.3.
s. 1, amended (S.): 1975, c.30, schs.6,7; 1980,
c.65, sch.6; repealed in pt.: *ibid.*, sch.34;
1988, c.29, sch.2.
s. 4, repealed: 1974, c.7, schs.7,8.
s. 5, amended: 1973, c.65, sch.27; 1974, c.7,
schs.7,8.
ss. 5, 6, amended (S.): 1982, c.45, sch.3.
s. 9, repealed in pt.: S.L.R. 1977.

61. Pensioners' Payments and National Insurance Act 1973.
Royal Assent, October 25, 1973.
repealed: 1986, c.50, sch.11.
ss. 8, 9, order 73/1969.

62. Powers of Criminal Courts Act 1973.
Royal Assent, October 25, 1973.
see *R.* v. *Riley* (1988) 87 Cr.App.R. 125, C.A.
s. 1, see *R.* v. *Gilby* [1975] 1 W.L.R. 924, C.A.;
R. v. *Fairhead* [1975] 2 All E.R. 737, C.A.; *R.*
v. *McQuaide* (1975) 60 Cr.App.R. 239, C.A.;
R. v. *Crosby; R.* v. *Hayes* (1975) 60 Cr.App.R.
234, C.A.; *R.* v. *Annesley* [1976] 1 W.L.R.
106, C.A.; *R.* v. *Head* (1976) 63 Cr.App.R.
157, C.A.; *R.* v. *Smith* (1976) 64 Cr.App.R.
116, C.A.; *R.* v. *Roberts, The Times,* January
19, 1978, C.A.; *R.* v. *Harling* (1977) 65
Cr.App.R. 320, C.A.; *R.* v. *George* [1984] 1
W.L.,R. 1082, C.A.; *R.* v. *Anderson* (1984) 78
Cr.App.R. 251, C.A.; *R* v. *West London Stipendiary Magistrate, ex p. Watts, The Times,*
May 30, 1987, D.C.; *R.* v. *Ross* (1988) 86
Cr.App.R. 337, Guildford Crown Ct.
s. 1, amended: 1977, c.45, sch.12; 1980, c.43,
sch.7; 1982, c.48, s.63.
s. 2, see *R.* v. *Barnett* (1986) 86 Cr.App.R. 365,
C.A.
s. 2, order 78/474; amended: 1977, c.45, s.57,
sch.12; order 78/474; 1982, c.48, sch.11;
repealed in pt.: 1977, c.45, sch.13; 1982,
c.48, sch.16.
ss. 2, 4, see *Cullen* v. *Rogers* [1982] 1 W.L.R.
729, H.L.
s. 3, amended: 1983, c.20, sch.4.
s. 4, repealed: 1982, c.48, schs.11, 16.
s. 4A, added: *ibid.*, sch.11.
s. 7, see *R.* v. *Wehner* [1977] 3 All E.R. 553,
C.A.; amended: 1977, c.45, s.57.
s. 8, see *R.* v. *Keelan* (1975) 61 Cr.App.R. 212,
C.A.
s. 9, amended: 1977, c.45, sch.12.
s. 11, amended: 1982, c.48, s.66.
s. 12, amended: 1988, c.33, s.69.
s. 13, see *R.* v. *Kitt* [1977] Crim.L.R. 220; *R.* v.
Robinson [1979] Crim.L.R. 785, C.A.; *R.* v.
*Statutory Committee of the Pharmaceutical
Society of Great Britain, ex p. Pharmaceutical
Society of Great Britain* [1981] 1 W.L.R. 886;
[1981] 2 All E.R. 805, D.C.; *R.* v. *Wilson* (1982)

CAP.

1973—cont.

62. Powers of Criminal Courts Act 1973—*cont.*
4 Cr.App.R.(S.) 75, C.A.; *R.* v. *Secretary of
State for the Home Department, ex p. Thornton* [1986] 3 W.L.R. 158, C.A.; *R.* v. *Barnes
(W.T.)* (1986) 83 Cr.App.R. 58, C.A.
s. 13, amended: 1982, c.48, sch.14; 1983, c.41,
sch.2.
s. 14, see *R.* v. *Evans* [1977] 1 W.L.R. 27; [1977]
1 All E.R. 228, C.A.; *R.* v. *Carnwell* (1978) 68
Cr.App.R. 58, C.A.; *R.* v. *Starie* (1979) 69
Cr.App.R. 239, C.A.; *Cooper* v. *Chief Constable of Lancashire* [1984] Crim.L.R. 99, Preston Crown Court; *Walsh* v. *Barlow; Thorpe* v.
Griggs (1984) 6 Cr.App.R.(S.) 286, D.C.;
[1985] 1 W.L.R. 90, D.C.
s. 14, amended: 1982, c.48, sch.12; repealed in
pt.: *ibid.*, schs.12,16.
ss. 14, 15, see *R.* v. *Dugdale* [1981] Crim.L.R.
105, Preston Crown Ct.
s. 15, see *R.* v. *Tebbutt, The Times,* February 2,
1988, C.A.
s. 15, amended: 1977, c.45, sch.12.
s. 16, see *R.* v. *Gainsborough JJ., ex p. Green,
The Times,* June 20, 1983, D.C.; *R.* v. *Worcester Crown Court, ex p. Lamb* (1985) 7
Cr.App.R.(S.) 44, D.C.; *Jones* v. *Kelsey* [1987]
Crim.L.R. 392; (1987) 85 Cr.App.R. 226, D.C.
s. 16, amended: 1982, c.48, sch.4.
s. 17, see *R.* v. *Adair* (1978) 123 S.J. 32, C.A.;
R. v. *Harding (Bernard), The Times,* June 15,
1983, C.A.; *R.* v. *Newcastle upon Tyne Crown
Court, ex p. Bradley, The Times,* April 17,
1984, D.C.; *R.* v. *Grays JJ., ex p. Adwinkle,
The Times,* December 1, 1984, D.C.
s. 17, amended: 1977, c.45, sch.12; 1982, c.48,
sch.12.
ss. 17A, 17B, 17C, added: *ibid.*, sch.13.
s. 18, repealed in pt.: 1981, c.47, sch.
s. 19, see *R.* v. *Ankers* (1975) 61 Cr.App.R. 170,
C.A.; *R.* v. *Foster,* February 10, 1976, C.A.;
R. v. *Genese* [1976] 2 All E.R. 600, C.A.;
Veator v. *Glennon* [1981] 1 W.L.R. 567, D.C.;
Lewisham London Borough v. *W. & P.,* May
15, 1987, Pearlman J.
s. 19, repealed: 1982, c.48, sch.16.
s. 20, see *R.* v. *Ampleford* (1975) 61 Cr.App.R.
325, C.A.
s. 20, amended: 1982, c.48, sch.14.
s. 20A, added: *ibid.*, s.62.
s. 21, see *R.* v. *Birmingham JJ., ex p. Wyatt*
[1975] 3 All E.R. 897, D.C.; *R.* v. *McGinlay; R.*
v. *Ballantyne* (1975) 62 Cr.App.R. 156, C.A.;
R. v. *Newbury JJ., ex p. Du Pont* (1984) 78
Cr.App.R. 255, D.C.; *R.* v. *Cardiff JJ., ex p.
Salter* (1986) 1 F.L.R. 162, Wood J.
s. 21, repealed in pt.: 1982, c.48, sch.16.
s. 22, see *R.* v. *Ipswich Crown Court, ex p.
Williamson* (1982) 4 Cr.App.R.(S.) 348, D.C.;
R. v. *Bangs* (1983) 5 Cr.App.R.(S.) 453, C.A.
s. 22, repealed in pt.: 1988, c.33,-sch.16.
ss. 22, 23, see *R.* v. *Barnes (W.T.)* (1986) 83
Cr.App.R. 58, C.A.
s. 23, see *R.* v. *Burn* (1976) 63 Cr.App.R. 289,
C.A.; *R.* v. *Tyson* (1979) 68 Cr.App.R. 314,
C.A.; *R.* v. *Folan* (1979) 69 Cr.App.R. 93, C.A.

1973—cont.

62. Powers of Criminal Courts Act 1973—cont.

s. 23, repealed in pt.: 1982, c.48, s.31, sch.16.

s. 26, see *R. v. Barnes (W.T.)* (1986) 83 Cr.App.R. 58, C.A.; *R. v. Seafield, The Times,* May 21, 1988, C.A.

s. 27, amended: 1982, c.48, sch.4.

s. 28, see *R. v. Gooden, The Times,* December 5, 1979, C.A.; *R. v. Bangs* (1983) 5 Cr.App.R.(S.) 453, C.A.; *R. v. Bourton, The Times,* November 21, 1984, C.A.

s. 29, repealed in pt.: 1982, c.48, sch.16.

s. 30, see *R. v. Carnwell* (1978) 68 Cr.App.R. 58, C.A.

s. 30, repealed in pt.: 1977, c.45, sch.13.

s. 31, amended: 1979, c.2, sch.4; 1982, c.48, s.69; 1988, c.33, s.60.

s. 32, amended: 1979, c.2, sch.4; c.55, sch.2; 1980, c.43, sch.7; 1982, c.48, sch.14; repealed in pt.: *ibid.,* sch.16.

s. 33, repealed: 1977, c.45, sch.13.

s. 34, see *R. v. Bunce* (1977) 66 Cr.App.R. 109, C.A.

s. 34A, added: 1977, c.45, s.49; 1988, c.33, sch.15; repealed in pt.: *ibid.,* schs. 15,16.

s. 35, see *R. v. Brogan* [1975] 1 W.L.R. 393; [1975] 1 All E.R. 879, C.A.; *R. v. Inwood* (1974) 60 Cr.App.R. 70, C.A.; *R. v. Hier* (1976) 62 Cr.App.R. 233, C.A.; *Quigley v. Stokes* [1977] 1 W.L.R. 434, D.C.; *R. v. Bunce* (1977) 66 Cr.App.R. 109, C.A.; *R. v. O'Donoghue and Dallas-Cope* (1974) 66 Cr.App.R. 116, C.A.; *R. v. Schofield* [1978] 2 All E.R. 705, C.A.; *R. v. Howell* (1978) 66 Cr.App.R. 179, C.A.; *R. v. Vivian* [1979] 1 All E.R. 48, C.A.; *Malone v. Met. Police Comr.* [1979] 1 All E.R. 256, C.A.; *M. (A Minor)* v. *Oxford* [1981] R.T.R. 246, D.C; *R. v. Donovan* [1982] R.T.R. 126, C.A.; *R. v. Hunt, The Times,* December 14, 1982, C.A.; *R. v. Amey* [1983] 1 W.L.R. 345, C.A.; *Bond v. Chief Constable of Kent* [1983] 1 W.L.R. 40, D.C.; *R. v. James (Michael); R. v. Meath* [1983] R.T.R. 192, C.A.; *R. v. Swann (Alan) and Webster (Alan)* (1984) 6 Cr.App.R.(S.) 22, C.A.; *R. v. Chappell* (1985) 80 Cr.App.R. 31, C.A.; *R. v. Horsham JJ., ex p. Richards* [1985] 1 W.L.R. 986, D.C.

s. 35, amended: 1977, c.45, s.60; 1988, c.33, s.104; repealed in pt.: 1980, c.43, sch.9.

s. 36, see *Gooch v. Ewing (Allied Irish Bank, Garnishee)* [1985] 3 All E.R. 654, C.A.

ss. 36–38, see v. *Bunce* (1977) 66 Cr.App.R. 109, C.A.

ss. 36–38, substituted: 1988, c.33, s.105.

s. 38, see *Berry v. Cooper, The Times,* March 30, 1983, C.A.

s. 39, see *D.P.P. v. Anderson* [1978] 2 All E.R. 512, H.L.; *R. v. Saville* [1980] 1 All E.R. 561, C.A.; *R. v. Downing* (1980) 71 Cr.App.R. 316, C.A.; *R. v. Reilly* [1982] 3 W.L.R. 149; [1982] 3 All E.R. 27, C.A.; *R. v. Raeburn* (1982) 74 Cr.App.R. 21, C.A.; *R. v. Mayer* (1984) 6 Cr.App.R.(S.) 193 C.A.; *R. v. Cannon* (1986) 82 Cr.App.R. 286, C.A.; *R. v. Riley* (1988) 152 J.P. 399, C.A.

s. 39, repealed: 1988, c.33, s.101, sch.16.

1973—cont.

62. Powers of Criminal Courts Act 1973—cont.

s. 40, see *R. v. Cain* [1984] 3 W.L.R. 393, H.L.; *R. v. Prefas, The Times,* November 12, 1986, C.A.

s. 41, repealed: 1985, c.65, sch.10.

s. 42, amended: 1980, c.43, sch.7; 1982, c.48, sch.14.

s. 43, see *R. v. Miele* [1976] R.T.R. 238, C.A.; *R. v. Taverner* [1976] R.T.R. 242, C.A.; *R. v. Lucas* [1976] R.T.R. 235, C.A.; *R. v. Lidster* [1976] R.T.R. 240, C.A.; *R. v. Hinde* [1977] R.T.R. 328, C.A.; *R. v. Thompson* (1978) 66 Cr.App.R. 130, C.A.; *R. v. Chester Justices, ex p. Smith* [1978] R.T.R. 373, D.C.; *Malone v. Met. Police Comr.* [1979] 1 All E.R. 256, C.A.; *R. v. Menocal* [1979] 2 W.L.R. 876, H.L.; *R. v. Kingston-upon-Hull JJ., ex p. Hartung* (1980) 72 Cr.App.R. 26, D.C.; *R. v. Khan (Sultan Ashraf); R. v. Crawley* [1982] 1 W.L.R. 1405, C.A.; *R. v. Thibeault* [1983] Crim.L.R. 102, C.A.; *R. v. Ribeyre* (1982) Cr.App.R.(S.) 165, C.A.; *R. v. McFarlane* (1982) 4 Cr.App.R.(S.) 264, C.A.; *Mercer v. Oldham* [1984] Crim.L.R. 232, D.C.; *R. v. Savage* (1983) Cr.App.R.(S.) 216, C.A.; *R. v. Bramble* (1984) 6 Cr.App.R.(S.) 80, C.A.; *R. v. Slater (J. K.)* [1986] 1 W.L.R. 1340, C.A.; *R. v. Boothe* [1987] Crim.L.R. 347, C.A.; *R. v. Neville* [1987] Crim.L.R. 585, C.A.; *R. v. Stratton, The Times,* January 15, 1988, C.A.

s. 43, amended: 1988, c.33, s.69, sch.15.

s. 43A, added: *ibid.,* s.107.

s. 44, see *R. v. Kent, The Times,* May 13, 1983, C.A.; *R. v. Riley* [1984] Crim.L.R. 40; (1984) 78 Cr.App.R. 121, C.A.; *R. v. Powell (M. B.)* (1984) 6 Cr.App.R.(S.) 354, C.A.; *R. v. Arif Mohammed* (1985) 7 Cr.App.R.(S) 92, C.A.; *R. v. Parrington* (1985) 7 Cr.App.R.(S.) 18, C.A.

s. 44, amended: 1980, c.43, sch.7; 1988, c.54, sch.3.

s. 45, repealed in pt.: 1982, c.48, sch.16.

s. 47, amended: *ibid.,* sch.11; repealed in pt.: *ibid.,* sch.16.

s. 48, repealed in pt.: *ibid.*

s. 49, amended: 1977, c.45, sch.12; repealed in pt.: *ibid.,* sch.13; 1982, c.48, schs.11, 16.

s. 50, repealed: *ibid.*

s. 51, amended: 1977, c.45, sch.12; 1979, c.55, sch.2; repealed in pt.: 1982, c.48, sch.16; 1985 c.51, sch.17.

s. 53, repealed in pt.: 1975, c.21, sch.10.

s. 54, orders 75/59, 297, 873, 1077, 1180, 1994; 76/179, 400, 1641, 1973; 77/139, 853, 1672, 1863, 1884; 78/652, 813, 814, 1192, 1400; 79/1285; 80/224, 391, 1020, 1162, 1261, 1449, 1656, 1828; 81/390, 1341, 1449; 82/728, 1812; 83/843, 1669, 1845, 1914, 1915; 84/426, 577, 1204, 1628; 85/1084, 1156, 1759, 1870, 1964, 1965, 2004, 2031; 86/464, 945, 1280, 1713, 2316–2318; 87/356, 1855, 2135, 2136, 2140, 2141, 2181, 2222, 2223; 88/258, 612.

s. 54, amended: 1977, c.45, s.57.

s. 57, see *R. v. Bangs* (1983) 5 Cr.App.R.(S.) 453, C.A.

CAP.

1973—cont.

62. Powers of Criminal Courts Act 1973—cont.
s. 57, amended: 1977, c.45, sch.12; 1980, c.43,
sch.7; repealed in pt.: 1977, c.45, sch.13;
1982, c.48, sch.16; 1988, c.33, sch.16.
s. 58, amended: 1982, c.48, sch.13; repealed in
pt.: 1975, c.21, sch.10 (S.); 1977, c.45,
sch.12.
s. 59, amended: 1982, c.48, sch.13; repealed in
pt.: S.L.R. 1977.
s. 60, order 74/941.
s. 64, amended: 1982, c.48, schs.4,14.
sch. 1, amended: *ibid.*, s.66, sch.11; repealed
in pt.: 1977, c.45, schs.12,13; 1982, c.48,
sch.16.
sch. 2, see *R.* v. *Raeburn* (1982) 74 Cr.App.R.
21, C.A.
sch. 2, repealed: 1985, c.65, sch.10.
sch. 3, rules 74/1352, 1569, 1954, 1955; 75/592,
910; 76/116, 1314, 2119; 84/647; orders
75/59, 297, 873, 1077, 1180, 1994; 76/179,
400, 1641, 1973; 77/139, 853, 1672, 1863,
1884; 78/652, 813, 814, 1192, 1400; 79/1285;
80/224, 391, 1020, 1162, 1261, 1449, 1656,
1828; 81/390, 1341, 1449; 82/728, 1812;
83/843, 1669, 1845, 1914, 1915; 84/426, 577,
1204, 1628; 85/1084, 1156, 1506, 1759,
1870, 1964, 1965, 2004, 2031; 86/464, 945,
1280, 1713, 2316–2318; 87/356, 1855, 2135,
2136, 2140, 2141, 2181, 2222, 2223; 88/258.
sch. 3, amended: 1977, c.38, sch.2; c.45,
sch.12; 1982, c.48, sch.11; 1988, c.33,
schs.11,15; repealed in pt.: 1977, c.38, sch.5;
c.45, schs.12,13; 1982, c.48, schs.11,16;
1985, c.51, sch.17; 1988, c.33, schs.11,16.
sch. 5, amended: 1974, c.4, sch.5; c.23, sch.3;
c.47, sch.4; repealed in pt.: 1975, c.21, sch.10
(S.); 1977, c.45, sch.13; 1980, c.43, sch.9;
1982, c.48, sch.16; 1983, c.41, sch.10; 1988,
c.33, sch.16; c.54, sch.1.

63. Government Trading Funds Act 1973.
Royal Assent, October 25, 1973.
ss. 1, 2, orders 74/1106; 75/501.
ss. 1, 2, 6, order 76/508.
ss. 1, 6, order 85/927.

64. Maplin Development Act 1973.
Royal Assent, October 25, 1973.
repealed: 1976, c.51, sch.

65. Local Government (Scotland) Act 1973.
Royal Assent, October 25, 1973.
orders 75/129; 77/1385, 1961; 78/1166, 1607;
79/465.
ss. 2, 5, amended: 1984, c.31, sch.2.
s. 3, amended: 1981, c.23, sch.2.
s. 3A, added: 1980, c.65, s.27.
s. 4, amended: 1983, c.2, sch.8.
ss. 6–10, repealed: *ibid.*, sch.9.
s. 7, rules 74/82; 77/1385, 1961; 79/656.
s. 11, repealed in pt.: 1983, c.2, sch.9.
s. 15, order 80/127.
s. 16, regs. 84/1652.
s. 17, orders 76/340; 77/9–11, 13–16, 22, 378;
84/1855, 1856, 1938–1941, 2030; 86/209,
210; 87/112, 334, 1943; 88/48—50, 218–221,
347–349, 746, 1877.
s. 23, modified: order 75/236; amended: 1981,
c.23, sch.2; repealed in pt.: *ibid.*, schs.2,4.

CAP.

1973—cont.

65. Local Government (Scotland) Act 1973—
cont.
s. 24, regs. 77/8.
s. 31, modified: order 75/236; amended: 1982,
c.43, sch.3; 1983, c.2, sch.8; 1985, c.65,
s.31.
s. 37, amended: 1984, c.31, sch.2.
s. 38, modified: order 75/236; amended: 1982,
c.43, sch.3.
s. 42, amended: 1986, c.60, sch.16.
s. 44, repealed: 1985, c.43, sch.3.
s. 45, regs. 75/686, 1941; 77/119, 1776;
78/1816, 1879; 79/1562; 80/98; 81/172;
82/115; 83/579; 84/691; 85/395; 86/588;
87/1381; 88/372.
s. 45, amended: 1982, c.43, s.60.
s. 45A, regs. 82/1396.
s. 45A, added: 1982, c.43, s.60.
s. 46, repealed in pt.: 1980, c.65, sch.34.
s. 48, modified: order 75/236.
s. 49, regs. 75/332; 81/1388; 87/308; amended:
1975, c.30, sch.6; 1982, c.43, s.60; repealed
in pt.: 1975, c.30, sch.7; 1982, c.43, s.60,
sch.4.
s. 49A, regs. 81/333; 82/115; 83/579; 84/691;
85/395; 86/588; 87/1381; 88/372.
s. 49A, added: 1980, c.65, s.26.
s. 50, regs. 75/686, 1941; 77/119, 1776;
78/1816, 1879; 79/1562; 80/98; 81/172, 333;
82/115, 1396; 83/579; 84/691; 85/395;
87/1381; 88/372.
ss. 50A–50K, added: 1985, c.43, s.2.
s. 50G, order 86/1433.
ss. 53 (in pt.), 54, repealed: 1981, c.23, sch.4.
s. 55, repealed in pt.: 1982, c.43, s.23, sch.4.
s. 56, amended: *ibid.*, s.32; 1987, c.47, s.28.
ss. 57, 62, 64–69, modified: order 75/236.
s. 64, amended: 1983, c.2, sch.8; c.39, s.7;
repealed in pt.: 1985, c.72, sch.13.
ss. 67, 69, amended: 1982, c.43, sch.3.
s. 69, see *Commission for Local Authority
Accounts in Scotland* v. *City of Edinburgh
District Council, The Times,* April 18, 1988.
ss. 69, 83, see *Meek* v. *Lothian Regional Council*
(O.H.), 1980 S.L.T.(Notes) 61.
s. 73, amended: 1981, c.23, sch.2.
s. 74, amended: *ibid.*,sch.3.
s. 74A, repealed: 1980, c.65, schs.23,34.
s. 75, see *East Lothian District Council* v.
National Coal Board (O.H.), 1982 S.L.T. 460.
ss. 81, 83, 88, 89, modified: order 75/236.
s. 83, amended: 1982, c.43, ss.6,50; 1984,
c.31, sch.9; 1986, c.10, s.3; 1987, c.47, sch.1.
s. 88, see *Meek* v. *Lothian Regional Council*
(O.H.), 1983 S.L.T. 494; *Commission for Local
Authority Accounts in Scotland* v. *City of Edinburgh District Council, The Times,* April 18,
1988.
s. 88, amended: 1986, c.10, s.3.
s. 90, amended: 1982, c.43, s.11.
s. 90A, added: *ibid.*
s. 91, see *Assessor for Dumfries and Galloway*
v. *Wigtown District Council,* 1977 S.C. 299.
s. 91, repealed: 1982, c.43, sch.4.
s. 94, order 87/943.
s. 94, amended: 1975, c.30, sch.6; 1981, c.23,
s.26; 1982, c.43, sch.3.

CAP.

1973—cont.

65. Local Government (Scotland) Act 1973—
cont.

s. 96, amended: 1976, c.66, ss.18,19.

s. 97, amended: 1975, c.30, sch.6; 1988, c.9, s.35.

ss. 97A, 97B, added: 1988, c.9, s.35.

s. 98, regs. 75/662; 88/133.

s. 99, amended: 1988, c.9, s.35.

s. 101, amended: 1984, c.31, s.10.

ss. 102, 103, 108A, see *Commission for Local Authority Accounts in Scotland* v. *Stirling District Council,* 1984 S.L.T. 442.

s. 105, regs. 75/663; 85/267.

s. 105, amended: 1984, c.31, s.10.

s. 106, amended: 1980, c.45, sch.10.

ss. 107–108C, repealed: 1987, c.47, sch.6.

ss. 108, 108A, see *Lord Advocate* v. *Stirling District Council,* 1986 S.L.T. 179.

s. 109, amended: 1982, c.43, sch.3; 1987, c.47, sch.1.

s. 110, amended: *ibid.*

s. 110A, regs. 88/1977.

s. 110A, added: 1981, c.41, sch.12.

s. 111, regs. 75/650, 652, 661, 2233; 76/648; 79/227, 235, 1597, 1598; 80/2050, 2051; 81/1045, 1046; 82/51, 1843; 83/862, 1095; 85/246; 86/407, 411; 87/2167; 88/19.

s. 111, amended: 1980, c.45, sch.10; 1982, c.43, sch.3; 1987, c.47, sch.1; repealed in pt.: *ibid.,* schs.1,6.

s. 112, regs. 74/600, 1317, 1602; 75/382, 1724; 76/1756; 77/1576; 78/1399; 79/1307; 80/1596; 81/1512; 82/1504.

ss. 112–115, repealed: 1982, c.24, sch.5.

s. 116, see *Glasgow Assessor* v. *Fine Fare,* Lands Val. Appeal Ct., December 4, 1975.

s. 116, orders 74/1056, 1565.

s. 116, amended: 1987, c.47, sch.1.

s. 117, repealed: S.L.R. 1986.

s. 118, amended: 1980, c.45, sch.10; 1987, c.47, sch.1.

ss. 119, 120, repealed: *ibid.,* sch.6.

s. 121, repealed: 1981, c.23, sch.2,4.

s. 125, amended: 1975, c.30, sch.6; 1978, c.4, sch; 1988, c.47, sch.4; repealed in pt.: *ibid.*

s. 126, amended: 1978, c.4, sch.; 1988, c.47, sch.4; repealed in pt.: *ibid.*

s. 129, repealed: 1980, c.44, sch.5.

s. 130, amended: 1987, c.26, sch.23.

s. 131, amended: 1974, c.44, sch.3; repealed in pt.: 1987, c.26, schs.23,24.

s. 133, amended: 1984, c.54, sch.9.

s. 134, regs. 80/1756.

s. 135, orders 75/231–237, 310; 76/418; amended: 1974, c.40, sch.4.

s. 136, repealed: *ibid.*

ss. 137 (in pt.), 139, repealed: 1982, c.43, sch.4.

s. 144, repealed in pt.: 1981, c.22, sch.6.

s. 147, repealed in pt.: S.L.R. 1981.

s. 148, repealed in pt.: 1980, c.45, sch.11.

s. 149, repealed: 1985, c.72, sch.13.

s. 150, order 75/177.

s. 150 (in pt.), 151, repealed: 1985, c.67, schs.3,8.

s. 152, repealed: 1982, c.16, sch.16.

CAP.

1973—cont.

65. Local Government (Scotland) Act 1973—
cont.

s. 154, amended: 1982, c.43, s.20.

ss. 154A, 154B, added: *ibid.,* s.7.

ss.158, 162, repealed: *ibid.,* sch.4.

s. 163, amended: *ibid.,* sch.3.

s. 164, repealed: *ibid.,* sch.4.

s. 167, repealed: S.L.R. 1981.

s. 170, amended: 1982, c.43, s.31.

s. 171, repealed in pt.: S.L.R. 1978.

s. 172, amended: 1975, c.77, sch.9.

ss. 172, 176, amended: 1982, c.43, sch.3.

ss. 177, 179, see *Bellway* v. *Strathclyde Regional Council* (O.H.), August 17, 1978.

s. 178, repealed: 1982, c.43, sch.4.

s. 179, substituted: *ibid.,* sch.3; amended: 1986, c.63, sch.11.

s. 180, repealed: 1982, c.43, s.5.

s. 181, amended: *ibid.,* sch.3.

s. 182, amended: 1979, c.46, sch.4.

s. 183, amended: 1975, c.30, sch.6.

ss. 185, 186, repealed: 1976, c.66, sch.8.

s. 188, repealed in pt.: 1985, c.13, sch.3.

ss. 189–191, 193, modified: order 75/236.

s. 194, modified: order 75/236; amended: 1975, c.30, sch.6.

ss. 195, 196, modified: order 75/236.

s. 197, modified: order 75/236, amended: 1978, c.29, sch.16; repealed in pt.: 1985, c.43, sch.3.

ss. 198, 199, modified: order 75/236.

s. 201, amended: 1976, c.66, ss.18,19.

s. 202, amended: order 75/1543; 1975, c.30, sch.6; 1980, c.45, sch.10; 1982, c.45, s.110.

ss. 202A, 202B, 202C, added: *ibid.*

s. 203, 204, amended: order 75/1543.

s. 205, orders 75/428, 669.

s. 205, repealed: 1980, c.9, sch.10.

s. 210, amended: 1986, c.63, sch.11; repealed in pt.: 1975, c.30, sch.7.

s. 210A, added: 1986, c.63, sch.11.

s. 211, see *Lord Advocate* v. *Stirling District Council,* First Division, July 3, 1985.

s. 213, repealed in pt.: S.L.R. 1981.

s. 215, see *McPhail* v. *Cunninghame District Council, William Loudon & Son* v. *Cunninghame District Council* (O.H.), 1985 S.L.T. 149.

s. 215, orders 74/653, 1804; 75/60, 177, 250, 574, 618, 676, 703; 76/211, 610, 619, 629, 651, 660, 684, 777, 779, 826, 1973, 2191; 78/419, 1070.

s. 216, orders 75/60. 574, 676, 703; 77/8.

s. 216, modified: order 25/236; repealed in pt.: 1982, c.43, sch.4.

s. 218, repealed: *ibid.,* s.62, sch.4.

s. 219, see *Gordon District Council* v. *Hay* (O.H.), 1978 S.L.T. 2.

s. 219, regs. 75/734, 838, 1800; 83/263, 264.

ss. 219–221, repealed: 1982, c.43, sch.4.

s. 220, regs. 74/1754.

s. 222, orders 75/659; 77/277.

s. 224, repealed in pt.: 1975, c.24, sch.3; 1982, c.43, s.63, sch.4.

s. 225, orders 78/584, 585, 1934; 79/92, 93, 672, 776; 84/780, 1926; 85/1629, 2034; 87/2090.

1973—cont.

65. Local Government (Scotland) Act 1973—
cont.
s. 229, orders 79/239, 356, 671, 775, 878–880,
1195, 1391, 1564; 80/603, 1153, 1154, 1218,
1219; 81/132.
s. 229, amended: 1978, c.4, s.5; 1982, c.45,
s.134.
s. 233, regs. 74/600, 1317; 75/382, 1724;
76/1756; 85/246; 86/407; orders 77/277;
78/1070, 1934; 79/92, 93, 239, 356, 671, 672,
775, 776, 878–880, 1564; 80/603, 1153, 1154,
1218, 1219; 81/132; 82/329; 86/1433; rules
74/82; 77/120; 79/656, 1195, 1391, 1564.
s. 233, amended: 1986, c.49, sch.4.
s. 235, regs. 81/1388; 87/1381; 88/1977.
s. 235, amended: 1980, c.45, sch.10.
s. 236, amended: *ibid.*; 1981, c.23, sch.3; 1987,
c.26, sch.23.
s. 238, repealed in pt.: 1975, c.24, sch.3; order
73/1886, 2181.
sch. 1, amended: 1984, c.31, sch.2.
schs. 2, 3, repealed in pt.: 1983, c.2, sch.9.
ssh. 3, regs. 84/1652.
sch. 4, repealed in pt.: 1975, c.24, sch.3.
sch. 7, amended: 1975, c.30, sch.6; 1982, c.43,
sch.3.
sch. 7A, added: 1985, c.43, s.2, sch.1.
sch. 8, amended: 1975, c.30, s.17.
sch. 9, repealed in pt.: *ibid.*, sch.7; 1976, c 71,
sch.8; order 78/1173; 1987, c.26, schs.23,24.
sch. 10, repealed in pt.: 1988, c.47, sch.4.
sch. 11, repealed: 1980, c.44, sch.5.
sch. 12, amended: 1974, c.44, sch.13; repealed
in pt.: 1980, c.52, sch.5; 1985, c.71, sch.1;
1987, c.26, schs.23,24.
sch. 13, repealed in pt.: 1985, c.71, sch.1.
sch. 14, amended: 1975, c.30, sch.6; repealed
in pt.: 1975, c.30, sch.7; S.L.R. 1976; 1980,
c.65, sch. 34; 1984, c.27, sch. 14; c.54,
sch.11; 1988, c.54, sch.1.
sch. 15, regs. 80/1756; repealed in pt.: S.L.R.
1977; 1980, c.45, sch.11.
sch. 16, amended: 1974, c.40, sch.4.
sch. 17, repealed in pt.: 1975, c.30, sch.7; 1980,
c.45, sch.11; 1983, c.23, sch.5.
sch. 18, repealed in pt.: 1978, c.55, sch.4; 1980,
c.34, sch.9; 1985, c.67, schs.3,7,8.
sch. 20, see *Lothian Regional Council* v. *B.,*
1984 S.L.T.(Sh.Ct.) 83.
sch. 22, amended: 1982, c.43, sch.3; repealed
in pt.: *ibid.*, sch.4.
sch. 23, amended: 1974, c.32, ss.4,13, sch.;
c.39, sch.5; c.40, sch.3; 1975, c.30, sch.6;
repealed in pt.: 1979, c.46, sch.4; 1980, c.45,
sch.11; 1982, c.43, sch.4; c.52, sch.3.
sch. 24, repealed in pt.: 1976, c.32, sch.5; c.66,
sch.8; 1982, c.30, sch.7; c.33, sch.2; c 45,
sch.4; 1985, c.13, sch.3.
sch. 25, repealed in pt.: 1980, c.45, sch.11;
1984, c.27, sch.14; 1985, c.72, sch.13.
sch. 27, amended: 1974, c.32, ss.4,13, sch.;
c.39, sch.5; c.40, sch.3; repealed in pt.: 1975,
c.21, sch.10; c.78, sch.6; S.L.R. 1976; 1976,
c.71, sch.8; 1978, c.3, sch.2; c.28, sch.4;
c.38, sch.3; 1980, c.9, sch.10; c.45, sch.11;
1981, c.68, sch.9; c.69, sch.17; 1982, c.16,

1973—cont.

65. Local Government (Scotland) Act 1973—
cont.
sch.16; c.45, sch.4; 1983, c.35, sch.2; 1984,
c.56, sch.3; 1986, c.49, sch.4; 1987, c.43,
sch.5; 1988, c.9, sch.7.
sch. 28, see *Loyal Orange Lodge No.* 493
Hawick First Purple v. *Roxburgh District Council,* Second Division, December 14, 1979.
sch. 28, amended: 1974, c.32, ss.4,13, sch.;
c.39, sch.5; c.40, schs.3,4; repealed in pt.:
S.L.R. 1977; 1984, c.12, sch.7.
sch. 29, amended: 1974, c.32, ss.4,13, sch.;
c.39, sch.5; c.40, sch.3.

66. Channel Tunnel (Initial Finance) Act 1973.
Royal Assent, November 13, 1973.

67. Fuel and Electricity (Control) Act 1973.
Royal Assent, December 6, 1973.
ss. 1–8, continued in force: orders 84/1691;
85/1639.
s. 2, orders 73/2068, 2080, 2087, 2091, 2092,
2119; 74/948, 986, 1225, 2151, 2159, 2160;
76/1204.
ss. 2, 5, orders 73/2120, 2137, 2146, 2172,
2188; 74/78, 117, 137, 197, 198, 245, 377,
511, 620, 1898, 2017, 2150; 76/1840.
s. 4, order 73/2051; S.R. 1977 No. 342.
s. 4, amended: order 81/154.
s. 9, orders 73/2053, 2054, 2160.
s. 10, orders 74/1893, 1897; 75/1705, 1835;
76/1917; 77/1874; 78/1626; 80/1722;
81/1673; 82/1529; 83/1522; 84/1691;
85/1639; 86/1885; 88/1848.

68. International Sugar Organisation Act 1973.
Royal Assent, December 19, 1973.

**69. Northern Ireland Constitution (Amendment)
Act 1973.**
Royal Assent, December 19, 1973.
s. 1, repealed in pt.: 1982, c.38, sch.3.

1974

1. Consolidated Fund Act 1974.
Royal Assent, January 22, 1974.
repealed: 1976, c.43, sch.D.

2. Appropriation Act 1974.
Royal Assent, February 8, 1974.
repealed: 1976, c.43, sch.D.

3. Slaughterhouses Act 1974.
Royal Assent, February 8, 1974.
see *R.* v. *Rabbinical Commission for the Licensing of Shochetim, ex p. Cohen, The Times,*
December 22, 1987, C.A.
s. 2, amended: 1984, c.30, sch.10; repealed in
pt.: 1980, c.65, schs.1,34.
s. 4, amended: 1984, c.30, sch 10.
s. 6, amended: 1980, c.43, sch.7.
ss. 12, 16, amended: 1984, c.30, sch.10;
repealed in pt.: 1980, c.65, schs.1,34.
s. 18, repealed in pt.: 1974, c.7, schs.6, 8.
s. 20, amended: 1981, c.22, sch.5.
s. 28, repealed in pt.: 1984, c.22, sch.3.
s. 30, amended: 1981, c.67, sch.4.
s. 32, repealed in pt.: 1976, c.57, sch.2.
s. 35, amended: 1981, c.22, sch.5.
s. 38, regs. 83/688, 689; 84/1310, 1311.

1974—cont.

3. Slaughterhouses Act 1974—cont.

s. 38, amended: 1980, c.43, sch.7; 1981, c.22, sch.5.

s. 40, amended: 1974, c.7, sch.6; 1981, c.22, sch.5.

s. 42, amended: ibid.

s. 43, amended: 1980, c.43, sch.7.

s. 46, repealed in pt.: 1984, c.30, sch.11.

sch. 3, repealed in pt.: 1974, c.7, sch.8; 1984, c.30, sch.11.

4. Legal Aid Act 1974.

Royal Assent, February 8, 1974.

repealed: 1988, c.34, sch.6.

regs. 75/1866.

s. 1, regs. 74/1302; 75/1866; 76/1894; 77/446, 1934; 78/1568; 79/350, 1395; 82/236; 83/618, 1784; 84/1837; 85/1614; 86/643; 87/627; order 88/666.

s. 2, see R. v. Worthing JJ., ex p. Stevenson [1976] 2 All E.R. 194, D.C.; Parry v. Parry [1986] 16 Fam.Law 211, C.A.

s. 2, regs. 80/477, 1898.

s. 2A, regs. 80/477, 1898; 82/1592; 83/470, 1142, 1963; 84/241, 637; 88/461.

s. 3, regs. 77/182; 80/1119; 83/1785; 85/1840.

s. 4, regs. 74/1184; 75/634, 1684; 76/1681; 77/183, 1635; 78/1567; 79/166, 1164; 80/477; 82/237; 83/392, 618, 1652, 1784; 84/1715; 85/1694; 87/396; 88/459, 461.

s. 4, amended: regs. 88/459.

s. 5, regs 77/182, 1716; 80/477, 1059.

s. 6, regs. 74/1403; 75/855, 1867; 77/1935; 78/1571; 79/351, 1394; 82/238; 83/617, 1783; 84/1838; 85/1615; 87/628; 88/667.

s. 7, see Johnson v. Ribbins (Sir Francis Pittis & Son (A Firm, Third Party) [1977] 1 All E.R. 806, C.A.

s. 7, regs. 76/499; 77/447; 80/1894.

ss. 7, 8, see Lye v. Marks and Spencer, The Times, February 15, 1988, C.A.

s. 8, see McDonnell v. McDonnell [1977] 1 W.L.R. 34, C.A.; Miller v. Littner (1979) 123 S.J. 473, Oliver J.; Ford v. Ford, The Times, January 16, 1981, C.A.; The Debtor v. Law Society, The Times, February 20, 1981, C.A.; Boorman v. Godfrey, The Times, March 12, 1981, C.A.; Gokholl v. Budaly, August 10, 1982, Bow County Ct.; Littaur v. Steggles Palmer [1985] 1 W.L.R. 1208, Sir Neil Lawson.

s. 8, regs. 80/1894.

s. 9, see Hanlon v. The Law Society [1980] 2 W.L.R. 756; [1980] 2 All E.R. 199, H.L.; Manley v. The Law Society [1981] 1 W.L.R. 335; [1981] 1 All E.R. 401, C.A.; Simmons v. Simmons [1984] 1 All E.R. 83; (1983) 13 Fam.Law 179, C.A.; Jones v. The Law Society (1983) 13 Fam.Law 117, Sir John Arnold P.; R. v. The Law Society, ex p. Saxton [1983] 3 W.L.R. 830, C.A.; Van Hoorn v. The Law Society [1983] 3 W.L.R. 199, Balcome J.; Curling v. The Law Society [1985] 1 All E.R. 705, C.A.; Simpson v. The Law Society [1987] 2 W.L.R. 1390, H.L.

s. 9, regs. 74/1403; 75/855, 1867; 76/628; 77/1293, 1715, 1935; 78/1571; 79/351, 1394;

1974—cont.

4. Legal Aid Act 1974—cont.

80/477, 1894, 1898; 81/173; 82/238, 1892; 83/617, 1783; 84/1838; 87/628; 88/460, 667.

s. 10, see Storer v. Wright [1981] 2 W.L.R. 208, C.A.; Harris v. Harris, February 11, 1987, H.H. Judge Whitley, Portsmount Crown Ct.

s. 11, regs. 77/1715–17; 78/1569, 1570; 79/280, 281; 80/477, 1894, 1898; 83/423, 424, 1683; 86/274, 276; 88-/461, 467.

s. 13, see McDonnell v. McDonnell [1977] 1 W.L.R. 34, C.A.; Maynard v. Osmond, The Times, October 5, 1978, C.A.; Maynard v. Osmond (No. 2) [1979] 1 W.L.R. 31, C.A.; Miller v. Littner (1979) 123 S.J. 473, Oliver J.; Millican v. Tucker [1980] 1 All E.R. 1083, C.A.; Dupree v. Downshire Properties, May 8, 1979, Hayman J., West London County Ct.; Gayways Linings v. Toczek, The Times, March 1, 1980, C.A.; Megarity v. D. J. Ryan & Sons (No. 2) [1980] 1 W.L.R. 1318; [1980] 3 All E.R. 602, C.A.; Din v. Wandsworth London Borough Council (No. 2) [1982] 1 All E.R. 1022, H.L.; Kelly v. London Transport Executive [1982] 1 W.L.R. 1055, C.A.; Davy-Chiesman v. Davy-Chiesman [1984] 1 All E.R. 321, C.A.; Lee v. South West Thames Regional Health Authority (No. 2), The Times July 22, 1985, C.A.; Landau v. Purvis, The Times, August 12, 1986, G. Godfrey Q.C.; Adams v. Riley [1988] 1 All E.R. 89, Hutchison J.; Aire Property Trust v. Treekweek, The Times, June 29, 1988, C.A.

ss. 13, 14, see S. v. S. (Unassisted Party's Costs) [1978] 1 W.L.R. 11, C.A.; R. & T. Thew v. Rees [1981] 3 W.L.R. 190; [1981] 2 All E.R. 964, C.A.; Megarity v. The Law Society; Galway Linings v. The Law Society [1982] A.C. 81, H.L.

s. 14, regs. 80/477, 1894, 1898; order 80/476.

s. 20, regs. 74/1184, 1302, 1403; 75/634, 855, 1684, 1867; 76/338, 499, 628, 1681, 1894; 77/182, 183, 446, 447, 1293, 1635, 1715, 1716, 1934, 1935; 79/166, 280, 281, 350, 351, 1164, 1394, 1395; 80/477, 1059, 1119, 1628–1630, 1894, 1898; 81/173; 82/236–238, 1592; 83/392, 423, 424, 470, 617, 618, 1142, 1451, 1652, 1783–1785, 1935, 1963; 84/241, 637, 1715, 1837, 1838; 85/1491, 1614, 1615, 1694, 1840, 1879, 1880; 86/272, 275, 276, 445, 643, 1186, 1559, 2135; 87/388, 396, 443, 627, 628, 2098; 85/446, 447, 459–461, 467, 666, 667.

s. 25, regs. 87/2098; 88/446, 447, 459–461, 467, 666, 667.

s. 28, see R. v. Tullett [1976] 1 W.L.R. 241; R. v. Rogers [1979] 1 All E.R. 693, Master Matthews; R. v. Gravesham Juvenile Court, ex p. B. (1982) 12 Fam.Law 207, Forbes J.

ss. 28–30, see Welch v. Redbridge Justices, The Times, April 4, 1984, D.C.

ss. 28, 31, see R. v. Huntingdon Magistrates' Court, ex p. Yapp [1986] Crim.L.R. 689; (1987) 84 Cr.App.R. 90, D.C.

s. 29, see R. v. Cambridge City Justices, ex p. L. (An Infant) (1979) 124 S.J. 187, D.C.

CAP.

1974—cont.

4. Legal Aid Act 1974—cont.

s. 30, see *R. v. Guildhall JJ., ex p. Marshall* [1976] 1 W.L.R. 335; [1976] 1 All E.R. 767, D.C.; *R. v. Gibson (Ivano), The Times,* May 21, 1983, C.A.; *R. v. Maurice Kirk* (1983) 76 Cr.App.R. 194, C.A.; *R. v. Kearney, The Times,* July 16, 1983, C.A.

s. 30, regs. 86/273.

s. 31, see *R. v. Maurice Kirk* (1983) 76 Cr.App.R. 194, C.A.

s. 34, regs. 75/64; 79/61; 80/1651, 1652.

s. 37, see *R. v. Boswell; R. v. Halliwell* [1987] 1 W.L.R. 705, Leggatt J.

s. 39, regs. 76/790; 77/875; 79/360; 80/661, 1651, 1652; 82/1197; 83/235, 1049, 1863; 84/112, 264, 1716; 85/333, 1632; 86/273, 274, 444, 1515, 1835; 87/369, 422; 88/423, 468.

s. 43, order 74/709.

sch. 2, see *Storer v. Wright* [1981] 2 W.L.R. 208, C.A.

sch. 2, regs. 87/2098.

5. Horticulture (Special Payments) Act 1974.

Royal Assent, February 8, 1974.

s. 1, schemes 74/1003; 75/1999.

6. Biological Weapons Act 1974.

Royal Assent, February 8, 1974.

s. 2, repealed in pt.: 1975, c.59, sch.6; 1978, c.23, sch.7.

s. 4, repealed in pt.: 1984, c.60, sch.7.

s. 6, orders 74/1110–1112; 75/240.

7. Local Government Act 1974.

Royal Assent, February 8, 1974.

see *R. v. Local Commissioner for Administration for the North and North East Area of England, ex p. Bradford City Metropolitan Council* [1979] 2 W.L.R. 1, C.A.

s. 1, amended: 1976, c.32, sch.4; 1979, c.55, sch.2; 1980, c.65, s.69, sch.32; repealed in pt.: 1975, c.2, sch.; 1980, c.65, sch.34; 1985, c.71, sch.1.

s. 1, regs. 74/1060.

s. 2, see *R. v. Secretary of State for the Environment, ex p. Hackney L.B.C. and Camden L.B.C.,* (1984) 81 L.S.Gaz. 664, C.A.

s. 2, regs. 74/788; 75/5; 76/214; 78/171, 1701; 79/1514; 80/37; 84/85; 88/1951.

s. 3, orders 74/550, 2109; 75/2149; 76/2201–2203; 77/2113; 78/1867; 80/57.

s. 4, orders 74/2108; 75/2150; 76/2201–2203; 77/2114, 2115; 78/1868, 1869; 80/58, 59, 2048, 2049; 82/186.

s. 5, regs. 75/1054; 78/1144; 81/1086; 82/106.

s. 6, amended: 1978, c.55, s.22; 1985, c.51, s.8; repealed in pt.: 1978, c.55, s.22, sch. 4; 1980, c.66, sch.25; 1985, c.51, sch. 17; 1988, c.41, s.125, sch.13 (prosp.).

s. 7, amended: 1985, c.51, sch.3.

s. 8, amended: *ibid.*; repealed in pt.: 1975, c.2, sch.; 1982, c.24, sch.5; 1988 c.40, sch.13.

s. 9, amended: 1982, c.24, sch.5.

s. 10, regs. 74/428, 1987; 75/1950; 76/2071; 77/1342, 1941, 2002; 78/1701; 79/337, 1514; 80/877; 81/311.

s. 10, amended: 1980, c.65, s.68.

CAP.

1974—cont.

7. Local Government Act 1974—cont.

s. 11, regs. 74/411, 412, 1086, 1321; 75/327; 76/1458, 1745; 77/1500; 78/387, 1504; 79/417, 1309; 80/1625; 81/1474; 82/1491.

ss. 11–14, repealed: 1982, c.25, sch.5.

s. 13, orders 14/411, 412.

s. 15, see *Investors in Industry Commercial Properties v. Norwich City Council* [1986] 2 W.L.R. 925, H.L.

ss. 15, 16, see *Windsor Securities v. Liverpool City Council* (1979) 250 E.G. 57, C.A.

s. 19, orders 75/540; 76/206, 207, 490, 535; 77/2083; 79/1516; 83/547; 85/102; 88/974; amended: 1977, c.11, s.4.

s. 20, repealed: 1978, c.40, sch.2.

s. 21, see *White v. Bromidge* (1979) 251 E.G. 469, C.A.; *Wright, Re; Maudsley, Re; Smith, Re, The Times,* January 16, 1985; (1985) 274 E.G. 717, C.A.; *Appeal of Maudsley (V.O.), Re* (Ref. LVC/184/1982) (1986) 26 R.V.R. 181.

s. 21, order 74/629.

s. 22, orders 76/206, 207, 535; 79/1516; 83/547.

s. 23, order 76/490.

ss. 23, 24, amended: 1988, c.9, sch.3.

s. 24, orders 74/683, 707; 83/1661.

s. 25, amended: 1975, c.77, sch.10; 1980, c.20, s.7; 1985, c.51, sch.14; order 85/1884; 1988, c.9, sch.3; c.50, sch.17; repealed in pt.: 1980, c.65, sch.34; 1988, c.40, sch.13 (prosp.).

s. 26, see *Croydon London Borough Council v. Commissioner for Local Administration, The Times,* June 9, 1988, D.C.

s. 26, order 88/242.

s. 26, amended: 1985, c.51, sch.14; order 85/1884; 1988, c.9, sch.3.

ss. 26, 34, see *R. v. Local Commissioner for Administration for North Area of England, ex p. Bradford City Metropolitan Council* [1979] 2 W.L.R. 1, C.A.; *R. v. Local Commissioner for Administration for the South, the West Midlands, Leicestershire, Lincolnshire and Cambridgeshire, ex p. Eastleigh Borough Council* [1988] 3 W.L.R. 113, C.A.

s. 29, amended: 1977, c.49, sch.15.

s. 30, amended: 1975, c.77, sch.10; 1988, c.9, sch.3.

s. 31, amended: 1975, c.77, sch.10.

s. 32, see *Re A Complainant against Liverpool City Council* [1975] 2 All E.R. 650, D.C.

s. 32, amended: 1980, c.65, sch.34; 1988, c.9, sch.3.

s. 33, amended: 1977, c.49, sch.15.

s. 34, see *R. v. Local Commissioner for Administration for the South, the West Midlands, Leicestershire, Lincolnshire and Cambridgeshire, ex p. Eastleigh Borough Council, The Times,* July 14, 1987, Nolan J.

s. 34, amended: 1988, c.4, sch.6; repealed in pt.: 1985, c.51, sch.17.

s. 37, repealed: 1985, c.71, sch.1.

s. 40, repealed: 1980, c.66, sch.25.

s. 43, order 78/1583.

s. 43, repealed in pt.: 1975, c.24, sch.3; c.25, sch.3; orders 74/335; 77/943.

1974—cont.

7. Local Government Act 1974—*cont.*
s. 103, regs. 80/37.
sch. 1, orders 74/2108; 80/660.
sch. 1, amended: 1984, c.32, sch.6; repealed in pt.: 1980, c.65, sch.34; c.66, sch.25; 1984, c.32, sch.6,7.
sch. 2, regs. 74/428, 1987; 75/1950; 76/1939, 2071; 77/1432, 1941, 2002; 78/1701; 79/337, 1514.
sch. 2, amended: 1980, c.20, s.32, sch.6.
sch. 3, order 79/1516.
sch. 3, amended: 1984, c.12, s.31; c.33, sch. 1; 1986, c.44, sch.7; 1987, c.3, sch.1; c.53, s.30; repealed in pt.: 1981, c.38, sch. 6; 1984, c.12, sch.7.
sch. 4, orders 74/2024; 75/176; 81/1857; 83/1480.
sch. 4, amended: 1985, c.51, sch.8; repealed in pt.: 1975, c.24, sch.3; c.25, sch.3; 1988, c.9, schs.3,7.
sch. 5, amended: 1986, c.61, sch.4; 1988, c.9, sch.3; c.40, sch.12.
sch. 6, repealed in pt.: 1977, c.49, sch.16; 1980, c.66, sch.25; 1981, c.22, sch.6.; 1984, c.27, sch.14; c.30, sch.11; c.32, sch.7; 1985, c.12, sch.2; c.67, sch.8; c.72, sch.13; 1986, c.63, sch.12.
sch. 7, repealed in pt.: 1976, c.70, sch.8; 1980, c.65, sch.34; c.66, sch.25; 1984, c.32, sch.7.

8. Statutory Corporations (Financial Provisions) Act 1974.
Royal Assent, February 8, 1974.
s. 1, repealed: 1975, c.55, sch.5.
s. 2, orders 74/1959, 1960, 1965, 2065; repealed: 1975, c.55, sch.5; repealed in pt.: 1977, c.13, sch.2.
s. 3, repealed: 1975, c.55, sch.5.
s. 5, amended: 1974, c.21, sch.3; repealed in pt.: 1975, c.55, sch.5.
sch. 1, repealed: *ibid.*
sch. 2, repealed in pt.: *ibid.*; c.64, sch.7; c.78, sch.6; 1976, c.51, sch.; 1980, c.34, sch.9; c 60, sch.3; 1981, c.38, sch.6.
sch. 3, repealed in pt.: 1975, c.42, s.3; 1981, c.64, sch.13.

9. Pensions (Increase) Act 1974.
Royal Assent, February 8, 1974.
ss. 1, 4, regs. 74/715, 813, 882, 914, 940, 975, 985, 1531, 1532, 1702, 1729, 1778, 1805.
s. 3, repealed in pt.: 1975, c.60, sch.5.
s. 4, amended: orders 74/1264, 1759; repealed in pt.: order 79/1451.
s. 6, repealed in pt.: 1985, c.58, sch.4.
sch., amended: regs. 74/715.

10. Representation of the People Act 1974.
Royal Assent, February 8, 1974.

11. Charlwood and Horley Act 1974.
Royal Assent, February 8, 1974.
s. 2, orders 74/772, 1353.

12. Consolidated Fund (No. 2) Act 1974.
repealed: 1976, c.43, sch.D.

13. Representation of the People (No. 2) Act 1974.
Royal Assent, April 10, 1974.
repealed: 1977, c.9, sch.

1974—cont.

14. National Insurance Act 1974.
Royal Assent, May 13, 1974.
ss. 1–4, repealed: 1975, c.18, sch.1.
s. 5, repealed: 1975, c.11, sch.6.
s. 6, regs. 84/451, 614; 86/2218; 87/214.
s. 6, amended: 1975, c.18, sch.2; c.60, sch.4; c.61, sch.4; 1976, c.71, sch.7; 1982, c.24, sch.4; regs. 75/572; 1986, c.50, sch.10; repealed in pt.: 1975, c.18, sch.1; 1986, c.50, sch.11.
s. 7, repealed: 1975, c.1, sch.1; repealed in pt.: 1975, c.11, sch.6.
s. 8, order 74/841; repealed in pt.: 1975, c.18, sch.1; 1976, c.71, sch.8.
sch. 1, repealed: 1975, c.11, sch.6.
sch. 2, repealed: 1975, c.18, sch.1.
sch. 3, repealed: 1975, c.11, sch.6.
sch. 4, repealed in pt.: 1975, c.11, sch.6; c.18, sch.1; c.60, sch.5; order 75/1503.
sch. 5, order 74/841; repealed: 1975, c.18, sch.1.
sch. 6, repealed: *ibid.*

15. Consolidated Fund (No. 3) Act 1974.
Royal Assent, May 23, 1974.
repealed: 1976, c.43, sch.D.

16. Independent Broadcasting Authority Act 1974.
Royal Assent, May 23, 1974.
repealed: 1981, c.68, sch.9.

17. Rabies Act 1974.
Royal Assent, May 23, 1974.
repealed: 1981, c.22, sch.6.
see *R. v. Sands* (1976) 63 Cr.App.R. 297, C.A.

18. Contingencies Fund Act 1974.
Royal Assent, May 23, 1974.

19. Lord High Commissioner (Church of Scotland) Act 1974.
Royal Assent, June 27, 1974.

20. Dumping at Sea Act 1974.
Royal Assent, June 27, 1974.
repealed: 1985, c.48, s.15.
s. 15, orders 75/810, 811, 1831, 2180.

21. Ministers of the Crown Act 1974.
Royal Assent, June 27, 1974.
repealed: 1975, c.27, sch.3.
s. 3, sch. 1, regs. 74/1867.

22. Statute Law (Repeals) Act 1974.
Royal Assent, June 27, 1974.
s. 3, orders 83/763; 84/1692.

23. Juries Act 1974.
Royal Assent, July 9, 1974.
s. 1, amended: 1988, c.33, s.119.
s. 2, amended: 1982, c.53, s.61.
s. 3, amended: 1983, c.2, sch.8; 1988, c.33, sch.15; repealed in pt.: 1983, c.2, sch.9.
s. 6, amended: 1988, c.33, sch.15.
s. 9, rules 82/1109.
s. 9, repealed in pt.: 1981, c.55, sch.5.
s. 9A, added: 1988, c.33, s.120.
s. 11, see *R. v. Binns* [1982] Crim.L.R. 522, Stocker J.
s. 12, see *R. v. Harrington* (1976) 64 Cr.App.R. 1, C.A.; *R. v. Paling* (1978) 67 Cr.App.R. 299, C.A.; amended: 1977, c.45, s.43.
s. 12, repealed in pt.: 1988, c.33, sch.16.

CAP.

1974—cont.

23. Juries Act 1974—cont.

s. 16, see *R.* v. *Hambery* [1977] 2 W.L.R. 999, C.A.; *R.* v. *Richardson* [1979] 3 All E.R. 247, C.A.

s. 16, repealed in pt.: 1988, c.33, s.121, sch.16.

s. 17, see *R.* v. *Barry* (*Christopher*) [1975] 1 W.L.R. 1190; [1975] 2 All E.R. 760, C.A.; *R.* v. *Reynolds* [1981] Crim.L.R. 706; [1981] 3 All E.R. 849, C.A.; *R.* v. *Pigg* [1983] 1 W.L.R. 6, H.L.; *R.* v. *Thornton, The Times,* June 7, 1988, C.A.

s. 18, see *R.* v. *Chapman* (1976) 63 Cr.App.R. 75, C.A.; *R.* v. *Bliss* [1986] Crim.L.R. 467; (1987) 84 Cr.App.R. 1, C.A.

s. 19, regs. 74/1461; 75/2016; 78/1579.

s. 19, amended: 1977, c.38, sch.2; 1988, c.13, sch.3; repealed in pt.: 1975, c.18, sch.1; 1977, c.38, sch.5; regs. 75/750; 77/4.

s. 20, amended: 1988, c.33, sch.15.

sch. 1, amended: 1982, c.48, sch.14; c.51, sch.3; 1983, c.20, sch.4; 1984, c.34, sch.1; 1988, c.33, s.119, sch.8; repealed in pt.: 1976, c.52, sch.10; 1978, c.51, s.75; c.52, s.33; 1981, c.55, sch.5.

sch. 2, repealed: 1988, c.13, sch.4.

24. Prices Act 1974.

Royal Assent, July 9, 1974.

order 76/1269.

s. 1, orders 74/1240, 1323, 1487, 1913, 1985; amended: 1975, c.32, s.1; orders 76/358, 952.

s. 2, orders 74/1711, 1984; 75/38, 166, 279, 527, 551, 713, 715, 1074, 1083, 1243–45, 1499, 1721, 1740, 1953, 1954, 2020; 76/97, 511, 873, 1250, 1268, 1658, 1737, 1929, 1937, 1938, 1975, 2128; 77/192, 193, 360, 535, 769, 786, 934, 935, 1166, 1929; 78/97, 98, 516, 545, 835, 971, 1014, 1790; 79/34, 384, 660; 80/4; 81/1019; 82/1169; 85/995; 86/175.

s. 2, amended: 1975, c.32, s.2; order 75/527.

s. 3, repealed: 1977, c.33, s.16, sch.3.

s. 4, see *Warinco A.G.* v. *Samor S.p.A.* [1979] 1 Lloyd's Rep. 450, C.A.

s. 4, orders 74/1368, 1369; 75/1317, 1737; 76/796; 77/293, 1057, 1334, 1412; 78/133, 738; 79/4, 361, 364, 1124; 80/1121; S.Rs. 1978 No. 60; 1979 Nos. 293, 294, 405, 408, 414, 427; 1980 Nos. 263, 337; 87/8.

s. 4, amended: 1977, c.33, s.16.

s. 6, order 74/1218; repealed in pt.: 1975, c.24, sch.3; c.25, sch.3.

s. 7, see *South London Tyre and Battery Centre* v. *Bexley London Borough* [1981] R.T.R. 258, D.C.

s. 8, order 74/1323.

sch., orders 74/1566; 76/1205; 77/934, 935; amended: 1975, c.32, ss.1,2; 1977, c.33, s.16; regs. 77/1224; repealed in pt.: 1980, c.21, sch.2.

25. Lord Chancellor (Tenure of Office and Discharge of Ecclesiastical Functions) Act 1974.

Royal Assent, July 9, 1974.

CAP.

1974—cont.

26. Solicitors (Amendment) Act 1974.

Royal Assent, July 17, 1974.

repealed: 1974, c.47, sch.4.

s. 19, order 75/534.

27. Education (Mentally Handicapped Children) (Scotland) Act 1974.

Royal Assent, July 17, 1974.

s. 1, orders 75/307, 748.

28. Northern Ireland Act 1974.

Royal Assent, July 17, 1974.

Commencement orders: 85/60; 87/449; 88/1, 2, 4; S.Rs. 1984 No. 143, 300, 422; 1987, Nos. 6, 20, 308.

s. 1, orders 77/1165; 78/957; 79/816; 81/998; 82/957, 1078; 83/779; 85/1054; 86/1047; 87/1207; 88/1181.

ss. 1 (in pt.), 2, repealed: 1982, c.38, sch.3.

sch. 1, orders 77/177, 228, 315, 610, 1245–1249, 1250–1254, 2151–2154, 2156–2158; 78/1036–1051, 1406, 1585, 1906–1909; 79/294, 296, 297, 922–926, 1572, 1573, 1574, 1575, 1710, 1713, 1714; 80/396, 397, 561, 563, 704, 869, 870, 993, 1083–1088, 1626, 1709, 1957–1959; 81/154–156, 158, 159, 226–228, 230, 231, 435–438, 607–610, 838, 839, 1114–1118, 1675, 1799, 1813; 82/155–158, 337–339, 528, 712, 713, 846, 1080–1084, 1534–1537, 1831, 1833, 1840; 83/147–150, 419–421, 764, 766, 767, 1117–1121, 1524, 1895, 1896, 1899, 1900, 1905; 84/359, 702–704, 1156–1159, 1167; 1821, 1822, 1983, 1984, 1986; 85/60, 170, 171, 452, 453, 754–756, 957–959; S.Rs. 1978 Nos. 11, 12, 17, 21, 42, 199, 232, 245, 271, 309, 348, 362, 406; 1979 Nos. 191, 213, 270, 292, 325, 334; 1980 Nos. 128, 165, 212, 463; 1981 Nos. 20, 85, 221, 227, 284, 401; 1982 Nos. 207, 238, 249, 261, 267, 286, 290, 299, 380; 1983 Nos. 93, 165, 202; 1984 Nos. 15, 143, 291, 300, 422; 1985 Nos. 82, 136, 188, 218, 247; 1986 Nos. 107, 124, 169, 363; 1987 Nos. 6, 20, 21, 121, 137, 161, 184, 185, 200, 271, 308, 449; 1988 Nos. 1, 2, 4, 116, 180, 216, 254, 380, 594.

sch. 1, amended: order 79/1573.

sch. 2, repealed: 1982, c.38, s.3.

29. Parks Regulation (Amendment) Act 1974.

Royal Assent, July 17, 1974.

30. Finance Act 1974.

Royal Assent, July 31, 1974.

s. 1, amended: 1984, c.43, ss.22, 24, 25; repealed in pt.: 1975, c.45, sch.14; 1977, c.36, sch.9; 1979, c.2, sch.6; 1984, c.43, sch.23.

s. 2, repealed in pt.: 1981, c.35, sch.19; c.63, sch.7; 1986, c.41, sch.23.

s. 3, repealed: 1977, c.36, sch.9.

s. 4, repealed: 1979, c.4, sch.4.

s. 5, repealed: 1977, c.36, sch.9.

s. 6, repealed: 1983, c.55, sch.11.

ss. 7–16, repealed: 1988, c.1, sch.31.

s. 8, see *James* v. *I.R.C.* [1977] 1 W.L.R. 835, Slade J.

s. 17, repealed in pt.: 1985, c.54, schs. 14, 17.

CAP.

1974—cont.

30. Finance Act 1974—cont.
ss. 18–23, repealed: 1988, c.1, sch.31.
s. 20, repealed in pt.: 1988, c.39, sch.14.
s. 24, amended: 1978, c.42, sch.9.
ss. 25–28, 30, repealed: 1988, c.1, sch.31.
ss. 31–33, repealed: 1979, c.14, sch.8.
s. 34, repealed: 1978, c.42, sch.13.
s. 35, order 80/114; repealed: 1980, c.48, sch.20.
ss. 36, 37, repealed: 1988, c.1, sch.31.
s. 38, see *Pogson* v. *Lowe* [1983] S.T.C. 365, C.A.
ss. 38–47, repealed: 1985, c.54, sch.27.
s. 48, repealed: 1979, c.14, sch.8.
s. 49, repealed in pt.: 1982, c.39, sch.22.
s. 51, repealed in pt.: 1975, c.7, sch.13.
s. 52, repealed in pt.: *ibid.*; 1988, c.1, sch.31.
s. 53, repealed: S.L.R. 1986.
s. 55, orders 74/2054; 79/722, 761 (S.); 80/496, 504 (S.); 81/400, 458 (S.).
s. 57, amended: 1979, c.14, sch.7; repealed in pt.: 1979, c.2, sch.6; c.14, sch.8; 1983, c.55, sch.11; 1985, c.54, sch.27.
sch. 1, see *Hendy* v. *Hadley* [1980] 2 All E.R. 554, Vinelott J.; *Frost* v. *Feltham* [1981] 1 W.L.R. 452, Nourse J.; *Hughes (Inspector of Taxes)* v. *Viner* [1985] 3 All E.R. 40; [1985] S.T.C. 235, Walton J.
sch. 1, repealed: 1988, c.1, sch.31.
sch. 2, see *Cooke* v. *Blacklaws* [1985] S.T.C. 1, Gibson J.
sch. 2, repealed: 1988, c.1, sch.31.
sch. 3, repealed: 1985, c.54, sch.27.
sch. 4, see *Pogson* v. *Lowe* [1984] 1 W.L.R. 183, H.L.; *Furniss* v. *Ford* (1981) 55 T.C. 561; [1981] T.R. 255, Vinelott J.
sch. 4, repealed: 1985, c.54, sch.27.
sch. 5, repealed: 1976, c.40, sch.15.
schs. 6–10, repealed: 1985, c.54, sch.27.
sch. 11, repealed: 1984, c.43, s.109, sch.23; repealed in pt.: 1986, c.41, sch.23.
sch. 12, repealed in pt.: 1975, c.7, sch.13; 1986, c.41, sch.23; 1988, c.1, sch.31.
schs. 13, 14 (in pt.), repealed: S.L.R. 1986.

31. Appropriation (No. 2) Act 1974.
Royal Assent, July 31, 1974.
repealed: 1976, c.43, sch.D.

32. Town and Country Amenities Act 1974.
Royal Assent, July 31, 1974.
regs. 77/228.
ss. 1, 2, 10, 11, repealed in pt.: 1981, c.19, sch.1.
ss. 3 (in pt.), 5, repealed: 1986, c.63, sch.12.
s. 5, repealed (S.): *ibid.*
s. 7, regs. 74/1336.
s. 13, orders 75/147, 1202.
s. 13, repealed in pt.: 1979, c.46, sch.5.

33. Northern Ireland (Young Persons) Act 1974.
Royal Assent, July 31, 1974.
repealed: 1978, c.5, sch.6.
s. 3, orders 77/2142, 2155.

34. Pakistan Act 1974.
Royal Assent, July 31, 1974.

CAP.

1974—cont.

35. Carriage of Passengers by Road Act 1974.
Royal Assent, July 31, 1974.
s. 8, amended: 1979, c.28, s.3; 1983, c.14, sch.2; repealed in pt.: 1979, c.28, ss.3,6.
s. 11, amended: order 81/226.
sch., amended: 1979, c.28, s.4.

36. Mines (Working Facilities and Support) Act 1974.
Royal Assent, July 31, 1974.
s. 1, see *Re W. J. King & Sons' Application* [1976] 1 W.L.R. 521; [1976] 1 All E.R. 770, C.A.
s. 2, repealed: S.L.R. 1977.

37. Health and Safety at Work etc. Act 1974.
Royal Assent, July 31, 1974.
see *Page* v. *Freighthire Tank Haulage, The Times,* November 5, 1980, E.A.T.
s. 1, regs. 83/943.
s. 1, amended: 1975, c.71, sch.15; repealed in pt.: *ibid.,* sch.18.
s. 2, see *R.* v. *Swan Hunter Shipbuilders* [1981] I.C.R. 831, C.A.; *Page* v. *Freight Hire (Tank Haulage)* [1981] I.C.R. 299; [1981] 1 All E.R. 394, E.A.T.; *Osborne* v. *Bill Taylor of Huyton* [1982] I.C.R. 168, D.C.; *Briggs Amasco* v. *Smith,* 1981 S.C.C.R. 274; *West Bromwich Building Society* v. *Townsend* [1983] I.C.R. 257, McNeill J.; *Dutton & Clark* v. *Daly* [1985] I.R.L.R. 363, E.A.T.; *Tudhope* v. *City of Glasgow District Council,* 1986 S.C.C.R. 168; *Tesco Stores* v. *Seabridge, The Times,* April 29, 1988, D.C.
s. 2, regs. 75/1584; 77/500; 82/1496; 84/1244; 86/890; 88/766.
s. 2, amended: 1975, c.71, sch.15; repealed in pt.: *ibid.,* sch.18.
s. 3, see *Skinner* v. *John G. McGregor (Contractors),* 1977 S.L.T.(Sh.Ct.) 83; *Aitchison* v. *Howard Doris,* 1979 S.L.T.(Notes) 22; *R.* v. *Swan Hunter Shipbuilders* [1981] I.C.R. 831, C.A.; *Carmichael* v. *Rosehall Engineering Works* [1983] I.R.L.R. 480, High Court of Justiciary, 1983 S.C.C.R. 353, 415; *R.* v. *Mara* [1987] 1 W.L.R. 87, C.A.; *Sterling-Winthrop Group* v. *Allan,* 1987 S.C.C.R. 25.
s. 4, see *B.P. Oil* v. *Smith,* 1982 S.C.C.R. 482; *T. Kilroe & Sons* v. *Gower* [1983] Crim.L.R. 548, Liverpool Crown Ct.; *Westminster City Council* v. *Select Management* [1985] 1 All E.R. 897, C.A.
s. 5, regs. 83/943.
s. 6, modified: regs. 80/907; amended: 1987, c.43, sch.3.
s. 7, see *Coult* v. *Szouba* [1982] R.T.R. 376, D.C.
s. 10, amended: 1975, c.71, sch.15.
ss. 10, 11, see *Hadley* v. *Hancox, The Times,* November 18, 1986, D.C.
s. 11, regs. 76/455, 1246, 2005; 77/746, 913, 918, 1841; 78/209, 270, 635, 752, 807, 1126, 1516, 1702; 79/318, 427, 1203, 1298, 1378; 80/907, 942, 1100; 81/16, 270, 686, 687, 695, 792, 917, 1011, 1059, 1152, 1327, 1332, 1333, 1486, 1652; 82/247, 630, 695, 827, 877, 1418, 1496, 1503; 83/17, 70, 219, 484,

395

CAP.

1974—cont.
37. Health and Safety at Work etc. Act 1974—
cont.

644, 710, 714, 1140, 1450, 1640, 1919;
84/310, 569, 605, 1114, 1244, 1593, 1598,
1890, 1902; 85/279, 910, 1107, 1108, 1333,
1601, 2023; 87/605.

s. 11, amended: 1975, c.71, sch.15; repealed in pt.: *ibid.*, sch.18.

s. 14, regs. 75/335; 76/1246; amended: 1975, c.71, sch.15; 1976, c.14, sch.1 (S.); 1978, c.51, sch.16; c.52, sch.11; repealed in pt.: 1975, c.71, sch.18.

s. 15, regs. 74/1775, 1776, 1820, 1821, 1840, 1841, 1885–87, 1941–43, 1986, 2166; 75/45, 46, 282, 303, 1011, 1012, 1102, 1695; 76/455, 881, 1247, 1908, 2003–05, 2063; 77/500, 746, 913, 918, 1205, 1841; 78/209, 270, 635, 752, 807, 1126, 1516, 1648, 1702, 1723, 1951; 79/318, 427, 1203, 1298, 1378; 80/804, 907, 942, 1036, 1100, 1248, 1314, 1471, 1980; 81/399, 792, 917, 1011, 1059, 1333, 1498, 1652; 82/630, 695, 1357, 1418, 1496, 1503; 83/17, 19, 710, 943, 977, 978, 1130, 1140, 1450, 1502, 1640, 1649; 84/510, 605, 1114, 1244, 1593, 1598, 1890, 1902; 85/910, 1107, 1108, 1333, 1601, 2023; 86/890, 1709, 1922, 1951; 87/180, 2115; 88/711, 766, 1462, 1655–1657, 1729, 1930; orders 87/37, 52.

s. 15, amended: 1975, c.71, sch.15; 1977, c.45, sch.12.

ss. 15, 18, see *Hadley* v. *Hancox, The Times,* November 18, 1986, D.C.

s. 16, amended: 1975, c 71, sch.15; repealed in pt.: *ibid.*, sch.18.

s. 18, regs. 77/746; 79/427; 85/1107; amended: 1975, c.71, sch.15; repealed in pt.: *ibid.*, sch.18.

s. 20, see *Skinner* v. *John G. McGregor (Contractors),* 1977 S.L.T.(Sh.Ct.) 83; *Tudhope* v. *Laws,* 1982 S.L.T.(Sh.Ct.) 85; *Laws* v. *Keane,* 1983 S.L.T. 40; [1982] I.R.L.R. 500, High Ct. of Scotland.

s. 22, amended: 1987, c.43, sch.3.

s. 24, see *Chrysler United Kingdom* v. *McCarthy* [1978] I.C.R. 939, D.C.; *British Airways Board* v. *Henderson* [1979] I.C.R. 77, Industrial Tribunal.

s. 24, regs. 74/1925, 1926.

ss. 25A, 27A, added: 1987, c.43, sch.3.

s. 27, amended: 1988, c.19, sch.3.

s. 28, amended: 1975, c.71, sch.15; 1985, c.51, sch.14; order 85/1884; 1987, c.43, sch.3; 1988, c.4, sch.6; repealed in pt. (prosp.): 1988, c.40, sch.13.

s. 29, repealed: 1975, c.71, schs.15,18.

s. 30, regs. 75/45, 46, 282; repealed: 1975, c.71, schs.15,18.

ss. 31, 32, repealed: *ibid.*

s. 33, see *Skinner* v. *John G. McGregor (Contractors),* 1977 S.L.T.(Sh.Ct.) 83; *Aitchison* v. *Howard Doris,* 1979 S.L.T.(Notes) 22; *R.* v. *Swan Hunter Shipbuilders* [1981] I.C.R. 831, C.A.; *Coult* v. *Szouba* [1982] R.T.R. 376, D.C.; *Carmichael* v. *Rosehall Engineering Works,* 1983 S.C.C.R. 353; *Kemp* v. *Liebherr—Great*

CAP.

1974—cont.
37. Health and Safety at Work etc. Act 1974—
cont.

Britain, The Times, November 5, 1986, D.C.; *Tesco Stores* v. *Seabridge, The Times,* April 29, 1988, D.C.

s. 33, amended: 1975, c.71, sch.15; 1977, c.45, ss.15,30,31, schs.1,6; 1987, c.43, sch.3; repealed in pt.: 1975, c.71, sch.18; 1981, c.45, sch.

ss. 33, 36, see *West Cumberland By Products* v. *D.P.P., The Times,* November 12, 1987, D.C.

ss. 33, 37, see *Briggs Amasco* v. *Smith,* 1981 S.C.C.R. 274.

ss. 33, 40, see *Deary* v. *Mansion Hyde Upholsteries* [1983] I.R.L.R. 195, Q.B.D.; *B.P. Oil* v. *Smith,* 1982 S.C.C.R. 482.

s. 34, amended: 1986, c.44, sch.7.

s. 37, see *Armour* v. *Skeen,* 1977 S.L.T. 71; *Wotherspoon* v. *H.M. Advocate,* 1978 J.C. 74; *Dutton & Clark* v. *Daly* [1985] I.C.R. 780, E.A.T.

s. 38, see *Campbell* v. *Wallsend Slipway and Engineering Co.* [1978] I.C.R. 1015, D.C.

s. 43, regs. 78/1723; 79/1553; 80/1233; 81/270, 334; 82/247; 83/70, 484, 714, 1140, 1450, 1649; 84/310, 569, 1890, 1902; 85/279, 1333, 86/392, 669; 87/605, 2115; 88/712; orders 87/37, 52.

ss. 43, 44, 47, amended: 1975, c.71, sch.15; repealed in pt.: *ibid.*, sch.18.

s. 47, regs. 82/630; 83/1140.

s. 49, regs. 74/1775, 1776, 1820, 1821, 1840, 1841, 1885–87, 1941–43, 1986; 76/455, 2063; 78/1648; 80/1690; 81/16, 686, 687, 695, 917, 1152, 1327, 1332, 1414, 1486; 82/827, 877; 83/644, 943, 977–979, 994, 1026; 84/510, 1593.

s. 49, amended: 1975, c.71, sch.15; repealed in pt.: *ibid.*, sch.18.

s. 50, regs. 75/45, 46; 76/455, 1246, 2005; 77/746, 888–890, 913, 918; 78/270, 635, 752, 807, 1126, 1516, 1702; 79/1203, 1298, 1378; 80/907, 942, 1100, 1471; 81/16, 686, 695, 792, 917, 1011, 1059, 1152, 1327, 1332, 1333, 1486, 1652; 82/630, 695, 827, 877, 1357, 1418, 1496, 1503; 83/17, 219, 644, 710, 1140, 1919; 84/510, 605, 1593, 1598, 1890, 1902; 85/910, 1107, 1108, 1333, 1601, 2023; 87/180.

s. 50, amended: 1975, c.71, sch.15; repealed in pt.: *ibid.*, sch.18.

s. 52, see *Coult* v. *Szouba* [1982] R.T.R. 376, D.C.

s. 52, regs. 78/752; 81/1011, 1059; 83/1919; 85/1333; 88/1222.

s. 52, amended: 1975, c.71, sch.15.

s. 53, see *Westminster City Council* v. *Select Management* [1985] 1 All E.R. 897, C.A.

s. 53, regs. 81/687.

s. 53, amended: 1975, c.71, sch.15; 1987, c.43, sch.3; repealed in pt.: 1975, c.71, sch.15; 1985, c.51, sch.17; 1987, c.43, sch.5.

s. 55, amended: 1988, c.19, sch.3.

1974—cont.

37. Health and Safety at Work etc. Act 1974— *cont.*

s. 60, regs. 70/1553.

s. 60, amended: 1980, c.53, sch.1; 1981, c.54, sch.5; repealed in pt.: *ibid.*, sch.7; S.L.R. 1986.

s. 61, regs. 81/1338; 83/195.

s. 62, regs. 79/601; 80/286; 82/577; 83/195.

ss. 61–74, 76, repealed: 1984, c.55, sch.7.

s. 72, regs. 80/286.

s. 76, regs. 82/577; 83/1611.

s. 78, repealed in pt.: 1987, c.27, sch.4.

s. 79, repealed: 1985, c.9, sch.1.

s. 80, regs. 74/1775, 1776, 1820, 1821, 1840, 1841, 1885–87, 1941–43, 1986, 2056, 2170; 76/2007; 77/500; 83/943; 84/1244; 85/1333; order 87/37.

s. 80, amended: 1975, c.71, sch.15; 1978, c.44, sch.16; regs. 81/399.

s. 82, regs. 74/1775, 1776, 1820, 1821, 1840, 1841, 1885–87, 1941–43, 1986, 2011–13, 2056, 2170; 76/2003–05, 2063; 77/500, 746; 78/209, 752, 1648, 1723; 80/1471; 81/399, 792, 1152, 1327, 1332, 1333, 1414, 1486, 1652; 82/827, 877, 1357, 1418, 1496, 1503; 83/17, 70, 644, 710, 978, 994, 1026, 1140, 1640, 1649; 84/510, 1114, 1244, 1593, 1890, 1902; 85/1333; 86/392, 1922, 1951; 87/180, 605, 2115; 88/712, 766, 1462, 1655–1657, 1930; orders 87/37, 52.

s. 84, order 77/1232; amended: 1975, c.71, sch.15; repealed in pt.: 1975, c.24, sch.3; c.71, sch.18.

s. 85, orders 74/1439; 75/344; 77/294; 80/208, 269 (S.).

sch. 1, amended: 1975, c.65, sch.5; 1986, c.59, sch.

sch. 2, see *Campbell* v. *Wallsend Slipway and Eng. Co.* [1978] I.C.R. 1015, D.C.

sch. 3, regs. 76/2063; 77/913; 78/209, 752, 1702, 1723; 79/318, 1203; 80/804, 942, 1248, 1471; 81/399, 917, 1011, 1059; 82/630, 695, 1357, 1496; 83/710, 1130, 1649; 84/510, 1114, 1244, 1890, 1902; 85/910, 1333, 2023; 86/890, 1951; 87/2115; 88/711, 1462, 1655–1657, 1729, 1930; order 87/37.

sch. 3, amended: 1979, c.2, sch.4.

sch. 5, regs. 81/1338; 83/195.

schs. 5, 6, repealed: 1984, c.55, sch.7.

sch. 9, repealed in pt.: 1987, c.39, sch.2; 1988, c.4, sch.4.

sch. 10, repealed in pt.: 1984, c.29, sch.12; c.55, sch.7; 1985, c.51, sch.17.

38. Land Tenure Reform (Scotland) Act 1974.

Royal Assent, July 31, 1974.

s. 1, see *George Packman & Sons* v. *Dunbar's Trs.* (O.H.), 1977 S.L.T. 140.

s. 8, amended: 1985, c.73, s.1; 1987, c.26, sch.23; repealed in pt.: 1986, c.65, sch.2.

39. Consumer Credit Act 1974.

Royal Assent, July 31, 1974.

Commencement order: 84/436.

s. 8, amended: order 83/1878.

ss. 9, 15, see *Moorgate Mercantile Leasing* v. *Isobel Gell and Ugolini Dispensers (U.K.),*

1974—cont.

39. Consumer Credit Act 1974—*cont.*

October 21, 1985, H.H. Judge Rice, Grays Thurrock County Court.

ss. 11, 12, see *United Dominions Trust* v. *Taylor,* 1980 S.L.T.(Sh.Ct.) 28; *U.D.T.* v. *Whitfield,* June 12, 1986, Judge Vos, Newcastle County Ct.

s. 14, see *Elliott* v. *Director-General of Fair Trading* [1980] 1 W.L.R. 977, D.C.

s. 15, amended: order 83/1878.

s. 16, orders 77/326, 1493; 78/126, 1616; 79/1099; 80/52; 81/964; 82/1029; 83/434, 917; 85/620, 757, 1736, 1918; 86/1105, 2186; 87/1578; 88/707, 991.

s. 16, amended: 1981, c.38, sch.3; 1984, c.12, sch.4; 1986, c.53, sch.18; c.63, c.22; 1987, c.22, s.88; c.26, sch.23(S.); 1988, c.50, sch.17; repealed in pt.: 1975, c.71, sch.18; 1986, c.53, sch.19.

s. 17, amended: order 83/1878.

s. 19, regs. 83/1560; 85/1192.

s. 20, regs. 77/327; 80/51.

s. 22, regs. 75/2124; 76/1002; 79/796; 86/1016.

s. 26, regs. 77/330; 83/1565.

s. 37, regs. 76/1002; 81/614.

s. 39, see *Hicks* v. *Walker* [1984] Crim.L.R. 495, D.C.; *Brookes* v. *Retail Credit Cards* [1986] Crim.L.R. 327, D.C.

s. 41, regs. 76/837.

s. 43, orders 80/53, 1359; 85/621.

s. 43, amended: order 83/1878.

ss. 43, 44, see *Jenkins* v. *Lombard North Central* [1984] 1 W.L.R. 307, D.C.

s. 44, regs. 80/54, 1360; 83/110, 1721; 84/1055, 85/619.

ss. 44, 47, see *Lockhart* v. *British School of Motoring,* 1983 S.L.T.(Sh.Ct.) 73.

s. 46, see *Home Insulation* v. *Wadsley* [1988] CCLR 25, D.C.

s. 51, see *Elliott* v. *Director-General of Fair Trading* [1980] 1 W.L.R. 977, D.C.

s. 52, regs. 80/55, 1361; 83/110, 1721; 84/1055; 85/619.

s. 56, see *Moorgate Mercantile Leasing* v *Isobel Gell and Ugolini Dispensers (U.K.),* October 21, 1985, H.H. Judge Rice, Grays Thurrock County Court.

s. 57, regs. 83/1559.

s. 58, regs. 83/1557.

s. 59, regs. 83/1552.

s. 60, regs. 84/1600.

ss. 60, 61, regs. 83/1553.

s. 64, regs. 83/1557, 1558; 84/1108.

s. 69, regs. 83/1560.

s. 70, Act of Sederunt 85/705.

s. 70, amended: order 83/1571.

s. 71, regs. 83/1559.

s. 73, Act of Sederunt 85/705.

s. 74, regs. 83/1554.

s. 74, amended: 1979, c.37, s.38.

s. 75, see *United Dominions Trust* v. *Taylor,* 1980 S.L.T.(Sh.Ct.) 28; *Porter* v. *General Guarantee Corp.; Howard Baugh & Sons (Third Party)* [1982] R.T.R. 384, Kilner-Brown J.

s. 75, Act of Sederunt 85/705.

1974—cont.

39. Consumer Credit Act 1974—*cont.*
s. 75, amended: order 83/1878.
s. 76, regs. 83/1561.
s. 77, regs. 83/1569, 1571.
s. 77, amended: order 83/1571.
s. 78, regs. 83/1569–1571.
s. 78, amended: order 83/1571.
s. 79, regs. 83/1569, 1571.
s. 82, regs. 77/328; 79/661, 667.
s. 84, regs. 83/1555, 1571.
ss. 87, 88, regs. 83/1561.
s. 88, regs. 84/1109.
s. 93A, added (S.): 1987, c.18, sch.6.
s. 95, regs. 83/1562.
s. 96, regs. 83/1560.
s. 97, see *Home Insulation* v. *Wadsley* [1988] CCLR 25, D.C.
s. 98, regs. 83/1561.
s. 101, amended: order 83/1571.
s. 103, regs. 83/1569.
s. 105, regs. 83/1553, 1556.
ss. 107–110, regs. 83/1569, 1571.
s. 113, amended: 1987, c.13, s.4.
s. 114, regs. 83/1553, 1566.
s. 114, amended: 1979, c.37, s.38.
s. 118, regs. 83/1567.
ss. 118, 120, amended: order 83/1571.
s. 121, regs. 83/1568.
s. 123, order 84/435.
s. 127, regs. 83/1553.
s. 129, amended (S.): 1987, c.18, sch.6.
s. 137, see *Wills* v. *Wood, The Times,* March 24, 1984, C.A.
s. 138, see *Coldunell* v. *Gallon* [1986] 1 All E.R. 429, C.A.; *Davies* v. *Directloans* [1986] 1 W.L.R. 823, Edward Nugee Q.C. sitting as a deputy High Court judge.
ss. 138, 139, see *A. Ketley* v. *Scott* [1981] I.C.R. 241, Foster J.
s. 139, amended: orders 75/816; 77/600; 81/1123; 1982, c.53, sch.3; 1984, c.28, sch.2.
s. 141, Act of Sederunt 85/705.
s. 141, amended: 1982, c.27, sch.12.
s. 143, S.R. 1985 No. 102.
s. 145, see *Hicks* v. *Walker, The Times,* May 28, 1984, D.C.
ss. 145, 147, see *Brookes* v. *Retail Credit Cards* [1986] Crim.L.R. 327, D.C.
s. 146, amended: order 79/1576.
s. 147, regs. 75/2124; 76/837, 1002; 77/330; 79/796; 81/614; 86/1016.
s. 150, regs. 76/837.
s. 151, regs. 80/54, 1360; 83/110, 1721; 84/1055; 85/619.
s. 152, regs. 80/55, 1361; 83/110, 1721; 84/1046; 85/619.
ss. 155, 158, amended: order 83/1571.
ss. 157–160, regs. 77/329.
s. 161, repealed in pt.: 1980, c.65, schs.4,34.
s. 162, regs. 77/331; 84/1046.
s. 165, see *Aitchison* v. *Rizza,* 1985 S.C.C.R. 297.
s. 167, see *Lockhart* v. *British School of Motoring,* 1983 S.L.T.(Sh.Ct.) 73; *Jenkins* v. *Lom-*

1974—cont.

39. Consumer Credit Act 1974—*cont.*
bard North Central [1984] 1 W.L.R. 307, D.C.; *Jessop* v. *First National Securities,* (Sh.Ct.), 1988 S.C.C.R. 1.
ss. 170, 174, see *Brookes* v. *Retail Credit Card, The Times,* October 19, 1985, D.C.
s. 173, amended: 1987, c.22, s.87.
s. 174, amended: 1979, c.38, s.10; 1984, c.12, sch.4; 1986, c.31, sch.4; c.44, sch.7; 1987, c.43, sch.4.
s. 178, order 84/1107; S.R. 1985 No. 90.
s. 180, regs. 83/1557; 84/1108; 85/666.
s. 181, order 83/1571, 1878.
s. 182, regs. 76/837, 1002; 77/327–329; 79/661, 667, 1099, 1685; 80/51, 54, 55, 1360, 1361; 81/614; 83/110, 1553–1557, 1561, 1562, 1565, 1570, 1721; 84/1055, 1108, 1109, 1600; 85/619, 666, 1192, 1918; orders 75/816; 77/325, 326, 802, 1493, 2163; 78/1616; 79/1685; 80/50, 52, 1359; 81/964; 82/1029; 83/1551; 84/434, 435, 917; 85/620, 757, 1736; 86/1105, 2186; 87/1578; 88/707.
s. 185, amended: 1979, c.37, s.38.
s. 187, amended: 1987, c.22, s.89.
s. 189, regs. 75/2124; 76/837, 1002; 77/328–331; 79/661, 667, 796; 83/1552–1562, 1564–1570, 1721; 84/1046, 1055, 1108, 1109, 1600; 85/619, 666; 86/1016.
s. 189, amended: 1979, c.54, sch.2; 1982, c.50, sch.5; 1986, c.53, sch.18; 1987, c.22, s.88; repealed in pt.: 1985, c.51, sch.17.
s. 191, S.R. 1985 No. 90.
s. 191, amended: order 79/1573.
s. 192, orders 75/816; 77/325, 802, 2163; 79/1685; 80/50; 83/1551; 84/436.
sch. 3, amended: orders 77/325, 802, 2163; 80/50.
sch. 4, repealed: 1979, c.54, sch.3; repealed in pt.: 1982, c.52, sch.3; orders 81/158; 82/1083; 1985, c.66, sch.10; c.71, sch.1; 1988, c.1, sch.31.

40. Control of Pollution Act 1974.
Royal Assent, July 31, 1974.
Commencement orders: 82/624; 83/1182; 84/853; 85/70; 88/818.
see *Hammersmith London B.C.* v. *Magnum Automated Forecourts, The Times,* June 1, 1977, C.A.
order 81/196.
s. 2, amended: 1985, c.51, sch.6; order 85/1884; repealed in pt.: 1980, c.65, schs.2,34.
s. 3, see *Long* v. *Brooke* [1980] Crim.L.R. 109, Bradford Crown Ct.; *Ashcroft* v. *Cambro Waste Products* [1981] 1 W.L.R. 1349, D.C.; *R.* v. *London Waste Regulation Authority, ex p. Specialist Waste Management, The Times,* November 1, 1988, Farquharsen J.
s. 3, regs. 76/732; 77/1185, 2006; 87/402; 88/819.
s. 5, see *R.* v. *Derbyshire County Council, ex p. North East Derbyshire District Council* (1979) 77 L.G.R. 389, D.C.

1974—cont.

40. Control of Pollution Act 1974—cont.

s. 5, amended: 1985, c.51, sch.6; order 85/1884; repealed in pt.: 1980, c.65, schs.2,34.

ss. 5, 6, regs. 76/732; 77/2006.

s. 6, amended: 1980, c.65, sch.2; repealed in pt.: ibid., schs.2,34.

s. 10, regs. 76/732; 77/1185, 2006; 88/819.

s. 11, regs. 76/732; 77/2006.

s. 11, amended: 1985, c.51, sch.6; order 85/1884; repealed in pt.: 1980, c.65, schs.2,34.

s. 12, regs. 88/819.

s. 12, amended: 1985, c.51, sch.6; order 85/1884.

s. 13, amended: 1980, c.65, sch.2; 1984, c.54, sch.9 (S.); 1985, c.51, sch.6; order 85/1884.

s. 14, amended: order 85/1884.

s. 17, regs. 80/1709; 87/402.

s. 22, amended: 1980, c.66, sch.24.

ss. 22, 23, repealed (S.): 1982, c.43, sch.4.

s. 23, amended: 1980, c.65, sch.2; 1984, c.27, sch.13; repealed in pt.: 1980, c.65, schs.2,34.

s. 24, repealed: 1983, c.35, sch.2.

s. 25, amended: 1987, c.3, sch.1.

s. 27, amended: 1980, c.65, sch.2; repealed in pt.: ibid., schs.9,11 (S.).

s. 28, repealed: 1984, c.55, sch.7.

s. 30, regs. 76/732, 959; 77/1185, 2006; 80/1709; 84/863; 85/708; 87/402; 88/819.

s. 30, amended: 1985, c.51, sch.6; order 85/1884, repealed in pt.: ibid.

s. 31, amended: 1980, c.45, sch.10 (S.); regs.84/863; 1985, c.48, s.15.

s. 32, orders 83/1182; 86/1623; 87/1782.

s. 32, amended: 1980, c.66, sch.24; 1984, c.54, sch.9 (S.), regs. 84/863; 1985, c.48, s.15.

s. 33, amended (S.): 1980, c.45, sch.10.

s. 34, amended: regs. 84/863.

s. 35, regs. 84/865.

s. 35, amended: regs. 84/863.

s. 36, regs. 84/864, 865.

s. 36, repealed in pt.: 1985, c.51, sch.17.

ss. 36–38, amended: regs. 84/863.

s. 39, regs. 84/865

s. 39, amended: order 78/272; 1981, c.54, sch.5; regs. 84/863.

s. 40, regs. 84/865; 85/5.

ss. 40, amended: regs. 84/863.

s. 41, regs. 85/813.

s. 42, regs. 84/865.

s. 42, amended: regs. 84/863.

s. 43, regs. 76/958.

s. 44, order 76/957; regs. 76/958.

s. 51, amended: order 78/272.

s. 52, amended: 1983, c.23, sch.4; 1988, c.15, sch.2.

ss. 54, 55, amended: regs. 84/863.

s. 55, regs. 84/1200; 85/813.

s. 56, regs. 76/959; 84/582, 854, 863, 866 (S.), 867 (S.); 85/178 (S.), 507, 708.

Pt. 3 (ss. 57–74), s.60, see Lloyds Bank v. Guardian Assurance and Trollope & Colls (1987) 35 Build.L.R. 34, C.A.

1974—cont.

40. Control of Pollution Act 1974—cont.

ss. 57, 63, see Morganite Special Carbons v. Secretary of State for the Environment (1980) 256 E.G. 1105, D.C.

s. 58, see Hammersmith Borough Council v. Magnum Automated Forecourts [1978] 1 W.L.R. 50, C.A.; Lambert Flat Management v. Lomas (1981) 125 S.J. 218, D.C.; Strathclyde Regional Council v. Tudhope, 1983 S.L.T. 22; Tudhope v. Lee, 1982 S.C.C.R. 409; Tower Hamlets London Borough Council v. Manzoni [1984] J.P.L. 437, McCullough J.; Wycombe District Council v. Jeffways & Pilot Coaches (H.W.) (1983) 81 L.G.R. 662, C.A.; R. v. Birmingham Justices, ex p. Guppy (1988) 86 L.G.R. 264, D.C.

s. 60, see City of London Corporation v. Bovis Construction, The Times, April 21, 1988, C.A.

s. 61, repealed in pt.: 1984, c.55, sch.7.

s. 62, see Tower Hamlets, London Borough of v. Creitzman (1985) 83 L.G.R. 72, D.C.

s. 62, amended (S.): 1984, c.54, sch.9; repealed in pt. (S.): ibid., sch.11.

s. 63, repealed in pt.: 1980, c.65, schs.2,34.

s. 64, regs. 76/37; 82/600 (S.).

s. 70, regs. 75/2116; 76/945; 83/1455.

s. 71, orders 75/2115; 81/1828–1830; 82/601 (S.); 84/1992; 85/145 (S.); 87/1730.

s. 73, repealed in pt.: 1980, c.65, schs.2,34; 1984, c.12, sch.4; 1986, c.44, sch.9.

s. 75, see Budden v. B.P. Oil and Shell Oil; Albery-Speyer v. B.P. Oil and Shell Oil [1980] J.P.L. 586, C.A.

s. 75, regs. 76/1866, 1988, 1989; 79/1; 81/1523; 85/1728.

s. 76, regs. 76/1988, 1989.

s. 77, regs. 76/1866, 1988, 1989; 81/1523; 85/1728.

s. 78, amended: 74/2170; 1977, c.45, s.31, sch.6.

s. 79, repealed in pt.: 1980, c.65, schs.2,34.

s. 80, regs. 77/18; 82/602 (S.).

s. 81, regs. 77/17; 82/604 (S.).

s. 82, regs. 77/19; 82/603 (S.).

s. 87, amended: 1980, c.43, sch.7; repealed in pt.: 1977, c.45, sch.13.

s. 88, amended: 1980, c.58, sch.3.

s. 90, amended: 1980, c.65, sch.2.

s. 98, amended: order 85/1448; repealed in pt.: 1985, c.51, sch.17.

s. 100, regs. 80/638; 85/2011; 86/902, 1992, 2300; 87/783.

s. 104, orders 75/2115; 76/1638; 84/853, 1992; 85/70, 145 (S.); 86/1623; 87/1730, 1782; regs. 75/2116; 76/37, 732, 945, 958, 1988, 1989; 77/17–19, 1185, 2006; 80/1709; 81/1828–1830; 82/600 (S.)–604 (S.); 83/1455; 84/582, 864, 865, 866 (S.), 1200; 85/5, 813, 2011; 86/902, 1992; 87/783; 88/819.

s. 105, see R. v. London Waste Regulation Authority, ex p. Specialist Waste Management, The Times, November 1, 1988, Farquharson J.

s. 105, regs. 82/600 (S.), 602 (S.); 88/819.

CAP.

1974—cont.

40. Control of Pollution Act 1974—*cont.*
s. 105, amended (S.): 1984, c.54, sch.9.
s. 106, repealed in pt. (S.): *ibid.*, sch.9.
s. 108, orders 76/1638; 79/1085; 80/1497; 81/166.
s. 109, orders 74/2039, 2169; 75/230, 2118; 76/731, 956, 1080; 77/336, 476, 1587, 2164; 78/816, 954; 82/624; 83/1175; 84/853; 85/70; 88/818.
sch. 1, substituted: 1980, c.65, sch.2.
sch. 2, repealed in pt.: 1980, c.45, sch.11 (S.); 1984, c.55, sch.7.
sch. 3, orders 79/1085; 80/1497; 81/166
sch. 3, repealed in pt.: 1975, c.51, sch.5; 1978, c.3, sch.2; 1980, c.65, schs.2,34; 1984, c.22, sch.3.
sch. 4, repealed in pt. (S.): 1982, c.43, sch.4.

41. Policing of Airports Act 1974.
Royal Assent, July 31, 1974.
repealed: 1982, c.36, sch.3.
s. 1, see *British Airports Authority* v. *Fenerty* [1976] I.C.R. 361.
s. 1, orders 74/1671, 1672; 75/168, 375, 443, 445, 447, 1769; 76/590, 1045.
s. 6, orders 75/169, 376, 444, 446, 448; 76/591, 1046; 80/92–94, 156 (S.), 157 (S.).

42. Independent Broadcasting Authority (No. 2) Act 1974.
Royal Assent, July 31, 1974.
repealed: 1980, c.64, sch.7.
s. 2, order 76/1778.

43. Merchant Shipping Act 1974.
Royal Assent, July 31, 1974.
amended: 1982, c.48, s.49.
Pt. I, ss.22–24, sch.1, extended: 75/2181, 2182, 2183; 76/53.
s. 1, orders 78/1468; 80/867, 1872; 81/1240; 83/36, 415, 582; 84/1548; 85/230, 1430; 86/1777, 2038, 2223.
s. 1, substituted: 1988, c.12, sch.4.
s. 2, amended: 1979, c.2, sch.4; c.39, s.38; 1985, c.9, sch.2; 1988, c.12, sch.4.
s. 3, amended: 1979, c.39, sch.6.
s. 4, amended: *ibid.*, s.38; 1988, c.12, sch.4; repealed in pt.: 1979, c.39, sch.7; 1988, c.12, schs.4,7.
s. 4A, added: *ibid.*, sch.4.
s 5, orders 78/1467; 85/1665; 86/296; 87/220.
s. 5, repealed: 1988, c.12, schs.4,7.
s. 6, Act of Sederunt 79/670.
s. 6, amended: 1979, c.39, s.38; 1981, c.54, sch.5; repealed in pt.: 1988, c.12, schs.4,7.
s. 7, regs. 81/363; 83/1167.
s. 7, amended: 1988, c.12, sch.4; repealed in pt.: *ibid.*, schs.4,7.
s. 8, amended: *ibid.*, sch.4; repealed in pt.: *ibid.*, schs.4,7.
s. 8A, added: *ibid.*, sch.4.
s. 9, orders 78/54, 1468.
s. 9, repealed: 1979, c.39, sch.7.
ss. 10–13, repealed: order 83/1106.
s. 14, orders 86/310; 88/1899.
s. 14, amended: 1979, c.39, s.40, sch.6; 1988, c.12, s.38.
s. 15, amended: *ibid.*

CAP.

1974—cont.

43. Merchant Shipping Act 1974—*cont.*
s. 16, regs. 75/116, 2026; 76/940; 81/1098; 87/306, 311.
s. 17, regs. 75/116, 2026; 76/940; 81/1098; 82/120; 85/1607; 87/63, 306, 311, 548, 854, 1603; 88/1485.
s. 19, repealed in pt.: 1979, c.39, sch.7.
s. 20, orders 75/2164–2175, 2181, 2182, 2183; 76/2143; 77/1241, 1242; 81/214–223, 225, 1111; 83/1519; 84/543; 85/1197; 87/1263; 88/789.
s. 23, orders 77/1241, 1242.
s. 23, repealed in pt.: 1988, c.12, schs.4,7.
s. 24, orders 74/1792; 75/866; 78/1466; 79/808.
s. 24, repealed in pt.: S.L.R. 1986.
sch. 1, substituted: 1988, c.12, sch.4.
schs. 2, 3, repealed: order 83/1106.
sch. 4, amended: 1979, c.2, sch.4; c.39, s.40; 1988, c.12, s.38.
sch. 5, regs. 75/116, 2026; 76/940; 79/1519; 81/363, 1098; 82/120; 83/1167; 85/1607; 87/63, 306, 311, 548, 854, 1603; 88/1485.
sch. 5, amended: 1979, c.39, sch.6.

44. Housing Act 1974.
Royal Assent, July 31, 1974.
extended and modified: order 75/512.
Pts. I (ss.1–12) (exc. s.11), II–VIII (ss.13–104), repealed: 1985, c.71, sch.1.
repealed, except ss.11, 18 (in pt.), 129–131, sch.3 (in pt.), (S.): 1987, c.26, sch.24.
s. 5, orders 82/1809; 83/493.
s. 5, repealed in pt.: 1985, c.51, sch.17.
s. 7, orders 79/1586; 82/1810; 83/429, 664.
s. 10A, orders 82/1810; 83/493.
s. 10B, order 83/493.
s. 12, order 82/1810.
s. 12, amended: 1985, c.9, sch.2.
s. 13, see *Peabody Housing Association* v. *Green* (1978) 38 P. & C.R. 644, C.A.
ss. 13, 15, see *Goodman* v. *Dolphin Square Trust* (1979) 38 P. & C.R. 257, C.A.
s. 18, orders 75/314, 320.
s. 18, repealed in pt. (S.): 1980, c.52, s.41, sch.5.
s. 19, see *Ashby* v. *Ebdon* [1984] 3 All E.R. 869, Warner J.
s. 29, see *Peabody Housing Association* v. *Green* (1978) 38 P. & C.R. 644, C.A.
s. 36, see *Varsani* v. *Secretary of State for the Environment* (1980) 40 P. & C.R. 354, Sir Douglas Frank Q.C.; *R.* v. *Camden London Borough Council, ex p. Comyn Ching & Co. (London)* [1984] 47 P. & C.R. 417, Woolf J.
s. 43, see *Varsani* v. *Secretary of State for the Environment* (1980) 40 P. & C.R. 354, Sir Douglas Frank Q.C.; *Mullins* v. *Secretary of State for the Environment and Islington London Borough Council* [1981] J.P.L. 577, Woolf J.; *R.* v. *Camden London Borough Council, ex p. Comyn Ching & Co. (London)* [1984] 47 P. & C.R. 417, Woolf J.
s. 46, order 80/855.
s. 47, see *Fawcett* v. *Newcastle-upon-Tyne City Council* (1977) 75 L.G.R. 841, D.C.; amended: 1977, c.42, sch.23.

1974—cont.

44. Housing Act 1974—*cont.*
s. 48, order 83/429.

s. 49, orders 82/1809, 1810; 83/493.

s. 56, see *R. v. Kerrier District Council, ex p. Guppys (Bridport)* (1985) 274 E.C. 924, C.A.

s. 58, orders 77/1212; 80/856, 1736; 83/613.

s. 59, orders 80/1735; 81/1712; 82/581, 1763; 83/95; 84/1880.

s. 62, orders 74/1931; 76/526; 77/1213.

s. 63, orders 80/1737; 82/1205.

s. 64, orders 74/2004; 77/1211; 80/1736; 81/1461; 83/613.

s. 68, orders 77/1212; 80/856, 1736; 83/613.

s. 70, orders 80/1736; 83/613.

s. 71, orders 80/1737; 82/1205; 83/4; 84/1718.

s. 71A, see *R. v. Lambeth London Borough, ex p. Clayhope Properties* (1987) 283 E.G. 739, C.A.

s. 72, orders 77/1212; 80/856, 1736; 82/1895; 83/613; 84/1700.

s. 75, see *R. v. Westminster City Council, ex p. Hazan* [1988] 09 E.G. 57, C.A.

s. 78, orders 80/1735; 82/581, 1763; 83/95; 85/1880.

s. 79, order 77/2066.

s. 89, see *W. & J. Venmore v. Metropolitan Borough of Sefton* [1977] J.P.L. 308; *F.F.F. Estates v. Hackney London Borough Council* [1980] 3 W.L.R. 909, C.A.

s. 90, see *Canterbury City Council v. Bern, The Times,* February 11, 1981; (1982) 44 P. & C.R. 178, D.C.

ss. 105–117, repealed: 1985, c.71, sch.1.

s. 114, see *Elliott v. Southwark L.B.C.* [1976] 1 W.L.R. 499; [1976] 2 All E.R. 781, C.A.

s. 119, regs. 75/1114; 79/1515.

s. 120, repealed: 1988, c.1, sch.31.

s. 128, orders 76/526; 77/1211, 1213; 80/856, 1735–1737; 81/1461, 1712; 82/581, 1205, 1763, 1895; 83/4, 95, 613; 84/1700, 1718, 1880.

s. 129, see *R. v. Camden London Borough Council, ex p. Comyn Ching & Co. (London)* [1984] 47 P. & C.R. 417, Woolf J.

s. 131, orders 74/1406, 1562, 1791; 75/374, 1113; 79/1214; amended (S.): 1975, c.28, sch.3; repealed in pt.: 1985, c.71, sch.1.

schs. 1–7, repealed: *ibid.*

sch. 2, see *Wood v. South Western Co-operative Housing Society* (1982) 44 P. & C.R. 1983, C.A.

sch. 4, see *Arieli v. Duke of Westminster* (1984) 269 E.G. 535, C.A.

sch. 5, repealed in pt.: 1985, c.51, sch.17.

sch. 6, see *Canterbury Council v. Bern, The Times,* February 11, 1981, C.A.

sch. 8, see *Pearlman v. Keepers and Governors of Harrow School* [1978] 3 W.L.R. 736, C.A.; *Pollock v. Brook Shepherd* (1983) 45 P. & C.R. 357, C.A.; *Duke of Westminster v. Oddy* (1984) 270 E.G. 945, C.A.; *Johnston v. Duke of Devonshire* (1984) 272 E.G. 661, C.A.; *Mayhew v. Governors of Harrow Road Trust,* December 14, 1984, Judge Wild, Bloomsbury County Court; *Johnson v. Duke of Westmins-*

1974—cont.

44. Housing Act 1974—*cont.*
ter (1984) 17 H.L.R. 136, C.A., *R. v. Westminster Valuation Officer, ex p. Rendall* (1986) 26 R.V.R. 220, C.A.

sch. 8, amended: 1980, c.51, sch.21; repealed in pt.: *ibid.,* schs.21,26.

schs. 9–12, repealed: 1985, c.71, sch.1.

sch. 10, see *Elliott v. Southwark L.B.C.* [1976] 1 W.L.R. 499; [1976] 2 All E.R. 781, C.A.; repealed (S.): 1975, c.28, schs.3,4.

sch. 10A, added: 1975, c.28, sch.3; amended (S.): 1978, c.14, sch.2.

sch. 11, regs. 75/1114.

sch. 13, repealed in pt.: 1975, c.6, sch.6; (S.) c.28, sch.3; 1977, c.42, sch.25; c.45, sch.13; 1984, c.59, sch.10 (S.); 1985, c.71, sch.1; c.71, sch.1 (S.); 1987, c.26, sch.24 (S.).

sch. 14, repealed: 1985, c.71, sch.1.

sch. 14, amended (S.): 1975, c.28, sch.3; repealed in pt. (S.): 1985, c.71, sch.1.

sch. 15, repealed: *ibid.*

45. Housing (Scotland) Act 1974.
Royal Assent, July 31, 1974.

repealed: 1987, c.26, sch.24.

s. 2, regs. 78/965.

s. 3, orders 75/546; 76/350; 77/523, 1757; 78/381, 964; 85/297.

s. 5, orders 75/6; 77/2074; 78/1179; 80/2029; 84/514; regs. 80/851; 81/638.

s. 7, orders 77/1687; 80/852; 81/637; 82/596.

s. 9, regs. 78/965.

s. 10A, regs. 78/965; 80/851; 81/638; orders 82/596, 1154; 84/514; 85/297.

s. 11, order 77/2074.

s. 12, order 82/596.

s. 14A, regs. 78/965.

s. 29, see *O'Donnell v. Edinburgh District Council,* 1980 S.L.T.(Lands Tr.) 13.

s. 48, orders 76/350; 77/523, 1757, 2074; 78/381; 81/638; 85/297.

s. 49, orders 75/6, 546; 76/350; 77/523, 1757, 2074; 78/381, 964, 1179; 81/2029; 84/514; regs. 78/965; 80/851; 81/638; 82/596, 1154.

s. 51, order 74/1755.

sch. 2, regs. 78/965.

46. Friendly Societies Act 1974.
Royal Assent, July 31, 1974.

s. 2, amended: 1981, c.50, s.1.

s. 7, amended: 1975, c.45, sch.9; 1980, c.48, s.57; 1988, c.1, sch.29; repealed in pt.: 1985, c.54, s.41, sch.27.

s. 28, amended: 1984, c.28, sch.2.

s. 36, amended: 1985, c.9, sch.2.

s. 42, regs. 85/1919.

s. 46, amended: 1981, c.65, sch.6; repealed in pt.: 1985, c.58, sch.4.

s. 51, amended: 1985, c.71, sch.2.

s. 54, repealed: 1981, c.35, sch.19.

s. 59, repealed in pt. (S.): 1985, c.66, sch.8.

s. 64, orders 78/920; 80/1142; 82/1353; 84/513.

s. 64, repealed: 1988, c.1, sch.31.

ss. 66–68, amended: orders 75/1137; 84/539.

s. 87, amended: 1985, c.9, sch.2; 1986, c.45, sch.14.

s. 93, amended: 1988, c.1, sch.29.

1974

CAP.

1974—cont.

46. Friendly Societies Act 1974—cont.

s. 102, amended: 1980, c.43, sch.7.

s. 104, regs. 75/205; 76/353; 77/2001; 78/1717; 79/1555, 1750; 81/1831; 83/351; 84/309; 85/343; 86/620; 87/392; 88/449.

s. 105, repealed in pt.: 1985, c.54, sch.27.

s. 106, order 82/1353; amended: orders 75/1291, 1808; 77/1861, 1891; 81/241.

s. 108, repealed in pt.: 1981, c.55, sch.5.

s. 109, regs. 85/1919.

s. 111, amended: 1985, c.9, sch.2.

s. 112, order 75/420.

s. 113, order 75/419.

s. 117, order 75/204.

sch. 5, order 82/222; regs. 87/2088; amended: orders 75/1291, 1808; 77/1861, 1891; 81/241.

sch. 8, repealed: 1981, c.55, sch.5.

sch. 9, repealed in pt.: 1984, c.36, sch.5; 1985, c.54, sch.27; 1988, c.1. sch.31.

sch. 10, repealed in pt.: 1986, c.53, sch.19.

47. Solicitors Act 1974.

Royal Assent, July 31, 1974.

see *Solicitor, A, Re, The Times,* July 7, 1987, C.A.

s. 3, amended: 1985, c.61, sch.1.

s. 4, order 76/1155.

ss. 7, 8, repealed in pt.: 1985, c.61, schs.1,8.

s. 11, amended: 1985, c.23, s.4; c.61, sch.1.

s. 12, amended: 1983, c.20, sch.4; 1985, c.61, s.4; c.65, sch.8; repealed in pt.: *ibid.,* sch.10.

s. 13, amended: 1985, c.61, sch.1.

s. 13A, added: *ibid.,* s.5; repealed in pt.: 1985, c.65, sch.10.

s. 19, amended: 1981, c.54, sch.5; 1984, c.28, sch.33.

s. 20, see *Reiss Engineering* v. *Harris* [1987] R.P.C. 171, Patents Ct.

s. 21, amended: 1985, c.61, sch.1.

s. 22, see *Powell* v. *Ely, The Times,* May 22, 1980, D.C.; *Reynolds* v. *Hoyle (No. 2)* (1980) 124 S.J. 543, D.C.; *Reiss Engineering* v. *Harris* [1987] R.P.C. 171, Patents Ct.

s. 22, amended: 1985, c.61, s.6.

s. 23, substituted: *ibid.,* s.7.

s. 24, amended: *ibid.,* sch.1.

ss. 25, 27, see *Reiss Engineering* v. *Harris* [1987] R.P.C. 171, Patents Ct.

s. 26, amended: 1980, c.43, sch.7.

ss. 28, 34, amended: 1985, c.61, sch.1.

s. 32, amended: 1986, c.53, sch.18; repealed in pt.: *ibid.,* schs.18,19.

s. 33, amended: *ibid.,* sch.18.

s. 35, see *Yogarajah* v. *The Law Society* (1982) 126 S.J. 430, Walton J.; *Buckley* v. *Law Society* [1983] 1 W.L.R. 985, Sir Robert Megarry, V.-C.; *Cove* v. *The Law Society, The Times,* July 26, 1988, C.A.

s. 37, see *Swain* v. *The Law Society* [1982] 3 W.L.R. 261, H.L.

s. 38, amended: 1979, c.55, sch.2.

s. 39, see *Reiss Engineering* v. *Harris* [1987] R.P.C. 171, Patents Ct.

s. 42, amended: 1980, c.43, sch.7.

s. 43, see *B. (A Solicitor's Clerk), Re, The Times,* April 19, 1988, D.C.

CAP.

1974—cont.

47. Solicitors Act 1974—cont.

s. 43, amended: 1985, c.61, sch.1; repealed in pt.: *ibid.,* schs. 1, 8.

s. 44, amended: 1980, c.43, sch.7.

s. 44A, added: 1985, c.61, s.1

s. 44B, added: *ibid.,* s.2.

s. 45, amended: *ibid.,* s.3.

s. 46, rules 75/727; 85/226.

ss. 46, 50–53, see *Re A Solicitor, The Times,* October 19, 1983, Vinelott J.

s. 47, amended: 1982, c.53, s.56; 1985, c.61, s.44, sch.7.

s. 47A added: 1985, c.61, s.3.

ss. 48, 49, amended: *ibid.,* sch.7.

s. 50, see *McKernan's Application, Re, The Times,* October 26, 1985, C.A.

s. 50, amended: 1981, c.54, s.147; repealed in pt.: *ibid.,* sch.7.

s. 56, rules 83/370.

s. 57, see *Walton* v. *Egan* [1982] 3 W.L.R. 352, Mustill J.

ss. 59, 60, 70, see *Chamberlain* v. *Boodle & King (A Firm)* [1982] 3 All E.R. 188, C.A.

ss. 59, 69, see *Martin Boston & Co. (A Firm)* v. *Levy* [1982] 3 All E.R. 193, Warner J.

s. 62, amended: 1983, c.20, sch.4.

s. 69, see *Bartletts de Reya* v. *Byrne, The Times,* January 14, 1938, C.A.

s. 69, amended: orders 77/600; 81/1123; 1982, c.53, sch.3; 1984, c.28, sch.2.

s. 70, see *Davidsons* v. *Jones-Fenleigh, The Times,* March 11, 1980, C.A.; *Leo Abse & Cohen* v. *Evan G. Jones (Builders) The Times,* April 21. 1984, C.A.; *Symbol Park Lane* v. *Steggles Palmer (A Firm)* [1985] 1 W.L.R. 668, C.A.; *Harrison* v. *Tew* [1987] 3 All E.R. 865, C.A.

s. 71, see *Ingrams* v. *Sykes, The Independent,* November 12, 1987, C.A.

s. 74, see *Tarrant* v. *Speechly Bircham,* May 19, 1986, H.H. Judge Birks, Slough County Ct.

s. 75, repealed: 1988, c.34, sch.6.

s. 79, amended: 1985, c.61, sch.1.

s. 81A, orders 84/481; 88/743, 998.

s. 81A, added: 1981, c.54, sch.5.

s. 85, see *Lipkin Gorman* v. *Karpnale and Lloyds Bank* [1986] F.L.R. 271, Alliott J.

s. 85, amended: 1986, c.53, sch.18.

s. 87, see *Reiss Engineering* v. *Harris* [1987] R.P.C. 171, Patents Ct.

s. 87, amended: 1975, c.45, s.74; 1979, c.37, sch.6; 1981, c.31, sch.4; c.65, sch.6; 1982, c.50, sch.5; 1985, c.61, sch.1; 1986, c.53, sch.18; 1987, c.22, sch.6; repealed in pt.: 1985, c.58, sch.4; 1987, c.22, schs.6,7.

s. 88, amended: 1985, c.23, s.4.

s. 90, order 75/534.

s. 90, repealed in pt.: 1975, c.24, sch.3.

sch. 1, see *Yogarajah* v. *The Law Society* (1982) 126 S.J. 430, Walton J.; *Buckley* v. *The Law Society (No. 2)* [1984] 1 W.L.R. 1101, Megarry V.-C.; *Cove* v. *The Law Society, The Times,* July 26, 1988, C.A.

sch. 1, amended: 1983, c.20, sch.4; 1985, c.61, sch.1.

1974—cont.

47. Solicitors Act 1974—cont.

sch. 2, amended: 1985, c.23, s.4; repealed in pt.: 1985, c.61, schs.1,8.

sch. 3, repealed in pt.: 1975, c.24, sch.3; 1977, c.37, sch.6; 1981, c.45, sch.; c.54, sch.7; 1988, c.34, sch.6.

48. Railways Act 1974.

Royal Assent, July 31, 1974.

see *R.* v. *Secretary of State for Transport, ex p. Sherrif and Sons Ltd., The Times,* December 18, 1986, Taylor J.

s. 2, repealed: 1982, c.6, sch.

s. 3, orders 77/421; 86/1891; amended: 1978, c.55, s.14; 1982, c.6, s.2; 1984, c.32, s.37.

s. 4, amended: *ibid.*

ss. 5, 6, orders 74/2005; 75/2063; 76/2117; 77/2039; 78/1295, 1763; 79/1724.

ss. 5–7, repealed: 1980, c.34, sch.9.

s. 6, order 74/2002.

s. 8, see *R.* v. *Secretary of State for Transport, ex p. Sheriff & Sons, The Independent,* January 12, 1988, Taylor J.

s. 8, amended: 1978, c.55, s.16.

s. 9, repealed in pt.: 1974, c.24, sch.3.

s. 10, amended: 1984, c.32, s.37.

49. Insurance Companies Act 1974.

Royal Assent, July 31, 1974.

repealed: except ss.88 (in pt.), 90, sch.1; 1982, c.50, sch.6.

see *Stewart* v. *Oriental Fire & Marine Insurance Co.* [1984] 3 W.L.R. 741, Leggatt J.

ss. 1–11, repealed: 1981, c.31, sch.5.

ss. 2, 11, see *Bedford Insurance Co.* v. *Instituto do Resseguros do Brasil* [1984] 3 W.L.R. 726, Parker J.

s. 3, see *Phoenix General Insurance Co. of Greece S.A.* v. *Halvanon Insurance Co.; Same* v. *Administratia Asigurarilor de Stat* [1987] 2 W.L.R. 512, C.A.

s. 12, see *Medical Defence Union* v. *Department of Trade* [1979] 2 W.L.R. 686, Megarry V.-C.

s. 13, regs. 75/1996; 76/549, 869, 2040; 78/721; 80/6, 1129, 1820; 81/1656, 82/305, 1795.

s. 14, regs. 80/6, 1129, 1820; 82/305.

s. 16, regs. 75/1996; 76/549, 869, 2040; 78/721; 80/6, 1129; 82/305.

s. 17, regs. 75/1996; 76/549, 869, 2040; 78/721; 80/6, 1129, 1820; 82/305, 1795.

s. 17, amended: 1976, c.69, sch.2; 1980, c.22, sch.3; 1981, c.62, sch.3; modified: regs. 78/720.

s. 18, regs. 81/1656; 82/305.

s. 18, modified: regs. 78/720; 1981, c.31, s.18.

s. 20, amended: 1980, c.25, sch.1; repealed in pt.: *ibid.,* schs.1,5.

ss. 21, 22, amended: *ibid.,* sch.1.

s. 22A, added: 1981, c.31, s.18.

s. 23, amended: *ibid.,* sch.4; repealed in pt.: *ibid.,* sch.5.

s. 24, amended: 1980, c.25, sch.1; 1981, c.31, s.19; repealed in pt.: 1980, c.25, schs.1,5.

s. 25, amended: 1980, c.25, sch.1; 1981, c.31, s.20; repealed in pt.: *ibid.,* sch.5.

s. 26, amended: 1980, c.25, sch.1; 1981, c.31, sch.4.

1974—cont.

49. Insurance Companies Act 1974—cont.

s. 26A, regs. 82/305.

ss. 26A–26C, added: 1980, c.25, s.21.

s. 28, amended: 1980, c.25, sch.1; 1981, c.31, s.22; modified: regs. 78/720; repealed in pt.: 1980, s.22, sch.5.

s. 29, repealed: 1981, c.31, s.23, sch.5.

s. 30, amended: *ibid.,* s.23.

s. 31, amended: *ibid.*

s. 34, amended: *ibid.,* sch.4; repealed in pt.: *ibid.,* sch.5.

s. 37, amended: 1981, c.31, s.23.

s. 38, repealed: *ibid.,* sch.5.

s. 39, amended: *ibid.,* sch.4.

s. 40, amended: 1980, c.25, sch.1; 1981, c.31, sch.4; repealed in pt.: 1980, c.25, schs.1,5; 1981, c.31, sch.5.

s. 41, amended: 1980, c.25, sch.1; 1981, c.31, sch.4.

s. 42, amended: 1980, c.25, sch.1; 1981, c.31, s.27; repealed in pt.: 1980, c.25, schs.1,5; 1981, c.31, s.27, sch.5.

s. 43, amended: 1980, c.25, sch.1.

s. 44, regs. 75/1996; 76/549, 869, 2040; 78/721; 80/6, 1129.

s. 44, repealed: 1981, c.31, sch.5.

s. 45, amended: 1980, c.25, sch.1.

s. 46, amended: 1976, c.69, sch.2; 1980, c.25, sch.1; 1981, c.31, sch.4.

ss. 47, 48, amended: 1980, c.25, sch.1.

s. 50, see *Re Capital Annuities* [1978] 3 All E.R. 704, Slade J.

s. 51, amended: 1980, c.25, sch.1.

ss. 52–54, regs. 78/722; 81/1654; modified: regs. 78/720.

s. 54A, added: 1981, c.31, s.29.

s. 55A, added: 1980, c.25, sch.1.

s. 56, amended: 1975, c.75, s.22; 1981, c.31, sch.5.

s. 57, amended: *ibid.,* sch.4.

s. 58, repealed: *ibid.,* sch.5.

s. 60, amended: 1980, c.25, sch.1; repealed in pt.: 1981, c.31, sch.5.

s. 61, amended: *ibid.,* sch.4; repealed in pt.: *ibid.,* sch.5.

s. 62, regs. 81/1654; 83/48.

s. 63, see *R.* v. *Clegg,* March 15, 1977, Judge Beaumont, Central Criminal Court.

s. 64, regs. 76/521; 81/1654.

s. 64, amended: 1980, c.25, sch.1; repealed in pt.: 1981, c.31, sch.5.

s. 65, regs. 78/1304; 81/1654.

s. 65, amended: 1981, c.31, sch.4; repealed in pt.: *ibid.,* s.30.

s. 68, regs. 81/1654; 82/675.

s. 68, amended: 1980, c.25, sch.1; 1981, c.31, sch.4; repealed in pt.: *ibid.,* sch.5.

s. 69, amended: 1980, c.25, sch.1.

s. 72, amended: 1980, c.25, sch.1; 1981, c.31, s.30; repealed in pt.: 1980, c.25, schs.1,5.

s. 72, amended: *ibid.;* repealed in pt.: *ibid.,* schs.1,5.

s. 73, regs. 82/136.

ss. 73–75, repealed in pt.: 1981, c.31, sch.5.

s. 75, amended: 1976, c.69, sch.2; 1980, c.25, sch.1.

CAP.

1974—cont.

49. Insurance Companies Act 1974 *cont.*
s. 76, amended: *ibid.*
s. 78, regs. 74/2203; 76/87, 2039; 80/5; 81/710, 725, 1654.
s. 78, amended: 1981, c.31, s.33.
ss. 79–82, amended: *ibid.*, sch.4.
ss. 80, 81, amended: 1980, c.25, sch.1.
s. 82, amended: *ibid.*; c.43, sch.7.
s. 83, see *Bedford Insurance Co.* v *Instituto do Resseguros do Brasil* [1984] 3 W.L.R. 726, Parker J.; *Phoenix General Insurance Co. of Greece S.A.* v. *Halvanon Insurance Co.*; *Same* v. *Administratia Asigurarilor de Stat* [1987] 2 W.L.R. 512, C.A.
ss. 83, 84, repealed: 1981, c.31, sch.5.
s. 85, see *Medical Defence Union* v. *Department of Trade* [1979] 2 W.L.R. 686, Megarry V.-C.
s. 85, regs. 78/721, 722, 1304; 80/6, 1129, 81/1654, 1656; 82/136, 305, 1795.
s. 85, amended: 1980, c.25, sch.1; 1981, c.31, sch.4; repealed in pt.: *ibid.*, sch.5.
s. 86, regs. 74/2203; 75/959, 1996; 76/87, 521, 549, 869, 2039, 2040; 78/721, 722, 1304; 80/5, 6, 1129, 1820; 81/710, 725, 1654–1656; 82/136, 305, 675, 1795; 83/48.
s. 86, amended: 1981, c.31, s.33; repealed in pt.: *ibid.*, sch.5.
s. 87, amended: *ibid.*, sch.4.
s. 89, amended: 1980, c.25, sch.1.
s. 90, repealed in pt.: *ibid.*, schs.1,5.
sch. 1, repealed in pt.: 1981, c.31, sch.5; 1985, c.71, sch.1; 1988, c.1, sch.31.

50. Road Traffic Act 1974.
Royal Assent, July 31, 1974.
Commencement order: 84/811.
s. 1, see *Hedges* v. *Wray* [1977] R.T.R. 433, Goff J.; *R.* v. *Wells Street JJ., ex p. Collett* [1981] R.T.R. 272, D.C.
ss. 1–3, 5, regs. 75/324, 706.
ss. 1–5, repealed: 1984, c.27, sch.14.
ss. 6–15, repealed: 1988, c.54, sch.1.
s. 9, regs. 81/1042; 88/1036.
s. 17, repealed: 1981, c.56, sch.12; amended: 1984, c.27, sch.13.
s. 19, repealed: *ibid.*
ss. 20–22, repealed: 1988, c.54, sch.1.
s. 21, see *Traffic Commissioners for the South Wales Traffic Area* v. *Snape* [1977] R.T.R. 367, D.C.; *R.* v. *Petersfield JJ., ex p. Levy* [1981] R.T.R. 204, D.C.; *Westacott* v. *Centaur Overland Travel* [1981] R.T.R. 182, D.C.
s. 24, see *Ward* v. *Rawson* [1978] R.T.R. 498, D.C.; *Bulman* v. *Lakin* [1981] R.T.R. 1, D.C.; *Freight Transport Association* v. *Royal Berkshire County Council* [1981] R.T.R. 95, C.A. *Bentley* v. *Dickinson* [1983] R.T.R. 356, D.C.; *Mutton* v. *Bates (Nos. 1 & 2)* [1984] R.T.R. 256, D.C.; *Bentley* v. *Mullen* [1986] R.T.R. 7, D.C.; *Selby* v. *Chief Constable of Avon and Somerset* [1988] R.T.R. 216, D.C.
s. 24, orders 74/2075; 75/489, 756, 1154, 1479, 1653; 79/85 (S.).
s. 24, amended: 1980, c.34, sch.5; repealed in pt.: order 81/160.

CAP.

1974—cont.

50. Road Traffic Act 1974--*cont.*
sch. 1, regs. 75/324, 706.
sch. 1, repealed: 1984, c.27, sch.14.
schs. 2, 3, repealed: 1988, c.54, sch.1.
sch. 5, see *R.* v. *Petersfield JJ, ex p. Levy* [1981] R.T.R. 204, D.C.; *Westacott* v. *Centaur Overland Travel* [1981] R.T.R. 182, D.C.
sch. 5, repealed: 1988, c.54, sch.1.
sch. 6, see *Ward* v. *Rawson* [1984] R.T.R. 498, D.C.; *Bentley* v. *Dickinson* [1983] R.T.R. 356, D.C.; *Mutton* v. *Bates (Nos. 1 & 2)* [1984] R.T.R. 256, D.C.; *Bentley* v. *Mullen* [1986] R.T.R. 7, D.C.; *Selby* v. *Chief Constable of Avon and Somerset* [1988] R.T.R. 216, D.C.
sch. 6, repealed in pt.: 1975, c.78, sch.6; 1977, c.45, sch.13; 1980, c.34, sch.9; 1981, c.14, sch.8; 1982, c.49, sch.6.; 1984, c.27, sch.14; 1988, c.54, sch.1.
sch. 7, repealed in pt.: 1980, c.34, sch.9.
sch. 15, see *Traffic Commissioners for the South Wales Traffic Area* v. *Snape* [1977] R.T.R. 367, D.C.

51. Rent Act 1974.
Royal Assent, July 31, 1974.
repealed (S.): 1984, c.58, sch.10.
see *R.* v. *South Middlesex Rent Tribunal, ex p. Beswick* (1976) 32 P. & C.R. 67, D.C.; *Campbell* v. *Gardner* (1976) 238 E.G. 115, D.C.
s. 1, see *John Sainesbury & Co.* v. *Roberts* [1975] 1 W.L.R. 1104; [1975] 2 All E.R. 801, C.A.; *Metrobarn* v. *Gehring* [1976] 1 W.L.R. 776, C.A.; *Stubbs* v. *Assopardi* [1978] 1 W.L.R. 646, C.A.
s. 1, repealed in pt. (S.): 1980, c.52, sch.5.
ss. 1–5, repealed in pt.: 1977, c.42, sch.25.
s. 5, see *Metrobarn* v. *Gehring* [1976] 1 W.L.R. 776, C.A.; *Dominal Securities* v. *McLeod* (1978) 37 P. & C.R. 411, C.A.
ss. 6–8, repealed: 1977, c.42, sch.25.
s. 11, order 74/1442.
ss. 11, 12, repealed: 1982, c.24, sch.5.
s. 12, order 74/1483.
s. 13, amended: 1976, c.80, sch.8; repealed in pt.: 1977, c.42, sch.25.
ss. 14, 15, repealed in pt.: *ibid.*
s. 17, amended: 1977, c.42, sch.23; repealed in pt.: *ibid.*, sch.25.
sch. 1, amended: 1977, c.42, sch.23.
schs. 1, 2, repealed in pt.: *ibid.*, sch.25.
sch. 3, see *John Sainesbury & Co.* v. *Roberts* [1975] 1 W.L.R. 1104; [1975] 2 All E.R. 810, C.A.; *Stubbs* v. *Assopardi* [1978] 1 W.L.R. 646, C.A.; regs. 74/1499.
sch. 3, repealed in pt.: 1982, c.24, sch.5.

52. Trade Union and Labour Relations Act 1974.
Royal Assent, July 31, 1974.
see *Davis* v. *New England College of Arundel* [1977] I.C.R. 6; *Land* v. *West Yorkshire Metropolitan County Council, The Times,* November 5, 1980, C.A.; *Monie* v. *Coral Racing, The Times,* November 1, 1980, C.A.; *Mercury Communications* v. *Stanley, The Times,* November 10, 1983, C.A.
s. 1, repealed in pt.: 1978, c.44, sch.17; S.L.R. 1986.

1974—cont.

52. Trade Union and Labour Relations Act 1974—cont.

s. 1A, repealed: 1980, c.42, s.19, sch.2.

s. 2, see NWL v. Nelson (1979) 123 S.J. 488, C.A.; Associated Newspapers Group v. Wade [1979] 1 W.L.R. 697, C.A.; Electrical, Electronic, Telecommunication and Plumbing Union v. Times Newspapers [1980] 1 All E.R. 1097, O'Connor J.; Hughes v. Transport and General Workers' Union [1985] I.R.L.R. 382, Vinelott J.; Burnley Nelson and Rossendale and District Textile Workers' Union v. Amalgamated Textile Workers' Union [1986] 1 All E.R. 885, Tudor Price J.; News Group Newspapers v. Society of Graphical and Allied Trades 1982 [1986] I.R.L.R. 227, C.A.; British Association of Advisers and Lecturers in Physical Education v. National Union of Teachers [1986] I.R.L.R. 497, C.A.; Goring v. British Actors Equity Association [1987] I.R.L.R. 122, Browne-Wilkinson V.-C.

ss. 2, 3, amended: 1985, c.9, sch.2; repealed in pt.: 1982, c.46, sch.4.

s. 4, amended: 1985, c.9, sch.2.

ss. 5, 6, repealed: 1976, c.7, s.1.

s. 6, see Taylor v. Co-operative Retail Services, The Times, July 13, 1982, C.A.

s. 7, amended: 1976, c.7, s.3.

s. 8, regs. 78/1344; 79/1385; 80/1708; 81/1631; 85/300; 86/302; 87/258; 88/310.

s. 8, amended: 1975, c.71, sch.16; 1978, c.14, sch.16; regs. 79/1385; 80/1708; 86/302; 88/310; repealed in pt.: 1976, c.7, s.1, sch.18.

s. 11, amended: 1975, c.71, sch.16.

s. 13, see Camellia Tanker SA v. International Transport Workers' Federation [1976] I.C.R. 274, C.A.; B.B.C. v. Hearn [1977] 1 W.L.R. 1004, C.A.; Examite (trading as Cleveland Cranehire) v. Whittaker [1977] I.R.L.R. 312, C.A.; Beaverbrook Newspapers v. Keys [1978] I.C.R. 582, C.A.; Star Sea Transport Corp. of Monrovia v. Slater, Laughton and Collarbone [1978] I.R.L.R. 507, C.A.; United Biscuits (U.K.) v. Fall [1979] I.R.L.R. 110, Ackner J.; Associated Newspapers Group v. Wade [1979] 1 W.L.R. 697, C.A.; NWL v. Woods; NWL v. Nelson [1979] 1 W.L.R. 1294, H.L.; P.B.D.S. (National Carriers) v. Filkins [1979] I.R.L.R. 356, C.A.; Duport Steels v. Sirs [1980] 1 W.L.R. 142; [1980] 1 All E.R. 529, H.L.; Health Computing v. Meek, The Times, March 5, 1980, Goulding J.; Express Newspapers v. McShane [1980] 2 W.L.R. 89, H.L.; Express Newspapers v. Keys [1980] I.R.L.R. 247, Griffiths J.; Hadmor Productions v. Hamilton [1982] 2 W.L.R. 322, H.L.; Universe Tankships Inc. of Monrovia v. International Transport Workers' Federation [1982] 2 W.L.R. 803, H.L.; The Plessey Co. P.L.C. v. Wilson, First Division, March 23, 1982; Merkur Island Shipping Corp. v. Laughton [1983] 2 All E.R. 189, H.L.; Phestos Shipping Co. v. Kurmiawan, Second Division, December 8, 1982; St. Stephen Shipping Co. v. Guinane (O.H.), September 23, 1982; Mer-

1974—cont.

52. Trade Union and Labour Relations Act 1974—cont.

cury Communications v. Scott-Garner [1983] 3 W.I.R. 914, C.A.; Dimbleby & Sons v. National Union of Journalists [1984] 1 W.L.R. 427, H.L.; Galt v. Philp, 1984 S.L.T. 28; (1984) 134 New L.J. 257, High Ct. of Justiciary; Thomas v. National Union of Mineworkers [1985] 2 All E.R. 1, C.A.; Shipping Company Uniform Inc. v. International Transport Workers Federation [1985] I.C.R. 245, Staughton J.; Barretts & Baird (Wholesale) v. Institution of Professional Civil Servants, Financial Times, November 26, 1986, Henry J.

s. 13, amended: 1976, c.7, s.3; repealed in pt.: 1980, c.42, s.17, sch.2; 1982, c.46, s.19, sch.4.

ss. 13, 15, see News Group Newspapers v. Society of Graphical and Allied Trades '82 (No.2) [1987] I.C.R. 181, Stuart-Smith J.

s. 14, see Camellia Tanker SA v. International Transport Workers' Federation [1976] I.C.R. 274, C.A.; Gouriet v. Union of Post Office Workers [1977] 3 W.L.R. 300, H.L.; News Group Newspapers v. Society of Graphical and Allied Trades 1982 [1986] I.R.L.R. 227, C.A.

s. 14, repealed: 1982, c.46, s.15, sch.4.

s. 15, see British Airways Authority v. Ashton [1983] 3 All E.R. 6, D.C.; News Group Newspapers v. Sogat 1982, The Times, August 1, 1986, Stuart-Smith J.

s. 15, substituted: 1980, c.42, s.16; amended: 1982, c.46, sch.3.

s. 17, see Gouriet v. Union of Post Office Workers [1977] 3 W.L.R. 300, H.L.; British Broadcasting Corp. v. Hearn [1977] 1 W.L.R. 1004, C.A.; Examite (trading as Cleveland Cranehire) v. Whittaker [1977] I.R.L.R. 312, C.A.; Beaverbrook Newspapers v. Keys [1978] I.C.R. 582, C.A.; Associated Newspapers Group v. Wade [1979] 1 W.L.R. 697, C.A.; NWL v. Woods; NWL v. Nelson [1979] 1 W.L.R. 1294, H.L.; Duport Steels v. Sirs [1980] 1 W.L.R. 142; [1980] 1 All E.R. 529, H.L.; Express Newspapers v. McShane [1980] 2 W.L.R. 89, H.L.; Scotsman Publications v. Society of Graphical and Allied Trades (O.H.), 1986 S.L.T. 646 .

s. 17, amended: 1975, c.71, sch.16; repealed in pt.: 1982, c.46, sch.4.

s. 18, see Monterosso Shipping Co. v. International Transport Workers' Federation [1982] 3 All E.R. 841, C.A.; Gibbons v. Associated British Ports [1985] I.R.L.R. 376, Tudor Price J.; Marley v. Forward Trust Group [1986] I.R.L.R. 43, E.A.T; National Coal Board v. National Union of Mineworkers, The Times, June 21, 1986, Scott J.

ss. 20–24, repealed: S.L.R. 1986.

s. 21, see Riley v. Tesco Stores, The Times, January 30, 1980, C.A.

s. 28, see NWL v. Woods: NWL v. Nelson [1979] 1 W.L.R. 1294, H.L.; British Associ-

CAP.

**52. Trade Union and Labour Relations Act
1974**—*cont.*

*ation of Advisers and Lecturers in Physical
Education* v. *National Union of Teachers*
[1986] I.R.L.R. 497, C.A.

s. 29, see *Camellia Tanker SA* v. *International
Transport Workers' Federation* [1976] I.C.R.
274, C.A.; *Transport and General Workers
Union* v. *Dyer* [1977] I.R.L.R. 93; *B.B.C.* v.
Hearn [1977] 1 W.L.R. 1004, C.A.; *National
Union of Gold, Silver and Allied Trades* v.
Albury Brothers [1978] I.R.L.R. 504, C.A.;
NWL v. *Woods; NWL* v. *Nelson* [1979] 1
W.L.R. 1294, H.L.; *Health Computing* v. *Meek*
[1981] I.C.R. 24, Goulding J.; *USDAW* v.
Sketchley [1981] I.R.L.R. 291, E.A.T.; *R.* v.
C.A.C., ex p. B.T.P. Tioxide [1981] I.C.R. 843,
Forbes J.; *Hadmor Productions* v. *Hamilton*
[1982] 2 W.L.R. 322, H.L.; *Universe Tankships
Inc. of Monrovia* v. *International Transport
Workers' Federation* [1982] 2 W.L.R. 803,
H.L.; *Mercury Communications* v. *Scott-
Garner* [1983] 3 W.L.R. 914, C.A.; *Cleveland
County Council* v. *Springett* (1985) I.R.L.R.
131, E.A.T.

s. 29, amended: 1982, c.46, s.18; repealed in
pt.: 1977, c.45, sch.13; 1982, c.46, s.18.

s. 30, see *Blue Circle Staff Association* v. *Cer-
tification Officer* [1977] 1 W.L.R. 239; *Home
Counties Dairies* v. *Woods* [1977] 1 All E.R.
869; *Airfix Footwear* v. *Cope* [1978] I.C.R.
1210, E.A.T.; *Parsons* v. *Albert J. Parsons and
Sons* [1979] I.C.R. 271, C.A.; *Squibb U.K.
Staff Association* v. *Certification Officer* [1979]
I.C.R. 235, C.A.; *Wiltshire Police Authority* v.
Wynn [1980] 3 W.L.R. 445, C.A.; *Taylor* v.
Co-operative Retail Services, The Times, July
13, 1982, C.A.; *The National Society of Oper-
ative Printers, Graphical and Media Personnel*
v. *Kirkham* [1983] I.R.L.R. 70, E.A.T.; *Gibbons*
v. *Associated British Ports* [1985] I.R.L.R. 376,
Tudor Price J.; *Falconer* v. *A.S.L.E.F. and
N.U.R.* [1986] I.R.L.R. 331, Sheffield County
Ct.

s. 30, amended: 1978, c.29, sch.16 (S.); 1980,
c.53, sch.1; 1982, c.46, s.19; 1985, c.9,
sch.2; repealed: 1978, c.44, sch.17; repealed
in pt.: 1981, c.55, sch.5.

s. 31, order 74/1385; repealed in pt.: 1975,
c.24, sch.3; c.25, sch.3.

sch. 1, see *Cooper* v. *British Steel Corporation*
[1975] I.C.R. 454; *Treganovan* v. *Robert Knee
& Co.* [1975] I.C.R. 405; *Beardmore* v. *Westinghouse Brake and Signal Co.* [1976] I.C.R.
49; *Stock* v. *Frank Jones* [1976] I.C.R. 237;
Lyon v. *St. James Press* [1976] I.R.L.R. 215;
Grundy (Teddington) v. *Willis* [1976] I.C.R.
323; *Coulson* v. *City of London Polytechnic*
[1976] 1 W.L.R. 834; *Barrel Plating and Phos-
phating Co.* v. *Danks* [1976] 1 W.L.R. 879;
Barclay v. *Roach* [1976] I.C.R. 356; *Thompson*
v. *Eaton* [1976] I.C.R. 336; *Modern Injection
Moulds* v. *J. Price* [1976] I.C.R. 370; *Watling*
v. *Wm. Bird & Son Contractors* [1976] I.T.R.

CAP.

**52. Trade Union and Labour Relations Act
1974**—*cont.*

70; *Jackson* v. *General Accident Fire and Life
Assurance Co.* [1976] I.R.L.R. 338; *Portec
(U.K.)* v. *Mogensen* [1976] I.C.R. 396; *Lyon* v.
St. James Press [1976] I.C.R. 413; *Beardmore*
v. *Westinghouse Brake and Signal Co. (No. 2)*
[1976] I.C.R. 402; *Tomczynski* v. *J. K. Millar*
[1976] I.T.R. 127; *Fougère* v. *Phoenix Motor
Co.* [1976] I.C.R. 495; *Norgett* v. *Luton Industrial Co-operative Society* [1976] I.C.R. 442;
Brennan and Ging v. *Ellward (Lancs)* [1976]
I.R.L.R. 378; *Ferodo* v. *Barnes* [1976] I.C.R.
439; *Fred Shearer* v. *Buttress,* 1976 S.L.T.
242; *Home Counties Dairies* v. *Woods* [1977]
1 All E.R. 869; *Gentles* v. *Harvey Fabrication*
[1976] I.T.R. 228; *Cohen* v. *London Borough
of Barking* [1976] I.R.L.R. 416; *Ellis* v. *Brighton
Co-operative Society* [1976] I.R.L.R. 419;
Terry v. *East Sussex C.C.* [1976] I.C.R. 536;
W. Devis & Sons v. *Atkins* [1977] 3 W.L.R.
214, H.L.; *Council of Engineering Institutions*
v. *Madison* [1977] I.C.R. 30; *Lowndes* v.
Specialist Heavy Engineering [1977] I.C.R. 1;
Gilbert v. *Goldstone* [1977] 1 All E.R. 423;
Bengey v. *North Devon District Council* [1977]
I.C.R. 15; *Wilson* v. *Maynard Shipbuilding
Consultants A.B.* [1978] 2 W.L.R. 466, C.A.;
Moon v. *Homeworthy Furniture (Northern)*
[1977] I.C.R. 117; *Logabax* v. *Titherley* [1977]
I.C.R. 369, E.A.T.; *Donald Cook & Son* v.
Carter [1977] I.R.L.R. 88; *Help the Aged Hous-
ing Association (Scotland)* v. *Vidler* [1977]
I.R.L.R. 104; *Burton* v. *Field, Sons & Co.*
[1977] I.C.R. 106; *Conway* v. *Matthew Wright
& Nephew* [1977] I.R.L.R. 89; *Elliott* v. *Uni-
versity Computing Co. (Great Britain)* [1977]
I.C.R. 147; *Trend* v. *Chiltern Hunt* [1977]
I.R.L.R. 66; *Singh* v. *London County Bus Services* [1976] I.R.L.R. 176; *Whiley* v. *Anderson*
[1977] I.C.R. 167; *Gallagher* v. *Wragg* [1977]
I.C.R. 174; *Scott, Brownrigg & Turner* v.
Dance [1977] I.R.L.R. 141; *Associated Tyre
Specialists (Eastern)* v. *Waterhouse* [1977]
I.C.R. 218, E.A.T.; *Spencer* v. *Paragon Wall-
papers* [1977] I.C.R. 301, E.A.T.; *Bristol Chan-
nel Ship Repairers* v. *O'Keefe* [1977] 2 All E.R.
258, E.A.T.; *Buskin* v. *Vacutech Successors*
(1977) 12 I.T.R. 107, E.A.T.; *Bromsgrove Cast-
ing and Machining* v. *Martin* [1977] I.C.R. 417,
E.A.T.; *Union Cartage Co.* v. *Blunden* [1977]
I.C.R. 420, E.A.T.; *City of Birmingham District
Council* v. *Beyer* [1977] I.R.L.R. 211, E.A.T.;
Gale v. *John Wilkinson & Sons (Saltley) and
Transport and General Workers' Union* [1977]
I.R.L.R. 208, E.A.T.; *Express Lift Co.* v.
Bowles [1977] I.C.R. 474, E.A.T.; *Royle* v.
Globtik Management [1977] I.C.R. 552,
E.A.T.; *I.P.C. Business Press* v. *Gray* (1977)
12 I.T.R. 148, E.A.T.; *Trend* v. *Chiltern Hunt*
[1977] I.C.R. 612, E.A.T.; *Nelson* v. *B.B.C.*
[1977] I.C.R. 649, C.A.; *Saggers* v. *British
Railways Board* [1977] 1 W.L.R. 1090, E.A.T.;
British United Trawlers (Grimsby) v. *Carr*
[1977] I.C.R. 622, E.A.T.; *H. Goodwin* v. *Fitz-*

CAP.

52. Trade Union and Labour Relations Act 1974—*cont.*

maurice [1977] I.R.L.R. 393, E.A.T.; *Stock* v. *Frank Jones (Tipton)* [1977] 1 W.L.R. 1288, C.A.; *Wilson* v. *Maynard Shipbuilding Consultants A.B.* [1977] I.R.L.R. 491; [1978] 2 W.L.R. 466, C.A.; *Wailes Dove Bitumastic* v. *Woolcocks* [1977] I.C.R. 817, E.A.T.; *Cruickshank* v. *Hobbs* [1977] I.C.R. 725, E.A.T.; *Jeffrey* v. *Laurence Scott & Electromotors* [1977] I.R.L.R. 466, E.A.T.; *I.P.C. Business Press* v. *Gray* [1977] I.C.R. 858, E.A.T.; *I.T.T. Components Group (Europe)* v. *Kolah* [1977] I.C.R. 740, E.A.T.; *102 Social Club and Institute* v. *Bickerton* [1977] I.C.R. 911, E.A.T.; *East African Airways Corp.* v. *Foote* [1977] I.C.R. 776, E.A.T.; *Lake* v. *Essex County Council* [1979] I.C.R. 577, C.A.; *Throsby* v. *Imperial College of Science and Technology; Gwent County Council* v. *Lane* [1978] 2 W.L.R. 50, E.A.T.; *Chant* v. *Aquaboats* [1978] I.C.R. 643, E.A.T.; *Ladbroke Racing* v. *Mason* [1978] I.C.R. 49, E.A.T.; *Scott* v. *Aveling Barford* [1978] 1 W.L.R. 208, E.A.T.; *Wetherall (Bond St.)* v. *Lynn* [1978] 1 W.L.R. 200, E.A.T.; *Western Excavating (E.C.C.)* v. *Sharp* [1978] 2 W.L.R. 344, C.A.; *Nothman* v. *Barnet London Borough Council* [1979] 1 W.L.R. 67, H.L.; *Ford Motor Co.* v. *Hudson* [1978] I.C.R. 482, E.A.T.; *Stock* v. *Frank Jones (Tipton)* [1978] 1 W.L.R. 231, H.L.; *Cox* v. *Wildt Mellor Bromley* [1978] I.C.R. 736, E.A.T.; *Warner* v. *Barbers Stores* [1978] I.R.L.R. 109, E.A.T.; *Walker* v. *Josiah Wedgwood & Sons* [1978] I.C.R. 744, E.A.T.; *Smith* v. *Post Office* [1978] I.C.R. 283, E.A.T.; *Avon County Council* v. *Haywood-Hicks* [1978] I.C.R. 646, E.A.T.; *Nudds* v. *W. & J. B. Eastwood* [1978] I.C.R. 171, E.A.T.; *D. G. Moncrieff (Farmers)* v. *MacDonald* [1978] I.R.L.R. 112, E.A.T.; *Fox Maintenance* v. *Jackson* [1978] I.C.R. 110, E.A.T.; *The Open University* v. *Triesman* [1978] I.C.R. 524, E.A.T.; *Williamson* v. *Alcan (U.K.)* [1978] I.C.R. 104, E.A.T.; *Priddle* v. *Dibble* [1978] I.C.R. 149, E.A.T.; *City of Birmingham District Council* v. *Beyer* [1978] 1 All E.R. 910, E.A.T.; *Gayle* v. *John Wilkinson and Sons (Saltley)* [1978] I.C.R. 154, E.A.T.; *Hollister* v. *National Farmers' Union* [1979] I.C.R. 542, C.A.; *Dixon* v. *West Ella Developments* [1978] I.C.R. 865, E.A.T.; *Himpfen* v. *Allied Records* [1978] I.C.R. 689, E.A.T.; *Bullock* v. *Merseyside County Council* [1979] I.C.R. 79, C.A.; *Alidair* v. *Taylor* [1978] I.C.R. 445, C.A.; *Retarded Children's Aid Society* v. *Day* [1978] I.C.R. 437, C.A.; *Claisse* v. *Keydril* [1978] I.C.R. 812, E.A.T.; *Earl of Bradford* v. *Jowett (No. 2)* [1978] I.C.R. 431, E.A.T.; *Gorman* v. *London Computer Training Centre* [1978] I.C.R. 394, E.A.T.; *Cheek* v. *Santa Fe (U.K.)*, 1978 S.L.T.(Sh.Ct.) 60; *Lakhani* v. *Hoover* [1978] I.C.R. 1063, E.A.T.; *Redbridge London Borough Council* v. *Fishman* (1978) 76 L.G.R. 408, E.A.T.; *Todd* v. *British Midland Airways* [1978] I.C.R. 959, C.A.; *Naqvi* v. *Stephens*

CAP.

52. Trade Union and Labour Relations Act 1974—*cont.*

Jewellers [1978] I.C.R. 631, E.A.T.; *Moody* v. *Telefusion* [1978] I.R.L.R. 311, E.A.T.; *British Aircraft Corp.* v. *Austin* [1978] I.R.L.R. 322, E.A.T.; *Bristol Channel Ship Repairers* v. *O'Keefe* [1978] I.C.R. 691, E.A.T.; *Blue Star Ship Management* v. *Williams* [1978] I.C.R. 770, E.A.T.; *Porter* v. *Banbridge* [1978] 1 W.L.R. 1145, C.A.; *Smith* v. *Hayle Town Council* [1978] I.C.R. 996, C.A.; *Winnitt* v. *Seamarks Brothers* [1978] I.C.R. 1240, E.A.T.; *Zucker* v. *Astrid Jewels* [1978] I.C.R. 1088, E.A.T.; *Constanti* v. *British Broadcasting Corp., The Times*, October 6, 1978, C.A.; *Beaumont* v. *McNeill, The Times*, October 10, 1978, E.A.T.; *Wall's Meat Co.* v. *Khan* [1979] I.C.R. 52, C.A.; *Saggers* v. *British Railways Board (No. 2)* [1978] I.C.R. 1111, E.A.T.; *Palmanor* v. *Cedron* [1978] I.C.R. 1008, E.A.T.; *Keys* v. *Shoefayre* [1978] I.R.L.R. 476; *N. C. Watling & Co.* v. *Richardson* [1978] I.C.R. 1049, E.A.T.; *Wynne* v. *Hair Control* [1978] I.C.R. 870, E.A.T.; *Wilkins* v. *Cantrell and Cochrane (G.B.)* [1978] I.R.L.R. 483, E.A.T.; *Rawlings* v. *Lionweld* [1978] I.R.L.R. 481, E.A.T.; *R.* v. *Greater London Council, ex p. Burgess* [1978] I.C.R. 991, D.C.; *Adams* v. *Charles Zub Associates* [1978] I.R.L.R. 551, E.A.T.; *Nelson and Woollett* v. *The Post Office* [1978] I.R.L.R. 548, E.A.T.; *Sutton & Gates (Luton)* v. *Boxall* [1979] I.C.R. 67, E.A.T.; *Harris (Ipswich)* v. *Harrison* [1978] I.C.R. 1256, E.A.T.; *Bentley Engineering Co.* v. *Mistry* [1979] I.C.R. 47, E.A.T.; *Larkin* v. *Cambos Enterprises (Stretford)* [1978] I.C.R. 1247, E.A.T.; *Khanum* v. *Mid-Glamorgan Area Health Authority* [1979] I.C.R. 40, E.A.T.; *Beard* v. *St. Joseph's School Governors* [1978] I.C.R. 1234, E.A.T.; *Edwards* v. *Petbow* [1978] 13 I.T.R. 431, E.A.T.; *Winnett* v. *Seamarks Brothers* [1978] I.C.R. 1240, E.A.T.; *Courtaulds Northern Textiles* v. *Andrew* [1979] I.R.L.R. 84, E.A.T.; *O'Brian* v. *Prudential Assurance Co.* [1979] I.R.L.R. 140, E.A.T.; *Marsden* v. *Fairey Stainless* [1979] I.R.L.R. 103, E.A.T.; *Thames Television* v. *Wallis* [1979] I.R.L.R. 136, E.A.T.; *Banerjee* v. *City and East London Area Health Authority* [1979] I.R.L.R. 147, E.A.T.; *Crown Agents for Overseas Governments and Administration* v. *Lawal* [1979] I.C.R. 103, E.A.T.; *Leonard* v. *Fergus & Haynes Civil Engineering*, 1979 S.L.T.(Notes) 38; *Stepney Cast Stone Co.* v. *Macarthur* [1979] I.R.L.R. 181, E.A.T.; *Dixon* v. *British Broadcasting Corp.* [1979] 2 All E.R. 112, C.A.; *Presley* v. *Llanelli Borough Council* [1979] I.C.R. 419, E.A.T.; *International Paint Co.* v. *Cameron* [1979] I.C.R. 429, E.A.T.; *Lowson* v. *Percy Main & District Social Club & Institute* [1979] I.R.L.R. 227, E.A.T.; *Cookson & Zinn* v. *Morgan* [1979] I.C.R. 425, E.A.T.; *Parker* v. *Clifford Dunn* [1979] I.C.R. 463, E.A.T.; *Howard* v. *Department of*

1974—cont.

52. Trade Union and Labour Relations Act 1974—*cont.*

National Savings [1979] I.C.R. 584, E.A.T.; *Edwards* v. *Cardiff City Council* [1979] I.R.L.R. 303, E.A.T.; *Nelson* v. *British Broadcasting Corpn.* [1979] I.R.L.R. 346, C.A.; *A.E.I. Cables* v. *McLay*, 1979 S.L.T.(Notes) 66; *Derby City Council* v. *Marshall* [1979] I.C.R. 731, E.A.T., *Winfield* v. *London Philharmonic Orchestra* [1979] I.C.R. 726, E.A.T.; *Duff* v. *Evan Thomas Radcliffe & Co.* [1979] I.C.R. 720, E.A.T.; *Fisher* v. *York Trailer Co.* [1979] I.C.R. 834, E.A.T.; *Pillinger* v. *Manchester Area Health Authority* [1979] I.R.L.R. 430, E.A.T.; *Wiltshire County Council* v. *National Association of Teachers in Further and Higher Education and Guy* [1980] I.C.R. 455, C.A.; *Marley Tile Co.* v. *Shaw* [1980] I.C.R. 72, C.A.; *Nelson* v. *B.B.C. (No. 2)* [1980] I.C.R. 110, C.A.; *Rasool* v. *Hepworth Pipe Co. (No. 1)* [1980] I.C.R. 494, E.A.T.; *Rasool* v. *Hepworth Pipe Co. (No. 2)* [1980] I.R.L.R. 137, E.A.T.; *Atkinson* v. *George Lindsay & Co.*, First Division, March 14, 1980; *Riley* v. *Tesco Stores* [1980] I.C.R. 323, C.A.; *British Home Stores* v. *Burchell (Note)* [1980] I.C.R. 303, E.A.T.; *W. Weddell & Co.* v. *Tepper* [1980] I.C.R. 286, C.A., *Williams* v. *Western Mail and Echo* [1980] I.C.R. 366, E.A.T.; *Thomas Betts Manufacturing* v. *Harding* [1980] I.R.L.R. 255, C.A.; *Brown* v. *Southall and Knight* [1980] I.C.R. 617, E.A.T.; *Bailey* v. *B.P. Oil (Kent Refinery)* [1980] I.C.R. 642, C.A.; *Sainsbury (J.)* v. *Savage* [1981] I.C.R. 1, C.A.; *Post Office* v. *Wallser* [1981] 1 All E.R. 668, C.A.; *Howard* v. *Department of National Savings* [1981] I.C.R. 208, [1981] 1 All E.R. 674, C.A.; *Monie* v. *Coral Racing* [1981] I.C.R. 109, C.A.; *Janata Bank* v. *Ahmed* [1981] I.C.R. 791, C.A.; *Duport Furniture Products* v. *Moore* [1982] I.C.R. 84, H.L.; *Taylor* v. *Co-operative Retail Services* [1982] I.C.R. 600, C.A.; *Ladbroke Racing* v. *Arnott*, 1981 S.C. 159; *Waite* v. *Government Communications Headquarters* [1983] 2 All E.R. 1013, H.L.

sch. 1, regs. 74/1386, 1387, 1925, 1926; 75/2098, 2099; 76/660–662; 77/789, 911, 912, 1094, 1095; 78/991, 992; 84/1290.

sch. 1, amended: 1975, c.65, sch.5; c.71, s.29, schs.3,16; 1976, c.7, s.3; 1980, c.9, sch.9; c.42, schs.1,2; order 84/539; repealed in pt.: 1976, c.7, s.1, sch.18; c.74, sch.5; c.79, sch.6; 1978, c.44, sch.17.

sch. 2, amended: 1975, c.71, sch.16; 1980, c.9, sch.1; 1985, c.9, sch.2.

sch. 3, see *Nelson* v. *British Broadcasting Corp.* [1979] I.R.L.R. 346, C.A.

sch. 3, repealed in pt.: 1975, c.24, sch.3; c.25, sch.3; 1976, c.7, sch.18; 1978, c.44, sch.17; 1979, c.12, sch.7; 1980, c.9, sch.2; c.25, sch.5; 1982, c.46, sch.4; 1988, c.12, sch.7.

sch. 4, repealed in pt.: 1978, c.44, sch.17; S.L.R. 1986.

1974—cont.

53. Rehabilitation of Offenders Act 1974.
Royal Assent, July 31, 1974.

see *R.* v. *Kitt* [1977] Crim.L.R. 220; *Torr* v. *British Railways Board* [1977] I.C.R. 785, E.A.T.; *D.* v. *Yates, The Times*, December 3, 1986, C.A.

s. 1, see *Herbage* v. *Pressdram* [1984] 2 All E.R. 769, C.A.

s. 1, amended: 1977, c.45, sch.9; 1988, c.33, sch.15.

s. 2, amended: 1976, c.52, s.17, sch.9; 1981, c.55, sch.4.

s. 4, see *Practice Direction* [1975] 1 W.L.R. 1065; *R.* v. *Smallman* [1982] Crim.L.R. 175, C.A.; *Property Guards* v. *Taylor and Kershaw* [1982] I.R.L.R. 175, E.A.T.

s. 4, orders 75/1023, 86/1249, 2268.

ss. 4, 7, see *Francey* v. *Cunninghame District Council* (Sh.Ct.), 1987 S.C.L.R. 6.

s. 5, amended: 1976, c.52, sch.9; 1980, c.62, schs.7,8(S.); 1981, c.55, sch.4; 1982, c.48, sch.14; c.51, sch.3; 1983, c.20, sch.4; 1988, c.33, sch.8; repealed in pt.: 1982, c.48, sch.16; 1984, c.36, sch.3.

ss. 5, 6, see *Arif* v. *Excess Insurance Group* (O.H.), June 16, 1981.

s. 6, amended: 1977, c.45, sch.12; 1980, c.43, sch.7.

s. 7, see *Reynolds* v. *Phoenix Assurance Co., The Times*, February 16, 1978, C.A.

s. 7, orders 75/1023; 86/2268.

s. 7, amended: 1979, c.37, s.43; repealed in pt.: 1987, c.22, sch.7.

s. 9, see *X.* v. *Commissioner of Police of the Metropolis* [1985] 1 W.L.R. 420, Whitford J.

s. 10, order 86/2268.

54. Pensioners' Payments Act 1974.
Royal Assent, November 14, 1974.
repealed: 1986, c.50, sch.11.

55. Prevention of Terrorism (Temporary Provisions) Act 1974.
Royal Assent, November 29, 1974.
ss. 1–8 continued: order 75/874.
s. 6, order 74/2037.
s. 8, orders 74/1975, 2038.
s. 11, orders 74/2025, 2026, 2027.
s. 12, orders 75/874, 1955.
sch. 3, orders 74/1975, 2037, 2038; repealed in pt.: 1975, c.59, sch.6.

56. National Theatre Act 1974.
Royal Assent, November 29, 1974.
repealed: 1976, c.8, s.18.

57. Consolidated Fund (No. 4) Act 1974.
Royal Assent, December 12, 1974.
repealed: 1976, c.43, sch.D.

58. Social Security Amendment Act 1974.
Royal Assent, December 12, 1974.
repealed: 1975, c.18, sch.1.
s. 6, order 75/3.

1975

1. Consolidated Fund Act 1975.
Royal Assent, January 30, 1975.
repealed: 1977, c.35, sch.C.

CAP

2. Education Act 1975.
Royal Assent, February 25, 1975.
ss. 1, 2, repealed: 1980, s.20, sch.7.
s. 5, repealed in pt.: *ibid.*

3. Arbitration Act 1975.
Royal Assent, February 25, 1975.
s. 1, see *Nova (Jersey) Knit* v. *Kammgarn Spinnerei G.m.b.H.* [1977] 1 W.L.R. 713, H.L.; *Lonrho* v. *Shell Petroleum Co., The Times,* February 1, 1978, Brightman J.; *The Rena K., The Times,* March 1, 1978, Brandon J.; *Associated Bulk Carriers* v. *Koch Shipping Inc.; The Fuohsan Maru* [1978] 2 All E.R. 254, C.A.; *Paczy* v. *Haendler & Natermann GmbH* [1979] F.S.R. 420, Whitford J.; *H. Kruidenier (London)* v. *The Egyptian Navigation Co.; The El Amria (No. 2)* [1980] 2 Lloyd's Rep. 166, Sheen J.; *Paczy* v. *Haendler and Natermann GmbH* [1980] F.S.R. 526, Whitford J.; *Ellerine Bros. (Pty.)* v. *Klinger* [1982] 2 All E.R. 737, C.A.; *Cleobulos Shipping Co.* v. *Intertanker; The Cleon* [1983] 1 Lloyd's Rep. 586, C.A.; *Qatar Petroleum Producing Authority and Qatar General Petroleum Corp.* v. *Shell International Petroleum Maatschappij BV and Whessoee* [1983] 2 Lloyd's Rep. 35, C.A.; *Afia Worldwide Insurance Co.* v. *Deutsche Ruck Versicherung AG* (1983) 133 New L.J. 621, Mustill J.; *Michael I. Warde* v. *Feedex, International Inc.* [1984] 1 Lloyd's Rep. 210, Staughton J.; *The Tuyuti* [1984] 3 W.L.R. 231, C.A., *Rumput (Panama) S.A. and Belzetta Shipping Co. S.A.* v. *Islamic Republic of Iran Shipping Lines; Leage, The* [1984] 2 Lloyd's Rep. 259; *S.L. Sethia Liners* v. *State Trading Corp. of India* [1985] 1 W.L.R. 1398, C.A.; *World Star, The* [1986] 2 Lloyd's Rep. 274, Sheen J.; *Zambia Steel & Building Supplies* v. *Clark (James) Eaton* [1986] 2 Lloyd's Rep. 225, C.A.; *Etri Fans Co.* v. *NMB (U.K.)* [1987] 2 All E.R. 763, C.A.; *Metal Scrap Trade Corp.* v. *Kate Shipping Co.; Gladys, The, The Times,* April 5, 1988, C.A.; *First Steamship Co.* v. *C.T.S. Commodity Transport Shippng Schiffahrtsgesellschaft mbH; Ever Splendor, The* [1988] 1 Lloyd's Rep. 245, Phillips J.
s. 3, see *Agromet Motoimport* v. *Maulden Engineering Company (Beds.)* [1985] 2 All E.R. 436, Otton J.
s. 7, see *Government of the State of Kuwait* v. *Sir Frederick Snow & Partners* [1984] 2 W.L.R. 340, H.L.; *Zambia Steel & Buildings Supplies* v. *James Clark & Eaton, Financial Times,* August 15, 1986, C.A.
s. 7, orders 75/1709; 79/304; 84/455; 86/949; 87/1029.
s. 8, order 75/1662.

4. Biological Standards Act 1975.
Royal Assent, February 25, 1975.
s. 1, order 76/917.
s. 3, order 77/950.
s. 9, order 76/885.

5. General Rate Act 1975.
Royal Assent, February 25, 1975.
repealed: 1980, c.65, sch.34.
s. 1, order 78/993.

CAP.

6. Housing Rents and Subsidies Act 1975.
Royal Assent, February 25, 1975.
repealed: 1985, c.71, sch.1.
s. 16, repealed in pt.: 1985, c.51, sch.17.
ss. 15, 17, sch.1, regs. 75/909; 76/271; order 75/2001.
sch. 1, regs. 75/909; 76/271; order 75/2001.

7. Finance Act 1975.
Royal Assent, March 13, 1975.
s. 1, repealed: 1979, c.47, sch.5.
s. 2, repealed: 1975, c.45, s.17, sch.14.
s. 3, repealed: 1983, c.55, sch.11.
s. 4, repealed: 1979, c.2, sch.6.
ss. 5–12, repealed: 1988, c.1, sch.13.
s. 14, repealed in pt.: 1985, c.54, schs.14, 27.
ss. 16, 17, repealed: 1988, c.1, sch.13.
s. 18, repealed: 1981, c.35, sch.19.
s. 19, see *Clore (Deceased) (No. 3); Re I.R.C.* v. *Stype Trustees (Jersey)* [1985] S.T.C. 394, Walton J.
s. 19, repealed in pt.: 1984, c.52, sch.9.
s. 20, see *I.R.C.* v. *MacPherson* [1988] 2 W.L.R. 1261, H.L.
ss. 20, 21, repealed: 1984, c.52, sch.9.
s. 22, see *Moore* v. *I.R.C., The Times,* February 23, 1984, Gibson J.
ss. 22, 23, see *Miller* v. *I.R.C.* [1987] S.T.C. 108, Ct. of Session; *sub nom. Robertson's Trs.* v. *I.R.C.,* 1987 S.L.T. 543.
ss. 22–27, repealed: 1984, c.51, sch.9.
s. 25, see *I.R.C.* v. *Stype Investments (Jersey); Re Clore, decd.* [1982] 3 W.L.R. 228, C.A.
ss. 25, 27, see *I.R.C.* v. *Stannard* [1984] 2 All E.R. 105, Scott J.
s. 28, see *Re Dougal* [1981] S.T.C. 514, Ct. of Session, *Cowie's Trs., Petrs.,* First Division, June 5, 1981.
ss. 28–47, repealed: 1984, c.51, sch.9.
s. 44, see *I.R.C.* v. *MacPherson* [1988] 2 W.L.R. 1261, H.L.
s. 48, amended: 1985, c.9, sch.2.
s. 49, amended: 1984, c.51, sch.8; repealed in pt.: *ibid.,* sch.9.
s. 51, repealed: *ibid.*
s. 53, repealed: 1979, c.14, sch.8.
s. 55, orders 76/419; 77/2091.
s. 55, repealed: 1984, c.43, sch.23.
s. 59, repealed in pt.: 1983, c.55, sch.11.
schs. 1, 2, repealed: 1988, c.1, sch.13.
sch. 2, order 76/70.
sch. 3, repealed: 1981, c.35, sch.19.
sch. 4, see *Cowie's Trs., Petrs.,* First Division, June 5, 1981; *Fetherstonhaugh* v. *I.R.C. (formerly Finch* v. *I.R.C.)* [1984] S.T.C. 261, C.A.; *Clore (dec'd) (No. 3), Re; I.R.C.* v. *Stype Trustee (Jersey)* [1985] 2 All E.R. 819; [1985] S.T.C. 394, Walton J.
sch. 4, order 79/1688; functions transferred: orders 81/207; 86/600; amended: 1976, c.40, ss.83,124, schs.11,14; 1978, c.42, ss.66,68; 1979, c.46, sch.4; 1980, c.17, ss.12,13; c.48, s.94; 1981, c.35, ss.96,99; 1982, c.39, sch.17; 1983, c.28, sch.9; c.49, s.11; orders 79/1688; 81/207; 82/1585; 83/879; 1984, c.43, ss.105, 106, sch.2; repealed in pt.:

CAP.

1975—cont.

7. Finance Act 1975—cont.

1978, c.42, s.66, sch.13; order 79/1575; 1981, c.35, s.95, sch.19; c.54, sch.7; 1982, c.39, sch.22; 1983, c.49, sch.2; 1984, c.43, schs.21, 23; c.51, sch.9.

sch. 5, see *Re Hampden Settlement Trusts* [1977] T.R. 177, Walton J.; *Pearson* v. *I.R.C.* [1979] 3 W.L.R. 112, C.A.; *Von Ernst & Cie S.A.* v. *I.R.C.* [1979] S.T.C. 478, Browne-Wilkinson J.; *Pearson* v. *I.R.C.* [1980] 2 W.L.R. 872; [1980] 2 All E.R. 479, H.L.; *Thomas* v. *I.R.C.* [1981] S.T.C. 382, Vinelott J.; *Maitland's Trs.* v. *Lord Advocate* (O.H.), January 22, 1982; *I.R.C.* v. *Brandenburg* [1982] S.T.C. 555, Nourse J.; *Lord Inglewood* v. *I.R.C.* [1983] S.T.C. 133; [1983] 1 W.L.R. 366, C.A.; *Egerton* v. *I.R.C.* [1983] S.T.C. 531, C.A.; *I.R.C.* v. *Trustees of Sir John Aird's Settlement* [1983] S.T.C. 700; [1983] 3 All E.R. 481, C.A.; *'I.R.C.* v. *Trustees of Sir John Aird's Settlement (No. 2)* [1984] S.T.C. 81, C.A.; *Moore* v. *I.R.C., The Times*, February 23, 1984, Gibson J.; *Stenhouse Trustees* v. *Lord Advocate* [1984] S.T.C. 195, Ct. Session; *Swales* v. *I.R.C.* [1984] 3 All E.R. 16, Nicholls J.; *Cholmondeley* v. *I.R.C.* [1986] S.T.C. 384, Scott J.; *Robertsons Trs.* v. *I.R.C.*, 1987 S.L.T. 534; *I.R.C.* v. *MacPherson* [1988] 2 W.L.R. 1261, H.L.

sch. 5, orders 75/610; 80/1000.

schs. 5, 6, see *Von Ernst & Cie S.A.* v. *I.R.C.* [1980] 1 All E.R. 677, C.A.

schs. 5, 6, repealed: 1984, c.51, sch.9.

sch. 7, see *Von Ernst & Cie S.A.* v. *I.R.C.* [1980] 1 All E.R. 677, C.A.; *Minden Trust (Cayman)* v. *I.R.C.* [1985] S.T.C. 758, C.A.

sch. 7, orders 78/1107; 79/1454, 1979; 80/706; 81/840.

sch. 7, repealed: 1984, c.51, sch.9.

sch. 8, order 76/2184; amended: 1976, c.40, ss.74,75; repealed in pt.: *ibid.*,sch.15; 1981, c.35, s.96, sch.19.

schs. 9, 10, repealed: 1984, c.51, sch.9.

sch. 12, repealed: 1980, c.17, sch.2; 1981, c.28, sch.2; order 81/233; repealed in pt.: 1984, c.51, sch.9; 1988, c.1, sch.13.

8. Offshore Petroleum Development (Scotland) Act 1975.

Royal Assent, March 13, 1975.

s. 1, amended: 1982, c.23, s.26.

s. 3, order 75/1134.

s. 5, repealed in pt.: 1985, c.30, sch.

s. 6, regs. 76/1060.

s. 6, repealed in pt.: 1987, c.21, schs.2,3.

s. 10, amended: 1975, c.69, sch.4; 1982, c.23, s.26.

s. 18, amended: 1983, c.21, sch.3; 1985, c.48, s.15; 1987, c.21, sch.2; repealed in pt.: 1985, c.48, s.15.

s. 19, regs. 76/1060.

s. 20, repealed in pt.: 1975, c.69, sch.5.

9. Supply Powers Act 1975.

Royal Assent, March 13, 1975.

10. Statute Law (Repeals) Act 1975.

Royal Assent, March 13, 1975.

CAP.

1975—cont.

11. Social Security Benefits Act 1975.

Royal Assent, March 13, 1975.

ss. 1–7, repealed: 1975, c.18, sch.1.

s. 8, repealed in pt.: *ibid.*; order 78/1040.

s. 9, order 75/1504; repealed in pt.: 1975, c.18, sch.1.

s. 10, repealed: *ibid.*

s. 11, repealed: 1976, c.71, sch.8; order 77/2156.

ss. 12, 14, repealed in pt.: 1975, c.18, sch.1.

s. 14, orders 75/400, 1336, 1504.

schs. 1, 2, repealed: 1975, c.18, sch.1.

sch. 3, repealed: 1976, c.71, sch.8; order 77/2156.

sch. 4, order 75/1504; repealed in pt.: 1975, c.18, sch.1; order 77/2156.

sch. 5, orders 75/400, 1013, 1336, 1504; 76/408, 77/241, 1311; repealed in pt.: 1975, c.18, sch.1.

12. Consolidated Fund (No. 2) Act 1975.

Royal Assent, March 20, 1975.

repealed: 1977, c.35, sch.C.

13. Unsolicited Goods and Services (Amendment) Act 1975.

Royal Assent, March 20, 1975.

s. 4, order 75/731.

14. Social Security Act 1975.

Royal Assent, March 20, 1975.

modified: order 77/51; amended: 1975, c.71, s.40.

s. 1, see *WHPT Housing Association* v. *Secretary of State for Social Services* [1981] I.C.R. 737, Nourse J.

s. 1, regs. 75/492; 76/88; 77/1755; 78/507; 79/591; orders 84/1904, 1914; 87/48; 88/676.

s. 1, amended: 1975, c.71, s.40; 1981, c.1, s.1; 1982, c.2, s.2; orders 84/14, 1904; 1985, c.53, sch.5; order 87/48; repealed in pt.: 1986, c.50, sch.11.

s. 2, see *Midland Sinfonia Concert Society* v. *Secretary of State for Social Services, The Times*, November 11, 1980, Glidewell J.; *Warner Holidays* v. *Secretary of State for Social Services* [1983] I.C.R. 440, McNeill J.

s. 2, regs. 75/528; 77/1015, 1987; 78/1462, 1689; 80/1713; 84/350; order 87/935.

s. 3, regs. 75/492; 76/88; 77/638, 1987; 78/433, 1698, 1703, 1877; 79/359, 591; 83/10, 395; 84/77, 1697; 87/413, 606, 1590, 2111; 88/860, 992.

s. 3, amended: 1982, c.24, s.37, sch.4.

s. 4, regs. 75/492, 528, 1855; 76/404; 77/543, 1015, 1987; 78/1689; 79/358, 591; 80/13; 84/350; 85/1398; 87/413, 2111; 88/299.

s. 4, amended: 1975, c.60, s.2, sch.4; c.71, s.40; 1976, c.5, s.2; 1979, c.18, s.14, sch.3; 1981, c.1, s.1; 1982, c.2, sch.1; orders 75/1829; 77/113, 2180; 79/1694, 1736; 82/1790; 1985, c.53, ss.7,8; order 86/25; 1986, c.50, s.74, sch.10; orders 87/46; 88/675; repealed in pt.: 1975, c.60, sch.5; 1982, c.24, sch.5.

s. 5, regs. 75/492.

ss. 5, 6, repealed: 1975, c.60, sch.5.

s. 7, regs. 75/492; 79/591; orders 75/1683; 76/1976; 88/675.

1975—cont.

14. Social Security Act 1975—cont.

s. 7, amended: orders 75/1829; 77/113, 2180; 78/1840; 79/1694; 82/1790; 84/15; 1976, c.5, s.2; 1981, c.1, s.1; 1982, c.2, s.1; 1984, c.48, s.17; 1985, c.53, s.7; orders 86/25; 87/46; repealed in pt.: 1975, c.60, sch.5.

s. 7A, regs. 85/397.

s. 7A, added: 1984, c.48, s.17; amended: regs. 85/1398; order 87/46.

s. 8, regs. 75/492; 76/88, 507; 77/1755; 79/591; 80/1975; 84/77; 85/397; orders 87/46, 675.

s. 8, amended: orders 75/1829; 77/113, 2180; 78/1840; 79/1694; 82/1790; 84/15; 1976, c.5, s.2; 1981, c.1, s.1; 1982, c.2, s.1; 1984, c.48, s.18; 1985, c.53, s.7; regs. 85/1398; order 86/25; repealed in pt.: 1975, c.60, sch.5.

s. 9, regs. 75/492, 1855; 77/543, 1755; 78/1703; 79/591; amended: orders 75/1829; 77/113, 2180; 78/1840; 79/993, 1694; 82/1790; 84/15; 1975, c.60, s.4; 1981, c.1, s.1; 1982, c.2, s.1; order 86/25; 1986, c.41, s.41; orders 87/46; 88/675; repealed in pt.: 1975, c.60, sch.5.

s. 10, regs. 84/77.

s. 10, amended: orders 82/1790; 84/15.

s. 11, regs. 75/492; 76/88; 77/1755; 78/410; 79/591; 85/398, 399; 87/2111.

s. 12, see *Nabi* v. *British Leyland (U.K.), The Times,* December 1, 1979, C.A.

s. 12, amended: 1975, c.60, ss.17,18, sch.4; 1980, c.30, s.5; 1984, c.48, sch.5; repealed in pt.: 1980, c.30, s.5; c.39, sch; 1984, c.48, schs.5, 8; 1986, c.50, sch.11.

Pt. II (ss.12–92), modified: regs. 75/470.

s. 13, regs. 75/468, 492, 556, 562; 76/409, 1736; 77/788, 1484, 1706, 1755; 78/409; 79/591, 676; 81/1501; 83/197, 463, 1610; 85/1398, 1417; 87/316, 411, 413, 687, 914; 88/429, 516, 623, 1230, 1439, 1545.

s. 13, amended: 1975, c.60, ss.17,18, sch.4; 1979, c.18, sch.3; order 82/1790; 1985, c.53, sch.5; 1986, c.50, sch.8; 1988, c.7, sch.2; repealed in pt.: 1980, c.30, s.5; c.39, sch.; 1986, c.50, schs.8,11.

s. 14, see *Decision No. R(S) 6/86.*

s. 14, amended: 1975, c.60, ss.17,18, sch.4; 1979, c.18, sch.3; 1982, c.24, s.39, sch.4; 1986, c.50, sch.10; repealed in pt.: 1980, c.39, sch.

ss. 14, 17, see *Sun and Sand* v. *Fitzjohn* [1979] I.C.R. 268, E.A.T.; *Rodrigues* v. *Rodrigues, The Times,* April 6, 1988, C.A.

s. 15, regs. 83/186, 1598.

s. 15, amended: 1975, c.60, ss.17,18, sch.4; 1979, c.18, schs.1,3; 1982, c.24, sch.4.

s. 15A, regs. 86/484.

s. 15A, added: 1985, c.53, s.18.

s. 16, regs. 75/564; 83/1598; 86/484.

s. 16, amended: 1975, c.60, ss.17,18, sch.4; 1979, c.18, sch.1; 1985, c.53, s.9.

s. 17, see *Decisions Nos. R(S) 2/78; R(U) 5/80; R(U) 10/80; R(S) 3/81; R(U) 4/81; R(G) 1/82; R(S) 2/82; R(U) 1/82; R(S) 3/82; R(U) 2/83; R(S) 6/86; R(U) 3/86.*

s. 17, regs. 75/553, 564; 76/328, 677, 1245; 77/1362; 78/394, 608, 1123, 1213; 79/1278,

1975—cont.

14. Social Security Act 1975—cont.

1299; 80/1505; 81/1510; 82/642, 1345, 1492; 83/463, 1587, 1598; 84/551, 1703; 85/1571; 86/1011, 1118; 87/317, 327, 688, 878; 88/436, 689, 1674.

s. 17, amended: orders 76/1267; 1980, c.39, s.3; 1988, c.7, sch.4; repealed in pt.: 1980. c.39, sch.

s. 18, see *Decision No. R(U) 3/82.*

s. 18, amended: 1977, c.5, s.17; 1985, c.53, sch.5; 1986, c.50, s.43.

s. 19, see *Decision No. R (U) 5/77; R.* v. *National Insurance Commissioner, ex p. Thompson, Appendix to Social Security Decision No. R (U) 5/77,* D.C.; *Decisions Nos. R (U) 4/79; R (U) 5/79; R (U) 8/80; R (U) 15/80; Presho* v. *Insurance Officer* [1984] 2 W.L.R. 29, H.L.(E.); *Cartlidge* v. *Chief Adjudication Officer* [1986] 2 W.L.R. 558, C.A.; *Decisions Nos. R(U) 5/86; R(U) 1/87; R(U) 5/87.*

s. 19, amended; 1986, c.50, s.44; repealed in pt.: 1975, c.71, s.111, sch.18.

s. 20, see *Decision No. R(U) 2/77; Crewe* v. *Social Security Commissioner* [1982] 2 All E.R. 745, C.A.; *Decision No. R(U) 1/83.*

s. 20, regs. 75/564; 79/934, 940, 1299; 82/1105; 83/1598; order 88/487.

s. 20, amended: 1981, c.57, sch.2; 1985, c.53, s.10; 1986, c.50, s.43; order 88/487; 1988, c.19, s.27, sch.3; repealed in pt.: *ibid.,* sch.4.

s. 21, regs. 75/553, 563; 81/1157.

s. 21, repealed: 1986, c.50, s.38, sch.11.

s. 22, regs. 75/553; 86/903; 87/416.

s. 22, substituted: 1986, c.50, sch.4; amended: 1988, c.7, sch.4.

s. 23, regs. 75/553.

s. 23, substituted: 1986, c.50, sch.4.

s. 24, see *Decision No. R (G) 2/79; R.* v. *Chief National Insurance Commissioner, ex p. Connor* [1981] 2 W.L.R. 412; [1981] 1 All E.R. 769, D.C.; *Burns* v. *Secretary of State for Social Services,* 1985 S.L.T. 351.

s. 24, substituted: 1986, c.50, s.36.

s. 25, amended: 1975, c.60, ss.19,20, sch.4; c.61, sch.4; 1977, c.5, s.22; 1987, c.42, sch.2; repealed in pt.: 1986, c.50, sch.11.

s. 26, amended: 1975, c.60, ss.19,20, sch.4; 1977, c.5, s.22; repealed in pt.: 1986, c.50, sch.11.

s. 27, see *Decision No. R(P) 2/85.*

s. 27, regs. 85/600; 86/903.

s. 27, repealed in pt.: 1975, c.60, sch.5.

s. 28, regs. 75/566; 77/1509.

s. 28, amended: 1975, c.60, ss.19,20, sch.4; 1980, c.39, s.3; order 79/993; 1985, c.53, s.9; repealed in pt.: 1975, c.60, sch.5; 1985, c.53, sch.6; 1986, c.50, schs.10,11.

s. 29, regs. 76/1736; 79/642; 87/1854.

s. 29, amended: 1975, c.60, ss.19,20, sch.4; 1977, c.5, s.4; order 79/993; 1985, c.53, s.9; repealed in pt.: 1975, c.60, sch.5.

s. 30, regs. 75/563, 566, 588, 2126; 77/1509; 78/392; 79/642; 84/451.

s. 30, amended: 1975, c.60, ss.19,20, sch.4; 1977, c.5, s.5; 1979, c.18, s.4; orders

1975—cont.

14. Social Security Act 1975 —cont.

77/1325; 78/912; 79/993; 82/1130; 83/1244; 84/1104; 85/1245; repealed in pt.: 1977, c.55, s.22.

s. 31, regs. 75/497; 77/342; amended: 1975, c.61, sch.4; 1977, c.5, s.22.

s. 32, regs. 75/563, 565.

s. 32, repealed: 1986, c.50, sch.11.

s. 33, regs. 75/564, 598; 77/342, 343, 1362, 1509; 78/392, 508; 79/642; 83/1598.

s. 33, amended: 1975, c.60, ss.19,20, sch.4; repealed in pt.: 1986, c.50, s.42, sch.11.

s. 34, amended: 1975, c.60, ss.19,20, sch.4; 1984, c.48, sch.4; repealed in pt.: 1986, c.50, sch.11.

s. 35, see *R.* v. *National Insurance Commissioner, ex p. Secretary of State for Social Services, The Times,* February 26, 1981, D.C.; *Decision No. R (A) 2/80; R.* v. *National Insurance Commissioner, ex p. Secretary of State for Social Services, The Times,* April 15, 1981, C.A.; *Pearson* v. *Secretary of State for Social Services,* Second Division, November 20, 1981; *Decision No. R(A) 1/83; Jones (Receiver) (on behalf of H.W. Wilde)* v. *D.H.S.S., The Times,* February 20, 1984, C.A.; *Decision No. R(A) 3/83; Woodline* v. *Secretary of State for Social Services* [1984] 1 All E.R. 593, H.L.; *Decision No. R(A) 3/86; Moran* v. *Secretary of State for Social Services, The Times,* March 14, 1987, C.A.

s. 35, regs. 75/496, 598; 77/342, 417, 1361, 1679; 79/375, 1684; 80/1136; 83/1015, 1137, 1741; 87/1426; 88/531; amended: 1977, c.49, sch.15; 1979, c.18, s.2; 1980, c.30, sch.1; 1988, c.7, s.1.

s. 36, see *White* v. *Chief Adjudication Officer* [1986] 3 All E.R. 905, C.A.; *Ruddick* v. *Secretary of State for Social Services,* 1988 S.L.T. 707.

s. 36, regs. 75/1058; 76/1245; 77/342, 1312, 1363; 78/1123, 1340; 79/1278; 80/1505; 81/1510; 82/1492; 83/1587, 1683; 84/1303; 86/1933.

s. 36, substituted: 1984, c.48, s.11; amended: 1985, c.53, sch.4.

s. 37, regs. 76/409; 77/342; 81/655; 82/1493; amended: 1977, c.5, s.22; repealed in pt.: 1986, c.50, s.37, sch.11.

s. 37A, see *Insurance Officer* v. *Hemmant* [1984] 1 W.L.R. 857, C.A.; *Lees* v. *Secretary of State for the Social Services* [1985] 2 W.L.R. 805, H.L.; *Decisions Nos. R(M) 1/85; R/M 3/86; R/M 4/86.*

s. 37A, regs. 75/1573; 77/342, 1229, 1679; 79/172; 81/1817; 86/1541; orders 82/1130; 84/1104; 85/1245.

s. 37A, added: 1975, c.60, s.22; amended: 1977, c.49, sch.15; 1978, c.29, sch.16(S.); 1979, c.18, s.3; 1986, c.50, s.71; repealed in pt.: *ibid.,* sch.11.

s. 38, see *Decision No. R(G) 2/80; Decision No. R(G) 2/83; Secretary of State for Social Services,* v. *S* [1983] 3 All E.R. 173, C.A.; *Secretary of State* v. *The Insurance Officer* (1984) 14 Fam.Law 55, C.A.

1975—cont.

14. Social Security Act 1975—cont.

s. 38, regs. 75/515; 77/342; 85/1327; amended: 1975, c.61, sch.4; 1986, c.50, s.45.

s. 39, regs. 75/566; 79/642; 84/1704; 87/1854.

s. 39, amended: 1979, c.18, sch.1; 1985, c.53, s.12; repealed in pt.: *ibid.,* s.12, sch.6.

s 40, regs. 75/1058, 1166; 76/409; 79/642.

s. 41, see *Decision No. R (S)* 11/79.

s. 41, regs. 84/1699; 88/556, order 85/1570.

s. 41, amended: 1975, c.61, sch.4; 1980, c.30, sch.1; 1984, c.48, sch.5; order 85/1570; 1986, c.50, sch.11; order 87/45; repealed in pt.: 1980, c.30, schs.1,5; 1984, c.48, schs.5,8.

s. 42, repealed: 1975, c.61, schs.4,5.

s 43, regs. 77/620; amended: 1975, c.61, sch.4; 1977, c.5, s.22; repealed in pt.: 1975, c.61, sch.5.

s. 44, see *Decision No. R (S)* 11/79.

s. 44, regs. 75/564; 77/342, 343, 1509; 80/585; 84/1698, 1699; 88/554.

s. 44, amended: 1975, c.61, sch.4; 1980, c.30, sch.1; 1988, c.7, sch.4; repealed in pt.: 1980, c.30, schs.1,5.

s. 45, regs. 75/560, 2126; 79/628; 84/550; 85/1190.

s. 45, amended: 1975, c.61, sch.4; 1977, c.5, s.5; orders 77/1325; 78/912; 1985, c.53, s.13; 1988, c.7, sch.4; repealed in pt.: 1977, c.5, sch.2; 1985, c.53, sch.6; 1988, c.7, schs.4, 5.

s. 45A, see *Decision No. R(P) 3/88.*

s. 45A, regs. 85/1190; added: 1984, c.48, s.12.

s. 45A, amended: 1985, c.53, s.13; 1988, c.7, sch.4; repealed in pt.: *ibid.,* schs.4,5.

s. 46, regs. 75/2126; 77/342, 343, 84/1698, 1699; 85/1190; 88/554.

s. 46, amended: 1975, c.61, sch.4; 1980, c.30, sch.1; 1985, c.53, s.13; repealed in pt.: 1988, c.7, schs.4,5.

s. 47, regs. 75/564; 77/343, 1509; 85/1190.

s. 47, amended: 1975, c.61, sch.4; 1980, c.30, sch.1; 1985, c.53, s.13; repealed in pt.: 1980, c.30, schs.1,5.

s. 47A, regs. 80/827; added: 1980, c.30, sch.1.

s. 47B, added: 1984, c.48, s.14; repealed in pt.: 1988, c.7, sch.5.

s. 48, amended: 1982, c.24, sch.4; 1984, c.48, sch.7.

s. 49, regs. 75/1058; 76/409; 77/342, 343, 1509; 78/433; 80/585; 84/1698, 1699, 1728; 85/1190, 1618; 87/355; 88/436, 554.

s 49, amended: 1984, c.48, sch.4.

s. 49A, added: 1986, c.50, s.44.

s. 50, see *R.* v. *National Insurance Comr., ex p. Reed,* June 18, 1980, D.C.; *Nancollas* v. *Insurance Officer; Ball* v. *Insurance Officer* [1985] 1 All E.R. 833, C.A.

s. 50, regs. 76/1245; 82/1408; 83/186; order 75/559.

s. 50, amended: 1982, c.24, sch.4; 1986, c.50, sch.3; 1988, c.7, sch.4; repealed in pt.: 1982, c.24, s.39, sch.5; 1986, c.50, schs. 3,11.

1975—cont.

14. Social Security Act 1975—*cont.*

s. 50A, regs. 83/186, 1598.

s. 50A, added: 1982, c.24, s.39.

s. 51, regs. 75/467; 80/1714; 82/1738; 84/303; 86/1545.

ss. 53, 54, modified: regs. 75/470.

s. 56, regs. 76/1736; 77/342; 80/1631; 82/1408; 83/186; order 75/559.

s. 56, repealed: 1982, c.24, s.39, sch.5.

s. 57, order 75/559; regs. 82/1408.

s. 57, amended: 1982, c.24, s.39; order 79/993; repealed in pt.: 1984, c.48, sch.9; 1986, c.50, sch.11.

s. 58, orders 75/559; 76/1245; 77/1362; regs. 78/1123; 79/1278; 80/1505, 1510; 82/1408, 1494; 83/981; 84/1703; 85/1571; 86/1118; 87/327; 88/436.

ss. 58, 59, repealed: 1986, c.50, schs.3,11.

s. 59A, regs. 87/415; 88/553.

s. 59A, added: 1986, c.50, sch.31; amended: 1988, c.7, sch.4; repealed in pt.: *ibid.*, sch.5.

s. 59B, added: *ibid.*, s.2.

s. 60, see *Decision No. R (I)* 6/77; *R. v. National Insurance Commissioners, ex p. Steel* [1978] 3 All E.R. 78, D.C.; *Decisions Nos. R (I)* 8/80, 9/80; *R (I)* 3/83; *Smith (John Michael) v. Insurance Officer*, October 16, 1984, C.A.

s. 60, order 75/559; regs. 82/1408; 83/186.

s. 60, repealed: 1986, c.50, sch.11.

ss. 61, 62, order 75/559; regs. 82/1408.

s. 62, amended: 1986, c.50, schs.3,11.

s. 64, regs. 84/1699; 88/554; order 85/1570.

s. 64, amended: 1975, c.61, sch.5; 1984, c.48, sch.9; order 85/1570; 1986, c.50, schs.3,11; repealed in pt.: 1975, c.61, sch.5; 1982, c.24, sch.5.

s. 65, amended: 1975, c.61, sch.5; 1977, c.5, s.22; 1980, c.30, sch.1; 1986, c.50, schs.3,11; repealed in pt.: 1975, c.61, sch.5; 1980, c.30, schs.1,5; 1982, c.24, sch.5.

s. 66, regs. 76/1736; 77/341–343; 80/585; 84/1698; orders 75/559, 2126; 77/1325; 78/1698; 79/359; 83/186, 1001; 85/1190; 88/554.

s. 66, amended: 1975, c.61, sch.4; 1977, c.5, s.5; orders 77/1325; 78/912; 1980, c.30, sch.1; 1986, c.50, schs.3,11; repealed in pt.: 1977, c.5, sch.2; 1980, c.30, schs.1,5; 1982, c.24, sch.5; 1988, c.7, schs.4,5.

s. 66A, added: 1984, c.48, s.14.

s. 67, order 75/559; regs. 82/1408; amended: 1977, c.5, s.22; 1986, c.50, schs.3,11.

s. 68, regs. 77/342; 82/1408.

s.68, amended: 1975, c.61, sch.4; 1986, c.50, schs.3,11; repealed in pt.: 1975, c.61, sch.5.

s. 69, repealed: 1988, c.7, schs.1,5.

s. 70, regs. 77/342; 82/1408.

s. 70, substituted: 1984, c.48, sch.5; amended: 1986, c.50, schs.3,11.

s. 71, amended: 1977, c.5, s.22; 1986, c.50, schs.3,11; repealed in pt.: 1975, c.72, sch.4.

s. 72, regs. 76/1736; 82/1408; order 75/559; amended: 1977, c.5, s.22; 1986, c.50, schs.3,11.

1975—cont.

14. Social Security Act 1975—*cont.*

s. 73, amended: 1975, c.61, sch.4; 1977, c.5, s.22; 1986, c.50, schs.3,11; repealed in pt.: 1975, c.61, sch.5.

s. 74, regs. 76/1736; 82/1408; order 75/559.

ss. 74, 75, amended: 1986, c.50, schs.3,11.

s. 76, regs. 75/1537, 2241; 77/250; 79/265, 632, 992, 1569; 80/377, 1493; 83/185, 1094, 1095; 84/458, 1659; 85/159, 967; 87/335, 2112; 88/553.

s. 77, regs. 75/1537, 2241; 77/250, 342; 79/632, 992, 1569; 80/377, 1493; 83/185, 1094, 1095; 84/458, 1659; 85/159, 167; 87/335, 2112; 88/553.

s. 77, amended: 1986, c.50, sch.3; repealed in pt.: 1982, c.24, sch.5.

s. 78, regs. 75/1537; 80/377; 85/967.

s. 78, repealed in pt.: 1982, c.24, sch.5.

s. 79, see *Decisions Nos. R (S)* 5/80; *R (S)* 6/83; *R (S)* 11/83.

s. 79, regs. 75/560, 564, 1058, 1573; 76/409, 1736; 77/342, 1288, 1289, 1342, 1444, 1509; 78/433, 1000; 79/628, 781; 80/1136, 1943; 81/1101, 1817; 82/699, 1344, 1362; 83/186, 1598; 84/550, 1699; 86/1772; 87/878.

ss. 79–81, repealed: 1986, c.50, sch.11.

s. 80, regs. 75/560, 1058, 1166; 76/409; 77/361; 78/433; 79/628; 83/186; 85/600.

s. 81, regs. 75/555, 560, 1058, 1573; 76/409, 1736; 77/342, 1361, 1693; 78/1131; 79/223, 628, 1199; 80/1136, 1621, 1631; 82/1241, 1408, 1629; 83/1015; order 75/559; 87/1683.

s. 82, see *Decisions Nos. R (S)* 8/79; *R (U)* 5/80; *R (S)* 5/83, 6/83, 10/83; *R (G)* 3/83; *R (U)* 7/83; *R (S)* 11/83; *White v. Chief Adjudication Officer* [1986] 2 All E.R. 905, C.A.

s. 82, regs. 75/469, 470, 496, 555, 563, 565, 1573; 76/409, 1736; 77/342, 1312, 1679, 1693; 78/1698; 79/223; 80/1621, 1631; 81/1157; 82/1362, 1398, 1408, 1738; 83/186; 87/1683; 88/435, 553; order 75/559.

s. 82, repealed in pt.: 1985, c.53, sch.6; 1986, c.50, sch.11.

s. 83, regs. 75/554, 1058; 77/342; 82/1408; orders 75/559; 79/597.

s. 83, substituted: 1985, c.53, sch.5.

s. 84, regs. 75/1058; 76/409, 1736; 77/342, 343; 78/433; 80/1580; 83/1001; 84/1698, 1699; 85/1505; 87/355; 88/554; order 75/559.

s. 84, amended: 1985, c.53, s.13; repealed in pt.: 1986, c.50, sch.11.

s. 85, see *Decisions Nos. R (S)* 8/83; *R (U)* 6/83.

s. 85, regs. 75/496, 554, 555, 598, 1573; 76/409, 1736; 77/342, 1693; 78/433, 524, 1511; 79/223, 359, 597, 642; 80/1136, 1927; 82/1173, 1408; 83/186, 1015, 1137, 1186; 84/1699; 86/903; 87/31, 1683; 88/1446.

s. 85, amended: 1975, c.61, sch.4; 1979, c.18, s.15; repealed in pt.: 1975, c.61, sch.5.

s. 86, regs. 76/409; 77/342; 82/1408.

s. 86, repealed: 1986, c.50, sch.11.

s. 87, repealed in pt.: 1982, c.24, sch.5.

s. 88, regs. 75/469, 470, 560; 79/628.

s. 88, repealed in pt.: 1986, c.50, sch.11.

1975—cont.

14. Social Security Act 1975—*cont.*

s. 89, regs. 75/560; 79/628; 83/186; 84/458.

s. 89, repealed in pt.: 1982, c.24, sch.5.

s. 90, regs. 75/560; 79/628; 82/1408; order 75/559; 83/186.

s. 90, amended: 1986, c.50, sch.10; repealed in pt.: 1982, c.24, sch.5; 1985, c.53, sch.6; 1986, c.50. sch.11.

s. 91, order 75/559; regs. 82/1408.

s. 91, amended: 1982, c.24, sch.4; repealed in pt.: *ibid.*, sch.5.

s. 92, repealed: 1986, c.50, s.69, sch.11.

s. 93, see *WHPT Housing Association* v. *Secretary of State for Social Services* [1981] I.C.R. 737, Nourse J.

s. 93, amended: 1975, c.61, sch.4; 1977, c.5, s.22; repealed in pt.: 1975, c.61, sch.5.

s. 94, Acts of Sederunt 76/779; 83/397; repealed in pt.: 1977, c.38, sch.5; 1981, c.54, sch.7.

s. 95, see *Ruddick* v. *Secretary of State for Social Services*, 1988 S.L.T. 707.

s. 95, repealed: 1986, c.50, schs.5,11.

s. 96, amended: 1980, c.30, sch.1; 1986, c.50, sch.5.

s. 97, amended: 1979, c.18, s.9; 1983, c.41, sch.8; 1984, c.48, s.16.

ss. 97–99, see *R.* v. *Secretary of State for Social Services, ex p. Child Poverty Action Group, The Independent*, October 11, 1988, C.A.

s. 98, amended: 1984, c.48, s.16; 1986, c.50, sch.5.

s. 99, see *Decision No. R (S)* 5/80.

s. 100, regs. 86/2218; 88/1725.

s. 100, amended: 1980, c.30, sch.1; 1984, c.48, sch.4; 1986, c.50, sch.5; repealed in pt.: *ibid.*, schs.5,11.

s. 101, regs. 86/2218; 87/214.

s. 101, amended: 1984, c.48, sch.4; 1986, c.50, sch.5; repealed in pt.: *ibid.*, sch.11.

s. 102, amended: 1984, c.48, sch.4; 1986, c.50, sch.5.

s. 103, substituted: *ibid.*

s. 104, see *R.* v. *National Insurance Comr., ex p. Browning, The Times*, May 13, 1983, C.A.; *Insurance Officer* v. *Hemmant, The Times*, March 20, 1984, C.A., *Decisions Nos. R(G)1/84; R(M)1/85; R(I)3/87.*

s. 104, regs. 84/451; 87/1424, 1973; 88/1725.

s. 104, amended: 1983, c.41, sch.8; 1984, c.48, sch.4; 1986, c.50, sch.5; 1988, c.7, sch.4; repealed in pt.: 1986, c.50, schs.5,11.

s. 105, regs. 75/496, 598; 80/1136; 86/2218.

s. 106, see *R.* v. *Secretary of State for Social Services, ex p. Connolly* (1986) 83 L.S.Gaz. 786, C.A.

s. 106, regs. 75/496, 598, 1684; 80/1622; 82/38, 84/451; 86/2218; 87/214.

s. 106, amended: 1986, c.50, sch.5; repealed in pt.: *ibid.*, sch.11.

s. 107, see *Fraser* v. *Secretary of State for Social Services*, 1986 S.L.T. 386.

s. 107, amended: 1986, c.50, sch.5; repealed in pt.: *ibid.*, sch.11.

s. 108, regs. 84/451; 86/2218; 88/1725.

1975—cont.

14. Social Security Act 1975—*cont.*

s. 108, amended: 1983, c.41, sch.8; 1984, c.48, sch.4; 1986, c.50, sch.3.

s. 109, regs. 75/588; 84/451; 86/2218.

s. 109, amended: 1983, c.41, sch.8; 1984, c.48, sch.4; 1986, c.50, sch.5; repealed in pt.; 1983, c.41, schs.8,10.

s. 110, regs. 75/588; 82/38; 84/451; 86/2218.

s. 110, amended: 1979, c.18, sch.8; 1983, c.41, sch.8; 1984, c.48, sch.4; 1986, c.50, sch.5; repealed in pt.: *ibid.*, schs.5,11.

ss. 110, 112, see *Saker* v. *Secretary of State for Social Services, The Times*, January 16, 1988, C.A.

s. 111, regs. 75/588; 80/1561.

s. 111, amended: 1980, c.30, sch.1; repealed in pt.: 1983, c.41, sch.10.

s. 112, regs. 75/588; 80/1622; 84/454, 1991; 86/2218; 87/214; modified: order 75/1573; amended: 1983, c.41, sch.8; 1984, c.48, sch.4; 1986, c.50, sch.5.

s. 113, regs. 75/588, 1537; 76/1628; 79/264; 80/377; 83/185, 1094, 1095; 84/451, 458; 85/159, 967; 86/2218; 87/335.

s. 113, amended: 1983, c.41, sch.8.

s. 114, regs. 75/563, 588, 1573; 77/1229, 1679; 81/1817; 83/1186; 84/451, 1991; 86/1541, 2172, 2218; 87/214, 1967, 1970; Act of Sederunt 76/779.

s. 114, amended: 1978, c.44, sch.16; 1986, c.50, sch.5; repealed in pt.: *ibid.*, schs.5,11.

s. 115, regs. 75/468, 531; 76/615; 77/1444, 1706; 79/628, 676, 781; 80/1136, 1622; 82/38, 699; 83/186; 84/451, 613, 1991; 86/1933, 2218; 87/214, 409, 1970.

s. 115, amended: 1983, c.41, sch.8.

s. 116, regs. 87/1967.

s. 117, see *Jones* v. *Department of Environment* [1988] 2 W.L.R. 493.

s. 117, amended: 1983, c.41, sch.8; repealed in pt.: *ibid.*, sch.10; 1986, c.50, sch.11.

s. 118, repealed: 1975, c.61, sch.5.

s. 119, see *Sadiq* v. *Chief Adjudication Officer, The Times*, March 28, 1988, C.A.

s. 119, regs. 75/565, 588, 1058, 1250; 76/409, 962, 963; 77/342, 1325; 78/1698; 79/1067, 1163; 80/15, 1621, 1622, 1631, 1640; 81/849; 82/1408; 83/104, 186; 84/451, 458, 1259; 86/2218, 87/1970.

s. 119, amended: 1975, c.60, sch.4; c.61, sch.4; 1979, c.18, s.8, sch.3; 1980, c.30, sch.1; 1982, c.24, s.41; repealed in pt.: 1986, c.50, sch.11.

s. 120, orders 75/1829; 77/113, 2180; 78/1840; 79/1694; 82/1790; 84/15; 86/25; 87/46; 88/675; amended: 1975, c.60, sch.4; repealed in pt.: *ibid.*, sch.5.

s. 121, orders 79/1694; 82/1790; 84/15; 86/25; 87/46;88/675.

s. 122, orders 75/1829; 77/2180; 79/1694, 1736; 82/1790; 84/15; amended: 1975, c.71, s.40; 1977, c.5, s.1; 1980, c.30, sch.1; 1981, c.1, s.1; 1982, c.2, sch.1; 1985, c.53, sch.5; 1986, c.50, sch.10; repealed in pt.: 1982, c.2, sch.2; 1986, c.50, sch.11.

1975—cont.

14. Social Security Act 1975—*cont.*
s. 123, orders 79/1736, 88/675.
s. 123A, orders 86/25; 87/46.
s. 123A, added: 1985, c.53, s.7; amended: 1986, c.50, s.74.
s. 124, orders 75/1096; 78/475, 912; 79/993, 1429; 80/1245, 1302; 81/1195; 82/1130, 1178; 83/1244; 84/1104; 85/1245; regs. 82/1495; 86/1117.
ss. 124–126A, repealed: 1986, c.50, sch.11.
s. 125, see *Metzger* v. *Department of Health and Social Security* [1978] 1 W.L.R. 1046, C.A.
s. 125, orders 77/1325; 82/1130; 84/1104; 85/1245.
s. 126, regs. 75/598; 76/1069.
s. 126A, orders 79/993; 80/1245; 81/1195; 82/1130; 83/1244; 85/1245; regs. 82/1495; 84/1104; 86/1117.
s. 128, regs. 75/492, 493, 1058, 1855; 76/507; 77/543; 78/70; 79/591; 80/13, 1975; 83/1691; 88/269, 299.
s. 129, regs. 75/1, 467, 469, 470, 492, 494, 1058, 1855; 77/114, 543; 78/70, 507, 1877; 79/9, 591; 80/13; 83/73, 186; 1948; 84/146; 85/143, 400; 86/198; 88/553, 674.
s. 129, amended: 1977, c.5, s.1; repealed in pt.: *ibid.*, sch.2.
s. 130, regs. 75/492, 562; 78/508; 79/591, 1431; 80/1168; repealed in pt.: 1975, c.60, sch.5.
s. 131, regs. 75/467, 492, 563, 564, 598, 1058; 76/1069; 77/342, 1362, 1509, 1679, 1755; 78/433, 1123, 1698; 79/463, 591, 1278, 1432; 80/1505, 1975; 81/1157, 1510; 82/388, 1495; 83/1508, 1598, 1610; 84/1703; 85/1571; 86/485, 486, 1118, 1545; 87/327, 417, 2111; 88/435, 436.
s. 132, regs. 75/467, 492, 563; 79/591; 82/1738.
s. 132, amended: 1982, c.23, sch.3.
s. 133, orders 80/1408; 88/529.
s. 133, repealed in pt.: 1975, c.60, sch.15.
s. 134, regs. 75/492; 78/821; 79/358, 591; orders 87/48, 676.
s. 134, amended: 1975, c.71, s.40; 1979, c.18, s.14; order 79/1736; 1981, c.1, s.1; 1982, c.2, s.3; 1985, c.53, sch.5; 1986, c.50, s.74; orders 87/48, 676; modified: regs. 79/591; repealed in pt.: 1986, c.50, sch.11.
s. 135, amended: 1975, c.60, sch.4; 1980, c.30, s.5; 1984, c.48, sch.4; repealed in pt.: 1986, c.50, sch.11.
s. 136, repealed: *ibid.*
s. 138, repealed: 1981, c.1, sch 5.
s. 139, regs. 76/88; 77/638, 788, 1229, 1361, 1362, 1755, 1987; 78/392, 393, 409, 423, 508, 524, 821, 1123, 1669, 1877; 79/345, 375, 597, 628, 642, 1278, 1483; 80/1136, 1505, 1561.
s. 139, repealed: 1980, c.30, sch.5.
s. 140, regs. 77/1361.
s. 141, regs. 79/628; 80/1505, 1561; 82/1408.
s. 141, amended: 1981, c.33, sch.2; 1982, c.24, sch.4; 1986, c.50, sch.10; repealed in pt.: *ibid.*, sch.11.
s. 142, regs. 75/566; 76/1003.

1975—cont.

14. Social Security Act 1975—*cont.*
s. 142, amended: 1975, c.60, sch.4; 1986, c.50, s.65; repealed in pt.: 1980, c.30, sch.5.
s. 143, orders 75/812; 76/1916; 77/51, 1873, 2150; 78/1527; 79/290, 921; 81/605, 1542; 82/1527, 1528; 83/604, 1698, 1894; 84/125, 354, 1817; 85/1202; 87/935, 1830, 1831; 88/590, 591.
s. 143, amended: 1975, c.60, sch.4; 1977, c.5, s.20; 1981, c.33, s.6; 1986, c.50, s.65; repealed in pt.: *ibid.*, s.65, sch.11.
ss. 144, 145, repealed: *ibid.*, sch.11.
s. 146, see *Barras* v. *Reeve* [1980] 3 All E.R. 705, D.C.; *R.* v. *Highbury Corner Stipendiary Magistrate, ex p. D.H.S.S., The Times,* February 4, 1987, D.C.
s. 146, regs. 75/146, 560; 79/591; 82/1241; 83/53; amended: 1975, c.60, sch.4; 1981, c.33, sch.1; reepaled in pt.: 1986, c.50, sch.11.
ss. 146, 150, 151, 152, see *R.* v. *Melksham JJ., ex p. Williams, The Times,* March 15, 1983, D.C.
s. 147, repealed: 1986, c.50, sch.11; repealed in pt. (S.): 1980, c.62, sch.8.
s. 148, amended: 1975, c.60, sch.4.
s. 149, see *I.R.C.* v. *Findlay McClure & Co.* (O.H.), 1986 S.L.T. 417.
s. 150, amended: 1975, c.60, sch.4.
s. 151, amended: *ibid.*; repealed in pt.: 1986, c.50, sch.11.
ss. 151, 152, see *Department of Health and Social Security* v. *Milner and Brown; The Times,* July 27, 1982, Sir Douglas Frank, Q.C.
s. 152, see *Department of Health and Social Security* v. *Evans* [1984] I.C.R. 317, Hirst J.
s. 152, amended: 1975, c.60, sch.4; 1980, c.43, sch.7; repealed in pt.: 1985, c.65, s.216, sch.10; 1986, c.50, sch.11.
s. 153, repealed: 1985, c.65, sch.10.
s. 155, regs. 75/1537; 80/377; 84/458; 85/967.
s. 155, repealed in pt.: 1983, c.41, sch.10.
s. 157, regs. 75/467.
s. 158, repealed: 1980, c.30, schs.1,5.
s. 159, order 75/559; regs 82/1408.
s. 160, amended: orders 75/1291; 77/1861, 1891; 81/241.
s. 161, repealed in pt.: 1975, c.72, sch.4.
s. 162, regs. 75/497, 515, 561; 79/642; 84/458.
s. 164, repealed: 1986, c.50, sch.11.
s. 165A, regs. 85/1250; 86/903; 87/878, 1968.
s. 165A, added: 1985, c.53, s.17; amended: 1986, c.50, sch.10; substituted: *ibid.*
s. 166, regs. 77/619; 84/451, 458; 86/2171; orders 76/1916; 77/51, 619, 1618, 1619, 1778, 1873; 82/903–905, 1124, 1519, 1520; 83/438, 1003; 84/111; 85/677, 1305, 1327, 1570, 1618; 86/485, 486, 903, 1009, 1011, 1259, 1961; 87/36, 317, 355, 358, 606, 659, 687, 878, 1325, 1440, 1854, 1917, 1968, 1970, 1973, 2111; 88/299, 516, 522, 524, 660, 661, 663, 674, 803, 909, 999, 1228, 1230, 1438, 1439, 1444–1446, 1545, 1724, 1725, 1890(S.), 1908, 1970; order 87/1910.

1975—cont.

14. Social Security Act 1975—cont.
s. 166, amended: 1986, c.50, s.62, sch.5; repealed: 1980, c.30, sch.5.
s. 167, regs. 77/1618, 1619, 1778; 82/206; 83/496; orders 84/14, 1904; 87/48.
s. 167, amended: 1977, c.5, s.1; 1979, c.18, s.4; 1980, c.30, sch.1; 1981, c.1, s.1; 1985, c.53, sch.5; 1986, c.50, ss.43, 62,74, sch.10; repealed in pt.: 1975, c.60, sch.5.
s. 168, regs. 77/1509; 84/77, 107, 240, 350, 380, 550, 1259, 1659, 1704, 1921, 1926; 85/397–399, 600, 1398, 1926–1931; 86/198, 317, 485, 715, 1046, 1545, 1716, 1717; 87/106, 411, 413, 657, 687, 914, 1099–1107, 1110–1114, 1590, 1854, 2111; 88/429, 474–476, 523, 647, 689, 1016.
s. 168, repealed in pt.: 1980, c.30, sch.5.
sch. 1, regs. 75/1, 492, 528, 1855; 76/88, 507; 77/114, 543, 638, 1755; 78/423, 1689, 1703, 1877; 79/591; 80/1975; 81/82; 82/1033; 83/10, 395, 408; 84/77; 85/396, 399, 1411; 87/413, 2111; 88/992.
sch. 1, amended: 1975, c.60, ss.17–19,22, sch.4; 1980, c.62, sch.1; 1982, c.24, s.37; 1985, c.53, sch.5; 1986, c.50, sch.8.
sch. 2, regs. 84/77.
sch. 2, amended: 1978, c.42, s.30, sch.4; 1985, c.54, s.42; 1988, c.1, sch.29 (prosp.); c.39, sch.3; repealed in pt.: 1984, c.43, sch.23; 1988, c.39, sch.14 (prosp.).
sch. 3, regs. 78/508; 88/623; amended: 1975, c.60, ss.17–19,22, sch.4; 1979, c.18, schs.1,3; 1986, c.50, schs.4,8,10; 1988, c.7, s.6; repealed in pt.: 1980, c.62, s.5; 1986, c.50, sch.11; 1988, c.7, s.5, sch.5.
sch. 4, see *WHPT Housing Association* v. *Secretary of State for Social Services* [1981] I.C.R. 737, Nourse J.
sch. 4, regs. 80/1505; 81/1510.
sch. 4, amended: 1975, c.60, ss.17–19, 22, sch.4; 1979, c.18, schs.4,5; 1984, c.48, schs.4,5; orders 76/1029; 77/1325; 78/475, 912; 82/1130; 84/1104; 85/1245; 1986, c.50, s.36; order 87/45; 1988, c.7, sch.1; repealed in pt.: 1975, c.60, sch.5; c.61, schs.4,5; 1980, c.30, sch.5; 1982, c.24, sch.5; 1984, c.48, sch.9; 1985, c.53, sch.6; 1986, c.50, s.38, sch.11.
sch. 5, repealed: *ibid.*
schs. 5, 6, regs. 84/77.
sch. 6, amended: 1980, c.39, s.4; repealed: *ibid.*, sch.
sch. 7, repealed: 1975, c.60, s.20, sch.5.
sch. 8, order 75/559; regs. 82/1408.
sch. 8, amended: 1982, c.24, sch.4; 1984, c.48, sch.4; 1986, c.50, sch.3; repealed in pt.: *ibid.*, sch.11.
sch. 9, regs. 76/1736; 82/1408; 83/186; order 75/559; repealed in pt.: 1975, c.61, sch.5; 1986, c.50, schs.3,11.
sch. 10, amended: 1983, c.41, sch.8; order 84/1818; repealed in pt.: 1981, c.20, sch.4.
sch. 11, repealed in pt.: 1982, c.24, sch.5.
sch. 12, regs. 75/588; 84/451; 86/2218.
sch. 12, amended: 1983, c.41, sch.8; 1986, c.50, sch.5.

1975—cont.

14. Social Security Act 1975—cont.
sch. 13, regs. 75/468, 531, 588; 77/1444, 1706; 79/628, 676, 781; 80/1136, 1622; 82/699; 84/451, 1991; 86/1933, 2218; 87/409, 1970.
sch. 13, amended: 1983, c.41, sch.8; 1986, c.50, sch.5.
sch. 14, regs. 75/598; 76/1069; 77/1362; 78/1123; 79/1278; 82/1408, 1495; 83/1588; order 75/559; 84/1703, 85/1571; 86/1118.
sch. 14, repealed: 1986, c.50, sch.11.
sch. 15, regs. 77/1361, 1362; 79/375, 597, 628, 642, 1278; 80/1136.
sch. 15, repealed: 1980, c.30, sch.5.
sch. 16, regs. 77/341; 79/628; 82/1408, 1495.
sch. 16, amended: 1986, c.50, sch.10; repealed in pt.: *ibid.*, sch.11.
sch. 18, amended: 1985, c.19, sch.2; repealed: 1985, c.65, sch.10; c.66, sch.8 (S.).
sch. 19, repealed: 1980, c.30, schs.1,5.
sch. 20, regs. 75/1058; 77/343, 1509; 78/433; 80/585; 84/77, 107, 240, 303, 350, 380, 451, 550, 551, 1259, 1659, 1697–1699, 1703, 1704, 1728, 1921, 1991; 85/397, 398, 600, 967, 1190, 1305, 1323, 1327, 1398, 1618, 1926–1931; 86/198, 317, 485, 486, 751, 1011, 1046, 1118, 1541, 1545, 1716, 1717, 1772, 2171, 2218; 87/31, 106, 214, 316, 327, 335, 409, 411, 413, 415–417, 606, 657, 688, 878, 914, 1100, 1102, 1106, 1110–1112, 1424, 1590, 1683, 1854, 2112; 88/269, 299, 429, 435, 436, 474–476, 516, 523, 531, 553, 556, 647, 674, 689, 860, 992, 1016, 1545, 1647.
sch. 20, amended: 1975, c.60, sch.4; c.71, s.40; 1980, c.30, sch.1; 1983, c.41, sch.8; 1984, c.48, schs.4,5,7; 1985, c.53, sch.5; 1986, c.50, sch.5; repealed in pt.: 1975, c.60, sch.5; c.61, schs.4,5; c.72, sch.4; 1976, c.5, sch.; 1977, c.5, sch.2; 1980, c.30, schs.1,5.
sch. 27, repealed in pt.: order 82/158.

15. Social Security (Northern Ireland) Act 1975.
Royal Assent, March 20, 1975.
s. 1, regs. 77/318; S.Rs. 1979 No. 186; 1984 Nos. 4, 425; 1987 No. 25; 1987, No. 123.
s. 1, amended: orders 81/230; 82/158.
s. 2, S.Rs. 1977 No. 349; 1978 Nos. 308, 401; 1980 No. 405; 1984 No. 81.
s. 3, regs. 77/280; S.Rs. 1977 No. 349; 1978 Nos. 79, 90, 369, 371, 400; 1979 No. 186; 1982 No. 69; 1983 Nos. 8, 64; 1984 Nos. 43, 317, 378; 1987 Nos. 143, 201, 348, 468; 1988 Nos. 169, 204; amended: order 82/1084.
s. 4, S.Rs. 1977 No. 349; 1978 No. 401; 1979 No. 186; 1980 No. 93; 1984 No. 81; 1985 No: 260; 1987 Nos. 143, 468.
s. 4, amended: orders 75/1503; 81/230; 82/158; repealed in pt.: orders 75/1503; 82/1084.
ss. 5, 6, repealed: 75/1503.
s. 7, S.R. 1979 No. 186; amended: orders 81/230; 82/158; repealed in pt.: order 75/1503.
s. 7A, S.R. 1985 No. 61.
s. 8, regs. 77/318; S.Rs. 1979 No. 186; 1980 No. 463; 1984 No. 43; 1985 No. 61; amended: orders 81/230; 82/158; repealed in pt.: order 75/1503.

1975—cont.

15. Social Security (Northern Ireland) Act 1975—*cont.*

s 9, regs. 77/318; S.Rs. 1978 No. 369; 1979 No. 186.

s. 9, amended: orders 75/1503; 81/230; 82/158; 1986, c.41, s.41; repealed in pt.: order 75/1503.

s. 10, S.Rs. 1979 No. 186; 1984 No. 43.

s. 10, amended: order 81/230.

s. 11, regs. 77/318; S.Rs. 1978 No. 86; 1979 No. 186; 1982 No. 69; 1985 No. 61; 1987 No. 468.

s. 12, amended: order 75/1503.

ss. 12, 13, repealed in pt.: order 80/1087.

s. 13, regs. 77/275, 318; 82/96; S.Rs. 1977 No. 332; 1978 No. 77; 1979 Nos. 186, 193; 1981 No. 367; 1982 No. 42; 1983 Nos. 31, 76, 348; 1985 Nos. 260, 263; 1987 Nos. 115, 138, 143, 220; 1988 Nos. 73, 105, 125, 276, 298, 326.

s. 14, amended: orders 75/1503; 82/1084; repealed in pt.: order 80/1087.

s. 15, S.Rs. 1983 No. 36; 1984 No. 245; 1988 No. 355.

s. 15, amended: orders 75/1503; 82/1084.

s. 15A, S.R. 1986 No. 82.

s. 16, S.Rs. 1979 No. 211; 1984 No. 245; 1986 No. 82.

s. 16, amended: order 75/1503.

s. 17, regs. 82/96; S.Rs. 1978 Nos. 120, 262; 1979 Nos. 211, 371, 377; 1980 No 357; 1981 Nos. 345, 367; 1982 Nos. 42, 147, 301, 345; 1983 Nos. 76, 343; 1984 Nos. 245, 376; 1985 No. 278; 1986 Nos. 212, 266, 275; 1987 Nos. 90, 128, 221; 1988 Nos. 98, 169, 355.

s. 17, amended: orders 80/1087; 81/1118; repealed in pt.: order 81/1118.

s. 20, S.Rs. 1979 Nos. 211, 286, 377; 1982 No. 247; 1984 No. 245; 1988 No. 83.

s. 21, S.Rs. 1978 No. 114; 1981 No. 278.

s. 22, S.Rs. 1986 No. 157; 1987 No. 170.

ss. 22, 24, repealed in pt.: order 80/1087.

s. 25, amended: orders 75/1503, 1504.

s. 26, amended: order 75/1503.

s. 27, S.Rs. 1977 No. 351; 1985 No. 92; 1986 No. 157; 1987 No. 465.

s. 27, repealed in pt.: order 75/1503.

s. 28, regs. 77/280; amended: orders 75/1503; 80/1087; repealed in pt.: order 75/1503.

s. 29, S.Rs. 1979 No. 243; 1987 No. 404.

s. 30, regs. 77/280; S.Rs. 1978 Nos. 101, 114; 1979 No. 243; 1984 No. 144.

s. 32, S.R. 1978 No. 114.

s. 33, regs. 77/280; S.Rs. 1978 Nos. 101, 102; 1979 Nos. 211, 243; 1984 No. 245.

s. 35, regs. 77/305; S.Rs. 1978 No. 90; 1979 Nos. 102, 458; 1980 No. 267; 1983 Nos. 203, 217; 1984 No. 418; 1987 Nos. 322, 413; 1988 No. 129.

s. 36, see *Social Security Decision No. RI/83* (N.C.I.P.); *Insurance Officer* v. *McCaffrey* [1984] 1 W.L.R. 1353, H.L.

s. 36, S.Rs. 1978 Nos. 262, 275, 385; 1979 No. 371; 1980 No. 357; 1981 No. 345; 1982 No. 345; 1983 No. 370; 1984 No. 317.

1975—cont.

15. Social Security (Northern Ireland) Act 1975—*cont.*

s. 37, S.Rs. 1981 Nos. 142, 144; 1982 No. 342.

s. 37A, see *Social Security Decision No. R I/83* (MOB).

s. 37A, regs. 77/305; S.Rs. 1978 No. 90; 1979 No. 47; 1980 No. 385; 1981 No. 407; 1984 No. 174; 1987 No. 465.

s. 38, S.R. 1985 No. 227.

s. 39, S.Rs. 1979 No. 243; 1984 No. 372; 1987 No. 404.

s. 40, S.Rs. 1979 No. 243; 1984 No. 317.

s. 41, S.Rs. 1984 No. 382; 1985 No. 281.

s. 42, repealed: order 75/1504.

s. 43, amended and repealed in pt.: order 75/1504.

s. 44, S.Rs. 1980 No. 144; 1984 Nos. 373, 382; 1988, No. 138.

ss. 44–47, amended: order 75/1504.

s. 45, S.Rs. 1978 No. 351; 1984 Nos. 123, 382; 1985 No. 229.

s. 45A, S.R. 1985 No. 229.

s. 46, S.Rs. 1984 Nos. 373, 382; 1985 No. 229; 1988, No. 138.

s. 47, S.R. 1985 No. 229.

s. 47A, S.R. 1980 No. 216.

s. 48, amended: order 82/1084.

s. 49, regs. 77/280; S.Rs. 1978 No. 90; 1980 No. 144; 1984 Nos. 373, 377, 382; 1985 Nos 229, 300; 1987 No. 129; 1988 Nos. 98, 138.

s. 50, S.R. 1983 No. 36.

s. 50, amended and repealed in pt.: order 82/1084.

s. 50A, S.Rs. 1983 No. 36; 1984 No. 245.

s. 51, S.R. 1980 No. 406; 1984 No. 80; 1986, No. 303.

s. 56, order 75/1504; S.R. 1983 No. 36.

s. 56, repealed: order 82/1084.

s. 57, S.R. 1984 No. 92.

s. 58, S.Rs. 1978 No. 262; 1979 No. 371; 1980 No. 357; 1981 No. 345; 1982 No. 344; 1983 No. 218; 1984 No. 92; 1985 No. 278; 1986 No. 212; 1987 No. 128; 1988 No. 98.

s. 59A, S.Rs. 1987 No. 142; 1988 No. 148.

s. 59, amended: order 80/1087.

s. 64, S.R. 1985 No. 281.

ss. 64–66, order 75/1504.

ss. 64–66, repealed in pt.: order 82/1084.

s. 66, S.Rs. 1978 Nos. 97, 371; 1980 No. 144; 1983 Nos. 36, 193; 1984 Nos. 373, 382; 1985 No. 229; 1988 No. 138.

ss. 67, 68, 70, 72, 74, S.R. 1984 No. 92.

ss. 68, 70, 73, amended and repealed in pt.: order 75/1504.

ss. 76, 77, S.Rs. 1979 Nos. 78, 208, 275, 429; 1980 No. 355; 1982 No. 59; 1983 Nos. 19, 37, 260; 1984 Nos. 174, 371; 1985 No. 41; S.Rs. 1986 Nos. 179, 270; 1987 Nos. 116, 454; 1988 No. 148.

ss. 76–78, regs. 77/272.

s. 77, repealed in pt.: order 82/1084.

s. 78, S.Rs. 1983 No. 19; 1986 No. 179.

s. 79, see *Insurance Officer* v. *McCaffrey* [1984] 1 W.L.R. 1353, H.L.

CAP.

1975—cont.

15. Social Security (Northern Ireland) Act 1975—cont.

s. 79, regs. 77/280; S.Rs. 1977 No. 351; 1978 No. 90; 1979 Nos. 211, 259, 446; 1980 Nos. 267, 452; 1981 Nos. 7, 407; 1982 Nos. 153, 302, 318; 1983 No. 36, 1984 Nos. 123, 245, 317, 382.

s. 79, amended: order 82/1084; repealed in pt.: order 80/1087.

s. 80, S.Rs. 1977 No. 351; 1978 No. 90; 1983 No. 36; 1984 No. 317; 1985 No. 92; amended: orders 75/1504; 77/2156; repealed in pt.: order 75/1504.

s. 81, S.Rs. 1977 Nos. 316, 351; 1978 No. 222; 1979 No. 68; 1980 Nos. 267, 385; 1982 Nos. 284, 381; 1983 Nos. 36, 203; 1984 Nos. 92, 144, 317; 1985 No. 92; 1987 No. 391.

s. 81, repealed in pt.: order 82/1084.

s. 82, regs. 77/305; S.Rs. 1977 Nos. 316, 351; 1978 No. 114; 1979 Nos. 68, 371; 1980 No. 385; 1981 No. 278; 1982 Nos. 318, 322; 1983 No. 36; 1984 Nos. 92, 317; 1987 No. 391; 1988 Nos. 77, 148.

s. 83, S.Rs. 1979 No. 242; 1984 Nos. 92, 317.

s. 84, S.Rs. 1978 No. 90; 1980 No. 396; 1983 No. 36; 1984 Nos. 373, 382; 1985 No. 229; 1987 No. 129; 1988 No. 138.

s. 85, regs. 77/280; S.Rs. 1977 No. 316; 1978 Nos. 90, 107, 326; 1979 Nos. 68, 97, 242, 243; 1980 No. 451; 1982 No. 272; 1983 Nos. 36, 203, 217, 233; 1984 Nos. 92, 317, 382; 1986 No. 157; 1987 Nos. 12, 391, 413; 1988 No. 312; amended and repealed in pt.: order 75/1504.

s. 86, S.R. 1984 No. 92.

s. 86, amended and repealed in pt.: order 75/1504.

s. 87, amended: order 81/234; repealed in pt.: order 82/1084.

s. 88, S.R. 1977 No. 351.

s. 89, S.Rs. 1977 No. 351; 1984 No. 174.

ss. 89, repealed in pt.: order 82/1084.

s. 90, S.Rs. 1977 No. 351; 1983 No. 36; 1984 No. 92.

s. 90, repealed in pt.: order 82/1084.

s. 91, S.R. 1984 No. 92.

s. 91, amended: order 82/1084; repealed in pt.: ibid.

s. 92, repealed in pt.: orders 80/1087; 82/1084.

s. 93, amended and repealed in pt.: order 75/1504.

s. 94, amended: 1978, c.23, sch.5.

s. 95, amended: order 75/1504.

s. 96, amended: 1975, c.60, sch.4.

s. 97, S.R. 1987 No. 61.

s. 97, amended: 1979, c.18, s.9.

s. 98, S.R. 1987 No. 82.

s. 100, S.Rs. 1987 Nos. 82, 466; 1988 No. 369.

s. 101, S.Rs. 1987 Nos. 82, 112.

s. 104, S.Rs. 1984 No. 144; 1987 Nos. 325, 463; 1988 Nos. 82, 369.

s. 105, S.R. 1980 No. 267; 1984 No. 144; 1987 No. 82.

s. 106, S.Rs. 1979 No. 458; 1980 No. 383; 1982 No. 29; 1984 No. 144; 1987 Nos. 82, 112.

CAP.

1975—cont.

15. Social Security (Northern Ireland) Act 1975—cont.

s. 108, S.Rs. 1984 Nos. 144, 317; 1987 No. 82.

ss. 109, 110, S.R. 1984 No. 144; 1987 No. 82.

s. 111, S.Rs. 1980 No. 362; 1982 No. 29.

s 112A, S.Rs. 1987 Nos. 81, 112.

s. 112A, added: 1986, c.50, sch.9

s. 113, regs. 77/272; 82/249, 566; S.Rs. 1979 No. 77; 1982 Nos. 59, 128; 1983 Nos. 19, 37, 260; 1984 Nos. 144, 174; 1985, No. 41; 1986 Nos. 179, 270; 1987 Nos. 82, 116.

s. 114, regs. 77/305; S.Rs. 1978 No. 114; 1981 No. 407; 1983 Nos. 36, 233; 1984 Nos. 144, 174, 445; 1987 Nos. 82, 100, 112, 459, 466; 1988 Nos. 147, 369.

s. 115, regs. 77/272; S.Rs. 1977 Nos. 332, 351; 1979 No. 193; 1980 Nos. 267, 363, 426; 1982 Nos. 29, 153; 1983, No. 36; 1984 Nos. 144, 317, 445; 1987 Nos. 82, 112, 117, 466.

s. 118, repealed: order 75/1504.

s. 119, see R. (D.H.S.S.) v. National Insurance Comrs. [1980] 8 N.I.J.B., Hutton J.

s. 119, S.Rs. 1978 No. 371; 1979 Nos. 314, 354; 1980 Nos. 18, 382, 383, 385; 1981 No. 187; 1982 No. 322; 1983 Nos. 12, 36; 1984 Nos. 92, 144, 174, 299, 317; 1987 Nos. 82, 466; amended: orders 75/1503, 1504.

s. 120, S.Rs. 1978 Nos. 10, 96, 202, 387; 1979 Nos. 273, 459; 1980 Nos. 89, 294; 1981 No. 274; 1982 Nos. 242, 413; 1983 No. 243; 1984 Nos. 5, 424; 1985 No. 230; 1986 Nos. 16, 211; 1987 No. 26; 1988 No. 122.

s. 123, regs. 75/492, 493, 1855; 78/70; 79/591; 80/13, 1975; 83/1691; 88/269, 299.

s. 124, S.Rs. 1978 Nos. 41, 91, 400; 1979 No. 14; 1980 No. 93; 1983 Nos. 9, 36, 430; 1984 Nos. 46, 317; 1985 Nos. 25, 61; 1986 No. 45; 1988 Nos. 121, 148.

s. 125, S.Rs. 1978 No. 102; 1979 No. 394; 1980 No. 267; repealed in pt.: order 75/1503.

s. 126, regs. 77/280, 305, 318; S.Rs. 1978 Nos. 90, 114, 262, 371; 1979 Nos. 131, 211, 371, 392; 1980 Nos. 357, 463; 1981 Nos. 278, 345; 1982 Nos. 82, 343; 1983 No. 341; 1984 Nos. 245, 317, 376; 1985 No. 278; 1986 Nos. 71, 72, 212, 303; 1987 Nos. 128, 151, 468; 1988 Nos. 77, 98.

s. 127, S.R. 1988 No. 149.

s. 127, repealed in pt.: order 75/1503; S.R. 1980 No. 316.

s. 128, S.Rs. 1978 No. 400; 1979 No. 186; 1987 No. 25; 1988 No. 123.

s. 128, amended: orders 81/230; 82/158; repealed in pt.: ibid.

ss. 129, 130–132, S.R. 1979 No. 186; amended: order 75/1503.

s. 130, amended: 1981, c.38, sch.3.

s. 133, amended: 1975, c.60, sch.4.

s. 134, S.Rs. 1977 Nos. 336, 378; 1979 Nos. 92, 186, 303; 1981 No. 363; 1982 Nos. 370, 378; 1983 Nos. 98, 387, 432; 1984 Nos. 68, 90, 449; 1985 No. 205; 1987 Nos. 231, 399, 402; 1988 Nos. 119, 120.

s. 134, amended: order 75/1503; 1977, c.5, s.20; order 81/1118.

1975—cont.

15. Social Security (Northern Ireland) Act 1975—*cont.*

s. 135, amended: order 75/1503.

s. 137, S.Rs. 1977 No. 351; 1982 No. 284; 1983 No. 10; amended: orders 75/1503; 81/1118.

s. 138, amended: 1975, c.60, sch.4.

ss. 139, 141–143, amended: order 75/1503.

s. 146, regs. 77/272; S.Rs. 1979 No. 186; 1983 No. 19; 1984 No. 174; 1986 No. 179.

s. 150, S.R. 1984 No. 92.

s. 152, S.R. 1979 No. 243.

s. 154A, S.Rs. 1985 No. 226; 1986 No. 157; 1987 No. 465.

s. 155, S.Rs. 1985 Nos. 227, 229; 1987, No. 61.

s. 155, amended: order 79/1573; repealed in pt.: 1977, c.5, sch.2.

s. 156, amended: order 81/230; repealed in pt.: order 75/1503.

s. 157, S.Rs. 1984 Nos. 31, 43, 60, 80, 81, 92, 144, 245, 299, 332, 371–373, 376–378, 382, 444; 1985 No. 41.

s. 157, repealed in pt.: 1977, c.5, sch.2.

sch. 1, regs. 77/318; S.Rs. 1977 Nos. 332, 351; 1978 Nos. 369, 400, 401; 1979 No. 186; 1981 No. 30; 1982 Nos. 69, 267; 1983 Nos. 8, 64; 1984 Nos. 31, 43; 1985 Nos. 59, 61, 257; 1987 Nos. 143, 468; 1988 No. 204.

sch. 2, amended: 1978, c.42, sch.4; 1985, c.54, s.42; 1988, c.1, sch.29; c.39, sch.3 (prosp.); repealed in pt.: 1984, c.23; 1988, c.39, sch.14 (prosp.).

sch. 3, S.Rs. 1978 No. 102; 1988 No. 125; amended: order 75/1503.

sch. 4, amended: orders 75/1503, 1504; repealed in pt.: orders 75/1503, 1504; 82/1084.

sch. 6, amended: order 80/1087; repealed *ibid.*

sch. 7, repealed: order 75/1503.

sch. 8, S.Rs. 1984 Nos. 92, 174.

sch. 8, amended: order 82/1084.

sch. 9, S.R. 1984 No. 92.

sch. 9, repealed in pt.: order 75/1504.

sch. 10, S.R. 1987 No. 61.

sch. 10, amended: 1980, c.30, s.13; 1986, c.50, sch.9.

sch. 11, repealed in pt.; order 82/1084.

sch. 12, S.Rs. 1982 No. 59; 1983 No. 19; 1984, No. 144; 1987 No. 82.

sch. 13, regs. 77/272; S.Rs. 1977 Nos. 332, 351; 1979 No. 193; 1980 Nos. 267, 383; 1982 Nos. 29, 153; 1983 Nos. 19, 36; 1984 Nos. 144, 445; 1987 Nos. 112, 117, 466.

sch. 14, S.Rs. 1978 No. 262; 1979 No. 371; 1980 No. 357; 1981 No. 345; 1982 No. 343; 1983 No. 341; 1984 No. 92; 1985 No. 278; 1986 No. 212.

sch. 17, regs. 77/280; 88/269; S.Rs. 1978 No. 90; 1979 No. 243; 1980 No. 144; 1984 Nos. 31, 60, 80, 81, 92, 123, 245, 299, 332, 371–373, 376–378, 382, 444; 1985 No. 41; 1987 Nos. 112, 129, 404; amended and repealed in pt.: orders 75/1503, 1504.

16. Industrial Injuries and Diseases (Old Cases) Act 1975.

Royal Assent, March 13, 1975.

1975—cont.

16. Industrial Injuries and Diseases (Old Cases) Act 1975—*cont.*

s. 2, schemes 75/1138; 76/1277; 77/991, 1063, 1607; 83/1361; 86/1174; amended: orders 77/1325; 79/993; 82/1130; 87/45, 1978; repealed in pt.: 1986, c.50, sch.10.

ss. 2, 4, schemes 79/1190; 80/1556; 81/1516; 82/1489, 1490; 84/452, 453; 85/1446; 87/419, 429; 88/574.

ss. 2, 7, amended: orders 76/1029; 78/912; 80/1245; 83/1244; 84/1104; 85/1245.

s. 3, scheme 82/1489.

s. 4, schemes 77/380, 991, 992, 1063, 1104, 1607; 83/136, 1361; 86/1174; amended: 1977, c.5, s.11; 1986, c.50, sch.10; repealed in pt.: 1977, c.5, sch.2; 1986, c.50, sch.11.

s. 5, schemes 79/996; 83/136, 504; 85/491; 87/400.

ss. 5, 7, scheme 75/1139.

s. 6, amended: 1980, c.30, s.4; repealed in pt.: *ibid.*, s.4, sch.5.

s. 7, scheme 77/380; amended: 1975, c.61, sch.4; 1977, c.5, s.11; 1982, c.24, sch.4; orders 77/1325; 79/993; scheme 82/1490; 1986, c.50, sch.10; orders 87/45, 1978; repealed in pt.: 1977, c.5, sch.2; 1986, c.50, sch.10.

s. 8, schemes 77/380, 992, 1063; 83/136, 84/453; amended: 1977, c.5, s.11; repealed in pt.: *ibid.*, sch.2.

s. 9, repealed in pt.: 1986, c.50, sch.11.

ss. 9, 10, schemes 82/1489; 83/136; 84/453.

s. 10, repealed: 1986, c.50, sch.11.

s. 11, order 77/1325; repealed in pt.: 1977, c.5, sch.2.

ss. 12, 13, schemes 82/1489; 83/136.

s. 14, scheme 83/136.

s. 14, amended: 1977, c.5, s.11.

17. Industrial Injuries and Diseases (Northern Ireland Old Cases) Act 1975.

Royal Assent, March 20, 1975.

s. 2, regs. 77/273, 287; 82/341; S.Rs. 1978 No. 315; 1979 No. 346; 1980 No. 361; 1981 No. 346; 1983 Nos. 101, 277; 1984 No. 145; 1985 No. 253; 1986 No. 222; 1987 Nos. 118, 152; 1988 No. 104; scheme 84/277.

s. 3, S.R. 1983 No. 101.

s. 4, regs. 77/287; 82/341; S.Rs. 1978 No. 315; 1979 No. 346; 1980 No. 361; 1981 No. 346; 1983 Nos. 101, 277; 1984 No. 145; 1985 No. 253; 1987 Nos. 118, 152; 1988 No. 104; scheme 84/277.

s. 4, amended: order 79/1573.

ss. 5–8, S.R. 1983 No. 101.

18. Social Security (Consequential Provisions) Act 1975.

Royal Assent, March 20, 1975.

s. 1, see *Peter Willows* v. *Lewis* [1981] T.R. 439, Sir Douglas Frank, Q.C.

s. 1, adopted: order 76/1003.

s. 2, regs. 75/515, 553–559, 562, 564–566, 598, 812, 813, 1747, 1860; 76/533, 1069, 1736; 77/272, 1693; 78/393, 1123; 79/643, 940; 83/118; orders 76/225; 77/425; 87/935; S.Rs. 1978 Nos. 114, 262; 1979 No. 244; 1983 No 16; 1984 No 245.

1975—cont.

18. Social Security (Consequential Provisions) Act 1975—*cont.*

ss. 87, 144, 146–153, 160, 163, sch. 1; adopted: order 76/1003.

sch. 2, see *Peter Willows* v. *Lewis* [1981] T.R. 439, Sir Douglas Frank, Q.C.

sch. 2, repealed in pt.: 1975, c.24, sch.3; c.25, sch.3; c.60, sch.5; c.61, sch.5; c.71, sch.18; 1976, c.71, sch.8; 1977, c.36, sch.9; c.42, sch 25; 1978, c.44, sch.17; 1979, c.47, sch.5; 1980, c.5, sch.6; c.42, sch.2; 1981, c 20, sch.4; 1982, c.9, sch.3; c.10, sch.4; 1984, c.22, sch.3; orders 75/1503, 1504; 76/1041, 1043; 77/2156; 78/1042; 82/158; 1985, c.9, sch.1; c.65, sch.10; c.66, sch.8 (S.); c.71, sch.1; 1986, c.50, sch.; 1988, c.1, sch.31.

sch. 3, regs. 75/467, 469, 470, 492, 496, 515, 552–558, 560, 562, 564–567, 598, 812, 813, 1747, 1855, 1860; 76/533, 1069, 1736; 77/272, 543, 544, 1693; 78/393, 1123, 1877; 79/591, 628, 643, 940; 83/118; S.Rs. 1977 Nos. 316, 351; 1978 Nos. 105, 114, 262, 400; 1979 Nos. 186, 211, 242; 1983 Nos. 16, 101, 277; 1984 No. 245; 1987 No. 413; orders 76/225; 77/425, 1131; 1986, c.50, sch.

sch. 3, amended: 1975, c.26, sch.4; repealed in pt.: 1975, c.60, sch.5; 1980, c.30, sch.5; orders 75/1503, 1504.

19. Export Guarantees Amendment Act 1975.

Royal Assent, March 27, 1975.

repealed: 1975, c.38, s.12.

20. District Courts (Scotland) Act 1975.

Royal Assent, March 27, 1975.

s. 1A, order 86/1836.

s. 1A, added: 1985, c.73, s.33.

s. 2, amended: 1980, c.4, sch.1.

s. 3, repealed in pt.: 1977, c.45, sch.13.

s. 8, see *Strathclyde Regional Council* v. *City of Glasgow District Council* (O.H.), 1988 S.L.T. 144.

s. 10, repealed in pt.: 1976, c.66, sch.8.

s. 11, amended: 1985, c.73, s.34; repealed in pt.: 1976, c.66, sch.8.

s. 13, repealed in pt.: *ibid.*

s. 15, amended: 1985, c.73, s.34.

s. 17, regs. 75/674, 1940; 77/40.

s. 17, amended: 1977, c.38, sch.3; repealed in pt.: *ibid.*; 1976, c.66, sch.8.

s. 19, regs. 75/734; 83/264.

s. 19, repealed: 1985, c.73, sch.4.

s. 21, repealed: 1986, c.47, sch.5.

s. 22, repealed: 1976, c.66, sch.8.

s. 26, repealed in pt.: *ibid.*

s. 27, repealed in pt.: 1977, c.45, sch.13.

sch. 1, repealed in pt.: 1976, c.66, sch.8; c.67, sch 2; 1977, c.45, sch.13.

21. Criminal Procedure (Scotland) Act 1975.

Royal Assent, May 8, 1975.

s. 1, see *MacDougall* v. *Russell*, 1986 S.L.T. 403.

s. 2, amended: 1987, c.41, s.58.

s. 5, amended: *ibid.*, sch.1; repealed in pt.: *ibid.*, schs.1,2.

s. 8, repealed in pt.: 1982, c.48, sch.16.

s. 13, amended: 1982, c.51, sch.3; 1983, c.20, sch.4; 1984, c.36, sch.3.

1975—cont.

21. Criminal Procedure (Scotland) Act 1975—*cont.*

s. 17, repealed: 1977, c.45, sch.13.

s. 18, amended: 1980, c.4, s.7.

s. 19, amended: 1980, c.62, sch.7.

ss. 19, 20, see *Carmichael* v. *Armitage*, 1983 S.L.T. 316.

s. 20, amended: 1980, c.62, s.6.

s. 20A, see *Carmichael* v. *Armitage*, 1983 S.L.T. 316; *H.M. Advocate* v. *Cafferty*, 1984 S.C.C.R. 444; *Walker* v. *H.M. Advocate*, 1985 S.C.C.R 150.

s. 20A, added: 1980, c.62, s.6.

s. 20B, see *Carmichael* v. *Armitage*, 1983 S.L.T. 316.

s. 20B, added 1980, c.62, s.6.

ss. 23, 24, amended: 1975, c.72, s.70.

s. 25, amended: 1984, c.36, sch.3.

s. 26, amended: 1980, c.4, sch.1.

s. 28, see *H.M. Advocate* v. *Keegan*, 1981 S.L.T.(Notes) 35; *Tin Fan Lau, Petr.*, 1986 S.L.T. 535; *Gibbons, Petr.*, 1988 S.L.T. 657.

s. 28, amended: 1980, c.62, sch.7.

s. 29, repealed: 1980, c.4, sch.2.

s. 30, see *Long* v. *H.M.Advocate*, 1984 S.C.C.R. 161.

s. 30, amended: 1980, c.4, sch.1; repealed in pt.: *ibid.*, sch.2.

ss. 34, 36, repealed: *ibid.*

s. 50, see *Andrew* v. *H.M. Advocate*, 1982, S.C.C.R. 539.

s. 60, see *McHugh* v. *H.M. Advocate*, 1978 J.C. 12.

s. 67, see *H.M. Advocate* v. *J.M.R.*, 1985 S.C.C.R. 330; *Varey* v. *H.M. Advocate*, 1986 S.L.T. 321.

s. 68, amended: 1980, c.62, sch.4; repealed in pt.: *ibid.*, sch.8.

s. 69, amended: *ibid.*, sch.4.

s. 70, see *McAllister* v. *H.M. Advocate*, 1985 S.L.T. 399.

s. 71, amended: 1980, c.62, sch.7.

s. 74, amended: *ibid.*, sch.4; repealed in pt.: *ibid.*, sch.8.

s. 75, see *Welsh* v. *H.M. Advocate*, 1986 S.L.T. 664.

ss. 75, 76, see *H.M. Advocate* v. *McDonald*, 1984 S.L.T. 426.

ss. 75, 76, substituted: 1980, c.62, sch.4.

s. 76A, see *Templeton* v. *H.M. Advocate*, 1988 S.L.T. 171.

s. 76A, added: 1980, c.62, sch.4.

s. 77, substituted: *ibid.*

s. 77A, added: *ibid.*

s. 78, see *H.M.Advocate* v. *Cafferty*, 1984 S.C.C.R. 444; *H.M.Advocate* v. *Graham*, High Court of Justiciary, April 19, 1985.

ss. 78, 80, substituted: 1980, c.62, sch.4.

ss. 78, 81, see *H.M. Advocate* v. *Swift*, 1983, S.C.C.R. 204.

s. 81, amended: 1980, c.62, sch.7.

ss. 81, 82, see *Monaghan* v. *H.M. Advocate*, 1984 S.L.T. 262.

s. 82, amended: 1980, c.62, s.13, sch.4.

s. 82A, added: *ibid.*, s.27.

s. 83, see *MacNeil* v. *H.M. Advocate*, 1986 S.C.C.R. 288.

CAP.

1975—cont.
21. Criminal Procedure (Scotland) Act 1975— cont.

ss. 83, 84, amended: 1980, c.62, sch.4.
s. 86, amended: 1987, c.41, sch.1.
ss. 87, 88, repealed: *ibid.*, sch.2.
ss. 89, 90, amended: 1985, c.73, s.23, sch.2.
s. 91, amended: 1980, c.55, sch.2; 1985, c.73, s.23, sch.2.
s. 96, amended: 1980, c.62, sch.4.
s. 98, amended: *ibid.*, sch.7; 1985, c.73, s.23, sch.2.
s. 99, amended: 1980, c.55, s.2.
s. 100, amended: 1980, c.62, sch.7.
s. 101, see *H.M. Advocate* v. *McCann*, 1977 S.L.T.(Notes) 19; *H.M. Advocate* v. *Walker*, 1981 S.L.T.(Notes) 111; *Gildea* v. *H.M. Advocate*, 1983 S.L.T. 458; *Watson* v. *H.M. Advocate*, 1983 S.L.T. 471; 1983 S.C.C.R. 115; *H.M. Advocate* v. *Swift*, High Court of Justiciary, June 28, 1984; *H.M. Advocate* v. *Brown*, 1984 S.C.C.R. 347; *McGinty* v. *H.M. Advocate*, 1985 S.L.T. 25; *Farrell* v. *H.M. Advocate*, 1985 S.L.T. 58; *Welsh* v. *H.M. Advocate*, 1986 S.L.T. 664; *MacDougall* v. *Russell*, 1986 S.L.T. 403; *Dobbie* v. *H.M. Advocate*, 1986 S.L.T. 648; *H.M. Advocate* v. *Sinclair*, 1987 S.L.T. 161; *H.M. Advocate* v. *Shevlin*, 1987 S.L.T. 314; *Sandford* v. *H.M. Advocate*, 1987 S.L.T. 339; *Mallison* v. *H.M. Advocate*, 1987 S.C.C.R. 320; *H.M. Advocate* v. *Campbell*, 1988 S.L.T. 72; *McDonald* v. *H.M. Advocate*, 1988 S.L.T. 693; *Berry* v. *H.M. Advocate*, 1989 S.L.T. 71.
s. 101, substituted: 1980, c.62, s.14.
s. 102, substituted: *ibid.*, s.16.
s. 103, substituted: *ibid.*, sch.4.
s. 104, substituted: *ibid.*; amended: 1987, c.41, s.58.
ss. 105–107, repealed: 1980, c.62, schs.4,8.
s. 108, see *H.M.Advocate* v. *Cafferty*, 1984 S.C.C.R. 444; *McAllister* v. *H.M.Advocate*, 1985 S.L.T. 399.
s. 108, amended: 1980, c.62, sch.4; 1985, c.73, sch.2.
ss. 108, 111A, see *H.M. Advocate* v. *McDonald*, 1984 S.L.T. 426.
s. 110, amended: 1980, c.62, sch.4.
s. 111A, added: *ibid.*, sch.7.
s. 112, substituted: 1987, c.41, s.57.
s. 113, amended: 1980, c.62, sch.7; 1987, c.41, sch.1.
s. 114, Acts of Adjournal 77/1724; 78/1425; 79/1155; 80/1441; 81/948, 1420; 82/1364; 83/1442; 85/1534; 86/1687.
s. 114, substituted: 1987 c.41, s.57.
ss. 115–119, repealed: *ibid.*, sch.2.
ss. 120–122, repealed: 1980, c.62, schs.4,8.
s. 123, see *Keane* v. *H.M. Advocate*, 1987 S.L.T. 220.
s. 127, amended: 1980, c.62, s.18, sch.4.
s. 129, amended: 1987, c.41, sch.1.
s. 130, amended: 1980, c.62, s.23, sch.2.
s. 139A, added: 1987, c.41, s.63.
s. 140A, added: 1980, c.62, s.19.
s. 140A, see *McAvoy* v. *H.M. Advocate*, High Court of Justiciary, May 28, 1982; *Little* v.

CAP.

1975—cont.
21. Criminal Procedure (Scotland) Act 1975— cont.

H.M. Advocate, 1983 S.L.T. 489; 1983 S.C.C.R. 56.
s. 141, see *McCourtney* v. *H.M. Advocate*, High Court of Justiciary, July 12, 1977; *Burton* v. *H.M. Advocate*, 1979 S.L.T.(Notes) 59; *McHugh* v. *H.M. Advocate*, 1978 J.C. 12; *Sandlan* v. *H.M. Advocate*, 1983 S.L.T. 519; *H.M. Advocate* v. *Ferrie*, 1983 S.C.C.R. 1; *Monaghan* v. *H.M. Advocate*, 1984 S.L.T. 262; *Upton* v. *H.M. Advocate*, 1986 S.L.T. 594; *Fleming* v. *H.M. Advocate* 1986 S.C.C.R. 577; *Dodds* v. *H.M. Advocate*, 1988 S.L.T. 194; *Leggate* v. *H.M. Advocate*, The Scotsman, August 12, 1988.
s. 141, amended: 1979, c.16, s.1; 1980, c.62, s.28, sch.7; 1987, c.41, sch.1; repealed in pt.: 1980, c.62, sch.8.
ss. 141A, 141B, added 1985, c.73, s.36.
s. 143, see *Hunter* v. *H.M. Advocate*, 1984, S.L.T. 434; *B.* v. *Kennedy*, 1987 S.L.T. 765.
s. 143, substituted: 1980, c.62, s.29.
s. 145, see *Bennett* v. *H.M. Advocate*, 1980 S.L.T.(Notes) 73; *Cunningham* v. *H.M. Advocate*, 1984 S.L.T. 249.
s. 145, amended: 1980, c.62, s.21.
s. 147, see *Low* v. *H.M. Advocate*, 1988 S.L.T. 97.
s. 148A, see *Thomson* v. *H.M. Advocate*, 1988 S.C.C.R. 354.
s. 148A, added: 1982, c.48, s.73.
s. 149, substituted: *ibid.*, s.30; amended: 1987, c.41, sch.1.
s. 149A, see *Sandlan* v. *H.M. Advocate*, 1983 S.L.T. 519.
s. 149A, added: 1982, c.48, s.30; amended: 1985, c.73, s.37.
s. 151, substituted: 1982, c.48, s.6.
s. 153, see *Cunningham* v. *H.M. Advocate*, 1984 S.L.T. 249; *MacKenzie* v. *H.M. Advocate*, 1986 S.L.T. 389; 1986 S.C.C.R. 94.
s. 153, amended: 1982, c.48, s.24.
s. 154, repealed in pt.: *ibid.*
s. 160, see *Cordiner* v. *H.M. Advocate*, High Ct. of Justiciary, February 24, 1978; *Murphy* v. *H.M. Advocate*, 1978 J.C. 1; *McColl* v. *Skeen*, 1980 S.L.T.(Notes) 53; *McAvoy* v. *H.M. Advocate*, High Court of Justiciary, May 28, 1982; *Graham* v. *H.M. Advocate*, 1984 S.L.T. 67; *Slane* v. *H.M. Advocate*, 1984 S.L.T. 293; *Varey* v. *H.M. Advocate*, 1986 S.L.T. 321; *Deeney* v. *H.M. Advocate*, 1986 S.C.C.R. 393.
s. 168, amended: 1980, c.62, sch.7.
s. 169, substituted: 1980, c.62, s.22, amended 1984, c.46, sch.5.
s. 170, see *Merrin* v. *S.*, 1987 S.L.T. 193.
s. 171, amended: 1976, c.67, sch.1; 1986, c.36, sch.1; 1988 c.33, sch.15.
s. 173, amended: 1980, c.62, sch.7.
s. 174, amended: 1983, c.39, sch.2.
ss. 174, 175, see *Smith* v. *H.M. Advocate*, 1980 S.L.T.(Notes) 56.
s. 174A, added: 1983, c.39, s.34; amended: 1984, c.36, sch.3.

1975—cont.

21. Criminal Procedure (Scotland) Act 1975— cont.

s 175, see *Allan* v. *H.M. Advocate*, 1983 S.C.C.R. 183.

s. 175, amended: 1983, c.39, sch.2; 1984, c.36, sch.3.

s 176, amended: 1983, c.39, s.35, sch.2; 1984, c.36, sch.3.

s. 178, amended: 1983, c.39, s.22, sch.2; 1984, c.36, s.76, sch.3.

s. 179, see *Long* v. *H.M. Advocate*, 1984 S.C.C.R. 161.

s. 179, amended: 1980, c.4, s.5; c.62, sch.7.

s. 180, amended: 1980, c.4, s.6, sch.1; repealed in pt.: *ibid.*,s.6, sch.2.

s. 183, amended: 1978, c.49, s.7; 1982, c.48, sch.13; 1987, c.41, s.65, sch.1.

s. 184, amended: 1983, c.39, s.36; 1984, c.36, sch. 3; repealed in pt.: 1983, c.39, s.36, sch.3.

s. 186, amended: 1980, c.62, s.46; 1982, c.48, sch.7; 1987, c.41, s.65.

s. 188, amended: 1978, c.49, sch.2.

s. 191, repealed in pt.: 1980, c.62, sch.8.

s. 193, amended: *ibid.*, s.46.

s. 193A, added: 1977, c.45, s.11; 1980, c.62, sch.7; amended: 1982, c.48, sch.15.

s. 193B, repealed: 1987, c.41, sch.8.

s. 194, substituted: 1980, c.62, s.47; amended: *ibid.*, s.66.

s. 195, repealed: *ibid.*, sch.8.

s. 196, amended: *ibid.*, ss.48,66.

ss. 197–202, repealed: *ibid.*, sch.8.

s. 204, repealed: *ibid.*, s.45, sch.8.

s. 205, substituted: *ibid.*, s.43.

s. 205A, added: *ibid.*

s. 206, substituted: *ibid.*, s.44.

s. 206A, added: 1985, c.73, s.45.

s. 207, substituted: 1980, c.62, s.45; amended: 1985, c.73, s.43; 1988, c.33, s.124.

s. 208, repealed: 1980, c.62, sch.8.

s. 209, repealed: *ibid.*, s.45.

ss. 210, 211, repealed: *ibid.*, sch.8.

s. 212, amended: *ibid.*, sch.7; 1987, c.41, sch.1; repealed in pt.: *ibid.*

s. 215, substituted: 1980, c.62, sch.7; amended: 1987, c.41, sch.1.

s. 216, see *Vaughan* v. *H.M. Advocate*, 1979 S.L.T. 49; *Templeton* v. *H.M. Advocate*, 1988 S.L.T. 171.

s. 216, amended: 1987, c.41, s.64.

s. 218, see *Muir* v. *H.M. Advocate*, 1985 S.C.C.R. 402; *Campbell* v. *H.M. Advocate*, 1986 S.C.C.R. 403.

s. 218, repealed in pt.: 1980, c.62, schs.7,8.

s. 219, amended: *ibid.*, s.54.

s. 221, amended: 1987, c.41, s.58.

s. 223, see *Donnelly* v. *H.M. Advocate*, 1984 S.C.C.R. 93.

s. 227A, added: 1980, c.62, s.20.

s. 228, see *Boyle* v. *H.M. Advocate*, 1976 S.L.T. 126; *McAvoy* v. *H.M. Advocate*, High Court of Justiciary, May 28, 1982; *Green* v. *H.M. Advocate*, 1983 S.C.C.R. 42; *Moffat* v. *H.M. Advocate*, 1983 S.C.C.R. 121; *Graham* v. *H.M. Advocate*, 1984 S.L.T. 67; *Rubin* v. *H.M. Advocate*, High Court of Justiciary, March 9,

1975—cont.

21. Criminal Procedure (Scotland) Act 1975— cont.

1984, *Morland* v. *H.M. Advocate*, 1985 S.C.C.R. 316; *Allison* v. *H.M. Advocate*, 1985 S.C.C.R. 408; *McDonald* v. *H.M. Advocate*, 1987 S.C.C.R. 153; *Salusbury-Hughes* v. *H.M. Advocate*, 1987 S.C.C.R. 38; *Cameron* v. *H.M. Advocate*, 1988 S.L.T. 169; *Williamson* v. *H.M. Advocate*, 1988 S.C.C.R. 56.

s. 228, substituted: 1980, c.62, sch.2; repealed in pt.: *ibid.*, sch.8.

s. 229, repealed: *ibid.*, schs.2,8.

s. 231, see *Little* v. *H.M. Advocate*, 1983 S.L.T. 489; 1983 S.C.C.R. 56; *Smith* v. *H.M. Advocate*, 1983 S.C.C.R. 30.

s. 231, substituted: 1980, c.62, sch.2; 1987, c.41, s.45.

s. 232, repealed: 1980, c.62, schs.2,8.

s. 233, see *Ferguson, Petitioner*, 1980 S.L.T. 21; *Smith* v. *H.M. Advocate*, 1983 S.C.C.R. 30.

s: 233, substituted: 1980, c.62, sch.2.

ss. 234, 236, repealed in pt.: *ibid.*, schs.2,8.

ss. 236A, 236B, 236C, added: *ibid.*, sch.2.

s. 237, substituted: *ibid.*

ss. 238, 239, amended: *ibid.*

s. 240, repealed in pt.: *ibid.*, schs.2,8.

ss. 241–243, amended: *ibid.*, sch.7.

s. 244, see *Ferguson, Petitioner*, 1980 S.L.T. 21.

s. 244, substituted: 1980, c.62, sch.2.

s. 245, amended: 1987, c.41, sch.1; repealed in pt.: 1980, c.62, schs.2,8.

s. 246, amended: 1987, c.41, sch.1.

s. 247, amended: 1980, c.62, sch.2; repealed in pt.: *ibid.*, schs.2,8.

s. 251, amended: *ibid.*, sch.7.

s. 252, see *Green* v. *H.M. Advocate*, 1983 S.C.C.R. 42; *Moffat* v. *H.M. Advocate*, 1983 S.C.C.R. 121; *Rubin* v. *H.M. Advocate*, High Court of Justiciary, March 9, 1984; *Morland* v. *H.M. Advocate*, 1985 S.C.C.R. 316; *McCadden* v. *H.M. Advocate*, 1986 S.L.T. 138; *Allison* v. *H.M. Advocate*, 1985 S.C.C.R. 408.

s. 252, substituted: 1980, c.62, sch.2.

s. 253, repealed in pt.: *ibid.*, schs.2,8.

s. 254, see *Boyle* v. *H.M. Advocate*, 1976 J.C. 32, High Ct. of Justiciary; *O'Neil* v. *H.M. Advocate*, 1976 S.L.T.(Notes) 7; *Cordiner* v. *H.M. Advocate*, High Ct. of Justiciary, February 24, 1978; *McAvoy* v. *H.M. Advocate*, High Court of Justiciary, May 28, 1982; *Burns* v. *H.M. Advocate*, 1983 S.L.T. 38; *Mackenzie* v. *H.M. Advocate*, High Court of Judiciary, November 3, 1982; *Sweeney* v. *X*, 1982 S.C.C.R. 509; *King* v. *H.M. Advocate*, 1985 S.C.C.R. 322; *Grant* v. *H.M. Advocate*, 1985 S.C.C.R. 431; *Jamieson* v. *H.M. Advocate*, 1987 S.C.C.R. 484; *Cameron* v. *H.M. Advocate*, 1988 S.L.T. 169; *Slater* v. *H.M. Advocate*, 1987 S.C.C.R. 745.　-

ss. 254, 255, substituted: 1980, c.62, sch.2.

s. 255, see *Mackenzie* v. *H.M. Advocate*, High Court of Judiciary, November 3, 1982.

s. 256, amended: 1980, c.62, sch.2.

s. 257, repealed in pt.: *ibid.*, schs.2,8.

1975—cont.

21. Criminal Procedure (Scotland) Act 1975— cont.

s. 261, amended: *ibid.*, sch.7.

s. 262, see *Ferguson, Petitioner,* 1980 S.L.T. 21.

s. 263, see *Preece* v. *H.M. Advocate* [1981] Crim.L.R. 783, High Court of Justiciary; *Leitch* v. *Secretary of State for Scotland,* 1983 S.L.T. 394.

s. 263, repealed in pt.: 1980, c.62, schs.2,8; 1987, c.41, sch.2.

s. 263A, see *Lord Advocate's Reference (No. 1 of 1985),* 1987 S.L.T. 187.

s. 263A, added: 1980, c.62, s.37.

s. 264, amended: *ibid.*,sch.2; 1987, c.41, s.68.

s. 265, amended: 1980, c.62, sch.2; repealed in pt.: *ibid.*, schs.2,8.

s. 268, amended: *ibid.*,sch.7; 1987, c.41, sch.1.

ss. 269, 270, amended: 1980, c.62, sch.2.

s. 271, amended: *ibid.*; 1985, c.73, sch.2.

s. 272, amended: 1980, c.62, sch.2.; repealed in pt.: *ibid.*, sch.8.

s. 273, amended and repealed in pt.: *ibid.*,sch.2.

s. 274, repealed in pt.: *ibid.*, schs.2,8.

s. 277, amended: *ibid.*, sch.2; repealed in pt.: *ibid.*, schs.2,8.

s. 280, see *Smith* v. *H.M. Advocate,* 1980 S.L.T.(Notes) 56.

s. 280, amended: 1980, c.62, sch.2.

s. 280A, see *H.M. Advocate* v. *Sinclair,* 1987 S.L.T. 161.

s. 280A, added: 1980, c.62, s.35.

s. 282, Acts of Adjournal 76/172, 339, 371, 1062; 78/123, 125, 491, 1686; 79/95, 232, 612, 1632, 80/425, 1929; 81/22, 386–388, 1151, 1443, 1766, 1786; 82/121, 468; 83/972; 84/19, 820; 85/316, 1565; 87/1328; 88/110.

ss. 282, 283, amended: 1980, c.62, sch.7.

s. 283, see *City of Glasgow District Licensing Board* v. *MacDonald,* 1978 S.L.T.(Sh.Ct.) 74.

s. 283A, added: 1977, c.45, sch.11; amended: 1980, c.62, sch.7.

s. 284, amended: 1977, c.45, sch.11; 1982, c.48, sch.7.

s. 285, amended: 1980, c.62, sch.7, 1982, c.48, sch.7; repealed in pt.: 1980, c.62, s.7, sch.8.

s. 289, amended: 1977, c.45, sch.11.

ss. 289A–289D, added: 1977, c.45, sch.11.

s. 289B, regs. 88/1484.

s. 289B, substituted: 1982, c.48, s.55; amended: 1987, c.41, sch.1; repealed in pt.: *ibid.*, sch.2.

s. 289C, amended: 1982, c.48, s.55; repealed in pt.: 1985, c.72, sch.13.

s. 289D, order 84/526.

s. 289D, amended: 1980, c.62, sch.7; 1982, c.48, s.53; 1985, c.13, sch.2.; repealed in pt.: 1980, c.62, sch.8; 1982, c.48, s.53, sch.16; 1987, c.41, sch.2.

ss. 289E–289H, added: 1982, c.48, s.54.

ss. 289F, 289G, regs. 84/1576.

s. 289G, amended: 1987, c.41, s.66; 1988, c.33, sch.15.

ss. 289GA, 289GB, added: 1987, c.41, s.66.

s. 289GC, added: 1988, c.33, s.56.

s. 289GD, added: *ibid.*, s.54.

1975—cont.

21. Criminal Procedure (Scotland) Act 1975— cont.

s. 290, see *Thomson* v. *Smith, Morgan* v. *Smith,* 1982 S.C.C.R. 57; *Sharp* v. *Tudhope,* 1986 S.C.C.R. 64.

s. 291, amended: 1980, c.62, s.38; repealed in pt.: 1982, c.48, sch.16.

s. 294, amended: 1980, c.4, s.7.

s. 295, see *Skeen* v. *Speirs,* 1980 S.L.T.(Notes) 86.

s. 295, substituted: 1980, c.4, s.8.

s. 296, amended: *ibid.*, s.9; repealed in pt.: *ibid.*, sch.2.

s. 297, amended: 1975, c.72, s.70.

s. 298, amended: 1980, c.62, sch.7.

s. 299, amended: 1980, c.4, sch.1; repealed in pt.: *ibid.*, sch.2.

s. 300, amended: 1987, c.41, s.6; repealed in pt.: *ibid.*, sch.2.

ss. 301, 302, repealed: 1980, c.4, sch.2.

s. 303, repealed in pt.: *ibid.*

s. 305, amended: 1980, c.62, sch.7.

s. 310, repealed in pt.: *ibid.*, schs.7,8.

s. 311, see *Smith* v. *Moffat,* 1981 S.C.C.R. 291; *Scott* v. *Mackay,* 1983 S.C.C.R. 210; *Aitchison* v. *Wringe,* 1985 S.L.T. 449; *Cardle* v. *Campbell,* 1985 S.C.C.R. 309; *Geddes* v. *Hamilton,* 1986 S.L.T. 536; *Muir* v. *Carmichael,* 1988 S.C.C.R. 79.

s. 312, see *Joseph Johnston & Sons* v. *Ingram,* 1976 S.L.T. (Notes) 30; *Blair* v. *Keane,* 1981 S.L.T. (Notes) 4; *Lockhart* v. *National Coal Board,* 1981 S.L.T. 161; *Aitchison* v. *Tudhope,* High Court of Justiciary, January 29, 1981; *Skinner* v. *Patience,* 1982 S.L.T.(Sh.Ct.) 81; *Elsey* v. *Smith,* 1982 S.C.C.R. 218; *Dyce* v. *Aitchison,* 1985 S.C.C.R. 184; *Smith* v. *Allan,* 1985 S.L.T. 565; *Anderson* v. *Allan,* 1985 S.C.C.R. 339; *Davidson* v. *Aitchison,* 1986 S.L.T. 402; *Allan* v. *McGraw,* 1986 S.C.C.R. 257; *MacLennan* v. *MacKenzie,* 1988 S.L.T. 16; *Wood* v. *Allan,* 1988 S.L.T. 341; *Cruickshanks* v. *McPhail,* 1988 S.C.C.R. 165; *Walkingshaw* v. *Robinson & Davidson,* High Court of Justiciary, June 14, 1988.

s. 312, amended: 1977, c.45, sch.11; 1980, c.62, s.46; 1982, c.48, sch.7.

s. 314, see *Skeen* v. *Evans,* 1979 S.L.T.(Notes) 55; *Smith* v. *Bernard,* 1980 S.L.T.(Notes) 81; *Tudhope* v. *Buckner,* 1985 S.C.C.R. 352.

s. 314, amended: 1980, c.62, s.11; repealed in pt.: *ibid.*, s.11, sch.8.

ss. 314, 315, see *Kelly* v. *Tudhope,* 1987 S.L.T. 99.

s. 316, see *Skeen* v. *Fullarton,* 1980 S.L.T.(Notes) 46; *Aitchison* v. *Wringe,* 1985 S.L.T. 449; *Muir* v. *Carmichael,* 1988 S.C.C.R. 79.

ss. 316, 319, see *Lockhart* v. *Bradley,* 1977 S.L.T. 5.

s. 321, amended: 1980, c.4, sch.1; repealed in pt.: *ibid.*,sch.2.

s. 322, amended: 1982, c.51, sch.3; 1983, c.20, sch.4; 1984, c.36, sch.3.

s. 325, repealed: 1977, c.45, sch.13.

1975—cont.

21. Criminal Procedure (Scotland) Act 1975—*cont.*

s. 326, see *Mackinnon* v. *Virhia*, High Court of Justiciary, November 28, 1979; *Donlon* v. *Mackinnon*, 1982 S.L.T. 93; *Muir* v. *Carmichael*, 1988 S.C.C.R. 79.

s. 326, repealed in pt.: 1980, c.43, sch.9.

s. 328, see *H.M. Advocate* v. *McGrade*, 1982 S.L.T.(Sh.Ct.) 13.

s. 328, amended: 1987, c.41, s.62.

s. 329, amended: 1975, c.72, s.70; 1987, c.41, s.62.

s. 330, amended. 1984, c.36, sch.3.

s. 331, see *Skeen* v. *Ives Cladding*, 1976 S.L.T.(Notes) 31; *Lockhart* v. *Bradley*, 1977 S.L.T. 5; *Smith* v. *Peter Walker & Son (Edinburgh)*, 1978 J.C. 44; *Young* v. *Smith*, 1981 S.L.T. (Notes) 101; *Tudhope* v. *Mathieson*, 1981 S.C.C.R. 231; *Carmichael* v. *Sardar & Sons*, 1983 S.C.C.R. 433; *Tudhope* v. *Lawson*, 1983 S.C.C.R. 435; *Beattie* v. *Tudhope* 1984 S.L.T. 423; *Tudhope* v. *Brown*, 1984 S.C.C.R. 163; *Tudhope* v. *Buckner*, 1985 S.C.C.R. 352; *McCartney* v. *Tudhope*, 1986 S.L.T. 159; *Stagecoach* v. *McPhail*, 1986 S.C.C.R.184; *Kelly* v. *Tudhope*, 1987 S.L.T. 99; *Ross Inns* v. *Smith*, 1987 S.L.T. 121.

s. 331, amended: 1986, c.36, sch.1.

ss. 331, 334, see *Beattie* v. *McKinnon*, 1977 J.C. 64.

s. 331A, see *Lockhart* v. *Robb*, 1988 S.C.C.R. 381.

s. 331A, added: 1980, c.62, s.14.

s. 333, see *Valentine* v. *Thistle Leisure*, 1983 S.C.C.R. 515.

s. 334, see *Scott* v. *Annan*, 1982 S.L.T. 90; *Henderson* v. *Ingram*, 1982 S.C.C.R. 135; *Mackinnon* v. *Craig*, 1983 S.L.T. 475; *Aitchison* v. *Wringe*, 1985 S.L.T. 449; *Jessop* v. *Christie*, 1986 S.C.C.R. 7.

s. 334, amended: 1980, c.62, s.36, sch.7.

ss. 334, 335, see *Skeen* v. *Fullarton*, 1980 S.L.T.(Notes) 46.

s. 335, see *Cochrane* v. *West Calder Co-operative Society*, 1978 S.L.T.(Notes) 22; *Craig* v. *Keane*, 1981 S.C.C.R. 166; *MacNeill* v. *Robertson*, 1982 S.C.C.R. 468; *Valentine* v. *Thistle Leisure*, 1983 S.C.C.R. 515; *Mackenzie* v. *Brougham*, 1985 S.L.T. 276; *Dyce* v. *Aitchison*, 1985 S.C.C.R. 184; *MacArthur* v. *MacNeill*, 1987 S.L.T. 299; *Tudhope* v. *Fulton*, 1986 S.C.C.R. 567; *Belcher* v. *MacKinnon*, 1987 S.L.T. 298; *Brown* v. *McLeod*, 1986 S.C.C.R. 615; *Duffy* v. *Ingram*, 1987 S.C.C.R. 286.

s. 336, see *Skeen* v. *Sullivan*, 1980 S.L.T.(Notes) 11; *Milne* v. *Guild*, 1986 S.L.T. 431.

s. 337, amended: 1980, c.4, sch.1; 1987, c.41, s.62; repealed in pt.: 1980, c.4, sch.2; c.62, sch.8.

s. 337A, added: *ibid.*, s.15.

s. 338, see *Skeen* v. *Sullivan*, 1980 S.L.T.(Notes) 11; *Skeen* v. *Fullarton*, 1980 S.L.T.(Notes) 46.

s. 338, amended: 1980, c.62, s.17; repealed in pt.: 1980, c.4, sch.2.

s. 338A, see *Tudhope* v. *Gough*, 1982 S.C.C.R. 157.

1975—cont.

21. Criminal Procedure (Scotland) Act 1975—*cont.*

s. 338A, added: 1980, c.62, s.18.

s. 342A, added: 1987, c.41, s.63.

s. 344, amended: 1980, c.62; s.46, sch.7; 1982, c.48, sch.7.

s. 345A, see *Williamson* v. *Wither*, 1981 S.C.C.R. 214; *Keane* v. *Bathgate*, 1983 S.L.T. 651; *Taylor* v. *Douglas*, 1984 S.L.T. 69.

s. 345A, added: 1980, c.62, s.19.

s. 346, see *MacLean* v. *Tudhope*, 1982 S.C.C.R. 555; *Templeton* v. *MacLeod*, 1986 S.L.T. 149; *Conner* v. *Lockhart*, 1986 S.C.C.R. 360; *Leggate* v. *H.M. Advocate*, *The Scotsman*, August 12, 1988.

s. 346, amended: 1979, c.16, s.1; 1980, c.62, s.28, sch.7; 1987, c.41, sch.1; repealed in pt.: 1980, c.62, sch.8.

ss. 346A, 346B, added: 1985, c.73, s.36.

s. 348, substituted: 1980, c.62, s.29.

s. 349A, added: 1982, c.48, s.73.

s. 350, see *Brown* v. *Smith*, 1981 S.C.C.R. 206.

s. 350, substituted: 1980, c.62, s.30.

s. 350A, see *Campbell* v. *Allen*, 1988 S.C.C.R. 47.

s. 350A, added: 1980, c.62, s.30; amended: 1985, c.73, s.37.

s. 352, substituted: 1980, c.62, s.6.

s. 353, see *Andrews* v. *McLeod*, 1982 S.L.T. 456.

s. 354, see *Evans* v. *Wilson*, 1981 S.C.C.R. 60.

s. 357, see *Mitchell* v. *Dean* 1979 S.L.T.(Notes) 12; *Boustead* v. *MacLeod*, 1979 S.L.T.(Notes) 48; *McColl* v. *Skeen*, 1980 S.L.T.(Notes) 53; *Moffat* v. *Smith*, 1983 S.C.C.R. 392; *Johnson* v. *Allan*, 1984 S.L.T. 261; *O'Neill* v. *Tudhope*, 1984 S.L.T. 424; *Anderson* v. *Allan*, 1985 S.C.C.R. 262; *Carmichael* v. *Monaghan*, 1987 S.L.T. 338.

s. 357, amended: 1980, c.62, s.40.

ss. 357, 358, see *Robertson* v. *Aitchison*, 1981 S.L.T.(Notes) 127.

ss. 359, 360, see *Scott* v. *MacKay*, 1983 S.C.C.R. 210.

s. 364, amended: 1980, c.62, sch.7.

s. 365, repealed: *ibid.*, sch.8.

s. 368, amended: 1976, c.67, sch.1; 1986, c.36, sch.1; 1988, c.33, sch.15.

s. 369, see *Merrin* v. *S.*, 1987 S.L.T. 193.

s. 370, amended: 1980, c.62, sch.7.

s. 374, amended: 1977, c.45, s.31, sch.6; 1984, c.46, sch.5.

ss. 375–377, amended: *ibid.*, sch.3.

ss. 375, 376, 379, see *Bain* v. *Smith* 1980 S.L.T.(Notes) 69.

s. 375A, added: 1983, c.20, s.34.

s. 376, see *Smith* v. *M.*, 1983 S.C.C.R. 67.

s. 376, amended: 1983, c.39, sch.2.

s. 377, amended: *ibid.*, s.35, sch.2.

s. 379, amended: *ibid.*, s.22, sch.2; 1984, c.36, s.76, sch.3.

s. 380, see *McGoldrick* v. *Normand*, 1988 S.L.T. 273.

s. 380, amended: 1980, c.4, s.5; c.62, sch.7.

s. 381, amended: 1980, c.4, s.6, sch.1; repealed in pt.: *ibid.*, s.6, sch.2.

1975—cont.

21. Criminal Procedure (Scotland) Act 1975— *cont.*

s. 384, amended: 1978, c.49, s.7; 1980, c.62, s.53; 1982, c.48, sch.13; 1987, c.41, s.65, sch.1.

s. 385, amended: 1983, c.39, s.36; 1984, c.36, sch.3; repealed in pt.: 1983, c.39, s.36, sch.3.

s. 387, amended: 1978, c.49, s.8; 1980, c.62, s.46; 1982, c.48, sch.7; 1987, c.41, s.65.

s. 389, amended: 1978, c.49, sch.2.

s. 392, repealed in pt.: *ibid.*, sch.8.

s. 394, amended: 1982, c.48, sch.7.

s. 395, amended: 1978, c.49, s.66, sch.7.

s. 395A, added: *ibid.*, s.49; amended: *ibid.*, s.66.

s. 396, see *Sullivan* v. *McLeod* 1980 S.L.T.(Notes) 99; *Dunlop* v. *Allan*, 1984 S.C.C.R. 329; *Buchanan* v. *Hamilton*, 1988 S.C.C.R. 379.

s. 396, amended: 1980, c.62, s.66.

ss. 396, 397, see *Campbell* v. *Jessop*, 1988 S.L.T. 160.

ss. 396, 398, see *Finnie* v. *McLeod*, 1983 S.C.C.R. 387.

s. 397, amended: 1977, c.45, sch.11; 1980, c.43, sch.7; c.62, s.66.

s. 398, amended: *ibid.*, s.66, sch.7.

s. 399, amended: *ibid.*; repealed in pt.: *ibid.*, schs.7,8.

s. 400, amended: *ibid.*, s.66.

s. 401, amended: *ibid.*, s.66, sch.7.

s. 402, amended: *ibid.*, s.66.

s. 403, amended: 1977, c.45, sch.7; 1980, c.43, sch.7; c.62, s.66; repealed in pt.: 1977, c.45, schs.7,13.

s. 404, amended: 1980, c.62, s.66.

s. 405, repealed: *ibid.*, sch.8.

s. 406, amended: *ibid.*, s.66, sch.7.

s. 407, see *Campbell* v. *Jessop*, 1988 S.L.T. 160.

s. 407, amended: 1980, c.62, ss.50,66, sch.7; 1985, c.73, s.40; 1987, c.41, s.67.

ss. 408, 409, amended: 1980, c.62, s.66, sch.7.

s. 410, repealed: *ibid.*, sch.8.

s. 411, amended: *ibid.*, ss.52,66, sch.7; 1987, c.18, sch.6; repealed in pt.: 1980, c.62, s.52, sch.8.

s. 413, regs. 88/294.

s. 413, substituted: 1987, c.41, s.59.

s. 414, repealed: 1980, c.62, s.45, sch.8.

s. 415, see *Milligan* v. *Jessop*, 1988 S.C.C.R. 137.

s. 415, amended: 1985, c.73, s.43; 1988, c.33, s.124.

s. 416, see *Devlin* v. *Macfarlane*, 1976 S.L.T.(Notes) 5; *Deasley* v. *Hogg*, 1976 S.L.T.(Notes) 7.

ss. 416, 417, see *Mackay* v. *Tudhope*, 1979 S.L.T.(Notes) 43; *Sullivan* v. *McLeod*, 1980 S.L.T.(Notes) 99.

ss. 416, 417, repealed: 1980, c.62, sch.8.

s. 418, repealed: *ibid.*, s.45, sch.8.

ss. 419, 420, repealed: *ibid.*, sch.8.

s. 421, amended: *ibid.*, sch.7; 1982, c.48, sch.15; repealed in pt.: *ibid.*, sch.16.

1975—cont.

21. Criminal Procedure (Scotland) Act 1975— *cont.*

s. 424, see *Strathclyde Regional Council* v. *City of Glasgow District Council* (O.H.), 1988 S.L.T. 144.

s. 424, amended: 1980, c.62, sch.7.

s. 426, substituted: *ibid.*; amended: 1987, c.41, sch.1.

s. 428, amended: 1980, c.62, s.64.

s. 430, see *Pettigrew* v. *Ingram*, 1982 S.L.T. 435; *Noble* v. *Guild*, 1987 S.C.C.R. 518; *Cartledge* v. *McLeod*, 1988 S.L.T. 389.

ss. 430, 434, see *Tudhope* v. *Colbert*, 1978 S.L.T.(Notes) 57.

s. 431, see *Morrison* v. *Scott*, 1987 S.C.C.R. 376.

s. 431, repealed in pt.: 1980, c.62, sch.7.

s. 432, amended: *ibid.*, ss.53,54.

s. 433, see *Campbell* v. *Jessop*, 1988 S.L.T. 160.

s. 434, repealed in pt.: 1980, c.62, sch.8.

s. 435, amended: *ibid.*, s.46.

s. 436, substituted: *ibid.*, sch.7.

s. 439, see *Tudhope* v. *Senatti Holdings*, 1984 S.C.C.R. 251.

s. 439, substituted: 1980, c.62, s.20.

s. 442, see *Tudhope* v. *Mathieson*, 1981 S.C.C.R. 231; *McLean* v. *Tudhope*, 1982 S.C.C.R. 555; *Courtney* v. *Mackinnon*, 1986 S.C.C.R. 545; *Marshall* v. *Macdougall*, 1987 S.L.T. 123; *Moore* v. *Tudhope*, 1987 S.C.C.R. 370.

s. 442, substituted: 1980, c.62, sch.3.

ss. 442A, 442B, added: *ibid.*

s. 443, amended: *ibid.*; 1983, c.39, s.34.

s. 443A, added: 1987, c.41, s.68.

s. 444, see *Galloway* v. *Hillary*, 1983 S.C.C.R. 119; *Elliot, Applicant*, High Court of Justiciary, February 10, 1984; *Durant* v. *Lockhart*, 1986 S.L.T. 312; *MacDougall, Petr.*, 1986 S.C.C.R. 128; *Singh, Petr.*, 1987 S.L.T. 63; *Dickson* v. *Valentine*, 1988 S.C.C.R. 325.

s. 444, amended: 1980, c.4, sch.1; c.62, sch.3; repealed in pt.: *ibid.*, sch.8.

ss. 444, 447, see *McTaggart, Pctr.*, 1987 S.C.C.R. 638.

s. 445, repealed: 1980, c.62, schs.3,8.

s. 446, see *Fenton, Petr.*, 1982 S.L.T. 164.

s. 446, amended: 1980, c.4, sch.1; c.62, sch.3; repealed in pt.: 1980, c.4, sch.2.

s. 447, see *Gordon* v. *Allen*, 1987 S.L.T. 400.

s. 447, amended: 1980, c.62, sch.3; 1985, c.73, sch.2; repealed in pt.: 1980, c.62, sch.8.

ss. 447, 451, see *Mackinnon* v. *McGarry*, 1988 S.L.T.(Sh.Ct.) 15.

s. 448, see *Barry, Petr.*, 1985 S.C.C.R. 106.

s. 448, amended: 1980, c.4, sch.1; c.62, sch.3; repealed in pt.: *ibid.*, schs.3,8; 1985, c.73, sch.4.

s. 449, amended: 1980, c.62, sch.3.

ss. 451, 452, substituted: *ibid.*

s. 452, see *Aitchison* v. *Rizza*, 1985 S.C.C.R. 297; *Marshall* v. *Macdougall*, 1987 S.L.T. 123.

s. 452A, see *McLean* v. *Tudhope*, 1982 S.C.C.R. 555.

ss. 452A, 452B, see *Courtney* v. *Mackinnon*, 1986 S.C.C.R. 545.

1975—cont.

21. Criminal Procedure (Scotland) Act 1975—cont.

ss. 452A, 452B, added: 1980, c.62, sch.3.

s. 453, amended: *ibid.*, s.46, sch.3.

s. 453A, see *Pettigrew* v. *Ingram,* 1982 S.L.T. 435.

ss. 453A–453E, added: 1980, c.62, sch.3.

s. 435C, see *Briggs* v. *Guild,* 1987 S.C.C.R. 141.

s. 454, see *Skeen* v. *Murphy,* 1978 S.L.T.(Notes) 2; *McLeary* v. *Douglas,* 1979 S.L.T. 140; *Aitchison* v. *Tudhope,* High Court of Justiciary, January 29, 1981.

s. 454, repealed in pt.: 1980, c.62, schs.3,8

s. 457, Acts of Adjournal 76/172, 339, 371, 1062; 78/123, 125, 491, 1686; 79/95, 232, 612, 1632; 80/425; 81/22, 386–388, 1443, 1766, 1786, 82/121, 468; 83/972; 84/1955; 85/43, 316, 1565; 86/1191, 1686, 2184; 88/110.

ss. 457–459, amended: 1980, c.62, sch.7.

s. 457A, added: 1982, c.48, s.55.

s. 460, repealed in pt.: 1980, c.62, schs.7,8.

s. 462, see *Smith* v. *H.M. Advocate,* 1980 S.L.T.(Notes) 56; *Sullivan* v. *McLeod,* 1980 S.L.T.(Notes) 99; *Cartledge* v. *McLeod,* 1988 S.L.T. 389.

s. 462, amended: 1977, c.45, sch.11; 1978, c.29, sch.16(S.); 1980, c.4, sch.1; c.62, s.25, sch.7; 1982, c.48, sch.15; 1983, c.39, sch.2; 1984, c.36, sch.3; repealed in pt.: 1983, c.39, schs.2,3.

s. 463, amended: 1980, c.62, sch.7; 1987, c.41, s.59; repealed in pt.: 1977, c.45, sch.13; 1980, c.43, sch.9.

sch. 1, see *B.* v. *Kennedy,* 1987 S.L.T. 765; *F.* v. *Kennedy,* 1988 S.L.T. 404.

sch. 1, amended: 1976, c.67, sch.1; repealed in pt.: *ibid.*, sch.2; 1986, c.36, sch.1.

sch. 2, repealed: 1980, c.55, sch.3.

sch. 3, amended: 1980, c.4, sch.1; repealed in pt.: *ibid.*, sch.2; amended: 1980, c.62, sch.7.

sch. 4, repealed: 1980, c.55, sch.8.

sch. 5, amended: 1983, c.39, s.36.

sch. 7, amended: 1980, c.62, s.66.

sch. 7A, repealed in pt.: 1983, c.2, sch.9, 1984 c.24, sch.6; 1986, c.48, sch.5.

schs. 7A–7C, added: 1977, c.45, sch.11.

sch. 7B, repealed: 1980, c.62, sch.8.

sch. 7C, repealed in pt.: 1979, c.39, sch.7; 1980, c.52, s.65, sch.5; 1981, c.69, sch.17; 1984, c.12, sch.7; c.27, sch.4; 1987, c.26, sch.24.

sch. 7D, added: 1982, c.48, s.56, sch.6; repealed in pt.: 1982, c.33, sch.2; 1984, c.27, sch.4; 1987, c.26, sch.24; 1988, c.54, sch.1.

sch. 9, repealed in pt.: 1984, c.36, sch.5.

22. Oil Taxation Act 1975.

Royal Assent, May 8, 1975.

s. 1, amended: 1979, c.47, ss.18,21; 1980, c.48, s.104; 1982, c.39, s.132; 1988, c.1, sch.29.

s. 2, see *R.* v. *Att.-Gen., ex p. I.C.I.,* The Financial *Times,* January 29, 1985, Woolf J.

s. 2, amended: 1980, c.48, ss.19,22; 1982, c.39, s.133, sch.19; 1983, c.28, sch.8; 1987, c.16, sch.13; repealed in pt.: *ibid.*, s.62, sch.16.

1975—cont.

22. Oil Taxation Act 1975—cont.

s. 3, see *I.R.C.* v. *Mobil North Sea* [1987] 1 W.L.R. 389, C.A.

s. 3, amended: 1981, c.35, s.119; 1982, c.39, s.20; 1983, c.28, sch.8; c.56, s.5; 1984, c.43, s.124; 1987, c.16, sch.13; repealed in pt.: 1984, c.43, s.24, sch.23.

s. 4, amended: 1982, c.39, s.20.

s. 5, amended: 1983, c.28, sch.8; 1988, c.1, sch.29; repealed in pt.: 1980, c.48, sch.20.

s. 5A, added: 1983, c.28, s.37, sch.8; amended: 1985, c.54, s.90; repealed in pt.: 1987, c.16, s.62, sch.16.

s. 5B, added: *ibid.*, s.64, sch.13.

s. 6, amended: 1988, c.1, sch.29.

s. 8, amended: 1979, c.47, s.21; 1983, c.28, s.36.

s. 9, substituted: 1981, c.35, s.114; amended: 1983, c.28, sch.8; 1985, c.54, s.90; 1987, c.16, s.64, sch.13.

s. 10, amended: 1979, c.47, s.21.

s. 12, amended: 1980, c.48, s.109; 1983, c.28, s.39; repealed in pt.: 1982, c.39, s.135, sch.22.

ss. 13–20, repealed: 1988, c.1, sch.31.

s. 20, repealed in pt.: 1988, c.39, sch.14.

s. 21, amended: 1988, c.1, sch.29.

sch. 2, see *Amoco (U.K.) Exploration Co.* v. *I.R.C.* [1983] S.T.C. 634, Walton J.

sch. 2, amended: 1976, c.40, s.130; 1980, c.1, ss.1,2; 1982, c.39, sch.19; 1983, c.28, sch.8; c.56, s.10; 1987, c.16, s.62, schs. 10, 13; c.51, s.101; repealed in pt.: 1987, c.16, s.62, sch.16; 1988, c.39, sch.14.

sch. 3, see *R.* v. *Att.-Gen., ex p. I.C.I.,* The Financial *Times,* January 29, 1985, Woolf J.

sch. 3, amended: 1977, c.36, s.54; 1980, c.48, s.100; 1981, c.35, s.116; 1982, c.23, sch.3; c.39, sch.19; 1983, c.28, s.38, sch.10; 1986, c.44, sch.7; 1987, c.16, s.62, sch.11; 1988, c.1, sch.29; repealed in pt.: 1982, c.23, schs.3,4; c.39, s.137, sch.22; 1987, c.62, schs.11,16.

sch. 4, amended: 1988, c.1, sch.29; repealed in pt.: 1983, c.56, sch.6.

sch. 5, amended: 1980, c.1, s.2; 1983, c.28, s.40.

sch. 6, amended: *ibid.*, s.40.

sch. 7, amended: *ibid.*, sch.8; 1987, c.62, s.67, sch.13; repealed in pt.: 1983, c.28, s.37.

sch. 9, repealed: 1988, c.1, sch.31.

23. Reservoirs Act 1975.

Royal Assent, May 8, 1975.

Commencement orders; 83/1666; 85/176; 86/466, 2202.

s. 2, amended: 1985, c.51, s.11.

ss. 2, 3, regs. 85/177.

s. 4, regs. 84/1874; 85/175, 1086; 86/853; 88/69.

s. 5, regs. 84/1874; 85/175, 177, 548, 1086; 86/468, 853.

s. 11, regs. 85/177, 548.

s. 12, regs. 84/1874.

s. 19, rules 86/467.

CAP.

1975—cont.

23. Reservoirs Act 1975—*cont.*
ss. 20, 21, regs. 86/468.
s. 23, regs. 86/468; rules 86/467.
s. 29, orders 83/1666; 85/176; 86/466, 2202.

24. House of Commons Disqualification Act 1975.
Royal Assent, May 8, 1975.
s. 1, amended: 1976, c.52, s.20; 1978, c.23, sch.5.
s. 5, orders 82/160; 83/608; 84/705; 85/1212; 86/2219; 87/449.
s. 6, amended: 1975, c.66, s.5; 1983, c.2, sch.8.
ss. 6, 7, modified: order 82/1135.
s. 10, substituted: 1983, c.2, sch.8; repealed in pt.: *ibid.*, sch.9.
sch. 1, amended: 1975, c.30, schs.4,6,7; 1975, c.55, sch.3; 1975, c.65, sch.3; c.68, schs.1,3; c.69, sch.1; c.70, sch.1; c.71, sch.16; c.74, s.1; 1976, c.6, s.7; c.25, sch.6; c.46, sch.; c.68, s.14; c.71, sch.7; c.74, sch.1; c.75, sch.1; c.83, sch.1; 1978, c.21, sch.1; c.23, sch.5; c.29, sch.16(S.); c.51, sch.16; c.52, sch.11; 1979, c.10, sch.; c.12, sch.6; c.18, sch.3; c.39, s.1; c.43, sch.1; 1980, c.33, s.7; c.53, sch.1; 1982, c.10, sch.3; c.32, sch.3; c.33, sch.1; c.49, sch.5; c.52, sch.2; 1983, c.2, sch.8; c.3, s.1; c.20, sch.4; c.21, s.2; c.23, s.1; c.25, sch.2; c.41, sch.9; c.44, sch.2; c.47, sch.3; orders 82/160; 83/608; 1984, c.12, s.60, sch.1; c.28, sch.2; c.32, sch.3; c.35, sch.2; c.46, sch.1; order 84/705; 1985, c.17, sch.4; c.51, sch.13; c.56, sch.1; c.62, schs.1,4; c.65, sch.1; order 85/1212; 1986, c.31, s.2; c.39, sch.2; c.44, s.49, schs.1,2; c.47, sch.3(S.); c.48, sch.4; c.49, sch.4; c.53, sch.1; c.56, sch.3; c.60, sch.11; order 86/2219; 1987, c.1, sch.1; c.3, sch.1; order 87/449; 1988, c.19, sch.3; c.34, sch.5; c.35, schs. 1,2 (prosp.); c.40, sch.2; c.43, sch.2; c.48, sch.7; c.50, schs.7,17; repealed in pt.: 1975, c.60, sch.5; c.71, sch.18; c.77, sch.3; S.L.R. 1976; 1976, c.51, sch.; c.55, sch.4; c.74, sch.5; 1977, c.3, ss.1,42; c.49, sch.15; 1978, c.23, sch.7; S.L.R. 1978; 1979, c.36, sch.8; 1980, c.21, sch.2; c.26, sch.3; c.30, s.9, sch.5; c.34, sch.9; c.53, sch.7; c.60, sch.3; c.64, sch.1; c.65, schs.26,34; 1981, c.28, s.2; c.29, schs.1,5; c.38, sch.3; c.54, sch.5; c.56, sch.12; c.57, schs.2,3; 1983, c.3, sch.3; c.23, sch.5; c.29, schs.1,3; c.41, sch.10; orders 82/160; 83/608; 1984, c.12, s.60, sch.1; c.60, sch.7; orders 84/705; 85/1212; 1986, c.31, sch.6; c.44, sch.9; c.60, sch.17; order 86/2219; 1987, c.3, sch.3; c.21, sch.3; 1988, c.19, sch.4; c.43, schs.2,10; c.48, sch.8.
sch. 3, repealed: S.L.R. 1977.

25. Northern Ireland Assembly Disqualification Act 1975.
Royal Assent, May 8, 1975.
s. 1, amended: 1976, c.52, s.20; 1978, c.23, sch.5.
s. 5, repealed in pt.: 1976, c.52, sch.10; S.L.R. 1977.

CAP.

1975—cont.

25. Northern Ireland Assembly Disqualification Act 1975—*cont.*
sch. 1, amended: 1975, c.30, schs.5,6,7; c.68, schs.1,3; c.74, s.1; 1976, c.5, sch.6; c.46, sch.; c.74, sch.1; 1977, c.3, ss.1,42; 1978, c.21, sch.1; c.23, sch.5; c.51, sch.16; c.52, sch.11; orders 75/814; 76/1042, 1043; 1980, c.33, s.7; 1981, c.29, schs.1,5; c.38, sch.3; c.54, sch.5; c.56, sch.12; order 82/1083; 1983, c.3, s.1; c.21, s.2; c.12, s.60, sch.1; c.28, sch.2; c.35, sch.2; c.46, sch.1; c.60, sch.6; 1985, c.17, sch.4; c.62, schs.1,4; c.65, sch.1; 1986, c.31, s.2; c.44, s.49, schs.1,2; c.45, sch.3 (S.); c.48, sch.4; c.49, sch.4; c.53, sch.1; c.56, sch.3; c.60, sch.11; 1987, c.3, sch. 1; 1988, c.19, sch.3; c.34, sch.5; c.35, sch.1; c.48, sch.7; repealed in pt.: orders 75/1503; 76/1043; 1975, c.71, sch.18; S.L.R. 1976; 1976, c.55, sch.4; c.74, sch. 5; 1978, c.52, sch.7; 1979, c.10, sch.; c.12, sch.6; c.36, sch.8; c.39, s.1; c.43, sch.1; order 79/294; 1980, c.21, sch.2; c.26, sch.3; c.30, s.9, sch.5; c.34, sch.9; c.60, sch.3; orders 80/1085; 81/435; 1983, c.3, sch.3; c.44, sch.2; 1984, c.60, sch.7; 1985, c.21, sch.2; 1987, c.3, sch. 3; c.21, sch.3; repealed in pt.: 1988, c.19, sch.4; c.48, sch.8.
sch. 2, repealed in pt.: 1982, c.38, sch.3; c.39, sch.1.
sch. 3, repealed: S.L.R. 1977.

26. Ministers of the Crown Act 1975.
s. 1, orders 76/229, 1775; 78/272, 274; 79/571, 578, 907; 80/705, 1719; 81/207, 238, 239 (S.), 834, 1670; 82/159; 83/879, 1127; 84/1814, 1818; 85/166, 442, 1778, 1779; 86/600, 2237; 87/465, 2039; 88/1836, 1984.
s. 2, orders 76/1775; 79/578, 907; 83/146, 1127; 85/1778; 88/1843.
s. 5, order 79/1451.
s. 7, sch. 2, regs. 75/1260; 76/1519, 1830; 2013; 77/320, 1675; 79/1276, 1277; repealed: order 79/1451.
s. 8, regs. 77/2186.
sch. 2, regs. 77/2186.

27. Ministerial and other Salaries Act 1975.
Royal Assent, May 8, 1975.
s. 1, orders 76/1215; 77/1295; 78/1102; 79/905; 80/1073; 82/848; 83/1128; 84/1171, 1818; 85/1214; 86/1169; 88/2253; amended: orders 77/1295; 78/1102; 82/848; 86/1169; 87/941, 1836; 88/1088, 2253.
schs. 1, 2, amended: orders 77/1295; 78/1102; 82/848; 88/2253.

28. Housing Rents and Subsidies (Scotland) Act 1975.
Royal Assent, May 8, 1975.
repealed, except sch.3 (in pt.): 1987, c.26, sch.24.
s. 2, orders 79/378, 669.
sch. 3, repealed in pt.: 1980, c.52, sch.5; 1982, c.24, sch.5; 1984, c.58, sch.10; 1985, c.71, sch.1.

29. Mental Health (Amendment) Act 1975.
Royal Assent, May 8, 1975.
repealed: 1982, c.51, sch.4.
s. 2, order 75/1218.

CAP.

1975—cont.

30. Local Government (Scotland) Act 1975.
Royal Assent, May 8, 1975.
orders 77/1385, 1961; 78/1166, 1607; 79/455.
s. 1, orders 77/1691; 82/540, 1122; 84/1505.
s. 1, amended: 1981, c.23, s.2; repealed in pt.: 1987, c.47, sch.2.
s. 2, see *Assessor for Strathclyde Region* v. *Dass Nicholas*, 1981 S.L.T.(Notes) 116; *Symington* v. *Assessor for Strathclyde Region*, 1983 S.L.T. 660; *B.P. Oil Grangemouth Refinery* v. *Assessor for Lothian Region*, 1985 S.L.T. 228; *Assessor for Strathclyde Region* v. *Scottish Special Housing Association*, 1986 S.L.T. 421; *Assessor for Borders Region* v. *A.M.S. Leisure*, 1986 S.L.T. 689; *Assessor for Strathclyde Region* v. *B.S.R.*, 1987 S.L.T. 250; *Assessor for Central Region* v. *Fleming's Trs.*, 1987 S.L.T. 793.
s. 2, amended: 1981, c.23, s.9, sch.3; repealed in pt.: S.L.R. 1986; 1987, c.47, sch.2.
ss. 2, 3, see *Assessor for Lothian Region* v. *Wilson*, 1979 S.L.T. 93; *Prestonfield House Hotel Co.* v. *Lothian Regional Assessor*, 1983 S.L.T. 96; *W.R. Whitwell* v. *Assessor for Strathclyde Region*, 1988 S.L.T. 64.
s. 3, see *W.R. Whitwell* v. *Assessor for Strathclyde Region*, 1988 S.L.T. 64; *Scott* v. *Assessor for Strathclyde Region*, 1988 S.L.T. 89.
s. 3, orders 77/1691; 84/1505.
s. 3, amended: 1976, c.64, s.1; 1984, c.31, s.11.
s. 4, order 75/1220.
s. 5, regs. 82/915.
s. 5, amended: orders 78/1173–76, repealed in pt. S.L.R. 1986.
s. 6, see *Assessor for Orkney* v. *Post Office*, 1982 S.C. 32.
s. 6, orders 78/1173–77; 79/951; 82/697; 85/193–200, 588; 88/1219, 1220.
s. 6, amended: 1988, c.41, sch.12.
s. 7, amended: 1987, c.47, sch.1.
s. 8, amended: 1981, c.23, s.7, sch.3; 1982, c.24, sch.4; 1986, c.50, sch.10.
s. 9, amended: 1981, c.23, s.8; 1988, c.41, sch.12.
s. 9A, added: *ibid.*
s. 14, amended: *ibid.*, sch.3; repealed in pt.: 1984, c.54, sch.9.
s. 15, order 86/672.
s. 16, regs. 75/825, 827.
s. 16, amended: 1981, c.23, sch.3; repealed in pt.: 1987, c.47, sch.6.
s. 20, repealed: 1984, c.54, sch.9.
s. 21, amended: 1981, c.23, sch.1.
s. 22, order 75/1974; regs. 75/1975; 88/187.
s. 22, repealed in pt.: 1981, c.23, schs.1,4.
s. 23, amended: 1975, c.77, sch.10; 1985, c.73, s.55; 1988, c.9, sch.3; c.43, sch.2; repealed in pt.: 1980, c.65, sch.34.
s. 24, order 88/1306.
s. 24, amended: 1985, c.73, s.55; 1988, c.9, sch.3.
s. 28, amended: 1981, c.23, sch.1; repealed in pt.: *ibid.*, schs.1,4; 1988, c.9, sch.3, 7.
s. 29, amended: 1978, c.39, s.1; 1981, c.23, sch.1; 1988, c.9, sch.3.

CAP.

1975—cont.

30. Local Government (Scotland) Act 1975—cont.
s. 30, amended: 1980, c.65, s.184; 1981, c.23, sch.1; 1988, c.9, sch.3.
s. 34, order 75/800.
s. 35, orders 77/1691, 1692; 78/1173–1177; 82/697, 1122; 84/1505; 85/193–200, 588; 88/1219, 1220.
s. 37, see *Assessor for Lothian Region* v. *Wilson*, 1979 S.L.T. 93; *Symington* v. *Assessor for Strathclyde Region*, 1983 S.L.T. 660; *W.R. Whitwell* v. *Assessor for Strathclyde Region*, 1988 S.L.T. 64; *Dalgleish* v. *Assessor for Strathclyde Region*, 1988 S.L.T. 57; *Scott* v. *Assessor for Strathclyde Region*, 1988 S.L.T. 89.
s. 37, orders 82/1122; 84/1505.
s. 37, amended: 1981, c.23, s.1; order 82/1122, 1984, c.31, s.20; 1987, c.47, sch.1; repealed in pt.: 1984, c.31, s.20; 1987, c.47, sch.6
s. 39, see *Glasgow Assessor* v. *Fine Fare*, Lands Val. Appeal Ct., December 4, 1975.
s. 39, orders 75/824, 1055.
sch. 1, repealed: 1988, c.41, sch.13.
sch. 3, regs. 75/825, 827.
sch. 3, amended: 1981, c.23, s.27, sch.3; 1982, c.41, s.5; 1986, c.65, s.17; 1987, c.47, sch.1; 1988, c.9, sch.6; repealed in pt.: 1987, c.26, schs.23,24.
sch. 4, amended: 1978, c.4, s.4; repealed in pt.: 1988, c.9, schs.3,7.
sch. 6, amended: orders 78/1173, 1176; 1980, c.45, sch.10; repealed in pt.: *ibid.*, sch.11.

31. Malta Republic Act 1975.
Royal Assent, May 8, 1975.
s. 1, repealed in pt.: 1981, c.61, sch.9.

32. Prices Act 1975.
Royal Assent, May 8, 1975.
s. 1, orders 76/358, 952.
s. 2, order 76/410.

33. Referendum Act 1975.
Royal Assent, May 8, 1975.
repealed: S.L.R. 1986.
s. 1, order 75/801.

34. Evidence (Proceedings in Other Jurisdictions) Act 1975.
Royal Assent, May 22, 1975.
see *Ukley* v. *Ukley* (1977) V.R. 121, Vict.Sup.Ct.; *Halcon International Inc.* v. *The Steel Transport and Trading Co.* [1979] R.P.C. 97, C.A; *International Power Industries Incorporated, Re, The Times*, July 5, 1984; Woolf J.; *R.* v. *Rathbone, ex p. Dikko* [1985] 2 W.L.R. 375, Forbes J.; *Jahre (Anders) Re*, [1986] 1 Lloyd's Rep. 496, C.A.; *Barber (J.) & Sons (A Firm)* v. *Lloyd's Underwriters* [1986] 2 All E.R. 845, Evans J.; *R.* v. *Secretary of State for the Home Department, ex p. Spermacet Whaling and Shipping Co. S.A., The Times*, November 14, 1986, D.C.; *Boeing Co.* v. *P.P.G. Industries Inc., The Independent*, July 14. 1988, C.A.
ss. 1, 2, 9, see *State of Norway's Application, Re* [1986] 3 W.L.R. 452, C.A.

CAP.

1975—cont.

34. Evidence (Proceedings in Other Jurisdictions) Act 1975—cont.
ss. 1–3, see *Re Westinghouse Electric Corporation Uranium Contract Litigation M.D.L. Docket No. 235 (No. 1) (No. 2)*; *Rio Tinto Zinc Corp.* v. *Westinghouse Electric Corp.* [1978] 2 W.L.R. 81, H.L.
s. 2, see *H.M. Advocate, Petitioner*, 1978 S.L.T.(Notes) 17; *Lord Advocate* v. *Sheriffs*, 1978 S.C. 56; *Asbestos Insurance Coverage Cases, Re, The Times*, December 1, 1984, C.A.; *R.* v. *Rathbone, ex p. Dikko* [1985] 2 W.L.R. 375, Forbes J.; *Asbestos Insurance Coverage Cases, Re, The Financial Times*, March 6, 1985, H.L.
ss. 2, 3, see *Overseas Programming Co.* v. *Cinématographische Commerz-Anstalt and Iduna Film GmbH, The Times*, May 16, 1984, French J.
ss. 2, 5, Act of Sederunt 76/283.
s. 3, see *R.* v. *Rathbone, ex p. Dikko* [1985] 2 W.L.R. 375, Forbes J.
s. 4, repealed in pt.: 1978, c.23, sch.7.
ss. 4, 7, amended: 1981, c.54, sch.5.
s. 6, order 76/428; amended: order 79/1714.
s. 9, see *State of Norway's Application (No. 2), Re* [1988] 1 FTLR 293, C.A.
s. 9, amended: 1984, c.28, sch.2.
s. 10, orders 76/429; 77/589; 78/1890–1892, 1920; 79/1711; 80/1956; 83/1700; 86/218; 87/622, 1266.
sch. 1, repealed in pt.: order 79/1714.

35. Farriers (Registration) Act 1975.
Royal Assent, May 22, 1975.
s. 7, substituted: 1977, c.31, sch.
ss. 8, 10, amended: *ibid.*
s. 11, amended: *ibid.*; repealed in pt.: *ibid.*, s.1.
s. 15A, added: *ibid.*, sch.
s. 16, amended: *ibid.*; repealed in pt.: *ibid.*, s.1.
s. 19, orders 75/2018; 78/1928; 81/767 (S.).
sch. 1, amended: 1975, c.69, sch.4; 1985, c.9, sch.2.
sch. 3, rules 76/700, 701; amended: 1977, c.31, sch.; 1981, c.54, sch.5.

36. Air Travel Reserve Fund Act 1975.
Royal Assent, May 22, 1975.
s. 1, amended: order 83/1127.
s. 4, regs. 75/1196; 77/1331.
s. 6, order 86/155.
s. 7, amended: 1982, c.1, sch.1.

37. Nursing Homes Act 1975.
Royal Assent, July 3, 1975.
repealed: 1984, c.23, sch.3.
ss. 1, 5, 6, 19, regs. 84/958.
ss. 3, 5, 6, 8, 19, regs. 81/933.
s. 6, regs. 83/901.
s. 24, order 75/1281.

38. Export Guarantees Act 1975.
Royal Assent, July 3, 1975.
repealed: 1978, c.18, sch.
s. 5, orders 77/436; 78/322.
s. 6, orders 75/1854; 76/1251.

39. Hearing Aid Council (Extension) Act 1975.
Royal Assent, July 3, 1975.
s. 2, order 75/1882.

CAP.

1975—cont.

40. Diseases of Animals Act 1975.
Royal Assent, July 3, 1975.
order 76/708.
repealed: 1981, c.22, sch.6.
s. 5, orders 76/159, 596, 775; 77/1124.

41. Industrial and Provident Societies Act 1975.
Royal Assent, July 3, 1975.
s. 2, order 81/395.
s. 6, amended: *ibid.*

42. New Towns Act 1975.
Royal Assent, July 3, 1975.
repealed: 1981, c.64, sch.13.

43. British Leyland Act 1975.
Royal Assent, July 3, 1975.

44. Appropriation Act 1975.
Royal Assent, August 1, 1975.
repealed: 1977, c.35, sch.C.

45. Finance (No. 2) Act 1975.
Royal Assent, August 1, 1975.
s. 1, repealed in pt.: 1975, c.45, sch.14; 1977, c.36, sch.9; 1979, c.2, sch.6.
s. 2, repealed: 1980, c.48, sch.20.
ss. 3, 4, repealed in pt.: *ibid.*; 1981, c.63, sch.7.
ss. 5, 6, repealed in pt.: 1977, c.36, sch.9; 1981, c.35, sch.19.
s. 7, repealed: 1976, c.40, sch.15.
s. 8, repealed: 1979, c.2, sch.6.
ss. 9, 10, repealed: 1979, c.4, sch.4.
s. 11, repealed: 1979, c.5, sch.7
ss. 12, 13, repealed: 1979, c.6, sch.
ss. 14, 15, repealed: 1979, c.4, sch.4.
s. 16, regs. 75/1789; 76/1223; 78/893.
s. 16, repealed: 1979, c.2, sch.6.
s. 17, see *Customs and Excise Commissioners* v. *Mechanical Services (Trailer Engineers)* [1979] 1 All E.R. 501, C.A.
s. 17, repealed: 1979, c.47, s.1, sch.5.
s. 18, regs. 75/1275, 2014, 2015, 2204; 80/1536.
ss. 18–21, repealed: 1983, c.55, sch.11.
ss. 22–24, repealed: 1983, c.53, sch.3.
s. 25, repealed: 1988, c.1, sch.31.
s. 29, repealed: 1977, c.36, sch.9.
s. 30, repealed in pt.: 1976, c.40, sch.15, 1981, c.35, sch.19.
s. 32, repealed: *ibid.*, s.32, sch.15.
s. 34, amended: 1978, c.45, sch.2; repealed in pt.: 1980, c.48, sch.20.
s. 35, repealed: 1976, c.40, sch.15.
s. 36, amended: 1981, c.35, s.70; 1982, c.39, s.44; 1985, c.9, sch.2; 1988, c.39, s.47; repealed in pt.: 1981, c.35, sch.19; 1982, c.39, sch.22.
s. 36A added: 1981, c.35, s.71; amended: 1982, c.39, s.45; 1988, c.39, s.48, repealed in pt.: 1982, c.39, sch.22.
s. 37, amended: 1976, c.40, s.71; repealed in pt.: *ibid.*, sch.15.
s. 38, see *Brady* v. *Hart (trading as Jaclyn Model Agency)* [1985] S.T.C. 498, D.C.; *Bhadra* v. *Ellam (Inspector of Taxes)* [1988] S.T.C. 239, Knox J.
s. 39, repealed: 1975, c.45, sch.14.
s. 41, repealed: 1987, c.16, sch.16.

CAP.

1975—cont.

45. Finance (No. 2) Act 1975—*cont.*
s. 42, amended: 1979, c.14, sch.7; 1987, c.16, sch.15.
s. 43, repealed: 1988,c.1, sch.31.
s. 44, repealed in pt.: 1979, c.14, sch.8; 1987, c.16, sch.16; 1988, c.1, sch.31.
s. 45, repealed in pt.: 1988, c.39, sch.14.
s. 46, repealed in pt.: 1980, c.48, sch.20.
s. 47, regs. 75/1283; orders 79/1687; 82/1587; 85/563; 86/1181, 1832; 87/513, 898, 1492, 1988.
s. 47, amended: 1988, c.1, sch.29; repealed in pt.: 1987, c.16, sch.16; 1988, c.1, sch.31; c.39, sch.14; restored in pt.: *ibid.*, sch.13.
s. 48, orders 79/1687; 82/1587; 85/563; 86/1181, 1832; 87/513, 898, 1492, 1988.
s. 48, repealed: 1988, c.1, sch.31.
s. 49, amended: 1988, c.39, s.93; repealed in pt.: 1985, c.54, schs. 14, 27.
ss. 50–53, repealed: 1988, c.1, sch.31.
s. 54, see *I.R.C.* v. *Clydebridge Properties* [1980] S.T.C. 68, Ct. of Session.
s. 54, repealed: 1981, c.35, sch.19.
s. 55, repealed: 1978, c.45, sch.13.
s. 56, repealed: 1976, c.40, schs.11,15; repealed in pt.: 1988, c.1, sch.31.
s. 57, repealed: 1979, c.14, sch.8.
s. 58, amended: *ibid.*, sch.7;1988, c.1, sch.29; repealed in pt.: 1985, c.54, sch.27.
ss. 59–64, repealed: 1979, c.14, sch.8.
s. 65, repealed: 1976, c.40, s.49, sch.15.
s. 68, order 76/1126.
ss. 68–71, repealed: 1988, c.39, sch.31.
s. 69, regs. 75/1960; 80/1135; 85/158, 351.
s. 69, repealed in pt. (S.): 1985, c.71,sch.1.
ss. 69, 70, see *R.* v. *Downes* (1983) 77 Cr.App.R. 260, C.A.
ss. 69, 70, regs. 88/636.
s. 70, see *Cooper* v. *Sercombe* [1976] T.R. 373; (1982) 53 T.C. 278, Fox J.; *Phelps* v. *Moore* [1980] S.T.C. 568, Browne-Wilkinson J.; *Kirvell* v. *Guy* [1979] S.T.C. 312, Walton J.; *Kington* v. *Reilly* [1981] S.T.C. 121, Goulding J.
s. 70, regs. 75/1960; 80/1135; 84/2008; 85/185, 351; 86/1240.
s. 70, amended: 1980, c.48, sch.8; 1982, c.39, s.47, sch.8; order 81/160; 1987, c.51, s.93; repealed in pt.: 1980, c.48, schs.8,20.
s. 70A, added: 1982, c.39, sch.8.
s. 71, order 80/1171.
s. 71, amended: 1982, c.39, sch.8; 1985, c.71, sch.2; repealed in pt.: 1980, c.48, sch.20; 1985, c.65, sch.10; c.71, sch.1.
s. 71, repealed in pt. (S.): 1985, c.66, sch.8; c.71, sch.1.
s. 75, repealed in pt.: 1979, c.2, sch.6; c.14, sch.8; 1983, c.55, sch.11.
schs. 1, 2, repealed: 1977, c.36, sch.9.
sch. 3, repealed in pt.: 1976, c.40, sch.15; 1979, c.2, sch.6; c.3, sch.3; c.4, sch.4; c.5, sch.7; c.6, sch.
schs. 4, 5, repealed: 1979, c.4, sch.4.
sch. 6, repealed in pt.: 1979, c.2, sch.6; c.4, sch.4.

CAP.

1975—cont.

45. Finance (No. 2) Act 1975—*cont.*
sch. 7, see *Customs and Excise Comrs.* v. *Mechanical Services (Trailer Engineers)* [1979] 1 All E.R. 501, C.A.
sch. 7, repealed: 1979, c.47, s.1, sch.5.
sch. 7, order 77/1786.
sch. 8, repealed: 1988, c.1, sch.31.
sch. 9, repealed: 1985, c.54, sch.27.
sch. 10, see *I.R.C.* v. *Clydebridge Properties* [1980] S.T.C. 68, Ct. of Session.
sch. 10, repealed: 1981, c.35, sch.19.
sch. 11, repealed: *ibid.*, s.49, sch.15.
sch. 12, see *Kirvell* v. *Guy* [1979] S.T.C. 312, Walton J.; *Phelps* v. *Moore* [1980] S.T.C. 568, Browne-Wilkinson J.; *Kington* v. *Reilly* [1981] S.T.C. 121, Goulding J.; *Jones* v. *Lonnen* [1981] S.T.C. 337, Vinelott J.; *Cooper* v. *Sercombe* (1982) 53 T.C. 278, Fox J.
sch. 12, regs. 80/1135; 84/2008; 86/1240.
sch. 12, repealed: 1988, c.1, sch.31.
sch. 13, repealed: 1988, c.1, sch.31.

46. International Road Haulage Permits Act 1975.
Royal Assent, August 1, 1975.
s. 1, amended: order 81/160; 1988, c.54, sch.3.
s. 1, regs. 75/2234.
s. 3, see *Holloway* v. *Brown* [1978] R.T.R. 537, D.C.
s. 3, repealed in pt.: 1988, c.54, sch.1.

47. Litigants in Person (Costs and Expenses) Act 1975.
Royal Assent, August 1, 1975.
see *Hart* v. *Aga Khan Foundation (UK)* [1984] 1 All E.R. 239, Lloyd J.
orders 80/1158, 1159.
s. 1, see *MacBeth Currie & Co.* v. *Matthew,* 1985 S.L.T.(Sh.Ct.) 44.
s. 1, Acts of Sederunt, 76/1606; 83/1438.
s. 2, orders 76/364, 1432; 80/1152.

48. Conservation of Wild Creatures and Wild Plants Act 1975.
Royal Assent, August 1, 1975.
repealed: 1981, c.69, sch.17.
s. 7, order 77/1700.
s. 14, order 77/1700.
sch. 1, order 79/353.

49. Mobile Homes Act 1975.
Royal Assent, August 1, 1975.
see *Taylor* v. *Calvert, The Times,* February 3, 1978, C.A.; *Stroud* v. *Weir Associates,* (1987) 19 H.L.R. 151, C.A.
s. 1, see *Lamb* v. *Adams,* (1981) 42 P. & C.R. 145, C.A.
ss. 1, 2, 4, see *Brice* v. *National By-Products* (1983) 46 P. & C.R. 281, C.A.
ss. 1–6, 9 (in pt.), repealed: 1983, c.34, sch.2.
ss. 3, 4, see *Grant* v. *Allen* [1980] 1 All E.R. 720, C.A.
ss. 4, 9, see *Faulkner* v. *Love (Trading as W. Love & Son)* [1977] 2 W.L.R. 477; [1977] 1 All E.R. 791, C.A.
s. 6, order 76/3065.

50. Guard Dogs Act 1975.
Royal Assent, August 1, 1975.
s. 1, see *Hobson* v. *Gledhill* [1978] 1 W.L.R. 215; [1978] 1 All E.R. 945, D.C.

1975—cont.

50. Guard Dogs Act 1975—cont.
s. 5, amended: 1982, c.48, ss.37,38,46.
s. 8, order 75/1767.

51. Salmon and Freshwater Fisheries Act 1975.
Royal Assent, August 1, 1975.
s. 4, see *Wrothwell (F. J. H.)* v. *Yorkshire Water Authority* [1984] Crim.L.R. 43, D.C.
s. 6, see *Champion* v. *Maughan* [1984] 1 W.L.R. 469, D.C.
s. 6, amended: 1986, c.62, s.33; 1987, c.49, sch.1.
s. 19, see *Cain* v. *Campbell* [1978] Crim.L.R. 292, D.C.; *Thames Water Authority* v. *Homewood, The Times,* November 25, 1981, D.C.
s. 25, amended: 1986, c.62, s.36.
s. 26, see *R.* v. *South West Water Authority, ex p. Cox, The Times,* January 2, Woolf J.; *R.* v. *Minister of Agriculture, Fisheries and Food, ex p. Graham, The Times,* April 16, 1988, McCowan J.
s. 28, orders 76/435, 673, 722, 1544, 2245; 77/254, 1585, 1586; 82/1420; 83/1350; 85/783; 87/99, 612, 745, 1054.
s. 28, amended: 1983, c.23, sch.4.
s. 30, amended: 1986, c.62, s.34.
s. 39, amended: *ibid.,* s.26 (S.), sch.4.
s. 41, orders, 76/673; 77/254.
s. 41, amended: 1983, c.23, sch.4.
3. 43, amended: 1986, c.62, s.26 (S.), sch.4.
sch. 2, amended: *ibid.,* s.36.
sch. 3, see *R.* v. *Minister of Agriculture Fisheries and Food, ex p. Wear Valley District Council, The Times,* March 26, 1988, D.C.A.
sch. 3, orders 83/1350; 85/783; 88/1668.
sch. 3, amended: 1985, c.51, sch.8; 1986, c.62, s.33.
sch. 4, amended: 1977, c.45, s.31, sch.6; 1979, c.2, sch.4; 1986, c.62, s.35.

52. Safety of Sports Grounds Act 1975.
Royal Assent, August 1, 1975.
s. 1, orders 76/1264, 1285; 77/1323, 1345 (S.); 78/1091, 1099; 79/1022, 1026; 80/1021, 1034; 81/949; 82/60 (S.), 1052; 83/962, 1013; 84/942, 1014 (S.); 85/1063, 1064; 86/1243 (S.), 1296; 87/1689; 88/1975.
s. 1, amended: 1987, c.27, s.20, sch.2.
s. 2, amended: *ibid.,* ss.19,21, sch.2.
ss. 3,4, amended: 1985, c.51, sch.8; 1987, c.27, sch.2.
s. 5, amended: 1985, c.51, sch.8; 1987, c.27, s.22; repealed in pt.: *ibid.,* s.22, sch.4.
s. 6, regs. 76/1263, 1300; 86/1045; 87/1941.
s. 6, amended: 1987, c.27, s.22.
s. 7, amended and repealed in pt.: *ibid.*
s. 8, amended: *ibid.,* sch.2.
s. 9, amended: 1984, c.55, sch.6; 1987, c.27, sch.2.
s. 10. substituted: *ibid.,* s.23.
s. 10A, regs. 87/1941.
s. 10A, added: 1987, c.27, s.24.
s. 10B, added: *ibid.,* s.25.
s. 11, amended: 1982, c.43, schs.3,4(S.); 1985, c.51, sch.8.
s. 12, amended: 1987, c.27, ss.23, 25, sch.2; repealed in pt.: *ibid.,* schs.2,4.

1975—cont.

52. Safety of Sports Grounds Act 1975—cont.
s. 15, order 86/1044.
s. 15, repealed: 1987, c.27, s.15, sch.4.
s. 15A, added: *ibid.,* s.15.
s. 17, amended: 1984, c.54, sch.9(S.); 1985, c.51, sch.8; 1987, c.27, sch.2; repealed in pt.: *ibid.,* schs. 2,4.
s. 18, orders 78/1091; 82/60 (S.); 83/962; 84/942; 85/1063, 1064; 86/1044, 1296; 88/1975.
s. 18, amended: 1987, c.27, s.15.

53. Public Service Vehicles (Arrest of Offenders) Act 1975.
Royal Assent, August 1, 1975.
ss. 1, 2, repealed in pt.: 1981, c.14, sch.8.

54. Limitation Act 1975.
Royal Assent, August 1, 1975.
repealed: 1980, c.58, sch.3.
see *Walford* v. *Richards* [1976] 1 Lloyd's Rep. 526, C.A.; *Biss* v. *Lambeth Southwark and Lewisham Area Health Authority (Teaching), The Times,* November 16, 1977, C.A.
s. 1, see *McCafferty* v. *Metropolitan Police Receiver* [1977] 2 All E.R. 756, C.A.; *Thompson* v. *Brown (trading as George Albert Brown (Builders) & Co.), The Times,* May 13, 1981, H.L.; *Arnold* v. *Central Electricity Generating Board* [1987] 2 W.L.R. 245, C.A.
s. 2, see *Casey* v. *J. Murphy & Sons,* December 13, 1979, C.A.
s. 3, see *Walkley* v. *Precision Forgings* [1978] 1 W.L.R. 1228, C.A.

55. Statutory Corporations (Financial Provisions) Act 1975.
Royal Assent, August 1, 1975.
s. 1, orders 75/1903, 1909, 1911; 76/1108; 77/23, 197.
s. 4, repealed: 1982, c.6, sch.
s. 6, repealed in pt.: 1986, c.44, sch.9.
sch. 2, amended: 1987, c.3, sch.1; 1988, c.50, sch.17.
schs. 2, 4, repealed in pt.: 1975, c.78, sch. 6; 1977, c.13, sch.2; 1979, c.11, sch.12; 1980, c.60, sch.3.
sch. 3, repealed in pt.: 1979, c.11, sch.12; 1986, c.44, sch.9.
sch. 4, repealed in pt.: 1981, c.38, sch.6; 1985, c.71, sch.1.

56. Coal Industry Act 1975.
Royal Assent, August 1, 1975.
s. 1, amended: 1980, c.50, s.8; 1987, c.3, sch.1.
s. 3, regs. 76/478.
s. 3, repealed: 1975, c.64, sch.7.
s. 5, repealed: 1986, c.63, sch.12.
sch. 1, amended: 1986, c.44, sch.7; 1987, c.3, sch.1.
sch. 2, regs. 76/478.
sch. 2, repealed in pt.: *ibid.*
sch. 3, repealed in pt.: 1981, c.67, sch.6; 1986, c.63, sch.12.
sch. 4, repealed: *ibid.*

57. Remuneration, Charges and Grants Act 1975.
Royal Assent, August 1, 1975.
s. 1, orders 77/1294, 1302; amended: orders 76/1097, 1161; 1977, c.33, s.17.

CAP.

1975—cont.

57. Remuneration, Charges and Grants Act 1975—cont.
s. 2, orders 76/228, 1161; 77/1302, repealed in pt.: 1977, c.33, s.17, sch.3; 1980, c.31, sch.2.
s. 3, orders 75/1293; 76/1170.
s. 3, repealed: 1980, c.21, sch.2.
s. 5, repealed: 1980, c.51, sch.26.

58. Lotteries Act 1975.
Royal Assent, August 7, 1975.
repealed, except s. 20 in pt. and sch. 4 in pt.: 1976, c.32, sch.5.
s. 10, regs. 77/238, 256.
ss. 10, 18, 20, order 77/409.
s. 11, sch.2, order 77/410.

59. Criminal Jurisdiction Act 1975.
Royal Assent, August 7, 1975.
s. 4, amended: 1978, c.5, s.34; repealed in pt.: ibid., sch.6.
s. 6, see R. v. Smyth [1982] 12 N.I.J.B., Hutton J.
s. 8, repealed: order 81/155.
s. 9, repealed in pt.: order 79/1714.
s. 12, repealed: 1979, c.31, sch.2.
s. 14, repealed in pt.: ibid.
s. 14, orders 75/1347; 76/813.
sch. 1, amended: orders 81/154, 155; 1982, c.36, sch.2.
sch. 2, amended: 1975, c.62, s.6; repealed in pt.: 1978, c.5, sch.6.
sch. 3, amended: 1978, c.26, s.6.
sch. 4, amended: 1980, c.47, sch.4.
sch. 5, repealed in pt.: order 81/609.

60. Social Security Pensions Act 1975.
Royal Assent, August 7, 1975.
see Mono Pumps v. Froggatt and Radford [1987] I.R.L.R. 368, E.A.T.
regs. 78/524; order 81/598.
s. 1, regs. 75/1855; 77/543, 1953; 78/1669; 79/591, 1483; 82/1573; 83/1689; 84/1756; 85/1726; 88/299.
s. 1, amended: 1986, c.50, s.74.
s. 2, repealed: 1975, c.5, sch.2.
s. 3, regs. 75/1855; 77/544; 79/591; 82/1739.
s. 3, amended: 1986, c.50, sch.8.
s. 4, regs. 85/397.
s. 4, amended: 1984, c.48, sch.7; repealed in pt.: ibid., schs.7,8.
s. 5, regs. 79/501; 84/77.
s. 5, amended: 1986, c.50, sch.8.
s. 6, regs. 85/1417; 87/316; 88/429.
s. 6, amended: orders 76/1029; 77/1325; 78/912; 79/993; 80/1245; 82/1130; 83/1244; 1979, c.18, sch.3; order 84/1104; 1985, c.53, sch.5; order 85/1245; 1986, c.50, s.18, sch.8; orders 87/45, 1978; repealed in pt.: 1979, c.18, sch.3; 1986, c.50, schs.8,11.
s. 8, amended: 1979, c.18,sch.1.
s. 9, regs. 78/949; 79/1428.
s. 11, amended: 1977, c.5, s.5; 1979, c.18, sch.3; 1980, c.30, s.3.
s. 12, regs. 87/1854.
s. 13, amended: 1986, c.50, sch.10.
s. 15, regs. 78/529.
s. 15, amended: 1977, c.5, s.4; regs. 78/529; 1986, c.50, sch.10.

CAP.

1975—cont.

60. Social Security Pensions Act 1975—cont.
s. 16, amended: 1977, c.5, s.4; 1982, c.24, sch.4; regs. 78/529.
s. 17, repealed: 1979, c.18, sch.1.
s. 19, repealed in pt.: 1986, c.50, sch.11.
s. 20, regs. 78/392; 79/642; amended: 1979, c.18, sch.1.
s. 21, orders 79/832; 80/728; 82/607; 83/655; 84/581; 85/688; 86/809; 87/861; 88/867; amended: 1979, c.18, s.10; 1980, c.30, s.3; 1985, c.53, sch.3; repealed in pt.: 1980, c.30, sch.5.
s. 22, regs. 84/458.
s. 22, repealed in pt.: 1980, c.30, sch.5; 1986, c.50, sch.11.
s. 23, orders 76/1029; 79/993; 80/1245, 1302; 81/1195; 82/1178; 84/1307.
s. 23, amended: 1979, c.18, sch.3; 1986, c.50, sch.10; repealed in pt.: 1980, c.30, s.3; 1986, c.50, sch.11.
s. 24, regs. 78/393; 81/330.
s. 24, amended: 1986, c.50, sch.10.
s. 26, amended: ibid., s.9, schs.2,10; repealed in pt.: 1985, c.53, sch.6.
s. 27, regs. 75/1855; 77/543; 79/591.
s. 27, amended: order 82/493; 1985, c.53, sch.5; 1986, c.50, sch.10; order 87/656.
s. 28, orders 82/493; 87/656.
s. 28, amended: 1985, c.53, sch.5.
s. 29, regs. 87/1113.
s. 29, amended: 1986, c.50, schs.2,10.
s. 30, regs. 75/1927; 84/380; 87/1101.
s. 30, adapted: order 77/2038; amended: 1986, c.50, schs.2,10; order 87/1978; repealed in pt.: 1978, c.44, sch.17; 1986, c.50, sch.11.
s. 31, regs. 75/1927; 78/1827; 84/380; 86/1716; 87/1104, 1114; 88/475.
s. 31, amended: 1975, c.71, sch.16; repealed in pt.: 1980, c.42, sch.2.
s. 32, regs. 75/2101; 83/722; 84/380; 85/1323; 86/1716; 87/1101, 1114.
s. 32, amended: 1982, c.24, sch.4; 1986, c.50, s.9, schs.2,10; repealed in pt.: 1986, c.50, sch.11.
s. 33, regs. 76/1069.
s. 33, amended: 1986, c.50, schs.2,10; repealed in pt.: ibid., sch.11.
s. 34, repealed: ibid.
s. 35, regs. 77/1706; 79/676; 85/1417, 1930; 86/1716; 87/411; 88/387, 429, 475, 1618, 1652, 1656(S.), 1956(S.); order 87/1978.
s. 35, amended 1977, c.5, ss.3,22; 1979, c.18, sch.3; 1985, c.53, sch.3; 1986, c.50, s.9, sch.8; 1988, c.7, sch.2.
s. 36, regs. 87/1100.
s. 36, amended: order 83/1244; 1985.c.53, sch.5.; 1986, c.50, s.9, sch.2; repealed in pt.: ibid., sch.11.
s. 37, amended: order 83/1244; 1986, c.50, sch.11.
s. 37A, added: ibid., s.9.
s. 38, regs. 75/2101; 78/1089; 84/380; 85/1323; 86/317, 1716; 87/1099, 1114; 88/475.

1975—cont.

60. Social Security Pensions Act 1975—cont.

s. 38, amended: 1980, c.30, s.3; c.48, s.19; 1986, c.50, s.9, sch.10; repealed in pt.: 1980, c.30, sch.8.

s. 39, regs. 75/2101; 76/143; 84/380; 87/1114.

s. 39, amended: 1986, c.50, s.9; repealed in pt.: *ibid.*, sch.11.

s. 40, regs. 75/2101; 77/1188; 78/250; 84/107, 240, 380.

s. 40, amended: 1977, c.5, s.22; 1986, c.50, sch.2.

s. 41, regs. 83/338; 84/380; 88/475.

s. 41, amended: 1980, c.30, s.3; 1985, c.53, sch.5; order 87/1978; repealed in pt.: 1986, c.50, schs.10,11.

ss. 41A–41E, added: 1984, c.48, sch.6.

s. 41A, amended: 1985, c.53, s.6, sch.5; 1986, c.50, schs.2,10; repealed in pt.: 1985, c.53, sch.6.

s. 41B, regs. 85/1927; 87/1114.

s. 41B, amended: 1985, c.53, s.6, sch.5; 1986, c.50, sch.9; repealed in pt.: 1985, c.53, sch.6.

s. 41C, regs. 84/1921; 85/1926; 87/1114.

s. 41C, amended: 1985, c.53, sch.3.

s. 41D, repealed in pt.: *ibid.*, sch.6.

s. 41E, amended: 1986, c.50, sch.2.

s. 42, regs. 86/317

s. 42, amended: 1985, c.53, schs.3,5; 1986, c.50, schs.2,10.

s. 43, regs. 76/143; 78/250; 84/107, 380; 85/1323, 86/317; 87/1106, 1114; 88/475.

s. 43, amended: 1984, c.48, sch.7; 1985, c.53, schs.3,5; 1986, c.50, sch.10.

s. 44, regs. 76/143, 1217; 78/134, 250; 82/492; 83/338; 84/380; 85/1323; 87/657.

s. 44, amended: 1984, c.48, s.19; 1985, c.53, schs.3,5; 1986, c.50, s.9, sch.2,10; repealed in pt.: *ibid.*, sch.11.

s. 44A, regs. 85/1928; 87/657.

s. 44D, added: 1985, c.53, sch.1.

s. 44ZA, regs. 87/657, 1103; 88/475, 647.

s. 44ZA, added: 1986, c.50, sch.2.

s. 45, regs. 76/143, 1217; 78/134, 250; 82/492; 83/338; 84/380; 86/317, 1716; 87/657, 1114; 88/475.

s. 45, amended: 1985, c.53, schs.3,5; 1986, c.50, sch.2,8.

s. 46, regs. 76/1217; 78/134; 82/492.

s. 46, repealed: 1986, c.50, sch.11.

s. 47, regs. 76/143; 84/380; 86/317.

s. 47, amended: 1977, c.5, s.22; 1985, c.53, sch.5.

s. 48, amended: 1985, c.53, sch.5; 1986, c.50, sch.2

s. 49, amended: *ibid.*, s.9, schs.2,10; regs. 87/1116; repealed in pt.: 1986, c.50, schs.10,11.

s. 50, amended: *ibid.*, s.9, schs.2,10.

s. 51, regs. 75/2101; 84/107, 380; 87/1114; 88/475.

s. 51, amended: 1986, c.50, sch.2.

s. 51A, regs. 82/1032, 1033; 83/338; 84/380.

s. 51A, added: 1982, c.24, s.40.

1975—cont.

60. Social Security Pensions Act 1975—cont.

s. 52, regs. 75/2101; 77/1118, 1119, 1618, 1619, 1625, 1678, 1680, 1681, 1778, 1921; 84/107, 380; 85/1928; 86/317, 1716; 87/1104, 1111, 1114; 88/475.

s. 52A, orders 86/2070; 87/1981; 88/2118.

ss. 52A–52D, added: 1985, c.53, sch.1.

s. 52C, regs. 85/1929; 86/2171; 87/1106; 88/474, 476.

s. 52C, amended: 1986, c.50, sch.10.

s. 52D, amended: *ibid.* s.9, sch.10; repealed in pt.: *ibid.*, sch.11.

ss. 53, 55, regs. 76/142.

s. 55, amended: 1985, c.53, sch.5.

s. 56A, regs. 86/1046, 1717; 87/1105, 1110; 88/474, 476.

ss. 56A–56N, added: 1985, c.53, sch.5.

s. 56E, regs. 86/1046, 1717; 88/476.

s. 56K, repealed in pt.: 1986, c.50, sch.11.

s. 56P, regs. 87/1102.

s. 56P, added: 1986, c.50, s.11.

s. 58, amended: 1985, c.65, sch.8; c.66, sch.7 (S.); 1986, c.45, sch.14.

s. 59, orders 79/1047; 81/1217; 82/1178; 83/1264; 84/1307; 85/1575; 86/1116; 87/130; 88/217.

s. 59, amended: 1979, c.18, s.11, sch.3; 1986, c.50, s.9, sch.10; repealed in pt.: 1985, c.53, schs.5,6.

s. 59A, added: 1979, c.18, s.11; amended: 1986, c.50, s.9.

s. 60, Act of Sederunt, 76/779.

s. 60, amended: 1985, c.53, sch.5.

s. 60A, added: 1979, c.18, s.18.

s. 60B, added: 1988, c.7, sch.2.

s. 61, regs. 77/1118, 1119, 1680; 78/392, 393, 529, 1669; 79/345, 1483; 82/1033; amended: 1979, c.18, sch.3; 1986, c.50, sch.10; repealed in pt.: 1980, c.30, sch.5.

s. 62, regs. 83/338; 84/380; 85/1323; 86/1046; 87/1099.

s. 62, repealed in pt.: 1980, c.30, s.3, sch.5.

s. 63, regs. 75/1855; 77/543, 544, 1615; 78/409, 79/345, 591, 643; 81/1627.

s. 65, order 76/1029.

s. 66, regs. 75/1927; 76/142; 77/1618, 1619, 1778; 78/289, 1355; 79/1645; 80/288; 84/380, 1921; 86/317, 1046; 87/1114.

s. 66, amended: 1979, c.18, sch.3; 1980, c.30, s.4; 1984, c.48, sch.7; 1986, c.50, schs.2,10; repealed in pt.: 1985, c.53, sch.6; 1986, c.50, sch.11.

s. 67, orders 75/1318, 1572, 1689, 2079; 76/141, 1173, 2129; 77/778, 1403, 1485, 1617, 2038; 78/367; 79/171, 367, 394, 1030.

s. 68, amended: 1979, c.18, sch.3; 1985, c.53, sch.5.

sch. 1, regs. 78/392; 79/642; 87/1854; amended: 1979, c.18, schs.1,3; orders 79/993; 83/1244; 84/1104; 1980, c.30, s.4; 1985, c.53, s.9; 1986, c.50, s.18, sch.10; orders, 87/45, 1978.

sch. 1A, regs. 85/1930, 1931; 86/751, 2171; 87/1107, 1112; 88/474, 476, 523, 1016.

CAP.

1975—cont.

60. Social Security Pensions Act 1975—*cont.*

sch. 1A, added: 1985, c.53, sch.1; amended: 1986, c.50, sch.10; repealed in pt.: *ibid.*, schs.10,11.

sch. 2, regs. 75/1927, 2101; 76/143; 77/1618, 1619, 1625, 1678, 1680, 1681, 1778, 1921; 78/250, 1089, 1827; 83/338, 380; 84/107, 380; 85/1323, 1928; 86/317, 1716; 87/657, 1104, 1111; 88/475.

sch. 2, amended: 1976, c.35, sch.2; 1986, c.50, sch.2; regs. 87/1116; repealed in pt.: 1986, c.50, sch.11.

sch. 3, amended: 1985, c.53, sch.5; c.65, sch.8; c.66, sch.7(S.); 1986, c.45, sch.14; c.50, sch.2; order 87/656.

sch. 4, order 76/1029; amended: orders 83/1244; 87/1978; repealed in pt.: 1976, c.71, sch.8; 1977, c.42, sch.25; 1979, c.47, sch.5; c.55, sch.3; 1980, c.30, sch.5; 1982, c.24, sch.; 1985, c.9, sch.1; c.53, sch.6; c.65, sch.10; c.66, sch.8 (S.); 1986, c.50, sch.2.

61. Child Benefit Act 1975.

Royal Assent, August 7, 1975.

s. 2, regs. 75/1926; 76/965; 77/534; 82/470; 83/3; 87/357; 88/1227.

s. 2, amended: 1986, c.50, s.70; 1988, c.7, s.4; repealed in pt.: 1980, c.30, s.4, sch.5.

ss. 2–4, regs. 80/1045.

s. 3, see *Decision No. R (F.) 2/79.*

s. 3, regs. 76/965, 1758; amended: 1977, c.49, sch.15.

s. 4, regs. 77/534; 78/1275; 82/470; 83/3; 87/357; 88/1227.

s. 4, amended: 1988, c.7, s.4.

s. 4A, added: 1979, c.18, s.15.

s. 5, order 76/966; regs. 77/1328; 78/914; 79/998; 80/110; 84/1106.

s. 5, repealed in pt.: 1986, c.50, sch.11.

s. 6, see *Decision No. R (S) 3/80.*

s. 6, regs. 75/1924; 76/963, 964, 1758; 78/540; 81/1772; 82/1242; 84/1960; 87/1968; 88/1227.

s. 6, amended: 1986, c.50, sch.10; repealed in pt.: *ibid.*, sch.11.

s. 7, regs. 76/962, 964; 78/540; 80/1640; 82/39; 84/451, 458, 1960.

s. 7, repealed: 1986, c.50, sch.11.

s. 8, regs. 76/962; 82/1242; 84/458.

s. 8, repealed: 1986, c.50, sch.11.

s. 9, regs. 76/965.

ss. 9 (in pt.), 10, repealed: 1986, c.50, sch.11.

s. 11, regs. 75/1924; 76/964; 82/1242; 84/1960.

s. 11, repealed: 1986, c.50, sch.11.

s. 12, adopted: order 77/7.

s. 13, regs. 75/1926; 76/963, 1758; 84/458, 875.

s. 14, regs. 77/7.

s. 15, orders 79/921; 81/605, 1542; 83/1894; 84/125, 354; 87/1831; 88/590; amended: 1977, c.5, s.20; orders 77/425, 592, 593; 1981, c.33, s.6; repealed in pt.: 1986, c.50, s.65, sch.11.

s. 16, regs. 75/1924–1926; 76/308; order 75/1690; repealed: 1975, c.61, sch.5.

s. 17, regs. 76/965; 77/1327, 1328; 78/914; order 78/912.

CAP.

1975—cont.

61. Child Benefit Act 1975—*cont.*

s. 17, amended: 1984, c.48, sch.4; repealed in pt.: 1986, c.50, sch.11.

s. 18, repealed: 1975, c.61, sch.5.

s. 19, repealed in pt.: 1976, c.71, sch.8.

s. 20, regs. 75/1924; 76/962–965, 1758, 2194; 84/875.

s. 21, order 76/961; repealed in pt.: 1975, c.61, sch.5; 1976, c.71, sch.8; amended: 1980, c.30, sch.4.

s. 22, regs. 81/1194; 82/1128; 83/1243; 84/451, 458, 875, 939, 1106, 1960; 85/1243; 86/1172; 87/357; 88/1227.

s. 22, amended: 1986, c.50, s.62.

s. 24, see *Decisions Nos. R. (F) 1/79; R. (F) 1/82; R (S) 9/83.*

s. 24, regs. 75/1924, 1926; 76/963, 965; 78/540; 84/337, 875, 939, 1106; 85/1243; 87/357; 88/1227; order 76/961; repealed in pt.: 1975, c.72, sch.4; 1983, c.41, sch.10; 1986, c.50, sch.11.

s. 32, amended: 1981, c.33, s.6.

sch. 1, regs. 76/965, 1758; 78/540, 1275; 83/3; 84/337; 87/357.

sch. 1, amended: 1984, c.48, sch.4.

sch. 2, regs. 80/1045.

sch. 3, amended: 1986, c.50, sch.10.

sch. 4, repealed in pt.: 1976, c.5, sch.; c.71, sch.8; 1980, c.30, sch.5; 1982, c.24, sch.5; 1984, c.48, sch.8.

sch. 5, repealed in pt.: 1976, c.5, sch.; 1986, c.50, sch.11.

62. Northern Ireland (Emergency Provisions) Amendment Act 1975.

Royal Assent, August 7, 1975.

s. 1, repealed in pt.: order 79/1714.

ss. 2–5, 6 (in pt.), 8, 9 (in pt.), 10–13, 14 (in pt.), 15–19, repealed: 1978, c.5, sch.6.

ss. 21, 22, order 77/2142; repealed: 1978, c.5, sch.6.

s. 23 (in pt.), sch.1 (in pt.), schs.2,3, repealed: *ibid.*

63. Inheritance (Provision for Family and Dependants) Act 1975.

Royal Assent, November 12, 1975.

see *F. (decd.) Re, The Times,* February 11, 1985, Balcome J.

s. 1, see *Re Wilkinson (decd.)* [1977] 3 W.L.R. 514, Arnold J.; *Kaur* v. *Kaur, The Times,* April 29, 1978, Foster J.; *Re Christie (decd.); Christie* v. *Keeble* [1979] 2 W.L.R. 105, Vivian Price, Q.C.; *Re Sehota (decd.)* [1978] 3 All E.R. 385, Foster J.; *C.A.* v. *C.C., The Times,* November 17, 1978, Sir George Baker; *Jelley* v. *Iliffe, The Times,* December 19, 1980, C.A.; *Re Kirkby (decd.)* (1981) 11 Fam.Law 210, Purchas J.; *Re Harmsworth (decd.),* March 12, 1982, Michael Wheeler Q.C.; *Bunning (decd.), Re* [1984] 3 W.L.R. 266, Vinelott J.; *Besterman (decd.), Re* [1984] 3 W.L.R. 280, C.A.; *Williams* v. *Roberts* (1984) 14 Fam.Law 210, Wood J.; *Royse (decd.), Re* [1984] 3 W.L.R. 784, C.A.; *Callaghan (decd.), Re* [1984] 3 W.L.R. 1076, Booth J.; *Leach (decd.) (Leach*

434

1975—cont.

63. Inheritance (Provision for Family and Dependants Act 1975—*cont.*

v. *Linderman*), *Re* (1984) 14 Fam.Law 274,
Michael Wheeler Q.C.; *Whytte* v. *Ticehurst*
[1986] 2 W.L.R. 700, Booth J.: *Debenham
Decd., Re* (1986) 16 Fam.Law 101, Ewbank
J.

ss. 1–3, see *Re Coventry (decd.)*; *Coventry* v.
Coventry [1979] 3 W.L.R. 802, C.A.

ss. 1, 2, see *Re McC.* (1979) 9 Fam.Law 26, Sir
George Baker P.; *Re Fullard (decd.)* (1981) 11
Fam.Law 116, C.A.; *Leach (decd.), Re* [1985]
2 All E.R. 754, C.A.

ss. 1, 3, see *Re Christie (decd.)*; *Christie* v.
Keeble [1979] 2 W.L.R. 105, Vivian Price Q.C.;
Re Beaumont (decd.); *Martin* v. *Midland Bank
Trust Co.* [1979] 3 W.L.R. 818, Sir Robert
Megarry V.-C.; *Malone* v. *Harrison* [1979] 1
W.L.R. 1353, Hollings J.; *Kourkey* v. *Lusher*
(1982) 12 Fam.Law 86, Wood J.; *Re Snoek
(decd.)* (1983) 13 Fam.Law 19, Wood J.; *Re
Crawford (decd.)* (1983) 4 F.L.R 273, Eastham
J.; *Harrington* v. *Gill* (1983) 4 F.L.R. 265, C.A.

ss. 1, 3, 6, see *Stead* v. *Stead* (1985) 15
Fam.Law 154, C.A.

ss. 1, 4, see *Re Dennis (decd.)* [1981] 2 All E.R.
140, Browne-Wilkinson J.

s. 2, see *Royse (decd.). Re* [1984] 3 W.L.R. 784,
C.A.; *Debenham Decd., Re* (1986) 16
Fam.Law 101, Ewbank J.

ss. 2, 3, see *Rajabally* v. *Rajahally* [1987] 2 F.L.R.
390, C.A.

s. 3, see *Re Christie (decd.)*; *Christie* v. *Keeble*
[1979] 2 W.L.R. 105, Vivian Price, Q.C.; *Re
Clark*; *Clark* v. *Clark*, December 18, 1980,
Winchester Crown Ct., Hollings J.; *Re Fullard
(decd.)* (1981) 11 Fam.Law 116, C.A.; *Bunning
(decd.), Re* [1984] 3 W.L.R. 266, Vinelott J.;
Besterman (decd.), Re [1984] 3 W.L.R. 280,
C.A.; *Callaghan (decd.), Re* [1984] 3 W.L.R.
1076, Booth J.; *Rowlands (decd.), Re*; *Row-
lands* v. *Rowlands* (1984) 14 Fam.Law 280,
C.A.; *R. (decd.), Re: R.* v. *O.* (1986) 16
Fam.Law 589; Mr Registrar Garland; *Deben-
ham (decd.), Re* (1986) 16 Fam.Law 101,
Ewbank J.

s. 4, see *Re Salmon (decd.)*, *Coard* v. *National
Westminster Bank, The Times*, July 12, 1980,
Robert Megarry V.-C.; *Re Dennis (decd.)*;
Dennis v. *Lloyds Bank, The Times*, November
14, 1980, Browne-Wilkinson J.; *Freeman
(decd.), Re* [1984] 3 All E.R. 906, H.H. Judge
Thomas; *Johnson (Paul Anthony) Decd., Re*,
May 8, 1987, Latey J.

s. 9, see *Re Crawford (decd.)* (1983) 4 F.L.R.
273, Eastham J.

s. 10, see *Re Kennedy (decd.)*; *Kennedy* v. *The
Official Solicitor to the Supreme Court*, May
22, 1980, Judge Willis, Shoreditch County Ct.

s. 15, *Re Fullard (decd.)* (1981) 11 Fam.Law 116,
C.A.; *Whiting* v. *Whiting* [1988] 1 W.L.R. 565,
C.A.

s. 15, amended: 1984, c.42, s.8.

s. 15A, added: *ibid.*

s. 19, amended 1982, c.53, s.52.

1975—cont.

63. Inheritance (Provision for Family and Dependants Act 1975—*cont.*

s. 22, order 81/1636.

s. 22, repealed: 1982, c.53, sch.9.

s. 25, see *Re Cairnes (decd.)* (1982) 12 Fam.Law
177, Lincoln J.

s. 25, amended: 1984, c.42, s.25.

64. Iron and Steel Act 1975.

Royal Assent, November 12, 1975.

repealed: 1982, c.25, sch.7.

ss. 19, 36, orders 77/1267; 80/764.

sch. 6, repealed in pt.: 1984, c.29, sch.12.

65. Sex Discrimination Act 1975.

Royal Assent, November 12, 1975.

see *Bick* v. *Royal School for the Deaf*, May 20,
1976; *Shields* v. *E. Coomes (Holdings), The
Times*, April 28, 1978, C.A.; *Noble* v. *David
Gold & Sons (Holdings), The Times*, January
16, 1980, C.A.

s. 1, see *Peake* v. *Automotive Products* [1977]
3 W.L.R. 853; [1977] I.R.L.R. 365, C.A.; *Price*
v. *Civil Service Commission* [1977] 1 W.L.R.
1417, E.A.T.; *Steel* v. *Union of Post Office
Workers* [1978] 1 W.L.R. 64, E.A.T.; *Saunders*
v. *Richmond-upon-Thames London Borough
Council* [1978] I.C.R. 75, E.A.T.; *Roberts* v.
Cleveland Area Health Authority; *Garland* v.
British Rail Engineering; *MacGregor Wallcov-
erings* v. *Turton* [1979] 1 W.L.R. 754, C.A.;
Ministry of Defence v. *Jeremiah* [1979] 3
W.L.R. 857, C.A.; *Durrant* v. *North Yorkshire
Area Health Authority and Secretary of State
for Social Services* [1979] I.R.L.R. 401, E.A.T.;
Turley v. *Allders Department Stores* [1980]
I.C.R. 66, E.A.T.; *Quinn* v. *Williams Furniture*
[1981] I.C.R. 328, C.A.; *Page* v. *Freight Hire
(Tank Haulage)* [1981] I.C.R. 299; [1981] 1 All
E.R. 394, E.A.T.; *Skyrail Oceanic* v. *Coleman*
[1981] I.C.R. 864, C.A.; *Francis* v. *British Air-
ways Engineering Overhaul* [1982] I.R.L.R. 10,
E.A.T.; *Horsey* v. *Dyfed County Council* [1982]
I.C.R. 755, E.A.T.; *Clarke* v. *Eley (IMI) Kynoch*
[1983] I.C.R. 765, E.A.T.; *Barber* v. *Guardian
Royal Exhange Assurance Group*; *Roberts* v.
Tate & Lyle Food and Distribution, The Times,
April 14, 1983, E.A.T.; *Gill* v. *El Vino Co.*
[1983] 2 W.L.R. 155, C.A.; *Watches of Switz-
erland* v. *Savell* [1983] I.R.L.R. 141, E.A.T.; *R.*
v. *Entry Clearance Officer, Bombay,* ex p.
Amin [1983] 3 W.L.R. 258, H.L.; *Home Office*
v. *Holmes* [1984] I.R.L.R. 299, E.A.T.; *New-
stead* v. *Department of Transport and H.M.
Treasury* [1985] I.R.L.R. 299, E.A.T.; *Rainey* v.
Greater Glasgow Health Board, 1985 S.L.T.
518; *Kidd* v. *D.R.G. (U.K.)* [1985] I.C.R. 405,
E.A.T.; *Hayes* v. *Malleable Working Men's
Club and Institute*; *Maughan* v. *North East
London Magistrates' Court Committee* [1985]
I.C.R. 703, E.A.T.; *Greencroft Social Club and
Institute* v. *Mullen* [1985] I.C.R. 796, E.A.T.;
Porcelli v. *Strathclyde Regional Council* [1986]
I.C.R. 564, Court of Session, First Division;
Rainey v. *Greater Glasgow Health Board*,
1987 S.L.T. 146; *Secretary of State for Edu-
cation, ex p. Schaffter* [1987] I.R.L.R. 53,

1975—cont.

65. Sex Discrimination Act 1975—cont.

Schiemann J.; *Francis* v. *Tower Hamlets Borough Council* (1987) L.S.Gaz. 2530, E.A.T.; *Turner* v. *Labour Party and the Labour Party Superannuation Society* [1987] I.R.L.R. 101, E.A.T.; *Cornelius* v. *University College of Swansea* [1987] I.R.L.R. 141, C.A.; *Balgobin & Francis* v. *London Borough of Tower Hamlets* [1987] I.R.L.R. 401, E.A.T.; *Greater Glasgow Health Board* v. *Carey* [1987] I.R.L.R. 484, E.A.T.; *R.* v. *Immigration Appeal Tribunal and the Department of Employment, ex p. Bernstein* [1987] Imm.A.R. 182, Taylor J.; *R.* v. *Birmingham City Council, ex p. Equal Opportunities Commission* [1988] I.R.L.R. 96, McCullough J.; *Duke* v. *G.E.C. Reliance (formerly Reliance Systems)* [1988] 2 W.L.R. 359, H.L.; *Oakes* v. *Sidney Sussex, Cambridge* [1988] 1 W.L.R. 431, Browne-Wilkinson V.-C.
ss. 1, 3, see *Hurley* v. *Mustoe, The Times,* March 14, 1981, E.A.T.
ss. 3, 5, see *Kidd* v. *DRG (UK)* [1985] I.C.R. 405, E.A.T.
s. 4, see *British Airways Engine Overhaul* v. *Francis* [1981] I.C.R. 278, E.A.T.
ss. 4, 5, see *Cornelius* v. *University College of Swansea* [1987] I.R.L.R. 141, C.A.
ss. 4, 6, see *Wileman* v. *Minilec Engineering* [1988] I.C.R. 318, E.A.T.
s. 6, see. *Peake* v. *Automotive Products* [1977] 3 W.L.R. 853; [1977] I.R.L.R. 365, C.A.; *Amies* v. *Inner London Education Authority* [1977] 2 All E.R. 100; [1977] I.C.R. 308, E.A.T.; *Moberly* v. *Commonwealth Hall (University of London)* [1977] I.C.R. 791, E.A.T.; *Oxford* v. *Department of Health and Social Security* [1977] I.C.R. 884, E.A.T.; *Steel* v. *Union of Post Office Workers* [1978] 1 W.L.R. 64, E.A.T.; *Roberts* v. *Cleveland Area Health Authority* [1978] I.C.R. 370, E.A.T.; *Hebbes* v. *Rank Precision Industries (Trading as Rank Hilger)* [1978] I.C.R. 489, E.A.T.; *Humphreys* v. *Board of Managers of St. George's Church of England (Aided) Primary School* [1978] I.C.R. 546, E.A.T.; *Knight* v. *Att.-Gen.* [1979] I.C.R. 194, E.A.T.; *Department of the Environment* v. *Fox* (1979) 123 S.J. 404, E.A.T.; *Roberts* v. *Cleveland Area Health Authority; Garland* v. *British Rail Engineering; MacGregor Wallcoverings* v. *Turton* [1979] 1 W.L.R. 754, C.A.; *Hugh-Jones* v. *St. John's College, Cambridge* [1979] I.C.R. 818, E.A.T.; *Jeremiah* v. *Ministry of Defence* [1979] 3 W.L.R. 857, C.A.; *Turley* v. *Allders Department Stores* [1980] I.C.R. 66, E.A.T.; *Noble* v. *David Gold & Son (Holdings)* [1980] I.C.R. 543, C.A.; *Page* v. *Freight Hire (Tank Haulage)* [1981] I.C.R. 209; [1981] 1 All E.R. 394, E.A.T.; *Burton* v. *British Railways Board* [1981] I.R.L.R. 17, E.A.T.; *Garland* v. *British Rail Engineering* [1982] 2 W.L.R. 918, H.L.; *Southampton & South West Hampshire Health Authority (Teaching)* v. *Marshall* [1983] I.R.L.R. 236, E.A.T.; *Roberts* v. *Tate & Lyle Food and*

1975—cont.

65. Sex Discrimination Act 1975—cont.

Distribution; Barber v. *Guardian Royal Exchange Assurance Group* [1983] I.C.R. 521, E.A.T.; *Oliver* v. *J. P. Malnick & Co. (a firm)* [1983] 3 All E.R. 795, E.A.T.; *E.C. Commission* v. *United Kingdom of Great Britain and Northern Ireland (No. 165/82)* [1984] I.R.L.R. 29, European Ct.; *Brennan* v. *J. H. Dewhurst* [1984] I.C.R. 52, E.A.T.; *Home Office* v. *Holmes* [1984] I.R.L.R. 299, E.A.T.; *Oliver* v. *Malnick (J. P.) & Co. (No. 2)* [1984] I.C.R. 458, Industrial Tribunal; *Newstead* v. *Department of Transport and H.M. Treasury* [1985] I.R.L.R. 299, E.A.T.; *Hayes* v. *Malleable Working Men's Club and Institute: Maughan* v. *North East London Magistrates' Court Committee* [1985] I.C.R. 703, E.A.T.; *Gunning* v. *Mirror Group Newspapers* [1986] 1 All E.R. 385, C.A.; *Haughton* v. *Olau Line (U.K.)* [1986] 1 W.L.R. 504, C.A.; *Porcelli* v. *Strathclyde Regional Council* [1986] I.C.R. 564, Court of Session, First Division; *Gloucester Working Men's Club & Institute* v. *James* [1986] I.C.R. 603, E.A.T.; *Parsons* v. *East Surrey Health Authority* [1986] I.C.R. 837, E.A.T.; *Foster* v. *British Gas* [1987] I.C.R. 52, Industrial Tribunal; *Francis* v. *Tower Hamlets Borough Council* (1987) L.S.Gaz. 2530, E.A.T.; *Turner* v. *Labour Party and the Labour Party Superannuation Society* [1987] I.R.L.R. 101, E.A.T.; *Cornelius* v. *University College of Swansea* [1987] I.R.L.R. 141, C.A.; *Snowball* v. *Gardner Merchant* [1987] I.C.R. 719, E.A.T.; *Rolls Royce* v. *Doughty* [1987] I.R.L.R. 447, E.A.T.; *Balgobin & Francis* v. *London Borough of Tower Hamlets* [1987] I.R.L.R. 401, E.A.T.; *Greater Glasgow Health Board* v. *Carey* [1987] I.R.L.R. 484, E.A.T.; *R.* v. *Birmingham City Council, ex p. Equal Opportunities Commission* [1988] I.R.L.R. 96, McCullough J.; *Duke* v. *G.E.C. Reliance (formerly Reliance Systems)* [1988] 2 W.L.R. 359, H.L.
s. 6, amended: 1986, c.59, s.2; repealed in pt.: *ibid.*, s.1, sch.
ss. 6, 7, see *Timex Corp.* v. *Hodgson* [1982] I.C.R. 63, E.A.T.
s. 7, see *Sisley* v. *Britannia Security Systems* [1983] I.C.R. 628, E.A.T.; *Williams* v. *Dyffed County Council* [1986] I.C.R. 449, E.A.T.
s. 7, amended: 1986, c.59, s.1.
s. 8, see *Oliver* v. *Malnick (J. P.) & Co. (No. 2)* [1984] I.C.R. 458, Industrial Tribunal.
ss. 9, 15, see *Rice* v. *Fon-A-Car* [1980] I.C.R. 133, E.A.T.
s. 10, see *Haughton* v. *Olau Line (U.K.)* [1986] 1 W.L.R. 504, C.A.
s. 10, order 87/930.
s. 10, amended: 1978, c.46, s.1.; 1982, c.23, sch.3.
s. 11, amended: 1986, c.59. s.2; repealed in pt.: *ibid.*, s.1, sch.
s. 13, see *British Judo Association* v. *Petty* [1981] I.C.R. 660, E.A.T.; *R.* v. *Immigration Appeal Tribunal and the Department of Employment, ex p. Bernstein* [1987] Imm.A.R. 182, Taylor J.

CAP.

1975—cont.

65. Sex Discrimination Act 1975—cont.

s. 14, amended: 1982, c.10, sch.3; 1988, c.19, sch.3, repealed in pt.: 1981, c.57, schs.2,3.

s. 16, amended: *ibid.*, sch.2; 1988, c.19, sch.3.

s. 20, see *E.C. Commission* v. *United Kingdom of Great Britain and Northern Ireland (No. 165/82)* [1984] I.R.L.R. 29, European Ct.

s. 20, amended: order 83/1202; repealed in pt.: 1979, c.36, sch.8.

s. 22, amended (S.): 1980, c.44, sch.4; 1988, c.40, sch.12; repealed in pt.: 1980, c.20, sch.1.

s. 23, see *R.* v. *Secretary of State for Education and Science, ex p. Keating, The Times,* December 3, 1985, Taylor J.; *Oakes* v. *Sidney Sussex, Cambridge* [1988] 1 W.L.R. 431, Browne-Wilkinson V.-C.

s 23, amended: 1980, c.20, s.33; c.44, sch.4 (S.); 1981, c.60, sch.3.

ss. 23, 25, 38, see *R.* v. *Birmingham City Council, ex p. Equal Opportunities Commission* [1988] I.R.L.R. 96, McCullough J.

s. 24, orders 75/1902, 2113; 80/1860.

ss. 24, 25, amended: 1988, c.40, sch.12; repealed in pt.: *ibid.*, schs.12,13.

s. 25, amended (S.): 1980, c.44, sch.4.

s. 28, amended: 1988, c.40, sch.12; repealed in pt.: 1985, c.47, s.4.

s. 29, see *Decision No. R (S)* 11/79; *Quinn* v. *Williams Furniture* [1981] I.C.R. 328, C.A.; *R.* v. *Immigration Appeal Tribunal, ex p. Kassam* [1980] W.L.R. 1037; [1980] 2 All E.R. 330, C.A.; *Jones* v. *Royal Liver Friendly Society, The Times,* December 2, 1982, C.A.; *Gill* v. *El Vino Co.* [1983] 2 W.L.R. 155, C.A.; *R.* v. *Entry Clearance Officer Bombay, ex p. Amin* [1983] 3 W.L.R. 258, H.L.; *R.* v. *Immigration Appeal Tribunal and the Department of Employment, ex p. Bernstein* [1987] Imm.A.R. 182, Taylor J.

s. 35, amended: 1980, c.30, sch.4.

s. 41, see *Balgobin & Francis* v. *London Borough of Tower Hamlets* [1987] I.R.L.R. 401, E.A.T.

s. 42, see *G.L.C.* v. *Farrar* [1980] I.C.R. 266, E.A.T.; *R.* v. *Birmingham City Council, ex p. Equal Opportunities Commission* [1988] I.R.L.R. 96, McCullough J.

s. 43, see *Hugh-Jones* v. *St. John's College, Cambridge* [1979] I.C.R. 848, E.A.T.

s. 43, amended: order 77/528.

s. 44, see *G.L.C.* v. *Farrar* [1980] I.C.R. 266, E.A.T.; *British Judo Association* v. *Petty* [1981] I.C.R. 660, E.A.T.

s. 47, amended: 1986, c.59, s.4.

s. 51, see *Decision No. R (S)* 11/79; *Hugh-Jones* v. *St. John's College, Cambridge* [1979] I.C.R. 848, E.A.T.; *G.L.C.* v. *Farrar* [1980] I.C.R. 266, E.A.T.; *Page* v. *Freight Hire (Tank Haulage)* [1981] I.C.R. 299; [1981] 1 All E.R. 394, E.A.T.; *R.* v. *Secretary of State for Education, ex p. Schaffter* [1987] I.R.L.R. 53, Schiemann J.

s. 51, amended: 1986, c.61, sch.4.

CAP.

1975—cont.

65. Sex Discrimination Act 1975—cont.

s. 53, see *R.* v. *Birmingham City Council, ex p. Equal Opportunities Commission* [1988] I.R.L.R. 96, McCullough J.

s. 56, amended: 1976, c.74, sch.4.

s. 56A, order 85/387.

s. 58, amended: 1976, c.74, sch.4; regs. 75/1993.

s. 59, regs. 75/1993.

s. 59, amended: 1984, c.28, sch.2.

s. 60, see *Schmidt* v. *Austicks Bookshops* [1978] I.C.R. 85, E.A.T.

s. 62, amended: 1976, c.74, sch.4.

s. 65, see *Nelson* v. *Tyne and Wear Passenger Transport Executive* [1978] I.C.R. 183, E.A.T.; *Ministry of Defence* v. *Jeremiah* [1979] 3 W.L.R. 857, C.A.; *Prestcold* v. *Irvine* [1981] I.C.R. 777, C.A.; *Hurley* v. *Mustoe (No. 2)* [1983] I.C.R. 422, E.A.T.

s. 65, amended: 1975, c.71, sch.16; 1976, c.74, sch.4; 1978, c.44, sch.16.

ss. 65, 66, see *Turner* v. *Labour Party and the Labour Party Superannuation Society* [1987] I.R.L.R. 101, E.A.T.

s 66, see *Skyrail Oceanic* v. *Coleman* [1982] I.C.R. 864, C.A.; *R.* v. *Birmingham City Council, ex p. Equal Opportunities Commission* [1988] I.R.L.R. 96, McCullough J.

s. 66, amended: 1976, c.74, sch.4; 1984, c.28, sch.2; Acts of Sederunt, 76/1851; 77/973.

s. 67, regs. 75/1993; 77/843.

s. 72, repealed in pt.: 1976, c.74, sch.5; amended: *ibid.*, sch.4.

s. 74, see *Oxford* v. *Department of Health and Social Security* [1977] I.C.R. 884, E.A.T.; *Greater Glasgow Health Board* v. *Carey* [1987] I.R.L.R. 484, E.A.T.

s. 74, order 75/2048; regs. 77/844.

s. 75, amended: 1976, c.74, sch.4; 1978, c.44, sch.16; Act of Sederunt 76/374; 1986, c.47, sch.3 (S.); 1988, c.34, sch.5.

s. 76, see *Hutchinson* v. *Westward Television* [1977] I.C.R 279, E.A.T.; *Gloucester Working Men's Club & Institute* v. *James* [1986] I.C.R. 603, F.A.T.

s. 76, amended: 1976, c.74, sch.4.

s. 77, see *E.C. Commission* v. *United Kingdom of Great Britain and Northern Ireland (No. 165/82)* [1984] I.R.L.R. 29, European Ct.

s. 79, amended (S.): 1980, c.44, sch.4; repealed in pt. (S.): *ibid.*, sch.5.

s. 80, orders 77/528; 83/1202.

s. 80, repealed in pt.: 1986, c.59, sch.

s. 81, orders 75/2048, 2112; 80/1860; regs. 77/844; 87/930.

s. 81, amended (S.): 1980, c.44, sch.4; repealed in pt.: 1986, c.59, sch.

s. 82, see *Hugh-Jones* v. *St. John's College, Cambridge* [1979] I.C.R. 848, E.A.T.; *Quinnen* v. *Hovell* [1984] I.C.R. 525, E.A.T.; *Gunning* v. *Mirror Group Newspapers* [1986] 1 All E.R. 385, C.A.

s. 82, regs. 75/1993; 77/843; repealed in pt.: 1975, c.71, sch.18; 1982, c.10, schs.3,4; amended: 1980, c.44, sch.4 (S.); 1986, c.59, s.2; 1988, c.40, sch.12.

1975—cont.

65. Sex Discrimination Act 1975—cont.
s. 83, orders 75/1845, 2112.
s. 85, see *Department of the Environment* v. *Fox* [1979] I.C.R. 736, E.A.T.; *R.* v. *Entry Clearance Officer, Bombay, ex p. Amin* [1983] 3 W.L.R. 258, H.L.; *R.* v. *Immigration Appeal Tribunal and the Department of Employment, ex p. Bernstein* [1987] Imm.A.R. 182, Taylor J.
s. 85, repealed in pt.: 1981, c.55, sch.5.
ss. 85, 86, see *Knight* v. *Att.-Gen.* [1979] I.C.R. 194, E.A.T.
sch. 1, see *Rainey* v. *Greater Glasgow Health Board,* 1987 S.L.T. 146.
sch. 1, amended: 1975, c.71, sch.16; repealed in pt.: 1986, c.59, sch.
sch. 2, repealed: *ibid.*; amended: 1988, c.40, sch.12.
sch. 3, amended: 1976, c.74, sch.4.
sch. 4, amended: 1979, c.36, sch.7; repealed in pt.: *ibid.*, sch.8.
sch. 5, repealed in pt.: 1975, c.71, sch.18; 1979, c.36, sch.8.

66. Recess Elections Act 1975.
Royal Assent, November 12, 1975.
s. 1, amended: 1985, c.65, sch.8; 1986, c.45, sch.14; repealed in pt.: 1985, c.65, sch.10.
s. 5, repealed in pt.: *ibid.*

67. Housing Finance (Special Provisions) Act 1975.
Royal Assent, November 12, 1975.
repealed: 1985, c.71, sch.1.

68. Industry Act 1975.
Royal Assent, November 12, 1975.
s. 1, amended: 1980, c.33, s.7; repealed in pt.: *ibid.*, s.7, sch.2.
s. 2, amended: *ibid.*,s.1; repealed in pt.: *ibid.*,s.1, sch.2.
s. 3, amended: *ibid.*, s.8.
s. 4, repealed: *ibid.*, s.9, sch.2.
s. 7, see *Booth & Co. (International)* v. *National Enterprise Board* [1978] 3 All E.R. 624, Forbes J.
s. 8, amended: 1979, c.32, s.1, sch.; order 78/580; 1980, c.33, s.5; order 80/1211; 1981, c.6, s.1; repealed in pt.: 1980, c.33, s.5, sch.2; 1981, c.6, s.1, sch.
s. 8, orders 78/580; 80/1211.
s. 9, amended: 1984, c.46, sch.5.
s. 10, amended: 1980, c.33, s.6; repealed in pt.: *ibid.*, s.6, sch.2.
s. 21, repealed *ibid.*, s.19, sch.2.
s. 22, repealed: 1982, c.52, sch.3.
ss. 28–34, repealed: 1980, s.33, s.19, sch.2.
s. 37, amended: 1982, c.52, sch.2; 1984, c.57, sch.1; 1985, c.9, sch.2; repealed in pt.: 1980, c.33, sch.2.
s. 38, order 78/580.
s. 39, order 75/1881.
s. 39, repealed in pt.: 1980, c.33, sch.2; 1982, c.52, sch.3.
sch. 1, amended: 1985, c.9, sch.2; 1986, c.60, sch.16; repealed in pt.: *ibid.*, sch.17.
sch. 2, amended: order 78/1042; 1980, c.33, s.4; 1983, c.29, s.4, sch.2; 1985, c.9, sch.2; repealed in pt.: 1980, c.33, sch.2.

1975—cont.

68. Industry Act 1975—cont.
sch. 4, repealed in pt.: *ibid.*, sch.2; 1982, c.52, sch.3.
sch. 5, repealed in pt.: 1982, c.52, sch.2.
sch. 6, repealed: 1980, c.33, sch.2.
sch. 7, repealed in pt.: 1982, c.52, sch.3.

69. Scottish Development Agency Act 1975.
Royal Assent, November 12, 1975.
s. 2, amended: 1980, c.33, s.1; repealed in pt.: *ibid.*, s.1, sch.2.
s. 5, repealed: *ibid.*, s.8, sch.2.
ss. 8, 15, 28, order 75/1898.
s. 10, amended: 1981, c.38, sch.3; 1984, c.12, sch.4; repealed in pt.: 1982, c.43, sch.4; 1984, c.12, sch.4.
s. 11, amended: 1988, c.19, sch.3.
s. 13, amended: 1979, c.32, s.1, sch.; 1981, c.6, s.2; 1987, c.56, s.1; repealed in pt.: 1980, c.33, s.5, sch.2.
s. 14, amended: 1980, c.33, s.6; repealed in pt.: *ibid.*, s.6, sch.2.
s. 15, regs. 76/2182; 83/265.
s. 17, amended: 1984, c.46, sch.5; repealed in pt.: 1980, c.33, sch.2.
s. 18, repealed: *ibid.*, s.9, sch.2.
s. 20, amended: 1982, c.52, sch.2; repealed in pt.: 1980, c.33, sch.2.
s. 21, repealed: 1980, c.19, s.4.
s. 25, amended: 1985, c.9, sch.2.
sch. 1, amended: *ibid.*; 1986, c.60, sch.16; repealed in pt.: *ibid.*, sch.17.
sch. 2, amended: 1978, c.51, sch.16; 1980, c.33, s.4; 1983, c.29, s.4, sch.2; repealed in pt.: 1980, c.33, sch.2.
sch. 3, regs. 76/2182; 83/265.
sch. 3, amended: 1978, c.44, sch.16.
sch. 4, repealed in pt.: 1980, c.33, sch.2.

70. Welsh Development Agency Act 1975.
Royal Assent, November 12, 1975.
s. 1, amended: 1980, c.33, s.1; repealed in pt.: *ibid.*, s.1, sch.2.
ss. 2, 5, amended: 1976, c.75, s.23.
ss. 3, 12, repealed: *ibid.*, s.8, sch.2.
s. 13, amended: 1982, c.52, sch.2; 1987, c.3, sch.1.
s. 16, substituted: 1982, c.42, s.2.
s. 18, amended: 1979, c.32, s.1, sch.; 1981, c.6, s.2; 1988, c.5, s.1; repealed in pt.: 1980, c.33, s.5, sch.2.
s. 19, amended: 1984, c.46, sch.5; repealed in pt.: 1980, c.33, sch.2.
s. 20, amended: *ibid.*, s.6; repealed in pt.: *ibid.*, s.6, sch.2.
s. 22, amended: 1981, c.67, sch.4; repealed in pt.: *ibid.*, sch.6.
s. 24, amended: 1988, c.19, sch.3.
s. 27, amended: 1985, c.9, sch.2; repealed in pt.: 1984, c.12, sch.4; 1986, c.44, sch.9.
s. 29, order 75/228.
sch. 1, amended: 1985, c.9, sch.2; 1986, c.60, sch.16; repealed in pt.: *ibid.*, sch.17.
sch. 2, regs. 76/2107; amended: 1978, c.44, sch.16.
sch. 3, amended: 1978, c.52, sch.11; 1980, c.33, s.4; 1983, c.29, s.4, sch.2; 1985, c.25, s.5; repealed in pt.: 1980, c.33, sch.2.

1975—cont.

71. Employment Protection Act 1975.
Royal Assent, November 12, 1975.
s. 1, see *U.K. Association of Professional Engineers* v. *A.C.A.S.* [1980] 2 W.L.R. 254; [1980] 1 All E.R. 612, H.L.
s. 6, orders 77/867, 937, 2076; amended: 1978, c.44, sch.16; 1980, c.42, sch.1; repealed in pt.: 1978, c.44, sch.17.
s. 8, see *Blue Circle Staff Association* v. *Certification Officer* [1977] 1 W.L.R. 239; *General and Municipal Workers Union* v. *Certification Officer* [1977] 1 All E.R. 771; *A. Monk & Co. Staff Association* v. *Certification Officer and Association of Scientific, Technical and Managerial Staffs* [1980] I.R.L.R. 431, E.A.T.
s. 8, regs. 78/1329; 79/1385; 80/1708; 81/1631; 85/300; 86/302; 87/258; 88/310; amended: 1978, c.44, sch.16; regs. 86/302; 88/310.
s. 11, see *Powley* v. *A.C.A.S.* [1977] I.R.L.R. 190, Browne-Wilkinson J.; *Grunwick Processing Laboratories* v. *A.C.A.S.* [1978] 2 W.L.R. 277, H.L.; *National Union of Gold, Silver and Allied Trades* v. *Albury Brothers* [1979] I.C.R. 84, C.A.; *National Employers Life Assurance Co.* v. *A.C.A.S. and A.S.T.M.S.* [1979] I.R.L.R. 282, Browne-Wilkinson J.; *Engineers' and Managers, Association* v. *A.C.A.S.* [1980] 1 W.L.R. 302, H.L.; *USDAW* v. *Sketchley* [1981] I.C.R. 644, E.A.T.; *R.* v. *C.A.C., ex p. B.T.P. Tioxide* [1981] I.C.R. 843, Forbes J.
ss. 11–16, repealed: 1980, c.42, s.19, sch.2.
s. 12, see *U.K. Association of Professional Engineers* v. *A.C.A.S.* [1980] 2 W.L.R. 254; [1980] 1 All E.R. 612, H.L.; *Engineers' and Managers' Association* v *A.C.A.S.* [1980] 1 W.L.R. 302, H.L.
ss. 12, 14, see *Grunwick Processing Laboratories* v. *A.C.A.S.* [1978] 2 W.L.R. 277, H.L.; *Powley* v. *A.C.A.S.* [1978] I.C.R. 123, Browne-Wilkinson J.; *National Employers Life Assurance Co.* v. *A.C.A.S.* [1979] I.C.R. 620, Browne-Wilkinson J.
s. 14, see *National Employers Life Assurance Co.* v. *A.C.A.S. and A.S.T.M.S.* [1979] I.R.L.R. 282, Browne-Wilkinson J.
ss. 17, 18, see *Civil Service Union* v. *Central Arbitration Committee* [1980] I.R.L.R. 274, Forbes J.
ss. 17, 19, see *R.* v. *C.A.C., ex p. B.T.P. Tioxide* [1981] I.C.R. 843, Forbes J.
ss. 17, 21, repealed in pt.: 1980, c.42, sch.2.
Pt. II (ss. 22–88): repealed; except s.40: 1978, c.44, sch.17.
s. 22, see *Mailway (Southern)* v. *Willsher* [1978] I.C.R. 511, E.A.T.
s. 22, orders 77/1322, 1601, 2032; 78/826.
s. 25, orders 77/2031; 78/737, 826.
s. 28, orders 77/156–158, 902, 1096, 1158, 1322, 1349, 1522, 1523, 1583, 1601, 2032; 78/153, 429.
s. 29, order 76/659.
s. 35, see *Hughes* v. *Gwynedd Area Health Authority* [1978] I.C.R. 161, E.A.T.; *Nu-Swift International* v. *Mullinson* [1979] I.C.R. 157, E.A.T.; *Lloyds Bank* v. *Secretary of State for Employment* [1979] I.C.R. 258, E.A.T.

1975—cont.

71. Employment Protection Act 1975—*cont.*
s. 36, see *Inner London Education Authority* v. *Nash* [1979] I.C.R. 229, E.A.T.
s. 40, repealed in pt.: 1977, c.5, sch.2; 1986, c.50, sch.11.
s. 42, regs. 77/322, 668.
s. 48, see *Bovey* v. *Board of Governors of the Hospital for Sick Children, The Times,* May 5, 1978, E.A.T.
s. 53, see *Brassington* v. *Cauldon Wholesale* [1977] I.C.R. 405, E.A.T.; *Robb* v. *Leon Motor Services* [1978] I.C.R. 506, E.A.T.; *Cheall* v. *Vauxhall Motors* [1979] I.R.L.R. 253.
s. 56, see *Brassington* v. *Cauldon Wholesale* [1978] I.C.R. 405, E.A.T.
s. 57, see *Vine* v. *D.R.G. (U.K.)* [1978] I.R.L.R. 475; *McCormack* v. *Shell Chemicals U.K.* [1979] I.R.L.R. 40; *Sood* v. *G.E.C. Elliott Process Automation* [1980] I.C.R. 1, E.A.T.; *Young* v. *Carr Fasteners* [1979] I.C.R. 844, E.A.T.
s. 59, see *Ratcliff* v. *Dorset County Council* [1978] I.R.L.R. 191.
s. 60, see *Corner* v. *Buckingham County Council* [1978] I.C.R. 836, E.A.T.
s. 61, see *Dutton* v. *Hawker Siddeley Aviation* [1978] I.C.R. 1057, E.A.T.
s. 64, see *Fox Brothers (Clothes) (In Liquidation)* v. *Bryant* [1979] I.C.R. 64, E.A.T.; *Secretary of State for Employment* v. *Haynes* [1980] I.C.R. 371, E.A.T.
s. 64, order 77/2031.
ss. 64, 66, see *Secretary of State for Employment* v. *Wilson* [1978] I.C.R. 200, E.A.T.
s. 70, see *Horsley Smith & Sherry* v. *Dutton* [1977] I.C.R. 594; [1977] I.R.L.R. 172, E.A.T.; *Charles Lang & Sons* v. *Aubrey* [1978] I.C.R. 168, E.A.T.; *Daynecourt Insurance Brokers* v. *Iles* [1978] I.R.L.R. 335, E.A.T.; *Lowson* v. *Percy Main & District Social Club & Institute* [1979] I.C.R. 568, E.A.T.; *Marchant* v. *Earley Town Council* [1979] I.C.R. 891, E.A.T.
s. 71, see *Meridian* v. *Gomersall* [1977] I.C.R. 597, F.A.T.; *Gupta* v. *Burroughs Machines* 1978, S.L.T.(Notes) 42.
s. 72, see *Enessy Co. S.A., T/A The Tulcan Estate* v. *Minoprio* [1978] I.R.L.R. 489, E.A.T.
ss. 72, 73, see *Cadbury* v. *Doddington* [1977] I.C.R. 982, E.A.T.
s. 74, see *Brownson* v. *Hire Service Shops* [1978] I.C.R. 517, E.A.T.
s. 75, see *Brown's Cycles* v. *Brindley* [1978] I.C.R. 467, E.A.T.; order 77/2031.
s. 76, see *Weatherill* v. *Shipton Automation* (1977) 12 I.T.R. 123, E.A.T.; *Robert Whiting Designs* v. *Lamb* [1978] I.C.R. 89, E.A.T.; *Brown's Cycles* v. *Brindley* [1978] I.C.R. 467, E.A.T.; *Brownson* v. *Hire Service Shops* [1978] I.C.R. 517, E.A.T.; *Manning* v. *R. & H. Wale (Export)* [1979] I.C.R. 433, E.A.T.; *Gallear* v. *J. F. Watson & Son* [1979] I.R.L.R. 306, E.A.T.; *Peara* v. *Enderlin* [1979] I.C.R. 804, E.A.T.
s. 78, see *Barley* v. *Amey Roadstone Corp.* (1976) 11 I.T.R. 283; [1977] I.C.R. 546, E.A.T.;

1975—cont.

71. Employment Protection Act 1975—cont.
Stone v. Charrington & Co. [1977] I.C.R. 248,
E.A.T.; Forsyth v. Fry's Metals [1977] I.R.L.R.
243; Taplin v. C. Shippam [1978] I.C.R. 1068,
E.A.T.
ss. 81, 84, see Scott v. Creager [1979] I.C.R.
403, E.A.T.
s. 85, see Barrett v. National Coal Board [1978]
I.C.R. 1101, E.A.T.
s. 86, order 77/2031.
s. 88, see General and Municipal Workers Union
v. Certification Officer [1977] 1 All E.R. 771;
Kurnchyk v. Derby City Council [1978] I.C.R.
1116, E.A.T.; Squibb U.K. Staff Association v.
Certification Officer [1979] I.C.R. 235, C.A.;
Mackay v. Highland Regional Council, 1984,
S.L.T. 146.
ss. 89–96, repealed: 1979, c.12, sch.7.
s. 98, repealed: 1980, c.42, s.19, sch.2.
s. 99, see Amalgamated Society of Boilermak-
ers, Shipwrights, Blacksmiths and Structural
Workers v. George Wimpey M.E. & Co. [1977]
I.R.L.R. 95; Kelly v. Upholstery and Cabinet
Works (Amesbury) [1977] I.R.L.R. 91; National
Union of Tailors and Garment Workers v.
Charles Ingram & Co. [1977] I.R.L.R. 147;
[1977] I.C.R. 530, E.A.T.; Sir Alfred McAlpine
& Son (Northern) v. Foulkes [1977] I.C.R. 748,
E.A.T.; Barratt Developments (Bradford) v.
Union of Construction, Allied Trades and Tech-
nicians [1978] I.C.R. 319, E.A.T.; National
Union of Gold, Silver and Allied Trades v.
Albury Brothers [1978] I.R.L.R. 504, C.A.;
Union of Construction, Allied Trades and Tech-
nicians v. H. Rooke & Son [1978] I.C.R. 818,
E.A.T.; National Union of Teachers v. Avon
County Council (1978) 76 L.G.R. 403, E.A.T.;
Bakers' Union v. Clarks of Hove [1978] 1
W.L.R. 1207, C.A.; National and Local Gov-
ernment Officers Association v. National
Travel (Midlands) [1978] I.C.R. 598, E.A.T.;
Joshua Wilson and Bros v. Union of Shop,
Distributive and Allied Workers [1978] I.C.R.
614, E.A.T.; Association of Patternmakers and
Allied Craftsmen v. Kirvin [1978] I.R.L.R. 318,
E.A.T.; Transport and General Workers Union
v. Gainsborough Distributors (U.K.) [1978]
I.R.L.R. 450, E.A.T.; Hamish Armour (Receiver
of Barry Staines) v. A.S.T.M.S. [1979] I.R.L.R.
24, E.A.T.; Spillers-French (Holdings) v. Union
of Shop, Distributive and Allied Workers
[1980] I.C.R. 31, E.A.T.; USDAW v. Leancut
Bacon [1981] I.R.L.R. 295, E.A.T.; Decision
No. R (U) 3/83; Association of University
Teachers v. University of Newcastle-upon-
Tyne [1987] I.C.R. 317, E.A.T.
ss. 99–101, amended: order 79/958.
ss. 99, 101, see National Union of Gold, Silver
and Allied Trades v. Albury Brothers [1979]
I.C.R. 84, C.A.; G.K.N. Sankey v. National
Society of Metal Mechanics [1980] I.C.R. 148,
E.A.T.; Green and Son (Castings) v. Associ-
ation of Scientific, Technical and Managerial
Staffs [1984] I.C.R. 352, E.A.T.; Jowett
(Angus) & Co. v. National Union of Tailors and

1975—cont.

71. Employment Protection Act 1975—cont.
Garment Workers [1985] I.R.L.R. 326; [1985]
I.C.R. 646; E.A.T.; Transport & General Work-
ers Union v. Ledbury Preserves (1928) [1986]
I.C.R. 855, E.A.T.
s. 100, see Secretary of State for Employment
v. Helitron [1980] I.C.R. 523, E.A.T.
s. 101, see Talke Fashions v. Amalgamated
Society of Textile Workers and Kindred Trades
[1977] I.C.R. 833, E.A.T.; Sir Alfred McAlpine
& Son (Northern) v. Foulkes [1977] I.C.R. 748,
E.A.T.; National Union of Gold, Silver and
Allied Trades v. Albury Brothers [1978] I.R.L.R.
504, C.A.; Transport and General Workers
Union v. Gainsborough Distributors (U.K.)
[1978] I.R.L.R. 460, E.A.T.; USDAW v. Sketchley [1981] I.C.R. 644, E.A.T.
ss. 101, 102, see Spillers-French (Holdings) v.
Union of Shop, Distributive and Allied Workers
[1980] I.C.R. 31, E.A.T.
s. 102, amended: 1978, c.44, sch.16.
s. 103, see Sir Alfred McAlpine & Son (Northern)
v. Foulkes [1977] I.C.R. 748, E.A.T.
ss. 104, 106, amended: 1978, c.44, sch.16.
s. 106, order 79/958.
s. 106, repealed in pt.: 1980, c.42, sch.2.
s. 108, amended: 1978, c.44, sch.16; repealed
in pt.: ibid., sch.17.
s. 109, repealed: 1978, c.44, sch.17.
s. 111, repealed in pt.: 1976, c.71, sch.8.
s. 112, regs. 76/677; 77/674; repealed: 1978,
c.44, sch.17.
s. 113, repealed: 1977, c.5, sch.2.
s. 118, repealed in pt.: 1978, c.44, sch.17; 1980,
c.42, sch.2.
s. 119, see National Association of Teachers in
Further and Higher Education v. Manchester
City Council [1978] I.C.R. 1190, E.A.T.
s. 119, amended: 1978, c.44, sch.16; 1982,
c.46, sch.2; repealed in pt.: 1976, c.79, sch.9;
1978, c.44, sch.17; 1982, c.46, sch.4.
s. 120, repealed: 1978, c.44, sch.17.
s. 121, see R. v. Secretary of State for the
Foreign and Commonwealth Office, ex p.
Council of Civil Service Unions, The Times,
July 17, 1984, Glidewell J.
s. 121, amended: 1978, c.44, sch.12; 1980,
c.42, sch.1; repealed in pt.: 1978, c.44,
sch.13; 1980, c.42, sch.2; 1981, c.55, sch 5.
s. 122, amended: 1976, c.74, sch.3; 1978, c.36,
sch.2; repealed in pt.: ibid., sch.3; c.44,
sch.17.
s. 123, regs. 77/668; orders 76/766, 1379;
77/82, 588, 2031; 84/1149.
s. 123, repealed in pt.: 1978, c.44, sch.17.
s. 124, repealed in pt.: ibid.
s. 125, amended: ibid., sch.16.
s. 126, see National Union of Tailors and Garment Workers v. Charles Ingram & Co. [1977]
I.C.R. 530, E.A.T.; R. v. C.A.C., ex p. B.T.P.
Tioxide [1981] I.C.R. 843, Forbes J.
s. 126, amended: 1978, c.44, sch.16; 1980,
c.42, sch.1; 1982, c.46, sch.3; repealed in
pt.: 1978, c.44, sch.17; 1982, c.46, sch.4.
s. 126A, added: ibid., sch.3.

CAP.

71. Employment Protection Act 1975—*cont.*

s. 127, orders 76/766; 77/588; 81/208; 84/1149.

s. 127, amended: 1978, c.46, s.1; 1980, c.42, sch.1, 1982, c.9, s.11; c.10, sch.3; c.23, sch.3; c.46, sch.3; repealed in pt.: 1978, c.44, sch.17; 1979, c.12, sch.7; 1980, c.42, sch.2; order 81/839.

s. 128, repealed in pt.: 1978, c.44, sch.17; order 81/839.

s. 129, orders 75/1938; 76/144, 321, 530, 1379, 1996; 77/82, 433, 936, 2075.

s. 129, repealed in pt.: 1978, c.44, sch.17.

sch. 1, amended: 1988, c.19, s.22; repealed in pt.: 1978, c.44, sch.17.

schs. 1, 2, order 77/1601.

schs. 2-6, repealed: 1978, c.44, sch.17.

sch. 3, see *Bovey* v. *Board of Governors of the Hospital for Sick Children* [1978] I.C.R. 934, E.A.T.

sch. 4, see *Palmanor* v. *Cedron* [1978] I.C.R. 1008, E.A.T.; *Barrett* v. *National Coal Board* [1978] I.C.R. 1101, E.A.T.

schs. 4, 5, see *Secretary of State for Employment* v. *Haynes* [1980] I.C.R. 371, E.A.T.

sch. 6, see *Askew* v. *Victoria Sporting Club* [1976] I.C.R. 302; *International Aviation Services (U.K.)* v. *Jones* [1979] I.R.C. 371, E.A.T.; rules 76/322.

schs. 7, 8, repealed: 1979, c.12, sch.7.

sch. 11, see *R.* v. *Central Arbitration Committee, ex p. Deltaflow* [1978] I.C.R. 534, D.C.; *R.* v. *Central Arbitration Committee, ex p. T.I. Tube Division Services* [1978] I.R.L.R. 183, D.C.; *R.* v. *Central Arbitration Committee, ex p. N. W. Regional Health Authority* [1978] I.C.R. 1228, D.C.; *R.* v. *C.A.C., ex p. The Banking Insurance and Finance Union* [1983] I.C.R. 27, C.A.

sch. 11, repealed: 1980, c.42, s.19, sch.2.

sch. 12, regs. 76/663.

sch. 14, order 77/898; repealed in pt.: 1978, c.6, s.3; 1988, c.19, sch.4.

sch. 16. see *Dhami* v. *Top Spot Night Club* [1977] I.R.L.R. 231, E.A.T.; *Active Elderly Housing Association* v. *Sparrow* (1978) 13 I.T.R. 395, E.A.T.; *Dimbleby & Sons* v. *National Union of Journalists, The Times,* March 2, 1984, H.L.

sch. 16, repealed in pt.: 1976, c.74, sch.5; 1978, c.44, sch.17; 1980, c.42, sch.2; c.44, sch.5 (S.); c.60, sch.3; 1981, c.57, sch.3; c.68, sch.9; 1982, c.46, sch.4; 1985, c.21, sch.2; 1986, c.48, sch.5; c.59, sch.; 1987, c.1, sch.2.

sch. 17, repealed in pt.: 1978, c.44, sch.17; 1979, c.12, sch.7; 1980, c.42, sch.2.

72. Children Act 1975.

Royal Assent, November 12, 1975.

Commencement orders: 77/227 (S.33); 78/1440 (S.131); 82/33 (S.2); 83/1946; 85/779, 1557 (S.); 87/1242.

Pt. I (ss. 1–32), repealed: 1976, c.36, sch.4.

ss. 1–32, repealed (S.): 1978, c.28, sch.4.

s. 3, see *Re P. (An Infant) (Adoption: Parental Consent)* [1976] 3 W.L.R. 924, C.A.; *Re B (An Infant)* [1976] 2 W.L.R. 755; *A. and B.* v. *C.,* 1977 S.C. 27; *Re M. (A Minor),* June 5, 1980.

CAP.

72. Children Act 1975—*cont.*

C.A.; *Re D. (Minors)* (1980) 10 Fam.Law 246, C.A.; *Re H. (A Minor)* [1982] 3 W.L.R. 501, Hollings J.; *El-G.* v. *El.-G. (Minors: Adoption)* (1982) 12 Fam.Law 251, Wood J.; *W (A Minor: Adoption), Re* (1984) 14 Fam.Law 179, C.A.; *R.* v. *Tower Hamlets Juvenile Justices, ex p. London Borough of Tower Hamlets* (1984) 14 Fam.Law 307, Bush J.; *P.B. (A Minor) (Application to Free for Adoption), Re* (1985) 15 Fam.Law 198, Sheldon J.; *V. (A Minor) (Adoption: Consent), Re* [1986] 1 All E.R. 752, C.A.; *S. (A Minor) (Adoption), Re; The Times,* August 26, 1987, C.A.; *C. (A Minor) (Adoption Order: Conditions), Re* [1988] 2 W.L.R. 474, H.L.; *P. (Minors) (Adoption by Step-Parent), Re* [1988] F.C.R. 401, C.A.

ss. 3–12, see *Re H.; Re W. (Minors)* (1983) 13 Fam.Law 144, C.A.

s. 4, regs. 81/1818; 82/34 (S.); 83/1964.

s. 4, amended: 1983, c.41, sch.2.

s. 8, see *Secretary of State* v. *The Insurance Officer* (1984) 14 Fam.Law 55, C.A.; *M. (A Minor) (Adoption Order: Access), Re* (1985) 15 Fam.Law 321, C.A.; *V. (A Minor) (Adoption: Consent), Re* [1986] 1 All E.R. 752, C.A.; *C. (A Minor) (Adoption Order: Condition), Re* (1986) 1 F.L.R. 315, C.A.; *C. (A Minor) (Adoption Order: Conditions), Re* [1988] 2 W.L.R. 474, H.L.

s. 8, repealed in pt.: 1976, c.31, sch.3; amended (S.): 1976, c.36, sch.3.

s. 9, see *S. (A Minor) (Adoption), Re* (1985) 15 Fam.Law 132, C.A.; *Y. (Minors) (Adoption: Jurisdiction), Re* [1985] 3 W.L.R. 601, Sheldon J.

s. 10, see *Re S. (Infants) (Adoption by Parent)* [1977] 2 W.L.R. 919, C.A.; *Re S.* (1978) Fam.Law 88, C.A.; *Re D. (Minors)* (1980) 10 Fam.Law 246, C.A.; *Re Howes (A Minor)* (1981) 11 Fam.Law 246, Hollings J.; *Re H. (Adoption by Step-Parent: Preliminary Examination)* (1983) 4 F.L.R. 261, Hollings J.; *P. (Minors) (Adoption by Step-Parent), Re* [1988] F.C.R. 401, C.A.

s. 12, see *Re A. (A Minor)* (1979) 10 Fam. Law 49, C.A.; *Re F. (A Minor)* [1982] 1 W.L.R. 102, C.A.; *Re H. (B) (An Infant); W. (N) (An Infant)* (1982) 127 S.J. 86, C.A.; *K. (A Minor), Re, The Times,* March 7, 1985, C.A.; *V. (Adoption: Parental Consent), Re* (1985) 15 Fam.Law 56, C.A.; *C. (A Minor), Re, The Times,* July 22, 1985, C.A.; *P.B. (A Minor), Re* (1985) 15 Fam.Law 198, Sheldon J.; *A.B.* v. *C.B.,* 1985 S.L.T. 514.; *G.B. (Adoption: Parental Agreement) Re* (1985) 15 Fam.Law 314, C.A.; *V. (A Minor) (Adoption: Consent), Re* [1986] 1 All E.R. 752, C.A.; *S. (A Minor) (Adoption: Procedure), Re* (1986) 1 F.L.R. 302, C.A.; *J. (A Minor) (Adoption Application), Re* (1987) 151 J.P.N. 62, Sheldon J.; *A. (A Minor) (Adoption: Parental Consent), Re* [1987] 1 W.L.R. 153, C.A.; *M. (A Minor) (Custodianship: Juris-*

CAP.

72. Children Act 1975—*cont.*
diction), Re [1987] 1 W.L.R. 162, C.A.; *R. (A Minor) (Adoption or Custodianship), Re* (1987) 151 J.P.N. 175, Sheldon J.
ss. 12, 14, see *Hampshire County Council* v. *C.* [1988] F.C.R. 133, C.A.
ss. 12, 23, 25, amended (S.): 1976, c.36, sch.3.
s. 14, see *Adoption Application No. 118/1984, Re, The Times,* February 15, 1985, *sub nom., M.* v. *Berkshire C.C.* (1985) 15 Fam.Law 161, C.A.; *W. (A Minor) (Wardship Jurisdiction), Re* [1985] 2 W.L.R. 892, H.L.; *sub nom. W.* v. *Hertfordshire C.C.* [1985] 2 All E.R. 301, H.L.; *P.B. (A Minor) (Application to Free for Adoption), Re,* (1985) 15 Fam.Law 198, Sheldon J.; *T.D. (A Minor) (Wardship: Jurisdiction), Re* (1986) 16 Fam.Law 18, Sheldon J.
s. 16, amended (S.): 1976, c.36, sch.3.
s. 17, repealed in pt.: 1978, c.22, s.72, sch.3.
s. 18, see *Y. (Minors) (Adoption: Jurisdiction) Re* [1985] 3 W.L.R. 601, Sheldon J.
s. 19, see *O. (A Minor) (Adoption by Grandparents), Re* (1985) 15 Fam.Law 305, D.C.
s. 21, amended: 1978, c.22, s.73; repealed in pt.: *ibid.,* s.73, sch.3.
s. 24, orders 78/1431, 1442; amended: 1978, c.22, s.74.
s. 28, see *Re K. (A Minor),* December 20, 1982, Eastham J.; *S. (A Minor) (Adoption), Re* (1985) 15 Fam.Law 132, C.A.; *A (Adoption: Placement), Re* [1988] 1 W.L.R. 229, Lincoln J.
s. 30, amended: 1983, c.41, sch.2.
s. 33, see *J. (A Minor) (Adoption Application), Re* (1987) 151 J.P.N. 62, Sheldon J.
s. 33, amended: 1987, c.42, sch.2; repealed in pt.: 1986, c.55, schs.1,2.
ss. 33, 37, see *M. (A Minor), Re, The Times,* October 13, 1986, C.A.; *Hampshire County Council* v. *C* [1988] F.C.R. 133, C.A.
s. 34, substituted: 1978, c.22, s.64; amended: 1987, c.42, sch.2; repealed in pt.: *ibid.,* schs. 2,4.
ss. 34A, 34B, added: 1978, c.22, s.65.
s. 35, order 88/1069.
s. 35, amended: 1978, c.22, s.66; 1987, c.42, sch.2.
s. 35A, added: 1987, c.22, s.67.
s. 36, amended: *ibid.,* s.68, sch.2; repealed in pt.: 1987, c.42, schs.2,4.
s. 37, see *J. (A Minor) (Adoption Application), Re* (1987) 151 J.P.N. 82, Sheldon J.; *A. (A Minor) (Adoption: Parental Consent), Re* [1987] 1 W.L.R. 153, C.A.; *M. (A Minor) (Custodianship: Jurisdiction), Re* [1987] 1 W.L.R. 162, C.A.; *R. (A Minor) (Adoption or Custodianship). Re* (1987) 151 J.P.N. 175, Sheldon J.; *S. (A Minor) (Adoption or Custodianship), Re* [1987] 2 W.L.R. 977, C.A.
s. 37, amended: 1976, c.36, sch.3; 1978, c.22, s.69; 1983, c.41, sch.2; 1987, c.42, sch.2.
s. 40, regs. 85/792, 1494.
ss. 41, 42, amended: 1983, c.41, sch.2.
s. 43, amended: 1978, c.22, sch.2; 1987, c.42, sch.2.
s. 43A, added: 1978, c.22, s.70; amended: 1983, c.41, sch.2.

CAP.

72. Children Act 1975—*cont.*
s. 45, repealed: 1987, c.42, schs.2,4.
s. 46, amended: 1978, c.22, sch.2; 1980, c.43, sch.7.
s. 47, amended (S.): 1978, c.28, sch.3; 1986, c.9, sch.1; repealed in pt. (S.): *ibid.,* sch.2.
ss. 47, 48, Acts of Sederunt 86/513, 515.
s. 48, repealed in pt. (S.): 1986, c.9, sch.2.
s. 49, amended: *ibid.,* sch.1.
ss. 51, 52, amended: 1983, c.41, sch.2.
s. 53, repealed in pt. (S.): *ibid.,* sch.2.
ss. 53 (in pt.), 54, repealed: 1986, c.55, sch.2.
s. 55, amended (S.): 1986, c.9, sch.1.
ss. 56–63, repealed: 1980, c.5, sch.6.
s. 57, see *Lewisham London Borough Council* v. *Lewisham Juvenile Court Justices, The Times,* November 1, 1978, C.A.; *O'Dare A.* v. *South Glamorgan County* (1980) 10 Fam.Law 215, D.C.
s. 65, see *R.* v. *Worthing JJ., ex p. Stevenson* [1976] 2 All E.R. 194, D.C.
s. 65, repealed: 1988, c.34, sch.6.
s. 67, see *R.* v. *Leicester Juvenile Court, ex p. K.D.C.* (1985) 80 Cr.App.R. 320, D.C.
ss. 67, 71, repealed: 1980, c.5, sch.6.
s. 69, order 77/1037.
s. 72, repealed in pt.: 1983, c.41, sch.10.
s. 85, see *C* v. *H.* (1979) 123 S.J. 537, D.C.
s. 85, repealed in pt.: 1987, c.42, sch.4.
ss. 85, 86, see *M. and H. (Minors) (No. 2), Re* (1988) 152 J.P.N. 127, Booth J.
s. 89, repealed: 1978, c.30, sch.3.
s. 92, regs. 76/2080.
s. 93, repealed in pt.: 1987, c.42, sch.4.
ss. 95–97, repealed: 1980, c.6, sch.3; 1984, c.56, sch.3 (S.).
s. 98, repealed: 1980, c.5, sch.6; amended: 1983, c.20, sch.4.
s. 100, rules 88/329.
s. 100, amended: 1984, c.28, sch.2; c.42, sch.1; 1986, c.55, sch.1; repealed in pt.: 1976, c.36, sch.4; 1978, c.28, sch.4 (S.); 1986, c.55, schs.1,2.
s. 101, amended: 1978, c.22, s.71, sch.2; 1983, c.41, sch.2; repealed in pt.: 1984, c.42, sch.3.
s. 102, repealed in pt.: 1976, c.36, sch.4; 1978, c.28, sch.4 (S.).
s. 103, regs. 83/1908; 84/566 (S.), 1442 (S.); 85/1556 (S.); 86/3.
s. 103, amended: 1976, c.36, sch.3; 1978, c.28, sch.3 (S.); 1980, c.5, sch.5; 1983, c.41, sch.2.
s. 105, amended: 1978, c.28, sch.3 (S.).
s. 106, orders 83/86, 107 (S.), 1946.
s. 107, see *Y. (Minors) (Adoption: Jurisdiction), Re* [1985] 3 W.L.R. 601, Sheldon J.
s. 107, orders 78/1431, 1432, 1441, 1442.
s. 107, amended (S.): 1976, c.36, sch.3; 1978, c.28, sch.3; repealed in pt.: 1976, c.36, sch.4; 1978, c.28, sch.4 (S.); 1985, c.51, sch.17.
s. 108, orders 76/1744; 77/227, 1036; 78/1433; 80/1475; 81/1792, 82/33 (S.); 83/86, 107 (S.), 1946; 84/554 (S.); 85/779, 1557 (S.); 87/1242; repealed in pt. (S.): 1978, c.28, sch.4.
s. 109, repealed in pt.: 1981, c.61, sch.9; 1983, c.41, sch.10.

1975—cont.

72. Children Act 1975—*cont.*
sch. 1, see *Secretary of State for Social Services v. S.* [1983] 3 All E.R. 173, C.A.; *Secretary of State* v. *The Insurance Officer* (1984) 14 Fam.Law 55, C.A.
sch. 1, repealed: 1976, c.36, sch.4; repealed in pt.: 1976, c.31, sch.2; 1981, c.61, sch.1; amended: 1976, c.31, sch.2; order 86/948.
sch. 2, repealed: 1976, c.36, sch.4; amended: 1976, c.36, sch.3 (S.); 1981, c.61, sch.1; order 86/948; repealed in pt. (S.): 1978, c.28, sch.4.
sch. 3, see *Re D. (A Minor) (Justices' Decision; Review)* [1977] 2 W.L.R. 1006, Dunn J.; *Re H. (A Minor), The Times,* October 29, 1977, C.A.
sch. 3, repealed in pt.: 1976, c.36, sch.4; S.L.R. 1977; 1978, c.22, s.74, sch.3; c.28, sch.4 (S.); 1980, c.5, sch.6; c.6, sch.3; 1981, c.54, sch.7; c.61, sch.9; 1984, c.56, sch.3 (S.); 1985, c.71, sch.1; 1987, c.42, sch.4; c.45, sch.4; 1988, c.34, sch.6.

73. Cinematograph Films Act 1975.
Royal Assent, November 12, 1975.
repealed: 1980, c.41, sch.

74. Petroleum and Submarine Pipe-Lines Act 1975.
Royal Assent, November 12, 1975.
s. 1, regs. 75/2122.
s. 1, repealed (prosp.): 1985, c.62, sch.4.
s. 1, amended: 1982, c.23, sch.3; repealed in pt.: *ibid.*, schs.3,4.
Pt. I (ss.1–16), repealed (exc. s.1, sch.1): 1985, c.62, sch.4.
s. 6, order 82/1819.
s. 16, order 76/860.
s. 22, amended: 1982, c.23, s.25, repealed in pt.: *ibid.*, s.25, sch.4.
s. 23, amended: *ibid.*, s.25.
s. 26, regs. 76/923; 86/1985.
s. 26, repealed in pt.: 1982, c.23, s.25, sch.4.
s. 27, regs. 77/835; 86/1985; amended (S.): 1976, c.14, sch.1.
s. 30, amended: order 77/1251.
s. 31, regs. 81/750; 85/1051.
s. 32, regs. 76/923; 77/835; 86/1985.
s. 33, orders, 88/634, 741, 804, 805, 881–883, 911, 912, 981–983, 1232–1238, 1554, 1559–1561, 1740–1744, 1900–1903
s. 33, amended: 1982, c.23, s.25.
ss. 34–39, repealed: 1987, c.12, s.28, sch.3.
s. 40, repealed in pt.: 1982, c.23, sch.4.
s. 41, repealed in pt.: *ibid.*, s.30, sch.4.
s. 44, repealed in pt.: *ibid.*, schs.3,4.
s. 45, amended: 1985, c.48, s.15; repealed in pt.: 1982, c.23, schs.3,4.
s. 46, regs. 75/2122; order 76/860.
s. 46, amended: 1982, c.23, sch.3; repealed in pt.: 1985, c.62, sch.4.
s. 48, amended: 1985, c.9, sch.2; repealed in pt.: 1985, c.62, sch.4.
s. 49, order 75/2120.
sch. 1, regs. 75/2122.
sch. 1, amended: 1982, c.23, sch.3; repealed (prosp.): 1985, c.62, sch.4.
schs. 2, 3, amended and repealed in pt.: 1987, c.12, sch.1.

1975—cont.

75. Policyholders Protection Act 1975.
Royal Assent, November 12, 1975.
s. 3, amended: 1980, c.25, sch.3; 1981, c.31, sch.4; 1982, c.50, sch.5; repealed in pt: 1980, c.25, sch.5.
s. 5, amended: 1985, c.9, sch.2; 1986, c.45, sch.14; repealed in pt.: 1985, c.65, sch.10.
ss. 6, 7, amended: order 81/160; 1988, c.54, sch.3.
s. 8, amended: 1981, c.31, sch.4.
s. 9, amended: order 81/160; 1988, c.54, sch.3.
s. 10, repealed in pt.: 1981, c.31, sch.5.
s. 15, see *Policyholders Protection Board* v. *Official Receiver* [1976] 1 W.L.R. 447; [1976] 2 All E.R. 58.
ss. 15, 16, amended: 1985, c.9, sch.2; 1986, c.45, sch.14.
s. 19, repealed in pt.: 1981, c.31, sch.5.
s. 20, amended: 1985, c.9, sch.2.
s. 22, repealed in pt.: 1980, c.25, sch.5; 1982, c.50, sch.6.
s. 27, amended: 1980, c.25, sch.3., 1985, c.9, sch.2.
s. 28, amended: 1982, c.50, sch.4.
s. 29, amended: 1980, c.25, sch.3; 1982, c.50, sch.4; 1985, c.9, sch.2.
s. 32, amended: 1982, c.50, sch.5; repealed in pt.: 1980, c.25, sch.5.
sch. 1, amended: 1985, c.9, sch.2.
sch. 3, amended: 1982, c.50, sch.5; repealed in pt.: 1980, c.25, sch.5.

76. Local Land Charges Act 1975.
Royal Assent, November 12, 1975.
s. 1, amended: 1980, c.66, sch.24; 1984, c.55, sch.6; 1988, c.4, sch.6.
s. 3, amended: 1982, c.30, s.34.
s. 4, repealed in pt.: 1978, c.30, sch.3.
s. 8, amended: 1982, c.30, s.34.
s. 10, amended: *ibid.*; 1984, c.28, sch.2.
s. 14, rules 77/985; 78/1638; 79/1404; 81/78; 82/461; 85/221; 86/424; 87/389.
s. 20, order 77/984.
sch. 1, see *Barber* v. *Shah* (1985) 17 H.L.R. 584, D.C.
sch. 1, rules 86/424.
sch. 1, repealed in pt.: 1976, c.70, sch.8; 1980, c.51, sch.26; c.66, sch.25; 1981, c.64, sch.13; 1982, c.16, sch.16; c.30, sch.7; 1985, c.71, sch.1.

77. Community Land Act 1975.
Royal Assent, November 12, 1975.
repealed: 1980, c.65, s.101, schs.17,34.
s. 2, orders 77/480; 80/393.
s. 3, regs. 76/331; 77/743.
s. 4, orders 76/19; 77/148.
s. 5, orders 76/18, 110, 198, 199, 405
s. 7, orders 76/330, 622.
s. 15, see *Davis* v. *Secretary of State for the Environment and North Norfolk District Council* [1980] J.P.L. 324, Sir Douglas Frank, Q.C.
s. 16, order 76/383; modified: order 77/480.
ss 19, 21, regs. 76/230, 397, 513, 1083.
s. 26, orders 76/1218, 2210; 77/741; 80/1172.
s. 40, orders 76/1219, 2211; 77/742
s. 46, regs. 76/417, 777; orders 76/1871; 77/450.

1975—cont.

77. Community Land Act 1975—*cont.*
s. 53, regs. 76/230, 331, 397, 417, 513, 777, 1083; 77/743; orders 76/18, 19, 110, 198, 199, 330, 383, 405, 622, 1218, 1219, 1871, 2210, 2211; 77/148, 450, 480, 741, 742; 80/393, 1172.
sch. 4, regs. 76/513, 1083.
sch. 6, regs. 76/230, 397.
schs. 7, 8, regs. 76/230, 397, 513, 1083.
sch. 8, amended: 1985, c.9, sch.2

78. Airports Authority Act 1975.
Royal Assent, November 12, 1975.
repealed: 1986, c.31, sch.6.
ss. 1, 9, see *R.* v. *British Airports Authority, ex p. Wheatley* [1983] R.T.R. 466, C.A.
s. 2, see *Air Canada* v. *Secretary of State for Trade* [1981] 3 All E.R. 336, Parker J.
ss. 2, 9, see *Cinnamond* v. *British Airports Authority* [1980] 1 W.L.R. 582; [1980] 2 All E.R. 368, C.A.
ss. 13, 14, orders 76/789, 1494–1496.

79. Consolidated Fund (No. 3) Act 1975.
Royal Assent, December 19, 1975.
repealed: 1977, c.35, sch.C.

80. OECD Support Fund Act 1975.
Royal Assent, December 19, 1975.

81. Moneylenders (Crown Agents) Act 1975.
Royal Assent, December 19, 1975.
repealed: 1979, c.43, sch.7.

82. Civil List Act 1975.
Royal Assent, December 19, 1975.

83. Northern Ireland (Loans) Act 1975.
Royal Assent, December 19, 1975.
s. 1, order 84/1915.
s. 1, amended: *ibid.*; 1985, c.76, sch.1.

1976

1. National Coal Board (Finance) Act 1976.
Royal Assent, March 4, 1976.
s. 1, repealed: 1977, c.39, sch.5.
s. 2, orders 78/416; 79/374; 80/433; 81/470; 82/406; 83/459; 84/456; 85/522.
s. 2, amended: orders 77/542; 82/406; 84/456; 85/522; 1987, c.3, sch.1; repealed in pt.: 1977, c.39, sch.4; order 81/470, 1987, c.3, sch.3.
s. 3, repealed: 1977, c.39, sch.5.
s. 4, amended: 1987, c.3, sch.1.

2. Consolidated Fund Act 1976.
Royal Assent, March 25, 1976.
repealed: 1978, c.57, sch.(C.).

3. Road Traffic (Drivers' Ages and Hours of Work) Act 1976.
Royal Assent, March 25, 1976.
see *Brady* v. *Licensing Authority for North West Traffic Area* [1981] Crim.L.R. 407, C.A.; *Paterson* v. *Richardson* [1982] R.T.R. 49, D.C.
s. 1, see *G. (A Minor)* v. *Jarrett* [1981] R.T.R. 186, D.C.
s. 1, repealed: 1988, c.54, sch.1.
s. 1, sch. 1, see *Ferrymasters* v. *Adams* [1980] R.T.R. 139, D.C.; *Anderton* v. *Frost* [1984] R.T.R. 106, D.C.

1976—cont.

3. Road Traffic (Drivers' Ages and Hours of Work) Act 1976—*cont.*
s. 2, see *Pearson* v. *Rutherford* [1982] R.T.R. 54, D.C.; *Oxford* v. *Spencer* [1983] R.T.R. 63, C.A.; *Carter* v. *Walton* [1985] R.T.R. 378, D.C.
s. 2, regs. 78/1938; repealed in pt.: 1979, c.12, sch.7; 1980, c.42, sch.2
s. 4, orders 76/471; 78/6.
s. 4 (in pt.), schs. 1, 2, repealed: 1988, c.54, sch.1.
sch. 2, see *R.* v. *Southend-on-Sea Justices, ex p. Sharp* [1980] R.T.R. 25, D.C.

4. Trustee Savings Banks Act 1976.
Royal Assent, March 4, 1976.
Commencement order: 86/1221.
order 76/1054.
s. 3, order 78/1718.
s. 16, orders 79/551, 1183; 81/319.
s. 37, orders 76/2149, 2150.
s. 38, orders 76/642, 1829; 77/1740; 78/533, 1079; 79/1475; 81/848; 86/1221.

5. Education (School-Leaving Dates) Act 1976.
Royal Assent, March 25, 1976.

6. Solicitors (Scotland) Act 1976.
Royal Assent, March 25, 1976.
repealed, except s.9: 1980, c.46, sch.7.
s. 5, amended: 1981, c.65, sch.6.

7. Trade Union and Labour Relations (Amendment) Act 1976.
Royal Assent, March 25, 1976.
ss. 1, 3, repealed: 1978, c.44, sch.17.
s. 2, repealed: 1980, c.42, sch.2.
s. 3, see *Taylor* v. *Co-operative Retail Services, The Times,* October 24, 1980, E.A.T.

8. Prevention of Terrorism (Temporary Provisions) Act 1976.
Royal Assent, March 25, 1976.
repealed: 1984, c.8, s.18.
see *R.* v. *Secretary of State for the Home Office, ex p. Stitt, The Times,* February 3, 1987, D.C.
s. 1, order 79/745.
ss. 10, 11, see *H.M. Advocate* v. *Von,* 1979 S.L.T.(Notes) 62.
s. 12, see *Ex p. Lynch* [1980] 8 N.I.J.B. Lord Lowry L.C.J.
ss. 12, 14, see *R.* v. *Durham Prison Governor, ex p. Carlisle* [1979] Crim.L.R. 175, D.C.
ss. 13, 14, orders 76/465; 77/271, 1605; 79/168, 169; 80/1336; 82/1521.
ss. 16, 18, orders 76/772, 895, 896.
s. 17, orders 76/499; 78/487; 79/352; 80/406; 81/467; 82/426; 83/414.
sch. 3, orders 76/465; 77/1605; 79/168, 169; 80/1336; 82/1521.

9. Water Charges Act 1976.
Royal Assent, March 25, 1976.
s. 1, see *Hart District Council* v. *Plumbe* (1979) 78 L.G.R. 388, D.C.
s. 2, see *Anglian Water Authority* v. *Castle, The Times,* February 23, 1983, C.A.; *South West Water Authority* v. *Rumble's* [1985] 2 W.L.R. 405, H.L.

10. Post Office (Banking Services) Act 1976.
Royal Assent, March 25, 1976.
s. 1, repealed in pt.: 1979, c.37, sch.7.
ss. 2, 3 (in pt.), repealed: 1981, c.38, sch.

1976—cont.

11. Housing (Amendment) (Scotland) Act 1976.
Royal Assent, April 13, 1976.
repealed: 1981, c.72, s.1.

12. Statute Law Revision (Northern Ireland) Act 1976.
Royal Assent, April 13, 1976.

13. Damages (Scotland) Act 1976.
Royal Assent, April 13, 1976.
see *Cunningham* v. *National Coal Board* (O.H) 1981 S.L.T.(Notes) 74.
s. 1, see *Hartley* v. *Scottish Omnibuses,* 1978 S.L.T.(Sh.Ct.) 35; *Finnie* v. *Cameron* (O.H.), 1979 S.L.T. 57; *Plaxton* v. *Aaron Construction (Dundee)* (O.H.) 1980 S.L.T.(Notes) 6; *Watt* v. *Grampian Regional Council,* 1980 S.L.T(Sh.Ct.) 80; *McArthur* v. *Raynesway Plant* (O.H.), 1980 S.L.T.(Notes) 79; *Bell* v. *Hay* (O.H.), December 20, 1978; *McAllister* v. *Abram,* Second Division, January 28, 1980; *Dingwall* v. *Walter Alexander & Sons (Midland),* Second Division, March 20, 1981; *Porter* v. *Dickie* (O.H.), 1983 S.L.T. 234; *Prentice* v. *Chalmers,* 1985 S.L.T. 168; *Donald* v. *Strathclyde Passenger Transport Executive,* 1986 S.L.T. 625; *Forbes* v. *House of Clydesdale* (O.H.), 1987 S.C.L.R. 136; *Phillips* v. *Grampian Health Board* (O.H.), 1988 S.L.T. 628.
s. 1, amended: 1982, c.53, s.14; 1983, c.14, sch.1.
ss. 1, 10, see *Quinn* v. *Reed* (O.H) 1981 S L T.(Notes) 117.
ss. 1, 12, see *Cunningham* v. *National Coal Board* (O.H.), 1981 S.L.T.(Notes) 74; *Clark* v. *J. M. J. Contractors* (O.H.), 1982 S.I T 299.
s. 2, see *Allison* v. *British Rail Engineering* (O.H.), 1978 S.L.T.(Notes) 34.
s. 4, repealed in pt.: 1982, c.53, s.14.
s. 5, see *McArthur* v. *Raynesway Plant* (O.H.), 1980 S.L.T. 74; *Marshall* v. *Black* (O.H.), June 20, 1980.
s. 5, repealed: 1982, c.53, s.14, sch.9; amended: 1983, c.14, sch.1.
ss. 6, 10, amended: 1982, c.53, s.14.
s. 12, see *Watt* v. *Grampian Regional Council,* 1980 S.L.I.(Sh.Ct.) 80, *McArthur* v. *Raynesway Plant* (O.H.), 1980 S.L.T.(Notes) 79.
sch. 1, see *Hartley* v. *Scottish Omnibuses,* 1978 S.L.T.(Sh.Ct.) 35; *Bell* v. *Hay* (O.H.), December 20, 1978; *Quinn* v. *Reed* (O.H) 1981 S.L.T.(Notes) 117; *Forbes* v. *House of Clydesdale* (O.H.), 1987 S.C.L.R. 136.
sch. 1, amended: 1986, c.9, sch.1.

14. Fatal Accidents and Sudden Deaths Inquiry (Scotland) Act 1976.
Royal Assent, April 13, 1976.
s. 2, amended: 1982, c.48, sch.7.
s. 7, rules 77/191.
s. 9, amended: 1982, c.23, sch.3.
s. 10, order 77/190.
sch. 3, order 77/271; amended: 1977, c.45, s.31, sch.6.

15. Rating (Caravan Sites) Act 1976.
Royal Assent, April 13, 1976.
s. 1, repealed in pt.: 1976, c.70, sch.8; 1980, c.65, sch.34.

1976—cont.

15. Rating (Caravan Sites) Act 1976—*cont.*
s. 3, see *Bourne Leisure (Seton Sands)* v. *Lothian Regional Assessor,* 1983 S.L.T. 298.
s. 3, amended: 1984, c.31, s.14; 1987, c.47, sch.1 (S.); repealed in pt.: 1978, c.40, sch.2; 1987, c.47, sch.6 (S.).
s. 3A, order 84/1881.
s. 3A, added: 1978, c.40, s.15; repealed in pt. (S.): 1987, c.47, sch.6.
s. 4, amended (S.): *ibid.,* sch.1; repealed in pt. (S.): *ibid.,* sch. 6.

16. Statute Law (Repeals) Act 1976.
Royal Assent, May 27, 1976.
s. 3, orders 79/111; 84/1692.
sch. 2, repealed in pt.: S.L.R. 1977; S.L.R. 1978; 1981, c.69, sch.17.

17. Land Drainage (Amendment) Act 1976.
Royal Assent, May 27, 1976.
order 76/2244.
repealed: 1976, c.70, sch.8.

18. Licensing (Amendment) Act 1976.
Royal Assent, May 27, 1976.

19. Seychelles Act 1976.
Royal Assent, May 27, 1976.
order 76/894.
ss. 3, 4, repealed: 1981, c.61, sch.9.
s. 5, repealed in pt.: *ibid.*
s. 6, repealed: S.L.R. 1986.
sch., repealed in pt.: 1981, c.9, sch.

20. Education (Scotland) Act 1976.
Royal Assent, June 10, 1976.
repealed: 1980, c.44, sch.5.
s. 7, orders 76/925; 78/970.

21. Crofting Reform (Scotland) Act 1976.
Royal Assent, June 10, 1976.
see *Macphee* v. *South Uist Estates,* 1985 S.C.C.R. 108.
s. 1, see *Fraser* v. *Noble,* 1977 S.L.T. (Land Ct.) 8; *Campbell* v. *Duke of Argyll's Trs.,* 1977 S.L.T.(Land Ct.) 22; *Gillies* v. *Countess of Sutherland's Trs.,* 1978 S.L.T.(Land Ct.) 2; *Gilmour* v. *Master of Lovat,* 1979 S.L.T.(Land Ct.) 2; *Fulton* v. *Noble,* 1983 S.L.T.(Land Ct.) 40; *Duke of Argyll's Trs.* v. *Macneill,* 1983 S.L.T.(Land Ct.) 35; *MacLennan* v. *Duke of Argyll Trs.,* 1982 S.L.C.R. 119; *Geddes* v. *Martin,* 1987 S.C.L.R. 104.
ss. 1–4, see *Cameron* v. *Duke of Argyll's Trustees,* 1981 S.L.T.(Land Ct.) 2.
s. 2, see *Ferguson* v. *Ross Estates Co.* 1977 S.L.T.(Land Ct.) 19; *Mackintosh* v. *Countess of Seafield's Trs.,* 1979 S.L.T.(Land Ct.) 6; *Robertson* v. *Secretary of State for Scotland,* 1983 S.L.T.(Land Ct.) 38; *Foxley* v. *Forestry Commission,* 1982 S.L.C.R. 73; *MacLennan* v. *Duke of Argyll's Trs.,* 1982 S.L.C.R. 119; *MacAskill* v. *Basil Baird & Sons,* 1987 S.L.T.(Land Ct.) 34.
ss. 3, 4, see *Fraser* v. *Noble,* 1977 S.L.T. (Land Ct.) 8; *Ferguson* v. *Ross Estates Co.,* 1977 S.L.T.(Land Ct.) 19; *Gilmour* v. *Master of Lovat,* 1979 S.L.T.(Land Ct.) 2.
s. 4, see *Galbraith* v. *Bray's Trs.,* 1978 S.L.T.(Land Ct.) 3; *MacLugash* v. *Islay Estates Co,* 1985 S.L.C.R. 99.

CAP.

1976—cont.

21. Crofting Reform (Scotland) Act 1976—cont.
s. 6, see *Macleod* v. *Viscount Thursoe*, 1982 S.L.C.R 123.
s. 7, see *Fraser* v. *Noble* 1977 S.L.T.(Land Ct.) 8.
s. 9, see *Maclean* v. *Secretary of State for Scotland*, 1980 S.L.T.(Land Ct.) 18; *Macrae* v. *Secretary of State*, *Cameron* v. *Secretary of State*, *Macleod* v. *Secretary of State*, 1981 S.L.T.(Land Ct.) 18; *Duke of Argyll's Trs.* v. *Macneill*, 1983 S.L.T.(Land Ct.) 35; *Cameron* v. *Corpach Common Graziers*, 1984 S.L.T.(Land Ct.) 41; *Enessy Co. S.A.* v. *Shareholders in Tarbert Common Grazings*, 1984 S.L.T.(Land Ct.) 7; *Highland Regional Council* v. *Macaulay*, 1984 S.L.C.R. 70; *Galson Estate* v. *Saunders*, 1984 S.L.C.R. 74; *Wester Ross Salmon* v. *Maclean*, 1985 S.L.C.R. 124; *Trustees of Tenth Duke of Argyll* v. *MacKay*, 1985 S.L.C.R. 121; *Vestey* v. *Blunt*, 1986 S.L.C.R. 150; *Kershaw* v. *Mackenzie*, 1988 S.L.T.(Land Ct.) 41.
s. 9, amended: 1985, c.73, s.30.
s. 12, scheme 88/559.
s. 17, amended: 1987, c.18, sch. 6.

22. Freshwater and Salmon Fisheries (Scotland) Act 1976.
Royal Assent, June 10, 1976.
s. 1, orders 80/400; 82/377; 83/389–391; 85/384; 86/469, 473, 474, 1590; 88/437, 1516, 1733, 1734, 1913.
ss. 6, 7, 9, 10, amended: 1981, c.29, s.38.
s. 7, sch.3, amended and repealed in pt.: 1986, c.62, sch.4.
sch. 3, see *Taddale Properties* v. *I.R.C.* [1988] S.T.C. 303, C.A.

23. Atomic Energy Authority (Special Constables) Act 1976.
Royal Assent, June 10, 1976.

24. Development Land Tax Act 1976.
Royal Assent, July 22, 1976.
repealed: 1985, c.54, sch.27.
ss. 1, 7, sch. 2, see *Lowe* v. *Comr. of Inland Revenue*, 1985 S.L.T.(Lands Tr.) 12.
s. 28, see *I.R.C.* v. *Matthew's Executors* [1984] S.T.C. 386, Ct. of Session; *Worthing Rugby Football Club Trustees* v. *I.R.C.* [1987] 1 W.L.R. 1057, C.A.
s. 33, amended: 1986, c.45, sch.14.
s. 40, regs. 84/1172.
s. 42, repealed: 1985, c.65, sch.10; repealed in pt. (S.): 1985, c.66, sch.8.
s. 45, see *I.R.C.* v. *Metrolands (Property Finance)* [1982] 1 W.L.R. 341, H.L.
s. 47, order 76/1148.
sch. 1, see *R.* v. *I.R.C.*, *ex p. Harrow London Borough Council* [1983] S.T.C. 246, Stephen Brown J.
sch. 3, see *Taddale Properties* v. *I.R.C.* [1987] S.T.C. 411, Scott J.

25. Fair Employment (Northern Ireland) Act 1976.
Royal Assent, July 22, 1976.
see *Northern Ireland Electricity Service's Application, Re* [1987] 12 N.I.J.B. 24, Nicholson J.

CAP.

1976—cont.

25. Fair Employment (Northern Ireland) Act 1976—cont.
s. 9, amended: 1981, c.38, sch.3.
ss. 16, 17, 28, see *Fair Employment Agency* v. *Craigavon Borough Council* [1980] I.R.L.R. 316, N.I.C.A.
ss. 16, 17, 28, 52, see *Ministry of Defence* v. *Fair Employment Agency for Northern Ireland* [1988] I.R.L.R. 151, Belfast Recorder's Court.
s. 17, see *Armagh District Council* v. *Fair Employment Agency* [1983] 15 N.I.J.B., C.A.
s. 47, repealed: 1982, c.27, sch.14.
s. 49, amended: 1982, c.23, sch.3.
s. 50, repealed in pt.: 1981, c.55, sch.5.
s. 56, amended: order 79/1573.

26. Explosives (Age of Purchase) Act 1976.
Royal Assent, July 22, 1976.
s. 1, repealed in pt.: 1987, c.43, sch.5.

27. Theatres Trust Act 1976.
Royal Assent, July 22, 1976.
s. 2, amended (S.): 1978, c.24, s.1.
s. 6, repealed in pt. (S.): *ibid.*
s. 6, order 76/2236.
sch., amended: 1985, c.9, sch.2; functions transferred: order 86/600.

28. Congenital Disabilities (Civil Liability) Act 1976.
Royal Assent, July 22, 1976.
see *McKay* v. *Essex Area Health Authority* [1982] 2 W.L.R. 890, C.A.
s. 4, orders 83/1889–1893; 85/752; 87/668.

29. Representation of the People (Armed Forces) Act 1976.
Royal Assent, July 22, 1976.
repealed: 1983, c.2, sch.9.
s. 4, order 76/2044.

30. Fatal Accidents Act 1976.
Royal Assent, July 22, 1976.
see *Bailey* v. *Barking and Havering Area Health Authority*, The Times, July 22, 1978, Pain J.; *Nutbrown* v. *Rosier*, The Times, March 1, 1982, Aubrey Myerson Q.C.; *Clay* v. *Pooler* [1982] 3 All E.R. 570, Hodgson J.; *Robertson* v. *Lestrange* [1985] 1 All E.R. 950, Webster J.; *Holmes* v. *Bangladesh Biman Corp.*, Financial Times, March 9, 1988, C.A.
ss. 1–4, substituted: 1982, c.53, s.3.
s. 3, see *Benson* v. *Biggs Wall & Co.* [1982] 3 All E.R. 300, Pain J.
s. 4, see *Pidduck* v. *Eastern Scottish Omnibuses*, The Times, October 31, 1988, Sheen J.
s. 5, sch. 1, repealed in pt.: 1982, c.53, sch.9.
sch. 1, repealed in pt.: 1980, c.58, sch.4; 1983, c.14, sch.3.

31. Legitimacy Act 1976.
Royal Assent, July 22, 1976.
s. 1, see *F. and F.* v. *Att.-Gen. and F.* (1979) 10 Fam.Law 60, Eastman J.
s. 1, amended: 1987, c.42, s.28.
ss. 4, 6, amended: 1976, c.36, sch.3.
sch. 1, repealed in pt.: *ibid.*, sch.4.

32. Lotteries and Amusements Act 1976.
Royal Assent, July 22, 1976.
s. 2, amended: 1984, c.9, s.1.

1976—cont.

32. Lotteries and Amusements Act 1976—*cont.*
ss. 2, 14, see *Imperial Tobacco* v. *Att.-Gen.*
[1980] 2 W.L.R. 466; [1980] 1 All E.R. 866,
H.L.; *Express Newspapers* v. *Liverpool Daily
Post and Echo* [1985] 1 W.L.R. 1089, Whitford
J.
ss. 5, 10, 11, amended (S.): order 81/595.
s. 8, amended: 1980, c.65, s.68; repealed in
pt.: 1987, c.6, sch.5.
s. 12, regs. 81/109, 303 (S.).
s. 16, see *Brown* v. *Plant*, 1985 S.L.T. 371.
s. 16, amended: orders 80/29; 82/83, 132 (S.);
84/465 (S.); 88/1025, 1053.
s. 18, orders 77/1176, 1179 (S.); 80/29, 149,
298, 503 (S.); 81/110, 251, 252, 455, 547 (S.),
595 (S.), 596 (S.); 82/83, 132 (S.), 1170, 1172,
1254; 83/126; 84/245, 465 (S.); 85/262, 263,
480 (S.), 481 (S.); 87/243; 88/14, 108(S.), 335,
1025, 1053.
s. 19, repealed in pt.: 1984, c.60, sch.7.
s. 23, repealed in pt.: 1985, c.51, sch.17.
s. 24, orders 80/298, 503 (S.); 81/251, 455, 547
(S.); 82/83, 132 (S.), 1170, 1172, 1254;
83/126; 84/245, 465 (S.); 85/262, 263, 480
(S.), 481 (S.); 87/243; 88/14, 108(S.), 335,
1025, 1053.
sch. 1, amended: order 81/252.
sch. 2, amended (S.): order 81/595.
sch. 3, see *Hunt* v. *City of Glasgow District
Council* (Sh.Ct.), 1987 S.C.L.R. 244.
sch. 3, amended: orders 77/1179 (S.); 80/298;
1980, c.55, sch.2 (S.); orders 81/455;
82/1170, 1254; 88/14; repealed in pt. (S.):
1980, c.55, sch. 2; 1985, c.73, sch. 4.
sch. 4, repealed in pt.: 1981, c.63, sch.7.

33. Restrictive Practices Court Act 1976.
Royal Assent, July 22, 1976.
s. 9, rules 76/1897, 1898, 1899; 82/871.
s. 12, order 76/1896.

34. Restrictive Trade Practices Act 1976.
Royal Assent, July 22, 1976.
s. 1, see *Re Association of British Travel Agents
Agreement* [1984] I.C.R. 12, Restrictive Practices Court.
ss. 1, 6, 9, see *Vernon and Co. Pulp Products* v.
Universal Pulp Containers [1980] F.S.R. 179,
Megarry V.-C.
s. 2, see *National Daily and Sunday Newspapers
Proprietors' Agreement, Re* [1986] I.C.R. 44,
Restrictive Practices Ct.
s. 6, see *Academy Sound and Vision* v. *WEA
Records* [1983] I.C.R. 586, Vinelott J.
ss. 6, 9, see *Topliss Showers* v. *Gessey & Son*
[1982] I.C.R. 501, Neill J.
s. 7, amended: 1977, c.19, s.3.
s. 9, see *Agreements Relating to the Supply of
Diazo Copying Materials, Machines and Ancillary Equipment, Re* [1984] I.C.R. 429, Restrictive Practices Court.
s. 9, orders 83/382; 84/1269, 2031; 86/614.
s. 10, see *Agreement Between All Members of
the Building Employers Confederation, Re*
[1984] C.I.L.L. 109, McNeill J.
s. 11, see *Fisher* v. *Director General of Fair
Trading* [1982] I.C.R. 71, C.A.

1976—cont.

34. Restrictive Trade Practices Act 1976—*cont.*
s. 11, order 85/2044.
s. 11, repealed in pt.: 1981, c.20, sch.4.
ss. 11, 16, see *Royal Institution of Chartered
Surveyors' Application, Re; Royal Institution
of Chartered Surveyors* v. *Director General of
Fair Trading* [1986] I.C.R. 551, C.A.
s. 14, orders 85/2044, 2204.
s. 14, amended: 1977, c.19, s.1.
ss. 18, 19, see *Re Association of British Travel
Agents Agreement* [1984] I.C.R. 12, Restrictive Practices Court.
s. 19, see *Agreement Between All Members of
the Building Employers Confederation, Re*
[1984] C.I.L.L. 109, McNeill J.; *Association of
British Travel Agents Agreement (No. 2), Re*
[1985] I.C.R. 122, Restrictive Practices Court.
s. 19, amended: 1980, c.21, s.28.
s. 20, amended: 1985, c.67, s.116.
s. 22, rules 76/1897; 82/871.
ss. 23, 27, regs. 77/612; 84/392.
s. 24, see *Vernon and Co. Pulp Products* v.
Universal Pulp Containers [1980] F.S.R. 179,
Megarry V.-C.
s. 29, order 88/67.
s. 33, order 82/569.
s. 33, amended: 1985, c.9, sch.2.
s. 35, see *Re Agreements Relating to the Supply
of Bread* [1977] I.C.R. 946, R.P.Ct.; *Vernon
and Co. Pulp Products* v. *Universal Pulp Containers* [1980] F.S.R. 179, Megarry V.-C.;
*Agreements Relating to the Supply of Diazo
Copying Materials, Machines and Ancillary
Equipment, Re* [1984] I.C.R. 429, Restrictive
Practices Court.
s. 39, amended: 1980, c.43, sch.7.
s. 41, amended: 1979, c.38, s.10; 1980, c.21,
s.19; c.43, sch.7; 1984, c.12, sch.4; 1986,
c.31, sch.4; c.44, sch.7; c.60, sch.13.
s. 42, orders 85/2044; 86/614.
s. 43, amended: 1985, c.9, sch.2.
s. 45, order 76/1877.
sch. 1, amended: 1977, c.37, sch.5; 1979, c.36,
sch.7; 1984, c.24, sch.5; 1985, c.61, s.60;
c.65, s.217; 1986, c.45, sch.14.; 1988, c.48,
sch.7.
sch. 2, amended: 1980, c.21, s.27.
schs. 2, 3, see *Vernon and Co. Pulp Products* v.
Universal Pulp Containers [1980] F.S.R. 179,
Megarry V.-C.
sch. 3, see *Academy Sound and Vision* v. *WEA
Records* [1983] I.C.R. 586, Vinelott J.
sch. 3, amended: 1980, c.21, s.30; 1986, c.39,
sch.2; 1988, c.48, sch.7.
sch. 5, repealed in pt.: 1976, c.53, sch.3; 1986,
c.49, sch.4.

35. Police Pensions Act 1976.
Royal Assent, July 22, 1976.
s. 1, regs. 79/406.
s. 1, amended: 1980, c.10, s.2.
ss. 1, 3, regs. 76/1707; 77/1705, 1947, 2173;
78/375, 1348, 1578, 1691; 79/1259, 1287,
1406; 80/82, 272, 1485, 1616; 81/1322;
82/1151, 1315; 83/996, 1378; 84/1349;
85/156, 1318, 2029; 86/1379, 1380; 87/156,
256, 257, 341, 1462, 1907, 2215; 88/1339.

CAP.

1976—cont.
35. Police Pensions Act 1976—cont.
s. 2, regs. 87/256, 257.
s. 4, regs. 77/2173; 78/375, 1348, 1578; 79/406, 1259, 1287, 1406; 80/82, 272, 1616; 82/1151; 83/996; 85/156; 86/1379; 87/156, 256, 257, 341, 1907, 2215; 88/1339.
s. 5, regs. 76/1707; 77/1705, 1947; 78/1578, 1691; 79/1287, 1406; 80/1485; 81/1322, 82/1315; 83/1378; 84/1349; 85/1318; 86/1380; 87/256, 257, 1462.
s. 6, regs. 87/156, 256, 257, 341.
ss. 7, 8, regs. 87/256, 257.
sch. 2, repealed in pt.: 1980, c.10, s.3.
36. Adoption Act 1976.
Royal Assent, July 22, 1976.
Commencement orders: 83/1946; 87/1242.
s. 2, amended: 1980, c.6, sch.6.
s. 3, amended: 1983, c.41, sch.2.
s. 10, repealed: ibid., schs.2,10.
s. 18, amended: ibid., sch.2; 1987, c.42, s.7, sch.2.
ss. 22, 23, repealed (S.): 1978, c.28, sch.4.
s. 24, amended: 1983, c.41, sch.2.
s. 26, repealed in pt.: 1978, c.22, s.72, sch.3.
s. 27, amended: 1983, c.41, sch.2; repealed in pt.: ibid., schs.2,10.
s. 28, amended: 1977, c.45, sch.13; 1978, c.22, sch.2; 1983, c.41, sch.2; repealed in pt.: ibid., schs.2,10.
ss. 29, 30, amended: ibid., sch.2.
s. 31, amended: 1980, c.5, sch.5.
s. 32, amended: 1980, c.6, sch.2; c.7, sch.1; 1982, c.51, sch.3; 1983, c.20, sch.4; c.41, sch.9.
s. 34, amended: 1980, c.5, sch.5.
s. 40, repealed: 1981, c.61, sch.9.
s. 42, amended: ibid., sch.7.
s. 47, amended: order 86/948; repealed in pt.: 1981, c.61, sch.9; 1986, c.50, sch.11; 1988, c.7, sch.5.
s. 51, repealed in pt. (S.): 1978, c.28, sch.4.
s. 53, amended: ibid., s.74.
s. 57, amended: 1977, c.45, sch.13.
s. 58A, added: 1983, c.41, sch.2.
s. 62, amended: 1984, c.28, sch.2; c.42, sch.1.
s. 63, amended: 1983, c.41, sch.2; repealed in pt.: 1978, c.22, sch.2; 1983, c.41, sch.10; 1984, c.28, sch.3.
s. 64, amended: 1978, c.22, s.73; repealed in pt.: ibid., sch.3.
ss. 66, amended: 1980, c.43, sch.7.
s. 72, amended: ibid.; 1983, c.41, sch.2; 1987, c.42, s.7, sch.2.
ss. 73, 74, repealed in pt. (S.): 1978, c.28, sch.4.
s. 74, orders 83/1946; 84/1946; 87/1242.
s. 74, repealed in pt.: 1981, c.63, sch.9.
sch. 1, repealed in pt.: 1978, c.22, s.74, sch.3.
sch. 3, amended: ibid., sch.2; repealed in pt.: ibid., sch.3; (S.) 1978, c.28, sch.4; 1980, c.5, sch.6; c.6, sch.3; 1981, s.54, sch.7; 1983, c.41, sch.10; 1984, c.56, sch.3 (S.); 1987, c.42, sch.4; 1988, c.34, sch.6.
37. Food and Drugs (Control of Food Premises) Act 1976.
Royal Assent, July 22, 1976.
repealed: 1984, c.30, sch.11.
s. 7, regs. 79/27.

CAP.

1976—cont.
38. Dangerous Wild Animals Act 1976.
Royal Assent, July 22, 1976.
ss. 1, 4, see Halpern v. Chief Constable of Strathclyde (Sh.Ct.), 1988 S.L.C.R. 137.
s. 5, amended: 1981, c.37, s.22; 1986, c.14, sch.3.
ss. 5, 7, see Hemming v. Graham-Jones, The Times, October 23, 1980, D.C.
s. 7, repealed in pt.: 1981, c.37, s.22.
s. 8, orders 77/1940; 81/1173.
sch., substituted: order 81/1173.
39. Divorce (Scotland) Act 1976.
Royal Assent, July 22, 1976.
s. 1, Boyle v. Boyle (O.H.), 1977 S.L.T. (Notes) 69, Lord Maxwell; Craigie v. Craigie, 1979 S.L.T.(Notes) 60; Nolan v. Nolan (O.H.), 1979 S.L.T. 293; Duncan v. Duncan (O.H.), June 4, 1982; Hastie v. Hastie (O.H.), 1985 S.L.T. 146; Matthews v. Matthews, 1985 S.L.T.(Sh.Ct.) 68; Stewart v. Stewart, 1987 S.L.T. (Sh.Ct.) 48.
s. 1, Act of Sederunt 76/1994, 2160.
s. 5, see Cowie v. Cowie (O.H.), 1977 S.L.T.(Notes) 47; MacRae v. MacRae (O.H.), 1977 S.L.T.(Notes) 72; Wormsley v. Wormsley (O.H.), 1977 S.L.T.(Notes) 79; Gray v. Gray (O.H.), 1979 S.L.T.(Notes) 94; Jenkinson v. Jenkinson (O.H.), July 23, 1979; Henderson v. Henderson (O.H.), 1981 S.L.T.(Notes) 25; Chalmers v. Chalmers (O.H.) 1982 S.L.T. 79; Lambert v. Lambert, Second Division, June 17, 1981; Thomson v. Thomson, 1982 S.L.T. 521; Mitchell v. Mitchell (O.H.), March 25, 1982; Sandison's Exrx v. Sandison (O.H.), 1984 S.L.T. 111; Graham v. Graham (O.H.), 1984 S.L.T. 89; Bryan v. Bryan (O.H.), 1985 S.L.T. 444; Elder v. Elder (O.H.), December 4, 1984; Finlayson v. Finlayson Exrx (O.H.), July 17, 1984; Brodie v. Brodie (O.H.), 1986 S.L.T. 640; Stewart v. Stewart (O.H.), 1987 S.L.T. 246; Wilson v. Wilson, 1987 S.L.T. 721; Caven v. Caven (O.H.), 1987 S.L.T. 761; McCrae v. McCrae (O.H.), 1988 S.L.T. 248; MacPherson v. MacPherson, The Scotsman, October 28, 1988; Smith v. Smith, 1988 S.L.T. 840.
s. 5, Act of Sederunt 76/1994.
ss. 5–8, repealed: 1985, c.37, sch.2.
s. 6, see Leslie v. Leslie (O.H.), April 2, 1982; Chalmers v. Chalmers, First Division, February 11, 1983; Leslie v. Leslie (O.H.), 1987 S.L.T. 232.
s. 10, see McNaught v. McNaught, 1977 S.L.T. 75.
s. 11, Acts of Sederunt 76/1994, 2160.
s. 13, amended: 1983, c.12, sch.1.
40. Finance Act 1976.
Royal Assent, July 29, 1976.
s. 2, orders 76/1206, 1207; regs. 78/1786; repealed: 1979, c.4, sch.4.
s. 3, repealed: ibid.
s. 4, regs. 76/1197; 77/1779; 78/1156.
ss. 4, 5, repealed: 1979, c.7, sch.2.
s. 6, order 76/2134; amended: 1978, c.42, sch.12; repealed in pt.: 1979, c.7, sch.2; c.8, sch.2.

CAP.

1976—cont.

40. Finance Act 1976—cont.
s. 7, amended: 1978, c.42, s.9.
s. 8, regs. 76/1197; amended: 1977, c.36, s.1.
ss. 9, 10, repealed: 1979, c.5, sch.7.
s. 11, amended: 1988, c.54, sch.3.
s. 13, repealed: 1978, c.42, ss.8,9, sch 13.
s. 14, repealed in pt.: 1977, c.36, sch.9.
s. 15, regs. 76/1223, 78/1725; repealed: 1979, c.2, sch.6.
ss. 16, 18, repealed: 1977, c.36, sch.9.
s. 17, repealed: 1979, c.47, sch.5.
s. 19, repealed: 1983, c.50, sch.11.
s. 20, repealed: 1979, c.47, sch.9.
ss. 21–23, repealed: 1983, c.50, sch.11.
ss. 22, 25, 27, see *I.R.C.* v. *Stannard, The Times,* February 14, 1984, Scott J.
ss. 24–38, repealed: 1988, c.1, sch.31.
s. 41, amended: 1978, c.42, s.30; 1988, c.1, sch.31.
s. 43, repealed: 1979, c.47, sch.5.
ss. 44–50, repealed: 1988, c.1, sch.31.
s. 46, see *Tilcon* v. *Holland* [1981] S.T.C. 365, Vinelott J.
s. 51, repealed: 1979, c.47, sch.13.
ss. 52, 53, repealed: 1979, c.14, sch.8.
s. 54, amended: *ibid.,* sch.7.
ss. 55, 56, repealed: *ibid.,* sch.8.
ss. 60–71, repealed: 1988, c.1, sch 31.
s. 61, see *Wicks* v. *Firth (Inspector of Taxes); Johnson* v. *Firth* [1983] 2 W.L.R. 34, H.L.
s. 62, amended: 1988, c.39, s.49.
s. 64, see *Gilbert* v. *Hemsley, The Times,* July 11, 1981, Vinelott J.; *Wilson* v. *Alexander* [1986] S.T.C. 365, Harman J.
s. 64, orders 78/434; 80/889; 81/974; 82/1159; 83/1102; 84/1635; 85/1598; 86/703; 87/1897.
s. 64A, orders 83/1101; 84/1636; 85/1599; 86/702.
s. 66, see *Williams (Inspector of Taxes)* v. *Todd, The Times,* July 4, 1988, Peter Gibson J.
s. 66, orders 78/28; 80/439; 82/1982; 87/512, 886, 1493, 1989.
s. 72, amended: 1980, c.48, s.51; repealed in pt.: 1988, c.1, sch.31.
ss. 73–125, repealed: 1984, c.51, sch.9.
s. 126, repealed: 1986, c.41, s.79, sch.23.
s. 127, order 79/370.
s. 127, repealed in pt.: 1986, c.41, s.84, sch.23.
s. 128, repealed: 1988, c.39, sch.14.
s. 129, repealed: 1985, c.54, sch.27.
s. 131, amended: 1988, c.1, sch.29.
s. 132, amended: 1979, c.14, sch.7; repealed in pt.: 1979, c.2, sch.6; 1983, c.55, sch.11; 1984, c.51, sch.9.
schs. 1, 2, repealed: 1977, c.36, sch.9.
sch. 3, repealed in pt.: 1979, c.2, sch.6; c.4, sch.4; c.8, sch.2.
sch. 4, regs. 77/1143, 1144; 78/1159–1161; 79/346; 80/1947, 1948; 84/322, 323; S.Rs. 1978 Nos. 131, 285; 1981 No. 75, 76; 1984 Nos. 230, 231; amended: 1978, c.42, sch.3; 1980, c.48, s.29; 1982, c.39, s.35; c.50, sch.5; order 79/1576.
sch. 4, repealed: 1988, c.1, sch.31.

CAP.

1976—cont.

40. Finance Act 1976—cont.
sch. 5, see *D.I.K. Transmissions (Dundee)* v. *I.R.C.* [1980] S.T.C. 724, Ct. of Sessions; [1981] S.L.T. 87; *I.R.C.* v. *Watson and Philip* [1984] S.T.C. 184, Ct. of Session; *Purchase* v. *Tesco Stores* [1984] S.T.C. 304, Warner J.; *Payne* v. *Barratt Developments (Luton), The Times,* December 17, 1984, H.L.; *Fraser* v. *London Sports Car Centre, Financial Times,* July 17, 1985, C.A.; *Pobjoy Mint* v. *Lane* [1985] S.T.C. 314, C.A.; *General Motors Acceptance Corp. (U.K.)* v. *I.R.C.* [1987] S.T.C. 22, C.A.; *Ashworth (Inspector of Taxes)* v. *Mainland Car Deliveries* [1987] S.T.C. 481, Knox J.
sch. 5, substituted: 1981, c.35, sch.9; repealed: *ibid.,* sch.19.
sch. 7, order 80/889.
schs. 7, 8, repealed: 1988, c.1, sch.31.
sch. 9, amended: 1977, c.36, s.35; repealed in pt.: 1988, c.1, sch.31.
sch. 10, see *Finch* v. *I.R.C.* [1985] Ch. 1, C.A.
schs. 10–14, repealed: 1984, c.51, sch.9.

41. Iron and Steel (Amendment) Act 1976.
Royal Assent, July 29, 1976.
repealed: 1982, c.25, sch.7.

42. Protection of Birds (Amendment) Act 1976.
Royal Assent, July 29, 1976.
repealed: 1977, c.45, sch.13.

43. Appropriation Act 1976.
Royal Assent, August 6, 1976.
repealed: 1978, c.57, sch.(C).

44. Drought Act 1976.
Royal Assent, August 6, 1976.
s. 5 (in pt.), sch. 3, repealed: S.L.R. 1986.

45. Rating (Charity Shops) Act 1976.
Royal Assent, August 6, 1976.
s. 1, repealed in pt.: S.L.R. 1986; 1988, c.41, sch.13 (prosp.).

46. Police Act 1976.
Royal Assent, August 6, 1976.
ss. 1 (in pt.), 2–13, 14 (in pt.), sch. (in pt.), repealed: 1984, c.60, sch.7.
ss. 3, 11, see *R.* v. *Police Complaints Board, ex p. Madden; R.* v. *Police Complaints Board, ex p. Rhone* [1983] 1 W.L.R. 447, McNeill J.
s. 6, regs. 77/577–580.
s. 10, regs. 77/580, 581.
s. 11, see *R.* v. *Secretary of State for the Home Department, ex p. Thornton* [1986] 3 W.L.R. 158, C.A.
s. 12, see *R.* v. *Secretary of State for the Home Department, ex p. Chief Constable of Nottingham, The Times,* March 10, 1984, Hodgson J.
s. 13, orders: 76/1998; 77/576.

47. Stock Exchange (Completion of Bargains) Act 1976.
Royal Assent, October 12, 1976.
ss. 1–4, repealed: 1985, c.9, sch.1.
s. 3, regs. 79/53.
s. 4, regs. 80/926.
s. 5, amended: 1986, c.60, s.194.
s. 7, orders 79/55, 238.
s. 7, amended: 1985, c.9, sch.2; repealed in pt.: *ibid.,* sch.1; 1986, c.60, sch.17.

1976—cont.

48. Parliamentary and Other Pensions and Salaries Act 1976.
Royal Assent, October 12, 1976.
s. 1, repealed in pt.: 1984, c.52, sch.
s. 7, repealed: 1977, c.49, sch.16; 1978, c.29, sch.17(S.).
schs. 1–4, repealed: 1987, c.45, sch.4.

49. Chronically Sick and Disabled Persons (Amendment) Act 1976.
Royal Assent, October 26, 1976.

50. Domestic Violence and Matrimonial Proceedings Act 1976.
Royal Assent, October 26, 1976.
see *Re V. (A Minor) (Wardship)* (1979) 123 S.J. 201, Sir George Baker P.; *Leighton* v. *Case*, December 1, 1980, Judge McDonnell, O.B.E., Lambeth County Ct.; *Fairweather* v. *Kolosine* (1982) 11 H.L.R. 61, C.A.; *Lee* v. *Lee* (1983) 12 H.L.R. 116, C.A.
s. 1, see *P.* v. *P.*, August 19, 1977, Judge Hill-Smith, Bedford County Ct.; *Lewis* v. *Lewis, The Times,* November 1 and 3, 1977, C.A.; *Rennick* v. *Rennick* [1977] 1 W.L.R. 1455, C.A.; *B.* v. *B. (Domestic Violence: Jurisdiction)* [1978] 2 W.L.R. 160, C.A.; *Cantliff* v. *Jenkins* [1978] 2 W.L.R. 177, C.A.; *Crutcher* v. *Crutcher, The Times,* July 18, 1978, Payne J.; *Davis* v. *Johnson* [1978] 2 W.L.R. 553, H.L.; *Spindlow* v. *Spindlow* [1978] 3 W.L.R. 77, C.A.; *Hopper* v. *Hopper* (Note) [1978] 1 W.L.R. 1342, C.A.; *McLean* v. *Nugent* (1979) 123 S.J. 521, C.A.; *Adeoso* v. *Adeoso* [1980] 1 W.L.R. 1535, C.A; *Myers* v. *Myers* [1982] 1 W.L.R. 247, C.A.; *Whitter* v. *Peters; Peart* v. *Stewart* [1982] 1 W.L.R. 389, C.A.; *Horner* v. *Horner* [1982] 2 W.L.R. 914, C.A.; *Warwick* v. *Warwick* (1982) 12 Fam.Law 60, C.A.; *Freeman* v. *Collins* (1983) 13 Fam.Law 113, C.A.; *Spencer* v. *Camacho* (1983) 13 Fam.Law 114, C.A.; *O'Neill* v. *Williams* (1984) 14 Fam.Law 85, C.A.; *Wiseman* v. *Simpson* [1988] 1 W.L.R. 35, C.A.
s. 2, see *Davis* v. *Johnson* [1978] 2 W.L.R. 553, H.L.; *Lewis (A. H.)* v. *Lewis (R. W. F.)* [1978] 1 All E.R. 729, C.A.; *Cinderby* v. *Cinderby; Pekesin* v. *Pekesin, The Times,* April 27, 1978, C.A.; *Morgan* v. *Morgan* (1979) 9 Fam.Law 87, C.A.; *McLaren* v. *McLaren* [1978] 9 Fam.Law 153, C.A.; *Boylan* v. *Boylan* (1980) 11 Fam.Law 76, C.A.; *White* v. *White* [1983] 2 All E.R. 51, C.A.; *Thurley* v. *Smith* (1985) 15 Fam.Law 31, C.A.; *Wooton* v. *Wooton* (1985) 15 Fam.Law 31, C.A.; *Galan* v. *Galan* (1985) 15 Fam.Law 256, C.A.; *Newman* v. *Benesch, The Times,* September 22, 1986, C.A.
s. 2, amended: 1978, c.22, sch.2.
ss. 3, 4, repealed: 1983, c.19, s.3.
s. 5, order 77/559.

51. Maplin Development Authority (Dissolution) Act 1976.
Royal Assent, October 26, 1976.
repealed: 1981, c.19, sch.1.
s. 1, order 76/1844.

1976—cont.

52. Armed Forces Act 1976.
Royal Assent, October 26, 1976.
s. 1, repealed: 1981, c.55, s.1, sch.5.
s. 1, orders 77/1231; 80/1074.
s. 2, regs. 77/1097; 79/215.
s. 4, repealed in pt.: 1981, c.55, schs.3,5.
s. 6, order 77/89.
s. 7, amended: 1986, c.21, s.7; repealed in pt.: *ibid.,* s.7, sch.2.
s. 8, amended: 1982, c.48, sch.8.
s. 13, repealed in pt.: *ibid.,* sch.16.
s. 21, amended: 1981, c.55, sch.3.
s. 27, amended: 1985, c.9, sch.2.
s. 22, orders 77/897; 87/2173.
sch. 3, rules 77/91, 93; 79/1456; 80/2005; orders 82/367; 83/716; 84/1671; 87/2001, 2173; amended: order 79/1714; 1981, c.55, s.5, sch.1; 1984, c.60, sch.6; 1986, c.21, ss.9,12.
sch. 9, repealed in pt.: order 79/1714; 1981, c.55, sch.5; 1983, c.2, sch.9.
sch. 13, order 77/88.

53. Resale Prices Act 1976.
Royal Assent, October 26, 1976.
s. 10, amended: 1988, c.48, sch.7.
s. 21, rules 76/1899.
s. 27, amended: 1985, c.9, sch.2.
s. 30, order 76/1876.

54. Trinidad and Tobago Republic Act 1976.
Royal Assent, October 26, 1976.
s. 1, order 76/1914.
s. 2, order 76/1915.
s. 2, repealed in pt.: S.L.R. 1986.

55. Agriculture (Miscellaneous Provisions) Act 1976.
Royal Assent, November 15, 1976.
s. 1, orders 76/1963; 77/224.
s. 6, repealed: 1979, c.13, sch.2.
s. 7, regs. 77/899, 900, 1112, 1695, 2007; 78/244, 318, 319, 443, 446, 447, 583; 79/25, 26, 357; 81/8.
ss. 8–10, repealed: 1981, c.22, sch.6.
s. 9, order 77/1721.
ss. 11, 12, 16, repealed: 1977, c.12, sch.2.
ss. 17–24, repealed: 1986, c.5, sch.15.
s. 18, see *R.* v. *Agricultural Land Tribunal (Wales), ex p. Hughes* (1980) 225 E.G. 703, D.C.; *Moss* v. *National Coal Board* (1982) 264 E.G. 52, Stephen Brown J.; *Bailey* v. *Sitwell* (1986) 279 E.G. 1092, Hodgson J.
s. 18, orders 84/1309; 85/997.
ss. 18, 20, see *Littlewood* v. *Rolfe* (1982) 43 P. & C.R. 262, H.H. Judge Fay, Q.C.; *Saul* v. *Norfolk County Council* [1984] 3 W.L.R. 84, C.A.; *Trinity College Cambridge* v. *Caines* (1984) 272 E.G. 1287, C.A.
ss. 18, 20, 21, see *Wilson* v. *Earl Spencer's Settlement Trustees* (1985) 274 E.G. 1254, Hodgson J.
ss. 18, 20, 22, see *Hulme* v. *Earl of Aylesford and Trustees of Earl of Aylesford's Settlement (1965)* (1978) 246 E.G. 851, Agricultural Land Tribunal.
ss. 20, 21, see *Moses* v. *Hurst; R.* v. *Agricultural Land Tribunal for the Eastern Area, ex p. Moses* (1984) 269 E.G. 853, Hodgson J.

1976—cont.

55. Agriculture (Miscellaneous Provisions) Act 1976—*cont.*
s. 21, see *Jackson* v. *Hall; Williamson* v. *Thompson* [1980] 2 W.L.R. 118, H.L.; *Dagg* v. *Lovett* (1980) 256 E.G. 491, C.A.
s. 23, regs. 77/1215.
s. 27, orders 77/39; 78/402; repealed in pt.: 1977, c.12, sch.2; 1986, c.5, sch.15.
sch. 2, repealed: 1979, c.13, sch.2.
sch. 3, repealed in pt.: 1981, c.19, sch.1; c.22, sch.6; 1985, c.5, sch.15; S.L.R. 1986.
sch. 3A, repealed: 1986, c.5, sch.15.

56. Supplementary Benefit (Amendment) Act 1976.
Royal Assent, November 15, 1976.
repealed: 1976, c.71, sch.8.

57. Local Government (Miscellaneous Provisions) Act 1976.
Royal Assent, November 15, 1976.
ss. 1–6, repealed: 1980, c.66, sch.25.
s. 7, amended: 1984, c.27, sch.13; repealed in pt.: 1984, c.22, sch.3.
s. 8, repealed: 1982, c.30, sch.7.
ss. 9, 10, repealed: 1985, c.71, sch.1.
s. 12, amended: 1984, c.55, sch.6.
s. 13, amended: 1980, c.66, sch.24; 1981, c.67, sch.4; repealed in pt.: *ibid.*, sch.6.
s. 15, amended: 1980, c.66, sch.24; 1987, c.3, sch.1; repealed in pt.: 1986, c.31, sch 6
s. 19, amended: 1985, c.51, sch.14; repealed in pt. (prosp.): 1988, c.40, sch.13.
s. 20, amended: 1981, c.43, s.4.
s. 24, amended: 1980, c.65, sch.6.
s. 26, amended: 1987, c.3, sch.1.
s. 27, repealed in pt.: 1982, c.32, sch.6.
s. 33, amended: 1980, c.65, sch.6; 1986, c.4, sch.7.
s. 34, repealed: 1984, c.55, sch.7.
s. 35, repealed in pt.: 1985, c.51, sch.17.
s. 37, regs. 78/889.
s. 37, repealed: 1984, c.27, sch.14.
s. 39, repealed in pt.: 1982, c.32, sch.6.
s. 42, amended: 195, c.48, s.15; repealed in pt.: 1985, c.30, sch.
s. 43, repealed: 1982, c.30, sch.7.
s. 44, amended: 1980, c.66, sch.24; 1981, c.38, sch.3; 1984, c.27, sch.13; 1985, c.51, sch.14; order 85/1884; 1988, c.4, sch.6; repealed in pt.: 1980, c.66, sch.25; 1981, c.38, sch.3; 1984, c.12, schs.4,7; 1985, c.51, sch.17; 1988, c.40, sch.13 (prosp.).
s. 46, see *Pitts* v. *Lewis, The Times*, June 10, 1988, D.C.
s. 46, amended: 1985, c.67, sch.7.
s. 48, see *R.* v. *Bournemouth Borough Council* (1985) 83 L.G.R. 662, Mann J.
ss. 48, 50, 51, amended: 1988, c.54, sch.3.
s. 55, see *Challoner* v. *Evans, The Times*, November 2, 1986, D.C.
s. 59, amended: 1988, c.64, sch.3.
s. 63, amended: 1980, c.34, sch.5; 1981, c.14, sch.7; 1985, c.67, sch.1.
s. 64, amended: 1984, c.27, sch.13.
s. 75, see *Pitts* v. *Lewis, The Times*, June 10, 1988, D.C.; *Leeds City Council* v. *Azam, The Times*, July 13, 1988, D.C.

1976—cont.

57. Local Government (Miscellaneous Provisions) Act 1976—*cont.*
s. 75, amended: 1982, c.45, s.16; repealed in pt.: 1985, c.67, schs.7,8.
s. 80, amended: 1980, c.34, sch.5; 1981, c.14, sch.7; 1985, c.67, sch.7.
s. 81, orders 78/316, 651, 739; 79/805, 806; 80/1428; 81/895.
s. 83, order 77/68.
sch. 1, repealed in pt.: 1979, c.46, sch.5.
sch. 2, repealed in pt.: 1980, c.66, sch.25; 1981, c.67, sch.6.

58. International Carriage of Perishable Foodstuffs Act 1976.
Royal Assent, November 15, 1976.
ss. 1–3, regs. 81/521.
ss. 1–4, regs. 79/415; 85/1071.
ss. 2, 3, 6, 7, 9–11, amended: order 83/1123.
ss. 3, 4, regs. 79/416; 87/1066.
s. 9, repealed in pt.: 1981, c.45, sch.
s. 11, repealed in pt.: 1984, c.60, sch.7.
s. 16, order 83/1123.
s. 16, amended: 1983, c.14, sch.2.
s. 20, regs. 79/415, 416; 85/1071.
s. 21, order 79/413.

59. National Health Service (Vocational Training) Act 1976.
Royal Assent, November 15, 1976.
repealed: 1977, c.49, sch.16; 1978, c.29, sch.17 (S.).

60. Insolvency Act 1976.
Royal Assent, November 15, 1976.
s. 1, regs. 84/1199.
ss. 1, 2, repealed: 1985, c.65, sch.10.
s. 3, repealed: 1986, c.45, sch.12.
ss. 4, 5 (in pt.), 6–8, repealed: 1985, c.65, sch.10.
s. 5, repealed (S.): 1985, c.66, sch.8.
s. 7, see *Re Reed (A Debtor)* [1979] 2 All E.R. 22, D.C.; *Re A Debtor (No. 13 of 1964), ex p. Official Receiver* v. *The Debtor* [1979] 3 All E.R. 15, D.C.; *Re A Debtor (No. 1E of 1978)* (1979) 123 S.J. 602, D.C.
s. 9, repealed: 1985, c.9, sch.1.
s. 10, rules 77/364, 365; 78/543, 544, 1224; 79/209; 82/1148, 1437; 83/727, 1645; 84/1371; 85/95.
ss. 10, 11 repealed: 1985, c.65, sch.10.
s. 12, amended: 1984, c.28, sch.2; repealed in pt.: *ibid.*, sch.4; 1985, c.65, sch.10.
s. 14, orders 76/1960; 77/363, 1375; 78/139.
s. 14, repealed in pt.: 1985, c.9, sch.1; c.65, sch.10.
s. 19, amended: order 83/1123.
sch. 1, repealed: 1985, c.65, sch.10.
sch. 1, repealed in pt. (S.): 1985, c.66, sch.8.
sch. 2, repealed in pt.: 1985, c.9, sch.2.

61. Electricity (Financial Provisions) (Scotland) Act 1976.
Royal Assent, November 15, 1976.
s. 1, repealed: 1979, c.11, sch.12.
s. 2, orders 77/614, 1358; 79/412, 960; 80/1206; 81/1215.

62. Motor-Cycle Crash Helmets (Religious Exemption) Act 1976.
Royal Assent, November 15, 1976.
repealed: 1988, c.54, sch.1.

1976—cont.

63. Bail Act 1976.
Royal Assent, November 15, 1976.
s. 2, see *D.P.P. v. Richards* [1988] 3 W.L.R. 153, D.C.
s. 2, amended: 1977, c.45, sch.12; 1980, c.43, sch.7; 1988, c.33, sch.15; repealed in pt.: 1977, c.45, sch.13.
s. 3, see *R. v. Reader* (1987) 84 Cr.App.R. 294, C.A.
s. 3, amended: 1980, c.43, sch.7; 1982, c.51, s.34; 1983, c.20, sch.4; 1987, c.38, sch.2; 1988, c.33, s.131.
ss. 3, 4, see *R. v. Mansfield JJ., ex p. Sharkey* [1984] 3 W.L.R. 1328, D.C.; *R. v. Bournemouth Justices, ex p. Cross; R. v. Same, ex p. Griffin; R. v. Same ex p Pamment, The Times*, October 24, 1988, D.C.
s. 4, see *R. v. Slough JJ., ex p. Duncan* (1982) 75 Cr.App.R. 384, D.C.
s. 4, amended: 1980, c.43, sch.7.
s. 5, rules 78/251, 439; 82/1109.
s. 6, see *R. v. Harbax Singh* [1979] 2 W.L.R. 100, C.A.; *R. v. Tyson* (1979) 68 Cr.App.R. 314, C.A.; *R. v. Gateshead JJ., ex p. Usher* [1981] Crim.L.R. 491, D.C.; *Schiavo v. Anderton* [1986] 3 W.L.R. 177, D.C.; *Laidlaw v. Atkinson, The Times*, August 2, 1986, D.C.; *R. v. Reader* (1987) 84 Cr.App.R. 294, C.A.; *D.P.P. v. Richards* [1988] 3 W.L.R. 153, D.C.
s. 7, see *R. v. Ipswich Crown Court, ex p. Reddington* [1981] Crim.L.R. 618, D.C.; *R. v. Bournemouth Justices, ex p. Cross; R. v. Same, ex p. Griffin; R. v. Same ex p. Pamment, The Times*, October 24, 1988, D.C.
s. 8, see *R. v. Warwick Crown Court, ex p. Smalley* (1987) 84 Cr.App.R. 51, D.C.
s. 8, rules 78/251, 439; 82/1109.
s. 10, repealed: 1977, c.45, sch.13.
s. 11, repealed: 1988, c.34, sch.6.
sch. 1, see *R. v. Vernege* [1982] 1 W.L.R. 293, C.A.; *R. v. Slough JJ, ex p. Duncan* (1982) 75 Cr.App.R. 384, D.C.; *R. v. Mansfield Justices, ex p. Sharkey* [1984] 3 W.L.R. 1328, D.C.; *R. v. Bournemouth Justices, ex p. Cross; R. v. Same, ex p. Griffin; R. v. Same ex p. Pamment, The Times*, October 24, 1988, D.C.
sch. 1, amended: 1980, c.43, sch.7; 1982, c.51, s.34; 1988, c.33, ss.131, 153–155.
sch. 2, repealed in pt.: 1977, c.45, sch.13; 1978, c.30, sch.3; 1980, c.43, sch.9; 1981, c.22, sch.6; c.54, sch.7; 1982, c.48, sch.16; 1983, c.2, sch.9; 1985, c.23, sch.2.

64. Valuation and Rating (Exempted Classes) (Scotland) Act 1976.
Royal Assent, November 15, 1976.
s. 1, order 77/1163.
s. 1, repealed in pt.: 1987, c.47, sch. 6.

65. Retirement of Teachers (Scotland) Act 1976.
Royal Assent, November 15, 1976.
repealed: 1980, c.44, sch.5.

66. Licensing (Scotland) Act 1976.
Royal Assent, November 15, 1976.
s. 1, amended: 1981, c.23, sch.3.

1976—cont.

66. Licensing (Scotland) Act 1976—*cont.*
s. 5, see *Main v. City of Glasgow District Licensing Board* (O.H.), 1987 S.L.T. 305; *Najafian v. Glasgow District Licensing Board* (Sh.Ct.), 1987 S.C.L.R. 679.
s. 6, see *Knowles v. Stirling District Licensing Board*, 1980 S.L.T.(Sh.Ct.) 87; *Tuzi v. City of Edinburgh District Licensing Board* (O.H.), July 8, 1983; *Hart v. City of Edinburgh District Licensing Board*, 1987 S.L.T. (Sh.Ct.) 54; *Clive v. Nithsdale District Licensing Board*, 1987 S.L.T.(Sh.Ct.) 113.
s. 8, orders 77/1085; 87/1738; 88/1464.
s. 10, see *Tevan v. Motherwell District Licencing Board (No. 1)*, 1985 S.L.T.(Sh.Ct.) 14; *Ballantyne v. City of Glasgow District Licensing Board* (O.H.), 1987 S.L.T. 745.
ss. 10, 13, see *Tait v. City of Glasgow District Licensing Board* (O.H.), 1987 S.L.T. 340; *M. Milne v. City of Glasgow District Licensing Board*, 1987 S.L.T.(Sh.Ct.) 145.
ss. 10, 14, see *Fife and Kinross Motor Auctions v. Perth and Kinross District Licensing Board*, Second Division, April 10, 1980.
s. 11, see *Argyll Arms (McManus) v. Lorn, Mid-Argyll, Kintyre & Islay Divisional Licensing Board* (O.H.), 1988 S.L.T. 290.
s. 13, see *Purdon v. Glasgow District Licensing Board*, 1988 S.C.L.R. 466.
s. 14, see *Prime v. Hardie*, 1978 S.L.T.(Sh.Ct.) 71.
s. 15, see *Bury v. Kilmarnock and London District Licensing Board*, 1988 S.C.L.R. 436.
s. 16, see *Hutcheon v. Hamilton District Licensing Board*, 1978 S.L.T.(Sh.Ct.) 44; *Chief Constable of Grampian v. City of Aberdeen District Licensing Board*, 1979 S.L.T.(Sh.Ct.) 2.
s. 17, see *Khan v. City of Glasgow District Licensing Board*, 1980 S.L.T.(Sh.Ct.) 49; *Ahmed v. Stirling District Licensing Board*, 1980 S.L.T.(Sh.Ct.) 51; *Wolfson v. Glasgow District Licensing Board*, Second Division, December 14, 1979; *Ginera v. City of Glasgow District Licensing Board*, 1982 S.L.T. 136; *D. & A. Haddow v. City of Glasgow District Licensing Board*, 1983 S.L.T.(Sh.Ct.) 5; *Grolla v. City of Edinburgh District Licensing Board*, 1983 S.L.T.(Sh.Ct.) 12; *Tominey v. City of Glasgow District Licensing Board*, 1984 S.L.T.(Sh.Ct.) 2; *Collins v. Hamilton District Licensing Board*, 1984 S.L.T. 230; *Hart v. City of Edinburgh District Licensing Board*, 1987 S.L.T.(Sh.Ct.) 54; *Clive v. Nithsdale District Licensing Board*, 1987 S.L.T.(Sh.Ct.) 113; *Chief Constable, Strathclyde Police v. City of Glasgow District Licensing Board*, 1988 S.L.T. 128.
s. 18, see *Martin v. Ellis*, 1978 S.L.T.(Sh.Ct.) 38; *H. D. Wines (Inverness) v. Inverness District Licensing Board*, Second Division, June 11, 1981; *Troc Sales v. Kirkcaldy District Licensing Board*, 1982 S.L.T.(Sh.Ct.) 77; *Moughal v. Motherwell District Licensing Board*, 1983 S.L.T.(Sh.Ct.) 84; *R. W. Cairns v. Busby East Church Kirk Session*, Second Division, November 2, 1984.

1976—cont.

66. Licensing (Scotland) Act 1976—cont.

s. 22, repealed: 1983, c.28, s.9, sch.10.

s. 25, see Chief Constable of Tayside v. Angus District Licensing Board, 1980 S.L.T.(Sh.Ct.) 31; Paterson v. City of Glasgow District Licensing Board, 1982 S.L.T.(Sh.Ct.) 37; Tominey v. City of Glasgow District Licensing Board, 1984 S.L.T.(Sh.Ct.) 2; Archyield v. City of Glasgow Licensing Board (O.H.), 1987 S.L.T. 547.

ss. 25, 26, see Baljaffray Residents' Association v. Milngavie and Bearsden District Council Licensing Board, 1981 S.L.T.(Sh.Ct.) 106.

s. 26, see Ginera v. City of Glasgow District Licensing Board, 1982 S.L.T. 136; Lipoltan v. Glasgow District Licensing Board (Sh.Ct.), 1988 S.C.L.R. 443; Chief Constable, Strathclyde Police v. City of Glasgow District Licensing Board, 1988 S.L.T. 128.

s. 28, amended: 1984, c.54, sch.9.

s. 31, see Lightheart v. City of Edinburgh District Licensing Board, 1978 S.L.T.(Sh.Ct.) 41; Singh and Kaur v. Kirkcaldy District Licensing Board, 1988 S.L.T. 286.

s. 33, amended: 1980, c.55, s.21.

s. 35, see City of Glasgow District Licensing Board v. MacDonald, 1978 S.L.T.(Sh.Ct.) 74; Tennent Caledonian Breweries v. City of Aberdeen District Licensing Board, 1987 S.L.T. (Sh.Ct.) 2.

s. 37, see Coppola v. Midlothian District Licensing Board, 1983 S.L.T.(Sh.Ct.) 95.

s. 38, see Allied Breweries (U.K.) v. City of Glasgow District Licensing Board (O.H.), 1985 S.L.T. 307.

s. 39, see Hutcheon v. Hamilton District Licensing Board, 1978 S.L.T.(Sh.Ct.) 44; Lightheart v. City of Edinburgh District Licensing Board, 1978 S.L.T.(Sh.Ct.) 41; Martin v. Ellis, 1978 S.L.T.(Sh.Ct.) 38; Kieran v. Adams, 1979 S.L.T.(Sh.Ct.) 13; Robertson v. Inverclyde Licensing Board, 1979 S.L.T.(Sh.Ct.) 16; Charles Watson (Scotland) v. Glasgow District Licensing Board, 1980 S.L.T.(Sh.Ct.) 37; Ahmed v. Stirling District Licensing Board, 1980 S.L.T.(Sh.Ct.) 51; Freeland v. City of Glasgow District Board, 1980 S.L.T.(Sh.Ct.) 125; Ladbroke Racing (Scotland East) v. Midlothian District Licensing Board, 1981 S.L.T.(Sh.Ct.) 12; Johnson v. City of Edinburgh District Licensing Board, First Division, February 4, 1981; H. D. Wines (Inverness) v. Inverness District Licensing Board, Second Division, June 11, 1981; Joe Coral (Racing) v. Hamilton District Council, 1981 S.L.T.(Notes) 106; Troc Sales v. Kirkcaldy District Licensing Board, 1982 S.L.T.(Sh.Ct.) 77; Cigaro (Glasgow) v. City of Glasgow District Licensing Board, First Division, December 8, 1981; Moughal v. Motherwell District Licensing Board, 1983 S.L.T.(Sh.Ct.) 84; Coppola v. Midlothian District Licensing Board, 1983 S.L.T.(Sh.Ct.) 95; Sutherland v. City of Edinburgh District Licensing Board, 1984 S.L.T. 241; R. W. Cairns v. Busby East Church Kirk

1976—cont.

66. Licensing (Scotland) Act 1976—cont.

Session, Second Division, November 2, 1984; Botterills of Blantyre v. Hamilton District Licensing Board, Second Division, July 12, 1985; Padda v. Strathkelvin District Licensing Board (Sh.Ct.), 1988 S.C.L.R. 349.

s. 39, Acts of Sederunt 77/1622; 79/1520.

Pt. IV (ss. 47–52), repealed: 1981, c.23, s.8, sch.4.

s. 53, see Ginera v. City of Glasgow District Licensing Board, 1982 S.L.T. 136.

ss. 54, 58, see Stewart v. Dunphy, 1980 S.L.T.(Notes) 93.

s. 59, repealed in pt.: 1981, c.23, sch.4.

s. 62, see Wallace v. Kyle and Carrick Licensing Board, 1979 S.L.T.(Sh.Ct.) 12.

s. 63, orders 77/763; 87/838.

s. 63, amended: 1979, c.2, sch.4.

s. 64, see Sloan v. North-East Fife District Council Licensing Board, 1978 S.L.T.(Sh.Ct.) 62; Archyield v. City of Glasgow Licensing Board (O.H.), 1987 S.L.T. 547.

s. 64, amended: 1980, c.55, s.21.

s. 66, see Elantosh v. City of Edinburgh District Licensing Board, Second Division, July 8, 1983.

s. 67, see Byrne v. Tudhope, 1983 S.C.C.R. 337.

s. 68, see Wilson v. Allied Breweries, 1986 S.L.T. 549; Tudhope v. McDonald, 1986 S.C.C.R. 32; Paton v. Wilson, 1988 S.L.T. 634.

s. 77, see Dunning v. Cardle, 1981 S.L.T.(Notes) 107.

s. 85, see Chief Constable, Strathclyde Police v. City of Glasgow District Licensing Board, 1988 S.L.T. 128.

s. 90, see Macdonald v. Skinner, 1978 S.L.T.(Notes) 52.

s. 92, amended: 1985, c.67, sch.7.

s. 94, repealed: 1981, c.35, sch.19.

ss. 95, 103, amended: 1980, c.55, s.21.

s. 103, see Dick v. Stirling Lawn Tennis and Squash Club, 1981 S.L.T.(Sh.Ct.) 103.

ss. 103, 108, see Scottish Homosexual Rights Group, Petitioners, 1981 S.L.T.(Sh.Ct.) 18.

ss. 104, 106, see Royal British Legion Club, Petrs., 1984 S.L.T.(Sh.Ct.) 62.

s. 107, amended: 1980, c.55, sch.2.

ss. 111–113, amended: ibid., s.21.

s. 117, see Edinburgh North Constituency Association S.N.P. Club v. Thomas H. Peck, 1978 S.L.T.(Sh.Ct.) 76.

s. 122, see Macdonald v. Skinner, 1978 S.L.T.(Notes) 52.

s. 123, amended: regs. 79/1755.

s. 127, see Tudhope v. McDonald, 1986 S.C.C.R. 32.

s. 131, see D. & A. Haddow v. City of Glasgow District Licensing Board, 1983 S.L.T.(Sh.Ct.) 5.

s. 133, see Joe Coral (Racing) v. Hamilton District Council, 1981 S.L.T.(Notes) 106.

s. 133, amended: 1985, c.72, s.52.

ss. 133, 136, see Cigaro (Glasgow) v. City of Glasgow District Licensing Board, First Division, December 8, 1981.

1976—cont.
66. Licensing (Scotland) Act 1976—*cont.*
s. 135, orders 87/1738, 1464.
s. 138, amended: 1978, c.51, sch.16.
s. 139, see *Macdonald* v. *Skinner,* 1978 S.L.T.(Notes) 52; *Baljaffray Residents' Association* v. *Milngavie and Bearsden District Council Licensing Board,* 1981 S.L.T.(Sh.Ct.) 106; *Tuzi* v. *City of Edinburgh District Licensing Board* (O.H.), July 8, 1983; *Chief Constable, Northern Constabulary* v. *Lochaber District Licensing Board,* 1985 S.L.T. 410; *Tudhope* v. *McDonald,* 1986 S.C.C.R. 32.
s. 139, amended: 1979, c.4, sch.3; regs. 79/1755; 1984, c.54, sch.9; 1985, c.73, s.53; repealed in pt.: 1981, c.35, sch.19.
s. 140, amended: 1980, c.55, sch.2; repealed in pt.: *ibid.,* sch.3; 1981, c.23, sch.4.
s. 141, orders 76/2068; 77/212, 718.
sch. 1, see *Khan* v. *City of Glasgow District Licensing Board,* 1980 S.L.T.(Sh.Ct.) 49; *Chief Constable, Northern Constabulary* v. *Lochaber District Licensing Board,* 1985 S.L.T. 410.
sch. 3, repealed: 1981, c.23, s.8, sch.4.
sch. 4, see *Freeland* v. *City of Glasgow District Licensing Board,* 1980 S.L.T.(Sh.Ct.) 125; *Ginera* v. *City of Glasgow District Licensing Board,* 1982 S.L.T. 136; *R. W. Cairns* v. *Busby East Church Kirk Session,* Second Division, November 2, 1984.
sch. 5, see *Stewart* v. *Dunphy,* 1980 S.L.T.(Notes) 93.
sch. 5, repealed in pt.: 1981, c.28, sch.4.
sch. 7, repealed in pt.: 1979, c.4, sch.4.
sch. 8, see *Cigaro (Glasgow)* v. *City of Glasgow District Licensing Board,* First Division, December 8, 1981.
67. Sexual Offences (Scotland) Act 1976.
Royal Assent, November 15, 1976.
ss. 2A–2D, added: 1986, c.36, s.1.
s. 2D, repealed in pt.: 1987, c.41, sch.2.
s. 4, amended: 1986, c.36, sch.1.
s. 5, see *B.* v. *Kennedy,* 1987 S.L.T. 765; *F.* v. *Kennedy,* 1988 S.L.T. 404.
s. 13, repealed in pt.: 1982, c.45, sch.4
s. 14, amended: 1977, c.45, sch.11.
s. 15, see *Sweeney* v. *X,* 1982 S.C.C.R. 509.
sch. 1, repealed in pt.: 1984, c.36, sch.5.
68. New Towns (Amendment) Act 1976.
Royal Assent, November 15, 1976.
repealed: 1981, c.64, sch.13.
s. 13, regs. 77/1411.
69. Companies Act 1976.
Royal Assent, November 15, 1976.
Commencement orders; 76/2188; 77/165, 529, 774, 1348; 79/1544; 80/1748; 82/671; 84/683.
repealed: 1985, c.9, sch.1.
orders 79/1545, 1547.
s. 1, order 77/1367.
ss. 1, 4, see *Smith* v. *Inglis,* 1983 S.L.T. 160.
s. 2, order 77/166.
ss. 3, 6, order 77/1367.
s. 9, orders 77/1367, 1370; 80/1786; 82/676.
s. 10, orders 77/166, 1367.

1976—cont.
69. Companies Act 1976—*cont.*
s. 12, see *Taylor* v. *McGirr* [1986] Crim.L.R. 544, D.C.
s. 13, see *Secretary of State for Trade and Industry* v. *Hart* [1982] 1 W.L.R. 481, D.C.
s. 21, regs. 83/1021.
s. 23, regs. 83/1021.
s. 28, see *Re Civica Investments, The Times,* June 9, 1982, Nourse J.; *Arctic Engineering, Re* [1986] 1 W.L.R. 686, Hoffman J.
s. 29, regs. 77/776; orders 77/775; 82/673.
s. 37, regs. 80/1749, 1980; 82/105.
s. 44, order 82/673; regs. 83/1021.
s. 45, orders 76/2188; 77/165, 529, 774, 1348; 79/1544; 82/671; 84/683.
70. Land Drainage Act 1976.
Royal Assent, November 15, 1976.
s. 2, amended: 1985, c.51, sch.7; order 86/208; repealed in pt.: 1985, c.51, sch.17; order 86/208.
ss. 2, 3, order 88/566.
s. 3, amended: orders 86/613, 615; repealed in pt.: 1985, c.51, sch.17.
s. 5, amended: *ibid.,* sch.7; order 86/208; repealed in pt.: 1985, c.51, sch.17.
s. 7, regs. 77/366.
s. 10, order 81/74.
s. 11, orders 78/79, 506, 595, 843, 1288, 1371, 1588–1590, 1819; 79/266, 579, 1243; 80/60, 147, 159, 360, 793, 921, 1048, 1427, 1436; 81/398, 491, 492, 556, 557; 82/290, 501, 1407, 1758; 83/369, 633, 903; 84/162, 462, 497; 85/58, 210, 505, 681, 1124, 1393, 1559; 86/1266, 1919; 87/555, 815, 2230, 88/237.
s. 12, order 82/110.
s. 13, orders, 87/1928, 1929.
s. 16, amended: 1985, c.51, sch.7.
s. 17, see *Strutts Kingston Estate Settlement Trustees* v. *Kingston Brook International Drainage Board* (Ref. 138/1977) (1979) 251 E.G. 577; *Steel Stampings* v. *Severn Trent Water Authority* (Ref. 189/1980) (1982) 263 E.G. 359.
s. 19, amended: 1980, c.43, sch.7.
s. 23, amended: 1981, c.38, sch.3; 1984, c.12, sch.4.
s. 24, amended: 1985, c.51, sch.7.
s. 25, orders 78/1980; 79/511; 84/2064.
s. 28, amended: 1985, c.51, sch.7.
s. 30, amended: regs. 78/319.
s. 32, amended: 1981, c.38, sch.3; repealed in pt.: 1984, c.12, sch.7; 1985, c.51, sch.17.
s. 37, regs. 77/84.
s. 37, amended: 1981, c.67, sch.4; repealed in pt.: *ibid.,* sch.6.
s. 43, amended: 1986, c.49, sch.3.
s. 45, amended: 1985, c.51, sch.7; order 86/208.
s. 46, order 80/2017.
s. 46, amended: 1980, c.65, s.181; repealed in pt.: 1982, c.32, sch.6.
s. 48, amended: regs. 78/319.
s. 49, orders, 78/665; 81/247; 86/447; 87/318; amended: regs. 78/319; repealed in pt.: 1982, c.32, sch.6.

CAP.

1976—cont.

70. Land Drainage Act 1976—cont.
ss. 51, 52, amended: regs. 78/319.
s. 62, amended: 1988, c.15, sch.2.
s. 65, repealed in pt.: 1980, c.65, s.182, sch.34.
s. 72, regs. 77/357.
s. 92, repealed in pt.: 1985, c.51, sch.17.
s. 94, regs. 77/339.
s. 95, regs. 77/84, 357, 366.
s. 96, repealed in pt.: 1986, c.63, sch.12.
s. 97, repealed in pt.: 1985, c.51, sch.17.
s. 98, amended: *ibid.*, sch.7; repealed in pt.: *ibid.*, sch.17; order 86/208.
s. 99, amended: 1985, c.51, sch.7.
s. 101, repealed: *ibid.*, sch.17.
s. 104A, added: order 86/208.
s. 109, orders 78/79, 1371, 1980; 79/266; 80/360, 921, 1427, 1436; 81/74, 398, 491, 492; 82/110; 83/369, 466, 633; 84/162, 2064; 85/681, 1393; 86/1919; 87/555, 815, 1928, 1929, 2230; 88/237.
s. 109, amended: 1980, c.65, s.181.
s. 110, amended: 1985, c.51, sch.7; repealed in pt.: *ibid.*, sch.17.
s. 111, amended: 1979, c.46, sch.4.
s. 112, amended: 1981, c.38, sch.3; 1984, c.12, sch.4; c.32, sch.6; 1986, c.44, sch.7; 1987, c.3, sch.1; repealed in pt.: 1986, c.31, sch.6.
s. 116, amended: order 78/319; 1985, c.51, sch.7; order 86/208.
s. 117, orders 78/79, 506.
sch. 1, amended. 1982, c.32, sch.5; 1983, c.23, sch.4; 1985, c.65, sch.8; repealed in pt.: 1982, c.32, sch.6
sch. 2, order 78/319.
sch. 2, repealed in pt.: 1982, c.32, sch.6.
sch. 5, amended: order 86/208; repealed in pt.: 1983, c.23, sch.5; order 86/208.
sch. 6, orders 78/79, 506.
sch. 7, repealed in pt.: 1980, c.66, sch.25.

71. Supplementary Benefits Act 1976.
Royal Assent, November 15, 1976.
see *Supplementary Benefits Commission* v. *Riley, The Times,* November 15, 1978, Sheen J.; *Decision No. R(SB)*17/85.
s. 1, see *R.* v. *West London Supplementary Benefits Appeal Tribunal, ex p. Wyatt* [1978] 1 W.L.R. 240, D.C.; *Supplementary Benefits Commission* v. *Jull; Y.* v. *Supplementary Benefits Commission* [1980] 3 W.L.R. 436; [1980] 3 All E.R. 65, H.L.; *Lincoln* v. *Hayman* [1982] 1 W.L.R. 488, C.A.; *Decision No. R(SB)* 52/83.
s. 1, regs. 80/985, 1299, 1586, 1641; 81/815, 1526; 82/907, 1125; 83/1000, 1004, 1399; 84/938; 85/613, 1835; 86/1292; 87/659, 1325; amended: 1980, c.30, sch.2.
ss. 1, 3, see *Vaughan* v. *Social Security Adjudication Officer, The Times,* July 17, 1986, C.A.: *Kelly* v. *Supplementary Benefits Commission,* 1983, S.C. 32; *Scottish Old People's Welfare Council, Petrs.* (O.H.), 1987 S.L.T. 179.
ss. 1–21, repealed: 1986, c.50, sch.11.
s. 2, see *Decision No. R(SB)* 29/83; *R.* v. *Secretary of State for Social Services, ex p.*

CAP.

1976—cont.

71. Supplementary Benefits Act 1976—cont.
Cotton, The Times, December 14, 1985, C.A.; *Secretary of State for Social Services* v. *Elkington, The Independent,* March 18, 1987, C.A.; *Decision No. R(SB)* 22/86.
s. 2, regs. 77/1141, 1142, 1226, 1326; 78/913, 1459; 79/997; 80/982, 1299, 1300, 1634, 1774; 81/513, 815; 82/907, 914, 1125; 83/337, 1000, 1004; 84/451, 1102, 1103, 1991, 2034; 85/613, 614, 1136, 1246, 1247, 1835; 86/1259, 1292, 1293; 87/17, 49, 659, 660, 1325.
s. 2, amended: 1977, c.5, s.14; 1979, c.18, sch.3; 1980, c.30, sch.2; 1983, c.41, sch.8; repealed in pt.: 1980, c.30, schs.2,5.
s. 3, see *Decision No. R(SB)* 52/83; *Supplementary Benefits Officer* v. *Howell, The Times,* April 11, 1984, C.A.
s. 3, regs. 80/985, 1649; 81/815, 1196, 1528; 82/907, 914, 1127; 83/1000, 1004, 1240, 1245, 1630; 84/593, 938, 1103; 85/1247; 86/1259, 1261; 87/36, 481, 2010.
s. 3, amended: 1980, c.30, sch.2.
s. 4, regs. 80/1641, 1642; 81/815, 1529; 82/907, 914; 83/1000; 84/938; 85/1016; 86/1259; 87/481.
s. 4, substituted: 1980, c.30, sch.2.
s. 5, regs. 77/1141; 80/1586; 82/907; 83/463, 1000; 84/938; 86/1010; 87/358.
s. 5, amended: 1980, c.30, sch.2; 1982, c.24, s.38.
s. 5, regs. 81/99, 815, 1526.
s. 6, see *R.* v. *Manchester Supplementary Benefits Appeal Tribunal, ex p. Riley* [1979] 1 W.L.R. 426, Sheen J.; *Perrot* v. *Supplementary Benefits Commission* [1980] 1 W.L.R. 1153; [1980] 3 All E.R. 110, C.A.; *R.* v. *Supplementary Benefits Commission, ex p. Lewis, The Times,* November 5, 1981, C.A.; *Decision No. R(SB)* 26/82; *Chief Supplementary Benefit Officer* v. *Cunningham* [1985] I.C.R. 660, C.A.; *Decisions Nos. R(SB)* 22/85; *R(SB)* 34/85.
s. 6, regs. 77/1141; 80/1586; 81/99, 815, 1526; 82/907; 83/1000; 84/518, 938; 87/358.
ss. 6, 7, see *R.* v. *Peterborough Supplementary Benefits Appeal Tribunal, ex p. Supplementary Benefits Commission* [1978] 3 All E.R. 887, D.C.
ss. 6, 7, substituted: 1980, c.30, sch.2.
s. 7, see *Bloomfield* v. *Supplementary Benefits Commission* (1978) 123 S.J. 33, Sheen J.; *Sampson* v. *Supplementary Benefits Commission* (1979) 123 S.J. 284, Watkins J.
s. 8, see *R.* v. *Bolton Supplementary Benefits Appeal Tribunal, ex p. Fordham, The Times,* November 28, 1978, Sheen J.
s. 8, amended: 1980, c.30, sch.2; 1986, c.50, sch.10; repealed in pt.: 1980, c.30, schs.2,5.
s. 9, regs. 80/1641; 81/815; 82/907, 914; 83/1000; 84/458, 938.
s. 9, amended: 1980, c.30, sch.2; 1981, c.33, s.4; repealed in pt.: 1980, c.30, schs.2,5.
s. 10, regs. 80/1586; 81/1526; 82/907; 84/458.
s. 10, substituted: 1980, c.30, sch.2; 1982, c.24, s.38; amended: 1983, c.41, sch.8.

1976—cont.

71. Supplementary Benefits Act 1976—cont.

s. 11, regs. 80/1579; 81/815; 86/562, 1259.

s. 11, amended: 1980, c.30, sch.2.

s. 12, regs. 80/1580; 81/815.

s. 12, amended: 1980, c.30, sch.2; 1982, c.24, sch.4; repealed in pt.: ibid., schs.4,5; 1983, c.41, sch.10.

s. 14, regs. 77/1141, 1142; 80/983, 985, 1579, 1642, 1643, 1649; 81/815, 1525, 1528, 1529; 82/522, 907, 914, 1400; 83/337, 1000, 1004; 84/451, 458, 938; 85/1016; 86/562, 1259, 2154; 87/36, 2010.

s. 14, amended: 1979, c.18, s.6, sch.3; 1980, c.30, sch.2; 1982, c.24, sch.4; repealed in pt.: 1980, c.30, schs.2,5; 1983, c.41, sch.8.

s. 15, repealed: 1983, c.41, sch.8.

s. 15A, see Decision No. R(SB) 24/82.

s. 15A, rules 80/1605; 82/40.

s. 15A, repealed: 1983, c.41, sch.8.

s. 16, amended: 1980, c.30, sch.2; repealed in pt.: ibid., schs.2,5.

s. 17, see R. v. Bolton Supplementary Benefits Appeal Tribunal, ex p. Fordham, The Times, November 28, 1978, Sheen J.; Supplementary Benefits Commission v. Higgins, 1980 S.L.T.(Sh.Ct.) 20; Meikle v. Annan, 1984 S.C.C.R. 270.

s. 17, amended: 1980, c.30, sch.2; 1986, c.9, sch.1(S.); repealed in pt. (S.): ibid., sch.2.

ss. 17, 18, see Holley v. Thompson [1981] 1 W.L.R. 159, D.C.; Supplementary Benefits Commission v. Mitchell, Second Division, June 11, 1981.

s. 18, see McBurnie (Inspector of Taxes) v. Tacey [1984] 1 W.L.R. 1019, Peter Gibson J.; Tayside Regional Council v. Thaw, 1987 S.L.T. 69; Secretary of State for Social Services v. McMillan, 1987 S.L.T.(Sh.Ct.) 52; Secretary of State for Social Services v. Ritchie, 1987 S.L.T.(Sh.Ct.) 98.

s. 18, amended: 1980, c.30, sch.2; repealed in pt.: 1978, c.22, sch.3; 1980, c.30, schs.2,5.

s. 18, amended (S.): 1986, c.9, sch.1.

ss. 18, 19, see Robinson v. Lowther (1980) 10 Fam.Law 214, D.C.

s. 19, see Moore v. Ball [1984] 2 W.L.R. 865.

s. 19, amended: 1978, c.22, sch.2; 1979, c.55, sch.2; 1980, c.30, sch.2; 1982, c.24, sch.4; repealed in pt.: 1980, c.30, schs.2,5.

s. 19, repealed (S.): 1986, c.9, sch.2.

s. 20, see Decision Nos. R(SB) 21/82,28/83; R(SB) 34/83; R(SB) 44/83; Decisions Nos. R(SB) 12/84, R(SB) 40/84, R(SB) 15/87.

s. 20, regs. 80/1580, 1649; 81/815; 83/1000.

s. 20, amended: 1982, c.24, s.41, sch.4; 1983, c.41, sch.9; repealed in pt.: 1980, c.30, sch.2; 1983, c.41, sch.10.

s. 21, see Clear v. Smith [1981] 1 W.L.R. 399, D.C.

s. 21, amended: 1977, c.5, s.14; 1980, c.30, sch.2; 1981, c.33, sch.1.

s. 22, amended: 1977, c.5, s.14; 1980, c.30, sch.2; 1981, c.33, sch.1; order 88/1843; repealed in pt.: 1980, c.30, schs.2,5.

1976—cont.

71. Supplementary Benefits Act 1976—cont.

s. 23, amended: 1977, c.5, s.14; 1981, c.33, sch.1; order 88/1843.

ss. 24–27, repealed: 1986, c.50, sch.11.

s. 25, see Galt v. Turner, 1981 S.L.T. (Notes) 99; Meikle v. Annan, 1984 S.C.C.R. 270; R. v. Davis, The Times, May 20, 1986, D.C.

s. 27, see R. v. Secretary of State for Social Services, ex p. Child Poverty Action Group and G.L.C., The Times, August 8, 1985, C.A.; Decision No. R(SB) 27/85.

s. 28, rules 80/1605; 82/40.

s. 28, repealed: 1983, c.41, sch.10.

s. 29, repealed: 1977, c.5, sch.2.

s. 30, amended: 1980, c.30, sch.2; repealed in pt.: ibid., schs.2,5.

ss. 31–34, repealed: 1986, c.50, sch.11.

s. 32A, regs. 80/1774; 81/1524.

s. 33, see R. v. D.H.S.S., ex p. London Borough of Camden, The Times, March 5, 1986, D.C.

s. 33, regs. 81/1016, 1197; 82/1127; 84/451, 458, 1102, 1103; 85/1835; 86/1259, 1292; 87/1325.

ss. 33, 34, see R. v. Secretary of State for Social Services, ex p. Camden London Borough Council, The Times, March 6, 1987, C.A.

s. 34, see Decision No. R(SB) 30/83.

s. 34, regs. 80/982, 1774; 81/815, 1524; 83/1000; 84/458, 518, 593, 938, 1102, 1103, 2034; 85/613, 614, 1136, 1246, 1247, 1835; 86/562, 1010, 1259, 1292, 1293, 1961, 2154; 87/17, 36, 49, 358, 481, 659, 660, 1325, 2010, 2193.

s. 36, repealed in pt.: 1980, c.30, sch.5.

sch. 1, see R. v. West London Supplementary Benefits Appeal Tribunal, ex p. Wyatt [1978] 1 W.L.R. 240, D.C.; R. v. Greater Birmingham Supplementary Benefit Appeal Tribunal, ex p. Khan [1979] 3 All E.R. 759, D.C.; R. v. Bolton Supplementary Benefits Appeal Tribunal, ex p. Fordham [1981] 1 W.L.R. 28; [1981] 1 All E.R. 50, C.A.; McDougall v. Secretary of State for Social Services; McIntyre v. Secretary of State for Social Services, The Times, May 15, 1981, H.L.; Roberts v. Supplementary Benefits Commission, Second Division, November 26, 1980; Crake v. Supplementary Benefits Commission; Butterworth v. Supplementary Benefits Commission [1982] 1 All E.R. 498, Woolf J.; Pearson v. Secretary of State for Social Services, Second Division, November 20, 1981; Decision No. R(SB) 7/83; Chief Supplementary Benefits Officer v. Leary [1985] 1 W.L.R. 84, C.A.; R. v. Secretary of State for Social Services, ex p. Camden London Borough Council, The Times, March 6, 1987, C.A.

sch. 1, regs. 77/1141, 1142; 78/913; 80/1300, 1579, 1774; 81/513, 1196, 1524, 1525, 1527; 82/1126, 1127, 1634; 83/503, 505, 700, 1004, 1240, 1245, 1399; 84/282, 458, 938, 1102, 1103, 2034; 85/613, 614, 1136, 1246, 1247, 1835; 86/562, 1293; 87/17, 49, 659, 660, 1325.

CAP.

1976—cont.

71. Supplementary Benefits Act 1976—cont.

sch. 1, repealed: 1986, c.50, sch.11.

schs. 2, 3, repealed: 1980, c.30, sch.5.

sch. 4, rules 80/1605; 82/40.

sch. 4, repealed: 1983, c.41, sch.10.

sch. 5, amended: 1980, c.30, sch.2; repealed in pt.: *ibid.*, schs.2,5; 1985, c.51, sch.17; 1986, c.50, sch.11.

sch. 6, amended: 1980, c.30, sch.2; repealed in pt.: *ibid.*, schs.2,5.

sch. 7, repealed in pt.: 1977, c.5, sch.2; 1978, c.22, sch.3; c.44, sch.17; order 77/2158; 1980, c.30, sch.5; c.51, sch.26; 1982, c.24, sch 5; 1983, c.41, sch.10; 1986, c.50, sch.11; 1988, c.1, sch.31; c.34, sch.6.

sch. 16, amended: 1982, c.24, s.42.

72. Endangered Species (Import and Export) Act 1976.

Royal Assent, November 22, 1976.

s. 1, amended: 1979, c.2, sch.4.

ss. 1, 3, amended: 1981, c.69, sch.10.

s. 3, orders 77/153; 78/1280, 1939; 79/1054; 82/1230; 83/1609; 85/1502.

s. 4, amended and repealed in pt.: 1981, c.69, sch.10.

ss. 4, 5, amended: 1979, c.2, sch.4.

s. 10, amended: *ibid.*

s. 11, orders 77/153; 78/1939; 79/1054; 83/1609; 85/1502.

s. 13, order 77/24.

s. 13, amended: 1981, c.69, sch.10; repealed in pt.: *ibid.*, sch.17.

schs. 1–3, substituted: order 82/1230.

sch. 2, amended: order 79/1054.

sch. 3, amended: orders 78/1280; 79/1054; 83/1609.

schs. 4, 5, added: 1981, c.69, sch.10.

73. Industry (Amendment) Act 1976.

Royal Assent, November 22, 1976.

74. Race Relations Act 1976.

Royal Assent, November 22, 1976.

see *Kingston* v. *British Railways Board* [1984] I.R.L.R 146, C A

s. 1, see *Singh* v. *Rowntree Mackintosh* [1979] I.C.R. 554, E.A.T.; *Panesar* v. *Nestlé Co.* [1980] I.C.R. 144, C.A.; *Kingston and Richmond Area Health Authority* v. *Kaur* [1981] I.C.R. 631, E.A.T.; *Chattopadhyay* v. *The Headmaster of Holloway School* [1981] I.R.L.R. 487, E.A.T.; *Bayoomi* v. *British Railways Board* [1981] I.R.L.R. 431, Industrial Tribunal; *Chin* v. *British Aerospace P.L.C.* [1982] I.R.L.R. 56, E.A.T.; *Ojutiku* v. *Manpower Services Commission* [1982] I.C.R. 661, C.A.; *Owen & Briggs* v. *James* [1982] I.C.R. 618, C.A.; *Mandla (Sewa Singh)* v. *Dowell Lee* [1983] 2 W.L.R. 620, H.L.; *Perera* v. *The Civil Service Commission and the Department of Customs and Excise* [1983] I.R.L.R. 166, C.A.; *Showboat Entertainment Centre* v. *Owens* [1984] I.C.R. 65, E.A.T.; *Orphanos* v. *Queen Mary College* [1985] 2 All E.R. 233, H.L.; *Raval* v. *D.H.S.S.* [1985] I.C.R. 685, E.A.T.; *R.* v. *Commission for Racial*

CAP.

1976—cont.

74. Race Relations Act 1976—cont.

Equality, ex p. Westminster City Council [1985] I.C.R. 827, C.A.; *Singh* v. *British Rail Engineering* [1986] I.C.R. 22, E.A.T.; *McAlister* v. *Labour Party, The Times*, June 5, 1986, E.A.T.; *Tejani* v. *Superintendent Registrar for the District of Peterborough, The Times*, June 10, 1986, C.A.; *Gwynedd County Council* v. *Jones, The Times*, July 28, 1986, E.A.T.; *Tower Hamlets London Borough Council* v. *Qayyum* [1987] I.C.R. 729, E.A.T.; *Irving & Irving* v. *The Post Office* [1987] I.R.L.R. 289, C.A.; *North West Thames Regional Health Authority* v. *Noone* [1987] I.R.L.R. 357, E.A.T.; *Dhatt* v. *McDonalds Hamburgers, The Times*, May 17, 1988, E.A.T.; *Meer* v. *Tower Hamlets London Borough Council, The Times*, June 3, 1988, C.A.; *West Midlands Passenger Transport Executive* v. *Singh* [1988] I.R.L.R. 186, C.A.; *Alexander* v. *The Home Office* [1988] I.R.L.R. 190, C.A.; *Hampson* v. *Department of Education and Science* [1988] I.C.R. 278, E.A.T.; *Commission for Racial Equality* v. *Dutton, The Times*, July 29, 1988, C.A.

ss. 1, 3, see *Commission for Racial Equality* v. *Riley*, July 5, 1982, H.H. Judge Da Cunha (sitting with assessors) Manchester C.C.; *Raval* v. *D.H.S.S. and The Civil Service Commission* [1985] I.R.L.R. 370, E.A.T.; *Gwynedd County Council* v. *Jones* [1986] I.C.R 833, E.A.T.; *Tejani* v. *Superintendent Registrar for the District of Peterborough* [1986] I.R.L.R. 502, C.A

ss. 1, 4, see *Zarczynska* v. *Levy* [1979] 1 W.L.R. 125, E.A.T.; *Din (Ghulam)* v. *Carrington Viyella* [1982] I.C.R. 256, E.A.T.

s 2, see *Aziz* v. *Trinity Street Taxis, The Guardian*, March 9, 1988, C.A.

ss. 2, 4, see *Kirby* v. *Manpower Services Commission* [1980] I.C.R. 420; [1980] 1 W.L.R. 725, E.A.T.

s. 3, see *Mandla (Sewa Singh)* v. *Dowell Lee* [1983] 2 W.L.R. 620, H.L.; *Tower Hamlets London Borough Council* v. *Qayyum, The Times*, May 2, 1987, E.A.T.; *West Midlands Passenger Transport Executive* v. *Singh* [1988] I.R.L.R. 186, C.A.; *Alexander* v. *The Home Office* [1988] I.R.L.R. 190, C.A.

s. 4, see *Heron Corp* v. *Commis* [1980] I.C.R. 713, E.A.T.; *Tanna* v. *Post Office* [1981] I.C.R. 374, E.A.T.; *Eke* v. *Comrs. of Customs and Excise* [1981] I.R.L.R. 334, E.A.T.; *Kingston and Richmond Area Health Authority* v. *Kaur* [1981] I.C.R. 631, E.A.T.; *Khanna* v. *Ministry of Defence* [1981] I.C.R. 653, E.A.T.; *Chattopadhyay* v. *The Headmaster of Holloway School* [1981] I.R.L.R. 487, E.A.T.; *Owen & Briggs* v. *James* [1983] I.C.R. 618, C.A.; *B.L. Cars* v. *Brown* [1983] I.C.R. 143, E.A.T.; *Daley* v. *Allied Suppliers* [1983] I.C.R. 90, E.A.T.; *Showboat Entertainment Centre* v. *Owens* [1984] I.C.R. 65, E.A.T.; *Lupetti* v. *Wrens Old House* [1984] I.C.R. 348, E.A.T.; *Kingston* v. *British Railways Board* [1984]

1976—cont.

74. Race Relations Act 1976—*cont.*

I.C.R. 781, C.A.; *Wadi* v. *Cornwall and Isles of Scilly Family Practitioner Committee* [1985] I.C.R. 492, E.A.T.; *Raval* v. *D.H.S.S.* [1985] I.C.R. 685, E.A.T.; *R.* v. *Commission for Racial Equality, ex p. Westminster City Council* [1985] I.C.R. 827, C.A.; *Deria* v. *General Council of British Shipping* [1986] I.C.R. 172, C.A.; *De Souza* v. *The Automobile Association* [1986] I.C.R. 514, C.A.; *North West Thames Regional Health Authority* v. *Noone* [1987] I.R.L.R. 357, E.A.T.; *West Midlands Passenger Transport Executive* v. *Singh* [1988] I.R.L.R. 186, C.A.; *Sheikh* v. *Anderton, The Times,* July 18, 1988, E.A.T.

s. 7, see *B.L. Cars* v. *Brown* [1983] I.C.R. 143, E.A.T.; *Daley* v. *Allied Suppliers* [1983] I.C.R. 90, E.A.T.

s. 8, order 87/929.

s. 8, amended: 1978, c.46, s.1.

ss. 8, 9, amended: 1982, c.74, sch.3.

ss. 8, 14, see *Deria* v. *General Council of British Shipping* [1986] I.C.R. 172, C.A.

s. 13, see *Ojutiku* v. *Manpower Services Commission* [1982] I.C.R. 661, C.A.

s. 13, amended: 1982, c.10, sch.3; 1988, c.19, sch.3; repealed in pt.: 1981, c.57, schs.2,3.

s. 15, amended: *ibid.,* sch.2; 1988, c.19, sch.3.

s. 17, amended (S.): 1980, c.44, sch.4; 1988, c.40, sch.12; repealed in pt.: 1980, c.20, sch.1.

s. 18, amended: 1980, c.20, s.33; c.44, sch.4(S.); 1981, c.60, sch.3.

s. 19, amended: 1980, c.44, sch.4(S.); 1988, c.40, sch.12; repealed in pt.: *ibid.,* sch.13.

s. 19A, added: 1986, c.63, s.55; amended: 1988, c.4, sch.3.

s. 20, see *Savjani* v. *I.R.C.* [1981] 2 W.L.R. 636, C.A.; *Gurmit Singh Kambo* v. *Vaulkhard, The Times,* December 7, 1984, C.A.

s. 20, see *Alexander* v. *Home Office* 1099 I.R.L.R. 190, C.A.

ss. 20, 31, see *Commission for Racial Equality* v. *Riley,* July 5, 1982, H.H. Judge Da Cunha (sitting with assessors) Manchester C.C.

ss. 20, 43, see *Home Office* v. *Commission for Racial Equality* [1981] 2 W.L.R. 703; [1981] 1 All E.R. 1042, Woolf J.

s. 21, see *Alexander* v. *The Home Office* [1988] I.R.L.R. 190, C.A.

s. 30, see *Zarczynska* v. *Levy* [1979] 1 W.L.R. 125, E.A.T.; *Showboat Entertainment Centre* v. *Owens, The Times,* November 2, 1983, E.A.T.

ss. 30, 31, see *Commission for Racial Equality* v. *Imperial Society of Teachers of Dancing,* [1983] I.C.R. 473, E.A.T.

s. 32, see *Kingston* v. *British Railways Board* [1984] I.C.R. 781, C.A.; *Wadi* v. *Cornwall & Isles of Scilly Family Practitioner Committee* [1985] I.C.R. 492, E.A.T.; *Irving & Irving* v. *The Post Office* [1987] I.R.L.R. 289, C.A.

s. 37, amended: 1988, c.19, sch.3.

s. 41, see *Hampson* v. *Department of Education and Science* [1988] I.C.R. 278, E.A.T.

1976—cont.

74. Race Relations Act 1976—*cont.*

s. 47, see *West Midlands Passenger Transport Executive* v. *Singh* [1988] I.R.L.R. 186, C.A.

s. 47, order 83/1081.

s. 47, amended: 1988, c.50, s.137.

ss. 48–50, see *Hillingdon London Borough Council* v. *Commission for Racial Equality* [1982] 3 W.L.R. 159, H.L.

s. 49, see *R.* v. *The Commission for Racial Equality, ex p. Cottrell and Rothon* [1980] 3 All E.R. 265, D.C.

ss. 49, 50, see *Commission for Racial Equality* v. *Prestige Group* [1984] 1 W.L.R. 335, H.L.

ss. 49, 50, regs. 77/841.

s. 50, amended: 1984, c.28, sch.2.

s. 53, see *Alexander* v. *The Home Office* [1988] I.R.L.R. 190, C.A.

s. 54, see *Showboat Entertainment Centre* v. *Owens* [1984] I.C.R. 65, E.A.T.

s. 54, see *Zarczynska* v. *Levy* [1979] 1 W.L.R. 125, E.A.T.

s. 56, see *North West Thames Regional Health Authority* v. *Noone* [1987] I.R.L.R. 357, E.A.T.; *Noone* v. *North West Thames Regional Health Authority (No. 2), The Independent,* July 26, 1988, C.A.

s. 56, amended: 1978, c.44, sch.16.

ss. 56, 57, see *Bayoomi* v. *British Railways Board* [1981] I.R.L.R. 431, Industrial Tribunal.

s. 57, see *Gurmit Singh Kambo* v. *Vaulkhard, The Times,* December 7, 1984, C.A.; *Orphanos* v. *Queen Mary College* [1985] 2 All E.R. 233, H.L.; *Alexander* v. *The Home Office* [1988] I.R.L.R. 190, C.A.

s. 58, see *R.* v. *Commission for Racial Equality, ex p. Westminster City Council* [1985] I.C.R. 827, C.A.

s. 58, regs. 77/841.

s. 59, see *Commission for Racial Equality* v. *Amari Plastics* [1982] 2 All E.R. 499, C.A.

s. 63, see *Zarczynska* v. *Levy* [1979] 1 W.L.R. 125, E.A.T.; *Showboat Entertainment Centre* v. *Owens, The Times,* November 2, 1983, E.A.T.

ss. 63, 70, see *Commission for Racial Equality* v. *Riley,* July 5, 1982, H.H. Judge Da Cunha (sitting with assessors) Manchester C.C.

s. 65, see *Virdee* v. *E.C.C. Quarries* [1978] I.R.L.R. 296; *R.* v. *Wells Street JJ., ex p. Collett* [1981] R.T.R. 272, D.C.

s. 65, order 77/842.

s. 66, amended: 1978, c.44, sch.16; 1986, c.47, sch.8; 1988, c.34, sch.5.

s. 67, see *Alexander* v. *The Home Office* [1988] I.R.L.R. 190, C.A.

s. 67, orders 83/713; 84/297, 1075.

s. 68, see *Jalota* v. *Imperial Metal Industry (Kynoch)* [1979] I.R.L.R. 313, E.A.T.; *Lupetti* v. *Wrens Old House* [1984] I.C.R. 348, E.A.T.; *Doff* v. *British Telecom* [1988] I.R.L.R. 16, E.A.T.

s. 70, repealed: 1986, c.64, sch.3.

s. 71, see *Wheeler* v. *Leicester City Council* [1985] 3 W.L.R. 335, H.L.; *R.* v. *Lewisham Borough Council, ex p. Shell U.K.* [1988] 1 All E.R. 938, D.C.

1976—cont.

74. Race Relations Act 1976—cont.

s. 71, amended: 1985, c.51, sch.14; order 85/1884; 1988, c.4, sch.6; repealed in pt. (prosp.): 1988, c.40, sch.13.

s. 72, see Orphanos v. Queen Mary College [1985] 2 All E.R. 233, H.L.

s. 74, orders 77/842; 87/929.

s. 75, see Home Office v. Commission for Racial Equality [1981] 2 W.L.R. 703; [1981] 1 All E.R. 1042, Woolf J.; Alexander v. The Home Office [1988] I.R.L.R. 190, C.A.

s. 75, regs. 77/1774; 83/1773; 84/218; 85/1309, 1757.

s. 75, repealed in pt.: 1981, c.55, sch.5.

s. 78, see Tanna v. Post Office [1981] I.C.R. 374, E.A.T.; Daley v. Allied Suppliers [1983] I.C.R. 90, E.A.T.; Wadi v. Cornwall and Isles of Scilly Family Practitioner Committee [1985] I.C.R. 492, E.A.T.

s. 78, regs. 77/841.

s. 78, amended: 1980, c.44, sch.4 (S.); repealed in pt.: 1982, c.10, schs.3,4; 1988, c.40, sch.13.

s. 79, see Commission for Racial Equality v. Ealing London Borough Council [1978] 1 W.L.R. 112, C.A.

s. 79, orders 77/680, 840.

s. 79, repealed in pt.: 1986, c.64, sch.3.

sch. 2, see Commission for Racial Equality v. Ind Coope, May 9, 1978, Judge Ruttle, Westminster County Ct.; Commission for Racial Equality v. Ealing London Borough Council [1978] 1 W.L.R. 112, C.A.; amended: 1978, c.44, sch.16.

sch. 3, repealed in pt.: 1978, c.44, sch.17.

75. Development of Rural Wales Act 1976.

Royal Assent, November 22, 1976.

s. 3, regs. 77/1896.

s. 3, amended: 1978, c.52, sch.11.

ss. 5, 19, regs. 77/1378.

s. 6, amended: 1981, c.67, sch.4; repealed in pt.: ibid., sch.6.

s. 7, repealed: 1980, c.63, sch.2.

s. 8, amended: 1985, c.71, sch.2; 1988, c.50, sch.17.

s. 10, amended: 1983, c.29, s.4, sch.2.

s. 12, order 80/235

s. 12, amended: order 80/235; 1981, c.6, s.2; repealed in pt.: ibid., s.2, sch.

s. 13A, order 86/1509.

s. 13A, added: 1985, c.5, sch.2.

s. 17, amended: 1988, c.19, sch.3.

s. 18, repealed: 1980, c.51, sch.26.

ss. 19, 20, repealed: 1982, c 24, sch.5.

s. 22, repealed in pt.: 1980, c.51, sch.26; 1982, c.24, sch.5.

s. 25, regs. 77/1896.

s. 28, amended: 1981, c.67, sch.4.

s. 29, regs. 77/1896.

s. 31, repealed: 1985, c.54, sch.27.

s. 34, amended: 1987, c.3, sch.1; repealed in pt.: 1984, c.12, sch.4; 1986, c.31, sch.6; c.44, sch.9.

s. 35, orders 76/2038; 77/116.

1976—cont.

75. Development of Rural Wales Act 1976—cont.

sch. 1, amended: 1978, c.52, sch.11.

sch. 2, regs. 77/1896.

schs. 2, 6, amended: 1978, c.44, sch.16.

sch. 3, regs. 77/1378.

sch. 3, functions transferred: order 81/238; amended: 1980, c.66, sch.24; 1981, c.38, sch.3; 1984, c.12, sch.4; c.57, sch.1; 1987, c.3, sch.1; repealed in pt.: 1984, c.12, sch.7; 1985, c.71, sch.1; 1986, c.44, sch.9.

sch. 4, repealed in pt.: 1979, c.46, sch.5; 1981, c.67, sch.6.

sch. 5, repealed in pt.: 1980, c.51, sch.26; 1982, c.24, sch.5.

sch. 6, regs. 77/1896.

sch. 7, repealed in pt.: 1977, c.42, sch.25; 1980, c.65, sch.34; 1981, c.64, sch.13; 1983, c.23, sch.5; 1985, c.71, sch.1.

76. Energy Act 1976.

Royal Assent, November 22, 1976.

s. 1, orders 77/2; 79/199, 797, 1383; 80/1013, 1253.

s. 4, order 77/1870.

s. 6, orders 76/2162; 80/1609; 82/968; 83/909.

s. 7, order 80/1253.

s. 8, repealed: 1982, c.23, s.12, sch.4.

ss. 9–11, substituted: ibid., sch.3.

ss. 9, 12, amended: 1986, c.44, sch.7.

s. 13, repealed: 1980, c.37, s.1.

s. 14, order 87/2175.

s. 14, repealed in pt.: 1983, c.25, sch.4.

s. 15, order 77/1603.

s. 17, orders 76/2162; 77/2, 1870; 79/193.

s. 17, amended: 1982, c.23, sch.3.

s. 18, repealed in pt.: ibid., sch.4; 1986, c.44, sch.9.

s. 21, amended: 1982, c.52, sch.3; 1984, c.57, sch.1.

s. 22, orders 77/1870; 80/1253.

s. 23, orders 76/1964, 2127; 77/652.

sch. 1, amended: 1980, c.34, sch.5; 1981, c.14, sch.7; 1985, c.67, sch.1; 1988, c.54, sch.3; repealed in pt.: 1980, c 34, sch.9; 1985, c.67, schs.1,8.

sch. 4, order 80/1253.

77. Weights and Measures etc. Act 1976.

Royal Assent, November 22, 1976.

repealed, except ss. 12–14, 15 (in pt.), sch. 6: 1985, c.72, sch.13.

s. 8, sch. 4, see Gaunt v. Nelson [1987] R.T.R. 1, D.C.

s. 12, amended: order 81/231; 1984, c.30, sch.10; 1985, c.72, sch.12.

s. 13, amended: order 79/1573.

s. 14, amended: order 81/231; 1985, c.72, sch.12.

sch. 5, S.R. 1978 No. 20.

sch. 6, amended: order 81/231; 1984, c.30, sch.10; 1985, c.72, sch.12.

78. Industrial Common Ownership Act 1976.

Royal Assent, November 22, 1976.

s. 1, regs. 77/1386.

s. 2, amended: 1985, c.9, sch.2.

CAP.

1976—cont.

79. Dock Work Regulation Act 1976.
Royal Assent, November 22, 1976.
s. 2, amended: 1981, c.56, sch.5; repealed in pt.: *ibid.*, sch.12.
s. 3, orders 80/1703; 81/1556; amended: 1981, c.21, s.2; orders 80/1703; 81/1556.
ss. 7, 8, repealed in pt.: 1981, c.56, sch.12.
s. 14, sch. 1, amended: 1978, c.44, sch.16; repealed in pt.: *ibid.*, sch.17.
s. 15, repealed in pt.: 1980, c.42, sch.2.
s. 17, orders 77/1122, 1775.
sch. 1, amended: 1985, c.9, sch.2.

80. Rent (Agriculture) Act 1976.
Royal Assent, November 22, 1976.
s. 1, see *Lord Glendyne* v. *Rapley* [1978] 1 W.L.R. 601, C.A.; *Earl of Normanton* v. *Giles* [1980] 1 W.L.R. 28, H.L.
s. 1, order 76/2124.
ss. 2, 4, see *Skinner* v. *Cooper* [1979] 1 W.L.R. 666, C.A.
s. 3, amended: 1980, c.51, s.76.
s. 4, see *Durman* v. *Bell, The Times,* February 5, 1988, C.A.
s. 4, amended: 1977, c.42, sch.23; 1980, c.51, s.76; 1988, c.50, s.39, sch.4; repealed in pt.: *ibid.*, schs.4,18.
s. 5, amended: 1977, c.42, sch.23; 1980, c.51, s.73; 1981, c.64, sch.12; 1985, c.51, sch.14; c.71, sch.2; order 85/1884; 1988, c.4, sch.6; c.50, sch.17; repealed in pt.: 1985, c.51, sch.17, 1988, c.40, sch.13 (prosp.).
s. 7, amended: 1981, c.64, s.75, sch.25.
s. 8, amended: 1984, c.28, sch.2.
s. 9, amended: 1977, c.42, sch.23; 1986, c.5, sch.14.
s. 13, regs. 80/1697; 84/1391.
s. 13, amended: 1977, c.42, sch.23, 1980, c.51, s.61, sch.25; repealed in pt.: 1988, c.50, sch.18.
s. 15, repealed: order 87/264.
s. 19, amended: 1977, c.42, sch.23.
s. 25, amended: 1982, c.48, sch.3
s. 27, amended: 1977, c.42, sch.23; 1985, c.71, sch.2; 1988, c.50, s.26, repealed in pt.: 1985, c.51, sch.17.
ss. 27–29, see *R.* v. *Agricultural Dwelling-House Advisory Committee for Bedfordshire, Cambridgeshire and Northamptonshire, ex p. Brough* (1987) 282 E.G. 1542; (1987) 19 H.L.R. 367, Hodgson J.
s. 28, amended: 1977, c.17, s.1; 1988, c.50, sch.17.
s. 32, order 77/41.
s. 32, repealed: 1982, c.24, sch.5.
ss. 33, 34, amended: 1977, c.42, sch.23.
s. 40, repealed in pt.: *ibid.*, sch.25.
sch. 2, amended: *ibid.*, sch.23; 1986, c.63, sch.4.
sch. 3, order 77/1268.
sch. 4, amended: 1977, c.42, sch.23; 1985, c.71, sch.2; 1986, c.63, sch.4; repealed in pt.: 1980, c.51, sch.25; 1988, c.50, sch.18.
sch. 5, amended: 1977, c.42, sch.23; c.43, sch.1; 1985, c.71, sch.2.
sch. 6, repealed: order 87/264.

CAP.

1976—cont.

80. Rent (Agriculture) Act 1976—*cont.*
sch. 7, repealed: 1982, c.24, sch.5.
sch. 8, repealed in pt.: 1977, c.43, s.12, sch.3; 1981, c.24, sch.3; c.64, sch.13; c.67, sch.6; 1984, c.28, sch.4; 1985, c.71, sch.1.
sch. 9, see *Skinner* v. *Cooper* [1979] 1 W.L.R. 666, C.A.

81. Education Act 1976.
Royal Assent, November 22, 1976.
ss. 1–3, repealed: 1979, c.49, s.1.
s. 2, see *North Yorkshire County Council* v. *Secretary of State for Education and Science, The Times,* October 20, 1978, Browne-Wilkinson J.
ss. 4, 5, repealed: 1980, c.20, sch.7.
s. 5, regs. 77/1443.
s. 5, repealed in pt.: 1980, c.20, s.28.
ss. 7–9, repealed: *ibid.*, sch 7.
s. 10, repealed: 1981, c.60, sch.4.

82. Sexual Offences (Amendment) Act 1976.
Royal Assent, November 22, 1976.
s. 1, see *R.* v. *Gaston* (1981) 73 Cr.App.R. 164, C.A.; *R.* v. *Olugboja* [1981] 3 W.L.R. 585, C.A.; *R.* v. *Pigg* [1982] 1 W.L.R. 762; *R.* v. *Woods* (1982) 74 Cr.App.R. 312, C.A.; *R.* v. *Satnam*; *R.* v. *Kewal* (1984) 78 Cr.App.R. 149, C.A.
ss. 1, 2, see *R.* v. *Barton* (1987) 85 Cr.App.R. 5, C.A.
s. 2, see *R.* v. *Lawrence* [1977] Crim.L.R. 492, May J.; *R.* v. *Hinds and Butler* [1979] Crim.L.R. 111, Northampton Crown Ct.; *R.* v. *Mills* (1978) 68 Cr.App.R. 327, C.A.; *R.* v. *Fenton*; *R.* v. *Neal* [1980] Crim.L.R. 573; (1980) 71 Cr.App.R. 307, C.A.; *R.* v. *Viola* [1982] 1 W.L.R. 1138, C.A.; *R.* v. *Breckenridge* (1984) 79 Cr.App.R. 244, C.A.; *R.* v. *Taylor (R.P.)* (1985) 80 Cr.App.R. 327, C.A.; *R.* v. *Haughian* (1985) 80 Cr.App.R. 334, C.A.; *R.* v. *Cox (David)* (1987) 84 Cr.App.R. 132, C.A.
s. 3, amended: 1980, c.43, sch.7; 1981, c.55, sch.2.
s. 4, see *R.* v. *Gilligan* [1987] Crim.L.R. 501, Nottingham Crown Ct., Boreham J.
s. 4, amended: 1984, c.46, sch.5; 1988, c.33, s.158; repealed in pt.: 1984, c.46, schs.5,6; 1988, c.33, s.158, sch.16.
s. 5, amended: 1984, c.46, sch.5; 1988, c.33, sch.15; repealed in pt.: *ibid.*, sch.16.
s. 6, repealed: *ibid.*, s.158, sch.16.
ss. 5, 6, amended: *ibid.*, sch.5.
s. 7, see *R.* v. *Gaston* (1981) 73 Cr.App.R. 164, C.A.
s. 7, order 78/485.
s. 7, amended: 1988, c.33, s.158, sch.15; repealed in pt.: *ibid.*, sch.16.

83. Health Services Act 1976.
Royal Assent, November 22, 1976.
regs. 80/1202.
s. 1, regs. 77/323.
s. 1, repealed: 1980, c.53, s.9, sch.7.
s. 2, amended: 1977, c.49, sch.15; repealed: *ibid.*, sch.16.
ss. 2, 4, 5, 7–11, repealed (S.): 1978, c.29, sch.17.

CAP.

1976—cont.

83. Health Services Act 1976—cont.
ss. 3, 6, repealed: 1980, c.53, sch.7.
ss. 4, 5, repealed: 1977, c.49, sch.16.
ss. 7–11, repealed: ibid.
s. 12, amended: 1980, c.53, ss.12,13, sch.2.
s. 13, amended: 1977, c.49, sch.15; 1980, c.53, schs.2,3.
s. 14, regs. 77/643, 644; 80/1192, 1201.
s. 14, amended: 1977, c.49, sch.15; 1978, c.52, sch.11; 1980, c.53, s.14, sch.2; repealed in pt.: ibid., schs.2,7.
s. 16, regs. 77/644, 673; 80/1201, 1241; amended: 1980, c.53, schs.2,3; repealed in pt.: ibid., sch.7.
s. 17, amended: ibid., sch.2.
s. 18, amended: ibid., sch.3.
s. 19, repealed in pt.: 1984, c.23, sch.3; c.36, sch.5.
s. 20, amended: 1980, c.53, sch.3.
s. 21, repealed in pt.: ibid., sch.7.
s. 22, regs. 77/643, 644, 673.
s. 22, repealed in pt.: 1980, c.53, schs.2,7.
s. 23, order 81/1473.
s. 23, amended: 1978, c.29, sch.16(S.); 1980, c.53, sch.3; repealed in pt.: 1977, c.49, sch.16; 1978, c.29, sch.17; 1980, c.53, sch.7.
s. 24, repealed in pt.: ibid.
sch. 1, regs. 77/323.
sch. 1, repealed: 1980, c.53, s.9, sch.7.
sch. 2, repealed: ibid., sch.7.
sch. 3, repealed: 1977, c.49, sch.16; 1978, c.29, sch.17(S.).
sch. 4, repealed in pt.: 1977, c.49, sch.16; 1978, c.29, sch.17(S.).
84. Consolidated Fund (No. 2) Act 1976.
Royal Assent, December 22, 1976.
repealed: 1978, c.57, sch.(C.).
85. National Insurance Surcharge Act 1976.
Royal Assent, December 22, 1976.
repealed: 1984, c.43, sch.23.
86. Fishery Limits Act 1976.
Royal Assent, December 22, 1976.
s. 2, see Mackenzie v. Uribe, 1983 S.L.T. 492.
s. 2, orders 76/2216–2225; 77/623, 941, 1084, 1292, 1568, 1637; 78/191, 288, 490, 767, 772, 1168, 1650, 1651, 1950; 79/504; 85/244; 86/382.
s. 2, repealed in pt.: 1981, c.29, sch.5; 1984, c.26, sch.2; 1988, c.12, sch.7.
s. 6, orders 77/1292, 1568, 1637, 2087; 78/490, 767, 772, 1168, 1650, 1651, 1950; 79/504; 85/244; 86/382.
s. 8, amended: 1988, c.12, sch.6.
s. 11, orders 77/1244; 78/280, 281.
s. 12, orders 78/1404, 1405, 1525, 1526.
sch. 1, repealed in pt.: 1981, c.29, sch.5.
sch. 2, repealed in pt.: 1979, c.45, sch.7; 1981, c.29, sch.5; order 81/227; 1984, c.26, sch.2; 1988, c.12, sch.7.
sch. 3, order 85/244.

1977

1. Consolidated Fund Act 1977.
Royal Assent, March 17, 1977.

CAP.

1977—cont.

2. Covent Garden Market (Financial Provisions) Act 1977.
Royal Assent, March 17, 1977.
3. Aircraft and Shipbuilding Industries Act 1977.
Royal Assent, March 17, 1977.
order 81/1726.
s. 1, regs. 77/625, 626.
s. 1, amended: 1980, c.33, s.20; repealed in pt.: 1980, c.26, s.10, sch.3.
s. 2, repealed: 1983, c.15, s.1, sch.
s. 3, amended: 1983, c.15, s.1; order 83/1076; 1985, c.9, sch.2; 1986, c.60, sch. 16; repealed in pt.: 1980, c.26, s.10; c.63, sch.2; 1986, c.60, schs.16,17.
s. 4, repealed in pt.: 1980, c.26, s.10.
ss. 4A, 4B, added: 1983, c.15, s.2.
s. 5, repealed: ibid., sch.
s. 6, amended: 1982, c.46, sch.3; repealed in pt.: 1980, c.26, s.10.
s. 7, repealed in pt.: ibid., s.10, sch.3.
ss. 8, 9, repealed in pt.: ibid., sch.3.
s. 11, orders 79/961; 80/1203, 1208; 83/1076; 84/909; 85/327; 86/2258; 88/1401.
s. 11, amended: 1979, c.59, s.1; 1982, c.4, s.1; order 80/1208; 1983, c.58, s.1; orders 84/909; 85/327; 1986, c.19, s.1; 1987, c.52, s.1; order 88/1401; repealed in pt.: 1980, c.26, sch.3.
s. 13, amended: 1983, c.29, s.4, sch.2.
ss. 13–15, repealed in pt.: 1980, c.26, sch.3.
s. 17, amended: 1985, c.9, sch.2.
s. 18, amended: 1980, c.33, s.20; 1983, c.15, s.1; repealed in pt.: ibid., s.1, sch.
s. 20, see Anglomar Shipping Co. v. Swan Hunter Shipbuilders and Swan Hunter Group; The London Lion [1980] 2 Lloyd's Rep. 456, C.A.
s. 23, amended: 1985, c.9, sch.2.
ss. 23–25, see Hawker Siddeley Aviation v. Hawker Siddeley Group [1983] Com.L.R. 248, H.L.
s. 40, regs. 77/754.
ss. 40, 41, 44, repealed in pt.: 1980, c.26, s.10.
s. 42, rules 77/1020.
ss. 45, 46, repealed: 1980, c.26, sch.3.
s. 48, amended: 1983, c.15, s.1.
ss. 48, 49, repealed in pt.: 1980, c.26, s.10, sch.3.
s. 49, regs. 77/1329; 78/232; amended: 1978, c.44, sch.16.
s. 50, amended: ibid.; repealed in pt.: ibid., s.10.
s. 53, see Anglomar Shipping Co. v. Swan Hunter Shipbuilders and Swan Hunter Group; The London Lion [1980] 2 Lloyd's Rep. 456, C.A.
s. 53, repealed in pt.: 1980, c.26, s.10; 1983, c.15, s.2, sch.
s. 56, orders 77/539, 540.
s. 56, amended: 1985, c.9, sch.2; repealed in pt.: 1980, c.42, sch.2.
sch. 5, repealed in pt.: 1980, c.26, s.10.
sch. 7, rules 77/1020, 1022.
4. Roe Deer (Close Seasons) Act 1977.
Royal Assent, March 17, 1977.

1977—cont.

5. Social Security (Miscellaneous Provisions) Act 1977.
Royal Assent, March 30, 1977.
see *McDougall* v. *Secretary of State for Social Services; McIntyre* v. *Secretary of State for Social Services, House of Lords, May 14, 1981.*
s. 1, regs. 77/1707; 83/10; orders 77/2180; 79/676; 80/1975; 84/77.
s. 1, repealed in pt.: 1980, c.30, sch.5.
s. 3, repealed in pt.: 1979, c.18, sch.3.
s. 4, amended: *ibid.*, sch.1.
s. 5, repealed in pt.: *ibid.*, sch.3; 1985, c.53, sch.6.
s. 7, repealed: 1980, c.39, sch.
s. 8, repealed in pt.: 1980, c.30, sch.5.
s. 9, repealed: 1986, c.50, sch.11.
s. 10, schemes 77/993, 1063.
s. 11, scheme 77/1063.
s. 11, repealed in pt.: 1980, c.30, sch.5.
s. 12, orders 77/1630; 78/278, 1902; 79/113, 1312; 80/1080, 1081, 1955; 81/1110, 1672; 82/845, 1077; 83/883, 1116, 1521; 84/1154, 1687; 85/1201; 86/592; 87/165; 88/248.
s. 13, regs. 77/1229; 78/743; amended: 1977, c.49, sch.15; 1978, c.29, sch.16(S.); 1979, c.18, sch.3.
s. 14, repealed in pt.: 1980, c.30, sch.5; 1981, c.33, s.8.
ss. 14, 15, regs. 77/619.
s. 15, repealed: 1980, c.30, sch.5.
s. 16, repealed: 1978, c.44, sch.17.
s. 17, repealed in pt.: 1986, c.50, sch.11.
s. 18, regs. 77/622.
s. 18 amended: 1978, c.44, sch.16; 1986, c.50, sch.10; repealed in pt.: *ibid.*, sch.11.
s. 19, repealed: *ibid.*
s. 21, regs. 77/1188; 83/338; 84/380; 85/1323; 86/1716.
s. 21, amended: 1980, c.30, s.3; 1981, c.33, sch.2; 1985, c.53, sch.3; 1986, c.50, sch.8.
s. 22, regs. 77/956, 1188; 83/186, 338; 84/107, 240, 380; 85/1323; 86/1716.
s. 22, amended: 1980, c.30, s.3, sch.4; c.39, s.7; repealed in pt.: 1980, c.30, sch.5; 1981, c.33, s.8; c.57, schs.2,3; 1983, c.41, sch.10; 1984, c.48, sch.8; 1985, c.53, sch.6; 1986, c.50, sch.11; 1988, c.19, sch.4.
s. 24, regs. 77/619, 638, 1229; 84/107, 240, 380; 85/1323.
s. 24, repealed in pt.: 1980, c.30, sch.5.
s. 25, orders 77/617, 618.
sch. 1, scheme 77/1063; repealed in pt.: schemes 77/991, 992.

6. International Finance, Trade and Aid Act 1977.
Royal Assent, March 30, 1977.
repealed: 1980, c.63, sch.2.

7. Nuclear Industry (Finance) Act 1977.
Royal Assent, March 30, 1977.
s. 2, orders 81/487; 87/165; amended: 1981, c.71, s.1; orders 81/487; 87/165.
s. 3, amended: 1985, c.9, sch.2.

1977—cont.

8. Job Release Act 1977.
Royal Assent, March 30, 1977.
s. 1, continued in force: order 85/1128.
s. 1, orders 78/1007; 79/957; 80/937; 81/874; 82/910; 83/1214; 84/77, 950; 86/1291; 87/1339; continued in force: 81/874; 82/910; 83/1214; 84/77; 86/1291; 87/1339.

9. Representation of the People Act 1977.
Royal Assent, March 30, 1977.
repealed: 1983, c.2, sch.9.

10. Town and Country Planning (Scotland) Act 1977.
Royal Assent, March 30, 1977.
s. 4, see *Central Regional Council* v. *Clackmannan District Council,* 1983 S.L.T. 666; *Earl Car Sales (Edinburgh)* v. *City of Edinburgh District Council,* First Division, June 3, 1982.

11. General Rate (Public Utilities) Act 1977.
Royal Assent, March 30, 1977.

12. Agricultural Holdings (Notices to Quit) Act 1977.
Royal Assent, March 30, 1977.
repealed: 1986, c.5, sch.15.
s. 1, see *Parsons* v. *Parsons* [1983] 1 W.L.R. 1390, Donald Rattee Q.C.
s. 2, see *Thomas* v. *Official Solicitor* (1983) 265 E.G. 601, C.A.; *Harding* v. *Marshall* (1983) 267 E.G. 161, C.A.; *Parrish* v. *Kinsey* (1983) 268 E.G. 1113, C.A.; *Parsons* v. *Parsons* [1983] 1 W.L.R. 1390, Donald Rattee Q.C.; *Dickinson* v. *Boucher* (1984) 269 E.G. 1159, C.A.; *Sumnal* v. *Statt* (1984) 271 E.G. 628, C.A.; *Sykes* v. *Land* (1984) 271 E.G. 1265, C.A.; *Featherstone* v. *Staples* [1986] 2 All E.R. 461, C.A.; *Burton* v. *Timmis* (1987) E.G. 795, C.A.; *Cawley* v. *Pratt* [1988] 33 E.G. 54, C.A.; *Gisborne* v. *Burton* [1988] 38 E.G. 129, C.A.
s. 2, regs. 78/258; 84/1308.
ss. 2–4, see *Clegg* v. *Fraser* (1982) 264 E.G. 144, McCullough J.
s. 3, see *Wickington* v. *Bonney* (1983) 266 E.G. 434; (1984) 47 P. & C.R. 655, Stephen Brown J.; *Gisborne* v. *Burton* [1988] 38 E.G. 129, C.A.
s. 5, orders 78/257; 84/1300.
s. 11, order 78/257.
s. 15, order 78/246.

13. British Airways Board Act 1977.
Royal Assent, March 30, 1977.
repealed: 1980, c.60, sch.3.
s. 9, amended: 1980, c.60, s.2; 1982, c.1, s.2.
ss. 9, 21, order 80/500.
s. 11, amended: 1983, c.29, s.4, sch.2.

14. Returning Officers (Scotland) Act 1977.
Royal Assent, May 26, 1977.
repealed: 1983, c.2, sch.9.
s. 4, order 77/1162.

15. Marriage (Scotland) Act 1977.
Royal Assent, May 26, 1977.
s. 2, see *H.M. Advocate* v. *J.M.R.,* 1985, S.C.C.R. 330.
s. 2, amended: 1986, c.9, sch.1; c.16, sch.2; repealed in pt.: 1986, c.9, sch.2.
s. 3, regs. 77/1671, 1893; 79/144; 80/241; 81/204; 82/193; 83/1796; 85/1889; 86/1622, 1954, 2255.

1977—cont.

15. Marriage (Scotland) Act 1977—cont.
s. 3, amended: regs. 77/1893; 1986, c.16, sch.2; c.55, sch.1.
s. 4, regs. 77/1671.
s. 5, amended: 1986, c.16, sch.2.
s. 6, regs. 77/1671.
s. 6, amended: 1980, c.55, s.22; 1986, c.16, sch.2.
s. 7, regs. 77/1671.
s. 7, amended: 1986, c.16, sch.2.
s. 8, regs. 77/1670.
s. 8, amended: 1980, c.55, sch.3.
s. 13, repealed in pt.: 1980, c.55, s.22, sch.3.
ss. 13, 23A, see Saleh v. Saleh (O.H.), 1987 S.L.T. 633.
s. 16, regs. 77/1671.
s. 19, regs. 77/1893; 79/144; 80/241; 81/204; 82/193; 85/1889; 86/2255; amended: regs. 77/1893.
s. 23A, added: 1980, c.55, s.22.
s. 25, regs. 77/1893; 79/144; 80/241; 81/204; 82/193; 83/1796; 85/1889; 86/2255.
s. 26, regs. 77/1893; 80/241; 83/1796; 85/1889; 86/1622, 1954, 2255.
s. 26, amended: 1986, c.55, sch.1.
sch. 1, amended: 1986, c.16, sch.2.
s. 2, repealed in pt.: 1988, c.44, sch.

16. New Towns (Scotland) Act 1977.
Royal Assent, May 26, 1977.
s. 1, order 77/1343.
s. 3, regs. 79/98; amended: 1978, c.44, sch.16.

17. Rent (Agricultural) Amendment Act 1977.
Royal Assent, May 26, 1977.

18. Statute Law (Repeals) Act 1977.
Royal Assent, June 16, 1977.
s. 4, order 84/1692.
sch. 2, repealed in pt.: 1980, c.9, sch.10.

19. Restrictive Trade Practices Act 1977.
Royal Assent, June 30, 1977.

20. Transport (Financial Provisions) Act 1977.
Royal Assent, June 30, 1977.
s. 2, repealed: 1980, c.34, sch.9.
s. 3, repealed: 1981, c.12, s.1.

21. Passenger Vehicles (Experimental Areas) Act 1977.
Royal Assent, July 22, 1977.
repealed: 1981, c.14, sch.8.
s. 1, orders 77/1554, 1835; 80/413; 81/914, 1439.
s. 2, sch., amended: 1980, c.34, sch.5.

22. Redundancy Rebates Act 1977.
Royal Assent, July 22, 1977.
repealed: 1978, c.44, sch.17.
s. 1, order 77/1321.
s. 2, order 77/294; S.R. 1985 No. 146; amended: order 79/1573.

23. New Towns Act 1977.
Royal Assent, July 22, 1977.
repealed: 1981, c.64, sch.13.

24. Merchant Shipping (Safety Convention) Act 1977.
Royal Assent, July 23, 1977.
s. 1, order 81/1540.
s. 1, amended: regs. 81/568; 85/212; repealed in pt.: regs. 80/536.
s. 4, regs. 80/531, 532; order 80/528.

1977—cont.

25. Minibus Act 1977.
Royal Assent, July 22, 1977.
repealed: 1981, c.14, sch.8.
s. 1, regs. 77/1709; orders 78/1930; 80/1356; 81/1037; repealed in pt.: 1978, c.55, sch.4.
ss. 1, 3, amended: 1980, c.34, s.33.
s. 3, regs. 77/1708, 2103; 78/1931; orders 80/1357; 81/195.
s. 4, amended: 1980, c.34, s.33, sch.5.

26. Licensing (Amendment) Act 1977.
Royal Assent, July 22, 1977.

27. Presumption of Death (Scotland) Act 1977.
Royal Assent, July 22, 1977.
s. 12, regs. 78/160.
s. 15, see Horak v. Lord Advocate, 1984 S.L.T. 201.
s. 15, Acts of Sederunt 78/161, 162.
s. 20, order 78/159.

28. Control of Food Premises (Scotland) Act 1977.
Royal Assent, July 22, 1977.
s. 9, order 78/172.

29. Town and Country Planning (Amendment) Act 1977.
Royal Assent, July 22, 1977.
s. 1, see Scott Markets v. Waltham Forest London Borough [1979] J.P.L. 96, Mars-Jones J.

30. Rentcharges Act 1977.
Royal Assent, July 22, 1977.
ss. 4, 8, 9, 12, 15, regs. 78/16.
s. 10, amended: 1984, c.28, sch.2.
s. 18, order 78/15.

31. Farriers (Registration) (Amendment) Act 1977.
Royal Assent, July 22, 1977.

32. Torts (Interference with Goods) Act 1977.
Royal Assent, July 22, 1977.
s. 1, amended: 1987, c.43, sch.4.
ss. 2, 6, see Lewis Trusts v. Bambers Stores [1983] F.S.R. 453, C.A.
s. 3, see Hillesden Securities v. Ryjack, [1983] 2 All E.R. 184, Parker J.; Secretary of State for Defence v. Guardian Newspapers, The Times, October 26, 1984, H.L.; Rubycliff v. Plastic Engineers [1986] R.P.C. 573, Browne-Wilkinson V.-C.
s. 4, see Perry (Howard E.) & Co. v. British Railways Board [1980] 2 All E.R. 579, Megarry V.-C.; Thaper v. Singh [1987] FLR 369, C.A.
s. 4, amended: 1981, c.54, sch.5; 1984, c.28, sch.2.
s. 5, see Macaulay v. Screenkarn [1987] F.S.R. 257, Falconer J.
s. 6, see Highland Leasing v. Paul Field (T/A Field Machinery), December 6, 1985, R. M. Stewart Q.C.
s. 8, see De Franco v. Commissioner of Police for the Metropolis, The Times, May 8, 1987, C.A.
ss. 9, 14, amended: 1984, c.28, sch.2.
s. 10, see Adventure Film Productions v. Tully, The Times, October 14, 1982, Whitford J.
s. 17, orders 77/1910; 78/627; 80/2024.

CAP.
1977—cont.
33. Price Commission Act 1977.
Royal Assent, July 22, 1977.
repealed, except ss. 16, 17: 1980, c.21, sch.2.
s. 5, regs. 77/1221.
s. 7, order 78/445.
s. 9, regs. 77/1282; 79/229.
s. 11, orders 78/1307, 1716.
s. 12, orders 78/1307; 79/129.
s. 13, regs. 77/1224.
s. 15, regs. 77/1220.
s. 16, order 78/1389.
s. 17, order 77/1302.
s. 22, regs. 77/1220, 1221, 1224; 79/229; order 77/1285.
sch. 2, regs. 77/1220.
34. Northern Ireland (Emergency Provisions) (Amendment) Act 1977.
Royal Assent, July 22, 1977.
repealed: 1978, c.5, sch.6.
35. Appropriation Act 1977.
Royal Assent, July 29, 1977.
36. Finance Act 1977.
Royal Assent, July 29, 1977.
s. 1, repealed in pt.: 1977, c.36, sch.9; 1979, c.4, sch.4.
s. 2, order 77/1979; regs. 77/2042; repealed in pt.: 1977, c.36, sch.9; 1979, c.7, sch.2.
s. 3, amended: 1979, c.7, s.11; repealed in pt.: ibid., sch.2.
s. 4, repealed: 1979, c.5, sch.7.
ss. 5, 6, repealed in pt.: 1980, c.48, sch 20; 1985, c.54, sch.27.
s. 7, orders 77/1866, 1936; 79/241, 1489.
s. 8, regs. 77/2042.
ss. 8, 9, repealed: 1979, c.2, sch.6.
s. 10, regs. 77/1404.
s. 10, amended: 1979, c.3, sch.2.
s. 11, amended: 1980, c.48, s.17.
s. 12, repealed: 1979, c.3, sch.3.
ss. 13, 15, 21, repealed: 1978, c.42, sch.13.
ss. 14, 16, repealed: 1983, c.55, sch.11.
ss. 17–32, repealed: 1988, c.1, sch.31.
s. 31, sch. 7, see Robins (Inspector of Taxes) v. Durkin, The Times, May 12, 1988, Knox J.
s. 33, see Vertigan v. Brady (Inspector of Taxes) [1988] S.T.C. 91, Knox J.
s. 40, repealed: 1979, c.14, sch.8.
ss. 41, 42, amended: ibid., sch.7.
s. 43, repealed: ibid., sch.8.
s. 44, repealed: 1978, c.42, sch.13.
ss. 45–48, repealed: 1988, c.1, sch.31.
s. 49, repealed: 1983, c.49, sch.2.
s. 50, repealed: 1982, c.39, sch.22.
s. 51, repealed: 1981, c.35, sch.19; repealed in pt.: 1982, c.39, sch.22.
ss. 52, 53, repealed: 1984, c.51, sch.9.
s. 55, repealed: 1985, c.54, sch.27.
s. 57, repealed: 1984, c.43, sch.23.
s. 58, order 77/1937.
s. 58, repealed: 1987, c.16, sch.16.
s. 59, amended: 1979, c.2, sch.4; repealed in pt.: 1979, c.14, sch.8; 1983, c.49, sch.2; 1984, c.51, sch.9.
schs. 1, 2, repealed: 1979, c.4, sch.4.

CAP.
1977—cont.
36. Finance Act 1977—cont.
sch. 4, see R. v. Department of Transport, ex p. Lakeland Plastics (Windermere) [1983] R.T.R. 82, D.C.
schs. 4, 5, repealed: 1980, c.48, sch.20.
sch. 6, repealed: 1983, c.55, sch.11.
sch. 7, see Hoye v. Forsdyke, The Times, July 15, 1981, Vinelott J.; Varnum v. Deeble [1985] S.T.C. 308, C.A.; Platten v. Brown [1986] S.T.C. 514, Hoffmann J.
schs. 7, 8, repealed: 1988, c.1, sch.31.
37. Patents Act 1977.
Royal Assent, July 29, 1977.
see Wavin Pipes v The Hepworth Iron Co. [1982] F.S.R. 32, Costello J.; Agfa-Gevaert (Engelsmann) AG Application [1982] R.P.C. 441, Falconer J.; Pfizer Inc. v. Jiwa International (H.K.) Co. [1988] R.P.C. 15, Supreme Ct. of H.K.
s. 1, see Imperial Chemical Industries (Richardson's) Appn. [1981] F.S.R. 609, Falconer J.; Merrill Lynch Inc.'s Application [1988] R.P.C. 1, Falconer J.
ss. 1–3, see Ward's Applications [1986] R.P.C. 50, Patent Office.
ss. 1, 3, see Genentech Inc.'s Patent [1988] R.P.C. 553, Whitford J.
s. 2, see Sopharma S.A's Application [1983] R.P.C. 195, Patent Office; Furr v. Truline (C.D.) (Building Products) [1985] F.S.R. 553, Falconer J.; L'Oreal's Application [1986] R.P.C. 19, Whitford J.; James Industries' Patent [1987] R.P.C. 235, Patent Office.
s. 4, see Unilever (Davis's) Application [1983] R.P.C. 219, Falconer J.
ss. 4, 5, 14, see Rohde and Schwarz's Application [1980] R.P.C. 155, Patent Office.
s. 5, see Omron Tateisi Electronics Co.'s Application [1981] R.P.C. 125, Graham J.; U.K. Matsushita Electric Works' Application [1983] R.P.C. 105, Patent Office; L'Oreal's Application [1986] R.P.C. 19, Whitford J.
ss. 5, 14, see Hydroacoustics Incorporated Appns. [1981] F.S.R. 538, D.C.
s. 7, see James Industries' Patent [1987] R.P.C. 235, Patent Office.
ss. 7, 13, see Nippon Piston Ring Co.'s Applications [1987] R.P.C. 120, Patents Ct.
s. 12, see Kakkar v. Szelke, The Times, October 18, 1988, C.A.
s. 13, see Sonic Tape's Patent [1987] R.P.C. 251, Patent Office.
s. 14, see Imperial Chemical Industries (Richardson's) Appn. [1981] F.S.R. 609, Falconer J.; Protoned B.V.'s Application [1983] F.S.R. 110, Whitford J; Hollister Inc.'s Application [1983] R.P.C. 10, Whitford J.; Chinoin's Application [1986] R.P.C. 39, Falconer J.; Intera Corp.'s Application [1986] R.P.C. 45a, C.A.; Peabody International's Application [1986] R.P.C. 521, Patent Appeal; Raychem's Applications [1986] R.P.C. 547, Falconer J.; Genentech Inc.'s Patent [1988] R.P.C. 553, Whitford J.
s. 14, rules 78/216; 82/717.
s. 14, repealed in pt.: 1988, c.48, sch.8.

1977—cont.

37. Patents Act 1977—*cont.*

ss. 14, 17, see *General Motors Corp. (Longhouse's) Application* [1981] R.P.C. 41, Patent Office.

ss. 14, 20, see *Glatt's Application* [1983] R.P.C. 122, Whitford J.

s. 15, see *Fater S.p.A.'s Application* [1979] F.S.R. 647, Graham J.; *Rohde and Schwarz's Application* [1980] R.P.C. 155, Patent Office; *P's Application* [1983] R.P.C. 269, Patent Office; *Ogawa Chemical Industries* [1986] R.P.C. 63, Falconer J.; *Kiwi Coders Corporation's Application* [1986] R.P.C. 106, Whitford J.; *Raychem's Applications* [1986] R.P.C. 547, Falconer J.; *Van der Lely's Application* [1987] R.P.C. 61, Patents Ct.; *V.E.B. Kombinat Waczlager und Normtiele's Application* [1987] R.P.C. 405, Falconer J.

s. 15, amended: 1988, c.48, sch.5.

s. 16, see *Pierce Chemical Co.'s Application* [1980] R.P.C. 232, Graham J.; *Intera Corp.'s Application* [1986] R.P.C. 45a, C.A.: *Peabody International's Application* [1986] R.P.C. 521, Patent Appeal.

ss. 16–18, see *Rohde and Schwarz's Application* [1980] R.P.C. 155, Patent Office.

s. 17, see *Application Des Gaz's Application* [1987] R.P.C. 297, Falconer J.

ss. 17, 18, see *Hollister Inc's Application* [1983] R.P.C. 10, Whitford J.

ss. 17, 18, amended: 1988, c.48, sch.5.

s. 18, see *Jaskowski's Application* [1981] R.P.C. 197, Patent Office; *International Business Machines Corp. (Barclay & Bigar's) Application* [1983] R.P.C. 284, Patent Office; *Nippon Gaishi K.K's Application* [1983] R.P.C. 388, Whitford J.

ss. 18, 19, see *Ogawa Chemical Industries* [1986] R.P.C. 63, Falconer J.

s. 19, see *Intera Corp.'s Application* [1986] R.P.C. 45a, C.A.; *Merrill Lynch Inc.'s Application* [1988] R.P.C. 1, Falconer J.

s. 19, amended: 1986, c.39, sch.2.

ss. 19, 20, 25, see *P's Application* [1983] R.P.C. 269, Patent Office.

s. 25, rules 78/216; 82/717.

ss. 25, 28, see *Ling's Patent and Wilson's and Pearce's Patent* [1981] R.P.C. 85, Whitford J.; *Deforeit's Patent* [1986] R.P.C. 142, Patent Office; *Textron Inc., Re,* [1988] 1 FTLR 210, C.A.

s. 27, see *Braun A.G.'s Application* [1981] R.P.C. 355, Patents Office; *Waddington's Patent* [1986] R.P.C. 158, Patent Office; *Philips Electronic and Associated Industries Patent* [1987] R.P.C. 244, Patent Office.

s. 27, amended: 1986, c.39, sch.2.

s. 28, see *Dynamics Research and Manufacturing Inc.'s Patent* [1980] R.P.C. 179, Whitford J.; *Mead's Patent* [1980] R.P.C. 146, Whitford J.; *Convex's Patent* [1980] R.P.C. 423, C.A.; *Frazer's Patent* [1981] R.P.C. 53, Anthony Walton Q.C., sitting as a deputy judge of the Patent Court.

s. 28, amended: 1988, c.48, sch.5; repealed in pt.: *ibid.*, schs.5,8.

1977—cont.

37. Patents Act 1977—*cont.*

s. 28A, added: *ibid.*, sch.5.

s. 29, see *International Business Machines Corp. (Barclay & Bigar's) Application* [1983] R.P.C. 284, Patent Office.

s. 32, rules 78/216; 82/717; 85/1166.

s. 32, substituted: 1986, c.39, sch.1.

s. 34. Act of Sederunt 78/955.

s. 35, repealed: 1986, c.39, sch.3.

s. 37, see *James Industries' Patent* [1987] R.P.C. 235, Patent Office.

s. 37, amended: 1988, c.48, sch.5.

ss. 37, 39, see *Reiss Engineering Co. v. Harris* [1985] I.R.L.R. 232, Falconer J.

s. 38, see *Borg-Warner Corp.'s Patent* [1986] R.P.C. 137, Patent Office.

s. 39, amended: 1988, c.48, sch.5.

s. 40, Act of Sederunt 78/955.

s. 41, amended: order 78/621.

s. 42, amended: 1981, c.55, s.22.

s. 43, amended: 1988, c.48, sch.5.

s. 44, see *Ficherra v. Flogates* [1983] F.S.R. 198, Whitford J.

s. 46, see *R. v. Comptroller-General of Patents, Designs and Trade Marks, ex p. Gist-Brocades* [1986] 1 W.L.R. 51, H.L.; *Allen & Hanbury v. Generics (U.K.) and Gist Brocades, Brocades (Great Britain); Beecham Group; Comptroller General of Patents* [1986] R.P.C. 203, H.L.; *Ciba-Geigy A.G.'s Patent* [1986] R.P.C. 403, Patents Ct.; *Syntex Corporation's Patent* [1986] R.P.C. 585, Whitford J.; *Diamond Shamrock Technologies S.A.'s Patent* [1987] R.P.C. 91, Patents Ct.; *Roussel-Uclaf (Clemence & Le Martret's) Patent* [1987] R.P.C. 109, Patents Ct.; *Shiley Inc.'s Patent* [1988] R.P.C. 97, Whitford J.

s. 46, amended: 1988, c.48, sch.5.

ss. 46, 48, see *Hilti; A.G.'s Patent* [1987] F.S.R. 594, Falconer J.

ss. 46, 48, 50, 55, see *Allen & Hanburys (Salbutamol) Patent* [1987] R.P.C. 327, C.A.

s. 48, see *Extrude Hone Corp's Patent* [1984] F.S.R. 105, Patent Office; *Enviro Spray System Inc.'s Patents* [1986] R.P.C. 147, Patent Office; *Allen & Hanbury v. Generics (U.K.) and Gist Brocades, Brocades (Great Britain); Beecham Group; Comptroller General of Patents* [1986] R.P.C. 203, H.L.; *Ciba-Geigy A.G.'s Patent* [1986] R.P.C. 403, Patents Ct.; *Syntex Corporation's Patent* [1986] R.P.C. 585, Whitford J.

s. 49, repealed in pt.: 1988, c.48, schs.5,8.

s. 50, see *An Application by Generics (U.K.), Re, Financial Times*, March 26, 1986, Whitford J.; *Enviro Spray System Inc.'s Patents* [1986] R.P.C. 147, Patent Office; *Allen & Hanbury v. Generics (U.K.) and Gist Brocades, Brocades (Great Britain); Beecham Group; Comptroller General of Patents* [1986] R.P.C. 203, H.L.; *Ciba-Geigy A.G.'s Patent* [1986] R.P.C. 403, Patents Ct.; *Syntex Corporation's Patent* [1986] R.P.C. 584, Whitford J.

s. 51, substituted: 1988, c.48, sch.5.

1977—cont.

37. Patents Act 1977—cont.
s. 52, amended: order 78/621.
s. 53, amended: 1988, c.48, sch.5.
s. 56, amended: 1978, c.29, sch.16(S.).
s. 57, amended: 1988, c.48, sch.7.
s. 57A, added: ibid., sch.5.
s. 58, amended: order 78/621; 1988, c.48, sch. 5.
s. 60, see Smith Kline & French Laboratories v. R.D. Harbottle (Mercantile) [1979] F.S.R. 555, Oliver J.; Belegging-en-Exploitatiemaatschappij Lavender B.V. v. Witten Industrial Diamonds [1979] F.S.R. 59, C.A.; Rotocrop International v. Genbourne [1982] F.S.R. 241, Graham J.; Monsanto v. Stauffer Chemical Co. and Stauffer Chemical, Financial Times, June 18, 1985, C.A.; Furr v. Trueline (C.D.) (Building Products) [1985] F.S.R. 553, Falconer J.; Upjohn Co. v. Kerfoot (T.) & Co. [1988] F.S.R. 1, Whitford J., Rhone Poulenc A.G. v. Dikloride Herbicides [1988] F.S.R. 282, Malaysia H.C.: Dellareed v. Delkim Developments [1988] F.S.R. 329, Falconer J.
s. 60, amended: 1988. c.48, sch.5.
ss. 60, 61, see Kalman v. PCL Packaging (U.K.) [1982] F.S.R. 406, Falconer J.
ss. 60, 65, see Canon K.K.'s Application [1982] R.P.C. 549, Whitford J.
s. 61, see Hawker Siddeley Dynamics Engineering v. Real Time Developments [1983] R.P.C. 395, Whitford J.
s. 63. see Codex Corp. v. Racal-Milgo [1983] R.P.C. 369, C.A.
s 64, substituted: 1988, c.48, sch.5.
s. 65, see Brupat v. Smith [1985] F.S.R. 156, Court of Session.
ss. 66, 67, see PCUK v. Diamond Shamrock Industrial Chemicals [1981] F.S.R. 427, Falconer J.
s. 68, see Christian Salvesen (Oil Services) v. Odfjell Drilling and Consulting Co. (U.K.) (O.H.), 1985 S.L.T. 397.
s. 70, see Neild v. Rockley [1986] F.S.R. 3, Falconer J.; Johnston Electric Industrial Manufactory v. Mabuchi-Motor K.K. [1986] F.S.R. 280, Whitfield J.
s. 71, see Hawker Siddeley Dynamics Engineering v. Real Time Developments [1983] R.P.C. 395, Whitford J.; Martinez's Patent [1983] R.P.C. 307, Patent Office; Reckitt & Colman Products v. Biorex Laboratories [1985] F.S.R. 94, Falconer J.
s. 72, see James Industries' Patent [1987] R.P.C. 235, Patent Office; Genentech Inc.'s Patent [1988] R.P.C. 553, Whitford J.
s. 72, rules 78/216.
s. 72, amended: 1988, c.48, sch.5; repealed in pt.: ibid., sch.8.
s. 73, see International Business Machines Corp. (Barclay & Bigar's) Application [1983] R.P.C. 284, Patent Office.
s. 73, amended: 1988, c.48, sch.5.
s. 74, see Martinez's Patent [1983] R.P.C. 307, Patent Office, Dow Chemical Co. v. Ishihara Sangyo K.K. [1985] F.S.R. 4, Whitford J.;

1977—cont.

37. Patents Act 1977—cont.
Reckitt & Colman Products v. Biorex Laboratories [1985] F.S.R. 94, Falconer J.
s. 74, amended: 1988, c.48, sch.5.
s. 76, see Hydroacoustics Incorporated Appns. [1981] F.S.R. 538, D.C.; Protoned B.V.'s Application [1983] F.S.R. 110, Whitford J.; Waddington's Patent [1986] R.P.C. 158, Patent Office; Chinoin's Application [1986] R.P.C. 39, Falconer J.; Ward's Applications [1986] R.P.C. 50, Patent Office; Raychem's Applications [1986] R.P.C. 547, Falconer J.; Van der Lely's Application [1987] R.P.C. 61, Patents Ct.; Philips Electronic and Associated Industries Patent [1987] R.P.C. 244, Patent Office.
s. 76, substituted: 1988, c.48, sch.5.
s. 77, see Deforeit's Patent [1986] R.P.C. 142, Patent Office; Amersham International v. Corning [1987] R.P.C. 53, Patents Ct.
s. 77, rules 87/288.
s. 77, amended: 1988, c.48, sch.5.
s. 78, see L'Oreal's Application [1986] R.P.C. 19, Whitford J.
s. 78, rules 78/216; 82/717; 87/288.
ss. 78, 80, amended: 1988, c.48, sch.5.
s. 82, see Kakkar v. Szelke, The Times, October 18, 1988, C.A.
ss. 84, 85, repealed: 1988, c.48, sch.8.
s. 88, repealed: 1988, c.48, schs.5,8.
s. 89, see U.K.: Matsushita Electric Works' Application [1983] R.P.C. 105. Patent Office; Brossmann's Application, Re [1983] R.P.C. 109, Patent Office; Masuda's Application [1987] R.P.C. 37, Patents Ct.
s. 89, amended: 1988, c.48, sch.5; substituted: ibid.
ss. 89A, 89B, added: ibid.
s. 90, orders 82/162; 83/1709; 84/367, 1694; 85/173, 456, 457; 88/1856.
s. 90, repealed in pt.: S.L.R. 1986.
s. 91, see Rotocrop International v. Genbourne [1982] F.S.R. 241, Graham J.
s. 92, rules 78/216; 82/717; Act of Sederunt 78/955.
s. 92, amended: order 79/1714.
s. 93, amended: order 78/621; 1987, c.18, sch.6(S.).
s. 94, Act of Sederunt 78/955.
ss. 96, 97 (in pt.), repealed: 1981, c.54, sch.7.
ss. 96, 97, 99, see Omron Tateisi Electronics Co.'s Application [1981] R.P.C. 125, Graham J.
s. 97, see Standard Brands' Patent [1980] R.P.C. 187, C.A.; Nachf's Application [1983] R.P.C. 87, Whitford J.; Hawker Siddeley Dynamics Engineering v. Real Time Developments [1983] R.P.C. 395, Whitford J.
s. 97, rules 78/216; 82/717.
ss. 97, 99, see Allen & Hanburys (Salbutamol) Patent [1987] R.P.C. 327, C.A.
ss. 99A, 99B, added: 1988, c.48, sch.5.
s. 101, see Intera Corp.'s Application [1986] R.P.C. 45a, C.A.
s. 102, substituted: 1988, c.48, sch.8.

CAP.

1977—cont.

37. Patents Act 1977—cont.

ss. 102–104, see *Reiss Engineering* v. *Harris* [1987] R.P.C. 171, Patents Ct.

s. 102A, added: 1988, c.48, sch.5.

s. 104, see *"Dormeuil" Trade Mark* [1983] R.P.C. 132, Nourse J.; *Rockwell International* v. *Serck Industries* [1987] R.P.C. 89, Falconer J.; *Sonic Tape's Patent* [1987] R.P.C. 251, Patent Office.

s. 104, repealed: 1988, c.48, sch.8.

s. 105, see *Santa Fe International Corporation* v. *Napier Shipping S.A.* [1986] R.P.C. 22, Court of Session.

s. 105, amended: 1988, c.48, sch.7; repealed in pt.: *ibid.*, schs.7,8.

s. 107, see *Extrude Hone Corp's Patent* [1984] F.S.R. 105, Patent Office.

s. 107, amended: order 78/621; 1987, c.18, sch.6(S.).

s. 108, see *Allen & Hanburys (Salbutamol) Patent* [1987] R.P.C. 327, C.A.

s. 114, see *Frazer's Patent* [1981] R.P.C. 53, Anthony Walton Q.C., sitting as a deputy judge of the Patent Court.

s. 114, repealed: 1988, c.48, sch.8.

s. 115, rules 78/216; 82/717.

s. 115, repealed: 1988, c.48, sch.8.

s. 117, see *P's Application* [1983] R.P.C. 269, Patent Office; *Masuda's Application* [1987] R.P.C. 37, Patents Ct.; *V.E.B. (Kombinat Waczlager and Normteile's Application* [1987] R.P.C. 405, Falconer J.

s. 118, see *Diamond Shamrock Technologies S.A.'s Patent* [1987] R.P.C. 91, Patents Ct.

s. 118, amended: 1988, c.48, sch.5.

s. 120, rules 78/216; 80/1783; 82/717; 87/288.

s. 123, see *Fater S.p.A.'s Application* [1979] F.S.R. 647, Graham J.; *Omron Tateisi Electronics Co's Application* [1981] R.P.C. 125, Graham J.; *Waddington's Patent* [1986] R.P.C. 158, Patent Office; *Intera Corp.'s Application* [1986] R.P.C. 45a, C.A.

s. 123, rules 78/216, 1093; 80/137, 498, 1146, 1783; 81/72; 82/297, 717, 1428; 84/283; 85/785, 1099, 1166; 87/288, 753; 88/855.

s. 123, amended: 1986, c.39, sch.2; 1988, c.48, schs.5,7; repealed: *ibid.*, sch.8.

s. 124, rules 80/498, 1146; 81/72.

s. 125, see *Glatt's Application* [1983] R.P.C. 122, Whitford J.; *Philips Electronic and Associated Industries Patent* [1987] R.P.C. 244, Patent Office; *Genentech Inc.'s Patent* [1988] R.P.C. 553, Whitford J.

s. 125A, added: 1988, c.48, sch.5.

s. 127, see *Convex's Patent* [1980] R.P.C. 423, C.A.; *Hydroacoustics Incorporated Appns.* [1981] F.S.R. 538, D.C.; *Martinez's Patent* [1983] R.P.C. 307, Patent Office; *Santa Fe International Corporation* v. *Napier Shipping .A.* [1986] R.P.C. 22, Court of Session.

s. 127, rules 78/216; 82/717.

ss. 128, 130, sch. 1, see *Hydroacoustics Incorporated Appns.* [1981] F.S.R. 538, D.C.

s. 130, see *Pierce Chemical Co.'s Application* [1980] R.P.C. 232, Graham J.; *PCUK* v. *Dia-*

CAP.

1977—cont.

37. Patents Act 1977—cont.

mond Shamrock Industrial Chemicals [1981] F.S.R. 427, Falconer J.; *Kalman* v. *PCL Packaging (U.K)* [1982] F.S.R. 406, Falconer J.; *Sopharma S.A.'s Application* [1983] R.P.C. 195, Patent Office; *Intera Corp.'s Application* [1986] R.P.C. 45a, C.A.; *Van der Lely's Application* [1987] R.P.C. 61. Patents Ct.; *Philips Electronic and Associated Industries Patent* [1987] R.P.C. 244, Patent Office; *V.E.B. Kombinat Waczlager and Normteile's Application* [1987] R.P.C. 405, Falconer J.; *Upjohn Co.* v. *Kerfoot (T.) & Co.* [1988] F.S.R. 1, Whitford J.

s. 130, rules 82/717.

s. 130, amended: order 78/621; 1981, c.55, s.22; 1985, c.61, s.60; 1988, c.48, schs.5,7; repealed in pt.: *ibid.*, sch.8.

s. 131, amended: 1985, c.9, sch.2.

s. 132, orders 77/2090; 78/586, 621.

s. 132, amended: 1982, c.23, sch.3.

sch. 1, see *Reckitt & Colman Products* v. *Biorex Laboratories* [1985] F.S.R. 94, Falconer J.; *Allen & Hanbury's* v. *General (U.K.), Gist-Brocades N.V.* v. *Beecham Group, Financial Times*, June 7, 1985, C.A.; *R.* v. *Comptroller-General of Patents, Designs and Trade Marks, ex p. Gist-Brocades N.V.* [1986] 1 W.L.R. 51, H.L.; *Ciba-Geigy A.G.'s Patent* [1986] R.P.C. 403, Patents Ct.; *Masi A.G.* v. *Coloroll* [1986] R.P.C. 483, Patents Ct.; *Allen & Hanburys (Salbutamol) Patent* [1987] R.P.C. 327, C.A.; *Hilti A.G.'s Patent* [1987] F.S.R. 594, Falconer J.

sch. 1, amended: 1988, c.48, ss.293, 294.

schs. 1, 2, see *Martinez's Patent* [1983] R.P.C. 307, Patent Office.

sch. 2, see *Convex's Patent* [1980] R.P.C. 423, C.A.; *Santa Fe International Corporation* v. *Napier Shipping Co. S.A.* [1986] R.P.C. 22, Court of Session; *Allen & Hanbury* v. *Generics (U.K.) and Gist Brocades, Brocades (Great Britain); Beecham Group; Comptroller General of Patents* [1986] R.P.C. 203, H.L.

sch. 2, repealed in pt.: 1981, c.54, sch.1.

sch. 4, see *Belegging-en-Exploitatiemaatschappij Lavender B.V.* v. *Witten Industrial Diamonds* [1979] F.S.R. 59, C.A.; *Standard Oil Co. (Fahrig's) Application* [1980] R.P.C. 359, Whitford J.; *Convex's Patent* [1980] R.P.C. 423, C.A.; *International Business Machines Corp.'s Application* [1980] F.S.R. 565, Graham J.; *Rotocrop International* v. *Genbourne* [1982] F.S.R. 241, Graham J.; *Nachf's Application* [1983] R.P.C. 87, Whitford J.; *Martinez's Patent* [1983] R.P.C. 307, Patent Office; *Reckitt & Colman Products* v. *Biorex Laboratories* [1985] F.S.R. 94, Falconer J.; *Allen & Hanbury* v. *Generics (U.K.) and Gist Brocades, Brocades (Great Britain); Beecham Group; Comptroller General of Patents* [1986] R.P.C. 203, H.L.

sch. 4, rules 85/785, 1099; 87/610, 753; 88/855.

sch. 5, repealed in pt.: 1988, c.48, sch.8.

CAP.

CAP.

1977—cont.

38. Administration of Justice Act 1977.
Royal Assent, July 29, 1977.
s. 1, repealed in pt. (S.): 1986, c.47, sch.5.
s. 2, order 77/1405.
s. 6, repealed: 1978, c.44, sch.17.
s. 8, repealed: 1978, c.19, sch.
ss. 9, 10, 22 (in pt.), 27, repealed: 1981, c.54, sch.7.
s. 11, repealed: 1982, c.53, sch.9
ss. 13–16, 17 (in pt.), 18, 19 (in pt.) 20, repealed: 1984, c.28, sch.4.
s. 21, repealed: 1979, c.55, sch.3.
s. 25, repealed: 1988, c.3, sch.
s. 28, order 77/1491.
s. 29, Acts of Sederunt 78/106, 1373.
s. 29, repealed in pt.: 1988, c.36, sch.2.
s. 32, orders 77/1490, 1589, 2202; 79/972; 80/1981.
s. 32, repealed in pt.: 1978, c.19, sch.; order 78/810.
sch. 1, repealed in pt.: 1986, c.47, sch.5(S.); 1988, c.34, sch.6.
sch. 2, repealed in pt.: 1978, c.23, sch.7; 1979, c.55, sch.3; 1980, c.30, sch.5; 1988, c.13, sch.4.

39. Coal Industry Act 1977.
Royal Assent, July 29, 1977.
ss. 2, 3, repealed: 1983, c.60, s.2, sch.
ss. 4, 5, repealed: 1980, c.50, s.11.
s. 5, order 79/1011.
s. 6, repealed: 1987, c.3, sch. 3.
s. 7, orders 78/415; 79/385; 80/434, 835, 1984; 81/482; 82/407; 83/506; 84/457; 85/558; 86/625; 87/1258; 88/1252.
s. 7, amended: 1980, c.50, s.7; order 86/631; 1987, c.3, sch.1; repealed in pt.: 1980, c.50, ss. 7, 11; 1982, c.15, s.4; 1983, c.60, s.4; 1985, c.27, s.3.
s. 8, repealed: 1980, c.50, ss.5,11.
ss. 9–11, amended: 1987, c.3, sch.1.
s. 12, regs. 77/1452.
s. 14, amended: 1985, c.9, sch.2; 1987, c.3, sch.1.
sch. 1, amended: 1980, c.50, s.1.
sch. 2, repealed: 1987, c.3, sch.3.
sch.4, repealed in pt.: 1980, c.63, sch.2; 1987, c.3, sch.3.

40. Control of Office Development Act 1977.
Royal Assent, July 29, 1977.
repealed: 1986, c.63, sch.12.

41. Water Charges Equalisation Act 1977.
Royal Assent, July 29, 1977.
repealed: 1983, c.23, s.8, sch.5.
ss. 1–3, orders 77/2165; 78/1921; 79/1754.

42. Rent Act 1977.
Royal Assent, July 20, 1977.
see *R.* v. *Rent Officer for London Borough of Camden, ex p. Ebiri* (1981) 257 E.G. 604, D.C.; *Scrimgeour* v. *Waller* (1980) 257 E.G. 61, C.A.; *R.* v. *Camden London Borough Rent Officer, ex p. Plant* (1980) 257 E.G. 713, Glidewell J.; *Firstcross (formerly Welgelegen N.V.)* v. *East West (Export/Import)* (1980) 255 E.G. 355, C.A.; *Guppys Properties* v. *Knott (No. 3)* (1981) 258 E.G. 1083, Sir Douglas Frank Q.C.; *Midanbury Properties (Southampton)* v. *Houghton*

1977—cont.

42. Rent Act 1977—*cont.*
T. Clark and Son (1981) 259 E.G. 565, Sir Douglas Frank Q.C.; *Re Leeds Federated Housing Association* (1981) 260 E.G. 813, Sir Douglas Frank, Q.C.; *Metropolitan Properties Co. (F.G.C.)* v. *Good* (1981) 260 E.G. 67, Woolf J; *R.* v. *Rent Assessment Committee for London, ex p. Ellis Rees* (1982) 262 E.G. 1299, Forbes J.; *Sopwith* v. *Stutchbury* (1984) 17 H.L.R. 50, C.A.
s. 1, see *Russell* v. *Booker* (1982) 263 E.G. 513, C.A.; *Grosvenor (Mayfair) Estates* v. *Amberton* (1983) 265 E.G. 693, Leonard Hoffman Q.C.; *R.* v. *Rent Officer of Nottingham Registration Area, ex p. Allen* (1985) 275 E.G. 251; (1986) 52 P. & C.R. 41, Farquharson J.
ss. 1, 2, see *Regalian Securities* v. *Ramsden* [1981] 1 W.L.R. 611; [1981] 2 All E.R. 65, H.L.
ss. 1, 8, see *St. Catherine's College* v. *Dorling* [1979] 3 All E.R. 250, C.A.
s. 2, see *Lloyd* v. *Sadler, The Times*, January 20, 1978, C.A.; *Atyeo* v. *Fardoe* (1978) 37 P. & C.R. 494, C.A.; *Heath Estates* v. *Burchell* (1979) 251 E.G. 1173, C.A.; *Kyriacou* v. *Pandeli*, February 11, 1980, Deputy Circuit Judge Pryor, Shoreditch County Ct.; *Watson* v. *Lucas, The Times*, July 8, 1980, C.A.; *Fletcher* v. *Davies* (1981) 257 E.G. 1149, C.A.; *Metropolitan Properties Co.* v. *Cronan* (1982) 262 E.G. 1077, C.A.; *Regalian Securities* v. *Scheuer* (1982) 262 E.G. 973, C.A.; *Richards* v. *Green* (1983) 268 E.G. 443, C.A.; *Hampstead Way Investments* v. *Lewis-Weare* [1985] 1 W.L.R. 164, H.L.; *Kavanagh* v. *Lyroudias* [1985] 1 All E.R. 560, C.A.; *Duke and Duke* v. *Porter* (1987) 19 H.L.R. 1, C.A.; *Hall* v. *King* (1987) 19 H.L.R. 440, C.A.; *Sefton Holdings* v. *Cairns, The Times*, November 3, 1987, C.A.; *R.* v. *Kensington and Chelsea London Borough Council (Housing Benefits Review Board), ex p. Robertson* (1988) 28 R.V.R. 84, Kennedy J.
s. 2, amended: 1988, c.50, s.39.
s. 3, see *The British Bata Shoe Co.* v. *Snodlak*, February 26, 1982; H.H. Judge Rice, Southend County Ct.
s. 5, repealed in pt.: 1980, c.51, sch.26.
s. 5A, regs. 87/1940.
s. 5A, added: 1986, c.63, sch.4.
ss. 6, 10, see *Russell* v. *Booker* (1982) 263 E.G. 513, C.A.
s. 7, see *Rita Dale* v. *Adrahill and Ali Khan*, December 8, 1981, H.H. Judge Stuckley; *Otter* v. *Norman* [1988] 3 W.L.R. 321, H.L.
s. 8, regs. 88/1683, 2236.
s. 9, see *McHale* v. *Daneham* (1979) 249 E.G. 969, Judge Edwards; *Francke* v. *Hakmi*, November 4, 1983, Bloomsbury and Marylebone County Ct.
s. 10, amended: 1986, c.5, sch.14.
s. 12, see *Guppy* v. *O'Donnell*, July 27, 1979, Judge Rowland, Westminster County Court; *Landau* v. *Sloane*; *Midgalski* v. *Corvin, The Times*, April 1, 1980, C.A.; *Barnes* v. *Gorsuch* (1982) 43 P. & C.R. 294, C.A.; *Griffiths* v. *English* (1982) 261 E.G. 257, C.A.; *Williams* v.

1977—cont.

42. Rent Act 1977—*cont.*

Mate (1982) 263 E.G. 883; (1983) 46 P. & C.R. 43, C.A.; *Caldwell* v. *McAteer* (1984) 269 E.G. 1039, C.A.; *Cooper* v. *Tait* (1984) 271 E.G. 105; (1984) 48 P. & C.R. 460, C.A.; *R.* v. *Plymouth City Council and Cornwall County Council, ex p. Freeman* (1988) 28 R.V.R. 89, C.A.

s. 12, amended: 1980, c.51, ss.65,69.

s. 13, see *Crown Estate Comrs.* v. *Wordsworth* (1982) 264 E.G. 439; (1982) 44 P. & C.R. 302, C.A.; *Crown Estate Commissioners* v. *Connor and the London Rent Assessment Panel* (1987) 19 H.L.R. 35, McCowan J.

s. 13, substituted: 1980, c.51, s.73.

s. 14, amended: 1980, c.65, s.155; 1981, c.64, sch.12; 1985, c.51, sch.14; order 85/1884; 1988, c.4, sch.6; c.50, s.62; repealed in pt.: 1985, c.51, sch.17; 1988, c.40, sch.13 (prosp.).

s. 15, amended: 1985, c.71, sch.2; 1988, c.50, sch.17; repealed in pt.: 1980, c.51, s.74, sch.26.

s. 16, amended: *ibid.,* sch.25; 1985, c.71, sch.2; 1986, c.63, sch.5.

s. 16A, repealed: 1988, c.50, sch.18.

s. 17, repealed: 1980, c.51, sch.26.

s. 18, repealed in pt.: *ibid.,* schs.25,26.

s. 18A, added: *ibid.,* sch.25.

s. 19, see *Lambeth London Borough Council* v. *Udechuka, The Times,* April 30, 1980, C.A.; *Mann* v. *Cornella* (1980) 254 E.G. 403, C.A.; *Baldock* v. *Murray* (1980) 257 E.G. 281, C.A.

ss. 19–21, repealed: 1988, c.50, sch.18.

s. 24, see *Simmonds* v. *Egyed,* February 12, 1985, Bloomsbury County Court.

s. 24, repealed in pt.: 1980, c.51, sch.26.

s. 25, see *MacFarquhar* v. *Phillimore; Marks* v. *Phillimore* (1986) 18 H.L.R. 397, C.A.; *Griffiths* v. *Birmingham City District Council,* January 26, 1987; H.H. Judge Clive Taylor, Q.C., Stafford County Ct.; *Dixon* v. *Allgood* [1987] 1 W.L.R. 1689, H.L..

s. 26, see *Bradsman* v. *Smith* (1980) 255 E.G. 699, C.A.

ss. 27–43, repealed: 1980, c.51, sch.26.

s. 29, see *Yewbright Properties* v. *Stone* (1980) 40 P. & C.R. 402, C.A.

s. 34, amended: 1980, c.66, sch.24.

s. 44, see *Brecker* v. *Field,* July 12, 1982, H.H. Judge Wild, Bloomsbury and Marylebone County Court, *Kent* v. *Millmead Properties* (1983) 266 E.G. 899, C.A.; *Waddock* v. *Cheniston Investment, The Independent,* August 19, 1988, C.A.

s. 44, amended: order 87/264; repealed in pt.: 1980, c.51, sch.26.

s. 45, see *The British Bata Shoe Co.* v. *Snodlak,* February 26, 1982; H.H. Judge Rice, Southend County Ct.

s. 45, amended: 1980, c.51, s.61, sch.25; order 87/264; repealed in pt.: 1980, c.51, s.61, sch.26; order 87/264.

ss. 46, 49, see *Aristocrat Property Investments* v. *Harounoff* (1982) 43 P. & C.R. 284, C.A.

s. 48, repealed: 1980, c.51, s.63, sch.26.

1977—cont.

42. Rent Act 1977—*cont.*

s. 49, regs. 80/1697; 87/266.

s. 49, amended: 1980, c.51, sch.25.

s. 50, repealed: *ibid.,* sch.26; amended: 1980, c.66, sch.24.

s. 51, amended: 1980, c.51, s.68; repealed in pt.: *ibid.,* sch.26; order 87/264.

s. 52, substituted: *ibid.,* s.68.

s. 53, repealed: *ibid.,* sch.26.

s. 54, repealed in pt.: *ibid.*

s. 55, repealed: order 87/264.

s. 56, repealed: *ibid.,* s.60, sch.26.

s. 57, see *Brecker* v. *Field,* July 12, 1982, H.H. Judge Wild, Bloomsbury and Marylebone County Court.

s. 57, amended: 1980, c.51, s.68.

s. 60, regs. 78/495; 80/1697; 87/266.

s. 61, regs. 87/266.

s. 61, repealed in pt.: 1980, c.51, sch.26.

s. 62, amended and repealed in pt.: 1985, c.51, sch.8.

Pt. IV (ss. 62–75), see *Crown Estate Commissioners* v. *Connor and the London Rent Assessment Panel* (1987) 19 H.L.R. 35, McCowan J.

s. 63, amended: 1980, c.51, s.59; 1985, c.51, sch.8; 1988, c.50, ss.120, 121, sch.14; repealed in pt.: *ibid.,* s.120, schs.14,18.

ss. 64A, 64B, added: *ibid.,* s.120, sch.14.

s. 66, see *Kent* v. *Millmead Properties* (1983) 266 E.G. 899, C.A.

ss. 66, 67, regs. 80/1697; 84/1391.

s. 67, see *R.* v. *Chief Rent Officer for Kensington and Chelsea London Borough Council, ex p. Moberly* (1986) 278 E.G. 305, S.C.

s. 67, amended: 1980, c.51, ss.59–61; repealed in pt.: *ibid.,* sch.26; 1988, c.50, sch.18.

ss. 67, 70, see *Williams* v. *Khan* (1982) 43 P. & C.R. 1, C.A.; *Kovatis* v. *Corp. of Trinity House* (1982) 262 E.G. 445, Forbes J.

s. 68, regs. 82/1015.

ss. 68, 69, repealed: 1988, c.50, schs.17, 18.

s. 69, see *Guppy's Properties* v. *Knott* (1979) 253 E.G. 907, Sir Douglas Frank Q.C.; *Curry* v. *Ronan,* July 24, 1980, Judge Stock, Southampton County Ct.; *Ellis and Son Fourth Amalgamated Properties* v. *Southern Rent Assessment Panel* (1984) 270 E.G. 39, Mann J.

s. 69, amended: 1986, c.63, s.7; repealed in pt.: *ibid.,* sch 12.

s. 70, see *Guppy's Properties* v. *Knott* (1979) 253 E.G. 907, Sir Douglas Frank Q.C.; *Williams* v. *Khan, The Times,* April 12, 1980, Stocker J.; *Dennis* v. *McDonald* [1982] 2 W.L.R. 275, C.A.; *Firstcross* v. *Teasdale* (1983) 265 E.G. 305, McNeill J.; *Henry Smith's Charity Trustees* v. *Hemmings* (1983) 265 E.G. 383, C.A.; *Western Heritable Investment Co.* v. *Husband, The Times,* August 10, 1983, H.L.; *Wareing* v. *White* (1984) 270 E.G. 851, Woolf J.; *Crown Estates Comrs.* v. *Connor* (1986) 280 E.G. 532, McCowan J.; *R.* v. *London Rent Assessment Panel, ex p. Mota* [1988] 02 E.G. 66, Schiemann J.

CAP.

1977—cont.

42. Rent Act 1977—cont.

s. 70, amended: 1986, c.63, s.17; repealed in pt.: 1980, c.51, schs.25,26; 1986, c.63, s.17, sch.12.

ss. 70, 71, see *Perseus Property Co.* v. *Burberry* (1985) 273 E.G. 405, Nolan J.

s. 71, see *Firstcross* v. *Teasdale* (1983) 265 E.G. 305, McNeill J.; *Betts* v. *Vivamat Properties* (1984) 270 E.G. 849, Hodgson J.; *Wigglesworth* v. *Property Holding and Investment Trust* (1984) 270 E.G. 555, McCullough J.

s. 71, repealed in pt.: 1980, c.51, sch.26; order 87/264.

s. 72, substituted: *ibid.*,s.61.

s. 73, regs. 80/1697; 84/1391.

s. 73, amended: 1980, c.51, s.62, sch.25.

s. 74, regs. 74/494, 495; 80/1696–1700; 81/271, 1493, 1783; 82/1015; 84/1391; 88/2178.

s. 74, amended: 1988, c.50, s.41; repealed in pt.: *ibid.*, sch.18.

s. 76, repealed: 1980, c.51, s.72, sch.26.

s. 77, regs. 80/1697.

s. 77, repealed in pt.: 1980, c.51, sch.26; 1988, c.50, schs.17,18.

s. 78, amended: 1980, c.51, sch.25; 1985, c.71, sch.2; repealed in pt.: 1980, c.51, sch.26.

s. 79, regs. 80/1697; 84/1391.

s. 79, amended: 1980, c.51, sch.25; repealed in pt.: *ibid.*,schs.25,26.

s. 80, amended: *ibid.*,s.70; repealed in pt.: 1988, c.50, sch.18.

s. 81A, regs. 80/1697.

s. 81A, added: 1980, c.51, s.71; repealed in pt.: 1988, c.50, sch.18.

s. 84, regs. 80/1697.

s. 84, repealed in pt.: 1980, c.51, sch.26.

s. 85, amended: *ibid.*,sch.25.

s. 86, amended: *ibid.*,sch.10; 1985, c.71, sch.2; 1988, c.50, sch.17; repealed in pt.: 1980, c.51, sch.26.

s. 87, amended: *ibid.*,s.61; repealed in pt.: *ibid.*,s.61, sch.26; 1988, c.50, sch.18.

s. 88, amended: 1980, c.51, sch.25; 1985, c.71, sch.2; 1988, c.50, sch.18.

s. 89, repealed: *ibid.*, schs.17,18.

ss. 90, 91, repealed: 1975, c.51, schs.10,26.

s. 92, amended: 1985, c.71, sch.2; repealed in pt.: 1980, c.51, schs.10,26.

s. 93, amended: *ibid.*, sch.10; 1988, c.50, sch.17; repealed in pt.: 1980, c.51, schs.10,26.

s. 96, repealed in pt.: *ibid.*, s.61, sch.26.

s. 98, see *Kyriacou* v. *Pandeli*, February 11, 1980, Deputy Circuit Judge Pryor, Shoreditch County Ct.; *Yewbright Properties* v. *Stone* (1980) 254 E.G. 863, C.A.; *Siddiqui* v. *Rashid* [1980] 1 W.L.R. 1018, C.A.; *Patel* v. *Patel* [1981] 1 W.L.R. 1342, C.A.; *Kidder* v. *Birch* (1982) 126 S.J. 482, C.A.; *Yoland* v. *Reddington* (1982) 263 E.G. 157, C.A.; *Fernandes* v. *Parvardin* (1982) 264 E.G. 49, C.A.; *Leith Properties* v. *Springer* [1982] 3 W.L.R. 731, C.A.; *Leith Properties* v. *Byrne* [1983] 2 W.L.R. 67, C.A.; *Hill* v. *Rochard, The Times*, February 1, 1983, C.A.; *Gladyric* v. *Collinson*

CAP.

1977—cont.

42. Rent Act 1977—cont.

(1983) 267 E.G. 761, C.A.; *Battlespring* v. *Grates* (1983) 268 E.G. 355, C.A.; *Florent* v. *Horez* (1983) 268 E.G. 807, C.A.; *Cobstone Investments* v. *Maxim* [1984] 2 All E.R. 635, C.A.; *Pazgate* v. *McGrath* (1984) 272 E.G. 1069, C.A.; *R.* v. *Bloomsbury and Marylebone County Court, ex p. Blackburne* (1985) 275 E.G. 1273, C.A.; *Alexander* v. *Mohamedzadeh* (1985) 276 E.G. 1258, C.A.; *Minchburn* v. *Fernandez* (1987) 19 H.L.R. 29, C.A.; *Roberts* v. *Macilwraith-Christie* (1987) 1 E.G.L.R. 224, C.A.; *Appleton* v. *Aspin* [1988] 04 E.G. 123, C.A.; *R.* v. *Newcastle upon Tyne County Court, ex p. Thompson* [1988] 26 E.G. 112, McNeill J.

s. 98, amended: 1980, c.51, s.66.

s. 100, see *Kyriacou* v. *Pandeli*, February 11, 1980, Deputy Circuit Judge Pryor, Shoreditch County Ct.; *Kidder* v. *Birch* (1984) 46 P. & C.R. 362, C.A.

s. 100, amended: 1980, c.51, s.75.

s. 101, substituted: 1985, c.71, sch.2.

s. 102A, added: 1980, c.51, s.69.

s. 103, repealed in pt.: 1988, c.50, sch.18

s. 104, see *Lambeth London Borough Council* v. *Udechuka, The Times*, April 30, 1980, C.A.

s. 106A, see *Bryant* v. *Best* (1987) 283 E.G. 843, C.A.

s. 106A, added: 1980, c.51, s.69.

ss. 108–113, repealed: *ibid.*, sch.26.

s. 114, regs. 74/495.

s. 114, repealed: 1980, c.51, s.60, sch.26.

s. 115, repealed: *ibid.*, sch.26

s. 116, amended: *ibid.*, sch.25; 1985, c.71, sch.2; 1986, c.63, sch.3; repealed in pt., 1980, c.51, schs.25,26.

s. 117, repealed: *ibid.*, sch.26.

s. 118, repealed: 1985, c.71, sch.1.

ss. 119, 125, see *Saleh* v. *Robinson, The Times*, March 24, 1988, C.A.

ss. 120, 123, see *Nock* v. *Munk* (1982) 263 E.G. 1085, Donald Nicholls Q.C.

ss. 120, 125, see *Adair* v. *Murrell* (1982) 263 E.G. 66, Skinner J.

s. 127, amended: 1980, c.51, s.78; 1988, c.50, s.115, repealed in pt.: *ibid.*, s.115.

s. 128, amended: 1980, c.51, s.79.

s. 129, amended: *ibid.*, sch.25

ss. 130, 131 (in pt.): repealed: *ibid.*, sch.26.

s. 132, amended: *ibid.*, sch.25.

ss. 133–135, repealed: *ibid.*, sch.26.

s. 136, amended: 1980, c.51, sch.25.

s. 137, see *Metropolitan Properties* v. *Cordery* (1979) 39 P. & C.R. 10, C.A.; *Leith Properties* v. *Springer* [1982] 3 W.L.R. 731, C.A.; *Trustees of Henry Smith's Charity* v. *Wilson* [1983] 2 W.L.R. 77, C.A.; *Leith Properties* v. *Byrne* [1983] 2 W.L.R. 67, C.A.; *Patoner* v. *Alexandrakis* (1984) 272 E.G. 330, C.A.; *Patoner* v. *Lowe* (1985) 275 E.G. 540, C.A.

s. 137, amended: 1986, c.5, sch.14; repealed in pt.: 1988, c.50, schs.17,18.

s. 138, amended: 1980, c.51, sch.25.

CAP.

1977—cont.

42. Rent Act 1977—cont.

s. 141, see *Russell* v. *Booker* (1982) 263 E.G. 513, C.A.; *Tingey* v. *Sutton* [1984] 1 W.L.R. 1154, C.A.

s. 141, repealed in pt.: 1980, c.51, sch.26.

s. 142, rules 78/1961; 81/139.

s. 145, repealed: 1985, c.71, sch.2.

s. 147, amended: 1984, c.28, sch.2.

s. 149, amended: 1980, c.51, sch.25; 1985, c.71, sch.2; 1988, c.50, s.43; repealed in pt.: 1985, c.71, sch.1.

s. 150, repealed in pt.: 1980, c.51, sch.26.

s. 151, amended: 1982, c.48, sch.3.

s. 152, repealed in pt.: 1980, c.51, sch.26.

s. 153, amended: 1980, c.51, sch.25.

s. 155, repealed in pt.: *ibid.*, sch.26.

sch. 1, see *Helby* v. *Rafferty* [1978] 3 All E.R. 1016, C.A.; *Atyeo* v. *Fardoe* (1978) 37 P. & C.R. 494, C.A.; *Watson* v. *Lucas* [1980] 1 W.L.R. 1493; [1980] 3 All E.R. 647, C.A.; *General Management* v. *Locke* (1980) 255 E.G. 155, C.A.; *Swanbrae* v. *Elliott* (1987) 281 E.G. 917; (1987) 19 H.L.R. 87, C.A.; *Portman Registrars & Nominees* v. *Mohammed Latif*, April 23, 1987, H.H. Judge Hill-Smith, Willesden County Ct.; *Sefton Holdings* v. *Cairns, The Times*, November 3, 1987, C.A.; *Chios Investment Property Co.* v. *Lopez, The Times*, November 3, 1987, C.A.

sch. 1, amended: 1980, c.51, s.76; 1988, c.50, s.39; repealed in pt.: 1980, c.51, sch.26; 1988, c.50, schs.4,18.

sch. 2, see *Beebe* v. *Mason* (1980) 254 E.G. 987, C.A.; *Landau* v. *Sloane, The Times*, February 26, 1981, H.L.; *Barnes* v. *Gorsuch* (1982) 43 P. & C.R. 294, C.A.; *Williams* v. *Mate* (1982) 263 E.G. 883, C.A.; (1983) 46 P. & C.R. 43, C.A.; *Caldwell* v. *McAteer* (1984) 269 E.G. 1039, C.A.

sch. 2, amended: 1980, c.51, s.65; repealed in pt.: *ibid.*, s.65, sch.26; 1988, c.50, sch.18.

schs. 3, 4, 6, repealed: 1980, c.51, sch.26.

sch. 7, repealed in pt.: *ibid.*

sch. 8, repealed: 1988, c.50, sch.18.

sch. 9, repealed: 1980, c.51, sch.26.

sch. 10, amended: *ibid.*, ss.71,148; repealed in pt.: *ibid.*, schs.25,26.

sch. 11, amended: *ibid.*, s.61, sch.6; repealed in pt.: *ibid.*, sch.26; 1988, c.50, schs.17,18.

sch. 12, see *Guppy's Properties* v. *Knott* (1979) 253 E.G. 907, Sir Douglas Frank Q.C.

sch. 12, regs. 80/1697; 84/1391.

sch. 12, amended: 1986, c.63, sch.5; 1988, c.50, sch.17; repealed in pt.: 1980, c.51, sch.26; 1986, c.63, sch.12; repealed: 1988, c.50, sch.18.

sch. 13, repealed: 1980, c.51, sch.26.

sch. 14, repealed in pt.: *ibid.*; 1988, c.50, sch.18.

sch. 15, see *Ager* v. *Burnell*, October 26, 1978, Judge Corley, Ilford County Ct.; *Evans* v. *Engelson* (1979) 253 E.G. 577, C.A.; *Siddiqui* v. *Rashid* [1980] 1 W.L.R. 1018, C.A.; *Yewbright Properties* v. *Stone* (1980) 40 P. & C.R. 402, C.A.; *Mohan* v. *Manning*, April 1, 1981, Judge Gill, Middlesbrough County Ct.; *Patel*

CAP.

1977—cont.

42. Rent Act 1977—cont.

v. *Patel* [1981] 1 W.L.R. 1342, C.A.; *Harley* v. *Hood* (1981) 259 E.G. 159, C.A.; *Kidder* v. *Birch* (1982) 126 S.J. 482, C.A., *Yoland* v. *Reddington* (1982) 263 E.G. 157, C.A.; *Fernandes* v. *Parvardin* (1982) 264 E.G. 49, C.A.; *Leith Properties* v. *Springer* [1982] 3 W.L.R. 731, C.A.; *Leith Properties* v. *Byrne* [1983] 2 W.L.R. 67, C.A.; *Hill* v. *Rochard, The Times*, February 1, 1983, C.A.; *Kidder* v. *Birch* (1983) 265 E.G. 773; (1984) 46 P. & C.R. 362, C.A.; *Minay* v. *Sentongo* (1983) 266 E.G. 433, C.A.; *Florent* v. *Horez* (1983) 268 E.G. 807, C.A.; *Abiafo* v. *Lord*, January 3, 1984, H.H. Judge Tibber, Edmonton County Court; *Cobstone Investments* v. *Maxim* [1984] 2 All E.R. 635, C.A.; *Holloway* v. *Povey* (1984) 271 E.G. 195, C.A.; *Pocock* v. *Steel, The Times*, November 21, 1984, C.A.; *Pazgate* v. *McGrath* (1984) 272 E.G. 1069, C.A.; *R.* v. *Bloomsbury and Marylebone County Court, ex p. Blackburne* (1984) 14 H.L.R. 56, Glidewell J.; *Perseus Property Co.* v. *Burberry* (1985) 273 E.G. 405, Nolan J.; *Naish* v. *Curzon* (1985) 273 E.G. 1221, C.A.; *Bradshaw* v. *Baldwin-Wiseman* (1985) 274 E.G. 285; 49 P. & C.R. 382, C.A.; *Manaton* v. *Edwards* (1985) 276 E.G. 1257, C.A.; *Alexander* v. *Mohamedzadeh* (1985) 276 E.G. 1258; (1986) 51 P. & C.R. 41, C.A.; *Hewitt* v. *Lewis* [1986] 1 All E.R. 927, C.A.; *Naish* v. *Curzon* (1986) 51 P. & C.R. 229, C.A.; *Bissessar* v. *Ghosn* (1986) 18 H.L.R. 486, C.A.; *Fowler* v. *Minchin* (1987) 19 H.L.R. 224, C.A.; *Reid and Reid* v. *Andreou*, February 14, 1986, H.H. Judge Tibber; Edmonton County Ct.; *Bostock* v. *de la Pagerie, sub nom. Bostock* v. *Tacher de la Pagerie* (1987) 19 H.L.R. 358, C.A.; *Hodges* v. *Blee* (1987) E.C. 1215, C.A.; *Coombs* v. *Parry* (1987) 19 H.L.R. 384, C.A., *Roberts* v. *Macilwraith-Christie* (1987) 1 E.G.L.R. 224, C.A.; *Gent* v. *De La Mare* (1988) 20 H.L.R. 199, C.A.; *R.* v. *Newcastle upon Tyne County Court, ex p. Thompson* [1988] 26 E.G. 112, McNeill J.

sch. 15, amended: 1980, c.51, ss.55, 66, 67, schs.7, 8, 25; 1985, c.24, s.1; c.71, sch.2; 1986, c.63, s.13; repealed in pt.: 1980, c.51, sch.26; 1988, c.50, sch.18.

sch. 16, amended: 1985, c.71, sch.2; repealed in pt.: 1985, c.51, sch.17.

sch. 17, amended: 1980, c.51, sch.25; repealed in pt.: *ibid.*, schs. 25,26.

sch. 19, repealed: 1980, c.51, sch.26.

sch. 20, amended: order 87/264; repealed in pt.: 1980, c.51, sch.26; order 87/264; 1988, c.50, sch.18.

schs. 21, 22, repealed: 1980, c.51, sch.26.

sch. 23, repealed: 1983, c.19, sch.3; repealed in pt.: 1984, c.28, sch.4; 1985, c.71, sch.1.

sch. 24, see *Williams* v. *Mate* (1983) 46 P. & C.R. 43, C.A.

sch. 24, amended: 1980, c.51, sch.25; repealed in pt.: 1988, c.50, sch.18.

CAP.

1977—cont.

43. Protection from Eviction Act 1977.
Royal Assent, July 29, 1977.
see *Ashgar* v. *Ahmed* (1984) 17 H.L.R. 25, C.A.
s. 1, see *R.* v. *Davidson-Acres* [1980] Crim.L.R.
50, C.A.; *R.* v. *Phekoo* [1981] Crim.L.R. 399,
C.A.; *R.* v. *Yuthiwattana* [1984] Crim.L.R. 562;
(1985) 80 Cr.App.R. 55, C.A.; *R.* v. *A.M.K.
(Property Management)* [1985] Crim.L.R. 600,
C.A.; *Schon* v. *Camden London Borough
Council, The Times,* May 6, 1986, C.A.; *R.* v.
Ahmad [1986] Crim.L.R. 739, C.A.
s. 1, amended: 1988, c.50, s.29.
ss. 1, 4, see *Costelloe* v. *London Borough of
Camden* [1986] Crim.L.R. 249, D.C.
s. 3, see *Thompson* v. *Elmbridge Borough Council* [1987] 1 W.L.R. 1425, C.A
s. 3, amended: 1980, c.51, s.69; 1988, c.50,
s.30.
s. 3A, added: *ibid.,* s.31.
s. 4, amended: *ibid.,* s.30.
s. 5, see *Lambeth London Borough Council* v.
Udechuka, The Times, April 30, 1980, C.A.;
Wilsher v. *Foster,* September 30, 1981, Judge
Glanville Q.C., Brighton County Ct.; *Peckham
Mutual Building Society* v. *Registe* (1981) 42
P. & C.R. 186, Vinelott J.; *Meretune Investments* v. *Martin,* December 15, 1983, H.H.
Judge Figgis, Kingston-upon-Thames County
Court.
s. 5, regs. 80/1624.
s. 5, amended: 1988, c.50, s.32.
s. 7, amended: 1982, c.48, sch.3; repealed in
pt.: 1988, c.50, schs.17,18.
s. 8, amended: 1986, c.5, sch.14; 1988, c.50,
s.33.
sch. 1, repealed in pt.: 1984, c.28, sch.4.

44. Post Office Act 1977.
Royal Assent, July 29, 1977.
repealed: 1981, c.38, sch.6.

45. Criminal Law Act 1977.
Royal Assent, July 29, 1977.
Commencement orders: 77/1365, 1426, 1682,
1744 (S.131); 78/712, 900 (S.74); 80/487, 587
(S.52), 1632, 1701 (S.147); 82/243; 85/579.
s. 1, see *R.* v. *Quinn* [1978] Crim.L.R. 750,
Nottingham Crown Ct.; *R.* v. *Soul* (1970) 70
Cr.App.R 295, C.A.; *R.* v. *Barnard* (1979) 70
Cr.App.R. 28, C.A.; *R.* v. *Orpin* (1980) 124
S.J. 271, C.A.; *R.* v. *Molyneux; R* v. *Farm-
borough* (1980) 72 Cr.App.R. 111, C.A.; *R.* v.
Ayres [1984] 1 All E.R. 619, H.L.; *R.* v. *B.*
[1984] Crim.L.R. 352, C.A.; *R.* v. *Tonner; R.*
v. *Evans* [1984] Crim.L.R. 618, C.A.; [1985] 1
W.L.R. 344, C.A.; *R.* v. *Zemmel; R.* v. *Mecik*
[1985] Crim.L.R. 213, C.A.; *R.* v. *Lloyd; R.* v.
Bhuee; R. v. *Ali* [1985] 3 W.L.R. 30, C.A.; *R.*
v. *Hollinshead* [1985] 3 W.L.R. 159, H.L.; *R.*
v. *Anderson (William Ronald)* [1985] 3 W.L.R.
268, H.L.; *R.* v. *Elghazal* [1986] Crim.L.R. 52,
C.A.; *R* v *James and Ashford* [1986]
Crim.L.R. 118, C.A.; *R.* v. *Grant* (1986) 82
Cr.App.R. 324, C.A.; *R.* v. *Cooke* [1986] 3
W.L.R. 327, H.L.
s. 1, amended: 1981, c.47, s.5.
ss. 1, 4, see *R.* v. *Whitehead* [1982] 3 W.L.R.
543, C.A.

CAP.

1977—cont.

45. Criminal Law Act 1977.—*cont.*
ss. 1, 4, 5, see *R.* v. *McLaughlin* (1983) 76
Cr.App.R. 42, C.A.
ss. 1, 5, see *R.* v. *Duncalf* [1979] 1 W.L.R. 918,
C.A.; *R.* v. *Walters; R* v. *Tovey; R.* v. *Padfield*
[1979] R.T.R. 220, C.A.
s. 5, see *R.* v. *Holmes* [1980] 2 All E.R. 458,
C.A.; *R.* v. *Longman; R* v. *Cribben* (1980) 72
Cr.App.R. 121, C.A.; *R.* v. *Molyneux; R.* v.
Farmborough (1980) 72 Cr.App.R. 111, C.A.;
R. v. *Ayres* [1984] 1 All E.R. 619, H.L.; *R.* v.
Tonner; R. v. *Evans* [1985] 1 W.L.R. 344,
C.A.; *R.* v. *Zemmel, R.* v. *Mecik* [1985]
Crim.L.R. 213, C.A.; *R.* v. *Hollinshead* [1985]
3 W.L.R. 159, H.L.; *R.* v. *Grant (Alexander),
The Times,* December 24, 1985, C.A.; *R.* v.
Cooke [1986] 3 W.L.R. 327, H.L.; *R.* v. *Evans*
[1986] Crim.L.R. 470, C.A.; *R.* v. *Sirat
(Mohammed)* (1986) 83 Cr.App.R. 41; [1986]
Crim.L.R. 245, C.A.
s. 5, repealed in pt.: 1981, c.47, sch.; 1987,
c.38, sch.12.
s. 7, amended: 1985, c.71, sch.2; 1988, c.50,
sch.17.
s. 9, amended: 1987, c.46, s.7.
s. 11, repealed: 1984, c.60, sch.7.
s. 14, see *Cashen* v. *Fitzsimmons,* February 4,
1980, D.C.
s. 14, repealed: 1980, c.43, sch.9.
s. 15, see *R.* v. *South Western Magistrates'
Court, ex p. Beaton* [1980] R.T.R. 35, D.C.
ss. 15 (in pt.), 16, 18–22, repealed: 1980, c.43,
sch.9.
s. 16, see *R* v. *Brentwood JJ., ex p. Jones*
[1979] R.T.R. 155, D.C.
s. 18, amended (S.): 1979, c.39, s.42.
s. 19, see *R.* v. *St. Albans Juvenile Court, ex p.
Godman* [1981] 2 W.L.R. 882; [1981] 2 All
E.R. 311, D.C.; *R.* v. *Tottenham Juvenile
Court, ex p. A.R.C. (A Minor); R.* v. *Islington
North Juvenile Court, ex p. C. D. (A Minor);
R.* v. *Feltham Justices, ex p. N. C. (A Minor)*
[1982] 2 W.L.R. 945, D.C.
ss. 19–24, see *R.* v. *Tottenham JJ., ex p.
Arthur's Transport Services* [1981] Crim.L.R.
180, D.C.
ss. 20, 21, see *R.* v. *Horseferry Road Magistrates' Court, ex p. Constable* [1981] Crim.L.R.
504, D.C.
s. 23, see *R.* v. *Leicester Justices, ex p. Lord*
[1980] Crim.L.R. 581, D.C.; *R.* v. *Hatfield JJ.,
ex p. Castle* [1980] 3 All E.R. 509, D.C.; *R* v.
Considine (1979) Cr.App.R. 239, C.A.; *Re
Prescott (Note)* (1979) 70 Cr.App.R. 244, C.A.;
R v. *Tottenham JJ., ex p. Tibble* (1981) 73
Cr.App.R. 55, D.C.
ss. 23–27, repealed: 1980, c.43, sch 9.
s. 25, see *R.* v. *Coventry City JJ., ex p. Wilson*
[1982] Crim.L.R. 787, D.C.
s. 28, see *Tandridge District Council* v. *Powers*
(1982) L.G.R. 453, D.C.
s. 28, amended: 1980, c.43, sch.7; repealed in
pt.: *ibid.,* sch.9.
ss. 29, 30 (in pt.), repealed: *ibid.*
s. 31, repealed in pt.: 1982, c.48, sch.16; 1985,
c.72, sch.13.

1977—cont.

45. Criminal Law Act 1977—cont.
ss. 32 (in pt.), 34, 35 repealed: 1982, c.48, sch.16.
s. 36, amended: *ibid.*,sch.14, repealed in pt.: 1980, c.43, sch.9; 1982, c.48, sch.16.
s. 37, repealed in pt.: *ibid.*
s. 38, amended: 1980, c.43, sch.7; repealed in pt.: 1985, c.65, sch.10.
s. 38A, added (S.): 1980, c.62, s.51; amended: 1982, c.48, sch.14.
s. 38B, added: *ibid.*,s.52.
s. 39, rules 80/137.
s. 39, amended (S.): 1980, c.62, sch.7.
ss. 41, 42, repealed: 1980, c.43, sch.9.
s. 43, repealed: 1988, c.33, sch.16.
s. 44, see *R. v. Lidiard* (1978) 122 S.J. 743, C.A.; *R. v. Home Office, ex p. Graham, The Times,* August 8, 1983, D.C.; *R. v. Foster, The Times,* March 31, 1984, C.A.; *R. v. Lee* (1984) 81 L.S.Gaz. 970, C.A.
s. 44, repealed in pt.: 1980, c.47, sch.5.
s. 45, repealed: 1980, c.43, sch.9.
s. 47, see *R. v. Clarke* [1982] 1 W.L.R. 1090, C.A.; *R. v. Ipswich Crown Court, ex p. Williamson* (1982) 4 Cr.App.R.(S.) 348, D.C.; *R. v. Gow* (1983) 5 Cr.App.R.(S) 250, C.A.; *R. v. Taylor (J.S.)* (1984) 6 Cr.App.R.(S.) 448, C.A.; *R. v. Hannell* (1985) 82 Cr.App.R. 41, C.A.
s. 47, amended: 1982, c.48, s.30.
s. 48, rules 85/601.
s. 48, amended: 1980, c.43, sch.7.
s. 50, see *R. v. Eadie* (1978) 66 Cr.App.R. 234, C.A.; *R. v. Midgley* [1979] R.T.R. 1, C.A.; *Allan v. Patterson* [1980] R.T.R. 97, High Court of Justiciary; *Jarvis v. Norris* [1980] R.T.R. 424, D.C.; *R. v. Austin* [1981] R.T.R. 10, C.A.; *R. v. Ford* [1982] R.T.R. 5, C.A.; *R. v. Governor of Holloway Prison, ex p. Jennings* [1982] 3 W.L.R. 450; [1982] 3 All E.R. 104, H.L.; *R. v. Coventry Magistrates' Court, ex p. Wilson* [1982] R.T.R. 177, D.C.; *R. v. Seymour (Edward)* [1983] R.T.R. 202, C.A.; *R. v. McLaren* [1984] R.T.R. 126, C.A.; *Hughes v. Challes* [1984] R.T.R. 283, D.C.; *R. v. Krawec* [1985] R.T.R. 1, C.A.; *R. v. Hazell* [1985] R.T.R. 369, C.A.; *R. v. Khan* [1985] R.T.R. 365, C.A.
s. 50, regs. 80/222.
s. 50, repealed: 1988, c.54, sch.1.
s. 52, see *Taylor v. Chief Constable of Kent, The Times,* January 16, 1981, D.C.
s. 53, see *R. v. Wells Street Stipendiary Magistrates, ex p. Golding* [1979] Crim.L.R. 254, D.C.
s. 53, repealed in pt.: 1985, c.13, sch.3.
s. 54, repealed in pt.: 1984, c.60, sch.7.
s. 55, repealed in pt.: 1981, c.22, sch.6; order 81/1115.
s. 56, repealed: 1988, c.13, sch.4.
s. 57, order 78/474.
ss. 58 (in pt.), 59–61, repealed: 1980, c.43, sch.9.
s. 62, see *Grennan v. Wescott* [1988] R.T.R. 253, D.C.
s. 62, repealed: 1984, c.60, sch.7.

1977—cont.

45. Criminal Law Act 1977—cont.
s. 63, repealed in pt.: 1980, c.22, sch.4; c.43, sch.9.
s. 64, repealed in pt.: 1978, c.30, sch.3; 1980, c.43, sch.7.
s. 65, see *R. v. Adair* (1978) 123 S.J. 32, C.A.; *R. v. Brentwood JJ., ex p. Jones* [1979] R.T.R. 155, D.C.; *R. v. South Western Magistrates' Court, ex p. Beaton* [1980] R.T.R. 35, D.C.; *R. v. Wells Street JJ., ex p. Collett* [1981] R.T.R. 272, D.C.; *R. v. Krawec* [1985] R.T.R. 1, C.A.
s. 65, orders 77/1365, 1426, 1682, 1744; 78/712, 900; 80/487, 587 (S.), 1632, 1707 (S.); 82/243; 85/579.
s. 65, amended: 1980, c.43, sch.7; repealed in pt.: 1980, c.43, sch.9; c.47, sch.5; order 81/1115.
sch. 1, see *Allen v. Ireland* [1984] 1 W.L.R. 903, D.C.
sch. 1, repealed in pt.: 1983, c.2, sch.9; 1986, c.48, sch.5; 1988, c.54, sch.1.
sch. 2, repealed: 1980, c.43, sch.9; repealed in pt.: 1981, c.45, sch.
sch. 3, repealed: 1980, c.43, sch.9, repealed in pt.: 1980, c.51, sch.26; 1981, c.45, sch.
sch. 4, repealed: 1980, c.43, sch.9.
sch. 5, amended: *ibid.*, sch.7; repealed in pt.: 1979, c.2, sch.6; 1980, c.43, sch.9; 1988, c.33, sch.16; c.54, sch.1.
sch. 6, repealed in pt.: 1979, c.36, sch.8; c.39, sch.7; 1980, c.5, sch.6; c.7, sch.2; c.44, sch.5(S.); c.51, schs.23,26; c.66, sch. 25; 1981, c.69, sch.17; 1983, c.20, sch.6; 1984, c.12, sch.7; c.23, sch.3; c.27, sch.14; c.30, sch.11; c.55, sch.7; 1987, c.35, s.2; 1988, c.17, sch.4; c.33, sch.16; c.54, sch.1.
sch. 7, repealed in pt.: 1980, c.43, sch.9.
sch. 8, repealed: *ibid.*
sch. 9, amended: 1982, c.48, sch.14; repealed in pt.: *ibid.*, sch.16.
sch. 10, repealed: 1988, c.13, sch.4.
sch. 11, repealed in pt.: 1982, c.48, sch.16.
sch. 12, see *R. v. Adair* (1978) 123 S.J. 32, C.A.; *R. v. Wells Street JJ., ex p. Collett* [1981] R.T.R. 272, D.C.; *R. v. Krawec* [1985] R.T.R. 1, C.A.
sch. 12, repealed in pt. (S.): 1978, c.28, sch.4; 1980, c.22, sch.4; c.43, sch.9; c.51, sch.26; 1982, c.44, sch.; c.48, sch.16; c.49, sch.6.; 1983, c.2, sch.9; c.28, schs.10, 12; 1984, c.27, sch.14; 1988, c.17, sch.4; c.33, sch.16; c.34, sch.6; c.54, sch.1.
schs. 12, 14, see *R. v. Brentwood JJ., ex p. Jones* [1979] Crim.L.R. 115, D.C.
sch. 14, see *R. v. South Western Magistrates' Court, ex p. Beaton* [1980] R.T.R. 35, D.C; *R. v. Clarke* [1982] 1 W.L.R. 1090, C.A.
sch. 14, amended: 1980, c.43, sch.7; repealed in pt.: *ibid.*, sch.9.

46. Insurance Brokers (Registration) Act 1977.
Royal Assent, July 29, 1977.
ss. 3, 5, see *Pickles v. Insurance Brokers' Registration Council* [1984] 1 All E.R. 1073, D.C.
s. 11, amended: 1985, c.9, sch.2.
ss. 12, 15, amended: 1986, c.60, s.138.

1977—cont.

46. Insurance Brokers (Registration) Act 1977— cont.

ss. 15, 18, see *James* v. *Insurance Brokers' Registration Council, The Times,* February 16, 1984, H.L.

s. 19, amended: 1981, c.54, sch.5.

s. 20, rules 78/1503.

ss. 27, 28, orders 78/1394, 1395, 1456–1458: 79/408, 489, 490; 81/1630; 82/1406; 85/1804; 87/1496; 88/950.

s. 28, order 80/62.

s. 29, amended: 1981, c.31, sch.4; 1982, c.50, sch.5; 1985, c.9, sch.2; repealed in pt.: 1980, c.25, sch.5.

s. 30, orders 77/1782; 78/1393; 80/1824. sch., order 80/62.

47. Local Authorities (Restoration of Works Powers) Act 1977.

Royal Assent, July 29, 1977.

repealed: 1985, c.71, sch.1.

48. Housing (Homeless Persons) Act 1977.

Royal Assent, July 29, 1977.

repealed (S.): 1987, c.26, sch. 24.

see *R.* v. *Beverley Borough Council, ex p. McPhee* [1979] J.P.L. 94, D.C.; *R.* v. *Slough Borough Council, ex p. Ealing London Borough Council; R.* v. *Slough Borough Council, ex p. Jack; R.* v. *Ealing London Borough Council, ex p. Slough Borough Council; R.* v. *Hillingdon London Borough Council, ex p. Slough Borough Council, The Times,* December 23, 1980, C.A; *Cocks* v. *Thanet District Council* [1982] 3 W.L.R. 1121, H.L.; *R.* v. *Swansea City Council, ex p. Thomas, The Times,* April 14, 1983, Woolf J.; *R.* v. *Mole Valley District Council, ex p. Minnett* (1983) 12 H.L.R. 51, D.C.; *R.* v. *Wyre Borough Council, ex p. Joyce* (1983) 11 H.L.R. 73, D.C.; *R.* v. *Hillingdon London Borough, ex p. Wilson* (1983) 12 H.L.R. 63, D.C.; *R.* v. *Westminster City Council, ex p. Ali* (1983) 11 H.L.R. 85, D.C.; *R.* v. *Wandsworth London Borough, ex p. Rose* (1983) 11 H.L.R. 107, D.C.; *R.* v. *Exeter City Council, ex p. Gliddon and Draper* (1984) 14 H.L.R. 103, Woolf J., *R.* v. *Southampton City Council, ex p. Ward* (1984) 14 H.L.R. 119, McCullough J.; *R.* v. *Woodspring District Council, ex p. Walters* (1984) 16 H.L.R. 75, D.C.; *R.* v. *Surrey Heath Borough Council, ex p. Li* (1984) 16 H.L.R. 83, D.C.; *R.* v. *Ryedale District Council, ex p. Smith* (1984) 16 H.L.R. 69, D.C.; *R.* v. *Hambleton District Council, ex p. Geoghan (Thomas)* [1985] J.P.L. 394, Forbes J.; *R.* v. *Preseli District Council, ex p. Fisher* (1984) 17 H.L.R. 147, D.C.; *City of Gloucester* v. *Miles* (1985) 17 H.L.R. 292, C.A.; *R.* v. *West Dorset District Council, ex p. Phillips* (1984) 17 H.L.R. 336, Hodgson J.

s. 1, see *Williamson* v. *Moray District Council,* 1980 S.L.T.(Sh.Ct.) 32; *Brown* v. *Hamilton District Council,* 1980 S.L.T.(Sh.Ct.) 81; *Lambert* v. *Ealing London Borough Council* [1982] 1 W.L.R. 550, C.A.; *Stringer* v. *Halton Borough Council,* August 27, 1982, H.H. Judge

1977—cont.

48. Housing (Homeless Persons) Act 1977—cont.

Lloyd Jones; *R.* v. *South Herefordshire District Council, ex p. Miles* (1983) 17 H.L.R. 82, D.C.; *R.* v. *Borough of Dinefwr, ex p. Marshall* (1984) 17 H.L.R. 130, McCullough J.; *McAlinden* v. *Bearsden and Milngavie District Council* (O.H.),September 6, 1985; *Hynds* v. *Midlothian District Council* (O.H.), July 3, 1985; *R.* v. *Purbeck District Council, ex p. Cadney* (1985) 17 H.L.R. 534, Nolan J.; *R.* v. *Hillingdon London Borough Council, ex p. Pulhofer* [1986] 1 All E.R. 467, H.L.; *R.* v. *Hammersmith and Fulham London Borough Council, ex p. O'Brian* (1985) 84 L.G.R. 202, Glidewell J.

s. 1, amended(S.): 1985, c.71, sch.2; 1986, c.65, s.21.

ss. 1, 2, see *Re Islam (Taffazzul); R.* v. *Hillingdon London Borough Council, ex p. Islam (Taffazzul)* [1981] 3 W.L.R. 942, H.L.; *R.* v. *Waveney District Council, ex p. Bowers, The Times,* May 25, 1982, Stephen Brown J.; *R.* v. *Ealing London Borough Council, ex p. Sidhu* [1982] 80 L.G.R. 534, Hodgson J.; *Stewart* v. *Monklands District Council* (O.H.), 1987 S.L.T. 630.

s. 1, 4, see *R.* v. *Westminster City Council, ex p. Chambers* (1983) 81 L.G.R. 407, D.C.

s. 2, see *R.* v. *Waveney District Council, ex p. Bowers* [1982] 3 W.L.R. 661, C.A.; *Noble* v. *South Herefordshire District Council* (1983) 17 H.L.R. 80, C.A.; *R.* v. *Bath City Council, ex p. Sangermano* (1984) 17 H.L.R. 94; *Hynds* v. *Midlothian District Council* (O.H.), July 3, 1985; *Kelly* v. *Monklands District Council* (O.H.), 1986 S.L.T. 169; *R.* v. *Hammersmith and Fulham London Borough Council, ex p. O'Brian* (1985) 84 L.G.R. 202, Glidewell J.

s. 3, see *Thornton* v. *Kirklees Metropolitan Borough Council* [1979] 2 All E.R. 349, C.A.; *De Falco* v. *Crawley Borough Council; Silvestri* v. *Same, The Times,* December 13, 1979, C.A; *Miller* v. *Wandsworth London Borough Council, The Times,* March 19, 1980, Walton J.; *Delahaye* v. *Oswestry Borough Council, The Times,* July 29, 1980, Woolf J.; *Youngs* v. *Thanet District Council* (1980) 78 L.G.R. 474, Judge Davies, Q.C.; *City of Gloucester Council* v. *Miles* (1985) 17 H.L.R. 292, C.A.; *Eastleigh Borough Council* v. *Walsh* [1985] 2 All E.R. 112, H.L.

s. 3, amended(S.): 1985, c.71, sch.2.

s. 4, see *Lally* v. *Kensington and Chelsea Royal Borough, The Times,* March 27, 1980, Browne-Wilkinson J.; *Att.-Gen. (ex rel. Tilley)* v. *Wandsworth London Borough Council, The Times,* March 21, 1980, Judge Mervyn Davies; *Williamson* v. *Moray District Council,* 1980 S.L.T.(Sh.Ct.) 32; *Youngs* v. *Thanet District Council* (1980) 78 L.G.R. 474, Judge Davies, Q.C.; *Brown* v. *Hamilton District Council,* 1980 S.L.T.(Sh.Ct.) 81; *Dyson* v. *Kerrier District Council* [1980] 1 W.L.R. 1205; [1980] 3 All E.R. 313, C.A.; *MacKenzie* v.

1977—cont.

48. Housing (Homeless Persons) Act 1977—*cont.*
West Lothian District Council, 1979 S.C. 433;
Din (Taj) v. Wandsworth London Borough
Council [1981] 3 All E.R. 881, H.L.; Re Islam
(Taffazzul); R. v. Hillingdon London Borough
Council, ex p. Islam (Taffazzul) [1981] 3 W.L.R.
942, H.L.; R. v. Director of Housing and Com-
munity Services, Thurrock Borough Council,
ex p. R. L. Weslie, September 22, 1981,
Judge Phillips; R. v. Wyre Borough Council,
ex p. Parr, The Times, February 4, 1982, C.A.;
Robinson v. Torbay Borough Council [1982] 1
W.L.R. 726, Goddall J.; Restormel Borough
Council v. Buscombe (1982) 12 Fam.Law 207,
C.A.; R. v. Exeter City Council, ex p. Gliddon
[1985] 1 All E.R. 493, Woolf J.; R. v. Ham-
mersmith and Fulham London Borough Coun-
cil, ex p. O'Brian (1985) 17 H.L.R. 471,
Glidewell J.; Kensington and Chelsea Royal
Borough Council v. Hayden (1984) 17 H.L.R.
114, C.A.; Hynds v. Midlothian District Council
(O.H.), July 3, 1985; R. v. Ealing London
Borough Council, ex p. McBain [1985] 1
W.L.R. 1351, C.A.; Kelly v. Monklands District
Council (O.H.), 1986 S.L.T. 169; R. v. Hilling-
don London Borough Council [1986] 1 All E.R.
467, H.L.; R. v. East Hertfordshire District
Council, ex p. Hunt, (1985) 18 H.L.R. 51,
Mann J.; R. v. Camden London Borough
Council, ex p. Wait, The Times, July 12, 1986,
McCowan J.; Mazzacherini v. Argyll and Bute
District Council (O.H.), 1987 S.C.L.R. 475.
s. 4, amended (S.): 1986, c.65, s.21.
ss. 4, 5, see R. v. Slough Borough Council, ex
p. Ealing London Borough [1981] 2 W.L.R.
399; [1981] 1 All E.R. 601, C.A.; R. v. Westminster City Council, ex p. Chambers, The
Times, October 21, 1982, McCullough J.;
Brown v. Hamilton District Council (H.L.),
1983 S.L.T. 397.
ss. 4, 8, see R. v. Beverley Borough Council,
The Times, October 27, 1978, D.C.
s. 5, see R. v. Hillingdon London Borough Council, ex p. Streeting (No. 2) [1980] 3 All E.R.
413, C.A.; R. v. Director of Housing and
Community Services, Thurrock Borough
Council, ex p. R. L. Weslie, September 22,
1981, Judge Phillips; R. v. Eastleigh Borough
Council, ex p. Betts [1983] 2 All E.R. 1111; R.
v. Hammersmith and Fulham London Borough
Council, ex p. O'Brian (1985) 17 H.L.R. 471,
Glidewell J.; R. v. Vale of the White Horse
District Council, ex p. Smith (1985) 83 L.G.R.
437, Woolf J.; Hynds v. Midlothian District
Council (O.H.), July 3, 1985; R. v. Hammersmith and Fulham London Borough Council,
ex p. O'Brian (1985) 84 L.G.R. 202, Glidewell
J.
s. 5, orders 78/69, 661.
s. 5, amended(S.): 1985, c.71, sch.2.
ss. 5, 6, see R. v. Bristol City Council, ex p.
Browne [1979] 3 All E.R. 344, D.C.
ss. 6, 7, repealed(S.): 1985, c.71, sch.1.
s. 7, see R. v. Westminster City Council, ex p.
Chambers (1983) 81 L.G.R. 407, D.C.

1977—cont.

48. Housing (Homeless Persons) Act 1977—*cont.*
s. 9, see R. v. South Herefordshire District
Council, ex p, Miles (1983) 17 H.L.R. 82, D.C.
s. 9, amended(S.): 1985, c.71, sch.2.
ss. 10, 13, repealed(S.): ibid.,sch.1.
s. 12, see Kelly v. Monklands District Council
(O.H.), 1986 S.L.T. 169.
s. 14, orders 77/1821; 78/315; amended: 1978,
c.44, sch.16; repealed in pt.: ibid.,schs.16,17.
s. 16, see Re Islam (Taffazzul); R. v. Hillingdon
London Borough Council, ex p. Islam (Taffazzul) [1981] 3 W.L.R. 942, H.L.; R. v. Wimbourne District Council, ex p. Curtis, (1985)
18 H.L.R. 79, Mann J.
s. 17, see Re Falco and Silvestri v. Crawley
Borough Council [1980] 1 All E.R. 913; [1980]
1 C.M.L.R. 437, C.A.; Dyson v. Kerrier District
Council [1980] 1 W.L.R. 1205; [1980] 3 All
E.R. 313, C.A.; Lewis v. North Devon District
Council [1981] 1 All E.R. 27, Woolf J.; Krish-
nan v. Hillingdon London Borough Council,
January 21, 1981, Hugh Francis, Q.C., sitting
as a Deputy Judge, D.C.; R. v. Slough Bor-
ough Council, ex p. Ealing London Borough
[1981] 2 W.L.R 399; [1981] 1 All E.R. 601,
C.A.; Youngs v. Thanet District Council (1980)
78 L.G.R. 474, Judge Davies, Q.C.; Pin v.
Wandsworth London Borough Council, The
Times, June 30, 1981, C.A.; White v. Exeter
City Council, October 30, 1981, His Honour
Judge Cox sitting as a High Court Judge;
MacKenzie v. West Lothian District Council,
1979 S.C. 433; R. v. Thanet District Council,
ex p. Reeve, The Times, November 25, 1981,
Woolf J; Din (Taj) v. Wandsworth London
Borough Council [1981] 3 All E.R. 881, H.L.;
Re Islam (Taffazzul); R. v. Hillingdon London
Borough Council, ex p. Islam (Taffazzul) [1981]
3 W.L.R. 942, H.L.; Lambert v. Ealing Borough
Council [1982] 1 W.L.R. 550, C.A.; Robinson
v. Torbay Borough Council [1982] 1 All E.R.
726, Goddall J.; R. v. Westminster City Coun-
cil, ex p. Chambers, The Times, October 21,
1982, Cullough J.; R. v. Salford City Council,
ex p. Devenport, The Times, March 5, 1983,
C.A.; R. v. Hammersmith and Fulham London
Borough Council, ex p. Duro-Rama, The
Times, March 10, 1983, Woolf J.; R. v. Roch-
ester City Council, ex p. Trotman, The Times,
May 9, 1983, Forbes J.; Brown v. Hamilton
District Council (H.L.), 1983 S.L.T. 397; R. v.
Hillingdon London Borough Council, ex p.
Wilson, The Times, July 14, 1983, Woolf J.;
R. v. Basingstoke and Deane Borough Coun-
cil, ex p. Bassett (1984) 14 Fam.Law 90,
Taylor J.; R. v. Eastleigh Borough Council, ex
p. Beattie (1984) 14 Fam.Law 115, Woolf J.;
R. v. Wandsworth London Borough Council,
ex p. Nimako-Boateng (1984) 14 Fam.Law
117, Woolf J.; R. v. Portsmouth City Council,
ex p. Knight (1984) 82 L.G.R. 184, Woolf J.;
R. v. Salford City Council, ex p. Devenport
(1984) 82 L.G.R. 89, C.A.; R. v. Reigate and
Banstead Borough Council (1985) 15
Fam.Law 28, McCullough J.; R. v. Exeter City

1977—cont.

48. Housing (Homeless Persons) Act 1977—*cont.*
Council, ex p. Gliddon [1985] 1 All E.R. 493,
Woolf J.; R. v. South Herefordshire District
Council, ex p. Miles (1983) 17 H.L.R. 82, D.C.;
R. v. Ealing London Borough Council, ex p.
McBain, The Times, October 10, 1985, C.A.;
R. v. Gloucester City Council, ex p. Miles
(1985) 83 L.G.R. 607, C.A.; R. v. Eastleigh
Borough Council, ex p. Evans (1984) 17 H.L.R.
515, McNeil J.; R. v. Penwith District Council,
ex p. Trevena (1984) 17 H.L.R. 527, McNeil
J.; R. v. Wimbourne District Council, ex p.
Curtis, (1985) 18 H.L.R. 79, Mann J.: R. v.
Hammersmith and Fulham London Borough
Council, ex p. O'Brian (1985) 84 L.G.R. 202,
Glidewell J.; Stewart v. Monklands District
Council (O.H.), 1987 S.C.L.R. 630; Mazzacherini
v. Argyll and Bute District Council (O.H.), 1987
S.C.L.R. 475; Wincentzen v. Monklands Dis-
trict Council, 1988 S.L.T. 847.

s. 18, see Eastleigh Borough Council v. Betts
[1983] 2 All E.R. 1111, H.L.; R. v. Vale of
White Horse District Council, ex p. Smith
(1985) 83 L.G.R. 437, Woolf J.

s. 18A, added(S.): 1985, c.71, sch.2.

s. 19, amended(S.): ibid.; repealed in pt.(S.):
ibid.,sch.1.

s. 20, repealed in pt.(S.): ibid.

s. 21, amended(S.): ibid., sch.2; repealed in
pt.(S.): ibid.,sch.1.

49. National Health Service Act 1977.
Royal Assent, July 29, 1977.

see Hensman v. Traill, The Times, October 22,
1980, Bristow J.

ss. 1, 2, regs. 81/933.

ss. 1, 3, see R. v. Secretary of State for Social
Services, ex p. Hincks (1979) 123 S.J. 436,
Wien J.

s. 4, amended: 1982, c.51, sch.3; 1983, c.20,
sch.4.

s. 5, amended: 1979, c.23, s.1; 1984, c.48, s.9;
1988, c.40, sch.12; c.49, s.10; repealed in
pt.: 1988, c.7, sch.5; c.49, s.10, sch.3.

s. 6, orders 78/339, 489; 81/597; regs. 81/101.

s. 6, repealed in pt.: 1980, c.53, s.8, sch.7.

s. 8, orders 81/1836–1838; 82/343–345; 83/30,
31, 336, 1090; 84/328; 85/25, 26, 369, 370;
88/406, 407.

s. 8, amended: 1980, c.53, sch.1; repealed in
pt.: 1983, c.41, sch.10.

s. 9, order 81/1838.

s. 9, repealed: 1983, c.20, s.13, sch.10.

s. 10, orders 84/1213, 1946; 85/301.

s. 10, substituted: 1984, c.48, s.5.

s. 11, orders 78/331; 80/796; 81/727; 82/313,
314, 1515; 83/312, 892, 1351; 84/188, 190,
692; 85/996, 1345, 1877; 86/440, 963, 1015,
2004, 2006; 87/6, 151, 192, 808.

s. 11, amended: 1980, c.53, sch.1.

s. 12, regs. 80/797; 81/728, 1847; 82/10, 312,
315; 83/314, 1352; 84/189; 85/1876; 86/964,
2005, 2007.

s. 12, amended: 1980, c.53, sch.1; repealed in
pt.: 1984, c.48, sch.8.

1977—cont.

49. National Health Service Act 1977—*cont.*
s. 13, regs. 80/1204; 81/888; 82/37, 287, 315;
84/189, 1577; 85/304; 87/245; orders 81/728;
84/693; 86/964, 2005, 2007.

ss. 13, 14, see Linden v. D.H.S.S. [1986] 1
W.L.R. 164, Scott J.

ss. 13, 14, amended: 1980, c.53, sch.1.

s. 14, regs. 80/1204; 81/888; 82/37, 287;
85/304.

s. 15, regs. 88/864.

s. 15, amended: 1980, c.53, sch.1; 1984, c.48,
s.5; repealed in pt.: ibid., schs.3,8.

s. 16, regs. 79/739, 897; 81/774; 82/277, 287;
83/313; 85/213; 87/401.

s. 16, amended: 1980, c.53, sch.1.

s. 17, regs. 80/1204; 81/888; 82/287; order
84/1577.

s. 17, substituted: 1984, c.48, sch.2.

s. 18, regs. 82/287; 87/245; orders 84/693,
1577.

s. 18, amended: 1980, c.53, sch.1; repealed in
pt.: order 85/39.

s. 19, amended: 1980, c.53, sch.1; repealed in
pt.: 1984, c.48, sch.8.

s. 20, regs. 78/21; 82/37.

s. 20, amended: 1980, c.53, sch.1.

s. 21, see Decision No. R(A) 3/83.

s. 22, regs. 84/296; orders 82/314; 85/305.

s. 22, amended: 1980, c.53, sch.1; 1983, c.41,
sch.5; 1984, c.48, sch.3; repealed in pt.
(prosp.): 1988, c.40, sch.13.

s. 23, amended: 1988, c.54, sch.3; repealed in
pt.: 1980, c.53, sch.7.

s. 24, repealed: 1980, c.63, sch.2.

s. 25, amended: 1988, c.49, sch.2.

s. 26, amended: 1980, c.53, s.3.

s. 27, amended: 1988, c.54, sch.3.

s. 28, repealed in pt.: 1988, c.49, s.19, sch.3.

ss. 28A, 28B, substituted: 1983, c.41, s.1;
amended: 1985, c.71, sch.2; 1988, c.50,
sch.17.

s. 29, regs. 80/1503; 81/774; 83/313; 85/290,
540, 803, 1053, 1712; 86/381, 916, 1846;
87/5, 407, 1425; 88/866, 1106.

s. 29, amended: 1980, c.53, s.7, sch.1; 1983,
c.41, sch.6; c.54, sch.5; order 85/39.

s. 30, regs. 79/1644; amended: 1980, c.53,
sch.1; order 81/432; 1984, c.48, sch.3; order
85/39; repealed in pt.: 1980, c.53, schs.1,7.

s. 31, regs. 79/1644.

s. 31, amended: 1980, c.53, sch.1; order 85/39.

s. 32, regs. 79/1644; 80/1900; 81/1790; 84/215;
85/1353; 86/1642.

s. 32, amended: order 85/39.

s. 33, amended: 1980, c.53, sch.1; orders
81/432; 85/39; 1988, c.49, sch.2.

s. 34, amended: 1980, c.53, sch.1; order 85/39.

s. 35, regs. 80/986, 1503; 84/760, 1424;
85/1336; 86/1499; 87/445, 736, 1512, 1965;
88/576.

s. 35, amended: 1980, c.53, sch.1; 1983, c.41,
s.15; 1984, c.24, sch.5; order 85/39.

s. 36, regs. 80/986; 81/774; 84/760, 1424;
85/1336; 86/1499; 87/445, 1512, 1965;
88/576; order 81/432.

CAP.

CAP.

1977—cont.

49. National Health Service Act 1977—cont.

s. 36, amended: 1980, c.53, sch.1; 1984, c.48, sch.3; order 85/39; 1988, c.49, sch.2.

s. 37, regs. 84/1424; 85/1336; 87/445.

s. 37, amended: 1980, c.53, sch.1; 1988, c.49 s.12; repealed in pt.: *ibid.*, sch.3.

s. 38, regs. 77/1999; 85/298; 86/975; 88/486.

s. 38, amended: 1980, c.53, sch.1; 1984, c.48, sch.3; order 85/39; 1988, c.49, s.13; repealed in pt.: 1984, c.48, s.1, sch.8.

s. 39, regs. 77/1999; 81/305; 85/298; 86/975, 976; 88/428, 486.

s. 39, amended: 1980, c.53, sch.1; order 85/39.

s. 40, regs. 86/975.

s. 41, amended: 1980, c.53, s.20, sch.1; order 85/39; repealed in pt.: 1980, c.53, sch.7.

ss. 41, 42, regs. 80/1503; 83/313; 85/290, 540, 805, 955, 1053, 1712; 86/381, 916, 1486; 87/5, 401, 1425; 88/866, 1106.

s. 42, substituted: 1986, c.66, s.3; amended: order 87/2202.

s. 43, regs. 83/313; 85/290, 803, 955.

s. 43A, amended: 1988, c.49, s.15.

ss. 43A, 43B, added: 1984, c.48, sch.7.

s. 43B, amended: 1986, c.66, s.4.

s. 44, amended: 1980, c.53, s.21, sch.1; 1984, c.48, sch.3; repealed in pt.: *ibid.*, sch.8.

s. 45, amended: 1980, c.53, s.21, sch.1; 1984, c.48, sch.3; repealed in pt.: *ibid.*, schs.3,8.

s. 46, amended: 1980, c.53, s.21, sch.1; order 85/39; repealed in pt.: 1984, c.48, sch.8.

s. 49, regs. 85/1671.

s. 50, regs. 86/975.

ss. 54, 55, amended: 1980, c.53, sch.1; order 85/39.

s. 56, amended: 1980, c.53, sch.1; 1984, c.48, sch.3; order 85/39.

s. 58, repealed: 1988, c.49, sch.3.

ss. 59, 60, repealed: 1980, c.50, s.10, sch.7.

ss. 61, 62 (in pt.): repealed: 1988, c.49, sch.3.

s. 63, amended: *ibid.*, s.7, repealed in pt.: *ibid.*, s.7, sch.3.

ss. 65, 66, substituted: *ibid.*, s.7.

s. 66A, repealed: *ibid.*, sch.3.

ss. 67–71, repealed: 1980, c.53, c.9, sch.7.

s. 72, repealed in pt.: 1984, c.48, sch.2.

ss. 73–76, repealed: 1980, c.53, s.9, sch.7.

s. 77, regs. 78/950; 79/681; 80/26, 1503; 81/501, 1714; 82/289; 83/306, 1165; 84/298; 85/326; 86/432; 87/368; 88/427, 866.

s. 78, regs. 77/1999; 78/950; 79/677; 80/352, 986; 81/307; 82/284; 83/309; 84/298; 85/298, 352; 86/976, 1136; 88/473.

s. 78, amended: 1988, c.49, s.11, sch.2; repealed in pt.: *ibid.*, sch.3.

s. 79, regs. 78/950; 79/677; 80/352, 986, 987; 81/307; 82/284; 83/309; 85/352; 88/473.

s. 79, repealed: 1988, c.49, s.11; repealed in pt.: *ibid.*, s.11, sch.3.

s. 79A, added: *ibid.*, s.11.

s. 81, regs. 80/986; 86/976.

ss. 81, 82, repealed in pt.: 1984, c.48, sch.8.

s. 82, regs. 77/1999; 81/305, 307; 86/976.

s. 83, regs. 79/681; 80/264, 1503; 82/289; 83/306; 84/298; 85/326; 86/432; 87/368; 88/427.

1977—cont.

49. National Health Service Act 1977—cont.

s. 83, amended: 1980, c.53, sch.1; 1984, c.48, sch.8.

s. 83A, regs. 88/551.

s. 83A, added: 1988, c.7, s.14; amended: 1988, c.49, sch.2.

s. 85, amended: 1980, c.53, sch.1.

ss. 85, 86, see *R. v. Secretary of State for Social Services, ex p. Lewisham, Lambeth and Southwark London Borough Councils, The Times*, February 26, 1980, Woolf J.

s. 87, amended: 1981, c.67, sch.4.

ss. 88, 91, 95, amended: 1980, c.53, sch.1.

s. 92, orders 78/1072; 81/1837; 82/314, 83/307, 308; 84/281.

s. 96A, added: 1980, c.53, s.5.

s. 97, see *R. v. Hillingdon Health Authority, ex p. Goodwin, The Times*, December 13, 1983, Woolf J.

s. 97, substituted: 1980, c.53, s.6; amended: 1984, c.48, s.6, sch.3; 1988, c.49, s.16; repealed in pt.: 1984, c.48, sch.8.

s. 97A, substituted: 1980, c.53, s.6.

s. 97B, added: 1984, c.48, sch.3; amended: 1988, c.49, s.16.

s. 98, regs. 82/277, 315; 84/189.

s. 98, amended: 1980, c.53, sch.1; 1983, c.41, sch.5; 1984, c.48, s.6; repealed in pt.: *ibid.*, sch.8.

s. 99, regs. 82/277.

s. 99, amended: 1980, c.53, sch.1.

s. 100, repealed in pt.: 1980, c.3, sch.7; 1983, c.41, schs.9,10.

ss. 101, 102, repealed in pt.: 1980, c.53, sch.7.

s. 103, order 88/865.

s. 104, amended: 1980, c.53, sch.1.

s. 105, amended: 1982, c.51, s.65, sch.3; 1983, c.20, sch.4; repealed in pt.: *ibid.*, schs.4,6.

s. 106, amended: 1987, c.39, s.2.

s. 108, repealed in pt.: 1983, c.41, schs.9, 10.

s. 108A, added: 1987, c.39, s.6.

s. 109, orders 82/152; 83/1114, 1115; 84/124; 87/1272; 88/589, 597.

s. 109, amended: 1980, c.53, schs.1,2; 1988, c.49, s.12; repealed in pt.: 1980, s.53, schs.2,7.

s. 110, amended: *ibid.*, schs.1,2; repealed in pt.: *ibid.*, schs.2,7.

s. 111, amended: 1978, c.52, sch.11.

s. 117, amended: 1987, c.39, s.7.

s. 118, amended: *ibid.*, s.4.

s. 119, amended: *ibid.*, sch.11; 1980, c.53, sch.1; 1987, c.39, s.5; repealed in pt.: *ibid.*, schs.2,7; order 85/39.

s. 121, regs. 82/795, 863, 1577; 83/302; 84/300; 85/371, 508; 86/459, 950; 87/371; 88/8, 472.

s. 121, amended: 1988, c.49, s.7.

s. 123, amended: 1985, c.71, sch.2.

s. 124, regs. 82/286.

ss. 124, 125, amended: 1980, c.53, sch.1.

s. 126, orders 81/1837, 1838; 84/1213; 85/26, 301, 370; 87/736, 1512; 88/407.

ss. 126–128, regs. 86/975.

1977—cont.

49. National Health Service Act 1977—cont.

s. 128, amended: 1980, c.53, sch.1; 1983, c.2, sch.4; c.54, sch.5, 1984, c.24, sch.5; c.48, sch.3; repealed in pt.: 1979, c.36, schs.7,8; 1980, c.53, schs.2,7; 1984, c.48, sch.8; 1985, c.51, sch.17.

s. 129, regs. 82/295.

s. 130, orders 81/1473; 85/149.

sch. 1, amended: 1981, c.60, sch.1; 1988, c.40, sch.12; c.49, sch.2; repealed in pt.: 1980, c.20, sch.1; 1988, c.49, sch.3.

sch. 3, see *R.* v. *East Berkshire Health Authority, ex p. Walsh,* November 15, 1983, Hodgson J.

sch. 3, regs. 82/312.

sch. 3, amended: 1979, c.23, s.2.

sch. 4, regs. 81/101; 86/458.

sch. 4, amended: order 78/489.

sch. 5, see *Wadi* v. *Cornwall and Isles of Scilly Family Practitioner Committee* [1985] I.C.R. 492, E.A.T.; *R.* v. *Trent Regional Health Authority, ex p. Jones, The Times,* June 19, Macpherson J.

sch. 5, regs. 78/228, 332, 1090; 79/738, 739, 897; 80/797; 81/933; 82/10, 276, 315, 345, 1516; 83/314, 315, 894, 1091, 1275, 1352; 84/189, 693, 994, 1735; 85/47, 213, 1067, 1876; orders 81/728, 1577; 84/1213; 85/66, 303, 369; regs. 86/331, 524, 964, 1014, 2005, 2007; 87/7, 152, 401, 1425; order 88/406.

sch. 5, amended: 1980, c.53, s.22, sch.1; 1983, c.41, s.15, sch.6; 1984, c.24, sch.5; c.48, sch.3; order 85/39; repealed in pt.: 1983, c.41, s.13, sch. 10; 1984, c.48, schs.3,8; order 85/39; 1988, c.40, sch.13 (prosp.).

sch. 6, see *R,* v. *Hillingdon Health Authority, ex p. Goodwin, The Times,* December 13, 1983, Woolf J.

sch. 6, amended: 1980, c.53, sch.1.

sch. 7, regs. 78/21; 82/37, 277; 85/304.

sch. 7, amended: 1984, c.48, sch.3.

sch. 8, see *Decision No. R(A) 3/83.*

sch. 8, orders 81/1838, 1847.

sch. 8, amended: 1982, c.51, s.65, sch.3; 1983, c.20, sch.4; c.41, sch.9; 1988, c.40, sch.12, repealed in pt.: 1983, c.41, sch.10.

sch. 9, repealed in pt.: 1984, c.48, sch.8.

sch. 10, see *Kerr* v. *Morris* [1986] 3 W.L.R. 662, C.A.

sch. 11, amended: 1981, c.61, sch.7.

sch. 12, regs. 78/950; 79/677; 80/352, 986, 987, 1503, 1659; 81/305, 307, 1345; 82/284; 83/309, 1165; 84/299; 85/298, 326, 352; 86/976, 1136; 88/427, 428, 473, 552, 1435.

sch. 12, amended: 1980, c.53, sch.5; 1984, c.48, sch.1; 1988, c.49, ss.11,13, sch.2; repealed in pt.: 1980, c.53, schs.5,7; 1984, c.48, sch.8; 1988, c.7, sch.5; c.49, sch.3.

sch. 13, amended: 1978, c.52, sch.11; 1987, c.39, s.4.

sch. 14, regs. 82/295.

sch. 14, amended: 1978, c.44, sch.16; 1984, c.22, sch.2; c.24, sch.5; repealed in pt.: 1978, c.44, sch.16; S.L.R. 1978; 1980, c.9, sch.10; 1982, c.51, sch.4; 1983, c.54, sch.7; 1984, c.29, sch.12.

1977—cont.

49. National Health Service Act 1977—cont.

sch. 15, amended: 1980, c.53, sch.1; repealed in pt.: 1978, c.40, sch.2; S.L.R. 1978; 1979, c.36, sch.8; 1980, c.48, sch.20; c.53, sch.7; 1982, c.51, sch.4; 1983, c.20, schs.6, 10; c.54, sch.5; 1984, c.23, sch.3; c.24, sch.6, c.29, sch.12; S.L.R. 1986; 1988, c.1, sch.31; c.49, sch.3; c.54, sch.1.

50. Unfair Contract Terms Act 1977.

Royal Assent, October 26, 1977.

see *British Airports Authority* v. *British Airways Board, The Times,* May 8, 1981, Parker J.; *Boomsma* v. *Clark & Rose,* 1983 S.L.T.(Sh.Ct.) 67.

s. 1, amended: 1984, c.3, s.2.

s. 2, see *Thompson* v. *Lohan (T.) (Plant Hire), The Times,* February 12, 1987, C.A.; *Smith* v. *Eric S. Bush (A Firm), The Times,* March 18, 1987, C.A.; *Phillips Products* v. *Hyland (Note)* [1987] 1 W.L.R. 659, C.A.; *Davies* v. *Parry* [1988] 20 E.G. 92, and 21 E.G. 74, McNeill J.

ss. 2, 3, see *Waldron Kelly* v. *British Railways Board,* March 17, 1981, Judge Brown Q.C., Stockport County Ct.

s. 3, see *Stag Line* v. *Tyne Shiprepair Group, The Times,* April 19, 1984, Staughton J.

s. 6, see *Hughes* v. *Hall & Hall* [1981] R.T.R. 430, D.C.; *Cavendish-Woodhouse* v. *Mancey* (1984) 82 L.G.R. 376, D.C.

s. 6, amended: 1979, c.54, sch.2.

ss. 6, 12, see *R. & B. Customs Brokers Co.* v. *United Dominions Trust; Saunders Abbot (1980) (Third Party)* [1988] 1 W.L.R. 321, C.A.

s. 7, amended: 1982, c.29, s.17.

ss. 8, 11, see *South Western General Property* v. *Marton* (1982) 263 E.G. 1090, Croom-Johnson J.

s. 11, see *Waldron Kelly* v. *British Railways Board,* March 17, 1981, Judge Brown Q.C.; Stockport County Court; *Walker* v. *Boyle* [1982] 1 All E.R. 634, Dillon J.; *George Mitchell (Chesterhall)* v. *Finney Lock Seeds, The Times,* July 2, 1983, H.L.; *South Western General Property Co.* v. *Marton* (1983) 2 Tr.L. 14, Croom-Johnson J.; *Stevenson* v. *Nationwide Building Society* (1984) 272 E.G. 663, Mr. J. Wilmers, Q.C.; *Smith* v. *Eric S. Bush (A Firm), The Times,* March 18, 1987, C.A.; *Phillips Products* v. *Hyland (Note)* [1987] 1 W.L.R. 659, C.A.

ss. 11, 13, see *Davies* v. *Parry* [1988] 20 E.G. 92, and 21 E.G. 74, McNeill J.

s. 14, amended: 1979, c.54, sch.2.

s. 17, see *McCrone* v. *Boots Farm Sales* (O.H.), 1981 S.L.T. 103; *Macrae & Dick* v. *Philip,* 1982 S.L.T.(Sh.Ct.) 5.

ss. 17, 20, see *Border Harvesters* v. *Edwards Engineering (Perth)* (O.H.), 1985 S.L.T. 128.

s. 20, see *Landcatch* v. *Marine Harvest* (O.H.), December 3, 1983.

ss. 20, 24, see *Continental Tyre & Rubber Co.* v. *Trunk Trailer Co.,* 1987 S.L.T. 58.

ss. 20, 25, amended: 1979, c.54, sch.2.

CAP.

1977—cont.

50. Unfair Contracts Terms Act 1977—cont.
s. 28, orders 78/54, 1468; 80/1872; 81/1240; 83/36, 582; 84/1548; 85/230, 1430; 86/1777.
s. 30, repealed: 1978, c.38, sch.3.
sch. 1, amended: 1986, c.39, sch.2; 1988, c.48, sch.7.
sch. 3, repealed in pt.: 1979, c.54, sch.3.

51. Pensioners Payments Act 1977.
Royal Assent, November 24, 1977.
repealed: 1986, c.50, sch.11.
s. 1, regs. 77/1947–1949; 78/1691.

52. Consolidated Fund (No. 2) Act 1977.
Royal Assent, December 15, 1977.

53. Finance (Income Tax Reliefs) Act 1977.
Royal Assent, December 15, 1977.
repealed: 1988, c.1, sch.31.

1978

1. Participation Agreements Act 1978.
Royal Assent, February 28, 1978.
s. 1, amended: 1982, c.23, s.31; 1985, c.9, sch.2.

2. Commonwealth Development Corporation Act 1978.
Royal Assent, March 23, 1978.
s. 2, amended: 1986, c.25, s.1.
s. 3, order 87/1253.
s. 9, amended: 1982, c.54, ss.1,2; 1986, c.25, s.1.
s. 9A, added: 1982, c.54, s.2; 1985, c.9, sch.2; repealed in pt.: 1986, c.25, s.1.
s. 10, amended: 1982, c.54, s.3.
s. 10A, added: 1986, c.25, s.1.
s. 11, amended: 1982, c.54, s.1; 1983, c.29, s.4; 1986, c.25, s.1.
s. 12, amended: ibid.
s. 17, amended: ibid.; repealed in pt.: 1979, c.60, sch.3; 1980, c.16, sch.2; 1986, c.25, s.1.
sch. 1, regs. 79/495.

3. Refuse Disposal (Amenity) Act 1978.
Royal Assent, March 23, 1978.
s. 1, amended: 1985, c.51, sch.6; order 85/1884; repealed in pt.: order 85/1884.
s. 2, amended (S.): 1984, c.54, sch.9; repealed in pt. (S.): ibid., schs.9,11.
s. 3, regs. 86/183.
s. 3, amended: 1980, c.66, sch.24; 1984, c.54, sch.9 (S.); 1985, c.51, sch.6; order 85/1884; repealed in pt.: 1980, c.65, schs.3,34; 1985, c.51, sch.17.
s. 4, regs. 86/183.
s. 4, amended: 1985, c.51, sch.6; order 85/1884; repealed in pt.: 1980, c.65, schs.3,34.
ss. 4, 5, regs. 78/1346; 80/169; 81/989; 82/1682; 85/1661.
s. 5, amended: 1985, c.51, sch.6; order 85/1884; repealed in pt.: 1985, c.51, sch. 17.
s. 6, amended (S.): 1984, c.54, sch.9; repealed in pt.: 1980, c.65, schs.3,34; 1985, c.51, sch.17.
s. 7, amended: 1981, c.67, sch.4; repealed in pt.: ibid., sch.6; 1985, c.51, sch.17.

CAP.

1978—cont.

3. Refuse Disposal (Amenity) Act 1978—cont.
s. 8, amended: 1986, c.63, sch.11; repealed in pt.: 1982, c.43, sch.4.
s. 9, order 84/288.
s. 11, amended: 1984, c.54, sch.9 (S.); order 85/1884.
s. 12 (in pt.), sch. 1, repealed: 1986, c.31, sch.6.

4. Local Government (Scotland) Act 1978.
Royal Assent, March 23, 1978.
s. 2, repealed: 1988, c.41, sch.13.
sch., repealed in pt.: 1983, c.2, sch.9.

5. Northern Ireland (Emergency Provisions) Act 1978.
Royal Assent, March 23, 1978.
continued in force, except s.12, sch.1; orders 80/1938; 81/1846; 83/1864; 85/40, 1083; 86/74; 87/30; 88/426.
repealed (prosp.): 1987, c.30, s.13.
see Spratt v. Doherty, The Times, July 23, 1983, H.L.
s. 2, substituted: 1987, c.30, s.1.
s. 3, amended: 1978, c.23, sch.5; order 81/228.
s. 3A, added: 1987, c.30, s.2.
s. 5A, added: ibid., s.3.
s. 6, substituted: ibid., s.4.
s. 7, amended: 1978, c.23, sch.5; 1980, c.47, sch.4.
s. 8, see R. v. Brophy [1980] 4 N.I. J.B., Kelly J.; R. v. McGrath [1980] 5 N.I.J.B., N.I.C.A; R v. Culbert [1982] 1 N.I.J.B., C.A.; R. v. Cowan [1987] 1 N.I.J.B. 15, C.A.; R. v. Howell [1987] 5 N.I.J.B. 10, Hutton J.
s. 8, substituted: 1987, c.30, s.5.
s. 9, amended and repealed in pt.: order 81/155.
s. 11, see McKee v. Chief Constable of Northern Ireland [1984] 1 W.L.R. 1358, H.L.
s. 11, substituted: 1987, c.30, s.6.
s. 13, amended: ibid., sch.1.
s. 14, see Murray v. Ministry of Defence [1988] 1 W.L.R. 692, H.L.
s. 14, amended: 1987, c.30, sch.1.
s. 15, amended: ibid., s.7, sch.1.
s. 18, amended: ibid., sch.1.
s. 19A, added: ibid., s.8.
s. 21, order 79/746.
s. 21, amended: 1987, c.30, s.9.
s. 22, see R. v. Lorenc [1988] N.I.J.B. 94, C.A.
s. 22, amended: 1987, c.30, s.10; repealed in pt.: ibid., s.10, sch.2.
s. 25, substituted: ibid., s.11.
s. 26, amended: ibid.
s. 28, rules 1982 (unnumbered).
ss. 28, 28A, substituted: 1987, c.30, s.12.
s. 28A, S.R. 1988 No. 221.
s. 30, order 86/75.
s. 31, see McKee v. Chief Constable of Northern Ireland [1984] 1 W.L.R. 1358, H.L.
s. 31, repealed in pt.: 1987, c.30, schs.1,2.
s. 32, amended: ibid., sch.1.
s. 33, orders 78/958, 1865; 79/817, 1683; 80/1049, 1938; 81/997, 1846; 82/956, 1874; 83/778, 1864; 84/1033; 85/40; 86/74, 1146; 87/30; 88/426.
s. 33, amended: 1978, c.23, sch.5; 1987, c.30, s.13, sch.1.

1978—cont.

5. Northern Ireland (Emergency Provisions) Act 1978—cont.
s. 34, repealed in pt.: 1978, s.23; sch.7.
sch. 2, amended: order 79/746.
sch. 4, amended: 1982, c.28, s.2; c.36, sch.2; 1983, c.18, s.4; 1984, c.8, sch.3; order 86/75; 1987, c.30, ss.11,17, sch.1; repealed in pt.: order 81/155.
sch. 5, repealed in pt.: order 81/228.

6. Employment Subsidies Act 1978.
Royal Assent, March 23, 1978.
S.R. 1982 No. 387.
s. 1, continued in force: orders 85/1959; 87/1124.
s. 3, S.Rs. 1979 No. 382; 1981 No. 158; 1984 No. 172; 1985 No. 324; orders 79/1579; 81/910; 82/1788; 84/830; 85/1959; 87/1124; 88/2229; S.Rs. 1987 No. 215; 1988 No. 402; amended: order 79/1573.

7. Consolidated Fund Act 1978.
Royal Assent, March 23, 1978.
repealed: 1980, c.54, sch.(C.).

8. Civil Aviation Act 1978.
Royal Assent, March 23, 1978.
ss. 1–4, repealed: 1982, c.36, sch.2.
s. 2, regs. 78/769; 80/83; 81/1029; 82/220, 1065.
s. 5, repealed in pt.: 1980, c.60, sch.3; 1982, c.1, sch.2.
ss. 6, 7, 9, 11, repealed: 1982, c.16, sch.16.
s. 8, repealed: 1986, c.31, sch.6.
s. 12, repealed: 1980, c.60, sch.3.
s. 13, repealed in pt.: 1982, c.1, sch.2; c.36, sch.2.
s. 14, amended: 1982, c.1, sch.1; repealed in pt.: 1982, c.16, sch.16.
s. 15, repealed in pt.: *ibid.*
s. 16, repealed in pt.: 1982, c.1, schs.1,2; c.36, sch.2.
s. 16, order 78/486.
sch. 1, amended: 1982, c.1, sch.1; 1982, c.16, sch.16; repealed in pt.: 1980, c.60, sch.3; 1986, c.31, sch.6.

9. Gun Barrel Proof Act 1978.
Royal Assent, May 5, 1978.
s. 9, orders 78/1587; 80/640.

10. European Assembly Elections Act 1978.
Royal Assent, May 5, 1978.
s. 1, repealed in pt.: 1986, c.58, sch.
s. 3, see *Prince* v. *Secretary of State for Scotland* (O.H.), 1985 S.L.T. 74.
ss. 4, 7, amended: 1983, c.2, sch.8.
s. 8, repealed in pt. (S.): 1980, c.55, sch.3.
s. 9, orders 79/349 (S.); 84/571, 623 (S.).
sch. 1, orders 79/219, 220, 349 (S.); 84/571, 623 (S.); 87/20; regs. 79/322, 338, 1021; 83/1152; 84/137, 198; 86/2209, 2250; 88/1822, 1823.
sch. 1, amended: 1983, c.2, sch.8.
sch. 2, orders 78/1903, 1904.
sch. 2, amended: 1981, c.8, s.1; 1986, c.56, sch.3; repealed in pt.: 1981, c.8, s.1.

11. Shipbuilding (Redundancy Payments) Act 1978.
Royal Assent, May 5, 1978.

1978—cont.

11. Shipbuilding (Redundancy Payments) Act 1978—cont.
s. 1, orders 78/1127, 1191; 79/881, 898; 80/573, 630; 81/315, 325, 916, 924; 82/1090, 1118.
s. 1, amended: 1985, c.9, sch.2.
s. 2, orders 78/1127; 79/881, 898; 80/573, 630; 81/315, 325, 916, 924; 82/1090, 1118; amended: 1981, c.6, s.5; 1982, c.4, s.2.
s. 2, repealed in pt.: 1985, c.14, s.1.

12. Medical Act 1978.
Royal Assent, May 5, 1978.
repealed: 1983, c.54, sch.7.
s. 1, orders 79/112, 1358.
s. 4, order 79/289.
s. 6, rules 80/861.
s. 6, sch. 3, see *Crompton* v. *General Medical Council* [1981] 1 W.L.R. 1435, P.C.
s. 11, order 80/873.
s. 14, rules 80/941.
s. 27, order 79/29.
s. 32, orders 78/1035; 79/920; 80/868, 1524.
sch. 1, order 79/1358.
sch. 4, rules 80/858–860, 941.

13. Education (Northern Ireland) Act 1978.
Royal Assent, May 25, 1978.

14. Housing (Financial Provisions) (Scotland) Act 1978.
Royal Assent, May 25, 1978.
repealed, except sch. 2 (in pt.): 1987, c.26, sch.24.
ss. 1, 2, orders 79/100; 80/73, 75; 81/115–117; 82/241, 242; 83/105, 106; 84/174; 85/185, 186; 86/388, 389, 678; 87/331, 332.
s. 3, orders 80/75; 81/116, 117; 83/105; 85/185; 86/389, 678.
s. 11, order 78/1333.
sch. 2, repealed in pt.: 1985, c.71, sch.1.

15. Solomon Islands Act 1978.
Royal Assent, May 25, 1978.
ss. 2, 4, 5, repealed in pt.: 1981, c.61, sch.9.
s. 6, amended: *ibid.*, sch.7.
s. 7, repealed in pt.: 1978, c.30, sch.3.
s. 8, repealed: S.L.R. 1986.
sch., repealed in pt.: 1981, c.9, sch.9; 1982, c.1, sch.2.

16. Trustee Savings Banks Act 1978.
Royal Assent, June 30, 1978.
repealed: 1981, c.65, sch.8.

17. Internationally Protected Persons Act 1978.
Royal Assent, June 30, 1978.
s. 2, amended: 1983, c.18, s.4.
s. 3, orders 79/453; 81/732; 82/147; 85/1990; 86/2013; 87/454, 2042.
ss. 3, 3A, substituted: 1988, c.33, sch.15.
s. 4, orders 79/453, 456, 573–575; 81/211, 732; 82/147; 85/1990; 86/2013; 87/454, 2042.
s. 4, amended: 1988, c.33, sch.15.
s. 5, order 79/455.

18. Export Guarantees and Overseas Investment Act 1978.
Royal Assent, June 30, 1978.
see *Culford Metal Industries* v. *Export Credit Guarantee Department, The Times,* March 25, 1981, Neill J.

1978—cont.

18. Export Guarantees and Overseas Investment Act 1978—*cont.*
s. 6, orders 80/371; 81/1129; 83/278, 279; amended: orders 83/278, 279.
s. 11, order 83/281; amended: *ibid.*
s. 13, orders 79/180; 80/366, 371; 81/393, 1129, 1130; 82/415; 83/198, 278, 279, 281.

19. Oaths Act 1978.
Royal Assent, June 30, 1978.
s. 1, see *R.* v. *Chapman* [1980] Crim.L.R. 42, C.A.
s. 5, see *R.* v. *Bellamy, The Times,* October 4, 1985, C.A.

20. Tuvalu Act 1978.
Royal Assent, June 30, 1978.
ss. 2, 3, repealed: 1981, c.61, sch.9.
s. 4, repealed in pt.: 1978, c.30, sch.3.
s. 5, repealed in pt.: 1981, c.61, sch.9.
sch. 2, repealed in pt.: 1981, c.9, sch; 1982, c.1, sch.2.

21. Co-operative Development Agency Act 1978.
Royal Assent, June 30, 1978.
s. 2, amended: 1984, c.57, s.1.
s. 3, amended: *ibid.;* repealed in pt.: *ibid.,* s.2, sch.2.
s. 3A, added: *ibid.,* s.2.
s. 4, order 81/1141.
s. 4, amended: *ibid.;* 1984, c.57, s.1; repealed in pt.: *ibid.,* s.1, sch.2.
sch. 2, amended: 1985, c.9, sch.2.

22. Domestic Proceedings and Magistrates' Courts Act 1978.
Royal Assent, June 30, 1978.
Commencement order: 85/779.
s. 1, see *Bergin* v. *Bergin* [1982] 12 Fam.Law 212, [1983] 1 W.L.R. 279, D.C.
s. 1, repealed in pt.: 1984, c.42, sch.1.
s. 2, see *Nelson* v. *Nelson, The Times,* December 2, 1981, D.C; *Burridge* v. *Burridge* [1982] 3 W.L.R. 552, Lincoln J.
s. 2, order 88/1069.
ss. 2, 3, see *Robinson* v. *Robinson* [1983] 2 W.L.R. 146, C.A.; *Vasey* v. *Vasey* (1985) 15 Fam.Law 158, C.A.
s. 3, see *Macey* v. *Macey* (1981) 11 Fam.Law 248, Wood J.; *Blower* v. *Blower* (1986) 16 Fam.Law 56, Heilbron J.; *Day* v. *Day,* November 26, 1986, Wood J.
s. 3, substituted: 1984, c.42, s.9; amended: 1986, c.55, sch.1.
s. 5, amended: 1984, c.42, s.9.
s. 6, substituted: *ibid.,* s.10.
s. 7, amended: *ibid.,* sch.1.
s. 8, amended: 1980, c.5, sch.5; c.43, sch.7.
s. 9, amended: 1980, c.5, sch.5.
s. 10, repealed in pt.: 1983, c.41, sch.10.
s. 11, amended: 1980, c.5, sch.5; 1984, c.42, sch.1.
s. 12, amended: 1980, c.43, sch.7.
s. 16, see *McCartney* v. *McCartney* [1981] 2 W.L.R. 184; [1981] 1 All E.R. 597, D.C; *Head* v. *Head, The Times,* April 1, 1982, D.C.
s. 16, amended: 1980, c.43, sch.7.
ss. 16, 18, see *Widdowson* v. *Widdowson* (1982) 12 Fam.Law 153, D.C.; *Horner* v. *Horner* [1982] 2 W.L.R. 914, C.A.

1978—cont.

22. Domestic Proceedings and Magistrates' Courts Act 1978—*cont.*
s. 20, see *Whitton* v. *Devizes JJ.* (1985) 15 Fam.Law 125, Anthony Lincoln J.; *Blower* v. *Blower* (1986) 16 Fam.Law 56, Heilbron J.
s. 20, amended: 1984, c.42, ss.9,11, sch.1; repealed in pt.: 1987, c.42, sch.4.
s. 20A, added: *ibid.,* sch.2.
ss. 22–24, amended: 1980, c.43, sch.7.
s. 28, amended: 1983, c.19, sch.2.
s. 29, see *D.* v. *M. (Minor: Custody Appeal)* [1982] 3 W.L.R. 891, C.A.; *Snape* v. *Snape* (1983) 13 Fam.Law. 210, Waite J.; *Fletcher* v. *Fletcher* [1985] 2 All E.R. 260, D.C., *Berry* v. *Berry* [1986] 3 W.L.R. 257, C.A.
s. 29, amended: 1984, c.42, sch.1.
s. 30, amended: 1980, c.43, sch.7; 1986, c.55, sch.1.
s. 32, amended: 1980, c.43, sch.7; 1987, c.42, sch.2.
s. 33, amended: 1980, c.43, sch.7.
ss. 36 (in pt.), 38 (in pt.), 41, 45 (in pt.), repealed: 1987, c.42, sch.4.
s. 47, amended: 1980, c.43, sch.7.
s. 51, see *Boniface* v. *Harris* (1983) 13 Fam.Law 117, D.C.
s. 60, repealed in pt.: 1985, c.37, sch.2.
s. 74, repealed in pt. (S.): 1978, c.28, sch.4.
ss. 75–85, repealed: 1980, c.43, sch.9.
s. 84, see *Hutchinson* v. *Hutchinson* (1980) 11 Fam.Law 24, D.C.
s. 86, repealed: 1979, c.55, sch.3.
s. 88, amended: *ibid.,* sch. 2; 1980, c.43, sch.7; 1987, c.42, sch.2.
s. 89, orders 78/997, 1489, 1490; 79/731; 80/2036 (S.); 85/779.
s. 90, repealed in pt. (S.): 1978, c.28, sch.4.
sch. 1, amended 1984, c.42, sch.1; 1987, c.42, sch.2; repealed in pt.: 1980, c.43, sch.9.
sch. 2, repealed in pt.: 1978, c.28, sch.4 (S.); 1980, c.5, sch.6; c.43, sch.9; 1981, c.54, sch.7; 1984, c.42, sch.3; 1985, c.37, sch.2 (S.); 1987, c.42, sch.4; 1988, c.34, sch.6.

23. Judicature (Northern Ireland) Act 1978.
Royal Assent, June 30, 1978.
s. 3, amended: 1982, c.53, sch.8.
s. 13, amended and repealed in pt.: *ibid.*
s. 21, see *R. (Att.-Gen.)* v. *Belfast Justices* [1981] 4 N.I.J.B., Lord Lowry C.J. and Hutton J.
s. 22, repealed in pt.: 1981, c.61, sch.9.
s. 23, see *McParland* v. *John Tinnelly & Sons* [1982] 1 N.I.J.B., Kelly J.
s. 27, amended: 1982, c.53, sch.8.
s. 31, amended: *ibid.,* s.69, sch.7; repealed in pt.: order 82/1080.
s. 33A, added: 1982, c.53, s.69, sch.7.
s. 35, amended: 1983, c.2, sch.8.
s. 36, amended: 1980, c.47, sch.4; repealed in pt.: *ibid.,* sch.5.
s. 37, repealed in pt.: *ibid.*
ss. 39, 40, repealed: *ibid.*
s. 44, amended: *ibid.,* sch.4.
s. 49, amended: *ibid.;* 1988, c.33, sch.15.

CAP.

1978—cont.

23. Judicature (Northern Ireland) Act 1978—cont.
s. 53, amended: order 79/1573; 1982, c.53, sch.8.
s. 55, S.Rs. 1979 Nos. 86, 205, 206, 431–433, 444, 445; 1980 Nos. 255, 346, 433; 1981 Nos. 166, 224; 1982 Nos. 138, 217; 1983 Nos. 5, 114, 183, 407; 1984 Nos. 110, 162, 189, 354; 1985 Nos. 170, 347; 1986 Nos. 128, 184, 203; 1987 No. 304; 1988 Nos. 70, 71.
s. 56, amended: order 79/1573; 1982, c.53, sch.8; repealed in pt.: order 79/1573.
s. 62, see *Monteith* v. *Western Health and Social Services Board* [1984] 13 N.I.J.B., Carswell J.; *Kelly* v. *Quartey-Papafio* [1985] 5 N.I.J.B. 84, Hutton J.; *Coubrough* v. *Short Brothers* [1985] 13 N.I.J.B. 20, C.A.; *Clements* v. *Mallon* [1987] 4 N.I.J.B. 103, C.A.
s. 62, order: 87/1283.
s. 68, S.R. 1982 No. 300.
s. 69, S.R. 1979 No. 103.
s. 69, amended: order 81/226.
s. 70, S.Rs. 1982 No. 300; 1983 No. 270.
s. 70, repealed in pt.: 1985, c.61, s.62, sch.8.
ss. 78, 81, amended: 1982, c.53, sch.8.
s. 82, S.R. 1979 No. 105.
s. 82, amended: 1982, c.53, sch.8.
s. 83, repealed: *ibid.*, sch.9.
s. 84, amended: orders 79/1576; 81/160; repealed in pt.: 1986, c.60, sch.17.
ss. 85, 91, amended: 1982, c.53, sch.8.
s. 94A, added: *ibid.*; amended: 1984, c.46, s.54; 1986, c.39, sch.2; 1988, c.48, sch.7.
s. 103, amended: 1985, c.61, s.62.
s. 104, S.Rs. 1979 No. 122; 1982 No. 192.
s. 108, amended: 1983, c.2, sch.8.
s. 116, S.Rs. 1979 Nos. 59, 154, 158–161, 262; 1980 Nos. 238–240, 264, 437; 1981 Nos. 173–175, 195, 364; 1982 Nos. 325–327; 1983 Nos. 206, 207, 420; 1984 Nos. 23, 137–139, 223, 419, 420; 1986 Nos. 103, 140, 195, 232, 233, 348, 369; 1987 Nos. 270, 412; 1988 Nos. 249, 281; orders 80/87, 88.
s. 117, order 81/226.
s. 117A, added: 1982, c.53, sch.8.
s. 118, repealed in pt.: order 81/233.
s. 119, amended: order 79/1573.
s. 120, amended: 1980, c.47, sch.4.
s. 123, orders 78/1101; 79/124, 422.
sch. 5, amended: 1987, c.30, sch.1; repealed in pt.: order 79/1575; 1980, c.47, sch.5; 1981, c.19, sch.1; 1982, c.27, sch.14; 1983, c.2, sch.9; orders 81/226, 228, 233; 1986, c.53, sch.19; 1987, c.16, sch.16; c.30, sch.2; 1988, c.1, sch.31; c.39, sch.14.

24. Theatres Trust (Scotland) Act 1978.
Royal Assent, June 30, 1978.
25. Nuclear Safeguards and Electricity (Finance) Act 1978.
Royal Assent, June 30, 1978.
s. 2, amended: 1980, c.43, sch.7.
26. Suppression of Terrorism Act 1978.
Royal Assent, June 30, 1978.
s. 1, amended: 1988, c.33,sch.15.
s. 3, repealed in pt.: *ibid.*, sch.16.

CAP.

1978—cont.

26. Suppression of Terrorism Act 1978—cont.
s. 4, amended 1978, c.17, s.5; 1983, c.18, s.4; 1984, c.37, s.11; repealed in pt.: 1978, c.17, s.5.
s. 5, order 86/2146.
s. 5, amended: 1988, c.33, sch.15.
s. 7, orders 78/1529–1531; 86/2019; 87/2045.
s. 8, orders 78/1245; 79/497; 80/357 (S.), 1392; 81/1389, 1507; 86/271, 1137; 87/2137.
s. 9, order 78/1063.
sch. 1, amended: order 81/155; 1982, c.28, s.3; c.36, sch.2; 1984, c.37, s.11; 1988, c.33, s.22.

27. Home Purchase Assistance and Housing Corporation Guarantee Act 1978.
Royal Assent, June 30, 1978.
repealed: 1985, c.71, sch.1; 1987, c.26, sch.4 (S.).
s. 1, orders 80/1371; 81/1061, 1126; 83/82, 1646; 84/954; 85/937; 86/1511; 87/268 (S.).
s. 2, orders 78/1785; 80/1371; 81/1061, 1126; 82/976; 83/82, 1646; 84/954; 85/937; 86/1511; 87/268 (S.).
ss. 2, 3, amended (S): 1985, c.71, sch.2.
s. 3, amended: 1986, c.53, sch.18; repealed in pt.: *ibid.*, sch.19.
s. 3A, added (S.): 1985, c.71, sch.2.
ss. 4, 5, repealed (S.): *ibid.*, sch.1.
s. 6, order 78/1412.
s. 6, amended (S): 1985, c.71, sch.2; repealed in pt.: *ibid.*, sch.1.
sch., amended: 1979, c.37, sch.6; orders 78/1785; 82/976; 1981, c.65, sch.6; 1987, c.22, sch.6; repealed in pt.: 1985, c.51, sch.17; c.58, sch.4.

28. Adoption (Scotland) Act 1978.
Royal Assent, July 20, 1978.
Commencement order: 84/1050.
s. 2, amended: 1984, c.56, sch.2.
s. 3, amended: 1983, c.41, sch.2.
ss. 3, 9, regs. 84/988.
s. 10, repealed in pt.: 1983, c.41, schs.2,10.
s. 11, see *A.* v. *Children's Hearing for the Tayside Region,* 1987 S.L.T.(Sh.Ct.) 126; *A.* v. *B.,* 1987 S.L.T.(Sh.Ct.) 121; *A. and B.* v. *C.,* 1987 S.C.L.R. 514.
s. 18, see *Borders Regional Council* v. *M.,* 1986 S.L.T. 222.
s. 18, amended: 1986, c.9, sch.1.
ss. 27, 28, amended: 1983, c.41, sch.2; repealed in pt.: *ibid.*, schs.2,10.
s. 29, amended: *ibid.*, sch.2.
s. 32, amended: 1984, c.36, sch.3; c.56, sch.2.
s. 39, see *A.B.* v. *M.* (O.H.), 1987 S.C.L.R. 389.
s. 39, amended: 1986, c.9, sch.1.
s. 40, repealed: 1981, c.61, sch.9.
s. 41, amended: *ibid.*, sch.7; 1986, c.36, sch.1; order 86/948; repealed in pt.: 1981, c.61, sch.9.
s. 46, amended: 1986, c.9, sch.1.
s. 59, Acts of Sederunt 84/997, 1013.
s. 60, regs. 84/988.

1978—cont.

28. Adoption (Scotland) Act 1978—*cont.*
s. 65, see *A.* v. *Children's Hearing for the Tayside Region,* 1987 S.L.T.(Sh.Ct.) 126.
s. 65, amended: 1986, c.9, sch.1; 1983, c.41, sch.2; 1985, c.73, s.27; repealed in pt.: 1986, c.9, sch.2.
s. 67, sch.2, order 84/1050.
sch. 3, repealed in pt.: 1984, c.56, sch.3.

29. National Health Service (Scotland) Act 1978.
Royal Assent, July 20, 1978.
ss. 1, 2, see *British Medical Association* v. *Greater Glasgow Health Board,* 1988 S.L.T. 538.
s. 2, regs. 81/147; orders 81/106; 83/1027; 88/808.
s. 2, amended: 1983, c.41, sch.7.
s. 4, amended: 1988, c.49, s.12; repealed in pt.: *ibid.,* sch.3.
s. 7, amended: 1980, c.53, sch.6.
s. 9, regs. 88/878.
s. 9, repealed in pt.: 1984, c.48, sch.8.
s. 10, amended: 1980, c.53, sch.6.
ss. 13A, 13B, added: 1986, c.66, s.5.
s. 15, amended: 1980, c.44, sch.4; c.53, s.3.
s. 16, repealed in pt.: 1980, c.53, sch.7.
s. 16A, added: *ibid.,* s.4.
s. 16A, substituted: 1983, c.41, s.2; 1985, c.71, sch.2.
s. 16B, added: 1983, c.41, s.3.
s. 17, repealed: 1980, c.63, sch.2.
s. 19, regs. 80/1674; 81/56, 965; 82/1279; 85/296, 534, 804, 1625, 1713; 86/303, 925, 1507, 2310; 87/386, 1382; 88/1073, 1454.
s. 19, amended: 1980, c.63, s.7; 1983, c.41, sch.7; c.54, sch.5.
s. 20, regs. 80/30; 81/56; amended: 1980, c.53, sch.6; regs. 81/56; order 81/432; repealed in pt.: 1980, c.53, schs.6,7.
ss. 21, 22, regs. 80/30; 81/55; 82/770; 83/948.
s. 22, regs. 84/1258; 86/1657.
ss. 23, 25, amended: order 81/432; 1988, c.49, sch.2.
s. 25, regs. 80/1220, 1674; 81/900; 84/1491; 85/1552; 86/1571; 87/1634; 88/854, 878.
s. 25, amended: 1980, c.53, sch.6; 1983, c.41, s.16; 1984, c.24, sch.5; repealed in pt.: 1980, c.53, sch.7.
s. 26, regs. 80/107; 81/360; 85/355; 86/965, 966; 88/463, 543, 545, 878, 1425.
s. 26, amended: 1984, c.48, sch.1; 1988, c.49, s.13; repealed in pt.: 1984, c.48, s.1, sch.8.
s. 27, regs. 80/1674; 81/56; 85/296, 534, 804, 1713; 86/303, 925, 1507, 2310; 87/385, 1382, 2202; 88/1073.
s. 27, amended: 1980, c.53, s.20; 1986, c.66, s.3.
s. 28, regs. 81/56; 85/296, 534, 804.
s. 28, amended: 1986, c.66, s.3.
s. 28A, amended: 198, c.49, s.15.
ss. 28A, 28B, added: 1984, c.48, s.7.
s. 28B, amended: 1986, c.66, s.4.
s. 29, repealed in pt.: 1984, c.48, sch.8.
s. 34, regs. 81/56; 86/965.
s. 39, amended: 1980, c.44, sch.4; 1988, c.49, s.10; repealed in pt.: *ibid.,* s.10, sch.3.
s. 50, repealed: 1988, c.49, sch.3.
ss. 51, 52, repealed: 1980, c.53, s.10, sch.7.

1978—cont.

29. National Health Service (Scotland) Act 1978—*cont.*
ss. 53, 54 (in pt.), repealed: 1988, c.49, sch.3.
s. 55, amended: *ibid.,* s.7; repealed in pt.: *ibid.,* s.7, sch.3.
ss. 57, 58, substituted: *ibid.,* s.7.
s. 58A, repealed: *ibid.,* sch.3.
ss. 59–63, 65–68, repealed: 1980, c.53, s.9, sch.7.
s. 64, repealed in pt.: 1984, c.48, sch.8.
s. 68, regs. 81/675.
s. 69, regs. 79/704; 80/296, 1674; 81/1717; 82/332; 83/334, 1172; 85/353; 86/488; 87/367; 88/365, 1073.
s. 70, regs. 79/705; 80/369; 81/359; 1431; 82/333; 83/335; 84/293; 85/354, 355; 86/966, 1192; 88/464.
s. 70, amended: 1988, c.49, s.11; repealed in pt.: *ibid.,* schs.2,3.
s. 71, regs. 79/705; 80/369, 1221; 81/359; 82/333; 83/335; 84/293; 85/354; 88/464.
s. 71, amended: 1988, c.49, s.11; repealed in pt.: *ibid.,* s.11, sch.3.
s. 71A, added: *ibid.,* s.11.
s. 72, regs. 88/535.
ss. 73, 74, regs. 86/966.
ss. 73–75, repealed in pt.: 1984, c.40, sch.8.
s. 75, regs. 79/704; 80/296, 1674; 82/332; 83/334; 84/292; 85/353; 86/488; 87/367; 88/365.
s. 75A, regs. 88/546.
s. 75A, added: 1988, c.7, s.14; amended: 1988, c.49, sch.2.
s. 79, amended: 1983, c.41, sch.7.
s. 84A, added: 1980, c.53, s.5.
s. 85, amended: *ibid.,* s.6; 1984, c.36, s.2; c.48, s.6; 1988, c.49, s.16, sch.2; repealed in pt.: 1980, s.53, sch.7; 1984, c.48, sch.8; 1988, c.7, sch.5.
s. 85A, added: 1980, c.53, s.6; amended: 1984, c.48, s.2; 1988, c.49, s.16.
s. 86, amended: 1984, c.48, s.2.
s. 90, amended: 1987, c.39, s.2.
s. 92A, added: *ibid.,* s.6.
s. 93, amended: 1988, c.49, s.12; repealed in pt.: 1980, c.53, schs.2,7.
s. 94, amended: 1987, c.39, s.8.
s. 95A, added: *ibid.,* s.4.
s. 96, amended: *ibid.,* s.5; repealed in pt.: 1980, c.53, schs.2,7.
s. 98, regs. 82/898, 1743; 83/362; 84/295; 85/383; 86/516, 924; 87/387; 88/13, 462.
s. 98, amended: 1988, c.49, s.7.
s. 99A, added: 1984, c.48, s.9.
s. 100, amended: 1984, c.36, sch.3; 1987, c.26, sch.23.
s. 102, order 84/389.
s. 102, amended: 1984, c.36, sch.3; repealed in pt.: 1983, c.39, sch.3.
s. 105, order 83/1027; regs. 86/965; 88/543, 808.
s. 105, amended: 1980, c.53, sch.6; 1983, c.41, sch.9; repealed in pt.: 1980, c.53, schs.6,7.
s. 106, regs. 79/705; 81/56; 86/965.

1978—cont.

29. National Health Service (Scotland) Act 1978—cont.

s. 108, regs. 79/704, 705; 80/296, 396, 1674; 81/359, 360, 675, 1431, 1717; 82/332, 333, 1279; 83/334, 335, 1172; 84/292, 293, 295, 1258; 85/296, 353–355, 383, 534, 804, 1625, 1713; 86/303, 488, 516, 924, 965, 1507, 1571, 1657, 2310; 87/367, 386, 387; 88/13, 365, 462–464, 535, 543, 545, 546, 1073, 1425, 1454.

s. 108, amended: 1980, c.44, sch.4; c.53, sch.6; 1983, c.54, sch.5; repealed in pt.: 1979, c.36, schs.7,8; 1980, c.44, schs.2,7.

sch. 1, regs. 81/147; 85/208; 86/944.

sch. 1, amended: 1980, c.44, sch.6; 1983, c.41, s.16, sch.7; 1984, c.24, sch.5.

sch. 3, repealed in pt.: 1984, c.48, sch.8.

sch. 5, regs. 86/944.

sch. 5, amended: 1980, c.44, sch.6; 1983, c.41, sch.7.

sch. 6, regs. 81/147.

schs. 6, 7, amended: 1985, c.73, s.54.

sch. 8, repealed in pt.: 1984, c.48, sch.8.

sch. 9, amended: 1982, c.48, sch.15; repealed in pt.: *ibid.*, sch.16.

sch. 10, amended: 1981, c.61, sch.7; *ibid.*, sch.15; repealed in pt.: *ibid.*, sch.16.

sch. 11, regs. 79/704, 705; 80/296, 396, 1221, 1674, 1686; 81/359, 360, 1431; 82/333; 83/335, 1172; 84/293; 85/353–355; 86/965, 966, 1192; 88/463, 464, 545, 1425.

sch. 11, amended: 1980, c.53, sch.5; 1984, c.48, sch.1; 1988, c.49, ss.11, 12, sch.2; repealed in pt.: 1980, c.53, sch.7; 1984, c.48, sch.8, 1988, c.7, sch.5; 1988, c.49, sch.3.

sch. 14, amended: 1980, c.53, sch.6; 1984, c.36, sch.3; repealed in pt.: *ibid.*, schs.6,7.

sch. 15, amended: 1980, c.44, sch.4; c.53, sch.6; repealed in pt.: 1979, c.36, sch.8; 1980, c.9, sch.10; c.44, sch.5; 1983, c.20, sch.6.

sch. 16, amended: 1980, c.44, sch.5; repealed in pt.: 1980, c.48, sch.20; c.53, sch.7; 1983, c.54, sch.5; 1984, c.29, sch.6; c.36, sch.5; S.L.R. 1986; 1988, c.1, sch.31; c.49, sch.3.

30. Interpretation Act 1978.

Royal Assent, July 20, 1978.

s. 6, see *Skinner* v. *Patience,* 1982 S.L.T.(St.Ct.) 81; *Prior (Valuation Officer)* v. *Sovereign Chicken* (1984) 270 E.G. 221, C.A.; *Lewis* v. *Surrey County Council, The Times,* October 17, 1987, H.L.

s. 7, see *House* v. *Emerson Electric Industrial Controls* [1980] I.C.R. 795, E.A.T.; *Lenlyn* v. *Secretary of State for the Environment; R.* v. *Secretary of State for the Environment, ex p. Lenlyn* (1985) 50 P. & C.R. 129, Hodgson J.; *Austin Rover Group* v. *Crouch Butler Savage Associates, The Times,* April 1, 1986, C.A.; *Secretary of State for Employment* v. *Milk & General Haulage (Nottingham)* (1987) 84 L.S.Gaz. 2118, E.A.T.; *T. & D. Transport (Portsmouth)* v. *Limburn* [1987] I.C.R. 696, E.A.T.; *Adam* v. *Secretary of State for Scotland* (O.H.), 1988 S.L.T. 300.

1978—cont.

30. Interpretation Act 1978—cont.

s. 12, see *Wilson* v. *Colchester Justices* [1985] 2 All E.R. 97, H.L.

s. 16, see *Convex's Patent* [1980] R.P.C. 423, C.A.; *R.* v. *West London Stipendiary Magistrates, ex p. Simeon* [1982] 3 W.L.R. 289, H.L.; *Porter* v. *Manning, The Times,* March 23, 1984, D.C.; *Martinez's Patent* [1983] R.P.C. 307, Patent Office; *Lydcare* v. *Secretary of State for the Environment and Westminster City Council* [1984] J.P.L. 39, McCullough J.; *Taylor* v. *McGirr* [1986] Crim.L.R. 544, D.C.

s. 17, see *R.* v. *Corby Juvenile Court, ex p. M* [1987] 1 W.L.R. 55, Waite J.

ss. 17, 22, sch.2, see *Cakebread (V.O.)* v. *Severn Trent Water Authority* [1988] R.A. 290, C.A.

s. 24, amended: order 79/1573; repealed in pt.: 1981, c.61, sch.9.

sch. 1, see *Northern Ireland Electricity Service's Application, Re* [1987] 12 N.I.J.B. 24, Nicholson J.

sch. 1, amended: 1980, c.43, sch.7; 1983, c.54, sch.5; 1984, c.28, sch.2; c.55, sch.6; 1987, c.16, sch.15; c.42, sch.2; 1988, c.33, sch.15; repealed in pt.: 1981, c.61, sch.9.

sch. 2, amended: 1987, c.42, sch.2; repealed in pt.: 1981, c.61, sch.9; 1987, c.42, schs.2,4.

31. Theft Act 1978.

Royal Assent, July 20, 1978.

s. 1, see *R.* v. *Halai* [1983] Crim.L.R. 624,C.A.; *R.* v. *Widdowson, The Times,* January 7, 1986, C.A.

s. 2, see *R.* v. *Holt* [1981] 1 W.L.R. 1000; [1981] 2 All E.R. 834, C.A. *R.* v. *Sibartie* [1983] Crim.L.R. 470, C.A.; *R.* v. *Jackson* [1983] Crim.L.R. 617, C.A.

s. 3, see *R.* v. *McDavitt* [1981] Crim.L.R. 477, C.A.; *R.* v. *Brooks and Brooks* [1983] Crim.L.R. 188, C.A.; *R.* v. *Allen (Christopher)* [1985] 3 W.L.R. 107, H.L.; *Troughton* v. *Metropolitan Police* [1987] Crim.L.R. 138, D.C.

s. 4, amended: 1980, c.43, sch.7.

sch. 1, amended: 1988, c.33, sch.15.

sch. 4, amended: 1981, c.54, sch.5.

32. Representation of the People Act 1978.

Royal Assent, July 20, 1978.

repealed: 1983, c.2, sch.9.

s. 2, orders 80/375; 81/191; 82/363.

33. State Immunity Act 1978.

Royal Assent, July 20, 1978.

see *Intpro Properties (U.K.)* v. *Sauvel, The Times,* December 1, 1982, Bristow J.; *Alcom* v. *Republic of Colombia, The Times,* October 26, 1983, C.A.

ss. 1, 4, 23, see *Sengupta* v. *Republic of India* [1983] I.C.R. 221, E.A.T.

ss. 2, 3, 6, 13, 16, 17, see *Alcom* v. *Republic of Colombia* [1984] 2 W.L.R. 750, H.L.

s. 3, see *Rayner (J. H.) (Mincing Lane)* v. *Department of Trade and Industry, The Independent,* June 26, 1987, Staughton J.

ss. 3, 10, see *Planmount* v. *Republic of Zaire* [1981] 1 All E.R. 1110, Lloyd J.

1978—cont.

33. State Immunity Act 1978—cont.

s. 4, amended: 1981, c.61, sch.7; order 86/948; repealed in pt.: 1979, c.60, sch.3.

s. 5, repealed in pt.: 1988, c.33, sch.16.

ss. 6, 16, see Intro Properties (U.K.) v. Sauvel [1983] 2 W.L.R. 908, C.A.

s. 7, amended: 1986, c.39, sch.2.

s. 13, see Forth Tugs v. Wilmington Trust Co., 1987 S.L.T. 153.

ss. 13, 14, see Hispano Americana Mercantile C.A. v. Central Bank of Nigeria (1979) 123 S.J. 336, C.A.

s. 14, order 79/457.

s. 15, order 78/1524.

s. 21, see R. v. Secretary of State for Foreign and Commonwealth Affairs, ex p. Trawnik, The Times, February 21, 1986, C.A.

s. 23, orders 78/1572; 79/458; 80/871; 81/1112; 85/1642.

34. Industrial and Provident Societies Act 1978.

Royal Assent, July 20, 1978.

s. 2, order 81/394.

s. 7, amended: ibid.

35. Import of Live Fish (Scotland) Act 1978.

Royal Assent, July 20, 1978.

s. 1, order 80/376.

ss. 1, 3, amended: 1981, c.29, s.37.

s. 2, repealed in pt.: ibid., sch.5.

36. House of Commons (Administration) Act 1978.

Royal Assent, July 20, 1978.

sch. 1, repealed in pt.: 1980, c.42, sch.2.

sch. 2, amended: 1978, c.44, sch.16.

37. Protection of Children Act 1978.

Royal Assent, July 20, 1978.

s. 1, see R. v. Owen, The Times, October 10, 1987, C.A.; R. v. Graham-Kerr, The Times, July 12, 1988, C.A.

s. 1, repealed in pt.: 1988, c.33, sch.16.

ss. 1, 7, see R. v. Owen (Charles) [1988] 1 W.L.R. 134, C.A.

s. 2, repealed in pt.: 1980, c.43, sch.9; 1984, c.60, sch.7.

ss. 4, 5, amended: 1988, c.33, sch.15; repealed in pt.: ibid., schs. 15, 16.

s. 6, amended: 1980, c.43, sch.7.

38. Consumer Safety Act 1978.

Royal Assent, July 20, 1978.

Commencement order: 86/1297.

repealed: 1987, c.43, sch.5.

see R. v. Secretary of State for Trade and Industry, ex p. Ian Kynaston Ford (1985) 4 Tr.L. 150, Woolf J.; Sarwan Singh Deu v. Dudley Metropolitan Borough Council, July 10, 1987; Sedgley Crown Ct.

s. 1, regs. 80/136, 725, 958; 82/444; 83/519; 84/145, 1057, 1233, 1260, 1802; 85/99, 127, 128, 1129, 2042, 2043, 2045, 2047; 86/758, 1323; 87/286, 603, 1337.

s. 2, regs. 80/136; 84/1260; 85/2045.

ss. 2–4, repealed in pt.: 1986, c.29, sch.2.

s. 3, sch. 1, orders 78/1728; 79/44, 887; 82/523; 83/1366, 1696; 1791; 84/83.

s. 4, regs. 80/136.

1978—cont.

38. Consumer Safety Act 1978—cont.

s. 5, amended: 1986, c.29, s.16; repealed in pt.: ibid., sch.2.

s. 7, regs. 85/99, 127, 128.

s. 9, amended: 1980, c.43, sch.7; 1984, c.30, sch.10; repealed in pt.: 1986, c.29, sch.2.

s. 10, repealed in pt: ibid.

s. 11, regs. 85/2043.

s. 11, amended: 1980, c.43, sch.7; 1984, c.30, sch.10.

s. 12, orders 78/1445; 86/1297; 87/1681.

sch. 1, repealed in pt.: 1986, c.29, sch.2.

sch. 2, regs. 85/99, 2043, 2047; 87/286, 603.

sch. 2, substituted: 1986, c.29, s.14, sch.1.

39. Local Government Act 1978.

Royal Assent, July 20, 1978.

s. 179, see Bellway v. Strathclyde Regional Council [1980] J.P.L. 683, Ct. of Session.

40. Rating (Disabled Persons) Act 1978.

Royal Assent, July 20, 1978.

s. 1, see Williams v. Wirral Borough Council (1981) 79 L.G.R. 697, C.A.; Parham v. Portsmouth City Council, May 27, 1982, H.H. Judge E. McLellan, Portsmouth County Court.

s. 1, amended: 1982, c.24, sch.4; 1986, c.50, sch.10.

s. 2, see Sanders v. Cheltenham Borough Council, July 14, 1980, Judge Bulger, Cheltenham County Ct.; Morgan v. Windsor and Maidenhead Royal Borough Council; Glenherne Nursing Services v. Same (1982) 80 L.G.R. 313, C.A.; Hebbes v. Rother District Council (1984) 230 E.G. 325, C.A.; Samaritans of Tyneside v. Newcastle Upon Tyne City Council [1985] R.A. 219, C.A.; Nottinghamshire County Council v. Nottinghamshire City Council (1987) 27 R.V.R. 82, Nottingham County Ct.

ss. 2, 3, amended: 1984, c.33, sch.1.

s. 4, order 85/245.

s. 4, amended: 1982, c.24, sch.4; 1986, c.50, sch.10.

s. 5, see The Royal Blind Asylum and School v. Lothian Regional Council, (1982) S.L.T.(Sh.Ct.) 89.

ss. 5, 6, amended: 1984, c.31, s.5.

ss. 7, 8 (in pt.), repealed (S.): 1987, c.47, sch.6.

41. Iron and Steel (Amendment) Act 1978.

Royal Assent, July 20, 1978.

repealed: 1981, c.46, sch.2.

42. Finance Act 1978.

Royal Assent, July 31, 1978.

s. 1, regs. 78/1156.

s. 1, repealed: 1979, c.7, sch.2.

s. 2, regs. 78/1786; repealed: 1979, c.4, sch.4.

ss. 3, 5, repealed: 1979, c.2, sch.6.

s. 6, orders 78/1147, 1497; 79/104, 181, 191, 314, 492, 510, 566, 567, 627, 842, 1148, 1182; 80/35, 279; 81/899; 82/747, 1145, 1208, 1601, 1753, 1754; 83/168, 300, 859; repealed in pt.: 1979, c.3, sch.3; c.8, sch.2.

s. 7, repealed: 1980, c.48, sch.20.

s. 10, repealed in pt.: 1979, c.8, sch.2.

s. 11, repealed in pt.: 1980, c.48, sch.20; 1983, c.55, sch.11.

CAP.

1978—cont.

42. Finance Act 1978—cont.

s. 12, see *T. H. Knitwear (Wholesale), Re* [1988] 2 W.L.R. 276, C.A.

s. 12, regs. 78/1129; 81/1080.

s. 12, repealed: 1983, c.55, sch.11.

ss. 13–28, repealed: 1988, c.1, sch.31.

s. 22, regs. 78/1117.

s. 29, repealed in pt.: 1988, c.1, sch.31.

s. 30, see *Butt* v. *Haxby, The Times,* December 15, 1982; [1983] S.T.C. 239, Vinelott J.

ss. 30–36, repealed: 1988, c.1, sch.31.

s. 37, amended: *ibid.,* sch.29.

s. 39, repealed: 1986, c.41, sch.23.

s. 40, amended: 1988, c.39, s.93.

ss. 41–43, repealed: 1988, c.1, sch.31.

ss. 44, 45 (in pt.), 46–52, repealed: 1979, c.14, sch.8.

s. 53, amended: 1988, c.39, s.89.

ss. 53–61, repealed: 1988, c.1, sch.31.

ss. 62, 63, repealed: 1980, c.48, sch.20.

s. 64, amended: 1979, c.14, sch.7; repealed in pt.: 1984, c.51, sch.9.

ss. 65–74, repealed in pt.: *ibid.*

s. 68, see *Russell* v. *I.R.C.* [1988] S.T.C. 195, Knox J.

s. 71, see *Egerton* v. *I.R.C.* [1983] S.T.C. 531, C.A.

s. 75, repealed: 1984, c.43, sch.23.

s. 76, repealed: 1979, c.47, sch.5.

s. 77, amended: 1980, c.48, s.17.

s. 78, order 80/664; 81/749.

s. 78, repealed 1984, c.43, sch.23.

s. 79, repealed: 1979, c.2, sch.6.

s. 80, amended: 1979, c.2, sch.4; repealed in pt.: 1979, c.14, sch.8; 1983, c.55, sch.11; 1984, c.51, sch.9.

schs. 2–5, repealed: 1988, c.1, sch.31.

sch. 6, amended: 1981, c.35, s.73; repealed in pt.: *ibid.,* sch.19.

schs. 7, 8, repealed: 1979, c.14, sch.8. ·

sch. 9, repealed: 1988, c.1, sch.31.

sch. 10, repealed: 1980, c.48, sch.20.

sch. 11, repealed in pt.: 1979, c.14, sch.8; 1982, c.39, sch.22; 1984, c.51, sch.9.

sch. 12, repealed 1983, c.55, sch.11.

43. Independent Broadcasting Authority Act 1978.

Royal Assent, July 31, 1978.

repealed: 1981, c.68, sch.9; see *Chelsea Football and Athletic Co.* v. *Heath, The Times,* January 3, 1981, E.A.T.; *Newland* v. *Simons and Willer (Hairdressers), The Times,* April 16, 1981, E.A.T.; *Union of Construction, Allied Trades and Technicians* v. *Brain, The Times,* April 1, 1981, C.A.; *McCormick* v. *Horsepower, The Times,* April 16, 1981, C.A.

s. 1, see *Mears* v. *Safecar Security* [1981] 1 W.L.R. 1214, E.A.T.

ss. 1–4, see *System Floors (U.K.)* v. *Daniel* [1981] I.R.L.R. 475, E.A.T.

s. 3, orders 79/461; 81/910.

44. Employment Protection (Consolidation) Act 1978.

Royal Assent, July 31, 1978.

see *Capon* v. *Rees Motors, The Times,* February 20, 1980, E.A.T.; *Skyrail Oceanic* v. *Coleman,*

CAP.

1978—cont.

44. Employment Protection (Consolidation) Act 1978—cont.

The Times, April 23, 1980, E.A.T; *Webb* v. *Anglian Water Authority* [1981] I.C.R. 811, E.A.T.; *President of the Methodist Conference* v. *Parfitt* [1983] 3 All E.R. 747, C.A.; *Gorictree* v. *Jenkinson* [1985] I.C.R. 51, E.A.T.; *Notcutt* v. *Universal Equipment Co. (London), The Times,* March 26, 1986, C.A.; *Caledonian Mining Co.* v. *Bassett* [1987] I.C.R. 425, E.A.T.

s. 1, see *System Floors (U.K.)* v. *Daniel* [1982] I.C.R. 54, E.A.T.; *Mears* v. *Safecar Security* [1982] 3 W.L.R. 366, C.A.; *Howman & Son* v. *Blyth* [1983] I.C.R. 416, E.A.T.; *Robertson* v. *British Gas Corp.* [1983] I.C.R. 351, C.A.

ss. 1, 2, amended: 1982, c.46, sch.2.

s. 3, repealed: *ibid.,* sch.4.

s. 4, see *Igbo* v. *Johnson Matthey Chemicals* [1986] I.C.R. 82, E.A.T.

s. 4, amended: 1982, c.46, sch.2; repealed in pt.: *ibid.*

s. 5, repealed in pt.: *ibid.,* sch.4.

s. 5A, added: *ibid.,* sch.2.

s. 6, see *Ford* v. *Stakis Hotels and Inns* [1987] I.C.R. 943, E.A.T.

s. 7, repealed: 1982, c.46, sch.4.

s. 8, see *Cofone* v. *Spaghetti House* [1980] I.C.R. 155, E.A.T.; *Chapman* v. *CPS Computer Group, The Times,* June 30, 1987, C.A.

ss. 8, 11, see *Coales* v. *Wood (John) & Co.* [1986] I.C.R. 71, E.A.T.

s. 11, see *Addison* v. *London Philharmonic Orchestra, The Times,* October 21, E.A.T.; *Mears* v. *Safecar Security* [1982] 3 W.L.R. 366, C.A.

s. 12, orders 79/1403; 81/6.

ss. 12, 15, 16, see *Cartwright* v. *Clancy (G)* [1983] I.C.R. 552, E.A.T.

s. 13, amended: 1982, c.46, schs.2,3.

s. 15, orders 78/1777; 79/1722; 80/2019; 82/77, 1866; 83/1962; 84/2019; 85/2032; 86/2283; 88/276.

s. 15, amended: 1980, c.42, s.14, sch.1; orders 84/2019; 85/2032; 86/2283.

s. 16, repealed in pt.: 1980, c.30, sch.5.

s. 18, orders 79/1403; 80/1715; 81/6; 83/571; 85/1270; 87/1757.

s. 18, amended: 1979, c.12, sch.6; 1986, c.48, sch.4.

s. 19, orders 80/1581; 85/1787; 88/1746.

s. 20, amended: 1982, c.46, sch.2.

s. 23, see *British Airways Engine Overhaul* v. *Francis* [1981] I.C.R. 278, E.A.T.; *National Coal Board* v. *Ridgway, sub nom. Ridgway and Fairbrother* v. *National Coal Board* [1987] I.C.R. 641, C.A.

s. 23, amended: 1980, c.42, s.15; 1982, c.46, s.10, sch.3; 1988, c.19, sch.3; repealed in pt.: 1980, c.42, s.15, sch.2; 1988, c.19, s.11, sch.4.

ss. 23, 24, see *British Airways Board* v. *Clark and Havill* [1982] I.R.L.R. 238, E.A.T.; *Adlam* v. *Salisbury and Wells Theological College* [1985] I.C.R. 786, E.A.T.

CAP.

1978—cont.

44. Employment Protection (Consolidation) Act 1978—cont.

ss. 23, 25, see Carlson v. Post Office [1981] I.C.R. 343, E.A.T.

s. 25, repealed in pt.: 1980, c.30, s.15, sch.2.

s. 26A, substituted: 1982, c.46, s.11.

s. 27, see R.H.P. Bearings v. Brookes [1979] I.R.L.R. 452, E.A.T.; Menzies v. Smith & McLaurin [1980] I.R.L.R. 180, E.A.T.; Repledge v. Pye Telecommunications [1981] I.C.R. 82, E.A.T.; Beal v. Beecham Group [1982] 1 W.L.R. 1005, C.A. Ministry of Defence v. Crook and Irving [1982] I.R.L.R. 488, E.A.T.; Beecham Group v. Beal (No. 2) [1983] I.R.L.R. 317, E.A.T.; Thomas Scott & Sons (Bakers) v. Allen [1983] I.R.L.R. 329, C.A.; Ashley v. Ministry of Defence [1984] I.C.R. 298, E.A.T.; British Bakeries (Northern) v. Adlington [1988] I.R.L.R. 177, E.A.T.

s. 28, see Meek v. Lothian Regional Council (O.H.), 1980 S.L.T.(Notes) 61; Beecham Group v. Beal (No. 2) [1983] I.R.L.R. 317, E.A.T.; Wignall v. British Gas Corp. [1984] I.C.R. 716, E.A.T.

s. 29, amended: 1980, c.53, sch.1; order 85/39; 1988, c.4, sch.6; c.40, sch.12; repealed in pt.: ibid., sch.13.

s. 31A, see Gregory v. Tudsbury [1982] I.R.L.R. 267, Industrial Tribunal.

s. 31A, added: 1980, c.42, s.13.

s. 32, amended: ibid., sch.1; repealed in pt.: ibid., sch.2.

s. 33, see Satchwell Sunvic v. Secretary of State for Employment [1979] I.R.L.R. 455, E.A.T.; Mitchell v. Royal British Legion Club [1981] I.C.R. 18, E.A.T.; Community Task Force v. Rimmer [1986] I.R.L.R. 203, E.A.T.; Secretary of State for Employment v. Ford (A.) and Sons (Sacks) [1986] I.C.R. 882, E.A.T.

s. 33, amended: 1979, c.36, sch.7; 1980, c.42, s.11; 1986, c.50, sch.10; repealed in pt.: 1980, c.42, sch.2; 1986, c.50, sch.11.

ss. 33, 34, see Secretary of State for Employment v. Cox [1984] I.C.R. 867, E.A.T.

ss. 33, 39, 43, see Secretary of State for Employment v. Doulton Sanitaryware [1981] I.C.R. 477, E.A.T.

ss. 34–44, repealed: 1986, c.50, sch.11.

s. 35, see Cullen v. Creasey Hotels (Limbury) [1980] I.C.R. 236, E.A.T.; Cooner v. Doal (P. S.) [1988] I.C.R. 495, E.A.T.

s. 45, see Community Task Force v. Rimmer [1986] I.C.R. 491, E.A.T.

ss. 45–48, see Dowuona v. John Lewis [1987] I.R.L.R. 310, C.A.

ss. 45, 47, 48, see Lavery v. Plessey Telecommunications [1983] I.C.R. 534, C.A.

s. 47, amended: 1980, c.42, s.11.

ss. 47, 48, see Kolfor Plant v. Wright [1982] I.R.L.R. 311, E.A.T.

s. 48, see Dowuona v. John Lewis [1987] 2 FTLR 292, C.A.

s. 49, see Daley v. A. E. Dorsett (Almar Dolls) [1982] I.C.R. 1, E.A.T.; Lanton Leisure v. White and Gibson [1987] I.R.L.R. 119, E.A.T.;

CAP.

1978—cont.

44. Employment Protection (Consolidation) Act 1978—cont.

Rex Stewart Jefferies Parker Ginsberg v. Parker, December 2, 1966 (C.A.T. No. 1080); Staffordshire County Council v. Secretary of State for Employment [1988] I.R.L.R. 3, E.A.T.

ss. 49–51, see Westwood v. Secretary of State for Employment [1984] 2 W.L.R. 418, H.L.

ss. 49, 50, 53, amended: 1982, c.46, sch.2.

s. 50, see Notcutt v. Universal Equipment Co. (London) [1986] 1 W.L.R. 641, C.A.

s. 51, see Dobie v. Burns International Security Services (U.K.) [1983] I.C.R. 478, E.A.T.

s. 53, see Rowan v. Machinery Installations (South Wales), November 13, 1981, E.A.T.; Brown v. Stuart Scott & Co. [1980] I.C.R. 166, E.A.T.; Gilham v. Kent County Council (No. 1) [1985] I.C.R. 227, C.A.; Smith v. City of Glasgow District Council (H.L.), 1987 S.L.T. 605; Ladbroke Entertainments v. Clark [1987] I.C.R. 585, E.A.T.

s. 54, see Withers v. Flackwell Heath Football Supporters' Club [1981] I.R.L.R. 307, E.A.T.; Hughes v. D.H.S.S.; D.H.S.S. v. Coy; Jarnell v. Department of the Environment [1985] 2 W.L.R. 866, H.L.

ss. 54, 55, see Karim v. Sunblest Bakeries, The Daily Telegraph, November 2, 1987, C.A.

s. 55, see Gillies v. Richard Daniels & Co. [1979] I.R.L.R. 457, E.A.T.; Terinex v. D'Angelo [1981] I.C.R. 12, E.A.T.; Haseltine Lake & Co. v. Dowler [1981] I.C.R. 222, E.A.T.; Ready Case v. Jackson [1981] I.R.L.R. 312, E.A.T.; Pedersen v. Camden London Borough Council [1981] I.C.R. 674, C.A.; Cort (R.) & Son v. Charman [1981] I.C.R. 816, E.A.T.; The Post Office v. Strange [1982] I.R.L.R. 515, E.A.T.; Woods v. W. M. Car Services (Peterborough) [1982] I.C.R. 693, C.A.; T.B.A. Industrial Products v. Morland [1982] I.C.R. 685; Belling & Lee v. Burford [1982] I.C.R. 454, E.A.T.; Greater Glasgow Health Board v. Pate, Second Division, December 19, 1981; Ford v. Warwickshire County Council, The Times, February 19, 1983, H.L.; Wadham Stringer Vehicles v. Brown [1983] I.R.L.R. 46, E.A.T.; Martin v. M.B.S. Fastening (Glynwed) Distribution [1983] I.C.R. 511, C.A.; O'Kelly v. Trusthouse Forte plc [1983] 3 W.L.R. 605, C.A.; R. v. East Berkshire Health Authority, ex p. Walsh, The Times, May 15, 1984, C.A.; Holroyd v. Gravure Cylinders [1984] I.R.L.R. 259, E.A.T.; Charnock v. Barrie Muirhead [1984] I.C.R. 641, E.A.T.; Crank v. Her Majesty's Stationery Office [1985] I.C.R. 1, E.A.T.; Newham London Borough Council v. Ward, The Times, July 19, 1985, C.A.; Shepherd (F. C) & Co. v. Jerrom [1985] I.R.L.R. 275, E.A.T.; Delabole Slate v. Berriman [1985] I.R.L.R. 305, C.A.; Norwest Holst Group Administration v. Harrison [1985] I.C.R. 668, C.A.; Dutton & Clark v. Daly [1985] I.C.R. 780, E.A.T.; Lewis v. Motorworld Garages [1986] I.C.R. 157, C.A.; Newham London Borough v. Ward [1985] I.R.L.R. 509, C.A.; Shook v. London

CAP.

1978—cont.

44. Employment Protection (Consolidation) Act 1978—cont.

Borough of Ealing [1986] I.R.L.R. 46, E.A.T.; Fay v. North Yorkshire County Council [1986] I.C.R. 133, C.A.; Lewis v. Surrey County Council, The Times, August 15, 1986, C.A.; Bridgen v. Lancashire County Council [1987] I.R.L.R. 58, C.A.; Cardinal Vaughan Memorial School Governors v. Alie [1987] I.C.R. 406, E.A.T.; Batchelor v. British Railways Board [1987] I.R.L.R. 136, C.A.; Lanton Leisure v. White and Gibson [1987] I.R.L.R. 119, E.A.T.; Courtaulds Northern Spinning v. Sibson [1988] I.C.R. 451, C.A.

s. 55, amended: 1982, c.46, sch.3.
ss. 55, 56, see Kolfor Plant v. Wright [1982] I.R.L.R. 311, E.A.T.; Dowuona v. John Lewis [1987] I.R.L.R. 310, C.A.
ss. 55, 56, amended: 1980, c.42, sch.1.
s. 56, see Lavery v. Plessey Telecommunications [1983] I.C.R. 534, C.A.
s. 56A, added: 1980, c.42, s.12.
s. 57, see Hinckley and Bosworth Borough Council v. Ainscough [1979] I.R.L.R. 224, E.A.T.; Dixon v. Wilson Walton Engineering [1979] I.C.R. 438, Industrial Tribunal; Bailey v. B.P. Oil (Kent Refinery) [1980] I.R.L.R. 287, C.A.; Noble v. David Gold & Son (Holdings) [1980] I.C.R. 543, C.A.; Bouchaala v. Trust House Forte Hotels [1980] I.C.R. 721, E.A.T.; The Post Office v. Fennell [1981] I.R.L.R. 221, C.A.; The Board of Governors, The National Heart & Chest Hospitals v. Nambiar [1981] I.R.L.R. 196, E.A.T.; Union of Construction, Allied Trades and Technicians v. Brain [1981] I.C.R. 542, C.A.; Eagle Star Insurance Co. v. Hayward [1981] I.C.R. 860, E.A.T.; Kingston v. British Railways Board, The Times, April 6, 1982, E.A.T.; Timex Corp. v. Thomson [1982] I.R.L.R. 522, E.A.T.; Jagdeo v. Smiths Industries [1982] I.C.R. 47, E.A.T.; W. & J. Bass v. Binns, The Times, June 15, 1982, C.A.; Morley's of Brixton v. Minott [1982] I.C.R. 444, E.A.T.; W. & J. Bass v. Binns [1982] I.C.R. 486, C.A.; Greater Glasgow Health Board v Pate, Second Division, December 19, 1981; Sillifant v. Powell Duffryn Timber [1983] I.R.L.R. 91, E.A.T.; G.E.C. Machines v. Gilford [1982] I.C.R. 725, E.A.T.; The Maintenance Co. v. Dormer [1982] I.R.L.R. 491, E.A.T.; Maund v. Penwith District Council [1982] I.C.R. 732, E.A.T.; Clarke v. Eley (IMI) Kynoch [1983] I.C.R. 165, E.A.T.; Seymour v. British Airways Board [1983] I.C.R. 148, E.A.T.; Iceland Frozen Foods v. Jones [1983] I.C.R. 17, E.A.T.; Freud v. Bentalls [1983] I.C.R. 77, E.A.T.; Ladbroke Racing v. Arnott [1983] I.R.L.R. 154, Ct. of Session; Grundy (Teddington) v. Plummer [1983] I.C.R. 367, E.A.T.; Gair v. Bevan Harris, 1983 S.L.T. 487; Spook Erection v. Thackray, Second Division, May 4, 1983; Meikle v. McPhail (Charleston Arms) [1983] I.R.L.R. 351, E.A.T.; Thomson v. Accoa Motor Co. [1983] I.R.L.R. 403, E.A.T.; Canning v. Niaz and McLoughlin

CAP.

1978—cont.

44. Employment Protection (Consolidation) Act 1978—cont.

[1983] I.R.L.R. 431, E.A.T.; Kelman v. Oram [1983] I.R.L.R. 432, E.A.T; Buchanan v. Tilcon, [1984] S.L.T. 134; Linlafoam (Manchester) v. Fletcher, The Times, March 12, 1984, Waite J.; Yate Foundry v. Walters [1984] I.C.R. 445, E.A.T.; Dobie v. Burns International Security Services (U.K.) [1984] 3 All E.R. 333, C.A.; Grooton (U.K.) v. Keld [1984] I.R.L.R. 302, E.A.T.; R.S.P.B. v. Croucher [1984] I.C.R. 604, E.A.T.; Kingston v. British Railways Board [1984] I.C.R. 781, C.A.; Smith v. City of Glasgow District Council, 1985 S.L.T. 138; Hotson v. Wisbech Conservative Club [1984] I.C.R. 859, E.A.T.; Yusuf v. Aberplace [1984] I.C.R. 850, E.A.T; Murphy v. Epsom College [1985] I.C.R. 80, C.A.; Gilham v. Kent County Council (No. 2) [1985] I.C.R. 233, C.A.; Shepherd (F.C.) & Co. v. Jerrom [1985] I.R.L.R. 275, E.A.T.; Greenall Whitley v. Carr [1985] I.C.R. 451, E.A.T.; McGrath v. Rank Leisure [1985] I.C.R. 527, E.A.T.; Berriman v. Delabole Slate [1985] I.C.R. 546, C.A.; Rolls Royce Motors v. Dewhurst [1985] I.C.R. 869, E.A.T.; Pink v. White; Pink v. White & Co. (Earls Barton) [1985] I.R.L.R. 489, E.A.T.; Stacey v. Babcock Power [1986] 2 W.L.R. 207, E.A.T.; Holden v. Bradville [1985] I.R.L.R. 483, E.A.T.; Lafferty (F.) Construction v. Duthie [1985] I.R.L.R. 487, E.A.T.; West Midlands Co-operative Society v. Tipton [1986] 2 W.L.R. 306, H.L.; Saeed v. G.L.C. (I.L.E.A.) (1986) I.R.L.R. 23, Popplewell J.; Pritchett and Dyjasek v. J. McIntyre [1986] I.R.L.R. 97, E.A.T.; R.S.P.C.A. v. Cruden [1986] I.R.L.R. 83, E.A.T.; Wadley v. Eager Electrical [1986] I.R.L.R. 93, E.A.T.; MDH v. Sussex [1986] I.R.L.R. 123, E.A.T.; Graham v. ABF [1986] I.R.L.R. 90, E.A.T.; Fay v. North Yorkshire County Council [1986] I.C.R. 133, C.A.; Fenton v. Stablegold (t/a Chiswick Court Hotel) [1986] I.R.L.R. 64, E.A.T.; Hereford and Worcester County Council v. Neale [1986] I.R.L.R. 168, C.A.; Adams v. Derby City Council [1986] I.R.L.R. 163, E.A.T.; Shook v. Ealing London Borough Council [1986] I.C.R. 314, E.A.T.; Laughton and Hawley v. BAP Industrial Supplies [1986] I.R.L.R. 245, E.A.T.; Polkey v. Dayton (A. E.) Services [1987] 1 All E.R. 948, C.A.; Smiths Industries Aerospace and Defence Systems v. Brookes [1986] I.R.L.R. 434, E.A.T.; Moyes v. Hylton Castle Working Men's Social Club and Institute [1986] I.R.L.R. 482, E.A.T.; Pritchett v. McIntyre (J.) [1978] I.C.R. 359, C.A.; Polkey v. Edmund Walker (Holdings) [1987] I.R.L.R. 13, C.A.; Labour Party v. Oakley, The Daily Telegraph, October 30, 1987, C.A.; Smith v. City of Glasgow District Council [1987] I.R.L.R. 326, H.L.; B.B.C. Sports Club v. Morgan [1987] I.R.L.R. 391, E.A.T.; Polkey v. Dayton (A.E.) Services [1987] 3 W.L.R. 1153, H.L.; Whitbread & Co. v. Thomas [1988] I.C.R. 135, E.A.T.; Brown v. Stockton-on-Tees Borough Council [1988] 2 W.L.R. 935, H.L.; Dillett v. National Coal

1978—cont.

44. Employment Protection (Consolidation) Act 1978—cont.

Board [1988] I.C.R. 218, C.A.; Roadchef v. Hastings [1988] I.R.L.R. 142, E.A.T.

s. 57, amended: 1980, c.42, s.6.

s. 58, see Curry v. Marlow District Council [1979] I.C.R. 769, E.A.T.; Drew v. Edmundsbury Borough Council [1980] I.C.R. 513, E.A.T.; Leyland Vehicles v. Jones, The Times, February 21, 1981, E.A.T.; Rath v. Cruden Construction [1982] I.C.R. 60, E.A.T.; Therm-A-Stor v. Atkins, [1983] I.R.L.R. 78, C.A.; Carrington v. Therma-A-Stor [1983] 1 W.L.R. 138, C.A.; O'Kelly v. Trusthouse Forte [1983] 3 W.L.R. 605, C.A.; Home Delivery Services v. Shackcloth, [1958] I.C.R. 147, E.A.T.; Sakals v. United Counties Omnibus Co. [1984] I.R.L.R. 474, E.A.T.; McGhee v. Midland British Road Services [1985] I.R.L.R. 503, E.A.T.; Crossville Motor Services v. Ashfield [1986] I.R.L.R. 475, E.A.T.; National Coal Board v. McGinty (1987) 84 L.S.Gaz. 2455, E.A.T.; Ridgway and Fairbrother v. National Coal Board [1987] I.R.L.R. 80, C.A.

s. 58, substituted: 1982, c.46, s.3; amended: 1988, c.19, sch.3; repealed in pt.: ibid., s.11, sch.4.

s. 59A, repealed: ibid.

s. 59, see Evans and Morgan v. A. B. Electronic Components [1981] I.R.L.R. 11, E.A.T.; Powers and Villiers v. A. Clarke & Co. (Smethwick) [1981] I.R.L.R. 483, E.A.T.; GEC Machines v. Gilford [1982] I.C.R. 725, E.A.T.; Tilgate Pallets v. Barras [1983] I.R.L.R. 231, E.A.T.; Henry v. Ellerman Lines [1985] I.C.R 57, C.A.; Cross International v. Reid [1985] I.R.L.R. 387, C.A.; Suflex v. Thomas [1987] I.R.L.R. 435, E.A.T.; Rogers v. Vosper Thornycroft (U.K.) [1988] I.C.R. 305, E.A.T.

s. 59, amended: 1982, c.46, sch.3.

s. 60, see Del Monte Foods v. Mundon [1980] I.C.R. 694, E.A.T.; Grimsby Carpet Co. v. Bedford [1987] I.R.L.R. 438, E.A.T.; Brown v. Stockton-on-Tees Borough Council [1988] 2 W.L.R. 935, H.L.

s. 62, see Dixon v. Wilson Walton Engineering [1979] I.C.R. 438, Industrial Tribunal; McCormick v. Horsepower [1981] 1 W.L.R. 993; [1981] 2 All E.R. 746, C.A.; Coates v. Modern Methods and Materials [1982] 3 W.L.R. 764, C.A. Power Packing Casemakers v. Faust [1983] 2 W.L.R. 439, C.A.; Midland Plastics v. Till [1983] I.C.R. 118, E.A.T.; Williams v. National Theatre Board [1982] I.C.R. 715, C.A.; Naylor v. Orton & Smith [1983] I.C.R. 665, E.A.T.; Courtaulds Northern Spinning v. Moosa [1984] I.R.L.R. 43, E.A.T.; Hindle Gears v. McGinty [1985] I.C.R. 111, E.A.T.; Highlands Fabricators v. McLaughlin [1984] I.C.R. 183, E.A.T.; Campey & Sons v. Bellwood [1987] I.C.R. 311, E.A.T.; Munir v. Jang Publications (1987) 84 L.S.Gaz. 2450, E.A.T.; Bolton Roadways v. Edwards [1987] I.R.L.R. 392, E.A.T.; Express & Star v. Bunday [1987] I.R.L.R. 422, C.A.

1978—cont.

44. Employment Protection (Consolidation) Act 1978—cont.

s. 62, amended: 1982, c.46, s.9, sch.3; repealed in pt.: ibid., sch.4.

s. 63, see Colwyn Borough Council v. Dutton [1980] I.R.L.R. 420, E.A.T.

s. 64, see Coley v. Trust House Forte, January 22, 1980, Birmingham Industrial Tribunal; B.P. Chemicals v. Joseph [1980] I.R.L.R. 55, E.A.T.; Howard v. Department for National Savings, The Times, October 16, 1980, C.A.; Dixon v. London Production Tools and Phildon Instrumentation (London) [1980] I.R.L.R. 385, E.A.T.; Nicoll v. Nocorrode, The Times, February 10, 1981, E.A.T.; D.H.S.S. v. Randalls [1981] I.C.R. 100, E.A.T.; Jennings v. Salford Community Service Agency [1981] I.C.R. 399, E.A.T.; Cort (R.) & Son v. Charman [1981] I.C.R. 816, E.A.T.; Duke v. Reliance Systems [1982] I.C.R. 449, E.A.T.; Waite v. Government Communications Headquarters [1983] I.C.R. 359, C.A.; Secretary of State for Trade v. Douglas [1983] I.R.L.R. 63, E.A.T.; Age Concern Scotland v. Hines [1983] I.R.L.R. 477, E.A.T.; Hughes v. Department of Health and Social Security; Coy v. D.H.S.S.; Jarnell v. Department of the Environment [1985] 2 W.L.R. 866, H.L., Hyland v. Barker (J. H.) (North West) [1985] I.C.R. 861, E.A.T.; South West Launderettes v. Laidler [1986] I.R.L.R. 68, E.A.T.; Highlands and Islands Development Board v. MacGillivray, 1986 S.L.T. 363, [1986] I.R.L.R. 210, Court of Session; Secretary of State for Scotland v. Meikle [1986] I.R.L.R. 208, E.A.T.; Swaine v. Health and Safety Executive [1986] I.C.R. 498, E.A.T.; Lanton Leisure v. White and Gibson [1987] I.R.L.R. 119, E.A.T.; Mauldon v. British Telecommunications [1987] I.C.R. 450, E.A.T.; Express and Star v. Bunday [1987] I.R.L.R. 422, C.A.; Whittle v. Manpower Services Commission [1987] I.R.L.R. 441, E.A.T.; Sillars v. Charringtons Fuels [1988] I.R.L.R. 180, E.A.T.

s. 64, amended: order 79/959, 1982, c.46, schs.2,3; order 85/782; 1986, c.59, s.3.

s. 64A, see Wickens v. Champion Employment [1984] I.C.R. 365, E.A.T.; Charnock v. Barrie Muirhead [1984] I.C.R. 641, E.A.T.; Cox v. ELG Metals [1985] I.C.R. 310, C.A.; Keabeech v. Mulcahay [1985] I.C.R. 791, E.A.T.; Harford v. Swiftrim [1987] I.C.R. 439, E.A.T.

s. 64A, added: 1980, c.42, s.8; amended: order 85/782.

s. 66, amended: 1980, c.42, sch.1; repealed in pt.: ibid., schs.1,2.

s. 67, see Beanstalk Shelving v. Horn [1980] I.C.R. 273, E.A.T.; House v. Emerson Electric Industrial Controls [1980] I.C.R. 795, E.A.T.; Post Office v. Moore [1981] I.C.R. 623, E.A.T.; Bodha (Vishnudut) v. Hampshire Area Health Authority [1982] I.C.R. 200, E.A.T.; T.B.A. Industrial Products v. Morland [1982] I.C.R. 685, C.A.; Swainston v. Hetton Victory Club [1983] I.R.L.R. 164, C.A.; Churchill v.

CAP.

1978—cont.

44. Employment Protection (Consolidation) Act 1978—cont.

A. *Yeates & Sons* [1983] I.C.R. 380, E.A.T.; *Palmer* v. *Southend-on-Sea Borough Council* [1984] 1 All E.R. 945, C.A.; *Duffin* v. *Secretary of State for Employment* [1983] I.C.R. 766, E.A.T.; *Crank* v. *Her Majesty's Stationery Office* [1985] I.C.R. 1, E.A.T.; *Hennessey* v. *Craigmyle & Co. and A.C.A.S.* [1985] I.R.L.R. 446, E.A.T.; *Croydon Health Authority* v. *Jaufurally* [1986] I.C.R. 4, E.A.T.; *Lang* v. *Devon General, The Times,* August 19, 1986, E.A.T.; *Batchelor* v. *British Railways Board* [1987] I.R.L.R. 136, C.A.; *Alex Monro (Butchers)* v. *Nicol* [1988] I.R.L.R. 49, E.A.T.; *Machine Tool Industry Research Association* v. *Simpson* [1988] I.R.L.R. 212, C.A.
s. 67, amended: 1982, c.46, s.9.
s. 68, see *Freemans* v. *Flynn* [1984] I.C.R. 874, E.A.T.; *Artisan Press* v. *Strawley and Parker* [1986] I.R.L.R. 126, E.A.T.
s. 68, amended: 1982, c.46, sch.3.
ss. 68, 73, see *Chelsea Football Club & Athletic Co.* v. *Heath* [1981] I.C.R. 323, E.A.T.
s. 69, see *Timex Corp.* v. *Thomson* [1982] I.R.L.R. 522, E.A.T.; *Freemans* v. *Flynn* [1984] I.C.R. 874, E.A.T.; *Lilley Construction* v. *Dunn* [1984] I.R.L.R. 483, E.A.T.; *Electronic Data Processing* v. *Wright* [1986] I.C.R. 76, E.A.T.; *Boots Co.* v. *Lees-Collier* [1986] I.C.R. 728, E.A.T.
ss. 69, 71, see *Artisan Press* v. *Strawley* [1986] I.C.R. 328, E.A.T.; *Whitbread West Pennines* v. *Reedy, The Times,* July 23, 1988, C.A.; *Morganite Electrical Carbon* v. *Donne* [1987] I.R.L.R. 363, E.A.T.
s. 71, see *Freemans* v. *Flynn* [1984] I.C.R. 874, E.A.T.
s. 71, amended: 1980, c.42, sch.1; 1982, c.46, s.5, sch.3.; repealed in pt.: *ibid.,* sch.4.
s. 72, see *Fenton* v. *Stablegold (t/a Chiswick Court Hotel)* [1986] I.R.L.R. 64, E.A.T.
s. 72, substituted: 1982, c.46, s.5.
s. 72A, added: *ibid.,* s.6.
s. 73, see *Kunz Engineering* v. *Santi* [1979] I.R.L.R. 459, E.A.T.; *Colwyn Borough Council* v. *Dutton* [1980] I.R.L.R. 420, E.A.T.; *Courtaulds Northern Spinning* v. *Moosa* [1984] I.R.L.R. 43, E.A.T.; *R.S.P.C.A.* v. *Cruden* [1986] I.C.R. 205, E.A.T.; *Artisan Press* v. *Strawley and Parker* [1986] I.R.L.R. 126, E.A.T.; *Fenton* v. *Stablegold (t/a Chiswick Court Hotel)* [1986] I.R.L.R. 64, E.A.T.; *Morganite Electrical Carbon* v. *Donne* [1987] I.R.L.R. 363, E.A.T.
s. 73, orders 84/2021; 86/2281; 88/277.
s. 73, amended: 1980, c.42, s.9, 1982, c.46, s.4; orders 84/2021, 2033; 1986, c.59, s.3; repealed in pt.: 1980, c.42, s.9, sch.2; 1982, c.46, s.4, schs.2,4.
ss. 73, 74, see *Daley* v. *A. E. Dorsett (Almar Dolls)* [1982] I.C.R. 1, E.A.T.; *Courtaulds Northern Spinning* v. *Moosa, The Times,* November 15, 1983, E.A.T.

CAP.

1978—cont.

44. Employment Protection (Consolidation) Act 1978—cont.

s. 74, see *Parker & Farr* v. *Shelvey* [1979] I.C.R. 896, E.A.T.; *Allen* v. *Hammett* [1982] I.C.R. 227, E.A.T.; *M.B.S.* v. *Calo, The Times,* February 28, 1983, E.A.T.; *Lucas* v. *Lawrence Scott* [1983] I.C.R. 309, E.A.T.; *Tulsa (J. & L.)* v. *Leston-Rama,* September 6, 1983, E.A.T.; *Courtaulds Northern Spinning* v. *Moosa* [1984] I.R.L.R. 43, E.A.T.; *Warrilow* v. *Walker (Robert)* [1984] I.R.L.R. 304, E.A.T.; *Morris* v. *Acco. Co.* [1985] I.C.R. 306, E.A.T.; *Shepherd (F.C.) & Co.* v. *Jerrom* [1985] I.R.L.R. 275, E.A.T.; *Finnie* v. *Top Hat Frozen Foods* [1984] I.R.L.R. 365, E.A.T.; *Boots Co.* v. *Lees-Collier* [1986] I.C.R. 728, E.A.T.; *R.S.P.C.A.* v. *Cruden* [1986] I.C.R. 205, E.A.T.; *Scottish & Newcastle Breweries* v. *Halliday* [1986] I.C.R. 577, E.A.T.; *Crossville Motor Services* v. *Ashfield* [1986] I.R.L.R. 475, E.A.T.; *Moyes* v. *Hylton Castle Working Men's Social Club and Institute* [1986] I.R.L.R. 482, E.A.T.; *Polkey* v. *Edmund Walker (Holdings)* [1987] I.R.L.R. 13, C.A.; *Babcock F.A.T.A.* v. *Addison* [1987] 1 F.T.L.R. 505, C.A.; *Mono Pumps* v. *Froggatt and Redford* [1987] I.R.L.R. 368, E.A.T.; *Morganite Electrical Carbon* v. *Donne* [1987] I.R.L.R. 363, E.A.T.; *Kinzley* v. *Minories Finance* [1987] I.R.L.R. 490, E.A.T.; *Isleworth Studios* v. *Rickard* [1988] I.R.L.R. 137, E.A.T.; *Roadchef* v. *Hastings* [1988] I.R.L.R. 42, E.A.T.
s. 74, amended: 1982, c.46, sch.3.
s. 75, orders 78/1778; 79/1723; 82/76, 1868; 84/2020; 86/2284.
s. 75, amended: orders 82/76; 84/2020; 86/2234.
ss. 75, 75A, see *Artisan Press* v. *Strawley* [1986] I.C.R. 328, E.A.T.
s. 75A, orders 84/2021; 85/2033, 86/2281; 88/277.
s. 75A, added: 1982, c.46, s.5; order 84/2021; amended: order 85/2033.
s. 76A, substituted: 1982, c.46, s.7.
ss. 76A–76C, added: 1980, c.42, s.10.
ss. 76B, 76C, repealed: 1982, c.46, sch.4.
s. 77, see *Bradley* v. *Edward Ryde & Sons* [1979] I.C.R. 488, E.A.T.; *Sulemany* v. *Habib Bank* [1983] I.C.R. 60, E.A.T.; *O'Kelly* v. *Trusthouse Forte plc* [1983] 3 W.L.R. 605, C.A.; *Ridgway and Fairbrother* v. *National Coal Board* [1987] I.R.L.R. 80, C.A.
s. 77, amended: 1982, c.46, s.8, sch.3.
ss. 77, 79, see *National Coal Board* v. *McGinty* [1988] I.R.L.R. 7, E.A.T.
s. 80, repealed in pt.: 1980, c.44, sch.1.
s. 81, see *Ryan* v. *Shipboard Maintenance* [1980] I.C.R. 88, E.A.T.; *O'Hare* v. *Rotaprint* [1980] I.C.R. 94, E.A.T.; *Dal* v. *A. S. Orr* [1980] I.R.L.R. 413, E.A.T.; *Carry All Motors* v. *Pennington* [1980] I.C.R. 806, E.A.T.; *A. Dakri & Co.* v. *Tiffen* [1981] I.C.R. 256, E.A.T.; *Cowan* v. *Haden* [1983] I.C.R. 1, C.A.; *Moncrieff* v. *Tayside Regional Council,* Second Division, November 18, 1982.; *Secretary of State for Employment* v. *Deary* [1984] I.C.R. 413,

CAP.

1978—cont.

44. Employment Protection (Consolidation) Act 1978—*cont.*

E.A.T.; *Secretary of State for Employment* v. *Cheltenham Computer Bureau, The Times,* January 24, 1985, E.A.T.; *Murphy* v. *Epsom College* [1985] I.C.R. 80, C.A.; *Macfisheries* v. *Findlay* [1985] I.C.R. 160, E.A.T.; *Birch* v. *University of Liverpool* [1985] I.C.R. 470, C.A.; *North Yorkshire County Council* v. *Fay* [1985] I.R.L.R. 247, C.A.; *Morley* v. *Morley (C.T.)* [1985] I.C.R. 499, E.A.T.; *Pink* v. *White; Pink* v. *White & Co. (Earls Barton)* [1985] I.R.L.R. 489, E.A.T.; *Marley* v. *Forward Trust Group* [1986] I.R.L.R. 43, E.A.T.; *Flack* v. *Kodak* [1986] I.R.L.R. 255, C.A.; *Secretary of State for Employment* v. *Spence* [1986] I.R.L.R. 248, C.A.; *Willcox* v. *Hastings* [1987] I.R.L.R. 298, C.A.; *Chapman & Elkin* v. *CPS Computer Group* [1987] I.R.L.R. 462, E.A.T.; *Rank Xerox* v. *Churchill, The Daily Telegraph,* May 27, 1988, E.A.T.; *Scott* v. *Coalite Fuels and Chemicals* [1988] I.R.L.R. 131, E.A.T.; *Sillars* v. *Charringtons Fuels* [1988] I.R.L.R. 180, E.A.T.

s. 81, amended: 1982, c.46, sch.3; repealed in pt.: *ibid.,* schs.2,4.

s. 82, see *Executors of J. F. Everest* v. *Cox* [1980] I.C.R. 415, E.A.T.; *Halliday* v. *Bingley Foundries,* July 16, 1980, Industrial Tribunal, Leeds; *Standard Telephones and Cables* v. *Yates* [1981] I.R.L.R. 21, E.A.T.; *Gloucestershire County Council* v. *Spencer* [1985] I.R.L.R. 393, C.A

s. 82, amended: regs. 86/151.

s. 83, see *Wiltshire County Council* v. *National Association of Teachers in Further and Higher Education, The Times,* January 26, 1980, C.A.; *Ryan* v. *Shipboard Maintenance* [1980] I.C.R. 88, E.A.T.; *Ford* v. *Warwickshire County Council, The Times,* February 19, 1983, H.L.; *Birch* v. *University of Liverpool* [1985] I.C.R. 470, C.A.; *Scott* v. *Coalite Fuels and Chemicals* [1988] I.R.L.R. 131, E.A.T.

ss. 83, 85, see *International Computers* v. *Kennedy* [1981] I.R.L.R. 28, E.A.T.

s. 84, see *Singer Co. (U.K.)* v. *Ferrier* [1980] I.R.L.R. 300, E.A.T.; *Rowan* v. *Machinery Installations (South Wales),* November 13, 1980, E.A.T.; *Tocher* v. *General Motors Scotland* [1981] I.R.L.R. 55, E.A.T.; *Ross* v. *Delrosa Caterers* [1981] I.C.R. 393, E.A.T.; *S.I. (Systems & Instrumentation)* v. *Grist* [1983] I.C.R. 788, E.A.T.; *Mckindley* v. *Hill (William) (Scotland)* [1985] I.R.L.R. 492, E.A.T.; *Lucas* v. *Henry Johnson (Packers & Shippers)* [1986] I.C.R. 384, E.A.T.; *Hempell* v. *W.H. Smith & Sons* [1986] I.C.R. 365, E.A.T.; *Elliot* v. *Stump (Richard),* (1987) 84 L.S.Gaz. 1142, E.A.T.; *Benton* v. *Sanderson Kayser* [1988] I.C.R. 313, E.A.T.

s. 85, see *C.P.S. Recruitment* v. *Bowen and Secretary of State for Employment* [1982] I.R.L.R. 54, E.A.T.; *Scott* v. *Coalite Fuels and Chemicals* [1988] I.R.L.R. 131, E.A.T.

s. 87, see *Spinpress* v. *Turner* [1986] I.C.R. 433, E.A.T.

CAP.

1978—cont.

44. Employment Protection (Consolidation) Act 1978—*cont.*

s. 88, see *A. Dakri & Co.* v. *Tiffen* [1981] I.C.R. 256, E.A.T.; *Allinson* v. *Drew Simmons Engineering* [1985] I.C.R. 488, E.A.T.

s. 89, see *Halliday* v. *Bingley Foundries,* July 16, 1980, Industrial Tribunal, Leeds.

s. 90, see *Slater and Secretary of State for Employment* v. *Swain (John) and Son* [1981] I.C.R. 554, E.A.T.; *Secretary of State for Employment* v. *Cameron Iron Works* [1988] I.C.R. 297, E.A.T.; *Staffordshire County Council* v. *Secretary of State for Employment* [1988] I.R.L.R. 3, E.A.T.

s. 91, see *Secretary of State for Employment* v. *Cheltenham Computer Bureau, The Times,* January 24, 1985, E.A.T.; *Willcox* v. *Hastings* [1987] I.R.L.R. 298, C.A.

s. 94, see *Ross* v. *Delrosa Caterers* [1981] I.C.R. 393, E.A.T.; *Atkin* v. *Ward and Haines Watts* [1983] I.C.R. 231, E.A.T.; *S.I. (Systems and Instrumentation)* v. *Grist* [1983] I.C.R. 788, E.A.T.; *Jeetle* v. *Elster, The Times,* December 17, 1984, E.A.T.

s. 96, order 80/1052.

s. 97, repealed: 1980, c.42, sch.2.

ss. 99, 101, 102, see *Vosper Thornycroft (U.K.)* v. *Transport and General Workers' Union* [1988] L.S.Gaz., March 2, 46, E.A.T.

s. 100, repealed in pt.: 1982, c.46, sch.4.

s. 101, see *Secretary of State for Employment* v. *Banks* [1983] I.C.R. 48, E.A.T.; *Duffin* v. *Secretary of State for Employment* [1983] I.C.R. 766, E.A.T.

s. 104, see *Secretary of State for Employment* v. *John Woodrow & Sons (Builders)* [1983] I.C.R. 582, E.A.T.; *Secretary of State for Employment* v. *Cheltenham Computer Bureau* [1985] I.C.R. 381, E.A.T.

s. 104, regs. 84/1066.

s. 104, amended: 1980, c.43, sch.7; 1982, c.46, sch.2; 1986, c.48, s.27; repealed in pt.: *ibid.,* sch.5.

ss. 104, 104A, see *Secretary of State for Employment* v. *Milk & General Haulage (Nottingham)* (1987) 84 L.S.Gaz. 2118, E.A.T.

s. 104A, added: 1986, c.48, s.27.

s. 105, amended: 1982, c.2, sch.1.

s. 106, see *Secretary of State for Employment* v. *Spence* [1986] I.R.L.R. 248, C.A.

s. 106, amended: 1982, c.46, sch.2; 1985, c.65, sch.8; c.66, sch.7 (S.); 1986, c.45, sch.14; repealed in pt.: 1986, c.48, sch.5.

s. 107, amended: 1980, c.43, sch.7.

s. 108, amended: 1986, c.48, sch.4.

s. 109, order 81/1744.

s. 109, amended: 1981, c.5, s.1.

s. 113, repealed: 1986, c.48, sch.5.

s. 117, amended: *ibid.,* s.27.

s. 121, see *Jowett (Angus) & Co.* v. *National Union of Tailors and Garment Workers* [1985] I.R.L.R. 326, E.A.T.

s. 121, repealed: 1985, c.65, sch.10; repealed in pt. (S.): 1985, c.66, sch.8.

1978—cont.

44. Employment Protection (Consolidation) Act 1978—cont.

s. 122, see *Secretary of State for Employment v. Jobling* [1980] I.C.R. 380, E.A.T.; *Westwood v. Secretary of State for Employment* [1983] I.R.L.R. 419, C.A.; *Morris v. Secretary of State for Employment* [1985] I.C.R. 522, E.A.T.; *Jowett (Angus) & Co. v. National Union of Tailors and Garment Workers* [1985] I.R.L.R. 326, E.A.T.

s. 122, orders 78/1777; 79/1722; 80/2019; 82/1866; 83/1962; 84/2019; 85/2032; 86/2283; 88/276.

s. 122, amended: 1982, c.46, sch.3; orders 80/2019; 82/77; 84/2019; 1985, c.9, sch.2; c.65, s.218, sch.8; c.66, sch.7 (S.); orders 84/2019; 85/2032; 1986, c.45, sch.14; orders 86/2283; 88/276; repealed in pt.: 1986, c.50, sch.11.

ss. 122, 124, see *Secretary of State for Employment v. Cooper* [1987] I.C.R. 766, E.A.T.

s. 123, amended: 1982, c.46, sch.3; 1985, c.65, sch.8; 1986, c.45, sch.14; c.50, sch.10; repealed in pt.: *ibid.*, sch.11.

s. 124, see *Morris v. Secretary of State for Employment* [1985] I.C.R. 522, E.A.T.

s. 124, amended: 1986, c.45, sch.10.

s. 125, see *Urethane Engineering Products, Re* (1988) 4 BCC 23, Peter Gibson J.

s. 125, amended: 1985, c.9, sch.2; c.65, sch.8; c.66, sch.7 (S.); 1986, c.45, sch.14; c.50, sch.10; repealed in pt.: 1985, c.65, sch.10.

s. 126, amended: *ibid.*

s. 127, amended: 1986, c.45, sch. 14; c.50, sch. 10; repealed in pt.: *ibid.*, sch. 11.

s. 128, amended: 1980, c.42, sch.1.

s. 131, see *B.B.C. Sports Club v. Morgan* [1987] I.R.L.R. 391, E.A.T.

s. 132, regs. 84/458.

s. 132, amended: 1979, c.18, sch.3; 1980, c.30, sch.4; 1982, c.24, sch.4; 1986, c.45, sch.10; repealed in pt.: *ibid.*, sch.11.

s. 133, amended: 1980, c.42, sch.1; 1986, c.48, sch.4; 1988, c.19, sch.3; repealed in pt.: 1986, c.50, sch.11.

s. 134, see *Slack v. Greenham (Plant Hire)* [1983] I.C.R. 617, E.A.T.; *Hennessey v. Craigmyle & Co.* [1986] I.C.R. 461.

s. 134, amended: 1980, c.42, sch.1.

s. 135, repealed in pt.: 1980, c.42, sch.2.

s. 136, see *A. Monk & Co. Staff Association v. Certification Officer and Association of Scientific, Technical and Managerial Staffs* [1980] I.R.L.R. 431, E.A.T.; *Harrod v. Ministry of Defence* [1981] I.C.R. 8, E.A.T.; *Woods v. W. M. Car Services (Peterborough)* [1982] I.C.R. 693, C.A.; *National Graphical Association v. Howard, The Times,* June 1, 1983, E.A.T.; *Martin v. M.B.S. Fastening (Glynwed) Distribution* [1983] I.C.R. 511, C.A.; *O'Kelly v. Trusthouse Forte plc* [1983] 3 W.L.R. 605, C.A.; *Medallion Holidays v. Birch* [1985] I.R.L.R. 406, E.A.T.; *Smith v. City of Glasgow District Council* (H.L.), 1987 S.L.T. 605.

1978—cont.

44. Employment Protection (Consolidation) Act 1978—cont.

s. 136, amended: 1980, c.42, sch.1; 1986, c.48, sch.4; 1988, c.19, sch.3.

s. 137, order 81/208.

s. 137, amended: 1982, c.23, sch.3; repealed in pt.: *ibid.*, schs.3,4.

s. 138, see *R. v. Secretary of State for the Foreign and Commonwealth Office, ex p. Council of Civil Service Unions, The Times,* July 17, 1984, Glidewell J.

s. 138, amended: 1980, c.9, sch.9; repealed in pt.: 1981, c.55, sch.5; 1986, c.50, sch.11.

s. 139, repealed in pt.: *ibid.*

s. 140, see *Tocher v. General Motors Scotland* [1981] I.R.L.R. 55, E.A.T.; *Slack v. Greenham (Plant Hire)* [1983] I.C.R. 617, E.A.T.; *Hennessey v. Craigmyle & Co.* [1986] I.C.R. 461, C.A.; *Igbo v. Johnson Matthey Chemicals* [1986] I.C.R. 505, C.A.; *Karim v. Sunblest Bakeries, The Daily Telegraph,* November 2, 1987, C.A.; *Scott v. Coalite Fuels and Chemicals* [1988] I.R.L.R. 131, E.A.T.

s. 140, repealed in pt.: 1980, c.42, schs.1,2.

s. 141, see *Janata Bank v. Ahmed* [1981] I.R.L.R. 457, C.A.; *Cox v. E. L. G. Metals* [1984] I.C.R. 1, E.A.T.

s. 141, amended: regs. 83/624.

s. 142, amended: 1980, c.42, s.8.

s. 143, repealed: 1982, c.46, sch.4.

s. 144, see *Goodeve v. Gilson's (A Firm)* [1985] I.C.R. 401, C.A.

s. 144, amended: 1988, c.12, sch.6.

s. 146, see *Home Office v. Robinson* [1982] I.C.R. 31, E.A.T.; *Lewis v. Surrey County Council, The Times,* October 17, 1987, H.L.

s. 146, amended: 1982, c.46, sch.2; regs. 83/624; repealed in pt.: 1982, c.46, schs.3,4.

s. 147, repealed: *ibid.*, sch.4.

s. 148, orders 78/1777; 79/1722; 80/2019; 82/77; 83/1962; 84/2019; 85/2032; 86/2283; 88/276.

s. 149, see *Capon v. Rees Motors* [1980] I.C.R. 553, C.A.; order 79/959.

s. 149, orders 81/847; 83/1160; 85/782, 1872; 88/907.

s. 149, amended: 1980, c.42, sch.1; 1982, c.46, schs.2,3; repealed in pt.: *ibid.*, sch.4.

s. 151, see *Nicoll v. Nocorrode* [1981] I.C.R. 348, E.A.T.; *General of The Salvation Army v. Dewsbury* [1984] I.C.R. 498, E.A.T.; *Charnock v. Barrie Muirhead* [1984] I.C.R. 641, E.A.T.; *Jeetle v. Elster* [1985] I.R.L.R. 227, E.A.T.; *Flack v. Kodak, The Times,* May 31, 1986, C.A.

s. 151, substituted: 1982, c.46, sch.2.

s. 153, see *Gardiner v. Merton London Borough Council, The Times,* November 26, 1980, C.A.; *A. Monk & Co. Staff Association v. Certification Officer and Association of Scientific, Technical and Managerial Staffs* [1980] I.R.L.R. 431, E.A.T.; *Merton London Borough Council v. Gardiner* [1981] 2 W.L.R. 232; [1980] I.R.L.R. 472, C.A.; *Addison v. London Philharmonic Orchestra* [1981] I.C.R. 261,

1978—cont.

44. Employment Protection (Consolidation) Act 1978—cont.

E.A.T.; *Secretary of State for Employment* v. *Newbold and Joint Liquidators of David Armstrong (Catering Services)* [1981] I.R.L.R. 305, E.A.T.; *Umar* v. *Pliastar* [1981] I.C.R. 727, E.A.T.; *President of the Methodist Conference* v. *Parfitt, The Times,* November 18, 1982, E.A.T.; *Williams* v. *National Theatre Board* [1982] I.C.R. 715, C.A.; *Washington Arts Association* v. *Forster* [1983] I.C.R. 346, E.A.T.; *Cox* v. *E. L. G. Metals* [1984] I.C.R. 1, E.A.T.; *O'Kelly* v. *Trusthouse Forte plc.* [1983] 3 W.L.R. 605; [1983] I.R.L.R. 369, C.A.; *Nethermere (St. Neots)* v. *Gardiner* [1984] I.C.R. 612, C.A.; *Charnock* v. *Barrie Muirhead* [1984] I.C.R. 641, E.A.T.; *Hair Colour Consultants* v. *Mena* [1984] I.C.R. 671, E.A.T.; *Poparm* v. *Weekes* [1984] I.R.L.R. 388, E.A.T.; *Capron* v. *Capron, The Times,* February 5, 1985, White J.; *Hughes* v. *Department of Health and Social Security; Coy* v. *D.H.S.S.; Jarnell* v. *Department of the Environment* [1985] 2 W.L.R. 866, H.L.; *Jeetle* v. *Elster* [1985] I.R.L.R. 227, E.A.T.; *South West Laundrettes* v. *Laidler* [1986] I.C.R. 455, E.A.T.; *The Highlands and Islands Development Board* v. *MacGillivray,* 1986 S.L.T. 363; [1986] I.R.L.R. 210, Court of Session; *Secretary of State for Employment* v. *Ford (A.) & Son (Sacks)* [1986] I.C.R. 882, E.A.T.; *Batchelor* v. *British Railways Board* [1987] I.R.L.R. 136, C.A.; *Harford* v. *Swiftrim* [1987] I.C.R. 439, E.A.T.; *National Coal Board* v. *Ridgway, sub nom. Ridgway and Fairbrother* v. *National Coal Board* [1987] I.C.R. 641, C.A.; *Express & Star* v. *Bunday* [1987] I.R.L.R. 442, C.A.; *Eaton* v. *Robert Eaton and Secretary of State for Employment* [1986] I.R.L.R. 83, E.A.T.

s. 153, amended: 1982, c.46, sch.3; 1986, c.48, sch.4; repealed in pt.: 1979, c.36, schs.7,8; 1982, c.46, sch.4; 1986, c.50, sch.11; 1988, c.19, sch.4.

s. 154, orders 78/1777; 79/1722; 80/2019; 82/1866; 83/1160; 1962; 84/2019–21; 85/782, 2032, 2033; 86/2281, 2283, 2284; 88/276, 277, 907.

s. 154, amended: 1980, c.42, sch.1; order 85/2033; repealed in pt.: 1980, c.42, schs.1,2.

ss. 155, 156, repealed in pt.: 1986, c.50, sch.11.

s. 157, amended: 1982, c.46, sch.2; repealed in pt.: 1986, c.50, sch.11.

sch. 1, amended: orders 80/1581; 85/1787; 88/1746; repealed in pt.: orders 80/1581, 1746.

schs. 1, 2, 3, order 79/1403.

sch. 2, see *Kolfor Plant* v. *Wright* [1982] I.R.L.R. 311, E.A.T.; *Lavery* v. *Plessey Telecommunications* [1983] I.C.R. 534, C.A.; *Community Task Force* v. *Rimmer* [1986] I.R.L.R. 203, E.A.T.; *Dowuona* v. *John Lewis* [1987] I.R.L.R. 310, C.A.

sch. 2, order 81/6.

sch. 2, amended: 1980, c.42, sch.1; 1982, c.46, sch.3; repealed in pt.: *ibid.,* sch.4.

1978—cont.

44. Employment Protection (Consolidation) Act 1978—cont.

sch. 3, see *Westwood* v. *Secretary of State for Employment* [1984] 2 W.L.R. 418, H.L.; *Notcutt* v. *Universal Equipment Co. (London)* [1986] 1 W.L.R. 641, C.A.

sch. 3, amended: 1980, c.42, sch.1; 1982, c.24, sch.2.

sch. 4, see *Slater and Secretary of State for Employment* v. *Swain (John) and Son* [1981] I.C.R. 554, E.A.T.; *Secretary of State for Employment* v. *John Woodrow and Sons (Builders)* [1983] I.C.R. 582, E.A.T.

sch. 4, amended: regs. 86/151; repealed in pt.: 1982, c.46, schs.2,4.

schs. 4, 6, see *Secretary of State for Employment* v. *Cheltenham Computer Bureau, The Times,* January 24, 1985, E.A.T.

sch. 5, amended: 1980, c.53, sch.1.; 1983, c.39, schs.2,9; order 85/39.

sch. 6, order 85/260.

sch. 6, amended: *ibid.;* repealed in pt.: 1980, c.42, sch.2; 1986, c.48, sch.5.

sch. 9, regs. 80/884, 885; 83/1807; 85/16, 17(S.).

sch. 9, amended: 1980, c.42, sch.1; 1982, c.46, sch.3; repealed in pt.: 1981, c.20, sch.4.

sch. 11, see *International Aviation Services (U.K.) (Trading as I.A.S. Cargo Airlines)* v. *Jones* [1979] I.R.L.R. 155, E.A.T.; *R.* v. *C.A.C., ex p. Gloucestershire County Council* [1981] I.C.R. 95, D.C.; *Irvine* v. *Prestcold* [1981] I.R.L.R. 281, C.A.; *Burton* v. *British Railways Board, The Times,* October 27, 1982, E.A.T.; *Greater Glasgow Health Board* v. *Pate,* Second Division, December 19, 1981; *O'Kelly* v. *Trusthouse Forte plc* [1983] 3 W.L.R. 605, C.A.; *Medallion Holidays* v. *Birch* [1985] I.R.L.R. 406, E.A.T.

sch. 11, rules 80/2035; 85/29.

sch. 11, amended: 1980, c.42, sch.1; 1981, c.54, sch.5; 1982, c.46, sch.3; 1988, c.19, sch.3; repealed in pt.: 1981, c.49, s.16.

sch. 12, amended: 1982, c.46, sch.3.

sch. 13, see *Allen & Son* v. *Coventry* [1980] I.R.C. 9, E.A.T.; *Hanson* v. *Fashion Industries (Hartlepool)* [1980] I.R.L.R. 393, E.A.T.; *Corton House* v. *Skipper, The Times,* December 6, 1980, E.A.T.; *Merton London Borough Council* v. *Gardiner* [1981] 2 W.L.R. 232; [1980] I.R.L.R. 472, C.A.; *Hanson* v. *Fashion Industries (Hartlepool)* [1981] I.C.R. 35, E.A.T.; *Mitchell* v. *Royal British Legion Club* [1981] I.C.R. 118, E.A.T.; *Jennings* v. *Salford Community Service Agency* [1981] I.C.R. 399, E.A.T.; *Ross* v. *Delrosa Caterers* [1981] I.C.R. 393, E.A.T.; *Rowan* v. *Machinery Installations (South Wales)* [1981] I.C.R. 386, E.A.T.; *Corton House* v. *Skipper* [1981] I.C.R. 307, E.A.T.; *Nicoll* v. *Nocorrode* [1981] I.C.R. 348, E.A.T.; *Coates* v. *Modern Methods and Material, The Times,* July 7, 1982, C.A.; *Ford* v. *Warwickshire County Council* [1983] 2 W.L.R. 399, H.L.; *Moncrieff* v. *Tayside Regional*

CAP.

1978—cont.

44. Employment Protection (Consolidation) Act 1978—cont.

Council, Second Division, November 18, 1982; Washington Arts Association v. Forster [1983] I.C.R. 346, E.A.T.; S.I. (Systems and Instrumentation) v. Grist [1983] I.C.R. 788, E.A.T.; Ingram v. Foxon [1984] I.C.R. 685, E.A.T.; University of Aston in Birmingham v. Malik [1984] I.C.R. 492, E.A.T.; Secretary of State for Employment v. Deary [1984] I.C.R. 413, E.A.T.; Charnock v. Barrie Muirhead [1984] I.C.R. 641, E.A.T.; Jeetle v. Elster [1985] I.C.R. 389, E.A.T.; Flack v. Kodak [1986] 2 All E.R. 1003, C.A.; Secretary of State for Employment v. Ford (A.) & Son (Sacks) [1986] I.C.R. 882, E.A.T.; Girls' Public Day School Trust v. Khanna [1987] I.C.R. 339, E.A.T.; Secretary of State for Employment v. Cohen [1987] I.C.R. 570, E.A.T.; Byrne v. Birmingham City District Council [1987] I.C.R. 519, C.A.; Lewis v. Surrey County Council [1987] 3 W.L.R. 927, H.L.; Express & Star v. Bunday [1987] I.R.L.R. 422, C.A.; Royal Ordnance v. Pilkington, The Times, May 17, 1988, E.A.T.; Sillars v. Charringtons Fuels [1988] I.R.L.R. 180, E.A.T.; Brook Lane Finance Co. v. Bradley [1988] I.C.R. 423, E.A.T.; Letheby and Christopher v. Bond [1988] I.C.R. 480, E.A.T.

sch. 13, amended: 1980, c.9, sch.9; c.42, sch.1; 1982, c.46, schs.2,3; 1985, c.17, sch.4; repealed in pt.: 1981, c.55, sch.5; 1982, c.46, sch.4; 1985, c.17, sch.5.

sch. 14, see Secretary of State for Employment v. Jobling [1980] I.C.R. 380, E.A.T.; Leyland Vehicles v. Reston [1981] I.C.R. 403, E.A.T.; Lotus Cars v. Sutcliffe and Stratton [1982] I.R.L.R. 381, C.A.; Donelan v. Kerrby Constructions [1983] I.C.R. 237, E.A.T.; Secretary of State for Employment v. John Woodrow and Sons (Builders) [1983] I.C.R. 582, E.A.T.; Keywest Club T/A Veeraswarmys Restaurant v. Choudhury [1988] I.R.L.R. 51, E.A.T.; National Coal Board v. Cheeseborough and Secretary of State for Employment [1988] I.R.L.R. 84, E.A.T.; Secretary of State for Employment v. Crane [1988] I.R.L.R. 238, E.A.T.; Cooner v. Doal (P.S.) [1988] I.C.R. 495, E.A.T.

sch. 14, orders 78/1777; 80/2019; 82/77, 1866; 83/1962; 84/2019; 85/2032; 86/2283; 88/276.

sch. 14, amended: 1980, c.42, sch.1; 1982, c.46, sch.3; orders 80/2019; 82/77; 84/2019; 85/2032; 86/2283; 88/276; repealed in pt.: regs. 86/151; 1986, c.50, sch.11.

sch. 15, see White v. Pressed Steel Fisher [1980] I.R.L.R. 176, E.A.T.

sch. 15, repealed in pt.: 1983, c.41, sch.10; 1986, c.50, sch.11.

sch. 16, repealed in pt.: 1981, c.19, sch.1; c.64, sch.13; 1982, c.10, sch.4; c.16, sch.16; c.46, sch.4; 1984, c.29, sch.12; c.32, sch.7; 1985, c.71, sch.1; 1986, c.48, sch.5; 1988, c.1, sch.31.

CAP.

1978—cont.

45. Statute Law (Repeals) Act 1978.
Royal Assent, July 31, 1978.
s. 3, order 84/1692.

46. Employment (Continental Shelf) Act 1978.
Royal Assent, July 31, 1978.
repealed: 1982, c.23, sch.4.

47. Civil Liability (Contribution) Act 1978.
Royal Assent, July 31, 1978.
s. 1, see Logan v. Uttlesford District Council, The Times, February 21, 1984, Sheen J.; Benarty, The, The Times, June 23, 1987, Hobhouse J.; Kapetin Georgis, The; sub nom. Virgo Steamship Co. S.A. v. Skaarup Shipping Corp., The Financial Times, October 21, 1987, Hirst J.; Lister (R.A.) & Co. v. Thompson (E.G.) (Shipping) (No. 2) [1987] 1 W.L.R. 1614, Hobhouse J.; Nottingham Health Authority v. Nottingham City Council, The Times, April 5, 1988, C.A.; Kapetan Georgis, The [1988] 1 FTLR 180, Hirst J.
s. 2, see Fitzgerald v. Lane [1988] 3 W.L.R. 356, H.L.
sch. 1, repealed in pt.: 1980, c.58, sch.4.; 1983, c.14, sch.3.

48. Homes Insulation Act 1978.
Royal Assent, July 31, 1978.
repealed: 1985, c.71, sch.1; 1987, c.26, sch.24 (S.).
s. 1, orders 80/1062; 81/1695; 82/504, 1772; 83/285; 84/838.
s. 1, amended: 1985, c.51, sch.8; repealed in pt. (S.): 1985, c.71, sch.1.
s. 2, repealed in pt.: 1985, c.51, sch.1.
s. 2, repealed in pt.: ibid., sch.17.
s. 3, repealed (S.): 1985, c.71, sch.1.
s. 4, amended (S.): ibid., sch.2.

49. Community Service by Offenders (Scotland) Act 1978.
Royal Assent, July 31, 1978.
s. 1, see McQueen v. Lockhart, 1986 S.C.C.R. 20.
ss. 3–5, see H.M. Advocate v. Hood, 1987 S.C.C.R. 63.
s. 4, amended: 1982, c.48, sch.7.
s. 6, amended: ibid., sch.13; repealed in pt.: ibid., sch.16.
ss. 6A, 6B, added: ibid., sch.13.
s. 7, repealed in pt.: 1987, c.41, sch.2.
s. 15, orders 78/1944; 80/268.
s. 15, amended: 1982, c.48, sch.13.
sch. 1, repealed: ibid., sch.16.

50. Inner Urban Areas Act 1978.
Royal Assent, July 31, 1978.
ss. 1, 15, orders 78/1314, 1343, 1486; 83/289; 84/838; 87/115.
s. 2, amended: 1978, c.51, sch.16; c.52, sch.11.
s. 4, repealed in pt.: 1980, c.65, sch.34.
s. 6, amended: ibid., s.191.
s. 12, repealed: ibid., s.88, sch.34.
sch., amended: 1978, c.51, sch.16; c.52, sch.11; 1980, c.65, s.191.

51. Scotland Act 1978.
Royal Assent, July 31, 1978.
repealed: order 79/928.

CAP.

1978—cont.

51. Scotland Act 1978—*cont.*
ss. 1, 17, 18, 63, 83, 85, schs. 2, 17, 18, see *Sillars* v. *Smith*, 1982, S.L.T. 539.
s. 85, order 79/928.
sch. 17, order 78/1912.

52. Wales Act 1978.
Royal Assent, July 31, 1978.
repealed: order 79/933.
s. 80, order 79/933.
sch. 12, order 78/1915.

53. Chronically Sick and Disabled Persons (Northern Ireland) Act 1978.
Royal Assent, July 31, 1978.
ss. 4, 5, 6, 8, 18, amended: order 82/1535.
s. 7, substituted: *ibid.*
s. 8A, added: *ibid.*
s. 14, S.R. 1979 No. 365.
s. 19, amended: order 79/1573.
s. 21, S.Rs. 1979 Nos. 364, 365.

54. Dividends Act 1978.
Royal Assent, July 31, 1978.
repealed: 1980, c.21, sch.2.

55. Transport Act 1978.
Royal Assent, August 2, 1978.
ss. 1–4, repealed: 1985, c.67, sch.8.
s. 5, regs. 78/1313; 80/144, 1358; 81/263, 269, 886; amended: 1980, c.34, sch.5; repealed in pt.: *ibid.*,sch.9.
s. 6, repealed: *ibid.*, schs.5,9.
s. 7, amended: *ibid.*, sch.5; repealed in pt.: *ibid.*, sch.9.
s. 8, regs. 78/1313
ss. 8, 17, repealed: 1980, c.34, sch.9.
s. 9, repealed in pt.: 1988, c.54, sch.1.
s. 11, orders 78/1535; 79/119.
ss. 11, 12, repealed: 1984, c.27, sch.14.
s. 14, order 81/441.
s. 14, repealed: 1982, c.6, sch.
s. 19, orders 78/1294, 1764; 79/1416.
ss. 19, 20, repealed: 1980, c.34, s.58, sch.9.
s. 20, orders 78/1289, 1294, 1764; 79/1416.
s. 21, amended: 1984, c.32, sch.6.
s. 24, order 78/1289.
s. 24, repealed in pt.: 1981, c.14, sch.8; 1988, c.54, sch.1.
sch. 1, repealed: 1980, c.34, sch.9.
sch. 2, regs. 78/1313.
sch. 2, repealed in pt.: *ibid.*; 1981, c.14, sch.8.
sch. 3, repealed in pt.: 1982, c.49, sch.6; 1988, c.54, sch.1.

56. Parliamentary Pensions Act 1978.
Royal Assent, August 2, 1978.
repealed: 1987, c.45, sch.4.
s. 11, orders 78/1837; 81/800; 82/1155; 84/1907.

57. Appropriation Act 1978.
Royal Assent, August 2, 1978.
repealed: 1980, c.54, sch.(C.).

58. Pensioners Payments Act 1978.
Royal Assent, November 23, 1978.
s. 1, regs. 78/1691.

CAP.

1979

1. Price Commission (Amendment) Act 1979.
Royal Assent, February 12, 1979.
repealed: 1980, c.21, sch.2.

2. Customs and Excise Management Act 1979.
Royal Assent, February 22, 1979.
amended: 1984, c.60, s.114.
s. 1, regs. 87/2114.
s. 1, amended: 1979, c.58, sch.1; 1981, c.35, sch.8; c.63, sch.5; c.43, sch.4; 1984, c.49, sch.1; c.51, s.103; repealed in pt.: 1981, c.35, sch.19; 1987, c.49, sch.2.
s. 8, amended: 1982, c.39, s.12.
s. 16, see *R.* v. *George and Davies* [1981] Crim.L.R. 185, C.A.
s. 17, amended: 1979, c.58, sch.1.
s. 19, orders 80/81, 482–486, 1367, 1368, 1879–1882.
s. 20, amended: 1987, c.16, s.6.
s. 21, amended: 1979, c.58, sch.1.
s. 22, orders 82/204; 85/1730; 86/525, 971; 87/1982.
s. 25, amended: 1976, c.16, s.6.
s. 26, amended: 1983, c.28, s.7.
s. 27, amended: *ibid.*; 1987, c.16, sch.7; repealed in pt.: 1984, c.22, sch.3.
s. 28, amended: 1987, c.16, sch.7.
s. 31, regs. 80/761; 81/1257; 84/1176.
s. 31, amended: 1981, c.35, sch.7; 1984, c.43, sch.4.
s. 34, amended: 1979, c.58, sch.1.
s. 35, regs. 79/564, 565; 81/1259, 1260; 86/1819.
s. 35, amended: 1979, c.58, sch.1; 1987, c.49, sch.1.
s. 36, amended: 1979, c.58, sch.1.
s. 37, amended: 1981, c.35, sch.6; 1984, c.43, schs.4,5; repealed in pt.: 1981, c.35, schs.6,19.
s. 37A–37C, added: 1984, c.43, sch.5.
s. 38, substituted: 1981, c.35, sch.6.
ss. 38A, 38B, added: *ibid.*
ss. 40, 41, amended: *ibid.*
s. 42, regs. 79/564; 81/1259, 1260; 86/1819.
s. 43, amended: 1979, c.58, sch.1; 1981, c.35, sch.6; regs. 82/1324; repealed in pt.: 1981, c.35, sch.19.
s. 45, regs. 88/1810.
s. 48, regs. 87/1781.
s. 49, see *R.* v. *Bow Street Magistrates' Court, ex p. Noncyp*, The Times, May 14, 1988, D.C.
s. 50, see *McNeil* v. *H.M. Advocate*, 1986 S.C.C.R. 288.
s. 50, amended: 1981, c.45, s.23; 1988, c.39, s.12.
s. 51, repealed in pt.: 1983, c.28, s.7, sch.10.
s. 52, amended: 1981, c.35, sch.7.
s. 53, substituted: *ibid.*, s.10, sch.7; amended: 1988, c.39, s.12.
ss. 54–58, substituted: 1981, c.35, s.10, sch.7.
ss. 58A–58E, added: *ibid.*, sch.7.
ss. 58A, 58D, amended: 1987, c.16, s.8.
s. 59, amended: 1981, c.35, sch.7.
s. 60, repealed in pt.: *ibid.*, sch.19.
s. 61, amended: 1979, c.58, sch.1; 1981, c.35, sch.7; 1987, c.51, s.103.

CAP.

1979—cont.

2. Customs and Excise Management Act 1979—cont.

s. 63, amended: 1979, c.58, sch.1; 1988, c.39, s.12.

s. 64, amended: 1979, c.58, sch.1; 1987, c.49, sch.1.

s. 66, regs. 81/1259, 1260.

s. 66, amended: 1979, c.58, sch.1; 1981, c.35, sch.7.

s. 68, see *R* v. *Uxbridge J.J., ex p. Sofaer, The Times,* December 4, 1986, D.C.

s. 68, amended: 1981, c.45, s.23; 1988, c.39, s.12.

s. 68A, added: 1982, c.39, s.11; 1988, c.39, s.12.

s. 68B, added: 1983, c.28, s.8.

ss. 69, 70, 74, amended: 1979, c.58, sch.1.

s. 75A, added: 1987, c.16, s.9.

s. 76, repealed: 1981, c.35, sch.19.

s. 77, repealed in pt.: 1987, c.16, s.10, sch.16.

s. 77A, added: *ibid.*, s.10.

s. 78, see *Customs and Excise Commissioners* v. *Claus* [1987] Crim.L.R. 756; (1988) 86 Cr.App.R. 189, D.C.

s. 78, amended: 1979, c.58, sch.1.

s. 81, amended: 1988, c.12, sch.6.

s. 81, regs. 79/564.

s. 83, amended: 1979, c.58, sch.1.

s. 86, see *R.* v. *Jones (Keith Desmond)* [1987] 1 W.L.R. 692, C.A.

ss. 88, 89, amended: 1987, c.49, sch.1.

s. 90, amended: 1979, c.58, sch.1.

s. 92, amended: *ibid.*, 1988, c.39, s.9.

s. 93, see *R.* v. *Customs and Excise Comrs., ex p. Hedges and Butler* [1986] 2 All E.R. 164, D.C.

s. 93, regs. 79/207, 208, 1146; 80/992; 82/611, 612, 964; 83/947; 85/252, 1627; 86/79, 910; 88/809, 1760.

s. 93, amended: 1981, c.35, sch.8; 1986, c.41, sch.3; repealed in pt.: 1988, c.39, s.9, sch.14.

s. 94, repealed in pt.: 1981, c.35, schs.8,19.

s. 95, repealed in pt.: *ibid.*, sch.19.

s. 98, amended: *ibid.*, sch.8.

s. 100, amended: 1988, c.39, s.12.

s. 100A, orders 84/1206–1211; 86/1643; 88/533.

Pt. VIIIA (ss. 100A–100F), added: 1984, c.43, s.8, sch.4.

ss. 100B–100D, regs. 84/1177; 88/710.

s. 101, amended: 1986, c.41, sch.5.

s. 102, amended: *ibid.*; 1987, c.16, sch.1.

s. 104, amended: 1986, c.41, sch.5.

ss. 105, 106, repealed: 1981, c.35, schs.8,19.

s. 110, see *R.* v. *Taafe* [1983] 1 W.L.R. 627, C.A.

s. 112, amended: 1981, c.35, sch.8.

s. 114, order 85/252.

s. 116A, added: 1981, c.35, sch.8.

s. 117, amended: *ibid.*; 1987, c.18, sch.6 (S.); repealed in pt.: 1981, c.35, sch.19.

s. 119, amended: *ibid.*, sch.6; 1984, c.43, sch.4; repealed in pt.: 1981, c.35, sch.19.

s. 120, regs. 87/2107; 88/1.

s. 123, amended: regs. 80/1825.

CAP.

1979—cont.

2. Customs and Excise Management Act 1979—cont.

s. 125, regs. 84/1177.

s. 127A, regs. 83/947; 86/910; 88/1810.

s. 127A, added: 1983, c.28, s.6.

s. 128, repealed in pt.: 1981, c.35, schs.6,19.

s. 136, amended: 1982, c.39, s.11; 1988, c.39, s.12.

s. 138, amended: 1984, c.60, sch.6; 1988, c.39, s.11; repealed in pt.: 1984, c.60, sch.7.

s. 140, repealed in pt.: 1981, c.35, schs.6,19.

s. 141, see *Lord Advocate* v. *DAF Trucks Finance (U.K.),* 1984 S.L.T.(Sh.Ct.) 6.

s. 142, amended: 1987, c.49, sch.1.

s. 147, amended: 1980, c.43, sch.7; 1988, c.39, s.11; repealed in pt.: 1982, c.48, schs.14,16.

s. 151, see *R.* v. *Clacton Justices, ex p. Commissioners of Customs and Excise, The Times,* October 5, 1987, D.C.

s. 151, amended: 1980, c.43, sch.7.

s. 152, see *C.B.S. Inc.* v. *Blue Suede Music* [1982] R.P.C. 523, Falconer J.

s. 153, amended: 1981, c.35, sch.8.

s. 156, amended: 1981, c.63, sch.5; 1982, c.48, sch.14; repealed in pt.: *ibid.*, sch.14,16.

s. 159, amended: 1979, c.58, sch.1; 1984, c.43, sch.4; 1988, c.39, s.12.

s. 161, see *McNeil* v. *H.M. Advocate,* 1986 S.C.C.R. 288.

s. 161, amended: 1984, c.60, sch.6.

s. 164, amended: 1984, c.43, sch.4; 1988, c.39, s.10.

s. 167, see *R.* v. *Cross* [1987] Crim.L.R. 43, C.A.; *Napier* v. *H.M. Advocate,* 1988 S.L.T. 271.

s. 170, see *Att.-Gen's Reference (No. 1 of 1982)* [1982] 2 W.L.R. 875, C.A.; *R.* v. *Neal* [1983] Crim.L.R. 677; (1983) 77 Cr.App.R. 283, C.A.; *R* v. *S. Jakeman* (1983) 76 Cr.App.R. 223, C.A.; *R.* v. *Taafe* [1984] 2 W.L.R. 326, H.L.; *R.* v. *Tonner, R.* v. *Evans, The Times,* July 6, 1984, C.A.; *R.* v. *Shivpuri* [1986] 2 W.L.R. 988, H.L.; *R.* v. *Collins* [1987] Crim.L.R. 256, C.A.; *R.* v. *Ellis, Street and Smith* [1987] Crim.L.R. 44; (1987) 84 Cr.App.R. 235, C.A.; *R.* v. *Ciappara* [1988] Crim.L.R. 172, C.A.

s. 170, amended: 1981, c.45, s.23; 1988, c.48, sch.8.

s. 171, amended: 1984, c.43, sch.5; repealed in pt.: S.L.R. 1986.

s. 175, repealed in pt. (S.): 1980, c.55, sch.3.

s. 177, repealed in pt.: S.L.R. 1986.

sch. 1, see *R.* v. *S. Jakeman* (1983) 76 Cr.App R. 223, C.A.

sch. 1, amended: 1985, c.39, s.1.

sch. 2, order 79/1393.

sch. 3, see *R.* v. *Bow Street Magistrates' Court, ex p. Noncyp, The Times,* May 14, 1988, D.C.

sch. 3, amended: 1979, c.58, sch.1.

sch. 4, repealed in pt.: 1979, c.58, sch.2; 1981, c.16, sch.2; c.22, sch.6; c.63, sch.7; c.69, sch.17; order 81/231; 1982, c.16, sch.16; c.23, sch.4; c.48, sch.16; c.53, sch.9; 1983, c.21, schs.3,4; c.53, sch.3; c.55, sch.11; 1984, c.30, sch.11; 1985, c.72, sch.13; S.L.R. 1986; 1987, c.16, sch.16; 1988, c.48, sch.8.

1979—cont.

2. Customs and Excise Management Act 1979—cont.

sch. 7, repealed in pt.: 1979, c.58, sch.2; 1983, c.53, sch.3; c.55, sch.11.

3. Customs and Excise Duties (General Reliefs) Act 1979.

Royal Assent, February 22, 1979.

orders 79/1718; 80/2032; 81/1228.

amended: 1984, c.60, s.114.

s. 1, orders 79/1142, 1717, 1747; 80/479, 665, 1303, 1800, 1867, 1884; 81/1363, 1415, 1777, 1778; 82/1189, 1466, 1475, 1760, 1782; 83/501, 1038, 1819; 84/810, 2006; 85/19, 112, 2041; 86/787, 2141; 87/1785, 2126; 88/185.

s. 2, regs. 79/554, 555; 82/793; 83/877; 84/1500; 86/2141.

s. 4, orders 79/737, 1717, 1747; 80/211, 245, 905, 1884; 81/621, 911, 1777, 1778; 82/116, 884, 1760, 1782, 1783; 83/876, 1819; 84/10, 898, 2006; 85/135, 283, 989, 2041; 86/495, 1102, 2174, 2292; 87/134, 1122, 1785, 2126; 88/238, 1127.

s. 6, repealed: 1979, c.58, sch.2.

s. 7, orders 84/895; 85/1378.

s. 7, substituted: 1984, c.43, s.14.

ss. 8, 10, 11, amended: 1979, c.58, sch.1.

s. 11A, added: 1988, c.39, s.5.

s. 13, orders 79/655, 1551; 82/1591; 83/1828, 1829; 84/718, 719; 85/1375, 1376; 86/2105.

s. 13, amended: 1984, c.43, s.15.

s. 17, orders 83/1828, 1829; 84/718, 719, 895.

s. 17, amended: 1984, c.43, ss.14,15; 1988, c.39, s.5.

sch. 1, repealed: 1979, c.58, sch.2.

sch. 2, repealed in part.: 1983, c.55, sch.11.

4. Alcoholic Liquor Duties Act 1979.

Royal Assent, February 22, 1979.

amended: 1984, c.60, s.114.

s. 1, amended: order 79/241; 1984, c.43, s.1; 1988, c.39, sch.1; repealed in pt.: ibid., schs.1,14.

s. 2, regs. 79/1146; 82/611, 612; 85/1627; 87/314; 88/809.

s. 2, substituted: order 79/241; amended: 1981, c.35, sch.8.

s. 3, regs. 79/1146; 82/611; 85/252, 1627; 87/314; amended: order 79/241.

s. 4, amended: 1980, c.43, sch.7; 1981, c.35, sch.8; order 79/241; 1987, c.49, sch.1; repealed in pt.: 1981, c.35, sch.19; order 79/241; 1986, c.41, sch.23; 1987, c.49, sch.2.

s. 5, amended: order 79/241; 1980, c.48, s.1; 1981, c.35, s.1; 1982, c.39, s.1; 1983, c.28, s.1; 1984, c.43, s.1; 1985, c.54, s.1.

s. 8, regs. 79/1146; 81/1258.

s. 8, substituted: 1988, c.39, s.6.

s. 12, amended: order 79/241; 1986, c.41, sch.5; repealed in pt.: ibid, s.8, sch.23.

s. 13, regs. 79/1146; 81/1258; 82/611; 83/947.

s. 13, amended: 1981, c.35, sch.8; 1985, c.54, s.1.

s. 14, amended: order 79/241; 1981, c.35, sch.8; 1985, c.54, s.1.

1979—cont.

4. Alcoholic Liquor Duties Act 1979—cont.

s. 15, regs. 79/1146; 82/611, 612; 83/947; 86/79; 88/809.

s. 15, amended: 1981, c.35, sch.8; repealed in pt.: 1986, c.41, schs.3,23.

s. 16, regs. 79/1146; amended: order 79/241.

s. 18, repealed in pt.: 1986, c.41, s.8, sch.23.

s. 19, regs. 79/1146; 81/1258; 88/1760.

s. 19, amended: 1981, c.35, sch.8.

s 20, repealed: order 79/241.

s. 21, amended: ibid.; repealed in pt.: 1981, c.35, sch.19.

s. 22, regs. 79/1146; 88/1760; amended: order 79/241; 1979, c.58, sch.1; 1981, c.35, sch.8; repealed in pt.: 1988, c.39, s.6, sch.14.

s. 23, amended: order 79/241.

s. 24, amended: 1981, c.35, sch.8.

s. 25, repealed in pt.: 1986, c.41, sch.23.

s. 26, amended: order 79/241; 1987, c.49, sch.1.

s. 27, repealed: 1981, c.35, schs.8,19.

s. 28, regs. 79/1146.

ss. 28, 29, repealed: 1981, c.35, schs.8,19.

s. 30, repealed in pt.: ibid.

s. 31, regs. 79/1146.

s. 31, amended: order 82/1575; 1988, c.39, s.6; repealed in pt.: order 82/1575

s. 32, repealed in pt.: 1981, c.35, schs.8,19.

s. 33, regs. 79/1146.

s. 33, amended and repealed in pt.: 1988, c.39, s.6.

s. 36, regs. 87/314.

s. 36, amended: order 79/241; 1980, c.48, s.1; 1981, c.35, s.1; 1982, c.39, s.1; 1983, c.28, s.1; 1984, c.43, s.1; 1985, c.54, s.1; 1988, c.39, s.6.

s. 37, amended: order 79/241.

s. 38, amended: 1985, c.54, sch.3.

s. 40, amended: 1982, c.39, s.9.

s. 42, repealed in pt.: 1988, c.39, s.1, sch.14.

s. 43, regs. 85/252, 1627.

s. 43, amended: 1979, c.58, sch.1; repealed in pt.: 1988, c.39, s.1, sch.14.

s. 45, amended: order 79/241; 1988, c.39, sch.1.

s. 46, regs. 79/1146; 85/252, 1627.

s. 46, amended: 1986, c.41, s.4; repealed in pt.: ibid., s.4, sch.23.

ss. 47, 48; repealed in pt.: ibid., s.8, sch.23.

s. 49, regs. 79/1146; 85/252, 1627.

s. 49, amended: 1985, c.54, sch.3.

s. 49A, added: 1986, c.41, s.4.

s. 50, regs. 85/1627.

s. 52, amended: 1985, c.54, sch.3; 1988, c.39, sch.1.

s. 54, see Cinzano (U.K.) v. Customs and Excise Comrs. [1985] 1 W.L.R. 484, H.L.

s. 54, amended: 1985, c.54, s.4; 1988, c.39, sch.1; repealed in pt.: 1986, c.41, sch.23.

s. 55, amended: 1984, c.43, s.1; 1988, c.39, sch.1; repealed in pt.: 1986, c.41, sch.23.

s. 55A, added: 1988, c.39, sch.1.

s. 56, regs. 79/1146, 1240; 80/992; 83/947; 85/403, 404; 88/809.

s. 56, repealed in pt.: 1986, c.41, sch.23.

ss. 57, 58, amended: order 79/241; 1979, c.58, sch.1.

1979—cont.

4. Alcoholic Liquor Duties Act 1979—cont.
s. 59, amended: *ibid.*; 1988, c.1, sch.1.
s. 60, regs. 79/1146, amended: order 79/241; 1988, c.1, sch.1.
s. 61, regs. 79/1240; 85/404.
s. 62, regs. 79/1146, 1218, 1240; 80/902; 83/947; 85/404.
s. 62, amended: order 79/241; 1980, c.48, s.1; 1981, c.35, s.1; 1982, c.39, s 1; 1983, c.28, s.1; 1984, c.43, s.1; 1985, c.54, s.1; 1988, c.1, s.1.
s. 63, regs. 79/1146; amended: order 79/241; 1988, c.1, s.1.
s. 65, repealed: 1981, c.35, schs.8,19.
s. 66, repealed: *ibid.*, sch.19.
s. 68, repealed: *ibid.*, schs.8,19.
s. 69, amended: *ibid.*, sch.8.
s. 70, repealed: *ibid.*, schs.8,19.
s. 71, amended: order 79/241; 1988, c.1, sch.1.
s. 71A, regs. 85/1627.
s. 71A, added: 1985, c.54, sch.3; amended: 1988, c.1, sch.1.
s. 72, amended: *ibid.*; repealed in pt.: 1985, c.54, schs.3,27.
s. 73, amended: 1988, c.1, sch.1.
s. 74, amended: order 79/241.
s. 75, amended: *ibid.*; repealed in pt.: 1986, c.41, s.8, sch.23.
s. 76, repealed: 1981, c.35, schs.8,19.
s. 77, regs. 79/1146; 83/252; 87/2009.
s. 77, amended: 1981, c.35, sch.8; repealed in pt.: *ibid.*, schs.8,19.
s. 78, amended: order 79/241.
s. 81, repealed: 1986, c.41, s.8, sch.23.
s. 82, regs. 79/1146; 86/1820.
s. 82, amended: order 79/241.
s. 83, repealed: 1986, c.41, sch.23.
s. 84, repealed: 1981, c.35, sch.19.
ss. 85–89, repealed: *ibid.*, schs.8,19.
s. 92, repealed in pt.: 1983, c.28, s.9, sch.10.
sch. 1, substituted: 1984, c.43, s.1, sch.1; amended: 1985, c.54, s.1, sch.1; 1988, c.1, ss.1, 7, sch.3.
sch. 2, repealed: 1984, c.43, sch.23.
sch. 3, repealed in pt.: *ibid.*, sch.19; order 81/231; 1985, c.72, sch.13; 1988, c.25, s.3.

5. Hydrocarbon Oil Duties Act 1979.
Royal Assent, February 22, 1979.
s. 6, amended: 1979, c.47, s.2; 1980, c.48, s.3; 1981, c.35, s.4; 1982, c.39, ss.3,4; 1984, c.43, s.3; 1985, c.54, s.3; 1986, c.41, s.2; 1988, c.39, s.3.
ss. 7, 8, amended: 1980, c.48, s.3; 1981, c.35, s.4.
s. 10, amended: 1988, c.39, s.12.
s. 11, amended: 1979, c.47, s.2; 1980, c.48, s.3; 1984, c.43, s.3; 1986, c.41, s.2.
s. 13, amended: 1988, c.39, s.3.
s. 13A, added: 1987, c.16, s.1; amended: 1988, c.39, s.3.
s. 14, amended: 1979, c.47, s.2; 1980, c.48, s.3; 1988, c.39, s.12.
ss. 17–19, amended: 1980, c.48, s.6; repealed in pt.: *ibid.*, sch.19.
s. 19A, added: *ibid.*, s.5.

1979—cont.

5. Hydrocarbon Oil Duties Act 1979—cont.
s. 20, substituted: 1985, c.54, sch.4.
s. 20A, regs. 85/1450.
s. 20A, added: 1985, c.54, sch.4.
s. 21, regs. 81/1134; 85/1450.
s. 24, regs. 81/1134; 85/1033, 1450.
s. 24, amended: 1981, c.35, s.6; 1982, c.39, s.4; 1987, c.16, s.1.
s. 27, amended: 1980, c.43, sch.7; 1981, c.35, s.5; 1982, c.39, s.4; 1985, c.54, sch.4; 1987, c.16, s.1.
sch. 1, amended: 1982, c.39, s.3.
sch. 3, regs. 81/1134.
sch. 3, amended: 1982, c.39, s.3; 1986, c.41, s.2; repealed in pt.: 1985, c.54, schs.4,27.
sch. 4, amended: 1981, c.35, s.6; 1982, c.39, s.4; repealed in pt.: 1981, c.35, sch.19.
sch. 5, amended: 1984, c.30, sch.10.
sch. 6, repealed in pt.: 1983, c.55, sch.11.

6. Matches and Mechanical Lighters Duties Act 1979.
Royal Assent, February 22, 1979.
amended: 1984, c.60, s.114.
s. 1, amended: 1981, c.35, s.3.
s. 2, repealed in pt.: 1986, c.41, s 8, sch.23.
s. 3, regs. 80/992; 83/947.
s. 3, amended: 1979, c.58, sch.1.
s. 6, amended: 1981, c.35, s.3.
s. 7, regs. 80/992; 83/947.
s. 7, amended: 1979, c.58, sch.1; 1986, c.41, sch.5.
s. 9, repealed in pt.: 1983, c.55, sch.11.

7. Tobacco Products Duty Act 1979.
Royal Assent, February 22, 1979.
amended: 1984, c.60, s.114.
s. 2, regs. 79/904; 80/992.
s. 2, repealed in pt.: 1981, c.35, sch.19.
s. 3, repealed: 1981, c.35, s.1, schs.2,19.
ss. 4, 6, repealed in pt.: *ibid.*, sch.19.
s. 7, regs. 79/904; 80/992; 82/964.
sch. 1, substituted: 1988, c.39, s.2.

8. Excise Duties (Surcharges or Rebates) Act 1979.
Royal Assent, February 22, 1979.
s. 1, amended: 1980, c.48, s.10; 1982, c.39, s.10.
s. 2, amended: 1979, c.47, s.4; 1980, c.48, s.10.
s. 3, repealed in pt.: 1979, c.58, sch.2.
sch. 1, repealed in pt.: S.L.R. 1986.

9. Films Act 1979.
Royal Assent, February 22, 1979.
repealed: 1985, c.21, s.1, sch.2.

10. Public Lending Right Act 1979.
Royal Assent, March 22, 1979.
functions transferred: order 86/600.
s. 2, orders 85/201; 88/609; amended: orders 85/201; 88/609.
s. 3, orders 82/719; 84/1847; 85/1581; 86/2103; 87/1908.
s. 5, orders 80/83; 83/480, 1688.

11. Electricity (Scotland) Act 1979.
Royal Assent, March 22, 1979.
s. 2, order 81/1048.
s. 4, amended: 1983, c.25, sch.3.

1979—cont.

11. Electricity (Scotland) Act 1979—*cont.*
s. 5, amended: 1982, c.43, sch.3; 1986, c.62, s.4.
s. 7, repealed in pt.: 1983, c.25, sch.4.
s. 8, amended: *ibid.*, sch.3.
s. 9, repealed in pt.: *ibid.*, sch.4.
s. 12, amended: 1981, c.28, sch.3; 1984, c.12, sch.4; c.54, sch.9.
s. 13, amended: *ibid.*; repealed in pt.: 1984, c.12, sch.4.
s. 15, substituted: 1983, c.25, s.19.
s. 16, regs. 88/1057.
s. 16, repealed: 1980, c.63, sch.2.
s. 22, amended: *ibid.*, s.17, sch.3; repealed in pt.: *ibid.*, sch.4.
s. 25, amended: 1983, c.29, s.4.
s. 27, repealed in pt.: 1987, c.16, sch.16.
s. 29, amended: 1982, c.56, s.1; 1988, c.37, s.1.
s. 29, order 82/748.
s. 35, amended: 1983, c.25, s.4; 1986, c.62, s.4; repealed in pt.: 1983, c.25, s.4, sch.4.
s. 40, regs. 88/1057.
s. 40, repealed in pt.: 1988, c.37, s.1.
s. 41, amended: 1982, c.48, sch.15; repealed in pt.: *ibid.*, schs.15,16.
s. 45, repealed in pt.: 1984, c.12, sch.7.
sch. 2, amended: 1982, c.43, sch.3; repealed in pt.: *ibid.*, schs.3,4.
sch. 3, amended: 1981, c.28, sch.3; 1984, c.12, sch.4.
sch. 4, amended: 1986, c.62, s.4.
sch. 9, amended: 1983, c.25, sch.3.
sch. 10, repealed in pt.: *ibid.*, sch.4.

12. Wages Councils Act 1979.
Royal Assent, March 22, 1979.
repealed: 1986, c.48, s.12, sch.5.
s. 4, orders 79/864, 865; 80/1495; 81/791, 82/384, 739, 1597.
s. 15, see *Cooner* v. *Doal (P.S.)* [1988] I.C.R. 495, E.A.T.
sch. 1, order 80/1495; 82/384, 739, 1597.

13. Agricultural Statistics Act 1979.
Royal Assent, March 22, 1979.
s. 1, amended and repealed in pt.: 1984, c.20, s.2.
s. 6, amended: 1980, c.43, sch.7.
sch. 1, repealed in pt.: 1982, c.9, sch.2.

14. Capital Gains Tax Act 1979.
Royal Assent, March 22, 1979.
amended: 1988, c.1, sch.29.
s. 1, amended: *ibid.*
ss. 3, 4 (in pt.) (prosp.), 5 (in pt.) (prosp.), repealed: 1988, c.39, sch.14.
s. 4, repealed in pt.: *ibid.*, s.104.
s. 5, orders 83/402; 84/343; 85/428; 86/527; 87/436; 88/506.
s. 5, amended: 1980, c.48, s.77; 1982, c.39, s.80; orders 84/402; 87/436; 88/506.
s. 6, repealed: 1984, c.43, s.63, sch.23.
s. 7, amended: 1980, c.48, s.61.
ss. 8, 9, repealed: 1984, c.43, s.63, sch.23.
s. 9, amended: 1985, c.9, sch.2.
ss. 10, 14–16, amended: 1988, c.1, sch.29.
s. 17, repealed: 1981, c.35, sch.19; amended: 1984, c.43, s.70.

1979—cont.

14. Capital Gains Tax Act 1979—*cont.*
s. 18, amended: *ibid.*, s.69; 1988, c.1, sch.29; c.48, sch.7.
s. 19, see *Spencer-Nairn* v. *I.R.C.*, 1985 S.L.T.(Lands Tr.) 46.
s. 19, repealed in pt.: 1981, c.35, s.90, sch.19.
s. 26, amended: 1988, c.1, sch.29.
s. 27, see *Lyon* v. *Pettigrew* [1985] S.T.C. 369, Walton J.
s. 28, amended: 1982, c.39, s.86.
s. 29A, added: 1981, c.35, s.90; amended: 1984, c.43, s.66; 1988, c.1, sch.29; repealed in pt.: 1984, c.43, s.66, sch.23.
s. 31, amended: 1980, c.48, s.83; 1986, c.41, s.56; 1988, c.1, sch.29.
s. 32, see *Chaney* v. *Watkis* [1986] S.T.C. 89, Nicholls J.
s. 32, amended: 1980, c.48, s.83; 1988, c.1, sch.29; repealed in pt.: 1984, c.43, sch.23.
s. 32A, added: 1988, c.1, sch.29.
s. 33, amended: *ibid.*
s. 33A, added: *ibid.*
s. 34, amended: 1983, c.49, s.6; 1986, c.41, s.56; 1988, c.1, sch.29; c.39, sch.13.
s. 35, amended: 1988, c.1, sch.29.
s. 45, repealed: 1988, c.39, s.104; repealed in pt. (prosp.): *ibid.*, sch.14.
s. 49, amended: 1980, c.48, s.83.
s. 53, amended: *ibid.*, s.86.
s. 54, amended: *ibid.*, s.87.
s. 55, amended: 1982, c.39, s.84; repealed in pt.: *ibid.*, s.84, sch.22.
s. 56, amended: 1980, c.48, s.87; 1982, c.39, s.84; repealed in pt.: *ibid.*, s.84, sch.22.
s. 56A, added: *ibid.*, s.84.
s. 60, amended: 1988, c.1, sch.29.
s. 62, amended: 1980, c.48, s.90.
ss. 62, 63, see *Spencer-Nairn* v. *I.R.C.*, 1985 S.L.T.(Lands Tr.) 46.
s. 63, amended: 1988, c.1, sch.29.
s. 64, amended: 1984, c.48, sch.13.
ss. 65, 66, amended: 1982, c.39, s.88; repealed in pt.: 1985, c.54, sch.27.
s. 67, substituted: 1986, s.41, s.59.
s. 68, amended: 1982, c.39, s.88; repealed in pt.: 1985, c.54, sch.27.
s. 69, repealed in pt.: *ibid.*
s. 70, amended: 1984, c.48, sch.13; repealed in pt.: 1985, c.54, sch.27.
ss. 74, 75, amended: 1988, c.1, sch.29.
s. 79, amended: 1980, c.48, s.91.
s. 84, amended: 1985, c.54, s.67; 1988, c.1, sch.29; repealed in pt.: 1985, c.54, sch.27.
s. 85, amended: 1988, c.1, sch.29.
s. 87, amended: 1987, c.51, sch.6; 1988, c.1, sch.29.
s. 89, amended: 1980, c.48, s.91; 1988, c.1, sch.29.
s. 90, amended: *ibid.*
s. 92, regs. 88/266.
s. 92, amended: 1987, c.16, s.40; 1988, c.1, sch.29.
s. 94, repealed: 1980, c.48, s.81, sch.20.
ss. 95, 97, repealed: *ibid.*, sch.20.
s. 98, amended: *ibid.*, s.81; 1988, c.1, sch.29.
s. 99, amended: 1982, c.53, s.46.

CAP.

1979—cont.

14. Capital Gains Tax Act 1979—cont.
s. 100, repealed: 1980, c.48, sch.20.
s. 101, see *Moore* v. *Thompson* [1986] S.T.C. 170, Millett J.
s. 101, amended: 1988, c.1, sch.29, repealed in pt.: 1988, c.39, sch.14.
ss. 101, 102, see *Batey (Inspector of Taxes)* v. *Wakefield* [1982] 1 All E.R. 61, C.A.; *Markey (Inspector of Taxes)* v. *Sanders* [1987] 1 W.L.R. 864, Walton J.; *Williams (Inspector of Taxes)* v. *Merrylees* [1987] 1 W.L.R. 1511, Vinelott J.
s. 102, amended: 1980, c.48, s.20; 1988, c.39, sch.8.
s. 105, repealed: *ibid.*, s.111.
s. 107, amended: 1984, c.48, s.63; 1986, c.41, s.59; 1988, c.1, sch.29.
s. 111A, added: 1982, c.39, s.83.
s. 113, amended: 1988, c.39, sch.6.
s. 114, repealed: 1985, c.54, sch.27.
s. 115, see *Todd (Inspector of Taxes)* v. *Mudd* [1987] S.T.C. 141, Vinelott J.; *Richart (Inspector of Taxes)* v. *Lyons (J.) & Co., The Times,* June 8, 1988, Millett J.
s. 115, amended: 1988, c.39, sch.8.
s. 118, see *Williams* v. *Evans* [1982] 1 W.L.R. 972, Nourse J.
s. 118, amended: 1988, c.39, s.112.
s. 119, amended: 1988, c.1, sch.29.
s. 120, amended: 1985, c.54, s.70.
s. 123A, added: 1988, c.1, sch.29.
s. 124, see *Atkinson (Inspector of Taxes)* v. *Dancer; Mannion (Inspector of Taxes)* v. *Johnston, The Times,* July 22, 1988, Peter Gibson J.
s. 124, amended: 1988, c.1, sch.29; repealed: 1985, c.54, s.69, sch.27.
s. 125, repealed: *ibid.*
s. 126, amended: *ibid.*, s.70; 1988, c.1, sch.29.
s. 128, amended: 1982, c.39, s.81.
s. 132A, added: 1988, c.1, sch.29.
s. 136, amended: *ibid.*
s. 137, amended: 1980, c.48, s.84; 1984, c.48, s.65; 1985, c.54, s.72; 1987, c.51, s.81; 1988, c.1, sch.29; repealed in pt.: 1984, c.48, s.65, sch.23.
s. 138, amended: 1987, c.51, s.81; repealed in pt.: 1984, c.48, s.65, sch.23.
s. 142, amended: 1988, c.39, s.101.
ss. 142A, 144A, added: 1988, c.1, sch.29.
s. 145, amended: *ibid.*
s. 146, amended: 1984, c.51, sch.8; repealed in pt.: 1982, c.39, sch.22.
s. 147, amended: 1984, c.51, sch.8; 1985, c.54, s.95; repealed in pt.: 1982, c.39, sch.22.
s. 148, repealed: 1984, c.43, s.68, sch.23.
s. 149, amended: 1984, c.51, sch.8; 1985, c.9, sch.2; 1988, c.1, sch.29.
ss. 149A–149D, added: *ibid.*
s. 149B, amended: 1988, c.39, sch.13.
s. 149D, regs. 88/1348.
s. 149D, amended: 1988, c.39, s.116.
s. 150, repealed in pt.: 1987, c.16, sch.16.
s. 151, repealed: 1985, c.54, sch.27.
s. 152, amended: 1988, c.1, sch.29.

CAP.

1979—cont.

14. Capital Gains Tax Act 1979—cont.
s. 155, amended: 1985, c.54, s.72; 1988, c.1, sch.29; c.39, sch.13; repealed in pt.: 1988, c.1, sch.31.
s. 157, amended: *ibid.*, sch.29.
sch. 1, amended: 1980, c.48, ss.77,78; 1981, c.35, s.89; 1982, c.39, s.80; 1983, c.20, sch.4; 1988, c.1, sch.29; repealed in pt.: 1988, c.39, s.104, sch.14 (prosp.).
sch. 2, orders 79/1231, 1676; 80/507, 922, 1910; 81/615, 1879; 82/413, 1774; 84/1774, 1996; 86/12; 87/259; 88/360.
sch. 2, repealed in pt.: 1986, c.44, sch.9.
sch. 3, see *Clarke (Inspector of Taxes)* v. *United Real (Moorgate)* [1988] S.T.C. 273, Walton J.
sch. 3, amended: 1988, c.1, sch.29.
sch. 4, amended: 1981, c.35, s.91; 1984, c.51, sch.8; 1985, c.54, s.70; repealed in pt.: 1981, c.35, sch.19; 1982, c.39, sch.22.
sch. 5, amended: *ibid.*, sch.13; 1988, c.1, sch.29.
sch. 6, amended: *ibid.*
sch. 7, repealed in pt.: 1984, c.51, sch.9; 1985, c.54, sch.27; 1988, c.1, sch.31; c.39, sch.14.
sch. 9, repealed in pt.: 1984, c.51, sch.9.

15. House of Commons (Redistribution of Seats) Act 1979.
Royal Assent, March 22, 1979.
repealed: 1986, c.56, sch.4.

16. Criminal Evidence Act 1979.
Royal Assent, March 22, 1979.

17. Vaccine Damage Payments Act 1979.
Royal Assent, March 22, 1979.
s. 1, regs. 79/1441; order 85/1249.
s. 1, amended: 1985, c.53, s.23.
ss. 2–5, 7, 8, regs. 79/432.
s. 4, regs. 84/442; 88/1169.
s. 8, regs. 88/1169.
ss. 10, 11, repealed: 1981, c.19, sch.1.

18. Social Security Act 1979.
Royal Assent, March 22, 1979.
ss. 4, 15, repealed in pt.: 1980, c.30, sch.5.
s. 16, repealed: 1984, c.60, sch.7.
s. 17, repealed: 1980, c.30, sch.5.
s. 20, repealed in pt.: 1981, c.19, sch.1.
s. 21, orders 79/369, 1031.
sch. 1, repealed in pt.: 1985, c.53, s.11, sch.6.
sch. 3, repealed in pt.: 1980, c.30, sch.5.

19. Administration of Justice (Emergency Provisions) (Scotland) Act 1979.
Royal Assent, March 22, 1979.
s. 1, order 79/550.
s. 4, see *Smith* v. *Bernard,* 1980 S.L.T.(Notes) 81.

20. Consolidated Fund Act 1979.
Royal Assent, March 22, 1979.
repealed: 1981, c.51, sch.(C.).

21. Forestry Act 1979.
Royal Assent, March 29, 1979.
s. 2, regs. 79/836.

22. Confirmation to Small Estates (Scotland) Act 1979.
Royal Assent, March 29, 1979.
s. 3, order 80/734.
s. 3, repealed in pt.: 1981, c.19, sch.1.

CAP.

1979—cont.

23. Public Health Laboratory Service Act 1979.
Royal Assent, March 29, 1979.

24. Appropriation Act 1979.
Royal Assent, April 4, 1979.
repealed: 1981, c.51, sch.(C.).

25. Finance Act 1979.
Royal Assent, April 4, 1979.
repealed: 1988, c.1, sch.31.

26. Legal Aid Act 1979.
Royal Assent, April 4, 1979.
repealed: 1988, c.34, sch.6.
Pt. II (ss. 6–10), ss. 12 (in pt.), 14 (in pt.), sch.1 (in pt.), repealed (S): 1986, c.47, sch.5.
s. 14, orders 79/756, 826; 82/1678; 83/418 (S.).

27. Kiribati Act 1979.
Royal Assent, June 19, 1979.
s. 2, order 79/719.
s. 3, repealed in pt.: 1981, c.61, sch.9.
ss. 4, 5, repealed: *ibid.*
s. 6, orders 79/719, 720.
s. 6, repealed in pt.: S.L.R. 1986.
s. 7, repealed in pt.: 1981, c.61, sch.9.
sch., repealed in pt.: 1981, c.9, sch; 1982, c.1, sch.2.

28. Carriage by Air and Road Act 1979.
Royal Assent, April 4, 1979.
s. 2, see *Fothergill* v. *Monarch Airlines* [1980] 3 W.L.R. 809; [1980] 2 All E.R. 696, H.L.
s. 6, order 81/604.
s. 7, order 80/1966.

29. International Monetary Fund Act 1979.
Royal Assent, April 4, 1979.
s. 1, orders 80/1131; 83/998.
s. 2, amended: 1983, c.51, s.1.

30. Exchange Equalisation Account Act 1979.
Royal Assent, April 4, 1979.
s. 3, amended: 1986, c.41, s.113.

31. Prosecution of Offences Act 1979.
Royal Assent, April 4, 1979.
repealed: 1985, c.23, sch.2.
s. 4, see *R.* v. *D.P.P., ex p. Raymond* (1979) 70 Cr.App.R. 233, C.A; *Raymond* v. *Att.-Gen.* [1982] 2 W.L.R. 849, C.A.
s. 6, see *R.* v. *Elliott* (1985) 81 Cr.App.R. 115, C.A.
ss. 8, 9, regs. 85/243.
sch. 1, repealed in pt.: 1983, c.2, sch.9.

32. Industry Act 1979.
Royal Assent, April 4, 1979.
s. 1, repealed in pt.: 1981, c.6, ss.1, 2, sch.

33. Land Registration (Scotland) Act 1979.
Royal Assent, April 4, 1979.
Commencement order: 85/501.
ss. 2, 9, see *Hughes* v. *Frame,* 1985 S.L.T.(Lands Tr.) 12.
s. 6, amended: 1981, c.59, s.6.
s. 9, amended: *ibid.*; 1985, c.73, sch.2.
s. 12, see *Keay* v. *Renfrew District Council,* 1982 S.L.T.(Lands Tr.) 33.
s. 12, amended: 1984, c.42, sch.1; 1985, c.37, sch.1; c.66, sch.7; c.73, sch.2.
ss. 20, 21, see *McCann* v. *Anderson, More* v. *Anderson,* 1981 S.L.T.(Lands Tr.) 13; *Ferguson* v. *Gibbs,* 1987 S.L.T. (Lands Tr.) 32.
s. 22A, added: 1985, c.73, s.2.

CAP.

1979—cont.

33. Land Registration (Scotland) Act 1979—*cont.*
s. 27, rules 80/1413; 82/974; 88/1143.
s. 28, amended: 1981, c.59; s.6; 1982, c.1, sch.1; 1984, c.12, sch.4; repealed in pt.: 1981, c.19, sch.1; 1982, c.16, sch.16.
s. 30, orders 80/1412; 82/520; 83/745; 85/501.
sch. 2, repealed in pt.: 1987, c.26, sch.24.

34. Credit Unions Act 1979.
Royal Assent, April 4, 1979.
s. 6, amended: 1985, c.9, sch.2; 1986, c.45, sch.14.
s. 8, amended: 1987, c.22, sch. 6.
ss. 13, 29, orders 79/866.
s. 25, repealed: 1988, c.1, sch.31.
s. 31, regs. 84/308; 86/622; 88/451.
s. 31, amended: 1980, c.43, sch.7; 1981, c.65, sch.6; 1987, c.22, sch.6; repealed in pt.: 1985, c.58, sch.4; 1987, c.22, schs.6,7.
s. 33, orders 79/936; 80/481.
sch. 1, amended: 1982, c.50, sch.5.
sch. 3, order 80/736.
sch. 3, repealed: 1987, c.22, sch.7.

35. Independent Broadcasting Authority Act 1979.
Royal Assent, April 4, 1979.
repealed: 1980, c.64, s.40, sch.7.
s. 3, order 80/189.

36. Nurses, Midwives and Health Visitors Act 1979.
Royal Assent, April 4, 1979.
Commencement orders: 80/893; 82/963, 1565; 83/668, 723; 85/789.
see *Hefferon* v. *Committee of U.K. Central Council for Nursing, Midwifery and Health Visiting, The Guardian,* March 10, 1988, D.C.
s. 1, orders 80/894; 82/961; 85/789.
s. 3, orders 82/1566, 1567; 83/726.
s. 5, orders 80/895; 82/1569; S.R. 1982 No. 362; order 83/725.
s. 7, order 83/1219.
s. 8, orders 82/1568; 83/724.
s. 9, order 83/927 (S.); S.R. 1983 No. 132.
s. 10, order 83/667.
s. 11, orders 83/921; 85/1852.
s. 11, amended: orders 83/884; 84/1975.
s. 11A, added: order 84/884.
s. 12, order 83/839; S.R. 1983 No. 117.
ss. 12, 13, amended: order 83/884.
s. 13, see *Slater* v. *United Kingdom Central Council for Nursing Midwifery and Health Visitors, The Independent,* June 9, 1987, D.C.
s. 16, amended: 1980, c.53, sch.1.
s. 18, repealed (S.): 1980, c.55, sch.3.
s. 21, repealed in pt.: 1983, c.41, sch.10.
s. 22, orders 83/873, 887; 86/786, 1345, 1897, 2294; 87/446, 944, 2156; 88/1798; S.Rs. 1983 No. 153; 1987 No. 473.
ss. 22A, 22B, added: order 83/884.
s. 23, S.Rs. 1983 No. 153; 1987 No. 473.
s. 23, amended: order 79/1573.
s. 24, orders 80/893; 82/1565; 83/668.
sch. 1, orders 80/894; 82/961.
sch. 2, orders 82/962, 1104; 88/158.
sch. 3, order 83/839; S.R. 1983 No. 117.

CAP.

1979—cont.

36. Nurses, Midwives and Health Visitors Act 1979—cont.

sch. 4, amended: 1985, c.9, sch.2.

sch. 5, order 83/723.

sch. 6, S.R.s. 1982 No. 362; 1983 No. 153; 1987 No. 473.

sch. 7, amended: 1980, c.53, schs.4,6; repealed in pt.: *ibid.*, schs.4,7; 1981, c.19, sch.1; 1984, c.23, sch.3.

sch. 8, amended: 1981, c.19, sch.6.

37. Banking Act 1979.

Royal Assent, April 4, 1979.

Commencement orders: 79/938; 82/188; 85/797.

repealed, except ss. 38, 47, 51, sch.6, 1987, c.22, sch.7.

s. 1, see *S.C.F. Finance Co.* v. *Masri* [1986] 2 Lloyd's Rep. 366, C.A.; *S.C.F. Finance Co.* v. *Masri (No. 2)* [1987] 2 W.L.R. 58, C.A.

s. 2, regs. 79/1204; 80/345–347; 81/112, 1381; 83/510, 1865; 84/769; 86/769, 1712; 87/65; orders 82/1681; 85/564, 572, 1845.

s. 12, regs. 80/348 (S.), 353.

s. 18, see *Re Goodwin Squires Securities, The Times,* March 22, 1983, Vinelott J.

Pt. II (ss. 21–23), order 84/1990.

s. 23, orders 82/1808; 83/1100; 84/897; 86/772.

s. 28, amended (S.): 1985, c.66, sch.7; repealed in pt. (S.): *ibid.*, schs.7,8.

s. 34, regs. 85/220; 87/64.

s. 52, orders 79/938, 82/188; 85/797.

sch. 6, repealed in pt.: order 81/156; 1985, c.71, sch.1; 1986, c.53, sch.19; c.60, sch.17.

38. Estate Agents Act 1979.

Royal Assent, April 4, 1979.

s. 1, amended (S.): 1985, c.73, sch.1.

s. 6, regs. 82/637.

s. 7, regs. 81/1518.

s. 8, regs. 82/637.

s. 10, amended: 1980, c.21, s.19; 1984, c.12, sch.4; 1986, c.31, sch.4; c.44, sch.7; 1987, c.43, sch.4.

s. 11, regs. 81/1519.

s. 14, amended: 1985, c.9, sch.2.

s. 23, amended: 1985, c.65, sch.8; c.66, sch.7 (S.).

s. 26, repealed in pt.: 1980, c.65, schs.4,34.

s. 30, regs. 81/1518, 1520; 82/637.

s. 33, amended: 1980, c.43, sch.7.

s. 35, repealed: 1981, c.19, sch.1.

s. 36, order 81/1517.

39. Merchant Shipping Act 1979.

Royal Assent, April 4, 1979.

Commencement orders: 82/1616; 83/440, 1312; 85/1827; 86/1052; 87/635, 719.

amended: 1982, c.48, s.49.

modified: orders 80/569, 570.

ss.1–13, repealed: 1983, c.21, sch.4.

s. 2, orders 80/1350; 81/1410; 82/1212.

s. 7, regs. 80/1163.

s. 9, regs. 80/1234.

s. 11, regs. 80/1244.

s. 14, order 87/855.

s. 15, orders 80/569, 570, 1510–1517, 1526.

s. 16, orders 80/1092; 87/635, 670, 855.

CAP.

1979—cont.

39. Merchant Shipping Act 1979—cont.

s. 19, orders 80/569, 570, 1509–1519, 1526.

s. 20, orders 81/836; 82/1666; 83/1106; 84/862, 1153; 85/2002; 87/470, 664; 88/788, 1840.

s. 20, amended: 1982, c.48, s.49; 1988, c.12, sch.6.

s. 21, regs. 79/1659; 80/529, 530, 534–538, 540, 542–544, 686, 1227, 2025, 2026; 81/363, 571–574, 576–583, 589, 1065, 1076, 1472, 1729, 1747; 82/1699; 83/117, 708, 808, 1167; 84/93–97, 346, 408, 1115, 1203, 1216–1221, 1223; 85/211, 512, 659–661, 663, 855, 936, 1193, 1194, 1216–1218; 86/144, 837, 1066–1075, 1935; 87/63, 548, 549, 854, 884, 1298, 1591, 1961; 88/38, 191, 317, 641, 642, 1116, 1275, 1396, 1485, 1547, 1636–1639, 1641, 1693, 1716.

s. 21, amended: 1986, c.23, s.11.

ss. 21, 22, see *Smith* v. *Brown,* 1988 S.L.T. 150.

s. 22, regs. 79/1659; 80/529, 530, 535–540, 542–544, 1227; 81/406, 568, 571, 573, 574, 576–584, 589, 1065, 1076, 1472, 1729, 1747; 82/876, 1699; 83/117, 708, 808; 84/93–97, 346, 408, 1115, 1203, 1216–1221, 1223; 85/211, 212, 512, 659–661, 663, 855, 936, 1193, 1194, 1217, 1218, 1664; 86/144, 1066–1074; 87/549, 1591, 1886, 1961; 88/38, 191, 317, 641, 642, 1116, 1275, 1547, 1636–1639, 1641, 1693, 1716.

s. 22, amended: 1984, c.28, sch.2.

s. 28, amended: 1988, c.12, sch.6; repealed in pt.: *ibid.,* schs.6,7.

s. 30, regs. 79/1577.

s. 31, repealed: 1988, c.12, sch.7.

s. 32, order 86/1052.

s. 32, repealed in pt.: 1988, c.12, sch.7.

s. 34, order 86/2285.

s. 37, repealed in pt.: 1988, c.12, sch.7.

s. 38, orders 81/214–223, 405, 431; 83/1519; 84/543.

s. 38, repealed in pt.: 1988, c.12, sch.7.

s. 39, repealed in pt. (S.): 1987, c.18, sch.8.

s. 40, repealed in pt.: 1988, c.12, sch.7.

s. 42, amended: 1980, c.53, sch.7.

s. 43, regs. 79/1519.

s. 43, amended: 1980, c.53, sch.7; repealed in pt.: 1982, c.48, sch.16.

ss. 44–45 (in pt.), repealed: 1988, c.12, sch.7.

s. 46, amended: *ibid.,* sch.5.

s. 47, orders 80/569, 570, 1509–1519, 1526; 81/420–430, 1810, 1811; 83/762; 84/356, 1161, 1688; 86/1163; 88/790, 1851, 1991.

s. 49, regs. 82/1699; 83/708.

s. 49, amended: 1986, c.23, s.11; 1988, c.12, sch.5; repealed in pt.: 1986, c.23, s.11.

s. 50, amended: 1983, c.21, sch.3; repealed in pt.: 1987, c.21, sch.3.

s. 52, orders 79/807, 1578; 80/354, 923; 81/405; 82/1616; 83/439, 440, 1312; 85/1827; 86/1052; 87/635, 719.

s. 68, regs. 80/533.

s. 93, regs. 79/1577.

sch. 1, repealed: 1987, c.21, sch.3.

1979—cont.

39. Merchant Shipping Act 1979—*cont.*
sch. 2, repealed: 1983, c.21, sch.4.

sch. 3, orders 80/1125, 1872; 81/1249; 83/36, 582; 84/1548; 85/230, 1430; 86/1777; 87/703, 855, 931.

sch. 3, modified: order 80/1092; amended and repealed in pt.: order 87/670.

sch. 4, orders 86/1040, 1932, 2224.

sch. 5, repealed in pt.: 1983, c.21, sch.4.

sch. 6, regs. 79/1519, 1577.

sch. 6, amended: 1988, c.12, sch.6; repealed in pt.: *ibid.*, sch.7.

sch. 7, repealed in pt.: 1983, c.21, sch.4; 1984, c.5, sch.2.

40. Representation of the People Act 1979.
Royal Assent, April 4, 1979.

repealed: 1983, c.2, sch.9.

41. Pneumoconiosis etc. (Workers' Compensation) Act 1979.
Royal Assent, April 4, 1979.

s. 1, regs. 79/1726; 82/1867; 83/1861; 84/1972; 85/2034; 86/2035; 88/668.

s. 1, amended: 1985, c.53, s.24.

s. 2, amended: 1986, c.50, sch.3; repealed in pt.: *ibid.*, sch.11.

s. 4, regs. 79/727, 1726; 82/1867; 83/1861; 84/1972; 85/1645; 86/2035.

s. 5, regs. 79/727; 85/1645.

s. 7, regs. 79/727, 1726; 82/1867; 83/1816; 84/1972; 85/1645; 86/2035; 88/668.

42. Arbitration Act 1979.
Royal Assent, April 4, 1979.

see *S.L. Sethia Liners* v. *Naviagro Maritime Corp.; The Kostas Melas* [1980] Com.L.R. 3, Goff J.; *Westzucker GmbH* v. *Bunge GmbH; Bremer Handelgesellschaft GmbH* v. *Westzucker GmbH, The Times*, May 20, 1981, C.A.

s. 1, see *Mondial Trading Co. G.m.b.H.* v. *Gill & Duffus Zucherhandelsgesellschaft m.b.H.* [1980] 2 Lloyd's Rep. 376, Robert Goff J.; *Pioneer Shipping* v. *B.T.P. Tioxide* [1981] 3 W.L.R. 292, H.L.; *International Sea Tankers Inc. of Liberia* v. *Hemisphere Shipping Co. The Wenjiang*, [1982] 2 All E.R. 437, C.A.; *B.V.S. SA* v. *Kerman Shipping Co. SA* [1982] 1 W.L.R. 166, Parker J.; *Italmare Shipping Co.* v. *Ocean Tanker Co. Inc.* [1982] 1 W.L.R. 158, C.A.; *Hayn Roman & Co. SA* v. *Cominter (U.K.)* [1982] 1 Lloyd's Rep. 295, Robert Goff J.; *A. B. Bofors Vva, C.A.V. and George Kuikka* v. *A. B. Skandia Transport; The Felixstowe Dock and Rail Co. and Croxson European Transport* [1982] 1 Lloyd's Rep. 410, Bingham J.; *Oxford Shipping Co.* v. *Nippon Yusen Kaisha; The Eastern Saga* [1982] Com.L.R. 151, Mustill J.; *Schiffahrtsagentur Hamburg Middle East Line GmbH* v. *Virtue Shipping Corp.; The Oinoussian Virtue* [1981] 2 All E.R. 887, Goff J.; *Cobec International* v. *Sidi, The Times*, November 4, 1982, Bingham J. *Clea Shipping Corp.* v. *Bulk Oil International: The Alaskan Trader* [1983] 1 Lloyd's Rep. 315, Bingham J.; *Moran* v. *Lloyd's* [1983] 2 W.L.R. 672, C.A.; *Vinava Shipping Co.* v. *Finelvet AG:*

1979—cont.

42. Arbitration Act 1979—*cont.*
The Chrysalis [1983] 1 Lloyd's Rep. 503, Murtill J.; *Interbulk* v. *Aiden Shipping Co.; Icco International Corn Co. NV* v. *Interbulk* [1983] Com.L.R. 142, Lloyd J.; *Warde* v. *Feedex International Inc., The Times*, November 2, 1983, Staughton J.; *Antaios Compania Naviera SA* v. *Salen Rederierna SA; The Antaios (No. 2)* [1983] 2 Lloyd's Rep. 473, C.A.; *E. R. Dyer* v. *The Simon Build/Peter Lind Partnership* [1982] 23 Build.L.R. 28, Nolan J.; *Bulk Oil (Zug)* v. *Sun International* [1984] 1 W.L.R. 147, C.A.; *Sergama N. V.* v. *Penny Le Roy* (1984) 269 E.G. 322, Staughton J.; *99 Bishopgate* v. *Prudential Assurance Co.* (1984) 270 E.G. 950, Lloyd J.; *Antaios Compania Naviera SA* v. *Salen Redevierna AB* [1984] 3 W.L.R. 592, H.L.; *Pera Shipping Corp.* v. *Petroship S.A.; Pera, The, The Times*, May 7, 1985, Lloyd J.; *National Westminster Bank* v. *Arthur Young McClelland Moores & Co.* [1985] 2 All E.R. 817, C.A.; *Norwich Union Life Insurance Society* v. *Trustee Savings Bank Central Board* (1986) 278 E.G. 162, Hoffmann J.; *Trave Schiffahrtsgesellschaft mbh* v. *Ninemia Maritime Corp.* [1986] 2 W.L.R. 773, C.A.; *Lucas Industries* v. *Welsh Development Agency* [1986] 3 W.L.R. 80, Browne-Wilkinson V.-C.; *Gebr. Van Weelde Sch. b.v.* v. *Société Industrielle D'acide Phosphorique Et Déngrais; Dynashinky, The* [1986] 1 Lloyd's Rep. 435, Hobhouse J.; *Aden Refinery Co.* v. *Ugland Management Co.* [1986] 3 W.L.R. 949, C.A.; *Warrington and Runcorn Development Corp.* v. *Greggs* (1987) 281 E.G. 1075, Warner J.; *Universal Petroleum Co.* v. *Handels und Transport Gesellschaft M.b.H.,* [1987] 1 F.T.L.R. 429, C.A.; *Triumph Securities* v. *Reid Furniture Co.* (1987) 283 E.G. 1071, Harman J.; *Procter & Gamble Philippine Manufacturing Corp.* v. *Peter Cremer GmbH & Co.; Manila, The (No. 2), The Independent*, April 15, 1988, Hirst J; *Kansa General Insurance Co.* v. *Bishopsgate Insurance* [1988] 1 FILR 190, Hirst J.; *Petraco (Bermuda)* v. *Petromed International S.A.* [1988] 1 W.L.R. 896, C.A.

s. 1, amended: 1981, c.54, s.148.

s. 2, see *Chapman* v. *Charlwood Alliance Properties* (1981) 260 E.G. 1041, Hodgson J.; *Babanaft International Co. SA* v. *Avant Petroleum, The Times*, April 23, C.A.; [1982] 1 W.L.R. 871; *Gebr Broer BV* v. *Saras Chimica SpA, The Times*, July 27, 1982, Parker J.

s. 2, amended: 1981, c.54, s.148, sch.5.

s. 3, see *Arab African Energy Corp.* v. *Olie Produkten Nederland BV, The Times*, May 18, 1983, Leggat J.; *Marine Contractors* v. *Shell Petroleum Development Co of Nigeria* [1983] Com.L.R. 251, Staughton J.

s. 4, order 79/754.

s. 7, see *Warde* v. *Feedex International Inc., The Times*, November 2, 1983, Staughton J.

s. 7, amended: 1984, c.28, sch.2.

s. 8, order 79/750.

CAP.

1979—cont.

42. Arbitration Act 1979—cont.
s. 20, amended: 1982, c.39, s.153.
sch. 1, amended: 1982, c.46, sch.3.

43. Crown Agents Act 1979.
Royal Assent, April 4, 1979.
s. 1, order 79/1672.
s. 4, orders 80/689; 81/1160.
s. 8, amended: 1987, c.22, sch.6; repealed in pt.: 1987, c.16, sch.16.
s. 17, order 84/2036.
s. 17, amended and repealed in pt.: 1986, c.43, s.1.
ss. 22, 31, amended: 1985, c.9, sch.2.
s. 31, order 79/1673.

44. Leasehold Reform Act 1979.
Royal Assent, April 4, 1979.

45. Weights and Measures Act 1979.
Royal Assent, April 4, 1979.
repealed: order 81/231; 1985, c.72, sch.13.
s. 1, regs. 79/1613; 80/1064; S.Rs. 1979 No. 435; 1980 No. 403.
ss. 1–3, see *Bakerboy (Hot Bread)* v. *Barnes*, March 23, 1984, D.C., Nolan J.
s. 3, regs. 79/1613; S.R. 1979 No. 435.
s. 5, regs. 79/1613; 80/1064; S.Rs. 1979 No. 435; 1980 No. 403.
s. 10, amended: 1985, c.9, sch.2.
ss. 13–15, regs. 79/1613; 80/1064; S.Rs. 1979 No. 435; 1980 No. 403.
s. 15, regs. 82/144; 84/1317; 85/573.
s. 24, order 79/1228.
sch. 1, regs. 79/1613; S.R. 1979 No. 435.

46. Ancient Monuments and Archaeological Areas Act 1979.
Royal Assent, April 4, 1979.
Commencement orders: 79/786; 81/1300, 1466 (S.146); 82/362.
s. 1, amended: 1983, c.47, sch.4.
s. 1A, added: *ibid.*
s. 2, regs. 81/1467.
ss. 2–6, amended: 1983, c.47, sch.4.
s. 3, orders 81/1302, 1468; 84/222.
s. 6A, added: 1983, c.47, sch.4.
ss. 7–21, amended: 1983, c.47, sch.4.
ss. 10, 16, amended: 1981, c.67, sch.4, repealed in pt.: *ibid.*, sch.6.
ss. 22, 23, repealed in pt.: 1983, c.47, sch.6.
ss. 24, 25, 28–30, 32, amended: *ibid.*, sch.4.
ss. 33, 34, amended: *ibid.*; 1985, c.51, sch.2.
s. 35, regs. 84/1285.
s. 35, amended: 1988, c.4, sch.3.
s. 37, order 84/1286.
ss. 37–39, 41, 45, 46, 49, 53, 54, 57, amended: 1983, c.47, sch.4.
ss. 38, 60, regs. 84/1285.
ss. 47, 61, regs. 81/1469.
s. 52A, added: 1988, c.4, sch.3.
s. 61, amended: 1983, c.47, sch.4; 1987, c.3, sch.1; repealed in pt.: 1984, c.12, sch.4; 1985, c.51, sch.17; 1986, c.31, sch.6; c.44, sch.9.
s. 62, repealed in pt.: 1981, c.19, sch.1.
s. 63, repealed: *ibid.*
s. 65, orders 79/786; 81/1300, 1466; 82/362.

CAP.

1979—cont.

46. Ancient Monuments and Archaeological Areas Act 1979—cont.
sch. 1, regs. 81/1301, 1467.
sch. 2, amended: 1985, c.51, sch.2.
sch. 4, repealed in pt.: 1984, c.51, sch.9; 1988, c.41, sch.13 (prosp.).
sch. 5, amended: 1981, c.67, sch.4.

47. Finance (No. 2) Act 1979.
Royal Assent, July 29.
s. 1, repealed: 1983, c.55, sch.11.
ss. 2–4, repealed: 1980, c.48, sch.20.
ss. 5–12, repealed: 1988, c.1, sch.31.
s. 9, amended: order 88/1843.
s. 13, repealed: 1981, c.35, sch.19; 1988, c.1, sch.13.
ss. 15, 16, 17 (in pt.), repealed: *ibid.*
s. 18, repealed: 1980, c.48, sch.20.
s. 22, repealed: 1985, c.62, sch.4.
s. 23, repealed: 1982, c.39, sch.22.
s. 24, repealed: 1985, c.54, sch.27.
schs. 1, 2, repealed: 1988, c.1, sch.31.
sch. 4, repealed in pt.: 1980, c.48, sch.20; 1985, c.54, sch.27.

48. Pensioners' Payments and Social Security Act 1979.
Royal Assent, July 26, 1979.
repealed: 1986, c.50, sch.11.
order 80/1169.
s. 1, regs. 80/1485, 1486; 82/1315, 1316.
ss. 1–3, amended: orders 81/1158; 82/1106; 83/1200; 84/1082.
s. 2, amended: 1980, c.9, sch.9; c.30, sch.4; 1984, c.48, sch.4.
s. 3, regs. 80/71; S.R. 1980 No. 39.
s. 4, orders 81/1158; 82/1106; 83/1200; 84/1082; 85/1189; 86/1119; 87/1305.

49. Education Act 1979.
Royal Assent, July 26, 1979.
s. 1, repealed in pt.: 1980, c.20, sch.1.

50. European Assembly (Pay and Pensions) Act 1979.
Royal Assent, July 26, 1979.
ss. 3, 3A, substituted: 1984, c.52, s.14.
s. 4, orders 82/1142; 85/1116.
s. 8, amended: 1987, c.45, sch.3; 1988, c.1, sch.29; repealed in pt.: 1986, c.58, sch.

51. Appropriation (No. 2) Act 1979.
Royal Assent, July 27, 1979.
repealed: 1981, c.51, sch.(C.).

52. Southern Rhodesia Act 1979.
Royal Assent, November 14, 1979.
s. 1, orders 79/1600; 80/395.
s. 2, orders 79/1654; 80/243.
s. 3, orders 79/1445, 1571, 1601; 80/565.
s. 3, repealed in pt.: 1979, c.60, sch.3.

53. Charging Orders Act 1979.
Royal Assent, December 6, 1979.
s. 1, see *First National Securities* v. *Hegerty* [1984] 3 W.L.R. 769, C.A.; *Mercantile Credit Co.* v. *Ellis, The Independent,* March 17, 1987, C.A.
s. 1, amended: order 81/1123; 1982, c.53, s.34, sch.3; 1984, c.28, sch.2.
ss. 1, 3, see *Harman* v. *Glencross* [1986] 1 All E.R. 545, C.A.

CAP.

1979—cont.

53. Charging Orders Act 1979—cont.

s. 2, see *National Westminster Bank* v. *Stockton* [1981] 1 W.L.R. 67, Russell J.

ss. 2, 3, 6, 17, see *Perry* v. *Phoenix Assurance, The Times*, March 26, 1988, Browne-Wilkinson V.-C.

s. 3, see *Ancocharm* v. *Greville and Greville*, March 1, 1982, Kingham J., Luton County Ct.

s. 4, repealed: 1985, c.65, s.10.

s. 5, amended: 1981, c.54, sch.5; 1984, c.28, sch.2.

s. 6, amended: 1986, c.53, sch.18.

s. 7, repealed in pt.: 1981, c.54, sch.7; 1984, c.28, sch.4.

s. 8, order 80/627.

54. Sale of Goods Act 1979.

Royal Assent, December 6, 1979.

Commencement order: 83/1572.

s. 2, see *National Employers Mutual General Insurance Association* v. *Jones* [1987] 3 All E.R. 385, C.A.

s. 11, see *Bernstein* v. *Pamson Motors (Golders Green)* [1987] 2 All E.R. 220, Rougier J.

ss. 13, 14, see *Border Harvesters* v. *Edwards Engineering (Perth)* (O.H.), 1985 S.L.T. 128.

s. 14, see *Buchanan-Jardine* v. *Hamilink* First Division, March 26, 1982; *Keeley* v. *Guy McDonald* (1984) 134 New L.J. 522, Mustill J.; *Lancashire Textiles (Jersey)* v. *Thompson Shepherd & Co.* (O.H.) November 20, 1984; *M/S Aswan Engineering Establishment Co.* v. *Lupdine* [1987] 1 W.L.R. 1, C.A.; *Rogers* v. *Parish (Scarborough)* [1987] 2 W.L.R. 353, C.A.; *N.V. Devos Gebroeder* v. *Sunderland Sportswear* (O.H.), 1987 S.L.T. 331; *Bernstein* v. *Pamson Motors (Golders Green)* [1987] 2 All E.R. 220, Rougier J.; *Shine* v. *General Guarantee Corporation, The Times*, August 18, 1987, C.A.; *Wormell* v. *R.H.M. Agriculture (East)* [1987] 1 W.L.R. 1091, C.A.; *Lutton* v. *Saville Tractors (Belfast)* [1986] 12 N.I.J.B. 1, Carswell J.; *R. & B. Customs Brokers Co.* v. *United Dominions Trust: Saunders Abbot (1980) (Third Party)* [1988] 1 W.L.R. 321, C.A.; *Business Application Specialists* v. *Nationwide Credit Corp., The Times*, April 27, 1988, C.A.; *Shine* v. *General Guarantee Corp. (Reeds Motor Co. (A Firm), Third Party)* [1988] 1 All E.R. 911, C.A.

s. 14, order 83/1572.

ss. 17–19, see *Mitsui & Co.* v. *Flota Mercante Grancolumbiana S.A., The Times*, April 27, 1988, C.A.

s. 21, see *Shaw* v. *Commissioner of Police for the Metropolis* [1987] 1 W.L.R. 1332, C.A.

ss. 24, 25, see *National Employer's Mutual General Insurance Association* v. *Jones* [1988] 2 W.L.R. 952, H.L.

ss. 25, see *Ladbroke Leasing (South West)* v. *Reekie Plant* (O.H.), May 5, 1982; *Archivent Sales & Development* v. *Strathclyde Regional Council*, 1985 S.L.T. 154; [1984] Build.L.R. 98, Court of Session (Outer House) Lord Mayfield; *Martin* v. *Duffy* [1985] 11 N.I.J.B. 80,

CAP.

1979—cont.

54. Sale of Goods Act 1979—cont.

Lord Lowry L.C.J.; *Harrison (W.) (Harrow)* v. *Rapid Civil Engineering and Usborne Developments* (1987) 38 Build.L.R. 106, His Honour Judge Davies Q.C.

s. 25, order 83/1572.

s. 32, see *D. L. Electrical Supplies (Mitcham)* v. *G. L. Group*, 1987 S.L.T. (Sh.Ct.) 36.

s. 35, see *Bernstein* v. *Pamson Motors (Golders Green)* [1987] 2 All E.R. 220, Rougier J.

s. 40, repealed (S.): 1987, c.18, sch.8.

ss. 46, 48, see *Re U.S., The Times*, October 10, 1983, Nourse J.

s. 50, see *Gebruder Metelmann GmbH & Co. KG* v. *N.B.R. (London)* (1983) 133 New L.J. 642, Mustill J.

s. 51, see *Allen* v. *W. (Burns) (Tractors)* (O.H.), 1985 S.L.T. 252.

s. 53, see *Procter & Gamble Philippine Manufacturing Corp.* v. *Kurt A. Becher GmbH* [1988] FTLR 450, C.A.

s. 55, see *George Mitchell (Chesterhall)* v. *Finney Lock Seeds* [1983] 3 W.L.R. 163, H.L.; *Landcatch* v. *Marine Harvest* (O.H.) December 3, 1983.

s. 61, see *National Employers Mutual General Insurance Association* v. *Jones* [1987] 3 All E.R. 385, C.A.

s. 61, repealed in pt.: 1985, c.65, sch.10; c.66, sch.8 (S.).

ss. 61, 62, see *Ladbroke Leasing (South West)* v. *Reekie Plant* (O.H.), May 5, 1982.

s. 62, see *Armour* v. *Thyssen Edelstahlwerke, The Scotsman*, August 5, 1988.

sch. 2, repealed in pt.: 1981, c.19, sch.1.

55. Justices of the Peace Act 1979.

Royal Assent, December 6, 1979.

s. 2, repealed in pt.: 1985, c.51, sch.17.

s. 4, amended: *ibid.*, s.12.

s. 6, amended: 1982, c.53, s.65.

s. 12, amended: 1985, c.51, s.12.

s. 18, rules 86/923.

ss. 16, 18, amended: 1980, c.43, sch.7.

s. 18, rules 87/1137.

s. 19, amended: 1985, c.51, s.12.

s. 21, regs. 80/1258.

s. 22, amended: 1985, c.51, s.12.

s. 23, orders 81/389, 1299; 82/1720; 83/828, 1628, 1837; 84/391, 568, 1528; 85/1078, 1117, 1633, 1673, 1796, 1863, 1961; 86/231, 765, 1057, 2113, 2114, 2192; 87/154, 519, 1201, 1688, 1739, 1786, 1796, 1797, 1912, 1913, 1925, 1962; 88/575, 1665, 1717.

s. 23, amended: 1985, c.51, s.12.

ss. 23, 24, orders 80/381, 940, 1804, 1818; 82/469.

s. 24, orders 82/1720; 83/828, 1628; 84/391, 568, 1528; 85/1078, 1117; regs. 88/1698.

s. 24, amended: 1985, c.51, s.12; repealed in pt.: *ibid.*, sch.17.

ss. 24A, 24B, added: 1988, c.33, s.164.

s. 24B, regs. 88/1698.

ss. 27–30, amended: 1980, c.43, sch.7.

s. 33, amended: 1983, c.21, sch.3; repealed in pt.: 1987, c.21, sch.3.

CAP.   CAP.

1979—cont.

55. Justices of the Peace Act 1979—*cont.*
s. 36A, added: 1988, c.33, s.164.
s. 37, amended: *ibid.*
s. 41, amended (prosp.): 1988, c.41, sch.12.
s. 44, see *R.* v. *Cardiff JJ., ex p. Salter* (1986) 1 F.L.R. 162, Wood J.
s. 52, see *R.* v. *Waltham Forest JJ., ex p. Solanke* [1986] 3 W.L.R. 315, C.A.; *R.* v. *Manchester City Magistrates' Court, ex p. Davies (No. 2)* [1988] 1 All E.R. 930, Simon Brown J.
s. 57, amended: 1985, c.51, s.2; order 85/1383; repealed in pt.: 1985, c.51, sch.17.
s. 58, amended: *ibid.*, s.60.
s. 59, amended: *ibid.*, s.12.
s. 60, repealed: *ibid.*, sch.17.
s. 61, amended: 1980, c.43, sch.7; 1988, c.33, sch.15.
s. 64, amended: 1985, c.51, sch.14; order 85/1884; 1988, c.4, sch.6; c.50, sch.17; repealed in pt.: 1985, c.51, sch.17; 1988, c.40, sch.13 (prosp.).
sch. 2, repealed in pt.: 1980, c.43, sch.9; 1982, c.49, sch.6; 1985, c.51, sch.17; 1988, c.34, sch.6.

56. Consolidated Fund (No. 2) Act 1979.
Royal Assent, December 20, 1979.
repealed: 1981, c.51, sch.(C.).

57. European Communities (Greek Accession) Act 1979.
Royal Assent, December 20, 1979.

58. Isle of Man Act 1979.
Royal Assent, December 20, 1979.
ss. 1, 6, amended: 1983, c.55, sch.9.
s. 5, amended: 1980, c.43, sch.7.
s. 6, orders 80/183, 866; 82/1067, 1068.
s. 7, orders 80/182; 83/140.
s. 7, amended: 1983, c.53, s.10.
s. 8, amended: 1984, c.43, s.15.
s. 9, regs. 88/1760.
s. 9, amended: 1981, c.45, s.21; 1984, c.43, s.15.
s. 11, order 80/399.
sch. 1, repealed in pt.: 1981, c.35, sch.19; 1983, c.55, sch.11; 1984, c.43, sch.23.

59. Shipbuilding Act 1979.
Royal Assent, December 20, 1979.
s. 1, repealed: 1982, c.4, s.1.

60. Zimbabwe Act 1979.
Royal Assent, December 20, 1979.
s. 1, order 80/394.
s. 2, repealed: 1981, c.61, sch.9.
ss. 4, 5, order 80/701.
s. 5, repealed in pt.: 1981, c.61, sch.9.
sch. 1, repealed: *ibid.*
schs. 1, 2, repealed in pt.: order 80/701.

1980

1. Petroleum Revenue Tax Act 1980.
Royal Assent, January 31, 1980.
s. 1, amended: 1982, c.39, sch.19.
sch., amended: 1983, c.28, sch.8; c.56, s.10; 1987, c.16, sch.13; repealed in pt.: 1981, c.35, sch.19.

1980—cont.

2. Papua New Guinea, Western Samoa and Nauru (Miscellaneous Provisions) Act 1980.
Royal Assent, January 31, 1980.
ss. 1, 3, repealed in pt.: 1981, c.61, sch.9.
s. 2, repealed: *ibid.*

3. Representation of the People Act 1980.
Royal Assent, January 31, 1980.
repealed: 1983, c.2, sch.9.
s. 2, see *Lockhart* v. *Stokes,* 1981 S.L.T.(Sh.Ct.) 71.
s. 3, see *Aitchinson* v. *Tudhope,* High Court of Justiciary, January 29, 1981; *H.M. Advocate* v. *Brown,* 1983 S.L.T. 136.
s. 3, order 80/1030.

4. Bail etc. (Scotland) Act 1980.
Royal Assent, January 31, 1980.
s. 1, see *Smith* v. *M.,* 1982 S.L.T. 421; *McNeill* v. *Milne,* 1984 S.C.C.R. 427.
s. 2, see *Welsh* v. *H.M. Advocate,* 1986 S.L.T. 664.
ss. 2, 3, see *H.M. Advocate* v. *Crawford,* 1985 S.L.T. 242.
s. 3, see *Rowley* v. *H.M. Advocate,* 1983 S.C.C.R. 413; *MacNeill* v. *Smith,* 1984 S.L.T.(Sh.Ct.) 63; *Baird* v. *Lockhart,* 1986 S.C.C.R. 514; *Allan* v. *Lockhart,* 1986 S.C.C.R. 395; *H.M. Advocate* v. *Kerr,* 1987 S.C.C.R. 283; *Montgomery* v. *H.M. Advocate,* 1987 S.C.C.R. 264.
s. 10, amended: 1985, c.73, s.21.
s. 13, order 80/315.

5. Child Care Act 1980.
Royal Assent, January 31, 1980.
see *R.* v. *Tower Hamlets London Borough Council, ex p. Monaf, Ali and Miah, The Times,* April 28, 1988, C.A.
s. 2, see *W.* v. *Hertfordshire C.C.* [1985] 2 All E.R. 301, H.L.; *G.* v. *Hounslow London Borough Council* (1988) 86 L.G.R. 186, Crawford Q.C.
ss. 2, 3, see *W.* v. *Nottinghamshire County Council* (1986) 12 Fam.Law 185, C.A.
s. 3, see *Crosby (A Minor)* v. *Northumberland County Council* (1982) 12 Fam.Law 92, D.C.; *Re T. (A Minor)* (1982) 12 Fam.Law 218, Hollings J.; *R.* v. *Sunderland Juvenile Court, ex p. G. (A Minor), The Times,* December 5, 1987, C.A.; *P. (A Minor) (Child Abuse: Evidence), Re* [1987] 2 F.L.R. 467, C.A.; *Staffordshire County Council* v. *C. and M.* (1988) 152 J.P.N. 238, Latey J.; *M.* v. *H.* [1988] 3 All E.R. 5, H.L.
s. 3, amended: 1983, c.20, sch.4; c.41, sch.2.
s. 5, amended and repealed in pt.: 1985, c.60, s.25.
s. 8, amended: 1987, c.42, s.8.
s. 10, see *R.* v. *Befordshire County Council, ex p. C.; R.* v. *Hertfordshire County Council, ex p. B.* (1987) 85 L.G.R. 218, Ewbank J.
s. 10, amended: 1982, c.48, sch.14; 1983, c.41, sch.2; repealed in pt.: *ibid.*, sch.10.
s. 12, see *Hereford and Worcester County Council* v. *E.H.* (1985) 15 Fam.Law 229, Wood J.

CAP.

5. Child Care Act 1980—*cont.*

s. 12A, see *W.* v. *Nottinghamshire County Council* (1986) 12 Fam.Law 185, C.A.

ss. 12A–12G, see *M.* v. *Berkshire C.C.* (1985) 15 Fam.Law 161, C.A.; *T.D. (A Minor) (Wardship: Jurisdiction), Re,* (1986) 16 Fam.Law 18, Sheldon J.

s. 12A–12G, added: 1983, c.41, sch.1.

ss. 12A, 12C, see *R.* v. *Corby Juvenile Court, ex p. M* [1987] 1 W.L.R. 55, Waite J.

s. 12B, see *R.* v. *Bolton Metropolitan Borough Council, ex p. B.* (1985) 15 Fam.Law 193, Wood J.

s. 12B, order 83/1860.

ss. 12B–12D, see *Devon County Council* v. *C.* (1986) 16 Fam.Law 20, C.A.

s. 12C, see *R.* v. *Slough Justices, ex p. B.* (1985) 15 Fam.Law 189, Wood J.; *Y.* v. *Kirklees Borough Council, The Times,* February 23, 1985, Waterhouse J.; *Southwark London Borough Council* v. *H.* [1985] 1 W.L.R. 861, D.C.; *Devon County Council* v. *C., The Times,* May 18, 1985, C.A.; *Hereford and Worcester County Council* v. *Jah* (1985) 15 Fam.Law 324, C.A.; *A.* v. *Wigan Metropolitan Borough Council* (1986) 16 Fam.Law 162, Ewbank J.; *P. (Minors: Access), Re; P.* v. *P. (Gateshead Metropolitan Borough Council Intervening), The Times,* February 19, 1988, C.A.

s. 13, amended: 1983, c.41, sch.2; 1987, c.42, s.8.

s. 18, see *Liddle* v. *Sunderland Borough Council* (1983) 13 Fam.Law 250, Latey J.; *M.* v. *Lambeth London Borough Council, The Times,* March 27, 1984, Balcombe J.; *R.* v. *Slough Juvenile Court, ex p. Royal Berkshire County Council* [1984] 2 W.L.R. 45, D.C.; *F. M. (A Minor), Re* (1984) 14 Fam.Law 146, Balcombe J.; *R.* v. *Solihull Metropolitan Borough Council, ex p. C.* (1984) 14 Fam.Law 175, D.C.; McCullough J.; *M.* v. *Lambeth London Borough Council (No. 2), The Times,* December 20, 1984, Sheldon J.; *R.* v. *Avon County Council, ex p. K.* [1986] 1 F.L.R. 433, Heilbron J.

ss. 18, 21, see *G.* v. *Hounslow London Borough Council* (1986) 86 L.G.R. 186, Crawford Q.C.

s. 21, see *R.* v. *F. (A Child), The Times,* March 20, 1985, C.A.; *R.* v. *F. (A Child), The Times,* April 20, 1985, C.A.; *S.* v. *Walsall Metropolitan Borough Council* [1985] 3 All E.R. 294, C.A.; *Kininmonth* v. *Chief Adjudication Officer, The Times,* October 17, 1986, C.A.

s. 21, amended: 1982, c.20, s.15; c.48, sch.14; 1983, c.41, sch.2.

s. 21A, see *L. (A Minor), Re, The Times,* July 25, 1984, Hollings J.; *M.* v. *Lambeth Borough Council and Liverpool City Council* (1984) 14 Fam.Law 211, Balcombe J.; *K. (A Minor), Re, The Times,* December 20, 1984, Heilbron J.; *L. (A Minor), Re, The Times,* November 2, 1984, Hollings J.; *M.* v. *Lambeth Borough Council* (1985) 83 L.G.R. 185, Balcombe J.; *R.* v. *Northampton Juvenile Court, ex p. Ham-*

CAP.

5. Child Care Act 1980—*cont.*

mersmith and Fulham London Borough (1985) 15 Fam.Law 124, Ewbank J.; *M. (A Minor), Re, The Times,* January 24, 1986, C.A.; *M.* v. *Lambeth Borough Council (No. 3)* (1986) 2 F.L.R. 136, C.A.; *Liverpool City Council* v. *H.K.* (1985) 83 L.G.R. 421, Heilbron J.

s. 21A, regs. 83/652, 1808; 86/1591.

s. 21A, added: 1982, c.48, s.25.

s. 21A, substituted: 1983, c.41, sch.2; 1988, c.34, sch.5.

Pt. IA (ss. 21A–21G) see *Devon County Council* v. *C., The Times,* February 21, 1985, Sheldon J.; *M. (A Minor), Re* [1985] 1 All E.R. 745, C.A.; *P. (Minors: Access), Re* (1988) 18 Fam.Law 333, C.A.

s. 22, regs. 82/447.

s. 22A, added: 1986, c.28, s.1.

s. 24, amended: 1983, c.41, sch 2; 1987, c.42, s.8.

s. 25, repealed in pt.: 1986, c.50, sch.11.

s. 30, amended: order 88/1843.

ss. 31–34, substituted: 1983, c.41, s.4.

s. 35, amended: *ibid.,* sch.2.

s. 36, repealed in pt.: *ibid.,* sch.10.

s. 39, regs. 83/652, 1808; 86/1591.

s. 39, amended: 1982, c.48, sch.14; 1988, c.40, sch.1; repealed in pt.: 1983, c.41, sch.10.

s. 40, see *R.* v. *Secretary of State for Social Services, ex p. The Official Custodian of Charities, The Times,* February 28, 1984, D.C.

s. 42, amended: 1988, c.40, sch.1.

s. 43, orders 81/633, 762, 763, 1224, 1225; 82/567, 784, 785, 994, 1265, 1343; 83/51.

s. 43, repealed in pt.: 1983, c.41, sch.10.

s. 43A, added: *ibid.,* s.5.

s. 44, amended: *ibid.,* sch.2; repealed in pt.: *ibid.,* sch.10.

s. 45, amended: *ibid.,* s.19, sch.2; 1986, c.50, sch.10; repealed in pt.: 1983, c.41, s.9, sch.10.

s. 46, see *R.* v. *Essex County Council, ex p. Washington, The Times,* July 12, 1986, C.A.; *R.* v. *Essex County Council, ex p. Washington* (1987) 85 L.G.R. 210, McCowan J.

s. 46, substituted: 1983, c.41, s.19.

s. 47, amended: 1987, c.42, sch.2.

s. 48, amended: 1980, c.43, sch.7.

ss. 49, 50, repealed: 1987, c.42, schs.2,4.

ss. 52, 54, 55, repealed in pt.: *ibid.,* sch.2.

s. 56, amended: 1983, c.41, sch.4; 1984, c.23, sch.1.

s. 57, amended: 1983, c.41, sch.4.

ss. 57A–57D, added: *ibid.,* sch.4.

s. 58, repealed *ibid.,* sch.10.

s. 60, amended: 1983, c.41, sch.4.

s. 61, regs. 82/447.

s. 62, regs. 82/13.

s. 64, amended: 1983, c.41, sch.1; 1987, c.42, s.8.

s. 64A, added: 1983, c.41, sch.1.

s. 71, repealed: *ibid.,* s.27, s.10.

s. 73, amended: 1984, c.60, sch.6; 1988, c.33, sch.15.

s. 76, amended: 1983, c.41, sch.4.

1980—cont.

5. Child Care Act 1980—*cont.*
s. 79, amended: 1983, c.20, sch.4; c.41, sch.2; 1984, c.36, sch.3; repealed in pt.: 1983, c.41, sch.10.
s. 82, amended: *ibid.,* sch.2.
s. 85, regs. 86/1591.
s. 85, amended: 1983, c.41, sch.2; 1986, c.28, s.1.
s. 86, amended: 1987, c.42, sch.2.
s. 87, see *T.D. (A Minor) (Wardship: Jurisdiction), Re,* (1986) 16 Fam.Law 18, Sheldon J.
s. 87, amended: 1983, c.41, sch.4; 1987, c.42, sch.2; repealed in pt.: 1983, c.41, sch.10.
s. 90, order 80/1935.
sch. 1, repealed: 1983, c.41, sch.10.
sch. 2, repealed in pt.: 1987, c.42, sch.4.
sch. 3, repealed: 1983, c.41, sch.10.
sch. 4, amended: *ibid.,* sch.2.
sch. 5, repealed in pt.: 1980, c.43, sch.9; 1982, c.32, s.15; 1983, c.41, schs.6,10; 1984, c.36, sch.5; c.56, sch.2 (S.); 1988, c.34, sch.6.

6. Foster Children Act 1980.
Royal Assent, January 31, 1980.
s. 2, amended: 1982, c.51, sch.3; 1983, c.20, schs.4, 9; 1984, c.23, sch.1.
s. 7, amended: 1984, c.56, sch.2.
s. 16, amended: 1980, c.43, sch.7.
sch. 2, repealed in pt. (S.): 1984, c.56, sch.3.

7. Residential Homes Act 1980.
Royal Assent, March 20, 1980.
repealed: 1983, c.41, sch.10.
s. 4, amended: 1980, c.43, sch.7.
s. 12, order 80/947.

8. Gaming (Amusement) Act 1980.
Royal Assent, March 20, 1980.

9. Reserve Forces Act 1980.
Royal Assent, March 20, 1980.
s. 5, amended: 1982, c.14, s.1.
s. 6, repealed in pt.: 1986, c.21, sch.2.
s. 98, amended and repealed in pt.: 1982, c.14, s.1.
s. 117, repealed in pt.: 1986, c.21, sch.2.
s. 122, order 83/1966.
s. 143, amended: 1981, c.55, s.12.
s. 144, amended: 1980, c.43, sch.7.
s. 145, amended: 1985, c.17, sch.4.
s. 150, amended: 1982, c.14, s.2.
s. 153, repealed: *ibid.*
s. 156, amended: 1980, c.43, s.20; 1982, c.14, s.2; repealed in pt.: *ibid.,* s.1, sch.6.
s. 158, order 86/2026.
sch. 1, repealed in pt.: 1988, c.33, sch.16.
sch. 2, amended: 1984, c.36, sch.3.
sch. 5, amended: 1980, c.43, sch.7.
sch. 7, amended and repealed in pt.: 1984, c.36, sch.3.
sch. 8, amended: 1983, c.20, schs.4,9; repealed in pt.: 1980, c.43, sch.5; 1982, c.14, s.1.
sch. 9, repealed in pt.: 1980, c.30, sch.5; 1985, c.71, sch.3.

10. Police Negotiating Board Act 1980.
Royal Assent, March 20, 1980.
s. 2, regs. 81/477, 1371; 82/271, 350, 1486, 1487; 83/1348, 1934; 84/1590, 1633, 1808; 85/130, 686, 885, 1045.

1980—cont.

11. Protection of Trading Interests Act 1980.
Royal Assent, March 20, 1980.
s. 1, see *British Airways Board* v. *Laker Airways* [1984] 3 W.L.R. 413, H.L.
s. 1, orders 82/885; 83/900.
s. 3, amended: 1980, c.43, sch.7.
s. 7, amended: 1982, c.27, s.38.
s. 8, orders 83/607, 1700, 1703, 1704.
s. 8, repealed in pt.: 1980, c.43, sch.9.

12. Bees Act 1980.
Royal Assent, March 20, 1980.
s. 1, orders 80/792; 82/107; 87/867.
s. 4, order 82/107.
s. 5, order 80/791.

13. Slaughter of Animals (Scotland) Act 1980.
Royal Assent, March 20, 1980.
s. 8, repealed in pt.: 1981, c.23, sch.2.
ss. 9, 18, regs. 83/874; 84/1205.
ss. 13, 15, 16, amended: 1981, c.22, sch.5.

14. Consolidated Fund Act 1980.
Royal Assent, March 20, 1980.
repealed: 1982, c.40, sch.(C.)

15. National Health Service (Invalid Direction) Act 1980.
Royal Assent, March 20, 1980.
repealed: S.L.R. 1986.

16. New Hebrides Act 1980.
Royal Assent, March 20, 1980.
s 1, order 80/1079.
s. 1, repealed: 1981, c.61, sch.9.
s. 3, repealed: S.L.R. 1986.
s. 4, repealed in pt.: 1981, c.61, sch.9.
sch. 1, repealed in pt.: 1981, c.9, sch.

17. National Heritage Act 1980.
Royal Assent, March 31, 1980.
functions transferred: orders 81/207; 86/600.
ss. 2, 4, 5, 7, 9, 10, 12, 14, 16, amended: orders 81/207; 83/879.
ss. 2, 12, 18, repealed in pt.: order 81/207.
s. 8, amended: 1984, c.51, sch.8.
s. 8, sch.1, order 83/879.
ss. 12, 13, amended: 1984, c.51, sch.8; repealed in pt.: *ibid.,* sch.9.
s. 14, amended: *ibid.,* sch.8.

18. Betting, Gaming and Lotteries (Amendment) Act 1980.
Royal Assent, March 31, 1980.
repealed: 1985, c.18, sch.

19. Highlands and Islands Air Services (Scotland) Act 1980.
Royal Assent, April 3, 1980.

20. Education Act 1980.
Royal Assent, April 3, 1980.
see *R.* v. *Inner London Education Authority, ex p. Palomar, The Times,* September 24, 1982, McNeill J.
ss. 2–4, repealed: 1986, c.61, sch.6.
s. 4, regs. 81/809, 1180.
s. 5, see *R.* v. *Hampshire County Council, ex p. Martin, The Times,* November 20, 1982, McNeill J.
s. 6, amended: 1988, c.40, s.30.
s. 7, see *R.* v. *Surrey County Council Education Committee, ex p. H.* (1985) 83 L.G.R. 219, C.A.

1980—cont.

20. Education Act 1980—*cont.*
s. 8, regs. 81/630; 83/41; 88/1023.
s. 8, amended: 1988, c.40, sch.31.
s. 9, amended: 1981, c.60, sch.3; 1988, c.40, s.31; repealed in pt.: *ibid.*, s.31, sch.13.
s. 10, amended: 1981, c.60, sch.3; repealed in pt.: *ibid.*, sch.4.
s. 11, amended: *ibid.*, sch.3.
s. 12, see *R.* v. *Secretary of State for Education and Science, ex p. Birmingham District Council* (1985) 83 L.G.R. 79, McCullough J.; *R.* v. *Gwent Borough Council, ex p. Bryant, The Times,* April 18, 1988, Hodgson J.; *R.* v. *Secretary of State for Education and Science, ex p. Hardy, The Times,* July 28, 1988, D.C.
s. 12, amended: 1988, c.40, s.31; repealed in pt.: *ibid.*, s.31, sch.13.
ss. 12, 13, regs. 80/490, 658.
s. 13, amended: 1988, c.40, s.31.
s. 14, repealed in pt.: 1984, c.55, sch.7.
s. 15, regs. 80/490, 658; order 81/1133.
s. 15, repealed: 1988, c.40, s.31, sch.13.
s. 16, amended: *ibid.*, s.31.
s. 17, see *Marina Shipping* v. *Laughton* [1982] 1 All E.R. 481, C.A.
s. 17, regs. 80/1743; 81/1861; 83/189; 84/147; 85/685; 86/991; 87/1312; 88/1210.
s. 18, regs. 81/174, 1868; 83/205; 84/148; 85/830; 86/990; 87/1313; 88/1211.
ss. 20, 23, 25, repealed (S.): 1980, c.44, sch.5.
s. 21, regs. 80/1011.
s. 22, amended: 1986, c.50, s.77; 1988, c.40, sch.12.
s. 27, regs. 81/1086; 82/106; 83/262; 86/542; 87/879; 88/542.
s. 27, amended: 1988, c.40, sch.12; repealed: *ibid.*, sch.13.
s. 31, regs. 80/917; repealed in pt. (S.): 1980, c.44, sch.5.
ss. 31, 32, repealed: 1986, c.61, sch 6.
s. 33, repealed in pt. (S.): 1980, c.44, sch.5; 1981, c.60, sch.4.
s. 35, regs. 80/917, 1011, 1743, 1862; 81/174, 630, 809, 1086, 1180, 1861, 1868; 82/106; 83/41, 189, 205, 260, 262; 84/147, 148; 85/685, 830; 86/542, 990, 991; 87/879, 1312, 1313; 88/542, 1210, 1211.
s. 35, repealed in pt.: 1980; c.44, sch.5 (S.); 1986, c.61, sch.6; 1988, c.40, sch.13.
s. 37, orders 80/489, 959; 81/1064; repealed (S.): 1980, c.44, sch.5.
s. 38, regs. 80/917, 1862; 83/260; amended: 1988, c.40, sch.13; repealed (S.): 1980, c.44, sch.5.
sch. 1, repealed in pt.: 1988, c.40, sch.13.
sch. 3, repealed in pt.: *ibid.*; (prosp.) *ibid.*
sch. 5, see *R.* v. *Leeds City Council, ex. p. Datta, The Times,* November 25, 1982, C.A.; *R.* v. *Barnet London Borough Council, ex p. Nilish Shah* [1983] 2 W.L.R. 16, H.L.; *R.* v. *Hereford and Worcester County Council, ex p. Wimbourne* (1984) 82 L.G.R. 251, D.C.
sch. 6, repealed: 1986, c.61, sch.6.

1980—cont.

21. Competition Act 1980.
Royal Assent, April 3, 1980.
s. 2, orders 80/979; 84/1919.
s. 2, amended: 1988, c.54, sch.3.
ss. 3, 4, regs. 80/980.
s. 11, orders 80/981; 82/1080.
s. 11, amended: 1984, c.32, sch.6; 1985, c.9, sch.2; c.67, s.114.
s. 12, amended: 1985, c.9, sch.2.
s. 14, repealed: 1988, c.48, sch.8.
ss. 15, 19, order 82/1080.
s. 19, amended: 1980, c.43, sch.7; 1984, c.12, sch.4; 1986, c.31, sch.4; c.44, sch.7, c.60, sch.13; 1987, c.43, sch.4; repealed in pt.: 1984, c.12, sch.7.
s. 24, order 82/1889.
s. 26, see *Association of British Travel Agents Agreement (No. 2), Re* [1985] I.C.R. 122, Restrictive Practices Court.
s. 33, orders 80/497, 978.

22. Companies Act 1980.
Royal Assent, May 1, 1980.
Commencement order: 83/1002.
repealed: 1985, c.9, sch.1.
s. 3, see *Baby Moon (U.K.), Re, The Times,* November 12, 1984, Harman J.
ss. 3–5, 8, 10–13, 33, 37, 41, regs. 80/1826.
s. 11, regs. 82/104, 674.
s. 12, see *Minster Assets. Re, The Times,* November 12, 1984, Harman J.
s. 13, regs. 83/1021.
ss. 29–43, see *Precision Dippings* v. *Precision Dippings Marketing* [1985] 3 W.L.R. 812, C.A.
s. 48, see *Joint Receivers and Managers of Niltan Carson* v. *Hawthorne* (1987) 3 B.C.C. 454, Hodgson J.
s. 75, see *Gammack, Petr.* (O.H.), July 7, 1982; 1983 S.L.T. 246; *Re A Company (No. 004475 of 1982)* [1983] 2 W.L.R. 381, Lord Grantchester Q.C.; *Re Carrington Viyella Plc, Financial Times,* February 16, 1983, Vinelott J.; *Re A Company (No. 002567 of 1982)* [1983] 2 All E.R. 854, Vinelott J.; *Re A Company (No. 003420 of 1981), The Times,* November 4, 1983, Nourse J.; *Re A Company (No. 003420 of 1981), The Times,* November 30, 1983, Nourse J.; *Re O. C. Transport Services* (1984) 81 L.S.Gaz. 1044, Mervyn Davies J.; *Re Garage Door Associates* [1984] 1 W.L.R. 35, Mervyn Davies J.; *A Company (No. 001424 of 1983), Re, The Times,* June 21, 1984, Vinelott J.; *Whyte, Petr.,* 1984 S.L.T. 330.; *London School of Electronics, Re* [1985] 3 All E.R. 474, Nourse J.; *Bird Precision Bellows, Re* [1985] 3 All E.R. 523, C.A.
s. 87, regs. 80/1055; 82/674; 83/1021.
s. 88, regs. 80/1826.
s. 90, orders 80/745, 1785; 81/1683; 83/1022.

23. Consular Fees Act 1980.
Royal Assent, May 1, 1980.
s. 1, orders 81/419, 476; 83/1518; 84/1155, 1819, 1979; 85/1984; 86/1881; 87/1264; 88/925.

1980—cont.

24. Limitation Amendment Act 1980.
Royal Assent, May 1, 1980.
ss. 1–9, 11–13, schs. 1, 2, repealed: 1980, c.58, sch.4.

25. Insurance Companies Act 1980.
Royal Assent, May 1, 1980.
s. 3, schs. 1, 2, repealed in pt.: 1981, c.31, sch.5.
s. 5, order 80/678.
sch. 3, repealed in pt.: 1981, c.31, sch.5; orders 81/154, 226; 82/1534.
sch. 3, repealed (N.I.): 1986, c.53, sch.19.

26. British Aerospace Act 1980.
Royal Assent, May 1, 1980.
s. 1, order 80/1989.
s. 3, amended: 1985, c.9, sch.2; repealed in pt.: 1988, c.39, sch.14.
s. 4, amended: 1985, c.9, sch.2.
s. 7, orders 81/622; 86/848.
s. 9, amended: 1985, c.9, sch.2; 1986, c.45, sch.14.
s. 10, order 81/1793.
s. 14, order 80/1988.
sch. 1, amended: 1982, c.52, sch.2.

27. Import of Live Fish (England and Wales) Act 1980.
Royal Assent, May 15, 1980.
s. 1, amended: 1981, c.29, s.37.
s. 2, repealed in pt.: *ibid.*, s.37, sch.5.
s. 3, amended: *ibid.*, s.37.

28. Iran (Temporary Powers) Act 1980.
Royal Assent, May 15, 1980.
s. 1, order 80/737.
s. 2, order 81/161.

29. Concessionary Travel for Handicapped Persons (Scotland) Act 1980.
Royal Assent, May 23, 1980.
s. 1, amended: 1985, c.67, sch.7; repealed in pt.: *ibid.*, schs.7,8.
s. 2, amended: 1984, c.36, sch.3; 1985, c.67, sch.7; repealed in pt.: *ibid.* schs.7,8.

30. Social Security Act 1980.
Royal Assent, May 28, 1980.
Commencement orders: 83/1002; 84/1492.
s. 1, repealed: 1986, c.50, sch.11.
s. 2, amended: 1980, c.39, s.6.
s. 3, repealed in pt.: 1984, c.48, sch.8; 1985, c.53, sch.6.
s. 4, repealed in pt.: 1986, c.50, sch.11.
s. 5, order 81/1156.
s. 5, repealed in pt.: 1986, c.50, s.38, sch.11.
s. 7, repealed: *ibid.*, sch.11.
s. 8, regs. 80/984, 1023, 1641, 1649; 82/907; 83/1004; 84/458.
s. 8, repealed in pt.: 1986, c.50, sch.11.
s. 9, regs. 80/1874.
s. 9, amended: 1982, c.24, sch.4; order 82/1084; 1984, c.48, sch.7; 1985, c.53, sch.5; 1986, c.50, sch.10; repealed in pt.: *ibid.*, sch.11.
s. 10, regs. 81/73; 82/1408; 83/1015, 1137.
s. 10, amended: 1986, c.50, sch.10; repealed in pt.: *ibid.*, sch.11.
s. 11, regs. 80/1561.
s. 11, repealed in pt.: regs. 80/1874.

1980—cont.

30. Social Security Act 1980—*cont.*
s. 13, amended: 1981, c.20, sch.3.
s. 14, see *Bland* v. *Chief Supplemenatary Benefit Appeal Tribunal* [1983] 1 All E.R. 537, C.A.; *White* v. *Chief Adjudication Officer*, [1986] 3 All E.R. 905, C.A.
s. 14, regs. 80/1321; 84/451; 87/214; order 84/1818; S.Rs. 1980 No. 329; 1984 No. 144; 1987 No. 112.
s. 14, amended: 1986, c.50, sch.9; repealed in pt.: *ibid.*, sch.11.
s. 15, see *Decision No. R (S) 4/82.*
s. 15, regs. 80/1622; 84/451; 87/214.
s. 15, repealed: 1986, c.50, sch.11.
s. 16, order 80/1082.
s. 18, amended: 1982, c.24, sch.4; 1986, c.50, sch.10; repealed in pt.: *ibid.*, sch.11.
s. 20, repealed in pt.: *ibid.*
s. 21, orders 80/729; 81/1438; 83/1002; 84/1492.
sch. 1, repealed in pt.: 1982, c.24, sch.5; 1986, c.50, sch.11; 1988, c.7, sch.5.
sch. 2, repealed in pt.: *ibid.*
sch. 3, regs. 82/1408, 1495; 83/1015, 1137.
sch. 3, amended: 1982, c.24, s.42, sch.4; order 82/1084; 1986, c.50, sch.10, repealed in pt.: *ibid.*, sch.11.
sch. 4, repealed in pt.: 1982, c.44, sch.; 1986, c.47, sch.5(S.)

31. Port of London (Financial Assistance) Act 1980.
Royal Assent, June 30, 1980.

32. Licensed Premises (Exclusion of Certain Persons) Act 1980.
Royal Assent, June 30, 1980.

33. Industry Act 1980.
Royal Assent, June 30, 1980.
ss. 2, 3, amended: 1985, c.9, sch.2.
s. 5, orders 80/1211; 87/520.
s. 5, amended: 1981, c.6, s.1; order 87/520; repealed in pt.: 1981, c.6, s.1, sch.
ss. 10–15, repealed: 1981, c.13, sch.2.
ss. 16–18, sch.1, repealed: 1982, c.52, sch.3.

34. Transport Act 1980.
Royal Assent, June 30, 1980.
ss. 1–11, repealed: 1981, c.14, sch.8.
ss. 3, 5–7, 11, 28, regs. 80/1354.
s. 5, see *R.* v. *Secretary of State for Transport, ex p. Cumbria County Council* [1983] R.T.R. 129, C.A.
s. 12, orders 81/373, 885.
ss. 12, 13, repealed: 1981, c.14, sch.8.
s. 14, regs. 81/262, 886.
ss. 14–16, repealed: 1981, c.14, sch.8.
s. 17, regs. 81/257; repealed: 1981, c.14, sch.8.
s. 18, regs. 81/262.
ss. 18–21, repealed: 1981, c.14, sch.8.
s. 22, regs. 81/258.
ss. 22, 23, repealed: 1981, c.14, sch.8.
s. 24, regs. 81/258.
ss. 24–27, repealed: 1981, c.14, sch.8.
s. 28, regs. 81/257, 258.
ss. 28, 29, repealed: 1981, c.14, sch.8.
s. 30, regs. 81/259; repealed: 1981, c.14, sch.8.
s. 31, regs. 81/258, 264.

CAP.

1980—cont.

34. Transport Act 1980—cont.
s. 31, amended: 1983, c.20, sch.4.
ss. 31, 32 (in pt.), 33, 36, 37 (in pt.), 38–41, 42, repealed: 1981, c.14, sch.8.
s. 35, repealed: 1984, c.32, sch.7.
s. 37, repealed in pt.: 1988, c.54, sch.1.
s. 43, orders 81/197, 694; amended: 1981, c.14, sch.7.
s. 44, repealed: 1981, c.14, sch.8.
s. 45, order 80/1380.
s. 46, repealed in pt.: 1988, c.39, sch.14.
ss. 47, 48, amended: 1985, c.9, sch.2.
s. 54, orders 81/346, 347, 1646.
s. 61, repealed: 1988, c.54, sch.1.
s. 62, repealed in pt.: 1984, c.32, sch.7.
s. 63, repealed: 1988, c.54, sch.1.
s. 64, see Yakha v. Tee [1984] R.T.R. 122, D.C.
s. 64, amended: 1985, c.67, sch.7.
s. 66, repealed in pt.: 1982, c.49, sch.6.
s. 70, orders 80/913, 1353, 1424; 81/256.
schs. 1–3, repealed: 1981, c.14, sch.8.
schs. 4, 5, repealed in pt.: ibid.
sch. 5, repealed in pt.: 1984, c.27, sch.14; c.32, sch.7; 1985, c.67, sch.8.

35. Sea Fish Industry Act 1980.
Royal Assent, June 30, 1980.
repealed: 1981, c.29, sch.5.

36. New Towns Act 1980.
Royal Assent, June 30, 1980.
repealed: 1981, c.64, sch.13.

37. Gas Act 1980.
Royal Assent, June 30, 1980.
repealed: 1986, c.44, sch.9.

38. Coroners Act 1980.
Royal Assent, July 17, 1980.
repealed: 1988, c.13, sch.4.
s. 2, see R. v. West Yorkshire Coroner, ex p. Smith, The Times, November 6, 1982, Webster J.

39. Social Security (No. 2) Act 1980.
Royal Assent, July 17, 1980.
ss. 1, 2, repealed: 1986, c.50, sch.11.
s. 2, regs. 83/1598.
s. 3, repealed in pt.: 1982, c.24, sch.5.
s. 4, repealed in pt.: 1986, c.50, sch.11.
s. 5, see Decisions No. R (U) 5/82; R (U) 4/83; R (U) 8/83.
s. 5, regs. 81/73, 815; order 81/1383.
s. 5, amended: 1982, c.24, sch.4; 1988, c.7, s.7.
s. 6, see Decisions Nos. R(SB) 17/85; R (SB) 29/85.
s. 6, regs. 80/1641; orders 82/1350; 83/1433; 84/1800; 85/1454.
s. 6, repealed: 1986, c.50, sch.11.
s. 7, regs. 80/1730.
s. 7, repealed in pt.: 1988, c.19, sch.4.
s. 8, order 80/1025.
sch. 3, regs. 83/1598.

40. Licensing (Amendment) Act 1980.
Royal Assent, July 17, 1980.
Commencement order: 82/1382.
s. 4, order 82/1382.

CAP.

1980—cont.

41. Films Act 1980.
Royal Assent, July 17, 1980.
Commencement order: 82/1020.
ss. 1, 3, repealed: 1981, c.15, sch.3.
ss. 2, 4, repealed: 1981, c.16, sch.2.
s. 7, order 82/1894.
s. 9, order 82/1020.
s. 9, repealed in pt.: 1981, c.15, sch.3; c.16, sch.2.

42. Employment Act 1980.
Royal Assent, August 1, 1980.
order 80/1926.
s. 1, regs. 80/1252; 82/953, 1108; 84/1654; 88/1123.
s. 1, amended: 1984, c.49, s.20; repealed in pt.: ibid.
s. 2, amended: 1988, c.19, sch.3; repealed in pt.: 1984, c.49, s.20.
s. 3, orders 80/1757, 1758; 83/584.
s. 3, amended: 1988, c.19, s.18.
s. 4, see National Graphical Association v. Howard (No. 2), The Times, July 23, 1983, E.A.T.; National Society of Operative Printers Graphical and Media Personnel v. Kirkham [1983] I.C.R. 241, E.A.T.; Goodfellow v. National Society of Operative Printers Graphical and Media Personnel, The Times, October 16, 1984, E.A.T.; National Graphical Association v. Howard [1985] I.C.R. 97, C.A.; Howard v. National Graphical Association [1985] I.C.R. 101, E.A.T.; Goodfellow v. NATSOPA [1985] I.C.R. 187, E.A.T.; McGhee v. Transport and General Workers Union (1985) 82 L.S.Gaz. 3696, C.A.; Clark v. Society of Graphical and Allied Trades 1982 [1986] I.C.R. 12, E.A.T.; Transport and General Workers' Union v. Tucker, The Times, March 2, 1988, C.A.
ss. 4, 5, see Day v. Society of Graphical and Allied Trades 1982 [1986] I.C.R. 640, E.A.T.
s. 5, see Howard v. National Graphical Association [1985] I.C.R. 101, E.A.T.; Saunders v. Bakers Food and Allied Workers Union [1986] I.R.L.R. 16, E.A.T.
s. 5, amended: 1988, c.19, sch.3.
ss. 7, 10, repealed: 1982, c.46, sch.4.
s. 11, see Secretary of State for Employment v. Cox, The Times, August 15, 1984, E.A.T.
s. 15, amended: 1988, c.19, sch.4; repealed in pt.: 1982, c.46, sch.4.
s. 16, see Thomas v. National Union of Mineworkers (South Wales), The Times, February 18, 1985, Scott J.
s. 17, see Hadmor Productions v. Hamilton [1981] 3 W.L.R. 139; [1981] 2 All E.R. 724, C.A.; Marina Shipping v. Laughton and Shaw [1982] I.R.L.R. 20, C.A.; Express Newspapers v. Mitchell, The Times, August 14, 1982, Leonard J.; Merkur Island Shipping Corp. v. Laughton [1983] 2 All E.R. 189, H.L.; St. Stephen Shipping Co. v. Guinane (O.H.) September 23, 1982; Dimbleby & Sons v. National Union of Journalists [1984] 1 W.L.R. 427, H.L.; Shipping Co. Uniform Inc. v. International Transport Workers Federation, Allen, Ross and Davies [1985] 1 Lloyd's Rep. 173,

CAP.

1980—cont.

42. Employment Act 1980—*cont.*
Staughton J.; *Thomas* v. *National Union of Mineworkers* [1985] 2 All E.R. 1, C.A.; *Star Offshore Services* v. *National Union of Seamen* (O.H.) May 10, 1988.
s. 18, repealed: 1982, c.46, sch.4.
s. 21, order 80/1170.
s. 24, see *National Society of Operative Printing, Graphical and Media Personnel* v. *Kirkham, The Times,* November 23, 1982, E.A.T.
sch. 1, repealed in pt.: 1981, c.40, s.16; 1982, c.46, sch.4; 1985, c.65, sch.10.

43. Magistrates' Courts Act 1980.
Royal Assent, August 1, 1980.
rules 81/1842, 1843.
ss. 1, 2, see *R.* v. *Intervision and Norris* [1984] Crim.L.R. 350, Knightsbridge Crown Court.
ss. 2, 3, see *R.* v. *Avon Magistrates' Court Committee, ex p. Bath Law Society* [1988] 2 W.L.R. 137, D.C.
ss. 2, 6, see *R.* v. *Cambridgeshire Justices, ex p. Fraser* [1984] 1 W.L.R. 1391, D.C.
s. 5, amended: 1982, c.48, sch.9.
s. 6, see *R.* v. *Hall* [1982] 1 All E.R. 75, C.A.; *R.* v. *Gallagher* [1983] Crim.L.R. 335, C.A.; *R.* v. *South Hackney Juvenile Court, ex p. R. B. (A Minor) and C. B. (A Minor)* (1983) 77 Cr.App.R. 294, D.C.; *R.* v. *Horseferry Road Metropolitan Stipendiary Magistrate, ex p. O'Regan, The Times,* May 17, 1986, D.C.; *R.* v. *Newcastle-under-Lyme JJ., ex p. Hemmings* [1987] Crim.L.R. 416, D.C.
s. 6, amended: 1982, c.48, s.61; 1988, c.33, sch.15.
s. 8, see *R.* v. *Horsham JJ., ex p. Farquharson* [1982] 2 W.L.R. 430; (1983) 76 Cr.App.R. 87; C.A.; *R.* v. *Leeds Justices, ex p. Sykes* [1983] 1 W.L.R. 132, D.C.
s. 8, amended: 1981, c.27, s.1; 1984, c.46, sch.5; repealed in pt.: 1981, c.49, s.4.
s. 9, see *R.* v. *Manchester Crown Court, ex p. Hill, The Times,* November 2, 1984, D.C.
ss. 9, 10, 15, see *R.* v. *Dorking JJ., ex p. Harrington* [1984] 3 W.L.R. 142, H.L. *sub nom. Harrington* v. *Roots* [1984] 2 All E.R. 474, H.L.
s. 10, see *R.* v. *Ali, The Times,* July 6, 1987, D.C.; *Arthur* v. *Stringer* (1987) 84 Cr.App.R. 361, C.A.
s. 10, amended: 1982, c.48, sch.9.
s. 10, 11, see *R.* v. *Afan JJ., ex p. Chaplin* [1983] R.T.R. 168, D.C.; *R.* v. *Macclesfield JJ., ex p. Jones* [1983] R.T.R. 143, D.C.
s. 11, see *R.* v. *Seisdon JJ., ex p. Dougan* [1982] 1 W.L.R. 1476, D.C.
s. 12, see *R.* v. *Epping and Ongar JJ., ex p. Breach; R.* v. *Same, ex p. Shippam (C.)* [1986] Crim.L.R. 810; [1987] R.T.R. 233, D.C.
s. 12, amended: 1985, c.23, sch.1.
s. 18, amended: 1982, c.48, sch.9.
ss. 18–20, see *R.* v. *Birmingham Justices, ex p. Hodgson* [1985] 2 W.L.R. 630, D.C.
ss. 18, 24, see *R.* v. *Islington North Juvenile Court, ex p. Daley* [1982] 3 W.L.R. 344, H.L.

CAP.

1980—cont.

43. Magistrates' Courts Act 1980—*cont.*
s. 19, see *R.* v. *South Hackney Juvenile Court, ex p. R. B. (A Minor) and C. B. (A Minor)* (1983) 77 Cr.App.R. 294, D.C.
s. 19, amended: 1985, c.23, sch.1.
s. 22, see *R.* v. *St. Helens JJ., ex p. McClorie* [1983] 1 W.L.R. 1332, C.A.; *R.* v. *Salisbury Magistrates' Court, ex p. Mastin* [1986] Crim.L.R. 545, D.C.; *R.* v. *Braden* [1988] Crim.L.R. 54, C.A.
s. 22, amended: 1988, c.33, s.38; repealed in pt.: *ibid.,* sch.16.
s. 24, see *R.* v. *South Hackney Juvenile Court, ex p. R. (A Minor) and C. B. (A Minor), The Times,* March 23, 1983, D.C.; *R.* v. *Vale of Glamorgan JJ., ex p. Beattie* (1984) 148 J.P.N. 749, D.C.; *R.* v. *Newham Juvenile Court, ex p. F. (A Minor)* [1986] 1 W.L.R. 939, D.C.; *R.* v. *Hammersmith Juvenile Court, ex p. O. (A Minor), The Times,* April 7, 1987, D.C.; *R.* v. *Crown Court at Doncaster, ex p. South Yorkshire Prosecution Service, sub nom. R.* v. *Doncaster Crown Court, ex p. Crown Prosecution Service* (1987) 85 Cr.App.R. 1; [1987] Crim.L.R. 395, D.C.
ss. 24, 25, see *R.* v. *South Hackney Juvenile Court, ex p. R. B. (A Minor) and C. B. (A Minor)* (1983) 77 Cr.App.R. 294, D.C.; *R.* v. *Hammersmith Juvenile Court, ex p. O.* (1988) 86 Cr.App.R. 342, D.C.
s. 25, see *R.* v. *Cambridgeshire Justices, ex p. Fraser* [1984] 1 W.L.R. 1391, D.C.; *Gillard, Re, (sub nom. R.* v. *Dudley JJ., ex p. Gillard)* [1985] 3 W.L.R. 936, H.L.; *R.* v. *Southend JJ., ex p. Wood, The Times,* March 8, 1986, D.C.
s. 25, amended: 1985, c.23, sch.1; repealed in pt.: *ibid.,* sch.2.
s. 30, repealed in pt.: *ibid.*
s. 32, repealed in pt.: 1981, c.47, sch.; 1988, c.33, sch.16.
ss. 34, 35, see *Chief Constable of Kent* v. *Mather* [1986] R.T.R. 36, D.C.
s. 37, see *R.* v. *Folkestone and Hythe Juvenile Court, ex p. R. (A Juvenile),* [1981] 1 W.L.R. 1501; (1982) 74 Cr.App.R. 58, D.C.
s. 37, amended: 1982, c.48, sch.14; 1988, c.33, sch.15.
s. 38, see *R.* v. *Guildhall JJ., ex p. Cooper, The Times,* May 6, 1983, Glidewell J.
s. 39, amended: 1988, c.54, sch.3.
s. 43, substituted: 1984, c.60, s.47.
s. 43A, added: 1981, c.54, sch.5.
s. 44, see *Bentley* v. *Mullen* [1986] R.T.R. 7, D.C.; *Smith* v. *Mellors and Soar* (1987) 84 Cr.App.R. 279, D.C.
s. 48, see *R.* v. *Southampton Magistrates' Court, ex p. Newman, The Guardian,* July 28, 1988, D.C.
s. 49, see *R.* v. *Marylebone Magistrates' Court and the Commissioner of Police for the Metropolis, ex p. Ryser* [1985] Crim.L.R. 735, D.C.; *R.* v. *Tottenham JJ., ex p. M.L.* (1986) 82 Cr.App.R. 277, C.A.
s. 49, repealed: 1984, c.60, sch.7.
s. 58, amended: 1987, c.42, sch.2.
s. 59, repealed in pt.: 1987, c.42, sch.4.

CAP.

1980—cont.

43. Magistrates' Courts Act 1980—cont.

s. 59, see *R.* v. *Camberwell Green JJ., ex p. Brown* (1983) 13 Fam.Law 212, Woolf J.

s. 60, see *Boniface* v. *Harris* (1983) 13 Fam.Law 117, D.C.; *Moore* v. *Ball* [1984] 2 W.L.R. 865, D.C.; *Fernandez* v. *Fernandez* (1984) 14 Fam. Law 177, D.C.

s. 61, rules 83/523.

s. 63, see *Head* v. *Head* [1982] 1 W.L.R. 1186, D.C.; *P.* v. *W. (Access Order: Breach)* [1984] 2 W.L.R. 439, D.C.; *Tilmouth* v. *Tilmouth* (1095) 15 Fam.Law 92, D.C.; *Thomason* v. *Thomason* (1985) 15 Fam.Law 91, D.C.

s. 64, see *R.* v. *Uxbridge JJ., ex p. Commissioner of Police of the Metropolis, The Times,* June 13, 1981, C.A.; *Wycombe District Council* v. *Jeffways & Pilot Coaches (H.W.)* (1983) 81 L.G.R. 662, C.A.; *R.* v. *Salisbury and Tilsbury and Mere Combined Juvenile Court, ex p. Ball* (1985) 15 Fam. Law 313, Kennedy J.

s. 64, amended: 1987, c.42, sch.2.

s. 65, amended: 1982, c.27, sch.12; 1984, c.42, s.44; 1986, c.50, sch.10; 1987, c.42, sch.2; repealed in pt.: *ibid.*, schs.2,4.

s. 67, rules 83/676, 677.

Pt. III (ss. 75–96) see *Snape* v. *Snape* (1983) 13 Fam.Law 210, Waite J.

s. 76, see *R.* v. *Birmingham JJ, ex p. Bennett* [1983] 1 W.L.R. 114; *R.* v. *Midhurst JJ., ex p. Seymour, The Times,* March 24, 1983, C.A.

s. 76, repealed in pt.: 1982, c.48, sch.16.

s. 77, see *R.* v. *Chichester JJ., ex p. Collins* [1982] 1 W.L.R. 334, D.C.; *Wilson* v. *Colchester JJ.* [1985] 2 All E.R. 97, H.L.

s. 77, amended: 1982, c.48, sch.14; 1988, c.33, s.61.

s. 80, amended: 1987, c.42, sch.2.

s. 81, amended: 1982, c.48, sch.14; repealed in pt.: *ibid.*, sch.16.

s. 82, see *R.* v. *Steyning Magistrates' Court, ex p. Hunter, The Times,* November 22, 1985, D.C.; *R.* v. *Norwich JJ., ex p. Tigger (formerly Lilly), The Times,* June 26, 1987, D.C.; *R.* v. *Birmingham Magistrates' Court, ex p. Mansell* [1988] 28 R.V.R. 112, D.C.

s. 82, amended: 1982, c.48, sch.16; 1988, c.33, s.61.

s. 85, substituted: *ibid.*

s. 85A, added: 1982, c.48, s.51.

s. 86, amended: *ibid.*

s. 87, see *Gooch* v. *Ewing (Allied Irish Bank, Garnishee)* [1985] 3 All E.R. 654, C.A.

s. 87, amended: 1981, c.54, sch.5; 1984, c.28, sch.2.

s. 87A, added: 1988, c.33, s.62.

s. 88, amended: 1982, c.48, sch.14.

s. 92, amended: 1988, c.34, sch.5; repealed in pt.: 1987, c.42, sch.4.

s. 93, see *R.* v. *Waltham Forest Justices, ex p. Solanke, The Times,* January 12, 1985, Woolf J.

ss. 93–95, amended: 1987, c.42, sch.2.

s. 95, see *R.* v. *Dover Magistrates' Court, ex p. Kidner* [1983] 1 All E.R. 475, D.C.; *Allen* v.

CAP.

1980—cont.

43. Magistrates' Courts Act 1980—cont.

Allen [1985] 2 W.L.R. 65, Booth J.; *Fletcher* v. *Fletcher* [1985] 2 All E.R. 260, D.C.; *Parry* v. *Meugens* (1986) 1 F.L.R. 125, Reeve J.; *Berry* v. *Berry* [1986] 3 W.L.R. 257, C.A.

s. 96A, added: 1982, c.48, sch.14.

s. 97, see *R.* v. *Barking Justices, ex p. Goodspeed* [1985] R.T.R. 70, D.C.; *R.* v. *Skegness Magistrates' Court, ex p. Cardy; R.* v. *Manchester Crown Court, ex p. Williams* [1985] R.T.R. 49, D.C.; *R.* v. *Coventry Magistrates' Court, ex p. Perks* [1985] R.T.R. 74, D.C.; *R.* v. *Sheffield JJ., ex p. Wrigley* [1985] R.T.R. 78, D.C.; *R.* v. *Peterborough Magistrates' Court, ex p. Willis and Amos* [1987] Crim.L.R. 692, D.C.

s. 97, amended: 1981, c.49, sch.2.

s. 100, amended: 1987, c.42, sch.2.

s. 101, see *Oxford* v. *Lincoln, The Times,* March 1, 1982, D.C.; *Guyll* v. *Bright* [1987] R.T.R. 104, D.C.

s. 102, see *R.* v. *Gallagher* [1983] Crim.L.R. 335, C.A.

s. 102, amended: 1985, c.33, sch.15.

ss. 102, 104, see *R.* v. *Governor of Ashford Remand Centre, ex p. Postlethwaite, The Times,* July 14, 1987, H.L.

s. 103, substituted: 1985, c.33, s.33.

s. 108, see *R.* v. *Battle JJ., ex p. Shepherd, The Times,* April 26, 1983, D.C

s. 108, amended: 1982, c.48, s 66; repealed in pt.: *ibid.*, sch.16.

s. 111, see *Universal Salvage* v. *Boothby, The Times,* December 14, 1983, D.C.; *R.* v. *Clerkenwell Metropolitan Stipendiary Magistrate, ex p. D. P. P.* [1984] 2 W.L.R. 244, D.C.; *Streames* v. *Copping, The Times,* February 25, 1984, D.C.; *Fletcher* v. *Fletcher* [1985] 2 All E.R. 260, D.C.; *Berry* v. *Berry* [1986] 3 W.L.R. 257, C.A.

s. 114, see *R.* v. *Newcastle upon Tyne JJ., ex p. Skinner* [1987] 1 All E.R. 349, D.C.

s. 114, rules 83/526.

s. 115, see *Chief Constable of the Surrey Constabulary* v. *Ridley and Steel* [1985] Crim.L.R. 725, D.C.; *Howley* v. *Oxford* (1985) 81 Cr.App.R. 246, D.C.; *Lanham* v. *Bernard, The Times,* June 23, 1986, D.C.

s. 119, amended: 1982, c.48, sch.14.

s. 120, see *R.* v. *Uxbridge JJ., ex p. Heward-Mills* [1983] 1 W.L.R. 56, McCullough J.; *R.* v. *Bow Street Magistrates' Court, ex p. Hall, The Times,* October 27, 1986, C.A.

s. 121, see *R.* v. *Malvern JJ., ex p. Evans; R.* v. *Evesham JJ., ex p. McDonagh* [1988] 1 All E.R. 371, D.C.

s. 121, amended: 1988, c.33, s.61.

s. 122, see *R.* v. *Croydon Crown Court, ex p. Claire, The Times,* April 3, 1986, D.C.

s. 123, see *Thornley* v. *Clegg* [1982] R.T.R. 405, D.C.; *Marco (Croydon)* v. *Metropolitan Police* [1983] Crim.L.R. 395; [1984] R.T.R. 24, D.C.; *Shah* v. *Swallow, The Times,* November 9, 1983, D.C.; *R.* v. *Eastbourne Justices, ex p. Kisten, The Times,* December 22, 1984, D.C.

CAP.

1980—cont.

43. Magistrates' Courts Act 1980—cont.

s. 125, see *Jones* v. *Kelsey* [1987] Crim.L.R. 392; (1987) 85 Cr.App.R. 226, D.C.

s. 125, amended: 1984, c.60, s.33; 1988, c.33, s.65.

s. 127, see *R.* v. *Manchester Stipendiary Magistrate, ex p. Hill; R.* v. *Dartford JJ., ex p. Dhesi; R.* v. *Edmonton JJ., ex p. Hughes* [1982] 3 W.L.R. 331, H.L.; *Marco (Croydon)* v. *Metropolitan Police* [1984] R.T.R. 24, D.C.; *R.* v. *Bow Street Acting Stipendiary Magistrate, ex p. Spiteri, The Times,* October 16, 1984, D.C.; *Y.* v. *Kirklees Borough Council, The Times,* February 23, 1985, Waterhouse J.; *R.* v. *Dacorum Magistrates' Court, ex p. Gardner (Michael)* [1985] Crim.L.R. 394, D.C.; *Hertsmere Borough Council* v. *Dunn Alan Building Contractors* [1985] Crim.L.R. 726, D.C.; *Patel* v. *Blakey* [198] R.T.R. 65, D.C.; *R.* v. *Pontypridd Juvenile Magistrates' Court, ex p. B., The Times,* July 28, 1988, D.C.

s. 128, see *R.* v. *Governor of Brixton Prison, ex p. Walsh* [1984] 3 W.L.R. 205, H.L.

s. 128, amended: 1982, c.48, sch.9; 1984, c.60, s.48; 1988, c.33, sch.15.

s. 128A, added: *ibid.,* s.155.

s. 130, amended: 1982, c.48, sch.9.

ss. 130, 148, see *R.* v. *Avon Magistrates' Courts Committee, ex p. Bath Law Society* [1988] 2 W.L.R. 137, D.C.

s. 131, repealed in pt.: 1982, c.48, schs.9,16.

s. 133, see *Head* v. *Head* [1982] 1 W.L.R. 1186, D.C.

s. 133, amended: 1982, c.48, sch.14; 1988, c.33, sch.15.

s. 134, repealed: *ibid.,* s.49, sch.16.

s. 135, amended: 1982, c.48, sch.14.

s. 136, amended: 1988, c.33, s.65.

s. 142, see *Morris* v. *Grant* [1983] Crim.L.R. 620, D.C.; *R.* v. *Camberwell Green Magistrates' Court, ex p. Ibrahim* (1984) 148 J.P.N. 316, D.C.; *Jane* v. *Broome, The Times,* November 2, 1987, D.C.

s. 143, order 84/447.

s. 143, amended: 1982, c.48, s.48; 1985; c.13, sch.2; repealed in pt.: 1988, c.33, sch.16.

s. 144, rules 81/552, 553; 82/245, 246; 83/523–525, 527, 675–677, 1148, 1793; 84/567, 611, 1542, 1552; 85/601, 1695, 1944, 1945; 86/367, 1079, 1141, 1332, 1333, 1498, 1962; 88/329, 868, 869, 913, 1701.

s. 145, rules 81/552, 553; 82/245, 246; 83/523–526; 84/1542, 1552; 85/1944; 86/1498, 1962; 88/329.

s. 146, rules 83/675.

s. 150, see *Head* v. *Head* [1982] 1 W.L.R. 1186, D.C.; *Chief Constable of Kent* v. *Mather* [1986] R.T.R. 36, D.C.

s. 150, amended: 1987, c.42, sch.2; repealed in pt.: *ibid.,* schs.2,4.

s. 155, order 81/457.

sch. 1, repealed in pt.: 1981, c.47, sch.; 1985, c.71, sch.1; 1986, c.48, sch.5.; 1988, c.33, sch.16.

CAP.

1980—cont.

43. Magistrates' Courts Act 1980—cont.

sch. 2, see *R.* v. *Braden, The Times,* October 14, 1987, C.A.

sch. 4, see *R.* v. *Midhurst JJ., ex p. Seymour* (1983) 5 Cr.App.R.(S) 99.

sch. 4, amended: 1982, c.48, sch.14; 1988, c.33, s.60.

sch. 5, amended: 1982, c.48, sch.9

sch. 6, amended: 1983, c.21, sch.3; 1985, c.13, sch.2; repealed in pt.: 1982, c.30, sch.7; 1987, c.19, sch; c.21, sch.3.

sch. 6A, added: 1982, c.48, s.48; amended: 1984, c.28, sch.2; 1988, c.13, sch.3; repealed in pt.: 1984, c.28, sch.4; 1988, c.13, sch.4.

sch. 7, repealed in pt.: 1980, c.66, sch.25; 1982, c.36, sch.3; c.48, sch.16; c.50, sch.6; c.51, sch.4; 1983, c.38, sch.3; 1984, c.30, sch.11; c.60, sch.7; 1985, c.71, sch.1; c.72, sch.13; 1987, c.22, sch.7; c.43, sch.7; 1988, c.17, sch.4; c.34, sch.6; c.41, sch.13 (prosp.); c.54, sch.1.

sch. 8, see *R.* v. *Folkestone and Hythe Juvenile Court JJ., ex p. R. (A Juvenile),* [1981] 1 W.L.R. 1501, D.C.; (1982) 74 Cr.App.R. 58, D.C.; *R.* v. *Hall* [1982] 1 All E.R. 75, C.A.

44. Education (Scotland) Act 1980.

Royal Assent, August 1, 1980.

Trust schemes 80/1817, 1865, 2037; 81/645, 739, 752, 760, 761, 841, 857, 1182, 1323, 1583, 1858, 1859; 82/48, 73, 109, 340, 647.

s. 1, see *Walker* v. *Strathclyde Regional Council (No. 1)* (O.H.), 1986 S.L.T. 523.

s. 1, amended: 1981, c.58, s.3; 1982, c.43, sch.3; repealed in pt.: *ibid.,* schs.3,4.

s. 2, regs. 82/56, 57, 1735; 87/290.

s. 4, amended: 1981, c.58, sch.2; 1986, c.33, s.14; repealed in pt.: 1981, c.58, schs.2,9; 1986, c.33, ss.14.

s. 5, repealed: 1981, c.58, schs.2,9.

s. 6, amended: 1982, c.43, sch.3.

s. 7, amended: 1981, c.58, s.8; repealed in pt.: *ibid.,* s.8, sch.9.

s. 14A, added: *ibid.,* s.12.

s. 16, amended: *ibid.,* sch.7.

s. 17, amended: *ibid.,* ss.7,8; repealed in pt.: *ibid.,* s.8, sch.9.

s. 18, amended: 1984, c.54, sch.9.

s. 19A, regs. 84/668.

s. 19A, added: 1984, c.6, s.1.

ss. 21, 22, 22C, 22D, see *Scottish Hierarchy of the Roman Catholic Church* v. *Highland Regional Council,* 1987 S.L.T. 169, 708.

s. 22, see *Deane* v. *Lothian Regional Council,* Second Division, July 6, 1985.

s. 22, amended: 1981, c.58, s.7; repealed in pt.: *ibid.,* s.7, schs.7,9.

s. 22A, regs. 87/2076.

ss. 22A–22D, added: 1981, c.58, s.6.

s. 22B, regs. 87/2076; 88/107.

s. 23, amended: 1981, c.58, sch.7; repealed in pt.: *ibid.,* sch.9; 1986, c.61, sch.6.

s. 28, see *Harvey* v. *Strathclyde Regional Council, First Division, The Times,* October 13, 1988.

CAP.

1980—cont.

44. Education (Scotland) Act 1980—cont.

ss. 28, 28A, see *Keeney* v. *Strathclyde Regional Council* (O.H.), 1986 S.L.T. 490.

s. 28, repealed in pt.: 1981, c.58, s.1, sch.9.

s. 28A, regs. 81/1558, 1561, 1733.

ss. 28A–28H, added: 1981, c.58, s.1.

ss. 28A, 28F, see *Lamont* v. *Strathclyde Regional Council*, 1988 S.L.T.(Sh.Ct.) 9.

s. 28B, regs. 81/1558, 1559; 82/950.

s. 28D, regs. 81/1560, 1561; 82/1733, 1736.

s. 28H, regs. 82/1733, 1736.

s. 29, order 80/1687.

s. 29, repealed: 1981, c.58, s.8, sch.9.

s. 35, see *Buchanan* v. *Price*, 1982 S.C.C.R. 534; *Neeson* v. *Lunn*, 1985 S.C.C.R. 102.

ss. 35, 42, see *Kiely* v. *Lunn*, 1983 S.L.T. 207.

ss. 38, 40, amended: 1981, c.58, sch.2.

s. 42, amended: *ibid.*, s.2.

s. 43, amended: 1982, c.48, sch.6.

s. 48A, order 87/1140.

s. 48A, added: 1986, c.61, s.48.

s. 49, regs. 81/966; 82/936; 83/1051, 1535; 84/990; 85/1120; 86/1227; 87/1366; 88/1042, 1423.

ss. 50, 51, amended: 1981, c.58, s.2.

s. 53, amended: 1986, c.50, s.77.

s. 54, see *Shaw* v. *Strathclyde Regional Council* (O.H.), 1987 S.C.L.R. 439.

s. 54, amended: 1981, c.58, sch.2.

s. 59, repealed: *ibid.*, schs.2,9.

ss. 60–65, substituted: *ibid.*, s.4.

ss. 61–64, amended: 1986, c.33, s.14.

s. 63, regs. 82/1736.

s. 65A, 65B, regs. 82/1734.

s. 65D, regs. 82/1222.

s. 66, amended: 1982, c.48, sch.6; repealed in pt.: 1981, c.58, s.16, sch.9.

s. 70, see *Walker* v. *Strathclyde Regional Council (No. 1)* (O.H.), 1986 S.L.T. 523.

s. 70, amended: 1988, c.47, sch.4.

s. 73, regs. 81/488, 625, 626; 82/891, 965; 83/798, 908, 1150, 1536; 84/381, 432, 751, 841, 1183; 85/506, 1183; 86/410, 510, 1103; 87/208, 291, 309, 644, 864, 1146, 1801; 88/328, 437, 1163, 1424.

s. 74, regs. 81/488, 1221; 82/965; 83/798, 908, 1150, 1536; 84/751, 841, 1183; 85/506, 1183; 86/410, 510, 1103; 87/291, 309, 644, 864, 1146, 1801; 88/328, 437, 1163, 1424, 1715.

s. 75, regs. 87/291, 644.

ss. 75A, 75B, added: 1981, c.58, s.5.

ss. 75A, 75B, regs. 82/949; 83/1080; 84/840; 85/1076; 86/1104; 87/1147; 88/1164.

s. 77, regs. 81/1071, 1221; 85/543, 679, 866, 1163, 1164; 86/1353; 87/309; 88/1448, 1449, 1715.

s. 77, amended: 1981, c.58, sch.6.

s. 86, see *Neeson* v. *Lunn*, 1985 S.C.C.R. 102.

s. 87, see *Connor* v. *Strathclyde Regional Council* (O.H.), 1986 S.L.T. 530.

s. 88, see *Nahar* v. *Strathclyde Regional Council* (O.H.), 1986 S.L.T. 570.

ss. 91–97, substituted: 1981, c.58, s.14.

s. 92, orders 81/967, 1691.

s. 97, orders 80/1687; 81/967, 1691.

CAP.

1980—cont.

44. Education (Scotland) Act 1980—cont.

s. 98, amended: 1981, c.58, ss.9,10; 1982, c.48, sch.6; repealed in pt.: 1981, c.58, s.9.

s. 101, amended: 1982, c.48, sch.6.

s. 104, regs. 81/1563, 1564.

s. 104, amended: 1981, c.58, sch.8; repealed in pt.: *ibid.*, schs.6,9.

s. 105, orders 81/841, 1676.

s. 105, amended: 1981, c.58, sch.8; repealed in pt.: *ibid.*, schs.6,9.

ss. 106, 107, amended: *ibid.*, sch.6.

s. 108, amended: 1981, c.58, sch.6; repealed in pt.: *ibid.*, schs.6,9.

s. 109, amended: *ibid.*, sch.6.

s. 110, amended: *ibid.*; repealed in pt.: *ibid.*, schs. 6, 9.

s. 111, amended: *ibid.*; 1985, c.8, sch.2; repealed in pt.: 1981, c.58, schs.6, 9.

s. 112, amended: *ibid.*, sch.6; repealed in pt.: *ibid.*, schs.6,9.

s. 113, orders 81/841, 1676.

s. 113, repealed: 1981, c.58, schs.6,9.

s. 114, amended: *ibid.*, sch.6; repealed in pt.: *ibid.*, schs.6,9.

s. 115, repealed: *ibid.*, schs.6,9.

s. 117, amended: *ibid.*, sch.6; repealed in pt.: *ibid.*, schs.6,9.

s. 118, substituted: *ibid.*, sch.6.

s. 118A, added: *ibid.*

s. 120, amended: *ibid.*

s. 121, amended: *ibid.*; repealed in pt.: *ibid.*, schs.6,9.

s. 122, amended: *ibid.*, sch.6.

s. 126, order 81/549.

s. 129, regs. 81/1562.

s. 129, amended: 1981, c.58, s.13; repealed in pt.: *ibid.*, s.13, sch.9.

s. 132, repealed in pt.: *ibid.*, sch.9.

s. 133, regs. 81/1221.

s. 135, regs. 85/542, 678; 88/1447.

s 135, amended: 1981, c.58, s.1, sch.2; 1987, c.40, s.2; repealed in pt.: 1981, c.58, schs.2,9.

s. 137, order 80/1287.

sch. 1, amended: 1987, c.18, sch.6.

sch. A1, added: 1981, c.58, s.1, sch.1; amended: 1988, c.47, sch.4.

sch. A2, see *Lamont* v. *Strathclyde Regional Council*, 1988 S.L.T.(Sh.Ct.). 9.

sch. A2, added: 1981, c.58, s.4, sch.3.

sch. 1A, added: *ibid.*, s.5, sch.4.

sch. 1B, added: *ibid.*, s.14, sch.5.

sch. 2, amended: *ibid.*, s.11; repealed in pt.: *ibid.*, s.11, sch.9.

sch. 3, amended: *ibid.*, sch.2.

sch. 4, repealed in pt.: 1984, c.36, sch.5; c.56, sch.3.

sch. 6, amended: 1981, c.23, s.38.

45. Water (Scotland) Act 1980.

Royal Assent, August 1, 1980.

s. 1, repealed in pt.: 1981, c.23, s.32, sch.4.

s. 2, repealed: *ibid.*, schs.2,4.

ss. 6, 8, see *McColl* v. *Strathclyde Regional Council* (O.H.), 1983 S.L.T. 616.

s. 9, amended: 1984, c.54, sch.9; 1987, c.47, sch.5; repealed in pt.: *ibid.*, sch.6.

1980—cont.

45. Water (Scotland) Act 1980—cont.

s. 9A, added: 1982, c.43, s.59; amended: 1987, c.47, sch.6.

s. 10, amended: ibid., s.57; 1984, c.54, sch.9.

s. 13, amended: 1984, c.54, sch.9.

s. 17, orders 80/1266, 1267, 1270–1272, 1501; 81/143, 171, 1014, 1500, 1718; 82/61, 183, 484, 849, 1640, 1791, 1871; 83/172, 467, 651, 1300–1302, 1371, 1612, 1805, 1806, 1825; 84/844, 891, 989, 1421; 86/693; 87/1032, 1390–1392, 1763, 1879; 88/20, 21, 222.

s. 18, order 83/1371.

s. 19, repealed: 1981, c.23, schs.2,4.

s. 20, amended: ibid., sch.3; repealed in pt.: ibid., schs.3,4.

ss. 23–25, amended: 1984, c.54, sch.9.

s. 28, repealed in pt.: 1984, c.12, sch.7.

s. 29, orders 80/1266, 1267, 1270–1272, 1501; 81/143, 171, 1014, 1500, 1718; 82/61, 849, 1640, 1791, 1871; 83/467, 1300, 1302, 1612, 1805, 1806, 1825; 84/844, 891, 989, 1421; 87/1390–1392, 1763, 1879; 88/20, 222.

s. 33, amended: 1984, c.54, sch.9.

s. 38, amended: 1982, c.48, schs.6,15.

s. 39, repealed: 1987, c.47, sch. 6.

s. 40, regs. 87/2167.

s. 40, substituted: 1987, c.47, sch. 5.

s. 41, regs. 86/411.

s. 41, amended: 1987, c.47, sch.5; repealed in pt.: ibid., sch. 6.

ss. 42, 43, substituted: ibid., sch. 5.

ss. 44, 45, repealed: ibid., sch. 6.

ss. 46–49, amended: ibid., sch. 5.

s. 53, repealed in pt.: ibid., sch. 6.

ss. 54, 55, amended: ibid., sch. 5.

s. 57, repealed: ibid., sch. 6.

s. 58, amended: ibid., sch. 5; repealed in pt.: 1981, c.23, schs.2,4.

s. 60, regs. 86/411.

s. 60, repealed in pt.: 1987, c.47, sch.6.

s. 61, amended: ibid., sch.5; repealed in pt.: ibid., sch.6.

s. 62, repealed: 1981, c.23, sch.4.

s. 64, amended: 1982, c.48, sch.6.

s. 65, amended: 1981, c.23, sch.2.

s. 66, amended: ibid.; repealed in pt.: ibid., schs.2,4.

s. 70, amended: ibid., s.33.

s. 72, orders 81/1801; 88/327; amended: 1982, c.48, sch.6.

ss. 75, 76, amended: 1984, c.54, sch.9.

s. 77, amended: 1981, c.23, s.33; 1984, c.54, sch.9.

s. 85, regs. 86/411.

s. 93, amended: 1984, c.54, sch.6.

ss. 94, 95, amended: ibid., sch.15.

s. 96, repealed: 1985, c.73, sch.4.

s. 107, orders 81/1718; 82/61, 484; 83/172, 651, 1300, 1301, 1422, 1612; 84/891, 989; 86/693; 87/1032, 1879; 88/21.

s. 109, amended: 1981, c.23, sch.3; 1984, c.54, sch.9; 1987, c.47, sch.5; repealed in pt.: 1984, c.54, schs.9,11; 1987, c.47, sch.6.

s. 110, amended: 1984, c.54, sch.9.

1980—cont.

45. Water (Scotland) Act 1980—cont.

sch. 1, repealed in pt.: ibid., sch.4.

sch. 3, amended: 1982, c.43, s.58; 1984, c.54, sch.9; repealed in pt.: 1982, c.43, s.58, sch. 4; 1984, c.54, schs. 9, 11.

sch. 4, amended: 1981, c.38, sch.3; 1982, c.48, schs.6, 15; 1984, c.12, sch.4; c.54, sch.9; repealed in pt.: 1982, c.48, schs. 15, 16; 1984, c.12, schs. 4, 7.

sch. 5, regs. 87/2167.

sch. 10, repealed in pt.: 1982, c.16, sch.16; 1983, c.23, sch.5; 1988, c.41, sch.13.

46. Solicitors (Scotland) Act 1980.

Royal Assent, August 1, 1980.

s. 6, amended: 1985, c.73, sch.1; repealed in pt.: ibid., schs.1, 4.

ss. 7, 9, amended: 1988, c.42, sch.1.

s. 10, amended: ibid.; repealed in pt.: ibid., schs.1,2.

ss. 11 (in pt.), 12, repealed: ibid., sch.2.

s. 15, amended: ibid., sch.1; repealed in pt.: 1985, c.73, schs.1,4.

s. 16, amended: 1985, c.73, sch.1.

s. 18, amended: 1984, c.36, sch.3; 1985, c.73, sch.1; repealed in pt.: 1985, c.73, sch.2.

s. 19, amended: 1988, c.42, sch.1; repealed in pt.: ibid., sch.2.

s. 25, amended: 1986, c.47, sch.3.

ss. 26–28, 30, 31, amended: 1985, c.73, sch.1.

s. 32, amended: ibid.; 1988, c.42, sch.1.

s. 33, repealed in pt.: ibid., schs.1,2.

s. 33A, added: 1985, c.73, sch.1.

s. 34, amended: ibid.

s. 35, amended: 1987, c.22, sch.6; 1988, c.42, sch.1; repealed in pt.: 1985, c.58, sch.4; c.73, sch.4; 1987, c.22, schs.6,7; 1988, c.42, sch.2.

s. 36, amended: 1980, c.55, s.25; 1985, c.73, sch.1; 1988, c.42, sch.1; repealed in pt.: 1980, c.55, s.25; 1988, c.42, sch.1.

s. 37, amended: 1985, c.73, sch.1.

s. 38, amended: ibid.; 1988, c.42, sch.1.

s. 39, amended: 1985, c.73, sch.1.

s. 39A, added: 1988, c.42, sch.1.

s. 40, amended: 1985, c.73, sch.1; 1988, c.42, sch.1.

s. 41, amended: 1985, c.73, sch.1; repealed in pt.: 1988, c.42, schs.1,2.

s. 42, amended: 1980, c.55, s.25; 1985, c.73, sch.1; repealed in pt.: 1988, c.42, sch.2.

ss. 42A, 42B, added: ibid., s.1.

s. 42C, added: ibid., s.2.

ss. 43–45, 47, amended: 1985, c.72, sch.1.

s. 48, repealed: ibid.

s. 51, amended: 1985, c.73, sch.1; 1986, c.47, sch.3; 1988, c.42, sch.1.

s. 52, amended: 1985, c.73, sch.1; 1988, c.42, sch.1.

s. 53, order 87/333.

s. 53, amended: 1980, c.55, s.24; 1985, c.71, sch.1; 1988, c.42, sch.1.

ss. 53A–53C, added: ibid., s.3.

s. 53D, added: ibid.

s. 54, amended: 1985, c.71, sch.1.

s. 57, see Chiene, Petr., 1984 S.L.T. 323.

CAP.

46. Solicitors (Scotland) Act 1980—*cont.*

s. 57, amended: 1988, c.42, sch.1; repealed in pt. *ibid.*, sch.2.

s. 60, repealed: *ibid.*

s. 61, amended: 1985, c.73, sch.1; 1988, c.42, sch.1.

s. 62A, added: 1985, c.73, sch.1.

s. 64, amended: *ibid.*

s. 65, amended: 1980, c.55, s.25; 1985, c.73, sch.1; 1988, c.42, s.5, sch.1; repealed in pt.: *ibid.*, sch.2.

sch. 1, amended: 1985, c.73, sch.1; 1988, c.42, sch.1; repealed in pt.: 1985, c.73, sch.4.

sch. 2, amended: 1988, c.42, sch.1; repealed in pt.: *ibid.*, sch.2.

sch. 3, amended: 1985, c.73, sch.1; repealed in pt.: *ibid.*, schs. 1,4.

sch. 4, amended: 1980, c.55, s.24; 1985, c.73, sch.1; 1988, c.42, sch.1.

sch. 6, amended: *ibid.*

47. Criminal Appeal (Northern Ireland) Act 1980.

Royal Assent, August 1, 1980.

s. 8, see *R.* v. *Ferguson* [1980] 11 N.I. J.B., C.A.

s. 10, amended: 1988, c.33, sch.15.

ss. 14, 25, see *R.* v. *Mullan* [1983] 12 N.I.J.B., C.A.; *R.* v. *McGrady* [1984] 8 N.I.J.B., C.A.

s. 16A, added: 1988, c.33, sch.15.

ss. 17, 18, substituted: *ibid.*

s. 28, see *Weir and Higgins Application, Re* [1986] 16 N.I.J.B. 46, Murray J.

ss. 28, 37, amended: order 82/159.

s. 29, see *R.* v. *Ellis* [1986] 10 N.I.J.B. 117, C.A.

ss. 44, 45, amended: 1988, c.33, sch.15.

sch. 1, amended: order 81/228.

sch. 4, repealed in pt.: order 82/159.

48. Finance Act 1980.

Royal Assent, August 1, 1980.

ss. 1, 2, 4 (in pt.), 5 (in pt.) repealed: 1981, c.35, sch.19.

s. 6, repealed: 1981, c.63, sch.7.

s. 7, repealed in pt.: *ibid.*; 1985, c.54, sch.27.

s. 8, repealed: 1981, c.35, sch.19.

s. 9, repealed: 1983, c.28, sch.10.

ss. 11–16, repealed: 1983, c.55, sch.11.

ss. 18–23, repealed: 1988, c.1, sch.31.

s. 24, orders 81/351; 82/320; 83/404; 84/344; 85/430; 86/529; 87/434; 88/503.

ss. 24–56, repealed: 1988, c.1, sch.31.

s. 47, orders 80/546.

s. 47, amended: 1988, c.39, s.89.

s. 57, repealed in pt.: 1985, c.54, sch.27; 1988, c.1, sch.31.

s. 58, repealed: 1984, c.43, sch.23.

ss. 69, 60, 61 (in pt.), 63, repealed: 1988, c.1, sch.31.

s. 64, order 84/2060.

s. 64, amended: 1986, c.41, s.57, sch.16; 1988, c.1, sch.29; repealed in pt.: 1986, c.41, sch.16.

s. 65, amended: 1985, c.54, sch.14; 1986, c.41, s.57, sch.16; 1981, c.1, sch.29; repealed in pt.: 1985, c.54, schs.14,27; 1986, c.41, sch.16.

ss. 66, 67, repealed: *ibid.*

CAP.

48. Finance Act 1980—*cont.*

s. 68, amended and repealed in pt.: *ibid.*

s. 69, amended: *ibid.*

s. 70, amended: 1988, c.1, sch.29; repealed in pt.: *ibid.*, sch.31.

s. 71, repealed: 1988, c.39, s.94, sch.14.

s. 73, amended: 1988, c.1, sch.29.

s. 74, amended: 1981, c.35, ss.74–76.

s. 77, repealed in pt. (prosp.): 1988, c.39, sch.14.

s. 79, amended: 1981, c.35, s.78; 1982, c.39, s.82; 1985, c.54, sch.70; 1986, c.41, s.101; repealed in pt.: 1982, c.39, s.82, sch.22.

s. 80, amended: 1984, c.43, ss.63,70.

s. 82, repealed in pt.: *ibid.*, sch.23.

s. 83, amended: *ibid.*, s.71.

s. 84, repealed in pt.: 1987, c.51, sch.9.

ss. 85–87, repealed: 1984, c.51, sch.9.

s. 88, repealed in pt.: 1984, c.51, sch.22; 1988, c.1, sch.31.

ss. 89–91, repealed: 1984, c.51, sch.22.

ss. 92, 93, repealed: *ibid.*, sch.9.

s. 94, regs. 81/880, 881 (S.), 1440, 1441; 83/1040 (S.), 1911.

s. 94, amended: 1981, c.54, sch.5; repealed in pt.: 1984, c.51, sch.9.

s. 95, repealed in pt.: 1984, c.43, sch.23.

s. 96, repealed: 1986, c.41, sch.23.

s. 97, amended: 1981, c.35, s.108; 1985, c.71, sch.2; 1987, c.16, s.54; 1988, c.39, s.142; repealed in pt : 1985, c.71, sch.1.

s. 98, amended: 1982, c.39, s.131; 1984, c.51, sch.8.

s. 99, repealed: 1985, c.54, sch.27.

s. 100, repealed: 1986, c.41, sch.23.

s. 101, amended: 1988, c.39, sch.13.

s. 105, repealed: 1982, c.39, sch.22.

s. 107, amended: 1988, c.1, sch.29; repealed in pt.: 1983, c.56, sch.6.

s. 108, regs. 82/92,1858.

s. 108, amended: 1988, c.1, sch.29.

s. 109, repealed: *ibid.*, sch.31; amended: 1988, c.33, sch.13.

ss. 110–116, repealed: 1985, c.54, sch.27.

s. 117, see *Combined Technologies Corp.* v. *I.R.C.* [1985] S.T.C. 348, Vinelott J.

s. 118, amended: 1988, c.1, sch.29; repealed in pt.: 1982, c.39, sch.22; 1984, c.43, sch.23; c.51, sch.9; 1985, c.54, sch.27; 1988, c.1, sch.31.

ss. 119, 121, repealed: *ibid.*

s. 122, amended: *ibid.*, sch.29; repealed in pt.: 1984, c.51, sch.9.

schs. 1–4, repealed: 1981, c.35, sch.19.

sch. 5, repealed: 1981, c.63, sch.7.

sch. 6, repealed in pt.: *ibid.*; 1982, c.39, sch.22; 1985, c.54, sch.27.

sch. 7, repealed: 1981, c.35, sch.19.

schs. 8–11, repealed: 1988, c.1, sch.31.

sch. 12, amended: 1982, c.39, s.77; 1983, c.28, s.33; repealed in pt.: 1982, c.39, s.77; 1983, c.28, s.33, sch.10.

sch. 13, amended: 1981, c.35, s.73; repealed in pt.: *ibid.*, sch.19.

schs. 14, 15, repealed: 1984, c.51, sch.9.

CAP.

1980—cont.

48. Finance Act 1980—*cont.*
sch. 15, see *Combined Technologies Corp.* v. *I.R.C.* [1985] S.T.C. 348, Vinelott J.
sch. 16, repealed: 1982, c.39, sch.22.
sch. 17, amended: 1981, c.35, s.114; 1983, c.28, s.41, sch.8; c.56, sch.6; 1987, c.16, sch.13; 1988, c.1, sch.29.
sch. 18, amended: 1986, c.41, s.73; 1988, c.1, sch.29; repealed in pt.: 1985, c.54, sch.27; 1986, c.41, s.74, sch.23; 1988, c.1, sch.31.
sch. 20, amended: 1982, c.39, s.157.

49. Deer Act 1980.
Royal Assent, August 8, 1980.
s. 3, amended: 1982, c.19, sch.2.
s. 4, amended: 1984, c.60, sch.6; repealed in pt.: *ibid.*, sch.7.

50. Coal Industry Act 1980.
Royal Assent, August 8, 1980.
s. 2, amended: 1987, c.3, sch.1.
s. 3, order 84/1888.
s. 3, amended: 1982, c.15, s.2; 1983, c.60, s.2, order 84/1888.
s. 4, orders 81/1131; 82/966.
s. 4, repealed: 1983, c.60, s.2.
s. 5, repealed: *ibid.*, s.2, sch.
ss. 6, 10 (in pt.), repealed: 1987, c.3, sch.3.
s. 7, order 84/1889.
s. 7, repealed in pt.: 1983, c.60, sch.

51. Housing Act 1980.
Royal Assent, August 8, 1980.
order 81/119.
repealed (S.): 1987, c.26, sch.24.
see *R.* v. *Secretary of State for the Environment, ex p. Enfield London Borough Council, The Times,* April 5, 1988, McNeill J.
s. 1, see *R.* v. *Plymouth City Council and Cornwall County Council, ex p. Freeman* (1988) 28 R.V.R. 89, C.A.
Pt. I (ss. 1–27), repealed: 1985, c.71, sch.1.
s. 2, see *Wood* v. *South Western Co-operative Housing Society* (1982) 44 P. & C.R. 198, C.A.
s. 2, order 83/672.
ss. 2, 5, see *Enfield London Borough Council* v. *McKeon* [1986] 2 All E.R. 730, C.A.; *R.* v. *Plymouth City Council and Cornwall County Council, ex p. Freeman* (1988) 28 R.V.R. 89, C.A.
s. 7, order 80/1342.
s. 8, orders 84/1554; 85/1979.
s. 9, regs. 80/1423.
ss. 10, 11, 23, see *Norwich City Council* v. *Secretary of State for the Environment* [1982] 1 All E.R. 737, C.A.
ss. 10, 16, see *Enfield London Borough Council* v. *McKeon* [1986] 2 All E.R. 730, C.A.
s. 11, see *R.* v. *Plymouth City Council and Cornwall County Council, ex p. Freeman* (1988) 28 R.V.R. 89, C.A.
s. 16, see *Sutton London Borough Council* v. *Swann, The Times,* November 30, 1985, C.A.
s. 17, see *Sutton (Hastoe) Housing Association* v. *Williams* [1986] 16 E.G. 75, C.A.
s. 19, orders 80/1345, 1375; 81/397, 940; 82/21, 187.

CAP.

1980—cont.

51. Housing Act 1980—*cont.*
s. 19, amended: 1985, c.51, sch.14; order 85/1884.
s. 21, order 80/1390.
s. 22, see *Wansbeck District Council* v. *Charlton* (1981) 79 L.G.R. 523, C.A.
s. 22, orders 80/1391, 1620, 1930; 84/1175; 85/36.
s. 28, see *Clays Lane Housing Co-operative* v. *Patrick, The Times,* December 1, 1984, C.A.; *R.* v. *Plymouth City Council, ex p. Freeman* (1988) 28 R.V.R. 89, C.A.
s. 28, amended: 1984, c.29, s.36; 1985, c.51, sch.14; repealed in pt.: 1984, c.29, s.36, sch.12.
ss. 28, 32, see *Greenwich London Borough Council* v. *McGrady* (1983) 81 L.G.R. 288, C.A.
ss. 28, 33, 34, see *Harrison* v. *Hammersmith and Fulham Borough Council; Haringey London Borough Council* v. *Mosuer; Watson* v. *Hackney London Borough Council* [1981] 1 W.L.R. 650, C.A.
s. 30, see *Reading Borough Council* v. *Ilsley,* June 2, 1981, Judge Blomefield, Reading County Ct.; *Peabody Donation Fund Governors* v. *Grant* (1982) E.G. 925, C.A.; *Harrogate Borough Council* v. *Simpson* [1986] 2 F.S.R. 91, C.A.; *South Northamptonshire District Council* v. *Power* [1987] 1 W.L.R. 1433, C.A.
s. 31, amended: 1984, c.29, sch.11.
s. 33, see *Wansbeck District Council* v. *Charlton* (1981) 79 L.G.R. 523, C.A.; *South Buckinghamshire County Council* v. *Francis,* October 1, 1985, Slough County Ct., P. S. J. Langan Q.C.; *Torridge District Council* v. *Jones* (1985) 276 E.G. 1253, C.A.
s. 33, order 80/1339.
s. 34, see *Woodspring District Council* v. *Taylor, The Times,* May 15, 1982, C.A.; *Enfield London Borough Council* v. *French* (1985) 49 P. & C.R. 223, C.A.
s. 37, see *Peabody Donation Fund Governors* v. *Higgins* [1983] 3 All E.R. 122, C.A.
ss. 37, 37A, 37B, substituted 1984, c.29, s.26.
s. 39, amended: *ibid.*, s.27.
s. 40, see *Palmer* v. *Sandwell Metropolitan Borough* (1987) 284 E.G. 1487, C.A.
s. 41A, regs. 85/1493.
s. 41A, added: 1984, c.29, s.28.
s. 41B, added: *ibid.*, s.29.
s. 48, see *Harrison* v. *Hammersmith and Fulham Borough Council; Haringey London Borough Council* v. *Mosuer; Watson* v. *Hackney London Borough Council* [1981] 1 W.L.R. 650, C.A.; *Restormel Borough Council* v. *Buscombe* (1982) 12 Fam.Law 207, C.A.; *Kensington and Chelsea Royal Borough Council* v. *Hayden* (1984) 17 H.L.R. 114, C.A.
s. 50, see *Reading Borough Council* v. *Isley,* June 2, 1981, Judge Blomefield, Reading County Ct.; *Harrogate Borough Council* v. *Simpson* [1986] 2 F.S.R. 91, C.A.; *R.* v. *Plymouth City Council and Cornwall County Council, ex p. Freeman* (1988) 28 R.V.R. 89, C.A.

CAP.

1980—cont.

51. Housing Act 1980—cont.

s. 50, amended: 1984, c.29, sch.11; repealed in pt.: 1985, c.51, sch.17.

s. 52, see *Paterson* v. *Aggio* (1987) 284 E.G. 508, C.A.

s. 52, regs. 80/1707; 81/1578, 1579; order 87/265.

s. 52, repealed in pt.: 1988, c.50, sch.18.

s. 56, orders 80/1694; 81/590, 1009; 82/582, 850, 1016, 1229, 1481, 1551, 1638, 1815; 83/19, 88, 364, 511, 840, 1079, 1375, 1537, 1675, 1856; 84/276, 638, 1312, 1443, 1827; 85/812, 1311, 1312; 86/864, 866, 1208, 1209, 1729, 2240; 87/737, 822, 1164, 1525; 88/28, 919, 1240, 1646, 2018; regs 81/591.

ss. 56–58, repealed: 1988, c.50, sch.18.

s. 58, regs. 83/132.

s. 59, repealed in pt.: 1988, c.50, sch.18.

s. 60, order 87/264.

s. 60, repealed: 198, c.50, sch.18.

s. 65, see *Williams* v. *Mate* (1982) 263 E.G. 883; (1983) 46 P. & C.R. 43, C.A.; *Caldwell* v. *McAteer* (1984) 269 E.G. 1039, C.A.

s. 66, see *Bradshaw* v. *Baldwin-Wiseman, The Times,* January 24, 1985, C.A.

s. 73, see *Crown Estate Comrs.* v. *Wordsworth, The Times,* June 17, 1982, C.A.

ss. 73, 76, repealed in pt.: 1988, c.50, sch.18.

ss. 80, 81 (in pt.), 83 (in pt.), 85 (in pt.), repealed: 1985, c.71, sch.1.

s. 86, see *R.* v. *Plymouth City Council and Cornwall Couty Council, ex p. Freeman* (1988) 28 R.V.R. 89, C.A.

s. 86, amended: 1984, c.29, sch.11; 1985, c.71, sch. 2.

s. 87, repealed: *ibid.,* sch.1.

Pts. V–VIII (ss.90–133), repealed: *ibid.*

ss. 105, 108, repealed in pt.: 1985, c.51, sch. 17.

s. 106, order 82/1039.

s. 108, order 81/723.

ss. 110, 111, amended: 1985, c.51, sch.14; repealed in pt.: *ibid.,* sch.17.

s. 118, order 81/297.

Pt. VIII (ss.120–133), repealed (S.): 1985, c.71, sch.1.

s. 124, orders 82/828; 83/112; 84/1833.

s. 130, order 81/722; 84/1803.

ss. 134–137, repealed: 1985, c.71, sch. 1.

s. 136, see *Sutton (Hastoe) Housing Association* v. *Williams* [1986] 16 E.G. 75, C.A.

s. 139, repealed: 1985, c.71, sch.1.

s. 140, regs. 82/62.

s. 140, repealed: 1986, c.63, schs.4, 12.

ss. 144–149, 149, 150 (in pt.), repealed: 1985, c.71, sch.1.

s. 147, see *Berg* v. *Trafford Borough Council, The Times,* July 14, 1987, C.A.

s. 147, order 81/1576.

s. 151, see *Wansbeck District Council* v. *Charlton* (1981) 79 L.G.R. 523, C.A.

s. 151, orders 80/1339, 1342, 1345, 1375, 1390, 1391, 1406, 1407, 1423, 1466, 1557, 1620, 1693, 1694, 1706, 1707, 1781; 81/119, 296, 297, 397, 590, 722, 723, 940, 1009, 1578,

CAP.

1980—cont.

51. Housing Act 1980—cont.

1579; 82/21, 187, 582, 850, 1016, 1039, 1229, 1481, 1551, 1638, 1815; 83/19, 88, 207, 364, 511, 672, 840, 1079, 1375, 1537, 1675, 1856; 84/1173, 1803, 1833; regs. 80/1930; 81/591; 84/1175; 85/36; 87/264.

s. 151, amended: 1984, c.29, sch.11; repealed in pt.: 1985, c.71, sch.1.

s. 153, orders, 80/1406, 1466, 1557, 1693, 1706, 1781; 81/119, 296.

ss. 153, 154, repealed in pt.: 1985, c.71, sch.1.

s. 155, amended: order 83/1122.

s. 158, order 80/1693.

sch. 1, see *Freeman* v. *Wansbeck District Council* (1984) 82 L.G.R. 131, C.A.; *Campbell* v. *City of Edinburgh District Council,* Second Division, February 7, 1986; *Enfield London Borough Council* v. *McKeon* [1986] 2 All E.R. 730, C.A.; *Dyer* v. *Dorset County Council* [1988] 3 W.L.R. 213, C.A.; *R.* v. *Plymouth City Council and Cornwall County Council, ex p. Freeman* (1988) 28 R.V.R. 89, C.A.

sch. 1, amended: 1985, c.51, sch.14; order 85/1884; 1986, c.65, sch.1; repealed: 1985, c.71, sch.1; repealed in pt.: 1986, c.65, s.10.

schs. 1–4A, repealed: 1985, c.71, sch.1.

sch. 1A, order 84/1173.

sch. 1A, amended: 1985, c.51, sch.14; order 85/1884; repealed: 1985, c.71, sch.1.

sch. 2, see *Charing Cross and Kelvingrove Housing Association* v. *Kraska,* 1986 S.L.T.(Sh.Ct.) 42; *Sutton (Hastoe) Housing Association* v. *Williams* [1988] 16 E.G. 75, C.A.

sch. 2, amended: 1986, c.65, s.11, schs.1,3; repealed: 1985, c.71, sch.1.

sch. 3, see *Eastleigh Borough Council* v. *Walsh* [1985] 2 All E.R. 112, H.L.; *Kensington and Chelsea Royal Borough Council* v. *Hayden* (1984) 17 H.L.R. 114, C.A.; *South Holland District Council* v. *Keyte* (1985) 19 H.L.R. 97, C.A.

sch. 3, order 80/1407.

sch. 3, repealed: 1985, c.71, sch.1.

sch. 4, see *Enfield London Borough Council* v. *French, The Times,* January 2, 1985; (1985) 49 P. & C.R. 223, C.A.; *Enfield London Borough Council* v. *McKeon* [1986] 2 All E.R. 730, C.A.

sch. 5, amended: 1980, c.65, sch.33; 1986, c.63, s.13.

sch. 7, see *Bradshaw* v. *Baldwin-Wiseman, The Times,* January 24, 1985, C.A.

sch. 8, see *Crown Estate Commissioners* v. *Connor and the London Rent Assessment Panel* (1986) 19 H.L.R. 35, McCowan J.

sch. 9, amended: 1985, c.71, sch.2; repealed in pt.: 1988, c.50, sch.18.

sch. 10, repealed in pt.: 1985, c.71, sch.1.

schs. 11–13, repealed: *ibid.,* sch.1.

sch. 14, repealed: 1982, c.39, sch.22.

sch. 15, repealed: 1982, c.24, sch.5.

sch. 16, amended: 1985, c.9, sch.2; repealed in pt. (S.): 1985, c.71, sch.1.

schs. 16–20, repealed: *ibid.*

schs. 17 (in pt.), 18, repealed (S.): *ibid.*

CAP.

1980—cont.

51. Housing Act 1980—cont.

sch. 19, amended: 1985, c.9, sch. 2; c.51, sch. 14.

sch. 21, see *Duke of Westminster* v. *Oddy* (1984) 270 E.G. 945, C.A.

schs. 23, 24, repealed: 1985, c.71, sch.1.

sch. 24, see *Berg* v. *Trafford Borough Council, The Times,* July 14, 1987, C.A.

sch. 24, order 81/1576.

sch. 25, repealed in pt.: 1981, c.24, sch.3; c.54, sch.7; 1983, c.19, sch.3; 1985, c.71, sch.1; 1988, c.50, sch.18.

sch. 25, repealed in pt. (S.): 1985, c.71, sch.1.

52. Tenants' Rights, etc. (Scotland) Act 1980.

Royal Assent, August 8, 1980.

Pts. I–III (ss.1–32), V (ss.66–81), except s.74, VI (ss.82–86), except s.86, schs. A1, 1–4, repealed: 1987, c.26, sch. 24.

s. 1, see *Kinghorn* v. *City of Glasgow District Council,* 1984 S.L.T. (Lands Tr.) 9; *Graham* v. *Motherwell District Council; Robertson* v. *The Same,* 1985 S.L.T.(Lands Tr.) 44; *Murdoch* v. *Gordon District Council,* 1985 S.L.T.(Lands Tr.) 42; *Docherty* v. *City of Edinburgh District Council,* 1985 S.L.T.(Lands Tr.) 61; *Motherwell District Council* v. *Gliori,* 1986 S.L.T. 444; *Campbell* v. *City of Edinburgh District Council,* 1987 S.L.T. 51; *McGroarty* v. *Stirling District Council* (O.H.), 1987 S.L.T. 85.

s. 1, order 86/2140.

ss. 1, 3, see *McDonald* v. *Renfrew District Council,* 1982 S.L.T.(Lands Tr.) 30; *Fraser* v. *City of Glasgow District Council,* 1982 S.L.T.(Lands Tr.) 46; *Hill* v. *Orkney Islands Council,* 1983 S.L.T.(Lands Tr.) 2.

ss. 1, 3, 4, see *Crilly* v. *Motherwell District Council,* 1908 S.L.T.(Lands Tr.) 7.

ss. 1, 7, see *Thomson* v. *City of Edinburgh District Council,* 1982 S.L.T.(Lands Tr.) 39.

s. 1A, order 81/1860.

s. 2, see *Neave* v. *City of Dundee District Council,* 1986 S.L.T. (Lands Tr.) 18; *McGroarty* v. *Stirling District Council* (O.H.), 1987 S.L.T. 85; *Hannan* v. *Falkirk District Council,* 1987 S.L.T. (Lands Tr.) 18.

s. 2, orders 80/1388; 84/1005; 86/2140.

ss. 2, 3, see *Stevenson* v. *West Lothian District Council,* 1985 S.L.T.(Lands Tr.) 9.

ss. 2, 4, see *Keay* v. *Renfrew District Council,* 1982 S.L.T.(Lands Tr.) 33; *MacLeod* v. *Ross and Cromarty District Council,* 1983 S.L.T. (Lands Tr.) 5; *Pollock* v. *Dumbarton District Council,* 1983 S.L.T.(Lands Tr.) 17.

ss. 2, 7, see *Fullerton* v. *Monklands District Council,* 1983 S.L.T.(Lands Tr.)15; *Thomson* v. *Stirling District Council,* 1985 S.L.T.(Lands Tr.) 4.

s. 3, see *Douglas* v. *Falkirk District Council.* 1983 S.L.T.(Lands Tr.) 21.; *Thomson* v. *City of Glasgow District Council,* 1986 S.L.T. (Lands Tr.) 6.

s. 4, see *Popescu* v. *Banff and Buchan District Council,* 1987 S.L.T. (Lands Tr.) 20; *Morrison* v. *Stirling District Council,* 1987 S.L.T. (Lands Tr.) 22.

CAP.

1980—cont.

52. Tenants' Rights, etc. (Scotland) Act 1980—cont.

s. 5, orders 80/1430, 1492.

s. 7, see *Murdoch* v. *Gordon District Council,* 1985 S.L.T.(Lands Tr.) 42; *Neave* v. *City of Dundee District Council,* 1986 S.L.T. (Lands Tr.) 18; *Hannan* v. *Falkirk District Council,* 1987 S.L.T. (Lands Tr.) 18.

s. 8, see *McGroarty* v. *Stirling District Council* (O.H.), 1987 S.L.T. 85.

s. 10, see *Hill* v. *Orkney Islands Council,* 1983, S.L.T.(Lands Tr.) 2; *Douglas* v. *Falkirk District Council,* 1983 S.L.T.(Lands Tr.) 21; *Kinghorn* v. *City of Glasgow District Council,* 1984 S.L.T. (Lands Tr.) 9; *Docherty* v. *City of Edinburgh District Council,* 1985 S.L.T.(Lands Tr.) 61; *Campbell* v. *City of Edinburgh District Council,* 1987 S.L.T. 51; *Thomson* v. *City of Glasgow District Council,* 1986 S.L.T. (Lands Tr.) 6.

ss. 12, 14, see *Monklands District Council* v. *Johnstone* (Sh.Ct.), 1987 S.C.L.R. 480.

ss. 12, 14, 15, see *Charing Cross and Kelvingrove Housing Association* v. *Kraska,* 1986 S.L.T.(Sh.Ct.) 42.

s. 14, see *City of Edinburgh District Council* v. *Davis,* 1987 S.L.T. (Sh.Ct.) 33.

s. 14, order 80/1389.

s. 15, see *Scottish Special Housing Association* v. *Lumsden,* 1984 S.L.T.(Sh.Ct.) 71; *City of Glasgow District Council* v. *Brown* (Sh.Ct.), 1988 S.C.L.R. 433.

s. 19, order 82/981.

s. 31, order 87/1388.

s. 34, order 80/1666.

ss. 34–36, 37 (in pt.), repealed: 1984, c.58, sch.10.

s. 37, order 80/1664.

ss. 38, 40, 41 (in pt.), 42–45, repealed in pt.: 1984, c.58, sch.10.

s. 46, amended: *ibid.,* sch.8; repealed in pt.: *ibid.,* sch.10.

s. 47, see *Western Heritable Investment Co.* v. *Husband, The Times,* August 10, 1983, H.L.

ss. 47, 48, 49 (in pt.), 50–63, 64 (in pt.): repealed: 1984, c.58, sch.10.

s. 52, regs. 82/259.

ss. 63, 65, amended: 1980, c.61, s.2.

s. 82, see *Thomson* v. *City of Glasgow District Council,* 1986 S.L.T. (Lands Tr.) 6; *Neave* v. *City of Dundee District Council,* 1986 S.L.T. (Lands Tr.) 18; *Hannan* v. *Falkirk District Council,* 1987 S.L.T. (Lands Tr.) 18.

s. 86, order 80/1387.

sch. 1, see *Douglas* v. *Falkirk District Council,* 1983 S.L.T.(Lands Tr.) 21; *Kinghorn* v. *City of Glasgow District Council,* 1984 S.L.T. (Lands Tr.) 9; *Stevenson* v. *West Lothian District Council,* 1985 S.L.T.(Lands Tr.) 9; *Docherty* v. *City of Edinburgh District Council,* 1985 S.L.T.(Lands Tr.) 61; *Campbell* v. *City of Edinburgh District Council* 1987 S.L.T. 51; *Barron* v. *Borders Regional Council,* 1987 S.L.T. (Lands Tr.) 36; *Campbell* v. *Western Islands Council,* 1988 S.L.T.(Lands Tr.) 4; *Burns* v.

CAP.

1980—cont.

52. Tenants' Rights, etc. (Scotland) Act 1980—cont.
Central Regional Council, 1988 S.L.T.(Lands Tr.) 46.
sch. 2, see *Scottish Special Housing Association* v. *Lumsden,* 1984 S.L.T.(Sh.Ct.) 71; *City of Glasgow District Council* v. *Brown* (Sh.Ct.), 1988 S.C.L.R. 433.

53. Health Services Act 1980.
Royal Assent, August 8, 1980.
Commencement order: 83/303.
s. 1, orders 82/288; 85/305.
ss. 1 (in pt.), 2, repealed: 1984, c.48, sch.8.
s. 4, repealed: 1983, c.41, sch.10.
s. 6, see *R.* v. *Hillingdon Health Authority, ex p. Goodwin, The Times,* December 13, 1983,Woolf J.
ss. 10, 11, repealed: 1988, c.49, sch.3.
s. 16, repealed in pt.: 1984, c.23, sch.3.
s. 17, repealed: 1988, c.49, sch.3.
s. 18, repealed: 1984, c.48, sch.8.
s. 19, repealed: 1988, c.49, sch.3.
s. 21, repealed in pt.: 1986, c.66, s.8.
s. 26, orders 80/1257; 81/306, 884; 83/303.
ss. 53, 64, order 84/1169.
sch. 1, repealed in pt.: 1982, c.51, sch.4; 1983, c.20, sch.4; c.41, sch.10; 1984, c.22, sch.3; c.23, sch.3; c.48, sch.8; order 85/39; 1986, c.66, s.8; 1988, c.54, sch.1.
sch. 4, repealed in pt.: 1984, c.23, sch.3.
sch. 5, repealed in pt.: 1984, c.48, sch.8.

54. Appropriation Act 1980.
Royal Assent, August 8, 1980.
repealed: 1982, c.40, sch.(C.)

55. Law Reform (Miscellaneous Provisions) (Scotland) Act 1980.
Royal Assent, October 29, 1980.
s. 1, see *H.M. Advocate* v. *Leslie,* 1985 S.C.C.R. 1.
s. 1, repealed in pt.: 1988, c.36, sch.2.
s. 2, repealed in pt.: S.L.R. 1986.
s. 6, see *MacMillan, Petr.,* 1987 S.L.T. (Sh.Ct.) 50.
s. 12, repealed: 1985, c.66, sch.8.
s. 16, see *Butler* v. *Thom,* 1982 S.L.T.(Sh.Ct.) 57.
s. 17, order 80/1823.
s. 22, see *Saleh* v. *Saleh* (O.H.), 1987 S.L.T. 633.
s. 23, repealed in pt.: 1984, c.45, sch.2.
s. 25, repealed in pt.: 1988, c.42, sch.2.
s. 26, repealed: 1986, c.47, sch.5.
s. 29, order 80/1726.
sch. 1, amended: 1988, c.33, sch.9.

56. Married Women's Policies of Assurance (Scotland) (Amendment) Act 1980.
Royal Assent, October 29, 1980.

57. Imprisonment (Temporary Provisions) Act 1980.
Royal Assent, October 29, 1980.
Pt. I (ss. 1–5), continued in force: order 80/1822.
s. 5, repealed: 1982, c.48, s.32, sch.16.
s. 6, see *R.* v. *Commissioner of Police of the Metropolis, ex p. Nahar, The Times,* May 28, 1983, D.C.
s. 8, orders 80/1822, 1998; 81/96, 1358.

CAP.

1980—cont.

58. Limitation Act 1980.
Royal Assent, October 29, 1980.
see *Arnold* v. *Central Electricity Generating Board, The Times,* October 23, 1987, H.L.
s. 2, see *Sevcon* v. *Lucas Cav* [1986] 1 W.L.R. 462, H.L.; *Kitney* v. *Jones Land Wootton* [1988] 20 E.G. 88, Nolan J.
s. 4A, added: 1985, c.61, s.57.
s. 7, see *Agromet Motoimport* v. *Maulden Engineering Company (Beds.)* [1985] 2 All E.R. 436, Otton J.
s. 8, see *Collin* v. *Duke of Westminster* [1985] 1 All E.R. 463, C.A.
s. 11, see *Deerness* v. *John R. Keeble & Son (Brantham)* [1983] 2 Lloyd's Rep. 260, H.L.; *Conry* v. *Simpson* [1983] 3 All E.R. 369, C.A.; *Pattison* v. *Hobbs, The Times,* November 11, 1985, C.A.; *Wilkinson* v. *Ancliff (B.L.T.)* [1986] 1 W.L.R. 1352, C.A.
ss. 11, 14, see *Brooks* v. *J. & Coates (U.K.)* [1984] I.C.R. 158, Boreham J.; *Pilmore* v. *Northern Trawlers* [1986] 1 Lloyd's Rep. 552, Eastham J.
s. 11A, added: 1987, c.43, sch.1.
s. 12, amended: *ibid.*
s. 14, see *Cornish* v. *Kearley & Tonge* (1983) 133 New L.J. 870, Hirst J.; *Davis* v. *Ministry of Defence, The Times,* August 7, 1985, C.A.; *Fowell* v. *National Coal Board, The Times,* May 28, 1986, C.A.; *Bristow* v. *Grout, The Times,* November 3, 1986, Jupp J.; *Rule* v. *Atlas Stone Co.,* December 11, 1984, Simon Brown J.; *Wilkinson* v. *Ancliff (B.L.T.)* [1986] 1 W.L.R. 1352, C.A.; *Young* v. *G.L.C. and Massey,* December 19, 1986, Owen J.
s. 14, amended: 1987, c.43, sch.1.
ss. 14A, 14B, added: 1986, c.37, s.1.
s. 15, see *BP Properties* v. *Buckler* (1987) 284 E.G. 375, C.A.; *Boosey* v. *Davis* (1988) 55 P. & C.R. 83, C.A.
ss. 15, 17, see *Buckinghamshire County Council* v. *Moran* (1988) 86 L.G.R. 472, Hoffmann J.
ss. 21, 23, see *Att.-Gen.* v. *Cocke* [1988] 2 W.L.R. 542, Harman J.
s. 25, repealed: 1986, No. 3, s.4.
s. 28, amended: 1985, c.61, s.57; 1987, c.43, sch.1.
s. 28A, added: 1986, c.37, s.2.
s. 29, see *Amantilla* v. *Telefusion* (1987) 9 Con.L.R. 139, H.H. Judge Davies Q.C.
s. 32, see *Peco Arts Ltd.* v. *Hazlitt Gallery* [1983] 3 All E.R. 193, Webster J.; *UBAF* v. *European American Banking Corp.* [1984] 2 W.L.R. 508, C.A.
s. 32, amended: 1986, c.37, s.2; 1987, c.43, sch.1.
s. 32A, added: 1985, c.61, s.57.
s. 33, see *Deerness* v. *John R. Keeble & Son (Brantham)* [1983] 2 Lloyd's Rep. 260, H.L.; *Cornish* v. *Kearley & Tonge* (1983) 133 New L.J. 870, Hirst J.; *Conry* v. *Simpson* [1983] 3 All E.R. 369, C.A.; *Taylor* v. *Taylor, The Times,* April 14, 1984, D.C.; *Brooks* v. *J. & P. Coates (U.K.)* [1984] I.C.R. 158, Boreham J.; *Eastman* v. *London County Bus Services, The Times,*

CAP.

1980—cont.

58. Limitation Act 1980—cont.
November 23, 1985, C.A.; *Pilmore* v. *Northern Trawlers* [1986] 1 Lloyd's Rep. 552, Eastham J.; *Bradley* v. *Hanseatic Shipping* [1986] 2 Lloyd's Rep. 34, C.A.; *Rule* v. *Atlas Stone Co.*, December 11, 1984, Simon Brown J.; *Young* v. *G.L.C. and Massey*, December 19, 1986, Owen J.; *Lye* v. *Marks and Spencer, The Times*, February 15, 1988, C.A.
s. 33, amended: 1987, c.43, sch.1.
s. 35, see *Charles Barrett (Shopfitters)* v. *Marley Retail*, July 29, 1982, H.H.Judge Stabb, Q.C., sitting as a High Court Judge; *Sorata* v. *Gardex* [1984] F.S.R. 81, Falconer J.; *Grimsby Cold Stores* v. *Jenkins & Potter* (1985) Const.L.J. 362, C.A.; *Steamship Mutual Underwriting Association* v. *Trollope & Colls (City)* (1985) 2 Const.L.J. 75, H.H. Judge Newey, Q.C., O.R.; *Kenya Railways* v *Antares Pte., The Times*, February 12, 1987, C.A.; *Fannon* v. *Backhouse, The Times*, August 22, 1987, C.A.; *Birmingham City District Council* v. *Bryant (C.) & Son and Bison Concrete* (1987) 9 Con L.R. 128, H.H. Judge Davies Q.C.; *Kennett* v. *Brown* [1988] 1 W.L.R. 582, C.A.
s. 35, repealed in pt.: 1981, c.54, sch.7.
s. 36, amended: 1985, c.61, s.57.
s. 38, amended: 1982, c.51, sch.3; 1983, c.20, sch.4.
s. 41, order 81/588.
sch. 1, see *Buckinghamshire County Council* v. *Moran* (1988) 86 L.G.R. 472, Hoffmann J.

59. Statute Law Revision (Northern Ireland) Act 1980.
Royal Assent, November 13, 1980.

60. Civil Aviation Act 1980.
Royal Assent, November 13, 1980.
Commencement order: 83/1940.
s. 3, order 83/1939.
s. 4, amended: 1985, c.9, sch.2; order 88/1984; repealed in pt.: 1988, c.39, sch.14.
s. 5, amended: 1985, c.9, sch.2.
s. 6, see *H.M. Advocate* v. *Cafferty*, 1984 S.C.C.R. 444.
ss. 6, 7, transfer of functions: order 88/1984; amended: *ibid.*
s. 7, order 87/747.
s. 10, order 83/1940.
ss. 11–19, 21, 26, repealed: 1982, c.16, sch.16.
s. 12, order 81/671.
ss. 22, 23, repealed: 1982, c.36, sch.3.
ss. 24, 25, repealed: 1986, c.31, sch.6.
s. 30, orders 84/130–132, 355.

61. Tenants' Rights, etc. (Scotland) Amendment Act 1980.
Royal Assent, November 13, 1980.
repealed: 1987, c.26, sch.24.

62. Criminal Justice (Scotland) Act 1980.
Royal Assent, November 13, 1980.
Commencement orders: 81/1751; 83/1580.
s. 2, see *Cummings* v. *H.M. Advocate*, 1982 S.C.C.R. 108; *H.M. Advocate* v. *Mair*, 1982 S.L.T. 471; *Tonge* v. *H.M. Advocate*, 1982 S.L.T. 506; *Smith* v. *Dudgeon*, 1983 S.L.T. 324; *Wilson* v. *Robertson*, 1986 S.C.C.R. 700.

CAP.

1980—cont.

62. Criminal Justice (Scotland) Act 1980—cont.
s. 2, amended: 1987, c.41, sch.1.
s. 3, amended: 1985, c.73, s.35.
ss. 3A–3D, added: *ibid.*
s. 4, see *Burke* v. *Mackinnon*, 1983 S.L.T. 487.
s. 6, see *Walker* v. *H.M. Advocate*, 1985 S.C.C.R. 150.
s. 7, amended: 1982, c.48, sch.7; repealed in pt.: *ibid.*, sch.16; 1988, c.54, sch.1.
s. 8, repealed: 1982, c.48, sch.16.
s. 9, see *Low* v. *MacNeill*, 1981 S.C.C.R. 243; *Brady* v. *Lockhart*, 1985 S.C.C.R. 349; *Cirignaco, Petr.*, 1986 S.L.T.(Sh.Ct.) 11.
s. 9, amended: 1982, c.48, schs.6,7.
s. 10, see *Wilson* v. *Tudhope*, 1985 S.C.C.R. 339.
s. 10, repealed in pt.: 1986, c.47, sch.5.
s. 14, see *MacDougall* v. *Russell*, 1986 S.L.T. 403; *Sandford* v. *H.M. Advocate*, 1986 S.C.C.R. 573; *Grugen* v. *Jessop*, 1985 S.C.C.R. 182; *Lockhart* v. *Robb*, 1988 S.C.C.R. 381.
s. 18, see *Tudhope* v. *Gough*, 1982 S.C.C.R. 157.
s. 20, see *Tudhope* v. *Senatti Holdings*, 1984 S.C.C.R. 251.
s. 23, amended: 1987, c.41, s.61.
s. 25, see *Rollo* v. *Wilson*, 1988 S.L.T. 659.
s. 26, see *Smith* v. *Paterson*, 1982 S.L.T. 437; *Smith* v. *Allan*, 1985 S.L.T. 565; *Allan* v. *Taylor*, 1986 S.C.C.R. 202; *McMillan* v. *H.M. Advocate*, 1988 S.L.T. 211.
s. 26, repealed in pt.: 1988, c.54, sch.1.
s. 30, see *Campbell* v. *Allen*, 1988 S.C.C.R. 47.
s. 31, repealed: 1982, c.49, sch.6; 1984, c.27, sch.14.
s. 32, see *H.M. Advocate* v. *Lesacher*, 1982 S.C.C.R. 418; *Muirhead, Petr.*, High Court of Justiciary, March 18, 1983.
s. 37, see *Lord Advocate's Reference (No. 1 of 1985)*, 1987 S.L.T. 187.
s. 41, amended: 1987, c.41, sch.1; 1988, s.33, sch.9.
ss. 41, 45, see *Milligan* v. *Jessop*, 1988 S.C.C.R. 137.
s. 46, repealed in pt.: 1982, c.49, sch.16.
s. 55, repealed: 1988, c.54, sch.1.
s. 58, see *Stewart* v. *H.M. Advocate*, 1982 S.C.C.R. 203; *Carmichael* v. *Siddique*, 1985 S.C.C.R. 145.
ss. 58, 60, 66, see *Tudhope* v. *Furphy*, 1984 S.L.T.(Sh.Ct.) 33.
s. 59, amended: 1982, c.48, sch.7.
s. 68, orders 80/2030; 85/1224.
ss. 68, 69, amended: 1985, c.57, s.10.
s. 70A, added: 1986, c.64, sch.1.
s. 71, amended: *ibid.*
s. 72A, added: *ibid.*
s. 74, see *Barrett* v. *Allan*, 1986 S.C.C.R. 479.
s. 75, amended: 1986, c.64, sch.1; repealed in pt.: *ibid.*, sch.3.
s. 77, amended: 1985, c.57, s.10.
s. 78, see *Sillars* v. *Smith*, 1982 S.L.T. 539; *Black* v. *Allen*, 1985 S.C.C.R. 11; *MacDougall* v. *Yuk-Sun Ho*, 1985 S.C.C.R. 199.

1980—cont.

62. Criminal Justice (Scotland) Act 1980—*cont.*
s. 80, see *Glover* v. *Tudhope*, 1986 S.C.C.R. 49.
s. 80, repealed in pt.: 1984, c.36, sch.5.
s. 84, orders 81/50, 444, 766, 1751.
sch. 1, see *Allan* v. *Taylor*, 1986 S.C.C.R. 202.
sch. 1, amended: 1981, c.45, s.26; 1984, c.27, sch.13; c.39, s.20; 1987, c.41, sch.1; repealed in pt.: 1984, c.27, sch.14.
sch. 2, see *Sweeney* v. *X*, 1982, S.C.C.R. 509; *Green* v. *H.M. Advocate*, 1983 S.C.C.R. 42; *Moffat* v. *H.M. Advocate*, 1983 S.C.C.R. 121; *Morland* v. *H.M. Advocate*, 1985 S.C.C.R. 316; *King* v. *H.M. Advocate*, 1985 S.C.C.R. 322; *Allison* v. *H.M. Advocate*, 1985 S.C.C.R. 408; *Salusbury-Hughes* v. *H.M. Advocate*, 1987 S.C.C.R. 38; *McDonald* v. *H.M. Advocate*, 1987 S.C.C.R. 153; *Briggs* v. *Guild*, 1987 S.C.C.R. 141; *Jamieson* v. *H.M. Advocate*, 1987 S.C.C.R. 484; *Slater* v. *H.M. Advocate*, 1987 S.C.C.R. 745; *Williamson* v. *H.M. Advocate*, 1988 S.C.C.R. 56.
sch. 3, see *McLean* v. *Tudhope*, 1982 S.C.C.R. 555; *Galloway* v. *Hillary*, 1983 S.C.C.R. 119; *Aitchison* v. *Rizza*, 1985 S.C.C.R. 297; *Courtney* v. *Mackinnon*, 1986 S.C.C.R. 545; *McTaggart, Petr.*, 1987 S.C.C.R. 638; *Dickson* v. *Valentine*, 1988 S.C.C.R. 325.
sch. 4, see *H.M. Advocate* v. *Cafferty*, 1984 S.C.C.R. 444.
sch. 7, see *Donlon* v. *Mackinnon*, 1982 S.L.T. 93.
sch. 7, repealed in pt.: 1981, c.56, sch.12; 1982, c.48, sch.16; 1988, c.54, sch.1.
sch. 8, repealed in pt.: S.L.R. 1986.

63. Overseas Development and Co-operation Act 1980.
Royal Assent, November 13, 1980.
order 81/1504.
s. 2, amended: 1981, c.29, s.3; 1987, c.3, sch.1.
s. 4, orders 82/1288, 1798; 83/697, 816, 1297–1299, 1952; 84/30; 85/592, 1289; 86/1587, 2328; 87/1252; 88/906, 1486.
s. 6, orders 81/517; 88/750.
s. 7, order 86/286, amended: *ibid.*
s. 8, amended: 1983, c.29, s.4.
sch. 1, amended: 1981, c.29, s.3; c.38, sch.3; 1987, c.3, sch.1; repealed in pt.: 1983, c.41, schs.9,10; 1986, c.44, sch.9.

64. Broadcasting Act 1980.
Royal Assent, November 13, 1980.
order 80/1907.
repealed: 1981, c.68, sch.9.
s. 17, see *R.* v. *Broadcasting Complaints Commission, ex p. Owen, The Times*, January 26, 1985, D.C.
s. 41, orders 81/759, 1262, 1806, 1807.

65. Local Government, Planning and Land Act 1980.
Royal Assent, November 13, 1980.
Commencement orders: 80/1871, 1893, 2014; 81/194, 341, 1251, 1618; 82/317(S.40); 83/673; 84/1493.
see *R.* v. *Secretary of State for the Environment, ex p. Birmingham City Council, The Independent*, February 25, 1987, D.C.

1980—cont.

65. Local Government, Planning and Land Act 1980—*cont.*
s. 1, repealed in pt.: 1985, c.72, sch.13.
s. 2, see *ILEA* v. *Secretary of State for the Environment, The Times*, May 26, 1984, C.A.
s. 2, regs: 83/8, 615.
s. 2, amended: 1982, c.32, sch.5; 1985, c.51, sch.14; order 85/1884; 1988, c.41, sch.12; repealed in pt.: 1985, c.51, sch.17; 1988, c.40, sch.13 (prosp.); c.41, sch.12.
s. 3, order 81/764; regs. 83/8, 615.
s. 3, amended: 1984, c.33, sch.1.
s. 4, repealed in pt.: 1984, c.32, sch.7; 1985, c.67, sch.8.
s. 5, repealed in pt.: 1985, c.51, sch.14.
Pt. III (ss. 5–23), see *I.L.E.A.* v. *Department of the Environment, The Times*, April 14, 1983, Woolf J.
s. 6, repealed in pt.: 1988, c.9, schs.6,7.
ss. 7, 9, regs. 81/340; 82/318 (S.), 325, 1036; 83/685; 84/159; 87/181; 88/160, 956; amended: 1988, c.9, sch.6.
s. 10, regs. 81/339; order 82/319 (S.); amended: regs. 81/339; order 82/319 (S.); 1988, c.9, sch.6.
s. 13, amended: *ibid.*; repealed in pt.: *ibid.*, schs.6,7.
s. 14, amended: 1982, c.32, sch.5.
s. 16, repealed in pt.: 1985, c.51, sch.14.
s. 17, see *R.* v. *Secretary of State for the Environment, ex p. Hackney London Borough Council, The Independent*, July 19, 1988, D.C.
s. 18, amended: 1988, c.9, sch.6.
s. 19, repealed in pt.: *ibid.*, sch.7.
ss. 19A, 19B, added: *ibid.*, sch.6.
s. 20, see *Inner London Education Authority* v. *Department of the Environment* (1985) 83 L.G.R. 24, C.A.; *Wilkinson* v. *Doncaster Metropolitan District Council* (1986) 84 L.G.R. 257, C.A.
s. 20, amended: 1982, c.30, s.38; c.43, s.56 (S.); 1984, c.54, sch.9 (S.); 1985, c.51, sch.14; order 85/1884; 1988, c.9, sch.6; c.19, sch.3; repealed in pt.: 1985, c.51, sch.17; 1988, c.9, sch.7; c.40, sch.13 (prosp.).
s. 23, orders 81/341; 82/317 (S.).
s. 25, amended: 1983, c.23, sch.4; repealed in pt.: *ibid.*, sch.5.
s. 33, repealed in pt.: 1982, c.32, sch.6.
s. 34, repealed in pt.: 1984, c.33, sch.1.
s. 41, order 80/2015.
s. 45, repealed: 1982, c.24, sch.5.
ss. 45, 47, order 80/2014.
s. 47, repealed in pt.: 1985, c.71, sch.1.
ss. 48–50, see *R.* v. *Secretary of State for the Environment, ex p. Brent London Borough Council* [1982] 2 W.L.R. 693; [1983] 3 All E.R. 321, D.C.; *R.* v. *Secretary of State for the Environment, ex p. Hackney L.B.C. and Camden L.B.C.* (1984) 81 L.S.Gaz. 664, C.A.
ss. 49, 50, order 80/2047.
s. 51, orders 81/1770; 84/1863.
s. 53, order 82/208.
s. 53, amended: 1985, c.51, s.69; repealed in pt.: *ibid.*, s.69, sch.17.

1980—cont.

65. Local Government, Planning and Land Act 1980—cont.

s. 54, amended: 1982, c.24, sch.4; 1985, c.51, s.69; 1986, c.50, sch.10; 1987, c.6, sch.4; repealed in pt.: 1982, c.24, schs.4,5; 1985, c.71, sch.1; 1987, c.6, schs.4,5.

s. 55, amended: 1985, c.51, s.69; repealed in pt.: *ibid.*, sch.17.

s. 56, regs. 81/295; 84/85; 88/1951.

s. 56, amended: 1985, c.71, sch.16; 1987, c.6, sch.4; repealed in pt.: 1982, c.32, sch.6; 1985, c.71, sch.17; 1987, c.6, sch.5.

ss. 56, 59, see *Smith* v. *Skinner; Gladden* v. *McMahon* (1986) 26 R.V.R. 45, D.C.

s. 57, amended: 1986, c.54, sch.1.

s. 58, amended: 1987, c.6, sch.4.

s. 59, see *R.* v. *Secretary of State for the Environment, ex p. London Borough of Hackney, The Times,* May 11, 1985, C.A.; *Nottinghamshire County Council* v. *Secretary of State for the Environment; City of Bradford Metropolitan Council* v. *The Same* [1986] 2 W.L.R. 1, H.L.; *R.* v. *Secretary of State for the Environment, ex p. Hackney London Borough Council* (1986) 84 L.G.R. 32, C.A.; *R.* v. *Secretary of State for the Environment, ex p. Greenwich London Borough Council, The Times,* February 27, 1987, Taylor J.

s. 59, amended: 1982, c.32, s.8; 1985, c.51, s.69; 1986, c.54, sch.1; repealed in pt.: 1982, c.32, sch.6; 1985, c.51, s.69; 1986, c.54, schs.1,2.

ss. 59–62, see *R.* v. *Hackney London Borough Council, ex p. Fleming* (1986) 26 R.V.R. 182, Woolf J.

s. 60, see *R.* v. *Secretary of State for the Environment, ex p. Leicester City Council* (1985) 25 R.V.R. 31, Woolf J.

s. 60, amended: 1986, c.54, sch.1.

s. 61, amended: *ibid.*; repealed in pt.: 1988, c.41, s.126.

s. 62, repealed: 1987, c.5, s.1.

s. 63, see *R.* v. *Secretary of State for Education and Science, ex p. ILEA, The Times,* June 20, 1985, D.C.

s. 63A, added: 1985, c.51, s.83.

s. 64, repealed: 1982, c.32, sch.6.

s. 65, see *R.* v. *Hackney London Borough Council, ex p. Fleming* (1986) 26 R.V.R. 182, Woolf J.

s. 65, substituted: 1987, c.5, sch. 4.

s. 67, regs. 85/23.

s. 68, regs. 81/311.

s. 68, amended: 1985, c.51, s.69; repealed in pt.: 1985, c.71, sch.1; 1986, c.61, sch.4; 1987, c.5, sch.5.

s. 69, order 84/239.

s. 70, amended (S.): 1982, c.43, sch.3; repealed in pt. (S.): *ibid.*, schs.3,4.

s. 71, see *R.* v. *Greater London Council, ex p. London Residuary Body* (1987) 19 H.L.R. 175, Macpherson J.

s. 71, amended: 1985, c.51, sch.14; order 85/1884; 1988, c.4, sch.6; c.40, s.131; repealed in pt. (prosp.): *ibid.*, sch.13.

1980—cont.

65. Local Government, Planning and Land Act 1980—cont.

Pt. VIII (ss.71–85), see *R.* v. *Secretary of State for the Environment, ex p. Newham London Borough Council* (1987) 19 H.L.R. 298, C.A.

s. 72, amended: 1985, c.51, sch.14; 1988, c.4, sch.6; c.40, sch.12 (prosp.); c.50, s.136; repealed in pt.: 1986, c.31, sch.6.

ss. 72, 75, regs. 81/348; 82/302; 83/296; 84/223; 85/257; 87/351, 2186; 88/1534.

ss. 72, 78, see *Smith* v. *Skinner; Gladden* v. *McMahon* (1986) 26 R.V.R. 45, D.C.

s. 75, regs. 88/434.

s. 78, amended and repealed in pt.: 1987, c.44, sch.

s. 79, amended: *ibid.*

s. 79A, added: 1988, c.41, s.130.

s. 80, amended: 1982, c.32, sch.5; 1987, c.44, sch.; 1988, c.41, ss.131, 132; repealed in pt.: *ibid.*, s.131.

s. 80A, regs. 87/1583, 2186; 88/1534.

s. 80A, amended: 1988, c.41, s.131.

ss. 80A, 80B, added: 1987, c.44, s.1, sch.

s. 81, repealed: 1985, c.51, sch.17.

s. 82, amended: *ibid.*, sch.14; c.67, sch.3; 1987, c.44, sch.1; repealed in pt.: 1985, c.67, schs.3,8.

s. 84, regs. 81/348; 82/302; 83/296, 1191; 84/223; 85/257; 87/351, 1583, 2186; 88/434, 1534.

ss. 84, 85, functions transferred: order 81/238; amended: 1987, c.44, sch.

s. 86, order 80/1946.

s. 86, repealed in pt.: 1985, c.51, sch.17.

s. 87, regs. 81/369, 443 (S.); 82/716, 759(S.); 83/1674, 1697; 85/1180(S.), 1182; 87/101.

s. 88, repealed: 1986, c.63, sch.12.

s. 94, orders 81/194, 1251, 1618; 83/94; 84/1493.

s. 96A, added: 1988, c.9, sch.5.

s. 97, substituted: *ibid.*

s. 98, see *Manchester City Council* v. *Secretary of State for the Environment* (1987) 54 P. & C.R. 212, C.A.

s. 98, amended: 1988, c.9, sch.5.

s. 99, order 81/15.

s. 99, amended: 1985, c.51, sch.14; order 85/1884; 1988, c.9, sch.5; repealed in pt.: 1985, c.51, sch.17; 1988, c.40, sch.13 (prosp.).

s. 99A, added: 1988, c.9, sch.5.

s. 100, amended: 1985, c.9, sch.2.

s. 104, amended: 1981, c.67, sch.14; repealed in pt.: *ibid.*, sch.6.

s. 108, amended: 1987, c.3, sch.1; repealed in pt.: 1986, c.31, sch.4; c.44, sch.9.

s. 109, amended: 1981, c.67, sch.4.

s. 116, repealed in pt.: 1985, c.51, sch.17.

s. 117, repealed: 1982, c.42, sch.

s. 119, amended: 1982, c.30, s.35.

s. 120, amended: 1981, c.67, sch.4; 1987, c.3, sch.1; repealed in pt.: 1981, c.67, sch.6; 1986, c.31, sch.6; c.44, sch.9.

ss. 126–130, repealed: 1981, c.64, sch.13.

s. 133, repealed in pt.: *ibid.*

1980—cont.

65. Local Government, Planning and Land Act 1980—*cont.*

s. 134, regs. 88/1147, 1967.

s. 134, repealed in pt.: 1986, c.63, s.47, sch.12.

s. 134, repealed in pt. (S.); *ibid.*, sch.12.

ss. 134, 135, orders 81/481, 936, 937; 87/179, 646, 922–924; 88/1144–1146.

s. 136, see *London Docklands Corp.* v. *Rank Hovis* (1985) 84 L.G.R. 101, C.A.

s. 139, orders 88/1147, 1967.

s. 141, see *Mersey Docks and Harbour Co.* v. *Merseyside Development Corporation* (Ref./12/1983) (1987) 27 R.V.R. 97.

s. 141, orders 81/941, 942, 999–1003, 1145, 1146, 1719, 1720; 82/514; 88/1308–1313, 1315–1321.

s. 141, amended: 1981, c.66, sch.3; 1985, c.9, sch.2.

ss. 142, 143, amended: 1981, c.67, sch.4; repealed in pt.: *ibid.*, sch.6.

s. 144, amended: *ibid.*, sch. 4.

s. 148, orders 81/560, 1082; 87/738, 1343–1345; 88/1400.

s. 149, regs. 81/558; orders 81/561, 1081; 87/739, 1340–1342; 88/1399, 1551–1553, 1968.

s. 150, order 81/1082.

ss. 152, 153, amended: 1985, c.71, sch.2; 1987, c.26, sch.23 (S).

s. 154, amended: 1982, c.24, sch.4; 1986, c.50, sch.10.

s. 155, repealed in pt. (S.): 1984, c.58, sch.10.

s. 156, amended (S.): 1987, c.26, sch.23; repealed in pt.: 1984, c.29, sch.12; 1985, c.71, sch.1; 1986, c.63, schs.4,12.

s. 158, repealed in pt.: 1983, c.23, sch.5.

s. 159, order 81/560.

s. 159, amended: 1984, c.22, sch.2; 1987, c.3, sch.1; repealed in pt.: 1985, c.71, sch.1.

s. 165, repealed in pt.: 1985, c.51, sch.17.

s. 170, order 83/900.

s. 170, amended: 1985, c.9, sch.2; 1987, c.3, sch.1; repealed in pt.: 1986, c.31, sch.6; c.44, sch.9; 1988, c.35, sch.2.

s. 171, amended: 1981, c.67, sch.4.

s. 179, see *Addis* v. *Clement (Valuation Officer)* (1987) 85 L.G.R. 489, C.A.

s. 179, orders 81/757, 764, 852, 950, 975 (S.), 1024, 1025, 1069 (S.), 1070–1072; 82/462; 83/896, 1359; 83/1816, 1817.

s. 181, order 80/2017.

sch. 1, repealed in pt.: 1984, c.30, sch.11.

sch. 3, see *International Military Services* v. *Capital and Counties P.L.C.* [1982] 2 All E.R. 20, Slade J.

sch. 3, repealed in pt.: 1984, c.32, sch.7.

sch. 4, repealed in pt.: 1985, c.67, sch.3.

sch. 6, repealed in pt.: 1982, c.30, sch.7; 1985, c.71, sch.1.

sch. 7, amended: 1984, c.27, sch.13; repealed in pt.: 1980, c.66, sch.25; 1983, c.35, sch.2; 1984, c.27, sch.14.

sch. 10, see *R.* v. *Secretary of State for Education and Science, ex p. ILEA, The Times,* June 20, 1985, D.C.

1980—cont.

65. Local Government, Planning and Land Act 1980—*cont.*

sch. 10, regs. 81/304, 312, 1840; 82/267, 304; 83/238, 261, 310; 84/224, 284; 85/2030; 86/314; 87/347, 359; 88/1563.

sch. 10, amended: 1986, c.61, sch.4; 1987, c.44, s.2; repealed in pt.: *ibid.*; 1988, c.40, sch.13.

sch. 11, repealed: 1982, c.32, sch.6.

sch. 12, see *R.* v. *Greater London Council, ex p. London Residuary Body* (1987) 19 H.L.R. 175, Macpherson J.

sch. 12, regs. 81/348; 82/302; 83/1191; 84/223; 87/351; 88/1534.

sch. 12, amended: 1985, c.71, sch.2; 1988, c.41, s.132; repealed in pt.: *ibid.*

sch. 13, repealed in pt.: 1985, c.51, sch.17.

sch. 14, repealed in pt.: 1982, c.30, sch.7; 1985, c.51, sch.17; 1986, c.63, sch.12.

sch. 15, repealed in pt.: 1985, c.51, sch.17; 1986, c.63, sch.12.

sch. 16, amended: 1981, c.38, sch.3; 1985, c.51, sch.14; order 85/1884; 1987, c.3, sch.1; 1988, c.50, sch.17; repealed in pt.: 1985, c.51, sch.17; 1986, c.31, sch.6, c.44, sch.9; 1988, c.35, sch.2; c.40, sch.13 (prosp.).

sch. 17, order 83/673.

sch. 17, repealed in pt.: 1981, c.67, sch.6.

sch. 19, repealed in pt.: 1986, c.44, sch.9.

sch. 20, amended: 1981, c.67, sch.4; repealed in pt.: *ibid.*, sch.6.

sch. 21, regs. 80/1856.

sch. 21, amended: 1981, c.67, sch.4; 1983, c.29, s.4, sch.2; repealed in pt.: 1981, c.67, sch.6.

sch. 22, regs. 84/2048.

sch. 23, repealed in pt.: 1981, c.67, sch.6.

sch. 25, repealed in pt.: 1981, c.64, sch.13.

sch. 26, orders 81/481, 936; 87/179, 646, 922–924; 88/1144–1146.

sch. 27, see *Mersey Docks and Harbour Co.* v. *Merseyside Development Corporation* (Ref./12/1983) (1987) 27 R.V.R. 97.

sch. 27, repealed in pt.: 1981, c.66, sch.5; 1985, c.71, sch.1.

sch. 28, amended: 1981, c.38, sch.3; 1984, c.12, sch.4; c.58, sch.8 (S.); 1988, c.43, sch.9; c.50, sch.17; repealed in pt.: 1981, c.67, sch.6.

sch. 29, repealed in pt.: 1986, c.63, sch.12.

sch. 30, repealed in pt. (S.): *ibid.*

sch. 31, orders 84/35; 87/1238.

sch. 31, amended: 1983, c.29, s.4, sch.2; 1985, c.5, s.12; c.9, sch.2; 1987, c.57, s.1.

sch. 32, see *Addis* v. *Clement (Valuation Officer)* (1987) 85 L.G.R. 489, C.A.

sch. 32, orders 81/757, 764, 852, 950, 975(S.), 1024, 1025, 1069(S.), 1070–1072, 1378; 82/462; 83/896, 907, 1007, 1304, 1305, 1331, 1359, 1452, 1473, 1639, 1816, 1817, 1852; 84/347, 443, 444, 1403; 85/137; 86/1557.

sch. 32, amended: 1982, c.32, s.6; c.43, sch.3 (S.); 1986, c.63, s.54; 1987, c.47, sch.1 (S.); repealed in pt.: 1985, c.71, sch.1.

1980—cont.

65. Local Government, Planning and Land Act 1980—*cont.*

sch. 33, see *Cardshops* v. *John Lewis Properties* [1982] 3 W.L.R. 803, C.A.; *Sperry* v. *Hambro Life Assurance* (1983) 265 E.G. 233, Goulding J.

sch. 33, repealed in pt.: 1985, c.71, sch.1.

66. Highways Act 1980.

Royal Assent, November 13, 1980.

s. 1, amended: 1985, c.51, sch. 4; repealed in pt: *ibid.*, sch. 17.

ss. 2, 4, amended: *ibid.*, sch. 4.

s. 6, amended: *ibid.*: repealed in pt.: *ibid.*, schs. 4, 17.

s. 7, repealed: *ibid.*, sch. 17.

s. 8, amended: *ibid.*, sch. 4.

s. 9, amended: 1982, c.49, sch.5.

s. 10, see *R.* v. *Secretary of State for the Environment, ex p. Binney, The Times,* October 8, 1983, Webster J.; *Burton* v. *Secretary of State for Transport, The Times,* February 12, 1988, C.A.

ss. 11 (in pt.), 15, 18 (in pt.), repealed: *ibid.*, sch.17.

s. 16, schemes 86/1646; 87/1429.

s. 20, amended: 1981, c.38, sch.3; 1985, c.51, sch.4; repealed in pt.: 1984, c.12, sch.4.

s. 24, repealed in pt.: 1985, c.12, sch.17.

s. 25, amended: 1981, c.69, s.64; repealed in pt.: 1985, c.51, sch.17.

ss. 26, 28, regs. 83/23.

s. 31, see *R.* v. *Secretary of State for the Environment, ex p. Blake* [1984] J.P.L. 101, Walton J.; *Gloucestershire County Council* v. *Farrow* [1985] 1 All E.R. 878, C.A.

s. 31, amended: 1981, c.69, s.72; 1985, c.51, sch.4; repealed in pt.: 1981, c.69, s.72, sch.17.

s. 34, amended: 1985, c.51, sch.4.

s. 35, amended: 1981, c.38, sch.3; 1984, c.12, sch.4; 1985, c.51, sch.4.

s. 36, amended: *ibid.*, c.71, sch.2.

s. 38, repealed in pt.: 1985, c.51, sch.17.

s. 39, repealed: S.L.R. 1986.

s. 40, amended: 1985, c.51, sch.4.

s. 42, amended: 1984, c.27, sch.13; 1985, c.51, sch.4.

ss. 43, 50, amended: *ibid.*

s. 52, amended: 1982, c.49, sch.5.

s. 59, amended: 1982, c.53, sch.3.

s. 60, amended: 1984, c.27, sch.13.

s. 61, amended: 1985, c.51, sch.4.

s. 62, amended: 1981, c.56, sch.10; repealed in pt.: 1985, c.51, sch.17.

s. 64, amended: *ibid.*, sch.4; repealed in pt.: *ibid.*, sch.17.

s. 66, amended: *ibid.*, sch.4.

ss. 67, 69, repealed in pt.: *ibid.*, sch.17.

s. 79, amended: *ibid.*, sch.4; repealed in pt.: *ibid.*, sch.17.

s. 80, amended: 1981, c.69, s.72; 1985, c.51, sch.4; repealed in pt.: *ibid.*, sch.17.

s. 82, amended: 1982, c.49, sch.5.

ss. 90A–90F, added: 1981, c.56, sch.10.

1980—cont.

66. Highways Act 1980—*cont.*

ss. 90A, 90B, repealed in pt.: 1985, c.51, sch.17.

s. 90C, regs. 83/1087; 86/1858.

s. 90D, regs. 83/1087.

s. 90F, amended: 1984, c.27, sch.13.

s. 95, amended: 1985, c.51, sch.4; repealed in pt.: *ibid.*, sch.17.

s. 100, amended: *ibid.*, sch.4.

s. 105A, added: regs. 88/1241.

s. 106, instruments 81/291, 1073, 1881; 82/585, 649, 952, 1003, 1035, 1443; 83/1658, 1786; 84/11, 25, 696, 700, 874, 1341, 1373, 1432, 1591, 1626, 1646, 1743, 1864; 85/731, 1429; 87/251, 1954, 2241; orders 84/1381, 1476.

s. 113, repealed in pt.: 1984, c.55, sch.7.

s. 114, amended: 1985, c.51, sch.4; repealed in pt.: 1984, c.55, sch.7.

s. 115, amended: 1984, c.27, sch.13; 1988, c.54, sch.3.

s. 115A, amended: 1984, c.27, sch.13.

ss. 115A–115K, added: 1982, c.30, sch.5.

s. 115D, amended: 1984, c.12, sch.4.

s. 115H, amended: 1984, c.66, sch.6; 1985, c.51, sch.4; repealed in pt.: *ibid.*, sch.17.

s. 115J, amended: 1984, c.66, sch.6.

s. 116, see *Gravesham Borough Council* v. *Wilson and Straight* [1983] J.P.L. 607, Woolf J.

s. 116, amended: 1985, c.51, sch.4; repealed in pt.: *ibid.*, sch.17.

s. 117, repealed in pt.: *ibid.*

ss. 118–121, regs. 83/23.

s. 119, see *Lake District Special Planning Board, ex p. Bernstein, The Times,* February 3, 1982, Hodgson J.

s. 119, amended: 1981, c.69, sch.16.

s. 131, see *Greenwich London Borough Council* v. *Millcroft Construction* (1987) 85 L.G.R. 66, D.C.

s. 134, amended: 1981, c.69, s.61; 1985, c.51, sch.4; repealed in pt.: 1981, c.69, s.61, sch.17.

s. 135, amended: *ibid.*, s.61; 1986, c.49, s.21; repealed in pt.: 1981, c.69, s.16, sch.17.

s. 136, amended: *ibid.*, s.72.

s. 137, see *R.* v. *Bierton* [1983] Crim. L.R. 392, Southwark Crown Ct.; *Waite* v. *Taylor* (1985) 82 L.S.Gaz. 1092, D.C.; *Cooper* v. *Metropolitan Police Comr.* (1986) 82 Cr.App.R. 238, D.C.; *Hertfordshire County Council* v. *Bolden, The Times,* December 9, 1986, D.C.; *Pugh* v. *Pidgen; Same* v. *Powley, The Times,* April 2, 1987, D.C.; *Hirst and Agu* v. *Chief Constable of West Yorkshire* [1987] Crim.L.R. 330; (1987) 85 Cr.App.R. 143, D.C.

s. 137, repealed in pt.: 1984, c.60, sch.7.

s. 139, see *Craddock* v. *Green* [1983] R.T.R. 479, D.C.: *Marco (Croydon) trading as A. & J. Bull Containers* v. *Metropolitan Police* [1984] R.T.R. 24, D.C.

s. 139, regs. 84/1933.

s. 139, amended: 1982, c.49, s.65.

s. 140, see *R.* v. *Worthing Magistrates, ex p. Waste Management, The Times,* February 16, 1988, D.C.

1980—cont.

66. Highways Act 1980—cont.

s. 142, amended: 1981, c.38, sch.3; 1984, c.12, sch.4.

s. 143, see *R.* v. *Welwyn Hatfield District Council, ex p. Brinkley* (1982) 80 L.G.R. 727; [1983] J.P.L. 378, Forbes J.

s. 143, amended: 1985, c.51, sch.4.

s. 144, amended: 1981, c.38, sch.3; 1984, c.12, sch.4; repealed in pt.: *ibid.*, schs.4,7; 1985, c.51, sch.4.

ss. 146, 147, amended: *ibid.*, sch.4.

s. 147A, added: 1982, c.30, s.23.

s. 148, see *Putnam* v. *Colvin* [1984] R.T.R. 150, D.C.

s. 151, amended: 1985, c.51, sch.4; repealed in pt.: *ibid.*, sch.17.

s. 154, amended: *ibid.*, sch.4.

s. 155, see *D.P.P.* v. *Turton, The Guardian*, June 8, 1988, D.C.

s. 156, amended: 1984, c.12, sch.4; 1985, c.51, sch.4; repealed in pt.: 1984, c.12, sch.7; 1985, c.51, sch.17.

ss. 157–159, repealed: *ibid.*

s. 160, amended: *ibid.*; repealed in pt.: *ibid.*, sch.17.

s. 161, amended: 1986, c.13, s.1.

s. 161A, added: *ibid.*

s. 168, amended: 1984, c.55, sch.6.

s. 169, amended: 1981, c.38, sch.3; 1984, c.12, sch.4; c.66, sch.6.

s. 170, amended: 1981, c.38, sch.3; 1984, c.12, sch.4; repealed in pt.: *ibid.*, schs.4,7; 1985, c.51, sch.17.

s. 172, amended: *ibid.*, sch.4.

s. 174, amended: 1981, c.38, sch.3.

s. 175, amended: 1985, c.51, sch.4.

s. 175A, added: 1981, c.43, s.1.

s. 177, amended: 1981, c.38, sch.3; 1984, c.12, sch.4.

ss. 178, 181, amended: 1981, c.38, sch.3; 1984, c.12, sch.4; repealed in pt.: 1981, c.38, sch.3.

s. 179, amended: 1982, c.30, s.22.

ss. 186, 188–200, 203, 205, 210, amended: 1985, c.51, sch.4.

s. 219, amended: 1984, c.66, sch.6; repealed in pt.: 1981, c.38, sch.12; 1984, c.32, sch.7; 1985, c.51, sch.17.

s. 220, amended: *ibid.*, sch.4.

s. 223, amended: 1984, c.55, sch.6; 1985, c.51, sch.4.

s. 230, amended: *ibid.*

ss. 238, 246, 247, amended: 1981, c.67, sch.4.

s. 250, amended: *ibid.*, repealed in pt.: *ibid.*, sch.6.

s. 254, amended: 1981, c.38, sch.3; c.67, sch.4; 1985, c.51, sch.4; repealed in pt.: 1984, c.12, sch.4; 1985, c.51, sch.17.

s. 257, amended: 1981, c.67, sch.4.

s. 258, functions transferred: order 81/238.

ss. 258, 259, amended: 1981, c.67, sch.4.

s. 263, amended: 1985, c.51, sch.4.

s. 264, amended: *ibid.*; repealed in pt.: *ibid.*, sch.17.

s. 265, amended: 1984, c.27, sch.13.

1980—cont.

66. Highways Act 1980—cont.

s. 269, repealed: 1985, c.51, sch.17.

s. 271, amended: *ibid.*, sch.4.

s. 285, amended: 1984, c.27, sch.13; 1985, c.51, sch.4; repealed in pt.: *ibid.*, sch.17.

s. 287, repealed in pt.: *ibid.*

s. 290, amended: 1981, c.38, sch.3; 1987, c.3, sch.1; repealed in pt.: 1984, c.12, sch.4.

s. 298, amended: 1985, c.51, sch.4; repealed in pt.: *ibid.*, sch.17.

s. 300, functions transferred: order 81/238.

s. 307, amended: 1984, c.38, s.5.

s. 312, amended: 1982, c.30, s.21.

s. 322, amended: 1981, c.67, sch.4.

s. 325, instruments: 84/696; 87/1954, 2241.

ss. 325, 326, regs. 83/23.

s. 326, repealed in pt.: 1985, c.51, sch.17.

s. 329, amended: 1981, c.38, sch.10; order 81/238; 1984, c.12, sch.4; c.27, sch.13; c.38, s.1; c.66, sch.6; 1988, c.54, sch.3; repealed in pt.: 1981, c.67, sch.6.; 1984, c.32, sch.7; 1985, c.51, sch.17.

s. 330, amended: *ibid.*, sch.4.

s. 334, substituted: 1984, c.12, sch.4.

s. 340, repealed in pt.: 1981, c.67, sch.6; c.69, sch.17; 1984, c.27, sch.24.

sch. 1, see *R.* v. *Secretary of State for the Environment, ex p. Binney, The Times*, October 8, 1983, Webster J.

sch. 1, functions transferred: order 81/238; repealed in pt.: 1985, c.51, sch.17.

sch. 2, see *Rea* v. *Minister of Transport* (1984) 48 P. & C.R. 239, C.A.; *Burton* v. *Secretary of State for Transport* [1988] 31 E.G. 50, C.A.

sch. 4, amended: 1988, c.54, sch.3.

sch. 6, regs. 83/23.

sch. 6, amended: 1981, c.38, sch.3; c.69, sch.16; 1988, c.50, sch.17; repealed in pt.: 1984, c.12, sch.4.

sch. 7, amended: 1985, c.51.sch.4.

sch. 9, repealed in pt.: *ibid.*, sch.17.

schs. 12, 15, amended: *ibid.*; repealed in pt.: *ibid.*, sch.17.

sch. 19, repealed in pt.: 1981, c.67, sch.6.

sch. 23, orders 83/483; 86/610.

sch. 24, repealed in pt.: 1981, c.64, sch.13; 1983, c.35, sch.2; 1984, c.27, sch.24; S.L.R. 1986; 1988, c.54, sch.1.

67. Anguilla Act 1980.

Royal Assent, December 16, 1980.

s. 1, orders 80/1953; 81/603; 82/334; 83/1107, 1108; 87/450.

68. Consolidated Fund (No. 2) Act 1980.

Royal Assent, December 18, 1980.

repealed: 1982, c.40, sch.(C.).

1981

1. Social Security (Contributions) Act 1981.

Royal Assent, January 29, 1981.

ss. 1, 2–5 (in pt.), repealed: 1982, c.2, sch.2.

2. Iron and Steel (Borrowing Powers) Act 1981.

Royal Assent, February 26, 1981.

repealed: 1981, c.46, sch.2.

CAP.

1981—cont.

3. Gas Levy Act 1981.
Royal Assent, March 19, 1981.
s. 1, amended: 1986, c.44, sch.6.
s. 2, order 82/548.
s. 3, substituted: 1986, c.44, sch.6.
ss. 4, 5, amended: *ibid.*
s. 5A, added: *ibid.*
ss. 6, 7, amended: *ibid.*

4. Consolidated Fund Act 1981.
Royal Assent, March 19, 1981.
repealed: 1983, c.27, sch.(C).

5. Redundancy Fund Act 1981.
Royal Assent, March 19, 1981.

6. Industry Act 1981.
Royal Assent, March 19, 1981.
s. 5, repealed: 1982, c.4, s.3.
s. 6, repealed: 1982, c.52, sch.3.

7. House of Commons Members' Fund and Parliamentary Pensions Act 1981.
Royal Assent, March 19, 1981.
s. 1, amended: 1987, c.45, sch.3.
s. 2, resolutions 85/2082; 87/511; 88/742.
s. 2, amended: order 84/2065.
s. 3, order 81/748.
ss. 4, 5 (in pt.), repealed: 1987, c.45, sch. 4.

8. European Assembly Elections Act 1981.
Royal Assent, March 19, 1981.

9. International Organisations Act 1981.
Royal Assent, April 15, 1981.

10. Merchant Shipping Act 1981.
Royal Assent, April 15, 1981.
Commencement order: 84/1695.
s. 4. order 82/1662–1664.
s. 5, orders 81/1677; 83/1906; 84/1695.

11. Parliamentary Commissioner (Consular Complaints) Act 1981.
Royal Assent, April 15, 1981.

12. Water Act 1981.
Royal Assent, April 15, 1981.
s. 2, amended: 1985, c.15, sch.2.
s. 5, repealed in pt.: 1984, c.55, sch.7.
s. 6, order 81/1755.

13. English Industrial Estates Corporation Act 1981.
Royal Assent, April 15, 1981.
s. 2, amended: 1982, c.52, sch.2; 1985, c.25, s.1.
s. 3, amended: 1985, c.21, sch; repealed in pt.: 1983, c.29, sch.3.
s. 4, amended: 1985, c.21, s.2.
s. 5, amended: 1983, c.29, s.4, sch.2.
s. 6, amended: 1985, c.25, s.3; repealed in pt.: *ibid.*, sch.
s. 7, amended: 1985, c.9, sch.2; c.25, s.4.
s. 8, amended: 1982, c.52, sch.2.
ss. 9, 10, repealed in pt.: 1982, c.52, sch.3.

14. Public Passenger Vehicles Act 1981.
Royal Assent, April 15, 1981.
s. 1, repealed in pt.: 1985, c.67, sch.8.
s. 2, see *R.* v. *Traffic Comrs., ex p. Licensed Taxi Drivers' Association* [1984] R.T.R. 197, D.C.
s. 2, repealed: 1985, c.67, sch.8.
s. 3, order 83/1714.

CAP.

1981—cont.

14. Public Passenger Vehicles Act 1981—*cont.*
s. 3, amended: 1985, c.67, sch.2.
ss. 4, 5, substituted: *ibid.*, s.3.
s. 5, regs. 86/1030, 1629, 1691.
s. 5, amended: 1985, c.51, sch.5.
s. 6, regs. 82/1058; 86/1812.
s. 6, amended: 1982, c.49, s.10; 1988, c.54, sch.3.
s. 8, amended: 1985, c.67, sch.7.
s. 9, regs. 87/1150.
s. 9, amended: 1982, c.49, ss.10, 21; 1985, c.67, schs.2,7; repealed in pt.: 1982, c.49, s.21, sch.6.
s. 9A, added: 1985, c.67, s.33.
s. 10, regs. 82/1058; amended: 1982, c.49, ss.10,11.
ss. 12, 14, amended: 1985, c.67, schs.1,2.
s. 14, regs. 86/1668.
s. 14A, added: 1985, c.67, s.25.
s. 15, amended: *ibid.*, schs.1,2.
s. 16, regs. 85/1905; 86/1668.
s. 16, amended: 1985, c.67, s.24, schs.2,7; repealed in pt.: *ibid.*, sch.8.
s. 17, amended: *ibid.*, schs.2,7.
s. 17A, added: *ibid.*, s.5.
s. 18, regs. 86/994, 1668.
s. 18, amended: 1985, c.67, s.24, sch.2.
s. 19, amended: 1985, c.65, sch.8; c.67, sch.2; 1986, c.45, sch.14.
s. 20, amended: 1982, c.49, s.10; 1985, c.67, s.29, sch.2.
s. 21, amended: *ibid.*, sch.2.
s. 22, regs. 85/214, 833.
s. 22, amended: 1985, c.67, schs.1,7.
s. 23, amended: *ibid.*, sch.2.
s. 23A, added: 1983, c.43, s.3.
s. 25, repealed in pt.: 1984, c.60, sch.7.
s. 26, regs. 84/1406.
s. 27, amended: 1983, c.20, sch.4; 1984, c.32, sch.6.
s. 28, repealed: 1985, c.67, s.32, sch.8.
Pt. III (ss.30–41), repealed: 1985, c.67, s.1, sch.8.
ss. 30, 31, see *R.* v. *Traffic Comrs. for the Metropolitan Traffic Area, ex p. Licensed Taxi Drivers' Association* [1984] R.T.R. 197, D.C.; *Strathclyde Passenger Executive* v. *McGill Bus Service,* Second Division, March 23, 1984.
s. 31, regs. 85/1907.
s. 31, amended: 1985, c.51, sch.5; repealed in pt.: *ibid.*, sch.17.
s. 35, repealed in pt.: *ibid.*
s. 37, regs. 85/1907.
s. 38, order 82/1243.
ss. 38, 40, amended: 1985, c.51, sch.5.
ss. 42–45, repealed: 1985, c.67, sch.8.
s. 44, regs. 81/1599; 82/1484; 86/1813.
s. 45, regs. 82/1482.
s. 46, repealed in pt.: 1985, c.67, schs.1,8.
s. 47, orders 82/221; 83/917, 1453; 84/204; 85/1010.
ss. 47, 48, repealed: 1985, c.67, s.32, sch.8.
s. 49, repealed: *ibid.*, sch.8.
s. 50, regs. 85/1907.

CAP.

1981—cont.

14. Public Passenger Vehicles Act 1981—cont.
ss. 50, 51, see Strathclyde Passenger Executive v. McGill Bus Service, 1984 S.L.T. 377.
ss. 50, 51, substituted: 1985, c.67, sch.31.
s. 51, regs. 87/1150.
s. 52, regs. 82/999; 83/916; 84/1763; 85/214, 833; 86/370, 869, 972, 1245, 1668, 1671, 1691; 88/340, 408, 960, 1104, 1879.
s. 52, amended: 1985, c.67, sch.2; repealed in pt.: ibid., schs.1,8.
s. 53, amended: ibid., sch.1; repealed in pt.: ibid., sch.8.
s. 54, regs. 86/1629.
s. 54, substituted: 1985, c.67, s.4.
s. 55, substituted: ibid., s.4.
s. 55, amended: ibid., sch.2.
s. 56, regs. 86/1629.
s. 56, amended: 1985, c.67, schs.2,7; repealed in pt.: ibid., sch.8.
s. 57, regs. 86/1668, 1691.
s. 57, amended: 1985, c.67, sch.2; repealed in pt.: ibid., schs.1,8.
s. 58, regs. 85/1906; 86/1628.
s. 58, repealed in pt.: 1985, c.67, schs.1,8.
s. 59, regs. 85/214, 1905, 1907; 86/994, 1668, 1691.
s. 59, repealed in pt.: 1985, c.67, schs.1, 8.
s. 60, see H. v. Traffic Comrs. for the Metropolitan Traffic Area, ex p. Licensed Taxi Drivers' Association [1984] R.T.R. 197, D.C.
s. 60, regs. 81/1623; 82/20, 999, 1482, 1483; 83/916; 84/32, 748, 1406, 1763; 85/214, 833, 1905, 1907; 86/370, 753, 869, 972, 1030, 1245, 1629, 1668, 1671, 1691; 87/1150, 88/340, 408, 960, 1104, 1809.
s. 60, amended: 1982, c.49, s.21; 1985, c.67, s.134, schs.2,7; repealed in pt.: ibid., s.134, sch.8.
s. 61, regs. 82/1058, 1482; 83/916; 84/32, 748, 1406, 1763; 85/833, 1906; 86/370, 567, 1030, 1628, 1779; 87/1150.
s. 61, repealed in pt.: 1985, c.67, s.135, sch.8.
s. 62, order 84/31.
s. 62, repealed: 1985, c.67, sch.8.
s. 65, amended: 1981, c.45, s.12; 1982, c.49, s.23; repealed in pt.: 1985, c.67, sch.8.
s. 66, repealed in pt.: ibid.
s. 66A, added: 1982, c.49, s.24.
s. 67, repealed in pt.: 1985, c.67, sch.8.
s. 68, amended: ibid., sch.1; repealed in pt.: ibid., sch.8.
s. 69, amended: ibid., sch.2; repealed in pt.: ibid., sch.8.
ss. 70–72, 74, 76, repealed in pt.: ibid., sch.8.
s. 78, orders 81/1823 (S.); 85/1477; 86/1504.
s. 79, amended: 1982, c.45, sch.3 (S.); 1985, c.67, sch.7.
s. 80, order 83/1714.
s. 81, regs. 85/1905; 86/1668.
s. 81, repealed in pt.: 1985, c.67, schs.1, 8.
s. 82, regs. 85/1905; 86/1668.
s. 82, amended: 1984, c.54, sch.9 (S.); 1985, c.67, sch.2; repealed in pt.: ibid., schs.1, 8.
s. 83, repealed in pt.: ibid.

CAP.

1981—cont.

14. Public Passenger Vehicles Act 1981—cont.
s. 87, amended: ibid., sch.7.
s. 89, order 81/1387.
sch. 1, amended: 1985, c.51, sch.5; c.67, sch.1; repealed in pt.: ibid., sch.8.
sch. 2, substituted: ibid., s.3, sch.2.
sch. 3, amended: ibid., sch.2.
sch. 4, amended: 1985, c.51.sch.5.
schs. 4, 5, repealed: 1985, c.67, sch.8.
sch. 7, repealed in pt.: 1981, c.56, s.39, sch. 12; 1982, c.49, sch. 6; 1984, c.27, sch. 14; c.32, sch. 7; 1988, c.54, sch.1.
sch. 8, amended: 1981, c.56, s.39; repealed in pt.: ibid., s.39, sch.12.

15. National Film Finance Corporation Act 1981.
Royal Assent, April 15, 1981.
s. 1, order 85/1943.
s. 7, amended: 1985, c.9, sch.2.
s. 9, order 85/1942.
sch. 1, order 85/1943.
sch. 1, repealed in pt.: 1985, c.21, s.3, sch.2.
sch. 2, amended: 1985, c.9, sch.2.

16. Film Levy Finance Act 1981.
Royal Assent, April 15, 1981.
s. 6, regs. 82/1022.
sch. 1, order 88/37.
sch. 1, amended: 1985, c.9, sch.2.

17. Energy Conservation Act 1981.
Royal Assent, May 21, 1981.

18. Disused Burial Grounds (Amendment) Act 1981.
Royal Assent, May 21, 1981.

19. Statute Law (Repeals) Act 1981.
Royal Assent, May 21, 1981.
s. 2, order 84/1692.

20. Judicial Pensions Act 1981.
Royal Assent, May 21, 1981.
s. 13, amended: order 84/1818.
s. 14, amended: regs. 88/1417.
s. 16A, added: ibid.
s. 21, orders 81/1555; 82/1455; 83/1459; 84/1625; 85/1691; 86/814; 87/209; 88/223; amended: 82/1455; 83/1459; 84/1625; 85/1691; 88/223.
ss. 23, 24, amended: regs. 88/1417.
s. 23, regs. 87/375.
s. 34, amended: 1981, c.54, sch.5; 1984, c.28, sch.2.
sch. 1, amended: 1981, c.54, sch.5; order 84/539; repealed in pt.: 1981, c.54, sch.5.
sch. 2, amended: regs. 88/1417.
sch. 3, repealed in pt.: 1981, c.54, sch.7.

21. Ports (Financial Assistance) Act 1981.
Royal Assent, June 11, 1981.
s. 1, amended: 1982, c.6, s.5; 1985, c.30, s.2.

22. Animal Health Act 1981.
Royal Assent, June 11, 1981.
order 81/1238.
s. 1, orders 81/1050, 1051, 1056 (S.), 1190; 82/35, 207 (S.), 234, 459, 608, 947, 948; 83/32, 210, 344, 941, 1071, 1382, 1401; 84/55, 561, 770, 1182, 1326, 1338, 1512, 1943, 2063 (S.); 85/24, 328, 1174, 1542, 1765, 1766; 86/5, 498, 862, 1290, 2061, 2062,

1981—cont.

22. Animal Health Act 1981—*cont.*
2265, 2295; 87/74, 135 (S.), 232, 233, 790,
836, 905, 1447, 1601; 88/224, 815, 851, 1039,
1345, 1453, 2264.
s. 6, orders 81/1455; 86/2295; 87/135 (S.).
s. 7, orders 81/1050, 1051, 1239, 1455; 82/35,
947; 83/32, 344, 941, 1071, 1401; 84/55, 561,
1338, 1943, 2063 (S.); 85/24, 1174; 86/5, 862,
1290, 1755, 2295; 87/74, 233, 790, 836;
88/224, 851, 1039, 1453, 2264.
s. 8, orders 81/1051, 1056 (S.), 1190, 1239;
82/207 (S.), 234, 608; 83/210, 344, 941, 1382,
1401; 84/561, 770, 1512, 1943, 2063 (S);
85/328, 1542, 1765, 1766; 86/498, 862, 1755;
87/135 (S), 232, 233, 790, 836, 1601; 88/815,
851, 1039, 1345, 2264.
s. 10, see *R. v. Secretary of State for Agriculture,
Fisheries and Food, ex p. Avi Centre (London),
The Times,* May 22, 1985, Kennedy J.
s. 10, orders 82/459, 948; 84/1182, 1326, 1943,
2063 (S); 86/2062, 2265.
s. 11, orders 83/872; 85/217; 86/1528, 1734;
87/211, 248, 1808; 88/6, 953, 1678.
s. 14, orders 83/210; 84/770; 86/862; 87/836.
s. 15, order 81/1239; 82/207 (S.), 234, 608;
83/344, 941, 1401; 84/561, 1943, 2063 (S);
85/328; 86/862, 1755; 87/790, 836; 88/2264.
s. 17, order 81/1239; 82/207 (S.), 234; 83/210,
344, 941, 1382; 84/561, 770, 1512; 85/328,
1542; 86/862, 1755; 87/790, 836.
s. 17, repealed in pt.: 1984, c.40, s.4, sch.2.
s. 21, order 86/2061.
s. 23, orders 81/1050, 1239; 82/35, 207 (S.),
234, 947; 83/32, 210, 344, 941, 1071, 1382;
84/55, 561, 770, 1338, 1512; 85/24, 328,
1174, 1542; 86/5, 862, 1290, 1755; 87/74,
790, 836, 1447; 88/224, 1453.
s. 25, orders 81/1239; 82/207 (S.), 234; 83/344,
941, 1382, 1401; 84/561, 1512, 1943, 2063
(S.); 85/328, 1542; 86/498, 862, 1755;
87/233, 836.
s. 26, order 83/1950.
s. 28, orders 81/1455; 82/207 (S.), 234; 85/328,
2295; 87/790.
s. 29, order 88/2264.
s. 32, orders 81/1412, 1448 (S.), 1455; 83/344,
345, 1943, 2063 (S.); 88/1345, 1346.
s. 34, see *R. v. Secretary of State for Agriculture,
Fisheries and Food, ex p. Avi Centre (London),
The Times,* May 22, 1985, Kennedy J.
s. 34, orders 81/1412, 1448 (S.), 1455; 86/2295;
88/1346.
s. 35, orders 81/1455; 86/2295; 87/790.
ss. 35, 36, order 83/346.
ss. 35, 36, amended: 1984, c.40, s.1.
ss. 37, 38, orders 88/815, 851.
ss. 37–39, order 81/1051.
s. 38, amended: 1984, c.32, sch.6.
s. 50, order 87/709.
s. 50, amended: 1985, c.51, sch.8.
s. 55, amended: 1981, c.67, sch.4; repealed in
pt.: *ibid.,* sch.6.
s. 60, amended: 1984, c.60, sch.6; repealed in
pt.: *ibid.,* sch.7.

1981—cont.

22. Animal Health Act 1981—*cont.*
s. 63, amended: 1984, c.40, s.2, sch.1.
s. 70, repealed: 1982, c.48, sch.16.
s. 72, orders 84/2063 (S.); 86/1755; 87/790,
905; 88/851, 1039, 2264.
s. 83, order 83/344; 84/1943, 2063 (S).
s. 84, orders 81/1728; 87/361.
s. 86, orders 81/1190; 84/2063 (S.); 87/135 (S.),
1601; 88/815, 851, 1039, 1345, 1346, 1453,
1678, 2264.
s. 87, orders 81/1239; 82/948; 83/344, 872,
941, 1401; 84/1943, 2063 (S.); 85/1765,
1766; 86/498, 1755, 2295; 87/135 (S.), 790;
88/815, 851; amended: 1984, c.40, s.2;
orders 85/1765.
s. 88, orders 82/207 (S.), 234, 608, 948; 83/344,
1382, 1401; 84/1943, 2063 (S.); 85/328, 1765,
1766; 86/1755; 87/790, 905; 88/1039, 2264.
s. 95, orders 84/1182; 86/2062.
sch. 2, see *R. v. Secretary of State for Agriculture, Fisheries and Food, ex p. Avi Centre
(London), The Times,* May 22, 1985, Kennedy
J.
sch. 5, repealed in pt.: 1981, c.69, sch.17; 1984,
c.30, sch.11.

**23. Local Government (Miscellaneous Pro-
visions) (Scotland) Act 1981.**
Royal Assent, June 11, 1981.
ss. 2–4, 9, Pt. II (ss.14–20), repealed: 1987,
c.47, sch.6.
s. 10, repealed: 1988, c.41, sch.13.
ss. 21–23, repealed: 1987, c.26, sch.24.
s. 23, orders 86/388, 389.
ss. 34, 35, repealed: 1987, c.26, sch.24.
s. 43, order 81/1402.
sch. 2, repealed in pt.: 1984, c.54, sch.9; 1987,
c.26, sch.24.
sch. 3, repealed in pt.: 1984, c.18, sch.; c.54,
sch.9; 1987, c.26, sch.24; c.47, sch.6.

24. Matrimonial Homes and Property Act 1981.
Royal Assent, July 2, 1981.
Commencement order: 83/50.
ss. 1–3, 5, 6, repealed: 1983, c.19, sch.3.
s. 4, repealed in pt.: *ibid.;* 1988, c.3, sch.
ss. 7, 8, see *Norman* v. *Norman* (1983) 13
Fam.Law 17, Wood J.
s. 8, repealed in pt.: 1984, c.42, sch.3.
s. 9, orders 81/1275; 83/50.
schs. 1, 2, repealed: 1983, c.19, sch.3.
sch. 2, see *Lewis* v. *Lewis, The Times,* March
10, 1984, C.A.

25. Industrial Diseases (Notification) Act 1981.
Royal Assent, July 2, 1981.
s. 1, regs. 85/568, 569, 1133, 1134; 87/2088.

26. Food and Drugs (Amendment) Act 1981.
Royal Assent, July 2, 1981.

27. Criminal Justice (Amendment) Act 1981.
Royal Assent, July 2, 1981.

**28. Licensing (Alcohol Education and Research)
Act 1981.**
Royal Assent, July 2, 1981.
s. 3, amended: 1986, c.60, sch.16.
s. 9, scheme 83/497.
s. 10, amended: 1985, c.9, sch.2.
s. 13, order 81/1324.

1981—cont.

29. Fisheries Act 1981.
Royal Assent, July 2, 1981.
s. 4, order 82/168.
ss. 15, 18, schemes 81/1765; 82/498, 1686; 83/1883; 84/1879; 85/987; 87/1135, 1136.
s. 30, orders 81/1165, 1871; 82/1161; 83/720, 1818; 84/173, 291 (S.), 516, 1956; 85/215, 313, 487; 86/110, 250, 251, 779, 926, 2090, 2329; 87/213, 292, 1536, 2234; 88/77, 136.
s. 31, schemes 81/1653; 83/626; 84/341; 87/1134.
s. 46, orders 81/1357, 1640.
sch. 2, amended: 1982, c.30, s.39.
sch. 4, amended: 1984, c.26, sch.1; repealed in pt.: *ibid.*, sch.2; S.L.R. 1986.

30. Horserace Betting Levy Act 1981.
Royal Assent, July 2, 1981.

31. Insurance Companies Act 1981.
Royal Assent, July 2, 1981.
repealed, except ss. 36 (in pt.), 38, sch.4 (in pt.): 1982, c.50, sch.6.
see *Bedford Insurance Co.* v. *Instituto do Resaguros do Brasil* (1984) 134 New L.J. 35, Parker J.
ss. 2, 5, 7, 9, 16, regs. 81/1654.
s. 9, amended: 1982, c.53, s.46.
s. 31, regs. 81/1655.
s. 37, order 81/1657.
sch. 4, repealed in pt.: 1987, c.22, sch.7; 1988, c.54, sch.1.

32. Transport Act 1962 (Amendment) Act 1981.
Royal Assent, July 2, 1981.

33. Social Security Act 1981.
Royal Assent, July 2, 1981.
ss. 1, 4, sch. 1 (in pt.), repealed: 1986, c.50, sch.11.
s. 7, order 81/1541.
s. 8, order 81/953.
sch. 2, repealed in pt.: 1985, c.53, sch.6.

34. Representation of the People Act 1981.
Royal Assent, July 2, 1981.
s. 3, sch., repealed in pt.: 1983, c.2, sch.9.

35. Finance Act 1981.
Royal Assent, July 27, 1981.
Commencement order: 82/205.
ss. 1 (in pt.), 2, repealed: 1982, c.39, sch.22.
ss. 7, 8, repealed in pt.: 1982, c.39, sch.22; 1985, c.54, sch.27.
s. 9, repealed in pt.: 1981, c.63, sch.7; 1982, c.39, sch.22.
s. 10, order 82/205.
ss. 12–15, repealed: 1983, c.55, sch.11.
ss. 16–18, repealed: 1983, c.53, sch.3.
ss. 19–37, 38 (in pt.), 39–72, repealed: 1988, c.1, sch.31.
s. 28, amended: order 88/1843.
s. 78, amended: 1982, c.39, s.82; repealed in pt.: *ibid.*, sch.22.
ss. 83, 84, amended: 1988, c.1, sch.31.
ss. 92–95 repealed: 1984, c.51, sch.9.
s. 96, amended: 1982, c.39, sch.17; repealed in pt.: 1984, c.51, sch.9.
ss. 97–106, repealed: *ibid.*

1981—cont.

35. Finance Act 1981—*cont.*
s. 107, amended: 1984, c.43, s.110; 1985, c.71, sch.2; 1986, c.63, sch.5; 1988, c.39, s.142, c.50, sch.17; repealed in pt.: 1985, c.54, sch.27.
s. 109, repealed: 1986, c.41, sch.23.
s. 110, amended: 1988, c.39, sch.13; repealed in pt.: *ibid.*, sch.14.
s. 111, see *Mobil North Sea* v. *I.R.C.* [1987] 1 W.L.R. 1065, H.L.
s. 111, amended: 1982, c.39, sch.19; 1983, c.28, sch.8; 1985, c.54, s.91; repealed in pt.: 1987, c.16, schs.13,16.
ss. 112, 113, amended: 1982, c.39, sch.19.
s. 120, repealed: 1988, c.1, sch.31.
s. 122, amended: 1982, c.39, ss.132,133; repealed in pt.: *ibid.*, sch.22.
ss. 123–128, repealed: *ibid.*
s. 127, see *Ellis* v. *I.C.I. Petroleum* [1983] S.T.C. 675, Gibson J.
s. 135, amended: 1985, c.54, sch.25; repealed in pt.: 1984, c.51, sch.9.
s. 136, repealed in pt.: 1987, c.16, sch.16.
s. 138, repealed 1988, c.1, sch.31.
s. 139, amended: *ibid.*, sch.29; repealed in pt.: 1984, c.51, sch.9.
schs. 1–4, repealed: 1982, c.39, sch.22.
sch. 5, repealed: 1981, c.63, sch.7.
sch. 6, repealed in pt.: regs. 82/1324.
sch. 8, repealed in pt.: 1986, c.41, sch.23; 1988, c.25, s.3.
schs. 9–12, repealed: 1988, c.1, sch.11.
schs. 13, 14, repealed: 1984, c.51, sch.9.
sch. 15, repealed: 1982, c.39, s.97, sch.22.
sch. 16, repealed: *ibid.*, sch.22.
sch. 17, repealed in pt.: 1988, c.39, sch.14.
sch. 18, repealed: 1987 c.16, sch.16.

36. Town and Country Planning (Minerals) Act 1981.
Royal Assent, July 27, 1981.
Commencement orders: 82/86, 1177; 86/760; 87/2002(S.).
see *Pioneer Aggregates (U.K.)* v. *Secretary of State for the Environment, The Times,* May 26, 1984, C.A.
s. 2, repealed in pt.: 1985, c.51, sch.17.
s. 33, repealed; 1987, c.12, sch.13.
s. 35, orders 82/86, 1177, 86/760; 87/2002(S.).

37. Zoo Licensing Act 1981.
Royal Assent, July 27, 1981.
Commencement order: 84/423.
s. 3, repealed in pt.: 1985, c.51, sch.17.
s. 4, amended: 1981, c.69, s.72; repealed in pt.: *ibid.*, s.72, sch.17.
s. 23, order 84/423.

38. British Telecommunications Act 1981.
Royal Assent, July 27, 1981.
s. 1, order 81/1274.
s. 1, amended: 1984, c.12, s.100; repealed (prospectively): *ibid.*, s.100, sch.7.
ss. 2, 4, 5, 6 (in pt.), 7, 8, repealed (prospectively): *ibid.*, sch.7.
ss. 3, 6 (in pt.), 9, 11–23, repealed: *ibid.*
s. 17, orders 82/491; 83/1846.
s. 18, order 82/490.

CAP.

1981—cont.

38. British Telecommunications Act 1981—*cont.*
ss. 24–34, repealed (prospectively): 1984, c.12, sch.7.
s. 29, amended: 1983, c.29, s.4, sch.2.
s. 33, orders 81/1800; 83/326.
ss. 35–53, repealed: 1984, c.12, sch.7.
s. 36, repealed: 1988, c.41, sch.13.
s. 37, S.R. 1983 No. 35.
ss. 54, 56, 57, repealed (prospectively): 1984, c.12, sch.7.
ss. 55, 58 (in pt.) repealed: *ibid.*
s. 63, amended: *ibid.*, sch.4.
s. 65, order 83/65.
s. 67, amended: 1987, c.22, sch.6; repealed in pt.: 1985, c.58, sch.4.
s. 69, orders 81/1483; 84/761.
s. 80, repealed in pt.: 1984, c.12, sch.7.
s. 81, repealed in pt.: 1988, c.39, sch.14.
s. 85, amended: 1985, c.9, sch.2; repealed in pt.: 1984, c.12, schs.4,7.
sch. 1, repealed in pt. (prospectively): *ibid.*, sch.7.
sch. 3, regs. 82/1211.
sch. 3, repealed in pt.: 1981, c.64, sch.13; c.67, sch.6; c.68, sch.9; 1982, c.16, sch.16; order 82/1083; 1984, c.12, sch.7, c.29, sch.12.
sch. 4, repealed in pt.: 1984, c.12, sch.7; 1985, c.65, sch.10; repealed (prospectively): 1984, c.12, sch.7.
sch. 5, amended: 1988, c.48, sch.7; repealed in pt.: 1984, s.12, sch.7.
sch. 7, repealed (prospectively): *ibid.*

39. Forestry Act 1981.
Royal Assent, July 27, 1981.

40. Licensing (Amendment) Act 1981.
Royal Assent, July 27, 1981.
Commencement order: 82/1383.
s. 3, order 82/1383.

41. Local Government and Planning (Amendment) Act 1981.
Royal Assent, July 27, 1981.
s. 1, sch., see *Tandridge District Council v. Powers* (1982) 80 L.G.R. 453, D.C.
s. 87, see *Hughes (H.T.) v. Secretary of State for the Environment and Fareham Borough Council* [1985] J.P.L. 486, Hodgson J.

42. Indecent Displays (Control) Act 1981.
Royal Assent, July 27, 1981.
s. 1, amended: 1982, c.33, sch.1; 1984, c.46, sch.5; 1985, c.13, sch.2.
s. 2, repealed in pt.: 1984, c.60, sch.7.
s. 5, amended (S.): 1982, c.45, s.5.

43. Disabled Persons Act 1981.
Royal Assent, July 27, 1981.
s. 2, repealed in pt.: 1984, c.27, sch.14.

44. Countryside (Scotland) Act 1981.
Royal Assent, July 27, 1981.
s. 18, order 81/1614.
s. 48A, order 81/1613.

45. Forgery and Counterfeiting Act 1981.
Royal Assent, July 27, 1981.
s. 1, see *R. v. Utting* [1987] 1 W.L.R. 1375, C.A.
ss. 1, 8, see *R. v. Gold; R. v. Schifreen* [1988] 2 W.L.R. 984, H.L.

CAP.

1981—cont.

45. Forgery and Counterfeiting Act 1981—*cont.*
ss. 1, 8, 9, see *R. v. Donnelly (Ian)* [1984] 1 W.L.R. 1017, C.A.
ss. 1, 9, see *R. v. More* [1987] 1 W.L.R. 1578, H.L.
ss. 1, 10, see *R. v. Campbell* (1985) 80 Cr.App.R. 47; [1984] Crim.L.R. 683, C.A.
s. 3, see *R. v. Tobierre* [1986] 1 W.L.R. 125, C.A.; *Chief Constable of West Mercia Police v. Williams* [1987] R.T.R. 188, D.C.
ss. 3, 10, see *R. v. Garcia* [1988] Crim.L.R. 115, C.A.
s. 9, see *R. v. Lack* (1987) 84 Cr.App.R. 342, C.A.
s. 10, see *R. v. Tobierre* [1986] 1 W.L.R. 125, C.A.
s. 11, repealed in pt.: 1983, c.20, sch.4.
s. 12, repealed in pt.: 1988, c.54, sch.1.
s. 15, see *McLeod v. Allan*, 1986 S.C.C.R. 666.
s. 27, order 81/1505.

46. Iron and Steel Act 1981.
Royal Assent, July 27, 1981.
repealed: 1982, c.25, sch.7.

47. Criminal Attempts Act 1981.
Royal Assent, July 27, 1981.
s. 1, see *R. v. Dunnington* [1984] 2 W.L.R. 125, C.A.; *R. v. Mucklow*, January 4, 1984, H.H. Judge Galpin, Newport, Isle of Wight Crown Court; *Chief Constable of Greater Manchester v. Ryan* (1984) 148 J.P.N. 429, C.A.; *R. v. Toye* [1984] Crim.L.R. 555, Southwark Crown Court; *R. v. Brown (Raymond Andrew)* [1984] 1 W.L.R. 1211, C.A.; *R. v. Pearman* [1985] R.T.R. 39, C.A.; *Anderton v. Ryan* [1985] 2 W.L.R. 968, H.L.; *R. v. Widdowson, The Times*, January 7, 1986, C.A.; *R. v. Webster*, February 12, 1986, Turner J.; *Bullivant (Roger) v. Ellis, Financial Times*, April 16, 1986, Falconer J.; *R. v. Shivpuri* [1986] 2 W.L.R. 988, H.L.; *Chief Constable of Hampshire v. Mace* (1987) 84 Cr.App.R. 40, D.C.; *R. v. Gullefer* [1987] Crim.L.R. 195, C.A.; *R. v. Millard and Vernon* [1987] Crim.L.R. 393, C.A., *R. v. Boyle (G.) and Boyle (J.)* (1987) 84 Cr.App.R. 270, C.A.
s. 5, see *R. v. Grant* (1986) 82 Cr.App.R. 324, C.A.
ss. 8, 10, see *R. v. West London Stipendiary Magistrate, ex p. Simeon* [1982] 3 W.L.R. 289, H.L.
s. 9, see *Reynolds and Warren v. Metropolitan Police* [1982] Crim.L.R. 831, Acton Crown Ct.
s. 9, amended: 1988, c.54, sch.3; repealed in pt.: 1984, c.60, sch.7.

48. Atomic Energy (Miscellaneous Provisions) Act 1981.
Royal Assent, July 27, 1981.

49. Contempt of Court Act 1981.
Royal Assent, July 27, 1981.
s. 1, see *Att.-Gen. v. English; Same v. Oakley, The Independent*, October 21, 1988, D.C.
ss. 1, 2, 4, 6, see *R. v. Horsham JJ., ex p. Farquharson* [1982] 2 W.L.R. 430; (1983) 76 Cr.App.R. 87, C.A.

CAP.

1981—cont.

49. Contempt of Court Act 1981—cont.

s. 2, see *Bullivant (Roger)* v. *Ellis, Financial Times*, April 16, 1986, Falconer J.; *Att.-Gen.* v. *News Group Newspapers* [1986] 2 All E.R. 833, C.A.

s. 2, amended: 1984, c.46, sch.5.

ss. 2, 5, see *Att.-Gen.* v. *English* [1982] 3 W.L.R. 278, H.L.

ss. 2, 7, see *Peacock* v. *London Weekend Television, The Times*, November 27, 1985, C.A.

s. 4, see *R.* v. *Rhuddlan JJ., ex p. H.T.V.* [1986] Crim.L.R. 329, D.C.; *Keane* v. *H.M. Advocate*, 1986 S.C.C.R. 491.

ss. 6, 7, see *Bullivant (Roger)* v. *Ellis, Financial Times*, April 16, 1986, Falconer J.

s. 8, see *McCadden* v. *H.M. Advocate*, 1986 S.L.T. 138.

s. 10, see *Secretary of State for Defence* v. *Guardian Newspapers* [1984] 3 W.L.R. 986, H.L.; *Francome* v. *Mirror Group Newspapers* [1984] 2 All E.R. 408, C.A.; *Handmade Films (Productions)* v. *Express Newspapers* [1986] F.S.R. 463, Browne-Wilkinson V.-C.; *Maxwell* v. *Pressdram* [1987] 1 W.L.R. 298, C.A.; *Inquiry under the Company Securities (Insider Dealing) Act 1985, An, Re* [1988] 2 W.L.R. 33, H.L.; *X* v. *Y* [1988] 2 All E.R. 648, Rose J.

s. 11, see *R.* v. *Reigate JJ., ex p. Argus Newspapers, The Times*, May 20, 1983, D.C.; *R.* v. *Central Criminal Court, ex p. Crook, The Times*, November 8, 1984, D.C.; *R.* v. *Arundel Justices, ex p. Westminster Press* [1985] 1 W.L.R. 708, D.C.; *R.* v. *Malvern JJ., ex p. Evans; R.* v. *Evesham JJ., ex p. McDonagh, The Times*, August 1, 1987, D.C.; *R.* v. *Tower Bridge JJ., ex p. Osborne, The Times*, December 4, 1987, D.C.

s. 12, see *R.* v. *Newbury JJ., ex p. Du Pont* (1984) 78 Cr.App.R. 255, D.C.; *R.* v. *Havant Magistrates' Court and Portsmouth Crown Court, ex p. Palmer* [1985] Crim.L.R. 658, D.C.

s. 12, repealed in pt.: 1982, c.48, sch.16.

s. 13, repealed: 1988, c.34, sch.6; repealed in pt. (S.): 1986, c.47, sch. 5.

s. 14, see *Peart* v. *Stewart* [1983] 2 W.L.R. 451, H.L.; *Enfield London Borough Council* v. *Mahoney* [1983] 1 W.L.R. 749, C.A.; *R.* v. *Phillips* (1984) 78 Cr.App.R. 88, C.A.; *Lee* v. *Walker, The Times*, December 14, 1984, C.A.; *H (A Minor) (Injunction: Breach), Re*, (1986) 16 Fam. Law 139, C.A.; *C. (A Minor) (Wardship: Contempt), Re*, (1986) 16 Fam. Law 187, C.A.; *Linnett* v. *Coles* [1986] 3 W.L.R. 843, D.C.; *Lewisham London Borough* v. *W. & P.*, May 15, 1987, Pearlman J., *R.* v. *Reader* (1987) 84 Cr.App.R. 294, C.A.; *S. & A. Conversions, Re* (1988) 4 BCC 384, C.A.

s. 14, amended: 1982, c.51, schs.3,14; 1983, c.20, sch.4; c.45, s.1; repealed in pt.: 1982, c.51, sch.16.

s. 15, amended: 1982, c.48, sch.7; 1987, c.41, sch.1(A).

s. 16, repealed in pt.: 1981, c.54, sch.7.

CAP.

1981—cont.

49. Contempt of Court Act 1981—cont.

s. 19, see *Peart* v. *Stewart* [1983] 2 W.L.R. 451, H.L.; *Att.-Gen.* v. *English; Same* v. *Oakley, The Independent*, October 21, 1988, D.C.

s. 19, amended: 1984, c.46, sch.5.

sch. 1, see *Peacock* v. *London Weekend Television, The Times*, November 27, 1985, C.A.

sch. 1, amended: 1983, c.20, sch.4; 1984, c.36, sch.3; 1985, c.23, sch.1.

sch. 2, repealed: 1984, c.28, sch.4; repealed in pt.: 1988, c.34, sch.6.

sch. 2, repealed in pt. (S.): 1986, c.47, sch.5.

50. Friendly Societies Act 1981.

Royal Assent, July 27, 1981.

repealed: 1983, c.27, sch.(C).

51. Appropriation Act 1981.

Royal Assent, July 28, 1981.

repealed: 1983, c.27, sch.(C).

52. Belize Act 1981.

Royal Assent, July 28, 1981.

ss. 2, 6, order 81/1107.

s. 4, repealed in pt: 1981, c.61, sch.9.

sch. 2, repealed in pt.: 1982, c.1, sch.2.

53. Deep Sea Mining (Temporary Provisions) Act 1981.

Royal Assent, July 28, 1981.

Commencement order: 82/52.

s. 1, amended: 1981, c.61, sch.7; order 86/948.

s. 2, regs. 82/58; 84/1230.

s. 3, orders 81/1814; 82/176–1/8; 84/1170; 85/2000.

s. 12, regs. 82/58; 84/1230.

s. 14, amended: 1981, c.61, sch.7.

s. 16, amended: 1985, c.48, s.15.

s. 18, order 82/52.

54. Supreme Court Act 1981.

Royal Assent, July 28, 1981.

see *Rover International* v. *Cannon Films Sales, The Times*, March 30, 1987, Harman J.

s. 2, orders 83/1705; 87/2059.

s. 2, amended: *ibid.*

s. 4, order 87/2059; amended: *ibid.*

s. 9, see *R.* v. *Williams (Carl)* [1982] 1 W.L.R. 1398, C.A.

s. 9, amended: 1982, c.53, s.58.

s. 16, see *WEA Records* v. *Visions Channel 4* [1983] 1 W.L.R. 721, C.A.; *R.* v. *Secretary of State for the Home Department, ex p. Dew, The Independent*, February 19, 1987, McNeill J.; *Bokhari* v. *Mahmood, The Independent*, April 19, 1988, C.A.

s. 18, see *R.* v. *Lambeth Metropolitan Stipendiary Magistrate, ex p. McComb* [1983] 2 W.L.R. 259, C.A.; *Moran* v. *Lloyd's* [1983] 2 W.L.R. 672, C.A.; *Beale* v. *Governors of Edgehill College, The Times*, January 12, 1984, C.A.; *Alltrans Express* v. *CVA Holdings* [1984] 1 W.L.R. 394, C.A.; *Nuadi* v. *Cotson, The Times*, May 15, 1984, C.A.; *R.* v. *Secretary of State for the Home Department, ex p. Dannenberg* [1984] 2 W.L.R. 855, C.A.; *White* v. *Brunton* [1984] 3 W.L.R. 105, C.A.; *Hall* v. *Wandsworth Health Authority, The Times*, February 16, 1985, Tudor Price J.; *Bonalumi*

CAP.   CAP.

1981—cont.

54. Supreme Court Act 1981—cont.
v. *Secretary of State for the Home Depart-
ment* [1985] 1 All E.R. 797, C.A.; *Marshall* v.
Levine [1985] 2 All E.R. 177, C.A.; *Thompson*
v. *Fraser* [1985] 3 All E.R. 511, C.A.; *Day* v.
Grant: R. v. *Manchester Crown Court, ex p.
Williams* [1985] R.T.R. 299, C.A.; *Gooch* v.
Ewing (Allied Irish Bank, Garnishee) [1985] 3
All E.R. 654, C.A.; *Aiden Shipping Co.* v.
Interbulk [1985] 1 W.L.R. 1222, C.A.; *R.* v.
Bolton JJ., ex p. Graeme, The Times, March
14, 1986, C.A.; *McCarney* v. *McCarney* (1986)
1 F.L.R. 312, C.A.; *Smith* v. *Middleton* [1986]
1 W.L.R. 598, C.A.; *Parry* v. *Parry* [1986] 16
Fam.Law 211, C.A.; *Crosby* v. *Crosby* (1986)
16 Fam.Law 328, C.A.; *Allette* v. *Allette*
(1986) 2 F.L.R. 427, C.A.; *Warren* v. *Kilroe (T.)
& Sons, The Times,* July 3, 1987, C.A.; *Carr*
v. *Atkins* [1987] 3 W.L.R. 529, C.A.; *Infabrics*
v. *Jaytex* [1987] F.S.R. 529, C.A.; *Bankamer-
ica Finance* v. *Nock* [1987] 3 W.L.R. 1191,
H.L.; *Warren* v. *Kilroe (T.) & Sons* [1988] 1 All
E.R. 638, C.A.; *Shine, Re, The Times,* August
8, 1988, C.A.
s. 19, see *Re Fletcher, The Times,* June 12,
1984, C.A.
s. 20, see *The Saint Anna* [1983] 2 All E.R. 691,
Sheen J.; *The Sonia S.* [1983] 2 Lloyd's Rep.
63, Sheen J.; *Sarnick Liner* v. *Owners of the
Antonis P. Lemos* [1985] 2 W.L.R. 468, H.L.;
River Rima, The [1986] 1 W.L.R. 758, H.L.
s. 20. amended: 1988, c.12, sch.6.
s. 21, see *Stephan J., The* [1985] 2 Lloyd's Rep.
344, Sheen J.; *Evpo Agnic, The Times,* July
21, 1988, C.A.
s. 26, repealed in pt.: 1986, c.55, schs.1,2.
s. 28, see *Smalley, Re* [1985] 2 W.L.R. 538,
H.L.; *Westminster City Council* v. *Lunepalm,
The Times,* December 10, 1985 (and correction December 13, 1985), Woolf J.; *R.* v.
Croydon Crown Court, ex p. Miller (1987) 85
Cr.App.R. 152, D.C.
s. 28, amended: 1982, c.30, sch.3.
s. 29, see *Tozer* v. *National Greyhound Racing
Club, The Times,* May 16, 1983, Walton J.; *R.*
v. *Preston Crown Court, ex p. Fraser* [1984]
Crim.L.R. 624, D.C.; *R.* v. *Chichester Crown
Court, ex p. Abodunrin* (1984) 79 Cr.App.R.
293, D.C.; *Smalley, Re* [1985] 2 W.L.R. 538,
H.L.; *R.* v. *Central Criminal Court, ex p. Ray-
mond* [1986] 1 W.L.R. 710, C.A.; *R.* v. *Maid-
stone Crown Court, ex p. Gill* [1986] 1 W.L.R.
1405, D.C.; *R.* v. *Inner London Crown Court,
ex p. Benjamin* (1987) 85 Cr.App.R. 267, D.C.
s. 31, see *O'Reilly* v. *Mackman, The Times,*
November 26, 1982, H.L.; *R.* v. *B.B.C., ex p.
Lavelle* [1983] 1 W.L.R. 23, Woolf J.; *Tozer* v.
National Greyhound Racing Club, The Times,
May 16, 1983, Walton J.; *Law* v. *National
Greyhound Racing Club* [1983] 3 All E.R. 300;
R. v. *Secretary of State for the Environment,
London Borough of Hammersmith and
Fulham, Royal Borough of Kensington and
Chelsea and G.L.C., ex p. Ward* [1984] J.P.L.

1981—cont.

54. Supreme Court Act 1981—cont.
90, Woolf, J.; *Wandsworth London Borough
Council* v. *Winder, The Times,* April 5, 1984,
C.A.; *Hall* v. *Wandsworth Health Authority,
The Times,* February 16, 1985, Tudor Price J.;
R. v. *Beverley County Court, ex p. Brown,
The Times,* January 25, 1985, C.A.; *R.* v.
*West Devon Borough Council, ex p. North
East Essex Building Co.* [1985] J.P.L. 291,
Mann J.; *R.* v. *Secretary of State for the
Environment, ex p. G.L.C., The Times,*
December 30, 1985, Woolf J.; *R.* v.
*Stratford-on-Avon District Council, ex p. Jack-
son* [1985] 1 W.L.R. 1319, C.A.; *R.* v. *Secre-
tary of State for the Environment, ex p.
Nottinghamshire County Council, The Times,*
November 10, 1986, D.C.; *R.* v. *Secretary of
State for the Home Department, ex p. Her-
bage* [1986] 3 W.L.R. 504, Hodgson J.; *R.* v.
*Secretary of State for the Home Department,
ex p. Dew* [1987] 2 All E.R. 1049, McNeill J.;
R. v. *H.M. Coroner for North Northumberland,
ex p. Armstrong* (1987) 151 J.P. 773, D.C.
s. 32, see *Powney* v. *Coxage, The Times,* March
8, 1988, Schiemann J.
s. 32A, added: 1982, c.53, s.6.
s. 33, see *Jacob (A Minor)* v. *Wessex Regional
Health Authority,* September 11, 1984,
Master Turner; *Hall* v. *Wandsworth Health
Authority, The Times,* February 16, 1985,
Tudor Price J.; *Taylor* v. *Anderton, The Times,*
October 21, 1986, Scott J.; *Huddleston* v.
Control Risks Information Services [1987] 1
W.L.R. 701, Hoffmann J.
ss. 33, 34, repealed in pt.: 1984, c.28, sch.4.
s. 35, amended: 1982, c.53, sch.6; repealed in
pt.: 1984, c.28, sch.4.
s. 35A, see *President of India* v. *La Pintada
Compania Navigacion S.A.* [1984] 3 W.L.R.
10, H.L.; *Allied London Investments* v.
Hambro Life Assurance (1985) 274 E.G. 148,
C.A.; *Fansa* v. *American Express International
Banking Corp., The Times,* June 26, 1985,
Russell J.; *Edmunds* v. *Adas, Financial Times,*
February 12, 1986, C.A.; *Edmunds* v. *Lloyds
Italico & L'Ancora Compagnia di Assicurazione
e Riassicurazione S.p.A.* [1986] 1 W.L.R. 492,
C.A.; *Coastal States Trading (U.K.)* v. *Mebro
Minaeraloel GmbH* [1986] 1 Lloyd's Rep. 465,
Hobhouse J.; *Mewis* v. *Woolf,* September
12, 1986, Sir Hugh Park sitting as a Deputy
High Court Judge at Exeter; *R.* v. *Secretary
of State for Transport, ex p. Sheriff & Sons,
The Independent,* January 12, 1988, Taylor J.;
Metal Box Co. v. *Currys; Massey Ferguson
(U.K.)* v. *Same; Reckitt & Colman (Products)*
v. *Same* [1988] 1 W.L.R. 175, McNeill J.; *R.*
v. *I.R.C., ex p. Woolwich Equitable Building
Society, The Times,* July 26, 1988, Nolan J.
s. 35A, added: 1982, c.53, s.15, sch.1.
s. 37, see *Z.* v. *A-Z and AA-LL* [1982] 2 W.L.R.
288, C.A.; *Chief Constable of Kent* v. *V.*
[1982] 3 W.L.R. 462, C.A.; *Astro Exito Navegacion SA* v. *Southland Enterprise Co., The
Times,* April 8, 1982, C.A.; *Hart* v. *Emelkirk;*

1981—cont.

54. Supreme Court Act 1981—cont.
Howroyd v. Emelkirk [1983] 3 All E.R. 15, Goulding J.; Ninemia Maritime Corp. v. Trave Schiffahrtgese Uschaft mbH und Co. KG [1983] 1 W.L.R. 1412, C.A.; Chief Constable of Hampshire v. A. [1984] 2 W.L.R. 954, C.A.; Orwell Steel (Erection and Fabrication) v. Asphalt and Tarmac (U.K.) [1984] 1 W.L.R. 1097, Farquharson J.; Hill Samuel & Co. v. Littaur (1985) 135 New L.J. 57, Bingham J.; House of Spring Gardens v. Waite [1985] F.S.R. 173, C.A.; Parker v. Camden London Borough Council [1985] 2 All E.R. 141, C.A.; Daiches v. Bluelake Investments (1985) 275 E.G. 462; (1986) 51 P. & C.R. 51, Harman J.; Peacock v. London Weekend Television, The Times, November 27, 1985, C.A.; Ainsbury v. Millington [1986] 1 All E.R. 73, C.A.; Bayer AG v. Winter [1986] 1 All E.R. 733, C.A.; South Carolina Insurance Co. v. Assurantie Maatschappij "De Zeven Provincien" N.V. [1986] 3 W.L.R. 398, H.L.; Company, A (No. 00596 of 1986), Re [1987] BCLC 133, Harman J.; I. (A Minor) (Surrogacy), Re (1987) 151 J.P.N. 334, Sir John Arnold P.; Company, A (No. 003318 of 1987), Re [1987] 3 BCC 564, Harman J.; Oriental Credit, Re [1988] 2 W.L.R. 172, Harman J.; Maclaine Watson & Co. v. International Tin Council (No. 2), The Times, May 5, 1988, C.A.; Associated Newspapers Group v. Insert Media [1988] 1 W.L.R. 509, Hoffmann J.; J. (Wardship) (A Minor) (1988) 18 Fam.Law 91, Sheldon J.; Leisure Data v. Bell [1988] F.S.R. 367, C.A.

s. 40, amended: 1987, c.22, sch.6.

s. 40A, order 88/1621

s. 40A, added: 1982, c.53, s.55, sch.4; amended: order 83/1621; 1985, c.9, sch.2; c.61, s.51; c.65, sch.8; 1986, c.45, sch.14; repealed in pt.: 1985, c.61, s.51, sch.8.

s. 42, see Re Fletcher, The Times, June 12, 1984, C.A.; Rohrberg v. Charkin, The Times, January 30, 1985, C.A.

s. 43, see R. v. Newcastle upon Tyne Crown Court, ex p. Bradley, The Times, April 17, 1984, D.C.; R. v. Croydon Crown Court, ex p. Miller (1987) 85 Cr.App.R. 152, D.C.

s. 47, see R. v. Kent, The Times, May 13, 1983, C.A.; R. v. Hart (1983) Cr.App.R.(S.) 25; R. v. Nodjoumi (1985) 7 Cr.App.R. (S.) 183, C.A.

s. 47, amended: 1988, c.33, sch.15; c.34, sch.5.

s. 48, see R. v. Plymouth JJ., ex p. Hart [1986] 2 W.L.R. 976, D.C.; Dutta v. Westcott [1986] 3 W.L.R. 746, D.C.; Arthur v. Stringer (1987) 84 Cr.App.R. 361, C.A.

s. 48, amended: 1982, c.51, sch.3; 1983, c.20, sch.4; 1988, c.34, s.156.

s. 49, see Williams & Glynn's Bank v. Astro Dinamico Compania Naviera S.A. [1984] 1 W.L.R. 438, H.L.; Att.-Gen. v. Arthur Anderson & Co., The Times, October 13, 1987, Steyn J.

s. 51, see Re G. (Minors) (Costs: Official Solicitors) (1982) 126 S.J. 135, C.A.; Re G. (Minors)

1981—cont.

54. Supreme Court Act 1981—cont.
(Wardship: Costs) [1982] 1 .W.L.R. 438, C.A; E.M.I. Records v. Ian Cameron Wallace [1982] 3 W.L.R. 245, Megarry V.-C.; Re A Solicitor, The Times, October 19, 1983, Vinelott J.; Aiden Shipping Co. v. Interbulk [1986] 2 W.L.R. 1051, H.L.; Davies (Joseph Owen) v. Eli Lilley & Co., The Times, June 6, 1987, C.A.; Goscott (Groundworks), Re, The Times, March 28, 1988, Mervyn Davies J.

s. 52, rules 82/1109.

s. 52, amended: 1985, c.23, sch.1.

s. 54, see Coldunell v. Gallon, The Times, November 21, 1985, C.A.

s. 54, order 82/543.

s. 55, amended: 1988, c.33, s.156.

s. 56, see Day v. Grant; R. v. Manchester Crown Court, ex p. Williams [1985] R.T.R. 299, C.A.

s. 58, see C. M. Stillevoldt B.V. v. E. L. Carriers Inc. [1983] 1 W.L.R. 207, C.A.

s. 68, amended: 1982, c.53, s.59.

s. 69, see Goldsmith v. Pressdram [1987] 3 All E.R. 485, C.A.; Viscount de L'Isle v. Times Newspapers [1987] 3 All E.R. 499, C.A.

s. 72, see Universal City Studios Inc. v. Hubbard [1984] 2 W.L.R. 492, C.A.; Overseas Programming Co. v. Cinematographische Comerz-Anstalt and Iduna Film GmbH, The Times, May 16, 1984, French J.; Thorn E.M.I. Video Programmes v. Kitching and Busby [1984] F.S.R. 342, New Zealand H.C.; Charles of the Ritz Group v. Jory [1986] F.S.R. 14, Scott J.; Crest Homes v. Marks [1987] 3 W.L.R. 293, H.L.

s. 72, amended: 1984, c.46, s.54; 1986, c.39, sch.2; 1988, c.48, sch.7.

s. 73, rules 82/1109.

ss. 74, rules 82/1109; 88/1635.

s. 75, see Practice Direction, (C.A.) (Crown Court Business: Classification) [1987] 1 W.L.R. 1671.

s. 76, amended: 1987, c.38, sch.2.

s. 77, see R. v. Spring Hill Prison Governor, ex p. Sohi [1988] 1 All E.R. 424, D.C.

s. 77, rules 82/1109.

s. 77, amended: 1985, c.23, sch.1; 1987, c.38, sch.2; repealed in pt.: 1985, c.23, sch.2.

s. 79, see R v. Williams (Carl) [1982] 1 W.L.R. 1398, C.A., R. v. Croydon Crown Court, ex p. Claire, The Times, April 3, 1986, D.C.

s. 81, rules 82/1109.

s. 81, amended: 1982, c.48, ss.29,60; 1987, c.38, sch.2.

s. 84, rules 81/1734; 82/375, 1109, 1111, 1786; 83/531, 1181; 84/699, 1051; 85/69, 846; 86/632, 1187, 2151, 2289; 87/716, 1423, 1977; 88/298, 1322, 1635, 1695, 1699, 1700.

s. 85, rules 88/298, 1340.

s. 86, rules 82/1109; 84/699; 86/2151; 87/716, 1977; 88/1322, 1635, 1695, 1699, 1700.

s. 87, rules 82/1109; 87/1177.

s. 89, orders 82/1188, 1755.

s. 89, amended: 1982, c.48, s.60; repealed in pt.: order 82/1188.

CAP.

1981—cont.

54. Supreme Court Act 1981—*cont.*
ss. 93, 97, amended: 1986, c.57, sch.
s. 99, orders 82/1367; 83/713; 84/297, 1075; 85/511; 86/1361, 2207.
s. 100, amended: 1984, c.28, sch.2.
s. 104, order 82/379.
s. 106, repealed in pt.: 1985, c.61, s.51, sch.8.
s. 109, amended: 1984, c.51, sch.8.
ss. 116, 121, see *Re Mathew (decd.)* [1984] 2 All E.R. 396, Lincoln J.
s. 126, repealed in pt.: 1982, c.53, sch.9.
s. 127, rules 82/449; 83/623; 85/1232; 87/2042.
s. 130, orders 82/1707; 83/1180; 84/340, 887; 86/637, 705, 2144, 2185; 87/2042.
s. 133, regs. 83/680.
s. 138, see *Bankers Trust Co. v. Galadari; Chase Manhattan Bank N.A. (Intervener)* [1986] 3 W.L.R. 1099, C.A.
s. 142, amended: 1983, c.2, sch.8.
s. 143, repealed in pt.: 1982, c.53, sch.9.
s. 144, repealed: 1983, c.20, sch.6.
s. 149, repealed: 1984, c.28, sch.4.
s. 150, orders 84/540; 85/1197; 87/1263.
s. 151, see *Re A Solicitor, The Times*, October 19, 1983, Vinelott J.; *Dorval Tankships Pty v. Two Arrows Maritime and Port Services; Pakistan Edible Oils Corp. intervening, The Times*, August 9, 1984, C.A.
s. 152, sch.2, repealed in pt.: order 82/1188.
sch. 1, amended: 1986, c.16, s.5; c.39, sch.2; c.55, sch.1; 1988, c.48, sch.7; repealed in pt.: 1987, c.42, sch.4.
sch. 3, repealed: 1984, c.28, sch.4.
sch. 5, repealed in pt.: 1982, c.27, sch.14; c.51, sch.4; c.53, sch.9; 1983, c.20, s.35, sch.3; c.54, sch.7; 1984, c.28, sch.4; c.51, sch.9; 1985, c.9, sch.1; c.65, sch.10; c.71, sch.1; 1987, c.16, sch.16.
sch. 6, repealed in pt.: 1983, c.54, sch.6.
sch. 7, repealed in pt.: 1984, c.28, sch.4.

55. Armed Forces Act 1981.
Royal Assent, July 28, 1981.
order 81/1503.
s. 1, orders 82/1069; 83/1104; 84/1147; 85/196.
ss. 1, 6 (in pt.), repealed: 1986, c.21, sch.2.
s. 9, repealed: 1984, c.60, sch.7.
s. 13, amended: 1982, c.51, sch.3; 1983, c.20, sch.4.
s. 14, amended: 1986, c.21, s.13.
s. 29, orders 81/1503; 82/497.

56. Transport Act 1981.
Royal Assent, July 31, 1981.
Commencement orders: 81/1333, 1617; 82/300, 310, 866, 1341, 1451, 1803; 83/576, 1089; 88/1037, 1170.
see *Jones v. Thomas (John Barrie)* [1987] Crim.L.R. 133, D.C.
s. 5, order 82/1887.
s. 10, regs. 83/559; amended: *ibid.*
ss. 11, 13, 14, amended: 1985, c.9, sch.2.
s. 15, orders 81/1364, 1665.
s. 17, scheme 82/9.
s. 18, orders 83/930; 86/2130.

CAP.

1981—cont.

56. Transport Act 1981—*cont.*
s. 19, see *R. v. Kent (Peter)* [1983] 1 W.L.R. 794, C.A.; *Johnson v. Finbow* [1983] 1 W.L.R. 879, D.C.; *MacNeill v. Low, MacNeill v. Wright*, 1983 S.C.C.R. 6; *Donnelly v. Shotton*, 1983 S.L.T. 657; *R. v. Thomas (Kevin), The Times*, October 17, 1983, C.A.; *Drummond v. Mackinnon*, 1983 S.L.T. 681; *R. v. Thomas* [1983] R.T.R. 437, C.A.; *Tudhope v. Eadie*, 1984 S.L.T. 178; *King v. Lnongo, The Times*, March 10, 1984, Goff J.; *Porter v. Manning, The Times*, March 23, 1984, D.C.; *Scott v. Scott*, 1983 S.C.C.R. 458; *Miller v. Allan*, 1984 S.L.T. 280; *Stephens v. Gibb*, 1984 S.C.C.R. 195; *R. v. Sandbach JJ., ex p. Pescud* (1983) Cr.App.R. (S.) 177, D.C.; *Pender v. Keane*, 1984 S.C.C.R. 325; *R. v. Sandwell* [1985] R.T.R. 45, C.A.; *Luongo v. King* [1985] R.T.R. 186, D.C.; *Johnston v. Over* [1985] R.T.R. 240, D.C.; *North v. Tudhope*, 1985 S.C.C.R. 161; *R. v. Yates* [1986] R.T.R. 68, C.A.; *Allan v. Barclay*, 1986 S.C.C.R. 111; *Middleton v. Tudhope*, 1986 S.C.C.R. 241; *Owen v. Jones, The Times*, January 28, 1987, D.C.; *Railton v. Houston*, 1986 S.C.C.R. 428; *Miller v. Ingram*, 1986 S.C.C.R. 437; *Robinson v. Aitchison*, 1986 S.C.C.R. 511; *McFadyen v. Tudhope*, 1986 S.C.C.R. 712; *Briggs v. Guild*, 1987 S.C.C.R. 141; *Gray v. Jessop*, 1988 S.C.C.R. 71; *Richardson v. McPhail*, 1988 S.C.C.R. 27.
s. 19, order 88/1906.
Pt. IV (ss.19–31), repealed: 1988, c.54, sch.1.
ss. 20, 21, see *Porter v. Manning, The Times*, March 23, 1984, D.C.
s. 25, see *Gaimster v. Marlow, The Times*, December 9, 1983, D.C.; *Cotter v. Kamil* [1984] R.T.R. 371, D.C.; *Howard v. Hallett* [1984] R.T.R. 353, D.C.; *Vaughan v. Dunn* [1984] R.T.R. 376, D.C.; *Hayward v. Eames* [1985] R.T.R. 12, D.C.; *Anderton v. Royle* [1985] R.T.R. 91, D.C.; *R. v. Skegness Magistrates' Court, ex p. Cardy; R. v. Manchester Crown Court, ex p. Williams* [1985] R.T.R. 49, D.C.; *Owen v. Chesters* [1985] R.T.R. 191, D.C.; *Snelson v. Thompson* [1985] R.T.R. 220, D.C.; *Hughes v. McConnell* [1985] R.T.R. 244, D.C.; *Chief Constable of Surrey v. Wickens* [1985] R.T.R. 277, D.C.; *Pine v. Collacott* [1985] R.T.R. 282, D.C.; *Stepniewski v. Comr. of Police of the Metropolis* [1985] R.T.R. 330, D.C.; *Woon v. Maskell* [1985] R.T.R. 289, D.C.; *Graham v. Albert* [1985] R.T.R. 352, D.C.; *Bunyard v. Hayes* [1985] R.T.R. 348, D.C.; *Duddy v. Gallagher* [1985] R.T.R. 401, D.C.; *Broadbent v. High* [1985] R.T.R. 359, D.C.; *Sivyer v. Parker, The Times*, January 23, 1986, D.C.; *Anderton v. Kinnard* [1986] R.T.R. 11, D.C.; *Patterson v. Charlton* [1986] R.T.R. 18, D.C.; *Walton v. Rimmer* [1986] R.T.R. 31, D.C.; *Archbold v. Jones* [1986] R.T.R. 178, D.C.; *Johnson v. West Yorkshire Metropolitan Police* [1986] R.T.R. 167, D.C.; *Beck v. Scammell* [1986] R.T.R. 162, D.C.; *Price v. Nicholls* [1986] R.T.R. 155, D.C.; *Owen v. Morgan*

1981—cont.

56. Transport Act 1981—cont.

[1986] R.T.R. 151, D.C.; *Redmond* v. *Parry* [1986] R.T.R. 146, D.C.; *Sutch* v. *Crown Prosecution Service*, January 30, 1987, H.H. Judge Compton, Wood Green Crown Ct.; *Newton* v. *Woods* [1987] R.T.R. 41, D.C.; *McKeon* v. *Ellis* [1987] R.T.R. 26, D.C.; *Matto* v. *Wolverhampton Crown Court, sub nom. Matto* v. *D.P.P.* [1987] R.T.R. 337, D.C.; *McGrath* v. *Field* [1987] R.T.R. 349, D.C.; *Nugent* v. *Ridley* [1987] R.T.R. 412, D.C.; *Hobbs* v. *Clark* [1986] R.T.R. 36, D.C.; *D.P.P.* v. *Singh* [1988] R.T.R. 209, D.C.; *Francis* v. *Chief Constable of Avon and Somerset Constabulary* [1988] R.T.R. 250, D.C.; *Grennan* v. *Wescott* [1988] R.T.R. 253, D.C.; *Pearson* v. *Comr. of Police of the Metropolis* [1988] R.T.R. 276, D.C.; *Mayon* v. *D.P.P.* [1988] R.T.R. 281, D.C.

ss. 26, 30, see *Porter* v. *Manning, The Times,* March 23, 1984, D.C.

s. 30, see *Johnston* v. *Over* [1985] R.T.R. 240, D.C.; *R.* v. *Preston* [1986] R.T.R. 136, C.A.; *Redmond* v. *Parry* [1986] R.T.R. 146, D.C.; *Barnett* v. *Fieldhouse* [1987] R.T.R. 266, D.C.; *Mawson* v. *Oxford, sub nom. Mawson* v. *Chief Constable of Merseyside* [1987] R.T.R. 398, D.C.

s. 31, orders 81/1617; 82/300, 866, 1341, 1451, 1803; 83/576; 88/1037, 1170.

s. 32, repealed (S.): 1984, c.54, sch.11.

s. 32, 40, order 83/1089.

ss. 33, 34, repealed: 1982, c.39, sch.22.

ss. 35, 40, orders 81/1331; 82/300, 310.

sch. 1, order 84/1747.

schs. 1, 4, repealed in pt.: 1988, c.39, sch.14.

sch. 3, amended: 1984, c.32, sch.6.

sch. 5, order 81/1665; scheme 82/9.

sch. 6, order 86/2130.

sch. 6, repealed in pt.: 1985, c.30, sch.

sch. 7, see *R.* v. *Sandwell* [1985] R.T.R. 45, C.A.; *Johnston* v. *Over* [1985] R.T.R. 240, D.C.

sch. 7, amended: order 88/1906; repealed: 1988, c.54, sch.1.

sch. 8, see *Gaimster* v. *Marlow, The Times,* December 9, 1983, D.C.; *Annan* v. *Mitchell,* 1984 S.C.C.R. 32; *Aitchison* v. *Matheson,* 1984 S.C.C.R. 83; *Bunyard* v. *Hayes, The Times,* November 3, 1984, D.C.; *Tudhope* v. *Quinn,* 1984 S.C.C.R. 255; *Stewart* v. *Aitchison,* 1984 S.C.C.R. 357; *Cotter* v. *Kamil* [1984] R.T.R. 371, D.C.; *Howard* v. *Hallett* [1984] R.T.R. 353, .D.C.; *Vaughan* v. *Dunn* [1984] R.T.R. 376, D.C.; *Reeves* v. *Enstone, The Times,* January 15, 1985, D.C.; *Walton* v. *Rimmer, The Times,* February 11, 1985, D.C.; *Hayward* v. *Eames* [1985] R.T.R. 12, D.C.; *Anderton* v. *Waring, The Times,* March 11, 1985, D.C.; *Annan* v. *Crawford,* 1984 S.C.C.R.

1981—cont.

56. Transport Act 1981—cont.

382; *Morgan* v. *Lee, The Times,* April 17, 1985, D.C.; *Anderton* v. *Royle* [1985] R.T.R. 91, D.C.; *R.* v. *Skegness Magistrates' Court, ex p. Cardy; R.* v. *Manchester Crown Court, ex p. Williams* [1985] R.T.R. 49, D.C.; *Owen* v. *Chesters* [1985] R.T.R. 191, D.C.; *Kelly* v. *MacKinnon,* 1985 S.C.C.R. 97; *McDerment* v. *O'Brien,* 1985 S.C.C.R. 50; *Snelson* v. *Thompson* [1985] R.T.R. 220, D.C.; *Hughes* v. *McConnell* [1985] R.T.R. 244, D.C.; *Chief Constable of Surrey* v. *Wickens* [1985] R.T.R. 277, D.C.; *Pine* v. *Collacott* [1985] R.T.R. 282, D.C.; *Tudhope* v. *Craig,* 1985 S.C.C.R. 214; *Allan* v. *Miller,* 1985 S.C.C.R. 227; *Reid* v. *Tudhope,* 1985 S.C.C.R. 268; *Green* v. *Lockhart,* 1985 S.C.C.R. 257; *Stepniewski* v. *Comr. of Police of the Metropolis* [1985] R.T.R. 330, D.C.; *Woon* v. *Maskell* [1985] R.T.R. 289, D.C.; *Gull* v. *Scarborough, The Times,* November 15, 1985, D.C.; *McCormick* v. *Hitchins, The Times,* December 10, 1985, D.C.; *Graham* v. *Albert* [1985] R.T.R. 352, D.C.; *Bunyard* v. *Hayes* [1985] R.T.R. 348, D.C.; *Duddy* v. *Gallagher* [1985] R.T.R. 401, D.C.; *Broadbent* v. *High* [1985] R.T.R. 359, D.C.; *Sivyer* v. *Parker, The Times,* January 23, 1986, D.C.; *Anderton* v. *Kinnard* [1986] R.T.R. 11, D.C.; *Patterson* v. *Charlton* [1986] R.T.R. 18, D.C.; *Walton* v. *Rimmer* [1986] R.T.R. 31, D.C.; *Harris* v. *Tudhope,* 1985 S.C.C.R. 305; *Bain* v. *Tudhope,* 1985 S.C.C.R. 412; *Archbold* v. *Jones* [1986] R.T.R. 178, D.C.; *Johnson* v. *West Yorkshire Metropolitan Police* [1986] R.T.R. 167, D.C.; *Owen* v. *Morgan* [1986] R.T.R. 151, D.C.; *Beck* v. *Scammell* [1986] R.T.R. 162, D.C.; *Price* v. *Nicholls* [1986] R.T.R. 155, D.C.; *Redmond* v. *Parry* [1986] R.T.R. 146, D.C.; *O'Brien* v. *Ferguson,* 1986 S.C.C.R. 155; *Houston* v. *McLeod,* 1986 S.C.C.R. 219; *Sutch* v. *Crown Prosecution Service,* January 30, 1987, H.H. Judge Compton, Wood Green Crown Ct.; *Douglas* v. *Stevenson,* 1986 S.C.C.R. 519; *Tudhope* v. *Fulton,* 1986 S.C.C.R. 567; *Newton* v. *Woods* [1987] R.T.R. 41, D.C.; *McKeon* v. *Ellis* [1987] R.T.R. 26, D.C.; *Gallagher* v. *Mackinnon,* 1986 S.C.C.R. 704; *Fraser* v. *McLeod,* 1987 S.C.C.R. 294; *Matto* v. *Wolverhampton Crown Court, sub nom. Matto* v. *D.P.P.* [1987] R.T.R. 337, D.C.; *McGrath* v. *Field* [1987] R.T.R. 349, D.C.; *Nugent* v. *Ridley* [1987] R.T.R. 412, D.C.; *Hobbs* v. *Clark* [1988] R.T.R. 36, D.C.; *Mackinnon* v. *Westwater,* 1987 S.C.C.R. 730; *D.P.P.* v. *Singh* [1988] R.T.R. 209, D.C.; *Francis* v. *Chief Constable of Avon and Somerset Constabulary* [1988] R.T.R. 250, D.C.; *Pearson* v. *Comr. of Police of the Metropolis* [1988] R.T.R. 276, D.C.; *Mayon* v. *D.P.P.* [1988] R.T.R. 281, D.C.; *MacMillan* v. *Scott,* 1988 S.C.C.R. 219.

sch. 8, repealed: 1988, c.54, sch.1.

sch. 9, see *R.* v. *Kent (Peter)* [1983] 1 W.L.R. 794, C.A.; *McLellan* v. *Tudhope,* 1984 S.C.C.R. 397; *Johnstone* v. *Over* [1985] R.T.R. 240, D.C.; *Cardle* v. *Campbell,* 1985 S.C.C.R. 309; *R.* v. *Preston* [1986] R.T.R. 136, C.A.;

CAP.
1981—cont.

56. Transport Act 1981—*cont.*
Redmond v. *Parry* [1986] R.T.R. 146, D.C.;
Aird v. *Valentine*, 1986 S.C.C.R. 353; *Barnett*
v. *Fieldhouse* [1987] R.T.R. 266, D.C.;
Mawson v. *Oxford, sub nom. Mawson* v.
Chief Constable of Merseyside [1987] R.T.R.
398, D.C.
sch. 9, repealed in pt.: 1988, c.54, sch.1.
sch. 10, amended: 1984, c.27, sch.13; repealed
(S.): 1984, c.54, sch.11.
sch. 11, repealed: 1982, c.39, sch.22.

57. Employment and Training Act 1981.
Royal Assent, July 31, 1981.
Commencement order: 82/126, 951.
ss. 1–8, repealed: 1982, c.10. sch.4.
s. 10, amended: 1988, c.19, sch.3.
s. 11, order 82/126.
s. 11, repealed in pt.: 1982, c.10, sch.4.
s. 22, order 82/951.
sch. 1, repealed: 1982, c.10, sch.4.
sch. 2, repealed in pt.: *ibid.*, c.52, sch.3.

58. Education (Scotland) Act 1981.
Royal Assent, October 30, 1981.
Commencement order: 82/951.
s. 21, regs. 82/1734.
s. 22, orders 81/1557; 82/951. 1737; 83/371.
sch. 8, regs. 82/1734.

59. Matrimonial Homes (Family Protection) (Scotland) Act 1981.
Royal Assent, October 30, 1981.
Commencement order: 82/972.
s. 1, amended: 1985, c.73, s.13.
ss. 1, 3, see *Tattersall* v. *Tattersall*, 1983 S.L.T.
506.
s. 3, see *Welsh* v. *Welsh*, 1987 S.L.T. (Sh.Ct.)
30.; *Berry* v. *Berry* (O.H.), 1988 S.L.T. 650.
s. 4, see *Bell* v. *Bell*, 1983 S.L.T. 224; *Smith* v.
Smith, 1983 S.L.T. 275; *Ward* v. *Ward*, 1983
S.L.T. 472; *Tattersall* v. *Tattersall*, 1983 S.L.T.
506; *Colagiascomo* v. *Colagiascomo*, 1983
S.L.T. 559; *Brown* v. *Brown*, 1985 S.L.T. 376;
Matheson v. *Matheson*, 1986 S.L.T. (Sh.Ct.)
2; *McCafferty* v. *McCafferty*, 1986 S.L.T. 650;
Boyle v. *Boyle* (O.H.), 1986 S.L.T. 656; *Mather*
v. *Mather* (O.H.), 1987 S.L.T. 565; *Nelson* v.
Nelson, 1988 S.L.T.(Sh.Ct.) 26.
s. 4, amended: 1985, c.73, s.13.
s. 6, regs. 82/971.
s. 6, amended and repealed in pt.: 1985, c.73,
s.13.
s. 7, see *Longmuir* v. *Longmuir*, 1985
S.L.T.(Sh.Ct.) 33; *Dunsmore* v. *Dunsmore*,
1986 S.L.T.(Sh.Ct.) 9; *O'Neill* v. *O'Neill*, 1987
S.L.T. (Sh.Ct.) 26; *Fyfe* v. *Fyfe*, 1987 S.L.T.
(Sh.Ct.) 38.
s. 7, repealed in pt.: 1985, c.37, sch.2.
s. 8, amended: 1985, c.73, s.13.
s. 10, repealed: 1985, c.66, sch.8.
s. 13, see *McGowan* v. *McGowan* (O.H.), 1986
S.L.T. 112.
s. 13, amended: 1983, c.12, sch.1; 1985, c.37,
sch.1; 1987, c.26, sch.23; repealed in pt.:
1984, c.18, s.8, sch.

CAP.
1981—cont.

59. Matrimonial Homes (Family Protection) (Scotland) Act 1981—*cont.*
s. 14, see *Tattersall* v. *Tattersall*, 1983 S.L.T.
506; *Brown* v. *Brown*, 1985 S.L.T. 376; *Boyle*
v. *Boyle* (O.H.), 1986 S.L.T. 656.
s. 18, see *McAlinden* v. *Bearsden and Milngavie
District Council* (O.H.), 1986 S.L.T. 191; *Clarke*
v. *Hatten* (Sh.Ct.), 1987 S.C.L.R. 527.
ss. 18, 22, amended: 1985, c.73, s.13.
s. 19, see *Crow* v. *Crow* (O.H.), 1986 S.L.T.
270; *Hall* v. *Hall*, 1987 S.L.T. (Sh.Ct.) 15;
Berry v. *Berry* (O.H.), 1988 S.L.T. 650.
s. 22, amended: 1988, c.43, sch.9.
s. 23, order 82/972.

60. Education Act 1981.
Royal Assent, October 30, 1981.
s. 1, see *R.* v. *Hampshire County Council, The
Times*, December 5, 1985, Taylor J.
ss. 1, 2, 4, 5, 7, 9, see *R.* v. *Secretary of State
for Education and Science, ex p. L.* (1988) 86
L.G.R. 13, C.A.
ss. 1, 5, 7, 9, see *D. (A Minor), Re*, [1987] 1
W.L.R. 1400, C.A.
s. 2, amended: 1988, c.40, sch.12.
ss. 5, 7, see *R.* v. *Hereford and Worcester
County Council, ex p. Lashford, The Times*,
November 10, 1986, C.A.; *R.* v. *Secretary of
State for Education and Science, ex p. L.*
(1988) 152 L.G.Rev. 110, C.A.
s. 7, see *R.* v. *Oxfordshire Education Authority,
ex p. W., The Times*, November 22, 1986,
D.C.; *R.* v. *Hereford and Worcester County
Council, ex p. Lashford, The Times*, May 13,
1987, C.A.
s. 7, regs. 83/29.
ss. 7, 8, amended: 1988, c.40, sch.12.
s. 12, regs. 83/1499.
s. 12, amended: 1988, c.40, sch.1.
ss. 15, 16, amended: *ibid.*, sch.12.
s. 19, regs. 83/29, 1499.
s. 20, orders 81/1711; 83/7.
s. 21, sch. 3, see *R.* v. *Birmingham City Council,
ex p. Equal Opportunities Commission* [1988]
I.R.L.R. 96, McCullough J.
sch. 1, regs. 83/29; 88/1067.
sch. 1, amended: 1988, c.40, sch.1.
sch. 4, repealed in pt.: *ibid.*, sch.13.

61. British Nationality Act 1981.
Royal Assent, October 30, 1981.
Commencement order: 82/933.
see *R.* v. *Secretary of State for the Home
Department, ex p. Bibi (Mahaboob)* [1985]
Imm.A.R. 134, Mann J.
s. 1, see *Kamal Pravin Bhatt, Re*, September 28,
1984, H.H. Judge Hickman, St. Albans County
Ct.
s. 2, orders 82/1004, 1709; 84/1766; 87/611.
s. 4, amended: order 86/948.
s. 8, see *R.* v. *Secretary of State for the Home
Department, ex p. Dinesh, The Times*,
December 11, 1986, Russell J.
s. 16, order 82/1710.
s. 37, order 83/1699.
s. 37, amended: 1983, c.6, s.4; order 86/948.

1981—cont.

61. British Nationality Act 1981—cont.

s. 38, orders 82/1070; 83/1699.

s. 39, amended: 1988, c.14, s.3; repealed in pt.: 1983, c.20, sch.6; 1988, c.14, s.3.

s. 40, regs. 82/988, 989; rules 86/2176.

s. 40, amended: 1983, c.6, s.4.

s. 41, regs. 82/986, 987, 1011, 1123, 1526, 1647; 83/479; 84/230; 85/1574; 86/378, 2175.

ss. 41–43, 45–48, 50, 51, amended: order 86/948.

s. 49, repealed: 1981, c.61, sch.9.

s. 51, amended: 1983, c.6, s.4.

s. 52, order 82/1832.

s. 53, orders 82/933, 1834–1836.

sch. 1, amended: 1983, c.20, sch.4.

sch. 3, amended: order 83/882; 1985, c.3, sch.

sch. 6, repealed in pt.: ibid. (prosp): order 86/948.

sch. 7, repealed in pt.: 1982, c.16, sch.16; c.36, sch.3; 1988, c.1, sch.31.

sch. 8, see *Gowa* v. *Att.-Gen.* [1985] 1 W.L.R. 1003, H.L.

62. Companies Act 1981.

Royal Assent, October 30, 1981.

Commencement orders: 81/1621, 1684; 82/103, 672; 83/1024; 84/684.

repealed: 1985, c.9, sch.1.

s. 23, order 82/1654.

s. 25, regs. 82/104.

ss. 31, 32, regs. 81/1685; 82/1653.

s. 41, regs. 84/2007.

s. 43, regs. 81/1622; 82/104.

s. 72, regs. 85/622.

ss. 74, 77, see *House of Fraser, Petrs.,* 1983 S.L.T. 500; *Lloyd (F.H.) Holdings, Re,* [1985] P.C.C. 268, Nourse J.

s. 77, see *Westminster Property Group, Re, The Times,* July 10, 1984, Nourse J.

s. 96, see *R.* v. *Sutcliffe-Williams and Gaskell* [1983] Crim.L.R. 255, Oxford Crown Ct.; *R.* v. *Redmond and Redmond* [1984] Crim.L.R. 292, C.A.

s. 116, order 84/134, 1169.

s. 118, regs. 81/1622; 82/104, 674.

s. 119, orders 81/1621, 1684; 82/103, 672; 83/1024; 84/684.

sch. 2, amended: 1982, c.50, sch.5.

sch. 3, repealed in pt.: *ibid.,* sch.6.

63. Betting and Gaming Duties Act 1981.

Royal Assent, October 30, 1981.

s. 1, amended: 1986, c.41, sch.4; 1987, c.16, s.3; repealed in pt.: *ibid.,* s.3, sch.16.

s. 3, repealed: *ibid.,* sch. 16.

s. 6, order 85/515.

s. 6, amended: 1986, c.41, sch.4.

s. 7, amended: 1982, c.39, sch.6.

ss. 9, 12, amended: 1986, c.41, sch.4; repealed in pt.: *ibid.,* schs.4,23.

s. 12, regs. 83/1770; 84/261; 86/400, 404; 87/312, 1963.

s. 14, amended: 1982, c.39, sch.6; 1984, c.43, s.6.

s. 15, amended: 1984, c.60, sch.6.

1981—cont.

63. Betting and Gaming Duties Act 1981—cont.

s. 17, amended: 1982, c.39, sch.6; 1986, c.41, sch.4.

ss. 19, 20, amended: *ibid.;* repealed in pt.: *ibid.,* schs.4,23.

s. 20, regs. 88/333.

s. 21, substituted: 1984, c.43, sch.3; amended: 1985, c.54, sch.5; 1987, c.16, s.5; repealed in pt.: *ibid.,* sch. 16.

s. 21A, regs. 84/1178; 88/1602.

s. 21A, added: 1984, c.43, sch.3; amended: 1985, c.54, sch.5; repealed in pt.: *ibid.,* schs.5,27.

s. 22, order 86/2069.

s. 22, amended: 1982, c.39, sch.6; 1984, c.43, sch.3; 1985, c.54, sch.5; order 86/2069; repealed in pt.: 1982, c.39, schs.6,22.

s. 23, amended: *ibid.,* sch.6; 1984, c.39, sch.6; 1985, c.54, sch.5; 1987, c.16, s.4; repealed in pt.: 1985, c.54, schs.5,27.

s. 24, amended: 1982, c.39, sch.6; 1984, c.39, sch.6; 1985, c.54, sch.5; repealed in pt.: 1984, c.39, schs.3,23.

s. 25, amended: 1982, c.39, sch.6; repealed in pt.: *ibid.,* schs.6,22.

s. 26, regs. 88/1602.

s. 26, amended: 1982, c.39, sch 6; 1985, c.54, sch.5; 1987, c.16, s.5.

s. 28, amended: 1986, c.41, sch.4.

s. 29, amended: *ibid.;* 1987, c.18, sch 6 (S.).

ss. 28, 29, amended: 1986, c.41, sch.4.

s. 29A, added: *ibid.,* s.7.

s. 30, repealed: 1985, c.65, sch.10; c.66, sch.8 (S.).

s. 33, amended: 1985, c.54, sch.5.

s. 35, amended: *ibid.;* 1986, c.41, sch.4; repealed in pt.: *ibid.,* schs.4,23.

sch. 1, regs. 86/400, 404; 87/312, 1963.

sch. 1, amended: 1984, c.60, sch.6; 1986, c.41, sch.4; 1987, c.16, s.3; 1988, c.39, s.12; repealed in pt.: *ibid.,* s.12, sch.14.

sch. 2, amended: *ibid.,* s.12; repealed in pt.: *ibid.,* s.12, sch.14.

sch. 3, order 82/166; regs. 88/333.

sch. 3, amended: *ibid.;* 1982, c.39, sch.6; 1983, c.28, s.5; 1984, c.60, sch.6; 1986, c.41, sch.4; 1988, c.39, s.12.

sch. 4, orders 83/1838; 86/2069; regs. 84/1178.

sch. 4, amended: 1982, c.39, sch.6; 1983, c.28, s.5; order 83/1838; 1984, c.43, sch.3; c.60, sch.6; 1985, c.54, sch.5; order 86/2069; 1987, c.16, s.3; repealed in pt.: 1984, c.43, schs.3,23; 1987, c.16, s.3.

64. New Towns Act 1981.

Royal Assent, October 30, 1981.

s. 1, 5, repealed in pt.: 1985, c.5, sch.4.

s. 2, orders 84/84; 87/104.

s. 7, order 86/435.

s. 7, amended: 1985, c.51, sch.8.

s. 16, amended: 1984, c.12, sch.4.

s. 17, amended: 1985, c.5, sch.3.

s. 19, amended: 1984, c.12, sch.4.

s. 22, amended: 1988, c.50, sch.17.

s. 23, repealed in pt.: 1984, c.12, sch.7.

CAP.

1981—cont.

64. New Towns Act 1981—cont.

s. 24, substituted: *ibid.*, sch.4.

s. 26, amended: *ibid.*, sch.4.

s. 34, amended: 1984, c.55, sch.6.

s. 35, amended: 1985, c.5, sch.3.

s. 36, amended: *ibid.*, s.1, sch.3; repealed in pt.: *ibid.*, s.1, sch.4.

ss. 36, 37, see *R. v. Commission for New Towns, ex p. Tomkins and Leach* (1988) 28 R.V.R. 107, Kennedy J.

s. 37, amended: 1985, c.5, s.1, sch.3; repealed in pt.: *ibid.*, sch.4.

s. 39, amended: 1984, c.12, sch.4; 1985, c.5, sch.3.

s. 41, orders 82/184; 85/321–323, 1951; 86/502; 88/265, 412, 413, 1410.

s. 43, repealed in pt.: 1986, c.63, s.20, sch.12.

s. 44, amended: 1985, c.5, s.3; repealed in pt.: *ibid.*, s.3, sch.4.

s. 45, amended: 1985, c.51, sch.8.

s. 47, amended: 1985, c.5, s.3; c.71, sch.2.

s. 48, repealed: 1985, c.5, sch.4.

s. 49, repealed in pt.: 1986, c.63, s.20, sch.12.

s. 50, amended: 1985, c.5, sch.3; c.71, sch.2; repealed in pt.: *ibid.*, sch.1.

s. 51A, added; 1985, c.5, s.4.

s. 54, regs. 85/274.

s. 54, repealed in pt.: 1985, c.5, sch.4.

s. 56, amended: *ibid.*, sch.2; repealed in pt.: *ibid.*, schs.2,4.

s. 57, amended: *ibid.*, s.3; 1985, c.71, sch.2.

s. 57A, added: 1986, c.63, s.20.

s. 58, amended: 1985, c.5, sch.3; repealed in pt.: *ibid.*, sch.4.

s. 58A, added: *ibid.*, s.6.

s. 60, order 84/42.

s. 60, amended: 1982, c.7, s.1; 1985, c.5, s.7.

s. 61, repealed in pt.: *ibid.*, schs.3,4.

s. 62, amended: 1983, c.29, s.4.

s. 62A, order 86/1382.

s. 62A, 62B, added: 1985, c.5, s.8.

s. 62B, order 86/1436.

s. 63, repealed in pt.: 1985, c.5, sch.4; repealed (S.): *ibid.*, sch.3.

s. 64, amended: *ibid.*, repealed in pt.: *ibid.*, schs, 3, 4; repealed (S.): *ibid.*, sch.3.

s. 66, repealed in pt.: *ibid.*, sch.4, repealed (S.); *ibid.*, sch.3.

s. 67, amended: *ibid.*, s.9.

s. 68, amended: 1985, c.9, sch.2.

s. 72, amended: 1981, c.67, sch.4.

s. 74, amended: 1985, c.5, sch.3.

s. 77, order 82/184.

s. 77, amended: 1985, c.5, s.8, sch.3; repealed in pt.: *ibid.*, schs.3, 4.

s. 78, repealed in pt.: 1984, c.12, sch.7; 1986, c.31, sch.6; c.44, sch.9.

s. 79, repealed in pt.: 1984, c.12, schs.4,7; 1986, c.31, sch.6; c.44, sch.9.

s. 80, amended: 1985, c 5, sch. 3; repealed in pt.: 1985, c.71, sch. 1.

s. 82, amended: 1985, c.5, sch. 3, repealed in pt.: *ibid.*, schs. 3, 4.

sch. 2, amended: *ibid.*, sch. 3; repealed in pt.: *ibid.*, schs. 3, 4.

CAP.

1981—cont.

64. New Towns Act 1981—cont.

sch. 4, amended and repealed in pt.: order 85/442.

sch. 9, amended: 1985, c.5, s.2.

sch. 10, orders 82/184; 85/321–323, 1951; 86/502; 88/265, 412, 413, 1410.

sch. 10, amended: 1985, c.5, sch.3; repealed in pt.: 1985, c.71, sch.1.

sch. 11, repealed in pt.: *ibid.*

sch. 12, repealed in pt.: 1982, c.16, sch.16; 1983, c.23, sch.5; 1985, c.71, sch.1; 1986, c.31, sch.6; 1988, c.1, sch.31.

65. Trustee Savings Banks Act 1981.

Royal Assent, October 30, 1981.

repealed; 1985, c.58, sch.4.

ss. 1, 4, 32, see *Ross v. Lord Advocate* [1986] 1 W.L.R. 1077, H.L.

s. 28, order 84/539.

s. 31, amended: 1986, c.45, sch.14.

s. 53, orders 83/636; 86/841.

s. 54, amended: 1986, c.45, sch.14.

s. 56, orders, 82/711; 83/1126.

sch. 5, orders 82/235; 83/636, 647, 1353, 1584; 84/612, 1971; 85/798, 1274, 1501, 1830; 86/453.

sch. 6, repealed in pt.: 1985, c.65, sch.10; c.71, sch.1.

66. Compulsory Purchase (Vesting Declarations) Act 1981.

Royal Assent, October 30, 1981.

ss. 2–4, 6, regs. 82/6.

sch. 2, amended: 1988, c.50, sch.9.

sch. 3, repealed in pt.: 1984, c.51, sch.9.

67. Acquisition of Land Act 1981.

Royal Assent, October 30, 1981.

ss. 7, 10, 11, regs. 82/6; 87/1915.

s. 8, repealed in pt.: 1984, c.12, schs.4,7; 1986, c.31, sch.6; c.44, sch.7.

s. 12, regs. 82/6; 87/1915.

s. 12, amended: 1988, c.50, sch.17.

s. 13, see *R. v. Secretary of State for Transport, ex p. De Rothschild, The Times,* July 23, 1988, C.A.

s. 15, regs. 82/6; 87/1915.

s. 17, amended: 1985, c.51, sch.14; order 85/1884; 1987, c.3, sch.1; 1988, c.4, sch.6; repealed in pt.: 1985, c.51, sch.14; 1988, c.40, sch.13 (prosp.)

s. 22, regs. 82/6; 87/1915.

s. 25, see *R. v. Camden London Borough Council, ex p. Comyn Ching & Co. (London)* (1984) 47 P. & C.R. 417.

s. 28, amended: 1984, c.12, sch.4; 1986, c.44, sch.7.

s. 29, regs. 87/1915.

s. 29, amended: 1986, c.63, sch.8; 1987, c.3, sch.1.

s. 32, amended: 1984, c.12, sch.4; 1986, c.31, sch.6.

s. 38, regs. 83/23.

sch. 1, amended: 1988, c.50, sch.17.

schs. 1, 3, regs. 82/6.

sch. 4, repealed in pt.: 1982, c.16, sch.16; c.25, sch.7; c.52, sch.2; 1983, c.25, sch.4; 1984,

CAP.

67. Acquisition of Land Act 1981—*cont.*
c.27, sch.14; c.30, sch.11; 1985, c.12, sch.2; c.71, sch.1; S.L.R. 1986; c.31, sch.6; c.63, sch.12.

68. Broadcasting Act 1981.
Royal Assent, October 30, 1981.
s. 2, order 87/673.
s. 2, amended: 1984, c.46, s.45; order 87/673.
ss. 2, 4, see *R.* v. *Broadcasting Complaints Commission, ex p. Owen, The Times,* January 26, 1985, D.C.; *Wilson* v. *Independent Broadcasting Authority (No. 2)* (O.H.), 1988 S.L.T. 276.
s. 3, amended: 1984, c.12, sch.4; c.46, sch.5.
s. 4, see *R.* v. *Independent Broadcasting Authority, ex p. Whitehouse, The Times,* April 4, 1985, C.A.; *R.* v. *Horseferry Road Magistrates, ex p. Independent Broadcasting Authority* [1986] 3 W.L.R. 132, D.C.
s. 4, amended: 1988, c.40, sch.12 (prosp.); c.48, sch.7.
s. 9, amended: 1984, c.46, sch.5.
s. 12, amended: 1985, c.9, sch.2.
s. 14, amended: 1984, c.46, sch.5.
s. 18, repealed in pt.: 1985, c.51, sch.17.
s. 19, amended: 1984, c.46, s.38; 1987, c.10, s.1.
s. 20, see *R.* v. *Independent Broadcasting Authority, ex p. Rank Organisation, The Times,* March 14, 1986, Mann J.
s. 20, repealed in pt.: 1988, c.48, schs.7,8.
s. 25, repealed in pt.: 1984, c.46, s.50, sch.6.
s. 32, orders 82/1522; 86/629.
s. 32, amended: order 82/1522; 1984, c.46, s.40; order 86/626; 1986, c.41, sch.22; repealed in pt.: *ibid.,* schs.22,23.
ss. 33, amended: 1984, c.46, sch.5.
s. 34, repealed in pt.: 1986, c.41, sch.23.
s. 35, amended: *ibid.,* sch.22; repealed in pt.: *ibid.,* schs.22,23.
s. 42, amended: 1984, c.46, sch.5; 1985, c.9, sch.2.
ss. 53, 54, amended: *ibid.,* sch.2.
ss. 54, 55, see *R.* v. *Broadcasting Complaints Commission, ex p. Owen* [1985] 2 W.L.R. 1025, D.C.
s. 55, see *R.* v. *Broadcasting Complaints Commission, ex p. Thames Television, The Times,* October 8, 1982, Stephen Brown J.; *R.* v. *Broadcasting Complaints Commission, ex p. BBC, The Times,* May 17, 1984, C.A.
ss. 55–59, amended: 1984, c.46, sch.2.
s. 60, regs. 82/1413.
s. 63, amended: 1984, c.46, sch.5; 1985, c.9, sch.2; repealed in pt.: 1984, c.46, sch.6.
s. 66, order 87/2205.
sch. 3, repealed in pt.: 1984, c.46, sch.6.
sch. 4, amended: 1982, c.39, s.144; 1984, c.46, sch.5; 1986, c.41, sch.22.
sch. 7, amended: 1984, c.46, sch.5; 1985, c.9, sch.2.

69. Wildlife and Countryside Act 1981.
Royal Assent, October 30, 1981.
Commencement orders: 82/44, 327, 990, 1136, 1217; 83/87.

69. Wildlife and Countryside Act 1981—*cont.*
s. 1, see *Kirkland* v. *Robinson* [1987] Crim.L.R. 643, D.C.
ss. 1, 4, see *Robinson* v. *Everett, The Times,* May 20, 1988, D.C.
s. 3, orders 83/1685; 84/578, 1471; 87/1163; 88/324, 1479.
s. 5, see *Robinson* v. *Hughes* [1987] Crim.L.R. 644, D.C.
s. 6, regs. 82/1219, 1220.
s. 7, regs. 82/1221.
s. 19, amended: 1984, c.60, sch.6; repealed in pt.: *ibid.,* sch.7.
s. 22, order 88/288.
s. 26, orders 84/578, 1471.
s. 27, repealed in pt.: 1985, c.51, sch. 17.
s. 28, amended: 1985, c.31, s.2; 1988, c.4, sch.3; repealed in pt.: 1985, c.31, s.2; c.59, s.1.
s. 30, regs. 82/1346.
s. 32, amended: 1986, c.49, s.20.
s. 34, amended: 1985, c.51, sch. 3.
s. 36, amended: 1987, c.49, sch.1; repealed in pt.: 1985, c.51, sch.17.
s. 37, regs. 86/143.
s. 39, amended: 1985, c.51, sch.3; 1988, c.4, sch.3; repealed in pt.: 1985, c.51, sch. 17.
s. 41, amended: 1986, c.49, s.20, sch.3; 1988, c.4, sch.3; repealed in pt.: 1986, c.49, sch.4.
s. 42, amended: 1985, c.51, sch.3.
s. 43, amended: 1985, c.31, s.3; c.51, sch. 3.
s. 44, amended: *ibid.;* 1988, c.4, sch.3.
ss. 51, 52, amended: 1985, c.51, sch.3.
ss. 53, 56, see *Rubenstein* v. *Secretary of State for the Environment* [1988] J.P.L. 85, Taylor J.
s. 54, amended: 1984, c.27, sch.13.
s. 57, regs. 83/21.
s. 60, repealed in pt.: 1984, c.27, sch.14.
s. 66, amended: 1985, c.51, sch.3.
s. 68, order 83/512.
s 70A, added: 1985, c.59, s.1.
s. 71, amended: 1988, c.4, sch.3.
s. 72, amended: 1984, c.54, sch.9 (S.); 1985, c.51, sch.3.
s. 74, orders 82/44, 327, 990, 1136, 1217; 83/20, 87.
sch. 5, amended and repealed in pt.: order 88/288.
sch. 8, amended: *ibid.*
schs. 14, 15, regs. 83/21.
schs. 14, 15, amended: 1985, c.51, sch.3.

70. Consolidated Fund (No. 2) Act 1981.
Royal Assent, December 22, 1981.
repealed: 1983, c.27, sch.(C).

71. Nuclear Industry (Finance) Act 1981.
Royal Assent, December 22, 1981.

72. Housing (Amendment) (Scotland) Act 1981.
Royal Assent, December 22, 1981.
repealed: 1987, c.26, sch.24.

1982

1. Civil Aviation (Amendment) Act 1982.
Royal Assent, February 2, 1982.
s. 1, repealed: 1986, c.31, sch.6.
s. 4, schs.1, 2, repealed: 1982, c.16, sch.16.

CAP.

1982—cont.

2. Social Security (Contributions) Act 1982.
Royal Assent, February 2, 1982.
sch. 1, repealed in pt.: 1985, c.53, sch.6; 1986, c.48, sch.5.

3. Currency Act 1982.
Royal Assent, February 2, 1982.

4. Shipbuilding Act 1982.
Royal Assent, February 25, 1982.
s. 1, repealed: 1983, c.58, s.1.

5. Hops Marketing Act 1982.
Royal Assent, February 25, 1982.
Commencement order: 82/463.
s. 1, order 82/463.
ss. 2, 4, order 82/1120.

6. Transport (Finance) Act 1982.
Royal Assent, February 25, 1982.

7. New Towns Act 1982.
Royal Assent, February 25, 1982.
repealed: 1985, c.5, sch.4.

8. Consolidated Fund Act 1982.
Royal Assent, March 22, 1982.
repealed: 1984, c.44, sch.(C.).

9. Agricultural Training Board Act 1982.
Royal Assent, March 29, 1982.
s. 1, order 88/1100.
s. 4, amended: 1987, c.29, s.1; 1988, c.19, sch.3; c.40, sch.12.
s. 5, amended: 1985, c.36, s.1; 1988, c.40, sch.12.
s. 5A, added: 1987, c.29, s.1.
s. 7, amended: *ibid.*
s. 7A, added: 1985, c.36, s.2.
s. 8, amended: 1985, c.9, sch.2; c.36, s.1; 1987, c.29, s.1.
ss. 13, 14, amended: 1988, c.40, sch.12.
sch. 1, amended: 1988, c.19, sch.3.

10. Industrial Training Act 1982.
Royal Assent, March 29, 1982.
s. 1, orders 82/920–922.
s. 1, amended: 1988, c.19, sch.3.
s. 3, order 85/1662.
s. 5, amended: 1988, c.19, sch.3.
s. 10, amended: 1986, c.15, s.1.
s. 11, orders 83/1679, 1956.
s. 12, order 83/1956.
s. 18, amended: 1982, c.24, sch.4; 1985, c.9, sch.2.
sch. 1, amended: 1988, c.19, s.29, sch.3.
sch. 2, order 82/921.

11. Canada Act 1982.
Royal Assent, March 29, 1982.
preamble, see *Manuel* v. *Att.-Gen.* [1982] 3 W.L.R. 821, C.A.

12. Travel Concessions (London) Act 1982.
Royal Assent, March 29, 1982.
repealed: 1984, c.32, sch.7.

13. Fire Service College Board (Abolition) Act 1982.
Royal Assent, April 7, 1982.
repealed: S.L.R. 1986.

14. Reserve Forces Act 1982.
Royal Assent, April 7, 1982.
s. 3, order 86/2026.

CAP.

1982—cont.

15. Coal Industry Act 1982.
Royal Assent, April 7, 1982.
ss. 1, 2, 4, 5 (in pt.), repealed: 1983 c.60, sch.
s. 3, amended and repealed in pt.: 1987, c.3, sch.1.

16. Civil Aviation Act 1982.
Royal Assent, May 27, 1982.
s. 2, regs. 83/550.
s. 2, amended: 1986, c.31, s.72.
s. 4, see *Air Ecosse* v. *Civil Aviation Authority,* 1987 S.L.T. 751.
s. 7, regs. 83/550; 86/1544; 87/379.
s. 11, regs. 83/550.
s. 14, amended: 1983, c.29, s.4, sch.2.
s. 15, order 84/65.
s. 15, amended: *ibid.*; 1985, c.9, sch.2.
s. 23, amended: 1985, c.9, sch.2; 1986, c.31, sch.4.
s. 24, amended: 1983, c.11, s.3.
ss. 27, 29, 32, repealed: 1986, c.31, sch.6.
s. 33, order 86/311.
ss. 33, 34 (in pt.), repealed: 1986, c.31, sch.6.
s. 35, order 86/1348.
s. 35, repealed in pt.: 1986, c.31, sch.6.
s. 36, repealed in pt.: 1984, c.22, sch.3.
ss. 37, 38 (in pt.), 40, repealed: 1986, c.31, sch.6.
s. 48, amended: 1984, c.12, sch.4.
s. 58, repealed: 1986, c.31, sch.6.
s. 60, orders 83/1905; 84/368, 1988; 85/458, 1643; 86/599, 1304, 2238; 87/2062, 2212; 88/251.
s. 60, repealed in pt.: 1986, c.31, sch.6.
s. 61, orders 83/1905; 84/368; 85/458, 1643; 86/599, 1304, 2238; 87/2062, 2212.
s. 61, repealed in pt.: 1986, c.31, sch.6.
ss. 64, 66, see *Air Ecosse* v. *Civil Aviation Authority,* 1987 S.L.T. 751.
ss. 64, 66, 67, regs. 83/550.
s. 73, regs. 82/1261, 1784; 83/332, 349, 969, 1833; 84/641, 1916, 1920; 85/160, 349, 510, 1916, 1917; 86/403, 1202, 2120, 2153, 2170; 87/269, 2083, 2100; 88/388, 772.
s. 73, amended: 1983, c.11, s.3.
s. 74, see *Civil Aviation Authority, ex p. Emery Air Freight Corp., The Times,* November 10, 1986, C.A.; *R.* v. *Civil Aviation Authority, ex p. Emery Air Freight Corp., The Times,* January 13, 1988, C.A.
s. 74, regs. 82/1784; 83/349, 969, 1833; 84/641, 1916, 1920; 85/160, 349, 510, 1916, 1917; 86/403, 1202, 2120, 2153, 2170; 87/269, 2083, 2100; 88/388, 772.
s. 74A, added: 1983, c.11, s.1.
s. 75, regs. 83/551; 86/1953.
s. 77, order 85/1643.
s. 82, regs. 83/1885; 84/474.
ss. 84, 85, regs. 83/550.
s. 88, orders 86/312, 1347; 87/1377, 2229.
ss. 88, 89, repealed in pt.: 1986, c.31, sch.6.
s. 93, order 86/2016.
s. 93, repealed in pt.: 1988, c.33, sch.16.
ss. 93A, 93B, added: *ibid.*, sch.15.
s. 97, order 86/1892.
s. 101, orders 84/368; 85/1643; 86/599, 1304; 87/2212.

1982—cont.

16. Civil Aviation Act 1982—*cont.*

s. 102, orders 83/1905; 84/368, 1988; 85/458, 1648; 86/599, 1304, 2238; 87/2062, 2212; 88/251; regs. 83/551.

s. 105, amended: 1984, c.54, sch.9(S.); 1985, c.9, sch.2; order 86/948; repealed in pt.: 1984, c.12, schs.4,7; 1985, c.15, sch.17; 1986, c.31, sch.6; c.44, sch.9.

s. 108, orders 86/1162; 87/456.

s. 108, amended: 1986, c.31, sch.4.

sch. 1, regs. 83/550.

sch. 2, regs. 84/575.

sch. 2, amended: 1984, c.29, sch.11; c.54, sch.9(S.); 1985, c.71, sch.2; repealed in pt.: 1984, c.54, schs.9,11(S.); c.55, sch.7.

sch. 4, amended: 1983, c.11, s.2.

schs. 5, 13 (in pt.), repealed: 1986, c.31, sch.6.

sch. 14, repealed in pt.: 1982, c.36, sch.3; 1986, c.31, sch.6.

sch. 15, repealed in pt.: 1982, c.36, sch.3; 1984, c.12, sch.7; 1986, c.31, sch.6.

17. Harbours (Scotland) Act 1982.

Royal Assent, May 27, 1982.

ss. 1, 2, order 83/316.

18. Industry Act 1982.

Royal Assent, May 27, 1982.

repealed: 1982, c.52, sch.3.

19. Deer (Amendment) (Scotland) Act 1982.

Royal Assent, June 28, 1982.

20. Children's Homes Act 1982.

Royal Assent, June 28, 1982.

s. 1, amended: 1983, c.41, sch.4; 1984, c.23, sch.1.

s. 3, repealed in pt.: *ibid.*, sch.10.

s. 4, amended: *ibid.*, sch.4.

s. 6, repealed in pt.: 1983, c.41, sch.10.

ss. 6A–6E, added: *ibid.*, sch.4.

s. 7, repealed: *ibid.*, sch.10.

s. 12, substituted: *ibid.*, sch.4.

s. 15, repealed in pt.: *ibid.*, sch. 10.

s. 16, amended: *ibid.*, sch.4.

21. Planning Inquiries (Attendance of Public) Act 1982.

Royal Assent, June 28, 1982.

22. Gaming (Amendment) Act 1982.

Royal Assent, June 28, 1982.

s. 2, sch. 2, repealed: 1987, c.19, sch.

23. Oil and Gas (Enterprise) Act 1982.

Royal Assent, June 28, 1982.

Commencement orders: 82/895, 1059, 1431; 87/2272.

s. 1–7, repealed: 1985, c.62, sch.4.

s. 3, orders 82/924, 1415.

ss. 9–17, repealed: 1986, c.44, sch.9.

s. 11, directions 82/1131; 86/980; orders 83/967, 968, 1096, 1667, 1668.

s. 21, orders 82/1606, 1622, 1648, 1684, 1685, 1766, 1797, 1851, 1852; 83/37–39, 67–69, 79, 131, 171, 222, 330, 347, 348, 413, 502, 543, 575, 595, 620, 646, 648, 669, 776, 777, 811–814, 835, 836, 852–855, 861, 933, 934, 997, 1011, 1012, 1097, 1134, 1256, 1257, 1261, 1262, 1273, 1288–1290, 1316, 1317, 1369, 1407, 1408, 1416, 1493, 1494, 1507, 1527, 1576–1578, 1585, 1586, 1617, 1618,

1982—cont.

23. Oil and Gas (Enterprise) Act 1982—*cont.*

1647, 1693, 1722, 1765, 1813, 1814, 1834, 1875–1877, 1921, 1922; 84/1, 21, 22, 29, 47, 48, 184–186, 211–214, 332–336, 377–379, 398–400, 429, 430, 486, 487, 527–530, 586–588, 625–630, 650–653, 685, 732–734, 795, 796, 833–837, 868–872, 900–904, 911–913, 970–975, 1007–1012, 1038, 1043–1045, 1058–1061, 1079, 1080, 1137, 1138, 1256, 1257, 1267, 1268, 1295, 1297–1299, 1351, 1352, 1385, 1386, 1426–1430, 1444, 1445, 1507–1509, 1570–1574, 1601–1603, 1620–1624, 1641–1645, 1662–1664, 1683, 1721–1726, 1771–1776, 1789–1791, 1828, 1849, 1870, 1895–1901, 1911–1914, 1947, 1948, 1999–2001, 2011; 85/13, 22, 82–87, 106–109, 114–117, 141, 188, 189, 280, 346–348, 391–394, 469–473, 483, 484, 514, 516, 517, 523–527, 603–609, 628–632, 690–692, 763–773, 790, 791, 793–795, 869, 870, 894–903, 928, 929, 946–954, 968–971, 1017–1022, 1041–1043, 1060–1062, 1080, 1081, 1225–1229, 1331, 1332, 1334, 1335, 1379–1382, 1385–1389, 1431–1437, 1462–1464, 1495–1498, 1509–1512, 1522–1524, 1647–1649, 1692, 1693, 1720–1723, 1750–1752, 1767–1771, 1810, 1811, 1813, 1814, 1824, 1825, 1867–1869, 1894, 1895, 1984–1950, 1972–1974; 86/27–51, 89–93, 106–109, 117, 118, 130–134, 157, 163–166, 200–206, 215, 236, 353–363, 433, 434, 460–462, 546, 548–550, 552, 605, 606, 815, 816, 818–822, 824, 826–830, 865, 889, 915, 941–943, 1007, 1008, 1012, 1092, 1101, 1130–1132, 1193–1200, 1281–1284, 1392–1396, 1462–1466, 1577–1586, 1665–1667, 1741–1747, 1838–1845, 2050–2052, 2055–2059, 2271–2274; 87/4, 53–59, 61, 62, 66–72, 199, 200–206, 591–595, 812–814, 974–989, 1094, 1095, 1399–1416, 1418–1420.

s. 21, repealed: 1987, c.12, s.24, sch.3.

s. 22, order 87/2198

s. 22, amended: 1987, c.12, s.24; c.49, sch. 1.

s. 23, order 87/2197.

s. 27, amended: 1983, c.21, sch.3; 1987, c.12, s.24; c.21, sch.2; repealed in pt.: 1987, c.12, s.24, sch.3.

s. 28, amended: 1987, c.49, sch.1.

s. 32, repealed in pt.: 1985, c.62, sch.4; 1986, c.44, sch.9.

ss. 33, 34, repealed: *ibid.*

s. 36, repealed in pt.: 1985, c.62, sch.4; 1986, c.44, sch.9.

s. 38, orders 82/895, 1059, 1431; 87/2272.

sch. 1, repealed: 1986, c.44, sch.9.

sch. 3, repealed in pt.: 1985, c.62, sch.4; 1986, c.44, sch.9; c.48, sch.5; 1987, c.12, sch.3; 1988, c.41, sch.13.

24. Social Security and Housing Benefits Act 1982.

Royal Assent, June 28, 1982.

Commencement orders: 82/893, 906.

see *R. v. Secretary of State for Health and Social Security, ex p. Sheffield City Council* (1985)

1982—cont.

24. Social Security and Housing Benefits Act 1982—*cont.*
18 H.L.R. 6, Forbes J.; *R.* v. *Housing Benefits Review Board of the London Borough of Ealing, ex p. Saville* (1986) 18 H.L.R. 349, Kennedy J; *R.* v. *Housing Benefit Review Board for Sedgemoor District Council, ex p. Weaden* (1986) 18 H.L.R. 355, Schiemann J.
s. 1, see *Palfrey* v. *Greater London Council* [1985] I.C.R. 437, D.C.
s. 1, regs. 82/894, 1349; 83/376; 87/372.
s. 1, amended: 1986, c.50, s.68.
s. 2, regs. 86/477.
s. 2, amended: 1985, c.53, s.18; regs. 86/477.
s. 3, regs. 82/894, 1349; 86/477; 87/868.
s. 3, amended: 1985, c.53, s.18, sch.4; 1986, c.50, sch.10.
s. 4, regs. 82/894.
s. 4, amended: 1984, c.48, sch.7.
s. 5, regs. 82/894; 84/385.
s. 5, amended: 1985, c.53, s.18; repealed in pt.: *ibid.*, s.18, sch.6.
s. 6, regs. 82/894; 84/385.
s. 7, orders 83/123, 1947; 84/2037; 86/67; regs. 87/33.
s. 7, amended: orders 83/123; 84/2037; 86/67; 1986, c.50, s.67; regs. 87/33; orders 87/45, 1978; repealed in pt.: 1986, c.50, sch.11.
s. 8, regs. 82/894.
s. 8, repealed: 1986, c.50, sch.11.
s. 9, regs. 83/376, 395; 85/1411; 86/318; 87/92, 413; 88/431.
s. 9, amended: 1985, c.53, s.19; 1986, c.50, s.67; repealed in pt.: *ibid.*, sch.11.
s. 11, Act of Sederunt 83/397.
ss. 11–16, regs. 82/1400.
ss. 11–16, repealed: 1986, c.50, sch.11.
s. 17, regs. 82/894; 85/1604; 86/477.
s. 17, amended: 1985, c.53, s.19.
s. 18, regs. 82/894.
s. 18, amended: 1984, c.48, sch.4.
ss. 19–21, repealed: 1986, c.50, sch.11.
s. 20, regs. 82/894.
s. 22, regs. 82/1349, 1738.
s. 22, amended: 1982, c.23, sch.3.
s. 22A, added: 1984, c.48, sch.7.
s. 23A, repealed in pt.: 1986, c.48, sch.5.
s. 24, repealed: 1985, c.53, schs.4,6.
s. 25, regs. 84/1965.
s. 25, repealed: 1986, c.50, sch.11.
s. 26, regs. 82/849, 1349; 83/376; 84/385; 86/318, 477; 87/92, 372, 868; 88/431.
s. 26, amended: 1985, c.53, sch.4; repealed in pt: 1983, c.41, sch.8.
s. 28, see *R.* v. *Secretary of State for Social Services, ex p. Association of Metropolitan Authorities* (1985) 17 H.L.R. 487, Webster J.; *R.* v. *Kensington and Chelsea London Borough Council, ex p. Woolrich, The Times,* September 1, 1987, Kennedy J.; *R.* v. *Kensington and Chelsea London Borough Council (Housing Benefits Review Board), ex p. Robertson* (1988) 28 R.V.R. 84, Kennedy J.
s. 28, regs. 82/1124, 1519, 1520; 83/57, 438, 912, 1014, 1239, 1242; 84/103, 104, 940,

1982—cont.

24. Social Security and Housing Benefits Act 1982—*cont.*
941, 1105, 1728; 85/368, 677, 1100, 1244, 1445; 86/84, 852, 1009, 1156, 2183; 87/1440.
ss. 28, 32, see *R.* v. *Secretary of State for Social Services, ex p. Cynon Valley Borough Council; R.* v. *Kensington and Chelsea (Royal) London Borough Council, ex p. Goodson* (1988) 86 L.G.R. 390, D.C.
Pt. II (ss. 28–36), repealed: 1986, c.50, sch.11.
s. 29, regs. 83/1242; 84/1105; 85/1244.
s. 30, regs. 82/1519.
s. 32, see *R.* v. *Secretary of State for Social Services, ex p. Waltham Forest London Borough Council; Same* v. *Same, ex p. Worcester City Council* (1987) 27 R.V.R. 265, D.C.
s. 32, orders 82/903, 904; 84/110; 85/440; 86/430, 2042; 87/1805.
s. 34, orders 82/905; 84/111.
s. 34, amended: 1987, c.6, sch.4.
s. 36, see *R.* v. *Secretary of State for Social Services, ex p. Association of Metropolitan Authorities* [1986] 1 W.L.R. 1, Webster J.
s. 36, regs. 82/914, 1126; orders 82/903, 904; 85/440; 86/430, 2042.
ss. 38, 41, 42 (in pt.), 44 (in pt.), repealed: 1986, c.50, sch.11.
s. 39, regs. 83/185, 186, 1598.
s. 45, regs. 82/1124; 83/438; 85/677; 86/1009; 87/92; orders 82/903–905.
s. 45, amended: 1986, c.50, sch.10; repealed in pt.: *ibid.*, sch.11.
s. 47, regs. 86/318; 87/92, 372, 413, 868; 88/431.
s. 47, repealed in pt.: 1986, c.50, sch.11.
s. 48, orders 82/893, 906.
s. 97, regs. 84/385.
sch. 1, regs. 82/894, 1349; 87/868.
sch. 1, amended: 1984, c.48, sch.4; repealed in pt.: 1985, c.53, sch.6.
sch. 2, regs. 82/894.
sch. 2, amended: 1983, c.41, sch.8; 1985, c.53, s.18; repealed in pt: 1983, c.41, schs.8,10; 1985, c.53, schs.4,6, c.65, sch.10; 1986, c.50, sch.11.
sch. 3, regs. 82/894, 1400.
sch. 3, amended: 1983, c.41, sch.8; 1984, c.48, sch.8.
sch. 4, regs. 82/894, 1126, 1400; 83/186, 197, 376, 505.
sch. 4, repealed in pt.: 1985, c.71, sch.1; 1986, c.50, sch.11; 1987, c.42, sch.4.

25. Iron and Steel Act 1982.
Royal Assent, July 13, 1982.
ss. 1 (in pt.), 2–32, 33 (in pt), 34 (in pt.), 35–38, schs. 1 (in pt.), 2–7, repealed: 1988, c.35, sch.2.
s. 1, sch. 1, repealed (prosp.): *ibid.*
s. 13, amended: 1988, c.1, sch.9; repealed in pt.: 1988, c.39, sch.14.
s. 18, order 82/1817.
s. 19, orders 82/1817; 84/1110; 85/1079.
s. 36, orders 84/1110; 85/1079.

CAP.

26. Food and Drugs (Amendment) Act 1982.
Royal Assent, July 13, 1982.
repealed: 1984, c.30, sch.11.
see *R. v. Uxbridge JJ., ex p. Gow, The Times,*
October 17, 1985, D.C.

27. Civil Jurisdiction and Judgments Act 1982.
Royal Assent, July 13, 1982.
Commencement orders; 84/1553; 86/1781,
2044.
see *Silver Athens (No. 1), The* [1986] 2 Lloyd's
Rep. 580, Sheen J.
s. 2, see *Porzelack K.G. v. Porzelack (U.K.)*
[1987] 1 W.L.R. 420, Browne-Wilkinson V.-C.;
Nordglimt, The [1987] FTLR 438, Hobhouse J.
s. 5, amended: 1987, c.42, sch.2; repealed in
pt.: *ibid.,* sch.2.
s. 9, orders 86/2027; 87/468.
s. 12, S.R. 1986 No. 359.
s. 18, amended: 1985, c.65, sch.8; 1986, c.32,
s.39; c.45, sch.14; 1987, c.41, s.45(S.); 1988,
c.33, sch.15; repealed in pt.: 1985, c.65,
sch.10.
s. 26, see *Silver Athens (No. 2), The* [1986] 2
Lloyd's Rep. 583; *Jalamatsya, The* [1987] 2
Lloyd's Rep. 164, Sheen J.
s. 27, see *World Star, The* [1986] 2 Lloyd's Rep.
274, Sheen J.; *Clipper Shipping Co. v. San
Vincente Partners,* 1998 S.L.T. 204.
s. 28, amended (S.): 1985, c.73, sch.2.
ss. 31, 32, amended: 1983, c.14, s.11.
ss. 32, 33, sch.13, see *Tracomin SA v. Sudan
Oil Seeds (No. 1)* [1983] 1 All E.R. 404, C.A.;
Tracomin SA v. Sudan Oil Seeds (No. 2) [1983]
3 All E.R. 140, C.A.
s. 40, repealed in pt.: 1986, c.47, sch.5(S.);
1988, c.34, sch.6.
ss. 41–46, see *St. Michael Financial Services v.
Michie* (Sh.Ct.), 1987 S.C.L.R. 376.
s. 48, Acts of Sederunt 84/1941, 1946, 1947;
S.R. 1986 No. 359.
s. 52, orders 83/607, 1703, 1704.
s. 53, orders 84/1553; 86/1781, 2044.
sch. 1, see *St. Michael Financial Services v.
Michie* (Sh.Ct.), 1987 S.C.L.R. 376; *Clipper
Shipping Co. v. San Vincente Partners,* 1918
S.L.T. 204; *Rich (Marc) & Co. A.G. v. Societa
Italiana Impianti PA; Atlantic Emperor, The,
Financial Times,* November 9, 1988, Hirst J.
sch. 5, amended: 1982, c.23, sch.3; 1985, c.9,
sch.2; 1986, c.39, sch.2; c.45, sch.14; c.50,
sch.10; c.60, s.188.
sch. 8, amended: 1986, c.39, sch.2; repealed in
pt.: 1984, c.15, sch.1.
sch. 9, amended: 1982, c.23, sch.3; 1987, c.47,
s.16(S.); repealed in pt.: 1985, c.37, sch.2.
sch. 13, order 84/1553.
sch. 14, amended: 1983, c.12, sch.1.

28. Taking of Hostages Act 1982.
Royal Assent, July 13, 1982.
Commencement order: 82/1532.
s. 3, orders 85/751; 87/455.
s. 3, repealed in pt.: 1988, c.33, sch.16.
s. 3A, added: *ibid.,* sch.15.

CAP.

28. Taking of Hostages Act 1982—*cont.*
s. 5, orders 82/1533, 1539, 1540, 1674, 1839;
85/751, 1992; 86/2015; 87/455, 2044.
s. 5, amended: 1988, c.33, sch.15.
s. 6, order 82/1532.

29. Supply of Goods and Services Act 1982.
Royal Assent, July 13, 1982.
Commencement order: 82/1770.
s. 12, orders 82/1771; 83/902.
s. 13, see *Metaalhandel Ja Magnus BV v. Ard-
fields Transport, Financial Times,* July 21,
1987, Gatehouse J.
s. 20, order 82/1770.

**30. Local Government (Miscellaneous Pro-
visions) Act 1982.**
Royal Assent, July 13, 1982.
Commencement orders: 82/1119, 1160.
see *Lambeth London Borough Council v. Grewal*
(1986) 82 Cr.App.R. 301, C.A.
Pt. I (s.1), see *R. v. Huntingdon District Council,
ex p. Cowan* [1984] 1 All E.R. 58, Glidewell J.
s. 1, amended: 1985, c.13, sch.2.
s. 2, see *R. v. Preston Borough Council, ex p.
Quietlynn; R. v. Trafford Borough Council, ex
p. Quietlynn; R. v. Chester City Council, ex p.
Quietlynn; R. v. Watford Borough Council, ex
p. Quietlynn, The Times,* March 22, 1984,
C.A.; *R. v. Bow Street Acting Stipendiary
Magistrate, ex p. Spiteri, The Times,* October
16, 1984, D.C.; *R. v. Birmingham City Council
v. ex p. Quietlynn* (1985) 83 L.G.R. 471,
Forbes J.; *Tunbridge Wells Borough Council
v. Quietlynn; South Tyneside Borough Council
v. Private Alternative Birth Control Information
and Education Centres; Watford Borough
Council v. The Same* [1985] Crim.L.R. 594,
D.C.; *Sheptonhurst v. Newham London Borough Council* (1985) 84 L.G.R. 97, C.A.; *R. v.
Peterborough City Council, ex p. Quietlynn*
(1987) 85 L.G.R. 249, C.A.; *Plymouth City
Council v. Quietlynn; Portsmouth City Council
v. Quietlynn; Quietlynn v. Oldham Borough
Council* [1987] 3 W.L.R. 189, D.C.
s. 5, see *Penwith District Council v. McCartan-
Mooney, The Times,* October 20, 1984, Taylor
J.
s. 8, repealed in pt.: 1984, c.55, sch.7.
s. 10, amended: 1987, c.27, s.47.
Pt. IX (ss.18, 19), repealed: 1984, c.30, sch.11.
s. 19, see *Dodds v. Spear, The Times,* October
31, 1985, D.C.
ss. 24, 25, repealed: 1984, c.55, sch.7.
s. 25, order 82/1160.
s. 28, repealed: 1984, c.55, sch.7.
s. 29, repealed in pt.: 1985, c.51, sch.17.
s. 30, repealed in pt.: 1986, c.44, sch.9.
s. 33, amended: 1985, c.51, sch.14; order
85/1884; 1988, c.4, sch.6; repealed in pt.:
1985, c.51, sch.17; 1988, c.40, sch.13
(prosp.).
s. 40, see *Sykes v. Holmes and Maw* [1985]
Crim.L.R. 791, D.C.
s. 40, amended: 1988, c.40, sch.12.
s. 41, amended: 1984, c.32, sch.6; 1985, c.51,
sch.14; order 85/1884; 1988, c.4, sch.6;
repealed in pt. (prosp.): 1988, c.40, sch.13.

1982—cont.

30. Local Government (Miscellaneous Provisions) Act 1982—cont.

s. 42, repealed: 1984, c.22, sch.3.

s. 45, amended: 1988, c.9, s.34; c.19, sch.3; repealed in pt. (prosp.): 1988, c.40, sch.13.

s. 48, order 88/66.

sch. 1, see *Manchester City Council* v. *Pryor, The Times,* December 23, 1983, Woolf J.; *Penwith District Council* v. *McCartan-Mooney, The Times,* October 20, 1984, Taylor J.; *R.* v. *North Hertfordshire District Council, ex p. Cobbold* [1985] 3 All E.R. 486, Mann J.; *R.* v. *Tyneside Justices, ex p. North Tyneside Borough Council, The Times,* November 7, 1987, Schiemann J.

sch. 1, amended: 1985, c.13, sch.2; 1987, c.27, ss.43, 46.

sch. 3, see *R.* v. *Preston Borough Council, ex p. Quietlynn; R.* v. *Trafford Borough Council, ex p. Quietlynn; R.* v. *Chester City Council, ex p. Quietlynn; R.* v. *Watford Borough Council, ex p. Quietlynn, The Times,* March 22, 1984, C.A.; *R.* v. *Bow Street Acting Stipendiary Magistrate, ex p. Spiteri, The Times,* October 16, 1984, D.C.; *R.* v. *Birmingham City Council, ex p. Quietlynn* (1985) 83 L.G.R. 461, Forbes J.; *Tunbridge Wells Borough Council* v. *Quietlynn; South Tyneside Borough Council* v. *Private Alternative Birth Control Information and Education Centres; Watford Borough Council* v. *The Same* [1985] Crim. L.R. 594, D.C.; *Lambeth London Borough Council* v. *Grewal, The Times,* November 26, 1985, C.A.; *Westminster City Council* v. *Croyalgrange* [1986] 1 W.L.R. 674, H.L.; *Sheptonhurst* v. *Newham London Borough Council* (1985) 84 L.G.R. 97, C.A.; *R.* v. *Peterborough City Council, ex p. Quietlynn* (1987) 85 L.G.R. 249, C.A.; *Plymouth City Council* v. *Quietlynn; Portsmouth City Council* v. *Quietlynn; Quietlynn* v. *Oldham Borough Council* [1987] 3 W.L.R. 189, D.C.; *Sheptonhurst* v. *City of Wakefield Metropolitan District Council, The Times,* November 18, 1987, C.A.; *Sierbein* v. *Westminster City Council* (1988) 86 L.G.R. 431, C.A.

sch. 3, order 82/1119.

sch. 3, amended: 1985, c.13, sch.2.

sch. 4, see *R.* v. *Bristol City Police, ex p. Pearce* (1985) 83 L.G.R. 711, Glidewell J.; *Watson* v. *Oldrey; Watson* v. *Malloy, The Times,* May 7, 1988, D.C.

sch. 4, amended: 1984, c.30, sch.10.

sch. 6, repealed in pt.: 1984, c.22, sch.3; 1986, c.63, sch.12.

31. Firearms Act 1982.

Royal Assent, July 13, 1982.

Commencement order: 83/1440.

s. 2, rules 83/1441, 1495(S.).

s. 4, order 83/1440.

32. Local Government Finance Act 1982.

Royal Assent, July 13, 1982.

Commencement order: 83/165.

s. 3, amended: 1987, c.6, sch.4.

s. 5, repealed in pt.: 1985, c.51, sch.17.

1982—cont.

32. Local Government Finance Act 1982—cont.

ss. 5, 8, see *R.* v. *Hackney London Borough Council, ex p. Fleming* (1986) 26 R.V.R. 182, Woolf J.

s. 8, see *R.* v. *Secretary of State for the Environment, ex p. Hammersmith and Fulham London Borough Council, The Times,* May 18, 1985, D.C.; *R.* v. *Secretary of State for the Environment, ex p. London Borough of Hackney, The Times,* May 11, 1985, C.A.

s. 8, amended: 1986, c.54, sch.1; 1987, c.6, sch.4; repealed in pt.: 1982, c.32, sch.6; 1986, c.54, schs.1,2.

s. 9, repealed in pt.: 1987, c.6, sch.5.

s. 12, amended: 1985, c.51, s.72; 1988, c.4, s.17; c.33, sch.11; c.41, sch.12; repealed in pt. (prosp.): 1988, c.40, sch.13.

ss. 15, 19, see *R.* v. *District Auditor for Leicester, ex p. Leicester City Council* (1985) 25 R.V.R. 191, Woolf J.

s. 16, amended: 1988, c.9, sch.4.

s. 17, see *Oliver* v. *Northampton Borough Council, The Times,* May 8, 1986, D.C.

s. 18, amended: 1985, c.43, sch.2.

ss. 19, 20, repealed in pt. (prosp.): 1988, c.40, sch.13.

ss. 19, 20, 22, see *Smith* v. *Skinner, Gladden* v. *McMahon* (1986) 26 R.V.R. 45, D.C.

s. 20, see *Hood* v. *McMahon, The Times,* August 1, 1986, C.A.; *Lloyd* v. *McMahon* [1987] 2 W.L.R. 821, H.L.

s. 23, regs. 83/1761, 1849; 86/1271.

ss. 25A–25D, added: 1988, c.30, sch.4.

s. 25AA, added: 1988, c.41, sch.12.

s. 29, amended: *ibid.*

s. 31, regs. 83/1849.

s. 31, amended: 1985, c.9, sch.2; c.67, sch.7; repealed in pt.: 1984, c.32, schs.6, 7.

s. 33, repealed in pt.: *ibid.,* sch.7.

ss. 33, 35, orders 82/1881; 83/165; regs. 83/249.

s. 35, regs. 83/1761, 1849; 86/1271.

s. 36, amended: 1988, c.4, sch.17.

sch. 2, amended: 1986, c.54, sch.1; repealed in pt.: *ibid.,* schs.1,2; 1987, c.6, sch.5.

sch. 3, amended: 1983, c.29, s.4, sch.2; 1985, c.67, sch.7.

sch. 5, repealed in pt.: 1984, c.32, sch.7.

33. Cinematograph (Amendment) Act 1982.

Royal Assent, July 13, 1982.

repealed: 1985, c.13, sch.3.

see *British Amusement Catering Trades Association* v. *Westminster City Council, The Times,* March 27, 1987, C.A.

sch. 2, repealed in pt. (S.): 1985, c.73, sch.2.

34. Forfeiture Act 1982.

Royal Assent, July 13, 1982.

Commencement order: 82/1731.

ss. 1, 2, see *Patterson, Petr.* (O.H.), 1986 S.L.T. 121.

s. 2, see *Cross, Petr.* (O.H.), 1987 S.L.T. 384.

ss. 2, 3, see *Royse (decd.), Re* [1984] 3 W.L.R. 784, C.A.

ss. 2, 7, see *K. (decd.), Re* [1985] 3 W.L.R. 234, C.A.

CAP.

1982—cont.

34. Forfeiture Act 1982—cont.
s. 4, see Decisions No. R(G) 1/84; No. R(G) 2/84.
s. 4, regs. 82/1732; 84/451; 87/214; order 84/1818.
s. 4, amended: 1986, c.50, ss.4,76.
s. 5, amended: ibid., s.76.
s. 7, order 82/1731.

35. Copyright Act 1956 (Amendment) Act 1982.
Royal Assent, July 13, 1982.
repealed: 1988, c.48, sch.8.

36. Aviation Security Act 1982.
Royal Assent, July 23, 1982.
s. 9, orders 85/1989, 1991; 86/2012, 2014; 87/451, 2041, 2043.
s. 9, amended: 1988, c.33, sch.15; repealed in pt.: ibid., sch.16.
s. 9A, added: ibid., sch.15.
s. 27, repealed in pt.: 1986, c.31, sch.6.
s. 29, amended: ibid., sch.4; repealed in pt.: ibid., sch.6.
s. 30, repealed in pt.: ibid.
s. 36, orders 83/81, 1644.
s. 38, amended: order 86/948; repealed in pt.: 1986, c.31, sch.6.
s. 39, orders 85/81, 1644; 86/2012, 2014; 87/451, 456, 2041, 2043.
s. 39, amended: 1988, c.33, sch.15.

37. Merchant Shipping (Liner Conferences) Act 1982.
Royal Assent, July 23, 1982.
Commencement order: 85/182.
ss. 2, 3, 13, regs. 85/405, 406.
s. 9, Act of Sederunt 86/799.
s. 15, orders 85/182, 447, 448.

38. Northern Ireland Act 1982.
Royal Assent, July 23, 1982.
s. 5, order 86/1036.

39. Finance Act 1982.
Royal Assent, July 30, 1982.
ss. 1 (in pt.), 2, repealed: 1984, c.43, sch.23.
ss. 5, 6, repealed in pt.: 1988, c.39, sch.14.
s. 9, order 82/1575.
ss. 13–17, repealed: 1983, c.55, sch.11.
s. 15, regs. 82/1088.
ss. 20–26, repealed: 1988, c.1, sch.31.
s. 27, repealed: ibid., sch.29.
s. 28, orders 82/1630; 83/93.
ss. 28–67, repealed: 1988, c.1, sch.31.
s. 29, regs. 82/1236; 83/311, 368; 84/1653; 85/1252; 87/404.
s. 41, repealed in pt.: 1988, c.39, sch.14.
s. 65, regs. 88/88.
s. 70, amended: 1986, c.41, sch.16; 1988, c.1, sch.29; repealed in pt.: 1986, c.41, sch.16.
s. 72, amended: 1983, c.28, s.32; 1984, c.43, s.62; 1985, c.21, s.6; 1988, c.1, sch.29; repealed in pt.: 1984, c.43, s.62, sch.23; 1985, c.21, s.6, sch.2.
s. 76, amended: 1987, c.51, s.72.
s. 77, repealed in pt.: 1983, c.28, sch.10.
s. 78, repealed: 1988, c.1, sch.31.
s. 80, repealed in pt.: ibid.; c.39, sch.14 (prosp.).
s. 85, repealed: 1984, c.43, sch.23.
ss. 86, 87, amended: 1985, c.54, sch.18; repealed in pt.: ibid., schs.18, 27.

CAP.

1982—cont.

39. Finance Act 1982—cont.
s. 88, amended: 1983, c.28, s.34; 1985, c.54, sch.18; 1988, c.1, sch.29; repealed in pt.: 1985, c.54, schs.18,27.
s. 89, repealed: ibid.
s. 90, repealed: 1984, c.43, sch.23.
s. 91, orders 83/403; 84/345.
ss. 91–127, repealed: 1984, c.51, sch.9.
s. 128, repealed in pt.: 1984, c.43, sch.23.
s. 129, repealed in pt.: 1985, c.54, sch.27.
s. 131, repealed: 1984, c.51, sch.9.
s. 134, see R. v. Att.-Gen., ex p. I.C.I., The Financial Times, January 29, 1985, Woolf J.
s. 136, repealed: 1988, c.1, sch.31.
s. 137, amended: 1982, c.52, sch.2; repealed in pt.: 1988, c.1, sch.31.
s. 138, repealed: ibid.
s. 139, amended: 1983, c.28, s.35.
s. 142, repealed in pt.: 1987, c.16, sch. 16.
s. 143, repealed: 1984, c.43, sch.23.
s. 144, order 82/1522.
s. 146, repealed: 1985, c.62, sch.4.
s. 147, amended: 1988, c.1, sch.29; repealed: 1986, c.44, sch.9.
s. 153, repealed in pt.: 1985, c.71, sch.1.
s. 154, orders 83/958; 84/194.
s. 154, repealed: 1984, c.43, sch.23.
s. 155, repealed: 1985, c.54, sch.27.
s. 157, amended: 1988, c.1, sch.29; repealed in pt.: 1984, c.51, sch.9; 1988, c.1, sch.31.
sch. 2, repealed: 1984, c.43, sch.23.
sch. 5, repealed in pt.: 1983, c.28, sch.10.
sch. 6, repealed in pt.: 1984, c.43, sch.23; 1985, c.54, sch.27; 1987, c.16, sch.16.
sch. 7, orders 82/1202, 1807; 83/1907; 84/1945; 85/1697; 86/386, 1440, 2191; 87/1224, 2127.
schs. 7–10, repealed: 1988, c.1, sch.31.
sch. 11, amended: 1988, c.1, sch.29; repealed in pt.: 1986, c.41, sch.16.
sch. 12, amended: 1983, c.49, s.6; 1984, c.43, sch.12; 1985, c.71, sch.2; 1986, c.41, s.56; 1988, c.1, sch.29; repealed in pt.: 1985, c.54, sch.27.
sch. 13, amended: 1983, c.49, s.7; 1985, c.54, sch.18; c.58, sch.2; 1988, c.1, sch.29; repealed in pt.: 1985, c.54, schs.18,27.
schs. 14–17, repealed: 1984, c.51, sch.9.
sch. 18, see R. v. Att.-Gen., ex p. I.C.I., The Financial Times, January 29, 1985, Woolf J.
sch. 18, amended: 1986, c.41, sch.21; repealed in pt.: ibid.
sch. 19, amended: 1983, c.28, s.35, sch.7; repealed in pt. ibid., s.35, schs.7,10.
sch. 21, amended: 1988, c.1, sch.29; repealed in pt.: ibid., sch.31.

40. Appropriation Act 1982.
Royal Assent, July 30, 1982.
repealed: 1984, c.44, sch.(C).

41. Stock Transfer Act 1982.
Royal Assent, July 30, 1982.
Commencement order: 85/1137.
s. 1, regs. 85/1145; 87/1294; 88/232.
s. 1, repealed: 1986, c.44, sch.9.
s. 2, order 88/231.

CAP.

1982—cont.

41. Stock Transfer Act 1982—cont.
s. 3, regs. 85/1144; 87/1293.
s. 6, order 85/1137.
s. 6, repealed in pt.: 1987, c.16, sch.16.
sch. 1, amended: 1985, c.51, sch.14; order 85/1884; repealed in pt.: 1985, c.51, sch.17; 1988, c.40, sch.13 (prosp.).
sch. 2, repealed in pt.: 1985, c.9, sch.1; 1987, c.16, sch.16.

42. Derelict Land Act 1982.
Royal Assent, July 30, 1982.
s. 1, orders 84/778; 85/1102–1104, 1653.
s. 1, amended: 1982, c.52, sch.2; 1984, c.57, sch.1; repealed in pt.: 1985, c.51, sch.17.

43. Local Government and Planning (Scotland) Act 1982.
Royal Assent, July 30, 1982.
Commencement order: 82/1137, 1397.
ss. 1–3, repealed: 1987, c.47, sch.6.
s. 4, order 83/120.
s. 5, regs. 83/534.
s. 8, amended: 1988, c.19, sch.3.
ss. 14, 34, see *Caithness District Council* v. *Highland Regional Council*, 1986 S.L.T. 519.
s. 22, regs. 83/270.
s. 24, amended: 1987, c.26, sch.23.
ss. 25, 30, amended: 1984, c.54, sch.9.
ss. 51–55, repealed: 1987, c.26, sch.24.
s. 65, order 83/120; regs. 83/534.
s. 69, orders 82/1137, 1397.
sch. 3, repealed in pt.: 1987, c.26, s.47, sch.6.

44. Legal Aid Act 1982.
Royal Assent, October 28, 1982.
repealed: 1988, c.34, sch.6.
s. 1, regs. 83/1451; 85/1880; 86/445, 1559; 87/388, 433.
ss. 5, 6, regs. 83/1863.
s. 7, regs. 83/1863; 84/1716; 85/1632; 87/422; 88/468.
ss. 7, 8, see *Sampson, Re* [1987] 1 W.L.R. 194, H.L.
s. 9, see *R.* v. *Huntingdon Magistrates' Court, ex p. Yapp* (1987) 84 Cr.App.R. 90, D.C.
s. 11, regs. 83/1863.
s. 16, orders 82/1893; 84/220, 730; regs. 88/468.

45. Civic Government (Scotland) Act 1982.
Royal Assent, October 28, 1982.
Commencement order: 83/201.
s. 3, see *Cunninghame District Council* v. *Payne*, 1988 S.L.J.(Sh.Ct.) 21.
s. 7, see *Gregan* v. *Tudhope*, 1987 S.C.C.R. 57; *Joseph Dunn (Bottlers)* v. *MacDougall*, 1987 S.C.C.R. 290; *McInnes* v. *Tudhope*, 1987 S.C.C.R. 368; *Normand* v. *Campbell* (Sh.Ct.), 1988 S.C.C.R. 142.
s. 9, amended: 1987, c.27, s.44.
s. 10, see *City Cabs (Edinburgh)* v. *City of Edinburgh District Council* (O.H.), 1988 S.L.T. 194; *Aitken* v. *City of Glasgow District Council* (Sh.Ct.), 1988 S.C.L.R. 287.
s. 10, amended: 1985, c.67, sch.7.
ss. 10, 13, see *McDowall* v. *Cunninghame District Council*, 1987 S.L.T. 662.

CAP.

1982—cont.

45. Civic Government (Scotland) Act 1982—cont.
s. 13, repealed in pt.: 1984, c.54, sch.11.
s. 18, amended: 1985, c.67, schs.2,7.
s. 19, amended: 1984, c.54, sch.9; repealed in pt.: *ibid.*, schs.9,11.
s. 20, regs. 83/1029; 86/1238.
ss. 20, 21, amended: 1985, c.67, sch.7.
s. 39, see *Joseph Dunn (Bottlers)* v. *MacDougall*, 1987 S.C.C.R. 290; *McInnes* v. *Tudhope*, 1987 S.C.C.R. 368.
ss. 39, 41, see *Thomson* v. *Kirkcaldy District Council* (O.H.), 1987 S.L.T. 372.
s. 40, see *Normand* v. *Campbell* (Sh.Ct.), 1988 S.C.C.R. 142.
s. 41, amended: 1985, c.13, sch.2; 1987, c.27, s.44.
s. 41A, added: *ibid.*
s. 46, see *White* v. *Allan*, 1985 S.C.C.R. 85; *Allan* v. *McGraw*, 1986 S.C.C.R. 257.
s. 48, amended: 1984, c.54, sch.9.
s. 51, see *MacNeill, Complainer*, 1984 S.L.T. 157.
s. 51, amended: 1984, c.46, s.26.
s. 52, amended: 1988, c.33, sch.15.
s. 52A, added: *ibid.*, s.161.
s. 54, amended: 1984, c.54, sch.9.
s. 58, see *Allan* v. *Bree*, 1987 S.C.C.R. 228.
ss. 62, 63, amended: 1986, c.64, sch.2; repealed in pt.: *ibid.*, sch.3.
s. 64, see *Aberdeen Bon-Accord Loyal Orange Lodge* v. *Grampian Regional Council*, 1988 S.L.T.(Sh.Ct.) 58.
ss. 64, 65, amended: 1986, c.64, sch.2.
s. 66, amended: *ibid.*; repealed in pt.: *ibid.*, sch.3.
ss. 67–69, see *Fleming* v. *Chief Constable of Strathclyde* (Sh.Ct.), 1987 S.C.L.R. 303.
ss. 67, 80, 83, see *Caithness* v. *Bowman* (Sh.Ct.), 1987 S.C.L.R. 642.
s. 87, see *University Court of the University of Edinburgh* v. *City of Edinburgh District Council*, 1987 S.L.T.(Sh.Ct.) 103.
s. 87, amended: 1987, c.26, sch.23.
s. 90, amended: 1987, c.47, sch.1.
s. 96, amended: 1984, c.54, sch.9.
s. 97, repealed in pt.: *ibid.*, sch.11.
s. 98, amended: 1987, c.27, s.48.
ss. 99, 103, see *Purves* v. *City of Edinburgh District Council*, 1987 S.L.T. 366.
s. 108, amended: 1987, c.26, sch.23.
s. 119, regs. 84/565; 88/1323.
s. 123, amended: 1987, c.3, sch.1.
ss. 124, 125, repealed (prospectively): 1982, c.45, s.126.
ss. 125, 128, amended: 1984, c.54, sch.9.
s. 129, repealed in pt.: 1987, c.9, sch.
s. 133, amended: 1984, c.54, sch.9.
s. 136, orders 83/202; 84/775.
s. 136, sch. 1, see *Seath* v. *City of Glasgow District Council*, 1985 S.L.T. 407.
s. 137, orders 83/201; 84/573, 774.
sch. 1, see *McDowall* v. *Cunninghame District Council*, 1987 S.L.T. 662; *Holmes* v. *Hamilton District Council* (Sh.Ct), 1987 S.C.L.R. 407;

1982—cont.

45. Civic Government (Scotland) Act 1982—*cont.*
Piper v. *Kyle and Carrick District Council,* 1988
S.L.T. 267; *Aitken* v. *City of Glasgow District
Council* (Sh.Ct.), 1988 S.C.L.R. 287.
sch. 3, repealed in pt.: 1987, c.26, sch.24.

46. Employment Act 1982.
Royal Assent, October 28, 1982.
Commencement order: 82/1656.
s. 1, repealed: 1985, c.9, sch.1.
s. 10, repealed in pt: 1988, c.19, sch.4.
s. 14, amended: *ibid.,* sch.3.
s. 15, see *Express and Star* v. *National Graphical
Association (1982)* [1986] I.C.R. 589, C.A.
ss. 15–18, see *Dimbleby and Sons* v. *National
Union of Journalists, The Times,* March 2,
1984, H.L.
s. 16, amended: 1987, c.43, sch.4.
s. 20, sch. 2, see *Salvation Army* v. *Dewsbury,
The Times,* March 1, 1984, E.A.T.
s. 22, order 82/1656.
sch. 3, repealed in pt.: 1985, c.65, sch.10; 1988,
c.19, sch.4.

47. Duchy of Cornwall Management Act 1982.
Royal Assent, October 28, 1982.
s. 6, amended: 1987, c.22, sch.6.
s. 9, amended: 1985, c.9, sch.2.

48. Criminal Justice Act 1982.
Royal Assent, October 28, 1982.
Commencement orders: 82/1857; 83/24(S.),
182, 627, 758(S.).
see *R.* v. *Lewis, The Times,* February 10, 1984,
C.A.
s. 1, see *R* v. *Power, The Times,* May 25, 1983,
C.A.; *R.* v. *Ardani* (1983) 77 Cr.App.R. 302,
C.A.; *R.* v. *Bates (John)* (1985) 7 Cr.App.R.(S.)
105, C.A.; *R.* v. *Bradbourn* (1985) 7
Cr.App.R.(S.) 180, C.A.; *R.* v. *Grimes* (1985) 7
Cr.App.R.(S.) 137, C.A.; *R* v. *Jeoffrey* (1985)
7 Cr.App.R.(S.) 135, C.A.; *R.* v. *Passmore*
(1985) 7 Cr.App.R.(S.) 377, C.A.; *R.* v. *Munday*
(1985) 7 Cr.App.R.(S.) 216, C.A.; *R.* v. *Roberts*
[1987] Crim.L.R. 581, C.A.; *R.* v. *Hayes* [1987]
Crim.L.R. 788, C.A.; *R.* v. *Hough* (1986) 8
Cr.App.R.(S.) 359, C.A.; *R.* v. *Reid; R.* v. *Cox,
The Times,* February 26, 1988, C.A.; *R.* v.
Stanley (1986) 8 Cr.App.R.(S.) 404, C.A.
s. 1, amended: 1988, c.33, sch.123.
ss. 1A–1C, added: *ibid.*
s. 2, see *R.* v. *Massheder* (1983) 5 Cr.App.R.
(S.) 442, C.A.; *R.* v. *Hayes* [1987] Crim.L.R.
788, C.A.
s. 2, amended: 1988, c.33, s.123.
ss. 4–6, repealed: *ibid.,* sch.16.
s. 7, see *R.* v. *Oakes* (1983) 5 Cr.App.R. (S.)
389, C.A.; *R.* v. *Oliver* (1983) 5 Cr.App.R. (S.)
477, C.A.; *R.* v. *Iqbal* (1985) 81 Cr.App.R. 145,
C.A.; *R.* v. *Fairhurst* [1986] 1 W.L.R. 1374,
C.A.; *R.* v. *Ealand and Standing* (1986) 83
Cr.App.R. 241, C.A.; *R.* v. *Learmouth, The
Times,* June 13, 1988, C.A.
s. 7, repealed: 1988, c.33, sch.16.
s. 9, see *R.* v. *Phillips* (1984) 78 Cr.App.R. 88,
C.A.; *Chief Constable of the Surrey Constabulary* v. *Ridley and Steel* [1985] Crim.L.R.

1982—cont.

48. Criminal Justice Act 1982—*cont.*
725, D.C.; *Howley* v. *Oxford* [1985] Crim.L.R.
724; (1985) 81 Cr.App.R. 246, D.C.
s. 12, see *R.* v. *Secretary of State for the Home
Department, ex p. H, The Times,* August 21,
1985, D.C.
ss. 12 (in pt.), 14, repealed: 1988, c.33, sch.16.
s. 15, amended: *ibid.,* sch.15.
s. 16, rules 83/621.
s. 17, amended: 1988, c.33, sch.8.
s. 20, repealed in pt.: *ibid.,* sch.16.
s. 21, see *R.* v. *Horrocks, The Times,* February
8, 1986, C.A.
s. 22, see *R.* v. *F. (A Child), The Times,* March
20, 1985, C.A.; *R.* v. *F. (A Child), The Times,*
April 20, 1985, C.A.
s. 25, repealed in pt.: 1983, c.41, sch.10; 1988,
c.34, sch.6.
s. 29, repealed in pt.: *ibid.*
s. 34, repealed in pt.: 1984, c.60, sch.7.
s. 39, amended: 1984, c.32, sch.6; repealed in
pt: 1988, c.54, sch.1.
s. 43, amended: 1988, c.33, s.58; repealed in
pt.: *ibid.,* sch.16.
ss. 44, 45, repealed: 1985, c.31, sch.6.
s. 46, repealed in pt.: 1985, c.9, sch.1.
s. 60, repealed in pt.: 1988, c.34, sch.6.
s. 69, repealed in pt.: 1986, c.21, sch.2.
s. 72, see *R.* v. *Tonner; R.* v. *Evans* [1984]
Crim.L.R. 618; [1985] 1 W.L.R. 344, C.A.
s. 73, see *Thomson* v. *H.M. Advocate,* 1988
S.C.C.R. 354.
ss. 74, 75, repealed in pt.: 1988, c.33, sch.16.
s. 80, orders 82/1857; 83/24(S.), 182, 627,
758(S.).
s. 80, repealed in pt.: 1988, c.33, sch.16.
s. 81, orders 83/1897, 1898; 84/1690; 86/1884.
s. 81, repealed in pt.: 1985, c.31, sch.6.
sch. 1, amended: 1986, c.32, s.24; c.64, sch.2;
1988, c.33, sch.15; c.54, sch.3; repealed in
pt.: 1986, c.64, sch.3.
sch. 2, repealed in pt.: 1988, c.54, sch.1.
sch. 3, repealed in pt.: 1982, c.33, sch.2; 1984,
c.27, sch.14; c.30, sch.11; 1985, c.71, sch.1;
1988, c.54, sch.1.
sch. 4, repealed in pt.: 1984, c.28, sch.4.
sch. 6, repealed in pt.: 1988, c.54, sch.1.
sch. 8, repealed in pt.: 1988, c.33, sch.16.
sch. 14, repealed in pt: 1983, c.53, sch.3; c.55,
sch.11; 1984, c.34, s.2.
sch. 15, repealed in pt.; 1984, c.58, sch.10(S.);
1988, c.54, sch.1.
sch. 17, see *R.* v. *Power, The Times,* May 25,
1983, C.A.; *R.* v. *Ardani* (1983) 77 Cr.App.R.
302, C.A.

49. Transport Act 1982.
Royal Assent, October 28, 1982.
Commencement orders: 82/1561, 1804;
83/276, 577, 650(S.); 86/1326.
Pt. I (ss. 1–7), repealed: 1985, c.67, sch.8.
s. 7, amended: 1985, c.9, sch.2.
ss. 9, 10, amended (prosp.): 1988, c.54, sch.2.
s. 13, amended: 1985, c.9, sch.2; 1988, c.54,
sch.2 (prosp.)
s. 16, repealed: *ibid.,* sch.1.

1982—cont.
49. Transport Act 1982—cont.
s. 17, amended (prosp.): *ibid.*, sch.2, repealed in pt.: *ibid.*, sch.1.
ss. 18–23, amended (prosp.): *ibid.*, sch.2.
s. 24, amended (prosp.): *ibid.*, sch.2; repealed in pt.: *ibid.*, sch.1.
s. 26, amended (prosp.): *ibid.*, sch.2.
Pt. III (ss.27–51), repealed: *ibid.*, sch.1.
s. 28, amended: 1988, c.33, s.63.
s. 29, orders 86/555(S.), 1327.
s. 29, amended: order 86/555(S.).
ss. 34, 35, 47, 50, amended: 1988, c.33, sch.15.
ss. 42, 43, amended (S.): 1985, c.73, sch.2.
s. 49, regs. 86/1330.
s. 53, regs. 83/220.
ss. 53–55, repealed: 1984, c.27, sch.14.
s. 55, order 83/218.
ss. 56–60, repealed: 1988, c.54, sch.1.
ss. 61, 62, repealed: 1984, c.27, sch.14.
ss. 63, 64, repealed: 198, c.54, sch.1.
ss. 64 (in pt.), 69, repealed: 1984, c.27, sch.14.
s. 70, order 84/1996; amended: *ibid.*; 1986, c.50, sch.10.
s. 72, amended (S.): 1984, c.54, sch.9; repealed in pt.: 1984, c.27, sch.13.
s. 73, orders 83/218; 86/1327, 1330.
s. 73, repealed in pt.: 1984, c.27, sch.13; 1985, c.67, sch.8.
s. 76, orders 82/1561, 1804; 83/276, 577, 650(S.); 84/175; 86/1326.
s. 76, repealed in pt.: 1984, c.27, sch.14.
schs. 1–3, repealed: 1988, c.54, sch.1.
sch. 2, amended (S.): 1984, c.54, sch.9; repealed in pt.(S.): *ibid.*, sch.11.
sch. 5, repealed in pt.: *ibid.*; 1988, c.54, sch.1.

50. Insurance Companies Act 1982.
Royal Assent, October 28, 1982.
amended: 1985, c.9, sch.2.
s. 2, regs. 85/1419; 87/2130.
s. 2, amended: *ibid.*
s. 5, regs. 85/1419; 87/2130.
s. 7, regs. 85/1419.
s. 7, amended: 1985, c.9, sch.2; 1986, c.60, s.134.
s. 9, regs. 85/1419.
s. 10, amended: 1985, c.9, sch.2.
s. 15, regs. 85/1419; 87/2130.
s. 15, amended: *ibid.*
s. 17, regs. 83/469, 1192, 1811; 87/2130; 88/672.
s. 18, regs. 83/1192, 1811; 88/672.
s. 20, regs. 83/1811.
s. 21, regs. 83/469, 1192, 1811.
s. 21, amended: 1985, c.9, sch.2.
s. 21A, added: 1986, c.60, s.135.
s. 31A, added: *ibid.*, s.136.
ss. 32, 33, regs. 85/1419; 87/2130.
s. 35, regs. 85/1419.
ss. 47A, added: 1985, c.9, s.25; amended: 1986, c.60, sch.13.
s. 47B, added: 1985, c.9, s.25.
s. 48, amended: *ibid.*
s. 49, amended: *ibid.*; regs. 87/2118.
s. 50, amended: 1985, c.9, s.25.
ss. 53, 54, amended: *ibid.*; 1986, c.45, sch.14.

1982—cont.
50. Insurance Companies Act 1982—cont.
ss. 55, 56, amended: 1985, c. 65, sch.8; 1986, c.45, sch.14.
s. 57, amended: 1985, c.65, sch.8; repealed in pt.: *ibid.*, sch.10.
s. 59, rules 85/95; 86/341, 1918, 2002.
s. 59, amended: 1985, c.9, sch.2; c.65, sch.8; 1986, c.45, sch.14.
ss. 60–62, regs. 85/1419.
s. 71, amended: 1985, c.9, sch.2; 1986, c.60, ss.135,136.
s. 72, regs. 83/396; 85/1419.
s. 72, amended: 1984, c.46, sch.5.
s. 73, repealed: 1986, c.60, s.137.
ss. 74, 75, regs. 85/1419.
s. 78, regs. 85/1419; 88/673.
s. 78, amended: 1986, c.60, s.137.
s. 79, repealed: *ibid.*, sch. 17.
ss. 83, 84, 86, regs. 83/224.
ss. 87, 89, amended: 1985, c.9, sch.2.
s. 90, regs. 83/224; 85/1419; 88/673.
s. 94A, added: 1985, c.46, s.1.
s. 94A, regs. 86/446; 87/350; 88/352.
s. 96, regs. 83/224, 469, 1192, 1811; 88/672.
s. 96, amended: 1985, c.9, sch.2; 1986, c.45, sch.14.
s. 97, regs. 83/224, 396, 469, 1192, 1811; 85/1419; 86/446; 87/350, 2130; 88/352, 672, 673.
s. 100, amended: 1985, c.9, sch.2.
sch. 2, amended: regs. 87/2130.
sch. 4, repealed in pt.: 1985, c.9, sch.1.
sch. 5, repealed in pt.: 1984, c.43, sch.23; c.51, sch.9; 1985, c.71, sch.1; 1986, c.53, sch.19; 1987, c.22, sch.7; 1988, c.1, sch.31; c.54, sch.1.

51. Mental Health (Amendment) Act 1982.
Royal Assent, October 28, 1982.
Commencement order: 83/890.
ss. 1–33, 35–61, repealed: 1983, c.20, sch.6.
s. 62, repealed: 1983, c.2, sch.9.
s. 63, repealed in pt.: 1983, c.20, sch.6; c.23, sch.3.
s. 64, repealed in pt.: 1982, c.51, sch.4; 1983, c.20, sch.6.
ss. 66, 68, repealed: *ibid.*
s. 69, order 83/890.
s. 69, repealed in pt.: 1983, c.2, sch.9; c.20, sch.6.
s. 70, amended: 1983, c.2, sch.8; c.20, sch.4; repealed in pt.: 1983, c.2, sch.9; c.20, schs.4,6; S.L.R. 1986.
sch. 1, repealed: 1983, c.20, sch.6.
sch. 2, repealed: 1983, c.2, sch.9.
sch. 3, repealed in pt.: 1983, c.20, sch.6; 1984, c.36, sch.5.
sch. 5, repealed in pt.: 1983, c.20, sch.6.

52. Industrial Development Act 1982.
Royal Assent, October 28, 1982.
s. 1, orders 84/1844; 88/322.
s. 1, amended: 1984, c.57, s.4, sch.1.
Pt. II (ss.2–6), substituted: *ibid.*, s.5, sch.1.
s. 5, orders 84/1843, 1846.
s. 14, amended: 1986, c.63, sch.11.
s. 14A, added: *ibid.*
s. 15, repealed in pt.: *ibid.*, sch.12.

CAP.

1982—cont.

52. Industrial Development Act 1982—cont.
s. 15, repealed in pt. (S.): *ibid.*
s. 16, repealed in pt.: 1985, c.25, s.4, sch.
s. 18, repealed in pt. (prospectively): 1984, c.57, sch.2.
sch. 1, amended: *ibid.*, sch.1; repealed in pt. (prospectively): *ibid.*, sch.2.
sch. 2, repealed in pt.: 1986, c.63, sch.11; 1988, c.1, sch.31.
sch. 2, repealed in pt.(S.): 1986, c.63, sch.11.

53. Administration of Justice Act 1982.
Royal Assent, October 28, 1982.
Commencement orders: 83/236; 84/1142, 1237(S.); 85/858.
see *Food Corporation of India* v. *Marastro Cia. Naviera S.A.: the Trade Fortitude* [1985] 2 Lloyd's Rep. 579, Leggatt J.
s. 3, repealed in pt.: 1983, c.14, sch.3.
ss. 7–9, see *Denheen* v. *British Railways Board* (O.H.), 1986 S.L.T. 249.
s. 8, see *Forsyth's Curator Bonis* v. *Govan Shipbuilders*, 1989 S.L.T. 91.
ss. 8, 9, see *Lynch* v. *W. Alexander & Sons (Midlands)* (Sh.Ct.) 1987 S.C.L.R. 780.
s. 12, see *Potter* v. *McCulloch* (O.H.), 1987 S.L.T. 308; *White* v. *Inveresk Paper Co.* (O.H.), 1987 S.L.T. 586; *White* v. *Inveresk Paper Co. (No. 2)* (O.H.), 1988 S.L.T. 2.
s. 13, amended (S.): 1986, c.9, sch.1.
s. 15, repealed in pt.: 1984, c.28, sch.2.
s. 21, see *Williams (decd.), Re* [1985] 1 All E.R. 964, Nicholls J.
s. 29, orders 84/297, 1075.
ss. 29 33, repealed: 1984, c.28, sch.2.
s. 35, rules 88/817.
s. 35A, see *Edmunds* v. *Lloyds Italico, The Times*, February 15, 1986, C.A.
s. 36, repealed: 1984, c.28, sch.2.
s. 38, rules 87/821.
s. 38, repealed in pt.: 1986, c.57, s.4.
s. 39, amended: *ibid.*, s.5.
s. 42, repealed in pt.: 1986, c.60, sch.17.
s. 46, repealed in pt.: 1988, c.1, sch.31.
s. 55, repealed in pt.: 1984, c 28, sch.2.
s. 62, see *Duke* v. *Plessey* (O.H.), 1987 S.L.T. 638.
s. 62, repealed: 1988, c.13, sch.4.
s. 63, see *R.* v. *Elliott* [1985] Crim.L.R. 310; (1985) 81 Cr.App.R. 115, C.A.
s. 67, see *R.* v. *Horsham JJ., ex p. Richards, The Times*, May 25, 1985, D.C.
s. 71, repealed: 1985, c.61, s.64, sch.8.
s. 76, orders 84/1142, 1287(S.); 85/858.
sch. 1, repealed in pt.: 1984, c.28, sch.4.
sch. 3, amended: *ibid.*, sch.2; repealed in pt.: *ibid.*, sch.4.
sch. 4, repealed in pt.: *ibid.*
sch. 5, repealed in pt.: 1988, c.3, sch.

54. Commonwealth Development Corporation Act 1982.
Royal Assent, December 22, 1982.

55. National Insurance Surcharge Act 1982.
Royal Assent, December 22, 1982.
repealed: 1984, c.43, sch.23

CAP.

1982—cont.

56. Electricity (Financial Provisions) Act 1982.
Royal Assent, December 22, 1982.
repealed: 1988, c.37, s.1.

57. Lands Valuation Amendment (Scotland) Act 1982.
Royal Assent, December 22, 1982.

1983

1. Consolidated Fund Act 1983.
Royal Assent, February 8, 1983.
repealed: 1984, c.44, sch. (C.).

2. Representation of the People Act 1983.
Royal Assent, February 8, 1983.
Commencement order: 83/153.
regs. 83/435, 436; 86/1091.
s. 1, see *Hipperson* v. *Newbury District Electoral Registration Officer* [1985] 3 W.L.R. 61, C.A.
s. 3, amended: 1985, c.50, sch.4.
s. 5, see *Hipperson* v. *Newbury District Electoral Registration Officer* [1985] 3 W.L.R. 61, C.A.
s. 7, regs. 83/548(S.); 86/1081, 1111(S).
s. 9, amended: 1985, c.50, s.4.
s. 10, regs. 86/1081, 1111(S.).
s. 10, amended: 1985, c.50, s.4.
s. 11, see *Cook* v. *Trist, The Times*, July 15, 1983, Comyn J.
s. 11, amended: 1985, c.50, sch.4.
s. 12, amended: *ibid.*, s.4.
ss. 14–16, regs. 83/548(S.); 86/1081, 1111(S.).
s. 15, amended: 1985, c.50, sch.4.
s. 18, regs. 85/548(S.); 86/1081, 1111(S).
s. 18, amended: 1985, c.50, sch 4; repealed in pt.: *ibid.*, s.4, schs.4,5.
s. 19, see *MacCorquodale* v. *Bovack*, 1984 S.L.T. 328.
ss. 19, 20, repealed: 1985, c.50, sch.5.
s. 20, regs. 83/548(S.).
s. 21, repealed: 1985, c.50, sch.5; repealed in pt.: 1985, c.54, sch.27.
s. 22, repealed: 1985, c.50, sch.5; amended: 1985, c.51, sch.16.
s. 24, order 83/468.
s. 26, amended: 1985, c.50, sch.4.
s. 28, order 83/468.
s. 28, amended: 1985, c.50, sch.4.
s. 29, regs. 83/735–737; 84/721 (S.), 723; 87/899, 900.
s. 31, amended: 1985, c.51, sch.9; repealed in pt.: *ibid.*, sch.17; 1988, c.40, sch.13 (prosp.).
ss. 32–34, repealed: 1985, c.50, sch.5.
s. 33, regs. 83/548(S.)
s. 35, amended: 1988, c.40, sch.12 (prosp.); repealed in pt.: 1985, c.51, sch.17; 1988, c.40, sch.13 (prosp.).
s. 36, rules 83/1153, 1154; 85/1848; 86/2214, 2215; 87/260, 261; regs. 86/1081, 1111(S.).
s. 36, amended: 1985, c.50, s.17; c.51, sch.9; repealed in pt.: *ibid.*, sch.17; 1988, c.40, sch.13 (prosp.).
s. 37, amended: 1985, c.51, s.18.
s. 38, repealed: *ibid.*, schs.4,5.
s. 39, amended: *ibid.*, s.19; c.51, sch.9; repealed in pt.: 1985, c.50, schs.4,5; c.51, sch.17; 1988, c.40, sch.13 (prosp.).

1983—cont.

2. Representation of the People Act 1983—*cont.*
s. 40, amended: 1985, c.50, ss.16, 19; c.51,
  sch. 9; 1988 c.40, sch.12 (prosp.); repealed
  in pt.: 1985, c.50, s.19, sch.5.
s. 42, rules 84/352; 86/2213(S.).
s. 43, amended: 1985, c.50, s.19; repealed in
  pt.: *ibid.*, sch.5.
s. 44, repealed: *ibid.*, schs.4,5.
s. 47, amended: 1985, c.51, sch.9; repealed in
  pt.: 1988, c.40, sch.13 (prosp.).
s. 49, amended: 1985, c.50, s.4; repealed in
  pt.: *ibid.*, schs.4,5.
s. 51, repealed: *ibid.*, schs.4,5.
s. 52, amended: *ibid.*, sch.4; repealed in pt.:
  ibid., schs.4,5.
s. 53, regs. 83/548(S.); 86/104, 105, 139, 1081,
  1111(S).
s. 53, amended: 1985, c.50, sch.4; repealed in
  pt.: *ibid.*, sch.5.
s. 54, amended: *ibid.*, sch.4.
s. 55, repealed: *ibid.*, schs.4,5.
s. 56, regs. 83/548(S.); 86/1081, 1111(S.).
s. 56, amended: 1985, c.50, schs.2,4; repealed
  in pt.: *ibid.*, schs.4,5.
s. 57, regs. 86/1111(S.).
s. 58, amended: 1985, c.50, sch.4.
s. 60, see *R.* v. *Phillips (C. K.)* (1984) 6
  Cr.App.R.(S.) 293, C.A.
s. 61, amended: 1985, c.50, sch.2; repealed in
  pt.: *ibid.*, schs.2,5.
s. 62, amended: *ibid.*, schs.3,4.
s. 63, substituted: *ibid.*, sch.4.
ss. 65, 66, amended: *ibid.*, sch.3.
ss. 67, 70, amended: *ibid.*, sch.4.
ss. 73, 74, amended: *ibid.*, s.14.
s. 75, regs. 83/548(S.); 86/1081, 1111(S).
s. 75, amended: 1984, c.46, sch.5; 1985, c.50,
  s.14, sch.4.
s. 76, amended: 1985, c.51, sch.9; repealed in
  pt.: 1985, c.50, schs.4,5; c.51, sch.17; 1988,
  c.40, sch.13.
s. 76A, added: 1985, c.50, s.14.
s. 76A, orders 86/383; 87/903.
s. 78, amended: 1985, c.50, sch. 4; order
  87/903.
s. 81, amended: 1985, c.50, sch.4.
s. 82, amended: *ibid.*; c.51, sch.9; repealed in
  pt.: *ibid.*, sch.17; 1988, c.40, sch.13.
ss. 85–89, amended: 1985, c.50, sch.4.
s. 89, regs. 83/548(S.); 86/1081, 1111(S.).
s. 90, amended: 1985, c.50, s.14.
s. 91, amended: *ibid.*, sch.4.
s. 93, see *Hobson* v. *Fishburn, The Guardian,*
  November 1, 1988, D.C.
s. 93, amended: 1984, c.46, sch.5; 1985, c.50,
  sch.4.
s. 94, amended: *ibid.*
s. 95, amended: *ibid.*; 1988, c.40, sch.12.
s. 96, substituted: 1985, c.50, sch.4; 1988,
  c.40, sch.12.
s. 97, amended: 1985, c.50, sch.4; repealed in
  pt.: 1984, c.60, sch.7.
s. 98, repealed in pt. (prosp.): 1988, c.41,
  sch.13.
ss. 99, 100, amended: 1985, c.50, sch.3.

1983—cont.

2. Representation of the People Act 1983—*cont.*
s. 103, repealed in pt.: *ibid.*, schs.4,5.
s. 104, repealed in pt.: *ibid.*, sch.5.
s. 106, see *Barrett* v. *Tuckman, The Times,*
  November 5, 1984, D.C.
ss. 106, 108, repealed in pt.: 1985, c.50,
  schs.4,5.
s. 110, amended: *ibid.*, sch.3.
s. 118, amended: *ibid.*, sch.4.
s. 119, amended: *ibid.* s.19.
ss. 121, 122, see *Hobson* v. *Fishburn, The
  Guardian,* November 1, 1988, D.C.
s. 122, amended: 1985, c.50, sch.4.
ss. 124, 125, repealed in pt.: *ibid.*, schs.4,5.
s. 126, amended: *ibid.*, sch.4; repealed in pt.:
  ibid., sch.5.
s. 127, see *Gilham* v. *Tall,* July 24, 1985, Mr.
  Bruce Loughland, Q.C., The Election Court.
s. 136, rules 85/1278; 88/557.
ss. 136, 140, amended: 1985, c.50, sch.4;
  repealed in pt.: *ibid.*, schs.4,5.
ss. 141 (in pt.), 142, repealed: *ibid.*
s. 148, repealed in pt.: *ibid.*, sch.5.
s. 149, amended: *ibid.*, sch.3.
s. 156, amended: *ibid.*, sch.4, repealed in pt.:
  ibid., schs.4,5.
s. 160, amended: *ibid.*, sch.4; repealed in pt.:
  ibid., schs.4,5.
ss. 161–163, amended: *ibid.*, sch.4; repealed in
  pt.: *ibid.*, sch.5.
s. 167, amended: *ibid.*, sch.4.
s. 168, amended: *ibid.*, sch.3; repealed in pt.:
  ibid., schs.4,5.
s. 169, see *Hobson* v. *Fishburn, The Guardian,*
  November 1, 1988, D.C.
s. 169, amended: 1985, c.50, sch.3; repealed in
  pt.: *ibid.*, sch.5.
ss. 171, 172, 173 (in pt.), repealed: *ibid.*,
  schs.4,5.
s. 176, amended: *ibid.*, sch.4; repealed in pt.:
  ibid., schs.4,5.
s. 178, substituted: *ibid.*, sch.4.
s. 181, amended: *ibid.*; sch.4; repealed in pt.:
  1985, c.23, sch.2; c.50, schs.4,5.
s. 182, rules 85/1278; Acts of Sederunt
  85/1426, 1427; 88/557.
s. 187, amended: 1985, c.50, sch.4; repealed in
  pt.: *ibid.*, schs.4,5.
s. 190, repealed: *ibid.*, schs.4,5.
s. 191, amended: *ibid.*, sch.4; repealed in pt.:
  ibid., sch.5.
ss. 192, 196 (in pt.), repealed: *ibid.*
s. 197, orders 86/383; 87/903.
s. 197, amended: 1985, c.50, sch.4; order
  87/903.
s. 199, repealed: 1985, c.50, s.22, sch.5.
s. 200, amended: *ibid.*, sch.4.
s. 201, regs. 83/548(S.); 86/104, 105, 139, 1081,
  1111(S.).
s. 201, amended: 1985, c.50, sch.4.
s. 202, regs. 83/548(S.); 86/1111(S.).
s. 202, amended: 1985, c.50, s.4, sch.2;
  repealed in pt.: *ibid.*, schs.4,5.
s. 203, amended: *ibid.*, sch.4; c.51, sch.9;
  repealed in pt.: 1985, c.50, schs.4,5; c.51,
  sch.17; 1988, c.40, sch.13 (prosp.).

CAP.

1983—cont.

2. Representation of the People Act 1983—cont.
s. 205, amended: 1985, c.50, sch.4.
s. 207, order 83/153.
sch. 1, regs. 83/548(S.); 86/1081, 1111(S.);
orders 83/605, 606.
sch. 1, amended: 1985, c.2, ss.1, 2 (N.I.); c.50,
ss.4, 13, 19, schs.2,4; repealed in pt.: 1984,
c.60, sch.7; 1985, c.50, s.19, schs.2,4,5; c.51,
sch.17; 1988, c.41, sch.13.
sch. 2, regs. 86/104, 105, 139, 1081, 1111(S).
sch. 2, amended: 1985, c.50, s.4, schs.2–4;
repealed in pt.: *ibid.*, schs.2,4,5.
sch. 3, amended: *ibid.*, sch.4.
sch. 4, regs. 86/1081; 1111(S.).
sch. 4, amended: 1985, c.50, s.14, sch.4.
sch. 5, amended: 1988, c.40, sch.12.
sch. 7, amended: 1985, c.50, sch.4; repealed in
pt.: *ibid.*, schs.4,5.
sch. 8, repealed in pt.: *ibid.*, sch.5; S.L.R. 1986.

3. Agricultural Marketing Act 1983.
Royal Assent, March 1, 1983.
Commencement order: 83/366.
s. 1, amended: 1986, c.49, s.8.
s. 7, amended: *ibid.*; repealed in pt.: *ibid.*, sch.4.
s. 9, order 83/366.
sch. 1, amended: 1986, c.49, s.8; repealed in
pt.: *ibid.*, s.8, sch.4.

4. Pig Industry Levy Act 1983.
Royal Assent, March 1, 1983.

5. Consolidated Fund (No. 2) Act 1983.
Royal Assent, March 28, 1983.
repealed: 1985, c.55, sch.(C.)

**6. British Nationality (Falkland Islands) Act
1983.**
Royal Assent, March 28, 1983.
s. 2, amended. order 86/948.
s. 4, regs. 83/479.

**7. Conwy Tunnel (Supplementary Powers) Act
1983.**
Royal Assent, March 28, 1983.

8. British Fishing Boats Act 1983.
Royal Assent, March 28, 1983.
s. 1, order 83/482.
s. 5, amended (S.): 1987, c.18, sch.6.
s. 9, amended: 1988, c.12, sch.6.
s. 10, order 85/1203.
s. 11, repealed in pt.: 1988, c.12, sch.7.

9. Currency Act 1983.
Royal Assent, March 28, 1983.

10. Transport Act 1983.
Royal Assent, March 28, 1983.
s. 1, amended: 1984, c.32, sch.6; 1985, c.51,
sch.12; c. 67, sch.3.
s. 2, amended: 1984, c.32, sch.6; repealed in
pt.: *ibid.*, schs.6,7.
s. 3, amended: 1985, c.67, s.102, sch.3;
repealed in pt.: 1984, c.32, sch.7; 1985, c.51,
schs.12,17; c.67, s.102, sch.8.
s. 4, amended: 1985, c.67, s.102; repealed in
pt.: 1984, c.32, sch.7; 1985, c.51, schs.12,17.
s. 5, repealed in pt.: *ibid.*
s. 6, amended: *ibid.*, sch.12; repealed in pt.:
1984, c.32, sch.7; 1985, c.51, schs.12,17.
ss. 7, 8, repealed in pt.: 1984, c.32, sch.7.
s. 9, repealed in pt.: *ibid.*; 1985, c.67, schs.3,8.
s. 10, repealed in pt.: 1984, c.32, sch.7.

CAP.

1983—cont.

11. Civil Aviation (Eurocontrol) Act 1983.
Royal Assent, April 11, 1983.
Commencement orders: 83/1886; 85/1915.
s. 4, orders 83/1886; 85/1915.

**12. Divorce Jurisdiction, Court Fees and Legal
Aid (Scotland) Act 1983.**
Royal Assent, April 11, 1983.
Commencement order: 84/253.
s. 2, order 83/949.
s. 2, repealed: 1988, c.32, sch.
s. 7, order 84/253.
sch. 1, repealed in pt.: 1985, c.37, sch.2; 1986,
c.9, sch.2; S.L.R. 1986; 1986, c.47, sch.5;
1988, c.32, sch.; c.36, sch.2.

13. Merchant Shipping Act 1983.
Royal Assent, April 11, 1983.
Commencement orders: 83/1435, 1601.
ss. 1–3, repealed: 1988, c.12, schs.6,7.
s. 4, repealed: *ibid.*, sch.7.
s. 5, regs. 83/1470, 1471; 85/1727; 88/1485.
s. 5, amended: 1988, c.12, sch.6; repealed in
pt.: *ibid.*, schs 6,7.
s. 6, repealed: *ibid.*, sch.7.
s. 8, orders 83/1701, 1702; 84/1985.
s. 9, repealed in pt.: 1984, c.5, sch.2; 1988,
c.12, schs.6,7.
s. 11, orders 83/1435, 1601.
sch. regs. 83/1470, 1471; 85/1727; 88/1485.

**14. International Transport Conventions Act
1983.**
Royal Assent, April 11, 1983.
s. 11, order 85/612.

15. British Shipbuilders Act 1983.
Royal Assent, May 9, 1983.

16. Level Crossings Act 1983.
Royal Assent, May 9, 1983.
s. 1, amended: 1984, c.27, sch.13; c.54, sch.9
(S.); repealed in pt.: 1985, c.51, sch.17.

17. Plant Varieties Act 1983.
Royal Assent, May 9, 1983.

18. Nuclear Materials (Offences) 1983.
Royal Assent, May 9, 1983.
s. 5, repealed in pt.: 1988, c.33, sch.16.
s. 5A, added: *ibid.*, sch.15.
s. 7, amended: *ibid.*

19. Matrimonial Homes Act 1983.
Royal Assent, May 9, 1983.
see *Lee* v. *Lee* (1983) 12 H.L.R. 116, C.A.
s. 1, see *Harris* v. *Harris* (1986) 1 F.L.R. 12,
C.A.; *Summers* v. *Summers* (1986) 16
Fam.Law 56, C.A.; *Hall* v. *King* (1987) 283
E.G. 1400; (1987) 19 H.L.R. 440, C.A.; *Kaur*
v. *Gill, The Independent,* March 16, 1988,
C.A.; *Wiseman* v. *Simpson* [1988] 1 W.L.R.
35, C.A.; *Whitlock* v. *Whitlock, The Independent,* October 6, 1988, C.A.
s. 1, amended: 1985, c.71, sch.2; 1988, c.50,
sch.17.
ss. 1, 9, see *Anderson* v. *Anderson* (1984) 14
Fam. Law 183, C.A.
s. 2, see *Kaur* v. *Gill, The Independent,* March
16, 1988, C.A.
s. 2, repealed in pt.: 1985, c.65, sch.10.
s. 7, sch. 1, see *Thompson* v. *Elmbridge Borough Council* [1987] 1 W.L.R. 1245, C.A.

1983—cont.

19. Matrimonial Homes Act 1983—*cont.*
s. 19, see *Seray-Wurie* v. *Seray-Wurie, The Times,* March 25, 1986, C.A.; *Essex County Council* v. *T., The Times,* March 15, 1986, C.A.
sch. 1, amended: 1985, c.71, sch.2; 1988, c.50, sch.17; repealed in pt.: 1984, c.42, sch.3.
sch. 2, repealed in pt.: S.L.R. 1986; 1988, c.3, sch.

20. Mental Health Act 1983.
Royal Assent, May 9, 1983.
Commencement order: 84/1357.
see *Crompton* v. *General Medical Council (No. 2)* (1985) 82 L.S.Gaz. 1864, P.C.
s. 1, see *R.* v. *Mental Health Review Tribunal, ex p. Clatworthy* [1985] 3 All E.R. 699, Mann J.; *R.* v. *Mental Health Commission, ex p. W, The Times,* May 27, 1988, D.C.
s. 3, see *Waldron, Ex p.* [1985] 3 W.L.R. 1090, C.A.; *R.* v. *Hallstrom, ex p. W.; R.* v. *Gardner, ex p. L.* [1986] 2 W.L.R. 883, McCullogh J.
s. 5, order 83/891.
s. 9, regs. 83/893.
ss. 17, 20, see *R.* v. *Hallstrom, ex p. W.; R.* v. *Gardner, ex p. L.* [1986] 2 W.L.R. 883, McCullough J.
s. 19, regs. 83/893.
s. 24, amended: 1984, c.23, sch.1.
s. 29, see *B., Re,* November 29, 1985, Liverpool County Ct.
s. 32, regs. 83/893.
s. 34, amended: 1984, c.23, sch.1.
s. 37, see *R.* v. *Nordon, The Times,* November 29, 1984, C.A.; *R.* v. *Ramsgate JJ., ex p. Kazmarek* (1985) 80 Cr.App.R. 366, D.C.
ss. 37, 47, 49, see *R.* v. *Castro* (1985) 81 Cr.App.R. 212, C.A.
s. 41, see *R.* v. *Courtney* [1988] Crim.L.R. 130, C.A.
s. 57, see *R.* v. *Mental Health Commission, ex p. W, The Times,* May 27, 1988, D.C.
ss. 57, 58, 64, regs. 83/893.
s. 69, amended: 1984, c.36, sch.3.
s. 70, see *R.* v. *Mental Health Review Tribunal, ex p. Secretary of State for the Home Department, The Times,* March 25, 1987, Farquharson J.
s. 72, see *R.* v. *Mental Health Review Tribunal, ex p. Pickering* [1986] 1 All E.R. 99, Forbes J.; *Grant* v. *Mental Health Review Tribunal, The Times,* April 28, 1986, McNeil J.; *Secretary of State for the Home Department* v. *Mental Health Review Tribunal for Mersey Regional Health Authority* [1986] 1 W.L.R. 1170, Mann J.; *R.* v. *Mersey Mental Health Review Tribunal, ex p. D., The Times,* April 13, 1987, D.C.
ss. 72, 73, see *Bone* v. *Mental Health Review Tribunal* [1985] 3 All E.R. 330, Nolan J.; *R.* v. *Mental Health Review Tribunal, ex p. Kaye, The Times,* May 25, 1988, D.C.
s. 73, see *Secretary of State for the Home Department* v. *Mental Health Review Tribunal for Mersey Regional Health Authority* [1986]

1983—cont.

20. Mental Health Act 1983—*cont.*
1 W.L.R. 1170, Mann J.; *R.* v. *Oxford Regional Mental Health Review Tribunal, ex p. Secretary of State for the Home Department* [1986] 1 W.L.R. 1180, C.A.; *Grant* v. *Mental Health Review Tribunal, The Times,* April 28, 1986, McNeil J.; *Campbell* v. *Secretary of State for the Home Department, sub nom. R.* v. *Oxford Regional Mental Health Review Tribunal, ex p. Secretary of State for the Home Department* [1987] 3 W.L.R. 522, H.L.; *R.* v. *Nottinghamshire Mental Health Review Tribunal, ex p. Secretary of State for the Home Department; R.* v. *Trent Mental Review Tribunal, ex p. Secretary of State for the Home Department, The Times,* October 12, 1988, C.A.
s. 78, see *Bone* v. *Mental Health Review Tribunal* [1985] 3 All E.R. 330, Nolan J.
s. 78, rules 83/942.
s. 79, amended: 1984, c.36, sch.3.
s. 80, amended: 1983, c.39, sch.2; 1984, c.36, sch.3.
ss. 88, 90, 92, amended: 1984, c.36, sch.3.
s. 94, amended: 1986, c.57, s.2.
s. 95, see *Re E. (Mental Health Patient) Re* [1985] 1 W.L.R. 245, C.A.
s. 96, see *B. (Court of Protection: Notice of Proceedings), Re* [1987] 1 W.L.R. 552, Millett J.
ss. 106–108, rules 84/2035; 86/127.
s. 111, amended: 1986, c.57, s.2.
s. 116, amended: 1984, c.36, sch.3.
s. 120, repealed in pt.: 1984, c.23, sch.3.
s. 121, amended: 1984, c.48, s.6.
s. 134, regs. 83/893.
s. 135, amended: 1984, c.36, sch.3; c.60, sch.6; repealed in pt.: *ibid.,* sch.7.
s. 139, see *Winch* v. *Jones* [1985] 3 W.L.R. 729, C.A.; *Waldron, Ex p.* [1985] 3 W.L.R. 1090, C.A.; *Furber* v. *Kratter, The Times,* July 21, 1988, Henry J.
s. 145, see *Secretary of State for the Home Department* v. *Mental Health Review Tribunal for Mersey Regional Health Authority* [1986] 1 W.L.R. 1170, Mann J.; *R.* v. *Mersey Mental Health Review Tribunal, ex p. D., The Times,* April 13, 1987, D.C.; *R.* v. *Mental Health Review Tribunal, ex p. Kay, The Times,* May 25, 1988, D.C.
s. 145, amended: 1984, c.23, sch.1.
s. 149, order 84/1357.
sch. 4, repealed in pt.: 1984, c.23, sch.3; c.36, sch.5; c.51, sch.9; S.L.R. 1986; 1987, c.45, sch.4.
sch. 5, regs. 83/893.

21. Pilotage Act 1983.
Royal Assent, May 9, 1983.
Commencement order: 86/1051.
repealed: 1987, c.21, sch.3.
s. 3, orders 83/1340; 85/251; 86/402; 87/295, 297.
s. 4, amended: 1985, c.9, sch.2.
s. 9, orders 85/831; 86/568; 87/843(S.), 1484, 1756(S.).
ss. 55, 58, order 86/1051.
sch. 3, repealed in pt.: 1988, c.1, sch.31.

1983—cont.

22. Ports (Reduction of Debt) Act 1983.
Royal Assent, May 9, 1983.

23. Water Act 1983.
Royal Assent, May 9, 1983.
Commencement orders: 83/1173, 1174, 1234, 1235.
s. 1, order 83/1234.
ss. 3, 9, orders 83/1174, 1235, 1320.
s. 11, orders 83/1173, 1234.
sch. 1, order 83/1234.
sch. 2, regs. 83/1267, 1319, 1320; order 83/1927.
sch. 4, order 83/1234.
sch. 10, order 83/1720.

24. Licensing (Occasional Permissions) Act 1983.
Royal Assent, May 9, 1983.
s. 1, see *R.* v. *Bromley Licensing JJ., ex p. Bromley Licensed Victuallers' Association* [1984] 1 All E.R. 794, Woolf J.
s. 4, order 83/1032.

25. Energy Act 1983.
Royal Assent, May 9, 1983.
Commencement orders: 83/790; 88/1587.
ss. 2, 5, regs. 84/136.
s. 9, regs. 84/135.
s. 16, regs. 88/1057.
s. 26, repealed in pt.: 1985, c.51, sch.17.
s. 33, orders 83/1889–1893; 85/752; 86/2018; 87/668.
s. 37, orders 83/790; 88/1587.
sch. 2, regs. 83/1129, 1748.

26. Pet Animals Act 1951 (Amendment) Act 1983.
Royal Assent, May 9, 1983.

27. Appropriation Act 1983.
Royal Assent, May 13, 1983.
repealed: 1985, c.55, sch.(C.).

28. Finance Act 1983.
Royal Assent, May 13, 1983.
ss. 1 (in pt.), 2, repealed: 1984, c.43, sch.23.
s. 4, repealed in pt.: 1988, c.39, sch.14.
s. 7, repealed in pt.: 1987, c.16, sch.16.
ss. 10–28, repealed: 1988, c.1, sch.31.
ss. 29, 34 (in pt.), repealed: 1985, c.54, sch.27.
s. 42, repealed: 1984, c.43, sch.23.
s. 45, order 83/1377.
s. 46, amended: 1988, c.1, sch.29; repealed in pt.: 1984, c.43, sch.23; c.51, sch.9; 1985, c.54, sch.27; 1988, c.1, sch.31.
s. 47, repealed: 1984, c.51, sch.9.
sch. 2, repealed: 1984, c.43, sch.23.
schs. 4, 5, repealed: 1988, c.1, sch.31.
sch. 5, amended: 1988, c.39, s.51.
sch. 6, amended: 1985, c.54, sch.19; 1988, c.1, sch.29.
sch. 8, amended: *ibid.*; repealed in pt.: 1987, c.16, sch.16.
sch. 9, repealed in pt.: 1983, c.53, sch.3; c.54, sch.11; 1984, c.51, sch.9.

29. Miscellaneous Financial Provisions Act 1983.
Royal Assent, May 13, 1983.
Commencement order: 83/1338.
s. 9, order 83/1338.
sch. 1, amended: 1988, c.16, s.3.
sch. 2, repealed in pt.: 1985, c.62, sch.4; c.71, sch.1; 1986, c.44, sch.9; 1988, c.35, sch.2.

1983—cont.

30. Diseases of Fish Act 1983.
Royal Assent, May 13, 1983.
Commencement order: 84/302.
s. 7, order 85/1391.
s. 9, amended: 1986, c.62, s.38.
s. 11, order 84/302.

31. Coroners' Juries Act 1983.
Royal Assent, May 13, 1983.
repealed: 1988, c.13, sch.4.
s. 3, order 83/1454.

32. Marriage Act 1983.
Royal Assent, May 13, 1983.
Commencement order: 84/413.
s. 9, S.R. 1984 No. 106.
s. 10, S.R. 1984 No. 96.
s. 12, order 84/413.

33. Solvent Abuse (Scotland) Act 1983.
Royal Assent, May 13, 1983.

34. Mobile Homes Act 1983.
Royal Assent, May 13, 1983.
s. 1, see *Balthasar* v. *Mullane* (1985) 17 H.L.R. 561; (1986) 84 L.G.R. 55, C.A.
s. 1, order 83/749.
ss. 1, 5, sch. 1, see *West Lothian District Council* v. *Morrison*, 1987 S.L.T. 361.
s. 5, see *Greenwich London Borough Council* v. *Powell, The Times,* February 24, 1988, C.A.
sch. 1, order 83/748.

35. Litter Act 1983.
Royal Assent, May 13, 1983.
s. 1, see *Camden London Borough Council* v. *Shinder* (1987) 86 L.G.R. 129, D.C.
s. 1, repealed in pt.: 1985, c.51, sch.17.
ss. 4, 6, amended: *ibid.,* sch.6.
s. 7, amended (S.): 1984, c.54, sch.9.

36. Social Security and Housing Benefits Act 1983.
Royal Assent, May 13, 1983.
repealed: 1986, c.50, sch.11.

37. Importation of Milk Act 1983.
Royal Assent, May 13, 1983.
s. 1, regs. 83/1545(S.), 1563; 85/1089, 1167(S.), 1324(S.); 88/1803, 1814(S.); S.Rs. 1983 No. 338; 1986 Nos. 21, 119.
s. 2, regs. 88/1814(S.).

38. Dentists Act 1983.
Royal Assent, May 13, 1983.
repealed: 1984, c.24, sch.6.
s. 34, order 83/1520.

39. Mental Health (Amendment) (Scotland) Act 1983.
Royal Assent, May 13, 1983.
Commencement orders: 83/1199, 1983.
repealed: 1984, c.36, sch.5.
s. 41, orders 83/1199, 1983.

40. Education (Fees and Awards) Act 1983.
Royal Assent, May 13, 1983.
s. 1, amended: 1988, c.40, sch.12.
ss. 1, 2, regs. 83/973, 1215; 84/1201; 1361(S.); 85/219, 1223(S.); 87/1364, 1383(S.); 88/1391.

41. Health and Social Services and Social Security Adjudications Act 1983.
Royal Assent, May 13, 1983.
Commencement orders: 83/974, 1862; 84/216, 957, 1347, 1767; 85/704.

1983—cont.

41. Health and Social Services and Social Security Adjudications Act 1983—cont.
s. 11, repealed in pt.: 1984, c.23, sch.3.
s. 19, repealed in pt.: 1986, c.50, sch.11.
s. 25, regs. 84/451.
s. 26, repealed in pt.: 1984, c.22, sch.3.
s. 27, repealed in pt.: 1984, c.30, sch.11.
s. 31, order 83/1798.
s. 32, orders 83/974, 1862; 84/216, 957, 1347, 1767; 85/704.
sch. 1, see *Southwark London Borough Council* v. *H.*, *The Times*, April 6, 1985, D.C.
sch. 1, repealed in pt.: 1988, c.34, sch.6.
sch. 2, repealed in pt.: 1984, c.56, sch.3.
sch. 4, repealed in pt.: 1984, c.23, sch.3.
sch. 6, repealed in pt.: 1983, c.54, sch.7.
sch. 8, regs. 84/451, 613; 86/2218; amended: 1984, c.48, sch. 7; 1986, c.50, sch.11.
sch. 9, repealed in pt.: 1984, c.22, sch.3; c.23, sch.3; 1986, c.50, sch.11.

42. Copyright (Amendment) Act 1983.
Royal Assent, May 13, 1983.
repealed: 1988, c.48, sch.8.

43. Road Traffic (Driving Licences) Act 1983.
Royal Assent, May 13, 1983.
ss. 1, 2 (in pt.), repealed: 1988, c.54, sch.1.

44. National Audit Act 1983.
Royal Assent, May 13, 1983.
sch. 4, amended: 1985, c.62, s.7; 1987, c.3, sch.1; repealed in pt.: 1984, c.12, sch.7 (prospectively); 1985, c.62, sch.4; 1986, c.31, sch.6; c.44, sch.9; 1987, c.3, sch.3; 1988, c.35, sch.2 (prosp.).

45. County Court (Penalties for Contempt) Act 1983.
Royal Assent, May 13, 1983.
s. 1, see *Lee* v. *Walker*, *The Times*, December 14, 1984, C.A.

46. Agricultural Holdings (Amendment) (Scotland) Act 1983.
Royal Assent, May 13, 1983.

47. National Heritage Act 1983.
Royal Assent, May 13, 1983.
Commencement orders: 83/1062, 1183, 1437; 84/208, 217, 225.
ss. 1–16, sch. 1, functions transferred: order 86/600.
s. 4, order 84/226.
s. 30, orders 84/422; 85/1818, 1850.
s. 31, orders 84/422; 85/1850; 87/1945.
s. 41, orders 83/1062, 1183, 1437; 84/208, 217, 225.
sch. 2, order 84/422.
sch. 3, amended: 1985, c.9, sch.2.
schs. 4, 5, repealed in pt.: 1986, c.63, sch.12.

48. Appropriation (No. 2) Act 1983.
Royal Assent, July 26, 1983.
repealed: 1985, c.55, sch.(C).

49. Finance (No. 2) Act 1983.
Royal Assent, July 26, 1983.
s. 7, amended: 1984, c.51, sch.8; 1986, c 56, sch.3; repealed in pt.: 1985, c.54, sch.27.
ss. 8–13, repealed: 1984, c.51, sch.9.
s. 14, repealed: 1985, c.54, sch.27.

1983—cont.

49. Finance (No. 2) Act 1983—cont.
s. 15, amended: *ibid.*, s.82; repealed in pt.: *ibid.*, sch.27.
s. 16, repealed in pt.: 1984, c.51, sch.9.

50. Companies (Beneficial Interests) Act 1983.
Royal Assent, July 26, 1983.
repealed: 1985, c.9, sch.1.

51. International Monetary Arrangements Act 1983.
Royal Assent, July 26, 1983.
Commencement order: 83/1643.
s. 1, orders 83/1643; 85/2038(S.).

52. Local Authorities (Expenditure Powers) Act 1983.
Royal Assent, July 26, 1983.
s. 1, orders 84/477; 85/547.

53. Car Tax Act 1983.
Royal Assent, July 26, 1983.
s. 2, see *R.* v. *Customs and Excise Comrs.,* ex p. *Nissan (U.K.)*, *The Times*, November 23, 1987, C.A.
s. 2, order 84/488; amended: *ibid.*
ss. 3, 5, 7, regs. 85/1737.
s. 8, sch. 1, regs. 83/1781; 85/1737; 86/306.
sch. 1, amended: 1984, c.43, s.16, c.60, sch.6; 1985, c.9, sch.2; 1987, c.18, sch.4; 1988, c.39, s.12; repealed in pt.: 1985, c.9, sch.1; c.65, sch.10; c.66, sch.8(S.).

54. Medical Act 1983.
Royal Assent, July 26, 1983.
order of council 84/62.
s. 1, order 87/457.
s. 17, amended: order 86/23.
s. 32, orders 86/149; 87/102, 2166.
s. 36, see *Finegan* v. *General Medical Council* [1987] 1 W.L.R. 121, P.C.
ss. 36, 41, see *Frempong* v. *G.M.C.* (1984) New L.J. 745, P.C.
s. 37, see *Crompton* v. *General Medical Council (No. 2)* [1985] 1 W.L.R. 885, P.C.
sch. 1, orders 86/1390; 87/457, 1120.
sch. 1, amended: 1985, c.9, sch.2.
sch. 2, amended: order 86/23.
sch. 4, order 87/2174.
sch. 5, repealed in pt.: 1984, c.24, sch.6.

55. Value Added Tax Act 1983.
Royal Assent, July 26, 1983.
s. 2, see *Nasim (Trading as Yasmine Restaurant)* v. *Customs and Excise Comrs.* [1987] S.T.C. 387, Simon Brown J.; *Customs and Excise Commissioners* v. *Fine Art Developments* [1988] S.T.C. 178, C.A.
s. 2, amended: 1987, c.16, s.13; 1988, c.39, s.14.
s. 3, see *Customs and Excise Comrs.* v. *Diners Club* [1988] S.T.C. 416, Kennedy J.
s. 3, orders 85/1646; 86/896, 1989; 87/1806.
s. 5, see *Customs and Excise Comrs.* v. *West Yorkshire Independent Hospital (Contract Services)* [1988] S.T.C. 443, Henry J.; *Tas-Stage* v. *Customs and Excise Comrs.* [1988] S.T.C. 436, Macpherson J.
s. 5, regs. 85/866.
s. 6, orders 84/1685; 87/1806.
s. 6, amended: 1987, c.16, s.12.

CAP.

1983—cont.

55. Value Added Tax Act 1983—*cont.*

s. 7, regs. 85/866; order 85/799.

s. 7, amended: 1987, c.16, s.19, sch.2.

s. 10, see *Boots Co. v. Customs and Excise Commissioners* [1988] S.T.C. 138, Macpherson J.

s. 14, see *Flockton (Ian) Developments v. Customs and Excise Comrs.* [1987] S.T.C. 394, Stuart-Smith J.; *R. v. Customs and Excise Commissioners, ex p. Strangewood* [1987] S.T.C. 502, Otton J.; *Customs and Excise Commissionrs v. Fine Arts Developments* [1988] S.T.C. 178, C.A.

s. 14, orders 84/33, 606, 736, 919; regs. 84/929, 1376; 85/866; 87/510, 781, 1072, 1427, 1916; 88/866, 1124.

s. 14, amended: 1987, c.16, s.11; 1988, c.39, sch.14.

s. 15, regs. 84/155; 85/105; order 87/510.

s. 15, amended: 1987, c.16, s.12.

s. 16, orders 83/1717; 84/489, 631, 766, 767, 959; 85/18, 431, 919; 86/530; 87/437, 518, 781, 1072, 1806; regs. 85/105, 866, 1650; 87/150, 1916; 88/507.

s. 16, amended: 1986, c.41, s.12; repealed in pt.: 1984, c.43, s.13, sch.23.

s. 17, orders 84/1784; 85/432, 1900; 86/704, 716; 87/517, 860, 1259; 88/1282.

s. 19, regs. 84/929, 1376; 85/693, 866, 1384, 1646; 87/1916; orders 86/939, 1989; 87/154, 155, 2108; 88/1174, 1193.

s. 19, amended: 1986, c.41, s.13.

s. 20, orders 85/1101; 86/336, 532.

s. 20, repealed in pt.: 1984, c.32, sch.7; 1985, c.51, sch.17.

s. 22, see *Euro-Academy v. Comrs. of Customs and Excise* [1987] 3 C.M.L.R. 29, VAT Tribunal.

s. 22, regs. 86/335.

s. 22, substituted: 1985, c.54, s.32; amended (S.): 1985, c.66, sch.7.

s. 23, regs. 87/2015.

s. 23, amended: 1987, c.16, sch.2.

s. 24, regs. 84/929, 1177, 1376; 85/886.

s. 24, repealed in pt.: 1984, c.43, sch.23.

s. 25, regs. 84/929, 1376; 85/105, 886.

s. 27, amended: 1984, c.43, s.11.

s. 29, amended: 1985, c.9, sch.2.

s. 29A, added: 1987, c.16, s.15.

s. 31, regs. 85/886, 1650.

s. 31, amended: 1985, c.54, s.31.

s. 33, regs. 85/886.

s. 33, amended: 1987, c.16, sch.2.

s. 34, orders, 84/202; 85/1046; 87/806.

s. 35, regs. 85/886.

s. 35, amended: 1987, c.16, s.12.

s. 37A, order 87/1806.

s. 37A, added: 1987, c.16, s.16.

s. 39, see *Aikman v. White*, 1985 S.L.T. 535; *Hayman v. Griffiths; Walker v. Hanby* [1987] 3 W.L.R. 1125, D.C.

s. 39, amended: 1985, c.54, sch.6; repealed in pt.: *ibid.*, s.12, schs.6,27.

CAP.

1983—cont.

55. Value Added Tax Act 1983—*cont.*

s. 40, see *R. v. London Value Added Tax Tribunal, ex p. Minster Associates* [1988] S.T.C. 386, Webster J.; *Lyons (I.) v. Customs and Excise Comrs.* (1987) V.A.T.T.R. 187, V.A.T. Tribunal.

s. 40, amended: 1985, c.54, s.24; 1986, c.41, s.10; 1987, c.16, sch.2; 1988, c.39, sch.14.

s. 41, regs. 85/886.

s. 45, orders 85/1646; 86/1989.

s. 45, amended: 1985, c.54, s.27; 1987, c.16, s.16.

s. 48, regs. 84/929, 1376; 85/886; orders 84/766, 767, 959; 85/18, 431, 432, 799, 919, 1900; 86/530, 704, 716; 87/437, 517, 518, 781, 1072, 1259, 1806; 88/507.

s. 48, amended: 1987, c.16, s.13.

sch. 1, see *Customs and Excise Commissioners v. Shingleton, The Times*, December 8, 1987, Brown J.; *Neal v. Customs and Excise Commissioners* [1988] S.T.C. 131, Simon Brown J.

sch. 1, regs. 85/886, 1650; 87/1916, orders 84/342; 85/433; 86/631; 87/438; 88/508.

sch. 1, amended: 1984, c.43, s.12; orders 85/433; 86/631; 1986, c.41, s.10; order 87/438; 1987, c.16, ss.13, 14; order 88/508; 1988, c.39, s.14; repealed in pt.: 1987, c.16, s.14, sch.16.

sch. 3, amended: order 85/799.

sch. 4, amended: 1986, c.41, s.11; 1987, c.16, s.17.

sch. 5, see *Pimblett (John) and Sons v. Comrs. of Customs and Excise* [1987] S.T.C. 202, Taylor J.; *Customs and Excise Comrs. v. Great Shelford Free Church (Baptist)* [1987] S.T.C. 249, Kennedy J.; *Customs and Excise Commissioners v. Quaker Oats* [1987] S.T.C. 638, Kennedy J; *Customs and Excise Commissioners v. Willmott (John) Housing* [1987] S.T.C. 692, Webster J.; *Wimpey Group Services v. Customs and Excise Commissioners* [1988] S.T.C. 1, Mann J.; *R. v. Customs and Excise Commissioners, ex p. Sims (T/A Supersonic Snacks)* [1988] S.T.C. 210, Taylor J.; *Customs and Excise Commissioners v. Lawson-Tancred* [1988] S.T.C. 326, Macpherson J.; *Pimblett (John) and Sons v. Customs and Excise Commissioners* [1988] S.T.C. 358, C.A.

sch. 5, order 88/1843.

sch. 5, amended: order 83/1717; 1984, c.43, s.10, schs.5,6; orders 84/489, 631, 766, 959; 85/18, 431, 799, 919; 86/530; 87/437, 518, 718, 1072, 1806; repealed in pt.: 1984, c.43, sch. 23; orders 84/489, 767; 85/799; 1985, c.54, s.11, sch.27; 1987, c.16, s.13, sch.16; orders 87/437, 518; 88/507.

sch. 6, see *Customs and Excise Commissioners v. Zinn* [1988] S.T.C. 57, Nolan J.; *Customs and Excise Commissioners v. Bell Concord Educational Trust* [1988] S.T.C. 143, Taylor J.; *E.C. Commission v. U.K. (No. 353/85)* (1988) S.T.C. 251, European Ct.

sch. 6, amended: 1984, c.24, sch 5; c.51, sch.8; orders 84/1784; 86/704, 716; 1987, c.16, s.18; orders 87/517, 860, 1259; 1988, c.39,

CAP.

1983—cont.

55. Value Added Tax Act 1983—cont.

s.13; order 88/1282; repealed in pt.: order 87/860.

sch. 7, see *Aikman* v. *White*, 1985 S.L.T. 535; *E.M.I. Records* v. *Spillane* [1986] 1 W.L.R. 967, Browne-Wilkinson, V.C.; *Schlumberger Inland Services Inc.* v. *Customs and Excise Comrs.* [1987] S.T.C. 288, Taylor J.; *Grunwick Processing Laboratories* v. *Customs and Excise Comrs.* [1987] S.T.C. 357, C.A.; *Hayman* v. *Griffiths; Walker* v. *Hanby* [1987] 3 W.L.R. 1125, D.C.; *R.* v. *Epsom Magistrates Court, ex p. Bell, The Times*, May 28, 1988, D.C.

sch. 7, regs. 85/105, 886, 1650; 86/71, 305; 87/1427, 1712, 1916; 88/886.

sch. 7, amended: 1984, c.43, s.16; c.60, sch.6; 1985, c.9, sch.2; c.54, s.23, sch.7; 1987, c.16, s.11; c.18, sch.8(S.); 1988, c.39, s.15; repealed in pt.: 1984, c.60, sch.7; 1985, c.9, sch.1; c. 54, s.23, schs.7,27; c.65, sch.10; c.66, sch.8(S.).

sch. 8, rules 86/590, 2290.

sch. 8, amended: 1985, c.54, ss.27, 28, sch.8; repealed in pt.: *ibid.*, s.27, schs.8, 27.

56. Oil Taxation Act 1983.

Royal Assent, December 1, 1983.

s. 8, amended: 1985, c.54, s.92; 1986, c.41, s.110.

ss. 9, 12, orders 86/1644, 1645; 87/545.

s. 11, repealed: 1988, c.1, sch.31.

s. 15, amended: 1985, c.54, s.92; 1988, c.1, sch.29.

sch. 1, amended: 1986, c.41, s.110; 1988, c.39, s.139.

sch. 2, amended: 1985, c.54, s.92; 1988, c.1, sch.29.

57. Consolidated Fund (No. 3) Act 1983.

Royal Assent, December 21, 1983.

repealed: 1985, c.55, sch. (C).

58. British Shipbuilders (Borrowing Powers) Act 1983.

Royal Assent, December 21, 1983.

59. Petroleum Royalties (Relief) Act 1983.

Royal Assent, December 21, 1983.

60. Coal Industry Act 1983.

Royal Assent, December 21, 1983.

s. 3, repealed: 1987, c.3, sch.3.

1984

1. Consolidated Fund Act 1984.

Royal Assent, March 13, 1984.

repealed: 1986, c.42, sch. (C).

2. Restrictive Trade Practices (Stock Exchange) Act 1984.

Royal Assent, March 13, 1984.

repealed: 1986, c.60, sch.17.

3. Occupiers' Liability Act 1984.

Royal Assent, March 13, 1984.

4. Tourism (Overseas Promotion) (Scotland) Act 1984.

Royal Assent, March 13, 1984.

CAP.

1984—cont.

5. Merchant Shipping Act 1984.

Royal Assent, March 13, 1984.

s. 2, amended: 1988, c.12, sch.5.

s. 12, repealed in pt.: *ibid.*, sch.7.

s. 13, order 84/1985.

sch. 1, amended: 1986, c.23, s.5; 1988, c.12, sch.6.

6. Education (Amendment) (Scotland) Act 1984.

Royal Assent, March 13, 1984.

7. Pensions Commutation Act 1984.

Royal Assent, March 13, 1984.

Commencement order: 84/1140.

s. 3, order 84/1140.

8. Prevention of Terrorism (Temporary Provisions) Act 1984.

Royal Assent, March 22, 1984.

cont'nued in force: orders 85/378; 87/273.

see *R.* v. *Secretary of State for the Home Office, ex p. Stitt, The Times*, February 3, 1987, D.C.

ss. 1, 13, 14 (in pt.), 17 (in pt.)., schs.1–3, continued in force: order 88/274.

s. 2, amended (S.): 1984, c.54, sch.9.

s. 12, see *Hanna* v. *Chief Constable of the Royal Ulster Constabulary* [1986] 13 N.I.J.B. 71, Carswell J.; *Fox's Application, Re* [1987] 1 N.I.J.B. 12, Lord Lowry L.C.J.

s. 12, sch.3, see *H.M. Advocate* v. *Copeland*, 1988 S.L.T. 249.

ss. 13, 14, orders 84/417, 418; 87/119, 1209.

ss. 16, 18, orders 84/860, 1165, 1166.

s. 17, orders 85/378; 86/417; 87/273; 88/274.

sch. 3, see *H.M. Advocate* v. *Copeland*, 1988 S.L.T. 249.

sch. 3, orders 84/417, 418; 87/119, 1209.

sch. 3, amended: 1984, c.60, sch.6.

9. Lotteries (Amendment) Act 1984.

Royal Assent, April 12, 1984.

10. Town and Country Planning Act 1984.

Royal Assent, April 12, 1984.

s. 1, regs. 84/996 (S.), 1015; 87/1529 (S.).

s. 1, amended: 1986, c.63, sch.7.

s. 1, amended: (S.): *ibid.*

s. 3, regs. 84/995 (S.), 1016.

s. 6, regs. 84/1015, 1016; 87/1529 (S.).

s. 6, amended: 1988, c.4, sch.3.

11. Education (Grants and Awards) Act 1984.

Royal Assent, April 12, 1984.

s. 1, regs. 85/2028; 86/1031; 88/1214.

ss. 1–3, regs. 84/1098.

s. 1, 3, regs. 85/1070; 87/1960.

s. 2, amended: 1986, c.1, s.1.

12. Telecommunications Act 1984.

Royal Assent, April 12, 1984.

Commencement orders: 84/749, 876.

s. 2, order 84/876.

s. 7, orders 85/694, 882; 87/3, 827; 88/831.

s. 7, amended: 1984, c.46, sch. 5.

s. 8, orders 85/694, 882.

s. 9, orders 84/855, 856, 1741; 85/788, 822, 998, 999, 1594–1597; 86/1113; 87/2094; 88/1763.

s. 10, amended (S.): 1984, c.54, sch.9.

s. 11, order 84/960.

s. 28, orders 85/717, 718, 1031.

1984—cont.

12. Telecommunications Act 1984—*cont.*
s. 28, amended: 1987, c.43, sch.4.
s. 29, orders 85/719, 1030.
s. 42, amended: 1984, c.46, sch.5.
s. 43, repealed in pt.: *ibid.*, schs.5,6.
s. 45, substituted: 1985, c.56, s.11, sch.2.
s. 52, amended: 1988, c.34, sch.5.
Pt. IV (ss.56–59), repealed: 1984, c.46, sch.6.
s. 57, order 84/980.
s. 60, orders 84/876, 886; 85/496.
s. 60, amended: 1985, c.9, sch.2.
s. 61, amended: *ibid.*; repealed in pt.: 1988, c.39, sch.14.
s. 62, amended: 1988, c.1, sch.29.
s. 63, repealed in pt.: 1988, c.39, sch.14.
s. 65, order 85/496.
s. 66, amended: 1985, c.9, sch.2.
s. 68, amended: *ibid.*; 1986, c.45, sch.14.
s. 70, amended: 1985, c.9, sch.2.
s. 72, amended: 1988, c.1, sch.29.
s. 73, amended: 1985, c.9, sch.2.
s. 82, see *Rudd* v. *Department of Trade and Industry, The Times,* April 16, 1986, D.C.
s. 85, order 87/774.
s. 85, amended: 1987, c.43, sch.4.
s. 92, repealed in pt.: 1984, c.46, sch.6.
s. 97, repealed in pt.: 1985, c.51, sch.17.
s. 98, order 85/61.
s. 98, amended (S.): 1984, c.54, sch.9.
s. 100, repealed (prospectively): 1984, c.12, s.100, sch.7.
s. 101, amended: 1987, c.43, sch.4; repealed in pt.: *ibid.*, sch.5.
s. 104, orders 84/855, 856, 886, 960, 980, 1741, 85/61, 496, 788, 822, 998, 999, 1594–1597; 86/1113.
s. 108, order 84/861.
s. 110, orders 84/749, 876.
sch. 1, repealed in pt.: 1987, c.39, sch.1.
sch. 2, amended (S.): 1984, c.54, sch.9; repealed in pt.: *ibid.*, schs.9,11 (S.); 1986, c.44, sch.9.
sch. 4, orders 85/1011, 1014 (S.); S.R. 1985 No. 366.
sch. 4, repealed in pt.: 1984, c.46, sch.6; c.54, sch.11 (S.); 1985, c.13, sch.3; c.71, sch.1; 1986, c.31, sch.6; 1987, c.26, sch.24 (S.); 1988, c.1, sch.31.
sch. 5, orders 84/980; 86/1275.
sch. 5, amended: 1985, c.9, sch.2.

13. Road Traffic (Driving Instruction) Act 1984.
Royal Assent, April 12, 1984.
repealed: 1988, c.54, sch.1.
s. 5, orders 85/578; 86/1336.

14. Anatomy Act 1984.
Royal Assent, May 24, 1984.
Commencement order: 88/81.
ss. 3, 5, regs. 88/44, 198.
ss. 8, 11, regs. 88/44.
s. 13, order 88/81.

15. Law Reform (Husband and Wife) (Scotland) Act 1984.
Royal Assent, May 24, 1984.
sch. 1, repealed in pt.: 1985, c.37, sch.2.

1984—cont.

16. Foreign Limitation Periods Act 1984.
Royal Assent, May 24, 1984.
Commencement order: 85/1276.
s. 7, order 85/1276.

17. Fosdyke Bridge Act 1984.
Royal Assent, May 24, 1984.

18. Tenants' Rights, Etc. (Scotland) Amendment Act 1984.
Royal Assent, May 24, 1984.
repealed: 1987, c.26, sch.24.

19. Trade Marks (Amendment) Act 1984.
Royal Assent, May 24, 1984.
Commencement order: 86/1273.
s. 1, amended: 1986, c.39, s.2; repealed in pt.: *ibid.*, sch.3.
s. 2, order 86/1273.
s. 2, amended: 1986, c.39, sch.2; repealed in pt.: *ibid.*, sch.3.
sch. 1, amended: *ibid.*, sch.2; repealed in pt.: *ibid.*, sch.3.
sch. 2, repealed in pt.: *ibid.*

20. Agriculture (Amendment) Act 1984.
Royal Assent, May 24, 1984.

21. Somerset House Act 1984.
Royal Assent, June 26, 1984.

22. Public Health (Control of Diseases) Act 1984.
Royal Assent, June 26, 1984.
ss. 2–4, order 85/707.
s. 3, amended: 1984, c.30, sch.10.
s. 6, amended: 1987, c.49, sch.1.
s. 7, amended: 1984, c.30, sch.10; c.55, sch.6.
s. 8, repealed in pt.: 1985, c.51, sch.17.
s. 13, regs. 85/434; 88/1546.
s. 14, repealed in pt.: 1986, c.31, sch.6.
s. 20, amended: 1984, c.30, sch.10.
s. 46, repealed in pt.: 1986, c.50, sch.11.
s. 58, regs. 88/1546.
sch. 2, repealed in pt.: 1985, c.71, sch.2.

23. Registered Homes Act 1984.
Royal Assent, June 26, 1984.
Commencement order: 84/1348.
ss. 5, 8, 16, regs. 84/1345; 86/457; 88/1192.
ss. 10, 11, 15, see *Lyons* v. *East Sussex County Council* (1988) 86 L.G.R. 369, C.A.
s. 17, regs. 84/1345; 88/1192.
s. 21, regs. 84/1578.
s. 23, regs. 84/1578; 86/456; 88/1192.
s. 26, regs. 84/1578.
s. 27, regs. 84/1578; 88/1191.
ss. 29, 35, regs. 84/1578.
s. 43, rules 84/1346.
s. 56, regs. 84/1578; 86/456; 88/1192.
s. 57, regs. 84/1345.
s. 59, order 84/1348.
sch. 2, regs. 84/1345, 1578.

24. Dentists Act 1984.
Royal Assent, June 26, 1984.
Commencement order: 84/1815.
s. 2, order 84/1816.
s. 3, repealed in pt.: order 87/2047.
s. 4, amended and repealed in pt.: *ibid.*
s. 27, see *Doughty* v. *General Medical Council* [1987] 3 W.L.R. 769, P.C.
s. 29, order 85/172.

1984—cont.

24. Dentists Act 1984—cont.
s. 45, regs. 85/1850; 86/887.
s. 49, order 87/2047.
s. 55, order 84/1815.
sch. 1, amended: orders 87/2047; 88/1843.
sch. 2, amended: order 86/23.
sch. 3, orders 84/1517, 2010.
schs. 3, 5, repealed in pt.: order 87/2047.

25. Betting, Gaming and Lotteries (Amendment) Act 1984.
Royal Assent, June 26, 1984.
Commencement order: 86/102.
s. 4, order 86/102.

26. Inshore Fishing (Scotland) Act 1984.
Royal Assent, June 26, 1984.
Commencement order: 85/961.
s. 1, orders 85/1569; 86/59.
s. 2, order 86/60.
ss. 2, 4, see *Procurator Fiscal Stranraer* v. *Marshall* [1988] 1 C.M.L.R. 657.
s. 8, amended: 1987, c.18, sch.6.
s. 9, amended: 1988, c.12, sch.6.
s. 11, order 85/961.
sch. 1, repealed in pt.: 1988, c.12, sch.7.

27. Road Traffic Regulation Act 1984.
Royal Assent, June 26, 1984.
Commencement order: 86/1147.
see *Rodgers* v. *Taylor, The Times,* October 28, 1986, D.C.
s. 1, amended: 1984, c.54, sch.9 (S.); 1985, c.51, sch.5; repealed in pt. (S.): 1984, c.54, schs.9,11.
s. 2, amended: *ibid.,* sch.9(S.); 1988, c.54, sch.3.
s. 5, see *Rodgers* v. *Taylor* [1987] R.T.R. 86, D.C.
s. 6, see *Greater London Council* v. *Secretary of State for Transport* [1986] J.P.L. 513, C.A.
s. 6, orders 87/897, 2168.
s. 6, amended: 1985, c.51. sch.5.
s. 7, amended: 1985, c.67, sch.1.
s. 9, amended: 1984, c.54, sch.9 (S.); 1985, c.51, sch.5.
s. 10, amended: 1984, c.54, sch.9 (S.); 1985, c.67, sch.1.
s. 12, amended: 1985, c.51, sch.5.
s. 14, amended (S.): 1984, c.54, sch.9.
ss. 15, 19, amended: 1985, c.51, sch.5.
s. 17, see *Mawson* v. *Oxford, sub nom. Mawson* v. *Chief Constable of Merseyside* [1987] Crim.L.R. 131; [1987] R.T.R. 398, D.C.
ss. 17–19, 21, 23, amended (S.): 1984, c.54, sch.9.
s. 23, amended: 1985, c.51, sch.5; repealed in pt.: *ibid.,* sch.17.
s. 24, amended (S.): 1984, c.54, sch.9.
s. 25, regs. 87/16.
s. 26, amended: 1985, c.51, sch.5.
s. 28, regs. 85/713.
s. 29, amended: 1984, c.54, sch.9 (S.); 1985, c.51, sch.5.
s. 30, amended: *ibid.;* repealed in pt.: *ibid.,* sch.17.
s. 31, amended: *ibid.,* sch.5.

1984—cont.

27. Road Traffic Regulation Act 1984—cont.
s. 32, amended (S.): 1984, c.54, sch.8; repealed in pt.: 1985, c.51, sch.17.
s. 34, amended (S.): 1984, c.54, sch.9; repealed in pt. (S.): *ibid.,* s.125, sch.11.
s. 35, repealed in pt.: 1988, c.54, sch.1.
s. 36, amended: 1985, c.51, sch.5.
s. 37, amended: 1984, c.54, sch.9 (S.); 1985, c.51, sch.5.
s. 38, amended: 1984, c.54, sch.9 (S.); 1985, c.67, sch.2.
s. 39, amended: 1985, c.51, sch.5; repealed in pt.: *ibid.,* sch.17.
s. 43, amended: *ibid.,* sch.5; repealed in pt.: *ibid.,* sch. 17; 1986, c.31, sch.6.
s. 44, order 86/225.
s. 44, amended: 1985, c.51, sch.5.
s. 45, amended: 1984, c.54, sch.9 (S.); 1985, c.51, sch.5; 1986, c.27, s.1; repealed in pt.: 1985, c.51, sch.17; 1986, c.27, s.1.
s. 47, repealed in pt.: 1985, c.51, sch.17; 1988, c.54, sch.1.
s. 50, repealed: 1985, c.51, sch.17.
s. 51, substituted: 1986, c.27, s.2.
s. 52, repealed in pt.: 1988, c.54, sch.1.
s. 53, amended: 1984, c.54, sch.9 (S.); 1985, c.51, sch.5; repealed in pt.: 1988, c.54, sch.1.
s. 55, amended: 1984, c.54, sch.9 (S.); 1985, c.51, sch.5; 1988, c.41, sch.12 (prosp.); repealed in pt.: 1984, c.54, schs.9, 11; 1985, c.51, sch.17.
ss. 58, 59, amended: *ibid.,* sch.5.
s. 61, amended: *ibid.;* 1988, c.54, sch.3.
s. 64, regs. 85/463, 713; 86/1859; 87/16.
s. 64, amended: 1988, c.54, sch.3.
s. 65, regs. 85/713; 87/16; directions 87/1706.
ss. 65–71, 77–80, amended (S.): 1984, c.54, sch.9.
ss. 66, 67, amended: 1988, c.54, sch.3.
s. 67, regs. 85/463.
ss. 73, 74, amended: 1985, c.51, sch.5; order 86/315.
s. 75, amended: *ibid.*
s. 78, repealed: 1988, c.54, sch.1.
s. 79, repealed in pt.: 1985, c.51, sch.17.
ss. 81, 89, see *Crossland* v. *D.P.P., The Independent,* June 10, 1988, D.C.
s. 82, regs. 85/1888(S.).
s. 82, amended (S.): 1984, c.54, sch.7.
ss. 83, 84, amended (S.): *ibid.,* sch.9.
s. 85, amended (S.): *ibid.,* schs.7,9.
s. 86, regs. 86/1175.
s. 90, repealed: 1988, c.54, sch.1.
s. 91, amended: 1985, c.51, sch.5.
ss. 92, 93, amended (S.): 1984, c.54, sch.9.
s. 94, substituted: 1985, c.51, sch.5.
s. 95, orders 86/1328, 2107 (S.).
s. 96, amended: 1988, c.54, sch.1.
s. 98, see *Mawson* v. *Oxford, sub nom. Mawson* v. *Chief Constable of Merseyside* [1987] R.T.R. 398, D.C.
s. 98, repealed: 1988, c.54, sch.1.
s. 99, regs. 86/183.
s. 100, amended: 1984, c.54, sch.9 (S.); 1985, c.51, sch.5; repealed in pt.: *ibid.,* sch.17.

CAP.

1984—cont.

27. Road Traffic Regulation Act 1984—cont.
ss 101, regs. 85/1661; 86/183.
s. 102, regs. 85/1661.
s. 102, amended: 1985, c.51, sch.5.
s. 103, regs. 86/184.
s. 104, regs. 85/1660.
s. 106, order 86/1177.
s. 106, amended: 1984, c.54, sch.9 (S.); 1985, c.51, sch.5.
s. 112, repealed in pt.: *ibid.*, sch.17.
ss. 113, 114, repealed: 1988, c.54, sch.1.
s. 115, amended: 1986, c.27, s.2.
s. 118, 120, 121, repealed: 1988, c.54, sch.1.
s. 120, amended (S.): 1984, c.54, sch.9; 1985, c.73, s.38.
s. 122, see *Greater London Council* v. *Secretary of State for Transport* [1986] J.P.L. 513, C.A.
s. 122, amended: 1984, c.54, sch 9 (S.); 1985, c.51, sch.5; repealed in pt.: *ibid.*, sch.17.
s. 123, repealed: *ibid.*
s. 124, regs. 86/178–181, 259; 87/2244, 2245.
s. 125, amended: 1985, c.51, sch.5.
s. 129, amended: *ibid.*: repealed in pt.: *ibid.*, sch.17; 1986, c.63, sch.12.
s. 129, repealed in pt. (S.): *ibid.*
s. 130, repealed in pt.: 1988, c.45, sch.1.
s. 131, orders 86/1224; 87/363.
ss 131, 132, amended (S.): 1984, c.54, sch.9.
s. 132A, added (S.): *ibid.*, s.127.
s. 134, regs. 85/463, 713, 1888 (S); 86/178–180.
s. 134, amended (S.): 1984, c.54, schs.7,9
ss. 138, 140, amended: 1988, c.45, sch.3.
s. 142, amended (S.): 1985, c.51, sch.5: c.67, sch.1; repealed in pt : 1984, c.54, schs.9,11; 1985, c.51, sch.17.
s. 145, order 86/1147.
s. 145, repealed in pt.: 1988, c.54, sch.1.
s. 146, see *Mawson* v. *Oxford, sub nom. Mawson* v. *Chief Constable of Merseyside* [1987] R.T.R. 398, D.C.
sch. 4, regs. 86/262.
sch. 4, amended: 1985, c.51, sch.5; repealed in pt.: *ibid.*, sch.17.
sch. 6, amended: regs. 86/1175; 1988, c.54, sch.3.
sch. 7, repealed: *ibid.*, sch.1.
schs. 7, 13, see *Mawson* v. *Oxford, sub nom. Mawson* v. *Chief Constable of Merseyside* [1987] R.T.R. 398, D.C.
sch. 9, see *R.* v. *Secretary of State for Transport, ex p. G.L.C., The Times,* October 31, 1985, C.A.
sch. 9, regs. 86/178–181, 259; 87/2245; orders 87/897, 2168.
sch. 9, amended: 1984, c.54, sch.9; 1985, c.51, sch.5; c.67, schs.1,2,3.
sch. 10, orders 84/1575, 1936 (S.); 85/464.
sch. 10, repealed in pt.: 1984, c.54, sch.11(S.); 1988, c.54, sch.1.
sch. 12, see *McInnes* v. *Allan,* 1987 S.C.L.R. 99.
sch. 12, orders 86/56, 1329, 1875 (S.).
sch. 12, amended: 1988, c.54, sch.3.
sch. 13, repealed in pt.: 1984, c.32, sch.7; 1985, c.67, sch.8; 1986, c.31, sch.6; 1988, c.54, sch.1.

CAP.

1984—cont.

28. County Courts Act 1984.
Royal Assent, June 26, 1984.
s. 2, orders 86/754, 2207.
s. 12, see *R.* v. *Stokes* [1988] Crim.L.R. 110, C.A.
s. 12, regs. 88/488.
s. 14, see *Stilwell* v. *Williamson, The Times,* September 1, 1986, C.A.
s 14, repealed in pt.: S.L.R. 1986.
s. 15, see *Doyle* v. *Talbot Motor Co.* [1988] 1 W.L.R. 980, C.A.
s. 32, substituted: 1985, c.61, s.51.
s. 33, amended: *ibid.*, sch.7; repealed in pt.: *ibid.*, schs.7,8.
s. 38, see *Lee* v. *Walker* [1985] 1 All E.R. 781, C.A.; *Ainsbury* v. *Millington* [1986] 1 All E.R. 73, C.A.
ss. 38, 39, see *Bush* v. *Green* [1985] 1 W.L.R. 1143, C.A.
s. 40, see *Weston* v. *Briar,* May 15, 1987, Hoffmann J.; *Practice Direction (Ch.D.) (Transfer of Business)* [1988] 1 W.L.R. 741.
ss. 40–42, amended: 1984, c.42, sch.1.
s. 41, see *Nissim* v. *Nissim, The Times,* December 11, 1987, C.A.
s. 42, see *Habib Bank A.G. Zurich* v. *Mindi Investments, The Times,* October 9, 1987, C.A.
s. 50, see *H.H. Property Co.* v. *Rahim* (1987) 282 E.G. 455, C.A.
s. 58, amended: 1985, c.61, sch 7; repealed in pt.: *ibid.*, schs.7,8.
s. 60, amended: 1985, c.51, sch.14; 1988, c.4, sch.6; repealed in pt.: 1985, c.51, sch.17; 1988, c.40, sch.13 (prosp.).
s. 66, amended: 1985, c.71, sch.2; 1988, c.50, sch.17.
s. 69, see *Ward* v. *Chief Constable of Avon and Somerset, The Times,* July 17, 1985, C.A.
s. 73, regs. 85/1807.
s. 73, amended: 1985, c.61, s.54.
s. 73A, added: *ibid.*
s. 75, see *Sharma* v. *Knight* (1986) 1 W.L.R. 757, C.A.
s. 75, rules 85/1269; 87/1119, 1397.
s. 77, amended: 1985, c.71, sch.2; 1988, c.50, sch.17.
ss. 79, 92, repealed in pt.: S.L.R. 1986.
s. 80, see *Ewing* v. *Hartley, The Times,* April 7, 1988, C.A.
s. 86, see *Mercantile Credit Co.* v. *Ellis, The Independent,* March 17, 1987, C.A.
s. 98, amended: 1985, c.9, sch.2; c.65, sch.8; 1986, c.45, sch.14.
s. 102, amended: 1985, c.65, sch.8; 1986, c.45, sch.14.
s. 109, see *Webb (Gerry) Transport* v. *Brenner (T/A Russell Brenner Metals and Midland Bank),* April 16, 1985, H.H. Judge Barr, Brentford County Court.
s. 109, amended: 1985, c.61, s.52; c.65, sch.8; 1986, c.45, sch.14; repealed in pt.: 1985, c.61, s.52, sch.8.
s. 112, amended: 1985, c.65, s.220.
s. 113, repealed in pt.: 1985, c.61, sch.8.
s. 115, amended: 1985, c.65, s.220.

CAP.

1984—cont.

28. County Courts Act 1984—cont.
s. 118, repealed in pt.: S.L.R. 1986.
s. 128, orders 85/574, 1834, 2143; 88/509.
s. 138, see *Gadsby and Mitchell* v. *Price and Harrison*, April 19, 1985, H.H. Judge Taylor, Harlow County Court; *Di Palma* v. *Victoria Square Property Co., The Times,* May 7, 1985, C.A.
s. 138, amended: 1985, c.61, s.55; repealed in pt.: *ibid.,* s.55, sch.8.
s. 139, amended: *ibid.,* s.55.
s. 141, repealed: S.L.R. 1986.
s. 147, amended: 1987, c.22, sch.6; repealed in pt.: 1984, c.42, sch.3.
sch. 2, repealed in pt.: 1985, c.65, sch.10; c.71, sch.1; 1986, c.53, sch.19; 1988, c.1, sch.31.

29. Housing and Building Control Act 1984.
Royal Assent, June 26, 1984.
ss. 1–38, repealed: 1985, c.71, sch.1.
s. 1, sch. 1, see *R.* v. *Plymouth City Council and Cornwall County Council, ex p. Freeman* (1988) R.V.R. 89, C.A.
s. 16, regs. 85/758.
s. 18, amended: 1985, c.51, sch.14.
s. 20, orders 84/1555; 85/1978.
s. 20, amended: 1985, c.51, sch.14; repealed in pt.: *ibid.,* sch.17.
s. 21, order 84/1174.
sch. 1–7, 11 (in pt.), repealed: 1985, c.71, sch.1.
sch. 3, order 84/1280.
sch. 4, amended: 1985, c.9, sch.2; c.51, sch.14.

30. Food Act 1984.
Royal Assent, June 26, 1984.
see *R.* v. *Uxbridge JJ., ex p., Gow, The Times,* October 17, 1985, D.C.
s. 2, see *R.* v. *Uxbridge JJ., ex p., Co-operative Retail Services, The Times,* October 23, 1985, D.C.; *McDonald's Hamburgers* v. *Windle* [1987] Crim.L.R. 200, D.C.
s. 4, regs. 84/1566; 85/912, 2026; 86/720, 721, 987, 2299; 87/1986, 1987.
s. 7, regs. 84/1566; 85/2026; 86/987, 2299; 87/1986, 1987.
s. 8, see *Barton* v. *Unigate Dairies* [1987] Crim.L.R. 121, D.C.; *Gateway Foodmarkets* v. *Simmonds* [1987] Crim.L.R. 696, D.C.
s. 11, amended: 1984, c.32, sch.6.
s. 13, regs. 84/1917, 1918; 85/216; 86/720; 87/2235–2237.
s. 30, regs. 86/722.
s. 33, regs. 85/68; 86/721; 87/212; 88/1804.
s. 34, regs. 85/68.
s. 38, regs. 85/530; 86/723; 87/212; 88/1805.
s. 45, regs. 85/530.
s. 51, amended: 1985, c.9, sch.2.
s. 68, orders 85/308; 86/429; 87/310; 88/336.
s. 71, amended: 1985, c.51, sch.8.
s. 73, regs. 87/133.
s. 74, regs. 85/530; 86/722, 723; 88/1804, 1805.
s. 100, see *R.* v. *Uxbridge JJ., ex p. Co-operative Retail Services, The Times,* October 23, 1985, D.C.
s. 102, see *Gateway Foodmarkets* v. *Simmonds* [1987] Crim.L.R. 696, D.C.

CAP.

1984—cont.

30. Food Act 1984—cont.
s. 118, regs. 84/1566, 1917, 1918; 85/68, 216, 530, 912, 2026; 86/720–723, 987, 2299; 87/212, 1986, 1987, 2235–2237; 88/1804, 1805.
s. 119, regs. 85/2026; 86/2299; 87/1986.
s. 132, amended: order 88/1843.
s. 135, regs. 84/1917.
s. 135, amended: order 88/1843.
sch. 10, repealed in pt.: 1984, c.32, sch.7; 1985, c.72, sch.13; 1987, c.43, sch.5.
sch. 11, amended: 1984, c.32, sch.6.

31. Rating and Valuation (Amendment) (Scotland) Act 1984.
Royal Assent, June 26, 1984.
ss. 1–4, repealed: 1987, c.47, sch.6.
s. 8, repealed: 1986, c.26, sch.24.
s. 12, see *Imperial Chemical Industries* v. *Central Region Valuation Appeal Committee* (O.H.), 1988 S.L.T. 106; *Civil Aviation Authority* v. *Argyll & Bute Valuation Appeal Committee* (O.H.), 1988 S.L.T. 119; *Distillers Co. (Bottling Services)* v. *Assessor for Fife Region,* 1988 S.L.T. (Lands Tr.) 49.
ss. 13, 21, repealed in pt.: S.L.R. 1986.
s. 20, see *Scott* v. *Assessor for Strathclyde Region,* 1988 S.L.T. 89.
sch. 1, repealed: 1987, c.47, sch.6.
sch. 2, repealed in pt.: 1988, c.41, sch.13.
sch. 3, repealed: S.L.R. 1986.

32. London Regional Transport Act 1984.
Royal Assent, June 26, 1984.
Commencement order: 84/877.
s. 1, order 84/877.
ss. 7, 10, repealed in pt.: 1985, c.51, sch.17.
s. 13, orders 85/165; 86/156; 87/125; 88/138.
ss. 13, 14, repealed (prosp.): 1988, c.41, sch.13.
s. 20, see *Dalgleish* v. *Assessor for Strathclyde Region,* 1988 S.L.T. 57; *W. R. Whitwell* v. *Assessor for Strathclyde Region,* 1988 S.L.T. 64.
s. 28, repealed in pt.: 1985, c.67, sch.8.
s. 30, repealed in pt.: 1985, c.51, sch.17.
s. 35, amended: 1985, c.67, sch.7.
ss. 43–45, repealed: *ibid.,* sch.8.
s. 49, see *R.* v. *Secretary of State for Transport, ex p. G.L.C.* [1985] 3 W.L.R. 574, McNeill J.
s. 49, amended: 1985, c.10, s.1.
s. 50, repealed in pt.: 1985, c.51, sch.17; c.67, sch.8.
s. 55, amended: *ibid.,* sch.7.
s. 64, repealed in pt.: 1988, c.39, sch.14.
s. 68, repealed in pt.: 1985, c.67, schs.7,8.
sch. 4, repealed in pt.: 1984, c.33, sch.1.
sch. 5, amended: 1985, c.67, schs.2,7; repealed in pt.: *ibid.,* schs.7,8.
sch. 6, repealed in pt.: *ibid.,* s.114, sch.8; 1986, c.5, sch.15; 1988, c.54, sch.1.

33. Rates Act 1984.
Royal Assent, June 26, 1984.
s. 1, orders 85/147, 256; 86/212, 230, 265, 329; 88/178, 192–194, 199, 286.
s. 1, amended: 1985, c.51, s.68; repealed in pt.: *ibid.:* sch.17.

CAP.

1984—cont.

33. Rates Act 1984—cont.
ss. 1–3, 6, 8, see *R.* v. *Hackney London Borough Council, ex p. Fleming* (1986) 26 R.V.R. 182, Woolf J.
s. 2, orders 85/823, 863; 86/265, 344; 87/785, 786, 1251; 88/729, 968.
s. 2, amended: orders 85/823, 863; 1985, c.51, s.68; orders 86/344; 87/1251; 88/968; repealed in pt.: 1985, c.51, s.68, sch.17.
s. 4, see *R.* v. *Secretary of State for the Environment, ex p. Leicester City Council* (1985) 25 R.V.R. 31, Woolf J.; *R.* v. *Secretary of State for the Environment, ex p. Greenwich London Borough Council, The Times*, December 19, 1985, C.A.
s. 4, orders 85/147, 256; 86/212, 230, 265, 329.
s. 5, repealed in pt.: 1985, c.51, sch.17.
s. 6, order 85/32.
s. 6, repealed in pt.: 1985, c.51, sch.17.
s. 7, amended: 1987, c.6, sch.4; repealed in pt.: 1985, c.51, sch.17.
s. 13, regs. 84/1355.
s. 14, rules 85/1486.
s. 15, rules 85/6, 1486.
s. 19, amended: 1987, c.6, sch.4.

34. Juries (Disqualification) Act 1984.
Royal Assent, July 12, 1984.
Commencement order: 84/1599.
s. 2, order 84/1599.

35. Data Protection Act 1984.
Royal Assent, July 12, 1984.
Commencement order: 85/1055.
s. 6, regs. 85/1465; 87/1304; 88/1969.
s. 8, regs. 85/1465; 87/272, 1304; 88/1969.
s. 9, regs. 86/1899.
s. 21, regs. 87/1507.
s. 29, orders 87/1903, 1904.
s. 30, order 87/1905.
s. 34, order 87/1906.
s. 37, order 87/2028.
s. 40, regs. 85/1465; 86/1899; 87/272, 1304, 1906; 88/1969.
s. 41, regs. 87/272, 1304, 1507; 88/1969.
s. 42, order 85/1055.
sch. 3, rules 85/1568.

36. Mental Health (Scotland) Act 1984.
Royal Assent, July 12, 1984.
s. 9, order 86/374.
ss. 18, 24, 26, see *B.* v. *Forsey* (H.L.), 1988 S.L.T. 572.
ss. 21, 40, amended: 1985, c.73, s.15; repealed in pt.: *ibid.*
s. 25, order 84/1095.
s. 29, see *T.* v. *Secretary of State for Scotland* (Sh.Ct.), 1987 S.C.L.R. 65; *F.* v. *Management Committee and Managers, Ravenscraig Hospital*, 1989 S.L.T. 49.
ss. 33, 34, see *A.B. and C.B.* v. *E.* (Sh.Ct.), 1987 S.C.L.R. 419.
s. 43, regs. 84/1494.
ss. 58, 74, 86, 96, regs. 84/1495.
ss. 97, 98, regs. 84/1494.
s. 113, see *F.* v. *Management Committee and Managers, Ravenscraig Hospital*, 1989 S.L.T. 49.

CAP.

1984—cont.

37. Child Abduction Act 1984.
see *R.* v. *Mousir* [1987] Crim.L.R. 561, C.A.
Royal Assent, July 12, 1984.
s. 1, amended: 1986, c.55, s.65.
s. 6, see *Deans* v. *Deans* (Sh.Ct.) 1988, S.C.L.R. 192.
s. 6, amended (S.): 1986, c.9, sch.1.

38. Cycle Tracks Act 1984.
Royal Assent, July 12, 1984.
s. 2, repealed: 1988, c.54, sch.1.
s. 3, regs. 84/1431.
s. 3, amended: 1986, c.5, sch.14.
s. 8, amended: 1988,c.54, sch.3.

39. Video Recordings Act 1984.
Royal Assent, July 12, 1984.
Commencement orders: 85/883, 904 (S.), 1264; 86/1125, 1182 (S.); 87/123, 160, 1142, 1249 (S.), 2155, 2273 (S.); 88/1018, 1079 (S.).
s. 3, amended: 1984, c.46, sch.5; 1985, c.13, sch.2.
s. 8, regs. 85/911.
s. 15, repealed in pt.: 1988, c.33, sch.16.
s. 16A, added: *ibid.*, s.162.
s. 23, orders 85/883, 904 (S.), 1264, 1265 (S.); 86/1125, 1182 (S.); 87/123, 160, 1142, 1249 (S.), 2155, 2273 (S.); 88/1018, 1079 (S.).

40. Animal Health and Welfare Act 1984.
Royal Assent, July 12, 1984.
see *Malins* v. *Cole & Attard*, Knightsbridge Crown Court.
s. 10, regs. 84/1325; 85/1857 (S.), 1858 (S.), 1861, 1862; 87/390, 904.
s. 11, regs. 87/390.
s. 17, order 85/1267.

41. Agricultural Holdings Act 1984.
Royal Assent, July 12, 1984.
Commencement order: 85/1644.
repealed: 1986, c.5, sch.15.
s. 8, order 85/1967.
s. 11, orders 85/1644, 1829.
sch. 5, order 85/1829.

42. Matrimonial and Family Proceedings Act 1984.
Royal Assent, July 12, 1984.
Commencement orders: 84/1589; 85/1316; 86/635, 1049, 1226 (S.).
ss. 5, 6, Pt. II (ss.3–11), see *Sandford* v. *Sandford* (1986) 16 Fam.Law 104, C.A.
s. 6, see *Morris* v. *Morris, The Times*, June 17, 1985, C.A.
s. 12, see *Chebarow* v. *Chebarow* [1987] 1 All E.R. 999, C.A.
s. 22, amended: 1988, c.50, sch.17.
s. 29A, added: 1985, c.37, sch.1.
s. 30, amended: *ibid.*
s. 32, amended: 1986, c.55, sch.11.
s. 38, amended: 1988, c.18, s.1.
s. 39, see *N. and L. (Minors) (Adoption Proceedings: Venue), Re* [1987] 1 W.L.R. 829, C.A.; *Nissim* v. *Nissim, The Times*, December 11, 1987, C.A.
s. 47, orders 84/1589; 85/1316; 86/635, 1049, 1226 (S.).
sch. 1, repealed in pt.: 1986, c.55, sch.2; 1988, c.34, sch.6.

1984—cont.

43. Finance Act 1984.
Royal Assent, July 26, 1984.
Commencement orders: 84/1180, 1836.
s. 4, repealed: 1985, c.54, sch.27.
s. 12, repealed: 1988, c.39, sch.14.
s. 16, repealed (S.): 1987, c.18, sch.8.
ss. 17–25, repealed: 1988, c.1, sch.31.
s. 26, orders 84/1674; 86/2147; 87/2075.
ss. 26–43, repealed: 1988, c.1, sch.31.
s. 38, amended: 1987, c.51, s.59; 1988, c.39, s.89.
s. 39, order 84/1180.
ss. 40–41, repealed: *ibid.*, sch.14.
ss. 44 (in pt.), 45–49, repealed: 1988, c.1, sch.31.
s. 50, amended: *ibid.*, sch.29; repealed in pt.: *ibid.*, sch.31.
s. 51, repealed: *ibid.*, c.39, sch.14.
ss. 52–55, 56 (in pt.), repealed: 1988, c.1, sch.31.
s. 60, amended: *ibid.*, sch.29.
s. 62, repealed in pt.: 1985, c.21, sch.2.
s. 65, repealed: 1987, c.51, sch.9.
s. 72, repealed: 1988. c.1, sch.31.
s. 73, repealed in pt.: 1985, c.54, sch.2; 1988, c.1, sch.31.
ss. 74–77, repealed: *ibid.*
s. 79, amended: 1987, c.51, s.76; 1988, c.1, sch.29; repealed in pt.: 1987, c.51, sch.9; 1988, c.1, sch.31.
s. 80, amended: 1988, c.39, sch.13.
ss. 82–100, repealed: 1988, c.1, sch.13.
s. 111, see *Ingram* v. *I.R.C., The Times,* November 18, 1985, Vinelott J.
s. 113, amended: 1987, c.51, sch.13; 1988, c.1, sch.29; repealed in pt.: 1987, c.51, schs.13,16.
s. 115, amended: 1988, c.1, sch.29.
ss. 118–123, repealed: 1985, c.54, sch.27.
s. 126, orders 84/1634; 85/1172, 1836.
s. 126, amended and repealed in pt.: 1985, c.54, s.96.
s. 127, order 84/1836.
s. 128, amended: 1988, c.1, sch.29; repealed in pt.: 1984, c.51, sch.9.
sch. 2, repealed in pt.: 1985, c.54, sch.27.
sch. 3, repealed in pt.: 1987, c.51, sch.16.
schs. 7–9, repealed: 1988, c.1, sch.31.
sch. 8, orders 84/1801; 86/711; regs. 85/1696, 1702.
sch. 10, amended: 1986, c.41, ss.22, 23; 1987, c.51, s.33, sch.4; 1988, c.39, s.69; repealed: 1988, c.1, sch.31.
sch. 11, amended: 1985, c.54, s.70; 1987, c.51, sch.2; repealed in pt.: 1988, c.1, sch.31.
sch. 13, amended: 1985, c.51, s.67; repealed in pt.: *ibid.*, sch. 27; 1986, c.41, sch.23; repealed in pt.: 1988, c.1, sch.31.
sch. 14, amended: *ibid.*, sch.29; repealed in pt.: 1984, c.51, sch.9; 1988, c.1, sch.31.
schs. 15–20, repealed: *ibid.*
sch. 21, repealed in pt.: 1984, c.51, sch.9; 1985, c.54, sch.27.
sch. 22, repealed in pt.: 1984, c.51, sch.9.

1984—cont.

44. Appropriation Act 1984.
Royal Assent, July 26, 1984.
repealed: 1986, c.42, sch. (C.).
45. Prescription and Limitation (Scotland) Act 1984.
Royal Assent, July 26, 1984.
46. Cable and Broadcasting Act 1984.
Royal Assent, July 26, 1984.
Commencement orders: 84/1796; 86/537; 87/672.
s. 2, orders 84/1994; 86/900.
s. 3, order 88/1370.
s. 8, repealed in pt.: 1988, c.48, schs.7,8.
s. 13, order 84/1993.
ss. 16 (in pt.), 22–24, repealed: 1988, c.48, sch.8.
s. 27, repealed: 1986, c.64, schs.2,3.
s. 28, amended: *ibid.*, sch.2.
s. 33, repealed in pt.: *ibid.*, schs.2,3.
s. 35, repealed in pt.: 1988, c.48, sch.8.
s. 36, repealed in pt.: 1985, c.51, sch.17.
s. 40, repealed in pt.: 1986, c.41, sch.23.
s. 49, amended: 1988, c.48, sch.7.
ss. 53, 54, repealed: *ibid.*, sch.8.
s. 56, repealed in pt.: *ibid.*, schs. 7, 8.
s. 58, order 88/1370.
s. 59, orders 84/1796; 86/537; 87/672.
sch. 5, repealed in pt.: 1985, c.13, sch.3; 1987, c.22, sch.7; 1988, c.33, sch.16; c.48, sch.8.
47. Repatriation of Prisoners Act 1984.
Royal Assent, July 26, 1984.
Commencement order: 85/550.
ss. 1, 3, 10, see *R.* v. *Secretary of State for the Home Department, ex p. Read* [1988] 2 W.L.R. 236.
s. 9, orders 85/550; 86/598; 87/1828.
sch. 1, repealed in pt.: 1988, c.33, sch.16.
48. Health and Social Security Act 1984.
Royal Assent, July 26, 1984.
Commencement orders: 84/1302, 1467; 86/974.
s. 5, orders 85/39, 302, 497.
s. 7, see *R.* v. *Secretary of State for Social Services, ex p. Westhead, The Times,* October 17, 1985, D.C.
s. 8, repealed: 1988, c.49, sch.3.
s. 11, regs. 84/1303.
s. 22, regs. 85/126.
s. 22, repealed: 1986, c.50, sch.11.
s. 26, amended: 1985, c.53, sch.5.
s. 27, orders 84/1302, 1467; 86/974.
s. 27, repealed in pt.: 1986, c.50, sch.11.
s. 28, regs. 84/1372, 1696, 1735; 85/298, 355 (S.); 86/965, 975, 976.
sch. 1, repealed in pt.: 1988, c.49, sch.3.
sch. 4, orders 84/1302, 1467.
sch. 4, repealed in pt.: 1986, c.50, sch.11; 1988, c.1, sch.31.
sch. 5, regs. 84/1699.
sch. 5, repealed in pt.: 1986, c.50, sch.11.
sch. 7, regs. 85/126.
sch. 7, repealed in pt.: 1985, c.53, sch.6.
49. Trade Unions Act 1984.
Royal Assent, July 26, 1984.
Commencement order: 84/1490.

CAP.

49. Trade Unions Act 1984—*cont.*

s. 1, amended: 1988, c.19, sch.3; repealed in pt.: *ibid.,* s.12, sch.4.

s. 2, amended: *ibid.,* sch.3.

s. 3, repealed: *ibid.,* s.14, sch.4.

ss. 4, 5, amended: *ibid.,* sch.3.

s. 6, repealed in pt.: *ibid.,* sch.4.

s. 8, amended: *ibid.,* sch.3; repealed in pt.: *ibid.,* schs.3,4.

s. 9, amended: *ibid.,* sch.3; repealed in pt.: *ibid.,* sch.4.

s. 10, see *Shipping Co. Uniform Inc.* v. *International Transport Workers Federation, Allen, Ross and Davies* [1985] 1 Lloyd's Rep. 173; [1985] I.C.R. 245, Staughton J.; *Monsanto* v. *Transport and General Workers' Union* [1987] 1 All E.R. 358, C.A.; *Longley* v. *National Union of Journalists* [1987] I.R.L.R. 109, C.A.

ss. 10, 11, see *Express & Star* v. *NGA (1982)* [1985] I.R.L.R. 455, Skinner J.; *Falconer* v. *A.S.L.E.F. and N.U.R.* [1986] I.R.L.R. 331, Sheffield County Ct.

ss. 10, 11, amended: 1988, c.19, s.17, sch.3.

s. 11, see *Austin Rover Group* v. *Amalgamated Union of Engineering Workers (TASS)* [1985] I.R.L.R. 162, Hodgson J.

s. 22, order 84/1490.

s. 22, amended: 1988, c.19, sch.3.

50. Housing Defects Act 1984.

Royal Assent, July 31, 1984.

Commencement order: 84/1701.

repealed: 1985, c.71, sch. 1; 1987, c.26, sch.24 (S.)

ss. 2, 27, see *McSweeney* v. *Dumbarton District Council,* 1987 S.L.T.(Sh.Ct.) 129.

s. 23, regs. 86/843(S.).

s. 29, order 84/1701.

sch. 1, order 84/1705.

sch. 4, amended: 1985, c.51, sch.14; 1987, c.3, sch.1.

51. Inheritance Tax Act 1984.

Royal Assent, July 31, 1984.

Capital Transfer Tax Act renamed: 1986, c.41, s.100.

amended: *ibid.*

s. 2, repealed: 1985, c.54, sch.27.

s. 3A, added: 1986, c.41, sch.19; amended: 1987, c.51, s.96; repealed in pt.: *ibid.,* s.96, sch.9.

s. 6, amended: 1988, c.1, sch.29.

s. 7, amended: 1986, c.41, sch.19; repealed in pt: *ibid.,* schs.19,23.

s. 8, orders 85/429; 86/528; 87/435; 88/505.

s. 8, amended: 1986, c.41, sch.19; repealed in pt.: 1988, c.39, s.136, sch.14.

s. 9, amended: 1986, c.41, sch.19.

s. 10, amended: 1987, c.16, sch.8.

s. 12, amended: 1987, c.51, s.98; 1988, c.1, sch.29.

s. 13, amended: 1985, c.9, sch.2; 1988, c.1, sch.29.

s. 18, amended: 1985, c.54, s.95.

s. 19, amended: *ibid.;* 1986, c.41, sch.19.

CAP.

51. Inheritance Tax Act 1984—*cont.*

s. 20, amended: 1985, c.54, s.95.

s. 21, amended: *ibid.;* 1988, c.1, sch.29.

ss. 22, 23, amended: 1985, c.54, s.95.

s. 24, amended: *ibid.;* repealed in pt.: 1988, c.39, s.137, sch.4.

ss. 25, 26, amended: 1985, c.54, s.95.

s. 26A, added: 1986, c.41, sch.19.

ss. 27, 28, amended: 1985, c.54, s.95.

s. 29, amended: *ibid.;* repealed in pt.: 1988, c.39, sch.14.

ss. 30, 31, amended: 1985, c.54, s.95, sch.26; 1986, c.41, sch.19.

s. 31, sch. 4, see *Raikes* v. *Lygon* [1988] 1 W.L.R. 281, Peter Gibson J.

s. 32, amended: 1986, c.41, sch.19; repealed in pt.: 1985, c.9, schs.26,27.

s. 32A, added: *ibid.,* sch.26; amended: 1986, c.41, sch.19.

s. 33, amended: 1985, c.9, s.95, sch.26; 1986, c.41, sch.19.

s. 34, amended: 1985, c.9, s.95, sch.26.

s. 35, amended: *ibid.;* 1986, c.41, sch.19.

ss. 36–37, amended: 1985, c.9, s.95.

s. 38, amended: *ibid.;* 1986, c.41, sch.19.

s. 39, amended: 1985, c.9, s.95.

s. 39A, added: 1986, c.41, s.105.

ss. 40–42, amended: 1985, c.9, s.95.

s. 49, amended: 1986, c.41, sch.19; repealed in pt.: 1987, c.51, s.96, sch.9.

ss. 54A, 54B, added: *ibid.,* sch.7.

s. 55, amended: 1986, c.41, sch.19; repealed in pt.: 1987, s.96, sch.9.

s. 56, amended: *ibid.,* sch.7.

s. 57A, added: 1987, c.16, sch.9.

ss. 66–68, amended: 1986, c.41, sch.19.

s. 72, amended: 1988, c.1, sch.29.

s. 76, amended: 1985, c.9, s.95.

s. 78, amended: *ibid.,* sch.26; 1986, c.41, sch.19.

s. 79, amended: 1985, c.9, sch.26.

ss. 86, 91, 94, 96, 97, amended: 1988, c.1, sch.29.

s. 98, amended: 1986, c.41, sch.19; 1987, c.16, sch.8.

s. 100, amended: *ibid.*

s. 102, amended: 1988, c.1, sch.29.

s. 103, amended: 1985, c.9, sch.2.

s. 104, amended: 1987, c.16, sch.8.

s. 105, amended: 1986, c.41, s.106; 1987, c.16, sch.8.

s. 107, amended: *ibid.*

s. 109A, added: *ibid.*

s. 113A, added: 1986, c.41, sch.19; amended: 1987, c.16, sch.8.

s. 113B, added: 1986, c.41, sch.19.

s. 124A, added: *ibid.;* amended: 1987, c.16, sch.8.

s. 124B, added: 1986, c.41, sch.19.

s. 131, amended: *ibid.*

ss. 136, 140, amended: 1987, c.16, sch.8.

s. 142, amended: 1986, c.41, sch.19.

ss. 148, 149, repealed: *ibid.,* sch.23.

ss. 151, 152, amended: 1987, c.51, s.98; 1988, c.1, sch.29.

CAP.

51. Inheritance Tax Act 1984—*cont.*
s. 155, amended: order 86/948.
s. 157, amended: 1987, c.22, sch.6.
s. 158, amended: 1987, c.16, s.70.
s. 167, repealed in pt.: 1986, c.41, sch.23.
s. 168, amended: 1987, c.16, sch.8; repealed in pt.: *ibid.*, schs.8,16.
s. 174, amended: 1988, c.1, sch.29.
s. 178, amended: 1987, c.16, sch.8; 1988, c.1, sch.29; repealed in pt.: 1987, c.16, schs.8,16.
s. 180, amended: *ibid.*, sch.8.
s. 199, amended: 1986, c.41, sch.19.
s. 201, amended: *ibid.*; 1987, c.51, sch.7.
s. 204, amended: 1986, c.41, sch.19; 1988, c.1, sch.29; repealed in pt.: 1986, c.41, schs.19,23.
s. 206, repealed: 1988, c.39, sch.14.
s. 207, amended: 1985, c.54, sch.26.
s. 216, amended: *ibid.*; 1986, c.41, sch.19; 1987, c.51, sch.7.
s. 225, repealed in pt.: S.L.R. 1986.
s. 226, amended: 1985, c.54, sch.26; 1986, c.41, sch.19; repealed in pt.: 1988, c.39, sch.14.
s. 227, amended: *ibid.*; 1987, c.16, sch.8.
s. 228, amended: *ibid.*
s. 230, functions transferred: order 86/600.
s. 233, orders 85/560; 86/1944; 87/887; 88/1280, 1623.
s. 233, amended: 1985, c.54, sch.26; 1986, c.41, sch.19; order 86/1944.
s. 234, amended: 1985, c.9, sch.2; 1986, c.41, s.107.
s. 236, amended: *ibid.*, sch.19; repealed in pt.: *ibid.*, sch.23; 1988, c.39, sch.14.
ss. 237, 239, amended: 1986, c.41, sch.19.
s. 256, regs. 87/1127, 1128(S.), 1129(N.I.).
s. 265, amended: 1987, c.51, sch.7.
s. 272, amended: 1987, c.16, sch.8; 1988, c.1, sch.29.
sch. 1, substituted: 1986, c.41, sch.19; amended: order 87/435; 1987, c.16, s.57; order 88/505; substituted: 1988, c.39, s.36.
sch. 2, amended: 1986, c.41, sch.19; repealed in pt.: *ibid.*, schs.19,23.
sch. 3, amended: 1985, c.16, sch.2 (S.); c.54, s.95.
sch. 4, amended: *ibid.*, s.95, sch.26; 1986, c.41, sch. 19; 1987, c.16, sch.9.
sch. 5, amended: 1985, c.54, s.95.
sch. 6, amended: *ibid.*, sch.26; 1986, c.41, sch.19.
sch. 8, repealed in pt.: 1985, c.54, sch.27; 1988, c.1, sch.31.

52. Parliamentary Pensions etc. Act 1984.
Royal Assent, July 31, 1984.
ss. 1–11, 15 (in pt.), 16, sch., repealed: 1987, c.45, sch.4.
ss. 1, 2, 4, order 84/1909.
s. 5, order 84/1908.

53. Local Government (Interim Provisions) Act 1984.
Royal Assent, July 31, 1984.
Commencement order: 85/2.

CAP.

53. Local Government (Interim Provisions) Act 1984—*cont.*
repealed (except ss.4, 6 (in pt.), 10, 11, 13): 1985, c.51, sch.17.
s. 1, order 85/2.
s. 6, see *R.* v. *Secretary of State for the Environment, ex p. Greater London Council* [1985] J.P.L. 543, Taylor J.
s. 6, orders 85/176; 86/466, 2202.
s. 7, see *R.* v. *District Auditor No. 3 Audit District of West Yorkshire Metropolitan County Council, ex p. West Yorkshire Metropolitan County Council* [1986] 26 R.V.R. 24, D.C.
s. 11, regs. 84/1760.

54. Roads (Scotland) Act 1984.
Royal Assent, October 31, 1984.
s. 1, repealed in pt.: 1987, c.47, sch.6.
s. 17, regs. 85/2080.
s. 21, regs. 86/509.
s. 34, see *Grant* v. *Lothian Regional Council* (O.H.), 1988 S.L.T. 533.
ss. 59, 87, 141, see *Lord Advocate* v. *Strathclyde Regional Council*, 1988 S.L.T. 546.
s. 60, regs. 86/642.
s. 71, regs. 86/252.
s. 140, amended: 1987, c.3, sch.1.
s. 143, regs. 85/1165, 2080; 86/252, 509, 642; orders 85/1471, 1953.
s. 144, regs. 85/1165.
s. 152, regs. 86/252.
s. 154, order 85/1471.
s. 157, order 85/1953.
sch. 9, repealed in pt.: 1986, c.44, sch.9; 1988, c.54, sch.1.

55. Building Act 1984.
Royal Assent, October 31, 1984.
Commencement orders: 85/1602, 1603.
s. 1, regs. 85/488, 1065, 1066, 1576; 86/2287; 87/798, 1445; 88/871.
s. 3, regs. 85/1065, 1576; 86/2287; 87/798, 1445; 88/871.
s. 4, amended: 1988, c.40, sch.12; repealed: 1986, c.31, sch.6.
s. 8, regs. 85/1065; 87/798, 1445.
ss. 11, 12, repealed in pt.: 1985, c.51, sch.17.
s. 14, regs. 85/1936.
s. 16, regs. 85/1066, 1576; 86/2287; order 85/1603; 86/2287; 87/798; 88/871.
s. 17, regs. 85/1066; 87/798.
s. 18, repealed in pt.: 1985, c.51, sch.17.
s. 30, order 85/1603.
s. 34, regs. 85/1576; 86/2287; 88/871.
s. 35, regs. 85/1066, 1576; 86/2287; 87/798; 88/871.
s. 36, see *Rickards* v. *Kerrier District Council, The Times*, April 7, 1987, Schiemann J.
s. 47, regs. 85/1066; 87/798.
s. 48, amended: 1987, c.27, s.7; regs. 87/798.
s. 50, regs. 86/2287; 88/871.
ss. 49–54, 56, regs. 85/1066; 87/798.
s. 59, repealed: 1986, c.31, sch.6.
s. 68, repealed in pt.: 1985, c.51, sch.17.
s. 76, amended: 1985, c.71, sch.2.
ss. 77, 79, amended: 1986, c.63, sch.9.

1984—cont.

55. Building Act 1984—cont.

s. 80, amended: 1985, c.71, sch. 2; 1986, c.44, sch.7; c.63, sch.5.

s. 81, amended: 1985, c.71, sch.2; 1986, c.63, sch.5.

s. 88, repealed in pt.: 1985, c.51, sch.17.

s. 89, repealed in pt.: 1985, c.71, sch.1.

s. 91, repealed in pt.: 1985, c.51, sch.17.

s. 120, orders 85/1602, 1603.

s. 126, regs. 88/871.

s. 126, amended: 1985, c.51, sch.8; repealed in pt.: ibid., sch.17; 1986, c.44, sch.9.

sch. 1, regs. 85/488, 1065, 1066, 1576; 86/2287; 87/798, 1445; 88/871.

sch. 1, amended: order 86/452.

sch. 3, regs. 87/798.

sch. 3, amended: 1985, c.51, sch.8; repealed in pt.: ibid., sch.17.

sch. 4, regs. 85/1066; 87/798.

sch. 5, repealed in pt.: 1985, c.71, sch.1.

sch. 6, repealed in pt.: 1984, c.55, s.4 (prospectively); 1985, c.71, sch.1.

56. Foster Children (Scotland) Act 1984.

Royal Assent, October 31, 1984.

ss. 3, 4, 14, regs. 85/1789.

57. Co-operative Development Agency and Industrial Development Act 1984.

Royal Assent, October 31, 1984.

Commencement order: 84/1845.

s. 7, orders 84/1845; 86/128.

58. Rent (Scotland) Act 1984.

Royal Assent, October 31, 1984.

s. 1, order 85/314.

s. 3, amended: 1988, c.43, s.46.

s. 3A, added: ibid.

s. 5, amended: 1985, c.71, sch.2; .1987, c.26, sch.23; 1988, c.43, s.47; repealed in pt.: 1987, c.26, sch.24.

s. 6, amended: ibid., sch.23.

s. 22, amended: 1988, c.43, s.38.

s. 23, amended: ibid., s.39.

s. 23A, added: ibid., s.40.

s. 24, amended: ibid.

ss. 28 (in pt.), 29 (in pt.), 30, 32 (in pt.), repealed: ibid., sch.10.

s. 33, amended: ibid., s.41.

s. 34, repealed in pt.: ibid., sch.10.

s. 37, see North v. Allan Properties (Edinburgh), 1987 S.L.T. (Sh.Ct.) 141.

ss. 40, 42, 49, repealed in pt.: 1988, c.43, sch.10.

s. 53, amended: ibid., s.48.

s. 54, repealed in pt.: ibid., sch.10.

s. 55, amended: ibid., s.47.

s. 56, amended: 1985, c.73, sch.2; repealed in pt.: 1988, c.43, sch.10.

s. 57, repealed in pt.: ibid.

s. 58, amended: ibid., s.41; repealed in pt.: ibid., sch.10.

s. 59, amended: 1987, c.26, sch.23; repealed in pt.: ibid., sch.24.

s. 61, amended: 1985, c.71, sch.2; 1988, c.43, s.69; repealed in pt.: ibid., schs.2,10.

s. 63, amended: ibid.; 1987, c.26, sch.23; repealed in pt.: ibid., sch.24.

1984—cont.

58. Rent (Scotland) Act 1984—cont.

s. 64, order 85/314.

s. 65, repealed in pt.: 1988, c.43, s.68, sch.10.

s. 66, amended: 1987, c.26, sch.23; repealed in pt.: 1988, c.43, sch.10.

ss. 67–69, repealed in pt.: ibid.

s. 70, repealed in pt.: ibid., s.44, sch.10.

ss. 71, 95, 98, repealed in pt.: ibid., sch.10.

s. 101, amended: 1987, c.26, sch.23.

s. 103, amended: 1988, c.43, sch.9; repealed in pt.: ibid., sch.10.

s. 105, repealed in pt.: ibid.

s. 106, amended: 1985, c.73, sch.2; 1987, c.26, sch.23.

sch. 1, amended: 1988, c.43, sch.9.

schs. 1A, 1B, added: ibid., s.46, sch.6.

sch. 2, amended: 1985, c.24, s.1; 1987, c.26, sch.23.

schs. 3, 7 (in pt.), repealed: 1988, c.43, sch.10.

sch. 9, amended: 1985, c.73, sch.2.

59. Ordnance Factories and Military Services Act 1984.

Royal Assent, October 31, 1984.

s. 10, order 84/2022.

s. 11, sch.3, repealed: 1987, c.4, s.7.

s. 13, repealed in pt.: 1988, c.39, sch.14.

s. 15, order 85/927.

60. Police and Criminal Evidence Act 1984.

Royal Assent, October 31, 1984.

Commencement orders: 84/2002; 85/623, 1934.

see R. v. Foster [1987] Crim.L.R. 821, Kingston Crown Ct.

s. 1, amended: 1988, c.33, s.140.

s. 4, amended: 1988, c.54, sch.3.

s. 5, amended: 1988, c.33, s.140.

s. 9, see R. v. Central Criminal Court, ex p. Adegbesan [1986] Crim.L.R. 691; [1986] 3 All E.R. 113, D.C.; R. v. Bristol Crown Court, ex p. Bristol Press and Picture Agency [1987] Crim.L.R. 329; (1987) 85 Cr.App.R. 190, D.C.; Carr v. Atkins [1987] 3 W.L.R. 529, C.A.; R. v. Leicester Crown Court, ex p. D.P.P. [1987] 1 W.L.R. 1371; [1987] 3 All E.R. 654, D.C.; R. v. Maidstone Crown Court, ex p. Waitt, The Times, January 4, 1988, D.C.; R. v. Central Criminal Court, ex p. D.P.P., The Independent, March 31, 1988, D.C.; Application under s.9 of the Police and Criminal Evidence Act 1984, Re, The Independent, May 27, 1988, Alliott J.; R. v. Manchester Crown Court, ex p. Taylor [1988] 1 W.L.R. 705, D.C.

s. 10, see R. v. Crown Court, ex p. Baines and White (1987) 137 New L.J. 945, D.C.; R. v. Snaresbrook Crown Court, ex p. D.P.P. [1987] 3 W.L.R. 1054, D.C.; R. v. Central Criminal Court, ex p. Francis & Francis (A Firm) [1988] 3 W.L.R. 989; [1988] 3 All E.R. 775, D.C.

s. 14, see R. v. Maidstone Crown Court, ex p. Waitt, The Times, January 4, 1988, D.C.; R. v. Manchester Crown Court, ex p. Taylor [1988] 1 W.L.R. 705, D.C.

s. 16, see R. v. Longman [1988] 1 W.L.R. 619, C.A.

CAP.

1984—cont.

60. Police and Criminal Evidence Act 1984—cont.

s. 17, see *Kynaston* v. *D.P.P.; Heron (Joseph)* v. *D.P.P.; Heron (Tracey)* v. *D.P.P., The Times,* November 4, 1987, D.C.

s. 17, amended: 1986, c.64, sch.2; repealed in pt.: *ibid.,* schs.2,3.

s. 18, see *R.* v. *Badham* [1987] Crim.L.R. 202, Wood Green Crown Court.

s. 24, amended: 1988, c.33, sch.15; repealed in pt: 1985, c.44, sch.5; 1988, c.33, sch.16.

ss. 25, 28, see *Nicholas* v. *Parsonage* [1987] R.T.R. 199, D.C.

s. 26, amended: 1985, c.50, s.25.

s. 27, regs. 85/1941.

s. 32, see *R.* v. *Badham* [1987] Crim.L.R. 202, Wood Green Crown Ct.

ss. 34, 36, amended: 1988, c.54, sch.3.

s. 43, see *R.* v. *Slough Justices, ex p. Stirling* [1987] Crim.L.R. 576, D.C.

s. 46, see *R.* v. *Avon Magistrates' Courts Committee, ex p. Broome, The Times,* May 14, 1988, D.C.

s. 51, see *Crown Prosecution Service* v. *Hawkins, The Guardian,* June 4, 1988, D.C.

s. 54, amended: 1988, c.33, s.147.

s. 55, amended: *ibid.,* sch.15.

s. 56, see *R.* v. *McIvor* [1987] Crim.L.R. 409, Sheffield Crown Ct.

s. 56, amended: 1986, c.32, s.32; 1988, c.33, s.99.

s. 58, see *D.P.P.* v. *Billington, Chappell, Rumble and East, The Independent,* July 22, 1987, D.C.; *Walters, Re* [1987] Crim.L.R. 577, D.C.; *R.* v. *Smith (Eric)* [1987] Crim.L.R. 579, Stafford Crown Ct.; *R.* v. *Samuel* [1988] 2 W.L.R. 920, D.C.; *D.P.P.* v. *Billington; Chappell* v. *D.P.P.; D.P.P.* v. *Rumble; Corywright* v. *East* [1987] Crim.L.R. 772, D.C.; *R.* v. *Alladice, The Times,* May 11, 1988, C.A.

s. 58, amended: 1986, c.32, s.32; 1988, c.33, s.99.

s. 59, repealed: 1988, c.34, sch.6.

s. 62, amended: 1988, c.54, sch.3.

s. 64, amended: 1988, c.33, s.148.

s. 65, amended: 1986, c.32, s.32; 1988, c.33, sch.15; repealed in pt.: *ibid.,* sch.16.

s. 66, see *Walters, Re* [1987] Crim.L.R. 577, D.C.; *R.* v. *Delaney, The Times,* August 30, 1988, C.A.; *Grennan* v. *Wescott* [1988] R.T.R. 253, D.C.

s. 67, orders 85/1937; 88/1200.

s. 68, see *R.* v. *O'Loughlin and McLaughlin* (1987) 85 Cr.App.R. 157, Central Criminal Ct.: *R.* v. *Martin, The Times,* December 21, 1987, C.A.; *R.* v. *Feest* [1987] Crim.L.R. 766, C.A.; *R.* v. *Bray, The Times,* July 4, 1988, C.A.; *R.* v. *Martin* [1988] 1 W.L.R. 655, C.A.

s. 68, repealed: 1988, c.33, sch.16.

s. 69, see *Sophocleous* v. *Ringer* [1987] R.T.R. 52, D.C.

s. 74, see *R.* v. *Robertson; R.* v. *Golder* [1987] 3 W.L.R. 327, C.A.

ss. 74, 75, see *R.* v. *O'Connor* [1987] Crim.L.R. 260; (1987) 85 Cr.App.R. 298, C.A.

CAP.

1984—cont.

60. Police and Criminal Evidence Act 1984—cont.

s. 76, see *R.* v. *Oxford City JJ., ex p. Berry* [1987] 1 All E.R. 244, Q.B.D.; *R.* v. *Fulling* [1987] 2 W.L.R. 923, C.A.; *R.* v. *Millard* [1987] Crim.L.R. 196, Central Criminal Ct.; *R.* v. *McIvor* [1987] Crim.L.R. 409, Sheffield Crown Ct.; *R.* v. *Liverpool Juvenile Court, ex p. R.* [1987] 2 All E.R. 668, D.C.; *R.* v. *Mason (Carl)* [1987] 3 All E.R. 481, C.A.; *R.* v. *Sat-Bhambra, The Times,* March 17, 1988, C.A.; *R.* v. *Goldenberg, The Times,* May 27, 1988, C.A.; *R.* v. *Harvey* [1988] Crim.L.R. 241, C.C.C.

s. 77, amended: order 85/1800.

s. 78, see *R.* v. *H.* [1987] Crim.L.R. 47, Winchester Crown Court, Gatehouse J.; *R.* v. *O'Connor* [1987] Crim.L.R. 260, C.A.; *R.* v. *Deacon* [1987] Crim.L.R. 404, Guildford Crown Ct.; *R.* v. *Beveridge* [1987] Crim.L.R. 401, C.A.; *Vel* v. *Owen, sub nom. Vel (Kevin)* v. *Chief Constable of North Wales* [1987] Crim.L.R. 496, D.C.; *R.* v. *Robertson; R.* v. *Golder* [1987] 3 W.L.R. 327, C.A.; *R.* v. *Smith (Eric)* [1987] Crim.L.R. 579, Stafford Crown Ct.; *R.* v. *Mason (Carl)* [1987] 3 All E.R. 481, C.A.; *R.* v. *O'Loughlin and McLaughlin* [1987] Crim.L.R. 632; (1987) 85 Cr.App.R. 157, Central Criminal Ct.; *Matto* v. *Wolverhampton Crown Court, sub nom. Matto* v. *D.P.P.* [1987] R.T.R. 337, D.C.; *R.* v. *O'Connor (P.S.)* (1987) 85 Cr.App.R. 298, C.A.; *R.* v. *Beveridge* (1987) 85 Cr.App.R. 255, C.A.; *R.* v. *Lunnon, The Times,* March 25, 1988, C.A.; *Kinsella* v. *Marshall, The Times,* April 19, 1988, D.C.; *R.* v. *O'Leary, The Times,* May 18, 1988, C.A.; *R.* v. *Samuel* [1988] 2 W.L.R. 920, C.A.; *R.* v. *Gaynor* [1988] Crim.L.R. 242, Liverpool Crown Ct.

s. 81, rules 87/716.

s. 82, see *R.* v. *Sat-Bhambra, The Times,* March 17, 1988, C.A.

s. 84, see *Vel (Kevin)* v. *Chief Constable of North Wales, The Times,* February 14, 1987, D.C.

s. 87, regs. 85/673.

s. 89, regs. 85/520, 673.

s. 94, regs. 85/518, 519.

s. 99, regs. 85/520, 671, 672; 88/1762.

s. 100, regs. 85/520, 671–673.

s. 101, regs. 85/518, 519.

s. 102, regs. 85/518.

s. 113, orders 85/1881, 1882; 86/307.

s. 114, orders 85/1800; 87/439.

s. 114, amended: 1988, c.33, s.150.

s. 116, see *R.* v. *McIvor* [1987] Crim.L.R. 409, Sheffield Crown Ct.; *R.* v. *Smith (Eric)* [1987] Crim.L.R. 579, Stafford Crown Ct.

s. 116, amended: 1986, c.32, s.36.

s. 120, amended: 1988, c.33, sch.15.

s. 121, orders 84/2002; 85/623, 1934.

sch. 1, see *R.* v. *Central Criminal Court, ex p. Adegbesan* [1986] Crim.L.R. 691; [1986] 3 All E.R. 113, D.C.; *R.* v. *Crown Court, ex p. Baines and White* (1987) 137 New L.J. 945, D.C.; *Carr* v. *Atkins* [1987] 3 W.L.R. 529, C.A.;

CAP.

1984—cont.

60. Police and Criminal Evidence Act 1984—cont.
R. v. *Leicester Crown Court, ex p. D.P.P.*
[1987] 1 W.L.R. 1371, D.C.; *R.* v. *Maidstone
Crown Court, ex p. Waitt, The Times,* January
4, 1988, D.C.; *R.* v. *Bristol Crown Court, ex p.
Bristol Press and Picture Agency* [1987]
Crim.L.R. 329; (1987) 85 Cr.App.R. 190, D.C.;
R. v. *Inner London Crown Court, ex p. Baines
& Baines (A Firm)* [1987] 3 All E.R. 1025,
D.C.; *Application under s.9 of the Police and
Criminal Evidence Act 1984, Re, The Independent,* May 27, 1988, Allott J.; *R.* v. *Manchester Crown Court, ex p. Taylor* [1988] 1 W.L.R.
705, D.C.
sch. 2, repealed in pt.: 1988, c.54, sch.1.
sch. 3, repealed in pt.: 1988, c.33, sch.16.
sch. 5, see *R.* v. *Smith (Eric)* [1987] Crim.L.R.
579, Stafford Crown Ct.
sch. 5, amended: 1988, c.33, sch.15; c.54,
sch.3; repealed in pt.: *ibid.,* sch.1.
sch. 7, repealed in pt.: 1985, c.50, sch.5.
61. Consolidated Fund (No. 2) Act 1984.
Royal Assent, December 20, 1984.
repealed: 1986, c.42, sch. (C).
62. Friendly Societies Act 1984.
Royal Assent, December 20, 1984.
s. 2, repealed in pt.: 1988, c.1, sch.31.
s. 4, orders 86/768, 1276.

1985

1. Consolidated Fund Act 1985.
Royal Assent, January 24, 1985.
repealed: 1987, c.17, sch. (C).
2. Elections (Northern Ireland) Act 1985.
Royal Assent, January 24, 1985.
Commencement order: 85/1221.
s. 1, amended: 1988, c.54, sch.3.
s. 3, amended: 1985, c.50, s.25.
s. 7, order 85/1221.
3. Brunei and Maldives Act 1985.
Royal Assent, March 11, 1985.
4. Milk (Cessation of Production) Act 1985.
Royal Assent, March 11, 1985.
s. 1, schemes 86/1612, 1614 (S.); 87/882 (S.),
908.
s. 5, scheme 87/882 (S.).
**5. New Towns and Urban Development Corpor-
ations Act 1985.**
Royal Assent, March 11, 1985.
s. 12, repealed: 1987, c.57, s.1.
6. Companies Act 1985.
Royal Assent, March 11, 1985.
see *Taylor* v. *McGirr, The Times,* April 11, 1986,
D.C.
ss. 2, 18, 45, see *Scandinavian Bank Group, Re*
[1987] 2 W.L.R. 752, Harman J.
s. 3, regs. 85/805.
s. 6, regs. 85/854; 87/752.
s. 8, regs. 85/805, 1052.
ss. 10, 12, regs. 85/854.
s. 13, amended: 1986, c.45, sch.13.
ss. 21, 30, regs. 85/854.

CAP.

1985—cont.

6. Companies Act 1985—cont.
s. 36, see *Rover International* v. *Cannon Film
Sales* (1987) 3 B.C.C. 369, Harman J.; *Osh-
kosh B'Gosh Inc.* v. *Dan Marbel, The Times,*
October 12, 1988, C.A.
s. 43, regs. 85/854.
s. 44, amended: 1986, c.45, sch.13.
ss. 49, 51, 53, regs. 85/854.
s. 54, regs. 85/854; 87/752.
Pt. III (ss.56–79), repealed: 1986, c.60, sch.17.
ss. 65, 72, 77, regs. 85/854.
ss. 81–83, 84 (in pt.), 85 (in pt.), 86, 87,
repealed: 1986, c.60, sch.17.
s. 88, regs. 85/854; 87/752; 88/1359.
s. 97, regs. 85/854.
s. 97, amended: 1986, c.60, sch.16; repealed in
pt.: *ibid.,* sch.17.
s. 103, amended: 1986, c.45, sch.13.
ss. 103, 108, 113, see *Ossory Estates, Re,*
[1988] BCLC 213, Harman J.
s. 112AA, added: 1985, c.65, s.215.
s. 117, regs. 85/854.
s. 121, see *Scandinavian Bank Group, Re* [1987]
2 W.L.R. 752, Harman J.
ss. 122, 123, regs. 85/854; 87/752.
s. 125, see *Cumbrian Newspapers Group* v.
*Cumberland & Westmorland Herald News-
paper & Printing Co.* [1986] 3 W.L.R. 26, Scott
J.
ss. 128, 129, regs. 85/854; 87/752.
s. 130, see *Tip-Europe, Re* [1987] BCC 647,
Gibson J.; *European Home Products, Re, Financial Times,* March 23, 1988, Mervyn Davies
J.
s. 131, amended: 1986, c.45, sch.13.
s. 135, see *Willaire Systems, Re* [1987] B.C.L.C.
67, C.A.; *Transfesa Terminals, Re* [1987] 3
BCC 647, Harman J; *Tip-Europe, Re* [1987] 3
BCC 647, Gibson J.; *European Home Products, Re, Financial Times,* March 23, 1988,
Mervyn Davies J.
s. 136, see *House of Fraser* v. *A.C.G.E. Investments,* [1987] 2 W.L.R. 1083, H.L.(Sc.).
ss. 136, 137, see *European Home Products, Re,
Financial Times,* March 23, 1988, Mervyn
Davies J.
s. 137, see *Willaire Systems, Re* [1987] B.C.L.C.
67, C.A.
s. 139, regs. 85/854.
s. 140, amended: 1986, c.45, sch.13.
s. 147, regs. 85/854.
ss. 151, 153, see *Brady* v. *Brady* [1988] 2 W.L.R.
1308, H.L.
s. 153, amended: 1985, c.65, sch.6; 1986, c.45,
sch.13; c.60, s.196.
ss. 155, 156, regs. 85/854.
s. 156, amended: 1986, c.45, sch.13.
s. 157, regs. 85/854; 87/752.
s. 158, see *Cornhill Insurance* v. *Improvement
Services* [1986] 1 W.L.R. 114, Harman J.
s. 161, repealed: 1988, c.39, sch.14.
s. 163, amended: 1986, c.60, sch.16.
s. 169, regs. 85/854; 87/752.
s. 173, regs. 85/854.
s. 173, amended: 1986, c.45, sch.13.

CAP.

1985—cont.

6. Companies Act 1985—cont.

s. 176, regs. 85/854; 87/752.

s. 178, repealed in pt.: 1985, c.65, sch.10.

s. 185, order 85/806.

s. 185, amended: 1986, c.60, s.194.

s. 190, regs. 85/854; 87/752.

s. 196, see *Brightlife, Re* [1987] 3 W.L.R. 197, Hoffmann J.

s. 196, substituted: 1986, c.45, sch.13.

s. 204, see *T.R. Technology Investment Trust, Re* (1988) 4 BCC 244, Hoffmann J.

s. 209, regs. 88/706.

s. 209, amended: 1986, c.60, s.197, sch.16; 1987, c.22, sch.6; 1988, c.1, sch.29.

s. 212, see *Lonrho, Re, The Times,* November 16, 1988, Vinelott J.

ss. 212, 216, see *Geers Gross, Re* (1987) 2 B.C.C. 528, C.A.; *Lonhro, Re,* 1987 P.C.C. 355, Vinelott J.; *T.R. Technology Investment Trust, Re,* (1988) 4 BCC 244, Hoffmann J.

s. 216, amended: 1985, c.65, sch.6.

s. 222, amended: *ibid.;* 1986, c.45, sch.13.

ss. 224, 225, regs. 85/854; 87/752.

s. 225, modified: 1985, c.65, sch.6; amended: 1985, c.45, sch.13.

s. 232, amended: 1987, c.22, sch.6.

s. 233, amended: *ibid.,* s.90.

s. 234, amended: *ibid.,* sch.6.

ss. 241, 242, regs. 85/854.

s. 247, amended: 1987, c.22, sch.6.

s. 248, amended: regs. 86/1865.

s. 251, regs. 86/1865.

s. 257, amended: 1987, c.22, sch.6.

s. 266, amended: 1988, c.1, sch.29; s.39, s.117.

ss. 266, 272, 273, 287, 288, regs. 85/854.

s. 295, amended: 1985, c.65, sch.6; 1986, c.53, sch.18.

ss. 295–299, repealed: 1986, c.46, sch.4.

s. 297, see *Arctic Engineering, Re, Financial Times,* October 30, 1985, Hoffmann J.

s. 300, see *Eurosystem Maritime, Re,* 1987 P.C.C. 190, Mervyn Davies J.; *Dawson Print Group, Re* (1987) 3 B.C.C. 322, Hoffmann J.; *Stanford Services, Re* (1987) 3 B.C.C. 326, Vinelott J.; *Lo-Line Electric Motors, Re* [1988] 3 W.L.R. 26, Browne-Wilkinson V.-C.; *Churchill Hotel, Re,* 1988 PCC 220, Peter Gibson J; *Majestic Recording Studios, Re* (1988) 4 BCC 519, Mervyn Davies J.

s. 300, repealed: 1985, c.65, sch.10.

s. 301, regs. 85/829; 86/2067.

ss. 301, 302, repealed: 1986, c.46, sch.4.

s. 302, amended: 1986, c.53, sch.18.

s. 317, see *Guinness* v. *Saunders* [1988] 1 W.L.R. 863; [1988] 2 All E.R. 940, C.A.

s. 318, regs. 85/854; 87/752.

s. 324, regs. 85/802.

s. 325, regs. 85/854; 87/752.

s. 329, amended: 1986, c.60, sch.16.

s. 331, repealed in pt.: 1987, c.22, sch.7.

ss. 338, 339, 344, amended: *ibid.,* sch.6.

s. 349, see *Lindholst & Co. A/S* v. *Fowler* [1988] BCLC 166, C.A.; *Blum* v. *O.C.P. Repartition S.A.* [1988] BCLC 170, C.A.

CAP.

1985—cont.

6. Companies Act 1985—cont.

s. 353, regs. 85/854; 87/752.

s. 359, see *Willaire Systems, Re* [1987] B.C.L.C. 67, C.A.; *Barbor* v. *Middleton* (O.H.), 1988 S.L.T. 288.

s. 362, regs. 85/854; 87/752.

ss. 363, 364, regs. 85/854.

s. 368, see *McGuinness* v. *Bremner,* 1988 S.L.T. 891.

s. 380, amended: 1986, c.45, sch.13.

s. 386, regs. 85/854; 87/752.

s. 395, see *Annangel Glory Compania Naviera S.A.* v. *Golodetz, Middle East Marketing Corp. (U.K.) and Hammond,* 1988 PCC 37, Saville J.; *Sugar Properties (Derisley Wood), Re,* [1988] BCLC 146, Mervyn Davies J.

s. 395, regs. 85/854.

s. 395, amended: 1985, c.65, sch.6.

ss. 395, 396, see *Specialist Plant Services* v. *Braithwaite* [1987] B.C.L.C. 1, C.A.; *Pfeiffer (E.) Weinkellerei–Weinenkauf GmbH & Co.* v. *Arbuthnot Factors* [1987] BCLC 522, Phillips J.

s. 396, amended: 1986, c.39, sch.2; 1988, c.48, sch.7.

ss. 397, 398, regs. 85/854.

s. 400, regs. 85/854; 87/752.

s. 401, regs. 85/854.

s. 403, regs. 85/854; 87/752.

ss. 405, 409, 410, regs. 85/854.

s. 410, amended: 1985, c.65, sch.6; 1986, c.39, sch.2; 1988, c.48, sch.7.

s. 413, regs. 85/854.

s. 416, regs. 85/854; 87/752.

s. 417, regs. 85/854.

s. 419, regs. 85/854; 87/752.

s. 424, regs. 85/854.

s. 425, amended: 1985, c.65, sch.6; repealed in pt.: 1988, c.36, sch.2.

s. 426, amended: 1985, c.65, sch.6.

s. 427A, added: regs. 87/1991.

ss. 428, 429, regs. 85/854; 87/752.

ss. 428–430, substituted: 1986, c.60, s.172, sch.12.

s. 433, repealed in pt.: *ibid.,* sch.17.

s. 437, amended: *ibid.,* sch.13.

s. 440, amended: *ibid.,* s.198; 1987, c.41, s.55; 1988, c.33, s.145.

s. 441, amended: 1985, c.65, sch.6; 1986, c.45, sch.13.

s. 446, amended: *ibid.,* schs.13,16; repealed in pt.: *ibid.,* schs.13,17.

s. 447, see *Gomba Holdings UK* v. *Homan* [1986] 3 All E.R. 94, Hoffmann J.

s. 449, orders 86/2046; 87/859, 1141; 88/1058, 1334.

s. 449, amended: 1985, c.65, sch.6; 1986, c.45, sch.13; c.60, sch.13; 1987, c.22, sch.6; repealed in pt.: 1986, c.60, sch.17.

s. 451A, added: *ibid.,* sch.13.

ss. 454, 456, see *Geers Gross, Re,* (1987) 3 B.C.C. 528, C.A.; *T.R. Technology Investment Trust, Re,* (1988) 4 BCC 244, Hoffmann J.

s. 456, see *Lonrho, Re,* 1987 P.C.C. 355, Vinelott J.

1985—cont.

6. Companies Act 1985—*cont.*

s. 459, see *Ward* v. *Coulson, Sanderson and Ward* [1986] P.C.C. 57, C.A.; *Company, A, (No. 00477 of 1986), Re,* 1986 P.C.C. 372, Hoffmann J.; *Company, A, (No. 004377 of 1986), Re* [1987] 1 W.L.R. 102, Hoffmann J.; *Company, A, (No. 005136 of 1986), Re* [1987] B.C.L.C. 82, Hoffmann J.; *Postgate & Denby (Agencies), Re* [1987] B.C.L.C. 8, Hoffmann J.; *Company, A (No. 001761 of 1986), Re* [1987] B.C.L.C. 141, Harman J.; *XYZ, Re,* 1987 P.C.C. 92, Hoffmann J.; *Mossmain, Re,* 1987 P.C.C. 104, Hoffmann J.; *Company, A (No. 00596 of 1986), Re* [1987] B.C.L.C. 133, Harman J.; *Company, A (No. 004175 of 1986), Re* [1987] 1 W.L.R. 585, Scott J.; *Malaga Investments, Petrs.* (V.C.), 1987 S.L.T. 603; *Company No. 007281 of 1986, Re* (1987) 3 B.C.C. 375, Vinelott J.; *Blue Arrow, Re* [1987] B.C.L.C. 585, Vinelott J.; *Kenyon Swansea, Re,* 1987 P.C.C. 333, Vinelott J.; *Company (No. 003843 of 1986), Re* [1987] B.C.L.C. 562, Millett J.; *McGuinness* v. *Bremner,* 1988 S.L.T. 891; *Quickdome, Re* (1988) 4 BCC 296, Mervyn Davis J.; *Company, A (No. 00370 of 1987;, Re, The Times,* July 5, 1988, Harman J.

s. 461, see *Company, A, Re (No. 005287 of 1985)* [1986] 1 W.L.R. 281, Hoffmann J.; *Company, A (No. 004175 of 1986), Re* [1987] 1 W.L.R. 585, Scott J

s. 461, amended: 1985, c.65, sch.6; 1986, c.45, sch.13.

s. 462, amended: *ibid.*

s. 463, amended: 1985, c.65, sch.6; 1986, c.45, sch.13; repealed in pt.: *ibid.,* sch.12.

s. 464, amended: 1985, c.65, sch.6; 1986, c.45, sch.13.

s. 466, regs. 85/854.

s. 467, repealed: 1985, c.65, sch.10; 1986, c.45, sch.12.

s. 468, repealed: *ibid.*

s. 469, regs. 85/854; 86/2097.

s. 469, repealed: 1986, c.45, sch.12.

ss. 469, 471, 473, see *Callaghan (Myles J.) (In Receivership)* v. *City of Glasgow District Council* (1987) 3 B.C.C. 337, Ct. of Session.

s. 470, regs. 85/854; 86/2097.

s. 470, repealed: 1985, c.65, sch.10; 1986, c.45, sch.12.

ss. 471, 472, repealed: *ibid.*

s. 473, see *Inverness District Council* v. *Highland Universal Fabrications* (O.H.), 1986 S.L.T. 556.

ss. 473–480, repealed: 1986, c.45, sch.12.

s. 481, regs. 85/854; 86/2097.

s. 481, repealed: 1986, c.45, sch.12.

s. 482, regs. 85/854; 86/2097.

ss. 482–485, 486 (in pt.), repealed: 1986, c.45, sch.12.

ss. 485, 486, regs. 85/854; 86/2097.

ss. 488–650, repealed: 1986, c.45, sch.12.

s. 494, see *Potter Oils, Re, Financial Times,* November 22, 1985, Hoffmann J.

1985—cont.

6. Companies Act 1985—*cont.*

ss. 495–498, regs. 85/854; 86/2097.

s. 499, see *Gomba Holdings UK* v. *Homan* [1986] 3 All E.R. 94, Hoffmann J.

s. 502, see *Barbor* v. *Middleton* (O.H.), 1988 S.L.T. 288.

s. 512, order 86/1361.

s. 517, see *Palmer Marine Surveys, Re, The Times,* October 26, 1985, Hoffman J.; *Ward* v. *Coulson, Sanderson and Ward* [1986] P.C.C. 57, C.A.; *Martin Coulter Enterprises, Re* [1988] BCLC 12, Vinelott J.

s. 518, see *Byblos Bank* v. *Al Khudhairy, Financial Times,* November 7, 1986, C.A.

ss. 518, 519, amended: 1985, c.65, sch.6; repealed in pt.: *ibid.,* sch.10.

s. 520, see *Company, A, Re,* May 20, 1986, H.H. Judge Cox; Exeter County Court; *Ward* v. *Coulson, Sanderson and Ward* [1986] P.C.C. 57, C.A.

s. 522, see *Company, A (No. 007523 of 1986), Re* [1987] B.C.L.C. 200, Mervyn Davies J.; *French's (Wine Bar), Re* [1987] B.C.L.C. 499, Vinelott J.; *McGuinness Bros. (U.K.), Re* (1987) 3 BCC 571, Harman J.; *Sugar Properties (Derisley Wood), Re,* [1988] BCLC 146, Mervyn Davies J.

s. 525, amended: 1985, c.65, sch.6.

ss. 526–531, 533, 534, repealed: *ibid.,* sch.10.

s. 535, substituted: *ibid.,* sch 6

s. 536, repealed: *ibid.,* sch.10.

s. 539, amended: *ibid.,* sch.6; repealed in pt.: *ibid.,* schs.6, 10.

ss. 540 (in pt.), 541–548, 551; repealed: *ibid.,* sch.10.

s. 552, amended: *ibid.,* sch.6.

ss. 553 (in pt.), 556, 560 (in pt.), 561, repealed: *ibid.,* sch.10.

s. 560, see *Linda Marie (in Liquidation), Re* (1988) 4 BCC 463, Warner J.

s. 561, see *Rhodes (John T.), Re, The Times,* July 12, 1986, Hoffmann J.; *Company, A (No. 003318 of 1987), Re* [1987] 3 B.C.C. 564, Harman J.; *Embassy Art Products, Re; Collinson, Sherratt and Robinson* v. *Parry, Parry and Brodie,* 1987 P.C.C. 389, Hoffman J; *Oriental Credit, Re* [1988] 2 W.L.R. 172, Hoffmann J.; *Esal Commodities (In Liquidation), Re, The Times,* May 30, 1988, C.A.

s. 562, amended: 1985, c.65, sch.6.

ss. 563, 564, 565 (in pt.), repealed: *ibid.,* sch.10.

s. 567, amended: *ibid.,* sch.6.

ss. 568, 570, 571 (in pt.), repealed: *ibid.,* sch.10.

s. 577, amended: *ibid.,* sch.6.

ss. 580 (in pt.), 582 (in pt.), 583, repealed: *ibid.,* sch.10.

s. 584, amended: *ibid.,* sch.6.

ss. 586, 588, repealed: *ibid.,* sch.10.

s. 589, amended: *ibid.,* sch.6.

ss. 590, 591, amended: *ibid.;* repealed in pt.: *ibid.,* sch.10.

s. 593, amended: *ibid.,* sch.6.

s. 598, amended: *ibid.;* repealed in pt.: *ibid.,* sch.10.

s. 600, regs. 85/854.

CAP.

1985—cont.

6. Companies Act 1985—cont.

ss. 601, 604 (in pt.), Pt. XX, Chap. IV (ss.606–610), 611–618, 619 (in pt.), 620, repealed: 1985, c.65, sch.10.

s. 602, see Barbor v. Middleton (O.H.), 1988 S.L.T. 288.

s. 613, amended (S.): 1985, c.66, sch.7.

s. 614, see Brightlife, Re [1987] 2 W.L.R. 197, Hoffmann J.

ss. 615A, 615B, added (S.): 1985, c.66, sch.7.

ss. 618, 619, see A.E. Realisations (1985), Re [1987] B.C.L.C. 486, Vinelott J.

s. 622, amended: 1985, c.65, sch.6; repealed in pt.: ibid., sch.10.

s. 623, amended (S.): 1985, c.66, sch.7.

s. 624, amended: 1985, c.65, sch.6.

ss. 625, 626, amended: ibid.; repealed in pt.: ibid., sch.10.

ss. 628, 629, repealed in pt.: ibid.

s. 630, see Augustus Barnett and Son, Re [1986] P.C.C. 167, Hoffmann J.

s. 630, amended: 1985, c.65, sch.6; repealed in pt.: ibid., sch.10.

s. 631, repealed: ibid.

s. 632, amended: ibid., 6; repealed in pt.: ibid., sch.10.

ss. 634, 637 (in pt.), repealed: ibid.

s. 638, repealed in pt.: 1985, c.54, sch.27.

ss. 640, 642, repealed: 1985, c.65, sch.10.

s. 643, amended (S.): 1985, c.66, sch.7.

s. 645, see Palmer Marine Surveys, Re [1986] 1 W.L.R. 573, Hoffmann J.

s. 651, amended: 1985, c.65, sch.6.

s. 653, see Clarkson (H.) (Overseas), Re (1987) 3 BCC 606, Hoffmann J.

ss. 657, 658, amended: 1985, c.65, sch.6; 1986, c.45, sch.13.

ss. 659–674, repealed: 1985, c.65, sch.12.

s. 663, order 85/1784; rules 86/341.

s. 664, amended: 1985, c.65, sch.6; repealed in pt.: ibid., sch.10.

s. 665, see International Tin Council, Re, The Times, April 29, 1988, C.A.

s. 665, repealed in pt.: 1985, c 58, sch.4; c.65, sch.10; c.66, sch. (S.).

s. 666, repealed in pt.: 1985, c.58, sch.4; c.65, sch.10.

ss. 667–669, amended: ibid., sch.6.

s. 671, repealed in pt.: ibid., sch.10.

ss. 680, 681, 684–686, 690–692, regs. 85/854.

s. 693, repealed in pt.: 1986, c.60, sch.17.

s. 694, regs. 85/854.

s. 695, see Rome v. Punjab National Bank, The Times, November 1, 1988, Hirst J.

ss. 698, 700, 701, regs. 85/854.

s. 708, regs. 88/887.

s. 709, repealed in pt.: 1986, c.45, sch.12; c.60, sch.17.

s. 710, repealed in pt.: 1986, c.45, sch.12.

s. 711, amended: ibid., sch.13; regs. 87/1991.

ss. 716, 717, amended: 1986, c.60, sch.16.

s. 718, regs. 85/680.

s. 723, regs. 85/725.

s. 724, repealed: 1986, c.43, sch.12.

CAP.

1985—cont.

6. Companies Act 1985—cont.

s. 726, see Jenred Properties v. Ente Nazionale Italiano per il Turismo, Financial Times, October 29, 1985, C.A.; Speed Up Holdings v. Gouch [1986] F.S.R. 330, Evans-Lombe Q.C.; Stewart v. Steen, 1987 S.L.T. (Sh.Ct.) 60; Aquila Design (GRB) Products v. Cornhill Insurance (1987) 3 B.C.C. 364, C.A.; Property Protection Services (Timber Preservation Specialists) v. Kerr, 1988 S.L.T. (Sh.Ct.) 41.

s. 733, amended: 1985, c.65, sch.6; 1986, c.45, sch.13; repealed in pt.: ibid..

s. 735, see Rover International v. Cannon Film Sales (1987) 3 B.C.C. 369, Harman J.

s. 735A. added: 1986, c.45, sch.13.

s. 738, see Scandinavian Bank Group, Re [1987] 2 W.L.R. 752, Harman J.

s. 741, see Eurostem Maritime, Re, 1987 P.C.C. 190, Mervyn Davies J.

s. 744, regs. 85/854; 86/2097; 88/1359.

s. 744, amended: 1987, c.22, sch.6; repealed in pt.: 1985, c.65, sch.10; 1986, c.60, sch.17, 1987, c.22, sch.7.

sch. 3, repealed: 1986, c.60, sch.17.

sch. 4, amended: 1986, c.39, sch.2; c.60, sch.16.

sch. 6, amended: 1987, c.22, sch.6; repealed in pt.: ibid., sch.7.

sch. 9, amended: 1986, c.39, sch.2; c.60, sch.16.

sch. 12, repealed: 1986, c.46, sch.4.

sch. 13, amended: 1986, c.60, sch.16.

schs. 13, 14, regs. 85/854; 87/752.

sch. 15A, added: regs. 87/1991.

sch. 16, repealed: 1986, c.45, sch.12.

schs. 17–19, 20 (in pt.), repealed: 1985, c.65, sch.10.

sch. 22, regs. 85/680.

sch. 22, amended: 1986, c.60, sch.16; repealed in pt.: ibid., sch.17.

sch. 24, amended: 1985, c.65, sch.6; 1986, c.60, sch.16; repealed in pt.: 1985, c.65, sch.10; 1986, c.45, sch.12; c.46, sch.4, c.60, sch.17.

7. Business Names Act 1985.

Royal Assent, March 11, 1985.

8. Company Securities (Insider Dealing) Act 1985.

Royal Assent, March 11, 1985.

s. 1, see R. v. Fisher (1988) 4 BCC 360, Southwark Crown Ct.

ss. 1, 2, see Att.-Gen.'s Reference (No. 1 of 1988), The Times, October 19, 1988, C.A.

s. 2, amended: 1986, c.60, s.173.

s. 3, amended: ibid., s.174; repealed in pt.: ibid., sch.17.

s. 4, amended: ibid., s.174.

s. 6, substituted: ibid., s.175.

s. 8, amended: 1988, c.33, s.48.

s. 13, amended: 1988, c.60, ss.174, 176; repealed in pt.: ibid., sch.17.

s. 15, repealed: ibid.

s. 16, amended: ibid., sch.16.

1985—cont.

9. Companies Consolidation (Consequential Provisions) Act 1985.
Royal Assent, March 11, 1985.
s. 2, regs. 85/854.
s. 4, regs. 85/854; 87/752.
s. 7, repealed: 1986, c.60, sch.17.
s. 20, repealed: 1987, c.22, sch.7.
s. 31, see *Taylor* v. *McGirr* [1986] Crim.L.R. 544, D.C.
sch. 2, repealed in pt.: 1985, c.65, sch.10; c.71, sch.1; c.72, sch.13; 1986, c.53, sch.19; c. 59, sch.; c.60, sch.17; 1987, c.22, sch.7; 1988, c.39, sch.14; c.41, sch.13 (prosp.); c.39, sch.3.

10. London Regional Transport (Amendment) Act 1985.
Royal Assent, March 11, 1985.

11. Consolidated Fund (No. 2) Act 1985.
Royal Assent, March 27, 1985.
repealed: 1987, c.17, sch. (C.).

12. Mineral Workings Act 1985.
Royal Assent, March 27, 1985.
ss. 2, 3 (in pt.), repealed in pt.: 1988, c.35, sch.2.
s. 8, regs. 85/814.

13. Cinemas Act 1985.
Royal Assent, March 27, 1985.
s. 3, orders 86/207, 320; amended; order 86/207.
ss. 17, 18, 21, amended: 1985, c.51, sch.8.

14. Shipbuilding Act 1985.
Royal Assent, March 27, 1985.

15. Hong Kong Act 1985.
Royal Assent, April 4, 1985.
sch., orders 86/948, 1160, 1298.

16. National Heritage (Scotland) Act 1985.
Royal Assent, April 4, 1985.
Commencement order: 85/851.
s. 25, order 85/851.

17. Reserve Forces (Safeguard of Employment) Act 1985.
Royal Assent, May 9, 1985.
s. 13, repealed: 1985, c.65, sch.10.
s. 13, repealed in pt.(S.): 1985, c.66, sch.8.
s. 22, order 86/2025.

18. Betting, Gaming and Lotteries (Amendment) Act 1985.
Royal Assent, May 9, 1985.
Commencement order: 85/1475.
s. 3, order 85/1475.

19. Town and Country Planning (Compensation) Act 1985.
Royal Assent, May 9, 1985.

20. Charities Act 1985.
Royal Assent, May 23, 1985.
Commencement order: 85/1583.
s. 7, order 85/1583.

21. Films Act 1985.
Royal Assent, May 23, 1985.
s. 2, order 85/811.
s. 3, order 85/1943.
s. 6, order 85/2001.
s. 7, repealed in pt.: 1988, c.48, sch.8.
sch. 1, regs. 85/994; orders 85/960, 2001.

22. Dangerous Vessels Act 1985.
Royal Assent, May 23, 1985.

1985—cont.

23. Prosecution of Offences Act 1985.
Royal Assent, May 23, 1985.
Commencement orders: 85/1849; 86/1029, 1334.
s. 1, see *R.* v. *Liverpool Crown Court, ex p. Bray* [1987] Crim.L.R. 51, D.C.
s. 3, orders 85/1956, 2010; 88/1121.
s. 3, amended: 1987, c.38, sch.2.
s. 11, regs. 85/1846.
s. 14, regs. 86/405, 842, 1250, 1818; 87/902, 1636, 1851; 88/807, 1054, 1862.
s. 14, amended: 1988, c.33, s.166.
s. 16, see *R.* v. *Jain, The Times,* December 10, 1987, C.A.
s. 16, amended: 1987, c.38, sch.2; 1988, c.33, sch.15; repealed in pt.: 1988, c.34, sch.6.
s. 18, amended: 1987, c.38, sch.2.
s. 19, amended: 1988, c.34, sch.5; repealed in pt.: *ibid.,* schs.5,8.
ss. 19, 20, regs. 86/1335.
s. 20, amended: 1988, c.34, sch.5.
s. 21, amended: *ibid.;* repealed in pt.: *ibid.,* schs.5,6.
s. 22, regs. 87/299; 88/164.
s. 22, amended: 1988, c.33, sch.15.
s. 29, regs. 85/1846; 87/299; 88/164.
s. 31, orders 85/1849; 86/1029, 1334.

24. Rent (Amendment) Act 1985.
Royal Assent, May 23, 1985.
s. 1, see *Hewitt* v. *Lewis* [1986] 1 All E.R. 927.

25. Industrial Development Act 1985.
Royal Assent, June 13, 1985.

26. Intoxicating Substances (Supply) Act 1985.
Royal Assent, June 13, 1985.

27. Coal Industry Act 1985.
Royal Assent, June 13, 1985.
s. 2, repealed: 1987, c.3, sch.3.
s. 3, order 86/631.

28. Motor-Cycle Crash-Helmets (Restriction of Liability) Act 1985.
Royal Assent, June 13, 1985.
repealed: 1988, c.54, sch.1.

29. Enduring Powers of Attorney Act 1985.
Royal Assent, June 26, 1985.
Commencement order: 86/125.
ss. 1, 4, 6, see *K., Re; F., Re, The Independent,* November 3, 1987, Hoffmann J.
s. 2, regs. 86/126; 87/1612.
s. 6, see *K., Re; F., Re* [1988] 1 All E.R. 358, Hoffmann J.
s. 7, amended: order 87/1628.
s. 10, rules 86/127.
s. 14, order 86/125.

30. Ports (Finance) Act 1985.
Royal Assent, June 26, 1985.
Commencement order: 85/1153.
s. 1, orders 86/714; 88/152; amended: order 86/714.
s. 7, order 85/1153.

31. Wildlife and Countryside (Amendment) Act 1985.
Royal Assent, June 26, 1985.
s. 2, repealed in pt.: 1985, c.59, s.1.

32. Hill Farming Act 1985.
Royal Assent, June 26, 1985.

1985—cont.

33. Rating (Revaluation Rebates) (Scotland) Act 1985.
Royal Assent, June 26, 1985.
s. 1, orders 85/1170; 86/150; 87/345; 88/114.

34. Road Traffic (Production of Documents) Act 1985.
Royal Assent, July 16, 1985.
repealed: 1988, c.54, sch.1.

35. Gaming (Bingo) Act 1985.
Royal Assent, July 16, 1985.
Commencement order: 86/832.
s. 3, regs. 86/834.
s. 5, order 86/832.
sch. , order 86/833.

36. Agricultural Training Board Act 1985.
Royal Assent, July 16, 1985.

37. Family Law (Scotland) Act 1985.
Royal Assent, July 16, 1985.
Commencement orders: 86/1237; 88/1887.
see *Conlon* v. *O'Dowd* (Sh.Ct.), 1988 S.C.L.R. 119.
s. 1, see *Nixon* v. *Nixon* (O.H.), 1987 S.L.T. 602; *Inglis* v. *Inglis* (Sh.Ct.), 1987 S.C.L.R. 608.
s. 2, see *Matheson* v. *Matheson* (O.H.), 1988 S.L.T. 238.
ss. 3, 5, see *Hannah* v. *Hannah* (O.H.), 1988 S.L.T. 82.
s. 4, see *Inglis* v. *Inglis* (Sh.Ct.), 1987 S.C.L.R. 608.
s. 5, see *Nixon* v. *Nixon* (O.H.), 1987 S.L.T. 602.
s. 6, see *Neill* v. *Neill*, 1987 S.L.T. (Sh.Ct.) 143; *Donaldson* v. *Donaldson* (O.H.), 1988 S.L.T. 243.
s. 7, see *Mackenzie* v. *Mackenzie* (Sh.Ct.), 1987 S.C.L.R. 671.
s. 8, see *Dever* v. *Dever* (Sh.Ct.), 1988 S.C.L.R. 352; *McKeown* v. *McKeown* (Sh.Ct.), 1988 S.C.L.R. 355; *Petrie* v. *Petrie* (Sh.Ct.), 1988 S.C.L.R. 390; *Atkinson* v. *Atkinson* (Sh.Ct.), 1988 S.C.L.R. 396; *Maclellan* v. *Maclellan* (Sh.Ct.), 1988 S.C.L.R. 399; *Bell* v. *Bell* (Sh.Ct.), 1988 S.C.L.R. 457.
ss. 8, 9, see *Thirde* v. *Thirde* (Sh.Ct.), 1987 S.C.L.R. 335; *Wilson* v. *Wilson*, 1987 S.L.T. 721.
s. 9, see *Dever* v. *Dever* (Sh.Ct.), 1988 S.C.L.R. 352; *Petrie* v. *Petrie* (Sh.Ct.), 1988 S.C.L.R. 390; *Atkinson* v. *Atkinson* (Sh.Ct.), 1988 S.C.L.R. 396; *Maclellan* v. *Maclellan* (Sh.Ct.), 1988 S.C.L.R. 399; *Phillip* v. *Phillip* (Sh.Ct.), 1988 S.C.L.R. 427; *Bell* v. *Bell* (Sh.Ct.), 1988 S.C.L.R. 457.
s. 10, see *Petrie* v. *Petrie* (Sh.Ct.), 1988 S.C.L.R. 390; *Maclellan* v. *Maclellan* (Sh.Ct.), 1988 S.C.L.R. 399; *Phillip* v. *Phillip* (Sh.Ct.), 1988 S.C.L.R. 427; *Bell* v. *Bell* (Sh.Ct.), 1988 S.C.L.R. 457.
s. 11, see *Petrie* v. *Petrie* (Sh.Ct.), 1988 S.C.L.R. 390.
ss. 11, 13, see *Thirde* v. *Thirde* (Sh.Ct.), 1987 S.C.L.R. 335.
s. 12, see *Bell* v. *Bell* (Sh.Ct.), 1988 S.C.L.R. 457.
s. 13, see *Petrie* v. *Petrie* (Sh.Ct.), 1988 S.C.L.R. 390; *Dever* v. *Dever* (Sh.Ct.), 1988 S.C.L.R. 352; *Bell* v. *Bell* (Sh.Ct.), 1988 S.C.L.R. 457.

1985—cont.

37. Family Law (Scotland) Act 1985—*cont.*
s. 14, see *McKeown* v. *McKeown* (Sh.Ct.), 1988 S.C.L.R. 355.
s. 14, amended: 1985, c.66, sch.7.
s. 25, see *Bell* v. *Bell* (Sh.Ct.), 1988 S.C.L.R. 457.
s. 27, see *Matheson* v. *Matheson* (O.H.), 1988 S.L.T. 238; *Donaldson* v. *Donaldson* (O.H.), 1988 S.L.T. 243.
s. 27, amended: 1985, c.73, sch.2; 1986, c.9, sch.2.
s. 28, see *Smith* v. *Smith* (O.H.), 1987 S.L.T. 199; *Grindlay* v. *Grindlay* (O.H.), 1987 S.L.T. 264; *Collins* v. *Collins* (O.H.), 1987 S.L.T. 224; *Wilson* v. *Wilson*, 1987 S.L.T. 721; *Caven* v. *Caven* (O.H.), 1987 S.L.T. 761; *Gow* v. *Gow* (O.H.), 1987 S.L.T. 798; *McCrae* v. *McCrae* (O.H.), 1988 S.L.T. 248; *Ross* v. *Ross* (O.H.), 1988 S.C.L.R. 267; *Macpherson* v. *Macpherson*, 1989 S.L.T. 231; *Smith* v. *Smith*, 1988 S.L.T. 840.
s. 29, orders 86/1237; 88/1887.

38. Prohibition of Female Circumcision Act 1985.
Royal Assent, July 16, 1985.
s. 3, repealed in pt.: 1988, c.33, sch.16.

39. Controlled Drugs (Penalties) Act 1985.
Royal Assent, July 16, 1985.

40. Licensing (Amendment) Act 1985.
Royal Assent, July 16, 1985.

41. Copyright (Computer Software) Amendment Act 1985.
Royal Assent, July 16, 1985.
ss. 1, 2, see *M.S. Associates* v. *Power* [1988] F.S.R. 242, Falconer J.

42. Hospital Complaints Procedure Act 1985.
Royal Assent, July 16, 1985.

43. Local Government (Access to Information) Act 1985.
Royal Assent, July 16, 1985.

44. Sexual Offences Act 1985.
Royal Assent, July 16, 1985.
s. 1, amended: 1988, c.54, sch.3.

45. Charter Trustees Act 1985.
Royal Assent, July 16, 1985.

46. Insurance (Fees) Act 1985.
Royal Assent, July 16, 1985.

47. Further Education Act 1985.
Royal Assent, July 16, 1985.
Commencement orders: 85/1429; 87/1335 (S.).
ss. 1, 2, amended: 1988, c.40, sch.12.
s. 3, amended: order 86/452; repealed in pt. (prosp.): 1988, c.40, sch.13.
s. 7, orders 85/1429; 87/1335 (S.).

48. Food and Environment Protection Act 1985.
Royal Assent, July 16, 1985.
Commencement orders: 85/1390, 1698.
s. 1, orders 86/1027, 1059, 1121, 1179, 1185, 1232, 1247, 1294, 1331, 1344, 1360, 1384, 1410–1413, 1422, 1431, 1432, 1435, 1479, 1483, 1491, 1508, 1535, 1540, 1547, 1552, 1574, 1576, 1592, 1595, 1615, 1616, 1621, 1662, 1664, 1681, 1688, 1689, 1707, 1720, 1756, 1765, 1775, 1837, 1849, 1900, 1993; 86/1993 (S.), 2208, 2242, 2248; 87/153, 182, 249, 263, 885, 906, 1165 (S.), 1181, 1436,

CAP.

1985—cont.

48. Food and Environment Protection Act 1985—cont.

1450, 1515, 1555, 1567, 1568, 1638, 1682, 1687, 1696, 1697, 1802, 1837, 1888, 1893, 1894; 88/7, 9, 11, 951, 954, 964, 1292, 1329, 1353, 1675, 1679, 1680, 1881; S.Rs. 1988 Nos. 3, 194, 280, 349.

s. 7, orders 85/1699; 86/1510.

s. 16, order 85/1516; regs. 85/1517; 86/1510; 88/1378; S.Rs. 1987 Nos. 341, 342, 414; 1988 No. 313.

s. 24, orders 86/1059, 1247, 1294, 1331, 1344, 1360, 1411, 1413, 1422, 1431, 1432, 1435, 1479, 1483, 1491, 1508, 1535, 1540, 1547, 1552, 1574, 1576, 1592, 1595, 1615, 1616, 1621, 1662, 1664, 1681, 1688, 1689, 1707, 1720, 1756, 1765, 1775, 1837, 1849, 1900, 1993, 2208, 2242, 2248; 87/153, 182, 249, 263, 270, 885, 906, 1165 (S.), 1181, 1436, 1450, 1515, 1555, 1567, 1568, 1638, 1682, 1687, 1696, 1697, 1802, 1837, 1888, 1893; regs. 86/1510; S.Rs. 1987 No. 367, 395, 414; orders 88/7, 9, 11, 951, 954, 964, 1292, 1329, 1353, 1675, 1679, 1680, 1881; regs. 88/1378; S.Rs. 1988 Nos. 3, 194, 313, 349.

s. 26, orders 87/665–667; 88/1084.

s. 27, orders 85/1390, 1698.

sch. 5, regs. 85/1517; S.R. 1987 No. 342.

49. Surrogacy Arrangements Act 1985.
Royal Assent, July 16, 1985.

50. Representation of the People Act 1985.
Royal Assent, July 16, 1985.
Commencement orders: 85/1185; 86/639, 1080; 87/207.

regs. 86/1091.

ss. 2, 3, 6–8, regs. 86/1081, 1111 (S.).

s. 8, repealed in pt.: 1985, c.54, sch.27.

ss. 9, 15, regs. 86/1081, 1111 (S.).

s. 27, regs. 86/1111 (S.).

s. 27, repealed in pt.: 1986, c.58, sch.

s. 29, orders 85/1185; 86/639, 1080; 87/207.

sch. 4, amended: 1985, c.73, sch.2.

51. Local Government Act 1985.
Royal Assent, July 16, 1985.
Commencement orders: 85/1175, 1177, 1263, 1283, 1285, 1286, 1295, 1342, 1362, 1408; 88/1179.

s. 3, repealed in pt.: 1986, c.63, sch.12.

s. 4, regs. 88/139, 140; order 88/1179.

s. 8, repealed in pt. (prosp.): 1988, c.41, sch.13.

s. 10, orders 85/1884; 86/413, 564.

s. 11, order 86/208.

s. 13, order 85/1933.

s. 13, repealed: 1988, c.13, sch.4.

CAP.

1985—cont.

51. Local Government Act 1985—cont.

s. 15, orders 85/1408, 1409.

s. 15, amended: 1988, c.33, sch.15; repealed in pt.: *ibid.*, sch.16.

s. 16, order 86/265.

ss. 18–22, repealed (prosp.): 1988, c.40, sch.13.

ss. 18, 23, order 85/1283.

ss. 24, 25, rules 85/1184.

ss. 31, 32, amended: 1986, c.10, s.10.

s. 40, order 86/425.

s. 40, amended: 1986, c.31, sch.4.

s. 42, repealed in pt.: 1985, c.67, sch.8.

s. 43, repealed in pt.: 1986, c.8, ss.1, 3, sch.

s. 44, order 86/148.

s. 45, order 86/413.

s. 46, order 86/226.

ss. 46, 47, functions transferred: order 86/600.

s. 47, order 86/148.

s. 48, see *R.* v. *London Boroughs Grants Committee, ex p. Greenwich London Borough Council, The Times*, May 6, 1986, D.C.

s. 49, orders 87/118; 88/359.

s. 52, orders 86/192, 297, 298, 399, 425, 426, 523, 573, 582.

s. 56, see *R.* v. *Secretary of State for the Environment, ex p. Camden London Borough Council, The Times*, July 14, 1987, D.C.

s. 56, regs. 86/867.

s. 57, orders 85/1175, 1263, 1285, 1286, 1295, 1342, 1362.

s. 58, orders 86/436, 439; 88/452.

s. 60, amended: 1988, c.12, sch.3.

s. 62, orders 86/148, 573.

s. 63, order 87/1220.

s. 66, orders 86/96, 437, 471, 501, 553, 563, 1398.

s. 67, orders 86/1774; 87/15, 117, 651, 1077, 1288, 1446, 1451, 1463, 1579, 2219; 88/233, 323, 452, 713, 751, 783, 1019, 1093, 1335, 1590, 1615, 1745, 1747.

s. 68, orders 86/212, 265.

s. 68, repealed in pt. (prosp.): 1988, c.40, sch.13.

s. 69, repealed in pt.: 1986, c.54, sch.2; 1987, c.6, sch.5.

s. 77, orders 86/2063, 2093; 87/118; 88/359.

s. 80, repealed in pt.: 1986, c.54, sch.2.

s. 81, repealed in pt. (prosp.): 1988, c.40, sch.13.

s. 83, repealed in pt. (prosp.): 1988, c.41, sch.13.

s. 84, repealed in pt. (prosp.): 1988, c.40, sch.13.

s. 85, regs. 85/1302, 1303.

s. 89, order 86/442.

s. 90, repealed in pt. (prosp.): 1988, c.40, sch.13.

s. 97, see *Westminster City Council, Re* [1986] 2 W.L.R. 807, H.L.

s. 98, orders 85/1341; 86/148, 452, 564.

s. 100, orders 86/148, 211, 256, 297, 298, 330, 413, 442, 564, 624; 87/117, 2219; 88/323.

s. 101, orders 85/1320, 1383, 1410, 1506; 86/1, 81, 148, 208, 227, 297, 298, 300, 330, 379, 399, 413, 425, 442, 452, 454, 564, 613,

CAP.

1985—cont.

51. Local Government Act 1985—*cont.*
615–618, 711, 1929, 2063, 2092, 2093;
87/118, 1463; 88/166, 167, 359, 565, 1542,
1955.
s. 101, amended: 1988, c.50, sch.17.
s. 103, orders 86/208, 227, 613, 615–618, 711;
88/565.
sch. 1, regs. 88/139.
sch. 1, amended: 1986, c.63, schs.10, 11;
repealed in pt.: *ibid.*, sch.11.
sch. 2, repealed in pt.: *ibid.*, sch.12.
sch. 3, order 86/561.
sch. 4, see *Richmond Borough Council* v. *Secretary of State for Transport*, (1986) 136 New L.J. 941, Sir Neil Lawson.
sch. 4, orders 85/1177; 86/256, 278.
sch. 5, orders 86/154, 315, 316.
sch. 5, repealed in pt.: 1986, c.27, s.3; 1988, c.40, sch.13 (prosp.).
sch. 8, amended: 1985, c.72, sch.12; repealed in pt.: 1985, c.71, sch.1; c.72, sch.13.
sch. 9, repealed (prosp.): 1988, c.40, sch.13.
sch. 12, repealed in pt.: 1985, c.67, sch.8.
sch. 13, see *R.* v. *Secretary of State for the Environment, ex p. Camden London Borough Council, The Times*, July 14, 1987, D.C.
sch. 13, amended: 1985, c.71, sch.2; 1986, c.10, s.9; c.63, schs.4, 5; 1987, c.31, sch.4; 1988, c.54, sch.3; repealed in pt.: 1985, c.71, sch.1; 1986, c.63, schs.4, sch.12; 1987, c.31, schs.4,5; c.39, sch.2; 1988, c.50, sch.18.
sch. 14, amended: 1986, c.10, s.11; repealed in pt.: 1985, c.67, sch.8; c.71, sch.1; 1986, c.63, schs.4,12; 1988, c.40, sch.13 (prosp.); c.54, sch.1.
sch. 17, repealed in pt.: 1986, c.8, sch.

52. Town and Country Planning (Amendment) Act 1985.
Royal Assent, July 22, 1985.

53. Social Security Act 1985.
Royal Assent, July 22, 1985.
Commencement orders: 85/1125, 1364.
s. 5, regs. 86/1718; 88/476.
s. 5, amended: 1986, c.50, sch.10.
s. 6, regs. 85/1927; order 85/1622.
s. 7, regs. 85/1398, 1417.
s. 9, amended: 1986, c.50, sch.10.
s. 13, regs. 85/1305.
ss. 13 (in pt.), 14, repealed: 1988, c.7, sch.5.
ss. 15–17, repealed: 1986, c.50, sch.11.
s. 17, regs. 85/1250.
s. 22, repealed: 1986, c.50, sch.11.
s. 27, regs. 85/1190.
s. 27, repealed in pt.: 1986, c.50, sch.11.
s. 32, orders 85/1125, 1364; regs. 85/1398, 1417; 86/478; 88/429.
s. 32, schs.4,5, repealed in pt.: 1986, c.50, sch.11.

54. Finance Act 1985.
Royal Assent, July 25, 1985.
Commencement orders: 85/1451, 1622; 86/337, 365, 934, 968–970; 88/1354.
s. 2, repealed: 1986, c.41, sch.23.
s. 6, order 85/1622; regs. 85/1927.
s. 7, order 85/1451.

CAP.

1985—cont.

54. Finance Act 1985—*cont.*
s. 12, order 86/969.
s. 12, repealed: 1988, c.39, sch.14.
s. 13, see *Neal* v. *Customs and Excise Commissioners* [1988] S.T.C. 131, Simon Brown J.
s. 14, amended: 1988, c.39, s.14; repealed in pt.: *ibid.*, sch.14.
s. 14A, added: *ibid.*, s.17.
s. 15, see *Customs and Excise Commissioners* v. *Shingleton* [1988] S.T.C. 190, Simon Brown J.; *Neal* v. *Customs and Excise Commissioners* [1988] S.T.C. 131, Simon Brown J.
s. 15, amended: 1988, c.39, sch.14.
s. 16, amended: 1986, c.41, s.47.
s. 17, amended: *ibid.*, s.15; 1988, c.39, s.19.
s. 18, amended: *ibid.*, ss.14, 18; repealed in pt.: *ibid.*, sch.14.
s. 20, orders 86/906, 909, 970; regs. 88/1343, 1354.
s. 20, substituted: 1988, c.39, s.20.
s. 21, amended: *ibid.*, s.19.
s. 26, order 86/2288.
s. 27, order 86/934.
s. 30, order 86/365.
s. 32, order 86/337.
s. 33, see *Neal* v. *Customs and Excise Commissioners* [1988] S.T.C. 131, Simon Brown J.
s. 33, repealed in pt.: 1988, c.39, sch.14.
ss. 39–49, 51–54, repealed: 1988, c.1, sch.31.
s. 56, amended: 1986, c.41, s.57, sch.13; 1988, c.1, sch.29.
s. 57, amended: 1986, c.41, s.57; 1988, c.1, sch.29, repealed in pt.: 1986, c.41, s.57.
s. 60, repealed: 1988, c.1, sch.31.
s. 62, repealed: 1986, c.41, sch.23.
ss. 64, 65, repealed: 1988, c.1, sch.31.
s. 67, repealed in pt.: 1986, c.41, sch.23.
s. 68, amended: 1988, c.1, sch.29; c.39, s.118, sch.3; repealed in pt.: *ibid.*, sch.14.
s. 71, amended: 1988, c.1, sch.29.
s. 72, amended: 1987, c.51, s.81; 1988, c.1, sch.29; repealed in pt.: 1987, c.51, sch.9; 1988, c.1, sch.31.
ss. 73–77, repealed: *ibid.*
s. 78, amended and repealed in pt.: 1986, c.41, s.73; repealed (prosp.): *ibid.*, s.74, sch.23.
s. 79, amended: *ibid.*, s.73; c.45, sch.14; repealed in pt.: 1986, c.41, s.73; c.45, sch.14; repealed (prosp.): 1986, c.41, s.74, sch.23.
s. 80, amended: 1988, c.1, sch.29; repealed: 1986, c.41, s.74, sch.23.
s. 87, regs. 87/516.
s. 96, order 85/1172.
s. 98, amended: 1988, c.39, sch.14.
sch. 5, repealed in pt.: 1986, c.41, s.74, sch.23; 1987, c.16, sch.16.
sch. 7, repealed in pt.: 1988, c.39, sch.14.
schs. 9–13, 14 (in pt.), repealed: 1988, c.1, sch.31.
sch. 17, amended: *ibid.*, sch.29.
sch. 18, repealed: *ibid.*, sch.31.
sch. 19, regs. 86/387.
sch. 19, amended: 1988, c.1, sch.29.

CAP.

1985—cont.

54. Finance Act 1985—*cont.*
sch. 20, amended: 1987, c.16, s.47; 1988, c.1, sch.29; c.39, s.110; repealed in pt.: *ibid.,* s.110, sch.14.
schs. 22, 23, 25 (in pt.), repealed: 1988, c.1, sch.31.

55. Appropriation Act 1985.
Royal Assent, July 25, 1985.
repealed: 1987, c.17, sch. (C).

56. Interception of Communications Act 1985.
Royal Assent, July 25, 1985.
Commencement order: 86/384.
s. 12, order 86/384.

57. Sporting Events (Control of Alcohol etc.) Act 1985.
Royal Assent, July 25, 1985.
ss. 1A, 2A, 5A–5D, added: 1986, c.64, sch.1.
ss. 2, 3, 7, amended: *ibid.*
s. 8, amended: *ibid.;* repealed in pt.: *ibid.,* sch.3.
s. 9, orders 85/1151; 87/1520.

58. Trustee Savings Banks Act 1985.
Royal Assent, July 25, 1985.
Commencement orders: 86/1219–1223; 88/1168
s. 1, order 86/1222.
s. 4, orders 86/1220, 1223; 88/1168.
s. 6, order 86/100.
s. 6, repealed: 1987, c.22, sch.7.
s. 7, orders 85/1210, 1211.
sch. 1, order 86/1219.
sch. 1, amended: 1986, c.53, sch.19; 1987, c.22, sch.6; repealed in pt.: *ibid.,* schs.6, 7.
sch. 2, amended: 1988, c.1, sch.29; repealed in pt.: *ibid.,* sch.31.
sch. 3, repealed: 1987, c.22, sch.7.
sch. 5, order 86/1221.

59. Wildlife and Countryside (Service of Notices) Act 1985.
Royal Assent, July 25, 1985.

60. Child Abduction and Custody Act 1985.
Royal Assent, July 25, 1985.
Commencement order: 86/1048.
see *A. (A Minor) (Abduction), Re* (1988) 18 Fam.Law 54, C.A.
s. 1, see *Viola* v. *Viola* (O.H.), 1987 S.C.L.R. 529.
s. 2, see *Kilgour* v. *Kilgour* (O.H.), 1987 S.L.T. 568.
s. 2, orders 86/1159; 87/163, 1825; 88/588, 1083, 1839.
s. 2, sch. 1, see *B.* v. *B. (Minors: Enforcement of Access Abroad)* [1988] 1 All E.R. 652, Waterhouse J.
s. 9, amended: 1986, c.55, sch.1.
s. 10, S.Rs. 1986 Nos. 203, 218, 219; Act of Sederunt 86/1955.
s. 11, amended: 1988, c.34, sch.5.
s. 20, amended: 1986, c.55, s.67, sch.1.
s. 24, S.Rs. 1986 Nos. 203, 218, 219; Acts of Sederunt 86/1955, 1966.
s. 24A, added: 1986, c.55, s.67.
s. 27, amended: *ibid.,* s.67, sch.1.
s. 29, order 86/1048.
sch. 1, see *Kilgour* v. *Kilgour* (O.H.), 1987 S.L.T. 568; *A.* v. *A.; A (A Minor), Re, The Times,* June 13, 1987, C.A.; *Viola* v. *Viola* (O.H.),

CAP.

1985—cont.

60. Child Abduction and Custody Act 1985—*cont.*
1987 S.C.L.R. 529; *B. (Minors), Re, The Times,* October 29, 1987, Waterhouse J.; *Campins-Coll, Petr.,* (O.H.), 1989 S.L.T. 33.
sch. 3, amended: 1987, c.42, sch.2.

61. Administration of Justice Act 1985.
Royal Assent, October 30, 1985.
Commencement orders: 86/364, 1503; 87/787; 88/1341.
s. 16, amended: 1985, c.65, sch.8; repealed in pt.: *ibid.,* sch.10.
s. 17, repealed in pt.: *ibid.*
s. 40, amended: 1988, c.34, sch.5.
ss. 41, 42, substituted: *ibid.,* s.33.
ss. 43, 44, amended: *ibid.,* sch.5.
ss. 45, 46, repealed: *ibid.,* sch.7.
s. 48, see *Practice Direction (Ch.D.) (No. 1 of 1987),* January 28, 1987.
s. 53, order 88/1342.
s. 60, repealed: 1988, c.48, sch.8.
s. 66, repealed: 1986, c.53, sch.19.
s. 69, orders 86/364, 1503; 87/787; 88/1341.
sch. 2, amended: 1988, c.1, sch.29.
sch. 4, rules 87/788, 789.
sch. 7, repealed in pt.: 1988, c.34, sch.7.

62. Oil and Pipelines Act 1985.
Royal Assent, October 30, 1985.
Commencement orders: 85/1748, 1749.
s. 3, orders 85/1749; 86/585.
s. 7, repealed in pt.: 1986, c.44, sch.9.
s. 8, order 85/1748.

63. Water (Fluoridation) Act 1985.
Royal Assent, October 30, 1985.

64. European Communities (Finance) Act 1985.
Royal Assent, October 30, 1985.

65. Insolvency Act 1985.
Royal Assent, October 30, 1985.
Commencement orders: 86/6, 185, 463, 840, 1924.
s. 1, amended: 1986, c.53, sch.18.
ss. 1–11, repealed: 1986, c.45, sch.12.
s. 3, order 86/1764.
ss. 4, 5, regs. 86/951, 1995.
s. 10, regs. 86/951, 1764, 1995.
s. 12, amended: 1986, c.53, sch.18.
ss. 12–14, repealed: 1986, c.46, sch.4.
s. 15, repealed: 1986, c.45, sch.12.
s. 16, repealed: 1986, c.46, sch.4.
s. 17, repealed: 1986, c.45, sch.12.
s. 18, repealed: 1986, c.46, sch.4.
ss. 19, 20–107, repealed: 1986, c.45, sch.12.
s. 106, rules 86/304, 385, 611, 612, 619, 626 (S.), 1916 (S.), 2134.
s. 108, repealed in pt.: 1986, c.45, sch.12; c.46, sch.4.
ss. 109–214, repealed: 1986, c.45, sch.12.
s. 215, repealed: 1988, c.3, sch.
ss. 216, 217 (in pt.), 221–234, repealed: 1986, c.45, sch.12.
s. 226, rules 86/385.
s. 235, repealed in pt.: 1986, c.45, sch.12.
s. 236, orders 86/6, 185, 463, 840, 1924.
s. 236, repealed in pt.: 1986, c.45, sch.12.

CAP.

65. Insolvency Act 1985—*cont.*
sch. 1, rules 86/952.
sch. 1, repealed in pt.: 1986, c.45, sch.12.
sch. 2, repealed: 1986, c.46, sch.4; amended:
1986, c 53, sch.18.
schs. 3–5, repealed: 1986, c.45, sch.12.
sch. 4, repealed in pt.: 1986, c.50, schs.10, 11.
sch. 5, rules 86/304.
sch. 6, repealed in pt.: 1986, c.45, sch.12; c.46,
sch.4.
sch. 7, repealed: 1986, c.45, sch.12.
sch. 8, repealed in pt.: 1986, c.5, sch.15; 1987,
c.16, sch.16; 1988, c.3, sch.; c.33, sch.16.
sch. 9, repealed in pt.: 1986, c.45, sch.12; c.46,
sch.4.
sch. 10, repealed: 1986, c.45, sch.12.

66. Bankruptcy (Scotland) Act 1985.
Royal Assent, October 30, 1985.
Commencement orders: 85/1924; 86/1913.
s. 1, Acts of Sederunt 86/514, 517.
ss. 5, 7, amended: 1987, c.41, s.45; 1988, c.33,
sch.15.
ss. 6–8, 11, order 85/1925.
s. 10, amended: 1986, c.60, sch.16.
s. 12, see *Royal Bank of Scotland* v. *Forbes*
(O.H.), 1988 S.L.T. 73.
s. 14, Acts of Sederunt 86/514, 517.
ss. 15, 19, 22, 23, order 85/1925.
s. 25, see *Inland Revenue Commissioners* v.
McDonald, 1988 S.L.T.(Sh.Ct.) 7.
s. 25, order 85/1925; Act of Sederunt 86/517.
s. 31, amended: 1988, c.50, s.118.
s. 37, amended: 1987, c.18, sch.6.
s. 45, order 85/1925.
s. 47, see *Holmes, Petr.*, 1988 S.L.T.(Sh.Ct.) 47.
ss. 48, 49, 51, 54, order 85/1925.
s. 62, Act of Sederunt 86/514.
s. 67, order 85/1925; regs. 86/1914.
s. 69, order 85/1925.
s. 70, amended: 1986, c.44, sch.7.
s. 73, order 85/1925; regs. 86/1914.
s. 73, amended: 1987, c.22, sch.6.
s. 74, order 85/1925.
s. 75, see *Watson* v. *Henderson* (Sh.Ct.), 1988
S.C.L.R. 439.
s. 78, orders 85/1924; 86/78, 1913.
sch. 2, Act of Sederunt 86/517.
sch. 3, regs. 86/1914; 87/2093.
sch. 3, amended: 1988, c.1, sch.29; repealed in
pt.: 1986, c.50, schs.10, 11.
sch. 4, order 85/1925.
sch. 5, order 85/1925; Acts of Sederunt 86/514,
517.
sch. 7, amended: 1987, c.18, sch.6; repealed in
pt.: 1986, c.45, sch.12; 1987, c.16, sch.16;
1988, c.54, sch.1.

67. Transport Act 1985.
Royal Assent, October 30, 1985.
Commencement orders: 85/1887; 86/80, 414,
1088, 1450, 1794, 1874; 87/1228; 88/2294.
s. 6, regs. 86/1671; 88/1879.
s. 7, regs. 86/1030.
s. 8, regs. 86/1671.
s. 9, regs. 86/1030.
s. 10, regs. 86/1779; orders 87/784, 839, 1535.

CAP.

67. Transport Act 1985—*cont.*
s. 12, regs. 86/566, 567, 1239 (S.).
s. 13, orders 86/1386, 1387.
s. 16, see *Tudor* v. *Ellesmere Port and Neston
B.C., The Times*, May 8, 1987, D.C.; *R.* v.
Reading Borough Council, ex p. Egan; Same
v. *Same, ex p. Sullman, The Times*, June 12,
1987, Nolan J.; *R.* v. *Great Yarmouth Borough
Council, ex p. Sawyer, The Times*, June 18,
1987, C.A.
s. 17, regs. 86/1188.
s. 23, regs. 86/1245.
s. 27, regs. 86/1668.
s. 42, regs. 86/1691.
s. 47, order 87/1613.
s. 60, orders 86/1287 (S.), 1648–1653,
1672–1677, 1880 (S.).
s. 66, order 85/1902.
ss. 69, 70, orders 86/1702, 1703, 1780.
s. 71, order 85/1902.
s. 73, order 85/1901.
s. 76, order 86/1874 (S.).
ss. 90, 91, order 85/1921.
ss. 93, 94, 97, 100, regs. 86/77.
s. 129, orders 85/1903; 87/337.
s. 131, repealed in pt.: 1988, c.39, sch.14.
s. 134, regs. 86/77.
s. 140, orders 85/1887; 86/80, 414, 1088, 1450,
1794; 87/1228; 88/2294.
sch. 2, repealed in pt.: 1988, c.54, sch.1.
sch. 4, rules 86/1547.
sch. 6, regs. 85/1904; 86/1523.
sch. 7, amended: 1988, c.54, sch.3.

68. Housing Act 1985.
Royal Assent, October 30, 1985.
amended: 1988, c.50, sch.17.
see *R.* v. *Hillingdon London Borough Council, ex
p. Tinn, The Times*, January 14, 1988, Kennedy J.; *R.* v. *Secretary of State for the
Environment, ex p. Enfield London Borough
Council, The Times*, April 5, 1988, McNeill J.;
R. v. *Tower Hamlets London Borough Council,
ex p. Monaf, Ali and Miah, The Times*, April
28, 1988, C.A.
s. 4, amended: orders 85/1884; 86/1; 1986,
c.63, sch.5; 1988, c.4, sch.6; c.50, s.62;
repealed in pt. (prosp.): 1988, c.40, sch.12.
s. 6A, added: 1988, c.50, sch.17.
Pt. II (ss. 8–57), see *R.* v. *Hammersmith and
Fulham London Borough, ex p. Beddowes*
(1986) 18 H.L.R. 458, C.A.; *R.* v. *Plymouth
City Council and Cornwall County Council, ex
p. Freeman* (1987) 19 H.L.R. 328, C.A.
s. 17, see *R.* v. *Secretary of State for the
Environment, ex p. Kensington and Chelsea
Royal Borough Council, The Times*, January
30, 1987, Taylor J.
ss. 20, 21, amended: 1986, c.63, sch.5.
ss. 21, 24, see *Wandsworth London Borough
Council* v. *Winder (No. 2)* (1987) 19 H.L.R.
204, Mervyn Davies J.
s. 22, see *R.* v. *Canterbury City Council, ex p.
Gillespie* (1987) 19 H.L.R. 7, Simon Brown J.
ss. 27, 27A, 27B, substituted: 1986, c.63, s.10.
s. 27C, added: *ibid.*, s.11.

CAP.

1985—cont.

68. Housing Act 1985—cont.

s. 30, repealed in pt.: *ibid.*, schs.5, 12.

s. 32, see *R. v. Hammersmith and Fulham London Borough, ex p. Beddowes* (1986) 18 H.L.R. 458, C.A.

s. 32, amended: 1988, c.50, sch.17.

s. 34, amended: *ibid.*, s.132.

s. 36, amended: 1986, c.63, sch.5.

s. 37, amended: 1988, c.50, s.125.

s. 43, amended: *ibid.*, s.132, sch.17.

s. 45, amended: 1987, c.31, sch.4; 1988, c.50, s.79; repealed in pt.: 1987, c.31, schs.4,5.

s. 46, repealed: 1986, c.63, schs.5, 12.

ss. 47, 48, amended: *ibid.*, sch.5.

ss. 49, 50 (in pt.), repealed: 1987, c.31, schs.4, 5.

s. 52, repealed in pt.: 1988, c.9, s.19, sch.7.

s. 57, amended: 1986, c.63, sch.5; 1988, c.50, sch.17.

s. 58, see *R. v. Kensington and Chelsea London Borough Council, ex p. Minton, The Guardian,* August 4, 1988, Macpherson J.

s. 58, amended: 1986, c.63, sch.5.

Pt. III (ss. 58–78), see *R. v. Lambeth London Borough, ex p. Ly* (1987) 19 H.L.R. 51, Simon Brown J.; *R. v. Wandsworth Borough Council, ex p. Banbury* (1987) 19 H.L.R. 76, Russell J.; *South Holland District Council v. Keyte* (1985) 19 H.L.R. 97, C.A.; *R. v. Hillingdon London Borough, ex p. Thomas* (1987) 19 H.L.R. 197, Taylor J.; *R. v. Christchurch Borough Council, ex p. Conway* (1987) 19 H.L.R. 238, Taylor J.; *R. v. Hillingdon London Borough Council, ex p. H., The Times,* May 17, 1988, Kennedy J.

s. 59, see *R. v. Reigate and Banstead Borough Council, ex p. Di Domenico, The Independent,* October 21, 1987, Mann J.; *R. v. Lambeth London Borough Council, ex p. Carroll, The Guardian,* October 8, 1987, Webster J.

s. 60, see *R. v. East Hertfordshire District Council, ex p. Bannon* (1986) 18 H.L.R. 515, Webster J.; *R. v. London Borough of Wandsworth, ex p. Henderson and Hayes* (1986) 18 H.L.R. 525, McNeill J.; *R. v. London Borough of Croydon, ex p. Toth* (1986) 18 H.L.R. 493, Simon Brown J.; *R. v. Christchurch Borough Council, ex p. Conway* (1987) 19 H.L.R. 238, Taylor J.; *R. v. Mole Valley District Council, ex p. Burton, The Times,* April 5, 1988, Hutchison J.; *R. v. Kensington and Chelsea London Borough Council, ex p. Cunha, The Guardian,* July 13, 1988, Otton J.

ss. 60, 62, see *R. v. Gravesham Borough Council, ex p. Winchester* (1986) 18 H.L.R. 207, Simon Brown J.

ss. 62, 63, see *R. v. Camden London Borough Council, ex p. Gillan, The Independent,* October 13, 1988, D.C.

s. 64, see *R. v. Kensington and Chelsea Royal London Borough Council, ex p. Hammell, The Times,* August 25, 1988, C.A.

s. 65, see *R. v. Croydon London Borough, ex p. Wait* (1986) 18 H.L.R. 434, McCowan J.; *R. v. London Borough of Wandsworth, ex p. Lindsay* (1986) 18 H.L.R. 502, Simon Brown J.

CAP.

1985—cont.

68. Housing Act 1985—cont.

s. 69, see *R. v. Camden London Borough, ex p. Wait* (1986) 18 H.L.R. 434, McCowan J.

s. 69, amended: 1986, c.63, s.14.

s. 72, amended: 1988, c.50, s.70.

s. 76, amended: 1986, c.26, sch.23.

ss. 79, 81–84, see *R. v. London Borough of Croydon, ex p. Toth* (1986) 18 H.L.R. 493, Simon Brown J.

s. 80, amended: 1986, c.63, sch.5; 1988, c.50, s.83; repealed in pt.: *ibid.*, sch.18.

s. 81A, added: *ibid.*, s.128.

s. 82, see *Thompson v. Elmbridge Borough Council* [1987] 1 W.L.R. 1425, C.A.

s. 83, regs. 87/755.

s. 84, see *Second W.R.V.S. Housing Society v. Blair* (1986) 19 H.L.R. 104, C.A.; *Wandsworth London Borough Council v. Fadayomi* [1987] 3 All E.R. 474, C.A.; *Wansbeck District Council v. Marley, The Times,* November 30, 1987, C.A.

s. 85, see *Governors of the Peabody Donation Fund v. Hay* (1986) 19 H.L.R. 145, C.A.

ss. 100, 101, amended: 1986, c.63, sch.3.

s. 105, see *R. v. Hammersmith and Fulham London Borough, ex p. Beddowes* (1986) 18 H.L.R. 458, C.A.

s. 106, see *R. v. Canterbury City Council, ex p. Gillespie* (1987) 19 H.L.R. 7, Simon Brown J.

s. 106A, added: 1986, c.63, s.6.

s. 108, amended: 1988, c.50, s.83.

s. 109A, added: 1986, c.63, sch.5.

s. 114, amended: 1988, c.50, s.83.

s. 115, amended: 1986, c.63, sch.4; 1988, c.50, sch.17.

s. 117, amended: 1986, c.63, sch.5; 1988, c.50, sch.17.

s. 121, repealed in pt.: 1985, c.65, sch.10.

s. 125, amended: 1986, c.63, s.4, sch.5.

ss. 125A–125C, added: *ibid.*, s.4.

s. 127, amended: *ibid.*, s.4; repealed in pt.: *ibid.*, schs.5, 12.

s. 129, amended: *ibid.*, s.2.

s. 130, amended: *ibid.*, sch.5.

s. 131, order 86/2193.

s. 131, amended: 1988, c.50, s.122.

ss. 137, 140, 142, 151, 152, amended: 1986, c.63, sch.5.

ss. 153A, 153B, added: 1988, c.50, s.124.

s. 154, amended: 1986, c.26, s.2.

s. 155, amended: 1988, c.50, sch.17.

s. 156, orders 87/1203, 1810; 88/85.

s. 156, amended: 1986, c.63, sch.5.

s. 157, orders 86/1695; 88/2057.

s. 158, amended: 1986, c.63, sch.5.

s. 160, see *R. v. Rushmoor Borough Council, ex p. Barrett* [1988] 2 All E.R. 268, C.A.

ss. 165, 168, repealed in pt.: 1988, c.3, sch.

s. 170, amended: 1988, c.34, sch.5.

s. 171, order 87/1732.

s. 171, amended: 1988, c.50, s.83.

ss. 171A–171H, added: 1986, c.63, s.8.

ss. 171B, 171C, amended: 1988, c.50, s.127.

s. 717F, amended: *ibid.*, sch.17.

s. 176, regs. 86/2194.

1985—cont.

68. Housing Act 1985—cont.

s. 187, repealed in pt. (S.): 1987, c.26, schs.23, 24.

s. 187, amended: 1986, c.63, sch.5.

s. 188, amended: ibid.; 1988, c.50, sch.17.

ss. 189–194, amended: ibid., sch.15.

Pt. VI (ss. 189–208), see R. v. London Borough of Lambeth, ex p. Clayhope Properties (1986) 18 H.L.R. 541, Hodgson J.

s. 190, see R. v. London Borough of Lambeth, ex p. Clayhope Properties (1986) 18 H.L.R. 541, Hodgson J.

s. 198, amended: 1988, c.50, sch.15.

s. 198A, added: ibid.

ss. 199–201, repealed: ibid., schs.15, 18.

s. 203, amended: ibid., sch.15.

s. 205, amended and repealed in pt.: ibid.

s. 207, amended: 1986, c.63, sch.5; 1988, c.50, sch.15.

s. 231, repealed: 1986, c.5, sch.15.

ss. 236, 238, amended: 1988, c.50, sch.17.

s. 239, amended: 1986, c.63, s.21.

s. 240, amended and repealed in pt.: ibid.

s. 244, amended: ibid., sch.3.

s. 245, order 88/1258.

s. 247, amended: 1988, c.50, sch.17.

s. 250, repealed in pt.: 1986, c.63, s.21.

s. 251, amended: ibid., sch.5.

s. 255, amended: ibid., sch.3.

s. 256, amended: ibid., sch.5.

ss. 257, 258, amended: ibid., s.21.

s. 259, order 88/1258.

ss. 259A, 259B, added: 1986, c.63, s.21.

ss. 263, 264, amended: 1988, c.50, sch.17.

ss. 268, 270, 276, 304, see Beaney v. Branchett (1987) 283 E.G. 1063, C.A.

ss. 270, 276, 286, 309, amended: 1988, c.50, sch.17.

s. 322, amended: 1986, c.63, sch.5.

s. 323, amended: 1988, c.50, sch.17.

Pt. XI (ss. 345–400), see Mayor and Burgesses of Wandsworth London Borough v. Orakpo (1987) 19 H.L.R. 57, C.A.; R. v. Secretary of State for the Environment, ex p. Royal Borough of Kensington and Chelsea (1987) 19 H.L.R. 161, Taylor J.

s. 352, see Thrasyvoulou v. London Borough of Hackney (1986) 18 H.L.R. 370, C.A.

s. 368, amended: 1988, c.50, sch.17.

s. 369, see Wandsworth London Borough Council v. Sparling, The Times, November 21, 1987, D.C.

ss. 381, 382, amended: 1988, c.50, sch.17.

s. 395, see Wandsworth London Borough Council v. Sparling (1985) 20 H.L.R. 169, D.C.

s. 400, amended: 1988, c.50, sch.17.

Pt. XIII (ss. 417–434), see Hemsted v. Lees and Norwich City Council (1986) 18 H.L.R. 424, McCowan J.

s. 425, amended: 1986, c.50, sch.10.

s. 427A, added: 1986, c.63, sch.5.

s. 429A, added: ibid., s.16; amended: 1988, c.50, sch.17.

s. 430, amended: ibid., ss.132, 136.

s. 434, amended: 1986, c.63, sch.5; 1988, c.50, sch.17.

1985—cont.

68. Housing Act 1985—cont.

s. 442, amended: 1986, c.52, sch.18.

s. 444, orders 87/1204, 1811; 88/87, 1727.

s. 444, amended: 1986, c.63, sch.5.

s. 445, orders 86/1511; 87/268; 88/270.

s. 447, orders 86/1489; 87/1202, 1809; 88/1723.

s. 447, amended: 1986, c.52, sch.18.

s. 448, order 86/1490.

s. 450, substituted: 1986, c.53, sch.18.

ss. 450A, 450B, amended: 1988, c.50, sch.17.

ss. 450A–450C, added: 1986, c.63, s.5.

ss. 452, 453, repealed in pt.: ibid., schs.5, 12.

s. 458, amended (S.): 1987, c.26, sch.23.

s. 458, amended: 1986, c.63, sch.5; repealed in pt.: 1986, c.53, sch.19.

s. 459, amended: 1986, c.63, sch.5; 1988, c.50, sch.17; repealed in pt.: 1986, c.53, sch.19.

s. 460, amended and repealed in pt.: 1986, c.63, sch.3.

ss. 462, 463, amended: ibid.

s. 464, amended: 1988, c.50, s.131.

s. 464A, added: 1986, c.63, sch.3.

s. 466, amended: ibid.

ss. 472, 481, 489, 497, orders 88/1263, 1467.

ss. 498A–489G, added: 1986, c.63, sch.3.

s. 498C, order 88/32.

s. 498F, order 87/2276.

s. 499, amended: 1986, c.63, sch.3.

s. 501, amended: 1988, c.50, s.131.

ss. 503, 504, see R. v. Camden London Borough Council, ex p. Christey (1987) 19 H.L.R. 420, Macpherson J.

ss. 503, 504, amended: 1988, c.50, s.131.

s. 508, orders 88/1263, 1467.

s. 509, orders 87/1379; 88/33, 1475.

s. 511, amended: 1986, c.63, sch.3.

s. 513, amended and repealed in pt.: ibid.

ss. 514, 515, amended: ibid.

s. 517, orders 87/1809; 88/33, 1475.

ss. 518, 519, amended: 1986, c.63, sch.3.

s. 521, orders 87/1285; 88/1239.

s. 526, amended: 1986, c.63, sch.3; 1988, c.50, s.131.

s. 533, amended: ibid., sch.17.

s. 535, amended: 1986, c.63, sch.3.

s. 538, order 88/884.

s. 543, orders 86/1494; 88/820, 923.

ss. 553, 554, amended: 1988, c.50, sch.17.

s. 568, regs. 86/797.

s. 573, amended: 1987, c.3, sch.1.

s. 577, amended: 1988, c.50, sch.17.

s. 604, amended: ibid., s.130.

s. 612, amended: ibid., sch.17.

s. 614, regs. 88/2189.

s. 618, amended: 1986, c.63, sch.5.

s. 621A, added: ibid.

s. 622, amended: 1986, c.53, sch.18; 1987, c.22, sch.6; 1988, c.50, sch.17.

sch. 1, amended: 1986, c.5, sch.14; 1988, c.40, sch.12; c.50, s.83.

sch. 2, see R. v. London Borough of Croydon, ex p. Toth (1986) 18 H.L.R. 493, Simon Brown J.; Second W.R.V.S. Housing Society v. Blair (1986) 19 H.L.R. 104, C.A.; Wandsworth

CAP.

1985—cont.
68. Housing Act 1985—cont.
London Borough Council v. *Fadayomi* [1987] 3 All E.R. 474, C.A.; *Wansbeck District Council* v. *Marley, The Times,* November 30, 1987, C.A.
sch. 2, amended: 1986, c.63, s.9; 1988, c.50, s.83, sch 17.
sch. 3, amended: 1986, c.63, sch.5; 1988, c.50, s.83.
sch. 3A, added: *ibid.,* s.6, sch.1.
sch. 4, amended: *ibid.,* sch.5; 1987, c.26, sch.23 (S.); 1988, c.50, s.83; repealed in pt.: 1987, c.26, schs.5, 12.
sch. 5, amended: *ibid.,* sch.1; 1988, c.50, ss.83, 123, sch.17; repealed in pt.: *ibid.,* s.123, sch.18.
sch. 6, order 86/2195.
sch. 6, amended: 1986, c.63, s.4, sch.5; repealed in pt.: *ibid.,* schs.5, 12.
sch. 9A, added: *ibid.,* s.8, sch.2.
sch. 11, amended: *ibid.,* sch.5.
sch. 14, see *Hemsted* v. *Lees and Norwich City Council* (1986) 18 H.L.R. 424, McCowan J.
sch. 14, amended: 1986, c.50, sch.10.
sch. 18, amended: 1985, c.65, sch.8; 1986, c.63, sch.5.
schs. 22, 24, amended: 1986, c.63, sch.5.
69. Housing Associations Act 1985.
Royal Assent, October 30, 1985.
s. 1, amended (S.): 1988, c.43, sch.2.
s. 2A, added: 1988, c.50, sch.6.
s. 3, amended: 1988, c.43, sch.2; c.50, sch.6; repealed in pt.: *ibid.,* schs.6,18.
s. 4, amended: 1986, c.63, s.19; c.65, s.13 (S.); 1988, c.43, sch.2; c.50, s.48.
ss. 5–7, amended: 1988, c.43, sch.2; c.50, sch.6.
s. 8, amended (S.): 1986, c.65, s.13; 1987, c.26, sch.23.
s. 9, amended: 1988, c.43, sch.3; c.50, sch.6.
s. 10, amended: 1986, c.63, sch.5; 1987, c.26, sch.23; 1988, c.43, schs.3,9; c.50, sch.6.
ss. 13, 14, amended: 1988, c.43, sch.3.
s. 15, amended: 1986, c.65, sch.2; 1988, c.50, sch.6.
s. 15A, added (S.): 1986, c.65, s.14; amended: 1988, c.43, sch.3; repealed in pt.(S.): *ibid.,* schs.9,10; substituted: 1988, c.50, sch.6.
ss. 16, 17, amended: 1988, c.43, sch.3; c.50, sch.6.
s. 18, amended: 1988, c.9, s.24; 1988, c.50, sch.6; repealed in pt.: *ibid.,* sch.18.
ss. 19, 21, 22, amended: 1988, c.43, sch.3; c.50, sch.6.
s. 23, amended: 1988, c.43, sch.3.
s. 24, order 88/395.
s. 27, amended: 1988, c.50, sch.6.
ss. 28–30, amended: 1988, c.43, sch.3; c.50, sch.6.
s. 31, amended: *ibid.*
s. 32, amended: 1988, c.43, sch.3.
s. 33, amended: 1988,c.50, sch.3.
s. 33A, added: *ibid.*
s. 36A, added: *ibid.,* s.49.
s. 39, amended: 1987, c.26, sch.23(S.); 1988, c.43, sch.9; c.50, sch.6.

CAP.

1985—cont.
69. Housing Associations Act 1985—cont.
s. 40, amended: 1986, c.65, sch.2; 1988, c.43, sch.3; c.50, sch.6; repealed in pt.: *ibid.,* sch.18.
ss. 41–57, repealed: *ibid.*
ss. 44, 45, 52, amended (S.): 1986, c.65, s.16; 1987, c.26, sch.23.
s. 46, amended: 1988, c.9, s.24.
s. 52, repealed in pt. 1988, c.3, sch.
s. 59, amended (S.): 1987, c.26, sch.23.
s. 62, amended: 1988, c.1, sch.29; repealed: 1988, c.50, sch.18.
s. 63, amended: *ibid.,* sch.6.
ss. 63–66, repealed: 1986, c.53, schs.18, 19.
ss. 67, 68, amended: 1986, c.63, sch.5.
s. 69, amended: 1988, c.9, s.24; c.50, sch.6.
s. 69A, added: 1986, c.63, sch.5; amended: 1987, c.26, sch.23(S.); 1988, c.50, sch.6.
s. 72, repealed in pt.: 1986, c.53, schs.18, 19.
s. 73, amended: 1986, c.63, sch.5; repealed in pt.: 1986, c.53, schs.18, 19; 1988, c.50, sch.18.
s. 74, amended: *ibid.,* sch.6.
s. 75, amended: *ibid.,* s.56, sch.6; repealed in pt.: *ibid.,* sch.18.
ss. 77, 83, amended: *ibid.,* sch.6.
s. 84, amended: 1986, c.53, sch.18.
s. 86, order 87/1389 (S.).
s. 86, amended: 1986, c.53, sch.18; c.65, sch.2.
s. 87, repealed in pt.: 1988, c.50, sch.18.
s. 88, amended (S.): 1987, c.26, sch.23.
s. 93, amended: 1988, c.50, sch.6.
s. 100, repealed (S.): 1986, c.65, sch.3.
s. 101, amended: 1986, c.53, sch.18.
s. 106, amended: 1986, c.65, s.13, sch.2 (S.); 1987, c.22, sch.6; 1988, c.43, sch.9; c.50, sch.6; repealed in pt.: 1986, c.65, sch.3; 1988 c.40, sch.13 (prosp.).
s. 107, amended: 1986, c.65, sch.2; 1987, c.31, sch.4; repealed in pt.: 1986, c.65, sch.3; 1988, c.50, sch.18.
sch. 2, amended: 1986, c.63, sch.5; 1988, c.43, sch.3.
sch. 5, amended: 1988, c.50, sch.6; repealed in pt.: *ibid.,* schs.6,18.
sch. 6, repealed in pt.: *ibid.*
70. Landlord and Tenant Act 1985.
Royal Assent, October 30, 1985.
see *Boldmark* v. *Cohen and Cohen* (1985) 19 H.L.R. 135, C.A.
s. 3, amended: 1987, c.31, s.50.
s. 4, amended: *ibid.,* s.45.
s. 5, amended: 1988, c.50, sch.17.
s. 11, see *Davies* v. *Brenner,* July 31, 1986; H.H. Judge Tibber, Edmonton County Ct.; *Al Hassani* v. *Merrigan* [1988] 03 E.G. 88, C.A.
s. 11, amended: 1985, c.50, s.116.
s. 14, amended: 1986, c.5, sch.14; 1988, c.50, s.116.
s. 18, amended: 1987, c.31, s.50.
s. 19, see *Delahay* v. *Maltlodge,* March 9, 1987; P. St. J. Langan Q.C.; *West London County Court; McClean* v. *Liverpool City Council* (1987) 283 E.G. 1395, C.A.; *Dinefwr Borough Council* v. *Jones* (1987) 19 H.L.R. 445, C.A.

581

CAP.

1985—cont.

70. Landlord and Tenant Act 1985—*cont.*
s. 19, amended: 1987, c.31, sch.2.
s. 20, order 88/1285.
s. 20, substituted: 1987, c.31, sch.2.
s. 20A, added: 1986, c.63, sch.5.
ss 20B, 20C, added: 1987, c.31, sch.2.
s. 21, amended: 1986, c.63, sch.5; 1987, c.31, sch.2.
ss. 22, 24, amended: *ibid.*
s. 26, amended: 1988, c.50, sch.17.
ss. 27, 28, amended: 1987, c.31, sch.2.
s. 29, see *R.* v. *London Rent Assessment Panel, ex p. Trustees of Henry Smith's Charity Kensington Estate, The Independent,* October 30, 1987, Schiemann J.
s. 29, amended: 1987, c.31, sch.2.
s. 30, amended: *ibid.;* repealed in pt.: *ibid.,* schs.2, 5.
s. 30A, added: *ibid.,* s.43, sch.3.
s. 30B, added: *ibid.,* s.44.
s. 38, amended: order 85/1884; 1988, c.4, sch.6; repealed in pt. (prosp.): 1988, c.40, sch.13.

71. Housing (Consequential Provisions) Act 1985.
Royal Assent, October 30, 1985.
sch. 2, amended: 1986, c.63, sch.5; repealed in pt.: 1986, c.5, sch.15; c.31, sch.6; c.53, sch.19; c.63, sch.12; 1987, c.26, sch.24 (S.); 1988, c.1, sch.31.
sch. 3, amended: 1986, c.63, sch.5.

72. Weights and Measures Act 1985.
Royal Assent, October 30, 1985.
ss. 4, 5, orders 86/1684, 1685; regs. 87/51.
s. 10, regs. 88/120.
s. 11, regs. 86/1210, 1320, 1682, 1683, 2109; 88/120, 128, 876, 997; order 88/558.
s. 12, regs. 86/1210, 1320; 88/128, 876, 997.
s. 15, regs. 86/1210, 1320, 1682, 1683, 2109; 87/1538; 88/120, 128, 876, 997.
s. 22, orders 87/216; 88/985, 2040.
s. 23, regs. 87/1538; 88/627.
s. 24, orders 87/216; 88/2040.
s. 47, regs. 86/2049.
s. 48, regs. 86/2049; 87/1538.
s. 49, regs. 86/2049.
ss. 51, 54, regs. 86/2049.
s. 62, order 87/2187.
ss. 63, 65, regs. 86/2049.
ss. 66, 68, regs. 86/2049; 87/1538.
s. 86, regs. 86/1210, 1260, 1320, 1682–1685, 2049, 2109; 87/51, 1538; 88/120, 128, 627, 997; orders 87/216, 2187; 88/895, 2040.
s. 94, regs. 86/1210, 1320, 1682–1685, 2049, 2109; 87/51, 1538; 88/120, 129, 765, 876, 997; order 88/558.
sch. 4, regs. 88/765.
sch. 5, amended: 1987, c.3, sch.1.

73. Law Reform (Miscellaneous Provisions) (Scotland) Act 1985.
Royal Assent, October 30, 1985.
Commencement orders: 85/1908, 1945, 2055; 88/1819.
s. 8, see *Shaw* v. *William Grant (Minerals),* 1988 S.C.L.R. 416.

CAP.

1985—cont.

73. Law Reform (Miscellaneous Provisions) (Scotland) Act 1985—*cont.*
s. 15, amended: 1986, c.39, sch.2; 1988, c.48, sch.7.
s. 16, repealed: 1986, c.55, sch.2.
s. 38, repealed: 1988, c.54, sch.1.
s. 39, repealed: 1987, c.41, sch.2.
s. 60, orders 85/1908, 1945, 2055; 88/1819.
sch. 1, amended: 1988, c.1, sch.20; repealed in pt.: *ibid.,* sch.31.
sch. 2, repealed in pt.: 1988, c.36, sch.2; 1988, c.54, sch.1.
sch. 3, repealed in pt.: *ibid.*

74. Consolidated Fund (No. 3) Act 1985.
Royal Assent, December 19, 1985.
repealed: 1987, c.17, sch. (C).

75. European Communities (Spanish and Portuguese Accession) Act 1985.
Royal Assent, December 19, 1985.

76. Northern Ireland (Loans) Act 1985.
Royal Assent, December 19, 1985.

1986

1. Education (Amendment) Act 1986.
Royal Assent, February 17, 1986.
s. 2, repealed: 1987, c.1, sch.2.

2. Australia Act 1986.
Royal Assent, February 17, 1986.
Commencement order: 86/319.
s. 17, order 86/319.

3. Atomic Energy Authority Act 1986.
Royal Assent, February 19, 1986.
s. 8, amended: 1988, c.48, sch.7.

4. Consolidated Fund Act 1986.
Royal Assent, March 18, 1986.
repealed: 1988, c.38, sch. (C.).

5. Agricultural Holdings Act 1986.
Royal Assent, March 18, 1986.
Commencement order: 86/1596.
s. 1, see *Short* v. *Greeves* [1988] 08 E.G. 109, C.A.
s. 7, regs. 88/281.
s. 9, regs. 88/282.
s. 12, see *Buckinghamshire County Council* v. *Gordon* (1986) E.G. 853, H.H. Judge Barr.
s. 24, order 86/1596.
sch. 3, see *Cawley* v. *Pratt* [1988] 33 E.G. 54, C.A.
sch. 3, regs. 87/711.
sch. 3, amended: 1987, c.3, sch.1; 1988, c.50, sch.17.
sch. 4, order 87/710.
sch. 5, amended: 1988, c.50, sch.17.
sch. 6, orders 86/1256; 87/1465; 88/1428.
sch. 6, amended: 1988, c.40, sch.12.
sch. 14, repealed in pt.: 1986, c.63, sch.12.

6. Prevention of Oil Pollution Act 1986.
Royal Assent, March 18, 1986.

7. Marriage (Wales) Act 1986.
Royal Assent, March 18, 1986.

8. Museum of London Act 1986.
Royal Assent, March 26, 1986.

1986—cont.

9. Law Reform (Parent and Child) (Scotland) Act 1986.
Royal Assent, March 26, 1986.
Commencement order: 86/1983.
see *McCann* v. *McCann* (Sh.Ct.), 1987 S.C.L.R. 742; *Conlon* v. *O'Dowd* (Sh.Ct.), 1988 S.C.L.R. 119.
ss. 2–4, see *Montgomery* v. *Lockwood* (Sh.Ct.) 1987 S.C.L.R. 525.
s. 3, see *Sinclair* v. *Sinclair* (O.H.), 1988 S.L.T. 87; *McEachan* v. *Young* (Sh.Ct.), 1988 S.C.L.R. 98; *M., Petr., The Scotsman*, November 11, 1988.
ss. 3, 8, see *A.B.* v. *M. (O.M.)*, 1987 S.C.L.R. 389.
s. 7, repealed in pt.: 1988, c.32, sch.
s. 11, order 86/1983.
sch. 1, repealed in pt.: 1986, c.50, sch.11; 1988, c.36, sch.2.
sch. 2, repealed in pt.: 1986, c.50, sch.11.

10. Local Government Act 1986.
Royal Assent, March 26, 1986.
Commencement order: 87/2003.
s. 1, repealed in pt. (prosp.): 1988, c.41, sch.13.
s. 2, amended: 1988, c.9, s.29.
s. 2A, added: *ibid.*, s.28.
s. 4, amended: *ibid.*, s.27.
s. 5, order 87/2004; 88/332(S.).
s. 6, amended: 1988, c.4, sch.6; repealed in pt. (prosp.): 1988, c.40, sch.13.
ss. 9, 11, repealed in pt. (prosp.): *ibid.*
s. 12, order 87/2003.
s. 12, repealed in pt. (prosp.): 1988, c.41, sch.13.

11. Gaming (Amendment) Act 1986.
Royal Assent, May 2, 1986.
Commencement order: 88/1250.
s. 3, order 88/1250.

12. Statute Law (Repeals) Act 1986.
Royal Assent, May 2, 1986.
sch. 2, repealed in pt.: 1986, c.56, sch.4.

13. Highways (Amendment) Act 1986.
Royal Assent, May 2, 1986.

14. Animals (Scientific Procedures) Act 1986.
Royal Assent, May 20, 1986.
Commencement orders: 86/2088; S.R. 1986, No. 364.
s. 8, order 86/2089.
s. 12, rules 86/1911; S.R. 1987 No. 2.
s. 28, order 86/2089.
s. 29, S.Rs. 1986 No. 364; 1987, No. 2.
s. 30, orders 86/2088; S.R. 1986 No. 364.

15. Industrial Training Act 1986.
Royal Assent, May 20, 1986.

16. Marriage (Prohibited Degrees of Relationship) Act 1986.
Royal Assent, May 20, 1986.
Commencement order: 86/1343.
s. 6, order 86/1343.

17. Drainage Rates (Disabled Persons) Act 1986.
Royal Assent, June 26, 1986.

18. Corneal Tissue Act 1986.
Royal Assent, June 26, 1986.

1986—cont.

19. British Shipbuilders (Borrowing Powers) Act 1986.
Royal Assent, June 26, 1986.
repealed: 1987, c.52, s.1.

20. Horticultural Produce Act 1986.
Royal Assent, June 26, 1986.

21. Armed Forces Act 1986.
Royal Assent, June 26, 1986.
Commencement orders: 86/2071, 2124; 87/1998.
s. 1, orders 87/1262; 88/1293.
s. 2, regs. 88/1395.
s. 17, orders 86/2071, 2124; 87/1998.

22. Civil Protection in Peacetime Act 1986.
Royal Assent, June 26, 1986.

23. Safety at Sea Act 1986.
Royal Assent, June 26, 1986.
Commencement order: 86/1759.
s. 13, amended: 1988, c.12, sch.6.
s. 15, order 86/1759.

24. Health Service Joint Consultative Committee (Access to Information) Act 1986.
Royal Assent, June 26, 1986.
s. 1, amended: 1988, c.40, sch.12.

25. Commonwealth Development Corporation Act 1986.
Royal Assent, June 26, 1986.

26. Land Registration Act 1986.
Royal Assent, June 26, 1986.
Commencement order: 86/2117.
s. 6, order 86/2117.

27. Road Traffic Regulation (Parking) Act 1986.
Royal Assent, July 8, 1986.

28. Children and Young Persons (Amendment) Act 1986.
Royal Assent, July 8, 1986.
Commencement orders: 88/1262, 2188.
ss. 2, 3, see *R.* v. *Newcastle City Juvenile Court, ex p. S. & T., The Times*, December 21, 1987.
s. 3, repealed in pt.: 1988, c.34, sch.6.
s. 4, rules 88/952.
s. 5, orders 88/1262, 2188.

29. Consumer Safety (Amendment) Act 1986.
Royal Assent, July 8, 1986.
repealed: 1987, c.43, sch.5.
s. 12, see *Rotherham Metropolitan Borough Council* v. *Raysun (U.K)*, *The Times*, April 27, 1988, D.C.

30. Forestry Act 1986.
Royal Assent, July 8, 1986.

31. Airports Act 1986.
Royal Assent, July 8, 1986.
Commencement orders: 86/1228, 1487.
s. 2, orders 86/1228, 1229.
s. 7, order 87/2232.
s. 10, repealed: 1986, c.60, sch.17.
s. 32, order 87/874.
ss. 36, 38, order 86/1544.
s. 40, order 86/1502.
s. 41, regs. 86/1544.
s. 47, regs. 86/1543.
ss. 48, 51, regs. 86/1544.
s. 63, orders 87/380, 1132, 2246.
s. 74, amended: 1987, c.43, sch.4; repealed in pt.: *ibid.*, sch.5.

1986—cont.

31. Airports Act 1966—*cont.*
s. 75, order 86/1801.
s. 77, amended: 1988, c.1, sch.29.
s. 79, orders 86/1228; 87/874.
s. 85, orders 86/1228, 1487.
sch. 2, amended (S.): 1987, c.26, sch.23.

32. Drug Trafficking Offences Act 1986.
Royal Assent, July 8, 1986.
Commencement orders: 86/1488, 1546, 2145, 2266(S.).
see *R.* v. *Small (Michael), The Times,* April 16, 1988, C.A.
ss. 2, 8, amended (S.): 1987, c.41, s.45.
s. 6, repealed in pt.: 1988, c.33, sch.16.
ss. 7–9, amended: *ibid.,* sch.5.
ss. 8, 9, see *Defendant, A, Re, The Independent,* April 2, 1987, Webster J.
ss. 8, 13, see *Peters, Re* [1988] 3 W.L.R. 182, C.A.
s. 10, repealed in pt.: 1988, c.33, sch.16.
s. 12, amended: *ibid.,* sch.5.
ss. 13, 15, repealed in pt. (S.): 1987, c.41, sch.2.
s. 15, amended: 1988, c.33, sch.5; c.50, sch.17; repealed in pt.: *ibid.,* sch.16.
s. 16, amended: 1987, c.41, sch.2(S.); 1988, c.33, sch.5; c.50, sch.17; repealed in pt. (S.): 1987, c.41, sch.2.
s. 17, repealed in pt.: *ibid.* (S.); 1988, c.33, sch.16.
s. 17A, added: *ibid.,* sch.5.
s. 18, amended: *ibid.*
s. 19, amended: 1987, c.41, s.45(S.); 1988, c.33, sch.5, repealed in pt.: *ibid.,* schs.5,16.
ss. 20–23, repealed (S.): 1987, c.41, sch.2.
s. 24, amended: 1988, c.33, sch.5.
s. 24A, order 88/593.
s. 24A, amended (S.): 1987, c.41, s.31.
s. 25, amended: 1988, c.33, sch.5; repealed in pt.: *ibid.,* schs.5,16.
s. 26, substituted: *ibid.,* sch.5.
s. 26A, added: *ibid.*
s. 27, see *R.* v. *Central Criminal Court, ex p. Francis & Francis (A Firm)* [1988] 1 All E.R. 677, D.C.
s. 27, rules 86/2151; Act of Adjournal 86/2184.
ss. 27–29, repealed in pt. (S.): 1987, c.41, sch.2.
s. 33, repealed: 1988, c.3, sch.
ss. 33, amended (S.): 1987, c.41, s.45; repealed in pt. (S.): *ibid.,* sch.2.
s. 38, amended: 1988, c.33, sch.5; repealed in pt.: *ibid.,* sch.16.
s. 40, orders 86/1488, 1546, 2145, 2266 (S.).
s. 40, amended: 1987, c.41, s.45(S.); 1988, c.33, sch.5; repealed in pt. (S.): 1987, c.41, sch.2.

33. Disabled Persons (Services, Consultation and Representation) Act 1986.
Royal Assent, July 8, 1986.
Commencement orders: 87/564, 729, 911 (S.); 88/51, 94.
ss. 5–7, amended: 1988, c.40, sch.12.
s. 15, repealed: 1986, c.66, s.5.
s. 18, orders 87/564, 729, 911 (S.); 88/51, 94.

34. Protection of Children (Tobacco) Act 1986.
Royal Assent, July 8, 1986.

1986—cont.

35. Protection of Military Remains Act 1986.
Royal Assent, July 8, 1986.
s. 10, order 87/1281.

36. Incest and Related Offences (Scotland) Act 1986.
Royal Assent, July 18, 1986.
Commencement order: 86/1803.
s. 3, order 86/1803.

37. Latent Damage Act 1986.
Royal Assent, July 18, 1986.

38. Outer Space Act 1986.
Royal Assent, July 18, 1986.

39. Patents, Designs and Marks Act 1986.
Royal Assent, July 18, 1986.
Commencement orders: 86/1274; 88/1824.
s. 4, orders 86/1274; 88/1824.
sch. 2, repealed in pt.: 1988, c.1, sch.31; c.48, sch.8.

40. Education Act 1986.
Royal Assent, July 18, 1986.
ss. 4, 8, see *R.* v. *Westminster Roman Catholic Diocesan Trustees, ex p. Mars, The Times,* January 9, 1988, Simon Brown J.

41. Finance Act 1986.
Royal Assent, July 25, 1986.
s. 9, amended: 1988, c.54, sch.3.
ss. 16–23, repealed: 1988, c.1, sch.31.
s. 23, repealed in pt.: 1988, c.39, sch.14.
s. 24, amended: 1988, c.1, sch.29; repealed in pt.: *ibid.,* sch.31.
ss. 25–32, repealed: *ibid.*
s. 26, repealed in pt.: 1988, c.39, sch.14.
ss. 34–54, 56 (in pt.), repealed: 1988, c.1, sch.31.
s. 58, amended: *ibid.,* sch.29.
ss. 61–63, repealed: *ibid.,* sch.31.
s. 66, order 87/512.
s. 69, amended: 1988, c.1, sch.29.
s. 70, amended: 1987, c.16, s.52.
s. 78, amended: 1988, c.1, sch.29.
s. 81, regs. 88/654; amended: *ibid.*
s. 82, amended: 1987, c.16, s.53.
ss. 87–89, amended: *ibid.,* sch.7.
s. 89, regs. 88/654; amended: *ibid.*
s. 89A, added: 1987, c.51, s.100.
s. 90, amended: 1987, c.16, sch.7.
s. 91, repealed in pt.: 1987, c.51, s.100, sch 9.
s. 92, orders 86/1710, 1833; 87/514, 883, 888, 1494, 1900; 88/758, 1281, 1624, 2187.
s. 92, amended: orders 86/1710, 1833; 1987, c.16, sch.7.
s. 94, amended: 1988, c.39, sch.13.
s. 98, regs. 86/1711; 88/835.
s. 99, amended: 1988, c.39, s.144.
s. 104, regs. 87/1130.
s. 114, amended: 1988, c.1, sch.29.
sch. 7, repealed: *ibid.,* sch.31.
sch. 8, regs. 86/1948; 87/2128; 88/657.
sch. 8, repealed: 1988, c.1, sch.31.
sch. 9, amended: 1987, c.16, sch.5; repealed in pt.: 1988, c.1, sch.31.
schs. 10–12, repealed: 1988, c.1, sch.31.
sch. 11, regs. 87/530.
sch. 12, regs. 87/352, 412.

1986—cont.

41. Finance Act 1986—cont.
sch. 13, amended: 1988, c.1, sch.29; repealed in pt: *ibid.*, sch.31.
s. 15, amended: *ibid.*, sch.29.
sch. 16, amended: *ibid.*; repealed in pt.: *ibid.*, sch.31.
schs. 17, 18 (in pt.), repealed: *ibid.*
sch. 19, repealed in pt.: 1987, c.51, sch.9; 1988, c.39, sch.14.
sch. 20, amended: 1987, c.16, s.58, sch.8; repealed in pt.: *ibid.*, sch.16.

42. Appropriation Act 1986.
Royal Assent, July 25, 1986.
repealed: 1988, c.38, sch. (C.).

43. Crown Agents (Amendment) Act 1986.
Royal Assent, July 25, 1986.

44. Gas Act 1986.
Royal Assent, July 25, 1986.
Commencement orders: 86/1315, 1316, 1809.
s. 3, order 86/1316.
s. 10, regs. 86/1448.
s. 17, regs. 88/296, 980.
s. 36, order 88/159.
s. 42, amended: 1987, c.43, sch.4; repealed in pt.: *ibid.*, sch.5.
s. 47, regs. 86/1448; 88/296.
s. 49, orders 86/1317, 1318.
ss. 51, 52, repealed in pt.: 1988, c.39, sch.14.
s. 54, order 87/866.
s. 58, repealed: 1986, c.60, sch.17.
ss. 62, 64, order 86/1810.
s. 63, amended: 1988, c.1, sch.29.
s. 68, orders 86/1315, 1809.
sch. 1, repealed in pt.: 1987, c.39, sch.2.
sch. 7, amended: 1986, c.63, sch.7; repealed in pt.: 1986, c.45, sch.12; 1988, c.41, sch.13.
sch. 7, amended (S.): 1986, c.63, sch.7; 1988, c.41, sch.13 (prosp.).

45. Insolvency Act 1986.
Royal Assent, July 25, 1986.
s. 8, see *Charnley Davies Business Services, Re* (1987) 3 B.C.C. 408, Harman J.; *Consumer and Industrial Press, Re* [1988] BCLC 177, Peter Gibson J.
s. 8, amended: 1987, c.22, sch.6.
Pt. II (ss. 8–27), see *Company A, (No. 00175 of 1987), Re* [1987] B.C.L.C. 467, Vinelott J.; *Newport County Association Football Club, Re* [1987] B.C.L.R. 582, Harman J.
ss. 8, 18, see *St. Ives Windings* [1987] 3 BCC 634, Harman J.
s. 9, amended: 1988, c.33, s.62.
s. 11, see *Air Ecosse* v. *Civil Aviation Authority,* 1987 S.L.T. 751; (1987) 3 BCC 492, Ct. of Session.
ss. 14, 17, 23, 27, see *Charnley Davies, Re* (1988) 4 BCC 152, Peter Gibson J.
ss. 23, 27, see *Charnley Davies Business Services, Re* (1987) 3 B.C.C. 408, Harman J.
ss. 53, 54, 62, 65–67, 70, 71, regs. 86/1917 (S.).
s. 108, see *Keypak Homecare, Re* [1987] B.C.L.C. 409, Millett J.
s. 109, regs. 87/752.
s. 115, see *Sandwell Copiers, Re* (1988) 4 BCC 227, Mervyn Davies J.

1986—cont.

45. Insolvency Act 1986—cont.
s. 120, repealed in pt.: 1988, c.36, sch.2.
ss. 122, 123, see *Craig* v. *Iona Hotels* (Sh.Ct.), 1988 S.C.L.R. 130.
ss. 122–124, see *Walter L. Jacob & Co.* v. *Financial Intermediaries, Managers and Brokers Regulatory Association* (Sh.Ct.), 1988 S.C.L.R. 184.
s. 124, see *Quickdome, Re* (1988) 4 BCC 296, Mervyn Davies J.; *Instrumentation Electrical Services, Re* (1988) 4 B.C.C. 301, Mervyn Davies J.
s. 124, amended: 1988, c.33, s.62.
s. 127, see *Company, A (No. 007523 of 1986), Re* [1987] BCLC 200, Mervyn Davies J.; *French's (Wine Bar), Re* [1987] B.C.L.C. 499, Vinelott J.; *McGuinness Bros. (U.K.), Re* (1987) 3 BCC 571, Harman J.; *Webb Electrical, Re* (1988) 4 BCC 230, Harman J.
s. 140, see *Charnley Davies Business Services, Re* (1987) 3 B.C.C. 408, Harman J.
ss. 178, 179, see *A. E. Realisations (1985), Re* [1987] B.C.L.C. 486, Vinelott J.
s. 162, repealed in pt.: 1988, c.36, sch.2.
ss. 184, 206, amended: order 87/1996.
s. 214, see *Bath Glass, Re* (1988) 4 BCC 130, Peter Gibson J.; *Company, A (No. 005009 of 1987), Re,* (1988) 4 BCC 424, Knox J.
s. 221, see *Company, A (No. 00359 of 1987), Re* [1987] 3 W.L.R. 339, Gibson J.
s. 230, see *Company, A (No. 003318 of 1987), Re* [1987] 3 B.C.C. 564, Harman J.; *Aveline Barford, Re, The Times,* August 25, 1988, Hoffmann J.
ss. 242, 243, see *Bank of Scotland, Petrs.,* 1988 S.L.T. 690.
s. 253, see *Peake, Re,* July 16, 1987, Mr. Registrar Ashworth, Blackburn County Ct
ss. 264, 266, 267, repealed in pt.: 1988, c.33, sch.16.
s. 273, amended: order 86/1996.
s. 277, repealed: 1988, c.33, sch.16.
s. 281, amended: 1987, c.43, sch.4.
s. 282, repealed in pt.: 1988, c.33, sch.16.
s. 283, amended: 1988, c.50, s.117.
s. 285, see *Smith (S. J.) (A Bankrupt), ex p. Braintree District Council; Braintree District Council* v. *The Bankrupt* [1988] 3 W.L.R. 327, Warner J.
ss. 293, 297, repealed in pt.: 1988, c.33, sch.16.
s. 308, amended: 1988, c.50, sch.17.
s. 308A, added: *ibid.*, s.117.
ss. 309, 315, amended: *ibid.*
s. 327, repealed: 1988, c.33, sch.16.
s. 335, amended: 1988, c.50, sch.17.
s. 341, repealed in pt.: 1988, c.33, sch.16.
s. 346, amended: order 86/1996.
s. 351, amended: 1988, c.50, sch.17.
ss. 354, 358, 360, 361, 364, amended: order 86/1996.
ss. 382, 383, 385, repealed in pt.: 1988, c.33, sch.16.
s. 386, regs. 87/2093.
s. 390, regs. 86/1995, 2247.

CAP.

1986—cont.

45. Insolvency Act 1986—cont.
ss. 392, 393, regs. 86/1995.
s. 402, repealed: 1988, c.33, sch.16.
s. 411, rules 86/1915 (S.), 1916 (S.), 1918 (S.),
1925, 2000, 2002; 87/1919, 1021 (S.), 2023;
regs. 86/1994, 2134.
s. 412, regs. 86/1994; rules 87/1919.
s. 414, orders 86/2030, 2143, 2144; 88/95.
s. 415, orders 86/2030, 2143, 2144; 88/95.
ss. 416, 418, order 86/1996.
s. 419, regs. 86/1995, 2247.
s. 420, order 86/2142.
s. 421, order 86/1999.
s. 422, amended: 1987, c.22, sch.6.
s. 426, order 86/2123.
s. 439, orders 86/2001, 2245; 87/1398.
s. 441, order 86/2001; 87/1398.
sch. 6, order 86/1996, regs. 87/2093.
sch. 6, amended: 1988, c.1, sch.29.
sch. 8, regs. 86/1994.
sch. 14, repealed in pt.: 1987, c.16, sch.16;
1988, c.1, sch.31; c.3, sch.; c.54, sch.1.

46. Company Directors Disqualification Act 1986.
Royal Assent, July 25, 1986.
s. 2, see R. v. Georgiou (1988) 4 BCC 322, C.A.
ss. 4, 6, 10, sch. 1, see Bath Glass, Re (1988)
4 BCC 130, Peter Gibson J.
ss. 6–9, see Majestic Recording Studios, Re
(1988) 4 BCC 519, Mervyn Davies J.
s. 8, amended: 1986, c.60, s.198; 1987, c.42,
s.55; 1988, c.3, s.145.
s. 18, regs. 86/2067.
s. 21, order 86/2142; rules 86/2134; 87/2023.

47. Legal Aid (Scotland) Act 1986.
Royal Assent, July 25, 1986.
Commencement orders: 86/1617; 87/289.
s. 4, amended: 1988, c.39, sch.4; repealed in
pt.: ibid., schs.4,6.
s. 8, amended: 1986, c.50, sch.10.
s. 9, regs. 87/642; 88/1390.
s. 11, regs. 87/704; 88/685.
s. 11, amended: 1986, c.50, sch.10.
s. 12, regs. 87/382, 883; 88/489, 1131.
ss. 14A, 15, regs. 87/825, 826.
s. 16, repealed in pt.: 1988, c.34, schs.4,6.
s. 17, regs. 87/381; 88/490, 1171, 1891(S.).
ss. 17, 18, amended: 1988, c.34, sch.4;
repealed in pt.: ibid., schs. 4,6.
ss. 19, 20, regs. 87/381.
ss. 19, 20, amended: 1988, c.34, sch.4.
s. 31, regs. 87/307; 88/1126.
s. 32, repealed in pt.: 1988, c.34, sch.4.
s. 33, regs. 87/365, 366, 382, 823, 824, 883,
895, 1356, 1358; 88/420, 421, 1107, 1109,
1131.
s. 33, amended: 1988, c.34, sch.4.
s. 36, regs. 87/307, 381, 382, 384, 431, 704,
705; 88/685, 686, 1126, 1131, 1171, 1389,
1891(S.).
s. 36, amended: 1988, c.34, sch.4.
s. 37, regs. 87/883; 88/489, 490, 685, 1131,
1171, 1390, 1891(S.).
s. 38, Acts of Sederunt 87/427, 492; Acts of
Adjournal 87/430; 88/110.

CAP.

1986—cont.

47. Legal Aid (Scotland) Act 1986—cont.
s. 42, regs. 87/381, 382; 88/489, 490, 1131.
s. 45, regs. 87/894; 88/422.
s. 46, orders 86/1617; 87/289.
sch. 1, repealed in pt.: 1988, c.34, schs.4,6.
sch. 2, amended: 1987, c.18, s.98.
sch. 4, regs. 87/894; 88/422.

48. Wages Act 1986.
Royal Assent, July 25, 1986.
Commencement order: 86/1998.
see Staffordshire County Council v. Secretary of
State for Employment, The Times, August 19,
1987, E.A.T.
s. 1, see Patterson v. Pename, The Times,
October 25, 1988, E.A.T.
ss. 1, 5, amended: 1988, c.19, sch.3.
s. 7, amended: 1986, c.50, sch.10.
s. 13, order 87/801.
s. 19, regs. 87/863, 1852.
s. 25, regs. 87/862, 863, 1852.
s. 27, sch.6, see Secretary of State for Employment v. Milk & General Haulage (Nottingham)
(1987) 84 L.S.Gaz. 2118, E.A.T.
s. 33, order 86/1998.
sch. 2, regs. 87/862.
sch. 3, regs. 87/863, 1852.
sch. 6, see Secretary of State for Employment
v. Cameron Iron Works [1988] I.C.R. 297,
E.A.T.; Staffordshire County Council v. Secretary of State for Employment [1988] I.R.L.R.
3, E.A.T.
sch. 8, order 86/2282.

49. Agriculture Act 1986.
Royal Assent, July 25, 1986.
Commencement orders: 86/1419, 1484, 1485
(S.), 1596, 2301.
s. 9, orders 86/1419, 2302.
s. 18, orders 86/2249, 2251–2254, 2257; 87/653
(S.), 654 (S.); 2026, 2027, 2029, 2030–2034;
88/173, 174, 176, 491(S.)–495(S.).
s. 24, orders 86/1484, 1485 (S.), 1596, 2301.
sch. 1, orders 86/1530; 87/626; 88/653.
sch. 2, orders 86/1475; 87/870 (S.); 88/714.

50. Social Security Act 1986.
Royal Assent, July 25, 1986.
Commencement orders: 86/1609, 1719, 1958,
1959; 87/354, 543, 1096, 1853; 88/567.
s. 1, regs. 87/1109, 1933; 88/137.
s. 2, regs. 87/1101, 1109, 1118, 1933; 88/137.
s. 3, regs. 87/1109, 1115, 1933; 88/137.
s. 4, regs. 87/1113.
s. 5, regs. 87/657, 658, 1111; 88/647.
s. 7, regs. 87/1115.
s. 9, regs. 87/1100.
s. 12, regs. 87/1108, 1933; 88/830.
s. 14, regs. 87/1115, 1117; 88/475.
s. 15, regs. 87/1108; 88/647.
s. 16, regs. 87/657, 658; 88/647.
s. 17, regs. 87/1116; 88/474, 1016, 1377, 1417.
s. 17, amended: 1988, c.7, sch.4; repealed in
pt.: 1987, c.45, sch.4.
s. 20, regs. 87/1967, 1971, 1973; 88/660, 663,
1228, 1438, 1444, 1445, 1890(S.).
s. 20, amended: 1988, c.7, ss.3,4; c.41, sch.10;
order 88/1843; repealed in pt.: 1988, c.7, s.3,
sch.5; c.41, sch.10.

1986—cont.

50. Social Security Act 1986—cont.

s. 21, regs. 87/1968, 1971, 1973; 88/660, 663, 1445, 1890(S.).

s. 21, amended: 1988, c.7, sch.4; c.41, sch.10; c.43, s.70(S.); c.50, 121.

s. 22, regs. 87/1967, 1971, 1973; 88/660, 661, 663, 908, 910, 999, 1228, 1438, 1444, 1445, 1890(S.), 1970.

s. 22, amended: 1988, c.41, sch.10.

ss. 22A, 22B, added: *ibid.*

s. 23, regs. 87/1967; 88/660, 663, 664.

s. 23, amended: 1988, c.1, s.29; c.7, sch.

s. 23A, regs. 88/688.

s. 23A, added: 1988, c.7, sch.4.

s. 24, amended: 1987, c.42, sch.2; repealed in pt.: *ibid.*, sch.4.

s. 25, repealed: *ibid.*, schs.2, 4.

s. 25A, added (S.): 1987, c.18, s.68.

s. 26, amended: 1987, c.42, sch.2.

s. 27, regs. 86/2217; 87/491; 88/664, 688.

s. 28, regs. 87/1971; 88/1890(S.); order 88/471.

s. 29, regs. 87/1971; 88/661, 1890(S.).

s. 29, amended: 1988, c.7, sch.4.

s. 30, order 87/1910.

s. 30, amended: 1987, c.6, sch.4; 1988, c.7, sch.4; c.43, s.70(S.); c.50, s.121; regs. 88/458.

s. 31, regs. 88/662, 1890(S.).

s. 31, amended: 1988, c.50, sch.17.

ss. 31A–31G, added: 1988, c.41, sch.10.

s. 32, regs. 86/2173; 87/481; 88/36, 1724, 1908.

s. 32, amended: 1987, c.7, s.1; 1988, c.7, sch.3; repealed in pt.: *ibid.*, schs.3,5.

s. 33, regs. 88/35, 524.

s. 33, amended: 1988, c.7, schs.3,4; repealed in pt.: *ibid.*, sch.5.

s. 34, regs. 88/34.

s. 34, amended: *ibid.*, sch.3; repealed in pt.: *ibid.*, sch.5.

s. 39, regs. 86/1561.

s. 46, regs. 86/1960; 88/532.

ss. 46, 48, amended: 1988, c.7, sch.4.

ss. 47, 48, regs. 86/1960.

s. 49, regs. 87/235.

s. 50, regs. 86/1960.

s. 50, repealed in pt.: 1988, c.7, schs.4,5.

s. 51, regs. 86/1541, 1960, 2172, 2217; 87/372, 491, 1967, 1968, 1971, 1973; 88/522, 661, 664, 1725, 1890(S.).

s. 51, amended: 1988, c.7, sch.3; c.50, s.121; repealed in pt.: 1988, c.7, sch.5; c.41, sch.10.

ss. 51A, 51B, added: *ibid.*

s. 52, regs. 86/2218; 87/1970.

s. 52, amended: 1988, c.7, sch.3; repealed in pt.: *ibid.*, sch.5.

s. 53, regs. 86/2217; 87/491; 88/664, 688, 1725.

s. 53, amended: 1988, c.7, schs.3,4; repealed in pt.: *ibid.*, sch.5.

s. 54, regs. 86/1960, 2172; 87/1102; 88/536.

s. 56, amended: 1988, c.41, sch.10.

s. 60, regs. 87/250.

s. 61, amended: 1988, c.41, sch.10.

s. 63, orders 87/45, 1978.

s. 63, amended: regs. 88/961.

1986—cont.

50. Social Security Act 1986—cont.

s. 64, regs. 87/327; 88/436.

s. 67, regs. 87/33.

s. 74. regs. 87/413.

s. 80, regs. 87/418.

s. 83, regs 86/1960; 87/250, 491; 88/544, 664; orders 86/1609; 87/45.

s. 83, amended: 1988, c.41, sch.10.

s. 84, regs. 86/1541, 1716, 1960, 2172, 2173, 2217; 87/235, 250, 372, 406, 411, 413, 415, 416, 418, 481, 491, 914, 1100–1102, 1108, 1109, 1111, 1113, 1115–1118, 1692, 1933, 1967–1970, 1972, 1974; 88/34–36, 137, 239, 429, 458, 474, 475, 521, 522, 524, 532, 544, 660–663, 664, 670, 688, 908–910, 999, 1228, 1438, 1444, 1445, 1724, 1890(S.), 1970.

s. 84, amended: 1988, c.1, sch.29, repealed in pt.: 1988, c.7, sch.5.

s. 85, order 88/529.

s. 85, amended: 1988, c.41, sch.10.

s. 86, regs. 88/430.

s. 88, orders 86/1609, 1719, 1958, 1959; 87/354, 543, 1906, 1853; 88/567.

s. 89, regs. 86/1541, 2173, 2217, 2218; 87/33, 372, 406, 411, 415, 416, 481, 491, 914, 1109, 1692, 1854, 1969, 1970, 1972, 1974; 88/239, 429, 458, 521, 522, 544, 664, 670, 961.

sch. 1, regs. 87/1117; 88/474, 830.

sch. 3, regs. 88/544.

sch. 3, amended: 1988, c.7, sch.1; repealed in pt.: *ibid.*, schs.1,5.

sch. 4, regs. 86/1960; 87/235, 413, 430, 532.

sch. 4, amended: 1988, c.7, sch.4.

sch. 6, amended: 1988, c.1, sch.29.

sch. 7, regs. 86/2218.

sch. 10, repealed in pt.: 1987, c.6, sch.5; c.16, sch.16; 1988, c.1, sch.31; c.7, sch.5; c.34, sch.6.

51. British Council and Commonwealth Institute Superannuation Act 1986.

Royal Assent, July 25, 1986.

Commencement orders: 86/1860; 87/588.

s. 3, orders 86/1860; 87/588.

52. Dockyard Services Act 1986.

Royal Assent, July 25, 1986.

s. 1, orders 86/2243, 2244.

ss. 1, 2, see *Institution of Professional Civil Servants* v. *Secretary of State for Defence, The Times,* April 30, 1987, Millett J.

s. 3, repealed in pt.: 1987, c.4, s.7.

53. Building Societies Act 1986.

Royal Assent, July 25, 1986.

Commencement order: 86/1560.

order 87/1872.

s. 2, regs. 86/2155; 87/391.

s. 7, regs. 87/378, 1670; order 87/2131; rules 87/2133.

s. 7, amended: orders 87/378, 1670; repealed in pt.: order 87/378.

s. 8, rules 87/2133.

s. 10, order 86/2099.

s. 12, order 87/1671.

s. 14, orders 87/1498; 88/1394.

s. 15, orders 86/1877; 88/1197.

s. 15, amended: orders 87/1975; 88/1141, 1197.

CAP.

1986—cont.

53. Building Societies Act 1986—cont.
s. 16, order 88/1197.
s. 16, amended: orders 87/1975; 88/1141, 1197.
s. 17, order 87/1942.
s. 18, orders 86/1715; 87/1871, 2018; 88/23, 1196 1393.
s. 18, amended: 1987, c.22, sch.6.
s. 19, orders 87/1975; 88/1141.
s. 20, rules 87/2133; order 88/1124.
s. 20, amended: order 88/1142.
s. 21, regs. 87/1499.
s. 23, orders 86/2098; 88/1344.
s. 25, amended: 1987, c.22, sch.6; repealed in pt.: *ibid.*, schs.6, 7.
s. 27, order 87/1349.
s. 27, amended: 1987, c.22, sch.6; order 87/1349.
s. 34, orders 87/172, 1670, 1848, 1976, 2019; 88/1141.
s. 45, orders 86/1878; 88/22, 777.
s. 48, regs. 87/891.
s. 53, orders 87/1500; 88/630.
s. 53, amended: 1987, c.22, sch.6.
s. 54, repealed in pt.: *ibid.*, sch.7.
ss. 73–76, regs. 87/2072.
s. 96, regs. 86/2152; order 87/2005.
s. 98, amended: 1987, c.22, sch.6.
s. 101, amended: 1986, c.60, sch.16.
s. 102, regs. 88/1153.
ss. 102, 107, amended: 1987, c.22, sch.6.
s. 109, amended: 1988, c.39, sch.12.
s. 116, regs. 86/2155; 87/395; 88/448.
s. 121, orders 86/2168, 2169; 87/395, 426.
s. 126, order 86/1560.
sch. 1, repealed in pt.: 1987, c.39, sch.2.
sch. 4, rules 86/2216.
sch. 8, orders 86/1763; 87/1848.
sch. 8, amended: orders 87/172, 1670, 1976, 2019, 1987, c.22, sch.6; 1988, c.1, sch.29; order 88/1141; repealed in pt.: 1987, c.22, schs.6, 7.
sch. 10, order 87/723.
sch. 17, regs. 88/1153.
sch. 18, repealed in pt.: 1987, c.22, sch.24(S.); 1988, c.1, sch.31.

54. Rate Support Grants Act 1986.
Royal Assent, October 21, 1986.
ss. 1–3, sch.1, see *R. v. Secretary of State for the Environment, ex p. Greenwich London Borough Council* (1987) 27 R.V.R. 48, Taylor J.
sch. 1, repealed in pt.: 1987, c.5, s.1; c.6, sch.5.

55. Family Law Act 1986.
Royal Assent, November 7, 1986.
Commencement order: 88/375.
s. 1, Act of Sederunt 88/615.
ss. 1, 3, amended: 1987, c.42, sch.2
s. 27, rules 88/329; Acts of Sederunt 88/613, 615; S.Rs. 1988 Nos. 11, 113.
s. 28, Acts of Sederunt 88/613, 615.
s. 39, rules 88/329; S.Rs. 1988 Nos. 112, 113.
s. 42, rules 88/329.
s. 56, substituted: 1987, c.42, s.22.

CAP.

1986—cont.

55. Family Law Act 1986—cont.
s. 60, amended: *ibid.*, sch.2.
s. 64, rules 88/1328.
s. 64, repealed: 1988, c.34, schs.5,6.
s. 69, order 88/375.
sch. 1, repealed in pt.: 1988, c.36, sch.2.

56. Parliamentary Constituencies Act 1986.
Royal Assent, November 7, 1986.
s. 4, orders 87/462, 469, 937, 2050, 2208, 2209.

57. Public Trustee and Administration of Funds Act 1986.
Royal Assent, November 7, 1986.
Commencement order: 86/2261.
s. 6, order 86/2261.
sch., repealed in pt.: 1987, c.39, sch.2.

58. European Communities (Amendment) Act 1986.
Royal Assent, November 7, 1986.

59. Sex Discrimination Act 1986.
Royal Assent, November 7, 1986.
Commencement orders: 86/2313; 88/99.
s. 2, see *Duke v. Reliance Systems, The Times,* February 23, 1987, C.A.
s. 10, orders 86/2313; 88/99.

60. Financial Services Act 1986.
Royal Assent, November 7, 1986.
Commencement orders: 86/1940, 2031, 2246; 87/623, 907, 1997, 2157, 2158; 88/723, 740, 995, 1960, 2148, 2149.
s. 2, orders 88/318, 496, 803.
s. 41, regs. 87/2142.
s. 46, orders 88/350, 723.
s. 48, order 88/171; amended: *ibid.*
s. 58, orders 88/316, 716.
s. 75, orders 88/496, 803.
s. 75, amended: 1987, c.22, sch.6.
s. 81, regs. 88/280, 284.
s. 87, regs. 88/1961; order 88/2015.
s. 105, amended: 1987, c.22, sch.6.
s. 113, regs. 87/2143.
s. 114, orders 87/942; 88/738.
s. 118, orders 87/942, 2035, 2069; 88/738; S.R. 1987 No. 440.
s. 130, order 88/439.
s. 172, regs. 87/752.
s. 177, see *Inquiry under the Company Securities (Insider Dealing) Act 1985, An, Re, The Times,* January 27, 1988, Browne-Wilkinson V.-C.
s. 178, see *Inquiry under the Company Securities (Insider Dealing) Act 1985, An, Re* [1988] 2 W.L.R. 33;[1988] 1 All E.R. 203, H.L.
s. 178, order 87/942.
s. 180, orders 86/2046; 87/859, 1141; 88/1058.
s. 180, amended: 1987, c.22, sch.6.
s. 185, amended: *ibid.*; repealed in pt.: *ibid.*, sch.6.
s. 186, amended: *ibid.*, sch.6; repealed in pt.: *ibid.*, schs.6, 7.
s. 190, order 87/1905.
s. 191, orders 88/41, 724.
s. 193, repealed: 1987, c.22, sch.7.
s. 195, repealed: 1986, c.60, sch.17.
ss. 199, 201, order 87/942.
s. 205, order 88/1961.

CAP.

1986—cont.

60. Financial Services Act 1986—*cont.*
s. 206, order 87/942.
s. 207, regs. 88/1961.
s. 211, orders 86/1940, 2031, 2246; 87/623, 907, 1997, 2158; 88/740, 995, 1960, 2285.
sch. 1, amended: orders 88/318, 496, 803; repealed in pt.: orders 88/318, 496.
sch. 5, amended: 1987, c.22, sch.6.
sch. 6, rules 88/351.
sch. 11, orders 87/925, 2069; S.R. 1987 Nos. 228, 440.
sch. 13, repealed in pt.: 1987, c.22, sch.7.
sch. 15, orders 87/925, 2157; 88/2258.
sch. 15, amended: 1988, c.1, sch.29.

61. Education (No. 2) Act 1986.
Royal Assent, November 7, 1986.
Commencement orders: 86/2203; 87/344, 1159.
s. 8, regs. 87/1359.
s. 8, amended: 1988, c.40, s.116.
s. 16, regs. 87/1359.
s. 17, repealed in pt.: 1988, c.40, sch.13.
s. 18, repealed in pt.: *ibid.*, schs.12, 13.
ss. 19 (in pt.), 20, repealed: *ibid.*, sch.13.
s. 21, substituted: *ibid.*, s.115.
s. 29, repealed: *ibid.*, s.51, sch.13.
s. 30, amended: *ibid.*, s.51.
s. 36, regs. 87/1359.
s. 43, amended: 1988, c.40, sch.12.
s. 46A, added: *ibid.*
s. 47, regs. 87/1103.
ss. 47, 49, amended: 1988, c.40, sch.12.
s. 50, regs. 87/96; 88/355, 1365, 1397.
s. 54, regs. 87/34
s. 54, amended: 1988, c.40, sh.12.
s. 56, repealed in pt.: 1988, c.40, sch.13.
s. 58, amended: *ibid.*, sch.12.
s. 61, regs. 87/1160.
s. 61, amended: 1988, c.40, sch.12.
s. 62, regs. 87/1160, 1359.
s. 62, amended: 1988, c.40, sch.12.
s. 63, regs. 87/96, 1160, 1359; 88/355, 1365, 1397.
s. 65, amended: 1988, c.40, sch.12.
s. 66, orders 86/2203; 87/344, 1159.
sch. 2, regs. 87/1359.
sch. 2, amended: 1988, c.40, sch.12.
sch. 4, repealed in pt.: *ibid.*, sch.13.

62. Salmon Act 1986.
Royal Assent, November 7, 1986.
ss. 1, 2, order 88/994.
s. 3, regs. 88/390.
ss. 8, 10, regs. 88/235.

63. Housing and Planning Act 1986.
Royal Assent, November 7, 1986.
Commencement orders: 86/2262; 87/304, 348, 754, 1554, 1607 (S.), 1759, 1939, 2277; 88/283, 1787.
s. 3, repealed: 1987, c.26, sch.24.
ss. 7, 12, 13 (in pt.), 19, repealed: 1988, c.50, sch.18.
s. 42, regs. 88/1788.
s. 57, orders, 86/2262; 87/1554, 1607 (S.), 1759, 1939, 2277; 88/283, 1787.

CAP.

1986—cont.

63. Housing and Planning Act 1986—*cont.*
sch. 4, repealed in pt.: 1988, c.50, sch.18.
sch. 5, repealed in pt.: 1987, c.26, sch.24, c.50, sch.18.

64. Public Order Act 1986.
Royal Assent, November 7, 1986.
Commencement orders: 86/2041; 87/198, 852.
s. 5, see *D.P.P.* v. *Orum, The Times,* July 25, 1988, D.C.; *Lodge* v. *D.P.P., The Times,* October 26, 1988, D.C.
s. 14, see *Police* v. *Reid (Lorna)* [1987] Crim.L.R. 702, Bow Street Magistrates' Court.
ss. 34, 36, order 87/853.
s. 41, orders 86/2041; 87/198, 852.

65. Housing (Scotland) Act 1986.
Royal Assent, November 7, 1986.
Commencement order: 86/2137.
ss. 1–12, repealed: 1987, c.26, sch.24.
ss. 13 (in pt.), 14–16; repealed: 1988, c.50, sch.18.
ss. 18–21, repealed: 1987, c.26, sch.24.
s. 23, order 86/2139.
s. 26, order 86/2137.
sch. 1, repealed: 1987, c.26, sch.24.
sch. 2, repealed in pt.: *ibid.*; 1988, c.50, sch.18.

66. National Health Service (Amendment) Act 1986.
Royal Assent, November 7, 1986.
Commencement order: 87/399.
s. 1, regs. 87/2 (S.), 18.
s. 8, order 87/399.

67. Consolidated Fund (No. 2) Act 1986.
Royal Assent, December 18, 1986.
repealed: 1988, c.38, sch. (C.).

68. Advance Petroleum Revenue Tax Act 1986.
Royal Assent, December 18, 1986.

1987

1. Teachers' Pay and Conditions Act 1987.
Royal Assent, March 2, 1987.
s. 3, orders 87/650, 1433; 88/1055.
s. 3, amended: 1988, c.40, sch.12; order 88/2074.
s. 7, amended: 1988, c.40, sch.12.

2. Licensing (Restaurant Meals) Act 1987.
Royal Assent, March 2, 1987.
repealed: 1988, c.17, sch.4.

3. Coal Industry Act 1987.
Royal Assent, March 5, 1987.
s. 2, order 88/455; amended: *ibid.*
s. 3, orders 87/770; 88/456.
s. 3, amended: *ibid.*

4. Ministry of Defence Police Act 1987.
Royal Assent, March 5, 1987.
s. 1, regs. 88/1088.
s. 4, regs. 88/1099.

5. Rate Support Grants Act 1987.
Royal Assent, March 12, 1987.

6. Local Government Finance Act 1987.
Royal Assent, March 12, 1987.
ss. 13, 14, repealed (S.): 1987, c.47, sch.6.
sch. 1, amended: 1988, c.9, sch.16.

CAP.

CAP.

1987—cont.

26. Housing (Scotland) Act 1987—cont.
s. 194, repealed in pt.: 1988, c.43, schs.2, 10.
s. 196, repealed: *ibid.*, sch.10.
s. 200, amended: *ibid.*, sch.7, repealed: *ibid.*, sch.10.
s. 202, amended: *ibid.*, sch.2.
s. 204, order 88/123.
s. 207, amended: 1988, c.43, sch.9.
s. 208, amended: 1988, c.50, s.132.
s. 216, amended: 1988, c.43, sch.9.
s. 222, order 88/270.
s. 239A, added: 1988, c.43, s.2.
ss. 240, 242–244, amended: *ibid.*, sch.7.
ss. 242, 244, order 87/2269.
s. 248, amended: 1988, c.43, schs.7, 8.
s. 249, order 87/2269.
s. 254, amended: 1988, c.43, sch.7; repealed: *ibid.*, sch.10.
s. 255, order 88/10.
s. 255, amended: 1988, c.43, sch.7, 8; repealed: *ibid.*, sch.10.
s. 256A, added: *ibid.*, s.2.
s. 266, order 88/978.
s. 268, amended: 1988, c.43, sch.7.
s. 276, amended: *ibid.*, schs.2, 7.
ss. 281–283, 285, amended: *ibid.*, sch.7.
s. 296, amended: *ibid.*, sch.7; repealed: *ibid.*, sch.10.
s. 297, repealed: *ibid.*
s. 299, amended: *ibid.*, sch.7.
ss. 311, 328, amended: *ibid.*, sch.9.
s. 337, repealed: 1988, c.9, s.19, sch.7.
s. 338, amended: 1988, c.43, schs.7, 9.
sch. 3, amended: *ibid.*, sch.9.
sch. 6A, added: 1988, c.50, s.135, sch.16.
sch. 7, amended: 1988, c.43, sch.7.
sch. 10, amended: *ibid.*, sch.8.
sch. 12, repealed in pt.: *ibid.*, schs.2, 10.
schs. 13, 14, repealed in pt.: *ibid.*, sch.10.
sch. 16, repealed in pt.: *ibid.*, s.67, sch.10.
schs. 20, 24, amended: *ibid.*, sch.7.
27. Fire Safety and Safety of Places of Sport Act 1987.
Royal Assent, May 15, 1987.
Commencement orders: 87/1762; 88/485, 626(S.), 1806.
s. 31, regs. 88/1807.
s. 50, orders 87/1762; 88/485, 626(S.), 1806.
28. Deer Act 1987.
Royal Assent, May 15, 1987.
29. Agricultural Training Board Act 1987.
Royal Assent, May 15, 1987.
30. Northern Ireland (Emergency Provisions) Act 1987.
Royal Assent, May 15, 1987.
Commencement orders: 87/1241; 88/1105.
continued in force: order 88/426.
repealed in pt. (prosp.): 1987, c.30, s.26.
s. 26, orders 87/1241; 88/426, 1105.
31. Landlord and Tenant Act 1987.
Royal Assent, May 15, 1987.
Commencement orders: 87/2177; 88/480, 1283.
s. 2, amended: 1988, c.50, sch.13.

CAP.

1987—cont.

31. Landlord and Tenant Act 1987—cont.
s. 3, amended: *ibid.*; repealed in pt.: *ibid.*, schs.13, 18.
s. 4, amended: *ibid.*, sch.13; repealed in pt.: *ibid.*, sch.18.
s. 13, regs. 87/2178.
s. 20, order 88/1285.
ss. 26, 35, 40, amended: 1988, c.50, sch.13.
s. 42, order 88/1284.
s. 45, repealed: 1988, c.50, sch.18.
s. 51, repealed: 1988, c.3, sch.
s. 58, amended: 1988, c.4, sch.6; c.50, schs. 13, 17; repealed in pt. (prosp.): 1988, c.40, sch.13.
s. 60, repealed in pt.: 1988, c.50, sch.18.
s. 62, orders 87/2177; 88/480, 1283.
sch. 4, repealed in pt.: 1988, c.50, sch.18.
32. Crossbows Act 1987.
Royal Assent, May 15, 1987.
33. AIDS (Control) Act 1987.
Royal Assent, May 15, 1987.
s. 1, orders 88/117, 1047.
sch., amended: order 88/1047.
34. Motor Cycle Noise Act 1987.
Royal Assent, May 15, 1987.
sch., amended: 1987, c.43, sch.4.
35. Protection of Animals (Penalties) Act 1987.
Royal Assent, May 15, 1987.
36. Prescription (Scotland) Act 1987.
Royal Assent, May 15, 1987.
37. Access to Personal Files Act 1987.
Royal Assent, May 15, 1987.
sch. 1, amended: 1988, c.50, sch.17.
38. Criminal Justice Act 1987.
Royal Assent, May 15, 1987.
Commencement orders: 87/1061; 88/397, 1564.
see *R.* v. *Director of Serious Fraud, ex p. Saunders, The Independent*, July 29, 1988, D.C.
s. 1, regs. 88/1863.
s. 2, amended: 1988, c.33, s.143, sch.15.
s. 3, amended: *ibid.*, sch.15.
s. 4, amended: *ibid.*, s.144; c.34, sch.5.
s. 5, regs. 88/1691.
s. 5, amended: 1988, c.33, s.144.
s. 6, rules 88/1695.
s. 6, substituted: 1988, c.33, s.144.
ss. 7, 9, rules 88/1699.
s. 9, repealed in pt.: 1988, c.33, sch.16.
s. 11, amended: *ibid.*, sch.15; repealed in pt.: *ibid.*, sch.16.
s. 13, amended: *ibid.*, sch.15.
s. 16, orders 87/1061; 88/397, 1564.
sch. 1, amended: 1988, c.33, s.166, sch.15.
sch. 2, repealed in pt.: *ibid.*, sch.16; c.34, sch.6.
39. Parliamentary and Health Service Commissioners Act 1987.
Royal Assent, May 15, 1987.
40. Registered Establishments (Scotland) Act 1987.
Royal Assent, May 15, 1987.
41. Criminal Justice (Scotland) Act 1987.
Royal Assent, May 15, 1987.
Commencement orders: 87/1468, 1594, 2119; 88/482, 483, 1710.

1987—cont.

41. Criminal Justice (Scotland) Act 1987—cont.
ss. 1, 11, 16, amended: 1988, c.13, sch.5.
s. 33, amended: 1988, c.50, sch.17.
s. 34, amended: 1988, c.13, sch.5; c.50, sch.17.
s. 38, amended: 1988, c.13, sch.5.
s. 45, repealed in pt.: ibid., sch.16.
ss. 52, 54, amended: ibid., sch.15.
s. 56, order 87/2025.
s. 56, amended: 1988, c.54, sch.3.
s. 72, orders 87/1468, 1594, 2119; 88/482, 483, 1710.
sch. 1, regs. 88/1863.
sch. 1, repealed in pt.: 1988, c.54, sch.1.

42. Family Law Reform Act 1987.
Royal Assent, May 15, 1987.
Commencement order: 88/425.
ss. 1, 18, 21, see Practice Direction (Fam.D.) (Probate: Grants of Representation: Oath) [1988] 2 All E.R. 308.
s. 34, order 88/425.

43. Consumer Protection Act 1987.
Royal Assent, May 15, 1987.
Commencement orders: 87/1680, 1681, 2116; 88/802, 2041, 2076.
s. 11, regs. 87/1911, 1920, 1979, 2116; 88/802, 1324, 1647.
s 12, order 87/1681.
s. 45, amended: 1988, c.54, sch.3.
s. 50, orders 87/1680; 88/2041, 2076.

44. Local Government Act 1987.
Royal Assent, May 15, 1987.
s. 2, repealed: 1988, c.40, sch.13.

45. Parliamentary and other Pensions Act 1987.
Royal Assent, May 15, 1987.
Commencement order: 87/1311.
s. 7, order 87/1311.
sch. 3, repealed in pt.: 1988, c.1, sch.31.

46. Diplomatic and Consular Premises Act 1987.
Royal Assent, May 15, 1987.
Commencement orders: 87/1022, 2248; 88/106.
s. 2, see R. v. Secretary of State for Foreign and Commonwealth Affairs, ex p. Samuel, The Times, September 10, Henry J.
s. 2, order 88/30.
s 9, orders 87/1022, 2248; 88/106.
sch. 1, repealed in pt.: 1988, c.3, sch.8.

47. Abolition of Domestic Rates Etc. (Scotland) Act 1987.
Royal Assent, May 15, 1987.
Commencement order: 87/1489.
s. 2, regs. 87/2179; 88/1477.
s. 2, amended: 1988, c.41, sch.12; repealed in pt.: ibid., sch.13.
s. 3, regs.88/1904.
s. 3, amended: 1988, c.1, sch.29; c.41, sch.12.
s. 4, repealed in pt.: ibid., sch.13.
s. 5, regs. 88/1477.
s. 5, amended: 1988, c.41, sch.12.
s. 8, regs. 88/632.
s. 8, amended: 1988, c.41, s.129, sch.12.
s. 10, regs. 88/631, 1540.
s. 10, amended: 1988, c.41, sch.12.
s. 11, regs. 88/631.

1987—cont.

47. Abolition of Domestic Rates Etc. (Scotland) Act 1987—cont.
s. 11, amended: 1988, c.41, sch.12; repealed in pt.: ibid., sch.13.
ss. 11A, 11B, added: ibid., sch.12.
s. 13, amended: ibid.
ss. 13, 14, regs. 88/157, 1539.
s. 14, amended: 1988, c.41, sch.21; repealed in pt.: ibid.
s. 15, regs. 88/157, 1539, 1611.
s. 15, amended: 1988, c.41, sch.12
s. 16, regs. 88/157, 1539.
s. 17, regs. 88/1539
s. 17, amended: 1988, c.41, sch.12; repealed in pt.: ibid., sch.13.
s. 18, regs. 88/157, 1539.
s. 18, amended: 1988, c.41, sch.12.
s. 18A, added: ibid.
s. 20, regs. 88/157, 1539.
s. 20, amended: 1988, c.41, sch.12; repealed in pt.: ibid., sch.13.
s. 20A, regs. 88/1539.
ss. 20A, 20B, added: 1988, c.41, sch.12.
s. 20B, regs. 88/1889
s. 24, regs. 88/1483.
s. 24, amended: 1988, c.41, sch.12; repealed in pt.: ibid., sch.13.
s. 26, regs. 87/2179; 88/157, 631, 632, 1477, 1538–1540, 1880, 1889, 1904.
s. 26, amended: 1988, c.41, sch.12.
s. 30, amended: ibid.; repealed in pt.: ibid., sch.13.
s. 31, regs. 88/157, 1477, 1538–1540, 1880.
s. 32, regs. 88/1889
s. 35, order 87/1489.
sch. 1, regs. 87/2179; 88/1477.
sch. 1A, regs. 88/1541.
sch. 1A, added: 1988, c.41, sch.12.
sch. 2, amended: ibid.; repealed in pt.: ibid., sch.13.
sch. 4, amended: ibid., sch.12.
sch. 5, regs. 88/157, 631, 632, 1538–1541, 1611, 1880, 1889.
sch. 5, amended: 1988, c.41, sch.12.

48. Irish Sailors and Soldiers Land Trust Act 1987.
Royal Assent, May 15, 1987.
Commencement order: 87/1909.
s. 3, order 87/1909.

49. Territorial Sea Act 1987.
Royal Assent, May 15, 1987.
Commencement order: 87/1270.
s. 1, order 87/1269.
s. 4, order 87/1270.

50. Appropriation (No. 2) Act 1987.
Royal Assent, July 23, 1987.

51. Finance (No. 2) Act 1987.
Royal Assent, July 23, 1987.
Commencement order: 88/744.
ss. 1–63, 64 (in pt.), 65–68, 70, 71, 73 (in pt.), 74–77, repealed: 1988, c.1, sch.31.
ss. 20, 54–56, amended: 1988, c.39, s.54.
s. 56, regs. 87/1765.
s. 81, order 88/744.

CAP.

1987—cont.

51. Finance (No. 2) Act 1987—*cont.*
s. 84, amended: 1988, c.1, sch.29.
ss. 87, 88 (in pt.), 90, 92, 93, repealed: *ibid.*, sch.31.
s. 102, orders 88/93, 643.
schs. 1–5, 6 (in pt.), repealed: 1988, c.1, sch.31.
sch. 3, regs. 87/1513.

52. British Shipbuilders (Borrowing Powers) Act 1987.
Royal Assent, July 23, 1987.

53. Channel Tunnel Act 1987.
Royal Assent, July 23, 1987.
s. 33, orders 87/2068; 88/67, 68.

54. Consolidated Fund (No. 2) Act 1987.
Royal Assent, November 17, 1987.

55. Consolidated Fund (No. 3) Act 1987.
Royal Assent, December 10, 1987.

56. Scottish Development Agency Act 1987.
Royal Assent, December 17, 1987.

57. Urban Development Corporations (Financial Limits) Act 1987.
Royal Assent, December 17, 1987.

1988

1. Income and Corporation Taxes Act 1988.
Royal Assent, February 9, 1988.
Commencement orders: 88/745, 1002.
s. 1, amended: 1988, c.39, s.24; repealed in pt.: *ibid.*, s.24, sch.14.
s. 6, repealed in pt. (prosp.): *ibid.*, sch.14.
s. 15, amended: *ibid.*, sch.6; repealed in pt.: *ibid.*, sch.14.
s. 16, repealed: *ibid.*
s. 17, amended: *ibid.*, s.76.
s. 18, repealed in pt.: *ibid.*, sch.14.
s. 20, amended: *ibid.*, s.61.
s. 39, repealed in pt.: *ibid.*, s.75, sch.14.
s. 45, amended: *ibid.*, s.76.
s. 53, amended: *ibid.*, sch.6.
s. 54, repealed: *ibid.*, schs.6, 14.
s. 61, amended: *ibid.*, sch.13.
ss. 62, 63, amended: *ibid.*, sch.3.
ss. 83, 103, amended: 1988, c.48, sch.7.
ss. 123, 124, amended: 1988, c.39, s.76.
s. 127, amended: 1988, c.19, sch.3.
s. 138, repealed: 1988, c.39, s.88, sch.14.
s. 139, repealed: *ibid.*, sch.14.
s. 141, amended: *ibid.*, ss. 46, 47.
s. 142, amended: *ibid.*, s.46.
s. 152, amended: order 88/1843.
s. 155, amended: 1988, c.39, ss.46, 49.
s. 160, orders 88/757, 1279, 1622, 2186.
ss. 162, 178, amended: 1988, c.39, sch.13.
ss. 185, 186, amended: *ibid.*, s.89.
s. 188, amended: *ibid.*, s.74.
s. 189, amended: *ibid.*, s.57.
s. 202, amended: *ibid.*, s.70.
s. 203, amended: *ibid.*, s.128, sch.3.
s. 256, repealed in pt. (prosp.): *ibid.*, sch.14.
s. 257, amended: *ibid.*, s.25; substituted (prosp.): *ibid.*, s.33.

CAP.

1988—cont.

1. Income and Corporation Taxes Act 1988—*cont.*
ss. 257A–257E, added (prosp.): *ibid.*, s.33.
s. 258, repealed: *ibid.*, s.25, sch.14.
s. 259, amended: *ibid.*, s.30, sch.3, (prosp.).
s. 260, amended: *ibid.*, s.134.
s. 261, repealed in pt.: *ibid.*, sch.14; substituted (prosp.): *ibid.*, sch.3.
s. 262, substituted (prosp.): *ibid.*
ss. 263, 264, repealed: *ibid.*, s.25, sch.14.
s. 265, repealed in pt.: *ibid.*, sch.14; substituted: *ibid.*
s. 266, amended (prosp.): *ibid.*, s.29, sch.3.
s. 273, substituted (prosp.): *ibid.*, sch.3.
s. 274, amended (prosp.): *ibid.*, s.29.
s. 275, repealed: *ibid.*, sch.14.
s. 278, amended (prosp.): *ibid.*, s.31; repealed in pt. (prosp.): *ibid.*, s.31, sch.14.
s. 279, order 88/1002.
s. 279, repealed (prosp.): 1988, c.39, s.32, sch.14.
s. 280, repealed in pt.: *ibid.*; repealed (prosp.): *ibid.*
s. 281, amended: *ibid.*, s.134: repealed (prosp.): *ibid.*, sch.14.
s. 282, substituted (prosp.): *ibid.*, sch.3.
ss. 282A, 282B, added (prosp.): *ibid.*, s.34.
s. 283, repealed (prosp.): *ibid.*, sch.14.
s. 284, repealed in pt.: *ibid.*; repealed (prosp.): *ibid.*
ss. 285–288, repealed (prosp.): *ibid.*
s. 289, amended: *ibid.*, s.51; repealed in pt.: *ibid.*, sch.14.
s. 290A, added: *ibid.*, sch.3.
s. 294, amended: *ibid.*, s 52.
s. 304, amended (prosp.): *ibid.*, sch.3; repealed in pt. (prosp.): *ibid.*, schs.3, 14.
s. 311, amended: *ibid.*, s.53.
s. 313, amended: *ibid.*, s.73.
s. 315, amended: order 88/1843.
s. 318, order 88/1843.
s. 325, repealed in pt. (prosp.): 1986, c.39, sch.14.
s. 347A, added: *ibid.*, s.36.
s. 347B, added: *ibid.*; amended (prosp.): *ibid.*, sch.3; repealed in pt. (prosp.): *ibid.*, sch.14.
ss. 348 (in pt.), 349 (in pt.), 351, repealed (prosp.): *ibid.*
s. 355, amended: *ibid.*, s.44; repealed in pt.: *ibid.*, s.44, sch.14.
s. 356A, added: *ibid.*, s.42.
s. 356B, added: *ibid.*; amended (prosp.): *ibid.*, sch.3.
ss. 356C, 356D, added: *ibid.*, s.42.
s. 357, amended: *ibid.*, s.42; repealed in pt.: *ibid.*, ss.43, 44, sch.14.
s. 358, amended: *ibid.*, s.44; repealed in pt.: *ibid.*, sch.14.
s. 361, amended (prosp.): *ibid.*, sch.3; repealed in pt. (prosp.): *ibid.*, schs.3, 14.
ss. 367, 370, 373, amended: *ibid.*, s.43.
s. 376, orders 88/781, 1962.
s. 376, amended: 1988, c.50, sch.17.
s. 378, regs. 88/1347.

1988—cont.

1. Income and Corporation Taxes Act 1988—
cont.
s. 380, amended: 1988, c.39, sch.6; repealed in pt. (prosp.): *ibid.*, sch.14.
s. 382, repealed in pt. (prosp.): *ibid.*, sch.14.
ss. 383, 385, amended: *ibid.*, sch.6; repealed in pt. (prosp.): *ibid.*, sch.14.
s. 387, amended: 1988, c.48, sch.7.
s. 389, repealed in pt. (prosp.): 1988, c.39, sch.14.
s. 420, repealed in pt. (prosp.): *ibid.*, schs.3, 14.
s. 450, amended: *ibid.*, ss.58–60.
s. 451, amended: *ibid.*, s.61.
s. 452, repealed in pt.: *ibid.*, s.61, sch.14.
s. 467, amended (prosp.): *ibid.*, schs.3, 14.
s. 469, amended: *ibid.*, s.71.
s. 470, order 88/745.
s. 476, regs. 88/1011.
s. 483, order 88/2145.
s. 491, repealed in pt. (prosp.): 1988, c.39, sch.14.
ss. 505, 512, repealed in pt.: *ibid.*
ss. 525, 527, repealed in pt (prosp.): *ibid.*
s. 533, amended: *ibid.*, sch.13.
s. 535, repealed in pt. (prosp.): *ibid.*, sch.14.
s. 536, amended: 1988, c.48, sch.7.
ss. 537A, 537B, added: *ibid.*
s. 559, amended: 1988, c.39, s.28.
s. 560, amended: 1988, c.50, sch.17.
s. 574, repealed in pt. (prosp.): *ibid.*, sch.14.
s. 577, repealed in pt.: *ibid.*, s.72, sch.14.
s. 590, amended (prosp.): *ibid.*, sch.3.
s. 591, amended *ibid.*, sch.13.
s. 617, amended: 1988, c.7, sch.4.
s. 618, amended: 1988, c.39, s.54.
s. 623, repealed in pt.: *ibid.*, sch.14; (prosp.) sch. 14.
s. 628, amended (prosp.): *ibid.*, sch.3.
s. 630, amended: *ibid.*, s.55.
s. 632, order 88/993.
s. 632, amended: *ibid.*; 1988, c.39, s.54.
s. 638, regs. 88/1014.
s. 638, amended: 1988, c.39, s.55.
s. 639, regs. 88/1013.
ss. 644, 646, repealed in pt. (prosp.): 1988, c.39, sch.14.
s. 649, regs. 88/1012.
s. 655, regs. 88/1437.
s. 655, amended: 1988, c.39, s.54.
s. 683, amended (prosp.): *ibid.*, sch.3.
s. 686, amended: *ibid.*, s.55.
s. 694, amended: *ibid.*, s.24; repealed in pt.: *ibid.*, s.24, sch.14.
s. 703, repealed in pt. (prosp.): *ibid.*
s. 729, order 88/1002.
s. 765, amended: *ibid.*, s.105; repealed in pt.: *ibid.*, s.105, sch.14.
s. 767, repealed in pt.: *ibid.*, sch.14.
s. 780, repealed in pt.: *ibid.*, s.75, sch.14.
s. 788, orders 88/932, 933.
s. 810, repealed in pt. (prosp.): 1988, c.39, sch.14.
s. 821, amended: 1988, c.48, sch.7.
ss. 824, 825, orders 88/756, 1278, 1621, 2185.

1988—cont.

1. Income and Corporation Taxes Act 1988—
cont.
ss. 824, 825, amended: 1988, c.39, sch.13.
s. 832, amended: *ibid.*, s.24; repealed in pt.: *ibid.*, sch.14.
ss. 833, 835, amended (prosp.): *ibid.*, sch.3; repealed in pt. (prosp.): *ibid.*, sch.14.
s. 842, amended: *ibid.*, s.117.
sch. 2, repealed: *ibid.*, s.75, sch.14.
sch. 6, amended: *ibid.*, s.45.
sch. 9, amended: *ibid.*, s.69.
sch. 10, amended: *ibid.*, sch.13.
sch. 11, repealed in pt.: *ibid.*, s.74, sch.14.
sch. 12, amended: *ibid.*, s.67.
sch. 14, repealed in pt. (prosp.): *ibid.*, sch.14.
sch. 15, amended: *ibid.*, sch.13.
sch. 19, amended: 1988, c.48, sch.7.
sch. 19A, added: 1988, c.39, s.58.
sch. 23, regs. 88/1436.
sch. 23, amended: 1988, c.39, s.56.
sch. 25, amended: 1988, c.48, sch.7.
sch. 27, amended: 1988, c.39, sch.13.
sch. 29, amended: *ibid.*; repealed in pt.: *ibid.*, schs.13, 14; (prosp.) sch. 14; c.48, sch.8.

2. Arms Control and Disarmament (Privileges and Immunities) Act 1988.
Royal Assent, February 9, 1988.
s. 1, order 88/792.

3. Land Registration Act 1988.
Royal Assent, March 15, 1988.

4. Norfolk and Suffolk Broads Act 1988.
Royal Assent, March 15, 1988.
Commencement order: 88/955.
s. 26, sch.7, order 88/955.
sch. 6, amended: 1988, c.54, sch.6.

5. Welsh Development Agency Act 1988.
Royal Assent, March 15, 1988.

6. Consolidated Fund Act 1988.
Royal Assent, March 15, 1988.

7. Social Security Act 1988.
Royal Assent, March 15, 1988
Commencement orders: 88/520, 1226, 1857.
ss. 13, 17, regs. 88/536
s. 18, orders 88/520, 554, 1226, 1229, 1363, 1857.

8. Multilateral Investment Guarantee Agency Act 1988.
Royal Assent, March 24, 1988.
Commencement order: 88/715.
s. 9, orders 88/715, 791, 1300.

9. Local Government Act 1988.
Royal Assent, March 24, 1988.
Commencement order: 88/979.
s. 1, amended: 1988, c.43, sch.2; repealed in pt. 1988, c.40, sch.13 (prosp.); c.43, schs.2, 10.
s. 2, order 88/1372; regs. 88/1415, 1469.
s. 6, regs. 88/1371, 1413, 1468.
s. 8, regs. 88/1373, 1414, 1470.
s. 15, order 88/1372; regs. 88/1371, 1373, 1413–1415, 1468–1470.
s. 24, repealed in pt.: 1988, c.50, sch.18.
s. 26, amended: *ibid.*, s.132.
s. 32, orders 88/979, 1043(S.).

CAP.

1988—cont.

9. Local Government Act 1988—cont.
sch. 1, amended: 1988, c.40, sch.12.
sch. 2, repealed in pt.: *ibid.*, sch.13 (prosp.);
c.50, schs.2, 10.

10. Duchy of Lancaster Act 1988.
Royal Assent, May 3, 1988.

11. Regional Development Grants (Termination) Act 1988.
Royal Assent, May 3, 1988.

12. Merchant Shipping Act 1988.
Royal Assent, May 3, 1988.
Commencement orders: 88/1010, 1907.
ss. 13, 19, 21, 53, regs. 88/1926.
s. 56, order 88/1841.
s. 58, orders 88/1010, 1907.
schs. 2, 3, regs. 88/1926.

13. Coroners Act 1988.
Royal Assent, May 10, 1988.
ss. 16–18, amended: 1988, c.54, sch.3.
sch. 3, repealed in pt.: 1988, c.33, sch.16.

14. Immigration Act 1988.
Royal Assent, May 10, 1988.
Commencement order: 88/1133.
s. 5, orders 88/1134, 1203.
s. 12, order 88/1133.

15. Public Utility Transfers and Water Charges Act 1988.
Royal Assent, May 10, 1988.
Commencement order: 88/879, 1165.
s. 5, regs. 88/1048, 1288.
s. 8, orders 88/879, 1165.

16. Farm Land and Rural Development Act 1988.
Royal Assent, May 10, 1988.
s. 1, scheme, 88/1125.
s. 2, scheme 88/1291.

17. Licensing Act 1988.
Royal Assent, May 19, 1988.
Commencement orders: 88/1187, 1333.
s. 20, orders 88/1187, 1333.

18. Matrimonial Proceedings (Transfers) Act 1988.
Royal Assent, May 19, 1988.

19. Employment Act 1988.
Royal Assent, May 26, 1988.
Commencement orders: 88/1118, 2042.
s. 15, order 88/2117.
s. 26, order 88/1409.
s. 34, orders 88/1118, 2042.

20. Dartford–Thurrock Crossing Act 1988.
Royal Assent, June 28, 1988.
Commencement order: 88/1129.
s. 4, order 88/1129.
s. 17, order 88/1364.

21. Consumer Arbitration Agreements Act 1988.
Royal Assent, June 28, 1988.
Commencement orders: 88/1598, 2291.
s. 9, orders 88/1598, 2291.

22. Scotch Whisky Act 1988.
Royal Assent, June 28, 1988.

23. Motor Vehicles (Wearing of Rear Seat Belts by Children) Act 1988.
Royal Assent, June 28, 1988.
s. 1. repealed: 1988, c.54, sch.1.
s. 2, amended: *ibid.*, sch.3.
s. 3, repealed in pt.: *ibid.*, sch.1.

CAP.

1988—cont.

24. Community Health Councils (Access to Information) Act 1988.
Royal Assent, July 29, 1988.

25. Licensing (Retail Sales) Act 1988.
Royal Assent, July 29, 1988.
Commencement order: 88/1670.
s. 4, order 88/1670.

26. Landlord and Tenant Act 1988.
Royal Assent, July 29, 1988.

27. Malicious Communications Act 1988.
Royal Assent, July 29, 1988.

28. Access to Medical Reports Act 1988.
Royal Assent, July 29, 1988.

29. Protection of Animals (Amendment) Act 1988.
Royal Assent, July 29, 1988.

30. Environment and Safety Information Act 1988.
Royal Assent, July 29, 1988.

31. Protection against Cruel Tethering Act 1988.
Royal Assent, July 29, 1988.

32. Civil Evidence (Scotland) Act 1988.
Royal Assent, July 29, 1988.

33. Criminal Justice Act 1988.
Royal Assent, July 29, 1988.
Commencement orders: 88/1408, 1676, 1817(S.), 2073.
s. 37, repealed in pt.: 1988, c.54, sch.1.
s. 40, amended: *ibid.*, sch.3.
ss. 63, 68, repealed: *ibid.*, sch.1.
ss. 84, 85, amended: 1988, c.50, sch.17.
s. 138, orders 88/2242, 2247.
s. 141, order 88/2019.
s. 171, orders 88/1408, 1676, 1817(S.), 2073.
sch. 15, repealed in pt.: 1988, c.54, sch.1.

34. Legal Aid Act 1988.
Royal Assent, July 29, 1988.
Commencement orders: 88/1361, 1388(S.).
s. 47, orders 88/1361, 1388(S.).

35. British Steel Act 1988.
Royal Assent, July 29, 1988.
Commencement order: 88/1375.
s. 1, orders 88/1375, 1376.

36. Court of Session Act 1988.
Royal Assent, July 29, 1988.
s. 5, Acts of Sederunt 88/2059, 2060.
s. 5, amended: 1988, c.32, s.2.

37. Electricity (Financial Provisions) (Scotland) Act 1988.
Royal Assent, July 29, 1988.

38. Appropriation Act 1988.
Royal Assent, July 29, 1988.

39. Finance Act 1988.
Royal Assent, July 29, 1988.
Commencement order: 88/1634.
s. 1, order 88/1634.
s. 38, amended (prosp.): 1988, c.39, sch.3.
s. 40, repealed in pt. (prosp.): *ibid.*, sch.14.
sch. 6, repealed in pt.: *ibid.*
sch. 10, repealed in pt. (prosp.): *ibid.*

40. Education Reform Act 1988.
Royal Assent, July 29, 1988.
Commencement orders: 88/1459, 1794, 2002, 2271.
s. 28, regs. 88/1515.

CAP.
1988—cont.

40. Education Reform Act 1988—*cont.*
s. 46, order 88/2074.
s. 61, regs. 88/1474.
s. 73, order 88/1981.
s. 121, order 88/1799.
s. 122, orders 88/1800, 1801.
s. 126, orders 88/1799–1801.
s. 214, order 88/2035.
s. 216, orders 88/2034, 2035.
s. 232, order 88/1799.
s. 236, orders 88/1459, 1794, 2002, 2271.
sch. 7, orders 88/1799–1801.

41. Local Government Finance Act 1988.
Royal Assent, July 29, 1988.
Commencement order: 88/1456.
order 88/1456.
s. 111, repealed in pt. (prosp.): 1988, c.40, sch.13.
s. 147, orders 88/2146, 2153.
sch. 6, order 88/2146.

42. Solicitors (Scotland) Act 1988.
Royal Assent, July 29, 1988.

43. Housing (Scotland) Act 1988.
Royal Assent, November 2, 1988.
Commencement order: 88/2038.
s. 4, repealed in pt.: 1988, c.50, sch.18.
ss. 19, 36, amended: *ibid.,* sch.17.
s. 38, amended: *ibid.*; repealed in pt.: *ibid.,* schs.17, 18.
s. 63, amended: *ibid.,* sch.17.
s. 74, order 88/2038.
sch. 3, repealed: 1988, c.50, sch.18.
sch. 4, amended: *ibid.,* sch.17.
schs. 9, 10, repealed in pt.: *ibid.,* sch.18.

44. Foreign Marriage (Amendment) Act 1988.
Royal Assent, November 2, 1988.

45. Firearms (Amendment) Act 1988.
Royal Assent, November 15, 1988.
Commencement order: 88/2209.
s. 27, order 88/2209.

CAP.
1988—cont.

46. European Communities (Finance) Act 1988.
Royal Assent, November 15, 1988.

47. School Boards (Scotland) Act 1988.
Royal Assent, November 15, 1988.

48. Copyright, Designs and Patents Act 1988.
Royal Assent, November 15, 1988.

49. Health and Medicines Act 1988.
Royal Assent, November 15, 1988.
Commencement order: 88/2107.
s. 26, order 88/2107.

50. Housing Act 1988.
Royal Assent, November 15, 1988.
Commencement orders: 88/2056, 2152.
s. 141, orders 88/2056, 2152.
sch. 1, regs. 88/2236.

51. Rate Support Grant 1988.
Royal Assent, November 15, 1988.

52. Road Traffic Act 1988.
Royal Assent, November 15, 1988.
ss. 17, 19, amended (prosp.): 1988, c.54, sch.2.
s. 19A, added (prosp.): *ibid.*
ss. 46, 47, 51, 61, 67, amended (prosp.): *ibid.*
ss. 67A, 67B, added (prosp.): *ibid.*
ss. 84, 85, 122, 172, 174, amended (prosp.): *ibid.*
s. 183, amended and repealed in pt. (prosp.): *ibid.*
s. 192, amended (prosp.): *ibid.*

53. Road Traffic Offenders Act 1988.
Royal Assent, November 15, 1988.
ss. 13, 91, 95, sch.2, amended (prosp.): 1988, c.54, sch.2.

54. Road Traffic (Consequential Provisions) Act 1988.
Royal Assent, November 15, 1988.

55. Consolidated Fund (No. 2) Act 1988.
Royal Assent, December 20, 1988.

CURRENT LAW

LEGISLATION NOT YET IN FORCE TABLE

The following table alphabetically lists Statutes which have received the Royal Assent and remain on the Statute Book but which, in whole or in part, are not yet in force and for which no coming-into-force date has yet been fixed. Please note that provisions which have been prospectively repealed are not included.

This table is **up to date to December 31, 1988.** Subscribers to Current Law Monthly Digests should also consult the "Dates of Commencement" table in the most recent issue for the latest information on commencement orders.

Note: This table does not deal with Finance Acts, the commencement dates of which are usually contained within the text of the relevant Act (additional commencement orders are listed in the Dates of Commencement section of Current Law Monthly Digest).

Statute	Provisions not yet in force
Administration of Justice Act 1982 (c.53)	ss.23–25, s.27, s.28, s.73(8), s.75 (part), Sched. 2, Sched. 6, para. 10, Sched. 8, paras. 6–8; Sched. 9, Pt. I (part), Pt. II (part)
Administration of Justice Act 1985 (c.61)	ss.9–10, s.34(3), ss.40–44, s.53, s.67(1) (part), Sched. 2, Sched. 7, paras. 1–6, Sched. 8, Pt. III (part)
Agriculture Act 1970 (c.40)	Sched. 5, Pt. V (part)
Agriculture Act 1986 (c.49)	s.8(1)(3)–(6).
Animal Health and Welfare Act 1984 (c.40)	s.5(1) (part)
Banking Act 1979 (c.37)	s.51(1) (part) (2) (part), Sched. 6, paras. 8, 10, 18
British Steel Act 1988 (c.35)	s.1, ss.3–14, s.15(2), s.16, Scheds. 1–3
Building Act 1984 (c.55)	s.12 (part), s.13 (part), s.20, s.31 (part), s.33, s.38 (part), s.42(1)–(3), (4)–(6) (part), s.43(1)(2), (3) (part), s.44, s.45, s.133(2) (part), Sched. 1, para. 9, Sched. 7 (part)
Building Societies Act 1986 (c.53)	s.18 (part), s.35, ss.38–40 (part), s.90 (part), s.124, Sched. 21
Cable and Broadcasting Act 1984 (c.46)	ss.42–44, 51, 57(1) (part), Scheds. 3, 4, 5 (part)
Carriage by Air and Road Act 1979 (c.28)	s.1, s.3(1)(2)(4), s.4(1)(3), (4) (part), s.5 (part), s.6(1)(a)(c), (2)–(4), s.7, Sched. 1, 2
Carriage of Passengers by Road Act 1974 (c.35)	ss.1–6

Legislation not yet in force table

Statute	Provisions not yet in force
Child Care Act 1980 (c.5)	s.20
Children Act 1975 (c.72)	s.70, Sched. 3, para. 71, para. 74(*b*) (part), Sched. 4, Pt. VII (part)
Children and Young Persons Act 1969 (c.54)	s.4, s.5(1)–(7), (9) (part), s.8, Sched. 4, paras. 2, 3, 5(1)
Children's Homes Act 1982 (c.20)	All provisions
Civil Evidence Act 1968 (c.64)	ss.1–10 (in relation to bankruptcy proceedings)
Civil Evidence Act 1972 (c.30)	s.1 (part), s.4(2)–(5) (part)
Civil Evidence (Scotland) Act 1988 (c.32)	All provisions
Consumer Arbitration Agreements Act 1988 (c.21)	All provisions
Contempt of Court Act 1981 (c.49)	s.21(2)
Control of Pollution Act 1974 (c.40)	s.1, s.12(10), s.28 (part), s.33, s.34(3), s.38(3)–(5), s.39(3)(6)–(8) (part), s.45, s.46(1)–(3)(8), s.47, s.48, s.52, Sched. 3, paras. 7, 30, Sched. 4 (part)
Co-operative Development Agency and Industrial Development Act 1984 (c.57)	Sched. 2, Part II
Credit Unions Act 1979 (c.34)	s.3(2), (3)
Criminal Justice Act 1972 (c.71)	s.49, Sched. 6 (part)
Criminal Justice Act 1982 (c.48)	Sched. 16 (part)
Criminal Justice Act 1988 (c.33)	ss.1–32, s.35, s.36, s.43, s.50, ss.60–62, s.65, ss.71–95, ss.98–102, s.103(1) (part), (2), ss.108–120, s.130, s.146, ss.150–154, s.159, s.170(1) (part), (2) (part), Scheds. 1–7, 9, 13, 14, 15 (part), 16 (part)
Criminal Procedure (Scotland) Act 1975 (c.21)	s.23, s.214, s.329, s.423
Crofters (Scotland) Act 1961 (c.58)	s.12
Dartford-Thurrock Crossing Act 1988 (c.20)	All provisions
Disabled Persons (Services, Consultation and Representation) Act 1986 (c.33)	ss.1–3, s.4 (part), s.7, s.8 (part), s.11, s.12 (part), s.13 (part), s.14 (part), s.15
Docks and Harbours Act 1966 (c.28)	s.1 (part), Sched. 1 (part)

598

Statute	Provisions not yet in force
Dock Work Regulation Act 1976 (c.79)	s.2, s.4(6)–(8), s.5(4) (part), ss.7–10, s.11(2)(*b*), (3)–(15), s.14, s.16(2) (part), (3), s.17(4), Sched. 2, Scheds. 4–6
Education Reform Act 1988 (c.40)	s.5, s.7, s.10(2), s.12, s.16, s.23(2), s.24, s.26 (part), s.27(4)–(8) (part), (9) (part), s.28 (part), s.29, s.31(1) (part), (2) (part), (3)–(6), s.32 (part), s.115, s.152, ss.209–211, s.219 (part), s.237(1) (part), Scheds. 1, 7, 9, 10, Sched. 12, paras. 1–39, 54–59, 61–63, 65–67, 69–79, 86–101, 103–107, Sched. 13, Pt. II (part)
Employment Act 1988 (c.19)	s.33 (part)
Employment and Training Act 1973 (c.50)	s.9(3)(4)
Employment of Children Act 1973 (c.24)	All provisions
Energy Act 1983 (c.25)	Sched. 4, Part I (part)
Estate Agents Act 1979 (c.38)	s.16, s.17, s.19, s.22
European Communities Act 1972 (c.68)	Sched. 3, Part II (part)
Family Law Act 1986 (c.55)	Sched. 1, para. 10(3)
Family Law Reform Act 1987 (c.42)	ss.2–17, s.23, s.25, s.30, s.32, s.33 (part), Sched. 1, Sched. 2 (part), Sched. 3 (part), Sched. 4 (part)
Financial Services Act 1986 (c.60)	s.12, s.20, s.24 (part), s.37 (part), s.39 (part), s.40, s.53 (part), s.57 (part), s.58 (part), s.86 (part), s.96, s.123 (part), s.125 (part), ss.142–153, ss.155–159, s.160 (part), s.161, s.162 (part), ss.163–168, s.170 (part), s.171, s.174 (part), s.193, s.196, s 206 (part), s.212 (part), s.213 (part), Scheds. 1 (part), 6, 11 (part), 14 (part), 16 (part), 17 (part)
Fire Precautions Act 1971 (c.40)	s.3, s.4, s.12(2), (9), (11), (12), s.16(1)(*b*), (2)(*b*), s.19(3)(*c*), s.34, s.36, s.40 (part)
Fire Safety and Safety of Places of Sport Act 1987 (c.27)	ss.1–2, ss.5–7, s.10, s.15, s.16 (part), s.18 (part), s.47, s.49 (part), Scheds. 1 (part), 4 (part), 5 (part)
Guard Dogs Act 1975 (c.50)	ss.2–4, s.5 (part), s.6
Health and Medicines Act 1988 (c.49)	s.8, s.9, s.11(1)–(6)(8), ss.12–14, s.25(1) (part), (2) (part), Sched. 2, paras. (1) (part), 3–5, 8, 9 (part), 10–12, 15, Sched. 3 (part)
Health and Safety at Work etc. Act 1974 (c.37)	Sched. 10 (part)
Health and Social Security Act 1984 (c.48)	s.7(1)(3), Sched. 8 (part)
Health and Social Services and Social Security Adjudications Act 1983 (c.41)	s.21, s.22, s.24, Sched. 10, Part I (part)

Legislation not yet in force table

Statute	Provisions not yet in force
Horse Race (Totalisator and Betting Levy Board) Act 1972 (c.69)	s.3
Hospital Complaints Procedure Act 1985 (c.42)	All provisions
Housing Act 1980 (c.51)	s.141 (part), Sched. 6, Sched. 21, para. 7, Sched. 26 (part)
Housing Act 1988 (c.50)	ss.1–45, s.46(3)–(5), s.47(1)(3), (6) (part), ss.48–59, ss.93–131, ss.135–137, s.140(1) (part), Scheds. 1–4, 6–16, Sched. 17, paras. 1–90, 97, 103, 106–113
Housing and Planning Act 1986 (c.63)	s.5, s.7, s.8, s.18 (part), s.24 (part), ss.27–38, s.41(3), s.43, s.53, Sched. 2, Sched. 4, para. 10, Sched. 5, paras. 9, 16, 18–20, 27, 29, 31, 34–38, 40, Sched. 7, Sched. 10, Pt. II, Sched. 11, paras. 19, 39, 40, 57, 58, Sched. 12, Pt. I (part), Pt. III (part), Pt. IV (part)
Immigration Act 1988 (c.14)	s.7(1), Sched., para. 1
Land Registration Act 1988 (c.3)	All provisions
Land Registration (Scotland) Act 1979 (c.33)	s.2(1)(2) (part), s.3(3) (part)
Landlord and Tenant Act 1987 (c.31)	s.61 (part), Sched. 5
Law Reform (Miscellaneous Provisions) (Scotland) Act 1985 (c.73)	Sched. 2 (part)
Legal Aid Act 1974 (c.4)	s.16, s.26, Sched. 1, paras. 1(c), 4
Legal Aid Act 1982 (c.44)	s.11(1), s.12(2), s.12(3)(b), s.13
Legal Aid Act 1988 (c.34)	s.1, s.2, s.3(2)–(4), ss.4–34, ss.36–43, s.44 (in part), s.45, Sched. 2, Sched. 3, Sched. 4, para. 3, para. 10, Sched. 5, Sched. 6, Sched. 7, paras. 1–5, 9–11, Sched. 8
Legal Aid (Scotland) Act 1967 (c.43)	s.7(4)–(7)
Legal Aid (Scotland) Act 1986 (c.47)	ss.26–28, 30
Licensing Act 1988 (c.17)	Sched. 3, paras. 2, 8 (part), 10, 16–18, Sched. 4, (in part)
Litter Act 1983 (c.35)	s.4, Sched. 2 (part)
Local Government Finance Act 1988 (c.41)	Sched. 12, paras. 7, 11–13, Sched. 13, Pt. IV (part)
Local Government (Miscellaneous Provisions) (Scotland) Act 1981 (c.23)	s.37, Sched. 4 (part)

Legislation not yet in force table

Statute	Provisions not yet in force
Maintenance Orders (Reciprocal Enforcement) Act 1972 (c.18)	s.22(2)
Matrimonial and Family Proceedings Act 1984 (c.42)	ss.28–31, s.40, s.41, Sched. 1, para. 1 (part), paras. 14, 19(a), 20(a), Sched. 2, para. 3, Sched. 3 (part)
Medicines Act 1968 (c.67)	Sched. 5, paras. 16, 17, Sched. 6 (part)
Merchant Shipping Act 1970 (c.36)	s.6, s.36, s.51, s.87, s.95(2), (3), Sched. 2, Pt. I, paras. 3–5, Sched. 4, paras. 5–7, para. 10
Merchant Shipping Act 1974 (c.43)	s.12, s.13, s.24(4), Sched. 2, paras. 3, 4, Sched. 3
Merchant Shipping Act 1979 (c.39)	s.14(3)(7), s.15(3), s.23(1)–(6), s.24, s.25, s.35(1) (part), (2) (part), s.37(6), s.38(4), s.51(2) (part), Sched. 2, para. 13(1)(2)
Merchant Shipping Act 1983 (c.13)	ss.1–4, 9 (part)
Merchant Shipping Act 1988 (c.12)	ss.1–10, ss.12–25, s.34, s.48 (part), s.52, s.54, s.57(4)(part), (5) (part), s.58(4) (part), Sched. 1, Sched. 2, Sched. 3, Sched. 4, Sched. 5 (part), Sched. 6 (part), Sched. 7 (part), Sched. 8 (part)
Motor Cycle Noise Act 1987 (c.34)	All provisions
Motor Vehicles (Wearing of Rear Seat Belts by Children) Act 1988 (c.23)	s.1
National Health Service Act 1966 (c.8)	s.10
National Health Service (Amendment) Act 1986 (c.66)	ss.4, 5 (to the extent that it inserts s.13B of the National Health Service (Scotland) Act 1978 into that Act)
Northern Ireland (Emergency Provisions) Act 1987 (c.30)	s.12
Nuclear Material (Offences) Act 1983 (c.18)	All provisions
Nurses, Midwives and Health Visitors Act 1979 (c.36)	s.18
Offices, Shops and Railway Premises Act 1963 (c.41)	ss.4–19, s.23, s.42(1)–(7), s.43(1)–(5), s.44, s.46, s.63, s.69, ss.72–75, s.76, s.78, s.80, s.82, s.83, s.84, s.90, s.91, Sched. 2 (all in relation to covered market places only)
Oil and Gas (Enterprise) Act 1982 (c.23)	s.26, s.37(part), Sched. 3, paras. 24, 25, 35–36, 38, 40–41, Sched. 4 (part)
Outer Space Act 1986 (c.38)	All provisions

Legislation not yet in force table

Statute	Provisions not yet in force
Parliamentary and other Pensions Act 1987 (c.45)	All provisions except s.4(1)(3)
Patents Act 1977 (c.37)	s.53(1), s.60(4), ss.86–88
Patents, Designs and Marks Act 1986 (c.39)	s.1 (part), s.3 (part), Sched. 1, paras. 3, 4, Sched. 3, Pt. I (part)
Police Act 1969 (c.63)	s.3
Police and Criminal Evidence Act 1984 (c.60)	s.37(11)–(14), s.60(1)(*b*), (2)
Ports (Finance) Act 1985 (c.30)	Sched.
Powers of Criminal Courts Act 1973 (c.62)	s.6(3)(*b*), (6)(*b*), (10)
Prosecution of Offences Act 1985 (c.23)	Sched. 1, para. 11, Sched. 2 (part)
Public Service Vehicles (Arrest of Offenders) Act 1975 (c.53)	s.1 (part)
Rates Act 1984 (c.33)	s.10, s.11, Sched. 1, paras. 5, 6
Representation of the People Act 1985 (c.50)	ss.1–4, s.12 (part), s.19(1)–(5), (6)(*b*)(*c*), Sched. 1, Sched. 4, para. 34 (part), 5 (part)
Road Traffic Act 1960 (c.16)	s.266
Road Traffic Act 1974 (c.50)	s.7(1) (part), s.7(2), Sched. 6, paras. 13, 21, 24, Sched. 7 (part)
Road Traffic Regulation Act 1984 (c.27)	Sched. 8, para. 3
Roads (Scotland) Act 1984 (c.54)	ss.36–40
Safety at Sea Act 1986 (c.23)	ss.1–9, 12, 13, 14(1), (4) (part)
Salmon Act 1986 (c.62)	s.21
Science and Technology Act 1965 (c.4)	Sched. 4 (part)
Scotch Whisky Act 1988 (c.22)	ss.1–3, s.5
Sea Fisheries Act 1968 (c.77)	Sched. 2, Pt. II (part)
Social Security Act 1973 (c.38)	s.51(1)(2)(8)(9), s.69(7), s.86 (part), s.92(1)(5)–(7), Sched. 27, paras. 24 (part), 64 (part), 78 (part), 80 (part), 85, 88, Sched. 28 (part)
Social Security Act 1980 (c.30)	Sched. 1, Pt. I, para. 5 (part)

Legislation not yet in force table

Statute	Provisions not yet in force
Social Security Act 1985 (c.53)	Sched. 2 (part), Sched. 5, para. 35
Social Security Act 1986 (c.50)	s.30 (part), s.37, s.45, s.46 (part), s.49 (part), s.61, ss.63–64, s.65 (part), s.67 (part), s.70, s.71 (part), s.72 (part), s.74, s.76, s.79 (part), s.80 (part), s.81, ss.83–85, s.86 (part), Scheds. 3 (part), 4 (part), 5 (part), 7 (part), 10 (part), 11 (part)
Social Security Act 1988 (c.7)	s.1, s.2(3), s.5, s.8, s.10, s.12, s.15, s.16(1) (part), (2) (part), Sched. 4, paras. 4, 6–10, 11 (part), 12, 13, 19, 22, 26–28, Sched. 5 (part)
Social Security and Housing Benefits Act 1982 (c.24)	Sched. 5 (part)
Telecommunications Act 1984 (c.12)	s.96, Sched. 7, Pt. III
Transport Act 1968 (c.73)	s.81, s.82(1)–(3), (6) (part), s.83, s.91 (part), s.92 (part), s.99(1)–(9) (part), (10)
Transport Act 1981 (c.56)	Sched. 12, Pt. III (part)
Transport Act 1982 (c.49)	ss.8–15, ss.17–26, s.39, s.66, s.72(a), Sched. 2, Sched. 5, paras. 5, 7–9, 10(a), 11, 12, 14–17, 20–24
Transport Act 1985 (c.67)	s.139(3) (part), Sched. 8 (part)
Universities (Scotland) Act 1966 (c.13)	s.17(2) (part)
Unsolicited Goods and Services (Amendment) Act 1975 (c.13)	s.1 (part), s.2(1)
Vehicle and Driving Licences Act 1969 (c.27)	s.2(8) (part), Sched. 3 (part)
Water Act 1981 (c.12)	s.2
Water Act 1983 (c.23)	Sched. 5, Pt. I (part)
Weights and Measures Act 1985 (c.73)	s.43

TABLE OF STATUTORY INSTRUMENTS AFFECTED
1947–1988

This table lists all amendments and revocations to post-1946 Statutory Instruments effected by subsequent Statutory Instruments.

The first entry under 1947, for example, shows that S.I. No. 1 of 1947 was amended by S.I. No. 641 of 1977. Brief digests of Statutory Instruments are contained in Current Law Year Books.

1947

1 amended 77/641
31 revoked 80/804
138 revoked 64/639
145 revoked 61/1214
165 revoked 59/298
184 amended 86/2312
187 amended 59/1331
195 revoked 62/640
248 revoked 65/1776
486 revoked 65/1776
493 amended 60/159; 61/158
567 amended 65/1049; 67/143
568 revoked 65/294
579 amended 65/1097
580 amended 65/1152
612 revoked 59/734
656 revoked 61/139
661 amended 68/254
749 revoked 61/2307
772 revoked 59/2238
806 revoked 68/305
845 revoked 67/136
865 revoked 68/780
871 revoked 86/1755
885 amended 68/917
931 amended 60/62; 65/688
988 revoked 65/1776
1026 revoked 67/364
1047 revoked 62/1939
1048 revoked 62/467
1065 revoked 87/1758
1093 revoked 64/1771
1134 revoked 59/2106
1148 revoked 64/1467
1149 amended 62/2143; 64/171; 71/538
1170 revoked 59/377
1176 revoked 86/1755
1189 amended 61/2107; 80/1940; 88/1492
1245 revoked 69/793
1354 revoked 77/549
1355 revoked 64/709
1358 amended 70/1831
1426 amended 59/1788; 63/1102; 63/2150; 64/2006; 65/78; 67/790
1433 revoked 88/1664
1443 amended 68/570; 70/1945; revoked 86/1951
1486 revoked 62/1874
1490 revoked 61/281
1513 revoked 62/546
1531 amended 64/572
1562 amended 59/1541; 61/565; 62/79; 63/216
1594 revoked 59/1919
1597 revoked 63/660
1608 revoked 61/1841
1622 revoked 66/579
1659 amended 86/390

1947—*cont.*

1675 revoked 69/793
1697 revoked 70/1307
1731 revoked 87/801
1733 revoked 77/1689
1742 amended 61/801; 61/1530; revoked 84/108
1750 amended 68/1780
1755 amended 67/949; 80/362
1774 amended 68/1097
1792 revoked 70/1215
1829 revoked 64/903
1920 revoked 65/1776
1938 amended 69/1462
2034 amended 79/1660
2037 revoked 79/1331
2040 revoked 66/438
2042 revoked 61/276
2043 amended 63/1050; 63/1924; 63/2091
2045 revoked 77/1938
2049 revoked 79/1331
2050 revoked 71/516
2051 revoked 79/1333
2080 revoked 59/61
2161 amended 82/877
2177 revoked 64/1895
2192 amended 64/489
2214 amended 59/2204; 61/335; 61/995; 62/404; 62/634; 62/1336; 62/1872; 64/1656
2243 revoked 71/128
2244 revoked 70/1738
2248 amended 63/1641
2275 amended 84/108
2304 revoked 87/1758
2313 amended 70/1216
2439 amended 61/1983
2441 amended 69/1330
2499 revoked 59/1915
2501 revoked 59/529
2515 revoked 75/60
2530 revoked 65/1776
2547 amended 62/2543; 71/259
2576 amended 64/1974
2600 amended 86/2312
2652 revoked 62/1595
2662 amended 63/684; 74/595
2691 revoked 61/276
2722 revoked 61/2307
2737 revoked 75/60
2741 revoked 61/1189
2855 revoked 61/258
2863 revoked 61/2315
2865 amended 68/1096
2866 amended 68/573
2867 amended 68/1099
2869 amended 68/576
2873 amended 68/1104
2874 amended 68/578

STATUTORY INSTRUMENTS AFFECTED 1947–1988

1948—*cont.*
1451 revoked 72/827
1452 revoked 72/828
1453 revoked 67/1102
1454 revoked 66/1066
1456 revoked 72/1433
1462 revoked 78/425
1466 amended 71/1419
1467 revoked 67/386
1469 revoked 75/469
1470 revoked 73/693
1471 revoked 75/470
1475 amended 60/772; 74/188
1480 revoked 61/543
1488 amended 69/1774
1494 revoked 69/1612
1505 revoked 74/284
1506 amended 66/756; 71/1684; 73/1200
1531 revoked 62/2756
1547 amended 81/917
1551 revoked 60/2178
1559 revoked 70/1307
1564 amended 61/203; 63/777; 65/284
1579 revoked 59/748
1589 revoked 80/326
1592 revoked 73/482
1596 amended 69/1641; 74/521
1609 revoked 75/60
1613 revoked 60/695
1643 revoked 59/1
1663 revoked 67/560
1674 revoked 60/1794
1677 revoked 74/548
1681 revoked 67/1928
1687 revoked 81/1155
1691 revoked 65/321
1716 amended 74/433
1721 amended 72/1069
1727 revoked 60/1347
1739 revoked 62/1924
1741 revoked 67/190
1766 revoked 64/1382
1767 revoked 65/1453
1768 amended 71/1833; 73/1219
1781 revoked 75/1204
1794 revoked 63/934
1801 amended 61/158
1831 revoked 60/1338
1842 amended 64/57
1844 amended 76/225
1875 amended 70/684
1880 revoked 65/1776
1888 amended 79/1087
1907 amended 60/1875
1932 revoked 65/1666
1938 revoked 61/1865
1943 amended 78/444; 85/1829
1949 revoked 86/214
1954 revoked 86/214
2026 revoked 61/865
2038 revoked 69/1611
2045 revoked 65/1681
2061 revoked 60/2202
2062 revoked 63/791
2064 revoked 59/105
2066 revoked 61/2274
2092 revoked 87/856
2093 revoked 87/857
2094 revoked 87/858
2096 amended 68/434

1948—*cont.*
2132 revoked 73/1311
2146 revoked 64/1895
2162 amended 65/868
2188 revoked 71/1894
2222 revoked 80/545
2223 revoked 77/1443
2231 revoked 74/1910
2233 amended 68/1779
2282 amended 75/663
2324 revoked 68/1480
2333 revoked 62/62
2340 revoked 66/1218
2350 revoked 77/2150
2355 revoked 65/540
2361 amended 59/42; 63/1068; 63/1108; 65/1769
2372 revoked 66/95
2391 amended 71/307
2399 amended 63/260
2422 revoked 61/276
2434 amended 65/1159
2462 amended 67/1036
2471 revoked 66/579
2517 revoked 68/1624
2523 revoked 59/552
2530 revoked 60/1410
2571 revoked 67/364
2573 amended 62/400; 64/1397; 72/668; 73/598;
        75/1706; 76/52; 77/423; 85/444
2581 revoked 67/488
2595 revoked 69/1622
2600 revoked 70/150
2664 revoked 61/248
2677 amended   63/2115;   69/1137;   74/1962;
        75/1777;   76/1992;   80/592;   81/1737;
        82/1813
2687 amended 62/1270; 65/40
2704 revoked 61/2307
2711 revoked 72/604
2713 revoked 59/258
2721 revoked 65/1753
2723 revoked 59/467
2763 revoked 65/1681
2748 amended 75/1135; 76/1431
2768 amended 75/1135; 76/1431; 77/953
2770 amended 61/597; 77/1353
2771 amended 68/1585
2774 amended 64/1085; 67/1130; 81/1142
2791 revoked 60/1052
2792 amended 76/1774; 83/141
2801 revoked 53/287
2802 revoked 62/2756
2817 amended 79/199
2821 amended 77/2195
2837 revoked 74/2136
2845 revoked 62/2125

1949
  35 amended 86/2312
  74 revoked 75/677
  86 revoked 72/555
 104 revoked 62/1371
 137 revoked 63/85
 140 revoked 65/1864
 168 revoked 72/1693
 189 revoked 61/1345
 221 revoked 61/1754
 247 amended 60/2044; 64/584
 253 revoked 61/1465
 277 revoked 65/384

607

STATUTORY INSTRUMENTS AFFECTED 1947–1988

1655 revoked 65/762
1656 revoked 62/1405
1658 amended 59/378
1660 revoked 61/2307
1668 revoked 69/1622
1697 revoked 59/467
1718 revoked 60/1688
1762 revoked 62/1561
1774 revoked 68/562
1794 revoked 64/1702
1815 amended 59/1426
1816 amended 79/1254; 79/1641
1831 revoked 61/836
1832 revoked 60/972
1836 revoked 81/233
1847 revoked 60/1777
1852 revoked 64/2058
1853 revoked 64/2985
1857 amended 59/2024
1858 revoked 63/572
1879 amended 61/2399
1884 amended 82/1188
1885 amended 80/1005; 82/1182
1888 revoked 76/820
1897 revoked 77/402
1905 revoked 64/466
1912 amended 69/1155
1945 revoked 75/308
1981 revoked 67/520
1983 revoked 67/330
1984 revoked 70/1981
1989 revoked 70/1307
2007 amended 59/2180
2025 revoked 62/787
2033 revoked 84/108
2042 revoked 71/516
2058 revoked 70/16
2059 revoked 66/1541
2060 revoked 66/1548
2102 revoked 61/281
2105 amended 59/1340; 62/1614
2115 revoked 67/364
2120 amended 68/542
2121 revoked 67/1114
2139 revoked 75/849
2140 revoked 75/849
2145 amended 74/70
2146 revoked 67/1104
2147 amended 74/70
2161 revoked 85/930
2163 revoked 65/376
2166 revoked 67/1180
2167 amended 68/548
2168 amended 59/715
2189 revoked 72/2003
2191 revoked 61/2274
2192 revoked 61/2274
2197 amended 68/1868
2198 amended 70/953
2199 amended 69/380
2224 amended 83/977
2225 amended 81/1332
2230 revoked 59/1262
2239 revoked 71/2124
2247 revoked 62/1562
2252 revoked 70/1853
2259 amended 68/1366
2275 revoked 71/1095
2285 amended 75/1696; 76/1461; 77/1836

2292 amended 72/1979
2309 amended 66/839
2315 revoked 75/182
2318 revoked 70/1981
2328 amended 69/1601
2360 amended 59/591
2368 amended   59/1924;   61/1184;   62/2729;
          64/229;   64/1336;   65/1551;   67/393;
          71/262; 74/86; 74/2043; 75/890; 75/1440;
          78/907; 78/1151; 80/96; 80/1794; 81/71;
          revoked 84/1989
2369 amended 70/1147
2393 amended 59/733
2397 revoked 59/504
2399 revoked 65/1776
2401 revoked 59/525
2404 amended 77/2195
2413 revoked 74/519
2414 revoked 68/2049
2419 revoked 59/529
2423 amended 74/271
2441 amended 77/537
2452 amended 62/2320
2455 revoked 59/1866

1950
  16 revoked 65/443
  21 amended 61/2418
  36 revoked 75/60
  37 amended 59/552; 60/494; 60/623; 60/644
  51 revoked 65/904
  65 amended 63/879; 80/1248; 82/877
  69 revoked 62/549
  76 revoked 60/473
  80 revoked 59/479
 123 revoked 84/455
 142 revoked 59/394
 145 revoked 68/72
 152 revoked 63/1142
 189 revoked 68/97
 198 revoked 68/1181
 211 revoked 65/1000
 216 revoked 70/260
 228 revoked 78/1326
 283 revoked 66/1163
 330 revoked 69/1696
 332 revoked 60/1775
 333 revoked 63/1026
 346 revoked 59/479
 359 amended 71/936
 364 revoked 66/1143
 376 amended 68/748; 71/914; 77/1452
 378 revoked 67/364
 388 amended 59/2327
 391 revoked 70/16
 392 revoked 72/1940
 409 revoked 60/1542
 410 amended 60/1542
 411 revoked 87/1758
 425 amended 64/790
 430 amended 70/1075
 453 revoked 62/1003
 458 revoked 70/529
 478 revoked 67/212
 479 revoked 74/778
 497 amended 80/362
 510 revoked 61/1192
 512 revoked 60/975
 515 revoked 74/1261

STATUTORY INSTRUMENTS AFFECTED 1947–1988

521 revoked 60/974
531 revoked 81/1155
533 amended 68/1408; 80/6; 82/136; revoked 83/224
534 revoked 64/1382
572 revoked 65/1776
579 revoked 88/957
590 revoked 61/2307
593 amended 65/1730
594 revoked 68/1997; 68/2052
601 amended 60/623
610 amended 70/1831
619 revoked 61/814
627 revoked 61/427
637 revoked 60/2320
643 revoked 68/1408
673 revoked 62/2786
677 revoked 66/507
687 revoked 78/1848
692 revoked 75/1803
718 revoked 59/1241
728 revoked 63/709
741 revoked 65/1201
742 amended 71/915
748 amended 68/574; 74/1270
749 amended 68/308
750 amended 68/309
765 revoked 72/555
718 revoked 62/2756
752 revoked 67/1925
786 amended 61/2399
804 revoked 78/1093
820 revoked 70/1464
824 revoked 62/62
826 revoked 75/182
827 revoked 70/1792
830 revoked 72/555
836 revoked 64/1848
838 revoked 87/1273
839 amended 87/1273
840 amended 62/2852; 72/752; 88/1758
842 revoked 71/746
861 amended 60/241
862 revoked 72/982
896 amended 60/1047; 61/2101; revoked 83/156
914 revoked 62/1562
942 revoked 75/679
947 revoked 68/711
948 amended 59/1239; 59/2276; 64/1420
964 revoked 87/1758
980 amended 76/1234
984 revoked 70/189
1021 revoked 60/2406
1023 revoked 59/2099
1031 amended 63/793
1042 amended 60/466; revoked 66/1189
1050 revoked 67/1928
1066 amended 59/2245; 63/968; 70/675
1073 revoked 61/276
1108 revoked 61/1895
1119 revoked 65/1588
1120 amended 82/915
1131 revoked 63/708
1133 revoked 73/1165
1136 revoked 65/1681
1142 revoked 63/934
1162 amended 66/602
1172 revoked 78/1614

1183 amended 61/999; 62/635; 62/2182; 63/884; 63/1926; 64/918
1184 amended 64/1397; 72/668; 75/1706; 76/52; 77/423; revoked 85/444
1186 revoked 62/640
1195 amended 69/1068; 73/1326
1220 amended 74/1243
1222 revoked 88/551
1224 revoked 60/1792
1231 amended 64/1974; 74/1354; 75/1345
1239 revoked 64/1289
1250 revoked 69/912
1251 revoked 74/486
1254 revoked 69/904
1255 revoked 69/905
1258 amended 74/486
1259 revoked 66/569
1268 revoked 60/442
1272 revoked 70/189
1275 amended 60/503
1284 revoked 73/1311
1286 revoked 84/463
1298 revoked 75/849
1287 amended 78/583
1300 revoked 83/1718
1304 revoked 82/1419
1326 amended 62/622; 66/828; 77/1695; 80/1238
1327 revoked 64/32
1343 revoked 63/1972
1351 revoked 74/529
1358 revoked 60/1471
1359 revoked 60/408
1368 revoked 59/637
1386 amended 74/215; 74/219; 79/1085; 80/1320; 80/1330; 81/166
1416 revoked 59/1
1435 revoked 66/579
1442 amended 67/1063
1468 revoked 72/1433
1474 revoked 61/2328
1483 revoked 70/16
1500 amended 63/1159
1514 amended 59/1244
1517 amended 66/312
1524 amended 62/1047
1533 amended 61/98; 62/2550
1539 revoked 72/1693
1544 revoked 69/1654
1555 amended 65/2091
1556 revoked 61/1087
1560 amended 73/995
1565 revoked 59/467
1579 revoked 67/1186
1595 revoked 63/38
1596 revoked 68/752
1603 revoked 74/507
1643 amended 60/1372; 61/2464
1645 revoked 60/1060
1650 amended 73/1759; 83/609
1695 amended 82/224
1681 amended 72/1979
1724 amended 78/583
1725 amended 79/973
1731 amended 59/347
1747 revoked 74/312
1753 revoked 62/1562
1754 revoked 59/308
1768 revoked 59/1262
1794 revoked 74/529

  1807 revoked 60/723
  1818 revoked 60/1777
  1837 revoked 86/2312
  1847 amended 63/866
  1850 revoked 62/1319; 76/856
  1867 revoked 65/899
  1908 revoked 64/1107
  1915 amended 60/1210
  1941 revoked 65/1776
  1945 revoked 74/504
  1947 revoked 69/1696
  1968 revoked 61/2323
  1977 amended 68/306
  1979 revoked 67/1925
  1987 revoked 78/1739
  1993 amended 64/353; 64/1974; 71/836; 75/1345;
       75/2040
  1999 revoked 60/2144
  2005 revoked 64/1150
  2006 revoked 64/1151
  2007 revoked 64/1151
  2028 revoked 60/1175
  2032 revoked 66/184
  2035 amended 80/1895
  2071 revoked 66/1151
  2097 revoked 65/1530
  2108 revoked 63/1026
  2136 revoked 59/1901
  2140 amended 59/786
  2144 amended 78/117; 80/1727

1951
    34 revoked 82/545
    55 revoked 63/572
    67 revoked 59/734
    69 revoked 66/579
    71 revoked 62/271
    78 revoked 61/139
   135 revoked 60/1708
   141 revoked 70/260
   144 revoked 64/489
   146 revoked 59/377
   149 amended 60/494
   165 revoked 72/828
   185 revoked 66/579
   187 amended 60/2278
   207 amended 59/506; 60/2172; 63/186; 64/418;
       68/1543; 70/927
   209 amended 76/241
   210 revoked 75/1803
   232 amended 65/2187; 84/108
   239 amended 59/2024
   264 revoked 70/71
   265 amended 64/222
   266 revoked 69/757
   267 revoked 69/756
   290 revoked 75/470
   306 revoked 59/467
   309 amended 69/710
   334 revoked 62/640
   335 amended 75/1024
   342 amended 64/1297
   343 amended 64/1548; 68/1735; 83/1923
   346 revoked 70/16
   353 revoked 72/828
   354 amended 64/2090
   384 revoked 63/793
   420 amended 65/1013
   423 revoked 65/1753

   429 revoked 59/377
   444 revoked 67/364
   483 revoked 62/813
   513 revoked 64/903
   514 revoked 59/525
   520 amended 84/618
   536 revoked 65/723
   545 amended 60/1688
   548 revoked 81/1563
   549 revoked 81/1564
   562 revoked 63/1333
   565 amended 81/1222
   574 amended 74/484
   578 amended 81/1733
   579 revoked 63/1159
   590 revoked 73/1311
   596 revoked 61/42
   609 revoked 62/2601
   610 revoked 61/741
   634 revoked 62/1939
   635 revoked 65/1588
   638 revoked 66/737
   668 revoked 70/752; 70/1191
   674 revoked 71/986; amended 83/1216
   700 amended 59/1386
   701 revoked 66/1507
   716 revoked 63/855
   725 revoked 75/1280
   738 revoked 66/223
   743 revoked 74/73
   764 amended 63/1333
   768 revoked 61/2495
   784 revoked 62/790
   807 revoked 59/2309
   808 revoked 62/621
   809 amended 63/1333
   812 revoked 60/1321
   813 revoked 66/579
   824 revoked 61/1795
   833 revoked 64/504
   836 revoked 62/1003
   839 revoked 65/1776
   843 revoked 74/248
   852 revoked 73/1113
   861 revoked 74/507
   862 revoked 74/522
   901 amended 60/2144
   918 revoked 59/467
   922 revoked 74/1169
   935 revoked 65/1588
   936 amended 68/1671
   938 revoked 62/787
   954 revoked 75/2138
   960 revoked 62/1562
   962 revoked 66/100
   971 revoked 59/537
   980 amended 76/1236
   993 revoked 72/555
  1005 revoked 61/212
  1006 revoked 81/1473
  1020 revoked 59/962
  1021 revoked 59/962
  1022 revoked 59/962
  1027 revoked 61/139
  1036 revoked 66/12
  1038 revoked 60/695
  1063 revoked 70/16
  1068 amended 60/623; 62/979
  1069 amended 60/1410; 73/498

1951—*cont.*
1071 amended 60/1473
1081 revoked 68/1366
1108 revoked 59/2099
1146 revoked 66/1548
1150 revoked 66/165
1157 amended 67/1831
1167 revoked 62/1874
1196 revoked 79/1254; 79/1641
1207 amended 60/1402
1208 amended 61/557
1216 revoked 67/530
1219 revoked 59/1605
1220 revoked 62/2297
1222 revoked 74/595
1223 amended 65/362; 74/70
1232 amended 60/2422; 67/1265; 71/707; 71/1220; 71/1419; 72/603; 72/604; 72/606
1258 revoked 67/1114
1259 revoked 68/541
1261 revoked 67/65
1274 amended 69/23
1284 revoked 74/529
1305 revoked 59/1241
1309 revoked 68/1676
1343 revoked 64/388
1351 revoked 67/1944
1353 amended 71/333
1355 revoked 74/1992
1372 revoked 61/1520
1380 revoked 64/404
1389 revoked 60/1651
1392 revoked 59/2199
1393 revoked 59/2200
1394 revoked 59/2201
1403 revoked 59/1262
1411 revoked 67/386
1414 revoked 75/308
1417 amended 63/2021
1426 revoked 63/982
1450 revoked 83/1634
1454 revoked 77/217
1456 revoked 68/430; 70/1065
1457 revoked 68/430; 70/1065
1464 revoked 74/548
1465 revoked 74/276
1486 amended 59/1459; 65/1089
1504 revoked 62/1937
1508 amended 65/559
1542 revoked 59/467
1543 amended 84/108
1564 amended 63/572
1586 revoked 61/139
1589 revoked 65/635
1606 revoked 64/504
1609 amended 64/241; 72/752; 88/1758
1644 revoked 65/963
1653 revoked 69/833
1663 amended 64/1297
1697 amended 60/1515
1701 revoked 60/1503
1720 revoked 68/827
1725 revoked 79/792
1726 revoked 79/791
1738 amended 63/660
1741 amended 59/1131; 74/76
1743 amended 59/364; 59/1832
1748 revoked 61/2258
1759 amended 82/695
1775 revoked 59/1980

1951—*cont.*
1783 revoked 61/623
1786 revoked 59/82
1787 revoked 59/84
1798 amended 67/1488
1806 amended 81/708
1828 amended 59/187
1846 revoked 61/1389
1848 revoked 61/546
1852 revoked 65/1023
1855 revoked 74/529
1899 amended 61/2030
1936 amended 59/88
1942 revoked 82/1538
1946 amended 64/1397; 72/668; 75/1706; 76/52; 77/423; 1946 revoked 85/444
1949 amended 63/1491
1982 revoked 64/1107
1995 amended 70/392
2003 revoked 73/1522
2051 revoked 59/1334
2057 revoked 74/504
2069 revoked 64/1382
2072 amended 66/514
2076 revoked 72/1433
2078 revoked 62/1562
2091 revoked 60/1581
2126 revoked 61/2315
2128 revoked 62/640
2149 amended 60/226; 71/25
2173 revoked 71/2054
2192 revoked 62/2756
2241 revoked 68/430; 70/1065
2242 revoked 68/430; 70/1065

1952
1 amended 74/1262
3 revoked 64/1895
52 amended 61/1929
60 amended 65/1024; 67/876; 71/1209
72 amended 67/619
75 revoked 84/1232
88 revoked 59/2099
91 revoked 70/201
114 revoked 86/401
119 amended 62/2169; 62/2410; 64/1388
137 amended 64/935
154 revoked 59/377
158 revoked 67/480
159 revoked 64/926
170 revoked 69/1704
194 amended 61/1015; 64/489
196 amended 59/281; 59/1745; 60/2015
225 revoked 87/1758
231 revoked 60/513
289 amended 60/73; 61/781; 61/2210; 63/1769; 65/611
293 revoked 60/779
341 revoked 60/2147
344 revoked 63/934
345 revoked 62/2786
347 revoked 63/885
368 revoked 70/201
373 revoked 66/164
381 revoked 60/1505
385 amended 85/1383; revoked 88/1698
387 revoked 59/61
389 revoked 65/723
405 revoked 74/529
422 revoked 72/604

430 revoked 64/1348
437 amended 63/1956
452 amended 60/458
454 revoked 59/377
457 revoked 65/1864
458 amended 61/1505; 65/1306
459 revoked 70/1434
460 revoked 59/537
494 revoked 72/555
495 revoked 72/1433
518 revoked 84/2028
520 amended 61/2418
525 amended 62/2696
526 revoked 72/604
531 amended 60/1195
550 revoked 61/1346
554 revoked 59/504
561 amended 62/738
565 amended 70/2103; 76/1889; 79/1630; 81/1222; 84/2058; 87/2231; 88/537
582 revoked 65/1753
586 revoked 72/2025
635 amended 62/2784
649 revoked 68/827
660 revoked 67/29
687 revoked 60/1338
699 revoked 60/20
704 revoked 68/1366
719 revoked 64/1269
740 revoked 59/2148
744 revoked 70/1479
747 revoked 59/1109
752 revoked 62/405
755 amended 61/1011
775 revoked 77/217
777 revoked 77/217
791 revoked 61/546
804 revoked 84/989
815 revoked 59/734
834 revoked 63/2059
835 revoked 67/364
868 amended 59/1052; 61/2317; 65/980; 68/1864; 69/592
870 revoked 59/261
873 amended 59/1241; 60/2395; 64/2003
874 revoked 62/787
878 revoked 65/1176
882 revoked 65/1312
883 revoked 65/1189
889 amended 64/1898; 71/823
896 revoked 65/1238
897 revoked 65/1186
900 amended 60/1504; 61/2128; 62/921; 62/1058; 69/32; 76/1113; 78/1315; 80/635; 80/1354; 81/258
906 revoked 65/2136
917 revoked 72/1693
918 revoked 63/1343
919 revoked 66/44
924 revoked 74/529
930 revoked 74/778
937 amended 69/710
938 revoked 69/793
944 amended 59/1495; 64/1148; 71/1329; 71/1468; 73/1814; 74/1797; 75/1717; 76/1708; 77/1704; 78/1577; 79/1286; 80/1615
957 revoked 60/1676
958 revoked 74/529

961 revoked 76/1544
989 amended 64/1765
992 revoked 67/520
993 revoked 65/899
997 amended 59/1131
1004 revoked 62/1003
1012 revoked 65/1023
1023 revoked 65/54
1024 revoked 72/555
1031 amended 63/1627
1032 amended 69/594
1046 amended 69/1154; revoked 72/1309
1062 revoked 65/1776
1077 amended 63/1169
1092 revoked 68/1154
1106 revoked 62/1049
1113 revoked 66/638
1161 revoked 65/2045
1168 amended 70/392
1207 revoked 71/707
1208 revoked 64/73
1219 revoked 61/1194
1220 revoked 59/377
1221 revoked 60/1052
1223 revoked 75/849
1224 revoked 61/713
1233 amended 71/914
1250 revoked 64/504
1252 amended 60/2422
1256 revoked 62/1562
1258 revoked 59/480
1284 revoked 83/1718
1299 revoked 68/125
1301 revoked 66/164
1310 revoked 62/326
1330 revoked 72/1693
1331 revoked 59/410
1343 amended 61/334
1346 revoked 64/926
1349 revoked 71/2116
1351 revoked 62/787
1366 revoked 59/1334
1368 revoked 60/301
1380 revoked 70/16
1383 revoked 61/203
1393 revoked 69/1696
1394 revoked 61/167
1405 revoked 64/388
1406 revoked 64/387
1410 revoked 66/256
1411 revoked 66/262
1412 revoked 61/1519
1417 revoked 65/1864
1422 revoked 61/814
1432 amended 68/1014; 72/1012; 75/1263; revoked 83/569
1447 amended 71/1329
1454 revoked 72/555
1457 amended 69/212
1464 amended 72/2013; 83/134
1466 amended 74/1243
1467 revoked 63/1262
1469 revoked 69/1219
1481 revoked 63/1229
1503 amended 59/772; 64/71; 71/824
1524 amended 73/1984
1560 revoked 67/1632
1584 revoked 61/1580
1587 revoked 74/389

STATUTORY INSTRUMENTS AFFECTED 1947–1988

1952—cont.
1589 revoked 60/503
1596 revoked 80/499
1616 revoked 67/1326
1617 revoked 69/1704
1633 revoked 64/504
1639 amended 67/398
1664 revoked 65/723
1689 amended 83/979
1690 amended 60/2106
1697 revoked 67/1865; 70/1284
1703 amended 60/660; 64/255; 66/538
1704 revoked 65/538
1705 revoked 65/543
1706 revoked 65/544
1713 revoked 82/1787
1720 revoked 75/663
1721 revoked 75/825
1722 revoked 75/663
1723 revoked 75/663
1724 revoked 75/663
1737 revoked 62/1562
1745 revoked 60/2112
1746 revoked 64/418
1758 revoked 62/1003
1771 revoked 62/1562
1792 revoked 69/1453
1798 amended 65/853
1800 revoked 81/892
1808 revoked 61/623
1815 revoked 59/1832
1859 revoked 83/609
1869 amended 65/528; 71/1216; 74/573; 86/1444
1894 revoked 69/905
1895 amended 60/494
1899 amended 67/1280
1900 amended 67/1279; 69/1369
1906 amended 71/375; 76/773; 79/1409
1918 revoked 63/1094
1929 revoked 65/2121
1933 amended 65/565
1937 revoked 63/1450
1948 revoked 65/1103
1950 revoked 65/1106
1951 revoked 65/1113
1952 revoked 65/1046
1953 revoked 65/1114
1956 revoked 65/1107
1957 revoked 65/1112
1959 revoked 65/1062
1965 revoked 74/529
1977 revoked 65/1067
1994 amended 60/2343; 63/2075
1998 revoked 64/21
1999 revoked 69/212
2004 revoked 63/2040
2026 revoked 59/622
2031 revoked 65/131
2035 revoked 78/186
2059 amended 60/2207; 84/108
2086 revoked 60/699
2088 revoked 62/1504
2103 amended 61/70
2106 revoked 63/885
2108 revoked 59/1035
2113 amended 61/317; 62/295; 63/2067; 65/1571;
    67/371; 68/1935; 69/1007; 69/1162;
    70/1868; 72/529; 73/715; 74/205;
    74/1236; 75/213; 76/1932; 77/364;

1952—cont.
    77/1394; 78/544; 78/1224; 79/1590;
    80/2044; 82/1148; 82/1437; 84/1371
2114 revoked 65/1622
2115 revoked 71/448
2116 revoked 74/529
2117 revoked 69/519
2122 revoked 65/1776
2138 amended 74/70
2144 amended 60/2422; 67/1265; 72/606
2159 revoked 65/1995
2160 revoked 61/36
2162 revoked 62/2756
2166 amended 71/1329; 74/1797; 75/1717
2168 revoked 60/2191
2171 amended 59/2180
2176 revoked 67/65
2179 revoked 72/603
2180 amended 59/786
2184 revoked 68/827
2190 revoked 68/1920
2191 revoked 68/1920
2198 amended 64/1974; 71/836; 75/1345
2209 revoked 68/219
2221 revoked 61/1525
2222 revoked 61/1523
2224 revoked 65/1993
2226 amended 67/1094
2228 revoked 71/848
2229 amended 60/1349; 67/1094; 79/1146;
    81/1258; 1982/611; 88/1760
2230 amended 79/1446; 83/252
2231 amended 79/1146; revoked 86/1820
2232 revoked 78/893
2233 revoked 63/1596
2236 revoked 60/1349
2244 revoked 63/1333
2253 revoked 61/141
2259 revoked 66/863
2268 revoked 60/699
2273 amended 63/1508
2274 amended 61/630; 66/1372; 70/643; 79/1168

1953
    3 revoked 63/1333
  16 revoked 64/1837
  19 revoked 79/291
  25 amended 82/1514
  42 revoked 75/825
  60 revoked 60/785
  65 revoked 71/1537
  87 revoked 65/2090
115 amended 63/1875
117 revoked 72/1139
118 revoked 72/1139
130 amended 62/1614
135 revoked 61/2423
143 revoked 67/1166
148 revoked 80/499
151 revoked 66/1319
168 revoked 75/2232
179 revoked 74/595
205 amended 70/1403; 74/2128; 77/1881;
    80/557; 83/1539; revoked 84/552
214 revoked 63/1658
246 revoked 84/1566; 84/1714
250 revoked 66/579
264 revoked 75/1803
269 revoked 64/1178
276 revoked 64/242

1953—*cont.*

280 revoked 61/1637
299 amended 60/1989; 65/528
317 revoked 59/335
336 revoked 60/1146
337 revoked 72/1693
354 revoked 77/217
355 revoked 77/217
365 revoked 74/2003
392 revoked 72/456
393 amended 66/688
395 revoked 60/707
399 revoked 59/2199
400 revoked 59/2200
401 revoked 59/2201
417 revoked 70/1792
420 amended 61/184; 66/1553
421 revoked 71/2054
422 revoked 59/2148
433 revoked 70/16
435 revoked 64/853
437 revoked 74/768
439 revoked 61/1520
443 amended 73/2203
447 revoked 70/1307
452 amended 61/1631
456 revoked 69/1704
471 amended 60/624
472 amended 59/785; 66/563; 71/25
473 amended 63/657
474 revoked 60/587
476 revoked 64/004
480 revoked 62/8
489 revoked 60/2148
493 revoked 73/579
495 revoked 69/1696
499 revoked 64/1043
507 amended 59/448; 73/1676
526 amended 73/2106
536 revoked 70/400; amended (Scotland) 70/1127; 70/1284; 70/1285; 70/1286
557 revoked 62/1562
564 amended 74/1716
565 amended 61/1836; 62/1256
581 revoked 59/899
586 revoked 61/1188
588 revoked 60/1960
589 revoked 61/741
591 amended 69/592
592 revoked 81/1540
593 amended 79/1707
597 revoked 64/903
622 revoked 62/2735
624 revoked 67/386
636 revoked 65/543
640 revoked 79/564
643 revoked 75/1790
645 revoked 73/1311
650 revoked 71/1503
651 revoked 63/1381
657 revoked 2423
669 revoked 59/467
691 revoked 81/1063; 81/1320
696 revoked 75/825
720 amended 75/743
732 revoked 65/538
735 revoked 62/2786
739 revoked 64/1652
742 revoked 71/2115
743 amended 60/461

1953—*cont.*

748 amended 59/1301
756 revoked 72/604
813 revoked 61/315
828 revoked 59/472
851 revoked 64/21
884 amended 76/225; 88/591
886 amended 64/241; 72/752; 73/589; 88/1758
887 revoked 70/117
888 amended 64/350
893 revoked 65/538
894 revoked 62/787
900 amended 61/376; 68/57; 68/646
920 revoked 67/1876
934 revoked 62/2812
951 amended 77/1743
961 revoked 66/184
965 amended 59/1131; 61/2192; 67/36; 69/1776; 72/594
966 amended 59/425; 67/507
968 revoked 59/797
975 revoked 61/2315
979 revoked 72/606
980 revoked 60/2291
985 revoked 65/1776
986 revoked 65/1776
995 revoked 66/1548
998 amended 61/1045
1014 amended 71/407
1033 revoked 74/529
1036 amended 60/1967; 61/393; 65/1047; 75/341; 76/346; 76/1098
1045 revoked 60/1505
1059 revoked 69/212
1060 revoked 62/1562
1062 revoked 65/1420
1065 amended 64/1441
1079 revoked 60/498
1083 revoked 74/768
1084 revoked 67/77
1085 revoked 74/768
1086 revoked 85/1758
1107 revoked 69/904
1108 revoked 69/905
1114 amended 62/699
1138 amended 61/602
1156 revoked 59/365; 59/366
1162 revoked 59/2099
1172 revoked 63/1450
1174 revoked 71/303; 71/459
1196 revoked 83/609
1201 amended 59/2210
1202 revoked 61/2323
1203 revoked 60/1060
1204 amended 59/1768
1205 revoked 63/1042
1206 amended 61/2318; 67/810
1208 revoked 61/2274
1211 revoked 59/1036
1212 revoked 59/1038
1213 revoked 59/35
1215 revoked 59/377
1227 amended 60/2430; 64/73; 64/504; 67/1169
1228 amended 59/1594; 62/737; 64/790
1230 revoked 68/615
1232 revoked 62/271
1236 revoked 77/1585
1241 revoked 66/1548
1275 revoked 70/16
1287 revoked 61/281

1953—*cont.*
1301 revoked 60/699
1307 revoked 81/1063; 81/1320
1310 revoked 67/1119
1311 revoked 67/1119
1314 revoked 64/504
1345 revoked 62/376
1347 revoked 68/2049
1360 amended 62/1031; 63/660
1369 amended 62/2871
1393 revoked 59/397
1396 revoked 59/1334
1403 amended 61/760; 67/522
1411 revoked 74/529
1415 revoked 73/267
1419 revoked 74/529
1428 revoked 60/258
1429 revoked 60/260
1430 revoked 60/259
1440 revoked 62/1562
1441 revoked 74/529
1444 revoked 64/1859
1446 amended 61/1045
1447 revoked 59/2148
1449 amended 60/583
1459 revoked 70/16
1464 amended 81/1332
1466 revoked 61/2000
1472 revoked 62/1562
1474 amended 67/809
1478 revoked 61/1188
1479 revoked 61/1188
1484 revoked 59/544
1488 revoked 74/529
1492 revoked 79/712
1521 revoked 72/752
1525 amended 71/915
1526 revoked 67/190
1531 revoked 87/2114
1532 amended 60/2186; 65/1031
1544 revoked 69/1696
1545 amended 63/879; 73/36
1551 amended 67/311; 79/1457
1555 revoked 78/186
1557 revoked 65/1525
1560 revoked 64/1577
1564 revoked 61/1188
1575 revoked 59/1110
1576 revoked 60/1349
1587 revoked 74/529
1598 amended 74/1885
1609 revoked 59/1098
1631 revoked 61/2000
1640 revoked 60/1555
1642 amended 60/995
1646 amended 63/1772
1669 amended 69/592
1671 amended   60/2214;   64/2034;   67/1282;
    67/1288; 68/1649; 72/1689; 72/1758
1679 revoked 66/1189
1702 amended 71/1333; 71/2133; 73/474; 79/711;
    revoked 83/1917
1708 revoked 67/1001
1709 amended 64/1033; 71/1130
1710 revoked 65/1500
1712 revoked 65/1338
1720 amended 64/477
1721 revoked 60/1519
1728 amended   64/353;   74/1354;   75/1345;
    75/2040

1953—*cont.*
1732 revoked 59/498
1748 revoked 60/723
1755 amended 67/1755
1759 revoked 74/529
1773 revoked 65/1864
1776 amended 71/91
1777 amended 67/1978; 74/69; 87/622
1800 revoked 62/2756
1804 amended 87/677
1805 revoked 61/476
1813 amended 62/761; 76/974
1818 revoked 59/1
1820 revoked 62/1532
1821 revoked 60/1542
1828 revoked 63/844; 63/849; 64/760
1832 amended 69/1807; 73/462
1837 revoked 61/1520
1849 amended 64/654; 67/1370
1871 revoked 74/778
1889 revoked 67/1864; 70/400
1896 revoked 60/1913
1906 revoked 60/977
1907 revoked 59/105
1908 revoked 62/405
1909 amended 60/1367
1910 revoked 61/1188
1915 amended 73/938
1919 revoked 65/1707
1923 amended 62/177
1928 revoked 68/1366
1937 amended 84/108

1954
4 amended 64/1910; 69/1601
5 revoked 59/467
14 revoked 69/1511
21 revoked 60/1227
23 amended 75/2117; 78/806
27 revoked 65/538
49 amended 60/2449
55 revoked 64/941
64 revoked 59/2213
87 revoked 62/1562
103 revoked 65/1687
104 revoked 65/1051
105 revoked 65/1550
117 revoked 67/330
144 revoked 80/699
145 revoked 59/105
162 revoked 72/1404
163 revoked 73/693
165 revoked 70/786
166 revoked 60/408
171 revoked 65/510
189 amended 59/847; 59/1803; 61/557; 62/300;
    63/394; 65/40; 66/1010; 67/330; 67/520;
    67/1168;   67/1265;   68/827;   69/1696;
    71/707;   71/1220;   71/1419;   72/604;
    72/1302
198 revoked 61/2455
211 amended 69/1385
212 revoked 61/713
224 amended 67/278; 69/352
234 revoked 60/2112
235 revoked 73/1060
243 revoked 75/182
253 revoked 64/242
263 revoked 72/1693
265 revoked 70/107

1954—*cont.*

267 revoked 60/699
268 revoked 71/405
304 revoked 68/512
320 revoked 65/509
325 revoked 59/374
332 revoked 74/529
333 revoked 59/1901
350 revoked 74/529
352 revoked 67/1169
361 revoked 59/1832
363 revoked 62/1562
370 revoked 71/1524
383 amended 60/984; 74/484; 76/515
384 amended 66/337
391 revoked 59/2108
392 amended 62/837
395 revoked 70/623
396 revoked 63/2133
397 revoked 70/87
400 revoked 70/107
405 amended 65/987
413 revoked 63/793
436 revoked 74/529
438 revoked 65/1822
439 revoked 68/1314
448 amended 71/1454
452 amended 60/722; 61/1233
454 revoked 70/1047
461 amended 70/1224
463 revoked 74/171
473 revoked 59/890
481 revoked 62/1874
482 revoked 59/105
484 revoked 62/2786
493 revoked 70/1737
497 amended 63/1943
498 revoked 69/904
499 revoked 69/905
516 amended 70/910
519 amended 61/1556; 66/1149
534 revoked 60/2149
549 revoked 60/211
565 revoked 70/16
574 amended 60/1353
577 revoked 64/583
585 revoked 72/555
601 revoked 66/579
609 revoked 70/606
613 revoked 67/1867; 70/1286
625 revoked 81/679
627 amended 75/2117
628 amended 64/368
635 revoked 65/1536
636 amended 59/874; 60/1061; 62/1638; 67/811; 67/1481
637 amended 59/875; 62/1639; 67/812; 67/1482
641 revoked 69/384
643 revoked 60/1824
665 revoked 68/512
669 revoked 62/2248
670 amended 73/974; 75/1547
671 amended 73/975; 75/1548
672 amended 73/990; 75/1577
674 revoked 66/256
675 revoked 66/262
678 revoked 64/303
687 revoked 61/543
689 amended 69/454
694 revoked 71/307

1954—*cont.*

699 revoked 62/2528
700 revoked 62/2529
711 revoked 65/756
712 amended 70/619
726 revoked 62/1562
740 revoked 65/533
742 revoked 64/755
761 revoked 65/1776
762 revoked 64/1151
779 revoked 70/1099
782 amended 72/1433
796 amended 61/72; 62/2653; 67/748; 68/1675; 69/1689; 71/1977; 76/1362; 83/623; 85/1232
796 revoked 87/2024
807 revoked 65/509
809 amended 59/1095; 62/1296; 65/1543
810 revoked 59/2001
813 amended 60/583; 77/1598
814 revoked 59/410
815 amended 59/448; 65/512; 71/1821; 75/1569; 76/376
824 amended 63/1333
829 revoked 60/972
830 amended 69/592
849 revoked 60/1477
853 revoked 72/287
863 revoked 73/1085
865 amended 84/908
869 amended 62/596; 74/1462
879 revoked 74/520
888 revoked 74/812
898 amended 60/784; 66/1164; 66/1556; 68/1217; 71/189; 72/51; 74/2045
900 revoked 60/1069
904 revoked 62/513
909 revoked 59/410
911 revoked 59/1029
916 revoked 62/1562
923 revoked 75/470
925 revoked 60/1069
933 revoked 65/1453
950 amended 71/887
957 amended 61/1621
962 revoked 67/1104
996 revoked 83/1176
974 amended 59/1405
976 revoked 63/558
981 revoked 72/1693
982 amended 61/1295
983 revoked 60/1321
985 revoked 61/1389
991 amended 59/448
1017 amended 67/1643
1025 revoked 63/683
1027 revoked 65/1776
1029 revoked 63/885
1037 revoked 59/2199
1038 revoked 59/2200
1039 revoked 59/2201
1040 revoked 59/2197
1041 amended 67/1482
1044 revoked 64/1289
1048 amended 63/2060; 68/44; 68/68; 68/128; 73/313; 74/73; 74/520; 77/1341; 82/1514
1049 amended 59/1288; 65/422; 74/520; 82/1514
1050 amended 74/520
1059 amended 73/503; 74/812
1074 amended 64/2097

STATUTORY INSTRUMENTS AFFECTED 1947–1988

1089 revoked 63/844; 63/849; 64/760
1096 revoked 60/699
1105 revoked 59/1869
1106 revoked 59/1262
1110 amended 67/964
1133 revoked 59/374
1138 revoked 59/81
1142 amended 61/335
1145 revoked 60/701
1146 revoked 60/1652; 60/1654
1147 revoked 60/1652; 60/1654; 60/1656
1158 amended 59/905
1192 revoked 74/520; 77/1341
1205 revoked 64/904
1206 revoked 64/853
1207 revoked 69/793
1211 revoked 77/1341
1212 revoked 77/1341; 86/24
1215 revoked 66/214
1222 revoked 61/1983
1224 revoked 74/520
1227 revoked 77/1341; 86/24
1229 revoked 74/520
1230 revoked 74/520
1237 revoked 74/520; 77/1341
1241 revoked 74/812
1242 revoked 74/812
1243 revoked 74/812
1244 revoked 70/1307
1256 amended 70/1307
1258 revoked 84/1232
1259 amended 74/812
1261 amended 74/812
1262 amended 65/283
1267 amended 60/1542
1268 revoked 59/277
1277 revoked 62/1562
1281 revoked 59/1869
1319 amended 61/2172
1350 revoked 65/1192
1366 amended 66/312
1367 revoked 63/885
1369 amended 64/1187; 65/133; 65/978; 66/1180
1370 amended 65/132
1373 revoked 59/1980
1374 amended 61/335
1375 revoked 59/105
1376 revoked 59/105
1378 amended 66/898
1382 amended 72/681; revoked 86/401
1401 amended 61/352
1417 revoked 64/1971
1419 amended 88/1758
1426 revoked 59/1901
1429 revoked 59/1901
1437 amended 64/1794
1437 amended 64/1794
1442 revoked 59/467
1443 revoked 66/164
1444 revoked 66/164
1457 amended 77/1585
1468 revoked 61/63
1470 revoked 60/442
1471 revoked 74/1257
1482 revoked 75/182
1483 revoked 70/201
1484 revoked 69/757
1485 revoked 69/756
1504 revoked 59/1262

1505 revoked 65/1500
1552 revoked 74/529
1557 revoked 61/1015
1566 revoked 59/1620
1568 revoked 62/405
1577 revoked 62/1003
1578 amended 63/1178; 68/1731; 73/1407; 74/1935
1585 revoked 65/1776
1595 amended 61/1046
1596 amended 59/528; 60/1604; 64/2065; 65/528; 68/1241; 68/2049
1597 revoked 62/1562
1600 revoked 63/798
1610 amended 64/1548
1611 revoked 79/1146
1612 amended 66/674; 80/76; 81/260; revoked 84/1406
1614 revoked 80/1354
1616 revoked 69/1219
1622 revoked 59/190
1627 revoked 67/72
1630 revoked 61/814
1635 revoked 68/1232
1637 amended 59/1965; 62/2747
1644 revoked 68/2049
1645 revoked 63/1450
1647 revoked 71/303; 71/459
1656 revoked 61/1637
1663 amended 71/1329
1666 amended 60/1410
1675 amended 64/1974; 71/836
1677 revoked 66/579
1686 revoked 65/538
1687 revoked 65/543
1688 revoked 65/544
1691 revoked 68/1366
1699 amended 60/2172
1702 revoked 59/1036
1703 revoked 62/1874
1704 revoked 59/1241
1705 revoked 60/661
1706 amended 63/1221; 82/975
1711 amended 76/1505; 79/952; 83/675
1719 revoked 59/1901
1720 revoked 63/798
1723 revoked 67/377
1725 revoked 59/2108
1726 revoked 65/1776
1728 revoked 65/1776
1741 revoked 68/630
1743 amended 63/559

1955
  2 amended 60/451
  3 amended 60/462
  9 amended 59/454
 10 amended 60/452
 11 amended 60/460; 64/274
 13 amended 64/277
 15 amended 60/463
 16 amended 73/606
 38 revoked 63/798
 47 amended 60/2422
 48 revoked 64/504
 49 revoked 62/787
 57 revoked 64/1285
 75 revoked 69/1453
 78 revoked 62/1024

1955—*cont.*

81 revoked 65/1426
87 revoked 68/1503
91 revoked 59/1551
109 revoked 61/213
112 revoked 66/1250
113 revoked 66/1250
116 amended 62/2729; 64/229; revoked 84/1989
120 revoked 80/1468
125 revoked 78/1739
127 revoked 72/1693
133 revoked 61/782
143 revoked 67/330
147 revoked 71/1593
162 amended 66/1188
164 revoked 66/1189
170 amended 60/464
175 amended 60/465
177 amended 60/450
181 amended 60/449
182 amended 60/455
199 revoked 61/203
209 revoked 64/1895
222 amended 71/1821; 75/1569
224 revoked 74/389
226 revoked 77/217
235 revoked 68/1503
242 revoked 60/205
243 revoked 60/1060
245 revoked 62/405
255 revoked 72/211
259 revoked 61/2249
260 amended 61/163
266 amended 65/1483
279 revoked 74/529
280 revoked 74/529
291 revoked 78/1267
292 revoked 78/1267
337 revoked 59/2052
346 revoked 71/778
350 revoked 63/660
354 revoked 82/1218
360 revoked 71/986; amended 83/1216
365 revoked 60/2254
367 revoked 73/309
370 revoked 61/946
382 revoked 66/821
383 revoked 74/529
385 revoked 62/1562
390 revoked 65/733
391 revoked 59/821
399 amended 66/1401
400 revoked 59/2148
401 revoked 65/527
402 revoked 64/1972
405 amended 64/409
407 amended 65/514
408 revoked 59/358
411 revoked 61/200
419 amended   63/1178;   68/173;   73/1407;
     74/1935
420 amended 76/225; 88/591
422 amended 64/26
426 revoked 82/1538
428 revoked 59/1295
430 revoked 61/2274
431 revoked 60/1652; 60/1654; 60/1656
432 revoked 60/1652; 60/1654; 60/1656
435 amended 64/790
436 amended 65/247

1955—*cont.*

442 amended 60/503; 64/1301; 66/382
443 revoked 61/281
445 revoked 70/16
447 amended 60/637; 63/895
448 revoked 60/637
451 revoked 60/2448
452 revoked 66/1250
461 revoked 82/718
469 amended 61/2333
473 revoked 64/903
476 revoked 77/1341
480 revoked 62/2756
481 revoked 62/2756
482 revoked 63/1646
487 amended 76/602
493 amended 60/2422; 67/1265; 72/606
494 revoked 63/934
496 revoked 62/1234
498 revoked 65/40
503 revoked 88/1162
543 revoked 76/435
545 revoked 63/812
550 revoked 61/2315
552 revoked 61/1189
553 amended 73/1758
560 revoked 64/279
585 revoked 70/911
588 revoked 80/74
589 revoked 78/683
604 revoked 64/755
608 revoked 74/509
613 revoked 68/630
627 revoked 66/727
639 revoked 59/1901
651 revoked 62/1562
659 revoked 61/526
662 revoked 59/973
679 revoked 60/656
680 revoked 60/657
690 amended 62/833; 76/133; 85/312; 87/282
692 revoked 59/177
701 revoked 62/2786
702 revoked 62/2786
705 revoked 62/405
706 revoked 60/1652; 60/1654; 60/1656
709 amended 69/592
710 amended 67/810
711 amended 59/1051; 61/2316
732 revoked 59/1145
741 amended 80/863
782 amended 62/145
806 amended 66/514
812 revoked 59/748
814 revoked 87/1781
828 revoked 62/1405
830 revoked 59/67
832 amended 71/1282
835 revoked 62/1003
842 revoked 70/1056; amended 71/1316
846 revoked 61/1757
853 revoked 59/1854
857 amended 76/241
862 revoked 64/21
865 revoked 59/1262
872 revoked 63/885
873 revoked 59/1312
874 amended 76/225; 88/591
882 revoked 65/538
884 revoked 61/1286

886 revoked 61/628
926 amended 79/1457
927 amended 60/583
929 amended 76/241
930 amended 59/1661
931 revoked 59/374
932 revoked 61/427
933 revoked 62/1862
962 revoked 64/840
982 revoked 78/425
987 revoked 59/748
990 amended 59/2053; 84/817; 84/1811; revoked 86/1078
992 amended 59/2327
996 revoked 63/286
1010 revoked 59/410
1037 revoked 63/1172
1038 revoked 62/1585
1040 revoked 59/397
1041 revoked 82/1514
1047 revoked 68/1163
1050 amended 82/1514
1051 revoked 59/1029
1054 revoked 59/983
1059 revoked 61/1242
1069 revoked 59/1824
1082 revoked 65/510
1084 amended 61/1441; 80/362
1125 amended 69/1575; 71/471; 76/1621; 83/367
1129 amended 65/282; 76/1315, 83/1856
1135 revoked 60/699
1137 revoked 59/394
1141 revoked 65/1500
1146 revoked 60/491
1157 amended 61/1045
1158 revoked 62/1586
1162 revoked 63/934
1190 revoked 62/1616
1203 amended 67/25
1207 revoked 59/1296
1209 revoked 60/444; amended 76/221
1215 amended 64/918
1216 revoked 61/2274
1217 revoked 61/2323
1221 revoked 62/405
1226 amended 73/503; 74/812
1240 revoked 59/1
1243 amended 61/2399
1247 revoked 59/1536
1250 revoked 63/261
1280 revoked 59/190
1293 amended 59/519, 64/1712; 65/1393
1296 revoked 59/374
1310 revoked 77/944
1329 revoked 62/1924
1342 revoked 70/16
1346 amended 65/2041; 87/1781
1347 revoked 74/520
1350 revoked 66/693
1363 revoked 72/557
1370 revoked 68/427
1371 revoked 67/1121
1372 amended 80/1250
1382 revoked 64/504
1390 revoked 80/12
1395 revoked 59/377
1411 revoked 74/812
1427 revoked 72/1693
1449 revoked 64/1151

1452 amended 60/1410; 62/2116; 73/498
1460 revoked 61/814
1470 revoked 70/16
1474 revoked 60/513
1479 amended 70/392; 74/8
1494 amended 69/710; 74/520
1495 revoked 59/1105
1496 revoked 74/520
1509 amended 61/1171
1518 revoked 74/812
1532 amended 63/1808
1542 revoked 68/72
1547 amended 61/2349
1562 revoked 62/1562
1602 revoked 69/1696
1613 amended 62/1978
1629 revoked 70/1521
1630 revoked 63/211
1641 amended 59/1037; 62/168
1650 amended 64/1397; 72/668; 75/1706; 76/52; 77/423; revoked 85/444
1654 amended 62/2177
1655 revoked 66/10
1660 revoked 70/1853
1664 revoked 64/1178
1666 revoked 64/404
1668 revoked 66/11
1673 revoked 60/1165
1680 revoked 62/2584
1681 revoked 62/2584
1693 amended 65/1960
1698 revoked 77/217
1699 revoked 62/1562
1704 revoked 59/2052
1739 revoked 61/713
1750 revoked 77/217
1751 revoked 76/1416
1761 revoked 63/576
1769 revoked 65/510
1778 revoked 61/315
1799 amended 63/403; 64/1974; 71/836; 74/1354; 75/1345
1800 revoked 59/1901
1815 revoked 59/2199
1816 revoked 59/2200
1817 revoked 59/2201
1818 revoked 61/2315
1821 revoked 59/1977
1822 revoked 59/1978
1826 amended 59/905
1829 revoked 60/408
1853 amended 71/333
1857 amended 73/491
1859 revoked 60/2149
1861 revoked 64/302
1866 revoked 67/434
1867 revoked 65/540
1877 revoked 61/141
1878 revoked 59/498
1882 revoked 74/529
1883 revoked 61/1015
1884 revoked 65/1776
1885 revoked 65/1776
1890 revoked 64/755
1891 revoked 63/558
1892 amended 63/559
1893 amended 71/61
1895 revoked 61/546
1899 revoked 67/1867

1955—cont.

1900 amended 67/1864; 67/1867
1901 revoked 64/1289
1905 revoked 59/1241
1906 revoked 60/1601
1907 revoked 59/396
1911 amended 86/693
1913 revoked 65/538
1916 revoked 70/16
1941 revoked 63/1094
1954 amended 76/221
1963 amended 60/358
1973 amended 59/2054; 60/547; 61/2336
1978 revoked 60/699
1984 revoked 59/1869
1986 revoked 62/478
1993 amended 83/874; 84/1205
2006 amended 61/244; 63/1100; 67/1928
2007 amended 67/1928

1956

3 revoked 59/410
25 revoked 82/1218
41 revoked 74/507
82 revoked 60/972
84 revoked 72/1992
85 revoked 59/537
88 revoked 70/150
90 revoked 59/1039
91 revoked 59/1980
101 revoked 67/1839; 84/1950
104 revoked 65/531
105 revoked 61/1983
117 amended 62/295
118 revoked 59/467
125 revoked 63/1159
126 revoked 60/1069
131 revoked 68/1535
133 revoked 70/1737
142 amended 59/1341; 60/1238
151 amended 62/2871
154 revoked 65/538
155 revoked 62/1562
162 revoked 72/316
163 revoked 72/419
168 amended 63/871
192 revoked 65/510
202 amended 59/97
227 revoked 67/330
231 revoked 61/1189
232 amended 64/918
235 revoked 83/609
265 revoked 61/1792
280 revoked 68/1405
289 revoked 65/532
297 amended 63/919; 84/108
299 revoked 74/529
305 amended 59/42
321 revoked 60/119
324 revoked 60/645
327 revoked 74/519
328 revoked 74/519
330 revoked 59/2108
332 revoked 82/1234
336 revoked 62/1562
350 revoked 59/1901
353 revoked 77/217
357 amended 87/1285; 88/1185
363 amended 76/95
376 revoked 60/398

1956—cont.

381 revoked 59/386
385 revoked 62/2756
401 amended 59/1131
405 amended 64/398
413 revoked 64/926
414 revoked 66/1458
419 revoked 83/609
421 revoked 60/972
422 revoked 65/318
445 revoked 63/845
466 amended 68/62
467 amended 71/1011
469 amended 65/721; revoked 83/1634
470 revoked 72/1940
479 revoked 59/2108
500 revoked 82/1218
501 revoked 59/1262
503 revoked 61/2307
521 revoked 62/2379
527 amended 62/270
529 revoked 74/418
530 amended 68/2062
531 revoked 61/542
540 revoked 63/1646
551 revoked 65/1776
559 revoked 80/545
577 revoked 59/190
579 amended 61/2436
580 amended 61/1837
582 revoked 59/2148
587 amended 63/1516; revoked 83/1718
588 revoked 65/177
608 revoked 62/1562
615 amended 61/2316
617 amended 59/1293; 61/1195
618 amended 59/1967; 61/1196
619 revoked 72/1721
630 amended 61/2469; 71/1257; 72/847
647 revoked 75/1803
657 amended 61/2009
658 revoked 59/150
685 revoked 70/786
711 revoked 74/595
715 amended 60/929; 63/922; 64/562; 67/579; 68/428
716 revoked 62/1939
723 revoked 63/230
725 revoked 61/141
731 amended 60/1652; 63/88; 64/916; 64/1652
732 amended 71/189
731 amended 74/1262
741 revoked 72/557
770 amended 66/770
771 amended 66/770
775 revoked 82/1419
779 revoked 59/719
780 amended 66/507
782 revoked 86/113
792 revoked 60/86
800 revoked 67/65
807 revoked 63/1509
817 revoked 63/885
818 amended 64/273
821 amended 64/275
827 revoked 59/1035
828 revoked 59/1036
829 revoked 59/1038
830 revoked 59/1039
834 revoked 61/1189

1956—*cont.*

835 revoked 61/1192
836 revoked 60/1652; 60/1654; 60/1656
854 amended 72/776
855 amended 60/1473
866 revoked 61/814
868 revoked 60/1913
882 revoked 64/1548
894 amended 67/1162; 68/1055; 71/1079;
    75/1135; 76/475; 82/57
897 revoked 67/710
899 revoked 67/709
907 revoked 60/1322
919 amended 62/1288; 83/1703; 85/68
927 amended 60/45
930 revoked 61/1150
932 revoked 62/1585
938 revoked 60/1601
947 revoked 77/1113
948 revoked 77/763
953 revoked 59/986
959 amended 59/2249
962 amended 64/638; 68/164
976 revoked 72/1693
977 revoked 61/141
989 revoked 62/1562
1000 revoked 59/537
1001 revoked 59/1312
1002 revoked 67/1764; 71/383
1010 revoked 65/1588
1022 amended 64/1148; 71/1468; 73/1814;
    74/1797; 75/1717; 76/1708; 77/1704;
    78/1577; 79/1286; 80/1615
1038 revoked 77/217
1039 amended 65/1268
1045 revoked 82/544
1046 revoked 73/985
1048 revoked 69/18
1049 revoked 69/19
1050 revoked 69/20
1060 revoked 70/557
1061 revoked 63/1169
1062 revoked 62/1562
1066 revoked 72/583
1070 revoked 62/787
1075 revoked 69/352
1076 revoked 62/2248
1077 revoked 74/455
1078 revoked 74/287
1103 revoked 60/2259
1113 amended 66/514; 68/1
1127 revoked 75/1024
1131 revoked 63/1450
1135 revoked 62/1586
1136 revoked 72/641
1139 amended 60/1410
1145 revoked 70/1286
1146 revoked 70/1286
1147 amended 62/301
1148 revoked 61/1528
1149 revoked 67/1579
1158 revoked 62/2756
1163 revoked 59/374
1166 revoked 79/1254
1168 revoked 75/1970
1169 revoked 62/1616
1179 revoked 72/583
1183 revoked 63/1435
1185 revoked 82/1176
1188 revoked 64/298; 64/504

1956—*cont.*

1189 revoked 66/727
1191 revoked 65/1776
1197 amended 62/295
1199 amended 60/2422; 61/557; 62/12; 63/394;
    64/297; 67/1265; 72/606
1202 revoked 61/542
1205 revoked 67/1763
1207 revoked 63/791
1210 revoked 60/1652; 60/1654; 60/1656
1212 revoked 60/972
1217 amended 64/489
1229 amended 65/1435; 67/375
1230 amended 60/2308
1231 revoked 70/16
1239 amended 64/1149; 66/1046; 71/146
1243 amended 64/1974; 75/1345; 75/2040
1262 amended 62/528; 66/1372; 70/643
1265 revoked 62/1585
1316 revoked 60/300
1320 revoked 59/409
1321 revoked 59/410
1329 revoked 74/529
1345 revoked 65/1500
1355 revoked 79/1641
1368 amended 67/1482
1379 revoked 64/1794
1387 revoked 59/288
1394 revoked 59/713
1403 revoked 72/820
1423 revoked 83/1106
1424 revoked 74/418
1426 revoked 66/693
1427 revoked 69/1139
1428 amended 64/128; 69/1138
1431 amended 59/1673
1438 revoked 75/182
1440 revoked 59/1586
1441 revoked 59/1585
1442 revoked 59/1584
1443 revoked 59/396
1454 amended 84/108
1455 amended 63/698; 84/108
1456 revoked 71/1316
1466 revoked 68/234
1467 amended 68/233
1468 amended 68/232
1469 amended 68/231
1470 revoked 65/540
1471 revoked 68/230
1472 revoked 60/161
1473 revoked 63/1508
1480 revoked 61/623
1482 revoked 67/489
1484 revoked 65/527
1490 amended 63/1370
1493 revoked 63/261
1494 revoked 68/512
1509 revoked 63/660
1511 revoked 61/623
1512 amended 63/2108; 65/513
1513 amended 64/935
1519 revoked 65/1426
1520 revoked 59/1901
1532 revoked 66/636
1556 revoked 65/538
1571 revoked 59/1334
1578 revoked 60/972
1579 revoked 72/1992
1580 revoked 59/2199

STATUTORY INSTRUMENTS AFFECTED 1947–1988

1956—*cont.*

1581 revoked 59/2200
1582 revoked 59/2201
1588 amended 71/1821; 75/1569
1602 revoked 63/1026
1611 amended 83/941
1615 revoked 59/1686
1616 revoked 65/510
1619 amended 62/2234
1641 revoked 60/1069
1654 revoked 68/1755
1655 revoked 72/196
1657 revoked 72/765
1668 amended 72/1181; 74/2061
1670 revoked 88/1167
1672 revoked 61/2000
1674 revoked 70/16
1685 revoked 59/433
1688 revoked 75/216
1690 revoked 74/389
1691 revoked 84/552
1692 amended 65/1973
1698 revoked 74/389
1700 revoked 59/1977
1734 revoked 63/483
1738 revoked 78/1269
1743 revoked 64/755
1744 revoked 65/54
1745 revoked 62/2248
1750 amended 77/944
1757 revoked 65/613
1758 amended 61/817; 62/594; 63/1617; 66/882; 75/1102; 78/1648; 88/1729
1759 revoked 65/1559
1760 amended 78/1648
1761 amended 78/1648
1762 revoked 60/69
1763 revoked 66/881
1764 amended 60/1116; 66/1139; 75/1102
1765 amended 78/1648; 83/710
1766 amended 67/1083; 74/1853; 75/1102; 77/1205; 78/1648
1767 revoked 61/854
1768 amended 78/1648; 80/942
1769 amended 60/1738; 74/2124; 77/913
1770 revoked 79/318
1771 amended 78/1648
1773 amended 78/1648
1774 revoked 62/1423
1775 revoked 64/209
1778 amended 64/209; 74/2013; 79/318; 81/917; 83/994
1779 amended 83/994; 83/1130
1780 amended 81/917; 83/1026; 88/1930
1781 amended 83/1026
1782 amended 78/1648
1793 revoked 69/297
1794 reroked 65/531
1797 revoked 70/16
1809 amended 69/437
1813 revoked 63/1069
1825 revoked 61/201
1826 revoked 65/533
1827 revoked 72/765
1844 revoked 64/227
1845 revoked 60/1069
1851 amended 64/353; 64/1974; 71/836; 75/285
1853 revoked 60/1165
1873 revoked 64/302

1956—*cont.*

1875 amended 60/1553; 68/1785; 72/878; 77/2195; 82/1224
1878 amended 61/2216
1891 revoked 61/2315
1897 amended 76/225; 88/591
1901 revoked 71/1316
1905 revoked 75/1543
1907 revoked 59/1262
1914 revoked 79/1456
1929 revoked 70/1839
1933 revoked 16/330
1934 revoked 60/1913
1940 revoked 88/1729
1942 amended 78/1648
1943 amended 78/1648
1944 revoked 65/358
1953 revoked 62/2248
1963 amended 65/942
1966 revoked 74/418
1975 revoked 62/1562
1978 revoked 87/918
1981 revoked 80/2005
1984 revoked 60/1601
1986 revoked 64/388
1987 revoked 64/387
1993 amended 61/2399
1999 revoked 68/716
2000 revoked 70/16
2001 revoked 65/1776
2009 revoked 62/2204
2011 revoked 65/1500
2014 amended 64/1148; 71/1329
2017 revoked 67/82
2018 revoked 74/2013
2020 revoked 69/1696
2027 revoked 82/449
2030 revoked 61/1188
2033 revoked 59/1035
2034 revoked 59/1036
2035 revoked 59/1038
2036 revoked 59/1009
2042 revoked 65/1536
2047 amended 61/81
2050 revoked 72/765
2053 revoked 73/1812; 73/1814
2060 revoked 60/160
2077 revoked 62/2753
2087 revoked 59/374
2088 revoked 59/375
2108 revoked 73/693
2118 revoked 75/284
2124 revoked 72/1740

1957

6 revoked 60/234
8 revoked 68/1366
13 revoked 64/1857; 75/1536
63 revoked 65/533
84 amended 66/209
87 revoked 71/927
99 amended 61/2316
114 revoked 65/509
115 amended 61/281
116 revoked 62/787
123 amended 80/1354
126 revoked 61/2000
132 revoked 60/12
138 amended 59/545
163 revoked 59/548

STATUTORY INSTRUMENTS AFFECTED 1947–1988

1957—*cont.*

832 revoked 60/1639
838 revoked 70/1100
845 amended 59/775
846 revoked 74/418
855 revoked 69/1494
856 amended 76/225; 82/1528; revoked 88/590;
    amended 88/591
860 revoked 64/1000
862 revoked 62/405
866 amended 62/2076; 73/409
875 amended 82/766
891 revoked 63/436
909 revoked 59/2108
924 revoked 65/1506
926 revoked 59/2135
929 revoked 83/1730
931 amended 60/1553; 61/859; 71/968; 72/878
940 amended 81/1414
940 revoked 81/917
947 revoked 64/364
948 revoked 77/1260
964 revoked 59/467
966 amended 71/1011
971 revoked 63/1646
972 revoked 86/1078
973 amended 62/296
976 amended 64/2097
977 amended 64/2097
978 revoked 68/1314
981 amended 61/2239; 64/1119; 65/1933
984 amended 69/764; 72/1034
985 revoked 70/786
1012 amended 60/414
1024 amended 75/1807
1026 revoked 59/644
1027 revoked 59/645
1031 revoked 75/1803
1032 revoked 62/1562
1037 revoked 64/504
1045 revoked 70/16
1057 revoked 74/337
1058 amended 75/1412
1066 amended 62/1287; 62/1532; 66/1203
1068 revoked 62/941
1072 revoked 60/972
1074 revoked 75/1208
1076 revoked 60/1054
1080 revoked 61/1792
1081 revoked 60/119
1089 amended 70/106
1094 revoked 67/82
1095 revoked 59/2117
1099 revoked 59/2029
1109 revoked 60/719
1113 amended 59/2282; 60/1875
1118 amended 26/1058
1119 revoked 60/1505
1122 amended 70/392
1125 revoked 64/462
1128 revoked 60/79
1136 amended 64/1974; 71/836
1137 revoked 70/1851
1138 amended 59/1984
1140 revoked 60/2259
1145 revoked 77/1585
1146 revoked 59/1262
1150 amended 66/629
1153 amended 63/572
1154 amended 86/13

1957—*cont.*

1155 amended 69/710
1156 revoked 59/1262
1157 amended 63/795; 69/1771; 73/792; 83/133
1172 revoked 67/1766
1173 revoked 78/467
1175 revoked 62/1586; 62/1616
1177 revoked 68/219
1178 revoked 65/1776
1195 amended 59/772; 59/2055; 64/71; 71/824
1199 revoked 60/2291
1200 revoked 60/1338
1219 amended 62/1284
1222 revoked 72/1693
1232 revoked 59/228
1234 revoked 59/2
1244 revoked 63/1026
1245 revoked 63/436
1246 revoked 63/437
1254 revoked 64/704
1257 amended 60/1948; 61/1213
1261 revoked 59/2071
1262 revoked 59/150
1282 revoked 59/190
1289 revoked 61/139
1297 amended 65/1022
1299 revoked 69/1696
1304 amended 62/596; 74/1462
1305 revoked 59/1334
1309 revoked 72/606
1310 revoked 59/1901
1315 revoked 79/72
1319 revoked 67/330
1322 revoked 73/693
1327 amended 61/751; 70/968
1328 revoked 59/498
1330 revoked 61/141
1332 amended 63/394; 64/2001
1333 amended 64/2001
1334 revoked 61/1983
1340 revoked 67/1168
1341 revoked 60/726
1342 revoked 60/727
1343 revoked 71/2126
1349 revoked 60/1349
1353 revoked 78/1739
1354 amended 67/876; 71/1209
1357 revoked 71/707
1358 revoked 82/975
1363 revoked 60/1652; 60/1654; 60/1656
1366 amended 59/1293
1367 amended 59/1967
1370 revoked 60/972
1378 revoked 70/349
1379 amended 66/202
1383 amended 61/911; 63/657; 67/676
1385 amended 81/1414
1386 amended 76/1247; 81/1414
1391 revoked 63/1026
1392 revoked 73/693
1399 amended 61/2511
1400 revoked 60/1069
1402 revoked 60/1146
1403 revoked 60/1146
1404 amended 62/1695
1405 amended 62/1695
1406 amended 62/1695
1421 revoked 71/778
1422 revoked 70/1100
1423 revoked 68/357

1957—*cont.*

1424 revoked 83/1106
1426 revoked 61/1841
1428 revoked 74/529
1429 revoked 68/1920
1432 revoked 62/2248
1437 revoked 66/579
1440 revoked 63/1722
1455 amended 60/784; 74/2045
1476 revoked 61/1520
1480 amended 63/186; 64/418
1506 revoked 60/600
1523 revoked 64/690
1524 amended 60/847; 61/60; 67/974; 72/1724
1525 revoked 61/2030
1526 revoked 59/1036
1527 revoked 62/1086
1528 revoked 62/405
1529 revoked 62/1874
1530 revoked 60/1652; 60/1654; 60/1656
1531 revoked 60/1652; 60/1654; 60/1656
1542 amended 59/1341; 60/1238
1557 revoked 59/719
1579 revoked 63/1026
1605 amended 64/1608
1612 revoked 59/1456
1614 revoked 59/1457
1622 revoked 59/986
1624 revoked 59/1536
1649 amended 60/2472
1657 revoked 64/2029
1658 revoked 59/177
1683 revoked 84/108
1684 amended 66/339; 71/568
1685 revoked 74/820
1694 revoked 59/2099
1697 amended 66/898
1715 revoked 60/2178
1716 revoked 63/793
1717 revoked 65/1023
1729 revoked 62/1255
1733 revoked 72/765
1734 revoked 72/641
1740 revoked 61/332
1741 amended 61/2316
1742 revoked 59/2199
1743 revoked 59/2200
1745 revoked 59/2201
1746 revoked 62/1086
1748 revoked 62/405
1749 revoked 62/2601
1750 revoked 59/537
1759 amended 61/352
1760 revoked 68/427
1763 revoked 64/755
1764 amended 67/1001
1772 amended 61/595; 66/557
1775 amended 59/1331; 64/1898; 71/823
1780 amended 68/1003
1781 revoked 68/716
1788 revoked 59/1097
1789 revoked 59/1097
1790 revoked 60/491
1797 revoked 59/2238
1798 revoked 65/533
1807 amended 62/1766
1827 amended 62/1614
1834 revoked 66/1250
1835 amended 59/1803; 60/1282; 61/557; 62/300;

1957—*cont.*

   67/1168;   69/1696;   70/1981;   71/707;
   72/603; 72/604; 73/1124
1842 revoked 66/253
1849 revoked 72/603
1859 amended 84/354
1861 revoked 83/1718
1862 revoked 64/504
1870 revoked 67/330
1871 revoked 59/1854
1872 revoked 59/1027
1875 revoked 61/2274
1879 amended 76/225; 88/591
1880 amended 62/977; 64/38
1888 revoked 70/1981
1889 revoked 72/604
1894 revoked 62/1677
1896 amended 61/1495
1907 revoked 59/396
1919 amended 61/958
1925 revoked 63/1159
1931 revoked 60/1754
1934 revoked 59/1145
1937 amended 62/417
1949 revoked 72/606
1950 amended 60/2422; 71/1220; 74/1128
1951 amended 74/1128
1954 revoked 77/1230
1961 revoked 61/485
1970 amended 61/729
1972 revoked 71/2124
1976 revoked 60/1069
1993 revoked 62/787
2004 revoked 65/538
2011 revoked 68/694
2022 amended 60/920
2027 revoked 86/401
2039 revoked 68/716
2050 revoked 60/972
2051 amended 78/1062; 83/771
2059 amended 71/1239
2072 revoked 59/1241
2074 revoked 64/504
2075 revoked 61/203
2077 amended   60/2422;   67/1265;   71/1220;
   71/1419; 72/603; 72/604; 72/606; 74/1128
2091 revoked 68/1769
2094 revoked 65/1500
2097 revoked 64/242
2109 revoked 59/668
2133 amended 71/825
2141 amended 62/2477; 64/1419
2146 revoked 70/1981
2149 revoked 64/1857
2150 amended 60/1096
2151 revoked 63/230
2152 revoked 63/522
2157 revoked 60/1601
2160 amended 62/123
2167 revoked 59/2197
2168 revoked 62/405
2170 revoked 59/190
2172 revoked 64/302
2173 amended 70/392
2174 revoked 59/397
2175 revoked 72/555
2176 revoked 69/1696
2177 revoked 62/300
2179 revoked 73/1124
2180 revoked 72/1433

STATUTORY INSTRUMENTS AFFECTED 1947–1988

1957—*cont.*
2182 revoked 66/727
2191 revoked 82/688
2197 amended 69/710
2198 revoked 59/1585
2200 revoked 70/16
2201 revoked 71/1894
2202 revoked 68/219
2203 revoked 59/1
2208 amended 74/2170; 87/180
2210 revoked 62/1562
2212 revoked 66/164
2214 amended 59/2024
2215 revoked 60/398
2216 revoked 75/1647
2220 revoked 63/791
2224 amended 80/714; 81/1124; 83/1676
2225 amended 64/489; 72/966
2226 amended 71/936
2228 amended 81/1763
2229 revoked 72/1693
2232 revoked 62/1939
2233 amended 86/136; 87/613
2240 revoked 66/1168
2242 amended 72/681; revoked 86/401
2243 revoked 67/386
2245 amended 62/215
2248 revoked 76/820
2249 revoked 59/1069
2251 amended 67/735

1958
2 revoked 59/918
4 revoked 74/2078
5 revoked 60/235
17 revoked 68/1366
42 revoked 61/213
43 revoked 64/418
44 amended 62/489; 68/125
48 revoked 62/2756
55 revoked 65/532
61 amended 60/1307; 71/1060; 73/36; 84/1593
73 revoked 68/1389
80 revoked 68/1463
90 revoked 63/261
98 amended 60/1771
101 revoked 71/1469
135 revoked 64/690
136 revoked 87/52
142 revoked 80/699
144 amended 62/168
151 revoked 63/1026
153 revoked 59/1869
154 revoked 60/1146
155 revoked 65/1707
158 revoked 62/2735
160 revoked 61/2307
161 revoked 70/1869
163 amended 64/255
165 amended 86/58
166 revoked 63/548
182 revoked 61/1792
183 revoked 60/119
184 amended 65/1509
197 revoked 59/1901
214 amended 65/1673
216 revoked 61/2399
217 revoked 61/623
218 revoked 59/588
239 revoked 68/1012

1958—*cont.*
251 amended 65/1638
257 amended 68/257; revoked 86/1951
258 amended 61/2316
259 revoked 65/1864
261 amended 59/1292
262 revoked 59/537
263 amended 63/2085; 65/2013
268 revoked 68/1525
270 revoked 60/727
271 revoked 63/1508
276 revoked 74/389
279 revoked 61/542
285 revoked 66/11
288 revoked 60/2259
299 revoked 66/1351
301 amended 82/41; 83/561
302 revoked 61/2376
304 revoked 60/1125
305 revoked 71/1524
308 revoked 73/1060
309 revoked 60/559
310 revoked 71/1524
313 amended 62/2527; 79/427; 81/1059; 84/1244; revoked 86/1951
326 amended 60/327
331 revoked 67/65
342 revoked 61/36
343 revoked 63/318
357 revoked 60/1473
358 amended 62/655
359 amended 65/2142
364 revoked 65/1995
365 revoked 61/019
368 revoked 74/418
370 revoked 64/1148
371 revoked 59/1778
392 amended 65/634
399 revoked 60/1143
403 revoked 59/1628
416 revoked 67/1485
417 revoked 59/1312
420 revoked 62/2786
422 amended 88/591
423 amended 76/225; 88/591
426 amended 69/369
427 amended 61/2322
428 revoked 61/1192
429 revoked 60/1652; 60/1654; 60/1656
430 revoked 60/1652; 60/1654; 60/1656
434 amended 63/773; 65/58; 70/1845
440 amended 61/2399
441 revoked 59/1535
459 revoked 60/503
468 revoked 60/2178
469 revoked 62/271
471 revoked 62/36
472 revoked 84/1406
473 revoked 72/751
496 revoked 75/1733
497 revoked 66/1143
501 revoked 61/2349
502 revoked 61/654
503 revoked 63/793
505 revoked 74/32
507 revoked 66/1250
518 amended 62/610; 71/537
519 amended 68/588; 72/42; 74/563; 74/1574; 74/1972; 75/854; 75/1298
523 amended 72/503

STATUTORY INSTRUMENTS AFFECTED 1947–1988

524 amended 62/156
531 revoked 66/1163
532 revoked 62/1796
533 revoked 59/644
534 revoked 59/645
535 revoked 61/1441
543 revoked 59/623
544 revoked 59/547
549 revoked 58/726
554 amended 65/420; 83/1646
557 revoked 60/2178
558 amended 78/17; 80/1563
560 revoked 64/242
564 revoked 61/213
565 revoked 59/1899
566 revoked 63/845
568 revoked 68/1595
581 revoked 60/1363
583 amended 64/418
586 revoked 70/1737
587 amended 60/1229; 62/1489
589 revoked 60/1071
590 revoked 65/1864
591 revoked 59/2206
592 revoked 61/2274
594 revoked 63/1148
595 amended 59/1967
597 amended 76/225; 88/591
599 amended 83/1676; revoked 85/172
600 amended 59/1302; 60/703; 60/1276; 60/2201; 61/2036; 61/2272; 61/2273; 62/2599; 63/791
602 revoked 65/1105
605 revoked 62/2756
617 revoked 59/161
620 revoked 59/2238
621 revoked 68/1089
627 revoked 59/1555
642 revoked 59/2090
644 amended 62/1376
646 revoked 61/2483
650 revoked 65/1776
652 revoked 68/1262
655 revoked 65/1753
656 revoked 59/2010
658 amended 67/848; 69/1627; 82/942
659 amended 60/395; 63/1389; 65/606
660 revoked 61/1996
662 revoked 62/1562
664 revoked 71/986; 83/1216
666 revoked 61/1524
670 revoked 60/676
685 revoked 79/1050
701 revoked 67/1168
702 revoked 67/1169
706 revoked 62/1562
708 revoked 59/1454
709 revoked 62/1787
714 revoked 66/1066
718 revoked 60/2151
724 amended 66/324; 72/867; 77/1608; 80/1106; revoked 83/1216
744 revoked 69/1139
750 revoked 59/1508
752 revoked 60/1794
765 revoked 71/214
767 revoked 63/885
769 revoked 61/1194
771 amended 76/225; 88/591

772 amended 76/225; 88/591
787 revoked 71/981
788 amended 61/860; 64/710
817 revoked 61/901
819 revoked 59/1869
820 revoked 59/2108
828 revoked 62/1585
829 revoked 65/1734
830 amended 59/502
831 revoked 59/501
832 amended 67/1012
837 revoked 60/726
844 revoked 59/161
847 amended 71/915
849 revoked 61/1101
865 revoked 62/1670
872 revoked 65/1316
892 revoked 60/234
893 revoked 59/288
899 revoked 59/986
907 revoked 60/856
908 revoked 59/2135
915 revoked 59/1772
917 revoked 61/2315
923 amended 59/300; 60/954; 62/2577; 64/62; 65/1068; 67/1003; 68/1221
924 revoked 61/751
926 revoked 72/751
928 revoked 63/1193
932 revoked 59/702
949 revoked 70/16
956 revoked 71/290
957 revoked 68/1986
958 revoked 76/250
961 revoked 59/330
962 revoked 86/1951
970 revoked 62/611
973 amended 59/313; 59/391; 59/423; 59/520; 59/736; 59/1004; 59/1215; 59/1250; 59/1591; 59/1957; 59/2133; 60/252; 60/381; 60/541; 60/737; 60/811; 60/908; 60/1074; 60/1218; 60/1219; 60/1533; 60/1764; 60/1970; 60/2309; 61/128; 61/279
979 revoked 60/513
980 revoked 60/770
1002 revoked 60/12
1006 revoked 62/1562
1008 revoked 60/121
1015 amended 60/698
1016 revoked 60/699
1017 revoked 64/613
1041 amended 59/1343; 69/1888
1049 revoked 60/2202
1050 revoked 60/442
1051 revoked 78/186
1052 amended 61/60; 72/1724
1055 revoked 59/1
1056 revoked 60/1688
1060 revoked 67/711
1061 revoked 87/730
1063 revoked 60/221
1064 revoked 63/2128
1065 revoked 71/1148
1068 revoked 59/467
1069 revoked 64/1178
1071 revoked 60/79
1074 amended 65/324
1082 revoked 59/1125

1083 revoked 64/504
1092 revoked 59/1686
1093 revoked 61/1996
1094 revoked 60/594
1095 amended 65/932
1103 amended 66/629
1106 amended 59/1480; 60/1832; 60/2188
1107 revoked 67/1022
1109 revoked 60/185
1110 revoked 60/96
1122 revoked 62/1685
1126 revoked 81/1142
1138 revoked 65/1426
1140 revoked 59/386
1142 amended 64/1895
1143 revoked 62/1868
1150 revoked 60/6
1156 revoked 63/1160
1166 revoked 62/1003
1172 amended 59/1341; 60/1238
1174 revoked 59/83
1180 revoked 59/161
1181 amended 69/1327
1182 revoked 60/1754
1192 revoked 68/694
1206 revoked 62/1679
1208 amended 59/445; 67/69; 70/708; 72/1218;
        75/12; 77/1602; 79/794; 85/565; 85/1150;
        86/770; 88/295
1212 revoked 59/1266
1217 revoked 60/181
1219 revoked 63/934
1223 revoked 61/1062
1226 revoked 70/1100
1232 revoked 60/1
1235 revoked 74/768
1237 revoked 67/386
1238 amended 71/1419
1240 revoked 66/1641
1243 revoked 65/1192
1244 revoked 62/2248
1246 revoked 65/1776
1249 revoked 62/1371
1250 revoked 88/1082
1251 revoked 60/972
1252 revoked 61/834
1254 revoked 64/690
1255 revoked 61/2323
1256 revoked 62/2601
1257 revoked 60/1652; 60/1654; 60/1656
1258 revoked 60/1652; 60/1654; 60/1656
1259 amended   60/1056;   60/1960;   60/2415;
        61/741
1260 revoked 61/741
1262 amended 67/1482
1263 amended 76/225; 88/591
1264 revoked 75/1704
1269 amended 59/1171
1270 amended 60/1971
1271 revoked 66/509
1273 revoked 74/520
1281 revoked 59/1279
1283 revoked 63/1781
1286 revoked 61/814
1287 revoked 67/1725
1289 amended 60/364
1301 revoked 75/308
1319 revoked 62/1532
1323 revoked 66/579

1324 amended 62/1939
1328 revoked 74/812
1327 revoked 60/1045
1335 revoked 59/644
1336 revoked 59/645
1349 revoked 59/1586
1350 revoked 70/1851
1390 revoked 70/786
1391 revoked 60/1413
1402 revoked 69/1642
1407 revoked 60/160
1411 revoked 67/1022
1416 revoked 69/975
1417 revoked 59/161
1444 amended 88/1758
1454 amended 62/1287
1460 revoked 63/709
1472 amended 61/545
1473 revoked 60/719
1478 revoked 64/884
1479 revoked 64/885
1486 amended 62/1694
1487 amended 63/634
1492 amended 62/2047
1506 revoked 70/16
1514 amended 69/592
1516 revoked 62/405
1519 amended 60/1367
1520 revoked 59/105
1522 revoked 60/1652; 60/1654; 60/1656
1523 revoked 60/1653
1524 revoked 61/741
1525 revoked 59/1977
1526 revoked 83/1106
1527 revoked 81/612
1530 amended 76/1315
1535 revoked 60/600
1548 revoked 60/929
1553 revoked 61/1581
1562 amended 60/625; 71/1148
1565 revoked 60/220
1574 revoked 62/417
1575 amended 62/937
1583 revoked 59/1457
1595 revoked 69/77
1597 revoked 65/1559
1606 revoked 67/422
1607 amended 62/2613; 62/2691; 68/1154
1615 amended 64/474
1617 revoked 83/1718
1620 amended 68/508
1624 revoked 63/1094
1632 amended 85/1677
1634 revoked 67/29
1642 revoked 73/997
1644 amended 62/2163
1649 amended 62/1696
1650 revoked 59/1262
1653 revoked 75/679
1659 revoked 59/2071
1660 revoked 63/401
1675 amended 62/2871
1676 amended 64/1604; 74/894
1690 revoked 61/946
1697 revoked 59/396
1706 revoked 65/635
1716 revoked 66/11
1717 revoked 66/10
1718 revoked 67/1022

1958—cont.

1721 amended 59/751
1728 amended 62/1939
1737 revoked 67/72
1745 revoked 62/760
1746 revoked 63/483
1747 amended 62/2177
1750 revoked 59/1312
1751 amended 66/1188
1765 revoked 80/6
1766 revoked 59/574
1767 revoked 60/137
1780 revoked 75/1722
1790 revoked 59/644
1791 revoked 59/645
1802 revoked 60/1312
1803 revoked 60/1311
1804 revoked 60/1883
1807 revoked 72/1693
1808 amended 61/631; 72/1464; 84/108
1814 amended 60/1557; 66/162; revoked 87/1758
1819 revoked 86/2312
1822 amended 63/1136
1846 revoked 61/1996
1848 revoked 62/1320
1849 revoked 60/1025
1851 amended 60/798; 63/1679; 64/368
1860 revoked 74/418
1872 amended 71/174; 71/1796; 73/1774; 76/373; revoked 87/492
1881 revoked 63/230
1882 revoked 65/538
1913 amended 59/1965
1923 amended 78/963
1924 amended 78/962
1935 revoked 75/182
1936 amended 60/499
1937 revoked 59/161
1939 revoked 63/2047
1941 revoked 61/403
1953 revoked 59/537
1957 revoked 59/104
1958 revoked 60/1652; 60/1654; 60/1656
1966 revoked 60/667
1971 amended 83/689; 84/1310
1975 amended 77/971; revoked 84/810
1976 amended 69/1339
1979 revoked 84/810
1981 revoked 60/739
1983 revoked 59/1147
1988 amended 64/418
1990 amended 78/1919; 83/525
1991 amended 62/1591; 88/2132
2009 revoked 68/716
2011 revoked 62/1562
2024 revoked 74/287
2039 revoked 62/2584
2041 amended 60/328
2045 revoked 60/1649
2046 amended 63/465; 71/1398
2048 revoked 74/507
2049 revoked 59/1938
2050 revoked 65/1321
2055 revoked 75/2054
2060 amended 63/657
2062 revoked 85/831
2063 revoked 85/831
2066 amended 62/2736; 77/822; 71/1771
2076 revoked 59/1842
2078 revoked 62/1685

1958—cont.

2082 revoked 68/219
2083 amended 59/2162
2084 amended 60/2293
2089 amended 61/495
2092 revoked 72/1693
2093 revoked 65/527
2094 revoked 65/1776
2095 revoked 60/809
2096 revoked 60/1189
2109 revoked 60/96
2110 amended 83/1026
2112 revoked 59/467
2116 revoked 64/302
2122 amended 60/698
2123 revoked 60/699
2124 amended 60/2422
2125 amended 62/622
2127 revoked 59/622
2129 revoked 62/742
2134 revoked 64/2056
2141 amended 62/918; revoked 87/1787
2148 amended 64/105; 71/333
2149 revoked 62/2248
2151 revoked 74/418
2152 revoked 59/1584
2153 revoked 59/1585
2154 revoked 59/1262
2166 amended   59/1493;   60/911;   60/1540;
      60/2154; 61/443; 62/568; 66/699; 67/303;
      67/885; 83/688; 84/1311
2167 revoked 62/1532
2168 revoked 77/1805
2169 revoked 64/755
2171 revoked 62/389
2173 revoked 59/809
2181 revoked 63/1323
2184 revoked 64/690
2186 revoked 60/1054
2187 amended 61/2316
2190 revoked 61/834
2191 revoked 69/734
2192 revoked 59/748
2194 amended 65/2195; 73/630
2198 revoked 65/261
2200 amended 70/392
2215 revoked 60/2263
2216 revoked 62/1562
2221 revoked 65/2197
2222 revoked 61/794
2223 revoked 61/403
2224 revoked 59/1842
2225 revoked 59/1842
2226 amended 64/1974; 71/836; 75/1545
2233 amended 63/988; 71/514; 72/1506; 76/1142
2262 revoked 78/1684
2268 revoked 60/251
2270 revoked 61/1117
2271 revoked 59/2238
2276 revoked 62/2125

1959

1 revoked 67/1875
2 revoked 60/1675
3 amended   71/809;   77/1890;   80/1896;
      86/1962
18 revoked 61/2420
29 revoked 79/72
40 revoked 74/768
47 amended 60/729; 70/785

1959—*cont.*

48 revoked 63/1159
60 amended 68/1571
61 revoked 73/270
62 amended 64/489
81 revoked 78/259
82 revoked 72/1207
83 amended 60/1885; 64/17; 64/366; 67/174;
   67/396
86 revoked 64/404
89 amended 62/213
95 amended 64/1895
96 revoked 74/1817
104 revoked 60/205
105 revoked 62/1874
106 revoked 63/1148
119 revoked 74/529
121 revoked 68/512
136 revoked 59/1239
148 revoked 59/1586
150 revoked 60/983
151 revoked 60/235
161 revoked 60/1296
162 revoked 80/1468
170 revoked 74/418
174 amended 70/806; 70/1064; 72/1755
177 revoked 60/615
178 revoked 60/334
179 revoked 60/1363
180 amended 67/396
190 revoked 61/2242
192 revoked 60/119
204 amended 60/342
207 amended 71/1421
213 revoked 68/1366
220 revoked 65/1426
221 revoked 64/409
225 revoked 62/2735
228 amended 60/844; 60/845; 62/2341; 62/2436
235 revoked 59/1457
237 revoked 59/1456
238 revoked 59/1457
239 revoked 59/1457
243 revoked 61/281
244 revoked 63/798
258 revoked 68/491
259 amended 62/8; 66/1131
260 revoked 65/260
261 revoked 65/936
270 revoked 59/1842
272 revoked 63/1876
277 amended   62/1288;   73/1064;   77/171;
   79/1567; 83/1703; 85/68
278 revoked 71/394
279 amended 64/2099; 64/2100
286 amended 62/1296
287 revoked 61/946
288 revoked 59/2232
290 revoked 60/281
291 revoked 60/281
292 amended 61/1388; 65/1538
293 amended 61/1834; 65/1541
296 amended 64/268; 74/1654
297 revoked 64/1000
300 revoked 60/954
301 revoked 70/1961
302 revoked 71/593
306 amended 64/20
313 revoked 61/403
314 revoked 59/1842

1959—*cont.*

330 revoked 59/2079
337 amended 71/534
338 revoked 66/214
358 amended 66/249
359 revoked 78/259
362 revoked 81/1086
363 revoked 74/259
364 revoked 82/106
365 amended 62/2073; 71/342; 73/2021; 73/340;
   75/1962;   77/278;   78/1146;   80/888;
   81/1087; 82/129; revoked 83/1499
366 amended 64/1083; 69/410; 77/278; revoked
   83/74
367 revoked 59/1586
368 revoked 60/1652; 60/1654; 60/1656
369 revoked 60/1652; 60/1654; 60/1656
370 revoked 61/623
373 revoked 59/847
374 revoked 67/1189
375 revoked 65/756
377 amended 74/557; 75/2188; 83/1124
379 amended 60/1464
381 amended 62/2515
382 revoked 72/751
384 revoked 63/1468
386 revoked 59/2256
391 revoked 61/403
393 revoked 69/403
394 revoked 69/403
395 revoked 67/792
396 revoked 67/792
397 revoked 59/1832
400 amended 70/684
406 amended 63/1624; 88/1295
408 revoked 59/1307
409 revoked 69/483
411 amended 60/625, 71/1148
413 amended 78/173; 85/1068
423 revoked 61/403
425 amended 62/469; 68/507
426 amended 74/1422
427 amended 76/1247; 81/1414
428 amended 76/1247; 81/1414
429 revoked 65/726
430 revoked 69/757
431 revoked 70/201
433 amended 61/2099; 64/1874; 69/925; 84/108
444 revoked 59/1901
447 amended 66/1088
450 revoked 65/1776
452 amended 61/152
466 revoked 71/311
467 revoked 75/1537
469 amended 62/467
471 revoked 67/1864; 70/400
472 revoked 67/1866
474 amended 62/1690
476 revoked 71/1537
477 amended   68/1849;   72/1753;   73/321;
   79/1185
479 revoked 71/1520
480 revoked 76/1644
481 revoked 66/579
493 revoked 62/2871
496 revoked 69/1704
498 revoked 65/1735
499 revoked 65/1734
500 revoked 61/141
501 amended 61/144; 62/1097; 63/563

STATUTORY INSTRUMENTS AFFECTED 1947–1988

1959—*cont.*
503 revoked 61/714
504 revoked 76/1768
518 revoked 74/32
520 revoked 61/403
521 revoked 59/1842
522 revoked 59/1842
524 revoked 64/228
525 amended 64/374
526 revoked 63/1109
528 revoked 68/2049
529 revoked 68/2050
531 revoked 62/2786
537 revoked 68/114
538 revoked 64/1000
539 amended 66/1; 68/331
547 revoked 60/627
548 revoked 62/623
549 revoked 60/278
552 amended 60/644; 61/507; 61/551; 62/1047;
    62/2851; 63/782; 66/142; 70/676; 71/1572
568 amended 69/118
569 amended 64/1899; 66/1401
570 amended 69/23
572 revoked 70/1285
574 revoked 60/135
588 amended 61/1812; 62/2371; 63/1898; 65/58;
    70/1548
589 amended 60/1872; 83/1718
615 revoked 59/1278
622 revoked 68/137
623 revoked 60/269
625 revoked 62/2187
629 amended 62/1817
639 revoked 76/1796
640 amended   59/1887;   60/597;   61/1527;
    62/1138; 62/2406; 63/2054; 64/2031;
    68/163
644 revoked 60/1151
645 revoked 60/1151
668 revoked 60/2250
670 amended 63/225
677 revoked 67/212
678 revoked 65/904
679 amended 73/2202
685 revoked 65/1635
686 revoked 67/330
702 revoked 60/596
705 revoked 75/182
707 revoked 72/1833
713 revoked 59/1832
719 revoked 61/773
725 revoked 60/727
726 revoked 65/538
731 revoked 60/1069
734 amended 62/1287; 63/1083; 83/1727; 85/67
736 revoked 61/403
747 revoked 68/716
748 amended 64/476; 65/64; 65/1663; 69/759;
    70/426; 70/1289; 71/152; 71/1437;
    72/1779
759 revoked 67/386
761 revoked 64/1857
763 amended 71/1163; 77/977; revoked 84/1013
765 amended 74/275; 77/939
766 revoked 74/32
771 revoked 74/418
772 amended 59/2055; 64/71; 71/824
773 revoked 82/34
785 amended 71/25

1959—*cont.*
787 revoked 60/6
789 revoked 62/1685
802 amended   64/1148; 71/1329; 74/1797;
    75/1717
804 revoked 61/1996
809 revoked 60/95
813 revoked 74/595
829 amended 70/1847
831 amended   60/2261; 62/1287; 63/1435;
    66/1203; 72/1391; 73/1052; 73/1340;
    75/1486; 83/1727; 85/67
833 revoked 76/475
834 revoked 87/2233
835 revoked 85/1799
836 revoked 67/1022
837 revoked 61/523
847 revoked 69/1696
848 revoked 67/1168
849 amended 61/239
861 amended 70/1437; revoked 86/1299
862 revoked 62/1550
863 revoked 62/1646
864 revoked 62/1649
869 revoked 81/612
872 amended 70/484; 75/805
874 amended 59/1979
875 amended 67/1482
876 amended 60/769; 62/2455
877 revoked 62/787
886 revoked 63/1937
890 revoked 72/2051
892 revoked 64/409
899 revoked 70/1126
906 revoked 81/917
909 revoked 66/569
910 revoked 59/1578
917 revoked 73/2037
920 amended 60/494; 76/241
921 revoked 62/1685
928 amended   72/1489; 73/1039; 73/1310;
    75/1597; 83/270; 84/1518; 85/1068
937 revoked 64/504
939 revoked 63/286
940 amended 63/743; 74/607; 83/327
942 revoked 59/1290
949 amended 62/562; 71/822; 71/1771
955 amended 71/1525
956 revoked 74/149
961 amended 69/630; 62/562
962 revoked 74/595
963 revoked 74/595
972 revoked 71/986; amended 83/1216
975 revoked 65/163
976 amended 64/441
977 revoked 62/417
978 revoked 65/1105
979 amended 63/1256
981 amended   60/402;   60/1248;   60/2394;
    61/1620
982 amended   60/402;   60/1248;   60/2394;
    61/1620
983 amended 61/1119; revoked 85/63
984 revoked 85/64
986 revoked 60/2130
999 amended 67/677
1002 revoked 65/723
1003 revoked 59/1842
1004 revoked 61/403
1010 revoked 64/1354

1959—*cont.*

1018 amended 60/273
1027 revoked 61/22
1028 amended 66/455
1029 revoked 75/203
1035 amended 67/24; 69/855
1036 revoked 61/1001
1037 amended 62/168
1038 amended 62/406; 63/2093; 69/856
1039 amended 63/2095; 69/859
1040 revoked 62/1338
1041 revoked 63/1148
1044 revoked 61/1192
1047 revoked 61/2274
1048 revoked 61/2274
1049 revoked 60/1652; 60/1654; 60/1656
1050 revoked 60/1652; 60/1654; 60/1656
1051 amended 61/2316
1052 amended 69/592
1053 revoked 60/1296
1060 revoked 60/408
1063 amended 77/273
1076 revoked 61/1996
1077 revoked 60/594
1078 revoked 60/594
1079 amended 61/2211; 62/1005; 64/569
1080 revoked 65/243
1081 revoked 65/243
1082 revoked 61/276
1083 revoked 62/1562
1094 revoked 74/1940
1095 amended 62/1296
1096 revoked 67/1199
1097 revoked 60/1588
1098 revoked 77/928
1099 revoked 65/2197
1105 revoked 65/537
1106 revoked 64/1637
1113 revoked 59/1842
1114 revoked 62/1685
1115 revoked 77/1027
1123 revoked 64/2003
1125 revoked 60/754
1130 amended 66/34
1131 amended 62/2130; 67/36; 87/750
1133 revoked 61/2101
1135 revoked 64/418
1145 revoked 60/1256
1147 revoked 82/1163
1148 revoked 62/2126
1149 revoked 64/464
1150 revoked 64/349
1151 revoked 62/2708
1154 revoked 67/1168
1155 revoked 70/1524
1156 revoked 67/1169
1157 revoked 67/1170
1169 revoked 69/212
1170 revoked 65/1506
1175 amended 61/1481
1176 revoked 61/2499
1192 amended 66/629
1204 revoked 59/1842
1207 revoked 70/615
1214 revoked 62/1685
1215 revoked 61/403
1216 amended 76/1247; 81/1414
1217 amended 75/1102
1226 revoked 69/628
1240 amended 60/1220; 61/1100

1959—*cont.*

1241 amended 60/2395; 63/396; 64/2003
1243 amended 65/537
1250 revoked 61/403
1251 amended 71/836; 74/1354; 75/1345
1253 revoked 68/458
1262 revoked 71/1649
1265 revoked 62/1586
1266 revoked 70/1100
1271 revoked 70/1100
1274 revoked 62/1616
1277 revoked 65/194
1278 revoked 67/330
1279 revoked 66/980
1280 revoked 61/1210
1281 revoked 62/1585
1282 revoked 70/107
1286 revoked 63/709; 63/749
1287 revoked 64/1382
1290 revoked 72/604
1291 revoked 63/365
1294 revoked 59/1967
1296 revoked 68/1862
1298 revoked 63/87
1299 revoked 63/86
1302 revoked 63/791
1310 revoked 60/1652; 63/88
1312 revoked 62/1652
1318 revoked 73/425
1324 amended 61/1484
1325 amended 61/1487
1326 amended 61/1488
1331 amended 60/2409; 64/1898; 71/823
1333 revoked 61/542
1334 amended 66/914
1336 revoked 66/508
1341 amended 60/1238
1346 amended 71/1106; 83/1646
1348 revoked 84/1936
1349 revoked 68/1463
1350 revoked 60/1471
1360 revoked 60/1778
1361 revoked 75/679
1362 amended 71/1634
1363 amended 70/597
1375 amended 62/717; 63/262; 65/155; 65/1847;
     67/1940; 71/1855; 72/345
1388 revoked 69/1437
1391 revoked 65/538
1396 revoked 62/1562
1398 revoked 70/718
1399 amended 63/976; 67/963
1400 revoked 66/253
1424 revoked 70/16
1432 amended 63/1222; 68/379
1433 amended 60/2094
1454 revoked 62/1786
1455 revoked 60/555
1456 revoked 60/1708
1457 revoked 60/1708
1458 amended 66/249; 72/258
1459 amended 62/981; 65/1089; 66/500; 73/497;
     75/852
1460 revoked 64/1150
1461 revoked 64/1151
1468 amended 71/1041
1474 revoked 62/141
1482 amended 61/624; 67/1928
1484 revoked 64/1381
1485 revoked 68/1405

1495 revoked 64/1148
1501 amended 62/2116; 73/498
1507 amended 72/97
1508 revoked 60/1870
1509 revoked 59/1938
1530 revoked 59/1842
1534 revoked 71/1316
1535 revoked 60/2030
1536 revoked 61/1130
1541 amended 61/565; 62/79
1542 revoked 72/990
1543 revoked 77/1805
1551 revoked 63/42
1555 revoked 60/931
1556 revoked 60/930
1557 revoked 60/2151
1569 revoked 64/2029
1571 amended 60/245; 60/625; 71/1148
1573 amended 69/710
1575 amended 64/1895
1578 revoked 67/65
1581 revoked 65/1453
1584 revoked 61/2379
1585 revoked 61/2360
1586 revoked 61/2361
1589 amended 64/409
1591 revoked 61/403
1592 revoked 60/95
1596 revoked 67/1169
1597 revoked 62/1936
1602 revoked 70/260
1605 revoked 62/2463
1607 revoked 59/1842
1608 revoked 66/907
1609 amended 64/572
1610 revoked 64/875
1619 amended 62/2730
1620 revoked 63/1626
1663 revoked 67/964
1685 revoked 71/282
1686 revoked 61/1309
1692 amended 67/522
1693 revoked 70/786
1714 revoked 60/1151
1715 revoked 60/1151
1717 revoked 60/796
1732 revoked 63/483
1733 revoked 66/579
1770 revoked 67/480
1772 revoked 60/1652; 60/1654; 60/1656
1773 revoked 62/2187
1774 revoked 64/926
1775 revoked 63/1323
1778 revoked 60/1811
1787 revoked 71/1593
1788 amended 63/2150; 64/2006
1788 revoked 72/2025
1793 amended 67/847
1800 amended 83/118
1803 amended 69/1696
1805 revoked 60/408
1823 revoked 60/1296
1831 amended 64/1149; 66/1046
1832 amended 61/2203; 63/1379; 64/1312; 65/1;
    65/1978; 68/1148; 75/1964; 78/1145;
    80/1861; 81/1788; 83/74; 87/1182
1842 amended 59/2086; 60/216; 60/294; 60/542
1854 revoked 60/1986
1860 amended 61/2176; 63/676; 65/40; 74/2058

1861 amended 60/1104; 61/137; 72/428; 72/1031
1868 revoked 65/936
1869 revoked 64/205
1879 revoked 62/1685
1899 revoked 60/2082
1900 revoked 69/79
1901 revoked 60/717
1904 revoked 65/538
1915 revoked 64/1382
1916 amended 70/392
1917 revoked 68/716
1924 revoked 64/229
1925 revoked 64/227
1933 amended 62/2818
1936 revoked 63/1646
1938 revoked 61/955
1942 revoked 61/1996
1947 revoked 65/1776
1948 revoked 67/530
1950 revoked 64/242
1957 revoked 61/403
1958 revoked 65/1776
1964 revoked 65/435
1965 amended 62/191; 62/980; 62/2746; 65/298;
    65/1096
1968 amended 64/1197
1972 amended 61/568; 61/1828
1976 revoked 61/1194
1977 amended 60/440
1978 revoked 61/742
1981 revoked 60/1652; 60/1654; 60/1656
1982 revoked 60/1654; 60/1656
1983 revoked 60/205
1985 amended 61/1376
1991 amended 61/628
1992 revoked 70/16
1994 revoked 63/1114
1999 revoked 60/1151
2000 revoked 60/1151
2001 amended 62/2141; 63/630; 63/1786; 67/404
2005 revoked 63/1159
2010 revoked 60/1917
2011 revoked 60/2310
2015 revoked 72/1693
2024 amended 62/656; 68/1154
2026 revoked 63/1
2027 revoked 70/2021
2028 revoked 70/2022
2042 revoked 61/1792
2043 revoked 60/119
2052 revoked 63/985
2053 revoked 86/1078
2054 amended 60/547
2055 amended 64/71; 71/824
2063 revoked 65/1500
2067 revoked 71/2124
2068 revoked 60/1754
2069 amended 64/21
2070 revoked 60/664
2071 revoked 60/1713
2073 revoked 61/1316
2079 revoked 61/759
2080 revoked 66/95
2081 revoked 81/917
2084 amended 63/1674
2086 amended 60/542
2090 revoked 60/1916
2091 revoked 70/1130
2098 revoked 73/1388

1959—cont.

2102 revoked 65/726
2103 revoked 65/726
2104 revoked 65/726
2105 revoked 65/726
2106 amended 62/1287; 75/1484; 83/1727; revoked 84/1304
2108 revoked 69/840
2115 amended 62/1404; 68/1039; 76/335; 83/560; revoked 86/401
2117 revoked 80/804
2118 revoked 80/804
2119 amended 83/118
2131 revoked 74/418
2133 revoked 61/403
2135 revoked 61/903
2146 revoked 60/584
2147 revoked 60/584
2148 revoked 70/294
2164 revoked 62/1562
2175 revoked 62/2756
2182 amended 75/1594; 83/270; revoked 84/1518
2194 amended 60/1088; 62/2871
2197 amended 60/1658; 67/162; 67/223; 67/231; 73/2155
2198 revoked 67/226
2199 amended 60/202; 67/226
2200 revoked 67/227
2201 amended 67/232; 67/587; 68/1093
2202 revoked 62/1550
2203 revoked 61/2315
2204 amended 61/335
2205 revoked 63/88
2206 amended 67/225; 67/228; 67/472
2209 amended 62/827
2211 revoked 63/885
2214 revoked 61/2460
2216 amended 76/225; 77/1873
2231 revoked 63/1646
2232 revoked 61/922
2238 amended 61/599; 61/1116; 61/1920; 64/753; 65/1575; 67/173; 67/1619
2239 revoked 60/258
2240 revoked 60/260
2245 revoked 69/269
2252 revoked 60/1151
2253 revoked 60/1151
2254 revoked 65/1707
2255 revoked 72/1188
2256 revoked 61/1007
2257 revoked 68/716
2258 amended 83/994
2259 amended 83/1026
2261 revoked 65/1622
2262 revoked 61/2307
2264 revoked 70/1190
2274 revoked 65/538
2275 revoked 66/908
2277 revoked 62/1562
2282 amended 61/1953; 67/938; 72/147; 86/1733
2285 amended 60/1244
2286 amended 61/14
2296 revoked 71/1524
2310 revoked 68/512
2328 amended 62/1030

1960

1 revoked 61/921
6 revoked 61/942
12 revoked 61/1

1960—cont.

13 revoked 71/1524
20 revoked 65/2155
41 revoked 74/529
46 revoked 62/389
62 amended 61/1051; 63/1563
63 revoked 62/417
65 amended 63/1537
66 revoked 60/695
68 revoked 60/2178
69 amended 68/1037; 78/1648
74 revoked 63/1209
75 amended 62/1152
77 revoked 62/503
79 revoked 61/531
86 revoked 65/711
87 revoked 64/1151
89 amended 63/304; 66/1369; 68/909; 71/900
95 revoked 60/968
96 revoked 61/1026
105 amended 61/1493; 77/944
117 revoked 88/1930
119 revoked 74/235
121 revoked 61/653
122 amended 74/413
130 revoked 61/814
135 revoked 60/1196
136 amended 60/542; 60/829
137 revoked 60/1197
144 revoked 64/853
154 amended 62/348; 70/995; 83/1646
155 amended 62/718; 63/747; 67/688
157 revoked 61/278
160 revoked 61/514
161 amended 68/1659
167 revoked 62/1585
169 revoked 64/904
180 revoked 74/514
181 revoked 60/1871
185 revoked 61/252
191 revoked 60/1151
192 revoked 60/1151
199 amended 67/1919
200 revoked 64/690
202 revoked 67/226
*203 revoked 60/1654; 60/1656
204 revoked 62/1874
205 revoked 60/1060
206 revoked 61/2274
207 revoked 61/1001
208 amended 64/2035
209 amended 64/2036
210 amended 64/2037; 73/2160
211 amended 76/225; 88/591
212 amended 76/225; 82/1528; revoked 84/125
220 revoked 60/2206
227 revoked 66/11
228 revoked 66/10
233 revoked 67/72
234 revoked 60/1412
235 revoked 61/345
241 amended 67/784
242 revoked 67/1928
243 revoked 67/1928
245 amended 71/1148
246 revoked 80/1106; 83/1718
247 revoked 62/2871
250 amended 63/348; 63/929; 65/109; 66/102; 66/220; 67/179; 67/305; 68/188; 69/111;

635

STATUTORY INSTRUMENTS AFFECTED 1947–1988

1960—cont.

70/302; 71/336; 72/274; 74/401; 75/202; 76/247; 78/254; 80/225; 80/1185; 88/215

251 revoked 61/2437
252 revoked 61/403
253 revoked 62/1685
254 revoked 64/504
255 revoked 60/1708
256 revoked 60/1708
258 amended 63/1309
259 amended 63/1310
260 amended 63/36
261 amended 63/37
262 revoked 61/1983
265 amended 60/2474
269 revoked 61/179
270 amended 69/850; 82/1639 (S. 177)
276 revoked 60/594
278 revoked 63/946
281 amended 61/278
282 revoked 63/708
283 revoked 63/709
293 revoked 76/250
301 revoked 62/467
302 amended 70/1406
312 revoked 65/936
313 revoked 61/1996
323 revoked 67/1928
327 revoked 62/395
335 revoked 60/1296
347 revoked 83/1422
350 amended 71/346
359 revoked 63/1911
360 revoked 63/1660
361 revoked 70/16
369 revoked 68/716
380 revoked 67/1022
381 revoked 61/403
402 revoked 60/1248
406 amended 60/2239
408 revoked 62/148
409 revoked 61/1520
421 amended 68/1530
426 revoked 62/1936
427 revoked 64/462
428 revoked 64/4623
436 revoked 78/186
439 revoked 60/1653
441 revoked 63/1626
466 revoked 66/1189
473 revoked 63/1159
475 amended 60/2152
476 revoked 60/968
477 revoked 68/219
491 revoked 61/2456
494 amended 60/644; 60/1574; 76/241
497 amended 60/756; 60/1559; 70/812; 72/1757
498 revoked 65/2114
500 revoked 63/1333
502 amended 74/70
503 amended 62/550
513 amended 62/127; 63/566; 70/115
514 revoked 65/1824
540 revoked 62/1685
541 revoked 61/403
543 amended 79/543; 85/1278
545 revoked 65/1776
546 revoked 64/903
551 revoked 61/558
553 revoked 64/1895

1960—cont.

554 revoked 62/1786
555 revoked 62/1787
559 revoked 61/1827
560 revoked 66/1034
568 revoked 83/1718
569 amended 71/430; revoked 83/1718
570 revoked 83/1718
579 revoked 72/1309
587 revoked 63/1159
588 revoked 63/572
593 amended 64/1732
594 revoked 61/2004
595 revoked 61/1996
596 revoked 63/552
600 revoked 60/2253
601 revoked 83/1718
612 amended 64/644; 84/108
615 revoked 61/1927
623 amended 60/644; 76/241
624 amended 62/1924; 84/108
625 amended 61/1153; 71/1148
627 revoked 63/818
630 amended 62/562
637 amended 63/895
641 amended 65/419
645 revoked 71/307
660 amended 64/255
662 amended 63/744; 63/1256
663 revoked 64/1895
664 amended 60/1766; 62/2849; 63/586
667 revoked 61/344
669 revoked 60/1069
670 revoked 63/1145
676 revoked 61/1528
679 revoked 62/787
688 revoked 81/399
695 amended 65/555
696 revoked 73/1856
698 amended 61/1611
699 amended 61/1612; 62/2670; 63/1299; 64/141; 64/582
703 revoked 63/791
704 revoked 60/1654; 60/1656
707 amended 6/225; 88/591
708 revoked 77/792
712 revoked 61/1825
717 revoked 65/722
719 revoked 61/6
722 revoked 62/500
725 revoked 60/2195
726 revoked 68/1077
727 revoked 63/1376
728 revoked 75/1803
730 revoked 62/148
736 revoked 66/856
737 revoked 61/403
738 revoked 62/1685
747 revoked 74/529
754 revoked 60/2183
756 amended 60/1559
757 amended 70/806; 70/1064
762 revoked 64/942
763 revoked 64/943
764 revoked 69/1307
769 amended 62/2455
770 revoked 60/2295
771 revoked 60/1241
779 revoked 69/939
780 revoked 64/1966

STATUTORY INSTRUMENTS AFFECTED 1947–1988

1960—*cont.*

781 revoked 67/330
782 revoked 69/1696
784 amended 72/51; 74/2045
792 revoked 60/2206
793 revoked 63/845
806 amended 70/1064
809 revoked 61/1926
811 revoked 61/403
819 revoked 72/1693
827 revoked 72/555
831 revoked 74/1066
839 revoked 72/1433
847 amended 85/1986
848 revoked 60/1060
849 amended 61/585; 64/698
856 revoked 61/442
870 amended 69/253
882 revoked 70/16
885 amended 61/689; 62/1251
888 revoked 61/525
897 revoked 61/1401
906 revoked 62/1685
907 revoked 62/1685
908 revoked 61/403
910 revoked 68/955
921 revoked 67/844
922 revoked 70/1770
929 revoked 63/922
941 revoked 66/223
954 revoked 62/2577
959 revoked 63/1594
963 revoked 61/1422
967 amended 62/1324; 64/1059; 67/1610; 72/1295
968 revoked 60/2294
971 revoked 78/1881
972 revoked 66/1184
974 revoked 77/55
977 revoked 78/1914
983 revoked 61/1347
993 revoked 61/1996
1014 revoked 66/224
1023 amended 60/1640; 61/774
1025 revoked 61/2081
1026 revoked 62/1562
1043 revoked 64/1966
1045 revoked 61/160
1046 revoked 64/755
1047 amended 61/2101; 65/1088; revoked 83/156
1054 amended 61/2274
1055 revoked 60/1653
1056 revoked 61/741
1057 revoked 61/741
1058 revoked 61/2274
1059 amended 61/739; 61/1190
1063 revoked 62/2786
1064 revoked 69/384
1065 revoked 63/1646
1069 revoked 66/1256
1070 revoked 66/1257
1071 revoked 68/1029
1072 revoked 62/907
1074 revoked 61/403
1075 revoked 62/1685
1083 revoked 68/1714
1087 amended 66/556
1088 revoked 62/2871
1089 revoked 62/1677
1095 revoked 64/1857

1960—*cont.*

1096 amended 60/1208
1099 revoked 71/1316
1100 revoked 84/108
1101 amended 65/1806
1103 amended 61/1378; 63/676; 63/1265; 63/1988; 66/1048; 74/2057
1104 amended 72/428
1105 revoked 80/1468
1108 revoked 66/792
1117 amended 66/629
1118 revoked 66/1241
1124 revoked 61/2375
1128 amended 61/726; 63/744; 63/1256
1132 amended 61/1692; 61/1912; 62/1601; 63/1584; 65/523
1139 amended 71/1772; 74/241; 76/447; 82/288
1143 amended 68/955; 68/1502
1146 amended 62/553; 73/791; 75/1253; 75/1399; 80/1164
1150 revoked 65/1753
1151 amended 60/1783; 61/112; 61/928; 61/1641; 61/2348
1153 amended 64/457
1154 revoked 67/479
1155 revoked 64/404
1165 revoked 68/218
1175 revoked 65/1267
1178 revoked 61/441
1183 amended 60/2390
1185 revoked 68/1077
1186 revoked 63/1376
1187 amended 67/1173; 68/32; 69/196; 73/624
1189 revoked 62/2547
1191 amended 62/115
1195 amended 82/102; 84/108
1196 revoked 60/1488
1197 revoked 60/1489
1199 amended 76/1247; 81/1414
1207 revoked 62/2465
1210 amended 62/300; 66/1048; 67/330; 67/1168; 69/1696; 70/1981; 71/555; 71/606; 73/1124; 74/2057
1213 revoked 68/219
1216 revoked 83/585
1217 revoked 61/403
1218 revoked 61/403
1219 revoked 61/403
1220 revoked 62/1685
1230 revoked 77/217
1231 revoked 77/217
1232 revoked 77/217
1233 revoked 77/217
1234 revoked 77/217
1235 revoked 77/217
1236 revoked 71/593
1240 revoked 69/297
1241 amended 62/1593; 68/44; 68/68; 68/128; 71/1962; 71/2078; 74/24; 75/1337; 82/288; revoked 83/893
1248 revoked 60/2394
1249 revoked 70/16
1253 amended 62/1369; 63/1680
1255 revoked 65/1825
1256 revoked 61/1623
1260 revoked 68/1262
1261 revoked 68/219
1262 revoked 65/1776
1263 revoked 65/1776
1264 amended 61/1485

1960—*cont.*

1265 amended 61/1486
1268 revoked 69/871
1270 revoked 72/1954
1272 revoked 81/932
1274 revoked 62/2248
1275 amended 64/353; 64/197; 71/836; 75/1345; 75/2040
1276 revoked 63/701
1277 amended 60/1396
1282 amended 70/1981
1283 revoked 72/603
1284 revoked 64/504
1285 revoked 69/1696
1286 revoked 67/330
1290 revoked 60/1654; 60/1656
1295 revoked 62/1585
1296 revoked 63/3
1298 revoked 70/1100
1305 revoked 73/1030
1306 revoked 72/765
1311 revoked 61/1652
1318 revoked 70/1100
1321 revoked 67/1060
1322 revoked 74/932
1325 revoked 61/2242
1329 amended 62/2081
1337 amended 79/800; 83/1073
1338 revoked 61/1824
1348 revoked 75/182
1349 revoked 67/1094
1350 amended 75/1891; 80/992
1363 revoked 61/887
1366 revoked 65/1864
1367 revoked 64/1572
1369 amended 66/1415
1371 amended 66/84
1373 revoked 61/2274
1374 revoked 61/2274
1383 amended 76/221
1385 amended 62/78
1395 amended 60/2194; 73/1561; 75/1372; 77/1761; 78/1566; 79/324; 80/1793
1404 amended 67/1928
1410 amended 86/1176
1411 revoked 61/368
1412 revoked 62/701
1422 revoked 64/1966
1423 amended 62/2041
1424 revoked 63/1026
1426 revoked 66/1254
1431 revoked 68/1920
1443 revoked 65/723
1444 revoked 69/18
1445 revoked 69/19
1446 revoked 69/20
1453 amended 65/1081
1466 revoked 72/1693
1469 amended 61/663
1471 revoked 80/1630
1472 revoked 62/148
1473 revoked 66/69
1475 revoked 64/1382
1476 revoked 63/709
1485 revoked 61/1401
1488 revoked 61/1040
1489 revoked 61/1041
1503 revoked 80/1354
1505 amended 62/927; 67/252; 69/1638; 69/1799; 71/2020

1960—*cont.*

1506 revoked 80/1354
1515 amended 61/853; 62/678
1524 revoked 65/726
1525 revoked 65/726
1526 revoked 69/1437
1529 revoked 70/1269
1530 revoked 68/491
1531 revoked 67/1022
1533 revoked 61/403
1534 revoked 62/1685
1538 revoked 65/722
1539 revoked 64/1382
1542 revoked 63/1571
1545 revoked 64/1753
1553 amended 61/859; 63/62; 71/968; 86/136
1557 revoked 87/1758
1567 amended 68/1553; 82/102
1582 revoked 70/1958
1583 amended 63/1235
1588 revoked 62/51
1596 revoked 62/667
1597 revoked 66/223
1598 revoked 68/1843
1600 revoked 70/198
1601 revoked 70/1172
1602 amended 62/1287; 83/1727; 85/67
1603 revoked 68/2049
1604 revoked 68/2049
1605 revoked 65/538
1612 revoked 81/917
1621 revoked 61/1825
1622 revoked 68/716
1640 amended 61/774
1647 revoked 66/224
1648 revoked 64/1178
1649 revoked 63/817
1654 amended 61/997; 61/1504
1656 amended 61/998
1659 revoked 63/1148
1661 amended 83/1676
1669 revoked 60/2291
1672 revoked 66/765
1675 revoked 61/1310
1676 revoked 65/2036
1682 revoked 71/986; amended 83/1216
1688 amended 66/299; 72/524
1689 revoked 75/308
1690 revoked 81/917
1691 revoked 81/917
1695 revoked 69/77
1701 amended 63/859
1703 amended 62/1383; 63/384
1713 revoked 61/1209
1714 revoked 64/1150
1721 revoked 61/260
1734 amended 61/781
1736 revoked 61/1996
1737 revoked 61/2004
1738 amended 74/2124
1745 revoked 61/281
1746 amended 67/676
1754 revoked 61/1373
1761 revoked 63/708
1763 revoked 61/2398
1764 revoked 61/403
1765 revoked 62/1685
1772 revoked 75/679
1775 revoked 65/855
1777 amended 64/688

638

1960—*cont.*

1793 amended 61/2301; 73/938
1794 amended 74/427
1811 revoked 64/70
1824 revoked 65/631
1826 revoked 62/2042
1827 revoked 62/2043
1840 revoked 65/1293
1848 revoked 64/1148
1854 amended 63/1306
1855 revoked 62/1679
1870 revoked 62/251
1883 revoked 61/177
1885 revoked 74/66
1887 revoked 62/1685
1888 revoked 61/171
1911 amended 62/332
1913 revoked 63/1952
1916 revoked 62/875
1917 revoked 62/876
1926 amended 61/1850
1931 revoked 75/1803
1932 amended 61/114; 61/115; 61/116; 61/117;
     69/690; 74/903; 80/1248; 81/917; 83/644
1934 amended 71/1526
1935 amended 71/1528; 73/1561; 83/545
1943 revoked 65/726
1944 revoked 65/726
1949 revoked 61/1520
1959 revoked 61/741
1960 revoked 61/741
1961 revoked 61/1192
1962 revoked 62/402
1965 revoked 61/2315
1969 revoked 62/621
1970 revoked 61/403
1971 amended 71/1767
1973 revoked 75/539
1979 revoked 62/417
1981 revoked 72/641
1982 revoked 72/765
1984 revoked 88/1167
1986 revoked 62/16
1989 revoked 68/1366
1997 revoked 74/418
2014 revoked 73/1165
2029 amended 61/2107
2030 amended 62/790; 62/841
2045 revoked 63/3
2057 revoked 62/148
2067 revoked 64/1895
2070 amended 63/464; 83/1646
2082 revoked 64/163
2091 revoked 62/2044
2094 revoked 72/287
2105 revoked 65/726
2109 revoked 61/1996
2110 revoked 61/2004
2111 revoked 61/1996
2112 amended 61/2200; 64/1794
2121 revoked 62/1562
2130 revoked 61/2331
2131 revoked 64/1966
2137 amended 61/145
2138 revoked 61/403
2139 revoked 62/1685
2140 revoked 67/1900
2147 revoked 77/988
2148 amended 63/746
2149 amended 63/631; 64/503; 65/569; 72/937

1960—*cont.*

2150 amended 71/986; 71/1908
2151 revoked 63/381
2153 revoked 80/1255
2162 revoked 63/1937
2163 revoked 61/2398
2171 revoked 61/2307
2178 amended 63/715; 72/501
2183 revoked 61/1928
2185 amended 85/1988
2186 revoked 65/1031
2191 amended 61/781
2194 revoked 80/1793
2195 amended 71/194; 71/1914; 73/2125; 76/333;
     78/622;   80/1791;   84/519;   86/1358;
     revoked 87/381
2201 revoked 63/791
2202 revoked 63/791
2206 amended 61/1272; 62/1772
2210 revoked 61/1189
2211 revoked 64/1848
2212 revoked 63/365
2213 revoked 63/1148
2214 amended 64/2034; 72/1758
2217 amended 72/2001
2219 revoked 61/1827
2220 revoked 67/1900
2229 revoked 80/1582
2230 revoked 63/2030
2240 revoked 63/2108
2250 revoked 61/2118
2251 revoked 62/1786
2252 revoked 62/1787
2253 revoked 61/1640
2254 revoked 62/2465
2259 amended 62/2850
2261 amended 62/1287
2263 revoked 63/635
2269 amended 76/373; revoked 87/492
2284 amended 74/423
2286 revoked 62/2755
2287 revoked 61/1309
2289 revoked 62/2755
2291 revoked 70/1858
2292 amended 62/624; 62/144
2294 revoked 61/2285
2295 revoked 62/2563
2309 revoked 61/403
2310 revoked 62/1685
2311 amended 63/1754; 65/1680; 69/1773
2319 revoked 65/269
2320 amended 61/1629
2322 amended 61/423; 61/424; 62/263
2325 revoked 68/1262
2327 revoked 65/1776
2328 revoked 65/1776
2329 revoked 70/16
2330 revoked 70/16
2331 amended 62/1287; 66/850; 68/1474; 73/161;
     76/103; 80/1849; 81/1174; 83/1727; 85/67
2332 revoked 86/103
2335 revoked 72/583
2336 revoked 62/2282
2343 revoked 65/538
2350 amended 63/658; 64/587
2367 revoked 62/2248
2368 revoked 61/1623
2369 revoked 62/148
2384 revoked 62/2576
2385 revoked 64/1148

639

1960—*cont.*

2392 revoked 64/1070
2393 revoked 66/1548
2394 revoked 61/1620
2396 amended 71/2125
2397 revoked 78/1684
2404 revoked 68/716
2405 revoked 65/331
2406 revoked 63/1279
2408 revoked 64/1090
2409 amended 64/1898; 71/823
2410 revoked 66/1184
2412 revoked 61/1188
2414 revoked 61/1189
2415 revoked 61/741
2416 revoked 65/134
2417 revoked 63/1626
2418 revoked 62/2187
2422 amended 61/2352; 63/394; 63/676; 67/1265;
　　　72/606
2424 amended 64/241; 72/752; 77/564; 88/1758
2428 revoked 65/1506
2429 revoked 73/693
2430 revoked 64/504
2431 revoked 67/386
2433 revoked 68/392
2437 amended 68/1495; 73/249; 76/294; 81/137;
　　　81/1319; 83/270; 85/1068
2438 amended 70/684
2440 revoked 63/977
2448 amended 63/568; 64/1259; 64/1272; 69/118;
　　　70/929
2449 amended 66/249; 72/258; 73/1629
2450 revoked 84/108
2456 revoked 64/1733

1961

　1 revoked 64/801
　6 revoked 64/104
　12 revoked 66/256
　13 revoked 66/262
　21 revoked 69/793
　22 revoked 63/908
　33 revoked 74/786
　34 revoked 69/297
　36 revoked 61/2045
　52 amended 62/1939
　53 revoked 62/2311
　54 revoked 64/943
　61 revoked 63/88
　62 revoked 62/405
　63 revoked 74/1253
　64 revoked 68/114
　65 revoked 74/1256
　72 revoked 87/2024
　87 revoked 61/2379
　88 revoked 61/2360
　89 revoked 61/2361
　90 revoked 68/1986
　99 revoked 62/787
124 revoked 69/1452
125 amended 69/437
127 revoked 64/227
128 revoked 61/403
129 revoked 61/2398
130 revoked 62/234
136 revoked 72/1204
138 amended 74/2058
139 revoked 67/801
141 revoked 63/2137

1961—*cont.*

142 revoked 65/1735
143 revoked 65/1734
144 amended 62/1097; 63/563
145 revoked 64/1116
153 revoked 71/831
156 revoked 65/726
160 revoked 62/843
169 revoked 68/1920
170 revoked 73/578
171 revoked 73/578
177 revoked 61/1654
179 revoked 62/149
181 revoked 62/1562
182 revoked 64/755
183 revoked 65/54
187 amended 63/711, 68/1570; 72/1196
194 revoked 65/2179
195 revoked 84/467
196 revoked 70/1464
200 revoked 64/370
201 revoked 65/1002
202 revoked 65/1753
203 revoked 63/777
206 revoked 70/1307
209 amended　61/2108;　62/2254;　63/827;
　　　66/1240; 67/261
212 revoked 74/897
213 revoked 63/434
225 revoked 78/1836
231 amended 65/1487; 84/108
243 amended 71/1196; 75/629; 75/685; 76/874;
　　　79/1563;　81/996;　83/702;　85/1068;
　　　revoked 88/1484
244 revoked 67/1928
247 revoked 66/1254
248 amended 62/2319
249 revoked 66/219
251 revoked 71/819
252 revoked 64/685
257 revoked 86/120
260 revoked 69/915
264 amended 62/2796; 65/1596; 65/2107
266 revoked 70/1194
272 amended 61/1346
274 amended 73/944; 73/1049; 74/897
275 revoked 68/716
276 revoked 63/1529
277 revoked 64/1043
278 revoked 62/1685
279 revoked 61/403
280 revoked 61/2398
281 amended 62/477; 63/482; 64/1678; 68/44;
　　　71/2030; 83/1646
292 revoked 65/538
293 revoked 71/557
294 amended 63/970
305 revoked 65/531
315 revoked 65/950
316 amended 69/710
317 amended 62/295; 74/1236; 75/213
318 revoked 72/1404
323 amended 63/1862
329 revoked 72/287
332 revoked 64/56
343 revoked 73/1230
344 revoked 63/978
345 revoked 62/1359
355 revoked 71/1649
367 revoked 68/427

STATUTORY INSTRUMENTS AFFECTED 1947–1988

368 revoked 74/391
375 revoked 66/1257
377 revoked 72/1693
383 revoked 72/1433
391 amended 63/1987
402 revoked 71/1469
403 revoked 64/1986
405 revoked 69/793
407 amended 83/1646
408 revoked 66/1253
420 revoked 72/555
422 revoked 61/2004
431 amended 64/530; 83/644
434 revoked 61/1996
435 revoked 61/1996
437 revoked 79/1035
439 amended 63/2117; 66/1120
440 revoked 67/1864
441 amended 63/1621; 64/502; 68/1616
442 revoked 62/1464
468 revoked 62/2000
470 revoked 66/1575
471 revoked 69/77
476 amended 75/328
477 revoked 67/489
478 amended 77/2195
482 revoked 82/1218
485 revoked 68/172
486 revoked 70/16
489 amended 69/74
492 revoked 70/1307
505 revoked 69/487
507 amended 62/2851
508 revoked 64/463
513 revoked 63/2030
514 revoked 62/1613
522 revoked 61/2398
523 revoked 62/1685
524 revoked 64/1986
525 revoked 65/2179
526 revoked 64/1230
527 revoked 66/1257
531 revoked 62/1355
532 revoked 65/723
542 revoked 62/620
543 revoked 68/1618
546 amended 62/924; 62/937
551 amended 62/2851
553 revoked 61/1022
555 revoked 80/1630
556 revoked 12/148
557 amended 62/12; 65/40; 66/1010; 67/1168; 71/707; 71/1419; 72/604; 75/1748; 76/409
558 revoked 62/623
559 amended 66/1145; 71/189
560 amended 62/1308
565 amended 62/79
570 revoked 62/401
571 revoked 62/1550
576 revoked 62/1652
577 amended 68/1105; 68/2034; 74/558; 80/1532
584 amended 76/225; 88/591
591 revoked 62/1003
598 revoked 62/2374
599 amended 61/1116
602 revoked 63/934
611 revoked 63/1333

623 amended 61/1299; 63/419; 63/1541; 64/1325; 66/287; 82/102; 84/108
624 revoked 67/1928
625 revoked 62/2756
626 revoked 63/845
628 amended 69/1804; 76/863
630 amended 70/643
635 revoked 65/869
653 revoked 64/1383
655 amended 67/1632
656 revoked 74/2
661 revoked 64/1383
669 revoked 69/487
670 revoked 70/1737
691 revoked 75/1537
692 revoked 69/1452
702 revoked 62/1685
705 revoked 84/1575
706 amended 64/598
711 revoked 66/219
726 amended 63/744; 63/1256
731 amended 64/107
737 revoked 61/2315
738 revoked 61/2274
739 revoked 61/1190
740 revoked 61/2274
743 revoked 65/135
745 revoked 65/1023
751 amended 70/968
759 revoked 62/2224
760 revoked 67/522
765 revoked 65/731
770 revoked 69/975
771 revoked 66/214
773 revoked 63/215
778 revoked 61/2004
779 revoked 61/1996
780 revoked 61/1996
782 revoked 61/2423
794 revoked 65/1559
803 revoked 64/1986
810 revoked 80/1468
814 revoked 65/577
819 revoked 69/1122
834 revoked 62/2186
835 revoked 63/791
836 revoked 74/1258
837 revoked 63/885
838 revoked 62/2350
854 amended 75/1102; 78/1648
856 revoked 79/950
857 amended 77/1385
859 revoked 71/968
860 revoked 67/1928
861 revoked 64/1349
867 revoked 62/300
868 revoked 62/1562
873 revoked 61/1373
874 revoked 65/1192
887 revoked 62/2546
888 revoked 67/1022
889 revoked 71/986; 83/1216
899 revoked 71/2054
900 revoked 76/1796
901 revoked 63/958
902 revoked 62/701
903 revoked 62/2629
904 revoked 65/867
906 revoked 81/1473

STATUTORY INSTRUMENTS AFFECTED 1947–1988

1961—*cont.*

907 revoked 64/755
908 amended 61/947; 71/340; 74/287
909 revoked 74/284
915 revoked 74/507
917 revoked 74/522
920 revoked 66/1257
921 revoked 62/2478
922 revoked 61/2072
929 revoked 61/2285
930 revoked 61/1401
942 revoked 64/1094
943 revoked 74/1329
944 revoked 65/722
946 revoked 79/1703
947 revoked 74/287
950 revoked 75/60
955 revoked 62/999
958 amended 72/1181; 74/2061
959 revoked 64/1986
961 revoked 61/2398
962 revoked 64/404
964 amended 88/1758
973 revoked 74/507
986 revoked 63/2074
988 revoked 81/748
993 revoked 64/690
996 revoked 62/1874
997 amended 61/1504
999 amended 64/918
1000 revoked 76/219
1007 revoked 62/2269
1008 revoked 81/612
1011 amended 75/92
1012 amended 69/851; 71/860
1016 revoked 72/1940
1026 revoked 62/2295
1033 revoked 62/2547
1034 revoked 63/3
1037 revoked 65/726
1038 revoked 65/726
1039 revoked 65/726
1040 revoked 61/1521
1041 revoked 61/1522
1042 revoked 74/1948
1071 revoked 71/290
1072 revoked 64/840
1081 revoked 70/1237
1082 revoked 68/219; 68/1244
1084 revoked 65/1776
1085 revoked 61/2307
1086 revoked 74/897
1087 amended 64/397; 67/1110; 74/989; 82/1089
1091 amended 69/1326
1099 revoked 64/251
1100 revoked 62/1685
1104 revoked 61/2004
1106 revoked 67/1185
1110 revoked 64/1966
1116 revoked 64/753
1117 revoked 62/569
1130 amended 62/2061
1143 amended 66/543
1152 revoked 64/755
1156 revoked 69/1642
1163 revoked 61/2351
1172 revoked 65/728
1183 amended 61/2245
1184 revoked 64/229
1185 revoked 63/1982

1961—*cont.*

1188 revoked 66/575
1189 amended 61/2272; 63/883; 64/916
1190 revoked 61/2274
1191 revoked 61/2274
1192 revoked 62/1875
1193 revoked 62/405
1194 revoked 67/815
1197 revoked 68/114
1198 revoked 72/120
1200 revoked 62/2786
1202 amended 76/225; 88/591
1209 revoked 62/1894
1210 revoked 71/1156
1214 amended 68/101; 78/1443; 81/1574; 86/1414
1215 revoked 63/1026
1219 amended 68/247
1220 amended 66/629
1229 revoked 64/409
1233 revoked 62/500
1236 revoked 64/409
1237 revoked 62/1936
1241 revoked 74/389
1244 revoked 63/985
1246 amended 64/40
1248 amended 62/467
1249 amended 64/71; 71/824
1250 amended 81/917
1251 amended 85/2023
1259 revoked 61/1792
1260 amended 64/1965
1269 revoked 67/65
1270 revoked 82/34
1271 revoked 64/559
1272 revoked 62/1772
1283 revoked 65/538
1299 amended 61/1870; 63/774; 63/1560; 65/108; 66/651; 68/205; 68/1820; 72/261; 84/108
1300 revoked 63/1419
1309 revoked 62/2205
1310 revoked 63/121
1311 revoked 68/716
1313 revoked 63/1646
1320 revoked 65/760
1322 revoked 69/487
1330 amended 65/1588
1337 revoked 61/2004
1338 revoked 61/1996
1339 revoked 61/1996
1346 amended 61/2209; 62/14
1347 revoked 63/856
1348 revoked 63/1781
1352 amended 73/1856
1358 revoked 72/1954
1361 amended 85/1677
1364 amended 64/722
1365 revoked 68/357
1369 revoked 61/1373
1370 revoked 63/2137
1371 amended 63/561
1373 revoked 65/225
1377 revoked 63/204
1378 amended 63/676; 74/2057
1389 revoked 71/1652
1391 revoked 70/1100
1392 amended 61/2417
1393 revoked 62/1685
1394 revoked 61/2398
1398 revoked 80/1177

STATUTORY INSTRUMENTS AFFECTED 1947-1988

1401 revoked 63/1247
1405 revoked 71/311
1421 revoked 70/1792
1422 revoked 62/2735
1441 revoked 80/362
1443 revoked 70/1100
1461 revoked 62/2756
1462 revoked 67/1900
1464 amended 71/986; 84/1319
1465 revoked 72/1217
1470 revoked 69/808
1471 revoked 62/1581
1473 revoked 67/1900
1489 revoked 75/2182
1494 amended 62/44; 64/7
1496 revoked 64/690
1498 revoked 64/691
1499 amended 70/1953
1501 revoked 64/2050
1502 revoked 61/2315
1506 amended 70/1435; 75/1511; 75/1514
1507 amended 63/1042
1510 revoked 68/114
1512 revoked 65/1536
1513 amended 76/225; 88/591
1515 revoked 74/897
1516 revoked 62/1050
1519 revoked 69/1674
1520 revoked 69/1675
1521 revoked 61/1954
1522 revoked 61/1955
1524 revoked 68/1852
1525 revoked 68/1852
1526 amended 64/353; 64/1974; 75/1345
1527 amended 62/2406; 64/2031
1528 revoked 72/641
1529 revoked 61/2004
1530 amended 63/1483; 64/501; 84/108
1532 amended 61/2144; 62/287; 62/1385; 62/2150; 64/1472; 64/1933
1533 revoked 61/1966
1534 revoked 61/1996
1546 revoked 76/1237
1549 amended 76/373; revoked 87/492
1566 revoked 69/1046
1580 amended 66/94; 74/903; 84/1593
1581 amended 84/1593
1582 revoked 69/403
1587 revoked 63/1646
1593 amended 62/1852
1596 revoked 62/1003
1604 revoked 63/3
1611 amended 62/2669
1612 revoked 64/582
1613 revoked 67/1022
1614 revoked 62/1685
1619 revoked 63/1982
1621 revoked 62/1868
1622 revoked 67/792
1623 revoked 63/1116
1631 amended 73/623; 81/1658
1636 revoked 62/251
1637 revoked 64/1446
1640 revoked 62/2465
1642 revoked 67/1875
1643 revoked 63/1646
1652 revoked 61/2280
1653 revoked 61/2327

1676 amended 62/911; 63/193; 63/1539; 64/84; 65/47; 65/726
1692 amended 61/1912; 62/1601
1703 amended 64/1307
1751 amended 69/390
1754 amended 63/1542
1755 revoked 78/259
1757 revoked 65/961
1768 amended 74/903
1781 revoked 75/216
1782 revoked 62/417
1792 amended 62/1303; 62/2106; 63/1349; 64/1964; 65/2178; 66/901; 67/961; 67/1612
1793 revoked 66/636
1795 amended 62/1209; 62/1416; 65/176; 65/688
1796 revoked 61/2004
1801 revoked 62/787
1807 revoked 61/1996
1810 revoked 65/538
1812 amended 62/2375
1823 revoked 62/2044
1824 amended 70/985; 72/1926; 74/2129; 75/1656; 76/1255; 77/1668; 80/1180; 80/1819
1825 amended 64/1281; 70/987; 74/2130; 75/1658; 76/1253; 77/1666
1826 revoked 70/1858
1827 amended 70/986; 74/2132; 75/1659; 76/1252; 77/1669; 80/1188
1829 revoked 61/2315
1832 amended 64/494; 66/444
1838 revoked 62/1685
1839 revoked 61/2398
1841 revoked 64/17
1849 revoked 64/205
1868 amended 64/478
1877 amended 84/108
1894 revoked 71/1649
1900 revoked 61/2423
1902 revoked 68/716
1912 amended 62/1601
1912 amended 62/1602; 63/1585; 65/524
1919 revoked 65/726
1925 revoked 63/1172
1926 revoked 63/1052
1927 revoked 63/1157
1928 revoked 62/2775
1931 revoked 79/1254
1932 revoked 67/112
1933 revoked 69/1826
1942 revoked 79/1641
1952 revoked 65/731
1953 revoked 72/143
1954 revoked 61/2148
1955 revoked 61/2149
1962 revoked 65/726
1963 revoked 65/726
1966 revoked 72/1636
1974 revoked 67/1557
1983 amended 66/323; 66/1564; 84/108
1995 revoked 64/1794
1996 revoked 63/165
2000 amended 61/2172; 61/2501; 63/982; 63/1569; 63/1769
2003 revoked 62/211
2004 revoked 63/194
2020 revoked 64/1986
2021 revoked 61/2398

STATUTORY INSTRUMENTS AFFECTED 1947–1988

2022 revoked 62/1685
2024 amended 62/1329
2031 revoked 87/1263
2032 revoked 76/894
2033 amended 65/130
2034 revoked 62/405
2036 revoked 63/791
2038 revoked 62/405
2039 revoked 64/1202
2040 revoked 71/1234
2059 amended 65/995
2064 revoked 62/1562
2070 revoked 63/1145
2072 revoked 62/2318
2074 revoked 68/427
2080 revoked 63/817
2081 revoked 63/1690
2084 revoked 63/1646
2099 amended 64/1874; 84/108
2100 amended 86/58
2101 revoked 65/1681
2102 revoked 71/1968
2107 amended 67/1252
2112 amended 68/1368
2118 revoked 63/317
2128 revoked 80/1354
2131 revoked 62/1562
2144 amended 62/1385
2148 revoked 62/726
2149 revoked 62/727
2152 revoked 72/419
2163 revoked 72/1309
2171 revoked 72/1467
2176 amended 74/2058
2187 revoked 62/1464
2192 amended 62/2130; 87/750
2193 amended 68/166; 72/1270
2200 amended 63/1477; 64/955
2201 revoked 63/194
2202 revoked 63/165
2203 revoked 63/1379
2205 revoked 71/2089
2205 amended 82/1506 (S. 170)
2209 revoked 65/760
2210 amended 63/1770
2211 amended 62/230
2213 amended 73/2200; revoked 86/647
2223 revoked 72/316
2224 revoked 62/1685
2225 revoked 64/1986
2242 revoked 67/983
2243 revoked 87/2233
2244 revoked 62/1586; 62/1616
2247 amended 1059; 62/1384
2249 revoked 62/2216
2251 revoked 79/1095
2254 revoked 70/16
2255 revoked 62/384
2256 revoked 62/1691
2261 revoked 66/1143
2271 revoked 74/32
2272 amended 63/613; 63/1967; 63/2085; 64/1657
2273 revoked 63/791
2276 revoked 63/365
2277 revoked 81/612
2279 revoked 62/2224
2280 revoked 62/802
2285 revoked 63/1433

2291 amended 68/1752
2293 revoked 63/1529
2299 revoked 75/1803
2307 revoked 70/1870
2314 revoked 80/395
2316 revoked 76/421
2317 amended 69/592
2318 amended 67/810
2323 revoked 62/2598
2324 revoked 62/2601
2325 revoked 65/1864
2326 revoked 62/1652
2327 revoked 62/803
2328 amended 64/74, 66/541; 68/1670; 70/948
2330 revoked 64/104
2331 revoked 63/1735
2351 revoked 67/1057
2352 revoked 68/827
2353 revoked 62/1562
2354 revoked 65/445
2360 revoked 63/1233
2361 revoked 63/1234
2364 revoked 68/219
2365 revoked 65/1776
2366 revoked 66/1257
2368 revoked 68/356
2375 revoked 62/2388
2376 revoked 62/2388
2379 revoked 63/1232
2381 revoked 70/1981
2395 revoked 79/1456
2396 revoked 63/1061
2397 revoked 80/2005
2398 revoked 63/2048
2399 amended 63/339; 84/108
2402 revoked 77/1261
2412 revoked 69/939
2413 revoked 74/932
2414 revoked 72/583
2415 revoked 64/1986
2416 revoked 62/1685
2418 amended 64/489; 66/770
2419 revoked 65/1500
2420 revoked 65/1929
2423 amended 65/292
2434 revoked 81/917
2435 revoked 81/917
2437 revoked 62/834
2446 revoked 63/1529
2447 amended 71/825
2448 revoked 70/1100
2450 revoked 66/727
2456 revoked 65/236
2460 amended 67/974; 72/1724
2461 revoked 64/690
2463 amended 62/629
2469 amended 71/1257
2470 revoked 62/2628
2482 amended 62/1561
2483 revoked 64/1579
2498 revoked 73/693
2510 revoked 64/205
2515 amended 76/913

1962

8 revoked 74/1169
9 revoked 63/978
12 amended 69/1696; 71/1419; 72/604; 72/606
16 revoked 64/586

1962—cont.

24 revoked 67/1022
25 revoked 69/212
37 revoked 65/1825
42 revoked 85/149
43 revoked 74/520
51 revoked 63/1530
63 revoked 76/1858
75 amended 88/1188
76 revoked 63/635
98 revoked 65/1707
109 amended 64/151
110 revoked 62/2269
112 revoked 88/1167
140 revoked 64/1986
141 revoked 62/1685
146 revoked 68/694
147 revoked 80/1630
148 revoked 71/62
149 revoked 64/1217
163 revoked 72/1096
164 revoked 62/1936
165 revoked 64/690
166 revoked 64/911
173 amended 76/225
174 revoked 81/612
180 amended 62/759
196 amended 68/1979
204 amended 66/981
212 revoked 63/165
220 revoked 65/330
226 amended 62/1747
227 amended 64/531
228 revoked 70/1172
232 revoked 64/1986
233 revoked 64/1986
234 revoked 62/1685
236 revoked 65/330
238 revoked 66/69
241 revoked 81/917
251 revoked 64/667
252 revoked 70/1737
260 revoked 74/591
270 amended 64/458; 67/541; 68/441
271 amended 64/644; 65/402; 65/1645; 66/366
272 revoked 64/888
280 revoked 88/46
281 revoked 66/164
282 revoked 66/164
283 revoked 65/165
287 amended 62/1385; 64/1472; 64/1933
290 revoked 63/381
299 revoked 64/1966
300 revoked 69/1696
308 revoked 62/2815
321 revoked 73/24
323 amended 73/589; 88/1758
326 amended 64/73; 64/504; 66/1006; 67/1168;
    67/1169; 67/1170; 70/1981
327 revoked 62/2563
330 revoked 62/1050
331 amended 64/787
347 revoked 69/469
349 revoked 66/1022
350 revoked 62/1685
351 revoked 63/2048
366 revoked 82/1384
371 revoked 63/194
385 revoked 72/192
389 amended 63/679; 67/541; 71/494

1962—cont.

391 amended 63/797; 68/1319; 71/538
395 revoked 64/253
397 revoked 64/690
400 amended 64/1396
404 amended 63/1050; 63/1328
406 amended 63/2093; 69/856
407 revoked 67/407
417 amended   62/989;   62/1150;   62/1807;
    62/1851; 62/1913; 62/2089; 62/2654;
    63/39; 63/509; 63/867; 63/1267; 63/1408;
    63/1750; 63/1814; 64/6; 64/259; 64/553;
    64/976; 64/1334; 64/1714; 64/1982;
    65/208; 65/330; 65/607; 65/727; 65/728;
    65/954
419 revoked 64/301
425 revoked 67/178
433 amended 67/1928
440 amended 62/2128
466 amended 67/1808; 83/1818
467 amended 65/1009
469 amended 68/507
478 amended 63/572; 67/104; 84/108
487 revoked 65/760
489 amended 68/125
490 revoked 63/382
500 revoked 62/2813
503 amended 67/541; 67/1623
513 revoked 63/740
519 revoked 83/1718
528 amended 64/1062
538 revoked 70/863
543 revoked 63/940
545 revoked 67/384
546 revoked 65/244
552 amended 63/514; 67/1632
553 amended 75/1399
554 revoked 75/1803
561 revoked 65/1753
569 revoked 64/754
572 revoked 63/1247
579 amended 64/952
595 revoked 63/1433
596 amended 74/1462
608 revoked 83/1718
609 revoked 83/1718
610 amended 65/518
611 amended 63/568; 69/118
613 revoked 84/1495
614 amended 75/828; revoked 84/1494
615 revoked 62/1685
616 revoked 64/1986
619 revoked 63/845
620 revoked 63/235
623 amended 63/402; 64/206; 65/345; 66/200;
    67/334; 68/407; 69/501; 70/377
624 amended 62/1414
625 revoked 62/2175
626 revoked 62/1874
628 revoked 64/690
640 revoked 64/279
645 amended 67/512; 72/595
648 amended 84/108
652 amended 66/247
656 revoked 68/1154
667 revoked 68/1163
675 revoked 83/1718
679 amended 71/1148
687 revoked 74/32
692 revoked 63/165

1962—cont.

700 amended 68/1431; 72/1387
701 revoked 63/1593
705 amended 64/550
715 amended 67/759; 83/1579
720 revoked 74/1486
721 revoked 76/1883
726 revoked 62/1794
727 revoked 62/1795
729 revoked 64/1148
737 revoked 86/1532
739 amended 63/793; 64/16
742 revoked 63/1464
745 revoked 63/1247
748 revoked 64/1739
750 amended 65/651
757 revoked 77/944
758 revoked 64/1579
760 revoked 64/1580
761 amended 64/1348; 68/1862; 83/1818; 87/234
766 revoked 80/1468
767 revoked 86/1738
779 revoked 75/1597
780 amended 62/2569; revoked 70/1737
787 revoked 64/2077
790 revoked 69/641
792 revoked 64/211
795 revoked 80/916
800 amended 68/1010; 79/508
801 revoked 62/2488
802 revoked 62/2487
803 revoked 62/2062
813 amended 63/63; 65/407; 71/538
823 revoked 65/538
824 revoked 68/219
825 revoked 71/846
826 revoked 65/135
827 revoked 63/1148
834 revoked 63/634
835 amended 62/2844
838 revoked 65/1776
839 revoked 68/219
840 amended 67/746; 68/813; 71/538
841 revoked 63/302
842 revoked 62/1355
843 revoked 63/869
844 revoked 62/1357
845 revoked 64/70
846 revoked 64/143
847 revoked 67/1022
848 revoked 62/1685
849 revoked 64/1986
850 revoked 63/2048
862 amended 62/942
864 revoked 72/532
865 revoked 62/2044
874 revoked 68/716
875 revoked 64/80
876 revoked 64/627
882 amended 62/1978
883 amended 76/133
884 revoked 77/167
885 revoked 64/1986
895 revoked 64/1890
907 revoked 65/1472
909 revoked 65/726
910 revoked 65/726
911 revoked 65/726
912 revoked 73/1856

1962—cont.

913 revoked 63/1247
918 revoked 87/1781
920 revoked 85/214
927 revoked 71/2020
934 revoked 66/579
935 amended 70/106
940 amended 73/2139
941 revoked 66/970
959 revoked 66/579
960 revoked 63/165
978 revoked 77/295
981 revoked 69/1661
982 revoked 65/331
987 revoked 69/1696
991 amended 62/2170
999 revoked 64/192
1000 revoked 71/2025
1001 revoked 71/1894
1003 revoked 65/516
1005 amended 65/649
1014 revoked 73/579
1021 revoked 66/253
1024 revoked 63/1509
1030 amended 67/91
1038 revoked 64/801
1040 revoked 63/194
1050 amended 63/1305; 63/1771
1055 revoked 62/1685
1056 revoked 64/1986
1059 amended 62/1384
1076 revoked 67/801
1084 amended 62/1647; 62/1875; 67/221; 69/1502
1085 amended 62/1551
1086 amended 62/1245; 62/1550; 62/1870; 62/1875; 66/575; 67/223; 67/231
1087 amended 66/575; 67/224; 67/233; 67/234
1089 revoked 62/2187
1092 revoked 81/612
1093 revoked 63/511
1097 revoked 63/563
1103 revoked 64/755
1105 revoked 65/1753
1106 revoked 64/211
1148 amended 63/1018; 66/629
1150 revoked 65/954
1153 revoked 63/1247
1154 revoked 63/1247
1155 revoked 63/165
1157 amended 88/21
1158 revoked 62/2311
1168 revoked 63/1116
1172 amended 63/655; 67/1318; 71/494
1175 revoked 63/1781
1197 revoked 70/1238
1198 revoked 70/1076
1208 revoked 65/936
1210 revoked 65/1002
1213 revoked 74/529
1220 revoked 71/2089
1221 revoked 64/416
1231 amended 71/1196
1244 revoked 65/2162
1267 revoked 70/201
1268 revoked 69/757
1269 revoked 69/756
1271 revoked 71/374
1287 amended 63/1435; 66/1203; 67/1866; 69/871; 70/1172; 77/1805; 79/1254

STATUTORY INSTRUMENTS AFFECTED 1947–1988

1289 amended 71/1619; 79/1091
1293 amended 64/353; 64/1974; 74/2040
1301 revoked 70/623
1302 revoked 79/1545
1304 amended 62/2107
1312 revoked 79/1456
1313 revoked 64/1986
1314 revoked 62/1685
1315 revoked 63/2048
1316 revoked 65/153
1318 revoked 64/1817
1319 amended 71/1706
1324 amended 64/1059
1332 revoked 66/1184
1333 revoked 65/1864
1334 revoked 62/1874
1337 revoked 74/1252
1338 revoked 68/1863
1340 amended 63/2096; 68/300
1341 amended 63/2097; 68/301
1342 amended 63/2098; 68/302
1344 revoked 74/1208
1345 revoked 81/612
1347 amended 67/596
1355 revoked 64/728
1357 amended 70/786; 72/499
1359 revoked 63/1583
1361 amended 67/210
1364 revoked 63/165
1369 revoked 63/909
1380 revoked 64/2077
1385 amended 64/1473; 64/1933
1389 revoked 80/2005
1393 amended 64/1963; 65/2023; 66/1546; 68/1974
1394 amended 64/1962; 65/2024; 66/1545; 68/1975
1402 revoked 68/955
1404 revoked 86/401
1412 amended 62/2871
1414 amended 62/2803
1423 amended 78/1648
1424 revoked 76/746
1425 revoked 65/473
1426 amended 64/243
1428 revoked 67/1170
1450 amended 84/108
1464 revoked 64/574
1471 revoked 64/388
1472 amended 76/1247; 81/1414
1481 revoked 66/219
1504 revoked 69/1676
1529 revoked 63/1376
1531 revoked 76/1883
1532 amended 67/1119; 67/1864; 70/400; 71/882; 73/1340
1535 revoked 65/936
1540 amended 71/294
1547 revoked 85/1197
1548 revoked 63/2094
1561 amended 69/1012; 83/1646
1563 revoked 62/1685
1564 revoked 64/1986
1565 revoked 67/844
1571 revoked 66/1257
1583 revoked 64/205
1584 revoked 63/1646
1585 revoked 63/1670
1586 amended 64/321; 67/372; revoked 87/1135

1587 revoked 70/1100
1591 revoked 70/1792
1592 revoked 68/1920
1593 amended 74/1337; 83/893
1598 revoked 74/1323
1610 revoked 64/1178
1612 revoked 64/1383
1613 revoked 64/1326
1615 revoked 70/1100
1616 revoked 87/1135
1617 amended 63/396
1633 revoked 69/905
1639 amended 67/1482
1641 revoked 64/690
1642 amended 85/1985
1645 revoked 65/1862
1646 revoked 65/1860
1648 revoked 63/791
1649 revoked 65/1861
1652 amended 63/787; 63/1322
1657 revoked 81/612
1659 revoked 66/1523
1666 amended 67/1874
1667 amended 81/1332
1668 amended 70/1285
1669 amended 65/214; 66/118; 67/135; 69/167
1677 revoked 64/1222
1679 revoked 65/882
1685 revoked 64/1988
1689 revoked 65/1404
1690 amended 65/1554
1691 revoked 63/404
1714 revoked 71/62
1718 revoked 63/194
1719 revoked 65/255
1722 amended 65/987
1753 revoked 65/951
1756 revoked 65/227
1765 amended 66/1111; 67/266; 68/1973; 74/1691; 79/365; 80/968; 81/178; 86/660
1782 revoked 70/87
1783 revoked 65/722
1784 revoked 67/1928
1786 revoked 65/1411
1787 amended 63/974; 64/470
1789 amended 64/1370
1794 revoked 62/2037
1795 revoked 62/2036
1797 amended 63/1097; 63/1672; 64/1363
1814 revoked 64/685
1816 revoked 65/877
1819 revoked 64/754
1821 amended 62/2811
1824 revoked 65/950
1834 revoked 70/107
1847 revoked 65/757
1849 amended 66/382
1850 amended 64/1048
1851 revoked 65/954
1867 revoked 67/742
1868 amended 66/408
1869 amended 87/935; 88/591
1870 amended 66/575
1871 revoked 63/1629
1874 revoked 63/2088
1877 revoked 1967/792
1878 revoked 63/1233
1879 revoked 63/1234
1885 revoked 70/16

1962—*cont.*

1886 revoked 63/2048
1887 revoked 64/1986
1892 revoked 74/1836
1894 revoked 63/400
1913 revoked 65/731
1924 amended 63/599; 84/108
1926 amended 71/988; 73/1310
1939 amended 67/541; 71/538
1941 revoked 63/165
1942 amended 65/1641
1959 revoked 63/165
1962 revoked 70/214
1977 revoked 74/504
1978 amended 86/2210
1999 revoked 81/932
2017 revoked 74/529
2029 revoked 83/1718
2030 revoked 83/1718
2033 revoked 64/941
2036 revoked 62/2211
2037 revoked 62/2210
2041 amended 65/1377
2042 revoked 64/1475
2043 revoked 64/1475
2044 revoked 77/851
2045 amended 71/449; 74/1305; 76/342; 77/2000;
  78/1752; 79/1550; 80/1741; 81/1753;
  83/372; 84/279; 85/339; 86/609
2060 revoked 63/1593
2061 revoked 64/1487
2062 revoked 64/800
2069 revoked 66/11
2070 revoked 64/853
2071 revoked 64/904
2072 revoked 66/10
2077 amended 73/1856
2086 revoked 71/124
2087 revoked 65/538
2089 revoked 65/7.6
2099 revoked 63/194
2106 amended 64/1964
2107 amended 64/1965
2112 revoked 67/72
2116 revoked 73/498
2123 revoked 64/1986
2124 revoked 64/749
2125 revoked 63/1209
2126 amended 65/448
2130 amended 67/36; 69/1766
2132 revoked 70/1194
2133 revoked 63/165
2142 revoked 68/512
2143 amended 64/171
2145 revoked 65/1776
2146 revoked 65/1776
2147 revoked 65/1776
2150 amended 64/1472
2153 revoked 64/1753
2158 revoked 87/217
2159 revoked 77/1397
2160 revoked 77/1397
2162 revoked 77/1397
2168 amended 64/1469
2169 amended 64/424; 64/1388
2171 revoked 63/1509
2174 revoked 62/2598
2177 revoked 67/1763
2178 revoked 67/1763
2183 revoked 64/690

1962—*cont.*

2186 revoked 65/127
2189 revoked 81/612
2195 revoked 70/1737
2203 revoked 64/1966
2204 revoked 65/432
2210 revoked 62/2309
2211 revoked 62/2310
2214 revoked 63/165
2216 revoked 65/485
2224 revoked 64/756
2229 revoked 64/17
2230 revoked 63/942
2240 revoked 64/1986
2248 revoked 66/1210
2254 revoked 63/827
2269 revoked 64/1214
2279 revoked 66/66
2282 revoked 63/1026
2295 revoked 64/1132
2298 revoked 63/236
2309 revoked 62/2667
2310 revoked 62/2668
2311 revoked 64/942
2318 revoked 64/1108
2334 amended 71/91
2336 revoked 64/1988
2337 revoked 63/2048
2340 amended 65/640
2349 revoked 63/885
2352 amended 67/1489; 67/1490
2354 revoked 81/612
2368 amended 63/692
2374 revoked 70/1770
2377 revoked 63/1670
2387 revoked 79/1456
2388 revoked 67/1890
2410 amended 64/1388
2443 revoked 64/1178
2463 amended 65/612
2464 revoked 65/726
2465 revoked 63/604
2477 amended 64/1419
2478 revoked 64/1313
2487 revoked 65/238
2489 revoked 69/1622
2497 revoked 77/988
2498 revoked 64/1094
2501 amended 63/1409; 64/1328; 65/1424;
  65/2106
2506 revoked 63/194
2508 revoked 63/165
2518 revoked 64/211
2522 revoked 71/2124
2527 revoked 86/1951
2531 revoked 63/1773
2543 revoked 75/1803
2544 revoked 68/1077
2546 revoked 64/430
2547 revoked 64/757
2556 revoked 77/357
2557 amended 73/308; 82/1627; revoked 83/6
2562 revoked 74/768
2563 revoked 63/1413
2569 revoked 70/1737
2570 revoked 63/1646
2571 revoked 63/1670
2572 revoked 63/194
2573 revoked 63/165
2576 amended 64/1900; 86/995

1962—cont.
2577 revoked 64/62
2582 revoked 68/2049
2584 amended 72/1612
2585 revoked 64/1986
2586 revoked 64/1182
2591 revoked 82/1234
2592 revoked 82/1218
2597 revoked 76/421
2599 revoked 63/791
2600 amended 63/612; 63/1048
2601 amended 63/609; 63/1920
2610 revoked 66/1189
2613 amended 68/1154
2614 revoked 65/1600
2615 revoked 68/219
2628 revoked 63/1917
2629 revoked 64/1277
2631 revoked 64/1992
2640 revoked 67/1796
2641 revoked 86/1002
2642 revoked 67/1797
2643 revoked 85/1049
2644 revoked 85/1048
2647 revoked 63/1831
2650 revoked 64/1043
2653 revoked 87/2024
2654 revoked 65/954
2667 revoked 63/273
2668 revoked 63/274
2669 revoked 63/1298
2670 revoked 64/582
2681 revoked 63/2074
2682 revoked 74/520
2683 revoked 66/1548
2691 revoked 68/1154
2704 revoked 65/1776
2705 revoked 76/1897
2706 revoked 73/7
2708 amended 63/484; 64/954
2713 revoked 68/218
2730 revoked 64/228
2735 revoked 63/1172
2736 amended 71/822; 71/1771
2738 revoked 65/538
2739 revoked 64/229
2741 revoked 68/716
2742 revoked 64/422
2743 revoked 63/2012
2744 revoked 64/1986
2745 revoked 63/2048
2756 revoked 66/1582
2758 amended 68/2011; 71/1128; 73/2019
2760 revoked 64/2077
2761 revoked 85/1048
2764 revoked 85/1049
2767 revoked 86/1002
2770 revoked 67/1804
2773 revoked 67/1803
2774 revoked 65/1500
2775 revoked 64/537
2785 revoked 69/733
2786 revoked 66/1590
2804 amended 63/1976
2806 revoked 65/1753
2812 amended 65/490
2813 revoked 63/542
2814 revoked 65/936
2817 revoked 65/731
2835 amended 65/2105

1962—cont.
2842 amended 68/2062
2848 revoked 66/69
2850 revoked 65/2197
2852 amended 88/1758
2854 revoked 66/219
2871 amended 69/642; 72/1311

1963
1 revoked 87/1781
2 revoked 87/1781
3 revoked 65/1324
20 revoked 83/156
38 amended 69/919; 83/1646
39 revoked 64/954
42 amended 63/1248; 65/300
62 amended 71/968; 72/878
63 amended 71/538
64 amended 68/1912
79 amended 69/23
82 revoked 67/1763
85 revoked 67/1763
86 revoked 67/1763
87 revoked 67/1763
88 amended 63/1633; 64/267; 64/916; 64/1199;
   64/1652; 74/1262
90 revoked 63/1861
91 revoked 64/1966
100 revoked 68/408
121 revoked 64/557
133 revoked 77/402
153 amended 66/279; 67/447; 69/122
165 revoked 63/2043
167 revoked 63/791
168 revoked 63/791
169 revoked 63/791
170 revoked 63/791
171 revoked 63/791
174 revoked 64/1652
179 revoked 64/1467
186 amended 64/418
187 revoked 65/722
190 revoked 63/2137
192 revoked 65/726
193 revoked 65/726
194 amended 63/341; 63/469; 63/931; 63/1337;
   63/1586; 63/1823; 64/113; 64/347;
   64/1179; 64/1751; 64/1914; 65/205;
   65/291; 65/397; 65/520; 65/729; 65/765
200 revoked 63/2043
209 amended 63/528; 64/474
210 revoked 76/929
215 revoked 64/2018
224 revoked 72/1644
230 revoked 68/1257
231 revoked 79/72
235 revoked 64/421
236 revoked 64/619
260 amended 72/257; 75/1840; 83/1646
261 amended 65/684; 65/1729; 66/499; 66/1165;
   67/541; 67/1414; 68/1528; 71/564;
   71/1336; 84/108
262 amended 65/155; 67/1940
263 revoked 64/227
284 revoked 70/1194
286 amended 76/919
298 revoked 65/726
299 revoked 65/726
301 revoked 77/1397
302 revoked 64/626

1963—*cont.*

303 revoked 64/574
304 amended 71/538
317 revoked 65/703
318 revoked 65/704
323 amended 67/676
339 amended 84/108
341 amended 64/113; 64/1179
352 revoked 64/2077
354 revoked 64/1988
355 revoked 63/2048
356 revoked 65/1201
364 revoked 65/1201
372 amended 71/213
375 amended 80/699; 80/700
379 revoked 77/1113
381 revoked 64/516
382 revoked 69/209
394 amended 64/297; 64/2001; 65/40; 67/330;
      67/1265; 70/1981; 72/260
395 revoked 64/504
396 revoked 64/2003
398 revoked 77/1397
400 revoked 63/2005
401 revoked 64/849
402 revoked 64/206
403 amended 64/353; 72/1156; 75/1345
404 revoked 66/973
409 revoked 65/726
411 revoked 68/125
417 amended 65/730
418 revoked 65/1472
421 revoked 66/139
434 revoked 65/224
436 revoked 69/668
437 revoked 65/329
439 revoked 65/1116
444 revoked 63/2048
450 revoked 65/942
452 revoked 65/2114
453 amended 63/962; 66/514
454 revoked 65/726
466 revoked 65/1622
467 revoked 69/519
468 revoked 64/388
469 amended 64/113; 64/1179; 64/1914
483 amended 68/1700; 70/858; 70/1850; 75/299
492 amended 67/522
493 revoked 66/1143
494 revoked 64/404
501 revoked 69/1696
505 amended 63/1333
508 revoked 63/2043
509 revoked 65/954
514 revoked 67/801
515 revoked 65/1588
516 revoked 65/1588
525 revoked 68/354
541 revoked 64/17
542 revoked 64/1333
550 revoked 66/1582
552 revoked 65/920
556 revoked 63/2137
557 revoked 65/225
560 revoked 67/801
561 revoked 65/1735
562 revoked 65/1734
567 revoked 83/1718
569 revoked 69/401
572 amended 84/108

1963—*cont.*

576 revoked 74/2213
580 amended 67/1521
582 revoked 66/165
585 revoked 68/1405
595 revoked 67/1022
596 amended 68/659
598 revoked 65/159
602 revoked 64/1986
603 revoked 64/1988
604 revoked 64/1633
606 revoked 73/425
607 revoked 68/1257
608 revoked 66/1184
609 amended 63/1920
610 revoked 63/791
611 revoked 63/791
612 amended 63/1048
616 amended 71/391
617 revoked 82/1538
629 revoked 86/1755
634 revoked 64/1633
635 revoked 65/1249
636 revoked 77/2083
640 revoked 67/983
656 amended 69/68
660 amended 67/104; 72/1688; 83/1646
661 revoked 66/214
676 amended 67/844; 74/2057; 74/2058
677 amended 66/24
682 revoked 65/1776
685 revoked 79/1230
686 revoked 65/722
688 revoked 64/67
697 revoked 66/1257
698 revoked 84/108
700 revoked 68/1714
708 amended 65/229; 72/1385
709 revoked 73/31
710 amended 66/514
735 revoked 63/2048
736 revoked 77/944
738 revoked 63/2043
742 revoked 67/1875
743 amended 74/607; revoked 83/327
745 revoked 68/512
748 amended 82/270
749 revoked 74/539
751 revoked 64/763
752 revoked 64/763
753 revoked 63/2048
767 revoked 65/1995
770 revoked 70/1100
772 amended 72/642
786 amended 64/57
788 amended 84/1153
791 revoked 63/1968
792 revoked 80/560
793 amended 67/136; 67/541; 71/371
794 amended 72/260
795 revoked 83/133
796 revoked 66/907
797 amended 68/1318
798 revoked 74/1242
803 revoked 75/60
813 revoked 78/1954
814 revoked 63/1172
817 revoked 64/1447
827 revoked 67/261
831 revoked 66/1582

1963—cont.

836 revoked 63/2048
842 revoked 64/1966
844 revoked 64/760
845 revoked 66/1063
846 revoked 67/1022
848 revoked 84/1153
858 revoked 65/1294
866 amended 65/1111
867 revoked 65/954
869 revoked 64/2079
879 revoked 73/36
881 revoked 72/990
882 revoked 64/914
883 revoked 64/916
886 amended 64/507; 66/1590
897 revoked 71/1649
901 revoked 71/1316
902 revoked 64/916
908 revoked 67/1308
909 revoked 64/667
910 revoked 66/216
911 revoked 72/287
912 revoked 64/409
915 amended 64/1934
917 revoked 63/2043
919 amended 71/538; 84/108
920 revoked 71/1469
921 amended 88/1758
922 revoked 67/579
926 amended 74/70
928 revoked 64/409
929 amended 68/177; 71/346; 75/202; 76/247
930 amended 64/1533; 65/2112
931 amended 64/1179
933 revoked 76/1678
934 revoked 70/376
936 revoked 72/641
940 revoked 65/377
947 revoked 67/386
948 revoked 75/652
949 revoked 70/597
953 amended 63/1205
958 revoked 65/1803
962 amended 65/514
963 revoked 75/849
965 amended 63/1578
968 revoked 69/675
969 revoked 66/908
973 revoked 64/469
974 amended 64/470
978 revoked 64/1127
989 revoked 68/219; 68/1244
992 revoked 64/755
993 amended 69/437
999 amended 65/571; 67/346; 68/44; 68/68;
   68/128; 68/913; 70/1889; 71/341
1004 revoked 69/915
1007 revoked 65/348
1008 revoked 64/751
1009 revoked 64/751
1010 revoked 64/421
1011 revoked 72/69
1012 revoked 64/421
1013 revoked 64/1986
1014 revoked 63/2048
1015 revoked 64/1988
1017 revoked 69/297
1018 amended 63/1230; 66/629
1023 revoked 65/1139

1963—cont.

1025 revoked 76/1076
1026 revoked 70/170
1029 revoked 63/2043
1030 amended 63/1390; 65/2116
1042 revoked 64/943
1045 amended 63/2090
1047 revoked 63/1968
1050 amended 63/2091
1051 revoked 65/135
1052 revoked 64/1080
1058 revoked 65/1822
1063 revoked 65/722
1064 revoked 71/907
1070 revoked 83/1718
1071 amended 69/850
1076 revoked 64/205; 64/751
1082 revoked 65/516
1090 revoked 67/65
1091 revoked 66/1257
1094 amended 67/1208
1100 revoked 67/1928
1102 revoked 72/2025
1111 revoked 88/568
1112 revoked 64/2058
1116 revoked 64/880
1125 revoked 65/527
1132 revoked 69/841
1133 revoked 78/1240
1134 revoked 67/1425
1138 revoked 65/851
1139 revoked 64/1182
1140 revoked 64/1986
1141 revoked 63/2048
1142 revoked 77/665
1143 revoked 74/529
1145 amended 65/857
1148 amended 64/506; 65/982; 66/397; 67/813
1149 revoked 81/612
1150 revoked 81/612
1157 revoked 65/1190
1159 amended 63/1439; 67/541; 72/256
1160 revoked 64/1890
1165 revoked 68/392
1166 revoked 63/2043
1169 revoked 70/117
1170 revoked 64/1986
1175 revoked 64/751
1177 revoked 64/751
1178 amended 68/1731; 73/1407; 74/1935
1193 revoked 65/736
1209 revoked 65/851
1223 revoked 78/1096
1228 amended 75/1024
1229 amended 65/1497; 66/915; 71/1179; 75/654;
   76/882; 81/454; 83/174; 83/1727; 85/67;
   revoked 87/2236
1230 amended 66/629
1231 amended 75/685; 76/874; revoked 88/1484
1232 revoked 65/2029
1233 revoked 65/2030
1234 revoked 65/1682
1244 revoked 82/1218
1247 revoked 65/739
1256 amended 67/147
1257 revoked 66/256
1258 revoked 66/262
1262 revoked 70/1792
1263 revoked 68/1920
1265 amended 74/2057

1963—*cont.*

1267 revoked 65/954
1274 revoked 70/1100
1277 revoked 70/1100
1280 revoked 64/17
1283 revoked 68/79
1291 revoked 68/282
1292 revoked 66/856
1295 revoked 64/1047
1296 revoked 64/1966
1298 amended 64/581
1299 revoked 64/582
1311 amended 64/1149; 66/1046
1317 revoked 81/612
1323 amended 63/2102
1330 revoked 64/1986
1331 revoked 64/1988
1332 amended 63/1639; 67/508; 69/29; 69/938; 71/421; 83/1332
1339 revoked 71/986; 83/1216
1341 amended 67/1616
1342 revoked 74/703
1353 revoked 76/1954
1354 revoked 76/1674
1355 revoked 63/2137
1357 revoked 78/893
1358 revoked 65/1824
1360 revoked 64/756
1366 revoked 65/326
1367 revoked 64/17
1368 revoked 65/936
1374 revoked 78/215
1375 revoked 68/1077
1376 revoked 69/1146
1379 revoked 72/1678
1380 revoked 67/792
1381 amended 80/992
1388 revoked 66/1256
1392 revoked 64/751
1393 revoked 64/751
1394 revoked 64/751
1403 revoked 64/942
1407 revoked 63/2043
1408 revoked 65/954
1409 amended 64/1328
1413 revoked 64/972
1414 revoked 65/2170
1415 revoked 64/205
1418 revoked 77/1397
1419 revoked 67/1022
1420 revoked 67/65
1423 revoked 70/1194
1433 revoked 64/1721
1434 revoked 81/932
1435 amended 70/400; 72/1391; 80/1849; 83/1727; revoked 84/1304
1442 revoked 65/227
1446 revoked 72/686
1447 revoked 82/544
1450 amended 64/1076; 66/498; 66/501; 66/502; 66/505; 66/506
1451 revoked 66/505
1453 revoked 65/506
1454 revoked 66/501
1455 revoked 65/502
1456 amended 66/503; 68/908
1457 amended 64/1077
1458 amended 64/1433
1459 amended 64/1434; 65/1005; 66/504; 67/1196; 71/118

1963—*cont.*

1461 amended 72/1489; 81/137; 83/270; revoked 84/1518
1464 revoked 64/1341
1465 revoked 64/1986
1466 revoked 64/1988
1467 revoked 63/2048
1468 revoked 81/1086
1483 amended 64/501
1488 revoked 66/1184
1489 revoked 63/2088
1490 revoked 67/1763
1503 amended 83/1727; 85/67
1504 amended 66/514
1507 revoked 64/1214
1508 amended 70/1992
1514 revoked 64/211
1516 revoked 80/1106
1519 revoked 64/751
1520 revoked 64/751
1521 revoked 64/751
1528 revoked 64/1290
1529 revoked 64/1718
1530 revoked 65/1657
1538 revoked 65/726
1540 revoked 65/726
1543 revoked 70/1737
1547 revoked 70/1287
1552 revoked 70/170
1553 revoked 70/170
1568 amended 64/590
1571 revoked 77/1033
1579 revoked 65/744
1583 revoked 64/1889
1591 amended 83/270; 85/1068
1593 revoked 64/1452
1595 revoked 71/846
1600 revoked 64/1986
1601 revoked 63/2048
1602 revoked 64/1988
1603 revoked 64/1108
1613 amended 65/1009
1614 revoked 68/512
1622 amended 66/316; 67/541; 68/417
1625 revoked 64/690
1626 revoked 64/1186
1628 revoked 65/134
1629 revoked 65/135
1630 revoked 63/2094
1631 amended 65/1867; 67/1903; 78/1628; 85/1200
1632 amended 64/1658; 77/1629
1633 amended 64/267; 64/916; 64/1199; 64/1652
1635 revoked 63/2085
1636 revoked 78/1881
1640 revoked 65/731
1644 revoked 68/512
1646 revoked 66/1288
1656 revoked 64/1277
1657 revoked 64/537
1658 revoked 69/762
1659 amended 66/711
1665 revoked 72/751
1670 revoked 66/1289
1671 revoked 63/2043
1684 revoked 76/1857
1690 revoked 65/1392
1691 revoked 64/211
1692 revoked 67/364
1702 revoked 64/751

1963—*cont.*
1703 revoked 64/751
1704 revoked 64/751
1706 revoked 65/100
1707 revoked 79/1605
1708 amended 77/99
1709 amended 68/267; 68/1541; 70/179; 76/1330
1710 amended 64/76; 68/338; 69/81; 70/1370; 72/767; 74/1326; 77/1932; 79/1612; 80/1070; 84/1446; 85/1532; 86/1682; 88/120
1711 amended 68/339
1712 revoked 64/755
1713 revoked 72/863
1722 revoked 72/1204
1723 revoked 65/726
1735 revoked 65/1295
1741 revoked 64/1993
1744 revoked 67/1022
1745 revoked 64/751
1746 revoked 64/751
1747 revoked 64/751
1748 revoked 65/726
1749 revoked 65/726
1750 revoked 65/954
1752 amended 74/954
1755 revoked 70/1194
1756 revoked 87/2233
1760 revoked 72/1693
1767 revoked 75/679
1773 amended 64/1235; 65/626
1777 revoked 65/1557
1781 revoked 68/844
1787 revoked 64/751
1788 revoked 64/751
1789 revoked 64/751
1790 revoked 70/1238
1791 revoked 63/2048
1792 revoked 64/1988
1796 amended 63/2000
1809 revoked 64/752
1810 revoked 64/751
1811 revoked 64/751
1813 revoked 65/936
1814 revoked 65/726
1819 revoked 83/1718
1820 revoked 65/1201
1822 revoked 65/1201
1823 amended 64/1179
1830 amended 82/829; 83/72
1833 amended 74/501
1834 amended 74/500; revoked 86/1002
1838 revoked 63/2043
1843 revoked 64/211
1864 revoked 70/92
1871 revoked 69/840
1876 revoked 67/1961
1879 amended 74/487
1880 amended 74/488; revoked 86/1002
1881 revoked 86/1002
1888 amended 83/874; 84/1205
1890 amended 65/1465; 67/622
1891 revoked 68/1615
1892 revoked 64/1966
1894 amended 67/1808; 83/1818
1897 revoked 70/1137
1901 revoked 64/751
1902 revoked 64/751
1903 revoked 64/751
1904 revoked 82/449

1963—*cont.*
1905 revoked 73/807
1908 revoked 64/1988
1909 revoked 64/2077
1917 revoked 64/1891
1918 amended 65/1871; 67/1483; 67/1919; 70/287; 73/957
1919 amended 69/865
1921 amended 67/816; 67/1480
1922 revoked 63/2088
1925 revoked 64/269
1931 revoked 81/612
1932 revoked 70/16
1935 revoked 66/223
1937 revoked 66/597
1950 revoked 65/1296
1951 amended 71/928; 71/498; 76/241; 77/1526
1952 revoked 65/817
1959 revoked 549
1960 revoked 64/159
1964 revoked 64/1718
1966 amended 72/445; 76/421
1975 revoked 67/1875
1976 amended 64/2004
1977 revoked 66/1548
1979 revoked 71/1316
1981 revoked 70/1194
1982 revoked 64/1337
1988 amended 74/2057
1989 revoked 65/1776
1990 revoked 68/219
1992 revoked 67/1022
1994 revoked 73/268
2001 amended 75/629; 78/1273; 85/1060
2004 revoked 65/2179
2005 revoked 64/1763
2006 revoked 71/311
2009 revoked 64/1986
2010 revoked 64/1986
2011 revoked 64/1988
2012 revoked 64/1988
2027 revoked 64/751
2028 revoked 64/751
2029 revoked 64/751
2030 revoked 67/489
2038 revoked 66/1547
2040 revoked 68/1358
2043 revoked 65/160
2048 revoked 64/1987
2049 revoked 70/1307
2053 revoked 64/1966
2058 amended 81/686
2059 revoked 67/635
2060 revoked 69/793
2069 revoked 64/755
2073 revoked 64/1148
2075 revoked 65/538
2076 revoked 74/529
2077 revoked 68/716
2084 amended 64/2041
2085 amended 64/1407
2087 revoked 63/2088
2088 amended 64/919; 64/1191; 64/1652
2089 amended 64/1652
2092 revoked 64/916
2093 amended 69/856
2094 amended 64/1192; 65/1305; 66/1178; 66/1180
2095 amended 69/859
2097 amended 68/301

STATUTORY INSTRUMENTS AFFECTED 1947–1988

1963—cont.
2104 revoked 66/1189
2111 revoked 69/77
2112 revoked 67/1861
2115 amended 74/1962; 75/1777
2117 revoked 66/1120
2120 revoked 70/1792
2121 revoked 68/1920
2122 revoked 64/1718
2123 revoked 70/1057
2126 amended 66/864
2131 revoked 81/1562
2133 amended 65/159
2136 revoked 67/65
2137 revoked 67/1416
2138 amended 75/1799
2149 revoked 71/1593
2150 revoked 72/2025

1964
2 revoked 65/160
4 revoked 64/1313
5 revoked 77/1397
6 revoked 65/954
12 amended 65/1796
14 revoked 74/1836
15 revoked 64/1624
17 revoked 65/856
19 amended 83/1727; 85/67
21 amended 64/1951; 67/2; 67/523; 67/541; 68/515; 83/1646
22 revoked 72/828
23 revoked 74/504
24 revoked 65/1557
26 amended 66/339; 68/125; 68/912
39 revoked 79/729
41 revoked 64/751
42 revoked 64/751
43 revoked 64/751
44 amended 83/270; 85/1068
52 revoked 64/1987
55 revoked 66/1184
56 revoked 66/188
60 revoked 81/612
61 revoked 81/612
62 revoked 64/1068
64 revoked 72/863
68 revoked 65/160
70 revoked 64/1185
71 amended 71/824
72 revoked 67/1887
73 revoked 75/560
75 revoked 67/788
76 amended 70/1370; 72/767; 77/1932; revoked 88/876
77 revoked 70/1100
78 revoked 73/482
80 revoked 65/1188
81 revoked 69/101
82 revoked 65/726
83 revoked 65/726
84 revoked 65/726
91 revoked 65/584
92 revoked 75/182
100 revoked 64/1986
101 revoked 64/1988
104 revoked 65/681
110 amended 67/1848
122 revoked 72/1309
125 revoked 64/127

1964—cont.
126 revoked 64/128
127 revoked 69/1139
130 revoked 64/1987
133 revoked 65/538
141 revoked 64/582
142 revoked 68/218
143 revoked 65/1237
147 revoked 67/1169
149 revoked 68/716
150 amended 66/514
163 revoked 75/60
167 amended 81/522
168 revoked 68/1920
172 revoked 64/751
173 revoked 64/751
174 revoked 64/751
180 revoked 76/1559
181 revoked 80/1676
193 revoked 68/1676
197 revoked 65/326
205 amended 64/489; 65/870; 66/30; 67/1640; 67/1934; 70/48; 70/233
206 revoked 65/345
209 amended 74/2013
211 revoked 65/1837
222 revoked 70/92; 70/131
223 revoked 64/1987
227 amended 64/1835; 71/261; 74/1314; 75/229; 75/576; 75/1532; 86/691; revoked 86/1319
228 revoked 68/1389
229 amended 64/1336; 71/262; 74/2043; 75/890; 75/1440; revoked 84/1989
232 revoked 65/160
241 amended 67/1005; 72/1483
242 amended 67/541; 73/453
249 revoked 88/110
250 revoked 64/1986
251 revoked 67/1022
252 revoked 64/1988
253 revoked 66/207
256 revoked 64/2086
259 revoked 65/954
263 amended 66/692
264 revoked 78/1880
267 amended 64/1199; 64/1652
268 amended 64/1654
269 revoked 64/493
272 amended 73/760
277 amended 67/1366
279 amended 65/315
280 revoked 81/612
281 revoked 81/612
283 revoked 64/2077
295 revoked 74/529
297 amended 64/2001; 67/1265; 72/603; 72/604; 72/606; 74/1128
308 amended 67/541; 70/1843; 71/494; 73/260
319 revoked 74/529
321 revoked 87/1135
323 revoked 65/1837
324 revoked 64/751
325 revoked 64/751
326 revoked 64/751
330 revoked 66/1256
346 amended 69/904
347 amended 64/1179
348 revoked 65/348
353 amended 75/1345; 75/2040
354 revoked 70/1194

654

359 revoked 69/85
364 revoked 67/1514
366 amended 64/1249
367 amended 64/1250; 65/2175
369 revoked 73/6
371 revoked 64/751
372 revoked 64/751
373 revoked 64/751
377 revoked 64/1987
387 amended 74/1923; 76/502
388 amended 68/440; 71/2019; 74/713; 76/503;
    81/70; 82/260; 83/568; 87/1256; 87/2176;
    88/89; 88/747; 88/1421
389 revoked 74/529
390 revoked 65/225
397 revoked 67/1110
402 revoked 64/1986
404 revoked 71/450
407 revoked 74/529
408 revoked 65/703
409 revoked 71/438
418 amended 66/1153; 67/320; 67/541; 67/1391
419 revoked 66/1257
421 revoked 64/1603
422 revoked 68/2076
423 revoked 65/733
430 revoked 65/1091
436 revoked 65/723
448 amended 72/1024
453 revoked 74/32
454 revoked 70/92
455 revoked 64/1116
456 amended 65/622
458 amended 67/211
461 revoked 68/716
462 revoked 69/401
463 revoked 73/352
464 amended 65/663
466 revoked 65/664
468 amended 68/735
469 revoked 65/77
471 revoked 66/1582
476 amended 71/1437; 72/1779
488 amended 72/1922; 72/1955
489 amended 72/316
492 revoked 64/921
493 revoked 64/916
497 amended 65/421
504 revoked 75/559
507 revoked 66/1590
516 revoked 67/1759
536 revoked 84/463
537 revoked 64/1716
544 revoked 65/851
548 revoked 74/1948
553 revoked 65/954
554 revoked 65/160
557 revoked 65/1392
559 revoked 80/1248
561 revoked 70/1393
562 revoked 67/579
563 amended 67/577
564 revoked 66/216
574 revoked 64/1646
581 amended 64/1436
582 revoked 66/709
586 revoked 67/619
594 amended 73/938
600 amended 71/349

613 amended 65/560
619 amended 64/1461; 65/947
626 revoked 65/1574
627 revoked 65/1175
628 revoked 64/1987
629 revoked 64/1988
631 revoked 66/1288
632 revoked 69/1349
633 revoked 64/1986
634 revoked 73/7
641 revoked 66/1257
644 amended 82/102
654 amended 67/1370
655 revoked 73/292
656 revoked 67/1869
658 revoked 64/1986
662 revoked 71/2054
663 revoked 66/1063
667 revoked 64/1445
670 amended 84/108
671 revoked 77/851
673 amended 67/624
674 revoked 67/625
675 revoked 65/160
676 revoked 65/726
682 revoked 65/1753
685 revoked 65/1337
686 revoked 65/1426
687 revoked 68/1132
690 amended   64/1194;   64/1651;   65/1303;
    65/1857;   65/1858;   65/1859;   65/2159;
    66/684;   66/685;   66/1409;   66/1185;
    67/877;   67/974;   67/1151;   68/1858;
    70/290; 70/637; 71/1850
693 revoked 67/480
694 revoked 67/815
696 revoked 79/116
699 revoked 74/1821
704 revoked 81/1051
706 revoked 78/257
707 revoked 78/258
708 amended 66/898
711 revoked 71/747
712 revoked 71/746
713 revoked 74/389
720 revoked 65/1139
728 revoked 65/1147
729 revoked 65/760
735 amended 65/990
736 revoked 67/602
737 amended 65/988
738 revoked 67/603
744 revoked 67/1875
749 revoked 64/1988
750 revoked 64/1986
753 revoked 67/1619
754 amended 64/953; 64/1058
755 revoked 67/937
756 revoked 65/281
757 revoked 65/1342
760 amended   69/1818;   70/1596;   72/1510;
    76/295; 77/927; 80/1849; 83/1727; 85/67
766 revoked 70/1194
767 amended   69/1847;   70/1619;   72/1790;
    76/442; 77/1026; 81/137 (S. 20); 85/1068
769 revoked 65/160
776 revoked 66/575
781 amended 81/687
784 revoked 65/1324

STATUTORY INSTRUMENTS AFFECTED 1947–1988

790 amended 68/204
800 revoked 65/240
801 revoked 65/1311
802 revoked 70/1137
803 amended 70/1224
809 revoked 66/936
810 revoked 68/1132
812 amended 67/938
814 revoked 73/294
818 revoked 65/160
827 revoked 65/326
830 revoked 66/636
831 revoked 65/538
840 revoked 71/289
844 revoked 75/1405
849 revoked 68/1485
852 amended 67/245
853 revoked 71/413
857 revoked 65/363
870 revoked 65/584
872 revoked 71/490
875 revoked 68/189
876 revoked 70/1194
879 revoked 71/1542
880 revoked 65/1076
886 revoked 65/1249
889 revoked 68/1920
894 amended 66/1344
896 amended 66/1345
903 revoked 66/794
904 revoked 71/414
907 revoked 82/665
908 revoked 64/1988
909 revoked 64/1986
910 revoked 64/1987
913 revoked 64/914
917 amended 64/999
919 revoked 64/1652
920 revoked 67/1763
921 revoked 66/575
923 revoked 80/395
926 amended 67/1143
930 revoked 65/1881
931 revoked 81/612
939 amended 68/271
940 amended 68/270
942 revoked 69/1308
943 revoked 69/1307
944 amended 67/683; 71/270; 74/997; revoked 83/78
949 revoked 82/661
953 revoked 64/1058
961 amended 66/629
965 amended 82/827
966 amended 82/827
970 revoked 81/917
972 revoked 65/2169
973 revoked 68/716
974 revoked 65/1324
976 revoked 65/954
979 amended 64/2111
983 revoked 74/519
986 revoked 74/32
989 revoked 65/1208
990 revoked 68/1132
991 revoked 65/726
995 revoked 74/549
996 amended 68/280
997 revoked 74/667

1000 amended 65/137
1001 amended 83/1676
1002 amended 68/960
1006 revoked 72/316
1010 revoked 65/169
1015 amended 70/1562
1016 amended 68/985
1024 amended 66/1346
1025 amended 68/1742
1032 revoked 67/1002
1033 amended 67/1658; 74/1837; 75/1007; 77/1149
1039 revoked 66/1163
1043 revoked 64/1811
1050 revoked 65/726
1051 revoked 65/726
1052 revoked 65/726
1055 amended 65/1981
1056 amended 72/1472
1058 revoked 67/1611
1059 revoked 67/1610
1071 71/1135
1072 revoked 66/1582
1074 amended 66/1294
1079 amended 67/263; 67/279; 67/648; 67/924; 67/1062; 74/684; 74/2081; 88/1100
1080 revoked 65/2073
1083 revoked 83/74
1085 revoked 81/1142
1086 amended 67/263; 67/279; 67/648; 67/924; 67/1062; 69/1333; 74/684; 74/1082; 88/1100
1087 amended 64/1338; 64/1521; 64/1775
1089 revoked 72/287
1094 revoked 65/1082
1096 revoked 80/402
1100 revoked 67/1121
1104 revoked 70/16
1106 amended 68/1291
1107 amended 69/1272; 78/1163; revoked 86/923
1108 revoked 65/787
1109 amended 73/2101; 77/957; revoked 84/2063
1110 revoked 71/707
1111 revoked 75/560
1112 revoked 67/330
1116 amended 66/55; 66/241; 69/1374; 71/1981
1119 revoked 65/1933
1123 revoked 65/227
1125 revoked 68/219
1126 revoked 74/520
1127 revoked 65/2135
1128 revoked 65/1404
1129 revoked 65/936
1132 revoked 65/1407
1133 revoked 64/1390
1134 revoked 70/2
1135 revoked 70/2
1136 revoked 70/2
1138 revoked 64/1718
1139 revoked 70/350
1140 revoked 70/350
1142 revoked 70/1059
1144 revoked 69/101
1146 revoked 66/936
1148 amended 66/1045; 71/1329; 71/1468; 73/1814; 74/1797; 75/1717; 76/1708; 77/1704; 78/1577; 79/1286; 80/1615
1150 revoked 78/1483
1151 amended 73/2030; 77/948; revoked 84/1943

STATUTORY INSTRUMENTS AFFECTED 1947–1988

1964—cont.

1152 revoked 78/1485
1153 revoked 67/839
1168 revoked 70/1146
1169 revoked 66/1288
1170 revoked 66/1289
1173 revoked 87/1135
1174 revoked 78/215
1175 revoked 70/1100
1177 amended 66/254; 67/85; 67/1048; 68/73;
    68/191; 68/545; 68/791; 68/972; 68/973;
    68/1027; 68/1334; 68/1435; 68/1540
1179 amended 64/1751
1182 revoked 64/1988
1185 revoked 65/168
1189 revoked 65/134
1190 revoked 65/135
1191 revoked 64/1652
1193 amended 65/1203
1194 amended 64/1651
1198 amended 67/244
1199 amended 64/1652
1202 revoked 79/114
1211 revoked 68/1262
1212 revoked 68/219
1213 revoked 65/1776
1214 revoked 65/1069
1215 revoked 70/16
1216 revoked 69/1632
1217 revoked 69/1211
1219 revoked 65/743
1222 revoked 68/742
1223 revoked 78/215
1226 revoked 64/1361
1228 revoked 70/1100
1229 revoked 70/1194
1230 revoked 68/1434
1231 revoked 66/975
1232 revoked 66/1582
1239 revoked 73/31
1247 revoked 67/1668
1248 revoked 65/1155
1251 amended 65/530; 74/607
1254 revoked 64/1763
1255 amended 72/2041; 83/346
1259 amended 66/1209
1276 revoked 80/1894
1277 revoked 65/1077
1282 revoked 72/419
1283 revoked 64/1652
1289 revoked 66/1073
1290 amended 68/709
1291 amended 79/1457
1294 revoked 77/1443
1295 revoked 70/891
1301 revoked 66/382
1308 revoked 67/792
1309 revoked 69/403
1310 revoked 69/403
1313 revoked 65/1236
1321 revoked 81/917
1322 revoked 81/917
1323 revoked 81/917
1325 amended 66/287
1326 revoked 65/1737
1329 amended 68/2011
1334 revoked 65/954
1335 revoked 64/1986
1337 revoked 68/1389
1338 revoked 65/160

1964—cont.

1341 revoked 68/1381
1342 revoked 64/1988
1343 revoked 64/1987
1346 revoked 86/401
1347 amended 73/938
1349 revoked 73/1311
1350 revoked 73/1311
1351 amended 70/1451
1353 revoked 67/792
1354 revoked 72/1577
1367 revoked 65/227
1374 revoked 66/343
1382 revoked 69/17; 69/286
1383 revoked 65/1270
1384 revoked 66/1521
1386 amended 71/1874; 81/19; revoked 84/1943
1390 revoked 64/1877
1391 revoked 65/1753
1394 revoked 67/1763
1397 amended 72/668; 75/1706; 76/52; 77/423;
    revoked 85/444
1401 amended 68/1101
1402 amended 68/1106
1403 revoked 82/1538
1407 revoked 66/1256
1409 amended 75/835; 76/371; 81/387 (S. 37);
    81/1443 (S. 145); revoked 87/430
1410 amended 65/1788; 68/1933; 71/926;
    73/1145; 75/836; 76/339; 76/1062; 79/95;
    79/1632; 81/388 (S. 38); 82/121; 82/468;
    83/972; revoked 87/430
1413 revoked 70/1194
1416 amended 88/1758
1423 revoked 65/1411
1430 revoked 66/505
1431 revoked 66/501
1432 revoked 66/502
1436 amended 65/1149
1437 revoked 66/709
1438 amended 64/1915
1442 revoked 65/326
1445 revoked 65/1423
1446 revoked 66/20
1447 revoked 65/1156
1451 revoked 65/225
1452 revoked 66/266
1454 revoked 72/467
1462 revoked 65/577
1463 revoked 65/1208
1464 amended 65/654
1466 revoked 66/579
1467 revoked 80/1163
1468 revoked 72/1608
1475 revoked 68/1954
1487 revoked 66/43
1513 revoked 87/381
1514 revoked 69/403
1515 revoked 69/403
1516 revoked 67/792
1517 revoked 71/1502
1521 revoked 65/160
1526 revoked 73/807
1529 amended 65/753; 86/399
1530 amended 73/641
1532 amended 65/354
1536 revoked 75/717
1537 revoked 64/1986
1538 revoked 64/1988
1539 revoked 66/1241; 70/786

1548 amended 76/911; 85/60
1550 amended 74/1310
1551 revoked 80/12
1556 revoked 71/2048
1566 revoked 66/936
1567 revoked 65/1646
1572 revoked 67/477
1579 revoked 70/298
1580 revoked 70/299
1581 revoked 70/300
1582 revoked 65/2135
1584 revoked 74/529
1588 amended 73/261
1596 revoked 65/1569
1597 revoked 72/2026
1598 revoked 65/1241
1599 revoked 66/371
1600 revoked 85/244
1601 revoked 67/1932
1602 revoked 65/1448
1603 revoked 65/2131
1604 amended 74/894
1606 revoked 74/529
1615 revoked 74/529
1622 amended 76/60; revoked 87/492
1624 revoked 65/431
1633 revoked 65/1119
1634 revoked 74/529
1637 revoked 65/551
1644 revoked 64/1725
1646 revoked 65/1693
1650 revoked 65/100
1657 amended 67/244
1662 revoked 68/1647
1664 revoked 69/858
1666 revoked 66/1590
1668 revoked 66/214
1673 amended 67/541; 69/27; 71/494
1679 revoked 66/1288
1681 revoked 65/726
1682 revoked 65/726
1683 revoked 65/726
1712 amended 71/539; 83/1646
1714 revoked 65/954
1716 revoked 65/1073
1718 revoked 66/809
1719 revoked 72/1693
1721 revoked 66/208
1722 revoked 64/1987
1723 revoked 64/1988
1724 revoked 67/1022
1725 revoked 64/1877
1728 revoked 80/1248
1729 revoked 68/937
1736 amended 83/644
1751 amended 64/1914
1753 amended 65/2110; 66/1340; 67/1464
1763 revoked 65/2065
1767 revoked 65/951
1771 amended 69/353
1775 revoked 65/160
1779 amended 84/108
1782 amended 67/263; 67/279; 67/648; 67/924; 67/1062; 68/1614; 74/684
1783 revoked 66/1254
1784 revoked 67/574
1791 revoked 75/679
1798 revoked 65/1825
1800 revoked 72/1693

1808 revoked 68/2076
1811 amended 65/1570; 70/2004
1813 amended 65/605
1817 revoked 66/749
1819 revoked 65/1002
1835 amended 67/1366
1841 revoked 65/538
1842 revoked 68/1920
1845 revoked 88/1842
1848 amended 65/1713; 69/1503; 76/1155; 87/1986
1851 revoked 69/1674
1852 revoked 65/723
1854 revoked 72/419
1855 amended 73/1124
1857 revoked 75/1536
1858 revoked 69/1270
1859 revoked 68/1826
1864 revoked 72/316
1874 amended 82/102; revoked 84/108
1877 revoked 65/169
1882 revoked 65/1837
1889 revoked 66/1517
1890 revoked 68/937
1891 revoked 65/1927
1892 revoked 77/339
1893 revoked 71/62
1894 revoked 65/538
1895 amended 67/541; 71/538; 72/1436; 73/378; 83/1646
1898 amended 71/823
1899 revoked 66/1401
1902 amended 68/1368
1903 revoked 68/1367
1907 revoked 80/1630
1909 revoked 68/512
1916 revoked 73/2114
1926 amended 77/518
1944 revoked 65/1776
1946 revoked 65/79
1947 revoked 65/80
1953 amended 68/911
1958 revoked 66/1288
1966 amended 65/1603; 65/1731; 65/2148; 66/221; 66/601; 67/433; 67/932; 67/1584; 68/653; 69/1347; 71/2040
1967 amended 71/608
1969 revoked 68/716
1970 revoked 66/575
1971 revoked 69/1676
1972 revoked 69/1676
1974 amended 71/836; 75/1345
1977 revoked 70/16
1978 revoked 66/1548
1979 revoked 68/165
1980 revoked 65/1404
1981 revoked 65/160
1982 revoked 65/954
1986 revoked 66/1555
1987 revoked 65/2099
1988 amended 65/95; 65/265; 65/699; 65/1172; 65/1328; 65/1462; 65/1627; 65/1832; 65/1985; 65/2100; 66/61; 66/173; 66/482; 66/605; 66/746; 66/921
1990 amended 69/849
1993 revoked 65/764
1998 amended 67/57
2001 amended 70/1981; 71/1220; 72/606; 74/1128

1964—*cont.*

2002 revoked 71/2084
2005 amended 65/2117
2006 revoked 67/790
2007 amended 72/1435; 81/1876
2015 revoked 68/1826
2018 revoked 66/637
2028 revoked 65/722
2029 revoked 78/1093
2030 revoked 68/373
2040 revoked 66/575
2042 amended 73/108
2043 amended 65/1124; 67/474; 70/635
2045 revoked 82/1526
2049 revoked 66/1189
2058 amended 72/1434; 87/585; 88/639
2065 revoked 68/2049
2077 revoked 76/585
2079 revoked 67/1513
2095 revoked 65/1837
2097 amended 67/541; 68/372; 68/1810; 73/353

1965

2 revoked 69/403
3 revoked 81/1086
5 revoked 68/1132
8 revoked 65/2099
22 revoked 76/1897
28 revoked 75/825
30 revoked 65/936
34 amended 65/2075; 65/2120
35 amended 67/1265; 71/1220
36 revoked 75/559
38 revoked 66/1548
40 amended 67/330; 67/1265; 68/827; 70/1981;
    71/1220; 72/606; 74/2058
42 revoked 65/1208
44 amended 65/2109; 67/669
46 revoked 65/726
47 revoked 65/726
50 revoked 65/726
55 amended 67/1162; 75/1135; 76/475
60 amended 71/939
64 amended 72/1779
65 revoked 69/1021
66 revoked 68/619
71 revoked 70/1194
74 revoked 66/165
76 revoked 66/1063
77 revoked 65/1411
78 revoked 67/790; 72/2025
79 revoked 65/80; 65/174
80 revoked 65/175
84 revoked 70/1100
85 revoked 65/726
86 revoked 65/726
87 revoked 65/726
92 revoked 65/1426
94 revoked 66/1555
95 revoked 66/921
96 amended 65/654
98 revoked 66/253
100 revoked 65/1428
123 amended 70/1370; 72/1551; 80/1070;
    revoked 88/876
126 revoked 66/1184
127 revoked 66/441
134 amended 65/1718; 66/687
150 amended 73/8
151 revoked 84/108

1965—*cont.*

155 amended 67/1940
169 revoked 65/1209
170 revoked 78/852
173 revoked 65/1646
174 revoked 65/175; 65/288
175 revoked 65/289
188 revoked 65/951
194 revoked 70/87
195 amended 81/1223
196 revoked 70/107
197 amended 75/1712
198 revoked 67/1197
208 revoked 65/954
209 revoked 65/726
211 revoked 66/1250
216 revoked 80/499
217 revoked 66/809
224 revoked 67/1312
225 revoked 68/1256
229 revoked 72/1353
230 revoked 73/1165
236 revoked 76/1899
237 revoked 71/450
238 revoked 67/1159
239 revoked 67/1160
240 revoked 66/1039
247 amended 72/346
249 revoked 66/69
253 revoked 80/1866
259 revoked 73/1119
260 revoked 74/362
261 revoked 74/363
262 revoked 65/538
265 revoked 66/921
266 revoked 65/2099
278 revoked 70/170
281 amended 65/1809; 67/618
282 amended 76/1315
283 amended 78/1682
288 revoked 65/289; 65/479
289 revoked 65/480
294 revoked 74/351
307 amended 80/804; 81/917; 82/827
308 revoked 69/483
315 amended 66/309
318 revoked 68/580
319 amended 67/156; 67/486
321 amended 65/1090; 65/1266; 66/335; 66/868;
    66/1283; 66/1531; 66/1620; 67/387;
    67/487; 67/1090; 67/1789; 68/1016;
    68/1150; 68/1602; 68/1759; 68/1760;
    69/474; 69/475; 69/1702; 69/1703;
    69/1819; 70/134; 70/682; 70/1058;
    71/166; 71/202; 71/203; 71/265; 71/1161;
    71/1162; 71/1215; 71/1797; 71/1809;
    72/164; 72/1530; 73/145; 73/360; 73/540;
    73/541; 73/1991; 74/845; 74/1603;
    74/1628; 74/1686; 74/2090; 75/89;
    75/1106; 75/1585; 75/1850; 76/137;
    76/282; 76/283; 76/372; 76/467; 76/745;
    76/779; 76/847; 76/867; 76/1061;
    76/1326; 76/1605; 76/1849; 76/1994;
    76/2020; 76/2196; 76/2197; 77/71;
    77/472; 77/974; 77/978; 77/1621; 78/106;
    78/113; 78/161; 78/690; 78/799; 78/925;
    78/947; 78/955; 78/1373; 78/1804;
    79/348; 79/516; 79/670; 79/1033;
    79/1410; 79/1438; 79/1631; 80/290;
    80/388; 80/891; 80/892; 80/909; 80/1016;

1965—cont.

80/1144; 80/1754; 80/1801; 80/1803;
81/496; 81/497; 81/1137; 82/174; 82/467;
82/654; 82/804; 82/1381; 82/1679;
82/1723; 82/1824; 82/1825; 83/397;
83/398; 83/656; 83/826; 83/971; 83/1210;
83/1824; 83/1825; 84/235; 84/472;
84/499; 84/919; 84/920; 84/997; 84/1132;
84/1133; 85/227; 85/500; 85/555; 85/760;
85/1178; 85/1426; 85/1600; 86/514;
86/694; 86/799; 86/1128; 86/1231;
87/871; 87/1079; 87/1206; 87/2160;
88/420; 88/615; 88/684; 88/1032; 88/1521

326 amended 65/934
327 revoked 65/739; amended 87/2160
328 revoked 65/1002
329 revoked 71/937
340 revoked 74/954
345 revoked 66/200
348 revoked 65/1324
362 amended 74/70
363 revoked 77/928
364 revoked 80/321
365 revoked 80/321
366 revoked 80/321
390 revoked 70/1194
395 revoked 71/1649
396 revoked 67/937
403 revoked 78/252
404 revoked 75/1446
411 revoked 67/386
422 amended 74/520; 82/1514
430 revoked 82/739
431 revoked 67/640
432 revoked 67/641
438 revoked 70/557
444 revoked 77/366
450 amended 71/2089; 82/1506
454 revoked 70/1047
470 revoked 65/882
473 revoked 69/1092
477 revoked 77/1113
478 revoked 72/1330
479 revoked 65/480
481 amended 66/236
491 revoked 65/882
492 revoked 66/1606
498 revoked 73/31
499 revoked 69/286
500 revoked 71/1469
502 revoked 67/1416
503 revoked 65/1735
508 amended 66/1250
509 amended 66/1250
510 amended 66/1250
515 revoked 66/636
516 revoked 73/334
517 amended 71/1122
527 amended 69/451
531 amended 66/1250
532 amended 66/1250
533 amended 66/1250
534 amended 65/2082; 74/607
535 revoked 70/376
536 amended 68/899
537 amended 74/520; 82/1514
538 revoked 68/26
540 amended 66/1250; 86/452
542 revoked 69/438
543 revoked 77/580

1965—cont.

544 revoked 77/581
551 revoked 70/702
552 revoked 73/1812
556 revoked 88/1167
563 amended 68/44; 68/68; 68/128; 71/1121
564 amended 70/969
565 revoked 81/555
571 amended 71/341
572 revoked 66/734
573 revoked 65/72
574 amended 69/942
575 revoked 65/1837
576 amended 68/44; 68/68; 68/128
577 revoked 78/436
578 revoked 85/930
579 revoked 74/418
584 revoked 75/1385
585 revoked 66/1582
586 revoked 78/186
587 revoked 66/575
588 revoked 76/421
589 revoked 85/444
591 revoked 85/445
595 amended 75/1506; 75/1509
601 revoked 76/1778
604 revoked 66/1045
607 revoked 65/954
617 amended 80/215
618 revoked 77/759
619 revoked 69/1787
620 amended 68/44; 68/68; 68/128; 71/1120
621 amended 66/1216; 67/1330; 68/488; 69/413;
    74/520; 77/1341
636 amended 66/312
638 revoked 68/514
641 revoked 67/1900
645 revoked 74/520
654 amended 65/1444; 67/1197; 77/293
655 revoked 74/519
679 revoked 78/602
681 revoked 66/551
682 amended 65/1885
684 amended 71/1336
699 revoked 66/921
700 revoked 66/1555
703 revoked 65/2076
704 revoked 68/1847
705 revoked 73/579
717 revoked 70/891
718 amended 72/1181; 74/2061
721 revoked 83/1634
722 revoked 75/910
723 amended 67/1884; 71/480; 72/1208;
    revoked 84/647
739 amended 65/1415
740 revoked 65/945
742 amended 65/887
753 revoked 86/399
755 revoked 66/1351
756 revoked 67/556
757 revoked 70/789
787 revoked 67/745
790 revoked 66/1257
826 revoked 68/716
827 revoked 68/219
828 revoked 65/1776
836 amended 68/914
839 revoked 80/2005
854 amended 73/1856

STATUTORY INSTRUMENTS AFFECTED 1947–1988

865 revoked 71/62
871 revoked 66/1288
898 revoked 75/560
899 amended 66/27; 74/464
900 revoked 67/520
901 revoked 71/1095
902 amended 77/938
904 revoked 67/212
936 amended 65/937
940 amended 75/1135; 76/475
953 revoked 65/1411
970 revoked 67/625
971 amended 67/626
976 revoked 81/612
979 revoked 66/575
980 amended 69/592
981 revoked 74/1259
989 revoked 67/603
991 revoked 67/602
992 amended 66/460; 67/604
993 amended 66/462; 67/605
998 revoked 74/351
1000 amended 78/1248
1004 revoked 70/1194
1007 revoked 77/1027
1014 revoked 74/529
1016 revoked 74/529
1021 amended 78/1248
1023 revoked 68/1120
1024 amended 67/876; 71/1209
1026 revoked 79/680
1028 revoked 66/936
1034 revoked 66/1555
1035 revoked 65/2099
1046 amended 72/531; 77/252; 81/581
1050 amended 72/1146
1051 revoked 80/534
1059 revoked 65/1837
1061 revoked 65/1209
1067 revoked 78/1543
1069 revoked 67/907
1073 revoked 66/554
1074 revoked 65/1822
1076 revoked 65/2044
1077 revoked 67/758
1082 revoked 67/926
1083 revoked 66/159
1084 revoked 70/1194
1088 amended 67/1064; 71/1718; revoked 83/156
1089 amended 68/923; 69/1661
1091 revoked 65/2154
1098 revoked 65/1500
1099 revoked 65/1636
1100 revoked 65/1637
1101 amended 67/301; 70/941; 71/1660; 74/31
1102 revoked 65/2035; 65/2036
1103 amended 75/927; 77/252
1104 revoked 81/572
1105 amended 66/744; 69/409; 75/330; 77/229; 77/252; 78/1872; 81/577
1106 amended 74/2185; 75/330; 77/252; 80/541; 81/1472; 81/1747; 84/1222; revoked 85/1218
1107 amended 69/1315
1108 revoked 74/1919
1113 revoked 80/542
1113 amended 81/578
1114 revoked 80/540
1119 revoked 66/1516

1121 revoked 77/1876
1128 revoked 68/114
1132 amended 82/408
1140 revoked 65/1707
1147 revoked 66/820
1148 revoked 66/1590
1149 amended 66/708
1150 revoked 66/709
1151 revoked 70/1958
1152 revoked 74/351
1156 revoked 67/639
1157 amended 67/302; 71/1661; 72/638; 77/1474
1164 revoked 69/297
1166 revoked 69/77
1167 revoked 69/77
1168 amended 69/1537
1170 revoked 66/1555
1171 revoked 66/1555
1172 revoked 66/921
1175 amended 66/786
1176 revoked 66/787
1179 amended 66/629
1184 revoked 78/505
1185 revoked 66/779
1186 revoked 66/1493
1188 revoked 66/803
1189 revoked 66/804
1190 revoked 67/939
1191 revoked 68/1256
1192 amended 68/1258
1196 revoked 66/1257
1197 revoked 70/1737
1203 revoked 68/1377
1208 revoked 66/936
1209 revoked 65/1610
1214 revoked 66/113
1215 revoked 66/114
1216 revoked 68/137
1217 revoked 67/1626
1222 revoked 74/514
1227 revoked 68/716
1228 revoked 66/113
1229 revoked 65/1776
1230 revoked 67/1611
1234 revoked 67/889
1236 revoked 66/1494
1237 revoked 66/1494
1238 revoked 66/1495
1239 revoked 75/910
1240 revoked 70/1194
1241 amended 65/1667; 67/1931; 72/2026
1249 revoked 65/2089
1250 revoked 67/627
1251 amended 74/102
1252 revoked 70/16
1255 amended 70/775
1256 amended 73/2005
1257 amended 73/2006
1262 revoked 70/774
1264 revoked 75/1537
1267 revoked 70/776
1270 revoked 66/1520
1276 revoked 67/65
1283 revoked 77/759
1284 revoked 70/1190
1288 amended 74/520
1289 revoked 79/1678
1290 amended 67/541; 73/258
1294 revoked 67/644

1965—*cont.*

1295 revoked 67/645
1296 revoked 72/1954
1297 amended 67/960
1298 revoked 69/841
1301 revoked 86/401
1307 amended 77/50
1311 revoked 66/855
1312 revoked 66/1492
1314 amended 68/692
1321 revoked 67/628
1324 revoked 67/675
1328 revoked 66/921
1329 revoked 66/1555
1331 revoked 65/2099
1337 revoked 66/1505
1338 revoked 66/1506
1339 revoked 74/1948
1342 revoked 70/296
1346 amended 88/57
1343 revoked 71/1089
1352 revoked 68/694
1354 revoked 65/1693
1355 revoked 66/1256
1356 revoked 65/1837
1360 revoked 74/1943
1362 revoked 75/1385
1366 revoked 74/455
1371 revoked 70/1194
1373 revoked 72/317
1391 amended 67/263; 67/279; 67/648; 67/924;
    67/1062; 69/689; 74/684
1392 revoked 68/54
1394 revoked 66/794
1400 revoked 69/414
1404 revoked 70/497
1407 revoked 67/838
1411 revoked 67/455
1412 revoked 71/1037
1414 revoked 69/414
1415 amended 66/1312
1417 revoked 68/600
1418 revoked 68/77
1419 revoked 68/239
1420 amended 81/1004; 82/670; 85/1146
1421 revoked 71/907
1422 amended 83/629
1423 revoked 67/757
1426 revoked 71/438
1428 revoked 66/185
1435 revoked 67/375
1437 revoked 71/1652
1441 amended 72/1512
1442 revoked 66/1501
1448 amended 72/2026
1449 revoked 70/1340
1456 revoked 78/215
1457 revoked 78/215
1462 revoked 66/921
1463 amended 74/1408
1464 revoked 73/482
1467 amended 72/528
1468 amended 70/177
1469 revoked 78/215
1470 revoked 78/215
1471 revoked 69/1308
1472 revoked 66/1255
1473–1484 revoked 77/217
1485 revoked 69/1675

1965—*cont.*

1487 amended 84/108
1490 revoked 73/63
1496 revoked 66/159
1497 amended 71/1179; 75/654; revoked 87/2236
1500 amended 66/875; 68/107; 69/204; 69/1547;
    70/228; 71/260; 72/334; 73/230; 74/206;
    78/750; 79/105; 79/1619; 80/1857;
    81/1588; 82/124; 82/786; 83/291; revoked
    87/821
1501 revoked 67/1611
1506 amended 71/636
1508 revoked 65/1951
1513 revoked 70/1100
1514 revoked 70/1100
1519 amended 70/572
1520 revoked 75/910
1521 revoked 71/414
1522 revoked 71/413
1523 revoked 70/1194
1524 revoked 70/1981
1525 revoked 77/982
1526 revoked 77/1876
1532 revoked 78/1105
1533 revoked 74/1255
1535 amended 87/927
1536 amended 87/928
1537 revoked 73/1329
1542 revoked 78/1177
1544 revoked 70/350
1545 amended 68/1931
1550 revoked 77/1010
1551 revoked 84/1989
1554 revoked 68/1283
1555 revoked 77/1033
1556 revoked 73/292
1557 revoked 66/1273
1559 amended 75/1102; 78/1648
1561 revoked 66/1035
1564 revoked 70/1823
1567 revoked 65/1776
1568 revoked 66/1063
1569 amended 65/1982; 66/59; 67/1930; 72/2026
1571 amended 74/1236; 75/213
1572 revoked 72/1404
1574 revoked 66/854
1575 revoked 67/1619
1576 revoked 68/1300
1578 revoked 68/1132
1588 amended 69/22
1590 revoked 69/286
1599 revoked 71/2001
1601 revoked 68/1920
1602 revoked 68/1920
1603 revoked 70/815
1608 revoked 75/1803
1611 amended 71/90
1621 amended 69/1053
1622 revoked 70/2007
1623 revoked 74/1136
1624 revoked 66/1289
1625 revoked 66/1288
1626 revoked 65/2099
1627 revoked 66/921
1635 amended 72/2045
1636 revoked 65/1637; 65/1781
1637 revoked 65/1782
1645 amended 82/102; revoked 84/108
1655 revoked 69/715
1656 revoked 66/809

STATUTORY INSTRUMENTS AFFECTED 1947–1988

1657 revoked 67/1528
1659 revoked 77/665
1660 revoked 78/1739
1663 revoked 70/1289
1666 revoked 74/1351
1667 revoked 67/1931
1671 revoked 67/937
1676 amended 69/710
1679 revoked 67/675
1681 amended 71/1718; 83/156; 86/249
1682 revoked 67/1305
1685 revoked 70/1400
1687 amended 70/491; 73/934
1693 revoked 68/1534
1701 revoked 67/455
1703 revoked 75/216
1707 amended 66/874; 68/105; 69/205; 69/1869; 70/229; 71/453
1722 revoked 68/26
1729 revoked 67/1414
1731 revoked 70/815
1734 amended 65/2172; 66/913; 68/1255; 69/784
1735 amended 65/2173; 66/912; 68/1254; 69/783
1737 revoked 67/634
1741 revoked 85/1758
1742 revoked 68/1745
1744 revoked 67/1763
1745 amended 67/380
1747 revoked 70/1194
1748 revoked 67/1751
1753 revoked 69/760
1754 revoked 66/1256
1776 amended 66/559; 66/1055; 66/1514; 67/829; 68/1244; 69/1105; 69/1894; 70/671; 70/944; 70/1208; 70/1861; 71/354; 71/835; 71/1269; 71/1955; 72/813; 72/1194; 73/1384; 73/2016; 73/2046; 74/295; 74/1360; 75/128; 75/911; 76/337; 76/1196; 77/532; 77/960; 77/1955; 78/251; 78/359; 78/579; 78/1066; 79/35; 79/402; 79/522; 79/1542; 79/1716; 79/1725; 80/1010; 80/1908; 80/2000; 81/1734; 82/1111; 83/531; 83/1181; 83/1786; 84/1051; 85/69; 85/846; 86/632; 86/1187; 86/2001; 86/2289; 87/1423; 88/298; 88/1340
1777 amended 73/1356
1781 revoked 65/1782; 65/1943
1782 revoked 65/1944
1783 revoked 74/1598
1788 amended 73/1145; 75/836; 76/339; 76/1062; revoked 87/430
1800 revoked 67/640
1803 revoked 68/765
1804 revoked 75/559
1809 revoked 67/618
1815 amended 69/67; 79/41
1816 revoked 73/807
1819 revoked 74/32
1821 revoked 67/792
1823 amended 69/64
1824 amended 74/2056
1825 revoked 71/381
1826 revoked 78/1779
1827 revoked 72/1693
1828 revoked 75/1704
1830 revoked 65/2099
1831 revoked 66/1555
1832 revoked 66/921

1837 revoked 66/1249
1838 amended 84/267
1839 amended 71/1158; 77/1671; 83/43; 84/266; 86/21; 87/1984
1840 revoked 70/1431
1841 revoked 71/1160
1842 revoked 74/1502
1843 revoked 71/1159
1847 amended 67/1940
1958 amended 85/1987
1860 amended 67/970; 72/808; 72/1101
1861 revoked 69/736
1862 revoked 84/1151
1863 amended 73/1084
1864 revoked 69/1832
1869 revoked 78/1880
1872 revoked 78/1881
1873 revoked 75/1704
1884 revoked 66/1184
1886 revoked 66/1255
1887 amended 68/848
1893 amended 65/2067; revoked 84/1066
1895 revoked 68/844
1898 revoked 67/745
1899 revoked 68/716
1900 revoked 68/512
1901 amended 68/1502
1903 revoked 67/1182
1905 revoked 66/1045
1907 revoked 67/1416
1919 revoked 66/159
1920 revoked 76/893
1927 revoked 67/1729
1929 revoked 77/288
1933 revoked 72/1827
1934 revoked 67/793
1939 revoked 79/1661
1940 revoked 67/1189
1941 revoked 66/809
1943 revoked 65/1944
1947 revoked 88/110
1952 amended 79/1571
1954 amended 65/1987
1956 revoked 72/1583
1964 amended 74/991
1971 revoked 74/1555
1976 amended 67/1648; 68/1080
1978 revoked 72/1678
1981 amended 76/919
1982 revoked 72/2026
1985 revoked 66/921
1992 revoked 78/560
1993 revoked 81/1260
1995 amended 67/1310; 74/1299; 76/355; 77/2022; 78/1729; 79/1558; 80/1751; 81/1833; 83/350; 84/307; 85/344Z; 86/621; 87/394; 88/450
2006 amended 67/541; 71/538; 72/427; 82/102
2011 revoked 81/1540
2012 revoked 77/1876
2017 revoked 71/2124
2018 amended 67/361
2019 amended 67/359
2020 revoked 67/362
2021 revoked 67/360
2028 amended 67/263; 67/279; 67/648; 67/924; 67/1062; 69/1290; 73/1224; 74/684
2029 revoked 68/345
2030 revoked 68/197

1965—*cont.*

2034 revoked 77/80
2035 revoked 67/1215
2036 revoked 67/1360
2039 revoked 79/1662
2041 revoked 87/1781
2042 revoked 69/1419
2043 revoked 72/1333
2044 revoked 66/668
2045 revoked 66/669
2046 revoked 68/1947
2049 amended 67/478
2054 revoked 76/1796
2062 revoked 70/1194
2063 revoked 66/373
2065 revoked 67/644
2067 revoked 84/1066
2070 revoked 76/1644
2071 revoked 71/1520
2072 revoked 76/1768
2073 revoked 68/8
2074 revoked 67/758
2075 revoked 66/1540
2076 revoked 67/744
2079 revoked 79/72
2082 amended 74/607
2083 revoked 66/375
2085 revoked 75/1536
2089 revoked 67/988
2090 revoked 70/1033
2093 revoked 70/16
2098 revoked 66/1555
2099 revoked 66/1556
2100 revoked 66/921
2108 revoked 66/1606
2110 amended 67/1464
2117 amended 66/1611
2119 revoked 80/1941
2120 amended 67/49
2121 revoked 80/449
2122 revoked 70/197
2131 revoked 66/1560
2135 revoked 68/1355
2136 revoked 68/1356
2137 revoked 68/219
2138 revoked 67/561
2139 amended 66/303; 66/304; 67/742
2140 revoked 68/885
2142 amended 72/504
2147 amended 74/1354
2148 revoked 70/815
2149 amended 76/795
2153 revoked 82/1419
2154 revoked 66/533
2155 revoked 70/312
2161 revoked 66/575
2162 revoked 67/227
2168 revoked 67/17
2169 revoked 69/901
2176 amended 69/849
2179 revoked 76/1450
2181 revoked 82/1234
2184 revoked 66/1144
2187 revoked 84/108
2188 amended 73/1136
2192 revoked 67/926
2196 revoked 77/1725
2197 amended 67/541; 68/5; 68/6
2199 revoked 70/94

1966

1 amended 66/500
10 revoked 71/107
11 revoked 71/108
12 revoked 68/1366
13 revoked 67/1887
19 revoked 67/757
20 revoked 68/1051
25 revoked 66/817
26 revoked 67/520
29 revoked 67/72
31 revoked 66/1288
32 revoked 66/1289
35 revoked 74/529
37 revoked 72/287
40 revoked 67/17
41 revoked 68/885
42 revoked 68/885
43 amended 68/4; 68/1926
44 revoked 68/1927
48 amended 68/815; 75/1680
50 revoked 66/1249
51 amended 66/218
52 revoked 76/1742
59 revoked 67/1930
60 revoked 66/1555
61 revoked 66/921
62 revoked 74/351
66 revoked 69/1399
67 revoked 66/166
68 revoked 66/167
70 revoked 67/937
71 revoked 67/675
75 revoked 66/1449
94 amended 84/1593
95 amended 74/209; 81/917
98 revoked 70/108
99 amended 72/653
100 revoked 79/1662
101 revoked 74/351
105 revoked 70/1194
113 revoked 69/1308
115 revoked 68/885
119 revoked 70/1238
121 revoked 75/1970
132 revoked 75/630
136 revoked 66/992
137 revoked 66/992
143 amended 67/263; 67/279; 67/648; 67/924; 67/1062; 74/684; 82/663
144 revoked 66/886
146 revoked 68/26
149 amended 75/1087
150 revoked 67/1001
153 revoked 67/207
158 revoked 74/351
159 revoked 69/553
162 revoked 87/1758
163 revoked 76/585
164 amended 66/581; 67/1205; 67/1233; 69/772; 69/1196; 70/46; 71/1222; 72/1289; 75/514; 75/1139; 77/380; 77/992; 77/1063; 77/1104; 79/996; revoked 83/136
165 amended 67/1204; 67/1232; 69/1195; 70/46; 71/1223; 72/1288; 73/1439; 73/1440; 74/943; 75/513; 75/1138; 76/1277; 77/991; 77/1063; 77/1607; 78/1460; 79/1190; 80/1556; 81/1516; 82/1489
166 revoked 66/167

168 revoked 67/907
171 revoked 66/1566
172 revoked 66/1555
173 revoked 66/921
175 revoked 67/838
178 revoked 66/1253
179 revoked 66/1254
185 revoked 66/1549
188 revoked 69/150
189 revoked 81/612
191 revoked 72/1992
193 revoked 67/1900
200 revoked 67/334
203 revoked 70/214
207 amended 68/259
208 revoked 67/886
214 amended 67/541; 68/287
216 revoked 72/641
217 revoked 70/615
219 amended 67/438; 68/1813; 69/138
221 revoked 70/815
222 revoked 71/374
223 amended 70/1323; 72/1574; 74/2184; 86/455
224 revoked 71/1628
229 revoked 66/739
237 revoked 79/1752
238 amended 79/955; 85/435
242 revoked 81/1736
243 revoked 71/1649
245 amended 67/263; 67/279; 67/648; 67/924; 67/1062; 68/1882; 74/684; 82/658
246 amended 67/263; 67/279; 67/648; 67/924; 67/1062; 74/684; 82/662
249 amended 72/258
250 revoked 71/450
253 revoked 72/228
254 amended 68/545
255 revoked 69/1675
256 revoked 70/1880
262 revoked 70/1881
266 revoked 70/702
270 amended 76/225; 88/591
273 revoked 75/910
274 revoked 66/1582
277 revoked 74/32
285 revoked 74/529
286 revoked 74/529
288 revoked 74/32
289 revoked 67/65
292 revoked 68/885
310 revoked 69/1027
312 revoked 70/488
317 amended 71/1619
319 revoked 73/2037
324 revoked 83/1718
325 revoked 74/529
332 revoked 70/16
335 amended 69/1703; 70/96
338 revoked 75/559
346 revoked 71/131
347 revoked 69/646
348 revoked 69/647
349 revoked 69/648
352 amended 67/1534; revoked 69/970
357 revoked 70/862
358 amended 71/538
371 revoked 66/743
376 revoked 66/1519

387 revoked 73/8
388 revoked 70/1981
389 revoked 75/559
390 revoked 82/1085
391 revoked 77/1876
392 revoked 81/612
402 revoked 72/1588
407 revoked 68/885
409 revoked 68/844
420 revoked 70/1858
421 revoked 66/1566
424 amended 68/1842
428 revoked 68/898
431 revoked 69/840
437 revoked 68/1257
438 revoked 71/516
439 revoked 66/1249
440 revoked 67/1626
441 amended 66/574
442 revoked 66/1184
446 revoked 72/990
447 revoked 72/1693
448 revoked 70/1464
449 revoked 72/1693
450 revoked 72/1693
451 revoked 72/1693
452 revoked 72/1693
453 revoked 72/1693
454 revoked 72/1693
461 amended 67/626
464 revoked 70/1194
465 revoked 71/1135
467 amended 70/1267
476 revoked 71/1524
479 revoked 69/401
482 revoked 66/921
483 revoked 66/1566
484 revoked 71/289
485 revoked 71/290
489 revoked 75/1536
490 revoked 75/1536
491 revoked 69/1270
492 revoked 71/1524
499 amended 82/102; revoked 84/108
502 amended 68/907
503 amended 68/908
505 amended 67/1195; 68/906; 69/1707; 71/888
507 revoked 73/1178
508 revoked 69/1742
509 revoked 69/1784
510 revoked 67/1900
514 amended 83/1646
518 revoked 68/551
519 revoked 71/1524
520 amended 71/825
530 revoked 71/1087
533 revoked 70/311
538 amended 75/79
539 amended 85/474
542 revoked 69/1787
544 revoked 68/219
545 revoked 69/1674
546 revoked 66/1590
549 revoked 67/844
551 revoked 68/422
554 revoked 68/1130
560 revoked 68/219
564 revoked 69/553
569 revoked 69/163

1966—cont.

579 amended 68/1212; 69/1152; 73/1862; 74/424; 76/48
581 amended 83/136
588 revoked 77/167
597 revoked 69/1008
599 revoked 70/1194
600 revoked 66/740
601 revoked 70/815
602 amended 67/1813
604 revoked 66/1555
605 revoked 66/921
635 revoked 68/26
636 revoked 67/765
637 revoked 69/610
638 revoked 69/611
641 revoked 68/619
642 revoked 85/1093
648 revoked 76/585
649 revoked 66/1257
654 amended 67/1290
660 revoked 68/885
661 revoked 68/885
667 amended 66/1098; 68/988; 68/1223; 72/338; 73/2067
668 revoked 67/1198
669 revoked 69/929
670 amended 67/510
673 revoked 75/559
674 revoked 84/1406
675 revoked 72/751
676 revoked 72/751
683 revoked 67/937
701 revoked 69/1326
705 revoked 72/1693
708 amended 67/525
709 revoked 68/75
714 revoked 82/449 (S. 56)
715 revoked 70/1190
719 amended 66/1092
720 amended 66/1093
721 revoked 67/627
724 revoked 66/1288
727 revoked 72/764
728 revoked 72/1309
732 revoked 66/1449
734 revoked 69/940
735 revoked 78/1839
737 revoked 76/305
738 revoked 70/1194
739 amended 67/196
741 revoked 72/1291
743 revoked 72/2026
745 revoked 66/1555
746 revoked 66/921
749 revoked 67/980
750 revoked 69/941
754 amended 71/183
756 amended 71/1684
757 revoked 66/1249
758 amended 75/631
759 amended 68/1087
760 revoked 82/183 (S. 27)
764 amended 69/118
769 revoked 72/1693
779 revoked 68/660
783 revoked 66/1566
785 revoked 69/1437
786 revoked 70/998
787 revoked 67/1361

1966—cont.

791 amended 66/1487; 83/172/; 85/67
794 amended 74/595
803 revoked 68/1420
804 revoked 67/1362
809 revoked 67/1767
810 revoked 71/1316
813 revoked 79/883
815 revoked 84/1314
818 revoked 66/1625
820 revoked 68/260
821 revoked 69/1173
822 amended 66/1046
823 amended 67/263; 67/279; 67/648; 67/924; 67/1062
829 revoked 67/675
831 revoked 68/420
834 revoked 67/937
836 revoked 70/1238
842 revoked 67/792
844 revoked 75/1722
846 revoked 67/1900
849 revoked 75/1647
850 revoked 68/1474
851 amended 69/132
854 revoked 68/133
855 revoked 68/1327
856 revoked 68/282
857 revoked 68/1256
858 revoked 68/1257
870 revoked 70/89
874 amended 71/453
875 amended 71/260
876 revoked 75/1803
881 amended 74/1075; 75/1102
883 revoked 67/1360
885 revoked 66/1351
886 revoked 67/1292
887 revoked 69/1308
888 amended 69/173; 70/1823; 74/1054
891 revoked 66/1449
893 revoked 68/1714
894 amended 66/931; 66/1314
896 amended 67/274
897 revoked 86/399
898 amended 71/814; 72/1522; 76/276
899 amended 70/106
905 revoked 79/72
910 revoked 67/1305
911 revoked 67/1416
915 amended 71/1179; 75/654; 76/882; revoked 87/2236
916 revoked 72/486
917 revoked 72/487
919 revoked 74/703
920 amended 71/1419
921 revoked 68/1881
922 revoked 66/1555
923 revoked 66/1555
933 revoked 68/1495
935 revoked 76/585
936 revoked 71/631
944 amended 73/2093; revoked 88/195
946 revoked 77/1876
951 revoked 71/311
959 amended 70/1580; 71/1497; 72/909
961 revoked 70/1100
963 revoked 77/1397
966 revoked 68/716

1966—cont.

969 amended 67/263; 67/279; 67/648; 67/924;
    67/1062; 74/684; 75/985
970 amended 72/603; 72/604
973 revoked 82/1550
975 revoked 68/1183
980 revoked 71/601
982 amended 88/1519
985 revoked 70/497
987 revoked 75/1537
989 revoked 77/1725
997 revoked 68/781
1000 revoked 66/1582
1002 revoked 75/560
1003 revoked 68/827
1004 amended 67/1168; 67/1169
1005 revoked 67/1169
1006 amended 67/1168; 72/1301; 74/1128
1010 amended 69/1696; 70/1981; 71/707
1011 revoked 70/376
1012 revoked 67/386
1014 revoked 69/1028
1016 revoked 72/1992
1017 revoked 74/1251
1020 amended 80/1531
1021 revoked 66/1477
1023 revoked 68/1954
1028 revoked 70/1194
1032 revoked 79/837
1033 revoked 81/1826
1034 revoked 81/1826
1035 revoked 70/1849
1036 revoked 66/1253
1038 revoked 66/1257
1039 revoked 67/206
1043 revoked 74/1016
1044 amended 86/1532
1045 amended 67/1230; 68/157; 68/397; 69/1001;
    70/250; 71/145; 71/1329; 71/1468;
    73/1814; 74/1797; 75/1717; 76/1708;
    77/1704; 78/1577; 79/1286; 80/1615
1048 amended 67/844; 74/2057
1049 revoked 67/330
1051 amended 67/1582; 80/1849; 83/1727; 85/67
1054 revoked 70/423
1055 amended 71/1269
1056 revoked 70/16
1063 revoked 75/282
1065 revoked 77/1141
1067 revoked 77/1142
1069 revoked 69/414
1073 amended 85/67
1074 amended 73/1340; 80/1849; 85/67
1080 revoked 66/1555
1081 revoked 68/1881
1082 revoked 66/1566
1083 revoked 68/716
1089 revoked 67/792
1092 amended 66/1093
1095 revoked 67/190
1096 amended 67/541; 71/494; 73/259
1098 revoked 73/2067
1099 revoked 67/844
1101 revoked 70/1270
1102 revoked 69/1101
1107 amended 73/121; 75/1269
1111 amended 75/1691
1112 amended 67/163; 67/279; 67/648; 67/924;
    67/1062; 69/879; 73/860; 74/684; 88/1100
1116 amended 67/127

1966—cont.

1123 amended 81/166
1124 revoked 66/1590
1129 revoked 69/793
1130 revoked 74/1169
1132 revoked 68/491
1138 revoked 67/455
1142 amended 71/145
1143 amended 71/960
1144 revoked 72/317
1152 revoked 78/1844
1153 revoked 67/1391
1156 revoked 68/26
1157 revoked 73/118
1162 revoked 74/1555
1163 amended 69/121; 71/530
1164 amended 66/1556; 71/189; 74/526; 75/361
1165 revoked 67/1414
1174 amended 69/367
1176 amended 69/368
1180 amended 67/241
1181 revoked 67/246
1182 amended 69/370; 83/1676
1184 revoked 70/954
1189 revoked 71/392
1190 revoked 86/1951
1191 amended 73/1590
1192 revoked 67/489
1197 revoked 74/529
1203 revoked 73/1340
1206 amended 81/137; 83/270; 85/1068
1210 revoked 72/1602
1214 revoked 69/1472
1216 amended 74/520
1218 revoked 73/482
1219 revoked 66/1555
1220 revoked 68/1881
1224 revoked 68/619
1226 revoked 80/331
1227 revoked 76/1742
1228 revoked 70/1307
1229 revoked 69/77
1230 revoked 66/1625
1232 amended 67/1299
1233 revoked 74/506
1236 revoked 67/1767
1241 revoked 70/786
1244 revoked 68/716
1245 amended 67/448
1248 revoked 75/1537
1249 amended 67/516; 67/1099; 67/1583
1252 amended 73/1310; 81/137; 83/270; 85/1068
1253 revoked 70/1084
1254 revoked 70/1083
1255 revoked 70/1085
1256 revoked 70/1081
1257 revoked 69/216
1261 amended 67/559
1263 amended 83/270; 85/1068
1273 revoked 73/536
1281 revoked 70/489
1287 revoked 86/399
1288 revoked 69/321
1289 amended 68/438; 68/839
1299 amended 71/2166
1302 revoked 68/219
1304 revoked 68/2061
1308 revoked 71/438
1309 revoked 67/1767
1318 revoked 77/1805

667

STATUTORY INSTRUMENTS AFFECTED 1947–1988

1322 amended 66/1467; 67/607
1327 revoked 69/915
1334 revoked 66/1566
1335 revoked 68/1881
1336 revoked 75/910
1338 revoked 77/851
1340 amended 67/1464
1347 amended 67/263; 67/279; 67/648; 67/924; 67/1062; 74/684; 88/1100
1348 revoked 80/1630
1349 revoked 69/915
1351 revoked 79/1333
1352 revoked 70/789
1365 revoked 67/1105
1373 revoked 73/334
1376 revoked 70/1081
1377 revoked 69/216
1379 amended 75/1372; revoked 80/1793
1384 revoked 73/1310
1387 revoked 78/1844
1390 revoked 67/65
1400 revoked 85/2023
1404 revoked 67/815
1408 revoked 70/954
1412 revoked 77/1876
1420 revoked 76/1899
1425 amended 67/541; 69/749
1428 amended 72/1367
1432 revoked 69/403
1440 revoked 80/1304
1441 revoked 70/1085
1445 revoked 67/1621
1449 revoked 74/505
1454 revoked 70/16
1458 amended 67/1138; 87/1268; revoked 88/1842
1459 revoked 70/1434
1462 revoked 68/1881
1467 revoked 67/607
1468 revoked 67/1035
1469 revoked 66/1555
1470 amended 70/383
1471 amended 68/658; 68/989; 70/1996; 80/1195; 82/210
1472 revoked 66/1555
1474 revoked 80/1854
1475 revoked 68/1714
1477 revoked 67/642
1479 amended 67/128
1480 amended 67/129
1481 amended 68/100; 68/2001; 69/1797; 70/265
1482 revoked 68/1389
1483 revoked 74/768
1484 revoked 73/2114
1490 amended 67/541; 71/494; 73/263
1491 revoked 68/422
1492 revoked 67/1601
1493 revoked 73/221
1494 revoked 68/1320
1495 revoked 67/1363
1500 revoked 74/1120
1501 revoked 67/1759
1502 revoked 67/664
1503 revoked 68/1609
1504 revoked 68/173
1505 revoked 70/783
1506 revoked 67/1631
1514 amended 71/1269; 75/128
1515 revoked 67/645

1516 revoked 68/525
1517 revoked 68/328
1518 revoked 69/1188
1519 revoked 69/35
1520 revoked 68/1562
1521 revoked 68/1563
1522 revoked 80/1177
1523 amended 74/1047; 75/1292; 80/362
1528 revoked 70/1194
1533 revoked 80/499
1540 revoked 78/1834
1544 amended 67/1260
1547 revoked 71/1152
1548 revoked 71/656
1549 revoked 67/1027
1555 amended 67/79; 67/203; 67/468; 67/469; 67/953; 67/1112; 67/1562; 67/1718; 68/77; 68/642; 68/643; 68/679
1556 amended 74/526; 75/361
1560 revoked 67/1859
1563 revoked 68/1881
1565 amended 67/1290
1566 revoked 69/1847
1570 revoked 71/132
1572 revoked 68/26
1573 amended 75/1997; revoked 80/1866
1575 revoked 82/1218
1576 revoked 83/1499
1577 revoked 81/1086
1578 revoked 71/2054
1579 revoked 80/623
1582 revoked 71/232
1586 revoked 72/1693
1587 revoked 70/875
1588 revoked 73/8
1590 revoked 71/233
1595 revoked 68/885
1596 revoked 67/477
1600 amended 81/232
1603 amended 67/993
1604 amended 67/1054
1605 revoked 67/1724
1609 amended 69/1845
1616 revoked 74/351
1617 revoked 74/351
1618 revoked 74/506
1619 revoked 68/716
1625 amended 67/1553; revoked 71/234
1628 revoked 67/1583
1629 amended 73/1792
1640 revoked 70/94

1967

10 amended 85/1476
11 amended 67/1029
18 amended 67/248; 68/1094; 69/593
19 revoked 69/915
20 revoked 69/861
24 amended 69/855
27 revoked 71/2124
29 amended 69/1460; 72/1891; 75/640; 75/1135; 77/634; 81/1017; 86/1353; revoked 87/309
34 revoked 82/34
38 revoked 71/108
39 revoked 71/107
46 revoked 72/316
62 revoked 72/419
63 amended 85/1513

1967—*cont.*

65 amended 68/418
68 revoked 74/351
71 revoked 70/198
72 revoked 71/136
77 revoked 74/768
78 revoked 68/1881
79 revoked 68/679
80 amended 68/1701
81 amended 85/1068
82 amended 78/1648
89 revoked 72/1693
94 revoked 69/1787
99 revoked 68/885
102 revoked 74/351
104 amended 71/25; 74/433
105 revoked 74/1339
112 amended 84/1593
115 revoked 68/1801
127 amended 67/1242
128 revoked 81/1113
130 revoked 74/351
131 revoked 70/1194
136 amended 68/387
143 revoked 74/351
144 revoked 71/220
145 revoked 73/118
153 revoked 67/1169
154 revoked 67/1168
155 amended 67/156
159 amended 67/249
160 revoked 67/815
167 amended 80/1987
169 revoked 75/2132
171 revoked 77/944
172 amended 67/1093; 75/594; 79/1519; 80/282
173 amended 67/1619
176 revoked 69/414
178 revoked 69/888
181 revoked 68/1337
184 revoked 70/198
185 revoked 77/580
186 revoked 77/581
196 amended 67/1244
203 revoked 68/679
204 revoked 68/1881
205 revoked 67/1847
206 revoked 67/1051
207 revoked 68/196
209 revoked 70/497
213 revoked 70/1238
223 amended 73/2155; 83/1107; 83/1108
224 amended 73/2155; 78/1030; 83/1109
225 revoked 91/1106
226 revoked 78/1027
227 revoked 73/2155
229 revoked 78/1901
230 amended 83/1112
231 amended 83/1112
232 amended 67/547
240 revoked 69/1064
241 revoked 68/1377
246 revoked 68/1377
247 revoked 69/1832
248 amended 68/1094; 69/593
252 revoked 69/1423
253 amended 70/1224
255 amended 67/1267
259 revoked 67/937
263 revoked 82/657

1967—*cont.*

266 amended 75/1691
267 revoked 77/1724
270 amended 68/516
274 amended 67/1213
276 amended 71/836; 72/1156; 76/314
278 revoked 69/352
279 revoked 68/1333
283 amended 74/195
286 amended 67/1211
292 revoked 82/107
298 amended 70/644
301 amended 71/1660
313 revoked 72/38
314 revoked 72/39
315 revoked 71/450
316 amended 67/1290; revoked 84/316
318 amended 70/271
324 amended 70/717
327 revoked 70/1194
330 amended 67/1265; 69/292; 71/807; 71/1220; 71/1419; 71/1633; 72/1301; 72/1302; 74/593; 74/1243
331 amended 68/1882
333 revoked 74/351
334 amended 68/407
346 amended 71/2067
347 revoked 74/351
354 amended 67/935
357 revoked 67/1847
359 revoked 72/38
360 revoked 72/39
361 revoked 72/38
362 revoked 72/39
363 amended 69/105; 70/1010; 71/1898; 73/895
364 amended 68/2071; 72/1762; 82/1207
366 revoked 67/554
372 amended 67/1131; 73/116; 74/194; 74/360; 81/1765; revoked 87/1135
376 revoked 77/763
379 amended 67/1686
381 revoked 70/16
385 amended 69/1039; 72/205; 83/1727; 85/67
386 amended 67/594; 67/1573; 69/1277; 71/1420; 72/1300; 73/1444; 74/1129
388 amended 69/1038; 72/307; 83/270; 85/1068
392 revoked 68/1389
393 revoked 84/1989
394 revoked 68/885
395 amended 75/70; 75/2212; 78/1809; 80/2004; 84/2009; 88/2099
396 amended 68/526
400 revoked 70/1858
415 revoked 69/414
416 revoked 67/633
417 amended 67/1046
422 revoked 77/1142
424 revoked 67/1105
430 revoked 78/602
431 revoked 74/351
432 revoked 74/351
433 revoked 68/1256
434 revoked 77/293
439 revoked 69/414
446 revoked 68/348
448 amended 67/1316
449 amended 67/588
451 revoked 75/1379
453 revoked 71/232
455 revoked 71/1038

1967—*cont.*
463 revoked 74/1750
467 amended 69/403; 69/1107; 71/1654
468 revoked 68/679
469 revoked 68/679
470 revoked 68/1881
471 amended 69/1065; 70/1942
476 revoked 77/1876
477 revoked 70/482
480 amended 67/806; 67/807; 67/808; 69/1083; 74/528; 79/931; 81/440
484 amended 70/483; 71/2117
486 amended 72/494
488 revoked 69/403
489 revoked 76/1987
490 revoked 68/26
494 amended 67/1074; 70/459
496 amended 70/483
512 amended 72/595; 74/645
516 revoked 67/1583
517 revoked 85/197
520 amended 71/1419; 74/416
523 revoked 68/515
525 amended 68/74
526 revoked 68/75
530 amended 71/538
533 revoked 69/216
534 amended 71/822; 71/1771
552 revoked 70/1194
553 revoked 71/2
554 revoked 67/786
555 revoked 67/1847
556 revoked 79/1331
561 revoked 67/1189
562 revoked 72/604
563 revoked 67/1168
574 revoked 68/405
575 revoked 67/1292
576 revoked 67/1293
578 amended 68/425
579 amended 68/428
593 revoked 69/1027
594 amended 71/1420; 74/1129
599 amended 76/1168; 80/999; 84/1072
601 amended 71/1212; revoked 85/197
606 revoked 72/287
613 revoked 70/1100
614 revoked 72/1693
618 revoked 70/60
627 revoked 67/1806
628 revoked 73/157
633 revoked 71/510
634 revoked 68/1421
635 revoked 68/1422
637 amended 81/326
639 revoked 68/1357
640 revoked 69/428
641 revoked 70/723
642 revoked 68/616
643 revoked 69/216
644 revoked 70/1105
645 revoked 69/655
646 revoked 71/934
647 revoked 67/1667
648 amended 67/924; 67/1062; 74/684; 82/921; 88/1100
651 revoked 68/1881
652 revoked 67/1847
655 revoked 73/284
657 amended 85/266

1967—*cont.*
663 revoked 68/751
664 revoked 68/1484
668 revoked 71/450
675 revoked 70/1288
677 amended 73/2141
678 amended 77/1915
683 amended 71/270; 74/997
685 revoked 74/351
694 revoked 67/1622
706 revoked 69/414
709 amended 67/891; 67/1120; 67/1625; 70/585; 71/1822; 72/676; 72/1592
711 revoked 72/1928
712 revoked 72/1929
713 revoked 74/713
714 amended 69/1396
715 revoked 75/653
718 revoked 74/351
719 amended 68/1490
734 revoked 67/1687
743 revoked 72/316
744 revoked 68/1846
745 revoked 70/617
748 revoked 87/2024
753 amended 70/753
754 revoked 70/1194
757 revoked 69/654
758 revoked 70/624
760 amended 70/1981; 71/1419
765 revoked 68/1074
766 revoked 68/26
772 amended 68/1968; 70/1366
773 revoked 68/733
774 revoked 68/1534
780 revoked 68/1881
786 revoked 67/1652
788 amended 70/194
790 revoked 72/2025
791 revoked 71/1842
792 amended 75/1054; 82/559
793 revoked 73/1311
794 revoked 68/282
799 amended 68/1592; 72/908
802 revoked 88/1082
810 amended 84/701
812 amended 67/1482
814 revoked 81/612
815 revoked 71/1237
816 revoked 68/294
817 revoked 72/1588
820 amended 81/604
823 revoked 75/60
824 amended 71/1258; 73/701
826 amended 68/851
828 amended 71/1419
829 amended 71/1269; 76/337
830 revoked 67/1106
832 revoked 75/559
839 revoked 85/2043
840 revoked 70/350
844 revoked 73/1013
853 revoked 76/820
859 amended 68/1851; revoked 70/428
860 amended 67/1864; 70/400; 83/1727; revoked 84/1566
861 amended 67/1864; 68/2046; 70/400; 80/1849; 83/1727; revoked 84/1566
862 amended 67/1864; 68/2047; 70/400; 80/1849; 83/1727; revoked 84/1566

STATUTORY INSTRUMENTS AFFECTED 1947–1988

865 revoked 67/1292
866 revoked 67/1293
867 amended 67/882
868 amended 67/883
869 revoked 75/910
870 revoked 75/60
876 amended 71/1209
879 amended 71/1060; 73/36
882 amended 67/883
886 revoked 68/1511
887 revoked 70/1194
889 revoked 68/1077
890 revoked 70/1146
901 revoked 69/78
902 revoked 67/1688
907 revoked 70/917
912 revoked 68/929
913 revoked 68/91
915 revoked 70/1085
922 revoked 74/351
923 revoked 68/26
924 revoked 71/1766
926 revoked 70/573
928 amended 68/1730; 70/645
932 revoked 70/815
934 amended 70/644
937 revoked 73/1468
938 amended 72/147
939 revoked 69/691
940 revoked 87/1781
944 revoked 68/716
947 revoked 74/505
948 revoked 76/1987
949 revoked 74/778
952 revoked 68/1881
953 revoked 68/679
954 amended 86/2001
964 revoked 71/846
965 amended 76/1286
966 revoked 70/1238
967 revoked 70/1238
970 revoked 72/1101
971 revoked 79/1316
972 revoked 19/1315
975 revoked 68/1377
976 revoked 72/970
977 revoked 69/736
997 revoked 67/1847
980 revoked 68/991
981 revoked 71/253
987 revoked 74/1329
988 revoked 69/562
993 amended 67/1958
994 revoked 67/1890
1001 amended 75/1087
1002 amended 75/135; 87/2266
1004 revoked 73/1311
1005 amended 72/752; 72/1483
1008 revoked 78/1177
1010 amended 67/1283
1018 amended 68/245; 71/502; 71/1585; 72/517; 72/1955; 75/281; 77/701; 80/746; 80/1494; 81/404
1019 revoked 73/22
1020 revoked 73/22
1021 amended 71/843; 75/1544; 76/1073; 82/902; 87/2226
1022 revoked 81/1233
1024 revoked 70/1194

1025 revoked 70/198
1027 revoked 67/1385
1030 revoked 68/1139
1031 revoked 74/529
1036 amended 71/1279
1039 revoked 73/2059
1041 revoked 73/2059
1044 revoked 73/2059
1045 revoked 77/1141
1051 revoked 67/1651
1052 revoked 70/439
1054 revoked 68/124
1059 revoked 73/1311
1061 revoked 70/457
1062 amended 74/684; 79/1595; 82/923; 88/1100
1064 revoked 83/156
1071 revoked 67/1847
1072 amended 73/1977
1076 revoked 73/31
1077 amended 83/270; revoked 84/1714
1078 amended 68/139; 69/327; 81/137; 83/270; revoked 84/1714
1079 amended 69/326; 81/137; 83/270; revoked 84/1714
1080 revoked 81/612
1081 revoked 69/216
1082 amended 70/1163; 71/916
1083 amended 74/1853
1087 revoked 70/1824
1088 revoked 70/1714
1093 amended 75/594
1094 amended 81/1258; revoked 88/1760
1098 amended 67/1226
1099 revoked 67/1583
1104 amended 74/70
1110 amended 74/989
1111 revoked 72/1693
1112 revoked 68/679
1113 revoked 68/1881
1114 amended 74/70
1119 revoked 69/1817
1124 amended 68/769
1125 revoked 71/707
1126 amended 68/770
1127 amended 68/1118
1130 revoked 81/1142
1131 amended 73/116; 75/360; revoked 87/1135
1132 amended 70/1100
1136 revoked 70/1137
1138 revoked 88/1842
1139 revoked 69/736
1140 amended 67/1919; 72/443
1141 amended 67/1919; 71/210; 73/1890; 83/878
1148 amended 68/117
1150 amended 83/1676
1152 revoked 77/1876
1153 revoked 81/612
1157 revoked 74/1367
1159 revoked 67/1649
1160 revoked 67/1650
1162 amended 69/77; 69/1341; 71/903; 73/864; 75/1135; 76/475
1163 revoked 72/1138
1164 revoked 71/1213
1165 revoked 68/599
1166 revoked 70/810
1171 revoked 68/1389
1173 amended 67/1808; 69/746; 83/1818
1176 revoked 72/1544

STATUTORY INSTRUMENTS AFFECTED 1947–1988

1967—*cont.*

1180 revoked 75/849
1181 revoked 82/1234
1182 revoked 73/7
1183 revoked 76/955
1186 amended 71/1632
1187 revoked 75/1537
1188 revoked 69/35
1189 amended 71/1632; 79/1331; 79/1335
1192 revoked 68/26
1195 amended 68/906; 71/888
1194 amended 88/488
1198 revoked 68/626
1199 amended 73/322; 76/475; 79/1186; 80/100;
    82/965
1200 amended 75/216
1203 revoked 69/1848
1204 revoked 82/1489
1205 revoked 83/136
1211 revoked 68/347
1215 revoked 68/1987
1216 revoked 70/1194
1221 amended 70/531
1223 revoked 75/559
1228 amended 68/17
1230 amended 71/145
1234 amended 67/1380; 68/325
1241 revoked 69/17; 69/286
1242 amended 60/246
1243 revoked 70/786
1250 revoked 76/585
1254 revoked 67/1847
1255 revoked 68/1881
1260 revoked 74/1203
1265 amended 68/524; 68/827; 69/1696; 71/906;
    71/1220; 72/606; 73/693
1267 revoked 68/493
1269 revoked 72/751
1270 revoked 69/321
1271 revoked 69/1832
1279 amended 69/1369
1280 amended 68/118
1286 revoked 76/1987
1289 amended 68/325
1292 revoked 69/1307
1293 revoked 69/1308
1294 amended 68/1166; 71/90
1303 amended 67/1904–1916; 68/112; 68/113;
    68/183; 68/184; 68/185; 68/884; 68/1091
1305 revoked 69/618
1308 revoked 70/809
1310 amended 76/355; 78/1729; 80/1751; 83/350;
    86/621; 87/394
1312 revoked 69/1265
1315 revoked 68/1074
1316 amended 68/245
1322 revoked 69/1423
1324 revoked 69/1423
1330 amended 69/413; 74/520; 77/1341
1342 revoked 68/716
1345 amended 67/1447; revoked 86/399
1347 revoked 70/1238
1350 revoked 70/1194
1360 amended 68/1987
1361 revoked 73/184
1362 revoked 73/219
1363 revoked 68/1321
1369 revoked 69/1349
1385 revoked 67/1929; 68/344
1386 revoked 82/659

1967—*cont.*

1390 revoked 69/1443
1392 revoked 77/1725
1406 revoked 69/1028
1413 revoked 83/1718
1414 revoked 68/1528
1416 revoked 68/1253
1427 amended 68/1477
1435 revoked 68/1881
1439 revoked 72/752
1441 revoked 68/125; 68/512
1442 revoked 79/1546
1447 revoked 86/399
1455 revoked 68/619
1456 revoked 80/319
1457 revoked 80/319
1462 amended 73/4; 83/622
1466 revoked 72/419
1468 revoked 69/1696
1469 revoked 72/316
1470 revoked 68/558
1472 revoked 70/1194
1475 revoked 69/647
1476 revoked 69/646
1477 revoked 69/648
1480 revoked 76/894
1485 amended 84/510
1489 revoked 69/864
1500 revoked 71/232
1501 revoked 71/1469
1513 revoked 69/868
1514 revoked 69/869
1515 revoked 68/1745
1516 amended 70/392
1522 revoked 69/963
1523 revoked 69/964
1524 amended 74/1310
1527 revoked 79/1456
1528 revoked 70/110
1530 revoked 69/1021
1533 revoked 74/778
1534 revoked 69/970
1546 revoked 71/233
1550 revoked 70/376
1553 revoked 71/234
1555 amended 69/693; 71/1025
1556 revoked 69/216
1559 amended 68/967; 69/694; 70/2024
1560 amended 70/1650; 71/1190
1561 amended 68/983; 69/708; 70/1651
1562 revoked 68/679
1564 revoked 68/1881
1566 revoked 70/548
1570 revoked 75/558
1571 revoked 75/558
1572 amended 75/1250; 75/1661
1582 amended 67/1939; 80/1832; 83/1727; 85/67
1583 amended 67/1946; 68/668; 68/1002
1584 revoked 70/815
1594 revoked 85/802
1601 revoked 68/1328
1609 amended 70/2026
1611 revoked 71/643
1612 amended 67/1877
1614 revoked 76/748
1615 amended 69/849
1621 amended 68/1686
1622 revoked 68/559
1626 revoked 71/1666
1631 revoked 73/1141

1967—*cont.*

1645 revoked 72/317
1648 revoked 69/1184
1649 revoked 67/1845
1650 revoked 67/1853
1651 revoked 67/1855
1652 revoked 67/1765
1653 revoked 69/297
1658 amended 74/1837; 75/1087; 77/1149
1659 revoked 71/809
1660 revoked 70/1792
1661 revoked 68/1920
1665 revoked 69/321
1666 revoked 69/321
1667 revoked 75/19
1678 revoked 70/954
1683 amended 80/697
1688 revoked 68/919
1689 revoked 78/436
1692 revoked 79/563
1699 amended 69/1256; 75/1528; 76/237; 78/1325
1702 revoked 69/1307
1703 revoked 69/1308
1704 revoked 69/1675
1714 amended 68/266; revoked 84/1950
1715 amended 68/131
1718 revoked 68/679
1719 revoked 68/1881
1723 revoked 84/1950
1724 revoked 82/1234 (S. 146)
1729 revoked 68/2002
1730 amended 68/937
1734 revoked 71/2084
1736 revoked 69/77
1747 amended 68/343
1753 revoked 69/321
1754 revoked 70/1194
1759 amended 69/208; 69/209; 69/909
1767 amended 68/333; 68/1399; 72/386
1768 amended 69/1481
1771 revoked 70/1238
1776 revoked 71/107
1792 revoked 83/40
1793 revoked 72/287
1796 revoked 80/953
1798 revoked 70/1238
1799 revoked 74/529
1802 amended 68/1932
1804 revoked 80/1599
1805 revoked 72/287
1806 revoked 69/131
1808 amended 83/1818
1809 amended 71/1269; 76/1196
1810 revoked 68/219
1811 revoked 68/1262
1819 amended 68/2049; 69/203
1820 amended 71/25
1821 amended 70/539; 71/517; 72/558; 73/916; 76/729; 79/192; 80/61; 80/748
1822 amended 67/1840
1824 amended 67/1874
1831 amended 83/133
1832 revoked 70/16
1835 revoked 68/1881
1842 revoked 72/316
1844 revoked 71/450
1845 revoked 72/419
1847 revoked 68/1948
1853 revoked 69/459

1967—*cont.*

1854 revoked 69/458
1855 revoked 69/460
1856 revoked 70/862
1859 revoked 68/2075
1860 revoked 75/282
1861 revoked 71/1067
1862 amended 71/1818
1863 amended 70/1985; 71/1819
1864 revoked 70/400
1865 revoked 78/1420
1866 amended 80/1849; 83/1727; 85/67
1867 amended 80/1849; 83/1727; 85/67
1869 amended 69/697
1870 amended 71/945
1872 revoked 75/2223
1873 amended 68/2006; 71/2070; 75/2222; 77/2121; 79/1668; 83/1882; revoked 87/2224
1875 amended 70/1109; 74/482; revoked 86/724
1876 revoked 75/597
1878 revoked 70/1194
1882 revoked 72/328
1884 amended 72/1208; revoked 84/647
1885 revoked 74/1992
1887 revoked 82/1234
1890 revoked 69/1487
1895 revoked 74/357
1898 revoked 69/428
1900 amended 75/1949; 76/363
1904 amended 68/292; 68/1375
1905 amended 68/292; 68/1375; 81/1803
1906 amended 68/292; 68/1375
1907 amended 68/292; 68/1375
1908 amended 68/292; 68/1375
1909 amended 68/292; 68/1375; 81/1803
1910 amended 68/292; 68/1375; 75/1508; 75/1512
1911 amended 68/292; 68/1375; 75/2163; 81/1803
1912 amended 68/292
1913 amended 68/292; 68/1375; 81/1803
1914 amended 68/292; 68/1375
1915 amended 68/292; 68/1375; 81/1803
1916 amended 68/292; 68/1375; 81/1803
1919 amended 75/1704; 78/1880; 78/1881
1927 revoked 74/351
1928 amended 71/538
1929 revoked 68/344
1930 revoked 72/2026
1931 revoked 72/2026
1933 revoked 69/1647
1935 revoked 71/593
1936 revoked 71/592
1946 amended 68/159
1958 amended 68/1067
1960 revoked 81/988
1965 revoked 74/363
1976 amended 69/698; 71/942
1977 amended 68/968; 70/1446
1978 amended 74/69; revoked 83/1633

1968

7 revoked 73/22
8 revoked 69/761
10 revoked 68/1843
21 revoked 69/1219
24 revoked 69/1787
25 amended 69/408; 69/1786; 70/418; 70/1402; 71/151; 71/804; 73/1156; 75/933;

STATUTORY INSTRUMENTS AFFECTED 1947–1988

75/1361; 76/1595; 77/1005; 77/1989; 78/1239; 79/1543
26 amended 68/552; 68/766; 68/1207; 68/1761; 69/137; 69/911; 70/66; 70/417; 70/601; 71/156; 71/659
30 amended 68/1882
32 amended 71/566
35 amended 75/1303
43 amended 74/1809; 75/1894; 76/363; 76/1494; 76/1495; 76/1496; 78/1346; 80/169; 81/989; 83/1682; 85/1661; revoked 86/183
46 revoked 69/647
47 revoked 69/646
48 revoked 69/648
50 revoked 68/716
51 revoked 84/1950
54 revoked 69/753
61 revoked 82/636
69 revoked 77/1370
71 amended 71/195
72 amended 74/520
74 amended 68/1682
75 amended 68/1683
77 revoked 68/679
78 revoked 68/1881
80 revoked 68/1232
83 revoked 70/376
84 revoked 69/970
94 revoked 65/585
97 amended 73/1351; 79/1426; 81/1085; 83/1727; revoked 84/1918
98 amended 73/1350; 79/1427; 81/1084; 83/1727; revoked 84/1917
100 revoked 69/1797
105 amended 71/453
106 revoked 75/1803
107 amended 71/260
110 revoked 70/*238
111 revoked 76/893
112 amended 68/292; 68/1375; 81/1803
113 amended 68/292; 68/1375; 81/1803
114 revoked 71/211
118 revoked 81/1113
121 revoked 74/351
123 revoked 68/1130
128 amended 71/538; 73/549
132 revoked 70/1288
133 revoked 69/640
135 revoked 69/1453
137 revoked 68/456
139 amended 69/327; revoked 84/1714
145 revoked 72/1333
155 revoked 70/1194
157 amended 70/145; 71/1329
165 revoked 71/438
170 amended 70/1954; 75/605; 78/1387; 80/580; 82/572
172 amended 68/363; 68/364; 68/365
173 revoked 68/1610
174 revoked 70/1238
176 revoked 76/585
182 amended 68/463; 68/726; 73/233; 79/452; 79/1310
183 amended 68/292; 68/1375; 81/1803
184 amended 68/292; 68/1375; 81/1803
185 amended 68/292; 68/1375; 81/1803
189 amended 69/1594; 85/1152
190 revoked 70/351

196 revoked 69/224
197 revoked 69/1713
200 revoked 70/1100
205 revoked 72/261
207 amended 79/882
208 amended 69/493; 69/1820; 70/424; 70/1413; 71/185; 71/810; 72/778; 73/1138; 75/1452; 76/621; 77/1131; 77/2009; 78/999; 78/1171; 79/1698; 81/361; 82/273; 82/1768; 83/318; 83/1368; 83/1768; 87/424; 87/1878
218 revoked 73/1521
219 revoked 71/953
225 revoked 72/467
237 amended 74/595
238 revoked 68/1011
245 revoked 68/1569
248 amended 75/666; 78/1545; 82/680 (S. 103)
251 revoked 68/1881
252 revoked 68/1948
255 revoked 69/1021
256 revoked 68/619
258 amended 82/1099
259 revoked 70/281
260 revoked 69/1172
263 amended 80/1887; 83/270; 84/1518; 85/1068
264 revoked 75/60
266 revoked 84/1950
267 revoked 68/1541
279 revoked 74/549
281 revoked 71/987
282 amended 69/1430; 71/193
285 amended 68/586
286 amended 68/587
287 amended 71/538
295 revoked 76/984
314 revoked 71/1954
323 revoked 73/284
327 revoked 69/901
328 revoked 69/1187
332 revoked 78/1543
333 revoked 72/386
338 revoked 70/1370
344 revoked 69/115
345 revoked 69/1780
347 revoked 68/1478
354 revoked 73/7
355 revoked 71/450
357 amended 74/544; 78/1128; 85/1850; revoked 86/887
362 revoked 69/321
363 revoked 69/647
364 revoked 69/646
365 revoked 69/648
370 revoked 70/1288
371 revoked 74/529
373 revoked 71/447
375 revoked 69/618
378 revoked 69/1704
385 revoked 70/1194
386 revoked 78/910
387 revoked 74/351
388 revoked 71/102
389 revoked 71/457
390 amended 69/636; 76/15; 80/1724
392 amended 83/108
397 amended 71/145
398 revoked 73/352

1968—*cont.*
399 revoked 76/250
404 revoked 70/16
405 revoked 68/1381
407 revoked 69/501
414 amended 88/1603
420 revoked 70/993
422 revoked 70/605
423 revoked 71/1135
424 revoked 70/1085
426 revoked 69/321
430 amended   70/400;   80/1849;   83/1727;
      revoked 84/1566
431 revoked 71/161
435 revoked 75/1204
440 amended 74/713; 76/503
441 amended 71/494
445 revoked 81/87
448 revoked 69/760
449 revoked 76/475
454 amended 71/562
456 revoked 70/504
457 revoked 69/972
464 revoked 71/1237
467 revoked 77/1876
468 revoked 81/612
471 revoked 72/1693
475 revoked 74/351
480 revoked 72/1577
481 revoked 68/1881
488 amended 74/520
491 revoked 74/364
492 revoked 72/752
496 amended 71/2076; 74/339
497 revoked 70/131
505 amended 74/1309; 76/127; 80/1864
507 revoked 69/1409
512 amended 71/538
523 revoked 69/321
524 amended 70/1981; 72/606; 75/559
525 revoked 69/1476
527 amended 71/538
530 revoked 71/232
532 amended 85/1449; 85/1504
533 revoked 68/1253
534 revoked 69/483
544 revoked 73/1468
545 revoked 74/32
549 revoked 68/1591
552 amended 71/156
555 revoked 74/351
557 revoked 74/557
560 amended 68/1462
563 revoked 71/557
570 revoked 71/1040
571 revoked 86/1951
574 amended 74/1270
575 amended 74/2149
579 revoked 71/392
580 revoked 69/386
585 revoked 75/979
586 amended 68/587; 68/999
588 amended 74/1574; 74/1941; 75/1298
590 revoked 75/630
592 revoked 75/1385
593 revoked 68/1256
594 revoked 71/450
596 revoked 70/1194
600 revoked 68/1013
601 revoked 71/352

1968—*cont.*
602 revoked 69/321
611 revoked 74/529
614 revoked 79/436
616 revoked 69/1891
617 revoked 85/1093
618 revoked 80/331
619 revoked 72/506
621 revoked 80/331
622 revoked 69/1021
626 revoked 69/930
641 revoked 68/1948
642 revoked 68/679
643 revoked 68/679
644 revoked 68/1881
645 revoked 75/1647
653 revoked 70/815
655 amended 70/1237; 79/1457
656 amended 79/569; 80/1612
657 revoked 77/851
660 revoked 70/1480
674 revoked 83/1718
676 revoked 75/1722
677 revoked 70/1188
678 revoked 70/1187
679 amended   68/950;   68/1030;   68/1158;
      68/1383;   68/1509;   68/1510;   68/1778;
      68/1880; 69/1338; 69/1413
686 revoked 73/22
687 revoked 73/22
694 revoked 80/1968
710 revoked 75/650
711 revoked 75/930
716 revoked 72/777
717 amended 71/3449; 76/1073; 81/86; 84/648;
      88/260
727 revoked 68/1377
728 revoked 69/736
729 amended 74/1941; 74/1943
730 revoked 81/612
736 revoked 79/72
742 revoked 69/894
745 revoked 69/553
746 revoked 86/399
747 revoked 70/1194
748 amended 71/914
751 revoked 69/546
752 revoked 69/547
754 amended 78/631
759 revoked 74/285
763 amended 81/1229
764 revoked 74/2191
765 revoked 69/687
766 amended 68/1761; 71/156
767 revoked 71/289
779 revoked 72/1693
780 amended 71/1060; 73/36; 81/917; revoked
      85/1333
787 amended 74/684
790 revoked 84/108
796 amended 78/25
799 revoked 75/862
813 amended 71/538
815 amended 75/1680
816 amended 68/1168; 68/1607
818 revoked 74/506
824 revoked 72/751
826 revoked 72/751
827 amended   69/1508;   71/1419,   71/1422;
      72/1363; 73/776; 73/1547

1968—*cont.*

830 amended 69/702
831 amended 71/946
841 revoked 72/1693
844 revoked 74/2000
845 revoked 70/1288
849 amended 74/1943; 83/1579
850 revoked 69/973
861 revoked 68/1366
864 revoked 82/677
865 revoked 68/1533; 85/802
874 revoked 80/2005
875 amended 69/695; 71/940
876 amended 69/696
884 amended 68/1375; 73/761; 81/1803
885 revoked 68/1020
887 revoked 77/1234
888 amended 77/1235; 88/587
892 revoked 80/184
898 revoked 82/665
906 amended 71/888
913 amended 71/341
919 amended 68/1990
927 revoked 71/1061
928 revoked 71/1062
930 revoked 68/1881
931 revoked 69/1399
935 revoked 86/1002
936 revoked 86/1002
937 amended 68/1771; 69/813; 69/1633
938 revoked 70/16
939 revoked 71/656
941 amended 74/595
942 amended 82/723
947 revoked 70/170
948 amended 81/275
950 revoked 69/1413
953 revoked 86/1002
954 revoked 86/1002
955 revoked 69/1420
962 revoked 70/1194
965 amended 69/700
966 amended 69/701; 70/1445
978 revoked 68/1948
981 amended 70/1648; 70/1649; 71/1188; 72/725
982 amended 69/707
987 amended 71/553; 73/1268
989 amended 70/384
991 revoked 69/851
994 revoked 72/765
995 revoked 72/641
1007 revoked 75/559
1014 amended 75/1263; revoked 83/569
1020 revoked 72/1583
1026 revoked 74/351
1030 revoked 69/1413
1032 amended 71/1876; 74/684
1033 amended 74/684
1039 revoked 86/401
1040 revoked 73/22
1041 revoked 73/22
1043 revoked 70/87
1045 revoked 70/1083
1047 revoked 69/1323
1048 revoked 74/67
1051 revoked 70/979
1053 amended 70/1003; 75/595; 79/1267; 80/641
1055 amended 75/1135; 76/475
1064 revoked 72/764

1968—*cont.*

1065 revoked 74/351
1066 amended 73/143
1071 amended 72/798
1073 revoked 70/1288
1074 revoked 79/991
1076 revoked 70/1146
1077 amended 70/1145; 71/1206; 75/1885; 77/1330; 78/1092; 79/1751; 80/1178
1079 revoked 70/336
1080 revoked 73/176
1081 revoked 69/1419
1090 revoked 76/421
1091 amended 77/47
1094 revoked 79/1655
1097 amended 73/1325
1106 revoked 72/1721
1109 revoked 77/1875
1111 revoked 69/1086
1117 revoked 75/341
1118 amended 71/1054
1120 revoked 74/778
1130 revoked 69/1714
1132 revoked 71/632
1137 revoked 69/946
1147 amended 69/867
1148 revoked 72/1678
1154 amended 73/625
1157 revoked 68/1881
1158 revoked 69/1413
1163 amended 70/515; 74/734; 74/1441; 77/108; 78/1257; 83/1052
1164 revoked 74/1555
1168 revoked 69/1423
1169 revoked 71/352
1170 amended 74/908
1173 revoked 72/419
1177 revoked 72/890
1180 revoked 72/316
1181 amended 73/1471; 79/1537; 81/1035; revoked 85/913
1201 revoked 73/1281
1206 revoked 76/585
1207 amended 71/156
1211 revoked 75/1538
1213 revoked 68/1587
1214 revoked 69/1413
1220 amended 72/1975
1225 revoked 68/1467
1230 revoked 82/1197
1231 amended 70/1980; 76/790; 80/661; 80/1651; 83/1863; 84/1716; 85/1632; 86/274; 87/422; 88/468
1232 revoked 79/1333
1233 revoked 79/1331
1235 revoked 71/1295
1240 revoked 71/2001
1242 revoked 77/1861
1244 amended 71/835; 71/1269; 72/1194; 76/1196
1248 revoked 69/321
1249 amended 74/2045
1251 revoked 69/483
1262 amended 78/1118; 87/1977
1265 revoked 78/30
1266 revoked 73/579
1271 revoked 71/626
1281 revoked 82/129
1282 revoked 75/60
1284 amended 69/1720

1968—*cont.*

1285 amended 69/1447
1296 revoked 70/497
1298 amended 69/1881
1299 amended 69/1878
1309 revoked 77/1861
1314 amended 75/1693; 76/2031; 78/12; 80/1848; 80/1850; 81/1432; 83/670; revoked 86/1039
1315 amended 71/1; 78/1388
1316 revoked 73/1189
1319 revoked 70/998
1320 amended 70/1150
1321 revoked 73/191
1327 revoked 70/1136
1328 revoked 73/312
1333 revoked 71/1530
1334 revoked 74/32
1337 revoked 74/351
1338 revoked 70/1194
1353 revoked 76/1987
1354 revoked 68/1467
1355 revoked 69/632
1357 revoked 69/1739
1358 revoked 69/1740
1363 amended 68/2071; 75/1183; revoked 87/376
1366 amended 69/844; 74/274; 76/1226; 82/288; revoked 88/1546
1374 revoked 71/1237
1381 revoked 79/1393
1383 revoked 69/1413
1384 revoked 68/1948
1385 revoked 68/1881
1388 amended 68/1622
1389 amended 70/955; revoked in part 78/216; amended in part 82/717; amended 85/785
1390 revoked 68/1391
1391 revoked 68/1713
1397 revoked 74/773
1399 revoked 72/386
1404 revoked 68/1467
1405 amended 71/538; 72/251; 83/1646
1406 revoked 71/86
1408 revoked 80/6; 81/1657
1420 revoked 70/940
1421 revoked 70/1227
1422 revoked 70/1228
1425 revoked 68/1545
1428 revoked 70/60
1429 revoked 70/702
1442 revoked 70/16
1443 revoked 72/765
1444 revoked 72/641
1448 amended 69/849
1452 amended 71/175; 79/1544
1455 revoked 70/1194
1470 revoked 74/778
1471 amended 70/1996
1474 revoked 76/103
1484 revoked 69/1261
1485 revoked 69/1841
1492 amended 71/8234
1493 revoked 75/308
1495 revoked 76/294
1502 revoked 73/757
1504 amended 70/445; 76/863
1508 revoked 68/1881
1509 revoked 69/1413
1510 revoked 69/1413
1511 revoked 70/364

1968—*cont.*

1526 revoked 72/751
1533 revoked 85/802
1536 revoked 70/617
1541 revoked 79/1605
1542 revoked 78/1538
1545 revoked 68/1587
1558 amended 70/625; 71/911; 78/1883; 79/1551; 82/1591; 84/718; 85/1375; 86/2105
1559 revoked 70/558
1560 revoked 70/558
1561 revoked 73/955
1562 revoked 70/883
1563 revoked 74/811
1570 revoked 72/1196
1571 revoked 80/1820
1571 amended 81/1657
1576 revoked 70/1881
1578 revoked 70/809
1587 revoked 68/1713
1588 revoked 74/285
1591 revoked 69/440
1592 amended 72/908
1596 revoked 70/16
1597 revoked 70/1105
1598 revoked 69/655
1605 revoked 71/457
1606 revoked 74/1995
1607 revoked 74/508
1609 revoked 71/87
1610 revoked 74/211
1617 revoked 68/1939
1618 revoked 69/741
1623 revoked 73/31
1632 revoked 69/321
1633 revoked 70/624
1634 revoked 69/517
1645 revoked 86/724
1646 revoked 77/1875
1655 amended 76/225; 88/591
1667 revoked 73/807
1669 amended 76/608
1675 revoked 87/2024
1676 amended 81/726
1677 revoked 69/1307
1678 revoked 69/1308
1682 amended 70/797
1684 revoked 72/555
1695 revoked 70/1194
1700 revoked 75/299
1702 revoked 70/955
1713 revoked 68/1746
1714 revoked 76/1977
1721 revoked 68/1948
1722 revoked 68/1881
1723 revoked 72/1433
1729 revoked 70/573
1730 revoked 70/645
1731 amended 73/1407; 74/1935
1736 revoked 69/1307
1737 revoked 69/1308
1740 revoked 70/283
1741 revoked 75/1467
1745 revoked 78/1727
1746 revoked 68/1803
1753 revoked 75/956
1755 revoked 76/183
1758 revoked 81/721
1761 amended 71/156
1763 revoked 82/660

STATUTORY INSTRUMENTS AFFECTED 1947–1988

1968—*cont.*

1771 revoked 69/1633
1775 revoked 73/807
1778 revoked 69/1413
1786 revoked 74/351
1795 revoked 70/783
1798 revoked 69/1713
1799 revoked 69/618
1801 revoked 72/1955
1802 revoked 76/1897
1803 revoked 68/1939
1807 revoked 70/548
1810 amended 71/494
1826 revoked 75/1536
1837 revoked 69/216
1841 revoked 77/1774
1842 revoked 72/1291
1843 revoked 70/1194
1846 revoked 70/497
1847 revoked 70/499
1848 revoked 70/1083
1851 revoked 70/428
1854 revoked 71/352
1857 revoked 70/954
1859 amended 75/1033
1862 amended 72/118; 75/1209; 82/709
1863 amended 65/1209
1869 amended 73/1328; 87/466; 87/2055
1871 revoked 70/1085
1880 revoked 69/1413
1881 revoked 71/274
1882 revoked 82/658
1885 revoked 69/60
1889 revoked 75/653
1890 revoked 70/917
1896 revoked 70/376
1898 revoked 72/316
1899 revoked 74/351
1901 amended 75/216
1910 revoked 72/1362
1913 revoked 71/132
1914 revoked 70/862
1915 revoked 74/389
1917 amended 68/2072
1919 revoked 81/553
1920 revoked 81/552
1921 revoked 72/419
1926 revoked 70/1599
1927 revoked 74/538
1929 amended 71/333
1930 revoked 69/1647
1933 amended 73/1145; 75/836; 76/339; 76/1062; revoked 87/430
1934 revoked 71/1954
1939 revoked 69/45
1944 revoked 76/1987
1945 revoked 74/32
1947 amended 82/827
1948 revoked 69/1751
1952 revoked 74/420
1953 revoked 69/1092
1954 amended 69/1597
1956 amended 70/1875; 71/2031
1961 revoked 75/991
1963 revoked 72/777
1964 revoked 80/401
1965 revoked 71/2128
1966 revoked 71/1156
1968 revoked 70/1366
1969 amended 73/938

1968—*cont.*

1972 revoked 70/1454
1973 amended 75/1691
1978 amended 71/1958; revoked 83/713
1986 revoked 69/187
1989 revoked 71/233
1995 revoked 71/234
2003 revoked 75/910
2006 amended 75/2222; revoked 87/2224
2007 revoked 75/2223
2009 amended 69/1509
2011 amended 71/1128
2019 revoked 69/517
2042 amended 78/647
2044 revoked 69/1787
2046 revoked 84/1566
2047 revoked 84/1566
2049 amended 69/1811; 71/1218; 74/571; 77/1912; 82/955; 82/265; 84/460; 85/568; 85/1133; 86/1442; 87/2088
2050 revoked 87/2088
2051 amended 82/102; 84/108
2052 amended 69/76
2062 revoked 74/1720
2063 revoked 70/593
2070 revoked 69/216
2071 amended 72/1762; 75/1183; revoked 87/376
2075 revoked 69/1823
2077 revoked 82/1094

1969

2 amended 80/178
17 amended 75/148; 81/14; 88/963
18 revoked 77/890
19 revoked 77/889
20 revoked 77/888
26 revoked 73/1415
32 revoked 80/1354
34 revoked 72/1693
35 revoked 71/1443
37 revoked 74/529
38 revoked 74/529
45 revoked 69/211
52 revoked 69/321
55 amended 71/538; 72/1360
67 revoked 79/41
77 revoked 77/1360
78 revoked 71/1775
80 revoked 76/1987
81 amended 70/1370; 72/767
85 revoked 77/1043
86 amended 70/967
94 amended 73/1731
95 amended 73/1727
96 amended 73/1732
101 revoked 70/1897
102 amended 71/1094
104 amended 71/1436
115 revoked 70/865
129 revoked 69/517
131 amended 70/139
137 amended 71/156
142 revoked 71/1237
147 revoked 88/1850
148 revoked 75/2192
150 revoked 72/969
151 revoked 77/1875
152 revoked 77/1876
163 revoked 74/361; 82/276
164 revoked 70/615

STATUTORY INSTRUMENTS AFFECTED 1947-1988

1969—cont.
165 revoked 74/529
168 revoked 72/777
170 revoked 73/334
174 revoked 70/1824
176 revoked 82/1197
187 revoked 71/475
189 revoked 74/351
195 revoked 73/284
196 amended 73/624
197 revoked 74/529
200 revoked 72/577
201 revoked 85/1919
203 amended 74/572; 82/266; 85/569; 85/1134;
    revoked 87/2089
204 amended 71/260
205 amended 71/453
206 revoked 75/1803
208 revoked 69/909
209 revoked 70/657
211 revoked 69/314
212 amended 70/24; 70/506; 76/651
213 revoked 71/108
214 revoked 71/107
216 revoked 70/1082
217 revoked 73/1468
224 revoked 71/248
231 revoked 81/1086
232 revoked 69/1751
233 amended 71/470; 72/262
245 revoked 81/404
252 revoked 70/170
254 revoked 74/506
257 revoked 72/467
258 amended 70/230; 86/1079
268 revoked 74/529
269 revoked 83/23
270 amended 69/1767; 82/1639
276 revoked 73/31
278 revoked 69/517
284 amended 86/1558
286 amended 74/596
288 revoked 70/1524
289 revoked 71/707
290 revoked 75/558
291 revoked 75/560
293 revoked 77/1142
294 revoked 77/1141
295 revoked 70/16
297 amended 70/79; 71/264; 74/248; 80/1204
305 revoked 75/60
310 amended 70/811; 77/931
312 revoked 82/648
314 revoked 69/329
315 revoked 69/1751
318 revoked 69/329
319 amended 71/562
321 amended 69/1042; 69/1456; 69/1761; 70/49;
    70/777; 71/444; 71/979; 72/805; 72/843;
    72/987; 72/1473; 72/1690
322 revoked 71/352
324 revoked 71/501
326 revoked 84/1714
327 revoked 84/1714
329 revoked 69/407
339 revoked 71/707
344 amended 69/1457; 72/1609
351 revoked 74/287
354 revoked 74/455
355 revoked 81/1473

1969—cont.
360 amended 71/538; 73/256
365 revoked 83/1676
370 amended 83/1676
371 revoked 71/1235
384 amended 76/225; 88/591
386 revoked 72/456
387 revoked 81/612
388 amended 71/2071
399 revoked 73/1468
400 amended 71/822; 71/1771
401 revoked 71/474
403 revoked 75/1054
407 revoked 69/473
410 revoked 83/74
411 revoked 71/474
413 revoked 74/520; 77/1341
414 amended   74/1674;   76/1657;   78/481;
    82/1103
419 revoked 76/1977
420 revoked 71/2020
425 revoked 72/1313
428 revoked 70/722
433 revoked 72/2051
436 revoked 74/505
438 revoked 74/375
439 revoked 71/371
458 revoked 69/896
459 revoked 69/897
460 revoked 69/1513
463 amended   71/1493;   73/1103;   75/2030;
    76/1494; 76/1496; revoked 86/179
467 amended 70/1986
471 revoked 71/1295
473 revoked 69/571
475 amended 70/682
480 amended 71/530
481 revoked 71/262
482 revoked 71/263
483 amended 69/1093; 70/339; 70/511; 70/1417;
    71/1368;   72/1098;   73/271;   73/1299;
    74/1125;   75/311;   75/1619;   76/402;
    76/1705;   77/385;   77/1193;   77/1684;
    78/959; 78/1301; 79/695; 79/1689
484 revoked 74/351
487 amended 71/1521; 76/363; 79/213; 82/615;
    revoked 87/2245
493 amended 75/1452; 76/621
500 revoked 72/1940
501 revoked 70/377
505 revoked 72/777
506 revoked 76/475
510 revoked 71/1135
511 amended 69/999
513 revoked 75/287
517 revoked 70/691
519 revoked 75/1351
521 revoked 71/438
522 revoked 71/261
525 revoked 74/529
535 amended 74/966
536 amended 74/974
537 revoked 69/571
541 revoked 70/1401
546 revoked 69/1645
547 revoked 70/1410
550 amended 73/355; 75/606; 76/1902
552 amended 73/359; 75/665; 76/1924
553 revoked 72/550
554 revoked 78/1096

1969—*cont.*

562 revoked 70/1032
571 revoked 69/664
572 revoked 69/1751
573 revoked 69/1751
575 revoked 83/22
583 revoked 70/1081
585 amended 71/836; 72/1156; 75/1345
586 revoked 70/523
590 revoked 73/1080
591 revoked 69/736
595 revoked 72/454
610 revoked 71/922
611 revoked 71/923
618 revoked 71/1539
619 revoked 75/1537
625 revoked 74/1761
628 revoked 71/1172
632 revoked 70/1336
636 amended 76/15
637 revoked 72/1204
638 revoked 72/1204
639 revoked 72/317
640 revoked 70/855
641 revoked 70/856
646 revoked 76/1495
647 revoked 76/1494
648 revoked 76/1496
654 revoked 70/978
655 revoked 70/1105
659 revoked 77/1360
664 revoked 69/779
667 revoked 71/937
670 revoked 75/653
672 revoked 71/289
676 revoked 69/779
677 revoked 71/438
679 revoked 72/419
680 revoked 72/316
686 revoked 70/1190
687 revoked 70/1052
688 revoked 73/334
690 revoked 87/2115
691 revoked 69/1726
692 revoked 70/1887
693 amended 71/1025
695 amended 71/940
698 amended 71/942
713 revoked 77/1043
715 revoked 70/1194
716 revoked 70/376
721 revoked 77/1164
722 revoked 83/136
723 revoked 71/232
724 revoked 71/233
728 revoked 74/351
730 amended 71/183
732 revoked 72/990
733 amended 75/1209
734 amended 75/1209
735 amended 71/1738
736 revoked 76/1156
740 revoked 84/1160
748 revoked 80/1304
753 revoked 70/1447
756 revoked 73/79
757 revoked 73/79
758 revoked 71/631
759 revoked 70/1447
760 revoked 72/2061

1969—*cont.*

761 revoked 70/1314
762 revoked 70/1315
763 revoked 71/953
770 revoked 69/1136
776 revoked 71/913
779 revoked 69/878
785 revoked 77/1360
793 revoked 74/520; 77/1341
808 amended 71/1060; 73/36; revoked 85/1333
813 revoked 69/1633
817 revoked 77/285
822 revoked 69/878
833 revoked 83/551
839 revoked 69/1751
840 amended 70/795
841 revoked 78/998
842 amended 69/1865
843 revoked 75/282
844 amended 74/274; revoked 88/1546
848 revoked 75/1054
849 revoked 74/703
851 amended 71/860
854 revoked 77/1235
857 amended 83/1113; revoked 88/1842
860 revoked 79/1655
861 revoked 79/1655
868 revoked 70/1070
869 revoked 73/2076
871 revoked 82/1018
875 revoked 70/567
878 revoked 69/1020
879 revoked 72/772
882 amended 79/1740
884 revoked 82/661
888 amended 74/797; 79/401; revoked 87/16
892 revoked 73/1134
894 revoked 70/1478
895 revoked 73/2037
896 revoked 70/554
897 revoked 70/543
903 revoked 75/739
904 revoked 74/648
905 amended 77/96; 78/198; 79/322; 79/1657; 80/1033; 83/436
906 revoked 74/248
909 revoked 70/656
911 amended 71/156
912 revoked 75/850
915 revoked 73/470
918 revoked 74/522
922 revoked 80/1630
923 revoked 71/62
927 revoked 72/777
929 revoked 71/1697
930 revoked 71/1696
936 revoked 73/22
937 revoked 73/22
939 amended 69/1699; 87/330
940 revoked 74/931
941 revoked 74/932
945 amended 74/787
954 revoked 70/560
955 revoked 87/381
963 revoked 80/804
964 revoked 80/804
970 revoked 76/789
972 revoked 71/1038
973 revoked 71/1037
974 revoked 70/1082

988 revoked 70/1288
989 revoked 71/234
997 amended 70/1124; 71/114; 72/933
1000 revoked 80/361
1001 amended 71/148; 71/1329
1008 revoked 70/1968
1013 amended 72/921
1015 revoked 72/1171
1020 revoked 69/1244
1021 revoked 78/294
1022 revoked 72/506
1023 amended 85/1090
1024 amended 71/1093; 85/1091
1027 revoked 72/507
1028 amended 70/1991; 72/647
1034 revoked 71/274
1035 revoked 76/585
1038 revoked 72/307
1039 revoked 72/205
1042 revoked 73/24
1045 amended 72/956
1046 revoked 74/1992
1047 revoked 70/1237
1048 revoked 70/786
1049 revoked 72/147
1050 revoked 76/241
1054 revoked 74/529
1063 amended 77/2149
1068 amended 73/1326
1070 amended 73/2099
1071 revoked 88/1082
1073 amended 81/1105
1075 amended 78/1030
1076 amended 73/2156
1082 revoked 70/954
1084 revoked 77/1875
1085 revoked 81/612
1086 revoked 75/1208
1090 revoked 70/993
1100 revoked 88/333
1101 revoked 84/1178
1105 amended 71/1269; 74/496
1107 revoked 70/1267
1110 amended 70/242; 71/1538
1115 amended 71/1557
1119 amended 85/474
1126 revoked 69/1167
1127 amended 72/1790
1132 revoked 69/1603
1133 revoked 73/1013
1135 amended 70/1524; 71/707; 71/1421; 72/555; 75/560
1137 amended 70/1246; 74/1962; 75/1777
1141 revoked 71/1377
1143 revoked 83/1718
1149 amended 71/823
1154 revoked 72/1309
1161 amended 74/6
1162 amended 74/1236; 75/213
1167 revoked 69/1244
1168 revoked 75/559
1169 revoked 77/1142
1170 revoked 71/656
1171 revoked 76/1977
1172 revoked 70/1202
1173 revoked 71/1569
1174 revoked 81/1174
1177 revoked 72/1404
1178 revoked 70/16

1179 revoked 78/1600
1184 revoked 73/176
1195 revoked 82/1489
1196 amended 71/1222; revoked 83/136
1201 revoked 80/1106
1210 revoked 82/663
1211 revoked 72/229
1215 revoked 69/1751
1216 revoked 70/256
1219 amended 83/1441
1220 amended 70/549
1240 amended 71/1876
1244 revoked 69/1275
1254 revoked 69/1751
1256 amended 75/1528; 76/237
1261 revoked 70/1281
1264 amended 73/1727
1265 revoked 71/1404
1269 revoked 75/1536
1270 revoked 75/1536
1272 revoked 86/923
1277 amended 71/1420; 74/1129
1290 amended 70/1634; 74/684
1292 revoked 70/1194
1294 revoked 69/1518
1296 amended 74/595
1307 revoked 71/1146
1308 revoked 71/1147
1311 revoked 88/1167
1316 revoked 74/1919
1322 revoked 73/284
1325 revoked 79/1678
1329 revoked 69/1518
1331 revoked 71/450
1333 revoked 72/765
1334 revoked 72/641
1335 revoked 72/764
1339 revoked 77/971
1342 amended 75/1193; 77/1456; 84/599; 86/2002; 88/1358
1344 revoked 70/1210
1345 revoked 70/1211
1346 revoked 71/62
1347 revoked 70/815
1348 revoked 77/1725
1361 amended 71/1220; 72/606
1362 amended 71/1421; 72/555
1365 revoked 81/1543
1368 amended 73/960
1370 revoked 79/114
1372 revoked 76/1778
1375 amended 74/684; 74/719; 82/920; 88/1100
1376 revoked 71/1530
1380 revoked 84/980
1382 revoked 72/1693
1397 revoked 70/16
1398 revoked 72/937
1399 revoked 71/1057
1402 revoked 77/1725
1405 amended 74/684
1407 revoked 75/1330
1413 revoked 70/1522
1414 revoked 70/691
1415 revoked 81/1281
1416 revoked 69/1781
1419 revoked 72/1221
1420 revoked 74/1982
1424 revoked 73/757
1430 amended 71/193

STATUTORY INSTRUMENTS AFFECTED 1947–1988

1432 revoked 83/680
1437 revoked 86/1953
1440 amended 74/496
1441 revoked 70/557
1443 revoked 71/1500
1444 revoked 84/1950
1445 revoked 84/1950
1446 revoked 84/1950
1451 revoked 74/878
1452 revoked 70/1806
1454 revoked 81/1752
1456 revoked 73/24
1457 amended 72/1609
1460 revoked 75/640
1462 revoked 75/1110
1464 amended 72/1761
1470 amended 70/1404
1472 revoked 76/1450
1473 revoked 77/1585
1475 amended 71/494
1476 revoked 70/1240
1479 revoked 70/577
1484 revoked 71/232
1487 amended 77/952
1493 amended 76/225; revoked 84/1817
1494 amended 76/225; revoked 83/1698
1495 revoked 74/1821
1500 revoked 79/916
1508 amended 71/1422
1511 revoked 75/1126
1513 revoked 70/542
1514 revoked 71/233
1517 revoked 71/1469
1518 revoked 69/1550
1519 revoked 69/1751
1529 revoked 71/1880
1532 amended 72/489; 75/898; revoked 84/421
1547 revoked 87/821
1549 amended 71/1441
1550 revoked 69/1677
1563 revoked 77/1341
1564 revoked 71/631
1570 revoked 76/820
1572 revoked 74/1203
1574 revoked 70/1194
1575 amended 71/471
1578 amended 77/2082
1580 amended 73/154; 73/1732
1581 amended 74/282; 74/541
1582 amended 71/1962; 71/2078; 72/1779
1585 revoked 71/2124
1586 revoked 72/777
1589 revoked 71/450
1596 amended 83/1818
1597 revoked 88/110
1603 revoked 70/399
1605 revoked 75/1331
1611 revoked 74/468
1612 revoked 74/468
1614 revoked 70/170
1624 revoked 70/691
1622 revoked 88/1673
1626 revoked 78/1699
1632 amended 76/1073
1633 revoked 71/1060
1634 revoked 72/895
1636 revoked 77/1737
1638 revoked 71/2020
1643 amended 70/456

1644 amended 70/455
1645 revoked 70/1409
1646 revoked 70/376
1649 revoked 84/1232
1653 revoked 73/1007
1654 amended 74/493
1658 revoked 71/274
1661 amended 75/852
1674 amended 70/1026; 76/1188; 80/1837; 81/1532
1675 amended 70/1027; 73/1077; 76/1188; 79/49; 80/1837; 81/1532
1676 amended 74/320; 75/167
1677 amended 69/1889
1684 revoked 75/1703
1686 amended 76/225; 88/591
1689 revoked 87/2024
1696 amended 70/1580; 71/1421; 74/1243
1700 revoked 72/583
1701 revoked 74/931
1704 revoked 78/809
1706 revoked 71/263
1707 amended 71/888
1710 revoked 81/553
1711 revoked 81/552
1712 revoked 86/724
1713 revoked 72/255
1714 revoked 70/1268
1719 revoked 70/1522
1728 revoked 73/1311
1729 revoked 70/1495
1732 revoked 70/1194
1733 revoked 72/1217
1737 revoked 71/2045
1739 revoked 71/207
1740 revoked 73/1017
1743 revoked 74/2211
1745 amended 71/968
1746 amended 72/1672
1749 revoked 75/558
1750 revoked 70/1851
1751 amended 70/934
1753 revoked 88/558
1754 amended 77/2195
1758 revoked 72/764
1761 revoked 73/24
1762 revoked 71/352
1771 revoked 83/133
1774 amended 74/248
1777 revoked 82/129
1780 revoked 72/276
1781 amended 74/1781
1782 revoked 71/1628
1787 amended 71/1498; 73/1252; 75/1739; 77/583; 85/809; 86/1846; 87/1062
1791 revoked 70/1522
1799 revoked 71/149
1800 revoked 71/450
1806 amended 70/1875
1813 amended 70/643
1816 revoked 71/1954
1817 amended 80/1849; 83/1211; 83/1727
1818 amended 76/295
1820 amended 75/1452
1821 revoked 73/176
1822 amended 72/758; 73/127; 73/789
1823 revoked 71/1171
1824 amended 80/1351
1826 revoked 85/1580

STATUTORY INSTRUMENTS AFFECTED 1947–1988

1969—*cont.*

1829 amended 87/2210
1831 revoked 70/482
1835 revoked 70/824
1836 revoked 72/1221
1837 amended 72/774
1841 revoked 73/1256
1845 revoked 72/861
1847 amended 70/1619; 76/442
1848 amended 81/137; 83/270
1849 revoked 71/232
1850 revoked 71/233
1851 revoked 82/449
1852 revoked 74/2003
1853 revoked 74/2003
1858 amended 73/2019; 88/962
1859 revoked 70/1082
1861 amended 71/1987
1864 revoked 72/1955
1871 revoked 72/772
1880 revoked 71/234
1883 revoked 77/1734
1887 amended 70/796
1890 revoked 70/786
1892 amended 81/275
1894 amended 75/911

1970

  2 revoked 80/485
 10 revoked 76/1987
 16 amended 70/191; 70/904; 70/2031; 71/1081;
     72/1941; 73/699; 73/2045; 75/244; 76/29;
     76/201; 76/281; 76/604; 76/797; 76/830;
     76/890;   77/149;   77/348;   77/1189;
     77/1911;   78/397;   78/817;   80/694;
     80/1215; 80/1918; revoked 83/713
 20 revoked 70/214
 25 revoked 70/691
 28 revoked 71/1539
 29 revoked 71/953
 46 amended 70/507; 70/977; 71/1201; 71/1202;
     71/1220;   71/1222;   71/1223;   71/1420;
     71/1497;   72/603;   72/604;   72/606;
     72/1231;   72/1301;   73/1013;   73/1124;
     74/1129; 74/2057; 75/1537
 49 revoked 73/24
 50 revoked 75/1647
 57 revoked 79/1456
 58 revoked 80/2005
 60 revoked 71/845
 66 amended 71/156
 71 revoked 73/79
 73 revoked 77/454
 87 revoked 72/1566
 89 revoked 71/2096
 92 revoked 73/79
 94 amended   74/1122;   75/1486;   80/1849;
     83/1727; 84/649; 85/1560
 95 revoked 71/274
 98 revoked 71/2
 99 amended 71/1601
102 revoked 78/436
106 amended 71/2130; 73/1031; 74/1464
107 amended   71/2131;   72/1572;   73/1300;
     74/652; 75/628
108 amended   74/1337;   75/1597;   76/2232;
     81/137; 83/270; 84/847; 85/1068
109 revoked 72/317
110 revoked 72/264
120 revoked 72/2061

1970—*cont.*

121 revoked 75/1803
123 revoked 76/1447
124 revoked 72/507
128 revoked 75/1722
131 revoked 73/79
138 revoked 74/778
140 revoked 70/1737
141 revoked 70/1737
142 revoked 80/1695
143 revoked 76/585
144 revoked 72/574
145 amended 70/649
147 amended 78/782; 78/1886; 81/209; 82/145;
     86/2011; 87/453
148 amended 87/453
150 amended 76/225; revoked 83/1894
153 amended 73/1327; 85/1997
154 amended 80/1962
156 revoked 70/954
158 revoked 77/1875
159 revoked 77/1876
170 revoked 71/451
171 revoked 70/486
174 revoked 71/108
175 revoked 71/136
176 revoked 71/107
179 revoked 79/1605
189 revoked 73/1911
191 revoked 83/713
197 revoked 74/595
198 revoked 74/476
201 revoked 73/166
202 amended 71/353
204 amended 73/345; 74/1354; 75/285; 76/314
205 amended 74/684
213 revoked 70/745
214 revoked 70/297
217 revoked 72/555
222 revoked 72/1433
226 revoked 71/2128
227 revoked 77/1164
228 amended 71/260
229 amended 71/453
230 revoked 86/1079
231 amended 71/809; 75/300; 76/1767; 78/754
234 revoked 70/548
239 amended 71/324
242 revoked 71/1538
249 amended 82/1370
250 amended 71/145
251 revoked 71/1539
252 revoked 82/657
255 revoked 73/552
256 revoked 70/593
257 revoked 86/1459
260 amended 72/1778
262 revoked 71/220
264 revoked 72/316
270 revoked 71/274
274 revoked 81/1736
283 revoked 71/1136
285 revoked 81/1540
287 amended   73/1890;   75/1704;   78/1880;
     78/1881
293 amended 71/538; 73/628
294 amended 75/341; 76/346; 76/1098; 81/363;
     84/97
296 revoked 71/1088
297 revoked 70/570

683

STATUTORY INSTRUMENTS AFFECTED 1947–1988

298 revoked 74/179
299 revoked 74/181
300 revoked 74/180
301 revoked 77/1316
303 revoked 75/1330
308 revoked 79/837
309 amended 72/421; 74/1372
311 revoked 71/868
312 revoked 73/1160
326 amended 71/562
335 revoked 74/163
339 amended 71/1368
341 revoked 73/292
342 revoked 70/745
348 amended 71/880
349 amended 71/881
350 revoked 75/1319
356 revoked 71/818
358 revoked 74/2211
359 revoked 73/292
360 revoked 71/473
361 revoked 74/351
363 revoked 70/1268
364 revoked 71/1166
365 amended 71/470
370 amended 73/2196
376 amended 70/1879
380 revoked 87/1785
400 amended 72/1510; 74/1119; 74/1121; 75/1485; 76/509; 76/541; 76/859; 76/1832; 77/927; 77/928; 78/646; 78/420; 79/1576; 80/1834; 80/1849; 83/1727; revoked 84/1305
409 revoked 71/450
411 revoked 71/1148
416 revoked 73/1309
417 amended 71/156
419 revoked 74/389
422 revoked 72/419
423 revoked 87/1781
425 revoked 72/777
426 amended 72/1779
428 revoked 71/1023
429 revoked 70/2014
441 revoked 74/2211
446 revoked 71/474
447 revoked 74/1992
448 revoked 71/2124
449 revoked 70/1209
453 revoked 72/507
454 revoked 72/506
462 revoked 70/1522
464 revoked 71/274
466 revoked 75/287
468 revoked 75/1536
470 amended 73/623
472 revoked 70/1238
473 revoked 70/993
475 revoked 71/1398
477 amended 73/2019
479 revoked 70/1082
482 revoked 74/1262
484 amended 75/805
489 revoked 73/317
497 revoked 71/1297
498 revoked 71/1393
499 revoked 71/1394
500 amended 71/538
503 revoked 71/561

504 revoked 71/398
507 amended 71/1420; 74/1129
511 amended 71/1368
515 amended 74/732
521 revoked 70/599
522 revoked 70/570
529 amended 73/164; 73/165
539 amended 76/729
542 revoked 70/721
543 revoked 70/1389
544 revoked 70/1390
545 revoked 79/1007
548 amended 71/13; 71/295; 75/212; 77/1286; 78/1680; 79/841; 79/1490; 80/798; 81/882; 81/1706; revoked 84/1053
557 revoked 76/1333
558 amended 72/838; revoked 83/1710; 84/1828
561 revoked 70/691
562 revoked 71/1443
567 revoked 71/309
569 revoked 70/1194
570 revoked 70/641
573 revoked 71/1058
577 revoked 70/1288
579 revoked 73/118
586 revoked 75/1054
587 revoked 71/232
596 amended 78/1796
597 revoked 76/2022
599 revoked 70/631
600 revoked 75/679
601 amended 71/156
605 revoked 72/1858
606 revoked 72/1859
612 revoked 72/341
615 amended 74/855
617 revoked 71/990
620 revoked 70/1137
623 amended 70/1348
624 revoked 72/1819
625 revoked 72/1770
629 revoked 70/1522
631 revoked 70/764
633 amended 73/588
638 revoked 81/612
639 revoked 72/456
641 revoked 70/898
645 revoked 71/1483
654 revoked 73/983
656 revoked 71/859
666 revoked 73/334
670 revoked 80/506
671 amended 71/354; 75/911
673 amended 74/1354
677 revoked 75/910
678 revoked 82/1218
679 revoked 70/1148
690 revoked 71/62
691 revoked 71/477
697 amended 73/938
702 revoked 71/885
703 revoked 72/819
705 revoked 75/653
706 amended 77/1980
708 amended 72/1218; revoked 85/1150
716 revoked 82/1234
719 revoked 70/1209
720 revoked 84/667
722 revoked 71/150

723 revoked 71/1605
728 amended 72/1349
739 revoked 71/1549
740 revoked 72/276
741 revoked 72/255
743 revoked 71/1666
744 revoked 72/1693
745 revoked 71/2051
748 revoked 72/386
752 amended 75/1486; 80/1849; 83/1727; 85/67
753 revoked 76/1987
758 revoked 71/451
764 revoked 70/879
771 revoked 71/274
772 revoked 70/1522
774 revoked 80/904
775 revoked 70/1085
776 revoked 80/897
777 revoked 73/24
781 amended 73/359; 75/671; 76/1921; 78/76; 80/143; 82/130; 83/80; revoked 84/470
782 amended 71/496
783 revoked 71/830
786 amended 71/307; 76/911; 84/1923
787 revoked 71/62
788 amended 78/76
789 revoked 79/1331
795 revoked 70/898
796 revoked 70/1288
799 amended 73/355; 75/604; 76/1964; 78/38; 80/27; 82/84; 83/5; revoked 84/248
807 revoked 70/1545
809 revoked 71/1381
810 amended 75/1910
816 amended 71/1054
820 revoked 82/711
821 amended 75/802, revoked 88/1082
822 revoked 70/1950
823 revoked 79/930
824 revoked 81/612
825 revoked 71/2118
828 amended 70/1804
830 revoked 80/623
833 amended 71/1304
834 revoked 75/1329
847 amended 73/143
850 revoked 74/179
851 revoked 74/180
852 revoked 74/181
858 revoked 75/299
860 amended 71/1023
862 revoked 76/1987
863 revoked 74/778
865 revoked 73/131
867 revoked 71/1297
877 amended 71/940
878 amended 72/628
879 amended 70/964; 71/941
882 amended 75/1848
883 revoked 71/1022
887 amended 75/1848; 77/72; 80/390; 81/498; 82/653; revoked 84/234
891 revoked 75/1330
897 revoked 75/1385
898 revoked 70/1014
904 amended 71/1081; 76/29; 76/201; 76/850; 76/890; revoked 83/713
905 revoked 71/656
906 revoked 82/61

917 revoked 70/1640
920 revoked 70/1641
924 revoked 70/1340
926 revoked 74/32
933 revoked 70/1522
940 revoked 70/1529
944 amended 71/1269
950 amended 73/1758
952 amended 73/2096
954 amended 70/1442; 70/1951; 71/1733
955 revoked 78/216
961 amended 82/1448
962 revoked 73/275
966 revoked 77/1043
977 amended 71/1420; 71/1422; 72/555; 74/1129
978 revoked 71/750
979 revoked 75/1117
985 amended 72/1926; 74/2129; 80/1819
986 revoked 74/2132
987 revoked 74/2130
988 revoked 70/1855
991 revoked 71/477
995 revoked 71/1148
998 revoked 70/1528
1002 amended 78/1833
1003 amended 75/595
1004 revoked 81/552
1008 revoked 76/391
1013 revoked 71/2001
1014 revoked 70/1239
1021 revoked 87/376
1023 revoked 70/1288
1032 revoked 72/16
1033 revoked 73/342
1035 revoked 73/1742
1038 revoked 71/413
1039 revoked 71/414
1040 revoked 72/1086
1046 revoked 81/142
1047 revoked 74/399
1049 amended 76/2001
1051 amended 74/396
1052 revoked 70/1616
1053 amended 71/1876; 74/684
1055 revoked 70/1209
1056 amended 72/495; 72/1029
1057 revoked 75/73
1059 revoked 75/74
1065 amended 81/137; 83/270; revoked 84/1714
1066 revoked 70/1324
1067 revoked 70/2014
1068 revoked 82/648
1070 revoked 71/1454
1074 revoked 72/1940
1076 amended 74/1235
1078 revoked 71/1038
1079 revoked 71/1037
1080 revoked 70/1288
1081 revoked 72/322
1082 revoked 72/321
1083 revoked 72/320
1085 amended 71/468; 71/1105; 71/1980; 71/2162
1089 revoked 72/507
1090 revoked 81/926
1091 revoked 70/1522
1095 revoked 75/1597
1096 revoked 73/1310

STATUTORY INSTRUMENTS AFFECTED 1947–1988

1097 revoked 71/490
1099 revoked 75/675
1101 revoked 75/1486
1102 revoked 73/1340
1105 revoked 71/991
1106 revoked 71/992
1109 revoked 86/724
1113 revoked 72/1992
1115 revoked 81/439
1116 amended 85/752
1123 revoked 78/1739
1125 revoked 74/520
1126 revoked 86/214
1127 revoked 81/137; 82/1779; 84/1519
1129 revoked 72/1223
1130 revoked 72/1224
1135 revoked 80/1793
1136 revoked 71/308
1137 revoked 71/2052
1142 revoked 73/334
1145 revoked 80/1178
1146 revoked 82/1022
1148 revoked 71/2001
1150 amended 70/1848
1160 revoked 71/987
1161 revoked 71/953
1162 revoked 80/1630
1163 amended 71/916
1166 revoked 70/1288
1169 revoked 75/287; 83/1727
1172 amended 85/67
1177 revoked 75/60
1187 revoked 75/1314
1188 amended 74/1287
1190 revoked 82/448
1191 amended 75/1597; 81/137; 83/270; 85/1068
1201 amended 71/836; 74/1354; 76/314
1202 revoked 71/1679
1208 amended 71/1269; 76/337
1209 revoked 72/333
1210 revoked 71/1591
1211 revoked 75/100
1214 revoked 71/333
1217 amended 75/1773
1220 revoked 71/450
1221 revoked 71/1626
1227 revoked 71/1280
1228 revoked 74/632
1237 revoked 75/967
1238 revoked 70/1610
1239 revoked 70/1332
1240 revoked 71/1698
1245 amended 71/251
1246 revoked 74/1962
1247 revoked 81/275
1253 amended 84/1383
1256 amended 82/1335
1259 revoked 7i/274
1265 amended 72/1387
1266 revoked 71/1297
1267 amended 71/1654
1268 revoked 72/581
1270 revoked 80/1147
1271 revoked 74/2211
1277 amended 71/532; 72/1645; 76/387
1281 revoked 71/1415
1284 revoked 79/383
1285 amended 81/137; 83/270; 85/1068
1286 amended 81/137; 83/270; 85/1068

1287 revoked 87/1758
1298 amended 73/1390
1301 revoked 71/1058
1307 amended 74/812
1314 revoked 71/2129
1315 revoked 73/954
1322 amended 71/1876
1323 amended 72/1574
1324 revoked 70/1350
1329 revoked 73/1468
1332 revoked 70/1496
1335 revoked 72/317
1337 revoked 82/677
1340 revoked 74/505
1341 revoked 83/6
1348 revoked 70/1489
1349 revoked 71/953
1350 revoked 70/1425
1351 revoked 71/352
1352 revoked 81/1436
1356 amended 76/335; revoked 86/401
1357 revoked 72/1693
1366 revoked 71/649
1368 revoked 75/1446
1369 revoked 75/1447
1370 amended 71/40; 72/1551; 74/1326; 76/1981; 80/1070; revoked 86/1683
1372 revoked 72/1413
1374 amended 71/825
1384 revoked 70/1641
1388 revoked 70/1522
1389 revoked 71/65
1390 revoked 71/64
1392 revoked 72/863
1393 amended 75/1939
1400 amended 78/468
1402 amended 71/804
1407 revoked 73/1468
1409 revoked 71/1369
1410 revoked 73/44
1413 amended 75/1452
1417 amended 71/1368
1425 revoked 70/1596
1431 revoked 74/1501
1432 revoked 75/1704
1435 amended 75/1505; 75/1507; 75/1510; 75/1513
1437 revoked 86/1299
1440 revoked 83/1126
1441 amended 72/1103
1444 revoked 71/1968
1445 amended 71/944; 72/629
1446 amended 71/943
1447 revoked 72/757
1448 revoked 72/321
1449 revoked 72/322
1452 amended 72/1483
1454 revoked 72/1652
1455 revoked 72/386
1459 amended 71/1072; 73/644
1460 revoked 77/1725
1463 revoked 72/777
1464 revoked 74/1738
1478 revoked 74/674
1479 revoked 74/675
1480 revoked 71/1651
1488 amended 73/1992
1490 revoked 79/1227
1493 revoked 82/1234

1495 revoked 72/869
1498 amended 70/1883
1514 revoked 74/529
1519 revoked 71/451
1522 revoked 71/1813; amended 71/1891
1528 revoked 71/1919
1529 revoked 71/1918
1536 amended 78/274
1537 amended 71/2119
1538 revoked 78/1881
1551 revoked 75/559
1558 revoked 71/2001
1559 revoked 71/477
1561 revoked 72/247
1563 revoked 72/1693
1570 revoked 71/232
1571 revoked 71/233
1580 amended 71/1419; 72/604; 72/606; 73/693
1583 revoked 71/234
1584 revoked 74/1659
1587 amended 71/617
1596 revoked 70/1669
1599 revoked 72/9
1615 revoked 72/1750
1616 revoked 72/1751
1621 amended 71/363; 86/1532
1633 revoked 80/850
1634 amended 74/684
1640 revoked 71/1518
1641 revoked 71/2001
1645 revoked 73/176
1646 amended 74/520
1648 amended 71/1187
1650 amended 71/1189
1659 amended 71/156
1674 amended   71/2106;   71/2108–2114;
    73/604–608
1681 amended 73/67; 74/692; 76/1775
1683 revoked 71/211
1686 revoked 71/1297
1700 amended 72/842
1704 revoked 72/555
1706 amended 75/631
1707 amended 73/1782
1709 amended 80/1742
1710 amended   80/1070;   80/1742;   83/1653;
    83/1654;   revoked   86/1684;   amended
    87/51
1711 amended 86/1682
1712 revoked 78/1962
1713 revoked 75/1381
1714 amended   79/1719;   80/1070;   80/1742;
    83/1653;   83/1654;   revoked   86/1684;
    amended 87/51
1716 amended 73/1802
1724 revoked 71/1836
1731 revoked 72/419
1732 revoked 72/316
1737 amended 73/1443; 76/587; 80/1695
1738 amended 75/1567
1742 amended 72/291; 73/124; 75/388; 75/1454
1743 revoked 82/659
1746 amended 73/984
1747 revoked 70/1884
1759 amended 71/1077; 72/368; 73/492; 73/1965;
    76/547
1762 revoked 82/448
1775 amended 76/48
1780 revoked 86/1442

1783 amended 75/1399
1784 revoked 77/1141
1790 amended 71/986; 71/1908; 83/1216
1791 revoked 81/552 (L.1)
1792 amended 76/1769; 78/869; 83/526; 84/567;
    revoked 88/913
1798 amended 71/353
1800 amended 71/946
1801 amended 71/945
1805 amended 71/1076; 72/362; 73/476; 73/1395;
    76/547
1806 revoked 78/229
1807 revoked 82/449
1814 revoked 75/670
1815 amended 80/809
1818 revoked 71/274
1824 revoked 76/652
1826 revoked 74/1735
1827 amended 75/1522; revoked 85/1333
1832 revoked 75/788
1833 revoked 75/991
1839 revoked 77/288
1840 revoked 71/102
1844 amended 73/262
1846 revoked 71/2001
1848 revoked 71/1922
1849 revoked 72/903; 72/996
1850 revoked 75/299
1853 amended 71/1031; 81/1681
1858 revoked 82/1021
1861 amended 71/1269
1863 amended 71/860
1865 revoked 71/987
1866 revoked 71/1900
1869 revoked 75/1344
1870 revoked 75/1343
1871 amended 71/836; 75/1345; 76/314
1876 amended 71/2032; 72/2033; 73/2180
1879 amended 71/1263
1880 revoked 79/1434
1881 revoked 79/1435
1882 revoked 73/485
1884 revoked 70/1993
1886 amended 74/684; 75/985
1887 revoked 71/643
1889 amended 71/341
1897 amended 76/1664
1919 revoked 78/275
1933 revoked 78/1028
1940 amended 75/1209; 80/1076; 84/127
1945 revoked 86/1951
1946 revoked 79/1316
1948 amended 80/1530
1950 revoked 72/1104
1951 amended 71/1733
1953 amended 74/2145
1958 amended 86/1328
1959 revoked 71/222
1967 amended 74/1462
1968 revoked 72/1078
1972 revoked 75/1536
1974 amended 73/938
1977 amended 73/2206
1979 revoked 76/1987
1981 amended   71/621;   71/1018;   71/1419;
    71/1478;   71/633;   72/394;   73/1478;
    74/1128
1982 revoked 71/477
1987 revoked 75/1385

STATUTORY INSTRUMENTS AFFECTED 1947–1988

1970—*cont.*

1988 amended 73/319
1990 amended 73/1390
1994 revoked 78/30
1995 revoked 72/322
1996 revoked 80/1195
2007 revoked 75/1350
2008 revoked 75/1351
2014 revoked 72/574
2020 revoked 78/796
2021 revoked 72/1139
2022 revoked 72/1189
2023 amended 71/1025
2024 amended 71/1026
2031 amended 71/1081; 76/29; 76/850; 76/890; revoked 83/713
2032 revoked 71/1954
2033 amended 83/629
2038 revoked 79/1333

1971

1 revoked 78/1388
7 revoked 71/37
11 revoked 76/1544
13 amended 71/295; revoked 84/1053
21 revoked 73/334
29 revoked 71/991
30 revoked 71/992
37 revoked 71/166
40 amended 76/1981; revoked 86/1683
52 revoked 74/1748
62 revoked 80/1894
63 revoked 80/1630
65 revoked 71/675
67 revoked 75/1849
76 revoked 71/993
77 revoked 71/457
80 amended 81/499
87 revoked 72/207
90 amended 73/461; 75/1148; 76/1119; 78/948; 78/1167; 79/1633; 80/1678; 81/1408; 82/466; 83/970; 84/471; 84/1135; 85/544; revoked 86/978
92 amended 72/1621; 80/1443; 85/781. 1976
100 revoked 75/1208
101 revoked 71/1649
102 revoked 72/194
103 revoked 80/1630
107 revoked 74/831
108 revoked 75/1090
113 revoked 78/796
115 revoked 71/1813
124 amended 74/1187; 83/798; revoked 87/864
129 amended 71/1217; 74/572; 84/461; revoked 86/1445
131 amended 74/1017; 78/370
132 amended 74/1008; 78/369
133 revoked 77/580
134 revoked 77/581
136 revoked 72/1001
145 amended 71/1329; 71/1468; 72/522; 73/318; 73/1814; 74/1797; 75/1717; 76/1708; 77/1704; 78/1577; 79/1286; 80/1615
149 revoked 74/2060
150 revoked 72/1430
154 revoked 71/2001
156 amended 71/659; 71/1141; 71/1901; 72/74; 72/339; 72/1195; 73/33; 73/356; 73/734; 73/1368; 73/1583; 74/649; 74/1365; 74/1973; 75/211; 75/915; 75/1324;

1971—*cont.*

76/538; 76/1274; 77/582; 77/1006; 77/1988; 78/1169; 79/694; 79/1216; 79/1470
157 revoked 79/991
165 revoked 76/1977
166 revoked 71/192; amended 71/201
169 amended 71/1368; 75/311
174 amended 76/373; revoked 87/492
175 revoked 78/1544
185 amended 76/621
192 revoked 71/327
194 revoked 87/381
196 revoked 72/777
197 amended 72/1673
207 revoked 72/854
211 revoked 76/215
212 revoked 81/233
213 amended 76/899
214 revoked 71/393
216 revoked 77/1875
217 revoked 77/1876
218 amended 77/432; 81/632; 83/1428; 85/581; 87/1139
219 amended 71/1796; 73/1774; 76/373; revoked 87/492
220 amended 73/1129; 73/1686; 74/666; 74/1484; 75/747; 75/1434; 75/1936; revoked 77/445
222 revoked 72/241
226 revoked 80/1437
227 revoked 80/1438
231 amended 86/442; 88/233
232 amended 71/583; 71/1327; 71/1328; 71/1380; 71/1466; 73/428; 73/1773; 74/1533; 74/1534; 74/1535; 74/1629; 74/1796; 76/1707; 77/1705; 77/1947; 78/1578; 79/1287; 79/1406; 80/1616; 81/1322; 83/1378; 87/256
233 amended 71/584; 71/1328; 71/1467; 73/431; 74/1535; 77/1948
234 amended 71/585; 71/1402; 71/1501; 72/1847; 73/433; 74/1630
239 amended 73/430; 74/1534
246 amended 73/434; 74/1629
249 amended 72/466; 74/169; 75/369; 76/270; 77/656; 79/320; 81/285; 82/331; 83/430; 84/1713; 85/1514
253 amended 76/1016; 79/748; 83/1149; 88/2177
254 revoked 74/1869
259 revoked 75/1803
260 revoked 87/821
261 amended 74/1314
262 revoked 74/86
263 amended 74/87
271 revoked 72/322
272 revoked 71/1813
273 amended 71/499
274 revoked 73/1029
275 amended 75/1372; revoked 80/1793
283 revoked 84/108
287 amended 71/1795; revoked 87/427
288 amended 71/554; revoked 87/384
289 amended 73/501
290 amended 73/502
291 revoked 75/287
295 amended 75/212; revoked 84/1053
300 revoked 74/32
303 revoked 71/459

STATUTORY INSTRUMENTS AFFECTED 1947–1988

304 amended 71/1405; 72/190; 72/1687; 73/1733; 74/242; 75/1906
306 revoked 76/986
308 revoked 72/168
311 amended 71/1036; 72/1375; 73/2173; revoked 86/498
317 revoked 87/381
327 revoked 71/603
329 revoked 79/837
333 amended 74/601; 75/1216
340 revoked 78/950
342 revoked 82/129
343 amended 74/604
349 amended 77/799
350 revoked 75/978
351 revoked 77/1043
352 revoked 82/1478
354 amended 71/1269
362 revoked 74/32
364 revoked 71/518
374 amended 87/2107
375 amended 76/778
383 amended 71/447
392 revoked 80/1216
394 revoked 72/1940
398 revoked 78/692
403 revoked 76/1987
404 amended 74/534
406 revoked 80/69
409 revoked 83/1718
413 revoked 76/117
414 amended 71/1976; 72/1400; 73/1175; 73/1746; 74/746; 74/1569; 74/1954; 75/592; 76/116
415 amended 77/846; 80/1382; 83/1157; 84/1949
420 revoked 74/522
421 amended 83/1646
437 revoked 71/1539
444 revoked 73/24
446 revoked 88/110
447 revoked 73/278
448 revoked 74/1306
450 amended 71/1285; 71/1628; 73/870; 75/1089; 75/1342; 76/1680; 76/230; 78/1536; 81/366; 83/1248; 83/1802; 84/814; 86/607; 86/1177; 86/2101; 87/2085; 87/2123
451 revoked 76/1076
454 revoked 83/713
457 revoked 75/1686
460 amended 71/1070
461 revoked 75/205
462 revoked 74/1301
463 revoked 74/1299
468 amended 71/1105
469 amended 72/263; 73/667; 74/613
472 revoked 74/506
473 revoked 73/292
475 revoked 72/492
477 amended 71/1028; 71/1370; 71/1566; 71/2034
479 revoked 72/333
480 revoked 84/647
490 revoked 75/674
492 amended 83/1424; 84/100; 84/1867; 85/843, 1724; 86/518
495 revoked 86/399
497 amended 74/622

498 amended 76/241
500 amended 73/533; 73/717
501 revoked 73/1309
502 revoked 81/404
503 revoked 72/1955
510 revoked 77/1097
511 revoked 80/623
516 revoked 75/609
519 revoked 71/1048
532 amended 72/1645; 76/387
533 revoked 77/1284
545 revoked 73/79
546 revoked 73/79
547 revoked 74/595
548 revoked 73/166
549 revoked 72/641
550 revoked 72/765
551 revoked 76/789
554 revoked 87/384
558 revoked 76/475
560 amended 72/1910; 77/2083; revoked 83/547
561 amended 73/654
564 amended 82/102
571 revoked 78/207
583 amended 71/1328; 71/1466; 73/428; 74/1535
584 amended 71/1328; 73/431
585 amended 73/433
591 revoked 75/2232
592 amended 77/804; 78/670
595 revoked 82/1085
596 revoked 75/2192
601 revoked 73/748
602 revoked 73/747
603 revoked 71/684
618 amended 79/429; 81/1059; 84/1244; revoked 86/1951
621 amended 71/707; 71/1419; 71/1854; 72/604; 72/1232; 74/416
622 revoked 80/1605
627 revoked 73/112; 73/210
631 revoked 73/292
632 revoked 73/292
633 amended 72/1735
643 revoked 75/341
644 revoked 75/341
648 amended 74/684
649 revoked 71/1531
656 amended 71/1983; 76/852; 77/151; 77/350; 81/1624; revoked 83/713
659 revoked 79/1470
661 amended 83/687
673 revoked 71/1544
674 revoked 71/1551
675 revoked 71/1545
679 revoked 76/1987
680 revoked 80/1605
683 revoked 72/777
686 amended 72/431
691 revoked 77/1113
694 amended 73/1006; 75/239; 75/1736; 77/1560; 78/1261; 79/803; 80/116; 80/1855; 81/1042; revoked 84/812
701 amended 71/1821; 75/1569
707 amended 71/1219; 71/1419; 74/1243
708 amended 71/1823
714 revoked 78/1027
719 amended 74/692
720 revoked 79/305

STATUTORY INSTRUMENTS AFFECTED 1947–1988

721 revoked 80/184
724 revoked 72/531
725 amended 72/1938
726 revoked 72/1939
728 revoked 73/1007
736 revoked 75/739
741 revoked 73/1405
746 revoked 75/550
747 revoked 75/548
748 revoked 71/2052
750 revoked 72/782
752 revoked 72/1693
753 revoked 74/2044
756 amended 82/975
767 revoked 75/663
769 revoked 80/1120
770 amended 72/1181; 74/2061
778 amended 82/973
781 amended 75/1345
792 amended 77/895
797 amended 73/116; 75/360; revoked 87/1135
801 revoked 73/352
802 revoked 73/292
803 revoked 73/292
808 amended 73/981; 75/694
810 amended 75/1452
814 amended 76/276
817 revoked 71/912
818 amended 86/1459
819 revoked 74/1169
822 amended 71/1771
827 revoked 78/1962
830 revoked 72/680
835 amended 71/1269
836 amended 72/1156; 75/1345
844 amended 74/614
845 revoked 72/35
846 amended 72/2050
847 revoked 76/1447
848 revoked 81/1259
851 revoked 71/1813
854 revoked 73/292
855 revoked 72/254
856 revoked 73/292
857 revoked 73/292
858 revoked 71/1813
868 revoked 72/718
869 revoked 75/1208
870 amended 75/407
871 amended 75/414
884 revoked 71/1297
885 revoked 71/818
887 revoked 76/748
904 amended 71/1810; 72/1673
905 revoked 71/2094
906 revoked 73/693
907 revoked 74/778
911 revoked 72/1770
912 revoked 71/952
913 revoked 72/815
922 revoked 73/1514
923 amended 74/1620
926 amended 73/1145; 75/836; 76/339; 76/1062;
     revoked 87/430
928 revoked 76/241
934 amended 74/796
937 revoked 85/610
947 revoked 73/292
952 revoked 71/985

953 amended 71/1923; 72/1095; 73/1413
968 amended 72/878; revoked 87/613
969 revoked 79/72
972 amended 72/1226; 74/1523; 77/675;
     77/1039; 77/1053; 83/1730
973 amended 72/1201; 75/681; 77/1051;
     79/1760; 83/1726
974 amended 77/1052; 78/1140; 83/1725
975 amended 74/1877; revoked 81/1375
979 revoked 73/24
980 amended 72/1609
981 revoked 74/2003
984 revoked 73/1468
985 revoked 71/1027
986 amended 71/1908; 74/1464
987 revoked 77/345
988 revoked 74/1340
991 revoked 72/943
992 revoked 72/944
997 revoked 82/648
998 amended 74/999
1003 revoked 75/341
1017 revoked 75/1350
1019 revoked 75/559
1020 revoked 75/1351
1022 revoked 73/155
1023 revoked 72/165
1027 revoked 71/1157
1028 amended 71/1370; 71/2034
1029 amended 74/1844
1032 revoked 71/2052
1033 revoked 73/294
1036 revoked 86/498
1037 revoked 77/2055
1038 revoked 77/2054
1040 revoked 86/1951
1048 revoked 71/2001
1054 amended 72/1145
1056 revoked 71/1813
1057 amended 73/411
1058 amended 72/2018
1060 revoked 79/1553
1061 amended 79/427; 81/1059; 84/1244;
     revoked 86/1951
1062 amended 79/427; 81/1059; 84/1244;
     revoked 86/1951
1065 amended 80/1699; 81/1783; 87/2178;
     88/2200
1067 revoked 75/1025
1069 revoked 71/1264
1072 amended 73/644
1075 amended 71/1348; 71/1635
1076 amended 76/547
1077 amended 76/547
1079 amended 75/1135; 77/475
1081 amended 76/850; revoked 83/713
1082 revoked 76/1333
1083 revoked 71/1649
1087 revoked 82/1163
1088 revoked 72/1087
1090 revoked 80/319
1094 revoked 78/294
1101 revoked 80/1665
1102 revoked 72/506
1103 amended 72/868; 74/701; 74/1807
1109 revoked 72/1154
1111 amended 73/1727
1113 amended 73/1732
1114 amended 73/1731

STATUTORY INSTRUMENTS AFFECTED 1947–1988

1971—*cont.*

1117 amended 74/208; 75/194; 75/1443
1124 revoked 73/292
1130 amended 74/1837
1135 revoked 75/1184
1137 revoked 73/470
1141 revoked 79/1470
1142 revoked 77/1496
1148 amended 80/1421; 83/1646
1150 revoked 85/1471
1152 amended 71/1984; 75/2119; 76/851; 77/150;
    77/349; revoked 83/713
1156 amended   71/1932;   71/1940;   71/1941;
    71/1958; 71/1959; 71/1960
1157 revoked 71/1271
1158 amended 77/1671; 84/266
1160 revoked 75/2091
1164 revoked 71/1655
1166 revoked 72/1745
1170 revoked 73/807
1171 revoked 76/1324
1172 amended 74/192
1173 amended 72/1174
1178 revoked 76/585
1179 amended 75/654
1183 revoked 73/1007
1186 revoked 73/1029
1194 amended 71/1876
1196 revoked 76/874
1197 revoked 86/1537
1201 amended 72/1231; 75/559; 75/560
1202 revoked 73/1013
1203 revoked 72/777
1206 revoked 75/1885
1210 amended 76/177
1212 revoked 78/1178
1217 revoked 86/1445
1218 revoked 86/1442
1220 amended 72/603; 72/606; 74/1128
1222 amended 75/514; 75/1139; revoked 83/136
1223 revoked 82/1489
1234 amended 74/1775; 82/1148
1235 revoked 76/50
1237 amended 74/109; 74/1709; 76/51; 77/1627;
    84/1977; revoked 85/1983
1245 revoked 75/1343
1257 amended 72/847
1259 revoked 74/831
1260 revoked 75/1090
1264 revoked 71/1429
1269 amended 72/813; 72/1194; 73/2046; 75/911;
    76/337; 76/1196
1271 revoked 71/1319
1279 amended 72/1387
1280 revoked 73/175
1281 revoked 82/448
1284 revoked 71/1628
1285 revoked 72/1865
1287 revoked 72/242
1292 revoked 82/1109
1297 revoked 75/1207
1299 revoked 81/1259
1300 revoked 81/1260
1303 revoked 77/339
1319 revoked 71/1401
1326 amended 77/640
1327 amended 71/1328; 71/1466
1328 amended 71/1467; 73/431; 74/1535
1329 amended 74/1797; 75/1717
1330 amended 73/432; 73/965

1971—*cont.*

1331 revoked 77/1142
1333 revoked 84/1917
1348 amended 71/1635
1352 revoked 75/341
1353 revoked 75/341
1356 revoked 87/1781
1357 revoked 71/1897
1368 amended 72/1098; 75/311; 75/1619
1369 revoked 73/43
1380 revoked 74/778
1381 revoked 75/1910
1387 revoked 71/1813
1393 revoked 72/1820
1394 revoked 74/2022
1401 revoked 71/1475
1402 amended 73/433; 74/1630
1404 revoked 72/1240
1405 amended 72/1687
1406 revoked 72/386
1407 revoked 72/1608
1410 amended 73/2079
1415 revoked 72/928
1418 amended 77/892
1419 amended 71/1478; 71/1633; 72/603; 72/604;
    72/606; 73/693; 74/1243; 75/558
1420 amended 74/1129
1421 amended 72/555
1426 revoked 72/255
1427 revoked 71/1539
1429 revoked 71/1465
1430 revoked 74/1992
1437 amended 72/1779
1441 revoked 72/1954
1443 amended 71/1942
1449 revoked 75/366
1450 amended 78/1139; 79/1585
1454 revoked 72/1312
1465 revoked 71/1607
1466 amended 73/428; 74/1535
1467 amended 73/431; 74/1535
1469 amended   72/1310;   73/1481;   74/1055;
    75/484;   77/1949;   79/1407;   81/1321;
    83/1379
1475 revoked 71/1506
1478 revoked 72/1301
1482 revoked 72/1819
1483 revoked 72/1959
1492 revoked 75/266
1493 amended   73/1103;   75/267;   76/1562;
    revoked 86/178
1498 amended 75/1739
1500 revoked 72/1347
1501 amended 73/433; 74/1630
1505 revoked 72/333
1506 revoked 71/1541
1518 revoked 72/1116
1520 revoked 76/1645
1521 amended 75/881; 75/1586
1524 amended 74/797; 76/363; 76/1494; 76/1495;
    76/1496
1527 revoked 74/149
1530 revoked 80/1273
1531 revoked 72/1279
1536 revoked 73/807
1537 amended 72/1220; 73/423; 73/1258; 74/708;
    74/1134;   75/296;   75/1629;   76/1702;
    77/362;   77/1203;   77/1654;   78/504;
    78/969; 78/1278; 79/824; 79/1682
1538 amended 71/2029; 74/595

STATUTORY INSTRUMENTS AFFECTED 1947–1988

1539 revoked 72/1082
1541 revoked 71/1584
1542 revoked 75/536
1544 revoked 71/1993
1545 revoked 71/1994
1549 revoked 77/1141
1551 revoked 72/373
1553 revoked 72/2051
1554 revoked 73/292
1555 revoked 73/292
1556 revoked 72/386
1557 amended 75/629
1569 amended 74/42
1570 amended 75/1939
1577 amended 75/1303
1584 revoked 71/1621
1585 revoked 81/404
1591 revoked 72/1606
1593 revoked 80/14
1600 revoked 72/317
1602 revoked 73/79
1603 revoked 73/79
1604 revoked 72/1430
1605 revoked 72/1431
1607 revoked 71/1629
1615 revoked 75/910
1621 revoked 71/1650
1623 revoked 80/1809
1628 revoked 72/850
1629 revoked 71/1647
1631 revoked 72/35
1632 revoked 79/1331
1633 amended 72/604
1634 revoked 78/324
1635 revoked 71/2001
1642 revoked 73/292
1647 revoked 71/1697
1649 revoked 75/1328
1650 revoked 71/1689
1651 revoked 73/220
1652 revoked 81/1218
1661 revoked 77/1474
1666 revoked 73/147
1668 revoked 71/1695
1679 amended 74/41
1685 revoked 79/1188
1686 revoked 78/1303
1687 revoked 81/651
1689 revoked 71/1720
1690 revoked 72/1654
1695 revoked 71/1713
1696 revoked 73/146
1697 amended 73/146; 74/686
1698 revoked 73/122
1708 revoked 72/1437
1713 revoked 71/1774
1715 revoked 73/1678
1716 revoked 77/1284
1717 revoked 77/1284
1718 revoked 83/156
1720 revoked 71/1778
1728 revoked 72/555
1729 revoked 72/1433
1730 revoked 75/1184
1731 revoked 74/1821
1735 revoked 81/612
1736 revoked 80/1093
1737 revoked 72/1098
1739 amended 73/1757; 73/1893

1742 amended 88/591
1743 revoked 86/1882
1747 amended 73/236
1750 revoked 72/322
1751 revoked 72/321
1752 revoked 78/1875
1766 revoked 73/160
1769 amended 71/1964
1774 revoked 71/1937
1775 revoked 77/1360
1778 revoked 71/1895
1788 revoked 72/1678
1795 revoked 87/427
1796 amended 73/1774; 76/373; revoked 87/492
1811 revoked 71/2052
1813 amended 71/1891
1814 revoked 76/1977
1821 amended 75/1569
1823 revoked 72/1937
1835 revoked 72/1939
1836 revoked 73/156
1839 revoked 72/242
1842 revoked 73/845
1848 revoked 86/1299
1849 amended 81/1676
1854 amended 72/1232
1856 revoked 80/1120
1861 amended 75/896; 78/1266; 79/1226; 80/887;
     82/1244; 83/1346; 85/1416; 86/1357;
     87/1199; 88/1198
1870 revoked 72/765
1871 revoked 77/1724
1874 revoked 84/522
1877 revoked 80/1894
1879 revoked 78/425
1880 revoked 76/1766
1882 amended 71/2021; 72/1620; 72/1791; 73/16;
     73/892; 73/1166
1883 amended 72/1658; 74/977
1891 revoked 73/1845
1894 revoked 75/1189
1895 revoked 71/1938
1896 revoked 73/334
1897 revoked 71/2001
1900 amended 71/1956
1901 revoked 79/1470
1908 amended 73/1837
1912 revoked 87/381
1914 revoked 87/381
1916 revoked 74/351
1917 revoked 78/216
1918 revoked 73/218
1919 revoked 73/183
1920 revoked 75/1686
1921 amended 73/2227
1922 revoked 73/190
1923 amended 72/1095; 73/777; 73/1973
1930 revoked 86/129
1933 amended 74/208; 81/1489
1936 revoked 73/906
1937 revoked 71/1986
1938 revoked 72/21
1947 revoked 73/334
1953 amended 73/1973
1954 revoked 78/1759
1955 amended 72/1194; 75/911; 76/1196
1956 revoked 75/205
1963 revoked 72/1937
1964 amended 71/2082

1971—*cont.*

1965 amended 71/2083
1968 revoked 84/1885
1970 revoked 74/1992
1971 revoked 73/1845
1972 revoked 72/321
1974 revoked 73/1845
1975 revoked 73/1174
1976 revoked 73/1175
1977 revoked 87/2024
1979 revoked 76/1076
1983 amended 76/852; revoked 83/713
1984 amended 76/851; revoked 83/713
1985 revoked 83/713
1986 revoked 71/2154
1990 revoked 75/674
1993 revoked 72/949
1994 revoked 72/950
1995 revoked 77/1360
2001 revoked 73/2037
2002 revoked 72/386
2008 amended 73/2009
2009 revoked 73/1029
2010 revoked 72/1829
2012 amended 72/1984
2013 revoked 72/1693
2019 amended 74/713; 76/503
2020 revoked 87/1149
2021 revoked 73/1845
2023 revoked 75/663
2024 revoked 74/1992
2025 revoked 74/1992
2026 amended 74/908
2029 revoked 74/595
2035 revoked 74/1094
2041 revoked 72/1909
2042 revoked 72/1829
2043 revoked 73/1845
2044 revoked 79/1618
2045 revoked 74/2211
2046 revoked 72/1976
2048 revoked 73/733
2051 revoked 75/547
2052 amended 73/794; 75/404; 79/310; revoked 81/1596
2055 revoked 74/351
2061 revoked 74/351
2062 revoked 74/351
2063 revoked 74/351
2064 revoked 74/351
2065 revoked 74/351
2066 amended 74/351
2067 revoked 74/351
2068 revoked 74/351
2070 amended 75/2222; revoked 87/2224
2071 revoked 75/2223
2074 revoked 82/1478
2075 revoked 74/351
2077 revoked 74/351
2082 amended 71/2083
2084 amended 83/284; 88/1738
2085 revoked 77/789
2089 revoked 82/1506
2095 revoked 75/1536
2096 revoked 73/1047
2100 revoked 72/1098
2101 revoked 72/1992
2102 amended 72/1102; 74/1107; 75/803; 76/769; 77/1237; 78/1887; 81/210; 81/731;

1971—*cont.*

82/146; 85/1989; 86/2012; 87/451; 87/2041
2103 amended 72/960; 73/762; 77/1239; 78/1889; 81/213; 81/734; 81/149; 85/1993; 86/2016; 87/456
2104 amended 72/219
2118 revoked 77/1258
2122 revoked 74/351
2123 revoked 74/351
2124 amended 72/1783; 73/1714; 74/1968; 75/519; 75/1764; 75/2198; 78/977; 79/94; 80/389
2125 amended 78/1791
2127 amended 75/285; 75/2040; 76/314
2128 revoked 73/1450
2129 revoked 73/953
2130 amended 74/1464
2131 amended 72/1572; 75/628
2133 revoked 84/2133
2142 revoked 74/351
2143 revoked 74/351
2144 revoked 78/207
2146 revoked 73/1238
2147 revoked 74/778
2152 amended 75/1345
2154 revoked 72/15
2155 revoked 74/351
2156 revoked 74/351
2157 revoked 74/351
2158 revoked 74/351
2159 revoked 74/351
2160 revoked 74/351
2161 revoked 79/72
2163 revoked 74/351
2164 revoked 74/351
2165 revoked 74/351

1972

3 revoked 73/807
4 revoked 73/807
8 revoked 72/1955
9 amended 73/521
14 revoked 70/1437
15 revoked 72/57
16 revoked 73/342
21 revoked 72/58
23 revoked 80/1809
24 amended 75/1056
25 revoked 72/58
35 revoked 72/1297
38 revoked 74/1386
39 revoked 74/1387
42 amended 74/563; 74/1574; 74/1972; 75/854; 75/1298
49 revoked 74/831
51 amended 74/2045
52 revoked 72/1829
57 revoked 72/83
60 revoked 74/2
66 amended 72/356
67 amended 72/357
69 revoked 73/820
70 revoked 76/1935
71 amended 73/495; 74/984; 74/2029; 78/1808
74 revoked 79/1470
81 amended 73/143
82 revoked 73/1468
83 revoked 72/94
84 revoked 78/294

STATUTORY INSTRUMENTS AFFECTED 1947–1988

1972—*cont.*

87 revoked 79/594
89 amended 73/106
91 revoked 79/792
92 amended 72/1735
94 revoked 72/149
95 amended 74/1045
96 revoked 74/505
107 revoked 77/1164
108 revoked 73/1678
113 amended 75/1209
120 amended 75/1209
129 revoked 74/1114
132 revoked 73/42
135 amended 73/177; 74/905
136 revoked 72/777
146 revoked 72/386
149 revoked 72/170
150 revoked 76/1396
153 revoked 73/39
160 amended 72/273
161 revoked 77/1284
165 amended 72/1856; revoked 73/61
166 amended 72/1301; 74/1128; 74/1243
168 revoked 73/311
169 revoked 72/306
171 amended 86/442; 88/233
172 revoked 72/557; amended 86/442; 88/233
173 amended 86/442; 88/233
177 revoked 81/961
178 amended 73/1929; 74/1389; 75/532; 76/1026; 79/514; 81/61; revoked 83/550
188 revoked 75/1184
190 amended 72/1687; 73/1733; 75/1906
193 revoked 72/277
194 revoked 75/1346
195 revoked 82/1478
196 revoked 77/612
207 revoked 72/1532
210 revoked 77/134
211 revoked 74/1053
215 revoked 72/230
223 amended 74/1802; 75/1049; 79/5; 81/314
225 revoked 72/305
226 revoked 72/1829
227 revoked 88/110
228 amended 75/500; 81/1347; 88/2189
230 revoked 72/299
235 revoked 73/1013
237 revoked 76/2008
239 revoked 72/306
240 revoked 72/305
241 revoked 73/558
242 revoked 72/1413
245 revoked 72/305
254 revoked 73/292
263 amended 73/667; 74/613
264 revoked 73/264
265 revoked 72/305
266 revoked 72/938
273 revoked 72/306
274 revoked 73/1856
275 amended 76/817
276 revoked 72/771
277 revoked 72/399
287 revoked 80/14
288 revoked 76/748
291 revoked 73/124
299 revoked 72/347
301 revoked 81/1106

1972—*cont.*

303 revoked 82/648
308 amended 73/672; 84/232; revoked 88/110
314 revoked 73/807
316 amended 73/761; 77/92; 81/1220; 83/719; 84/1670; 86/2126
317 amended 73/1276; 74/1944; 75/1370
320 revoked 74/1402
321 revoked 74/1401
322 revoked 74/1403
328 revoked 74/1992
330 revoked 77/1141
333 revoked 74/476
334 revoked 87/821
335 amended 76/495
339 revoked 79/1470
340 revoked 74/805
341 revoked 73/806
347 revoked 72/372
355 revoked 77/1097
356 amended 72/432
357 amended 72/432
360 revoked 76/1987
362 amended 76/547
366 revoked 75/180
367 amended 74/565; 74/1549
368 amended 76/547
372 revoked 72/488
373 revoked 72/1216
375 revoked 75/560
385 revoked 86/312
386 revoked 72/930
390 amended 74/510; 74/859
391 revoked 74/861
392 revoked 76/2008
393 revoked 75/559
394 amended 72/603; 72/604
395 amended 73/1068; 84/1751
399 revoked 72/609
400 revoked 72/488
403 revoked 82/1094
406 revoked 73/1029
407 revoked 88/559
419 amended 74/752; 76/1772; 77/94; 81/1219; 83/718; 84/1669; 86/2125; 87/2000
421 amended 72/585; 74/1372; 77/683; 79/837
428 revoked 72/1031
429 revoked 78/1772
431 revoked 78/1303
442 revoked 77/1360
445 revoked 76/421
454 revoked 79/929
455 revoked 79/930
456 amended 73/964; 74/868; 75/2194; 77/430
457 revoked 79/253
466 amended 74/169
474 revoked 74/32
475 revoked 74/32
482 revoked 73/122
488 revoked 72/530
489 amended 74/185; 75/898; revoked 84/489
492 revoked 73/591
509 amended 72/1392
517 revoked 81/404
518 amended 72/1728; revoked 74/529
519 revoked 74/529
527 revoked 74/1992
529 amended 74/1236; 75/213
530 revoked 72/678
532 revoked 74/1992

1972—cont.

545 amended 86/690
550 revoked 77/320
551 revoked 77/1360
552 revoked 72/334
554 revoked 75/1363
555 amended 72/1287; 73/1441; 74/10; 74/46;
74/1036
556 revoked 73/42
557 revoked 75/1494
558 amended 76/729
567 amended 77/1867
568 revoked 76/1987
569 revoked 73/2037
570 amended 81/1323
574 revoked 78/1364
581 revoked 73/1563
583 amended 75/1802; 79/259; 80/1061
585 revoked 79/837
595 amended 74/645
597 revoked 82/660
598 amended 72/649
599 amended 72/650
603 amended 74/416; 74/1128
604 amended 73/1478; 74/593
606 amended 72/1302; 74/1128
609 revoked 72/790
611 revoked 82/448
620 revoked 73/292
640 amended 78/1139; 79/1585
641 amended 73/389; 74/552; 75/714; 75/1192;
76/1962;   76/2111;   77/545;   77/1448;
77/1916;   78/1334;   78/1855;   79/1388;
79/1533;   80/45;   80/1614;   80/1986;
81/372;   81/486;   81/1460;   81/670;
81/1172;   81/1482;   82/488;   82/1013;
82/1227;   82/1574;   83/495;   83/1063;
84/388;   84/603;   84/1052;   84/1564;
85/146; 85/891; 85/1479; 86/2001
648 revoked 72/1829
649 amended 72/659
650 amended 72/660
652 revoked 73/292
656 amended 75/594
665 amended 74/1298; 75/1284; 76/1227
666 revoked 78/1543
668 amended 75/1706; 76/52; 77/423; 85/444
672 revoked 74/1114
673 revoked 79/1715
675 revoked 81/612
677 revoked 72/1909
678 revoked 72/824
680 revoked 73/1140
681 amended 76/335; revoked 86/401
683 revoked 73/1223
699 revoked 74/1401
700 amended 74/1999
716 revoked 75/1046
718 revoked 73/1159
727 amended 73/865; 74/1905
729 amended   75/2031;   76/1495;   78/707;
revoked 86/259
734 revoked 73/1190
738 revoked 78/1875
751 revoked 81/257
757 revoked 73/2171
759 revoked 78/1875
760 revoked 78/1875
761 revoked 73/470
764 amended   74/553;   75/1190;   75/2153;

1972—cont.

77/1807;   78/888;   78/1594;   80/619;
81/484;   82/487;   82/1282;   83/1367;
83/1762; 83/1750; 84/9; 84/602; 85/342;
86/2001; 88/1166 .
765 amended   75/1191;   76/1543;   77/1447;
78/1297; 80/452; 80/767; 81/310; 84/601;
85/861; 86/2001; 88/1356
767 amended 88/876
771 revoked 73/1222
772 revoked 82/664
775 revoked 72/1829
776 amended 75/1135; 76/475
777 revoked 76/1073
778 amended 75/1452
779 amended 74/1998
782 revoked 73/1115
790 revoked 72/851
791 amended 76/241
803 revoked 75/910
805 revoked 73/24
806 revoked 82/1478
808 revoked 72/1098
809 revoked 77/982
813 amended 72/1194; 73/2046; 76/1196
814 revoked 78/1483
815 amended 73/976
818 revoked 74/834
819 revoked 74/835
820 revoked 79/1038
821 amended 72/976
822 amended 72/977
824 revoked 72/991
825 revoked 78/1485
827 revoked 74/504
828 amended 74/503; 74/504
838 revoked 83/1710; 83/1828
843 revoked 73/24
844 revoked 78/998
846 amended 77/1869
849 revoked 72/1829
850 revoked 81/931
851 revoked 72/998
852 revoked 78/483
854 revoked 73/1016
857 amended 73/464
863 revoked 76/988
864 revoked 78/809
867 revoked 80/1106
869 revoked 74/45
872 revoked 73/955
877 amended 74/737; 75/1383; 77/863; 80/1869
878 amended 77/744; 87/613
879 revoked 73/1443
883 revoked 73/284
887 amended 77/286
890 revoked 75/1808
898 revoked 76/1977
903 revoked 72/996
904 revoked 79/838
905 revoked 73/1678
906 amended 75/266
910 revoked 74/1414; 74/1415
911 revoked 75/1291
917 amended 74/1587
918 amended 72/1876; 77/45; 78/1756; 79/1519;
81/1789
919 amended 72/1877; 77/45; 79/1519; 83/478
920 revoked 72/1608
928 revoked 73/1255

1972—cont.

930 amended 72/2040
931 amended 75/503
932 revoked 78/436
938 revoked 78/796
941 amended 86/1434
943 revoked 74/11
944 revoked 74/12
949 revoked 72/1126
950 revoked 72/1127
951 revoked 72/1829
959 revoked 74/1262
960 revoked 77/1239
969 revoked 77/829
970 revoked 75/430
971 amended 77/1257; 78/1913; 79/1309, 82/715; 83/769
973 amended 87/2070
980 revoked 73/1173; 75/1090
986 revoked 82/449
987 revoked 73/24
990 amended 73/1794; 79/1276
991 revoked 72/1137
996 revoked 74/1283
998 revoked 72/1406
1001 revoked 75/1091
1005 revoked 82/448
1011 revoked 73/42
1012 revoked 83/569
1014 revoked 73/2114
1019 revoked 73/380
1021 revoked 73/1845
1024 amended 73/290
1029 amended 73/1405
1030 revoked 72/1603
1042 revoked 72/1829
1046 amended 76/231
1048 revoked 72/1909
1054 revoked 75/1350
1055 revoked 75/1351
1057 revoked 72/1829
1061 revoked 85/214
1066 revoked 74/1402
1072 amended 78/1042
1073 amended 74/1267; 81/228
1076 revoked 75/1247
1077 revoked 72/1608
1082 revoked 73/956
1087 revoked 74/439
1088 revoked 74/440
1090 revoked 75/653
1092 revoked 76/1987
1094 amended 75/177; 76/457
1096 revoked 83/370
1101 amended 84/126; 87/2199
1102 revoked 77/1237
1115 revoked 78/1177
1116 revoked 73/1198
1117 revoked 77/1033
1124 revoked 75/1207
1126 revoked 72/2016
1127 revoked 72/2017
1137 revoked 72/1350
1147 amended 73/244; 73/595; 73/1882; 73/2123
1148 amended 75/274; 77/1759; 79/224; 87/1712
1154 revoked 74/1486
1156 amended 75/1345
1165 revoked 77/1796
1166 revoked 72/1534
1167 revoked 77/1796

1972—cont.

1168 revoked 72/1970
1169 revoked 77/1796
1170 revoked 77/1796
1173 revoked 77/1284
1174 revoked 77/1284
1175 revoked 77/1284
1176 amended 73/987
1177 revoked 76/585
1178 amended 76/1882; 80/1851; 84/1358
1181 amended 74/2061
1186 revoked 73/334
1188 revoked 75/1972
1189 revoked 75/1350
1190 revoked 75/1343
1191 revoked 75/1344
1193 amended 74/595; 74/1891
1194 amended 74/295
1195 revoked 79/1470
1200 amended 74/498; 77/161; 78/1139; 79/1585
1201 amended 75/681
1203 amended 79/1319
1206 revoked 76/1073
1207 revoked 78/257
1208 revoked 84/647
1209 revoked 72/1829
1211 revoked 80/1670
1215 revoked 72/1829
1216 revoked 72/2015
1217 amended 73/1821; 74/792; 74/2187; 81/1567
1218 revoked 85/1150
1219 revoked 78/1875
1220 amended 74/708; 75/296; 75/1629
1221 revoked 80/1672
1222 revoked 76/1451
1223 revoked 74/1009
1224 revoked 74/1010
1226 amended 74/1523
1231 amended 75/559; 75/560
1233 revoked 74/1401
1234 revoked 79/837
1239 revoked 77/1360
1240 revoked 73/1500
1242 revoked 72/1937
1244 revoked 76/1034
1245 revoked 74/399
1246 revoked 72/1829
1255 revoked 72/2051
1257 revoked 73/1013
1258 revoked 75/1537
1263 amended 75/1504; 76/58; 76/1042; 78/1040; 78/1041; 78/1050
1265 amended 77/2156; 78/1045; 78/1907; 81/154; 81/432
1266 revoked 74/1114
1268 amended 81/611; 86/2001
1272 revoked 76/1396
1274 revoked 76/1082
1275 revoked 75/675
1277 revoked 79/668
1279 revoked 73/1484
1280 amended 73/1635
1282 revoked 80/1438
1287 amended 74/1036
1288 revoked 82/1489
1289 amended 75/514; 75/1139; revoked 83/136
1291 revoked 75/917
1294 amended 72/1876; 74/2047; 78/1754; 79/1519; revoked 85/1828

1972—*cont.*

1295 amended 74/1734; 77/1181; 78/107; 78/979; 78/1758; 79/1519; 81/313; revoked 87/408
1300 amended 74/1129
1301 amended 74/1128; 75/558
1306 revoked 73/176
1307 revoked 82/1015
1313 revoked 76/300
1329 amended 75/2211
1333 revoked 76/1469
1336 revoked 73/1468
1344 amended 74/1708; 74/1934; 77/1017; 77/1760; 78/273; revoked 86/590
1345 amended 73/418; 73/594; 81/356; 81/1079; 83/140
1347 revoked 73/1497
1348 revoked 74/505
1350 revoked 72/1465
1354 revoked 76/1690
1355 amended 75/2045
1356 revoked 73/1713
1361 revoked 73/2037
1362 revoked 77/228
1368 revoked 73/807
1371 revoked 77/1072
1375 revoked 86/498
1377 amended 73/1411
1385 amended 83/1614; revoked 87/764
1387 amended 83/1188
1388 revoked 73/292
1391 revoked 84/1304
1398 revoked 73/42
1399 revoked 74/476
1400 amended 74/746; 75/592
1401 revoked 76/117
1404 amended 74/1237; 75/214
1406 revoked 72/1767
1413 revoked 78/32
1416 revoked 72/1829
1425 revoked 75/674
1430 revoked 73/2134
1431 revoked 75/67
1433 amended 74/8; 74/464
1461 amended 73/1579
1466 revoked 80/1120
1471 revoked 72/1829
1473 revoked 73/24
1477 amended 73/2000
1481 revoked 86/399
1483 amended 77/564; 86/1277
1484 revoked 74/11
1485 revoked 74/12
1489 revoked 84/1518
1493 revoked 77/1141
1496 revoked 72/1829
1500 revoked 78/1483
1502 revoked 77/890
1503 revoked 77/889
1504 revoked 77/888
1510 amended 74/1121; 76/295; 76/509; 76/541; 76/859; 80/1849
1511 revoked 75/1537
1521 revoked 77/1284
1522 amended 76/276
1523 revoked 79/1577
1532 revoked 73/539
1535 revoked 75/1046
1536 revoked 78/196
1537 amended 80/362
1538 revoked 78/1485

1972—*cont.*

1539 revoked 78/1875
1544 revoked 75/1446
1551 revoked 88/876
1556 revoked 74/595
1566 amended 73/1463; 73/1464; 74/125
1572 amended 75/628
1574 amended 74/2184
1577 amended 77/1207; 82/36; 84/1577
1580 amended 73/2088; 75/1035
1584 revoked 79/1655
1585 revoked 79/1655
1586 revoked 81/605
1587 amended 76/225; 88/591
1588 revoked 78/1527
1589 revoked 85/1172
1591 revoked 81/612
1596 amended 75/177
1602 revoked 74/160
1603 revoked 73/142
1604 revoked 80/1177
1606 revoked 73/1883
1610 amended 79/730; 80/1859; 82/1028; 85/1854; 87/2092
1613 amended 75/617; 77/693; 83/1649; 85/1809
1614 revoked 72/1829
1615 revoked 73/176
1616 revoked 75/1951
1617 amended 74/1794; 75/1140
1618 revoked 75/1952
1619 amended 74/1795; 75/1141
1625 revoked 76/391
1633 revoked 77/2157
1634 amended 78/1048; 81/156; 81/437; 81/600; 82/1535; 82/1537
1635 amended 72/1875; 88/479
1636 revoked 79/1545
1642 amended 73/428; 74/1534; 74/1629
1644 revoked 76/597
1645 amended 76/387
1652 revoked 81/804
1653 amended 79/762
1655 amended 73/1838
1656 revoked 72/1829
1657 revoked 75/910
1658 amended 74/977
1659 amended 74/1863; revoked 75/1958
1660 amended 74/1864; 75/1418
1664 revoked 73/1029
1666 revoked 75/65
1667 amended 75/980
1668 amended 75/2221; 79/1635
1675 revoked 77/320
1677 amended 75/806
1678 revoked 73/1535
1679 amended 88/1000
1683 amended 82/1027; revoked 84/2040
1684 amended 82/1026; revoked 84/2041
1688 amended 83/1646; revoked 87/177
1689 amended 82/1025
1690 revoked 73/24
1691 revoked 76/489
1634 revoked 72/1829
1697 amended 72/1876; 72/1877; 79/1519
1698 amended 72/1876; 72/1877
1699 amended 72/1876; 72/1877
1700 amended 72/1876; 78/1757; 85/340
1701 amended 72/1877; 88/2064
1704 amended 76/817
1719 amended 83/1834; 83/1897

STATUTORY INSTRUMENTS AFFECTED 1947–1988

1720 amended 80/399; 83/1835; 83/1898
1721 amended 81/1816
1722 revoked 76/128
1723 revoked 74/1114
1724 amended 79/910
1728 revoked 74/529
1729 revoked 74/1401
1739 amended 76/1223
1741 revoked 78/483
1743 amended 75/1442
1746 revoked 78/1759
1748 revoked 80/1630
1749 revoked 80/1894
1751 revoked 73/835
1753 amended 74/1410; 85/866
1756 revoked 80/1793
1758 amended 75/999; 76/2018; 78/24; 80/451; 81/534; 82/1502; 82/1024
1761 revoked 74/1738
1764 revoked 74/389
1765 amended 83/1749
1769 revoked 72/1883
1771 revoked 74/478
1778 revoked 74/777
1782 revoked 82/1109
1783 revoked 81/500
1789 amended 84/728
1790 amended 74/1338; 76/442; 76/914; 76/946; 76/1176; 81/137
1804 amended 78/230; 80/1851; revoked 83/363
1805 revoked 79/97
1813 amended 83/1836; 84/1690
1816 amended 73/960
1817 revoked 82/1085
1819 revoked 74/139
1820 revoked 74/234
1821 revoked 73/42
1827 revoked 76/378
1828 revoked 74/529
1833 amended 84/621
1839 revoked 72/2019
1842 revoked 73/1468
1843 revoked 79/1254
1845 amended 73/431
1847 revoked 73/433
1848 amended 73/647
1852 amended 73/774
1856 amended 73/285; 73/556
1857 amended 73/1702
1858 revoked 74/1479
1859 revoked 74/1480
1860 amended 74/713; 76/503
1862 revoked 74/505
1865 amended 75/1089; 75/1342
1871 amended 72/1876; 75/733; 78/36
1872 amended 72/1877; 75/733
1873 revoked 81/570
1874 revoked 81/569
1876 amended 87/884
1878 amended 74/847; 80/1851
1880 revoked 73/55
1883 revoked 72/2067
1887 revoked 76/260
1891 revoked 87/309
1898 amended 76/337
1899 revoked 73/1468
1906 revoked 79/1641
1907 revoked 73/2037
1909 revoked 73/1845

1910 revoked 77/2083
1913 amended 73/647
1917 revoked 74/1401
1922 revoked 77/1097
1925 revoked 82/1021
1926 revoked 80/1819
1928 revoked 83/1106
1929 amended 83/1106
1930 revoked 75/1692
1931 amended 76/1067
1934 amended 84/108
1936 amended 85/1472
1938 amended 74/1556; 75/1072; 76/479
1939 revoked 78/1
1941 amended 76/850; revoked 83/713
1955 revoked 81/404
1956 revoked 75/739
1959 revoked 74/714
1960 revoked 76/1987
1966 amended 75/639; 83/58
1970 revoked 77/1795
1971 revoked 77/1976
1976 revoked 74/1461
1980 amended 73/101; 77/944
1987 revoked 80/1698
1988 revoked 74/305
1991 revoked 88/784
1996 amended 78/1038
1997 amended 77/2153
1998 amended 77/2157; 78/1050; 78/1907; 78/1041
1999 amended 77/2157; 78/1041
2000 revoked 85/1213
2015 revoked 73/75
2016 revoked 73/76
2017 revoked 73/77
2018 revoked 74/46
2019 revoked 73/140
2023 revoked 77/1796
2024 revoked 73/2037
2025 revoked 79/1702
2034 amended 73/2187
2042 revoked 73/587
2050 amended 77/295
2051 revoked 81/909
2059 revoked 74/1286
2061 revoked 75/225
2062 revoked 73/587
2067 revoked 73/85
2076 amended 79/1760; 81/1633

1973
6 revoked 85/2023
7 amended 80/804; 81/917; 83/978; 85/2023
8 amended 80/804; 81/917; 85/2023
15 amended 78/272; 78/1248; 83/1600; revoked 85/1271
22 amended 83/1053
24 revoked 78/1017
31 revoked 77/289
33 revoked 79/1470
36 amended 80/1248; 85/1333
37 amended 82/877
39 amended 73/285; 73/1218; 74/261
42 amended 73/451; 73/615; 73/775; 73/1154; 73/1623
43 revoked 74/1542
44 revoked 74/1543
61 revoked 74/98

1973—*cont.*

63 revoked 74/485
66 revoked 78/216
70 amended 78/1049
71 revoked 74/1114
72 revoked 79/1715
74 revoked 79/1553
75 revoked 73/572
76 revoked 73/573
77 revoked 73/574
79 amended 74/648; 76/2065; 83/1154; 85/1848; revoked 86/2214
85 revoked 73/117
86 amended 73/544; 74/1721; 75/1928
92 revoked 76/1396
94 amended 74/595
98 revoked 73/557
100 revoked 78/1875
106 revoked 78/796
112 revoked 73/210
116 amended 75/360; revoked 87/1135
117 revoked 73/141
118 amended 84/261; revoked 86/400
119 revoked 76/1073
120 revoked 79/883
122 revoked 74/732
123 amended 87/1372
124 revoked 75/388
131 revoked 74/445
144 revoked 73/1845
146 amended 74/684; 74/686
147 revoked 74/174
148 revoked 73/557
149 revoked 79/838
152 amended 74/1408
153 amended 73/1732
155 revoked 74/810
156 revoked 74/331
157 revoked 74/332
160 revoked 80/1274
161 revoked 76/103
162 revoked 73/807
166 revoked 73/1910
173 amended 75/385; 80/304; 81/338; 81/955; 84/202; 85/1046; 87/806
175 revoked 74/631
176 amended 73/1539; 75/541; revoked 78/495
177 revoked 73/1362
178 revoked 82/1228
183 revoked 74/743
184 revoked 74/744
188 amended 83/59
190 revoked 74/754
191 revoked 74/755
194 amended 88/1729
195 revoked 80/804
198 amended 73/300
204 revoked 73/288
207 amended 75/844; 83/60
215 amended 74/260
218 revoked 74/437
219 revoked 74/438
220 revoked 73/2148
221 revoked 73/2149
229 revoked 74/595
231 revoked 75/1803
237 amended 73/1887; 77/1244
239 revoked 75/1803
244 amended 73/595
249 revoked 76/294

1973—*cont.*

264 amended 74/278
268 revoked 83/1842; amended 87/897
270 amended 75/227; 76/892; 80/724
273 revoked 77/289
278 revoked 75/1254
284 revoked 76/332
285 amended 73/556
288 amended 78/1660; 79/1541; 80/1562
289 revoked 75/1686
290 amended 73/366
304 revoked 80/1177
311 revoked 74/574
313 revoked 74/520
319 revoked 74/476
322 amended 76/475
326 revoked 77/1796
327 amended 74/1708; 78/273
328 revoked 77/1796
329 revoked 77/1796
333 revoked 84/108
334 amended 74/340; 74/2102; 75/91; 75/728; 76/381; 76/950; 77/700; 78/326; 78/1196; 81/44; 82/66; 84/1858; 85/350; 86/2212; 88/637
335 revoked 77/1796
336 amended 77/1795; 77/1796
340 revoked 81/1086; 1499
342 revoked 74/1042
343 amended 75/580
348 amended 84/108
349 revoked 80/4777
350 revoked 77/345
352 revoked 76/249
355 amended 75/604; 75/606; 84/248
356 revoked 79/1470
359 amended 75/665; 75/671; 84/470
362 amended 75/1056
369 revoked 76/1883
370 revoked 81/786
379 revoked 78/1157
380 revoked 76/1447
386 revoked 74/542
387 amended 74/822
388 revoked 77/1795
389 revoked 74/552
390 amended 73/1562; 77/1762; 78/1565; 79/325; 80/1792; 82/622; 84/210; 85/337; 86/254; 86/673; 86/1359; revoked 87/382; amended 87/1355; 88/1110
391 revoked 76/1073
392 revoked 73/2150
393 revoked 73/1845
398 revoked 73/1106
399 amended 74/1135; 74/1993; revoked 74/1135
400 revoked 75/1405
403 revoked 75/1247
408 revoked 75/287
412 revoked 73/2155
414 amended 78/1042
415 revoked 81/155
416 revoked 81/438; 86/442
417 amended 86/442; 88/233
418 amended 73/594
419 revoked 73/2037
423 amended 75/1629
424 amended 74/980; 77/1287; 78/1330; 80/1565
427 revoked 74/648

STATUTORY INSTRUMENTS AFFECTED 1947–1988

1973—*cont.*

428 amended 73/429; 73/1773; 74/1533; 74/1534; 74/1535; 74/1629; 74/1796; 75/1718; 76/306; 76/1707; 77/1705; 77/2173; 78/375; 78/1348; 78/1578; 79/406; 79/1287; 80/82; 80/272; 80/1411; 80/1616; 82/1157; 83/996; 85/156; 86/1379; 87/156; revoked 87/256
429 revoked 87/256
430 amended 74/1534; 79/75; 80/1260; 83/990; 87/157
431 amended 74/1535; 79/76
433 amended 74/1630; 79/784; 80/1411
434 amended 74/1629; 79/783; 80/1410; 82/1660; 87/1699; 87/1700
435 amended 82/1660
444 amended 73/2025
450 amended 78/125; revoked 88/110
452 revoked 74/32
465 revoked 85/223
467 amended 85/225; 87/1070
468 revoked 85/222
474 revoked 83/1917
476 amended 76/547
484 revoked 74/139
490 amended 77/231; 86/706
492 amended 76/547
495 amended 74/984
497 amended 75/852; 79/1527; 80/2020; 85/819
498 amended 86/1776
503 revoked 74/812
515 revoked 74/32
519 revoked 74/601
521 revoked 74/537
539 revoked 74/210
544 amended 74/1721; 75/1928
545 amended 73/1803
546 amended 73/1517; 75/1725
547 revoked 77/1360
548 amended 73/1013
558 revoked 74/497
573 revoked 73/848
574 revoked 73/849
590 revoked 77/1284
593 revoked 75/1385
594 revoked 80/182
595 revoked 74/1708
596 revoked 80/697
597 revoked 76/215
598 amended 75/1706; 76/52; 77/423; revoked 85/444
599 revoked 76/1156
600 amended 76/1041
613 revoked 81/612
614 amended 75/1441
617 revoked 75/916
621 revoked 77/1222
623 amended 81/1658; 85/1677
645 revoked 73/1065
648 revoked 73/1845
650 amended 73/832
651 revoked 73/1845
652 revoked 73/1034
653 revoked 75/2082
659 amended 73/1801; 74/1223; 75/615; 75/1081; 75/1674; 78/1454
660 revoked 77/1225
662 revoked 73/1788
663 revoked 73/1789
664 revoked 73/1786

1973—*cont.*

666 amended 74/614; 75/252
667 amended 74/613
672 revoked 88/110
673 amended 73/1145; 75/836; 76/339; 76/1062; revoked 87/430
681 amended 75/1109; 75/2082
686 amended 74/735
687 revoked 79/1188
688 amended 73/943; 73/1466
690 revoked 75/203
691 amended 74/266
699 revoked 75/33
702 revoked 79/1393
707 amended 82/1500
722 amended 73/832
728 revoked 79/1751
731 amended 80/362
734 amended 74/339
739 amended 81/1577
740 amended 79/1573
741 amended 75/21
747 revoked 81/202; 84/325
748 amended 73/2058; 74/619; 81/1372; revoked 84/325
753 amended 82/1112
755 revoked 75/1247
756 revoked 78/1017
757 revoked 74/1982
762 revoked 77/1239
763 amended 76/225
772 revoked 79/1715
777 amended 73/1973
778 revoked 73/1787
780 amended 75/177
784 revoked 73/1786
790 revoked 81/552
791 amended 75/1399
792 revoked 83/133
793 revoked 75/1046
794 amended 75/404; revoked 81/1596
796 revoked 77/1379
797 amended 74/402; 75/499; 75/1623; 77/1380; 79/326; 83/788; 84/1143; revoked 85/2066
798 amended 74/1449; 75/294; 84/1146; 85/2067; 86/2332
799 amended 83/1909
806 revoked 80/1459
807 revoked 88/1766
812 revoked 75/1098
828 amended 74/1997; 75/2131
830 revoked 75/2130
832 amended 73/945
835 revoked 74/1912
845 revoked 75/1233
847 amended 75/1345
848 revoked 73/1542
849 revoked 73/1543
850 revoked 73/1544
856 revoked 75/751
860 revoked 82/664
861 amended 88/1024
865 amended 74/1905
866 amended 74/1906; revoked 75/1957
871 revoked 73/1856
875 revoked 73/1856
905 revoked 75/560
914 revoked 76/1883
916 amended 76/729
921 revoked 75/1090

STATUTORY INSTRUMENTS AFFECTED 1947–1988

STATUTORY INSTRUMENTS AFFECTED 1947–1988

1756 amended 74/1108; 75/804; 76/770; 77/1238;
78/1888; 81/212; 81/733; 82/148;
85/1991; 86/2014; 87/451; 87/2043
1758 amended 77/49
1767 revoked 82/449
1773 amended 74/1796
1774 amended 76/373; revoked 87/492
1776 amended 76/185; 87/1114
1777 amended 74/1650
1778 amended 74/1645
1779 revoked 75/149
1784 amended 74/1324; revoked 84/614
1785 revoked 74/2113
1786 revoked 74/2114
1787 revoked 74/2115
1793 revoked 77/320
1801 amended 74/1223; 75/615; 75/1081;
75/1674
1802 amended 74/1311
1805 revoked 74/1403
1809 amended 74/1647
1811 amended 74/102
1812 revoked 75/1098
1814 amended 74/1797
1818 amended 75/751
1820 revoked 73/2143
1821 amended 74/792; 74/2187
1822 amended 76/667; 77/511; 77/2077; 80/1806;
81/1713; 83/1719; 84/1886; 85/1878;
87/2099; 88/2113
1838 amended 76/348
1844 revoked 73/2152
1845 amended 73/2169; 73/2179; 73/2208;
73/2218; 74/166; 74/608; 74/887; 74/889;
74/1020
1850 revoked 74/977
1856 amended 77/1148; 77/1599
1861 amended 74/142; 74/273; 74/339; 74/406;
74/482; 74/520; 74/1351; 74/2044;
75/244; 76/315
1863 amended 74/142; 74/404; 74/482; 74/520;
74/1351; 74/2044; 75/244; 76/315
1864 revoked 78/1017
1866 revoked 74/1042
1867 revoked 74/880
1871 revoked 77/1113
1879 revoked 73/2104
1881 revoked 73/2089
1883 revoked 74/999
1887 revoked 77/1244
1888 revoked 78/281
1890 amended 78/1881
1891 amended 73/2175
1892 amended 75/806
1896 amended 77/2157; 81/437; 81/608; 82/1537
1897 amended 73/2221; revoked 86/1951
1898 revoked 75/1091
1899 revoked 75/1090
1900 revoked 73/2110
1901 revoked 73/2110
1910 amended 73/1911; 74/84; 76/2066; 83/1153;
revoked 86/2215
1911 amended 76/2067; 83/1151; revoked 87/1
1913 revoked 73/2110
1914 amended 74/1947
1915 amended 74/1751
1916 amended 74/1814
1928 revoked 78/1699
1929 amended 74/1389; revoked 83/550

1936 amended 87/232
1937 amended 74/1961
1943 revoked 73/2111
1944 amended 73/2024
1945 amended 76/761; 80/104; 80/929
1946 amended 74/143; 74/1349
1947 revoked 75/1943
1948 revoked 74/2036
1949 amended 74/588; 74/838; 74/1199
1950 revoked 75/1537
1951 amended 73/2023
1955 revoked 74/1297
1958 amended 83/1136
1964 revoked 79/1702
1965 amended 76/547; 76/1870; 78/380; 78/768;
80/930
1967 amended 78/1080; revoked 84/1316
1968 revoked 84/1316
1970 amended 74/1859
1978 revoked 76/1396
1979 amended 84/1164
1993 revoked 80/509
1996 ceased to have effect 74/520; amended
83/178
1997 amended 75/313; 76/212
2001 amended 81/92; 82/991
2010 revoked 76/1898
2012 revoked 79/739
2013 revoked 77/1043
2015 revoked 76/1076
2016 revoked 77/344
2017 amended 74/1883
2018 amended 74/1723
2021 revoked 82/129
2030 revoked 84/1943
2036 revoked 80/1894
2037 amended 74/277; 74/724; 75/113; 75/987;
76/697; 76/737; 76/763; 76/1193;
77/1072; 77/1073; 77/1767; 81/899
2038 revoked 79/1393
2045 amended 76/29; 76/850; 76/890; revoked
83/713
2051 revoked 77/1870
2052 revoked 73/2090
2058 revoked 74/619
2059 revoked 74/502
2060 revoked 75/596
2061 amended 81/91; 82/992; 86/561
2063 amended 74/398
2065 amended 74/1133
2068 revoked 74/511
2069 revoked 77/2047
2070 revoked 78/693
2071 revoked 77/972
2072 revoked 74/721
2073 revoked 74/722
2074 revoked 74/888
2075 revoked 75/690
2076 revoked 75/691
2078 revoked 77/1360
2080 amended 74/511
2082 revoked 80/482
2084 revoked 83/1206
2085 revoked 75/1943
2086 revoked 75/1943
2087 revoked 74/245
2088 amended 75/1035
2091 amended 74/511
2092 amended 74/511

1973—*cont.*

2095 amended 75/2157
2099 revoked 88/1082
2100 revoked 76/2062
2101 revoked 84/2063
2106 amended 77/167
2114 amended 79/1255
2117 revoked 84/255
2119 revoked 74/2151
2120 amended 73/2137; 73/2146
2124 amended 75/928; 84/1640; 86/26
2125 amended 76/333; revoked 87/381
2126 amended 75/149
2127 amended 74/1882
2129 revoked 76/1135
2130 revoked 77/770
2131 revoked 74/512
2132 revoked 74/512
2133 amended 73/2211
2134 revoked 75/66
2135 amended 88/1519
2137 amended 73/2172
2143 amended 74/791; 87/2171
2146 amended 73/2172
2148 revoked 74/1898
2149 amended 74/1898
2150 revoked 77/1791
2152 amended 74/756
2153 amended 74/161
2163 amended 78/1041; 79/1573; 81/155; 81/228; 82/713
2167 revoked 76/1324
2169 amended 74/889
2171 revoked 74/1411
2172 revoked 74/59
2173 revoked 86/498
2178 revoked 74/889
2179 amended 74/887
2182 revoked 78/1875
2188 revoked 76/1204
2192 revoked 81/1836
2193 revoked 74/32
2199 revoked 86/1201
2200 revoked 86/647
2205 revoked 81/1707
2208 revoked 76/976
2209 amended 74/166; 74/885
2210 amended 74/132; 74/1063; 74/1350
2212 revoked 76/1679
2215 amended 75/51; 76/157
2217 amended 76/791; 78/21; 82/137; revoked 85/304
2218 revoked 75/2094
2219 amended 74/161
2221 amended 79/427; 81/1059; 84/1244; revoked 86/1951
2226 amended 74/1014; 74/1376
2227 revoked 74/2076
2229 revoked 77/2047

1974

1 revoked 80/449
2 revoked 77/901
3 amended 76/187
9 revoked 78/331
11 revoked 74/1927
12 revoked 75/42
14 revoked 75/1247
22 revoked 81/93
24 revoked 82/287

1974—*cont.*

28 revoked 77/104
29 amended 82/288
32 amended 74/188; 74/341
35 amended 74/318; 74/378; 75/203
36 revoked 82/287
39 amended 74/425
41 revoked 74/1874
42 revoked 74/1875
44 amended 74/229; 79/210; revoked 87/375
45 revoked 75/1136
46 revoked 74/1162
48 amended 75/23
53 amended 74/285; 74/455; 85/39
54 amended 74/678
62 revoked 77/1033
63 amended 82/75; 84/168
64 revoked 78/1017
65 revoked 76/316
66 revoked 82/97
67 revoked 78/259
69 amended 83/1633
70 revoked 83/1634
76 amended 75/83
77 amended 75/82
78 amended 74/117; 74/137
79 amended 75/47
80 amended 74/1556; 75/1072
81 revoked 78/1
82 amended 77/120; 79/656; 84/352; revoked 87/2213
83 revoked 82/448
84 revoked 86/2215
86 revoked 75/372
87 revoked 75/371
88 amended 76/1175
98 revoked 74/976
99 revoked 82/1478
101 revoked 77/1164
102 amended 74/1410; 75/520; 81/1221; 81/1323; 85/866
109 amended 74/1704; 76/51; revoked 85/1983
111 revoked 74/1114
114 amended 75/105
125 revoked 74/595
134 revoked 74/909
139 revoked 74/1401
141 amended 75/1747
152 amended 75/81
153 amended 75/78
154 amended 75/77
160 amended 74/285; 74/455; 75/719; 76/690; 76/1407; 81/774; 82/288; 82/1283; 83/313; 85/39; 85/290; 85/540; 85/803; 85/955; 85/1053; 85/1712; 86/381; 86/916; 86/1486; 87/5; 87/401; 87/407; 87/1425; 88/866; 88/1106; 88/2297
163 amended 74/349; 74/414
164 amended 74/823
165 revoked 75/992
166 amended 74/889
167 revoked 74/2072
169 amended 75/359
172 revoked 77/285
174 revoked 75/435
177 amended 74/968; 75/289
179 revoked 79/429
180 revoked 79/430
181 revoked 79/431
182 amended 74/824; 75/7

STATUTORY INSTRUMENTS AFFECTED 1947–1988

1974—*cont.*

183 amended 82/288
185 amended 75/898; revoked 84/421
186 amended 78/339
187 revoked 81/101
189 amended 74/801; 75/302
190 amended 82/288
194 amended 75/360; revoked 87/1135
196 revoked 81/597
197 revoked 74/2151
198 revoked 76/1204
207 revoked 75/1803
208 amended 75/1443
209 revoked 81/917
210 revoked 74/1000
211 revoked 74/1001
213 revoked 78/796
217 revoked 74/1404
219 amended 81/679
228 amended 75/80
229 revoked 87/375
234 revoked 74/2021
235 amended 82/288
241 amended 75/1337; 76/447; revoked 83/893
243 amended 83/468
248 amended 82/75; 84/168
250 amended 75/160
260 revoked 76/1987
261 revoked 74/1619
268 revoked 79/1434
269 revoked 79/1435
273 amended 83/893
274 revoked 88/1546
275 amended 75/939
278 revoked 75/914
282 revoked 74/541
284 amended 74/609; 78/950; 82/288; 86/976;
    88/473
285 revoked 80/1503
287 amended 74/1377; 77/199; 78/950; 81/305;
    82/288; 85/39; 85/298; revoked 86/975
295 amended 75/128
296 amended 82/288; 85/39
305 revoked 75/964
306 revoked 75/1047
307 amended 75/1945
308 amended 75/35
310 revoked 75/287
318 amended 75/784; 75/1765; 82/288
330 amended 75/325; 76/273
331 revoked 74/118
340 amended 81/44
361 revoked 82/276
362 revoked 81/329
363 revoked 81/328
364 revoked 81/327
376 revoked 77/1360
378 amended 75/984
380 amended 74/1928
381 amended 74/434; 74/1988
382 amended 74/1924
383 amended 74/1482
390 revoked 76/1987
391 revoked 78/884
393 amended 75/96
397 revoked 80/1808
399 revoked 76/1035
402 amended 75/499; 75/1623; revoked 85/2066
404 amended 74/595; 74/1351; 74/2044;
    75/1636; 76/315

1974—*cont.*

405 revoked 76/232
406 amended 74/595; 74/1351; 74/2044;
    75/1636; 76/315
411 revoked 78/1504
418 revoked 77/289
419 amended 86/420; revoked 88/944
420 amended 86/420; revoked 88/945
423 revoked 76/300
434 amended 74/1988
437 revoked 75/509
438 amended 75/509
441 amended 74/1357
444 revoked 81/553
445 revoked 74/1304
447 amended 74/1808; 75/1984; 77/107;
    77/1745; 78/1795; 78/1917; 79/1565;
    81/180; 81/316; 82/125; 83/574; 84/698;
    85/426; revoked 86/724
448 amended 74/1081
450 revoked 78/602
455 amended 74/907; 82/288; 85/39; 87/445
458 revoked 79/6
462 amended 75/106
465 revoked 76/516
466 amended 81/106; revoked 83/1027
474 revoked 74/2066
476 revoked 74/1475
477 amended 82/288; revoked 83/1275
478 revoked 75/934
479 revoked 77/890
482 amended 74/968
483 amended 74/595; 74/968; 74/2044; 75/944;
    76/315
484 amended 74/1081; 85/777
488 revoked 86/1002
489 revoked 76/1073
494 amended 78/1090; 82/288
495 amended 82/288; 85/47
496 revoked 80/1468
497 revoked 75/465
500 revoked 86/1002
503 revoked 88/808
504 amended 74/1031; 74/2048; 88/878
505 amended 74/508; 79/705; 80/1220; 81/900;
    84/1491; 85/1552; 86/1571; 87/1634;
    88/854
506 amended 74/508; 75/696; 76/733; 76/1574;
    78/1762; 81/56; 81/965; 82/1279; 85/296;
    85/534; 85/804; 85/1625; 85/1713;
    86/925; 86/1507; 87/385; 87/386;
    87/1382; 88/1073; 88/1454
507 amended 74/1522; 75/789; 76/1825; 80/107;
    81/360; 85/355; revoked 86/965
508 revoked 80/1674
515 amended 81/9; 81/179
518 amended 75/1131; 86/282
519 amended 74/595; 75/1131; 83/529; 85/1148;
    86/345
520 amended 77/1121; 77/1341; 77/1845;
    78/266; 78/822; 78/1738; 78/1739; 79/2;
    79/592; 79/1534; 80/216; 80/233; 80/234;
    81/1250; 81/1509; 82/908; 82/1514;
    83/178; 83/1269; 83/1270; 84/201;
    85/489; 85/1515; 85/1920; 86/24
522 amended 74/1440; 75/1987; 77/471; 79/704;
    79/705
526 amended 75/361
527 revoked 77/1999
528 revoked 75/1613

705

1974—*cont.*

529 amended 75/59; 75/873; 75/1077; 75/1994;
76/179; 76/400; 76/1641; 76/1973;
77/139; 77/853; 77/1672; 77/1863;
77/1884; 78/652; 78/813; 78/814;
78/1192; 79/1285; 80/391; 80/1020;
80/1162; 80/1261; 80/1449; 80/1656;
81/390; 81/1449; 82/728; 82/1812;
83/843; 83/1669; 84/426; 84/577;
84/1204; 84/1628; 85/1084; 85/1759;
85/1870; 85/1964; 85/1965; 85/2004;
86/464; 86/945; 86/1280; revoked 86/1713

530 revoked 76/117
536 revoked 75/1615
537 revoked 75/1424
538 revoked 75/1425
539 amended 86/435
541 revoked 82/277
543 revoked 74/2114
544 revoked 86/887
547 revoked 78/1844
548 revoked 76/540
*552 revoked 75/714; 76/1962
554 revoked 74/1708
555 amended 76/225; 88/591
556 amended 83/1125
559 amended 75/160
563 amended 76/854; 75/1296
564 revoked 75/1184
565 amended 74/1549
566 amended 74/1548; 74/1706; 75/180
572 amended 86/1445; revoked 87/2089
574 revoked 75/323
588 amended 74/838; 74/1199
595 amended 74/968; 74/1557; 75/1073;
75/1636
596 revoked 76/1419
597 revoked 87/2024
600 amended 74/1317; 74/1602; 75/382;
75/1724; 76/1756; 77/1576; 78/222;
78/1399; 79/1307; 80/1596; 81/1512;
82/1504
601 amended 75/1216
607 amended 83/327
612 amended 75/253; 75/1149
614 amended 75/252
615 revoked 74/1884; 74/1909
616 revoked 75/120
618 amended 84/224
620 revoked 74/2151
627 revoked 80/1503
628 revoked 77/204
630 amended 74/1282; 75/535
631 revoked 75/8
632 revoked 75/9
633 revoked 78/1844
636 amended 75/285; 76/314
637 revoked 75/1350
638 revoked 75/1351
647 revoked 80/1674
648 amended 75/1329; 77/105; 78/197; 79/338;
79/1679; 80/1031; 83/435
649 revoked 79/1470
651 revoked 75/850
652 amended 75/628
655 revoked 74/1695
660 amended 74/2157
661 revoked 74/2113
667 amended 85/1208

1974—*cont.*

668 amended 75/2236; 79/170; 83/1148;
86/1962
673 revoked 75/674
674 revoked 74/1718
675 revoked 75/1531
682 amended 74/756; 74/1007
688 revoked 74/1249
692 amended 76/1775
702 revoked 79/1456
706 amended 76/953; 80/1585
707 amended 83/1661
708 amended 75/1629
711 revoked 77/2127
713 amended 76/503
714 revoked 75/1357
721 revoked 75/209
722 revoked 75/210
731 revoked 75/1986
733 revoked 74/1461
734 amended 74/1441
736 revoked 75/1348
737 amended 75/1383
743 revoked 74/1664
745 revoked 79/883
746 amended 75/592
747 amended 74/1664
754 revoked 74/2134
755 amended 74/2134
760 amended 75/720; 75/1665; 81/1699;
revoked 85/980
762 amended 74/855
763 revoked 80/1182
764 amended 75/635
765 revoked 78/1017
767 revoked 75/1904
768 amended 84/688; 86/1342
769 revoked 74/1994
770 revoked 75/93
771 revoked 75/94
772 amended 74/1353
775 revoked 74/2114
776 revoked 74/2115
785 revoked 74/2113
788 amended 84/85; revoked 88/1951
791 amended 74/2186
792 amended 74/2187
796 revoked 75/18
797 revoked 77/548
799 revoked 78/32
801 amended 75/302
810 revoked 75/365
811 amended 75/365; 75/1641
812 amended 75/638; 78/425; 78/1378; 78/1794;
78/1926; 80/198; 80/342; 80/1885;
81/1892; 82/1303; 82/305; 82/1303;
83/1421; 84/254; 84/581; 86/1449;
revoked 87/1850
817 revoked 75/1161
818 revoked 77/1097
830 revoked 77/1074
831 revoked 75/1026
832 amended 77/180; 83/1789
834 amended 74/1558
838 amended 74/1199
839 revoked 78/1875
840 revoked 74/2114
848 amended 75/1071; 75/1873; 80/1851;
81/564; 82/1565; 83/684
853 revoked 75/1116

1974—*cont.*
1265 revoked 77/1240
1266 revoked 78/1906
1275 revoked 76/1783
1276 revoked 79/1715
1278 revoked 75/1482
1282 amended 75/535
1283 revoked 74/2028
1286 amended 86/2001
1287 revoked 75/1315
1297 revoked 75/992
1298 amended 75/1284; 76/1227
1299 revoked 76/355
1300 revoked 75/205
1301 revoked 76/354
1302 amended 75/856; revoked 88/666
1303 amended 75/855: revoked 88/667
1304 revoked 78/1162
1305 revoked 76/342
1306 revoked 76/341
1309 amended 76/127
1311 amended 75/901
1312 amended 75/902
1313 revoked 75/1046
1314 revoked 75/576
1316 amended 75/1725
1317 amended 75/1724; 76/1756
1318 revoked 74/2072
1321 revoked 75/327
1324 amended 76/140; revoked 84/1324
1325 revoked 82/448
1331 revoked 76/128
1332 amended 75/246
1336 revoked 77/228
1337 amended 75/1597
1338 revoked 80/1889
1339 revoked 78/492
1340 revoked 75/1598
1343 revoked 75/1348
1345 amended 75/244
1346 revoked 76/1073
1348 revoked 76/1073
1350 amended 74/1498
1352 revoked 74/1955
1355 revoked 75/94
1356 amended 83/940; 85/1068; 86/791
1357 revoked 80/1177
1360 amended 75/911
1365 revoked 79/1470
1366 amended 75/1054; revoked 86/541
1368 revoked 77/1412
1369 revoked 75/1317
1372 amended 79/837
1377 amended 75/1687; 75/1948; 76/1823;
      77/434; 80/1659; 81/307; 81/1345;
      83/309; 85/298; 86/976; revoked 88/551
1379 revoked 75/2204
1381 revoked 75/1344
1382 revoked 75/1328
1383 revoked 75/1346
1384 revoked 75/1343
1386 revoked 80/884
1387 revoked 80/885
1388 revoked 76/1987
1389 amended 76/1026; revoked 83/550
1401 revoked 76/1983
1402 revoked 76/1986
1403 revoked 76/1982
1404 revoked 76/1985
1410 amended 75/520; 81/1221; 81/1323

1974—*cont.*
1411 revoked 75/1571
1414 revoked 75/1537
1415 revoked 75/1537
1416 revoked 77/1141
1418 revoked 77/682
1419 revoked 74/2028
1440 amended 75/1715; 75/1988; 76/1874;
      80/1686; 81/359; 81/1431; 83/335;
      85/355; 86/966; revoked 88/546
1441 revoked 78/1257
1447 revoked 75/390
1449 amended 75/294
1461 revoked 77/4
1474 revoked 75/674
1475 revoked 77/1711
1477 revoked 76/1242
1479 revoked 75/2051
1481 revoked 83/1190
1484 amended 75/747; 75/1936
1486 revoked 82/555
1490 revoked 80/184
1492 revoked 75/739
1493 revoked 75/1171
1494 amended 75/1865
1497 revoked 79/429; 79/430; 79/431
1499 amended 75/342
1500 revoked 74/2114
1501 revoked 75/1809
1502 revoked 75/1810
1504 amended 75/1322
1507 revoked 76/117
1511 amended 75/500
1514 revoked 75/1132
1515 revoked 76/1073
1522 revoked 76/1825
1533 amended 74/1534; 74/1535; 74/1796;
      75/1718; 87/256
1540 revoked 75/1207
1541 amended 74/2069
1542 revoked 74/2067
1543 amended 75/579
1547 amended 82/288; 85/39; 85/1626
1548 revoked 77/2055
1549 revoked 77/2054
1552 revoked 78/1504
1555 amended 83/159
1556 amended 75/1072
1557 revoked 78/1
1558 revoked 75/256
1559 revoked 75/67
1566 revoked 75/1074
1567 revoked 75/304
1569 revoked 74/1954
1572 revoked 75/571
1574 revoked 75/854
1580 revoked 75/1026
1581 revoked 75/1090
1582 revoked 75/1091
1584 revoked 75/1385
1585 amended 75/389
1586 revoked 75/1424
1595 revoked 79/186
1598 amended 79/383
1603 amended 75/89
1612 revoked 75/581
1618 revoked 75/99
1619 revoked 75/1648
1620 revoked 75/1826
1652 amended 80/1870

1974—*cont.*

1659 revoked 75/1009
1665 revoked 81/1634
1673 revoked 87/256
1681 amended 75/303
1695 revoked 75/1779
1696 amended 75/1779
1697 revoked 75/1927
1698 revoked 75/42
1699 revoked 75/218
1706 amended 75/180
1707 amended 75/179
1708 revoked 78/273
1709 revoked 85/1983
1711 revoked 75/1245
1718 revoked 75/1530
1720 amended 75/778
1721 amended 75/1928
1734 revoked 87/408
1735 amended 85/1729
1740 amended 83/1315; 86/391
1748 amended 81/1263; 81/1875; 82/288
1757 revoked 79/643
1764 revoked 80/1120
1767 revoked 76/1983
1769 revoked 74/2021
1777 revoked 75/1692
1779 revoked 79/1198
1793 revoked 74/2114
1794 amended 75/1140
1795 amended 75/1141
1796 amended 75/1718; 87/256
1797 amended 75/1717
1806 revoked 78/884
1808 amended 75/1984; 80/193
1809 amended 75/1894; revoked 85/1661
1813 revoked 75/571
1816 revoked 77/1074
1817 revoked 79/792
1825 revoked 75/1482
1836 revoked 82/569
1837 amended 77/1149; 80/952
1838 amended 86/587
1846 revoked 87/1369
1847 revoked 87/1370
1851 amended 76/39
1863 revoked 75/1958
1867 revoked 77/320
1868 amended 75/2130
1869 amended 81/1785
1876 revoked 75/2204
1877 revoked 81/1375
1885 amended 74/2166
1886 revoked 80/804
1890 revoked 77/982
1895 revoked 78/1026
1898 revoked 74/2151
1906 revoked 75/1957
1910 amended 79/705
1911 revoked 75/560
1912 revoked 75/1256
1919 amended 82/1292
1923 amended 76/502
1927 amended 75/1825
1931 revoked 76/526
1934 revoked 86/590
1935 amended 75/692
1936 amended 75/342
1937 revoked 83/680
1942 amended 86/1951

1974—*cont.*

1943 amended 81/917
1944 amended 75/1370
1954 amended 76/116
1955 revoked 75/910
1962 amended 75/1777
1968 revoked 81/500
1971 revoked 75/2082
1973 revoked 79/1470
1974 revoked 77/580
1975 revoked 76/465
1982 amended 75/1644; 78/965
1984 revoked 75/1243
1993 revoked 77/1360
1996 revoked 75/2130
1997 amended 75/2131
2000 revoked 80/1279
2003 revoked 76/738; amended 77/482
2004 revoked 77/1211
2005 amended 76/2117; 77/2039; 78/1763; 79/1724
2008 revoked 78/1698
2009 revoked 75/492
2010 amended 75/562; 77/1484; 78/508; 79/345; 80/1168; 84/458
2020 revoked 75/1744
2021 revoked 75/936
2024 amended 81/1857
2025 revoked 76/896
2026 revoked 76/772
2027 revoked 76/895
2028 revoked 76/565
2032 revoked 76/260
2034 amended 76/1247; 80/1036; 81/1414; 84/605
2035 revoked 75/492
2036 revoked 75/1943
2038 revoked 76/466
2042 revoked 83/587
2043 revoked 84/1989
2044 amended 75/944; 75/1636; 76/315
2051 revoked 75/917
2057 amended 83/118; 86/2001
2058 amended 83/118
2059 revoked 79/642
2060 revoked 79/642
2064 revoked 78/554
2066 revoked 75/205
2067 revoked 75/1423
2071 revoked 75/2094
2073 revoked 76/976
2074 amended 75/1064; 75/1266
2076 revoked 75/2100
2079 amended 75/485; 75/1573; 75/2126; 77/342; 77/343; 77/956; 79/1067; 80/1621; 81/849; 82/1241; 82/1398; 82/1408
2080 revoked 76/128
2081 revoked 80/1274
2082 revoked 80/1273
2083 revoked 87/671
2087 amended 75/637
2095 revoked 75/1350
2096 revoked 75/1351
2100 revoked 77/1142
2102 amended 75/91; 75/728; 76/381; 76/950
2110 amended 75/85; 75/974
2113 revoked 76/1170
2114 revoked 76/1171
2115 revoked 76/1172
2120 revoked 75/1744

1974—cont.

2128 revoked 84/552
2129 revoked 75/1656
2130 revoked 75/1658
2131 revoked 75/1657
2132 amended 75/1659
2136 amended 79/1072
2142 revoked 78/1906
2143 amended 76/226; 79/124
2144 amended 81/839
2150 revoked 76/1204
2158 revoked 76/1170
2160 amended 80/1013
2163 amended 75/972; 75/1266; 75/1320; 75/1529
2167 revoked 77/2127
2168 revoked 77/344
2170 amended 87/180
2171 revoked 75/492
2178 revoked 75/1090
2179 revoked 75/1026
2182 amended 76/1753
2185 revoked 85/1218
2188 amended 75/1290
2189 revoked 77/796
2191 amended 80/177
2192 amended 75/458; 75/566; 75/1747; 76/1069
2203 revoked 76/87
2204 revoked 78/796
2206 revoked 75/571
2208 revoked 81/1184
2211 amended 77/361; 84/1182; 86/2062
2227 amended 87/1032

1975

1 revoked 75/1883
3 amended 76/1240
5 amended 81/295; revoked 88/1951
8 revoked 75/626
9 amended 75/2247
10 revoked 76/1396
11 revoked 78/809
18 revoked 75/2246
20 revoked 75/1648
26 amended 75/207
30 revoked 77/1164
33 revoked 83/713
34 amended 76/562
35 amended 76/562
36 revoked 82/1478
38 revoked 75/1244
42 revoked 75/1824
49 revoked 80/1854
51 amended 76/157
55 amended 77/1074
56 revoked 77/1970
59 revoked 86/1713
62 amended 80/1253
64 revoked 78/30
66 amended 75/2248; 80/98
67 amended 75/2248
70 amended 75/2212
73 amended 75/1300; 77/568
74 amended 75/1147; 77/567
75 revoked 75/492
79 amended 76/83
91 amended 81/44
92 revoked 83/1188
95 revoked 78/32
96 amended 76/176

1975—cont.

98 revoked 77/1360
99 revoked 75/2097
105 amended 76/84
106 amended 76/108
107 amended 76/33
108 amended 76/148
110 amended 76/1175
112 revoked 83/425
113 revoked 75/1714
116 amended 75/2062; 79/1519; 81/399
122 revoked 75/1184
125 revoked 75/559
126 revoked 81/552
127 revoked 81/553
133 revoked 84/39
134 amended 76/313
135 revoked 87/2266
136 amended 77/1146
137 revoked 75/965
140 revoked 75/373
142 revoked 80/623
143 revoked 77/1284
149 revoked 78/796
154 revoked 78/1875
158 amended 75/1209; 76/216; 81/1109
159 revoked 79/912
160 revoked 76/1782
166 revoked 75/715
176 amended 83/1480
177 amended 76/457
179 revoked 75/1230
180 revoked 75/1229
181 revoked 76/106
183 revoked 79/991
186 revoked 78/1017
197 amended 81/147
203 amended 75/346; 77/944; 87/233
205 amended 76/353; 77/2001; 78/1717; 79/1555; 80/1750; 81/1831; 83/351; 84/309; 85/343; 86/620; 87/392; 88/449
207 revoked 75/2094
208 revoked 75/603
209 revoked 75/602
210 revoked 75/601
211 revoked 79/1470
218 revoked 75/1357
219 revoked 75/528
224 revoked 77/1097
225 amended 76/1520; 78/91; 79/240; 80/358; 81/1571; 82/283
229 revoked 86/1319
238 revoked 78/1017
239 revoked 84/812
241 revoked 75/1247
244 amended 75/944; 76/315; 76/850
245 amended 75/1736; 78/1262; revoked 84/812
253 amended 75/1149
255 revoked 75/1685
263 revoked 75/1744
265 amended 75/1696
266 revoked 83/1740
267 amended 75/1562; revoked 86/178
269 revoked 76/1073
276 revoked 76/1987
277 revoked 75/1227
278 revoked 75/1226
279 revoked 75/1243
280 revoked 75/1558
281 revoked 81/404

1975—*cont.*

282 amended 76/1247; revoked 84/1114
287 revoked 77/508
292 revoked 78/861
296 revoked 75/1629
297 revoked 86/1713
299 amended 77/1820; 81/105; 84/793; 86/1322
301 revoked 81/553
304 revoked 75/1118
305 revoked 75/1116
308 amended 76/1240; 77/206; 83/1008; revoked 88/1550
310 amended 76/418
311 amended 75/1619
312 revoked 77/1711
317 amended 76/564
318 amended 76/240
323 revoked 75/2096
325 amended 76/273
327 revoked 78/1504
330 amended 75/471; 76/432; 77/252; 77/313; 77/498; 78/1598; 78/1873; 81/567
335 amended 76/1246
340 revoked 83/1206
341 revoked 76/346
343 revoked 76/1242
345 amended 83/249
347 revoked 75/1325
357 revoked 78/17
359 amended 76/270
360 revoked 87/1135
362 revoked 75/2051
363 revoked 75/1288
364 amended 75/984; 82/203; 82/1288
365 revoked 75/1641
366 revoked 76/347
368 revoked 81/899
369 revoked 79/1333
371 revoked 75/1262
372 amended 75/890; 75/1440
381 amended 75/1725
382 revoked 78/222
383 amended 76/155
388 revoked 75/1454
389 revoked 75/2050
390 revoked 75/1778
392 revoked 76/585
403 revoked 84/140
404 revoked 81/1596
411 amended 75/1209
415 amended 76/225; 88/591
416 revoked 78/1906
423 amended 78/279; 82/1423
425 amended 80/1529
429 revoked 76/1783
431 revoked 79/1715
432 revoked 75/2194
458 amended 75/2126; 77/343
465 revoked 76/474
467 amended 80/1714; 83/1738; 84/303
468 revoked 79/676
469 amended 83/186; 88/553
470 amended 83/186; 88/553
472 revoked 75/1628
473 revoked 88/110
476 revoked 83/1820
485 revoked 77/777
488 amended 79/1561; 80/1584
490 revoked 75/1828
492 revoked 79/591

1975—*cont.*

493 amended 75/1058; 84/1303; 88/269
494 amended 75/1058; 84/1303
496 revoked 75/598
497 amended 77/342
498 revoked 77/1379
499 amended 75/1623; 77/1380; 83/788; revoked 85/2066
508 revoked 75/1530
511 revoked 76/332
513 revoked 82/1489
514 amended 75/1139; revoked 83/136
515 amended 77/342; 85/1327
516 revoked 75/528
517 revoked 76/128
518 revoked 81/552
519 revoked 81/500
520 amended 81/1221; 81/1323
521 revoked 76/1076
528 revoked 78/1698
529 amended 75/1058; 84/1303
530 amended 80/1408; revoked 88/529
531 revoked 76/615
532 revoked 83/550
536 amended 78/1344; 79/1385; 81/1631; 85/300; 86/302; 87/258; 88/310
538 amended 80/1708
539 amended 78/1509; 79/1405; 84/969; 86/267
541 revoked 78/495
544 revoked 76/1983
546 revoked 77/523
547 revoked 85/1272
548 amended 81/1522
550 revoked 81/1499
551 revoked 75/1244
553 amended 77/343; 77/1509; 81/1157; 87/416
554 revoked 79/597
555 amended 75/1058; 77/342; 77/956; 77/1693; 79/223; 83/186; 84/1303; 84/1699; 87/31; 87/1683
556 amended 76/409; 76/533; 76/1736; 77/788; 78/409; 81/1501; 82/96; 83/197; 83/463; 83/1610; 85/1398; 87/414; 87/681; 88/516; 88/1230; 88/1439; 88/1545
557 amended 78/393; 78/1123
558 amended 75/1058; 76/409; 79/1163; 80/1561; 80/1622; 82/138; revoked 84/451
559 revoked 82/1408
560 revoked 79/628
562 amended 78/508
563 amended 75/1058; 75/1573; 76/409; 77/342; 77/1679; 79/463; 79/1278; 79/1432; 80/1505; 81/1157; 83/186; 83/1738; 85/1571; 86/486; 86/1545; 86/1561; 88/435
564 amended 75/1058; 76/328; 76/533; 76/677; 76/1245; 77/342; 77/343; 77/1362; 77/1509; 78/394; 78/608; 78/1123; 78/1213; 79/934; 79/940; 79/1299; 80/1505; 81/1501; 81/1510; 82/96; 82/1105; 82/1345; 82/1492; 83/463; 83/1598; 84/1303
565 amended 76/533; 77/342; 82/1398
566 amended 75/1747; 76/1003; 79/642; 79/643
570 revoked 77/4
571 revoked 77/501
572 revoked 84/451
576 revoked 75/1532
579 revoked 75/1423
593 revoked 76/117

STATUTORY INSTRUMENTS AFFECTED 1947–1988

594 amended 80/642; 80/744
595 revoked 80/641
596 revoked 80/1749
597 amended 80/1784; revoked 84/682
598 amended 77/342; 77/1361; 77/1679; 79/375;
79/1684; 80/1136; 80/1622; 82/38;
83/1015; 83/1137; 83/1741; 84/451;
87/1426; 88/531
601 revoked 75/1857
602 revoked 75/1856
603 revoked 75/1858
604 revoked 76/1904
605 amended 76/593
606 revoked 76/1902
608 revoked 80/28
609 revoked 79/648
615 amended 75/1081; 75/1674
616 revoked 75/2204
622 revoked 88/1082
624 revoked 77/1795
625 revoked 75/1824
626 amended 75/2247
630 revoked 85/1531
632 amended 82/231
634 amended 75/1684; revoked 88/459
637 amended 75/1539; 77/672; 78/152; 78/1926;
83/1028
638 amended 77/1360; 78/425; 78/1378; 80/198;
80/342; 81/1892; 82/1303; 83/1421;
revoked 87/1850
640 revoked 87/309
641 revoked 78/1017
642 revoked 76/316
649 amended 75/2158; 78/273
650 amended 79/235; 79/1597; 80/2051
652 amended 79/227; 79/1597; 80/2050; 82/51;
82/1843; 83/1843; revoked 85/246
653 amended 76/456; 77/1862
654 revoked 76/882
655 amended 76/406
659 amended 77/277
660 revoked 82/329
662 revoked 88/133
663 revoked 85/267
664 revoked 80/148
665 revoked 76/1924
666 amended 76/616
670 amended 76/1903; 80/1127; 81/1; 84/246;
88/1028
671 revoked 76/1921
674 amended 75/1940; 77/40
675 revoked 76/1081
677 revoked 81/829
678 amended 75/1746
679 amended 76/693; 76/1307
680 amended 76/563
685 revoked 76/874
686 amended 75/1941; 77/119; 77/1776;
78/1816; 78/1879; 79/1562; 81/172;
81/333; 82/115; 83/579; 84/691; 85/395;
87/1381; 88/372
694 revoked 82/89
695 revoked 80/1674
696 amended 76/733
697 amended 76/66; 81/760; 85/866
698 amended 76/66; 81/761; 85/866; 88/1448
703 amended 76/211
711 revoked 76/1135
712 revoked 77/770

713 revoked 75/1083
714 amended 79/1388
715 revoked 75/1245
717 amended 82/1553; 83/717; 84/520 revoked
87/307
718 revoked 80/1503
719 amended 76/690; 85/1053; revoked 87/401
720 revoked 85/980
722 amended 76/683
726 revoked 84/2
727 revoked 85/226
728 amended 76/381; 76/950
729 revoked 77/2066
734 amended 75/1864; 83/264
739 revoked 77/1309
740 revoked 77/2102
741 revoked 85/616
745 revoked 77/1796
746 revoked 76/128
747 amended 75/1434
750 revoked 81/572
757 revoked 76/1076
778 revoked 75/1776
784 amended 76/864
785 amended 76/643
788 amended 76/1922; 80/1161; 81/59; 84/469;
88/1051
789 revoked 86/965
791 revoked 80/1672
802 revoked 88/1082
803 revoked 77/1237
804 revoked 77/1238
806 revoked 76/215
807 revoked 78/783
808 amended 75/1832; 76/422; 78/783
812 amended 87/935; 88/591
813 revoked 76/225
816 amended 81/226
824 amended 75/1055
825 amended 84/1652
826 amended 76/610
828 revoked 84/1494
829 amended 82/232; 83/282
835 revoked 87/430
836 revoked 87/430
837 amended 86/1911; revoked 88/110
850 amended 77/111; 78/205; 79/338; 79/1770;
80/1133; 83/548
855 amended 75/1867; revoked 88/667
856 amended 75/1866; revoked 88/666
864 revoked 76/1170
865 revoked 76/1172
868 revoked 75/1614
869 revoked 77/85
872 revoked 77/1360
873 revoked 86/1713
879 revoked 77/586
880 revoked 80/1437
881 amended 75/1586
882 revoked 75/2231
888 revoked 87/790
889 revoked 87/790
890 revoked 84/1989
891 revoked 78/216
896 revoked 78/1266
898 revoked 84/421
901 amended 75/1862
902 amended 75/1863
908 revoked 75/1517

STATUTORY INSTRUMENTS AFFECTED 1947–1988

909 amended 76/271
910 amended 76/1314
912 amended 76/644
914 amended 75/1608
915 revoked 79/1470
916 amended 77/814; 78/1797
917 amended 77/813; 78/1798
918 revoked 82/648
919 revoked 82/648
920 revoked 77/1113
928 revoked 86/26
929 revoked 81/1654
931 revoked 77/1360
933 amended 75/1361
940 revoked 78/1096
944 amended 76/315
947 revoked 75/1530
949 revoked 76/260
954 revoked 76/346
956 revoked 76/1400
958 revoked 84/451
959 revoked 78/722
967 amended 79/1457
972 amended 75/1320; 75/1529
975 amended 76/719
976 revoked 75/1943
981 revoked 76/332
983 revoked 76/1073
984 revoked 82/203
989 revoked 75/1111
991 revoked 76/1446
993 revoked 80/1106
998 revoked 81/1295
1002 revoked 78/1759
1003 amended 75/1005; 76/719
1004 revoked 75/1943
1005 amended 75/1066; 76/719
1009 revoked 76/468
1018 amended 76/774
1019 amended 76/862
1020 amended 76/947
1021 revoked 78/216
1023 amended 86/1249; 86/2268
1024 amended 79/1013; 88/815
1025 revoked 76/986
1026 revoked 77/2069
1032 revoked 82/1467
1036 amended 76/1039; 77/48; 77/826; 79/1450; 83/416
1037 revoked 82/1526
1038 amended 81/435
1042 revoked 76/1044
1046 revoked 80/637
1051 revoked 78/32
1054 amended 75/1929; 76/1191; 77/887; 81/1086; 82/106; 83/74; revoked 86/541
1058 amended 76/409; 76/615; 76/1245; 77/342; 77/343; 77/1312; 77/1362; 78/1123; 78/1340; 78/1698; 79/359; 79/597; 79/628; 79/642; 79/1278; 80/1505; 81/1510; 82/1408; 82/1492; 83/1587; 83/1683; 84/451; revoked 84/1303
1060 amended 76/1089
1062 revoked 75/1943
1064 revoked 75/1744
1065 amended 75/1266
1067 revoked 75/2094
1069 amended 76/1140
1070 amended 76/948

1071 amended 75/1873; 83/684
1074 revoked 76/1268
1075 revoked 78/1
1077 revoked 86/1713
1080 revoked 76/332
1081 amended 75/1674
1083 revoked 76/1269
1086 revoked 79/1456
1087 amended 77/1149; 80/952; 88/1273
1090 amended 75/2066; 77/406
1091 amended 75/2068; 77/408
1092 amended 81/1088
1096 amended 76/1029
1097 amended 76/1030
1098 revoked 85/542
1099 revoked 81/1838
1100 revoked 81/1836
1101 revoked 77/1103
1103 amended 76/1078
1104 amended 76/1049
1107 revoked 76/1069
1109 revoked 77/2047
1121 amended 79/1248
1126 revoked 80/969
1130 revoked 76/1977
1132 amended 76/684; 78/1882; 79/655
1135 amended 76/475; 82/56; 82/1735; 87/290
1137 revoked 84/539
1138 revoked 82/1489
1139 revoked 83/136
1153 revoked 82/137
1161 amended 77/1201
1163 revoked 77/1074
1166 amended 76/409; 79/628; 79/642; revoked 84/1303
1167 amended 76/1048
1168 amended 76/949
1170 amended 78/558
1171 revoked 75/1865
1173 revoked 80/1058
1177 revoked 84/1316
1178 amended 78/1080; revoked 84/1316
1179 amended 78/1080; 81/1780; revoked 84/1316
1180 revoked 86/1713
1183 revoked 87/376
1184 revoked 77/1437
1185 revoked 76/128
1188 revoked 80/1120
1189 amended 76/836; 81/358
1190 revoked 84/602
1191 revoked 84/601
1192 revoked 84/603
1193 revoked 84/599
1196 amended 77/1331
1198 amended 77/1443; 79/1552
1204 amended 81/1385; 84/329
1205 revoked 79/1639
1207 revoked 77/1307
1208 amended 80/1095; 85/459
1211 revoked 88/1842
1212 revoked 78/1906
1225 revoked 77/1308
1226 revoked 76/824
1227 revoked 76/824
1228 revoked 78/998
1229 revoked 75/1663
1230 revoked 75/1664
1234 revoked 77/85

1975—*cont.*

1235 revoked 76/1984
1236 revoked 76/1984
1240 revoked 78/1699
1241 revoked 88/1647
1243 revoked 76/873
1244 revoked 76/1929
1245 revoked 75/1954
1253 amended 75/1399
1254 revoked 87/1537
1256 revoked 76/1202
1260 revoked 77/320
1261 revoked 78/252
1262 revoked 78/216
1263 revoked 83/569
1265 revoked 78/861
1266 revoked 75/1744
1267 revoked 75/1943
1274 revoked 76/1926
1275 revoked 75/2204
1280 amended 87/1937
1284 revoked 76/1227
1286 revoked 76/1073
1291 revoked 77/1291
1292 amended 80/362
1293 revoked 76/1170
1294 revoked 76/1171
1295 revoked 76/1172
1297 revoked 76/128
1299 revoked 81/1752
1305 revoked 76/1985
1308 amended 78/1041
1309 revoked 79/294
1313 amended 83/1599; 88/1667
1314 revoked 85/372
1315 revoked 85/358
1316 revoked 76/1333
1319 amended 77/1638; 80/8; revoked 87/1538
1320 amended 75/1529
1322 amended 76/1288; 77/1310; 78/1011; 79/1041; 80/1109; 81/1162
1324 revoked 79/1470
1325 revoked 76/1659
1326 amended 79/1760
1328 revoked 78/1243
1329 amended 77/106; 79/434; 80/1032; 81/63
1331 revoked 80/1771
1332 revoked 78/1875
1333 revoked 78/1875
1334 revoked 78/1875
1335 revoked 77/1141
1337 revoked 83/893
1341 revoked 81/931
1343 revoked 80/821
1344 amended 76/1363; 78/1298; 80/820; 81/861
1346 revoked 80/819
1348 revoked 75/1665
1350 revoked 80/2007
1351 revoked 80/2008
1352 revoked 77/1360
1357 revoked 77/344
1358 revoked 80/1630
1360 revoked 80/1437
1362 amended 76/924
1366 amended 76/1208; revoked 87/603
1372 revoked 80/1793
1376 revoked 80/1177
1379 amended 76/293; 83/1287
1381 revoked 76/1807
1385 amended 84/713

1975—*cont.*

1386 revoked 82/448
1393 revoked 78/693
1394 revoked 79/318
1401 revoked 81/812
1402 revoked 81/813
1405 amended 77/1318
1416 revoked 76/824
1417 revoked 76/824
1419 amended 76/1141
1420 amended 76/1183
1421 revoked 76/1242
1432 revoked 77/1796
1433 amended 78/807
1434 amended 75/1936
1437 amended 76/1050
1440 revoked 78/1151
1442 amended 80/1205
1446 revoked 77/1694
1447 revoked 77/1691
1450 revoked 78/1504
1463 revoked 75/1953
1464 revoked 76/873
1465 revoked 76/1322
1466 revoked 76/1323
1467 revoked 78/1093
1471 revoked 76/1076
1473 amended 79/1535
1475 revoked 79/221
1484 revoked 84/1304
1485 amended 76/509; 80/1834; revoked 84/1305
1486 revoked 80/1833
1487 revoked 79/752
1491 revoked 80/1009
1494 revoked 84/812
1495 revoked 77/501
1498 revoked 77/1711
1499 revoked 75/1954
1503 amended 75/1504; 76/1042; 76/1043; 77/2151; 77/2156; 78/1042; 79/396
1504 amended 76/427; 76/1041; 77/2156; 81/234; 82/1504
1510 revoked 78/783
1511 revoked 78/783
1513 revoked 79/720
1515 revoked 75/1783
1518 revoked 76/585
1526 revoked 79/186
1527 revoked 84/485
1528 amended 76/237
1532 revoked 78/1120
1536 revoked 81/859
1537 revoked 80/377
1543 revoked 84/918
1558 revoked 77/915
1562 revoked 86/178
1569 amended 76/376
1573 amended 76/409; 77/342; 77/1679; 79/172; 79/597; 80/1622; 81/1817; 82/1241; 82/1408; 83/1186; 83/1186; 84/451; 84/458; 86/1541; 86/2217; 87/491; 87/1968
1583 revoked 76/1171
1594 revoked 84/1518
1596 amended 76/946; 84/1519
1597 revoked 80/1888
1598 revoked 79/1073
1607 revoked 80/1685
1612 revoked 77/1725
1613 revoked 76/1032

1975—*cont.*

1614 revoked 76/1031
1615 revoked 76/1031
1618 revoked 75/1904
1619 amended 76/402
1623 revoked 83/788
1628 revoked 76/1670
1631 revoked 77/1437
1643 revoked 82/448
1646 revoked 77/290
1647 amended 82/53; 88/2111
1656 revoked 76/1255
1657 revoked 76/1254
1658 revoked 76/1253
1659 revoked 76/1252
1663 revoked 76/1272
1664 revoked 77/2045
1673 revoked 76/1396
1684 revoked 88/459
1686 revoked 77/25
1687 amended 75/1946; revoked 88/551
1688 revoked 80/1503
1689 amended 77/1485; 77/2038
1692 revoked 78/600
1694 revoked 79/774
1696 amended 76/1461
1697 revoked 77/1307
1702 revoked 78/1875
1703 revoked 84/1148
1704 amended 80/1075
1706 amended 76/52; 77/423; revoked 85/444
1708 revoked 78/454
1709 revoked 79/304
1713 revoked 80/637
1715 amended 75/1988; revoked 88/546
1716 revoked 80/1674
1718 amended 87/256
1721 revoked 75/1954
1722 amended 82/91
1724 revoked 76/1756
1725 amended 76/1755
1730 revoked 76/1076
1731 revoked 77/1309
1732 revoked 76/2062
1736 revoked 75/1830
1740 revoked 76/410
1744 revoked 75/2073; 75/2203; 76/125; 76/370; 76/912; 76/1012; 76/1017; 76/1382; 76/1677; 76/1687; 76/2019; 77/616; 77/713
1747 amended 75/1860; 76/1170
1748 amended 76/409
1756 amended 83/78
1758 revoked 76/260
1759 revoked 77/85
1763 amended 88/2000
1764 revoked 81/500
1771 amended 83/1818
1781 revoked 80/1216
1782 revoked 80/1120
1789 revoked 79/207
1790 revoked 79/1240
1791 revoked 77/971
1800 amended 83/263
1803 amended 78/751; 79/106; 80/1858; 81/1589; 82/123; 82/787; 83/290; 84/285; 86/1142; 86/2115; revoked 87/821
1808 revoked 77/1891
1809 revoked 77/1892
1828 amended 80/1987

1975—*cont.*

1829 revoked 79/1694
1831 revoked 88/1084
1832 revoked 78/783
1836 revoked 76/1783
1837 revoked 79/1715
1839 revoked 82/1085
1842 revoked 87/1758
1844 revoked 79/1470
1845 amended 75/2112
1846 revoked 76/1983
1848 revoked 77/72
1849 revoked 77/73
1850 revoked 77/71
1855 revoked 79/591
1856 revoked 76/233
1857 revoked 76/234
1858 revoked 76/235
1859 amended 76/1175
1866 revoked 88/666
1867 revoked 88/667
1868 revoked 80/558
1869 revoked 78/1759
1873 amended 79/1224
1874 amended 79/1257; 81/505
1884 amended 79/395
1885 amended 79/1751
1894 revoked 85/1661
1900 revoked 77/1097
1902 amended 80/1860
1904 revoked 77/1075
1905 revoked 77/1074
1925 amended 76/308
1927 amended 77/1618; 78/250, 78/1827; revoked 84/380
1929 amended 76/1191; 81/1086; revoked 83/74
1941 revoked 77/1776
1943 revoked 77/921
1945 revoked 78/950
1946 revoked 88/551
1947 revoked 76/1171
1948 revoked 76/1172
1953 amended 76/97
1954 revoked 76/511
1956 revoked 76/1982
1960 amended 80/1135; 84/1857; 85/351; 86/1240; 88/636
1962 revoked 81/1087
1964 revoked 80/1861
1968 revoked 77/1437
1972 revoked 80/70
1975 revoked 88/187
1976 revoked 76/375
1977 amended 76/251; 76/588
1978 amended 76/719; 76/912; 76/976
1984 revoked 77/107
1987 revoked 79/705
1988 revoked 88/546
1992 revoked 86/260
1993 amended 77/843
1994 amended 86/1713
1995 revoked 77/851
1996 revoked 80/6
1997 revoked 80/1866
1998 revoked 76/125
2000 amended 76/1643; 87/897
2002 revoked 77/85
2004 revoked 77/1796
2005 revoked 77/1796
2006 revoked 77/1796

STATUTORY INSTRUMENTS AFFECTED 1947–1988

1975—*cont.*
2007 revoked 77/1796
2008 revoked 76/128
2009 revoked 76/128
2010 revoked 76/128
2011 revoked 76/128
2012 revoked 76/128
2013 revoked 76/128
2016 revoked 77/4
2017 revoked 76/1204
2020 revoked 76/1268
2027 amended 75/2238; 76/173
2029 revoked 86/180
2030 revoked 86/179
2031 revoked 86/259
2037 revoked 76/1076
2047 revoked 76/260
2048 amended 77/844
2054 revoked 87/1915
2056 amended 77/616; 77/1046
2057 amended 77/838
2058 revoked 76/976
2063 amended 78/1763
2067 revoked 77/2069
2069 amended 77/255; revoked 87/1529
2070 revoked 76/1073
2071 revoked 78/554
2072 amended 76/1786
2073 amended 75/2203
2074 amended 77/616
2077 revoked 77/1093
2079 amended 76/1173
2080 revoked 77/104
2081 amended 76/868; 76/1862
2082 revoked 77/2047
2085 amended 83/1941
2093 revoked 77/1499
2094 amended 77/616; 77/713
2095 revoked 77/921
2098 revoked 77/1094
2099 revoked 77/1095
2100 revoked 77/1081
2101 amended 76/143; 77/1188; 78/250; 78/1089; 81/129; 83/338; 84/107; revoked 84/380
2113 revoked 80/1860
2115 revoked 84/1992
2119 amended 76/851; revoked 83/713
2124 amended 79/796; 86/1016
2125 amended 88/1128
2126 amended 77/343
2129 amended 75/2238
2136 revoked 87/862
2137 revoked 87/862
2138 revoked 87/863
2139 revoked 76/1135
2140 revoked 77/770
2157 revoked 80/182
2158 revoked 78/273
2160 revoked 81/1106
2161 revoked 76/215
2164 amended 81/214
2165 amended 81/215
2166 amended 81/217
2167 amended 81/218
2169 amended 81/220; revoked 85/1197
2170 amended 81/221
2171 amended 81/222; 84/543
2175 amended 81/216
2176 revoked 78/1906
2178 revoked 81/155

1975—*cont.*
2179 revoked 77/2157
2181 amended 77/1242
2182 revoked 81/225
2183 revoked 81/1111
2184 revoked 81/434
2185 revoked 81/224
2186 revoked 81/433
2192 amended 78/185; 80/1967; 83/612
2193 revoked 79/1715
2194 revoked 77/430
2196 revoked 80/1624
2198 revoked 81/500
2204 revoked 77/1759
2208 revoked 76/1171
2209 revoked 76/1172
2210 revoked 79/1748
2221 revoked 87/177
2222 revoked 87/2224
2223 amended 77/2122; 79/1669; 83/1883; 87/2225
2225 revoked 87/1758
2232 amended 78/1464; revoked 85/62
2233 amended 79/1597; 81/1046; 83/862; revoked 86/411
2239 revoked 77/921
2241 revoked 80/377

1976
1 revoked 79/591
11 amended 78/27
16 revoked 77/501
17 revoked 78/1759
19 amended 77/148
26 revoked 78/1303
29 amended 76/850; 76/890; revoked 83/713
30 amended 77/1584; revoked 83/62
32 revoked 78/32
42 revoked 78/1614
46 revoked 80/1667
51 revoked 85/1983
53 amended 81/219
55 revoked 88/247
59 amended 78/1042; 79/1574
60 revoked 87/492
71 revoked 76/1170
72 revoked 76/1172
73 revoked 76/1171
87 revoked 81/1654
88 revoked 79/591
90 amended 76/477; 76/588
91 amended 83/140
97 revoked 76/1929
98 amended 85/2044; 86/2204
106 revoked 77/133
107 revoked 77/134
111 revoked 84/1316
117 amended 85/1383
123 revoked 77/359
124 revoked 77/358
125 amended 76/510; 76/977
128 revoked 77/2092; 78/1064
138 revoked 77/2140
140 revoked 84/614
143 amended 77/1188; 78/250; 81/129; 83/338; revoked 84/380
148 amended 78/27
154 revoked 77/85
172 revoked 88/110
179 revoked 86/1713

716

STATUTORY INSTRUMENTS AFFECTED 1947–1988

717

583 revoked 76/1783
585 amended 76/1167; 77/404; 77/1640; 78/384; 79/1426; 79/270; 79/1232; 80/1102; 80/1103; 80/1950; 81/1143; 81/1678; 82/1047; revoked 83/686
587 revoked 80/1695
589 amended 76/1005
592 revoked 77/1213
595 amended 76/762
597 revoked 77/944
604 amended 76/797; 76/850; revoked 83/713
605 amended 76/850; revoked 83/713
606 revoked 77/345
607 revoked 77/344
612 revoked 79/1121
613 revoked 78/1096
614 revoked 77/1284
615 amended 79/628; 82/699; 84/1303; 87/409
620 revoked 76/1073
623 revoked 77/633
625 revoked 76/2062
628 revoked 80/1894
630 revoked 76/1170
637 revoked 77/763
638 amended 76/1179
639 revoked 76/1271
652 revoked 77/848
656 revoked 77/915
658 amended 76/1170
659 revoked 80/1581
661 revoked 80/884
662 revoked 80/885
666 revoked 78/796
667 amended 77/511
674 amended 76/780
676 revoked 78/1759
677 revoked 83/1598
684 revoked 79/655
687 revoked 80/2007
688 revoked 80/2008
692 revoked 78/1747
693 revoked 81/830
695 revoked 77/1173
702 amended 87/950
708 revoked 80/14
713 revoked 78/390
720 revoked 84/802
726 revoked 81/257
730 amended 81/559; 83/1389; 83/1608; 84/1131; 87/1892
732 amended 77/1185; 85/1884; revoked 88/819
734 revoked 77/1075
738 amended 78/615; 79/258; 79/1761
743 revoked 81/1707
748 amended 76/938; 80/130
766 amended 77/588; 81/208; 84/1149
769 revoked 77/1237
770 revoked 77/1238
772 revoked 84/1165
776 revoked 77/944
791 revoked 82/37
794 revoked 79/1752
797 amended 76/850; revoked 83/713
801 revoked 77/586
818 revoked 78/809
824 revoked 78/1409
838 revoked 79/555
840 amended 77/1489; 78/1108
841 revoked 76/1987

850 amended 76/890; revoked 83/713
851 revoked 83/713
852 revoked 83/713
856 revoked 85/1165
857 revoked 77/85
859 revoked 80/1849
863 amended 85/88
869 revoked 80/6
873 revoked 77/786
874 revoked 88/1484
882 revoked 87/2236
883 revoked 78/554
890 revoked 83/713
891 revoked 80/1216
895 revoked 84/860
896 revoked 84/1166
901 revoked 79/555
905 revoked 86/541
910 revoked 77/1360
911 revoked 85/60
912 amended 76/2014
914 amended 80/1888; 80/1889; 81/137; 82/108; 83/270; 84/1519; 85/1068
929 revoked 82/288
937 revoked 79/1092
938 amended 80/130
940 amended 79/1519; 87/306
944 revoked 76/1080
945 revoked 83/1455
946 amended 76/1176; 80/1889; 81/137; 82/410; 83/270; 85/1068
954 revoked 78/260
960 revoked 76/1586
962 amended 78/540; 80/15; 80/1640; 82/39; 82/1242; revoked 84/451
963 amended 76/1758; 84/458; 84/875; 86/2217; 87/491
964 amended 75/1758; 78/540; 81/1772; 82/1242; 84/458; revoked 84/1960
965 amended 76/1758; 77/534; 78/540; 78/1275; 80/1045; 82/965; 83/3; 84/337; 84/939; 86/2217; 87/357; 87/491; 88/521; 88/1227
974 revoked 87/234
975 revoked 77/1074
976 amended 77/1093
977 revoked 77/1499
978 revoked 78/1
988 revoked 78/1188
1002 amended 81/614
1008 revoked 78/1117
1018 revoked 76/1073
1019 amended 84/419
1120 revoked 84/1314
1026 revoked 83/550
1029 revoked 77/1325
1032 revoked 77/1
1035 amended 79/607
1039 revoked 77/48
1040 amended 77/1251
1041 amended 79/574
1042 amended 81/228; 88/249
1043 amended 77/2156; 79/396; 82/528
1055 revoked 80/850
1061 revoked 76/1326
1062 revoked 78/1686
1068 amended 79/1004; revoked 85/978
1069 revoked 77/1362
1073 amended 82/681; 82/902; 82/1113; 82/1628; 83/317; 83/1354; 84/1651; 85/111;

1976—*cont.*

85/1325; 85/1733; 86/576; 87/423; 87/1914; 88/1501

1075 revoked 77/1309
1076 amended 76/1764; 77/871; 78/697; 78/1109; 79/1412; 80/180; 80/1734
1076 revoked 81/952
1077 revoked 77/1043
1081 amended 79/614; 81/927
1087 revoked 77/1308
1093 revoked 78/32
1098 revoked 77/2049
1099 revoked 87/1781
1100 revoked 77/695
1104 revoked 78/998
1112 amended 79/194
1113 revoked 80/1354
1114 revoked 85/214
1117 revoked 78/1875
1118 revoked 78/1875
1119 revoked 78/948
1124 revoked 76/1660
1125 revoked 76/1661
1129 revoked 82/1000
1133 revoked 80/900
1135 revoked 82/1034
1142 amended 87/2073
1145 revoked 78/1121
1149 revoked 83/1888
1151 revoked 77/46
1156 amended 79/919; 82/1075; 87/1271; 87/1829; revoked 88/247
1158 amended 77/1251
1160 revoked 81/612
1167 revoked 83/686
1170 revoked 77/1272
1171 revoked 77/1281
1172 revoked 77/1281
1176 revoked 81/137
1177 revoked 77/85
1179 amended 77/1073
1190 amended 84/1172
1191 revoked 83/74
1192 revoked 77/915
1197 revoked 77/1779
1200 amended 76/1570
1202 revoked 77/216
1203 revoked 79/1748
1204 revoked 79/797; 79/1383
1206 amended 79/1218
1207 amended 79/1146; 80/992
1208 revoked 87/603
1209 amended 79/693; 81/1168; 83/1727; 85/67
1210 revoked 78/1906
1212 amended 78/1041; 81/839
1215 revoked 77/1295
1217 revoked 78/134
1218 revoked 80/1172
1219 amended 76/2211; 77/742
1221 amended 79/768; 81/1169; 85/1068
1222 revoked 78/1759
1223 amended 78/1725
1226 revoked 88/1546
1234 revoked 77/1759
1237 revoked 82/1464
1240 revoked 88/1550
1242 amended 77/1290; 78/1078; 79/1014; 80/1141; 81/1150; 82/1061
1245 revoked 77/1362
1247 amended 84/1114

1976—*cont.*

1250 revoked 76/1658
1252 revoked 77/1669
1254 revoked 77/1667
1255 revoked 77/1668
1256 revoked 78/1017
1257 revoked 77/1737
1263 amended 86/1045; revoked 87/1941
1265 revoked 79/954
1267 amended 77/1327; 77/1328; 78/914; 79/998; 80/110; 80/1246; 81/1194; 82/1128; 83/1243; 84/1106; 85/1243; 86/1172; 87/1978
1268 revoked 77/935
1269 revoked 77/934
1271 revoked 76/2059
1272 revoked 76/2060
1274 revoked 79/1470
1275 revoked 77/501
1277 revoked 82/1489
1283 revoked 80/899
1284 revoked 79/1715
1288 revoked 77/1310
1289 amended 82/117; 85/124; 85/125
1290 amended 86/1987
1294 revoked 84/1316
1295 revoked 84/1316
1296 revoked 78/741
1297 revoked 77/2059
1300 revoked 87/1941
1307 revoked 81/830
1308 revoked 78/260
1322 revoked 77/1388
1323 revoked 77/1389
1324 revoked 77/440
1326 revoked 78/947
1330 revoked 79/1605
1333 revoked 81/54
1341 revoked 81/155
1362 revoked 87/2024
1363 revoked 81/861
1366 revoked 84/1480
1377 revoked 77/1281
1378 revoked 77/1281
1389 revoked 76/1831
1396 revoked 78/1633
1400 revoked 76/2157
1401 revoked 77/1711
1403 revoked 77/1284
1416 revoked 82/1234
1419 amended 86/443
1420 amended 80/1849
1440 revoked 77/85
1446 revoked 76/2158
1447 amended 78/1878; 78/1938; 86/1493; revoked 87/1421
1450 revoked 80/362
1458 revoked 78/1504
1461 amended 77/1836
1465 revoked 80/223
1466 revoked 80/222
1469 amended 80/1671
1479 revoked 78/1243
1497 revoked 78/260
1507 revoked 78/1017
1517 revoked 80/184
1519 revoked 77/320
1532 revoked 82/1109
1533 revoked 85/831
1541 amended 87/843

1976—*cont.*

1542 amended 84/419
1586 revoked 76/1799
1595 revoked 79/1727
1597 amended 81/1593
1600 revoked 83/587
1604 revoked 78/1875
1606 amended 83/1438
1628 revoked 80/377
1640 revoked 77/1284
1641 revoked 86/1713
1644 amended 78/1518; 79/978; 82/4; revoked 84/265
1645 amended 78/1519; 82/3; revoked 84/265
1658 revoked 76/1975
1659 revoked 77/1069
1660 revoked 76/1798
1661 revoked 76/1800
1670 revoked 77/1359
1674 revoked 80/1070
1676 amended 78/723; 81/1338; 83/195; 85/488; 85/1065
1679 revoked 86/944
1681 revoked 88/459
1682 revoked 77/25
1701 revoked 79/1376
1707 amended 87/256
1709 revoked 77/1164
1726 amended 77/996; 77/2168; 78/41; 78/1140; 81/1791; 83/1729; 85/1558; 85/2008; 88/1009
1736 amended 77/343; 79/597; 79/628; 79/642; 82/1408
1742 revoked 80/1177
1745 revoked 78/1504
1756 revoked 78/1399
1758 amended 84/1960; 86/2217; 87/491
1764 revoked 81/952
1768 amended 79/1222; 81/1842; revoked 84/611
1769 revoked 88/913
1773 revoked 78/273
1776 revoked 77/422
1779 amended 84/358
1780 amended 77/2157; 78/1050; 81/155; 81/608
1781 revoked 77/2156
1782 amended 77/828
1783 revoked 80/1965
1784 revoked 79/1715
1791 revoked 85/81
1796 amended 81/1818; revoked 84/1964
1798 revoked 77/300
1799 revoked 77/302
1800 revoked 77/301
1807 revoked 79/1359
1813 amended 78/127
1818 amended 81/137; 83/270; 85/1068
1821 revoked 80/1503
1823 revoked 88/551
1825 revoked 86/965
1826 revoked 81/535
1830 revoked 77/320
1831 revoked 77/1049
1832 amended 80/1849; 83/1727; 85/67
1840 revoked 79/797; 79/1383
1850 revoked 82/1506
1853 revoked 77/1284
1856 revoked 77/25
1858 revoked 78/1644
1866 revoked 81/1523
1871 amended 77/450

1976—*cont.*

1873 revoked 80/1674
1874 revoked 88/546
1882 revoked 83/1575
1883 amended 83/1703; 85/68
1885 amended 87/546
1886 revoked 80/1833
1890 revoked 78/1832
1894 revoked 88/666
1895 revoked 88/667
1897 amended 82/871
1901 revoked 81/2
1903 revoked 81/1
1904 revoked 78/38
1906 revoked 81/899
1911 revoked 80/1888
1916 revoked 88/591
1921 revoked 78/76
1922 revoked 81/59
1923 revoked 81/58
1925 revoked 78/44
1926 amended 81/20
1929 revoked 78/98
1935 revoked 81/1497
1937 revoked 77/786
1938 amended 77/192
1939 amended 77/1342; 77/2002; 79/337; 80/877; 81/311
1951 revoked 83/1718
1954 amended 78/1065
1955 revoked 88/1546
1956 revoked 77/2030
1959 revoked 78/1747
1961 amended 77/511
1962 revoked 76/2111
1970 revoked 77/1399
1973 revoked 86/1713
1975 revoked 76/2128
1977 revoked 81/1694
1981 revoked 86/1683
1982 revoked 81/57
1983 revoked 81/34
1984 revoked 81/33
1985 revoked 81/31
1986 revoked 81/30
1987 amended 78/422; 78/1422; 78/1512; 79/47; 79/1206; 80/919; 80/1043; 81/934; 82/496; 82/967; 85/1844; 86/2001; 88/387; 88/816; 88/1374; 88/1652
2003 amended 85/1333; 87/37
2012 amended 79/1677; 81/485; 83/1103; 84/600; 86/2001; 87/1635; 88/1355
2013 revoked 77/320
2017 revoked 78/436
2019 amended 79/1101; 80/495; 83/354; 87/346
2021 amended 80/1051
2024 revoked 77/2092; 78/1064
2025 revoked 77/2092; 78/1064
2026 revoked 77/2092; 78/1064
2027 revoked 77/2092; 78/1064
2029 revoked 77/2092; 78/1064
2031 revoked 86/1039
2039 revoked 81/1654
2040 revoked 80/6
2056 revoked 79/1203
2059 revoked 77/859
2060 revoked 77/858
2061 revoked 88/876
2062 revoked 80/615
2063 amended 88/1729

1976—*cont.*

2065 revoked 86/2214
2066 revoked 86/2215
2067 revoked 87/1
2072 revoked 77/1499
2077 amended 77/435; 77/616; 77/713; 77/1087
2080 revoked 87/2088
2081 revoked 87/2088
2084 revoked 77/1437
2085 revoked 78/554
2092 revoked 87/2089
2094 revoked 80/1657
2095 amended 80/1657
2096 amended 77/155; 77/274; 77/653
2100 revoked 88/1167
2105 amended 81/911; revoked 86/2174
2111 revoked 79/1388
2112 revoked 83/1806
2113 amended 77/274
2117 amended 78/1763
2126 amended 81/1709; 83/2126
2128 revoked 79/384
2136 revoked 87/1135
2144 amended 86/2020
2145 amended 79/1603; 82/151
2146 revoked 78/1906
2147 amended   77/2151;   78/1039;   78/1042; 82/528
2149 revoked 83/1126
2150 revoked 82/711
2153 revoked 79/1715
2154 revoked 81/612
2155 revoked 81/1694
2156 amended 79/396
2157 revoked 78/267
2158 revoked 78/360
2159 revoked 78/1727
2162 amended 80/1609; 82/968; 83/909
2163 revoked 79/221
2164 revoked 82/1109
2165 revoked 80/2005
2166 revoked 77/344
2167 revoked 77/345
2177 revoked 77/954
2181 revoked 84/921
2182 amended 83/265
2183 amended 79/259; 84/1301
2186 amended 83/1703; 85/68
2187 revoked 81/1707
2189 revoked 78/54
2199 revoked 80/615
2204 revoked 77/320
2205 revoked 77/2049
2206 amended 77/1722
2207 revoked 77/1272
2208 revoked 77/501
2226 revoked 79/1088
2228 revoked 77/915
2233 revoked 78/1759
2234 revoked 87/821
2235 revoked 87/821
2241 revoked 80/1279
2242 revoked 77/129
2243 revoked 84/1319

1977

  1 revoked 78/31
 *2 revoked 79/797; 79/1383
  4 revoked 78/1579
 10 revoked 77/603

1977

 25 revoked 80/1648
 27 revoked 80/1058
 36 revoked 78/32
 38 revoked 79/1203
 44 revoked 78/1447
 46 revoked 78/177
 48 revoked 77/826
 51 revoked 81/605
 56 revoked 79/1715
 61 revoked 78/1409
 71 revoked 78/113
 72 revoked 81/498
 73 revoked 84/235
 85 revoked 81/912
 87 amended 83/717; 86/1241; 87/1999
 88 amended 83/716; 84/1671; 87/2001
 90 revoked 79/1456
 91 revoked 79/1456
 93 revoked 80/2005
 96 revoked 83/436
 99 revoked 83/1918
104 revoked 78/796
105 revoked 83/435
111 revoked 83/548
113 revoked 79/1694
114 revoked 79/591
119 revoked 77/1776
120 revoked 87/2213
128 revoked 80/1279
129 revoked 80/1279
133 revoked 78/196
134 revoked 78/195
136 revoked 78/211
139 revoked 86/1713
146 revoked 78/294
149 revoked 83/713
150 revoked 83/713
151 revoked 83/713
152 revoked 80/1216
153 revoked 78/1939
154 revoked 79/1017
166 revoked 79/1545
176 amended 79/1638; 80/1936; 81/1821; 83/1; 85/2024; 87/1887
182 revoked 80/477
183 revoked 88/459
184 amended 79/497
192 revoked 77/535
193 revoked 78/98
200 revoked 77/1291
204 amended 86/1782
205 revoked 77/1759
206 revoked 88/1550
208 revoked 87/1757
216 revoked 78/605
218 amended 77/381
228 amended 86/443; revoked 87/349
238 amended 81/303
240 amended 77/1631; revoked 88/243
248 amended 77/709; 84/330; revoked 86/1335
250 revoked 80/377
252 amended 77/632; 78/801; 84/995; revoked 87/1591
255 revoked 87/1529
256 amended 81/109; 88/2161
271 revoked 84/418
278 amended 83/74; revoked 83/1499
279 revoked 78/950
288 revoked 86/697

STATUTORY INSTRUMENTS AFFECTED 1947–1988

289 amended 77/1781; 80/1946; 81/245; 81/246;
81/1569; 83/1615; 85/1011; 86/435;
87/702; 87/765; 88/1272; revoked 88/1813
290 revoked 77/1377
291 revoked 81/1298
295 amended 85/240
300 revoked 77/720
301 revoked 77/721
302 revoked 77/722
311 revoked 77/1711
314 amended 78/245; 79/237; 81/803; 85/510;
revoked 86/1202
320 amended 77/1675; 79/1227; 82/686
322 revoked 77/668
324 revoked 80/1437
326 revoked 80/52
327 revoked 80/51
328 amended 79/661; 79/667
331 amended 84/1046
340 revoked 77/1437
341 revoked 77/343
342 amended 77/343; 77/417; 78/433; 79/597;
79/628; 79/642; 80/377; 82/1408; 84/1303
343 amended 77/620; 77/1509; 78/433; 78/1698;
80/585; 80/827; 80/1580; 83/186;
83/1001; 84/1698; 84/1699; 84/1728;
85/1190; 85/1305; 85/1618; 87/355;
88/436; 88/554; 88/556
344 amended 78/527; 79/400; 80/977; 80/1484;
81/1099; 83/1853; 84/1511; 85/144;
85/1315; 86/634; 88/226
345 revoked 79/399
348 revoked 83/713
349 revoked 83/713
350 revoked 83/713
351 revoked 80/1216
354 revoked 85/1661
358 revoked 78/296
359 revoked 78/295
360 revoked 77/769
377 revoked 78/1188
380 revoked 83/136
402 revoked 82/652
403 revoked 82/1218
404 amended 81/1143; revoked 83/686
407 revoked 77/2069
410 revoked 81/251
416 revoked 82/89
420 revoked 79/125
422 amended 77/820, 1520
423 revoked 85/444
426 amended 81/155
427 amended 82/155
428 amended 85/169; 85/454
429 amended 87/668
432 amended 83/1428
434 amended 78/950; revoked 88/551
440 revoked 80/393
446 revoked 88/666
454 revoked 81/327
455 revoked 84/417
471 amended 79/705; revoked 88/546
477 revoked 81/804
480 revoked 80/393
482 revoked 78/615
484 revoked 79/1203
486 amended 78/931; 79/1023; 81/364; 84/419;
85/1612; 87/129
496 revoked 82/1218

497 revoked 81/912
501 revoked 78/1599
508 revoked 80/370
523 revoked 77/1757
530 revoked 79/1545
531 revoked 79/1545
535 revoked 77/935
543 revoked 79/591
544 revoked 79/591
545 amended 79/1388
548 amended 83/217; 86/1224; revoked 87/363
558 revoked 84/1316
564 amended 86/1277
567 revoked 78/1424
568 revoked 78/1423
569 amended 77/1080
570 revoked 80/299
578 revoked 85/520
579 revoked 85/520
580 revoked 85/518
581 revoked 85/519
582 revoked 79/1470
586 revoked 77/1324
587 revoked 79/218
590 revoked 78/783
597 revoked 81/155
598 amended 77/2157
600 revoked 81/1123
601 amended 81/1122
602 revoked 85/1213
610 amended 77/2156; 79/396; 80/1087
621 revoked 77/1141
627 revoked 77/2049
628 revoked 81/570
632 revoked 87/1591
633 revoked 79/380
634 revoked 87/309
638 revoked 79/591
643 revoked 80/1192
644 revoked 80/1201
647 revoked 78/1633
654 revoked 77/2056
655 amended 81/1323
665 amended 85/1579; 86/435
673 revoked 80/1202
674 amended 84/458
682 revoked 79/838
683 revoked 79/837
691 amended 82/264; 83/1727; 85/67
692 revoked 77/1284
701 revoked 81/404
705 revoked 79/838
706 revoked 79/837
712 revoked 78/260
713 amended 77/1087
716 revoked 80/279
717 amended 77/2185; 86/111; 86/946; revoked
87/374
720 revoked 77/876
721 revoked 77/877
722 revoked 77/878
741 revoked 80/1172
744 revoked 87/613
746 amended 80/1744; 85/1107; 86/294
759 revoked 85/576
769 revoked 77/878
770 revoked 82/1034
771 revoked 82/771
775 revoked 82/673

1977—*cont.*

776 revoked 86/2067
777 revoked 79/1746
781 revoked 78/1286
786 revoked 78/97
789 amended 84/1290
790 revoked 78/1017
791 revoked 78/1017
792 revoked 78/1017
799 amended 79/801
809 revoked 78/1017
817 revoked 80/182
818 revoked 78/273
824 amended 80/1096
826 revoked 79/1450
827 amended 79/289; 81/432; 86/23
830 revoked 79/1715
833 revoked 86/724
835 amended 82/1513
851 revoked 77/2052
853 revoked 80/224
858 revoked 77/2055
859 revoked 77/1441
871 revoked 81/952
876 revoked 77/1656
877 revoked 77/1657
878 revoked 77/1466
879 revoked 79/1203
880 revoked 79/1203
887 revoked 83/74
888 amended 83/1140
889 amended 83/1140
890 amended 83/1140; revoked 87/37
891 amended 77/1264
901 revoked 80/449
910 amended 78/1148; 83/877; 84/1500; revoked 86/2141
911 revoked 80/884
912 revoked 80/885
915 revoked 78/1019
918 revoked 83/219
920 revoked 79/1331
921 amended 77/1058; 77/1315
927 amended 79/1254; 80/1849; 82/1311; 83/1727; 85/67; 86/2299
928 amended 80/1849; 82/1066; 83/1727; 85/67; 86/2299
939 revoked 78/1759
942 revoked 79/503
946 revoked 78/1483
947 revoked 78/1483
948 revoked 84/1943
949 revoked 77/1284
956 amended 83/186; 84/1303
957 revoked 84/2063
958 revoked 78/1875
962 revoked 78/1188
966 revoked 78/260
967 revoked 79/1203
968 revoked 79/1203
971 revoked 84/810
972 revoked 87/2107; 88/1
976 revoked 79/804
982 amended 77/1301; 78/462; 78/1059; 79/462; 79/1659; 83/708; 83/768; 83/769; revoked 86/1892
983 revoked 77/2056
985 amended 78/1638; 79/1404; 81/78; 83/1591; 85/221; 86/424; 87/389
988 revoked 87/1758

1977—*cont.*

989 revoked 78/1485
990 revoked 78/1485
991 revoked 82/1489
992 revoked 83/136
1005 revoked 79/1727
1006 revoked 79/1470
1010 amended 83/708
1015 revoked 78/1689
1016 amended 77/2008
1017 revoked 86/590
1021 revoked 81/199
1026 amended 77/1883; 79/1641; 81/137; 82/1619; 83/270; 85/1068
1027 amended 81/137; 82/1209; 83/270; 85/1068; 87/26
1028 amended 82/18; 83/270; 85/1068
1033 amended 80/488; 80/1863; 82/1359; 83/1510; 83/1702; 85/530; revoked 86/723
1035 revoked 78/260
1043 amended 78/1316; 82/1206; 84/1834; 85/577; revoked 86/882; amended 86/1338
1044 revoked 78/54
1048 revoked 84/451
1049 revoked 78/1010
1054 amended 83/1728
1056 revoked 78/1121
1057 revoked 78/1389
1063 amended 82/1489; revoked 83/136
1067 revoked 83/587
1069 revoked 78/1073
1074 amended 79/638; revoked 84/687
1075 amended 79/639; revoked 84/686
1079 revoked 86/13
1081 revoked 77/2047
1083 revoked 79/503
1084 revoked 79/504
1085 revoked 87/1738
1092 revoked 77/2041
1097 amended 79/215; 80/747; 83/343; 83/898; revoked 85/1820
1102 revoked 78/331
1103 revoked 79/738
1113 revoked 83/1217
1117 revoked 77/2041
1118 amended 77/1680
1119 amended 77/1681
1121 revoked 86/24
1131 amended 84/2029
1132 revoked 78/1875
1133 revoked 78/1875
1134 revoked 79/104
1135 amended 81/980
1139 revoked 78/32
1140 revoked 80/136
1140 amended 81/1549; 85/1279
1142 revoked 80/1579
1143 amended 78/1160; 84/323
1144 amended 78/1161; 84/322
1149 amended 80/952; 85/1050
1150 revoked 78/998
1152 revoked 80/2026
1166 revoked 77/1922
1173 amended 81/747; 83/210; 84/770; revoked 86/862
1174 revoked 81/552
1175 revoked 81/553
1176 revoked 80/298
1179 revoked 80/503

STATUTORY INSTRUMENTS AFFECTED 1947–1988

1977—*cont.*

1180 revoked 85/705
1185 revoked 88/819
1187 revoked 84/614; 87/408
1188 amended 78/250; 81/129; 83/338; 84/107;
    revoked 84/380
1189 revoked 83/713
1190 revoked 78/796
1195 revoked 79/1203
1210 amended 81/108; 84/640; 86/1217; 87/329;
    88/1030
1216 revoked 80/1216
1226 revoked 80/1643
1229 amended 78/743; 84/458
1230 revoked 80/453
1234 revoked 84/1150
1236 revoked 78/1885
1237 revoked 82/146
1238 revoked 82/148
1239 revoked 82/1353
1241 revoked 81/225
1245 amended 78/1039
1250 amended 79/1203
1252 revoked 81/228
1253 amended 78/1042
1254 amended 78/1042
1255 revoked 80/1965
1256 revoked 79/1715
1257 revoked 83/769
1259 revoked 77/1796
1272 revoked 78/1082
1281 revoked 78/1083
1282 revoked 79/229
1284 revoked 78/1480
1286 revoked 78/1680
1288 amended 79/628
1289 revoked 79/781
1291 revoked 77/1756
1292 revoked 79/504
1293 revoked 80/1894
1295 revoked 78/1102
1296 revoked 80/560
1301 amended 79/1659; 83/708; 83/768; 83/769;
    revoked 86/1892
1303 amended 78/594
1304 amended 78/272; 80/124; 80/1394
1307 revoked 78/1097
1308 revoked 78/1098
1309 amended   77/2174;   78/669;   80/1733;
    80/1810;   81/631;   81/1127;   82/1174;
    83/1232; 84/98; 84/1925; 85/832; 86/752;
    86/868; 88/959; 88/1101
1310 revoked 78/1011
1312 revoked 84/1303
1317 revoked 86/262
1319 amended 79/414
1324 revoked 78/1137
1325 revoked 78/912
1330 revoked 79/1751
1332 revoked 84/1316
1333 revoked 84/1316
1335 revoked 84/1315
1336 revoked 78/1699
1341 amended 78/1738; 78/1739; revoked 86/24
1344 revoked 78/260
1345 amended 82/60
1356 revoked 78/998
1359 revoked 78/1190
1360 amended   77/1808;   78/1507;   80/344;

1977—*cont.*

    82/1302;   83/639;   83/1431;   84/2028;
    88/1618
1361 amended 79/628; 79/1684
1362 revoked 78/1123
1367 revoked 79/1545
1368 amended 79/54; revoked 83/1023
1369 revoked 79/1545
1370 revoked 80/1786
1374 revoked 78/1121
1379 amended 84/1144; revoked 86/2331
1380 revoked 85/2066
1388 revoked 83/1206
1389 revoked 83/1204
1400 revoked 79/1088
1401 revoked 78/1017
1402 revoked 78/1832
1409 revoked 78/1097
1411 amended 85/274
1413 amended 85/1802; revoked 86/2128
1437 revoked 81/362
1438 revoked 79/1092
1439 revoked 80/222
1440 revoked 80/223
1441 revoked 77/2054
1443 amended 79/260; 79/5472
1444 amended 79/628
1451 revoked 78/1243
1461 revoked 81/266
1462 amended 77/1737; 80/1787; revoked 84/176
1466 revoked 78/255
1468 revoked 81/1736
1489 amended 78/1108; 80/1130; 84/1592
1491 revoked 83/1374
1492 revoked 80/1648
1493 revoked 80/52
1496 revoked 80/1354
1497 amended 78/1538; revoked 83/1206
1500 revoked 78/1504
1501 revoked 78/1409
1509 amended 79/628; 79/642; 83/1598; 87/416
1517 revoked 79/1135
1519 revoked 78/1
1521 revoked 86/399
1530 revoked 78/1747
1547 revoked 81/57
1548 revoked 81/34
1560 revoked 84/812
1568 revoked 79/504
1576 revoked 78/1399
1577 revoked 81/1339
1584 revoked 83/62
1602 revoked 85/1150
1603 revoked 83/1486
1605 revoked 80/1336; 84/418
1607 revoked 82/1489
1614 amended 78/1312
1615 amended 77/2038; revoked 84/380
1620 revoked 80/1648
1622 amended 79/1520
1624 revoked 78/1759
1627 amended 78/780; revoked 85/1983
1630 revoked 78/1525
1631 revoked 88/243
1635 revoked 88/459
1632 revoked 79/1715
1637 revoked 79/504
1638 revoked 79/504
1639 revoked 78/1017
1640 revoked 83/686

STATUTORY INSTRUMENTS AFFECTED 1947–1988

1977—*cont.*

1647 amended 81/1311
1653 amended 86/465; 86/940
1656 revoked 78/886
1657 revoked 78/887
1662 revoked 79/1203
1667 revoked 80/1181
1668 revoked 80/1180
1669 revoked 80/1188
1672 revoked 86/1713
1679 amended 78/433; 83/186
1683 revoked 87/1538
1687 revoked 80/852
1691 revoked 84/1505
1692 revoked 84/1505
1694 amended 80/267; 80/1875; 81/928; 84/1504
1705 amended 87/256
1706 amended 79/676
1707 revoked 79/676
1708 amended 78/1931; 80/1357; 81/195
1709 revoked 80/1356
1715 revoked 80/1894
1716 revoked 80/477
1717 revoked 80/1630
1721 revoked 86/2061
1724 revoked 78/1425
1727 amended 84/1633
1734 revoked 79/1333
1735 revoked 80/1601
1737 amended 80/637; 82/226; revoked 84/176
1745 amended 78/1795; 78/1917
1751 revoked 78/1480
1753 amended 83/530; 88/1128
1754 revoked 79/1342
1755 revoked 79/591
1756 revoked 80/1809
1757 revoked 78/381
1759 revoked 80/1536
1760 revoked 86/590
1761 revoked 80/1793
1762 revoked 87/382
1774 revoked 84/218
1776 revoked 78/1879
1777 amended 81/1054
1779 revoked 79/904
1781 revoked 77/2085
1786 revoked 77/2092; 78/1064
1787 revoked 77/2092; 78/1064
1788 revoked 77/2092; 78/1064
1789 revoked 77/2092; 78/1064
1790 amended 78/273
1791 revoked 77/2092; 78/1064
1792 revoked 77/2092; 78/1064
1793 revoked 77/2092; 78/1064
1794 revoked 77/1064; 78/2092
1795 revoked 80/442
1796 revoked 81/1741
1797 revoked 77/2092; 78/1064
1804 revoked 83/1372
1805 amended 83/1727; 85/67; 87/2235
1838 revoked 80/79
1845 amended 77/1956; revoked 86/24
1849 revoked 77/2092; 78/1064
1854 revoked 82/1602
1858 amended 85/1975; revoked 87/373
1881 revoked 84/552
1884 revoked 86/1713
1891 revoked 80/242
1892 revoked 79/143
1896 amended 78/211

1977—*cont.*

1905 revoked 78/1485
1906 revoked 78/1485
1908 revoked 78/1483
1909 revoked 78/1483
1911 revoked 83/713
1912 revoked 87/2088
1917 revoked 79/1092
1922 amended 80/1949
1929 revoked 78/516
1932 revoked 88/876
1933 revoked 78/1962
1934 revoked 88/666
1935 revoked 88/667
1939 revoked 81/804
1950 revoked 78/1772
1953 revoked 79/591
1954 revoked 79/792
1956 revoked 86/24
1957 revoked 78/1599
1960 revoked 79/1748
1970 revoked 82/1442
1971 revoked 83/1916
1987 revoked 79/591
1988 revoked 79/1470
1989 revoked 79/1727
1999 revoked 86/975
2000 revoked 78/1752
2001 revoked 78/1717
2010 revoked 80/1414
2021 revoked 79/648
2022 revoked 78/1729
2025 amended 79/1301
2028 revoked 87/2106
2030 revoked 79/706
2033 revoked 78/554
2039 amended 79/1724
2041 revoked 81/1769
2048 amended 78/820
2049 revoked 78/600
2052 amended 79/1301; 83/1761; 83/1769; amended 86/406
2054 revoked 80/48
2055 revoked 80/49
2056 revoked 81/1768
2059 revoked 84/1316
2069 revoked 86/1335
2072 revoked 80/2025
2079 revoked 82/1234
2080 revoked 84/484
2081 revoked 82/815
2086 revoked 79/503
2087 revoked 79/504
2092 revoked 78/1064
2102 revoked 87/374
2103 amended 80/142; 81/1599; 82/1484; 86/1813
2110 revoked 81/806
2112 amended 78/272; 83/641; 85/1310
2121 revoked 87/2224
2127 revoked 80/1921
2129 revoked 80/1922
2132 revoked 80/1923
2133 revoked 80/1924
2136 revoked 87/1135
2138 amended 81/1018
2140 revoked 81/1739
2150 amended 88/591
2154 revoked 82/155
2156 amended 79/1572; 80/1087

725

STATUTORY INSTRUMENTS AFFECTED 1947–1988

1977—*cont.*
2157 amended 78/1042; 78/1050; 79/297; 81/158;
    81/226; 81/227; 81/437; 82/156
2160 revoked 80/1965
2167 revoked 79/45
2171 revoked 79/318
2172 revoked 80/637
2173 amended 78/375; revoked 87/256
2180 amended 79/1694
2182 amended 81/1294
2184 revoked 78/1243
2185 revoked 87/374
2186 revoked 79/495
2189 revoked 80/1756
2196 revoked 80/615

1978
1 amended 78/272; 78/672; 80/127; 82/218
2 amended 80/126; 82/217
11 revoked 81/32
12 revoked 80/1850
21 revoked 82/37
25 revoked 78/1058
26 revoked 79/1342
30 amended 79/61; 80/1652; revoked 83/1863
32 amended 78/934; 79/37; 79/773; 80/25;
    80/955; 81/7; 81/1050; 82/35; 82/947;
    83/32; 83/1071; 84/55; 84/1338; 85/24;
    85/1174; 86/5; 86/1290; 87/74; 87/1447;
    88/224; 88/1453
37 revoked 81/2
38 revoked 80/27
44 revoked 81/21
54 revoked 78/1468
62 revoked 79/1376
68 revoked 78/1747
70 revoked 79/591
75 revoked 81/58
76 revoked 80/143
77 amended 78/598
78 revoked 78/1205
81 revoked 78/1142
82 revoked 78/640
83 revoked 78/1205
84 revoked 78/1205
85 revoked 78/1205
96 revoked 82/1234
97 revoked 81/1019
105 amended 80/1831; 83/1727; 85/67
107 revoked 87/408
109 revoked 78/1142
110 revoked 78/1142
111 revoked 78/1205
113 revoked 79/348
114 revoked 78/1424
115 revoked 78/1423
117 revoked 80/1727
123 amended 78/491; revoked 88/110
124 revoked 80/850
125 revoked 88/110
126 revoked 80/52
134 revoked 87/657
140 revoked 81/34
146 revoked 81/553
147 revoked 81/552
155 revoked 78/1205
171 revoked 88/1951
176 revoked 81/1636
177 revoked 81/419
179 amended 80/1096

1978—*cont.*
181 amended 80/1096
182 amended 83/1676
186 revoked 84/1168
188 revoked 81/612
189 revoked 80/1921
192 revoked 78/1205
193 revoked 78/1142
195 revoked 80/249
196 revoked 79/211
197 revoked 83/435
198 revoked 83/436
199 amended 79/56
205 revoked 83/548
206 revoked 78/1875
207 revoked 78/1875
209 amended 81/792; 83/17; revoked 84/1244
214 revoked 79/586
215 revoked 84/412
216 amended 80/137; 80/1146; 80/1783; 81/72;
    82/717; 86/583
222 amended 80/1596
224 revoked 80/192
228 revoked 79/738
237 revoked 78/1342
241 revoked 78/693
245 revoked 86/1202
246 revoked 78/1142
250 amended 83/338; revoked 84/380
252 revoked 84/1506
255 revoked 78/735
257 amended 84/1300; revoked 87/710
258 amended 84/1308
259 amended 84/1301
260 revoked 81/29
266 revoked 86/24
267 revoked 79/86; 80/574
269 revoked 80/1648
270 revoked 83/219
271 revoked 78/796
273 revoked 80/183
277 amended 78/1034; 78/1895; 81/1671
278 revoked 78/1525
284 revoked 80/1965
286 revoked 79/1434
287 revoked 79/1435
288 amended 78/490; 78/767
289 amended 78/1355; 80/288
293 revoked 79/1092
294 amended 80/316; 82/1101; 85/1092
295 revoked 80/351
297 revoked 80/319
298 revoked 80/319
299 revoked 80/319
300 revoked 80/319
303 revoked 80/321
304 revoked 80/319
306 revoked 80/319
317 revoked 81/362
324 revoked 85/291
327 revoked 79/839
331 amended 82/288; 85/39
339 revoked 78/489
345 amended 79/642; 79/643
360 revoked 79/91; 80/604
372 revoked 81/857
373 revoked 80/370
375 revoked 87/256
381 revoked 85/297
384 amended 81/1143; revoked 83/686

STATUTORY INSTRUMENTS AFFECTED 1947–1988

387 revoked 78/1504
390 revoked 79/770
391 amended 78/393
392 revoked 79/642
393 amended 78/1123; 81/330; 81/1195
394 revoked 83/1598
397 revoked 83/713
407 revoked 87/374
408 amended 78/1368; revoked 87/373
409 amended 79/345
411 revoked 79/318
415 amended 79/385; 80/434; 80/835; 80/1894;
    81/482; 83/506; 85/558; 86/625; 87/1258;
    88/1252
417 revoked 84/265
422 revoked 88/1652
423 revoked 79/591
425 amended 78/1378; 78/1926; 80/198; 80/342;
    81/1892; 82/1303; 83/1421
428 revoked 79/366
430 revoked 80/2026
433 amended 78/1698; 79/597; 79/628
436 amended 81/787; 85/1176; 88/31; 88/1362
438 amended 80/806
439 revoked 82/1109
454 revoked 80/184
457 revoked 81/155
462 revoked 79/1659
463 revoked 84/1318
469 revoked 78/1382
470 revoked 78/1491
475 revoked 87/1850
483 revoked 81/396
484 amended   80/1742;   86/1082;   revoked
    86/1082
491 revoked 88/110
492 amended   80/1886;   83/270;   84/1518;
    85/1068
493 revoked 84/1128
494 revoked 80/1697
495 revoked 80/1697
496 revoked 81/753
505 amended   81/1170;   83/1485;   revoked
    87/1758
507 revoked 79/591
508 amended 81/330; 88/623
516 revoked 78/1790
524 revoked 79/597
528 revoked 87/1914; 87/1850
532 revoked 80/1536
537 revoked 82/263
540 amended 84/451; 84/1960
541 revoked 78/1480
545 revoked 79/384
553 revoked 79/1223
554 amended   78/1799;   79/1599;   80/1892;
    81/1746; 82/175; revoked 83/1784
559 revoked 80/501
564 amended 78/1546; 84/1369; 86/560
569 revoked 80/2008
570 revoked 80/2007
581 revoked 78/1599
597 revoked 85/217
600 revoked 79/798
602 revoked 80/443
605 revoked 80/584
607 revoked 80/1120
608 revoked 83/1598
611 amended 81/364; 84/419; 85/1612; 87/129

622 revoked 87/381
635 revoked 81/1333
641 revoked 81/29
646 revoked 80/1849
652 revoked 86/1713
663 revoked 78/1875
672 revoked 82/218
673 revoked 81/29
683 revoked 80/792
689 revoked 78/1480
691 amended 80/1890
692 revoked 79/875
693 revoked 80/356
697 revoked 81/952
698 amended 79/155
704 revoked 80/2007
705 revoked 80/2008
707 revoked 86/259
708 revoked 80/751
721 revoked 80/6
722 revoked 81/1654
723 revoked 85/1065
733 revoked 81/29
735 revoked 78/1419
741 revoked 84/1316
750 revoked 87/821
756 revoked 79/1331
757 revoked 81/553
758 revoked 81/552
764 amended 79/56
769 amended 80/88; 80/1029; 82/220
772 revoked 79/504
775 revoked 83/1380
780 revoked 85/1983
782 revoked 82/145
788 revoked 79/1388
795 amended 79/491; 84/41
796 amended   78/945;   78/1219;   78/1496;
    78/1812;   79/164;   79/276;   79/1671;
    80/1370;   81/558;   81/925;   81/1206;
    81/1641; 82/153
801 revoked 87/1591
805 revoked 81/1481
809 amended 80/751; 81/822; 83/1475
812 amended 81/980
813 revoked 86/1713
814 revoked 86/1713
817 revoked 83/713
818 revoked 78/1759
821 revoked 79/591
822 revoked 86/24
834 amended 85/43; revoked 88/110
835 revoked 79/34
837 revoked 80/356
838 revoked 81/31
861 revoked 79/1094; 82/1478
869 revoked 88/913
873 revoked 81/57
877 revoked 81/34
881 revoked 87/750
884 revoked 87/133
886 revoked 78/1418
887 revoked 78/1417
890 revoked 81/29
892 revoked 80/1675
893 amended 78/1186; 79/1146; 80/992; 85/252;
    revoked 85/1627
907 revoked 78/1151
922 revoked 79/399

1978—*cont.*

924 revoked 82/1506
927 revoked 81/137
929 revoked 82/1000
930 revoked 81/585
931 revoked 79/1023
934 revoked 83/1071
935 revoked 81/29
939 amended 79/1258
943 revoked 78/1875
944 revoked 78/1875
945 revoked 78/1812
946 revoked 80/1810
947 revoked 82/467
948 amended 82/466
950 amended 79/677; 80/352; 80/987; 80/1503;
    81/307; 82/284; 82/288; 83/309; 84/299;
    85/298; 85/352; 86/976; revoked 88/473
960 revoked 79/586
964 revoked 85/297
965 revoked 80/1647
971 revoked 81/1019
972 revoked 80/1536
975 revoked 80/79
976 revoked 80/80
977 revoked 81/500
979 revoked 87/408
982 revoked 78/1019
986 revoked 87/750
987 revoked 80/1921
988 revoked 80/1924
989 revoked 80/1923
991 revoked 80/884
992 revoked 80/885
998 amended 79/840; 80/988; 81/966; 82/936;
    83/1051; 84/990; revoked 85/1120
1000 revoked 79/781
1001 revoked 79/45
1005 revoked 84/1261
1010 revoked 79/888
1011 revoked 79/1041
1014 amended 79/660; revoked 86/175
1017 amended   78/1233;   78/1234;   78/1235;
    78/1263;   78/1317;   79/843;   79/1062;
    80/139; 80/140; 80/287; 80/610; 80/1166;
    80/1789;   81/261; . 81/915;   81/1189;
    81/1580;   81/1663;   81/1688;   82/1057;
    82/1132;   82/1223;   82/1272;   82/1422;
    82/1480;   82/1576;   83/112;   83/471;
    84/195; 84/331; 84/386; 84/679; 84/813;
    84/1543;   84/1809;   85/91;   85/730;
    85/1363;   85/2039;   85/2051;   revoked
    86/1078
1024 revoked 80/184
1027 amended 78/1521
1030 amended 78/1622
1033 amended 80/1096
1041 amended 81/155
1042 amended 81/226; 82/1534
1043 revoked 81/155
1045 amended 78/1050; 79/924; 79/1573; 81/228
1046 revoked 81/155
1048 amended 81/437; 81/608; 82/1537
1049 amended 81/158; 81/438
1050 amended 81/155
1051 revoked 81/154
1052 amended 78/1896; 82/1531
1053 amended 78/1897
1054 amended 78/1898; 82/154
1055 revoked 81/1113

1978—*cont.*

1058 revoked 88/243
1059 revoked 79/1659
1060 revoked 79/1715
1070 revoked 82/329
1071 revoked 82/1234
1073 revoked 79/823
1081 revoked 84/1316
1083 revoked 79/568
1086 revoked 81/1707
1089 amended 84/380; revoked 84/614
1092 revoked 79/1751
1093 amended 82/1428
1096 amended 79/333; 83/188; 87/1365; 88/1392
1097 revoked 79/889
1098 revoked 79/900
1102 revoked 79/905
1105 amended 80/1096
1106 amended 80/398; 80/1525; 81/1544; 86/220;
    87/2206
1109 revoked 81/952
1110 revoked 80/637
1111 revoked 79/1088
1112 revoked 79/1832
1120 revoked 80/221
1121 amended 79/899; 80/16; 80/1126; 82/1121;
    83/1731; 85/123; 87/1439
1122 amended 79/954
1127 revoked 81/924
1128 revoked 79/1279; 86/887
1129 amended 81/1080; revoked 86/335
1131 amended 82/1629: revoked 87/1968
1133 amended 86/1512; 86/1513; 86/1514
1137 revoked 79/939
1141 revoked 79/837
1142 amended 78/1143; 82/106
1146 revoked 83/1499
1151 revoked 80/96
1157 revoked 86/1458
1158 amended 80/266; 80/2018; 81/1855; 85/615
1159 amended 79/346; 79/1576
1162 revoked 79/1019
1163 revoked 86/923
1166 amended 83/1301
1168 amended 78/1650
1169 revoked 79/1470
1173 revoked 85/193; 85/196
1174 amended 82/697
1175 revoked 85/200
1176 revoked 85/198
1177 revoked 85/199
1178 revoked 85/197
1179 revoked 80/2029
1188 revoked 79/1281
1190 revoked 79/1084
1191 revoked 81/916
1197 revoked 82/234
1205 amended 78/1941
1212 revoked 82/1218
1219 revoked 81/1641
1226 revoked 78/1406
1233 revoked 86/1078
1234 revoked 81/697
1235 revoked 86/1078
1236 revoked 78/1832
1237 revoked 78/1811
1240 revoked 86/1776
1243 amended 79/967; 79/1149; 80/773; 81/898;
    revoked 83/1706
1260 amended 79/1145; revoked 84/812

1978—*cont.*

1261 revoked 84/812
1262 revoked 84/812
1263 revoked 86/1078
1266 revoked 79/1226
1267 amended 85/808
1268 amended 85/807
1273 amended 84/842; 85/1068, 1856; 87/1957
1274 revoked 81/31
1279 revoked 82/207
1280 revoked 78/1939
1285 revoked 83/1206
1294 amended 78/1764
1295 amended 79/1724
1298 revoked 81/861
1304 revoked 81/1654
1307 amended 79/129
1313 amended 80/144; 80/1358; 81/263; 82/1483
1315 revoked 80/1354
1317 revoked 86/1078
1318 revoked 79/1092
1319 revoked 78/1811
1320 revoked 80/222
1321 revoked 80/223
1329 revoked 79/1385
1334 revoked 79/1388
1340 revoked 84/1303
1345 amended 81/990; 83/1696; 85/1661; revoked 86/184
1346 revoked 85/1661
1347 revoked 86/181
1348 revoked 87/256
1354 amended 83/1477; 84/1260; 85/1279
1357 amended 78/1846; 85/243
1364 amended 82/1554; revoked 86/1492
1368 revoked 87/373
1372 amended 85/2047
1378 amended 78/1926; 80/198; 80/432; 81/1892; 82/1303; 83/1421; revoked 87/1850
1379 revoked 80/1809
1387 revoked 80/1398
1389 revoked 80/1121
1391 revoked 81/34
1395 amended 79/490; 82/1406
1399 revoked 79/1307
1400 revoked 80/1261
1404 revoked 78/1525
1405 revoked 78/1525
1409 revoked 80/247
1411 revoked 81/29
1417 revoked 78/1742
1418 revoked 78/1741
1419 revoked 78/1802
1420 amended 82/254; 83/1727; 85/67; 87/1986
1422 revoked 88/1652
1423 amended 80/1553; 82/1167; 86/266; 88/1502
1424 amended 80/1554; 82/1166; 86/255; 88/1503
1425 revoked 79/1155
1426 revoked 83/686
1459 revoked 80/1643
1460 revoked 82/1489
1461 revoked 84/673
1462 revoked 78/1689
1464 revoked 85/62
1467 revoked 85/1665
1468 revoked 79/790
1480 revoked 81/1455
1482 amended 87/1434

1978—*cont.*

1483 amended 81/1412
1485 amended 81/1448
1491 revoked 79/600
1498 revoked 79/604
1504 amended 79/417; 79/1303; 80/1625; 81/1474; 82/1491
1508 revoked 80/1177
1511 revoked 79/597
1512 revoked 88/1652
1518 revoked 84/265
1519 revoked 84/265
1525 amended 78/1902; 79/113; 79/1312; 80/1080; 80/1081; 80/1955; 81/1110; 81/1672; 82/845; 82/1077
1527 amended 82/1527; 83/604; 88/591
1528 amended 85/1640
1537 revoked 83/1206
1538 revoked 83/1206
1543 revoked 81/1747
1545 revoked 80/1780
1564 revoked 82/216
1565 revoked 87/382
1566 revoked 80/1793
1567 revoked 88/459
1568 revoked 88/666
1569 revoked 80/477
1570 revoked 80/1630
1571 revoked 88/667
1574 revoked 81/1694
1578 amended 87/256
1592 revoked 79/586
1593 revoked 81/1768
1599 amended 78/1942; 79/321; 79/740; 79/1194; 79/1338; revoked 84/1459
1600 revoked 81/1135
1616 revoked 80/52
1621 revoked 80/183
1624 amended 78/1894
1627 revoked 80/1965
1631 revoked 81/250
1632 revoked 82/1021
1644 amended 80/1543; 88/1186
1649 revoked 82/1094
1651 revoked 79/504
1652 revoked 79/503
1653 revoked 80/2007
1654 revoked 80/2008
1660 revoked 79/591
1683 revoked 79/1331
1684 amended 81/1623
1696 revoked 79/1632
1689 amended 80/1713; 84/350
1698 amended 79/359; 84/1679; 87/606
1699 revoked 79/894
1702 revoked 81/1059
1703 revoked 79/591
1716 amended 79/364
1717 revoked 79/1555
1723 amended 87/605
1727 amended 85/1176
1738 revoked 86/24
1739 revoked 86/24
1741 revoked 79/616
1742 revoked 79/615
1747 revoked 80/1687
1748 amended 81/8
1752 revoked 79/1550
1755 revoked 81/569
1758 revoked 87/408

1978—*cont.*
1759 amended 80/790; 80/1217; 83/659; 83/1769;
    revoked 83/713
1764 amended 79/1416
1772 revoked 80/1779
1773 revoked 80/247
1778 amended 79/1723
1780 revoked 80/1120
1786 amended 79/1146
1790 revoked 79/384
1794 amended 78/1926; 80/198; 80/342; 81/1892;
    82/1303; 83/1421; revoked 87/1850
1795 revoked 79/1565
1799 revoked 83/1784
1800 amended 87/2020
1801 revoked 80/615
1802 revoked 79/942
1810 revoked 80/222
1811 revoked 79/1092
1812 revoked 81/1641
1813 revoked 80/223
1816 revoked 81/172
1817 amended 79/409
1820 revoked 87/1135
1823 revoked 86/401
1827 amended 84/380
1832 revoked 80/1182
1837 amended 81/800; 82/1155; 84/1907
1840 revoked 79/1694
1842 amended 79/1349
1845 revoked 84/1303
1847 revoked 80/299
1848 revoked 82/655
1855 revoked 79/1388
1866 amended 79/1718
1867 amended 80/2048
1870 revoked 79/1088
1872 revoked 82/1234
1875 revoked 79/1596
1876 revoked 80/1648
1877 revoked 79/591
1878 revoked 86/1493
1879 revoked 80/98
1880 revoked 83/1887
1886 revoked 82/145
1887 revoked 82/146
1888 revoked 82/148
1889 revoked 82/149
1893 amended 84/1982
1910 amended 80/1964; 81/228
1911 amended 84/548
1914 amended 83/770
1917 revoked 80/193
1926 amended 80/198; 80/342; 81/1892; 82/1303;
    83/1421; revoked 87/1850
1927 amended   80/1838;   83/1701;   revoked
    87/1523
1930 revoked 80/1356
1932 revoked 86/1532
1933 amended 79/153; 79/1142
1938 revoked 86/1493
1939 revoked 82/1250
1942 revoked 84/1459
1961 revoked 81/139
1962 amended 88/765

1979

  1 revoked 81/1523
  2 revoked 86/24
  9 revoked 79/591

1979—*cont.*
 12 revoked 79/48
 34 revoked 80/4
 36 revoked 80/1921
 37 revoked 83/1071
 42 revoked 80/615
 45 amended 79/1008; 80/283; 80/1650; 81/793;
    81/1872;   82/1019;   83/274;   83/1156;
    83/1805; 84/349; revoked 84/1861
 51 amended 80/1193; 81/1548; 82/244
 47 revoked 88/1652
 53 revoked 85/724
 54 revoked 83/1023
 60 revoked 79/178
 61 revoked 83/1863
 71 revoked 83/1206
 80 revoked 80/1058
 86 revoked 79/459
 91 revoked 79/411
 94 revoked 81/500
 95 revoked 87/430
 97 amended 79/1519
100 amended 80/75; 81/116
106 revoked 87/821
112 amended 87/457
113 amended 81/1110
135 revoked 82/844
136 revoked 81/1641
138 revoked 86/1078
142 revoked 86/887
143 revoked 80/244
144 revoked 80/241
145 revoked 82/220
146 revoked 81/1736
149 revoked 80/265
154 revoked 80/356
156 revoked 82/216
160 revoked 80/1437
166 revoked 88/459
168 revoked 84/417
169 revoked 84/418
178 revoked 79/568
181 amended 79/510
189 revoked 80/370
191 amended 79/492
193 revoked 79/797; 79/1383
194 amended 80/948
208 revoked 82/612
210 revoked 87/375
211 revoked 80/250
213 revoked 88/2245
214 revoked 87/2244
215 revoked 85/1820
218 amended 80/160; 81/152; 82/219; 83/196;
    84/165; 85/138; revoked 86/416
221 amended 81/669; 83/709; 87/1771; revoked
    88/1567
226 revoked 79/613
231 amended 79/510
232 revoked 79/612
237 revoked 86/1202
238 revoked 85/806
242 revoked 81/365
245 revoked 81/365
253 revoked 83/271
263 revoked 80/1894
264 revoked 80/377
265 revoked 80/377
267 revoked 81/362
268 revoked 83/1206

1979—*cont.*

269 revoked 79/837
270 amended 81/1143; revoked 83/686
276 revoked 81/1641
280 revoked 80/1630
281 revoked 80/477
290 amended 83/1698; 83/1894; 84/125; 88/590
296 amended 81/226
297 amended 81/437
301 amended 88/933
304 revoked 84/1168
305 revoked 86/1305
310 revoked 81/1596
314 revoked 79/1148
315 revoked 80/1922
321 revoked 84/1459
322 revoked 84/198
324 revoked 80/1793
326 revoked 85/2066
333 amended 83/1274
338 revoked 84/137
341 amended 88/1984
342 revoked 84/978
348 revoked 80/388; 84/623
350 revoked 88/666
351 revoked 88/667
358 revoked 79/591
359 amended 79/597
364 amended 79/633; 79/1124; revoked 88/2079
366 revoked 80/480
367 revoked 78/394
378 revoked 79/669
379 amended 80/1319; 83/1058; 87/643
380 revoked 80/502
382 amended 80/263
383 amended 81/137; 82/409; 83/270; 85/1068;
  87/2014
393 revoked 87/1303
398 revoked 80/1657
401 revoked 87/16
406 revoked 87/256
408 revoked 87/1496
409 amended 79/1521; 82/508
410 revoked 82/507
415 amended 81/521; revoked 85/1071
416 revoked 85/1071
423 revoked 82/1218
427 amended 81/1059; 82/1033; 84/1244;
  86/1951
429 revoked 83/735
430 revoked 83/736
431 revoked 83/737
432 amended 79/1441; 84/442; 88/1169
435 amended 80/1070
437 revoked 82/1218
438 revoked 82/1218
439 revoked 81/1694
446 amended 85/821
453 amended 81/211; 81/732; 82/147; 85/1990;
  86/2013; 87/454; 87/2042
462 revoked 79/1659
489 amended 81/1630
514 revoked 83/550
521 amended 88/557
551 revoked 79/1183
553 revoked 88/1167
555 amended 82/1793
557 amended 81/724
565 revoked 81/1260
571 revoked 80/1459

1979—*cont.*

577 revoked 79/1715
586 revoked 80/1990
587 revoked 80/792
588 revoked 84/723
591 amended 79/1483; 80/13; 80/1975; 81/82;
  82/206; 82/1033; 82/1573; 83/10; 83/53;
  83/73; 83/395; 83/496; 83/1689; 83/1691;
  83/1738; 83/1739; 84/77; 84/146;
  84/1756; 85/143; 85/396; 85/397; 85/398;
  85/399; 85/400; 85/1398; 85/1411;
  85/1726; 86/198; 86/485; 87/106; 87/413;
  87/417; 87/1590; 87/2111; 88/299;
  88/674; 88/860; 88/992
592 revoked 86/24
597 amended 80/1927; 82/1172; 83/186;
  84/1303; 88/1446
599 revoked 80/2025
600 revoked 80/49
604 revoked 80/48
607 revoked 81/293
614 revoked 81/927
615 revoked 79/1165
616 revoked 79/1166
628 amended 79/781; 79/1199; 80/1136;
  80/1621; 80/1943; 81/1101; 82/699;
  82/1241; 82/1344; 82/1362; 83/186;
  83/1015; 84/458; 84/550; 84/1303;
  85/600; 85/1250; 86/1561; 86/1772;
  86/2217; 87/416; 87/878; 87/1968
631 revoked 79/798
632 revoked 80/377
638 revoked 84/687
639 revoked 84/686
641 amended 79/1273
642 amended 84/1303; 84/1704; 87/1854
643 amended 81/1627
647 revoked 79/1333
648 revoked 79/1331
656 revoked 87/2213
660 revoked 86/175
668 revoked 87/376
676 amended 85/1417; 87/316; 87/411; 88/429
677 revoked 88/473
680 revoked 79/1275
681 revoked 80/1503
694 revoked 79/1470
700 revoked 80/48
704 revoked 80/1674
705 amended 80/369; 80/1221; 81/359; 82/333;
  83/335; 84/293; 85/354; 85/355; 86/966;
  revoked 88/464 [except reg. 12]
711 revoked 83/1917
721 revoked 81/612
727 revoked 85/1645
738 revoked 81/933
739 revoked 85/213
740 revoked 84/1459
741 revoked 80/1808
742 revoked 80/1808
744 revoked 80/1810
749 revoked 88/1349
751 revoked 80/1383
752 amended 80/731; 82/1382; 83/1727; 85/67
757 amended 83/676; 88/868
758 amended 83/677; 88/869
759 revoked 81/1750
770 revoked 82/142
773 revoked 83/1071
774 revoked 85/979

1979—*cont.*

779 revoked 80/2008
780 revoked 80/2007
781 amended 83/186
785 amended 82/917; 84/846; 86/409
789 revoked 79/1596
790 revoked 80/280
791 revoked 87/632
792 amended 81/1476; 85/1572; 88/970
794 revoked 85/1150
796 amended 79/1437
797 revoked 79/1375
798 revoked 80/270
800 revoked 83/1073
803 revoked 84/812
804 revoked 80/1442
815 revoked 82/608
819 revoked 80/442
823 revoked 80/954
825 revoked 80/850
837 amended 79/1642; 80/1110; revoked 84/1844
840 revoked 85/1120
841 revoked 84/1053
842 revoked 80/279
843 revoked 1078
847 revoked 80/1058
875 revoked 81/476
881 revoked 81/924
883 revoked 85/726
888 revoked 80/901
889 revoked 80/974
897 amended 81/933; revoked 85/213
898 revoked 81/916
900 revoked 80/1111
904 amended 80/992; 82/964
919 amended 82/1075; revoked 88/247
921 amended 82/1528; 87/1831; 88/591
923 revoked 81/155
930 revoked 84/368
934 revoked 83/1598
937 amended 79/1556; 80/1752; 81/1832; 83/352; 84/308; 85/345; 86/622; 87/393; 88/451
939 revoked 79/430
940 revoked 83/1598
941 revoked 79/1748
942 revoked 80/44
949 amended 79/1428
951 revoked 85/588
954 amended 80/1912; 81/1102; 81/1776; 82/1045; 83/1184; revoked 88/538
959 revoked 85/782
967 revoked 83/1706
974 revoked 84/1213
976 revoked 80/789
978 revoked 84/265
991 amended 81/919; 82/1607; 84/1214; 85/1808
992 revoked 80/377
993 revoked 82/1130
996 revoked 83/136
1003 revoked 80/900
1004 revoked 85/978
1005 amended 84/199; 84/1873; revoked 85/977
1008 revoked 84/1861
1019 revoked 80/1499
1023 revoked 80/322
1029 amended 85/92
1038 amended 80/2013

1979—*cont.*

1040 revoked 80/1921
1041 revoked 80/1109
1054 revoked 82/1230
1058 revoked 81/29
1062 revoked 86/1078
1067 revoked 82/1408
1073 amended 80/1232; 81/1320; 82/516; 82/1619; 83/270; 84/1518; 85/1068
1083 revoked 81/29
1084 revoked 80/1301
1088 amended 80/582; 81/126; 81/1732; 82/1479; 83/1602; 85/113; 86/369
1089 revoked 80/1182
1092 amended 80/879; 80/1165; 81/696; 81/1619; 82/8; 83/328; revoked 84/981
1094 revoked 82/578
1099 revoked 80/52
1101 revoked 80/495
1122 revoked 86/724
1127 revoked 81/42
1136 revoked 81/29
1145 revoked 84/812
1146 amended 85/1627; 86/1820
1149 revoked 83/1706
1155 revoked 80/1441
1163 revoked 84/451
1164 revoked 88/459
1165 revoked 79/1742
1166 revoked 79/1743
1168 amended 87/842
1175 revoked 80/1990
1176 amended 81/1296
1182 revoked 80/279
1183 amended 81/319; 83/636; 83/1584
1190 revoked 82/1489
1193 amended 80/967; 80/1197; 81/1236; 82/1232; 82/1416
1194 revoked 84/1459
1198 amended 81/1664; 84/1810; 85/745; 86/313; 87/1327; 87/2161
1204 amended 80/345; 80/346; 81/1381; 83/510; 83/1865
1205 revoked 80/754
1206 amended 88/1652
1215 revoked 81/1694
1216 revoked 79/1470
1220 revoked 81/553
1221 revoked 81/552
1222 revoked 84/611
1223 revoked 82/1034
1226 revoked 80/887
1230 amended 86/1696
1232 revoked 83/686
1240 amended 80/992; 85/404
1254 amended 83/1727; 85/67; 85/912
1259 amended 87/256
1273 revoked 81/29
1274 revoked 81/362
1275 revoked 80/1610
1278 revoked 80/1505
1280 revoked 81/396
1285 revoked 86/1713
1287 amended 87/256
1288 revoked 80/890
1289 revoked 80/49
1290 revoked 80/48
1299 revoked 83/1598
1307 amended 80/1596
1314 amended 81/606; 84/1824

1980

4 revoked 81/1019
5 revoked 81/1654
6 amended 81/1656; 63/1192; 83/1795; 83/1811
7 revoked 80/1922
8 revoked 87/1538
12 amended 84/1326
13 revoked 88/299
14 amended 80/1934; 81/1238; 82/948
15 revoked 84/451
24 revoked 80/1921
25 revoked 83/1071
27 revoked 82/84
28 revoked 82/85
29 revoked 82/83
30 amended 81/55; 82/770; 83/948; 84/1258
35 revoked 80/279
36 amended 83/1727; 85/67
44 revoked 80/1365
45 revoked 81/670
48 amended 80/1175; 80/1295; 80/2022
49 revoked 80/2023
51 amended 85/1192; revoked 85/620
52 amended 80/1361; 81/964; 82/1029; 84/434; 84/917; revoked 85/757
53 amended 80/1359; revoked 85/621
54 amended 80/1360; 83/110; 83/1721; 84/1055; 85/619
55 amended 83/110; 83/1721; 84/1055; 85/619
57 amended 80/2049; 82/186
70 revoked 84/481
73 amended 81/117
76 amended 84/1406
82 revoked 87/256
88 revoked 82/220
96 revoked 81/71
97 revoked 81/1707
98 revoked 81/172
107 revoked 86/965
108 amended 86/1962
109 amended 81/980
111 revoked 87/353
116 revoked 84/812
126 amended 82/217
127 revoked 82/218
136 amended 85/127
137 revoked 81/72
139 revoked 86/1078
140 revoked 86/1078
141 revoked 81/257
143 revoked 82/130
148 revoked 82/131
149 revoked 82/132
153 amended 81/652
154 amended 81/653
160 revoked 86/416
168 revoked 81/279
169 revoked 85/1661
170 amended 82/944
180 revoked 81/952; 87/1850
183 amended 82/1067; 82/1068
184 amended 80/559; 82/1523
192 revoked 82/198
193 revoked 81/180
198 amended 80/342; 81/1892; 82/1303; 83/198
216 revoked 86/24
221 revoked 91/248

1980—*cont.*

222 amended 81/1330; 81/1534; 83/836; revoked 84/1404
223 amended 81/1329; 81/1535; 83/537; revoked 84/1404
224 revoked 86/1713
229 amended 81/130
233 revoked 86/24
234 revoked 86/24
241 revoked 81/204
242 revoked 82/191
243 revoked 80/395
244 revoked 81/203
247 revoked 82/1417
250 revoked 81/277
251 revoked 81/29
264 revoked 80/1503
270 revoked 81/363
272 revoked 87/256
280 revoked 80/1872
281 revoked 80/1873
283 revoked 84/1861
286 revoked 82/577
287 amended 82/1576; revoked 86/1078
289 amended 83/270; 85/1068
295 amended 81/976; revoked 87/353
296 revoked 80/1674
298 revoked 81/455
299 revoked 81/456
316 revoked 82/1101
317 revoked 81/362
318 amended 82/1098
320 amended 85/993; 86/442; 88/233
321 amended 82/1095
322 revoked 81/364
330 amended 81/342; 83/293; 83/1500; 84/243; 85/356; 86/338; revoked 87/188
331 amended 82/1114; 84/242; 85/1096
332 revoked 83/1206
333 revoked 83/1206
334 revoked 83/1204
335 amended 83/1205; 83/1880; 84/92; 86/1437; revoked 87/1566
340 revoked 81/327
342 amended 81/1892; 82/1303; 83/1421; revoked 87/1850
343 revoked 80/1177
345 revoked 83/1865
346 revoked 83/1865
347 amended 86/100
350 revoked 83/587
351 amended 81/357; 82/1102; 83/292; 83/1501; revoked 85/357
352 revoked 88/473
355 revoked 81/354
356 amended 81/355; 81/1237; 82/1261; 83/332
362 amended 81/1205; 82/288; 83/1765; 85/39; 87/2218
369 revoked 84/293
370 amended 81/324; revoked 83/443
371 amended 81/1130
374 revoked 80/1809
377 amended 80/1493; 82/1249; 82/566; 83/185; 83/1094; 84/458; 84/1659; 85/159; revoked 85/967
388 revoked 81/496
389 revoked 81/500
397 amended 81/226
404 amended 80/944
405 revoked 87/851

STATUTORY INSTRUMENTS AFFECTED 1947–1988

413 revoked 81/1439
419 revoked 81/1707
420 amended 82/599; 84/306; 84/839; 85/873; 85/230; 86/195; 87/428; 87/1679; 87/1758
425 amended 88/110
439 revoked 82/1273
442 amended 80/866; 84/33; 85/919
443 revoked 86/443
448 revoked 85/1861
449 amended 83/807; 84/688; 84/1892; 86/196
450 amended 82/1457; 84/688; 86/197
453 revoked 85/1857
457 amended 83/483
477 revoked 80/1898
480 revoked 81/490
488 revoked 80/1863
490 revoked 80/658
495 revoked 83/354
498 revoked 81/72
499 amended 86/194; revoked 87/1758
501 revoked 81/548
502 revoked 81/546
503 revoked 81/547
508 revoked 80/1695
509 revoked 84/887
510 revoked 81/552
511 revoked 81/553
529 amended 81/582; 84/346; 84/1223; 85/1216; 86/1075
530 amended 81/579; 84/1203; revoked 85/659
532 revoked 81/568
533 revoked 81/569
534 amended 81/406
535 amended 81/580; 81/1472; 84/1220; 85/660; 87/1886; 88/1693
536 amended 81/576; revoked 85/1217
537 revoked 81/572
538 amended 81/577; 81/1472; 84/97; 86/1072
540 revoked 87/1298
541 amended 81/575; revoked 85/1218
542 amended 81/578; revoked 86/1071
543 amended 81/581; revoked 87/1961
544 amended 81/574; 81/1472; 81/1747; 84/1221; 85/1194
557 amended 80/668; revoked 84/552
561 amended 81/226; 82/528
563 amended 81/226; 81/228
572 revoked 81/363
573 revoked 81/924
574 revoked 86/986
580 revoked 81/1604
604 revoked 86/996
610 revoked 86/1078
615 amended 81/36; 83/1663; 83/1775; revoked 83/1831
616 revoked 81/1694
623 amended 80/2001; revoked 86/1372
630 revoked 81/916
634 revoked 85/214
635 amended 80/1354
637 amended 81/37; 81/527; 83/1713; 83/1832; 84/179; 84/1835; 85/30; 88/1811
638 revoked 86/902
642 revoked 80/744
645 amended 80/1306
656 revoked 82/1478
664 revoked 81/749
666 revoked 80/946
668 revoked 84/552

683 revoked 80/2007
687 revoked 85/1194
694 revoked 83/713
703 amended 81/432
704 amended 81/154; 81/155
709 amended 85/1996
714 revoked 83/1676
717 revoked 81/612
721 revoked 82/1000
725 amended 83/519; revoked 88/1324
735 revoked 81/60
746 revoked 81/404
747 revoked 85/1820
758 revoked 81/29
761 revoked 81/1257
762 revoked 87/763
765 amended 88/1640
766 amended 82/805
773 revoked 83/1706
776 revoked 84/1406
780 amended 87/2071
789 revoked 81/1747
790 revoked 83/713
792 amended 87/867
796 revoked 85/1877
797 revoked 85/1876
798 revoked 84/1053
800 amended 81/625; 82/891
803 revoked 87/851
804 amended 81/1059; 84/1114; 85/1333; revoked 85/2023
811 revoked 86/647
819 amended 81/1515; 83/1708; 86/696; 88/870
820 revoked 81/861
821 amended 80/1060; 83/1680; 83/1707; 86/637; 86/2144; 88/510
822 revoked 86/1201
850 revoked 81/758
851 revoked 81/638
852 revoked 81/637
861 revoked 86/1390
866 amended 82/1067; 82/1068
867 revoked 83/415
870 amended 80/1087; 81/228; 82/1084
873 amended 83/1676
877 amended 81/311
879 revoked 84/981
880 revoked 86/1078
884 revoked 85/16
885 revoked 85/17
887 revoked 82/1244
888 revoked 83/1499
890 revoked 81/1455
894 revoked 82/961
895 revoked 82/962; amended 83/725
898 revoked 82/844
899 amended 83/1759; 84/1872; revoked 85/975
900 amended 81/938; 83/1765; revoked 85/976
901 amended 81/939; 82/894; 84/910; revoked 85/981
903 revoked 85/831
914 revoked 85/214
917 amended 80/1862; 83/260
919 revoked 88/1652
926 revoked 85/680
928 revoked 81/1707
943 revoked 81/29
948 amended 81/960
952 amended 81/963; 82/939; 83/1048; 85/1050

STATUTORY INSTRUMENTS AFFECTED 1947–1988

1980—*cont.*

954 revoked 81/968
955 revoked 83/1071
958 amended 85/128; 87/2116
960 revoked 80/1393
961 revoked 80/1366
962 revoked 80/1426
965 amended 81/1236; 82/1416
966 amended 81/1188; 82/1417
969 revoked 81/1191
974 revoked 81/943
975 revoked 82/1234
979 amended 82/1919
982 amended 80/1774; 81/815
983 amended 80/1649; 81/815
984 amended 84/458
985 amended 81/815; 81/1196; 81/1528
987 revoked 88/473
988 revoked 85/1120
992 amended 85/1627
1003 revoked 83/1885
1004 revoked 82/1884
1009 amended 85/1384; revoked 86/939
1012 amended 85/1377; revoked 86/938
1020 revoked 86/1713
1026 revoked 80/1944
1027 revoked 80/1945
1031 revoked 83/435
1033 revoked 83/436
1036 revoked 84/605
1043 revoked 88/1652
1050 revoked 83/317; 85/1325; 85/1733; amended 87/1914
1058 amended 81/231; 81/1727; 83/530; 84/1618; 85/1871; 87/803; revoked 88/186
1059 revoked 80/1898
1062 amended 81/1695
1064 revoked 86/2049
1070 amended 80/1742; 85/777; 86/1082; revoked 86/1082
1071 revoked 82/1228
1072 amended 81/1533; 83/273; 83/1764; 84/619; 84/1923; 85/1029; 86/57
1073 revoked 81/834
1085 amended 81/154; 82/1535
1087 amended 82/1084
1097 revoked 81/257
1100 amended 81/1059; 84/1244; revoked 86/1951
1102 revoked 83/686
1103 revoked 83/686
1106 revoked 83/1718
1111 revoked 81/981
1120 amended 86/366
1121 revoked 87/8
1129 revoked 83/1811
1133 revoked 83/548
1136 amended 84/451
1143 revoked 81/363
1146 revoked 82/717
1149 revoked 81/943
1162 revoked 86/1713
1165 revoked 84/981
1166 revoked 86/1078
1167 revoked 81/1159
1175 revoked 80/2022
1176 revoked 80/2023
1177 amended 81/1680; 83/272
1179 revoked 82/1022
1181 revoked 82/1021

1980—*cont.*

1182 amended 82/7; 82/1623; 84/1927; 85/1072; 87/524; 88/1103; 88/1669
1186 revoked 80/2007
1187 revoked 80/2008
1192 revoked 80/1201
1197 revoked 82/1416
1204 revoked 82/287
1215 revoked 83/713
1216 amended 81/1625; 82/1367; revoked 83/713
1217 revoked 83/713
1221 revoked 84/293
1227 amended 81/1811; revoked 84/1115
1233 amended 81/270; 82/247; 83/484; 84/310; revoked 86/392
1239 amended 80/1770; 80/1979
1242 revoked 81/1283
1243 revoked 80/1350
1245 revoked 81/1195
1247 revoked 81/943
1252 amended 82/1108; revoked 88/1123
1254 amended 82/918; 84/845; 86/412
1261 revoked 86/1713
1279 amended 81/374; 86/472
1294 revoked 80/2022
1295 revoked 80/2022
1296 revoked 80/2023
1298 amended 81/1708; 83/508; 83/1763; 84/618; 84/1922; 85/1025
1299 amended 80/1774; 81/513; 81/1016; 81/1196; 81/1197; 82/1125; 82/1126; 82/1127; 82/1299; 83/505; 83/700; 83/1245; 83/1399
1300 revoked 81/1527
1301 revoked 81/1227
1319 revoked 83/1058
1321 revoked 84/451
1331 amended 81/1236; 82/1416
1336 revoked 84/418
1339 amended 84/1224; revoked 87/755
1342 revoked 86/2193
1349 revoked 81/362
1350 revoked 81/1410
1352 revoked 81/943
1354 amended 81/264; 85/1907; revoked 86/691
1356 amended 81/1037
1359 revoked 85/621
1365 revoked 80/1978
1370 revoked 81/1641
1371 revoked 81/1061
1374 revoked 80/1606
1383 amended 81/1728
1388 revoked 84/1005
1391 amended 80/1620; revoked 84/1175
1398 revoked 81/1411
1408 revoked 88/529
1413 amended 82/974
1417 revoked 80/1796
1418 revoked 81/29
1419 revoked 80/1456
1429 revoked 82/85
1437 amended 82/1035; 83/1003; 84/451; 84/458; 84/979; 85/1946; 86/2217; 87/281; 87/491
1438 amended 83/1003; revoked 87/1968
1441 revoked 81/1420
1442 amended 85/1815
1449 revoked 86/1713
1450 amended 82/133; 82/1142; 85/1116
1455 revoked 87/851
1456 amended 83/128

STATUTORY INSTRUMENTS AFFECTED 1947–1988

1980—*cont.*

1858 revoked 87/821
1866 amended 83/939; 86/788
1870 amended 88/1973
1872 revoked 81/1240
1873 revoked 81/1252
1878 revoked 83/592
1881 amended 81/751; 82/726
1884 amended 81/1228; 81/1415
1885 amended 81/1892; 82/1303; 83/1421; revoked 87/1850
1888 amended 82/514; 83/270; 84/847; 84/1518; 85/1068
1889 amended 81/137; 82/515; 83/270; 84/1518; 85/1068
1892 revoked 83/1784
1894 amended 81/173; 83/424; 83/1483; 83/1892; 86/272; 86/1186; 86/2001; 86/2135; 88/46; 88/1938
1898 amended 82/1237; 82/1592; 83/392; 83/470; 83/1142; 83/1652; 83/1935; 83/1963; 84/241; 84/637; 84/1715; 85/149; 85/694; 85/1879; 86/275; 87/396; 88/459; 88/461
1900 revoked 85/1353
1911 amended 81/905; 81/1768
1912 revoked 81/1776; 88/538
1918 revoked 83/713
1921 amended 81/80; 82/29; 82/1596; 83/341; 83/1212, 83/1801
1922 amended 82/26; 84/769
1923 amended 82/28
1924 amended 82/27
1929 revoked 88/110
1931 revoked 86/1319
1941 revoked 86/2187
1944 revoked 81/564
1945 revoked 81/563
1946 revoked 88/1813
1950 revoked 83/686
1952 revoked 82/1068
1965 revoked 82/161; 85/1643; amended 84/1988; 85/137
1973 revoked 87/1135
1978 revoked 81/599
1980 revoked 82/105
1986 revoked 81/670
1990 amended 81/1026; 82/1043; 83/1098; 83/1725; revoked 84/1739
1993 revoked 83/1390
1994 amended 81/98; 81/281; 81/465; 81/592; 81/1163
1996 revoked 81/1163
1999 revoked 81/1769
2001 revoked 86/1372
2003 revoked 82/1056
2005 amended 83/1854
2007 amended 81/1642; 82/859; 83/775; 83/1785; revoked 84/880
2008 amended 81/1643; 82/860; 83/774; revoked 84/881
2009 revoked 80/2032
2106 revoked 85/293
2022 amended 81/628; 81/1261; 80/1854
2023 revoked 81/1854
2025 amended 81/1812; revoked 86/1935
2026 amended 81/1812; revoked 85/1306
2030 revoked 85/1224
2035 amended 85/29; 88/2072
2049 amended 82/186

1981

1 revoked 84/246
2 amended 83/1740; 84/247
7 revoked 83/1071
16 amended 81/917
19 revoked 84/522
22 revoked 88/110
29 revoked 82/1606
30 revoked 83/640
31 amended 83/1781
32 revoked 83/1680
34 revoked 81/1669; 85/1714; amended 84/1884
36 revoked 83/1831
41 revoked 87/851
54 revoked 85/359
55 revoked 84/1258
57 amended 85/528; 87/2078
58 amended 84/468; 85/641
59 revoked 84/469
61 revoked 83/550
65 revoked 82/1416
66 revoked 82/1417
67 amended 85/111; 87/1914
69 revoked 84/1932
71 revoked 84/1989
72 revoked 82/717
73 revoked 83/1598
80 revoked 83/1212
86 revoked 84/648
91 revoked 86/561
99 revoked 81/1526
100 revoked 81/1164
101 amended 86/458
106 revoked 83/1027
112 revoked 83/1865
115 amended 82/242
121 amended 84/91; revoked 86/193
128 amended 82/194
129 amended 84/380; 84/614
137 amended 82/1619; 82/1779; 83/270; 83/1779; revoked 84/1519
148 amended 81/478; 82/1618
152 revoked 86/416
154 amended 82/157; 82/1535
172 revoked 82/115
174 amended 81/1808; 83/205; 84/148; revoked 85/830
176 revoked 82/811
180 revoked 82/125; revoked 86/724
193 revoked 86/568
199 revoked 83/61
202 revoked 84/325
203 revoked 82/192
204 revoked 82/193
209 revoked 82/145
210 revoked 82/146
211 revoked 82/147
212 revoked 82/148
213 revoked 82/149
222 amended 81/431
228 amended 82/159
229 revoked 85/454
231 amended 81/231
241 revoked 82/222
245 revoked 88/1813
246 revoked 85/1012
248 amended 82/718
249 revoked 82/448

STATUTORY INSTRUMENTS AFFECTED 1947–1988

1981—*cont.*

251 amended 82/1172; revoked 83/126
252 revoked 85/262
257 amended 82/20; 82/1058; 82/1482; 84/1763; 86/370; 86/1812; 87/1150; 88/340
258 amended 85/1905; 86/994; revoked 86/1668
259 amended 85/1906; revoked 86/1628
260 revoked 84/1406
261 revoked 82/1576; 86/1078
262 revoked 87/1150
263 amended 85/263
264 revoked 86/1691
265 amended 85/214
267 revoked 81/699
269 amended 81/886
270 revoked 82/247
271 revoked 87/2178
277 revoked 82/1248
279 revoked 81/1825
289 amended 86/442
295 revoked 88/1951
304 amended 81/1834
305 revoked 86/975
307 amended 86/976; revoked 88/473
312 amended 81/1840; 82/267
313 revoked 87/408
315 revoked 81/916
316 revoked 86/724
324 revoked 83/443
325 revoked 81/924
327 amended 83/268; 86/1236
328 amended 85/6; revoked 85/1486
334 revoked 83/714
340 revoked 82/1036
342 revoked 87/188
354 amended 83/573; 83/1080; 86/334; 87/244; 87/746; 88/330
357 revoked 85/357
359 amended 84/293; 86/966; revoked 88/464; 88/546
360 revoked 86/965
362 amended 82/1093; 83/349; 84/641; 85/349; revoked 86/403
363 amended 81/589; 81/624; 82/120
369 amended 83/1674
372 revoked 81/1172
386 revoked 88/110
387 revoked 87/430
388 amended 82/468; revoked 87/430
390 revoked 86/1713
396 revoked 83/1166
402 revoked 82/1606
404 amended 83/898; 85/1819
419 revoked 83/1518
437 amended 82/1537
443 amended 82/759
454 amended 83/173; 83/1727; 85/67; 85/216; revoked 87/2237
455 revoked 82/1170
456 revoked 82/1171
461 revoked 84/748
468 revoked 81/1272
488 revoked 82/949
490 revoked 82/698
496 revoked 82/654
497 amended 82/467
498 revoked 82/653
499 revoked 82/466
500 amended 86/373
501 revoked 87/368

1981—*cont.*

504 revoked 83/684
513 revoked 83/1399
521 revoked 85/1071
528 revoked 82/1312
530 revoked 81/1204
532 revoked 83/982
535 amended 83/552
536 amended 86/442; 88/233
546 revoked 82/1253
547 revoked 82/1254
548 revoked 82/721
551 revoked 85/100
552 amended 82/245; 83/523; 84/1552; 85/1695; 85/1944; 86/1332; 88/2132
553 amended 82/246; 83/524; 84/1542; 85/1945; 86/1333; 88/2132
560 amended 86/435
563 revoked 81/1154
564 revoked 81/1153
569 amended 85/1828
572 amended 84/1219; 85/663
573 amended 83/708; 85/211
575 revoked 85/1218
576 revoked 85/1217
579 amended 84/1203; 85/659
580 revoked 85/660
581 revoked 87/1961
585 revoked 81/1185
595 amended 85/481
596 revoked 85/480
599 revoked 81/1457
605 revoked 87/1830; amended 88/591
622 revoked 86/848
628 revoked 81/1854
629 revoked 81/1027
630 amended 83/41; 88/1023
632 revoked 83/1428
637 revoked 83/492
638 revoked 83/493
640 revoked 81/1144
641 revoked 82/1606
644 amended 85/828; 86/442; 88/233
650 revoked 82/1234
663 revoked 85/886
664 revoked 82/449
668 revoked 81/1641
669 revoked 88/1567
670 revoked 84/1052
675 revoked 84/292
679 amended 85/707
696 revoked 84/981
697 revoked 86/1078
710 revoked 81/1654
722 revoked 84/1803
725 revoked 81/1654
727 amended 84/692
728 amended 82/10; 84/693
731 revoked 82/146
732 revoked 82/147
733 revoked 82/148
734 revoked 82/149
740 amended 87/1284; 88/252
746 revoked 82/1034
747 revoked 86/862
781 revoked 84/1629
786 amended 83/169; 83/1017; 84/113; 85/684
792 revoked 84/1244
793 revoked 84/1861
803 revoked 86/1202

804 amended 86/443; 86/623
806 revoked 88/633
809 amended 81/1180; revoked 87/1359
815 revoked 81/1529; amended 84/451; 86/2217; 87/491
829 amended 84/238
830 amended 84/237; 85/1014; 2007; 88/977; 88/1249
834 revoked 82/848
836 revoked 83/1666
838 amended 82/1534
849 revoked 82/1408
854 revoked 82/1234
859 amended 83/1086; 83/1088; 83/1879; 83/1880; 84/966; 86/1859; 87/1706
861 amended 81/1103; 83/1180; 86/705; 86/2185
869 revoked 82/1606
870 revoked 82/1606
871 amended 81/1270; 82/1606
872 revoked 82/1606
873 revoked 82/1606
880 amended 87/1127
881 amended 83/1040; 87/1128
882 revoked 84/1053
887 revoked 84/615
888 revoked 82/287
898 revoked 83/1706
903 revoked 82/1606
904 revoked 81/1019
905 revoked 81/1768
912 amended 82/257
914 revoked 85/1010
915 revoked 86/1078
916 amended 82/1090
924 amended 82/1118
925 revoked 81/1641
929 revoked 87/353
930 amended 81/330
931 amended 86/2100; 88/847
932 amended 82/288; 83/901; 84/958
936 amended 81/937
938 revoked 85/976
939 revoked 85/981
943 revoked 82/942
948 revoked 81/1420
951 revoked 81/1694
952 amended 82/99; 82/230; 82/937; 83/1662; 84/274; 84/737; 85/1161; 86/748; 87/560; revoked 87/1378
955 revoked 85/1046
960 revoked 82/938
961 revoked 82/938
963 amended 82/939
964 revoked 85/620; 85/757
966 revoked 85/1120
968 revoked 82/1399
969 revoked 83/1855
974 revoked 82/1145
976 revoked 87/353
981 revoked 82/1041
989 revoked 85/1661
990 revoked 85/1661
996 revoked 88/1484
1016 amended 81/1527; revoked 83/1399
1017 amended 86/1353; revoked 87/309
1019 revoked 82/1169
1026 revoked 84/1739
1027 revoked 81/1854

1029 revoked 82/220
1034 amended 83/703; 84/1885; 85/1008; revoked 87/800
1035 revoked 85/913
1042 revoked 84/812
1045 amended 83/1095
1050 revoked 83/1071
1056 revoked 82/207
1059 amended 84/1244; 85/1333; 86/1951
1061 revoked 83/82
1063 amended 83/1700, 83/1727; 85/67; 88/2112
1066 revoked 87/1303
1077 amended 82/1637
1078 revoked 84/1885
1080 revoked 85/886; 86/335
1081 amended 86/435
1082 amended 86/435
1084 revoked 84/1917
1085 revoked 84/1918
1086 amended 83/262; 86/542; 87/879
1087 revoked 83/1499
1095 amended 85/1803
1098 amended 87/306
1102 revoked 88/538
1115 amended 82/1080
1121 amended 87/467
1126 revoked 83/82
1135 revoked 86/1536
1138 revoked 82/1507
1143 revoked 83/686
1151 revoked 88/110
1153 revoked 81/1491
1154 revoked 81/1492
1159 revoked 82/1107
1162 amended 82/1147
1165 revoked 81/1871
1170 revoked 87/1758
1180 revoked 87/1359
1183 revoked 83/1206
1188 revoked 82/1417
1189 revoked 82/1480; 86/1078
1190 revoked 82/234
1191 revoked 82/995
1193 revoked 82/942
1195 revoked 82/1130
1196 amended 81/1528
1197 amended 81/1526; 83/1399
1206 revoked 81/1641
1227 revoked 82/1552
1228 revoked 81/1363
1236 revoked 82/1416
1239 revoked 86/1735
1240 revoked 83/36
1250 revoked 86/24
1252 revoked 83/43
1257 revoked 84/1176
1258 revoked 88/1760
1260 amended 86/1819
1261 amended 81/1852; 82/456; 83/491
1263 revoked 82/1480; 85/39; 85/1659
1270 revoked 82/1606
1271 revoked 82/81
1293 revoked 83/1206
1295 amended 81/1662; revoked 83/1206
1302 amended 84/222
1306 revoked 83/592
1311 amended 86/1733
1320 amended 82/1779; 83/270; 83/1779; 85/1068

STATUTORY INSTRUMENTS AFFECTED 1947–1988

STATUTORY INSTRUMENTS AFFECTED 1947–1988

1982—*cont.*

345 amended 83/31
355 amended 82/864; revoked 83/1167
356 revoked 86/403
361 revoked 83/1166
373 revoked 82/1021
385 amended 82/1303; 83/1421; revoked 87/1850; 88/1850
402 revoked 82/1008
423 revoked 87/1378
430 revoked 84/812
442 revoked 82/945
443 revoked 82/946
446 revoked 87/2024
447 revoked 88/2184
456 revoked 83/491
460 revoked 82/782
461 revoked 83/1591
467 revoked 86/967
468 revoked 87/430
488 amended 84/1052
490 revoked 85/719
491 revoked 85/717
492 revoked 87/657
493 revoked 87/656
496 revoked 88/1652
498 amended 85/987
507 revoked 83/533
508 revoked 83/532
512 revoked 82/1296
533 revoked 83/1282
534 revoked 83/982
540 revoked 82/1122
541 revoked 84/880
542 revoked 84/881
555 amended 84/6; 86/443; 87/1760
565 revoked 83/684
566 amended 84/451; revoked 85/967
577 revoked 85/1576
578 amended 83/1042; revoked 87/1843
586 amended 83/1715; 84/879; 85/567; 85/1503; 86/1505; 86/2001; 87/1119; 88/279
587 revoked 1606
599 revoked 87/1758
601 revoked 85/145
608 revoked 83/344
612 amended 86/79; revoked 88/809
614 revoked 87/2244
615 revoked 87/2245
618 revoked 84/483
620 revoked 83/1423
621 revoked 83/982
622 revoked 84/210
626 amended 86/1980
635 amended 88/1216
636 amended 88/1215
638 revoked 84/1404
642 revoked 83/1598
652 revoked 84/233
674 revoked 85/854
681 amended 82/1628; 83/317
695 revoked 88/1657
697 revoked 85/196
698 revoked 83/707
703 revoked 82/1606
704 revoked 82/1184
705 revoked 82/1249
716 amended 83/1674
717 amended 83/180; 84/283; 85/785; 85/1166; 86/583; 87/288; 88/2089

1982—*cont.*

719 amended 83/480; 83/1688; 84/1847; 85/1581; revoked 86/1319; amended 86/2001; 86/2103; 87/1908; 88/2070
721 revoked 83/544
725 amended 84/785
747 amended 82/1145; revoked 83/1753
767 revoked 88/1349
770 revoked 84/1258
786 revoked 87/821
792 revoked 83/1282
795 revoked 82/863
805 revoked 84/1404
809 revoked 84/978
810 revoked 83/686
811 amended 85/576; 86/1043; 87/802
824 amended 83/1110; revoked 85/444
828 amended 83/207; 84/1833; revoked 88/395
829 amended 83/72
834 amended 83/897; 85/2003; 86/2074
841 amended 88/1910
844 amended 85/1529; 87/188
848 revoked 83/1128
859 revoked 84/880
860 revoked 84/881
863 amended 82/1577; 83/302; 84/300; 85/371; 85/508; 86/459; 86/950; 87/371; 88/8; 88/472
864 revoked 83/1167
876 amended 84/93
894 amended 83/376; 84/385; 85/126; 86/477; 87/372; 87/868
897 revoked 85/981
898 amended 82/1743; 83/362; 84/295; 85/1120; 86/516; 86/924; 87/387; 88/13; 88/462
908 revoked 86/24
914 amended 84/451
936 revoked 85/1120
937 revoked 87/1378
938 amended 84/1042; revoked 86/1148
939 amended 83/1048; 84/1041
945 revoked 82/1351
946 revoked 82/1352
947 revoked 83/1071
949 amended 83/1030; 84/840; 85/1076; revoked 86/1104
954 amended 82/1295; 83/114; 83/477; 83/1135
955 revoked 87/2088
967 revoked 88/1852
992 revoked 86/561
996 amended 84/1360; 85/498
999 revoked 85/214
1000 amended 84/397; 86/1021
1004 amended 83/1709; 84/1766; 87/611
1008 revoked 82/1298
1009 amended 84/740; 86/151; 88/466
1011 revoked 84/230
1013 revoked 84/1052
1016 amended 84/1443
1018 amended 83/1727; 84/604; 85/67
1019 revoked 84/1861
1026 revoked 84/2041
1029 revoked 85/620; 85/757
1032 revoked 84/380
1036 revoked 83/685
1040 revoked 82/1606
1041 revoked 83/686
1043 revoked 84/1739
1045 revoked 88/538
1057 revoked 86/1078

743

1982—cont.

1075 revoked 88/247
1079 amended 84/1823
1088 revoked 85/886
1093 revoked 86/403
1094 amended 85/1098
1102 revoked 85/357
1104 amended 88/158
1105 revoked 83/1598
1107 revoked 83/1201
1108 revoked 88/1123
1109 amended 84/699; 86/2151; 88/952; 88/1322;
    88/1635; 88/2131; 88/2160
1110 amended 85/697
1123 amended 83/1647; 85/1574
1124 amended 82/1519; 83/57; 83/1014; 83/1239;
    83/1242; 84/103; 84/104; 84/940; 84/941;
    84/1105; 84/1965; 85/368; 85/440; 85/667
1125 amended 83/1399
1126 amended 83/505; 83/1399
1127 amended 83/1399
1130 revoked 83/1244
1132 revoked 86/1078
1135 amended 85/1268; 86/1811
1142 revoked 85/1116
1143 amended 84/51; revoked 86/177
1144 amended 84/52; 85/1119
1151 revoked 87/256
1161 revoked 87/292
1163 amended 83/374; 84/1479
1169 revoked 85/995
1170 revoked 88/14
1171 revoked 83/127
1172 revoked 83/126
1194 revoked 87/353
1197 amended 83/235; 83/1049; 84/112; 84/264;
    85/333; 86/273; 86/444; 86/1515;
    86/1835; 87/369; revoked 88/423
1202 amended 83/1807
1208 amended 82/160; 83/1754
1212 revoked 83/1340
1214 revoked 82/1606
1215 revoked 82/1606
1223 revoked 86/1078
1227 revoked 83/1063
1229 amended 86/1208
1231 revoked 82/1417
1232 revoked 82/1416
1236 amended 83/311; 83/368; 85/1252; 88/1347
1239 revoked 84/150
1241 amended 86/217; 87/491
1242 amended 84/451; 84/1960
1244 revoked 83/1346
1250 revoked 82/1606
1251 revoked 82/1606
1252 revoked 87/353
1253 revoked 83/333
1254 revoked 88/108
1271 amended 84/697; 84/1402; 85/46; 86/427;
    87/1508; 88/1523
1272 revoked 86/1078
1283 amended 85/1053
1290 revoked 83/266
1291 revoked 83/267
1295 revoked 83/1135
1297 revoked 82/1307
1298 revoked 82/1543
1303 amended 83/1421; revoked 87/1850;
    88/1850
1345 revoked 83/1598

1982—cont.

1349 amended 83/1738
1350 revoked 83/1433
1351 revoked 82/1541
1352 revoked 82/1542
1364 revoked 83/1442
1367 revoked 83/713
1384 amended 88/1338
1391 amended 84/2008
1392 revoked 82/1606
1393 revoked 82/1606
1398 revoked 82/1408
1399 revoked 83/1492
1400 revoked 86/2218; 87/214
1406 revoked 85/1804
1408 amended 82/1494; 83/186; 84/458; 84/1259;
    84/1303; 84/1703; 85/1571; 86/1118;
    86/1561; 86/2217; 87/327; 87/491;
    87/1968; 88/436
1416 amended 83/385; revoked 83/1463
1417 amended 83/572; revoked 83/1464
1422 revoked 86/1078
1432 amended 84/255
1442 revoked 87/730
1446 revoked 85/849
1455 revoked 83/1459
1457 amended 84/688; 85/242; 86/476; 88/971
1471 revoked 85/886
1474 amended 88/2198
1478 amended 84/178; 84/402; 84/816; 84/1024;
    85/44; 85/1525; 86/371; 88/338; revoked
    88/1478
1480 revoked 86/1078
1486 revoked 87/851
1489 amended 82/1490; 83/1361; 84/452;
    84/1181; 85/1446; 87/419; 87/429; 88/574
1492 revoked 83/1587
1496 amended 84/1244; 85/1333; 86/890
1506 amended 85/499; 86/641
1513 amended 86/1985
1514 revoked 86/24
1519 amended 85/677
1520 amended 83/57; 83/438; 85/677
1521 revoked 84/418
1527 amended 88/591
1528 amended 84/125; 88/590
1540 revoked 87/455
1541 revoked 83/33
1542 revoked 83/34
1543 revoked 83/1642
1551 amended 85/1843
1552 revoked 83/1465
1554 revoked 86/1492
1556 revoked 85/849
1574 revoked 84/1052
1576 revoked 86/1078
1579 amended 86/1277
1590 amended 83/1184; 84/219; 84/1270; 85/475
1596 revoked 83/1212
1602 revoked 84/1145
1606 amended 83/222; 83/1797; 84/1352;
    84/1900; 84/1901; 85/470
1622 revoked 83/1684
1623 revoked 86/1501
1628 amended 83/1354
1634 revoked 83/1399
1642 revoked 83/1821
1665 revoked 85/443
1674 revoked 83/1839
1680 revoked 85/1422

744

STATUTORY INSTRUMENTS AFFECTED 1947–1988

1982—cont.
1682 revoked 85/1661
1684 revoked 83/39
1685 revoked 83/69
1696 revoked 85/1661
1697 amended 87/775
1701 revoked 87/1523
1706 amended 83/1681; 85/574; 85/1834; 86/633;
    86/2143; 88/509
1725 revoked 84/1739
1727 amended 84/2237
1732 revoked 87/451
1756 revoked 85/976
1757 revoked 85/975
1760 amended 83/1038
1766 revoked 83/38
1768 revoked 83/1368
1769 revoked 83/713
1773 revoked 85/1299
1775 revoked 83/1831
1782 amended 83/501
1784 amended   84/1916;   85/1917;   86/2153;
    87/2100; revoked 88/2151
1785 revoked 84/880
1794 amended 83/275
1795 amended 83/469; 83/1192; 83/1811
1801 revoked 83/1212
1805 revoked 84/1861
1806 revoked 85/1875
1808 amended 84/897
1812 revoked 86/1713
1817 revoked 84/1110
1821 revoked 83/1629
1847 revoked 83/15
1852 revoked 83/575
1867 revoked 83/1861
1868 revoked 84/2020
1877 revoked 87/381
1882 revoked 87/2224
1884 amended 87/114
1885 revoked 88/526
1895 amended 84/1700
1897 amended 84/102; 84/1686; 85/94

1983
4 revoked 84/1718
5 revoked 84/248
6 amended 88/1090
17 revoked 84/1244
29 amended 88/1067
32 revoked 83/1071
33 revoked 83/863
34 revoked 83/864
36 revoked 83/582
37 revoked 83/777
43 revoked 83/593
57 revoked 85/677
61 revoked 88/2135
62 revoked 85/273
68 revoked 83/347
70 revoked 86/392
71 amended 88/1672
74 amended 87/1126
78 amended 88/1094
79 revoked 83/502
80 revoked 84/470
82 revoked 83/1646
104 amended 84/458; revoked 86/2217; 87/491
111 revoked 86/724
112 revoked 86/1078

1983—cont.
114 revoked 83/1135
117 revoked 88/1637
123 revoked 84/1947
126 revoked 87/243
127 amended 84/166; revoked 88/15
126 revoked 87/243
131 revoked 83/646
132 revoked 86/2181
136 amended 83/504; 84/453; 85/491; 87/400
141 amended 84/123
160 revoked 87/851
169 revoked 85/684
171 revoked 83/620
173 revoked 87/2237
174 revoked 87/2236
181 revoked 84/459
182 amended 83/627
185 amended 84/451; revoked 85/685
186 amended 83/1598; 84/451
195 revoked 85/1065
196 revoked 86/416
201 amended 84/573; 84/774
202 amended 84/775
205 revoked 85/830
207 revoked 88/395
210 revoked 86/862
217 revoked 87/363
219 revoked 85/1108
220 revoked 85/1660
239 revoked 88/1478
250 amended 86/442; 88/233
252 revoked 87/2009
253 amended 86/382
256 amended 83/1818; 86/251; revoked 86/2090
258 revoked 87/292
261 amended 84/224
271 revoked 88/10
274 revoked 84/1861
280 revoked 85/852
290 revoked 87/821
291 revoked 87/821
292 revoked 85/357
293 revoked 87/188
295 amended 83/475; revoked 85/886
296 amended 84/223; 85/257; 87/351; revoked
    87/2186
302 amended 86/459; 88/472
306 amended 87/368, 88/551
309 amended 86/976; 88/473; revoked 88/551
312 amended 86/440
313 revoked 87/401
315 amended   85/1067;   revoked   85/1876;
    amended 86/2001
328 revoked 84/981
330 revoked 83/1134
333 amended 84/338; revoked 88/109
334 revoked 88/365
335 amended 84/293; revoked 88/546
338 revoked 84/380
341 revoked 83/1212
342 revoked 85/1299
343 revoked 85/1820
348 revoked 83/812
349 revoked 86/403
362 amended 86/516; 88/462
368 amended 84/1653; 87/404; revoked 88/1347
373 revoked 84/280
376 amended 85/1411
380 revoked 84/380

745

STATUTORY INSTRUMENTS AFFECTED 1947–1988

382 amended 84/1269; 86/614
385 revoked 83/1463
392 revoked 88/459
413 revoked 83/776
415 revoked 86/2223
416 revoked 86/2225
417 amended 85/1776; 86/597
422 amended 87/469
425 amended 83/1439; revoked 86/428
431 revoked 84/446
435 amended 86/104
436 amended 86/105
438 revoked 85/677
443 amended 84/390; revoked 85/373
463 amended 83/1598
469 amended 83/1192; 83/1811
471 revoked 86/1078
475 revoked 85/886
477 revoked 83/1135
480 revoked 84/1847
481 amended 84/893; 85/1220; 86/1346
483 amended 86/610
492 revoked 87/2269
493 revoked 87/2269
495 revoked 83/1063
505 amended 83/1399
506 amended 84/1889; 86/625; 87/1258; 88/1252
510 revoked 83/1865
519 revoked 88/1324
526 revoked 88/913
530 revoked 88/186
536 revoked 84/1404
537 revoked 84/1404
543 revoked 83/852
544 amended 84/661; 85/385
548 amended 86/139; revoked 86/1111
550 amended 87/379
560 revoked 86/401
569 revoked 88/1422
570 revoked 88/1422
572 revoked 83/1464; 85/1270
573 revoked 86/334
574 revoked 84/698
579 amended 84/691
582 revoked 84/1548
586 revoked 84/738
587 amended 86/2001
592 amended 85/209; revoked 88/128
593 revoked 84/1582
595 revoked 83/811
604 amended 88/591
607 amended 83/1700
618 amended 88/459; 88/666
623 revoked 87/2024
640 revoked 88/1138
641 revoked 85/1310
647 revoked 83/1353
648 revoked 83/835
659 revoked 83/713
667 amended 86/2294
669 revoked 84/1297
670 revoked 86/1039
684 amended 84/1785; 88/980
685 amended 87/177; 88/160
686 amended 83/1164; 83/1540; 84/1289; 84/1675; 85/1313; 86/628; 87/191; 88/367
688 revoked 84/1311
689 revoked 84/1310

700 revoked 83/1399
702 revoked 88/1484
704 amended 85/1068
707 revoked 84/445
708 amended 86/1163
709 revoked 88/1567
713 amended 84/297; 84/1075; 85/511; 86/2001; 86/754; 86/1361; 86/2207; 88/2165
714 revoked 84/569
720 revoked 87/292
722 revoked 84/380
733 revoked 84/1010
762 amended 84/1688
774 revoked 84/881
775 revoked 84/880
785 revoked 85/224
787 revoked 87/821
788 revoked 85/2066
789 revoked 83/805
793 revoked 87/800
798 revoked 87/864
808 amended 85/512
813 revoked 83/1316
814 revoked 84/184
843 revoked 86/1713
854 revoked 83/1257
855 revoked 83/1011
861 revoked 83/1585
863 revoked 83/1735
864 revoked 83/1736
873 amended 86/786; 86/1345; 86/1897; 87/446; 87/944; 88/1798
883 amended 83/1116; 83/1521; 84/1154; 84/1687; 85/1201; 86/592; 87/165; 88/248
884 amended 84/1975
887 revoked 87/2156
898 revoked 85/1820
899 revoked 85/1819
910 amended 87/1326
912 revoked 85/677
916 revoked 85/214
921 amended 85/1852
928 revoked 85/981
932 revoked 86/1078
938 amended 85/1068; revoked 86/791
939 revoked 86/788
941 amended 86/1755
947 amended 86/910
957 revoked 83/1212
968 amended 83/1668
969 revoked 86/1202
971 revoked 86/967
972 revoked 87/430
973 amended 84/1201; 85/1219; 87/1364; 88/1391
981 revoked 84/1703
996 revoked 87/256
1000 amended 84/451; 86/2217; 87/491
1006 revoked 85/849
1008 revoked 88/1550
1011 revoked 84/55
1012 revoked 83/1262
1014 revoked 85/677
1017 revoked 85/684
1021 revoked 85/854
1025 revoked 84/748
1029 revoked 86/1238
1030 revoked 86/1104
1042 revoked 87/1843

1983—*cont.*
1048 amended 84/1041
1051 revoked 85/1120
1058 revoked 87/643
1063 amended 84/1052
1078 revoked 84/1314
1080 revoked 86/334
1087 revoked 86/1856
1094 amended 84/451; 85/967
1097 revoked 84/332
1098 revoked 84/1739
1106 amended 84/1153; 85/2002
1110 revoked 85/444
1113 revoked 88/1842
1128 amended 84/1171; revoked 87/1836
1129 amended 83/1748
1135 revoked 84/1116
1140 amended 87/605
1150 amended 84/841; 85/1183; revoked 86/1103
1151 revoked 87/1
1153 revoked 86/2215
1154 revoked 86/2214
1156 revoked 84/1861
1158 revoked 87/949
1160 amended 85/1872; 88/907
1166 revoked 85/1605
1167 amended 83/1427; 83/1471; 85/936; 85/1607
1182 amended 86/1623
1185 amended 84/1179; 85/1160; 86/1325; revoked 87/1261
1186 amended 84/451
1190 amended 86/443
1191 revoked 87/2186
1192 revoked 83/1811
1204 amended 83/1879; 86/1439; 87/1564
1205 revoked 87/1566
1206 amended 83/1881; 86/1438; 87/1565
1209 amended 86/1244
1211 amended 85/67; 88/2112
1212 amended 84/756; 86/586; 87/674; 87/1250; 88/2017
1213 amended 83/1506; 84/1862; 85/309; revoked 85/1288
1215 amended 84/1361; 85/1223; 87/1383
1240 amended 83/1399
1242 revoked 84/1105
1244 revoked 84/1104
1245 amended 83/1399
1246 revoked 88/296
1261 revoked 83/1408
1266 revoked 85/849
1269 revoked 86/24
1270 revoked 86/24
1271 amended 86/24
1273 revoked 84/1
1289 revoked 83/1577
1290 revoked 83/1494
1314 amended 88/1654
1340 revoked 85/251
1343 revoked 84/141
1348 amended 83/1934
1349 revoked 87/851
1351 amended 86/1015
1352 amended 86/1014
1353 revoked 84/612
1354 amended 84/1651
1368 amended 84/2029
1369 revoked 83/1578
1372 amended 84/1576

1983—*cont.*
1375 amended 83/1675; 85/1311; 86/864
1382 amended 84/1983; 85/1542
1383 revoked 86/988
1384 revoked 84/1522
1389 revoked 87/1892
1390 amended 86/1210
1398 amended 85/2040; 87/470
1399 amended 84/1102; 84/1103; 84/2034; 85/613; 85/1136; 85/1247; 86/1173; 86/1292; 86/1293; 87/17; 87/49; 87/659; 87/1325; 87/1972; 87/2193
1407 revoked 84/22
1416 revoked 83/1877
1421 revoked 87/1850
1427 revoked 85/1067
1428 revoked 87/1139
1433 revoked 84/1800
1439 revoked 86/428
1445 revoked 85/626
1450 amended 86/392; revoked 87/52
1451 revoked 87/443
1459 revoked 84/1625
1463 amended 85/38; 85/944
1464 amended 84/2043
1465 revoked 84/1558
1471 amended 85/1727
1472 revoked 84/1649
1477 revoked 84/1260
1485 revoked 87/1758
1492 revoked 84/1356
1493 revoked 84/379
1500 revoked 87/188
1501 revoked 85/357
1506 revoked 85/1288
1507 revoked 84/1059
1508 amended 85/67; 86/720
1509 amended 85/68; 86/721
1514 amended 85/1068; 86/790
1515 amended 85/1068; 85/1222; 86/789
1518 amended 84/1154; 84/1819; 84/1979; 85/1984; 86/1881; revoked 87/1264
1535 revoked 85/1120
1536 revoked 87/864
1537 amended 84/1443
1539 revoked 84/552
1545 amended 85/1324; 85/1167
1553 amended 84/1600; 85/666; 88/2047
1557 amended 84/1108; 85/666; 88/2047
1561 amended 84/1109
1563 amended 85/1089; revoked 88/1803
1575 amended 84/1358
1576 revoked 84/48
1586 revoked 84/185
1587 amended 83/1598; 84/1303; revoked 84/1703
1588 revoked 84/1704
1589 revoked 85/2027
1598 amended 84/551; 84/1703; 85/1571; 86/484; 86/1011; 86/1118; 87/317; 87/327; 87/688; 88/436; 88/689; 88/1674; 88/2119
1609 amended 85/1494
1611 revoked 85/1576
1614 revoked 87/764
1615 revoked 88/1813
1616 revoked 85/74
1618 revoked 84/486
1626 revoked 85/2054
1629 revoked 84/607
1640 revoked 87/52

1983—*cont.*

1646 revoked 84/954
1649 amended 85/279; 86/392; 87/2115
1652 amended 84/1935; revoked 88/459
1653 revoked 86/1685
1654 amended 87/51
1655 revoked 88/120
1656 amended 84/1303
1662 amended 87/1378
1663 revoked 83/1831
1665 revoked 84/1677
1669 revoked 86/1713
1674 amended 85/1182; 87/101
1683 revoked 84/1303
1688 amended 84/1847
1691 revoked 88/299
1693 revoked 84/333
1697 amended 85/1180
1698 amended 88/591
1735 revoked 84/1096
1736 revoked 84/1097
1740 revoked 86/1981
1761 amended 86/1271
1765 revoked 84/1008
1766 revoked 84/8
1770 revoked 86/400
1773 revoked 84/218
1778 revoked 85/1960
1781 revoked 85/1737
1782 revoked 85/1299
1783 amended 88/667
1784 amended 88/459; 88/666
1792 revoked 85/1288
1793 revoked 88/913
1795 amended 85/268, 1890
1796 revoked 85/1889
1797 revoked 84/1920
1800 revoked 88/1478
1802 revoked 85/1299
1803 revoked 84/1754
1807 revoked 85/16
1808 amended 86/1591
1811 amended 87/2130; 88/672
1812 revoked 87/851
1813 revoked 84/1620
1814 revoked 84/586
1818 revoked 86/2090
1828 amended 85/1376
1830 revoked 86/453
1831 amended 87/2012; 88/1808
1833 revoked 88/2151
1835 revoked 84/1865
1836 revoked 84/1866
1838 revoked 86/2069
1842 amended 85/664
1845 revoked 86/1713
1846 revoked 85/718
1850 amended 85/1325
1859 revoked 84/812
1861 revoked 84/1972
1865 amended 84/396; 85/564; 85/572; 85/1845;
     86/769; 86/1712
1875 revoked 84/1008
1876 revoked 84/528
1880 revoked 84/92
1884 revoked 85/1714
1894 amended 88/591
1905 revoked 85/1643
1908 amended 86/3
1912 amended 88/841

1983—*cont.*

1914 revoked 86/1713
1915 revoked 86/1713
1916 revoked 87/1464
1917 revoked 88/2050
1919 revoked 88/1222
1921 revoked 84/587
1922 revoked 84/378
1947 revoked 84/2037
1948 revoked 88/674
1954 revoked 87/2035
1962 revoked 84/2019

1984

19 revoked 88/110
21 revoked 84/211
29 revoked 84/430
32 revoked 85/833
47 revoked 84/212
55 revoked 85/24
62 revoked 86/149
72 amended 85/503
85 revoked 88/1951
90 revoked 85/849
91 revoked 86/193
92 revoked 87/1566
102 amended 84/1686; 85/94
103 revoked 85/677
104 revoked 85/677
107 amended 84/240; revoked 84/380
113 revoked 85/684
116 amended 85/402
125 amended 88/591
129 amended 85/1994
137 revoked 86/2209
145 amended 84/1057
147 revoked 85/685
148 revoked 85/830
155 revoked 85/886
159 amended 88/956
165 revoked 86/416
166 revoked 87/242
174 amended 85/185; 86/678
176 amended 86/666; 86/1391; 87/841; 87/2170;
     88/2128
178 revoked 88/1478
186 revoked 84/970
195 revoked 86/1078
199 revoked 85/977
201 revoked 86/24
210 revoked 87/382
213 revoked 84/833
215 revoked 85/1353
218 amended 85/1309; 85/1757
221 revoked 85/258
223 revoked 85/257; 87/2186
224 amended 85/2030
230 amended 86/378
231 amended 84/1792
232 revoked 88/110
240 revoked 84/380
242 revoked 85/357
243 revoked 87/188
245 amended 88/1025
246 revoked 88/1028
247 amended 87/608; 88/1026
248 amended 87/609; 88/1027
252 amended 85/825; 86/449; 87/772; 88/798
254 revoked 87/1850
256 amended 85/826, 2072; 86/450; 87/38;
     87/771; 88/799; 88/969

1984—cont.

257 amended 84/466; revoked 85/827
261 revoked 86/400
266 amended 86/21 .
274 revoked 87/1378
280 revoked 85/280; 85/338
283 revoked 85/785
284 amended 86/314
285 revoked 87/821
292 amended 88/365
293 amended 86/966; revoked 88/464
295 revoked 86/516; 86/924
297 amended 86/2001
298 revoked 87/368
299 amended 86/976; revoked 88/473
300 amended 86/459; revoked 86/950
306 revoked 87/1758
307 revoked 85/344
308 revoked 85/345
309 revoked 85/343
310 amended 86/392
331 revoked 86/1078
334 revoked 84/912
335 revoked 84/527
336 revoked 84/650
338 revoked 87/255
341 amended 87/1134
349 revoked 84/1861
352 revoked 87/2213
354 amended 88/591
368 revoked 86/1304
377 revoked 84/588
380 amended 85/1323; 85/1928; 85/1930; 86/317; 86/1716; 87/657; 07/1100, 87/1103; 87/1104; 87/1106; 87/1114; 87/1117; 88/475
386 revoked 86/1078
388 revoked 84/1052
390 revoked 85/373
396 revoked 86/1712
398 revoked 84/834
399 revoked 84/868
400 revoked 84/836
402 revoked 88/1478
408 amended 88/1396
411 amended 85/634
412 amended 87/547; 88/1759
415 revoked 87/214
416 revoked 87/1758
418 amended 87/119; 87/1209
421 amended 86/443; 87/804; 87/2227
426 revoked 86/1713
429 revoked 84/734
432 revoked 87/291
434 revoked 85/620; 85/757
445 revoked 85/438
446 revoked 85/741
451 amended 84/613; 84/451; 84/1991; 86/1259; 86/1541; 86/1217; 86/2218; 87/335; 87/491; 87/1968
455 amended 86/538
457 amended 84/1889; 85/558; 86/625; 87/1258; 88/1252
458 amended 84/1960; 85/967; 86/2217; 87/491
459 revoked 85/921
460 revoked 86/1442
461 revoked 86/1445
464 amended 87/740
465 amended 88/1053
466 revoked 85/827

1984—cont.

468 amended 87/630; 88/1050
469 revoked 88/1051
470 amended 84/1804; 87/631; 88/1052
481 revoked 88/743
487 revoked 84/900
490 revoked 84/978
516 revoked 87/292
519 amended 85/557; 86/681; 87/825; 88/422; revoked 87/366
519 amended 88/1108
520 amended 85/554; 86/674; 87/826; 87/1357; 88/922; 88/1111; revoked 87/365
521 revoked 84/1963
529 revoked 84/1427
530 revoked 84/913
549 amended 86/2235
552 amended 85/1414
561 revoked 86/1755
565 amended 88/1323
566 amended 85/1556
567 revoked 88/913
569 revoked 85/279
577 revoked 86/1713
607 revoked 84/1049
612 revoked 84/1971
613 revoked 86/2218; 87/214
614 amended 85/1926; 86/1716; 86/2171; 87/1106; 88/476
626 revoked 84/1621
627 revoked 84/1298
628 revoked 85/632
629 revoked 84/835
630 revoked 84/1295
641 revoked 86/403
647 amended 85/1506
651 revoked 84/1038
652 revoked 84/1007
653 revoked 84/1060
661 revoked 85/385
679 revoked 86/1078
682 revoked 85/680
686 amended 88/605
687 amended 88/604
691 revoked 85/395
694 revoked 85/849
698 amended 85/426; revoked 86/724
720 revoked 87/899
721 revoked 87/899
722 revoked 87/900
737 revoked 87/1378
738 revoked 85/974
746 amended 87/155; 87/2108; 88/1193
748 amended 87/1755; 88/1809
751 amended 84/1740; revoked 85/506
769 amended 85/1540; 97/910
770 revoked 86/862
779 amended 85/1035; 86/2001; 88/1357
796 revoked 84/1570
812 amended 87/1315
813 revoked 86/1078
816 revoked 88/1478
817 revoked 86/1078
819 revoked 85/849
820 revoked 88/110
837 revoked 84/1426
839 revoked 87/1758
840 revoked 86/1104
841 revoked 86/1103
854 revoked 85/507

STATUTORY INSTRUMENTS AFFECTED 1947–1988

856 revoked 87/2094
863 amended 85/708
867 revoked 85/178
869 revoked 84/1257
870 revoked 84/1643
871 revoked 84/1351
872 revoked 84/1601
880 amended 85/1783; 86/2030
881 revoked 85/1784
887 amended 86/2001
895 amended 85/1378
901 revoked 84/1722
902 revoked 85/85
903 revoked 85/607
904 revoked 84/1061
910 revoked 85/981
911 revoked 84/1641
917 revoked 85/620; 85/757
929 amended 84/1376; revoked 85/886
938 amended 86/2217; 87/491
940 revoked 85/677
941 revoked 85/677
954 revoked 85/937
955 revoked 87/1591
972 revoked 84/1771
973 revoked 84/1772
974 revoked 84/1428
975 revoked 84/1999
980 revoked 88/1370
981 amended 84/1401; 84/1761; 85/1651;
    86/739; 87/1509; 88/1522
990 revoked 85/1120
996 amended 87/1529
1005 revoked 87/2138
1011 revoked 84/1430
1012 revoked 85/1522
1015 amended 87/349
1017 revoked 84/1296
1024 revoked 88/1478
1041 amended 85/1050
1042 revoked 86/1148
1043 revoked 84/1385
1045 revoked 86/815
1047 amended 84/1538; 84/1787; 85/509;
    revoked 86/740
1048 revoked 86/740
1049 revoked 84/1903
1053 amended 85/490; 88/376
1053 amended 88/899
1058 revoked 84/1429
1075 amended 86/2001
1079 revoked 85/87
1081 revoked 85/1188
1096 revoked 84/1456
1097 revoked 84/1457
1098 amended 85/1070; 85/2028; 86/1031;
    87/1960; 88/1214; 88/2037
1104 revoked 85/1245
1105 revoked 85/677
1110 revoked 85/1079
1114 revoked 88/1657
1116 amended 84/1240; revoked 85/1126
1132 revoked 86/967
1138 revoked 84/1999
1143 revoked 85/2066
1144 revoked 86/2231
1150 revoked 86/2221
1153 amended 88/1840
1155 revoked 87/1264

1168 amended 85/455
1170 revoked 85/2000
1171 revoked 85/1214
1175 amended 85/36; revoked 86/2194
1177 amended 88/710
1178 revoked 88/1602
1179 revoked 87/1261
1203 amended 85/659
1204 revoked 86/1713
1206 amended 86/1643
1209 amended 88/533
1216 amended 85/661; 86/1074; 87/1886
1217 amended 85/661; 86/1067
1218 amended 85/1193; 86/1070
1220 revoked 85/660
1221 revoked 85/1194
1222 revoked 85/1218
1224 revoked 87/755
1232 revoked 87/1850
1240 revoked 85/1126
1243 revoked 85/1416
1244 amended 86/1922; 86/1951; 88/766
1256 revoked 84/1723
1260 amended 85/2044; 87/1920; 88/802;
    88/2121
1267 revoked 84/1683
1268 revoked 86/550
1300 revoked 87/710
1303 amended 86/1933; 86/2218
1304 amended 85/67
1305 amended 85/67; 85/71; 85/2026; 87/1986
1306 revoked 85/1299
1308 revoked 87/711
1309 revoked 85/997
1314 amended 85/1980; revoked 88/2039
1315 amended 85/988
1316 amended 86/1260; revoked 88/2040
1317 amended 85/573; revoked 86/2049
1338 revoked 85/24
1345 amended 86/457; 88/1192
1347 amended 84/1767
1356 revoked 85/1317
1360 amended 85/498
1376 revoked 85/886
1383 revoked 86/1646
1386 revoked 84/1622
1387 revoked 84/1642
1404 amended 85/1656; 87/315; 87/1556
1444 revoked 84/1898
1445 revoked 85/770
1446 revoked 88/876
1452 revoked 85/1299
1456 revoked 84/1647
1457 revoked 84/1648
1471 amended 88/1479
1504 amended 85/195; 85/588; 87/432; 87/794;
    88/337
1507 revoked 85/471
1508 revoked 85/106
1509 revoked 85/951
1512 revoked 85/1542
1518 amended 85/1068
1519 amended 84/1714; 85/71; 85/1068; 86/836;
    87/26; 87/2014
1523 amended 86/988
1538 revoked 86/740
1543 revoked 86/1078
1548 revoked 85/230
1551 revoked 86/404

STATUTORY INSTRUMENTS AFFECTED 1947–1988

1984—*cont.*

1558 revoked 85/1530
1566 amended 85/67; 86/987
1572 revoked 85/894
1573 revoked 84/1721
1574 revoked 85/114
1578 amended 86/456; 88/1191
1579 revoked 87/360
1582 revoked 85/229
1590 revoked 87/851
1602 revoked 84/1849
1603 revoked 85/523
1618 revoked 88/186
1623 revoked 84/1773
1624 revoked 84/1895
1625 revoked 85/1691
1627 revoked 84/1935
1628 revoked 86/1713
1640 revoked 86/26
1647 revoked 84/19676
1648 revoked 84/1968
1649 amended 85/864
1650 amended 85/38
1651 amended 85/1733
1653 revoked 88/1347
1654 amended 88/1123; 88/2116
1658 amended 88/2137
1659 revoked 85/967
1663 revoked 84/1828
1664 revoked 85/392
1677 revoked 85/1628
1685 amended 87/1806
1686 amended 85/94
1703 revoked 85/1571
1705 revoked 86/1494
1714 amended 85/1068; 86/1288
1715 revoked 88/459
1717 revoked 85/805
1725 revoked 85/188
1726 revoked 84/1897
1727 revoked 85/188; 85/1534
1728 amended 85/677
1740 revoked 85/506
1774 revoked 84/1911
1775 revoked 85/773
1776 revoked 85/83
1787 revoked 86/740
1789 revoked 85/391
1790 revoked 85/606
1791 revoked 85/86
1800 revoked 85/1454
1802 amended 87/1979
1805 amended 85/315
1808 revoked 87/851
1809 revoked 86/1078
1811 revoked 86/1078
1814 amended 86/600
1817 amended 88/591
1819 revoked 87/1264
1823 amended 86/222
1829 revoked 85/84
1833 revoked 88/395
1837 revoked 88/666
1838 revoked 88/667
1847 revoked 85/1581
1861 amended 85/310; 85/857; 85/1823
1862 revoked 85/1288
1865 revoked 85/1859
1866 revoked 85/1860
1870 revoked 85/603

1984—*cont.*

1871 revoked 87/1758
1872 revoked 85/975
1873 revoked 85/977
1874 amended 86/853; 88/69
1885 revoked 87/800
1890 amended 86/392
1898 revoked 85/115
1902 amended 85/2023; 86/294; 88/1462
1903 revoked 85/187
1912 revoked 85/604
1913 revoked 85/768
1914 revoked 85/393
1916 revoked 88/2151
1920 amended 85/160; 85/1916; 86/2120; 87/2083; 88/2130
1921 amended 85/1926; 85/1927; 87/1114; 88/475
1927 revoked 86/1501
1934 amended 87/1057; 88/39
1947 revoked 85/524
1948 revoked 85/189
1955 revoked 88/110
1956 revoked 86/2090
1960 amended 86/2217; 87/491; 87/1968; revoked 88/1227
1965 revoked 85/677
1967 revoked 85/157
1968 revoked 85/158
1969 revoked 85/1299
1970 amended 86/701
1971 revoked 85/798
1972 revoked 85/2035
1977 revoked 85/1983
1979 revoked 87/1264
1980 revoked 88/1299
1988 revoked 85/1643
1989 amended 85/784; 86/584; 87/287; 88/2088
1991 revoked 86/2218; 87/214
2000 revoked 85/950
2001 revoked 85/525
2002 amended 85/623
2005 amended 85/1851; 86/1894
2006 amended 85/19; 85/112
2011 revoked 87/53
2019 amended 85/2028
2020 revoked 86/2284
2021 revoked 85/2033
2024 amended 85/2075; 87/2129
2034 amended 85/613
2037 revoked 86/67

1985

6 revoked 85/1486
12 revoked 85/1299
13 revoked 85/765
14 revoked 85/631
15 revoked 85/472
22 revoked 85/766
24 revoked 86/5
34 revoked 85/849
36 revoked 88/1265
39 amended 85/497
43 revoked 88/110
44 revoked 88/1478
67 amended 87/2237
91 revoked 86/1078
94 amended 85/556; 86/140
95 amended 86/2002
99 amended 85/191

1985—*cont.*
100 revoked 86/497
105 revoked 85/886
107 revoked 85/953
108 revoked 86/816
109 revoked 85/473
111 amended 87/1914
116 revoked 85/769
117 revoked 85/895
118 revoked 85/1299
122 revoked 85/1714
130 revoked 87/851
138 revoked 86/416
141 revoked 85/605
148 revoked 85/849
156 revoked 87/256
157 revoked 85/1131
158 revoked 85/1132
159 revoked 85/967; amended 86/2218
175 amended 86/853
177 amended 85/548
185 revoked 86/678
186 amended 86/466
187 revoked 85/1130
194 amended 88/1219
202 revoked 87/353
209 revoked 88/128
213 amended 86/2001
214 amended 85/833; 86/753; 86/869; 86/972;
        88/960; 88/1104
216 revoked 87/2237
220 amended 87/64; revoked 88/645
221 revoked 86/424
229 revoked 85/1428
230 revoked 85/1430
246 amended 86/407; 88/19
251 revoked 86/402
252 revoked 85/1627
257 amended 87/351; revoked 87/2186
263 amended 87/2168
268 revoked 85/1890
279 revoked 86/392
281 revoked 87/353
296 amended 85/804
298 revoked 86/975
300 revoked 86/302
306 amended 88/186
309 revoked 85/1288
310 revoked 85/1823
313 revoked 87/292
316 revoked 88/110
326 amended 87/368
337 revoked 87/382
338 revoked 86/608
343 revoked 86/620
344 revoked 86/621
345 revoked 86/622
346 revoked 85/771; 85/948
347 revoked 85/772
348 revoked 85/1229
349 revoked 86/403
352 revoked 88/473
353 amended 88/365
354 revoked 88/464
355 revoked 86/965
356 revoked 87/188
357 amended 86/339
359 revoked 86/1399
368 revoked 85/677
371 revoked 86/459

1985—*cont.*
373 amended 87/403; 88/571
383 amended 87/387
385 revoked 87/498
394 revoked 85/1723; 86/134
397 revoked 87/890
426 revoked 86/724
434 revoked 88/1546
438 revoked 87/649
440 amended 86/430
458 revoked 85/1643
464 revoked 86/1225
469 revoked 85/954; 87/536
487 amended 86/926; 87/1536
488 revoked 85/1065
489 revoked 86/24
506 revoked 86/510
508 revoked 86/459
509 revoked 86/740
510 revoked 86/1202
514 revoked 85/767
516 revoked 85/952
517 revoked 85/1335
520 amended 88/1762
527 revoked 85/1382
542 revoked 85/678
543 revoked 85/1163
554 revoked 87/365
555 (except para. 3) revoked 86/967
556 amended 86/140
557 revoked 87/366
564 revoked 86/1712
565 revoked 85/1150
568 revoked 87/2088
569 revoked 87/2089
572 revoked 86/1712
573 revoked 86/2049
575 amended 87/608
588 amended 88/1220
608 revoked 85/870
609 revoked 85/1017
613 revoked 85/1835
620 revoked 85/737
622 revoked 88/706
628 revoked 85/949
629 revoked 85/795
630 revoked 85/895
637 revoked 87/1758
641 amended 87/630
660 amended 87/1886
661 amended 87/1886
677 amended 85/1100; 85/1244; 85/1445; 86/84;
        86/852;   86/1009;   86/1156;   86/2183;
        87/1440
678 revoked 88/1447
679 revoked 85/1164
684 amended 86/989; 87/1314; 88/1212
685 amended 86/991; 87/1312; 88/1210
691 revoked 86/816
692 revoked 86/816
693 revoked 85/886
698 amended 88/726
699 revoked 86/1020
716 amended 87/1434
717 amended 85/1031
719 revoked 85/1030
730 revoked 86/1078
741 revoked 85/1883
750 revoked 88/1298

STATUTORY INSTRUMENTS AFFECTED 1947–1988

751 amended   85/1992;   86/2015;   87/455;
        87/2044
757 amended   85/1736;   85/1918;   86/2186;
        87/1578; 88/707; 88/991
763 revoked 85/1060
764 revoked 86/815
777 amended 86/1082; revoked 86/1082
784 revoked 86/584
785 amended 86/583
790 revoked 86/815
791 revoked 85/1389
792 amended 85/1494
793 amended 86/117
794 revoked 85/1380
798 revoked 85/1274
805 amended 85/1052
823 revoked 87/786
827 amended 86/451; 87/39; 88/966
829 revoked 86/2067
830 amended 86/990; 87/1313; 88/1211
849 amended 85/1085; 85/1293; 85/1294; 86/82;
        86/540;   86/1446;   86/1934;   87/215;
        87/271; 87/1350; revoked 87/2070
852 revoked 87/803
854 amended 86/2097; 87/752; 88/1359
856 amended 88/1305
857 revoked 85/1823
863 revoked 86/344
885 revoked 87/851
886 amended 85/1650; 86/71; 86/305; 86/335;
        87/150; 87/510; 88/2083; 88/2108
897 revoked 85/1334
898 revoked 85/1751
899 revoked 86/816
900 revoked 85/1041
901 revoked 85/1388
902 revoked 85/1332
903 revoked 85/1722
910 amended 88/711
921 amended 86/691; revoked 86/1319
928 revoked 86/92
929 revoked 85/1381
936 revoked 85/1067
937 revoked 86/1511
946 revoked 86/29
947 revoked 85/1386
960 amended 85/2001
962 amended 85/1569
967 amended 86/1561; 87/335; 87/2112; 88/553
968 revoked 85/1331
969 revoked 86/816
970 revoked 86/816
971 revoked 85/1495
975 amended 87/1092
976 amended 87/1091
977 amended 87/1097
979 amended 87/1093
980 amended 87/1098
981 amended 87/1148
988 amended 88/2040
993 revoked 86/442
995 revoked 87/401
996 amended 85/1332; 85/1345; 86/2001
997 revoked 86/1256
1011 revoked 88/1813
1012 amended 86/8; revoked 88/1813
1021 revoked 85/1387
1022 revoked 85/1228
1027 revoked 85/1299

1029 amended 88/1056; 88/1983; 88/2066
1042 amended 85/1379
1043 amended 85/1385
1045 revoked 87/851
1050 amended 86/1144
1061 revoked 85/1814
1062 revoked 85/1509; 86/34
1063 amended 88/1975
1065 amended 85/1936; 87/1445
1066 amended 85/1936; 87/798
1067 amended 87/798
1068 amended 87/800
1071 amended 87/1066
1072 revoked 86/1501
1076 revoked 86/1104
1080 revoked 85/1721
1081 revoked 85/1750
1084 revoked 86/1713
1086 amended 86/853
1089 revoked 88/1803
1108 revoked 87/52
1120 revoked 86/1227
1126 revoked 86/1306
1130 revoked 87/700
1131 revoked 87/405
1133 amended 87/2088
1134 revoked 87/2089
1136 revoked 85/1835
1144 amended 87/1293
1151 amended 87/1520
1156 revoked 86/1713
1160 revoked 87/1261
1161 revoked 87/1378
1163 amended 88/1449
1166 amended 86/583
1167 amended 85/1324
1174 revoked 86/5
1183 revoked 86/1103
1202 amended 88/591
1213 revoked 87/2233
1226 revoked 86/33
1227 revoked 85/1647
1230 revoked 87/1758
1232 revoked 87/2024
1266 amended   87/1950;   88/1201;   88/1982;
        88/2065
1274 revoked 85/1501
1293 revoked 87/2070
1294 revoked 87/2070
1306 amended 87/884
1317 revoked 86/861
1323 amended   86/317;   86/1716;   87/1099;
        87/1114; 88/475
1325 amended 86/576
1333 amended 86/392
1363 revoked 86/1078
1377 revoked 86/938
1383 amended 88/1698
1384 revoked 86/939
1411 amended 86/318; 87/92; 88/431
1416 amended 86/1357
1428 revoked 86/1778
1430 revoked 86/1777
1431 revoked 86/133
1432 revoked 85/1974
1433 revoked 86/118
1434 revoked 85/1869
1435 revoked 86/32
1436 revoked 85/1767

STATUTORY INSTRUMENTS AFFECTED 1947–1988

1437 revoked 86/215
1462 revoked 85/1813
1463 revoked 85/1825
1464 revoked 86/815
1465 amended 87/1304
1492 amended 86/199
1496 revoked 86/49
1497 revoked 86/90
1501 revoked 85/1830
1510 revoked 86/361
1511 revoked 86/165
1512 revoked 86/31
1515 revoked 86/24
1523 revoked 86/606
1524 revoked 86/1200
1525 revoked 88/1478
1530 revoked 86/1050
1532 revoked 88/876
1533 revoked 88/976
1565 revoked 88/110
1571 revoked 86/1118
1576 amended 85/1936; 86/2287; 87/798; 88/871
1577 revoked 87/851
1581 revoked 86/2103
1593 amended 87/675; 88/1031
1596 revoked 87/3
1605 amended 87/136; revoked 87/1637
1607 amended 85/1727; 86/837; revoked 87/63
1614 revoked 88/666
1615 revoked 88/667
1627 amended 87/314
1630 amended 85/2020; 86/348; 86/813; 86/1352; 86/2179; 87/973; 87/1053; 87/1125; 87/1218; 87/1804; 87/1902; revoked 87/2184
1643 amended 86/2238; 88/251
1646 revoked 86/1989
1648 revoked 86/28
1649 revoked 86/30
1650 amended 87/1916
1665 amended 86/296; revoked 87/220
1686 revoked 88/110
1691 revoked 86/814
1692 revoked 86/109
1693 revoked 86/816
1694 revoked 88/459
1712 revoked 87/1425
1705 amended 86/140
1712 revoked 87/1425
1713 amended 87/1382
1714 amended 86/544; 86/2121; 87/1145
1720 revoked 86/89
1727 revoked 87/63
1733 amended 87/423
1737 amended 86/306; 88/2082
1752 revoked 86/816
1759 revoked 86/1713
1768 revoked 86/51
1769 revoked 86/35
1770 revoked 86/91
1771 revoked 86/815
1777 amended 87/1826; 87/1833
1800 amended 87/439
1801 amended 86/2076
1802 revoked 86/2128
1804 revoked 88/1964
1807 amended 86/2001
1810 revoked 86/815

1811 revoked 86/865
1819 revoked 86/2072
1820 amended 86/2073
1823 amended 86/982; 86/1997; 87/1123; 87/1980; 88/1015; 88/2136
1824 revoked 86/50
1844 revoked 88/1652
1845 revoked 86/1712
1848 revoked 86/2214
1850 revoked 86/887
1857 amended 87/904
1858 revoked 87/904
1862 revoked 87/904
1867 revoked 86/816
1868 revoked 86/93
1870 revoked 86/1713
1871 revoked 88/186
1875 revoked 86/2161
1880 amended 86/445; 86/1559; 87/388; revoked 88/446
1881 revoked 86/307
1883 revoked 87/96
1884 amended 86/564
1890 revoked 87/2256
1894 revoked 86/164
1895 revoked 86/166
1903 amended 87/337
1905 revoked 86/1668
1906 revoked 86/1628
1907 revoked 86/1691
1917 revoked 88/2151
1919 amended 88/1959
1920 revoked 86/24
1924 amended 85/78
1928 amended 87/657
1929 amended 86/2171;87/1106; 87/1114; 88/474; 88/476; 88/1016
1930 amended 86/751; 87/1106; 88/476
1931 amended 86/751; 86/1046; 86/2171; 87/1107; 87/1114; 88/474; 88/476; 88/523; 88/1016
1936 amended 87/798
1939 amended 86/2129; 88/2133
1948 revoked 86/865
1949 revoked 86/362
1950 revoked 86/206
1960 revoked 87/50
1964 revoked 86/1713
1965 revoked 86/1713
1972 revoked 86/815
1973 revoked 86/815
1975 revoked 87/373
1979 amended 88/1726
1980 amended 88/2039; 88/2040
1981 revoked 88/1813
1982 revoked 86/8
1984 revoked 87/1264
2004 revoked 86/1713
2005 revoked 87/2256
2010 amended 88/1121
2011 amended 86/2300; revoked 87/783
2029 amended 87/256; 87/1907
2030 amended 87/347
2031 revoked 86/1713
2032 revoked 86/2283
2033 revoked 86/2281
2035 revoked 88/668
2039 revoked 86/1078
2041 amended 86/787

STATUTORY INSTRUMENTS AFFECTED 1947–1988

779 revoked 87/292
784 revoked 87/851
814 revoked 87/209
818 revoked 86/915
822 revoked 86/1396
823 revoked 86/915
824 revoked 86/1101
825 revoked 86/1101
826 revoked 86/1101
827 revoked 86/1667
828 revoked 86/1130
831 revoked 87/803
837 revoked 87/63
853 revoked 88/69
859 revoked 87/2174
861 revoked 87/370
862 amended 87/836
869 amended 86/972
924 amended 88/462
938 amended 87/149
939 amended 87/154
941 revoked 86/1101
942 revoked 86/1130
943 revoked 86/1130
945 revoked 86/1713
946 revoked 87/374
951 revoked 86/1995
963 amended 87/192
965 amended 88/543
966 amended 86/1192; 88/463; 88/464; 88/545; 88/546
975 amended 88/486
976 amended 88/428; 88/473; 88/623; 88/1435; 88/1935
977 revoked 88/1653
978 amended 87/865; revoked 88/681
994 revoked 86/1668
1007 revoked 86/1130
1027 revoked 86/1121
1032 amended 87/942
1039 amended 88/135
1043 revoked 87/802
1045 revoked 87/1941
1046 amended 86/1717; 87/1105; 88/476
1050 revoked 87/364
1059 revoked 86/1179
1078 amended 86/1597; 87/676; 87/1133; 88/271; 88/1102; 88/1177; 88/1178; 88/1287; 88/1524; 88/1871
1081 amended 86/1460
1090 revoked 88/1478
1092 revoked 86/1466
1103 amended 87/1146; 88/1163
1104 amended 87/1147; 88/1164
1115 revoked 86/1620
1117 revoked 87/45
1118 revoked 87/327
1120 revoked 87/32
1121 amended 86/1185; 86/1247; revoked 86/1294
1131 revoked 86/1396
1132 revoked 87/989
1135 revoked 87/1758
1142 revoked 87/821
1144 amended 87/1296; 87/1297
1148 revoked 88/1327
1154 revoked 87/381
1157 amended 87/934; 88/247
1158 revoked 88/247

1159 amended 87/163; 87/1825; 88/588; 88/1083; 88/1839
1169 revoked 87/941
1176 revoked 88/1813
1179 amended 86/1232; revoked 86/1331
1191 revoked 88/110; 88/1191
1195 revoked 86/2050
1196 revoked 86/1586
1199 amended 87/4
1202 amended 88/772
1224 revoked 87/363
1227 amended 87/1366; 88/1042
1233 revoked 88/1001
1250 revoked 87/902
1256 revoked 87/1465
1259 amended 86/2218
1260 revoked 88/2040
1279 revoked 88/1343
1280 revoked 86/1713
1284 revoked 86/2050
1290 revoked 87/74
1294 amended 86/1344; 86/1384; revoked 86/1412
1303 amended 86/1890; 86/2236; 87/170; 88/1856
1304 revoked 87/2212
1305 amended 87/1835
1306 amended 86/1397; revoked 87/1261
1310 amended 88/1112
1319 amended 88/894
1324 amended 87/499; 87/1393
1325 revoked 87/1261
1331 amended 86/1360; 86/1416; revoked 86/1422
1344 revoked 86/1412
1353 revoked 87/309
1357 revoked 87/1199
1358 revoked 87/381
1359 revoked 87/382
1360 revoked 86/1422
1361 amended 86/2001
1368 revoked 87/2216
1369 revoked 87/1378
1373 revoked 88/2110
1374 amended 86/2218
1379 revoked 87/256
1384 revoked 86/1412
1390 amended 87/1120
1395 revoked 86/2050
1397 revoked 87/1261
1410 revoked 86/1422
1411 amended 86/1435; 86/1483; 86/1535; 86/1576; 86/1616; 86/1662; revoked 86/1681
1413 revoked 86/1431; amended 86/1479; 86/1540; 86/1592; 86/1621; revoked 86/1689
1422 amended 86/1432; 86/1491; 86/1508; 86/1552; revoked 86/1574
1431 revoked 86/1689
1432 revoked 86/1574
1435 revoked 86/1681
1437 revoked 87/1566
1441 amended 88/287
1442 amended 86/1445; 87/2088
1446 revoked 87/2070
1447 revoked 87/751
1449 revoked 87/1850

STATUTORY INSTRUMENTS AFFECTED 1947–1988

1453 amended 88/64; 88/652
1456 amended 86/1669; 87/805; 88/760
1463 revoked 86/1838
1464 revoked 87/199
1475 revoked 87/870; amended 88/714
1479 revoked 86/1689
1483 revoked 86/1681
1491 revoked 86/1574
1493 revoked 87/1421
1494 revoked 88/820
1508 revoked 86/1574
1511 revoked 87/268
1528 revoked 86/1734
1530 amended 87/626; 88/653
1535 revoked 86/1681
1536 revoked 88/629
1540 revoked 86/1689
1541 amended 86/2218
1552 revoked 86/1574
1559 revoked 88/446
1574 amended 86/1595; 86/1615; 86/1664; 86/1688; 86/1720; 86/1765; 86/1837; 86/1900; revoked 86/1993
1576 revoked 86/1681
1577 revoked 86/2050
1581 revoked 86/1667
1583 revoked 86/1747
1585 revoked 86/1747
1592 revoked 86/1689
1595 revoked 86/1993
1611 amended 87/410; 87/909
1612 revoked 87/908
1613 amended 87/425; 87/881
1614 revoked 87/882
1615 revoked 86/1993
1616 revoked 86/1681
1621 revoked 86/1689
1623 amended 87/1782
1627 revoked 87/901
1662 revoked 86/1681
1664 revoked 86/1900
1671 amended 88/1879
1681 amended 86/1707; 86/1756; 86/1775; 86/1849; 86/2242; 87/182; 87/263; 87/885; revoked 87/1181
1682 amended 86/2109
1689 amended 86/2208; 87/249; 87/906; 87/1555; 87/1687; revoked 87/1893
1691 amended 88/408
1699 amended 87/153
1701 revoked 86/1780
1707 revoked 87/1181
1711 amended 88/835
1712 amended 87/65; revoked 88/646
1713 amended 86/2317; 86/2318; 87/356; 87/1855; 87/2222; 87/2223; 88/585; 88/612
1715 amended 87/2018; revoked 88/1196
1718 amended 88/476
1734 revoked 87/211
1735 revoked 88/396
1741 revoked 87/199
1742 revoked 86/2050
1744 revoked 86/2271
1746 revoked 87/595
1756 revoked 87/1181
1765 revoked 86/1900
1775 revoked 87/1181

1777 amended 86/2038; 87/855
1795 amended 87/876
1818 amended 87/1851; revoked 88/1862
1837 revoked 86/1900
1839 revoked 87/199
1841 revoked 87/53
1842 revoked 87/53
1843 revoked 86/2050
1844 revoked 87/989
1845 revoked 86/2050
1849 revoked 87/1181
1876 amended 88/705
1877 amended 87/1670
1881 revoked 87/1264
1900 revoked 86/1993
1915 amended 87/1921
1925 amended 86/2142; 87/1919
1934 revoked 87/2070
1948 amended 87/2128; 88/657; 88/1348
1960 amended 87/1978; 88/532
1965 amended 87/275
1982 revoked 86/2075
1993 revoked 86/2248; 87/2248
1994 amended 86/2142; 87/1959; 88/1739
1995 amended 86/2247
2001 amended 86/2245; 87/1398
2004 amended 87/192
2006 amended 87/192
2020 amended 87/2046
2027 revoked 87/468
2030 amended 86/2142; 88/95
2032 revoked 87/851
2049 amended 87/1538
2052 revoked 87/199
2057 revoked 87/595
2058 revoked 87/595
2059 revoked 87/595
2090 amended 88/77
2098 amended 87/1500; revoked 88/1344
2103 revoked 87/1908
2115 revoked 87/821
2128 amended 88/2043
2152 revoked 87/2005
2153 revoked 88/2151
2155 revoked 87/391
2161 revoked 87/2096
2172 revoked 87/1968
2173 revoked 87/481
2180 revoked 87/122
2184 revoked 88/110
2208 revoked 87/1893
2214 amended 87/261
2215 amended 87/260
2218 amended 87/335; 87/1424; 87/1970; 88/1725
2221 revoked 88/786
2226 amended 87/1828
2241 revoked 87/851
2242 revoked 87/1181
2248 revoked 87/270
2249 amended 88/174
2252 amended 88/176
2256 revoked 88/80
2257 amended 88/173
2281 revoked 88/277
2283 revoked 88/276
2300 revoked 87/783
2318 amended 88/258

STATUTORY INSTRUMENTS AFFECTED 1947–1988

1987

1 amended 87/262
19 revoked 87/1758
27 revoked 87/97
28 revoked 87/98
37 amended 88/712
45 revoked 87/1978
38 revoked 87/771
50 revoked 88/165
52 amended 87/605
63 amended 87/548; 87/854; 87/2113; 88/478;
　　revoked 88/1485
64 revoked 88/645
65 revoked 88/646
67 revoked 87/199
69 revoked 87/1399
70 revoked 87/989
71 revoked 87/199
74 revoked 88/224
91 amended 88/430
96 amended 88/355
102 revoked 87/2166
106 revoked 88/299
118 amended 88/359
136 revoked 87/1637
153 revoked 87/1893
156 amended 87/256; 87/341
158 amended 87/342
159 amended 87/343
163 revoked 87/1825
172 revoked 88/1141
178 revoked 87/304
182 revoked 87/1181
184 amended 87/519
188 amended 88/357
189 amended 88/356
202 revoked 87/989
208 revoked 88/437
209 revoked 88/223
211 amended 87/248; 87/1808
215 revoked 87/2070
243 revoked 88/335
244 revoked 88/330
248 revoked 87/1808
249 revoked 87/1893
255 revoked 88/373
256 amended 87/341
257 amended 87/341; 87/2215; 88/1339
263 revoked 87/1181
268 revoked 88/270
271 revoked 87/2070
272 revoked 87/1304
275 amended 87/1329; 87/2279
288 amended 87/610
291 revoked 87/644
292 revoked 88/136
295 revoked 88/297
299 amended 88/164
307 amended 88/1126
311 amended 87/1603
312 revoked 87/1963
327 revoked 88/436
332 amended 88/548
340 revoked 88/1427
347 amended 88/1563
350 revoked 88/352
351 revoked 87/2186
364 revoked 88/331
365 amended 87/824; 87/1358; 88/421; 88/1109
366 amended 87/823; 87/895; 88/420; 88/1107

1987—*cont.*

367 amended 88/365
368 amended 88/427
370 revoked 88/234
371 amended 88/472
373 revoked 88/1420
374 revoked 88/1418
377 revoked 88/453
381 amended 87/431; 88/1171
382 amended 87/883; 87/1356; 88/489; 88/1131
387 amended 88/489; 88/490
388 revoked 88/446
391 revoked 88/448
392 revoked 88/449
393 revoked 88/451
394 revoked 88/450
404 revoked 88/1347
405 revoked 87/889
415 amended 88/553
423 amended 87/1914; 87/1914
424 revoked 87/1878
428 revoked 87/1758
430 revoked 88/110
443 amended 88/447
444 revoked 88/1385
468 amended 87/2211; 88/1304; 88/1853
481 amended 88/36
491 amended 88/664
498 revoked 88/671
519 amended 87/894
548 revoked 87/854
560 revoked 87/1378
605 revoked 88/712
610 amended 87/753; revoked 88/855
625 revoked 88/1607
627 revoked 88/666
628 revoked 88/667
642 amended 88/1390
644 amended 87/1801
650 revoked 87/1433
653 amended 88/491
654 amended 88/492
657 amended 88/647
670 amended 87/855
700 revoked 88/890
702 revoked 88/1813
704 revoked 88/685
705 revoked 88/686
718 revoked 87/1978
734 revoked 87/870
747 amended 88/1984
751 amended 87/964
753 revoked 88/855
763 revoked 87/2105
765 revoked 88/1813
771 revoked 88/799
772 revoked 88/798
784 revoked 87/1535
785 revoked 88/729
786 revoked 87/1251
821 amended 88/817
823 revoked 88/420
839 revoked 87/1535
851 amended 87/1753; 88/727; 88/1821;
　　88/2162
854 revoked 88/1485
864 amended 88/1424
865 revoked 88/681
885 revoked 87/1181
890 revoked 87/1842

STATUTORY INSTRUMENTS AFFECTED 1947–1988

1988—*cont.*
165 revoked 88/2077
186 amended 88/1128
233 amended 88/1019
338 revoked 88/1478
359 amended 88/2202
387 revoked 88/1652
428 amended 88/1435
477 revoked 88/1360
525 revoked 88/538
536 amended 88/555
588 revoked 88/1083
590 amended 88/591
596 amended 88/1854
664 amended 88/688; 88/1725
683 amended 88/1761; revoked 88/2071
740 amended 88/995; 88/1960
743 revoked 88/998
791 amended 88/1300
807 revoked 88/1962
816 revoked 88/1652
820 revoked 88/923
856 amended 88/2083
874 revoked 88/2092
876 amended 88/2120

1988—*cont.*
890 revoked 88/2094
913 amended 88/2132
919 amended 88/1240
953 revoked 88/1678
1039 revoked 88/1345
1042 amended 88/1423
1048 amended 88/1288
1054 revoked 88/1862
1083 revoked 88/1839
1102 revoked 88/1177
1134 revoked 88/1203
1196 amended 88/1393
1263 revoked 88/1467
1272 revoked 88/1813
1374 revoked 88/1652
1485 amended 88/1929
1539 amended 88/1611
1562 amended 88/1790
1590 amended 88/1615
1724 amended 88/1908
1800 amended 88/1888
1801 amended 88/1888
1810 revoked 88/1898
1813 amended 88/2091